M000013216

ACCESS

FIND any word in the Bible...QUICKLY!

THE
EVERYDAY SERIES

Everyday Access: Your Bible Concordance

Copyright © 2006 by Thomas Nelson, Inc.

Published in Nashville, Tennessee, by Thomas Nelson, Inc., Publishers.

Interior design and typesetting by John Adams, ProtoType Graphics, Nashville, Tennessee.

ISBN 1-4185-0564-1

Library of Congress Cataloging-in-Publication data available on request.

1 2 3 4 5 6 7 — 10 09 08 07

were jealous of Moses and of A,.............. Ps 106:16
Family of A, trust the LORD;.............. Ps 115:10
he will bless the family of A. .... Ps 115:12
Family of A, praise the LORD. .... Ps 135:19
I sent Moses, A, and Miriam to .... Mic 6:4
came from the family of A.................... Lk 1:5
They said to A, 'Make us gods .... Ac 7:40
must be called by God as A was. .... Heb 5:4
priest like Melchizedek, not A. .... Heb 7:11

AARON'S

But A stick swallowed theirs. .... Ex 7:12
Then A sister Miriam, an .... Ex 15:20
they will be on A heart when he .... Ex 28:30
A son, who will become high .... Ex 29:30
the LORD, and A sons, the .... Le 1:5
special oil on A head to make.............. Le 8:12
clothes and on A sons and their .... Le 8:30
A sons Nadab and Abihu took .... Le 10:1
A uncle Uzziel had two sons .... Le 10:4
Now two of A sons had died while.......... Le 16:1
If one of A descendants has .... Le 21:21
If one of A descendants has a.............. Le 22:4
These were the names of A sons, ... Nu 3:3
stick from Levi, write A name. .... Nu 17:3
Tent, he saw that A stick (which.......... Nu 17:8
Put A walking stick back in .... Nu 17:10
Moses took off A clothes and put .... Nu 20:28
A sons were Nadab, Abihu, ... 1Ch 6:3
These were A sons: Eleazar was.......... 1Ch 6:50
priest of A family must be with .... Ne 10:38
A rod that once grew leaves, ... Heb 9:4

ABADDON

language is A and in the Greek .... Rev 9:11

ABANA

A and the Pharpar, the rivers 2Ki 5:12

ABANDON

I will never a you." .... Heb 13:5

ABANDONED

God, my God, why have you a me? .... Ps 22:1
You have a the agreement with .... Ps 89:39
his altar and a his Temple. .... La 2:7
empty ruins and a cities that .... Eze 36:4
shepherd who a the flock. .... Zch 11:17
God, my God, why have you a me?" .... Mt 27:46
God, my God, why have you a me?" .... Mk 15:34

ABARIM

mountain in the A Mountains, ... Nu 27:12
Go up the A Mountains, to Mount .... Dt 32:49

ABBA

prayed, "A, Father! You can do .... Mk 14:36

ABDA

Adoniram son of A was in charge 1Ki 4:6

ABDON

A son of Hillel from the city of .... Jdg 12:13
Then A son of Hillel died and.............. Jdg 12:15

ABEDNEGO

Meshach, and Azariah's was A. .... Da 1:7
and A leaders over the area of .... Da 2:49
are Shadrach, Meshach, and A. .... Da 3:12
and A were tied up and thrown .... Da 3:21
and A in the area of Babylon.................. Da 3:30

ABEL

gave birth to Cain's brother A. .... Ge 4:2
A took care of flocks, and Cain .... Ge 4:2
A brought the best parts from .... Ge 4:4
LORD accepted A and his gift, ... Ge 4:4
his brother A and killed him. .... Ge 4:8
"Where is your brother A?" .... Ge 4:9
He will take the place of A, ... Ge 4:25

of that good man A to the murder .... Mt 23:35
the killing of A to the killing .... Lk 11:51
was by faith that A offered God .... Heb 11:4
A died, but through his faith he .... Heb 11:4
message than the blood of A. .... Heb 12:24

ABIATHAR

But A, a son of Ahimelech, who 1Sa 22:20
David said to A the priest, ... 1Sa 30:7
So Zadok and A took the Ark of 2Sa 15:29
Zadok and A were the priests, ... 2Sa 20:25
son of Zeruiah and A the priest,.............. 1Ki 1:7
Solomon removed A from being the 1Ki 2:27
Jehoiada and A later took 1Ch 27:34
the time of A the high priest, ... Mk 2:26

ABIATHAR'S

the new high priest in A place. 1Ki 2:35

ABIB

in the month of A, you are .... Ex 13:4
the month of A, because in that .... Ex 34:18
your God during the month of A, ... Dt 16:1

ABIEL

son of A from the tribe of 1Sa 9:1

ABIEZER

all that my people of A did. .... Jdg 8:2

ABIEZRITE

to Joash, one of the A people.............. Jdg 6:11

ABIEZRITES

at Ophrah, where the A live. .... Jdg 6:24

ABIGAIL

His wife was named A. 1Sa 25:3
When A saw David, she quickly 1Sa 25:23
Then David sent a message to A, ... 1Sa 25:39
whose mother was A, the widow of 2Sa 3:3
mother was A daughter of Nahash.......... 2Sa 17:25
whose mother was A from Carmel. 1Ch 3:1

ABIHAIL

the daughter of Jerimoth and A.............. 2Ch 11:18
came for Esther daughter of A, ... Est 2:15
So Queen Esther daughter of A,.............. Est 9:29

ABIHU

gave birth to Nadab, A, Eleazar,.............. Ex 6:23
You, Aaron, Nadab, A, and .... Ex 24:1
Aaron, Nadab, A, and seventy .... Ex 24:9
with his sons Nadab, A, Eleazar, ... Ex 28:1
LORD and destroyed Nadab and A, ... Le 10:2
Nadab, the oldest, A, Eleazar,.............. Nu 3:2
the father of Nadab, A, Eleazar, ... Nu 26:60
sons were Nadab, A, Eleazar, and 1Ch 24:1

ABIHUD

Bela's sons were Addar, Gera, A, ... 1Ch 8:3

ABIJAH

and A were judges in Beersheba. 1Sa 8:2
son A became very sick. 1Ki 14:1
his wife A had his son, named 1Ch 2:24
Rehoboam's son was A. 1Ch 3:10
Rehoboam chose A son of Maacah 2Ch 11:22
and his son A became king in his 2Ch 12:16
A became the king of Judah 2Ch 13:1
But A became strong. He married 2Ch 13:21
Everything else A did—what he 2Ch 13:22
A died and was buried in 2Ch 14:1
mother's name was A daughter of 2Ch 29:1
Rehoboam was the father of A. .... Mt 1:7
A was the father of Asa. .... Mt 1:7

ABIJAH'S

A army chased Jeroboam's army 2Ch 13:19
who belonged to A group. .... Lk 1:5

ABIJAM

A became king of Judah during 1Ki 15:1
was war between A and Jeroboam 1Ki 15:6
A died and was buried in 1Ki 15:8

ABILENE

and Lysanias, the ruler of A. .... Lk 3:1

ABILITY

him the skill, a, and knowledge .... Ex 35:31
doesn't have the a to be wise................... Pr 17:16
some people the a to enjoy the .... Ec 5:19
GOD gave me the a to teach so .... Is 50:4
wisdom and the a to learn many .... Da 1:17
take away their a to understand. .... Hos 4:11
born without the a to become.................. Mt 19:12
demons and the a to heal .... Lk 9:1
one person the a to speak with 1Co 12:8
to another the a to prophesy. 1Co 12:10
give you the a to understand 2Ti 2:7

ABIMELECH

A king of Gerar heard this,...................... Ge 20:2
night God spoke to A in a dream .... Ge 20:3
as a punishment on A for taking .... Ge 20:18
Then A came with Phicol, the.................. Ge 21:22
town of Gerar to see A king of .... Ge 26:1
A called for Isaac and said, ... Ge 26:9
A son of Gideon went to his .... Jdg 9:1
There they made A their king. .... Jdg 9:6
A ruled Israel for three years.................. Jdg 9:22
to say, 'A woman killed A.'" .... Jdg 9:54
people of Israel saw A was dead, ... Jdg 9:55
remember who killed A son of 2Sa 11:21

ABINADAB

Jesse called A and told him to 1Sa 16:8
the second was A, and the third 1Sa 17:13
Jonathan, A, and Malki-Shua. 1Sa 31:2
Ahio, sons of A, led the new 2Sa 6:3
second son was A, his third was.............. 1Ch 2:13

ABINADAB'S

the LORD to A house on a hill. 1Sa 7:1
Ark of God from A house on a new 1Ch 13:7

ABINOAM

a message to Barak son of A.................. Jdg 4:6
Barak son of A had gone to Mount .... Jdg 4:12
Barak son of A sang this song: .... Jdg 5:1
capture your enemies, son of A!.............. Jdg 5:12

ABIRAM

Korah, Dathan, A, and On turned .... Nu 16:1
tents of Korah, Dathan, and A." .... Nu 16:24
It cost Hiel the life of A, ... 1Ki 16:34

ABISHAG

found a girl named A from Shunam 1Ki 1:3
him to give me A the Shunammite 1Ki 2:17
Why do you ask me to give him A? 1Ki 2:22

ABISHAI

Hittite and A son of Zeruiah, ... 1Sa 26:6
sons, Joab, A, and Asahel, were 2Sa 2:18
and his brother A killed Abner, ... 2Sa 3:30
the army under the command of A, ... 2Sa 10:10
A son of Zeruiah said to the 2Sa 16:9
David said to A, "Sheba son of 2Sa 20:6
A, brother of Joab son of 2Sa 23:18
A fought three hundred soldiers.............. 1Ch 11:20
A son of Zeruiah killed eighteen 1Ch 18:12

ABISHALOM

mother was Maacah daughter of A. 1Ki 15:2
was Maacah, the daughter of A............... 1Ki 15:10

ABISHUA

Phinehas was the father of A.................. 1Ch 6:4

ABISHUA'S

was A son. Uzzi was Bukki's 1Ch 6:51

ABIUD

Zerubbabel was the father of A................ Mt 1:13

ABLE

They will be a to do anything .... Ge 11:6
they will not be a to understand .... Ge 11:7
that I would be a to have....................... Ge 21:7
I will be a to return in peace .... Ge 28:21
when will I be a to do something .... Ge 30:30
am not a to stand up before you .... Ge 31:35
So you are a to break out first, ... Ge 38:29
she was not a to hide the baby .... Ex 2:3
magicians were a to do the same .... Ex 7:11
will not be a to drink the water .... Ex 7:18
no one will be a to see the .... Ex 10:5
dark you will be a to feel it." .... Ex 10:21
He is a to design pieces to be .... Ex 31:4
He is a to design pieces to be .... Ex 35:32
they are also a to weave things. .... Ex 35:35
or older who were a to serve in .... Nu 1:20
and she is not a to have another............ Nu 5:27
she will be a to have babies. .... Nu 5:28
'The LORD was not a to bring .... Nu 14:16
I am a to reward you well.".................... Nu 22:37
I am not a to take care of you................ Dt 1:9
No one will be a to stop you; .... Dt 7:24
the LORD was not a to take his .... Dt 9:28
and you will be a to gather your.............. Dt 11:14
you will not be a to keep them, ... Dt 28:41
will not be a to lend to them .... Dt 28:44
of them will be a to stand .... Jos 10:8
but a nation has been a to defeat you. .... Jos 10:20
nation has been a to defeat you. .... Jos 23:9
You are not a to serve the LORD, ... Jos 24:19
strong and a men from Moab; .... Jdg 3:29
have not been a to have children .... Jdg 13:3
will always be a to please you. 2Sa 16:4
so he was never a to build a 1Ki 5:3
they are a to hear your wisdom. 1Ki 10:8
so you will be a to obey the 1Ch 22:12
they are a to hear your wisdom.............. 2Ch 9:7
god is even less a to save you 2Ch 32:15
won't be a to save his people 2Ch 32:17
the wicked will not be a to see, ... Job 11:20
so who would be a to stand up .... Job 41:10
You are truly a to save. .... Ps 69:13
he is loving and a to save. .... Ps 130:7
Whenever you are a, do good to............. Pr 3:27
they aren't a to help you. .... Is 2:22
person will be a to keep only .... Is 7:21
A baby will be a to play near a .... Is 11:8
child will be a to put his hand .... Is 11:8
people will be a to eat safely, ... Is 14:30
in need will be a to lie down in .... Is 14:30
no one will be a to close it; .... Is 22:22
no one will be a to open it. .... Is 22:22
will not be a to understand." .... Is 29:14
will not be a to keep it away .... Is 47:11
they will not be a to help you. .... Is 47:15
think I am not a to save you? .... Is 50:2
You will be a to stand against................ Je 1:18
no one will be a to put it out, ... Je 4:4
they will not be a to escape. .... Je 11:11
idols will not be a to help when .... Je 11:12
who is not a to save anyone? .... Je 14:9
You will not be a to argue with .... Eze 3:26
will not be a to say anymore, ... Eze 28:9
they will not be a to live by.................... Eze 33:12
and a to serve in his palace. .... Da 1:4
Are you a to tell me what I .... Da 2:26
because you were a to tell these .... Da 2:47

the God we serve is **a** to save us .... Da 3:17
and he is **a** to make proud people .... Da 4:37
always worship been **a** to save .... Da 6:20
No one was **a** to save the sheep .... Da 8:7
one will be **a** to stand against .... Da 11:16
they will not be **a** to find him,................ Hos 5:6
no one will be **a** to save them. .... Hos 5:14
will not be **a** to save themselves .... Am 2:14
and you won't be **a** to save .... Mic 2:3
sacrifices will be **a** to take .... Zch 14:21
Then the men were **a** to see. .... Mt 9:30
the man, he was **a** to speak. .... Mt 9:33
has made some **a** to accept it.................. Mt 19:11
you will be **a** to do what I did .... Mt 21:21
So Jesus was not **a** to work any .... Mk 6:5
can't talk he makes **a** to speak."............. Mk 7:37
believe will be **a** to do these .... Mk 16:17
You will not be **a** to speak until .... Lk 1:20
but no one was **a** to heal her. .... Lk 8:43
there, but they will not be **a.** .... Lk 13:24
build but was not **a** to finish.' .... Lk 14:30
but he was not **a** because he was .... Lk 19:3
So they were not **a** to trap Jesus.............. Lk 20:26
enemies will be **a** to stand .... Lk 21:15
But no one was **a** to touch him, ... Jn 7:30
and will be **a** to come in and go .... Jn 10:9
in the world is **a** to save us." .... Ac 4:12
Then he is **a** to see again." .... Ac 9:12
had not been **a** to leave his bed .... Ac 9:33
they were barely **a** to keep the .... Ac 14:18
our ancestors were **a** to carry.................. Ac 15:10
It is **a** to give you strength, ... Ac 20:32
Immediately I was **a** to see him. .... Ac 22:13
think you will be **a** to escape .... Rm 2:3
that God was **a** to do what he had .... Rm 4:21
not even **a** to obey God's law. .... Rm 8:7
will ever be **a** to separate us .... Rm 8:39
God is **a** to put them back where .... Rm 11:23
you were not **a** to take solid 1Co 3:2
that you will be **a** to stand it. 1Co 10:13
He made us **a** to be servants of **a** 2Co 3:6
as they were **a** and even more 2Co 8:3
that you will be **a** to know that .... Eph 3:19
you will be **a** to stand strong .... Eph 6:13
will be **a** to work for the Lord. .... Php 1:22
so you will be **a** to answer .... Col 4:6
welcome guests, and **a** to teach. 1Ti 3:2
am sure he is **a** to protect what 2Ti 1:12
they will be **a** to teach others.............. 2Ti 2:2
they are never **a** to understand 2Ti 3:7
which are **a** to make you wise. 2Ti 3:15
he is **a** to be gentle with those .... Heb 5:2
he was **a** to give eternal .... Heb 5:9
So he is **a** always to save those .... Heb 7:25
Abraham was made **a** to become **a**........... Heb 11:11
perfect and **a** to control their .... Jam 3:2
so you will be **a** to pray. 1Pe 4:7
They are not **a** to go on sinning,.............. 1Jn 3:9
so that he is **a** to open the .... Rev 5:5

ABNER

of his army was **A** son of Ner, ... 1Sa 14:50
Goliath, Saul asked **A,** commander 1Sa 17:55
killing Goliath, **A** brought him 1Sa 17:57
saw where Saul and **A** son of Ner, ... 1Sa 26:5
A stabbed Asahel in the stomach, ... 2Sa 2:23
his brother Abishai killed **A,** 2Sa 3:30

ABNER'S

all the people cried at **A** grave. 2Sa 3:32
buried it in **A** tomb at Hebron. 2Sa 4:12

ABOARD

paid for the trip and went **a,** .... Jnh 1:3
took him **a** and went to Mitylene. .... Ac 20:14
so we went **a** and sailed away. .... Ac 21:2

ABRAHAM

name from Abram to **A** because I .... Ge 17:5
Then **A** gathered Ishmael, all the .... Ge 17:23
A was ninety-nine years old when .... Ge 17:24
A hurried to the tent where .... Ge 18:6
A and Sarah were very old. .... Ge 18:11
Should I tell **A** what I am going .... Ge 18:17
give **A** what I promised him."................. Ge 18:19
A stood there before the LORD. .... Ge 18:22
the LORD finished speaking to **A,** .... Ge 18:33
he left, and **A** returned home. .... Ge 18:33
he remembered what **A** had asked. .... Ge 19:29
A left Hebron and traveled to .... Ge 20:1
Then **A** prayed to God, and God.............. Ge 20:17
A named his son Isaac, the son .... Ge 21:3
A was one hundred years old when .... Ge 21:5
was the son of **A** by Hagar,.................. Ge 21:9
And **A** lived as a stranger in the.............. Ge 21:34
God said to him, "**A!**" .... Ge 22:1
On the third day **A** looked up and .... Ge 22:4
A answered, "God will give us .... Ge 22:8
Then **A** took his knife and was .... Ge 22:10
to him from heaven and said, "**A!** .... Ge 22:11
So **A** went and took the sheep and.............. Ge 22:13
So **A** named that place The LORD .... Ge 22:14
A was very sad and cried because .... Ge 23:2
A buried his wife Sarah in the .... Ge 23:19
So **A** bought the field and the.................. Ge 23:20
A was now very old, and the LORD .... Ge 24:1
A married again, and his new.................. Ge 25:1
A left everything he owned to.................. Ge 25:5
A lived to be one hundred .... Ge 25:7
So **A** was buried with his wife .... Ge 25:10
A had a son named Isaac. .... Ge 25:19
because your father **A** obeyed me. .... Ge 26:5
I am the God of your father **A.** .... Ge 26:24
blessing of **A** so that you may.................. Ge 28:4
the land God gave to **A.**........................ Ge 28:4
Let the God of **A,** who is the God .... Ge 31:53
A and Sarah his wife are buried............... Ge 49:31
to the land he promised to **A,** .... Ge 50:24
agreement he had made with **A,**.............. Ex 2:24
the God of **A,** the God of Isaac, ... Ex 3:6
appeared to **A,** Isaac, and Jacob .... Ex 6:3
who served you—**A,** Isaac, and .... Ex 32:13
my agreement with **A,** and I will .... Le 26:42
the land that I promised to **A,**................. Nu 32:11
your ancestors—**A,** Isaac, and .... Dt 1:8
your servants **A,** Isaac, and...................... Dt 9:27
the father of **A** and Nahor, ... Jos 24:2
are the God of **A,** Isaac, and 1Ki 18:36
because of his agreement with **A,** 2Ki 13:23
made with **A** and the promise he 1Ch 16:16
descendants of your friend **A.**.................. 2Ch 20:7
Ur in Babylonia and named him **A.** .... Ne 9:7
with the people of the God of **A,**.............. Ps 47:9
descendants of his servant **A,**.................. Ps 105:6
the LORD who set **A** free says to .... Is 29:22
from the family of my friend **A.** .... Is 41:8
Look at **A,** your ancestor, and.................. Is 51:2
'**A** was only one person, yet he .... Eze 33:24
the people of **A** as you promised .... Mic 7:20
David came from the family of **A.** .... Mt 1:1
yourselves, '**A** is our father.' .... Mt 3:9
children for **A** from these rocks................ Mt 3:9
and will sit and eat with **A,**...................... Mt 8:11
I am the God of **A,** the God of .... Mt 22:32
Isaac was the son of **A.** .... Lk 3:34

teeth with pain when you see **A**,.............. Lk 13:28
The rich man saw **A** far away with.......... Lk 16:23
answered, "Our father is **A**." .... Jn 8:39
father **A** was very happy that .... Jn 8:56
truth, before **A** was even born, I .... Jn 8:58
The God of **A**, Isaac, and Jacob, ... Ac 3:13
Our glorious God appeared to **A**, ... Ac 7:2
God said to **A**, 'Leave your .... Ac 7:3
the family of **A**, and others who .... Ac 13:26
So what can we say that **A**,.................... Rm 4:1
Scripture says, "**A** believed God, ... Rm 4:3
lives with faith like that of **A**, ... Rm 4:16
are true children of **A**............................ Rm 9:7
Israelite from the family of **A**, ... Rm 11:1
A believed God, and God accepted............ Gal 3:6
true children of **A** are those who .... Gal 3:7
News was told to **A** beforehand,.............. Gal 3:8
are blessed just as **A** was. .... Gal 3:9
promises both to **A** and to his.................. Gal 3:16
his blessings to **A** through the .... Gal 3:18
of the promise God made to **A**. .... Gal 3:29
say that **A** had two sons........................ Gal 4:22
but the people who are from **A**. .... Heb 2:16
God made a promise to **A**. .... Heb 6:13
Abraham when **A** was coming back .... Heb 7:1
they met, Melchizedek blessed **A**, ... Heb 7:1
and **A** gave him a tenth of .... Heb 7:2
paid it when **A** paid Melchizedek .... Heb 7:9
It was by faith **A** obeyed God's .... Heb 11:8
by faith that **A**, when God tested .... Heb 11:17
God made the promises to **A**, ... Heb 11:17
A, our ancestor, was made right .... Jam 2:21
A believed God, and God accepted............ Jam 2:23
Sarah obeyed **A**, her husband, and............ 1Pe 3:6

ABRAHAM'S

for taking **A** wife Sarah. .... Ge 20:18
He said, "I am **A** servant. .... Ge 24:34
history of Ishmael, **A** son. .... Ge 25:12
A sons were Isaac and Ishmael. 1Ch 1:28
We are **A** children, and we .... Jn 8:33
God accepted **A** faith and that .... Rm 4:9
Then all of **A** children can have .... Rm 4:16
A true children are those who .... Rm 9:8
so you are **A** descendants. .... Gal 3:29
God accepted **A** faith, and that .... Jam 2:23

ABRAM

old, his sons **A**, Nahor, and.................... Ge 11:26
Terah was the father of **A**, ... Ge 11:27
took his son **A**, his grandson Lot .... Ge 11:31
The LORD said to **A**, "Leave your .... Ge 12:1
At this time **A** was 75 years old.............. Ge 12:4
The LORD appeared to **A** and said, ... Ge 12:7
so **A** went down to Egypt to live.............. Ge 12:10
A was very rich in cattle, ... Ge 13:2
all made an agreement to help **A**. .... Ge 14:13
and blessed **A**, saying, "Abram, ... Ge 14:19
Then **A** gave Melchizedek a tenth .... Ge 14:20
The king of Sodom said to **A**, ... Ge 14:21
a vision: "**A**, don't be afraid. .... Ge 15:1
was going down, **A** fell into a .... Ge 15:12
an agreement with **A** and said, ... Ge 15:18
A did what Sarai said.............................. Ge 16:2
A was eighty-six years old when .... Ge 16:16
A was ninety-nine years old, ... Ge 17:1
your name from **A** to Abraham .... Ge 17:5
and **A**, who was called Abraham. 1Ch 1:27
God who chose **A** and brought him .... Ne 9:7

ABRAM'S

A wife was named Sarai, and.................. Ge 11:29
A nephew who was living in Sodom, ... Ge 14:12

ABSALOM

third son was **A**, whose mother 2Sa 3:3
a son named **A** and a son named 2Sa 13:1
A did not say a word, good or 2Sa 13:22
men killed Amnon as **A** commanded,........ 2Sa 13:29
A has killed all of the king's 2Sa 13:30
King David missed **A** very much. 2Sa 14:1
A was greatly praised for his 2Sa 14:25
A had three sons and one 2Sa 14:27
A stole the hearts of all Israel. 2Sa 15:6
'**A** is the king at Hebron!'" 2Sa 15:10
suggested to **A** and the elders................ 2Sa 17:15
A had made Amasa captain of the 2Sa 17:25
A was riding his mule, it went 2Sa 18:9
"I saw **A** hanging in an oak tree!" 2Sa 18:10

ABSALOM'S

So **A** servants set fire to 2Sa 14:30
A head got caught in the tree, ... 2Sa 18:9
Joab's men took **A** body and threw 2Sa 18:17
and it is called **A** Monument even 2Sa 18:18

ABSENT

Though I am **a** from you in my .... Col 2:5

ABUSE

evil people **a** women who cannot .... Job 24:21
not **a** poor people because they .... Pr 22:22
idols, or **a** others with words 1Co 5:11

ABUSED

mistreated and **a** all your life.................. Dt 28:33
and they **a** her all night long. .... Jdg 19:25
They are **a**, because there is no .... Zch 10:2
They were poor, **a**, and treated .... Heb 11:37
on as he did when we are **a**. .... Heb 13:13

ACACIA

dyed red; fine leather; **a** wood; .... Ex 25:5
Use a wood and build an Ark.................... Ex 25:10
on four posts of **a** wood that are.............. Ex 26:32
Make an altar of **a** wood, four .... Ex 27:1
Israel were still camped at **A**,.................. Nu 25:1
desert—cedars, **a**, myrtle, and................ Is 41:19
water to the valley of **a** trees. .... Joe 3:18

ACCEPT

but he did not **a** Cain and his .... Ge 4:5
well, I will **a** you, but if you .... Ge 4:7
I beg you to **a** the gift I give .... Ge 33:11
You must not **a** money from a.................. Ex 23:8
so the LORD will **a** the gifts .... Ex 28:38
and the LORD will **a** it to remove .... Le 1:4
they did and **a** punishment for .... Le 26:41
I will **a** your offering just as .... Nu 18:27
If they **a** your offer and open .... Dt 20:11
with me, let him **a** an offering. 1Sa 26:19
a my willing praise and teach me .... Ps 119:108
child, listen and **a** what I say. .... Pr 4:10
to advice and **a** correction, ... Pr 19:20
The LORD will not **a** me with his .... Is 56:3
So now the LORD will not **a** them............ Je 14:10
to me, I will not **a** them. .... Je 14:12
There I will **a** you. There I will .... Eze 20:40
Then I will **a** you, says the Lord .... Eze 43:27
wouldn't **a** you," says the LORD................ Mal 1:8
you and will not **a** your gifts," .... Mal 1:10
the LORD will **a** the offerings .... Mal 3:4
everyone can **a** this teaching, ... Mt 19:11
can marry should **a** this teaching .... Mt 19:12
They hear the teaching and **a** it................ Mk 4:20
you must **a** the kingdom of God as............ Mk 10:15
me refuses to **a** the One who sent .... Lk 10:16
you must **a** the kingdom of God as............ Lk 18:17
to all who did **a** him and believe.............. Jn 1:12
to me, and I will always **a** them................ Jn 6:37
because you don't **a** my teaching. .... Jn 8:37

ACCEPTED

in me and do not **a** my words. ....Jn 12:48
world cannot a him, because it ....Jn 14:17
they would not a Paul's teaching ....Ac 18:6
will not a the truth about me...................Ac 22:18
God will a us also because we ....Rm 4:24
people who a God's full grace.................Rm 5:17
So they did not a God's way of ....Rm 10:3
God again, he will a them back. ....Rm 11:23
Jews refuse to a the Good News, ...Rm 11:28
so you should a each other, ...Rm 15:7
be an offering that God would a— ....Rm 15:16
This helps you to a patiently 2Co 1:6
A God's salvation as your helmet, ...Eph 6:17
and you should fully a it: 1Ti 1:15
true, and you should fully a it. 1Ti 4:9
So I patiently a all these 2Ti 2:10
at all times, a troubles, do the................2Ti 4:5
it but did not a it with faith. ....Heb 4:2
and refused to a their freedom ....Heb 11:35
important that we a discipline ....Heb 12:9
in gentleness a God's teaching ....Jam 1:21
He will a those sacrifices 1Pe 2:5
and we do not a God's teaching..............1Jn 1:10
who does not a Jesus as the 1Jn 2:22

ACCEPTED

The LORD a Abel and his gift, ...Ge 4:4
And the LORD a Abram's faith, ...Ge 15:6
a goat—so it might be a for him. ....Le 22:19
with it, so that it will be a. ....Le 22:21
Then David a Abigail's gifts. 1Sa 25:35
David's sons a Solomon as king..............1Ch 29:24
burnt offerings will not be a; ....Je 6:20
prophet is not a in his hometown ....Lk 4:24
people who a what Peter said ....Ac 2:41
But Barnabas a Saul and took him...........Ac 9:27
and God a Abraham's faith, ...Rm 4:3
all the Jews a the good news. ....Rm 10:16
Christ a you, so you should ....Rm 15:7
to give, your gift will be a. 2Co 8:12
have already a the Good News. ....Gal 1:9
you a it as the word of God, ...1Th 2:13
But he a the shame as if it were ....Heb 12:2
and God a Abraham's faith, ...Jam 2:23

ACCEPTING

in a many hard things, in 2Co 6:4
patient, a each other in love. ....Eph 4:2

ACCEPTS

who loves learning a correction,..............Pr 12:1
but anyone who a correction is ....Pr 15:5
Whoever a you also accepts me,...............Mt 10:40
Whoever a a child in my name ....Mt 18:5
And whoever a me accepts the One ....Mk 9:37
little child in my name a me. ....Lk 9:48
Whoever a what he says has ....Jn 3:33
belongs to God a what God says. ....Jn 8:47
accepts anyone I send also a me. ....Jn 13:20
every country God a anyone who ....Ac 10:35
Then God a their faith, and that ....Rm 4:5
So when God a the Jews, surely ....Rm 11:15
Love patiently a all things. 1Co 13:7
who a that sacrifice and is ....Php 4:18
Religion that God a as pure and..............Jam 1:27

ACCIDENT

who caused the a must pay money— ....Ex 21:22
a person sins by a and does some ....Le 4:2

ACCIDENTALLY

But if a person kills someone a, ...Ex 21:13
If a person a sins and does ....Le 5:15
is for everyone who sins a— ....Nu 15:29
a person who a kills someone may...........Nu 35:11
killed someone a was to be....................Jos 20:9

ACCO

Canaanites from the cities of A, ...Jdg 1:31
Don't cry in A. Roll in the dust ....Mic 1:10

ACCOMPLISH

He will a my salvation and 2Sa 23:5
having fun doesn't a anything. ....Ec 2:2

ACCOMPLISHES

Moab's bragging a nothing. ....Je 48:30

ACCOUNT

David a complete a of the war. 2Sa 11:18
is the a of the forced labor 1Ki 9:15
in your faith on a of me, ...Mt 26:31
do all this to you on a of me, ...Jn 15:21

ACCUSE

do you a God of not answering ....Job 33:13
Let those who a me be disgraced ....Ps 109:29
don't a someone who has not ....Pr 3:30
I will not a forever, nor will I ....Is 57:16
the LORD will a all the nations. ....Je 25:31
find reasons to a Daniel about ....Da 6:4
people, and he will a Israel." ....Mic 6:2
by Joshua's right side to a him. ....Zch 3:1
looking for a reason to a Jesus, ...Mt 12:10
Sabbath day so they could a him. ....Lk 6:7
They began to a Jesus, saying, ...Lk 23:2
and Tertullus began to a him, ...Ac 24:2
who wanted to a Paul to come to ....Ac 24:8
They can a the man there in ....Ac 25:5

ACCUSED

a us of spying on his country, ...Ge 42:30
the men who had a Daniel be..................Da 6:24
priests and the elders a Jesus, ...Mt 27:12
leading priests a Jesus of many ....Mk 15:3
manager was a of cheating him................Lk 16:1
'When a man is a of a crime, ...Ac 25:16
they have a me because I hope ....Ac 26:7
who a them day and night before ....Rev 12:10

ACCUSER

and let an a stand against him. ....Ps 109:6
The a of our brothers and ....Rev 12:10

ACCUSERS

to face his a and defend himself..............Ac 25:16

ACCUSING

learn why the Jews were a Paul................Ac 22:30
to know why they were a him, ...Ac 23:28
Those who are a me did not find ....Ac 24:12

ACCUSTOMED

because you are a to doing evil. ....Je 13:23

ACHAICUS

Fortunatus, and A have come. 1Co 16:17

ACHAN

from the tribe of Judah named A. ....Jos 7:1
A answered, "It is true! ....Jos 7:20
threw stones at A and his family ....Jos 7:25
Remember how A son of Zerah ....Jos 22:20
Carmi's son was A, who caused 1Ch 2:7

ACHAN'S

They piled rocks over A body, ...Jos 7:26

ACHE

me, LORD, because my bones a................Ps 6:2
Stomachs a, and everyone's face ....Nah 2:10

ACHIEVEMENTS

about your a and wisdom is true 1Ki 10:6
about your a and wisdom is true 2Ch 9:5

ACHISH

Saul and went to A king of Gath. 1Sa 21:10
made their home in Gath with A. 1Sa 27:3
That day A gave David the town 1Sa 27:6

So A called David and said to................. 1Sa 29:6
ran away to A king of Gath, ... 1Ki 2:39

ACHOR
the Valley of A to Debir where .... Jos 15:7
the Valley of A will be a place .... Is 65:10

ACRE
over a half a of ground. 1Sa 14:14

ACROSS
who spread a the earth after .... Ge 10:32
It blew a the land all that day .... Ex 10:13
to face each other a the lid. .... Ex 25:20
Jordan River, a from Jericho. .... Nu 31:12
lead the people a the river and .... Dt 3:28
you will soon go a and take that.............. Dt 4:22
God will lead you a himself. .... Dt 31:3
of Mount Pisgah, a from Jericho. .... Dt 34:1
these people go a the Jordan .... Jos 1:2
Israel walked a the Jordan River .... Jos 3:17
Gilgal is a from the road that .... Jos 15:7
those who lived a the Jordan 1Sa 31:7
The people went a the Jordan to.............. 2Sa 19:18
placing gold chains a the front 1Ki 6:21
was six feet a and could hold 1Ki 7:38
They saw the water a from them, ... 2Ki 3:22
wings were thirty feet a. 2Ch 3:13
which is a from the Inspection .... Ne 3:31
Who stretched a ruler a it? .... Job 38:5
comes jumping a the mountains, ... Sng 2:8
people can walk a them with .... Is 11:15
land sends messengers a the sea; .... Is 18:2
the nations a the seas will be .... Is 60:5
on the shore a from the island. .... Eze 26:8
up to a place a from Lebo Hamath .... Eze 47:20
just to walk a it took a person .... Jnh 3:3
look back and forth a the earth.............. Zch 4:10
and go ahead of him a the lake. .... Mt 14:22
travel a land and sea to find .... Mt 23:15
from the lands a the Jordan .... Mk 3:8
"Let's go a the lake." .... Mk 4:35
to them, "Let's go a the lake." .... Lk 8:22
which flashes a the sky and .... Lk 17:24
a boat and started a the lake to .... Jn 6:17
his followers a the Kidron .... Jn 18:1
They went a the whole island to............. Ac 13:6
Satan's army marched a the earth .... Rev 20:9

ACSAH
I will give A, my daughter, as .... Jdg 1:12

ACSHAPH
Shimron, and to the king of A. .... Jos 11:1

ACT
he did not complete the sex a. .... Ge 38:9
don't a as if one person is more .... Dt 1:17
This a of kindness is greater .... Ru 3:10
careful how I a and will not sin .... Ps 39:1
are careless and quick to a. .... Pr 14:16
but those who a too quickly .... Pr 21:5
People who a with stubborn pride .... Pr 21:24
it is crazy to a like a fool. .... Ec 7:25
They a just like a nation that .... Is 58:2
rust. They all a dishonestly. .... Je 6:28
LORD, have spoken, and I will a. .... Eze 22:14
am going to a, but not for your .... Eze 36:22
In court they will a as judges................. Eze 44:24
Israel, you a like a prostitute, ... Hos 4:15
they a like this now when life .... Lk 23:31
one good a that Christ did makes .... Rm 5:18
must think and a like Christ .... Php 2:5
why do you a as if you still .... Col 2:20
in the way you a with people who .... Col 4:5
and will a as if they serve God 2Ti 3:5
animals that a without thinking 2Pe 2:12

ACTED
but he a as if he didn't know .... Ge 42:7
because you both a against my .... Nu 20:24
he a like a madman and clawed on 1Sa 21:13
the king of Israel a today! 2Sa 6:20
So Amnon went to bed and a sick........... 2Sa 13:6
Rehoboam a wisely. He spread his.......... 2Ch 11:23
But you have a like a prostitute .... Je 3:1
Their mother has a like a .... Hos 2:5
some spies who a as if they were .... Lk 20:20
and Jesus a as if he were going .... Lk 24:28
in the group a as though their .... Ac 4:32

ACTING
guilty of a like a prostitute,.................. Ge 38:24
that the people were a wildly................. Ex 32:25
that she was a like a prostitute .... Je 3:9
a like very important people. .... Ac 25:23
are a like people of the world. 1Co 3:3
you are a like people of the 1Co 3:4

ACTION
for every thing and every a, ... Ec 3:17
By your sinful a you have become .... Eze 24:13
will take a and then return to .... Da 11:28
Every good a and every perfect .... Jam 1:17

ACTIONS
have heard about the queen's a. .... Est 1:18
gives them what their a deserve. .... Job 34:11
Stop those wicked a done by evil .... Ps 7:9
thoughts, and evil a are sin. .... Pr 21:4
sins and for a that I hate, ... Eze 16:58
judge you by your ways and a, ... Eze 24:14
'Stop your evil ways and evil a.' .... Zch 1:4
greed, evil a, lying, doing .... Mk 7:22
judge his own a and not compare .... Gal 6:4
words, your a, your love, your 1Ti 4:12
but their a show they do not .... Tit 1:16
but by our a and true caring. 1Jn 3:18
their own shameful a like foam............... Jud 1:13

ACTIVELY
the Father too is a seeking such .... Jn 4:23

ACTS
perform the a to remove that .... Le 5:6
it to perform the a that remove .... Le 16:10
They will retell your mighty a, ... Ps 145:4
wise person a with good sense, ... Pr 13:16
your a of adultery and your .... Je 13:27
your hateful a and sexual sins .... Eze 16:22
doing good deeds and kind a.................. Ac 9:36
are proud of their shameful a, ... Php 3:19
from those a that lead to death. .... Heb 6:1
about the wonderful a of God, ... 1Pe 2:9

ACTUALLY
But a, those who explain the .... Je 8:8
mountain that you a worship the .... Jn 4:21
It is a being said that there is 1Co 5:1

ADAH
married two women, A and Zillah............. Ge 4:19
Esau's grandsons by his wife A............... Ge 36:12

ADAIAH
name was Jedidah daughter of A, ... 2Ki 22:1
Also there was A son of Jeroham. .... Ne 11:12

ADAM
LORD God forced A out of the .... Ge 3:23
This is the family history of A. .... Ge 5:1
and image, and A named him Seth. .... Ge 5:3
So A lived a total of 930 years, ... Ge 5:5
the son of Adam. A was the son .... Lk 3:38
from the time of A to the time .... Rm 5:14
So as one sin of A brought the .... Rm 5:18
In A all of us die. In the same................. 1Co 15:22

ADAM'S

But the last A became a spirit................. 1Co 15:45
because A was formed first and 1Ti 2:13
the seventh descendant from A, ... Jud 1:14

ADAM'S

free gift is not like A sin. .... Rm 5:15

ADAR

of the month of A in the sixth................. Ezr 6:15
the twelfth month, which was A. .... Est 3:13
twelfth month, the month of A. .... Est 9:1

ADD

A salt to it to keep it pure and .... Ex 30:35
LORD, but do not a to it. .... Le 10:12
Don't a to these commands, ...Dt 4:2
I will a fifteen years to your 2Ki 20:6
will a years to your life. .... Pr 9:11
People cannot a anything to what .... Ec 3:14
I will a fifteen years to your .... Is 38:5
You cannot a any time to your .... Mt 6:27
You cannot a any time to your .... Lk 12:25
to your faith, a goodness; 2Pe 1:5
patience, a service for God; 2Pe 1:6
God will a to that person the .... Rev 22:18

ADDAR

go to Hazar A and over to Azmon............. Nu 34:4
and continued past Hezron to A. .... Jos 15:3

ADDED

The angel a, "You are now .... Ge 16:11
dough before the yeast was a. .... Ex 12:34
and he a greatly to the wall at 2Ch 27:3
I a all these things together to .... Ec 7:27
and rumor will be a to rumor............... Eze 7:26
day the Lord a those who were .... Ac 2:47
the Lord and were a to the group .... Ac 5:14

ADDITION

worship these gods in a to me. .... Ex 20:23
offerings are in a to those for .... Le 23:38
In a, the priest must sacrifice .... Nu 5:8
Do it in a to the daily burnt .... Nu 28:24
in Moab in a to the agreement he .... Dt 29:1
a to what he had already given 1Ki 10:13

ADDS

Job now a to his sin by turning .... Job 34:37
If anyone a anything to these .... Rev 22:18

ADMAH

Sodom, Gomorrah, A, Zeboiim, and .... Ge 14:8
to make you like A or treat you .... Hos 11:8

ADMIN

Amminadab was the son of A. .... Lk 3:33

ADMIRE

They will not a the sparkling .... Job 20:17

ADMIRED

brightness nor a the moon moving........... Job 31:26

ADMIT

maybe they will a they turned .... Le 26:40
and must a the wrong that has .... Nu 5:7
We a that we are guilty and none .... Ezr 9:15
you have to do is a your sin—................. Je 3:13

ADONI-BEZEK

There they found A, the ruler of.............. Jdg 1:5

ADONI-ZEDEK

At this time A king of Jerusalem .... Jos 10:1

ADONIJAH

fourth son was A, whose mother 2Sa 3:4
A was the son of King David and 1Ki 1:5
Why then has A become king?' 1Ki 1:13
A was also afraid of Solomon, ... 1Ki 1:50
if this doesn't cost A his life! 1Ki 2:23
fourth son was A, whose mother 1Ch 3:2

ADONIJAH'S

all of A guests were afraid,..................... 1Ki 1:49

ADONIKAM

the descendants of A—666;..................... Ezr 2:13

ADONIRAM

A was in charge of the men who 2Sa 20:24
A man named A was in charge. 1Ki 5:14
A was in charge of the forced................. 2Ch 10:18

ADOPTED

and she a the baby as her own .... Ex 2:10
who had been a by Mordecai,.................. Est 2:15
king's daughter a him and raised .... Ac 7:21

ADRAMMELECH

them to A and Anammelech, ... 2Ki 17:31
his sons A and Sharezer killed 2Ki 19:37

ADRIATIC

carried around in the A Sea. .... Ac 27:27

ADRIEL

her instead to A of Meholah. 1Sa 18:19

ADULLAM

Hirah from A went with him. .... Ge 38:12
and escaped to the cave of A................. 1Sa 22:1
at the rock by the cave near A. 1Ch 11:15

ADULTERY

You must not be guilty of a. .... Ex 20:14
You must not be guilty of a. ....Dt 5:18
by a woman who takes part in a. .... Pr 5:20
takes part in a may cost you .... Pr 6:26
and those who take part in a!.................. Is 57:3
unclean and was guilty of a, ... Je 3:9
They are guilty of a and murder. .... Eze 23:37
stealing and a are everywhere. .... Hos 4:2
'You must not be guilty of a.' .... Mt 5:27
divorced woman is guilty of a. .... Mt 5:32
is guilty of a against her.......................... Mk 10:11
woman is also guilty of a." .... Lk 16:18
woman who had been caught in a........... Jn 8:3
the law says she is guilty of a. .... Rm 7:3
You must not be guilty of a. .... Rm 13:9
take part in a but you murder................. Jam 2:11
who take part in a with her will .... Rev 2:22
the wine of the anger of her a." .... Rev 14:8

ADULTS

all the a and little children .... Is 22:24
thinking you should be like a. 1Co 14:20

ADUMMIM

road that goes through A Pass, ... Jos 15:7

ADVANCE

God planned in a for us to live .... Eph 2:10
in a about the sufferings....................... 1Pe 1:11

ADVICE

and I will give you some a....................... Ex 18:19
or fortune-tellers for a, ... Le 19:31
followed Balaam's a and turned .... Nu 31:16
make Ahithophel's a foolish."................... 2Sa 15:31
But Rehoboam rejected this a. 1Ki 12:8
King Jeroboam asked for a. 1Ki 12:28
and he got a from mediums and 2Ki 21:6
to a medium and asked her for a 1Ch 10:13
rejected the a of the elders..................... 2Ch 10:13
their bad a led to his death. 2Ch 22:4
He got a from mediums and 2Ch 33:6
the king to ask for a from experts .... Est 1:13
and power, good a and .... Job 12:13
and waited quietly for my a. .... Job 29:21
way and follow their own a. .... Ps 81:12
had refused the a of God Most .... Ps 107:11
pleasure; they give me good a. .... Ps 119:24
do not forget your mother's a. .... Pr 1:8

ADVISE

right, but the wise listen to **a**. .... Pr 12:15
children take their parents' **a**, ... Pr 13:1
but those who take a are wise. .... Pr 13:10
Plans fail without good **a**, ... Pr 15:22
a that can succeed against the .... Pr 21:30
and so is good **a** from a friend. .... Pr 27:9
king who doesn't listen to **a**. .... Ec 4:13
heard, so I give my final **a**: .... Ec 12:13
They will ask **a** from their idols .... Is 19:3
gives wonderful **a**, who is very .... Is 28:29
and don't ask the LORD for **a**. .... Je 10:21
still have the **a** from the wise .... Je 18:18
priest and the **a** from the elders .... Eze 7:26
So, O king, please accept my **a**. .... Da 4:27
people ask wooden idols for **a**; .... Hos 4:12
has been able to give him **a**?" .... Rm 11:34

ADVISE

and those who **a** him have given .... Ezr 7:15
the wise men who **a** the king of .... Is 19:11
those sticks of wood to **a** them! .... Hos 4:12
I **a** you to buy from me gold made .... Rev 3:18

ADVISED

one of the people who **a** David, ... 2Sa 15:12
elders who had **a** Solomon during 1Ki 12:6
elders who had **a** Solomon during 2Ch 10:6
seven people who **a** the king, ... Je 52:25
people who **a** the king, keepers .... Da 3:2

ADVISER

was a priest and **a** to the king; 1Ki 4:5

ADVISES

praise the LORD because he **a** me. .... Ps 16:7

AENEAS

There he met a man named **A**, ... Ac 9:33

AENON

John was also baptizing in **A**, ... Jn 3:23

AFFECTS

A lazy person **a** the one he works .... Pr 10:26

AFFORD

He can **a** to use wine to wash his .... Ge 49:11
if the person cannot **a** a lamb, ... Le 5:7
young pigeons, which he can **a**. .... Le 14:22
making the vow can **a** to pay. .... Le 27:8
and even more than they could **a**. 2Co 8:3

AFRAID

and I was **a** because I was naked, ... Ge 3:10
Abram, don't be **a**. I will defend .... Ge 15:1
Sarah was **a**, so she lied and .... Ge 18:15
in the dream. They were very **a**. .... Ge 20:8
Hagar? Don't be **a**! God has heard .... Ge 21:17
I was **a** you would kill me so you .... Ge 26:9
Jacob was very **a** and worried. .... Ge 32:7
she said, "Don't be **a**, Rachel. .... Ge 35:17
father saw it, they were **a**. .... Ge 42:35
said to them, "Don't be **a**. .... Ge 50:19
because he was **a** to look at God. .... Ex 3:6
But Moses answered, "Don't be **a**! .... Ex 14:13
Don't be **a** of the people in that .... Nu 14:9
so don't be **a** and don't worry." .... Dt 1:21
spies we sent made us **a**, ... Dt 1:28
Don't be **a** of them, because the .... Dt 3:22
Don't be **a** of them, because the .... Dt 7:21
I was **a** of the LORD's anger and .... Dt 9:19
Don't lose your courage or be **a**. .... Dt 20:3
Your enemies will be **a** of you, ... Dt 33:29
Don't be **a**, because the LORD .... Jos 1:9
down! Don't be **a**! You will not .... Jdg 6:23
So Saul was **a** of David. 1Sa 18:12
all of Adonijah's guests were **a**, ... 1Ki 1:49
he was **a** and ran for his life, ... 1Ki 19:3
Elisha said, "Don't be **a**. 2Ki 6:16

'Don't be **a** of what you have 2Ki 19:6
LORD made all nations **a** of him. 1Ch 14:17
because he was **a** of the angel of 1Ch 21:30
Don't be **a** or discouraged, ... 1Ch 28:20
'Don't be **a** or discouraged ..:........... 2Ch 20:15
Don't be **a** of them. Remember .... Ne 4:14
because they were **a** of Mordecai. .... Est 9:3
you will not be **a** when .... Job 5:21
God has made me **a**; the Almighty .... Job 23:16
may surround me, but I am not **a**. .... Ps 3:6
I will not be **a**, because you are .... Ps 23:4
So why should I be **a**? .... Ps 27:1
surrounds me, I will not be **a**. .... Ps 27:3
be **a** of rich people because .... Ps 49:16
I trust God, so I am not **a**. .... Ps 56:4
when I think, I become **a**. .... Ps 77:3
You will not be **a** of diseases .... Ps 91:6
the Egyptians were **a** of them. .... Ps 105:38
will not be **a**, because the LORD .... Ps 118:6
When I am **a**, you, LORD, know the .... Ps 142:3
you lie down, you won't be **a**; .... Pr 3:24
they are **a** to say anything. .... Pr 29:24
and will be **a** to go for a walk. .... Ec 12:5
Don't be **a** of their anger or .... Is 7:4
I will trust him and not be **a**. .... Is 12:2
Everyone will be **a**. Pain and .... Is 13:8
They will be **a** of the LORD .... Is 19:16
Don't be **a**. Look, your God .... Is 35:4
Shout it out and don't be **a**. .... Is 40:9
Don't be **a**, because I am your .... Is 41:10
Don't be **a**, because I am with .... Is 43:5
Don't be **a** of the evil things .... Is 51:7
Surely you are **a** of me," says .... Je 5:22
I am very sad and when I am **a**. .... Je 8:18
It is not **a** when the days are .... Je 17:8
will not be **a** or terrified again .... Je 23:4
Do not be **a** to serve the .... Je 40:9
Babylon, but don't be **a** of him. .... Je 42:11
Jacob, my servants, don't be **a**; .... Je 46:27
poisonous insects, don't be **a**. .... Eze 2:6
Their kings are terribly **a**, ... Eze 27:35
king will be **a** for his own life .... Eze 32:10
land with no one to make them **a**. .... Eze 39:26
I had a dream that made me **a**. .... Da 4:5
I, Daniel, was very **a**. .... Da 7:28
Who wouldn't be **a**? The Lord GOD .... Am 3:8
The sailors were **a**, and each man .... Jnh 1:5
and cubs go without being **a**? .... Nah 2:11
you must be **a** because of what .... Hab 2:17
again be **a** of being harmed. .... Zph 3:15
still with you. So don't be **a**.' .... Hag 2:5
So don't be **a**; work hard." .... Zch 8:13
don't be **a** to take Mary as your .... Mt 1:20
Jesus answered, "Why are you **a**? .... Mt 8:26
don't be **a**. You are worth much .... Mt 10:31
courage! It is I. Do not be **a**." .... Mt 14:27
So I was **a** and went and hid your .... Mt 25:25
said to the women, "Don't be **a**. .... Mt 28:5
Jesus said to them, "Don't be **a**. .... Mt 28:10
synagogue leader, "Don't be **a**; .... Mk 5:36
because Herod was **a** of John and .... Mk 6:20
courage! It is I. Do not be **a**." .... Mk 6:50
the crowd who followed were **a**. .... Mk 10:32
They were **a** of him, because all .... Mk 11:18
You are not **a** of what other .... Mk 12:14
that are coming, don't be **a**. .... Mk 13:7
But the man said, "Don't be **a**. .... Mk 16:6
to him, "Zechariah, don't be **a**. .... Lk 1:13
said to her, "Don't be **a**, Mary; .... Lk 1:30
said to Simon, "Don't be **a**. .... Lk 5:10
The followers were **a** and amazed .... Lk 8:25
he said to Jairus, "Don't be **a**. .... Lk 8:50
But they were **a** to ask Jesus .... Lk 9:45

don't be a of people who can .... Lk 12:4
was a of you, because you are a .... Lk 19:21
riots, don't be a, because these .... Lk 21:9
nations will be a and confused .... Lk 21:25
were very a and bowed their .... Lk 24:5
the boat. The followers were a, ... Jn 6:19
they were a of the elders, ... Jn 9:22
Don't be a, people of Jerusalem! .... Jn 12:15
your hearts be troubled or a. .... Jn 14:27
because he was a of some of the .... Jn 19:38
and John were not a to speak, ... Ac 4:13
they were a the people would .... Ac 5:26
but they were all a of him. .... Ac 9:26
He became a and said, "What do .... Ac 10:4
Roman citizens, they were a. .... Ac 16:38
Don't be a. Continue talking .... Ac 18:9
Felix became a when Paul spoke .... Ac 24:25
The men were a that the ship .... Ac 27:17
But if you do wrong, then be a. .... Rm 13:4
am a that when I come, you will 2Co 12:20
from them. He was a of the Jews. .... Gal 2:12
They are a they will be attacked .... Gal 6:12
and are not a to speak the word .... Php 1:14
Encourage the people who are a. 1Th 5:14
thinking or a if you hear that 2Th 2:2
that makes us a but a spirit 2Ti 1:7
and they were not a to disobey .... Heb 11:23
will not be a, because the Lord .... Heb 13:6
do what is right and are not a. 1Pe 3:6
They are not a to speak against 2Pe 2:10
on me and said, "Do not be a. .... Rev 1:17
not be a of what you are about .... Rev 2:10
and were not a to speak my name .... Rev 3:8
who saw them became very a. .... Rev 11:11
much that they were a of death. .... Rev 12:11
her will be a of her suffering .... Rev 18:15

AFTERNOON

Wait until this a." .... Jdg 19:8
house in the a while he was 2Sa 4:5
The a passed, and the prophets 1Ki 18:29
Late in the a, the twelve .... Lk 9:12
until three o'clock in the a, ... Lk 23:44
was about four o'clock in the a. .... Jn 1:39
day for the a prayer service. .... Ac 3:1
One a about three o'clock, ... Ac 10:3
time—three o'clock in the a. .... Ac 10:30

AFTERWARDS

A I brought you out. .... Jos 24:5
Soon a Jesus went to a town .... Lk 7:11
But a, he thought to himself, '................ Lk 18:4

AGABUS

One of them, named A, stood up .... Ac 11:28
named A arrived from Judea. .... Ac 21:10

AGAG

king will be greater than A; .... Nu 24:7
He took King A of the Amalekites 1Sa 15:8
A came to Samuel in chains, ... 1Sa 15:32
And Samuel cut A to pieces 1Sa 15:33

AGAG'S

he killed all of A army with the 1Sa 15:8

AGAGITE

Haman son of Hammedatha the A. .... Est 3:1
Hammedatha, the A, was the enemy .... Est 9:24

AGATE

jacinth, an a, and an amethyst; .... Ex 28:19

AGE

and will be buried at an old a. .... Ge 15:15
Sarah was past the a when women .... Ge 18:11
a son for Abraham in his old a. .... Ge 21:2
At the a of fifty, they must .... Nu 8:25

Nun died at the a of one hundred .... Jos 24:29
at the a of one hundred ten. .... Jdg 2:8
in your old a because of your .... Ru 4:15
let him die peacefully of old a. 1Ki 2:6
than other young men your a, ... Da 1:10
carrying a cane because of a. .... Zch 8:4
time is the end of the a, ... Mt 13:39
when the a to come has arrived, ... Mt 19:28
even until the end of this a." .... Mt 28:20
in this a they will have life .... Mk 10:30
And in the a that is coming, ... Lk 18:30
much past the a for having .... Rm 4:19
past the best a to marry and he 1Co 7:36
than most other Jews of my a. .... Gal 1:14
children reach the a set by .... Gal 4:2

AGED

How is your a father you told me .... Ge 43:27
went in to see the a king in his 1Ki 1:15
a doors and the glorious King .... Ps 24:7

AGES

of him in order of their a, ... Ge 43:33
which stood for a, break into .... Hab 3:6
hidden for long a past but is .... Rm 16:25

AGREE

But we must a to one thing: .... Ge 34:22
"'The woman must say, "I a." .... Nu 5:22
He must a to give the older son .... Dt 21:17
Rahab answered, "I a to this." .... Jos 2:21
The men from Judah said, "We a. .... Jdg 15:13
said, "If you a to this, I will 1Ki 20:34
said, "If you a with this, don't 2Ki 9:15
I will never a you are right; .... Job 27:5
They will a that the Holy One of .... Is 29:23
you on earth a about something .... Mt 18:19
people did not a with each other .... Jn 7:43
they could not a with each other .... Jn 9:16
leaders did not a with each .... Jn 10:19
and your husband a to test the .... Ac 5:9
they are waiting for you to a." .... Ac 23:21
of the ship did not a with Paul, ... Ac 27:11
all of you a with each other 1Co 1:10
A with each other, and live in 2Co 13:11
makes everything a with what he .... Eph 1:11
teaching does not a with the 1Ti 6:3
and these three witnesses a. 1Jn 5:8

AGREED

Moses a to stay with Jethro, ... Ex 2:21
So Joshua a to make peace with .... Jos 9:15
Ben-Hadad a with King Asa, ... 1Ki 15:20
also a to make David king. 1Ch 12:38
Jehoshaphat a with Ahaziah to 2Ch 20:36
all the people a to stay seven 2Ch 30:23
the Jewish people a to do what .... Est 9:23
they a to free their male and .... Je 34:10
So the guard a to test them for .... Da 1:14
So John a to baptize Jesus .... Mt 3:15
The man a to pay the workers one .... Mt 20:2
You a to work for one coin. .... Mt 20:13
different things—none of them a. .... Mk 14:56
they all a that God's teaching .... Lk 7:29
knew about this and a to it. .... Ac 5:2
Saul a that the killing of .... Ac 8:1
We have all a to choose some .... Ac 15:25

AGREEING

I stood there a and holding the .... Ac 22:20
his purpose by a to give the .... Rev 17:17

AGREEMENT

But I will make an a with you— .... Ge 6:18
as the sign of the a between me .... Ge 9:13
LORD made an a with Abram and .... Ge 15:18
I will make an a between us, ... Ge 17:2

But I will make my **a** with Isaac, ... Ge 17:21
Let us make an **a**, and let us set .... Ge 31:44
remembered the **a** he had made .... Ex 2:24
if you obey me and keep my **a**, ... Ex 19:5
the Book of the **A** and read it so............... Ex 24:7
the Ark of the **A** containing the .... Ex 26:33
Sabbath day as an **a** between them .... Ex 31:16
don't make an **a** with the people............... Ex 34:12
tablets of the **A** in his hands. .... Ex 34:29
the Ark of the **A** in it and hang .... Ex 40:3
that had the **A** written on them .... Ex 40:20
I will keep my **a** with you. .... Le 26:9
I will remember my **a** with Jacob, ... Le 26:42
is a lasting **a** of salt before .... Nu 18:19
I am making my peace with him. .... Nu 25:12
He will keep his **a** of love for a .... Dt 7:9
Moses to make an **a** with the .... Dt 29:1
to enter into an **a** and a promise............... Dt 29:12
people broke the **A** of the LORD, ... Dt 29:25
the Ark of the **A** with the LORD............... Jos 3:3
had made a peace **a** with Israel .... Jos 10:1
'I will never break my **a** with you. .... Jdg 2:1
served before the Ark of the **A**. .... Jdg 20:28
Jonathan made an **a** with David, ... 1Sa 18:3
them made an **a** before the LORD 1Sa 23:18
God made a lasting **a** with me, ... 2Sa 23:5
Solomon made an **a** with the king 1Ki 3:1
have broken their **a** with you,.................. 1Ki 19:10
So the two kings made a peace **a**. 1Ki 20:34
made an **a** between the LORD 2Ki 11:17
not forget the **a** I made with you 2Ki 17:38
the Ark of the **A** was put there. 1Ch 6:31
He made an **a** with them in Hebron 1Ch 11:3
He will keep his **a** forever; 1Ch 16:15
This is the **a** I made with your 2Ch 7:18
Israel forever by an **a** of salt. 2Ch 13:5
Jerusalem obeyed the **a** of God, ... 2Ch 34:32
let us make an **a** before our God. .... Ezr 10:3
you keep your **a** with those who............... Ne 1:5
You keep your **a** of love. .... Ne 9:32
Will it make an **a** with you and .... Job 41:4
failed to keep our **a** with you.................. Ps 44:17
LORD made an **a** with Jacob and .... Ps 78:5
my **a** with him will never end. .... Ps 89:28
He will keep his **a** forever; .... Ps 105:8
He remembers his **a** forever. .... Ps 111:5
and the **a** with the LORD. .... Is 8:20
I will make an **a** with that .... Is 55:3
the Sabbath, and to keep my **a**. .... Is 56:6
I will make an **a** with them that .... Is 61:8
I commanded them to obey the **a**, ... Je 11:8
This is the **a** I will make with .... Je 31:33
cannot break the **a** ease. .... Eze 17:15
had made an **a** with Egypt will .... Eze 30:5
I will make an **a** of peace with .... Eze 34:25
You keep your **a** of love with all .... Da 9:4
make a peace **a** with the king.................. Da 11:17
have broken the **a** as Adam did; .... Hos 6:7
blood of the **a** with you I will .... Zch 9:11
respect for the **a** our ancestors .... Mal 2:10
is the new **a** that God makes .... Mt 26:28
is the new **a** that God makes .... Mk 14:24
This new **a** begins with my blood .... Lk 22:20
God made an **a** with Abraham, ... Ac 7:8
cup is the new **a** that is sealed 1Co 11:25
This new **a** is not a written law, ... 2Co 3:6
Even an **a** made between two .... Gal 3:15
God had an **a** with Abraham and .... Gal 3:17
And the new **a** is based on .... Heb 8:6
the stone tablets of the old **a**. .... Heb 9:4
blood of the **a** that made them .... Heb 10:29
all of you should be in **a**,...................... 1Pe 3:8

that holds the **a** God gave to his .... Rev 11:19
the Tent of the **A**) in heaven was .... Rev 15:5

AGREEMENTS
They make **a** with other nations, ... Is 30:1
sign and seal their **a** and call .... Je 32:44
will make **a** with that cruel .... Da 11:23
they make **a** with those who do .... Hos 7:5

AGREES
This **a** with the purpose God had .... Eph 3:11
for anything that **a** with what he 1Jn 5:14
and the truth **a** with what they 3Jn 1:12

AGRIPPA
days later King **A** and Bernice .... Ac 25:13
A said to Paul, "You may now .... Ac 26:1

AGUR
are the words of **A** son of Jakeh. .... Pr 30:1
Don't let them think, "**A**! .... Ps 35:25

AHAB
A son of Omri became king of 1Ki 16:29
Then **A** went to meet Elijah. 1Ki 18:16
King **A** told Jezebel every thing 1Ki 19:1
came to **A** king of Israel.......................... 1Ki 20:13
prophet said, "**A**, the LORD says 1Ki 20:13
the palace of **A** king of Israel................... 1Ki 21:1
One day **A** said to Naboth, ... 1Ki 21:2
Everything else **A** did is written 1Ki 22:39
Ahaziah son of **A** went to help 1Ki 22:49
Ahaziah son of **A** became king of 1Ki 22:51
After **A** died, Moab broke away 2Ki 1:1
Joram son of **A** became king over 2Ki 3:1
as the family of **A** had done, ... 2Ki 8:18
A had seventy sons in Samaria. 2Ki 10:1
who had helped **A** was left alive. 2Ki 10:11
and said to them, "**A** served Baal 2Ki 10:18
arrow which hit **A** king of Israel............... 2Ch 18:33
against God, as **A** and his family 2Ch 21:13
treat you like Zedekiah and **A**, ... Je 29:22

AHAB'S
All of **A** family must die.......................... 2Ki 9:8
appointed to destroy **A** family. 2Ch 22:7
the things that **A** family does;.................. Mic 6:16

AHAVA
the canal that flows toward **A**, ... Ezr 8:15

AHAZ
Then Jotham's son **A** became king............ 2Ki 15:38
A was the son of Jotham king of 2Ki 16:1
Then King **A** went to Damascus to 2Ki 16:10
A died and was buried with his 2Ki 16:20
Hezekiah son of **A** king of Judah 2Ki 18:1
the stairway of **A** that it had 2Ki 20:11
God handed over **A** to the king of 2Ch 28:5
The other things **A** did as king, ... 2Ch 28:26
Uzziah, Jotham, **A**, and Hezekiah .... Is 1:1
go and meet **A** at the place where .... Is 7:3
Then the LORD spoke to **A** again, ... Is 7:10
But **A** said, "I will not ask for.................. Is 7:12
in the year that King **A** died: .... Is 14:28
that Jotham, **A**, and Hezekiah .... Mic 1:1
A was the father of Hezekiah. .... Mt 1:9

AHAZ'S
and **A** son Hezekiah became king 2Ki 16:20
A son Hezekiah became king in 2Ch 28:27

AHAZIAH
and his son **A** became king in his 1Ki 22:40
A son of Ahab became king of 1Ki 22:51
A fell down through the wooden 2Ki 1:2
A son of Jehoram became king of 2Ki 8:25
A was twenty-two years old when 2Ki 8:26
A was wounded in his chariot on 2Ki 9:27

Joash son of **A** was king of Judah 2Ki 13:1
So **A** began to rule Judah. 2Ch 22:1
A was twenty-two years old when 2Ch 22:2
A did what the LORD said was 2Ch 22:4

AHAZIAH'S

became king in **A** place during 2Ki 1:17
A servants carried his body in a 2Ki 9:28
was Ahaziah. **A** son was Joash. 1Ch 3:11
God caused **A** death when he went 2Ch 22:7

AHEAD

master, you go on a of me, your .... Ge 33:14
sent me here a of you to save .... Ge 45:5
Jacob sent Judah a of him to see .... Ge 46:28
to Moses, "Go a of the people, ... Ex 17:5
I am sending an angel a of you, ... Ex 23:20
I am forcing out a of you the .... Le 20:23
the LORD went a again and stood .... Nu 22:26
God will go a of you and fight .... Dt 1:30
He will defeat them a of you, ... Dt 9:3
your God will destroy a of you. .... Dt 12:29
Jordan River a of your brothers .... Jos 1:14
and carried it a of the people.................. Jos 3:6
will push them out a of you. .... Jos 23:5
out the Amorites a of the people .... Jdg 11:23
he's here. He's a of you. Hurry 1Sa 9:12
Go a of me to Gilgal. 1Sa 10:8
have gone a of you to defeat 2Sa 5:24
him and ran a of King Ahab all 1Ki 18:46
Gehazi went on a and laid the 2Ki 4:31
God has hidden the road a.................... Job 3:23
days of suffering are a of me. .... Job 30:27
Then he sent a man a of them—.............. Ps 105:17
wise see danger a and avoid it, ... Pr 22:3
told us a of time so we could .... Is 41:26
They each went straight a. .... Eze 10:22
will send my messenger a of you, ... Mt 11:10
the boat and go a of him across .... Mt 14:22
will go a of you into Galilee." .... Mt 26:32
is going into Galilee a of you, ... Mt 28:7
will send my messenger a of you, ... Mk 1:2
the boat and go a of him to.................... Mk 6:45
were walking a of Jesus and .... Mk 11:9
don't worry a of time about what .... Mk 13:11
will send my messenger a of you, ... Lk 7:27
out in pairs a of him into every .... Lk 10:1
not to worry a of time about .... Lk 21:14
out, he goes a of them, and they.............. Jn 10:4
We went out a of Paul and sailed............. Ac 20:13
and straining toward what is a, ... Php 3:13
Jesus has gone a of us and for .... Heb 6:20

AHIJAH

A was a son of Ichabod's brother 1Sa 14:3
So Saul said to **A** the priest, ... 1Sa 14:18
Jerusalem, **A,** the prophet 1Ki 11:29
Jeroboam son of Nebat through **A,**........... 1Ki 12:15
Now **A** was very old and blind. 1Ki 14:4
his servant, the prophet **A.** 1Ki 14:18
Baasha son of **A,** from the tribe 1Ki 15:27
his servant **A** from Shiloh. 1Ki 15:29
Baasha son of **A** became king of 1Ki 15:33
the prophecy of **A** the Shilonite,............... 2Ch 9:29

AHIJAH'S

and went to **A** home in Shiloh. 1Ki 14:4

AHIKAM

the priest, **A** son of Shaphan, ... 2Ki 22:12
He appointed Gedaliah son of **A,** 2Ki 25:22
So **A** did not hand Jeremiah over .... Je 26:24
put Gedaliah son of **A** in charge.............. Je 40:7
up and killed Gedaliah son of **A,** .... Je 41:2

AHILUD

son of **A** was the recorder. 2Sa 8:16
Baana son of **A** was governor of 1Ki 4:12

AHIMAAZ

take your son **A** and Abiathar's 2Sa 15:27
A son of Zadok said to Joab, ... 2Sa 18:19
Then **A** ran by way of the Jordan 2Sa 18:23
A was the father of Azariah. 1Ch 6:9

AHIMAN

to Hebron, where **A,** Sheshai, and .... Nu 13:22

AHIMELECH

went to Nob to see **A** the priest. 1Sa 21:1
the king said, "**A,** you and all 1Sa 22:16
David asked **A** the Hittite and 1Sa 26:6
Abiathar son of **A** were priests. 1Ch 18:16
David, Zadok, **A,** the leaders 1Ch 24:31

AHIMELECH'S

and for all of **A** relatives who 1Sa 22:11
to him, "David is in **A** house." .... Ps 51:19

AHINOAM

Saul's wife was **A** daughter of 1Sa 14:50
also had married **A** of Jezreel. 1Sa 25:43
whose mother was **A** from Jezreel............ 1Ch 3:1

AHIO

Uzzah and **A,** sons of Abinadab, ... 2Sa 6:3
A was walking in front of it. 2Sa 6:4

AHISHAR

A was responsible for everything 1Ki 4:6

AHITHOPHEL

he sent for **A,** one of the people 2Sa 15:12
A is one of the people with 2Sa 15:31
Absalom said to **A,** "Tell us what 2Sa 16:20
good advice of **A** so the LORD 2Sa 17:14
A advised the king. 1Ch 27:33

AHITHOPHEL'S

you can make **A** advice useless. 2Sa 15:34

AHITUB

a son of Ichabod's brother **A.** 1Sa 14:3
Zadok son of **A** and Abiathar son 2Sa 8:17
A was the father of Zadok. 1Ch 6:8
A was the officer responsible 1Ch 9:11

AI

the west, and **A** was to the east .... Ge 12:8
before, between Bethel and **A,** .... Ge 13:3
sent some men from Jericho to **A,** .... Jos 7:2
"Go to **A** and spy out the area." .... Jos 7:2
three thousand men went up to **A,** .... Jos 7:4
The people of **A** killed about .... Jos 7:5
the city of **A** and made it a pile .... Jos 8:28
the king of **A** on a tree and left .... Jos 8:29
the town of **A** is destroyed!..................... Je 49:3

AIATH

of Assyria will enter near **A.** .... Is 10:28

AIDED

You have not a the weak! .... Job 26:2

AIJALON

still over the Valley of **A.**" .... Jos 10:12
in the city of **A** in the land .... Jdg 12:12

AIM

will string his bow and take a. .... Ps 7:12
backs when you a your arrows at .... Ps 21:12
dead with Christ, a at what is.................. Col 3:1

AIMS

but he a his bow well. His arms .... Ge 49:24

AIR

God made the a and placed some .... Ge 1:7
God named the a "sky." Evening .... Ge 1:8

Moses threw ashes into the **a**,................. Ex 9:10
the birds of the **a** and the wild 1Sa 17:44
or ask the birds of the **a**,....................... Job 12:7
wiser than the birds of the **a**?' .... Job 35:11
You will throw them into the **a**, ... Is 41:16
birds of the **a** and wild animals .... Je 15:3
the birds of the **a** and the fish................. Hos 4:3
Look at the birds in the **a**. .... Mt 6:26
something—not just the **a**. 1Co 9:26
You will be talking into the **a**!................. 1Co 14:9
to meet the Lord in the **a**. 1Th 4:17
high in the **a** cry out in a loud .... Rev 8:13
angel flying high in the **a**. .... Rev 14:6
poured out his bowl into the **a**. .... Rev 16:17

AKELDAMA
this so they named this place **A**............... Ac 1:19
In their language **A** means "Field .... Ac 1:19

AKIM
Zadok was the father of **A**...................... Mt 1:14
A was the father of Eliud. .... Mt 1:14

ALABASTER
him with an **a** jar filled with .... Mt 26:7
him with an **a** jar filled with .... Mk 14:3
she brought an **a** jar of perfume .... Lk 7:37

ALAMOTH
of music. By **a**. A psalm of the .... Ps 45:17

ALARM
the trumpets for giving the **a**. .... Nu 31:6

ALARMED
visions in my mind that **a** me.................. Da 4:5
All their neighbors became **a**,................. Lk 1:65

ALARMS
a day of **a** and battle cries. ' .... Zph 1:16

ALERT
Be **a**. Continue strong in the 1Co 16:13
praying, keeping **a**, and always .... Col 4:2
but we should be **a** and have 1Th 5:6

ALEXANDER
the father of **A** and Rufus, ... Mk 15:21
John, and **A** were there, as well .... Ac 4:6
They put a man named **A** in front .... Ac 19:33
when they saw that **A** was a Jew, ... Ac 19:34
Hymenaeus and **A** have done that,........... 1Ti 1:20
A the metalworker did many 2Ti 4:14

ALEXANDRIA
in the city of **A** and was a good .... Ac 18:24
a ship from **A** that was going to .... Ac 27:6

ALIVE
female. Keep them **a** with you. .... Ge 6:19
us, 'Is your father still **a**?.................... Ge 43:7
Joseph is still **a**, and I will go .... Ge 45:28
will be buried **a** and will go to .... Nu 16:30
all of us who are **a** here today. .... Dt 5:3
will always do well and stay **a**, ... Dt 6:24
leave nothing **a** in the cities .... Dt 20:16
one of the men of Ai was left **a**, ... Jos 8:22
none of the enemy was left **a**................... Jos 11:8
a man or woman **a** to Gath. 1Sa 27:11
to David while the baby was **a**, ... 2Sa 12:18
'My son is **a** and your son is dead. 1Ki 3:23
and said, "See! Your son is **a**!" 1Ki 17:23
In either case capture them **a**." 1Ki 20:18
Jehu did not leave anyone **a**. 2Ki 10:14
will come out of Jerusalem **a**;................. 2Ki 19:31
the Israelites who were left **a**,................. 2Ch 34:9
a few of us are left **a** today.................... Ezr 9:15
as long as I am **a** and God's .... Job 27:3
almost dead, you will keep me **a**. .... Ps 71:20
What person **a** will not die? .... Ps 89:48

they would have swallowed us **a**. .... Ps 124:3
swallow them **a**, as death does; .... Pr 1:12
But anyone still **a** has hope; .... Ec 9:4
people will be left **a** in Israel .... Is 10:20
will come out of Jerusalem **a**;................. Is 37:32
people of Israel who are left **a**. .... Is 49:6
left a few Jews **a** in the land. .... Je 40:11
you who are left **a** from Judah. .... Je 42:15
you escape **a** wherever you go. .... Je 44:5
leave a few people **a** from Israel .... Je 50:20
But I will leave some people **a**; .... Eze 6:8
who has been **a** forever, and he .... Da 7:13
on horses will not escape **a**. .... Am 2:15
those who escape **a** and turn them .... Ob 1:14
I will keep **a** those who were .... Mic 4:7
of your people who are left **a**................... Mic 7:18
who are left **a** will take .... Zph 2:9
who were left **a** obeyed the LORD .... Hag 1:12
that liar was still **a** he said, ' .... Mt 27:63
Mary told them that Jesus was **a**. .... Mk 16:11
which is a today but tomorrow is .... Lk 12:28
was dead, but now he is **a** again! .... Lk 15:24
was dead, but now he is **a**. .... Lk 15:32
who said that Jesus was **a**! .... Lk 24:23
and told him, "Your son is **a**."................. Jn 4:51
in many ways that he was **a**. .... Ac 1:3
man home **a** and were greatly .... Ac 20:12
Paul said that he is still **a**. .... Ac 25:19
You need it to stay **a**. .... Ac 27:34
of sin and **a** with God through .... Rm 6:11
I was **a** before I knew the law. .... Rm 7:9
all of us will be made **a** again. 1Co 15:22
you we will be **a** in Christ by 2Co 13:4
God made you **a** with Christ, ... Col 2:13
who are still **a** will be gathered 1Th 4:17
whether we are **a** or dead when he........... 1Th 5:10
God's word is **a** and working and .... Heb 4:12
but he was made **a** in the spirit. 1Pe 3:18
but look, I am **a** forever and .... Rev 1:18
People say that you are **a**, ... Rev 3:1
The beast that was once **a**, ... Rev 17:11
beast were thrown **a** into the .... Rev 19:20

ALL-POWERFUL
worship the LORD **A** and to offer 1Sa 1:3
the LORD God **A** was with him. 2Sa 5:10
of the LORD **A**, whose throne is 2Sa 6:2
'The LORD **A** is God over Israel!' 2Sa 7:26
As surely as the LORD **A** lives, ... 1Ki 18:15
of the LORD **A** will make this................... 2Ki 19:31
The LORD **A**—he is the glorious............... Ps 24:10
The LORD **A** is with us; .... Ps 46:11
are the LORD God **A**, the God of .... Ps 59:5
LORD God **A**, how long will you be .... Ps 80:4
LORD **A**, how lovely is your .... Ps 84:1
LORD God **A**, hear my prayer; .... Ps 84:8
LORD **A**, happy are the people who .... Ps 84:12
LORD God **A**, who is like you? .... Ps 89:8
the LORD God **A**, the Mighty One .... Is 1:24
The LORD **A** has a certain day .... Is 2:12
The LORD GOD **A** will take away............... Is 3:1
Holy, holy, holy is the LORD **A**. .... Is 6:3
that the LORD **A** is holy........................ Is 8:13
The LORD **A** is angry, so the land .... Is 9:19
LORD **A** has made this promise: .... Is 14:24
The LORD **A** will bless them, ... Is 19:25
The LORD **A** will prepare a feast .... Is 25:6
The Lord GOD **A** has told me how .... Is 28:22
The LORD **A** will come with .... Is 29:6
The LORD **A** will defend Jerusalem .... Is 31:5
is the LORD **A**, who saves Israel............... Is 44:6
Our Savior is named the LORD **A**; .... Is 47:4
His name is the LORD **A**. .... Is 54:5

is what the LORD **A**, the God of .... Je 7:3
called by your name, LORD God **A**. .... Je 15:16
God, the living God, the LORD **A**. .... Je 23:36
'The LORD **A**, the God of Israel,............... Je 27:4
says the Lord GOD, the God **A**. .... Am 3:13
The LORD **A** will send fire to .... Hab 2:13
This is what the LORD **A** says: .... Hag 1:2
This is what the LORD **A** says: ' .... Zch 1:3
that the LORD **A** has sent me to .... Zch 2:11
by my Spirit,' says the LORD **A**. .... Zch 4:6
this is what the LORD **A** says: ' .... Zch 6:12
The LORD **A** spoke his word, ... Zch 8:1
The LORD **A** says, "At that time I .... Zch 13:2
Honor my name," says the LORD **A**. .... Mal 2:3
me in this," says the LORD **A**. .... Mal 3:10
The Lord **A** allowed a few of our .... Rm 9:29
have been heard by the Lord **A**. .... Jam 5:4

ALLEYS

the streets and a of the town, ... Lk 14:21

ALLOW

This will **a** all these animals to .... Ge 7:3
I will **a** you to do this also. .... Ge 19:21
a me to find a wife for his son .... Ge 24:12
But we will **a** you to marry her .... Ge 34:15
I will not **a** Benjamin to go with .... Ge 42:38
the king will **a** you to settle................... Ge 46:34
I will **a** you to live long lives. .... Ex 23:26
The LORD did not **a** that, ... Dt 29:20
and **a** them to eat at your table. 1Ki 2:7
A Abishag the Shunammite to 1Ki 2:21
But I will **a** him to confront one 1Ki 11:32
I will **a** Solomon's son to....................... 1Ki 11:36
I cannot **a** this second command. 1Ki 20:9
So I will **a** you to defeat this 1Ki 20:28
So why did you **a** me to be born? .... Job 10:18
I will not **a** people to be proud .... Ps 101:5
I will **a** them to rebuild .... Je 12:16
you don't **a** on earth will be .... Mt 16:19
But he would not **a** the demons to .... Mk 1:34
refused to **a** anyone to carry .... Mk 11:16
and would not **a** them to speak, ... Lk 4:41
begged Jesus **a** them to go .... Lk 8:32
would not **a** the thief to enter .... Lk 12:39
Do not **a** what you think is good .... Rm 14:16
that come from God **a** you to live .... Rm 15:5
If you **a** yourselves to be .... Gal 5:3
But I do not **a** a woman to teach............. 1Ti 2:12

ALLOWED

and I may be **a** to live because .... Ge 12:13
So they **a** Rebekah and her nurse .... Ge 24:59
But God has not **a** your father to .... Ge 31:7
No one is **a** to touch him. .... Ex 19:13
God **a** that to happen, ... Ex 21:13
person will be **a** to enter the .... Jos 20:4
in Jerusalem and **a** him to have 1Ki 15:4
their widows were not **a** to cry. .... Ps 78:64
LORD All-Powerful **a** a few of our .... Is 1:9
The LORD **a** this to happen, ... Is 42:24
The Lord **a** Nebuchadnezzar to .... Da 1:2
food that they are not **a** to eat. .... Hos 9:3
Moses **a** you to divorce your .... Mt 19:8
So Jesus **a** them to do this. .... Mk 5:13
So Jesus **a** them to do this. .... Lk 8:32
they were **a** to recognize Jesus. .... Lk 24:31
he has **a** the Son to have life .... Jn 5:26
But we are not **a** to put anyone .... Jn 18:31
until he has been **a** to face his .... Ac 25:16
Rome, Paul was **a** to live alone, ... Ac 28:16
God left them and **a** them to have .... Rm 1:28
"I am **a** to do all things,"....................... 1Co 6:12
"We are **a** to do all things,".................... 1Co 10:23

they were not **a** to enter and .... Heb 3:19
it was **a** to use its power for .... Rev 13:5

ALLOWING

lives by not **a** the Israelites to .... Jos 9:26
pain without **a** something new to .... Is 66:9
So God is **a** even other nations .... Ac 11:18

ALLOWS

husband says and the court **a**. .... Ex 21:22
will be the things that God **a**. .... Mt 18:18
This **a** me to have Christ .... Php 3:8

ALMIGHTY

to him and said, "I am God **A**. .... Ge 17:1
May God **A** bless you and give you .... Ge 28:3
I pray that God **A** will cause the .... Ge 43:14
helps you. God **A** blesses you. He .... Ge 49:25
I see a vision from the **A**, ... Nu 24:4
because the **A** has made my life .... Ru 1:20
The arrows of the **A** are in me; .... Job 6:4
suffer the anger of the **A**. .... Job 21:20
Then the **A** will be your gold and .... Job 22:25
I wish the **A** would set a time .... Job 24:1
What has the **A** planned from on .... Job 31:2
breath of the **A** gave me life. .... Job 33:4
impossible for the **A** to do evil. .... Job 34:10
The **A** is too high for us to .... Job 37:23
The **A** scattered kings like snow............. Ps 68:14
voice of God **A** when he speaks.............. Eze 10:5
was and is coming. I am the **A**." .... Rev 1:8
holy, holy is the Lord God **A**. .... Rev 4:8
you, Lord God **A**, who is and who .... Rev 11:17
on the great day of God **A**. .... Rev 16:14
the terrible anger of the God the **A**. .... Rev 19:15
the Lord God **A** and the Lamb are .... Rev 21:22

ALMOND

from poplar, **a**, and plane trees .... Ge 30:37
shaped like **a** flowers on it..................... Ex 25:33
like the flowers on an **a** tree. .... Ec 12:5
"I see a stick of **a** wood." .... Je 1:11

ALMONDS

myrrh, pistachio nuts, and **a**. .... Ge 43:11
blossomed, and produced **a**. .... Nu 17:8

ALOES

smell like myrrh, **a**, and cassia. .... Ps 45:8
with myrrh, **a**, and cinnamon. .... Pr 7:17
myrrh, and **a**—all the best .... Sng 4:14
pounds of myrrh and **a**. .... Jn 19:39

ALONGSIDE

sailors came **a** to trade with you............. Eze 27:9
cattle which live **a** much water. .... Eze 32:13
The pavement ran **a** the gates and .... Eze 40:18
The walls **a** the entrance were .... Eze 41:2
A the land for the priests, ... Eze 48:13

ALOUD

Temple he read **a** the scroll that .... Je 36:8

ALPHA

I am the **A** and the Omega...................... Rev 1:8
I am the **A** and the Omega, the .... Rev 21:6
I am the **A** and the Omega, the .... Rev 22:13

ALPHAEUS

James son of **A**, and Thaddaeus; .... Mt 10:3
saw a man named Levi son of **A**, ... Mk 2:14
James the son of **A**, Thaddaeus, ... Mk 3:18
James son of **A**, Simon (known as .... Ac 1:13

ALTAR

Noah built an **a** to the LORD. .... Ge 8:20
them on the **a** as offerings to .... Ge 8:20
Abram built an **a** there to the .... Ge 12:7
Abraham built an **a** there. .... Ge 22:9
laid him on the wood on the **a**. .... Ge 22:9

an a to the God who appeared .... Ge 35:1
Jacob built an a and named the .... Ge 35:7
Moses built an a and named it .... Ex 17:15
Make an a of dirt for me, ... Ex 20:24
use stones to make an a for me, ... Ex 20:25
half of the blood on the a. .... Ex 24:6
Make an a of acacia wood, ... Ex 27:1
the a will become very holy, ... Ex 29:37
they approach the a to serve as .... Ex 30:20
Then he made the a of incense .... Ex 37:25
tools of bronze to use on the a: .... Ex 38:3
gold a, the special olive oil .... Ex 39:38
have put wood and fire on the a, ... Le 1:7
them on the east side of the a, ... Le 1:16
these parts on the a as food; .... Le 3:11
corners of the a of incense that .... Le 4:7
corners of the a that is before .... Le 4:18
Go to the a and offer sin .... Le 9:7
the LORD's a near the entrance .... Le 17:6
off the bronze a and spread a .... Nu 4:13
used for serving at the a— .... Nu 4:14
oil on the a and all its tools. .... Nu 7:1
will be used to cover the a. .... Nu 16:38
on the a of the LORD your .... Dt 12:27
Build an a of stones there to .... Dt 27:5
Joshua built an a for the LORD, ... Jos 8:30
There they built a beautiful a. .... Jos 22:10
down your father's a to Baal, ... Jdg 6:25
went up to the sky from the a. .... Jdg 13:20
Saul built an a to the LORD. 1Sa 14:35
Go and build an a to the LORD on 2Sa 24:18
hold of the corners of the a. 1Ki 1:50
stood facing the LORD's a, ... 1Ki 8:22
man said, "A, altar, the LORD 1Ki 13:2
The a also broke into pieces, ... 1Ki 13:5
rebuilt the a of the LORD, ... 1Ki 18:30
water ran off the a and filled 1Ki 18:35
Ahaz saw an a at Damascus, ... 2Ki 16:10
burned them on the a to ruin it. 2Ki 23:16
I can build an a to the LORD 1Ch 21:22
made a bronze a thirty feet long 2Ch 4:1
the LORD's a that was in front 2Ch 15:8
sprinkled their blood on the a. 2Ch 29:22
and burn incense on only one a 2Ch 32:12
began to build the a of the God .... Ezr 3:2
burning on the a of the LORD our .... Ne 10:34
and I come to your a, LORD. .... Ps 26:6
Then I will go to the a of God, ... Ps 43:4
bulls will be offered on your a. .... Ps 51:19
Come to the corners of the a. .... Ps 118:27
to take a hot coal from the a. .... Is 6:6
there will be an a for the LORD .... Is 19:19
the rocks of the a to dust, ... Is 27:9
place on my a will please me, ... Is 56:7
has rejected his a and abandoned .... La 2:7
the gate of the a was the idol .... Eze 8:5
between the porch and the a. .... Eze 8:16
the priests who serve at the a. .... Eze 40:46
is burned on the a is seven feet .... Eze 43:15
it on the four corners of the a, ... Eze 43:20
they will give the a to God. .... Eze 43:26
corners of the ledge of the a, ... Eze 45:19
of the a will be cut off, ... Am 3:14
saw the Lord standing by the a, ... Am 9:1
will be like the holy a bowls. .... Zch 14:20
bringing unclean food to my a. .... Mal 1:7
offer your gift to God at the a, ... Mt 5:23
leave your gift there at the a. .... Mt 5:24
swear by the a when they make .... Mt 23:18
between the a and the Temple. .... Lk 11:51
found an a that had these words .... Ac 17:23
the sacrifices share in the a? 1Co 10:18
In it was a golden a for burning .... Heb 9:4

offered his son Isaac on the a. .... Jam 2:21
I saw under the a the souls of .... Rev 6:9
the golden a before the throne. .... Rev 8:3
with fire from the a and threw .... Rev 8:5
over the fire, came from the a. .... Rev 14:18

ALTAR'S
the a fire must be kept burning. .... Le 6:9

ALTARS
Destroy their a, break their .... Ex 34:13
and cut down your incense a. .... Le 26:30
the lampstand, the a, the tools .... Nu 3:31
Build me seven a here, and .... Nu 23:1
destroyed your a, and killed 1Ki 19:10
of Baal, in front of the a. 2Ki 11:18
the LORD's a and the places 2Ki 18:22
He built a for Baal, and he made 2Ki 21:3
Manasseh built a in the Temple 2Ki 21:4
He built a to worship the stars 2Ki 21:5
of Judah had built a on the roof 2Ki 23:12
altars and the a Manasseh had 2Ki 23:12
destroyed the a and places for 2Ch 31:1
raise their young near your a, ... Ps 84:3
not trust the a they have made, ... Is 17:8
they burn incense on a of brick. .... Is 65:3
built as many a to burn incense .... Je 11:13
and they have destroyed your a. .... Rm 11:3

ALWAYS
evil and were a sinning against .... Ge 13:13
' This will a be my name, by .... Ex 3:15
You are a to remember this day .... Ex 12:14
that it is a there in front of .... Ex 25:30
Aaron must a wear this on his .... Ex 28:38
And if you a give the best part .... Nu 18:32
that they would a obey my .... Dt 5:29
things will a go well for you .... Dt 12:28
to respect the LORD your God a. .... Dt 14:23
These rocks will a remind the .... Jos 4:7
But Samuel a went back to Ramah, ... 1Sa 7:17
He sat where he a sat, near the 1Sa 20:25
let my family a be blessed." 2Sa 7:29
will a eat at my table. 2Sa 9:10
had a been David's friend. 1Ki 5:1
there will a be a descendant 1Ki 11:36
the jug will a have oil in it, ... 1Ki 17:14
descendants would a rule. 2Ki 8:19
he will keep his promises a. 1Ch 16:15
of Purim should a be celebrated .... Est 9:28
a succeed. They are far from .... Ps 10:5
I keep the LORD before me a. .... Ps 16:8
Good people a lend freely to .... Ps 37:26
He a helps in times of trouble. .... Ps 46:1
But I will a have hope and will .... Ps 71:14
people are wicked, a at ease, ... Ps 73:12
I will a sing about the LORD's .... Ps 89:1
He will not a accuse us, and he .... Ps 103:9
A remember what you have been .... Pr 4:13
let her love a hold you captive. .... Pr 5:19
Trouble a comes to sinners, ... Pr 13:21
Those who are a respectful will .... Pr 28:14
you will a be struggling for .... Ec 4:6
runner does a not win the race, ... Ec 9:11
People are a writing books, ... Ec 12:12
trust the LORD, a because he is .... Is 26:4
nor will I a be angry, because .... Is 57:16
The LORD will a lead you. .... Is 58:11
rain comes; it a produces fruit. .... Je 17:8
he a used stories to teach them. .... Mt 13:34
So a be ready, because you don't .... Mt 24:42
You will a have the poor with .... Mt 26:11
I will be with you a, even until .... Mt 28:20
A be ready, because you don't .... Mk 13:33
Don't a think about what you .... Lk 12:29

Son, you are **a** with me, and all .... Lk 15:31
they should **a** pray and never .... Lk 18:1
People **a** serve the best wine .... Jn 2:10
Sir, give us this bread **a**." .... Jn 6:34
I **a** do what is pleasing to him, ... Jn 8:29
I know that you **a** hear me, ... Jn 11:42
have **a** taught in synagogues and .... Jn 18:20
'I keep the Lord before me **a**. .... Ac 2:25
You are **a** against what the Holy .... Ac 7:51
This is why I **a** try to do what I .... Ac 24:16
Son, knows that I **a** mention you .... Rm 1:9
I **a** thank my God for you because 1Co 1:4
It **a** trusts, always hopes, and 1Co 13:7
A give yourselves fully to the 1Co 15:58
In Christ it has **a** been yes. 2Co 1:19
who **a** leads us as captives in 2Co 2:14
So we **a** have courage. 2Co 5:6
sadness, but we are **a** rejoicing. 2Co 6:10
Then you will **a** have plenty of 2Co 9:8
I **a** remember you in my prayers, ... Eph 1:16
A give thanks to God the Father............... Eph 5:20
A pray for all God's people. .... Eph 6:18
a praying with joy for all of you. .... Php 1:4
but there is one thing I **a** do. .... Php 3:13
Be full of joy in the Lord **a**................... Php 4:4
you need, **a** giving thanks. .... Php 4:6
prayers for you we **a** thank God, ... Col 1:3
to have peace. **A** be thankful. .... Col 3:15
should **a** be kind and pleasant .... Col 4:6
a thank God for all of you and 1Th 1:2
A be joyful. 1Th 5:16
We must **a** thank God for you, ... 2Th 1:3
That is why we **a** pray for you, ... 2Th 1:11
These women are **a** learning new 2Ti 3:7
he is able **a** to save those who .... Heb 7:25
a be willing to listen and slow .... Jam 1:19
A be ready to answer everyone 1Pe 3:15
I will **a** help you remember them. 2Pe 1:12
Doing wrong is a sin, but there 1Jn 5:17

AMALEK
and Eliphaz gave birth to **A**. .... Ge 36:12
Then Balaam saw **A** and gave this .... Nu 24:20
went to the city of **A** and set up 1Sa 15:5

AMALEKITE
an Egyptian, the slave of an **A**. 1Sa 30:13
I told him, 'I am an **A**.' 2Sa 1:8

AMALEKITES
defeated all the **A**, as well as .... Ge 14:7
his hands down, the **A** would win. .... Ex 17:11
Since the **A** and the Canaanites .... Nu 14:25
Midianites, the **A**, and other .... Jdg 6:33
Sidonians, **A**, and Maonites were .... Jdg 10:12
took King Agag of the **A** alive, ... 1Sa 15:8
all the **A**, and I brought 1Sa 15:20
"Bring me King Agag of the **A**."............... 1Sa 15:32
After David had defeated the **A**,............... 2Sa 1:1

AMARIAH
Azariah was the father of **A**. 1Ch 6:11

AMASA
Absalom had made **A** captain of 2Sa 17:25
hand he took **A** by the beard to 2Sa 20:9
Abigail was the mother of **A**, ... 1Ch 2:17

AMASA'S
pushed the sword into **A** stomach, ... 2Sa 20:10

AMAZE
will continue to **a** these people .... Is 29:14
place that will **a** and frighten .... Je 19:3

AMAZED
other because they were so **a**.................. Ge 43:33
All these things **a** her. 1Ki 10:5

All these things **a** her............................ 2Ch 9:4
who were **a** by Egypt's glory .... Is 20:5
Watch them and be **a** and shocked. .... Hab 1:5
I am **a** at what you have done. .... Hab 3:2
people were **a** at his teaching, ... Mt 7:28
All the people were **a** and said, ... Mt 12:23
The crowd was **a** when they saw .... Mt 15:31
people were **a** at his teaching .... Mk 1:22
Everyone was completely **a**. .... Mk 5:42
The followers were greatly **a**. .... Mk 6:51
people were **a** at his teaching. .... Mk 11:18
Pilate was **a** that Jesus would .... Mk 15:44
who heard him were **a** at his .... Lk 2:47
of Jesus and were **a** at the words .... Lk 4:22
They were **a** at his teaching, ... Lk 4:32
When Jesus heard this, he was **a**. .... Lk 7:9
The girl's parents were **a**, ... Lk 8:56
And being **a** at his answer, ... Lk 20:26
because they were **a** and happy,............... Lk 24:41
The people were **a** and said, ... Jn 7:15
people were **a** and ran to them .... Ac 3:11
the people who heard him were **a**. .... Ac 9:21
I saw the woman, I was very **a**. .... Rev 17:6

AMAZIAH
Jerusalem, and **A**, his son, ... 2Ki 12:21
his war against **A** king of Judah, ... 2Ki 13:12
A son of Joash became king of 2Ki 14:1
A son of Joash, the king of 2Ki 14:17
other things **A** did are written 2Ki 14:18
king in place of his father **A**. 2Ki 14:21
Uzziah son of **A** became king of............... 2Ki 15:1
Joash's son **A** became king in his 2Ch 24:27
A did what the LORD said was 2Ch 25:2
When **A** stopped obeying the LORD, ... 2Ch 25:27
A, a priest at Bethel, sent this .... Am 7:10
Then **A** said to Amos, "Seer, go .... Am 7:12
Amos answered **A**, "I do not make........... Am 7:14

AMAZIAH'S
There **A** army killed ten thousand 2Ch 25:11

AMAZING
to keep you alive in an **a** way.................. Ge 45:7
LORD will do **a** things among you............. Jos 3:5
Then an **a** thing happened as .... Jdg 13:19
the **a** things he has done on the .... Ps 46:8
You answer us in **a** ways, God our .... Ps 65:5
Say to God, "Your works are **a**! .... Ps 66:3
the **a** things he has done for .... Ps 66:5
in Egypt and **a** things by the Red .... Ps 106:22
Your knowledge is **a** to me;.................. Ps 139:6
made me in an **a** and wonderful............... Ps 139:14
because you have done **a** things. .... Is 25:1
before these **a** things come true? .... Da 12:6
in heaven that was great and **a**. .... Rev 15:1

AMBITIOUS
because they are jealous and **a**, ... Php 1:15

AMBUSH
to set up an **a** behind the city." .... Jos 8:2
and set up an **a** in the ravine. 1Sa 15:5
Let's **a** and kill someone; .... Pr 1:11

AMBUSHED
mountains and **a** us in the desert .... La 4:19

AMBUSHES
set up **a** all around Gibeah .... Jdg 20:29
the LORD set **a** for the people of 2Ch 20:22

AMEN
all the people will say, "**A**!" .... Dt 27:15
Jehoiada answered the king, "**A**! 1Ki 1:36
the people said "**A**" and praised 1Ch 16:36
group said, "**A**," and they .... Ne 5:13
up their hands and said, "**A**! .... Ne 8:6

A

will always be. **A** and amen. For .... Ps 41:13
the whole world. Amen and **a.** .... Ps 72:19
the LORD forever! **A** and amen. A .... Ps 89:52
Let all the people say, "**A!**" .... Ps 106:48
He said, "**A!** Let the LORD really .... Je 28:6
the glory are yours forever. **A.** .... Mt 6:13
should be praised forever. **A.** .... Rm 1:25
To him be the glory forever! **A!** .... Rm 11:36
gives peace be with you all. **A.** .... Rm 15:33
Christ be with all of you. **A.** .... Rm 16:24
cannot say a to your prayer of 1Co 14:16
to God forever and ever. **A.** .... Gal 1:5
Christ be with your spirit. **A.** .... Gal 6:18
all time, forever and ever. **A.** .... Eph 3:21
to him forever and ever. **A.** 1Pe 4:11
is his forever and ever. **A.** 1Pe 5:11
be to him now and forever! **A.** 2Pe 3:18
him. Yes, this will happen! **A.** .... Rev 1:7
The **A**, the faithful and true .... Rev 3:14
said, "**A**," and the elders .... Rev 5:14
to our God forever and ever. **A**!" .... Rev 7:12
They said: "**A**, Hallelujah!" .... Rev 19:4
am coming soon." **A.** Come, Lord .... Rev 22:20
the Lord Jesus be with all. **A.** .... Rev 22:21

AMETHYST
a jacinth, an agate, and an **a;** .... Ex 28:19
a jacinth, an agate, and an **a;** .... Ex 39:12
jacinth, and the twelfth was **a.** .... Rev 21:20

AMMIEL'S
David and Bathsheba, **A** daughter. 1Ch 3:5

AMMINADAB
tribe of Judah—Nahshon son of **A;** .... Nu 1:7
of Ram, who was the father of **A.** .... Ru 4:19
Ram was the father of **A.** .... Mt 1:4
Nahshon was the son of **A.** .... Lk 3:33

AMMINADAB'S
Ram was **A** father, and Amminadab 1Ch 2:10

AMMON
The men of **A** were winning. 2Sa 11:23
and **A** against Jehoiakim to 2Ki 24:2
But now here are men from **A,** 2Ch 20:10
ambushes for the people of **A,** 2Ch 20:22
the people of **A** will be under .... Is 11:14
the people of Edom, Moab, and **A;** .... Je 25:21
the people of **A** and prophesy .... Eze 25:2
the leaders of **A** will be saved .... Da 11:41
and **A** will be destroyed like .... Zph 2:9

AMMONITE
of all the **A** people who are .... Ge 19:38
still in the **A** city of Rabbah. .... Dt 3:11

AMMONITES
not go near the land of the **A,** .... Dt 2:37
the land of the **A** that went as .... Jos 13:25
A gathered for war and camped .... Jdg 10:17
So the **A** were defeated by the .... Jdg 11:33
of the Moabites, **A,** Edomites, ... 1Ki 11:1
When Nahash king of the **A** died, ... 1Ch 19:1
the capital city of the **A,** .... Je 49:2

AMNON
first was **A**, whose mother was 2Sa 3:2
named Absalom and a son named **A.** 2Sa 13:1
named Tamar, and **A** loved her. 2Sa 13:1
So **A** went to bed and acted sick. 2Sa 13:6
After that, **A** hated Tamar. 2Sa 13:15
he hated **A** for disgracing his 2Sa 13:22

AMON
Take Micaiah and send him to **A,** 1Ki 22:26
Manasseh's son **A** became king in 2Ki 21:18
had made plans to kill King **A,** 2Ki 21:24
Josiah son of **A** was king of .... Je 1:2

Josiah son of **A** was king of .... Zph 1:1
A was the father of Josiah. .... Mt 1:10

AMORITE
the great trees of Mamre the **A.** .... Ge 14:13
was king of the **A** people and .... Dt 1:4
the power to defeat Sihon the **A,** .... Dt 2:24
these five **A** kings—the kings .... Jos 10:5
father was an **A**, and your mother .... Eze 16:3
and your father was an **A**. .... Eze 16:45

AMORITES
the Jebusites, **A,** Girgashites, ... Ge 10:16
as well as the **A** who lived in .... Ge 14:7
to punish the **A** for their evil .... Ge 15:16
A, Canaanites, Girgashites, and .... Ge 15:21
Hittites, **A,** Perizzites, Hivites .... Ex 3:8
Hittites, **A,** Perizzites, Hivites .... Ex 3:17
the Canaanites, **A,** Hittites, ... Ex 33:2
and **A** live in the mountains; .... Nu 13:29
to Sihon, king of the **A,** saying, ... Nu 21:21
the kings of the **A,** when he .... Dt 31:4
the kings of the **A** west of the .... Jos 5:1
two kings of the **A** from the east .... Jos 9:10
Live in the land of the **A,** .... Jdg 6:10
of Gilead, where the **A** lived. .... Jdg 10:8
also between Israel and the **A.** 1Sa 7:14
Sihon king of the **A**, Og king of .... Ps 135:11
He defeated Sihon king of the **A.** .... Ps 136:19
give you the land of the **A.** .... Am 2:10

AMOS
are the words of **A,** one of the .... Am 1:1
said to me, "**A,** what do you see? .... Am 7:8
A is making evil plans against .... Am 7:10
Amaziah said to **A,** "Seer, go .... Am 7:12
Then **A** answered Amaziah, "I do .... Am 7:14
A was the son of Nahum. .... Lk 3:25

AMOUNT
whatever **a** the woman's husband .... Ex 21:22
This **a** is a gift to the LORD. .... Ex 30:13
total **a** of gold used to build .... Ex 38:24
supplied a large **a** of iron to be 1Ch 22:3
brought a large **a,** one-tenth 2Ch 31:5
Then the **a** of money your .... Ezr 4:13
back the extra **a** you charged— .... Ne 5:11
about the **a** of money Haman .... Est 4:7
men a certain **a** of food and wine .... Da 1:5
the **a** you give to others will .... Mt 7:2
the soldiers a large **a** of money .... Mt 28:12
they can get back the same **a!** .... Lk 6:34
are by the **a** of faith God has .... Rm 12:3

AMOUNTS
that you have equal **a** of each. .... Ex 30:34

AMOZ
the prophet, the son of **A.** 2Ki 19:2
Isaiah son of **A** sent a message 2Ki 19:20
by the prophet Isaiah son of **A.** 2Ch 26:22
Isaiah son of **A** prayed to heaven 2Ch 32:20
Isaiah son of **A** saw about what .... Is 1:1

AMPHIPOLIS
traveled through **A** and Apollonia .... Ac 17:1

AMRAM
The sons of Kohath were **A,** .... Ex 6:18
A lived one hundred thirty-seven .... Ex 6:20
and **A** had two sons, Aaron and .... Nu 26:59

AMRAM'S
A children were Aaron, Moses, ... 1Ch 6:3
A sons were Aaron and Moses. 1Ch 23:13

AMRAPHEL
Now **A** was king of Babylonia, ... Ge 14:1
king of Goiim, **A** king of .... Ge 14:9

ANAH
A is the man who found the hot .... Ge 36:24

ANAK
the descendants of A lived. .... Nu 13:22
Arba was the father of A. .... Jos 15:13
Talmai, the descendants of A. .... Jos 15:14
Arba was the father of A. .... Jos 21:11

ANAKITE
heard that the A people lived .... Jos 14:12
out the three A families living .... Jos 15:14

ANAKITES
A come from the Nephilim people. .... Nu 13:33
And we saw the A there!'" .... Dt 1:28
They were very tall, like the A. .... Dt 2:10
"No one can stop the A." .... Dt 9:2
Joshua fought the A who lived .... Jos 11:21
the greatest man among the A. .... Jos 14:15

ANANIAH
the son of A, made repairs .... Ne 3:23

ANANIAS
But a man named A and his wife .... Ac 5:1
of Jesus in Damascus named A. .... Ac 9:10
The Lord spoke to A in a vision, ... Ac 9:10
But A answered, "Lord, many .... Ac 9:13
But the Lord said to A, "Go! .... Ac 9:15
So A went to the house of Judas. .... Ac 9:17
There a man named A came to me. .... Ac 22:12
A, the high priest, heard this .... Ac 23:2
Five days later A, the high .... Ac 24:1

ANATH
Shamgar son of A saved Israel. .... Jdg 3:31
In the days of Shamgar son of A, ... Jdg 5:6

ANATHOTH
to go back to your fields in A. 1Ki 2:26
Gallim! Laishah, listen! Poor A! .... Is 10:30
in the town of A in the land .... Je 1:1
the people from A who plan to .... Je 11:21
from the city of A will be left .... Je 11:23
Jeremiah from A is acting like .... Je 29:27
buy my field near the town of A. .... Je 32:7
the field at A from my cousin .... Je 32:9

ANCESTOR
make you the a of many people." .... Ge 17:2
He is the a of all the Moabite .... Ge 19:37
will be the a of many nations .... Ge 35:11
He is the a of the Edomites, ... Ge 36:9
took your a Abraham from the .... Jos 24:3
the city of David, his a. 1Ki 15:24
not do as his a David had done. 2Ki 14:3
just as his a David had done. 2Ki 18:3
lived as his a David lived 2Ki 22:2
Unlike his a David, he did not 2Ch 28:1
just as his a David had done. 2Ch 29:2
to obey the God of his a David. 2Ch 34:3
Abraham, your a, and Sarah, who .... Is 51:2
cups that his a Nebuchadnezzar .... Da 5:2
Your a Jacob fled to Northwest .... Hos 12:12
Abraham, our a, in Mesopotamia .... Ac 7:2
Abraham, our a, was made right .... Jam 2:21

ANCESTORS
to the land where your a lived, ... Ge 31:3
bury me where my a are buried." .... Ge 47:30
My a Abraham and Isaac served .... Ge 48:15
Bury me with my a in the cave in .... Ge 49:29
'The God of your a sent me to you. .... Ex 3:13
he promised your a he would give .... Ex 13:5
the land I promised to their a. .... Nu 14:23
how our a went down into Egypt .... Nu 20:15
you are acting just like your a! .... Nu 32:14
The LORD promised it to your a— .... Dt 1:8

the Agreement with your a, ... Dt 4:31
the God of your a, has promised. .... Dt 6:3
land the LORD promised your a. .... Dt 8:1
to keep his promise to your a, ... Dt 9:5
you will die and join your a, ... Dt 32:50
promised their a to give them, ... Jos 5:6
God of your a, has given this .... Jos 18:3
time ago your a lived on the .... Jos 24:2
land I promised to give your a. .... Jdg 2:1
God of their a who had brought .... Jdg 2:12
Their a had obeyed the LORD's .... Jdg 2:17
They became worse than their a. .... Jdg 2:19
miracles our a told us he did .... Jdg 6:13
and brought your a out of Egypt. 1Sa 12:6
to the land you gave to their a. 1Ki 8:34
because our a did not obey the 2Ki 22:13
in this land you gave our a. 2Ch 6:31
God of their a, sent prophets 2Ch 36:15
But our a made the God of heaven .... Ezr 5:12
people whose a were from Israel .... Ne 9:2
You led our a with a pillar of .... Ne 9:12
find out what their a learned, ... Job 8:8
Our a told us what you did in .... Ps 44:1
There your a tested me and tried .... Ps 95:9
Sarah, who gave birth to your a. .... Is 51:2
Our a worshiped you in our holy .... Is 64:11
for your sins and your a' sins," .... Is 65:7
fair to your a, so why did they .... Je 2:5
I brought your a out of Egypt, ... Je 7:22
made with your a when I brought .... Je 11:4
a forgot me and worshiped Baal. .... Je 23:27
I brought your a into the desert .... Eze 20:35
the evil things done by our a, ... Da 9:16
you promised to our a long ago. .... Mic 7:20
Don't be like your a. .... Zch 1:4
agreement our a made with God? .... Mal 2:10
the sin that your a started. .... Mt 23:32
promised to our a, to Abraham .... Lk 1:55
the prophets whom your a killed! .... Lk 11:47
a worshiped on this mountain, ... Jn 4:20
Your a ate the manna in the .... Jn 6:49
agreement God made with your a. .... Ac 3:25
the God of our a, raised Jesus. .... Ac 5:30
But our a did not want to obey .... Ac 7:39
Joshua led our a to capture the .... Ac 7:45
'The God of our a chose you long .... Ac 22:14
promise that God made to our a. .... Ac 26:6
to the Jewish a are true. .... Rm 15:8
God spoke to our a through the .... Heb 1:1
made with their a when I took .... Heb 8:9

ANCHOR
So they pulled up the a, ... Ac 27:13
this hope as an a for the soul, ... Heb 6:19

ANCHORS
they threw four a into the water .... Ac 27:29

ANCIENT
since I set up my a people. .... Is 44:7

ANDREW
called Peter) and his brother A; .... Mt 10:2
and his brother A throwing a net .... Mk 1:16
John to the home of Simon and A. .... Mk 1:29
A, Philip, Bartholomew, Matthew, ... Mk 3:18
with Peter, James, John, and A. .... Mk 13:3
Then A took Simon to Jesus. .... Jn 1:42
his followers, A, Simon Peter's .... Jn 6:8
Philip told A, and then Andrew .... Jn 12:22
John, James, A, Philip, Thomas, ... Ac 1:13

ANER
was a brother of Eshcol and A, ... Ge 14:13
But give A, Eshcol, and Mamre .... Ge 14:24

ANGEL

The **a** of the L<small>ORD</small> found Hagar .... Ge 16:7
The **a** added, "You are now .... Ge 16:11
and God's **a** called to Hagar from .... Ge 21:17
The **a** said, "Don't kill your son .... Ge 22:12
will send his **a** before you to .... Ge 24:7
He was the **A** who saved me from .... Ge 48:16
There the **a** of the L<small>ORD</small> appeared........... Ex 3:2
My **a** will go ahead of you and .... Ex 23:23
the donkey saw the **a** of the L<small>ORD</small> .... Nu 22:23
The **a** of God said to Gideon, ... Jdg 6:20
He looked like an **a** from God; .... Jdg 13:6
are as good as an **a** from God. 1Sa 29:9
Like an **a** of God, you know what 2Sa 14:17
wise like an **a** of God who knows 2Sa 14:20
When the **a** raised his arm toward 2Sa 24:16
When David saw the **a** that killed 2Sa 24:17
"Get up and eat," the **a** said. 1Ki 19:5
But the L<small>ORD</small>'s **a** said to Elijah 2Ki 1:3
God sent an **a** to destroy 1Ch 21:15
L<small>ORD</small> sent an **a** who killed all 2Ch 32:21
The **a** of the L<small>ORD</small> camps around .... Ps 34:7
the wind as the **a** of the L<small>ORD</small> .... Ps 35:5
slippery as the **a** of the L<small>ORD</small>........... Ps 35:6
Then the **a** of the L<small>ORD</small> went out .... Is 37:36
He sent his own **a** to save them. .... Is 63:9
God has sent his **a** and saved his .... Da 3:28
holy **a** coming down from heaven. .... Da 4:13
My God sent his **a** to close the .... Da 6:22
wrestled with the **a** and won, ... Hos 12:4
The **a** who was talking with me .... Zch 1:9
Then they spoke to the L<small>ORD</small>'s **a**, ... Zch 1:11
Then the **a** said to Joshua, ... Zch 3:4
a said, "The woman stands for .... Zch 5:8
an **a** of the Lord came to him in .... Mt 1:20
said to the **a**, "How can I know .... Lk 1:18
God sent the **a** Gabriel to .... Lk 1:26
said to the **a**, "How will this .... Lk 1:34
The **a** said to them, "Do not be .... Lk 2:10
from heaven joined the first **a**, ... Lk 2:13
given by the **a** before the baby .... Lk 2:21
Sometimes an **a** of the Lord came .... Jn 5:4
a of the Lord opened the doors .... Ac 5:19
An **a** of the Lord said to Philip, ... Ac 8:26
A holy **a** spoke to Cornelius, ... Ac 10:22
us about the **a** he saw standing .... Ac 11:13
The **a** struck Peter on the side .... Ac 12:7
said, "It must be Peter's **a**.".................... Ac 12:15
Maybe an **a** or a spirit did speak .... Ac 23:9
Last night an **a** came to me from .... Ac 27:23
to look like an **a** of light........................ 2Co 11:14
or even an **a** from heaven, should .... Gal 1:8
welcomed me as an **a** from God, ... Gal 4:14
And God never said this to an **a**: .... Heb 1:13
Jesus sent his **a** to show it to .... Rev 1:1
this to the **a** of the church .... Rev 2:1
I saw a powerful **a** calling in a .... Rev 5:2
Then the **a** filled the incense .... Rev 8:5
The first **a** blew his trumpet, ... Rev 8:7
king who was the **a** of the .... Rev 9:11
another powerful **a** coming down .... Rev 10:1
The **a** was holding a small scroll .... Rev 10:2
the seventh **a** blew his trumpet .... Rev 11:15
Then the **a** swung his sickle over .... Rev 14:19
The second **a** poured out his bowl .... Rev 16:3
seventh **a** poured out his bowl .... Rev 16:17
Then the **a** carried me away by .... Rev 17:3
Then a powerful **a** picked up a .... Rev 18:21
And the **a** said to me, "Write .... Rev 19:9
The **a** grabbed the dragon, that .... Rev 20:2
The **a** also measured the wall. .... Rev 21:17
The **a** said to me, "These words .... Rev 22:6
have sent my **a** to tell you these .... Rev 22:16

ANGEL'S

up from the **a** hand to God with .... Rev 8:4
from the **a** hand and ate it .... Rev 10:10

ANGELS

The two **a** came to Sodom in the .... Ge 19:1
and he saw **a** of God going up and .... Ge 28:12
One day the **a** came to show .... Job 1:6
lower than the **a** and crowned .... Ps 8:5
So they ate the bread of **a**. .... Ps 78:25
against them, his destroying **a**. .... Ps 78:49
None of them **a** is like the L<small>ORD</small>. .... Ps 89:6
has put his **a** in charge of you................... Ps 91:11
You who are his **a**, praise the .... Ps 103:20
Praise him, all you **a**. .... Ps 148:2
thousands of **a** were serving him .... Da 7:10
one of the most important **a**, ... Da 10:13
'He has put his **a** in charge of .... Mt 4:6
and **a** came and took care of him. .... Mt 4:11
workers who gather are God's **a**. .... Mt 13:39
Son of Man will send out his **a**, ... Mt 13:41
Father's glory and with his **a**. .... Mt 16:27
that they have **a** in heaven who .... Mt 18:10
will be like the **a** in heaven. .... Mt 22:30
trumpet to send his **a** all around............... Mt 24:31
his great glory, with all his **a**. .... Mt 25:31
me more than twelve armies of **a**. .... Mt 26:53
will be like the **a** in heaven. .... Mk 12:25
When the **a** left them and went .... Lk 2:15
before the **a** of God that they .... Lk 12:8
presence of the **a** of God when .... Lk 15:10
the **a** carried him to the arms .... Lk 16:22
seen a vision of **a** who said that .... Lk 24:23
open and '**a** of God going up .... Jn 1:51
She saw two **a** dressed in white,............... Jn 20:12
God gave you through his **a**, ... Ac 7:53
nor life, nor **a**, nor ruling .... Rm 8:38
in the future we will judge **a**, ... 1Co 6:3
on her head, because of the **a**. 1Co 11:10
languages of people or even **a**. 1Co 13:1
from heaven with his powerful **a**. 2Th 1:7
right in spirit, and seen by **a**. 1Ti 3:16
became much greater than the **a**, ... Heb 1:4
lower than the **a** and crowned .... Heb 2:7
time was made lower than the **a**. .... Heb 2:9
it is not **a** that Jesus helps, ... Heb 2:16
to thousands of **a** gathered .... Heb 12:22
have welcomed **a** without knowing .... Heb 13:2
into which a desire to look........................ 1Pe 1:12
God's right side ruling over **a**, ... 1Pe 3:22
When **a** sinned, God did not let 2Pe 2:4
remember the **a** who did not keep .... Jud 1:6
stars are the **a** of the seven .... Rev 1:20
my Father and before his **a**. .... Rev 3:5
voices of many **a** around the .... Rev 5:11
a were holding the four winds .... Rev 7:1
I saw the seven **a** who stand .... Rev 8:2
dragon and his fought back. .... Rev 12:7
dragon with his **a** was thrown .... Rev 12:9
before the holy **a** and the Lamb............... Rev 14:10
were seven **a** bringing seven .... Rev 15:1
temple saying to the seven **a**, ... Rev 16:1
one of the seven **a** who had the .... Rev 17:1
one of the seven **a** who had the .... Rev 21:9
with twelve **a** at the gates, ... Rev 21:12

ANGER

May their **a** be cursed, because .... Ge 49:7
don't let your **a** destroy your .... Ex 32:11
saved the Israelites from my **a**. .... Nu 25:11
afraid of the L<small>ORD</small>'s **a** and rage, ... Dt 9:19
a will be like a burning fire .... Dt 29:20
My **a** has started a fire that.................... Dt 32:22
God's **a** will be against us for .... Jos 9:20

LORD held his a back and did not 2Ch 12:12
his a was like a burning fire. .... Est 1:12
A kills the fool, and jealousy .... Job 5:2
hide me until your a is gone. .... Job 14:13
God's a will bring punishment by .... Job 19:29
suffer the a of the Almighty. .... Job 21:20
that his a never punishes, ... Job 35:15
LORD, rise up in your a; .... Ps 7:6
In your a you will swallow them.............. Ps 21:9
His a lasts only a moment, ... Ps 30:5
the foreign nations in your a. .... Ps 56:7
Destroy them in your a; .... Ps 59:13
let your a catch up with them. .... Ps 69:24
sent his strong a against them, ... Ps 78:49
He found a way to show his a. .... Ps 78:50
knows the full power of your a? .... Ps 90:11
unkind answer will cause more a. .... Pr 15:1
A is cruel and destroys like a .... Pr 27:4
but wise people calm a down................. Pr 29:8
stirring up a causes trouble." .... Pr 30:33
use him like a rod to show my a; .... Is 10:5
time until God's a is finished. .... Is 26:20
crushed them because of my a. .... Is 63:3
a will be like a hot fire that.................... Je 7:20
have made my a burn like a hot .... Je 17:4
His a will be like a hurricane.................. Je 23:19
My a is like the wine in a cup. .... Je 25:15
footstool, on the day of his a. .... La 2:1
Then my a will come to an end. .... Eze 5:13
I will send my a against you. .... Eze 7:3
to pour out my a against them .... Eze 20:8
to pour out my a against them .... Eze 20:21
you in my hot a and put you .... Eze 22:20
happen in the time of God's a. .... Da 8:19
not die in a or in a battle. .... Da 11:20
I took him away in my great a. .... Hos 13:11
my a and rage, I will pay back .... Mic 5:15
no one can survive his strong a. .... Nah 1:6
That day will be a day of a,.................... Zph 1:15
on the day the LORD shows his a. .... Zph 2:3
God's a is shown from heaven .... Rm 1:18
on the day he shows his a. .... Rm 2:5
jealousy, a, selfish fighting 2Co 12:20
a, bad temper, doing or saying .... Col 3:8
manner, without a and arguments............ 1Ti 2:8
because a will not help you live .... Jam 1:20
will drink the wine of God's a, ... Rev 14:10
the great winepress of God's a. .... Rev 14:19
after them, God's a is finished. .... Rev 15:1
of the terrible a of God the .... Rev 19:15

ANGRILY

Then Moses very a left the king................. Ex 11:8
I a tore my robe and coat, ... Ezr 9:3
Do not speak a to an older man, ... 1Ti 5:1

ANGRY

Cain became very a and felt .... Ge 4:5
please don't be a with me, ... Ge 18:30
please don't be a with me, ... Ge 18:32
Jacob became very a and said, ... Ge 31:36
They were very a that Shechem .... Ge 34:7
The king became a with his .... Ge 40:2
if Joseph is still a with us? .... Ge 50:15
The LORD became a with Moses and......... Ex 4:14
LORD doesn't become a quickly, ... Nu 14:18
But God became a because Balaam .... Nu 22:22
The LORD was a with Israel, ... Nu 32:13
Mount Sinai you made the LORD a— ...... Dt 9:8
The LORD was a with the people .... Jdg 2:14
Some of our a men might attack .... Jdg 18:25
Saul, and he became very a. 1Sa 18:8
Jonathan was very a and left the 1Sa 20:34
Abner was very a because of what............ 2Sa 3:8

David was a because the LORD had 2Sa 6:8
They are as a as a bear that is 2Sa 17:8
The LORD was a with Solomon,............... 1Ki 11:9
Their sins have made me a, ... 1Ki 16:2
he was very a, even furious. .... Ne 4:1
Then the king became very a;............... Est 1:12
when King Xerxes was not so a,............. Est 2:1
became very a with Mordecai. .... Est 5:9
turns them over when he is a.................. Job 9:5
Ram, became very a with Job, ... Job 32:2
because he can quickly become a. .... Ps 2:12
When you are a, do not sin. .... Ps 4:4
have surrounded me like a bulls. .... Ps 22:12
Is he too a to pity us?" .... Ps 77:9
They made God a by building.................. Ps 78:58
Will you be a forever? .... Ps 79:5
He does not become a quickly, ... Ps 103:8
An a king can put someone to .... Pr 16:14
a king is like a roaring lion, ... Pr 19:12
gift will calm an a person; .... Pr 21:14
telling gossip brings a looks. .... Pr 25:23
An a person causes trouble; .... Pr 29:22
will become a with your words .... Ec 5:6
Don't become a quickly, because .... Ec 7:9
because your boss is a with you. .... Ec 10:4
So he became very a with us and .... Is 42:25
I became very a and hid from you .... Is 54:8
evil people are like the a sea, ... Is 57:20
Will you always be a at me? .... Je 3:5
'I will not be a with you .... Je 3:12
of Jerusalem have made me a. .... Je 32:32
to make me a by making idols .... Je 44:8
will be quiet and not a anymore. .... Eze 16:42
their answer, he became very a. .... Da 2:12
made the Lord a when they killed .... Hos 12:14
very unhappy, and he became a.............. Jnh 4:1
it is right for you to be a?" .... Jnh 4:4
LORD, were you a at the rivers, ... Hab 3:8
And I am very a with the nations .... Zch 1:15
says, "I am a at my shepherds .... Zch 10:3
if you are a with a brother or .... Mt 5:22
master was very a and put the .... Mt 18:34
if you are a with someone, ... Mk 11:25
older son was a and would not go .... Lk 15:28
why are you a at me for healing............... Jn 7:23
they became a and wanted to kill .... Ac 5:33
jealous, being a, being selfish, ... Gal 5:20
When you are a, do not sin, and.............. Eph 4:26
These things make God a. .... Col 3:6
I was a with them. I said, 'They .... Heb 3:10
whom was God a for forty years? .... Heb 3:17
Do not become a easily, ... Jam 1:19
The people of the world were a, ... Rev 11:18
dragon was very a at the woman, ... Rev 12:17

ANIMAL

plants as food for every wild a, ... Ge 1:30
clothes from a skins for the man .... Ge 3:21
destroy every a and everything .... Ge 6:7
kind of clean a, and take one .... Ge 7:2
Every a, everything that crawls .... Ge 8:19
'Kill an a and prepare some .... Ge 27:7
Some savage a has eaten him. .... Ge 37:33
firstborn male a to the LORD,.................. Ex 13:15
has sexual relations with an a. .... Ex 22:19
must cut the a into pieces, ... Le 1:12
You may eat any a that has split.............. Le 11:3
if the a has fins and scales, ... Le 11:9
must hate any a in the water .... Le 11:12
Whatever the a falls on must be .... Le 11:32
Every a that crawls on the .... Le 11:41
has sexual relations with an a, ... Le 20:15
the proudest a, which is strong .... Pr 30:30

the spirit of an a goes down .... Ec 3:21
Do you think a sacrifices will .... Je 11:15
No person or a will walk through .... Eze 29:11
mind of an a for seven years. .... Da 4:16
The first a looked like a lion, ... Da 7:4
This a had four heads and was .... Da 7:6
more than I want a sacrifices................... Hos 6:6
roar unless it has caught an a; .... Am 3:4
looked up and saw four a horns. .... Zch 1:18
to the Lord an a that has...................... Mal 1:14
more than I want a sacrifices.' .... Mt 12:7
be made clean by a sacrifices. .... Heb 9:23
can tame every kind of wild a, ... Jam 3:7

ANIMAL'S
The a inner organs and legs must .... Le 1:9
picks up the a dead body must .... Le 11:40
the a life is still in it. .... Le 17:14

ANIMALS
the large sea a and every living .... Ge 1:21
Let the earth be filled with a, ... Ge 1:24
made the wild a, the tame .... Ge 1:25
boat as food for you and the a." .... Ge 6:21
Lot had so many a that the land .... Ge 13:6
Abram killed the a and cut each........... Ge 15:10
When the came to drink, they .... Ge 30:38
the stronger a in the flock were .... Ge 30:41
the weaker a were Laban's, ... Ge 30:42
care of farm a all our lives...................... Ge 46:34
disease on your farm a that are .... Ex 9:3
All the farm a in Egypt died, ... Ex 9:6
become sores on people and a. .... Ex 9:10
let the wild a eat what is left .... Ex 23:11
'These are the land a you may eat: .... Le 11:2
Of all the a that walk on four .... Le 11:27
These crawling a are unclean for .... Le 11:29
birds, and other a on earth, as .... Le 11:46
between unclean a and clean .... Le 11:47
must bring those a to the LORD .... Le 17:5
Are we and our a to die here?................ Nu 20:4
These a chew the cud, but they .... Dt 14:7
You have many a, silver, gold, ... Jos 22:8
They took the a that belonged to 1Ch 5:21
skinned the a and gave the blood 2Ch 35:11
But ask the a, and they will .... Job 12:7
The a take cover from the rain .... Job 37:8
like wild a they feed on us..................... Ps 80:13
you large sea a and all the .... Ps 148:7
are no better off than the a, ... Ec 3:19
Only desert a will live there, ... Is 13:21
has made it a place for wild a, ... Is 23:13
about the a in southern Judah .... Is 30:6
Birds and small a will own that .... Is 34:11
flown away, and the a are gone. .... Je 9:10
in Jerusalem—both people and a. .... Je 21:6
Desert a and hyenas will live .... Je 50:39
The wild a will not eat them, ... Eze 34:28
It was a home for the wild a, ... Da 4:21
I saw four huge a come up from .... Da 7:3
of the other a had been taken.................. Da 7:12
'The four great a are four .... Da 7:17
his cave with the a he caught;................. Nah 2:12
you bring blind a as sacrifices, ... Mal 1:8
with the wild a, and the angels .... Mk 1:13
In it were all kinds of a, ... Ac 10:12
eating a that have been .... Ac 15:20
people, birds, a, and snakes. .... Rm 1:23
I fought wild a in Ephesus only 1Co 15:32
liars, evil a, and lazy people .... Tit 1:12
blood of a into the Most Holy.................. Heb 13:11
and by the wild a of the earth. .... Rev 6:8

ANKLE
their beautiful a bracelets, ... Is 3:18

ANKLES
water that came up to my a. .... Eze 47:3
man's feet and a became strong. .... Ac 3:7

ANNA
a prophetess, A, from the family .... Lk 2:36
tribe of Asher. A was very old. .... Lk 2:36
A never left the Temple but...................... Lk 2:37

ANNAS
A and Caiaphas were the high .... Lk 3:2
and led him first to A, the .... Jn 18:13
Then A sent Jesus, who was still .... Jn 18:24
A the high priest, Caiaphas, ... Ac 4:6

ANNOUNCE
you, and I will a my name, the .... Ex 33:19
priest must a that the person .... Le 13:3
'You will a the LORD's appointed .... Le 23:2
and a freedom for all the people............... Le 25:10
you are to a the blessings from .... Dt 11:29
I will a the name of the LORD. .... Dt 32:3
So now, a to the people, 'Anyone .... Jdg 7:3
prophets to a in Jerusalem:...................... Ne 6:7
and the skies a what his hands .... Ps 19:1
A that God is powerful. .... Ps 68:34
has sent me to a the time when .... Is 61:2
I will a my judgments against.................. Je 1:16
A this message to the family of .... Je 5:20
They a to the king of Babylon .... Je 51:31
to me said to me, "A this:...................... Zch 1:14
and to a the time when the Lord............... Lk 4:19
And now we a to you that he has 1Jn 1:2

ANNOUNCED
the priest has a him clean, ... Le 13:7
This prophet a the things you 2Ki 1:17
He a that everyone in Judah 2Ch 20:3
I a we would all fast and deny .... Ezr 8:21
king's order be a everywhere in .... Est 1:20
a a holiday for all the empire .... Est 2:18
God has a that he will destroy .... Is 10:22
destroy this land, as he has a................... Is 10:23
has a that disaster will come to .... Je 11:17
Josiah was king, a fast was a.................... Je 36:9
LORD your God a this disaster .... Je 40:2
to kill the wise men was a, ... Da 2:13
And it was a that Daniel was the .... Da 5:29
They a that they would fast for .... Jnh 3:5
They a the Good News there, ... Ac 14:7
the Temple and the a time when.............. Ac 21:26

ANNOUNCEMENT
So they made an a everywhere in 2Ch 30:5
had Cyrus send an a to his whole 2Ch 36:22
Cyrus to send an a to his whole .... Ezr 1:1
Dan makes an a and brings bad .... Je 4:15
He sent this a through Nineveh: .... Jnh 3:7
this vision and a I heard what .... Rev 19:1

ANNOUNCEMENTS
the man who made a for the king .... Da 3:4

ANNOUNCES
His thunder a the coming storm, ... Job 36:33
a peace and brings good news, ... Is 52:7
who a salvation and says to .... Is 52:7

ANNOUNCING
city streets, a before Mordecai .... Est 6:11
news! He is a peace! Celebrate .... Nah 1:15

ANTELOPE
goats, ibex, a, and mountain .... Dt 14:5

ANTIOCH
a man from A who had become a .... Ac 6:5
and A telling the message to .... Ac 11:19
In A the followers were called .... Ac 11:26

the church at **A** there were these .... Ac 13:1
trip from Perga and went to **A,** .... Ac 13:14
sailed away to **A** where the..................... Ac 14:26
went to **A** where they gathered .... Ac 15:30
Paul and Barnabas stayed in **A** .... Ac 15:35
The believers in **A** put Paul into .... Ac 15:40
Peter came to **A,** I challenged .... Gal 2:11
sent from James came to **A.** .... Gal 2:12
suffered, as in **A,** Iconium, and 2Ti 3:11

ANTIPAS
in me even during the time of **A,** .... Rev 2:13

ANTIPATRIS
him to the city of **A** that night. .... Ac 23:31

ANTS
Go watch the **a,** you lazy person. .... Pr 6:6
A have no commander, no leader .... Pr 6:7
A are not very strong, but they .... Pr 30:25

ANXIOUS
test me and know my **a** thoughts. .... Ps 139:23
Maroth will be **a** for good news .... Mic 1:12

ANYBODY
A who eats yeast during this .... Ex 12:19

ANYMORE
not grow good crops for you **a,** .... Ge 4:12
so the LORD will not be angry **a.** .... Dt 13:17
old, and I cannot lead you **a.** .... Dt 31:2
will not help you **a** unless you .... Jos 7:12
they did not cause trouble **a.** .... Jdg 8:28
He won't answer me **a,** either by 1Sa 28:15
They did not fight them **a.** 2Sa 2:28
And Elisha did not see him **a.**.................. 2Ki 2:12
did not come **a** into the land 2Ki 6:23
he will not be angry with us **a.** 2Ch 29:10
the king was not so angry **a.** .... Est 7:10
am guilty, but I will not sin **a.**.................. Job 34:31
grave whom you don't remember **a,** .... Ps 88:5
He may not be angry with them **a.**............ Pr 24:18
nor will they train for war **a.** .... Is 2:4
their stubborn, evil hearts **a.** .... Je 3:17
or the Valley of Ben Hinnom **a.** .... Je 7:32
will not remember their sins **a.**" .... Je 31:34
No one will live there **a.** .... Je 51:37
see false visions or prophesy **a,** .... Eze 13:23
will not leave me **a** or make .... Eze 14:11
your harps will not be heard **a.** .... Eze 26:13
not cause your nation to fall **a,** .... Eze 36:15
they will not burn it **a.** .... Mic 4:3
no one will live in Ashkelon **a.** .... Zch 9:5
no one will remember them **a.** .... Zch 13:2
may go now, but don't sin **a.**" .... Jn 8:11
the world will not see me **a,** .... Jn 14:19
I do not live **a**—it is Christ who .... Gal 2:20
not remember their sins **a.**" .... Heb 8:12
do—I will not remember **a.**" .... Heb 10:17
of the earth **a** until the .... Rev 20:3
and there was no sea **a.** .... Rev 21:1

ANYONE
If **a** kills you, I will punish .... Ge 4:15
If **a** could count the dust on the .... Ge 13:16
A who touches this man or his .... Ge 26:11
A who touches the mountain must .... Ex 19:12
You must not murder **a.** .... Ex 20:13
A who kidnaps someone and either .... Ex 21:16
Put to death **a** who has sexual .... Ex 22:19
If **a** treats the Sabbath like any .... Ex 31:14
show mercy to **a** to whom I want .... Ex 33:19
A who is clean may eat other meat. .... Le 7:19
and **a** who touches the dead body .... Le 11:24
When **a** loses hair from his head .... Le 13:40
A who touches the person who .... Le 15:7

A who touches something that was .... Le 15:10
A who eats blood must be cut off. .... Le 17:14
A who curses his father or .... Le 20:9
'If **a** curses his God, he is .... Le 24:15
If **a** is too poor to pay the .... Le 27:8
A else who goes near the Holy .... Nu 1:51
away from camp **a** with a harmful .... Nu 5:2
when a snake bit **a,** that person .... Nu 21:9
A who blesses you will be .... Nu 24:9
a who curses you will be cursed. .... Nu 24:9
may marry **a** you wish, as long .... Nu 36:6
You must not murder **a.** .... Dt 5:17
Don't let **a** use magic or .... Dt 18:10
The LORD hates **a** who does these .... Dt 18:12
Has **a** lost his courage? .... Dt 20:8
God hates **a** who is dishonest .... Dt 25:16
A will be cursed who has sexual .... Dt 27:21
A who takes Baal's side will be .... Jdg 6:31
'**A** who gives a wife to a man of .... Jdg 21:18
nation where you did not know **a.** .... Ru 2:11
still too dark to recognize **a.** .... Ru 3:14
was a head taller than **a** else. 1Sa 10:23
to the oxen of **a** who does not................. 1Sa 11:7
Did I hurt or cheat **a**? 1Sa 12:3
Is **a** left in Saul's family?...................... 2Sa 9:3
Bring me **a** who says anything bad 2Sa 14:10
the wine is for **a** to drink who 2Sa 16:2
the right to kill **a** in Israel.".................... 2Sa 21:4
He was wiser than **a** on earth. 1Ki 4:31
A who wanted to be a priest for 1Ki 13:33
evil than **a** who ruled before 1Ki 14:9
Elisha will kill **a** who escapes 1Ki 19:17
a who dies in the fields will 1Ki 21:24
If **a** greets you, don't respond. 2Ki 4:29
Jehu did not leave **a** alive. 2Ki 10:14
Don't let **a** miss this meeting, ... 2Ki 10:19
Kill **a** who comes near. 2Ki 11:8
me, and don't let **a** hurt me. 1Ch 4:10
Don't let **a** win against you." 2Ch 14:11
A who refused to obey the LORD, ... 2Ch 15:13
Don't let **a** come into the Temple 2Ch 23:6
with a sword **a** who follows her............... 2Ch 23:14
If **a** changes this order, a wood .... Ezr 6:11
I had not told **a** what God had .... Ne 2:12
A who enters must be put to .... Est 4:11
but how can **a** be right in the .... Job 9:2
wish I had died before **a** saw me. .... Job 10:18
How can **a** be pure? How can .... Job 15:14
Can **a** be of real use to God? .... Job 22:2
Can **a** put hooks in its nose? .... Job 40:24
a was looking to God for help. .... Ps 14:2
So why should I fear **a**? .... Ps 27:1
LORD did not let **a** hurt them; .... Ps 105:14
Then **a** can understand wise words .... Pr 1:6
A who loves learning accepts .... Pr 12:1
he will punish **a** who plans evil. .... Pr 12:2
but **a** who accepts correction is .... Pr 15:5
give true answers to **a** who asks. .... Pr 22:21
greater than **a** who had lived .... Ec 2:9
God, who is stronger than **a.** .... Ec 6:10
A who digs a pit might fall into .... Ec 10:8
A who climbs out of the hole .... Is 24:18
a builds a wall of thornbushes .... Is 27:4
A who trusts in it will never be .... Is 28:16
me to anyone? Is **a** equal to me?" .... Is 40:25
A who trusts in me will not be .... Is 49:23
A who lives as they live will .... Is 59:8
tear to pieces **a** who comes out .... Je 5:6
A who stays in Jerusalem will .... Je 21:9
curse will be on **a** who doesn't .... Je 48:10
Don't pity **a,** and don't show .... Eze 9:5
not mistreat **a** or keep something .... Eze 18:16
But I could not find **a.**........................... Eze 22:30

A who doesn't bow down and.................. Da 3:6
those kingdoms to a he chooses. .... Da 4:25
A who can read this writing and   Da 5:7
A who doesn't obey will be...................... Da 6:7
a who calls on the LORD will.................. Joe 2:32
will I find a to comfort you?" .... Nah 3:7
A from the nations who does not .... Zch 14:17
The LORD thinks a who does evil .... Mal 2:17
'A who divorces his wife must .... Mt 5:31
him, "Don't tell a about this. .... Mt 8:4
If a wants to enter a strong...................... Mt 12:29
A who speaks against the Son of .... Mt 12:32
not to tell a he was the Christ. .... Mt 16:20
You must not murder a; .... Mt 19:18
Don't tell a about this.............................. Mk 1:44
a who speaks against the Holy .... Mk 3:29
not to tell a who he was........................... Mk 8:30
A who divorces his wife and .... Mk 10:11
If a asks you why you are doing.............. Mk 11:3
They did not tell a about what .... Mk 16:8
A who believes and is baptized .... Mk 16:16
and I can give it to a I wish. .... Lk 4:6
If a slaps you on one cheek, ... Lk 6:29
A who is not with me is against .... Lk 11:23
a who speaks against the Holy .... Lk 12:10
If a comes to me but loves his................. Lk 14:26
He did not need a to tell him .... Jn 2:25
A who eats this bread will never .... Jn 6:50
Let a who is thirsty come to me .... Jn 7:37
If a believes in me, rivers of .... Jn 7:38
A here who has never sinned can .... Jn 8:7
standards. I am not judging a. .... Jn 8:15
ever heard of a giving sight to .... Jn 9:32
If a walks in the daylight, ... Jn 11:9
A who hears my words and does .... Jn 12:47
If you forgive a his sins, ... Jn 20:23
a who calls on the Lord will .... Ac 2:21
was given to a who needed it.................. Ac 4:35
power so that a on whom I lay my .... Ac 8:19
God accepts a who worships him .... Ac 10:35
Don't tell a that you have told .... Ac 23:22
A who has died is made free from .... Rm 6:7
A who trusts in him will never .... Rm 9:33
Scripture says "a" because there .... Rm 10:12
A who has the gift of serving .... Rm 12:7
If a destroys God's temple, ... 1Co 3:17
But if a says to you, "That food 1Co 10:28
if a speaks in a different 1Co 14:27
If a belongs to Christ, there is 2Co 5:17
We do not want a to find fault 2Co 6:3
patient with a who comes to you 2Co 11:4
A will be cursed who does not .... Gal 3:10
If a thinks he is important when............. Gal 6:3
Do not let a fool you by telling .... Eph 5:6
If a thinks he has a reason to .... Php 3:4
Do not let a disqualify you by................. Col 2:18
not let a fool you in any way. 2Th 2:3
A who refuses to work should not 2Th 3:10
Do not let a treat you as if you 1Ti 4:12
no evil about a, to live in........................ Tit 3:2
A who lives on milk is still a .... Heb 5:13
A who comes to God must believe .... Heb 11:6
A who doubts is like a wave in .... Jam 1:6
A who wants to be a friend of .... Jam 4:4
A who is sick should call the .... Jam 5:14
A who trusts in him will never 1Pe 2:6
A who serves should serve with 1Pe 4:11
He does not want a to be lost,................ 2Pe 3:9
But if a does sin, we have a 1Jn 2:1
A who says, "I am in the light," 1Jn 2:9
will not cause a to stumble in 1Jn 2:10
A who goes on sinning has never 1Jn 3:6
A who believes in the Son of God 1Jn 5:10

If a sees a brother or sister 1Jn 5:16
A who does not confess this is a.............. 2Jn 1:7
not given the power to kill a, ... Rev 9:5
A who has ears should listen: .... Rev 13:9
If a worships the beast and his .... Rev 14:9
And a whose name was not found .... Rev 20:15
of life to a who is thirsty. .... Rev 21:6
If a adds anything to these .... Rev 22:18

ANYONE'S
Did I steal a ox or donkey?..................... 1Sa 12:3
and don't guarantee a loan. .... Pr 22:26
and we have never been a slaves. .... Jn 8:33
I never wanted a money or fine .... Ac 20:33
believe without a saying a word 1Pe 3:1

ANYTHING
will be able to do a they want. .... Ge 11:6
Do a you want to her." .... Ge 16:6
Is a too hard for the LORD? .... Ge 18:14
Her son should not inherit a; .... Ge 21:10
Do not say a to Jacob, good or .... Ge 31:24
If you have found a, show it to .... Ge 31:37
I will give a you ask. .... Ge 34:11
He has not kept a from me except .... Ge 39:9
must not eat a made with yeast .... Ex 12:20
that looks like a in the sky .... Ex 20:4
a that makes someone unclean— .... Le 5:3
must not touch a that is holy .... Le 12:4
we never see a but this manna!"............. Nu 11:6
A the Israelites present as holy .... Nu 18:19
of a that crawls on the ground, ... Dt 4:18
a that belongs to your neighbor.............. Dt 5:21
Do not add a to it, and do not.................. Dt 12:32
Do not eat a the LORD hates................... Dt 14:3
don't send them away without a. .... Dt 15:13
Do not disobey a I command you .... Dt 28:14
She must not eat a that grows on .... Jdg 13:14
Let me give you a you need, ... Jdg 19:20
and did not hide a from him. 1Sa 3:18
If I have done a wrong, you must 1Sa 12:3
"I'll do a you want me to do."................ 1Sa 20:4
to him, "We will do a you say." 2Sa 15:15
I will do for him a you wish, ... 2Sa 19:38
you may take a you want for a 2Sa 24:22
Solomon will do a you ask him," 1Ki 2:17
prophesies a good about me, ... 1Ki 22:8
and I will pay a you ask." 2Ki 18:14
master the king, do a you want. 1Ch 21:23
prophesies a good about me, ... 2Ch 18:7
Give those people a they need—............. Ezr 6:9
had not yet said a to the Jewish .... Ne 2:16
A she asked for was given to her .... Est 2:13
hands have never done a cruel, ... Job 16:17
He does a he wants. .... Job 23:13
If you have a to say, answer me;............. Job 33:32
"Who will give us a good?" .... Ps 4:6
There is no one who does a good, ... Ps 14:3
They don't take a to the grave; .... Ps 49:17
I want more than a to be in the .... Ps 84:2
I will not look at a wicked. .... Ps 101:3
People can't do a to me. .... Ps 118:6
long before he made a else. .... Pr 8:22
will believe a, but the wise .... Pr 14:15
I have never done a wrong." .... Pr 20:9
an archer shooting at just a. .... Pr 26:10
having fun doesn't accomplish a. .... Ec 2:2
A I saw and wanted, I got for .... Ec 2:10
cannot add a to what God has .... Ec 3:14
feel happy, and money buys a. .... Ec 10:19
be worse than a that has........................ Is 7:17
Can you compare God to a? .... Is 40:18
there has ever been a like this. .... Je 2:10
I have not loaned or borrowed a, ... Je 15:10

you ever heard **a** like this?' .... Je 18:13
I cannot do **a** to stop you." .... Je 38:5
I will never do **a** like again, ... Eze 5:9
of the trumpet but didn't do **a**. .... Eze 33:5
Don't give us **a** but vegetables .... Da 1:12
could not find **a** wrong with him .... Da 6:4
has never been **a** like it before, ... Joe 2:2
will never be **a** like it again. .... Joe 2:2
Don't say **a**, even to your wife. .... Mic 7:5
get **a** you ask for in prayer. .... Mt 21:22
a you did for even the least of .... Mt 25:40
"We have never seen **a** like this!" .... Mk 2:12
Ask me for **a** you want, and I .... Mk 6:22
God can do **a**!" .... Lk 1:37
able to trap Jesus in **a** he said................ Lk 20:26
or sandals, did you need **a**?" .... Lk 22:35
"Can **a** good come from Nazareth?" .... Jn 1:46
If you ask me for **a** in my name,............. Jn 14:14
I never said **a** in secret. .... Jn 18:20
never eaten **a** that is unholy .... Ac 11:8
Stop and think before you do **a**. .... Ac 19:36
If I have really done **a** wrong,................. Ac 24:19
Can **a** separate us from the love .... Rm 8:35
potter can make **a** he wants to .... Rm 9:21
not owe people **a**, except always.............. Rm 13:8
A that is done without believing.............. Rm 14:23
I will not let **a** make me its 1Co 6:12
want you to share **a** with demons. 1Co 10:20
or if you do **a**, do it all for 1Co 10:31
Do not let **a** move you. 1Co 15:58
Satan would not win **a** from us, ... 2Co 2:11
free from **a** that makes body or 2Co 7:1
cannot do **a** against the truth,................. 2Co 13:8
one can stop it or add **a** to it. .... Gal 3:15
much more than **a** we can ask or .... Eph 3:20
to hurt others. Never do **a** evil. .... Eph 4:31
not worry about **a**, but pray and .... Php 4:6
He was there before **a** was made, ... Col 1:17
because of **a** we did ourselves................. 2Ti 1:9
are useless for doing **a** good. .... Tit 1:16
If he has done **a** wrong to you or .... Phm 1:18
Moses could not make **a** perfect. .... Heb 7:19
People can't do **a** to me." .... Heb 13:6
If people never said **a** wrong, ... Jam 3:2
are bold and do **a** they want. 2Pe 2:10
we ask God for **a** that agrees 1Jn 5:14
wealthy and do not need **a**.' .... Rev 3:17
If anyone adds **a** to these words, ... Rev 22:18

ANYTIME

A Moses went before the Lord to .... Ex 34:34
our king, come down **a** you want. 1Sa 23:20
Listen to them **a** they ask you................. 1Ki 8:52
you can help them **a** you want. .... Mk 14:7

ANYWAY

to them, but they prophesied **a**. .... Je 23:21

ANYWHERE

You may live **a** you want." .... Ge 20:15
there was no food **a** in the land, ... Ge 47:13
on any tree or plant **a** in Egypt. .... Ex 10:15
made with yeast **a** in your land. .... Ex 13:7
offerings just **a** you please. .... Dt 12:13
of your towns **a** in Israel where .... Dt 18:6
if you went out **a** you would die,.............. 1Ki 2:42
than a thousand days **a** else. .... Ps 84:10
the sheep will go **a** they want, ... Is 5:17
so there is not **a** clean place **a**. .... Is 28:8
he was free to go **a** he wanted. .... Je 37:4
Cut **a** your blade is turned. .... Eze 21:16
could be seen from **a** on earth. .... Da 4:11
there was no food **a** in the whole .... Lk 4:25
greatest faith I have found **a**, ... Lk 7:9
was no food **a** in the country, ... Lk 15:14

APARTMENT

was sitting in the winter **a**. .... Je 36:22

APES

silver, ivory, **a**, and baboons. 1Ki 10:22

APHEK

went up to **A** to fight against 1Ki 20:26

APIECE

fifteen pounds of silver **a**, ... 2Ch 1:17

APOLLOS

A Jew named **A** came to Ephesus. .... Ac 18:24
A began to speak very boldly in............... Ac 18:26
another says, "I follow **A**"; 1Co 1:12
the seed, and **A** watered it. 1Co 3:6
Now about our brother **A**: 1Co 16:12
lawyer and **A** on their journey .... Tit 3:13

APOLLYON

and in the Greek language is **A**. .... Rev 9:11

APOSTLE

So he became an **a** with the other .... Ac 1:26
me to be an **a** and chose me to .... Rm 1:1
I am an **a** to those who are not .... Rm 11:13
me to be an **a** of Christ Jesus 1Co 1:1
free man. I am an **a**. I have seen 1Co 9:1
good enough to be called an **a**, ... 1Co 15:9
I am an **a** because that is what 2Co 1:1
Paul, an **a**. I was not chosen .... Gal 1:1
I am an **a** because that is what .... Eph 1:1
From Paul, an **a** of Christ Jesus. .... Col 1:1
the Good News and to be an **a**. 1Ti 2:7
Peter, an **a** of Jesus Christ. 1Pe 1:1

APOSTLES

are the names of the twelve **a**: .... Mt 10:2
chose twelve and called them **a**. .... Mk 3:14
The **a** gathered around Jesus and .... Mk 6:30
and called the twelve **a** to him. .... Mk 9:35
the twelve **a** aside and began .... Mk 10:32
to Bethany with the twelve **a**. .... Mk 11:11
of the twelve **a**, Judas Iscariot................ Mk 14:10
to the eleven **a** while they were .... Mk 16:14
twelve of them, whom he named **a**: .... Lk 6:13
money to help Jesus and his **a**. .... Lk 8:3
He sent the **a** out to tell about................ Lk 9:10
When the **a** returned, they told .... Lk 9:10
send prophets and **a** to them. .... Lk 11:49
The **a** said to the Lord, "Give us .... Lk 17:5
took the twelve **a** aside and said.............. Lk 18:31
Jesus and the **a** were sitting at .... Lk 22:14
The **a** also began to argue about.............. Lk 22:24
who told the **a** everything that .... Lk 24:10
Jesus told the **a** he had chosen .... Ac 1:2
The **a** saw Jesus during the forty .... Ac 1:3
and asked Peter and the other **a**, ... Ac 2:37
The **a** were doing many miracles .... Ac 2:43
great power the **a** were telling .... Ac 4:33
The **a** called him Barnabas .... Ac 4:36
the money and gave it to the **a**. .... Ac 5:2
a did many signs and miracles .... Ac 5:12
took the **a** and put them in jail. .... Ac 5:18
They called the **a** in, beat them, ... Ac 5:40
except the **a**, were scattered .... Ac 8:1
the two **a** began laying their .... Ac 8:17
So he offered the **a** money, ... Ac 8:18
The **a** and the believers in Judea .... Ac 11:1
But when the **a**, Barnabas and .... Ac 14:14
The **a** and the elders gathered to .... Ac 15:6
They are very important **a**. .... Rm 16:7
God has put us **a** in last place, ... 1Co 4:9
has given a place first to **a**,...................... 1Co 12:28
Peter and then by the twelve **a**. 1Co 15:5
by James and later by all the **a**. 1Co 15:7

APPEAL

those "great **a**" are any better 2Co 11:5
I met no other **a**, except James, ... Gal 1:19
to his holy **a** and prophets. .... Eph 3:5
he made some to be **a**, some to be .... Eph 4:11
even though as **a** of Christ we 1Th 2:7
what the **a** of our Lord Jesus .... Jud 1:17
say they are **a** but really are .... Rev 2:2
holy people and **a** and prophets! .... Rev 18:20
of the twelve **a** of the Lamb. .... Rev 21:14

APPEAL

Our **a** does not come from lies or 1Th 2:3

APPEALING

right side, **a** to God for us. .... Rm 8:34

APPEALS

never refused the **a** of the poor .... Job 31:16

APPEAR

so the dry land will **a**." .... Ge 1:9
'The LORD did not **a** to you'?" .... Ex 4:1
the LORD will **a** to you today.'" .... Le 9:4
goes in when I **a** in a cloud over .... Le 16:2
LORD did not **a** to them again. .... Jdg 13:21
day's morning stars never **a**; .... Job 3:9
When you **a**, you will burn them .... Ps 21:9
hay, and let the new grass **a**. .... Pr 27:25
Blossoms **a** through all the land. .... Sng 2:12
Then the LORD will **a** above them,........... Zch 9:14
Son of Man will **a** in the sky. .... Mt 24:30
green and soft and new leaves **a**, ... Mk 13:28
kingdom would **a** immediately. .... Lk 19:11
their leaves **a**, you know that .... Lk 21:30
That Day will **a** with fire, ... 1Co 3:13
Evil so he will **a** at the right 2Th 2:6
Then that Man of Evil will **a**, ... 2Th 2:8

APPEARANCE

his **a** was frightening. .... Jdg 13:6
praised for his handsome **a**. 2Sa 14:25
you change their **a** and send them .... Job 14:20
His **a** was so damaged he did not .... Is 52:14
nothing in his **a** to make us .... Is 53:2
watched, Jesus' **a** was changed; .... Mt 17:2
the **a** of his face changed, ... Lk 9:29
to understand the **a** of the earth .... Lk 12:56

APPEARED

The LORD **a** to Abram and said, ... Ge 12:7
the LORD again **a** to Abraham near .... Ge 18:1
The LORD **a** to Isaac and said, ... Ge 26:2
The LORD **a** to him that night and .... Ge 26:24
to the God who **a** to you there .... Ge 35:1
a to him again and blessed him. .... Ge 35:9
of the LORD **a** to him in flames .... Ex 3:2
the God of the Hebrews, **a** to us. .... Ex 3:18
I **a** to Abraham, Isaac, and Jacob .... Ex 6:3
glory of the LORD **a** in a cloud. .... Ex 16:10
of the LORD **a** at the Meeting............... Nu 14:10
The LORD **a** at the Meeting Tent .... Dt 31:15
angel of the LORD **a** to Gideon .... Jdg 6:12
of the LORD **a** to Manoah's wife .... Jdg 13:3
Then the valleys of the sea **a**, ... 2Sa 22:16
the LORD **a** to him in a dream 1Ki 3:5
The LORD had **a** to Solomon twice, ... 1Ki 11:9
horses of fire **a** and separated............... 2Ki 2:11
That night God **a** to Solomon and 2Ch 1:7
where the LORD had **a** to David, ... 2Ch 3:1
Then the LORD **a** to Solomon at............. 2Ch 7:12
Then the valleys of the sea **a**, ... Ps 18:15
He commanded, and it **a**. .... Ps 33:9
a person's hand **a** and began .... Da 5:5
Then Moses and Elijah **a** to them, ... Mt 17:3
where they **a** to many people............... Mt 27:53
Then Elijah and Moses **a** to them, ... Mk 9:4
of the Lord **a** to Zechariah,................... Lk 1:11

a in heavenly glory, talking....../............ Lk 9:31
angel from heaven **a** to him to .... Lk 22:43
Remember when Theudas **a**? .... Ac 5:36
Our glorious God **a** to Abraham, ... Ac 7:2
years later an angel **a** to Moses .... Ac 7:30
But Philip **a** in a city called................. Ac 8:40
and Bernice **a** with great show, ... Ac 25:23
then a great wonder **a** in heaven: .... Rev 12:1
Then another wonder **a** in heaven: .... Rev 12:3

APPEARING

be cut off from **a** before me. .... Le 22:3

APPEARS

earth and a rainbow **a** in them, ... Ge 9:14
If mildew again **a** in his house, ... Le 14:43
the Lord Jesus **a** with burning 2Th 1:7
who is on his way to hell, **a**. 2Th 2:3

APPETITE

But now we have lost our **a**; .... Nu 11:6
Evil people never lack an **a**, ... Job 20:20
yourself if you have a big **a**. .... Pr 23:2
Your **a** will be gone. .... Ec 12:5

APPLAUD

they **a** others who do them. .... Rm 1:32

APPLAUDS

Everyone who hears about you **a**, ... Nah 3:19

APPLE

lover is like an **a** tree in the .... Sng 2:3
you under the **a** tree where you .... Sng 8:5
palm trees, the **a** trees—all the .... Joe 1:12

APPLES

as gold **a** in a silver bowl .... Pr 25:11
refresh me with **a**, because I am.............. Sng 2:5
the smell of your breath like **a**, ... Sng 7:8

APPLY

The same rules **a** to an Israelite .... Ex 12:49

APPOINT

the king also **a** officers over .... Ge 41:34
their heads to **a** them as priests .... Ex 28:41
is how you will **a** Aaron and his............. Ex 29:9
A Aaron and his sons to serve as .... Nu 3:10
A Joshua and help him be brave .... Dt 3:28
A judges and officers for your .... Dt 16:18
Let's **a** a king over us like the................ Dt 17:14
they should **a** commanders to lead........... Dt 20:9
really want to **a** me king over .... Jdg 9:15
A him to lead my people Israel. 1Sa 9:16
LORD sent me to **a** you king over 1Sa 15:1
You must **a** the one I show you." 1Sa 16:3
Samuel, "Go, **a** him, because he 1Sa 16:12
oil on Solomon to **a** him king 1Ch 29:22
oil on Zadok to **a** him as priest. 1Ch 29:22
A people who live in Jerusalem .... Ne 7:3
send them or **a** them or speak to .... Je 14:14
and to **a** a most holy place..................... Da 9:24
you going to **a** people as judges 1Co 6:4
so you could **a** elders in every .... Tit 1:5

APPOINTED

when they are **a** as priests. .... Ex 29:29
way that you **a** their father as................. Ex 40:15
If the **a** priest sins so that .... Le 4:3
man who has been **a** will lead the .... Le 16:21
'These are the LORD's **a** feasts, ... Le 23:4
who were **a** to serve as priests. .... Nu 3:3
the Passover at the **a** time. .... Nu 9:2
I **a** commanders over a thousand .... Dt 1:15
always serve before my **a** king. 1Sa 2:35
The LORD has **a** you to lead his 1Sa 10:1
He has **a** him to rule his people, ... 1Sa 13:14
The LORD **a** you to be king over 1Sa 15:17

Saul is the LORD's **a** king. 1Sa 24:6
to kill the LORD's **a** king?" 2Sa 1:14
to Hebron and **a** David king over 2Sa 2:4
The LORD **a** me to be over Israel. 2Sa 6:21
We **a** Absalom to rule us, but now 2Sa 19:10
He is the **a** king of the God of 2Sa 23:1
I have **a** you king over Israel.' 2Ki 9:3
They **a** him king and poured olive 2Ki 11:12
!Then David **a** some of the Levites 1Ch 16:4
Jehoshaphat **a** judges in all the 2Ch 19:5
the LORD had **a** to destroy Ahab's 2Ch 22:7
Hezekiah **a** groups of priests 2Ch 31:2
he has **a** me to build a Temple 2Ch 36:23
to our God and **a** guards to watch .... Ne 4:9
I was **a** governor in the land of .... Ne 5:14
son of Zicri was **a** over them, ... Ne 11:9
against the LORD and his **a** one. .... Ps 2:2
He is loyal to his **a** king, ... Ps 18:50
know the LORD helps his **a** king. .... Ps 20:6
I **a** him by pouring holy oil on .... Ps 89:20
and rejected your **a** king. .... Ps 89:38
do not reject your **a** king. .... Ps 132:10
LORD says to Cyrus, his **a** king: .... Is 45:1
a you as a prophet to the nations. .... Je 1:5
of Babylon had **a** Zedekiah son .... Je 37:1
I **a** a living creature to guard .... Eze 28:14
until the **a** leader comes will .... Da 9:25
years the **a** leader will be .... Da 9:26
who have been **a** to serve the .... Zch 4:14
because he **a** me to tell the Good .... Lk 4:18

APPOINTING
special oil used in **a** priests. .... Ex 29:21
holy olive oil for **a** the priests .... Ex 37:29
sheep used in **a** the priests, ... Le 8:29
The time of **a** will last seven .... Le 8:33

APPOINTMENT
offering for the **a** of priests, ... Le 7:37
asked for an **a** so that he could .... Da 2:16

APPRECIATE
we ask you to **a** those who work 1Th 5:12

APPROACH
Whenever they **a** the altar to .... Ex 30:20
when they **a** the Holy Place." .... Nu 8:19
When you **a** this town, a group of 1Sa 10:5

APPROACHED
Then Abraham **a** him and asked, ... Ge 18:23
As Barak **a**, the LORD confused .... Jdg 4:15
a the door of the tower to set .... Jdg 9:52
Saul **a** Samuel at the gate and 1Sa 9:18
Elijah **a** the people and said, ... 1Ki 18:21
Then the woman **a** him, dressed .... Pr 7:10
a woman **a** him with an alabaster .... Mt 26:7
a woman **a** him with an alabaster .... Mk 14:3

APPROACHES
If a woman **a** an animal and has .... Le 20:16

APPROVAL
haven't asked for the LORD's **a**.' 1Sa 13:12
and my **a** was important to them. .... Job 29:24
given the Son the **a** to judge, ... Jn 5:27
of you really have God's **a**. 1Co 11:19

APPROVE
you show that you **a** of what your .... Lk 11:48
whomever you **a** to take your gift 1Co 16:3
as the kind of person he will **a**. 2Ti 2:15

AQUILA
met a Jew named **A** who had been .... Ac 18:2
for Syria, with Priscilla and **A**. .... Ac 18:18
where Paul left Priscilla and **A**. .... Ac 18:19
my greetings to Priscilla and **A**, ... Rm 16:3

A and Priscilla greet you in the 1Co 16:19
Priscilla and **A** and the family 2Ti 4:19

AR
It destroyed **A** in Moab, and it .... Nu 21:28
have given **A** to the descendants .... Dt 2:9
Today you will pass by **A**, ... Dt 2:18
took the wealth from **A** in Moab, ... Is 15:1

ARAB
and Geshem the **A** heard about it, ... Ne 2:19
No **A** will put a tent there; .... Is 13:20
lovers, like an **A** in the desert. .... Je 3:2

ARABAH
flowing down to the Sea of **A** .... Jos 3:16

ARABIA
the kings of **A** and governors 1Ki 10:15
All the kings of **A** and the 2Ch 9:14
the night near some trees in **A**. .... Is 21:13
People of **A** and all the rulers .... Eze 27:21
had become Jews), Crete, and **A**. .... Ac 2:11
I went away to **A** and later went .... Gal 1:17
Sinai in **A** and is a picture .... Gal 4:25

ARABS
Some **A** brought him flocks: 2Ch 17:11
Philistines and **A** attacked Judah 2Ch 21:17
Philistines, the **A** living in Gur 2Ch 26:7
Tobiah, the **A**, the Ammonites, ... Ne 4:7

ARAD
Hormah, **A**, ... Jos 12:14
Judah near the city of **A**. .... Jdg 1:16

ARAM
Asshur, Arphaxad, Lud, and **A**. .... Ge 10:22
Balak brought me here from **A**; .... Nu 23:7
the gods of **A**, Sidon, Moab, ... Jdg 10:6
I was living in Geshur in **A**. 2Sa 15:8
was the king of **A** and ruled in 1Ki 15:18
The king of **A** will attack you 1Ki 20:22
was peace between Israel and **A**. 1Ki 22:1
The king of **A** was at war with 2Ki 6:8
Ben-Hadad king of **A** was sick. 2Ki 8:7
Hazael king of **A** attacked Gath 2Ki 12:17
LORD's arrow of victory over **A!** 2Ki 13:17
king of **A** ordered his chariot 2Ch 18:30
fought against Hazael king of **A**. 2Ch 22:5
over Ahaz to the king of **A** 2Ch 28:5
of Israel and **A** will be empty. .... Is 7:16
People of **A** became traders for .... Eze 27:16
The people of **A** will be taken .... Am 1:5

ARAMAIC
speak to us in the **A** language. 2Ki 18:26
It was written in the **A** language .... Ezr 4:7
speak to us in the **A** language. .... Is 36:11
the king in the **A** language, ... Da 2:4

ARAMEAN
and the sister of Laban the **A**. .... Ge 25:20
came to Laban the **A** in a dream .... Ge 31:24
My father was a wandering **A**. .... Dt 26:5
and forty thousand **A** horsemen. 2Sa 10:18
thoroughly defeated the **A** army. 1Ki 20:21
what Naaman the **A** brought. 2Ki 5:20
So he made the **A** army blind, ... 2Ki 6:18
twilight and went to the **A** camp, ... 2Ki 7:5
Manasseh had an **A** slave woman, ... 1Ch 7:14
seven thousand **A** chariot drivers 1Ch 19:18
the **A** army came against Joash. 2Ch 24:23
Babylonian army and the **A** army.' .... Je 35:11

ARAMEANS
A from Damascus came to help 2Sa 8:5
A became David's servants and 2Sa 8:6
Arameans, and the **A** ran away. 2Sa 10:13

ARARAT

The **A** had gone out to raid the 2Ki 5:2
A became David's servants and 1Ch 18:6
sent them out to fight the **A**. 1Ch 19:10
A defeated Ahaz and took many 2Ch 28:5
The **A** came from the east and the .... Is 9:12
from Crete, and the **A** from Kir. .... Am 9:7

ARARAT

they escaped to the land of **A**. 2Ki 19:37
they escaped to the land of **A**. .... Is 37:38
these kingdoms of **A**, Minni, and .... Je 51:27

ARAUNAH

floor of **A** the Jebusite. 2Sa 24:16
king answered **A**, "No, I will pay 2Sa 24:24
A was separating the wheat from 1Ch 21:20
So David paid **A** about fifteen 1Ch 21:25
him on the threshing floor of **A**, ... 1Ch 21:28
floor of **A** the Jebusite. 2Ch 3:1

ARAUNAH'S

A four sons who were with him hid. 1Ch 21:20

ARBA

died in Kiriath **A** (that is, ... Ge 23:2
past it was called Kiriath **A**, ... Jos 14:15
used to be called Kiriath **A** .... Jdg 1:10
lived in Kiriath **A** and its....................... Ne 11:25

ARCHANGEL

the voice of the **a**, and with the 1Th 4:16
Not even the **a** Michael, when he .... Jud 1:9

ARCHELAUS

But he heard that **A** was now king .... Mt 2:22

ARCHER

in the desert and became an **a**. .... Ge 21:20
by is like an **a** shooting at just .... Pr 26:10

ARCHERS

A attack him violently and shoot .... Ge 49:23
The **a** shot him, and he was badly 1Sa 31:3
The **a** on the city wall shot at 2Sa 11:24
were mighty warriors and good **a**. 1Ch 8:40
and the **a** shot him with their 1Ch 10:3
King Josiah was shot by **a**. 2Ch 35:23
his **a** surround me. He stabs my .... Job 16:13
that time only a few of the **a**, ... Is 21:17
the land of **a**), Tubal, Greece .... Is 66:19
sound of the horsemen and the **a**, ... Je 4:29
Call for the **a** to come against................. Je 50:29

ARCHIPPUS

Tell **A**, "Be sure to finish the .... Col 4:17
to **A**, a worker with us; .... Phm 1:2

AREA

lived in the **a** between Mesha .... Ge 10:30
light to the **a** in front of it. .... Ex 25:37
quail into the **a** all around the .... Nu 11:31
in the southern **a** of Canaan, ... Nu 33:40
the southern **a**, the seacoast, ... Dt 1:7
"Go to Ai and spy out the **a**." .... Jos 7:2
ambush in the west of the city............... Jos 8:12
Mount Hermon in the **a** of Mizpah. .... Jos 11:3
and all the **a** of Bashan up to .... Jos 12:5
You gave us only one **a** of land, ... Jos 17:14
David is in the **a**, I will track 1Sa 23:23
but the Arameans covered the **a**. 1Ki 20:27
lived in the **a** of Bashan all 1Ch 5:11
take her out of the Temple **a**. 2Ch 23:14
the people of the **a** who returned .... Ezr 2:1
the people of the **a** who returned .... Ne 7:6
That whole **a** will be an empty .... Je 25:11
the forest of the southern **a**. .... Eze 20:46
The private **a**, including the .... Eze 41:13
measuring inside the Temple **a**, ... Eze 42:15
leaders over the **a** of Babylon, ... Da 2:49

Abednego in the **a** of Babylon. .... Da 3:30
he went to the **a** of Galilee, ... Mt 2:22
in the desert **a** of Judea. .... Mt 3:1
and all the **a** around the Jordan .... Mt 3:5
begged him to leave their **a**. .... Mt 8:34
about Jesus all around that **a**................... Mt 9:31
went to the **a** of Tyre and Sidon. .... Mt 15:21
and went to the **a** of Magadan. .... Mt 15:39
Jesus came to the **a** of Caesarea .... Mt 16:13
everywhere in the **a** of Galilee. .... Mk 1:28
to beg Jesus to leave their **a**. .... Mk 5:17
villages in that **a** and taught. .... Mk 6:6
and went to the **a** around Tyre. .... Mk 7:24
to the **a** of the Ten Towns. .... Mk 7:31
and went to the **a** of Dalmanutha. .... Mk 8:10
and went into the **a** of Judea and .... Mk 10:1
all over the **a** around the Jordan............... Lk 3:3
to every place in the whole **a**. .... Lk 4:37
Galilee to the **a** of the Gerasene .... Lk 8:26
through the **a** between Samaria .... Lk 17:11
was traveling through all the **a**, ... Ac 9:32
and forced them out of their **a**. .... Ac 13:50
and asked Paul, "What **a** are you .... Ac 23:34
The first **a** in the Tent was .... Heb 9:2

AREAS

Canaan, all the **a** of Goshen, the............... Jos 11:16
All these **a** are the lands the .... Jos 18:28
Israelites in all the **a** of 1Ch 13:2
for kings and **a** controlled by .... Ezr 4:15
These are the **a** of the tribes .... Eze 48:1
The richest **a** will feel safe, ... Da 11:24
The **a** of Bashan and Carmel dry .... Nah 1:4
to the **a** around those cities. .... Ac 14:6
News in the **a** beyond your city 2Co 10:16
I went to the **a** of Syria and .... Gal 1:21

AREN'T

Why **a** you making as many bricks .... Ex 5:14
A you going to do something? .... Jdg 18:9
Why **a** you repairing the damage 2Ki 12:7
A they in your records? .... Ps 56:8
So why **a** the hurts of my people .... Je 8:22
said to Jesus, "**A** you going to.................. Mt 26:62
A you going to answer?"....................... Mk 15:4
at Jesus: "**A** you the Christ? .... Lk 23:39
you **a** looking for me because you .... Jn 6:26
A you also one of that man's .... Jn 18:17
A all these people that we hear .... Ac 2:7

AREOPAGUS

took him to a meeting of the **A**, ... Ac 17:19
a member of the **A**, a woman named .... Ac 17:34

ARETAS

under King **A** wanted to arrest me 2Co 11:32

ARGOB

and took the whole area of **A**, ... Dt 3:4

ARGUE

and Lot's herdsmen began to **a**. .... Ge 13:7
named that well **A** because they............... Ge 26:20
If two men **a**, and one hits the .... Ex 21:18
So how can I **a** with God, or even .... Job 9:14
Almighty and to **a** my case with .... Job 13:3
A my case and save me. .... Ps 119:154
Whoever loves to **a** loves to sin. .... Pr 17:19
No one can **a** with God, who is .... Ec 6:10
for those who **a** with the God who .... Is 45:9
He will not **a** or cry out; .... Mt 12:19
could not **a** with Jesus' answers .... Mt 22:34
that they could not **a** with him. .... Ac 6:10
often talk and **a** with the Jewish............... Ac 9:29
and do not **a** about opinions. .... Rm 14:1
presence not to **a** about words. 2Ti 2:14
want. So you **a** and fight. You................. Jam 4:2

ARGUED

herdsmen of Gerar **a** with them .... Ge 26:20
They **a** with Moses and said, ... Nu 20:3
the Israelites **a** with the LORD .... Nu 20:13
They **a** angrily with Gideon. .... Jdg 8:1
the two women **a** before the king 1Ki 3:22
I **a** with the officers, saying, ... Ne 13:11
They **a** about Jesus' question, ... Mk 11:31
They **a** about this, saying, "If .... Lk 20:5
all came and **a** with Stephen. .... Ac 6:9
things and **a** against what Paul .... Ac 13:45
Stoic philosophers **a** with him, ... Ac 17:18
He **a** very strongly with the Jews .... Ac 18:28
stood up and **a**, "We find nothing .... Ac 23:9
they **a** and began leaving after .... Ac 28:25
when he **a** with the devil about .... Jud 1:9

ARGUES

the person who **a** with the .... Job 40:2

ARGUING

should be no **a** between you and .... Ge 13:8
two people who are **a** must stand .... Dt 19:17
What makes you keep on **a?** .... Job 16:3
they are **a** and fighting. .... Hab 1:3
teachers of the law **a** with them............... Mk 9:14
were you **a** about on the road?" .... Mk 9:33
and heard Jesus **a** with the .... Mk 12:28
me did not find me **a** with anyone .... Ac 24:12
They were **a** very much with each .... Ac 28:29
without complaining or **a**. .... Php 2:14
with a love for **a** and fighting 1Ti 6:4
is true, and this ends all **a**. .... Heb 6:16

ARGUMENT

have an **a** and go to court, ... Dt 25:1
If you have an **a** with your .... Pr 25:9
person keeps an **a** going. .... Pr 26:21
He will settle his **a** with Israel .... Is 27:8
because their **a** on the road was .... Mk 9:34
to have an **a** about which one .... Lk 9:46
had an **a** with a Jew about .... Jn 3:25
followers had an **a** with the .... Ac 6:1
there was an **a** between the .... Ac 23:7
The **a** was beginning to turn into .... Ac 23:10

ARGUMENTS

come to her to settle their **a**. .... Jdg 4:5
and your **a** are as weak as clay. .... Job 13:12
and are always starting **a**. .... Pr 6:14
who starts **a** among families. .... Pr 6:19
and a separate people like the .... Pr 18:19
have told you my **a** against these .... Je 20:12
We destroy people's **a** 2Co 10:4
These things only bring **a;** 1Ti 1:4
away from foolish and stupid **a**, ... 2Ti 2:23
avoid someone who causes **a**. .... Tit 3:10
where your fights and **a** come .... Jam 4:1

ARIMATHEA

of Jesus from the town of **A**, ... Mt 27:57
Joseph from **A** was brave enough .... Mk 15:43
the town of **A** and was waiting .... Lk 23:51
Joseph from **A** asked Pilate if he .... Jn 19:38

ARIOCH

king of Babylonia, **A** was king of .... Ge 14:1
A, the commander of the king's .... Da 2:14
Daniel went to **A**, the man King............... Da 2:24
Very quickly **A** took Daniel to .... Da 2:25

ARISE

A and punish those people...................... Ps 59:5
God, **a** and defend yourself. .... Ps 74:22

ARISTARCHUS

The people grabbed Gaius and **A**, ... Ac 19:29
A, a man from the city of .... Ac 27:2

A, a prisoner with me, and Mark, ... Col 4:10
And also Mark, **A**, Demas, and .... Phm 1:24

ARISTOBULUS

who are in the family of **A**...................... Rm 16:10

ARK

and build an **A** forty-five inches .... Ex 25:10
a lid of pure gold for the **A;** .... Ex 25:17
Put this lid on top of the **A**,.................... Ex 25:21
made the **A** of acacia wood; .... Ex 37:1
Most Holy Place where the **A** is............... Le 16:2
They were responsible for the **A**, ... Nu 3:31
When the **A** left the camp, Moses .... Nu 10:35
mountain. Also make a wooden **A**........... Dt 10:1
put the new tablets in the **A**." .... Dt 10:2
carrying the **A** of the Agreement .... Jos 3:3
river where the **A** of the LORD .... Jos 4:5
them march in front of the **A**. .... Jos 6:4
before the **A** of the Agreement. .... Jdg 20:28
The **A** of God was taken by the 1Sa 4:11
had captured the **A** of God,.................... 1Sa 5:1
you send back the **A** of the God 1Sa 6:3
The **A** stayed at Kiriath Jearim a 1Sa 7:2
The **A** is called by the Name, ... 2Sa 6:2
died there beside the **A** of God. 2Sa 6:7
The **A** of the LORD stayed in 2Sa 6:11
up a tent for the **A** of the LORD,............. 2Sa 6:17
Take the **A** of God back into the 2Sa 15:25
inside the **A** were two stone 1Ki 8:9
had put in the **A** at Mount Sinai. 1Ki 8:9
to bring the **A** of God back from 1Ch 13:5
winged creatures on the **A**,.................... 1Ch 13:6
out his hand to steady the **A**. 1Ch 13:9
Levites may carry the **A** of God............... 1Ch 15:2
were also guards for the **A**..................... 1Ch 15:24
serve before the **A** of the LORD............... 1Ch 16:4
the Levites lifted up the **A**. 2Ch 5:4
inside the **A** were two stone 2Ch 5:10
Put the Holy **A** in the Temple 2Ch 35:3
He let the **A**, his power, be .... Ps 78:61
heard about the **A** in Bethlehem. .... Ps 132:6
come with the **A** that shows your .... Ps 132:8
remember the **A** of the Agreement. .... Je 3:16
Inside this **A** was a golden jar .... Heb 9:4
Above the **A** were the creatures .... Heb 9:5
The **A** that holds the agreement .... Rev 11:19

ARM

and two gold **a** bracelets .... Ge 24:22
a bands, bracelets, signet rings, ... Nu 31:50
raised his **a** toward Jerusalem 2Sa 24:16
Put down your **a!**" The angel 2Sa 24:16
said this, his **a** was paralyzed, ... 1Ki 13:4
and the king's **a** was healed, ... 1Ki 13:6
Put down your **a!**" The angel 1Ch 21:15
their **a** is raised to do harm, ... Job 38:15
a has great power. Your hand .... Ps 89:13
right hand and holy **a** he has won .... Ps 98:1
and his right **a** holds me tight. .... Sng 2:6
He will wave his **a** over the..................... Is 11:15
his powerful **a** come down with .... Is 30:30
The LORD will stretch out his **a**, ... Is 31:3
been cut off, and its **a** broken!" .... Je 48:25
With your **a** bare, you will .... Eze 4:7
both the strong **a** and the broken .... Eze 30:22
a will lose all its strength, ... Zch 11:17

ARMAGEDDON

that is called **A** in the Hebrew .... Rev 16:16

ARMED

and cross the Jordan River **a**, ... Nu 32:21
and **a** men walked behind the Ark. .... Jos 6:9
six hundred men **a** for war stood .... Jdg 18:17

eighty thousand men **a** for war. 2Ch 17:18
in majesty and **a** with strength. .... Ps 93:1

ARMIES
united their **a** in the Valley .... Ge 14:3
Gomorrah and their **a** ran away,............... Ge 14:10
kept the two **a** apart all night.................. Ex 14:20
caught between the **a** of Israel. .... Jos 8:22
confused those **a** when Israel .... Jos 10:10
gathered their **a** for war. 1Sa 17:1
against the **a** of the living God 1Sa 17:26
The **a** were camped across from.............. 1Ki 20:29
No one can count God's **a**. .... Job 25:3
Kings and their **a** run away. .... Ps 68:12
Praise him, all you **a** of heaven. .... Ps 148:2
it and put his **a** all around it. .... Ec 9:14
The **a** of Aram and Israel have .... Is 7:2
I will cause the **a** of Media to .... Is 13:17
In one night **a** took the wealth .... Is 15:1
I will send **a** to Babylon for.................... Is 43:14
Their **a** have bows and spears. .... Je 50:42
A will surround the city when .... Je 51:2
the Commander of heaven's **a**. .... Da 8:11
will attack the **a** of the king .... Da 11:7
my Temple from **a** who would come .... Zch 9:8
me more than twelve **a** of angels. .... Mt 26:53
When you see **a** all around .... Lk 21:20
in battle and defeated other **a**. .... Heb 11:34
The **a** of heaven, dressed in fine .... Rev 19:14

ARMONI
king did take **A** and Mephibosheth 2Sa 21:8

ARMOR
who carried his **a** and said,..................... Jdg 9:54
Jonathan's **a** said to him, ... 1Sa 14:7
who carried his **a** died together 1Sa 31:6
Saul's head and took off his **a**. 1Sa 31:9
They put Saul's **a** in the temple 1Sa 31:10
the officer who carried his **a**, ... 1Ch 10:4
put Saul's **a** in the temple of 1Ch 10:10
spears, helmets, **a**, bows, and 2Ch 26:14
Pick up the shield and **a**........................ Ps 35:2
himself with goodness like **a**. .... Is 59:17
your spears. Put on your **a**!.................... Je 46:4
Put on the full **a** of God so that .... Eph 6:11

ARMORY
across from the way up to the **a**,............. Ne 3:19

ARMREST
and each **a** had a lion beside it. 1Ki 10:19
and each **a** had a lion beside it. 2Ch 9:18

ARMS
the bracelets on his sister's **a**................. Ge 24:30
boys and put his **a** around them. .... Ge 48:10
bow well. His **a** are made strong .... Ge 49:24
when Moses' **a** became tired, ... Ex 17:12
and his **a** will hold you up .... Dt 33:27
held him in her **a**, and cared for .... Ru 4:16
from his cup and slept in his **a**. 2Sa 12:3
altar with his **a** raised toward................ 1Ki 8:54
you will hold a son in your **a**." 2Ki 4:16
about Leviathan's **a** and legs, ... Job 41:12
for battle so my **a** can bend a .... Ps 18:34
They have bitten my **a** and legs.............. Ps 22:16
into a bundle to fill one's **a**. .... Ps 129:7
energy, and her **a** are strong. .... Pr 31:17
their **a** hold men like chains. .... Ec 7:26
At that time your **a** will shake .... Ec 12:3
raise your a to me in prayer, ... Is 1:15
lambs in his **a** and carries them .... Is 40:11
a statue, using his powerful **a**. .... Is 44:12
sons back to you in their **a**,.................... Is 49:22
and held in my **a** and bounced on .... Is 66:12
and die in their mothers' **a**..................... La 2:12

tear those charms off your **a**, ... Eze 13:20
will break his **a**, both the .... Eze 30:22
will break the **a** of the king of .... Eze 30:24
Its chest and **a** were made of .... Da 2:32
His **a** and legs were shiny like .... Da 10:6
took them by the **a**, but they did............. Hos 11:3
Taking the child in his **a**,........................ Mk 9:36
took the children in his **a**, ... Mk 10:16
baby in his **a** and thanked God .... Lk 2:28
carried him to the **a** of Abraham. .... Lk 16:22
down, and put his **a** around him. .... Ac 20:10

ARMY
commander of his **a**, went back to .... Ge 21:32
will defeat the king and his **a**................. Ex 14:4
chariot drivers, and **a**—chased .... Ex 14:9
at the Egyptian **a** and made them .... Ex 14:24
will serve in the **a** of Israel,.................... Nu 1:3
and his whole **a** marched out to .... Nu 21:33
Og and his sons and all his **a**; .... Nu 21:35
Og king of Bashan and all his **a**;............. Dt 3:3
chariots and an **a** that is bigger .... Dt 20:1
to serve in the **a** died in the .... Jos 5:4
the commander of the LORD's **a**." .... Jos 5:14
king of Ai saw the **a** of Israel,................. Jos 8:14
Bethel chased the **a** of Israel. .... Jos 8:17
The **a** of Judah was not able to .... Jos 15:63
Sisera and his **a** and chariots................. Jdg 4:15
The enemy **a** ran away to the city .... Jdg 7:22
the men in his **a** were shaking 1Sa 13:7
Saul gathered his **a** and entered 1Sa 14:20
So the **a** saved Jonathan, ... 1Sa 14:45
Saul and the **a** let Agag live, ... 1Sa 15:9
Abner and the **a** were sleeping 1Sa 26:7
When he saw the Philistine **a**,................. 1Sa 28:5
at Hebron, the **a** said to Joab,................ 2Sa 3:23
defeated all the **a** of Hadadezer. 2Sa 8:9
David and all his **a** returned to 2Sa 12:31
There David's **a** defeated the 2Sa 18:7
The Philistine **a** had camped in 2Sa 23:13
and Joab the commander of the **a**, ... 1Ki 1:19
David defeated the **a** of Zobah, ... 1Ki 11:24
Israel led the **a** and destroyed................ 1Ki 20:21
defeated the Aramean **a**......................... 1Ki 20:21
So he made the Aramean **a** blind, ... 2Ki 6:18
chariots, horses, and a large **a**. 2Ki 7:6
his **a** ran away to their tents. 2Ki 8:21
the whole **a** ran away at night 2Ki 25:4
But the Babylonian **a** chased King 2Ki 25:5
men ready to serve in the **a**, ... 1Ch 7:4
became large, like the **a** of God. 1Ch 12:22
Joab led out the **a** of Israel.................... 1Ch 20:1
Abijah led an **a** of four hundred 2Ch 13:3
to sneak behind Judah's **a**. 2Ch 13:13
Abijah's **a** chased Jeroboam's................ 2Ch 13:19
with an enormous **a** and three 2Ch 14:9
killed that the **a** could not 2Ch 14:13
his heavenly **a** standing on his 2Ch 18:18
A large **a** is coming against you 2Ch 20:2
this large **a** that is attacking 2Ch 20:12
Jehoshaphat's **a** went out into 2Ch 20:20
The **a** of Judah also captured ten 2Ch 25:12
The Israelite **a** captured two 2Ch 28:8
Hezekiah put **a** commanders over 2Ch 32:6
The heavenly **a** worships you.................. Ne 10:9
wipe out the **a** of any state or .... Est 8:11
I lived like a king among his **a**, ... Job 29:25
If an **a** surrounds me, I will not .... Ps 27:3
No king is saved by his great **a**. .... Ps 33:16
Egypt and his **a** drowned in the .... Ps 136:15
a king when his **a** is around him. .... Pr 30:31
wonderful as an **a** flying flags. .... Sng 6:10
a will spread its wings like .... Is 8:8

This day the **a** will stop at Nob. .... Is 10:32
This **a** is coming from a faraway .... Is 13:5
He leads out the **a** of heaven one .... Is 40:26
escape from the Babylonian **a,** .... Je 32:4
The **a** of the king of Egypt had .... Je 37:5
the Babylonian **a** had surrounded .... Je 37:5
'The **a** of the king of Egypt came .... Je 37:7
But the Babylonian **a** chased them .... Je 39:5
An **a** is coming from the north. .... Je 50:41
But the Babylonian **a** chased King .... Je 52:8
The whole Babylonian **a,** led by .... Je 52:14
horsemen, and a great **a.** .... Eze 26:7
its treasures as pay for his **a.** .... Eze 29:19
the cruelest **a** of any nation, ... Eze 30:11
Egypt and his **a** will see these................. Eze 32:31
on their feet, a very large **a.** .... Eze 37:10
will be a large **a** with large and .... Eze 38:4
on Gog, his **a,** and the many .... Eze 38:22
Gog and all his **a** will be buried .... Eze 39:11
and surrounded it with his **a.** .... Da 1:1
soldiers in his **a** to tie up........................ Da 3:20
threw some of the **a** of heaven to .... Da 8:10
the North will have a large **a,** .... Da 11:11
His **a** will be swept away in .... Da 11:26
of Israel's **a** in the Valley...................... Hos 1:5
and powerful **a** will spread over .... Joe 2:2
LORD shouts out orders to his **a.** .... Joe 2:11
to be among the **a** groups from .... Mic 5:2
the **a** is dressed in red. .... Nah 2:3
you stabbed the leader of his **a.** .... Hab 3:14
Capernaum, an **a** officer came to .... Mt 8:5
furious and sent his **a** to kill .... Mt 22:7
When the **a** officer and the .... Mt 27:54
commanders of his **a,** and the.................. Mk 6:21
When the **a** officer who was .... Mk 15:39
he called the **a** officer who had .... Mk 15:44
There was an **a** officer who had a .... Lk 7:2
the **a** officer there saw what .... Lk 23:47
Italian group of the Roman **a.**.................. Ac 10:1
of the Roman **a** in Jerusalem .... Ac 21:31
who served in the emperor's **a,** .... Ac 27:1
serves in the **a** and pays his own 1Co 9:7
with me in the **a** of Christ. .... Php 2:25
serving in the **a** wastes time 2Ti 2:4
on horses were in their **a**—.................... Rev 9:16
rider on the horse and his **a.** .... Rev 19:19
And Satan's **a** marched across the .... Rev 20:9

ARNON

The **A** is the border between the................. Nu 21:13
Get up and cross the **A** Ravine. .... Dt 2:24
River from the **A** Ravine to Mount .... Jos 12:1
the cities along the **A** River. .... Jdg 11:26
cross the river **A** like little .... Is 16:2
Announce at the **A** River that .... Je 48:20

AROER

the cities of Dibon, Ataroth, **A,** .... Nu 32:34
We defeated **A** on the edge of the .... Dt 2:36
Gad the land from **A** by the Arnon............ Dt 3:12
the land from **A** at the Arnon .... Jos 12:2
in Heshbon and **A** and the towns .... Jdg 11:26
they camped near **A** on the south 2Sa 24:5
will leave the cities of **A.**...................... Is 17:2
people living in the town of **A,** .... Je 48:19

AROSE

I, Deborah, **a,** until I arose to .... Jdg 5:7
until I **a** to be a mother to .... Jdg 5:7
A great storm **a** on the lake so .... Mt 8:24

AROUND

flows **a** the whole land of .... Ge 2:11
flows **a** the whole land of Cush. .... Ge 2:13
fire that flashed **a** in every .... Ge 3:24

you will wander **a** on the earth." .... Ge 4:12
in the lands **a** the Mediterranean .... Ge 10:5
Lot looked all **a** and saw the .... Ge 13:10
The men **a** the house answered, ... Ge 19:9
said, "Look **a** you at my land.................... Ge 20:15
Canaanite girls who live **a** here. .... Ge 24:37
put his arms **a** him and hugged .... Ge 33:4
wheat gathered **a** it and bowed .... Ge 37:7
a gold chain **a** Joseph's neck. .... Ge 41:42
boys and put his arms **a** them. .... Ge 48:10
the morning dew lay **a** the camp. .... Ex 16:13
must set a limit **a** the mountain .... Ex 19:12
get up and walk **a** outside with .... Ex 21:19
gold, and put a gold strip **a** it.................. Ex 25:24
a courtyard **a** the Holy Tent. .... Ex 27:9
Put gold **a** the stones to hold .... Ex 28:11
they gathered **a** Aaron and said,............... Ex 32:1
Gold was put **a** these jewels to .... Ex 39:13
come from other nations **a** you; .... Le 25:44
make their camp **a** the Holy Tent .... Nu 1:53
they captured the towns **a** it, ... Nu 21:32
are the borders **a** your country.' .... Nu 34:12
But you must turn **a** and follow .... Dt 1:40
your God moves **a** through your .... Dt 23:14
March **a** the city with your army .... Jos 6:3
seventh time **a** the priests blew .... Jos 6:16
were all standing **a** the Ark of .... Jos 8:33
the villages **a** Kiriath Arba had .... Jos 21:12
Each town had pastures **a** it. .... Jos 21:42
peace from their enemies **a** them. .... Jos 23:1
I gave the land **a** the mountains .... Jos 24:4
who lived **a** them defeat them.................. Jdg 2:14
the ground **a** it gets wet with .... Jdg 6:39
their enemies living all **a** them. .... Jdg 8:34
explored the land **a** Laish said .... Jdg 18:14
set up ambushes all **a** Gibeah. .... Jdg 20:29
her gather even **a** the piles of .... Ru 2:15
you from your enemies **a** you, ... 1Sa 12:11
against Israel's enemies all **a.**.................. 1Sa 14:47
unsatisfied gathered **a** David, ... 1Sa 22:2
like a wall **a** us while we were 1Sa 25:16
the army were sleeping **a** Saul. 1Sa 26:7
The fighting was heavy **a** Saul. 1Sa 31:3
go **a** and attack them in front of 2Sa 5:23
bed and walked **a** on the roof of............... 2Sa 11:2
soldiers gathered all **a** David. 2Sa 16:6
The waves of death came **a** me; 2Sa 22:5
brightens the darkness **a** me. 2Sa 22:29
blood on the belt **a** his waist 1Ki 2:5
as well as a wall **a** Jerusalem................... 1Ki 3:1
wars with the countries **a** him, ... 1Ki 5:3
All the walls **a** the Temple were 1Ki 6:29
They danced **a** the altar they had 1Ki 18:26
Turn **a** and get me out of the 1Ki 22:34
a leather belt **a** his waist." 2Ki 1:8
and chariots all **a** the city. 2Ki 6:15
chariots of fire all **a** Elisha.................... 2Ki 6:17
of Baal, "Look **a,** and make sure 2Ki 10:23
Judah and the towns **a** Jerusalem. 2Ki 23:5
He made a camp **a** the city and 2Ki 25:1
The fighting was heavy **a** Saul, ... 1Ch 10:3
Gath and the small towns **a** it. 1Ch 18:1
When he turned **a,** he saw the 1Ch 21:20
Turn **a** and get me out of the 2Ch 18:33
and the Temple and **a** the king. 2Ch 23:10
Fish Gate and **a** the hill of 2Ch 33:14
Then the people **a** them tried to .... Ezr 4:4
separate from the people **a** us. .... Ezr 9:1
gathered **a** him who were also .... Ezr 10:1
The wall **a** Jerusalem is broken .... Ne 1:3
A report is going **a** to all the .... Ne 6:6
singers from all **a** Jerusalem, ... Ne 12:28
have been wandering **a** the earth, ... Job 1:7

You have put a wall a him, ...Job 1:10
you now turn a and destroy me? ....Job 10:8
They feel a in darkness with no ....Job 12:25
I have dark circles a my eyes. ....Job 16:16
So the poor go a naked without ....Job 24:10
scatters his lightning a him, ...Job 36:30
But the wicked are all a us;....................Ps 12:8
The ropes of death wrapped a me. ....Ps 18:5
God brightens the darkness a me. ....Ps 18:28
Terror is all a me. They make ....Ps 31:13
the LORD camps a those who fear ....Ps 34:7
waves are crashing all a me. ....Ps 42:7
Walk a Jerusalem and count its ....Ps 48:12
like lions, are all a me; ....Ps 57:4
Repay those a us seven times ....Ps 79:12
and burns up his enemies all a. ....Ps 97:3
all the wild animals creep a. ....Ps 104:20
and an iron ring a his neck. ....Ps 105:18
the light a me turn into night................Ps 139:11
They go a telling lies, ...Pr 6:12
that fly a and never land. ....Pr 26:2
Then it turns a and repeats the ....Ec 1:6
but fools walk a in the dark. ....Ec 2:14
I got up and went a the city, ...Sng 3:2
walk a with their heads held ....Is 3:16
has walked a naked and barefoot ....Is 20:3
will stumble a like someone who ....Is 24:20
wheat as a border a the field. ....Is 28:25
I will put armies all a you, ...Is 29:3
Look a you at the earth below. ....Is 51:6
I looked a, but I saw no one to ....Is 63:5
the city walls a Jerusalem and ....Je 1:15
Cut down the trees a Jerusalem,............Je 6:6
refuse to turn a and come back. ....Je 8:5
me with anger at the evil a me. ....Je 15:17
burn up everything a you!'" ....Je 21:14
Roll a in the dust, leaders of ....Je 25:34
Jeremiah, woke up and looked a. ....Je 31:26
Mizpah turned a and ran to ....Je 41:14
fall and roll a in its own vomit ....Je 48:26
Gomorrah and the towns a them," ....Je 49:18
You dance a like a young cow in ....Je 50:11
Soldiers a Babylon, shout the ....Je 50:15
together from all a the world. ....Je 50:41
be many dead people lying all a. ....Je 51:47
bronze pomegranates all a it. ....Je 52:22
that burns up everything a it. ....La 2:3
and wild dogs wander a it. ....La 5:18
a bright light a it and fire ....Eze 1:4
and were full of eyes all a. ....Eze 1:18
the nations a you will shame ....Eze 5:15
they come from all a for sexual ....Eze 16:33
made everyone a you afraid of ....Eze 26:17
all the nations a who hate them...............Eze 28:26
Rivers flowed a the bottom of................Eze 31:4
Assyria's army lies a its grave. ....Eze 32:23
He led me a among the bones, ...Eze 37:2
I will turn you a and put hooks ....Eze 38:4
Windows were all a the gateway ....Eze 40:33
Temple had a raised base all a. ....Eze 41:8
He measured the area all a. ....Eze 42:15
and light is all a him. ....Da 2:22
four men walking a in the fire. ....Da 3:25
a band of iron and bronze a it; ....Da 4:15
gold chain to wear a your neck. ....Da 5:16
a trench filled with water a it,................Da 9:25
build a wall a her so she cannot ....Hos 2:6
of cattle wander a confused, ...Joe 1:18
The water was all a me, and your ....Jnh 2:3
The deep sea was all a me; ....Jnh 2:5
seaweed was wrapped a my head. ....Jnh 2:5
going a barefoot and naked. ....Mic 1:8
Nile River with water all a her. ....Nah 3:8

they will walk a like the blind, ...Zph 1:17
I will be a wall of fire a it,' ....Zch 2:5
of poison to the nations a her. ....Zch 12:2
You will jump a, like well-fed ....Mal 4:2
When Jesus saw the crowd a him, ...Mt 8:18
this spread all a the area. ....Mt 9:26
stone tied a the neck and be ....Mt 18:6
put a wall a it and dug a hole ....Mt 21:33
send his angels all a the earth, ...Mt 24:31
people were sitting a Jesus, ...Mk 3:32
A great crowd gathered a him, ...Mk 4:1
he would wander a the burial ....Mk 5:5
and pushed very close a him. ....Mk 5:24
looking a to see who had ....Mk 5:32
and towns a here to buy ....Mk 6:36
they look like trees walking a." ....Mk 8:24
to the towns a Caesarea Philippi ....Mk 8:27
and John looked a, but they saw ....Mk 9:8
put a wall a it and dug a hole ....Mk 12:1
like to walk a wearing fancy ....Mk 12:38
his angels all a the earth to....................Mk 13:27
of the Lord was shining a them, ...Lk 2:9
over the area a the Jordan River ....Lk 3:3
Jesus looked a at all of them ....Lk 6:10
dig up the dirt a it and put on................Lk 13:8
you see armies all a Jerusalem, ...Lk 21:20
people, teaching all a Judea. ....Lk 23:5
this, Jesus traveled a Galilee. ....Jn 7:1
he wrapped it a his waist. ....Jn 13:4
towel that was wrapped a him. ....Jn 13:5
and put a purple robe a him. ....Jn 19:2
she turned a and saw Jesus ....Jn 20:14
he wrapped his coat a himself. ....Jn 21:7
from all the towns a Jerusalem, ...Ac 5:16
heaven suddenly flashed a him. ....Ac 9:3
all the widows stood a Peter, ...Ac 9:39
jumped up and began walking a. ....Ac 14:10
putting a heavy load a the necks ....Ac 15:10
search all a for him and find ....Ac 17:27
come from Jerusalem stood a him,...........Ac 25:7
they tied ropes a the ship to ....Ac 27:17
We have troubles all a us, ...2Co 4:8
with those who order you a, ...2Co 11:20
so he put guards a the city......................2Co 11:32
belt of truth tied a your waist ....Eph 6:14
and mean people all a you, ...Php 2:15
had marched a them for seven ....Heb 11:30
are living all a you and might.................1Pe 2:12
goes a like a roaring lion 1Pe 5:8
rain, which the wind blows a...................Jud 1:12
and had a gold band a his chest. ....Rev 1:13
All a the throne was a rainbow ....Rev 4:3
A the throne there were ....Rev 4:4
the center and a the throne were ....Rev 4:6
of many angels a the throne, ...Rev 5:11
will not walk a naked and have ....Rev 16:15
and gathered a the camp of God's ....Rev 20:9

ARPAD

are the kings of Hamath and A?.............2Ki 19:13
Hamath and A are put to shame, ...Je 49:23

ARPHAXAD

Elam, Asshur, A, Lud, and Aram. ....Ge 10:22
A was the son of Shem. ....Lk 3:36

ARRANGE

in the table and a everything ....Ex 40:4
duty was to a the king's food ....Je 51:59

ARRANGED

a according to their nations. ....Ge 10:32
two baskets of figs a in front ....Je 24:1
it out for you. I a it in order, ...Lk 1:3

ARRANGEMENTS

Make a because you are not going 2Ki 20:1
a, because you are not going .... Is 38:1

ARREST

You should a any madman who acts .... Je 29:26
son of Abdeel a Baruch the .... Je 36:26
they will a you and take you .... Mt 10:17
They wanted to a him, but they .... Mt 21:46
set a trap to a Jesus and kill .... Mt 26:4
The man I kiss is Jesus. A him." .... Mt 26:48
his soldiers to a John and put .... Mk 6:17
wanted to find a way to a Jesus, ... Mk 12:12
People will a you and take you .... Mk 13:9
find a trick to a Jesus and kill .... Mk 14:1
and you did not a me there. .... Mk 14:49
wanted to a Jesus at once, ... Lk 20:19
Those who came to a Jesus were .... Lk 22:52
and you didn't a me there. .... Lk 22:53
some Temple guards to a him. .... Jn 7:32
Then they could a him. .... Jn 11:57
he would a them and bring them .... Ac 9:2
him the power to a everyone who .... Ac 9:14
He came here to a the followers .... Ac 9:21
so he decided to a Peter, too. .... Ac 12:3
going there to a these people .... Ac 22:5
King Aretas wanted to a me, ... 2Co 11:32

ARRESTED

So Potiphar a Joseph and put him .... Ge 39:20
So Hanun a David's officers. 2Sa 10:4
So Hanun a David's officers. 1Ch 19:4
So why haven't you a him? .... Je 29:27
so he a Jeremiah and took him to .... Je 37:14
you are a, don't worry about .... Mt 10:19
this, Herod had a John, tied him .... Mt 14:3
and grabbed Jesus and a him. .... Mt 26:50
people who a Jesus led him to .... Mt 26:57
When you are a and judged, ... Mk 13:11
The people who a Jesus led him .... Mk 14:53
They a Jesus, and led him away, ... Lk 22:54
But no one a him, because the .... Jn 8:20
and the guards a Jesus. .... Jn 18:12
After Herod a Peter, he put him .... Ac 12:4
went to Paul and a him. .... Ac 21:33
a men and women and put them in .... Ac 22:4
But I was a in Jerusalem and .... Ac 28:17

ARRIVAL

year after their a at the Temple .... Ezr 3:8

ARRIVE

When you a, find Jehu son of 2Ki 9:2
when they a, they are .... Job 6:20
When I a, I will send whomever 1Co 16:3

ARRIVED

and in time they a there. .... Ge 12:5
Just before they a in Egypt, ... Ge 12:11
Mesopotamia and a safely at the .... Ge 33:18
When Joseph a, someone told .... Ge 48:2
people of Israel a at the Desert .... Nu 20:1
you left Egypt until you a here. .... Dt 9:7
from Moab and a at Bethlehem at .... Ru 1:22
When he a in Shiloh, Eli was by 1Sa 4:13
and his servant a at Gibeah, ... 1Sa 10:10
When they a, Samuel saw Eliab, ... 1Sa 16:6
When David a at the camp, the 1Sa 17:20
David and his men a at Ziklag, ... 1Sa 30:1
marching all day, a at Mahanaim. 2Sa 2:29
and all his army a at Hebron, ... 2Sa 3:23
king's sons a, crying loudly. 2Sa 13:36
all his people a at the Jordan, ... 2Sa 16:14
the king has a safely home." 2Sa 19:30
the king, Nathan the prophet a. 1Ki 1:22
When all the elders of Israel a, ... 1Ki 8:3

When Rehoboam a in Jerusalem, ... 1Ki 12:21
When they a at the Jordan, ... 2Ki 6:4
They a at night and surrounded 2Ki 6:14
But before the messenger a, ... 2Ki 6:32
him, "The man of God has a." 2Ki 8:7
When the king a from Damascus, ... 2Ki 16:12
When all the elders of Israel a, ... 2Ch 5:4
When they a at the Temple of the .... Ezr 2:68
Finally we a in Jerusalem where .... Ezr 8:32
come; the day has a. Don't let .... Eze 7:12
When Jesus a at the other side .... Mt 8:28
When he a, he saw a great crowd .... Mt 14:14
when the age to come has a, ... Mt 19:28
Jesus' mother and brothers a. .... Mk 3:31
When Jesus a in Galilee, the .... Jn 4:45
Simon Peter a and went into the .... Jn 20:6
Peter and John a, they prayed .... Ac 8:15
When they a in Antioch, Paul and .... Ac 14:27
When they a in Jerusalem, they .... Ac 15:4
when Apollos a, he helped them .... Ac 18:27
named Agabus a from Judea. .... Ac 21:10
When we a at Rome, Paul was .... Ac 28:16
they a, Peter stopped eating .... Gal 2:12

ARRIVES

not sit down to eat until he a." 1Sa 16:11
When she a, she will pretend to 1Ki 14:5
the messenger a, shut the door 2Ki 6:32
If he a soon, we will both come .... Heb 13:23

ARROW

Jonathan shot an a beyond him. 1Sa 20:36
a went through Joram's heart, ... 2Ki 9:24
The LORD's a of victory over 2Ki 13:17
city or even shoot an a here. 2Ki 19:32
soldier shot an a who hit Ahab 2Ch 18:33
but a bronze a will stab him. .... Job 20:24
be cut short like a broken a. .... Ps 58:7
by night or an a during the day. .... Ps 91:5
through the liver with an a. .... Pr 7:23
a club, a sword, or a sharp a. .... Pr 25:18
city or even shoot an a here. .... Is 37:33
He made me like a sharp a. .... Is 49:2

ARROWS

your bow and a and go hunting .... Ge 27:3
with stones or shot with a. .... Ex 19:13
they will shoot them with a. .... Nu 24:8
My a will be covered with their .... Dt 32:42
I will shoot three a to the side 1Sa 20:20
Elisha said, "Take the a." 2Ki 13:18
with their a and wounded him. 1Ch 10:3
used to shoot a and large rocks. 2Ch 26:15
The a of the Almighty are in me; .... Job 6:4
hurt it, nor the a, darts, and .... Job 41:26
he has made his flaming a. .... Ps 7:13
He shot his a and scattered his .... Ps 18:14
Your sharp a will enter the .... Ps 45:5
and shoot bitter words like a. .... Ps 64:3
There God broke the flaming a, ... Ps 76:3
man who has his bag full of a. .... Ps 127:5
shooting deadly, burning a .... Pr 26:18
Their a bring death. All their .... Je 5:16
lies from their mouths like a. .... Je 9:3
Shoot your a at Babylon! .... Je 50:14
kidneys with the a from his bag. .... La 3:13
throws lots with a and asks .... Eze 21:21
shields, bows and a, war clubs, ... Eze 39:9
with bows and a will not stand .... Am 2:15
of your flying a and the gleam .... Hab 3:11
and his a will shoot like .... Zch 9:14
the burning a of the Evil One. .... Eph 6:16

ARTAXERXES
When **A** became king of Persia, ... Ezr 4:7
From **A**, king of kings, to Ezra .... Ezr 7:12
gone back to **A** king of Babylon .... Ne 13:6

ARTEMIS
the temple of the goddess **A**. .... Ac 19:24
"Great is **A** of Ephesus!" .... Ac 19:34

ARTICLES
—silver, gold, and other **a**. 1Ki 7:51
the silver and gold and other **a**. 2Ch 5:1

ARTIST
are like jewels shaped by an **a**. .... Sng 7:1

ARVAD
from Sidon and **A** used oars to .... Eze 27:8
of **A** and Cilicia guarded your .... Eze 27:11

ASA
and his son **A** became king in his 1Ki 15:8
A ruled in Jerusalem for 1Ki 15:10
A did what the LORD said was 1Ki 15:11
A removed her from being queen 1Ki 15:13
Everything else **A** did—his 1Ki 15:23
After **A** died, he was buried with 1Ki 15:24
like his father **A**, and he did 1Ki 22:43
A called out to the LORD his God, ... 2Ch 14:11
A got a disease in his feet. 2Ch 16:12
made by King **A** as a part of his .... Je 41:9
Abijah was the father of **A**. .... Mt 1:7
A was the father of Jehoshaphat. .... Mt 1:8

ASA'S
Jehoshaphat, **A** son, became king 1Ki 15:24
A army also attacked the camps 2Ch 14:15
Jehoshaphat, **A** son, became king 2Ch 17:1

ASAHEL
Now **A** was a fast runner, as fast 2Sa 2:18
A chased Abner, going straight 2Sa 2:19
Abner stabbed **A** in the stomach, ... 2Sa 2:23
David's men took **A** and buried 2Sa 2:32
the Thirty: **A** brother of Joab; 2Sa 23:24

ASAHEL'S
to the place where **A** body lay. 2Sa 2:23
A son Zebadiah took his place as 1Ch 27:7

ASAPH
Joah son of **A** was the recorder. 2Ki 18:37
singers Heman, **A**, and Ethan 1Ch 15:19
A, who played the cymbals, was 1Ch 16:5
David first gave **A** and his 1Ch 16:7
chose some of the sons of **A**, ... 1Ch 25:1
King David chose **A** to preach, ... 1Ch 25:2
words David and **A** the seer had 2Ch 29:30
the sons of **A**, stood with their .... Ezr 3:10
animals that die. A psalm of **A**. .... Ps 49:20
son of Jesse. A psalm of **A**. .... Ps 72:20
A psalm of **A**. A song. .... Ps 75:10
skillful hands. A psalm of **A**. .... Ps 78:72
By the gittith. A psalm of **A**. .... Ps 80:19
Joah son of **A** was the recorder. .... Is 36:22

ASAPH'S
singers from **A** family stood 2Ch 35:15

ASENATH
also gave Joseph a wife named **A**, ... Ge 41:45
came, Joseph and **A** had two sons. .... Ge 41:50

ASHAMED
were naked, but they were not **a**. .... Ge 2:25
As slaves in Egypt you were **a**, ... Jos 5:9
Then all Israel will be **a**!" 1Sa 11:2
He was a of his father and upset 1Sa 20:34
felt **a** after he had counted 2Sa 24:10
at Elisha until he felt **a**. 2Ki 8:11
I was a to ask the king for .... Ezr 8:22

he was embarrassed and **a**. .... Est 6:12
enemies will be a and troubled. .... Ps 6:10
Let them be **a** and embarrassed, ... Ps 35:26
protection. Never let me be **a**. .... Ps 71:1
who worship idols should be **a**; .... Ps 97:7
proud people a because they lied .... Ps 119:78
the sea, be **a**, because the sea .... Is 23:4
you will be **a** and disgraced. .... Is 41:11
A thief is a when someone .... Je 2:26
They should be **a** of the terrible .... Je 6:15
are a of their poor harvest, ... Je 12:13
They will be a because they have .... Je 20:11
Your mother will be very **a**; .... Je 50:12
Feel a and suffer disgrace, ... Eze 16:52
Be a and embarrassed about your .... Eze 36:32
way, naked and **a**, you who live .... Mic 1:11
made your own houses a of you. .... Hab 2:10
are not a of what they do. .... Zph 3:5
will be a of their visions .... Zch 13:4
If people are **a** of me and my .... Mk 8:38
of Man will be **a** of them when he .... Lk 9:26
I am not a of the Good News, ... Rm 1:16
not trying to make you feel **a**. 1Co 4:14
God will make me **a** before you. 2Co 12:21
with them so they will feel **a**. 2Th 3:14
So do not be a to tell people 2Ti 1:8
and do not be a of me, in prison 2Ti 1:8
So he is not a to call them his .... Heb 2:11
So God is not a to be called .... Heb 11:16
life in Christ will be made **a**. 1Pe 3:16
are a Christian, do not be **a**. 1Pe 4:16
and not be a in his presence. 1Jn 2:28

ASHDOD
were left in Gaza, Gath, and **A**. .... Jos 11:22
A and the small towns and .... Jos 15:47
they took it from Ebenezer to **A**. 1Sa 5:1
the language of **A** to some other .... Ne 13:24
commander to **A** to attack that .... Is 20:1
A will be empty by noon, and the .... Zph 2:4
Foreigners will live in **A**, ... Zch 9:6

ASHER
me happy," so she named him **A**. .... Ge 30:13
Zilpah: Gad and **A**. These are .... Ge 35:26
Dan, Naphtali, Gad, and **A**. .... Ex 1:4
them the tribe of **A** will camp. .... Nu 2:27
A is the most blessed of .... Dt 33:24
of Phanuel in the tribe of **A**. .... Lk 2:36
the tribe of **A** twelve thousand, ... Rev 7:6

ASHER'S
A land will grow much good food; .... Ge 49:20
border touched **A** land on the .... Jos 17:10

ASHERAH
and cut down their **A** idols. .... Ex 34:13
and burn their **A** idols in the .... Dt 12:3
served the idols of Baal and **A**. .... Jdg 3:7
had made a terrible **A** idol, ... 1Ki 15:13
the four hundred prophets of **A**, ... 1Ki 18:19
made for Baal, **A**, and all the 2Ki 23:4
and he tore down the **A** idols. 2Ch 14:3
He broke up the **A** idols and the 2Ch 34:4

ASHES
Though I am only dust and **a**, ... Ge 18:27
hands with a from a furnace. .... Ex 9:8
and carry the a outside the camp .... Le 6:11
will collect the a from the cow .... Nu 19:9
Tamar put a on her head and tore 2Sa 13:19
rough cloth and **a**, and went out .... Est 4:1
and he sat in a in misery. .... Job 2:8
are worth no more than **a**, ... Job 13:12
I eat a for food, and my tears .... Ps 102:9
and scatters the frost like **a**. .... Ps 147:16

ASHKELON (continued)

them a crown to replace their **a**, ... Is 61:3
dead bodies and **a** are thrown, ... Je 31:40
turned you into a on the ground .... Eze 28:18
on rough cloth, and sat in **a**. .... Da 9:3
cloth and sat in a to show how .... Jnh 3:6
cloth and put a on themselves to .... Lk 10:13
and bulls and the a of a cow are.............. Heb 9:13
burning them until they were **a**. 2Pe 2:6

ASHKELON

Judah captured Gaza, **A**, Ekron,.............. Jdg 1:18
Gaza, **A**, Gath, and Ekron. 1Sa 6:17
announce in the streets of **A**. 2Sa 1:20
to attack **A** and the seacoast." .... Je 47:7
no one will live in **A** anymore. .... Zch 9:5

ASHKENAZ

sons of Gomer were **A**, Riphath,.............. Ge 10:3

ASHPENAZ

King Nebuchadnezzar ordered **A**, ... Da 1:3

ASHTAROTH

king of Bashan who ruled in **A**. .... Jos 9:10
of Golan in Bashan and **A**. 1Ch 6:71

ASHTEROTH

the Rephaites in **A** Karnaim, ... Ge 14:5

ASHTORETH

LORD and worshiped Baal and **A**. .... Jdg 2:13
Solomon worshiped **A**, the goddess 1Ki 11:5
worshiped the Sidonian god **A**, ... 1Ki 11:33
One was for **A**, the hated goddess 2Ki 23:13

ASIA

Judea, Cappadocia, Pontus, **A**, ... Ac 2:9
them preach the Good News in **A**. .... Ac 16:6
himself stayed in **A** for a while. .... Ac 19:22
that everyone in **A** and the whole .... Ac 19:27
person in **A** to follow Christ. .... Rm 16:5
the trouble we suffered in **A**. 2Co 1:8
that everyone in **A** has left me, ... 2Ti 1:15
Cappadocia, **A**, and Bithynia. 1Pe 1:1
To the seven churches in **A**: .... Rev 1:4

ASK

with me, but let me **a** you this. .... Ge 18:30
A him to sell me the cave of .... Ge 23:9
Agreed! We will do what you **a**." .... Ge 30:34
Esau will come to you and **a**, ' .... Ge 32:17
said, "Why do you a my name?" .... Ge 32:29
I will give anything you **a**. .... Ge 34:11
Each woman should a her Egyptian .... Ex 3:22
a him to stop this punishment .... Ex 10:17
When your children a you, ' .... Ex 12:26
I a heaven and earth to speak................. Dt 4:26
All the other nations will **a**, ... Dt 29:24
Today I a heaven and earth to be .... Dt 30:19
A your father and he will tell .... Dt 32:7
We a only that the LORD your God .... Jos 1:17
All the Israelites a you: .... Jos 22:16
Please a God if our journey will .... Jdg 18:5
husband went to a her to come .... Jdg 19:3
I a the LORD to punish me .... Ru 1:17
I will do everything you **a**, ... Ru 3:11
A him to save us from the 1Sa 7:8
the priest said, "Let's a God." 1Sa 14:36
All I a is that you remain brave 1Sa 18:17
with you, but I a you one thing. 2Sa 3:13
Maybe he will do what I **a**. 2Sa 14:15
Now I have one thing to a you; 1Ki 2:16
Please a him to give me Abishag 1Ki 2:17
"**A**, mother," the king answered............. 1Ki 2:20
A for whatever you want me to 1Ki 3:5
a that you give me a heart that 1Ki 3:9
give you what you did not a for:.............. 1Ki 3:13
Let's **a** him what we should do."............. 1Ki 22:7

We can a the LORD through him." 2Ki 3:11
Master, did I a you for a son? 2Ki 4:28
Don't a for trouble, or you and 2Ki 14:10
A for whatever you want me to 2Ch 1:7
Jehoshaphat did not a for help 2Ch 17:3
We could a the LORD through him, ... 2Ch 18:7
Don't a for trouble, or you and 2Ch 25:19
We would a God for a safe trip .... Ezr 8:21
What do you want to a me? .... Est 5:3
He had come to a the king about .... Est 6:4
A old people; find out what.................... Job 8:8
But a the animals, and they will .... Job 12:7
but you also **a**, 'What's the use? .... Job 35:3
Would a person a to be swallowed .... Job 37:20
I will a you questions, and you .... Job 38:3
If you a me, I will give you the .... Ps 2:8
Many people **a**, "Who will give us .... Ps 4:6
They do not a the LORD for help. .... Ps 14:4
a only one thing from the LORD. .... Ps 27:4
You do not a for burnt offerings .... Ps 40:6
they will not a the wise for .... Pr 15:12
I a two things from you, LORD. .... Pr 30:7
A for a sign from the LORD your .... Is 7:11
who are still alive a something .... Is 8:19
They will a advice from their .... Is 19:3
clay does not a the potter, ' .... Is 45:9
You a me about what will happen. .... Is 45:11
They a me to judge them fairly. .... Is 58:2
in the land who a for blessings .... Is 65:16
You might a yourself, "Why has .... Je 13:22
A the people in other nations .... Je 18:13
You sent me to a the LORD for .... Je 42:9
They a their mothers, "Where is .... La 2:12
Israel came to a about the LORD .... Eze 20:1
we a because of your mercy. .... Da 9:18
My people a wooden idols for................. Hos 4:12
now I a you, LORD, please kill .... Jnh 4:3
Rulers a for money, and judges' .... Mic 7:3
But you **a**, "How have you loved.............. Mal 1:2
You **a**, "Why?" It is because the .... Mal 2:14
You **a**, 'How have we robbed you?' .... Mal 3:8
A, and God will give to you. .... Mt 7:7
If your children a for bread, ... Mt 7:9
told her daughter what to a for, ... Mt 14:8
sinful people a for a miracle as .... Mt 16:4
anything you a for in prayer.".................... Mt 21:22
you know I could a my Father, ... Mt 26:53
the crowd to a for Barabbas to .... Mt 27:20
And you **a**, 'Who touched me?' "............... Mk 5:31
A me for anything you want, ... Mk 6:22
A for the head of John the .... Mk 6:24
do you people a for a miracle as............. Mk 8:12
the things you a for in prayer,.............. Mk 11:24
Pilate began to a him to .... Mk 15:8
to Pilate and a for Jesus' body .... Mk 15:43
were afraid to a Jesus about it. .... Lk 9:45
So I tell you, **a**, and God will .... Lk 11:9
Holy Spirit to those who a him!" .... Lk 11:13
that you a me for a drink, ... Jn 4:9
said, "He is old enough. **A** him." .... Jn 9:23
And if you a for anything in my .... Jn 14:13
anything you a for in my name. .... Jn 15:16
A and you will receive, so that .... Jn 16:24
of the followers dared a him, ... Jn 21:12
and a for a man named Saul from .... Ac 9:11
men to Joppa and a Simon Peter .... Ac 10:32
I do not a to be saved from .... Ac 25:11
But I a: Didn't people hear the .... Rm 10:18
a you to look out for those who .... Rm 16:17
The Jews a for miracles, and the 1Co 1:22
anything we can a or imagine. .... Eph 3:20
pray and a God for everything .... Php 4:6
I a that you do this for me in .... Phm 1:20

You do not a for burnt offerings .... Heb 10:6
wisdom, you should a God for it. .... Jam 1:5
But when you a God, you must .... Jam 1:6
when you a, you do not receive .... Jam 4:3
he hears us every time we a him, ... 1Jn 5:15
a you that we all love each other. 2Jn 1:5

ASKED

God a, "Who told you that you .... Ge 3:11
The LORD a Cain, "Why are you .... Ge 4:6
He a, "Who is your father? .... Ge 24:23
She a, "Why is this happening to .... Ge 25:22
Isaac a, "Are you really my son .... Ge 27:24
Then Jacob a him, "Please tell .... Ge 32:29
What they a seemed fair to Hamor........... Ge 34:18
She a, "What will you give me if .... Ge 38:16
He a us, 'Is your father still..................... Ge 43:7
Moses a the LORD about the frogs........... Ex 8:12
And the LORD did as Moses a. .... Ex 8:13
people grumbled to Moses and a, ... Ex 15:24
I have forgiven them as you a. .... Nu 14:20
The angel of the LORD a Balaam, ... Nu 22:32
facedown on the ground and a, ... Jos 5:14
he a for good things to happen .... Jos 24:10
Sisera a for water, but Jael .... Jdg 5:25
Then Manoah a the angel of the............... Jdg 13:17
Boaz a, "Who are you?" .... Ru 3:9
Eli a, "What happened, my son?" 1Sa 4:16
The Philistines a, "What kind of............ 1Sa 6:4
Saul's uncle a, "Please tell me. 1Sa 10:15
the LORD when you a for a king." 1Sa 12:17
Samuel a, "What have you done?" 1Sa 13:11
Then he a Jesse, "Are these all 1Sa 16:11
David a, "Now what have I done 1Sa 17:29
And Jonathan a David to repeat 1Sa 20:17
David a the LORD, "Should I go 1Sa 23:2
and I will do what you have a." 1Sa 25:35
The woman a, "Whom do you want 1Sa 28:11
a, "What wrong have I done? 1Sa 29:8
Then Saul a me, 'Who are you?' 2Sa 1:8
David a the LORD, "Should I 2Sa 5:19
he a them, "Is the baby dead?" 2Sa 12:19
king a, "Is young Absalom all 2Sa 18:29
She a him, "Are you Joab?" 2Sa 20:17
king?" Nathan a. "Our real king, ... 1Ki 1:11
Since you a for wisdom to make 1Ki 3:11
When Hiram heard what Solomon a, ... 1Ki 5:7
King Rehoboam a the elders who 1Ki 12:6
King Jeroboam a for advice. 1Ki 12:28
Elijah a her, "Would you bring 1Ki 17:10
down under a bush and a to die. 1Ki 19:4
Then the king a, "Who will 1Ki 20:14
So Ahab a King Jehoshaphat,................... 1Ki 22:4
The LORD a, 'How will you do it? 1Ki 22:22
said, "You have a a hard thing. 2Ki 2:10
He a, "Is everything all right?" 2Ki 5:21
Elisha a, "Where did it fall?" 2Ki 6:6
Hazael a, "Why are you crying, ... 2Ki 8:12
And God did what Jabez had a. 1Ch 4:10
to a medium and a her for advice 1Ch 10:13
Then David a the priests Zadok 1Ch 15:11
But since you have a for wisdom 2Ch 1:11
King Rehoboam a the elders who 2Ch 10:6
Why have you a their gods for 2Ch 25:15
We also a for their names, ... Ezr 5:10
I a them about Jerusalem and the .... Ne 1:2
they a the Levites to come from .... Ne 12:27
I a the king to let me leave. .... Ne 13:6
The king a them, "What does the .... Est 1:15
Anything she a was given to .... Est 2:13
The king a, "What is it, Queen .... Est 5:3
Then King Xerxes a Queen Esther,............ Est 7:5
You a, 'Who is this that made my .... Job 42:3

He a you for life, and you gave .... Ps 21:4
I a the LORD for help, and he................... Ps 34:4
He never a himself, "For whom am .... Ec 4:8
Hezekiah then a Isaiah, "What .... Is 38:22
Zedekiah a him in private, ... Je 37:17
Then he a me, "Human, can these .... Eze 37:3
The man a me, "Human, do you see .... Eze 47:6
Daniel a his friends to pray .... Da 2:18
Daniel a the king to make .... Da 2:49
holy angel a the first one, ... Da 8:13
he cried and a for his blessing. .... Hos 12:4
afraid, and they a Jonah, "What............... Jnh 1:10
I a the angel who was talking................... Zch 1:19
He a me, "What do you see?" .... Zch 4:2
Then I a the angel, "What are .... Zch 4:11
I a the angel who was talking................... Zch 5:10
They a, "Where is the baby who................ Mt 2:2
He a the men, "Do you believe .... Mt 9:28
They a him, "Are you the One who .... Mt 11:3
Jesus a his followers, "Do you .... Mt 13:51
his followers came to him and a, ... Mt 15:12
I will do what you a." .... Mt 15:28
His followers a him, "How can we .... Mt 15:33
Jesus a, "How many loaves of .... Mt 15:34
Then Jesus a them, "And who do .... Mt 16:15
Then Peter came to Jesus and a,............... Mt 18:21
They a, "Is it right for a man .... Mt 19:3
A man came to Jesus and a, ... Mt 19:16
Jesus a, "What do you want? .... Mt 20:21
The people a, "Who is this man?" .... Mt 21:10
They a, "How did the fig tree .... Mt 21:20
a Jesus this question to test him: .... Mt 22:35
They a, "Why waste that perfume?".......... Mt 26:8
and Pilate a him, "Are you .... Mt 27:11
to Pilate and a to have Jesus' .... Mt 27:58
so amazed they a each other, ... Mk 1:27
Then Jesus a the people, "Which .... Mk 3:4
Jesus a, "Who are my mother and .... Mk 3:33
Then Jesus a him, "What is your .... Mk 5:9
Jesus a them, "How many loaves .... Mk 6:38
a Jesus for a miracle from God. .... Mk 8:11
put his hands on the man and a, ... Mk 8:23
Then Jesus a, "But who do you .... Mk 8:29
Jesus a the boy's father, ... Mk 9:21
They a, "Is it right for a man .... Mk 10:2
Jesus a, "What do you want me to .... Mk 10:36
a coin, and he a, "Whose image .... Mk 12:16
to Jesus and a him a question. .... Mk 12:18
in the Temple, he a, "Why do the .... Mk 12:35
John, and Andrew. They a Jesus, ... Mk 13:3
The high priest a Jesus another .... Mk 14:61
Pilate a Jesus, "Are you the .... Mk 15:2
Pilate a, "Why? What wrong has .... Mk 15:14
Zechariah a for a writing tablet .... Lk 1:63
The people a John, "Then what .... Lk 3:10
a, "Isn't this Joseph's son? .... Lk 4:22
a him, "What is your name?" .... Lk 8:30
country a Jesus to leave,......................... Lk 8:37
Then Jesus a, "But who do you .... Lk 9:20
a Pharisee a Jesus to eat with .... Lk 11:37
He a the first one, 'How much do .... Lk 16:5
The followers a Jesus, "Where .... Lk 17:37
A certain leader a Jesus,......................... Lk 18:18
down the road, he a, "What is .... Lk 18:36
So the spies a Jesus, "Teacher, ... Lk 20:21
They a, "Where do you want us to .... Lk 22:9
Satan has a to test all of you .... Lk 22:31
Pilate a Jesus, "Are you the .... Lk 23:3
Herod a Jesus many questions, ... Lk 23:9
Prophet?" they a. He answered, ... Jn 1:21
But none of them a, "What do you .... Jn 4:27
The man a, "What time did my son .... Jn 4:52
the lake, they a him, "Teacher, ... Jn 6:25

So the people **a,** "What miracle .... Jn 6:30
Jesus **a** the twelve followers, ... Jn 6:67
So the Jews **a,** "Will he kill..................... Jn 8:22
His followers **a** him, "Teacher, ... Jn 9:2
They **a** him, "Where is this man?" .... Jn 9:12
They **a,** "What did he do to you? .... Jn 9:26
He **a,** "Who is the Son of Man, ... Jn 9:36
He **a,** "Where did you bury him?" .... Jn 11:34
leaned closer to Jesus and **a,** .... Jn 13:25
Peter **a** Jesus, "Lord, where .... Jn 13:36
Peter **a,** "Lord, why can't I .... Jn 13:37
now you have not **a** for anything .... Jn 16:24
question even before it is **a.** .... Jn 16:30
high priest **a** Jesus questions .... Jn 18:19
Pilate **a** them, "Do you want me .... Jn 19:15
from Arimathea **a** Pilate if he .... Jn 19:38
They **a** her, "Woman, why are you .... Jn 20:13
because Jesus **a** him the third.................. Jn 21:17
together, they **a** Jesus, "Lord, ... Ac 1:6
felt guilty and **a** Peter and the................. Ac 2:37
pleased God and **a** God to let him .... Ac 7:46
They **a,** "Is Simon Peter staying .... Ac 10:18
Then they **a** Peter to stay with .... Ac 10:48
a Barnabas and Saul to come to............... Ac 13:7
Then the people **a** for a king, ... Ac 13:21
a Pilate to have him killed. .... Ac 13:28
and **a** them, "Did you receive the .... Ac 19:2
I **a,** 'Who are you, Lord?' .... Ac 22:8
You have **a** to see Caesar, ... Ac 25:12
But he **a** to be kept in Caesarea............... Ac 25:21
So we **a** Titus to help you finish 2Co 8:6
I **a** Titus to go to you, and I..................... 2Co 12:18
to God and **a** God for help. .... Heb 5:7
Then one of the elders **a** me, ... Rev 7:13

ASKING

and that is why they are **a** me, ' .... Ex 5:8
sins the evil of **a** for a king." 1Sa 12:19
to Abigail, **a** her to be his wife 1Sa 25:39
message to you, **a** you to come 2Sa 14:32
during the war, **a** him to help 1Ch 5:20
"Now, what are you **a** for? .... Est 5:6
Without **a** questions, God breaks .... Job 34:24
brags a lot is **a** for trouble. .... Pr 17:19
nations, without **a** my Spirit. .... Is 30:1
to Egypt and **a** them for horses .... Eze 17:15
the king is **a** something that is .... Da 2:11
praying and **a** God for help. .... Da 6:11
don't understand what you are **a.** .... Mt 20:22
followers began **a** him privately,.............. Mk 9:28
it is that is **a** you for water,..................... Jn 4:10
They were **a** this to trick Jesus .... Jn 8:6
Are you **a** each other what I .... Jn 16:19
confused, each other, "What .... Ac 2:12
Are you **a** us who made him well? .... Ac 4:9
By **a** him questions yourself, ... Ac 24:8
a me to sentence him to death. .... Ac 25:15
a for everything you need. .... Eph 6:18
a God that you will know fully .... Col 1:9
a our God to help you live the 2Th 1:11
anything without **a** you first so .... Phm 1:14
the beast, **a,** "Who is like .... Rev 13:4

ASKS

now on when your son **a** you, ' .... Ex 13:14
Suppose a man **a** his neighbor to .... Ex 22:10
' If King David **a** that, tell him, ... 2Sa 11:21
He **a** if he will recover from his 2Ki 8:9
of heaven, whatever he **a** for. .... Ezr 7:21
so we may do what Esther **a.**"................... Est 5:5
I answer when he **a** me to explain .... Job 31:14
But no one **a,** 'Where is God, my .... Job 35:10
Someone **a,** "Why are your clothes .... Is 63:2
No man **a** you to be a prostitute, ... Eze 16:34

If a person **a** you for something,.............. Mt 5:42
everyone who **a** will receive. .... Mt 7:8
Give to everyone who **a** you, ... Lk 6:30
everyone who **a** will receive. .... Lk 11:10

ASLEEP

while he was **a,** God removed one .... Ge 2:21
While he was **a,** a very terrible .... Ge 15:12
Saul was **a** in the middle of the 1Sa 26:7
the LORD had put them sound **a.** 1Sa 26:12
during the night while I was **a,** 1Ki 3:20
of them gets sleepy and falls **a.** .... Is 5:27
woke me up as if I had been **a.** .... Zch 4:1
The girl is not dead, only **a.**" .... Mt 9:24
everyone was **a,** his enemy came .... Mt 13:25
stole the body while you were **a.** .... Mt 28:13
the person is **a** or awake, ... Mk 4:27
The child is not dead, only **a.**" .... Mk 5:39
and again he found them **a,** .... Mk 14:40
they were sailing, Jesus fell **a.** .... Lk 8:23
She is not dead, only **a.**"......................... Lk 8:52
found them **a** because of their .... Lk 22:45
Our friend Lazarus has fallen **a,**.............. Jn 11:11
if he is only **a,** he will be all .... Jn 11:12
he went sound **a** and fell to the .... Ac 20:9

ASSEMBLE

sound of the trumpet, **a** there.................. Ne 4:20
gather nations and **a** kingdoms. .... Zph 3:8

ASSEMBLED

shepherds may be **a** against it, ... Is 31:4

ASSEMBLY

all Israel, the **a** of the LORD, ... 1Ch 28:8

ASSISTANT

boy, Joshua had been Moses' **a.** .... Nu 11:28
to Joshua son of Nun, Moses' **a.** .... Jos 1:1
it back to the **a,** and sat down. .... Lk 4:20

ASSOCIATE

Jewish people to **a** with or visit .... Ac 10:28
letter not to **a** with those who.................. 1Co 5:9

ASSYRIA

flows out of **A** toward the east. .... Ge 2:14
he went to **A,** where he built .... Ge 10:11
Pul king of **A** came to attack the 2Ki 15:19
to Tiglath-Pileser king of **A,** 2Ki 16:7
king of **A** surrounded Samaria 2Ki 18:9
great king, the king of **A,** says: 2Ki 18:19
me about Sennacherib king of **A.** 2Ki 19:20
the king of **A** at the Euphrates 2Ki 23:29
time of Esarhaddon king of **A,** .... Ezr 4:2
the king of **A** to fight against .... Is 7:17
in anger I use **A** like a club. .... Is 10:5
be a highway from Egypt to **A,** .... Is 19:23
time Israel, **A,** and Egypt will.................. Is 19:24
are my people. **A,** I made you. .... Is 19:25
Sargon king of **A** sent a military .... Is 20:1
A will be defeated by a sword, ... Is 31:8
for help. Then they run to **A.** .... Hos 7:11
against the north and destroy **A.** .... Zph 2:13
of Egypt and gather them from **A.** .... Zch 10:10

ASSYRIA'S

the king of **A** army commanders to 2Ch 33:11
But **A** king doesn't understand .... Is 10:7
disease upon **A** soldiers. .... Is 10:16
A army lies around its grave. .... Eze 32:23
will defeat **A** pride and destroy .... Zch 10:11

ASSYRIANS

three years the **A** captured 2Ki 18:10
The **A** will be like water rising .... Is 8:7
Egyptians and **A** will worship God........... Is 19:23
had sexual relations with the **A,**............... Eze 16:28
All the **A** will attack you: .... Eze 23:23

will destroy the **A** with their .... Mic 5:6
us from the **A** when they come .... Mic 5:6

ASTONISHED
parents saw him, they were **a**. .... Lk 2:48

ASWAN
from **A** in southern Egypt." .... Is 49:12
in the north to **A** in the south, ... Eze 29:10
in the north to **A** in the south, ... Eze 30:6

ATAD
to the threshing floor of **A,** .... Ge 50:10
threshing floor of **A** and said, ... Ge 50:11

ATE
took some of its fruit and **a** it .... Ge 3:6
tricked me, so I **a** the fruit." .... Ge 3:13
While they **a,** he stood under the .... Ge 18:8
without yeast, and they **a** it. .... Ge 19:3
a it, and I blessed him, and it .... Ge 27:33
thin and ugly cows **a** the seven .... Ge 41:4
heads of grain **a** the seven full .... Ge 41:7
brothers **a** and drank freely .... Ge 43:34
They **a** everything that was left .... Ex 10:15
The Israelites **a** manna for forty .... Ex 16:35
the fish we **a** for free in Egypt. .... Nu 11:5
and the Israelites **a** food there .... Nu 25:2
You **a** no bread and drank no wine .... Dt 29:6
a the food grown in the land .... Jos 5:12
they **a** and drank and cursed .... Jdg 9:27
They **a** it, too, but Samson did .... Jdg 14:9
and she **a** until she was full; .... Ru 2:14
So Saul **a** with Samuel that 1Sa 9:24
So no Israelite soldier **a** food 1Sa 14:24
So Mephibosheth **a** at David's 2Sa 9:11
so Uriah **a** and drank with David. 2Sa 11:13
the people who **a** at his table: 1Ki 4:22
and he **a** and drank with him 1Ki 13:19
Elijah **a** and drank. 1Ki 19:8
After they **a** it, Elisha left and 1Ki 19:21
So we boiled my son and **a** him. 2Ki 6:29
of the tents and **a** and drank. 2Ki 7:8
of his life, he **a** at the king's 2Ki 25:29
The people **a** the feast for seven 2Ch 30:22
from captivity **a** the Passover .... Ezr 6:21
They **a** until they were full and .... Ne 9:25
friend, who **a** at my table, has .... Ps 41:9
So they **a** the bread of angels. .... Ps 78:25
Baal at Peor and **a** meat that had .... Ps 106:28
bread and water you **a** every day. .... Is 30:20
Those who once **a** fine foods are .... La 4:5
You **a** fine flour, honey, and .... Eze 16:13
he hunted, and he **a** people. .... Eze 19:3
young men who **a** the king's food. .... Da 1:15
It crushed and **a** what it killed, ... Da 7:7
locusts that **a** your crops— .... Joe 2:25
locusts **a** your fig and olive .... Am 4:9
And when you **a** and drank, it was .... Zch 7:6
he **a** locusts and wild honey. .... Mt 3:4
sinners" came and **a** with Jesus .... Mt 9:10
those with him **a** the holy bread, ... Mt 12:4
the birds came and **a** it all up. .... Mt 13:4
All the people **a** and were .... Mt 14:20
five thousand men there who **a**, ... Mt 14:21
four thousand men there who **a,** .... Mt 15:38
and **a** locusts and wild honey. .... Mk 1:6
and the birds came and **a** it up. .... Mk 4:4
were five thousand men who **a**. .... Mk 6:44
four thousand people who **a**. .... Mk 8:9
a nothing during that time, ... Lk 4:2
them in their hands, and **a** them. .... Lk 6:1
and took and **a** the holy bread, ... Lk 6:4
the seed, and the birds **a** it up. .... Lk 8:5
They all **a** and were satisfied, ... Lk 9:17

will say, 'We **a** and drank with .... Lk 13:26
Jesus took the fish and **a** it. .... Lk 24:43
me because you **a** the bread and .... Jn 6:26
Our ancestors **a** the manna in the .... Jn 6:31
'The man who **a** at my table has .... Jn 13:18
They **a** together in their homes, ... Ac 2:46
After he **a** some food, his .... Ac 9:19
witnesses who **a** and drank with .... Ac 10:41
again, broke bread, and **a**. .... Ac 20:11
all **a** the same spiritual food, ... 1Co 10:3
way, after they **a**, Jesus took 1Co 11:25
Peter **a** with the non-Jewish .... Gal 2:12
And when we **a** another person's 2Th 3:8
from the angel's hand and **a** it. .... Rev 10:10
but after I **a** it, it was sour .... Rev 10:10
all the birds **a** the bodies until .... Rev 19:21

ATHALIAH
mother, **A,** saw that her son 2Ki 11:1
in a bedroom to hide him from **A,** 2Ki 11:2
that time **A** ruled the land. 2Ki 11:3
Joash so **A** could not kill him. 2Ch 22:11
the sons of wicked **A** had broken 2Ch 24:7

ATHENS
leading Paul went with him to **A**. .... Ac 17:15
for Silas and Timothy in **A,** .... Ac 17:16
All the people of **A** and those .... Ac 17:21
said, "People of **A**, I can see .... Ac 17:22
Later Paul left **A** and went to .... Ac 18:1
it was best to stay in **A** alone 1Th 3:1

ATHLETE
rejoices like an **a** eager to run .... Ps 19:5
Also an **a** who takes part in a 2Ti 2:5

ATTACK
for the Ark and **a** them to its .... Ex 25:12
A one creature on one end of the .... Ex 25:19
together and **a** them to the .... Nu 15:38

ATTACHED
with wings and **a** them to each .... Ex 37:7
They **a** these gold pieces to the .... Ex 39:18
high and was **a** to the Temple 1Ki 6:10
but were not **a** to the Temple .... Eze 41:6

ATTACK
well, sin is ready to **a** you. .... Ge 4:7
made a surprise **a** against the .... Ge 14:15
made a surprise **a** on the city, ... Ge 34:25
Archers **a** him violently and .... Ge 49:23
will send wild animals to **a** you, ... Le 26:22
a lion, they lie waiting to **a;** .... Nu 24:9
When they march up to **a** a city, ... Dt 20:10
Israel, so we cannot **a** them now. .... Jos 9:19
from Gilgal for a surprise **a**. .... Jos 10:9
Go down and **a** the camp of the .... Jdg 7:9
will lead us to **a** the Ammonites? .... Jdg 10:18
I would **a** it and save the sheep 1Sa 17:35
As Goliath came near to **a** him, ... 1Sa 17:48
to Jerusalem to **a** the Jebusites 2Sa 5:6
Don't **a** the Philistines from the 2Sa 5:23
With your help I can **a** an army. 2Sa 22:30
Micaiah answered, "**A** and win! 1Ki 22:15
asked, "Which way should we **a**?" 2Ki 3:8
and Egyptian kings to **a** us!" 2Ki 7:6
Then he went to **a** Jerusalem. 2Ki 12:17
of Egypt, was coming to **a** him. 2Ki 19:9
a ramp to the city walls. 2Ki 19:32
was under **a** until Zedekiah's 2Ki 25:2
I go and **a** the Philistines 1Ch 14:10
of the balsam trees, then **a**. 1Ch 14:15
of his armies to **a** the towns of 2Ch 16:4
go with me to **a** Ramoth in Gilead 2Ch 18:3
the king of Babylon to **a** them. 2Ch 36:17
Will he even **a** the queen while I .... Est 7:8

They a like eagles swooping down .... Job 9:26
hide in the bushes waiting to a? .... Job 38:40
me from the wicked who a me, ... Ps 17:9
and those who hate me a me, ... Ps 27:2
Cruel people a me, but I have .... Ps 59:3
The lions roar as they a. .... Ps 104:21
They may a me, but they will be .... Ps 109:28
armies of Media to a Babylon. .... Is 13:17
Assyria built towers to a it; .... Is 23:13
will a Jerusalem, and that city .... Is 29:2
of Egypt, was coming to a him. .... Is 37:9
someone to a the Babylonians; .... Is 48:14
will defeat those who do a you. .... Is 54:15
Get up! We will a at noon! But .... Je 6:4
and build an a ramp to the top .... Je 6:6
poisonous snakes to a you. .... Je 8:17
'No enemy will a this country .... Je 14:15
and surrounded the city to a it. .... Je 39:1
He will come here and a Egypt. .... Je 43:11
Let a sword a her treasures, ... Je 50:37
Jordan River to a a strong pen .... Je 50:44
He is like a bear ready to a me, ... La 3:10
the days of your a on Jerusalem. .... Eze 4:8
build devices to a the cities .... Eze 17:17
and devices to a the walls. .... Eze 21:22
All the Assyrians will a you: .... Eze 23:23
An enemy will a Egypt, and Cush .... Eze 30:4
the king of Babylon will a you. .... Eze 32:11
the angry goat a the sheep and .... Da 8:7
the South and will a the armies .... Da 11:7
of the North will a the king of .... Da 11:9
the North will a with chariots, ... Da 11:40
I will a like a bear robbed of .... Hos 13:8
a destroying a from the Almighty .... Joe 1:15
come to a in the Valley Where .... Joe 3:12
sent a worm to a the plant so .... Jnh 4:7
will a you, ruining you because .... Mic 6:13
destroyer is coming to a you, ... Nah 2:1
Their horse soldiers a quickly; .... Hab 1:8
They a quickly, like an eagle .... Hab 1:8
'A the strong, walled cities! .... Zph 1:16
wolves that a in the evening, ... Zph 3:3
the nations that a Jerusalem. .... Zch 12:9

ATTACKED

Cain a his brother Abel and .... Ge 4:8
kings who were a united their .... Ge 14:3
They often a the descendants of .... Ge 25:18
a them and captured some of them. .... Nu 21:1
When Judah a, the Lord handed .... Jdg 1:4
The men of Joseph a with swords .... Jdg 1:25
Samson a the Philistines and .... Jdg 15:8
They a those peaceful people and .... Jdg 18:27
Jonathan a the Philistine camp 1Sa 13:3
When it a me, I caught it by its 1Sa 17:35
and given us the enemy who a us. 1Sa 30:23
They a me at my time of trouble, ... 2Sa 22:19
king of Egypt had a and captured 1Ki 9:16
home, a lion a and killed him. 1Ki 13:24
king of Aram a Gath and captured 2Ki 12:17
a Damascus and captured it and 2Ki 16:9
Assyria came and a all the land 2Ki 17:5
of Assyria a all the strong, ... 2Ki 18:13
The Philistines had a and robbed 1Ch 14:9
Asa's army from Judah a them, ... 2Ch 14:12
Baasha king of Israel a Judah. 2Ch 16:1
army surrounded and a Lachish. 2Ch 32:9
They a me at my time of trouble, ... Ps 18:18
the terror of death has a me. .... Ps 55:4
They a me, even though I loved .... Ps 109:4
of Assyria a all the strong, ... Is 36:1
a speckled bird a on all sides .... Je 12:9
When the enemy a, a woman with .... Je 15:9

sadness and a me with grief. .... La 3:5
to Jericho, some robbers a him. .... Lk 10:30
I a the church of God and tried .... Gal 1:13
why am I still being a? .... Gal 5:11
were hurt and a before crowds .... Heb 10:33

ATTACKER

to save her husband from his a, ... Dt 25:11
the a by his sex organs, ... Dt 25:11

ATTACKERS

three groups of a that swept .... Job 1:17

ATTACKING

enemy and a them from behind. .... Jos 10:19
enemy by a them at the waters .... Jos 11:7
The Philistines are a our land!" 1Sa 23:27
Judah and Ziklag, a Ziklag and 1Sa 30:1
all Israel were a the Philistine 1Ki 15:27
Jeroboam's army a both in front 2Ch 13:14
God, proud people are a me; .... Ps 86:14
king of Babylon is a us. .... Je 21:2
This man who was a us is now .... Gal 1:23

ATTACKS

an enemy who a you in your own .... Nu 10:9
the person who a and murders .... Dt 22:26
to the man who a and captures .... Jos 15:16
Again and again God a me; .... Job 16:14
Save my life from their a; .... Ps 35:17
On the day Gog a the land of .... Eze 38:18
When the spirit a him, it throws .... Mk 9:18
Then the wolf a the sheep and .... Jn 10:12

ATTENTION

warden paid no a to anything .... Ge 39:23
believe you or pay a to the .... Ex 4:8
Pay a to the angel and obey him. .... Ex 23:21
he refused to pay a to you. .... Dt 1:45
If you pay a to these laws and .... Dt 7:12
Pay careful a to all the words I .... Dt 32:46
kings. Pay a, rulers! I myself .... Jdg 5:3
But she did not answer or pay a. 1Sa 4:20
David paid a to these words and 1Sa 21:12
Give your a to my prayers and 1Ki 8:52
did not pay a to the commands .... Ne 9:34
Job, pay a and listen to me; .... Job 33:31
Pay a to my prayer, because I .... Ps 17:1
I will pay a to a wise saying; .... Ps 49:4
Pay a to me and answer me. .... Ps 55:2
He paid a to me. so I will call .... Ps 116:2
pay a so you will understand. .... Pr 4:1
My child, pay a to my words; .... Pr 4:20
teachers or pay a to my .... Pr 5:13
My son, pay a to me, and watch .... Pr 23:26
If a ruler pays a to lies, ... Pr 29:12
Pay a, you peoples! .... Is 34:1
God may die, but no one pays a. .... Is 57:1
pay a to the word of the Lord: .... Je 2:31
Pay a to the road on which you .... Je 31:21
Pay a to all that I will show .... Eze 40:4
Lord said to me, "Human, pay a. .... Eze 44:5
did not pay a to your order. .... Da 3:12
My God, pay a and hear me. .... Da 9:18
Pay a, people of Israel. .... Hos 5:1
pay a to the One who threatens .... Mic 6:9
The flock did not pay a to me, ... Zch 11:8
Pay a to what I say. .... Mal 2:2
you pay no a to who they are. .... Mt 22:16
Jesus paid no a to what they .... Mk 5:36
You pay no a to who people are, ... Lk 20:21
Pay a to what I have to say. .... Ac 2:14
her mind to pay a to what Paul .... Ac 16:14
without paying a to their deeds, ... Rm 4:6
give special a to those who are .... Gal 6:10

You show special **a** to the one.................Jam 2:3
is finished. Pay **a:** The third   ....Rev 11:14

ATTITUDE
a proud **a** brings ruin. ....Pr 16:18

ATTRACT
So I am going to **a** her;   ....Hos 2:14

ATTRACTED
the captives and are **a** to her, ...Dt 21:11

ATTRACTIVE
teaching of God our Savior **a.**..................Tit 2:10

AUGUSTUS
A Caesar sent an order that all ....Lk 2:1

AUNT
would shame him. She is your **a.** ....Le 18:14

AUTHORITIES
all rulers, **a,** and powers, and 1Co 15:24
over all rulers, **a,** powers, and.................Eph 1:21
the rulers and **a** and the powers ....Eph 6:12
all powers, **a,** lords, and rulers ....Col 1:16
over angels, **a,** and powers.....................1Pe 3:22

AUTHORITY
under the king's **a** they should ....Ge 41:35
He was given **a,** glory, and the ....Da 7:14
taught like a person who had **a.** ....Mt 7:29
am a man under the **a** of others,...............Mt 8:9
the Son of Man has **a** on earth to ....Mt 9:6
gave them **a** to drive out evil ....Mt 10:1
leaders love to use all their **a.**.................Mt 20:25
What **a** do you have to do these ....Mt 21:23
taught like a person who had **a,** ....Mk 1:22
the Son of Man has **a** on earth to ....Mk 2:10
to have the **a** to force demons.................Mk 3:15
and gave them **a** over evil ....Mk 6:7
Who gave you this **a?"** ....Mk 11:28
because he spoke with **a.** ....Lk 4:32
a and power he commands evil ....Lk 4:36
the Son of Man has **a** on earth to ....Lk 5:24
am a man under the **a** of others,...............Lk 7:8
them power and **a** over all demons...........Lk 9:1
Tell us what **a** you have to do ....Lk 20:2
was that **a** from God or just from ....Lk 20:4
hand him over to the **a** and power ....Lk 20:20
those who have **a** over others ....Lk 22:25
Since Jesus was under Herod's **a,** ....Lk 23:7
But I have not come by my own **a.** ....Jn 7:28
I did not come by my own **a;** ....Jn 8:42
who has the **a** to decide dates ....Ac 1:7
what power or **a** did you do this? ....Ac 4:7
We must obey God, not human **a!** ....Ac 5:29
I do not say this by human **a;** 1Co 9:8
have a symbol of **a** on her head,.............1Co 11:10
about the **a** the Lord gave us 2Co 10:8
But this **a** is to build you up, ...2Co 10:8
rulers and powers of their **a.** ....Col 2:15
yield to the **a** of your husbands, ...Col 3:18
could have used our **a** over you. 1Th 2:7
tell you by the **a** of the Lord to 1Th 5:27
the **a** of our Lord Jesus Christ 2Th 3:6
teach or to have **a** over a man, ...1Ti 2:12
to yield to the **a** of rulers and ....Tit 3:1
leaders and act under their **a.** ....Heb 13:17
people who have **a** in this world: 1Pe 2:13
and **a** through Jesus Christ our ....Jud 1:25
our God and the **a** of his Christ ....Rev 12:10
and his throne and great **a.**.....................Rev 13:2
their power and **a** to the beast. ....Rev 17:13

AUTUMN
The **a** rains fill it with pools ....Ps 84:6
who gives us **a** and spring rains ....Je 5:24

to receive the **a** and spring ....Jam 5:7
They are **a** trees without fruit ....Jud 1:12

AVOID
no one could **a** that question. 2Sa 14:19
A their ways, and don't follow ....Pr 4:15
It is safer to **a** such promises. ....Pr 11:15
a whatever would cause their ....Pr 15:24
the LORD you will **a** evil. ....Pr 16:6
so **a** people who talk too much. ....Pr 20:19
wise see danger ahead and **a** it, ...Pr 27:12
a someone who causes arguments............Tit 3:10
I beg you to **a** the evil things 1Pe 2:11

AVOIDED
I have **a** every evil way so I.....................Ps 119:101
Jesus was the Christ would be **a.** ....Jn 9:22

AVOIDING
but **a** quarrels will bring you ....Pr 20:3

AWAKE
I lie **a.** I am like a lonely bird ....Ps 102:7
stay **a** all night so I can think ....Ps 119:148
speak to you when you are **a.**.................Pr 6:22
If you stay **a,** you will have ....Pr 20:13
A, north wind. Come, south wind. ....Sng 4:16
I sleep, but my heart is **a.** ....Sng 5:2
A! Awake! Get up, Jerusalem. The ....Is 51:17
him and kept him **a** at night. ....Da 2:1
could not stay **a** with me for one ....Mt 26:40
Stay **a** and pray for strength ....Mt 26:41
the person is asleep or **a,** ....Mk 4:27
you stay **a** with me for one ....Mk 14:37
Stay **a** and pray for strength ....Mk 14:38
those who stay **a** and keep their ....Rev 16:15

AWAKEN
the deer not to **a** or excite my.................Sng 2:7

AWAKENED
"The boy has not **a,**" he said. 2Ki 4:31
not get up or be **a** until the ....Job 14:12

AWAKENS
but when he **a,** he is still ....Is 29:8

AWFUL
is dead, he may do something **a.**" 2Sa 12:18
trouble, darkness, and **a** gloom. ....Is 8:22
At that **a** time they will not see ....Je 18:17
end like the end of an **a** day." ....Am 8:10

AWHILE
me, please stay **a** with me, your ....Ge 18:3
you to stay **a** so we can cook ....Jdg 13:15
Even if I stay **a,** I would not ....Jdg 13:16
the guests have been drinking **a,** ....Jn 2:10

AWL
stick an **a** through his ear into ....Dt 15:17

AWOKE
morning Balaam **a** and said to ....Nu 22:13
he **a** like a man who had been ....Ps 78:65
but when they **a** fully, they saw ....Lk 9:32

AX
If the **a** head flies off the.........................Dt 19:5
not destroy its trees with an **a.** ....Dt 20:19
Abimelech took an **a** and cut some ....Jdg 9:48
the head of his **a** fell into the 2Ki 6:5
A dull **a** means harder work. ....Ec 10:10
An **a** is not better than the ....Is 10:15
a forest is cut down with an **a.** ....Is 10:34
The **a** is now ready to cut down ....Mt 3:10
The **a** is now ready to cut down ....Lk 3:9

AXES
plows, hoes, **a,** and sickles 1Sa 13:20
of hammers, **a,** or any other 1Ki 6:7

with saws, iron picks, and **a.** 1Ch 20:3
They came with **a** raised as if to .... Ps 74:5
Egypt with **a** like men who cut .... Je 46:22

AXHEAD
Elisha said, "Pick up the **a.**" 2Ki 6:7

AXLES
bronze wheels with bronze **a.** 1Ki 7:30

AZARIAH
A son of Zadok was the priest; 1Ki 4:2
Amaziah's son was **A.** 1Ch 3:12
A and eighty other brave priests 2Ch 26:17
A, the leading priest from 2Ch 31:10
King Hezekiah and **A** the officer 2Ch 31:13
and **A** from the people of Judah. .... Da 1:6
Hananiah, Mishael, and **A.** .... Da 1:11

AZARIAH'S
was Meshach, and **A** was Abednego. .... Da 1:7

AZAZIAH
Jeiel, and **A** played the harps.................. 1Ch 15:21

AZEKAH
yet been taken—Lachish and **A.** .... Je 34:7

AZOTUS
in a city called **A** and preached .... Ac 8:40
on the way from **A** to Caesarea. .... Ac 8:40

AZZUR
The prophet Hananiah son of **A,** .... Je 28:1

B

BAAL
Balak took Balaam to Bamoth **B;** .... Nu 22:41
began to worship **B** of Peor, ... Nu 25:3
and worshiped **B** and Ashtoreth. .... Jdg 2:13
the altar for **B** had been .... Jdg 6:28
If **B** is a god, let him fight for .... Jdg 6:31
means "let **B** fight against him, ... Jdg 6:32
to serve **B** and worship him. 1Ki 16:31
worshiping **B** and put an altar 1Ki 16:32
fifty prophets of **B** and the four 1Ki 18:19
him, but if **B** is the true God, ... 1Ki 18:21
down before **B** and whose mouths 1Ki 19:18
his father had made for **B.** 2Ki 3:2
A man from **B** Shalishah came to 2Ki 4:42
Ahab served **B** a little, but Jehu 2Ki 10:18
all the people who worship **B.** 2Ki 10:19
Jehu destroyed **B** worship in 2Ki 10:28
in worshiping **B** at Peor and ate .... Ps 106:28
had a vineyard at **B** Hamon. .... Sng 8:11
in the name of **B** and worshiped............. Je 2:8
to the god **B** and follow other .... Je 7:9
sacrifices to **B** on the roofs of .... Je 32:29
and gold, but she used it for **B.** .... Hos 2:8
But they sinned by worshiping **B,** .... Hos 13:1
have never bowed down before **B.**" .... Rm 11:4

BAAL'S
Anyone who takes **B** side will be .... Jdg 6:31
Now call for me all **B** prophets 2Ki 10:19

BAAL-BERITH
They made **B** their god. .... Jdg 8:33
from the temple of the god **B.**................. Jdg 9:4

BAAL-ZEBUB
them, "Go, ask **B,** god of Ekron,.............. 2Ki 1:2

BAALS
to God and followed the **B.** .... Jdg 8:33
You have gone after the **B.** 1Ki 18:18
she burned incense to the **B.** .... Hos 2:13
sacrifices to the **B** and burned .... Hos 11:2

BAASHA
between Asa and **B** king of Israel 1Ki 15:16
Everything else **B** did and all 1Ki 16:5
So **B** died and was buried in 1Ki 16:6
B king of Israel attacked Judah. 2Ch 16:1

BABEL
place is called **B** since that is .... Ge 11:9

BABIES
the **b** struggled inside her. .... Ge 25:22
flocks gave birth to streaked **b.** .... Ge 31:8
with many **b** born to your wives, ... Ge 49:25
they let all the boy **b** live. .... Ex 1:17
but let all the girl **b** live." .... Ex 1:22
"This is one of the Hebrew **b.**" .... Ex 2:6
so that you will eat your own **b,** .... Dt 28:53
and so will **b** and gray-haired................. Dt 32:25
will throw their **b** to the ground 2Ki 8:12
children and to sing praises..................... Ps 8:2
from the LORD; **b** are a reward. .... Ps 127:3
people are like **b** too old for .... Is 28:9
eat their own **b,** the children .... La 2:20
The **b** are so thirsty their .... La 4:4
that cannot feed their **b.** .... Hos 9:14
are pregnant or have nursing **b!** .... Mt 24:19
even their **b** to Jesus so he .... Lk 18:15
and who have no **b** to nurse.' .... Lk 23:29
to leave their **b** outside to die.................. Ac 7:19
without the Spirit—**b** in Christ. 1Co 3:1
things be like **b,** but in your 1Co 14:20
Then we will no longer be **b.** .... Eph 4:14
As newborn **b** want milk, you.................. 1Pe 2:2

BABOONS
silver, ivory, apes, and **b.**....................... 1Ki 10:22

BABY
now on when a **b** boy is eight.................. Ge 17:12
Circumcise every **b** boy whether.............. Ge 17:13
and I are too old to have a **b.**" .... Ge 18:12
The first **b** was born red....................... Ge 25:25
so that **b** was named Jacob. .... Ge 25:26
said, "This **b** came out first." .... Ge 38:28
the **b** with the red string on his .... Ge 38:30
the **b** is a girl, let her live, ... Ex 1:16
She put the **b** in the basket. .... Ex 2:3
Take this **b** and nurse him for.................. Ex 2:9
adopted the **b** as her own son. .... Ex 2:10
The price for a **b** boy one month .... Le 27:6
Sometimes a **b** is born with half.............. Nu 12:12
Do not cook a **b** goat in its .... Dt 14:21
She named the **b** Ichabod, saying, ... 1Sa 4:21
Samuel took a **b** lamb and offered 1Sa 7:9
David prayed to God for the **b.** 2Sa 12:16
On the seventh day the **b** died. 2Sa 12:18
he asked them, "Is the **b** dead?" 2Sa 12:19
this woman rolled over on her **b,** 1Ki 3:19
The living **b** is my son, and the 1Ki 3:22
Cut the living **b** into two pieces 1Ki 3:25
hurt like a woman having a **b.** .... Ps 48:6
peace, like a **b** with its mother .... Ps 131:2
say a **b** born dead is better off .... Ec 6:3
don't know how a **b** grows inside .... Ec 11:5
a woman giving birth to a **b;** .... Is 26:17
a woman forget the **b** she nurses? .... Is 49:15
a cry like a woman having a **b,** .... Je 4:31
a woman giving birth to a **b?** .... Je 13:21
they growl like **b** lions. .... Je 51:38
because the **b** in her is from the .... Mt 1:20
Where is the **b** who was born to .... Mt 2:2
to kill all the **b** boys in .... Mt 2:16
Elizabeth could not have a **b,** .... Lk 1:7
this reason the **b** will be holy .... Lk 1:35
thought she could not have a **b,** .... Lk 1:36

the unborn **b** inside her jumped,.............. Lk 1:41
the **b** inside me jumped with joy. .... Lk 1:44
When the **b** was eight days old, ... Lk 1:59
You will find a **b** wrapped in .... Lk 2:12
found Mary and Joseph and the **b**,.......... Lk 2:16
When the **b** was eight days old, ... Lk 2:21
Joseph brought the **b** Jesus to................. Lk 2:27
Simeon took the **b** in his arms .... Lk 2:28
circumcise a **b** boy on a Sabbath .... Jn 7:22
But when her **b** is born, she .... Jn 16:21
milk is still a **b** and knows .... Heb 5:13
that Moses was a beautiful **b**, ... Heb 11:23
he could eat her **b** as soon as it .... Rev 12:4

BABY'S
went and got the **b** own mother................ Ex 2:8

BABYLON
Nimrod's kingdom covered **B**, ... Ge 10:10
Assyria brought people from **B**,.............. 2Ki 17:24
from a faraway country—from **B**." 2Ki 20:14
day will be taken away to **B**. 2Ki 20:17
king of **B** came up to Jerusalem. 2Ki 24:10
king of **B** marched against 2Ki 25:1
Evil-Merodach became king of **B**, ... 2Ki 25:27
carried away to **B** all the things 2Ch 36:18
took captive to **B** the people who 2Ch 36:20
the Persian kingdom defeated **B**. 2Ch 36:20
went from **B** to Jerusalem. .... Ezr 1:11
the people in **B** as captives...................... Ezr 5:12
first year Cyrus was king of **B**, ... Ezr 5:13
had put them in the temple in **B**. .... Ezr 5:14
Ezra came to Jerusalem from **B**. .... Ezr 7:6
you receive from the area of **B**. .... Ezr 7:16
Artaxerxes king of **B** in the .... Ne 13:6
by Nebuchadnezzar king of **B**. .... Est 2:6
the rivers in **B** we sat and cried .... Ps 137:1
People of **B**, you will be .... Ps 137:8
of Amoz this message about **B**: .... Is 13:1
B is the most beautiful of all .... Is 13:19
this song about the king of **B**:................ Is 14:4
of **B**, morning star, you have .... Is 14:12
back the answer, "**B** has fallen. .... Is 21:9
carry out his wishes against **B**. .... Is 48:14
My people, leave **B**! Run from the .... Is 48:20
to Nebuchadnezzar king of **B**. .... Je 21:7
of the king of **B** for seventy .... Je 25:11
king of **B** and refuse to be under .... Je 27:8
B will be powerful for seventy .... Je 29:10
and to Nebuchadnezzar king of **B**, ... Je 32:28
king of **B** had appointed Zedekiah .... Je 37:1
and he took them all away to **B**. .... Je 39:9
Nebuchadnezzar king of **B**. .... Je 43:10
'**B** will be captured............................... Je 50:2
Shoot your arrows at **B**! .... Je 50:14
B, you are too proud, and I am .... Je 50:31
ready to attack you, city of **B**. .... Je 50:42
to destroy **B** like a wind that .... Je 51:2
B was like a gold cup in the LORD' .... Je 51:7
B has suddenly fallen and been .... Je 51:8
king of **B** has defeated .... Je 51:34
B will become a pile of ruins, ... Je 51:37
How **B** has been defeated! .... Je 51:41
The sea has risen over **B**; .... Je 51:42
I will punish the god Bel in **B**. .... Je 51:44
'In the same way **B** will sink and .... Je 51:64
will bring him to **B** in the land .... Eze 12:13
'The king of **B** came to Jerusalem .... Eze 17:12
He is Nebuchadnezzar king of **B**, ... Eze 26:7
king of **B** came to Jerusalem .... Da 1:1
all the wise men of **B** be killed. .... Da 2:12
charge of all the wise men of **B**. .... Da 2:48
plain of Dura in the area of **B**. .... Da 3:1
this great **B** as my royal home .... Da 4:30

first year as king of **B**, ... Da 7:1
You will go to **B**, but you will .... Mic 4:10
you who live right in **B**."...................... Zch 2:7
that the people were taken to **B**. .... Mt 1:11
were taken to **B** until Christ was .... Mt 1:17
I will send you away beyond **B**.' .... Ac 7:43
The church in **B**, who was chosen 1Pe 5:13
ruined is the great city of **B**! .... Rev 14:8
the sins of **B** the Great, ... Rev 16:19
GREAT **B** MOTHER OF PROSTITUTES ... Rev 17:5
ruined is the great city of **B**! .... Rev 18:2
the sea stood far away from **B**. .... Rev 18:17
great city of **B** will be thrown .... Rev 18:21

BABYLON'S
B gods will be put to shame, ... Je 50:2
nations drank **B** wine, so they .... Je 51:7
I will dry up **B** sea and make her .... Je 51:36

BABYLONIA
died in Ur in **B**, where he was .... Ge 11:28
him out of Ur in **B** and named him .... Ne 9:7
will put Egypt and **B** on the list .... Ps 87:4
terrible things I said about **B**— .... Je 25:13
did many more sexual sins in **B**,............ Eze 16:29
which he carried to **B** and put in .... Da 1:2
are going to **B** to build a temple .... Zch 5:11

BABYLONIAN
But the **B** army chased King 2Ki 25:5
The **B** army is already attacking............. Je 32:29
the **B** army had surrounded the............. Je 37:5
So the **B** army left Jerusalem to .... Je 37:11
But the **B** army chased King .... Je 52:8

BABYLONIANS
The **B** broke up the bronze 2Ki 25:13
The **B** sent three groups of .... Job 1:17
Look at the land of the **B**; .... Is 23:13
Run from the **B**! Tell this news .... Is 48:20
Even the **B** will have to serve .... Je 25:14
I am not leaving to join the **B**." .... Je 37:14
The **B** set fire to the palace and .... Je 39:8
take all the wealth from the **B**. .... Je 50:10
So the **B** captured Zedekiah and .... Je 52:9
The **B** broke into pieces the .... Je 52:17
language and writings of the **B**. .... Da 1:4
will use the **B**, those cruel and .... Hab 1:6
the nations the **B** have hurt will .... Hab 2:6

BACKBONE
fat tail cut off close to the **b**, ... Le 3:9

BACKED
the Israelites **b** up and led the................. Jdg 20:31

BACKS
them on the **b** of their donkeys. .... Jos 9:4
rested on the **b** of twelve bronze.............. 1Ki 7:25
them turn their **b** when you aim .... Ps 21:12
see and their **b** be forever weak .... Ps 69:23
pole from their **b** and the rod .... Is 9:4
their wealth on the **b** of donkeys .... Is 30:6
they have turned their **b** to me. .... Je 2:27
their **b** turned to the Temple .... Eze 8:16
and made all their **b** twist. .... Eze 29:7
see and their **b** be forever weak .... Rm 11:10

BACKWARD
and the rider is thrown off **b**. .... Ge 49:17
God, Eli fell **b** off his chair...................... 1Sa 4:18
They went **b**, not forward. .... Je 7:24

BACKWARDS
they walked **b** into the tent and .... Ge 9:23

BAD
they are as **b** as I have heard................... Ge 18:21
gave his father **b** reports about .... Ge 37:2

BADGER

eyesight was **b** because he was ....Ge 48:10
the people heard this **b** news, ...Ex 33:4
a good animal for a **b** one, ...Le 27:10
the Israelites a **b** report about...............Nu 13:32
an Israelite virgin a **b** name. ....Dt 22:19
You will have **b** growths, sores, ...Dt 28:27
Disobedience is as **b** as the sin 1Sa 15:23
water is so **b** the land cannot 2Ki 2:19
It was so **b** that a donkey's head...............2Ki 6:25
Though his disease was very **b**, ...2Ch 16:12
their **b** advice led to his death. 2Ch 22:4
Nothing **b** will ever happen to ....Ps 10:6
should I be afraid of **b** days? ....Ps 49:5
Nothing **b** will happen to you; ....Ps 91:10
storm was so **b** that they lost ....Ps 107:26
if there is any **b** thing in me. ....Ps 139:24
with those who have **b** tempers. ....Pr 22:24
Do not say **b** things about ....Pr 30:10
judge both good people and **b**. ....Ec 3:17
B dreams come from too much ....Ec 5:3
B things happen to good people, ...Ec 8:14
good things happen to **b** people...............Ec 8:14
there, but only **b** ones grew. ....Is 5:2
things bad and **b** things good, ...Is 5:20
new wine will be **b**, and the ....Is 24:7
a wild vine that grows **b** fruit? ....Je 2:21
a hot and dry land with **b** soil. ....Je 17:6
'Nothing **b** will happen to you.' ....Je 23:17
But the **b** figs are too rotten ....Je 24:8
Both **b** and good things come by ....La 3:38
make something **b** happen to them ....Eze 3:20
until all the **b** things have ....Da 11:36
The **b** things they do are all ....Hos 7:2
quiet, because it is a **b** time. ....Am 5:13
'Nothing **b** will happen to us.' ....Am 9:10
If you say **b** things to a brother ....Mt 5:22
though you are **b**, you know how ....Mt 7:11
but a **b** tree produces bad fruit. ....Mt 7:17
tree cannot produce **b** fruit, ...Mt 7:18
who planted the **b** seed is the ....Mt 13:39
and threw away the **b** fish. ....Mt 13:48
nothing as **b** will ever happen...............Mt 24:21
a **b** tree produce good fruit. ....Lk 6:43
though you are **b**, you know how ....Lk 11:13
b things happened to Lazarus. ....Lk 16:25
will happen when **b** times come?" ....Lk 23:31
There will be a **b** smell." ....Jn 11:39
good and **b**, will surely be ....Ac 24:15
storm was very **b**, we lost all ....Ac 27:20
or told us anything **b** about you. ....Ac 28:21
excuse for the **b** things they do. ....Rm 1:20
but I do the **b** things I do not ....Rm 7:19
"**B** friends will ruin good habits." 1Co 15:33
Good and **b** do not belong 2Co 6:14
anger, **b** temper, doing or saying ....Col 3:8
others will go from **b** to worse. 2Ti 3:13
good and **b** water flow from the ....Jam 3:11
friend, do not follow what is **b**; 3Jn 1:11
I know the **b** things some people ....Rev 2:9

BADGER

rock **b** chews the cud but does ....Le 11:5

BADGERS

eat camels, rabbits, or rock **b**...............Dt 14:7
are hiding places for the **b**. ....Ps 104:18
Rock **b** are not very powerful, ...Pr 30:26

BADLY

to treat her mistress Sarai **b**. ....Ge 16:4
the people of Ai beat them **b**. ....Jos 7:4
shot him, and he was **b** wounded. 1Sa 31:3
I am **b** hurt and am almost dead...............2Sa 1:9
room in Samaria and was **b** hurt. 2Ki 1:2
left, Joash was **b** wounded...............2Ch 24:25

have treated me **b** all my life. ....Ps 129:1
they have been hurt **b**. ....Je 14:17
treated Jeremiah the prophet **b**. ....Je 38:9
you are treated **b** in one city, ...Mt 10:23
way treated the other son **b**. ....Gal 4:29
being treated **b** and are 2Th 1:4
poor, abused, and treated **b**. ....Heb 11:37

BAG

and a leather **b** full of water. ....Ge 21:14
a leather **b** filled with wine. 1Sa 1:24
bread, a leather **b** full of wine, ...1Sa 16:20
his shepherd's **b** and grabbed his 1Sa 17:40
He took a stone from his **b**,...............1Sa 17:49
burst like a new leather wine **b**. ....Job 32:19
The **b** of arrows rattles against ....Job 39:23
I am like a wine **b** going up in ....Ps 119:83
who has his **b** full of arrows. ....Ps 127:5
lover is like a **b** of myrrh that ....Sng 1:13
with the arrows from his **b**...............La 3:13
Don't carry a **b** or extra clothes ....Mt 10:10
a third servant one **b** of gold, ...Mt 25:15
who got one **b** went out and dug ....Mt 25:18
no bread, no **b**, and no money ....Mk 6:8
walking stick, **b**, bread, money, ...Lk 9:3
a purse, a **b**, or sandals, did ....Lk 22:35
now if you have a purse or a **b**, ...Lk 22:36

BAGGAGE

He's hiding behind the **b**." 1Sa 10:22

BAGS

his brothers' **b** with grain and ....Ge 42:25
old leather wine **b** that were ....Jos 9:4
The food in our **b** is gone. 1Sa 9:7
and leather **b** full of wine. 2Sa 16:1
silver in two **b** with two changes 2Ki 5:23
new wine into old leather **b**. ....Mt 9:17
another servant two **b** of gold, ...Mt 25:15
money and earned five more **b**. ....Mt 25:16
the new wine will break the **b**, ...Mk 2:22
new wine into old leather **b**. ....Lk 5:37

BAIT

into a trap where there is no **b**; ....Am 3:5

BAKE

make bricks and **b** them to make ....Ge 11:3
of Egypt to **b** loaves of bread ....Ex 12:39
fine flour and **b** twelve loaves...............Le 24:5
perfume and cook and **b** for him. 1Sa 8:13
the hot coals to **b** my bread. ....Is 44:19
sin offering and the grain ....Eze 46:20

BAKED

He **b** bread without yeast, and ....Ge 19:3
all kinds of **b** food for the king ....Ge 40:17
offering that is **b** in an oven, ...Le 7:9
like bread **b** with olive oil. ....Nu 11:8
his head a loaf **b** over coals and 1Ki 19:6
of iron and partly of **b** clay...............Da 2:33

BAKER

to the king and the king's **b**. ....Ge 40:1
him wine and the **b** had a dream. ....Ge 40:5
the king hanged the **b** on a pole. ....Ge 40:22
are like an oven heated by a **b**. ....Hos 7:4

BAKING

your ovens and into your **b** pans. ....Ex 8:3
had the job of **b** the bread used 1Ch 9:31
b it over human dung where the...............Eze 4:12

BALAAM

messengers to **B** son of Beor at ....Nu 22:5
But the donkey said to **B**, ...Nu 22:30
Balak did what **B** asked, and he ....Nu 23:30
but I refused to listen to **B**. ....Jos 24:10
they had hired **B** to put a curse ....Ne 13:2

B

way, following the way **B** went. 2Pe 2:15
to doing the wrong that **B** did. .... Jud 1:11
who follow the teaching of **B**. .... Rev 2:14

BALAAM'S
crushing **B** foot against it. .... Nu 22:25
who followed **B** advice and turned .... Nu 31:16

BALAK
B son of Zippor saw everything .... Nu 22:2
king of Moab, **B** son of Zippor, ... Jos 24:9
the evil plans of **B** king of Moab............... Mic 6:5
He taught **B** how to cause the................. Rev 2:14

BALAK'S
awoke and said to **B** leaders, ... Nu 22:13

BALANCES
Your weights and **b** should weigh .... Le 19:36
LORD wants honest **b** and scales; .... Pr 16:11

BALCONIES
stories like steps and had **b**. .... Eze 42:3

BALD
hair from his head and is **b**, ... Le 13:40
in fancy ways, they will be **b**. .... Is 3:24
Make yourself **b** like the eagle, ... Mic 1:16

BALDHEAD
you baldhead! Go up too, you **b**!" 2Ki 2:23

BALL
a gold bell and a pomegranate **b**, ... Ex 28:34
a bell and a pomegranate **b**. .... Ex 39:26
tightly into a **b** and throw you .... Is 22:18

BALLS
b like pomegranates of blue, ... Ex 28:33
of the outer robe between the **b**.............. Ex 39:25

BALM
carrying spices, **b**, and myrrh. .... Ge 37:25
some **b**, some honey, spices, ... Ge 43:11
Isn't there **b** in the land of .... Je 8:22
Go up to Gilead and get some **b**, ... Je 46:11
b for her pain, and maybe she .... Je 51:8
and for honey, olive oil, and **b**. .... Eze 27:17

BALSAM
them in front of the **b** trees. 2Sa 5:23
in the tops of the **b** trees, ... 1Ch 14:15

BAND
b of shepherds may be assembled .... Is 31:4
the ground with a **b** of iron and .... Da 4:15
had a gold **b** around his chest. .... Rev 1:13

BANDAGE
has not been wrapped with a **b**, ... Eze 30:21
us, but he will **b** our wounds. .... Hos 6:1

BANDAGED
wine on his wounds, and **b** them. .... Lk 10:34

BANDAGES
God hurts, but he also **b** up; .... Job 5:18
and **b** their wounds. .... Ps 147:3
the LORD **b** his broken people .... Is 30:26
the sick or put **b** on those that .... Eze 34:4
put **b** on those that were hurt,............... Eze 34:16

BANDS
hooks and **b** on twenty bronze .... Ex 27:10
must have silver **b** and hooks and .... Ex 27:17
silver hooks and **b** on ten posts .... Ex 38:12
arm **b**, bracelets, signet rings,............... Nu 31:50
those important men in iron **b**. .... Ps 149:8
and wore golden **b** tied around .... Rev 15:6

BANK
cows on the **b** of the Nile. .... Ge 41:3
dug along the **b** of the river, ... Ex 7:24
stood on the **b** of the Jordan. 2Ki 2:13

bankers and those who owe the **b**. .... Is 24:2
me back to the **b** of the river. .... Eze 47:6
have put my gold in the **b**. .... Mt 25:27
you put my money in the **b**? .... Lk 19:23

BANKER
people owed money to the same **b**............ Lk 7:41

BANKERS
to **b** and those who owe the bank. .... Is 24:2

BANKS
the Jordan overflows its **b**. .... Jos 3:15
rising over the **b** of the river, ... Is 8:7
along the **b** of the Nile will .... Is 19:7
like a river overflowing its **b**. .... Is 66:12
grow on both **b** of the river, ... Eze 47:12

BANNER
and named it The LORD Is My **B**. .... Ex 17:15
have raised a **b** to gather those .... Ps 60:4
and his **b** over me is love. .... Sng 2:4
raises a **b** for the nations far .... Is 5:26
God will raise a **b** as a sign for .... Is 11:12
You will see a **b** raised on a .... Is 18:3
a hilltop, like a **b** on a hill. .... Is 30:17
I will raise my **b** for all the .... Is 49:22
Raise the **b** as a sign for the .... Is 62:10
Lift up a **b** and tell them. .... Je 50:2
Lift up a **b** in the land! .... Je 51:27

BANNERS
under their family flag and **b**." .... Nu 2:2

BANQUET
The **b** lasted one hundred eighty .... Est 1:4
On the seventh day of the **b**, ... Est 1:10
king gave a great **b** for Esther .... Est 2:18
Then go to the **b** with the king .... Est 5:14
He brought me to the **b** room,............... Sng 2:4
gave a big **b** for a thousand .... Da 5:1
guests, came into the **b** room................. Da 5:10
man gave a big **b** and invited .... Lk 14:16

BAPTISM
answer, 'John's **b** was from God,' .... Mt 21:25
and preaching a **b** of changed .... Mk 1:4
preaching a **b** of changed hearts .... Lk 3:3
I have a **b** to suffer through, ... Lk 12:50
preached to the people about **b**. .... Ac 10:37
Israel about a **b** of changed .... Ac 13:24
"What kind of **b** did you have?" .... Ac 19:3
John's **b** was a baptism of .... Ac 19:4
We shared his death in our **b**. .... Rm 6:3
one Lord, one faith, and one **b**. .... Eph 4:5
water is like **b** that now saves................. 1Pe 3:21

BAPTISMS
return to the teaching about **b**, ... Heb 6:2

BAPTIST
time John the **B** began preaching .... Mt 3:1
John the **B** was in prison, but he .... Mt 11:2
John the **B** is greater than any .... Mt 11:11
is John the **B**, who has risen .... Mt 14:2
of John the **B** here on a platter. .... Mt 14:8
Some say you are John the **B**................. Mt 16:14
"Ask for the head of John the **B**." .... Mk 6:24
Some say you are John the **B**................. Mk 8:28
John the **B** came and did not eat .... Lk 7:33
the **B** has risen from the dead." .... Lk 9:7

BAPTIZE
I **b** you with water to show that .... Mt 3:11
He will **b** you with the Holy .... Mt 3:11
River and wanted John to **b** him. .... Mt 3:13
B them in the name of the Father .... Mt 28:19
everyone, "I **b** you with water, ... Lk 3:16
He will **b** you with the Holy .... Lk 3:16

they did not let John **b** them. .... Lk 7:30
Prophet, why do you **b** people?" .... Jn 1:25
John answered, "I **b** with water, ... Jn 1:26
Jesus himself did not **b** people, ... Jn 4:2
I did not **b** any of you except 1Co 1:14

BAPTIZED

and he **b** them in the Jordan .... Mt 3:6
I need to be **b** by you!" .... Mt 3:14
as Jesus was **b**, he came up out .... Mt 3:16
their sins and were **b** by him in .... Mk 1:5
in Galilee and was **b** by John in .... Mk 1:9
And can you be **b** with the same .... Mk 10:38
believes and is **b** will be saved, ... Mk 16:16
collectors came to John to be **b**. .... Lk 3:12
When John **b** people, was that .... Lk 20:4
People were going there to be **b**............... Jn 3:23
days that will be **b** with the Holy .... Ac 1:5
accepted what Peter said were **b**. .... Ac 2:41
after he was **b**, he stayed very .... Ac 8:13
the water, and Philip **b** him. .... Ac 8:38
Then Saul got up and was **b**. .... Ac 9:18
people from being **b** with water? .... Ac 10:47
that they be **b** in the name of .... Ac 10:48
but you will be **b** with the Holy .... Ac 11:16
the people in her house were **b**. .... Ac 16:15
to Paul and believed and were **b**. .... Ac 18:8
Get up, be **b**, and wash your sins .... Ac 22:16
When we were **b**, we were buried .... Rm 6:4
Were you **b** in the name of Paul? 1Co 1:13
They were all **b** as followers of 1Co 10:2
But we were all **b** into one body 1Co 12:13
do who are being **b** for the dead? 1Co 15:29
When you were **b**, you were buried .... Col 2:12

BAPTIZING

place where John was **b** people. .... Mt 3:7
John was **b** people in the desert .... Mk 1:4
River, where John was **b** people. .... Jn 1:28
John was also **b** in Aenon, near .... Jn 3:23

BAR

them loose, along with the **b**. .... Jdg 16:3
break down the **b** of the gate to .... Am 1:5

BAR-JESUS

they met a magician named **B**. .... Ac 13:6
is the name for **B** in the Greek .... Ac 13:8

BARABBAS

prison, named **B**, who was known .... Mt 27:16
crowd to ask for **B** to be freed .... Mt 27:20
was a man named **B** in prison who .... Mk 15:7
people to ask Pilate to free **B**, ... Mk 15:11
this man away! Let **B** go free!" .... Lk 23:18
No, not him! Let **B** go free!" .... Jn 18:40

BARAK

was told that **B** son of Abinoam .... Jdg 4:12
Then Deborah said to **B**, "Get up! .... Jdg 4:14
So **B** entered her tent, and .... Jdg 4:22
a song! Get up, **B**! Go capture................ Jdg 5:12
about Gideon, **B**, Samson, ... Heb 11:32

BARBER'S

use it like a **b** razor to shave .... Eze 5:1

BARE

rest as it lies **b** without them. .... Le 26:43
the lion apart with his **b** hands. .... Jdg 14:6
Raise a flag on the **b** mountain. .... Is 13:2
barefoot, with their buttocks **b**. .... Is 20:4
your feet are **b** or until your .... Je 2:25
Go up to the **b** hilltop and cry................ Je 7:29
land will be stripped **b** because .... Eze 12:19
leaving you naked and **b**. .... Eze 16:39
poured the blood on the **b** rock. .... Eze 24:7

will make you a **b** rock, and you.............. Eze 26:14
What you sow is only a **b** seed, ... 1Co 15:37

BAREFOOT

He covered his head and went **b**. 2Sa 15:30
naked and **b** for three years .... Is 20:3
evil, going around **b** and naked. .... Mic 1:8

BARELY

you will **b** hear the millstone .... Ec 12:4
are like two **b** burning sticks .... Is 7:4
they could **b** tell he was human .... Is 52:14
they were **b** able to keep the .... Ac 14:18
we were **b** able to bring in the .... Ac 27:16

BARGAIN

try to **b** with you for it? .... Job 41:6

BARK

off some of the **b** so that the .... Ge 30:37
even a dog will **b** at the .... Ex 11:7
dogs will **b** in the beautiful .... Is 13:22
dogs that don't know how to **b**. .... Is 56:10
stripped all the **b** off my trees................ Joe 1:7

BARLEY

bloom, and the **b** had ripened, so .... Ex 9:31
six bushels of **b** seed needed. .... Le 27:16
a land that has wheat and **b**, ... Dt 8:8
that a loaf of **b** bread rolled .... Jdg 7:13
the beginning of the **b** harvest. .... Ru 1:22
gave me these six portions of **b**, ... Ru 3:17
at the beginning of **b** harvest.................. 2Sa 21:9
quarts of **b** will be sold for 2Ki 7:1
was a field of **b** at that place. 1Ch 11:13
sixty-two thousand bushels of **b**. 2Ch 27:5
let weeds come up instead of **b**." .... Job 31:40
Take wheat, **b**, beans, small .... Eze 4:9
Cry for the wheat and the **b**. .... Joe 1:11
five loaves of **b** bread and two .... Jn 6:9
left from the five **b** loaves. .... Jn 6:13
quarts of **b** for a day's pay .... Rev 6:6

BARN

no oxen, no food is in the **b**. .... Pr 14:4
seeds for crops still in the **b**? .... Hag 2:19
part of the grain into his **b**,...................... Mt 3:12
wheat and bring it to my **b**.'" .... Mt 13:30
part of the grain into his **b**,...................... Lk 3:17

BARNABAS

The apostles called him **B** .... Ac 4:36
But **B** accepted Saul and took him .... Ac 9:27
this, so they sent **B** to Antioch. .... Ac 11:22
Set apart for me **B** and Saul to .... Ac 13:2
Paul and **B** spoke very boldly,.................. Ac 13:46
Paul and **B** told the Good News in .... Ac 14:21
But Paul and **B** stayed in Antioch .... Ac 15:35
B wanted to take John Mark with .... Ac 15:37
B took Mark and sailed to Cyprus,.......... Ac 15:39
so they accepted **B** and me. .... Gal 2:9
the cousin of **B**, greet you. .... Col 4:10

BARNEA

them from Kadesh **B** to look at .... Nu 32:8
left Kadesh **B** until we crossed .... Dt 2:14
LORD said at Kadesh **B** when he .... Jos 14:6

BARNS

God will bless you with full **b**, ... Dt 28:8
Let our **b** be filled with crops .... Ps 144:13
Then your **b** will be full, and .... Pr 3:10
b are empty and falling down. .... Joe 1:17
the pens and no cattle in the **b**. .... Hab 3:17
or harvest or store food in **b**, ... Mt 6:26
tear down my **b** and build bigger .... Lk 12:18
they don't have storerooms or **b**, ... Lk 12:24

B

BARRED
people like the **b** gates of a .... Pr 18:19

BARRELS
and your wine **b** will overflow .... Pr 3:10
b will overflow with new wine .... Joe 2:24
is full and the **b** are spilling .... Joe 3:13

BARREN
have marched over those **b** hills. .... Je 12:12

BARS
high walls and gates with **b**. .... Dt 3:5
a town with gates and **b**." 1Sa 23:7
with bronze **b** on their gates. 1Ki 4:13
doors, bolts, and **b** in place. .... Ne 3:3
its legs are like **b** of iron. .... Job 40:18
gates and cuts apart iron **b**. .... Ps 107:16
and cut through their iron **b**. .... Is 45:2
The **b** of her gates are broken. .... Je 51:30
and smashed the **b** of the gates. .... La 2:9
when I break the **b** of their .... Eze 34:27
has burned the **b** of your gates. .... Nah 3:13

BARSABBAS
One was Joseph **B**, who was also .... Ac 1:23
They chose Judas **B** and Silas, ... Ac 15:22

BARTHOLOMEW
and **B**; Thomas and Matthew, ... Mt 10:3
Andrew, Philip, **B**, Matthew, ... Mk 3:18
Andrew, James, John, Philip, **B**, ... Lk 6:14
Philip, Thomas, **B**, Matthew, ... Ac 1:13

BARTIMAEUS
beggar named **B** son of Timaeus.............. Mk 10:46

BARUCH
I gave them to **B** son of Neriah, ... Je 32:12
B wrote those messages on the .... Je 36:4
and **B** wrote them on a scroll:................ Je 45:1

BARZILLAI
B were at Mahanaim when David 2Sa 17:27

BASE
Its **b**, stand, flower-like cups, ... Ex 25:31
set fire to the **b** of the .... Dt 32:22
and he put it on a stone **b**. 2Ki 16:17
had a raised **b** all around. .... Eze 41:8

BASED
b on their responsibilities and 2Ch 31:17
Their worship is **b** on nothing................. Is 29:13
The law is not **b** on faith. .... Gal 3:12
new agreement is **b** on promises .... Heb 8:6

BASES
forty silver **b** for the frames. .... Ex 26:19
The **b** for the posts were made of .... Ex 38:17
the Holy Tent and their **b**, ... Nu 3:37
standing on **b** of fine gold. .... Sng 5:15

BASHAN
went up the road toward **B**.................... Nu 21:33
of Og, king of **B**, as well as all .... Nu 32:33
Og was king of **B** and lived in................ Dt 1:4
and Golan in **B** in the land of .... Jos 20:8
and the East Manasseh in **B**. .... Jos 21:6
Like the strong bulls of **B**, ... Ps 22:12
and the great oak trees of **B**, ... Is 2:13
if they were fat animals from **B**:.............. Eze 39:18
you cows of **B** on the Mountain of .... Am 4:1
Let them feed in **B** and Gilead as .... Mic 7:14
areas of **B** and Carmel dry up, ... Nah 1:4
Cry, oaks in **B**, because the.................... Zch 11:2

BASHED
their children were **b** to death. .... Hos 10:14

BASKET
In the top **b** were all kinds of .... Ge 40:17
so she got a **b** made of reeds and .... Ex 2:3
She put the baby in the **b**. .... Ex 2:3
When she saw the **b** in the tall .... Ex 2:5
Then take the **b** of bread that .... Ex 29:23
not put any grapes into your **b**. .... Dt 23:24
Place the **b** before the LORD .... Dt 26:10
Your **b** and your kitchen will be .... Dt 28:17
But the other **b** had figs too .... Je 24:2
"It is a measuring **b** going out." .... Zch 5:6
a woman sitting inside the **b**. .... Zch 5:7
lifted up the **b** between earth .... Zch 5:9
lowering him in a **b** through an .... Ac 9:25
lowered me in a **b** through a hole 2Co 11:33

BASKETFULS
expecting to find twenty **b**, ... Hag 2:16

BASKETS
were three bread **b** on my head. .... Ge 40:16
three **b** stand for three days. .... Ge 40:18
I let them put down their **b**. .... Ps 81:6
showed me two **b** of figs arranged .... Je 24:1
good fish in **b** and threw away .... Mt 13:48
twelve **b** with the leftover .... Mt 14:20
filled seven **b** with the leftover .... Mt 15:37
twelve **b** with the leftover .... Mk 6:43
filled seven **b** with the leftover .... Mk 8:8
gathered up, filling twelve **b**. .... Lk 9:17
filled twelve **b** with the pieces............... Jn 6:13

BATCH
the whole **b** of dough rise."..................... 1Co 5:6
the whole **b** of dough rise."..................... Gal 5:9

BATH
came to the river to take a **b**, ... Ex 2:5
wash their clothes and take a **b**,............. Nu 19:19
sheep just coming from their **b**. .... Sng 4:2
is a tenth of a **b** from each cor. .... Eze 45:14
After a person has had a **b**,.................... Jn 13:10

BATHE
all his hair, and **b** in water. .... Le 14:8
from a man, he must **b** in water;............. Le 15:16
He will **b** his body in water in a .... Le 16:24
Let him **b** his feet in olive oil................. Dt 33:24

BATHED
in Samaria where prostitutes **b**, ... 1Ki 22:38
They seem to be **b** in cream and............. Sng 5:12
Then I **b** you with water, ... Eze 16:9
The two sisters **b** themselves for............. Eze 23:40

BATHING
on the roof, he saw a woman **b**. 2Sa 11:2

BATHSHEBA
That woman is **B** daughter of 2Sa 11:3
But **B** became pregnant and sent 2Sa 11:5
relations with **B** in secret, ... 2Sa 12:12
Then David comforted **B** his wife. 2Sa 12:24
this, he went to **B**, Solomon's 1Ki 1:11
B went in to see the aged king 1Ki 1:15
So **B** went to King Solomon to 1Ki 2:19
four children of David and **B**, ... 1Ch 3:5
David after David's sin with **B**. .... Ps 50:23

BATS
kind of heron, hoopoes, or **b**. .... Le 11:19
of heron, the hoopoes, or **b**. .... Dt 14:18
them away to the **b** and moles. .... Is 2:20

BATTLE
he had brought back from the **b**. .... Ge 14:20
Write about this **b** in a book so .... Ex 17:14
must go before the LORD into **b**............. Nu 32:20
prepare for **b** and cross the.................... Nu 32:29

people volunteered to go to **b**. .... Jdg 5:2
and I fought a great **b** against.................. Jdg 12:2
Gibeah. The **b** was very hard................... Jdg 20:34
Israel turned around in the **b**. .... Jdg 20:39
defeated the Philistines in **b**. 1Sa 7:10
going out to their **b** positions,................. 1Sa 17:20
So David led them in **b**. 1Sa 18:13
He cannot go with us into **b**. 1Sa 29:4
How the mighty have fallen in **b**! 2Sa 1:19
Let him be killed in **b**." 2Sa 11:15
Philistines were gathered for **b**, ... 2Sa 23:9
On the seventh day the **b** began.............. 1Ki 20:29
if you come back safely from **b**, ... 1Ki 22:28
In **b** Amaziah killed ten thousand 2Ki 14:7
say you have **b** plans and power.............. 2Ki 18:20
and prepared for **b** in the Valley 2Ch 14:10
The **b** continued all day. 2Ch 18:34
is not your **b**, it is God's....................... 2Ch 20:15
In the **b** King Josiah was shot by 2Ch 35:23
' It smells the **b** from far away; .... Job 39:25
You gave me strength in **b**. .... Ps 18:39
but he keeps me safe in **b**. .... Ps 55:18
the **b** has pressed me all day .... Ps 56:1
savior, you protect me in **b**..................... Ps 140:7
me for war, who trains me for **b**, ... Ps 144:1
can get the horses ready for **b**, ... Pr 21:31
that marched in **b** and every .... Is 9:5
Prepare the shields for **b** .... Is 21:5
when they see God's **b** flag," .... Is 31:9
say you have **b** plans and power.............. Is 36:5
like a horse charging into a **b**. .... Je 8:6
the morning and **b** cries at noon, ... Je 20:16
the enemy in the **b** on the LORD's .... Eze 13:5
He will fight a **b** and destroy .... Eze 26:8
army, but he will lose the **b**, ... Da 11:11
a powerful army lined up for **b**. .... Joe 2:5
It will come during a day of **b**, ... Am 1:14
marching to **b** through muddy .... Zch 10:5
were powerful in **b** and defeated .... Heb 11:34
like horses prepared for **b**. .... Rev 9:7
and chariots hurrying into **b**. .... Rev 9:9
for the **b** on the great day .... Rev 16:14
and Magog—to gather them for **b**. .... Rev 20:8

BATTLEFIELD

four thousand soldiers on the **b**............... 1Sa 4:2

BATTLES

and go with us and fight our **b**." 1Sa 8:20
brave and fight the LORD's **b**." 1Sa 18:17
to help us and to fight our **b**."................. 2Ch 32:8

BAY

started at the **b** of the sea at .... Jos 15:5
they saw a **b** with a beach and .... Ac 27:39

BDELLIUM

B and onyx are also found there. .... Ge 2:12

BEACH

The waves may pound the **b**, ... Je 5:22
all knelt on the **b** and prayed,................. Ac 21:5
the ship to the **b** if they could. .... Ac 27:39
wind and sailed toward the **b**................... Ac 27:40

BEACHES

who made the **b** to be a border .... Je 5:22

BEAM

wood **b** is to be pulled from his .... Ezr 6:11

BEAMS

roof made from **b** and cedar 1Ki 6:9
to the Temple by cedar **b**. 1Ki 6:10
were forty-five **b** on the roof, ... 1Ki 7:3
gold on the Temple's ceiling **b**, ... 2Ch 3:7
beautiful cedar **b** and throw them .... Je 22:7

BEANS

roasted grain, **b**, small peas, ... 2Sa 17:28
wheat, barley, **b**, small peas, ... Eze 4:9

BEAR

When a lion or **b** came and took a 1Sa 17:34
have killed both a lion and a **b**! 1Sa 17:36
as angry as a **b** that is robbed................. 2Sa 17:8
It is God who made the **B**, Orion, ... Job 9:9
stars of the **B** with its cubs? .... Job 38:32
better to meet a **b** robbed of her .... Pr 17:12
a roaring lion or a charging **b**. .... Pr 28:15
He is like a **b** ready to attack .... La 3:10
before me that looked like a **b**. .... Da 7:5
runs from a lion and meets a **b**, ... Am 5:19
B with each other, and forgive .... Col 3:13

BEAR'S

feet like a **b** feet and a mouth .... Rev 13:2

BEARD

his head, his **b**, his eyebrows, ... Le 14:9
or cut the edges of your **b**. .... Le 19:27
and let spit run down his **b**. 1Sa 21:13
took Amasa by the **b** to kiss him. 2Sa 20:9
pulled hair from my head and **b**, ... Ezr 9:3
head and running down his **b**. .... Ps 133:2
and legs and removing Judah's **b**. .... Is 7:20
Every head and **b** has been shaved........... Is 15:2
been shaved and every **b** cut off. .... Je 48:37
razor to shave your head and **b**............... Eze 5:1

BEARDS

shave off the edges of their **b**,................. Le 21:5
until your **b** have grown back. 2Sa 10:5
he shaved their **b** and cut off 1Ch 19:4
Samaria had shaved off their **b**, ... Je 41:5

BEARS

Then two mother **b** came out of 2Ki 2:24
Cows and **b** will eat together in .... Is 11:7
All of us growl like the **b**. .... Is 59:11

BEAST

b in the tall grass along the .... Ps 68:30
and hateful **b** and all the idols .... Eze 8:10
Then I saw a **b** coming up out of .... Rev 13:1
This **b** looked like a leopard, ... Rev 13:2
he had given his power to the **b**............... Rev 13:4
And they also worshiped the **b**, ... Rev 13:4
on earth worship the first **b**, ... Rev 13:12
And the second **b** does great .... Rev 13:13
And the second **b** was given power .... Rev 13:15
the name of the **b** or the number .... Rev 13:17
the mark of the **b** and who .... Rev 16:2
saw a woman sitting on a red **b**............... Rev 17:3
The **b** you saw was once alive but .... Rev 17:8
seven heads on the **b** are seven .... Rev 17:9
to rule with the **b** for one hour. .... Rev 17:12
But the **b** was captured and with .... Rev 19:20
the mark of the **b** and worshiped .... Rev 19:20
prophet and the **b** were thrown .... Rev 19:20
the mark of the **b** on their .... Rev 20:4
sulfur with the **b** and the false .... Rev 20:10

BEAST'S

idol and gets the **b** mark on the .... Rev 14:9

BEASTS

an animal was killed by wild **b**, ... Ge 31:39
saw animals, wild **b**, reptiles, ... Ac 11:6

BEAT

slave masters **b** these men and .... Ex 5:14
I will **b** you seven times harder. .... Le 26:21
When you **b** your olive trees to .... Dt 24:20
the people of Ai **b** them badly. .... Jos 7:4
the horses' hoofs **b** the ground. .... Jdg 5:22
the house and **b** on the door. .... Jdg 19:22

B

I **b** my enemies into pieces,.....................2Sa 22:43
My father **b** you with whips, ...1Ki 12:11
I **b** my enemies into pieces,.......................Ps 18:42
They make people want to **b** them............Pr 18:6
They **b** me up, but I don't ....Pr 23:35
B your breasts in grief, because ....Is 32:12
I **b** my breast with sorrow. ....Je 31:19
So **b** your chest in sadness.....................Eze 21:12
You will **b** many nations into ....Mic 4:13
like doves and **b** their breasts, ...Nah 2:7
at him and **b** him with whips ....Mt 20:19
the servants, **b** them, and killed ....Mt 22:6
Jesus' face and **b** him with their..............Mt 26:67
They will **b** him with whips and ....Mk 10:34
guards led Jesus away and **b** him. ....Mk 14:65
The soldiers **b** Jesus on the head ....Mk 15:19
off his clothes, **b** him, and left ....Lk 10:30
But he **b** on his chest because he ....Lk 18:13
But they **b** the servant and sent ....Lk 20:10
They **b** us in public without a ....Ac 16:37
b him there before the court. ....Ac 18:17
believers in jail and **b** them. ....Ac 22:19
up, preparing to **b** him, Paul ....Ac 22:25
the right to **b** a Roman citizen ....Ac 22:25
sent to **b** me and keep me from 2Co 12:7

BEATEN

you will be **b** by your enemies. ....Nu 14:42
Israel has been **b** by the enemy. ....Jos 7:8
He will be **b** up and disgraced, ...Pr 6:33
when you were only **b** with a rod. ....Eze 21:10
Israel is **b** down; its root is ....Hos 9:16
children were **b** to death at....................Nah 3:10
But Jesus was **b** with whips and ....Mt 27:26
After having Jesus **b** with whips, ...Mk 15:15
will be **b** with many blows!....................Lk 12:47
Silas and had them **b** with rods. ....Ac 16:22
We are often **b**, and we have no 1Co 4:11
We are **b** and thrown into prison. 2Co 6:5
times I was **b** with rods. 2Co 11:25
Some were laughed at and **b**. ....Heb 11:36
If you are **b** for doing wrong, ...1Pe 2:20

BEATING

saw an Egyptian **b** a Hebrew man,...........Ex 2:11
has to be punished with a **b**, ...Dt 25:2
your **b** is about to kill me. ....Ps 39:10
a rainstorm **b** against the wall ....Is 25:4
like the sea **b** its waves on your ....Eze 26:3
making fun of him and **b** him. ....Lk 22:63
b their chests because they were ....Lk 23:48
saw them, they stopped **b** Paul. ....Ac 21:32

BEATINGS

I have been hurt more in **b**.....................2Co 11:23

BEATS

If a man **b** his male or female.................Ex 21:20
With his hammer he **b** the metal ....Is 44:12
My heart **b** for you, and my love ....Hos 11:8

BEAUTIFUL

caused every **b** tree and every ....Ge 2:9
woman saw that the tree was **b**, ...Ge 3:6
God saw that these girls were **b**,..............Ge 6:2
saw that Sarai was very **b**. ....Ge 12:14
the king of Egypt how **b** she was. ....Ge 12:15
His wife Rebekah was very **b**,..................Ge 26:7
eyes, but Rachel was very **b**. ....Ge 29:17
cows ate the seven **b** fat cows. ....Ge 41:4
runs free, that has **b** fawns. ....Ge 49:21
Put four rows of **b** gems on the ....Ex 28:17
If you see a **b** woman among the ....Dt 21:11
things I saw was a **b** coat from ....Jos 7:21
There they built a **b** altar. ....Jos 22:10
Her younger sister is more **b**. ....Jdg 15:2

was wise and **b**, but Nabal was 1Sa 25:3
a woman bathing. She was very **b**...........2Sa 11:2
Absalom had a **b** sister named 2Sa 13:1
Tamar, and she was a **b** woman...............2Sa 14:27
in Israel for a **b** young woman, ...1Ki 1:3
girl was very **b**, and she cared 1Ki 1:4
to bring every **b** young girl to ....Est 2:3
all the land as **b** as Job's.......................Job 42:15
B words fill my mind. ....Ps 45:1
The princess is very **b**. ....Ps 45:13
It is high and **b** and brings joy ....Ps 48:2
because their houses are more **b**. ....Ps 49:16
to go into the **b** land of Canaan; ....Ps 106:24
and like a **b** crown on your head. ....Pr 4:9
desire her because she is **b**. ....Pr 6:25
A **b** woman without good sense is ....Pr 11:22
home with rare and **b** treasures...............Pr 24:4
time is as **b** as gold apples ....Pr 25:11
You are the most **b** of women. ....Sng 1:8
Oh, you are **b**, and your eyes are ....Sng 1:15
trading ships and the **b** ships..................Is 2:16
their **b** ankle bracelets, their ....Is 3:18
is the most **b** of all kingdoms................Is 13:19
That **b** crown of flowers is just ....Is 28:1
Jerusalem, that **b** place of rest. ....Is 33:20
as **b** as the hill of Carmel and...............Is 35:2
Be **b** again, holy city of ....Is 52:1
How **b** is the person who comes ....Is 52:7
make my beautiful Temple more **b**. ....Is 60:7
will be like a **b** crown in the ....Is 62:3
a land more **b** than that of any ....Je 3:19
tree, with **b** fruit and shape. ....Je 11:16
b cedar beams and throw them ....Je 22:7
Egypt is like a **b** young cow, ...Je 46:20
people called the most **b** city, ...La 2:15
tall and became like a **b** jewel. ....Eze 16:7
were very **b** and became a queen. ....Eze 16:13
have said, "I am like a **b** ship." ....Eze 27:3
So the tree was great and **b**, ...Eze 31:7
and has a **b** voice and plays ....Eze 33:32
The leaves of the tree were **b**.................Da 4:12
will attack the **b** land of Judah. ....Da 11:41
like the **b** olive trees and the ....Hos 14:5
You have planted **b** vineyards, ...Am 5:11
stone, shouting, 'It's **b**!' ....Zch 4:7
How **b** the buildings are!........................Mk 13:1
decorated with **b** stones and ....Lk 21:5
the Temple gate called **B** Gate, ...Ac 3:2
was born, and he was very **b**. ....Ac 7:20
How **b** is the person who comes to..........Rm 10:15
and pure and **b** and respected. ....Php 4:8
saw that Moses was a **b** baby,.................Heb 11:23
clothes that should make you **b**. 1Pe 3:3

BEAUTIFULLY

not dressed as **b** as one of these ....Mt 6:29

BEAUTY

Aaron to give him honor and **b**. ....Ex 28:2
for its greatness and **b**. 1Ch 22:5
giving Esther her **b** treatments ....Est 2:9
months of **b** treatments that ....Est 2:12
see the LORD's **b** and look with ....Ps 27:4
Jerusalem, whose **b** is perfect. ....Ps 50:2
fool you, and **b** can trick you,................Pr 31:30
had no special **b** or form to make ....Is 53:2
b of Jerusalem has gone away. ....La 1:6
Your **b** was perfect, because of ....Eze 16:14
full of wisdom and perfect in **b**. ....Eze 28:12
But the **b** of the heavenly bodies 1Co 15:40
The sun has one kind of **b**, ...1Co 15:41
like a bride in all her **b**. ....Eph 5:27
falls off, and its **b** is gone. ....Jam 1:11

b should come from within you— 1Pe 3:4
that will never lose its b. 1Pe 5:4

BECOMES

is married when he b your slave, ... Ex 21:3
on something, it b unclean. .... Le 11:35
days before she b clean from her .... Le 12:4
everything he sits on b unclean. .... Le 15:4
the woman who b unclean from her .... Le 15:33
holy offerings until he b clean. .... Le 22:4
person touches b unclean, ... Nu 19:22
But if he b angry, you will know 1Sa 20:7
from your son when he b king. 1Ki 11:12
Their body b so thin there is .... Job 33:21
when the water b hard as stone, ... Job 38:30
make it dark, and it b night. .... Ps 104:20
When he b angry, he will crush .... Ps 110:5
servant who b a king, a foolish .... Pr 30:22
sea, but the sea never b full. .... Ec 1:7
sister on the day she b engaged? .... Sng 8:8
Not one of them b tired or falls .... Is 5:27
not drink water, he b tired. .... Is 44:12
only to shout and the sea b dry. .... Is 50:2
his message b like a burning .... Je 20:9
comes, it b a roaring fire. .... Hos 7:6
everyone who eats it b unclean. .... Hos 9:4
the nation that b rich by doing .... Hab 2:9
seed grows and b the largest of .... Mk 4:32
his teeth, and b very stiff. .... Mk 9:18
The seed grows and b a tree, ... Lk 13:19
a prostitute b one body with 1Co 6:16
That old self b worse, because .... Eph 4:22
of the world b God's enemy. .... Jam 4:4

BECOMING

regular sacrifices for b clean." .... Le 14:32
unclean by b a prostitute, ... Le 21:9
arm was healed, b as it was 1Ki 13:6
because he was b a leader of .... Est 9:4
gone to prison before b king. .... Ec 4:14
at night, b drunk with wine. .... Is 5:11
the sea was b more stormy. .... Jnh 1:13
The LORD is b angry about what .... Mic 2:7
body is b older and weaker. 2Co 4:16
so that by his b poor you might 2Co 8:9
I was b a leader in the Jewish .... Gal 1:14
new and are b like the One who .... Col 3:10
selfish, or b angry quickly. .... Tit 1:7

BED

strength and sat up on his b. .... Ge 48:2
your father's b and shamed me .... Ge 49:4
killed might have to stay in b. .... Ex 21:18
the body fluid lies on a b, ... Le 15:4
every b he lies on will be .... Le 15:24
His b was made of iron, and it .... Dt 3:11
One night he was lying in b. 1Sa 3:2
So he told Samuel, "Go to b. 1Sa 3:9
me on his b so I can kill him. 1Sa 19:15
got up from his b and walked 2Sa 11:2
Amnon went to b and acted sick. 2Sa 13:6
down on his b to worship God, ... 1Ki 1:47
she put the dead baby in my b. 1Ki 3:20
will never get up from your b; 2Ki 1:16
the boy was lying dead on his b. 2Ki 4:32
they killed Joash in his own b. 2Ch 24:25
I think my b will comfort me .... Job 7:13
while in b in great pain; .... Job 33:19
I go to b and sleep in peace, ... Ps 4:8
my b is soaked from my crying. .... Ps 6:6
will never get out of b again." .... Ps 41:8
Let them sing for joy even in b! .... Ps 149:5
have made my b smell sweet with .... Pr 7:17
person turns over and over in b. .... Pr 26:14
so pleasant! Our b is the grass. .... Sng 1:16

to sleep on a b that was too .... Is 28:20
make your b on every hill and .... Is 57:7
sat on a fine b with a table set .... Eze 23:41
lying on my b, I saw pictures .... Da 4:5
the vision while lying on my b, ... Da 4:13
my servant is at home in b. .... Mt 8:6
was sick in b with a fever, ... Mk 1:30
went to her b, took her hand, ... Mk 1:31
lamp under a bowl or under a b? .... Mk 4:21
found her daughter lying in b; .... Mk 7:30
a bowl or hides it under a b. .... Lk 8:16
and my children and I are in b. .... Lk 11:7
will be sleeping in one b; .... Lk 17:34
able to leave his b for the past .... Ac 9:33
Stand up and make your b." .... Ac 9:34
throw her on a b of suffering. .... Rev 2:22

BEDROOM

into your b, on your bed, ... Ex 8:3
to see the aged king in his b, ... 1Ki 1:15
and his nurse in a b to hide him 2Ki 11:2
like a bridegroom from his b. .... Ps 19:5
of rich people, even in your b. .... Ec 10:20
his room, the bride from her b. .... Joe 2:16

BEDROOMS

even in the b of their rulers. .... Ps 105:30

BEDS

brought b, bowls, clay pots, ... 2Sa 17:28
a deep sleep, lying on their b. .... Job 33:15
His cheeks are like a bed of spices; .... Sng 5:13
with those whose b you love, ... Is 57:8
just lie on their b and cry. .... Hos 7:14
lie on b decorated with ivory .... Am 6:4
who lie on their b and make evil .... Mic 2:1
placed their sick on b and mats .... Ac 5:15

BEDTIME

Before b, men both young and old .... Ge 19:4

BEELZEBUL

head of the family is called B, ... Mt 10:25
Jesus uses the power of B, ... Mt 12:24
were saying, "B is living inside .... Mk 3:22
use the power of B to force out .... Lk 11:18

BEER

Bered, was called B Lahai Roi. .... Ge 16:14
was now living at B Lahai Roi. .... Ge 25:11
not drink wine or b when you go .... Le 10:9
or vinegar made from wine or b. .... Nu 6:3
sheep, wine, b, or anything you .... Dt 14:26
no bread and drank no wine or b. .... Dt 29:6
drink wine or b or eat anything .... Jdg 13:4
I have not drunk any wine or b. 1Sa 1:15
Wine and b make people loud and .... Pr 20:1
Give b to people who are dying .... Pr 31:6
The b will taste bitter to those .... Is 24:9
are drunk with b and are filled .... Is 28:7
let's drink all the b we want. .... Is 56:12
you if you give him wine and b. .... Mic 2:11
He will never drink wine or b, ... Lk 1:15

BEERSHEBA

and wandered in the desert of B. .... Ge 21:14
made the agreement at B, ... Ge 21:32
They all traveled back to B, ... Ge 22:19
that city is called B even now. .... Ge 26:33
left B and set out for Haran. .... Ge 28:10
Then Jacob left B. .... Ge 46:5
from Dan to B, knew Samuel was 1Sa 3:20
burned incense, from Geba to B. 2Ki 23:8
'As surely as the god of B lives, ... Am 8:14

BEES

chased you like b and defeated .... Dt 1:44
a swarm of b and honey in it. .... Jdg 14:8

surrounded me like a swarm of **b**, ... Ps 118:12
and they will come like **b**. .... Is 7:18

BEG

So I **b** you to accept the gift I .... Ge 33:11
we **b** you to forgive our wrong. .... Ge 50:17
I **b** you to let the man of God .... Jdg 13:8
Don't **b** me to leave you or to .... Ru 1:16
They will **b** for a little money 1Sa 2:36
Now, I **b** you, forgive my sin. 1Sa 15:25
LORD, I **b** you to forgive us, ... 2Sa 24:10
and went to **b** the king for her 2Ki 8:3
presence to **b** for mercy and to .... Est 4:8
could only **b** God, my Judge, for............. Job 9:15
The angel will **b** for mercy and .... Job 33:24
your neighbor and **b** to be free .... Pr 6:3
The poor **b** for mercy, but the .... Pr 18:23
for them or **b** me to help them, ... Je 7:16
made your enemies **b** you in times .... Je 15:11
Children **b** for bread, but no one .... La 4:4
people began to **b** Jesus to leave........... Mk 5:17
ditches, and I am ashamed to **b**.............. Lk 16:3
same man who used to sit and **b**?" .... Jn 9:8
to this gate to **b** for money .... Ac 3:2
Now I **b** you to eat something. .... Ac 27:34
I **b** you to offer your lives as a .... Rm 12:1
I **b** you to help me in my work by .... Rm 15:30
b you, brothers and sisters, by 1Co 1:10
so I **b** you, please follow my 1Co 4:16
so I **b** you to become like me. .... Gal 4:12
I especially **b** you to pray so .... Heb 13:19
I **b** you to avoid the evil things 1Pe 2:11

BEGGAR

blind **b** named Bartimaeus son of .... Mk 10:46

BEGGED

But Lot **b** them to come, so they............... Ge 19:3
the angels **b** Lot to hurry. .... Ge 19:15
because Jacob **b**, Esau accepted .... Ge 33:11
But Moses **b** the LORD his God and .... Ex 32:11
'David **b** me to let him go to his 1Sa 20:6
Although Absalom **b** David, ... 2Sa 13:25
his knees before Elijah and **b**, ... 2Ki 1:13
prophets had **b** Elisha until he 2Ki 2:17
She **b** Elisha to stay and eat. 2Ki 4:8
Then Jehoahaz **b** the LORD, and 2Ki 13:4
feet and cried and **b** him to stop.............. Est 8:3
The demons **b** Jesus, "If you make........... Mt 8:31
they **b** him to leave their area. .... Mt 8:34
They **b** Jesus to let them touch .... Mt 14:36
fell on his knees and **b**, '..................... Mt 18:26
Because you **b** me to forget what .... Mt 18:32
fell to his knees and **b** Jesus, ... Mk 1:40
demons Jesus, "Send us into .... Mk 5:12
b him to let them touch just .... Mk 6:56
She **b** Jesus to force the demon .... Mk 7:26
man to Jesus and **b** him to touch .... Mk 8:22
he bowed before him and **b** him, ... Lk 5:12
The men went to Jesus and **b** him, ... Lk 7:4
and the demons **b** Jesus to allow .... Lk 8:32
had healed **b** to go with him, ... Lk 8:38
I **b** your followers to force the .... Lk 9:40
father went out and **b** him to .... Lk 15:28
they **b** him to stay with them, ... Jn 4:40
He **b** them, "Save yourselves from .... Ac 2:40
They **b** him, "Hurry, please come .... Ac 9:38
the people there **b** Paul not to............... Ac 21:12
But they **b** and pleaded with us 2Co 8:4
I **b** the Lord three times to take 2Co 12:8
Israel heard and **b** not to hear .... Heb 12:19

BEGGING

Absalom kept **b** David until he 2Sa 13:27
Will it keep **b** you for mercy and .... Job 41:3

LORD, hear me **b** for fairness; .... Ps 17:1
or their children **b** for food. .... Ps 37:25
wander around, **b** for food..................... Ps 109:10
run after them, **b**, but they are .... Pr 19:7
'I was **b** the king not to send me............. Je 38:26
officer came to him, **b** for help. .... Mt 8:5
b him to come to his house. .... Lk 8:41
was sitting beside the road, **b**. .... Lk 18:35
his followers were **b** him, ... Jn 4:31
earlier seen this man **b** said, ... Jn 9:8
b him not to go into the theater. .... Ac 19:31
am **b** you with the gentleness and 2Co 10:1

BEGINNINGS

Your **b** and your ancestors were .... Eze 16:3
that small **b** are unimportant .... Zch 4:10

BEGINS

the blood that **b** the Agreement, ... Ex 24:8
Bread **b** on the fifteenth .... Le 23:6
the land that **b** at Gilead and .... Dt 3:16
to where the sea **b** or walked .... Job 38:16
you where the Jordan River **b**, ... Ps 42:6
moon is full, when our feast **b**. .... Ps 81:3
Wisdom **b** with respect for the .... Ps 111:10
Knowledge **b** with respect for the .... Pr 1:7
Wisdom **b** with respect for the .... Pr 9:10
and understanding **b** with knowing .... Pr 9:10
fool **b** by saying foolish things .... Ec 10:13
When the killing in Egypt, ... Eze 30:4
water before the long war **b**. .... Nah 3:14
from where the Nile River **b**; .... Zph 3:10
and he **b** to beat the other .... Mt 24:49
Anyone who **b** to plow a field but .... Lk 9:62
new agreement **b** with my blood .... Lk 22:20
that it **b** and ends with faith. .... Rm 1:17
the blood that **b** the Agreement .... Heb 9:20
God's grace and **b** to cause..................... Heb 12:15
And if that judging **b** with us,................ 1Pe 4:17
until the day **b** and the morning 2Pe 1:19

BEGS

He **b** God on behalf of a human as............. Job 16:21
as a person **b** for his friend. .... Job 16:21
even **b** God for us with deep .... Rm 8:26

BEHALF

He begs God on **b** of a human as a............. Job 16:21

BEHAVED

wanted men who **b** like animals .... Eze 23:20

BEHAVING

to stop **b** like an unfaithful .... Hos 2:2

BEHAVIOR

the Amorites for their evil **b**." .... Ge 15:16
Mordecai's **b** because Mordecai .... Est 3:4
children are known by their **b**; .... Pr 20:11
women to be holy in their **b**, ... Tit 2:3

BEHEMOTH

Look at **B**, which I made just as .... Job 40:15

BEINGS

Let us make human **b** in our image .... Ge 1:26
them and named them human **b**. .... Ge 5:2
destroy all human **b** that I made............. Ge 6:7
punishment come from human **b**!"........... 2Sa 24:14
Why do you take care of human **b**? .... Ps 8:4
What can human **b** do to me?................... Ps 56:4
The mind of human **b** is hard to .... Ps 64:6
Go back into dust, human **b**." .... Ps 90:3
Human **b**, whom I created, would .... Is 57:16
remove human **b** from the earth," .... Zph 1:3
power like this to human **b**. .... Mt 9:8
We are only human **b** like you. .... Ac 14:15
and human **b** have no right to................. Rm 9:20
nor was I sent from human **b**.................... Gal 1:1

B

you was not made up by human **b**............ Gal 1:11
so that human **b** can reach God................ 1Ti 2:5
Why do you take care of human **b**? .... Heb 2:6

BEL

The god **B** will be put to shame, ... Je 50:2
punish the god **B** in Babylon. .... Je 51:44

BELIAL

Christ and **B**, the devil, have 2Co 6:15

BELIEF

will also suffer for their **b**. .... Mk 10:30

BELIEFS

Your **b** about these things should .... Rm 14:22

BELIEVE

that you **b** I dug this well. .... Ge 21:30
you really **b** that your mother, ... Ge 37:10
was shocked and did not **b** them. .... Ge 45:26
Israelites will **b** that the LORD .... Ex 4:5
long will they not **b** me in spite .... Nu 14:11
Know and **b** today that the LORD .... Dt 4:39
Proof That We **B** the LORD Is God. .... Jos 22:34
know and fully **b** that the LORD............... Jos 23:14
I could not **b** it then, but now I 1Ki 10:7
been who did not **b** in the LORD 2Ki 17:14
I did not **b** it then, but now I 2Ch 9:6
or trick you, and do not **b** him. 2Ch 32:15
I truly **b** I will live to see the .... Ps 27:13
LORD protects those who truly **b**, ... Ps 31:23
to their followers who **b** them. .... Ps 49:13
did not **b** what God promised. .... Ps 106:24
Fools will **b** anything, and the .... Pr 14:15
You may **b** you are doing right, ... Pr 21:2
kind, but don't **b** them, because .... Pr 26:25
are wise and **b** they are clever. .... Is 5:21
but you should not **b** them. .... Is 8:12
They refuse to **b** the proof from .... Is 33:8
Don't **b** him when he says .... Is 37:10
next so we will **b** that you are................. Is 41:23
They **b** their own lies and refuse .... Je 8:5
world could not **b** that enemies .... La 4:12
b all the words I will speak to................ Eze 3:10
Don't **b** your neighbor or trust a.............. Mic 7:5
that you won't **b** even when you .... Hab 1:5
Do you **b** that I can make you see .... Mt 9:28
others and say they will **b**, ... Mt 10:32
you will **b** that John is Elijah, ... Mt 11:14
If you **b**, you will get anything .... Mt 21:22
because they all **b** that John was .... Mt 21:26
hate you because you **b** in me. .... Mt 24:9
There he is!' But don't **b** them. .... Mt 24:23
Then we will **b** in him. .... Mt 27:42
and lives and **b** the Good News!" .... Mk 1:15
Don't be afraid; just **b**." .... Mk 5:36
do believe! Help me to **b** more!"............. Mk 9:24
So I tell you to **b** that you have .... Mk 11:24
There he is!' But don't **b** them. .... Mk 13:21
the followers did not **b** them. .... Mk 16:13
who does not **b** will be punished. .... Mk 16:16
they cannot **b** it and be saved. .... Lk 8:12
They **b** for a while, but when .... Lk 8:13
Just **b**, and your daughter will .... Lk 8:50
and say they do not **b** in me, ... Lk 12:9
they **b** John was a prophet." .... Lk 20:6
I tell you, you will not **b** me. .... Lk 22:67
But they did not **b** the women, ... Lk 24:11
foolish and slow to **b** everything............. Lk 24:25
accept him and in him he gave .... Jn 1:12
Do you really **b** you can build it .... Jn 2:20
Jesus did not **b** in them because .... Jn 2:24
People who **b** in God's Son are .... Jn 3:18
Those who **b** in the Son have .... Jn 3:36
now we **b** because we heard him .... Jn 4:42

because you don't **b** in the One .... Jn 5:38
if you don't **b** what Moses wrote.............. Jn 5:47
we see a miracle, we will **b** you. .... Jn 6:30
But some of you don't **b**." .... Jn 6:64
We **b** and know that you are.................. Jn 6:69
if you don't **b** that I am he." .... Jn 8:24
"Do you **b** in the Son of Man?" .... Jn 9:35
He said, "Lord, I **b**!" .... Jn 9:38
my Father does, then don't **b** me. .... Jn 10:37
believe in me, **b** what I do. .... Jn 10:38
Those who **b** in me will have life .... Jn 11:25
Martha, do you **b** this?" .... Jn 11:26
I **b** that you are the Christ, ... Jn 11:27
B in the light while you still .... Jn 12:36
Or **b** because of the miracles I .... Jn 14:11
Those who **b** will do even greater .... Jn 14:12
Jesus answered, "So now you **b**? .... Jn 16:31
I will not **b** it until I see the................... Jn 20:25
Those who **b** without seeing me .... Jn 20:29
so that you may **b** that Jesus is .... Jn 20:31
I **b** that Jesus Christ is the Son .... Ac 8:37
that all who **b** in Jesus will be .... Ac 10:43
those who were not Jewish to **b**............. Ac 14:27
B in the Lord Jesus and you will .... Ac 16:31
They refused to **b** and said evil .... Ac 19:9
Sadducees do not **b** in angels or............. Ac 23:8
But the Pharisees do **b** in them all. .... Ac 23:8
you **b** what the prophets wrote? .... Ac 26:27
chain because I **b** in the hope .... Ac 28:20
is true for all who **b** in Christ,............... Rm 3:22
and if you **b** in your heart that .... Rm 10:9
with our mouths that we **b**,................... Rm 10:10
if the Jews will **b** in God again, ... Rm 11:23
I **b** I also have God's Spirit...................... 1Co 7:40
prophecy is for people who **b**,................. 1Co 14:22
We **b**, and so we speak. 2Co 4:13
live by what we **b**, not by what 2Co 5:7
So all who **b** as Abraham believed .... Gal 3:9
to people who **b** in Jesus Christ............... Gal 3:22
living like those who do not **b**. .... Eph 4:17
We **b** that Jesus died and that he 1Th 4:14
because not all people **b**........................ 2Th 3:2
people who **b** and know the truth. 1Ti 4:3
someone who does not **b** in God. 1Ti 5:8
Then those who do **b** in God will be .... Tit 3:8
to God must **b** that he is real .... Heb 11:6
God, you must **b** and not doubt. .... Jam 1:6
You **b** there is one God. .... Jam 2:19
But the demons **b** that, too, and .... Jam 2:19
Through Christ you **b** in God,................. 1Pe 1:21
But to the people who do not **b**, ... 1Pe 2:7
be persuaded to **b** without 1Pe 3:1
that we **b** in his Son, Jesus 1Jn 3:23
So do not **b** every spirit, but 1Jn 4:1
who does not **b** makes God a liar, ... 1Jn 5:10
all those who did not **b**. .... Jud 1:5
who refuse to **b**, who do evil .... Rev 21:8

BELIEVED

Abram **b** the LORD. And the LORD .... Ge 15:6
and the Israelites **b**............................... Ex 4:31
but I fully **b** the LORD would .... Jos 14:8
Then the people **b** what the LORD .... Ps 106:12
I **b**, so I said, "I am completely .... Ps 116:10
of Memphis have **b** false things. .... Is 19:13
Who would have **b** what we heard? .... Is 53:1
The people of Nineveh **b** God. .... Jnh 3:5
healed just as you **b** he would." .... Mt 8:13
are made well because you **b**." .... Mt 9:22
and prostitutes **b** him............................ Mt 21:32
you are made well because you **b**. .... Mk 5:34
you are healed because you **b**." .... Mk 10:52
all the people **b** that John was .... Mk 11:32

BELIEVER

Because you **b**, you are saved .... Lk 7:50
You were healed because you **b**." .... Lk 17:19
who **b** people would not rise from .... Lk 20:27
and his followers **b** in him. .... Jn 2:11
Then they **b** the Scripture and .... Jn 2:22
in that town **b** in Jesus because .... Jn 4:39
First we **b** in Jesus because of .... Jn 4:42
If you really **b** Moses, you would .... Jn 5:46
things, many people **b** in him. .... Jn 8:30
said to the Jews who **b** in him, ... Jn 8:31
in that place many **b** in Jesus. .... Jn 10:42
saw what Jesus did, **b** in him. .... Jn 11:45
But many **b** in Jesus, even many .... Jn 12:42
you loved me and **b** that I came .... Jn 16:27
and they **b** that you sent me. .... Jn 17:8
John preach the things they .... Ac 4:4
more men and women **b** in the Lord .... Ac 5:14
the Jewish priests **b** and obeyed. .... Ac 6:7
men and women **b** Philip and were .... Ac 8:12
Simon himself **b**, and after he .... Ac 8:13
this, and many **b** in the Lord. .... Ac 9:42
he gave us who **b** in the Lord .... Ac 11:17
group of people **b** and turned to .... Ac 11:21
b because he was amazed at the .... Ac 13:12
have life forever **b** the message. .... Ac 13:48
a great many Jews and Greeks **b**. .... Ac 14:1
and others **b** the apostles. .... Ac 14:4
and saw that he **b** God could heal .... Ac 14:9
happy because they now **b** in God. .... Ac 16:34
Among those who **b** was Dionysius, ... Ac 17:34
to Paul and **b** and were baptized. .... Ac 18:8
the Holy Spirit when you **b**?" .... Ac 19:2
and the officer **b** what the .... Ac 27:11
But Abraham **b** God and continued .... Rm 4:18
Lord, who **b** what we told them? .... Rm 10:16
thing, and this is what you **b**. 1Co 15:11
own hearts we **b** we would die. 2Co 1:9
Scriptures, "I **b**, so I spoke." 2Co 4:13
heard the Good News and **b** it. .... Gal 3:2
as Abraham **b** are blessed just .... Gal 3:9
your salvation—you **b** in Christ. .... Eph 1:13
but because I **b** in Christ. .... Php 3:9
Jesus, the One in whom I have **b**. 2Ti 1:12
We who have **b** are able to enter .... Heb 4:3
Abraham **b** that God could raise .... Heb 11:19
Abraham **b** God, and God accepted .... Jam 2:23

BELIEVER

If your fellow **b** sins against .... Mt 18:15
mother was Jewish and a **b**, ... Ac 16:1
I am truly a **b** in the Lord, ... Ac 16:15
goes to court against another **b**— 1Co 6:6
man has a wife who is not a **b**, ... 1Co 7:12
but she must marry another **b**. 1Co 7:39
This weak **b** for whom Christ died 1Co 8:11
because I am a **b** in Christ. .... Php 1:13
away from any **b** who refuses to 2Th 3:6
an elder must not be a new **b**, ... 1Ti 3:6
woman who is a **b** has widows in 1Ti 5:16
a person and as a **b** in the Lord. .... Phm 1:16

BELIEVERS

no true **b** are left on earth. .... Ps 12:1
there was a meeting of the **b** .... Ac 1:15
to the number of **b** that day. .... Ac 2:41
The **b** met together in the Temple .... Ac 2:46
five thousand in the group of **b**. .... Ac 4:4
The group of **b** were united in .... Ac 4:32
were added to the group of **b**. .... Ac 5:14
the Samaritan **b** might receive .... Ac 8:15
The Jewish **b** who came with Peter .... Ac 10:45
of the **b** were scattered when .... Ac 11:19
The Lord was helping the **b**, ... Ac 11:21
Antioch where the **b** had put them .... Ac 14:26

began teaching the non-Jewish **b**: .... Ac 15:1
The non-Jewish **b** must be .... Ac 15:5
Let's visit the **b** and see how .... Ac 15:36
Then they let the **b** go free. .... Ac 17:9
The **b** quickly sent Paul away to .... Ac 17:14
Many of the **b** began to confess .... Ac 19:18
Jerusalem the **b** were glad to see .... Ac 21:17
I put the **b** in jail and beat .... Ac 22:19
The **b** in Rome heard that we were .... Ac 28:15
The **b** in Macedonia and Southern .... Rm 15:26
call themselves **b** in Christ but 1Co 5:11
and you do this to other **b**! 1Co 6:8
who are not **b** decide to leave, ... 1Co 7:15
way you lived before you were **b**. 1Co 12:2
hundred of the **b** at the same 1Co 15:6
And these **b** praised God because .... Gal 1:24
some false **b** had come into our .... Gal 2:4
other Jewish **b** who joined with .... Gal 2:13
in Ephesus, **b** in Christ Jesus: .... Eph 1:1
most of the **b** have become more .... Php 1:14
Christ is in all **b**, and Christ .... Col 3:11
to all the **b** in Macedonia 1Th 1:7
read this letter to all the **b**. 1Th 5:27
Warn them as fellow **b**. 2Th 3:15
Tell the **b** to do these things so 1Ti 5:7
B who are poor should take pride .... Jam 1:9
as **b** in our glorious Lord Jesus .... Jam 2:1
your fellow **b** or judge them, ... Jam 4:11

BELIEVES

child who **b** his treasures will .... Je 49:4
these little children **b** in me, ... Mt 18:6
Anyone who **b** and is baptized .... Mk 16:16
everyone who **b** can have eternal .... Jn 3:15
so that whoever **b** in him may not .... Jn 3:16
and whoever **b** in me will never .... Jn 6:35
whoever **b** has eternal life. .... Jn 6:47
If anyone **b** in me, rivers of .... Jn 7:38
whoever **b** in me will do the same ...... Jn 14:12
that everyone who **b** in him may .... Rm 10:4
Anyone who **b** in the Son of God 1Jn 5:10

BELIEVING

But I had almost stopped **b**; .... Ps 73:2
leaving them and **b** in Jesus. .... Jn 12:11
in me is really **b** in the One who .... Jn 12:44
Then, by **b**, you may have life .... Jn 20:31
the governor from **b** in Jesus. .... Ac 13:8
have been made holy by **b** in me.' ...... Ac 26:18
promise, and he never stopped **b**. .... Rm 4:20
is made holy through his **b** wife. 1Co 7:14
made holy through her **b** husband. 1Co 7:14
you continue **b** what I told you 1Co 15:2
that by our **b** we could receive .... Gal 3:14
been saved by grace through **b**. .... Eph 2:8
honor not only of **b** in Christ .... Php 1:29
who have died **b** in Christ will 1Th 4:16
people will stop **b** the faith. 1Ti 4:1
When a **b** person prays, great .... Jam 5:16

BELL

a gold **b** and a pomegranate ball. .... Ex 28:34
robe there was a **b** and a............... Ex 39:26
am only a noisy **b** or a crashing 1Co 13:1

BELLIES

and their **b** are fat with flesh, ... Job 15:27

BELLS

ringing of the **b** will be heard .... Ex 28:35
They also made **b** of pure gold .... Ex 39:25
time the horses' **b** will have .... Zch 14:20

BELLY

sword deep into the king's **b**! .... Jdg 3:21

BELONG

children **b** to me, and these..................... Ge 31:43
'They **b** to your servant Jacob. .... Ge 32:18
and all our animals **b** to you. .... Ge 47:18
dead animal will **b** to the one .... Ex 21:34
for Aaron will **b** to his............................ Ex 29:29
grain offering will **b** to Aaron.................... Le 2:3
clean so he can **b** to the LORD .... Le 14:18
holy things that **b** to the LORD. .... Le 19:8
the land will **b** to the first .... Le 25:27
child slaves will **b** to you, ... Le 25:45
them, they **b** to the priest.' .... Nu 5:10
they **b** to the LORD in a special .... Nu 6:8
These things **b** to us and our .... Dt 29:29
your Thummim and Urim **b** to Levi, ... Dt 33:8
bronze and iron **b** to the LORD .... Jos 6:19
will **b** to the LORD all his life. 1Sa 1:28
of Israel will **b** to you and your 1Sa 9:20
'Your silver and gold **b** to me,................. 1Ki 20:3
he said: "We **b** to you, David. 1Ch 12:18
these utensils **b** to the LORD for.............. Ezr 8:28
the people who **b** to God with.................. Ezr 9:2
so they will **b** to God; .... Ne 10:33
and bring you back where you **b**. .... Job 8:6
You who **b** to the LORD, fear him! .... Ps 34:9
leaders of the earth's **b** to God............... Ps 47:9
and truth **b** to God's people; .... Ps 85:10
skies and the earth **b** to you. .... Ps 89:11
the highest mountains **b** to him. .... Ps 95:4
He made us, and we **b** to him; .... Ps 100:3
Canaan, and it will **b** to you."................. Ps 105:11
those who **b** to you will bless .... Ps 145:10
I **b** to my lover, and my lover .... Sng 6:3
will say, 'I **b** to the LORD,' .... Is 44:5
a land that does not **b** to you.'............... Je 5:19
our lives don't really **b** to us. .... Je 10:23
holy people who **b** to the Most .... Da 7:18
children who do not **b** to him. .... Hos 5:7
the other nations that **b** to me," .... Am 9:12
the kingdom will **b** to the LORD. .... Ob 1:21
take lands that don't **b** to them. .... Hab 1:6
It will **b** to the descendants of................ Zph 2:7
Those left alive will **b** to God.................. Zch 9:7
in heaven that they **b** to me. .... Mt 10:32
because you **b** to the Christ .... Mk 9:41
what kind of spirit you **b** to. .... Lk 9:55
angels of God that they **b** to me.............. Lk 12:8
things that **b** to someone else .... Lk 16:12
but I don't **b** to this world. .... Jn 8:23
You **b** to your father the devil, ... Jn 8:44
They don't **b** to the world, ... Jn 17:16
the other nations that **b** to me, ... Ac 15:17
from the God I **b** to and worship. .... Ac 27:23
called to **b** to Jesus Christ. .... Rm 1:6
doing things that **b** to darkness .... Rm 13:12
another says, "I **b** to Apollos." 1Co 3:4
And you **b** to Christ, and Christ 1Co 3:23
free persons who **b** to the Lord. 1Co 7:22
I am free and **b** to no one. 1Co 9:19
those people who **b** to heaven are 1Co 15:48
Good and bad do not **b** together. 2Co 6:14
remember that we **b** to Christ................. 2Co 10:7
You **b** to Christ, so you are .... Gal 3:29
Those who **b** to Christ Jesus have .... Gal 5:24
You **b** to God's family........................... Eph 2:19
because we all **b** to each other .... Eph 4:25
God's proof that you **b** to him. .... Eph 4:30
children who **b** to the light..................... Eph 5:8
as if you still **b** to this world .... Col 2:20
all people who **b** to the light 1Th 5:5
we **b** to the day, so we should 1Th 5:8
and power **b** to God forever. 1Ti 6:16
Power and glory **b** to him forever 1Pe 4:11

And they **b** to the world, so what 1Jn 4:5
will say they **b** to me before my .... Rev 3:5
glory, and power **b** to our God, ... Rev 19:1

BELONGED

stole the idols that **b** to him. .... Ge 31:19
everything that **b** to Potiphar, ... Ge 39:5
mirrors that **b** to the women who .... Ex 38:8
land that **b** to his ancestors. .... Nu 36:8
to the land that **b** to your .... Dt 30:5
This land now **b** to Joseph's .... Jos 24:32
that the field **b** to Boaz, ... Ru 2:3
everything that **b** to Elimelech .... Ru 4:9
and Ziklag has **b** to the kings of.............. 1Sa 27:6
everything that **b** to Saul and 2Sa 9:9
that **b** to Mephibosheth 2Sa 16:4
the throne that **b** to my father................. 1Ki 2:24
captured all that **b** to the king 2Ki 24:7
that **b** to the oldest son. 1Ch 5:2
the land that **b** to the 2Ch 34:33
so I rejected those who **b** to me. .... Is 47:6
the one that **b** to Simon, and .... Lk 5:3
If you **b** to the world, it would .... Jn 15:19
private property **b** to everyone .... Ac 4:32
b to the synagogue of Free Men .... Ac 6:9
some who **b** to the church. .... Ac 12:1
believers who **b** to the Pharisee .... Ac 15:5
who **b** to a different tribe. .... Heb 7:13
like Cain who **b** to the Evil One 1Jn 3:12

BELONGING

of the animals **b** to Israelites .... Ex 9:6
special time of **b** to the LORD, ... Nu 6:6
to the field **b** to Joshua of Beth 1Sa 6:14
The vineyard **b** to the LORD, ... Is 5:7
where the land **b** to Damascus and .... Eze 47:17
take something **b** to someone else .... Rm 7:7
make you pure, **b** only to him. 1Th 5:23
about priests **b** to that tribe. .... Heb 7:14

BELONGINGS

and all the **b** he had gotten in................. Ge 36:6
Esau and Jacob's **b** were becoming .... Ge 36:7
people did not take their **b**..................... Est 9:10
Their **b** will be carried off— .... Je 49:29
and whose **b** are in the house .... Lk 17:31

BELONGS

and now it **b** to us and our .... Ge 31:16
Everything you see here **b** to me, ... Ge 31:43
that the earth **b** to the LORD. .... Ex 9:29
that **b** to your neighbor. .... Ex 20:17
altar **b** completely to the LORD' .... Ex 30:10
of the grain offering **b** to Aaron .... Le 2:10
All the fat **b** to the LORD. .... Le 3:16
The land really **b** to me, ... Le 25:23
the LORD will show who **b** to him............. Nu 16:5
the land that **b** to your .... Dt 2:4
the older son **b** to the wife he .... Dt 21:15
of my harvest that **b** to God, ... Dt 26:13
Hebron still **b** to the family of.................. Jos 14:14
b to the tribe of Benjamin. .... Jdg 19:14
land to you. It **b** to my family." 1Ki 21:3
in heaven and on earth **b** to you. 1Ch 29:11
under the sky **b** to me. .... Job 41:11
The earth **b** to the LORD, and.................. Ps 24:1
our shield, **b** to the LORD, to .... Ps 89:18
joy **b** to those who are honest. .... Ps 97:11
The glory **b** to you because of................. Ps 115:1
of one that **b** to the LORD is .... Ps 116:15
each shield **b** to a strong........................ Sng 4:4
my lover, and my lover **b** to me. .... Sng 6:3
him as a bride **b** to her husband. .... Is 62:4
But that day **b** to the Lord GOD .... Je 46:10
Every living thing **b** to me. .... Eze 18:4

the kingdom of heaven **b** to them. .... Mt 5:3
of heaven **b** to people who are .... Mt 19:14
kingdom of God **b** to people who .... Mk 10:14
the kingdom of God **b** to you. .... Lk 6:20
the glory that **b** to the only Son .... Jn 1:14
The bride **b** only to the .... Jn 3:29
a son **b** to the family forever. .... Jn 8:35
The person who **b** to God accepts .... Jn 8:47
And everyone who **b** to the truth .... Jn 18:37
and each part **b** to all the other .... Rm 12:5
to Christ, and Christ **b** to God. 1Co 3:23
because the earth **b** to the Lord, ... 1Co 10:26
If anyone **b** to Christ, there is 2Co 5:17
The glory **b** to God forever and .... Gal 1:5
continues to sin **b** to the devil. 1Jn 3:8
The one who does good **b** to God. 3Jn 1:11
are a synagogue that **b** to Satan. .... Rev 2:9
Salvation **b** to our God, who .... Rev 7:10
rule the world now **b** to our Lord .... Rev 11:15
He **b** to the first seven kings, ... Rev 17:11

BELOVED
b is like a dove hiding in the .... Sng 2:14
What is my **b** Judah doing in my .... Je 11:15

BELOW
above the air and some **b** it. .... Ge 1:7
with water from springs **b**, ... Ge 49:25
on the earth **b** or in the water .... Ex 20:4
or of fish in the water **b**. .... Dt 4:18
heaven above and on the earth **b**. .... Dt 4:39
as the Dead Sea **b** Mount Pisgah. .... Dt 4:49
on the earth **b** or in the water .... Dt 5:8
with water from the springs **b**, ... Dt 33:13
heavens above and the earth **b**! .... Jos 2:11
who lived **b** Mount Hermon in the .... Jos 11:3
was in the valley **b** Gideon. .... Jdg 7:8
was **b** Jezreel from Beth Shan 1Ki 4:12
than the wall in the room **b**. 1Ki 6:6
in heaven above or on earth **b**. 1Ki 8:23
Their roots dry up **b** ground, ... Job 18:16
but **b** ground things are changed .... Job 28:5
Look around you at the earth **b**. .... Is 51:6
the secrets of the earth **b**, ... Je 31:37
live with the dead **b** the earth .... Eze 26:20
Eden in the place **b** the earth. .... Eze 31:18
You people are from here **b**, ... Jn 8:23
When we went **b** a small island .... Ac 27:16
us, nothing **b** us, nor anything .... Rm 8:39
go down into the world **b**?'" .... Rm 10:7

BELSHAZZAR
King **B** gave a big banquet for a .... Da 5:1
King **B** was very frightened. .... Da 5:6
Then **B** gave an order for Daniel .... Da 5:29

BELSHAZZAR'S
In **B** first year as king of .... Da 7:1

BELT
robe, a turban, and a cloth **b**. .... Ex 28:4
the woven **b** of the holy vest. .... Ex 28:27
His **b** will be the cloth belt, ... Le 16:4
including his sword, bow, and **b**. 1Sa 18:4
given you a **b** and four ounces 2Sa 18:11
blood on the **b** around his waist 1Ki 2:5
and wrap around him like a **b**." .... Ps 109:19
like a **b** around his waist. .... Is 11:5
and buy a linen **b** and put it .... Je 13:1
Don't let the **b** get wet." .... Je 13:1
and dug up the **b** and took it .... Je 13:7
clothes with a **b** of fine gold .... Da 10:5
wore a leather **b** around his .... Mt 3:4
a leather **b** around his waist, ... Mk 1:6
tied your own **b** and went where .... Jn 21:18
borrowed Paul's **b** and used it to .... Ac 21:11

tie up the man who wears this **b**. .... Ac 21:11
with the **b** of truth tied around .... Eph 6:14

BELTESHAZZAR
new name was **B**, Hananiah's was .... Da 1:7
I called him **B** to honor my god, ... Da 4:8
Daniel, whom the king named **B**. .... Da 5:12

BELTS
robes, cloth **b**, and headbands .... Ex 28:40
them, tied cloth **b** around them, ... Le 8:13
and provides **b** to the merchants .... Pr 31:24
of fine cloth **b**, they will wear .... Is 3:24
had **b** around their waists and .... Eze 23:15

BEN
through the Valley of **B** Hinnom, ... Jos 15:8
fire in the Valley of **B** Hinnom. 2Ch 33:6

BEN-HADAD
B was the king of Aram and ruled 1Ki 15:18
B agreed with King Asa, so he 1Ki 15:20
B king of Aram gathered together 1Ki 20:1
where **B** king of Aram was sick. 2Ki 8:7
B said to him, "What did Elisha 2Ki 8:14
the strong cities of King **B**." .... Je 49:27
destroy the strong towers of **B**. .... Am 1:4

BEN-HADAD'S
So Ahab said to **B** messengers, ... 1Ki 20:9
B men had wanted a sign from 1Ki 20:33
Hazael became king in **B** place. 2Ki 8:15

BEN-HUR
B was governor of the mountain 1Ki 4:8

BENAIAH
B son of Jehoiada was over the 2Sa 8:18
the prophet, **B**, his father's 1Ki 1:10
Solomon ordered **B** to go and kill 1Ki 2:29
B son of Jehoiada killed Joab, ... 1Ki 2:34
B killed an Egyptian who was 1Ch 11:23
and **B** played the lyres. 1Ch 15:20
B and Jahaziel were priests who 1Ch 16:6
B was a brave warrior who led 1Ch 27:6

BENAIAH'S
B son Ammizabad was in charge of 1Ch 27:6
Zechariah was **B** son. 2Ch 20:14

BENCHES
and he upset the **b** of those who .... Mt 21:12
and he upset the **b** of those who .... Mk 11:15

BEND
and those who **b** down to drink." .... Jdg 7:5
so my arms can **b** a bronze bow. 2Sa 22:35
to the armory, as far as the **b**. .... Ne 3:19
so my arms can **b** a bronze bow. .... Ps 18:34
their swords and **b** their bows to .... Ps 37:14

BENDING
B down and looking in, he saw .... Lk 24:12

BENDS
who **b** down to look at the skies .... Ps 113:6

BENEFIT
to be used for his own **b**. .... Php 2:6

BENJAMIN
but Jacob called him **B**. .... Ge 35:18
and now you want to take **B** away, ... Ge 42:36
Jacob, "Send **B** with me, and we .... Ge 43:8
When Joseph saw his brother **B**, ... Ge 43:29
but **B** was given five times more .... Ge 43:34
hugged his brother **B** and cried, ... Ge 45:14
The tribe of **B** totaled 35,400 .... Nu 1:37
This is the land chosen for **B**: .... Jos 18:11
The tribe of **B** also received .... Jos 18:25
B was among the people who .... Jdg 5:14
The women of **B** have been killed. .... Jdg 21:16

BENJAMIN'S

'Be kind to the men of **B**. .... Jdg 21:22
The men of **B** came to Abner, ... 2Sa 2:25
B had three sons: Bela, Beker, ... 1Ch 7:6
Abner was over the tribe of **B**. 1Ch 27:21
people of Judah and **B** heard that .... Ezr 4:1
Judah and **B** lived in Jerusalem. .... Ne 11:4
Run for your lives, people of **B**! .... Je 6:1
near Anathoth in the land of **B**. .... Je 32:8
got to the **B** Gate of Jerusalem, ... Je 37:13
B will have one share. .... Eze 48:23
first into battle, people of **B**. .... Hos 5:8
and **B** will take over Gilead. .... Ob 1:19
will reach from the **B** Gate and .... Zch 14:10
the tribe of **B** and was king for .... Ac 13:21
of Abraham, from the tribe of **B**. .... Rm 11:1
of Israel and the tribe of **B**. .... Php 3:5
the tribe of **B** twelve thousand .... Rev 7:8

BENJAMIN'S

and found the cup in **B** sack. .... Ge 44:12
Joseph's Gate, **B** Gate, and Dan's .... Eze 48:32

BENJAMINITE

So 18,000 brave **B** fighters were .... Jdg 20:44
our daughters to marry a **B**. .... Jdg 21:7
The **B** ran to Eli and told him 1Sa 4:14

BENJAMINITES

lived with the **B** in Jerusalem. .... Jdg 1:21
The **B** left their own cities and .... Jdg 20:14
the **B** killed 18,000 Israelites, ... Jdg 20:25
So that is what the **B** did. .... Jdg 21:23
With Shimei came a thousand **B**. 2Sa 19:17

BENT

where he **b** down to the ground 1Ki 18:42
I am **b** over and bowed down; .... Ps 38:6
can straighten what he has **b**. .... Ec 7:13
I hurt! I am **b** over in pain. Oh .... Je 4:19
The vine then **b** its roots toward .... Eze 17:7
their neck and **b** down and fed .... Hos 11:4
back was always **b**; she could not .... Lk 13:11
But Jesus **b** over and started .... Jn 8:6
she **b** down and looked inside the .... Jn 20:11

BEOR

to Balaam son of **B** at Pethor, ... Nu 22:5
Balaam son of **B** to curse you, ... Jos 24:9
Bela son of **B** was king of Edom, ... 1Ch 1:43
the son of **B**, who loved being. 2Pe 2:15

BERA

B king of Sodom, Birsha king of .... Ge 14:2

BERAKIAH

murder of Zechariah son of **B**, ... Mt 23:35

BEREA

and Silas to **B** where they went .... Ac 17:10
Silas and Timothy stayed in **B**. .... Ac 17:14

BEREANS

The **B** were eager to hear what .... Ac 17:11

BEREKIAH

the prophet Zechariah son of **B**, ... Zch 1:1

BERITH

room of the temple of El **B**. .... Jdg 9:46

BERNICE

Agrippa and **B** came to Caesarea .... Ac 25:13
day Agrippa and **B** appeared with .... Ac 25:23
Governor Festus, **B**, and all the .... Ac 26:30

BERYL

the eighth was **b**, the ninth was .... Rev 21:20

BEST

brought the **b** parts from some .... Ge 4:4
that you are the **b** person among .... Ge 7:1
and took one of his **b** calves. .... Ge 18:7

She took the **b** clothes of her .... Ge 27:15
Take some of the **b** foods in our .... Ge 43:11
give them the **b** land in Egypt, ... Ge 45:18
give them the **b** of what we have .... Ge 45:20
brothers the **b** land in Egypt, ... Ge 47:11
clothes and the **b** wine to wash .... Ge 49:11
and can't find the **b** words." .... Ex 4:10
six hundred of his **b** chariots, ... Ex 14:7
king's **b** officers are drowned .... Ex 15:4
must bring the **b** of the .... Ex 23:19
take the **b** part of the liver, ... Ex 29:22
Bring the **b** first crops that you .... Ex 34:26
give you all the **b** olive oil and .... Nu 18:12
Choose the **b** and holiest part .... Nu 18:29
Bashan and the **b** of the wheat. .... Dt 32:14
They chose the **b** land for .... Dt 33:21
thousand of his **b** fighting men .... Jos 8:3
wife was given to his **b** man. .... Jdg 14:20
to her, "Do what you think is **b**. 1Sa 1:23
Let him do what he thinks is **b**.". 1Sa 3:18
Do whatever you think is **b**. 1Sa 14:7
Why did you take the **b** things? 1Sa 15:19
The **b** thing I can do is escape 1Sa 27:1
killed two of the **b** warriors 2Sa 23:20
cedars and its **b** pine trees. 2Ki 19:23
I have done my **b** to prepare for 1Ch 29:2
thousand of the **b** soldiers from 2Ch 11:1
of Israel's **b** men were killed. 2Ch 13:17
purple robe made of the **b** linen. .... Est 8:15
your table full of the **b** food. .... Job 36:16
He will point them to the **b** way. .... Ps 25:12
My **b** and truest friend, who ate .... Ps 41:9
struck down the **b** young men of .... Ps 78:31
the **b** years of your life will .... Pr 5:9
The **b** that people can do is eat, ... Ec 2:24
and your mouth like the **b** wine. .... Sng 7:9
with all the **b** food and wine, ... Is 25:6
Her **b** young men will be killed!" .... Je 48:15
Fill it with the **b** bones. .... Eze 24:4
were paid with the **b** clothes, ... Eze 27:24
The **b** fruits of all the first .... Eze 44:30
You bring your **b** fellowship .... Am 5:22
people of the **b** nation in the .... Am 6:1
your **b** warriors will be afraid, ... Ob 1:9
the rich and enjoy the **b** food. .... Hab 1:16
he will eat the **b** sheep and tear .... Zch 11:16
watched for the **b** time to turn .... Mt 26:16
the tomb the **b** way you know." .... Mt 27:65
choosing the **b** places to sit, ... Lk 14:7
Bring the **b** clothes and put them .... Lk 15:22
always serve the **b** wine first. .... Jn 2:10
Do your **b** to live in peace with .... Rm 12:18
almost past the **b** age to marry 1Co 7:36
will show you the **b** way of all. 1Co 12:31
are doing, work the **b** you can. .... Col 3:23
Do your **b** to come to me as soon 2Ti 4:9
in the way they thought was **b**. .... Heb 12:10
do your **b** to add these things to 2Pe 1:5
do your **b** to be without sin and 2Pe 3:14

BETH

in the valley opposite **B** Peor. .... Dt 3:29
in the valley opposite **B** Peor, ... Dt 34:6
going up to **B** Horon and killed .... Jos 10:10
B Peor, the hills of Pisgah, and .... Jos 13:20
Jordan River as far as **B** Barah. .... Jdg 7:24
If it goes toward **B** Shemesh in 1Sa 6:9
went straight toward **B** Shemesh. 1Sa 6:12
his body on the wall of **B** Shan. 1Sa 31:10
below Jezreel from **B** Shan to. 1Ki 4:12
the cities of Lower **B** Horon 1Ki 9:17
in battle at **B** Shemesh in Judah. 2Ki 14:11
She built Lower **B** Horon, Upper 1Ch 7:24

B

go to Gilgal or go up to **B** Aven. .... Hos 4:15
the calf-shaped idol at **B** Aven. .... Hos 10:5

BETHANY
and went out of the city to **B,** .... Mt 21:17
Jesus was in **B** at the house of .... Mt 26:6
Bethphage and **B** near the Mount .... Mk 11:1
he went out to **B** with the twelve .... Mk 11:11
Jesus was in **B** at the house of .... Mk 14:3
Jesus came near Bethphage and **B,** .... Lk 19:29
all happened at **B** on the other .... Jn 1:28
B was about two miles from .... Jn 11:18
Jesus went to **B,** where Lazarus .... Jn 12:1

BETHEL
mountain east of **B** and set up .... Ge 12:8
camped before, between **B** and Ai, ... Ge 13:3
was Luz, but Jacob named it **B.** .... Ge 28:19
God who appeared to you at **B,** .... Ge 31:13
buried under the oak tree at **B,** .... Ge 35:8
wait in ambush between **B** and Ai, ... Jos 8:9
Jericho, Ai (near **B**), ... Jos 12:9
Jericho to the mountains of **B.** .... Jos 16:1
They sent some spies to **B** .... Jdg 1:23
which is north of the city of **B,** .... Jdg 21:19
year he went from **B** to Gilgal to 1Sa 7:16
chose priests in **B** to serve at 1Ki 12:32
of God from Judah to go to **B.** 1Ki 13:1
an old prophet was living in **B.** 1Ki 13:11
Hiel from **B** rebuilt the city of 1Ki 16:34
the golden calves in **B** and Dan. 2Ki 10:29
that god in the town of **B,** .... Je 48:13
you, people of **B,** because you. .... Hos 10:15
met with him at **B** and spoke with .... Hos 12:4
Come to the city of **B** and sin; .... Am 4:4
fire will burn **B,** and there will .... Am 5:6
a priest at **B,** sent this message .... Am 7:10
prophesy anymore here at **B.** .... Am 7:13

BETHESDA
which is called **B** in the Hebrew .... Jn 5:2

BETHLEHEM
to Ephrath, a district of **B,** .... Ge 35:19
Today Ephrath is **B.**............................. Ge 48:7
he died and was buried in **B.** .... Jdg 12:10
He left **B** to look for another .... Jdg 17:8
Ephrathahites from **B** in Judah. .... Ru 1:2
they came to the town of **B.** .... Ru 1:19
Boaz came from **B** and greeted his........... Ru 2:4
of Ephrathah and famous in **B.** .... Ru 4:11
you to Jesse who lives in **B,** 1Sa 16:1
son of Jesse of **B** play the harp. 1Sa 16:18
from **B** killed Goliath 2Sa 21:19
well near the city gate of **B!"** 2Sa 23:15
We heard about the Ark in **B.** .... Ps 132:6
But you, **B** Ephrathah, though you .... Mic 5:2
in the town of **B** in Judea during .... Mt 2:1
'But you, **B,** in the land of .... Mt 2:6
the baby boys in **B** and in the .... Mt 2:16
went to the town of **B** in Judea, ... Lk 2:4
to each other, "Let's go to **B.** .... Lk 2:15
from David's family and from **B,** .... Jn 7:42

BETHPHAGE
they stopped at **B** at the hill .... Mt 21:1
to the towns of **B** and Bethany .... Mk 11:1
Jesus came near **B** and Bethany, ... Lk 19:29

BETHSAIDA
How terrible for you, **B!** .... Mt 11:21
of him to **B** across the lake .... Mk 6:45
and his followers came to **B.** .... Mk 8:22
a town called **B** where they could .... Lk 9:10
Philip was from the town of **B,** .... Jn 1:44
who was from **B** in Galilee,................... Jn 12:21

BETHUEL
B became the father of Rebekah. .... Ge 22:23
B the Aramean was the father of .... Ge 28:5

BETHUEL'S
was **B** daughter and the sister .... Ge 25:20

BEWARE
B of evil thoughts. Don't think, ... Dt 15:9
B of the yeast of the Pharisees .... Mt 16:6
B of the yeast of the Pharisees .... Mk 8:15
B of the teachers of the law. .... Mk 12:38
B of the yeast of the Pharisees, ... Lk 12:1
B of the teachers of the law. .... Lk 20:46

BEZALEL
I have chosen **B** son of Uri from............... Ex 31:2
I have filled **B** with the Spirit .... Ex 31:3
So **B,** Oholiab, and every skilled.............. Ex 36:1
B made the Ark of acacia wood;............. Ex 37:1

BIG
is how **b** I want you to build .... Ge 6:15
hands and on the **b** toes of their............. Ex 29:20
He will make your stomach get **b,** .... Nu 5:21
The cities are **b,** with walls up .... Dt 1:28
cut off his thumbs and **b** toes................... Jdg 1:6
came together into one **b** army. 2Sa 10:15
altar that was **b** enough to hold 1Ki 18:32
else, "This is a very **b** job. .... Ne 4:19
marked off how **b** it should be? .... Job 38:5
at the sea, so **b** and wide, with .... Ps 104:25
if you have a **b** appetite. .... Pr 23:2
away your sins like a **b** cloud;................. Is 44:22
They have grown **b** and fat. .... Je 5:28
rocks in Babylon **b** enough for .... Je 51:26
giant eagle with **b** wings and .... Eze 17:3
Belshazzar gave a **b** banquet for .... Da 5:1
A **b** stone was brought and placed .... Da 6:17
his **b** horn broke off and four .... Da 8:8
LORD caused a **b** fish to swallow .... Jnh 1:17
Who are you, **b** mountain? .... Zch 4:7
don't notice the **b** piece of wood............. Mt 7:3
stomach of the **b** fish for three .... Mt 12:40
It becomes **b** enough for the wild .... Mt 13:32
your faith is as **b** as a mustard .... Mt 17:20
Levi gave a **b** dinner for Jesus .... Lk 5:29
don't notice the **b** piece of wood............. Lk 6:41
why worry about the **b** things? .... Lk 12:26
A man gave a **b** banquet and .... Lk 14:16
there is a **b** pit between you and............... Lk 16:26
It was full of **b** fish, one .... Jn 21:11
would not be **b** enough for all................. Jn 21:25
that looked like a **b** sheet being .... Ac 10:11
that looked like a **b** sheet being .... Ac 11:5
to break up from the **b** waves. .... Ac 27:41
a lot will have a **b** harvest. 2Co 9:6
rudder controls that **b** ship,................... Jam 3:4
A **b** forest fire can be started .... Jam 3:5
and he was given a **b** sword. .... Rev 6:4
like smoke from a **b** furnace. .... Rev 9:2
thunder, and a **b** earthquake—the .... Rev 16:18

BIGGER
nations that are **b** and stronger .... Dt 9:1
an army that is **b** than yours, ... Dt 20:1
finger is **b** than my father's..................... 1Ki 12:10
Give us a **b** place to live." .... Is 49:20
Make your tent **b;** stretch it out .... Is 54:2
down my barns and build **b** ones, ... Lk 12:18
on the lake were getting **b.** .... Jn 6:18

BIGGEST
the **b** troublemaker in Israel?" 1Ki 18:17

BILDAD
the Temanite, **B** the Shuhite, ... Job 2:11

BILHAH

his slave girl **B** to his daughter .... Ge 29:29
with Israel's slave woman **B,** .... Ge 35:22
These are Jacob's sons by **B,** .... Ge 46:25

BILL

him, 'Take your **b,** sit down.................... Lk 16:6
'Take your **b** and write eight .... Lk 16:7

BIRD

He also made every **b** that flies, ... Ge 1:21
animal and every **b** in the sky, ... Ge 2:19
Two of every kind of **b,** animal, ... Ge 6:20
and every **b** went out of the boat .... Ge 8:19
offering for the LORD is a **b,** .... Le 1:14
b must be for a sin offering, ... Le 5:7
Then he will take the living **b,** .... Le 14:6
You may eat any clean **b.** .... Dt 14:11
hunting a **b** in the mountains!.................. 1Sa 26:20
Fly like a **b** to your mountain.................... Ps 11:1
I know every **b** on the mountains, ... Ps 50:11
escaped like a **b** from the .... Ps 124:7
like a **b** flying away from a .... Pr 6:5
Like a **b** caught in a trap, ... Pr 7:23
home is like a **b** that leaves its .... Pr 27:8
in a net, or a **b** caught in a .... Ec 9:12
a **b** might fly and tell what you .... Ec 10:20
wake up when a **b** starts singing, ... Ec 12:4
wings like a **b** until it covers .... Is 8:8
I cried like a **b** and moaned like .... Is 38:14
Every **b** in the sky had flown .... Je 4:25
Like a **b** hatching an egg it did .... Je 17:11
food for every **b** that eats meat .... Eze 39:4
every kind of **b** and wild animal.............. Eze 39:17
grew like the claws of a **b.** .... Da 4:33
glory will fly away like a **b;**.................... Hos 9:11
A **b** will not fall into a trap .... Am 3:5
of wild animal, **b,** reptile, and................. Jam 3:7
every unclean **b** and unclean .... Rev 18:2

BIRD'S

the **b** blood must be drained out............... Le 1:15
He will pull the **b** head from its .... Le 5:8
a person reaching into a **b** nest. .... Is 10:14
back that looked like a **b** wings............... Da 7:6

BIRDS

and let **b** fly in the air above .... Ge 1:20
pairs of all the **b** of the sky, ... Ge 7:3
boat with you—the **b,** animals, ... Ge 8:17
large **b** flew down to eat the .... Ge 15:11
and the **b** will eat your flesh."................. Ge 40:19
these are the **b** you are to hate. .... Le 11:13
But do not eat these **b:** .... Dt 14:12
fields will be eaten by the **b.** 1Ki 14:11
The **b** brought Elijah bread and 1Ki 17:6
wiser than the **b** of the air?' .... Job 35:11
b in the sky, the fish in the .... Ps 8:8
The **b** were as many as the sand............... Ps 78:27
Wild **b** make nests by the water;............... Ps 104:12
b of the valley will peck out .... Pr 30:17
like little **b** that have fallen .... Is 16:2
B will feed on them all summer,............... Is 18:6
who make nets for catching **b,** .... Je 5:26
food for the **b** of the sky and .... Je 7:33
Even the **b** in the sky know the .... Je 8:7
trap people as if they were **b.** .... Eze 13:20
B of every kind will build nests .... Eze 17:23
All the **b** of the sky made their .... Eze 31:6
and the **b** lived in its branches. .... Da 4:12
wild animals and the **b** of the .... Hos 4:3
come swiftly like **b** from Egypt .... Hos 11:11
I will destroy the **b** in the air .... Zph 1:3
are worth much more than the **b.** .... Mt 6:26
for the wild **b** to come and build............. Mt 13:32

and the wild **b** can make nests in .... Mk 4:32
the seed, and the **b** ate it up. .... Lk 8:5
Look at the **b.** They don't plant .... Lk 12:24
of animals, reptiles, and **b.** .... Ac 10:12
earthly people, **b,** animals, and .... Rm 1:23
have another, **b** have another,................. 1Co 15:39
and all the **b** ate the bodies.................... Rev 19:21

BIRTH

and when you give **b** to children, ... Ge 3:16
pregnant and gave **b** to Cain. .... Ge 4:1
Eve gave **b** to Cain's brother .... Ge 4:2
pregnant and gave **b** to Enoch. .... Ge 4:17
Hagar gave **b** to a son for Abram, ... Ge 16:15
when Hagar gave **b** to Ishmael. .... Ge 16:16
daughter gave **b** to a son and .... Ge 19:37
Isaac, the son Sarah gave **b** to. .... Ge 21:3
came, Rebekah gave **b** to twins. .... Ge 25:24
pregnant and gave **b** to a son................. Ge 29:32
Then Leah gave **b** to another son. .... Ge 29:35
After the **b** of Joseph, Jacob .... Ge 30:25
the animals gave **b** to speckled .... Ge 31:8
Rachel gave **b** to the son, but .... Ge 35:18
time came for Tamar to give **b,** .... Ge 38:27
They gave **b** to their babies .... Ex 1:19
Zipporah gave **b** to a son. .... Ex 2:22
who gave **b** to Aaron and Moses. .... Ex 6:20
'If a woman gives **b** to a son, ... Le 12:2
She will give **b** to a baby, ... Dt 28:57
forgot the God who gave you **b.** .... Dt 32:18
a Nazirite, given to God from **b.** .... Jdg 13:5
I cannot give **b** to more sons to .... Ru 1:11
As Tamar gave **b** to Judah's son .... Ru 4:12
and in time she gave **b** to a son. 1Sa 1:20
had much trouble in giving **b.**................. 1Sa 4:19
I gave **b** to a baby while she was 1Ki 3:17
From my **b** I guided the widows.............. Job 31:18
when the mountain goats give **b?** .... Job 39:1
the pain of giving **b** is over.................... Job 39:3
In sin my mother gave **b** to me. .... Ps 51:5
From **b,** evil people turn away .... Ps 58:3
been dressed in holiness from **b;** .... Ps 110:3
My son, I gave **b** to you. .... Pr 31:2
is better than the day of **b.** .... Ec 7:1
there your mother gave **b** to you. .... Sng 8:5
like a woman giving **b** to a baby. .... Is 13:8
are like the pains of giving **b.**................. Is 21:3
like a woman giving **b** to a baby; .... Is 26:17
We gave **b,** but only to wind. .... Is 26:18
who gave **b** to your ancestors. .... Is 51:2
giving **b** to your new nation, ... Is 66:9
like a woman giving **b** to a baby? .... Je 13:21
wild animals gave **b** under its................ Eze 31:6
and gave **b** to Hosea's son. .... Hos 1:3
The pain of **b** will come for him, ... Hos 13:13
like a woman trying to give **b?** .... Mic 4:9
mother who gave **b** to him will .... Zch 13:3
is how the **b** of Jesus Christ .... Mt 1:18
will give **b** to a son, and you .... Mt 1:21
will give **b** to a son, and you .... Lk 1:13
will be happy because of his **b.** .... Lk 1:14
and even from **b,** he will be .... Lk 1:15
pregnant and give **b** to a son, ... Lk 1:31
time for Elizabeth to give **b,** .... Lk 1:57
mother who gave **b** to you and .... Lk 11:27
When a woman gives **b** to a baby, ... Jn 16:21
like a woman ready to give **b.**................. Rm 8:22
who never gave **b** to children.................. Gal 4:27
eight days after my **b.** .... Php 3:5
ready to give **b** so he could eat .... Rev 12:4

B

BIRTHDAY
later, on his **b**, the king gave .... Ge 40:20
On Herod's **b**, the daughter of .... Mt 14:6
On Herod's **b**, he gave a dinner .... Mk 6:21

BIT
Then when a snake **b** anyone, ... Nu 21:9
nose and my **b** in your mouth. 2Ki 19:28
He sent flies that **b** the people. .... Ps 78:45
their mouths a **b** that will lead .... Is 30:28
the heat and **b** him on the hand. .... Ac 28:3

BITE
head, and you will **b** his heel." .... Ge 3:15
love words that **b** and tongues .... Ps 52:4
quick, dangerous snake to **b** you. .... Is 14:29
and they will **b** you," says the .... Je 8:17
will command a snake to **b** them. .... Am 9:3

BITES
That snake **b** a horse's leg, ... Ge 49:17
Later it **b** like a snake with .... Pr 23:32
If a snake **b** the tamer before it .... Ec 10:11

BITHYNIA
to go into **B**, but the Spirit .... Ac 16:7
Cappadocia, Asia, and **B**. 1Pe 1:1

BITS
must be led with **b** and reins, ... Ps 32:9
gossip are like tasty **b** of food. .... Pr 18:8
gossip are like tasty **b** of food; .... Pr 26:22
and the small house into **b**. .... Am 6:11
When we put **b** into the mouths of .... Jam 3:3

BITTEN
anyone who is **b** looks at it, ... Nu 21:8
They have **b** my arms and legs. .... Ps 22:16
a wall might be **b** by a snake; .... Ec 10:8
wall, and then is **b** by a snake. .... Am 5:19

BITTER
he let out a loud and **b** cry. .... Ge 27:34
They made their lives **b**. .... Ex 1:14
eat it with **b** herbs and bread .... Ex 12:8
this **b** water that brings a curse .... Nu 5:19
the lamb with **b** herbs and bread .... Nu 9:11
you like a plant that grows **b**, ... Dt 29:18
their bunches of grapes are **b**. .... Dt 32:32
My complaint is still **b** today. .... Job 23:2
swords and shoot **b** words like .... Ps 64:3
even something **b** tastes sweet. .... Pr 27:7
beer will taste **b** to those who .... Is 24:9
of Judah eat **b** food and drink .... Je 9:15
prophets eat **b** food and drink .... Je 23:15
like a **b** cup to drink. .... Eze 23:31
you are full of **b** jealousy and .... Ac 8:23
Do not be **b** or angry or mad. .... Eph 4:31
and have **b** jealousy in your .... Jam 3:14
third of all the water became **b**, ... Rev 8:11

BITTERLY
loudly and **b** for his father. .... Ge 50:10
'B curse its people, because .... Jdg 5:23
I cried **b** because there was no .... Rev 5:4

BLACK
sheep, every **b** lamb, and every .... Ge 30:32
the whole land so that it was **b**. .... Ex 10:15
eagles, vultures, **b** vultures, ... Le 11:13
and **b** hair is growing in it, ... Le 13:37
the future by signs or **b** magic. .... Le 19:26
and **b** clouds made it very dark. .... Dt 4:11
eagles, vultures, **b** vultures, ... Dt 14:12
skin has become **b** and peels off, ... Job 30:30
hair is wavy and **b** like a raven. .... Sng 5:11
can make them **b** like clothes of .... Is 50:3
tusks and valuable **b** wood as .... Eze 27:15
dark, gloomy day, cloudy and **b**. .... Joe 2:2

B horses pulled the second .... Zch 6:2
on your head become white or **b**. .... Mt 5:36
there before me was a **b** horse, ... Rev 6:5
sun became **b** like rough black .... Rev 6:12

BLACKER
But now they are **b** than coal, ... La 4:8

BLACKEST
A place in the **b** darkness has 2Pe 2:17
A place in the **b** darkness has .... Jud 1:13

BLACKNESS
gloom, a day of clouds and **b**, ... Zph 1:15

BLACKSMITH
land of Israel had no **b** because 1Sa 13:19
See, I made the **b**. .... Is 54:16

BLACKSMITHS
The Philistine **b** charged about 1Sa 13:21

BLADE
and the **b** came out his back. .... Jdg 3:22
and its **b** weighed about fifteen 1Sa 17:7
break a crushed **b** of grass or .... Is 42:3
Cut anywhere your **b** is turned. .... Eze 21:16
break a crushed **b** of grass or .... Mt 12:20

BLADES
into plow **b** and their spears .... Mic 4:3

BLAME
on you, I will accept the **b**. .... Ge 27:13
you, you can **b** me all my life. .... Ge 43:9
or you will be partly to **b**. .... Le 19:17
Don't **b** your people, the .... Dt 21:8
no one will **b** me for hurting .... Jdg 15:3
Don't **b** me or any of my 1Sa 22:15
My master, let the **b** be on me! 1Sa 25:24
Let the **b** be on me and my 2Sa 14:9
this Job did not sin or **b** God. .... Job 1:22
you can **b** me for my suffering. .... Job 19:5
How can you **b** God who is both .... Job 34:17
in their minds they **b** the LORD. .... Pr 19:3
So they are to **b** for their own .... Eze 33:5
Don't **b** the people, you priests, ... Hos 4:4
why does God **b** us for our sins? .... Rm 9:19
honor us, but others **b** us. 2Co 6:8
people without **b** before him. .... Eph 1:4
without wrong or **b** until our 1Ti 6:14
people complain and **b** others, ... Jud 1:16

BLAMED
will be **b** if anything is wrong .... Ex 28:38

BLAMES
he **b** them for mistakes. .... Job 4:18

BLANKET
day Hazael took a **b** and dipped 2Ki 8:15
worms cover your body like a **b**. .... Is 14:11
short and with a **b** that was too .... Is 28:20
our disgrace cover us like a **b**. .... Je 3:25

BLANKETS
donkeys and sit on saddle **b**, ... Jdg 5:10
his servants covered him with **b**, ... 1Ki 1:1
trading saddle **b** for riding. .... Eze 27:20

BLASPHEMOUS
destroyer will do **b** things until .... Da 9:27
will set up a **b** object that .... Da 11:31
You will see 'a **b** object that .... Mk 13:14

BLASPHEMY
as if he were God. That is **b**!" .... Mt 9:3

BLAST
Just a **b** of your breath, and the .... Ex 15:8
a very loud **b** from a trumpet, ... Ex 19:16
make one long **b** on the trumpets. .... Jos 6:5
against you and **b** you with the .... Eze 21:31

BLASTS

Praise him with trumpet **b**; .... Ps 150:3

BLAZE

Flames **b** from its mouth; .... Job 41:19
like flames that **b** through the................. Ps 83:14
a **b** has spread from the hometown .... Je 48:45
has eyes that **b** like fire and .... Rev 2:18

BLAZED

it **b** with fire that reached to .... Dt 4:11

BLAZING

firepot and a **b** torch passed .... Ge 15:17
as the mountain was **b** with fire, ... Dt 5:23
pulling them out of a **b** furnace. 1Ki 8:51
to melt them down in a **b** fire. .... Eze 22:20
to be thrown into a **b** furnace. .... Da 3:11
of his throne were **b** with fire. .... Da 7:9
evil people into the **b** furnace, ... Mt 13:50

BLEATING

hear cattle mooing and sheep **b**?" 1Sa 15:14

BLEED

as long as she continues to **b**. .... Le 15:25
and twisting noses makes them **b**, ... Pr 30:33

BLEEDING

woman becomes clean from her **b**, ... Le 15:28
during her time of monthly **b**................... Eze 18:6
who had been **b** for twelve years .... Mt 9:20
Instantly her **b** stopped, and she.............. Mk 5:29
who had been **b** for twelve years .... Lk 8:43

BLEMISH

No **b** was on him from his head to 2Sa 14:25

BLESS

I will **b** those who bless you, ... Ge 12:3
I will **b** her and give her a son, ... Ge 17:16
I will surely **b** you and give you .... Ge 22:17
I will be with you and **b** you. .... Ge 26:3
I will **b** you and give you many .... Ge 26:24
Then I will **b** you before I die." .... Ge 27:4
I hunted for you. Then **b** me."................... Ge 27:19
Father? **B** me, too, Father! .... Ge 27:38
God Almighty **b** you and give you .... Ge 28:3
let you go if you will **b** me." .... Ge 32:26
sons to me so I may **b** them." .... Ge 48:9
asked, and go. And also **b** me." .... Ex 12:32
I will **b** your thread and your .... Ex 23:25
May the LORD **b** you and keep you. .... Nu 6:24
my name, and I will **b** them." .... Nu 6:27
I know that if you **b** someone, ... Nu 22:6
the LORD wanted to **b** Israel, ... Nu 24:1
continued to **b** them three times. .... Nu 24:10
He will love and **b** you. .... Dt 7:13
will richly **b** you in the land .... Dt 15:4
He will **b** you if you obey the .... Dt 15:5
your God will **b** everything you .... Dt 23:20
Mount Gerizim to **b** the people: .... Dt 27:12
He will **b** the land he is giving .... Dt 28:8
your God will **b** you in the land .... Dt 30:16
said, "The LORD **b** you, my son!" .... Jdg 17:2
answered, "May the LORD **b** you!" .... Ru 2:4
because he must **b** the sacrifice............... 1Sa 9:13
Saul said, "May the LORD **b** you! 1Sa 15:13
The LORD **b** you for helping me. 1Sa 23:21
Please, **b** my family. Let it 2Sa 7:29
saying, '**B** the LORD, the God of............. 1Ki 1:48
You have chosen to **b** my family. 1Ch 17:27
b those who do what is right; .... Ps 5:12
They **b** the greedy but hate the .... Ps 10:3
and will **b** them in the land. .... Ps 41:2
mercy on us and **b** us and show us........... Ps 67:1
for him and **b** him all day long .... Ps 72:15
They may curse me, but you **b** me........... Ps 109:28

LORD remembers us and will **b** us. .... Ps 115:12
He will **b** the family of Israel; .... Ps 115:12
God **b** the one who comes in the .... Ps 118:26
May the LORD **b** you from Mount .... Ps 128:5
I will **b** her with plenty; .... Ps 132:15
who belong to you will **b** you................... Ps 145:10
but he will **b** the home of those .... Pr 3:33
Good people **b** and build up their .... Pr 11:11
they **b** the one who is willing .... Pr 11:26
and do not **b** their mothers. .... Pr 30:11
I will **b** them and let them live .... Eze 34:26
But from now on I will **b** you!'" .... Hag 2:19
God **b** the One who comes in the .... Mt 21:9
God **b** the kingdom of our father .... Mk 11:10
b those who curse you, pray for .... Lk 6:28
God **b** the king who comes in the .... Lk 19:38
God **b** the King of Israel!" .... Jn 12:13
to you first to **b** you by turning .... Ac 3:26
When people curse us, we **b** them. 1Co 4:12
I will surely **b** you and give you .... Heb 6:14

BLESSED

God **b** them and said, "Have many........... Ge 1:22
God **b** the seventh day and made .... Ge 2:3
on that day he **b** them and named .... Ge 5:2
Then God **b** Noah and his sons and .... Ge 9:1
on earth will be **b** through you."............... Ge 12:3
and **b** Abram, saying, "Abram, may .... Ge 14:19
may you be **b** by God Most High, ... Ge 14:19
the LORD had **b** him in every way............. Ge 24:1
They **b** Rebekah and said, "Our .... Ge 24:60
died, God **b** his son Isaac. .... Ge 25:11
nations on the earth will be **b**. .... Ge 26:4
Now the LORD has **b** you." .... Ge 26:29
Esau's hands, so Isaac **b** him................... Ge 27:23
everyone who blesses you be **b**." .... Ge 27:29
that Isaac had **b** Jacob and sent .... Ge 28:6
Then he **b** Jacob there. .... Ge 32:29
And the LORD **b** everything that .... Ge 39:5
Then Jacob **b** the king and left. .... Ge 47:10
And Israel **b** Joseph and said,................... Ge 48:15
the LORD **b** the Sabbath day and .... Ex 20:11
who blesses you will be **b**, ... Nu 24:9
your God has **b** everything you .... Dt 2:7
the city and **b** in the country. .... Dt 28:3
your herds will be **b** with calves............. Dt 28:4
Asher is the most **b** of the sons; .... Dt 33:24
Israel, you are **b**! No one else .... Dt 33:29
Joshua **b** Caleb son of Jephunneh .... Jos 14:13
be **b** above all women who live in .... Jdg 5:24
B be whoever noticed you!" .... Ru 2:19
May you be **b** for your wisdom. 1Sa 25:33
and the LORD **b** Obed-Edom and all 2Sa 6:11
he **b** the people in the name of 2Sa 6:18
king kissed Barzillai and **b** him............... 2Sa 19:39
the LORD **b** Obed-Edom's family 1Ch 13:14
family, so it will always be **b**." 1Ch 17:27
the LORD has **b** his people. 2Ch 31:10
B be your wonderful name....................... Ne 9:5
dying person **b** me, and I made .... Job 29:13
person's heart **b** me, because I .... Job 31:20
so God has **b** you forever. .... Ps 45:2
the nations be **b** because of him, ... Ps 72:17
May you be **b** by the LORD, who .... Ps 115:15
who respects the LORD will be **b**. .... Ps 128:4
Generous people will be **b**, ... Pr 22:9
but I **b** him and gave him many .... Is 51:2
trusts in the LORD will be **b**. .... Je 17:7
All the nations will call you **b**, ... Mal 3:12
They are **b** who hunger and thirst .... Mt 5:6
They are **b** who are persecuted .... Mt 5:10
But you are **b**, because you see .... Mt 13:16
answered, "You are **b**, Simon son .... Mt 16:17

his work, the servant will be **b**. .... Mt 24:46
his hands on them, and **b** them. .... Mk 10:16
Christ, the Son of the **b** God?" .... Mk 14:61
and he has **b** the baby to which .... Lk 1:42
You are **b** because you believed .... Lk 1:45
Then Simeon **b** them and said to .... Lk 2:34
You people who are poor are **b**, ... Lk 6:20
faith because of me are **b**!" .... Lk 7:23
B is the mother who gave birth .... Lk 11:27
They will be **b** when their master .... Lk 12:37
B are the people who will share .... Lk 14:15
'**B** are the women who cannot have .... Lk 23:29
he raised his hands and **b** them. .... Lk 24:50
seeing me will be truly **b**." .... Jn 20:29
nations on the earth will be **b**.' .... Ac 3:25
And God **b** all the believers very .... Ac 4:33
was richly **b** by God who gave .... Ac 6:8
'It is more **b** to give than to .... Ac 20:35
B are they whose sins are .... Rm 4:7
aside money as you have been **b**. 1Co 16:2
first so you could be **b** twice. 2Co 1:15
believed as was Abraham .... Gal 3:9
He is the **b** and only Ruler, ... 1Ti 6:15
they met, Melchizedek **b** Abraham, ... Heb 7:1
he **b** Abraham, the man who had .... Heb 7:6
b each one of Joseph's sons. .... Heb 11:21
for doing right, you are **b**. 1Pe 3:14
Christ, you are **b**, because the.................. 1Pe 4:14
B is the one who reads the words .... Rev 1:3
B are the dead who die from now .... Rev 14:13
B are those who have been .... Rev 19:9
B and holy are those who share .... Rev 20:6
B is the one who obeys the words .... Rev 22:7
B are those who wash their robes .... Rev 22:14

BLESSES
everyone who **b** you be blessed. .... Ge 27:29
He **b** you with rain from above, ... Ge 49:25
who **b** you will be blessed, ... Nu 24:9
LORD **b** his people with peace. .... Ps 29:11
whom the LORD **b** will inherit .... Ps 37:22
gates strong and **b** your children .... Ps 147:13
important person **b** the less .... Heb 7:7

BLESSING
and you will be a **b** to others. .... Ge 12:2
too late now to take back my **b**." .... Ge 27:33
"Haven't you saved a **b** for me?" .... Ge 27:36
descendants the **b** of Abraham so .... Ge 28:4
When a **b** is given in Israel, ... Ge 48:20
them, so I cannot change the **b**. .... Nu 23:20
you choose a **b** or a curse. .... Dt 11:26
gave this **b** to the Israelites .... Dt 33:1
God turned the curse into a **b**. .... Ne 13:2
You pour oil of **b** on my head; .... Ps 23:5
their children are a **b**. .... Ps 37:26
will be remembered as a **b**, ... Pr 10:7
The LORD's **b** brings wealth, ... Pr 10:22
which will be a **b** for the earth. .... Is 19:24
and so bring a **b** on your family. .... Eze 44:30
he cried and asked for his **b**. .... Hos 12:4
and leave behind a **b** for you. .... Joe 2:14
you, and you will become a **b**. .... Zch 8:13
my Father has given you his **b**. .... Mt 25:34
your **b** of peace will stay with.................. Lk 10:6
Is this **b** only for those who are .... Rm 4:9
us into that **b** of God's grace .... Rm 5:2
We give thanks for the cup of **b**, ... 1Co 10:16
this so that God's **b** promised to .... Gal 3:14
law could give us Abraham's **b**, ... Gal 3:18
spiritual **b** in the heavenly .... Eph 1:3
share with the Jews in God's **b**. .... Eph 3:6
every **b** we have in Christ. .... Phm 1:6

he wanted to get his father's **b**, ... Heb 12:17
But repay with a **b**, because you.............. 1Pe 3:9

BLESSINGS
The **b** of your father are greater .... Ge 49:26
to announce the **b** from Mount .... Dt 11:29
you life or death, **b** or curses. .... Dt 30:19
You always gave him **b**; .... Ps 21:6
Good people will have rich **b**, ... Pr 10:6
will give you the **b** I promised .... Is 55:3
and pour out all the **b** you need.............. Mal 3:10
holy and sure **b** that I promised .... Ac 13:34
we will receive **b** from God...................... Rm 8:17
gives many **b** to all who trust .... Rm 10:12
shared in the Jews' spiritual **b**, ... Rm 15:27
give you more **b** than you need. 2Co 9:8
freely gave his **b** to Abraham .... Gal 3:18
are the **b** God has promised .... Eph 1:18
by bringing you **b** in this life 1Ti 4:8
receive the **b** he has promised .... Heb 9:15
hope for the **b** God has for his 1Pe 1:4

BLEW
and it **b** the locusts away into .... Ex 10:19
and it **b** quail into the area all .... Nu 11:31
the priests **b** their trumpets. .... Jos 6:16
of Gideon's men **b** their trumpets .... Jdg 7:20
Then Joab **b** a trumpet, and his 2Sa 2:28
The wind **b** from his nose. 2Sa 22:16
They **b** the trumpet and shouted, ... 2Ki 9:13
They shouted, **b** horns and 1Ch 15:28
and the priests **b** the trumpets. 2Ch 13:14
came up, which **b** up high waves. .... Ps 107:25
the wind **b** them away, and there .... Da 2:35
and the winds **b** and hit that .... Mt 7:25
strong wind **b** up on the lake,.................. Lk 8:23
The first angel **b** his trumpet, ... Rev 8:7
the seventh angel **b** his trumpet.............. Rev 11:15

BLIND
in front of a **b** person to make .... Le 19:14
b men, crippled men, men with .... Le 21:18
the LORD any animal that is **b**, ... Le 22:22
cursed who sends a **b** person down .... Dt 27:18
were so weak he was almost **b**. 1Sa 3:2
Even the **b** and the crippled can 2Sa 5:6
Now Ahijah was very old and **b**............... 1Ki 14:4
So he made the Aramean army **b**, ... 2Ki 6:18
the eyes of their children go **b**. .... Job 17:5
The LORD gives sight to the **b**. .... Ps 146:8
B yourselves so that you cannot .... Is 29:9
the **b** people will see again,...................... Is 35:5
You who are **b**, look and see. .... Is 42:18
are like the **b** feeling our way .... Is 59:10
the people are **b** and crippled. .... Je 31:8
the streets as if they were **b**. .... La 4:14
will walk around like the **b**, ... Zph 1:17
but I will **b** all the horses of .... Zch 12:4
When you bring **b** animals as .... Mal 1:8
there, two **b** men followed him. .... Mt 9:27
The **b** can see, the crippled can .... Mt 11:5
And if a **b** person leads a blind .... Mt 15:14
the lame, the **b**, the crippled, ... Mt 15:30
You are **b**! Which is greater: the .... Mt 23:19
Pharisees, you are **b**! First make .... Mt 23:26
So Jesus took the **b** man's hand .... Mk 8:23
a **b** beggar named Bartimaeus son .... Mk 10:46
The **b** man jumped up, left his .... Mk 10:50
Can a **b** person lead another .... Lk 6:39
The **b** can see, the crippled can .... Lk 7:22
a **b** man was sitting beside the .... Lk 18:35
The **b** man cried out, "Jesus, Son .... Lk 18:38
Some were **b**, some were crippled, ... Jn 5:3
saw a man who had been born **b**. .... Jn 9:1
giving sight to a man born **b**. .... Jn 9:32

BLINDED

a demon open the eyes of the **b**?" ....Jn 10:21
the bright light had made me **b.** ....Ac 22:11
darkness has made that person **b.** 1Jn 2:11
pitiful, poor, **b**, and naked. ....Rev 3:17

BLINDED

and the eye is **b**, the man is to ....Ex 21:26
He has **b** their eyes, and he has ....Jn 12:40
this world has **b** the minds of 2Co 4:4

BLINDFOLDED

They **b** him and beat him with ....Mk 14:65
They **b** him and said, "Prove that ....Lk 22:64

BLINDNESS

those outside the door with **b,** ....Ge 19:11
who gives a person sight or **b?** ....Ex 4:11
you madness, **b**, and a confused..............Dt 28:28

BLINDS

windows, looking through the **b.** ....Sng 2:9

BLINKS

quickly as an eye **b**—when the 1Co 15:52

BLOCK

I am worshiping a **b** of wood!" ....Is 44:19
will **b** the road for travelers. ....Eze 39:11
So I will **b** her road with........................Hos 2:6
large stone to **b** the entrance ....Mt 27:60
large stone to **b** the entrance ....Mk 15:46

BLOCKED

or if it is **b** from flowing;......................Le 15:3
God has **b** my way so I cannot ....Job 19:8
b my way with a stone wall and..............La 3:9

BLOCKING

Stop **b** our path. Get out of our ....Is 30:11

BLOCKS

to cut large **b** of fine stone to 1Ki 5:17
but he **b** the way of the wicked. ....Ps 146:9
Jeremiah out of the **b** of wood, ...Je 20:3
down between large **b** of wood. ....Ac 16:24

BLOOD

Your brother's **b** is crying out ....Ge 4:10
in it, because **b** gives life. ....Ge 9:4
"You are my own flesh and **b**." ....Ge 29:14
dipped Joseph's robe in its **b.** ....Ge 37:31
"You are a bridegroom of **b** to me." ....Ex 4:25
the water will change into **b.** ....Ex 7:17
take some of the **b** and put it ....Ex 12:7
But the **b** will be a sign on the ....Ex 12:13
half of the **b** on the altar. ....Ex 24:6
Kill it and take some of its **b.** ....Ex 29:20
must bring its **b** and sprinkle it ....Le 1:5
the bird's **b** must be drained out..............Le 1:15
The rest of the **b** he must pour ....Le 4:7
Dipping his finger in the **b,**....................Le 4:17
But if the **b** of the sin offering ....Le 6:30
Anyone who eats **b** must be cut ....Le 7:27
will sprinkle the **b** seven times ....Le 16:14
If **b** is still in the meat, ...Le 17:14
because the life is in the **b.** ....Dt 12:23
road, covered with his own **b.**.................2Sa 20:12
drinking the **b** of the men who 2Sa 23:17
and spears until their **b** flowed, ...1Ki 18:28
the dogs licked up Naboth's **b,** 1Ki 21:19
I saw the **b** of Naboth and his.................2Ki 9:26
filled Jerusalem with their **b.** 2Ki 24:4
drinking the **b** of the men who 1Ch 11:19
bulls or drink the **b** of goats. ....Ps 50:13
feet in the **b** of the wicked. ....Ps 58:10
can stick your feet in their **b,** ....Ps 68:23
rivers to **b** so no one could ....Ps 78:44
water into **b** and made their ....Ps 105:29
land was made unholy by their **b.** ....Ps 106:38

not pleased by the **b** of bulls, ...Is 1:11
in the sky is covered with **b.** ....Is 34:5
Their own **b** will be the wine ....Is 49:26
place with the **b** of innocent ....Je 19:4
were dirty with **b**, so no one ....La 4:14
and **b** will flow in her streets..................Eze 28:23
Israel. Eat flesh and drink **b!** ....Eze 39:17
b, fire, and thick smoke. ....Joe 2:30
dark, the moon red as **b**, before ....Joe 2:31
Their **b** will be poured out like ....Zph 1:17
of the **b** of the agreement ....Zch 9:11
This is my **b** which is the new................Mt 26:28
This **b** is poured out for many to ....Mt 26:28
is still called the Field of **B.**....................Mt 27:8
This is my **b** which is the new................Mk 14:24
This **b** is poured out for many. ....Mk 14:24
He mixed their **b** with the blood..............Lk 13:1
blood with the **b** of the animals ....Lk 13:1
begins with my **b** which is poured ....Lk 22:20
was like drops of **b** falling to ....Lk 22:44
the Son of Man and drink his **b.**..............Jn 6:53
at once **b** and water came out. ....Jn 19:34
Akeldama means "Field of **B**." ....Ac 1:19
b, fire, and thick smoke. ....Ac 2:19
dark, the moon red as **b**, before ....Ac 2:20
that have been strangled, and **b.**..............Ac 15:20
faith in the **b** of Jesus' death. ....Rm 3:25
with God by the **b** of Christ's ....Rm 5:9
is a sharing in the **b** of Christ. 1Co 10:16
the body and the **b** of the Lord. 1Co 11:27
Flesh and **b** cannot have a part 1Co 15:50
set free by the **b** of his death, ...Eph 1:7
near through the **b** of Christ's................Eph 2:13
to offer my own **b** with your ....Php 2:17
through the **b** of Christ's death ....Col 1:20
room without taking **b** with him, ...Heb 9:7
take with him the **b** of goats and ....Heb 9:12
His sacrifice was his own **b,** ....Heb 9:12
must be made clean by **b,** ....Heb 9:22
and spread the **b** on the doors so ....Heb 11:28
his people holy with his own **b.** ....Heb 13:12
with the precious **b** of Christ, ...1Pe 1:19
Then the **b** of Jesus, God's Son, ...1Jn 1:7
the One who came by water and **b.** 1Jn 5:6
sins with the **b** of his death. ....Rev 1:5
and with the **b** of your death you ....Rev 5:9
whole moon became red like **b.** ....Rev 6:12
them white in the **b** of the Lamb. ....Rev 7:14
fire mixed with **b** were poured ....Rev 8:7
And a third of the sea became **b,** ....Rev 8:8
to make the waters become **b,** ....Rev 11:6
him by the **b** of the Lamb's death ....Rev 12:11
b flowed out of the winepress................Rev 14:20
and it became **b** like that of a ....Rev 16:3
drunk with the **b** of God's holy ....Rev 17:6
dressed in a robe dipped in **b,**...............Rev 19:13

BLOODSHOT

bruises? Who has **b** eyes? ....Pr 23:29

BLOODSTAINS

will wash the **b** out of Jerusalem ....Is 4:4

BLOODY

land is full of **b** crimes and the ....Eze 7:23
their footprints are **b.** ....Hos 6:8

BLOOM

flax was in **b**, and the barley ....Ex 9:31
like a plant beginning to **b.**....................Is 27:6
grain, they will **b** like a vine, ...Hos 14:7

BLOOMED

if the pomegranate trees had **b.** ....Sng 6:11
flowers have **b** and before the.................Is 18:5

B

BLOOMS

nothing grows, and nothing **b.** .... Dt 29:23
will have many **b.** It will show .... Is 35:2

BLOSSOM

watched the branches bud and **b,** .... Ge 40:10
rim of a cup or like a lily **b.** 1Ki 7:26
rim of a cup or like a lily **b.** 2Ch 4:5
vineyards while they are in **b.**................... Sng 2:15
the next day you make them **b.** .... Is 17:11
and they will **b** like a lily. .... Hos 14:5

BLOSSOMED

had even budded, **b,** and produced .... Nu 17:8

BLOSSOMS

an olive tree that loses its **b.** .... Job 15:33
B appear through all the land. .... Sng 2:12
Let's see if the **b** have already .... Sng 7:12

BLOW

He made a wind **b** over the earth, ... Ge 8:1
strong wind to **b** from the east. .... Ex 10:13
when you **b** the trumpet for a .... Le 23:24
you must **b** the horn of a male .... Le 25:9
If you **b** only one trumpet, ... Nu 10:4
B them over your burnt offerings .... Nu 10:10
everyone with me **b** our trumpets, ... Jdg 7:18
B the trumpet and shout, 'Long 1Ki 1:34
wind began to **b**, and soon a 1Ki 18:45
priests **b** the trumpet to call 2Ch 13:12
the east winds **b** over the earth? .... Job 38:24
His anger will **b** them away alive .... Ps 58:9
B them away as smoke is driven .... Ps 68:2
B the trumpet at the time of the .... Ps 81:3
B the trumpets and the sheep's .... Ps 98:6
A storm will **b** the evil person................. Pr 10:25
know where the wind will **b**, ... Ec 11:5
B on my garden, and let its..................... Sng 4:16
Nile will dry up, **b** away, and .... Is 19:7
The wind will **b** them all away; .... Is 57:13
B the war trumpet in the town of .... Je 6:1
have received a terrible **b;** .... Je 14:17
punishment will **b** all your .... Je 22:22
everywhere the four winds **b;** .... Je 49:36
wind to **b** against Babylon .... Je 51:1
B the trumpet among the nations! .... Je 51:27
he will **b** the trumpet and warn .... Eze 33:3
B the horn in Gibeah and the .... Hos 5:8
B the trumpet in Jerusalem; .... Joe 2:1
sent a very hot east wind to **b,** .... Jnh 4:8
The Lord GOD will **b** the trumpet, ... Zch 9:14
b trumpets in the synagogues .... Mt 6:2
wind begin to **b** from the south, ... Lk 12:55
wind began to **b** from the south, ... Ac 27:13
trumpets prepared to **b** them. .... Rev 8:6
three angels are about to **b**!'' .... Rev 8:13
angel is ready to **b** his trumpet, ... Rev 10:7

BLOWING

priests were **b** their trumpets................... Jos 6:9
of the LORD, **b** their trumpets. .... Jos 6:13
priests were **b** their trumpets.................. Jos 6:13
very happy and were **b** trumpets. 2Ki 11:14
had the job of **b** trumpets in 1Ch 15:24
desert like wind **b** in the south. .... Is 21:1
the wind was **b** from all four .... Da 7:2
the wind was **b** against it. .... Mt 14:24
the wind was **b** against them. .... Mk 6:48
By now a strong wind was **b,** .... Jn 6:18
b wind came from heaven and .... Ac 2:2
the storm was **b** us so hard that .... Ac 27:18
to keep them from **b** on the land .... Rev 7:1

BLOWN

of a leaf being **b** by the wind. .... Le 26:36
both trumpets are **b,** the people .... Nu 10:3

trumpets were **b,** and the musical 2Ch 29:27
a leaf that is **b** by the wind;................... Job 13:25
chaff that is **b** away by a storm? .... Job 21:18
them like chaff **b** by the wind as.............. Ps 35:5
like chaff **b** away by the wind. .... Ps 83:13
of the forest **b** by the wind...................... Is 7:2
tumbleweeds **b** away by a storm.............. Is 17:13
time a great trumpet will be **b,** .... Is 27:13
be like chaff that is **b** away. .... Is 29:5
and they are **b** away like chaff. .... Is 41:2
chaff that is **b** away by the .... Je 13:24
like a bush being **b** through the .... Je 48:6
They have **b** the trumpet, and .... Eze 7:14
be like chaff **b** from the .... Hos 13:3
you are **b** away like chaff, ... Zph 2:2
to see? A reed **b** by the wind? .... Mt 11:7
to see? A reed **b** by the wind? .... Lk 7:24
a wave in the sea, **b** up and down .... Jam 1:6
water and clouds **b** by a storm. 2Pe 2:17

BLOWS

and **b** of punishment will fall on.............. Job 20:23
When the trumpet **b,** the horse .... Job 39:25
like chaff that the wind **b** away. .... Ps 1:4
like a wind that **b** and does not .... Ps 78:39
After the wind **b,** the flower is .... Ps 103:16
The wind **b** to the south; .... Ec 1:6
dies and **b** away like dust. .... Is 5:24
he **b** on them and they die, ... Is 40:24
A hot wind **b** from the bare .... Je 4:11
like a wind that **b** chaff away. .... Je 51:2
When a trumpet **b** a warning in a .... Am 3:6
will be beaten with many **b!** .... Lk 12:47
will be beaten with few **b.** .... Lk 12:48
The wind **b** where it wants to and .... Jn 3:8
rain, which the wind **b** around. .... Jud 1:12
from a fig tree when the wind **b.** .... Rev 6:13

BLUE

paved with **b** sapphire stones .... Ex 24:10
b, purple, and red thread; .... Ex 25:4
curtains of fine linen and **b,** .... Ex 26:1
craftsmen must use gold and **b,** .... Ex 28:5
Use gold and **b,** purple and red .... Ex 28:6
holy vest, using only **b** cloth. .... Ex 28:31
used her hands to make the **b,** .... Ex 35:25
of the courtyard was made of **b,** .... Ex 38:18
It was woven only of **b** cloth. .... Ex 39:22
they must spread a **b** cloth over .... Nu 4:7
Put a **b** thread in each one of .... Nu 15:38
royal clothes of **b** and white and.............. Est 8:15
They put **b** and purple clothes on .... Je 10:9
wore **b** uniforms. They were all .... Eze 23:6
over the deck were **b** and purple .... Eze 27:7
fiery red, dark **b,** and yellow .... Rev 9:17

BLUSH

know how to **b** about their sins .... Je 6:15

BOANERGES

Jesus named them **B,** which means .... Mk 3:17

BOARD

in the mud like a threshing **b.**.................. Job 41:30
is hammered into a strong **b.** .... Is 22:23
new threshing **b** with many sharp .... Is 41:15
everyone else on **b** sank into the .... Eze 27:27

BOARDS

made the altar of **b** and left the .... Ex 38:7
the threshing **b** and the yokes.................. 2Sa 24:22
beams and cedar **b** on the Temple. 1Ki 6:9
floor to ceiling with cedar **b.** 1Ki 6:15
The floor was made from pine **b.** 1Ki 6:15
the threshing **b** for the wood, ... 1Ch 21:23
need it to make **b** for the gates .... Ne 2:8
will protect her with cedar **b.** .... Sng 8:9

use heavy **b** to crush dill; ....Is 28:27
made all your **b** of fir trees ....Eze 27:5
with threshing **b** that had iron ....Am 1:3
and the **b** that support the roof ....Hab 2:11
the wooden **b** of the buildings ....Zph 2:14
follow using wooden **b** or pieces ....Ac 27:44

BOAT

Build a **b** of cypress wood for ....Ge 6:14
bring into the **b** two of every ....Ge 6:19
Noah in the **b** in groups of two. ....Ge 7:15
it lifted the **b** off the ground. ....Ge 7:17
the **b** floated on it above the ....Ge 7:18
sent out the dove from the **b**, ...Ge 8:10
went out of the **b** by families. ....Ge 8:19
left the **b** and their father, ...Mt 4:22
so that waves covered the **b**, ...Mt 8:24
Jesus got into a **b** and went back ....Mt 9:1
so he got into a **b** and sat down, ...Mt 13:2
he left in a **b** and went to a ....Mt 14:13
And Peter left the **b** and walked ....Mt 14:29
Jesus got into the **b** and went to ....Mt 15:39
the day Noah entered the **b**. ....Mt 24:38
They were in a **b**, mending their..............Mk 1:19
to get a **b** ready for him to ....Mk 3:9
sat down in a **b** near the shore. ....Mk 4:1
Jesus was at the back of the **b**, ...Mk 4:38
When Jesus got out of the **b**, ...Mk 5:2
they went in a **b** by themselves ....Mk 6:32
struggling hard to row the **b**, ...Mk 6:48
he got into the **b** with them, ...Mk 6:51
Gennesaret and tied the **b** there..............Mk 6:53
and went in the **b** to the other ....Mk 8:13
to teach the people from the **b**. ....Lk 5:3
the **b** to fill with water, ...Lk 8:23
the day Noah entered the **b**. ....Lk 17:27
got into a **b** and started across ....Jn 6:17
the water, coming toward the **b**. ....Jn 6:19
net on the right side of the **b**, ...Jn 21:6
and built a large **b** to save his.............Heb 11:7
while Noah was building the **b**. 1Pe 3:20

BOATS

They glide past like paper **b**. ....Job 9:26
on the water in **b** made of reeds. ....Is 18:2
be no enemy **b** on those rivers ....Is 33:21
The ropes on your **b** hang loose..............Is 33:23
were also other **b** with them. ....Mk 4:36
Jesus saw two **b** at the shore of ....Lk 5:2
and filled both **b** so full that ....Lk 5:7
But then some **b** came from ....Jn 6:23

BOAZ

that the field belonged to **B**, ...Ru 2:3
B handed her some roasted grain, ...Ru 2:14
So **B** took Ruth home as his wife ....Ru 4:13
Salmon was the father of **B**, ...Ru 4:21
B was the father of Obed, and 1Ch 2:12
B was the father of Obed. ....Mt 1:5
B was the son of Salmon. ....Lk 3:32

BOAZ'S

of Boaz. (**B** mother was Rahab. ....Mt 1:5

BODIES

Your **b** will be marked to show ....Ge 17:13
came upon the dead **b** and stole ....Ge 34:27
and carried the **b** of Nadab and ....Le 10:5
or even touch their dead **b**;..................Le 11:8
of their bodies, or cut their **b**.................Le 21:5
You will eat the **b** of your sons ....Le 26:29
shave their **b** and wash their ....Nu 8:7
Your dead **b** will be food for all ....Dt 28:26
and hung their **b** on five trees, ...Jos 10:26
The Philistines' **b** lay on the 1Sa 17:52
removed the **b** of Saul and his 1Sa 31:12

the rain fell on her sons' **b**.....................2Sa 21:10
had hung the **b** of Saul and.....................2Sa 21:12
they saw all the dead **b**. 2Ki 19:35
and got the **b** of Saul and his 1Ch 10:12
let the **b** of Haman's ten sons ....Est 9:13
and worms will eat their **b**. ....Job 24:20
and their **b** will rot in a grave ....Ps 49:14
their **b** rotted on the ground. ....Ps 83:10
Dead **b** lie in the streets like ....Is 5:25
or fall down among the dead **b**. ....Is 10:4
You are covered by **b** that died ....Is 14:19
their **b** will rise from death. ....Is 26:19
The stink will rise from the **b**,...............Is 34:3
Then the **b** of the dead will ....Je 7:33
dogs to drag the **b** away, and the ....Je 15:3
Their **b** will be food for the......................Je 16:4
will eat the **b** of their own sons ....Je 19:9
threw the **b** into a deep well. ....Je 41:7
Pile up her dead **b** like heaps of ....Je 50:26
its streets with their **b**. ....Eze 11:6
hearts of stone from your **b**, ...Eze 36:26
with the dead **b** of their kings. ....Eze 43:7
the fire had not harmed their **b**. ....Da 3:27
her cubs, ripping their **b** open. ....Hos 13:8
Their **b** will rot and stink. ....Joe 2:20
the stink from all the dead **b**, ...Am 4:10
will be dead **b** thrown everywhere ....Am 8:3
their **b** are piled up—too many ....Nah 3:3
it can look at their naked **b**. ....Hab 2:15
put into their **b** that makes them ....Mk 7:15
not want the **b** to stay on the ....Jn 19:31
Later their **b** were moved to ....Ac 7:16
using their **b** wrongly with each..............Rm 1:24
are not circumcised in their **b**, ...Rm 2:27
things that controlled our **b**, ...Rm 7:5
give life to your **b** that die. ....Rm 8:11
you know that your **b** are parts 1Co 6:15
sin against their own **b**. 1Co 6:18
So honor God with your **b**. 1Co 6:20
to give your **b** to each other, ...1Co 7:5
heavenly bodies and earthly **b**. 1Co 15:40
Jesus can also be seen in our **b**. 2Co 4:10
they themselves do on their **b**. ....Eph 2:11
wives as they love their own **b**. ....Eph 5:28
They do whatever their **b** want, ...Php 3:19
and make them punish their **b**, ...Col 2:23
many things our **b** wanted and ....Tit 3:3
are people with physical **b**,.....................Heb 2:14
this makes their **b** clean again. ....Heb 9:13
and our **b** have been washed with ....Heb 10:22
we can control their whole **b**. ....Jam 3:3
It will eat your **b** like fire. ....Jam 5:3
things your **b** want to do that 1Pe 2:11
The **b** of the two witnesses will ....Rev 11:8
birds ate the **b** until they were ....Rev 19:21

BODY

and the two will become one **b**. ....Ge 2:24
Two nations are in your **b**, ...Ge 25:23
He will hang your **b** on a pole, ...Ge 40:19
prepared Jacob's **b** to be buried...............Ge 50:2
They carried his **b** to the land ....Ge 50:13
must bring the **b** as proof, ...Ex 22:13
underclothes next to his **b**. ....Le 6:10
touches its **b** will be unclean ....Le 11:39
discharges the **b** fluid must wash ....Le 15:7
from semen coming out of his **b**. ....Le 15:32
not cut your **b** to show sadness ....Le 19:28
unclean from touching a dead **b**. ....Nu 9:6
go to where the **b** was found, ...Dt 21:2
don't leave his **b** hanging on the..............Dt 21:23
They piled rocks over Achan's **b**, ...Jos 7:26
look at the **b** of the dead lion ....Jdg 14:8

honey from the **b** of the dead .... Jdg 14:9
and hung his **b** on the wall of 1Sa 31:10
himself followed the **b** of Abner.............. 2Sa 3:31
men took Absalom's **b** and threw 2Sa 18:17
that road saw the **b** and the lion 1Ki 13:25
'Dogs will eat the **b** of Jezebel 1Ki 21:23
Her **b** will be like manure on the 2Ki 9:37
stripped Saul's **b** and took his 1Ch 10:9
He put painful sores on Job's **b**, ... Job 2:7
My **b** is covered with worms and .... Job 7:5
and my **b** is as thin as a shadow. .... Job 17:7
Then his **b** is made new like a .... Job 33:25
and am glad. Even my **b** has hope,.......... Ps 16:9
people may try to destroy my **b**. .... Ps 27:2
My **b** is sick from your .... Ps 38:3
to show that my **b** and life are .... Ps 40:6
b and my mind may become weak, ... Ps 73:26
like a **b** lying in a grave whom .... Ps 88:5
filled his **b** with his life, ... Ps 109:18
you formed me in my mother's **b**. .... Ps 139:13
Then your **b** will be healthy, ... Pr 3:8
bring health to the whole **b**. .... Pr 4:22
Peace of mind means a healthy **b**, ... Pr 14:30
b is like shiny ivory covered .... Sng 5:14
cover your **b** like a blanket. .... Is 14:11
formed you in your mother's **b**, ... Is 44:2
to come out of my mother's **b**? .... Je 20:18
dragging his **b** away and throwing .... Je 22:19
two wings that covered its **b**. .... Eze 1:11
offering your **b** for sex to .... Eze 16:25
uncovered your **b** in your sexual .... Eze 16:36
Its **b** was destroyed, and it was .... Da 7:11
His **b** was like shiny yellow .... Da 10:6
these things, and my **b** trembles; .... Hab 3:16
who touches a dead **b** will become .... Hag 2:13
are the deep cuts on your **b**? .... Zch 13:6
to become one **b** and one spirit .... Mal 2:15
your whole **b** thrown into hell. .... Mt 5:29
The eye is a light for the **b**. .... Mt 6:22
and the **b** is more than clothes. .... Mt 6:25
can't move his **b** and is in much .... Mt 8:6
can kill the **b** but cannot kill .... Mt 10:28
and got his **b** and buried it. .... Mt 14:12
part of your **b** and live forever .... Mt 18:8
and the two will become one **b**.' .... Mt 19:5
Wherever the dead **b** is, there .... Mt 24:28
perfume on my **b** to prepare me .... Mt 26:12
bread and eat it; this is my **b**." .... Mt 26:26
is right, but the **b** is weak." .... Mt 26:41
Joseph took the **b** and wrapped it .... Mt 27:59
see the place where his **b** was. .... Mt 28:6
she felt in her **b** that she was .... Mk 5:29
came and got John's **b** and put it .... Mk 6:29
lose part of your **b** and to live. .... Mk 9:45
and the two will become one **b**.' .... Mk 10:8
perfume on my **b** to prepare me .... Mk 14:8
said, "Take it; this is my **b**." .... Mk 14:22
is right, but the **b** is weak." .... Mk 14:38
to Pilate and ask for Jesus' **b**. .... Mk 15:43
He put the **b** in a tomb that was .... Mk 15:46
spices to put on Jesus' **b**. .... Mk 16:1
Your eye is a light for the **b**. .... Lk 11:34
your whole **b** is full of light, ... Lk 11:36
can kill the **b** but after that .... Lk 12:4
and the **b** is more than clothes. .... Lk 12:23
whose **b** was covered with sores, ... Lk 16:20
This is my **b**, which I am giving .... Lk 22:19
He took the **b** down from the .... Lk 23:53
find the **b** of the Lord Jesus. .... Lk 24:3
that Jesus' **b** had been wrapped .... Lk 24:12
they did not find his **b** there. .... Lk 24:23
Jesus meant was his own **b**. .... Jn 2:21
person's whole **b** on the Sabbath .... Jn 7:23

a bath, his whole **b** is clean. .... Jn 13:10
men took Jesus' **b** and wrapped it .... Jn 19:40
sitting where Jesus' **b** had been, ... Jn 20:12
to his death, his **b** burst open, ... Ac 1:18
I rejoice. Even my **b** has hope, ... Ac 2:26
the grave. His **b** did not rot.' .... Ac 2:31
Her **b** was washed and put in a .... Ac 9:37
he turned to the **b** and said, ... Ac 9:40
and his **b** did rot in the grave. .... Ac 13:36
is only a Jew in his physical **b**; .... Rm 2:28
parts of your **b** to be slaves to........... Rm 6:19
see another law working in my **b**, ... Rm 7:23
wrong things you do with your **b**, ... Rm 8:13
of us has a **b** with many parts........... Rm 12:4
but in Christ we are all one **b**. .... Rm 12:5
The **b** is not for sexual sin but 1Co 6:13
know that your **b** is a temple for 1Co 6:19
to be holy in **b** and spirit. 1Co 7:34
we who are many are one **b**, ... 1Co 10:17
bread and said, "This is my **b**; 1Co 11:24
against the **b** and the blood 1Co 11:27
The human **b** has many parts. 1Co 12:14
you are the **b** of Christ, ... 1Co 12:27
What kind of **b** will they have?" 1Co 15:35
But God gives it a **b** that he has 1Co 15:38
Our physical **b** is becoming older 2Co 4:16
away from this **b** and be at home 2Co 5:8
was in his body or out of his **b**, ... 2Co 12:2
I still live in my **b**, but I live .... Gal 2:20
There is one **b** and one Spirit, ... Eph 4:4
and the two will become one **b**." .... Eph 5:31
them like his own glorious **b**. .... Php 3:21
is the head of the **b**, which is .... Col 1:18
together in one **b** to have peace. .... Col 3:15
Don't use your **b** for sexual sin 1Th 4:5
Training your **b** helps you in 1Ti 4:8
he was in the **b** of his ancestor .... Heb 7:10
They were rules for the **b**, ... Heb 9:10
through the curtain—Christ's **b**. .... Heb 10:20
its evil through the whole **b**. .... Jam 3:6
our sins in his **b** on the cross 1Pe 2:24
as long as I am in this **b**. 2Pe 1:13
I know I must soon leave this **b**, ... 2Pe 1:14
who would have the **b** of Moses, ... Jud 1:9
will eat her **b** and burn her with .... Rev 17:16

BODYGUARD
I'll make you my permanent **b**." 1Sa 28:2
fifty men for his personal **b**. 1Ki 1:5

BODYGUARDS
-in-law and captain of your **b**. 1Sa 22:14
David made leader of his **b**. 2Sa 23:23
and all the king's **b** with him, ... 1Ki 1:44
Carites, the royal **b**, as well as 2Ki 11:19
David made him leader of his **b**. 1Ch 11:25

BOHAN
to the stone of **B** son of Reuben. .... Jos 15:6

BOIL
and **b** what you want to boil .... Ex 16:23
B the meat at the door of the .... Le 8:31
may have a **b** on his skin that .... Le 13:18
and **b** some stew for these men." 2Ki 4:38
it and put it on Hezekiah's **b**, ... 2Ki 20:7
figs and put it on Hezekiah's **b**. .... Is 38:21
like a fire that makes water **b**, ... Is 64:2
B the pieces of meat until even .... Eze 24:5
where the priests will **b** the. .... Eze 46:20

BOILED
eat the lamb raw or **b** in water. .... Ex 12:9
will give them a **b** shoulder from .... Nu 6:19
He won't accept **b** meat from you, ... 1Sa 2:15

So we **b** my son and ate him. 2Ki 6:29
and they **b** the holy offerings in 2Ch 35:13

BOILING

One day Jacob was **b** a pot of ....Ge 25:29
deep sea bubble like a **b** pot; ....Job 41:31
I see a pot of **b** water, tipping ....Je 1:13

BOILS

They will cause **b** to break out ....Ex 9:9
punish you with **b** like those ....Dt 28:27

BOLD

b and cruel king who tells lies ....Da 8:23
Then Isaiah is **b** enough to say: ....Rm 10:20
this hope, so we are very **b**. 2Co 3:12
with you and **b** when I am away. 2Co 10:1
have become more **b** in Christ and...........Php 1:14
will be very **b** in their faith 1Ti 3:13
I could be **b** and order you to do...............Phm 1:8
teachers are **b** and do anything 2Pe 2:10

BOLDLY

marched out **b** in front of all ....Nu 33:3
b in the name of the Lord. ....Ac 9:28
Paul and Barnabas spoke very **b**, ...Ac 13:46
speak very **b** in the synagogue, ...Ac 18:26
spoke out **b** for three months...................Ac 19:8
He **b** preached about the kingdom ....Ac 28:31

BOLDNESS

your **b** will make him get up and ....Lk 11:8
to use that same **b** with you. 2Co 10:2
And this is the **b** we have in 1Jn 5:14

BOLT

have them shut and **b** the doors...............Ne 7:3

BOLTED

of the room and **b** the door after 2Sa 13:18

BOLTS

His **b** of lightning confused them 2Sa 22:15
its doors, **b**, and bars in place.................Ne 3:3
send lightning **b** on their way? ....Job 38:35
His many **b** of lightning confused ....Ps 18:14
and forth like **b** of lightning. ....Eze 1:14

BONE

bone for broken **b**, eye for eye, ...Le 24:20
touches a human **b** or a grave, ...Nu 19:16
bones came together, **b** to bone. ....Eze 37:7
bury the **b** in The Valley ....Eze 39:15

BONES

whose bones came from my **b**, ...Ge 2:23
you will carry my **b** with you out ....Ge 50:25
Don't break any of the **b**. ....Ex 12:46
carried the **b** of Joseph with ....Ex 13:19
has broken **b** or is crippled, ...Le 22:22
and break their enemies' **b**; ....Nu 24:8
carried the **b** of Joseph with ....Jos 24:32
Then David took the **b** of Saul 2Sa 21:12
grave. Put my **b** next to his. 1Ki 13:31
When the man touched Elisha's **b**, ...2Ki 13:21
covered the places with human **b**. 2Ki 23:14
burned human **b** on the altars. 2Ki 23:20
He burned the **b** of their priests 2Ch 34:5
and destroy his flesh and **b**, ...Job 2:5
me together with **b** and muscles. ....Job 10:11
I am nothing but skin and **b**; ....Job 19:20
continual pain in their very **b**. ....Job 33:19
me, LORD, because my **b** ache. ....Ps 6:2
and my **b** are out of joint. ....Ps 22:14
and my **b** are getting weaker. ....Ps 31:10
me feel as if my **b** were broken. ....Ps 42:10
scatter the **b** of your enemies ....Ps 53:5
my grief, my skin hangs on my **b**. ....Ps 102:5
You saw my **b** being formed as I...............Ps 139:15

our **b** have been scattered at the...............Ps 141:7
and your **b** will be strong. ....Pr 3:8
wife is like a disease in his **b**. ....Pr 12:4
but jealousy will rot your **b**. ....Pr 14:30
until their **b** become like lime; ....Is 33:12
a lion, he crushed all my **b**.....................Is 38:13
and give strength to your **b**. ....Is 58:11
gather up the **b** and bury them. ....Je 8:2
inside me, deep within my **b**. ....Je 20:9
Their skin hangs on their **b**; ....La 4:8
will scatter your **b** around your ....Eze 6:5
until even the **b** are cooked. ....Eze 24:5
He led me around among the **b**, ...Eze 37:2
me, "Human, can these **b** live?" ....Eze 37:3
to them, 'Dry **b**, hear the word ....Eze 37:4
grew, and skin covered the **b**. ....Eze 37:8
these **b** are like all the people ....Eze 37:11
of the den and crushed their **b**. ....Da 6:24
They burned the **b** of the king of ....Am 2:1
and tear the flesh off their **b**. ....Mic 3:2
My **b** feel weak, and my legs ....Hab 3:16
are full of the **b** of dead people ....Mt 23:27
Not one of his **b** will be broken. ....Jn 19:36
the center of our joints and **b**...................Heb 4:12

BOOK

battle in a **b** so people will ....Ex 17:14
he took the **B** of the Agreement ....Ex 24:7
I will erase from my **b** the names ....Ex 32:33
That is why the **B** of the Wars of ....Nu 21:14
that are written in this **b**. ....Dt 28:58
in the **B** of the Teachings ....Jos 8:31
wrote them in a **b** and put it 1Sa 10:25
written in the **b** of the history...............1Ki 11:41
in the **B** of the Teachings 2Ki 14:6
read from the **b** to the king. 2Ki 22:10
in this **B** of the Agreement.....................2Ki 23:21
in the history **b** about King 1Ch 27:24
was written in the **B** of Moses, ...2Ch 25:4
written in the **b** of the kings. 2Ch 25:26
was written in the **b** of Moses. 2Ch 35:12
Ezra opened the **b** in full view ....Ne 8:5
day they read the **B** of Moses to ....Ne 13:1
It is written about me in the **b** ....Ps 40:7
their names from the **b** of life, ...Ps 69:28
written in your **b** before I was ....Ps 139:16
the words of a **b** that is closed ....Is 29:11
the warnings written in this **b**. ....Je 25:13
in God's **b** will be saved.......................Da 12:1
close up the **b** and seal it. ....Da 12:4
This is the **b** of the vision of ....Nah 1:1
presence in a **b** to be remembered ....Mal 3:16
In the **b** in which Moses wrote ....Mk 12:26
it is written in the **b** of Isaiah ....Lk 3:4
The **b** of Isaiah the prophet was ....Lk 4:17
the **b** of Psalms, David himself ....Lk 20:42
that are not written in this **b**. ....Jn 20:30
The first **b** I wrote was about ....Ac 1:1
"In the **B** of Psalms," Peter said,...............Ac 1:20
written in the **b** of the prophets ....Ac 7:42
reading from the **B** of Isaiah, ...Ac 8:28
is written in the **B** of the Law." ....Gal 3:10
are written in the **b** of life. ....Php 4:3
It is written about me in the **b**. ....Heb 10:7
their names from the **b** of life, ...Rev 3:5
written in the Lamb's **b** of life. ....Rev 13:8
written in the **b** of life since ....Rev 17:8
and the **b** of life was opened. ....Rev 20:12
the words of prophecy in this **b**, ...Rev 22:10

BOOKS

in the record **b** of the kings of ....Est 10:2
People are always writing **b**, ...Ec 12:12
to begin, and the **b** were opened. ....Da 7:10

B

of Moses, the **b** of the prophets .... Lk 24:44
for all the **b** that would be .... Jn 21:25
their magic **b** and burned them .... Ac 19:19
in the **b** of the Prophets. .... Ac 24:14
me, along with my **b**, ... 2Ti 4:13
Then **b** were opened, and the book .... Rev 20:12

BOOT
Every **b** that marched in battle .... Is 9:5

BOOTH
in the tax collector's **b**. .... Mt 9:9
in the tax collector's **b**. .... Mk 2:14
in the tax collector's **b**. .... Lk 5:27

BORDER
direction on its eastern **b**. .... Ge 3:24
near the **b** of Edom. There there .... Nu 20:23
your southern **b** will start at .... Nu 34:3
The **b** on the west was the Jordan .... Dt 3:17
The southern **b** of Judah's land .... Jos 15:2
The eastern **b** was the shore of .... Jos 15:5
Sea was the western **b**. .... Jos 15:12
The northern **b** started at the .... Jos 18:12
Jordan River a **b** between us and .... Jos 22:25
as far as the **b** of Egypt. 2Ch 9:26
an old stone that marks a **b**, ... Pr 22:28
to the LORD at the **b** of Egypt. .... Is 19:19
wheat as a **b** around the field .... Is 28:25
beaches to be a **b** for the sea, ... Je 5:22
you at the **b** of Israel so you .... Eze 11:10
So the **b** line will go from the .... Eze 47:17
Hamath, on the **b**, and against .... Zch 9:2

BORDERS
and expand the **b** of your land. .... Ex 34:24
These shall be the **b**: .... Nu 34:2
He set up **b** for the people and .... Dt 32:8
Inside these **b** lived the family .... Jos 15:12
desert around the **b** of the lands .... Jdg 11:18
all the way to Gaza and its **b**, ... 2Ki 18:8
You set **b** for the seas that they .... Ps 104:9
to go beyond the **b** he had set. .... Pr 8:29
You made the **b** of the land wide. .... Is 26:15
cities that border Moab's **b**, ... Eze 25:9
when they walk over our **b**. .... Mic 5:6
even outside the **b** of Israel!'" .... Mal 1:5

BORING
Everything is **b**, so boring that .... Ec 1:8

BORN
After Seth was **b**, Adam lived 800 .... Ge 5:4
Methuselah was **b**, Enoch walked .... Ge 5:22
After Noah was **b**, Lamech lived .... Ge 5:30
and daughters were **b** to them. .... Ge 6:1
Abram, Nahor, and Haran were **b**. .... Ge 11:26
so a slave **b** in my house will .... Ge 15:3
New nations will be **b** from you, ... Ge 17:6
includes any boy **b** among your .... Ge 17:12
old when his son Isaac was **b**. .... Ge 21:5
The first baby was **b** red. .... Ge 25:25
young that were **b** were streaked, ... Ge 30:39
Joseph was **b** when his father .... Ge 37:3
red string on his hand was **b**, ... Ge 38:30
of Leah and Jacob **b** in Northwest .... Ge 46:15
Joseph had two sons **b** in Egypt, ... Ge 46:27
when he was **b**, Moses said, "I am .... Ex 18:3
her baby die before it is **b**, ... Ex 23:26
or a goat is **b**, it must stay .... Le 22:27
the first son **b** to Israel, ... Nu 1:20
a baby is **b** with half of its .... Nu 12:12
The first one **b** to any family, ... Nu 18:15
the first son **b** to Israel, ... Nu 26:5
first animals **b** to your herds .... Dt 12:6
those who were **b** in the desert .... Jos 5:5
God as a Nazirite since I was **b**. .... Jdg 16:17

"This boy was **b** for Naomi." .... Ru 4:17
The child was **b**, but the mother 1Sa 4:19
Sons were **b** to David at Hebron. 2Sa 3:2
and daughters were **b** to David. 2Sa 5:13
B next after Absalom, Adonijah 1Ki 1:6
David's children **b** in Jerusalem: 1Ch 14:4
I was naked when I was **b**, ... Job 1:21
So why did you allow me to be **b**? .... Job 10:18
How can someone **b** to a woman be .... Job 15:14
on you since the day I was **b**; .... Ps 22:10
tell lies as soon as they are **b**, ... Ps 58:3
be like a child **b** dead who never .... Ps 58:8
depended on you since I was **b**; .... Ps 71:6
mountains were **b** and before you .... Ps 90:2
are not yet **b** will praise the .... Ps 102:18
was **b** before there were oceans, ... Pr 8:24
is a time to be **b** and a time to .... Ec 3:2
A baby **b** dead is useless. .... Ec 6:4
the apple tree where you were **b**; .... Sng 8:5
A child has been **b** to us; .... Is 9:6
as when a child should be **b**, ... Is 37:3
carried you since you were **b**; .... Is 46:3
Before I was **b**, the LORD called .... Is 49:1
Before you were **b**, I set you .... Je 1:5
day you were **b**, your cord was .... Eze 16:4
hated on the day you were **b**. .... Eze 16:5
the two of them were being **b**. .... Hos 12:3
to Babylon until Christ was **b**. .... Mt 1:17
When Jesus was **b**, some wise men .... Mt 2:1
than any other person ever **b**, ... Mt 11:11
Some men were **b** without the .... Mt 19:12
something new is about to be **b**, ... Mt 24:8
for him if he had never been **b**." .... Mt 26:24
She was Greek, **b** in Phoenicia, ... Mk 7:26
something new is about to be **b**, ... Mk 13:8
for him if he had never been **b**." .... Mk 14:21
your Savior was **b** in the town of .... Lk 2:11
desire. They were **b** of God. .... Jn 1:13
unless you are **b** again, you .... Jn 3:3
before Abraham was even **b**, ... Jn 8:58
saw a man who had been **b** blind. .... Jn 9:1
You were **b** full of sin! .... Jn 9:34
when her baby is **b**, she forgets .... Jn 16:21
is why I was **b** and came into .... Jn 18:37
Joseph, a Levite **b** in Cyprus. .... Ac 4:36
Moses was **b**, and he was very .... Ac 7:20
a man who had been **b** crippled; .... Ac 14:8
who had been **b** in the country .... Ac 18:2
He was **b** in the city of .... Ac 18:24
b in Tarsus in the country of .... Ac 22:3
Paul said, "I was **b** a citizen." .... Ac 22:28
family into which Christ was **b**, ... Rm 9:5
but also man is **b** from woman. 1Co 11:12
We were not **b** as non-Jewish .... Gal 2:15
The son who was **b** in the normal .... Gal 4:29
You were not **b** Jewish. You are .... Eph 2:11
was **b** as a man and became like .... Php 2:7
when he was **b**, or when he died .... Heb 7:3
Levi was not yet **b**, but he was .... Heb 7:10
for three months after he was **b**. .... Heb 11:23
You have been **b** again, and this 1Pe 1:23
her baby as soon as it was **b**. .... Rev 12:4

BORROW
will not need to **b** from them. .... Dt 15:6
The wicked **b** and don't pay back, ... Ps 37:21
to those who **b** and those who .... Is 24:2
someone who wants to **b** from you. .... Mt 5:42

BORROWED
the one who **b** it must pay the .... Ex 22:14
Oh, my master! I **b** that ax!" 2Ki 6:5
I have not loaned or **b** anything, ... Je 15:10
He came to us and **b** Paul's belt .... Ac 21:11

BORROWERS
and **b** are servants to lenders.................. Pr 22:7

BORROWING
We are **b** money to pay the king's .... Ne 5:4

BORROWS
If a man **b** an animal from his .... Ex 22:14

BOSS
because your **b** is angry with you .... Ec 10:4
said to the **b** of all the workers .... Mt 20:8

BOTHER
but let me **b** you this one last .... Ge 18:32
Don't **b** the people of Moab. .... Dt 2:9
the young men not to **b** you. .... Ru 2:9
will no longer **b** them as they 2Sa 7:10
Then he won't **b** you again." 2Sa 14:10
Why **b** yourself with order? 2Ki 9:18
Do not **b** the work on that Temple .... Ezr 6:7
of a problem to **b** the king." .... Est 7:4
My conscience will never **b** me. .... Job 27:6
there will be no one to **b** them. .... Is 17:2
Then he will not **b** the king of .... Da 11:8
the others said, "Don't **b** him................... Mt 27:49
is no need to **b** the teacher .... Mk 5:35
Don't **b** the teacher anymore." .... Lk 8:49
the house answers, 'Don't **b** me!............... Lk 11:7
will continue to **b** me until I am .... Lk 18:5
said, "Does this teaching **b** you?............... Jn 6:61
we should not **b** the other people .... Ac 15:19
But this did not **b** Gallio......................... Ac 18:17
you, do not let that **b** you. 1Co 7:21

BOTHERED
They will not be **b** anymore. 2Sa 7:10
Why should you be **b** with me? 2Sa 19:35
They will not be **b** anymore. 1Ch 17:9
The tents of robbers are not **b**, ... Job 12:6
people may be **b** by trouble seven .... Pr 24:16
had dreams that **b** him and kept.............. Da 2:1
John's preaching always **b** him, ... Mk 6:20
who were **b** by evil spirits, ... Ac 5:16
This **b** Paul, so he turned and .... Ac 16:18

BOTHERING
day, because she kept **b** him. .... Jdg 14:17
She kept **b** Samson about his .... Jdg 16:16
out what was **b** Mordecai and why .... Est 4:5
people who are **b** you would .... Gal 5:12

BOTHERS
a dream that **b** me, and I want .... Da 2:3

BOTHERSOME
wife is as **b** as a continual .... Pr 27:15

BOTTLE
take this small **b** of olive oil 2Ki 9:1

BOTTLED
am like wine that has been **b** up; .... Job 32:19

BOTTLES
waists, their **b** of perfume, ... Is 3:20

BOTTOM
they sank to the **b** like a rock. .... Ex 15:5
altar near the **b** of the mountain.............. Ex 24:4
is left at the **b** of the altar. .... Ex 29:12
them at the **b** of the mountain. .... Ex 32:19
the blood at the **b** of the altar .... Le 4:18
stood at the **b** of the mountain .... Dt 4:11
you will be on top and not on **b**............... Dt 28:13
went down to the **b** of the hill, ... Jos 18:16
the valley at the **b** of the hill .... Jdg 7:1
rooms on the **b** floor were seven.............. 1Ki 6:6
down to the **b** of the chariot. 1Ki 22:35
dig away at the **b** of the .... Job 28:9
spot from the **b** of your foot to .... Is 1:6

LORD, from the **b** of the pit. .... La 3:55
the sea and have sunk to the **b**. .... Eze 27:34
flowed around the **b** of the tree .... Eze 31:4
so that even the **b** of the doors .... Am 9:1
from me at the **b** of the sea, ... Am 9:3
pieces, from the top to the **b**. .... Mt 27:51
pieces, from the top to the **b**. .... Mk 15:38
of cloth, woven from top to **b**................... Jn 19:23

BOTTOMLESS
hole that leads to the **b** pit. .... Rev 9:1
who was the angel of the **b** pit. .... Rev 9:11
up from the **b** pit will fight .... Rev 11:7
up out of the **b** pit and go away .... Rev 17:8
the key to the **b** pit and a large .... Rev 20:1
he threw him into the **b** pit, ... Rev 20:3

BOUGHT
in your family or **b** as a slave.................. Ge 17:13
So Abraham **b** the field and the .... Ge 23:20
who had **b** Joseph had taken .... Ge 37:36
He **b** Joseph from the Ishmaelites .... Ge 39:1
Joseph **b** all the land in Egypt .... Ge 47:20
Abraham **b** the field and cave................. Ge 49:30
If the man who **b** her promises to .... Ex 21:9
lives have been **b** back." .... Ex 30:16
girl has not been **b** or given her .... Le 19:20
pay back the one who **b** it. .... Le 25:27
gift cannot be **b** back or sold. .... Le 27:28
land Jacob had **b** for a hundred .... Jos 24:32
traded or **b** back something, ... Ru 4:7
one little female lamb he had **b**. 2Sa 12:3
So David **b** the threshing floor 2Sa 24:24
His traders **b** them in Kue. 1Ki 10:28
He **b** the hill of Samaria from.................. 1Ki 16:24
his traders **b** them in Kue. 2Ch 1:16
we have **b** freedom for our fellow .... Ne 5:8
Wisdom cannot be **b** with gold, ... Job 28:15
God **b** my life back from death, ... Job 33:28
the people you **b** long ago. .... Ps 74:2
away and brag about what they **b**. .... Pr 20:14
I **b** male and female slaves,..................... Ec 2:7
So I **b** a linen belt, just as the .... Je 13:2
I **b** the field at Anathoth from.................. Je 32:9
So I **b** her for six ounces of..................... Hos 3:2
decisions are **b** for a price. .... Mic 7:3
sold everything he had and **b** it. .... Mt 13:46
Joseph **b** some linen cloth, ... Mk 15:46
and Salome **b** some sweet-smelling .... Mk 16:1
I have just **b** a field, and I .... Lk 14:18
Judas **b** a field with the money .... Ac 1:18
grave Abraham had **b** for a sum of........... Ac 7:16
which he **b** with the death of his.............. Ac 20:28
because you were **b** by God for a 1Co 6:20
You all were **b** at a great price, ... 1Co 7:23
You were **b**, not with something 1Pe 1:18
Jesus, who **b** their freedom. 2Pe 2:1
your death you **b** people for God .... Rev 5:9
who had been **b** from the earth. .... Rev 14:3

BOULDER
tries to roll a **b** down on others .... Pr 26:27

BOULDERS
anyone who moves **b** might be hurt .... Ec 10:9

BOUNCED
in my arms and **b** on my knees. .... Is 66:12

BOUNCING
galloping and chariots **b** along! .... Nah 3:2

BOUND
If people are **b** in chains, ... Job 36:8
ropes of death **b** me, and the .... Ps 116:3
in Ramah **b** in chains with .... Je 40:1
two soldiers, **b** with two chains. .... Ac 12:6

I am **b** with this chain because I .... Ac 28:20
the whole world is **b** by sin. .... Gal 3:22
point of being **b** with chains 2Ti 2:9
b with everlasting chains, ... Jud 1:6

BOUNDARY
That **b** continued until it was .... Jos 18:12

BOW
So take your **b** and arrows and go .... Ge 27:3
and I will **b** down to you?" .... Ge 37:10
brothers will **b** down to you. .... Ge 49:8
but he aims his **b** well. His arms .... Ge 49:24
They will **b** facedown to the .... Ex 11:8
You must not **b** down to their .... Ex 23:24
in your land to **b** down to, ... Le 26:1
But don't **b** down and worship .... Dt 4:19
will come and **b** down before him. 1Sa 2:36
his sword, **b**, and belt. 1Sa 18:4
Jonathan's **b** did not fail to 2Sa 1:22
come near Absalom to **b** to him. 2Sa 15:5
Ziba said, "I **b** to you. 2Sa 16:4
so my arms can bend a bronze **b**. 2Sa 22:35
You made my enemies **b** before me. 2Sa 22:40
Then I must **b** in that temple. 2Ki 5:18
captured with your sword and **b**. 2Ki 6:22
Jehu drew his **b** and shot Joram 2Ki 9:24
Do not **b** down to them or worship 2Ki 17:35
Mordecai would not **b** down to him .... Est 3:5
will string his **b** and take aim. .... Ps 7:12
so my arms can bend a bronze **b**. .... Ps 18:34
You made my enemies **b** before me. .... Ps 18:39
Everyone will **b** down to him, ... Ps 22:29
I don't trust my **b** to help me, ... Ps 44:6
of the desert **b** down to him, ... Ps 72:9
Let all kings **b** down to him and .... Ps 72:11
like a crooked **b** that does not .... Ps 78:57
the LORD would **b** before him. .... Ps 81:15
let's worship him and **b** down. .... Ps 95:6
I will **b** down facing your holy .... Ps 138:2
Evil people will **b** down to those .... Pr 14:19
the wicked will **b** down at the .... Pr 14:19
but will **b** low with shame. .... Is 2:9
and they will **b** low with shame. .... Is 2:11
been captured without using a **b**. .... Is 22:3
uses his **b**, and they are blown .... Is 41:2
They will **b** down before you and .... Is 45:14
Bel and Nebo **b** down. Their idols .... Is 46:1
These gods will all **b** down. .... Is 46:2
Then they **b** down and worship it. .... Is 46:6
leaders will **b** down before you, ... Is 49:7
people just to **b** their heads .... Is 58:5
hurt you will **b** down to you; .... Is 60:14
They use their tongues like a **b**, ... Je 9:3
I will soon break Elam's **b**, ... Je 49:35
he prepared to shoot his **b**, ... La 2:4
of Jerusalem **b** their heads to .... La 2:10
to shoot his **b** and made me .... La 3:12
will knock your **b** out of your .... Eze 39:3
who doesn't **b** down and worship .... Da 3:6
the land the **b** and the sword .... Hos 2:18
like a loose **b** that can't shoot .... Hos 7:16
when I **b** before God on high? .... Mic 6:6
uncovered your **b** and commanded .... Hab 3:9
Judah like a **b** and Ephraim like .... Zch 9:13
peg, the battle **b**, and every .... Zch 10:4
If you will **b** down and worship .... Mt 4:9
'Everyone will **b** before me; .... Rm 14:11
So they will **b** down and worship 1Co 14:25
So I **b** in prayer before the .... Eph 3:14
every knee will **b** to the name of .... Php 2:10
before you and **b** at your feet, ... Rev 3:9
twenty-four elders **b** down before .... Rev 4:10
The rider on the horse held a **b**, ... Rev 6:2

BOWED
Then Abram **b** facedown on the .... Ge 17:3
Abraham **b** facedown on the ground .... Ge 17:17
Abraham rose and **b** to the people .... Ge 23:7
and I **b** my head and thanked the .... Ge 24:48
came up to Esau and **b** down flat .... Ge 33:6
around it and **b** down to it." .... Ge 37:7
came to him and **b** facedown on .... Ge 42:6
And they **b** low before Joseph to .... Ge 43:28
Israel's lap and **b** facedown to .... Ge 48:12
went to him and **b** low before him .... Ge 50:18
they **b** down and worshiped him. .... Ex 4:31
Then the people **b** down and .... Ex 12:27
and **b** down and kissed .... Ex 18:7
Moses quickly **b** to the ground .... Ex 34:8
shouted with joy and **b** facedown .... Le 9:24
Moses and Aaron **b** facedown in .... Nu 14:5
Then Balaam **b** facedown on the .... Nu 22:31
Then I again **b** facedown on the .... Dt 9:18
other gods and **b** down to them or .... Dt 17:3
Then Joshua **b** facedown on the .... Jos 5:14
He **b** facedown on the ground .... Jos 7:6
Then Ruth **b** low with her face to .... Ru 2:10
He **b** facedown on the ground 1Sa 20:41
David **b** facedown on the ground. 1Sa 24:8
off her donkey and **b** facedown on 1Sa 25:23
He came and **b** facedown on the 2Sa 1:2
Mephibosheth **b** to David again 2Sa 9:8
She **b** facedown on the ground to 2Sa 14:4
Joab **b** facedown on the ground 2Sa 14:22
Absalom came and **b** facedown on 2Sa 14:33
The Cushite **b** to Joab and ran 2Sa 18:21
Bathsheba **b** and knelt before the 1Ki 1:16
And King David **b** down on his bed 1Ki 1:47
before King Solomon and **b** down. 1Ki 1:53
have never **b** down before Baal 1Ki 19:18
David and the elders **b** facedown 1Ch 21:16
they **b** down on the pavement with 2Ch 7:3
Jehoshaphat **b** facedown on the 2Ch 20:18
of Judah came and **b** down to King 2Ch 24:17
He **b** down to them and offered 2Ch 25:14
Then they **b** down and worshiped .... Ne 8:6
Then he **b** down to the ground to .... Job 1:20
I **b** in sadness as if I were .... Ps 35:14
I am bent over and **b** down; .... Ps 38:6
on earth **b** down before you .... Is 14:12
I **b** facedown on the ground and .... Eze 1:28
I **b** facedown on the ground and I .... Eze 9:8
Then I **b** facedown on the ground .... Eze 11:13
I **b** facedown on the ground. .... Eze 43:3
they **b** down and worshiped the .... Da 3:7
I was very afraid and **b** facedown .... Da 8:17
b facedown and could not speak. .... Da 10:15
and they **b** down and worshiped .... Mt 2:11
The man **b** down before him and .... Mt 8:2
He **b** down before Jesus and said, ... Mt 9:18
to Jesus again and **b** before him .... Mt 15:25
came to Jesus and **b** before him. .... Mt 17:14
She **b** before him and asked him .... Mt 20:20
Then the soldiers **b** before Jesus. .... Mt 27:29
he **b** down before Jesus and said, ... Lk 5:8
he **b** before him and begged him, ... Lk 5:12
Then he **b** down at Jesus' feet .... Lk 17:16
very afraid and **b** their heads to .... Lk 24:5
Then he **b** his head and died. .... Jn 19:30
have never **b** down before Baal. .... Rm 11:4
twenty-four elders **b** down before .... Rev 5:8
and the elders **b** down and .... Rev 5:14
They all **b** down on their faces .... Rev 7:11
b down on their faces and .... Rev 11:16
living creatures **b** down and .... Rev 19:4
I **b** down at the angel's feet .... Rev 19:10
I **b** down to worship at the feet .... Rev 22:8

B

BOWING

and eleven stars **b** down to me."............... Ge 37:9
about his brothers **b** to him. .... Ge 42:9
b down to the ground before him. 2Ki 2:15
at Elisha's feet, **b** facedown to 2Ki 4:37
fun of him by **b** on their knees .... Mk 15:19

BOWL

dip it into the **b** filled with .... Ex 12:22
Make a bronze **b**, on a bronze .... Ex 30:18
made the bronze **b** for washing, ... Ex 38:8
Moses put the **b** between the .... Ex 40:30
animal falls into a clay **b**, ... Le 11:33
in a clay **b** containing fresh .... Le 14:50
a body fluid touches a clay **b**, ... Le 15:12
got a full **b** of water from it. .... Jdg 6:38
from bronze a large round **b**, ... 1Ki 7:23
The **b** rested on the backs of 1Ki 7:25
sides of the **b** were four inches 1Ki 7:26
Each **b** was six feet across and 1Ki 7:38
me a new **b** and put salt in it. 2Ki 2:20
the large bronze **b**, which was 1Ch 18:8
the large **b** with twelve bulls 2Ch 4:15
as gold apples in a silver **b**..................... Pr 25:11
person like grain in a **b**, ... Pr 27:22
chain or break like a golden **b**. .... Ec 12:6
Who has used a **b** to measure all .... Is 40:12
large bronze **b**, which is called .... Je 27:19
large bronze **b**, called the Sea............... Je 52:17
put them in one **b**, and make them .... Eze 4:9
lampstand with a **b** at the top. .... Zch 4:2
be filled like a **b** used for .... Zch 9:15
don't hide a light under a **b**. .... Mt 5:15
with me into the **b** is the one .... Mt 26:23
a lamp under a **b** or under a bed? .... Mk 4:21
his bread into the **b** with me. .... Mk 14:20
covers it with a **b** or hides it .... Lk 8:16
in a secret place or under a **b**, ... Lk 11:33
water into a **b** and began to wash .... Jn 13:5
poured out his **b** on the land. .... Rev 16:2

BOWL-SHAPED

above the **b** section and next to 1Ki 7:20

BOWLFUL

wine by the **b** and use the best .... Am 6:6

BOWLS

wrapped the **b** for making dough .... Ex 12:34
blood from the **b** and sprinkled .... Ex 24:8
pots, shovels, **b** for sprinkling................ Ex 38:3
plates, pans, **b**, and the jars .... Nu 4:7
twelve silver **b**, and twelve gold .... Nu 7:84
brought basic **b**, clay pots, ... 2Sa 17:28
Huram also made ten bronze **b**, ... 1Ki 7:38
hot coals, the **b**, and everything 2Ki 25:15
make the forks, **b**, and pitchers 1Ch 28:17
gold to make a hundred other **b**. 2Ch 4:8
brought out the **b** and pans that .... Ezr 1:7
hundred ten matching silver **b**, ... Ezr 1:10
gold and silver **b** and pans that .... Ezr 5:14
of gold, 50 **b**, and 530 pieces .... Ne 7:70
will be like **b** and jars hanging .... Is 22:24
Then I put some **b** full of wine .... Je 35:5
and **b** used for drink offerings. .... Je 52:19
will be like the holy altar **b**. .... Zch 14:20
and golden **b** full of incense .... Rev 5:8
angels seven golden **b** filled .... Rev 15:7
out the seven **b** of God's anger .... Rev 16:1

BOWS

land without using swords and **b**. .... Jos 24:12
The **b** of warriors break, but 1Sa 2:4
shields and swords and **b**. 1Ch 5:18
They came with **b** for weapons and 1Ch 12:2
helmets, armor, **b**, and stones 2Ch 26:14

their swords, spears, and **b**. .... Ne 4:13
he wicked string their **b**; .... Ps 11:2
hearts, and their **b** will break.................. Ps 37:15
He breaks all **b** and spears and .... Ps 46:9
of Ephraim had **b** for weapons, ... Ps 78:9
and all of their **b** are ready to................ Is 5:28
to kill, from **b** ready to shoot, ... Is 21:15
makes the idol and **b** down to it! .... Is 44:15
The soldiers carry **b** and spears............... Je 6:23
soldiers from Lydia who use **b**. .... Je 46:9
prepare their **b** to shoot. .... Je 51:3
and their **b** are broken, because .... Je 51:56
small shields, **b** and arrows, war .... Eze 39:9
but not by using **b** or swords, ... Hos 1:7
Soldiers with **b** and arrows will .... Am 2:15
b used in war will be broken. .... Zch 9:10

BOWSTRINGS

Samson broke the **b** like pieces .... Jdg 16:9
they set their arrows on the **b**. .... Ps 11:2

BOX

offering in a **b** beside the Ark. 1Sa 6:8
the LORD and the **b** with the gold 1Sa 6:11
priest took a **b** and made a hole 2Ki 12:9
Temple of the LORD into the **b**. 2Ki 12:9
that the **b** was full of money, ... 2Ki 12:10
put it in the **b** until the box 2Ch 24:10
stay by your feeding **b** at night? .... Job 39:9
the Temple money **b** and watched .... Mk 12:41
cloth and lying in a feeding **b**." .... Lk 2:12
gifts into the Temple money **b**. .... Lk 21:1
the one who kept the money **b**, ... Jn 12:6

BOXER

I fight like a **b** who is hitting 1Co 9:26

BOXES

the little **b** holding Scriptures .... Mt 23:5

BOY

on when a baby **b** is eight days .... Ge 17:12
includes any **b** born among your .... Ge 17:12
heard the **b** crying, and God's................ Ge 21:17
was with the **b** as he grew up. .... Ge 21:20
she named the **b** Son of My .... Ge 35:18
and said, "The **b** is not there! .... Ge 37:30
I told you not to harm the **b**, ... Ge 42:22
sees the young **b** is not with us, ... Ge 44:31
they let all the **b** babies live. .... Ex 1:17
Every time a **b** is born to the .... Ex 1:22
the basket and saw the baby **b**. .... Ex 2:6
who gives birth to a **b** or girl. .... Le 12:7
price for a baby **b** one month to .... Le 27:6
Ever since he was a young **b**, ... Nu 11:28
was only a **b** and was afraid, ... Jdg 8:20
because the **b** will be a Nazirite .... Jdg 13:7
do for the **b** who will be born .... Jdg 13:8
gave birth to a **b** and named him .... Jdg 13:24
Naomi took the **b**, held him in .... Ru 4:16
When the **b** is old enough to eat 1Sa 1:22
but the **b** continued to serve the 1Sa 2:11
And the **b** Samuel grew up serving 1Sa 2:18
You're only a **b**. Goliath has 1Sa 17:33
and saw that he was only a **b**,................ 1Sa 17:42
The **b** picked up the arrow and 1Sa 20:38
But a **b** saw Jonathan and Ahimaaz 2Sa 17:18
time Hadad was only a young **b**, ... 1Ki 11:17
Elijah took the **b** from her, ... 1Ki 17:19
lay on top of the **b** three times. 1Ki 17:21
Elijah carried the **b** downstairs 1Ki 17:23
the **b** was lying dead on his bed. 2Ki 4:32
The **b** sneezed seven times and 2Ki 4:35
brought a dead **b** back to life. 2Ki 8:5
it was said, 'A **b** is born!'........................ Job 3:3
I was a young **b** in my father's .... Pr 4:3

A poor but wise **b** is better than .... Ec 4:13
Name the **b** .... Is 8:3
before the **b** learns to say 'my.................. Is 8:4
how to speak. I am only a **b**." .... Je 1:6
with you? Bring the **b** here." .... Mt 17:17
the demon inside the **b**. .... Mt 17:18
it made the **b** lose control of .... Mk 9:20
these things since I was a **b**." .... Mk 10:20
to give birth, she had a **b**. .... Lk 1:57
The **b** Jesus stayed behind in .... Lk 2:43
and healed the **b** and gave him .... Lk 9:42
these commands since I was a **b**." .... Lk 18:21
Here is a **b** with five loaves of............... Jn 6:9
a baby **b** on a Sabbath day..................... Jn 7:22
a baby **b** can be circumcise on .... Jn 7:23

BOY'S
the walking stick on the **b** face, ... 2Ki 4:31
Jesus asked the **b** father,...................... Mk 9:21
hold of the **b** hand and helped .... Mk 9:27

BOYHOOD
make me suffer for my **b** sins. .... Job 13:26

BOYS
When the **b** grew up, Esau became........... Ge 25:27
brought the **b** close to him, ... Ge 48:10
that he will bless these **b**. .... Ge 48:16
name be known through these **b**, ... Ge 48:16
Why did you let the **b** live?" .... Ex 1:18
the Midianite **b**, and kill all.................... Nu 31:17
forty-two of the **b** to pieces. 2Ki 2:24
to take my two **b** as his slaves!" 2Ki 4:1
Even the little **b** hate me and .... Job 19:18
will cause young **b** to be your................. Is 3:4
and **b** stumbled under loads of .... La 5:13
They traded **b** for prostitutes, ... Joe 3:3
filled with **b** and girls playing. .... Zch 8:5
kill all the baby **b** in Bethlehem .... Mt 2:16

BOZRAH
became king. Jobab was from **B.** .... Ge 36:33
became king. He was from **B.**................. 1Ch 1:44
the city of **B,** dressed in red .... Is 63:1
Kerioth and **B.** Judgment has come .... Je 48:24
its wings over the city of **B.** .... Je 49:22
the strong buildings of **B.**" .... Am 1:12

BRACED
He **b** himself between the two .... Jdg 16:29

BRACELET
his head and the **b** from his arm, ... 2Sa 1:10

BRACELETS
two gold arm **b** weighing about .... Ge 24:22
pins, earrings, rings, and **b**. .... Ex 35:22
arm bands, **b**, signet rings, ... Nu 31:50
beautiful ankle **b**, their .... Is 3:18
b on your arms, a necklace................... Eze 16:11
They put **b** on the wrists of the .... Eze 23:42

BRACES
the Holy Tent, the **b**, the posts, ... Nu 3:36
of silver and its **b** of gold. .... Sng 3:10

BRAG
I didn't want their enemy to **b;** .... Dt 32:27
Israelites to **b** that they saved .... Jdg 7:2
puts on his armor should not **b**. 1Ki 20:11
Stay at home and. Don't ask 2Ki 14:10
have become proud, and you **b**. 2Ch 25:19
They **b** about the things they .... Ps 10:3
are selfish and **b** about .... Ps 17:10
laugh at me or **b** when I am .... Ps 38:16
their money and **b** about their .... Ps 49:6
why do you **b** about the evil you............. Ps 52:1
They **b** to the sky. They say that .... Ps 73:9
are proud, 'Don't **b**,' and to the .... Ps 75:4

who do evil **b** about what they .... Ps 94:4
they **b** about their gods. .... Ps 97:7
go away and **b** about what they .... Pr 20:14
Don't **b** to the king and act as................ Pr 25:6
People who **b** about gifts they .... Pr 25:14
Don't **b** about tomorrow;..................... Pr 27:1
the proud and those who **b,** .... Is 2:12
are proud and **b** by saying, ... Is 9:9
message, you who **b,** you leaders .... Is 28:14
The wise must not **b** about their .... Je 9:23
rich must not **b** about their .... Je 9:23
He will **b** about himself and .... Da 11:36
their leaders **b** about their .... Hos 7:16
b about the special offerings .... Am 4:5
Do not **b** when cruel things are .... Ob 1:12
will no longer **b** about their .... Mic 7:16
this city those who like to **b;** .... Zph 3:11
conceited and **b** about themselves .... Rm 1:30
You **b** about having God's law, ... Rm 2:23
a reason to **b** about ourselves .... Rm 3:27
So do not **b** about those branches .... Rm 11:18
should be only about the Lord................. 1Co 1:31
it is true that I **b** about you in 1Co 15:31
I will **b** about the things that 2Co 11:30
must continue to **b**. It will do 2Co 12:1
I will **b** about a man like that,............... 2Co 12:5
so they can **b** about what they .... Gal 6:13
so you cannot **b** about it...................... Eph 2:9
So we **b** about you to the other 2Th 1:4
love money, **b,** and be proud. 2Ti 3:2
in your hearts, do not **b**. .... Jam 3:14
But now you are proud and you **b**. .... Jam 4:16
They **b** with words that mean 2Pe 2:18
b about themselves, and they .... Jud 1:16

BRAGGED
The enemy **b**, 'I'll chase them .... Ex 15:9
care for, the flock you **b** about? .... Je 13:20
b and called himself a great man. .... Ac 8:9
I **b** to Titus about you, and you 2Co 7:14

BRAGGER
proud," "b," and "mocker."..................... Pr 21:24

BRAGGING
to Gaal, "Where is your **b** now? .... Jdg 9:38
Don't continue **b**, don't speak 1Sa 2:3
and cut off those **b** tongues. .... Ps 12:3
hate pride and **b**, evil ways and .... Pr 8:13
but their **b** means nothing. .... Is 16:6
This kind of **b** pleases me,".................. Je 9:24
Moab's **b** accomplishes nothing. .... Je 48:30
a mouth, and the mouth was **b**. .... Da 7:8
because the little horn was **b**. .... Da 7:11
eyes and a mouth that kept **b**............... Da 7:20
way of faith that stops all **b**, ... Rm 3:27
Your **b** is not good. 1Co 5:6
have my reason for **b** taken away. 1Co 9:15
not give me any reason for **b**. 1Co 9:16
I have been **b** about this to the 2Co 9:2
you so that our **b** about you in 2Co 9:3
will limit our **b** to the work.................. 2Co 10:13
Christ is my only reason for **b**. .... Gal 6:14
b is a lie that hides the truth. .... Jam 3:14
All of this **b** is wrong. .... Jam 4:16

BRAGS
Whoever **b** a lot is asking for .... Pr 17:19
but it **b** about great things. .... Jam 3:5

BRAIDED
not using **b** hair or gold or 1Ti 2:9

BRAIDS
the seven **b** of Samson's hair. .... Jdg 16:19

BRANCH

his young donkey to the best **b**. .... Ge 49:11
Take a **b** of the hyssop plant, ... Ex 12:22
Each **b** must have three cups .... Ex 25:33
b had three cups shaped like .... Ex 37:19
they cut off a **b** of a grapevine .... Nu 13:23
stick, a hyssop **b,** and a red .... Nu 19:6
must take a hyssop **b** and dip it .... Nu 19:18
time the LORD's **b** will be very .... Is 4:2
away both the **b** and stalk in one .... Is 9:14
new **b** will grow from a stump of .... Is 11:1
your grave, like an unwanted **b**. .... Is 14:19
I will make a good **b** sprout from .... Je 33:15
also take a young **b** from the top .... Eze 17:22
spread from the vine's main **b,** .... Eze 19:14
bring my servant called the **B.** .... Zch 3:8
the Branch will **b** out from where .... Zch 6:12
not a root or **b** will be left,".................. Mal 4:1
A **b** cannot produce fruit alone .... Jn 15:4
they are like a **b** that is thrown .... Jn 15:6
the sponge on a **b** of a hyssop .... Jn 19:29
are like the **b** of a wild olive .... Rm 11:17
those Jews are like a **b** that.................. Rm 11:24
red wool and a **b** of the hyssop .... Heb 9:19

BRANCHED

there the river **b** out to become .... Ge 2:10

BRANCHES

Jacob cut green **b** from poplar, ... Ge 30:37
flocks mated in front of the **b**. .... Ge 30:39
I watched the **b** bud and blossom, ... Ge 40:10
Each of the six **b** going out from .... Ex 25:33
The **b**, buds, and lampstand must .... Ex 25:36
as well as **b** from palm trees, ... Le 23:40
all those men cut **b** and followed .... Jdg 9:49
under the thick **b** of a large oak 2Sa 18:9
and bring back **b** from olive and .... Ne 8:15
again and will send out new **b**. .... Job 14:7
A flame will dry up their **b;**.................. Job 15:30
dew will lie on the **b** all night. .... Job 29:19
Our **b** reached the Mediterranean .... Ps 80:11
they sing among the tree **b**. .... Ps 104:12
With **b** in your hands, join the .... Ps 118:27
like olive **b** that produce many .... Ps 128:3
olives are left in the top **b**. .... Is 17:6
there and eat leaves from the **b**. .... Is 27:10
her people as if they were **b,** .... Je 5:10
and its **b** will be burned up. .... Je 11:16
like thorny **b** and stickers all .... Eze 2:6
The **b** turned toward the eagle, ... Eze 17:6
it will grow **b** and give fruit .... Eze 17:23
in the shelter of the tree's **b**. .... Eze 17:23
vine had many **b** and gave much .... Eze 19:10
Its strong **b** were broken off and .... Eze 19:12
be like thorny **b** or sharp .... Eze 28:24
with beautiful **b** that shaded the .... Eze 31:3
animals gave birth under its **b**. .... Eze 31:6
will grow **b** and fruit for my .... Eze 36:8
and the birds lived in its **b**. .... Da 4:12
down the tree and cut off its **b**. .... Da 4:14
They will be like spreading **b,**............... Hos 14:6
my trees and left the **b** white. .... Joe 1:7
the two olive **b** beside the two .... Zch 4:12
come and build nests in its **b**." .... Mt 13:32
Others cut **b** from the trees and .... Mt 21:8
When its **b** become green and soft .... Mt 24:32
Using thorny **b,** they made a .... Mt 27:29
produces large **b,** and the wild .... Mk 4:32
Others cut **b** in the fields and .... Mk 11:8
When its **b** become green and soft .... Mk 13:28
used thorny **b** to make a crown .... Mk 15:17
birds build nests in its **b**." .... Lk 13:19
So they took **b** of palm trees and .... Jn 12:13

am the vine, and you are the **b**. .... Jn 15:5
from some thorny **b** and put it on .... Jn 19:2
then the tree's **b** are holy too. .... Rm 11:16
holding palm **b** in their hands. .... Rev 7:9

BRAND

will wear the **b** of a captive. .... Is 3:24

BRAVE

been **b** to speak to the Lord. .... Ge 18:27
and no one is **b** enough to wake........... Ge 49:9
no one would be **b** enough to wake .... Nu 24:9
and help him be **b** and strong. .... Dt 3:28
Be strong and **b**. Don't be afraid............ Dt 31:6
strong and **b,** because you will .... Dt 31:7
Be strong and **b,** because you .... Dt 31:23
Joshua, be strong and **b!**................... Jos 1:6
to his men, "Be strong and **b!**.............. Jos 10:25
So 18,000 **b** Benjaminite fighters .... Jdg 20:44
Be **b,** Philistines! Fight like 1Sa 4:9
hearts of certain **b** men who went 1Sa 10:26
the **b** men of Jabesh marched all 1Sa 31:12
be strong and **b**. Saul your 2Sa 2:7
am **b** enough to pray to you. 2Sa 7:27
men who are as **b** as lions will 2Sa 17:10
of Jehoiada was a **b** fighter from 2Sa 23:20
He was a mighty and **b** man, ... 2Ki 5:1
all strong, **b,** and famous men 1Ch 5:24
So the **b** men of Jabesh went and 1Ch 10:12
men of Manasseh were **b** soldiers, ... 1Ch 12:21
Be strong and **b**. Don't be afraid 1Ch 22:13
Benaiah was a **b** warrior who led 1Ch 27:6
Be strong and **b**. Don't be afraid........... 2Ch 32:7
And there were **b** men with .... Ne 11:14
No one is **b** enough to make it .... Job 41:10
strong and **b,** and wait for the .... Ps 27:14
You made me strong and **b**. .... Ps 138:3
good people are as **b** as a lion. .... Pr 28:1
b people are crying out in the.............. Is 33:7
We are **b** men in battle!' .... Je 48:14
you still be **b** and strong when I .... Eze 22:14
LORD says, 'Zerubbabel, be **b**. .... Hag 2:4
day no one was **b** enough to ask.......... Mt 22:46
no one was **b** enough to ask Jesus .... Mk 12:34
Arimathea was **b** enough to go to .... Mk 15:43
No one was **b** enough to ask him .... Lk 20:40
But no one was **b** enough to talk .... Jn 7:13
you will have trouble, but be **b!** .... Jn 16:33
He said, "Be **b!** You have told .... Ac 23:11
then I also will be **b** and brag. 2Co 11:21
helped us to be **b** and to tell 1Th 2:2

BRAVELY

whom had fought **b** with swords. .... Jdg 20:46
He fought **b** and defeated the 1Sa 14:48
We must fight **b** for our people 2Sa 10:12
We must fight **b** for our people 1Ch 19:13
time and spoke **b** for the Lord. .... Ac 14:3

BRAVEST

time even the **b** warriors will .... Am 2:16

BRAY

donkey does not **b** when it has .... Job 6:5

BREAD

of Salem brought out **b** and wine. .... Ge 14:18
and make it into loaves of **b**." .... Ge 18:6
He baked **b** without yeast, and .... Ge 19:3
Jacob gave Esau **b** and vegetable .... Ge 25:34
there were three **b** baskets on my .... Ge 40:16
bitter herbs and **b** made without .... Ex 12:8
the Feast of Unleavened **B,** .... Ex 12:17
not eat any **b** made with yeast .... Ex 13:7
bless your **b** and your water. .... Ex 23:25
bring loaves of **b** made without .... Le 7:12
If any of the meat or **b** is left, ... Le 8:32

B

Feast of Unleavened **B** begins on .... Le 23:6
That **b** will belong to Aaron and.............. Le 24:9
the table for the **b** that shows a .... Nu 4:7
bitter herbs and **b** made without .... Nu 9:11
tasted like **b** baked with olive .... Nu 11:8
Feast of Unleavened **B** begins on ...... Nu 28:17
I did not eat **b** or drink water.................. Dt 9:9
You ate no **b** and drank no wine.............. Dt 29:6
and they took some dry, moldy **b**. .... Jos 9:5
of flour, made **b** without yeast. .... Jdg 6:19
should we give your soldiers **b**? .... Jdg 8:6
Eat some of our **b** and dip it in .... Ru 2:14
be carrying three loaves of **b**. 1Sa 10:3
ten loaves of **b** to your brothers 1Sa 17:17
five loaves of **b** or anything you 1Sa 21:3
David the holy **b** from the 1Sa 21:6
You gave him **b** and a sword! 1Sa 22:13
with two hundred loaves of **b**,.............. 2Sa 16:1
The **b** and cakes of figs are for 2Sa 16:2
brought Elijah **b** and meat every 1Ki 17:6
Please bring me a piece of **b**, ... 1Ki 17:11
a small loaf of **b** from the flour 1Ki 17:13
and new wine, **b** and vineyards, ... 2Ki 18:32
the job of baking the **b** used for 1Ch 9:31
of Unleavened **B** for seven days 2Ch 30:21
you gave them **b** from heaven. .... Ne 9:15
people as if they were eating **b**. .... Ps 53:4
But can he give us **b** also? .... Ps 78:20
So they ate the **b** of angels.................... Ps 78:25
filled them with **b** from heaven. .... Ps 105:40
they were eating **b** and drinking............ Pr 4:17
will treat you like a loaf of **b**, ... Pr 6:26
dry crust of **b** in peace than to .... Pr 17:1
will sin for only a piece of **b**. .... Pr 28:21
eat our own **b** and make our own .... Is 4:1
The grain is ground to make **b**. .... Is 28:28
and new wine, **b** and vineyards.' .... Is 36:17
used the hot coals to bake my **b**. .... Is 44:19
make the dough for cakes of **b**, ... Je 7:18
guard and to be given **b** each day .... Je 37:21
there was no more **b** in the city. .... Je 37:21
people groan, looking for **b**. .... La 1:11
Children beg for **b**, but no one .... La 4:4
This is because **b** and water will............ Eze 4:17
of barley and pieces of **b**, ... Eze 13:19
He gives **b** to the hungry and .... Eze 18:7
days when you eat **b** made without ...... Eze 45:21
Offer **b** made with yeast as a .... Am 4:5
be hungry for **b** or thirsty for .... Am 8:11
who eat your **b** with you now are .... Ob 1:7
fold touches **b**, cooked food, ... Hag 2:12
tell these rocks to become **b**." .... Mt 4:3
If your children ask for **b**, ... Mt 7:9
those with him ate the holy **b**, ... Mt 12:4
five loaves of **b** and two fish.".............. Mt 14:17
"Bring the **b** and the fish to me." .... Mt 14:18
divided the **b** and gave it to.................. Mt 14:19
seven loaves of **b** and the fish.............. Mt 15:36
five loaves of **b** that fed the .... Mt 16:9
seven loaves of **b** that fed the .... Mt 16:10
yeast used in **b** but to beware .... Mt 16:12
of the Feast of Unleavened **B**, ... Mt 26:17
Jesus took some **b** and thanked .... Mt 26:26
Take no **b**, no bag, and no money .... Mk 6:8
money to buy that much **b**!" .... Mk 6:37
He divided the **b** and gave it to .... Mk 6:41
leftover pieces of **b** and fish. .... Mk 6:43
many loaves of **b** do you have?" .... Mk 8:5
to God, and divided the **b**. .... Mk 8:6
five loaves of **b** for the five .... Mk 8:19
seven loaves of **b** for the four .... Mk 8:20
Unleavened **B** when the Passover .... Mk 14:12

one who dips his **b** into the bowl .... Mk 14:20
tell this rock to become **b**." .... Lk 4:3
does not live on **b** alone.'" .... Lk 4:4
and took and ate the holy **b**, ... Lk 6:4
and did not eat **b** or drink wine, ... Lk 7:33
stick, bag, **b**, money, or extra .... Lk 9:3
five loaves of **b** and two fish, ... Lk 9:13
loan me three loaves of **b**. .... Lk 11:5
him get up to give you the **b**, ... Lk 11:8
for the Feast of Unleavened **B**, ... Lk 22:1
Day of Unleavened **B** came when .... Lk 22:7
Jesus took some **b**, gave thanks,.......... Lk 22:19
to buy enough **b** for each person .... Jn 6:7
of barley and two little......................... Jn 6:9
gave them **b** from heaven to eat............ Jn 6:31
I am the **b** that gives life. .... Jn 6:35
who eats this **b** will never die. .... Jn 6:50
Judas took the **b** Jesus gave him............ Jn 13:30
on the fire, and there was **b**. .... Jn 21:9
sharing, breaking **b**, and praying .... Ac 2:42
of the Feast of Unleavened **B**. .... Ac 12:3
we all met together to break **b**, ... Ac 20:7
Paul took some **b** and thanked God ...... Ac 27:35
first piece of **b** is offered to.................. Rm 11:16
with the **b** that has no yeast— 1Co 5:8
the **b** of goodness and truth. 1Co 5:8
And the **b** that we break is a 1Co 10:16
over to be killed, he took **b** 1Co 11:23
who eats the **b** or drinks the cup 1Co 11:27
o the farmer and **b** for food. 2Co 9:10
table with the **b** that was made .... Heb 9:2

BREAK

were ready to **b** down the door. .... Ge 19:9
you will **b** free from him." .... Ge 27:40
of us if we **b** this agreement." .... Ge 31:53
"So you are able to **b** out first," .... Ge 38:29
cause boils to **b** out and become............ Ex 9:9
Don't **b** any of the bones. .... Ex 12:46
donkey back, then **b** its neck. .... Ex 13:13
their altars, **b** their stones.................... Ex 34:13
I will **b** your great pride,...................... Le 26:19
enemies and **b** their enemies' .... Nu 24:8
they must **b** the young cow's .... Dt 21:4
reject me and **b** my Agreement. .... Dt 31:20
did you **b** your promise to the............... 1Ki 2:43
have chosen to **b** your agreement 1Ki 11:11
should not again **b** your commands .... Ezr 9:14
building, it would **b** it down." .... Ne 4:3
evil people **b** into houses. .... Job 24:16
the clouds do not **b** under their .... Job 26:8
Let's **b** the chains that hold us .... Ps 2:3
You will **b** them into pieces like .... Ps 2:9
B the power of wicked people. .... Ps 10:15
hearts, and their bows will **b**. .... Ps 37:15
b the teeth in their mouths! .... Ps 58:6
I will not **b** my agreement nor .... Ps 89:34
Don't let me **b** your commands. .... Ps 119:10
Let no one **b** in. Let there be .... Ps 144:14
but sadness can **b** a person's .... Pr 15:13
of three strings is hard to **b**. .... Ec 4:12
silver chain or **b** like a golden .... Ec 12:6
I will **b** down the stone wall, ... Is 5:5
It will **b** and fall, and .... Is 22:25
limbs will become dry and **b** off, ... Is 27:11
small stick to **b** open the dill, ... Is 28:27
will **b** down the bronze gates of .... Is 45:2
with us, and do not **b** it. .... Je 14:21
you are watching, **b** that jar. .... Je 19:10
I will **b** this nation and this................... Je 19:11
but I will **b** it before two years .... Je 28:11
I will soon **b** Elam's bow, ... Je 49:35
B open her storehouses of grain. .... Je 50:26

in place to **b** down the walls. .... Eze 4:2
He cannot **b** the agreement and .... Eze 17:15
to use logs to **b** down the city .... Eze 21:22
be dark when I **b** Egypt's power. .... Eze 30:18
the sheep and **b** the sheep's two .... Da 8:7
and **b** the power of Israel's army .... Hos 1:5
Thieves **b** into houses, and .... Hos 7:1
They **b** through all efforts to .... Joe 2:8
will **b** down the bar of the gate .... Am 1:5
The people will **b** through the .... Mic 2:13
and skin them and **b** their bones; .... Mic 3:3
stood for ages, **b** into pieces; .... Hab 3:6
they **b** God's teachings. .... Zph 3:4
Pleasant to **b** the agreement God .... Zch 11:10
why do people **b** their promises .... Mal 2:10
ago, 'Don't **b** your promises, ... Mt 5:33
thieves can **b** in and steal them. .... Mt 6:19
the bags will **b**, the wine will .... Mt 9:17
in the Temple **b** this law about .... Mt 12:5
He will not **b** a crushed blade of .... Mt 12:20
watch and not let the thief **b** .... Mt 24:43
the new wine will **b** the bags, ... Mk 2:22
fish that the nets began to **b**. .... Lk 5:6
the new wine will **b** the bags, ... Lk 5:37
dead, they did not **b** his legs. .... Jn 19:33
we all met together to **b** bread, ... Ac 20:7
ship began to **b** up from the big .... Ac 27:41
But if you **b** the law, it is as .... Rm 2:25
the bread that we **b** is a sharing 1Co 10:16
Who is worthy to **b** the seals and .... Rev 5:2

BREAKABLE
iron and partly **b** like clay. .... Da 2:42

BREAKING
b into pieces the stone pillars .... Ex 23:24
is a skin disease **b** out in those .... Le 13:42
He forgives sin and law **b**. .... Nu 14:18
b them into pieces right in .... Dt 9:17
evil and **b** the Agreement. .... Dt 17:2
b the Agreement I made with them. .... Dt 31:16
against us for **b** the oath we .... Jos 9:20
weren't thieves you caught **b** .... Je 2:34
the promise by **b** the agreement. .... Eze 17:18
my promise and **b** my agreement. .... Eze 17:19
groan with **b** heart and great .... Eze 21:6
ship was in danger of **b** apart. .... Jnh 1:4
First Jesus was **b** the law about .... Jn 5:18
sharing, **b** bread, and praying .... Ac 2:42
bring shame to God by **b** his law, ... Rm 2:23
against us as **b** a command when .... Rm 5:13
had not sinned by **b** a command, ... Rm 5:14
You are guilty of **b** God's law. .... Jam 2:9
is guilty of **b** all the commands .... Jam 2:10
are guilty of **b** all of God's law .... Jam 2:11

BREAKS
if she **b** her promise." .... Nu 30:15
on the spider's web, but it **b**. .... Job 8:15
b powerful people into pieces .... Job 34:24
If war **b** out, I will trust the .... Ps 27:3
The LORD's voice **b** the trees; .... Ps 29:5
He **b** all bows and spears and .... Ps 46:9
his friends and **b** his promises. .... Ps 55:20
its **b** because it is shaking. .... Ps 60:2
God **b** the spirits of great .... Ps 76:12
He **b** down bronze gates and cuts .... Ps 107:16
about the sin **b** up friendships. .... Pr 17:9
so stop it before a fight **b** out. .... Pr 17:14
suddenly and **b** into small pieces .... Is 30:13
will be like a clay jar that **b**, ... Is 30:14
to obey me as an ox **b** its yoke. .... Je 2:20
as someone **b** a clay jar that .... Je 19:11
The person who sins **b** God's law. 1Jn 3:4

BREAST
take the **b** of the male sheep .... Ex 29:26
the fat and the **b** of the animal .... Le 7:30
thigh and the **b** of the .... Le 10:15
to present the **b** and the thigh .... Nu 6:20
just as the **b** that is presented .... Nu 18:18
is grabbed from its mother's **b**; .... Job 24:9
nurse at their mother's **b**. .... Is 28:9
I beat my **b** with sorrow. .... Je 31:19

BREASTPLATES
Their chests looked like iron **b**, ... Rev 9:9
They had **b** that were fiery red, ... Rev 9:17

BREASTS
put them on the **b** of the bull .... Le 9:20
and my mother's **b** feed me? .... Job 3:12
lies all night between my **b**. .... Sng 1:13
Your **b** are like two fawns, ... Sng 4:5
and your **b** are like its bunches .... Sng 7:7
who fed at my mother's **b**. .... Sng 8:1
and her **b** are not yet grown. .... Sng 8:8
a wall, and my **b** are like towers .... Sng 8:10
Beat your **b** in grief, because .... Is 32:12
Your **b** formed, and your hair .... Eze 16:7
let men touch and hold their **b**. .... Eze 23:3
touched her **b** and had sexual .... Eze 23:8
touched and held your young **b**. .... Eze 23:21
them dried-up **b** that cannot feed .... Hos 9:14
still feed at their mothers' **b**. .... Joe 2:16
like doves and beat their **b**, ... Nah 2:7

BREATH
He breathed the **b** of life into .... Ge 2:7
land that had the **b** of life in .... Ge 7:22
breathed his last **b** and died at .... Ge 25:8
his last **b** and died when he .... Ge 35:29
bed, took his last **b**, and died. .... Ge 49:33
blast of your **b**, and the waters .... Ex 15:8
God's **b** destroys them, and a .... Job 4:9
God, that my life is only a **b**. .... Job 7:7
let me catch my **b** but would .... Job 9:18
we take our last **b** and are gone. .... Job 14:10
God's **b** will carry the wicked .... Job 15:30
can't stand my **b**, and my own .... Job 19:17
alive and God's **b** of life is in .... Job 27:3
a person, the **b** of the Almighty .... Job 32:8
The **b** of God makes ice, and the .... Job 37:10
Its **b** sets coals on fire, and .... Job 41:21
By the **b** from his mouth, he made .... Ps 33:6
Everyone's life is only a **b**. .... Ps 39:5
least of people are only a **b**, ... Ps 62:9
When you take away their **b**, ... Ps 104:29
I am nearly out of **b**. .... Ps 119:131
They have no **b** in their mouths. .... Ps 135:17
are like a **b**; their lives are .... Ps 144:4
they both have the same **b**, ... Ec 3:19
he spoke, he took my **b** away. .... Sng 5:6
the smell of your **b** like apples, ... Sng 7:8
His **b** is like a rushing river, ... Is 30:28
when the **b** of the LORD blows .... Is 40:7
driven by the **b** of the LORD. .... Is 59:19
of Jerusalem gasping for **b** .... Je 4:31
They have no **b** in them. .... Je 10:14
who has given us **b** and life, ... Je 38:16
They have no **b** in them. .... Je 51:17
who was our very **b**, was caught .... La 4:20
I will cause **b** to enter you so .... Eze 37:5
gives life, **b**, and everything .... Ac 17:25
kill him with the **b** that comes 2Th 2:8
God put the **b** of life into the .... Rev 11:11

BREATHE
When you **b** on them, they are .... Ps 104:30
She became weak and unable to **b**. .... Je 15:9

B

and **b** on these people who were .... Eze 37:9
and it is hard for me to **b**.” .... Da 10:17

BREATHED
He **b** the breath of life into the .... Ge 2:7
He **b** his last breath and died at .... Ge 25:8
So Isaac **b** his last breath and................. Ge 35:29
said this, he **b** on them and said .... Jn 20:22

BREATHES
He **b**, and the sky clears........................ Job 26:13
that **b** praise the LORD .... Ps 150:6

BREATHING
and worse and finally stopped **b**. 1Ki 17:17
boy began **b** again and was alive. 1Ki 17:22

BREEZES
He sends the **b**, and the waters .... Ps 147:18

BRICK
burn incense on altars of **b**. .... Is 65:3
the clay in the **b** pavement in .... Je 43:9
yourself a **b**, put it in front .... Eze 4:1

BRICKLAYERS
as well as the **b** and............................. 2Ki 12:12
the carpenters, builders, and **b**. 2Ki 22:6
cedar logs, **b**, and carpenters 1Ch 14:1
stonecutters, **b**, carpenters, ... 1Ch 22:15
money to the **b** and carpenters. .... Ezr 3:7

BRICKS
Let's make **b** and bake them to .... Ge 11:3
hard to make **b** and mortar and to .... Ex 1:14
straw to make **b** as you used to .... Ex 5:7
must make as many **b** as you made .... Ex 5:11
He also made them build with **b**. 2Sa 12:31
These **b** have fallen, but we will .... Is 9:10
Get mud, mix clay, make **b**! .... Nah 3:14

BRIDE
want for the payment for the **b**, ... Ge 34:12
payment for a **b** who has never .... Ex 22:17
doesn't want money for the **b**. 1Sa 18:25
Your **b** stands at your right side .... Ps 45:9
Come with me from Lebanon, my **b**. .... Sng 4:8
is so sweet, my sister, my **b**. .... Sng 4:10
My **b**, your lips drip honey;................... Sng 4:11
jewels that a **b** wears proudly. .... Is 49:18
like a **b** dressed in jewels. .... Is 61:10
will be called the **B** of God,................... Is 62:4
You loved me like a young **b**. .... Je 2:2
sounds of the **b** and bridegroom. .... Je 7:34
make you my promised **b** forever. .... Hos 2:19
his room, the **b** from her bedroom .... Joe 2:16
The **b** belongs only to the .... Jn 3:29
want to give you as his pure **b**. 2Co 11:2
himself like a **b** in all her .... Eph 5:27
a bridegroom and **b** will never be .... Rev 18:23
the Lamb's **b** has made herself .... Rev 19:7
prepared like a **b** dressed for .... Rev 21:2
The Spirit and the **b** say, ... Rev 22:17

BRIDEGROOM
“You are a **b** of blood to me.” .... Ex 4:25
as was the custom for the **b**. .... Jdg 14:10
out like a **b** from his bedroom................. Ps 19:5
a **b** dressed for his wedding, ... Is 61:10
happy sounds of the bride and **b**. .... Je 7:34
The **b** should come from his room, ... Joe 2:16
friends of the **b** are not sad.................... Mt 9:15
cried out, 'The **b** is coming! .... Mt 25:6
went to buy oil, the **b** came. .... Mt 25:10
friends of the **b** do not fast .... Mk 2:19
friends of the **b** fast while he .... Lk 5:34
of the wedding called the **b**.................... Jn 2:9
The bride belongs only to the **b**. .... Jn 3:29
the voices of a **b** and bride will .... Rev 18:23

BRIDEGROOM'S
he gets to hear the **b** voice....................... Jn 3:29

BRIDEGROOMS
of brides and **b** in this place. .... Je 16:9
the sounds of brides and **b**,.................... Je 25:10
happy sounds of brides and **b**. .... Je 33:11

BRIDES
sounds of **b** and bridegrooms .... Je 16:9
the sounds of **b** and bridegrooms, ... Je 25:10
sounds of **b** and bridegrooms .... Je 33:11

BRIDESMAIDS
b follow behind her, and they .... Ps 45:14
be like ten **b** who took their .... Mt 25:1
five foolish **b** went to buy oil .... Mt 25:10
b who were ready went in with .... Mt 25:10

BRIDLES
high as horses' **b** for a distance .... Rev 14:20

BRIEF
happiness of evil people is **b**, ... Job 20:5

BRIERS
thorns and **b** from the desert. .... Jdg 8:7

BRIGHT
swelling or a rash or a **b** spot. .... Le 13:2
life will be as **b** as the noonday .... Job 11:17
His **b** glory would scare you, ... Job 13:11
the moon is not **b** and the stars .... Job 25:5
when it is **b** in the sky after .... Job 37:21
can look forward to a **b** future, ... Pr 13:9
as the moon, as **b** as the sun, as .... Sng 6:10
during the day and with a **b**, ... Is 4:5
you were as **b** as the rising sun .... Is 14:12
the moon will be **b** like the sun, ... Is 30:26
and you will be **b** like sunshine .... Is 58:10
hope for a **b** light, but all we .... Is 59:9
goodness shines like a **b** light, ... Is 62:1
are your clothes **b** red as if you .... Is 63:2
Her **b** day became dark from .... Je 15:9
cloud with a **b** light around it .... Eze 1:4
It was **b**, and lightning flashed .... Eze 1:13
and a **b** light was all around. .... Eze 1:27
it looked like **b** glowing metal. .... Eze 8:2
His face was **b** like lightning, ... Da 10:6
justice comes out like **b** light. .... Hos 6:5
make the earth dark on a **b** day............... Am 8:9
He is like a **b** light. .... Hab 3:4
his face became **b** like the sun, ... Mt 17:2
was shining as **b** as lightning,................. Mt 28:3
you will shine **b**, as when a lamp .... Lk 11:36
a **b** light from heaven suddenly .... Ac 9:3
a **b** light from heaven suddenly .... Ac 22:6
Moses' face so **b** that the....................... 2Co 3:7
lives in light so **b** no one can 1Ti 6:16
and his glory made the earth **b**. .... Rev 18:1
Fine linen, **b** and clean, was .... Rev 19:8
and I am the **b** morning star.”................. Rev 22:16

BRIGHTENS
The LORD **b** the darkness around 2Sa 22:29
My God **b** the darkness around me. .... Ps 18:28

BRIGHTER
He made the **b** light to rule the .... Ge 1:16
growing **b** and brighter until .... Pr 4:18
will be seven times **b** than now, ... Is 30:26
was **b** than the sun and flashed .... Ac 26:13

BRIGHTEST
the **b** of the one who gave her .... Sng 6:9
the sun shining at its **b** time. .... Rev 1:16

BRIGHTNESS
of the **b** of his presence came 2Sa 22:13
the sun in its **b** nor admired the .... Job 31:26

of the **b** of his presence came .... Ps 18:12
In the **b** of day we trip as if it .... Is 59:10
come to the **b** of your sunrise .... Is 60:3
nor will the **b** from the moon be .... Is 60:19
was full of the **b** from the glory .... Eze 10:4
and its **b** made the earth shine. .... Eze 43:2
shine like the **b** of the sky. .... Da 12:3

BRINGS

not let the one who **b** death come .... Ex 12:23
sins so that he **b** guilt on the .... Le 4:3
If this person **b** a lamb as his .... Le 4:32
If a person **b** a fellowship .... Le 7:16
When an Israelite **b** a holy gift, ... Nu 5:9
the bitter water that **b** a curse. .... Nu 5:18
The one who **b** the offering shall .... Nu 15:4
LORD your God **b** you into the .... Dt 11:29
the best fruits that the sun **b**, ... Dt 33:14
sends death, and he **b** to life. 1Sa 2:6
me when the LORD **b** you success." 1Sa 25:31
my enemies and **b** people under my 2Sa 22:48
promises or **b** freely to the LORD 2Ki 12:4
If the whip **b** sudden death, ... Job 9:23
and long life **b** understanding. .... Job 12:12
b disgrace on important people .... Job 12:21
of darkness and **b** dark shadows .... Job 12:22
It **b** you praise in heaven above. .... Ps 8:1
my enemies and **b** people under my .... Ps 18:47
Keeping them **b** great reward. .... Ps 19:11
a river that **b** joy to the city .... Ps 46:4
beautiful and **b** joy to the whole .... Ps 48:2
He **b** the clouds from the ends of .... Ps 135:7
He **b** out the wind from his .... Ps 135:7
he **b** back the captured .... Ps 147:2
He **b** peace to your country and .... Ps 147:14
it **b** more profit than gold. .... Pr 3:14
The LORD's blessing **b** wealth, ... Pr 10:22
Doing right **b** freedom to honest .... Pr 11:6
Whoever **b** trouble to his family .... Pr 11:29
Doing evil **b** no safety at all, ... Pr 12:3
A wicked messenger **b** nothing but .... Pr 13:17
kind to the needy **b** happiness. .... Pr 14:21
a proud attitude **b** ruin. .... Pr 16:18
A foolish child **b** disaster to a .... Pr 19:13
the wicked and **b** ruin on every .... Pr 21:12
the north wind **b** rain, telling .... Pr 25:23
telling gossip **b** angry looks. .... Pr 25:23
mean. Wisdom **b** happiness; it .... Ec 8:1
to him, as one who **b** happiness............... Sng 8:10
rule in a way that **b** justice,.................... Is 32:1
or give up until he **b** justice to .... Is 42:4
announces peace and **b** good news, ... Is 52:7
an announcement and **b** bad news .... Je 4:15
with the rain and **b** out the wind .... Je 10:13
your God before he **b** darkness .... Je 13:16
but this only **b** me insults. .... Je 20:8
will be to me a name that **b** joy! .... Je 33:9
with the rain and **b** out the wind .... Je 51:16
Although he **b** sorrow, he also .... La 3:32
from God that **b** destruction, ... Da 8:13
object that **b** destruction. .... Da 11:31
object that **b** destruction will .... Da 12:11
The enemy **b** them in with hooks. .... Hab 1:15
goes out and **b** seven other .... Mt 12:45
He **b** out both new things and old .... Mt 13:52
object that **b** destruction.' .... Mt 24:15
object that **b** destruction' .... Mk 13:14
goes out and **b** seven other .... Lk 11:26
When he **b** all his sheep out, ... Jn 10:4
which **b** glory to my Father. .... Jn 15:8
excuses and **b** the whole world .... Rm 3:19
And that **b** true life for all. .... Rm 5:18
sin, which **b** spiritual death, ... Rm 6:16

from this body that **b** me death? .... Rm 7:24
the Spirit that **b** life made you .... Rm 8:2
the law that **b** sin and death. .... Rm 8:2
The God who **b** peace will soon .... Rm 16:20
covered **b** shame to his head. 1Co 11:4
head uncovered **b** shame to her 1Co 11:5
the smell of death that **b** death, ... 2Co 2:16
The written law **b** death, but the.............. 2Co 3:6
and it **b** praise to God because .... Eph 1:6
Light **b** every kind of goodness, ... Eph 5:9
in a way that **b** honor to the .... Php 1:27
This new life **b** you the true .... Col 3:10
This **b** jealousy, fighting,........................ 1Ti 6:4
And when God **b** his firstborn Son .... Heb 1:6
reason Christ **b** a new agreement .... Heb 9:15
so the one who **b** death would not .... Heb 11:28
then the sin grows and **b** death. .... Jam 1:15
Anyone who **b** a sinner back from .... Jam 5:20

BROAD

Jerusalem as far as the **B** Wall. .... Ne 3:8
of the Ovens to the **B** Wall, ... Ne 12:38

BROILED

They gave him a piece of **b** fish. .... Lk 24:42

BROKE

the fields and **b** all the trees .... Ex 9:25
your right hand **b** the enemy to .... Ex 15:6
was carrying and **b** them at the .... Ex 32:19
first two stones which you **b**. .... Ex 34:1
fight **b** out in the camp between .... Le 24:10
You **b** my agreement, and I will .... Le 26:25
which you **b**, and you will put.................. Dt 10:2
the people **b** the Agreement .... Dt 29:25
That one man **b** God's law, but .... Jos 22:20
If we **b** God's law, we ask the .... Jos 22:23
But Samson **b** the bowstrings.................. Jdg 16:9
But he **b** the ropes as easily as .... Jdg 16:12
beside the gate, **b** his neck, and 1Sa 4:18
When war **b** out again, David went 1Sa 19:8
So the three warriors **b** through 2Sa 23:16
The altar also **b** into pieces, ... 1Ki 13:5
Moab **b** away from Israel's rule. 2Ki 1:1
to Jerusalem and **b** down the wall 2Ki 14:13
But Hezekiah **b** it into pieces. 2Ki 18:4
They **b** his agreement and did not 2Ki 18:12
Josiah **b** down these altars and 2Ki 23:12
b the stones of the altar into 2Ki 23:15
and **b** away from his rule 2Ki 24:1
b down the walls around Jerusalem. 2Ki 25:10
The Babylonians **b** up the bronze 2Ki 25:13
Jehoash **b** down the wall of 2Ch 25:23
disease **b** out on his forehead. 2Ch 26:19
of God and **b** them into pieces 2Ch 28:24
b up the Asherah idols and the 2Ch 34:4
Josiah **b** down the altars and 2Ch 34:7
a curse in case they **b** the oath. .... Ne 10:29
me, but God **b** me into pieces; .... Job 16:12
I **b** the fangs of evil people and .... Job 29:17
by your power and **b** the heads of .... Ps 74:13
There God **b** the flaming arrows, ... Ps 76:3
he **b** their pride by hard work. .... Ps 107:12
The trap **b**, and we escaped. .... Ps 124:7
You **b** the ropes I used to hold .... Je 2:20
off Jeremiah's neck and **b** it. .... Je 28:10
but they **b** that agreement,'' .... Je 31:32
over the men who **b** my agreement, ... Je 34:18
and they **b** down the walls around .... Je 39:8
flesh and skin and **b** my bones. .... La 3:4
He **b** my teeth with gravel and .... La 3:16
of Babylon and **b** his agreement .... Eze 17:16
the east wind **b** you to pieces .... Eze 27:26
You **b** my agreement by all the .... Eze 44:7
The rock **b** the iron, bronze, ... Da 2:45

big horn **b** off and four horns .... Da 8:8
I **b** the stick named Pleasant .... Zch 11:10
You **b** your promise to her, ... Mal 2:14
and thanked God for it and **b** it. .... Mt 26:26
earth shook and rocks **b** apart. .... Mt 27:51
feet, but he always **b** them off. .... Mk 5:4
and thanked God for it and **b** it. .... Mk 14:22
gave thanks, **b** it, and gave it .... Lk 22:19
soldiers came and the legs of .... Jn 19:32
the doors of the jail **b** open, ... Ac 16:26
again, **b** bread, and ate. .... Ac 20:11
b off a piece and began eating. .... Ac 27:35
Then he **b** the bread and said, ... 1Co 11:24
but Christ **b** down that wall of .... Eph 2:14
But they **b** that agreement, ... Heb 8:9

BROKEN
because he has **b** my agreement." .... Ge 17:14
What law have I **b** to cause you .... Ge 31:36
offering that is **b** into pieces, ... Le 6:21
the meat is cooked in must be **b**, ... Le 6:28
that has **b** bones or is crippled, ... Le 22:22
Broken bone for **b** bone, eye for .... Le 24:20
you have **b** our agreement. .... Le 26:15
whose neck was **b** in the valley. .... Dt 21:6
I have not **b** your commands, ... Dt 26:13
they have **b** the agreement I .... Jos 7:11
people have the agreement I .... Jdg 2:20
and hands had **b** off and were 1Sa 5:4
LORD has **b** through my enemies 2Sa 5:20
laws and have not **b** his rules. 2Sa 22:23
of Israel have **b** their agreement 1Ki 19:14
Then the city was **b** into, and 2Ki 25:4
God has **b** through my enemies by 1Ch 14:11
Athaliah had **b** into the Temple 2Ch 24:7
rebuilt all the **b** parts of the 2Ch 32:5
wall around Jerusalem is **b** down, ... Ne 1:3
that had been **b** down and the .... Ne 2:13
took a piece of **b** pottery to .... Job 2:8
teeth of a strong lion are **b**, ... Job 4:10
many people are **b** to pieces; .... Job 4:20
and my skin is **b** and full of .... Job 7:5
What they hope in is easily **b**; .... Job 8:14
My spirit is **b**; the days of my .... Job 17:1
wickedness is **b** in pieces like .... Job 24:20
shoulder and be **b** at the joint. .... Job 31:22
paying or have **b** the spirit of .... Job 31:39
raised to do harm, but it is **b**. .... Job 38:15
its body is like **b** pieces of .... Job 41:30
you have **b** the teeth of the .... Ps 3:7
laws and have not **b** his rules. .... Ps 18:22
I am like a piece of a **b** pot. .... Ps 31:12
not one of them will be **b**. .... Ps 34:20
power of the wicked will be **b**, ... Ps 37:17
things, I speak with a **b** heart. .... Ps 42:4
me feel as if my bones were **b**. .... Ps 42:10
God wants is a **b** spirit. .... Ps 51:17
a heart that is **b** and sorry for .... Ps 51:17
be cut short like a **b** arrow. .... Ps 58:7
Insults have **b** my heart and left .... Ps 69:20
The ground is plowed and **b** up. .... Ps 141:7
but a **b** spirit drains your .... Pr 17:22
no one can live with a **b** spirit. .... Pr 18:14
eating with a **b** tooth or walking. .... Pr 25:19
a city whose walls are **b** down. .... Pr 25:28
You will be like a **b** pitcher at .... Ec 12:6
They will fall and be **b**; .... Is 8:15
her gods lie **b** on the ground." .... Is 21:9
The earth will be **b** up; .... Is 24:19
bandages his **b** people and heals .... Is 30:26
People have the agreements .... Is 33:8
and her ropes will never be **b**. .... Is 33:20
like a piece of **b** pottery among .... Is 45:9

and to those whose hearts are **b**. .... Is 57:15
repairing the **b** places and for. .... Is 58:12
because your spirits will be **b**. .... Is 65:14
which are **b** wells that cannot .... Je 2:13
they had **b** their ties with him. .... Je 5:5
ruined, and all its ropes are **b**. .... Je 10:20
and Judah have **b** the agreement I .... Je 11:10
is like a **b** pot someone threw .... Je 22:28
My heart is **b**. All my bones .... Je 23:9
like pieces of a **b** jar. .... Je 25:34
Hananiah had **b** the yoke off .... Je 28:12
the city wall was **b** through. .... Je 39:2
Moab will be **b** up. Her little .... Je 48:4
against me and **b** away from me. .... Eze 2:3
and your incense altars **b** down. .... Eze 6:4
But now you are **b** by the sea and .... Eze 27:34
the place of the **b** horn are four .... Da 8:22
kingdom will be **b** up and divided .... Da 11:4
holy people will finally be **b**, ... Da 12:7
Israelites have **b** my agreement .... Hos 8:1
for grain have been **b** down, ... Joe 1:17
let your heart be **b**. Come back .... Joe 2:13
house will be **b** into pieces, ... Am 6:11
up again and mend its **b** places. .... Am 9:11
her idols will be **b** into pieces; .... Mic 1:7
The bows used in war will be **b**. .... Zch 9:10
That day it was **b**. The weak ones .... Zch 11:11
have **b** the agreement with the .... Mal 2:8
of Judah have **b** their promises. .... Mal 2:11
falls on this stone will be **b**, ... Mt 21:44
he had **b** his chains and had been .... Lk 8:29
falls on that stone will be **b**, ... Lk 20:18
of the men be **b** and the bodies .... Jn 19:31
"Not one of his bones will be **b**." .... Jn 19:36
an olive tree have been **b** off. .... Rm 11:17
branches were **b** off because they .... Rm 11:20
when pottery is **b** into pieces.' .... Rev 2:27

BROKENHEARTED
The LORD is close to the **b**, ... Ps 34:18
heals the **b** and bandages their .... Ps 147:3

BRONZE
made tools out of **b** and iron. .... Ge 4:22
from them: gold, silver, **b**; .... Ex 25:3
cover the whole altar with **b**. .... Ex 27:2
Make a **b** bowl, on a bronze .... Ex 30:18
ashes off the **b** altar and spread .... Nu 4:13
Moses, "Make a **b** snake, and put .... Nu 21:8
looked at the **b** snake and lived. .... Nu 21:9
where they put **b** chains on him .... Jdg 16:21
with a **b** helmet on his head and.............. 1Sa 17:5
many things made of **b** from Tebah 2Sa 8:8
made of silver, gold, and **b**. 2Sa 8:10
had a **b** spearhead weighing about........... 2Sa 21:16
skilled in making things from **b**. 1Ki 7:14
Solomon and did all the **b** work. 1Ki 7:14
On the sides were **b** lions, ... 1Ki 7:29
Rehoboam made **b** shields to put 1Ki 14:27
Ahaz moved the **b** altar that was 2Ki 16:14
the **b** snake Moses had made. 2Ki 18:4
they carried the **b** to Babylon. 2Ki 25:13
supplied more **b** than could be 1Ch 22:3
fifty thousand pounds of **b**, ... 1Ch 29:7
He made a **b** altar thirty feet 2Ch 4:1
pieces of polished **b** that were .... Ezr 8:27
of stone; my flesh is not **b**. .... Job 6:12
but a **b** arrow will stab them. .... Job 20:24
it look as hard as polished **b**. .... Job 37:18
so my arms can bend a **b** bow. .... Ps 18:34
He breaks down **b** gates and cut .... Ps 107:16
break down the **b** gates of the .... Is 45:2
and your head was like **b**. .... Is 48:4
bring you gold in place of **b**, ... Is 60:17

city, an iron pillar, a **b** wall. .... Je 1:18
He put **b** chains on Zedekiah and .... Je 39:7
eyes, and put **b** chains on him, ... Je 52:11
broke into pieces the **b** pillars, ... Je 52:17
all the **b** pieces to Babylon....................... Je 52:17
and sparkled like polished **b**. .... Eze 1:7
in and stood by the **b** altar. .... Eze 9:2
goods for slaves and items of **b**. .... Eze 27:13
part of its legs were made of **b**. .... Da 2:32
and had iron teeth and **b** claws. .... Da 7:19
legs were shiny like polished **b**, ... Da 10:6
horns of iron and hoofs of **b**. .... Mic 4:13
two mountains, mountains of **b**. .... Zch 6:1
feet were like **b** that glows hot .... Rev 1:15
fire and feet like shining **b**,...................... Rev 2:18
gold, silver, **b**, stone, and wood .... Rev 9:20
expensive wood, **b**, iron, and .... Rev 18:12

BROOK

it will go to the **b** of Egypt, ... Nu 34:5
to Azmon, the **b** of Egypt, and .... Jos 15:4
as far as the **b** of Egypt and .... Jos 15:47
have already crossed the **b**." 2Sa 17:20
Lebo Hamath and the **b** of Egypt. 1Ki 8:65
from the **b** of Egypt to the 2Ki 24:7
Lebo Hamath and the **b** of Egypt. 2Ch 7:8
drink from the **b** on the way. .... Ps 110:7
River to the **b** of Egypt. .... Is 27:12
you be like a **b** that goes dry?................. Je 15:18
will run along the **b** of Egypt to .... Eze 47:19
will run along the **b** of Egypt to .... Eze 48:28

BROOM

and ate the root of the **b** tree. .... Job 30:4
as with a **b** of destruction,"..................... Is 14:23

BROTH

a basket and the **b** into a pot. .... Jdg 6:19
Then pour the **b** on them." .... Jdg 6:20

BROTHER

Eve gave birth to Cain's **b** Abel. .... Ge 4:2
attacked his **b** Abel and killed .... Ge 4:8
to Cain, "Where is your **b** Abel?" .... Ge 4:9
he thought Abram was her **b**. .... Ge 12:16
Your **b** Nahor and his wife Milcah .... Ge 22:20
Abraham's **b**, was the father. .... Ge 22:23
She had a **b** named Laban, who ran .... Ge 24:29
Rebekah's **b** and mother said, ... Ge 24:57
My **b** Esau is a hairy man, ... Ge 27:11
Your **b** came and tricked me. .... Ge 27:35
My **b** Laban is living in Haran. .... Ge 27:43
Now Laban was the **b** of Rebekah,............ Ge 29:10
Jacob's **b** Esau was living in the.............. Ge 32:3
My **b** Esau will come to you and .... Ge 32:17
to a land away from his **b** Jacob. .... Ge 36:6
they hated their **b** and could not.............. Ge 37:4
Benjamin, Joseph's **b**, with them, ... Ge 42:4
b is dead, and he is the only .... Ge 42:38
When Joseph saw his **b** Benjamin, ... Ge 43:29
in the sack of the youngest **b**,.................. Ge 44:2
I am your **b** Joseph, whom you .... Ge 45:4
Tell your **b** Aaron to come to .... Ex 28:1
Tell your **b** Aaron that there are .... Le 16:2
is shameful for a **b** to marry his .... Le 20:17
Her husband's **b** must marry her, ... Dt 25:5
Caleb's younger **b**, saved the .... Jdg 3:9
David's oldest **b** Eliab heard 1Sa 17:28
I cry for you, my **b** Jonathan. 2Sa 1:26
Tamar said to him, "No, **b**! 2Sa 13:12
Absalom, Tamar's **b**, said to her,............... 2Sa 13:20
Has Amnon, your **b**, forced you to 2Sa 13:20
may kill him for killing his **b**. 2Sa 14:7
I ran away from your **b** Absalom. 1Ki 2:7
to marry your **b** Adonijah."...................... 1Ki 2:21

man of God and said, "Oh, my **b**." 1Ki 13:30
Is he still alive? He is my **b**." 1Ki 20:32
Lahmi, the **b** of Goliath, who 1Ch 20:5
I have become a **b** to wild dogs .... Job 30:29
against your **b** and lie about .... Ps 50:20
a **b** helps in time of trouble. .... Pr 17:17
A **b** who has been insulted is .... Pr 18:19
will be more loyal than a **b**. .... Pr 18:24
who had no family, no son or **b**. .... Ec 4:8
you were like my **b** who fed at my .... Sng 8:1
that **b** will stand up and say, ... Is 3:7
try to save his **b** or sister. .... Is 9:19
'Oh, my **b**,' or 'Oh, my sister.' .... Je 22:18
robbed his **b** and did what was .... Eze 18:18
laugh at your **b** Israel in his .... Ob 1:12
called Peter) and his **b** Andrew. .... Mt 4:18
are angry with a **b** or sister, ... Mt 5:22
called Peter) and his **b** Andrew; .... Mt 10:2
son of Zebedee, and his **b** John; .... Mt 10:2
My true **b** and sister and mother .... Mt 12:50
the wife of Philip, Herod's **b**. .... Mt 14:3
and John, the **b** of James, up .... Mt 17:1
forgive your **b** or sister from .... Mt 18:35
his **b** must marry the widow and .... Mt 22:24
Then the second **b** also died. .... Mt 22:26
Simon and his **b** Andrew throwing........... Mk 1:16
My true **b** and sister and mother .... Mk 3:35
John the **b** of James go with him. .... Mk 5:37
son of Mary and the **b** of James,.............. Mk 6:3
Philip, Herod's **b**, but then .... Mk 6:17
wrote that if a man's **b** dies, ... Mk 12:19
Philip, Herod's **b**, the ruler of .... Lk 3:1
him Peter), his **b** Andrew, James, ... Lk 6:14
tell my **b** to divide with me the .... Lk 12:13
said, 'Your **b** has come back, ... Lk 15:27
if a man's **b** dies and leaves .... Lk 20:28
The first **b** married and died, ... Lk 20:29
him was Andrew, Simon Peter's **b**. .... Jn 1:40
Andrew, Simon Peter's **b**, said, ... Jn 6
Mary's **b** was Lazarus, the man .... Jn 11:2
my **b** would not have died." .... Jn 11:32
Saul and said, "**B** Saul, the Lord .... Ac 9:17
James, the **b** of John, to be .... Ac 12:2
said to Paul, "**B**, you can see .... Ac 21:20
will cause your **b** or sister to .... Rm 14:21
from Sosthenes, our **b** in Christ................. 1Co 1:1
Now about our **b** Apollos: 1Co 16:12
from Timothy our **b** in Christ..................... 2Co 1:1
I did not find my **b** Titus. 2Co 2:13
b was chosen by the churches 2Co 8:19
we are sending with them our **b**, ... 2Co 8:22
except James, the **b** of the Lord................ Gal 1:19
b whom we love and a faithful .... Eph 6:21
my **b** in Christ, works .... Php 2:25
Also from Timothy, our **b**. .... Col 1:1
Tychicus is my dear **b** in Christ .... Col 4:7
Timothy, our **b**, works with us 1Th 3:2
Jesus, and from Timothy, our **b**. .... Phm 1:1
and comfort, my **b**, because the .... Phm 1:7
than a slave, as a loved **b**. .... Phm 1:16
So, my **b**, I ask that you do this .... Phm 1:20
know that our **b** Timothy has been .... Heb 13:23
A **b** or sister in Christ might .... Jam 2:15
know is a faithful **b** in Christ.................... 1Pe 5:12
dear **b** Paul told you the same 2Pe 3:15
but hates a **b** or sister,........................... 1Jn 2:9
the Evil One and killed his **b**. 1Jn 3:12
the things his **b** did were good. 1Jn 3:12
Jesus Christ and a **b** of James. .... Jud 1:1
John, am your **b**. All of us share.............. Rev 1:9

BROTHER'S

Your **b** blood is crying out to me .... Ge 4:10
relations with your dead **b** wife. .... Ge 38:8
relations with your **b** wife. .... Le 18:16
for a man to marry his **b** wife. .... Le 20:21
not want to marry his **b** widow, ... Dt 25:7
together at the oldest **b** house. .... Job 1:13
held on to his **b** heel while the .... Hos 12:3
to be married to your **b** wife." .... Mk 6:18
If you hurt your **b** or sister's .... Rm 14:15

BROTHER-IN-LAW

which is his duty to her as a **b**. .... Dt 25:5
My **b** will not carry on his .... Dt 25:7
descendants of Hobab, Moses' **b**. .... Jdg 4:11

BROTHERHOOD

to break the **b** between Judah and .... Zch 11:14

BROTHERS

be the lowest slave to his **b**." .... Ge 9:25
and mine, because we are **b**. .... Ge 13:8
He will attack all his **b**." .... Ge 16:12
May you be master over your **b**, ... Ge 27:29
talked to Dinah's **b** and said, ... Ge 34:8
Jacob and to Dinah's **b** and said, ... Ge 34:11
So the **b** took the flocks, herds, ... Ge 34:28
father bad reports about his **b**. .... Ge 37:2
When Joseph's **b** saw that their .... Ge 37:4
His **b** hated him even more .... Ge 37:8
Joseph's **b** were jealous of him, ... Ge 37:11
So when Joseph came to his **b**, ... Ge 37:23
b took Joseph out of the well .... Ge 37:28
Joseph knew they were his **b**, ... Ge 42:8
to fill his **b'** bags with grain .... Ge 42:25
Leave one of your **b** with me, ... Ge 42:33
The **b** tore their clothes to show .... Ge 44:13
He said to his **b**, "I am Joseph. .... Ge 45:3
father and your **b** the best land; .... Ge 47:6
And his **b** went to him and bowed .... Ge 50:18
Joseph and his **b** died, along .... Ex 1:6
If he has no **b**, then everything .... Nu 27:10
If two **b** are living together, ... Dt 25:5
one who was blessed among his **b**. .... Dt 33:16
and murdered his seventy **b**, ... Jdg 9:5
Samson's **b** and his whole family .... Jdg 16:31
of bread to your **b** in the camp. 1Sa 17:17
please let me go to see my **b**.' 1Sa 20:29
You are my **b**, my own family. 2Sa 19:12
invited all his **b**, the other 1Ki 1:9
Joel's **b** and all his family 1Ch 5:7
he killed all his **b** with a sword 2Ch 21:4
Fight for your **b**, your sons and .... Ne 4:14
But my **b** cannot be counted on. .... Job 6:15
God has made my **b** my enemies, ... Job 19:13
I will tell my **b** and sisters .... Ps 22:22
as if they were my friends or **b**. .... Ps 35:14
My **b** were angry with me and made ...... Sng 1:6
grab one of his **b** from his own .... Is 3:6
Your **b** hated you and turned .... Is 66:5
are to call your **b**, 'my people,' .... Hos 2:1
said, "Esau and Jacob were **b**. .... Mal 1:2
give their own **b** to be killed, ... Mt 10:21
his mother and **b** stood outside, ... Mt 12:46
Who is my mother? Who are my **b**?" ..... Mt 12:48
is Mary, and his **b** are James, ... Mt 13:55
left houses, **b**, sisters, father .... Mt 19:29
they were angry with the two **b**. .... Mt 20:24
there were seven **b** among us. .... Mt 22:25
and you are all **b** and sisters .... Mt 23:8
saw two more **b**, James and John, ... Mk 1:19
Jesus' mother and **b** arrived. .... Mk 3:31
Here are my mother and my **b**! .... Mk 3:34
left houses, **b**, sisters, mother .... Mk 10:29
Once there were seven **b**. .... Mk 12:20

seven **b** married her and died, ... Mk 12:22
give their own **b** to be killed, ... Mk 13:12
mother and **b** came to see him, ... Lk 8:19
My mother and my **b** are those who ...... Lk 8:21
I have five **b**, and Lazarus could .... Lk 16:28
left houses, wives, **b**, parents, ... Lk 18:29
Once there were seven **b**. .... Lk 20:29
Help your **b** be stronger when you .... Lk 22:32
his mother, **b**, and followers. .... Jn 2:12
So Jesus' **b** said to him, "You .... Jn 7:3
Jesus' **b** did not believe in him. .... Jn 7:5
said to his **b**, "The right time .... Jn 7:6
But after Jesus' **b** had gone to .... Jn 7:10
But go to my **b** and tell them, ' .... Jn 20:17
mother of Jesus, and Jesus' **b**. .... Ac 1:14
B and sisters, I know you did .... Ac 3:17
So, **b** and sisters, choose seven .... Ac 6:3
Joseph told his **b** who he was, ... Ac 7:13
He said, 'Men, you are **b**. .... Ac 7:26
the apostles and elders, your **b**. .... Ac 15:23
me letters to the **b** in Damascus. .... Ac 22:5
to them, "My **b**, I am a Pharisee, ... Ac 23:6
of our Jewish **b** who have come .... Ac 28:21
B and sisters, all of you .... Rm 7:1
the same way, my **b** and sisters. .... Rm 7:4
firstborn of many **b** and sisters. .... Rm 8:29
help my Jewish **b** and sisters, ... Rm 9:3
B and sisters, the thing I want .... Rm 10:1
this secret, **b** and sisters, so .... Rm 11:25
each other like **b** and sisters. .... Rm 12:10
you judge your **b** or sisters in .... Rm 14:10
all the **b** and sisters who are .... Rm 16:14
B and sisters, I ask you to look .... Rm 16:17
I beg you, **b** and sisters, by the 1Co 1:10
B and sisters, this is what I 1Co 7:29
sin against your **b** and sisters 1Co 8:12
and the Lord's **b** and Peter? 1Co 9:5
B and sisters, do not think like 1Co 14:20
I ask you, **b** and sisters, ... 1Co 16:15
All the **b** and sisters here send 1Co 16:20
am sending the **b** to you so that 2Co 9:3
should ask these **b** to go to you 2Co 9:5
The **b** who came from Macedonia 2Co 11:9
B and sisters, I became like you, ... Gal 4:12
My **b** and sisters, you are God's .... Gal 4:28
My **b** and sisters, God called you .... Gal 5:13
B and sisters, if someone in .... Gal 6:1
My **b** and sisters, the grace of .... Gal 6:18
with faith to you **b** and sisters .... Eph 6:23
I want you **b** and sisters to know .... Php 1:12
My **b** and sisters, be full of joy .... Php 3:1
dear **b** and sisters, I love you .... Php 4:1
holy and faithful **b** and sisters .... Col 1:2
Greet the **b** and sisters in .... Col 4:15
B and sisters, God loves you, ... 1Th 1:4
B and sisters, now we encourage 1Th 4:10
God for you, **b** and sisters. 2Th 1:3
And now, **b** and sisters, pray for 2Th 3:1
Treat younger men like **b**, ... 1Ti 5:1
be made like his **b** and sisters .... Heb 2:17
all of you holy **b** and sisters, ... Heb 3:1
b and sisters, be careful that .... Heb 3:12
each other as **b** and sisters. .... Heb 13:1
My **b** and sisters, I beg you to .... Heb 13:22
My **b** and sisters, when you have .... Jam 1:2
Listen, my dear **b** and sisters! .... Jam 2:5
B and sisters, be patient until .... Jam 5:7
My **b** and sisters, if one of you .... Jam 5:19
your Christian **b** and sisters. 1Pe 1:22
Love the **b** and sisters of God's 1Pe 2:17
kindness for your **b** and sisters 2Pe 1:7
My **b** and sisters, try hard to be 2Pe 1:10
our lives for our **b** and sisters. 1Jn 3:16

but hate their **b** or sisters, ... 1Jn 4:20
that you help the **b** and sisters, ... 3Jn 1:5
accuser of our **b** and sisters, ... Rev 12:10
And our **b** and sisters defeated .... Rev 12:11
you and your **b** and sisters who .... Rev 19:10
like you, your **b** the prophets, ... Rev 22:9

BROWN
with red, **b,** and white horses .... Zch 1:8

BRUISE
for wound, and **b** for bruise. .... Ex 21:25

BRUISED
an animal has **b,** crushed, torn, ... Le 22:24

BRUISES
Who has unnecessary **b**?........................ Pr 23:29

BRUSH
among the **b** and ate the root .... Job 30:4
and huddled together in the **b.** .... Job 30:7

BRUSHED
and wafers **b** with olive oil...................... Ex 29:2

BUBBLE
the deep sea **b** like a boiling .... Job 41:31

BUCKET
are like one small drop in a **b;** .... Is 40:15

BUCKETS
in wooden **b** and in stone jars. .... Ex 7:19
Israel's water **b** will always be .... Nu 24:7

BUD
the branches **b** and blossom, ... Ge 40:10
cup must have a **b** and a petal. .... Ex 25:33
A **b** was under the place where .... Ex 37:21
water it will **b** and put out new .... Job 14:9

BUDDED
It had even **b,** blossomed, and .... Nu 17:8

BUDDING
grapes will be **b** and growing.................. Is 18:5

BUDS
cups, **b,** and petals must .... Ex 25:31
The branches, **b,** and lampstand.............. Ex 25:36
to look for **b** on the vines, ... Sng 6:11

BUILD
B a boat of cypress wood for .... Ge 6:14
Let's **b** a city and a tower for .... Ge 11:4
There I will **b** an altar to God, ... Ge 35:3
Israelites in the cities .... Ex 1:11
The people must **b** a holy place .... Ex 25:8
acacia wood and **b** an Ark .... Ex 25:10
as gifts to **b** the Holy Tent. .... Ex 36:3
to Balak, "**B** me seven altars .... Nu 23:1
We will **b** pens for our animals .... Nu 32:16
B cities for your children and .... Nu 32:24
all you want and **b** nice houses .... Dt 8:12
to the altar you **b** for the LORD .... Dt 16:21
B roads to these cities, and .... Dt 19:3
and use them to **b** devices to .... Dt 20:20
When you **b** a new house, build a .... Dt 22:8
b the altar of the LORD your God .... Dt 27:6
We did not **b** this altar to offer .... Jos 22:23
Then **b** an altar to the LORD your .... Jdg 6:26
You must **b** a new cart and get 1Sa 6:7
He will **b** a house for me, and I 2Sa 7:13
He also made them **b** with bricks. 2Sa 12:31
B a house for yourself in....................... 1Ki 2:36
was never able to **b** a house for.............. 1Ki 5:3
only ones used to **b** the Temple, ... 1Ki 6:7
David wanted to **b** a temple for 1Ki 8:17
Solomon used to **b** the Temple 1Ki 9:15
He will **b** a house for me, and I 1Ch 17:12
We should **b** a great Temple for 1Ch 22:5

B the holy place of the LORD God; 1Ch 22:19
son Solomon will **b** my Temple and 1Ch 28:6
I will **b** a temple for worshiping 2Ch 2:4
David wanted to **b** a temple for 2Ch 6:7
But you are not the one to **b** it. 2Ch 6:9
the one who will **b** my temple.' 2Ch 6:9
go to Jerusalem to **b** the Temple .... Ezr 1:5
houses the wicked **b** are like a .... Job 27:18
to fly and **b** its nest so high................... Job 39:27
b your room above the clouds. .... Ps 104:3
so they could **b** a city in which .... Ps 107:36
If the LORD doesn't **b** the house, ... Ps 127:1
bless and **b** up their city, ... Pr 11:11
that, you can **b** your house..................... Pr 24:27
time to destroy and a time to **b.** .... Ec 3:3
but we will **b** again with cut .... Is 9:10
and I will **b** your foundations .... Is 54:11
will use rubies to **b** your walls .... Is 54:12
Build a road! **B** a road! Prepare .... Is 57:14
will one person **b** a house and .... Is 66:1
think you can **b** a house for me?............. Is 66:1
and **b** an attack ramp to the top .... Je 6:6
his wisdom to **b** the world and .... Je 10:12
'I will **b** a great palace for .... Je 22:14
B houses and settle in the land. .... Je 29:5
I will **b** you up and not tear you .... Je 42:10
Even if you **b** your home as high .... Je 49:16
When the people **b** a weak wall,............. Eze 13:10
Babylonians will **b** devices to .... Eze 17:17
He will **b** a road of earth to the .... Eze 26:8
You **b** Jerusalem by murdering .... Mic 3:10
that kills people to **b** a city,................. Hab 2:12
They may **b** houses, but they will .... Zph 1:13
on top of stones to **b** the Temple............ Hag 2:15
will **b** the Temple of the LORD. .... Zch 6:12
One man will **b** the Temple of the .... Zch 6:13
birds to come and **b** nests in its .... Mt 13:32
On this rock I will **b** my church,............. Mt 16:18
You **b** tombs for the prophets,................ Mt 23:29
of God and **b** it again in three................ Mt 26:61
I will **b** another Temple not made .... Mk 14:58
down my barns and **b** bigger ones,........... Lk 12:18
the wild birds **b** nests in its .... Lk 13:19
If you want to **b** a tower, you .... Lk 14:28
I will **b** it again in three days................ Jn 2:19
-six years to **b** this Temple!................... Jn 2:20
believe you can **b** it again in .... Jn 2:20
to let him **b** a house for him, ... Ac 7:46
think you can **b** a house for me?............. Ac 7:49
this authority is to **b** you up, ... 2Co 10:8
be used to **b** a spiritual temple— 1Pe 2:5
holy faith to **b** yourselves up, ... Jud 1:20

BUILDER
b wore his sword at his side .... Ne 4:18
stands, the **b** will get a reward 1Co 3:14
The **b** will be saved, but it will 1Co 3:15
but the **b** of everything is God .... Heb 3:4

BUILDERS
and Hiram's **b** and the men 1Ki 5:18
carpenters and the **b** who worked 2Ki 12:11
The **b** finished laying the .... Ezr 3:10
stone that the **b** rejected became .... Ps 118:22
the **b** are working for nothing. .... Ps 127:1
Your **b** made your beauty perfect. .... Eze 27:4
stone that the **b** rejected became .... Mt 21:42
stone that the **b** rejected became .... Mk 12:10
stone that the **b** rejected became .... Lk 20:17
the stone that you **b** rejected, ... Ac 4:11
stone that the **b** rejected has 1Pe 2:7

BUILDING
At that time Cain was **b** a city, ... Ge 4:17
and they stopped **b** the city. .... Ge 11:8

like an eagle **b** its nest that .... Dt 32:11
God of Israel by **b** an altar for .... Jos 22:16
Solomon was still **b** his palace 1Ki 3:1
So he finished **b** the Temple 1Ki 6:9
had spent seven years **b** it. 1Ki 6:38
Every important **b** was burned. 2Ki 25:9
the materials for **b** the Temple 1Ch 22:14
Solomon began **b** in the second 2Ch 3:2
captives were **b** a Temple for the .... Ezr 4:1
to delay the **b** plans during .... Ezr 4:5
They finished **b** the Temple as .... Ezr 6:14
who were **b** the wall. .... Ne 4:17
God angry by **b** places to worship .... Ps 78:58
use for the foundation of a **b,** .... Je 51:26
every important **b** was burned. .... Je 52:13
wall around the **b** was about nine .... Eze 41:12
for the **b** of the Temple. .... Zch 8:9
is like a man **b** a house who dug .... Lk 6:48
to take Paul to the army **b.** .... Ac 21:34
into the army **b** and beat him. .... Ac 22:24
Others are **b** on that foundation, ... 1Co 3:10
ut if the **b** is burned up, ... 1Co 3:15
You are like a **b** that was built .... Eph 2:20
most important stone in that **b,** .... Eph 2:20
them while Noah was **b** the boat. 1Pe 3:20

BUILDINGS

David built more **b** around it, ... 2Sa 5:9
these **b** were made with blocks 1Ki 7:9
King Solomon had built two **b**— 1Ki 9:10
Hiram helped with the **b.** 1Ki 9:11
He built storage **b** for grain, ... 2Ch 32:28
Jerusalem, your **b** are destroyed .... Is 52:9
there were some **b** that looked .... Eze 40:2
He took me closer to the **b,** .... Eze 40:3
and destroy their strong **b.**" .... Hos 8:14
destroy the city's strong **b.** .... Am 1:7
and walk over our large **b.** .... Mic 5:5
boards of the **b** will be gone. .... Zph 2:14
up to show him the Temple's **b.** .... Mt 24:1
How beautiful the **b** are! .... Mk 13:1
Do you see all these great **b?** .... Mk 13:2

BUILDS

like a hut that a guard **b** .... Job 27:18
anyone **b** a wall of thornbushes .... Is 27:4
to him until he **b** up Jerusalem .... Is 62:7
be for one who **b** his palace by .... Je 22:13
The LORD **b** his upper rooms above .... Am 9:6
up with pride, but love **b** up. 1Co 8:1

BUILT

Noah **b** an altar to the LORD. .... Ge 8:20
he **b** the cities of Nineveh, ... Ge 10:11
So Abram **b** an altar there to .... Ge 12:7
Abraham **b** an altar there. .... Ge 22:9
Isaac **b** an altar and worshiped .... Ge 26:25
There Jacob **b** an altar and named .... Ge 35:7
Joseph was well **b** and handsome. .... Ge 39:6
Then Moses **b** an altar and named .... Ex 17:15
b an altar before the calf and .... Ex 32:5
Then he **b** the altar for burnt .... Ex 38:1
Hebron had been **b** seven years .... Nu 13:22
There Balak **b** seven altars and .... Nu 23:14
And they **b** sheep pens. .... Nu 32:36
Has anyone **b** a new house but not .... Dt 20:5
lived in was **b** on the city wall .... Jos 2:15
Joshua **b** an altar for the LORD, ... Jos 8:30
So Gideon **b** an altar there to .... Jdg 6:24
Saul **b** an altar to the LORD. 1Sa 14:35
They **b** a palace for David. 2Sa 5:11
King Solomon also **b** a palace for 1Ki 7:1
have truly a wonderful Temple 1Ki 8:13
and the Temple I have **b** for you. 1Ki 8:44
He also **b** the cities of Lower 1Ki 9:17

King Solomon also **b** cities for 1Ki 9:19
He **b** whatever he wanted in 1Ki 9:19
Solomon also **b** ships at Ezion 1Ki 9:26
She saw the palace he had **b,** 1Ki 10:4
Jeroboam **b** temples on the places 1Ki 12:31
Omri **b** a city on that hill and 1Ki 16:24
He **b** a temple in Samaria for 1Ki 16:32
Jehoshaphat **b** trading ships to 1Ki 22:48
So Uriah the priest **b** an altar, ... 2Ki 16:11
They **b** places to worship gods in 2Ki 17:9
b altars for Baal, and he made 2Ki 21:3
He **b** altars to worship the stars 2Ki 21:5
kings of Israel had **b** temples 2Ki 23:19
Temple Solomon **b** in Jerusalem. 1Ch 6:10
David **b** houses for himself in 1Ch 15:1
David **b** an altar to the LORD 1Ch 21:26
Solomon **b** the Temple on the 2Ch 3:1
and he **b** all the towns in Hamath 2Ch 8:4
He **b** all he wanted in Jerusalem, ... 2Ch 8:6
She saw the palace he had **b,** 2Ch 9:3
The king **b** a large throne of 2Ch 9:17
in Jerusalem and **b** strong cities 2Ch 11:5
He **b** up the cities of Bethlehem, ... 2Ch 11:6
He **b** strong, walled cities and 2Ch 17:12
they **b** in the town of Ezion 2Ch 20:36
Jehoram also **b** places to worship 2Ch 21:11
Uzziah **b** towers in Jerusalem at 2Ch 26:9
He also **b** towers in the desert 2Ch 26:10
b storage buildings for grain, ... 2Ch 26:10
also **b** many towns. He had many 2Ch 32:29
of Jericho **b** part of the wall .... Ne 3:2
They **b** shelters on their roofs, ... Ne 8:16
The singers had **b** villages for .... Ne 12:29
a seventy-five foot platform **b,** .... Est 5:14
He **b** it on the waters and set it .... Ps 24:2
he **b** his Temple high like the .... Ps 78:69
the earth, he **b** it to last .... Ps 78:69
The LORD **b** Jerusalem on the holy .... Ps 87:1
Your kingdom is **b** on what is .... Ps 89:14
kingdom is **b** on what is right .... Ps 97:2
You **b** the earth on its .... Ps 104:5
Jerusalem is **b** as a city with .... Ps 122:3
Wisdom has **b** her house; .... Pr 9:1
I **b** houses and planted vineyards .... Ec 2:4
David's tower, **b** with rows of .... Sng 4:4
He **b** a tower in the middle of it .... Is 5:2
of Judah, 'You will be **b** again!' .... Is 44:26
"You will be **b** again!" .... Is 44:28
Judah have **b** places of worship .... Je 7:31
have as many altars to burn .... Je 11:13
You **b** a place of worship at the .... Eze 16:25
You **b** your place to worship gods .... Eze 16:31
You will not be **b** again, because .... Eze 26:14
all that your wisdom has **b,** .... Eze 28:7
I have **b** this great Babylon as .... Da 4:30
where the holy Temple is **b.** .... Da 11:45
Although Israel **b** more altars to .... Hos 8:11
Judah has **b** many strong, walled .... Hos 8:14
they **b** more altars for idols. .... Hos 10:1
You have **b** fancy houses of cut .... Am 5:11
when your walls will be **b** again, ... Mic 7:11
what those people have **b;** .... Hab 2:13
Tyre has **b** a strong wall for .... Zch 9:3
city that is **b** on a hill cannot .... Mt 5:14
man who **b** his house on rock. .... Mt 7:24
for a winepress and **b** a tower. .... Mt 21:33
for a winepress and **b** a tower. .... Mk 12:1
cliff on which the town was **b.** .... Lk 4:29
is like a man who **b** his house. .... Lk 6:49
and he **b** us a synagogue." .... Lk 7:5
and guards had **b** a fire and were .... Jn 18:18
was the one who **b** the Temple. .... Ac 7:47
in temples **b** by human hands. .... Ac 17:24

that was **b** on the foundation .... Eph 2:20
strong in love and be **b** on love. .... Eph 3:17
and have your lives **b** on him................... Col 2:7
Every house is **b** by someone,................... Heb 3:4
obeyed God and **b** a large boat to .... Heb 11:7
the city planned and **b** by God. .... Heb 11:10
will be **b** on this important 1Pe 2:6
of the city were **b** on twelve .... Rev 21:14
The city was **b** in a square, ... Rev 21:16

BULL

If a man's **b** kills a man or .... Ex 21:28
the **b** must be stoned to death, ... Ex 21:29
If a man steals a **b** or a sheep .... Ex 22:1
are to offer a **b** to remove the .... Ex 29:36
offer a young **b** as a sin .... Le 4:14
carry the **b** outside the camp .... Le 4:21
Moses brought the **b** for the sin .... Le 8:14
Take a **b** calf and a male sheep .... Le 9:2
he will kill the **b** for the sin................... Le 16:11
one **b** will be a sin offering to .... Nu 8:12
prepare a young **b** as a burnt .... Nu 15:8
a grain offering with the **b**. .... Nu 15:9
the majesty of a firstborn **b;** .... Dt 33:17
and a second **b** seven years old. .... Jdg 6:25
of Baal choose one **b** and kill it 1Ki 18:23
altar, cut the **b** into pieces, ... 1Ki 18:33
Mount Hermon jump like a baby **b.** .... Ps 29:6
than sacrificing a **b** with horns .... Ps 69:31
a statue of a **b** that eats grass .... Ps 106:20
give a young **b** as a sin offering .... Eze 43:19
offer a young **b** and a male sheep .... Eze 43:23

BULL'S

put their hands on the **b** head. .... Ex 29:10
put some of the **b** blood on the .... Ex 29:12
Take the **b** meat, skin, and .... Ex 29:14
bring some of the **b** blood into .... Le 4:16
some of the **b** blood and put it .... Eze 43:20

BULLS

cows and ten **b,** twenty female .... Ge 32:15
pay back five **b** for the one bull .... Ex 22:1
sacrifice young **b** as fellowship .... Ex 24:5
the burnt offering was twelve **b,** .... Nu 7:87
the seventh day offer seven **b,** .... Nu 29:32
of twelve bronze **b** that faced 1Ki 7:25
bronze lions, **b,** and creatures................ 1Ki 7:29
were carvings of **b** under the rim 2Ch 4:3
so many sheep and **b** no one could........... 2Ch 5:6
killed the **b** and sprinkled 2Ch 29:22
gave one thousand **b** and seven 2Ch 30:24
to God by offering a hundred **b,** .... Ezr 6:17
this money buy **b,** male sheep, ... Ezr 7:17
twelve **b** for all Israel, ... Ezr 8:35
Their **b** never fail to mate; .... Job 21:10
Now take seven **b** and seven male .... Job 42:8
Like the strong **b** of Bashan, ... Ps 22:12
save me from the horns of the **b.** .... Ps 22:21
I do not need **b** from your stalls .... Ps 50:9
eat the meat of **b** or drink the................ Ps 50:13
will offer sheep, **b,** and goats................. Ps 66:15
not pleased by the blood of **b,**................ Is 1:11
and young **b** will eat together, ... Is 11:6
offer seven **b** and seven male .... Eze 45:23
people sacrifice **b** at Gilgal, ... Hos 12:11
killed my best **b** and calves for .... Mt 22:4
brought some **b** and flowers to .... Ac 14:13
of goats and **b** and the ashes .... Heb 9:13
for the blood of **b** and goats to .... Heb 10:4

BUNCH

cut off the **b** of grapes there. .... Nu 13:24
My lover is like a **b** of flowers .... Sng 1:14

BUNCHES

their **b** of grapes are bitter. .... Dt 32:32
breasts be like **b** of grapes, ... Sng 7:8
and gather the **b** of grapes .... Rev 14:18

BUNDLE

My **b** stood up, and your bundles .... Ge 37:7
bring the first **b** of grain from................ Le 23:10
present the **b** before the LORD .... Le 23:11
and leave behind a **b** of grain, ... Dt 24:19
to make into a **b** to fill one's .... Ps 129:7

BUNDLES

the field tying **b** of wheat .... Ge 37:7
and your **b** of wheat gathered................ Ge 37:7
like **b** of grain gathered at the .... Job 5:26
they carry **b** of grain but still .... Job 24:10
singing and carrying **b** of grain. .... Ps 126:6
gathered them like **b** of grain to .... Mic 4:12

BURDEN

The **b** that I ask you to accept................ Mt 11:30
and I will not be a **b** to you. 2Co 12:14
so we would not **b** any of you.................. 1Th 2:9

BURDENS

We had great **b** there that were 2Co 1:8
body, we have **b,** and we groan. 2Co 5:4

BURIAL

I am buying it as a **b** place." .... Ge 23:9
the Hittite to use as a **b** place................. Ge 50:13
Doctors prepared his body for **b,** .... Ge 50:26
gives him or have a proper **b?**................. Ec 6:3
thrown into the **b** place where .... Je 26:23
give Gog a **b** place in Israel .... Eze 39:11
lived in the **b** caves and were .... Mt 8:28
on my body to prepare me for **b.** .... Mt 26:12
came to him from the **b** caves. .... Mk 5:2
on my body to prepare me for **b.** .... Mk 14:8
and had lived in the **b** caves, ... Lk 8:27
day for me to be prepared for **b**.............. Jn 12:7

BURIED

and will be **b** at an old age...................... Ge 15:15
Abraham **b** his wife Sarah in the .... Ge 23:19
and Ishmael **b** him in the cave .... Ge 25:9
So Abraham was **b** with his wife .... Ge 25:10
and was **b** under the oak tree .... Ge 35:8
Rachel was **b** on the road to .... Ge 35:19
his sons Esau and Jacob **b** him. .... Ge 35:29
Rebekah his wife are **b** there, ... Ge 49:31
and I **b** my wife Leah there. .... Ge 49:31
prepared Jacob's body to be **b.** .... Ge 50:2
of Canaan and **b** it in the cave .... Ge 50:13
After Joseph **b** his father, ... Ge 50:14
They will be **b** alive and will go .... Nu 16:30
There Miriam died and was **b.** .... Nu 20:1
Aaron died there and was **b;** .... Dt 10:6
He **b** Moses in Moab in the valley .... Dt 34:6
They **b** him in his own land at .... Jos 24:30
They **b** them at Shechem, in the .... Jos 24:32
Aaron died and was **b** at Gibeah .... Jos 24:33
He was **b** in the tomb of Joash, ... Jdg 8:32
he died and was **b** in Shamir. .... Jdg 10:2
he died and was **b** in Bethlehem. .... Jdg 12:10
him back and had **b** him in the............... Jdg 16:31
will die, and there I will be **b**.................. Ru 1:17
Then they **b** him at his home in 1Sa 25:1
had **b** Samuel in his hometown 1Sa 28:3
their bones and **b** them under................ 1Sa 31:13
men of Jabesh Gilead had **b** Saul. 2Sa 2:4
Asahel and **b** him in the tomb 2Sa 2:32
b Abner in Hebron, and David 2Sa 3:32
head and **b** it in Abner's tomb at 2Sa 4:12
died and was **b** in his father's................ 2Sa 17:23
The people **b** the bones of Saul 2Sa 21:14

he will **b** near his home in the 1Ki 2:34
he died and was **b** in Jerusalem,..............1Ki 11:43
will not be **b** in your family 1Ki 13:22
prophet **b** the body in his own 1Ki 13:30
After the prophet **b** the body, ...1Ki 13:31
Jeroboam's family who will be **b**, ...1Ki 14:13
After they **b** him, all Israel had 1Ki 14:18
and was **b** with his ancestors 1Ki 14:31
died and was **b** in Jerusalem, ...1Ki 15:8
he was **b** with his ancestors in 1Ki 15:24
to Jerusalem and **b** him with his..............2Ki 9:28
Then Elisha died and was **b**. 2Ki 13:20
died and was **b** in Samaria with 2Ki 14:16
and he was **b** with his ancestors..............2Ki 14:20
Ahaz died and was **b** with his..............2Ki 16:20
died and was **b** in the garden of 2Ki 21:18
He was **b** in his grave in the 2Ki 21:26
and you will be **b** in peace. 2Ki 22:20
Jerusalem and **b** him in his own 2Ki 23:30
Then they killed and **b** him. 2Ch 22:9
Ahaz died and was **b** in the city 2Ch 28:27
died and was **b** on a hill,..............2Ch 32:33
died and was **b** in his palace. 2Ch 33:20
let you die and be **b** in peace. 2Ch 34:28
he died and was **b** in the graves 2Ch 35:24
where his ancestors were **b**. 2Ch 35:24
ancestors are **b** lies in ruins, ...Ne 2:3
was I not **b** like a child born ....Job 3:16
They are **b** next to each other, ...Job 21:26
are laid low and **b** like everyone..............Job 24:24
will die of disease and be **b**, ...Job 27:15
When people die, they are **b**. ....Ps 146:4
the earth has been **b** with honor, ...Is 14:18
bodies to be **b** in a rocky pit. ....Is 14:19
You will not be **b** with those ....Is 14:20
He was **b** with wicked men, and he ....Is 53:9
where you will die and be **b**, ...Je 20:6
place where poor people are **b**. ....Je 26:23
over these stones I have **b**, ...Je 43:10
you will not be picked up or **b**. ....Eze 29:5
they are not **b** with the other ....Eze 32:27
all his army will be **b** there, ...Eze 39:11
came and got his body and **b** it. ....Mt 14:12
rich man died, too, and was **b**. ....Lk 16:22
our ancestor, died and was **b**. ....Ac 2:29
The men who **b** your husband are ....Ac 5:9
her out and **b** her beside her ....Ac 5:10
religious people **b** Stephen and ....Ac 8:2
he died and was **b** beside his ....Ac 13:36
we were **b** with Christ and shared ....Rm 6:4
that he was **b** and was raised to 1Co 15:4
you were **b** with Christ, ...Col 2:12

BURN

lamb we will **b** as a sacrifice? ....Ge 22:7
you must **b** it with fire. ....Ex 12:10
b for burn, wound for wound, and ....Ex 21:25
olive oil to **b** in the lamps; ....Ex 25:6
B the whole sheep on the altar; ....Ex 29:18
You must **b** these things as an ....Ex 29:42
Aaron must **b** sweet-smelling ....Ex 30:7
the priest must **b** all its parts ....Le 1:13
must not **b** any yeast or honey ....Le 2:11
He must **b** it on a wood fire on ....Le 4:12
He must **b** all the goat's fat on ....Le 4:26
The priest must **b** the clothing. ....Le 13:52
The people must **b** that man and ....Le 20:14
This great fire will **b** us up. ....Dt 5:25
B up their idols in the fire. ....Dt 7:25
They even **b** their sons and..............Dt 12:31
Then completely **b** the city and ....Dt 13:16
After you take the city, **b** it. ....Jos 8:8
We will **b** your house down with ....Jdg 12:1

did your servants **b** my field?" 2Sa 14:31
You will **b** their strong, walled 2Ki 8:12
David ordered his men to **b** them. 1Ch 14:12
There we will **b** sweet-smelling 2Ch 2:4
to **b** in front of the Most Holy 2Ch 4:20
of the Lᴏʀᴅ to **b** incense as his 2Ch 27:2
you will **b** them as in a furnace. ....Ps 21:9
your jealousy **b** like a fire? ....Ps 79:5
will your anger **b** like a fire? ....Ps 89:46
died as quickly as thorns **b**. ....Ps 118:12
I hate the incense you **b**. ....Is 1:13
wind will **b** you like fire. ....Is 33:11
The fires will **b** night and day; ....Is 34:10
Those who **b** incense are like ....Is 66:3
Will you **b** incense to the god ....Je 7:9
made my anger **b** like a hot fire,..............Je 17:4
fire, and it will **b** forever." ....Je 17:4
where they **b** their children in ....Je 19:5
that will **b** up everything..............Je 21:14
Baal so they could **b** their sons ....Je 32:35
Babylon, and he will **b** it down! ....Je 34:2
set it on fire, and **b** it down. ....Je 34:22
and he will **b** down the temples ....Je 43:13
B one-third with fire in the ....Eze 5:2
They will **b** down your houses and..............Eze 16:41
then melt and its rust **b** away.....................Eze 24:11
the weapons to **b** in their fires ....Eze 39:9
b like an oven; their hearts ....Hos 7:6
their hearts **b** inside them. ....Hos 7:6
and was going to **b** up the land. ....Am 7:4
set them on fire and **b** them up. ....Ob 1:18
I will **b** up your chariots in ....Nah 2:13
There the fire will **b** you up. ....Nah 3:15
a fire that will **b** up the whole..............Zph 1:18
so fire may **b** your cedar trees ....Zch 11:1
coming that will **b** like a hot ....Mal 4:1
but he will **b** the chaff with a ....Mt 3:12
the murderers and **b** their city. ....Mt 22:7
more oil for the lamps to **b**. ....Mt 25:3
of the Lord and **b** incense. ....Lk 1:9
but he will **b** the chaff with a ....Lk 3:17
them into the fire, and **b** them. ....Jn 15:6
to marry than to **b** with sexual 1Co 7:9
them, and no heat will **b** them, ...Rev 7:16
given power to **b** the people with ....Rev 16:8
her body and **b** her with fire. ....Rev 17:16

BURNED

and he **b** them on the altar as ....Ge 8:20
out and let her be **b** to death." ....Ge 38:24
were thin and **b** by the hot east ....Ge 41:6
fire must pay for what was **b**. ....Ex 22:6
Then he **b** sweet-smelling incense ....Ex 40:27
offering must be **b** with fire. ....Le 6:30
sin offering and **b** them on the ....Le 9:10
the mildew must be **b** with fire. ....Le 13:57
She must be **b** with fire. ....Le 21:9
They **b** all the Midianite towns ....Nu 31:10
Then Israel **b** the whole city and ....Jos 6:24
Then Joshua **b** the city of Ai and ....Jos 8:28
horses and **b** their chariots. ....Jos 11:9
only that city was **b** by Joshua. ....Jos 11:13
As the fire **b**, the angel of the ....Jdg 13:20
the Philistines **b** Samson's wife ....Jdg 15:6
weakened like **b** strings and fell..............Jdg 16:14
swords and then **b** the city. ....Jdg 18:27
they **b** every city they found. ....Jdg 20:48
We **b** Ziklag, as well." 1Sa 30:14
There they **b** the bodies. 1Sa 31:12
Human bones will be **b** on you.'" 1Ki 13:2
that idol and **b** it in the Kidron 1Ki 15:13
came down and **b** the sacrifice, ...1Ki 18:38
the temple of Baal and **b** them. 2Ki 10:26

The Israelites **b** incense 2Ki 17:11
The Sepharvites **b** their children 2Ki 17:31
housetop that is **b** by the wind 2Ki 19:26
They **b** incense to Baal, the sun, ... 2Ki 23:5
Josiah **b** that place, broke the 2Ki 23:15
Every important building was **b**................ 2Ki 25:9
He **b** the bones of their priests 2Ch 34:5
and its gates have been **b**. .... Ne 2:17
It **b** up the sheep and the .... Job 1:16
I thought about it, my anger **b**. .... Ps 39:3
b your Temple to the ground; .... Ps 74:7
They **b** every place where God .... Ps 74:8
it is cut down and **b** with fire;................ Ps 80:16
and my bones are **b** up with fire. .... Ps 102:3
and flames **b** up the wicked. .... Ps 106:18
You have **b** the vineyard........................ Is 3:14
People will be **b** until their .... Is 33:12
housetop that is **b** by the wind .... Is 37:27
There they **b** their own sons and .... Je 7:31
whole scroll was **b** in the fire............... Je 36:23
King Jehoiakim **b** the scroll .... Je 36:27
Jerusalem will not be **b** down, ... Je 38:17
It **b** up the leaders of Moab and .... Je 48:45
He **b** against the people of Jacob .... La 2:3
sacrifice is **b** on the altar is.................... Eze 43:15
hair was not **b**, their robes were .... Da 3:27
and flames have **b** all the trees .... Joe 1:19
They **b** the bones of the king of .... Am 2:1
It **b** up the deep water and was .... Am 7:4
her idols will be **b** with fire. .... Mic 1:7
they will be **b** up quickly like .... Nah 1:10
and tie them together to be **b**................... Mt 13:30
are pulled up and **b** in the fire, ... Mt 13:40
magic books and **b** them before .... Ac 19:19
But if the building is **b** up, ... 1Co 3:15
my body as an offering to be **b**. 1Co 13:3
animals are **b** outside the camp............... Heb 13:11
a third of the trees were **b** up................. Rev 8:7
They were **b** by the great heat, ... Rev 16:9
down from heaven and **b** them up. .... Rev 20:9

BURNED-OUT

I will make you a **b** mountain. .... Je 51:25

BURNING

sent a rain of **b** sulfur down .... Ge 19:24
bush continue to burn without burning .... Ex 3:3
them, like fire **b** straw. .... Ex 15:7
looked like a fire **b** on top of .... Ex 24:17
the lamps on the lampstand **b**. .... Ex 27:20
keep the lamps **b** before the LORD........... Ex 27:21
of acacia wood for **b** incense. .... Ex 30:1
must be kept **b** on the altar; .... Le 6:12
take a pan full of **b** coals from .... Le 16:12
to the LORD, the fire stopped **b**............... Nu 11:2
and throw them onto the **b** cow. .... Nu 19:6
mountain that was **b** with fire, ... Dt 9:15
will be like a **b** fire against .... Dt 29:20
empty jar with a **b** torch inside. .... Jdg 7:16
attacking Ziklag and **b** it. 1Sa 30:1
b fire came out of his mouth. 2Sa 22:9
b the palace and himself with it............... 1Ki 16:18
LORD's anger is **b** against us,................ 2Ki 22:13
will send his **b** anger against .... Job 20:23
send hot coals and **b** sulfur on .... Ps 11:6
b fire came out of his mouth. .... Ps 18:8
faster than **b** thorns can heat .... Ps 58:9
Let **b** coals fall on them. .... Ps 140:10
chest without **b** your clothes, ... Pr 6:27
hot coals without **b** your feet. .... Pr 6:28
their words are like a **b** fire. .... Pr 16:27
be like pouring **b** coals on his................. Pr 25:22
madman shooting deadly, **b** arrows .... Pr 26:18
like two barely **b** sticks that .... Is 7:4

like a fire **b** until everything .... Is 10:16
at the time of his **b** anger. .... Is 13:13
and his tongue is like a **b** fire. .... Is 30:27
Its land will be like **b** tar. .... Is 34:9
The **b** desert will have pools of .... Is 35:7
becomes like a **b** fire inside me, ... Je 20:9
Jehoiakim out of **b** the scroll, ... Je 36:25
Babylon's houses are **b**. .... Je 51:30
looked like **b** coals of fire or .... Eze 1:13
because my **b** anger is against .... Eze 7:12
will pile the wood high for **b**. .... Eze 24:9
hailstones and **b** sulfur on Gog, ... Eze 38:22
it was thrown into the **b** fire. .... Da 7:11
of a roaring fire **b** dry stalks. .... Joe 2:5
You were like a **b** stick pulled................ Am 4:11
man was like a **b** stick pulled .... Zch 3:2
for her is like a fire **b** in me." .... Zch 8:2
like a fire **b** a stack of wood .... Zch 12:6
of wood or like a fire **b** straw................. Zch 12:6
Moses wrote about the **b** bush, ... Mk 12:26
and I wish it were already **b**! .... Lk 12:49
When he wrote about the **b** bush, ... Lk 20:37
like a fire **b** in us when Jesus .... Lk 24:32
John was like a **b** and shining .... Jn 5:35
that Moses saw in the **b** bush. .... Ac 7:35
pouring **b** coals on his head. .... Rm 12:20
can stop all the **b** arrows of the .... Eph 6:16
appears with **b** fire from heaven.............. 2Th 1:7
a golden altar for **b** incense and .... Heb 9:4
touched and that is **b** with fire. .... Heb 12:18
sun rises with **b** heat and dries .... Jam 1:11
Gomorrah by **b** them until they 2Pe 2:6
the throne seven lamps were **b**, ... Rev 4:5
a big mountain, **b** with fire, was .... Rev 8:8
a large star, **b** like a torch, ... Rev 8:10
smoke from their **b** pain will .... Rev 14:11
will see the smoke from her **b**. .... Rev 18:9
eyes are like **b** fire, and on his .... Rev 19:12
into the lake of **b** sulfur with .... Rev 20:10
a place in the lake of **b** sulfur.................. Rev 21:8

BURNS

If the fire **b** his neighbor's .... Ex 22:6
the one who **b** them must wash .... Le 16:28
The man who **b** the cow must wash .... Nu 19:8
a fire that **b** down to the place .... Dt 32:22
completely as fire **b** up manure. 1Ki 14:10
My anger **b** against this place................. 2Ki 22:17
His anger **b** against me, and he .... Job 19:11
and fire **b** up their wealth.' .... Job 22:20
and spears and **b** up the chariots .... Ps 46:9
A fire **b** in front of him, and a................. Ps 50:3
a fire that **b** a forest or like..................... Ps 83:14
before him and **b** up his enemies .... Ps 97:3
Her lamp **b** late into the night. .... Pr 31:18
flames and **b** like a hot fire..................... Sng 8:6
just as fire **b** straw or dry .... Is 5:24
The fire **b** away the great trees .... Is 10:18
a great fire that **b** everything,................. Is 30:30
can live near this fire that **b** .... Is 33:14
Then he **b** the tree. He uses some .... Is 44:15
her salvation **b** bright like a .... Is 62:1
Like a fire that **b** all the time, ... Is 65:5
will be like wood that it **b** up. .... Je 5:14
burn until it **b** even the strong .... Je 17:27
fire that **b** up everything .... La 2:3
and the fire **b** up both ends and .... Eze 15:4
in back of them a flame **b**..................... Joe 2:3
to his net and **b** incense to .... Hab 1:16
into the fire that **b** forever. .... Mt 18:8
the fire that **b** forever that was .... Mt 25:41
is like a fire that **b** things up. .... Heb 12:29
lake of fire that **b** with sulfur.................. Rev 19:20

B

BURNT

him as a whole **b** offering on one .... Ge 22:2
it as a whole **b** offering to God, ... Ge 22:13
as sacrifices and **b** offerings, ... Ex 10:25
a whole **b** offering and other .... Ex 18:12
it is a **b** offering made by fire .... Ex 29:18
near the altar for **b** offerings, ... Ex 40:32
offering is a whole **b** offering .... Le 1:3
will bring whole **b** offerings, ... Le 23:37
animals for the **b** offering was .... Nu 7:87
offer a lamb as a **b** offering or .... Nu 15:5
ashes from the **b** offering to .... Nu 19:17
This is the **b** offering for every .... Nu 28:10
Present your **b** offerings on the .... Dt 12:27
altar to offer **b** offerings or .... Jos 22:23
accepted our **b** offering or grain .... Jdg 13:23
Bring me the whole **b** offering 1Sa 13:9
David offered whole **b** offerings 2Sa 6:17
I'll not offer any **b** offering or 2Ki 5:17
for Israel's **b** offerings will be 1Ch 22:1
Solomon offered **b** offerings to 2Ch 8:12
and offer a **b** offering for .... Job 42:8
You do not ask for **b** offerings .... Ps 40:6
bring me your **b** offerings. .... Ps 50:8
You don't want **b** offerings. .... Ps 51:16
enough of your **b** sacrifices of .... Is 1:11
Your **b** offerings will not be .... Je 6:20
rules to offer **b** offerings and .... Eze 43:18
me more than I want **b** offerings. .... Hos 6:6
If you offer me **b** offerings and .... Am 5:22
before him with **b** offerings, ... Mic 6:6
You do not ask for **b** offerings .... Heb 10:6

BURST

I am ready to **b** like a new .... Job 32:19
b into songs and make music. .... Ps 98:4
hills will **b** into song before .... Is 55:12
death, his body **b** open, and all .... Ac 1:18

BURSTS

b into flames and burns like .... Sng 8:6

BURY

so that I can **b** my dead wife." .... Ge 23:4
me you will not **b** me in Egypt. .... Ge 47:29
B me with my ancestors in the .... Ge 49:29
So Joseph went to **b** his father. .... Ge 50:7
Kill him there and **b** him. 1Ki 2:31
went into Edom to **b** the dead, ... 1Ki 11:15
When I die, **b** me in this same 1Ki 13:31
The men went to **b** Jezebel, ... 2Ki 9:35
No one was left to **b** the dead. .... Ps 79:3
They will **b** the dead in Topheth .... Je 7:32
is no room to **b** anyone else. .... Je 7:32
gather up the bones and **b** them. .... Je 8:2
They will **b** him like a donkey, ... Je 22:19
up their bodies and **b** them. .... Je 25:33
B them in the clay in the brick .... Je 43:9
people in the land will **b** them, ... Eze 39:13
they will **b** Gog's soldiers still .... Eze 39:14
the gravediggers **b** the bone in .... Eze 39:15
Memphis will **b** them. Weeds will .... Hos 9:6
let me go and **b** my father." .... Mt 8:21
as a place to **b** strangers who .... Mt 27:7
who are dead **b** their own dead. .... Lk 9:60
He asked, "Where did you **b** him?" .... Jn 11:34
which is how they **b** the dead. .... Jn 19:40
and they will refuse to **b** them. .... Rev 11:9

BURYING

stop you from **b** your dead wife." .... Ge 23:6
Egyptians were **b** their firstborn .... Nu 33:4
to your master Saul by **b** him. 2Sa 2:5
as some Israelites were **b** a man, ... 2Ki 13:21
Israel will be **b** them for seven .... Eze 39:12

BUSH

Hagar put her son under a **b.** .... Ge 21:15
caught in a **b** by its horns. .... Ge 22:13
of fire coming out of a **b.** .... Ex 3:2
How can a **b** continue burning .... Ex 3:3
God called to him from the **b,** .... Ex 3:4
down under a **b** and asked to die 1Ki 19:4
They are like a **b** in a desert .... Je 17:6
Go like a **b** being blown through .... Je 48:6
Moses wrote about the burning **b,** .... Mk 12:26
he wrote about the burning **b,** .... Lk 20:37
that Moses saw in the burning **b.** .... Ac 7:35

BUSHEL

was about one-half **b** of barley. .... Ru 2:17
Take this half **b** of cooked grain 1Sa 17:17
sheep, a **b** of cooked grain 1Sa 25:18
offering one-half **b** for each .... Eze 45:24
oil for each half **b** of grain. .... Eze 46:5
and one-half **b** with the male .... Eze 46:7

BUSHELS

for each six **b** of barley seed .... Le 27:16
gathered at least sixty **b,** .... Nu 11:32
ninety-five **b** of fine flour, ... 1Ki 4:22
sixty-two thousand **b** of wheat, ... 2Ch 27:5
six hundred **b** of wheat, six .... Ezr 7:22
and ten **b** of seed will grow only .... Is 5:10
of silver and ten **b** of barley. .... Hos 3:2
bill and write eight hundred **b.'** .... Lk 16:7

BUSHES

went to hide in caves and **b,** 1Sa 13:6
animals among the **b** and huddled .... Job 30:7
or hide in the **b** waiting to .... Job 38:40
the larger **b** in the forest, ... Is 9:18
and wild **b** will grow in the .... Is 34:13
hide in the thick **b** and climb up .... Je 4:29
stands will be covered with **b.'** .... Je 26:18
from the thick **b** near the Jordan .... Je 49:19
stands will be covered with **b.** .... Mic 3:12
they don't get grapes from **b.** .... Lk 6:44

BUSINESS

The king's **b** was very important, ... 1Sa 21:8
in God's work and the king's **b.** 1Ch 26:32
to those who do the king's **b,** .... Est 3:9
in ships and did **b** on the great .... Ps 107:23
Those who are fair in their **b** .... Ps 112:5
along, minding their own **b.** .... Pr 9:15
and another went to his **b.** .... Mt 22:5
a manager to take care of his **b.** .... Lk 16:1
'Do **b** with this money until I .... Lk 19:13
I come back, that is not your **b.** .... Jn 21:22
make a lot of money from our **b.** .... Ac 19:25
of your own **b,** and do your own 1Th 4:11
they are still taking care of **b.** .... Jam 1:11
a year, do **b,** and make money. .... Jam 4:13

BUSINESSES

you have in several different **b,** .... Ec 11:2

BUSY

work harder and keep them **b;** .... Ex 5:9
is thinking, or **b,** or traveling! 1Ki 18:27
But I was **b** doing other things, ... 1Ki 20:40
God keeps them **b** with what they .... Ec 5:20
I saw how **b** people are, working .... Ec 8:16
This city was a very **b** city, ... Is 22:2
But Martha was **b** with all the .... Lk 10:40
not married is **b** with the Lord's 1Co 7:32
who is married is **b** with things 1Co 7:33
do nothing but **b** themselves in 2Th 3:11
to gossip and **b** themselves with 1Ti 5:13

BUTCHER

an ox led to the **b,** like a deer .... Pr 7:22

BUTCHERED
a gentle lamb waiting to be **b**..................Je 11:19
people away like sheep to be **b**. ....Je 12:3

BUTTER
His words are slippery like **b**, ...Ps 55:21
Just as stirring milk makes **b**,.................Pr 30:33

BUTTOCKS
and barefoot, with their **b** bare. ....Is 20:4

BUY
in Egypt to **b** grain because ....Ge 41:57
went down to **b** grain from Egypt. ....Ge 42:3
B back every firstborn donkey by ....Ex 13:13
You must **b** back from the LORD ....Ex 13:13
If you **b** a Hebrew slave, he will ....Ex 21:2
the LORD to **b** back your lives. ....Ex 30:15
If you want to **b** your neighbor's ....Le 25:15
the silver to **b** anything you ....Dt 14:26
If you want to **b** back the land, ...Ru 4:4
When you **b** the land from Naomi, ...Ru 4:5
to Boaz, "**B** the land yourself,.................Ru 4:8
To **b** the threshing floor from 2Sa 24:21
the money to **b** timber and cut 2Ki 12:12
and builders to **b** cut stone and 2Ch 34:11
With this money **b** bulls, male ....Ezr 7:17
We did not **b** any fields. ....Ne 5:16
but we will not **b** on the Sabbath ....Ne 10:31
God will **b** you back from death ....Job 5:20
B me back from the clutches of ....Job 6:23
and you cannot **b** it with jewels ....Job 28:17
No one can **b** back the life of ....Ps 49:7
any good to try to **b** wisdom, ...Pr 17:16
sell some goats to **b** a field.....................Pr 27:26
person cannot **b** those expensive ....Is 40:20
So you did not **b** incense for me; ....Is 43:24
not have money, come, **b** and eat! ....Is 55:1
Come **b** wine and milk without ....Is 55:1
Go and **b** a linen belt and put it ....Je 13:1
and **b** a clay jar from a potter. ....Je 19:1
of Jacob and will **b** them back ....Je 31:11
so **b** my field near the town of ....Je 32:7
use their money to **b** fields.....................Je 32:44
They will again **b** fields in the ....Je 32:44
We have to **b** the water we drink; ....La 5:4
sold girls to **b** wine to drink.................Joe 3:3
sell the poor to **b** a pair of ....Am 2:6
that money they **b** wine to drink.............Am 2:8
will **b** poor people for silver, ...Am 8:6
go there and **b** you back from.................Mic 4:10
he owned to **b** that field. ....Mt 13:44
to the towns and **b** food for....................Mt 14:15
enough to **b** back their souls. ....Mt 16:26
who sell oil and **b** some for....................Mt 25:9
bridesmaids went to **b** oil, ...Mt 25:10
the coins to **b** Potter's Field...................Mt 27:7
money to **b** that much bread! ....Mk 6:37
enough to **b** back their souls. ....Mk 8:37
unless we go **b** food for all ....Lk 9:13
sword, sell your coat and **b** one. ....Lk 22:36
Where can we **b** enough bread for ....Jn 6:5
telling him to **b** what was needed ....Jn 13:29
you could **b** God's gift with.....................Ac 8:20
Those who **b** things should live 1Co 7:30
this so he could **b** freedom for ....Gal 4:5
I advise you to **b** from me gold ....Rev 3:18
B from me white clothes so you ....Rev 3:18
No one could **b** or sell without ....Rev 13:17
is no one to **b** their cargoes— ....Rev 18:11

BUYER
Don't let the **b** be happy or the ....Eze 7:12

BUYERS
B say, "This is bad. It's no good................Pr 20:14
masters, to **b** and sellers, to ....Is 24:2
Their **b** kill them and are not ....Zch 11:5
will not be any **b** or sellers ....Zch 14:21

BUYING
that I am **b** it as a burial ....Ge 23:9
paid for the grain they were **b**, ...Ge 47:14
am **b** from Naomi everything that ....Ru 4:9
people who were **b** and selling ....Mt 21:12
those who were **b** and selling ....Mk 11:15
eating, drinking, **b**, selling, ...Lk 17:28
a place for **b** and selling!" ....Jn 2:16
were in town **b** some food. ....Jn 4:8

BUYS
If someone **b** a slave and........................Ex 12:44
a profit from the food he **b**......................Le 25:37
She inspects a field and **b** it. ....Pr 31:16
happy, and money **b** anything. ....Ec 10:19

BUZI
to Ezekiel son of **B** in the land ....Eze 1:3

BYBLOS
and the men from **B** carved the 1Ki 5:18
the people of **B**, Ammon, Amalek, ...Ps 83:7
Workers of **B** were with you, ...Eze 27:9

C

CABUL
So he named them the Land of **C**, ...1Ki 9:13

CAESAR
Give to **C** the things that are ....Mt 22:21
right to pay taxes to **C** or not? ....Mk 12:14
Give to **C** the things that are ....Mk 12:17
Augustus **C** sent an order that ....Lk 2:1
year of the rule of Tiberius **C**..................Lk 3:1
These men were under **C**: ....Lk 3:1
us to pay taxes to **C** or not?" ....Lk 20:22
Then give to **C** the things that ....Lk 20:25
we should not pay taxes to **C**,.................Lk 23:2
makes himself king is against **C**. ....Jn 19:12
do things against the laws of **C**, ...Ac 17:7
the Temple, or against **C**." ....Ac 25:8
I want **C** to hear my case!" ....Ac 25:11
asked to see **C**, so you will go................Ac 25:12
he asked to be judged by **C**, ...Ac 25:25
he has asked **C** to hear his case...............Ac 26:32
You must stand before **C**. ....Ac 27:24
Rome to have my trial before **C**...............Ac 28:19
those from the palace of **C**......................Php 4:22

CAESAR'S
The men answered, "**C**."...........................Mt 22:21
to Caesar the things that are **C**, ...Mt 22:21
to Caesar the things that are **C**, ...Mk 12:17
name are on it?" They said, "**C**." ....Lk 20:24
to Caesar the things that are **C**, ...Lk 20:25
I am standing at **C** judgment seat ....Ac 25:10

CAESAREA
came to the area of **C** Philippi, ...Mt 16:13
to the towns around **C** Philippi. ....Mk 8:27
took Saul to **C** and from there ....Ac 9:30
At **C** there was a man named ....Ac 10:1
following day they came to **C**, ...Ac 10:24
Judea and went to the city of **C**,..............Ac 12:19
Paul landed at **C**, he went and ....Ac 18:22
and went to the city of **C**. ....Ac 21:8
the followers from **C** went with ....Ac 21:16
I need some men to go to **C**. ....Ac 23:23
horsemen went with Paul to **C**, ...Ac 23:32

CAGE

went to the city of C with some .... Ac 24:1
he went from C to Jerusalem. .... Ac 25:1
came to C to visit Festus. .... Ac 25:13
came here to C for the trial, ... Ac 25:17
But he asked to be kept in C. .... Ac 25:21

CAGE

put him into a c with chains .... Eze 19:9

CAGES

Like c full of birds, their .... Je 5:27

CAIAPHAS

of the high priest, named C. .... Mt 26:3
Jesus led him to the house of C, ... Mt 26:57
Annas and C were the high .... Lk 3:2
One of the men there was C, ... Jn 11:49
C did not think of this himself. .... Jn 11:51
of C, the high priest .... Jn 18:13
C was the one who told the Jews .... Jn 18:14
the high priest, C, John, and .... Ac 4:6

CAIN

pregnant and gave birth to C. .... Ge 4:1
flocks, and C became a farmer. .... Ge 4:2
C brought some food from the .... Ge 4:3
did not accept C and his gift. .... Ge 4:5
So C became very angry and felt .... Ge 4:5
C attacked his brother Abel and .... Ge 4:8
LORD said to C, "Where is your .... Ge 4:9
put a mark on C warning anyone .... Ge 4:15
So C went away from the LORD and .... Ge 4:16
At that time C was building a .... Ge 4:17
a better sacrifice than C did. .... Heb 11:4
Do not be like C who belonged to 1Jn 3:12
the things C did were evil, ... 1Jn 3:12
They have followed the way of C, ... Jud 1:11

CAKE

of bread, a c made with olive .... Ex 29:23
piece of a fig c and two 1Sa 30:12
a loaf of bread, a c of dates, ... 2Sa 6:19
as you would eat a barley c, ... Eze 4:12

CAKES

make bread, c mixed with olive .... Ex 29:2
it in a pot or made c with it, ... Nu 11:8
two hundred c of pressed figs 1Sa 25:18
of her special c for me while I 2Sa 13:6
Tamar took the c she had made 2Sa 13:10
one hundred c of raisins, one 2Sa 16:1
The bread and c of figs are for 2Sa 16:2
of bread, some c, and a jar of 1Ki 14:3
flour, fig c, raisins, wine, ... 1Ch 12:40
for the raisin c they had in Kir .... Is 16:7
make the dough for c of bread, ... Je 7:18
were making c that looked like .... Je 44:19
and love to eat the raisin c." .... Hos 3:1

CALAMUS

and saffron, c, and cinnamon, ... Sng 4:14

CALEB

of Judah, C son of Jephunneh; .... Nu 13:6
son of Nun and C son of .... Nu 14:6
But my servant C thinks .... Nu 14:24
blessed C son of Jephunneh .... Jos 14:13
C forced out the three Anakite .... Jos 15:14
So C gave her the upper and .... Jdg 1:15
and he was a descendant of C. 1Sa 25:3
C had another slave woman named 1Ch 2:48

CALEB'S

son of Kenaz, C younger brother, ... Jdg 3:9
C first son was Mesha. 1Ch 2:42
C slave woman was named Ephah, ... 1Ch 2:46
C daughter was Acsah. 1Ch 2:49

CALF

three men the c that had been .... Ge 18:8
a tool and made a statue of a c. .... Ex 32:4
saw the gold c and the dancing .... Ex 32:19
did with the c Aaron had made. .... Ex 32:35
The c will be a sin offering, ... Le 9:2
an idol in the shape of a c. .... Dt 9:16
took that sinful c idol you had .... Dt 9:21
said, "Take a young c with you. 1Sa 16:2
sacrificed a bull and a fat c. 2Sa 6:13
put one golden c in the city of 1Ki 12:29
as Dan to worship the c there. 1Ki 12:30
goat and c idols he had made. 2Ch 11:15
an idol of a c for themselves. .... Ne 9:18
dance like a c and Mount Hermon .... Ps 29:6
made a gold c at Mount Sinai .... Ps 106:19
They cut a c into two pieces .... Je 34:18
Kiss those c idols and sacrifice .... Hos 13:2
your father killed the fat c, ... Lk 15:27
an idol that looked like a c. .... Ac 7:41
The second was like a c. .... Rev 4:7

CALF'S

feet were like a c hoofs and .... Eze 1:7

CALF-SHAPED

I hate the c idol of Israel! .... Hos 8:5
Israel's c idol will surely be .... Hos 8:6

CALIPERS

a statue and his c to measure .... Is 44:13

CALL

will c her 'woman,' because she .... Ge 2:23
We will c Rebekah and ask her .... Ge 24:57
That is why people c him Edom. .... Ge 25:30
Now women will c me happy," .... Ge 30:13
day you will c a holy meeting; .... Le 23:21
and use them to c the people .... Nu 10:2
c down evil on the people of .... Nu 23:7
They will c the people to the .... Dt 33:19
a trumpet to c the Abiezrites to .... Jdg 6:34
didn't c you c us when you went .... Jdg 8:1
So go c to them for help. .... Jdg 10:14
Why didn't you c us to help you .... Jdg 12:1
the people, "Don't c me Naomi. .... Ru 1:20
C me Mara, because the Almighty .... Ru 1:20
Again Eli said, "I didn't c you. 1Sa 3:6
We c the person a prophet 1Sa 9:9
is why people c this place Rock 1Sa 23:28
I will c to the LORD, who is 2Sa 22:4
my c for help reached his ears. 2Sa 22:7
C the people together, and give 1Ki 21:9
Gehazi, "C the Shunammite 2Ki 4:12
Now c for me all Baal's prophets 2Ki 10:19
the trumpet to c us to war 2Ch 13:12
C if you want to, Job, but no .... Job 5:1
Then c me, and I will answer, or .... Job 13:22
You will c, and I will answer .... Job 14:15
I c to you, God, and you answer .... Ps 17:6
I will c to the LORD, who is .... Ps 18:3
listens when they c out to him. .... Ps 22:24
LORD, hear me when I c; .... Ps 27:7
C to me in times of trouble. .... Ps 50:15
I c to God, and he will hear me. .... Ps 77:1
love for those who c to you. .... Ps 86:5
I c to you in times of trouble, ... Ps 86:7
They will c to me, and I will .... Ps 91:15
c to you. Save me so I can obey .... Ps 119:146
LORD, I c to you. Come quickly. .... Ps 141:1
and to the little birds that c. .... Ps 147:9
Then you will c to me, but I .... Pr 1:28
for people who c good things bad .... Is 5:20
time I will c for my servant. .... Is 22:20
So I c that country Rahab the .... Is 30:7

CALLED

wild goats will **c** to their .... Is 34:14
Cyrus, I **c** you by name, and I.................. Is 45:4
You **c** yourselves people of the .... Is 48:2
You will **c** for nations that you .... Is 55:5
you should **c** to him while he is .... Is 55:6
should **c** the Sabbath a joyful .... Is 58:13
They will **c** you The City of the .... Is 60:14
you would **c** me 'My Father' .... Je 3:19
They will **c** it The Valley of .... Je 7:32
Then you will **c** my name. .... Je 29:12
with silver and **c** in witnesses.' .... Je 32:25
C for the archers to come .... Je 50:29
Then I will **c** for a war against .... Eze 38:21
people will **c** it The Valley of .... Eze 39:11
hard problems. **C** for Daniel. He.............. Da 5:12
You are to **c** your brothers, ... Hos 2:1
she will **c** me 'my husband;................... Hos 2:16
First they **c** to Egypt for help. .... Hos 7:11
C for a day when everyone fasts! .... Joe 1:14
c for a day when everyone fasts. .... Joe 2:15
They will **c** the farmers to come .... Am 5:16
they **c** for a holy war against .... Mic 3:5
I will **c** my people and gather .... Zch 10:8
the nations will **c** you blessed, ... Mal 3:12
And if you **c** someone a fool, ... Mt 5:22
marketplace, who **c** out to each .... Mt 11:16
'C the workers and pay them................... Mt 20:8
Then why did David **c** him 'Lord'? .... Mt 22:43
to have people **c** them 'Teacher.' .... Mt 23:7
answered, "Why do you **c** me good? .... Mk 10:18
with this man you **c** the king of .... Mk 15:12
They began to **c** out to him, ... Mk 15:18
Why do you **c** me, 'Lord, Lord,' .... Lk 6:46
do you want us to **c** fire down .... Lk 9:54
she will **c** her friends and .... Lk 15:9
I no longer **c** you servants, ... Jn 15:15
But I **c** you friends, because I .... Jn 15:15
clean, so don't **c** them unholy!" .... Ac 10:15
began to **c** Barnabas "Zeus" .... Ac 14:12
more time, I will **c** for you." .... Ac 24:25
about you? You **c** yourself a Jew. .... Rm 2:17
with those who **c** themselves 1Co 5:11
Those who **c** you "uncircumcised" .... Eph 2:11
and with the trumpet **c** of God. 1Th 4:16
we preached to **c** you to be saved 2Th 2:14
not ashamed to **c** them his .... Heb 2:11
obeyed God's **c** to go to another .... Heb 11:8
words that **c** you his children:................ Heb 12:5
is sick should **c** the church's .... Jam 5:14
pray to God and **c** him Father, ... 1Pe 1:17
learned what some **c** Satan's deep .... Rev 2:24

CALLED

east, in a place **c** Eden, and put .... Ge 2:8
Whatever the man **c** each living .... Ge 2:19
the LORD God **c** to the man and .... Ge 3:9
The place is **c** Babel since that .... Ge 11:9
of Bela. (Bela is also **c** Zoar.) .... Ge 14:2
he **c** out his 318 trained men who .... Ge 14:14
They **c** to Lot, "Where are the .... Ge 19:5
Then Abimelech **c** Abraham to him .... Ge 20:9
and God's angel **c** to Hagar from .... Ge 21:17
that place was **c** Beersheba.................. Ge 21:31
angel of the LORD **c** to Abraham .... Ge 22:15
Mamre was later **c** Hebron in the .... Ge 23:19
Abimelech **c** for Isaac and said, ... Ge 26:9
that city is **c** Beersheba even .... Ge 26:33
One day he **c** his older son Esau.............. Ge 27:1
Isaac **c** Jacob and blessed him .... Ge 28:1
the place was **c** A Pile to Remind .... Ge 31:48
It was also **c** Mizpah, because .... Ge 31:49
you will not be **c** Jacob any .... Ge 35:10
be Israel." So he **c** him Israel.................. Ge 35:10

but Jacob **c** him Benjamin. .... Ge 35:18
history of Esau (also **c** Edom). .... Ge 36:1
So the king **c** for Joseph. .... Ge 41:14
he **c** his son Joseph to him and .... Ge 47:29
Then Jacob **c** his sons to him.................. Ge 49:1
God **c** to him from the bush, ... Ex 3:4
the king **c** in his wise men and .... Ex 7:11
The king **c** for Moses and Aaron .... Ex 8:8
Then Moses **c** all the elders of .... Ex 12:21
the night the king **c** for Moses .... Ex 12:31
of Israel **c** the food manna................... Ex 16:31
Moses went down and **c** the elders........... Ex 19:7
he **c** Moses to come up to the top .... Ex 19:20
he **c** it the "Meeting Tent." .... Ex 33:7
and the LORD **c** out his name: .... Ex 34:5
The LORD **c** to Moses and spoke to .... Le 1:1
Moses **c** for Aaron and his sons .... Le 9:1
This time will be **c** Jubilee. .... Le 25:10
and **c** all the people of Israel .... Nu 1:18
way, they will be **c** Nazirites. .... Nu 6:2
He **c** to Aaron and Miriam, and .... Nu 12:5
That place was **c** the Valley of .... Nu 13:24
Bashan is **c** the Towns of Jair.................. Dt 3:14
Moses **c** all the people of Israel .... Dt 5:1
is **c** the city of palm trees. .... Dt 34:3
Then he **c** the twelve men .... Jos 4:4
Joshua son of Nun **c** the priests .... Jos 6:6
That is why it is **c** the Valley .... Jos 7:26
the past it was **c** Kiriath Arba, ... Jos 14:15
city (which is **c** Jerusalem)..................... Jos 15:8
Jearim (also **c** Kesalon) and came .... Jos 15:10
Then Joshua **c** a meeting of all .... Jos 22:1
Luz, which it is **c** even today. .... Jdg 1:26
the LORD chose leaders **c** judges, ... Jdg 2:16
Barak **c** the people of Zebulun .... Jdg 4:10
So they **c** out all the men of .... Jdg 7:24
also **c** Gideon, for all .... Jdg 8:35
She **c** out to him, "Samson, the .... Jdg 16:12
Then she **c** in a man to shave off .... Jdg 16:19
Boaz **c** to him, "Come here, ... Ru 4:1
The LORD **c** Samuel for the third 1Sa 3:8
I am here. You **c** me." Then Eli 1Sa 3:8
people of Ashdod **c** all five 1Sa 5:8
So they **c** all the kings of the 1Sa 5:11
Then they **c** for their priests 1Sa 6:2
Samuel **c** to Saul on the roof. 1Sa 9:26
c all the people of Israel 1Sa 10:17
So Saul **c** the army together at 1Sa 15:4
but Jonathan **c**, "The arrow is 1Sa 20:37
So Achish **c** David and said to 1Sa 29:6
It is **c** "The Bow," and it is 2Sa 1:18
place in Gibeon is **c** the Field 2Sa 2:16
walled city and **c** it the City of 2Sa 5:9
The Ark is **c** by the Name, the 2Sa 6:2
that place is **c** the Punishment 2Sa 6:8
Then David **c** Uriah to come to 2Sa 11:13
Then the king **c** for Absalom.................. 2Sa 14:33
and it is **c** Absalom's Monument 2Sa 18:18
and he **c** to the gatekeeper,..................... 2Sa 18:26
They **c** for help, but no one came 2Sa 22:42
took him to the spring **c** Gihon. 1Ki 1:38
room, **c** the Most Holy Place, ... 1Ki 6:16
he judged people, **c** the Hall of 1Ki 7:7
round bowl, which was **c** the Sea. 1Ki 7:23
King Solomon **c** for the elders of 1Ki 8:1
and they are still **c** that today................. 1Ki 9:13
that hill and **c** it Samaria after 1Ki 16:24
Ahab **c** about four hundred 1Ki 22:6
The LORD has **c** us three kings 2Ki 3:10
Elisha the prophet **c** a man from 2Ki 9:1
So King Joash **c** for Jehoiada the 2Ki 12:7
He **c** it Joktheel, as it is still 2Ki 14:7
bowl, which was **c** the Sea, off 2Ki 16:17

C

They c for the king, so the king 2Ki 18:18
and Abram, who was c Abraham. 1Ch 1:27
Tent (also c the Meeting Tent)................. 1Ch 6:32
that time Jerusalem was c Jebus, ... 1Ch 11:4
and the Ark is c by his name.................. 1Ch 13:6
that place is c The Punishment 1Ch 13:11
Then David c for his son Solomon 1Ch 22:6
Solomon c for the elders of.................... 2Ch 5:2
people, who are c by my name, ... 2Ch 7:14
Asa c out to the LORD his God, ... 2Ch 14:11
So King Ahab c four hundred................. 2Ch 18:5
Hazazon Tamar is also c En Gedi. 2Ch 20:2
Then I c for the priests, ... Ne 5:12
Hadassah was also c Esther, ... Est 2:7
the royal secretaries were c, ... Est 3:12
Then Esther c for Hathach,.................... Est 4:5
Haman c together his friends .... Est 5:10
So these days were c Purim, ... Est 9:26
If I c to him and he answered, ... Job 9:16
In my trouble I c to the LORD. .... Ps 18:6
They c for help, but no one came .... Ps 18:41
This poor man c, and the LORD .... Ps 34:6
because I have c to you all day. .... Ps 86:3
was in trouble, I c to the LORD, ... Ps 120:1
On the day I c to you, you .... Ps 138:3
I c, but you refused to listen; .... Pr 1:24
stubborn pride are c "proud,"................ Pr 21:24
I c for him, but he did not .... Sng 5:6
women saw her and c her happy; .... Sng 6:9
you will be c the City That Is .... Is 1:26
in Jerusalem will be c holy, ... Is 4:3
I have c those warriors to carry .... Is 13:3
the lookout c out, "My master .... Is 21:8
highway will be c "The Road to .... Is 35:8
on the earth and c you from a .... Is 41:9
the north I have c by name a man .... Is 41:25
I, the LORD, c you to do right, ... Is 42:6
have c you by name, and you are .... Is 43:1
will no longer be c the queen of .... Is 47:5
I have c you to be my people. .... Is 48:12
spoken; I have c him. I have .... Is 48:15
the LORD c me to serve him. .... Is 49:1
But the LORD c you to be his," .... Is 54:6
my Temple will be c a house for.............. Is 56:7
they will be c Trees of Goodness .... Is 61:3
You will be c priests of the .... Is 61:6
You will be c the People God .... Is 62:4
land will be c the Bride of God .... Is 62:4
will be c the Holy People, ... Is 62:12
Jerusalem will be c the City God .... Is 62:12
a hundred years will be c young, ... Is 65:20
The LORD c you "a leafy olive .... Je 11:16
and we are c by your name so .... Je 14:9
the city that is c by my name................ Je 25:29
bowl, which is c the Sea, the .... Je 27:19
So Jeremiah c for Baruch son of .... Je 36:4
You came near when I c to you; .... La 3:57
He c to the man dressed in linen .... Eze 9:3
wheels being c "whirling wheels .... Eze 10:13
I knew they were c cherubim................ Eze 10:20
It is still c High Place today. .... Eze 20:29
very angry and c for Shadrach, ... Da 3:13
Daniel, who was c Belteshazzar, ... Da 4:19
The king c for the magicians, ... Da 5:7
He c out to Daniel, "Daniel, ... Da 6:20
the city that is c by your name. .... Da 9:18
later they will be c 'children .... Hos 1:10
and I c my son out of Egypt. .... Hos 11:1
was in danger, I c to the LORD, ... Jnh 2:2
I have c for a time without rain .... Hag 1:11
bring my servant c the Branch. .... Zch 3:8
month, which is c Kislev, the .... Zch 7:1
Then it will be c the City of .... Zch 8:3

will be c the Holy Mountain."................. Zch 8:3
I c one Pleasant and the other .... Zch 11:7
Jesus is c the Christ. .... Mt 1:16
Herod c a meeting of all the .... Mt 2:4
"I c my son out of Egypt." .... Mt 2:15
to a town c Nazareth, and lived .... Mt 2:23
"He will be c a Nazarene." .... Mt 2:23
brothers, Simon (c Peter) and .... Mt 4:18
they will be c God's children. .... Mt 5:9
Jesus c his twelve followers .... Mt 10:1
Simon (also c Peter) and his .... Mt 10:2
of the family is c Beelzebul, ... Mt 10:25
Jesus c his followers to him and.............. Mt 15:32
Jesus c a little child to him .... Mt 18:2
Then the master c his servant in .... Mt 18:32
Jesus c all the followers .... Mt 20:25
at the hill c the Mount of .... Mt 21:1
My Temple will be c a house for............. Mt 21:13
from the group c Herodians. .... Mt 22:16
But you must not be c 'Teacher,' .... Mt 23:8
to a place c Gethsemane. .... Mt 26:36
field is still c the Field of...................... Mt 27:8
or Jesus who is c the Christ?" .... Mt 27:17
came to the place c Golgotha, ... Mt 27:33
a mountain and c to him those he .... Mk 3:13
twelve and c them apostles. .... Mk 3:14
He c his twelve followers .... Mk 6:7
Then Jesus c the crowd to him, ... Mk 8:34
Jesus sat down and c the twelve............. Mk 9:35
So they c the blind man, ... Mk 10:49
My Temple will be c a house for.............. Mk 11:17
went to a place c Gethsemane. .... Mk 14:32
palace (c the Praetorium) .... Mk 15:16
Jesus to the place c Golgotha, ... Mk 15:22
great and will be c the Son of .... Lk 1:32
will be c a prophet of the Most .... Lk 1:76
Alphaeus, Simon (c the Zealot), ... Lk 6:15
Jesus went to a town c Nain, ... Lk 7:11
He c for two of his followers .... Lk 7:18
Mary, c Magdalene, from whom.............. Lk 8:2
hold of her hand and c to her, ... Lk 8:54
Jesus c the twelve apostles .... Lk 9:1
him to a town c Bethsaida where .... Lk 9:10
in the crowd c out to Jesus, ... Lk 11:27
saw her, he c her over and said .... Lk 13:12
longer worthy to be c your son, ... Lk 15:19
So he c the manager in and said .... Lk 16:2
c, 'Father Abraham, have mercy .... Lk 16:24
but c to him, "Jesus! .... Lk 17:13
But Jesus c for the children, ... Lk 18:16
So he c ten of his servants and .... Lk 19:13
near the hill c the Mount of .... Lk 19:29
Unleavened Bread, c the Passover .... Lk 22:1
others like to be c 'friends of .... Lk 22:25
came to a place c the Skull, ... Lk 23:33
You will be c Cephas." .... Jn 1:42
of the wedding c the bridegroom .... Jn 2:9
Jesus came to the town c Sychar, ... Jn 4:5
Messiah is the One c Christ. .... Jn 4:25
is c Bethesda in the Hebrew .... Jn 5:2
they c the man who had been................ Jn 9:24
Thomas (the one c Didymus) said .... Jn 11:16
and Pharisees c a meeting .... Jn 11:47
to a town c Ephraim and stayed .... Jn 11:54
seat at the place c The Stone .... Jn 19:13
Hebrew language is c Golgotha.............. Jn 19:17
Thomas (c Didymus), who was one .... Jn 20:24
who was also c Justus. .... Ac 1:23
Temple gate c Beautiful Gate,................. Ac 3:2
they c Peter and John in again .... Ac 4:18
The apostles c him Barnabas .... Ac 4:36
(a group c the Sadducees) .... Ac 5:17
they c a meeting of the leaders .... Ac 5:21

They **c** the apostles in, beat .... Ac 5:40
twelve apostles **c** the whole .... Ac 6:2
power of God, **c** 'the Great Power .... Ac 8:10
Then he **c** the saints and the .... Ac 9:41
named Simon who is also **c** Peter. .... Ac 10:5
Cornelius **c** two of his servants .... Ac 10:7
followers were **c** Christians for .... Ac 11:26
who was also **c** Paul, was filled .... Ac 13:9
that God had **c** us to tell the .... Ac 16:10
there is another king, **c** Jesus." .... Ac 17:7
to Ephesus and **c** for the elders .... Ac 20:17
Then Paul **c** one of the officers .... Ac 23:17
came to a place **c** Fair Havens, ... Ac 27:8
that the island was **c** Malta. .... Ac 28:1
God **c** me to be an apostle and .... Rm 1:1
in Rome are also **c** to belong to .... Rm 1:6
and those he **c**, he also made .... Rm 8:30
He **c** us not from the Jews only .... Rm 9:24
later they will be **c** 'children .... Rm 9:26
God **c** me to be an apostle of 1Co 1:1
You were **c** to be God's holy 1Co 1:2
who has **c** you into fellowship 1Co 1:9
God to those people God has **c**— 1Co 1:24
But God **c** us to live in peace. 1Co 7:15
circumcision when he was **c**, ... 1Co 7:18
you were a slave when God **c** you, ... 1Co 7:21
when the Lord **c** them are free 1Co 7:22
though there are things **c** gods, ... 1Co 8:5
good enough to be **c** an apostle, ... 1Co 15:9
c you to become his people. .... Gal 1:6
He **c** me through his grace .... Gal 1:15
sisters, God **c** you to be free, ... Gal 5:13
to the life to which God **c** you. .... Eph 4:1
and God **c** you to have one hope. .... Eph 4:4
which God **c** me through Christ .... Php 3:14
you were all **c** together in one .... Col 3:15
Jesus, who is **c** Justus, also .... Col 4:11
God **c** us to be holy and does not 1Th 4:7
kind of life he **c** you to live. 2Th 1:11
must be **c** by God as Aaron was. .... Heb 5:4
God **c** this a new agreement, ... Heb 8:13
the Tent was **c** the Holy Place. .... Heb 9:2
Those who are **c** by God can now .... Heb 9:15
offered and **c** Abel a good man .... Heb 11:4
And Abraham was **c** God's friend. .... Jam 2:23
who **c** you out of darkness into 1Pe 2:9
This is what you were **c** to do, ... 1Pe 2:21
husband, and **c** him her master. 1Pe 3:6
yourselves were **c** to do this so 1Pe 3:9
c you to share in his glory in 1Pe 5:10
you really are **c** and chosen by 2Pe 1:10
that we are **c** children of God 1Jn 3:1
To all who have been **c** by God. .... Jud 1:1
They **c** to the mountains and the .... Rev 6:16
And he **c** out in a loud voice to .... Rev 7:2
is that old snake the devil or .... Rev 12:9
This angel **c** to the angel with............. Rev 14:18
the place that is **c** Armageddon .... Rev 16:16
He will defeat them with his **c**, ... Rev 17:14
on the horse is **c** Faithful and .... Rev 19:11
he **c** with a loud voice to all .... Rev 19:17

CALLING

walked ahead of his chariot **c**, ... Ge 41:43
of Manasseh, **c** them to follow .... Jdg 6:35
realized the LORD was **c** the boy. 1Sa 3:8
"Who is **c** for the king? 1Sa 26:14
c out to the people of Jerusalem........... 2Ch 32:18
God is gently **c** you from the .... Job 36:16
I am tired from **c** for help; .... Ps 69:3
at the crossroads, she stands **c**. .... Pr 8:2
creature was **c** to the others: .... Is 6:3
I am **c** a man from the east to............. Is 46:11

Now you are **c** to me, 'My father, ... Je 3:4
a man's voice **c** from the Ulai .... Da 8:16
LORD, I am **c** to you for help,.............. Joe 1:19
Lord GOD was **c** for fire to come .... Am 7:4
this said, "He is **c** Elijah." .... Mt 27:47
to your feet. Jesus is **c** you." .... Mk 10:49
C his followers to him, Jesus .... Mk 12:43
said, "Listen! He is **c** Elijah." .... Mk 15:35
c to one another and saying, '............. Lk 7:32
the voice of one **c** out in the .... Jn 1:23
is as if God is **c** to you through 2Co 5:20
powerful angel **c** in a loud voice........... Rev 5:2

CALLS

the king **c** you, he will ask,............... Ge 46:33
If he **c** you again, say, 'Speak,............. 1Sa 3:9
He **c** to the sky above and to the .... Ps 50:4
Wisdom **c** to you like someone .... Pr 8:1
is the voice of one who **c** out: .... Is 40:3
one by one and **c** all the stars............. Is 40:26
of Israel, who **c** you by name. .... Is 45:3
Then anyone who **c** on the LORD .... Joe 2:32
He **c** for the waters of the sea............. Am 9:6
voice of the LORD **c** to the city, ... Mic 6:9
He **c** his officers, but they .... Nah 2:5
voice of one who **c** out in the .... Mt 3:3
David **c** the Christ 'Lord,' .... Mt 22:45
voice of one who **c** out in the .... Mk 1:3
himself **c** the Christ 'Lord, ... Mk 12:37
voice of one who **c** out in the .... Lk 3:4
c to his friends and neighbors .... Lk 15:6
David **c** the Christ 'Lord,' .... Lk 20:44
and he **c** himself the Christ, ... Lk 23:2
He **c** his own sheep by name and .... Jn 10:3
Then anyone who **c** on the Lord.............. Ac 2:21
Anyone who **c** on the Lord will be .... Rm 10:13
who **c** you to his glorious 1Th 2:12

CALM

You only need to remain **c**; .... Ex 14:14
LORD said to Gideon, "**C** down!............... Jdg 6:23
The Levites helped **c** the people,........... Ne 8:11
He leads me to **c** water. .... Ps 23:2
mighty sea and **c** the stormy .... Ps 89:9
I am **c** and quiet, like a baby .... Ps 131:2
answer will **c** a person's anger, ... Pr 15:1
those with understanding stay **c**. .... Pr 17:27
gift will **c** an angry person .... Pr 21:14
but wise people **c** anger down. .... Pr 29:8
Remaining **c** solves great .... Ec 10:4
careful. Be **c** and don't worry.............. Is 7:4
If you will be **c** and trust me, ... Is 30:15
and it will bring **c** and safety .... Is 32:17
the sea, and the sea became **c**. .... Jnh 1:15
The waves of the sea will be **c**, ... Zch 10:11
and it became completely **c**. .... Mt 8:26
the boat, the wind became **c**. .... Mt 14:32
and it became completely **c**. .... Mk 4:39
them, and the wind became **c**. .... Mk 6:51
They stopped, and it became **c**. .... Lk 8:24

CALMED

the storm and **c** the waves. .... Ps 107:29

CALVES

herd and took one of his best **c**. .... Ge 18:7
and all your cattle will have **c**. .... Dt 7:14
blessed with **c** and your flocks .... Dt 28:4
your cattle will have many **c**, ... Dt 30:9
two cows that have just had **c**. 1Sa 6:7
cart, and take the **c** home, away 1Sa 6:7
had just had **c** and hitched them 1Sa 6:10
and fat **c** for sacrifices at the 1Ki 1:9
many cows, fat **c**, and sheep for 1Ki 1:19
Then he made two golden **c**. 1Ki 12:28

CAMEL

They molded statues of two c, ... 2Ki 17:16
have the gold c Jeroboam made 2Ch 13:8
their cows have healthy c. .... Job 21:10
C, lions, and young bulls will .... Is 11:6
C will eat grass there. .... Is 27:10
in Egypt's army are like fat c, ... Je 46:21
jump around, like well-fed c. .... Mal 4:2
best bulls and c for the dinner, ... Mt 22:4
him the blood of goats and c. .... Heb 9:12

CAMEL

Then she jumped down from the c .... Ge 24:64
The c chews the cud but does not .... Le 11:4
is easier for a c to go through .... Mt 19:24
a drink and then swallows a c! .... Mt 23:24
is easier for a c to go through .... Mk 10:25
is easier for a c to go through .... Lk 18:25

CAMEL'S

idols inside her c saddle and .... Ge 31:34
clothes were made from c hair, ... Mt 3:4
wore clothes made from c hair, ... Mk 1:6

CAMELS

male and female servants, and c. .... Ge 12:16
ten of Abraham's c and left, ... Ge 24:10
he made the c kneel down at the .... Ge 24:11
will also give water to your c.' .... Ge 24:14
he looked up and saw c coming. .... Ge 24:63
Their c were carrying spices, ... Ge 37:25
you may not eat c, rabbits, or .... Dt 14:7
Their c could not be counted .... Jdg 7:12
men who rode off on their c. 1Sa 30:17
servants and c carrying spices 1Ki 10:2
a gift of forty c loaded with 2Ki 8:9
fifty thousand c, two hundred 1Ch 5:21
on donkeys, c, mules, and oxen 1Ch 12:40
with her and c carrying spices, ... 2Ch 9:1
lived and took many sheep and c. 2Ch 14:15
435 c, and 6,720 donkeys. .... Ezr 2:67
three thousand c, five hundred .... Job 1:3
down and stole your c and killed .... Job 1:17
six thousand c, a thousand teams .... Job 42:12
treasure on the backs of c. .... Is 30:6
Herds of c will cover your land, ... Is 60:6
c and in chariots and wagons. .... Is 66:20
steal their c and their large .... Je 49:32
a pasture for c and the land .... Eze 25:5
horses, mules, c, donkeys, and .... Zch 14:15

CAMP

all the males born in his c, ... Ge 17:23
in Abraham's c were circumcised .... Ge 17:27
had made his c in the mountains .... Ge 31:25
he said, "This is the c of God!" .... Ge 32:2
quail came and covered the c, ... Ex 16:13
morning dew lay around the c. .... Ex 16:13
the people in the c trembled. .... Ex 19:16
people out of the c to meet God, ... Ex 19:17
and burn them outside the c. .... Ex 29:14
sounds like war down in the c." .... Ex 32:17
the Meeting Tent outside the c. .... Ex 33:7
Moses would return to the c, ... Ex 33:11
ashes outside the c to a special .... Le 6:11
must live alone outside the c. .... Le 13:46
make their c around the Holy .... Nu 1:53
should not c too close to it .... Nu 2:2
They should c under their family .... Nu 2:2
and they will c by divisions .... Nu 2:3
the Ark left the c, Moses said, ... Nu 10:35
the people at the edge of the c. .... Nu 11:1
dew fell on the c each night, ... Nu 11:9
stayed in the c, but the Spirit .... Nu 11:26
and they prophesied in the c. .... Nu 11:26
outside the c for seven days. .... Nu 12:14

the people in the c began crying .... Nu 14:1
him outside the c and stoned him .... Nu 15:36
for you, so the c must be holy. .... Dt 23:14
Go through the c and tell the .... Jos 1:11
to Joshua in the c near Gilgal. .... Jos 9:6
Now the c of Midian was in the .... Jdg 7:8
and attack the c of the .... Jdg 7:9
When Gideon came to the enemy c, ... Jdg 7:13
Surround the enemy c. When I and .... Jdg 7:18
has defeated the Philistine c. 1Sa 13:4
Saul made his c beside the road 1Sa 26:3
and Abishai went into Saul's c. 1Sa 26:7
middle of the c with his spear 1Sa 26:7
from Saul's c came to Ziklag. 2Sa 1:2
"I escaped from the Israelite c." 2Sa 1:3
So let's go to the Aramean c. 2Ki 7:4
thousand men in the Assyrian c. 2Ki 19:35
He made a c around the city and 2Ki 25:1
me. They c around my tent. .... Job 19:12
c they divide the wealth taken .... Ps 68:12
the birds fall inside the c, ... Ps 78:28
They made a c around the city .... Je 52:4
are burned outside the c. .... Heb 13:11
around the c of God's people .... Rev 20:9

CAMPED

to Bethel where he had c before, ... Ge 13:3
time Abram was c near the great .... Ge 14:13
that place and c in the Valley .... Ge 26:17
There he c east of the city. .... Ge 33:18
they were c by the Red Sea, ... Ex 14:9
He was c in the desert near the .... Ex 18:5
of Sinai and c in the desert .... Ex 19:2
They c under their flags and .... Nu 2:34
Israelites c in their tribes, ... Nu 24:2
They c along the Jordan on the .... Nu 33:49
They c in the land and destroyed .... Jdg 6:4
The Israelites c at Ebenezer and 1Sa 4:1
to the place where Saul had c. 1Sa 26:5
c by the spring at Jezreel. 1Sa 29:1
came and c in the Valley 2Sa 5:18
where we c for three days. .... Ezr 8:15
the city where David c. .... Is 29:1

CAMPFIRES

who stayed by the c will share .... Ps 68:13

CAMPING

the tribes c on the south should .... Nu 10:6
his officers are c out in the 2Sa 11:11

CAMPS

to their settlements and c. .... Ge 25:16
herds, and camels into two c. .... Ge 32:7
also attacked the c where the 2Ch 14:15
will set up their c among you .... Eze 25:4
and all the animals in the c. .... Zch 14:15

CAN'T

But I c run to the mountains. .... Ge 19:19
you c do it by yourself. .... Ex 18:18
so you c sell it for all time. .... Le 25:23
c we join the other Israelites? .... Nu 9:7
We c attack those people; .... Nu 13:31
"I c buy back the land. .... Ru 4:6
I done wrong? C I even talk?" 1Sa 17:29
You c go out against this 1Sa 17:33
You c get inside our city. 2Sa 5:9
I c bring him back to life. 2Sa 12:23
"I c go home with you," the man 1Ki 13:16
I c eat or drink with you in 1Ki 13:16
he c save you from my power. 2Ki 18:29
"You c get inside our city." 1Ch 11:5
and this problem c be solved in .... Ezr 10:13
sins so that you c see them, ... Ne 4:5
My wife c stand my breath, ... Job 19:17

Horses **c** bring victory; .... Ps 33:17
they **c** save by their strength. .... Ps 33:17
C the maker of eyes see? .... Ps 94:9
People **c** do anything to me. .... Ps 118:6
things, and I **c** do miracles. .... Ps 131:1
Gossips **c** keep secrets, but a .... Pr 11:13
fools **c** keep from showing how .... Pr 12:23
but those who **c** be trusted want .... Pr 13:2
because they **c** teach you .... Pr 14:7
the person who **c** be paid to do .... Pr 15:27
is crooked, you **c** make it .... Ec 1:15
missing, you **c** say it is there .... Ec 1:15
I **c** stand your New Moons, ... Is 1:13
he will say, "I **c** read the book, ... Is 29:11
for water, but they **c** find any. .... Is 41:17
eyes are covered so they **c** see. .... Is 44:18
because they **c** hurt you, and .... Je 10:5
We **c** control our own lives. .... Je 10:23
c I do the same thing with you?" .... Je 18:6
like a loose bow that **c** shoot. .... Hos 7:16
and you **c** stand those who tell .... Am 5:10
makes idols that **c** even speak! .... Hab 2:18
it **c** be taught to do right. .... Zph 3:2
c move his body and is in much .... Mt 8:6
others, but he **c** save himself! .... Mt 27:42
And those who **c** talk he makes .... Mk 7:37
people, but he **c** save himself. .... Mk 15:31
where thieves **c** steal and moths .... Lk 12:33
I just got married; I **c** come.' .... Lk 14:20
who is a sinner **c** do miracles .... Jn 9:16
Lord, why **c** I follow you now .... Jn 13:37
People **c** do anything to me." .... Heb 13:6

CANA

in the town of **C** in Galilee. .... Jn 2:1
So in **C** of Galilee Jesus did his .... Jn 2:11
to visit **C** in Galilee where .... Jn 4:46
Nathanael from **C** in Galilee, ... Jn 21:2

CANAAN

Ham was the father of **C**. .... Ge 9:18
May there be a curse on **C**! .... Ge 9:25
May **C** be Shem's slave. .... Ge 9:26
Abram lived in the land of **C**, ... Ge 13:12
ten years in **C** that Sarai gave .... Ge 16:3
called Hebron in the land of **C**. .... Ge 23:19
women from the land of **C**: .... Ge 36:2
Jacob lived in the land of **C**, ... Ge 37:1
from the land of **C** to buy food." .... Ge 42:7
and we live in the land of **C**. .... Ge 42:13
no food grew in the land of **C**. .... Ge 43:1
arrived from **C** with their flocks .... Ge 47:1
in the land of **C** and blessed me .... Ge 48:3
Rachel died in the land of **C**, ... Ge 48:7
east of Mamre in the land of **C**. .... Ge 49:30
the people of **C** will lose all .... Ex 15:15
do as they do in the land of **C**, ... Le 18:3
give the land of **C** to you and to .... Le 25:38
cross over into **C** and go before .... Nu 32:32
the Jordan River and go into **C**, ... Nu 33:51
will soon enter **C** and it will be .... Nu 34:2
divide the land of **C** among the .... Nu 34:29
Jabin king of **C** in the sight of .... Jdg 4:23
will give the land of **C** to you, ... 1Ch 16:18
I will give you the land of **C**, ... Ps 105:11
go into the beautiful land of **C**; .... Ps 106:24
land of Egypt and **C** became so .... Ac 7:11
in the land of **C** and gave the .... Ac 13:19

CANAANITE

my son from the **C** girls who live .... Ge 24:3
You must not marry a **C** woman. .... Ge 28:1
Jacob not to marry a **C** woman .... Ge 28:6
Simeon's son by a **C** woman). .... Ge 46:10
and Shaul, the son of a **C** woman. .... Ex 6:15

The **C** king of Arad lived in the .... Nu 21:1
A **C** woman from that area came to .... Mt 15:22

CANAANITES

The families of the **C** scattered. .... Ge 10:18
The **C** were living in the land at .... Ge 12:6
is the land of the **C**, Hittites, ... Ex 3:8
lead you to the land of the **C**, ... Ex 3:17
and the **C** live near the sea and .... Nu 13:29
Amalekites and the **C** are living .... Nu 14:25
and he let them defeat the **C**. .... Nu 21:3
the **C** continued to live there. .... Jos 17:12
they forced the **C** to work for .... Jos 17:13
of Israel lived with the **C**, ... Jdg 3:5
will take the land of the **C**, ... Ob 1:20

CANAL

by the Ahava **C**, I announced we .... Ezr 8:21
I was standing by the Ulai **C** .... Da 8:2

CANALS

over the rivers, **c**, ponds, and .... Ex 7:19
The **c** will stink; the streams of .... Is 19:6

CANCEL

make her keep or **c** any promise .... Nu 30:13
money must **c** the loan and not .... Dt 15:2
the year to **c** what people owe." .... Dt 15:9
written to **c** the letters Haman .... Est 8:5

CANCELED

husband has **c** it, so the LORD .... Nu 30:12
with his signet ring can be **c**." .... Est 8:8
Medes and Persians cannot be **c**." .... Da 6:12
He **c** the debt, which listed all. .... Col 2:14

CANCELS

he **c** her pledge or the careless .... Nu 30:8
husband hears about it and **c** it, ... Nu 30:12

CANE

six pounds of sweet-smelling **c**, ... Ex 30:23
sweet-smelling **c** from a faraway .... Je 6:20
carrying a **c** because of age. .... Zch 8:4

CANYON

gate all the way down to the **c**, ... Jos 7:5

CAPABLE

But choose some **c** men from among ...... Ex 18:21
hundred thousand **c** soldiers. 2Ch 13:3
c of learning and understanding, ... Da 1:4
person who serves God will be **c**, ... 2Ti 3:17

CAPERNAUM

Nazareth and went to live in **C**, ... Mt 4:13
Jesus entered the city of **C**, ... Mt 8:5
And you, **C**, will you be lifted .... Mt 11:23
and his followers came to **C**, ... Mt 17:24
and his followers went to **C**. .... Mk 1:21
about the things you did in **C**. .... Lk 4:23
Jesus went to **C**, a city in .... Lk 4:31
to the people, he went to **C**. .... Lk 7:1
And you, **C**, will you be lifted .... Lk 10:15
the town of **C** with his mother, ... Jn 2:12
him to come to **C** and heal his .... Jn 4:47
started across the lake to **C**. .... Jn 6:17
teaching in the synagogue in **C**. .... Jn 6:59

CAPES

their fine robes, **c**, shawls, and .... Is 3:22

CAPITAL

net of seven chains for each **c**, ... 1Ki 7:17
bronze **c** on top of the pillar 2Ki 25:17
Ecbatana, the **c** city of Media. .... Ezr 6:2
was in the **c** city of Susa. .... Ne 1:1
the **c** city of the Ammonites, ... Je 49:2
The bronze **c** on top of the one .... Je 52:22
has crushed the **c** city of Judah. .... La 1:15

CAPPADOCIA

Judea, C, Pontus, Asia, ... Ac 2:9
Pontus, Galatia, C, Asia, and 1Pe 1:1

CAPTAIN

of Egypt and c of the palace .... Ge 37:36
prison of the c of the guard, ... Ge 40:3
had made Amasa c of the army 2Sa 17:25
Then he sent a c with his fifty 2Ki 1:9
The c went to Elijah, who was 2Ki 1:9
urned up the c and his fifty. 2Ki 1:10
The third c came and fell down 2Ki 1:13
of Joab made the c of the Three. 1Ch 11:20
the c in charge of the guards .... Je 37:13
The c of the ship came and said, ... Jnh 1:6
the c of the soldiers that .... Ac 4:1
the c of the Temple guards and .... Ac 5:24
believed what the c and owner of .... Ac 27:11
Every sea c, every passenger, ... Rev 18:17

CAPTAINS

men who were c in Saul's army 2Sa 4:2
leaders, officers, c, chariot 1Ki 9:22
So the guards and c killed the 2Ki 10:25
and to the c of the soldiers .... Est 3:12
handsome young c and lieutenants .... Eze 23:6
governors, c of the soldiers, ... Da 3:2

CAPTIVE

Assyria will keep you c." .... Nu 24:22
because they will be taken c. .... Dt 28:41
had taken a little girl as a c. 2Ki 5:2
They were taken c from Jerusalem............ 2Ki 24:15
Nebuchadnezzar took c to Babylon 2Ch 36:20
let her love always hold you c. .... Pr 5:19
don't be held c by a woman who .... Pr 5:20
he will be held c by his .... Pr 5:23
Why were they taken c? .... Je 2:14
Ishmael had taken c from Mizpah .... Je 41:14
whole earth has been taken c. .... Je 51:41
took c some of the poorest .... Je 52:15
all 4,600 people were taken c. .... Je 52:30
will not be led c by the nations .... Eze 34:28
burned, are taken c, or robbed of............. Da 11:33
will be taken c to the country .... Am 1:5
the city where they were held c. .... Mic 2:13

CAPTIVES

they brought the c, the animals, ... Nu 31:12
took the people to Babylon as c. .... Ezr 5:12
Then the c who returned made .... Ezr 8:35
snatched the c from their teeth .... Job 29:17
they will wear the ropes of c. .... Is 3:24
They growl as they grab their c. .... Is 5:29
down among the c or fall down .... Is 10:4
to tell the c they are free, ... Is 61:1
Jerusalem were taken away as c. .... Je 1:3
will be taken as c to a foreign............. Je 13:19
when he took as c Jehoiachin son .... Je 27:20
from Jerusalem as c to Babylon:............. Je 29:4
will become c in other lands. .... Je 30:16
When the c Ishmael had taken saw .... Je 41:13
its c will go to every nation. .... Je 49:36
Nebuchadnezzar took away as c: .... Je 52:28
Make chains for c, because the .... Eze 7:23
you one of the c my father the .... Da 5:13
Israelites will become c again, ... Hos 11:5
people will be taken away as c, ... Zch 14:2
me to tell the c they are free .... Lk 4:18
always leads us as c in Christ's 2Co 2:14
led a parade of c, and he gave .... Eph 4:8

CAPTIVITY

Jerusalem into c under the 1Ch 6:15
had returned from c to Jerusalem .... Ezr 3:8
returned from c ate the Passover .... Ezr 6:21

people who lived through the c. .... Ne 1:2
come back from c built shelters .... Ne 8:17
will not send you into c again. .... La 4:22
in the twelfth year of our c, ... Eze 33:21
he people of Jacob back from c, ... Eze 39:25
the twenty-fifth year of our c, ... Eze 40:1
my people Israel back from c;............. Am 9:14
was captured and went into c. .... Nah 3:10

CAPTURE

your descendants c the cities of .... Ge 24:60
Go c your enemies, son of .... Jdg 5:12
city and spy it out and c it!" 2Sa 10:3
Elijah said, "C the prophets 1Ki 18:40
In either case c them alive." 1Ki 20:18
of the city, we'll c them alive. 2Ki 7:12
the land and c it and spy it out 1Ch 19:3
away so they could c Jerusalem............. 2Ch 32:18
Let thick darkness c that night. .... Job 3:6
anyone blind its eyes and c it? .... Job 40:24
Don't let her c you by the way .... Pr 6:25
have dug a pit to c me and have............. Je 18:22
to the top of the walls to c it. .... Je 32:24
Jerusalem, c it, set it on fire .... Je 34:22
will c treasures and take loot.................. Eze 38:12
to c Jehoiakim king............................. Da 1:2
city walls and will c a strong,................. Da 11:15
Sea and will c them. .... Da 11:18
destroyed, Egypt will c them; .... Hos 9:6
Do not c those who escape alive............. Ob 1:14
led our ancestors to c the lands .... Ac 7:45
We c every thought and make it 2Co 10:5

CAPTURED

men who was not c went to Abram, ... Ge 14:13
learned that Lot had been c, ... Ge 14:14
killed the king and c his land .... Nu 21:24
went and c Gilead and forced .... Nu 32:39
We c all his cities at that time................. Dt 2:34
Then we c all of Og's cities, ... Dt 3:4
They c that city, its king, and .... Jos 10:39
Joshua c all the cities from .... Jos 10:41
He c all these cities and their .... Jos 10:42
Caleb's brother, c the city, so .... Jos 15:17
Philistines c Samson and tore............. Jdg 16:21
had c the Ark of God, ... 1Sa 5:1
They c the women and everyone, ... 1Sa 30:2
David c one thousand chariots, ... 2Sa 8:4
and have c its water supply. 2Sa 12:27
The people c all the prophets.................. 1Ki 18:40
He also c Gilead and Galilee and 2Ki 15:29
Damascus and c it and sent all 2Ki 16:9
so they c Zedekiah and took him 2Ki 25:6
c the people left in Jerusalem, ... 2Ki 25:11
They also c one hundred thousand........... 1Ch 5:21
of Judah also c ten thousand 2Ch 25:12
They c Manasseh, put hooks in 2Ch 33:11
They c strong, walled cities and .... Ne 9:25
the Philistines c him in Gath. .... Ps 55:23
He let the Ark, his power, be c; .... Ps 78:61
Those who c us asked us to sing; .... Ps 137:3
people will be c and taken away, ... Is 5:13
the LORD's people will be c. .... Je 13:17
This is how Jerusalem was c: .... Je 39:1
'Babylon will be c. .... Je 50:2
Nineveh will be c and carried .... Nah 2:7
But the beast was c and with him .... Rev 19:20

CAPTURES

who attacks and c the city of .... Jos 15:16

CAPTURING

c it and all the little towns .... Jos 10:37
king of Israel, c the cities of 2Ki 15:29
temper is better than c a city. .... Pr 16:32

CARCHEMISH

Egypt led an army to attack **C**, ... 2Ch 35:20
city Calno is like the city **C**. .... Is 10:9
the city of **C** on the Euphrates .... Je 46:2

CARE

no person to **c** for the ground, ... Ge 2:5
of Eden to **c** for it and work .... Ge 2:15
Abel took **c** of flocks, and Cain .... Ge 4:2
my job to take **c** of my brother?" .... Ge 4:9
was her job to **c** for the sheep. .... Ge 29:9
Jacob took **c** of all the flocks .... Ge 30:36
Joseph to take **c** of all the .... Ge 39:22
the two prisoners in Joseph's **c**, ... Ge 40:4
I will **c** for you during the next .... Ge 45:11
and take **c** of farm animals, ... Ge 46:32
but God will take **c** of you. .... Ge 50:24
Moses was taking **c** of Jethro's .... Ex 3:1
Take **c** of the animals until the .... Ex 12:6
to take **c** of the oil lamps. .... Ex 30:7
will take **c** of the Holy Tent .... Nu 1:53
will help you **c** for the people .... Nu 11:17
not have to **c** for them alone. .... Nu 11:17
You must take **c** of the Holy .... Nu 18:5
I cannot take **c** of your problems .... Dt 1:12
see if he will take **c** of you. .... Ru 3:13
they did not **c** about the LORD. 1Sa 2:12
is out taking **c** of the sheep." 1Sa 16:11
where he took **c** of his father's 1Sa 17:15
commanded to take **c** of my people 2Sa 7:7
women to take **c** of the palace. 2Sa 15:16
one more person for me to take **c** 2Sa 15:33
killed, Absalom's men won't **c**. 2Sa 18:3
He had taken **c** of the king when 2Sa 19:32
and I will take **c** of you." 2Sa 19:33
for a young woman to **c** for you. 1Ki 1:2
a widow there to take **c** of you." 1Ki 17:9
took **c** of the king's clothes. 2Ki 22:14
land to take **c** of the vineyards 2Ki 25:12
to take **c** of the furniture 1Ch 9:29
Levites took **c** of the Meeting 1Ch 23:32
relatives took **c** of all the holy 1Ch 26:28
who took **c** of King David's 1Ch 27:31
of Hacmoni took **c** of the king's 1Ch 27:32
took **c** of the valuable gems. 1Ch 29:8
You took **c** of them for forty .... Ne 9:21
you taken **c** of the Temple?" .... Ne 13:11
so Mordecai took **c** of her. .... Est 2:7
Don't let God **c** about it. .... Job 3:4
but I don't **c** about myself. .... Job 9:21
the LORD takes **c** of his people, ... Ps 1:6
do you take **c** of human beings .... Ps 8:4
because he has taken **c** of me. .... Ps 13:6
is all I need. He takes **c** of me. .... Ps 16:5
and he will take **c** of you. .... Ps 37:5
They do not **c** about God. .... Ps 54:3
You take **c** of the land and water .... Ps 65:9
goodness you took **c** of the poor. .... Ps 68:10
Take **c** of us, your vine. .... Ps 80:14
and we are the people he takes **c** .... Ps 95:7
they even **c** about her dust. .... Ps 102:14
the LORD takes **c** of you." .... Ps 116:7
he takes **c** of those who are .... Ps 138:6
because you have taken **c** of me. .... Ps 142:7
and it will take **c** of you. .... Pr 4:6
people take **c** of their animals. .... Pr 12:10
Fools don't **c** if they sin, ... Pr 14:9
whoever takes **c** of his master .... Pr 27:18
Good people **c** about justice for .... Pr 29:7
They don't **c** who sees it. .... Is 3:9
They do not **c** about silver or .... Is 13:17
He takes **c** of his people like a .... Is 40:11
I have taken **c** of you from your .... Is 46:3

hungry and take **c** of the needs .... Is 58:10
the flock God gave you to **c** for, ... Je 13:20
Remember me and take **c** of me. .... Je 15:15
They don't **c** about you. .... Je 30:14
land to take **c** of the vineyards .... Je 52:16
by on the road don't seem to **c**. .... La 1:12
I will take **c** of my sheep. .... Eze 34:12
You did not take **c** of my holy .... Eze 44:8
charge of taking **c** of the Temple .... Eze 44:14
North will not **c** about the gods .... Da 11:37
and I take **c** of sycamore trees. .... Am 7:14
stand and take **c** of his people .... Mic 5:4
All-Powerful, **c** for my flock, ... Zch 10:3
angels came and took **c** of him. .... Mt 4:11
You don't **c** about the things of .... Mt 16:23
servant to take **c** of everything .... Mt 24:47
trusted me to **c** for five bags .... Mt 25:20
will let you **c** for much greater .... Mt 25:21
or in prison and **c** for you?" .... Mt 25:39
and you did not **c** for me.' .... Mt 25:43
angels came and took **c** of him. .... Mk 1:13
you **c** that we are drowning! .... Mk 4:38
You don't **c** about the things of .... Mk 8:33
lets his servants take **c** of it, ... Mk 13:34
and said, 'Take **c** of this man. .... Lk 10:35
don't you **c** that my sister has .... Lk 10:40
to take **c** of his business .... Lk 16:1
respect God or **c** about people. .... Lk 18:2
not really **c** about the sheep .... Jn 10:13
did not really **c** about the poor; .... Jn 12:6
said, "Take **c** of my sheep." .... Jn 21:16
for taking **c** of all her money. .... Ac 8:27
put Paul into the Lord's **c**, ... Ac 15:40
I don't **c** about my own life. .... Ac 20:24
am putting you in the **c** of God .... Ac 20:32
worked to take **c** of my own needs ...... Ac 20:34
who took **c** of his needs. .... Ac 27:3
I do not **c** if I am judged by you 1Co 4:3
No person takes **c** of a flock 1Co 9:7
parts to **c** the same for each 1Co 12:25
me about your great **c** for me, ... 2Co 7:7
who are chosen to **c** for them. .... Gal 4:2
but feeds and takes **c** of it. .... Eph 5:29
You continued to **c** about me, ... Php 4:10
Take **c** of your own business, ... 1Th 4:11
worked to take **c** of ourselves so 2Th 3:9
Take **c** of widows who are truly 1Ti 5:3
Whoever does not **c** for his own 1Ti 5:8
she should **c** for them herself. 1Ti 5:16
do you take **c** of human beings .... Heb 2:6
are still taking **c** of business. .... Jam 1:11
judges rightly, take **c** of him. 1Pe 2:23
she would be taken **c** of for one .... Rev 12:6

CARED

The LORD **c** for Sarah as he had .... Ge 21:1
wives, **c** for the flocks. .... Ge 37:2
the LORD **c** for and loved your .... Dt 10:15
him in her arms, and **c** for him. .... Ru 4:16
had not **c** for his feet, ... 2Sa 19:24
is how God has **c** for my family. 2Sa 23:5
she **c** for the king and served 1Ki 1:4
They **c** for the Temple courtyard 1Ch 23:28
the children they have **c** for. .... La 2:20
I **c** for them in the desert where .... Hos 13:5
I was sick, and you **c** for me. .... Mt 25:36
to an inn where he **c** for him. .... Lk 10:34
months Moses was **c** for in his .... Ac 7:20
of the body are **c** for and held .... Col 2:19

CAREFUL

in a dream and said, "Be **c!** .... Ge 31:24
And I must be **c** with my flocks .... Ge 33:13
Be **c** that you don't make an .... Ex 34:12

C

they are **c**, they will not die. .... Le 22:9
But be **c**! Watch out and don't................. Dt 4:9
Be **c**. Don't forget the Agreement .... Dt 4:23
be **c**! Do not forget the LORD. .... Dt 6:12
c to obey all the commands and .... Dt 11:32
Be **c** that you don't sacrifice .... Dt 12:13
c not to forget the Levites as .... Dt 12:19
c to do everything they tell you. .... Dt 17:10
Pay **c** attention to all the words .... Dt 32:46
You must be **c** to obey everything .... Jos 23:6
you must be **c** to love the LORD .... Jos 23:11
c not to drink wine or beer or................. Jdg 13:4
wife must be **c** to do everything .... Jdg 13:13
'Be **c** not to hurt young Absalom.' 2Sa 18:12
Be **c**! Don't be led away from God .... Job 36:18
I will be **c** what I say around .... Ps 39:1
I will be **c** to live an innocent .... Ps 101:2
help me be **c** about what I say. .... Ps 141:3
c what you think, because your .... Pr 4:23
Be **c** what you do, and always do .... Pr 4:26
c to use good sense, and watch .... Pr 5:2
c about giving a guarantee for .... Pr 6:1
Wise people are **c** and stay out .... Pr 14:16
Be **c** when you go to worship at .... Ec 5:1
Tell Ahaz, 'Be **c**. Be calm and .... Is 7:4
Be **c** not to carry a load on the .... Je 17:21
So be **c**, and do not break your .... Mal 2:15
Be **c**! When you do good things,............... Mt 6:1
Be **c** of false prophets............................ Mt 7:15
c of people, because they will............... Mt 10:17
Jesus said to them, "Be **c**! .... Mt 16:6
Be **c**. Don't think these little .... Mt 18:10
Be **c** that no one fools you. .... Mt 24:4
Jesus warned them, "Be **c**! .... Mk 8:15
Be **c** that no one fools you. .... Mk 13:5
You must be **c**. People will .... Mk 13:9
So be **c**. I have warned you about .... Mk 13:23
So be **c** how you listen. .... Lk 8:18
Be **c** not to let the light in .... Lk 11:35
Be **c** and guard against all kinds .... Lk 12:15
Be **c** so you are not fooled. .... Lk 21:8
Be **c** not to spend your time .... Lk 21:34
be **c** what you are planning to do .... Ac 5:35
c! Don't let what the prophets .... Ac 13:40
be **c**! Always remember that for .... Ac 20:31
people should be **c** how they 1Co 3:10
But be **c** that your freedom does............... 1Co 8:9
you should be **c** not to fall. 1Co 10:12
We are being **c** so that no one................. 2Co 8:20
Be **c**! "Just a little yeast makes .... Gal 5:9
other apart, be **c**, or you will .... Gal 5:15
But be **c**, because you might be .... Gal 6:1
So be very **c** how you live. .... Eph 5:15
Be **c** in your life and in your 1Ti 4:16
great patience and **c** teaching, ... 2Ti 4:2
also should be **c** that he does 2Ti 4:15
in God will be **c** to use their .... Tit 3:8
we must be more **c** to follow what .... Heb 2:1
be **c** that none of you has an .... Heb 3:12
let us be very **c** so none of you .... Heb 4:1
Be very **c** to make everything by .... Heb 8:5
c that no one fails to receive .... Heb 12:15
Be **c** that no one takes part in................. Heb 12:16
So be **c** and do not refuse to .... Heb 12:25
Control yourselves and be **c**! 1Pe 5:8
Be **c** so you will not fall from 2Pe 3:17
Be **c** yourselves that you do not 2Jn 1:8

CAREFULLY
Look it over **c** and see if it is .... Ge 37:32
Obey these laws **c**, in order to .... Dt 4:6
Learn them and obey them **c**. .... Dt 5:1
C obey every command I give you .... Dt 8:1

children to obey **c** everything in .... Dt 32:46
orders: "Listen **c**. You must set .... Jos 8:4
Darius' order quickly and **c**. .... Ezr 6:13
Guard these things **c**. .... Ezr 8:29
Look and listen **c**. .... Ne 1:6
listen **c** to the prayer of your .... Ne 1:11
people listened to the Book .... Ne 8:3
Listen **c** to my words; .... Job 13:17
Listen **c** to wisdom;............................... Pr 2:2
people think **c** about what they .... Pr 21:29
c to what wise people say; .... Pr 22:17
and listen **c** to words of .... Pr 23:12
to me, and I listened **c** to them. .... Je 15:16
If you **c** obey these commands, ... Je 22:4
by my rules and **c** obey my laws. .... Eze 36:27
Think **c** about the words I will .... Da 10:11
saying, "Look **c** for the child. .... Mt 2:8
Think **c** about what you hear................. Mk 4:24
everything **c** from the beginning............... Lk 1:3
look **c** for the coin until she .... Lk 15:8
You **c** study the Scriptures .... Jn 5:39
was ordered to guard them **c**. .... Ac 16:23
who **c** taught me everything about .... Ac 22:3
tradition more **c** than any other .... Ac 26:5
c before you lay your hands 1Ti 5:22
are those who **c** study God's .... Jam 1:25
prophets searched **c** and tried to 1Pe 1:10

CARELESS
pledge or the **c** promise she made .... Nu 30:8
No wonder my words seem **c**................. Job 6:3
C words stab like a sword, ... Pr 12:18
fools are **c** and quick to act. .... Pr 14:16
but those who are **c** will die. .... Pr 19:16
for every **c** thing they have said .... Mt 12:36

CARES
a land the LORD your God **c** for. .... Dt 11:12
Jesse! No one **c** about me! No one 1Sa 22:8
and see. No one **c** about me. I................. Ps 142:4
'No one **c** about Jerusalem!'" .... Je 30:17
Timothy, who truly **c** for you. .... Php 2:20
to him, because he **c** about you. 1Pe 5:7

CARGO
full of heavy **c** in the middle .... Eze 27:25
throwing the **c** from the ship .... Jnh 1:5
needed to unload its **c** there. .... Ac 21:3
The ship, the **c**, and even our .... Ac 27:10

CARGOES
there is no one to buy their **c**— .... Rev 18:11

CARING
while he was **c** for his father's .... Ge 36:24
were with them **c** for the sheep............... 1Sa 16:11
girl from Shunam, was **c** for him. 1Ki 1:15
the ground or **c** for the sheep................. Lk 17:7
the work of **c** for and teaching .... Eph 4:11
like a mother **c** for her little 1Th 2:7
c for orphans or widows who need .... Jam 1:27
but by our actions and true **c**................. 1Jn 3:18
and have no fear, **c** only for .... Jud 1:12

CARMEL
Go to Nabal at **C**, and greet him............... 1Sa 25:5
and those prophets to Mount **C**. 1Ki 18:20
climbed to the top of Mount **C**, ... 1Ki 18:42
Your head is like Mount **C**, ... Sng 7:5
trees of Bashan and **C** are dying. .... Is 33:9
they hide at the top of Mount **C**,............... Am 9:3
areas of Bashan and **C** dry up, ... Nah 1:4

CARNELIAN
stones, like jasper and **c**........................ Rev 4:3
the sixth was **c**, the seventh was............... Rev 21:20

CARPENTER

He is just the son of a **c**. .... Mt 13:55
is just the **c**, the son of Mary .... Mk 6:3

CARPENTERS

with cedar logs, **c**, and 2Sa 5:11
they paid the **c** and the builders 2Ki 12:11
c to build a palace for David. 1Ch 14:1
stoneworkers and **c** to repair the 2Ch 24:12
money to the bricklayers and **c**. .... Ezr 3:7

CARPETS

sewed on, **c** of many colors, ... Eze 27:24

CARRIAGES

sheep, horses, **c**, slaves, and .... Rev 18:13

CARRIED

He **c** everything with him that he .... Ge 31:18
They **c** his body to the land of .... Ge 50:13
Moses **c** the bones of Joseph with .... Ex 13:19
saw how I **c** you out of Egypt, ... Ex 19:4
obeyed Moses and **c** the bodies of .... Le 10:5
Meeting Tent and who **c** the Tent. .... Nu 4:47
who **c** the holy things .... Nu 10:21
who **c** the Ark of the Agreement .... Dt 31:25
the priests who **c** the Ark of the .... Jos 3:14
The priests **c** the Ark of the .... Jos 3:17
obeyed Joshua and **c** twelve rocks .... Jos 4:8
They **c** the seven trumpets and .... Jos 6:8
of the LORD **c** around the city .... Jos 6:11
and the priests **c** the Ark of the .... Jos 6:12
They cut wood and **c** water for .... Jos 9:27
they **c** the bones of Joseph with .... Jos 24:32
shoulders and **c** them to the top .... Jdg 16:3
all of whom **c** swords. .... Jdg 20:25
Ruth **c** the grain into town, ... Ru 2:18
They **c** it into Dagon's temple 1Sa 5:2
The officer who **c** Jonathan's 1Sa 14:7
the officer who **c** his armor died. 1Sa 31:6
David and his men **c** them away. 2Sa 5:21
the Levites with him **c** the Ark 2Sa 15:24
young men who **c** Joab's armor 2Sa 18:15
and she **c** him to her bed. 1Ki 3:20
They **c** the Ark of the LORD, ... 1Ki 8:4
on his donkey and **c** it back to 1Ki 13:29
They **c** away all the stones and 1Ki 15:22
Elijah **c** the boy downstairs and 1Ki 17:23
His body was **c** to Samaria and 1Ki 22:37
They **c** things from this tent and. 2Ki 7:8
Ahaziah's servants **c** his body in 2Ki 9:28
Valley and **c** their ashes to 2Ki 23:4
Josiah's servants **c** his body in 2Ki 23:30
Nebuchadnezzar **c** away Jehoiachin 2Ki 24:15
they **c** the bronze to Babylon. 2Ki 25:13
They **c** shields and spears. 1Ch 12:24
with them who **c** shields and 1Ch 12:34
The people **c** the Ark of God from 1Ch 13:7
chariot and **c** him to Jerusalem. 2Ch 35:24
Nebuchadnezzar **c** away to Babylon 2Ch 36:18
workers **c** out King Darius'. .... Ezr 6:13
one hand and **c** a weapon with .... Ne 4:17
Has your heart **c** you away from .... Job 15:12
Their idols are **c** by animals. .... Is 46:1
But he **c** away the sins of many .... Is 53:12
like the wind, have **c** us away. .... Is 64:6
cannot walk, they must be **c**. .... Je 10:5
who had been **c** away as captives. .... Eze 1:1
After I have **c** out my anger .... Eze 5:13
you **c** on your prostitution. .... Eze 16:16
my anger against you is **c** out. .... Eze 24:13
Trading ships **c** the things you .... Eze 27:25
which he **c** to Babylonia and put .... Da 1:2
but it will be **c** off to Assyria .... Hos 10:6
You have **c** with you your king, ... Am 5:26

while strangers **c** Israel's .... Ob 1:11
money will be **c** off by others .... Mic 1:7
will be captured and **c** away. .... Nah 2:7
on him and **c** our diseases." .... Mt 8:17
he was **c** up into heaven, ... Mk 16:19
while her son was being **c** out. .... Lk 7:12
and the angels **c** him to the arms .... Lk 16:22
from them and **c** into heaven. .... Lk 24:51
day he was **c** to this gate to .... Ac 3:2
they **c** her out and buried her .... Ac 5:10
Then they **c** a message from Paul .... Ac 17:15
and he **c** out his plan through .... Eph 3:11
Christ **c** our sins in his body on 1Pe 2:24
Then the angel **c** me away by the .... Rev 17:3

CARRIES

And anyone who **c** these things .... Le 15:10
in my arms as a nurse **c** a baby? .... Nu 11:12
carried you, like one **c** a child. .... Dt 1:31
to catch them and **c** them on its .... Dt 32:11
in his arms and **c** them close to .... Is 40:11
Suppose a person **c** in the fold .... Hag 2:12
The high priest **c** the blood of. .... Heb 13:11

CARRY

and gave it to his son to **c**, ... Ge 22:6
as much grain as they can **c**, ... Ge 44:1
When I die, **c** me out of Egypt, ... Ge 47:30
remember to **c** my bones with you .... Ex 13:19
C with you the walking stick .... Ex 17:5
and use these poles to **c** it. .... Ex 25:14
on each side of the Ark to **c** it. .... Ex 37:5
on others and **c** the ashes .... Le 6:11
So the goat will **c** on itself all .... Le 16:22
They must **c** the Holy Tent and .... Nu 1:50
Tell each man exactly what to **c**. .... Nu 4:32
Must I **c** them in my arms as a .... Nu 11:12
the tribe of Levi to **c** the Ark .... Dt 10:8
C a tent peg with you, and when .... Dt 23:13
Tell the priests who **c** the Ark .... Jos 3:8
priests will **c** the Ark of the .... Jos 3:13
C the rocks and put them down .... Jos 4:3
seven priests **c** trumpets made .... Jos 6:4
C the Ark of the Agreement. .... Jos 6:6
why do you want to **c** the news? 2Sa 18:22
because you helped **c** the Ark of 1Ki 2:26
thousand men to **c** the stones. 1Ki 5:15
and dishes used to **c** coals; 1Ki 7:50
Then you may **c** it to Jerusalem." 2Ch 2:16
Do not **c** it from place to place 2Ch 35:3
flood will **c** their houses away, ... Job 20:28
The east wind will **c** them away, ... Job 27:21
C me away to a high mountain. .... Ps 61:2
For you, I **c** this shame, and my .... Ps 69:7
You cannot **c** hot coals against .... Pr 6:27
little bird might **c** your words; .... Ec 10:20
soldiers all **c** swords and have .... Sng 3:8
warriors to **c** out my anger. .... Is 13:3
and the wind will **c** them away; .... Is 41:16
People who **c** idols of wood don't .... Is 45:20
from the east to **c** out my plan; .... Is 46:11
he will **c** out his wishes against .... Is 48:14
he will **c** away their sins. .... Is 53:11
and I will **c** you to the high .... Is 58:14
The soldiers **c** bows and spears. .... Je 6:23
So I will **c** out my anger on the .... Eze 13:15
They must **c** their shame with .... Eze 32:24
I am not good enough to **c**. .... Mt 3:11
Don't **c** a bag or extra clothes. .... Mt 10:10
not willing to **c** the cross and .... Mt 10:38
load I give you to **c** is light." .... Mt 11:30
named Simon, to **c** the cross for .... Mt 27:32
allow anyone to **c** goods through .... Mk 11:16
forced Simon to **c** the cross for .... Mk 15:21

Don't **c** a purse, a bag, or .... Lk 10:4
not willing to **c** his cross and .... Lk 14:27
purse or a bag, **c** that with you. .... Lk 22:36
forced him to **c** Jesus' cross .... Lk 23:26
our law for you to **c** your mat on .... Jn 5:10
soldiers had to **c** him because................. Ac 21:35
trying and let the wind **c** us. .... Ac 27:15
and let the wind **c** the ship..................... Ac 27:17
We **c** the death of Jesus in our 2Co 4:10
His goal was to **c** out his plan, ... Eph 1:10
the waves **c** one way and then .... Eph 4:14
so the flood would **c** her away. .... Rev 12:15
horns want to **c** out his purpose .... Rev 17:17

CARRYING

c it on both their shoulders, ... Ge 9:23
C these things and her son, ... Ge 21:14
Rebekah was **c** her water jar on .... Ge 24:15
Their camels were **c** spices, ... Ge 37:25
that he was **c** and broke them at.............. Ex 32:19
c the two stone tablets with him. .... Ex 34:4
they held the poles for **c** it. .... Ex 37:14
priests and Levites **c** the Ark .... Jos 3:3
the priests **c** the Ark came to .... Jos 3:15
One man will be **c** three goats. 1Sa 10:3
Another will be **c** three loaves 1Sa 10:3
The **c** poles were so long that 2Ch 5:9
with her and camels **c** spices, ... 2Ch 9:1
singing and **c** bundles of grain. .... Ps 126:6
bowls, pans for **c** hot coals, ... Je 52:19
each **c** a cane because of age.................. Zch 8:4
people came, **c** a paralyzed man. .... Mk 2:3
city and a man **c** a jar of water .... Mk 14:13
many people **c** swords and clubs .... Mk 14:43
some men were **c** on a mat a man .... Lk 5:18
people who were **c** it stopped. .... Lk 7:14
a man **c** a jar of water will meet.............. Lk 22:10
They were **c** torches, lanterns, ... Jn 18:3
C his own cross, Jesus went out .... Jn 19:17

CART

every two leaders giving a **c**. .... Nu 7:3
build a new **c** and get two cows 1Sa 6:7
Watch the **c**. If it goes toward 1Sa 6:9
chopped up the wood of the **c**. 1Sa 6:14
Abinadab's house on a new **c**, ... 1Ch 13:7
wheat from the chaff with his **c**,.............. Is 28:28

CARTS

six covered **c** and twelve oxen—............... Nu 7:3
Moses accepted the **c** and the................. Nu 7:6

CARVE

C the name of one of the twelve .... Ex 28:21
pure right and words on .... Ex 28:36
I will **c** a message on it,' .... Zch 3:9

CARVED

of Israel were **c** on these twelve .... Ex 39:14
and **c** these words in the gold, ... Ex 39:30
the men from Byblos **c** the stones 1Ki 5:18
which was **c** with pictures of 1Ki 6:18
the Temple were **c** with pictures 1Ki 6:29
also **c** on the two olive wood 1Ki 6:32
Designs were **c** into the bronze 1Ki 7:31
Manasseh **c** an Asherah idol and 2Ki 21:7
and he **c** creatures with wings on 2Ch 3:7
pen into lead, or **c** into stone .... Job 19:24
were **c** all around the Temple .... Eze 41:19
and creatures with wings were **c**. .... Eze 41:20
C on the doors of the Holy Place .... Eze 41:25

CARVES

way a person **c** words and designs .... Ex 28:11
jewels as a person **c** a seal..................... Ex 39:14

CARVING

are you **c** out a tomb from the .... Is 22:16

CARVINGS

covered with **c** of creatures with............... 1Ki 7:36
There were **c** of bulls under the 2Ch 4:3
She saw **c** of Babylonian men on a........... Eze 23:14
C of palm trees were on each .... Eze 40:16
c of creatures with wings and................. Eze 41:18

CASE

man must bring his **c** to God. .... Ex 22:9
brought their **c** to the LORD, ... Nu 27:5
A **c** must be proved by two or................. Dt 19:15
In either **c**, her first husband .... Dt 24:4
the judges will decide the **c**. .... Dt 25:1
his sword fell out of its **c**. 2Sa 20:8
Judge the **c**, punish the guilty, ... 1Ki 8:32
they sat down to study each **c**. .... Ezr 10:16
tied to a curse in **c** they broke .... Ne 10:29
and to argue my **c** with God. .... Job 13:3
Argue my **c** and save me. .... Ps 119:154
The LORD says, "Present your **c**." .... Is 41:21
won't plead the **c** of the orphan .... Je 5:28
wronged. Now judge my **c** for me. .... La 3:59
with a writing **c** at his side.................... Eze 9:2
plead your **c** in front of the.................... Mic 6:1
listen to the LORD's legal **c**. .... Mic 6:2
'Every **c** may be proved by two or .... Mt 18:16
will hear your **c** when those who .... Ac 23:35
I want Caesar to hear my **c**!" .... Ac 25:11
and you will win your **c**." .... Rm 3:4
But in any **c** each one of you 1Co 7:17
Every **c** must be proved by two or 2Co 13:1

CASES

decide the simple **c** themselves. .... Ex 18:22
brought the hard **c** to Moses, ... Ex 18:26
In all these **c** you must warn the.............. 2Ch 19:10
know how to decide **c** fairly, ... Mic 3:1
you take sides in court **c**. .... Mal 2:9
able to judge small **c** as well? 1Co 6:2

CASSIA

and twelve pounds of **c**. .... Ex 30:24
smell like myrrh, aloes, and **c**. .... Ps 45:8

CASTRATE

you would **c** themselves!........................ Gal 5:12

CATCH

disaster will **c** me, and I will .... Ge 19:19
When you **c** up with them, say, '.............. Ge 44:4
chase you and **c** you and destroy .... Dt 28:45
quickly, maybe you can **c** them." .... Jos 2:5
"Saul will **c** me someday. 1Sa 27:1
I'll **c** him while he is tired and 2Sa 17:2
would not let me **c** my breath but .... Job 9:18
A trap will **c** them by the heel .... Job 18:9
Can you **c** Leviathan on a fish .... Job 41:1
They wait to **c** poor people; .... Ps 10:9
let your anger **c** up with them. .... Ps 69:24
They will **c** you in their hands .... Ps 91:12
The lazy **c** no food to cook,.................... Pr 12:27
C the foxes for us—the little .... Sng 2:15
and he will **c** them in his trap. .... Is 8:14
all those who **c** fish from the .... Is 19:8
chases her will easily **c** her; .... Je 2:24
they go, I will **c** them in a net, ... Hos 7:12
They will **c** you in their hands .... Mt 4:6
After you **c** the first fish,..................... Mt 17:27
'They will **c** you in their hands .... Lk 4:11
in the water to **c** some fish." .... Lk 5:4
hard all night trying to **c** fish,................. Lk 5:5
trying to **c** him saying something .... Lk 11:54
the darkness will not **c** you. .... Jn 12:35

Friends, did you **c** any fish?" .... Jn 21:5
I was tricky and lied to **c** you.................. 2Co 12:16

CATCHES
living among you **c** a wild animal .... Le 17:13
before he **c** us and destroys 2Sa 15:14
c the wise in their own clever .... Job 5:13
when someone **c** him stealing. .... Je 2:26
He **c** them in his net and drags .... Hab 1:15
He **c** those who are wise in their 1Co 3:19
who **c** them to do what he wants. 2Ti 2:26

CATCHING
those who make nets for **c** birds, ... Je 5:26

CATTLE
to live in tents and raise **c**. .... Ge 4:20
was very rich in **c**, silver, and .... Ge 13:2
gave Abimelech some sheep and **c**, ... Ge 21:27
in charge of my sheep and **c**." .... Ge 47:6
donkeys, camels, **c**, goats, and .... Ex 9:3
not eat any of the fat from **c**, ... Le 7:23
kinds of **c** or sow your field .... Le 19:19
Balak offered **c** and sheep as a .... Nu 22:40
But we kept the **c** and valuable .... Dt 2:35
your **c** will have many calves,.................. Dt 30:9
your best **c**, and your donkeys 1Sa 8:16
why do I hear **c** mooing and sheep........... 1Sa 15:14
best sheep and **c** to sacrifice to 1Sa 15:21
David took all the sheep and **c**, ... 1Sa 30:20
rich man had many sheep and **c**. 2Sa 12:2
they had too many **c** for the land 1Ch 5:9
sheep and **c** as a great feast 2Ch 18:2
think of us as **c**, as if we are .... Job 18:3
The **c** on a thousand hills are .... Ps 50:10
LORD more than offering him **c**, ... Ps 69:31
the grass for **c** and vegetables .... Ps 104:14
He gives food to **c** and to the .... Ps 147:9
as you let your **c** and donkeys .... Is 32:20
The mooing of **c** cannot be heard. .... Je 9:10
destroy all Egypt's **c** which live .... Eze 32:13
the hoofs of **c** will not muddy .... Eze 32:13
he found people selling **c**, ... Jn 2:14
both the sheep and **c**, to leave.................. Jn 2:15
flour, wheat, **c**, sheep, horses, ... Rev 18:13

CAUGHT
a male sheep **c** in a bush by its .... Ge 22:13
So Laban **c** up with Jacob. .... Ge 31:25
So the servant **c** up with the .... Ge 44:6
If the thief is **c**, he must pay .... Ex 22:7
gods, you will be **c** in a trap." .... Ex 23:33
no one saw it, and she wasn't **c**. .... Nu 5:13
If we **c** all the fish in the sea, ... Nu 11:22
men of Ai were **c** between the .... Jos 8:22
and when they **c** him, they cut .... Jdg 1:6
went out and **c** three hundred................. Jdg 15:4
leave, Saul **c** his robe, and it 1Sa 15:27
I **c** it by its fur and hit it and 1Sa 17:35
head got **c** in the tree,........................... 2Sa 18:9
So they **c** her when she came to.............. 2Ki 11:16
King Zedekiah and **c** up with him 2Ki 25:5
Jehu's men **c** him hiding in.................... 2Ch 22:9
So they **c** her when she came to.............. 2Ch 23:15
feet would be **c** in a net when.................. Job 18:8
Their feet are **c** in the nets .... Ps 9:15
them be **c** in their own traps. .... Ps 10:2
I chased my enemies and **c** them. .... Ps 18:37
My sins have **c** me so that I .... Ps 40:12
evil man will be **c** in his wicked .... Pr 5:22
might be **c** by your own words. .... Pr 6:2
But if he is **c**, he must pay back .... Pr 6:31
butcher, like a deer **c** in a trap .... Pr 7:22
but the dishonest will be **c**....................... Pr 10:9
Lizards can be **c** in the hand, ... Pr 30:28

but a sinner will be **c** by them. .... Ec 7:26
a net, or a bird **c** in a trap, ... Ec 9:12
they will be trapped and **c**." .... Is 8:15
everyone who is **c** will be killed .... Is 13:15
chased them and **c** up with...................... Je 39:5
the pits will be **c** in the traps. .... Je 48:44
Zedekiah and **c** him in the plains .... Je 52:8
of a hand and **c** me by the hair .... Eze 8:3
roar unless it has **c** an animal; .... Am 3:4
the lake and **c** many different.................. Mt 13:47
out his hand and **c** Peter......................... Mt 14:31
to catch fish, and we **c** nothing. .... Lk 5:5
c so many fish that the nets .... Lk 5:6
amazed at the many fish they **c**,.............. Lk 5:9
We **c** this man telling things .... Lk 23:2
who had been **c** in adultery. .... Jn 8:3
this woman was **c** having sexual .... Jn 8:4
fished that night but **c** nothing. .... Jn 21:3
and they **c** so many fish they .... Jn 21:6
The ship was **c** in it and could .... Ac 27:15
by others and **c** in the devil's 1Ti 3:7
themselves and are **c** in a trap. 1Ti 6:9
animals born to be **c** and killed. 2Pe 2:12

CAULK
putting **c** in your ship's seams. .... Eze 27:9

CAUSE
I will **c** you to have much .... Ge 3:16
And I will **c** their numbers to .... Ge 17:20
I broken to **c** you to chase me? .... Ge 31:36
Almighty will **c** the governor to .... Ge 43:14
We will **c** the great sorrow that .... Ge 44:31
I will **c** the Egyptians to think .... Ex 3:21
He will **c** your horses, donkeys, ... Ex 9:3
They will **c** boils to break out .... Ex 9:9
I will **c** food to fall like rain .... Ex 16:4
I will **c** all my goodness to pass .... Ex 33:19
if I **c** mildew to grow in .... Le 14:34
will **c** diseases to spread among .... Le 26:25
you see will **c** you to go mad. .... Dt 28:34
From now on it won't **c** death, ... 2Ki 2:21
it will **c** your intestines 2Ch 21:15
they have no **c** to hate me. .... Ps 35:19
They use the law to **c** suffering. .... Ps 94:20
with quick tempers **c** trouble, ... Pr 15:18
Those two can **c** great disaster! .... Pr 24:22
let your words **c** you to sin,.................... Ec 5:6
I will **c** proud people to lose .... Is 13:11
They **c** the plants to sprout and .... Is 55:10
sins **c** him to turn away from .... Is 59:2
They **c** trouble and create more .... Is 59:4
because I will **c** a disaster to .... Je 11:23
lies that will **c** you to be taken .... Je 27:10
reason for you to **c** Jerusalem to .... Je 27:17
I will soon **c** a destroying wind .... Je 51:1
things that **c** people to sin. .... Eze 14:3
Or I might **c** a disease to spread .... Eze 14:19
I will **c** an enemy to attack you .... Eze 29:8
He will **c** terrible destruction .... Da 8:24
when I will **c** a time of hunger .... Am 8:11
every horse and **c** its rider to .... Zch 12:4
that time the LORD will **c** panic. .... Zch 14:13
And do not **c** us to be tempted, ... Mt 6:13
will come and **c** many people to .... Mt 24:11
the people might **c** a riot." .... Mt 26:5
for Herodias to **c** John's death. .... Mk 6:21
own parents and **c** them to be put .... Mk 13:12
the people might **c** a riot." .... Mk 14:2
do not **c** us to be tempted.'" .... Lk 11:4
Things that **c** people to sin will .... Lk 17:1
your neck than to **c** one of these .... Lk 17:2
and will **c** you to remember all .... Jn 14:26
they go they **c** ruin and misery. .... Rm 3:16

their feasts **c** them to stumble.................. Rm 11:9
I will **c** the wise to lose their 1Co 1:19
freedom does not **c** those who are 1Co 8:9
like this and **c** them to do what 1Co 8:13
love will **c** people to forgive 1Pe 4:8
but to **c** pain to the people for .... Rev 9:5

CAUSED
The LORD God **c** every beautiful .... Ge 2:9
So the LORD God **c** the man to .... Ge 2:21
So the LORD **c** them to spread out........... Ge 11:9
But God **c** the people in the .... Ge 35:5
which **c** boils to break out and .... Ex 9:10
So he **c** hail to fall upon the .... Ex 9:23
and the LORD **c** a strong wind to .... Ex 10:13
So the LORD **c** terrible things to .... Ex 32:35
shook! God had **c** the panic. 1Sa 14:15
and he **c** David to turn against 2Sa 24:1
God also **c** another man to be............. 1Ki 11:23
LORD **c** this to happen to keep 1Ki 12:15
and this sin **c** its ruin and 1Ki 13:34
blew until it **c** the mountains to 1Ki 19:11
The Lord had **c** the Aramean army 2Ki 7:6
and he **c** David to count the 1Ch 21:1
God **c** Ahaziah's death when he 2Ch 22:7
God **c** this to happen so that 2Ch 25:20
the LORD **c** Cyrus to send an .... Ezr 1:1
He **c** the kings of Persia to be .... Ezr 9:9
what God had **c** me to do for .... Ne 2:12
Then my God **c** me to gather the .... Ne 7:5
Who **c** this to happen? .... Is 41:4
it **c** them to fall into sin. .... Eze 7:19
They have **c** many women to become........ Eze 22:25
The LORD **c** a big fish to swallow .... Jnh 1:17
went north have **c** my spirit to .... Zch 6:8
So I have **c** you to be hated and .... Mal 2:9
screamed and **c** the boy to fall .... Mk 9:26
whose sin **c** this man to be born.............. Jn 9:2
to life and **c** him to be seen, ... Ac 10:40
Lord immediately **c** him to become .... Ac 12:23
c all the people to be upset .... Ac 21:27
there among you has **c** sadness. 2Co 2:5
have not yet **c** you to be killed. .... Heb 12:4
mercy he has **c** us to be born 1Pe 1:3
They have **c** many people to 2Pe 2:13

CAUSES
And whoever **c** an injury to a .... Le 24:19
the spirit in me **c** me to speak. .... Job 32:18
angry with one who **c** him shame. .... Pr 14:35
A useless person **c** trouble, ... Pr 16:28
A greedy person **c** trouble, ... Pr 28:25
so stirring up anger **c** trouble." .... Pr 30:33
on earth that **c** serious problems .... Ec 6:1
a stone that **c** people to stumble .... Is 8:14
what I see **c** me to shake with............... Is 21:3
your greatness **c** the nations to .... Is 33:3
The earth **c** plants to grow, ... Is 61:11
and a garden **c** the seeds planted .... Is 61:11
great God who **c** fear and wonder .... Da 9:4
If your right eye **c** you to sin, ... Mt 5:29
If your right hand **c** you to sin, ... Mt 5:30
He **c** the sun to rise on good .... Mt 5:45
and someone **c** that child to sin, ... Mt 18:6
the one who **c** them to happen! .... Mt 18:7
hand or your foot **c** you to sin, ... Mt 18:8
your eye **c** you to sin, take it .... Mt 18:9
and someone **c** that child to sin, ... Mk 9:42
If your hand **c** you to sin, ... Mk 9:43
If your foot **c** you to sin, ... Mk 9:45
your eye **c** you to sin, take it .... Mk 9:47
It **c** him to lose control of .... Lk 9:39
the person who **c** them to happen! .... Lk 17:1
Faith **c** us to be what the law .... Rm 3:31

stone that **c** people to stumble. .... Rm 9:32
eat food that **c** someone else to .... Rm 14:20
This **c** the Jews to stumble and 1Co 1:23
if the food I eat **c** them to fall 1Co 8:13
love of money **c** all kinds of 1Ti 6:10
avoid someone who **c** arguments. .... Tit 3:10
is "a stone that **c** people to 1Pe 2:8

CAUSING
pregnant woman, **c** the baby to .... Ex 21:22
c much trouble to the people of .... Jdg 10:9
c the temple to fall on the .... Jdg 16:30
c Amasa's insides to spill onto 2Sa 20:10
c you pain like a two-edged .... Pr 5:4
You are the ones who are **c** it!" .... Mt 27:24
c the boat to fill with water, ... Lk 8:23
each other, **c** divisions among................ Gal 5:20

CAVE
to live in the mountains in a **c**. .... Ge 19:30
to sell me the **c** of Machpelah at.............. Ge 23:9
wife Sarah in the **c** in the field .... Ge 23:19
buried him in the **c** of Machpelah .... Ge 25:9
That **c** is in the field of .... Ge 49:30
them hiding in the **c** at Makkedah .... Jos 10:17
opening of the **c** with large................... Jos 10:18
the five kings out of the **c**— .... Jos 10:23
Judah went to the **c** in the rock .... Jdg 15:11
and escaped to the **c** of Adullam. 1Sa 22:1
were hiding far back in the **c**................. 1Sa 24:3
Saul left the **c** and went his way 1Sa 24:7
put you in my power in the **c**. 1Sa 24:10
hiding in a **c** or some other.................. 2Sa 17:9
to him in the **c** of Adullam 2Sa 23:13
fifty in one **c** and fifty in 1Ki 18:4
went into a **c** and stayed all 1Ki 19:9
stood at the entrance to the **c**................ 1Ki 19:13
the rock by the **c** near Adullam. 1Ch 11:15
he escaped from Saul in the **c**. .... Ps 56:13
of David when he was in the **c**. .... Ps 141:10
its nest at the entrance of a **c**................. Je 48:28
He filled his **c** with the animals .... Nah 2:12
It was a **c** with a large stone .... Jn 11:38

CAVES
the mountains, in **c**, and in safe .... Jdg 6:2
went to hide in **c** and bushes, ... 1Sa 13:6
hid a hundred of them in two **c**, ... 1Ki 18:4
up streambeds, in **c**, and among.............. Job 30:6
Go into the **c** of the cliffs; .... Is 2:10
people will hide in **c** and cracks .... Is 2:21
run away and hide in deep **c**, ... Je 49:8
strongholds and **c** will die of .... Eze 33:27
lived in the burial **c** and were .... Mt 8:28
man lived in the **c**, and no one .... Mk 5:3
and had lived in the burial **c**, ... Lk 8:27
living in **c** and holes in the .... Heb 11:38
and put them in **c** of darkness 2Pe 2:4
themselves in **c** and in the rocks.............. Rev 6:15

CEDAR
birds, a piece of **c** wood, a .... Le 14:4
alive, the **c** wood, the hyssop .... Le 14:51
the priest must take a **c** stick, ... Nu 19:6
like **c** trees growing by the .... Nu 24:6
along with **c** logs, carpenters 2Sa 5:11
in a palace made of **c** wood, ... 2Sa 7:2
the great **c** trees of Lebanon 1Ki 4:33
Solomon as much **c** and pine as he 1Ki 5:10
made from beams and **c** boards on............ 1Ki 6:9
to the Temple by **c** beams. 1Ki 6:10
the Temple was covered with **c**, ... 1Ki 6:18
had four rows of **c** columns which 1Ki 7:2
covered with **c** from the floor 1Ki 7:7
had given Solomon all the **c**, ... 1Ki 9:11

message to a c tree in Lebanon. 2Ki 14:9
also sent c logs, bricklayers, ... 1Ch 14:1
am living in a palace made of c, ... 1Ch 17:1
Much of the c had been brought 1Ch 22:4
Also send me c, pine, and 2Ch 2:8
they would float c logs from .... Ezr 3:7
Its tail is like a c tree; .... Job 40:17
limbs like the mighty c tree. .... Ps 80:10
He is like a c of Lebanon, ... Sng 5:15
will protect her with c boards. .... Sng 8:9
and the c trees of Lebanon .... Is 14:8
windows and uses c wood for the .... Je 22:14
branch from the top of a c tree, ... Eze 17:22
They took a c tree from Lebanon .... Eze 27:5
The c trees in the garden of God .... Eze 31:8
Like the c trees in Lebanon, ... Hos 14:5
who were tall like c trees and .... Am 2:9
so fire may burn your c trees................... Zch 11:1

CEDARS
and burn up the c of Lebanon!' .... Jdg 9:15
Built of c from the Forest of 1Ki 7:2
down its tallest and its best 2Ki 19:23
LORD breaks the c of Lebanon. .... Ps 29:5
be tall like the c of Lebanon. .... Ps 92:12
they are the c of Lebanon, ... Ps 104:16
smell like the c of Lebanon. .... Sng 4:11
but we will put great c there." .... Is 9:10
down its tallest and its best .... Is 37:24
the desert—c, acacia, myrtle, ... Is 41:19
the sweet-smelling c in Lebanon. .... Hos 14:6

CEILING
from floor to c with cedar 1Ki 6:15
and the c was covered with cedar 1Ki 7:3
gold on the Temple's c beams, ... 2Ch 3:7
our c is made of juniper wood. .... Sng 1:17
through the c into the middle .... Lk 5:19

CELEBRATE
You must c the Feast of .... Ex 12:17
c this feast every year at the .... Ex 13:10
You must c the Feast of Weeks. .... Ex 23:16
You must c the Feast of Shelters............. Ex 23:16
C the Feast of Unleavened Bread. .... Ex 34:18
And c the Feast of Shelters in................. Ex 34:22
c the LORD's festival for seven .... Le 23:39
will c it in the seventh month. .... Le 23:41
Israelites to c the Passover,.................... Nu 9:4
But c it at twilight on the .... Nu 9:11
When you c the Passover, follow .... Nu 9:12
C the Passover of the LORD your .... Dt 16:1
rulers gathered to c and to .... Jdg 16:23
So I will c in the presence of 2Sa 6:21
in Jerusalem to c the Passover 2Ch 30:1
They were to c with songs of .... Ne 12:27
small villages c on the .... Est 9:19
He told them to c every year on .... Est 9:21
first month you will c the Feast .... Eze 45:21
you c the Feast of Shelters,.................... Eze 45:25
C your feasts, people of Judah, ... Nah 1:15
and to c the Feast of Shelters................. Zch 14:16
it so we can have a feast and c. .... Lk 15:23
who harvests c at the same time. .... Jn 4:36
Let us c this feast with the 1Co 5:8

CELEBRATED
the month, they c the Passover .... Jos 5:10
the Israelites c the other 1Ki 8:65
had not been c like this since 2Ki 23:22
Then they c the festival for.................... 2Ch 7:9
in Jerusalem the Feast of 2Ch 30:21
King Josiah c the Passover to 2Ch 35:1
Passover was c in the eighteenth 2Ch 35:19
they c the Feast of Shelters. .... Ezr 3:4

from captivity c the Passover .... Ezr 6:19
For seven days they c the Feast .... Ezr 6:22
be remembered and c from now on .... Est 9:28
should always be c by the Jewish .... Est 9:28
I have not c my great wealth or .... Job 31:25

CELEBRATING
drinking and c with the things 1Sa 30:16
Israelites were c in the 2Sa 6:5
Israelites were c in the 1Ch 13:8
saw King David dancing and c, ... 1Ch 15:29
they were having feasts and c. .... Est 8:17

CELEBRATION
During that c, the land will go .... Le 25:28
the people were enjoying the c, ... Jdg 16:25
the Israelites had a great c.................... 1Sa 11:15
had not been a c like this since 2Ch 30:26
the Passover c was finished, ... 2Ch 31:1
for the dead was turned into c. .... Est 9:22
agreed to hold the c every year. .... Est 9:23

CELEBRATIONS
I will put an end to all her c: .... Hos 2:11

CELL
Jeremiah into a c in a dungeon, ... Je 37:16
and a light shined in the c. .... Ac 12:7

CEMETERY
the c, the childless mother, the .... Pr 30:16

CENCHREA
At C Paul cut off his hair, ... Ac 18:18
is a helper in the church in C.................. Rm 16:1

CENTER
a hole in the c for Aaron's head .... Ex 28:32
city, with the city in the c. .... Nu 35:5
down from the c of the land, ... Jdg 9:37
turned to the two c pillars that .... Jdg 16:29
outward from the c of the bowl. 1Ki 7:25
them into the c of this city. .... Je 21:4
metal was in the c of the fire. .... Eze 1:4
put her at the c of the nations................. Eze 5:5
Now we can be the trading c. .... Eze 26:2
who live at the c of the world." .... Eze 38:12
the c of our joints and bones. .... Heb 4:12
standing in the c of the throne .... Rev 5:6
the Lamb at the c of the throne .... Rev 7:17

CENTERS
as supply c for the king. .... Ex 1:11

CENTS
which were only worth a few c. .... Mk 12:42

CEPHAS
You will be called C." .... Jn 1:42
"C" means "Peter." .... Jn 1:42

CEREMONY
of the marriage c with Leah, ... Ge 29:27
a special c to cleanse away sin. .... Nu 19:9
Jews used in their washing c. .... Jn 2:6
and share in their cleansing c. .... Ac 21:24

CERTAIN
But you may eat c insects that .... Le 11:21
mother must bring c sacrifices .... Le 12:6
at a c unclean place outside the .... Le 14:40
out for a c number of years. .... Le 25:50
the hearts of c brave men who 1Sa 10:26
and learned for c that Saul had 1Sa 26:4
Each group had c duties. 1Ch 24:3
Each group had a c time to serve .... Ezr 6:18
There is a c group of people .... Est 3:8
has a c plan planned when .... Is 2:12
the young men a c amount of food........... Da 1:5
to live for a c period of time. .... Da 7:12
often fast for a c time,........................... Mt 9:14

the city to a c man and tell him .... Mt 26:18
often fasted for a c time......................... Mk 2:18
the people in a c place refuse .... Mk 6:11
fast for a c time and pray, ... Lk 5:33
Jesus was praying in a c place. .... Lk 11:1
In a c town there was a judge................. Lk 18:2
A c leader asked Jesus, "Good .... Lk 18:18
Lord and fasting for a c time. .... Ac 13:2
and fasting for a c time. .... Ac 14:23
Christ we feel c before God. 2Co 3:4
them not to eat c foods which................. 1Ti 4:3
try hard to be c that you really 2Pe 1:10
coming, and their ruin is c...................... 2Pe 2:3

CERTAINLY

I will c return to you about .... Ge 18:10
children will c become a great .... Ge 18:18
me for help, I c will hear their .... Ex 22:23
for ourselves. We can c do it." .... Nu 13:30
and I will c do these things to................. Nu 14:35
they should c get what their .... Nu 27:7
The LORD will c let your family............... 1Sa 25:28
I will c hand them over to you." 2Sa 5:19
through him will c come true." 1Ki 13:32
thought he was c the king of 1Ki 22:32
Evil people will c be punished, ... Pr 11:21
being wise is c better than .... Ec 2:13
will c destroy this land .... Is 10:23
We must c tell the king about .... Je 36:16
and we will c do everything we .... Je 44:17
You must c drink from the cup of .... Je 49:12
The LORD will c do what he has .... Je 51:12
man insisted, "C this man was .... Lk 22:59

CHAFF

wheat from the c in a winepress.............. Jdg 6:11
separated the grain from the c, ... Ru 2:17
them and made them like c. 2Ki 13:7
the wind or like c that is blown .... Job 21:18
from slings are like c to it. .... Job 41:28
They are like c that the wind .... Ps 1:4
Make them like c blown by the .... Ps 35:5
like c blown away by the wind. .... Ps 83:13
They will be like c on the hills .... Is 17:13
as grain is separated from c. .... Is 27:12
wheat from the c with his cart, ... Is 28:28
will be like c that is blown .... Is 29:5
the wind blows them away like c. .... Is 40:24
you will make the hills like c. .... Is 41:15
wind to separate grain from c. .... Je 4:11
scatter you like c that is blown .... Je 13:24
like a wind that blows c away. .... Je 51:2
became like c on a threshing .... Da 2:35
They will be like c blown from .... Hos 13:3
you are blown away like c, ... Zph 2:2
will burn the c with a fire that .... Mt 3:12
the good grain from the c. .... Lk 3:17

CHAIN

he put a gold c around Joseph's .... Ge 41:42
like a silver c or break like .... Ec 12:6
and a gold c around his neck .... Da 5:7
king and a gold c to wear around .... Da 5:16
tie him up, not even with a c. .... Mk 5:3
bound with this c because I .... Ac 28:20
pit and a large c in his hand. .... Rev 20:1

CHAINED

under guard and c hand and foot, ... Lk 8:29

CHAINS

and two c of pure gold, twisted .... Ex 28:14
Attach the c to the two gold .... Ex 28:14
the c from the camels' necks. .... Jdg 8:26
put bronze c on him and made .... Jdg 16:21
Agag came to Samuel in c, ... 1Sa 15:32

His feet were not in c............................. 2Sa 3:34
placing gold c across the front 1Ki 6:21
a net of seven c for each 1Ki 7:17
and put bronze c on him and took 2Ki 25:7
of palm trees and c in the gold. 2Ch 3:5
He made a net of c and put them 2Ch 3:16
placed bronze c on his hands, ... 2Ch 33:11
He takes off c that kings put on .... Job 12:18
put my feet in c and keep close .... Job 13:27
Let's break the c that hold us .... Ps 2:3
They put c around his feet and .... Ps 105:18
were prisoners suffering in c................... Ps 107:10
and darkness and broke their c................ Ps 107:14
You have freed me from my c. .... Ps 116:16
put those kings in c and those .... Ps 149:8
and their arms hold men like c. .... Ec 7:26
scarves, ankle c, the cloth .... Is 3:20
gold and makes silver c for it. .... Is 40:19
behind you, coming along in c. .... Is 45:14
from the c around your neck .... Is 52:2
unfairly and undo their c. .... Is 58:6
He put bronze c on Zedekiah and .... Je 39:7
in Ramah bound in c with all the .... Je 40:1
put bronze c on him, and took .... Je 52:11
he put heavy c on me............................ La 3:7
Make c for captives, because the .... Eze 7:23
a cage with c and brought him .... Eze 19:9
control and tear away your c." .... Nah 1:13
of her leaders were put in c. .... Nah 3:10
people had used c to tie the .... Mk 5:4
he had broken his c and had been .... Lk 8:29
two soldiers, bound with two c. .... Ac 12:6
the c fell off Peter's hands. .... Ac 12:7
were freed from their c. .... Ac 16:26
soldiers to tie Paul with two c. .... Ac 21:33
The commander took Paul's c off. .... Ac 22:30
except for these c I have." .... Ac 26:29
bound with c like a criminal 2Ti 2:9
But God's teaching is not in c. 2Ti 2:9
Others were put in c and thrown .... Heb 11:36
with everlasting c, to be judged .... Jud 1:6

CHAIR

As the king stood up from his c,.............. Jdg 3:20
was sitting on a c near the 1Sa 1:9
Eli fell backward off his c. 1Sa 4:18
armrests on both sides of the c, ... 1Ki 10:19
a table, a c, and a lampstand 2Ki 4:10
armrests on both sides of the c, ... 2Ch 9:18
an honored c in his father's .... Is 22:23

CHALCEDONY

the third was c, the fourth was .... Rev 21:19

CHALDEA

country of C and went to live .... Ac 7:4

CHALLENGE

for a way to c the Philistines, ... Jdg 14:4
He keeps coming out to c Israel............... 1Sa 17:25
and went to c the Philistines. 1Sa 23:28
c God and get away with it.' .... Mal 3:15

CHALLENGED

by the community, and c Moses............... Nu 16:2
When he c Israel, Jonathan son 2Sa 21:21
when they c the Philistines..................... 2Sa 23:9
to Antioch, I c him to his face, ... Gal 2:11

CHAMELEONS

lizards, sand reptiles, and c. .... Le 11:30

CHAMPION

the Philistine c from Gath, ... 1Sa 17:23
saw that their c was dead, ... 1Sa 17:51

CHAMPIONS

wine and are c at mixing drinks. .... Is 5:22

CHANCE

sickness just happened by c." 1Sa 6:9
is looking for a c to kill you. 1Sa 19:2
not find any c to be alone with 2Sa 13:2
By c, a soldier shot an arrow, ... 1Ki 22:34
By c, a soldier shot an arrow 2Ch 18:33
Time and c happen to everyone. .... Ec 9:11
He missed his c for glory!'" .... Je 46:17
Use every c you have for doing .... Eph 5:16

CHANGE

I will c the name of Sarai, ... Ge 17:15
we cannot c what must happen. .... Ge 24:50
clean, and c your clothes. .... Ge 35:2
and the water will c into blood. .... Ex 7:17
the dust will c into gnats." .... Ex 8:16
they might c their minds and go .... Ex 13:17
who will not c their decisions .... Ex 18:21
spot does not spread or c, ... Le 13:23
and he does not c his mind. .... Nu 23:19
so I cannot c the blessing. .... Nu 23:20
c the clothes she was wearing .... Dt 21:13
refused to c their evil ways. .... Jdg 2:19
put on perfume, c your clothes, ... Ru 3:3
He does not lie or c his mind. 1Sa 15:29
so he does not c his mind. 1Sa 15:29
that you will c their minds." 1Ki 18:37
person who tries to c this order .... Ezr 6:12
C your mind; do not be unfair; .... Job 6:29
I will c the look on my face and .... Job 9:27
I will wait until my c comes. .... Job 14:14
you c their appearance and send .... Job 14:20
you want when you refuse to c? .... Job 34:33
them to c from doing evil .... Job 36:10
I will c my heart and life. .... Job 42:6
If they do not c their lives, ... Ps 7:12
agreement like c what I have said .... Ps 89:34
you will c them and throw them .... Ps 102:26
But you never c, and your life .... Ps 102:27
promise and will not c his mind. .... Ps 110:4
he made a law that will never c. .... Ps 148:6
whippings can c an evil heart. .... Pr 20:30
they let money c their thinking. .... Ec 7:7
He does not c his warnings. .... Is 31:2
I will c the desert into a lake .... Is 41:18
do something, no one can c it." .... Is 43:13
I c rivers into a desert, and .... Is 50:2
I will c your punishment into .... Is 60:17
so easy for you to c your mind. .... Je 2:36
spoken and will not c my mind. .... Je 4:28
must c your lives and do what .... Je 7:5
he will c it into deep gloom. .... Je 13:16
Can a leopard c his spots? .... Je 13:23
If you c your heart and return .... Je 15:19
you must not c and be like them .... Je 15:19
I will c my mind and not carry .... Je 18:8
C your ways and do what is right.' .... Je 18:11
I will c my mind about bringing .... Je 26:3
Now c your lives and start doing .... Je 26:13
I will c their sadness into .... Je 31:13
If you could c that agreement, ... Je 33:20
C your hearts and lives, and .... Eze 14:6
you did not c when you were only .... Eze 21:10
Things will c. Those who are .... Eze 21:26
or feel pity or c my mind. .... Eze 24:14
things, hoping things will c. .... Da 2:9
He will try to c times and laws .... Da 7:25
He can c his mind about doing .... Joe 2:13
and we can c the scales to cheat .... Am 8:5
will c your festivals into days .... Am 8:10
Maybe God will c his mind. .... Jnh 3:9
I did not c my mind," says the .... Zch 8:14
I the LORD do not c. .... Mal 3:6

C your hearts and lives because .... Mt 3:2
preach, saying, "C your hearts .... Mt 4:17
the people did not c their lives .... Mt 11:20
must c and become like little .... Mt 18:3
you still refused to c your ways .... Mt 21:32
C your hearts and lives and .... Mk 1:15
people should c their hearts .... Mk 6:12
but sinners to c their hearts .... Lk 5:32
But unless you c your hearts and .... Lk 13:3
good people who don't need to c. .... Lk 15:7
would believe and c their hearts .... Lk 16:30
and that a c of hearts and lives .... Lk 24:47
C your hearts and lives and be .... Ac 2:38
all people could c their hearts .... Ac 5:31
that Jesus will c the customs .... Ac 6:14
C your heart! Turn away from .... Ac 8:22
always trying to c the Lord's .... Ac 13:10
in the world to c their hearts .... Ac 17:30
Jews and Greeks to c their lives .... Ac 20:21
to you so you will c your hearts .... Rm 2:4
are stubborn and refuse to c, ... Rm 2:5
that will c when many who are .... Rm 11:25
This c in us brings ever greater 2Co 3:18
and we do not c the teaching of 2Co 4:2
sorrow made you c your lives. 2Co 7:9
makes people c their hearts 2Co 7:10
They c themselves to look like 2Co 11:13
they want to c the Good News of .... Gal 1:7
you now and could c the way I am .... Gal 4:20
Do not c and go back into the .... Gal 5:1
This c did not come from the One .... Gal 5:8
he will c our humble bodies and .... Php 3:21
will let them c their minds so 2Ti 2:25
like clothes, you will c them. .... Heb 1:12
that his purposes never c, ... Heb 6:17
find no way to c what he had .... Heb 12:17
who does not c like their .... Jam 1:17
C your laughter into crying and .... Jam 4:9
all people to c their hearts 2Pe 3:9
C your hearts and do what you .... Rev 2:5
If you do not c, I will come to .... Rev 2:5
but she does not want to c. .... Rev 2:21
still did not c their hearts and .... Rev 9:20
people refused to c their hearts .... Rev 16:9

CHANGED

cheated me and c my pay ten .... Ge 31:7
water in the Nile c into blood. .... Ex 7:20
in Egypt the dust c into gnats. .... Ex 8:17
So the LORD c the wind. .... Ex 10:19
and his officers c their minds .... Ex 14:5
of Leshem and c its name to Dan, ... Jos 19:47
just after they had c guards. .... Jdg 7:19
and you will be c into a 1Sa 10:6
Samuel, God c Saul's heart. 1Sa 10:9
lotions on, and c his clothes. 2Sa 12:20
LORD c Jacob's name to Israel. 1Ki 18:31
Then Neco c Eliakim's name to 2Ki 23:34
He also c Mattaniah's name to 2Ki 24:17
and Jerusalem and c his name to 2Ch 36:4
and Media, which cannot be c. .... Est 1:19
to defeat them, but that was c. .... Est 9:1
things are c as if by fire. .... Job 28:5
You c my sorrow into dancing. .... Ps 30:11
So he c their water into blood .... Ps 105:29
He c rivers into a desert and .... Ps 107:33
what I say will not be c. .... Is 45:23
his form was so c they could .... Is 52:14
My people haven't c their ways. .... Je 15:7
You have c the words of our God, ... Je 23:36
So the LORD c his mind and did .... Je 26:19
But now you have c your minds. .... Je 34:16
all that crowd will not be c. .... Eze 7:13

C

and Abednego, and he **c** his mind. .... Da 3:19
to it so that it cannot be **c,** .... Da 6:8
you have **c** what is right into a .... Am 6:12
So the LORD **c** his mind about .... Am 7:3
c his mind and did not do what .... Jnh 3:10
you really have **c** your hearts .... Mt 3:8
people would have **c** their lives .... Mt 11:21
Jesus' appearance was **c;** .... Mt 17:2
later the son **c** his mind and .... Mt 21:29
a baptism of **c** hearts and lives .... Mk 1:4
Jesus' appearance was **c.** .... Mk 9:2
a baptism of **c** hearts and lives .... Lk 3:3
you really have **c** your hearts .... Lk 3:8
the appearance of his face **c,** .... Lk 9:29
themselves to show they had **c.** .... Lk 10:13
were sorry and **c** their lives. .... Lk 11:32
of a letter in the law to be **c.** .... Lk 16:17
' But you have **c** it into a ' .... Lk 19:46
where he had **c** the water into .... Jn 4:46
a baptism of **c** hearts and lives. .... Ac 13:24
those who had **c** to worship God .... Ac 13:43
to show they really had **c.** .... Ac 26:20
So they **c** their minds and said, ... Ac 28:6
made was **c** to become useless, ... Rm 8:20
instead be **c** within by a new way .... Rm 12:2
in death, but we will all be **c.** 1Co 15:51
we are being to be like him. 2Co 3:18
they have not **c** their hearts 2Co 12:21
He **c** places with us and put .... Gal 3:13
brought back again to a **c** life. .... Heb 6:4
them back to a **c** life again, ... Heb 6:6
comes, the law must be **c,** too. .... Heb 7:12
God and have the grace of our .... Jud 1:4

CHANGES
gave Benjamin five **c** of clothes .... Ge 45:22
it **c** the words of good people. .... Dt 16:19
shirts and thirty **c** of clothes. .... Jdg 14:12
of gold and ten **c** of clothes. 2Ki 5:5
If anyone **c** this order, a wood .... Ezr 6:11
dawn the earth **c** like clay being .... Job 38:14
c the times and seasons of the .... Da 2:21
he **c** darkness into the morning .... Am 5:8
one sinner who **c** his heart and .... Lk 15:7
God never **c** his mind about the .... Rm 11:29
But when a person **c** and follows 2Co 3:16
Satan **c** himself to look like 2Co 11:14

CHANGING
I am **c** your name from Abram to .... Ge 17:5
made them happy by **c** the mind of .... Ezr 6:22
' But you are **c** God's house into .... Mk 11:17

CHARACTER
character, and **c** produces hope. .... Rm 5:4

CHARCOAL
Just as **c** and wood keep a fire .... Pr 26:21

CHARGE
who was in **c** of everything he .... Ge 24:2
left Joseph in **c** of everything .... Ge 39:6
put Joseph in **c** of all of Egypt. .... Ge 41:43
C him nothing for using your .... Ex 22:25
of Aaron was in **c** of keeping it. .... Ex 38:21
Do not **c** him any interest on .... Le 25:36
Levites in **c** of the Holy Tent .... Nu 1:50
You may **c** foreigners, but not .... Dt 23:20
his servant in **c** of the workers, ... Ru 2:5
Adoniram was in **c** of the men who 2Sa 20:24
Nathan was in **c** of the district 1Ki 4:5
Arza was in **c** of the palace at 1Ki 16:9
people to be in **c** of the music 1Ch 6:31
chosen to be in **c** of the Holy 1Ch 24:5
King David was in **c** of Asaph, ... 1Ch 25:6
in **c** of storing the wine that 1Ch 27:27

They were in **c** of an army of 2Ch 26:13
Levite was in **c** of the special 2Ch 31:14
These men were in **c** of the work .... Ezr 3:9
the palace, in **c** of Jerusalem. .... Ne 7:2
king's eunuch in **c** of the women. .... Est 2:3
put Mordecai in **c** of everything .... Est 8:2
or put him in **c** of the whole .... Job 34:13
You put them in **c** of everything .... Ps 8:6
They do not **c** interest on money .... Ps 15:5
C them with crime after crime, ... Ps 69:27
his angels in **c** of you to watch .... Ps 91:11
Joseph was in **c** of his riches. .... Ps 105:21
I have put you in **c** of nations .... Je 1:10
Horsemen, **c** into battle! .... Je 46:9
and put him in **c** of all the wise .... Da 2:48
to put Daniel in **c** of the whole .... Da 6:3
They **c** like soldiers; .... Joe 2:7
We can **c** them more and give them .... Am 8:5
will be in **c** of my Temple and .... Zch 3:7
has put his angels in **c** of you. .... Mt 4:6
a sign with this **c** against Jesus .... Mk 15:26
his angels in **c** of you to watch .... Lk 4:10
could have some **c** against him. .... Jn 8:6
The soldiers took **c** of Jesus. .... Jn 19:16
will put them in **c** of this work. .... Ac 6:3
c was worthy of jail or death. .... Ac 23:29
But I have no **c** to bring against .... Ac 28:19
owes you anything, **c** that to me. .... Phm 1:18

CHARGED
blacksmiths **c** about one-fourth 1Sa 13:21
they **c** one-eighth of an ounce. 1Sa 13:21
back the extra amount you **c**— .... Ne 5:11
anger the goat **c** the sheep with .... Da 8:6

CHARGES
its strength, and **c** into battle. .... Job 39:21
say about their **c** against you?" .... Mt 26:62
What **c** do you bring against this .... Jn 18:29
had come to make **c** against Paul .... Ac 24:1
But if these **c** are not true, ... Ac 25:11

CHARGING
You are **c** your own brothers too .... Ne 5:7
stop **c** them so much for this. .... Ne 5:10
as a roaring lion or a **c** bear. .... Pr 28:15
like a horse **c** into a battle. .... Je 8:6
are **c,** swords are shining, ... Nah 3:3

CHARIOT
ride in the second royal **c,** .... Ge 41:43
king's horses, **c** drivers, and .... Ex 14:9
and **c** drivers followed them into .... Ex 14:23
Sisera left his **c** and ran away .... Jdg 4:15
run in front of the king's **c.** 1Sa 8:11
hundred Aramean **c** drivers and 2Sa 10:18
Absalom got a **c** and horses for 2Sa 15:1
for Solomon's **c** and work horses; 1Ki 4:28
c from Egypt cost about fifteen 1Ki 10:29
ran to his **c** and escaped to 1Ki 12:18
Ahab got in his **c** and started 1Ki 18:45
King Ahab said to his **c** driver, ... 1Ki 22:34
licked his blood from the **c.** 1Ki 22:38
The man in the **c** is driving like 2Ki 9:20
the servant got Joram's **c** ready. 2Ki 9:21
his body in a **c** to Jerusalem 2Ki 9:28
and Jehu pulled him into the **c.** 2Ki 10:15
his body in a **c** from Megiddo to 2Ki 23:30
to hire chariots and **c** drivers 1Ch 19:6
thousand Aramean **c** drivers and 1Ch 19:18
plans for the **c** of the golden 1Ch 28:18
ran to his **c** and escaped to 2Ch 10:18
God made the **c** commanders turn 2Ch 18:31
him in another **c** and carried him 2Ch 35:24
You make the clouds your **c,** .... Ps 104:3

me feel like a prince in a **c**....................... Sng 6:12
and their **c** wheels move like a .... Is 5:28
a man coming in a **c** with a team .... Is 21:9
and the rumbling **c** wheels...................... Je 47:3
all looked like **c** officers born .... Eze 23:15
the fastest horse to the **c**. .... Mic 1:13
Red horses pulled the first **c**. .... Zch 6:2
White horses pulled the third **c**, ... Zch 6:3
The **c** pulled by the black horses .... Zch 6:6
sitting in his **c** reading from .... Ac 8:28

CHARIOT'S
The wheels were like a **c** wheels. 1Ki 7:33

CHARIOTS
with Joseph in **c** and on horses. .... Ge 50:9
took six hundred of his best **c**, ... Ex 14:7
Egyptians, their **c**, and chariot .... Ex 14:26
horses and **c**, when he drowned .... Dt 11:4
horses and burn all their **c**." .... Jos 11:6
plain, because they had iron **c**. .... Jdg 1:19
nine hundred iron **c** and was very .... Jdg 4:3
men chased Sisera's **c** and army............. Jdg 4:16
thousand **c** and six thousand 1Sa 13:5
David captured one thousand **c**,............. 2Sa 8:4
fourteen hundred **c** and twelve 1Ki 10:26
sold horses and **c** to all the 1Ki 10:29
the Arameans' horses and **c**. 1Ki 20:21
his horses and **c** to Elisha's.................... 2Ki 5:9
of horses and **c** of fire all 2Ki 6:17
and all his **c** went to Zair. 2Ki 8:21
c of Israel and their horsemen! 2Ki 13:14
and burned the **c** that were for 2Ki 23:11
of silver to hire **c** and chariot 1Ch 19:6
They imported **c** from Egypt for 2Ch 1:17
stalls for horses and **c**, ... 2Ch 9:25
Some trust in **c**, others in .... Ps 20:7
and burns up the **c** with fire. .... Ps 46:9
God comes with millions of **c**; .... Ps 68:17
valleys will be filled with **c**. .... Is 22:7
who defeated the **c** and horses .... Is 43:17
and his **c** come like a tornado. .... Je 4:13
and the noisy **c** and the rumbling .... Je 47:3
their weapons, **c**, and wagons. .... Eze 23:24
of the North will attack with **c**, ... Da 11:40
the noise of **c** rumbling over .... Joe 2:5
from you and destroy your **c**. .... Mic 5:10
The metal on the **c** flashes like .... Nah 2:3
The **c** race through the streets .... Nah 2:4
your horses and **c** of victory? .... Hab 3:8
destroy the **c** and their riders .... Hag 2:22
and saw four **c** going out between .... Zch 6:1
of many horses and **c** hurrying .... Rev 9:9

CHARM
C can fool you, and beauty can .... Pr 31:30

CHARMED
snakes cannot be **c**, and they .... Je 8:17

CHARMER
of the snake **c** no matter how .... Ps 58:5

CHARMING
she was **c** and a lover of magic. .... Nah 3:4

CHARMS
their bottles of perfume, and **c**, ... Is 3:20
who sew magic **c** on their wrists .... Eze 13:18
I am against your magic **c**, ... Eze 13:20
away the magic **c** you use so you .... Mic 5:12

CHASE
relatives and began to **c** him. .... Ge 31:23
so they will **c** the Israelites, ... Ex 14:17
'I'll **c** them and catch them...................... Ex 15:9
You will **c** your enemies and .... Le 26:7
They will **c** you and catch you .... Dt 28:45

person cannot **c** a thousand .... Dt 32:30
were called to **c** Joshua and his .... Jos 8:16
Should I **c** the Philistines? 1Sa 14:37
The LORD answered, "**C** them. 1Sa 30:8
men and **c** David tonight. 2Sa 17:1
followed Joab to **c** Sheba son of 2Sa 20:13
the wind; don't **c** after straw. .... Job 13:25
Why do you **c** me as God does? .... Job 19:22
They **c** away the orphan's donkey .... Job 24:3
my enemy **c** me and capture me. .... Ps 7:5
the wicked **c** down those who.................. Ps 10:2
He punishes those who **c** me. .... Ps 57:3
c after those you have hurt, ... Ps 69:26
but those who **c** after evil will.................... Pr 11:19
but the ones who **c** empty dreams .... Pr 28:19
really know how to **c** after love. .... Je 2:33
I will **c** them with war, hunger, ... Je 29:18
C them, kill them, and .... Je 50:21
Those who **c** after us want to .... La 5:5
as I **c** them with a sword. .... Eze 5:12
Murder will **c** you. Since you did .... Eze 35:6
'I will **c** away my lovers, ... Hos 2:5
and **c** from town to town. .... Mt 23:34

CHASED
led the men and **c** the enemy all............. Ge 14:14
animals, but Abram **c** them away. .... Ge 15:11
came and **c** the girls away, ... Ex 2:17
The shepherds **c** us away, but an .... Ex 2:19
c you like bees and defeated .... Dt 1:44
army of Israel **c** the men of Ai .... Jos 8:24
They **c** them to Greater Sidon, ... Jos 11:8
and the Egyptians **c** them with .... Jos 24:6
but Gideon **c** and captured them .... Jdg 8:12
Abimelech and his men **c** them, ... Jdg 9:40
battle and **c** the Philistines...................... 1Sa 14:22
I **c** my enemies and destroyed 2Sa 22:38
Aram ran away as Israel **c** them, ... 1Ki 20:20
Babylonian army **c** King Zedekiah........... 2Ki 25:5
Abijah's army **c** Jeroboam's army 2Ch 13:19
Asa's army **c** them as far as the 2Ch 14:13
darkness and **c** out of the world .... Job 18:18
will be **c** away like a vision. .... Job 20:8
They have **c** me until they have .... Ps 17:11
My enemies have **c** me all day; .... Ps 56:2
Babylonian army **c** them and .... Je 39:5
scattered from being **c** by lions. .... Je 50:17
Babylonian army **c** King Zedekiah .... Je 52:8
Those who **c** her caught her when .... La 1:3
they have **c** after other gods and .... Hos 4:12
people of Ekron will be **c** away. .... Zph 2:4

CHASES
as the angel of the LORD **c** them. .... Ps 35:6
but the one who **c** empty dreams .... Pr 12:11
He **c** them and is never hurt, ... Is 41:3
Any male who **c** her will easily .... Je 2:24
he **c** the east wind all day. .... Hos 12:1

CHASING
fall even when no one is **c** them. .... Le 26:36
the Red Sea as they were **c** you............. Dt 11:4
Continue **c** the enemy and .... Jos 10:19
Saul stopped **c** the Philistines, ... 1Sa 14:46
So Saul stopped **c** David and went 1Sa 23:28
It's as if you are **c** a dead dog................. 1Sa 24:14
Asahel refused to stop **c** Abner. 2Sa 2:23
King Ahab, they stopped **c** him. 2Ch 18:32
threw the people **c** them into .... Ne 9:11
Save me from those who are **c** me,........... Ps 142:6
My enemies are **c** me; .... Ps 143:3
even though no one is **c** them, ... Pr 28:1
is all useless, like **c** the wind. .... Ec 1:14
so those who are **c** me will trip .... Je 20:11

CHEAPER (continued)
and went c after her lovers .... Hos 2:13
is as useless as c the wind; .... Hos 12:1

CHEAPER
awhile, they serve the c wine................... Jn 2:10

CHEAT
Do not c or hurt a foreigner, ... Ex 22:21
Do not c a widow or an orphan............... Ex 22:22
steal something or c someone. .... Le 6:2
You must not c your neighbor .... Le 19:13
Do not c when you measure the .... Le 19:35
Don't c hired servants who are .... Dt 24:14
Did I hurt or c anyone? 1Sa 12:3
and they are paid to c people................... Is 1:23
The people c others and steal. .... Eze 22:29
did not try to c the king. .... Da 6:2
the scales to c the people. .... Am 8:5
They c people to get their .... Mic 2:2
those who c workers of their pay .... Mal 3:5
must not c. Honor your father .... Mk 10:19
they c widows and steal their .... Mk 12:40
people who steal, c, or take .... Lk 18:11
or get drunk, or c people. 1Co 5:11
you yourselves do wrong and c, ... 1Co 6:8
Titus did not c you, did he? 2Co 12:18
fooled: You cannot c God. People .... Gal 6:7
do not wrong or c another 1Th 4:6
who are evil and c others will................. 2Ti 3:13

CHEATED
but he c me and changed my pay .... Ge 31:7
You have not c us, or hurt us,................. 1Sa 12:4
One officer is c by a higher.................... Ec 5:8
sees if someone is c in his case .... La 3:36
And if I have c anyone, I will .... Lk 19:8
Why not let yourselves be c? 1Co 6:7
and we have not c anyone. 2Co 7:2

CHEATER
because every relative is a c, ... Je 9:4

CHEATING
stole or whatever he took by c. .... Le 6:4
the people who get rich by c. .... Je 17:11
things you got by c others and .... Mt 23:25
manager was accused of c him. .... Lk 16:1
or try to get rich by c others. 1Ti 3:8
or try to get rich by c others. .... Tit 1:7

CHEATS
who c people so he can build its............... Je 22:13
The person who c will be cursed. .... Mal 1:14

CHECK
must come back and c the house. .... Le 14:39
The judges must c the matter .... Dt 19:18
"C to see who has left our camp." 1Sa 14:17
Let's c every spring and valley 1Ki 18:5
C each vine again, like someone .... Je 6:9

CHECKED
When they c, they learned that 1Sa 14:17
king of Israel c the place about 2Ki 6:10
We c everything by number and by .... Ezr 8:34
We have c this, and it is true, ... Job 5:27

CHECKING
the matter and c carefully .... Dt 13:14

CHECKS
the priest c it again and the .... Le 14:48

CHEEK
have struck my enemies on the c; .... Ps 3:7
He should let anyone slap his c;............... La 3:30
turn to him the other c also. .... Mt 5:39
If anyone slaps you on one c, ... Lk 6:29

CHEEKS
shoulder, the c, and the inner .... Dt 18:3
of me and hit my c to insult me. .... Job 16:10
Your c are beautiful with .... Sng 1:10
Your c behind your veil are like .... Sng 4:3
His c are like beds of spices; .... Sng 5:13
I offered my c to those who .... Is 50:6
night, and tears are on her c. .... La 1:2

CHEER
Get up, eat something, and c up............... 1Ki 21:7
I decided to c myself up with .... Ec 2:3
the blind man, saying, "C up! .... Mk 10:49
I tell you to c up because none .... Ac 27:22

CHEERS
load, but a kind word c you up. .... Pr 12:25

CHEESE
ten pieces of c to the commander 1Sa 17:18
and c made from cows' milk for............... 2Sa 17:29
my mother like c formed from .... Job 10:10

CHEMOSH
One was a place to worship C, ... 1Ki 11:7
the Moabite god C, and the.................... 1Ki 11:33

CHERUBIM
I knew they were called c. .... Eze 10:20

CHEST
holy vest and the c covering. .... Ex 25:7
gems on the c covering: .... Ex 28:17
the Thummim in the c covering................ Le 8:8
as if it will jump out of my c. .... Job 37:1
Its c is as hard as a rock, ... Job 41:24
against your c without burning .... Pr 6:27
So beat your c in sadness. .... Eze 21:12
Its c and arms were made of .... Da 2:32
he beat on his c because he was............... Lk 18:13
of right living on your c. .... Eph 6:14
had a gold band around his c. .... Rev 1:13

CHESTS
beating their c because they .... Lk 23:48
Their c looked like iron .... Rev 9:9
bands tied around their c. .... Rev 15:6

CHEW
animals only c the cud or only .... Le 11:4
land! We will c them up. They .... Nu 14:9
These animals c the cud, but .... Dt 14:7
who did not let them c us up. .... Ps 124:6
will fall out so you cannot c, ... Ec 12:3

CHEWS
divided and that c the cud. .... Le 11:3
The camel c the cud but does not .... Le 11:4
has a split hoof and c the cud, ... Dt 14:6

CHICKS
gathers her c under her wings .... Mt 23:37
gathers her c under her wings .... Lk 13:34

CHIEF
served his wine and the c baker. .... Ge 40:20
who was the c of a Midianite .... Nu 25:15
the c of Saul's shepherds. 1Sa 21:7
Thirty, David's c soldiers, came 2Sa 23:13
Seraiah the c priest, Zephaniah 2Ki 25:18
Thirty, David's c soldiers, came 1Ch 11:15
the c ruler of the nations of .... Eze 38:2
Ashpenaz, his c officer, to .... Da 1:3
Christ, the C Shepherd, comes 1Pe 5:4

CHILD
God has given me another c. .... Ge 4:25
If she has a c, maybe I can have............... Ge 16:2
birth to a c when she is ninety? .... Ge 17:17
be able to have Abraham's c, ... Ge 21:7
can give birth to a c for me. .... Ge 30:3

When the c grew older, the woman .... Ex 2:10
house where she lived as a c, ... Le 22:13
c slaves will belong to you, ... Le 25:45
every firstborn c and every .... Nu 18:15
you, like one carries a c. .... Dt 1:31
you as a parent corrects a c. .... Dt 8:5
was his only c; he had no other .... Jdg 11:34
prayed for this c, and the LORD 1Sa 1:27
The c was born, but the mother 1Sa 4:19
because the LORD loved the c. 2Sa 12:25
But I am like a little c; 1Ki 3:7
new again, like the skin of a c. 2Ki 5:14
let any male c in Ahab's family 2Ki 9:8
Canaan's first c was Sidon. 1Ch 1:13
I not buried like a c born dead, ... Job 3:16
The fatherless c is grabbed from .... Job 24:9
them be like a c born dead who .... Ps 58:8
you have the freshness of a c. .... Ps 110:3
My c, listen to your father's .... Pr 1:8
My c, if sinners try to lead you .... Pr 1:10
My c, do not forget my teaching, ... Pr 3:1
correct the c they delight .... Pr 3:12
My c, hold on to wisdom and good .... Pr 3:21
My c, pay attention to my words; .... Pr 4:20
I was like a c by his side. .... Pr 8:30
A foolish c brings disaster to a .... Pr 19:13
c who robs his father and sends .... Pr 19:26
Every c is full of foolishness, ... Pr 22:15
of a good c is very happy; .... Pr 23:24
My c, eat honey because it is .... Pr 24:13
whose king is a c and whose .... Ec 10:16
before the c learns to choose .... Is 7:16
A c has been born to us; .... Is 9:6
few that even a c could count .... Is 10:19
and a little c will lead them. .... Is 11:6
as when a c should be born, ... Is 37:3
a woman giving birth to a c. .... Is 42:14
like a c drinking milk from its .... Is 60:16
you as a mother comforts her c. .... Is 66:13
like a woman having her first c. .... Je 4:31
is my dear son, The c I love. .... Je 31:20
an unfaithful c who believes his .... Je 49:4
and the life of the c is mine. .... Eze 18:4
Israel was a c, I loved him, ... Hos 11:1
give my very own c for my sin?" .... Mic 6:7
over the death of an only c. .... Zch 12:10
mercy to his c who serves him, ... Mal 3:17
Look carefully for the c. .... Mt 2:8
above the place where the c was. .... Mt 2:9
Take the c and his mother and .... Mt 2:13
to look for the c so he can kill .... Mt 2:13
to kill the c are now dead." .... Mt 2:20
Joseph took the c and his mother .... Mt 2:21
called a little c to him and .... Mt 18:2
himself humble like this c. .... Mt 18:4
Whoever accepts a c in my name .... Mt 18:5
someone causes that c to sin, ... Mt 18:6
The c is not dead, only asleep." .... Mk 5:39
into the room where the c was. .... Mk 5:40
the c in his arms, he said, ... Mk 9:36
accepts a c like this in my .... Mk 9:37
God as if you were a little c, ... Mk 10:15
saying, "What will this c be?" .... Lk 1:66
Now you, c, will be called a .... Lk 1:76
And so the c grew up and became .... Lk 1:80
angels had said about this c. .... Lk 2:17
The little c grew and became .... Lk 2:40
called to her, "My c, stand up!" .... Lk 8:54
my son, because he is my only c. .... Lk 9:38
If your c or ox falls into a .... Lk 14:5
of God as if you were a c, ... Lk 18:17
Sir, come before my c dies." .... Jn 4:49
so happy that a c has been born .... Jn 16:21

even before Abraham had a c. .... Ac 7:5
When I was a c, I talked like a 1Co 13:11
you are God's c, and God will .... Gal 4:7
a true c to me because you 1Ti 1:2
then, Timothy, my c, be strong 2Ti 2:1
you were a c you have known 2Ti 3:15
my true c in the faith we share: .... Tit 1:4
with you for my c Onesimus, ... Phm 1:10
My c, don't think the Lord's .... Heb 12:5
everyone who accepts as his c." .... Heb 12:6
and every c must be disciplined .... Heb 12:8
become God's c and knows God. 1Jn 4:7
Jesus is the Christ is God's c, ... 1Jn 5:1
who is a c of God conquers 1Jn 5:4
her c was taken up to God and .... Rev 12:5

CHILD'S
his body is made new like a c. .... Job 33:25
not be punished for a c sin. .... Eze 18:20
Jesus took the c father and .... Mk 5:40

CHILDBIRTH
feel the pain of c for you until .... Gal 4:19

CHILDHOOD
because youth and c are useless. .... Ec 11:10

CHILDISH
a man, I stopped those c ways. 1Co 13:11

CHILDLESS
cemetery, the c mother, the land .... Pr 30:16

CHILDREN
Have many c and grow in number. .... Ge 1:28
and when you give birth to c, ... Ge 3:16
These women gave birth to c, ... Ge 6:4
and said to them, "Have many c; .... Ge 9:1
Sarai was not able to have c. .... Ge 11:30
wife, had no c, but she had a .... Ge 16:1
age when women normally have c, ... Ge 18:11
Abraham's c will certainly .... Ge 18:18
from having c as a punishment .... Ge 20:18
with me and my c and my .... Ge 21:23
and his wife Milcah have c now .... Ge 22:20
Isaac's wife could not have c, ... Ge 25:21
bless you and give you many c, ... Ge 28:3
it possible for Leah to have c, ... Ge 29:31
Jacob, "Give me c, or I'll die!" .... Ge 30:1
it possible for her to have c. .... Ge 30:22
my wives and my c and let me go. .... Ge 30:26
So Jacob put his c and his wives .... Ge 31:17
and will make your c as many as .... Ge 32:12
Jacob divided his c among Leah, ... Ge 33:1
These are the c God has given .... Ge 33:5
you know that the c are weak. .... Ge 33:13
animals and the c set the speed .... Ge 33:14
duty to provide c for your .... Ge 38:8
God has given me c in the land .... Ge 41:52
You are robbing me of all my c. .... Ge 42:36
to me, 'I will give you many c. .... Ge 48:4
the people of Israel had many c, ... Ex 1:7
and all of your c leave Egypt. .... Ex 10:10
punish your c, and even your .... Ex 20:5
and your c will become orphans. .... Ex 22:24
any of your c to be sacrificed .... Le 18:21
gives one of his c to Molech, ... Le 20:2
uncle's wife will die without c; .... Le 20:20
he and his c will become free. .... Le 25:54
all the firstborn c of Israel. .... Nu 3:12
the firstborn c of the Egyptians .... Nu 3:13
Your c will be shepherds here. .... Nu 14:33
Then our c will be in strong, ... Nu 32:17
Your little c that you said .... Dt 1:39
teach these things to their c." .... Dt 4:10
will go well for you and your c. .... Dt 4:40
for them and their c forever! .... Dt 5:29

he will bless you with c. ....Dt 7:13
you and your c will live a long ....Dt 11:21
to death if their c do wrong, ...Dt 24:16
Your c will be blessed, as well ....Dt 28:4
to us and our c forever so that ....Dt 29:29
I gave him many c, including his ....Jos 24:3
land now belonged to Joseph's c. ....Jos 24:32
LORD had kept her from having c............1Sa 1:5
Michal had no c to the day she 2Sa 6:23
David's c because of this, ...1Ki 11:39
burned their c in the fire, ...2Ki 17:31
which he gave to the c of Jacob,.............2Ki 17:34
the four c of David and 1Ch 3:5
These were the c of Joel:........................1Ch 5:4
Amram's c were Aaron, Moses, and 1Ch 6:3
names of David's c born in 1Ch 14:4
God blessed Obed-Edom with c...............1Ch 26:5
and she gave Rehoboam these c: 2Ch 11:20
He made his c pass through fire 2Ch 33:6
You made their c as many as the ....Ne 9:23
their c went into the land and................Ne 9:24
My c may have sinned and cursed ....Job 1:5
know that you will have many c, ...Job 5:25
Your c sinned against God,....................Job 8:4
Their c who are left will never ....Job 27:14
and leave much money to their c. ....Ps 17:14
and their c will inherit the ....Ps 25:13
C, come and listen to me. ....Ps 34:11
and their c are a blessing. ....Ps 37:26
We are the c of Jacob, whom he ....Ps 47:4
And they would tell their c. ....Ps 78:6
he was very angry with his c. ....Ps 78:62
c will live in your presence, ...Ps 102:28
Abraham, the c of Jacob, his ....Ps 105:6
Let his c become orphans and his ....Ps 109:9
the c of honest people will be ....Ps 112:2
He gives c to the woman who has ....Ps 113:9
he give you and your c success. ....Ps 115:14
C are a gift from the LORD; ....Ps 127:3
C who are born to a young man ....Ps 127:4
Your wife will give you many c, ...Ps 128:3
My c, listen to your father's ....Pr 4:1
Wise c make their father happy,.............Pr 10:1
Wise c take their parents' ....Pr 13:1
If you do not punish your c, ...Pr 13:24
but foolish c disrespect their ....Pr 15:20
c are proud of their parents. ....Pr 17:6
Correct your c while there is ....Pr 19:18
Even c are known by their ....Pr 20:11
Train c to live the right way, ...Pr 22:6
who have wise c are glad because ....Pr 23:24
C who obey what they have been ....Pr 28:7
Correct your c, and you will be ....Pr 29:17
Her c speak well of her. ....Pr 31:28
have a hundred c and live a long ....Ec 6:3
I raised my c and helped them ....Is 1:2
C treat my people cruelly, ...Is 3:12
Their little c will be beaten to...............Is 13:16
The c of evil people will never ....Is 14:20
When they see all their c, ...Is 29:23
c of Israel, come back to the ....Is 31:6
Even c become tired and need to ....Is 40:30
will bring your c from the east ....Is 43:5
Your c will grow like a tree in................Is 44:4
Your c will soon return to you, ...Is 49:17
All your c are gathering to ....Is 49:18
Abraham had no c when I called ....Is 51:2
Your c will take over other ....Is 54:3
You kill c in the ravines and ....Is 57:5
and their c will be known among ....Is 61:9
and their c will be blessed. ....Is 65:23
you as my own c and give you ....Je 3:19
The c gather wood, and the ....Je 7:18

My c have gone away and left me. ....Je 10:20
Have many c in Babylon; ....Je 29:6
Your c will return to their own ....Je 31:17
Her little c will cry for help. ....Je 48:4
My c are left sad and lonely, ...La 1:16
C beg for bread, but no one ....La 4:4
and c will eat their parents. ....Eze 5:10
You killed your c and offered ....Eze 16:36
and their c were thrown into the ....Da 6:24
woman and have unfaithful c, ...Hos 1:2
be called 'c of the living God.'...............Hos 1:10
I will kill the c they love." ....Hos 9:16
Tell your c about these things, ...Joe 1:3
you are sad for the c you love. ....Mic 1:16
Her small c were beaten to death ....Nah 3:10
Their c will see it and rejoice;..............Zch 10:7
love their c and children love ....Mal 4:6
Rachel crying for her c. ....Mt 2:18
God could make c for Abraham ....Mt 3:9
for they will be called God's c. ....Mt 5:9
will be true c of your Father ....Mt 5:45
If your c ask for bread, which ....Mt 7:9
They are like c sitting in the ....Mt 11:16
are all of God's c who belong to ....Mt 13:38
ate, not counting women and c. ....Mt 14:21
Then the c of the king don't ....Mt 17:26
change and become like little c. ....Mt 18:3
these little c believes in me, ...Mt 18:6
even the servant's wife and c...............Mt 18:25
Let the little c come to me. ....Mt 19:14
Jesus put his hands on the c, ...Mt 19:15
and that the c were praising him ....Mt 21:15
Since he had no c, his brother ....Mt 22:25
We and our c will be responsible ....Mt 27:25
let the c eat all they want. ....Mk 7:27
these little c believes in me, ...Mk 9:42
Let the little c come to me. ....Mk 10:14
Jesus took the c in his arms, ...Mk 10:16
sisters, mothers, c, and fields. ....Mk 10:30
a wife but no c, then that man ....Mk 12:19
and have c for his brother. ....Mk 12:19
give their own c to be killed. ....Mk 13:12
C will fight against their own ....Mk 13:12
But they had no c, because ....Lk 1:7
and their c and will bring ....Lk 1:17
Abraham and to his c forever." ....Lk 1:55
God could make c for Abraham ....Lk 3:8
and you will be c of the Most ....Lk 6:35
They are like c sitting in the ....Lk 7:32
to those who are like little c. ....Lk 10:21
and my c and I are in bed. ....Lk 11:7
If your c ask for a fish, which................Lk 11:11
mother, wife, c, brothers, or ....Lk 14:26
and giving their c to be married ....Lk 17:27
Let the little c come to me. ....Lk 18:16
or c for the kingdom of God ....Lk 18:29
dies and leaves a wife but no c, ...Lk 20:28
They are c of God, because they.............Lk 20:36
the right to become c of God. ....Jn 1:12
We are Abraham's c, and we have ....Jn 8:33
We are not like c who never knew ....Jn 8:41
God's scattered c to bring them ....Jn 11:52
you will become c of light." ....Jn 12:36
Jesus said, "My c, I will be ....Jn 13:33
you, for your c, and for all who ....Ac 2:39
died without c to continue his................Ac 8:33
we are God's c, you must not ....Ac 17:29
the women and c, came outside ....Ac 21:5
their c and not to obey ....Ac 21:21
all of Abraham's c can have that ....Rm 4:16
much past the age for having c, ...Rm 4:19
The true c of God are those who ....Rm 8:14
If we are God's c, we will ....Rm 8:17

C

descendants are God's true **c.** .... Rm 9:8
Abraham's true **c** are those who .... Rm 9:8
be called 'c of the living God. .... Rm 9:26
clean, but now your **c** are holy. 1Co 7:14
sisters, do not think like **c.** 1Co 14:20
to you as if you were my **c.** 2Co 6:13
should save to give to their **c.** 2Co 12:14
that the true **c** of Abraham are .... Gal 3:7
We were once like **c,** slaves to .... Gal 4:3
Since you are God's **c,** God sent .... Gal 4:6
make us his own **c** through Jesus .... Eph 1:5
You are God's **c** whom he loves, ... Eph 5:1
So live like **c** who belong to the .... Eph 5:8
C, obey your parents as the Lord .... Eph 6:1
not make your **c** angry, but raise .... Eph 6:4
will be God's **c** without fault. .... Php 2:15
C, obey your parents in all .... Col 3:20
mother caring for her little **c.** 1Th 2:7
as a father treats his own **c.** 1Th 2:11
leaders of their **c** and their own 1Ti 3:12
if a widow has **c** or 1Ti 5:4
works such as raising her **c,** 1Ti 5:10
not be known as **c** who are wild .... Tit 1:6
their husbands, to love their **c,** .... Tit 2:4
me are the **c** God has given me. .... Heb 2:13
too old to have **c,** and Sarah .... Heb 11:11
All **c** are disciplined by their .... Heb 12:7
the blessings God has for his **c.** 1Pe 1:4
you are obedient **c** of God do not 1Pe 1:14
women are true **c** of Sarah if you 1Pe 3:6
My dear **c,** these are the last 1Jn 2:18
Yes, my dear **c,** live in him so 1Jn 2:28
all who do right are God's **c.** 1Jn 2:29
that we are called **c** of God. 1Jn 3:1
are and who the devil's **c** are: 1Jn 3:10
My **c,** we should love people not 1Jn 3:18
My dear **c,** you belong to God and 1Jn 4:4
So, dear **c,** keep yourselves away 1Jn 5:21
To the chosen lady and her **c:** 2Jn 1:1
to hear that my **c** are following 3Jn 1:4
war against all her other **c—** .... Rev 12:17
God, and they will be my **c.** .... Rev 21:7

CHIN

a sore on the scalp or on the **c,** .... Le 13:29
skin disease of the head or **c.** .... Le 13:30

CHIP

be like a **c** of wood floating .... Hos 10:7

CHISEL

shaped by a worker with his **c.** .... Je 10:3

CHISELS

he uses his **c** to cut a statue .... Is 44:13

CHLOE'S

people from **C** family have told 1Co 1:11

CHOICE

The first **c** of towns was given .... Jos 21:10
and gave them a **c** place at the 1Sa 9:22
agreement with the man of my **c;** .... Ps 89:3
I have no other **c,** because my .... Je 9:7
his **c** does not depend on what .... Rm 9:16
I preach because it is my own **c,** 1Co 9:17

CHOICES

I offer you three **c.** 2Sa 24:12
you not decide between two **c?** 1Ki 18:21
I offer you three **c.** 1Ch 21:10

CHOKED

My throat prefers to be **c;** .... Job 7:15
grew and **c** the good plants. .... Mt 13:7
grew and **c** the good plants. .... Mk 4:7
with it and **c** the good plants. .... Lk 8:7

CHOKES

my clothing and **c** me with the .... Job 30:18

CHOOSE

So let the king **c** a man who is .... Ge 41:33
and you may **c** any place in Egypt .... Ge 47:6
C some men and go and fight the .... Ex 17:9
c some capable men from among .... Ex 18:21
me in every place that I **c,** .... Ex 20:24
If you **c** some of their daughters .... Ex 34:16
Let's **c** a leader and go back to .... Nu 14:4
He will **c** the man who is holy. .... Nu 16:7
I will **c** one man whose walking .... Nu 17:5
C the best and holiest part from .... Nu 18:29
he **c** a leader for these people, ... Nu 27:16
you must **c** cities to be cities .... Nu 35:11
So **c** some men from each tribe— .... Dt 1:13
care for you and **c** you because .... Dt 7:7
I am letting you **c** a blessing or .... Dt 11:26
place the LORD your God will **c—** .... Dt 12:5
your God will **c** a place where he .... Dt 12:11
in the place the LORD will **c.** .... Dt 12:14
the LORD will **c** to be worshiped .... Dt 14:24
days at the place he will **c,** .... Dt 16:15
I command you to **c** these three .... Dt 19:7
or curses. Now, **c** life! Then you .... Dt 30:19
To **c** life is to love the LORD .... Dt 30:20
Now **c** twelve men from among you, ... Jos 3:12
C three men from each tribe, ... Jos 18:4
you must **c** for yourselves today .... Jos 24:15
That way we will **c** ten men from .... Jdg 20:10
C a man and send him to fight me. 1Sa 17:8
prophets of Baal **c** one bull and 1Ki 18:23
C to live and not to die!' 2Ki 18:32
I will **c** a place for my people 1Ch 17:9
the LORD says: '**C** for yourself 1Ch 21:11
threw lots to **c** the time his 1Ch 25:8
before Haman to **c** a day and a .... Est 3:7
c a day to ruin and destroy them. .... Est 9:24
C my teaching instead of silver, ... Pr 8:10
These people **c** their own ways, ... Is 66:3
So I will **c** their punishments, ... Is 66:4
C a commander to lead the army .... Je 51:27
of Israel will **c** men to work .... Eze 39:14
be a good idea to **c** one hundred .... Da 6:1
again and will **c** one leader for .... Hos 1:11
you would **c** not to cause harm. .... Jnh 4:2
and I will again **c** Jerusalem.'" .... Zch 1:17
But I cannot **c** who will sit at .... Mt 20:23
the master will **c** that servant .... Mt 24:47
people **c** to do what God wants, ... Jn 7:17
You did not **c** me; I chose you. .... Jn 15:16
used lots to **c** between them, ... Ac 1:26
c seven of your own men who are .... Ac 6:3
all agreed to **c** some messengers .... Ac 15:25
So God will **c** the one to whom he .... Rm 9:16
and bad and will **c** the good; .... Php 1:10
It is hard to **c** between the two. .... Php 1:23
God did not **c** us to suffer his 1Th 5:9
God did not **c** angels to be the .... Heb 2:5
Christ did not **c** himself to have .... Heb 5:5
long ago to **c** you by making you 1Pe 1:2

CHOOSES

to himself the person he **c.** .... Nu 16:5
LORD your God **c** to be worshiped .... Dt 12:18
the king the LORD your God **c.** .... Dt 17:15
those kingdoms to anyone he **c.** .... Da 4:25
he sets anyone he **c** over those .... Da 5:21
those whom the Son **c** to tell. .... Mt 11:27
his wife for any reason he **c?"** .... Mt 19:3
those whom the Son **c** to tell." .... Lk 10:22
but no one **c** himself for this .... Heb 5:4
The law **c** high priests who are .... Heb 7:28

CHOOSING

I am c the Levites from all the .... Nu 3:12
c a leader to take them back to .... Ne 9:17
guests were c the best places .... Lk 14:7

CHOP

c your wood and carry your water............. Dt 29:11
great power will c them down .... Is 10:33
They will c down Egypt's army as .... Je 46:23
from the field or c firewood .... Eze 39:10
you c them up like meat for the .... Mic 3:3

CHOPPED

of Beth Shemesh c up the wood 1Sa 6:14
is left when the tree is c down. .... Is 6:13
small trees have been c down, ... Is 9:10

CHORUS

One c went to the right on top .... Ne 12:31
The second c went to the left, ... Ne 12:38

CHORUSES

two large c to give thanks. .... Ne 12:31
The two c took their places at................. Ne 12:40
The c sang, led by Jezrahiah. .... Ne 12:42

CHOSE

they married any of them they c. .... Ge 6:2
Lot c to move east and live in .... Ge 13:11
Judah c a girl named Tamar to be .... Ge 38:6
prison warden c Joseph to take .... Ge 39:22
Joseph c five of his brothers to .... Ge 47:2
He c capable men from all the .... Ex 18:25
I myself c your fellow Levites.................. Nu 18:6
so I c twelve of your men, ... Dt 1:23
Moses c three cities east of the .... Dt 4:41
But the LORD c you because he .... Dt 7:8
ancestors, and he c you, their................ Dt 10:15
you c to make the promise .... Dt 23:23
They c the best land for .... Dt 33:21
So Joshua c one man from each............. Jos 4:4
the LORD c the tribe of Judah. .... Jos 7:16
Then he c thirty thousand of his............. Jos 8:3
Joshua c about five thousand .... Jos 8:12
the LORD—wherever he c it to be. .... Jos 9:27
Then Micah c one of his sons to .... Jdg 17:5
they c five soldiers from the .... Jdg 18:2
I c them from all the tribes of................. 1Sa 2:28
out because of the king you c. 1Sa 8:18
the LORD who c Moses and Aaron 1Sa 12:6
Now here is the king you c, ... 1Sa 12:13
Saul c three thousand men from 1Sa 13:2
in his hand and c five smooth................. 1Sa 17:40
The LORD c me, not your father 2Sa 6:21
when I c judges for my people 2Sa 7:11
earth that God c to be his own. 2Sa 7:23
he c some of the best soldiers................. 2Sa 10:9
king, because the LORD c him. 1Ki 2:15
You c them from all the nations 1Ki 8:53
David, whom I c, who obeyed all 1Ki 11:34
city where I c to be worshiped. 1Ki 11:36
So Jeroboam c his own time for a 1Ki 12:33
Then the king c an officer to 2Ki 8:6
rule and c their own king. 2Ki 8:20
always c to do what the LORD 2Ki 17:17
David c some people to be in 1Ch 6:31
Samuel the seer c these men 1Ch 9:22
The LORD c them to carry the Ark 1Ch 15:2
when I c judges for my people 1Ch 17:10
group David c stonecutters to................. 1Ch 22:2
King David c Asaph to preach, ... 1Ch 25:2
He c the tribe of Judah to lead, ... 1Ch 28:4
gathered, "God c my son Solomon, ... 1Ch 29:1
He c seventy thousand men to 2Ch 2:2
he c you to be their king." 2Ch 2:11
Solomon c seventy thousand of 2Ch 2:18

Jehoiada c two wives for Joash, ... 2Ch 24:3
They c Levites twenty years old .... Ezr 3:8
Ezra the priest c men who were .... Ezr 10:16
the God who c Abram and brought .... Ne 9:7
No one c God to rule over the................... Job 34:13
people he c for his very own. .... Ps 33:12
He c the land we would inherit. .... Ps 47:4
c the tribe of Judah and Mount .... Ps 78:68
He c David to be his servant and .... Ps 78:70
People of Jacob, I c you. .... Is 41:8
He is the one I c, and I am .... Is 42:1
People of Israel, I c you." .... Is 44:1
I c a time to punish people,..................... Is 63:4
in your mother's womb, I c you............... Je 1:5
he c Israel to be his special.................... Je 10:16
he c Israel to be his special.................... Je 51:19
He c three men as supervisors .... Da 6:2
They c their own kings without .... Hos 8:4
one prisoner whom the people c. .... Mt 27:15
Jesus c twelve and called them .... Mk 3:14
one prisoner whom the people c. .... Mk 15:6
to him and c twelve of them, ... Lk 6:13
Lord c seventy-two others and .... Lk 10:1
answered, "I c all twelve of you .... Jn 6:70
I am the one God c and sent into .... Jn 10:36
choose me; I c you. And I gave .... Jn 15:16
the One he c to be the Christ. .... Ac 3:20
so they c these seven men: .... Ac 6:5
one whom God c to be the judge .... Ac 10:42
They c elders for each church, ... Ac 14:23
c Judas Barsabbas and Silas, ... Ac 15:22
but Paul c Silas and left. .... Ac 15:40
our ancestors c you long ago to .... Ac 22:14
be an apostle and c me to tell .... Rm 1:1
and he c them to be like his Son .... Rm 8:29
God c the Israelites to be his .... Rm 11:2
And if he c them by grace, ... Rm 11:6
the ones God c did become right .... Rm 11:7
But God c the foolish things of 1Co 1:27
He c what the world thinks is 1Co 1:28
not come from the One who c you............ Gal 5:8
c us before the world was made.............. Eph 1:4
God c you from the beginning to 2Th 2:13
a high priest, but God c him. .... Heb 5:5
He c to suffer with God's people .... Heb 11:25
God c the poor in the world to .... Jam 2:5
but he was the stone God c, ... 1Pe 2:4

CHOSEN

I have c him so he would command .... Ge 18:19
know the LORD has c her for my .... Ge 24:44
own possession, c from all .... Ex 19:5
I have c Bezalel son of Uri from .... Ex 31:2
the goat that was c for the LORD .... Le 16:9
which was c by lot to remove the .... Le 16:10
He has c you from all the people .... Dt 7:6
This is the land c for Benjamin: .... Jos 18:11
you have c to serve the LORD. .... Jos 24:22
See the man the LORD has c. 1Sa 10:24
because I have c one of his sons............. 1Sa 16:1
all the c men of Israel— 2Sa 6:1
belong to the one c by the LORD 2Sa 16:18
of Saul, the LORD's c king." 2Sa 21:6
until the c time to stop. 2Sa 24:15
But I have c David to lead my................. 1Ki 8:16
Jerusalem, the city I have c." 1Ki 11:13
Ahab who had c so often to do 1Ki 21:25
The towns were c by throwing 1Ch 6:61
Don't touch my c people, and................. 1Ch 16:22
I have c Solomon to be my son, ... 1Ch 28:6
The LORD has c you to build the 1Ch 28:10
now I have c Jerusalem as the 2Ch 6:6
and I have c David to lead my 2Ch 6:6

C

which you have **c** and the Temple 2Ch 6:34
I have **c** this Temple and made it 2Ch 7:16
God has **c** Jerusalem as the place .... Ezr 6:12
where I have **c** to be worshiped. .... Ne 1:9
days of Purim at the **c** times. .... Est 9:31
the LORD has **c** for himself those .... Ps 4:3
he gives victory to his **c** one. .... Ps 28:8
so God has **c** you from among your .... Ps 45:7
have come against your **c** people. .... Ps 79:1
the one you have **c** for yourself. .... Ps 80:17
children of Jacob, his **c** people. .... Ps 105:6
Don't touch my **c** people, and .... Ps 105:15
I have **c** the way of truth; .... Ps 119:30
The LORD has **c** Jerusalem; .... Ps 132:13
has **c** the people of Israel for .... Ps 135:4
The LORD has **c** a time for .... Is 34:8
My **c** people will live there and .... Is 65:22
where I have **c** to be worshiped? .... Je 7:10
You who are **c** to punish this .... Eze 9:1
your people, to save your **c** one. .... Hab 3:13
will be his **c** city again. .... Zch 2:12
LORD who has **c** Jerusalem says .... Zch 3:2
is my servant whom I have **c**. .... Mt 12:18
You have been **c** to know the .... Mt 13:11
invited, but only a few are **c**." .... Mt 22:14
to help the people he has **c**. .... Mt 24:22
fool even the people God has **c**, ... Mt 24:24
will gather his **c** people from .... Mt 24:31
says: "The **c** time is near. I .... Mt 26:18
to help the people he has **c**. .... Mk 13:20
fool even the people God has **c**, ... Mk 13:22
gather his **c** people from every .... Mk 13:27
he was **c** by lot to go into the .... Lk 1:9
God has **c** this child to cause .... Lk 2:34
You have been **c** to know the .... Lk 8:10
This is my Son, whom I have **c**. .... Lk 9:35
Mary has **c** the better thing, ... Lk 10:42
himself if he is God's **C** One, ... Lk 23:35
I know those I have **c**. .... Jn 13:18
But I have **c** you out of the .... Jn 15:19
apostles he had **c** what they .... Ac 1:2
I have **c** Saul for an important .... Ac 9:15
people who were **c** to have life .... Ac 13:48
have **c** you to be my servant and .... Ac 26:16
can accuse the people God has **c**? .... Rm 8:33
of Israel, God's **c** children. .... Rm 9:4
that God has **c** by his grace. .... Rm 11:5
Jews are still God's **c** people, ... Rm 11:28
God made us his **c** people. 2Co 1:21
brother was **c** by the churches 2Co 8:19
I was not **c** to be an apostle by .... Gal 1:1
those who are **c** to care for them .... Gal 4:2
In Christ we were **c** to be God's .... Eph 1:11
God has **c** you and made you his .... Col 3:12
you, and we know he has **c** you, ... 1Th 1:4
is why I was **c** to tell the Good 1Ti 2:7
Christ Jesus and the **c** angels, ... 1Ti 5:21
I was **c** to tell that Good News 2Ti 1:11
those whom God has **c** can have 2Ti 2:10
faith of God's **c** people and to .... Tit 1:1
God has **c** his Son to own all .... Heb 1:2
so God has **c** you from among your .... Heb 1:9
To God's **c** people who are away 1Pe 1:1
Christ was **c** before the world 1Pe 1:20
But you are a **c** people, royal 1Pe 2:9
You were **c** to tell about the 1Pe 2:9
who was **c** like you, sends 1Pe 5:13
really are called and **c** by God. 2Pe 1:10
To the **c** lady and her children: 2Jn 1:1
with his called, **c**, and faithful .... Rev 17:14

CHRIST

the family history of Jesus **C**. .... Mt 1:1
Jesus is called the **C**. .... Mt 1:16
to Babylon until **C** was born. .... Mt 1:17
the birth of Jesus **C** came about. .... Mt 1:18
them where the **C** would be born. .... Mt 2:4
about what the **C** was doing. .... Mt 11:2
You are the **C**, the Son of the .... Mt 16:16
not to tell anyone he was the **C**. .... Mt 16:20
"The **C** is the Son of David." .... Mt 22:42
you have only one Master, the **C**. .... Mt 23:10
I am the **C**,' and they will .... Mt 24:5
you, 'The **C** is in the desert, ... Mt 24:26
you are the **C**, the Son of God. .... Mt 26:63
Jesus, the one called the **C**?" .... Mt 27:22
of the Good News about Jesus **C**, ... Mk 1:1
Peter answered, "You are the **C**." .... Mk 8:29
belong to the **C** will truly get .... Mk 9:41
so how can the **C** be his son?" .... Mk 12:37
to you, 'Look, there is the **C**!' .... Mk 13:21
Are you the **C**, the Son of the .... Mk 14:61
he is really the **C**, the king of .... Mk 15:32
of David. He is **C**, the Lord. .... Lk 2:11
before he saw the **C** promised by .... Lk 2:26
they knew Jesus was the **C**. .... Lk 4:41
You are the **C** from God." .... Lk 9:20
say that the **C** is the Son of .... Lk 20:41
David calls the **C** 'Lord,' so how .... Lk 20:44
If you are the **C**, tell us." .... Lk 22:67
he is God's Chosen One, the **C**." .... Lk 23:35
Aren't you the **C**? Then save .... Lk 23:39
said that the **C** must suffer .... Lk 24:26
and truth came through Jesus **C**. .... Jn 1:17
He said, "I am not the **C**." .... Jn 1:20
"Messiah" means "**C**." .... Jn 1:41
I am not the **C**, but I am the one .... Jn 3:28
Messiah is the One called **C**. .... Jn 4:25
Yet when the real **C** comes, ... Jn 7:27
C will not come from Galilee. .... Jn 7:41
you are the **C**, tell us plainly. .... Jn 10:24
I believe that you are the **C**, ... Jn 11:27
the law that the **C** will live .... Jn 12:34
and that they know Jesus **C**, ... Jn 17:3
may believe that Jesus is the **C**, ... Jn 20:31
talked about the **C** rising from .... Ac 2:31
to the cross—both Lord and **C**." .... Ac 2:36
the name of Jesus **C** for the .... Ac 2:38
power of Jesus **C** from Nazareth, ... Ac 3:6
prophets that his **C** would suffer .... Ac 3:18
the One he chose to be the **C**. .... Ac 3:20
Good News—that Jesus is the **C**. .... Ac 5:42
and preached about the **C**. .... Ac 8:5
that Jesus **C** is the Son of God. .... Ac 8:37
him, "Aeneas, Jesus **C** heals you. .... Ac 9:34
peace has come through Jesus **C**. .... Ac 10:36
baptized in the name of Jesus **C**. .... Ac 10:48
believed in the name Jesus **C**, ... Ac 11:17
power of Jesus **C**, I command you .... Ac 16:18
proved that the **C** must die and .... Ac 17:3
them that Jesus is the **C**. .... Ac 18:5
Scriptures that Jesus is the **C**. .... Ac 18:28
talk about believing in **C** Jesus. .... Ac 24:24
that the **C** would die, and as the .... Ac 26:23
taught about the Lord Jesus **C**, ... Ac 28:31
From Paul, a servant of **C** Jesus. .... Rm 1:1
Through **C**, God gave me the .... Rm 1:5
our Father and the Lord Jesus **C**. .... Rm 1:7
God, through **C** Jesus, will judge .... Rm 2:16
through their faith in Jesus **C**. .... Rm 3:22
true for all who believe in **C**, ... Rm 3:22
free from sin through Jesus **C**. .... Rm 3:24
the right time, **C** died for us, ... Rm 5:6
C died for us while we were .... Rm 5:8

So through **C** we will surely be .... Rm 5:9
grace of the one man, Jesus **C**. .... Rm 5:15
were buried with **C** and shared .... Rm 6:4
just as **C** was raised from the .... Rm 6:4
C died, and we have been joined .... Rm 6:5
life died with **C** on the cross so .... Rm 6:6
forever in **C** Jesus our Lord. .... Rm 6:23
the law through the body of **C**. .... Rm 7:4
those who are in **C** Jesus are not .... Rm 8:1
of Christ does not belong to **C**. .... Rm 8:9
But if **C** is in you, then the .... Rm 8:10
C made you right with God. .... Rm 8:10
us from the love **C** has for us? .... Rm 8:35
God that is in **C** Jesus our Lord. .... Rm 8:39
C ended the law so that everyone .... Rm 10:4
but in **C** we are all one body. .... Rm 12:5
The reason **C** died and rose from .... Rm 14:9
wrong, because **C** died for him. .... Rm 14:15
Even **C** did not live to please .... Rm 15:3
the Father of our Lord Jesus **C**. .... Rm 15:6
C accepted you, so you should .... Rm 15:7
people have never heard of **C**, ... Rm 15:20
person in Asia to follow **C**. .... Rm 16:5
believers in **C** before I was..................... Rm 16:7
proved that he truly loves **C**. .... Rm 16:10
message about **C** is the secret.................. Rm 16:25
God has given you in **C** Jesus. 1Co 1:4
But we preach a crucified **C**. 1Co 1:23
C is the power of God and the 1Co 1:24
In **C** we are put right with God, ... 1Co 1:30
But we have the mind of **C**..................... 1Co 2:16
without the Spirit—babies in **C**. 1Co 3:1
to Christ, and **C** belongs to God. 1Co 3:23
think of us as servants of **C**, ... 1Co 4:1
For **C**, our Passover lamb, has 1Co 5:7
bodies are parts of **C** himself.................. 1Co 6:15
there is only one Lord—Jesus **C**. 1Co 8:6
believing the Good News of **C**. 1Co 9:12
them, and that rock was **C**...................... 1Co 10:4
is a sharing in the blood of **C**. 1Co 10:16
as I follow the example of **C**. 1Co 11:1
Together you are the body of **C**, ... 1Co 12:27
that **C** died for our sins, as the 1Co 15:3
we preached that **C** was raised 1Co 15:12
C was first to be raised. 1Co 15:23
When **C** comes again, those who 1Co 15:23
Paul, an apostle of **C** Jesus. 2Co 1:1
In **C** it has always been yes. 2Co 1:19
all of God's promises is in **C**, ... 2Co 1:20
to preach the Good News of **C**, ... 2Co 2:12
sweet smell of **C** among those who 2Co 2:15
all stand before **C** to be judged. 2Co 5:10
The love of **C** controls us, ... 2Co 5:14
C died for all so that those who 2Co 5:15
belongs to **C**, there is a new 2Co 5:17
C had no sin, but God made him 2Co 5:21
How can **C** and Belial, the devil,.............. 2Co 6:15
the grace of our Lord Jesus **C**. 2Co 8:9
we belong to **C** just as you do. 2Co 10:7
want proof that **C** is speaking.................. 2Co 13:3
be alive in **C** by God's power. 2Co 13:4
but by trusting in Jesus **C**. .... Gal 2:16
have put our faith in **C** Jesus, ... Gal 2:16
We Jews came to **C**, trying to be.............. Gal 2:17
anymore—it is **C** who lives in me. .... Gal 2:20
C took away the curse the law .... Gal 3:13
In **C**, there is no difference .... Gal 3:28
You are all the same in **C** Jesus. .... Gal 3:28
Those who belong to **C** Jesus have .... Gal 5:24
In **C**, God has given us every .... Eph 1:3
is, in **C**, he chose us before .... Eph 1:4
C we are set free by the blood .... Eph 1:7
In **C** we were chosen to be God's .... Eph 1:11

God has put **C** over all rulers,.................. Eph 1:21
C himself is our peace. .... Eph 2:14
C Jesus himself is the most...................... Eph 2:20
the secret about the **C**. .... Eph 3:4
Good News about the riches of **C**, ... Eph 3:8
In **C** we can come before God with .... Eph 3:12
I pray that **C** will live in your .... Eph 3:17
And **C** gave gifts to people— .... Eph 4:11
we become like **C** and have his .... Eph 4:13
just as God forgave you in **C**. .... Eph 4:32
death, and **C** will shine on you. .... Eph 5:14
as **C** is the head of the church. .... Eph 5:23
your wives as **C** loved the church .... Eph 5:25
when Jesus **C** comes again. .... Php 1:6
because I am a believer in **C**. .... Php 1:13
Spirit of Jesus **C** is helping me, ... Php 1:19
honor to the Good News of **C**. .... Php 1:27
that Jesus **C** is Lord and bring .... Php 2:11
and our pride is in **C** Jesus. .... Php 3:3
of knowing **C** Jesus my Lord. .... Php 3:8
I can do all things through **C**,.................. Php 4:13
but Jesus **C** is exactly like him. .... Col 1:15
This secret is **C** himself, who is .... Col 1:27
All of God lives fully in **C**. .... Col 2:9
God made you alive with **C**, ... Col 2:13
But **C** is in all believers, ... Col 3:11
your hope in our Lord Jesus **C**. 1Th 1:3
believing in **C** will rise first. 1Th 4:16
our Lord Jesus **C** will have glory 2Th 1:12
our Savior and **C** Jesus our hope. 1Ti 1:1
C Jesus came into the world to 1Ti 1:15
in the grace we have in **C** Jesus.............. 2Ti 2:1
Refresh my heart in **C**. .... Phm 1:20
So also **C** did not choose himself .... Heb 5:5
C offered his sacrifice only.................... Heb 7:27
C entered the Most Holy Place .... Heb 9:12
But **C** came only once and for all .... Heb 9:26
And now **C** waits there for his .... Heb 10:13
Jesus **C** is the same yesterday, ... Heb 13:8
Peter, an apostle of Jesus **C**. 1Pe 1:1
Jesus **C** rose from the dead. 1Pe 1:3
with the precious blood of **C**, ... 1Pe 1:19
C was chosen before the world 1Pe 1:20
Through **C** you believe in God, ... 1Pe 1:21
on the day when **C** comes again. 1Pe 2:12
because **C** suffered for you and 1Pe 2:21
C carried our sins in his body.................. 1Pe 2:24
Then when **C**, the Chief Shepherd,.......... 1Pe 5:4
you to share in his glory in **C**, ... 1Pe 5:10
sins are forgiven through **C**. 1Jn 2:12
that the enemy of **C** is coming, ... 1Jn 2:18
does not accept Jesus as the **C**. 1Jn 2:22
keep themselves pure like **C**. 1Jn 3:3
know that **C** came to take away 1Jn 3:5
Jesus **C** is the One who came by.............. 1Jn 5:6
false teacher and an enemy of **C**. 2Jn 1:7
is the revelation of Jesus **C**, ... Rev 1:1
it is the message from Jesus **C**. .... Rev 1:2
To Jesus **C** be glory and power .... Rev 1:6
and ruled with **C** for a thousand.............. Rev 20:4

CHRIST'S

found any followers of **C** Way, ... Ac 9:2
God by the blood of **C** death. .... Rm 5:9
I will bring **C** full blessing. .... Rm 15:29
All of **C** churches send greetings .... Rm 16:16
We are fools for **C** sake, but you.............. 1Co 4:10
were called are now **C** slaves. 1Co 7:22
God's law—I am ruled by **C** law.............. 1Co 9:21
Then **C** power can live in me. 2Co 12:9
then **C** death would be useless. .... Gal 2:21
which is **C** body. The church is .... Eph 1:23
through the blood of **C** death................... Eph 2:13

It was also **C** purpose to end the .... Eph 2:16
C love is greater than anyone .... Eph 3:19
the blood of **C** death on the .... Col 1:20
C great strength that works .... Col 1:29
It was through **C** circumcision, ... Col 2:11
into God's love and **C** patience. 2Th 3:5
through the curtain—**C** body. .... Heb 10:20
are sharing in **C** sufferings so................ 1Pe 4:13
who goes beyond **C** teaching and 2Jn 1:9

CHRISTIAN

me to become a **C** in such a short .... Ac 26:28
that will make another **C** sin. .... Rm 14:13
something against another **C,**................. 1Co 6:1
If a **C** man has a wife who is not 1Co 7:12
And if a **C** woman has a husband 1Co 7:13
or cheat another **C** in this way. 1Th 4:6
having love for your **C** family, ... 1Th 4:9
true love for your **C** brothers 1Pe 1:22
you suffer because you are a **C,** 1Pe 4:16
know that your **C** family all over 1Pe 5:9
other a kiss of **C** love when you 1Pe 5:14
your special **C** meals you share .... Jud 1:12

CHRISTIANS

called **C** for the first time. .... Ac 11:26
been in danger with false **C.** 2Co 11:26
about those **C** who have died so 1Th 4:13

CHRISTS

False **C** and false prophets will .... Mt 24:24
False **C** and false prophets will .... Mk 13:22

CHRYSOLITE

fourth must have a **c,** an onyx, ... Ex 28:20
in the fourth there was a **c,**................... Ex 39:13
They looked like sparkling **c.** .... Eze 1:16
wheels looked like shining **c.** .... Eze 10:9
sapphire, turquoise, and **c.** .... Eze 28:13
seventh was **c,** the eighth was................. Rev 21:20

CHRYSOPRASE

tenth was **c,** the eleventh was .... Rev 21:20

CHURCH

On this rock I will build my **c,** .... Mt 16:18
he refuses to listen to the **c,** .... Mt 18:17
The whole **c** and all the others .... Ac 5:11
On that day the **c** of Jerusalem .... Ac 8:1
also trying to destroy the **c,** .... Ac 8:3
The **c** everywhere in Judea, ... Ac 9:31
The **c** in Jerusalem heard about .... Ac 11:22
met with the **c** and taught many .... Ac 11:26
the **c** prayed earnestly to God................. Ac 12:5
In the **c** at Antioch there were .... Ac 13:1
They chose elders for each **c,** .... Ac 14:23
So the **c** decided to send Paul, ... Ac 15:2
called for the elders of the **c.** .... Ac 20:17
like shepherds to the **c** of God, ... Ac 20:28
greet for me the **c** that meets at .... Rm 16:5
To the **c** of God in Corinth, ... 1Co 1:2
together as a **c** you are divided, ... 1Co 11:18
In the **c** God has given a place 1Co 12:28
that the whole **c** can be helped. 1Co 14:5
that help the **c** grow stronger. 1Co 14:12
keep quiet in the **c** meetings. 1Co 14:34
woman to speak in the **c** meeting. 1Co 14:35
I persecuted the **c** of God. 1Co 15:9
attacked the **c** of God and tried .... Gal 1:13
head over everything for the **c,** .... Eph 1:22
The **c** is filled with Christ, ... Eph 1:23
as Christ is the head of the **c.** .... Eph 5:23
loved the **c** and gave himself .... Eph 5:25
died so that the **c** could be pure .... Eph 5:27
is what Christ does for the **c,** .... Eph 5:29
I tried to hurt the **c.**............................. Php 3:6
were the only **c** that gave me .... Php 4:15

of the body, which is the **c.** .... Col 1:18
suffer through his body, the **c.** .... Col 1:24
also read to the **c** in Laodicea. .... Col 4:16
To the **c** in Thessalonica, the 1Th 1:1
person take care of God's **c?** 1Ti 3:5
are not in the **c** so he will not 1Ti 3:7
family is the **c** of the living 1Ti 3:15
c should not have to care for 1Ti 5:16
who lead the **c** well should 1Ti 5:17
stay away from the **c** meetings, ... Heb 10:25
The **c** in Babylon, who was chosen............ 1Pe 5:13
They told the **c** about your love. 3Jn 1:9
them and puts them out of the **c.** 3Jn 1:10
the angel of the **c** in Ephesus:................. Rev 2:1
to the angel of the **c** in Smyrna: .... Rev 2:8
angel of the **c** in Philadelphia .... Rev 3:7
the angel of the **c** in Laodicea: .... Rev 3:14

CHURCH'S

sick should call the **c** elders. .... Jam 5:14

CHURCHES

giving strength to the **c.** .... Ac 15:41
So the **c** became stronger in the .... Ac 16:5
the non-Jewish **c** are thankful as .... Rm 16:4
All of Christ's **c** send greetings .... Rm 16:16
is a rule I make in all the **c.** 1Co 7:17
I told the Galatian **c** to do: 1Co 16:1
The **c** in Asia send greetings to 1Co 16:19
God gave the **c** in Macedonia................... 2Co 8:1
was chosen by the **c** to go with 2Co 8:19
sent from the **c,** and they bring 2Co 8:23
I accepted pay from other **c,** 2Co 11:8
To the **c** in Galatia: .... Gal 1:2
In Judea the **c** in Christ had .... Gal 1:22
about you to the other **c** of God............... 2Th 1:4
To the seven **c** in Asia: .... Rev 1:4
book and send it to the seven **c:** .... Rev 1:11
lampstands are the seven **c,** .... Rev 1:20
are the angels of the seven **c.** .... Rev 1:20
what the Spirit says to the **c.** .... Rev 2:7
Then all the **c** will know I am .... Rev 2:23
what the Spirit says to the **c.** .... Rev 3:6
tell you these things for the **c.** .... Rev 22:16

CILICIA

in Tarsus in the country of **C,** .... Ac 22:3
he learned that Paul was from **C,** .... Ac 23:34

CINDERS

nothing but burning **c** and salt. .... Dt 29:23

CINNAMON

of sweet-smelling **c,** six pounds .... Ex 30:23
sweet with myrrh, aloes, and **c.** .... Pr 7:17
calamus, and **c,** with trees .... Sng 4:14
c, spice, incense, myrrh, ... Rev 18:13

CIRCLE

horizon like a **c** on the water at .... Job 26:10
throne above the **c** of the earth, ... Is 40:22

CIRCLES

I have dark **c** around my eyes. .... Job 16:16

CIRCUMCISE

eight days old, you will **c** him. .... Ge 17:12
because she had to **c** her son. .... Ex 4:26
stones and **c** the Israelites." .... Jos 5:2
days old, they came to **c** him. .... Lk 1:59
And yet you **c** a baby boy on a .... Jn 7:22
them not to **c** their children .... Ac 21:21

CIRCUMCISED

Every male among you must be **c.** .... Ge 17:10
that day Abraham **c** every man and .... Ge 17:23
men in Abraham's camp were **c,** .... Ge 17:27
c Isaac when he was eight days .... Ge 21:4
you refuse to be **c,** we will take .... Ge 34:17

CIRCUMCISES

Shechem, and every man was **c**............... Ge 34:24
a flint knife and **c** her son. .... Ex 4:25
the males in his house become **c**. .... Ex 12:48
a man who is not **c** may not eat .... Ex 12:48
eighth day the boy must be **c**. .... Le 12:3
This is why Joshua **c** the men: .... Jos 5:4
all the Israelites had been **c**, ... Jos 5:8
all those countries are not **c**. .... Je 9:26
who were not **c** in the flesh..................... Eze 44:7
he was **c** and was named Jesus, ... Lk 2:21
baby boy can be **c** on a Sabbath............... Jn 7:23
Abraham **c** him when he was eight .... Ac 7:8
Isaac also **c** his son Jacob, ... Ac 7:8
who are not **c** and ate with them! .... Ac 11:3
non-Jewish believers must be **c**. .... Ac 15:5
So Paul **c** Timothy to please his .... Ac 16:3
it is as if you were never **c**. .... Rm 2:25
who are not Jews are not **c**, ... Rm 2:26
Abraham was **c** to show that he .... Rm 4:11
important if a man is **c** or not. 1Co 7:19
not teach that a man must be **c**. .... Gal 5:11
if a man is **c** or uncircumcised. .... Gal 6:15
call themselves "**c**."........................... Eph 2:11
We are the ones who are truly **c**. .... Php 3:3
I was **c** eight days after my..................... Php 3:5
those who are **c** and those who .... Col 3:11

CIRCUMCISES

someone buys a slave and **c** him, ... Ex 12:44

CIRCUMCISION

Moses gave you the law about **c**. .... Jn 7:22
Jews have the written law and **c**, ... Rm 2:27
true **c** is done in the heart by .... Rm 2:29
It was before his **c**. .... Rm 4:10
I still taught **c**, my preaching .... Gal 5:11
Their **c** is only something they .... Eph 2:11
you had a different kind of **c**, ... Col 2:11
It was through Christ's **c**, ... Col 2:11
who insist on **c** to be saved. .... Tit 1:10

CITIZEN

he will be like a **c** of Israel,.................... Ex 12:48
either a **c** or a foreigner, ... Le 17:15
your fellow **c** in your heart. .... Le 19:17
if he is a **c** or a foreigner........................ Le 20:2
This man is a Roman **c**."........................ Ac 22:26
But Paul said, "I was born a **c**." .... Ac 22:28
to Herodion, my fellow **c**. .... Rm 16:11

CITIZENS

are for the **c** of Israel and for .... Le 18:26
All **c** must do these things in .... Nu 15:13
of safety for **c** of Israel, ... Nu 35:15
with one of the **c** there who sent .... Lk 15:15
even though we are Roman **c**................... Ac 16:37
Paul and Silas were Roman **c**, ... Ac 16:38
were not **c** of Israel, and you .... Eph 2:12
but are **c** together with God's .... Eph 2:19

CITRON

kinds of **c** wood and all kinds.................. Rev 18:12

CITY

that time Cain was building a **c**,.............. Ge 4:17
the great **c** between Nineveh and .... Ge 10:12
Let's build a **c** and a tower for .... Ge 11:4
they reached the **c** of Haran, ... Ge 11:31
of Mamre at the **c** of Hebron. .... Ge 13:18
will save the **c** for the fifty .... Ge 18:24
good people in the **c** of Sodom, ... Ge 18:26
twenty good people in the **c**?" .... Ge 18:31
I will not destroy the **c**." .... Ge 18:31
Lot was sitting near the **c** gate. .... Ge 19:1
any other relatives in this **c**? .... Ge 19:12
we are about to destroy this **c**. .... Ge 19:13
he destroyed the **c** where Lot had .... Ge 19:29

down at the well outside the **c**. .... Ge 24:11
girls from the **c** are coming out .... Ge 24:13
came out of the **c** with her water .... Ge 24:45
safely at the **c** of Shechem .... Ge 33:18
made a surprise attack on the **c**,.............. Ge 34:25
Go to the **c** of Bethel and live .... Ge 35:1
In every **c** he stored grain that .... Ge 41:48
in Egypt, near the **c** of Rameses. .... Ge 47:11
I leave the **c**, I will raise my .... Ex 9:29
unclean place outside the **c**. .... Le 14:40
sells a home in a walled **c**, ... Le 25:29
flames came from Sihon's **c**. .... Nu 21:28
destroy those left in the **c**."..................... Nu 24:19
finds the killer outside the **c**, ... Nu 35:27
Destroy the **c** completely and .... Dt 13:15
in the middle of the **c** square. .... Dt 13:16
burn the **c** and everything they .... Dt 13:16
That **c** should never be rebuilt; .... Dt 13:16
When you march up to attack a **c**, ... Dt 20:10
devices to attack the **c** walls, ... Dt 20:20
a virgin in a **c** and has sexual.................. Dt 22:23
is called the **c** of palm trees. .... Dt 34:3
at the **c** of Jericho." .... Jos 2:1
it was time to close the **c** gate, ... Jos 2:5
in was built on the **c** wall, ... Jos 2:15
march around the **c** seven times............... Jos 6:4
the walls of the **c** will fall so .... Jos 6:5
The LORD has given you this **c**! .... Jos 6:16
set up an ambush behind the **c**." .... Jos 8:2
After you take the **c**, burn it. .... Jos 8:8
burned the **c** of Ai and made it .... Jos 8:28
captured that **c**, its king, and .... Jos 10:39
gave him the **c** of Hebron as his .... Jos 14:13
Nibshan, the **C** of Salt, and En .... Jos 15:62
the Jebusite **c** (Jerusalem), ... Jos 18:28
to the strong, walled **c** of Tyre. .... Jos 19:29
may go to a **c** of safety to hide .... Jos 20:3
(Hebron was a **c** of safety). .... Jos 21:13
in Galilee (a **c** of safety), ... Jos 21:32
Jericho, the **c** of palm trees. .... Jdg 1:16
showed them the way into the **c**. .... Jdg 1:25
men fought the **c** of Shechem all .... Jdg 9:45
But inside the **c** was a strong .... Jdg 9:51
Manasseh and the **c** of Mizpah in .... Jdg 11:29
down to the **c** of Timnah where .... Jdg 14:1
went down to the **c** of Ashkelon .... Jdg 14:19
a Levite from the **c** of Bethlehem .... Jdg 17:7
smoke began to rise from the **c**. .... Jdg 20:40
Boaz went to the **c** gate and sat .... Ru 4:1
people in the **c** were struck with............... 1Sa 5:11
Saul went to the **c** of Amalek and 1Sa 15:5
entrance of the **c** of Gath and to............... 1Sa 17:52
David could not enter their **c**. 2Sa 5:6
and it became the **C** of David. 2Sa 5:7
Hiram king of the **c** of Tyre sent 2Sa 5:11
Ark of the LORD came into the **c**, ... 2Sa 6:16
to study the **c** and spy it out 2Sa 10:3
Joab watched the **c** and saw where 2Sa 11:16
shoot arrows from the **c** wall? 2Sa 11:20
a royal **c** of the Ammonites, ... 2Sa 12:26
standing on the **c** wall saw many 2Sa 13:34
the Ark of God back into the **c**. 2Sa 15:25
Go back to the **c** in peace and 2Sa 15:27
bring ropes to that **c** and pull 2Sa 17:13
So the king went to the **c** gate. 2Sa 19:8
die in my own **c** near the grave 2Sa 19:37
an important **c** of Israel. 2Sa 20:19
followed Solomon into the **c**. 1Ki 1:40
all that noise from the **c** mean?"............... 1Ki 1:41
Now the whole **c** is excited, ... 1Ki 1:45
Jerusalem, the **c** I have chosen."............... 1Ki 11:13
c where I chose to be worshiped. 1Ki 11:36
Jerusalem, the **c** of David, his................. 1Ki 11:43

golden calf in the **c** of Bethel 1Ki 12:29
who dies in the **c** will be eaten 1Ki 14:11
Omri built a **c** on that hill and 1Ki 16:24
Israel in the **c** of Samaria for 1Ki 16:29
Bethel rebuilt the **c** of Jericho. 1Ki 16:34
begin work on the **c**, and it cost 1Ki 16:34
Enter that **c**, and pour olive oil 1Ki 19:15
ran away to the **c** and hid in a 1Ki 20:30
of Jezebel in the **c** of Jezreel.' 1Ki 21:23
this **c** is a nice place to live 2Ki 2:19
came out of the **c** and made fun 2Ki 2:23
was the only **c** with its stones 2Ki 3:25
at night and surrounded the **c**. 2Ki 6:14
and chariots all around the **c**. 2Ki 6:15
There is no food in the **c**. 2Ki 7:4
don't let anyone leave the **c**. 2Ki 9:15
This **c** won't be handed over to 2Ki 18:30
a ramp to attack the **c** walls. 2Ki 19:32
I will protect the **c** for my sake 2Ki 20:6
to bring water into the **c**— 2Ki 20:20
hunger was terrible in the **c**. 2Ki 25:3
and it became the **C** of David. 1Ch 11:5
strong, walled **c**, which is why 1Ch 11:7
why it was named the **C** of David. 1Ch 11:7
Jerusalem is the **c** that the LORD 2Ch 12:13
in Jerusalem, the **c** of David. 2Ch 27:9
in Jericho, the **c** of palm trees. 2Ch 28:15
buried in the **c** of Jerusalem, ... 2Ch 28:27
from the springs outside the **c**. 2Ch 32:3
and settled in the **c** of Samaria .... Ezr 4:10
that evil **c** that refuses to .... Ezr 4:12
sad because the **c** where my .... Ne 2:3
live in Jerusalem, the holy **c**. .... Ne 11:1
172 men who guarded the **c** gates. .... Ne 11:19
from his capital **c** of Susa. .... Est 1:2
horseback through the **c** streets, ... Est 6:11
people in every **c** have the right .... Est 8:11
Dying people groan in the **c**, ... Job 24:12
when my **c** was attacked. .... Ps 31:21
People from the **c** of Tyre have .... Ps 45:12
that brings joy to the **c** of God, ... Ps 46:4
God is in that **c**, and so it will .... Ps 46:5
be praised in the **c** of our God, ... Ps 48:1
it is the **c** of the Great King. .... Ps 48:2
God will always keep his **c** safe. .... Ps 48:8
It is the **c** of the LORD .... Ps 48:8
growl and roam around the **c**. .... Ps 59:6
my rock and my strong, walled **c**. .... Ps 71:3
C of God, wonderful things are .... Ps 87:3
Come into his **c** with songs of .... Ps 100:4
is built as a **c** with the .... Ps 122:3
If the LORD doesn't guard the **c**, ... Ps 127:1
He makes your **c** gates strong and .... Ps 147:13
her voice in the **c** squares. .... Pr 1:20
Beside the **c** gates, at the .... Pr 8:3
rom the highest place in the **c**. .... Pr 9:3
people succeed, the **c** is happy. .... Pr 11:10
bless and build up their **c**, ... Pr 11:11
is better than capturing a **c**. .... Pr 16:32
is like the high walls of a **c**. .... Pr 18:11
can defeat a **c** full of warriors .... Pr 21:22
are like a **c** whose walls are .... Pr 25:28
of wisdom cause trouble in a **c**, ... Pr 29:8
is known at the **c** meetings, ... Pr 31:23
than ten leaders in a **c**. .... Ec 7:19
I got up and went around the **c**, ... Sng 3:2
as lovely as the **c** of Jerusalem, ... Sng 6:4
Is Right with God, the Loyal **C**." .... Is 1:26
and sadness near the **c** gates. .... Is 3:26
and clean the **c** with the spirit .... Is 4:4
Samaria is like the **c** Damascus. .... Is 10:9
near the **c** gates, cry out! .... Is 14:31
The **c** of Damascus will be .... Is 17:1

be named the **C** of Destruction. .... Is 19:18
to Ashdod to attack that **c**. .... Is 20:1
This city was a very busy **c**, ... Is 22:2
Look at your old, old **c**! .... Is 23:7
People from that **c** have traveled. .... Is 23:7
harp and walk through the **c**. .... Is 23:16
The ruined **c** will be empty, ... Is 24:10
have made the **c** a pile of rocks .... Is 25:2
He will destroy the proud **c**, ... Is 26:5
walled **c** will be empty like a .... Is 27:10
That **c**, the pride of Israel's .... Is 28:3
for the **c** that once was happy. .... Is 32:13
This **c** won't be handed over to .... Is 36:15
and save this **c** for my sake and .... Is 37:35
will rebuild my **c** and set my .... Is 45:13
The LORD says, "**C** of Babylon, go .... Is 47:1
You poor **c**. Storms have hurt .... Is 54:11
c of the Holy One of Israel. .... Is 60:14
will be called the **C** God Wants, ... Is 62:12
am going to make you a strong **c**, ... Je 1:18
person from every **c** and two from .... Je 3:14
wealth of this **c** to its enemies— .... Je 20:5
people are like the **c** of Sodom. .... Je 23:14
about this Temple and this **c**. .... Je 26:12
c will be rebuilt on its hill .... Je 30:18
The **c** of Jerusalem will never .... Je 31:40
the god of the **c** of Thebes. .... Je 46:25
of Egypt attacked the **c** of Gaza, ... Je 47:1
message to the **c** of Damascus: .... Je 49:23
Damascus was a **c** of my joy. .... Je 49:25
Then the **c** wall was broken .... Je 52:7
called the most beautiful **c**, ... La 2:15
scatter the coals over the **c**." .... Eze 10:2
This **c** is like a cooking pot, ... Eze 11:3
see visions of peace for the **c**, ... Eze 13:16
You are a **c** that kills those who .... Eze 22:3
the **c** of Tyre has spoken against .... Eze 26:2
funeral song for the **c** of Tyre. .... Eze 27:2
of gods from the **c** of Memphis. .... Eze 30:13
The **c** will measure about six .... Eze 48:35
the name of the **c** will be The .... Eze 48:35
Jerusalem, your **c** on your holy .... Da 9:16
The end of the **c** will come like .... Da 9:26
voice will thunder from that **c**, ... Joe 3:16
trumpet blows a warning in a **c**, ... Am 3:6
Do not enter the **c** gate of my .... Ob 1:13
go to the great **c** of Nineveh, ... Jnh 1:2
He went to the **c** of Joppa, ... Jnh 1:3
concern for the great **c** Nineveh, ... Jnh 4:11
message for the **c** of Nineveh .... Nah 1:1
wicked, stubborn **c** of Jerusalem, ... Zph 3:1
People from one **c** will go and .... Zch 8:21
Jesus to the holy **c** of Jerusalem .... Mt 4:5
A **c** that is built on a hill .... Mt 5:14
that is the **c** of the great King. .... Mt 5:35
entered the **c** of Capernaum, ... Mt 8:5
When you enter a **c** or town, ... Mt 10:11
went out of the **c** to Bethany, ... Mt 21:17
the murderers and burn their **c**. .... Mt 22:7
Go into the **c** to a certain man .... Mt 26:18
dead and went into the holy **c**, ... Mt 27:53
tomb went into the **c** to tell the .... Mt 28:11
Go into the **c** and a man carrying .... Mk 14:13
left and went into the **c**. .... Mk 14:16
to Capernaum, a **c** in Galilee, ... Lk 4:31
came near the **c** of Jericho, ... Lk 18:35
he saw the **c** and cried for it, ... Lk 19:41
go into the **c**, a man carrying .... Lk 22:10
Jesus left the **c** and went to the .... Lk 22:39
a riot in the **c** and for murder. .... Lk 23:19
lived in the **c** of Capernaum. .... Jn 4:46
was crucified was near the **c**. .... Jn 19:20
they entered the **c**, they went to .... Ac 1:13

him out of the c and began to .... Ac 7:58
Philip went to the c of Samaria .... Ac 8:5
in that c were very happy. .... Ac 8:8
was a magus named Simon in that c............ Ac 8:9
synagogues in the c of Damascus. .... Ac 9:2
came near the c, a bright light .... Ac 9:3
Get up now and go into the c................... Ac 9:6
named Saul from the c of Tarsus. .... Ac 9:11
were watching the c gates day .... Ac 9:24
him leave the c by lowering him .... Ac 9:25
an opening in the c wall. .... Ac 9:25
In the c of Joppa there was a .... Ac 9:36
went to the c of Tarsus to look .... Ac 11:25
and went to the c of Caesarea, ... Ac 12:19
everyone in the c came to hear .... Ac 13:44
But the c was divided. Some of .... Ac 14:4
was near the c, brought some................. Ac 14:13
and flowers to the c gates. .... Ac 14:13
dragged them before the c rulers .... Ac 16:19
that the c was full of idols. .... Ac 17:16
was born in the c of Alexandria .... Ac 18:24
The whole c became confused. .... Ac 19:29
that Ephesus is the c that keeps .... Ac 19:35
and sailed for the c of Assos, ... Ac 20:13
that in every c the Holy Spirit................. Ac 20:23
and went to the c of Caesarea. .... Ac 21:8
a citizen of that important c. .... Ac 21:39
a c on the island of Crete, ... Ac 27:12
so he put guards around the c. 2Co 11:32
through a hole in the c wall. 2Co 11:33
of the earthly c of Jerusalem. .... Gal 4:25
This c and its people are slaves .... Gal 4:25
waiting for the c that has real................. Heb 11:10
the c planned and built by God. .... Heb 11:10
to the c of the living God, ... Heb 12:22
we do not have a c that lasts .... Heb 13:14
tomorrow we will go to some c. .... Jam 4:13
who was killed in your c, ... Rev 2:13
and the name of the c of my God, ... Rev 3:12
on the holy c for forty-two .... Rev 11:2
This c is named Sodom and Egypt, ... Rev 11:8
a tenth of the c was destroyed. .... Rev 11:13
is the great c of Babylon! .... Rev 14:8
in the winepress outside the c, ... Rev 14:20
The great c split into three .... Rev 16:19
so he gave that c the cup filled .... Rev 16:19
is the great c of Babylon! .... Rev 18:2
for you, great c, powerful city................. Rev 18:10
How terrible for the great c! .... Rev 18:16
How terrible for the great c! .... Rev 18:19
the great c of Babylon will be................. Rev 18:21
people and the c God loves. .... Rev 20:9
I saw the holy c, the new .... Rev 21:2
The c had a great high wall with .... Rev 21:12
made of gold to measure the c, ... Rev 21:15
The c was built in a square, ... Rev 21:16
The c was 1,500 miles long, ... Rev 21:16
and the c was made of pure gold, ... Rev 21:18
The c does not need the sun or .... Rev 21:23
book of life will enter the c. .... Rev 21:27
go through the gates into the c. .... Rev 22:14
Outside the c are the evil .... Rev 22:15
tree of life and of the holy c, ... Rev 22:19

CITY'S
night in the c public square." .... Ge 19:2
These are the c measurements: .... Eze 48:16
destroy the c strong buildings. .... Am 1:10
and the Lamb is the c lamp. .... Rev 21:23
The c gates will never be shut .... Rev 21:25

CLAIM
have no share, c, or memorial .... Ne 2:20
Many people c to be loyal, ... Pr 20:6

CLAIMED
because Job c he was right .... Job 32:2

CLAIMS
say, "Look, your c are right, ... 2Sa 15:3

CLAP
C your hands, all you people. .... Ps 47:1
Let the rivers c their hands; .... Ps 98:8
the fields will c their hands. .... Is 55:12
by on the road c their hands at .... La 2:15
C your hands, stamp your feet, ... Eze 6:11
prophesy and c your hands. .... Eze 21:14

CLAPPED
they c their hands and said, ... 2Ki 11:12
have c your hands and stamped .... Eze 25:6

CLAPPING
as if the wind is c its hands; .... Job 27:23

CLAPS
He c his hands in protest, ... Job 34:37

CLAUDIUS
This happened when C ruled.................... Ac 11:28
because C commanded that all .... Ac 18:2

CLAWED
like a madman and c on the doors 1Sa 21:13

CLAWS
nails grew like the c of a bird. .... Da 4:33
and had iron teeth and bronze c. .... Da 7:19

CLAY
The c pot the meat is cooked in .... Le 6:28
animal falls into a c bowl, ... Le 11:33
the unclean c bowl gets on any .... Le 11:34
a body fluid touches a c bowl, ... Le 15:12
take some holy water in a c jar, ... Nu 5:17
you molded me like a piece of c. .... Job 10:9
your arguments are as weak as c. .... Job 13:12
I too am made out of c. .... Job 33:6
changes like c being pressed .... Job 38:14
has dried up like a c pot,....................... Ps 22:15
like a shiny coating on a c pot. .... Pr 26:23
be like a c jar that breaks, ... Is 30:14
just as a potter walks on the c. .... Is 41:25
The c does not ask the potter, ' .... Is 45:9
We are like c, and you are the .... Is 64:8
hands like the c in the potter's .... Je 18:6
Bury them in the c in the brick .... Je 43:9
of iron and partly of baked c. .... Da 2:33
you saw iron was mixed with c. .... Da 2:41
Get mud, mix c, make bricks!................. Nah 3:14
it clearly on c tablets so .... Hab 2:2
can use the same c to make one .... Rm 9:21
but we are like c jars that hold 2Co 4:7
also things made of wood and c. 2Ti 2:20

CLEAN
of every kind of c animal, ... Ge 7:2
The c animals, the unclean .... Ge 7:8
shaved, put on c clothes, and .... Ge 41:14
the camp to a special c place................... Le 6:11
who is c may eat other meat. .... Le 7:19
keep what is c separate from .... Le 10:10
unclean animals and c animals; .... Le 11:47
then she will be c from her loss .... Le 12:2
and he will become c again. .... Le 13:6
head seven days later to be c................. Nu 6:9
A c person must take a hyssop .... Nu 19:18
Other things with wings are c, ... Dt 14:20
be healed, and you will be c."................ 2Ki 5:10
skin of a child. And he was c.................. 2Ki 5:14
Levites had made themselves c. .... Ezr 6:20
and I am c in God's sight.' .... Job 11:4
Only those with c hands and pure .... Ps 24:4

CLEANED

my guilt and make me c again. .... Ps 51:2
away my sin, and I will be c. .... Ps 51:7
against you and c away all your .... Is 1:25
of Jerusalem and c the city with.............. Is 4:4
there is not a c place anywhere. .... Is 28:8
c the evil from your hearts so .... Je 4:14
I will sprinkle c water on you, ... Eze 36:25
months to make the land c again. .... Eze 39:12
So they put a c turban on his .... Zch 3:5
incense and c offerings to me, ... Mal 1:11
will come ready to c the grain, ... Mt 3:12
empty, swept c, and made neat. .... Mt 12:44
make the inside of the cup c, ... Mt 23:26
of the cup can be truly c. .... Mt 23:26
wrapped it in a c linen cloth. .... Mt 27:59
food with hands that were not c, ... Mk 7:2
house swept c and made neat. .... Lk 11:25
You Pharisees c the outside of .... Lk 11:39
and then you will be fully c. .... Lk 11:41
had a bath, his whole body is c. .... Jn 13:10
he said, "Not all of you are c." .... Jn 13:11
You are already c because of the .... Jn 15:3
God has made these things c,................ Ac 10:15
that, but you were washed c. 1Co 6:11
your children would not be c,................ 1Co 7:14
make the church c by washing it .... Eph 5:26
make themselves c from evil will 2Ti 2:21
made people c from their sins .... Heb 1:3
this makes their bodies c again. .... Heb 9:13
must be made c by blood, ... Heb 9:22
The worshipers made be c, ... Heb 10:2
You sinners, c sin out of your .... Jam 4:8
and to be made c by the blood 1Pe 1:2
that he was made c from his past 2Pe 1:9
were dressed in c, shining linen .... Rev 15:6
bright and c, was given to her .... Rev 19:8

CLEANED

The men c Ahab's chariot at a 1Ki 22:38
that are not c and covered, ... Is 1:6

CLEANS

And he trims and c every branch .... Jn 15:2

CLEANSE

special ceremony to c away sin. .... Nu 19:9
I wanted to c you, but you are .... Eze 24:13
I will c you from all your .... Eze 36:25
on the day I c you from all your .... Eze 36:33
of Jerusalem to c them of their .... Zch 13:1
He will c us from all the wrongs.............. 1Jn 1:9

CLEANSED

the person being c from the skin .... Le 14:7
The person to be c must wash his .... Le 14:8
will never be c from your sin .... Eze 24:13

CLEANSER

yourself with c and use much................ Je 2:22

CLEANSES

God's Son, c us from every sin 1Jn 1:7

CLEANSING

until her time of c is finished................ Le 12:4
them for his c to the priest at .... Le 14:23
On the Day of C, you must blow.............. Le 25:9
Sprinkle the c water on them,................ Nu 8:7
ashes to use in the c water,.................. Nu 19:9
and share in their c ceremony. .... Ac 21:24
was already after the Day of C. .... Ac 27:9

CLEAR

and it was as c as the sky! .... Ex 24:10
Make the way c for my people."............... Is 57:14
it will be c they were fools.................... Je 17:11
the Egyptians' water become c. .... Eze 32:14
enough for you to drink c water? .... Eze 34:18

will be made c and every secret .... Mk 4:22
that is hidden will become c, ... Lk 8:17
of him has been made c to them. .... Rm 1:19
It has been made c through the .... Rm 16:26
so that it may be c which of you............. 1Co 11:19
do not make c musical notes, ... 1Co 14:7
trumpet does not give a c sound, ... 1Co 14:8
is c this does not include God................ 1Co 15:27
can say it with a c conscience: 2Co 1:12
It is c I was not a burden to 2Co 12:16
and it became c that we are .... Gal 2:17
Now it is c that no one can be .... Gal 3:11
God will make them c to you.................. Php 3:15
With a c conscience they must 1Ti 3:9
Everything is c and lies open .... Heb 4:13
It is c that our Lord came from .... Heb 7:14
that we have a c conscience, ... Heb 13:18
a c conscience so that those 1Pe 3:16
a sea of glass, c like crystal. .... Rev 4:6
made of pure gold as c as glass.............. Rev 21:21

CLEARED

has already c the way for you. .... Jdg 4:14
You c the ground for us. .... Ps 80:9
He dug and c the field of stones .... Is 5:2

CLEARLY

This is c from the LORD, ... Ge 24:50
was poor, so he could not see c. .... Ge 27:1
the message of a man who sees c; .... Nu 24:3
Then write c all the words of .... Dt 27:8
'I c showed myself to the family 1Sa 2:27
Show me c how you want me to.............. Ps 5:8
you c see our secret sins. .... Ps 90:8
and your eyes will not see c. .... Ec 12:3
cannot speak c now will then be .... Is 32:4
be able to speak c and quickly. .... Is 32:4
you will understand this c. .... Je 23:20
write it c on clay tablets so.................. Hab 2:2
you will see c to take the dust .... Mt 7:5
I will tell them c, 'Get away .... Mt 7:23
his tongue so that he spoke c.................. Mk 7:35
he was able to see everything c. .... Mk 8:25
you will see c to take the dust .... Lk 6:42
You are speaking c to us now and .... Jn 16:29
God c showed this to you by the.............. Ac 2:22
Cornelius c saw a vision. .... Ac 10:3
c proving with the Scriptures .... Ac 18:28
that shows more c that God is .... Rm 3:5
their work will be c seen, ... 1Co 3:13
mirror, but then we shall see c. 1Co 13:12
you speak c with your tongue................ 1Co 14:9
this to you c in every way. 2Co 11:6
were told very c about the death .... Gal 3:1
Now the Holy Spirit c says that 1Ti 4:1
C, it is not angels that Jesus .... Heb 2:16
to understand c that his .... Heb 6:17
words "once again" c show us .... Heb 12:27
think c and control yourselves 1Pe 4:7
have these things cannot see c. 2Pe 1:9

CLEARS

He breathes, and the sky c...................... Job 26:13

CLEOPAS

The one named C answered, ... Lk 24:18

CLERK

Then the city c made the crowd .... Ac 19:35

CLEVER

was the most c of all the wild .... Ge 3:1
I have heard that he is c........................ 1Sa 23:22
Jonadab was a very c man..................... 2Sa 13:3
in their own c traps and sweeps .... Job 5:13
By her c words she made him give........... Pr 7:21
are wise and believe they are c. .... Is 5:21

C

and all the c things they have .... Is 25:11
So be as c as snakes and as .... Mt 10:16
dishonest manager for being c. .... Lk 16:8
people are more c with their own .... Lk 16:8
are wise in their own c traps." 1Co 3:19
not telling just c stories that 2Pe 1:16

CLEVERLY

Uzziah made c designed devices. 2Ch 26:15
idols that are c made, the work .... Hos 13:2
You c ignore the commands of God .... Mk 7:9

CLIFF

is safe, like a nest on a c. .... Nu 24:21
The c on one side was named 1Sa 14:4
to the top of a c and threw them 2Ch 25:12
on a high c and stays there .... Job 39:28
in the secret places of the c. .... Sng 2:14
places of the c and control the .... Je 49:16
in the hollow places of the c. .... Ob 1:3
the edge of the c on which the .... Lk 4:29

CLIFFS

leaders are thrown down the c. .... Ps 141:6
Go into the caves of the c; .... Is 2:10
the deep ravines and in the c, ... Is 7:19
I will roll you off the c, ... Je 51:25
be thrown down, the c will fall, ... Eze 38:20

CLIMB

C this mountain in the Abarim .... Nu 27:12
C to the top of Mount Pisgah and .... Dt 3:27
On that mountain that you c, ... Dt 32:50
to us,' we will c up, and the................ 1Sa 14:10
to his officer, "C up behind me, ... 1Sa 14:12
I will c up the palm tree and .... Sng 7:8
thick bushes and c up into the .... Je 4:29
the wall and c into the houses .... Joe 2:9
If they c up into heaven, I will .... Am 9:2
Philip to c in and sit with .... Ac 8:31

CLIMBED

They c up Mount Hor, and all the .... Nu 20:27
Then Moses c Mount Nebo from the .... Dt 34:1
Then they c up to the roof of .... Jdg 9:51
Jonathan c up, using his hands 1Sa 14:13
his officer c just behind him 1Sa 14:13
and they c down into it. 2Sa 17:18
and Ahimaaz c out of the well 2Sa 17:21
same time Elijah c to the top of 1Ki 18:42
If a fox c up on the stone wall .... Ne 4:3
back the covers and c into bed. .... Is 57:8
Death has c in through our.................. Je 9:21
and he c a sycamore tree so he .... Lk 19:4

CLIMBS

Anyone who c out of the hole................ Is 24:18
Anyone who c out of the pits .... Je 48:44
by the door, but c in some other .... Jn 10:1

CLOPAS

Mary the wife of C, and Mary................ Jn 19:25

CLOSE

my husband will be c to me, ... Ge 29:34
said to them, "Come c to me." .... Ge 45:4
brought the boys c to Israel. .... Ge 48:13
let one of her c relatives buy .... Ex 21:8
When Moses came c to the camp, ... Ex 32:19
tail cut off c to the backbone .... Le 3:9
Aaron's sons c to the altar. .... Le 8:24
must go out and c up the house .... Le 14:38
that would shame a c relative. .... Le 20:19
should not camp too c to it. .... Nu 2:2
wife you love, or a c friend. .... Dt 13:6
it was time to c the city gate, ... Jos 2:5
Boaz is one of our c relatives,............. Ru 2:20
Boaz said to the c relative, ... Ru 4:3

The c relative answered, ... Ru 4:4
Jonathan felt very c to David................... 1Sa 18:1
to someone who is very c to you. 2Sa 12:11
the king is our c relative. 2Sa 19:42
She will lie c to you and keep.............. 1Ki 1:2
officer who was c to the king 2Ki 7:2
Stay c to the king when he goes.............. 2Ki 11:8
the Temple and c the doors, ... Ne 6:10
chains and keep c watch wherever........... Job 13:27
All my c friends hate me; .... Job 19:19
when God's c friendship blessed .... Job 29:4
Because he is c by my side, ... Ps 16:8
I stay c to you; you support me .... Ps 63:8
But I am c to God, and that is .... Ps 73:28
You have brought me c to death; .... Ps 88:6
c my eyes, or let myself sleep .... Ps 132:4
The LORD is c to everyone who .... Ps 145:18
A neighbor c by is better than a .... Pr 27:10
Their weapons are c at hand, ... Is 5:27
he should pay very c attention." .... Is 21:7
Come c and listen to me. .... Is 41:5
Do not c your ears and ignore my .... La 3:56
his angel to c the lions' mouths .... Da 6:22
c up the book and seal it. .... Da 12:4
of you would c the Temple doors .... Mal 1:10
your room and c the door and .... Mt 6:6
You c the door for people to .... Mt 23:13
on the shore c to the water................. Mk 4:1
and pushed very c around him. .... Mk 5:24
You are c to the kingdom of God. .... Mk 12:34
They did not come c to Jesus .... Lk 17:12
As he was coming c to Jerusalem, ... Lk 19:37
He came c to Jesus so he could .... Lk 22:47
those who were c friends of .... Lk 23:49
Son is very c to the Father, ... Jn 1:18
Because he is c by my side, ... Ac 2:25
he stayed very c to Philip. .... Ac 8:13
his relatives and c friends. .... Ac 10:24
corners. It came very c to me.............. Ac 11:5
thought we were c to land, ... Ac 27:27
and brag that you are c to God. .... Rm 2:17
opens a door, no one can c it. .... Rev 3:7
was following c behind him. .... Rev 6:8

CLOSED

Then God c up the man's skin at .... Ge 2:21
Then the LORD c the door behind .... Ge 7:16
c the city gates and guarded .... Jos 6:1
out of the room and locked .... Jdg 3:23
had windows that opened and c. 1Ki 6:4
he c the doors of the Temple 2Ch 28:24
holes in the wall were being c. .... Ne 4:7
My wrongs will be c up in a bag, ... Job 14:17
You have c their minds to .... Job 17:4
their eyes be c so they cannot............. Ps 69:23
people will hide behind c doors............. Is 24:10
deep sleep. He has c your eyes. .... Is 29:10
of a book that is c and sealed. .... Is 29:11
will not be c day or night so .... Is 60:11
people of Israel have c ears, ... Je 6:10
The message is c up and sealed .... Da 12:9
of the sea c around my throat.............. Jnh 2:5
and they have c their eyes. .... Mt 13:15
Then the door was c and locked. .... Mt 25:10
because their minds were c. .... Mk 6:52
or understand? Are your minds c? .... Mk 8:17
Jesus c the book, gave it back .... Lk 4:20
eyes, and he has c their minds. .... Jn 12:40
The jail was c and locked, ... Ac 5:23
Temple doors were c immediately. .... Ac 21:30
and they have c their eyes. .... Ac 28:27
He c their eyes so they could .... Rm 11:8
their eyes be c so they cannot............. Rm 11:10

minds were c, and even today.................2Co 3:14
and was kept c with seven seals. ....Rev 5:1
bottomless pit, c it, and locked ....Rev 20:3

CLOSED-UP

walled-in spring, a c fountain. ....Sng 4:12

CLOSELY

Moses looked c at all the work ....Ex 39:43
But do not follow too c. ....Jos 3:4
working c with the workers ....Ru 2:23
Saul watched David c from then..............1Sa 18:9
When I looked at him more c, ...1Ki 3:21
My feet have c followed his ....Job 23:11
look c into my heart and mind. ....Ps 26:2
listen c to what I say. ....Pr 4:20
to me, and watch c what I do.................Pr 23:26
Listen c to what I tell you; ....Is 28:23
Listen c to me, and you will eat ....Is 55:2
to be guarded c till the third ....Mt 27:64
watched Jesus c to see if he ....Mk 3:2
at the fire and looked c at him. ....Mk 14:67
synagogue was watching Jesus c. ....Lk 4:20
were watching c to see if Jesus ....Lk 6:7
were watching Jesus very c. ....Lk 14:1
people were listening c to him. ....Lk 19:48
and looking c at him, she said, ...Lk 22:56
Stephen c and saw that his.....................Ac 6:15
and you follow c the teachings 1Co 11:2
Look c at yourselves. 2Co 13:5
you to follow c what they said 2Pe 1:19

CLOSER

I will go c to this strange ....Ex 3:3
God said, "Do not come any c. ....Ex 3:5
you have a c relative than I. ....Ru 3:12
was coming c to David. 1Sa 17:41
in them were coming c to Saul. 2Sa 1:6
The enemy comes c and closer. ....Je 46:22
were coming c to Jerusalem, ...Mk 11:1
and as he came c to the house, ...Lk 15:25
follower leaned c to Jesus and ....Jn 13:25
amazed and went near to look c. ....Ac 7:31
food will not bring us c to God. 1Co 8:8

CLOSES

if he c a door, no one will be ....Is 22:22
house gets up and c the door,.................Lk 13:25
when he c it, no one can open ....Rev 3:7

CLOSEST

share it with his c neighbor, ...Ex 12:4
a stranger to my c relatives ....Ps 69:8
the people c to his heart.......................Ps 148:14
understanding your c friend. ....Pr 7:4

CLOSING

to them, c the door behind ....Ge 19:6
the eighth day have a c meeting, ...Nu 29:35
and his men were c in on them. 1Sa 23:26
You keep my eyes from c. ....Ps 77:4

CLOTH

put on rough c to show that he ....Ge 37:34
with wings on the pieces of c..................Ex 26:1
Make loops of blue c on the edge ....Ex 26:4
robe, a turban, and a c belt. ....Ex 28:4
holy vest, using only blue c. ....Ex 28:31
Moses spread the c over the Holy ....Ex 40:19
and tied the c belt around him. ....Le 8:7
the mildew has spread on the c ....Le 13:51
and spread a purple c over it. ....Nu 4:13
braids of my hair into the c, ...Jdg 16:13
wrapped in a c behind the holy 1Sa 21:9
put on rough c to show how sad..............2Sa 3:31
in a field, and put a c over it. 2Sa 20:12
took the rough c that was worn 2Sa 21:10

dress in rough c to show our 1Ki 20:31
his face in a c so no one could 1Ki 20:38
they wore rough c and put dust ....Ne 9:1
put on rough c and ashes, and ....Est 4:1
sewed rough c over my skin to ....Job 16:15
and your hair is like purple c;.................Sng 7:5
Instead of fine c belts, they.....................Is 3:24
like the c a weaver rolls up ....Is 38:12
are like filthy pieces of c. ....Is 64:6
So put on rough c, show how sad ....Je 4:8
Your c shades over the deck were ....Eze 27:7
turquoise, purple c, cloth with ....Eze 27:16
on rough c, and sat in ashes. ....Da 9:3
keep your rough c on all night ....Joe 1:13
with rough c and sat in ashes.................Jnh 3:6
patch of unshrunk c over a hole ....Mt 9:16
wrapped it in a clean linen c. ....Mt 27:59
patch of unshrunk c over a hole..............Mk 2:21
only a linen c, was following ....Mk 14:51
But the c he was wearing came ....Mk 14:52
Joseph bought some linen c, ...Mk 15:46
wrapped in pieces of c and lying ....Lk 2:12
No one takes c off a new coat to ....Lk 5:36
wrapped in a piece of c and hid..............Lk 19:20
he saw only the c that Jesus' ....Lk 24:12
feet wrapped with pieces of c, ...Jn 11:44
which was all one piece of c, ...Jn 19:23
the spices in pieces of linen c, ...Jn 19:40
strips of linen c lying there, ...Jn 20:5
whose job was selling purple c. ....Ac 16:14
became black like rough black c, ...Rev 6:12
dressed in rough c to show their ....Rev 11:3
linen, purple c, silk, red cloth ....Rev 18:12

CLOTHE

and you c yourselves with the ....Eze 34:3
more sure that God will c you. ....Mt 6:30
So how much more will God c you? ....Lk 12:28
But c yourselves with the Lord ....Rm 13:14
that dies must c itself with 1Co 15:53
because it will c us so we will.................2Co 5:3
should always c yourselves with..............Col 3:12

CLOTHED

still c in the special priest's.....................Le 10:5
Saul c you with red dresses and..............2Sa 1:24
sadness, and c me in happiness ....Ps 30:11
The LORD is c in majesty and ....Ps 93:1
are c with glory and majesty;.................Ps 104:1
sitting, c, and in his right ....Mk 5:15
at Jesus' feet, c and in his ....Lk 8:35
we want to be c with our 2Co 5:4
so you can be c and so you can ....Rev 3:18
A woman was c with the sun,..............Rev 12:1

CLOTHES

LORD God made c from animal ....Ge 3:21
took the best c of her older son ....Ge 27:15
When Isaac smelled Esau's c,.................Ge 27:27
tore his c to show he was upset.................Ge 37:29
Joseph fine linen c to wear, ...Ge 41:42
gave each brother a change of c, ...Ge 45:22
wine to wash his c and the best ....Ge 49:11
be able to see under your c." ....Ex 20:26
Make holy c for your brother ....Ex 28:2
c to show that he belongs to me ....Ex 28:3
Take the c and dress Aaron in ....Ex 29:5
They made the holy c for Aaron..............Ex 39:1
The person must wash his c, ...Le 13:6
He must wash his c and bathe his ....Le 14:9
and wash their c so they will be ....Nu 8:7
explored the land, tore their c. ....Nu 14:6
A woman must not wear men's c, ...Dt 22:5
a man must not wear women's c. ....Dt 22:5
Don't wear c made of wool and ....Dt 22:11

Joshua tore his **c** in sorrow. .... Jos 7:6
shirts and thirty changes of **c.** .... Jdg 14:12
Saul put his own **c** on David. 1Sa 17:38
Saul put on other **c** to disguise 1Sa 28:8
You took off your **c** in front of 2Sa 6:20
and cut off their **c** at the hips. 2Sa 10:4
lotions on, and changed his **c.** 2Sa 12:20
Put on funeral **c** and don't put 2Sa 14:2
and gold, **c,** weapons, spices 1Ki 10:25
So Ahab wore other **c** and went 1Ki 22:30
Why have you torn your **c?** 2Ki 5:8
words, he tore his **c** in grief. 2Ki 6:30
and **c** out of the camp and hid 2Ki 7:8
road was full of **c** and equipment 2Ki 7:15
tore her **c** and screamed, ... 2Ki 11:14
put away his prison **c.** 2Ki 25:29
But you wear your royal **c."** 2Ch 18:29
tore her **c** and screamed, ... 2Ch 23:13
were naked the **c** that the 2Ch 28:15
Their **c** did not wear out, and .... Ne 9:21
She sent **c** for Mordecai to put .... Est 4:4
wearing royal **c** of blue and .... Est 8:15
go around naked without any **c;** .... Job 24:10
die for lack of **c** or let a needy .... Job 31:19
They divided my **c** among them, ... Ps 22:18
You took away my **c** of sadness, ... Ps 30:11
I put on **c** of sadness and showed .... Ps 35:13
Your **c** smell like myrrh, aloes, ... Ps 45:8
When I wear **c** of sadness, they .... Ps 69:11
They will all wear out like **c.** .... Ps 102:26
chest without burning your **c,** .... Pr 6:27
Make **c** from the lambs' wool, ... Pr 27:26
She makes linen **c** and sells them .... Pr 31:24
Put on nice **c** and make yourself .... Ec 9:8
Your **c** smell like the cedars of .... Sng 4:11
they will wear **c** of sadness. .... Is 3:24
have plenty of food and nice **c.** .... Is 23:18
them black like **c** of sadness." .... Is 50:3
will become useless like old **c,** .... Is 51:6
and **c** of praise to replace their .... Is 61:3
covered me with **c** of salvation .... Is 61:10
Why are your **c** bright red as if .... Is 63:2
on your **c** you have the blood .... Je 2:34
shepherd wraps himself in his **c,** .... Je 43:12
put away his prison **c,** .... Je 52:33
tie them in the folds of your **c.** .... Eze 5:3
you were naked and without **c.** .... Eze 16:7
Your **c** were made of fine linen, ... Eze 16:13
They were paid with the best **c,** .... Eze 27:24
trousers, turbans, and other **c.** .... Da 3:21
receive purple **c** fit for a king .... Da 5:7
His **c** were white like snow, ... Da 7:9
dressed in linen **c** with a belt .... Da 10:5
Tearing your **c** is not enough to .... Joe 2:13
You put on **c,** but you are not .... Hag 1:6
the fold of his **c** some meat made .... Hag 2:12
wearing dirty **c** and was standing .... Zch 3:3
the prophet's **c** made of hair to .... Zch 13:4
John's **c** were made from camel's .... Mt 3:4
or about the **c** you need for your .... Mt 6:25
And why do you worry about **c?** .... Mt 6:28
God the grass in the field, ... Mt 6:30
If I can just touch his **c,** .... Mt 9:21
a bag or extra **c** or sandals .... Mt 10:10
A man dressed in fine **c?** .... Mt 11:8
who wear fine **c** live in kings' .... Mt 11:8
and his **c** became white as light. .... Mt 17:2
special prayer **c** very long. .... Mt 23:5
I was without **c,** and you gave me .... Mt 25:36
see you without **c** and give you .... Mt 25:38
I was without **c,** and you gave me .... Mt 25:43
he tore his **c** and said, "This .... Mt 26:65
They took off his **c** and put a .... Mt 27:28

and put his own **c** on him again. .... Mt 27:31
to decide who would get his **c.** .... Mt 27:35
and his **c** were white as snow. .... Mt 28:3
and asked, "Who touched my **c?"** .... Mk 5:30
take only the **c** you are wearing. .... Mk 6:9
His **c** became shining white, ... Mk 9:3
to walk around wearing fancy **c,** .... Mk 12:38
and divided his **c** among .... Mk 15:24
who have fine **c** and much wealth .... Lk 7:25
he had worn no **c** and had lived .... Lk 8:27
and his **c** became shining white. .... Lk 9:29
They tore off his **c,** beat him, ... Lk 10:30
or about the **c** you need for your .... Lk 12:22
and the body is more than **c.** .... Lk 12:23
God **c** the grass in the field, ... Lk 12:28
Bring the best **c** and put them on .... Lk 15:22
to decide who would get his **c.** .... Lk 23:34
men in shining **c** suddenly stood .... Lk 24:4
they took his **c** and divided them .... Jn 19:23
They divided my **c** among them, ... Jn 19:24
Peter had taken his **c** off. .... Jn 21:7
wearing white **c** stood beside .... Ac 1:10
before me wearing shining **c.** .... Ac 10:30
about it, they tore their **c.** .... Ac 14:14
tore the **c** of Paul and Silas .... Ac 16:22
dust from his **c** and said to them .... Ac 18:6
handkerchiefs and **c** that Paul .... Ac 19:12
wanted anyone's money or fine **c.** .... Ac 20:33
I have been cold and without **c.** 2Co 11:27
wear proper **c** that show respect 1Ti 2:9
gold or pearls or expensive **c.** 1Ti 2:9
we have food and **c,** we will be 1Ti 6:8
They will all wear out like **c.** .... Heb 1:11
And, like **c,** you will change .... Heb 1:12
wearing nice **c** and a gold ring. .... Jam 2:2
in Christ might need **c** or food. .... Jam 2:15
your **c** have been eaten by moths. .... Jam 5:2
or fine **c** that should make you 1Pe 3:3
even their **c** which are dirty .... Jud 1:23
with me and will wear white **c,** .... Rev 3:4
be dressed in white **c** like them. .... Rev 3:5
Buy from me white **c** so you can .... Rev 3:18
and keep their **c** on so that they .... Rev 16:15

CLOTHING
for gifts—silver, gold, and **c.** .... Ex 3:22
of silver and gold and for **c.** .... Ex 12:35
having food or **c** or sexual .... Ex 21:10
donkey, sheep, **c,** or something .... Ex 22:9
C might have mildew on it. .... Le 13:47
must not wear **c** made from two .... Le 19:19
supplies, much **c,** and other 2Ch 20:25
100 pieces of **c** for the priests .... Ezr 2:69
530 pieces of **c** for the priests. .... Ne 7:70
67 pieces of **c** for the priests. .... Ne 7:72
rotten, like **c** eaten by moths. .... Job 13:28
on right living as if it were **c;** .... Job 29:14
grabs hold of my **c** and chokes me .... Job 30:18
and greatness as if they were **c.** .... Job 40:10
and they threw lots for my **c.** .... Ps 22:18
and put on violence as their **c.** .... Ps 73:6
clothes, and I stained all my **c.** .... Is 63:3
up and took off his outer **c.** .... Jn 13:4
and they threw lots for my **c."** .... Jn 19:24

CLOTHS
with salt or wrapped in **c.** .... Eze 16:4

CLOUD
ahead of them in a pillar of **c,** .... Ex 13:21
The pillar of **c** was always with .... Ex 13:22
So the **c** kept the two armies .... Ex 14:20
from the pillar of **c** and fire at .... Ex 14:24
of the LORD appeared in a **c.** .... Ex 16:10
with a thick **c** on the mountain. .... Ex 19:16

near the dark **c** where God was. .... Ex 20:21
and the **c** covered it for six .... Ex 24:16
the pillar of **c** at the entrance .... Ex 33:10
Then the **c** covered the Meeting .... Ex 40:34
When the **c** rose from the Holy .... Ex 40:36
as long as the **c** stayed on the .... Ex 40:37
was a fire in the **c** at night. .... Ex 40:38
when I appear in a **c** over the .... Le 16:2
so that the **c** of incense will .... Le 16:13
The **c** stayed above the Tent, ... Nu 9:16
When the **c** moved from its place .... Nu 9:17
night and in a **c** during the day, ... Dt 1:33
to send up a **c** of smoke from .... Jdg 20:38
c filled the Temple of the LORD. 1Ki 8:10
said he would live in a dark **c**. 1Ki 8:12
I see a small **c**, the size of a 1Ki 18:44
of the LORD was filled with a **c**. 2Ch 5:13
their work because of the **c**, ... 2Ch 5:14
he would live in the dark **c**. 2Ch 6:1
a pillar of **c** by day and with .... Ne 9:12
that day. Let a **c** hide it. Let .... Job 3:5
As a **c** disappears and is gone, ... Job 7:9
my safety disappears like a **c**. .... Job 30:15
He led them with a **c** by day and .... Ps 78:14
to them from the pillar of **c**. .... Ps 99:7
covered them with a **c** and lit up .... Ps 105:39
who look at every **c** will never .... Ec 11:4
of the desert like a **c** of smoke? .... Sng 3:6
there with a **c** of smoke during .... Is 4:5
become dark in this thick **c**. .... Is 5:30
because a **c** of dust comes from .... Is 14:31
on a fast **c** to enter Egypt. .... Is 19:1
As a **c** cools a hot day, you .... Is 25:5
away your sins like a big **c**; .... Is 44:22
The enemy rises up like a **c**, ... Je 4:13
You wrapped yourself in a **c**, ... La 3:44
was a great **c** with a bright .... Eze 1:4
Inside the **c** was what looked .... Eze 1:5
sweet-smelling **c** of incense was .... Eze 8:11
Temple was filled with the **c**, ... Eze 10:4
A **c** will cover Egypt, and her .... Eze 30:18
I will cover the sun with a **c**, ... Eze 32:7
Israel like a **c** that covers the .... Eze 38:16
voice came from the **c** and said, ... Mt 17:5
Then a **c** came and covered them, ... Mk 9:7
a **c** came and covered them, ... Lk 9:34
of Man coming in a **c** with power .... Lk 21:27
a **c** hid him from their sight. .... Ac 1:9
Moses in the **c** and in the sea. 1Co 10:2
by a great **c** of people whose .... Heb 12:1
dressed in a **c** with a rainbow .... Rev 10:1
heaven in a **c** as their enemies .... Rev 11:12
there before me was a white **c**, ... Rev 14:14
the white **c** was One who looked .... Rev 14:14

CLOUDS

c in the sky poured out rain. .... Ge 7:11
and the **c** in the sky stopped .... Ge 8:2
my rainbow in the **c** as the sign .... Ge 9:13
and black **c** made it very dark. .... Dt 4:11
rides on the **c** in his majesty. .... Dt 33:26
rained, and the **c** dropped water. .... Jdg 5:4
surrounded by fog and **c**. 2Sa 22:12
dawn, like a morning without **c**. 2Sa 23:4
the sky was covered with dark **c**. 1Ki 18:45
and their heads may touch the **c**, ... Job 20:6
he judge us through the dark **c**? .... Job 22:13
Thick **c** cover him so he cannot .... Job 22:14
moon, spreading his **c** over it. .... Job 26:9
sky and see the **c** so high above .... Job 35:5
rain then pours down from the **c**, ... Job 36:28
God controls the **c** and makes his .... Job 37:15
wind has blown all the **c** away. .... Job 37:21

when I made the **c** like a coat .... Job 38:9
sea and wrapped it in dark **c**, ... Job 38:9
has the wisdom to count the **c**? .... Job 38:37
down with dark **c** under his feet. .... Ps 18:9
of his presence came **c** with hail. .... Ps 18:12
the skies, your truth to the **c**. .... Ps 57:10
The **c** poured down their rain. .... Ps 77:17
command to the **c** above and .... Ps 78:23
Thick, dark **c** surround him. .... Ps 97:2
You make the **c** your chariot, ... Ps 104:3
He brings the **c** from the ends of .... Ps 135:7
the sky with **c** and sends rain to. .... Ps 147:8
into rivers and the **c** drop rain .... Pr 3:20
when he made the **c** above and put .... Pr 8:28
give are like **c** and wind that .... Pr 25:14
If **c** are full of rain, they will .... Ec 11:3
will command the **c** not to rain .... Is 5:6
go up above the tops of the **c**. .... Is 14:14
The **c** in the sky will pour out .... Is 24:18
a fire with thick **c** of smoke. .... Is 30:27
c, pour down victory. .... Is 45:8
will disappear like **c** of smoke. .... Is 51:6
are returning to you like **c**, ... Is 60:8
and his armies with **c** of dust. .... Is 66:15
He makes **c** rise in the sky all. .... Je 10:13
it reaches to the **c**.' .... Je 51:9
He makes **c** rise in the sky all. .... Je 51:16
rainbow in the **c** on a rainy day. .... Eze 1:28
its top was among the **c**. .... Eze 31:3
coming on the **c** in the sky. .... Da 7:13
and the **c** are the dust beneath .... Nah 1:3
gloom, a day of **c** and blackness, ... Zph 1:15
LORD is the one who makes the **c**. .... Zch 10:1
Man coming on **c** in the sky with .... Mt 24:30
Man coming in **c** with great power .... Mk 13:26
When you see **c** coming up in the .... Lk 12:54
them in the **c** to meet the Lord 1Th 4:17
water and **c** blown by a storm 2Pe 2:17
They are **c** without rain, which .... Jud 1:12
Jesus is coming with the **c**, ... Rev 1:7

CLOUDY

is a **c** day and a time when the .... Eze 30:3
scattered on a **c** and dark day. .... Eze 34:12
a dark, gloomy day, **c** and black. .... Joe 2:2

CLUB

Benaiah had a **c**, but he grabbed 2Sa 23:21
Benaiah had a **c**, but he grabbed 1Ch 11:23
it hurts them as much as a **c**, ... Pr 25:18
in anger I use Assyria like a **c**. .... Is 10:5
You are my war **c**, my battle .... Je 51:20
of Israel in the face with a **c**. .... Mic 5:1

CLUBS

C feel like pieces of straw to .... Job 41:29
and arrows, war **c**, and spears. .... Eze 39:9
swords and **c** who had been sent .... Mt 26:47
with swords and **c** as if I were .... Mk 14:48
with swords and **c** as though I .... Lk 22:52

CLUMPS

hard and the **c** of dirt stick .... Job 38:38

CLUSTERS

a fig cake and two **c** of raisins. 1Sa 30:12

CLUTCHES

back from the **c** of cruel people. .... Job 6:23

CNIDUS

time reaching C because the wind .... Ac 27:7

COAL

to take a hot **c** from the altar. .... Is 6:6
this hot **c** has touched your. .... Is 6:7
But now they are blacker than **c**, ... La 4:8

C

COALS

full of burning **c** from the altar .... Le 16:12
scatter the **c** a long distance .... Nu 16:37
Burning **c** went before him. 2Sa 22:9
and dishes used to carry **c**; 1Ki 7:50
a loaf baked over **c** and a jar of 1Ki 19:6
the pans for carrying hot **c**, ... 2Ki 25:15
and dishes used to carry **c**, ... 2Ch 4:22
Its breath sets **c** on fire, ... Job 41:21
He will send hot **c** and burning .... Ps 11:6
Burning **c** went before him. .... Ps 18:8
and with burning **c** of wood. .... Ps 120:4
Let burning **c** fall on them. .... Ps 140:10
cannot carry hot **c** against your .... Pr 6:27
walk on hot **c** without burning .... Pr 6:28
pouring burning **c** on his head, ... Pr 25:22
small to take **c** from the fire .... Is 30:14
used the hot **c** to bake my bread.............. Is 44:19
are not like **c** that give warmth .... Is 47:14
for carrying hot **c**, large bowls, ... Je 52:19
like burning **c** of fire or like .... Eze 1:13
scatter the **c** over the city." .... Eze 10:2
pot on the **c** so it may become .... Eze 24:11
shore, they saw a fire of hot **c**. .... Jn 21:9
pouring burning **c** on his head." .... Rm 12:20

COAST

the whole Mediterranean Sea **c**. .... Jos 9:1
Egypt and along the **c** of the .... Jos 15:47
still alive on the **c** of the .... Eze 25:16
who live by the **c** tremble, ... Eze 26:18
trees from the **c** of Cyprus and .... Eze 27:6
to cities along the **c** of the .... Da 11:18
quickly sent Paul away to the **c**, ... Ac 17:14

COASTAL

the kings of the **c** countries to .... Je 25:22

COASTLANDS

selling your goods on many **c**. .... Eze 27:15
who live in safety on the **c**. .... Eze 39:6

COAT

Then Shem and Japheth got a **c** .... Ge 9:23
Joseph left his **c** in her hand .... Ge 39:12
Moses put his hand inside his **c**.............. Ex 4:6
gives you his **c** as a promise for .... Ex 22:26
find a donkey or **c** or anything .... Dt 22:3
Give the **c** back at sunset, ... Dt 24:13
was a beautiful **c** from Babylonia .... Jos 7:21
spread out a **c**, and everyone .... Jdg 8:25
made a little **c** for him and took 1Sa 2:19
his head and a **c** of bronze armor 1Sa 17:5
He took off his **c** and gave it to 1Sa 18:4
man wearing a **c** is coming up." 1Sa 28:14
Hushai's **c** was torn, and there 2Sa 15:32
Ahijah took his new **c** and tore 1Ki 11:30
took off his **c**, and put it 1Ki 19:19
took off his **c**, rolled it up, ... 2Ki 2:13
up Elijah's **c** that had fallen 2Ki 2:13
water with Elijah's **c** and said, ... 2Ki 2:14
man took off his own **c** and put 2Ki 9:13
I angrily tore my robe and **c**, ... Ezr 9:3
My robe and **c** were torn, and I .... Ezr 9:5
a needy person go without a **c**. .... Job 31:19
the clouds like a **c** for the sea .... Job 38:9
stand out like folds in a **c**. .... Job 38:14
and covered with shame like a **c**. .... Ps 109:29
Take the **c** of someone who.................... Pr 20:16
taking away his **c** on a cold day .... Pr 25:20
gather up the waters in his **c**?................. Pr 30:4
You have a **c**, so you will be .... Is 3:6
himself in the **c** of his strong .... Is 59:17
wrapped me with a **c** of goodness, ... Is 61:10
take hold of a Judean by his **c**. .... Zch 8:23

shirt, let him have your **c** also. .... Mt 5:40
cloth over a hole in an old **c**. .... Mt 9:16
shrink and pull away from the **c**, ... Mt 9:16
and touched the edge of his **c**. .... Mt 9:20
touch just the edge of his **c**, ... Mt 14:36
cloth over a hole in an old **c**. .... Mk 2:21
in the crowd and touched his **c**. .... Mk 5:27
touch just the edge of his **c**, ... Mk 6:56
up, left his **c** there, and went .... Mk 10:50
ruins the new **c**, and the cloth.................. Lk 5:36
takes your **c**, do not stop him .... Lk 6:29
and touched the edge of his **c**, ... Lk 8:44
sword, sell your **c** and buy one. .... Lk 22:36
he wrapped his **c** around himself. .... Jn 21:7
"Put on your **c** and follow me." .... Ac 12:8
I left my **c** there with Carpus. 2Ti 4:13
You will fold them like a **c**. .... Heb 1:12

COATING

like a shiny **c** on a clay pot. .... Pr 26:23

COATS

You take the **c** from people who .... Mic 2:8
spread their **c** on the road. .... Mt 21:8
must not go back to get their **c**. .... Mt 24:18
to Jesus and put their **c** on it, ... Mk 11:7
must not go back to get their **c**. .... Mk 13:16
their **c** on the colt's back, ... Lk 19:35
left their **c** with a young man .... Ac 7:58
shirts and Tabitha had made .... Ac 9:39
threw off their **c**, and threw .... Ac 22:23

COBRA'S

be able to play near a **c** hole, ... Is 11:8

COBRAS

like the deadly poison of **c**...................... Dt 32:33
like deaf **c** that stop up their .... Ps 58:4
You will walk on lions and **c**; .... Ps 91:13

COFFIN

they put him in a **c** in Egypt. .... Ge 50:26
He went up and touched the **c**, ... Lk 7:14

COILED

Leviathan, the **c** snake, with his .... Is 27:1

COIN

its mouth and you will find a **c**. .... Mt 17:27
their pay, each received one **c**. .... Mt 20:9
You agreed to work for one **c**. .... Mt 20:13
me a **c** used for paying the tax. .... Mt 22:19
image and name are on the **c**?" .... Mt 22:20
gave Jesus a **c**, and he asked, ... Mk 12:16
I have found the **c** that I lost.' .... Lk 15:9
and gave a **c** to each servant. .... Lk 19:13
Show me a **c**. Whose image and.............. Lk 20:24

COINS

they gave him thirty silver **c**. .... Mt 26:15
up the silver **c** in the Temple .... Mt 27:6
to use the **c** to buy Potter's .... Mt 27:7
They took thirty silver **c**........................ Mt 27:9
and put in two small copper **c**, ... Mk 12:42
five hundred **c** and the other .... Lk 7:41
the Samaritan brought out two **c**, ... Lk 10:35
a woman has ten silver **c**, ... Lk 15:8
I earned ten **c** with the one you .... Lk 19:16
two small copper **c** into the box.............. Lk 21:2
about fifty thousand silver **c**. .... Ac 19:19

COLD

and harvest, **c** and hot, summer .... Ge 8:22
at night I was **c** and could not .... Ge 31:40
to cover themselves in the **c**. .... Job 24:7
No one can stand the **c** he sends. .... Ps 147:17
his coat on a **c** day or pouring .... Pr 25:20
day and in the **c** frost of the .... Je 36:30
hang on the walls on a **c** day. .... Nah 3:17

COLLAPSE

will be no light, **c**, or frost. .... Zch 14:6
ones a cup of **c** water because .... Mt 10:42
It was **c**, so the servants and .... Jn 18:18
it was raining and very **c**, ... Ac 28:2
have been **c** and without clothes. 2Co 11:27
that you are not hot or **c**. .... Rev 3:15

COLLAPSE

When the foundations for good **c**, ... Ps 11:3

COLLAR

with a woven **c** around the hole .... Ex 28:32
with a woven **c** sewn around it so .... Ex 39:23
chokes me with the **c** of my coat. .... Job 30:18
and on to the **c** of his robes. .... Ps 133:2

COLLECT

c two ounces of silver for each .... Nu 3:47
who is clean will **c** the ashes .... Nu 19:9
but you must not **c** what another .... Dt 15:3
who will **c** these things in all .... Ne 10:37
they **c** things but don't know who .... Ps 39:6
from the plants and **c** the grain. .... Is 17:5
themselves and **c** for themselves .... Hab 2:5
of the earth **c** different kinds .... Mt 17:25
who decided to **c** the money his .... Mt 18:23
the king began to **c** his money, ... Mt 18:24
will not have to **c** money after I 1Co 16:2
become priests must **c** a tenth .... Heb 7:5

COLLECTED

Joseph **c** all the money that was.............. Ge 47:14
So Moses **c** the money for the .... Nu 3:49
The man who **c** the cow's ashes .... Nu 19:10
that had been **c** for the Temple 1Ch 26:26
from what was **c** to the other 2Ch 31:15
from taxes **c** from .... Ezr 6:8
is the one who **c** the taxes?.................... Is 33:18
nations around them will be **c**—.............. Zch 14:14
men who the Temple tax came .... Mt 17:24
but he **c** a tenth from Abraham. .... Heb 7:6

COLLECTION

part of the **c** to these priests 2Ch 31:19
written in the **c** of sad songs. 2Ch 35:25
write about the **c** of money for 1Co 16:1

COLLECTOR

send out a tax **c** so he will have .... Da 11:20
Thomas and Matthew, the tax **c**;.............. Mt 10:3
believe in God or like a tax **c**................... Mt 18:17
out and saw a tax **c** named Levi.............. Lk 5:27
Pharisee and a tax **c** both went .... Lk 18:10
who was a very important tax **c**, ... Lk 19:2

COLLECTOR'S

sitting in the tax **c** booth. .... Mt 9:9
sitting in the tax **c** booth. .... Mk 2:14
Levi sitting in the tax **c** booth. .... Lk 5:27

COLLECTORS

Even the tax **c** do that. .... Mt 5:46
eat with tax **c** and sinners?" .... Mt 9:11
a friend of tax **c** and sinners.' .... Mt 11:19
it to the tax **c** for you and me." .... Mt 17:27
the tax **c** and the prostitutes .... Mt 21:31
many tax **c** and "sinners" were .... Mk 2:15
he eat with tax **c** and sinners?" .... Mk 2:16
Even tax **c** came to John to be .... Lk 3:12
drink with tax **c** and sinners?" .... Lk 5:30
the tax **c**, heard this, they .... Lk 7:29
a friend of tax **c** and sinners!'................ Lk 7:34
The tax **c** and sinners all came .... Lk 15:1

COLLECTS

or well that **c** water will stay .... Le 11:36
your government **c** will be less. .... Ezr 4:13

COLONY

Roman **c** and the leading city in.............. Ac 16:12

COLOR

are dark like the **c** of wine,.................... Ge 49:12
are as white as the **c** of milk. .... Ge 49:12
Why do you put **c** around your .... Je 4:30
Cush change the **c** of his skin? .... Je 13:23
a rainbow the **c** of an emerald. .... Rev 4:3

COLORED

Holy Tent from sheepskins **c** red, ... Ex 26:14
male sheepskins that are **c** red. .... Ex 35:7
my bed with **c** sheets from Egypt .... Pr 7:16

COLORFUL

made your places of worship **c**. .... Eze 16:16

COLORS

gems of many different **c**, ... 1Ch 29:2
many different **c** came to Lebanon............. Eze 17:3
carpets of many **c**, and tightly .... Eze 27:24

COLOSSAE

in Christ that live in **C**: .... Col 1:2

COLT

a donkey, on the **c** of a donkey. .... Zch 9:9
a donkey tied there with its **c**................... Mt 21:2
donkey and the **c** to Jesus and .... Mt 21:7
tell him its Master needs the **c**, ... Mk 11:3
and found the **c** just as Jesus .... Lk 19:32
sitting on the **c** of a donkey." .... Jn 12:15

COLT'S

threw their coats on the **c** back, ... Lk 19:35

COLUMN

they all go up in a **c** of smoke. .... Is 9:18

COLUMNS

rows of cedar **c** which supported 1Ki 7:2
she has made its seven **c**. .... Pr 9:1
Jehudi had read three or four **c**, ... Je 36:23
king cut those **c** off of the .... Je 36:23

COMB

c your hair and wash your face. .... Mt 6:17

COME

but this time it did not **c** back. .... Ge 8:12
your people will **c** to this land .... Ge 15:16
slave girl, where have you **c** .... Ge 16:8
you, and kings will **c** from you. .... Ge 17:6
of nations will **c** from her.".................... Ge 17:16
please to my house and spend.............. Ge 19:2
sun had already **c** up when Lot .... Ge 19:23
and then we will **c** back to you." .... Ge 22:5
the girl won't **c** back with you, ... Ge 24:8
when the women **c** out to get .... Ge 24:11
Why have you **c** to see me?.................... Ge 26:27
C near so I can touch you, ... Ge 27:21
and I will **c** back and take care .... Ge 30:31
you must never **c** to my side of .... Ge 31:52
Esau might **c** and destroy one................ Ge 32:8
C and have sexual relations with .... Ge 39:12
seven more cows **c** out of the .... Ge 41:19
We have **c** from the land of.................... Ge 42:7
and Benjamin to **c** back with you. .... Ge 43:14
said to them, "**C** close to me." .... Ge 45:4
and your brothers have **c** to you, ... Ge 47:5
son Joseph has **c** to see you." .... Ge 48:2
will **c** from Judah's family;..................... Ge 49:10
Why have you **c** home early today? .... Ex 2:18
God said, "Do not **c** any closer. .... Ex 3:5
and I have **c** down to save them .... Ex 3:8
Make frogs **c** up out of the water .... Ex 8:5
brings death **c** into your houses .... Ex 12:23
and water will **c** out of it so .... Ex 17:6
the people **c** to me for God's .... Ex 18:15

C

the people who c to you will get .... Ex 18:18
will c down on Mount Sinai, ... Ex 19:11
called Moses to c up to the top .... Ex 19:20
priests, who may c near me, must .... Ex 19:22
people cannot c up on Mount .... Ex 19:23
because God has c to test you. .... Ex 20:20
and I will c and bless you. .... Ex 20:24
causing the baby to c out. .... Ex 21:22
No one is to c to worship me .... Ex 23:15
Then Moses alone must c near me; .... Ex 24:2
anytime they c near the altar .... Ex 28:43
No one is to c before me without .... Ex 34:20
C here and pick up your cousins' .... Le 10:4
the person must c to the priest. .... Le 13:16
he may c back into the camp. .... Le 16:26
must c and buy it back. .... Le 25:25
women slaves must c from other .... Le 25:44
C with us. We will share with .... Nu 10:32
three of you c to the Meeting .... Nu 12:4
The Anakites c from the Nephilim .... Nu 13:33
C to Heshbon and rebuild it; .... Nu 21:27
A nation has c out of Egypt that............. Nu 22:5
So c and put a curse on them. .... Nu 22:6
"Balaam refused to c with us." .... Nu 22:14
C with me to another place, ... Nu 23:13
A star will c from Jacob;...................... Nu 24:17
A ruler will c from the .... Nu 24:19
You have now c to the mountain .... Dt 1:20
Their gods do not c near them, ... Dt 4:7
that you will c back to the LORD .... Dt 4:30
dreams might c to you and say .... Dt 13:1
for ten generations may c .... Dt 23:3
two peoples may c into the .... Dt 23:8
blessings will c and stay with .... Dt 28:2
curses will c upon you and stay .... Dt 28:15
children who will c after you, ... Dt 29:22
Let those gods c to help you! .... Dt 32:38
They have c to spy out our whole .... Jos 2:3
said, "They did c here, but I .... Jos 2:4
"C up out of the Jordan. .... Jos 4:17
the city will c out to fight us .... Jos 8:5
we left home to c to you it was .... Jos 9:12
C with me and help me attack .... Jos 10:4
c over into our land where the .... Jos 22:19
LORD your God made us c true, ... Jos 23:15
said to him, "C into my tent, ... Jdg 4:18
C down and attack the .... Jdg 7:24
the fig tree, 'C and be king .... Jdg 9:10
c and find shelter in my shade! .... Jdg 9:15
army ready and c out to battle.' .... Jdg 9:29
have you c to attack our land? .... Jdg 11:12
We have c to make Samson our .... Jdg 15:10
We have c to tie you up and to .... Jdg 15:12
disaster was about to c to them. .... Jdg 20:34
or brothers c to us and complain .... Jdg 21:22
wings you have c for shelter."............... Ru 2:12
Boaz told Ruth, "C here........................ Ru 2:14
would then c carrying a fork 1Sa 2:13
servant would c to the person................ 1Sa 2:15
messages fail to c true. 1Sa 3:19
the LORD had c into the Hebrew 1Sa 4:6
A god has c into the Hebrew 1Sa 4:7
sickness has c on you and your 1Sa 6:4
of prophets will c down from the 1Sa 10:5
the LORD, "Has Saul c here yet?" 1Sa 10:22
we will c out to meet you 1Sa 11:10
Philistines will c against me at 1Sa 13:12
'Stay there until we c to you,' 1Sa 14:9
C back with me so I may worship 1Sa 15:25
'I have c to offer a sacrifice.................... 1Sa 16:2
answered, "Yes, I c in peace. 1Sa 16:5
I have c to make a sacrifice to 1Sa 16:5
You c to me using a sword and 1Sa 17:45

' you may c out of hiding. 1Sa 20:21
the son of Jesse c to the feast 1Sa 20:27
that Saul plans to c to Keilah 1Sa 23:10
'Evil things c from evil people.' 1Sa 24:13
that Saul had c to Hakilah. 1Sa 26:4
I have sinned. C back, David my 1Sa 26:21
Ark of the LORD c to me now?"............... 2Sa 6:9
called Uriah to c to see him, ... 2Sa 11:13
Please let my sister Tamar c in. 2Sa 13:6
c and have sexual relations with 2Sa 13:11
let my brother Amnon c with us." 2Sa 13:26
but Joab still refused to c. 2Sa 14:29
People would c near Absalom to 2Sa 15:5
C with me to Jerusalem, and I 2Sa 19:33
Tell Joab to c here. I want to 2Sa 20:16
has my master the king c to me?" 2Sa 24:21
King David, to c, as well as all 1Ki 1:9
king said, "Tell Bathsheba to c 1Ki 1:28
mother. "Do you c in peace?"................. 1Ki 2:13
now I have c and seen it with 1Ki 10:7
"C back to me in three days."................. 1Ki 12:12
Please c home and eat with me, ... 1Ki 13:7
the door, he said, "C in, wife 1Ki 14:6
that disaster should c to you." 1Ki 22:23
you c back safely from battle, ... 1Ki 22:28
let fire c down from heaven and............. 2Ki 1:10
Let Naaman c to me. Then he will 2Ki 5:8
would surely c out and stand 2Ki 5:11
disease will c on you and your 2Ki 5:27
did this crazy man c to you?"................. 2Ki 9:11
said, "Have you c in peace, you 2Ki 9:31
about Ahab's family will c true. 2Ki 10:10
C and save me from the king of 2Ki 16:7
I have not c to attack and 2Ki 18:25
prophet who had c from Samaria. 2Ki 23:18
first people to c back and live................ 1Ch 9:2
If you have c peacefully to help 1Ch 12:17
He has c to live in Jerusalem 1Ch 23:25
Riches and honor c from you................. 1Ch 29:12
will c from far away to pray 2Ch 6:32
C with the Ark of the Agreement 2Ch 6:41
saw the fire c down from heaven 2Ch 7:3
They will c up through the Pass 2Ch 20:16
Edom who had c to attack Judah 2Ch 20:22
cause your intestines to c out." 2Ch 21:15
robbers who had c with the Arabs 2Ch 22:1
let anyone c into the Temple 2Ch 23:6
these people to c to the Temple 2Ch 30:1
spoken by Jeremiah would c true. 2Ch 36:22
spoken by Jeremiah would c true. .... Ezr 1:1
C, let's rebuild the wall of .... Ne 2:17
all made plans to c to Jerusalem .... Ne 4:8
So c, let's discuss this .... Ne 6:7
This trouble has c to us, to our .... Ne 9:32
load could c in on the Sabbath. .... Ne 13:19
She was to c to show her beauty .... Est 1:11
c today with Haman to a banquet .... Est 5:4
He had c to ask the king about .... Est 6:4
said to Satan, "Where have you c .... Job 1:7
to die, but death does not c. .... Job 3:21
Hard times do not c up from the............. Job 5:6
and they c to an end without .... Job 7:6
Your armies c against me. .... Job 10:17
Terrors will c over them;...................... Job 20:25
often does trouble c to them? .... Job 21:17
me, I will c out like gold. .... Job 23:10
God. Who can c against him? He .... Job 23:13
New honors will c to me..................... Job 29:20
My words c from an honest heart, ... Job 33:3
and flames c out of its mouth. .... Job 41:21
rise up! My God, c save me! You .... Ps 3:7
love, I can c into your Temple................. Ps 5:7
that victory will c to Israel .... Ps 14:7

and the glorious King will c .... Ps 24:7
So I c to worship you, LORD. .... Ps 27:8
Children, c and listen to me. .... Ps 34:11
Quickly c and help me, my Lord .... Ps 38:22
the end will c and how long I .... Ps 39:4
They just c to get bad news. .... Ps 41:6
Troubles have c again and again, ... Ps 42:7
C and see what the LORD has done, ... Ps 46:8
we c into your Temple to think .... Ps 48:9
that victory will c to Israel .... Ps 53:6
They c back at night. Like dogs .... Ps 59:6
honor and salvation c from God. .... Ps 62:7
All people will c to you. .... Ps 65:2
C and see what God has done, ... Ps 66:5
Messengers will c from Egypt; .... Ps 68:31
C near and save me; rescue me .... Ps 69:18
God, c quickly and save me. .... Ps 70:1
gifts should c to the God we .... Ps 76:11
tell those who c later about................... Ps 78:4
nations have c against your .... Ps 79:1
God, c and judge the earth,................... Ps 82:8
good things c from Jerusalem. .... Ps 87:7
diseases that c in the dark or .... Ps 91:6
no disaster will c to your home. .... Ps 91:10
C, let's sing for joy to the .... Ps 95:1
c before him with singing. .... Ps 100:2
let my cry for help c to you. .... Ps 102:1
wild donkeys c there to drink. .... Ps 104:11
but where does my help c from?............. Ps 121:1
c with the Ark that shows your .... Ps 132:8
tear open the sky and c down. .... Ps 144:5
all of their plans c to an end. .... Ps 146:4
Wisdom will c into your mind, ... Pr 2:10
for, don't say, "C back later. .... Pr 3:28
C, let's make love until morning. .... Pr 7:18
in riches will c to nothing. .... Pr 11:7
But wishes that c true are like .... Pr 13:12
is so good when wishes c true, ... Pr 13:19
the LORD can make them c true. .... Pr 16:1
cruel anger will c to an end. .... Pr 22:8
and your wishes will c true. .... Pr 24:14
Let the praise c from a stranger .... Pr 27:2
Words c again and again to our .... Ec 1:8
Bad dreams c from too much .... Ec 5:3
too many words c from foolish .... Ec 5:3
People c into this world with .... Ec 5:15
days of trouble c and the years .... Ec 12:1
that c from one Shepherd. .... Ec 12:11
The time has c to sing; .... Sng 2:12
C with me from Lebanon, my bride. .... Sng 4:8
north wind. C, south wind. Blow .... Sng 4:16
C back, come back, woman of .... Sng 6:13
C, my lover, let's go out into .... Sng 7:11
The LORD says, "C, let us talk .... Is 1:18
people who c back to the LORD .... Is 1:27
nations will c streaming to it .... Is 2:2
and they will c like bees....................... Is 7:18
Then a new loyal king will c; .... Is 16:5
our enemies will c to our land, ... Is 17:14
They will c back to the LORD, ... Is 19:22
but then night will c again. .... Is 21:12
those people will c and worship .... Is 27:13
let the tired people c and rest. .... Is 28:12
It will c morning after morning; .... Is 28:19
your words will c like a whisper............. Is 29:4
All-Powerful will c down to .... Is 31:4
I have not c to attack and .... Is 36:10
someone to c out of the north I .... Is 41:25
C back to me because I saved you........... Is 44:22
and power c only from the LORD .... Is 45:24
But troubles will c to you, ... Is 47:11
who are thirsty, c and drink. .... Is 55:1
not have money, c, buy and eat!............. Is 55:1

my salvation will c to you soon. .... Is 56:1
The LORD will c quickly like a .... Is 59:19
a Savior will c to Jerusalem .... Is 59:20
Nations will c to your light; .... Is 60:3
Israelites will c on horses, ... Is 66:20
All people will c to worship me .... Is 66:23
Disaster will c from the north................... Je 1:14
Come back to me, you unfaithful .... Je 3:14
and all nations will c together .... Je 3:17
They will c together from a land .... Je 3:18
C back to me, you unfaithful .... Je 3:22
A lion has c out of his den; .... Je 4:7
his chariots c like a tornado. .... Je 4:13
flocks will c against Jerusalem .... Je 6:3
you who c through these gates .... Je 7:2
heal us, but only terror has c.................... Je 8:15
Let's see that message c true!" .... Je 17:15
the LORD will c like a storm. .... Je 23:19
the message you prophesy c true. .... Je 28:6
He will c near to me when I .... Je 30:21
Punishment will c like a storm .... Je 30:23
'C, let's go up to Jerusalem to.................. Je 31:6
about Jerusalem c true through .... Je 39:16
He will c here and attack Egypt. .... Je 43:11
They c against Egypt with axes .... Je 46:22
Judgment has c to these towns: .... Je 48:21
of God's anger will c to you; .... La 4:21
The end has c! The end has come! .... Eze 7:6
c near with your weapon in your .... Eze 9:1
when every vision will c true................... Eze 12:23
pay all your lovers to c to you. .... Eze 16:33
of your final punishment has c. .... Eze 21:25
The time has c for me to act. .... Eze 24:14
who escapes will c to you with .... Eze 24:26
command the grain to c and grow;........... Eze 36:29
and saw muscles c on the bones, ... Eze 37:8
Wind, c from the four winds, and .... Eze 37:9
You will c like a storm. .... Eze 38:9
Only they may c near my table to .... Eze 44:16
you thought about things to c. .... Da 2:29
Meshach, and Abednego, c out! .... Da 3:26
huge animals c up from the sea,............... Da 7:3
saw a male goat c from the west. .... Da 8:5
A command will c to rebuild .... Da 9:25
leader who is to c will destroy .... Da 9:26
the prince of Greece will c,................... Da 10:20
for God's promises to c true. .... Da 11:14
the king of the North will c. .... Da 11:15
all these things will c true." .... Da 12:7
They will c to worship the LORD, ... Hos 5:6
Nations will c together against .... Hos 10:10
punishment will c like a .... Joe 1:15
C back to the LORD your God, ... Joe 2:13
and to attack in the Valley .... Joe 3:12
will c during a day of battle, ... Am 1:14
the LORD's day of judging to c. .... Am 5:18
An end has c for my people .... Am 8:2
be anxious for good news to c, ... Mic 1:12
nations will c streaming to it. .... Mic 4:1
Should I c before him with burnt .... Mic 6:6
will not c a second time.......................... Nah 1:9
they c from places far away. .... Hab 1:8
to a wooden statue, 'C to life!' .... Hab 2:19
people will c with gifts for me. .... Zph 3:10
right time has not c to rebuild .... Hag 1:2
person used to c to the wine vat .... Hag 2:16
you still did not c back to me,' .... Hag 2:17
They have c to scare and throw .... Zch 1:21
They have just c from the .... Zch 6:5
far away will c and build the .... Zch 6:15
They will c and attack Jerusalem .... Zch 12:2
on earth will c together to .... Zch 12:3
Then I will c to you and judge .... Mal 3:5

C

c and put a curse on the land.................. Mal 4:6
east and have c to worship him. .... Mt 2:2
Jesus said, "C follow me, and I .... Mt 4:19
Jesus told them to c with him. .... Mt 4:21
think that I have c to destroy .... Mt 5:17
and then c and offer your gift. .... Mt 5:24
May your kingdom c and what you .... Mt 6:10
Grapes don't c from thornbushes, ... Mt 7:16
for you to c into my house. .... Mt 8:8
soldier, 'C,' and he comes. .... Mt 8:9
Many people will c from the east .... Mt 8:11
But the time will c when the .... Mt 9:15
I did not c to bring peace, ... Mt 10:34
I have c so that 'a son will be .... Mt 10:35
Are you the One who is to c, ... Mt 11:3
Elijah, whom they said would c. .... Mt 11:14
C to me, all of you who are. .... Mt 11:28
the kingdom of God has c to you. .... Mt 12:28
wild birds to c and build nests .... Mt 13:32
The angels will c and separate .... Mt 13:49
Jesus said, "C." And Peter left .... Mt 14:29
around there that Jesus had c, ... Mt 14:35
Out of the mind c evil thoughts, ... Mt 15:19
Son of Man will c again with his .... Mt 16:27
say that Elijah must c first?" .... Mt 17:10
or three people c together in my .... Mt 18:20
Let the little children c to me. .... Mt 19:14
heaven. Then c and follow me." .... Mt 19:21
when the age to c has arrived, ... Mt 19:28
of Man did not c to be served. .... Mt 20:28
did that c from God or just from .... Mt 21:25
people, but they refused to c. .... Mt 22:3
C to the wedding feast.' .... Mt 22:4
will c in my name, saying, ' .... Mt 24:5
prophets will c and cause many .... Mt 24:11
nation. Then the end will c. .... Mt 24:14
know the day your Lord will c. .... Mt 24:42
Son of Man will c at a time you .... Mt 24:44
The master will c when that .... Mt 24:50
C and share my joy with me.' .... Mt 25:23
Son of Man will c again in his .... Mt 25:31
on his right, 'C, my Father has .... Mt 25:34
time has c for the Son of Man .... Mt 26:45
C down from that cross if you .... Mt 27:40
C and see the place where his .... Mt 28:6
said to them, "C follow me, and .... Mk 1:17
Did you c to destroy us? .... Mk 1:24
Be quiet! C out of the man!" .... Mk 1:25
evil spirit, c out of the man. .... Mk 5:8
Please c and put your hands on .... Mk 5:23
these evil things c from inside .... Mk 7:23
kingdom of God go with power .... Mk 9:1
Elijah must c first and make .... Mk 9:12
command you to c out of this boy .... Mk 9:25
Let the little children c to me. .... Mk 10:14
heaven. Then c and follow me." .... Mk 10:21
of Man did not c to be served. .... Mk 10:45
Many people will c in my name, ... Mk 13:6
prophets will c and perform .... Mk 13:22
owner of the house will c back. .... Mk 13:35
he might c back suddenly .... Mk 13:36
to make the Scriptures c true." .... Mk 14:49
C down from that cross!" .... Mk 15:30
let him c down now from the .... Mk 15:32
for the kingdom of God to c. .... Mk 15:43
The Holy Spirit will c upon you, ... Lk 1:35
Be quiet! C out of that man!" .... Lk 4:35
other boat to c and help them. .... Lk 5:7
I have not c to invite good .... Lk 5:32
But the time will c when the .... Lk 5:35
to ask Jesus to c and heal his .... Lk 7:3
to have you c into my house. .... Lk 7:6
why I did not c to you myself. .... Lk 7:7

soldier, 'C,' and he comes. .... Lk 7:8
A great prophet has c to us! .... Lk 7:16
God has c to help his people." .... Lk 7:16
Are you the One who is to c, ... Lk 7:19
asked Jesus to c to his house .... Lk 7:39
evil spirit to c out of the man. .... Lk 8:29
please c and look at my son, ... Lk 9:38
Son of Man did not c to destroy .... Lk 9:56
blessing will c back to you. .... Lk 10:6
kept holy. May your kingdom c. .... Lk 11:2
the kingdom of God has c to you. .... Lk 11:20
Son of Man will c at a time when .... Lk 12:40
The master will c when that .... Lk 12:46
People will c from the east, ... Lk 13:29
I just got married; I can't c.' .... Lk 14:20
went out and begged him to c. .... Lk 15:28
the dogs would c and lick his .... Lk 16:21
They did not c close to Jesus .... Lk 17:12
"When will the kingdom of God c?" .... Lk 17:20
The time will c when you will .... Lk 17:22
Let the little children c to me. .... Lk 18:16
heaven. Then c and follow me." .... Lk 18:22
to a place where Jesus would c, ... Lk 19:4
Zacchaeus, hurry and c down! .... Lk 19:5
the time will c when not one .... Lk 21:6
Many people will c in my name, ... Lk 21:8
but the end will c later." .... Lk 21:9
great signs will c from heaven. .... Lk 21:11
me when you c into your kingdom. .... Lk 23:42
for the kingdom of God to c. .... Lk 23:51
women who had c from Galilee .... Lk 23:55
A man will c after me, but he .... Jn 1:30
anything good c from Nazareth?" .... Jn 1:46
Philip answered, "C and see." .... Jn 1:46
Dear woman, why c to me? .... Jn 2:4
My time has not yet c." .... Jn 2:4
The Light has c into the world, ... Jn 3:19
your husband and c back here." .... Jn 4:16
C and see a man who told me .... Jn 4:29
and begged him to c to Capernaum .... Jn 4:47
Teacher, when did you c here?" .... Jn 6:25
No one can c to me unless the .... Jn 6:44
time for me has not yet c." .... Jn 7:8
but they c from him who sent me. .... Jn 7:16
A demon has c into you. .... Jn 7:20
But I have not c by my own .... Jn 7:28
And you cannot c where I am." .... Jn 7:34
is thirsty c to me and drink. .... Jn 7:37
Christ will not c from Galilee. .... Jn 7:41
You cannot c where I am going." .... Jn 8:21
I did not c by my own authority; .... Jn 8:42
will be able to c in and go out .... Jn 10:9
A demon has c into him and made .... Jn 10:20
a loud voice, "Lazarus, c out!" .... Jn 11:43
crowd who had c to Jerusalem for .... Jn 12:12
told him to c out of the tomb .... Jn 12:17
The time has c for the Son of .... Jn 12:23
I have c as light into the world .... Jn 12:46
because I did not c to judge the .... Jn 12:47
Where I am going you cannot c. .... Jn 13:33
go away, the Helper will not c. .... Jn 16:7
the time will c when I will not .... Jn 16:25
prayed, "Father, the time has c. .... Jn 17:1
that the Scripture would c true. .... Jn 17:12
how he would die would c true. .... Jn 18:32
to make the Scripture c true: .... Jn 19:36
Jesus said to them, "C and eat." .... Jn 21:12
want him to live until I c back, ... Jn 21:22
will c back in the same way you .... Ac 1:11
glorious day of the Lord will c. .... Ac 2:20
C back to God, and he will .... Ac 3:19
to Abraham was soon to c true, ... Ac 7:17
cries and have c down to save .... Ac 7:34

the One who is good would **c**,................. Ac 7:52
had not yet **c** upon any of them................ Ac 8:16
Now he has **c** here to Damascus, ... Ac 9:14
him, "Hurry, please **c** to us!" .... Ac 9:38
asked the men to **c** in and spend .... Ac 10:23
Joppa and ask Simon Peter to **c**............... Ac 10:32
that peace has **c** through Jesus .... Ac 10:36
and invite Simon Peter to **c**. .... Ac 11:13
Barnabas and Saul to **c** to him, ... Ac 13:7
"**C** over to Macedonia and help us." .... Ac 16:9
Let them **c** themselves and bring .... Ac 16:37
I will **c** back to you again if .... Ac 18:21
the one who would **c** after him, ... Ac 19:4
about, I order you to **c** out!" .... Ac 19:13
people will **c** like wild wolves................. Ac 20:29
to accuse Paul to **c** to you. .... Ac 24:8
and prayed for daylight to **c**. .... Ac 27:29
had to ask to **c** to Rome to have .... Ac 28:19
planned many times to **c** to you,.............. Rm 1:13
who are not Jews have to **c** to God. .... Rm 11:25
The Savior will **c** from Jerusalem .... Rm 11:26
Lord Jesus Christ to **c** again. 1Co 1:7
truths that **c** from the Spirit 1Co 2:14
But I will **c** to you very soon if 1Co 4:19
Then **c** together again so Satan 1Co 7:5
Man did not **c** from woman, but 1Co 11:8
when you **c** together to eat,.................... 1Co 11:33
Did God's teaching **c** from you? 1Co 14:36
Death has **c** because of what one 1Co 15:21
and then the end will **c**. 1Co 15:24
C back to your right way of 1Co 15:34
Macedonia **c** with me and find 2Co 9:4
so it will be ready when we **c**.................. 2Co 9:5
to Abraham might **c** through Jesus .... Gal 3:14
Now the way of faith has **c**, ... Gal 3:25
the right to **c** to the Father .... Eph 2:18
Jesus Christ, to **c** from heaven. .... Php 3:20
not give up when troubles **c**, ... Col 1:11
like a shadow of what was to **c**. .... Col 2:17
true and real has **c** and is found.............. Col 2:17
from the dead, to **c** from heaven. 1Th 1:10
Timothy now has **c** back to us 1Th 3:6
himself will **c** down from heaven 1Th 4:16
like pains that **c** quickly to a 1Th 5:3
works that **c** from your faith. 2Th 1:11
day of the Lord has already **c**. 2Th 2:2
Lord will not **c** until the 2Th 2:3
Man of Evil will **c** by the power 2Th 2:9
I hope I can **c** to you soon, ... 1Ti 3:14
the time has **c** for me to leave................ 2Ti 4:6
Do your best to **c** to me as soon 2Ti 4:9
that knowledge **c** from the hope.............. Tit 1:2
that can save everyone has **c**. .... Tit 2:11
and I will be able to **c** to you. .... Phm 1:22
sure that we can **c** before God's .... Heb 4:16
a need for another priest to **c**,................ Heb 7:11
And he will **c** a second time, ... Heb 9:28
those who **c** near to worship .... Heb 10:1
let us **c** near to God with a .... Heb 10:22
have not **c** to a mountain that .... Heb 12:18
You have not **c** to darkness, ... Heb 12:18
have **c** to thousands of angels................ Heb 12:22
You have **c** to God, the judge of .... Heb 12:23
These good gifts **c** down from the .... Jam 1:17
and curses **c** from the same .... Jam 3:10
They **c** from the selfish desires .... Jam 4:1
C near to God, and God will come .... Jam 4:8
And the Judge is ready to **c**! .... Jam 5:9
These troubles **c** to prove that................ 1Pe 1:7
C to the Lord Jesus, the "stone".............. 1Pe 2:4
beauty should **c** from within you—............ 1Pe 3:4
Jesus promised to **c** again. 2Pe 3:4
of the Lord will **c** like a thief. 2Pe 3:10

we can **c** without fear into God's 1Jn 3:21
He did not **c** by water only,...................... 1Jn 5:6
in your loyalty until I **c**. .... Rev 2:25
up, or I will **c** like a thief, ... Rev 3:3
trouble that will **c** to the whole .... Rev 3:10
I will **c** in and eat with you, ... Rev 3:20
trumpet, said, "**C** up here, and I .... Rev 4:1
with a voice like thunder, "**C**!" .... Rev 6:1
great day for their anger has **c**, ... Rev 6:17
two other troubles that will **c**.................. Rev 9:12
time has **c** to judge the dead, ... Rev 11:18
The time has **c** to destroy those .... Rev 11:18
the time to harvest has **c**, ... Rev 14:15
nations will **c** and worship you .... Rev 15:4
the kings from the east to **c**. .... Rev 16:12
I will **c** as a thief comes! .... Rev 16:15
He said, "**C**, and I will show you .... Rev 17:1
disasters that will **c** to her. .... Rev 18:4
the wedding of the Lamb has **c**, ... Rev 19:7
C and gather together for the .... Rev 19:17
Spirit and the bride say, "**C**!" .... Rev 22:17
Let whoever is thirsty **c**; .... Rev 22:17
soon." Amen. **C**, Lord Jesus! .... Rev 22:20

COMES

which **c** from the ground the LORD .... Ge 5:29
other, "Here **c** that dreamer. .... Ge 37:19
Judah will rule until Shiloh **c**,................. Ge 49:10
ox or donkey **c** and falls into it .... Ex 21:33
When the time **c** to punish,..................... Ex 32:34
uncleanness that **c** from people,.............. Le 7:21
with a woman and semen **c** out, ... Le 15:18
Then when Aaron **c** in, he will .... Le 16:13
anyone else who **c** near the holy .... Nu 3:10
eat anything that **c** from the .... Nu 6:4
Anyone who even **c** near the Holy .... Nu 17:13
the LORD our God **c** near when we .... Dt 4:7
the owner **c** looking for it; .... Dt 22:2
But when evening **c**, he must wash........... Dt 23:11
Their vine **c** from Sodom, and .... Dt 32:32
If anyone **c** and asks you, ' .... Jdg 4:20
soon as the sun **c** up in the .... Jdg 9:33
other, "When dawn **c**, we will.................. Jdg 16:2
everything he says **c** true. 1Sa 9:6
and he **c** and doesn't find you, ... 1Ki 18:12
Then when he **c** by, he can stay 2Ki 4:10
Kill anyone who **c** near. 2Ki 11:8
Everything **c** from you; 1Ch 29:14
which **c** from the word "Pur" .... Est 9:26
wait for daylight that never **c**.................. Job 3:9
be afraid when destruction **c**. .... Job 5:21
When it **c** to strength, God is .... Job 9:19
The cry of the poor **c** to God; .... Job 34:28
What I know **c** from far away. .... Job 36:3
God **c** out of the north in golden .... Job 37:22
good thing I have **c** from you." .... Ps 16:2
The sun **c** out like a bridegroom .... Ps 19:5
night, but joy **c** in the morning .... Ps 30:5
not be ashamed when trouble **c**............... Ps 37:19
God **c** with millions of chariots; .... Ps 68:17
the Lord **c** from Mount Sinai to .... Ps 68:17
bless the one who **c** in the name............. Ps 118:26
help **c** from the LORD, who made .... Ps 121:2
Our help **c** from the LORD, who.............. Ps 124:8
when disaster **c** over you like a .... Pr 1:27
who goes to her **c** back or walks .... Pr 2:19
the ruin that **c** to the wicked, ... Pr 3:25
correction that **c** from them will.............. Pr 6:23
wealth, and no sorrow **c** with it. .... Pr 10:22
it **c** to the wicked instead. .... Pr 11:8
No harm **c** to a good person, ... Pr 12:21
Money that **c** easily disappears .... Pr 13:11
Trouble always **c** to sinners, ... Pr 13:21

but knowledge c easily to those .... Pr 14:6
but the answer c from the LORD. .... Pr 16:33
someone else c and asks...................... Pr 18:17
Wealth that c from telling lies................ Pr 21:6
If you give up when trouble c, ... Pr 24:10
family for help when trouble c. .... Pr 27:10
justice c only from the LORD................ Pr 29:26
With much wisdom c much .... Ec 1:18
is better when it c with money. .... Ec 7:11
Here he c jumping across the .... Sng 2:8
Look! The enemy c quickly! .... Is 5:26
destruction c from far away? .... Is 10:3
cloud of dust c from the north. .... Is 14:31
But if anyone c to me for safety .... Is 27:5
This lesson also c from the LORD .... Is 28:29
open, a poisonous snake c out. .... Is 59:5
of Israel c from the LORD our .... Je 3:23
what will you do when the end c? .... Je 5:31
A loud noise c from the north to .... Je 10:22
When that day c, you will .... Je 30:24
because no one c for the feasts. .... La 1:4
and every vision c to nothing'? .... Eze 12:22
When this c true, and it surely .... Eze 33:33
When the end c near for those .... Da 8:23
until the time of the end c. .... Da 11:35
to us as surely as the dawn c............... Hos 6:3
My justice c out like bright .... Hos 6:5
When the sun c up, the king of .... Hos 10:15
and terrible day of the LORD c. .... Joe 2:31
Salvation c from the LORD!" .... Jnh 2:9
morning light c, they do what................ Mic 2:1
He c from very old times, from .... Mic 5:2
The earth trembles when he c; .... Nah 1:5
the sun c up, they fly away,.................. Nah 3:17
are weak, and justice never c................ Hab 1:4
of the LORD's anger c to you................. Zph 2:2
no one can survive when he c. .... Mal 3:2
soldier, 'Come,' and he c. .... Mt 8:9
Israel before the Son of Man c. .... Mt 10:23
evil spirit c out of a person, ... Mt 12:43
When the spirit c back, it finds .... Mt 12:44
The Evil One c and takes away .... Mt 13:19
It is what c out of their mouths .... Mt 15:11
do to these farmers when he c?'' .... Mt 21:40
bless the One who c in the name .... Mt 23:39
must happen before the end c. .... Mt 24:6
Son of Man c, he will be seen .... Mt 24:27
the same when the Son of Man c. .... Mt 24:39
When the master c and finds the .... Mt 24:46
Satan quickly c and takes away .... Mk 4:15
bless the One who c in the name .... Mk 11:9
must happen before the end c. .... Mk 13:7
here c the man who has turned .... Mk 14:42
the mother of my Lord c to me? .... Lk 1:43
is like who c to me and hears my .... Lk 6:47
soldier, 'Come,' and he c. .... Lk 7:8
the devil c and takes it away .... Lk 8:12
stronger c and defeats him .... Lk 11:22
evil spirit c out of a person, ... Lk 11:24
blessed when he c in and finds .... Lk 12:38
If anyone c to me but loves his .... Lk 14:26
who c back from the dead. .... Lk 16:31
the servant c in from working .... Lk 17:7
When the Son of Man c again, ... Lk 17:24
bless the king who c in the name .... Lk 19:38
the vine until God's kingdom c." .... Lk 22:18
He is the One who c after me. .... Jn 1:27
Human life c from human parents,.......... Jn 3:6
life c from the Spirit. .... Jn 3:6
where the wind c from or where .... Jn 3:8
salvation c from the Jews. .... Jn 4:22
the Messiah c, he will explain .... Jn 4:25
Life c from the Father himself, ... Jn 5:26

Whoever c to me will never be .... Jn 6:35
the bread that c down from .... Jn 6:41
my teaching c from God and not .... Jn 7:17
Yet when the real Christ c, ... Jn 7:27
that no prophet c from Galilee." .... Jn 7:52
You don't know where he c from, ... Jn 9:30
A thief c to steal and kill and .... Jn 10:10
bless the One who c in the name .... Jn 12:13
that eternal life c from what .... Jn 12:50
of truth who c from the Father. .... Jn 15:26
But when the Spirit of truth c, ... Jn 16:13
when the Holy Spirit c to you, ... Ac 1:8
until the time c when all things .... Ac 3:21
If their plan c from human .... Ac 5:38
named Ananias c to him and lays .... Ac 9:12
So faith c from hearing the Good .... Rm 10:17
Be patient when trouble c, ... Rm 12:12
But everything c from God................. 1Co 11:12
the Lord's death until he c. 1Co 11:26
when perfection c, the things 1Co 13:10
death also c because of one man. 1Co 15:21
When Christ c again, those who 1Co 15:23
If Timothy c to you, see to it 1Co 16:10
you free when the final day c. .... Eph 4:30
when Jesus Christ c again. .... Php 1:6
the good that c from giving. .... Php 4:17
Everything c from him. .... Col 1:18
which c from the ruling spirits .... Col 2:8
and when he c again, you will .... Col 3:4
the joy that c from the Holy 1Th 1:6
in when our Lord Jesus Christ c. 1Th 2:19
a thief that c in the night. 1Th 5:2
we are alive or dead when he c. 1Th 5:10
That glory c from the grace of 2Th 1:12
the breath that c from his mouth 2Th 2:8
a love that c from a pure heart 1Ti 1:5
our Lord Jesus Christ c again. 1Ti 6:14
another priest c who is like............... Heb 7:15
Anyone who c to God must believe .... Heb 11:6
a poor person c in wearing old, ... Jam 2:2
the wisdom that c from God is .... Jam 3:17
patient until the Lord c again. .... Jam 5:7
trouble which now c to test you............ 1Pe 4:12
When that day c, the skies will 2Pe 3:12
that no lie c from the truth................... 1Jn 2:21
him so that when Christ c back, ... 1Jn 2:28
sword that c out of my mouth. .... Rev 2:16
that c down out of heaven from .... Rev 3:12
fire c from their mouths and .... Rev 11:5
the beast that c up from the .... Rev 11:7
I will come as a thief c! .... Rev 16:15
When he c, he must stay a short............ Rev 17:10
until what God has said c about. .... Rev 17:17
rider's mouth c a sharp sword .... Rev 19:15

COMFORT

He will c us in our work, ... Ge 5:29
and daughters tried to c him, ... Ge 37:35
and his family came to c him.................. 1Ch 7:22
show their concern and to c him. .... Job 2:11
would have this c and be glad .... Job 6:10
think my bed will c me or that .... Job 7:13
the c God gives you not enough .... Job 15:11
let this be the way you c me. .... Job 21:2
So how can you c me with this .... Job 21:34
and your shepherd's staff c me. .... Ps 23:4
I found no one to c me. .... Ps 69:20
promise. When will you c me? .... Ps 119:82
was no one to c those they hurt.............. Ec 4:1
hard work and will c them.................... Is 14:3
Don't hurry to c me about the .... Is 22:4
so God will not c them; .... Is 27:11
He wants to rise and c you. .... Is 30:18

God says, "Comfort, **c** my people. .... Is 40:1
So the LORD will **c** Jerusalem; .... Is 51:3
and fighting. No one can **c** you. .... Is 51:19
guide them and **c** them and those .... Is 57:18
He has sent me to **c** those whose .... Is 61:1
will **c** you as a mother comforts .... Is 66:13
you are my **c** when I am very sad .... Je 8:18
bring food to **c** those who are .... Je 16:7
will give them **c** and joy instead .... Je 31:13
There is no one to **c** her; .... La 1:2
of food and lived in great **c**, ... Eze 16:49
You even gave **c** to your sisters .... Eze 16:54
will I find anyone to **c** you?" .... Nah 3:7
The LORD will **c** Jerusalem again, ... Zch 1:17
c they give is worth nothing. .... Zch 10:2
who grieve, for God will **c** them. .... Mt 5:4
come there to **c** Martha and Mary .... Jn 11:19
strength, encouragement, and **c**........... 1Co 14:3
who is full of mercy and all **c**................ 2Co 1:3
forgive him and **c** him to keep 2Co 2:7
You give me much **c**, and in all 2Co 7:4
but also by the **c** you gave him. 2Co 7:7
Does his love **c** you? .... Php 2:1
and they have been a **c** to me. .... Col 4:11
great joy and **c**, my brother, ... Phm 1:7

COMFORTABLE

Those who are **c** don't care that .... Job 12:5
feeling completely safe and **c**.............. Job 21:23
Attack the nation that is **c**, ... Je 49:31
and helped him to be more **c**................. Jnh 4:6

COMFORTED

and so he was **c** after his .... Ge 24:67
him, but he could not be **c**. .... Ge 37:35
So Joseph **c** his brothers and .... Ge 50:21
Then David **c** Bathsheba his wife. 2Sa 12:24
words have **c** those who fell, ... Job 4:4
They **c** him and made him feel .... Job 42:11
out my hands, but I cannot be **c**. .... Ps 77:2
LORD, have helped me and **c** me. .... Ps 86:17
but you **c** me and made me happy........... Ps 94:19
with me now! You have **c** me. .... Is 12:1
the LORD has **c** his people.................... Is 52:9
you, and you have not been **c**. .... Is 54:11
You will be **c** in Jerusalem." .... Is 66:13
She refused to be **c**, because her .... Je 31:15
Then you will be **c** after the .... Eze 14:22
You will be **c** when you see what .... Eze 14:23
were **c** in the place of the dead .... Eze 31:16
Then he will be **c** for all his .... Eze 32:31
She refused to be **c**, because her .... Mt 2:18
Now he is **c** here, and you are .... Lk 16:25
home alive and were greatly **c**. .... Ac 20:12
were **c**, not only by his coming 2Co 7:7
were we very **c**, we were even 2Co 7:13

COMFORTERS

You are all painful **c**! .... Job 16:2

COMFORTING

brother Esau is **c** himself by .... Ge 27:42
and his words were **c** and good............ Zch 1:13
with Mary in the house, **c** her. .... Jn 11:31

COMFORTS

like a person who **c** sad people. .... Job 29:25
When I suffer, this **c** me:...................... Ps 119:50
God who **c** them will lead them .... Is 49:10
because the LORD **c** his people .... Is 49:13
you as a mother **c** her child. .... Is 66:13
He **c** us every time we have 2Co 1:4
who **c** those who are troubled, ... 2Co 7:6

COMING

the city are **c** out to get water. .... Ge 24:13
he looked up and saw camels **c**............ Ge 24:63

going up and **c** down the ladder. .... Ge 28:12
Rachel is **c** now with his sheep .... Ge 29:6
He is **c** to meet you and has four .... Ge 32:6
Jacob looked up and saw Esau **c**, ... Ge 33:1
saw many herds as I was **c** here. .... Ge 33:8
saw him **c** from far away. .... Ge 37:18
the good years that are **c**, ... Ge 41:35
flames of fire **c** out of a bush. .... Ex 3:2
king and his army **c** after them, ... Ex 14:10
am **c** to you with your wife and .... Ex 18:6
from semen **c** out of his body................ Le 15:32
The voice was **c** from between the .... Nu 7:89
Israelites were **c** on the road to .... Nu 21:1
Balak heard that Balaam was **c**, ... Nu 22:36
this food, the manna stopped **c**............... Jos 5:12
spies saw a man **c** out of the .... Jdg 1:24
Sisera's chariot so late in **c**? .... Jdg 5:28
There are people **c** down from the .... Jdg 9:36
Why are you **c** to me now that you......... Jdg 11:7
that disaster was **c** to them. .... Jdg 20:41
woman, who is **c** into your home, ... Ru 4:11
time is **c** when I will destroy 1Sa 2:31
Israelites heard they were **c**, ... 1Sa 7:7
young women **c** out to get water........... 1Sa 9:11
they saw Samuel **c** toward them on 1Sa 9:14
Saul was **c** home from plowing the 1Sa 11:5
and asked, "Are you **c** in peace?" 1Sa 16:4
He keeps **c** out to challenge 1Sa 17:25
was **c** closer to David........................... 1Sa 17:41
that Saul was **c** to kill him. 1Sa 23:15
I see a spirit **c** up out of the 1Sa 28:13
old man wearing a coat is **c** up."............ 1Sa 28:14
I have men **c** to cut the wool. 2Sa 13:24
king and his servants **c** to him. 2Sa 24:20
wife is **c** to ask you about 1Ki 14:5
because a heavy rain is **c**." 1Ki 18:41
a human fist, **c** from the sea.".............. 1Ki 18:44
When he saw her **c** from far away,........... 2Ki 4:25
when he saw Jehu's troops **c**. 2Ki 9:17
of Egypt, was **c** to attack him. 2Ki 19:9
because he is **c** to judge the 1Ch 16:33
A large army is **c** against you................ 2Ch 20:2
because men are **c** at night to................ Ne 6:10
thunder announces the **c** storm, ... Job 36:33
as if **c** from a large pot over a.................. Job 41:20
he sees that their day is **c**.................... Ps 37:13
He is **c** to judge the world; .... Ps 96:13
because he is **c** to judge the .... Ps 98:9
Who is this **c** out of the desert .... Sng 3:6
sheep just **c** from their bath. .... Sng 4:2
the LORD is **c** on a fast cloud to............. Is 19:1
Disaster is **c** from the desert .... Is 21:1
It is **c** from a terrible country.................. Is 21:1
see a man **c** in a chariot with a .... Is 21:9
Morning is **c**, but then night .... Is 21:12
The time is **c** when each of you .... Is 31:7
of Egypt, was **c** to attack him. .... Is 37:9
the Lord GOD is **c** with power to .... Is 40:10
behind you, **c** along in chains................ Is 45:14
you will not even see it **c**. .... Is 47:11
Your sons are **c** from far away, ... Is 60:4
Look, your Savior is **c**. .... Is 62:11
is this **c** from Edom, from the .... Is 63:1
the LORD is **c** with fire and his .... Is 66:15
so I am **c** to punish them. .... Is 66:18
Disaster is **c** from the north; .... Je 6:1
destruction is **c** to you. .... Je 6:1
That army is **c** lined up for .... Je 6:23
see the people **c** from the north. .... Je 13:20
the days are **c**, says the LORD, ... Je 19:16
The time is **c** when Jerusalem................ Je 31:38
Their time of destruction is **c**;............... Je 46:21
Someone is **c**, like an eagle.................. Je 48:40

C

a stormy wind c from the north............... Eze 1:4
say, "The terrible day is c."..................... Eze 30:2
The time I talked about is c. .... Eze 39:8
God of Israel c from the east................ Eze 43:2
and I saw water c out from under .... Eze 47:1
a holy angel c down from heaven. .... Da 4:13
a human being c on the clouds .... Da 7:13
the east, c from the desert, ... Hos 13:15
the LORD's day of judging is c; .... Joe 2:1
efforts to stop them and keep c. .... Joe 2:8
The days are c when I will cause .... Am 8:11
The time is c when there will be............. Am 9:13
day of judging is c soon to all................ Ob 1:15
the LORD is c out of his place; .... Mic 1:3
he is c down to walk on the tops .... Mic 1:3
destroyer is c to attack you, ... Nah 2:1
s right hand is c around to you. .... Hab 2:16
is c from Teman; the Holy One .... Hab 3:3
LORD's day of judging is c soon; .... Zph 1:14
am c, and I will live among you,............. Zch 2:10
of judging is c when the wealth .... Zch 14:1
There is a day c that will burn .... Mal 4:1
away from God's c punishment?............. Mt 3:7
there is one c after me who is .... Mt 3:11
God's Spirit c down on him like .... Mt 3:16
Son of Man c with his kingdom .... Mt 16:28
Elijah is c and that he will .... Mt 17:11
and stories of wars that are c, ... Mt 24:6
see the Son of Man c on clouds .... Mt 24:30
time of night a thief was c, ... Mt 24:43
cried out, 'The bridegroom is c! .... Mt 25:6
and c on clouds in the sky." .... Mt 26:64
There is one c after me who is .... Mk 1:7
as Jesus was c up out of the .... Mk 1:10
That kingdom is c! Praise to God .... Mk 11:10
and stories of wars that are c, ... Mk 13:7
the Son of Man c in clouds with .... Mk 13:26
was c from the fields to the.................... Mk 15:21
ready for the c of the Lord." .... Lk 1:17
away from God's c punishment?............. Lk 3:7
there is one c who is greater .... Lk 3:16
and people were c to Jesus from .... Lk 8:4
the boy was c, the demon threw .... Lk 9:42
the time was c near for Jesus to .... Lk 9:51
knew what time a thief was c, ... Lk 12:39
you see clouds c up in the west, ... Lk 12:54
God's kingdom is c, but not in a .... Lk 17:20
widow who kept c to this judge, ... Lk 18:3
As he was c close to Jerusalem, ... Lk 19:37
the Son of Man c in a cloud with .... Lk 21:27
from Cyrene, was c in from the .... Lk 23:26
The time is c when people will .... Lk 23:29
c to Jesus and offering him some .... Lk 23:36
to all was c into the world! .... Jn 1:9
day John saw Jesus c toward him. .... Jn 1:29
saw Nathanael c toward him, ... Jn 1:47
going up and c down' on the Son .... Jn 1:51
The time is c when neither in .... Jn 4:21
"I know that the Messiah is c." .... Jn 4:25
Jesus did after c from Judea to .... Jn 4:54
While I am c to the water, ... Jn 5:7
time is c when all who are dead .... Jn 5:28
saw a large crowd c toward him, ... Jn 6:5
who is c into the world." .... Jn 6:14
on the water, c toward the boat. .... Jn 6:19
is c, when no one can work. .... Jn 9:4
When the worker sees a wolf c, ... Jn 10:12
Martha heard that Jesus was c, ... Jn 11:20
of God, the One c to the world." .... Jn 11:27
other, "Is he c to the Feast? .... Jn 11:56
Your king is c, sitting on the .... Jn 12:15
going, but I am c back to you.' .... Jn 14:28
the ruler of this world is c. .... Jn 14:30

time is c when those who kill .... Jn 16:2
I am c to you now. But I pray .... Jn 17:13
and something c down that looked........... Ac 10:11
very hard time is c to the whole .... Ac 11:28
He is c later, and I am not .... Ac 13:25
the One who was c in the future. .... Rm 5:14
wrong for the c of Christ; .... Php 1:10
and kind. The Lord is c soon. .... Php 4:5
to say about the c of our Lord 2Th 2:1
and by his c and his kingdom: 2Ti 4:1
hope and the c of the glory .... Tit 2:13
of the new world that was c, ... Heb 2:5
when Abraham c back after .... Heb 7:1
the time is c, says the Lord, ... Heb 8:8
the good things c in the future; .... Heb 10:1
even more as you see the day c. .... Heb 10:25
The One who is c will come and............. Heb 10:37
they saw them c far in the .... Heb 11:13
c from lips that speak his name............... Heb 13:15
the troubles that are c to you.................... Jam 5:1
because the Lord is c soon...................... Jam 5:8
the grace that was c to you. 1Pe 1:10
the powerful c of our Lord Jesus 2Pe 1:16
them long ago is still c, ... 2Pe 2:3
forward to the c of the day of 2Pe 3:12
that the enemy of Christ is c, ... 1Jn 2:18
which you have heard is c, ... 1Jn 4:3
Lord is c with many thousands .... Jud 1:14
He is c to punish all who are .... Jud 1:15
the One who is and was and is c, ... Rev 1:4
Jesus is c with the clouds, ... Rev 1:7
the One who is and was and is c. .... Rev 1:8
I am c soon. Continue strong in .... Rev 3:11
He was, he is, and he is c." .... Rev 4:8
like a voice c from the middle.................. Rev 6:6
another angel c up from the east .... Rev 7:2
sulfur c out of their mouths. .... Rev 9:17
powerful angel c down from .... Rev 10:1
The third trouble is c soon. .... Rev 11:14
I saw a beast c up out of the .... Rev 13:1
I heard a voice c from the altar .... Rev 16:7
like frogs c out of the mouth .... Rev 16:13
another angel c down from heaven .... Rev 18:1
I saw an angel c down from .... Rev 20:1
Listen! I am c soon! Blessed is .... Rev 22:7
true, says, "Yes, I am c soon." .... Rev 22:20

COMMAND

him so he would c his children .... Ge 18:19
Joseph gave a c to the servant .... Ge 44:1
Israel gave them a c and said,................ Ge 49:29
gave this c before he died. .... Ge 50:16
the king gave a c to the slave .... Ex 5:6
brother everything that I c you, ... Ex 7:2
must keep this c as a law for .... Ex 12:24
C the Israelites to start moving. .... Ex 14:15
C the people of Israel to bring .... Ex 27:20
Obey the things I c you today, ... Ex 34:11
Moses sent this c throughout the .... Ex 36:6
Give this c to Aaron and the .... Le 6:9
priest will c that two living .... Le 14:4
I give this c to the people of .... Le 17:14
my c not to do these hateful .... Le 18:30
the LORD's c to be made clear .... Le 24:12
Moses obeyed the c of the LORD .... Nu 3:51
the c the LORD gave Moses. .... Nu 8:3
This c is for the Levites. .... Nu 8:24
camped, and at his c they moved. .... Nu 9:23
acted against my c at the waters .... Nu 20:24
Moses obeyed the LORD's c. .... Nu 20:27
acted against my c in the Desert .... Nu 27:14
will do what you, our master, c. .... Nu 32:25
At the LORD's c Moses recorded .... Nu 33:2

is the LORD's **c** to Zelophehad's.............. Nu 36:6
You would not obey the LORD's **c**............. Dt 1:43
Then I gave this **c** to Joshua: .... Dt 3:21
obey every **c** I give you today................. Dt 8:1
I **c** you to give freely to your .... Dt 15:11
Do exactly as I **c**, and do not .... Dt 28:14
LORD gave this **c** to Joshua son .... Dt 31:23
and **c** your children to obey .... Dt 32:46
Anything you **c** us to do, we will .... Jos 1:16
C the priests to bring the Ark................. Jos 4:16
as I had Moses **c** you to do..................... Jos 20:2
obeyed this **c** of the LORD and .... Jos 21:3
You have rejected the LORD's **c**.............. 1Sa 15:23
the army under the **c** of Abishai, ... 2Sa 10:10
why did you ignore the LORD's **c**? 2Sa 12:9
did not obey the LORD's **c**.................... 1Ki 11:10
"Who will **c** the main army?" 1Ki 20:14
of Jezreel obeyed Jezebel's **c**, ... 1Ki 21:11
and Obadiah was second in **c**. 1Ch 12:9
will obey every **c** you give." 1Ch 28:21
I may **c** the locusts to destroy 2Ch 7:13
We obey the **c** of the LORD our 2Ch 13:11
At the king's **c**, the messengers 2Ch 30:6
soon as the king's **c** went out to 2Ch 31:5
He gave a **c** to the seven eunuchs .... Est 1:10
not obeyed the **c** of King Xerxes, ... Est 1:15
At his **c** they swirl around over .... Job 37:12
sky was made at the LORD's **c**. .... Ps 33:6
Lord gave the **c**, and a great .... Ps 68:11
Give the **c** to save me, because .... Ps 71:3
But he gave a **c** to the clouds .... Ps 78:23
But at your **c**, the water rushed .... Ps 104:7
God gave the **c** and healed them, ... Ps 107:20
He gives a **c** to the earth, ... Ps 147:15
Then he gives a **c**, and it melts. .... Ps 147:18
they were created by his **c**. .... Ps 148:5
I say and remember what I **c** you. .... Pr 2:1
obeys the king's **c** will be safe. .... Ec 8:5
I will **c** the clouds not to rain .... Is 5:6
so I **c** Assyria to fight against .... Is 10:6
At his **c** evil people will be .... Is 11:4
A **c** here, a command there. .... Is 28:10
has given the **c**, so his Spirit .... Is 34:16
them everything I **c** you to say. .... Je 1:17
me and do everything I **c** you. .... Je 11:4
and that **c** has been obeyed. .... Je 35:14
the LORD's **c** to stay in Judah. .... Je 43:4
come by the **c** of the Most High .... La 3:38
I will **c** the grain to come and .... Eze 36:29
The king's **c** was very strict, ... Da 3:22
that no law or **c** given by the .... Da 6:15
A **c** will come to rebuild .... Da 9:25
Then you **c** your husbands,................... Am 4:1
I will **c** a snake to bite them. .... Am 9:3
By **c** of the king and his .... Jnh 3:7
The LORD has given you this **c**, ... Nah 1:14
Priests, this **c** is for you. .... Mal 2:1
not to obey that **c** will be the .... Mt 5:19
and I have soldiers under my **c**. .... Mt 8:9
got up and gave a **c** to the wind .... Mt 8:26
then **c** me to come to you on the.............. Mt 14:28
to obey God's **c** so that you can .... Mt 15:3
did Moses give a **c** for a man to .... Mt 19:7
the first and most important **c**. .... Mt 22:38
I **c** you by the power of the .... Mt 26:63
I **c** you in God's name not to .... Mk 5:7
I **c** you to come out of this boy .... Mk 9:25
"What did Moses **c** you to do?" .... Mk 10:3
The second **c** is this: ' .... Mk 12:31
But you only need to **c** it, ... Lk 7:7
got up and gave a **c** to the wind .... Lk 8:24
gave a strong **c** to the evil .... Lk 9:42
I give you a new **c**: .... Jn 13:34

This is my **c**: Love each other as.............. Jn 15:12
This is my **c**: Love each other. .... Jn 15:17
I **c** you to come out of her!" .... Ac 16:18
had not sinned by breaking a **c**,............. Rm 5:14
The **c** was meant to bring life, ... Rm 7:10
And by the **c** of the eternal God .... Rm 16:26
I give this **c** for the married 1Co 7:10
writing to you is the Lord's **c**................. 1Co 14:37
is made complete in this one **c**: .... Gal 5:14
The **c** says, "Honor your father .... Eph 6:2
down from heaven with a loud **c**, ... 1Th 4:16
Jesus Christ we **c** you to stay 2Th 3:6
c those people and beg them in 2Th 3:12
by the **c** of God our Savior and 1Ti 1:1
purpose of this **c** is for people 1Ti 1:5
C and teach these things. 1Ti 4:11
of Christ Jesus, I give you a **c**. 1Ti 6:13
C those who are rich with things 1Ti 6:17
give you a **c** in the presence of 2Ti 4:1
preached by the **c** of God our .... Tit 1:3
the people every **c** in the law. .... Heb 9:19
made by God's **c** so what we see .... Heb 11:3
They did not want to hear the **c**:............ Heb 12:20
to obey even one **c** is guilty of .... Jam 2:10
and remember the **c** our Lord and 2Pe 3:2
writing a new **c** to you but an 1Jn 2:7
And God gave us this **c**: 1Jn 4:21
is not a new **c** but is the same............... 2Jn 1:5
the beginning, his **c** is this: 2Jn 1:6
given power to **c** all who will .... Rev 13:15

COMMANDED

The LORD God **c** him, "You may eat .... Ge 2:16
from which I **c** you not to eat................ Ge 3:17
did everything that God **c** him. .... Ge 6:22
female, just as God had **c** Noah............. Ge 7:9
Then the king **c** his men to make .... Ge 12:20
was eight days old as God had **c**. .... Ge 21:4
Jacob and blessed him and **c** him, ... Ge 28:1
He **c** the doctors who served him .... Ge 50:2
sons did as their father **c**. .... Ge 50:12
So the king **c** all his people, ... Ex 1:22
which the LORD had **c** him to do. .... Ex 4:28
but we are **c** to make bricks. .... Ex 5:16
He **c** them to lead the Israelites .... Ex 6:13
as the LORD **c** Moses and Aaron .... Ex 12:28
did what the LORD had **c** Moses. .... Ex 16:34
words the LORD had **c** him to say........... Ex 19:7
Bread in the way I **c** you. .... Ex 23:15
things that I **c** you to do to .... Ex 29:35
all these things I have **c** you: .... Ex 31:6
made without yeast as I **c** you. .... Ex 34:18
This is what the LORD has **c**: .... Ex 35:4
the Ark, just as the LORD **c** him. .... Ex 40:21
the LORD has **c** not to be done, ... Le 4:2
the day he **c** the Israelites to .... Le 7:38
Moses did as the LORD **c** him, ... Le 8:4
Moses had **c** them to bring, ... Le 9:5
fire Moses had **c** them to use .... Le 10:1
goat in a holy place, as I **c**!" .... Le 10:18
'This is what the LORD has **c**................... Le 17:2
everything the LORD **c** Moses. .... Nu 2:34
obeyed what the LORD **c** him. .... Nu 17:11
Eleazar did as the LORD **c** Moses. .... Nu 31:31
The LORD **c** these men to divide .... Nu 34:29
The LORD **c** you, our master .... Nu 36:2
as the LORD our God **c** us." .... Dt 1:41
your God has **c** you not to do................ Dt 4:23
living as he has **c** you and .... Dt 8:6
to do everything I have **c** you................ Dt 12:32
The LORD **c** Moses to make an .... Dt 29:1
just as the LORD had **c** Joshua. .... Jos 4:8
destroy everything as I **c** you.................. Jos 7:12

C

to obey everything c in the Book .... Jos 23:6
do everything I have c her." .... Jdg 13:14
to work, Boaz c his workers, ... Ru 2:15
So David c his men to kill Recab 2Sa 4:12
So David did what the LORD c. 2Sa 5:25
whom I c to take care of my 2Sa 7:7
be afraid, because I have c you! 2Sa 13:28
men killed Amnon as Absalom c, ... 2Sa 13:29
Joab c one-third of the men. 2Sa 18:2
But the king c Joab and the 2Sa 24:4
him to do, just as the LORD c. 2Sa 24:19
King Solomon c them to cut large 1Ki 5:17
obey all I have c and keep my 1Ki 9:4
because he had c Solomon not to 1Ki 11:10
The LORD had c the man of God to 1Ki 13:2
LORD c me not to eat or drink 1Ki 13:9
and I have c ravens to bring you 1Ki 17:4
I have c a widow there to take 1Ki 17:9
Jehoiada the priest had c. 2Ki 11:9
The LORD had c: "Parents must 2Ki 14:6
King Ahaz c Uriah the priest, ... 2Ki 16:15
Then the king of Assyria c, ... 2Ki 17:27
The king c Hilkiah the high 2Ki 23:4
The LORD c this to happen to the 2Ki 24:3
did as God c, and he and his 1Ch 14:16
Then the LORD c the angel to put 1Ch 21:27
feast days c by the LORD our 2Ch 2:4
obey all I have c and keep my 2Ch 7:17
as David, the man of God, had c. 2Ch 8:14
Jehoshaphat c them, "You must 2Ch 19:9
joy and singing as David had c. 2Ch 23:18
King Joash c that a box for 2Ch 24:8
King Hezekiah c the priests, ... 2Ch 29:21
the Passover as the law c. 2Ch 30:5
Then Hezekiah c the priests to 2Ch 31:11
over the fire as they were c, ... 2Ch 35:13
of the LORD, as King Josiah c. 2Ch 35:16
all the festivals c by the LORD. .... Ezr 3:5
the king of Persia, c us to do." .... Ezr 4:3
God of Israel had c and as kings .... Ezr 6:14
as David, the man of God, had c. .... Ne 12:24
as David had c his son Solomon. .... Ne 12:45
'King Xerxes c Queen Vashti to .... Est 1:17
just as Mordecai had c her. .... Est 2:20
The King c Haman, "Go quickly. .... Est 6:10
the king had c was to be done .... Est 9:1
He c, and it appeared. .... Ps 33:9
he c our ancestors to teach .... Ps 78:5
He c the Red Sea, and it dried .... Ps 106:9
The rules you c are right and .... Ps 119:138
myself have c those people whom .... Is 13:3
because the LORD has c it. .... Is 24:3
and I c all the armies in the .... Is 45:12
sacrifices, something I never c. .... Je 7:31
I c them to obey the agreement, ... Je 11:8
holy day, as I c your ancestors. .... Je 17:22
the LORD had c him to say, ... Je 26:8
did not do everything you c. .... Je 32:23
Then King Zedekiah c Ebed-Melech .... Je 38:10
Do everything I c you!" .... Je 50:21
The LORD c the people of Jacob .... La 1:17
his word that he c long ago. .... La 2:17
"I have done just as you c me." .... Eze 9:11
When the LORD c the man dressed .... Eze 10:6
I did these things as I was c. .... Eze 12:7
morning I did as I had been c. .... Eze 24:18
I prophesied as the LORD c me. .... Eze 37:10
honored him and c that an .... Da 2:46
Then he c some of the strongest .... Da 3:20
High God has c these things to .... Da 4:24
Then the king c that the men who .... Da 6:24
your bow and c many arrows to be .... Hab 3:9
I c my words and laws to my .... Zch 1:6

the gift Moses c for people who .... Mt 8:4
Jesus c them not to tell anyone .... Mt 17:9
c the demon inside the boy. .... Mt 17:18
field, as the Lord c me." .... Mt 27:10
Jesus c the evil spirit, "Be .... Mk 1:25
stood up and c the wind and said .... Mk 4:39
This is what Jesus c them: .... Mk 6:8
Jesus c the people not to tell .... Mk 7:36
Jesus c them not to tell anyone .... Mk 9:9
the Lord c and were without .... Lk 1:6
the law of the Lord c, ... Lk 2:39
Jesus c the evil spirit, "Be .... Lk 4:35
for your healing, as Moses c. .... Lk 5:14
I did what you c, but we still .... Lk 14:22
for doing what his master c. .... Lk 17:9
rested, as the law of Moses c. .... Lk 23:56
is what my Father c me to do." .... Jn 10:18
Then the officer c the chariot .... Ac 8:38
the Lord has c you to tell us." .... Ac 10:33
because Claudius c that all Jews .... Ac 18:2
seat and c that the man be .... Ac 25:17
really against what God has c. .... Rm 13:2
the Lord has c that those who 1Co 9:14
Do what you were c to do without 1Ti 6:14
that God c you to obey." .... Heb 9:20
love each other, just as he c. 1Jn 3:23
of truth, as the Father c us. 2Jn 1:4
living the way God c us to live. 2Jn 1:6

COMMANDER

have come as the c of the LORD's .... Jos 5:14
The c of the LORD's army .... Jos 5:15
you made me c of these people, ... Jdg 9:29
leader and c of their army. .... Jdg 11:11
The c of his army was Abner son 1Sa 14:50
Saul asked Abner, c of the army, ... 1Sa 17:55
Joab was c of all the army of 2Sa 20:23
Joab, the c of David's army, ... 1Ki 11:15
Naaman was c of the army of the 2Ki 5:1
Assyria sent out his supreme c, ... 2Ki 18:17
Then the c stood and shouted 2Ki 18:28
The c of the king's special 2Ki 25:15
become the c over all my army. 1Ch 11:6
so he became the c of the army. 1Ch 11:6
He became their c even though he 1Ch 11:21
Zebadiah took his place as c, ... 1Ch 27:7
Joab was the c of the king's 1Ch 27:34
Adnah was the c of three hundred 2Ch 17:14
was the c of two hundred 2Ch 17:15
Hananiah, the c of the palace, ... Ne 7:2
Ants have no c, no leader or .... Pr 6:7
sent a military c to Ashdod to. .... Is 20:1
the c attacked and captured it. .... Is 20:1
Then the c stood and shouted .... Is 36:13
They didn't answer the c at all, ... Is 36:21
a ruler and c of many nations. .... Is 55:4
c of the king's special guards, ... Je 39:9
Nebuzaradan, c of the guards, ... Je 40:1
Choose a c to lead the army .... Je 51:27
led by the c of the king's .... Je 52:14
together to make you their c. .... Eze 38:7
the c of the king's guards, ... Da 2:14
equal to God, the C of heaven's .... Da 8:11
But a c will put an end to the .... Da 11:18
with their c and the guards .... Jn 18:12
The c went to Paul and arrested .... Ac 21:33
The c said, "Do you speak Greek? .... Ac 21:37
The c was frightened because he .... Ac 22:29
The c took Paul's chains off. .... Ac 22:30
When c Lysias comes here, ... Ac 24:22

COMMANDERS

the c over a thousand men, ... Nu 31:14
gold from the c of a thousand .... Nu 31:54

He said to the **c** of his army, ... Jos 10:24
heart is with the **c** of Israel. .... Jdg 5:9
group of Makir, the **c** came down. .... Jdg 5:14
of your sons **c** over thousands 1Sa 8:12
David make you **c** over thousands 1Sa 22:7
the Philistine **c** were angry with 1Sa 29:4
orders to the **c** about Absalom. 2Sa 18:5
Joab and the **c** of the army,..................... 2Sa 24:4
He killed the two **c** of Israel's 1Ki 2:5
chariot **c**, and drivers. 1Ki 9:22
When these **c** saw Jehoshaphat, ... 1Ki 22:32
The **c** over a hundred men obeyed 2Ki 11:9
became **c** in David's army. 1Ch 12:21
to Joab and **c** of the troops, ... 1Ch 21:2
captains, **c** of his chariots 2Ch 8:9
of Aram ordered his chariot **c**, ... 2Ch 18:30
God made the chariot **c** turn away 2Ch 18:31
and army **c** decided to cut 2Ch 32:3
officers and **c** helped Hezekiah. 2Ch 32:3
Assyria's army **c** to attack Judah 2Ch 33:11
the shouts of **c** and the battle .... Job 39:25
Their **c** will be terrified when .... Is 31:9
one of his **c** will become even .... Da 11:5
leaders, the **c** of his army, ... Mk 6:21

COMMANDING

must do everything I am **c** you. .... Dt 12:14
That is why I am **c** this to you............... Dt 15:15
is why I am **c** you to do this. .... Dt 24:18
Jesus was **c** the evil spirit .... Lk 8:29
I am not **c** you to give. 2Co 8:8

COMMANDMENTS

Agreement—the Ten **C**—on the stone .... Ex 34:28
about his Agreement, the Ten **C**. .... Dt 4:13
the Ten **C** that he had told you .... Dt 10:4
and to obey his teachings and **c**.............. 2Ch 14:4

COMMANDS

did what I said and obeyed my **c**, ... Ge 26:5
you obey all his **c** and keep his .... Ex 15:26
to obey my **c** and teachings? .... Ex 16:28
If you do this as God **c** you, ... Ex 18:23
who love me and obey my **c**. .... Ex 20:6
and the **c** I have written to .... Ex 24:12
The **c** were written on both sides .... Ex 32:15
written the **c** on the tablets. .... Ex 32:16
them all the **c** that the LORD had .... Ex 34:32
If you don't obey the LORD's **c**, ... Le 8:35
The LORD has given me these **c**." .... Le 8:35
Remember my **c** and obey them; .... Le 22:31
my laws and **c** and obey them, ... Le 26:3
These are the **c** the LORD gave to .... Le 27:34
are the LORD's **c** given to you .... Nu 15:23
will remember to obey all my **c**, ... Nu 15:40
the laws and **c** that the LORD................ Nu 36:13
to the laws and **c** I will teach .... Dt 4:1
those who love me and obey my **c**........... Dt 5:10
these **c** I give you today. .... Dt 6:6
you disobey the **c** of the LORD .... Dt 11:28
Keep all the **c** I have given you .... Dt 27:1
You have also obeyed all my **c**. .... Jos 22:2
keep the LORD's **c** as their .... Jdg 2:22
would obey the **c** the LORD had.............. Jdg 3:4
the God of Israel, **c** you: ' .... Jdg 4:6
and if you turn against his **c**, ... 1Sa 12:15
gave his son Solomon his last **c**............... 1Ki 2:1
following the **c** his father David 1Ki 3:3
If you obey all my laws and **c**, ... 1Ki 6:12
obey my laws and **c** as David did, ... 1Ki 11:38
he obeyed the **c** the LORD had 2Ki 18:6
of Solomon's **c** to the priests 2Ch 8:15
We have disobeyed your **c** .... Ezr 9:10
holy Sabbath and gave them **c**, ... Ne 9:14
He **c** the sun not to shine and .... Job 9:7

lightning and **c** it to strike its .... Job 36:32
the one that **c** the eagle to fly .... Job 39:27
have obeyed your **c**, so I have.................. Ps 17:4
The **c** of the LORD are pure; .... Ps 19:8
Your **c** led Jacob's people to .... Ps 44:4
the LORD, who want what he **c**................ Ps 112:1
be ashamed when I study your **c**. .... Ps 119:6
Don't let me break your **c**. .... Ps 119:10
Your **c** make me wiser than my .... Ps 119:98
I love your **c** more than the.................... Ps 119:127
teaching, but keep my **c** in mind. .... Pr 3:1
Keep my **c** and you will live. .... Pr 4:4
your father's **c**, and don't .... Pr 6:20
These **c** are like a lamp; .... Pr 6:23
what I say, and treasure my **c**. .... Pr 7:1
Obey my **c**, and you will live. .... Pr 7:2
who obey the **c** protect .... Pr 19:16
and obey his **c**, because this is .... Ec 12:13
He **c** that Canaan's strong, ... Is 23:11
that obeys the **c** of its God. .... Is 58:2
and give them **c** only about burnt .... Je 7:22
If you carefully obey these **c**, ... Je 22:4
have obeyed the **c** of your .... Je 35:18
it happen unless the Lord **c** it. .... La 3:37
who love you and obey your **c**. .... Da 9:4
you, your **c**, and your laws..................... Da 9:5
the LORD and did not keep his **c**; .... Am 2:4
obeys the **c** and teaches other................ Mt 5:19
have life forever, obey the **c**." .... Mt 19:17
The man asked, "Which **c**?" .... Mt 19:18
prophets depend on these two **c**." .... Mt 22:40
He even gives **c** to evil spirits, ... Mk 1:27
stopped following the **c** of God, ... Mk 7:8
You know the **c**: 'You must not .... Mk 10:19
These **c** are more important than .... Mk 12:33
and power he **c** evil spirits,..................... Lk 4:36
Who is this that **c** even the wind .... Lk 8:25
and have always obeyed your **c**. .... Lk 15:29
all these **c** since I was a boy. .... Lk 18:21
law of Moses **c** that we stone to .... Jn 8:5
comes from what the Father **c**. .... Jn 12:50
you love me, you will obey my **c**. .... Jn 14:15
you obey my **c**, you will remain .... Jn 15:10
He received **c** from God that give .... Ac 7:38
they freely do what the law **c**,................. Rm 2:14
that the law's **c** are for those .... Rm 3:19
All these **c** and all others are .... Rm 13:9
thing is obeying God's **c**............................ 1Co 7:19
Jewish law had many **c** and rules, ... Eph 2:15
are only human **c** and teachings. .... Col 2:22
stories and the **c** of people who .... Tit 1:14
all sacrifices that the law **c**. .... Heb 10:8
breaking all the **c** in that law. .... Jam 2:10
does not obey God's **c** is a liar, ... 1Jn 2:4
we obey God's **c** and do what 1Jn 3:22
Loving God means obeying his **c**. 1Jn 5:3
who obey God's **c** and who have .... Rev 12:17
must obey God's **c** and keep their .... Rev 14:12

COMMITTED

a rebel and had **c** murder during .... Mk 15:7

COMMON

made silver as **c** as stones and 1Ki 10:27
trees as **c** as the fig trees....................... 1Ki 10:27
on the graves of the **c** people................... 2Ki 23:6
made silver as **c** as stones and 2Ch 9:27
and the **c** people so I could .... Ne 7:5
and **c** people will not respect .... Is 3:5
and the **c** people will die of.................... Is 5:13
to **c** people and priests, to .... Is 24:2
people and **c** people will die .... Je 16:6
C people gathered, and drunkards .... Eze 23:42
in each person, for the **c** good. 1Co 12:7

C

COMMUNITY

Tell the whole c of Israel that .... Ex 12:3
be cut off from the c of Israel. .... Ex 12:19
whole Israelite c grumbled to .... Ex 16:2
to the whole of the Israelites .... Ex 16:9
Israelite c left the Desert...................... Ex 17:1
the Israelite c together and .... Ex 35:1
members of the c who were .... Ex 38:25
sin offering for the whole c. .... Le 4:21
person in the c sins by accident .... Le 4:27
leaders chosen by the c, ... Nu 16:2
died and were gone from the c. .... Nu 16:33
the c must judge between the .... Nu 35:24
member of the c of the returned.............. Ezr 10:8
person off from the c of Israel. .... Mal 2:12

COMPANION

like me, my c and good friend. .... Ps 55:13

COMPANIONS

So my c led me into Damascus. .... Ac 22:11

COMPANY

keeps c with those who do evil .... Job 34:8
I hate the c of evil people, ... Ps 26:5

COMPARE

How can I c what I did with what .... Jdg 8:3
from Cush cannot c to wisdom; .... Job 28:19
Can you c God to anything? .... Is 40:18
Can you c me to anyone? .... Is 46:5
What can I c you to? .... La 2:13
After ten days c how we look .... Da 1:13
What can I c God's kingdom with?........... Lk 13:20
do not dare to c ourselves with 2Co 10:12
actions and not c himself with .... Gal 6:4

COMPARED

the earth, and c to him, people .... Is 40:22
now are nothing c to the great .... Rm 8:18
glory when it is c to the much 2Co 3:10
are worth nothing c with the .... Php 3:8

COMPARING

is true by c you with others 2Co 8:8

COMPASS

uses a line and a c to draw on .... Is 44:13

COMPETE

All those who c in the games use 1Co 9:25

COMPLAIN

these evil people c about me? .... Nu 14:27
gathered to c against Moses .... Nu 16:42
Then they will c to the LORD .... Dt 15:9
may c to the LORD about you, ... Dt 24:15
or brothers come to us and c, ... Jdg 21:22
will c because I am so unhappy. .... Job 7:11
I will c without holding back;................. Job 10:1
who c will accept being taught. .... Is 29:24
People of Jacob, why do you c? .... Is 40:27
Why do you c to me? .... Je 2:29
No one should c when he is .... La 3:39
Pharisees began to c to Jesus' .... Lk 5:30
teachers of the law began to c: .... Lk 15:2
people saw this and began to c, ... Lk 19:7
people began to c about Jesus .... Jn 6:41
Do not c as some of them did; 1Co 10:10
do not c against each other or .... Jam 5:9
These people c and blame others, ... Jud 1:16

COMPLAINED

Abraham c to Abimelech about .... Ge 21:25
foremen went to the king and c,.............. Ex 5:15
Now the people c to the LORD .... Nu 11:1
the Israelites c against Moses................. Nu 14:2
and their wives c loudly against .... Ne 5:1

c to the man who owned the land. .... Mt 20:11
have c to me about him .... Ac 25:24

COMPLAINING

soon all the Israelites began c. .... Nu 11:4
the grumbling and c of these .... Nu 14:27
from always c against you." .... Nu 17:5
with a quarreling c wife. .... Pr 21:19
but a c fool is worse than .... Pr 27:3
answered, "Stop c to each other. .... Jn 6:43
his followers were c about this, ... Jn 6:61
you if you were c about a crime .... Ac 18:14
everything without c or arguing. .... Php 2:14
homes to each other, without c. 1Pe 4:9

COMPLAINS

Who fights? Who c? Who has................. Pr 23:29

COMPLAINT

Your c is not against Aaron." .... Nu 16:11
I say, 'I will forget my c; .... Job 9:27
My c is still bitter today. .... Job 23:2
when they had a c against me, ... Job 31:13
You have heard my c; .... Ps 9:4
God, listen to my c. .... Ps 64:1
learn how God will answer my c. .... Hab 2:1
to judge a c between believers 1Co 6:5

COMPLAINTS

I have heard many c against the.............. Ge 18:20
returned and spread c among all .... Nu 14:36
I heard their c about these .... Ne 5:6
and tells the LORD his c. .... Ps 101:8

COMPLETE

But c the full week of the .... Ge 29:27
Tamar he did not c the sex act. .... Ge 38:9
Joab sent David a c account of 2Sa 11:18
them and have c faith in me, ... 1Ki 2:4
she had to c twelve months of .... Est 2:12
the land and will enjoy c peace. .... Ps 37:11
He will c the things the LORD .... Is 53:10
Your punishment is c, Jerusalem. .... La 4:22
this Temple, and he will c it. .... Zch 4:9
judge with truth and c fairness. .... Zch 8:16
And you will c the sin that your .... Mt 23:32
thing is that I c my mission, ... Ac 20:24
God will be the c ruler over 1Co 15:28
we pray that you will become c. 2Co 13:9
to make it c by your own power .... Gal 3:3
whole law is made c in this one .... Gal 5:14
on working to c your salvation .... Php 2:12
c all the duties of a servant 2Ti 4:5
be perfect and c and will have .... Jam 1:4

COMPLETED

and when he had c the week with .... Ge 29:28
When the sacrifices were c, ... 2Ch 29:29
of Jerusalem was c on the .... Ne 6:15

COMPLETELY

second month the land was c dry. .... Ge 8:14
he will force you to leave c. .... Ex 11:1
because I will c destroy the..................... Ex 17:14
man until he is c healed........................ Ex 21:19
Destroy c any person who makes a .... Ex 22:20
altar belongs c to the LORD's................. Ex 30:10
but he will not pull it c off. .... Le 5:8
offering must be c burned to the .... Le 6:22
by a priest must be c burned; .... Le 6:23
a split hoof that is c divided, ... Le 11:7
but the hoofs are not c divided; .... Le 11:26
so much that I c destroy them .... Le 26:44
the Levites are given c to him. .... Nu 3:9
They will be given c to me from .... Nu 8:16
differently and follows me c. .... Nu 14:24
we will c destroy their cities."................. Nu 21:2

or you will be **c** destroyed along .... Dt 7:26
the Dead Sea) was **c** cut off. .... Jos 3:16
had told Joshua to **c** destroy all .... Jos 10:40
They **c** destroyed the city, ... Jdg 1:17
from the rock and **c** burned up .... Jdg 6:21
Abimelech and **c** burn you leaders .... Jdg 9:20
follow the LORD **c** as his father 1Ki 11:4
your family as **c** as fire burns 1Ki 14:10
if I don't **c** destroy Samaria. 1Ki 20:10
said he would **c** destroy Israel 2Ki 14:27
They have **c** defeated every 2Ki 19:11
They followed David **c**. 1Ch 12:33
give yourselves **c** to obeying the 1Ch 22:19
Serve him **c** and willingly, ... 1Ch 28:9
and **c** wipe out all the Jewish .... Est 3:13
and **c** wipe out the army of any .... Est 8:11
feeling **c** safe and comfortable. .... Job 21:23
I wish Job would be tested **c**, ... Job 34:36
they are **c** right. .... Ps 19:9
You want me to be **c** truthful, ... Ps 51:6
destroy them **c**! Then they will .... Ps 59:13
for your Temple **c** controls me. .... Ps 69:9
thought, "We will **c** crush them!" .... Ps 74:8
rejected the people of Israel **c**. .... Ps 78:59
Teach me to respect you **c**. .... Ps 86:11
are powerful and **c** trustworthy. .... Ps 89:8
make people forget about them **c**. .... Ps 109:15
so I said, "I am **c** ruined." .... Ps 116:10
gave your orders to be obeyed **c**. .... Ps 119:4
are right and **c** trustworthy. .... Ps 119:138
close to being **c** ruined in front .... Pr 5:14
follow the LORD understand it **c**. .... Pr 28:5
Her husband trusts her **c**. .... Pr 31:11
Useless! Useless! **C** useless! .... Ec 1:2
can never **c** understand what .... Ec 3:11
would have been **c** destroyed like .... Is 1:9
and they have **c** accepted those .... Is 2:6
destroy the land **c** and fairly. .... Is 10:22
The earth will be **c** empty. .... Is 24:3
the city will be **c** destroyed. .... Is 32:19
and joy will fill them **c**, ... Is 35:10
They have **c** defeated every .... Is 37:11
given myself **c** to you and have .... Is 38:3
against you will vanish **c**. .... Is 41:12
it will be **c** ruined. .... Is 60:12
I will not **c** destroy them. .... Is 65:8
the land become **c** unclean? .... Je 3:1
but I will not **c** destroy it. .... Je 4:27
eaten them up **c** and destroyed .... Je 10:25
they will be carried away **c**. .... Je 13:19
have you **c** rejected the nation .... Je 14:19
I will **c** destroy this city. .... Je 19:8
I will **c** destroy all those .... Je 25:9
but I will not **c** destroy you. .... Je 30:11
I will **c** destroy the many .... Je 46:28
She will be **c** empty. .... Je 50:13
C destroy Babylon and do not .... Je 50:26
God **c** destroyed the cities of .... Je 50:40
or have you **c** rejected us? .... La 5:22
them a desire to respect me **c**, ... Eze 11:19
When the fire has burned it **c**, ... Eze 15:5
will **c** dry up and die when the .... Eze 17:10
will teach you to respect me **c**, ... Eze 36:26
his kingdom will be **c** destroyed. .... Da 7:26
go to destroy **c** many nations .... Da 11:44
country have been **c** unfaithful .... Hos 1:2
they **c** give themselves to being .... Hos 4:18
as oaks—I destroyed them **c**. .... Am 2:9
but I will not **c** destroy Jacob's .... Am 9:8
'We are **c** ruined; .... Mic 3:1
he will **c** destroy Nineveh; .... Nah 1:8
The LORD will **c** destroy anyone .... Nah 1:9
the battle will **c** destroy you. .... Nah 3:15

happen if you **c** obey the LORD .... Zch 6:15
day they will be **c** burned up so .... Mal 4:1
the waves, and it became **c** calm. .... Mt 8:26
your house will be left **c** empty. .... Mt 23:38
stopped, and it became **c** calm. .... Mk 4:39
Everyone was **c** amazed .... Mk 5:42
fell and was **c** destroyed." .... Lk 6:49
Now your house is left **c** empty. .... Lk 13:35
for your Temple **c** controls me." .... Jn 2:17
me so that they will be **c** one. .... Jn 17:23
He was made **c** well because of .... Ac 3:16
The meeting was **c** confused; .... Ac 19:32
things we are **c** victorious .... Rm 8:37
will quickly and **c** punish the .... Rm 9:28
would have been **c** destroyed like .... Rm 9:29
that you be **c** joined together 1Co 1:10
much sadness and giving up **c**. 2Co 2:7
you will **c** destroy each other. .... Gal 5:15
we are **c** free to enter the Most .... Heb 10:19
So give yourselves **c** to God. .... Jam 4:7
you have left before it dies **c**. .... Rev 3:2

COMPOSE
you **c** songs on musical .... Am 6:5

CONCEITED
of Moab are proud and very **c**. .... Is 16:6
are rude and **c** and brag about .... Rm 1:30
They will be **c**, will love 2Ti 3:4

CONCERN
he had great **c** for the honor of .... Nu 25:13
This does not **c** you, sons of 2Sa 16:10
This does not **c** you, sons of 2Sa 19:22
show their **c** and to comfort him. .... Job 2:11
But I had **c** for my holy name, ... Eze 36:21
shouldn't I show **c** for the great .... Jnh 4:11
has shown his **c** for his humble .... Lk 1:48
Lord without **c** for other things 1Co 7:35
day the load of my **c** for all the 2Co 11:28

CONCERNED
and was not **c** about anything .... Ge 39:6
Israel, and he was **c** about them. .... Ex 2:25
I am **c** about their pain, ... Ex 3:7
that the LORD was **c** about them .... Ex 4:31
poor, but the wicked are not **c**. .... Pr 29:7
I am **c** about you; I am on your .... Eze 36:9
the LORD became **c** about his land .... Joe 2:18
You are so **c** for that plant even .... Jnh 4:10

CONCERNS
Only one thing **c** me: .... Php 1:27

CONDEMN
'I will **c** you by your own words, ... Lk 19:22

CONDITION
to the **c** of your cattle. .... Pr 27:23

CONFESS
and he will **c** over it all the .... Le 16:21
the people will **c** their sins .... Le 26:40
C to the LORD, the God of Israel. .... Jos 7:19
Now, **c** it to the LORD, the God .... Ezr 10:11
I **c** the sins we Israelites have .... Ne 1:6
"I will **c** my sins to the LORD," .... Ps 32:5
c my guilt; I am troubled by my .... Ps 38:18
If you **c** and reject them, you .... Pr 28:13
began to **c** openly and tell .... Ac 19:18
everyone will **c** that Jesus .... Php 2:11
C your sins to each other and .... Jam 5:16
But if we **c** our sins, he will 1Jn 1:9
now who do not **c** that Jesus 2Jn 1:7
who does not **c** this is a false 2Jn 1:7

CONFESSED
They **c**, "We have sinned against 1Sa 7:6
You **c** by saying, 'I have killed 2Sa 1:16

They stood and c their sins and .... Ne 9:2
of the day they c their sins .... Ne 9:3
Then I c my sins to you and .... Ps 32:5
They c their sins, and he .... Mt 3:6
They c their sins and were .... Mk 1:5
that life when you c the good 1Ti 6:12
to the hope that we have c, ... Heb 10:23

CONFESSES
But whoever c the Son has the 1Jn 2:23
Every spirit who c that Jesus 1Jn 4:2
Whoever c that Jesus is the Son 1Jn 4:15

CONFESSING
was praying and c and crying .... Ezr 10:1
c my sins and the sins of the .... Da 9:20

CONFESSION
confessed the good c before many 1Ti 6:12
made the good c when he stood 1Ti 6:13

CONFIDENCE
You should have c because you .... Job 4:6

CONFIDENT
They are c and will not be .... Ps 112:8

CONFIDENTLY
house if we c maintain our hope .... Heb 3:6

CONFUSE
us go down and c their language .... Ge 11:7
I will c any people you fight .... Ex 23:27
destroy and c their words, ... Ps 55:9
who do magic. I c even the wise; .... Is 44:25
that time I will c every horse .... Zch 12:4

CONFUSED
is where the LORD c the language .... Ge 11:9
blindness, and a c mind. .... Dt 28:28
The LORD c those armies when .... Jos 10:10
the LORD c Sisera and his army .... Jdg 4:15
so frightened they became c. 1Sa 7:10
They found the Philistines c, ... 1Sa 14:20
of lightning c them with fear. 2Sa 22:15
of lightning c them with fear. .... Ps 18:14
listening is foolish and c. .... Pr 18:13
sights, and your mind will be c. .... Pr 23:33
The LORD has made the leaders c. .... Is 19:14
You are c. You think the clay is .... Is 29:16
his c mind leads him the wrong .... Is 44:20
His royal guests were c. .... Da 5:9
herds of cattle wander around c, ... Joe 1:18
Now they will be c. .... Mic 7:4
women were c and shaking with .... Mk 16:8
that were happening and was c, ... Lk 9:7
will be afraid and c because of .... Lk 21:25
They were all amazed and c, ... Ac 2:12
priests were c and wondered what .... Ac 5:24
The whole city became c. .... Ac 19:29
The meeting was completely c; .... Ac 19:32

CONFUSING
c them until they are destroyed. .... Dt 7:23
But some people are c you; .... Gal 1:7
Whoever is c you with such ideas .... Gal 5:10

CONFUSION
you curses, c, and punishment .... Dt 28:20
the c in the Philistine camp was 1Sa 14:19
but the city of Susa was in c. .... Est 3:15
from the land of gloom and c, ... Job 10:22
laughs at the c in the city, ... Job 39:7
a special day of riots and c. .... Is 22:5
cries of much c and destruction. .... Je 48:3
the day of c is near. .... Eze 7:7
bad name, you city full of c. .... Eze 22:5
will see great c and people .... Am 3:9
of all this c and shouting, ... Ac 21:34

is not a God of c but a God of 1Co 14:33
evil talk, gossip, pride, and c. 2Co 12:20
there will be c and every kind .... Jam 3:16

CONGRATULATE
to greet and c King David for 2Sa 8:10
to greet and c King David for 1Ch 18:10

CONNECT
of acacia wood to c the upright .... Ex 26:26

CONNECTED
all the work c with these items .... Nu 3:26
do everything c with these .... Nu 4:26

CONNECTING
c it to the woven belt so the .... Ex 28:28
the holy vest, c it to the woven .... Ex 39:21

CONQUER
we explored is too large to c. .... Nu 13:32
They will c Edom and Moab, ... Is 11:14
they will c the land of Assyria .... Mic 5:6
you will c our sins. .... Mic 7:19

CONQUERED
Edom will be c, but Israel will .... Nu 24:18
Philistines, c them, and took 2Sa 8:1
surrounded it and c it, ... 2Ki 3:25
Philistines, c them, and took 1Ch 18:1

CONQUERS
is a child of God c the world. 1Jn 5:4
the one who c the world is the 1Jn 5:5

CONSCIENCE
My c will never bother me. .... Job 27:6
c is ruled by the Holy Spirit, ... Rm 9:1
Because their c is weak, when 1Co 8:7
be judged by someone else's c? 1Co 10:29
and I can say it with a clear c: 2Co 1:12
and a good c and a true faith. 1Ti 1:5
With a clear c they must follow 1Ti 3:9
cannot make the c of the .... Heb 9:9
been made free from a guilty c, ... Heb 10:22
are sure that we have a clear c, ... Heb 13:18
Keep a clear c so that those who 1Pe 3:16

CONSCIENCES
And they show this by their c. .... Rm 2:15
liars whose c are destroyed as 1Ti 4:2
and their c have been ruined. .... Tit 1:15
make our c pure from useless .... Heb 9:14

CONSIDER
the LORD does not c guilty and .... Ps 32:2
things you did and c your deeds. .... Ps 77:12
I c everything you have done. .... Ps 143:5
these things or c what would .... Is 47:7
Ask this question, and c it: .... Je 30:6
C how the lilies grow; .... Lk 12:27
gathered to c this problem. .... Ac 15:6
the Lord does not c guilty." .... Rm 4:8
So if you c me your partner, ... Phm 1:17

CONSIDERED
Egyptian people c Moses to be a .... Ex 11:3
of this as I c all that is done .... Ec 8:9
When he c this, he went to the .... Ac 12:12

CONSIDERING
closest neighbor, c the number .... Ex 12:4

CONSIDERS
he c me his enemy. .... Job 33:10

CONSTANT
The LORD has c love for Israel, ... 1Ki 10:9
and c quarrels from those who 1Ti 6:5

CONTAIN

place in heaven cannot **c** you................... 1Ki 8:27
which I have built cannot **c** you................ 2Ch 6:18
words of the wicked **c** nothing .... Pr 10:11

CONTAINED

each of which **c** about seven and 1Ki 10:16
of which **c** about four pounds.................. 1Ki 10:17
each of which **c** about seven and 2Ch 9:15

CONTAINER

Samuel took the **c** of olive oil 1Sa 16:13
priest took the **c** of olive oil 1Ki 1:39

CONTAINERS

table, all its **c**, and the bread .... Ex 39:36
bring in clean **c** to the Temple," .... Is 66:20

CONTAINING

of the Agreement **c** the two stone .... Ex 26:33
to me with anything **c** yeast, ... Ex 34:25
in a clay bowl **c** fresh water. .... Le 14:5
the scroll **c** Jeremiah's words .... Je 36:10

CONTENT

palace that day happy and **c**. .... Est 5:9
will be **c** as if I had eaten the .... Ps 63:5
is better to be **c** with what .... Ec 4:6

CONTENTS

crop and its **c** and throw them .... Le 1:16

CONTEST

the young men have a **c** here." 2Sa 2:14
said, "Yes, let them have a **c**." 2Sa 2:14
takes part in a **c** must obey all 2Ti 2:5

CONTINUAL

the kindness and **c** goodness you .... Ge 32:10
This will be a **c** reminder before.............. Ex 28:29
flour for a **c** grain offering,..................... Le 6:20
incense, the **c** grain offering, ... Nu 4:16
as your share, your **c** portion.................. Nu 18:8
they may have **c** pain in their .... Job 33:19
a happy heart is like a **c** feast. .... Pr 15:15
as bothersome as a **c** dripping on .... Pr 27:15

CONTINUALLY

eyes are on it **c**, and he watches .... Dt 11:12
We will **c** set out the holy bread 2Ch 2:4
New honors will come to me **c**, ... Job 29:20
they rejoice and **c** praise your................. Ps 89:16
My tears flow **c**, without .... La 3:49
violence and made me **c** angry. .... Eze 8:17
c want to do all kinds of evil. .... Eph 4:19
c recall before God our Father 1Th 1:3
Pray **c**, ... 1Th 5:17

CONTINUE

these animals to **c** living on the .... Ge 7:3
Then you may **c** your journey." .... Ge 18:5
was afraid to **c** living in Zoar,.................. Ge 19:30
How can a bush **c** burning without........... Ex 3:3
let them go and **c** to hold them, ... Ex 9:2
to a rule that will **c** from now .... Ex 29:9
them and me that will **c** from now .... Ex 31:16
know you and **c** to please you. .... Ex 33:13
This law will **c** for people .... Le 3:17
This law will **c** forever. .... Le 16:31
and it will **c** from that evening .... Le 23:32
of Israel that will **c** forever.................... Le 24:8
threshing will **c** until the grape .... Le 26:5
are going to **c** doing this to me .... Nu 11:15
them to you and will **c** from now .... Nu 15:23
The girl will **c** to be the man's .... Dt 22:19
man who won't **c** his brother's .... Dt 25:9
but **c** to watch and be ready. .... Jos 8:4
C chasing the enemy and .... Jos 10:19
to **c** to follow him and serve him .... Jos 22:5

You must **c** to follow the LORD .... Jos 23:8
children to **c** their families .... Jdg 21:17
but **c** following closely behind .... Ru 2:8
I hope I can **c** to please you, ... Ru 2:13
Don't **c** bragging, don't speak.................. 1Sa 2:3
make his family **c**, and he will 1Sa 2:35
your kingdom **c** in Israel always, ... 1Sa 13:13
long will you **c** to feel sorry 1Sa 16:1
kingdom will **c** always before me 2Sa 7:16
servant David will **c** before you.............. 2Sa 7:26
priests could not **c** their work, ... 1Ki 8:11
please to keep that promise 1Ki 8:26
son to **c** to rule over one 1Ki 11:36
If the people **c** going to the 1Ki 12:27
servant David will **c** before you.............. 1Ch 17:24
please to keep that promise 2Ch 6:17
because if they **c**, it will hurt .... Ezr 4:22
allow them to **c** living in your................. Est 3:8
who do right will **c** to do right, ... Job 17:9
'We will **c** to trouble Job, ... Job 19:28
their riches will not **c**............................. Job 20:21
you may **c** to make fun of me. .... Job 21:3
and I will **c** to enjoy life.'...................... Job 33:28
C to love those who know you and........... Ps 36:10
God's love will **c** forever........................ Ps 52:1
skulls of those who **c** to sin. .... Ps 68:21
Let peace **c** as long as there is .... Ps 72:7
punishment would **c** forever. .... Ps 81:15
will make your family **c** forever............... Ps 89:4
will **c** forever, like the moon, ... Ps 89:37
They will **c** forever. .... Ps 111:8
their goodness will **c** forever. .... Ps 112:3
All things **c** to this day because .... Ps 119:91
Truth will **c** forever, but lies .... Pr 12:19
only **c** if they are fair .... Pr 16:12
his government will **c** forever. .... Pr 29:14
All things **c** the way they have .... Ec 1:9
God does will **c** forever. .... Ec 3:14
Why should you **c** to be punished?........... Is 1:5
Don't **c** bringing me worthless .... Is 1:13
and will **c** to grow forever .... Is 9:7
They will not **c** to depend on the .... Is 10:20
They will **c** doing evil, even if................ Is 26:10
I will **c** to amaze these people................ Is 29:14
he will not **c** to hide from you, ... Is 30:20
This will **c** until God pours his .... Is 32:15
that salvation will **c** forever. .... Is 45:17
But my salvation will **c** forever, ... Is 51:6
children to **c** his family. .... Is 53:8
their happiness will **c** forever.................. Is 61:7
I will **c** to speak for her; .... Is 62:1
don't **c** to be angry with us; .... Is 64:9
Don't **c** making evil plans. .... Je 4:14
long will you **c** being unclean?" .... Je 13:27
We will **c** to do what we want. .... Je 18:12
long will this **c** in the minds .... Je 23:26
that will **c** forever with you. .... Eze 16:60
The vine will not **c** to grow. .... Eze 17:9
you will not **c** to dishonor my .... Eze 20:39
'Let them **c** their sexual sins .... Eze 23:43
an end, but it will **c** forever. .... Da 2:44
you might **c** to be successful. .... Da 4:27
and war will **c** until the end. .... Da 9:26
he will not **c** to be successful. .... Da 11:12
things will **c** for many days. .... Da 11:33
Should we **c** to do this?"........................ Zch 7:3
my agreement with Levi may **c**,"............... Mal 2:4
They **c** saying things that mean .... Mt 6:7
Then both will **c** to be good." .... Mt 9:17
and his kingdom will not **c**. .... Mt 12:26
How long must I **c** to be patient .... Mt 17:17
family that is divided cannot **c**. .... Mk 3:25
against itself will not **c**. .... Lk 11:17

C

in those homes that c forever..................Lk 16:9
she will c to bother me until ....Lk 18:5
If you c to obey my teaching, ...Jn 8:31
we must c doing the work of the ....Jn 9:4
If we let him c doing these ....Jn 11:48
orders not to c teaching in that ....Ac 5:28
Then we can c to pray and to ....Ac 6:4
children to c his family. ....Ac 8:33
them to c trusting in God's ....Ac 13:43
he did not c with them in the ....Ac 15:38
C talking to people and don't be............Ac 18:9
not only c to do these evil ....Rm 1:32
God will c to be true even when ....Rm 3:4
think we should c sinning so ....Rm 6:1
if you c following in his ....Rm 11:22
of you should c to live the way 1Co 7:17
So these three things c forever: 1Co 13:13
Good News and c strong in it. 1Co 15:1
by it if you c believing what I 1Co 15:2
C strong in the faith. 1Co 16:13
death, and he will c to save us. 2Co 1:10
could not c to look at it. 2Co 3:7
who live would not c to live for 2Co 5:15
are right and will c forever." 2Co 9:9
And I will c doing what I am 2Co 11:12
I must c to brag. It will do no 2Co 12:1
of the Good News or c for you. ....Gal 2:5
every effort to c together in ....Eph 4:3
This work must c until we are ....Eph 4:13
not c living like those who do ....Eph 4:17
am sure he will c it until it is ....Php 1:6
happy, and I will c to be happy. ....Php 1:18
If I c living in my body, I will ....Php 1:22
but I c trying to reach it and ....Php 3:12
So we c to preach Christ to each ....Col 1:28
the Lord, so c to live in him. ....Col 2:6
C praying, keeping alert, and ....Col 4:2
him that you c to be strong 1Th 1:3
and day we c praying with all...............1Th 3:10
about the way you c to be strong 2Th 1:4
stand strong and c to believe 2Th 2:15
teaching will c to spread 2Th 3:1
C to have faith and do what you 1Ti 1:19
c to read the Scriptures to the 1Ti 4:13
C to do those things; 1Ti 4:15
Tell those who c sinning that 1Ti 5:20
C teaching these things, warning 2Ti 2:14
But you should c following the............2Ti 3:14
he could not c being a priest. ....Heb 7:23
are tempted and still c strong, ...Jam 1:12
Creator as they c to do what is 1Pe 4:19
a glory that will c forever. 1Pe 5:10
but we c living in darkness, ...1Jn 1:6
you c to follow what you heard 1Jn 2:24
God's children do not c sinning,...........1Jn 3:9
does not c to follow only his 2Jn 1:9
help them to c their trip in a 3Jn 1:6
kingdom, and in patience to c. ....Rev 1:9
Only c in your loyalty until I ....Rev 2:25
C strong in your faith so no one.............Rev 3:11
is doing evil c to do evil. ....Rev 22:11
whoever is holy c to be holy."..................Rev 22:11

CONTINUED

water c to rise, and the boat ....Ge 7:18
The water c to go down so that ....Ge 8:5
Jacob c his journey and came.................Ge 29:1
Then Israel c his journey and ....Ge 35:21
and he c to be sad about his son ....Ge 37:34
The Israelites c to live in the ....Ge 46:27
time of sorrow c for seven days.................Ge 50:10
Joseph c to live in Egypt with..................Ge 50:22
Hebrew people c to grow in ....Ex 1:20

The people c to bring gifts each ....Ex 36:3
of Sinai and c until the cloud ....Nu 10:12
but you have c to bless them ....Nu 24:10
carrying the Ark c standing in ....Jos 4:10
near Jericho and c to the waters..............Jos 16:1
the Canaanites c to live there. ....Jos 17:12
Canaanites c to live with them. ....Jdg 1:32
and they c chasing the ....Jdg 7:25
And she c to live with Naomi, ...Ru 2:23
but the boy c to serve the LORD. 1Sa 2:11
And the LORD c to show himself 1Sa 3:21
Samuel c as judge of Israel all 1Sa 7:15
commanders c to go out to fight...............1Sa 18:30
and Abishai c chasing Abner.................2Sa 2:24
the tribe of Judah c to follow 1Ki 12:20
fought wars and c to rule the 1Ki 14:19
the prophets c to act like this 1Ki 18:29
The battle c all day..............................1Ki 22:35
so the people c offering 1Ki 22:43
he c to sin like Jeroboam son 2Ki 3:3
So they c to do all the sins 2Ki 17:22
The battle c all day............................2Ch 18:34
But the people c doing wrong. 2Ch 27:2
The people c to offer sacrifices 2Ch 33:17
And it c to the time Darius was ....Ezr 4:5
Jewish elders c to build and ....Ezr 6:14
we c to work with half the men ....Ne 4:21
was wrong, yet c to blame him. ....Job 32:3
But the people c to sin against ....Ps 78:17
but they c to turn against him. ....Ps 106:43
in anger and c to hurt them. ....Is 14:6
have c year after year............................Is 29:1
in anger, but they c to do evil. ....Is 57:17
That is why I have c showing you ....Je 31:3
You have c doing them in Israel ....Je 32:20
She c the prostitution she began ....Eze 23:8
So Daniel c to be the king's ....Da 1:21
the people there have c sinning...............Hos 10:9
As Jesus c walking by Lake ....Mt 4:21
sat there and c watching him....................Mt 27:36
Jesus c looking around to see.................Mk 5:32
Jesus c teaching and said, ...Mk 12:38
of Judea people c talking about ....Lk 1:65
And John c to preach the Good ....Lk 3:18
Jesus sat down and c to teach ....Lk 5:3
But they c to shout, demanding ....Lk 23:23
They all c praying together with..............Ac 1:14
in the morning and c teaching. ....Ac 5:21
Stephen c speaking: ....Ac 7:51
group of believers c to grow. ....Ac 9:31
Peter c to knock, and when they ....Ac 12:16
God's message c to spread and ....Ac 12:24
They c their trip from Perga and ....Ac 13:14
As Paul c talking, Eutychus was..............Ac 20:9
We c our trip from Tyre and ....Ac 21:7
believed God and c hoping, ...Rm 4:18
And it c until the special........................Gal 3:19
c to care about me, but there ....Php 4:10
we have c praying for you, ...Col 1:9
sufferings, but you c strong. ....Heb 10:32
Moses c strong as if he could ....Heb 11:27

CONTINUES

As long as the earth c, planting ....Ge 8:22
agreement that c forever between ....Ge 9:16
a law in Egypt, which c today: ....Ge 47:26
for as long as she c to bleed. ....Le 15:25
He c to be kind to us—both she ....Ru 2:20
for Israel, which c even today. 1Sa 30:25
His love c forever. 1Ch 16:34
he c to obey them, I will make 1Ch 28:7
his love c forever." 2Ch 5:13
his love for Israel c forever." ....Ezr 3:11

but he **c** to be without blame." .... Job 2:3
will say, "Your love **c** forever; .... Ps 89:2
and his goodness **c** to their .... Ps 103:17
His love **c** forever. .... Ps 106:1
and his goodness **c** forever. .... Ps 111:3
His love **c** forever. .... Ps 118:1
it **c** forever in heaven. .... Ps 119:89
goodness **c** forever, and your .... Ps 119:142
His love **c** forever. .... Ps 136:1
LORD, your love **c** forever. .... Ps 138:8
but a good person's family **c**. .... Pr 12:7
he **c** to rule if he is loyal. .... Pr 20:28
and knowledge, it **c** strong...................... Pr 28:2
die, but the earth **c** forever...................... Ec 1:4
His love **c** forever!' .... Je 33:11
an agreement that **c** forever. .... Eze 37:26
and his kingdom **c** for all time. .... Da 4:34
in goodness that **c** forever; .... Da 9:24
If a person **c** to prophesy, ... Zch 13:3
guilty of a sin that **c** forever." .... Mk 3:29
This **c** until today." .... Rm 11:8
and everything **c** through him and .... Rm 11:36
new way which **c** forever has much 2Co 3:11
that as your faith **c** to grow, ... 2Co 10:15
a destruction that **c** forever. 2Th 1:9
children if she **c** in faith,...................... 1Ti 2:15
hope in God and **c** to pray night 1Ti 5:5
hold of the life that **c** forever. 1Ti 6:12
strong foundation **c** to stand. 2Ti 2:19
he **c** being a priest forever. .... Heb 7:3
tenth from Abraham, **c** living, as .... Heb 7:8
of his life, which **c** forever. .... Heb 7:16
living message that **c** forever. 1Pe 1:23
but the world **c** the way it has 2Pe 3:4
that he has life that **c** forever. 1Jn 1:2
anyone who **c** to sin belongs to 1Jn 3:8
But whoever **c** to follow the 2Jn 1:9
the victory and **c** to be obedient .... Rev 2:26

CONTINUING

Jordan River and **c** to the end of .... Jos 13:27
walls were **c** and that the holes .... Ne 4:7
should do while **c** to do those .... Lk 11:42
By **c** to have faith you will save .... Lk 21:19
The word of God was **c** to spread. .... Ac 6:7
by always **c** to do good, live .... Rm 2:7

CONTRACT

we have a **c** with death. .... Is 28:15
your **c** with death will not help .... Is 28:18

CONTRIBUTIONS

that a box for **c** be made. 2Ch 24:8
giving out the **c** made to the 2Ch 31:14

CONTROL

could not **c** himself in front.................... Ge 45:1
them get out of **c** and become................. Ex 32:25
are under your **c**, to do all the .... Nu 18:3
the Spirit of God took **c** of him, ... Nu 24:2
anyone try to **c** others with.................... Dt 18:11
the city, took **c** of it, and .... Jos 8:19
the army had taken **c** of the city.............. Jos 8:21
had **c** of the mountains and the .... Jos 11:16
Joshua took **c** of all the land of .... Jos 11:23
Israelites took **c** of the land .... Jos 12:1
The land was now under their **c**. .... Jos 18:1
and you took **c** of that land. .... Jos 24:8
Take **c** of the Jordan River as .... Jdg 7:24
from Egypt's **c** and from other 1Sa 10:18
he went to take **c** again at the................. 2Sa 8:3
been cities under Hadadezer's **c**. 2Sa 8:8
he was in firm **c** of his kingdom. 1Ki 2:12
I will allow him to **c** one tribe. 1Ki 11:32
Amaziah took **c** of the kingdom, ... 2Ki 14:5

under the **c** of Nebuchadnezzar.............. 1Ch 6:15
been cities under Hadadezer's **c**. 1Ch 18:8
people are in **c** of this land. 1Ch 22:18
Jehoram took **c** of his father's 2Ch 21:4
power to take **c** of the kingdom 2Ch 22:9
put all things under their **c**: .... Ps 8:6
for us and put them under our **c**. .... Ps 47:3
and do not **c** their selfish .... Ps 73:7
the sea and **c** over the rivers .... Ps 89:25
put your enemies under your **c**." .... Ps 110:1
don't let any sin **c** me. .... Ps 119:133
LORD, help me **c** my tongue; .... Ps 141:3
helps me keep my people under **c**. .... Ps 144:2
because he does not **c** himself, ... Pr 5:23
and are under your neighbor's **c**, ... Pr 6:3
but those who **c** their tempers .... Pr 15:18
The LORD can **c** a king's mind as .... Pr 21:1
be wise enough to **c** yourself. .... Pr 23:4
Those who do not **c** themselves .... Pr 25:28
but when the wicked get **c**, ... Pr 28:12
but wise people **c** theirs........................ Pr 29:11
else will **c** everything for...................... Ec 2:19
one can **c** the wind or stop his .... Ec 8:8
A stick cannot **c** the person who .... Is 10:15
of Ammon will be under their **c**............. Is 11:14
never again take **c** of the earth; .... Is 14:21
We can't **c** our own lives. .... Je 10:23
and refuse to be under his **c**, ... Je 27:8
under the **c** of the king .... Je 27:11
Nebuchadnezzar **c** over the wild .... Je 28:14
to them, "Jeremiah is in your **c**. .... Je 38:5
Live in the towns you **c**." .... Je 40:10
the cliff and **c** the high places.................. Je 49:16
power and **c** in the beautiful .... Da 11:16
you from their **c** and tear away .... Nah 1:13
your enemies under your **c**." ' .... Mt 22:44
one was strong enough to **c** him. .... Mk 5:4
made the boy lose **c** of himself, ... Mk 9:20
your enemies under your **c**.' " .... Mk 12:36
Then Peter lost **c** of himself .... Mk 14:72
causes him to lose **c** of himself .... Lk 9:39
your enemies under your **c**." ' .... Lk 20:43
your enemies under your **c**.' " .... Ac 2:35
died is made free from sin's **c**. .... Rm 6:7
do not let sin **c** your life here .... Rm 6:12
But if they cannot **c** themselves,............. 1Co 7:9
and has his own desires under **c**, ... 1Co 7:37
are under the **c** of the prophets 1Co 14:32
God put all things under his **c**. 1Co 15:27
are not trying to **c** your faith. 2Co 1:24
do not really **c** the evil desires .... Col 2:23
letting evil thoughts **c** you, ... Col 3:5
Christ gives **c** your thinking, ... Col 3:15
you to learn to **c** your own body.............. 1Th 4:4
and will not **c** themselves. 2Ti 3:3
homes and get **c** of silly women 2Ti 3:6
But you should **c** yourself at all 2Ti 4:5
put your enemies under your **c**." .... Heb 1:13
put all things under their **c**." .... Heb 2:8
always trying to **c** your lives. .... Jam 2:6
we can **c** their whole bodies. .... Jam 3:3
clearly and **c** yourselves so you 1Pe 4:7
C yourselves and be careful! 1Pe 5:8
things and those things **c** them, ... 2Pe 2:20
who had **c** over these disasters. .... Rev 16:9

CONTROLLED

c himself and said, "Serve the .... Ge 43:31
Joshua **c** all the land from Mount .... Jos 11:17
These thirty sons **c** thirty towns .... Jdg 10:4
The Philistines **c** one hill while 1Sa 17:3
Solomon **c** all the countries west 1Ki 4:24
Jair **c** twenty-three cities in.................... 1Ch 2:22

for kings and areas c by Persia. .... Ezr 4:15
before me also c the people, ... Ne 5:15
he c his anger and went home. .... Est 5:10
Who has c history since the .... Is 41:4
were slaves to sin—sin c you. .... Rm 6:17
sinful things that c our bodies, ... Rm 7:5
thinking is c by the Spirit, ... Rm 8:6

CONTROLLING
C your temper is better than .... Pr 16:32

CONTROLS
Do you know how God c the clouds .... Job 37:15
The LORD c the flood. .... Ps 29:10
for your Temple completely c me. .... Ps 69:9
a king's mind as he c a river; .... Pr 21:1
I saw that God c good people and .... Ec 9:1
your Temple completely c me." .... Jn 2:17
love of Christ c us, because we 2Co 5:14
small rudder c that big ship, ... Jam 3:4
slaves of anything that c them. 2Pe 2:19
the Evil One c the whole world. 1Jn 5:19

CONVINCE
With patience you can c a ruler, ... Pr 25:15

CONVINCED
and elders c the crowd to ask .... Mt 27:20
of them were c and joined Paul .... Ac 17:4
He has c and turned away many .... Ac 19:26

CONVINCING
After c Blastus, the king's .... Ac 12:20

COOING
the c of doves is heard in our .... Sng 2:12

COOK
You must not c a young goat in .... Ex 23:19
will be able to c all your bread .... Le 26:26
Do not c a baby goat in its .... Dt 14:21
so we can c a young goat for .... Jdg 13:15
perfume and c and bake for him. 1Sa 8:13
said to the c, "Bring the meat I 1Sa 9:23
So the c took the thigh and put 1Sa 9:24
go home and c our last meal. 1Ki 17:12
The lazy catch no food to c, ... Pr 12:27
He uses the fire to c his meat,.................. Is 44:16
hands kind women c their own .... La 4:10
food from them and c in them. .... Zch 14:21

COOKED
that had been c and milk curds .... Ge 18:8
she c them in the special way .... Ge 27:14
offering is c on a griddle, ... Le 2:5
grain offering is c in a pan,.................... Le 2:7
It must not be c with yeast.................... Le 6:17
in an oven, c on a griddle, ... Le 7:9
After they c it in a pot or made .... Nu 11:8
went in and c a young goat, ... Jdg 6:19
the meat would be c in a pot. 1Sa 2:14
half bushel of c grain and ten 1Sa 17:17
of wine, five c sheep, a bushel 1Sa 25:18
the poor man and c it for his 2Sa 12:4
Then he c the meat and gave it 1Ki 19:21
my bread. I c and ate my meat .... Is 44:19
meat until even the bones are c................. Eze 24:5
like a pancake c only on one .... Hos 7:8
touches bread, c food, wine, ... Hag 2:12

COOKING
crackling of thorns in a c fire. .... Ec 7:6
This city is like a c pot, ... Eze 11:3
the fire. Finish c the meat. Mix .... Eze 24:10
and places for c were built in .... Eze 46:23
the pot, like meat in a c pan. .... Mic 3:3
The c pots in the Temple of the .... Zch 14:20

COOL
during the c part of the day, ... Ge 3:8
place is like a c drink when you .... Pr 25:25
a c shadow from a large rock .... Is 32:2
c, flowing streams do not dry .... Je 18:14
finger in water and c my tongue, ... Lk 16:24

COOLNESS
like the c of snow in the .... Pr 25:13

COOLS
As a cloud c a hot day, you .... Is 25:5

COOPERATE
being ready to c in everything. 1Ti 2:11
who c with full respect. 1Ti 3:4
who are wild and do not c. .... Tit 1:6

COPIED
wrote and c important papers. 1Ch 2:55
c by the men of Hezekiah king of .... Pr 25:1

COPIES
Then I took both c of the record .... Je 32:11
So the c of the real things in .... Heb 9:23

COPPER
you can dig c out of the hills .... Dt 8:9
and c is melted out of rocks. .... Job 28:2
put silver, c, iron, lead, ... Eze 22:20
become hot and its c sides glow............... Eze 24:11
with you—gold or silver or c. .... Mt 10:9
and put in two small c coins, ... Mk 12:42
putting two small c coins into.................. Lk 21:2

COPY
should write a c of the .... Dt 17:18
and gave him a c of the 2Ki 11:12
and gave him a c of the 2Ch 23:11
A c of the letter that King .... Ezr 4:23
c of the order was given out as .... Est 3:14
also gave him a c of the order .... Est 4:8
c of the king's order was to be .... Est 8:13
the sealed c and the copy that .... Je 32:14
example and to c those who live .... Php 3:17
priests is only a c and a shadow............... Heb 8:5
is only a c of the real one .... Heb 9:24
and died, and c their faith. .... Heb 13:7

COR
a tenth of a bath from each c.................. Eze 45:14

CORAL
C and jasper are not worth .... Job 28:18
on, fine linen, c, and rubies. .... Eze 27:16

CORBAN
you, but it is C—a gift to God.' .... Mk 7:11

CORD
Give me your seal and its c, ... Ge 38:18
Can you put a c through its nose .... Job 41:2
were born, your c was not cut. .... Eze 16:4
He had a c made of linen and a .... Eze 40:3

CORDS
courtyard, the c, pegs, and all.................. Ex 39:40
pillars by white and purple c.................. Est 1:6
I led them with c of human .... Hos 11:4
a whip out of c and forced all.................. Jn 2:15

CORINTH
Paul left Athens and went to C. .... Ac 18:1
Apollos was in C, Paul was...................... Ac 19:1
To the church of God in C, ... 1Co 1:2
To the church of God in C, ... 2Co 1:1
to you in C and have opened 2Co 6:11
Erastus stayed in C, and I left.................. 2Ti 4:20

CORMORANTS
little owls, c, great owls, ... Le 11:17
desert owls, ospreys, c, ... Dt 14:17

CORNELIUS

there was a man named **C**, ... Ac 10:1
C stared at the angel. .... Ac 10:4
the men **C** sent had found Simon's .... Ac 10:17
Peter entered, **C** met him, fell .... Ac 10:25
and we entered the house of **C**. .... Ac 11:12

CORNER

frames for each **c** at the rear. .... Ex 26:23
At each top **c** of this holy vest .... Ex 28:7
c that stuck out like a horn .... Ex 37:25
He made each **c** stick out like a .... Ex 38:2
cut off a **c** of Saul's robe. 1Sa 24:4
the southeast **c** of the Temple. 1Ki 7:39
Gate of Ephraim to the **C** Gate, ... 2Ki 14:13
the southeast **c** of the Temple. 2Ch 4:10
on every street **c** in Jerusalem. 2Ch 28:24
room above the **c** of the wall. .... Ne 3:31
fills every dark **c** of this land. .... Ps 74:20
street near the **c** on the road .... Pr 7:8
to live in a **c** on the roof than .... Pr 21:9
to live in a **c** on the roof than .... Pr 25:24
down and lie on every street **c**, ... Is 51:20
Tower of Hananel to the **C** Gate............. Je 31:38
as far as the **c** of the Horse.................... Je 31:40
with hunger on every street **c**. .... La 2:19
In each **c** of the courtyard was a............. Eze 46:21
to death at every street **c**. .... Nah 3:10
Attack the **c** towers!' .... Zph 1:16
to the First Gate to the **C** Gate, ... Zch 14:10
they did not happen off in a **c**. .... Ac 26:26

CORNERS

them to the four **c** of the table .... Ex 25:26
way that two **c** with their horns .... Ex 27:2
on the two upper **c** of the chest .... Ex 28:23
blood on the **c** of the altar, ... Ex 29:12
The **c** that stick out like horns .... Ex 30:2
sides, and its **c** with pure gold, ... Ex 30:3
God by putting blood on its **c**— .... Ex 30:10
on the two upper **c** of the chest .... Ex 39:16
the blood on the **c** of the altar .... Le 4:7
the way to the **c** of your fields. .... Le 19:9
them to the **c** of your clothes. .... Nu 15:38
on the four **c** of your coat. .... Dt 22:12
took hold of the **c** of the altar. 1Ki 1:50
At the **c** there were bronze 1Ki 7:30
the towers and **c** of the city.................... 2Ch 26:15
all four **c** of the house at .... Job 1:19
Come to the **c** of the altar. .... Ps 118:27
around on the **c** of the streets. .... Pr 7:12
cut into the **c** of their altars. .... Je 17:1
from the four **c** of the skies. .... Je 49:36
come on the four **c** of the land. .... Eze 7:2
its four **c** shaped like horns .... Eze 43:15
in the four **c** of the courtyard .... Eze 46:22
The **c** of the altar will be cut .... Am 3:14
blood at the **c** of the altar. .... Zch 9:15
and on the street **c** and pray so .... Mt 6:5
go to the street **c** and invite .... Mt 22:9
lowered to earth by its four **c**.................. Ac 10:11
at the four **c** of the earth. .... Rev 7:1

CORNERSTONE

on, or who put its **c** in place .... Job 38:6
builders rejected became the **c**. .... Ps 118:22
From Judah will come the **c**, ... Zch 10:4
builders rejected became the **c**. .... Mt 21:42
builders rejected became the **c**. .... Mk 12:10
rejected became the **c**'? .... Lk 20:17
which has become the **c**.' .... Ac 4:11
rejected has become the **c**." 1Pe 2:7

CORNERSTONES

in Babylon big enough for **c**. .... Je 51:26

CORRECT

silver must be **c** as set by the .... Le 5:15
and that is worth the **c** amount. .... Le 5:18
way the husband can be proven **c**, ... Nu 5:31
them or listen when they **c** him, ... Dt 21:18
Do you mean to **c** what I say?.................... Job 6:26
You **c** me and I am insulted, ... Job 20:3
argues with the Almighty **c** him? .... Job 40:2
don't **c** me when you are angry; .... Ps 6:1
don't **c** me when you are angry. .... Ps 38:1
c and punish people for their .... Ps 39:11
LORD, those you **c** are happy; .... Ps 94:12
just as parents **c** the child they .... Pr 3:12
If you **c** someone who makes fun .... Pr 9:7
your children, you will **c** them. .... Pr 13:24
C your children while there is .... Pr 19:18
It is better to **c** someone openly .... Pr 27:5
Those who **c** others will later be.............. Pr 28:23
C your children, and you will be .... Pr 29:17
Words alone cannot **c** a servant,............. Pr 29:19
people do nothing when I **c** them. .... Je 7:28
LORD, **c** me, but be fair. .... Je 10:24
I **c** and punish those whom I .... Rev 3:19

CORRECTED

I did, and last night he **c** you." .... Ge 31:42
not hate being **c** by the Almighty .... Job 5:17
People may be **c** while in bed in .... Job 33:19
If he **c** me, that would be like .... Ps 141:5
you had listened when I **c** you, ... Pr 1:23
who hates being **c** is stupid. .... Pr 12:1
one who hates to be **c** will die. .... Pr 15:10
after being **c** many times will .... Pr 29:1

CORRECTING

lives, for **c** faults, and for 2Ti 3:16

CORRECTION

and felt the **c** of the LORD your .... Dt 11:2
advice, and you rejected my **c**. .... Pr 1:30
I would not listen to **c**! .... Pr 5:12
And the **c** that comes from them .... Pr 6:23
Whoever accepts **c** is on the way .... Pr 10:17
who loves learning accepts **c**,................ Pr 12:1
who refuses **c** will end up poor .... Pr 13:18
anyone who accepts **c** is wise. .... Pr 15:5
Listen to advice and accept **c**,................ Pr 19:20
C and punishment make children .... Pr 29:15

CORRECTLY

and balances should weigh **c**,................ Le 19:36
could not say that word **c**. .... Jdg 12:6
will know that I have spoken **c**: .... Ps 141:6
You have seen **c**, because I am .... Je 1:12
people the law **c** wants us to be.............. Rm 8:4

CORRECTS

LORD your God **c** you as a parent .... Dt 8:5
The one whom God **c** is happy, ... Job 5:17
the one who **c** nations punish .... Ps 94:10
The LORD **c** those he loves, ... Pr 3:12
don't stop trying when he **c** you. .... Heb 12:5

COSMETICS

six months with perfumes and **c**. .... Est 2:12

COST

It will **c** about one and .... Le 27:16
offerings that **c** me nothing." 2Sa 24:24
doesn't **c** Adonijah his life!.................... 1Ki 2:23
and a horse **c** nearly four pounds 1Ki 10:29
and horses **c** nearly four pounds 2Ch 1:17
The **c** of the building is to be .... Ezr 6:8
and its **c** cannot be weighed in .... Job 28:15
in adultery may **c** you your life. .... Pr 6:26
him angry may **c** you your life. .... Pr 20:2
so you will be saved without **c**." .... Is 52:3

without money and without c. .... Is 55:1
Two sparrows c only a penny,................ Mt 10:29
and decide how much it will c, ... Lk 14:28

COSTS
offering that c me nothing." 1Ch 21:24
The c should be paid from the .... Ezr 6:4
If it c everything you have, ... Pr 4:7
about how much the food c. .... Pr 23:7

COUCH
falling on the c where Esther .... Est 7:8
me or that my c will stop my .... Job 7:13
out to the king on his c. .... Sng 1:12
it's Solomon's c with sixty .... Sng 3:7
Solomon had a c made for himself............ Sng 3:9

COUCHES
gold and silver c on a floor set .... Est 1:6
on their beds and on their c." .... Am 3:12
ivory and stretch out on your c. .... Am 6:4

COULDN'T
c stand to see my father that sad. .... Ge 44:34
food, but they c find any. .... Ex 16:27
on someone he c see and kill .... Nu 35:23
When we c find them, we went to 1Sa 10:14
hurt so badly I knew he c live. 2Sa 1:10
them so they c rise up again. 2Sa 22:39
Elisha until he c refuse them 2Ki 2:17
in the sky, that c happen." 2Ki 7:2
him, so many they c be counted. 2Ch 12:3
and they c speak the language of .... Ne 13:24
them so they c rise up again. .... Ps 18:38
for him, but he c be found. .... Ps 37:36
you c remove the foolishness.................. Pr 27:22
language you c understand. .... Is 33:19
they happened so you c say, ' .... Is 48:5
it c be made into anything. .... Eze 15:5
the king, he c do anything for .... Hos 10:3
"Why c we force the demon out?" .... Mt 17:19
wanted to kill him. But she c, ... Mk 6:19
c we force that evil spirit out?................ Mk 9:28
C you stay awake with me for one .... Mk 14:37
c he keep Lazarus from dying? .... Jn 11:37

COUNCIL
He had a c meeting with his 2Ki 6:8
not listen on God's secret c. .... Job 15:8
you will be judged by the c. .... Mt 5:22
the whole Jewish c tried to find .... Mt 26:59
But the c could find no proof of .... Mk 14:55
all the Jewish c decided what to.............. Mk 15:1
member of the Jewish c, ... Mk 15:43
the c of the elders of the .... Lk 22:66
who was a member of the c. .... Lk 23:50
called a meeting of the c. .... Jn 11:47
and the whole c of elders can .... Ac 22:5
Paul looked at the c and said,................ Ac 23:1
stood before her in Jerusalem................ Ac 24:20

COUNSELOR
He was a wise c and was chosen 1Ch 26:14
His name will be Wonderful C, ... Is 9:6

COUNSELORS
your c will be like those you .... Is 1:26
leaders, the c, the skilled .... Is 3:3

COUNT
anyone could c the dust on the .... Ge 13:16
so many stars you cannot c them. .... Ge 15:5
as hard to c as the stars in the .... Ge 26:4
There will be too many to c.'" .... Ge 32:12
When you c the people of Israel, ... Ex 30:12
the sacrifice c for the person .... Le 7:18
he must c seven days for himself .... Le 15:13
C seven full weeks from the .... Le 23:15

C off seven groups of seven .... Le 25:8
c the number of years since the .... Le 25:15
bought him must c the time from .... Le 25:50
the priest must c the years to .... Le 27:23
and Aaron must c all the people.............. Nu 1:2
Do not c the tribe of Levi or .... Nu 1:49
C every male one month old or .... Nu 3:15
C the men from thirty to fifty .... Nu 4:30
C all the people of Israel by .... Nu 26:2
C all the men who are twenty................ Nu 26:2
c the people of Israel and Judah. 2Sa 24:1
there are too many of them to c. 1Ki 3:8
cattle no one could c them all. 1Ki 8:5
he caused David to c the people 1Ch 21:1
But Joab did not c the tribes of 1Ch 21:6
and bulls no one could c them. 2Ch 5:6
bring them and c them out for .... Ezr 1:8
Don't c it among the days of the............ Job 3:6
Then you will c my steps, but .... Job 14:16
No one can c God's armies. .... Job 25:3
has the wisdom to c the clouds?.............. Job 38:37
Do you c the months until they .... Job 39:2
can c all my bones; people look .... Ps 22:17
there would be too many to c. .... Ps 40:5
Jerusalem and c its towers..................... Ps 48:12
the locusts were too many to c. .... Ps 105:34
If I could c them, they would be .... Ps 139:18
so many girls you cannot c them, ... Sng 6:8
that even a child could c them. .... Is 10:19
as a hired helper would c time. .... Is 16:14
will again c their sheep as .... Je 33:13
there are too many to c. .... Je 46:23
I will c you like sheep and will .... Eze 20:37
which no one can measure or c.............. Hos 1:10
with too many soldiers to c. .... Joe 1:6
are piled up—too many to c. .... Nah 3:3
also will be too many to c." .... Rm 4:18
Love does not c up wrongs that 1Co 13:5
many that no one could c them. .... Rev 7:9
c the people worshiping there. .... Rev 11:1

COUNTED
descendants they cannot be c." .... Ge 16:10
and they c the weight as the .... Ge 23:16
came, will be c as my own sons............... Ge 48:5
person who is c must pay .... Ex 30:13
years old or older were c. .... Ex 38:26
years must be c since the land .... Le 25:27
first son born to Israel, was c; .... Nu 1:20
obeyed the LORD and c them all. .... Nu 3:16
Moses and Aaron c the Levite men .... Nu 3:39
Each man was c as the LORD had .... Nu 4:49
and camels they could not be c. .... Jdg 6:5
The people of Israel c everyone,............. Jdg 21:9
Saul c the men who were still................ 1Sa 13:15
David c his men and placed over 2Sa 18:1
They c the money that had been............. 2Ki 12:10
order for the people to be c. 1Ch 21:17
more cedar logs than could be c. 1Ch 22:4
So David only c the men who were 1Ch 27:23
Solomon c all the foreigners 2Ch 2:17
many miracles they cannot be c. .... Job 5:9
But my brothers cannot be c on.............. Job 6:15
many miracles they cannot be c. .... Job 9:10
and small that cannot be c..................... Ps 104:25
You c the houses of Jerusalem, ... Is 22:10
me for more days than can be c. .... Je 2:32
God has c the days until your................. Da 5:26
but sin is not c against us as .... Rm 5:13
wants you to be c worthy of his 2Th 1:5
seashore, they could not be c................. Heb 11:12

COUNTING

COUNTLESS

COUNTRIES

COUNTRY

C

who live in the **c** to be eaten by .... Eze 33:27
be beaten back to his own **c.** .... Da 11:9
the people in this **c** have been.................. Hos 1:2
them like lambs in the open **c.** .... Hos 4:16
taken captive to the **c** of Kir," .... Am 1:5
ate all the crops in the **c,** .... Am 7:2
and you will die in a foreign **c.** .... Am 7:17
What is your **c**? Who are your .... Jnh 1:8
still in my own **c** this is what I .... Jnh 4:2
a pile of ruins in the open **c,** .... Mic 1:6
come into our **c** and walk over .... Mic 5:5
one good person left in this **c**............... Mic 7:2
again, when your **c** will grow.................. Mic 7:11
the insults of the **c** of Moab and .... Zph 2:8
will bring trouble to the **c,** .... Zch 11:6
to get a new shepherd for the **c.** .... Zch 11:16
his mountain **c** and left his land .... Mal 1:3
will say, 'Edom is a wicked **c.** .... Mal 1:4
you will have a pleasant **c,**" .... Mal 3:12
to their own **c** by a different .... Mt 2:12
At noon the whole **c** became dark,........... Mt 27:45
At noon the whole **c** became dark,........... Mk 15:33
they were walking in the **c,**.................. Mk 16:12
no food anywhere in the whole **c.** .... Lk 4:25
of the Gerasene **c** asked Jesus to .... Lk 8:37
'Go out to the roads and **c** lanes, ... Lk 14:23
traveled far away to another **c.** .... Lk 15:13
man went to a **c** far away to be .... Lk 19:12
to go through the **c** of Samaria. .... Jn 4:4
is not respected in his own **c.** .... Jn 4:44
Many from the **c** went up to .... Jn 11:55
were from every **c** in the world. .... Ac 2:5
Abraham left the **c** of Chaldea .... Ac 7:4
every **c** God accepts anyone who .... Ac 10:35
country got its food from his **c.** .... Ac 12:20
out of that **c** with great power. .... Ac 13:17
spreading through the whole **c.** .... Ac 13:49
they came near the **c** of Mysia. .... Ac 16:7
been born in the **c** of Pontus. .... Ac 18:2
governor of the **c** of Southern .... Ac 18:12
and went to the **c** of Macedonia.............. Ac 20:1
from Tarsus in the **c** of Cilicia. .... Ac 21:39
in Tarsus in the **c** of Cilicia. .... Ac 22:3
things in our **c** are being made .... Ac 24:2
beginning in my own **c** and later .... Ac 26:4
from the people of your own **c,** 1Th 2:14
and forced us to leave that **c.** 1Th 2:15
He left his own **c,** not knowing .... Heb 11:8
in the **c** God promised to...................... Heb 11:9
are looking for a **c** that will be .... Heb 11:14

COUNTRYSIDE

trees in the **c** will know that I.................. Eze 17:24
to all other trees in the **c.** .... Eze 31:4
trees in the **c** will give their .... Eze 34:27
went to the town and to the **c,** .... Mk 5:14
can go to the **c** and towns around .... Mk 6:36
this in the town and the **c.** .... Lk 8:34
to the towns and **c** around here .... Lk 9:12

COUNTS

first son she has **c** as the son .... Dt 25:6
sees my ways and **c** every step I............... Job 31:4
He **c** the stars and names each .... Ps 147:4
a year as a hired helper **c** time. .... Is 21:16

COURAGE

of Canaan will lose all their **c.** .... Ex 15:15
will lose their **c** in the land of.................. Le 26:36
Don't lose your **c** or be afraid. .... Dt 20:3
saw this, they lost their **c.** .... Jos 7:5
for you. Have **c.** May the LORD be 2Ch 19:11
me, I had **c,** and I gathered .... Ezr 7:28
support you. Have **c** and do it." .... Ezr 10:4
you say, 'Have **c,**' then the .... Job 22:29

my wonderful God who gives me **c.** .... Ps 3:3
my head, and I have lost my **c.** .... Ps 40:12
so bad that they lost their **c.** .... Ps 107:26
I am afraid; my **c** is gone. .... Ps 143:4
and their **c** will melt away. .... Is 13:7
and Egypt's **c** will melt away. .... Is 19:1
and officers will lose their **c.** .... Je 4:9
Don't lose **c**; rumors will spread............... Je 51:46
to stir up his strength and **c.** .... Da 11:25
lose their **c,** and their knees .... Nah 2:10
quickly spoke to them, "Have **c**!............... Mt 14:27
spoke to them and said, "Have **c**! .... Mk 6:50
So men, have **c.** I trust in God .... Ac 27:25
Have **c,** and be strong. 1Co 16:13
So we always have **c.** 2Co 5:6
but that I will have the **c** now,................. Php 1:20
So do not lose the **c** you had in .... Heb 10:35

COURAGEOUS

He is brave and **c.** 1Sa 16:18
strong now; be **c.**" When he spoke .... Da 10:19

COURSE

"Of **c** I will go with you," .... Jdg 4:9
Of **c,** its gods are not really............... Je 2:11
'Of **c,** we know all wine bags .... Je 13:12
of **c,** there is in every way. .... Rm 3:2
c he is, because there is only .... Rm 3:30

COURT

left the king's **c** and traveled .... Ge 41:46
the elders of his **c,** and all the............... Ge 50:7
husband says and the **c** allows. .... Ex 21:22
when you accuse someone in **c.** .... Ex 23:7
who wants you to lie in **c,** .... Ex 23:8
to tell in **c** what he has seen .... Le 5:1
he receives a fair trial in **c.** .... Nu 35:12
have an argument and go to **c,** .... Dt 25:1
the city until a **c** comes to a .... Jos 20:6
at the western **c** and four guards 1Ch 26:18
guards on the road to the **c.** 1Ch 26:18
down in the daily **c** record in .... Est 2:23
for the daily **c** record to be .... Est 6:1
entered the outer **c** of the .... Est 6:4
crushed in **c** with no defense.................. Job 5:4
We cannot meet each other in **c.**.............. Job 9:32
in prison or calls you into **c,** .... Job 11:10
he bring you into **c** for this? .... Job 22:4
when I knew I could win in **c.** .... Job 31:21
and invite to stay in your **c.** .... Ps 65:4
and will defend the needy in **c.** .... Ps 140:12
the rights of the needy in **c.** .... Pr 22:22
not quickly take someone to **c.** .... Pr 25:8
takes a foolish person to **c,**...................... Pr 29:9
If they have to testify in **c,** .... Pr 29:24
his place in **c** and stands to.................. Is 3:13
those who take about others in **c,** .... Is 29:21
let us go to **c** together.......................... Is 50:8
take each other to **c** unfairly, ... Is 59:4
officers of the **c,** the priests, ... Je 34:19
no one who can take me to **c.** .... Je 49:19
is cheated in his case in **c.** .... La 3:36
of stones all around the **c.** .... Eze 40:17
In **c** they will act as judges.................. Eze 44:24
who stayed at the royal **c.** .... Da 2:49
But the **c** will decide what .... Da 7:26
So people sue each other in **c;** .... Hos 10:4
poor from getting justice in **c.**............... Am 5:12
money to decide who wins in **c.** .... Mic 3:11
but he will defend my case in **c.** .... Mic 7:9
you take sides in **c** cases. .... Mal 2:9
your enemy is taking you to **c,** .... Mt 5:25
and take you to **c** and whip you .... Mt 10:17
and take you to **c** and beat you .... Mk 13:9
your enemy is taking you to **c,** .... Lk 12:58

led Jesus to their highest **c**...................... Lk 22:66
Paul and took him to the **c**...................... Ac 18:12
judged by you or by any human **c**. 1Co 4:3
goes to **c** against another 1Co 6:6
are the ones who take you to **c**. .... Jam 2:6

COURTS

recorded what happened in the **c**; 1Ki 4:3
the wine in the **c** of my Temple." .... Is 62:9
be fair in the **c**. Maybe the LORD .... Am 5:15
In the **c** judge with truth and .... Zch 8:16
goods through the Temple **c**. .... Mk 11:16
go to the **c** and judges where .... Ac 19:38

COURTYARD

to form a **c** around the Holy ...... Ex 27:9
east end of the **c** must also be................. Ex 27:13
The **c** must be one hundred fifty.............. Ex 27:18
eat it in the **c** of the Meeting .... Le 6:16
entry to the **c** around the Holy .... Nu 3:26
a well in his **c**, and they 2Sa 17:18
The inner **c** was enclosed by 1Ki 6:36
Even the **c** was made with blocks 1Ki 7:9
Isaiah had left the middle **c**, ... 2Ki 20:4
the LORD in the **c** near the room 2Ki 23:11
for the Temple **c** and side rooms, ... 1Ch 23:28
Temple and the **c** around the 1Ch 28:11
opened to the **c** and covered them 2Ch 4:9
front of the new **c** in the Temple.............. 2Ch 20:5
is near the **c** of the king's .... Ne 3:25
have a room in the Temple **c**. .... Ne 13:7
was held in the **c** of the palace .... Est 1:5
near the **c** where the king's................. Est 2:11
Queen Esther standing in the **c**, ... Est 5:2
"Haman is standing in the **c**.".................. Est 6:5
prophesying in the Temple **c**, ... Je 20:1
sitting in the **c** of the guard,................. Je 32:12
Jeremiah was guarded in the **c**, ... Je 39:15
the **c** was the idol that caused.............. Eze 8:3
And a cloud filled the inner **c**. .... Eze 10:3
The inner **c** had a gateway across .... Eze 40:23
The man measured the inner **c**. .... Eze 40:47
and brought me into the inner **c**. .... Eze 43:5
as Peter was sitting in the **c**, ... Mt 26:69
was in the **c**, a servant girl .... Mk 14:66
middle of the **c** and sat together .... Lk 22:55
Jesus into the high priest's **c**. .... Jn 18:15

COURTYARDS

stars in the two **c** of the Temple 2Ki 21:5
will build my Temple and its **c**. 1Ch 28:6
the **c** around the LORD's Temple 1Ch 28:12
stars in the two **c** of the Temple 2Ch 33:5
in the **c** of the Temple,........................... Ne 8:16
to be in the **c** of the LORD's .... Ps 84:2
One day in the **c** of your Temple............. Ps 84:10
grow strong in the **c** of our God............. Ps 92:13
and come into his Temple **c**. .... Ps 96:8
and into his **c** with songs of .... Ps 100:4
in the Temple **c** in Jerusalem. .... Ps 116:19
s Temple and in the Temple **c**............. Ps 135:2
and fill the **c** with those who .... Eze 9:7
like the pillars of the **c**. .... Eze 42:6
Small **c** were in the four corners .... Eze 46:22
in charge of my Temple and my **c**. .... Zch 3:7

COUSIN

Mordecai had a **c** named Hadassah, ... Est 2:7
My **c** Hanamel came to me in the .... Je 32:8
me, and Mark, the **c** of Barnabas, ... Col 4:10

COUSINS

here and pick up your **c**' bodies................. Le 10:4
married their **c**, their father's .... Nu 36:11
daughters married their **c**, ... 1Ch 23:22

COVER

made something to **c** themselves. .... Ge 3:7
Make rooms in it and **c** it inside .... Ge 6:14
continued to **c** the earth for one .... Ge 7:24
darkness will **c** the land of .... Ex 10:21
If a man takes the **c** off a pit, ... Ex 21:33
C the Ark inside and out with ...... Ex 25:11
acacia wood, **c** them with gold, ... Ex 25:28
tent that will **c** the Holy Tent, ... Ex 26:7
So he would **c** his face again .... Ex 34:35
and **c** the Ark of the Agreement.............. Nu 4:5
c everything with fine leather, ... Nu 4:8
the gold altar, **c** it with fine................... Nu 4:11
dig a hole and **c** up your dung. .... Dt 23:13
C the opening of the cave with .... Jos 10:18
and made the sea to **c** them. .... Jos 24:7
Spread your **c** over me, because.............. Ru 3:9
nets to **c** the two large bowls 1Ki 7:41
They will be used to **c** the walls 1Ch 29:4
nets to **c** the two large bowls 2Ch 4:12
so large they almost **c** the land. .... Job 1:10
Let thick darkness **c** its light. .... Job 3:5
a bag, and you will **c** up my sin. .... Job 14:17
please do not **c** up my blood. .... Job 16:18
other, and worms **c** them both. .... Job 21:26
Thick clouds **c** him so he cannot .... Job 22:14
nothing to **c** themselves in the .... Job 24:7
The animals take **c** from the rain .... Job 37:8
c their faces in the grave. .... Job 40:13
C them with shame and disgrace, ... Ps 35:26
C them with shame. Then people .... Ps 83:16
He will **c** you with his feathers, ... Ps 91:4
will never **c** the earth again .... Ps 104:9
So let curses **c** him like clothes .... Ps 109:19
I will **c** his enemies with shame,........... Ps 132:18
Then the LORD will **c** Mount Zion .... Is 4:5
It used two wings to **c** its face, ... Is 6:2
Shut their ears. **C** their eyes. .... Is 6:10
and worms **c** your body like a .... Is 14:11
it will not **c** the dead any .... Is 26:21
I will **c** you with my hands and .... Is 51:16
you can't **c** yourself with those .... Is 59:6
of camels will **c** your land, ... Is 60:6
let our disgrace **c** us like a .... Je 3:25
embarrassed and **c** their heads .... Je 14:3
so they **c** their heads in shame. .... Je 14:4
'I will rise up and **c** the earth.................. Je 46:8
stream and fill the whole .... Je 47:2
its roaring waves **c** her. .... Je 51:42
C your face so you cannot see .... Eze 12:6
the prophets **c** it with whitewash .... Eze 13:10
prophets try to **c** this up by .... Eze 22:28
ground where dust would **c** it. .... Eze 24:7
Do not **c** your face, and do not .... Eze 24:17
Mediterranean Sea will **c** you. .... Eze 26:19
A cloud will **c** Egypt, and her .... Eze 30:18
I will **c** the sun with a cloud, ... Eze 32:7
on you and **c** you with skin. .... Eze 37:6
say to the mountains, "**C** us!"................. Hos 10:8
all of them will **c** their mouths, ... Mic 3:7
You **c** the LORD's altar with your .... Mal 2:13
of the Most High will **c** you. .... Lk 1:35
a new coat to **c** a hole in an old .... Lk 5:36
will say to the hills, '**C** us!' .... Lk 23:30
do not **c** its mouth to keep it 1Co 9:9
If a woman does not **c** her head,.............. 1Co 11:6
But a man should not **c** his head, ... 1Co 11:7
do not **c** its mouth to keep it 1Ti 5:18
and so you can **c** your shameful .... Rev 3:18

COVERED

Darkness **c** the ocean, and God's .... Ge 1:2
under the sky were **c** by it. .... Ge 7:19

C

because water still c the earth,	Ge 8:9
the tent and c their father.	Ge 9:23
Nimrod's kingdom c Babylon,	Ge 10:10
So Rebekah c her face with her	Ge 24:65
A large stone c the mouth of the	Ge 29:2
was a widow and c her face with	Ge 38:14
of reeds and c it with tar so	Ex 2:3
Moses c his face because he was	Ex 3:6
water and c the land of Egypt.	Ex 8:6
Swarms of locusts c all the land	Ex 10:14
The deep waters c them, and they	Ex 15:5
quail came and c the camp,	Ex 16:13
Mount Sinai was c with smoke,	Ex 19:18
on the mountain, the cloud c it.	Ex 24:15
and the cloud c it for six days.	Ex 24:16
of acacia wood c with gold.	Ex 26:37
themselves a calf c with gold,	Ex 32:8
He c it with pure gold and put a	Ex 37:11
Then he c the altar with bronze.	Ex 38:2
curtain that c the entrance to	Ex 39:34
Then the cloud c the Meeting	Ex 40:34
and his sons have c the holy	Nu 4:15
to the Lord six c carts and	Nu 7:3
was set up, a cloud c it.	Nu 9:15
Then the earth c them.	Nu 16:33
Tent, and the cloud c it.	Nu 16:42
arrows will be c with their	Dt 32:42
Then they c it with a pile of	Jos 8:29
been hiding and c the opening	Jos 10:27
king's fat c the whole sword,	Jdg 3:22
tent, and she c him with a rug.	Jdg 4:18
on the bed, c it with clothes,	1Sa 19:13
He c his head and went barefoot.	2Sa 15:30
of the well and c it with grain.	2Sa 17:19
The king c his face and cried	2Sa 19:4
servants c him with blankets,	1Ki 1:1
the Temple was c with cedar,	1Ki 6:18
He c this room with pure gold,	1Ki 6:20
two creatures were c with gold.	1Ki 6:28
doors that were c with gold.	1Ki 6:32
the ceiling was c with cedar	1Ki 7:3
the sky was c with dark clouds	1Ki 18:45
but the Arameans c the area.	1Ki 20:27
Then he c the places with human	2Ki 23:14
Holy Place and c them with gold.	2Ch 3:10
hurried home with his head c,	Est 6:12
came in and c Haman's face.	Est 7:8
My body is c with worms and	Job 7:5
enemies will be c with shame,	Job 8:22
he has c my paths with darkness.	Job 19:8
' and they keep their faces c.	Job 24:15
as if my path were c with cream	Job 29:6
disgrace, and I am c with shame.	Ps 44:15
The desert is c with grass and	Ps 65:12
and my face is c with disgrace.	Ps 69:7
trying to hurt me be c with	Ps 71:13
and the hills be c with crops.	Ps 72:16
We c the mountains with our	Ps 80:10
the people and c all their sins	Ps 85:2
short and c him with shame.	Ps 89:45
You c the earth with oceans;	Ps 104:6
The Lord c them with a cloud and	Ps 105:39
and the water c their foes.	Ps 106:11
disgraced and c with shame like	Ps 109:29
I have c my bed with colored	Pr 7:16
are like paths c with thorns	Pr 22:5
The ground was c with weeds,	Pr 24:31
The seat was c with purple cloth	Sng 3:10
shiny ivory c with sapphires.	Sng 5:14
are c with wounds, hurts, and	Is 1:6
You are c by bodies that died in	Is 14:19
Every table is c with vomit,	Is 28:8
He has c your heads.	Is 29:10

You have statues c with silver	Is 30:22
in the sky is c with blood.	Is 34:5
dirt will be c with their fat.	Is 34:7
their eyes are c so they can't	Is 44:18
He c himself with goodness like	Is 59:17
He has c me with clothes of	Is 61:10
iron that became c with rust.	Je 6:28
stands will be c with bushes.'	Je 26:18
will become a hill c with ruins,	Je 49:2
and two wings that c its body.	Eze 1:11
those who c it with whitewash	Eze 13:15
over you and c your nakedness.	Eze 16:8
fine linen and c you with silk.	Eze 16:10
bare rock so it will not be c.	Eze 24:8
I c them and held back their	Eze 31:15
grew, and skin c the bones.	Eze 37:8
Temple were also c by a roof	Eze 41:26
and linen that c her nakedness.	Hos 2:9
so you will be c with shame and	Ob 1:10
and c himself with rough cloth	Jnh 3:6
stands will be c with bushes.	Mic 3:12
It is only a statue c with gold	Hab 2:19
live in a place c with the	Mt 4:16
lake so that waves c the boat,	Mt 8:24
talking, a bright cloud c them.	Mt 17:5
Then a cloud came and c them,	Mk 9:7
there was a man c with a skin	Lk 5:12
cloud came and c them, and they	Lk 9:34
whose body was c with sores,	Lk 16:20
is a pool with five c porches,	Jn 5:2
loudly and c their ears and all	Ac 7:57
with his head c brings shame to	1Co 11:4
Our faces, then, are not c.	2Co 3:18
dies will be fully c with life.	2Co 5:4
and the Ark c with gold that	Heb 9:4
wings and was c all over with	Rev 4:8
and darkness c its kingdom.	Rev 16:10
It was c with names against God	Rev 17:3

COVERING

Noah removed the c of the boat	Ge 8:13
water returned, c the chariots,	Ex 14:28
the holy vest and the chest c.	Ex 25:7
be spread upward, c the lid,	Ex 25:20
Make a c for the Holy Tent from	Ex 26:14
beautiful gems on the chest c:	Ex 28:17
he put a c over his face.	Ex 33:33
to attach them to the chest c,	Ex 39:13
the c made of male sheepskins	Ex 39:34
and the Thummim in the chest c.	Le 8:8
the fat c the inner organs,	Le 9:19
c his skin from his head to his	Le 13:12
Holy Tent, its c, the curtain at	Nu 3:25
must spread a c of fine leather	Nu 4:14
Tent, its c, and its outer	Nu 4:25
the rocks that are c the opening	Jos 10:22
for each net c the bowls for	1Ki 7:42
made darkness his c, his shelter	Ps 18:11
This c will protect the people	Is 4:6
The dew c you is like the dew of	Is 26:19
spread his c for shade above	Je 43:10
also had two wings c its body.	Eze 1:23
will be like a cloud c the land.	Eze 38:9
a large stone c the entrance.	Jn 11:38
hair is given to her as a c.	1Co 11:15
who put a c over his face so the	2Co 3:13
there is a c over their minds.	2Co 3:15

COVERINGS

made two more c for the outer	Ex 36:19
She makes c for herself;	Pr 31:22

COVERS

the rental price c the loss.	Ex 22:15
the fat that c the inner organs	Ex 29:13

of the lid that **c** that Ark. .... Ex 30:6
that is in them and that **c** them .... Le 3:3
the fat that **c** the inner organs, ... Le 7:3
the disease **c** the whole body .... Le 13:13
out of Egypt that **c** the land. .... Nu 22:5
Darkness **c** them up in the .... Job 5:14
he **c** the judges' faces so they .... Job 9:24
see and a flood of water **c** you. .... Job 22:11
thick darkness that **c** my face. .... Job 23:17
He **c** the face of the moon, ... Job 26:9
his majesty **c** the earth. .... Ps 57:5
deep water, and the flood **c** me. .... Ps 69:2
until it **c** your whole country. .... Is 8:8
the veil that **c** all nations, ... Is 25:7
and a goldsmith **c** it with gold .... Is 40:19
pulled back the **c** and climbed .... Is 57:8
Darkness now **c** the earth; .... Is 60:2
like a cloud that **c** the land.................... Eze 38:16
just as water **c** the sea, people .... Hab 2:14
Selah His glory **c** the skies,..................... Hab 3:3
us the stone that **c** the entrance .... Mk 16:3
lighting a lamp **c** it with a bowl .... Lk 8:16

COW

Bring me a three-year-old **c,** .... Ge 15:9
If it is a **c** or a sheep, it is .... Le 27:26
get a young red **c** that does not .... Nu 19:2
The whole **c** must be burned while........... Nu 19:5
take a young **c** that has never .... Dt 21:3
had not plowed with my young **c,** .... Jdg 14:18
only one young **c** and two sheep .... Is 7:21
is like a beautiful young **c,** .... Je 46:20
like a young **c** in the grain. .... Je 50:11
like a stubborn young **c.** .... Hos 4:16
young **c** that likes to .... Hos 10:11
the ashes of a **c** are sprinkled................. Heb 9:13

COW'S

collected the **c** ashes must wash............... Nu 19:10
must break the young **c** neck................... Dt 21:4
I will give you **c** dung instead................. Eze 4:15

COWARDS

But **c,** those who refuse to .... Rev 21:8

COWS

young, forty **c** and ten bulls, ... Ge 32:15
Then seven more **c** came up out of........... Ge 41:3
seven beautiful **c** on the bank................. Ge 41:3
The seven good **c** stand for seven .... Ge 41:26
milk curds from the **c** and milk .... Dt 32:14
and get two **c** that have just 1Sa 6:7
sacrificed the **c** as burnt 1Sa 6:14
made from **c'** milk for David 2Sa 17:29
has killed many **c,** fat calves, ... 1Ki 1:19
ten **c** that were fed on good 1Ki 4:23
to Gath to steal **c** and sheep and 1Ch 7:21
wine, oil, **c,** and sheep, because 1Ch 12:40
their **c** have healthy calves..................... Job 21:10
those bulls among the **c.** .... Ps 68:30
C and bears will eat together in .... Is 11:7
oil, young sheep, and young **c.** .... Je 31:12
you **c** of Bashan on the Mountain .... Am 4:1

COZY

in your palace, **c** in your rooms .... Je 22:23

CRACK

put you in a large **c** in the rock .... Ex 33:22
You made the earth shake and **c.** .... Ps 60:2
belt there in a **c** in the rocks.".................. Je 13:4
and the valleys will **c** open,..................... Mic 1:4

CRACKED

bags that were **c** and mended, ... Jos 9:4
but now they are **c** and old. .... Jos 9:13
The ground is dry and **c** open, ... Je 14:4

CRACKLING

of fools is like the **c** of thorns .... Ec 7:6

CRACKS

hiding in the **c** of the rock, ... Sng 2:14
hide in caves and **c** in the rocks .... Is 2:21
Jerusalem had many **c** that needed .... Is 22:9
high wall with **c** in it that .... Is 30:13
hill and in the **c** of the rocks. .... Je 16:16

CRAFTSMAN

Have a skilled **c** sew designs of .... Ex 26:1
formed by a **c,** and a goldsmith .... Is 40:19
The **c** encourages the goldsmith, ... Is 41:7
The idol is something a **c** made;............... Hos 8:6
cleverly made, the work of a **c.** .... Hos 13:2

CRAFTSMEN

The **c** must use gold and blue, ... Ex 28:5
about a thousand **c** and metal................. 2Ki 24:16
the people living there were **c.** 1Ch 4:14
You have more **c** than can be 1Ch 22:16
work with my skilled **c** in Judah............... 2Ch 2:7
will help your **c** and the 2Ch 2:14
and in the Valley of the **C.** .... Ne 11:35
the skilled **c,** and those who try .... Is 3:3
are made by **c** and goldsmiths. .... Je 10:9
and all the **c** and metalworkers .... Je 24:1
and the skilled **c** who were left .... Je 52:15
Then the LORD showed me four **c.**........... Zch 1:20

CRAFTSMEN'S

of the people from **C** Valley, ... 1Ch 4:14

CRASH

that its waves **c** on the shore. .... Je 31:35
and a loud **c** will echo from the .... Zph 1:10
and it fell with a big **c.**" .... Mt 7:27
But we will **c** on an island." .... Ac 27:26

CRASHING

Your waves are **c** all around me................ Ps 42:7
praise him with **c** cymbals. .... Ps 150:5
is like the **c** of great waves..................... Is 17:12
like a storm **c** down on the evil .... Je 30:23
only a noisy bell or a **c** cymbal. 1Co 13:1

CRAWL

You will **c** on your stomach, ... Ge 3:14
animals that **c** on the ground, ... Le 11:42
They will **c** in the dust like a .... Mic 7:17

CRAWLING

and small **c** animals and wild .... Ge 1:24
and **c** thing will come to you to .... Ge 6:20
man, animal, **c** thing, and bird .... Ge 7:23
animal or an unclean **c** animal. .... Le 5:2
These **c** animals are unclean .... Le 11:29
touching any unclean **c** animal, ... Le 22:5
The Hebrews are **c** out of the 1Sa 14:11
animals, birds, **c** things, and 1Ki 4:33
and all cattle, **c** animals and .... Ps 148:10
every kind of **c** thing and .... Eze 8:10
the birds, and the **c** things. .... Hos 2:18
like insects **c** on the ground. .... Mic 7:17

CRAWLS

everything that **c** on the earth................. Ge 6:7
of animal that **c** on the earth, ... Ge 7:14
animal that **c** on the ground is .... Le 11:41
anything that **c** on the ground, ... Dt 4:18
everything that **c** on the ground,............. Eze 38:20

CRAZY

pretended to be **c** in front of 1Sa 21:13
Why did this **c** man come to you?"........... 2Ki 9:11
the time he acted **c** so Abimelech .... Ps 33:22
foolish and doing **c** things. .... Ec 2:12
and it is **c** to act like a fool..................... Ec 7:25

CREAM

ends by saying c and wicked	Ec 10:13
the people go c with fear over	Je 50:38
Babylon's wine, so they went c.	Je 51:7
The rulers become c with wine;	Hos 7:5
say the spiritual person is c.	Hos 9:7
and cause its rider to go c,"	Zch 12:4
A man who is c with a demon does	Jn 10:21
They said to her, "You are c!"	Ac 12:15
excellent Festus, I am not c.	Ac 26:25
they will say you are c.	1Co 14:23
I am c to talk like this.	2Co 11:23
the prophet's c thinking.	2Pe 2:16

CREAM

for a ruler, she brought him c.	Jdg 5:25
rivers flowing with honey and c.	Job 20:17
covered with c and the rocks	Job 29:6
to be bathed in c and are set	Sng 5:12

CREATE

C in me a pure heart, God, and	Ps 51:10
Why did you c us? For nothing	Ps 89:47
cause trouble and c more evil.	Is 59:4

CREATED

In the beginning God c the sky	Ge 1:1
So God c the large sea animals	Ge 1:21
In the image of God he c them.	Ge 1:27
He c them male and female.	Ge 1:27
The Spirit of God c me, and the	Job 33:4
the moon and stars, which you c.	Ps 8:3
you c summer and winter.	Ps 74:17
You c the north and the south.	Ps 89:12
born and before you c the earth	Ps 90:2
and he c the land with his own	Ps 95:5
them, they are c, and you make	Ps 104:30
they were c by his command.	Ps 148:5
I was c in the very beginning,	Pr 8:23
doing, or how he c everything.	Ec 11:5
understand how the earth was c.	Is 40:21
Who c all these stars?	Is 40:26
c the skies and stretched them	Is 42:5
He c you, people of Jacob;	Is 43:1
I, the LORD, have c it.	Is 45:8
beings, whom I c, would die.	Is 57:16
in the place where you were c,	Eze 21:30
prepared on the day you were c.	Eze 28:13
good from the day you were c,	Eze 28:15
of the God who c those things,	Rm 1:25
He is the One who c everything.	Eph 3:9
foods which God c to be eaten	1Ti 4:3

CREATES

the mountains and c the wind and	Am 4:13
the dead and who c something out	Rm 4:17

CREATING

work he had done in c the world.	Ge 2:3

CREATION

is the story of the c of the sky	Ge 2:4
to Christ, there is a new c.	2Co 5:17

CREATOR

Can't the c of ears hear?	Ps 94:9
Remember your C while you are	Ec 12:1
Holy One, the C of Israel, your	Is 43:15
come down from the C of the sun,	Jam 1:17
to the faithful C as they	1Pe 4:19

CREATURE

Every c that had the breath of	Ge 7:15
every living c that is with you.	Ge 9:12
Attach one c on one end of the	Ex 25:19
He made one c on one end of the	Ex 37:8
He rode a c with wings and flew.	2Sa 22:11
Each c was fifteen feet tall	1Ki 6:23
One wing of one c was seven and	2Ch 3:11

life of every c and the breath	Job 12:10
desire the c your hands have	Job 14:15
it is a c without fear.	Job 41:33
He rode a c with wings and flew.	Ps 18:10
He gives food to every living c.	Ps 136:25
Each c had six wings:	Is 6:2
The c touched my mouth with the	Is 6:7
Each living c had a human face	Eze 1:10
Each living c had four faces.	Eze 10:14
a living c to guard you.	Eze 28:14
and every c had two faces.	Eze 41:18
first living c was like a lion.	Rev 4:7
I heard the second living c say,	Rev 6:3

CREATURE'S

One c wing touched one wall,	1Ki 6:27
The c other wing was also seven	2Ch 3:11

CREATURES

and c that swarm on the earth,	Ge 7:21
gold to make two c with wings,	Ex 25:18
the two winged c on the Ark	Ex 25:22
sewed designs of c with wings	Ex 36:8
gold to make two c with wings	Ex 37:7
between the gold c with wings.	2Sa 6:2
made two c from olive wood	1Ki 6:23
wings of these c were spread out	1Ki 8:7
between the gold c with wings,	2Ki 19:15
the golden, winged c on the Ark,	1Ch 13:6
of the gold c were thirty feet	2Ch 3:11
The c stood on their feet,	2Ch 3:13
it is king over all proud c."	Job 41:34
gave it to the desert c as food.	Ps 74:14
between the gold c with wings.	Ps 80:1
between the gold c with wings.	Ps 99:1
with c large and small that	Ps 104:25
Heavenly c of fire stood above	Is 6:2
of the heavenly c used a pair	Is 6:6
between the gold c with wings,	Is 37:16
what looked like four living c,	Eze 1:5
The living c had human hands	Eze 1:8
fire from between the living c,	Eze 10:2
the living c spread their wings	Eze 10:19
palm trees and c with wings were	Eze 41:20
the Ark were the c that showed	Heb 9:5
were four living c with eyes all	Rev 4:6
Then I heard all c in heaven and	Rev 5:13
The four living c said, "Amen,"	Rev 5:14
elders and the four living c.	Rev 7:11
four living c and the elders.	Rev 14:3
the four living c gave to the	Rev 15:7
and the four living c bowed down	Rev 19:4

CREDIT

will not get c for the victory	Jdg 4:9

CREEP

all the wild animals c around.	Ps 104:20

CREPT

Then David c up to Saul and	1Sa 24:4

CRETAN

The C people came from Crete and	Dt 2:23

CRETANS

the C destroyed them and took	Dt 2:23
prophets said, "C are always	Tit 1:12

CRETE

Casluhites, and the people of C.	Ge 10:14
people came from C and destroyed	Dt 2:23
left alive from the island of C.	Je 47:4
and the Philistines from C,	Am 9:7
had become Jews), C, and Arabia.	Ac 2:11
of the island of C near Salmone.	Ac 27:7
I left you in C so you could	Tit 1:5

CREWS

with Hiram's men as the c. 2Ch 9:21

CRICKETS

winged locusts, c, and .... Le 11:22

CRIED

very sad and c because of her. .... Ge 23:2
Then Jacob kissed Rachel and c. .... Ge 29:11
kissed him, and they both c. .... Ge 33:4
So Jacob c for his son Joseph. .... Ge 37:35
and the people c to the king for .... Ge 41:55
Then Joseph left them and c. .... Ge 42:24
his brothers and c as he hugged .... Ge 45:15
his father and c over him and .... Ge 50:1
When they c for help, God heard .... Ex 2:23
frightened and c to the Lord for .... Ex 14:10
So Moses c out to the Lord, ... Ex 15:25
Moses c to the Lord, "What can .... Ex 17:4
The people c out to Moses, ... Nu 11:2
c to the Lord, "We want meat! .... Nu 11:18
So Moses c out to the Lord, ... Nu 12:13
Aaron bowed facedown and c out, ... Nu 16:22
The Israelites c for Moses for .... Dt 34:8
the Israelites c for help. .... Jdg 2:18
the curtains and c out, ' .... Jdg 5:28
the Israelites c out to the Lord for .... Jdg 6:7
So Gideon c out, "Lord God!.................. Jdg 6:22
Samson's wife c for the rest of .... Jdg 14:17
The women c together out loud .... Ru 1:14
so sad that she c and prayed to 1Sa 1:10
all the people in town c loudly. 1Sa 4:13
your ancestors c to the Lord 1Sa 12:10
together, but David c the most. 1Sa 20:41
and his army c loudly until they.............. 1Sa 30:4
They c for Saul and his son 2Sa 1:12
all the people c at Abner's 2Sa 3:32
David c for his son every day................. 2Sa 13:37
As he went, he c out, "My son 2Sa 18:33
the other woman c. "The living 1Ki 3:22
The old prophet c out to the man 1Ki 13:21
he felt ashamed. Then Elisha c. 2Ki 8:11
Then Hezekiah c loudly. 2Ki 20:3
father Ephraim c for them many 1Ch 7:22
So they c out to the Lord, ... 2Ch 13:14
the first Temple c when they saw .... Ezr 3:12
I sat down and c for several .... Ne 1:4
our ancestors c out to you, ... Ne 9:27
They fasted and c out loud,.................... Est 4:3
king's feet and c and begged him .... Est 8:3
seven days Job c out and cursed.............. Job 3:1
I c for those who were in .... Job 30:25
I c out to my God for help. .... Ps 18:6
prayer when I c out to you for .... Ps 31:22
I c out to him with my mouth and .... Ps 66:17
misery they c out to the Lord, ... Ps 107:6
we sat and c when we remembered .... Ps 137:1
Then Hezekiah c loudly. .... Is 38:3
c like a bird and moaned like a .... Is 38:14
on the ground and I c out, ... Eze 9:8
he c and asked for his blessing. .... Hos 12:4
Then I c out, "Lord God, stop! .... Am 7:5
and each man c to his own god. .... Jnh 1:5
So the men c to the Lord, ... Jnh 1:14
to die, so I c to you, and you .... Jnh 2:2
you fasted and c in the fifth .... Zch 7:5
They c out, "Have mercy on us, ... Mt 9:27
a ghost!" and c out in fear. .... Mt 14:26
area came to Jesus and c out,................. Mt 15:22
At midnight someone c out, ... Mt 25:6
went outside and c painfully. .... Mt 26:75
But Jesus c out again in a loud .... Mt 27:50
he was a ghost and c out. .... Mk 6:49
Immediately the father c out, ... Mk 9:24

o'clock Jesus c in a loud voice, ... Mk 15:34
She c out in a loud voice, ... Lk 1:42
The blind man c out, "Jesus, Son .... Lk 18:38
he saw the city and c for it, ... Lk 19:41
went outside and c painfully. .... Lk 22:62
Jesus c out in a loud voice,..................... Lk 23:46
in the Temple, c out, "Yes, you .... Jn 7:28
Jesus c. .... Jn 11:35
he c out in a loud voice, ... Jn 11:43
Then Jesus c out, "Whoever .... Jn 12:44
But some in the crowd c out, ... Jn 19:12
his knees and c in a loud voice .... Ac 7:60
Stephen and c loudly for him. .... Ac 8:2
So he c out, "Stand up on your .... Ac 14:10
Lord unselfishly, and I often c. .... Ac 20:19
Remembering that you c for me, ... 2Ti 1:4
the blessing so much that he c. .... Heb 12:17
c bitterly because there was no .... Rev 5:4
pregnant and c out with pain,................. Rev 12:2
dust on their heads and c out, ... Rev 18:19

CRIES

the Lord has heard your c. .... Ge 16:11
God heard their c, and he .... Ex 2:24
If he c out to me for help, ... Ex 22:27
listen to their c when trouble .... Job 27:9
If my land c out against me and .... Job 31:38
not forget the c of those who .... Ps 9:12
my c are not hidden from you. .... Ps 38:9
I heard the c of those who are .... Ps 92:11
c out in the noisy street and .... Pr 1:21
but there were only c of pain. .... Is 5:7
My heart c with sorrow for Moab. .... Is 15:5
My heart c for Moab like a harp.............. Is 16:11
she c and has pain from the .... Is 26:17
will shout their c of sorrow. .... Is 43:14
nation of Judah c as if someone .... Je 14:2
morning and battle c at noon,................. Je 20:16
and your c fill all the earth. .... Je 46:12
Listen to the c from the town of .... Je 48:3
It c like a flute for the people .... Je 48:36
She c loudly at night, and tears .... La 1:2
a young woman c when the man she .... Joe 1:8
in the land c for the dead. .... Am 9:5
a day of alarms and battle c. '................. Zph 1:16
the truth about him and c out, ... Jn 1:15
have heard their c and have come .... Ac 7:34
And Isaiah c out about Israel:................. Rm 9:27
and the Spirit c out, "Father." .... Gal 4:6
prayed with loud c and tears to .... Heb 5:7
your fields c out against you, ... Jam 5:4

CRIME

accuse a person of a c or sin. .... Dt 19:15
of lashes should match the c. .... Dt 25:2
done? What is my c? How did I 1Sa 20:1
Because of his c, make his house .... Ezr 6:11
Charge them with c after crime,.............. Ps 69:27
What have I done against you .... Je 37:18
about a c or some wrong. .... Ac 18:14
'When a man is accused of a c, ... Ac 25:16
or any other c, nor because you 1Pe 4:15

CRIMES

it all the sins and c of Israel. .... Le 16:21
think up violent c in the land. .... Ps 58:2
forgive their c or erase their .... Je 18:23
full of bloody c and the city is .... Eze 7:23
they deserve to die for their c. .... Hos 12:14
For the many c of Damascus, ... Am 1:3
For the many c of Israel,....................... Am 2:6
know your many c, your terrible .... Am 5:12

CRIMINAL

life and was treated like a c. .... Is 53:12
and clubs as if I were a c. .... Mt 26:55
and clubs as though I were a c. .... Mk 14:48
'He was treated like a c,' .... Lk 22:37
and clubs as though I were a c. .... Lk 22:52
But the other c stopped him and .... Lk 23:40
If he were not a c, we wouldn't .... Jn 18:30
bound with chains like a c. 2Ti 2:9

CRIMINALS

and I will be treated as c." 1Ki 1:21
says, "They put him with c." .... Mk 15:28
crucified Jesus and the c— .... Lk 23:33
One of the c on a cross began to .... Lk 23:39

CRIPPLE

You will c their horses and burn .... Jos 11:6

CRIPPLED

and they c oxen just for fun. .... Ge 49:6
blind men, c men, men with .... Le 21:18
that has broken bones or is c, ... Le 22:22
an animal is c or blind or has .... Dt 15:21
he c their horses and burned .... Jos 11:9
who was c in both feet. 2Sa 4:4
blind and the c can stop you." 2Sa 5:6
blind and the c may not enter. 2Sa 5:8
And he was c in both feet. 2Sa 9:13
to Ziba, 'I am c, so saddle a 2Sa 19:26
He c all but a hundred of the 1Ch 18:4
tooth or walking with a c foot. .... Pr 25:19
as the legs of a c person. .... Pr 26:7
even the c people will carry .... Is 33:23
C people will jump like deer, ... Is 35:6
of the people are blind and c. .... Je 31:8
that time, I will gather the c; .... Mic 4:6
When you bring c and sick .... Mal 1:8
blind can see, the c can walk, ... Mt 11:5
there was a man with a c hand. .... Mt 12:10
blind, the c, those who could .... Mt 15:30
The blind and c people came to .... Mt 21:14
a man with a c hand was there. .... Mk 3:1
said to the man with the c hand, ... Lk 6:8
blind can see, the c can walk, ... Lk 7:22
spirit in her that made her c. .... Lk 13:11
in the poor, the c, the blind, ... Lk 14:21
blind, some were c, and some .... Jn 5:3
man who had been c all his life. .... Ac 3:2
Jesus that made this c man well. .... Ac 3:16
thing that was done to a c man? .... Ac 4:9
This man was c, but he is now .... Ac 4:10
many weak and c people there. .... Ac 8:7
sat a man who had been born c; .... Ac 14:8

CRISPUS

C was the leader of that .... Ac 18:8
any of you except C and Gaius 1Co 1:14

CRITICIZE

accuse and c the whole land. .... Je 15:10
that no one will c us for the 2Co 8:20
give people a reason to c him, ... 1Ti 3:2
so that no one can c them. 1Ti 5:7
will be able to c the teaching .... Tit 2:5

CRITICIZED

is better to be c by a wise .... Ec 7:5
Then Jesus c the cities where he .... Mt 11:20
and he c them because they had .... Mk 16:14
why am I c because of something 1Co 10:30
he will not be c by others and 1Ti 3:7
truth so that you cannot be c. .... Tit 2:8

CRITICIZING

those who were c him were .... Lk 13:17
give you wisdom without c you. .... Jam 1:5

CROCODILE

You are like a great c that lies .... Eze 29:3
You are like a c in the seas. .... Eze 32:2

CROCODILES

geckos, c, lizards, sand .... Le 11:30

CROOKED

They were like a c bow that does .... Ps 78:57
C leaders cannot be your friends. .... Ps 94:20
happy to do what is c and evil. .... Pr 2:14
nothing I say is c or false. .... Pr 8:8
something is c, you can't make .... Ec 1:15
Israel to show how c they are. .... Am 7:8
living with c and mean people .... Php 2:15

CROP

the loss from the best of his c. .... Ex 22:5
the bird's c and its contents .... Le 1:16
still be eating from the old c; .... Le 25:22
of that year's c and store it in .... Dt 14:28
because locusts will eat the c. .... Dt 28:38
of the first c and the second .... Am 7:1
where it grew and produced a c. .... Mt 13:8
share of the c at harvest time. .... Mt 21:41
plants did not produce a c. .... Mk 4:7
It got taller and produced a c. .... Mk 4:8
some land, which grew a good c. .... Lk 12:16
to harvest a c that you did not .... Jn 4:38
produces a good c for those who .... Heb 6:7
plant a good c of right-living .... Jam 3:18
for his valuable c to grow from .... Jam 5:7

CROPS

not grow good c for you anymore, ... Ge 4:12
years of good c and plenty to .... Ge 41:29
years of good c came to an end .... Ge 41:53
so these c were destroyed. .... Ex 9:31
and harvest c on your land. .... Ex 23:10
you harvest your c on your land, ... Le 19:9
You must not cut the c that grow .... Le 25:5
or harvest the c that grow by .... Le 25:11
You may eat only the c that come .... Le 25:12
don't plant seeds or gather c, ... Le 25:20
One-tenth of all c belongs to .... Le 27:30
from the first c they harvest. .... Nu 18:12
fields with good c and will give .... Dt 7:13
both c will be ruined. .... Dt 22:9
be blessed, as well as your c; .... Dt 28:4
destroy all your trees and c. .... Dt 28:42
the Israelites planted c, ... Jdg 6:3
and destroyed the c that the .... Jdg 6:4
farm the land and harvest the c. 2Sa 9:10
all the c will be destroyed 1Ki 8:37
so bad the land cannot grow c." 2Ki 2:19
keep the land from growing c.'" 2Ki 2:21
the c will be destroyed 2Ch 6:28
a tenth of our c to the Levites, ... Ne 10:37
and let my c be plowed up. .... Job 31:8
and then you bless it with c. .... Ps 65:10
you load the wagons with many c. .... Ps 65:11
The land has given its c. .... Ps 67:6
and the hills are covered with c. .... Ps 72:16
He gave their c to grasshoppers .... Ps 78:46
and the land will give its c. .... Ps 85:12
cry as they plant c will sing at .... Ps 126:5
be filled with c of all kinds. .... Ps 144:13
the firstfruits from all your c. .... Pr 3:9
who gather c on time are wise .... Pr 10:5
a hard rain that destroys the c. .... Pr 28:3
cloud will never harvest c. .... Ec 11:4
will eat good c from the land. .... Is 1:19
let you eat the c of the land .... Is 58:14
will eat your c and your food. .... Je 5:17
field and the c in the ground. .... Je 7:20

I will take away their **c,** .... Je 8:13
fields or vineyards, or plant **c.** .... Je 35:9
Babylon plant their **c** or gather .... Je 50:16
a place famous for its good **c,** .... Eze 34:29
cutting locusts that ate your **c**— .... Joe 2:25
of your **c** every three days .... Am 4:4
I made your **c** die from disease .... Am 4:9
ate all the **c** in the country, ... Am 7:2
harvesting **c** when it's time to .... Am 9:13
like grasshoppers eating **c,** .... Nah 3:15
and the ground holds back its **c** .... Hag 1:10
have seeds for **c** still in the .... Hag 2:19
the ground will give good **c,** .... Zch 8:12
and the tenth of your **c.** .... Mal 3:8
so they won't eat your **c.** .... Mal 3:11
You gather **c** where you did not .... Mt 25:24
that I gather **c** where I did not .... Mt 25:26
have no place to keep all my **c.**' .... Lk 12:17
is gathering **c** for eternal life .... Jn 4:36
from heaven and **c** at the right .... Ac 14:17
and the land produced **c** again. .... Jam 5:18

CROSS

the people can **c** it on dry land. .... Ex 14:16
that the people are not to **c.** .... Ex 19:12
make us **c** the Jordan River. .... Nu 32:5
and **c** the Jordan River armed, ... Nu 32:21
will **c** over into Canaan and go .... Nu 32:32
c south of Scorpion Pass, and go .... Nu 34:4
We want to **c** the Jordan River .... Dt 2:29
You will soon **c** the Jordan River .... Dt 9:1
When you **c** the Jordan River, ... Dt 27:12
now you will **c** the Jordan River .... Jos 1:11
the Israelites to **c** his land. .... Jdg 11:20
were too tired to **c** the ravine. 1Sa 30:10
desert but to **c** over the Jordan 2Sa 17:16
said, "Hurry, **c** over the river! 2Sa 17:21
but I will **c** the Jordan River 2Sa 19:36
there, and no lions **c** over it. .... Job 28:8
for the seas that they cannot **c,** .... Ps 104:9
of Moab try to **c** the river Arnon .... Is 16:2
Even if you **c** the sea to Cyprus, ... Is 23:12
When you **c** rivers, you will not .... Is 43:2
your legs and **c** the rivers. .... Is 47:2
your people to **c** over and be .... Is 51:10
where the roads **c** and look. .... Je 6:16
and he started to **c** over to the .... Je 41:10
was a river that no one could **c.** .... Eze 47:5
to carry the **c** and follow me is .... Mt 10:38
Simon, to carry the **c** for Jesus. .... Mt 27:32
down from that **c** if you are .... Mt 27:40
Simon to carry the **c** for Jesus. .... Mk 15:21
Come down from that **c!"** .... Mk 15:30
at a distance from the **c,** .... Mk 15:40
took the body down from the **c,** .... Mk 15:46
to carry his **c** and follow me .... Lk 14:27
so no one can **c** over to you, ... Lk 16:26
to carry Jesus' **c** and to walk .... Lk 23:26
criminals on a **c** began to shout .... Lk 23:39
took the body down from the **c,** .... Lk 23:53
a sign and put it on the **c.** .... Jn 19:19
Standing near his **c** were Jesus' .... Jn 19:25
to stay on the **c** on the Sabbath .... Jn 19:31
first man on the **c** beside Jesus. .... Jn 19:32
to death by nailing him to a **c.** .... Ac 2:23
Jesus by hanging him on a **c.** .... Ac 5:30
him by hanging him on a **c.** .... Ac 10:39
him down from the **c** and laid him .... Ac 13:29
Christ on the **c** so that our .... Rm 6:6
so that the **c** of Christ would 1Co 1:17
Christ and his death on the **c.** 1Co 2:2
when he was killed on the **c,** 2Co 13:4
to death on the **c** with Christ, ... Gal 2:20

death of Jesus Christ on the **c.** .... Gal 3:1
about the **c** would not be .... Gal 5:11
follow only the **c** of Christ. .... Gal 6:12
this with his death on the **c.** .... Eph 2:16
caused his death—death on a **c.** .... Php 2:8
like enemies of the **c** of Christ. .... Php 3:18
of Christ's death on the **c.** .... Col 1:20
rules and nailed it to the **c.** .... Col 2:14
With the **c,** he won the victory .... Col 2:15
Son of God to a **c** again and are .... Heb 6:6
He suffered death on the **c.** .... Heb 12:2
his body on the **c** so we would 1Pe 2:24

CROSSBAR

middle **c** is to be set halfway .... Ex 26:28
made the middle **c** run along the .... Ex 36:33

CROSSBARS

Make **c** of acacia wood to connect .... Ex 26:26
Next he put the **c** through the .... Ex 40:18
the Holy Tent, the **c,** the posts, ... Nu 4:31

CROSSED

left quickly, **c** the Euphrates .... Ge 31:21
rose and **c** the Jabbok River .... Ge 32:22
Israel **c** his arms and put his .... Ge 48:14
the Israelites **c** the sea on dry .... Ex 14:29
So we **c** the valley. .... Dt 2:13
After you have **c** the Jordan .... Dt 27:4
So the people **c** the river near .... Jos 3:16
The people **c** the Jordan on the .... Jos 4:19
stopped the water until we **c** it. .... Jos 4:23
Ammonites then **c** the Jordan .... Jdg 10:9
together and **c** the river to the .... Jdg 12:1
David **c** over to the other side 1Sa 26:13
They **c** the Jordan River, and 2Sa 2:29
King David **c** the Kidron Valley, ... 2Sa 15:23
Elijah and Elisha **c** over on dry 2Ki 2:8
to the left, and Elisha **c** over. 2Ki 2:14
They **c** the Jordan River and 1Ch 12:15
they **c** over the Jordan River. 1Ch 19:17
The people **c** the river on foot. .... Ps 66:6
c over the whole earth so fast .... Da 8:5
When they had **c** the lake, they .... Mt 14:34
When they had **c** the lake, they .... Mk 6:53
that the people **c** the Red Sea as .... Heb 11:29

CROSSES

he **c** the river, he and all his 2Sa 17:16
two robbers on **c** beside Jesus, ... Mk 15:27

CROSSING

the Jabbok River at the **c,** .... Ge 32:22
that you are **c** the Jordan River .... Dt 4:26
land you are **c** the Jordan River .... Dt 6:1
land you are **c** the Jordan River .... Dt 30:18
and camped there before **c** it. .... Jos 3:1
had finished **c** the Jordan, ... Jos 4:1
After they finished **c** the river, ... Jos 4:11
flowing until you finished **c** it, ... Jos 4:23
Gilead would kill him at the **c.** .... Jdg 12:6
As the king was **c** the river, ... 2Sa 19:18
After **c** the Jordan River, they 2Sa 24:5

CROSSINGS

leads to the **c** of the Jordan .... Jos 2:7
and captured the **c** of the Jordan .... Jdg 3:28
captured the **c** of the Jordan .... Jdg 12:5
wait near the **c** into the desert 2Sa 15:28
tonight at the **c** into the desert 2Sa 17:16
The river **c** have been captured, ... Je 51:32

CROSSROADS

along the road and at the **c,** .... Pr 8:2
stand at the **c** to destroy those .... Ob 1:14

CROSSWAYS

like one wheel c inside another .... Eze 1:16
like a wheel c inside another .... Eze 10:10

CROWD

said to the angry c around him, ... Jdg 6:31
month a large c came together 2Ch 30:13
people in the c had not made 2Ch 30:17
out the Teachings for the c .... Ne 8:2
so afraid of the c that I kept .... Job 31:34
walk with the c and lead them to .... Ps 42:4
sat with the c as they laughed .... Je 15:17
anger is against the whole c. .... Eze 7:12
will bring a c against you to .... Eze 16:40
of a reckless c in the city. .... Eze 23:42
sounded like the roar of a c. .... Da 10:6
When Jesus saw the c around him, ... Mt 8:18
After the c had been thrown out .... Mt 9:25
The c was amazed and said, ... Mt 9:33
Then Jesus left the c and went .... Mt 13:36
he saw a great c waiting. .... Mt 14:14
After Jesus called the c to him, ... Mt 15:10
The c was amazed when they saw .... Mt 15:31
followers came back to the c, ... Mt 17:14
The c said, "This man is Jesus, ... Mt 21:11
of what the c will do because .... Mt 21:26
Then Jesus said to the c, ... Mt 26:55
convinced the c to ask for .... Mt 27:20
get to Jesus because of the c, ... Mk 2:4
The whole c followed him there, ... Mk 2:13
and a large c from Galilee .... Mk 3:7
home, but again a c gathered. .... Mk 3:20
A great c gathered around him, ... Mk 4:1
to teach the c God's message— .... Mk 4:33
Leaving the c behind, they took .... Mk 4:36
c gathered around him there. .... Mk 5:21
A large c followed Jesus and .... Mk 5:24
him in the c and touched his .... Mk 5:27
he saw a great c waiting. .... Mk 6:34
Jesus called the c to him again, ... Mk 7:14
led the man away from the c, ... Mk 7:33
was a great c with Jesus that .... Mk 8:1
Then Jesus called the c to him, ... Mk 8:34
they saw a great c around them .... Mk 9:14
But as soon as the c saw Jesus, ... Mk 9:15
Jesus saw that a c was quickly .... Mk 9:25
others in the c who followed .... Mk 10:32
the c will be against us." .... Mk 11:32
The large c listened to Jesus .... Mk 12:37
The c came to Pilate and began .... Mk 15:8
through the c and went on his .... Lk 4:30
the middle of the c right before .... Lk 5:19
Turning to the c that was .... Lk 7:9
and a large c traveled with him. .... Lk 7:11
A large c from the town was with .... Lk 7:12
When a great c was gathered, ... Lk 8:4
to Galilee, a c welcomed him. .... Lk 8:40
woman was in the c who had been .... Lk 8:43
A man in the c shouted to him, ... Lk 9:38
a woman in the c called out to .... Lk 11:27
Someone in the c said to Jesus, ... Lk 12:13
but the entire c rejoiced at all .... Lk 13:17
too short to see above the c. .... Lk 19:3
the whole c of followers began .... Lk 19:37
when he was away from the c. .... Lk 22:6
was speaking, a c came up, and .... Lk 22:47
go free and told this to the c. .... Lk 23:20
large c of people was following .... Lk 23:27
and saw a large c coming toward .... Jn 6:5
Within the large c there, many .... Jn 7:12
heard the c whispering these .... Jn 7:32
A large c of people heard that .... Jn 12:9
day a great c who had come to .... Jn 12:12

The c said, "We have heard from .... Jn 12:34
went out to the c again and said .... Jn 18:38
But some in the c cried out, ... Jn 19:12
this noise, a c came together. .... Ac 2:6
a loud voice he spoke to the c: .... Ac 2:14
Seeing the c, the Jewish people .... Ac 13:45
able to keep the c from offering .... Ac 14:18
The c joined the attack against .... Ac 16:22
to go in and talk to the c, ... Ac 19:30
city clerk made the c be quiet. .... Ac 19:35
place where the c was gathered. .... Ac 21:32
Some in the c were yelling one .... Ac 21:34
The c listened to Paul until he .... Ac 22:22

CROWDED

all the people c around Jeremiah .... Je 26:9
and royal advisers c around them .... Da 3:27

CROWDING

keep people from c against him. .... Mk 3:9
people were c all around him. .... Lk 8:42

CROWDS

praise you among c of people. .... Ps 35:18
come to you in c as if they were .... Eze 33:31
When Jesus saw the c, he went up .... Mt 5:1
the hill, great c followed him. .... Mt 8:1
When he saw the c, he felt sorry .... Mt 9:36
Large c gathered around him, ... Mt 13:2
But the c heard about it and .... Mt 14:13
Great c came to Jesus, bringing .... Mt 15:30
Large c followed him, and he .... Mt 19:2
Jesus said to the c and to his .... Mt 23:1
When Jesus saw the c, he told .... Mk 3:9
C of people were coming and .... Mk 6:31
Again, c came to him, and he .... Mk 10:1
the c of people who came to be .... Lk 3:7
Large c were traveling with .... Lk 14:25
C came from all the towns around .... Ac 5:16
When the c saw what Paul did, ... Ac 14:11
and attacked before c of people, ... Heb 10:33

CROWED

At once, a rooster c. .... Mt 26:74
courtyard. And the rooster c. .... Mk 14:68
the rooster c the second time. .... Mk 14:72
was still speaking, a rooster c. .... Lk 22:60
true. At once a rooster c. .... Jn 18:27

CROWN

put the holy c on the turban. .... Ex 29:6
is the holy c, and carved these .... Ex 39:30
gold, the holy c, on the front .... Le 8:9
Then I took the c from his head 2Sa 1:10
took the c off their king's 2Sa 12:30
and put the c on him and gave 2Ki 11:12
David took the c off the head of 1Ch 20:2
That gold c weighed about 1Ch 20:2
and put the c on him and gave 2Ch 23:11
Vashti, wearing her royal c. .... Est 1:11
so he put a royal c on her head .... Est 2:17
with a royal c on its head, ... Est 6:8
and white and a large gold c. .... Est 8:15
and removed the c from my head. .... Job 19:9
I would put it on like a c. .... Job 31:36
and placed a gold c on his head. .... Ps 21:3
and thrown his c to the ground. .... Ps 89:39
shame, but his c will shine." .... Ps 132:18
a beautiful c on your head." .... Pr 4:9
is like a c for her husband, ... Pr 12:4
Gray hair is like a c of honor; .... Pr 16:31
is wearing the c his mother put .... Sng 3:11
That beautiful c of flowers is .... Is 28:1
give them a c to replace their .... Is 61:3
like a beautiful c in the LORD's .... Is 62:3
The c has fallen from our head. .... La 5:16

and a beautiful c on your head. .... Eze 16:12
royal turban, and remove the c. .... Eze 21:26
the silver and gold into a c, ... Zch 6:11
The c will be kept in the Temple............... Zch 6:14
in his land like jewels in a c. .... Zch 9:16
they made a c, put it on his.................... Mt 27:29
to make a c for his head. .... Mk 15:17
soldiers made a c from some .... Jn 19:2
wearing the c of thorns and the .... Jn 19:5
our c will never be destroyed.................. 1Co 9:25
and the c we will take pride in 1Th 2:19
Now, a c is being held for me—a 2Ti 4:8
he is wearing a c of glory and .... Heb 2:9
get a glorious c that will never 1Pe 5:4
I will give you the c of life. .... Rev 2:10
so no one will take away your c. .... Rev 3:11
he was given a c, and he rode................ Rev 6:2
and a c of twelve stars was on .... Rev 12:1
and there was a c on each horn.............. Rev 13:1
He had a gold c on his head and .... Rev 14:14

CROWNED
the angels and c them with glory .... Ps 8:5
the angels and c them with glory .... Heb 2:7

CROWNS
beautiful c have fallen from .... Je 13:18
and beautiful c on their heads. .... Eze 23:42
and had golden c on their heads. .... Rev 4:4
They put their c down before the .... Rev 4:10
wore what looked like c of gold,........... Rev 9:7
heads and seven c on each head. .... Rev 12:3
and on his head are many c. .... Rev 19:12

CROWS
The owls and c will sit on the .... Zph 2:14
the rooster c you will say three .... Mt 26:34
the rooster c twice you will say .... Mk 14:30
Before the rooster c twice, ... Mk 14:72
before the rooster c this day, ... Lk 22:34
the rooster c, you will say .... Jn 13:38

CRUCIFIED
given to his enemies to be c." .... Mt 26:2
Then they led him away to be c.............. Mt 27:31
When the soldiers had c him, ... Mt 27:35
Two robbers were c beside Jesus, ... Mt 27:38
for Jesus, who has been c. .... Mt 28:5
him out of the palace to be c. .... Mk 15:20
The soldiers c Jesus and divided .... Mk 15:24
who were being c beside Jesus .... Mk 15:32
from Nazareth, who has been c............... Mk 16:6
demanding that Jesus be c................... Lk 23:23
the soldiers c Jesus and the .... Lk 23:33
to sinful people, be c, and rise .... Lk 24:7
to death, and they c him. .... Lk 24:20
free and power to have you c?" .... Jn 19:10
Jesus over to them to be c. .... Jn 19:16
There they c Jesus. .... Jn 19:18
They also c two other men,.................... Jn 19:18
Jesus was c was near the city. .... Jn 19:20
You c him, but God raised him .... Ac 4:10
But we preach a c Christ. 1Co 1:23
not have c the Lord of glory. 1Co 2:8
Jesus have c their sinful .... Gal 5:24
cross of Jesus my world was c, ... Gal 6:14

CRUCIFY
beat him with whips and c him. .... Mt 20:19
of them you will kill and c...................... Mt 23:34
They all answered, "C him!" .... Mt 27:22
beat him with whips and c him. .... Mk 10:34
They shouted, "C him!" .... Mk 15:13
again, "Crucify him! C him!" .... Lk 23:21
Crucify him! C him!" But Pilate .... Jn 19:6

answered, "C him yourselves,.................. Jn 19:6
"Do you want me to c your king?" .... Jn 19:15

CRUEL
slaves and be c to them for four .... Ge 15:13
be cursed, because it is too c................. Ge 49:7
Anyone who says c things to his .... Ex 21:17
of Egypt were c to us and our.................. Nu 20:15
But the Egyptians were c to us, ... Dt 26:6
will become c to his brother, ... Dt 28:54
who hate you and are c to you. .... Dt 30:7
and was very c to the people .... Jdg 4:3
powerful and were c to Israel, ... Jdg 6:2
Rehoboam spoke c words to them,........... 1Ki 12:13
Rehoboam spoke c words to them,........... 2Ch 10:13
And Asa was c to some of the 2Ch 16:10
has seen the c way you killed 2Ch 28:9
from the clutches of c people.' .... Job 6:23
You write down c things against............... Job 13:26
c suffer during all the years .... Job 15:20
have never done anything c, ... Job 16:17
Almighty will give to c people: .... Job 27:13
The ostrich is c to its young, ... Job 39:16
you see these c and evil things; .... Ps 10:14
me and were c to me and ground .... Ps 35:16
a wicked and c man who looked .... Ps 37:35
and c people want to kill me. .... Ps 54:3
C people attack me, but I have .... Ps 59:3
the hold of evil and c people, ... Ps 71:4
save them from c people who try .... Ps 72:14
a gang of c people is trying to .... Ps 86:14
enemies were c to them and kept .... Ps 106:42
protect me from c people .... Ps 140:1
servant David from c swords. .... Ps 144:10
life will be given to someone c. .... Pr 5:9
but c men get only wealth. .... Pr 11:16
but c people bring trouble on .... Pr 11:17
acts of the wicked are c. .... Pr 12:10
C people trick their neighbors .... Pr 16:29
Liars pay attention to c words. .... Pr 17:4
so a c messenger will be sent .... Pr 17:11
Their c anger will come to an .... Pr 22:8
Anger is c and destroys like a .... Pr 27:4
ruler without wisdom will be c, ... Pr 28:16
person and the c person are .... Pr 29:13
C people had all the power, ... Ec 4:1
of those who are c to others. .... Is 13:11
The c king who ruled us is .... Is 14:4
The c people attack like a .... Is 25:4
if you stop using c words and................. Is 58:9
They are c and show no mercy. .... Je 6:23
rescue you from these c people." .... Je 15:21
The soldiers are c and have no .... Je 50:42
my people are c like ostriches .... La 4:3
I will hand you over to c men, ... Eze 21:31
priests do c things to my....................... Eze 22:26
learned to be c, and you sinned .... Eze 28:16
ruled the sheep with c force. .... Eze 34:4
Stop being c and hurting people, ... Eze 45:9
me a fourth animal that was c, ... Da 7:7
a bold and c king who tells lies .... Da 8:23
But that c king will be............................ Da 8:25
by a very c and hated man,.................... Da 11:21
because they were c to the .... Joe 3:19
not brag when c things are done .... Ob 1:12
people of the city do c things................. Mic 6:12
c and wild people who march................. Hab 1:6
people who do c things as easily .... Mal 2:16
Anyone who says c things to his .... Mt 15:4
Anyone who says c things to his .... Mk 7:10
pray for those who are c to you............... Lk 6:28
said many c things to Jesus. .... Lk 22:65

people and was c to our .... Ac 7:19
They will be c, will hate what 2Ti 3:3

CRUELEST

against you, the c nation. .... Eze 28:7
The c foreign nation cut it down.............. Eze 31:12

CRUELLY

must not rule c over your own .... Le 25:46
the foreigner rule c over him. .... Le 25:53
Children treat my people c, ... Is 3:12
treated their captives c. .... Je 50:16
and they will treat others c.' .... Lk 11:49
will arrest you and treat you c. .... Lk 21:12

CRUELTY

and much c from the proud. .... Ps 123:4
wickedness and c as if they were .... Pr 4:17
depended on c and lies to help .... Is 30:12
has felt your endless c. .... Nah 3:19

CRUMBLE

C it and pour oil over it; .... Le 2:6

CRUMBLES

A mountain washes away and c; .... Job 14:18
God shouts and the earth c. .... Ps 46:6

CRUMBLING

lives, which are c into ruins. .... Job 15:28

CRUMBS

dogs eat the c that fall from .... Mt 15:27
table can eat the children's c." .... Mk 7:28

CRUSH

descendants will c your head,.................. Ge 3:15
in handmills, or c it between .... Nu 11:8
He will c the heads of the .... Nu 24:17
wish God would c me and reach .... Job 6:9
He would c me with a storm and .... Job 9:17
you hurt me and c me with your .... Job 19:2
they c olives to get oil and .... Job 24:11
might step on them and c them; .... Job 39:15
C the wicked wherever they are. .... Job 40:12
God will c his enemies' heads, ... Ps 68:21
"We will completely c them!" .... Ps 74:8
me; all your waves c me. Selah .... Ps 88:7
I will c his enemies in front of .... Ps 89:23
they c your people and make your .... Ps 94:5
becomes angry, he will c kings. .... Ps 110:5
dishonest words c the spirit. .... Pr 15:4
you the right to c my people and .... Is 3:15
he will c our enemy Moab like .... Is 25:10
Israel will c the rocks of the .... Is 27:9
use a wagon wheel to c cumin. .... Is 28:27
walk on mountains and c them; .... Is 41:15
decided to c him and make him .... Is 53:10
last lion to c their bones was .... Je 50:17
where people c the grain at .... Je 51:33
Must you c the rest of the grass .... Eze 34:18
kingdom will c all the other .... Da 2:44
walk on and c the whole earth. .... Da 7:23
the poor and c people who are .... Am 4:1
You will c the grapes, but you... .... Mic 6:15
Then you will c the wicked like .... Mal 4:3
He will c out the wine in the .... Rev 19:15

CRUSHED

bring c heads of new grain .... Le 2:14
portion of the c grain and oil,................ Le 2:16
has bruised, c, torn, or cut sex .... Le 22:24
you pure oil from c olives. .... Le 24:2
I c it into a powder like dust .... Dt 9:21
c and pierced the side of his .... Jdg 5:26
I destroyed and c them so they 2Sa 22:39
they were c by the LORD and his 2Ch 14:13
dust, who can be c like a moth. .... Job 4:19
safety and are c in court with................ Job 5:4

he held me by the neck and c me. .... Job 16:12
in the night, and they are c. .... Job 34:25
The poor are thrown down and c; .... Ps 10:10
c them so they couldn't rise up .... Ps 18:38
those whose spirits have been c............. Ps 34:18
But you c us in this place where .... Ps 44:19
the bones you c be happy again. .... Ps 51:8
You c the sea monster Rahab; .... Ps 89:10
they c me to the ground. .... Ps 143:3
down on others will be c by it. .... Pr 26:27
people are c like grain on the .... Is 21:10
comes, you will be c by it. .... Is 28:18
Like a lion, he c all my bones. .... Is 38:13
not break a c blade of grass .... Is 42:3
he was c for the evil we did. .... Is 53:5
the nations and c them because .... Is 63:3
on your holy place and c it. .... Is 63:18
You c them, but they refused to .... Je 5:3
my people are c, I am crushed. .... Je 8:21
the Lord has c the capital city .... La 1:15
the earth is c under his feet; .... La 3:34
those nations on her side are c. .... Eze 30:8
ruin and have c you from all .... Eze 36:3
of the den and c their bones. .... Da 6:24
It c and ate what it killed, ... Da 7:7
the animal that c and ate what .... Da 7:19
Israel is c by the punishment, ... Hos 5:11
You c the leader of the wicked .... Hab 3:13
not break a c blade of grass .... Mt 12:20
falls, that person will be c." .... Mt 21:44
falls, that person will be c!" .... Lk 20:18
will be c by non-Jewish .... Lk 21:24

CRUSHES

way that iron c and smashes .... Da 2:40

CRUSHING

c Balaam's foot against it. .... Nu 22:25
stone on his head, c his skull.............. Jdg 9:53
walking on and c the thornbush. 2Ki 14:9
walking on and c the thornbush. 2Ch 25:18
do not ruin it by c it forever. .... Is 28:28

CRUST

to eat a dry c of bread in peace .... Pr 17:1

CRUTCH

someone who must lean on a c. 2Sa 3:29
you were like a c made out of a .... Eze 29:6

CRY

She sat there and began to c. .... Ge 21:16
he let out a loud and bitter c. .... Ge 27:34
Then Esau began to c out loud. .... Ge 27:38
and they c out to me for help,................ Ex 22:23
it is not a c of defeat. .... Ex 32:18
may c loudly about the LORD .... Le 10:6
the people not to give a war c. .... Jos 6:10
my friends go and c together." .... Jdg 11:37
they began to c out loud. .... Ru 1:9
until Hannah would c and not eat 1Sa 1:7
your eyes will c and your heart 1Sa 2:33
you will c out because of the 1Sa 8:18
positions, shouting their war c. 1Sa 17:20
they were too weak to c anymore. 1Sa 30:4
daughters of Israel, c for Saul. 2Sa 1:24
c for you, my brother Jonathan. 2Sa 1:26
sad you are. C for Abner." King 2Sa 3:31
Near sunset c went out through 1Ki 22:36
men of Judah gave a battle c. 2Ch 13:15
We will c out to you when we are 2Ch 20:9
Don't be sad or c." All the .... Ne 8:9
and heard them c out at the Red .... Ne 9:9
people should fast and c loudly. .... Est 9:31
They began to c loudly and tore............. Job 2:12
Don't let my c ever stop being .... Job 16:18

and the injured **c** out for help, ... Job 24:12
widows will not even **c** for them. .... Job 27:15
I **c** out to you, God, but you do .... Job 30:20
he hears the **c** of the needy. .... Job 34:28
evil people when they **c** out, ... Job 35:12
them, they do not **c** for help. .... Job 36:13
when their young **c** out to God .... Job 38:41
of commanders and the battle **c**.............. Job 39:25
Listen to my **c** for help, my King .... Ps 5:2
LORD has heard my **c** for help; .... Ps 6:9
listen to my **c** for help. .... Ps 17:1
when I **c** out to you for help. .... Ps 28:2
people when they **c** out to him, ... Ps 34:17
my prayer, and listen to my **c**................. Ps 39:12
He turned to me and heard my **c**. .... Ps 40:1
and do not ignore my **c** for help. .... Ps 55:1
I **c** out to God Most High, to the .... Ps 57:2
God, hear my **c**; listen to my .... Ps 61:1
When I **c** and fast, they make fun .... Ps 69:10
poor when they **c** out and will .... Ps 72:12
I **c** out to God; I call to God, ... Ps 77:1
widows were not allowed to **c**. .... Ps 78:64
I **c** out to you day and night. .... Ps 88:1
let my **c** for help come to you. .... Ps 102:1
misery when he heard their **c**. .... Ps 106:44
early in the morning and **c** out. .... Ps 119:147
Those who **c** as they plant crops............. Ps 126:5
Listen to my **c**, because I am .... Ps 142:6
listen to my **c** for mercy. .... Ps 143:1
listens when they **c**, and he.................... Ps 145:19
C out for wisdom, and beg for .... Pr 2:3
poor when they **c** for help will .... Pr 21:13
is a time to **c** and a time to .... Ec 3:4
C, because the LORD's day of .... Is 13:6
near the city gates, **c** out! .... Is 14:31
to the places of worship to **c**. .... Is 15:2
people of Moab **c** for the cities .... Is 15:2
from the Nile, will groan and **c**; .... Is 19:8
at me. Let me **c** loudly. Don't .... Is 22:4
told the people to **c** and be sad, ... Is 22:12
You trading ships, **c**! The houses .... Is 23:1
in Jerusalem will not **c** anymore. .... Is 30:19
C for the land of my people, ... Is 32:13
I said, "What shall I **c** out?" .... Is 40:6
He will not **c** out or yell or .... Is 42:2
out the battle **c** and defeat his................. Is 42:13
When you **c** out for help, let the .... Is 57:13
will **c** out, and he will say. '.................... Is 58:9
You will **c** loudly, because your .... Is 65:14
how sad you are, and **c** loudly. .... Je 4:8
in the land will **c** loudly, ... Je 4:28
I hear a **c** like a woman having a .... Je 4:31
C loudly for those who are dead, ... Je 6:26
They **c** from a faraway land: .... Je 8:19
will **c** loudly for the mountains .... Je 9:10
the women who **c** at funerals to .... Je 9:17
your daughters how to **c** loudly. .... Je 9:20
They will **c** to me for help, ... Je 11:11
will **c** secretly because of your .... Je 13:17
Let them **c** out in their houses .... Je 18:22
Don't **c** for the dead king or be .... Je 22:10
little children will **c** for help. .... Je 48:4
Cry, Moab, **c** out! Announce at .... Je 48:20
Their **c** will be heard all the .... Je 49:21
I **c** about these things;............................ La 1:16
The people **c** out to the Lord. .... La 2:18
I **c** out and beg for help, but he .... La 3:8
The king will **c** greatly, the..................... Eze 7:27
people who groan and **c** about all .... Eze 9:4
shout the battle **c** and give the .... Eze 21:22
do not **c** loudly for the dead. .... Eze 24:17
C and say, "The terrible day is .... Eze 30:2
he will **c** out in pain like a .... Eze 30:24

made the deep springs **c** loudly. .... Eze 31:15
c for the people of Egypt. .... Eze 32:18
just lie on their beds and **c**...................... Hos 7:14
They **c** out to me, 'Our God, we .... Hos 8:2
and the priests will **c** about it. .... Hos 10:5
wake up and **c**! All you people .... Joe 1:5
you people who drink wine, **c**! .... Joe 1:5
C because there will be no more .... Joe 1:13
should **c** between the altar and .... Joe 2:17
people should **c** loudly to God. .... Jnh 3:8
will moan and **c** because of this .... Mic 1:8
They will **c** to the LORD, but he .... Mic 3:4
Now, why do you **c** so loudly? .... Mic 4:9
ruins. Who will **c** for her?" .... Nah 3:7
I **c** out to you about violence, ... Hab 1:2
the walls will **c** out against you .... Hab 2:11
a **c** will be heard at the Fish .... Zph 1:10
the LORD; even soldiers will **c**. .... Zph 1:14
C, pine trees, because the cedar .... Zch 11:2
The land will **c**, each family by .... Zch 12:12
You **c** and moan, because he does .... Mal 2:13
people will **c** and grind their .... Mt 8:12
a sad song, but you did not **c**.' .... Mt 11:17
He will not argue or **c** out; .... Mt 12:19
people will **c** and grind their .... Mt 13:42
people will **c** and grind their .... Mt 22:13
the peoples of the world will **c**. .... Mt 24:30
gave a loud **c**, and then came out .... Mk 1:26
of himself and began to **c**. .... Mk 14:72
because you will be sad and **c**. .... Lk 6:25
for her and said, "Don't **c**."..................... Lk 7:13
a sad song, but you did not **c**.' .... Lk 7:32
You will **c** and grind your teeth .... Lk 13:28
to his people who **c** to him night .... Lk 18:7
then the stones would **c** out." .... Lk 19:40
of Jerusalem, don't **c** for me. .... Lk 23:28
going to the tomb to **c** there. .... Jn 11:31
truth, you will **c** and be sad, ... Jn 16:20
With that Spirit we **c** out, ... Rm 8:15
and it makes me **c** to tell you .... Php 3:18
Be sad, **c**, and weep! Change your .... Jam 4:9
C and be very sad because of the .... Jam 5:1
the earth will **c** loudly because .... Rev 1:7
elders said to me, "Do not **c**! .... Rev 5:5
high in the air **c** out in a loud .... Rev 8:13
Then they will **c** and be sad .... Rev 18:9
the earth will **c** and be sad .... Rev 18:11

CRYING

brother's blood is **c** out to me .... Ge 4:10
heard the boy **c**, and God's angel .... Ge 21:17
they named that place Oak of **C**. .... Ge 35:8
He was **c**, so she felt sorry for .... Ex 2:6
Moses, "Why are you **c** out to me?........... Ex 14:15
every family **c** as they stood .... Nu 11:10
keep **c** to me, 'We want meat!' .... Nu 11:13
in the camp began **c** loudly. .... Nu 14:1
to the Meeting Tent, **c** there. .... Nu 25:6
went to him, **c**, and said, "You .... Jdg 14:16
God until evening, **c** loudly. .... Jdg 21:2
why are you **c** and why won't you 1Sa 1:8
Eli heard the **c** and asked, ... 1Sa 4:14
oxen when he heard the people **c**. 1Sa 11:5
c as he followed her to Bahurim. 2Sa 3:16
Then she went away, **c** loudly. 2Sa 13:19
king's sons arrived, **c** loudly. 2Sa 13:36
who has been **c** many days for 2Sa 14:2
Mount of Olives, **c** as he went. 2Sa 15:30
king is sad and **c** because of 2Sa 19:1
to the ground, **c**, "The LORD is 1Ki 18:39
asked, "Why are you **c**, master?" 2Ki 8:12
joyful shouting and the sad **c**................. Ezr 3:13
confessing and **c** and throwing .... Ezr 10:1

people had been c as they .... Ne 8:9
and loud c among the Jewish .... Est 4:3
joy and their c for the dead was .... Est 9:22
My face is red from c; .... Job 16:16
my bed is soaked from my c. .... Ps 6:6
C may last for a night, but joy .... Ps 30:5
My eyes are weak from so much c, ... Ps 31:9
and my years are spent in c. .... Ps 31:10
as if I were c for my mother. .... Ps 35:14
My eyes are weak from c. .... Ps 88:9
You stopped my eyes from c; .... Ps 116:8
There will be c and sadness near .... Is 3:26
squares, they are c loudly. .... Is 15:3
C is heard everywhere in Moab. .... Is 15:8
Their c is like the crashing of .... Is 17:12
be filled with sadness and c. .... Is 29:2
The LORD will hear your c, ... Is 30:19
brave people are c out in the .... Is 33:7
the sounds of c and sadness. .... Is 65:19
of Israel and praying for .... Je 3:21
sound of loud c is heard from .... Je 9:19
They are c out against you. .... Je 12:6
those who are c for the dead. .... Je 16:7
him hear loud c in the morning .... Je 20:16
leaders of the people c loudly, ... Je 25:36
We hear people c from fear. .... Je 30:5
of painful c and deep sadness. .... Je 31:15
to meet them, c as he walked. .... Je 41:6
People are c on every roof in .... Je 48:38
Sounds of people c are heard in .... Je 51:54
women sitting and c for Tammuz. .... Eze 8:14
And in their loud c they sing a .... Eze 27:32
People will be c in all the .... Am 5:16
like a time of c for the death .... Am 8:10
to the shepherds c because their .... Zch 11:3
like someone c over the death .... Zch 12:10
will be much c in Jerusalem, ... Zch 12:11
of painful c and deep sadness. .... Mt 2:18
musicians and many people c. .... Mt 9:23
Why are you c and making so much .... Mk 5:39
who were very sad and were c. .... Mk 16:10
who are now c are blessed, ... Lk 6:21
behind Jesus at his feet, c. .... Lk 7:38
people were c and feeling sad. .... Lk 8:52
who were sad and c for him. .... Lk 23:27
Jesus saw Mary and the Jews .... Jn 11:33
Mary stood outside the tomb, c. .... Jn 20:11
her, "Woman, why are you c?" .... Jn 20:13
widows stood around Peter, c. .... Ac 9:39
Why are you c and making me so .... Ac 21:13
Those who are c should live as 1Co 7:30
your laughter into c and your .... Jam 4:9
death, and c, and great hunger, ... Rev 18:8
death, sadness, c, or pain, ... Rev 21:4

CRYSTAL
Gold and c are not as valuable .... Job 28:17
a sea of glass, clear like c. .... Rev 4:6
like a jasper, clear as c. .... Rev 21:11
shining like c and was flowing .... Rev 22:1

CUB
like a lion's c, who jumps out .... Dt 33:22
or a lion's c kills an animal. .... Is 31:4
This c roamed among the lions. .... Eze 19:6

CUBS
a bear that is robbed of its c. 2Sa 17:8
The c of the mother lion are .... Job 4:11
stars of the Bear with its c? .... Job 38:32
robbed of her c than to meet .... Pr 17:12
the young lions. She had many c. .... Eze 19:2
like a bear robbed of her c, ... Hos 13:8
lion killed enough for his c, ... Nah 2:12

CUCUMBERS
We also had c, melons, leeks, ... Nu 11:5

CUD
divided and that chews the c. .... Le 11:3
a split hoof and chews the c, ... Dt 14:6

CUMIN
the dill and scatters the c. .... Is 28:25
use a wagon wheel to crush c. .... Is 28:27
—even your mint, dill, and c. .... Mt 23:23

CUP
squeezed the juice into the c. .... Ge 40:11
he put the king's c of wine into .... Ge 40:21
Put my silver c in the sack of .... Ge 44:2
and found the c in Benjamin's .... Ge 44:12
each c had a bud and a petal. .... Ex 37:19
drank from his c and slept in 2Sa 12:3
the rim of a c or like a lily 2Ch 4:5
you fill my c to overflowing. .... Ps 23:5
LORD holds a c of anger in his .... Ps 75:8
will lift up the c of salvation, ... Ps 116:13
when it sparkles in the c, ... Pr 23:31
a round drinking c always filled .... Sng 7:2
punishment was like wine in a c. .... Is 51:17
anger is like the wine in a c. .... Je 25:15
to drink from the c of suffering .... Je 49:12
was like a gold c in the LORD's .... Je 51:7
The c of God's anger will come .... La 4:21
like a bitter c to drink. .... Eze 23:31
The c of anger from the LORD's. .... Hab 2:16
Jerusalem like a c of poison to .... Zch 12:2
little ones a c of cold water .... Mt 10:42
you drink the c that I am about .... Mt 20:22
make the inside of the c clean, ... Mt 23:26
Jesus took a c and thanked God .... Mt 26:27
not give me this c of suffering. .... Mt 26:39
drink the same c that I will .... Mk 10:39
Jesus took a c and thanked God .... Mk 14:23
Take away this c of suffering. .... Mk 14:36
outside of the c and the dish, ... Lk 11:39
Jesus took a c, gave thanks, ... Lk 22:17
This c is the new agreement that .... Lk 22:20
take away this c of suffering. .... Lk 22:42
drink the c the Father gave me? .... Jn 18:11
thanks for the c of blessing, ... 1Co 10:16
This c is the new agreement that 1Co 11:25
eat the bread and drink the c, ... 1Co 11:28
strength in the c of his anger. .... Rev 14:10
gave that city the c filled with. .... Rev 16:19
She had a golden c in her hand, ... Rev 17:4

CUPS
as well as the jars and c, ... Ex 25:29
must have three c shaped like .... Ex 25:33
be four more c made like almond .... Ex 25:34
Its flower-like c, buds, and .... Ex 37:17
branch had three c shaped like .... Ex 37:19
All of Solomon's drinking c, ... 1Ki 10:21
was not used to make silver c, ... 2Ki 12:13
All of Solomon's drinking c, ... 2Ch 9:20
served in gold c of various .... Est 1:7
wine and some c before the men .... Je 35:5
gold and silver c that his. .... Da 5:2
the drinking c from the Temple .... Da 5:23
outside of your c and dishes, ... Mt 23:25
as the washing of c, pitchers, ... Mk 7:4

CURDS
been cooked and milk c and milk. .... Ge 18:8
There were milk c from the cows .... Dt 32:14
honey, milk c, sheep, and cheese 2Sa 17:29
be eating milk c and honey when .... Is 7:15
eat the milk c, and you clothe .... Eze 34:3

CURE

He would c him of his disease."	2Ki 5:3
will suddenly be hurt beyond c.	Pr 29:1
There is no c for your pain.	Je 30:15
heal you or c your wounds.	Hos 5:13
but they could not c him."	Mt 17:16

CURED

and itches that can't be c.	Dt 28:27
knees and legs that cannot be c,	Dt 28:35
intestines that could not be c.	2Ch 21:18
my injury is not c or healed.	Je 15:18
have a wound that cannot be c;	Je 30:12

CURSE

So I will put a c on the ground,	Ge 3:17
May there be a c on Canaan!	Ge 9:25
I will place a c on those who	Ge 12:3
will place a c on me because I	Ge 27:12
against God or c a leader of	Ex 22:28
You must not c a deaf person or	Le 19:14
bitter water that brings a c.	Nu 5:18
and if you put a c on someone,	Nu 22:6
put a c on the people of Jacob	Nu 23:7
called you here to c my enemies,	Nu 24:10
you choose a blessing or a c.	Dt 11:26
Mesopotamia, to put a c on you.	Dt 23:4
He turned the c into a blessing	Dt 23:5
placed under a c to be our	Jos 9:23
for Balaam son of Beor to c you,	Jos 24:9
'Bitterly c its people, because	Jdg 5:23
So the c spoken by Jotham,	Jdg 9:57
I heard you speak a c about the	Jdg 17:2
used his gods' names to c David.	1Sa 17:43
did it, may the LORD c them!"	1Sa 26:19
Why should this dead dog c you,	2Sa 16:9
let him c me because the LORD	2Sa 16:11
and put a c on them in the name	2Ki 2:24
was tied to a c in case they	Ne 10:29
Balaam to put a c on Israel.	Ne 13:2
turned the c into a blessing.	Ne 13:2
and he will c you to your face."	Job 1:11
and he will c you to your face."	Job 2:5
stay innocent? C God and die!"	Job 2:9
Let those who c days curse that	Job 3:8
God has made my name a c word;	Ps 59:12
They c and tell lies, so let	Ps 59:12
but in their hearts they c.	Ps 62:4
fun of me use my name as a c.	Ps 102:8
They may c me, but you bless me.	Ps 109:28
LORD will c the evil person's	Pr 3:33
People c those who keep all the	Pr 11:26
Those who c their father or	Pr 20:20
people will c you, and nations	Pr 24:24
he will think of it as a c.	Pr 27:14
or they will c you, and you will	Pr 30:10
saved is a c to its owners.	Ec 5:13
will look up and c their king	Is 8:21
So a c will destroy the earth.	Is 24:6
A c is placed on those who trust	Je 17:5
there be a c on the day I was	Je 20:14
the world will c Jerusalem.'"	Je 26:6
will c them and be shocked	Je 29:18
in Babylon will use this c: '	Je 29:22
will become a c word, and people	Je 42:18
c will be on anyone who doesn't	Je 48:10
and put your c on them.	La 3:65
This is the c that will go all	Zch 5:3
I will send a c on you and on	Mal 2:2
So a c is on you, because the	Mal 3:9
come and put a c on the land."	Mal 4:6
began to place a c on himself	Mt 26:74
began to place a c on himself	Mk 14:71
bless those who c you, pray for	Lk 6:28

the law, are under God's c."	Jn 7:49
'You must not c a leader of your	Ac 23:5
them well and do not c them.	Rm 12:14
When people c us, we bless them.	1Co 4:12
make them right are under a c,	Gal 3:10
took away the c the law put on	Gal 3:13
us and put himself under that c.	Gal 3:13
but then we c people, whom God	Jam 3:9

CURSED

will be c as no other animal,	Ge 3:14
now you will be c in your work	Ge 4:11
from the ground the LORD has c."	Ge 5:29
everyone who curses you be c,	Ge 27:29
their anger be c, because it is	Ge 49:7
He has c his father or mother,	Le 20:9
person who had c outside the	Le 24:23
But God has not c them, so I	Nu 23:8
who curses you will be c."	Nu 24:9
But you will be c if you disobey	Dt 11:28
displayed on a tree is c by God.	Dt 21:23
Anyone will be c who dishonors	Dt 27:16
Anyone will be c who kills a	Dt 27:24
You will be c in the city and	Dt 28:16
Jericho will be c by the LORD.	Jos 6:26
ate and drank and c Abimelech.	Jdg 9:27
If he does, he will be c!"	1Sa 14:24
c David, saying, "Get out,	2Sa 16:7
should die because he c you,	2Sa 19:21
He c me the day I went to	1Ki 2:8
Now see about this c woman.	2Ki 9:34
said they would be c and would	2Ki 22:19
have sinned and c God in their	Job 1:5
cried out and c the day he had	Job 3:1
but I c his home immediately.	Job 5:3
Their part of the land is c;	Job 24:18
He c others as often as he wore	Ps 109:18
who ignore your commands are c.	Ps 119:21
'C is the person who does not	Je 11:3
of this, the LORD c the land.	Je 23:10
and the c false measure?	Mic 6:10
The person who cheats will be c.	Mal 1:14
I have already c them, because	Mal 2:2
fig tree you c is dry and dead!	Mk 11:21
wish that I were c and cut off	Rm 9:3
God's Spirit says, "Jesus be c."	1Co 12:3
is displayed on a tree is c."	Gal 3:13
is about to be c by God and will	Heb 6:8
and they c the name of God,	Rev 16:9
They also c the God of heaven	Rev 16:11
People c God for the disaster of	Rev 16:21

CURSES

everyone who c you be cursed,	Ge 27:29
Anyone who c his father or	Le 20:9
'If anyone c his God, he is	Le 24:15
write these c on a scroll,	Nu 5:23
anyone who c you will be cursed.	Nu 24:9
and the c from Mount Ebal.	Dt 11:29
on Mount Ebal to announce the c:	Dt 27:13
all these c will come upon you	Dt 28:15
LORD will send you c, confusion,	Dt 28:20
The c will be signs and miracles	Dt 28:46
life or death, blessings or c.	Dt 30:19
and the c, exactly as they	Jos 8:34
bring all the c that are written	2Ch 34:24
people, put c on them, hit some	Ne 13:25
Their mouths are full of c,	Ps 10:7
those he c will be sent away.	Ps 37:22
getting even with insults and c.	Ps 44:16
so let those same c fall on him.	Ps 109:17
C will not harm someone who is	Pr 26:2
the poor will receive many c.	Pr 28:27
will be like c to my servants,	Is 65:15

I made all the c of this .... Je 11:8
anything, but everyone c me. .... Je 15:10
brought on us the c and promises .... Da 9:11
been used as c in other nations .... Zch 8:13
Praises and c come from the same .... Jam 3:10

CURSING

woman began c and speaking .... Le 24:11
He kept c David and throwing 2Sa 16:13
my mouth sin by c my enemies' .... Job 31:30
C others filled his body and his .... Ps 109:18
C, lying, killing, stealing and .... Hos 4:2
are full of c and hate." .... Rm 3:14

CURTAIN

Make each c the same size— .... Ex 26:2
This c will separate the Holy .... Ex 26:33
The c was thirty feet long and .... Ex 38:18
he hung the c at the entrance .... Ex 40:28
in front of the c of the Most .... Le 4:6
the LORD in front of the c. .... Le 4:17
go behind the c into the Most .... Le 16:2
go through the c into the Most .... Le 21:23
is in front of the c of the Ark .... Le 24:3
the c at the entrance to the .... Nu 3:25
take down the c, and cover the .... Nu 4:5
the c for the entry to the .... Nu 4:26
at the altar or go behind the c. .... Nu 18:7
He made the c of blue, purple, ... 2Ch 3:14
the c in the Temple was torn .... Mt 27:51
c in the Temple was torn .... Mk 15:38
c in the Temple was torn in two. .... Lk 23:45
behind the c in the Most Holy .... Heb 6:19
the second c was a room called .... Heb 9:3
through the c—Christ's body. .... Heb 10:20

CURTAINS

Sew five c together for one set, ... Ex 26:3
Hang the c with silver hooks and .... Ex 27:10
must carry the c of the Holy .... Nu 4:25
through the c and cried out, ' .... Jdg 5:28
had fine white c and purple .... Est 1:6
of Kedar, like the c of Solomon. .... Sng 1:5
My c are torn down quickly. .... Je 4:20

CUSH

around the whole land of C. .... Ge 2:13
C also had a descendant named .... Ge 10:8
Then Joab said to a man from C, ... 2Sa 18:21
C was the father of Nimrod, ... 1Ch 1:10
that reached from India to C. .... Est 8:9
The topaz from C cannot compare .... Job 28:19
he sang to the LORD about C, ... Ps 6:10
people of C will pray to God. .... Ps 68:31
and C will be born there." .... Ps 87:4
the land beyond the rivers of C. .... Is 18:1
I gave C and Seba to make you .... Is 43:3
made in Egypt and C and the tall .... Is 45:14
a person from C change the color .... Je 13:23
the countries of C and Put who .... Je 46:9
all the way to the border of C. .... Eze 29:10
and C will tremble with fear. .... Eze 30:4
in ships to frighten C, ... Eze 30:9
Persia, C, and Put will be with .... Eze 38:5
to me than the people of C. .... Am 9:7
C and Egypt gave her endless. .... Nah 3:9

CUSHION

sleeping with his head on a c. .... Mk 4:38

CUSHITE

Moses because of his C wife .... Nu 12:1
The C bowed to Joab and ran to 2Sa 18:21
The C answered, "May your 2Sa 18:32
Tirhakah, the C king of Egypt, ... 2Ki 19:9
Tirhakah, the C king of Egypt, ... Is 37:9

a C and a servant in the palace, ... Je 38:7
commanded Ebed-Melech the C, ... Je 38:10

CUSHITES

and C from Egypt with him, ... 2Ch 12:3
defeated the C when Asa's army 2Ch 14:12
C and Libyans had a large and 2Ch 16:8
lived near the C to be angry 2Ch 21:16
You C also will be killed by my .... Zph 2:12

CUSTOM

this came a c in Israel that .... Jdg 11:39
as was the c for the bridegroom. .... Jdg 14:10
by the pillar, as the c was. 2Ki 11:14
It became a c in Israel to sing 2Ch 35:25
It was a c for the king to ask .... Est 1:13
the Jewish people set up this c. .... Est 9:27
to the c of the priests, ... Lk 1:9
But it is your c that I free one .... Jn 18:39

CUSTOMS

Do not follow their c. .... Le 18:3
Their c are different from those .... Est 3:8
nations and learned their c. .... Ps 106:35
The c of other people are worth .... Je 10:3
change the c Moses gave us." .... Ac 6:14
children and not to obey c. .... Ac 21:21
about all the c and the things .... Ac 26:3
people or the c of our ancestors .... Ac 28:17

CUT

the animals and c each of them .... Ge 15:10
he did not c the birds in half. .... Ge 15:10
C away your foreskin to show .... Ge 17:11
will be c off from his people .... Ge 17:14
After he c the wood for the .... Ge 22:3
So Jacob c green branches from .... Ge 30:37
was gone to c the wool from his .... Ge 31:19
to Timnah to c the wool from his .... Ge 38:13
the king will c off your head! .... Ge 40:19
place that he c out for himself. .... Ge 50:5
will be c off from Israel. .... Ex 12:15
must be c off from the community .... Ex 12:19
Then c it into pieces and wash .... Ex 29:17
to c jewels and put them in .... Ex 31:5
day must be c off from his .... Ex 31:14
Moses c two stone tablets like .... Ex 34:4
and c down their Asherah idols. .... Ex 34:13
to c stones and jewels and put .... Ex 35:33
are able to c designs in metal .... Ex 35:35
the animal and c it into pieces. .... Le 1:6
person must c the animal into .... Le 1:12
the whole fat tail c off close .... Le 3:9
So I will c him off from his .... Le 20:6
this day must be c off from the .... Le 23:29
Passover must be c off from the .... Nu 9:13
C two stone tablets like the .... Dt 10:1
not c yourselves or shave your .... Dt 14:1
you may c down trees that you .... Dt 20:20
of his sex organ c off may come .... Dt 23:1
any iron tool to c the stones; .... Dt 27:5
but they will c wood and carry .... Jos 9:21
they c off his thumbs and big .... Jdg 1:6
and c down the Asherah idol .... Jdg 6:25
of Baal and c down the Asherah ...... Jdg 6:30
took an ax and c some branches ...... Jdg 9:48
You must never c his hair, ... Jdg 13:5
I took her and c her into parts .... Jdg 20:6
no one will ever c his hair with 1Sa 1:11
And Samuel c Agag to pieces 1Sa 15:33
kill you and c off your head. 1Sa 17:46
I c off the corner of your robe, ... 1Sa 24:11
They c off Saul's head and took 1Sa 31:9
their beards and c off their 2Sa 10:4
me go over and c off his head!" 2Sa 16:9

cared for his feet, c his beard, ... 2Sa 19:24
They c off the head of Sheba son 2Sa 20:22
C the living baby into two 1Ki 3:25
commanded them to c large blocks 1Ki 5:17
c down that idol and burned it 1Ki 15:13
kill it and c it into pieces. 1Ki 18:23
You will c down every good tree.............. 2Ki 3:19
Then Elisha c down a stick and 2Ki 6:6
is sending men to c off my head. 2Ki 6:32
I have c down its tallest cedars 2Ki 19:23
He c up all the gold objects 2Ki 24:13
thousand men to c stone in the 2Ch 2:2
Asa c down that idol, smashed it 2Ch 15:16
was Hezekiah who c off the upper 2Ch 32:30
Then Josiah c down the incense 2Ch 34:4
they are c off like the heads of .... Job 24:24
They c tunnels through the rock............. Job 28:10
lips and c off those bragging .... Ps 12:3
oil, but they c like knives. .... Ps 55:21
them be c short like a broken .... Ps 58:7
raised as if to c down a forest................ Ps 74:5
Now it is c down and burned with .... Ps 80:16
remember anymore, c off from .... Ps 88:5
You have c his life short and .... Ps 89:45
grass that has been c and dried. .... Ps 102:4
living; he has c short my life. .... Ps 102:23
Let his life be c short, and let .... Ps 109:8
an evil person will be c short.................. Pr 10:27
of it and c out a winepress .... Is 5:2
will build again with c stones. .... Is 9:10
So the LORD c off Israel's head .... Is 9:14
who are great will be c down;.................. Is 10:33
one will ever c us down again." .... Is 14:8
but now you have been c down. .... Is 14:12
The workers c the wheat. .... Is 17:5
The enemy will c the plants with .... Is 18:5
aid you could c out a tomb for .... Is 22:16
chisels to c a statue and his .... Is 44:13
the rock from which you were c; .... Is 51:1
you c Rahab into pieces and .... Is 51:9
Go along and c down Judah's................. Je 5:10
C off your hair and throw it .... Je 7:29
They c a calf into two pieces .... Je 34:18
Moab's strength has been c off, ... Je 48:25
He c down his Temple like a .... La 2:6
am going to c off the supply of .... Eze 4:16
take one-third and c it up with .... Eze 5:2
as I live, I will c you off. .... Eze 5:11
and I will c off from you both................ Eze 21:3
tables made of c stone for the................ Eze 40:42
Then he will c off my head .... Da 1:10
you saw a rock c free, but no .... Da 2:34
saw a rock c from a mountain, ... Da 2:45
the tree and c off its branches .... Da 4:14
of the altar will be c off, ... Am 3:14
built fancy houses of c stone, ... Am 5:11
C off your hair to show you are .... Mic 1:16
mighty forest has been c down. .... Zch 11:2
LORD will still c that person .... Mal 2:12
now ready to c down the trees, ... Mt 3:10
c it off and throw it away. .... Mt 5:30
good fruit is c down and thrown............ Mt 7:19
the prison to c off John's head. .... Mt 14:10
c it off and throw it away. .... Mt 18:8
Others c branches from the trees .... Mt 21:8
the master will c him in pieces .... Mt 24:51
high priest and c off his ear. .... Mt 26:51
tomb that he had c out of a wall .... Mt 27:60
went and c off John's head .... Mk 6:27
causes you to sin, c it off. .... Mk 9:43
causes you to sin, c it off. .... Mk 9:45
Others c branches in the fields .... Mk 11:8
high priest and c off his ear. .... Mk 14:47

a tomb that was c out of a wall .... Mk 15:46
fruit will be c down and thrown.............. Lk 3:9
said, "I c off John's head, ... Lk 9:9
the master will c him in pieces .... Lk 12:46
I never find any. C it down. Why .... Lk 13:7
high priest and c off his right .... Lk 22:50
a tomb that was c out of a wall .... Lk 23:53
man whose ear Peter had c off. .... Jn 18:26
will die, c off from God's .... Ac 3:23
quiet while its wool is being c; .... Ac 8:32
At Cenchrea Paul c off his hair, ... Ac 18:18
So the soldiers c the ropes and .... Ac 27:32
So they c the ropes to the .... Ac 27:40
cursed and c off from Christ .... Rm 9:3
you will be c off from the tree. .... Rm 11:22
like a branch c from a wild.................... Rm 11:24
she should have her hair c off. 1Co 11:6
dogs, who demand to c the body. .... Php 3:2
death, they were c in half, and .... Heb 11:37

CUTS

Who c a waterway for the heavy .... Job 38:25
gates and c apart iron bars .... Ps 107:16
and anyone who c logs might be .... Ec 10:9
rolls up and c from the loom. .... Is 38:12
He c down cedars or cypress or .... Is 44:14
are the deep c on your body?'................ Zch 13:6
the farmer c it, because this .... Mk 4:29
He c off every branch of mine .... Jn 15:2
It c all the way into us, where................ Heb 4:12

CUTTING

his men who were c the wool from........... Ge 38:12
that the workers c the grain had.............. Ru 2:3
the workers c grain and gather .... Ru 2:7
killed him by c off his head. 1Sa 17:51
He was c the wool off his sheep 1Sa 25:2
that Nabal was c the wool from 1Sa 25:4
hill country, c stone, and he 1Ki 5:15
c themselves with swords and 1Ki 18:28
As one man was c down a tree, ... 2Ki 6:5
experienced at c down the trees 2Ch 2:8
person is like c off your feet .... Pr 26:6
You are c off the men and women, ... Je 44:7
What the c locusts have left, ... Joe 1:4
locusts and the c locusts that .... Joe 2:25
Swing the c tool, because the .... Joe 3:13
and c himself with stones. .... Mk 5:5
I killed John by c off his head. .... Mk 6:16
the high priest, c off his right .... Jn 18:10

CUZA

the wife of C (the manager .... Lk 8:3

CYMBAL

a noisy bell or a crashing c. 1Co 13:1

CYMBALS

tambourines, rattles, and c..................... 2Sa 6:5
tambourines, c, and trumpets. 1Ch 13:8
and c and to sing happy songs. 1Ch 15:16
and played c, lyres, and harps. 1Ch 15:28
played the c, was the leader. 1Ch 16:5
the trumpets and c and other 1Ch 16:42
and play harps, lyres, and c. 1Ch 25:1
the Temple of the LORD with c, ... 1Ch 25:6
in white linen and played c, ... 2Ch 5:12
their trumpets, c, and other 2Ch 5:13
the Temple of the LORD with c, ... 2Ch 29:25
of Asaph, stood with their c. .... Ezr 3:10
and with the music of c, ... Ne 12:27
Praise him with loud c; .... Ps 150:5

CYPRESS

Build a boat of c wood for .... Ge 6:14
and c trees growing together in .... Is 41:19
down cedars or c or oak trees. .... Is 44:14

CYPRUS

Large c trees will grow where .... Is 55:13
pine, fir, and c trees together. .... Is 60:13
made your deck from c trees from .... Eze 27:6

CYPRUS

the shores of C and defeat .... Nu 24:24
to the ships from the land of C. .... Is 23:1
sea to the island of C and see. .... Je 2:10
and came from the island of C. .... Eze 27:7
Joseph, a Levite born in C. .... Ac 4:36
far as Phoenicia, C, and Antioch .... Ac 11:19
they sailed to the island of C. .... Ac 13:4
took Mark and sailed to C, ... Ac 15:39
We sailed near the island of C, ... Ac 21:3
He was from C and was one of the .... Ac 21:16
sailed close to the island of C, ... Ac 27:4

CYRENE

a man from C, named Simon, to............. Mt 27:32
named Simon from C, the father .... Mk 15:21
Simon, a man from C, was coming........... Lk 23:26
the areas of Libya near C, ... Ac 2:10
which included people from C, ... Ac 6:9
were people from Cyprus and C. .... Ac 11:20
from the city of C), Manaen (who .... Ac 13:1

CYRUS

This is what C king of Persia 2Ch 36:23
In the first year C was king of .... Ezr 1:1
C king of Persia had given .... Ezr 3:7
C brought out from the temple in .... Ezr 5:14
King C gave an order about the .... Ezr 6:3
had commanded and as kings C, ... Ezr 6:14
I say of C, 'He is my shepherd .... Is 44:28
This is what the LORD says to C, ... Is 45:1
C, I call you by name, and I .... Is 45:4
will bring C to do good things, ... Is 45:13
until the first year C was king. .... Da 1:21
king and when C the Persian was .... Da 6:28
During C' third year as king of .... Da 10:1

D

DAGON

Gederoth, Beth D, Naamah, and.............. Jos 15:41
turned east and went to Beth D, ... Jos 19:27
great sacrifice to their god D .... Jdg 16:23
temple and put it next to D. 1Sa 5:2
they found that D had fallen on 1Sa 5:3
So they put D back in his place. 1Sa 5:3
they again found D fallen on the 1Sa 5:4
is punishing us and D our god." 1Sa 5:7
his head in the temple of D. 1Ch 10:10
will punish those who worship D, ... Zph 1:9

DAILY

This is the d burnt offering..................... Nu 28:6
addition to the d burnt offering .... Nu 28:10
Besides the d burnt offerings .... Nu 28:15
addition to the d burnt offering .... Nu 28:24
monthly and d burnt offerings .... Nu 29:6
the d burnt offering with its .... Nu 29:11
the priests do their d work..................... 2Ch 8:14
of the LORD for their d service, ... 2Ch 31:16
down in the d court record .... Est 2:23
order for the d court record to .... Est 6:1
They surround me d like a flood; .... Ps 88:17
It stopped the d sacrifices that .... Da 8:11
people stopped the d sacrifices. .... Da 8:12
vision last—the d sacrifices, ... Da 8:13
from offering the d sacrifice, ... Da 11:31
The d sacrifice will be stopped. .... Da 12:11
up their lives d to follow me. .... Lk 9:23
use and another thing for d use.............. Rm 9:21

DAMAGE

must repair any d they find in 2Ki 12:5
repairing the d of the Temple? 2Ki 12:7
to repair the d of the Temple 2Ki 12:12
do not d the olive oil and wine! .... Rev 6:6

DAMAGED

men, men with d faces, deformed .... Le 21:18
or men who have d sex glands. .... Le 21:20
was so d he did not look .... Is 52:14

DAMARIS

woman named D, and some others. .... Ac 17:34

DAMASCUS

the way to Hobah, north of D. .... Ge 14:15
slave Eliezer from D will get .... Ge 15:2
Arameans from D came to help 2Sa 8:5
groups of soldiers in D in Aram. 2Sa 8:6
went to D and settled there, ... 1Ki 11:24
and Rezon became king of D. 1Ki 11:24
Aram and ruled in the city of D. 1Ki 15:18
leads to the desert around D. 1Ki 19:15
And you may put shops in D, ... 1Ki 20:34
the rivers of D, are better than 2Ki 5:12
went to D, where Ben-Hadad 2Ki 8:7
with every good thing in D. 2Ki 8:9
the towns of D and Hamath for 2Ki 14:28
attacked D and captured it and 2Ki 16:9
Then King Ahaz went to D to meet 2Ki 16:10
saw an altar at D, and he sent 2Ki 16:10
When the king arrived from D, ... 2Ki 16:12
Arameans from D came to help 1Ch 18:5
groups of soldiers in D in Aram. 1Ch 18:6
king of Aram, who lived in D. 2Ch 16:2
things to their king in D........................ 2Ch 24:23
of Judah as prisoners to D. 2Ch 28:5
to the gods of the people of D, ... 2Ch 28:23
of Lebanon that looks down on D. .... Sng 7:4
Aram is led by the city of D, ... Is 7:8
and D is led by its weak king,................. Is 7:8
possessions of D and Samaria .... Is 8:4
city Samaria is like the city D. .... Is 10:9
This is a message about D: .... Is 17:1
The city of D will be destroyed; .... Is 17:1
The government in D will end. .... Is 17:3
message is to the city of D:..................... Je 49:23
The city of D has become weak. .... Je 49:24
D was a city of my joy. .... Je 49:25
will set fire to the walls of D, ... Je 49:27
the border between D and Hamath. .... Eze 47:16
belonging to D and Hamath lies .... Eze 47:17
a point between Hauran and D. .... Eze 47:18
where D lies to the north. .... Eze 48:1
For the many crimes of D, ... Am 1:3
bar of the gate to D and destroy.............. Am 1:5
you away as captives beyond D," .... Am 5:27
of Hadrach and the city of D. .... Zch 9:1
the synagogues in the city of D. .... Ac 9:2
So Saul headed toward D. .... Ac 9:3
his hand and led him into D. .... Ac 9:8
of Jesus in D named Ananias. .... Ac 9:10
Now he has come here to D, ... Ac 9:14
of Jesus in D for a few days. .... Ac 9:19
own people in D could not argue .... Ac 9:22
in the name of Jesus in D. .... Ac 9:27
me letters to the brothers in D. .... Ac 22:5
About noon when I came near D, ... Ac 22:6
answered, 'Get up and go to D. .... Ac 22:10
I told this first to those in D, ... Ac 26:20
When I was in D, the governor 2Co 11:32
Arabia and later went back to D. .... Gal 1:17

DAMPNESS

hair with the d of the night." .... Sng 5:2

DAN

all the way to the town of **D**. .... Ge 14:14
D will rule his own people like .... Ge 49:16
The tribe of **D** was counted; .... Nu 1:38
That was the family of **D**, ... Nu 26:42
D is like a lion's cub, who .... Dt 33:22
all the land from Gilead to **D**, ... Dt 34:1
and changed its name to **D**, ... Jos 19:47
tribe of **D** gave them Elteketh, ... Jos 21:23
People of **D**, why did you stay by .... Jdg 5:17
changed the name of Laish to **D**, ... Jdg 18:29
Israelites from **D** to Beersheba, ... Jdg 20:1
all Israel, from **D** to Beersheba, ... 1Sa 3:20
and Judah, from **D** to Beersheba!" 2Sa 3:10
surely as the god of **D** lives . . . '............... Am 8:14

DANCE

the man they **d** and sing about, ... 1Sa 21:11
the Israelites **d** and sing about, ... 1Sa 29:5
their little ones **d** about. .... Job 21:11
land of Lebanon **d** like a calf .... Ps 29:6
They will **d** and sing, "All good .... Ps 87:7
why did you **d** like sheep? .... Ps 114:6
why did you **d** like little lambs? .... Ps 114:6
time to be sad and a time to **d**. .... Ec 3:4
would at the **d** of two armies?................. Sng 6:13
again and **d** with those who are .... Je 31:4
of Israel will be happy and **d**, ... Je 31:13
You **d** around like a young cow in .... Je 50:11
for you, but you did not **d**; .... Mt 11:17
for you, but you did not **d**; .... Lk 7:32

DANCED

sang songs of joy, **d**, and played 1Sa 18:6
Then David **d** with all his might 2Sa 6:14
They **d** around the altar they had 1Ki 18:26
The mountains **d** like sheep and .... Ps 114:4
of Herodias **d** for Herod and his .... Mt 14:6
of Herodias came in and **d**,..................... Mk 6:22

DANCING

her, playing tambourines and **d**. .... Ex 15:20
he saw the gold calf and the **d**, ... Ex 32:19
playing a tambourine and **d**. .... Jdg 11:34
to come out to join the **d**. .... Jdg 21:21
While the young women were **d**, ... Jdg 21:23
jumping and **d** in the presence 2Sa 6:16
King David **d** and celebrating, ... 1Ch 15:29
You changed my sorrow into **d**. .... Ps 30:11
They should praise him with **d**. .... Ps 149:3
him with tambourines and **d**; .... Ps 150:4
our **d** has turned to sadness. .... La 5:15
heard the sound of music and **d**............... Lk 15:25

DANGER

put your neighbor's life in **d**. .... Le 19:16
will live with **d** and be afraid .... Dt 28:66
the LORD lives, there is no **d**.................. 1Sa 20:21
and no **d** threatens my people. 1Ki 5:4
I put myself in **d** and take my .... Job 13:14
you and sudden **d** frightens you. .... Job 22:10
During **d** he will keep me safe in .... Ps 27:5
for you we are in **d** of death all .... Ps 44:22
You have put them in **d**; .... Ps 73:18
will not fear any **d** by night or .... Ps 91:5
is always in **d**, but I haven't .... Ps 119:109
the poor will face no such **d**. .... Pr 13:8
The wise see **d** ahead and avoid .... Pr 22:3
Then you will be in real **d**. .... Pr 22:25
The wise see **d** ahead and avoid .... Pr 27:12
the helpless when they are in **d**. .... Is 25:4
So they will be in **d**. .... Je 23:12
ship was in **d** of breaking apart................ Jnh 1:4
When I was in **d**, I called to the .... Jnh 2:2
you will be in **d** of the fire of .... Mt 5:22

with water, and they were in **d**. .... Lk 8:23
There is a **d** that our business.................. Ac 19:27
but there is also another **d**: .... Ac 19:27
nakedness or **d** or violent death? .... Rm 8:35
For you we are in **d** of death all .... Rm 8:36
But because sexual sin is a **d**,.................. 1Co 7:2
put ourselves in **d** every hour? 1Co 15:30
are always in **d** of death so that 2Co 4:11
and have been in **d** from rivers, ... 2Co 11:26
I have been in **d** in cities, ... 2Co 11:26
And I have been in **d** with false 2Co 11:26

DANGEROUS

a **d** snake lying near the path. .... Ge 49:17
where the Canaanites live is **d**. .... Jos 17:16
of Bicri is more **d** to us than 2Sa 20:6
It's **d** to promise something to .... Pr 20:25
is as **d** as a deep pit, ... Pr 23:27
ruler is as **d** to poor people as .... Pr 28:15
death and are as **d** as traps. .... Ec 7:26
give birth to another **d** snake.................. Is 14:29
be like a quick, **d** snake to bite .... Is 14:29
Judah is a **d** place full of lions .... Is 30:6
nor will **d** animals be on that .... Is 35:9
through a dark and **d** land....................... Je 2:6
or like a dark and **d** land? .... Je 2:31
they are really **d** like wolves. .... Mt 7:15
and were so **d** that people could............... Mt 8:28
it was now **d** to sail, because .... Ac 27:9

DANGERS

will protect you from all **d**; .... Ps 121:7
is ready for the **d** of the night. .... Sng 3:8
us from these great **d** of death, ... 2Co 1:10

DANIEL

second son was **D**, whose mother 1Ch 3:1
of Ithamar: **D**. From the .... Ezr 8:2
D, Ginnethon, Baruch, ... Ne 10:6
men like Noah, **D**, and Job were............... Eze 14:14
even if Noah, **D**, and Job were .... Eze 14:20
You think you are wiser than **D**................ Eze 28:3
Among those young men were **D**, ... Da 1:6
D decided not to eat the king's .... Da 1:8
to be kind and merciful to **D**, ... Da 1:9
Ashpenaz said to **D**, "I am afraid .... Da 1:10
had ordered a guard to watch **D**, ... Da 1:11
D said to the guard, "Please .... Da 1:12
D could also understand visions............... Da 1:17
the young men were as good as **D**,........... Da 1:19
So **D** continued to be the king's .... Da 1:21
to look for **D** and his friends .... Da 2:13
But **D** spoke to him with wisdom .... Da 2:14
explained everything to **D**. .... Da 2:15
So **D** went to King Nebuchadnezzar .... Da 2:16
Then **D** went to his house and .... Da 2:17
D asked his friends to pray that .... Da 2:18
the secret to **D** in a vision. .... Da 2:19
D praised the God of heaven. .... Da 2:19
D said: "Praise God forever and............... Da 2:20
Then **D** went to Arioch, the man .... Da 2:24
D said to him, "Don't put the .... Da 2:24
quickly Arioch took **D** to the .... Da 2:25
The king asked **D**, who was also .... Da 2:26
D answered, "No wise man, ... Da 2:27
on the ground in front of **D**. .... Da 2:46
king said to **D**, "Truly I know .... Da 2:47
the king gave **D** many gifts plus .... Da 2:48
D asked the king to make .... Da 2:49
so the king did as **D** asked..................... Da 2:49
D himself became one of the .... Da 2:49
Finally, **D** came to me. .... Da 4:8
Then **D**, who was called .... Da 4:19
I am talking about is named **D**, ... Da 5:12
Call for **D**. He will tell you .... Da 5:12

So they brought **D** to the king, ... Da 5:13
the king asked, "Is your name **D?** .... Da 5:13
Then **D** answered the king, ... Da 5:17
an order for **D** to be dressed .... Da 5:29
announced that **D** was the third .... Da 5:29
D was one of the supervisors, ... Da 6:2
D showed that he could do the .... Da 6:3
king planned to put **D** in charge, ... Da 6:3
to accuse **D** about his work .... Da 6:4
reason to accuse **D** unless it is .... Da 6:5
Even though **D** knew that the new .... Da 6:10
times each day **D** would kneel .... Da 6:10
a group and found **D** praying and .... Da 6:11
said to the king, "**D**, one of the .... Da 6:13
D still prays to his God three .... Da 6:13
wanted to save **D**, and he worked .... Da 6:14
and **D** was brought in and thrown .... Da 6:16
The king said to **D**, "May the God .... Da 6:16
move the rock and bring **D** out. .... Da 6:17
He called out to **D**, "Daniel, ... Da 6:20
to Daniel, "**D**, servant of the .... Da 6:20
D answered, "O king, live forever! .... Da 6:21
to lift **D** out of the lions .... Da 6:23
D had trusted in his God. .... Da 6:23
who had accused **D** be brought to .... Da 6:24
fear and respect the God of **D**. .... Da 6:26
one who saved **D** from the power .... Da 6:27
So **D** was successful during the .... Da 6:28
king of Babylon, **D** had a dream. .... Da 7:1
D said: "I saw my vision at .... Da 7:2
I, **D**, was worried. The visions .... Da 7:15
I, **D**, was very afraid. .... Da 7:28
rule, I, **D**, saw another vision, ... Da 8:1
I, **D**, saw this vision and tried .... Da 8:15
I, **D**, became very weak and was .... Da 8:27
year as king, I, **D**, was reading .... Da 9:2
said to me, "**D**, I have come to .... Da 9:22
king of Persia, **D**, whose name .... Da 10:1
At that time I, **D**, had been very .... Da 10:2
I, **D**, was the only person who .... Da 10:7
said to me, "**D**, God loves you .... Da 10:11
man said to me, "**D**, do not be .... Da 10:12
He said, "**D**, don't be afraid. .... Da 10:19
Then he said, "**D**, do you know .... Da 10:20
Now then, **D**, I tell you the .... Da 11:2
But you, **D**, close up the book .... Da 12:4
Then I, **D**, looked, and saw two .... Da 12:5
He answered, "Go your way, **D**. .... Da 12:9
As for you, **D**, go your way until .... Da 12:13
D the prophet spoke about 'a .... Mt 24:15

DANITES
The **D** had not yet been given .... Jdg 18:1

DARE
Today I stand and **d** the army of 1Sa 17:10
How **d** you prophesy in the name .... Je 26:9
d you say that Jerusalem will .... Je 26:9
would **d** to come to me uninvited? .... Je 30:21
We do not **d** to compare ourselves 2Co 10:12

DARED
None of the followers **d** ask him, ... Jn 21:12
of the others **d** to join them, ... Ac 5:13
d to judge the devil guilty. .... Jud 1:9

DARIUS
the time **D** was king of Persia. .... Ezr 4:5
the second year **D** was king of .... Ezr 4:24
go to King **D** and his written .... Ezr 5:5
was sent to King **D** by Tattenai, ... Ezr 5:6
him: To King **D**. Greetings. May .... Ezr 5:7
King **D**, you should know that we .... Ezr 5:8
King **D** gave an order to search .... Ezr 6:1
I, **D**, have given this order. .... Ezr 6:12

out King **D'** order quickly .... Ezr 6:13
kings Cyrus, **D**, and Artaxerxes .... Ezr 6:14
in the sixth year **D** was king. .... Ezr 6:15
while **D** the Persian was king. .... Ne 12:22
D the Mede became the new king .... Da 5:31
D thought it would be a good .... Da 6:1
King **D**, live forever! .... Da 6:6
So King **D** signed the law. .... Da 6:9
So King **D** gave the order, and .... Da 6:16
Then King **D** went back to his .... Da 6:18
morning King **D** got up at dawn .... Da 6:19
King **D** was very happy and told .... Da 6:23
Then King **D** wrote a letter to .... Da 6:25
during the time **D** was king and .... Da 6:28
the first year **D** son of Xerxes .... Da 9:1
During **D'** first year as king, ... Da 9:2
first year that **D** the Mede was .... Da 11:1
the second year that **D** was king, ... Hag 1:1

DARK
sun went down, it was very **d**. .... Ge 15:17
the streaked and **d** animals in .... Ge 30:40
His eyes are **d** like the color of .... Ge 49:12
It will be so **d** you will be able .... Ex 10:21
them in the evening before **d**. .... Ex 12:6
This made it **d** for the Egyptians .... Ex 14:20
went near the **d** cloud where God .... Ex 20:21
other in the evening before **d**. .... Ex 29:39
and black clouds made it very **d**. .... Dt 4:11
it was still too **d** to recognize .... Ru 3:14
came down with **d** clouds under 2Sa 22:10
said he would live in a **d** cloud. 1Ki 8:12
sky was covered with **d** clouds. 1Ki 18:45
he would live in the **d** cloud. 2Ch 6:1
noon they found him in the **d**. .... Job 5:14
They are made **d** by melting ice .... Job 6:16
darkness and brings **d** shadows .... Job 12:22
I have **d** circles around my eyes. .... Job 16:16
when it is **d**, they say, 'Light .... Job 17:12
in their tents will grow **d**, ... Job 18:6
is why it is so **d** you cannot see .... Job 22:11
judge us through the **d** clouds? .... Job 22:13
In the **d**, evil people break into .... Job 24:16
There is no **d** place or deep .... Job 34:22
sea and wrapped it in **d** clouds, ... Job 38:9
shoot from **d** places at those .... Ps 11:2
came down with **d** clouds under .... Ps 18:9
I walk through a very **d** valley, ... Ps 23:4
their road be **d** and slippery as .... Ps 35:6
fills every **d** corner of this .... Ps 74:20
You walk in the **d**, while the .... Ps 82:5
am almost in the **d** place of the .... Ps 88:6
be known in the **d** grave? .... Ps 88:12
come in the **d** or sickness that .... Ps 91:6
Thick, **d** clouds surround him. .... Ps 97:2
You make it **d**, and it becomes .... Ps 104:20
darkness and made the land **d**, ... Ps 105:28
shines in the **d** for honest .... Ps 112:4
the darkness is not **d** to you. .... Ps 139:12
the wicked walk around in the **d**; .... Pr 4:19
it is still **d** and prepares food .... Pr 31:15
but fools walk around in the **d**. .... Ec 2:14
moon, and stars will grow **d**; .... Ec 12:2
I'm **d** but lovely, women of .... Sng 1:5
d like the tents of Kedar, ... Sng 1:5
look at how **d** I am, at how dark .... Sng 1:6
at how **d** the sun has made me. .... Sng 1:6
will become **d** in this thick .... Is 5:30
They lived in a **d** land, but a .... Is 9:2
skies will be **d**. The sun will .... Is 13:10
The sun will grow **d** as it rises, ... Is 13:10
hide my words in some **d** place. .... Is 45:19
I can make the skies **d**; .... Is 50:3

may walk in the **d** and have no .... Is 50:10
and your moon will never be **d**, ... Is 60:20
through a **d** and dangerous land. .... Je 2:6
Israel or like a **d** and dangerous .... Je 2:31
sky will grow **d**, because I have .... Je 4:28
slip and fall on the **d** hills. .... Je 13:16
day became **d** from sadness. .... Je 15:9
me sit in the **d**, like those who .... La 3:6
of Israel are doing in the **d**? .... Eze 8:12
and carry them out in the **d**. .... Eze 12:6
out in the **d** and carried them .... Eze 12:7
in the **d** and will leave. .... Eze 12:12
the day will be **d** when I break .... Eze 30:18
the sky and make the stars **d**. .... Eze 32:7
in the sky become **d** over you; .... Eze 32:8
scattered in a cloudy and **d** day.............. Eze 34:12
It will be a **d**, gloomy day. .... Joe 2:2
The sun and the moon become **d**, ... Joe 2:10
sun will become **d**, the moon red .... Joe 2:31
sun and the moon will become **d**, ... Joe 3:15
light, and the day into **d** night. .... Am 5:8
it will be very **d**, not light at .... Am 5:20
the earth **d** on a bright day..................... Am 8:9
It will become **d** for them, ... Mic 3:6
their day will become **d**. .... Mic 3:6
tell you these things in the **d**, ... Mt 10:27
because the sky is **d** and red. .... Mt 16:3
sun will grow **d**, and the moon .... Mt 24:29
noon the whole country became **d**,........... Mt 27:45
while it was still **d**, Jesus woke .... Mk 1:35
sun will grow **d**, and the moon .... Mk 13:24
the morning while it is still **d**,................. Mk 13:35
noon the whole country became **d**,........... Mk 15:33
none of it is **d**, then you will .... Lk 11:36
have said in the **d** will be heard .... Lk 12:3
whole land became **d** until three............. Lk 23:44
It was **d** now, and Jesus had not .... Jn 6:17
the tomb while it was still **d**. .... Jn 20:1
sun will become **d**, the moon red .... Ac 2:20
everything became **d** for Elymas, ... Ac 13:11
shine like stars in the **d** world. .... Php 2:15
a light shining in a **d** place,.................... 2Pe 1:19
So a third of them became **d**, ... Rev 8:12
sun and day became **d** because of .... Rev 9:2
were fiery red, **d** blue, and .... Rev 9:17

DARKEST
the land of **d** night, from the .... Job 10:22

DARKNESS
D covered the ocean, and God's .... Ge 1:2
he divided the light from the **d**. .... Ge 1:4
light "day" and the **d** "night,"............... Ge 1:5
separate the light from the **d**. .... Ge 1:18
asleep, a very terrible **d** came. .... Ge 15:12
and **d** will cover the land of .... Ex 10:21
and total **d** was everywhere in .... Ex 10:22
fire, the cloud, and the deep **d**; .... Dt 5:22
you heard the voice from the **d**, ... Dt 5:23
And I brought **d** between you and .... Jos 24:7
people will be silenced in **d**. 1Sa 2:9
made **d** his shelter, surrounded 2Sa 22:12
LORD brightens the **d** around me. 2Sa 22:29
Let that day turn to **d**. .... Job 3:4
Let **d** and gloom have that day. .... Job 3:5
Let thick **d** cover its light. .... Job 3:5
Let thick **d** capture that night. .... Job 3:6
D covers them up in the daytime; .... Job 5:14
from the land of **d** and gloom, ... Job 10:21
where even the light is **d**." .... Job 10:22
and **d** will seem like morning. .... Job 11:17
deep things of **d** and brings dark .... Job 12:22
feel around in **d** with no light; .... Job 12:25
up trying to escape from the **d**; .... Job 15:22

They know **d** will soon come. .... Job 15:23
They will not escape the **d**. .... Job 15:30
if I spread out my bed in **d**,..................... Job 17:13
from light into **d** and chased out .... Job 18:18
he has covered my paths with **d**. .... Job 19:8
d waits for their treasure. .... Job 20:26
But I am not hidden by the **d**, ... Job 23:17
by the thick **d** that covers my .... Job 23:17
D is like morning to all these .... Job 24:17
friends with the terrors of **d**. .... Job 24:17
place where light and **d** meet................. Job 26:10
the mines for ore in thick **d**. .... Job 28:3
I walked through **d** by his light. .... Job 29:3
when I looked for light, **d** came............... Job 30:26
seen the gates of the deep **d**? .... Job 38:17
home, and where does **d** live?................ Job 38:19
He made **d** his covering, his .... Ps 18:11
God brightens the **d** around me............... Ps 18:28
and you covered us with deep **d**. .... Ps 44:19
D is my only friend. .... Ps 88:18
LORD sent **d** and made the land.............. Ps 105:28
Some sat in gloom and **d**; .... Ps 107:10
gloom and **d** and broke their .... Ps 107:14
could say, "The **d** will hide me. .... Ps 139:11
But even the **d** is not dark to .... Ps 139:12
d and light are the same to you. .... Ps 139:12
me live in **d** like those long..................... Ps 143:3
the **d** of the night was just .... Pr 7:9
be like a light going out in **d**. .... Pr 20:20
just as light is better than **d**. .... Ec 2:13
to **d** without even a name. .... Ec 6:4
who think **d** is light and light .... Is 5:20
is light and light is **d**, ... Is 5:20
they will see only **d** and pain; .... Is 5:30
only trouble, **d**, and awful gloom .... Is 8:22
they will be forced into the **d**................. Is 8:22
Before those people lived in **d**, ... Is 9:2
LORD and who do their work in **d**. .... Is 29:15
Instead of having **d** and gloom, ... Is 29:18
those who live in **d** out of their .... Is 42:7
I will make the **d** become light .... Is 42:16
I made the light and the **d**. .... Is 45:7
sit in **d** and say nothing .... Is 47:5
' You will tell those in **d**, ' .... Is 49:9
your light will shine in the **d**, ... Is 58:10
light, but there is only **d** now. .... Is 59:9
light, but all we have is **d**. .... Is 59:9
D now covers the earth; .... Is 60:2
deep **d** covers her people. .... Is 60:2
before he brings **d** and before................. Je 13:16
he will turn it into thick **d**; .... Je 13:16
be forced into **d** where they will .... Je 23:12
He led me into **d**, not light. .... La 3:2
I will bring **d** over your land, ... Eze 32:8
he knows what is hidden in **d**, ... Da 2:22
the dawn into **d** and walks over .... Am 4:13
he changes **d** into the morning .... Am 5:8
It will bring **d** for you, not .... Am 5:18
s day of judging will bring **d**, ... Am 5:20
ruin, a day of **d** and gloom, a .... Zph 1:15
who live in **d** will see a great .... Mt 4:16
whole body will be full of **d**. .... Mt 6:23
only light you have is really **d**, ... Mt 6:23
then you have the worst **d**. .... Mt 6:23
be thrown outside into the **d**, ... Mt 8:12
him out into the **d**, where people .... Mt 22:13
into the **d** where people will cry .... Mt 25:30
the **d** lasted for three hours. .... Mt 27:45
the **d** lasted for three hours. .... Mk 15:33
shine on those who live in **d**, ... Lk 1:79
not to send them into eternal **d**. .... Lk 8:31
whole body will be full of **d**. .... Lk 11:34
let the light in you become **d**. .... Lk 11:35

time—the time when **d** rules." .... Lk 22:53
The Light shines in the **d,** .... Jn 1:5
the **d** has not overpowered it. .... Jn 1:5
They wanted **d,** because they were .... Jn 3:19
never live in **d** but will have .... Jn 8:12
Then the **d** will not catch you. .... Jn 12:35
you walk in the **d,** you will not .... Jn 12:35
in me would not stay in **d.** .... Jn 12:46
turn away from **d** to the light, ... Ac 26:18
minds were filled with **d.** .... Rm 1:21
a light for those who are in **d** .... Rm 2:19
that belong to **d** and take up .... Rm 13:12
things that are now hidden in **d,** 1Co 4:5
the light shine out of the **d!**" 2Co 4:6
and **d** cannot share together. 2Co 6:14
In the past you were full of **d,** .... Eph 5:8
to do with the things done in **d,** .... Eph 5:11
the powers of this world's **d,** .... Eph 6:12
freed us from the power of **d,** .... Col 1:13
not living in **d,** and so that day 1Th 5:4
not belong to the night or to **d.** 1Th 5:5
have not come to **d,** sadness, and .... Heb 12:18
called you out of **d** into his 1Pe 2:9
them in caves of where they 2Pe 2:4
in the blackest **d** has been kept 2Pe 2:17
and in him there is no **d** at all. 1Jn 1:5
but we continue living in **d,** 1Jn 1:6
because the **d** is passing away, ... 1Jn 2:8
or sister, is still in the **d,** 1Jn 2:9
a brother or sister is in **d,** 1Jn 2:11
lives in **d,** and does not know 1Jn 2:11
because the **d** has made that 1Jn 2:11
Lord has kept these angels in **d,** .... Jud 1:6
in the blackest **d** has been kept .... Jud 1:13
and **d** covered its kingdom. .... Rev 16:10

DARTING
poisonous snakes and **d** snakes. .... Is 30:6

DARTS
you stick **d** all over its skin .... Job 41:7
nor the arrows, **d,** and spears. .... Job 41:26

DATE
down today's **d,** this very date. .... Eze 24:2
down today's **d,** this very **d.** .... Eze 24:2
trees, the **d** palm trees, the .... Joe 1:12

DATES
bread, a cake of **d,** and a cake 2Sa 6:19
of bread, some **d,** and raisins to 1Ch 16:3
authority to decide **d** and times. .... Ac 1:7
to write you about times and **d.** 1Th 5:1

DATHAN
Korah, **D,** Abiram, and On turned .... Nu 16:1
D and Abiram were brothers, ... Nu 16:1
D, Abiram, and On were from the .... Nu 16:1
Then Moses called **D** and Abiram, ... Nu 16:12
tents of Korah, **D,** and Abiram." .... Nu 16:24
stood and went to **D** and Abiram; .... Nu 16:25
tents of Korah, **D,** and Abiram. .... Nu 16:27
D and Abiram were standing .... Nu 16:27
sons were Nemuel, **D,** and Abiram. .... Nu 26:9
D and Abiram were the leaders .... Nu 26:9
see what he did to **D** and Abiram, ... Dt 11:6
and swallowed **D** and closed over .... Ps 106:17

DAUGHTER
She was the **d** of Haran, who was .... Ge 11:29
One day the older **d** said to the .... Ge 19:31
and the older **d** went and had .... Ge 19:33
next day the older **d** said to the .... Ge 19:34
and the younger **d** went and had .... Ge 19:35
The older **d** gave birth to a son .... Ge 19:37
The younger **d** also gave birth to .... Ge 19:38
She is the **d** of my father, ... Ge 20:12

she is not the **d** of my mother. .... Ge 20:12
Rebekah, the **d** of Bethuel, came .... Ge 24:15
was Bethuel's **d** and the sister .... Ge 25:20
Judith **d** of Beeri and Basemath .... Ge 26:34
of Beeri and Basemath **d** of Elon. .... Ge 26:34
married Mahalath, Ishmael's **d.** .... Ge 28:9
his **d** Rachel is coming now with .... Ge 29:6
Jacob saw Laban's **d** Rachel and .... Ge 29:10
me marry your younger **d** Rachel. .... Ge 29:18
he brought his **d** Leah to Jacob, ... Ge 29:23
Zilpah to his **d** to be her .... Ge 29:24
the younger **d** to marry before .... Ge 29:26
to marry before the older **d.** .... Ge 29:26
gave him his **d** Rachel as a wife. .... Ge 29:28
Bilhah to his **d** Rachel to be her .... Ge 29:29
gave birth to a **d** and named her. .... Ge 30:21
time Dinah, the **d** of Leah and .... Ge 34:1
how Shechem had disgraced his **d,** .... Ge 34:5
sexual relations with Jacob's **d;** .... Ge 34:7
because he loved Jacob's **d.** .... Ge 34:19
Adah **d** of Elon the Hittite; .... Ge 36:2
Oholibamah **d** of Anah, the son .... Ge 36:2
Basemath, Ishmael's **d,** the .... Ge 36:3
was Oholibamah the **d** of Anah. .... Ge 36:14
wife Oholibamah the **d** of Anah. .... Ge 36:18
Dishon and Oholibamah **d** of Anah. .... Ge 36:25
name was Mehetabel **d** of Matred, ... Ge 36:39
who was the **d** of Me-Zahab. .... Ge 36:39
the **d** of a man named Shua, ... Ge 38:2
wife, the **d** of Shua, died. .... Ge 38:12
who was the **d** of Potiphera, ... Ge 41:45
wife was Asenath **d** of Potiphera, ... Ge 41:50
in addition to his **d** Dinah. .... Ge 46:15
whom Laban gave to his **d** Leah. .... Ge 46:18
Asenath, the **d** of Potiphera, ... Ge 46:20
whom Laban gave to his **d** Rachel. .... Ge 46:25
Then the **d** of the king of Egypt .... Ex 2:5
The king's **d** opened the basket .... Ex 2:6
sister asked the king's **d,** .... Ex 2:7
The king's **d** said, "Go!" .... Ex 2:8
The king's **d** said to the woman, ... Ex 2:9
woman took him to the king's **d,** .... Ex 2:10
The king's **d** named him Moses, ... Ex 2:10
and he gave his **d** Zipporah to .... Ex 2:21
d of Amminadab and the sister .... Ex 6:23
of Aaron married a **d** of Putiel, ... Ex 6:25
you, your son or **d,** your male or .... Ex 20:10
If a man sells his **d** as a slave, ... Ex 21:7
son, he must treat her as a **d.** .... Ex 21:9
bull kills a person's son or **d.** .... Ex 21:31
to allow his **d** to marry him, ... Ex 22:17
But if she gives birth to a **d,** .... Le 12:5
she has a son or **d** and her days .... Le 12:6
either the **d** of your father or .... Le 18:9
with your son's **d** or your .... Le 18:10
daughter or your daughter's **d;** .... Le 18:10
father and his wife have a **d,** .... Le 18:11
with both a woman and her **d.** .... Le 18:17
either the **d** of her son or her .... Le 18:17
daughter of her son or her **d;** .... Le 18:17
dishonor your **d** by making her .... Le 19:29
d of either his father or his .... Le 20:17
or father, son or **d,** brother .... Le 21:2
If a priest's **d** makes herself .... Le 21:9
If a priest's **d** marries a person .... Le 22:12
the priest's **d** becomes widowed .... Le 22:13
the **d** of Dibri from the family. .... Le 24:11
put to death was Cozbi **d** of Zur, ... Nu 25:15
the **d** of a Midianite leader. .... Nu 25:18
Asher also had a **d** named Serah. .... Nu 26:46
he owned should go to his **d.** .... Nu 27:8
If he has no **d,** then everything .... Nu 27:9
you, your son or **d,** your male or .... Dt 5:14

your son or **d,** the wife you love .... Dt 13:6
offer a son or **d** as a sacrifice .... Dt 18:10
I gave my **d** to this man to be .... Dt 22:16
man has told lies about my **d.**.................... Dt 22:17
not find your **d** to be a virgin,.................. Dt 22:17
proof that my **d** was a virgin." .... Dt 22:17
his father's **d** or his mother's .... Dt 27:22
daughter or his mother's **d.**" .... Dt 27:22
she loves and to her son and **d.** .... Dt 28:56
give Acsah, my **d,** as a wife to .... Jos 15:16
Caleb gave his **d** Acsah to .... Jos 15:17
give Acsah, my **d,** as a wife to .... Jdg 1:12
Caleb gave his **d** Acsah to .... Jdg 1:13
his **d** was the first one to come .... Jdg 11:34
Jephthah saw his **d,** he tore his .... Jdg 11:35
He said, "My **d!** You have made me .... Jdg 11:35
Then his **d** said, "Father, you .... Jdg 11:36
d never had a husband. .... Jdg 11:39
to remember the **d** of Jephthah .... Jdg 11:40
here are my **d,** who has never................. Jdg 19:24
of us will let his **d** marry a man .... Jdg 21:1
Naomi said, "Go, my **d.**" .... Ru 2:2
said to Ruth, "Listen, my **d.** .... Ru 2:8
said to her, "My **d,** I must find .... Ru 3:1
said, "The LORD bless you, my **d.** .... Ru 3:10
Now, my **d,** don't be afraid...................... Ru 3:11
asked, "How did you do, my **d?**" .... Ru 3:16
Ruth, my **d,** wait here until .... Ru 3:18
His older **d** was named Merab, ... 1Sa 14:49
his younger **d** was named Michal. 1Sa 14:49
wife was Ahinoam **d** of Ahimaaz. 1Sa 14:50
whoever kills him marry his **d.** 1Sa 17:25
Here is my older **d** Merab. 1Sa 18:17
came for Saul's **d** Merab to marry 1Sa 18:19
Saul's other **d,** Michal, loved 1Sa 18:20
gave him his **d** Michal for his 1Sa 18:27
and that his **d** Michal loved.................... 1Sa 18:28
Saul's **d** Michal was also David's 1Sa 25:44
mother was Maacah **d** of Talmai, ... 2Sa 3:3
Rizpah, who was the **d** of Aiah. 2Sa 3:7
bring Saul's **d** Michal to me." 2Sa 3:13
Saul's **d** Michal looked out the 2Sa 6:16
but Saul's **d** Michal came out to 2Sa 6:20
And Saul's **d** Michal had no 2Sa 6:23
woman is Bathsheba **d** of Eliam. 2Sa 11:3
The lamb was like a **d** to him.................... 2Sa 12:3
had three sons and one **d.** 2Sa 14:27
mother was Abigail **d** of Nahash 2Sa 17:25
Rizpah was the **d** of Aiah. 2Sa 21:8
the five sons of Saul's **d** Merab. 2Sa 21:8
Aiah's **d** Rizpah took the rough 2Sa 21:10
told David what Aiah's **d** Rizpah, ... 2Sa 21:11
by marrying his **d** and bringing 1Ki 3:1
married to Taphath, Solomon's **d.** 1Ki 4:11
to Basemath, Solomon's **d.** 1Ki 4:15
who was the **d** of the king of 1Ki 7:8
as a wedding present to his **d,** 1Ki 9:16
The **d** of the king of Egypt moved 1Ki 9:24
He loved the **d** of the king of 1Ki 11:1
was Maacah **d** of Abishalom. 1Ki 15:2
was Maacah, the **d** of Abishalom. 1Ki 15:10
He married Jezebel **d** of Ethbaal, ... 1Ki 16:31
name was Azubah **d** of Shilhi. 1Ki 22:42
because he married Ahab's **d**.................... 2Ki 8:18
because she is a king's **d.**" 2Ki 9:34
King Jehoram's **d** and Ahaziah's 2Ki 11:2
'Let your **d** marry my son.' 2Ki 14:9
name was Jerusha **d** of Zadok. 2Ki 15:33
name was Abijah **d** of Zechariah. 2Ki 18:2
was Meshullemeth **d** of Haruz, ... 2Ki 21:19
name was Jedidah **d** of Adaiah, ... 2Ki 22:1
his son or **d** to Molech. 2Ki 23:10
who was the **d** of Jeremiah from 2Ki 23:31

name was Zebidah **d** of Pedaiah, ... 2Ki 23:36
name was Nehushta **d** of Elnathan............ 2Ki 24:8
name was Hamutal **d** of Jeremiah 2Ki 24:18
and she was the **d** of Matred,................. 1Ch 1:50
who was the **d** of Me-Zahab. 1Ch 1:50
woman, the **d** of Shua, was their 1Ch 2:3
he married the **d** of Makir, ... 1Ch 2:21
sexual relations with Makir's **d,** 1Ch 2:21
Sheshan let his **d** marry his 1Ch 2:35
Caleb's **d** was Acsah. 1Ch 2:49
mother was Maacah **d** of Talmai, ... 1Ch 3:2
David and Bathsheba, Ammiel's **d**........... 1Ch 3:5
David also had a **d** named Tamar. 1Ch 3:9
Ephraim's **d** was Sheerah. 1Ch 7:24
Saul's **d** Michal watched from a 1Ch 15:29
Solomon brought the **d** of the.................. 2Ch 8:11
the **d** of Jerimoth and Abihail. 2Ch 11:18
and Abihail was the **d** of Eliab, ... 2Ch 11:18
married Absalom's **d** Maacah, ... 2Ch 11:20
His mother was Maacah **d** of Uriel........... 2Ch 13:2
name was Azubah **d** of Shilhi. 2Ch 20:31
because he married Ahab's **d**.................... 2Ch 21:6
King Jehoram's **d,** took Joash, ... 2Ch 22:11
King Jehoram's **d** and Ahaziah's 2Ch 22:11
'Let your **d** marry my son.' 2Ch 25:18
name was Jerusha **d** of Zadok. 2Ch 27:1
name was Abijah **d** of Zechariah. 2Ch 29:1
who had married a **d** of Barzillai .... Ezr 2:61
had married the **d** of Meshullam .... Ne 6:18
He had married a **d** of Barzillai .... Ne 7:63
sons married a **d** of Sanballat .... Ne 13:28
her as his own **d** when her father .... Est 2:7
came for Esther **d** of Abihail, ... Est 2:15
So Queen Esther **d** of Abihail, ... Est 9:29
He named the first **d** Jemimah, ... Job 42:14
Jemimah, the second **d** Keziah, ... Job 42:14
and the third **d** Keren-Happuch. .... Job 42:14
Listen to me, **d;** look and pay .... Ps 45:10
She is her mother's only **d,** .... Sng 6:9
in sandals, you **d** of a prince. .... Sng 7:1
You are an unfaithful **d.** .... Je 31:22
name was Hamutal **d** of Jeremiah, ... Je 52:1
could not save their son or **d.** .... Eze 14:20
"The **d** is like her mother." .... Eze 16:44
father, mother, son, **d,** brother, ... Eze 44:25
The **d** of the king of the South .... Da 11:6
married Gomer **d** of Diblaim, ... Hos 1:3
again and gave birth to a **d.** .... Hos 1:6
d will turn against her mother, ... Mic 7:6
and said, "My **d** has just died. .... Mt 9:18
a **d** will be against her mother, ... Mt 10:35
their son or **d** more than they .... Mt 10:37
the **d** of Herodias danced for .... Mt 14:6
told her **d** what to ask for, ... Mt 14:8
My **d** has a demon, and she is .... Mt 15:22
moment the woman's **d** was healed. .... Mt 15:28
again and again, "My **d** is dying. .... Mk 5:23
They said, "Your **d** is dead...................... Mk 5:35
When the **d** of Herodias came in .... Mk 6:22
A woman whose **d** had an evil .... Mk 7:25
to force the demon out of her **d.** .... Mk 7:26
The demon has left your **d.**" .... Mk 7:29
and found her **d** lying in bed; .... Mk 7:30
Jairus' only **d,** about twelve .... Lk 8:42
said to him, "Your **d** is dead. .... Lk 8:49
and your **d** will be well." .... Lk 8:50
mother against **d** and daughter .... Lk 12:53
daughter and **d** against mother, ... Lk 12:53
I healed, a **d** of Abraham, has.................. Lk 13:16
the king's **d** adopted him and .... Ac 7:21
son of the king of Egypt's **d.** .... Heb 11:24

DAUGHTER-IN-LAW

son), and his **d** Sarai (Abram's	Ge 11:31
Then Judah said to his **d** Tamar,	Ge 38:11
know that she was Tamar, his **d.**	Ge 38:16
Judah, "Tamar, your **d**, is guilty	Ge 38:24
sexual relations with your **d**;	Le 18:15
has sexual relations with his **d**,	Le 20:12
So Naomi and her **d** Ruth, the	Ru 1:22
told her, "The LORD bless	Ru 2:20
But Naomi said to her **d** Ruth,	Ru 2:22
because of your **d** who loves you.	Ru 4:15
Eli's **d**, the wife of Phinehas,	1Sa 4:19
Judah's **d** Tamar gave birth to	1Ch 2:4
made his **d** unclean sexually.	Eze 22:11
and a **d** will be against her	Mic 7:6
a **d** will be against her	Mt 10:35
mother-in-law against **d** and	Lk 12:53
daughter-in-law and **d** against	Lk 12:53

DAUGHTERS

to grow, and **d** were born to them	Ge 6:1
with the **d** of human beings.	Ge 6:4
have two **d** who have never slept	Ge 19:8
sons, **d**, or any other	Ge 19:12
who were pledged to marry his **d**,	Ge 19:14
and your two **d** with you so you	Ge 19:15
his two **d** and led them safely	Ge 19:16
so he and his two **d** went to live	Ge 19:30
both of Lot's **d** became pregnant	Ge 19:36
Marry one of his **d.**	Ge 28:2
Now Laban had two **d.**	Ge 29:16
me and took my **d** as if you had	Ge 31:26
grandchildren and my **d** good-bye.	Ge 31:28
would take your **d** away from me.	Ge 31:31
to get your two **d** and the last	Ge 31:41
to Jacob, "These girls are my **d.**	Ge 31:43
to keep my **d** and their children	Ge 31:43
if you harm my **d** or marry other	Ge 31:50
and his **d** and blessed them,	Ge 31:55
his sons, his **d**, and all the	Ge 36:6
of his sons and **d** tried to	Ge 37:35
grandsons, his **d** and	Ge 46:7
in Midian who had seven **d.**	Ex 2:16
His **d** went to that well to get	Ex 2:16
He asked his **d**, "Where is this	Ex 2:20
our sons and **d**, and our flocks	Ex 10:9
she gives birth to sons or **d**,	Ex 21:4
wives, sons, and **d** are wearing,	Ex 32:2
of their **d** as wives for your	Ex 34:16
sons and those **d** worship gods,	Ex 34:16
and your sons and **d** may eat the	Le 10:14
the bodies of your sons and **d.**	Le 26:29
your sons and **d** as your	Nu 18:11
sons and **d** as your continual	Nu 18:19
ran away and his **d** were captured	Nu 21:29
he had only **d**, and their names	Nu 26:33
Then the **d** of Zelophehad came	Nu 27:1
Zelophehad's **d** belonged to the	Nu 27:1
The **d**' names were Mahlah, Noah,	Nu 27:1
The **d** of Zelophehad are right;	Nu 27:7
fathers with **d** living at home.	Nu 30:16
our brother, to his **d.**	Nu 36:2
if his **d** marry men from other	Nu 36:3
's command to Zelophehad's **d:**	Nu 36:6
Zelophehad's **d** obeyed the LORD's	Nu 36:10
Zelophehad's **d**—Mahlah, Tirzah,	Nu 36:11
or let your **d** marry their sons,	Dt 7:3
or let your sons marry their **d.**	Dt 7:3
you, your sons and **d**, your male	Dt 12:12
you, your sons and **d**, your male.	Dt 12:18
their sons and **d** as sacrifices	Dt 12:31
you, your sons and **d**, your male.	Dt 16:11
you, your sons and **d**, your male.	Dt 16:14

Your sons and **d** will be given to	Dt 28:32
have sons and **d,** but you will	Dt 28:41
of the sons and **d** the LORD your	Dt 28:53
his sons and **d** had made him	Dt 32:19
sons, **d,** cattle, donkeys,	Jos 7:24
but he had five **d**, named Mahlah,	Jos 17:3
LORD and gave the **d** some land,	Jos 17:4
The **d** of Manasseh received land	Jos 17:6
to marry the **d** of those people,	Jdg 3:6
allowed their **d** to marry the	Jdg 3:6
he had no other sons or **d.**	Jdg 11:34
He had thirty sons and thirty **d.**	Jdg 12:9
He let his **d** marry men who were	Jdg 12:9
would not allow our **d** to marry a	Jdg 21:7
allow our **d** to marry them,	Jdg 21:18
Naomi said, "My **d,** return to	Ru 1:11
back, my **d,** to your own homes.	Ru 1:12
Don't do that, my **d.**	Ru 1:13
Peninnah and to her sons and **d.**	1Sa 1:4
mother of three sons and two **d.**	1Sa 2:21
will take your **d** to make perfume	1Sa 8:13
d had been taken as prisoners.	1Sa 30:3
sons and **d** had been captured,	1Sa 30:6
young and old, sons and **d.**	1Sa 30:19
The **d** of the Philistines will	2Sa 1:20
You **d** of Israel, cry for Saul.	2Sa 1:24
sons and **d** were born to David.	2Sa 5:13
king's virgin **d** wore this kind	2Sa 13:18
your sons, **d**, wives, and slave	2Sa 19:5
their sons and **d** pass through	2Ki 17:17
did not have any sons, only **d.**	1Ch 2:34
had sixteen sons and six **d,**	1Ch 4:27
Zelophehad, and he had only **d.**	1Ch 7:15
and had more sons and **d.**	1Ch 14:3
sons; he had only **d**. Eleazar's	1Ch 23:22
Eleazar's **d** married their	1Ch 23:22
him fourteen sons and three **d.**	1Ch 25:5
twenty-eight sons and sixty **d.**	2Ch 11:21
twenty-two sons and sixteen **d.**	2Ch 13:21
Joash, and Joash had sons and **d.**	2Ch 24:3
women, sons and **d,** and many	2Ch 28:8
and our sons, **d,** and wives were	2Ch 29:9
and **d** also got part of the	2Ch 31:18
do not let your **d** marry their	Ezr 9:12
not let their **d** marry your sons	Ezr 9:12
and his **d** made repairs.	Ne 3:12
your sons and **d,** your wives, and	Ne 4:14
many sons and **d** in our families.	Ne 5:2
sell our sons and **d** as slaves.	Ne 5:5
Some of our **d** have already been	Ne 5:5
and their sons and **d** who could	Ne 10:28
to let our **d** marry foreigners	Ne 10:30
to let our sons marry their **d.**	Ne 10:30
Do not let your **d** marry the sons	Ne 13:25
do not take the **d** of foreigners	Ne 13:25
Job had seven sons and three **d.**	Job 1:2
day Job's sons and **d** were eating	Job 1:13
Your sons and **d** were eating and	Job 1:18
also had seven sons and three **d.**	Job 42:13
land as beautiful as Job's **d.**	Job 42:15
Kings' **d** are among your honored	Ps 45:9
their sons and **d** as sacrifices	Ps 106:37
own sons and **d,** as sacrifices to	Ps 106:38
Let our **d** be like the decorated	Ps 144:12
Greed has two **d** named 'Give' and	Pr 30:15
Yes, **d** of Jerusalem, this is my	Sng 5:16
far away and my **d** from faraway	Is 43:6
will carry your **d** on their	Is 49:22
and **d** of kings will take care of	Is 49:23
and your **d** are coming with them.	Is 60:4
and herds, their sons and **d.**	Je 3:24
They will eat your sons and **d.**	Je 5:17
own sons and **d** as sacrifices,	Je 7:31

Teach your **d** how to cry loudly. .... Je 9:20
Their sons and **d** will die from .... Je 11:22
or their sons, or their **d**. .... Je 14:16
have sons or **d** in this place." .... Je 16:2
the sons and **d** born in this land .... Je 16:3
bodies of their own sons and **d**, ... Je 19:9
Get married and have sons and **d**. .... Je 29:6
let your **d** be married so they .... Je 29:6
they also may have sons and **d**. .... Je 29:6
their sons and **d** as sacrifices .... Je 32:35
sons, or **d** ever drink wine. .... Je 35:8
the king's **d** and all the other .... Je 41:10
and children, and the king's **d**. .... Je 43:6
and your **d** have been taken away. .... Je 48:46
not save their own sons or **d**. .... Eze 14:16
could not save their sons or **d**. .... Eze 14:18
some sons and **d** will be led out. .... Eze 14:22
took your sons and **d** who were my .... Eze 16:20
lived north of you with her **d**; .... Eze 16:46
lived south of you with her **d**, ... Eze 16:46
Sodom and her **d** never did what .... Eze 16:48
what you and your **d** have done. .... Eze 16:48
She and her **d** were proud and had .... Eze 16:49
Sodom and her **d** were proud and .... Eze 16:50
Sodom and her **d** the good things .... Eze 16:53
Samaria and her **d** the good .... Eze 16:53
Sodom with her **d** and Samaria .... Eze 16:55
and Samaria with her **d**, ... Eze 16:55
You and your **d** will also return .... Eze 16:55
I will give them to you like **d**, ... Eze 16:61
Human, a woman had two **d**. .... Eze 23:2
my wives and had sons and **d**. .... Eze 23:4
and took away her sons and **d**, ... Eze 23:10
will take away your sons and **d**, ... Eze 23:25
their sons and **d** and burn their .... Eze 23:47
your sons and **d** that you left .... Eze 24:21
take away their sons and **d** also.............. Eze 24:25
give one of his **d** as a wife to .... Da 11:17
So your **d** become prostitutes, ... Hos 4:13
not punish your **d** for becoming .... Hos 4:14
Your sons and **d** will prophesy. .... Joe 2:28
your sons and **d** to the people................. Joe 3:8
your sons and **d** will be killed. .... Am 7:17
Your sons and **d** will prophesy. .... Ac 2:17
unmarried **d** who had the gift .... Ac 21:9
and you will be my sons and **d**, ... 2Co 6:18

DAUGHTERS-IN-LAW
So she and her **d** got ready to.................. Ru 1:6
Naomi and her **d** left the place .... Ru 1:7
But Naomi said to her two **d**, ... Ru 1:8
and your **d** are guilty of .... Hos 4:13
nor your **d** for their sins of .... Hos 4:14

DAVID
and Jesse was the father of **D**. .... Ru 4:17
the LORD's Spirit worked in **D**. 1Sa 16:13
Send me your son **D**, who is with 1Sa 16:19
them with his son **D** to Saul. 1Sa 16:20
When **D** came to Saul, he began to 1Sa 16:21
Let **D** stay and serve me because 1Sa 16:22
D would take his harp and play. 1Sa 16:23
Now **D** was the son of Jesse, ... 1Sa 17:12
D was the youngest. Jesse's 1Sa 17:14
but **D** went back and forth from.............. 1Sa 17:15
said to his son **D**, "Take this 1Sa 17:17
in the morning **D** left the sheep 1Sa 17:20
D left the food with the man who 1Sa 17:22
as usual, and **D** heard him. 1Sa 17:23
D asked the men who stood near 1Sa 17:26
Israelites told **D** what would be 1Sa 17:27
Eliab heard **D** talking with 1Sa 17:28
D asked, "Now what have I done 1Sa 17:29
what **D** said was told to Saul, ... 1Sa 17:31

D said to Saul, "Don't let 1Sa 17:32
But **D** said to Saul, "I, your.................... 1Sa 17:34
Saul said to **D**, "Go, and may 1Sa 17:37
Saul put his own clothes on **D**. 1Sa 17:38
D put on Saul's sword and tried 1Sa 17:39
was coming closer to **D**. 1Sa 17:41
looked at **D** and saw that he 1Sa 17:42
used his gods' names to curse **D**. 1Sa 17:43
He said to **D**, "Come here. 1Sa 17:44
But **D** said to him, "You come to 1Sa 17:45
to attack him, **D** ran quickly to 1Sa 17:48
D defeated the Philistine with................. 1Sa 17:50
Then **D** ran and stood beside him. 1Sa 17:51
D took Goliath's head to 1Sa 17:54
When Saul saw **D** go out to meet 1Sa 17:55
When **D** came back from killing............. 1Sa 17:57
D answered, "I am the son of 1Sa 17:58
When **D** finished talking with................. 1Sa 18:1
Saul kept **D** with him from that 1Sa 18:2
made an agreement with **D**, ... 1Sa 18:3
off his coat and gave it to **D**, ... 1Sa 18:4
sent **D** to fight in different 1Sa 18:5
Then Saul put **D** over the 1Sa 18:5
After **D** had killed the 1Sa 18:6
D has killed tens of thousands. 1Sa 18:7
The women say **D** has killed tens 1Sa 18:8
So Saul watched **D** closely from.............. 1Sa 18:9
D was playing the harp as he 1Sa 18:10
I'll pin **D** to the wall." 1Sa 18:11
LORD was with **D** but had left 1Sa 18:12
He sent **D** away and made him 1Sa 18:13
he feared **D** even more. 1Sa 18:15
and Judah loved **D** because he led 1Sa 18:16
said to **D**, "Here is my older 1Sa 18:17
D answered Saul, saying, "Who 1Sa 18:18
daughter Merab to marry **D**, ... 1Sa 18:19
other daughter, Michal, loved **D**. 1Sa 18:20
"I will let her marry **D**. 1Sa 18:21
to talk with **D** in private and 1Sa 18:22
servants said these words to **D**, ... 1Sa 18:23
told him what **D** had said, ... 1Sa 18:24
Saul said, "Tell **D**, 'The king 1Sa 18:25
Saul's servants told this to **D**, ... 1Sa 18:26
D brought all their foreskins to 1Sa 18:27
the LORD was with **D** and that his........... 1Sa 18:28
he grew even more afraid of **D**, ... 1Sa 18:29
D was more skillful than Saul's 1Sa 18:30
and all his servants to kill **D**, ... 1Sa 19:1
So he warned **D**, "My father Saul 1Sa 19:2
he said good things about **D**. 1Sa 19:4
D risked his life when he killed 1Sa 19:5
the LORD lives, **D** won't be put 1Sa 19:6
Jonathan called to **D** and told 1Sa 19:7
D went out to fight the 1Sa 19:8
D was playing the harp. 1Sa 19:9
tried to pin **D** to the wall with................. 1Sa 19:10
So she let **D** down out of a 1Sa 19:12
messengers to take **D** prisoner. 1Sa 19:14
Saul sent them back to see **D**,................. 1Sa 19:15
D told me if I did not help him 1Sa 19:17
After **D** had escaped from Saul, ... 1Sa 19:18
Saul heard that **D** was in Naioth 1Sa 19:19
asked, "Where are Samuel and **D**?" 1Sa 19:22
Then **D** ran away from Naioth in 1Sa 20:1
D took an oath, saying, "Your 1Sa 20:3
Jonathan said to **D**, "I'll do 1Sa 20:4
D said, "Look, tomorrow is the 1Sa 20:5
'D begged me to let him go to...................... 1Sa 20:6
D asked, "Who will let me know 1Sa 20:10
said to **D**, "I promise this 1Sa 20:12
made an agreement with **D**. 1Sa 20:16
Jonathan asked **D** to repeat his 1Sa 20:17
Jonathan said to **D**, "Tomorrow is 1Sa 20:18

D

peace with **D** and served him. 1Ch 19:19
But **D** stayed in Jerusalem. 1Ch 20:1
D took the crown off the head of 1Ch 20:2
D did this to all the Ammonite 1Ch 20:3
were killed by **D** and his men. 1Ch 20:8
and he caused **D** to count the 1Ch 21:1
So **D** said to Joab and the 1Ch 21:2
the list of the people to **D**. 1Ch 21:5
D had done something God had 1Ch 21:7
Then **D** said to God, "I have 1Ch 21:8
Go and tell **D**, 'This is what the 1Ch 21:10
Gad went to **D** and said to him, ... 1Ch 21:11
' Now, **D**, decide which of these 1Ch 21:12
D said to Gad, "I am in great 1Ch 21:13
D looked up and saw the angel of 1Ch 21:16
D said to God, "I am the one who 1Ch 21:17
Gad to tell **D** that he should 1Ch 21:18
D did what Gad told him to do, ... 1Ch 21:19
D came to Araunah, and when 1Ch 21:21
D said to him, "Sell me your 1Ch 21:22
Araunah said to **D**, "Take this 1Ch 21:23
But King **D** answered Araunah, ... 1Ch 21:24
So **D** paid Araunah about fifteen 1Ch 21:25
D built an altar to the LORD 1Ch 21:26
When **D** saw that the LORD had 1Ch 21:28
But **D** could not go to the Holy 1Ch 21:30
D said, "The Temple of the LORD 1Ch 22:1
So **D** ordered all foreigners 1Ch 22:2
D supplied a large amount of 1Ch 22:3
been brought to **D** by the people 1Ch 22:4
D said, "We should build a great 1Ch 22:5
D called for his son Solomon 1Ch 22:6
D said to him, "My son, I wanted 1Ch 22:7
word to me, '**D**, you have killed 1Ch 22:8
D said, "Now, my son, may the 1Ch 22:11
Then **D** ordered all the leaders 1Ch 22:17
D said to them, "The LORD your 1Ch 22:18
After **D** had lived long and was 1Ch 23:1
D gathered all the leaders of 1Ch 23:2
D said, "Of these, twenty-four 1Ch 23:4
D separated the Levites into 1Ch 23:6
D had said, "The LORD, the God 1Ch 23:25
D, with the help of Zadok, a 1Ch 24:3
descendants in front of King **D**, ... 1Ch 24:6
lots in front of King **D**, ... 1Ch 24:31
D and the commanders of the army 1Ch 25:1
King **D** chose Asaph to preach, ... 1Ch 25:2
King **D** was in charge of Asaph, ... 1Ch 25:6
for the Temple by King **D**, ... 1Ch 26:26
King **D** gave them the 1Ch 26:32
So **D** only counted the men who............. 1Ch 27:23
David's uncle, and he advised **D**. 1Ch 27:32
D commanded all the leaders of............. 1Ch 28:1
King **D** stood up and said, ... 1Ch 28:2
D said, "Now, in front of all 1Ch 28:8
Then **D** gave his son Solomon the 1Ch 28:11
D gave him plans for everything 1Ch 28:12
D gave Solomon directions for 1Ch 28:13
D told Solomon how much gold or........... 1Ch 28:14
D told him how much gold to use 1Ch 28:15
D told how much gold should be 1Ch 28:16
D said, "All these plans were 1Ch 28:19
D also said to his son Solomon, ... 1Ch 28:20
D said to all the Israelites 1Ch 29:1
and King **D** was also very happy. 1Ch 29:9
D praised the LORD in front of 1Ch 29:10
Then **D** said to all the people 1Ch 29:20
D son of Jesse was king over all............. 1Ch 29:26
D died when he was old....................... 1Ch 29:28
Everything **D** did as king, from 1Ch 29:29
writings tell what **D** did as king 1Ch 29:30
D had brought the Ark of God 2Ch 1:4
been very kind to my father **D**, ... 2Ch 1:8

to my father **D** come true. 2Ch 1:9
helped my father **D** by sending 2Ch 2:3
whom my father **D** chose. 2Ch 2:7
He has given King **D** a wise son, ... 2Ch 2:12
the craftsmen of your father **D**. 2Ch 2:14
time his father **D** had counted 2Ch 2:17
the LORD had appeared to **D**,............... 2Ch 3:1
his father **D** had set apart for 2Ch 5:1
what he promised to my father **D**. 2Ch 6:4
I have chosen **D** to lead my................... 2Ch 6:6
My father **D** wanted to build a 2Ch 6:7
the LORD said to my father **D**, ' 2Ch 6:8
now in place of **D** my father. 2Ch 6:10
you made to your servant **D**, ... 2Ch 6:15
you made to your servant **D**, ... 2Ch 6:16
your love for your servant **D**." 2Ch 6:42
s music that King **D** had made for 2Ch 7:6
the LORD had been so good to **D**, ... 2Ch 7:10
serve me as your father **D** did. 2Ch 7:17
I made with your father **D**, ... 2Ch 7:18
each gate, as **D**, the man of God............ 2Ch 8:14
the city of **D**, his father. 2Ch 9:31
king, "We have no share in **D**! 2Ch 10:16
been against the family of **D**. 2Ch 10:19
lived the way **D** and Solomon had 2Ch 11:17
gave **D** and his sons the right to 2Ch 13:5
as his ancestor **D** had lived when 2Ch 17:3
in Jerusalem, the city of **D**. 2Ch 21:1
agreement he had made with **D**............. 2Ch 21:7
the God of your ancestor **D**, ... 2Ch 21:12
belonged to King **D** and that were 2Ch 23:9
D had given them duties in the 2Ch 23:18
and singing as **D** had commanded.......... 2Ch 23:18
in Jerusalem, the city of **D**. 2Ch 25:28
in Jerusalem, the city of **D**. 2Ch 27:9
his ancestor **D**, he did not do 2Ch 28:1
just as his ancestor **D** had done............. 2Ch 29:2
and lyres, as **D**, Gad, and Nathan 2Ch 29:25
instruments of **D** king of Israel 2Ch 29:27
using the words **D** and Asaph the 2Ch 29:30
of Solomon son of **D** and king of 2Ch 30:26
God had said to **D** and his son 2Ch 33:7
as his ancestor **D** had lived, ... 2Ch 34:2
obey the God of his ancestor **D**. 2Ch 34:3
the jobs that King **D** and his son 2Ch 35:4
chosen for them by King **D**, ... 2Ch 35:15
LORD just as **D** king of Israel................. Ezr 3:10
From the descendants of **D**: .... Ezr 8:2
a group **D** and the officers had .... Ezr 8:20
the tombs of **D** and as far as .... Ne 3:16
group, as **D**, the man of God .... Ne 12:24
the musical instruments of **D**,............... Ne 12:36
the house of **D** to the Water Gate .... Ne 12:37
D had commanded his son Solomon. .... Ne 12:45
in the time of **D** and Asaph, ... Ne 12:46
D sang this when he ran away .... Ps 2:12
instruments. A psalm of **D**. .... Ps 3:8
music. For flutes. A psalm of **D**. .... Ps 4:8
the sheminith. A psalm of **D**. .... Ps 5:12
shiggaion of **D** which he sang to .... Ps 6:10
On the gittith. A psalm of **D**. .... Ps 7:17
Death of the Son." A psalm of **D**. .... Ps 8:9
For the director of music. Of **D**. .... Ps 10:18
the sheminith. A psalm of **D**. .... Ps 11:7
director of music. A psalm of **D**............. Ps 12:8
For the director of music. Of **D**. .... Ps 13:6
will be glad. A psalm of **D**. .... Ps 14:7
be destroyed. A miktam of **D**................ Ps 15:5
pleasure forever. A prayer of **D**. .... Ps 16:11
By the LORD's servant, **D**, ... Ps 17:15
D sang this song to the LORD .... Ps 17:15
D and his descendants forever. .... Ps 18:50
director of music. A psalm of **D**............. Ps 18:50

director of music. A psalm of **D**.............. Ps 19:14
director of music. A psalm of **D**.............. Ps 20:9
The Doe of Dawn." A psalm of **D**. .... Ps 21:13
what God has done. A psalm of **D**............. Ps 22:31
the LORD forever. A psalm of **D**. .... Ps 23:6
the glorious King. Selah Of **D**. .... Ps 24:10
from all their troubles! Of **D**. .... Ps 25:22
you in the great meeting. Of **D**. .... Ps 26:12
wait for the LORD's help. Of **D**. .... Ps 27:14
them forever. A psalm of **D**. .... Ps 28:9
peace. A psalm of **D**. A song for............. Ps 29:11
director of music. A psalm of **D**............. Ps 30:12
strong and brave. A maskil of **D**. .... Ps 31:24
send him away, and **D** did leave. .... Ps 33:22
him will be judged guilty. Of **D**. .... Ps 34:22
Of **D**, the servant of the LORD. .... Ps 35:28
cannot do evil any longer. Of **D**............. Ps 36:12
A psalm of **D** to remember..................... Ps 37:40
For Jeduthun. A psalm of **D**. .... Ps 38:22
director of music. A psalm of **D**............. Ps 39:13
director of music. A psalm of **D**............. Ps 40:17
A psalm of **D** when the prophet .... Ps 50:23
Nathan came to **D** after David's .... Ps 50:23
music. A maskil of **D**. When Doeg .... Ps 51:19
"**D** is in Ahimelech's house." .... Ps 51:19
By mahalath. A maskil of **D**. .... Ps 52:9
A maskil of **D** when the Ziphites .... Ps 53:6
We think **D** is hiding among our.............. Ps 53:6
instruments. A maskil of **D**. .... Ps 54:7
A miktam of **D** when the .... Ps 55:23
A miktam of **D** when he escaped .... Ps 56:13
Do Not Destroy." A miktam of **D**. .... Ps 57:11
A miktam of **D** when Saul sent .... Ps 58:11
miktam of **D**. For teaching. When .... Ps 59:17
With stringed instruments. Of **D**. .... Ps 60:12
For Jeduthun. A psalm of **D**. .... Ps 61:8
A psalm of **D** when he was in the .... Ps 62:12
director of music. A psalm of **D**............. Ps 63:11
of music. A psalm of **D**. A song. .... Ps 64:10
of music. A psalm of **D**. A song. .... Ps 67:7
tune of "Lilies." A psalm of **D**. .... Ps 68:35
A psalm of **D**. To help people .... Ps 69:36
the prayers of **D** son of Jesse. .... Ps 72:20
He chose **D** to be his servant and .... Ps 78:70
And **D** led them with an innocent .... Ps 78:72
the way for him. A prayer of **D**. .... Ps 85:13
made a promise to my servant **D**. .... Ps 89:3
I have found my servant **D**;.................... Ps 89:20
not hold back my love from **D**, ... Ps 89:33
holiness, I will not lie to **D**. .... Ps 89:35
your loyalty you promised to **D**?.............. Ps 89:49
goes on and on. A psalm of **D**. .... Ps 100:5
will remain with you." Of **D**. .... Ps 102:28
the LORD. A song. A psalm of **D**. .... Ps 107:43
director of music. A psalm of **D**............. Ps 108:13
who accuse them. A psalm of **D**. .... Ps 109:31
for going up to worship. Of **D**. .... Ps 121:8
descendants of **D** set their .... Ps 122:5
for going up to worship. Of **D**. .... Ps 123:4
for going up to worship. Of **D**. .... Ps 130:8
D and all his suffering. .... Ps 132:1
For the sake of your servant **D**, ... Ps 132:10
The LORD made a promise to **D**, ... Ps 132:11
king come from the family of **D**.............. Ps 132:17
for going up to worship. Of **D**. .... Ps 132:18
against the rocks. A psalm of **D**............. Ps 137:9
director of music. A psalm of **D**............. Ps 138:8
director of music. A psalm of **D**............. Ps 139:24
in his presence. A psalm of **D**. .... Ps 140:13
A maskil of **D** when he was in the .... Ps 141:10
taken care of me. A psalm of **D**. .... Ps 142:7
because I am your servant. Of **D**. .... Ps 143:12
your servant **D** from cruel swords .... Ps 144:10

LORD. A psalm of praise. Of **D**. .... Ps 144:15
wise words of Solomon son of **D**, ... Pr 1:1
Teacher, a son of **D**, king in .... Ec 1:1
descendant of **D**, listen .... Is 7:13
will be from the family of **D**. .... Is 16:5
the house of **D** around his neck .... Is 22:22
the city where **D** camped. .... Is 29:1
this city for my sake and for **D**, ... Is 37:35
the God of your ancestor **D**, ... Is 38:5
the blessings I promised to **D**................. Is 55:3
I made **D** a witness of my power .... Is 55:4
Family of **D**, this is what the .... Je 21:12
throne of **D** or rule in Judah. .... Je 22:30
LORD their God and **D** their king, ... Je 30:9
my agreement with **D** and Levi. .... Je 33:21
my servant **D** and to the family .... Je 33:22
descendants of **D** my servant rule .... Je 33:26
them one shepherd, my servant **D**........... Eze 34:23
and my servant **D** will be a ruler .... Eze 34:24
My servant **D** will be their .... Eze 37:24
D my servant will be their king .... Eze 37:25
harps, and, like **D**, you compose.............. Am 6:5
The kingdom of **D** is like a .... Am 9:11
of them will be strong like **D**. .... Zch 12:8
the family of **D** will be like God .... Zch 12:8
the family of **D** by itself and .... Zch 12:12
He came from the family of **D**, ... Mt 1:1
and **D** came from the family of .... Mt 1:1
Jesse was the father of King **D**. .... Mt 1:6
generations from Abraham to **D**. .... Mt 1:17
descendant of **D**, don't be afraid............. Mt 1:20
Have mercy on us, Son of **D**!" .... Mt 9:27
you not read what **D** did when he .... Mt 12:3
this man is the Son of **D**!" .... Mt 12:23
Lord, Son of **D**, have mercy on me .... Mt 15:22
Son of **D**, have mercy on us! .... Mt 20:30
Son of **D**, have mercy on us! .... Mt 20:31
Praise to the Son of **D**! .... Mt 21:9
"Praise to the Son of **D**," .... Mt 21:15
"The Christ is the Son of **D**." .... Mt 22:42
Then why did **D** call him 'Lord'? .... Mt 22:43
D calls the Christ 'Lord,' .... Mt 22:45
you never read what **D** did when .... Mk 2:25
D went into God's house and ate .... Mk 2:26
D also gave some of the bread .... Mk 2:26
Son of **D**, have mercy on me! .... Mk 10:47
more, "Son of **D**, have mercy on.............. Mk 10:48
the kingdom of our father **D**! .... Mk 11:10
that the Christ is the son of **D**? .... Mk 12:35
D himself, speaking by the Holy............. Mk 12:36
D himself calls the Christ 'Lord,............. Mk 12:37
Joseph from the family of **D**. .... Lk 1:27
give him the throne of King **D**, ... Lk 1:32
the family of God's servant **D**. .... Lk 1:69
Judea, known as the town of **D**. .... Lk 2:4
he was from the family of **D**. .... Lk 2:4
was born in the town of **D**. .... Lk 2:11
Nathan was the son of **D**. .... Lk 3:31
D was the son of Jesse. .... Lk 3:32
you not read what **D** did when he .... Lk 6:3
Son of **D**, have mercy on me! .... Lk 18:38
more, "Son of **D**, have mercy on.............. Lk 18:39
that the Christ is the Son of **D**? .... Lk 20:41
of Psalms, **D** himself says: ' .... Lk 20:42
D calls the Christ 'Lord,' .... Lk 20:44
the town where **D** lived." .... Jn 7:42
For **D** said this about him: '.................... Ac 2:25
I can tell you truly that **D**, ... Ac 2:29
D talked about the Christ rising .... Ac 2:31
D was not the one who was lifted .... Ac 2:34
our father **D** your servant, ... Ac 4:25
kept it until the time of **D**, ... Ac 7:45
him away, God made **D** their king............. Ac 13:22

D

that **d** God defeated Jabin king .... Jdg 4:23
On that **d** Deborah and Barak son .... Jdg 5:1
So on that **d** Gideon got the name .... Jdg 6:32
One of the trees decided to .... Jdg 9:8
The next **d** the people of Shechem .... Jdg 9:42
of Shechem all **d** until they .... Jdg 9:45
the Towns of Jair to this **d**. .... Jdg 10:4
birth until the **d** of his death.' .... Jdg 13:7
to me the other **d** is here!'' .... Jdg 13:10
On the fourth **d** they said to .... Jdg 14:15
her the answer on the seventh **d,** .... Jdg 14:17
on the seventh **d** of the feast, ... Jdg 14:18
d Samson went to Gaza and saw .... Jdg 16:1
his secret **d** after day until .... Jdg 16:16
day after **d** until he felt he .... Jdg 16:16
is named Mahaneh Dan to this **d**. .... Jdg 18:12
the fourth **d** they got up early .... Jdg 19:5
On the fifth **d** the man got up .... Jdg 19:8
night. The **d** is almost gone. .... Jdg 19:9
As the **d** was almost over, they .... Jdg 19:11
In only one **d** the Benjaminites .... Jdg 20:15
during the battle that **d**. .... Jdg 20:21
the Benjaminites the second **d**. .... Jdg 20:24
and fasted all **d** until evening. .... Jdg 20:26
at Gibeah on the third **d**, ... Jdg 20:30
On that **d** the Israelites killed .... Jdg 20:35
On that **d** 25,000 Benjaminites .... Jdg 20:46
the next **d** the people built .... Jdg 21:4
One **d** Ruth, the Moabite, said to .... Ru 2:2
will die on the same **d**. 1Sa 2:34
That same **d** a man from the tribe 1Sa 4:12
d the people of Beth Shemesh 1Sa 6:15
went back to Ekron the same **d**. 1Sa 6:16
the LORD and fasted that **d**. 1Sa 7:6
The **d** before Saul came, the LORD 1Sa 9:15
So Saul ate with Samuel that **d**. 1Sa 9:24
these signs come true that **d**. 1Sa 10:9
'Before the **d** warms up tomorrow, ... 1Sa 11:9
them before the heat of the **d**. 1Sa 11:11
and that same **d** the LORD sent 1Sa 12:18
One **d** Jonathan, Saul's son, said 1Sa 14:1
saved the Israelites that **d**, ... 1Sa 14:23
miserable that **d** because Saul 1Sa 14:24
That **d** the Israelites defeated 1Sa 14:31
that **d** on, the LORD's Spirit 1Sa 16:13
him from that **d** on and did not 1Sa 18:2
The next **d** an evil spirit from 1Sa 18:10
that way all **d** and all night. 1Sa 19:24
same time the **d** after tomorrow, ... 1Sa 20:12
On the third **d** go to the place 1Sa 20:19
the third **d** I will shoot three 1Sa 20:20
That **d** Saul said nothing. 1Sa 20:26
the next **d** was the second **d** 1Sa 20:27
That second **d** of the month he 1Sa 20:34
Each **d** the holy bread was 1Sa 21:6
happened to be there that **d**. 1Sa 21:7
That **d** David ran away from Saul 1Sa 21:10
to ambush me this very **d**!'' 1Sa 22:8
Edomite was there at Nob that **d**. 1Sa 22:22
Every **d** Saul looked for David, ... 1Sa 23:14
Today is the **d** the LORD spoke of 1Sa 24:4
Night and **d** they protected us. 1Sa 25:16
d Achish gave David the town 1Sa 27:6
nothing all that **d** and night. 1Sa 28:20
Since the **d** you came to me, ... 1Sa 29:6
in me from the **d** I came to you 1Sa 29:8
On the third **d,** when David and 1Sa 30:1
until the evening of the next **d**. 1Sa 30:17
his armor died together that **d**. 1Sa 31:6
The next **d** when the Philistines 1Sa 31:8
On the third **d** a young man from 2Sa 1:2
That **d** there was a terrible 2Sa 2:17
after marching all **d,** arrived at 2Sa 2:29

to eat while it was still **d**. 2Sa 3:35
That **d** all the people of Judah 2Sa 3:37
That **d** David said to his men, ... 2Sa 5:8
was afraid of the LORD that **d,** 2Sa 6:9
no children to the **d** she died. 2Sa 6:23
Jerusalem that **d** and the next. 2Sa 11:12
On the seventh **d** the baby died. 2Sa 12:18
do you look so sad **d** after day? 2Sa 13:4
David cried for his son every **d**. 2Sa 13:37
Many died that **d**—twenty thousand 2Sa 18:7
but that **d** more men died in the 2Sa 18:8
army had won the battle that **d**. 2Sa 19:2
into the city quietly that **d**. 2Sa 19:3
During the **d** she did not let the 2Sa 21:10
for the Israelites that **d**. 2Sa 23:10
and killed a lion on a snowy **d**. 2Sa 23:20
That **d** Gad came to David and 2Sa 24:18
He cursed me the **d** I went to 1Ki 2:8
The very **d** you leave and cross 1Ki 2:37
One **d** two women who were 1Ki 3:16
much food each **d** to feed himself 1Ki 4:22
Night and **d** please watch over 1Ki 8:29
this prayer **d** and night and do 1Ki 8:59
On that **d** King Solomon made holy 1Ki 8:64
On the following **d** Solomon sent 1Ki 8:66
One **d** as Jeroboam was leaving 1Ki 11:29
on the fifteenth **d** of the eighth 1Ki 12:32
the fifteenth **d** of the eighth 1Ki 12:33
That same **d** the man of God gave 1Ki 13:3
of God had done there that **d**. 1Ki 13:11
So that **d** in the camp they made 1Ki 16:16
until the **d** the LORD sends rain 1Ki 17:14
Elijah had enough food every **d**. 1Ki 17:15
for a whole **d** into the desert. 1Ki 19:4
On the seventh **d** the battle 1Ki 20:29
Aramean soldiers in one **d**. 1Ki 20:29
One **d** Ahab said to Naboth, ... 1Ki 21:2
Declare a **d** during which the 1Ki 21:9
declared a special **d** on which 1Ki 21:12
find out on the **d** you go to hide 1Ki 22:25
The battle continued all **d**. 1Ki 22:35
healed to this **d** just as Elisha 2Ki 2:22
One **d** Elisha went to Shunem, ... 2Ki 4:8
One **d** Elisha came to the woman's 2Ki 4:11
grew up and one **d** went out to 2Ki 4:18
the New Moon or the Sabbath **d**.'' 2Ki 4:23
Then the next **d** I said to her, ' 2Ki 6:29
land from the **d** she left until 2Ki 8:6
But the next **d** Hazael took a 2Ki 8:15
To this **d** he has never wanted to 2Ki 13:23
he had until the **d** he died. 2Ki 15:5
they have been there to this **d**. 2Ki 17:23
Today is a **d** of sorrow and 2Ki 19:3
One **d** as Sennacherib was 2Ki 19:37
of the LORD on the third **d**?'' 2Ki 20:8
up until this **d** will be taken 2Ki 20:17
angry from the **d** their ancestors 2Ki 21:15
on the tenth **d** of the tenth 2Ki 25:1
By the ninth **d** of the fourth 2Ki 25:3
on the seventh **d** of the fifth 2Ki 25:8
twenty-seventh **d** of the twelfth 2Ki 25:27
Every **d,** for as long as 2Ki 25:30
from that time until this **d**. 1Ch 5:26
on the table every Sabbath **d**. 1Ch 9:32
they were on duty **d** and night, ... 1Ch 9:33
The next **d** when the Philistines 1Ch 10:8
and killed a lion on a snowy **d**. 1Ch 11:22
afraid of God that **d** and asked, ... 1Ch 13:12
That **d** David first gave Asaph 1Ch 16:7
Every **d** tell how he saves us. 1Ch 16:23
were to serve there every **d**. 1Ch 16:37
served before the LORD every **d**. 1Ch 23:31
guard every **d** at the East Gate 1Ch 26:17

join you on your **d** of battle. .... Ps 110:3
This is the **d** that the LORD has .... Ps 118:24
to this **d** because of your .... Ps 119:91
I think about them all **d** long. .... Ps 119:97
Seven times a **d** I praise you for .... Ps 119:164
cannot hurt you during the **d,** .... Ps 121:6
He made the sun to rule the **d.** .... Ps 136:8
did on the **d** Jerusalem fell..................... Ps 137:7
On the **d** I called to you, you .... Ps 138:3
The night is as light as the **d;** .... Ps 139:12
book before I was one **d** old. .... Ps 139:16
I will praise you every **d;** .... Ps 145:2
delighted every **d,** enjoying his .... Pr 8:30
watching at my door every **d,** .... Pr 8:34
Every **d** is hard for those who................. Pr 15:15
even prepared a **d** of disaster .... Pr 16:4
All **d** long they wish for more, ... Pr 21:26
coat on a cold **d** or pouring..................... Pr 25:20
continual dripping on a rainy **d.** .... Pr 27:15
give me enough food for each **d.** .... Pr 30:8
d of death is better than the .... Ec 7:1
is better than the **d** of birth. .... Ec 7:1
working **d** and night and hardly .... Ec 8:16
is good to see the light of **d.** .... Ec 11:7
to enjoy every **d** of their lives,............... Ec 11:8
the **d** dawns and the shadows................. Sng 2:17
on his head on his wedding **d,** .... Sng 3:11
the **d** dawns and the shadows .... Sng 4:6
our sister on the **d** she becomes .... Sng 8:8
has a certain **d** planned when he .... Is 2:12
smoke during the **d** and with a .... Is 4:5
that **d** they will roar like the .... Is 5:30
the branch and stalk in one **d.** .... Is 9:14
d the army will stop at Nob. .... Is 10:32
the LORD's **d** of judging is near .... Is 13:6
the LORD's **d** of judging is .... Is 13:9
On that **d** Israel will sing this .... Is 14:4
that **d** all their strong cities................... Is 17:9
grapevines one **d** and try to make .... Is 17:11
In that **d** the Egyptians will be .... Is 19:16
each **d** I stand in the watchtower .... Is 21:8
has chosen a special **d** of riots .... Is 22:5
cloud cools a hot **d,** you silence .... Is 25:5
with you at the dawn of every **d.** .... Is 26:9
you is like the dew of a new **d;** .... Is 26:19
I will guard it **d** and night. .... Is 27:3
defeat you by **d** and by night. .... Is 28:19
bread and water you ate every **d.** .... Is 30:20
The fires will burn night and **d;** .... Is 34:10
Today is a **d** of sorrow and .... Is 37:3
One **d** as Sennacherib was .... Is 37:38
In one **d** you brought me to this .... Is 38:12
In one **d** you brought me to this .... Is 38:13
up until this **d** will be taken .... Is 39:6
to you suddenly, in a single **d.** .... Is 47:9
the **d** of salvation I will help .... Is 49:8
All **d** long they speak against .... Is 52:5
on that future **d,** they will know .... Is 52:6
This **d** is like the time of Noah .... Is 54:9
still come every **d** looking for .... Is 58:2
kind of special **d** is not what I................. Is 58:5
yourselves on that holy **d.** .... Is 58:13
brightness of **d** we trip as if it .... Is 59:10
will not be closed **d** or night so .... Is 60:11
your light during the **d** nor will .... Is 60:19
must not be silent **d** or night. .... Is 62:6
All **d** long I stood ready to .... Is 65:2
saw a country begin in one **d;**................. Is 66:8
Since the **d** your ancestors left .... Je 7:25
I could cry **d** and night for my .... Je 9:1
again and again to this very **d:** .... Je 11:7
them aside for the **d** of killing. .... Je 12:3
filled with tears night and **d,** .... Je 14:17

Her bright **d** became dark from .... Je 15:9
serve other gods **d** and night, ... Je 16:13
want the terrible **d** to come. .... Je 17:16
Bring the **d** of disaster on my .... Je 17:18
on the Sabbath **d** or bring it .... Je 17:21
or do any work on that **d.** .... Je 17:22
keep the Sabbath as a holy **d,**................. Je 17:22
as a holy **d** and not do any .... Je 17:24
and not do any work on that **d.** .... Je 17:24
the Sabbath **d** as a holy day. .... Je 17:27
the Sabbath day as a holy **d.** .... Je 17:27
The next **d** when Pashhur took .... Je 20:3
makes fun of me all **d** long. .... Je 20:7
make fun of me all **d** long. .... Je 20:8
be a curse on the **d** I was born; .... Je 20:14
blessing on the **d** when my mother........... Je 20:14
When that **d** is over, you will .... Je 23:20
And so it has been to this **d.** .... Je 25:18
until the **d** I go to get them, ... Je 27:22
This will be a terrible **d!** .... Je 30:7
When that **d** comes, you will .... Je 30:24
sun shine in the **d** and the moon .... Je 31:35
From the **d** Jerusalem was built .... Je 32:31
agreement with **d** and night that .... Je 33:20
my agreement with **d** and night,............... Je 33:25
the LORD on a **d** when the people .... Je 36:6
heat of the **d** and in the cold .... Je 36:30
bread each **d** from the street .... Je 37:21
guard until the **d** Jerusalem was............... Je 38:28
until the ninth **d** of the fourth .... Je 39:2
that **d** he gave them vineyards .... Je 39:10
But I will save you on that **d,** .... Je 39:17
The **d** after Gedaliah was .... Je 41:4
Even to this **d** the people of .... Je 44:10
soldiers will die on that **d,**" .... Je 50:30
city when the **d** of disaster .... Je 51:2
month, and tenth **d** as king. .... Je 52:4
By the ninth **d** of the fourth .... Je 52:6
there until the **d** he died......................... Je 52:11
on the tenth **d** of the fifth .... Je 52:12
twenty-fifth **d** of the twelfth .... Je 52:31
Every **d** the king of Babylon gave .... Je 52:34
me on the **d** of his great anger .... La 1:12
and lonely that I am weak all **d.** .... La 1:13
Now bring that **d** you have .... La 1:21
on the **d** of his anger. .... La 2:1
was like that of a feast **d.** .... La 2:7
This is the **d** we were waiting .... La 2:16
flow like a river **d** and night. .... La 2:18
them on the **d** of your anger; .... La 2:21
alive on the **d** of the LORD's .... La 2:22
me again and again, all **d** long. .... La 3:3
fun of me with songs all **d** long. .... La 3:14
on the fifth **d** of the fourth .... Eze 1:1
It was the fifth **d** of the month .... Eze 1:2
in the clouds on a rainy **d.** .... Eze 1:28
against me until this very **d.** .... Eze 2:3
a **d** for each year of their sin. .... Eze 4:6
of food every **d** at set times. .... Eze 4:10
of water every **d** at set times. .... Eze 4:11
the **d** of confusion is near. .... Eze 7:7
Look, the **d** is here. It has .... Eze 7:10
has come; the **d** has arrived. .... Eze 7:12
the fifth **d** of the sixth month .... Eze 8:1
During the **d** when the people are .... Eze 12:8
on the LORD's **d** of judging? .... Eze 13:5
the **d** you were born, your cord .... Eze 16:4
hated on the **d** you were born. .... Eze 16:5
on the tenth **d** of the month. .... Eze 20:1
Their **d** of judging has come; .... Eze 21:29
on the tenth **d** of the month. .... Eze 24:1
Jerusalem this very **d.** .... Eze 24:2
on the first **d** of the month..................... Eze 26:1

DAY   177   **DAY**

don't know the **d** your Lord will .... Mt 24:42
you don't know the **d** or the hour .... Mt 25:13
know that the **d** after tomorrow .... Mt 26:2
On that **d** the Son of Man will be .... Mt 26:2
On the first **d** of the Feast of .... Mt 26:17
until that **d** when I drink it .... Mt 26:29
Every **d** I sat in the Temple .... Mt 26:55
The next **d**, the day after........................ Mt 27:62
closely till the third **d.** .... Mt 27:64
The **d** after the Sabbath day was .... Mt 28:1
On the Sabbath **d** He went to the .... Mk 1:21
One Sabbath **d,** as Jesus was .... Mk 2:23
is not lawful on the Sabbath **d?**" .... Mk 2:24
The Sabbath **d** was made to help .... Mk 2:27
is Lord even of the Sabbath **d.**" .... Mk 2:28
on the Sabbath **d** so they could .... Mk 3:2
is lawful on the Sabbath **d:** .... Mk 3:4
Night and **d,** whether the person .... Mk 4:27
D and night he would wander .... Mk 5:5
the Sabbath **d** he taught in the .... Mk 6:2
When it was late in the **d,** .... Mk 6:35
on the third **d,** he will rise to .... Mk 10:34
The next **d** as Jesus was leaving.............. Mk 11:12
when that **d** or time will be..................... Mk 13:32
was now the first **d** of the Feast .... Mk 14:12
until that **d** when I drink it .... Mk 14:25
Every **d** I was with you teaching.............. Mk 14:49
was Preparation **D.** (That means.............. Mk 15:42
That means the **d** before the .... Mk 15:42
the day before the Sabbath **d.** .... Mk 15:42
The **d** after the Sabbath day, ... Mk 16:1
The day after the Sabbath **d,** .... Mk 16:1
early on that **d,** the first day .... Mk 16:2
day, the first **d** of the week,.................... Mk 16:2
on the first **d** of the week, ... Mk 16:9
One **d** Zechariah was serving as a .... Lk 1:8
speak until the **d** these things .... Lk 1:20
a new **d** from heaven will dawn .... Lk 1:78
food and praying for a whole **d.** .... Lk 2:37
they traveled for a whole **d.** .... Lk 2:44
On the Sabbath **d** he went to the .... Lk 4:16
and on the Sabbath **d,** he taught.............. Lk 4:31
One **d** while Jesus was standing.............. Lk 5:1
One **d** as Jesus was teaching the .... Lk 5:17
One Sabbath **d** Jesus was walking .... Lk 6:1
is not lawful on the Sabbath **d?**" .... Lk 6:2
Man is Lord of the Sabbath **d.**" .... Lk 6:5
On another Sabbath **d** Jesus went .... Lk 6:6
on the Sabbath **d** so they could .... Lk 6:7
is lawful on the Sabbath **d:** .... Lk 6:9
d Jesus and his followers got .... Lk 8:22
The next **d,** when they came down .... Lk 9:37
on the Judgment **D** it will be .... Lk 10:12
on the Judgment **D** it will be .... Lk 10:14
next **d,** the Samaritan brought .... Lk 10:35
us the food we need for each **d.** .... Lk 11:3
On the Judgment **D** the Queen of .... Lk 11:31
On the Judgment **D** the people of .... Lk 11:32
will be a hot **d,**' and it happens .... Lk 12:55
the synagogues on the Sabbath **d.** .... Lk 13:10
Jesus healed on the Sabbath **d.** .... Lk 13:14
them to drink water every **d**— .... Lk 13:15
her sickness on a Sabbath **d!**" .... Lk 13:16
on the third **d,** I will reach my .... Lk 13:32
and tomorrow and the next **d.** .... Lk 13:33
On a Sabbath **d,** when Jesus went .... Lk 14:1
wrong to heal on the Sabbath **d?**" .... Lk 14:3
into a well on the Sabbath **d,** .... Lk 14:5
and lived in luxury every **d.** .... Lk 16:19
times in one **d** and says that he .... Lk 17:4
married until the **d** Noah entered .... Lk 17:27
But the **d** Lot left Sodom, fire .... Lk 17:29
On that **d,** a person who is on................. Lk 17:31

who cry to him night and **d,** .... Lk 18:7
on the third **d,** he will rise to .... Lk 18:33
taught in the Temple every **d.** .... Lk 19:47
One **d** Jesus was in the Temple, ... Lk 20:1
d might come on you suddenly, ... Lk 21:34
During the **d,** Jesus taught the .... Lk 21:37
The **D** of Unleavened Bread came .... Lk 22:7
before the rooster crows this **d,** .... Lk 22:34
with you every **d** in the Temple, ... Lk 22:53
Before the rooster crows this **d,** .... Lk 22:61
When **d** came, the council of the .... Lk 22:66
but on that **d** they became .... Lk 23:12
This was late on Preparation **D,** .... Lk 23:54
the Sabbath **d** would begin. .... Lk 23:54
On the Sabbath **d** they rested, ... Lk 23:56
on the first **d** of the week, ... Lk 24:1
from the dead on the third **d.**" .... Lk 24:7
That same **d** two of Jesus' .... Lk 24:13
is now the third **d** since this .... Lk 24:21
from the dead on the third **d** .... Lk 24:46
The next **d** John saw Jesus coming .... Jn 1:29
The next **d** John was there again .... Jn 1:35
stayed there with him that **d.** .... Jn 1:39
The next **d** Jesus decided to go .... Jn 1:43
d this happened was a Sabbath .... Jn 5:9
this happened was a Sabbath **d.** .... Jn 5:9
your mat on the Sabbath **d.**" .... Jn 5:10
was doing this on the Sabbath **d,** .... Jn 5:16
the law about the Sabbath **d.** .... Jn 5:18
The next **d** the people who had .... Jn 6:22
raise them all on the last **d.**................... Jn 6:39
I will raise them on the last **d.** .... Jn 6:40
that person up on the last **d.** .... Jn 6:44
raise them up on the last **d.**................... Jn 6:54
a baby boy on a Sabbath **d.** .... Jn 7:22
a Sabbath **d** to obey the law of .... Jn 7:23
most important **d** of the feast .... Jn 7:37
happy that he would see my **d.** .... Jn 8:56
He saw that **d** and was glad." .... Jn 8:56
The **d** Jesus had made mud and .... Jn 9:14
man does not keep the Sabbath **d,** .... Jn 9:16
there not twelve hours in the **d?** .... Jn 11:9
the resurrection on the last **d.**" .... Jn 11:24
That **d** they started planning to .... Jn 11:53
the **d** for me to be prepared for .... Jn 12:7
The next **d** a great crowd who had .... Jn 12:12
be their judge on the last **d.** .... Jn 12:48
that **d** you will know that I am .... Jn 14:20
that **d** you will not ask me for............... Jn 16:23
that **d** you will ask the Father .... Jn 16:26
on Preparation **D** of Passover .... Jn 19:14
This **d** was Preparation Day, ... Jn 19:31
to start their Sabbath **d.** .... Jn 19:42
on the first **d** of the week, ... Jn 20:1
on the first **d** of the week, ... Jn 20:19
until the **d** he was taken up into .... Ac 1:2
When the **d** of Pentecost came, ... Ac 2:1
and glorious **d** of the Lord will .... Ac 2:20
the number of believers that **d.** .... Ac 2:41
together in the Temple every **d.** .... Ac 2:46
Every **d** the Lord added those who .... Ac 2:47
One **d** Peter and John went to the .... Ac 3:1
Every **d** he was carried to this .... Ac 3:2
them in jail until the next **d.** .... Ac 4:3
The next **d** the rulers, then .... Ac 4:5
Every **d** in the Temple and in .... Ac 5:42
food that was given out every **d.**............. Ac 6:1
next **d** when Moses saw two men .... Ac 7:26
that **d** the church of Jerusalem .... Ac 8:1
the city gates at night, ... Ac 9:24
the next **d** as they came near .... Ac 10:9
The next **d** Peter got ready and .... Ac 10:23
On the following **d** they came to............. Ac 10:24

on the third **d,** God raised Jesus .... Ac 10:40
next **d** the soldiers were very .... Ac 12:18
On a chosen **d** Herod put on his .... Ac 12:21
On the Sabbath **d** they went into .... Ac 13:14
which are read every Sabbath **d.** .... Ac 13:27
next Sabbath **d,** almost everyone .... Ac 13:44
The next **d** he and Barnabas left............. Ac 14:20
the synagogue every Sabbath **d.**" .... Ac 15:21
faith and grew larger every **d.** .... Ac 16:5
next **d** we sailed to Neapolis. .... Ac 16:11
On the Sabbath **d** we went outside .... Ac 16:13
each Sabbath **d** for three weeks .... Ac 17:2
Scriptures every **d** to find out .... Ac 17:11
also talked every **d** with people .... Ac 17:17
God has set a **d** that he will .... Ac 17:31
Every Sabbath **d** he talked with .... Ac 18:4
Paul talked with people every **d** .... Ac 19:9
On the first **d** of the week, ... Ac 20:7
and the next **d** came to a place .... Ac 20:15
Jerusalem on the **d** of Pentecost. .... Ac 20:16
from the first **d** I came to Asia. .... Ac 20:18
for three years, and night, I.................. Ac 20:31
The next **d** we reached Rhodes, ... Ac 21:1
and stayed with them for a **d.**.............. Ac 21:7
The next **d** we left Ptolemais and .... Ac 21:8
The next **d** Paul went with us to .... Ac 21:18
next **d** Paul took the four men .... Ac 21:26
The next **d** the commander decided .... Ac 22:30
before God up to this **d.**"..................... Ac 23:1
next **d** the horsemen went with .... Ac 23:32
The next **d** he told the soldiers .... Ac 25:6
The next **d** I sat on the judge's .... Ac 25:17
The next **d** Agrippa and Bernice.............. Ac 25:23
as they serve God **d** and night. .... Ac 26:7
The next **d** we came to Sidon.................. Ac 27:3
after the **D** of Cleansing.......................... Ac 27:9
The next **d** the storm was blowing .... Ac 27:18
A **d** later with their own hands .... Ac 27:19
The next **d** a wind began to blow .... Ac 28:13
people chose a **d** for a meeting .... Ac 28:23
greater on the **d** he shows his.................. Rm 2:5
will happen on the **d** when God,.............. Rm 2:16
All **d** long I stood ready to .... Rm 10:21
and the "**d**" is almost here..................... Rm 13:12
like people who belong to the **d.**.............. Rm 13:13
think that one **d** is more .... Rm 14:5
think one **d** is more important .... Rm 14:6
in you on the **d** our Lord Jesus 1Co 1:8
because the **D** of Judgment will 1Co 3:13
be saved on the **d** of the Lord. 1Co 5:5
one **d** twenty-three thousand of 1Co 10:8
on the third **d** as the Scriptures 1Co 15:4
I die every **d.** That is true, ... 1Co 15:31
On the first **d** of every week, ... 1Co 16:2
inside us is made new every **d.** 2Co 4:16
the **d** of salvation I helped you. 2Co 6:2
and the "**d** of salvation" is now. 2Co 6:2
a night and a **d** in the sea. 2Co 11:25
is on me every **d** the load of my 2Co 11:28
angry before the end of the **d.** .... Eph 4:26
you free when the final **d** comes. .... Eph 4:30
Then on the **d** of evil you will .... Eph 6:13
from the first **d** you believed .... Php 1:5
since the **d** we heard about you, ... Col 1:9
Moon Festival, or a Sabbath **d.** .... Col 2:16
night and **d** so we would not 1Th 2:9
Night and **d** we continue praying 1Th 3:10
well that the **d** the Lord comes 1Th 5:2
and so that **d** will not surprise 1Th 5:4
to the light and to the **d.** 1Th 5:5
we belong to the **d,** so we should 1Th 5:8
happen on the **d** when the Lord 2Th 1:10
hear that the **d** of the Lord has 2Th 2:2

That **d** of the Lord will not come 2Th 2:3
hard night and **d** so we would not 2Th 3:8
pray night and **d** for God's help................. 1Ti 5:5
you in my prayers, **d** and night. 2Ti 1:3
trusted me with until that **d.** 2Ti 1:12
mercy from the Lord on that **d.** 2Ti 1:18
give the crown to me on that **d**— 2Ti 4:8
each other every **d** while it is .... Heb 3:13
about the seventh **d** of the week: .... Heb 4:4
another **d,** called "today. .... Heb 4:7
God spoke later about another **d.** .... Heb 4:8
had to offer sacrifices every **d,** .... Heb 7:27
first room every **d** to worship.................. Heb 9:6
Every **d** the priests stand and do .... Heb 10:11
more as you see the **d** coming. .... Heb 10:25
God on the **d** when Christ comes 1Pe 2:12
until the **d** begins and the 2Pe 1:19
lived with evil people every **d,** 2Pe 2:8
waiting for the Judgment **D.** 2Pe 2:9
for the Judgment **D** and the 2Pe 3:7
To the Lord one **d** is as a...................... 2Pe 3:8
But the **d** of the Lord will come 2Pe 3:10
to the coming of the **d** of God. 2Pe 3:12
fear on the **d** God judges us, ... 1Jn 4:17
to be judged on the great **d,** .... Jud 1:6
On the Lord's **d** I was in the .... Rev 1:10
D and night they never stop .... Rev 4:8
The great **d** for their anger has .... Rev 6:17
worship him **d** and night in his .... Rev 7:15
a third of the **d** was without .... Rev 8:12
this hour and **d** and month and .... Rev 9:15
accused them **d** and night before .... Rev 12:10
will be no rest, **d** or night, for.................. Rev 14:11
on the great **d** of God Almighty. .... Rev 16:14
will come to her in one **d:** .... Rev 18:8
will be punished **d** and night .... Rev 20:10
will never be shut on any **d,** .... Rev 21:25

DAYBREAK
At **d,** Jesus went to a lonely .... Lk 4:42

DAYLIGHT
them in open **d** in the presence .... Nu 25:4
around in the **d** like a blind.................... Dt 28:29
the door and lay there until **d.** .... Jdg 19:26
let it wait for **d** that never .... Job 3:9
and brighter until full **d.** .... Pr 4:18
walks in the **d,** he will not .... Jn 11:9
water and prayed for **d** to come................. Ac 27:29
When **d** came, the sailors saw .... Ac 27:39

DAYTIME
In the **d** the sun took away my .... Ge 31:40
did it at night, not in the **d.**.................. Jdg 6:27
covers them up in the **d;** .... Job 5:14
In the **d** they shut themselves up .... Job 24:16
captive in the **d** with the people .... Eze 12:3
In the **d** I brought what I had .... Eze 12:7
While it is **d,** we must continue .... Jn 9:4

DEACONS
including your overseers and **d:** .... Php 1:1
d must be respected by others, ... 1Ti 3:8
let them serve as **d** if you find 1Ti 3:10
D must have only one wife and be 1Ti 3:12
who serve well as **d** are making 1Ti 3:13

DEAD
of Siddim (now the **D** Sea)...................... Ge 14:3
the halves of the **d** animals. .... Ge 15:17
so that I can bury my **d** wife.".................. Ge 23:4
place we have to bury your **d**.................. Ge 23:6
to help me bury my **d** wife here,.............. Ge 23:8
as witnesses. Bury your **d** wife.".............. Ge 23:11
and I will bury my **d** there." .... Ge 23:13
the land, and bury your **d** wife.".............. Ge 23:15

I am almost **d** from hunger. .... Ge 25:32
came upon the **d** bodies and stole .... Ge 34:27
with your **d** brother's wife. .... Ge 38:8
His brother is **d**, and he is the .... Ge 42:38
youngest son's brother is **d**, ... Ge 44:20
wanted to kill you are **d** now." .... Ex 4:19
lying **d** on the seashore. .... Ex 14:30
family of the **d** person accepts .... Ex 21:30
The **d** animal will belong to the .... Ex 21:34
bull, and the **d** animal is his. .... Ex 21:36
such as the **d** body of an unclean .... Le 5:2
animal is found **d** or torn by .... Le 7:24
or even touch their **d** bodies; .... Le 11:8
or even touch their **d** bodies, ... Le 11:11
who touches the **d** body of one of .... Le 11:24
up one of these **d** insects must .... Le 11:25
who touches the **d** body of one of .... Le 11:26
who touches the **d** body of one of .... Le 11:27
picks up their **d** bodies must .... Le 11:28
touches their **d** bodies will be .... Le 11:31
If the **d**, unclean animal falls .... Le 11:33
any **d**, unclean animal falls .... Le 11:35
who touches the **d** body of any .... Le 11:36
If a **d**, unclean animal falls on .... Le 11:37
put water on some seeds and a **d**, ... Le 11:38
this animal's **d** body must wash .... Le 11:40
up the animal's **d** body must wash .... Le 11:40
unclean by touching a **d** person. .... Le 21:1
But if the **d** person was one of .... Le 21:2
unclean if the **d** person is his .... Le 21:2
unclean if the **d** person was only .... Le 21:4
a house where there is a **d** body. .... Le 21:11
unclean from touching a **d** body, ... Le 22:4
I will pile your **d** bodies on the .... Le 26:30
unclean by touching a **d** body. .... Nu 5:2
that person is **d** and does not .... Nu 5:8
must not go near a **d** body. .... Nu 6:6
because they were near a **d** body. .... Nu 6:11
unclean from touching a **d** body. .... Nu 9:6
because of touching a **d** body. .... Nu 9:7
unclean because of a **d** body, ... Nu 9:10
be like a baby who is born **d**. .... Nu 12:12
until you lie **d** in the desert. .... Nu 14:33
will go to the place of the **d**, ... Nu 16:30
going to the place of the **d**, ... Nu 16:33
between the **d** and the living, ... Nu 16:48
Those who touch a **d** person's .... Nu 19:11
those who touch a **d** person's .... Nu 19:13
was killed, or a **d** person, or a .... Nu 19:18
people learned that Aaron was **d**, ... Nu 20:29
or touched a **d** body must stay .... Nu 31:19
at the south end of the **D** Sea, ... Nu 34:3
River and end at the **D** Sea. .... Nu 34:12
be safe from the **d** person's. .... Nu 35:12
relative of the **d** person must .... Nu 35:19
relative of the **d** person must .... Nu 35:21
the relative of the **d** person and .... Nu 35:24
killer from the **d** person's .... Nu 35:25
a relative of the **d** person finds .... Nu 35:27
the camp until they were all **d**. .... Dt 2:15
Galilee to the **D** Sea west of .... Dt 3:17
as far as the **D** Sea below Mount .... Dt 4:49
meat or touch their **d** bodies. .... Dt 14:8
you find that is already **d**. .... Dt 14:21
with the spirits of **d** people. .... Dt 18:11
the **d** person's relative who has .... Dt 19:6
the son of the **d** brother so that .... Dt 25:6
not offered it for **d** people. .... Dt 26:14
Your **d** bodies will be food for .... Dt 28:26
down to the place of the **d**. .... Dt 32:22
said, "My servant Moses is **d**. .... Jos 1:2
Sea of Arabah (the **D** Sea) was .... Jos 3:16
from Lake Galilee to the **D** Sea. .... Jos 12:3

at the south end of the **D** Sea .... Jos 15:2
was the shore of the **D** Sea, ... Jos 15:5
at the north shore of the **D** Sea, ... Jos 18:19
their king lying **d** on the floor! .... Jdg 3:25
there Sisera lay **d**, with the .... Jdg 4:22
Sisera sank, there he fell, **d**! .... Jdg 5:27
of Israel saw Abimelech was **d**, ... Jdg 9:55
the body of the **d** lion and found .... Jdg 14:8
from the body of the **d** lion. .... Jdg 14:9
found the jawbone of a **d** donkey, ... Jdg 15:15
to me and my sons who are now **d**. .... Ru 1:8
both the living and the **d**!" .... Ru 2:20
the Moabite, the **d** man's wife. .... Ru 4:5
will stay in the **d** man's name." .... Ru 4:5
doing this so her **d** husband's .... Ru 4:10
two sons are both **d**, and the 1Sa 4:17
were both **d**, she began to give 1Sa 4:19
-in-law and husband were **d**. 1Sa 4:21
them until all of them are **d**.' 1Sa 15:18
saw that their champion was **d**, ... 1Sa 17:51
you will be **d** in the morning." 1Sa 19:11
are chasing a **d** dog or a flea. 1Sa 24:14
David heard that Nabal was **d**, ... 1Sa 25:39
Now Samuel was **d**, and all the 1Sa 28:3
the officer saw that Saul was **d**, ... 1Sa 31:5
that Saul and his sons were **d**, ... 1Sa 31:7
things from the **d** soldiers, ... 1Sa 31:8
three sons **d** on Mount Gilboa. 1Sa 31:8
Now Saul was **d**. After David had 2Sa 1:1
of them have fallen and are **d**. 2Sa 1:4
his son Jonathan are **d** also." 2Sa 1:4
and his son Jonathan are **d**?" 2Sa 1:5
hurt and am almost **d** already.' 2Sa 1:9
Jonathan is **d** on Gilboa's hills. 2Sa 1:25
your master is **d**, and the people. 2Sa 2:7
that Saul and Jonathan were **d**. 2Sa 4:4
When he told me, 'Saul is **d**!' 2Sa 4:10
I am no better than a **d** dog!" 2Sa 9:8
heard that her husband was **d**, ... 2Sa 11:26
to tell him that the baby was **d**. 2Sa 12:18
If we tell him the baby is **d**, ... 2Sa 12:18
he knew that the baby was **d**. 2Sa 12:19
that the baby is **d**, you get up 2Sa 12:21
But now that the baby is **d**, ... 2Sa 12:23
No, only Amnon is **d**! Absalom has 2Sa 13:32
all of the king's sons are **d**. 2Sa 13:33
I am a widow; my husband is **d**. 2Sa 14:5
Why should this **d** dog curse you, ... 2Sa 16:9
man you are looking for is **d**, ... 2Sa 17:3
because the king's son is **d**." 2Sa 18:20
had lived and all of us were **d**? 2Sa 19:6
he was already **d**. Then Joab and 2Sa 20:10
she put the **d** baby in my bed. 1Ki 3:20
my baby, I saw that he was **d**! 1Ki 3:21
son, and the **d** baby is yours!" 1Ki 3:22
son is alive and your son is **d**.' 1Ki 3:23
went into Edom to bury the **d**, ... 1Ki 11:15
of the army, was **d** also. 1Ki 11:21
Ahab, "Naboth of Jezreel is **d**. 1Ki 21:15
that Naboth of Jezreel was **d**, ... 1Ki 21:16
valuables from the **d** bodies!" 2Ki 3:23
Your servant, my husband, is **d**. 2Ki 4:1
the boy was lying **d** on his bed. 2Ki 4:32
brought a **d** boy back to life. 2Ki 8:5
her son was **d**, she killed her 2Ki 11:1
threw the **d** man into Elisha's 2Ki 13:21
from Lebo Hamath to the **D** Sea. 2Ki 14:25
they saw all the **d** bodies. 2Ki 19:35
the officer saw that Saul was **d**, ... 1Ch 10:5
that Saul and his sons were **d**, ... 1Ch 10:7
came to strip the **d** soldiers, ... 1Ch 10:8
the other side of the **D** Sea. 2Ch 20:2
But they only saw **d** bodies lying 2Ch 20:24

her son was **d**, she killed all 2Ch 22:10
were very sad because he was **d**. 2Ch 35:24
crying for the **d** was turned .... Est 9:22
people, and they are all **d**. .... Job 1:19
I would be lying **d** in peace; .... Job 3:13
not buried like a child born **d**, ... Job 3:16
Will the **d** live again? All my .... Job 14:14
The spirits of the **d** tremble, ... Job 26:5
and where there is something **d**,............. Job 39:30
D people don't remember you; .... Ps 6:5
down to the place of the **d**. .... Ps 30:3
I am forgotten as if I were **d**. .... Ps 31:12
like a child born **d** who never .... Ps 58:8
I am almost **d**, you will keep .... Ps 71:20
horses and riders fell **d**. .... Ps 76:6
No one was left to bury the **d**.............. Ps 79:3
of troubles, and I am nearly **d**. .... Ps 88:3
have been left as **d**, like a body .... Ps 88:5
in the dark place of the **d**. .... Ps 88:6
show your miracles for the **d**?.............. Ps 88:10
sad until they were nearly **d**. .... Ps 109:16
filling them with **d** bodies; .... Ps 110:6
D people do not praise the LORD; .... Ps 115:17
in darkness like those long **d**................. Ps 143:3
I will be like those who are **d**............... Ps 143:7
took that path are now all **d**. .... Pr 2:18
happening in the world of the **d**,............. Pr 15:11
sense will end up among the **d**. .... Pr 21:16
decided that the **d** are better .... Ec 4:2
say a baby born **d** is better off .... Ec 6:3
A baby born **d** is useless. .... Ec 6:4
After that, they join the **d**. .... Ec 9:3
dog is better off than a **d** lion! .... Ec 9:4
die, but the **d** know nothing. .... Ec 9:5
After people are **d**, they can no .... Ec 9:6
D flies can make even perfume .... Ec 10:1
You will be **d** a long time. .... Ec 11:8
place of the **d** wants more and .... Is 5:14
D bodies lie in the streets like .... Is 5:25
the place of the **d** or as high as .... Is 7:11
alive ask something from the **d**?............. Is 8:19
or fall down among the **d** bodies. .... Is 10:4
The place of the **d** is excited to .... Is 14:9
It wakes the spirits of the **d**, ... Is 14:9
sent down to the place of the **d**. .... Is 14:11
the deep places where the **d** are. .... Is 14:15
You are like a **d** body other.................. Is 14:19
king who struck you is now **d**. .... Is 14:29
up, and all the plants are **d**; .... Is 15:6
time everything will be **d**; .... Is 17:11
idols and spirits of the **d**, ... Is 19:3
Those masters are now **d**; .... Is 26:14
ground will give birth to the **d**. .... Is 26:19
will not cover the **d** any longer. .... Is 26:21
stands over the **d** animal and .... Is 31:4
will fall like **d** leaves from a .... Is 34:4
they saw all the **d** bodies. .... Is 37:36
he was almost **d**. The prophet .... Is 38:1
the place of the **d** cannot praise .... Is 38:18
send them to the place of the **d**. .... Is 57:9
We are like **d** men among the .... Is 59:10
All of us are like **d** leaves, ... Is 64:6
to get messages from the **d**. .... Is 65:4
go out and see the **d** bodies of .... Is 66:24
Cry loudly for those who are **d**, ... Je 6:26
will bury the **d** in Topheth until .... Je 7:32
bodies of the **d** will become food .... Je 7:33
who are not **d** will wish they .... Je 8:3
'The **d** bodies of people will lie .... Je 9:22
the grass in every field be **d**? .... Je 12:4
a desert that is wilted and **d**. .... Je 12:11
to cry for the **d** or to show your .... Je 16:5
those who are crying for the **d**. .... Je 16:7

will make their **d** bodies food .... Je 19:7
The **d** people will be buried here .... Je 19:11
cry for the **d** king or be sad .... Je 22:10
white like a **d** man's face? .... Je 30:6
because her children are **d**!" .... Je 31:15
valley where **d** bodies and ashes .... Je 31:40
the Ammonite people wants you **d**? .... Je 40:14
of Nethaniah put **d** bodies in it .... Je 41:9
Pile up her **d** bodies like heaps .... Je 50:26
will be many **d** people lying all .... Je 51:47
who have been **d** a long time. .... La 3:6
A third will fall **d** by the sword .... Eze 5:12
I will lay the **d** bodies of the .... Eze 6:5
people will lie **d** among their .... Eze 6:13
Like wolves tearing a **d** animal, ... Eze 22:27
do not cry loudly for the **d**................... Eze 24:17
will fall **d** by the sword. .... Eze 24:21
the place of the **d** to join those .... Eze 26:20
live with the **d** below the earth .... Eze 26:20
wounded in Sidon will fall **d**, ... Eze 28:23
with Egypt will fall **d** in war. .... Eze 30:5
Egypt will fall **d** in war from .... Eze 30:6
and Bubastis will fall **d** in war, ... Eze 30:17
gone down to the place of the **d**. .... Eze 31:14
went down to the place of the **d**,........... Eze 31:15
it down to the place of the **d**. .... Eze 31:16
tree to the place of the **d**. .... Eze 31:17
place of the **d** below the earth .... Eze 32:18
the place of the **d** the leaders .... Eze 32:21
and all its army lie **d** there................... Eze 32:22
parts of the place of the **d**. .... Eze 32:23
parts of the place of the **d**. .... Eze 32:24
gone down to the place of the **d**............ Eze 32:25
of war to the place of the **d**. .... Eze 32:27
gone down to the place of the **d**............ Eze 32:29
gone down to the place of the **d**............ Eze 32:30
you will fall **d** on the mountains .... Eze 39:4
Travelers, east of the **D** Sea. .... Eze 39:11
still lying **d** on the ground. .... Eze 39:14
or with the **d** bodies of their .... Eze 43:7
and take the **d** bodies of their................ Eze 43:9
must not go near a **d** person, ... Eze 44:25
it enters the **D** Sea, it will .... Eze 47:8
water goes the **D** Sea will become .... Eze 47:9
will stand by the **D** Sea. .... Eze 47:10
the town of Tamar on the **D** Sea. .... Eze 47:18
Tamar on the **D** Sea to the waters .... Eze 48:28
turned white like a **d** person, ... Da 10:8
them from the place of the **d**?.............. Hos 13:14
they lie dry and **d** in the dirt. .... Joe 1:17
will be forced into the **D** Sea, ... Joe 2:20
the stink from all the **d** bodies, ... Am 4:10
any other **d** bodies with you? .... Am 6:10
the valley south of the **D** Sea." .... Am 6:14
There will be **d** bodies thrown .... Am 8:3
into days of crying for the **d**, ... Am 8:10
Mediterranean Sea to the **D** Sea, ... Am 8:12
as deep as the place of the **d**, ... Am 9:2
in the land cries for the **d**. .... Am 9:5
very weak and wished he were **d**. .... Jnh 4:8
Many are **d**; their bodies are .... Nah 3:3
all the merchants will be **d**;................... Zph 1:11
who touches a **d** body will become........... Hag 2:13
Your ancestors are **d**, and those .... Zch 1:5
it will flow east to the **D** Sea, ... Zch 14:8
because her children are **d**." .... Mt 2:18
to kill the **d** children are now **d**." .... Mt 2:20
people who are **d** bury their own .... Mt 8:22
The girl is not **d**, only asleep." .... Mt 9:24
raise the **d** to life again, ... Mt 10:8
can hear, the **d** are raised to .... Mt 11:5
who has risen from the **d**. .... Mt 14:2
raised from the **d** on the third.............. Mt 16:21

Son of Man had risen from the **d.** .... Mt 17:9
he will be raised from the **d.**" .... Mt 17:23
would not rise from the **d.** .... Mt 22:23
when people rise from the **d,** .... Mt 22:28
When people rise from the **d,** .... Mt 22:30
to you about rising from the **d.** .... Mt 22:31
God of the living, not the **d.**" .... Mt 22:32
of the bones of **d** people and all .... Mt 23:27
Wherever the **d** body is, there.................. Mt 24:28
But after I rise from the **d,** .... Mt 26:32
had died were raised from the **d.** .... Mt 27:52
was raised from the **d** and went .... Mt 27:53
days I will rise from the **d.**' .... Mt 27:63
that he has risen from the **d.** .... Mt 27:64
and they became like **d** men. .... Mt 28:4
risen from the **d** as he said he................ Mt 28:6
'Jesus has risen from the **d.** .... Mt 28:7
They said, "Your daughter is **d.** .... Mk 5:35
child is not **d,** only asleep.".................... Mk 5:39
who has risen from the **d.** .... Mk 6:14
Now he has risen from the **d!**" .... Mk 6:16
from the **d** after three days. .... Mk 8:31
Son of Man had risen from the **d.** .... Mk 9:9
meant about rising from the **d.** .... Mk 9:10
The boy looked as if he were **d,** .... Mk 9:26
days, he will rise from the **d.**" .... Mk 9:31
they saw the fig tree dry and **d,** .... Mk 11:20
tree you cursed is dry and **d!**" .... Mk 11:21
would not rise from the **d.** .... Mk 12:18
when people rise from the **d,** .... Mk 12:23
When people rise from the **d,** .... Mk 12:25
about people rising from the **d.** .... Mk 12:26
God of the living, not the **d.** .... Mk 12:27
But after I rise from the **d,** .... Mk 14:28
told Pilate that he was **d,**....................... Mk 15:45
He has risen from the **d;** .... Mk 16:6
rose from the **d** early on the .... Mk 16:9
after he had risen from the **d.** .... Mk 16:14
was so sick he was nearly **d.** .... Lk 7:2
can hear, the **d** are raised to .... Lk 7:22
to him, "Your daughter is **d.** .... Lk 8:49
sad because the girl was **d,**..................... Lk 8:52
She is not **d,** only asleep." .... Lk 8:52
they knew the girl was **d.** .... Lk 8:53
Baptist has risen from the **d.**" .... Lk 9:7
long ago has risen from the **d.**" .... Lk 9:8
days will be raised from the **d.**" .... Lk 9:22
people who are **d** bury their own .... Lk 9:60
left him lying there, almost **d.**................ Lk 10:30
good people rise from the **d.**" .... Lk 14:14
son was **d,** but now he is alive .... Lk 15:24
because your brother was **d,** .... Lk 15:32
place of the **d,** he was in much .... Lk 16:23
someone goes to them from the **d,** .... Lk 16:30
who comes back from the **d.**'" .... Lk 16:31
Where there is a **d** body, there .... Lk 17:37
would not rise from the **d,** .... Lk 20:27
be when people rise from the **d?**" .... Lk 20:33
raised from the **d** and live again .... Lk 20:35
have been raised from the **d.** .... Lk 20:36
showed that the **d** are raised to .... Lk 20:37
living, not the **d,** because all .... Lk 20:38
person in this place for the **d?** .... Lk 24:5
he has risen from the **d.** .... Lk 24:6
rise from the **d** on the third day .... Lk 24:7
really has risen from the **d!**.................... Lk 24:34
rise from the **d** on the third day .... Lk 24:46
Jesus was raised from the **d,** .... Jn 2:22
because his son was almost **d.** .... Jn 4:47
raises the **d** and gives them .... Jn 5:21
here when the **d** will hear the................ Jn 5:25
when all who are **d** and in their .... Jn 5:28
Jesus meant that Lazarus was **d,** .... Jn 11:13

said plainly, "Lazarus is **d.** .... Jn 11:14
already been **d** and in the tomb .... Jn 11:17
the sister of the **d** man, said, ... Jn 11:39
d man came out, his hands and .... Jn 11:44
the man Jesus raised from the **d.** .... Jn 12:1
whom Jesus raised from the **d.** .... Jn 12:9
from the **d** and told him to .... Jn 12:17
People pick up **d** branches,................... Jn 15:6
and saw that he was already **d,** .... Jn 19:33
which is how they bury the **d.**............... Jn 19:40
that Jesus must rise from the **d.** .... Jn 20:9
after he was raised from the **d,** .... Jn 21:14
after he was raised from the **d,** .... Ac 1:3
Jesus from the **d** and set him .... Ac 2:24
the Christ rising from the **d.** .... Ac 2:31
One whom God raised from the **d.** .... Ac 2:32
but God raised him from the **d.** .... Ac 3:15
rise from the **d** through the................... Ac 4:2
but God raised him from the **d.** .... Ac 4:10
was truly raised from the **d.** .... Ac 4:33
came in and saw that she was **d,** .... Ac 5:10
raised Jesus up from the **d!**.................... Ac 5:30
after he was raised from the **d.** .... Ac 10:41
judge of the living and the **d.** .... Ac 10:42
God raised him up from the **d!** .... Ac 13:30
by raising Jesus from the **d.** .... Ac 13:33
God raised Jesus from the **d.** .... Ac 13:34
raised from the **d** did not rot .... Ac 13:37
die and then rise from the **d.** .... Ac 17:3
Jesus and his rising from the **d.** .... Ac 17:18
by raising that man from the **d!**" .... Ac 17:31
Jesus being raised from the **d,** .... Ac 17:32
they picked him up, he was **d.** .... Ac 20:9
people will rise from the **d.**" .... Ac 23:6
people will rise from the **d.** .... Ac 23:8
surely be raised from the **d.** .... Ac 24:15
People will rise from the **d!**'" .... Ac 24:21
God to raise people from the **d?** .... Ac 26:8
as the first to rise from the **d,** .... Ac 26:23
would swell up or fall down **d.** .... Ac 28:6
life to the **d** and who creates .... Rm 4:17
Jesus our Lord from the **d.** .... Rm 4:24
raised from the **d** to make us .... Rm 4:25
raised from the **d** by the .... Rm 6:4
by rising from the **d** as he did. .... Rm 6:5
Christ was raised from the **d,** .... Rm 6:9
as being **d** to the power of sin............... Rm 6:11
One who was raised from the **d**— .... Rm 7:4
will always be **d** because of sin. .... Rm 8:10
God raised Jesus from the **d,** .... Rm 8:11
he was also raised from the **d,** .... Rm 8:34
and bring Christ up from the **d?**" .... Rm 10:7
God raised Jesus from the **d,** .... Rm 10:9
rose from the **d** to live again .... Rm 14:9
Lord from the **d** and will also 1Co 6:14
Christ was raised from the **d,** 1Co 15:12
one is ever raised from the **d,** 1Co 15:13
he raised Christ from the **d.** 1Co 15:15
If the **d** are not raised, Christ 1Co 15:16
truly been raised from the **d**— 1Co 15:20
If the **d** are never raised,...................... 1Co 15:29
If the **d** are not raised, "Let us 1Co 15:35
may ask, "How are the **d** raised? 1Co 15:35
same with the **d** who are raised 1Co 15:42
who raises people from the **d,**.............. 2Co 1:9
the Lord Jesus from the **d,** 2Co 4:14
raised from the **d** so that they.............. 2Co 5:15
who raised Jesus from the **d.** .... Gal 1:1
Christ from the **d** and put him at .... Eph 1:20
spiritually **d** because of your .... Eph 2:1
we were spiritually **d** because of .... Eph 2:5
that raised him from the **d.** .... Php 3:10
will be raised from the **d.** .... Php 3:11

one who was raised from the **d**. ....Col 1:18
he raised Christ from the **d**. ....Col 2:12
spiritually **d** because of your ....Col 2:13
raised from the **d** with Christ, ...Col 3:1
whom God raised from the **d**, ...1Th 1:10
we are alive or **d** when he comes. 1Th 5:10
herself is really **d** while she is 1Ti 5:6
who was raised from the **d**, ...2Ti 2:8
rising from the **d** has already 2Ti 2:18
will judge the living and the **d**, ...2Ti 4:1
the raising of the **d** and eternal ....Heb 6:2
one who wrote that will is **d**. ....Heb 9:16
man was so old he was almost **d**, ...Heb 11:12
that God could raise the **d**, ...Heb 11:19
received their **d** relatives.........................Heb 11:35
itself—that does nothing—is **d**. ....Jam 2:17
does not have a spirit is **d**, ...Jam 2:26
Jesus Christ rose from the **d**. 1Pe 1:3
Christ from the **d** and gave him 1Pe 1:21
Christ was raised from the **d**. 1Pe 3:21
to judge the living and the **d**. 1Pe 4:5
preached to those who are now **d**. 1Pe 4:6
does not love is still **d**........................1Jn 3:14
the ground. So they are twice **d**.................Jud 1:12
among those raised from the **d**. ....Rev 1:5
down at his feet like a **d** man.................Rev 1:17
I was **d**, but look, I am alive ....Rev 1:18
are alive, but really you are **d**. ....Rev 3:1
happy because these two are **d**. ....Rev 11:10
time has come to judge the **d**, ...Rev 11:18
Blessed are the **d** who die from ....Rev 14:13
blood like that of a **d** man, ...Rev 16:3
others that were **d** did not live ....Rev 20:5
in this first raising of the **d**. ....Rev 20:6
I saw the **d**, great and small, ...Rev 20:12
gave up the **d** who were in them...............Rev 20:13

DEADLY

like the **d** poison of cobras.....................Dt 32:33
the **d** rivers overwhelmed me..................2Sa 22:5
He has prepared his **d** weapons;...............Ps 7:13
the **d** rivers overwhelmed me...................Ps 18:4
traps and from **d** diseases. ....Ps 91:3
shooting **d**, burning arrows. ....Pr 26:18
and evil and full of **d** poison. ....Jam 3:8
wounded by the **d** sword but ....Rev 13:14

DEAF

makes someone **d** or not able to ....Ex 4:11
must not curse a **d** person or put ....Le 19:14
help. Do not be **d** to me. If you ....Ps 28:1
I am like the **d**; I cannot hear.................Ps 38:13
like **d** cobras that stop up their ....Ps 58:4
Your ears will be **d** to the noise ....Ec 12:4
At that time the **d** will hear the ....Is 29:18
see again, and the **d** will hear. ....Is 35:5
You who are **d**, hear me........................Is 42:18
Israel or more **d** than the ....Is 42:19
The **d** can hear, the dead are ....Mt 11:5
to him who was **d** and could not..............Mk 7:32
He makes the **d** hear! And those ....Mk 7:37
The **d** can hear, the dead are ....Lk 7:22

DEAL

a large meeting to **d** with them. ....Ne 5:7
it all in a bad **d** and have ....Ec 5:14
years the LORD will **d** with Tyre, ...Is 23:17
will **d** with you for the sake of ....Eze 20:44
been sold for a great **d** of money ....Mt 26:9

DEALINGS

and had no **d** with anyone else. ....Jdg 18:7
and they had no **d** with anyone ....Jdg 18:28

DEAR

said to her, "**D** woman, you are ....Lk 8:48
to you with our **d** friends ....Ac 15:25
into the kingdom of his **d** Son. ....Col 1:13
Tychicus is my **d** brother in....................Col 4:7

DEATH

comforted after his mother's **d**. ....Ge 24:67
or his wife will be put to **d**." ....Ge 26:11
kill our brother and hide his **d**? ....Ge 37:26
out and let her be burned to **d**." ....Ge 38:24
two sons to **d** if I don't bring ....Ge 42:37
'When my father was near **d**, ...Ge 50:5
one who brings **d** come into your ....Ex 12:23
this desert to starve us to **d**." ....Ex 16:3
almost ready to stone me to **d**." ....Ex 17:4
the mountain must be put to **d** ....Ex 19:12
and kills him must be put to **d**. ....Ex 21:12
put him to **d**, even if he has run ....Ex 21:14
or his mother must be put to **d**. ....Ex 21:15
he is caught must be put to **d**..............Ex 21:16
or mother must be put to **d**. ....Ex 21:17
the bull must be stoned to **d**, ...Ex 21:29
bull must also be stoned to **d**..................Ex 21:32
Put to **d** any woman who does evil...........Ex 22:18
Put to **d** anyone who has sexual ....Ex 22:19
to be put to **d** as punishment, ...Ex 23:7
that person must be put to **d**; ....Ex 31:14
Sabbath day must be put to **d**. ....Ex 31:15
on that day must be put to **d**. ....Ex 35:2
about the **d** of his sons. ....Le 10:3
But they are not to be put to **d**, ...Le 19:20
or mother must be put to **d**. ....Le 20:9
brought his own **d** on himself. ....Le 20:9
adultery and must be put to **d**. ....Le 20:10
father's wife must be put to **d**. ....Le 20:11
both of them must be put to **d**. ....⋅........Le 20:12
They must be put to **d**. ....Le 20:13
an animal, he must be put to **d**. ....Le 20:15
They must be put to **d**. ....Le 20:16
fortune-teller must be put to **d**. ....Le 20:27
the LORD must be put to **d**; ....Le 24:16
another person must be put to **d**. ....Le 24:17
another person must be put to **d**. ....Le 24:21
back; he must be put to **d**. ....Le 27:29
the Holy Tent will be put to **d**. ....Nu 1:51
holy things must be put to **d**."...............Nu 3:10
Holy Place was to be put to **d**. ....Nu 3:38
me, put me to **d**, and then I....................Nu 11:15
these people to **d** all at once, ...Nu 14:15
the camp and stoned him to **d**, ...Nu 15:36
If these men die a normal **d**—.................Nu 16:29
Holy Place will be put to **d**." ....Nu 18:7
a sword or who died a natural **d**, ...Nu 19:16
must put to **d** your people who ....Nu 25:5
who was put to **d** was Cozbi ....Nu 25:15
a murderer. He must be put to **d**. ....Nu 35:16
a murderer. He must be put to **d**. ....Nu 35:17
a murderer. He must be put to **d**. ....Nu 35:18
must put the murderer to **d**; ....Nu 35:19
at someone and cause **d**.........................Nu 35:20
with his hand and cause **d**. ....Nu 35:21
be put to **d** only if there are ....Nu 35:30
murderer who should be put to **d**. ....Nu 35:31
for the murderer to be put to **d**. ....Nu 35:33
You must put them to **d**. ....Dt 13:9
before the person is put to **d**; ....Dt 17:6
LORD your God must be put to **d**. ....Dt 17:12
of allowing the **d** of innocent ....Dt 19:10
is guilty of a sin worthy of **d**, ...Dt 21:22
must put her to **d** by throwing ....Dt 22:21
and put them to **d** by throwing ....Dt 22:24
with her must be put to **d**. ....Dt 22:25

has not done a sin worthy of **d.** .... Dt 22:26
not be put to **d** if their .... Dt 24:16
and success, **d** and destruction. .... Dt 30:15
I am offering you life or **d,** .... Dt 30:19
I send life and **d;** I can hurt, ... Dt 32:39
against you will be put to **d.** .... Jos 1:18
to live. Save us from **d.**" .... Jos 2:13
birth until the day of his **d.**'" .... Jdg 13:7
wife and her father to **d.** .... Jdg 15:6
so that we can put them to **d.** .... Jdg 20:13
Not even **d** will separate us." .... Ru 1:17
The LORD sends **d,** and he brings 1Sa 2:6
had decided to put them to **d.** 1Sa 2:25
No one will be put to **d** today. 1Sa 11:13
Put to **d** men and women, children 1Sa 15:3
the threat of **d** has passed." 1Sa 15:32
lives, David won't be put to **d.**" 1Sa 19:6
I am only a step away from **d!**" 1Sa 20:3
responsible for the **d** of all 1Sa 22:22
are responsible for your own **d.** 2Sa 1:16
They are together even in **d.** 2Sa 1:23
forever of the **d** of Abner son of 2Sa 3:28
you evil men to **d** because you 2Sa 4:11
Hanun about his father's **d.** 2Sa 10:2
King David got over Amnon's **d,** 2Sa 13:39
sinned, he can put me to **d!**" 2Sa 14:32
whether it means life or **d.**" 2Sa 15:21
be put to **d** in Israel today. 2Sa 19:22
were put to **d** during the first 2Sa 21:9
The waves of **d** came around me; 2Sa 22:5
ropes of **d** wrapped around me. 2Sa 22:6
or the **d** of your enemies 1Ki 3:11
like this? He will put me to **d.** 1Ki 18:9
From now on it won't cause **d,** 2Ki 2:21
of God, there's **d** in the pot!" 2Ki 4:40
trampled the officer to **d.** 2Ki 7:17
put Athaliah to **d** in the Temple 2Ki 11:15
There she was put to **d.** 2Ki 11:16
had been put to **d** with the sword 2Ki 11:20
he did not put to **d** the children 2Ki 14:6
years after the **d** of Jehoash son 2Ki 14:17
so the LORD put him to **d.** 1Ch 2:3
LORD put Saul to **d** and gave the 1Ch 10:14
Hanun about his father's **d.** 1Ch 19:2
or for the **d** of your enemies, ... 2Ch 1:11
their bad advice led to his **d.** 2Ch 22:4
Ahaziah's **d** when he went to 2Ch 22:7
put Athaliah to **d** in the Temple 2Ch 23:14
There they put her to **d.** 2Ch 23:15
been put to **d** with the sword. 2Ch 23:21
did not put to **d** their children. 2Ch 25:4
years after the **d** of Jehoash son 2Ch 25:25
must be put to **d** unless the king .... Est 4:11
to die, but **d** does not come. .... Job 3:21
buy you back from **d** in times of .... Job 5:20
be choked; my bones welcome **d.** .... Job 7:15
soon lie down in the dust of **d.** .... Job 7:21
If the whip brings sudden **d,** .... Job 9:23
hope go down to the gates of **d?** .... Job 17:16
d gnaws at their arms and legs. .... Job 18:13
tents and dragged off to **D,** .... Job 18:14
lie with them in the dust of **d.** .... Job 20:11
D is naked before God; .... Job 26:6
of destruction and **d** say, ' .... Job 28:22
you will bring me down to **d,** .... Job 30:23
does this to save people from **d,** .... Job 33:18
They are near **d,** and their life .... Job 33:22
Save him from **d.** I have found a .... Job 33:24
God bought my life back from **d,** .... Job 33:28
the gates of **d** been opened to .... Job 38:17
the tune of "The **D** of the Son." .... Ps 8:9
me go through the gates of **d.** .... Ps 9:13
The ropes of **d** came around me; .... Ps 18:4

ropes of **d** wrapped around me. .... Ps 18:5
You laid me in the dust of **d.** .... Ps 22:15
saves them from **d** and spares .... Ps 33:19
are in danger of **d** all the time. .... Ps 44:22
Don't they all face **d?** .... Ps 49:9
and **d** will be their shepherd. .... Ps 49:14
the terror of **d** has attacked me. .... Ps 55:4
Let **d** take away my enemies. .... Ps 55:15
you have saved me from **d.** .... Ps 56:13
the LORD God saves us from **d.** .... Ps 68:20
as they lay asleep in **d.** .... Ps 76:5
You have saved me from **d.** .... Ps 86:13
You have brought me close to **d;** .... Ps 88:6
be told in the place of **d?** .... Ps 88:11
and sentence to **d** the innocent. .... Ps 94:21
The ropes of **d** bound me, and the .... Ps 116:3
LORD, you saved me from **d.** .... Ps 116:8
The **d** of one that belongs to the .... Ps 116:15
swallow them alive, as **d** does; .... Pr 1:12
Her house is on the way to **d;** .... Pr 2:18
She is on the way to **d;** .... Pr 5:5
Her house is on the road to **d,** .... Pr 7:27
Those who hate me love **d.**" .... Pr 8:36
living will save you from **d.** .... Pr 10:2
living will save you from **d.** .... Pr 11:4
is another way that leads to **d.** .... Pr 12:28
that can save people from **d.** .... Pr 13:14
but in the end it leads to **d.** .... Pr 14:12
that can save people from **d.** .... Pr 14:27
right are protected even in **d.** .... Pr 14:32
whatever would cause their **d.** .... Pr 15:24
angry king can put someone to **d,** .... Pr 16:14
but in the end it leads to **d.** .... Pr 16:25
What you say can mean life or **d.** .... Pr 18:21
like a mist and leads to **d.** .... Pr 21:6
you will save them from **d.** .... Pr 23:14
who are being led to their **d;** .... Pr 24:11
because you will starve to **d.** .... Ec 4:5
The day of **d** is better than the .... Ec 7:1
A wise person thinks about **d,** .... Ec 7:4
are worse than **d** and are as .... Ec 7:26
the wind or stop his own **d.** .... Ec 8:8
tell what will happen after **d.** .... Ec 10:14
Love is as strong as **d;** .... Sng 8:6
the wicked will be put to **d.** .... Is 11:4
be beaten to **d** in front of them .... Is 13:16
he will destroy **d** forever. .... Is 25:8
ghosts will not rise from **d.** .... Is 26:14
their bodies will rise from **d.** .... Is 26:19
have made an agreement with **d;** .... Is 28:15
contract with **d** will not help .... Is 28:18
to go through the gates of **d?** .... Is 38:10
He was put to **d;** he was punished .... Is 53:8
as God wants find rest in **d.** .... Is 57:2
the Lord GOD will put you to **d.** .... Is 65:15
arrows bring **d.** All their people .... Je 5:16
D has climbed in through our .... Je 9:21
war, or they will starve to **d.** .... Je 16:4
Judah be put to **d** and the young .... Je 18:21
Jeremiah must be put to **d!** .... Je 38:4
the city, he will starve to **d.**" .... Je 38:9
He will bring **d** to those who are .... Je 43:11
inside the houses, **d** destroys. .... La 1:20
we face **d** in the desert. .... La 5:9
you responsible for their **d.** .... Eze 3:18
Disease and **d** will sweep through .... Eze 5:17
I will put you to **d** because I am .... Eze 16:38
so he will surely be put to **d.** .... Eze 18:13
lies to cause the **d** of others. .... Eze 22:9
when they are sad about a **d.**" .... Eze 24:17
eat when they are sad about a **d.** .... Eze 24:22
die a terrible **d** like those who .... Eze 28:8
Go lie down in **d** with those who .... Eze 32:19

now they lie in **d** with those .... Eze 32:29
punish Gog with disease and **d.** .... Eze 38:22
died a natural **d** or one that has .... Eze 44:31
the wise men of Babylon to **d.** .... Da 2:24
their children were bashed to **d.** .... Hos 10:14
Will I rescue them from **d?** .... Hos 13:14
crying for the **d** of an only son, ... Am 8:10
you saved me from the pit of **d,** .... Jnh 2:6
were beaten to **d** at every street .... Nah 3:10
is like a grave's desire for **d,** .... Hab 2:5
crying over the **d** of an only .... Zch 12:10
covered with the shadows of **d,** .... Mt 4:16
parents and have them put to **d.** .... Mt 10:21
or mother must be put to **d.'** .... Mt 15:4
the power of **d** will not be able .... Mt 16:18
guilty for the **d** of all the good .... Mt 23:35
stone to **d** those who are sent .... Mt 23:37
of sorrow, to the point of **d.**................. Mt 26:38
it has paid for a man's **d.''** .... Mt 27:6
I am not guilty of this man's **d.** .... Mt 27:24
will be responsible for his **d.''** .... Mt 27:25
for Herodias to cause John's **d.** .... Mk 6:21
or mother must be put to **d.'** .... Mk 7:10
and cause them to be put to **d.** .... Mk 13:12
of sorrow, to the point of **d.**................. Mk 14:34
in darkness, in the shadow of **d.**............. Lk 1:79
stone to **d** those who are sent .... Lk 13:34
the people will stone us to **d,** .... Lk 20:6
out with Jesus to be put to **d,** .... Lk 23:32
him over to be sentenced to **d,** .... Lk 24:20
already left **d** and entered life. .... Jn 5:24
we stone to **d** every woman who............... Jn 8:5
This sickness will not end in **d.** .... Jn 11:4
to stone you to **d** only a short .... Jn 11:8
not allowed to put anyone to **d,''**............. Jn 18:31
After his **d,** he showed himself .... Ac 1:3
he fell to his **d,** his body burst .... Ac 1:18
you put him to **d** by nailing him .... Ac 2:23
set him free from the pain of **d,** .... Ac 2:24
people would stone them to **d.** .... Ac 5:26
responsible for this man's **d.''**................. Ac 5:28
Barnabas and to stone them to **d.** .... Ac 14:5
with the **d** of his own son. .... Ac 20:28
charge was worthy of jail or **d.** .... Ac 23:29
I do not ask to be saved from **d.** .... Ac 25:11
asking me to sentence him to **d.** .... Ac 25:15
found no reason to order his **d.** .... Ac 25:25
faith in the blood of Jesus' **d.** .... Rm 3:25
God by the blood of Christ's **d.** .... Rm 5:9
through the **d** of his Son. .... Rm 5:10
man did, and with sin came **d.** .... Rm 5:12
so **d** ruled all people because .... Rm 5:17
punishment of **d** to all people, ... Rm 5:18
Sin once used **d** to rule us, ... Rm 5:21
We shared his **d** in our baptism. .... Rm 6:3
with Christ and shared his **d.** .... Rm 6:4
D has no power over him now. .... Rm 6:9
spiritual **d,** or you can obey .... Rm 6:16
Those things only bring **d.** .... Rm 6:21
The payment for sin is **d.** .... Rm 6:23
we did were bringing us **d.** .... Rm 7:5
life, but for me it brought **d.** .... Rm 7:10
that is good brought **d** to me? .... Rm 7:13
from this body that brings me **d?** .... Rm 7:24
the law that brings sin and **d.** .... Rm 8:2
by the sinful self, there is **d.** .... Rm 8:6
or danger or violent **d?** .... Rm 8:35
are in danger of **d** all the time. .... Rm 8:36
that neither **d,** nor life, nor .... Rm 8:38
will bring them life after **d.**............... Rm 11:15
Christ and his **d** on the cross. 1Co 2:2
the world, life, **d,** the present, ... 1Co 3:22
sealed with the blood of my **d.** 1Co 11:25

the Lord's **d** until he comes. 1Co 11:26
those who sleep in **d** will also.................. 1Co 15:20
D has come because of what one 1Co 15:21
enemy to be destroyed will be **d.** 1Co 15:26
We will not all sleep in **d,** 1Co 15:51
D is destroyed forever in victory. 1Co 15:54
D, where is your victory? 1Co 15:55
from these great dangers of **d,** 2Co 1:10
are the smell of **d** that brings 2Co 2:16
law brings **d,** but the Spirit 2Co 3:6
law that brought **d** was written 2Co 3:7
We carry the **d** of Jesus in our 2Co 4:10
in danger of **d** so that the life 2Co 4:11
So **d** is working in us, but life................. 2Co 4:12
sorrow the world has brings **d.** 2Co 7:10
I have been near **d** many times. 2Co 11:23
time I was almost stoned to **d.** 2Co 11:25
It was the law that put me to **d,** .... Gal 2:19
I was put to **d** on the cross with .... Gal 2:20
Christ's **d** would be useless. .... Gal 2:21
about the **d** of Jesus Christ .... Gal 3:1
set free by the blood of his **d,** .... Eph 1:7
through the blood of Christ's **d.** .... Eph 2:13
this with his **d** on the cross. .... Eph 2:16
Rise from **d,** and Christ will .... Eph 5:14
even when that caused his **d—** .... Php 2:8
and become like him in his **d.**............. Php 3:10
of Christ's **d** on the cross. .... Col 1:20
through Christ's **d** in the body .... Col 1:22
that is, his **d,** that you were.................... Col 2:11
He destroyed **d,** and through the 2Ti 1:10
the one who has the power of **d—** .... Heb 2:14
because of their fear of **d.** .... Heb 2:15
One who could save him from **d,** .... Heb 5:7
from those acts that lead to **d.** .... Heb 6:1
begin without blood to show **d.** .... Heb 9:18
without blood to show **d.** .... Heb 9:22
of the blood of Jesus' **d.** .... Heb 10:19
He was put to **d** without mercy. .... Heb 10:28
Abraham got Isaac back from **d.** .... Heb 11:19
one who brings **d** would not kill............... Heb 11:28
were stoned to **d,** they were cut .... Heb 11:37
He suffered **d** on the cross. .... Heb 12:2
must be put to **d** with stones.'' .... Heb 12:20
then the sin grows and brings **d.** .... Jam 1:15
soul from **d** and will cause .... Jam 5:20
blood of the **d** of Jesus Christ 1Pe 1:2
we have left **d** and have come.................. 1Jn 3:14
that does not lead to eternal **d** 1Jn 5:16
that does not lead to eternal **d.** 1Jn 5:17
sins with the blood of his **d.** .... Rev 1:5
the keys to **d** and to the place.................. Rev 1:18
not be hurt by the second **d.** .... Rev 2:11
blood of your **d** you bought .... Rev 5:9
rider was named **d,** and Hades was .... Rev 6:8
but **d** will run away from them. .... Rev 9:6
of the Lamb's **d** and by the .... Rev 12:11
but this **d** wound was healed. .... Rev 13:3
had the **d** wound that was healed. .... Rev 13:12
d, and crying, and great hunger,............... Rev 18:8
cry and be sad because of her **d.** .... Rev 18:9
guilty of the **d** of the prophets .... Rev 18:24
back for the **d** of his servants. .... Rev 19:2
The second **d** has no power over .... Rev 20:6
and **D** and Hades gave up the dead .... Rev 20:13
And **D** and Hades were thrown into .... Rev 20:14
and there will be no more **d,** .... Rev 21:4
This is the second **d.''** .... Rev 21:8

DEATHS
their own **d** on themselves..................... Le 20:12
will pay him back for those **d.** 1Ki 2:32
be forever guilty for their **d,** 1Ki 2:33

Jezebel for the **d** of my servants 2Ki 9:7
mistake that will cause your **d.** .... Je 42:20
you responsible for their **d.**.................... Eze 3:20
be responsible for their **d.** .... Eze 33:4
are to blame for their own **d.** .... Eze 33:5
the watchman for their **d.**' .... Eze 33:6
I will punish you for their **d.** .... Eze 33:8
punished for the **d** of all the .... Lk 11:50

DEBATE
After a long **d,** Peter stood up .... Ac 15:7

DEBORAH
D, Rebekah's nurse, died and was .... Ge 35:8
prophetess named **D,** the wife of .... Jdg 4:4
D would sit under the Palm Tree .... Jdg 4:5
sit under the Palm Tree of **D,** .... Jdg 4:5
D sent a message to Barak son of .... Jdg 4:6
D said to Barak, "The LORD, the .... Jdg 4:6
Barak said to **D,** "I will go if .... Jdg 4:8
go with you," **D** answered, "but .... Jdg 4:9
So **D** went with Barak to Kedesh. .... Jdg 4:9
follow him, and **D** went with him .... Jdg 4:10
Then **D** said to Barak, "Get up! .... Jdg 4:14
On that day **D** and Barak son of .... Jdg 5:1
Israel until I, **D,** arose, until .... Jdg 5:7
Wake up, wake up, **D!** .... Jdg 5:12
princes of Issachar were with **D.** .... Jdg 5:15

DEBT
Use your wealth to pay my **d.** .... Job 6:22
things for a **d** they didn't owe; .... Job 22:6
you think I sold you to pay a **d?** .... Is 50:1
He canceled the **d,** which listed .... Col 2:14

DEBTS
promises to pay a stranger's **d,** .... Pr 20:16

DECAY
is "planted" will ruin and **d,** 1Co 15:42

DECEIVING
They delight in **d** you while 2Pe 2:13

DECISION
because your **d** comes from God. .... Dt 1:17
must follow the **d** they give you .... Dt 17:10
court comes to a **d** and until the .... Jos 20:6
speak up. What is your **d?**" .... Jdg 20:7
heard about King Solomon's **d,** 1Ki 3:28
be with you when you make a **d.** 2Ch 19:6
That was the **d** of the officers .... Ezr 10:8
officers make a **d** for the whole .... Ezr 10:14
From heaven you gave the **d,** .... Ps 76:8
People throw lots to make a **d,** .... Pr 16:33
I have made a **d,** and I will not .... Je 4:28
of people in the Valley of **D,** .... Joe 3:14
is near in the Valley of **D.** .... Joe 3:14
He wants a **d** from the emperor. .... Ac 25:21

DECK
middle, and lower **d** in it. .... Ge 6:16
They made your **d** from cypress .... Eze 27:6
shades over the **d** were blue and .... Eze 27:7
men were the sailors on your **d.** .... Eze 27:8

DECLARE
They should **d:** "We did not kill .... Dt 21:7
They will **d** one person right and .... Dt 25:1
Today I **d** before the LORD your .... Dt 26:3
but **d** that the innocent person 1Ki 8:32
D a day during which the people 1Ki 21:9
but **d** that the innocent person 2Ch 6:23
God, **d** them guilty! Let them .... Ps 5:10
The heavens **d** the glory of God, ... Ps 19:1
saves them will **d** them right. .... Ps 24:5
If you **d** with your mouth, ... Rm 10:9
And we **d** with our mouths that we .... Rm 10:10

DECLARED
the God of my master, has **d!** 1Ki 1:36
They **d** a special day on which 1Ki 21:12
tell you what the LORD has **d:** .... Ps 2:7
the holy ones **d** the sentence. .... Da 4:17

DECORATE
then **d** yourself with glory and .... Job 40:10
finest dress and **d** yourself with .... Je 4:30
They **d** their idols with silver .... Je 10:4

DECREASE
of Egypt will **d** and dry up. .... Is 19:6

DEDICATION
for the Feast of **D** at Jerusalem. .... Jn 10:22

DEEDS
the same evil **d** that Jeroboam's 1Ki 16:7
have done, for their evil **d.** .... Ps 28:4
you did and consider your **d.** .... Ps 77:12
to Moses and his **d** to the people .... Ps 103:7
not give up their **d** and return. .... Hos 5:4
I remember all their evil **d.** .... Hos 7:2
live in it because of their **d.** .... Mic 7:13
has done mighty **d** by his power. .... Lk 1:51
doing good **d** and kind acts. .... Ac 9:36
paying attention to their **d,** .... Rm 4:6
should do good **d,** which is right 1Ti 2:10
life to do all kinds of good **d.** 1Ti 5:10
So also good **d** are easy to see, ... 1Ti 5:25
to be rich in doing good **d,** 1Ti 6:18
be an example of doing good **d.** .... Tit 2:7
are always wanting to do good **d.** .... Tit 2:14
because of good **d** we did to be .... Tit 3:5
for doing good **d** to provide what .... Tit 3:14
to show love and do good **d.** .... Heb 10:24
You have faith, but I have **d.**" .... Jam 2:18

DEEP
Abram fell into a **d** sleep. .... Ge 15:12
The **d** waters covered them, ... Ex 15:5
the **d** waters became solid in the .... Ex 15:8
three feet **d** on the ground, ... Nu 11:31
the cloud, and the **d** darkness; .... Dt 5:22
the sword **d** into the king's .... Jdg 3:21
very tired, he was in a **d** sleep. .... Jdg 4:21
and went **d** into his forehead, ... 1Sa 17:49
he pulled me from the **d** water. 2Sa 22:17
fifteen feet **d** and thirty feet 1Ki 6:3
and seven and one-half feet **d.** 1Ki 7:23
round, twenty-seven inches **d.** 1Ki 7:31
of each stand was nine inches **d.** 1Ki 7:35
and seven and one-half feet **d.** 2Ch 4:2
chasing them into the **d** water, ... Ne 9:11
when people are in **d** sleep .... Job 4:13
God's wisdom is **d,** and his power .... Job 9:4
He uncovers the **d** things of .... Job 12:22
and search **d** into the mines .... Job 28:3
d ocean says, 'It's not in me; .... Job 28:14
when people are in a **d** sleep, ... Job 33:15
no dark place or **d** shadow where .... Job 34:22
the gates of the **d** darkness? .... Job 38:17
It makes the **d** sea bubble like a .... Job 41:31
he pulled me from the **d** water. .... Ps 18:16
myself, I felt weak **d** inside me. .... Ps 32:3
justice is as **d** as the great .... Ps 36:6
you covered us with **d** darkness. .... Ps 44:19
I am in **d** water, and the flood .... Ps 69:2
hate me and the **d** water. .... Ps 69:14
drown me or the **d** water swallow .... Ps 69:15
the **d** waters shook with fear. .... Ps 77:16
and paths through the **d** waters, ... Ps 77:19
water, as if from the **d** ocean. .... Ps 78:15
How **d** are your thoughts! .... Ps 92:5
them through the **d** sea as if it .... Ps 106:9

miracles he did in the **d** oceans. .... Ps 107:24
in the seas and the **d** oceans. .... Ps 135:6
above and put the **d** underground .... Pr 8:28
guests end up **d** in the grave. .... Pr 9:18
words can be like **d** water, ... Pr 18:4
thoughts can be like a **d** well, ... Pr 20:5
The LORD looks **d** inside people .... Pr 20:27
wife are like a **d** trap. .... Pr 22:14
is as dangerous as a **d** pit, ... Pr 23:27
Though your sins are **d** red, ... Is 1:18
be a sign from as **d** as the place .... Is 7:11
will camp in the **d** ravines .... Is 7:19
to the **d** places where the dead .... Is 14:15
has made you go into a **d** sleep. .... Is 29:10
It was made **d** and wide with much .... Is 30:33
tell the **d** waters, 'Become dry! .... Is 44:27
and the waters of the **d** ocean. .... Is 51:10
d darkness covers her people. .... Is 60:2
the people through the **d** waters? .... Is 63:13
he will change it into **d** gloom. .... Je 13:16
inside me, **d** within my bones .... Je 20:9
of painful crying and **d** sadness:.............. Je 31:15
threw the bodies into a **d** well. .... Je 41:7
Fear, **d** pits, and traps wait for .... Je 48:43
run away and hide in **d** caves, ... Je 49:8
Your ruin is as **d** as the sea. .... La 2:13
and that cup is as **d** and wide.................... Eze 23:32
I will bring the **d** ocean waters .... Eze 26:19
the **d** springs made it tall. .... Eze 31:4
I made the **d** springs cry loudly. .... Eze 31:15
It was ten and one-half feet **d.** .... Eze 40:6
was ten and one-half feet **d.** .... Eze 40:7
It was about fourteen feet **d,** .... Eze 40:9
gates and was as **d** as the gates .... Eze 40:18
it was **d** enough for swimming; .... Eze 47:5
secrets that are **d** and hidden;.................. Da 2:22
I fell into a **d** sleep with my .... Da 8:18
I fell into a **d** sleep with my .... Da 10:9
Israel have gone **d** into sin as .... Hos 9:9
It burned up the **d** water and was .... Am 7:4
they dig down as **d** as the place .... Am 9:2
sea, down, down into the **d** sea. .... Jnh 2:3
The **d** sea was all around me; .... Jnh 2:5
'What are the **d** cuts on your body? .... Zch 13:6
forming a **d** valley that runs .... Zch 14:4
of painful crying and **d** sadness:.............. Mt 2:18
because the ground was not **d.** .... Mt 13:5
they did not have **d** roots. .... Mt 13:6
the teaching go **d** into his life, ... Mt 13:21
because the ground was not **d.** .... Mk 4:5
they did not have **d** roots. .... Mk 4:6
teaching to go **d** into their .... Mk 4:17
Take the boat into **d** water, ... Lk 5:4
a house who dug **d** and laid the .... Lk 6:48
teaching to go **d** into their .... Lk 8:13
The well is very **d,** and you have .... Jn 4:11
was falling into a **d** sleep. .... Ac 20:9
was one hundred twenty feet **d.** .... Ac 27:28
again. It was ninety feet **d.** .... Ac 27:28
God for us with **d** feelings that .... Rm 8:26
even the **d** secrets of God. 1Co 2:10
how high and how **d** that love is. .... Eph 3:18
your roots **d** in him and have .... Col 2:7
some call Satan's **d** secrets. .... Rev 2:24
the key to the **d** hole that leads .... Rev 9:1

DEEPER

the sore seems **d** than the .... Le 13:3
does not seem **d** than the skin, ... Le 13:4
the spot seems **d** than the skin .... Le 13:20
the spot is not **d** than the skin .... Le 13:21
white spot seems **d** than the skin .... Le 13:25
the spot is no **d** than the skin .... Le 13:26

If it seems **d** than the skin and .... Le 13:30
it does not seem **d** than the skin .... Le 13:31
does not seem **d** than the skin, ... Le 13:32
does not seem **d** than the skin, ... Le 13:34
They are **d** than the grave; .... Job 11:8

DEEPLY

caused the man to sleep very **d,** .... Ge 2:21
My son Shechem is **d** in love with .... Ge 34:8
I am a troubled woman, and I 1Sa 1:15
yes, drink **d,** lovers................................. Sng 5:1
you look **d** into the heart and .... Je 20:12
Jesus sighed **d** and said, "Why do .... Mk 8:12
he was upset and was **d** troubled. .... Jn 11:33
love each other **d** with all your 1Pe 1:22
love each other **d,** because love 1Pe 4:8

DEER

like a female **d** that runs free,................. Ge 49:21
as if it were a **d** or a gazelle; .... Dt 12:15
you would eat gazelle or **d** meat. .... Dt 12:22
d, gazelle, roe deer, wild goats, ... Dt 14:5
gazelle, roe **d,** wild goats, ibex .... Dt 14:5
they would eat a gazelle or a **d.** .... Dt 15:22
as fast as a **d** in the field. 2Sa 2:18
makes me like a **d** that does not 2Sa 22:34
three kinds of **d,** and fattened.................. 1Ki 4:23
watch when the **d** gives birth to .... Job 39:1
makes me like a **d** that does not .... Ps 18:33
As a **d** thirsts for streams of .... Ps 42:1
as lovely and graceful as a **d.** .... Pr 5:19
free yourself like a **d** running .... Pr 6:5
butcher, like a **d** caught in a .... Pr 7:22
gazelles and the **d** not to awaken .... Sng 2:7
is like a gazelle or a young **d.** .... Sng 2:9
or a young **d** on the mountain .... Sng 2:17
gazelles and the **d** not to awaken .... Sng 3:5
or a young **d** on the mountains .... Sng 8:14
away like hunted **d** or like sheep .... Is 13:14
people will jump like **d,** .... Is 35:6
Even the mother **d** in the field .... Je 14:5
rulers are like **d** that cannot .... La 1:6
makes me like a **d** that does not .... Hab 3:19

DEFEAT

helped you to **d** your enemies." .... Ge 14:20
man saw he could not **d** Jacob, ... Ge 32:25
he will **d** them and drive them .... Ge 49:19
but I will **d** the king and his .... Ex 14:4
honored when I **d** the king and .... Ex 14:17
When I **d** the king, his chariot .... Ex 14:18
it is not a cry of **d.** .... Ex 32:18
chase your enemies and **d** them,.............. Le 26:7
You will **d** your enemies and kill .... Le 26:8
and your enemies will **d** you. .... Le 26:17
so that your enemy will **d** you. .... Le 26:25
you will help us **d** these people, ... Nu 21:2
he let them **d** the Canaanites. .... Nu 21:3
Maybe then I can **d** them and make .... Nu 22:6
They will **d** their enemies and.................. Nu 24:8
Cyprus and **d** Assyria and Eber,.............. Nu 24:24
and your enemies will **d** you.'" .... Dt 1:42
you the power to **d** Sihon the .... Dt 2:24
The LORD wanted you to **d** Sihon,........... Dt 2:30
and when you **d** them, you must.............. Dt 7:2
will help you **d** their kings, ... Dt 7:24
He will **d** them ahead of you, ... Dt 9:3
will help you **d** them so that you .... Dt 21:10
you and to **d** your enemies for .... Dt 23:14
will help you **d** the enemies that.............. Dt 28:7
will help your enemies **d** you.................... Dt 28:25
D those who attack them, and .... Dt 33:11
will be able to **d** you all your .... Jos 1:5
need all our people to **d** them. .... Jos 7:3
You will never **d** your enemies .... Jos 7:13

will help you **d** the king of Ai, ... Jos 8:1
was not able to **d** those cities, ... Jos 17:12
nation has been able to **d** you. .... Jos 23:9
Israelite could **d** a thousand, ... Jos 23:10
not help you **d** your enemies. .... Jos 23:13
who lived around them **d** them; .... Jdg 2:14
will no longer **d** the nations who .... Jdg 2:21
or help Joshua's army **d** them. .... Jdg 2:23
Moab power to **d** Israel because .... Jdg 3:12
helped you to **d** your enemies, ... Jdg 3:28
in the city of Hazor, **d** Israel. .... Jdg 4:2
LORD will let a woman **d** Sisera." .... Jdg 4:9
many men to **d** the Midianites. .... Jdg 7:2
a great **d** Jephthah struck them .... Jdg 11:33
LORD helped you **d** your enemies, ... Jdg 11:36
Israelites to **d** the Benjaminites .... Jdg 20:35
LORD let the Philistines **d** us? 1Sa 4:3
It was a great **d** for Israel, ... 1Sa 4:10
and the LORD will let us **d** them. 1Sa 14:10
Will you let us **d** them?" 1Sa 14:37
and the Philistines will **d** him." 1Sa 18:21
help you **d** the Philistines." 1Sa 23:4
To **d** the Jebusites you must go 2Sa 5:8
ahead of you to **d** the Philistine 2Sa 5:24
him to **d** all his enemies. 1Ki 5:3
their enemies will **d** them. 1Ki 8:33
"Who will you use to **d** them?" 1Ki 20:14
governors will **d** them.'" 1Ki 20:14
allow you to **d** this huge army, ... 1Ki 20:28
You will **d** the Arameans at Aphek 2Ki 13:17
But now you will **d** it only three 2Ki 13:19
Ahaz but could not **d** him. 2Ki 16:5
You cannot **d** one of my master's 2Ki 18:24
before you to **d** the Philistine 1Ch 14:15
I will **d** all your enemies. 1Ch 17:10
their enemies will **d** them. 2Ch 6:24
for war, but God will **d** you. 2Ch 25:8
power to help you or to **d** you." 2Ch 25:8
so that Jehoash would **d** Judah, ... 2Ch 25:20
people had hoped to **d** them, ... Est 9:1
You **d** people forever, and they .... Job 14:20
Because my enemies do not **d** me, ... Ps 41:11
You will **d** them, because God has .... Ps 53:5
He will help me **d** my enemies. .... Ps 59:10
power scatter them and **d** them. .... Ps 59:11
He will **d** our enemies. .... Ps 60:12
I would quickly **d** their enemies .... Ps 81:14
wicked people will not **d** him. .... Ps 89:22
I will **d** those who hate him. .... Ps 89:23
He will **d** our enemies. .... Ps 108:13
he will **d** rulers all over the .... Ps 110:6
peace, and nothing will **d** them. .... Ps 119:165
In your love **d** my enemies. .... Ps 143:12
the nations and **d** the people. .... Ps 149:7
A wise person can **d** a city full .... Pr 21:22
An enemy might **d** one person, ... Ec 4:12
were not able to **d** the city. .... Is 7:1
people and to **d** many nations. .... Is 10:7
I will also **d** Jerusalem and her .... Is 10:11
Israelites will **d** those nations .... Is 14:2
it will **d** you by day and by .... Is 28:19
You cannot **d** one of my master's .... Is 36:9
battle cry and **d** his enemies. .... Is 42:13
will help you **d** nations and take .... Is 45:1
and you will **d** those who do .... Is 54:15
is used against you will **d** you. .... Is 54:17
they will not **d** you, because I .... Je 1:19
they will not **d** you, because I .... Je 15:20
him so we can **d** him and pay him .... Je 20:10
they will not **d** me. They will be .... Je 20:11
town of Heshbon plan Moab's **d.** .... Je 48:2
against you and wants to **d** you. .... Je 49:30
that is sure no one will **d** it," .... Je 49:31

the time has come for their **d;** .... Je 50:27
Her **d** was surprising, and no one .... La 1:9
when they hear about your **d.** .... Eze 26:15
and he will **d** three of the other .... Da 7:24
the South so that he can **d** him. .... Da 11:17
sweep away in **d** large and .... Da 11:22
He will plan to **d** and destroy .... Da 11:24
army will be swept away in **d;** .... Da 11:26
He will **d** many countries, but .... Da 11:41
pride will cause their **d;** .... Hos 7:10
you will trick you and **d** you. .... Ob 1:7
will fight and **d** the horsemen. .... Zch 10:5
I will **d** Assyria's pride and .... Zch 10:11
death will not be able to **d** it. .... Mt 16:18
soldiers can **d** the other king .... Lk 14:31
died to **d** the power of sin one .... Rm 6:10
God is for us, no one can **d** us. .... Rm 8:31
not let evil **d** you, but defeat .... Rm 12:21
defeat you, but **d** evil by doing .... Rm 12:21
peace will soon **d** Satan and give .... Rm 16:20
give the devil a way to **d** you. .... Eph 4:27
He will **d** them and kill them. .... Rev 11:7
God's holy people and to **d** them. .... Rev 13:7
the Lamb will **d** them, because he .... Rev 17:14
He will **d** them with his called, ... Rev 17:14
he will use to **d** the nations, ... Rev 19:15

DEFEATED

him came and **d** the Rephaites .... Ge 14:5
They also **d** the Horites in the .... Ge 14:6
They **d** all the Amalekites, ... Ge 14:7
who had **d** Midian in the country .... Ge 36:35
So Joshua **d** the Amalekites in .... Ex 17:13
But we **d** those Amorites. .... Nu 21:30
the LORD had **d** Sihon and Og. .... Dt 1:4
like bees and **d** you from Edom to .... Dt 1:44
We **d** him, his sons, and all his .... Dt 2:33
We **d** Aroer on the edge of the .... Dt 2:36
and we **d** the town in the ravine, ... Dt 2:36
we **d** them and left no one alive. .... Dt 3:3
in Heshbon and was **d** by Moses .... Dt 4:46
out to fight us, but we **d** them. .... Dt 29:7
So the Israelites **d** that city. .... Jos 6:20
how Joshua had **d** Jericho and Ai, ... Jos 9:3
We heard that he **d** the two kings .... Jos 9:10
that Joshua had **d** Ai and .... Jos 10:1
so Israel **d** them in a great .... Jos 10:10
the people **d** their enemies. .... Jos 10:13
That day Joshua **d** Makkedah. .... Jos 10:28
but Joshua also **d** him and his .... Jos 10:33
So Joshua **d** all the kings of the .... Jos 10:40
Joshua **d** all the people in the .... Jos 11:16
the other cities were **d** in war. .... Jos 11:19
the kings whom the Israelites **d.** .... Jos 12:1
Israelites **d** all these kings, ... Jos 12:6
Israelites also **d** kings in the .... Jos 12:7
Israelites **d** the king of each .... Jos 12:18
Moses had **d** them and had taken .... Jos 13:12
Moses had **d** him along with the .... Jos 13:21
against Leshem, **d** it, and killed .... Jos 19:47
None of their enemies **d** them; .... Jos 21:44
and they **d** ten thousand men at .... Jdg 1:4
men of Judah **d** the Canaanites .... Jdg 1:5
And they **d** Sheshai, Ahiman, and .... Jdg 1:10
d the Canaanites who lived in .... Jdg 1:17
The LORD **d** them with the sword, ... Jdg 4:15
On that day God **d** Jabin the king of .... Jdg 4:23
are robbing the people they **d!** .... Jdg 5:30
Ammonites were **d** by the .... Jdg 11:33
saw that they were **d.** .... Jdg 20:36
spread, they **d** the Israelites, ... 1Sa 4:2
hard and **d** the Israelites, ... 1Sa 4:10
the Israelites **d** the Philistines 1Sa 7:10

D

Philistines were **d** and did not 1Sa 7:13
Ammonite camp and **d** them before 1Sa 11:11
Saul has **d** the Philistine camp. 1Sa 13:4
the Israelites **d** the Philistines 1Sa 14:31
Saul went he **d** Israel's enemies.............. 1Sa 14:47
bravely and **d** the Amalekites. 1Sa 14:48
Then Saul **d** the Amalekites. 1Sa 15:7
So David **d** the Philistine with 1Sa 17:50
d them, and they ran away from............. 1Sa 19:8
David had the Amalekites, ... 2Sa 1:1
and David's men **d** Abner and the 2Sa 2:17
Perazim and **d** the Philistines 2Sa 5:20
He **d** the Philistines and chased 2Sa 5:25
gone and have **d** your enemies for 2Sa 7:9
Later, David **d** the Philistines,................. 2Sa 8:1
He also **d** the people of Moab. 2Sa 8:2
David also **d** Hadadezer son of 2Sa 8:3
that David had **d** all the army................. 2Sa 8:9
from the other nations he had **d**. 2Sa 8:11
saw that Israel had **d** them,.................. 2Sa 10:15
that the Israelites had **d** them, ... 2Sa 10:19
David's army **d** the Israelites. 2Sa 18:7
The LORD has **d** those who were 2Sa 18:28
that had been **d** in battle and 2Sa 19:3
Earlier, David had **d** Edom. 1Ki 11:15
After David **d** the army of Zobah, ... 1Ki 11:24
let the people of Israel be **d**." 1Ki 14:16
They **d** the towns of Ijon, Dan, ... 1Ki 15:20
Ahab thoroughly **d** the Aramean 1Ki 20:21
Hazael the Israelites in all 2Ki 10:32
He **d** Ben-Hadad three times and 2Ki 13:25
You have **d** Edom, but you have 2Ki 14:10
or you and Judah will be **d**." 2Ki 14:10
Israel **d** Judah, and every man of 2Ki 14:12
He **d** them and ripped open all 2Ki 15:16
He **d** Samaria in the ninth year 2Ki 17:6
Hezekiah **d** the Philistines all 2Ki 18:8
have completely **d** every country, ... 2Ki 19:11
Hadad **d** Midian in the country of 1Ch 1:46
the Hagrite people and **d** them. 1Ch 5:10
Perazim and **d** the Philistines 1Ch 14:11
he and his men **d** the Philistine 1Ch 14:16
I have **d** your enemies for you. 1Ch 17:8
Later, David **d** the Philistines,................. 1Ch 18:1
He also **d** the people of Moab. 1Ch 18:2
David also **d** Hadadezer king of 1Ch 18:3
that David had **d** all the army................. 1Ch 18:9
saw that Israel had **d** them,.................. 1Ch 19:16
that the Israelites had **d** them, ... 1Ch 19:19
So those Philistines were **d**. 1Ch 20:4
the people of Israel were **d**..................... 2Ch 13:18
So the LORD **d** the Cushites when 2Ch 14:12
They **d** the towns of Ijon, Dan, ... 2Ch 16:4
attack Judah. And they were **d**. 2Ch 20:22
because their enemies were **d**. 2Ch 20:27
yourself that you have **d** Edom, ... 2Ch 25:19
or you and Judah will be **d**." 2Ch 25:19
Israel **d** Judah, and every man of 2Ch 25:22
of the Ammonites and **d** them. 2Ch 27:5
Arameans **d** Ahaz and took many 2Ch 28:5
Pekah **d** them because they had 2Ch 28:6
of Damascus, who had **d** him................. 2Ch 28:23
the Persian kingdom of Babylon................ 2Ch 36:20
you **d** them for our ancestors.................. Ne 9:24
themselves **d** those who hated .... Est 9:1
Jewish people **d** all their .... Est 9:5
friends are **d** and have no more .... Job 32:15
they are **d** because the others .... Ps 10:10
will rejoice that I've been **d**. .... Ps 13:4
They are overwhelmed and **d**,................. Ps 20:8
but they are overwhelmed and **d**. .... Ps 27:2
Those who do evil have been **d**. .... Ps 36:12
at me or brag when I am **d**." .... Ps 38:16

Nations will be **d** before you. .... Ps 45:5
He **d** nations for us and put them .... Ps 47:3
and I have seen my enemies **d**. .... Ps 54:7
for help, my enemies will be **d**. .... Ps 56:9
You have kept me from being **d**. .... Ps 56:13
returned and **d** twelve thousand .... Ps 59:17
is my defender; I will not be **d**. .... Ps 62:2
is my defender; I will not be **d**. .... Ps 62:6
lives and does not let us be **d**................... Ps 66:9
D, they will bring you their..................... Ps 68:30
never be **d**. Good people will .... Ps 112:6
you kept me from being **d**. .... Ps 116:8
so I will see my enemies **d**..................... Ps 118:7
but I **d** them in the name of the .... Ps 118:10
with the LORD's power I **d** them. .... Ps 118:11
By the LORD's power, I **d** them. .... Ps 118:12
chased me until I was almost **d**, ... Ps 118:13
He will not let you be **d**. .... Ps 121:3
will not be **d** when they fight .... Ps 127:5
my life, but they have not **d** me. .... Ps 129:2
He **d** many nations and killed .... Ps 135:10
He **d** great kings. His love .... Ps 136:17
He **d** Sihon king of the Amorites. .... Ps 136:19
He **d** Og king of Bashan. .... Ps 136:20
who have been **d** and takes care.............. Ps 145:14
expect to be **d** by God's anger. .... Pr 11:23
they are never **d**, but the wicked.............. Pr 24:16
be happy when your enemy is **d**; .... Pr 24:17
they end up sick, **d**, and angry. .... Ec 5:17
the fight, but they will be **d**. .... Is 8:10
Like the time you **d** Midian, ... Is 9:4
I **d** those kingdoms that worship .... Is 10:10
As I **d** Samaria and her idols, ... Is 10:11
my wisdom I have **d** many nations. .... Is 10:13
depend on the person who **d** them............ Is 10:20
with a whip as he **d** Midian at .... Is 10:26
The enemy will be **d**; .... Is 16:4
They will fall back and be **d**; .... Is 28:13
Assyria will be **d** by a sword, ... Is 31:8
have completely **d** every country, ... Is 37:11
people have been **d** and robbed. .... Is 42:22
He is the one who **d** the chariots .... Is 43:17
the people who **d** you and .... Is 49:17
You were destroyed and **d**, ... Is 49:19
d and separated from my people. .... Is 49:21
darkness where they will be **d**. .... Je 23:12
will come for Babylon to be **d**, ... Je 27:7
Even if you **d** all of the .... Je 37:10
which was **d** at the city of .... Je 46:2
Their warriors are **d**. .... Je 46:5
strong, walled cities will be **d**. .... Je 48:41
king of Babylon **d**. .... Je 49:28
of Babylon has **d** and destroyed .... Je 51:34
How Babylon has been **d**! .... Je 51:41
her people were **d** by the enemy, ... La 1:7
I let you be **d** by those who hate............. Eze 16:27
afraid because you have been **d**.' .... Eze 26:18
You let them be **d** in war when .... Eze 35:5
the king of the South will be **d**. .... Da 11:25
her and be glad we have **d** her." .... Mic 4:11
it will be **d** and brought to an .... Nah 1:12
I have **d** the world."............................... Jn 16:33
shows that you are already **d**................... 1Co 6:7
all around us, but we are not **d**. 2Co 4:9
their faith they **d** kingdoms. .... Heb 11:33
in battle and **d** other armies. .... Heb 11:34
because you have **d** the Evil One. 1Jn 2:13
and you have **d** the Evil One. 1Jn 2:14
belong to God and have **d** them;.............. 1Jn 4:4
and sisters **d** him by the blood .... Rev 12:11

DEFEND

will **d** you, and I will give you................. Ge 15:1
The LORD will **d** his people and.............. Dt 32:36
They **d** themselves with their .... Dt 33:7
Are you going to **d** him? .... Jdg 6:31
'I will **d** and save this city for 2Ki 19:34
strong cities in Judah to **d** it. 2Ch 11:5
I will still **d** my ways to his .... Job 13:15
LORD, **d** me because I am right,.............. Ps 7:8
d me because I have lived an .... Ps 26:1
Wake up! Come and **d** me! My God .... Ps 35:23
LORD my God, **d** me with your .... Ps 35:24
God, **d** me. Argue my case against .... Ps 43:1
God, arise and **d** yourself. .... Ps 74:22
How long will you **d** evil people? .... Ps 82:2
D the weak and the orphans; .... Ps 82:3
d the rights of the poor and .... Ps 82:3
the poor and will **d** the needy in.............. Ps 140:12
LORD will **d** them in court and .... Pr 22:23
d the rights of all those who .... Pr 31:8
and **d** the rights of the poor and .... Pr 31:9
together can **d** themselves; .... Ec 4:12
send someone to save and **d** them. .... Is 19:20
will **d** Jerusalem like .... Is 31:5
He will **d** and save it; .... Is 31:5
'I will **d** and save this city for .... Is 37:35
of Assyria; I will **d** this city. .... Is 38:6
Your God will **d** his people.................... Is 51:22
in your hands to **d** yourselves................ Je 21:4
He will surely **d** them with power .... Je 50:34
I will soon **d** you, Judah, and .... Je 51:36
are broken to **d** these people so .... Eze 22:30
do not need to **d** ourselves to .... Da 3:16
but he will **d** my case in court. .... Mic 7:9
about how to **d** yourself or what .... Lk 12:11
am happy to **d** myself before you. .... Ac 24:10
is what Paul said to **d** himself: .... Ac 25:8
accusers and **d** himself against .... Ac 25:16
may now speak to **d** yourself." .... Ac 26:1
these things to **d** himself, ... Ac 26:24
right living to **d** ourselves 2Co 6:7

DEFENDED

Moses **d** the girls and watered .... Ex 2:17
us away, but an Egyptian **d** us. .... Ex 2:19
border, which was strongly **d.**................. Nu 21:24
so he **d** the Israelite and .... Ac 7:24
The first time I **d** myself,...................... 2Ti 4:16

DEFENDER

my **d** and my place of safety. 2Sa 22:3
I know that my **D** lives, and in .... Job 19:25
and my saving strength, my **d.** .... Ps 18:2
the God of Jacob is our **d.** .... Ps 46:7
the God of Jacob is our **d.** .... Ps 46:11
he is known as its **d.** .... Ps 48:3
to you, because God is my **d.** .... Ps 59:9
You are my **d,** my place of safety .... Ps 59:16
God, my **d,** you are the God who .... Ps 59:17
He is my **d;** I will not be .... Ps 62:2
He is my **d;** I will not be .... Ps 62:6
But the LORD is my **d;** .... Ps 94:22
He is my **d** and my Savior, my .... Ps 144:2
God, their **d,** is strong; .... Pr 23:11

DEFENSE

are crushed in court with no **d.** .... Job 5:4
in charge of our **d** towers?" .... Is 33:18
to be used in **d** of the attack .... Je 33:4
The river was her **d;** .... Nah 3:8
fathers, listen to my **d** to you." .... Ac 22:1

DEFENSES

and tear down the **d** they trust .... Pr 21:22
us with its strong walls and **d.** .... Is 26:1

a part of his **d** against Baasha .... Je 41:9
He made the walls and **d** sad;................. La 2:8
and tear down all your **d.** .... Mic 5:11
Guard the **d.** Watch the road. .... Nah 2:1
All your **d** are like fig trees .... Nah 3:12
Make your **d** strong! .... Nah 3:14

DELAY

hired others to **d** the building .... Ezr 4:5

DELAYED

But Lot **d.** So the two men took .... Ge 19:16
of his chariots' horses **d?'** .... Jdg 5:28
be done, and it will not be **d.** .... Eze 12:25
of my words will be **d** anymore. .... Eze 12:28
surely come; it will not be **d.** .... Hab 2:3
even if I am **d,** you will know 1Ti 3:15
will come and will not be **d.** .... Heb 10:37

DELIGHT

parents correct the child they **d** .... Pr 3:12
care about silver or **d** in gold.................. Is 13:17
and I will make her people a **d.** .... Is 65:18
They **d** in deceiving you while 2Pe 2:13

DELIGHTED

I was **d** every day, enjoying his .... Pr 8:30
and **d** with all its people......................... Pr 8:31
and be **d** with my people. .... Is 65:19

DELIGHTS

Because he **d** in me, he saved me. 2Sa 22:20
Because he **d** in me, he saved me. .... Ps 18:19
my love, you are full of **d.** .... Sng 7:6
my lover, the old **d** and the new.............. Sng 7:13

DELILAH

in love with a woman named **D,** .... Jdg 16:4
rulers went to **D** and said, ... Jdg 16:5
D said to Samson, "Tell me why.............. Jdg 16:6
rulers brought **D** seven new .... Jdg 16:8
D said to him, "Samson, the .... Jdg 16:9
Then **D** said to Samson, "You made .... Jdg 16:10
So **D** took new ropes and tied.................. Jdg 16:12
Then **D** said to Samson, "Again .... Jdg 16:13
D wove the seven braids of his .... Jdg 16:13
Then **D** said to him, "How can you .... Jdg 16:15
When **D** saw that he had told her .... Jdg 16:18
came back to **D** and brought .... Jdg 16:18
D got Samson to sleep, lying in .... Jdg 16:19

DELIVER

with us when we **d** this gift of................. 2Co 8:19

DEMAND

I will **d** blood for life. .... Ge 9:5
I will **d** the life of any animal .... Ge 9:5
and I will **d** the life of anyone .... Ge 9:5
We cannot **d** silver or gold from 2Sa 21:4
They did not **d** to know how the.............. 2Ki 12:15
it back and not **d** anything more .... Ne 5:12
Get up and **d** fairness. .... Ps 7:6
try to do what you **d** forever, ... Ps 119:112
dogs, who **d** to cut the body. .... Php 3:2

DEMANDING

the tribe of Benjamin **d,** .... Jdg 20:12
d that Jesus be crucified........................ Lk 23:23

DEMANDS

the LORD your God **d** it from you. .... Dt 23:21
Follow him by obeying his **d,** 1Ki 2:3
who follow the **d** of his .... Ps 25:10
they ignore my **d** and disobey my .... Ps 89:31
more loyal in obeying your **d.**.................. Ps 119:5
will obey your **d,** so please .... Ps 119:8
be praised. Teach me your **d.** .... Ps 119:12
obeying your **d,** and I will not.................. Ps 119:16
will think about your **d.** .... Ps 119:23

answered me. Teach me your **d.** .... Ps 119:26
teach me your **d,** and I will keep .... Ps 119:33
love, and I think about your **d.** .... Ps 119:48
about your **d** whenever I live .... Ps 119:54
the earth. Teach me your **d.** .... Ps 119:64
what is good. Teach me your **d.** .... Ps 119:68
suffer so I would learn your **d.** .... Ps 119:71
Let me obey your **d** perfectly so .... Ps 119:80
smoke, I do not forget your **d.** .... Ps 119:83
I will always respect your **d.** .... Ps 119:117
reject those who ignore your **d,** .... Ps 119:118
servant, and teach me your **d.** .... Ps 119:124
your servant. Teach me your **d.** .... Ps 119:135
me, and I will keep your **d.** .... Ps 119:145
because they do not want your **d.** .... Ps 119:155
you have taught me your **d.** .... Ps 119:171
Jacob, his laws and **d** to Israel. .... Ps 147:19
of the land the payment he **d.** .... Is 16:1
sealed that had the **d** and limits .... Je 32:11
do to Edom what my hot anger **d.** .... Eze 25:14

DEMON

talk because he had a **d** in him. .... Mt 9:32
forced the **d** to leave the man .... Mt 9:33
So people say, 'He has a **d.**' .... Mt 11:18
not talk, because he had a **d.** .... Mt 12:22
My daughter has a **d,** and she is .... Mt 15:22
commanded the **d** inside the boy. .... Mt 17:18
Then the **d** came out, and the boy .... Mt 17:18
couldn't we force the **d** out?" .... Mt 17:19
Jesus to force the **d** out of her .... Mk 7:26
The **d** has left your daughter." .... Mk 7:29
lying in bed; the **d** was gone. .... Mk 7:30
you say, 'He has a **d** in him.' .... Lk 7:33
forced by the **d** out into a .... Lk 8:29
d threw him on the ground and .... Lk 9:42
sending out a **d** who could not .... Lk 11:14
When the **d** came out, the man who .... Lk 11:14
answered, "A **d** has come into you .... Jn 7:20
a Samaritan and have a **d** in you. .... Jn 8:48
answered, "I have no **d** in me. .... Jn 8:49
know that you have a **d** in you! .... Jn 8:52
A **d** has come into him and made .... Jn 10:20
is crazy with a **d** does not say .... Jn 10:21
a **d** open the eyes of the blind? .... Jn 10:21

DEMONS

They made sacrifices to **d,** .... Dt 32:17
daughters as sacrifices to **d.** .... Ps 106:37
great pain, some had a **d,** some .... Mt 4:24
you we forced out **d** and did many .... Mt 7:22
brought to Jesus many who had **d.** .... Mt 8:16
Jesus spoke and the **d** left them, ... Mt 8:16
men who had **d** in them met him .... Mt 8:28
The **d** begged Jesus, "If you make .... Mt 8:31
So the **d** left the men and went .... Mt 8:32
happened to the men who had **d.** .... Mt 8:33
The prince of **d** is the one that .... Mt 9:34
gives him power to force **d** out." .... Mt 9:34
and force **d** out of people. .... Mt 10:8
the ruler of **d,** to force demons .... Mt 12:24
to force **d** out of people." .... Mt 12:24
of Beelzebul to force out **d.** .... Mt 12:27
your people use to force out **d?** .... Mt 12:27
of God's Spirit to force out **d,** .... Mt 12:28
who were sick and had **d** in them. .... Mk 1:32
forced many **d** to leave people. .... Mk 1:34
would not allow the **d** to speak, ... Mk 1:34
synagogues and forcing out **d.** .... Mk 1:39
to force **d** out of people. .... Mk 3:15
the ruler of **d** to force demons .... Mk 3:22
to force **d** out of people." .... Mk 3:22
d begged Jesus, "Send us into .... Mk 5:12
man who had the **d** living in him, ... Mk 5:16

freed from the **d** begged to go................ Mk 5:18
They forced many **d** out and put............. Mk 6:13
name to force **d** out of a person............. Mk 9:38
had forced seven **d** out of her............... Mk 16:9
will use my name to force out **d.**............ Mk 16:17
D came out of many people, ... Lk 4:41
commanded the **d** and would not .... Lk 4:41
from whom seven **d** had gone out; .... Lk 8:2
town who had **d** inside him came .... Lk 8:27
because many **d** were in him. .... Lk 8:30
The **d** begged Jesus not to send .... Lk 8:31
and the **d** begged Jesus to allow .... Lk 8:32
When the **d** came out of the man, ... Lk 8:33
mind, because the **d** were gone. .... Lk 8:35
over all **d** and the ability to................. Lk 9:1
name to force **d** out of people. .... Lk 9:49
the **d** obeyed us when we used .... Lk 10:17
the ruler of **d,** to force demons .... Lk 11:15
to force **d** out of people." .... Lk 11:15
of Beelzebul to force out **d.**............... Lk 11:18
of Beelzebul to force out **d,**................ Lk 11:19
your people use to force **d** out? .... Lk 11:19
the power of God to force out **d,**............ Lk 11:20
I am forcing **d** out and healing .... Lk 13:32
to idols is offered to **d,** 1Co 10:20
you to share anything with **d.** 1Co 10:20
the Lord and the cup of **d** also. 1Co 10:21
Lord's table and the table of **d.** 1Co 10:21
that lie and teachings of **d.** 1Ti 4:1
But the **d** believe that, too, and .... Jam 2:19
stop worshiping **d** and idols made .... Rev 9:20
spirits are the spirits of **d,** .... Rev 16:14
a home for **d** and a prison for................ Rev 18:2

DEN

A lion has come out of his **d;** .... Je 4:7
Like a lion, he has left his **d.** .... Je 25:38
be thrown into the lions' **d.** .... Da 6:7
be thrown into the lions' **d?"** .... Da 6:12
in and thrown into the lions' **d.** .... Da 6:16
the opening of the lions' **d.** .... Da 6:17
and hurried to the lions' **d.** .... Da 6:19
came near the **d,** he was worried .... Da 6:20
lift Daniel out of the lions' **d.** .... Da 6:23
be brought to the lions' **d.** .... Da 6:24
children were thrown into the **d.** .... Da 6:24
the floor of the **d** and crushed .... Da 6:24
not growl in its **d** when it has .... Am 3:4
is the lions' **d** and the place .... Nah 2:11
he filled his **d** with meat he had .... Nah 2:12

DENS

the rain and stay in their **d.**................... Job 37:8
they lie in their **d** or hide in .... Job 38:40
go back to their **d** to lie down. .... Ps 104:22
Come from the lions' **d** and from .... Sng 4:8

DENY

you must **d** yourself and you must .... Le 16:29
and you must **d** yourselves...................... Le 16:31
and you will **d** yourselves and .... Le 23:27
and you must **d** yourselves. .... Le 23:32
all fast and **d** ourselves before .... Ezr 8:21

DEPART

was coming near for Jesus to **d,** .... Lk 9:51

DEPARTURE

about his **d** which he would .... Lk 9:31

DEPOSIT

to keep as a **d** until you send .... Ge 38:17
you want me to give you as a **d?"** .... Ge 38:18

DEPTH

the skies or the **d** of the earth. .... Pr 25:3

DEPTHS

them back from the **d** of the sea. .... Ps 68:22
the sky and fell low to the **d**. .... Ps 107:26
will be thrown down to the **d**. .... Mt 11:23
will be thrown down to the **d!** .... Lk 10:15

DERBE

they ran away to Lystra and **D**, ... Ac 14:6
left and went to the city of **D**. .... Ac 14:20
told the Good News in **D**, ... Ac 14:21
Paul came to **D** and Lystra, ... Ac 16:1
Gaius, from **D**; Timothy; and .... Ac 20:4

DESCENDANT

Cush also had a **d** named Nimrod, ... Ge 10:8
Any male **d** of Aaron may eat it .... Le 6:18
Jair, the **d** of Manasseh, took the .... Dt 3:14
Nabal, and he was a **d** of Caleb. 1Sa 25:3
will always be a **d** of David, ... 1Ki 11:36
Bani was a **d** of Perez, and Perez 1Ch 9:4
help of Zadok, a **d** of Eleazar, ... 1Ch 24:3
and Ahimelech, a **d** of Ithamar, ... 1Ch 24:3
Shubael was a **d** of Amram, and 1Ch 24:20
and Jehdeiah was a **d** of Shubael. 1Ch 24:20
and Jahath was a **d** of Shelomoth. 1Ch 24:22
Shubael, the **d** of Gershom, who 1Ch 26:24
Pelonites and a **d** of Ephraim. 1Ch 27:10
a Levite and a **d** of Asaph, ... 2Ch 20:14
Ahaziah is a **d** of Jehoshaphat, ... 2Ch 22:9
and Zechariah, a **d** of Iddo, ... Ezr 5:1
and Zechariah, a **d** of Iddo. .... Ezr 6:14
Mahalalel was a **d** of Perez. .... Ne 11:4
son of Zechariah, a **d** of Shelah. .... Ne 11:5
Meshezabel was a **d** of Zerah, ... Ne 11:24
said, "Ahaz, **d** of David, listen........... Is 7:13
David not have a **d** ruling as .... Je 33:21
will always be a **d** of Jonadab. .... Je 35:19
you are a **d** of Nebuchadnezzar .... Da 5:22
He was a **d** of the Medes. .... Da 9:1
said, "Joseph, **d** of David, don't .... Mt 1:20
both to Abraham and to his **d**. .... Gal 3:16
But God said, "and to your **d**." .... Gal 3:16
continued until the special **d**, ... Gal 3:19
the seventh **d** from Adam, said .... Jud 1:14
of Judah, David's **d**, has won the .... Rev 5:5
I am the **d** from the family of .... Rev 22:16

DESCENDANTS

Your **d** and her descendants will .... Ge 3:15
and her **d** will be enemies. .... Ge 3:15
One of her **d** will crush your .... Ge 3:15
One of his **d** was the father of .... Ge 10:21
will give this land to your **d**." .... Ge 12:7
give to you and your **d** forever. .... Ge 13:15
will make your **d** as many as the .... Ge 13:16
Your **d** also will be too many to .... Ge 15:5
sure that your **d** will be .... Ge 15:13
your **d** will leave that land, ... Ge 15:14
give to your **d** the land between .... Ge 15:18
give you so many **d** they cannot .... Ge 16:10
I will give you many **d**. .... Ge 17:6
and you and all your **d** from now .... Ge 17:7
God and the God of all your **d**. .... Ge 17:7
you and your **d** all this land .... Ge 17:8
I will be the God of your **d**." .... Ge 17:8
You and your **d** must keep this .... Ge 17:9
with you and all your **d**, ... Ge 17:10
slave, who is not one of your **d**. .... Ge 17:12
forever with all his **d**. .... Ge 17:19
bless him and give him many **d**. .... Ge 17:20
and his **d** to live the way .... Ge 18:19
d I promised you will be from............. Ge 21:12
will also make the **d** of Ishmael .... Ge 21:13
I will make his **d** into a great .... Ge 21:18
me and my children and my **d**. .... Ge 21:23

bless you and give you many **d**. .... Ge 22:17
Through your **d** all the nations .... Ge 22:18
will give this land to your **d**.' .... Ge 24:7
may your **d** capture the cities .... Ge 24:60
Dedan's **d** were the people of .... Ge 25:3
All these were **d** of Keturah. .... Ge 25:4
d lived from Havilah to Shur, ... Ge 25:18
attacked the **d** of his brothers. .... Ge 25:18
you and your **d** all these lands, ... Ge 26:3
give you many **d**, as hard to .... Ge 26:4
Through your **d** all the nations .... Ge 26:4
and give you many **d** because of .... Ge 26:24
give you and your **d** the blessing .... Ge 28:4
you and your **d** the land on which .... Ge 28:13
Your **d** will be as many as the .... Ge 28:14
blessed through you and your **d**. .... Ge 28:14
I will give to you and your **d**." .... Ge 35:12
pregnant and for Er to have **d**. .... Ge 38:9
you have some **d** left on earth .... Ge 45:7
will make your **d** a great nation .... Ge 46:3
went to Egypt with all his **d**— .... Ge 46:6
into Egypt (Jacob and his **d**). .... Ge 46:8
Jacob's direct **d** who went to .... Ge 46:26
give your **d** this land forever. .... Ge 48:4
they have many **d** on the earth." .... Ge 48:16
will be great and have many **d**. .... Ge 48:19
and his **d** will be enough to make .... Ge 48:19
people who were **d** of Jacob. .... Ex 1:5
d are to honor the LORD with .... Ex 12:14
So all of your **d** must celebrate .... Ex 12:17
law for you and your **d** from now .... Ex 12:24
quarts of this food for your **d**. .... Ex 16:32
LORD, and save it for your **d**." .... Ex 16:33
and their **d** must obey this rule .... Ex 27:21
now on for Aaron and all his **d**. .... Ex 28:43
Aaron and his **d** will be priests .... Ex 29:9
belong to his **d** so that they can .... Ex 29:29
which Aaron and his **d** are to .... Ex 30:21
you and your **d** a great nation." .... Ex 32:10
'I will make your **d** as many as .... Ex 32:13
'I will give that land to your **d**.' .... Ex 33:1
they and their **d** from now on." .... Ex 40:15
'If any of your **d** have something .... Le 21:17
one of Aaron's **d** has something .... Le 21:21
any one of your **d** from now on is .... Le 22:3
one of Aaron's **d** has a harmful .... Le 22:4
that all your **d** will know I made .... Le 23:43
'If you or your **d** become unclean .... Nu 9:10
law for you and your **d** from now .... Nu 10:8
and Talmai, the **d** of Anak lived............. Nu 13:22
that only **d** of Aaron should burn .... Nu 16:40
come from the **d** of Jacob and .... Nu 24:19
He and his **d** will always be .... Nu 25:13
The **d** of Makir son of Manasseh .... Nu 32:39
Isaac, and Jacob and their **d**." .... Dt 1:8
give him and his **d** the land he .... Dt 1:36
the **d** of Esau who live in Edom. .... Dt 2:4
the **d** of Esau who lived in Edom. .... Dt 2:8
Ar to the **d** of Lot as their .... Dt 2:9
the **d** of Esau forced them out................ Dt 2:12
given it to the **d** of Lot for .... Dt 2:19
same thing for the **d** of Esau, ... Dt 2:22
The **d** of Esau in Edom let us go .... Dt 2:29
you, their **d**, and he brought .... Dt 4:37
chose you, their **d**, over all the .... Dt 10:15
to your ancestors and their **d**, ... Dt 11:9
that he and his **d** may rule the .... Dt 17:20
and their **d** out of all your .... Dt 18:5
d for ten generations may not................ Dt 23:2
and none of their **d** for ten .... Dt 23:3
to you and your **d** forever. .... Dt 28:46
diseases to you and your **d**. .... Dt 28:59
you and your **d** to love him with.............. Dt 30:6

not be forgotten by their **d**. .... Dt 31:21
will give this land to your **d**.' .... Dt 34:4
and Talmai, the **d** of Anak. .... Jos 15:14
city of Hebron to the **d** of Aaron............... Jos 21:13
was to teach the **d** of the .... Jdg 3:2
Kenites, the **d** of Hobab, Moses' .... Jdg 4:11
I will destroy the **d** of both you 1Sa 2:31
because all your **d** will die. 1Sa 2:33
d cried to the LORD for help. 1Sa 12:8
and between our **d** always.'" 1Sa 20:42
will not kill my **d** and that you 1Sa 24:21
will make your **d** kings of Israel 2Sa 7:11
to David and his **d** forever." 2Sa 22:51
'If your **d** live as I tell them..................... 1Ki 2:4
about the priest Eli and his **d**. 1Ki 2:27
for David, his **d**, his family, ... 1Ki 2:33
They were **d** of people that the 1Ki 9:21
one of David's **d** would always 2Ki 8:19
your **d** as far as your 2Ki 10:30
All these were **d** of Keturah. 1Ch 1:33
All these were **d** of Makir, ... 1Ch 2:23
These were Jerahmeel's **d**. 1Ch 2:33
Shobal's **d** were Haroeh, half the 1Ch 2:52
Salma's **d** were Bethlehem, the 1Ch 2:54
His **d** included the families who 1Ch 2:55
Hananiah's **d** were Pelatiah and 1Ch 3:21
Judah's **d** were Perez, Hezron, ... 1Ch 4:1
These were the **d** of Naarah. 1Ch 4:6
Ham's **d** had lived there in the 1Ch 4:40
They were the **d** of Abihail. 1Ch 5:14
Aaron and his **d** offered the 1Ch 6:49
places where Aaron's **d** lived. 1Ch 6:54
His **d** from the Kohath family 1Ch 6:54
So the **d** of Aaron were given 1Ch 6:57
the family history of Tola's **d**, ... 1Ch 7:2
and Huppites were **d** of Ir, ... 1Ch 7:12
These are Manasseh's **d**. 1Ch 7:14
are the names of Ephraim's **d**. 1Ch 7:20
Ephraim's **d** lived in these lands............. 1Ch 7:28
The **d** of Joseph son of Israel 1Ch 7:29
these men were **d** of Asher and 1Ch 7:40
These were the **d** of Ehud and 1Ch 8:6
Ehud's **d** were Naaman, Ahijah, ... 1Ch 8:7
All these men were Benjamin's **d**. 1Ch 8:40
and their **d** had to guard 1Ch 9:23
called together the **d** of Aaron 1Ch 15:4
You are the **d** of his servant, ... 1Ch 16:13
will make your **d** kings of Israel 1Ch 17:10
was one of the **d** of the 1Ch 20:4
These **d** of Rapha from Gath were 1Ch 20:8
Aaron and his **d** were chosen to 1Ch 23:13
were Levi's **d** listed by their 1Ch 23:24
helping Aaron's **d** in the service 1Ch 23:28
Aaron's **d**, with the services 1Ch 23:32
names of those **d** in front of 1Ch 24:6
names of the rest of Levi's **d**: 1Ch 24:20
Merari's **d** were Mahli and Mushi. 1Ch 24:26
priests, Aaron's **d**, had done. 1Ch 24:31
All these were Obed-Edom's **d**. 1Ch 26:8
one of the **d** of Perez, was 1Ch 27:3
pass it on to your **d** forever. 1Ch 28:8
They were **d** of the people that 2Ch 8:8
forever to the **d** of your friend 2Ch 20:7
one of David's **d** would always 2Ch 21:7
LORD promised about David's **d**. 2Ch 23:3
priests, Aaron's **d**, should burn 2Ch 26:18
the priests, the **d** of Aaron, to 2Ch 29:21
Some of Aaron's **d**, the priests, ... 2Ch 31:19
for the priests, the **d** of Aaron. 2Ch 35:14
to be slaves for him and his **d**. 2Ch 36:20
These are the **d** of Judah who................. Ne 11:4
All the **d** of Perez who lived in .... Ne 11:6

are **d** of Benjamin who moved .... Ne 11:7
Uzzi was one of Asaph's **d**, ... Ne 11:22
The **d** of the Benjaminites from .... Ne 11:31
aside part for the **d** of Aaron. .... Ne 12:47
They and their **d** and all those .... Est 9:27
and their **d** should always .... Est 9:28
for themselves and their **d**: .... Est 9:31
your **d** will be like the grass .... Job 5:25
no children or **d** among their .... Job 18:19
to David and his **d** forever. .... Ps 18:50
All you **d** of Jacob, honor him; .... Ps 22:23
The **d** of his servants will .... Ps 69:36
the **d** of Jacob and Joseph. .... Ps 77:15
Ammon and Moab, the **d** of Lot............... Ps 83:8
If his **d** reject my teachings and .... Ps 89:30
are **d** of his servant Abraham, ... Ps 105:6
Let all his **d** die and be .... Ps 109:13
Their **d** will be powerful in the .... Ps 112:2
There the **d** of David set their................. Ps 122:5
make one of your **d** rule as king............... Ps 132:11
my appointed one **d** to rule after .... Ps 132:17
its children and their **d**," .... Is 14:22
and my blessing on your **d**. .... Is 44:3
blessed him and gave him many **d**........... Is 51:2
still see his **d** and live a long .... Is 53:10
And none of his **d** will be .... Je 22:30
who brought the **d** of Israel from .... Je 23:8
Their **d** will be as they were in .... Je 30:20
will Israel's **d** ever stop being .... Je 31:36
I reject all the **d** of Israel....................... Je 31:37
I will give many **d** to my servant .... Je 33:22
I turn away from Jacob's **d**..................... Je 33:26
'You and your **d** must never drink .... Je 35:6
ordered his **d** not to drink wine .... Je 35:14
The **d** of Jonadab son of Recab .... Je 35:16
Jehoiakim's **d** will not sit on .... Je 36:30
a promise to the **d** of Jacob. .... Eze 20:5
group of priests are **d** of Zadok, ... Eze 40:46
the only **d** of Levi who can come .... Eze 40:46
are Levites and **d** of Zadok took............... Eze 44:15
They are the **d** of Zadok who did .... Eze 48:11
kingdom will not go to his **d**, ... Da 11:4
to bring Jacob's **d** out of Egypt; .... Hos 12:13
fire against the **d** of Joseph. .... Am 5:6
where Isaac's **d** worship will be .... Am 7:9
against the **d** of Isaac.' .... Am 7:16
completely destroy Jacob's **d**," .... Am 9:8
will not have **d** to carry on your .... Nah 1:14
belong to the **d** of Judah who are .... Zph 2:7
open for David's **d** and for the .... Zch 13:1
I will punish your **d**. .... Mal 2:3
So you **d** of Jacob have not been .... Mal 3:6
proof that you are **d** of those .... Mt 23:31
You are **d** of the prophets. .... Ac 3:25
give this land to him and his **d**, ... Ac 7:5
'Your **d** will be strangers in a .... Ac 7:6
Then your **d** will leave that land............... Ac 7:7
one of David's **d**, to Israel to .... Ac 13:23
Abraham and his **d** received the............... Rm 4:13
Your **d** also will be too many to .... Rm 4:18
They are the **d** of our great..................... Rm 9:5
of Abraham's **d** are true children .... Rm 9:7
The **d** I promised you will be .... Rm 9:7
of Abraham's **d** are God's true .... Rm 9:8
allowed a few of our **d** to live................. Rm 9:29
did not say, "and to your **d**." .... Gal 3:16
Christ, so you are Abraham's **d**. .... Gal 3:29
bless you and give you many **d**." .... Heb 6:14
him came as many **d** as there are .... Heb 11:12
The **d** I promised you will be .... Heb 11:18

DESCRIBE

They will **d** in writing the land .... Jos 18:4
You should **d** the seven parts of .... Jos 18:6
the land and **d** it in writing. .... Jos 18:8

DESERT

Edom to El Paran (near the **d**). .... Ge 14:6
a spring of water in the **d,** .... Ge 16:7
wandered in the **d** of Beersheba. .... Ge 21:14
lived in the **d** and became an .... Ge 21:20
He lived in the **D** of Paran, ... Ge 21:21
springs in the **d** while he was .... Ge 36:24
into this well here in the **d,** .... Ge 37:22
the land will not become a **d.**" .... Ge 47:19
flock to the west side of the **d,** .... Ex 3:1
days into the **d** to offer .... Ex 3:18
Go out into the **d** to meet Moses. .... Ex 4:27
hold a feast for me in the **d.**'" .... Ex 5:1
days into the **d** to offer .... Ex 5:3
people go worship me in the **d.**' .... Ex 7:16
a three-day journey into the **d.** .... Ex 8:27
to the Lord your God in the **d,** .... Ex 8:28
them through the **d** toward the .... Ex 13:18
at Etham, on the edge of the **d.** .... Ex 13:20
are lost, trapped by the **d.**' .... Ex 14:3
us out of Egypt to die in the **d?** .... Ex 14:11
Now we will die in the **d.**" .... Ex 14:12
the Red Sea into the **D** of Shur. .... Ex 15:22
Elim and came to the **D** of Sin, ... Ex 16:1
to Moses and Aaron in the **d.** .... Ex 16:2
us into this **d** to starve us to .... Ex 16:3
they looked toward the **d.** .... Ex 16:10
like frost were on the **d** ground. .... Ex 16:14
to eat in the **d** when I brought .... Ex 16:32
community left the **D** of Sin and .... Ex 17:1
camped in the **d** near the .... Ex 18:5
they reached the **D** of Sinai. .... Ex 19:1
they came to the **D** of Sinai and .... Ex 19:2
would become a **d** and the wild .... Ex 23:29
and from the **d** to the Euphrates............. Ex 23:31
to the Lord in the Sinai **D.** .... Le 7:38
white owls, **d** owls, ospreys, ... Le 11:18
out into the **d** as a goat that .... Le 16:10
send the goat away into the **d,** .... Le 16:21
sins to a lonely place in the **d.** .... Le 16:22
into the **d** must wash his clothes............. Le 16:26
Meeting Tent in the **D** of Sinai. .... Nu 1:1
they were in the **D** of Sinai. .... Nu 1:19
the Lord in the **D** of Sinai. .... Nu 3:4
said to Moses in the **D** of Sinai, ... Nu 3:14
Moses in the **D** of Sinai in the .... Nu 9:1
it was in the **D** of Sinai at .... Nu 9:5
moved from the **D** of Sinai and .... Nu 10:12
know where we can camp in the **d,** .... Nu 10:31
and camped in the **D** of Paran. .... Nu 12:16
leaders out from the **D** of Paran. .... Nu 13:3
from the **D** of Zin all the way to .... Nu 13:21
at Kadesh, in the **D** of Paran. .... Nu 13:26
had died in Egypt or in this **d.** .... Nu 14:2
So he killed them in the **d.**' .... Nu 14:16
I did in Egypt and in the **d,** .... Nu 14:22
and follow the **d** toward the .... Nu 14:25
You will die in this **d.** .... Nu 14:29
for you, you will die in this **d.** .... Nu 14:32
until you lie dead in the **d.** .... Nu 14:33
will all die here in this **d.**" .... Nu 14:35
Israelites were still in the **d,** .... Nu 15:32
land to this **d** to kill us, ... Nu 16:13
Israel arrived at the **D** of Zin, ... Nu 20:1
the Lord's people into this **d?** .... Nu 20:4
out of Egypt to die in this **d?** .... Nu 21:5
Abarim, in the **d** east of Moab. .... Nu 21:11
in the **d** just inside the Amorite .... Nu 21:13

went from the **d** to Mattanah. .... Nu 21:18
Mount Pisgah looks over the **d.** .... Nu 21:20
out to meet Israel in the **d.** .... Nu 21:23
mountain that looks over the **d.** .... Nu 23:28
magic but looked toward the **d.** .... Nu 24:1
Israelites in the **D** of Sinai, ... Nu 26:64
they would all die in the **d,** .... Nu 26:65
Our father died in the **d.** .... Nu 27:3
my command in the **D** of Zin................... Nu 27:14
wander in the **d** for forty years. .... Nu 32:13
will add to their stay in the **d,**............... Nu 32:15
at Etham, at the edge of the **d.** .... Nu 33:6
through the sea into the **d.** .... Nu 33:8
Sea and camped in the **D** of Sin. .... Nu 33:11
left the **D** of Sin and camped .... Nu 33:12
and camped in the **D** of Sinai. .... Nu 33:15
They left the **D** of Sinai and .... Nu 33:16
at Kadesh in the **D** of Zin. .... Nu 33:36
get part of the **D** of Zin near .... Nu 34:3
through the **D** of Zin and south .... Nu 34:4
of Israel in the **d** east of the .... Dt 1:1
large and terrible **d** you saw, ... Dt 1:19
in the **d** you saw how the Lord............... Dt 1:31
and follow the **d** road toward the .... Dt 1:40
we traveled on the **d** road toward .... Dt 2:1
traveled through this great **d.** .... Dt 2:7
along the **d** road to Moab. .... Dt 2:8
from the **d** of Kedemoth to .... Dt 2:26
Bezer in the **d** high plain was .... Dt 4:43
led you in the **d** for these forty .... Dt 8:2
large and terrible **d** that was .... Dt 8:15
and manna to eat in the **d.** .... Dt 8:16
Lord your God angry in the **d.** .... Dt 9:7
them into the **d** to kill them.' .... Dt 9:28
for you in the **d** until you .... Dt 11:5
will go from the **d** to Lebanon .... Dt 11:24
d owls, ospreys, cormorants, ... Dt 14:17
through the **d** for forty years .... Dt 29:5
them in a **d,** a windy, empty .... Dt 32:10
Meribah Kadesh in the **D** of Zin, ... Dt 32:51
as the southern **d** and the whole .... Dt 34:3
land from the **d** in the south to .... Jos 1:4
army died in the **d** on the way .... Jos 5:4
were born in the **d** on the trip................ Jos 5:5
about in the **d** for forty years. .... Jos 5:6
Then they ran toward the **d.** .... Jos 8:15
the fields and **d** and killed all .... Jos 8:24
the slopes, the **d,** and southern .... Jos 12:8
time we all wandered in the **d.** .... Jos 14:10
the way to the **D** of Zin in the................ Jos 15:1
was given these towns in the **d:** .... Jos 15:61
Jericho in the **d** in the land .... Jos 20:8
lived in the **d** for a long time .... Jos 24:7
of Judah to the **D** of Judah to .... Jdg 1:16
thorns and briers from the **d.**" .... Jdg 8:7
thorns and briers from the **d.** .... Jdg 8:16
went into the **d** to the Red Sea .... Jdg 11:16
went into the **d** around the .... Jdg 11:18
from the **d** to the Jordan River. .... Jdg 11:22
the Israelites toward the **d,** .... Jdg 20:42
ran toward the **d** to the rock of .... Jdg 20:45
to the rock of Rimmon in the **d,** .... Jdg 20:47
all kinds of disasters in the **d**................. 1Sa 4:8
Valley of Zeboim toward the **d.** 1Sa 13:18
few sheep of yours in the **d?** 1Sa 17:28
David stayed in the **d** hideouts 1Sa 23:14
was at Horesh in the **D** of Ziph, ... 1Sa 23:15
his men were in the **D** of Maon in 1Sa 23:24
and stayed in the **D** of Maon. 1Sa 23:25
also left the **D** of Maon and 1Sa 23:29
"David is in the **D** of En Gedi." 1Sa 24:1
David was in the **d,** he heard 1Sa 25:4
from the **d** to greet our master 1Sa 25:14

over Nabal's property in the **d.** 1Sa 25:21
went down to the **D** of Ziph with 1Sa 26:2
but David stayed in the **d.** 1Sa 26:3
on the way to the **d** near Gibeon. 2Sa 2:24
all the people went on to the **d.** 2Sa 15:23
crossings into the **d** until I 2Sa 15:28
who might become weak in the **d.** 2Sa 16:2
into the **d** but to cross over 2Sa 17:16
and tired and thirsty in the **d.**" 2Sa 17:29
buried near his home in the **d.** 1Ki 2:34
as Tadmor, which is in the **d.** 1Ki 9:18
for a whole day into the **d.** 1Ki 19:4
leads to the **d** around Damascus. 1Ki 19:15
Through the **D** of Edom." 2Ki 3:8
as far as the edge of the **d,** 1Ch 5:9
at his stronghold in the **d.** 1Ch 12:8
were in the **d** and the altar of 1Ch 21:29
's servant had made in the **d,** 2Ch 1:3
the town of Tadmor in the **d,** 2Ch 8:4
that leads to the **D** of Jeruel. 2Ch 20:16
out into the **D** of Tekoa early 2Ch 20:20
where they could see the **d,** 2Ch 20:24
give while they were in the **d.** 2Ch 24:9
towers in the **d** and dug many 2Ch 26:10
you did not leave them in the **d.** .... Ne 9:19
them for forty years in the **d;** .... Ne 9:21
a great wind came from the **d,** .... Job 1:19
paths and go into the **d** and die. .... Job 6:18
wander through a pathless **d.** .... Job 12:24
donkeys in the **d** who go about .... Job 24:5
They gathered **d** plants among the .... Job 30:4
the **d** that has no one in it? .... Job 38:26
the donkey the **d** as its home; .... Job 39:6
The LORD's voice shakes the **d;** .... Ps 29:8
far away and stay in the **d.** .... Ps 55:7
when he was in the **d** of Judah. .... Ps 62:12
for him who rides through the **d,** .... Ps 68:4
when you marched through the **d.** .... Ps 68:7
people of the **d** bow down to him .... Ps 72:9
gave it to the **d** creatures as .... Ps 74:14
the west or the **d** can judge you. .... Ps 75:6
the rocks in the **d** and gave them .... Ps 78:15
in the **d** they turned against God .... Ps 78:17
Can God prepare food in the **d?** .... Ps 78:19
often in the **d** and grieved him .... Ps 78:40
them like a flock through the **d.** .... Ps 78:52
that day at Massah in the **d.** .... Ps 95:8
I am like a **d** owl, like an owl .... Ps 102:6
ran like a river through the **d.** .... Ps 105:41
the deep sea as if it were a **d.** .... Ps 106:9
became greedy for food in the **d,** .... Ps 106:14
that they would die in the **d.** .... Ps 106:26
had wandered in the **d** lands. .... Ps 107:4
rivers into a **d** and springs of .... Ps 107:33
He changed the **d** into pools of .... Ps 107:35
them wander in a pathless **d.** .... Ps 107:40
as you bring streams to the **d.** .... Ps 126:4
He led his people through the **d.** .... Ps 136:16
to live alone in the **d** than with .... Pr 21:19
coming out of the **d** like a cloud .... Sng 3:6
Who is this coming out of the **d,** .... Sng 8:5
Only **d** animals will live there, ... Is 13:21
who turned the world into a **d,** .... Is 14:17
through the **d** to the mountain .... Is 16:1
city of Jazer and into the **d;** .... Is 16:8
message about the **D** by the Sea: .... Is 21:1
like the heat in the **d.** .... Is 25:5
Like a hot **d** wind, he will drive .... Is 27:8
city will be empty like a **d.** .... Is 27:10
the **d** will be like a fertile .... Is 32:15
will be found even in the **d,** .... Is 32:16
of Sharon is dry like the **d,** .... Is 33:9
D animals will live with the .... Is 34:14

The **d** and dry land will become .... Is 35:1
will flow in the **d,** and streams .... Is 35:6
The burning **d** will have pools of .... Is 35:7
Prepare in the **d** the way for the .... Is 40:3
I will change the **d** into a lake .... Is 41:18
I will make trees grow in the **d—** .... Is 41:19
make a road in the **d** and rivers .... Is 43:19
I put water in the **d** and rivers .... Is 43:20
hot sun nor the **d** wind will hurt .... Is 49:10
rivers into a **d,** and their fish .... Is 50:2
a horse walking through a **d,** .... Is 63:13
cities are empty like the **d.** .... Is 64:10
You followed me through the **d,** .... Je 2:2
us through the **d,** through a dry .... Je 2:6
that lives in the **d** and sniffs .... Je 2:24
I been like a **d** to the people .... Je 2:31
lovers, like an Arab in the **d.** .... Je 3:2
of the **d** toward the LORD' .... Je 4:11
good, rich land had become a **d.**............. Je 4:26
wolf from the **d** will kill them. .... Je 5:6
land an empty **d** where no one can........... Je 6:8
the land will become an empty **d!** .... Je 7:34
I wish I had a place in the **d—** .... Je 9:2
like an empty **d** where no one .... Je 9:12
and the **d** people who cut their .... Je 9:26
Judah an empty **d** and a home for .... Je 10:22
beautiful field into an empty **d.** .... Je 12:10
my field into a **d** that is wilted .... Je 12:11
is blown away by the **d** wind. .... Je 13:24
like a bush in a **d** that grows in .... Je 17:6
country will become an empty **d.** .... Je 18:16
I will truly make you into a **d,** .... Je 22:6
whole area will be an empty **d,** .... Je 25:11
will make that land a **d** forever. .... Je 25:12
of the people who live in the **d;** .... Je 25:24
will be like an empty **d,** .... Je 25:37
will become a **d** without anyone .... Je 26:9
sword found help in the **d.** .... Je 31:2
is an empty **d,** without people................. Je 32:43
'Our country is an empty **d,** .... Je 33:10
he made your country an empty **d,**........... Je 44:22
bush being blown through the **d.** .... Je 48:6
it will be an empty **d** forever. .... Je 49:33
and make it like an empty **d.** .... Je 50:3
She will be an empty, dry **d.** .... Je 50:12
D animals and hyenas will live .... Je 50:39
He will make Babylon an empty **d,**........... Je 51:29
has become a dry, **d** land, a land .... Je 51:43
cruel like ostriches in the **d.** .... La 4:3
and ambushed us in the **d.** .... La 4:19
we face death in the **d.** .... La 5:9
and wasted from the **d** to Diblah, ... Eze 6:14
the vine is planted in the **d,**................... Eze 19:13
and brought them into the **d.** .... Eze 20:10
But in the **d** Israel turned .... Eze 20:13
And in the **d** I swore to the .... Eze 20:15
or put an end to them in the **d.** .... Eze 20:17
said to their children in the **d,**................ Eze 20:18
my anger against them in the **d.** .... Eze 20:21
And in the **d** I swore to the .... Eze 20:23
ancestors into the **d** with Moses. .... Eze 20:35
ancestors in the **d** of the land .... Eze 20:36
were brought from the **d.** .... Eze 23:42
I will leave you in the **d,** .... Eze 29:5
Egypt will become an empty **d.** .... Eze 29:9
make it an empty **d** from Migdol .... Eze 29:10
I will make the land an empty **d.** .... Eze 33:28
the land an empty **d** because of .... Eze 33:29
live safely in the **d** and sleep .... Eze 34:25
you and make you an empty **d.** .... Eze 35:3
I will make her dry like a **d,** .... Hos 2:3
lead her into the **d** and speak .... Hos 2:14
like finding grapes in the **d.** .... Hos 9:10

for them in the **d** where it was .... Hos 13:5
coming from the **d**, that will dry .... Hos 13:15
behind them is like an empty **d**. .... Joe 2:3
Edom an empty **d**, because they .... Joe 3:19
through the **d** so I could give .... Am 2:10
in the **d** for forty years .... Am 5:25
Nineveh a ruin as dry as a **d**. .... Zph 2:13
land to the wild dogs of the **d**." .... Mal 1:3
in the **d** area of Judea. .... Mt 3:1
of one who calls out in the **d**: ' .... Mt 3:3
Jesus into the **d** to be tempted .... Mt 4:1
you go out into the **d** to see? .... Mt 11:7
is in the **d**,' don't go there .... Mt 24:26
of one who calls out in the **d**: ' .... Mk 1:3
people in the **d** and preaching a .... Mk 1:4
Spirit sent Jesus into the **d**. .... Mk 1:12
He was in the **d** forty days and .... Mk 1:13
lived in the **d** until the time. .... Lk 1:80
John son of Zechariah in the **d**. .... Lk 3:2
of one who calls out in the **d**: ' .... Lk 3:4
The Spirit led Jesus into the **d** .... Lk 4:1
you go out into the **d** to see? .... Lk 7:24
of one calling out in the **d**: ' .... Jn 1:23
lifted up the snake in the **d**, ... Jn 3:14
ate the manna in the **d**. .... Jn 6:31
ate the manna in the **d**, ... Jn 6:49
and went to a place near the **d**, ... Jn 11:54
was in the **d** near Mount Sinai. .... Ac 7:30
then in the **d** for forty years. .... Ac 7:36
of the Israelites in the **d**. .... Ac 7:38
in the **d** for forty years .... Ac 7:42
was with them in the **d**. .... Ac 7:44
Gaza from Jerusalem—the **d** road." .... Ac 8:26
them for forty years in the **d**. .... Ac 13:18
thousand killers out to the **d**." .... Ac 21:38
of them, so they died in the **d**. 1Co 10:5
when you tested God in the **d**. .... Heb 3:8
who sinned, who died in the **d**. .... Heb 3:17
away into the **d** to a place God .... Rev 12:6
place prepared for her in the **d**. .... Rev 12:14
me away by the Spirit to the **d**. .... Rev 17:3

DESERTERS
are nothing but **d** from Ephraim— .... Jdg 12:4

DESERTS
The **d** and their cities should .... Is 42:11
when he led them through the **d**. .... Is 48:21
will change her **d** into a garden .... Is 51:3
wandered in **d** and mountains, ... Heb 11:38

DESERVE
nothing here to **d** being put in .... Ge 40:15
have punished us less than we **d**; .... Ezr 9:13
gives them what their actions **d**. .... Job 34:11
and give the proud what they **d**. .... Ps 94:2
So you will get what you **d**; .... Pr 1:31
and he punishes them as they **d**. .... Pr 20:26
in faraway places as they **d**. .... Is 59:18
nations; you **d** respect. Of all .... Je 10:7
give them the punishment they **d**. .... Je 11:20
give them the punishment they **d**. .... Je 20:12
give you the punishment you **d**, ... Je 21:14
punishment they **d** for all their .... Je 25:14
people the punishment they **d**. .... Je 46:10
people did not **d** to be punished, ... Je 49:12
of Edom, you **d** to be punished, ... Je 49:12
people the punishment they **d**. .... Je 50:15
them as they **d** for destroying .... Je 51:11
them the full punishment they **d**. .... Je 51:56
he will give them what they **d**. .... Hos 12:2
and they **d** to die for their .... Hos 12:14
what we **d** for what we did .... Lk 23:41
He doesn't **d** to live!" .... Ac 22:22

are wrong and **d** the punishment .... Rm 3:8
them blood to drink as they **d**." .... Rev 16:6

DESERVES
as this the punishment it **d**? .... Je 5:9
as this the punishment it **d**? .... Je 5:29
like this the punishment it **d**?" .... Je 9:9
So I can decide what each one **d**; .... Je 17:10
should give her what she **d**; .... Je 50:15
Babylon as it **d** for destroying. .... Je 50:28
Babylon the punishment she **d**. .... Je 51:6

DESERVING
think are less **d** are the parts 1Co 12:23

DESIGN
is able to **d** pieces to be made .... Ex 31:4
is able to **d** pieces to be made .... Ex 35:32
decorated with a net **d** and 2Ki 25:17
also had a net **d** and was like 2Ki 25:17
and can make any **d** you show him. 2Ch 2:14
decorated with a net **d** and .... Je 52:22
pomegranates above the net **d**. .... Je 52:23
them know the **d** of the Temple .... Eze 43:11

DESIGNED
ago I **d** them, and now I have 2Ki 19:25
Uzziah made cleverly **d** devices. 2Ch 26:15
ago I **d** them, and now I have .... Is 37:26

DESIGNER
he was a **d** and also skilled at .... Ex 38:23

DESIRE
You will greatly **d** your husband, ... Ge 3:16
master began to **d** Joseph, ... Ge 39:7
had a strong **d** for some water. 2Sa 23:15
had a strong **d** for some water. 1Ch 11:17
my son Solomon a **d** to serve you. 1Ch 29:19
you will of the creature your .... Job 14:15
not to look with **d** at a girl. .... Job 31:1
myself out with **d** for your laws .... Ps 119:20
Take away my **d** to do evil or to .... Ps 141:4
Don't **d** her because she is .... Pr 6:25
because their **d** to eat makes .... Pr 16:26
Lazy people's **d** for sleep will .... Pr 21:25
and rulers should not **d** beer. .... Pr 31:4
has given them a **d** to know the .... Ec 3:11
to kiss, and I **d** him very much. .... Sng 5:16
my **d** for you made me feel like a .... Sng 6:12
his appearance to make us **d** him. .... Is 53:2
horses filled with sexual **d**; .... Je 5:8
will give them a **d** to respect me .... Eze 11:19
You **d** strangers instead of your .... Eze 16:32
unfaithful and **d** their hateful .... Eze 20:30
great sexual **d** for her lovers, ... Eze 23:5
her sexual **d** and prostitution. .... Eze 23:11
like animals in their sexual **d**. .... Eze 23:20
you will not **d** it or remember .... Eze 23:27
but their hearts **d** their selfish .... Eze 23:31
their **d** is like a grave's .... Hab 2:5
is like a grave's **d** for death, ... Hab 2:5
by any human parents or human **d**. .... Jn 1:13
than to burn with sexual **d**. 1Co 7:9
And your of to give has made most 2Co 9:2
their own evil **d** leads them away .... Jam 1:14
This **d** leads to sin, and then .... Jam 1:15
into which angels **d** to look. 1Pe 1:12
It is God's **d** that by doing good 1Pe 2:15
and their **d** for sin is never 2Pe 2:14
the wine of the **d** of her sexual .... Rev 18:3

DESIRED
If I have **d** another woman or .... Job 31:9
I did not miss any pleasure I **d**. .... Ec 2:10
from me and **d** to worship their .... Eze 6:9
all the idols of everyone she **d**. .... Eze 23:7

She also **d** the Assyrians, who .... Eze 23:12
same way you **d** to do the sinful .... Eze 23:21
had made the **d** land a ruin.'" .... Zch 7:14
people who **d** sexual relations .... Jud 1:7

DESIRES

salvation and satisfy all my **d.** 2Sa 23:5
along with the **d** of my heart. .... Job 17:11
do not control their selfish **d.** .... Ps 73:7
will be caught by their own **d.** .... Pr 11:6
your heart **d,** whatever you want .... Ec 11:9
to my lover, and he **d** only me. .... Sng 7:10
many other evil **d** keep the .... Mk 4:19
and has his own **d** under control, ... 1Co 7:37
control the evil **d** of the sinful .... Col 2:23
an overseer **d** a good work 1Ti 3:1
from him by their physical **d,** 1Ti 5:11
away from the evil **d** of youth. 2Ti 2:22
sin and are led by many evil **d.** 2Ti 3:6
who wants to live as God **d,** 2Ti 3:12
the selfish **d** that war within .... Jam 4:1
sins, evil **d,** drunkenness, ... 1Pe 4:3
not ruin you with its evil **d.** 2Pe 1:4
By their evil **d** they lead people 2Pe 2:18
their own evil **d** which are .... Jud 1:18

DESPISE

I hate and **d** lies, but I love .... Ps 119:163

DESTROY

I will **d** all human beings that I .... Ge 6:7
And I will **d** every animal and .... Ge 6:7
d all of them from the earth. .... Ge 6:13
on the earth to **d** all living .... Ge 6:17
will never again **d** every living .... Ge 8:21
will never again **d** all living .... Ge 9:11
will never again **d** all life on .... Ge 9:15
Do you plan to **d** the good people .... Ge 18:23
Will you still **d** it? .... Ge 18:24
you will not **d** the good people .... Ge 18:25
Will you **d** the whole city for .... Ge 18:28
there, will you **d** the city?'" .... Ge 18:29
in the city, will you **d** it?" .... Ge 18:30
there, I will not **d** the city." .... Ge 18:31
ten there, I will not **d** it." .... Ge 18:32
we are about to **d** this city. .... Ge 19:13
The LORD is about to **d** it!" .... Ge 19:14
I will not **d** that town. .... Ge 19:21
I cannot **d** Sodom until you .... Ge 19:22
would you **d** an innocent nation? .... Ge 20:4
Esau might come and **d** one camp, ... Ge 32:8
the plants the hail did not **d.**' .... Ex 10:12
sword, and my hand will **d** them.' .... Ex 15:9
will completely **d** the Amalekites .... Ex 17:14
D completely any person who .... Ex 22:20
Jebusites, and I will **d** them. .... Ex 23:23
You must **d** their idols, breaking .... Ex 23:24
saw God, but God did not **d** them. .... Ex 24:11
them that I am going to **d** them. .... Ex 32:10
let your anger **d** your people, ... Ex 32:11
mountains and **d** them from the .... Ex 32:12
and did not **d** the people as he .... Ex 32:14
I might **d** you on the way, ... Ex 33:3
for a moment, I would **d** you. .... Ex 33:5
D their altars, break their .... Ex 34:13
I will **d** that person from among .... Le 23:30
and fever that will **d** your eyes .... Le 26:16
away from you and **d** your cattle. .... Le 26:22
I will **d** your places where gods .... Le 26:30
I will **d** your cities and make .... Le 26:31
pull out my sword and **d** you. .... Le 26:33
I completely **d** them and break my .... Le 26:44
men so I can **d** them quickly. .... Nu 16:21
people so I can **d** them quickly." .... Nu 16:45
will completely **d** their cities." .... Nu 21:2

Jacob and will **d** those left in .... Nu 24:19
you will **d** all these people." .... Nu 32:15
D all of their carved statues .... Nu 33:52
to the Amorites, who will **d** us. .... Dt 1:27
He will not leave you or **d** you. .... Dt 4:31
with you and **d** you from the .... Dt 6:15
you must **d** them completely. .... Dt 7:2
you, and he will quickly **d** you. .... Dt 7:4
He will **d** them, and he will not .... Dt 7:10
You must **d** all the people the .... Dt 7:16
be able to **d** them all at once .... Dt 7:22
stop you; you will **d** them all. .... Dt 7:24
before you to **d** them like a fire .... Dt 9:3
them out and **d** them quickly, ... Dt 9:3
angry—angry enough to **d** you. .... Dt 9:8
so that I may **d** them and make .... Dt 9:14
angry enough with you to **d** you, ... Dt 9:19
enough with Aaron to **d** him, ... Dt 9:20
LORD had said he would **d** you, ... Dt 9:25
Lord GOD, do not **d** your people, ... Dt 9:26
He did not want to **d** you. .... Dt 10:10
must completely **d** all the places .... Dt 12:2
their idols and **d** their names .... Dt 12:3
your God will **d** ahead of you. .... Dt 12:29
D the city completely and kill .... Dt 13:15
that he will **d,** you will force .... Dt 19:1
Completely **d** these people: .... Dt 20:17
do not **d** its trees with an ax. .... Dt 20:19
diseases and **d** you from the land .... Dt 28:21
Locusts will **d** all your trees .... Dt 28:42
you and catch you and **d** you, ... Dt 28:45
will be happy to ruin and **d** you, ... Dt 28:63
people may **d** all of your land .... Dt 29:19
The LORD will **d** any memory of .... Dt 29:20
He will **d** those nations for you, ... Dt 31:3
of you, saying, 'D the enemy!' .... Dt 33:27
and then let the Amorites **d** us? .... Jos 7:7
things I commanded them to **d.** .... Jos 7:11
unless you **d** everything as I .... Jos 7:12
things he commanded you to **d.** .... Jos 7:13
Ai, as a sign to **d** the city, and .... Jos 8:26
completely **d** all the people as .... Jos 10:40
could completely **d** them without .... Jos 11:20
and Gad and **d** those lands. .... Jos 22:33
and that he will **d** you from this .... Jos 23:15
against him, he will **d** you." .... Jos 24:20
You must **d** their altars.' .... Jdg 2:2
when I will **d** the descendants 1Sa 2:31
Amalekites and **d** everything they 1Sa 15:3
so that I won't **d** you with them, ... 1Sa 15:6
they did not want to **d** them. 1Sa 15:9
'Go and **d** those evil people, ... 1Sa 15:18
to Keilah to **d** the town because 1Sa 23:10
had planned to **d** the good advice 2Sa 17:14
are trying to **d** an important 2Sa 20:19
not to **d** or ruin anything! 2Sa 20:20
us and tried to **d** all our people 2Sa 21:5
arm toward Jerusalem to **d** it, ... 2Sa 24:16
I will **d** your family as 1Ki 14:10
who will **d** Jeroboam's family, ... 1Ki 14:14
I will soon **d** you and your 1Ki 16:3
if I don't completely **d** Samaria. 1Ki 20:10
says to you, 'I will soon **d** you. 1Ki 21:21
I will **d** you, because you have 1Ki 21:22
did not **d** the places where 1Ki 22:43
You will **d** every strong, walled 2Ki 3:19
LORD would not **d** Judah because 2Ki 8:19
You must **d** the family of Ahab 2Ki 9:7
so he could **d** the worshipers 2Ki 10:19
at Aphek until you **d** them." 2Ki 13:17
never wanted to **d** them or reject 2Ki 13:23
would completely **d** Israel from 2Ki 14:27
them and let others **d** them; 2Ki 17:20

to attack and **d** this place 2Ki 18:25
to this country and **d** it.'" 2Ki 18:25
against Jehoiakim to **d** Judah. 2Ki 24:2
sent an angel to **d** Jerusalem, ... 1Ch 21:15
when the angel started to **d** it, ... 1Ch 21:15
the locusts to **d** the land. 2Ch 7:13
So I will not **d** them but will 2Ch 12:7
and did not fully **d** Rehoboam. 2Ch 12:12
nation made **d** another nation, ... 2Ch 15:6
one city would **d** another city, ... 2Ch 15:6
turned away and did not **d** them. 2Ch 20:10
LORD will **d** what you have made. 2Ch 20:37
LORD would not **d** David's family 2Ch 21:7
appointed to **d** Ahab's family. 2Ch 22:7
has decided to **d** you because you 2Ch 25:16
fight God, or he will **d** you." 2Ch 35:21
this order and **d** this Temple. .... Ezr 6:12
would get angry enough to **d** us, ... Ezr 9:14
for a way to **d** all of Mordecai's .... Est 3:6
be given to **d** those people. .... Est 3:9
empire ordering them to **d,** .... Est 3:13
messages to **d** all the Jewish .... Est 8:5
They may **d,** kill, and completely .... Est 8:11
the Jewish people to **d** them, ... Est 9:24
choose a day to ruin and **d** them. .... Est 9:24
your hand and **d** everything he .... Job 1:11
your hand and **d** his flesh and .... Job 2:5
and reach out his hand to **d** me. .... Job 6:9
Do you now turn around and **d** me? .... Job 10:8
In the same way, you **d** hope. .... Job 14:19
But you even **d** respect for God .... Job 15:4
Fire will **d** the tents of those .... Job 15:34
people will **d** them and burn up .... Job 20:26
up my road and work to **d** me, ... Job 30:13
works, but its Maker can **d** it. .... Job 40:19
d liars; the LORD hates those .... Ps 5:6
hearts they want to **d** others. .... Ps 5:9
enemies and **d** those who try to .... Ps 8:2
D from your land those nations .... Ps 10:16
They **d** my people as if they were .... Ps 14:4
You will **d** their families from .... Ps 21:10
people may try to **d** my body. .... Ps 27:2
a moth, you **d** what they love. .... Ps 39:11
They **d** my people as if they were .... Ps 53:4
D them because you are loyal to .... Ps 54:5
d and confuse their words, ... Ps 55:9
To the tune of "Do Not **D.**" .... Ps 56:13
To the tune of "Do Not **D.**" .... Ps 57:11
To the tune of "Do Not **D.**" .... Ps 58:11
D them in your anger; .... Ps 59:13
your anger; **d** them completely! .... Ps 59:13
enemies want to **d** me for no .... Ps 69:4
you **d** those who are unfaithful. .... Ps 73:27
out in the open and **d** them! .... Ps 74:11
To the tune of "Do Not **D.**" .... Ps 74:23
their sins and did not **d** them. .... Ps 78:38
Come, let's **d** them as a nation .... Ps 83:4
Disgrace them and **d** them. .... Ps 83:17
sins and will **d** them for their .... Ps 94:23
morning I will **d** the wicked .... Ps 101:8
So God said he would **d** them. .... Ps 106:23
people did not **d** the other .... Ps 106:34
people are waiting to **d** me, ... Ps 119:95
D all those who trouble me, ... Ps 143:12
him, but he will **d** the wicked. .... Ps 145:20
has no sense; he will **d** himself. .... Pr 6:32
dishonesty will **d** those who are .... Pr 11:3
an evil person can **d** a neighbor, ... Pr 11:9
the wicked can **d** it with their .... Pr 11:11
do not let them **d** themselves. .... Pr 19:18
of the wicked will **d** them, ... Pr 21:7
king will quickly **d** such people. .... Pr 24:22
is a time to **d** and a time to .... Ec 3:3

words and will **d** everything you .... Ec 5:6
be too wise. Why **d** yourself? .... Ec 7:16
but one sinner can **d** much good. .... Ec 9:18
the words of a fool will **d** them. .... Ec 10:12
He only wants to **d** other people .... Is 10:7
that he will **d** the land .... Is 10:22
will certainly **d** this land, ... Is 10:23
will not hurt or **d** each other on .... Is 11:9
like a weapon to **d** the whole .... Is 13:5
He will **d** the land and the .... Is 13:9
and I will **d** the pride of those. .... Is 13:11
But God will **d** it like Sodom and .... Is 13:19
I will **d** Babylon and its people, ... Is 14:22
I will **d** the king of Assyria in .... Is 14:25
The LORD will **d** the earth and .... Is 24:1
So a curse will **d** the earth. .... Is 24:6
mountain God will **d** the veil .... Is 25:7
he will **d** death forever. .... Is 25:8
but God will **d** these walls. .... Is 25:12
He will **d** the proud city, and he .... Is 26:5
Hail will **d** the forest, and the .... Is 32:19
be for you who **d** others but have .... Is 33:1
will **d** them and kill them all. .... Is 34:2
Edom and **d** those people as .... Is 34:5
to attack and **d** this country .... Is 36:10
I will **d** the hills and mountains .... Is 42:15
trouble you and who want to **d?** .... Is 51:13
I have made the destroyer to **d.** .... Is 54:16
us and have let our sins **d** us. .... Is 64:7
people do not **d** them, because .... Is 65:8
will not hurt or **d** each other on .... Is 65:25
and he will **d** many people with .... Is 66:16
and tear down, **d** and overthrow, ... Je 1:10
left his home to **d** your land. .... Je 4:7
but I will not completely **d** it. .... Je 4:27
but do not completely **d** them. .... Je 5:10
They will **d** with their swords .... Je 5:17
I will not **d** you completely. .... Je 5:18
I will **d** you, you who are .... Je 6:2
We will **d** the strong towers of .... Je 6:5
So I will **d** the place where I .... Je 7:14
I will **d** the cities of Judah so .... Je 9:11
in your anger, or you will **d** me. .... Je 10:24
Let us **d** the tree and its fruit. .... Je 11:19
pull it up completely and **d** it," .... Je 12:17
will **d** the people of Judah with .... Je 14:12
animals to eat and **d** the bodies. .... Je 15:3
Don't **d** me while you remain .... Je 15:15
D them, and destroy them again. .... Je 17:18
that I will pull down to **d** it. .... Je 18:7
I will completely **d** this city. .... Je 19:8
I will send men to **d** the palace, ... Je 22:7
I will completely **d** all those .... Je 25:9
I will **d** my Temple in Jerusalem .... Je 26:6
use Nebuchadnezzar to **d** them. .... Je 27:8
will completely **d** all those .... Je 30:11
to **d** them and bring them .... Je 31:28
I will **d** it, because of all the .... Je 32:32
I will **d** the towns in Judah so .... Je 34:22
will surely come and **d** this land .... Je 36:29
He will **d** the stone pillars in .... Je 43:13
You will **d** yourselves. .... Je 44:8
d the whole family of Judah. .... Je 44:11
will **d** cities and the people in .... Je 46:8
I will completely **d** the many .... Je 46:28
But I will not completely **d** you. .... Je 46:28
time has come to **d** all the .... Je 47:4
It is time to **d** all who are left .... Je 47:4
will soon **d** the Philistines, ... Je 47:4
and **d** the people of the East. .... Je 49:28
enemies, who want to **d** them. .... Je 49:37
and I will **d** its king and its .... Je 49:38
them, and completely **d** them. .... Je 50:21

Completely **d** Babylon and do not .... Je 50:26
foreign people to **d** Babylon like............... Je 51:2
because he wants to **d** Babylon. .... Je 51:11
I use you to **d** kingdoms......................... Je 51:20
from the north to **d** Babylon," .... Je 51:48
I will send people to **d** her," .... Je 51:53
The army has come to **d** Babylon. .... Je 51:56
that you will **d** this place so .... Je 51:62
against me to **d** my young men. .... La 1:15
planned to **d** the wall around .... La 2:8
and **d** them from under your .... La 3:66
send a time of hunger to **d** you, ... Eze 5:16
and I will **d** your places of idol .... Eze 6:3
will **d** those in the city. .... Eze 7:15
Kill and **d** old men, young men .... Eze 9:6
Will you **d** everyone left alive .... Eze 9:8
you completely **d** the Israelites .... Eze 11:13
and hailstones will **d** the wall. .... Eze 13:13
against him and **d** him from among .... Eze 14:9
to **d** its people and animals. .... Eze 14:21
fire, fire will still **d** them. .... Eze 15:7
of worship and **d** other places .... Eze 16:39
against them and **d** them in the .... Eze 20:13
did not **d** them or put an end to .... Eze 20:17
you that will **d** all your green .... Eze 20:47
It is polished to kill and **d,** .... Eze 21:28
so I would not have to **d** them. .... Eze 22:30
be a nation, and I will **d** you. .... Eze 25:7
And I will **d** Edom all the way .... Eze 25:13
they have tried to **d** Judah. .... Eze 25:15
and I will **d** those people still .... Eze 25:16
They will **d** the walls of Tyre .... Eze 26:4
a battle and **d** your villages.................. Eze 26:8
your walls and **d** your nice .... Eze 26:12
their swords and **d** all that your .... Eze 28:7
I will **d** the land of Egypt and .... Eze 29:10
be brought in to **d** the land. .... Eze 30:11
I will **d** the land and everything .... Eze 30:12
I will **d** the idols and take away .... Eze 30:13
I will **d** great numbers of people .... Eze 30:15
They will **d** the pride of Egypt .... Eze 32:12
I will also **d** all Egypt's cattle .... Eze 32:13
when I **d** all those who live in .... Eze 32:15
I will **d** those sheep that are .... Eze 34:16
I will **d** your cities, and you .... Eze 35:4
empty ruin and **d** everyone who .... Eze 35:7
the LORD came to **d** the city and .... Eze 43:3
'Cut down the tree and **d** it. .... Da 4:23
and will **d** people all over .... Da 7:23
He will **d** powerful people and .... Da 8:24
He will **d** many people without .... Da 8:25
who is to come will **d** the city .... Da 9:26
and will have the power to **d** it. .... Da 11:16
to defeat and **d** strong cities, ... Da 11:24
good friends will try to **d** him. .... Da 11:26
He will go to **d** completely many .... Da 11:44
will **d** her vines and fig trees, ... Hos 2:12
I will also **d** your mother. .... Hos 4:5
worship will **d** them and their................ Hos 5:7
that I will kill you and **d** you. .... Hos 6:5
their cities and **d** their strong .... Hos 8:14
he will **d** their holy stone .... Hos 10:2
cities and will **d** them and kill .... Hos 11:6
and I won't **d** Israel again. .... Hos 11:9
Israel, I will **d** you. .... Hos 13:9
He will **d** from their treasure .... Hos 13:15
Hazael that will **d** the strong .... Am 1:4
Damascus and the king who is .... Am 1:5
Gaza that will **d** the city's .... Am 1:7
I will **d** the king of the city of .... Am 1:8
Tyre that will **d** the city's.................... Am 1:10
that will even **d** the strong .... Am 1:12
of Rabbah that will **d** its strong .... Am 1:14

on Moab that will **d** the strong .... Am 2:2
and it will **d** the strong .... Am 2:5
I will also **d** the altars at .... Am 3:14
are trying to **d** the poor people .... Am 8:4
I will **d** it from off the earth, ... Am 9:8
I will surely **d** the wise people .... Ob 1:8
crossroads to **d** those who are .... Ob 1:14
I will **d** all her idols, and .... Mic 1:7
you, saying, "Let's **d** Jerusalem. .... Mic 4:11
They will **d** the Assyrians with .... Mic 5:6
from you and **d** your chariots. .... Mic 5:10
I will **d** the cities in your .... Mic 5:11
will **d** your statues of gods and .... Mic 5:13
from you and **d** your cities..................... Mic 5:14
you store up, the sword will **d.** .... Mic 6:14
he will completely **d** Nineveh;................. Nah 1:8
will completely **d** anyone making .... Nah 1:9
I will **d** the idols and metal .... Nah 1:14
battle will completely **d** you. .... Nah 3:15
made plans to **d** many people, ... Hab 2:10
send fire to **d** what those people .... Hab 2:13
will **d** the birds in the air and .... Zph 1:3
I will **d** those who worship the .... Zph 1:5
I will **d** you so that no one will .... Zph 2:5
because he will **d** all the gods .... Zph 2:11
against the north and **d** Assyria. .... Zph 2:13
When you bring it home, I **d** it. .... Hag 1:9
will **d** the foreign kingdoms and.............. Hag 2:22
house and **d** it with its wood .... Zch 5:4
all she has and **d** her power on .... Zch 9:4
and I will **d** the pride of the .... Zch 9:6
they will **d** the enemy with .... Zch 9:15
pride and **d** Egypt's power over .... Zch 10:11
will **d** all the people around .... Zch 12:6
I will go to **d** all the nations .... Zch 12:9
rebuild them, I will **d** them..................... Mal 1:4
have come to **d** the law of Moses .... Mt 5:17
and rust will **d** them and thieves............. Mt 6:19
the one who can **d** the soul and .... Mt 10:28
'I can **d** the Temple of God and .... Mt 26:61
You said you could **d** the Temple .... Mt 27:40
Did you come to **d** us?......................... Mk 1:24
'I will **d** this Temple that .... Mk 14:58
You said you could **d** the Temple .... Mk 15:29
Did you come to **d** us?......................... Lk 4:34
to save a life or to **d** it?" .... Lk 6:9
from heaven and **d** those people?" .... Lk 9:54
did not come to **d** the souls of................ Lk 9:56
can't steal and moths can't **d.** .... Lk 12:33
They will **d** you and all your .... Lk 19:44
answered them, "**D** this temple, ... Jn 2:19
comes to steal and kill and **d,** .... Jn 10:10
from Nazareth will **d** this place .... Ac 6:14
was also trying to **d** the church, ... Ac 8:3
trying to **d** those who trust .... Ac 9:21
wolves and try to **d** the flock. .... Ac 20:29
So do we **d** the law by following.............. Rm 3:31
God used a human life to **d** sin. .... Rm 8:3
Jews fell, did that fall **d** them? .... Rm 11:11
Do not **d** someone's faith by .... Rm 14:15
of food is the work of God. .... Rm 14:20
in order to **d** what the world 1Co 1:28
temple, God will **d** that person, ... 1Co 3:17
but God will **d** them both. 1Co 6:13
time Christ will **d** all rulers, ... 1Co 15:24
from God that can **d** the enemy's 2Co 10:4
church of God and tried to **d** it. .... Gal 1:13
faith that he once tried to **d.**" .... Gal 1:23
and so **d** God's promise to .... Gal 3:17
will completely **d** each other. .... Gal 5:15
mouth and will **d** him with the 2Th 2:8
things that ruin and **d** people.................. 1Ti 6:9
he could **d** the one who has the .... Heb 2:14

fire that will **d** all those who .... Heb 10:27
the only One who can save and **d**. .... Jam 4:12
to **d** the devil's work. 1Jn 3:8
are the very things that **d** them. .... Jud 1:10
time has come to **d** those who .... Rev 11:18

DESTROYED

d from the earth every living .... Ge 7:23
before the LORD **d** Sodom and .... Ge 13:10
you will not be **d** when the city .... Ge 19:15
mountains, or you will be **d**." .... Ge 19:17
and **d** those cities. .... Ge 19:25
God **d** the cities in the valley, ... Ge 19:29
my people and I will be **d**." .... Ge 34:30
that would have **d** you and your .... Ex 9:15
The hail **d** all the people and .... Ex 9:25
ripened, so these crops were **d**. .... Ex 9:31
ripen later, so they were not **d**. .... Ex 9:32
victory you **d** those who were .... Ex 15:7
the LORD and **d** Nadab and Abihu, ... Le 10:2
for the purpose of being **d**, ... Le 27:29
you will be **d** because of their .... Nu 16:26
the LORD and **d** the two hundred .... Nu 16:35
to die! We are **d**. We are all .... Nu 17:12
completely **d** the Canaanites .... Nu 21:3
It **d** Ar in Moab, and it burned .... Nu 21:28
and we **d** them as far as Nophah, ... Nu 21:30
but Amalek will be **d** at last.'" .... Nu 24:20
Eber, but they will also be **d**." .... Nu 24:24
Esau forced them out and **d** them, ... Dt 2:12
The LORD **d** the Zamzummites, ... Dt 2:21
in Edom, when he **d** the Horites. .... Dt 2:22
from Crete and the Avvites, ... Dt 2:23
Cretans **d** them and took their .... Dt 2:23
that time and completely **d** them, ... Dt 2:34
We completely **d** them, just like .... Dt 3:6
LORD your God **d** everyone among .... Dt 4:3
but you will be completely **d**. .... Dt 4:26
confusing them until they are **d**. .... Dt 7:23
be completely **d** along with it. .... Dt 7:26
you today that you will be **d**. .... Dt 8:19
Just as the LORD **d** the other .... Dt 8:20
they will be **d** for you, but be .... Dt 12:30
will be **d** and suddenly ruined .... Dt 28:20
from the skies until you are **d**. .... Dt 28:24
load on you until he has **d** you. .... Dt 28:48
your field, and you will be **d**. .... Dt 28:51
the Teachings, until you are **d**. .... Dt 28:61
which the LORD because he was .... Dt 29:23
today that you will surely be **d**. .... Dt 30:18
when he **d** them and their land. .... Dt 31:4
from them, and they will be **d**. .... Dt 31:17
starved and sick, **d** by terrible .... Dt 32:24
heard how you **d** Sihon and Og, ... Jos 2:10
in it are to be **d** as an offering .... Jos 6:17
that are to be **d** as an offering .... Jos 6:18
They completely **d** with the sword .... Jos 6:21
I have commanded that they be **d**. .... Jos 7:12
have been **d** will himself be .... Jos 7:15
all the people of Ai were **d**. .... Jos 8:26
defeated Ai and completely **d** it, ... Jos 10:1
let us, your servants, be **d**. .... Jos 10:6
and completely **d** all the people .... Jos 10:28
and completely **d** everything in .... Jos 10:35
they completely **d** the city and .... Jos 10:37
and completely **d** everything in .... Jos 11:12
he completely **d** them and their .... Jos 11:21
about what must be completely **d**. .... Jos 22:20
d them before you, and you took .... Jos 24:8
They completely **d** the city, ... Jdg 1:17
Canaan until finally they **d** him. .... Jdg 4:24
in the land and **d** the crops that .... Jdg 6:4
for Baal had been **d** and that the .... Jdg 6:28

those people **d** the Israelites .... Jdg 10:8
saying, "This man **d** our country. .... Jdg 16:24
but we **d** all the other animals." 1Sa 15:15
I **d** all the Amalekites, and I 1Sa 15:20
the LORD has **d** all your enemies 1Sa 20:15
d the Ammonites and attacked 2Sa 11:1
and all his people won't be **d**." 2Sa 17:16
I chased my enemies and **d** them. 2Sa 22:38
I **d** and crushed them so they 2Sa 22:39
and I **d** those who hated me. 2Sa 22:41
the crops were **d** by locusts 1Ki 8:37
If the Temple is **d**, everyone who 1Ki 9:8
that the Israelites had not **d**. 1Ki 9:21
He **d** them all as the LORD had 1Ki 15:29
Zimri **d** all of Baasha's family 1Ki 16:12
with you, **d** your altars, ... 1Ki 19:10
with you, **d** your altars, ... 1Ki 19:14
led the army and **d** the Arameans' 1Ki 20:21
the one that was **d** and as many 1Ki 20:25
Arameans until they are **d**.'" 1Ki 22:11
He **d** all those who were left, ... 2Ki 10:17
Jehu **d** Baal worship in Israel, ... 2Ki 10:28
king of Aram had **d** them and made 2Ki 13:7
until you had completely **d** it. 2Ki 13:19
but Hezekiah the LORD's 2Ki 18:22
My ancestors **d** them, defeating 2Ki 19:12
Assyria have **d** these countries 2Ki 19:17
So the kings have **d** them. 2Ki 19:18
had **d** the places where gods were 2Ki 21:3
nations the LORD had **d** ahead of 2Ki 21:9
would be cursed and would be **d**. 2Ki 22:19
d the places of worship at the 2Ki 23:8
Josiah **d** the mediums, ... 2Ki 23:24
been given to the LORD to be **d**. 1Ch 2:7
there, and completely **d** them. 1Ch 4:41
army of Israel **d** the land of 1Ch 20:1
the crops will be **d** by locusts 2Ch 6:28
that the Israelites had not **d**. 2Ch 8:8
They **d** all the towns near Gerar, ... 2Ch 14:14
Arameans until they are **d**.'" 2Ch 18:10
Asherah idols and **d** the altars 2Ch 31:1
My ancestors **d** those nations; 2Ch 32:14
nations the LORD had **d** ahead of 2Ch 33:9
They took or **d** every valuable 2Ch 36:19
That is why it was **d**. .... Ezr 4:15
who **d** this Temple and took the .... Ezr 5:12
its gates had been **d** by fire." .... Ne 2:3
gates that had been **d** by fire. .... Ne 2:13
and I have been sold to be **d**, ... Est 7:4
killed and **d** five hundred men. .... Est 9:6
have killed and **d** five hundred .... Est 9:12
Let the day I was born be **d**, ... Job 3:3
honest people will never be **d**. .... Job 4:7
strength and **d** my whole family .... Job 16:7
my plans have been **d**, along with .... Job 17:11
Even after my skin has been **d**, ... Job 19:26
'Surely our enemies are **d**, ... Job 22:20
but the wicked will be **d**. .... Ps 1:6
or you will be **d** by his anger, ... Ps 2:12
nations and **d** the wicked; .... Ps 9:5
You **d** their cities; .... Ps 9:6
these things will never be **d**. .... Ps 15:5
did not quit until they were **d**. .... Ps 18:37
and I **d** those who hated me. .... Ps 18:40
Don't let them say, "We **d** him." .... Ps 35:25
But sinners will be **d**; .... Ps 37:38
You **d** those other nations, ... Ps 44:2
You **d** the large trading ships .... Ps 48:7
let the wicked be **d** before God. .... Ps 68:2
who accuse me be ashamed and **d**........ Ps 71:13
you cause them to be **d**. .... Ps 73:18
They are **d** in a moment; .... Ps 73:19
He sent frogs that **d** them. .... Ps 78:45

He **d** their vines with hail and .... Ps 78:47
of Jacob and **d** their land. .... Ps 79:7
you **d** us by your angry looks. .... Ps 80:16
and your terrors have **d** me. .... Ps 88:16
We are **d** by your anger; .... Ps 90:7
but they will be **d** forever. .... Ps 92:7
surely your enemies will be **d**, ... Ps 92:9
They will be **d**, but you will .... Ps 102:26
Let sinners be **d** from the earth, ... Ps 104:35
the land, and he **d** all the food. .... Ps 105:16
and he **d** every tree in the .... Ps 105:33
He **d** the firstborn sons in Egypt............ Ps 135:8
of Babylon, you will be **d**. .... Ps 137:8
they will be **d** because they do .... Pr 1:32
the wicked will be **d** by their .... Pr 11:5
wicked person's house will be **d**, ... Pr 14:11
never stop dying and being **d**,............... Pr 27:20
who do right will see them **d**. .... Pr 29:16
like a country **d** by enemies. .... Is 1:7
completely **d** like the cities .... Is 1:9
you will be **d** by your enemies' .... Is 1:20
who turn against him will be **d**; .... Is 1:28
The fine houses will be **d**; .... Is 5:9
will be **d** just as fire burns .... Is 5:24
no! I will be **d**. I am not pure, ... Is 6:5
the cities are **d** and the people .... Is 6:11
land, but it will be **d** again. .... Is 6:13
those who followed them were **d**. .... Is 9:16
a desert, who **d** its cities, who............... Is 14:17
from Ar in Moab, and it was **d**. .... Is 15:1
rulers have **d** the grapevines. .... Is 16:8
The city of Damascus will be **d**; .... Is 17:1
cities of Israel will be **d**. .... Is 17:3
hanging on it will be **d**." .... Is 22:25
houses and harbor of Tyre **d**. .... Is 23:1
strong, walled cities be **d**. .... Is 23:11
any longer, because you are **d**. .... Is 23:12
because your strong city is **d**. .... Is 23:14
of rocks and have **d** her walls. .... Is 25:2
punished and **d** them and erased .... Is 26:14
behind will be **d** as if by hail. .... Is 28:17
how the whole earth will be **d**. .... Is 28:22
All of them will be **d** together. .... Is 31:3
Assyria will be **d**, but not by a .... Is 31:8
and their protection will be **d**............... Is 31:9
the city will be completely **d**. .... Is 32:19
others but have not been **d** yet. .... Is 33:1
but Hezekiah **d** the LORD's .... Is 36:7
My ancestors **d** them, defeating .... Is 37:12
of Assyria have **d** all these .... Is 37:18
So the kings have **d** them. .... Is 37:19
They were **d** as a flame is put................ Is 43:17
You will be **d** quickly; .... Is 47:11
never have died out nor been **d**." .... Is 48:19
you and **d** you will leave. .... Is 49:17
You were **d** and defeated, and................ Is 49:19
buildings are **d** now, but shout .... Is 52:9
live in cities that once were **d**. .... Is 54:3
this reminder will never be **d**." .... Is 55:13
doesn't serve you will be **d**;................... Is 60:12
it will not be ruined or **d**. .... Is 60:18
restore the places **d** long ago................ Is 61:4
your land the Land that God **D**. .... Is 62:4
is like a desert; it is **d**. .... Is 64:10
our precious things have been **d**. .... Is 64:11
they will all be **d** together," .... Is 66:17
They have **d** the land of Israel. .... Je 2:15
towns will be **d** with no one left .... Je 4:7
the whole country has been **d**. .... Je 4:20
My tents are **d** in only a moment. .... Je 4:20
its towns had been **d** by the LORD .... Je 4:26
Judah, you **d** nation, what are................ Je 4:30
destroy it just as I **d** Shiloh. .... Je 7:14

They have come and **d** the land .... Je 8:16
will be **d** and disappear from .... Je 10:11
they are judged, they will be **d**. .... Je 10:15
Those nations have **d** the people............ Je 10:25
completely and **d** their homeland. .... Je 10:25
taken hold of you and **d** you. .... Je 15:6
So I have **d** them and taken away .... Je 15:7
at how the country was **d**. .... Je 18:16
they see how the city was **d**. .... Je 19:8
towns the LORD **d** without pity. .... Je 20:16
because all your friends are **d**! .... Je 22:20
badly I have **d** those countries. .... Je 25:9
Their land has been **d** because of .... Je 25:38
Jerusalem as I **d** my Holy Tent at .... Je 26:6
Temple will be **d** like the one at .... Je 26:9
nations that **d** you will now be .... Je 30:16
destroyed you will now be **d**. .... Je 30:16
never again be torn down or **d**." .... Je 31:40
or hunger until they are all **d**................. Je 44:27
because Memphis will be **d**. .... Je 46:19
and the high plain will be **d**, ... Je 48:8
is near, and she will soon be **d**. .... Je 48:16
And he has **d** your strong, walled .... Je 48:18
the Arnon River that Moab is **d**............... Je 48:20
The nation of Moab will be **d**, ... Je 48:42
of Moab and **d** those proud people........... Je 48:45
who worship Chemosh have been **d**. .... Je 48:46
because the town of Ai is **d**! .... Je 49:3
Edom will be **d**. People who pass .... Je 49:17
Edom will be **d** like the cities .... Je 49:18
God completely **d** the cities of .... Je 50:40
they are judged, they will be **d**. .... Je 51:18
You have **d** the whole land...................... Je 51:25
Babylon has defeated and **d** us. .... Je 51:34
her palaces and **d** all her........................ La 2:5
he **d** the meeting place. .... La 2:6
he **d** and smashed the bars of the .... La 2:9
because my people have been **d**.............. La 2:11
He has **d** without mercy, and he .... La 2:17
and fearful, ruined and **d**." .... La 3:47
eyes, because my people are **d**. .... La 3:48
Sodom was **d** suddenly, and no .... La 4:6
food when my people were **d**.................. La 4:10
disease or be **d** by hunger inside .... Eze 5:12
will be **d** and your incense .... Eze 6:4
falls, you will be **d** under it. .... Eze 13:14
places and **d** their cities. .... Eze 19:7
They have **d** lives and have taken .... Eze 22:25
I **d** them with an anger that was .... Eze 22:31
traded with the nations is **d**. .... Eze 26:2
the island will be **d** by war. .... Eze 26:6
famous city, you have been **d**!................ Eze 26:17
No one was ever **d** like Tyre, ... Eze 27:32
the **d** places will be rebuilt...................... Eze 36:33
The cities were **d**, empty, and .... Eze 36:35
what was **d** and have planted .... Eze 36:36
our hope has gone. We are **d**.'................ Eze 37:11
and so I **d** them in my anger. .... Eze 43:8
that will never be **d** or given to .... Da 2:44
His kingdom will never be **d**, ... Da 6:26
body was **d**, and it was thrown .... Da 7:11
and his kingdom will never be **d**. .... Da 7:14
kingdom will be completely **d**. .... Da 7:26
But that cruel king will be **d**, ... Da 8:25
that place to be completely **d**................. Da 9:26
end comes to the **d** city." .... Da 9:27
people will be **d**, because they .... Hos 4:6
They will be **d**, because they .... Hos 7:13
and for all this they will be **d**................. Hos 8:4
Even if the people are not **d**, ... Hos 9:6
Israel will be **d**; its king will .... Hos 10:7
of false worship will be **d**, ... Hos 10:8
strong, walled cities will be **d**. .... Hos 10:14

The grain is **d**, the new wine is .... Joe 1:10
But it was I who **d** the Amorites .... Am 2:9
as oaks—I **d** them completely. .... Am 2:9
decorated with ivory will be **d**, ... Am 3:15
I **d** some of you as I destroyed .... Am 4:11
descendants worship will be **d**, ... Am 7:9
with shame and **d** forever. .... Ob 1:10
people of Judah when they are **d**. .... Ob 1:12
forty days, Nineveh will be **d**!" .... Jnh 3:4
and all your enemies will be **d**. .... Mic 5:9
So I will let you be **d**. .... Mic 6:16
they have been completely **d**. .... Nah 1:15
Destroyers have **d** God's people .... Nah 2:2
open, and the palace is **d**. .... Nah 2:6
is robbed, ruined, and **d**. .... Nah 2:10
be stolen and their houses **d**. .... Zph 1:13
the city of Ashkelon will be **d**. .... Zph 2:4
Moab will be **d** like Sodom, ... Zph 2:9
I have **d** nations; .... Zph 3:6
where they lived would not be **d**, ... Zph 3:7
the Temple was before it was **d**? .... Hag 2:3
I **d** your work with diseases, ... Hag 2:17
That city will be **d** by fire. .... Zch 9:4
their rich pastures are **d**. .... Zch 11:3
that are to be **d** be destroyed. .... Zch 11:9
and it will never be **d** again. .... Zch 14:11
d his mountain country and left .... Mal 1:3
say, "We were **d**, but we will go .... Mal 1:4
of Jacob have not been **d**. .... Mal 3:6
cannot be **d** by moths or rust .... Mt 6:20
against itself will be **d**. .... Mt 12:25
and sky will be **d**, but the words .... Mt 24:35
until the flood came and **d** them. .... Mt 24:39
and sky will be **d**, but the words .... Mk 13:31
fell and was completely **d**." .... Lk 6:49
they themselves are **d** or lost. .... Lk 9:25
against itself will be **d**. .... Lk 11:17
you will be **d** as they were! .... Lk 13:3
lives, you will all be **d** too!" .... Lk 13:5
you will know it will soon be **d**. .... Lk 21:20
and sky will be **d**, but the words .... Lk 21:33
for the whole nation to be **d**." .... Jn 11:50
and your money should both be **d**, ... Ac 8:20
God **d** seven nations in the land .... Ac 13:19
will be **d**, and Artemis is .... Ac 19:27
who were made ready to be **d**. .... Rm 9:22
completely **d** like the cities .... Rm 9:29
and they have **d** your altars. .... Rm 11:3
So his sinful self will be **d**, ... 1Co 5:5
but our crown will never be **d**. 1Co 9:25
that we will not be **d** along with 1Co 11:32
enemy to be **d** will be death. 1Co 15:26
to a life that cannot be **d**. 1Co 15:42
body that can be **d** must clothe 1Co 15:53
body that can be **d** will clothe 1Co 15:54
sometimes, but we are not **d**. 2Co 4:9
live in here on earth—will be **d**. 2Co 5:1
enemies will be **d** but that you .... Php 1:28
In the end, they will be **d**. .... Php 3:19
safe," they will be **d** quickly. 1Th 5:3
consciences are **d** as if by a hot 1Ti 4:2
He **d** death, and through the Good 2Ti 1:10
They will be **d**, but you will .... Heb 1:11
by God and will be **d** by fire. .... Heb 6:8
that can be shaken—will be **d**. .... Heb 12:27
which cannot be **d** or be spoiled 1Pe 1:4
that will never be **d** and is very 1Pe 3:4
And God also **d** the evil cities 2Pe 2:6
these false teachers will be **d**. 2Pe 2:12
slaves of things that will be **d**. 2Pe 2:19
was flooded and **d** with water. 2Pe 3:6
have in order to be **d** by fire. 2Pe 3:7
in them will be **d** by fire, ... 2Pe 3:10

that way everything will be **d**. 2Pe 3:11
the skies will be **d** with fire, ... 2Pe 3:12
But later he **d** all those who did .... Jud 1:5
Korah, they surely will be **d**. .... Jud 1:11
and a third of the ships were **d**. .... Rev 8:9
and a tenth of the city was **d**. .... Rev 11:13
cities of the nations were **d**. .... Rev 16:19
pit and go away to be **d**. .... Rev 17:8
the kings have already been **d**, ... Rev 17:10
and he will go away to be **d**. .... Rev 17:11
and she will be **d** by fire, ... Rev 18:8
riches have been **d** in one hour!" .... Rev 18:17
But she has been **d** in one hour! .... Rev 18:19

DESTROYER
I have made the **d** to destroy. .... Is 54:16
a **d** of nations has begun to .... Je 4:7
because the **d** will soon come .... Je 6:26
brought a **d** at noontime against .... Je 15:8
The **d** will come against every .... Je 48:8
The **d** of Moab and her towns has .... Je 48:15
because the **d** of Moab has come .... Je 48:18
But the **d** has taken over your .... Je 48:32
A **d** will do blasphemous things .... Da 9:27
The **d** is coming to attack you, ... Nah 2:1

DESTROYERS
four kinds of **d** against them," .... Je 15:3
D have destroyed God's people .... Nah 2:2

DESTROYING
completely **d** everyone in Debir .... Jos 10:39
in Hazor, completely **d** them; .... Jos 11:11
the angel who was **d** the people, ... 2Sa 24:16
d the city and the area nearby. 2Ki 15:16
the Hamites, **d** their tents, ... 1Ch 4:41
those were the people God was **d**. 1Ch 5:25
go through Israel **d** the people.' 1Ch 21:12
he said to the angel who was **d**, ... 1Ch 21:15
they repay us for not **d** them! 2Ch 20:11
the Edomites, **d** them completely. 2Ch 20:23
enemies, killing and **d** them. .... Est 9:5
against them, his **d** angels. .... Ps 78:49
stopped God's anger from **d** them. .... Ps 106:23
rich farmlands, **d** everything. .... Is 10:18
I will turn my anger to **d** them." .... Is 10:25
When you stop **d**, others will .... Is 33:1
not becoming angry and **d** you. .... Is 48:9
would stop me from **d** them.'" .... Je 13:14
are scattering and **d** my people," .... Je 23:1
the LORD is **d** their land. .... Je 25:36
as it deserves for **d** his Temple. .... Je 50:28
will soon cause a **d** wind to blow .... Je 51:1
they deserve for **d** his Temple. .... Je 51:11
you are a **d** mountain, and I am .... Je 51:25
of people **d** things are heard .... Je 51:54
The LORD is **d** Babylon and making .... Je 51:55
did not stop himself from **d** it. .... La 2:8
a time of hunger, **d** both people .... Eze 14:13
' this way **d** its people and .... Eze 14:17
d and killing people and animals. .... Eze 14:19
vine's main branch, **d** its fruit. .... Eze 19:14
have left, the **d** locusts have .... Joe 1:4
will come like a **d** attack from .... Joe 1:15
the **d** locusts and the cutting .... Joe 2:25
People are **d** things and hurting .... Hab 1:3
Will he go on **d** people without .... Hab 1:17
d countries and cities and .... Hab 2:8
and so they are **d** the faith of 2Ti 2:18
but they are **d** themselves by 2Pe 3:16

DESTROYS
used for, it is a mildew that **d**; .... Le 13:51
it is a mildew that **d** things; .... Le 14:44
The LORD **d** his enemies; 1Sa 2:10

he catches us and **d** us and kills 2Sa 15:14
God's breath **d** them, and a blast .... Job 4:9
'God **d** both the innocent and the .... Job 9:22
away naked and **d** the powerful................ Job 12:19
nations great and then **d** them; .... Job 12:23
he **d** my hope like a fallen tree. .... Job 19:10
his wisdom he **d** Rahab, the sea .... Job 26:12
is like a fire that burns and **d**;................. Job 31:12
but having no money **d** the poor. .... Pr 10:15
a foolish woman **d** hers by what.............. Pr 14:1
just like someone who **d** things. .... Pr 18:9
knowledge, but he **d** false words. .... Pr 22:12
is cruel and **d** like a flood, ... Pr 27:4
a hard rain that **d** the crops. .... Pr 28:3
just like someone who **d** things. .... Pr 28:24
strong winds, and a fire that **d**. .... Is 29:6
He **d** the poor with lies, even .... Is 32:7
live through this fire that **d**? .... Is 33:14
inside the houses, death **d**. .... La 1:20
In front of them a fire **d**; .... Joe 2:3
He **d** the protected city; .... Am 5:9
If anyone **d** God's temple, God 1Co 3:17
were killed by the angel that **d**. 1Co 10:10

DESTRUCTION
life and success, death and **d**. .... Dt 30:15
add to the **d** by killing my son. 2Sa 14:11
its ruin and **d** from the earth. 1Ki 13:34
will not be afraid when **d** comes. .... Job 5:21
You will laugh at **d** and hunger, ... Job 5:22
eyes should see their own **d**, ... Job 21:20
d is uncovered before him. .... Job 26:6
The places of **d** and death say, ' .... Job 28:22
fear **d** from God, and I fear his .... Job 31:23
lifted me out of the pit of **d**, ... Ps 40:2
D is everywhere in the city; .... Ps 55:11
Pride leads to **d**; .... Pr 16:18
do when your **d** comes from far .... Is 10:3
the Almighty is sending **d**. .... Is 13:6
Babylon as with a broom of **d**," .... Is 14:23
Horonaim, crying over their **d**. .... Is 15:5
will be named the City of **D**. .... Is 19:18
me about the **d** of Jerusalem." .... Is 22:4
Who planned Tyre's **d**? .... Is 23:8
them through the strainer of **d**. .... Is 30:28
I will bring **d** on the people of .... Is 43:28
they go they cause ruin and **d**. .... Is 59:7
north There will be terrible **d**." .... Je 4:6
terrible **d** is coming to you....................... Je 6:1
of violence and **d** are heard .... Je 6:7
shouting about violence and **d**. .... Je 20:8
Their time of **d** is coming; .... Je 46:21
cries of much confusion and **d**. .... Je 48:3
it is the noise of much **d**........................ Je 50:22
over to cruel men, experts in **d**. .... Eze 21:31
away from God that brings **d**, ... Da 8:13
will cause terrible **d** and will .... Da 8:24
object that brings **d**. .... Da 11:31
that brings **d** will be set up .... Da 12:11
unclean, and it is doomed to **d**. .... Mic 2:10
a day of **d** and ruin, a day .... Zph 1:15
object that brings **d**.' .... Mt 24:15
that brings **d'** standing where it .... Mk 13:14
one worthy of **d**, was lost so .... Jn 17:12
punished with a **d** that continues 2Th 1:9
Day and the **d** of all who are 2Pe 3:7

DESTRUCTIVE
d wind will burn you like fire. .... Is 33:11

DETERMINED
Canaanites were **d** to stay there.............. Jdg 1:27
Amorites were **d** to stay in Mount .... Jdg 1:35
I will be **d**, and I know I will .... Is 50:7
am **d** to bring disasters on you. .... Je 44:11

from Judah were **d** to go to Egypt .... Je 44:12
They are **d** to be unfaithful to .... Hos 5:4
he was **d** to go to Jerusalem. .... Lk 9:51
and he rode out, **d** to win the .... Rev 6:2

DEVELOP
years, a new friendship will **d**. .... Da 11:6

DEVICES
them to build **d** to attack the .... Dt 20:20
Uzziah made cleverly designed **d**. 2Ch 26:15
d on the towers and corners 2Ch 26:15
towers and with **d** to attack you. .... Is 29:3
the city and built **d** all around .... Je 52:4
build **d** to attack the cities .... Eze 17:17
of the walls and **d** to attack the .... Eze 21:22
He will set up **d** to attack you. .... Eze 26:8

DEVIL
desert to be tempted by the **d**................. Mt 4:1
d came to Jesus to tempt him, ... Mt 4:3
Then the **d** led Jesus to the holy .... Mt 4:5
The **d** said, "If you are the Son .... Mt 4:6
Then the **d** led Jesus to the top .... Mt 4:8
d said, "If you will bow down.................. Mt 4:9
said to the **d**, "Go away from me .... Mt 4:10
So the **d** left Jesus, and angels .... Mt 4:11
planted the bad seed is the **d**. .... Mt 13:39
for the **d** and his angels. .... Mt 25:41
where the **d** tempted Jesus for .... Lk 4:2
The **d** said to Jesus, "If you are .... Lk 4:3
Then the **d** took Jesus and showed........... Lk 4:5
d said to Jesus, "I will give .... Lk 4:6
the **d** led Jesus to Jerusalem .... Lk 4:9
After the **d** had tempted Jesus in .... Lk 4:13
the **d** comes and takes it away .... Lk 8:12
of you, but one of you is a **d**."................. Jn 6:70
You belong to your father the **d**,............... Jn 8:44
d had already persuaded Judas .... Jn 13:2
those who were ruled by the **d**, ... Ac 10:38
and said, "You son of the **d!** .... Ac 13:10
The **d** who rules this world has 2Co 4:4
and Belial, the **d**, have any 2Co 6:15
not give the **d** a way to defeat............... Eph 4:27
was afraid the **d** had tempted you 1Th 3:5
judged guilty just as the **d** was. 1Ti 3:6
escape from the trap of the **d**,............... 2Ti 2:26
has the power of death—the **d**—............... Heb 2:14
not spiritual; it is from the **d**.................. Jam 3:15
against the **d**, and the devil.................. Jam 4:7
and the **d** will run from you. .... Jam 4:7
The **d**, your enemy, goes around............... 1Pe 5:8
The **d** has been sinning since the 1Jn 3:8
to sin belongs to the **d**. 1Jn 3:8
is greater than the **d**, who is in 1Jn 4:4
argued with the **d** about who .... Jud 1:9
dared to judge the **d** guilty. .... Jud 1:9
the **d** will put some of you in .... Rev 2:10
old snake called the **d** or Satan, ... Rev 12:9
because the **d** has come down to .... Rev 12:12
snake who is the **d** and Satan, ... Rev 20:2

DEVOUR
I will **d** them like a lion and .... Hos 13:8

DEW
and in the morning **d** lay around .... Ex 16:13
When the **d** was gone, thin flakes .... Ex 16:14
When the **d** fell on the camp each .... Nu 11:9
my words will fall like **d**. .... Dt 32:2
with wonderful **d** from heaven, ... Dt 33:13
where the skies drop their **d**. .... Dt 33:28
If there is **d** only on the wool .... Jdg 6:37
around it gets wet with **d**." .... Jdg 6:39
ground around it was wet with **d**. .... Jdg 6:40
May there be no **d** or rain on the 2Sa 1:21

fall on him as **d** falls on the 2Sa 17:12
rain or **d** will fall during the 1Ki 17:1
The **d** will lie on the branches................Job 29:19
Who is father to the drops of **d**? ....Job 38:28
It is like the **d** of Mount Hermon ....Ps 133:3
is like the **d** on the grass. ....Pr 19:12
head is wet with **d,** and my hair ....Sng 5:2
the **d** in the heat of harvest....................Is 18:4
The **d** covering you is like the................Is 26:19
you is like the **d** of a new day; ....Is 26:19
Let the man become wet with **d,**..........Da 4:15
become wet with **d** and live like ....Da 4:23
and **d** from the sky will make you ....Da 4:25
became wet from **d.** His hair grew ....Da 4:33
an ox and became wet with **d.** ....Da 5:21
like the **d** that goes away early ....Hos 6:4
disappear like the morning **d.** ....Hos 13:3
I will be like the **d** to Israel, ...Hos 14:5
other people like **d** from the ....Mic 5:7

DIAMOND

I am making you as hard as a **d,**..............Eze 3:9

DIE

from that tree, you will **d!**"....................Ge 2:17
even touch it, or you will **d.**'"................Ge 3:3
to the woman, "You will not **d.** ....Ge 3:4
and don't know when I might **d.**............Ge 27:2
Give me children, or I'll **d!**" ....Ge 30:1
the fish in the Nile will **d,** ....Ex 7:18
time you see me, you will **d.**"................Ex 10:28
son in the land of Egypt will **d—** ....Ex 11:5
out of Egypt to **d** in the desert? ....Ex 14:11
God speak to us, or we will **d.**" ....Ex 20:19
have her baby **d** before it is ....Ex 23:26
wife will **d** without children ....Le 20:20
Let me **d** like good men, and let ....Nu 23:10
the children of Korah did not **d.** ....Nu 26:11
they would all **d** in the desert, ...Nu 26:65
I will **d** here in this land and ....Dt 4:22
now, we will **d!** This great fire ....Dt 5:25
fire anymore, or we will **d.**" ....Dt 18:16
relations with her must **d.** ....Dt 22:22
Or the second husband might **d.**............Dt 24:3
Let me **d** with these Philistines! ....Jdg 16:30
tribe in Israel will not **d** out. ....Jdg 21:17
And where you **d,** I will die, and............Ru 1:17
you and your men should **d.** 1Sa 26:16
Did Abner **d** like a fool? 2Sa 3:33
son who was born to you will **d.**" 2Sa 12:14
eat it and then **d** from hunger." 1Ki 17:12
prayed. "Let me **d.** I am no 1Ki 19:4
freed the man I said should **d,**............1Ki 20:42
Each must **d** for his own sins." 2Ki 14:6
Each must **d** for his own sins." 2Ch 25:4
stay innocent? Curse God and **d!**" ....Job 2:9
Why didn't I **d** as soon as I was ....Job 3:11
you die, wisdom will **d** with you! ....Job 12:2
we **d,** and our bodies are laid ....Job 14:10
powerful people **d** without help. ....Job 34:20
They **d** while they are still ....Job 36:14
to save those sentenced to **d.** ....Ps 79:11
But you will **d** like any other ....Ps 82:7
breath, they **d** and turn to dust ....Ps 104:29
but fools will **d** because they ....Pr 10:21
hates to be corrected will **d.** ....Pr 15:10
will not go free, liars will **d.** ....Pr 19:9
those who are careless will **d.**................Pr 19:16
If you spank them, they won't **d.** ....Pr 23:13
time to be born and a time to **d.** ....Ec 3:2
be foolish. Why **d** before your ....Ec 7:17
because tomorrow we will **d.**"................Is 22:13
There you will **d,** and there your ....Is 22:18
they will not **d** in prison,......................Is 51:14

that eat them will never **d,** ....Is 66:24
Their young men will **d** in war. ....Je 11:22
They will **d** in war, or they will ....Je 16:4
common people will **d** in the land ....Je 16:6
where you will **d** and be buried, ...Je 20:6
They said, "You must **d!** ....Je 26:8
will **d** this year, because you ....Je 28:16
person will **d** for his own sin ....Je 31:30
You will **d** in a peaceful way. ....Je 34:5
a well and left him there to **d!**................Je 38:9
They starve in pain and **d,** ....La 4:9
will surely **d,**' you must warn ....Eze 3:18
ways, they will **d** in their sin. ....Eze 3:18
who sins is the one who will **d.** ....Eze 18:4
do you want to **d,** people of ....Eze 18:31
want any who are wicked to **d.** ....Eze 33:11
one house, but they will also **d.** ....Am 6:9
'Jeroboam will **d** by the sword, ...Am 7:11
for me to **d** than to live." ....Jnh 4:3
for me to **d** than to live."......................Jnh 4:8
We will not **d.** LORD, you have ....Hab 1:12
I will even **d** with you!" ....Mt 26:35
In hell the worm does not **d;** ....Mk 9:44
are like angels and cannot **d.** ....Lk 20:36
eats this bread will never **d.** ....Jn 6:50
but you will **d** in your sins. ....Jn 8:21
will have life even if they **d.** ....Jn 11:25
and believes in me will never **d.** ....Jn 11:26
for one man to **d** for the people ....Jn 11:50
Jesus would **d** for their nation ....Jn 11:51
this to show how he would **d.** ....Jn 12:33
how he would **d** would come true. ....Jn 18:32
a law that says he should **d,** ....Jn 19:7
that this one would not **d.** ....Jn 21:23
ready to **d** for the Lord Jesus!............Ac 21:13
few people will **d** to save the ....Rm 5:7
person someone might possibly **d.** ....Rm 5:7
want, you will **d** spiritually................Rm 8:13
Lord, and if we **d,** we are dying ....Rm 14:8
I would rather **d** than to have my 1Co 9:15
Adam all of us **d.** In the same 1Co 15:22
I **d** every day. That is true, ...1Co 15:31
because tomorrow we will **d.**"..............1Co 15:32
on earth, whether I live or **d.** ....Php 1:20
everyone must **d** once and then be ....Heb 9:27
are the dead who **d** from now on ....Rev 14:13

DIED

of 930 years, and then he **d.** ....Ge 5:5
that moved on the earth **d.** ....Ge 7:21
last breath and at an old age, ...Ge 25:8
breathed his last breath and **d.** ....Ge 25:17
to the son, but she herself **d.** ....Ge 35:18
Joseph and his brothers **d,** ....Ex 1:6
long time, the king of Egypt **d.** ....Ex 2:23
in the Nile **d,** and the river ....Ex 7:21
The frogs **d** in the houses, ...Ex 8:13
All the farm animals in Egypt **d,** ....Ex 9:6
belonging to Israelites **d.**....................Ex 9:6
and they **d** in front of the LORD. ....Le 10:2
animal that **d** by itself or was ....Le 17:15
who gave a very bad report **d;** ....Nu 14:37
a sword or who **d** a natural death ....Nu 19:16
There Miriam **d** and was buried. ....Nu 20:1
Then Aaron **d** there on top of the ....Nu 20:28
of the LORD, **d** there in Moab, as ....Dt 34:5
twenty years old when he **d.** ....Dt 34:7
stabbed Abimelech, and he **d.**................Jdg 9:54
Elimelech, **d,** and she was left ....Ru 1:3
his neck, and **d,** because he was..............1Sa 4:18
Now Samuel **d,** and all the 1Sa 25:1
the LORD struck Nabal and he **d.** 1Sa 25:38
own sword, and he **d** with Saul. 1Sa 31:5

who had **d** in the battle. 2Sa 1:12
Uriah the Hittite also **d**.'" 2Sa 11:21
Uriah the Hittite also **d**."........................2Sa 11:24
On the seventh day the baby **d**. 2Sa 12:18
I wish I had **d** and not you.....................2Sa 18:33
over on her baby, and he **d**.....................1Ki 3:19
threw stones at him until he **d**. 1Ki 12:18
over Ben-Hadad's face, and he **d**. 2Ki 8:15
Then Elisha **d** and was buried. 2Ki 13:20
evening. Then he **d** at sunset. 2Ch 18:34
Jehoshaphat **d** and was buried 2Ch 21:1
and he **d** in terrible pain. 2Ch 21:19
Then Job **d**; he was old and had ....Job 42:17
In the year that King Uzziah **d**, ...Is 6:1
in the year that King Ahaz **d**: ....Is 14:28
and my wife **d** in the evening.................Eze 24:18
said, "My daughter has just **d**. ....Mt 9:18
Finally, the woman **d**. ....Mt 22:27
Later, Lazarus **d**, and the angels..............Lk 16:22
The rich man **d**, too, and was ....Lk 16:22
The first brother married and **d**,..............Lk 20:29
my brother would not have **d**...............Jn 11:21
my brother would not have **d**." ....Jn 11:32
has been four days since he **d**. ....Jn 11:39
Egypt, where he and his sons **d**...............Ac 7:15
and he was eaten by worms and **d**............Ac 12:23
time, Christ **d** for us, although ....Rm 5:6
Many people **d** because of the sin ....Rm 5:15
We **d** to our old sinful lives, ...Rm 6:2
d, and we have been joined.....................Rm 6:5
Yes, when Christ **d**, he died to ....Rm 6:10
and I **d**. The command was meant ....Rm 7:10
wrong, because Christ **d** for him. ....Rm 14:15
for whom Christ **d** is ruined 1Co 8:11
that Christ **d** for our sins, ...1Co 15:3
we know that One **d** for all, ...2Co 5:14
and I **d** to the law so that I can ....Gal 2:19
Jesus **d** so that by our believing ....Gal 3:14
Your old sinful self has **d**, ...Col 3:3
that Jesus **d** and that he rose 1Th 4:14
these great people **d** in faith. ....Heb 11:13
the living things in the sea **d**, ...Rev 8:9

DIES

unclean for her if she **d**. ....Le 21:3
'If a man **d** and has no son,...................Nu 27:8
When someone **d**, do not cut ....Dt 14:1
at that person until he **d**........................Dt 17:5
throw stones at him until he **d**, ...Dt 21:21
that lion **d** of hunger. The cubs ....Job 4:11
and its stump **d** in the dirt, ...Job 14:8
One person **d** while he still has ....Job 21:23
another person **d** with an unhappy...........Job 21:25
wicked die, hope **d** with them; ....Pr 11:7
a married man **d** without having ....Mt 22:24
wrote that if a man's brother **d**, ...Mk 12:19
a man's brother **d** and leaves a ....Lk 20:28
Sir, come before my child **d**." ....Jn 4:49
But if it never **d**, it remains ....Jn 12:24
if her husband **d**, she is free ....Rm 7:2
this body that **d** must clothe 1Co 15:53
this body that **d** will clothe 1Co 15:54

DIFFERENCE

know the **d** between unclean ....Le 11:47
will know the **d** between right 1Ki 3:9
could tell the **d** between the ....Ezr 3:13
I can tell the **d** between right ....Job 6:30
They make no **d** between holy and...........Eze 22:26
there is no **d** between clean ....Eze 22:26
my people the **d** between what is ....Eze 44:23
again see the **d** between good................Mal 3:18
there is no **d** between those who ....Rm 10:12
to know the **d** between good 1Co 12:10

there is no **d** between Jew and ....Gal 3:28
you will see the **d** between good.............Php 1:10
there is no **d** between Greeks ....Col 3:11
There is no **d** between slaves and ....Col 3:11
enough to know the **d** between ....Heb 5:14

DIFFERENCES

to have **d** among you so that 1Co 11:19

DIFFERENT

think they are **d** from other ....Nu 23:9
Don't plant two **d** kinds of seeds ....Dt 22:9
customs are **d** from those of all ....Est 3:8
animal was **d** from any animal I.............Da 7:7
to speak in **d** kinds of languages 1Co 12:10
gospel that is **d** from the Spirit 2Co 11:4
something **d** than the Good News. ....Gal 1:6

DIFFICULT

attack, may be too **d** to judge...................Dt 17:8
understand, whose language is **d**. ....Eze 3:5
language is **d**, whose words you ....Eze 3:6
may think it is too **d** to happen, ...Zch 8:6
but it is not too **d** for me," ....Zch 8:6

DIFFICULTIES

in troubles, in **d**, and in great 2Co 6:4
remember our hard work and **d**...............1Th 2:9

DIG

you did not **d**, and vineyards ....Dt 6:11
and where you can **d** copper out ....Dt 8:9
me, "Human, **d** through the wall. ....Eze 8:8
If they **d** down as deep as the ....Am 9:2
Let me **d** up the dirt around it.................Lk 13:8

DIM

afraid, and now our eyes are **d**. ....La 5:17
Now we see a **d** reflection, ...1Co 13:12

DIMNAH

D, and Nahalal, and the pastures ....Jos 21:35

DIMONAH

Kinah, **D**, Adadah, ...Jos 15:22

DINAH

Shechem fell in love with **D**, ...Ge 34:3
had disgraced their sister **D**. ....Ge 34:13

DINNER

until he has finished his **d**. ....Ru 3:3
Jesus was having **d** at Matthew's ....Mt 9:10
and his **d** guests had heard him................Mt 14:9
best bulls and calves for the **d**, ...Mt 22:4
was having **d** at Levi's house ....Mk 2:15
he gave a **d** party for the most ....Mk 6:21
and his **d** guests had heard it.................Mk 6:26
Levi gave a big **d** for Jesus at ....Lk 5:29
When you give a lunch or a **d**, ...Lk 14:12
There they had a **d** for Jesus. ....Jn 12:2

DIONYSIUS

Among those who believed was **D**,............Ac 17:34

DIP

d it into the bowl filled with ....Ex 12:22
The priest is to **d** his finger.....................Le 4:6
these he will **d** into the blood ....Le 14:6
He will **d** a finger of his right ....Le 14:16
he will **d** them into the blood ....Le 14:51
branch and **d** it into the water ....Nu 19:18
our bread and **d** it in our sauce. ....Ru 2:14
Send Lazarus to **d** his finger in ....Lk 16:24
I will **d** this bread into the ....Jn 13:26

DIPPED

killed a goat and **d** Joseph's ....Ge 37:31
and he **d** his finger in the blood ....Le 9:9
he **d** the end of his stick into 1Sa 14:27
went down and **d** in the Jordan 2Ki 5:14

DIPPING
a blanket and **d** it in water. 2Ki 8:15
The man who has **d** his hand with .... Mt 26:23
piece of bread, **d** it, and gave .... Jn 13:26
is dressed in a robe **d** in blood, ... Rev 19:13

DIPPING
D his finger in the blood, ... Le 4:17

DIPS
the one who **d** his bread into the .... Mk 14:20

DIRECT
of Jacob's **d** descendants who................. Ge 46:26
the priest, will **d** their work. .... Nu 4:28
the priest, will **d** their work." .... Nu 4:33
thousand Levites will **d** the work 1Ch 23:4
hundred men to **d** the workers. 2Ch 2:2
of them to **d** the workers and to 2Ch 2:18
fifty of them to **d** the people. 2Ch 8:10
he can **d** it as he pleases. .... Pr 21:1

DIRECTED
the priest, **d** the work of all.................... Nu 7:8
hundred men who **d** the workers. 1Ki 5:16
to preach, and Asaph **d** his sons. 1Ch 25:2
of them, and Jeduthun **d** them. 1Ch 25:3
Heman **d** all his sons in making 1Ch 25:6
for the Baal gods as Josiah **d**.................. 2Ch 34:4
in every town, as I **d** you. .... Tit 1:5

DIRECTING
responsibility of **d** the tribes 1Ch 26:32

DIRECTION
around in every **d** on its eastern .... Ge 3:24
land of Egypt in the **d** of Zoar. .... Ge 13:10
quail a day's walk in any **d**. .... Nu 11:31
feet in each **d** outside the city .... Nu 35:5
They will attack you from one **d**, ... Dt 28:7
You will attack them from one **d**, ... Dt 28:25
who could not escape in any **d**. .... Jos 8:20
soldiers running in every **d**. 1Sa 14:16
Ahab went in one **d** and Obadiah 1Ki 18:6
came from the **d** of Edom and 2Ki 3:20
blows from one **d** and then .... Ec 1:6
people led them in the wrong **d**, ... Is 9:16
and will start in that **d**. .... Je 50:5
wall and led me in the wrong **d**. .... La 3:9
in every **d** as I chase them .... Eze 5:12
came from the **d** of the upper .... Eze 9:2
I will scatter in every **d**, ... Eze 12:14
LORD and praying to him for **d**............... Zph 1:6

DIRECTIONS
will run from you in seven **d**. .... Dt 28:7
will run from them in seven **d**. .... Dt 28:25
gave Solomon **d** for the groups 1Ch 28:13
went in any one of the four **d**,................. Eze 1:17
in any of the **d** that the four .... Eze 10:11
was blowing from all four **d**, ... Da 7:2
four different **d** and were easy .... Da 8:8

DIRECTLY
did not speak **d** to people very 1Sa 3:1
had not spoken **d** to him yet. 1Sa 3:7

DIRT
back like **d** for them to walk .... Is 51:23

DISAPPEAR
Let them **d** like water that flows............. Ps 58:7
when you rise up, they will **d**.................. Ps 73:20
their teeth in anger and then **d**. .... Ps 112:10

DISAPPEARS
As a cloud **d** and is gone, people .... Job 7:9
Water from a lake, and a river .... Job 14:11

DISAPPOINT
protection will only **d** you. .... Is 30:3
And this hope will never **d** us, ... Rm 5:5

DISAPPROVED
They **d** of Saul and refused to................ 1Sa 10:27

DISASTER
evil people and **d** for those who .... Job 31:3
I am bringing **d** from the north .... Je 4:6
out my plans to bring **d** to them. .... Je 18:8
Disaster will come on top of **d**, ... Eze 7:26
God for the **d** of the hail, ... Rev 16:21
because this **d** was so terrible. .... Rev 16:21

DISASTERS
will see the **d** that come to this .... Dt 29:22
bringing the seven **d** came out of .... Rev 15:6
not receive the **d** that will come .... Rev 18:4

DISCHARGE
for a man or woman who has a **d**, ... Le 15:33

DISCIPLINE
but fools hate wisdom and **d**. .... Pr 1:7
do not reject the LORD's **d**,..................... Pr 3:11
the Lord's **d** is worth nothing .... Heb 12:5
they are like a father's **d**. .... Heb 12:7
that we accept **d** from the Father .... Heb 12:9

DISCIPLINED
children are **d** by their fathers. .... Heb 12:7
you are never **d** (and every child .... Heb 12:8
child must be **d**), you are not .... Heb 12:8
fathers here on earth who **d** us, ... Heb 12:9
fathers on earth **d** us for a .... Heb 12:10
We do not enjoy being **d**. .... Heb 12:11

DISCIPLINES
he **d** us so that we will not be 1Co 11:32
The Lord **d** those he loves, ... Heb 12:6
But God **d** us to help us, so we .... Heb 12:10

DISCOURAGE
You will **d** the Israelites from .... Nu 32:7
them tried to **d** the people of .... Ezr 4:4

DISCOURAGED
They were **d**, and their slavery .... Ex 6:9
they **d** the Israelites from going .... Nu 32:9
to Saul, "Don't let anyone be **d**. 1Sa 17:32
Don't be afraid or **d**. 1Ch 22:13
be afraid or **d**, because the LORD 1Ch 28:20
be afraid or **d** because of this 2Ch 20:15
be afraid or **d**, because the LORD 2Ch 20:17
comes to you, and you are **d**; .... Job 4:5
when he is **d** and tells the LORD .... Ps 101:8
and thirsty, and they were **d**. .... Ps 107:5
news. They are **d**. They are..................... Je 49:23
ask you not to become **d** because .... Eph 3:13

DISCUSS
So come, let's **d** this together. .... Ne 6:7
I will **d** your rules with kings .... Ps 119:46
I will **d** the things you wrote 1Co 7:1

DISCUSSION
They have nothing to say in a **d**............... Pr 24:7

DISEASE
you to have **d** and fever that .... Le 26:16
with the skin **d** came to the edge 2Ki 7:8
struck Uzziah with a skin **d**, ... 2Ki 15:5
became sick with a terrible **d**.................. Ps 106:29
Immediately the **d** disappeared. .... Lk 5:13
who had a skin **d** met him there. .... Lk 17:12
starvation, by **d**, and by the .... Rev 6:8

DISEASES
give you all the **d** of Egypt that .... Dt 28:60
all my sins and heals all my **d**. .... Ps 103:3
from different kinds of **d**. .... Mt 4:24
people with skin **d** are healed. .... Lk 7:22

DISGRACE
young, and their lives end in **d**. .... Job 36:14
D them and destroy them. .... Ps 83:17
left alone will **d** their mother. .... Pr 29:15
will be filled with **d**, ... Hab 2:16
did not want to **d** her in public, ... Mt 1:19
honor of suffering **d** for Jesus. .... Ac 5:41

DISGRACED
to you, so do not let me be **d**. .... Ps 31:17
the wicked be **d** and lie silent .... Ps 31:17
with you will be ashamed and **d**. .... Is 41:11
and I know I will not be **d**. .... Is 50:7
you to be hated and **d** in front .... Mal 2:9

DISGRACEFUL
She has done a **d** thing in Israel .... Dt 22:21
and has done a **d** thing among .... Jos 7:15
but a **d** wife is like a disease .... Pr 12:4
wicked do shameful and **d** things. .... Pr 13:5
the master's **d** child and will .... Pr 17:2
they love these **d** ways. .... Hos 4:18
pay for the **d** things they have .... Hos 12:14

DISGUISE
on other clothes to **d** himself, ... 1Sa 28:8

DISGUST
he looked down on David with **d**. 1Sa 17:42
and you sniff at it in **d**," .... Mal 1:13

DISGUSTED
other people to be **d** with them. 2Ch 30:7

DISH
or baked in a **d** belongs to the .... Le 7:9
a person wipes a **d** and turns it 2Ki 21:13
be used to make each gold **d**. 1Ch 28:17
be used to make each silver **d** 1Ch 28:17
person puts his hand in the **d**, ... Pr 19:24
may put their hands in the **d**, ... Pr 26:15
outside of the cup and the **d**, ... Lk 11:39
will dip this bread into the **d**. .... Jn 13:26

DISHONEST
anyone who is **d** and uses .... Dt 25:16
dishonest and uses **d** measures. .... Dt 25:16
If I have been **d** or lied to .... Job 31:5
No one who is **d** will live in my .... Ps 101:7
Don't let me be **d**; .... Ps 119:29
They are liars; they are **d**. .... Ps 144:8
They are liars; they are **d**. .... Ps 144:11
is wrong, and their ways are **d**. .... Pr 2:15
but the **d** will be caught. .... Pr 10:9
The Lord hates **d** scales, but he .... Pr 11:1
but a **d** witness tells lies. .... Pr 12:17
but a foolish person is **d**. .... Pr 14:8
but **d** words crush the spirit. .... Pr 15:4
right than to be wealthy and **d**. .... Pr 16:8
d weights and dishonest measures. .... Pr 20:10
weights and **d** measures. .... Pr 20:10
The Lord hates **d** weights, and .... Pr 20:23
and **d** scales do not please him. .... Pr 20:23
Guilty people live **d** lives, ... Pr 21:8
refuses to take **d** money will .... Pr 28:16
those who are **d** will suddenly be .... Pr 28:18
people hate those who are **d**, ... Pr 29:27
Keep me from lying and being **d**. .... Pr 30:8
they were **d** in order to make .... Is 57:17
lives. They are **d**. Anyone who .... Is 59:8
Why do **d** people have such easy .... Je 12:1
your many sins and **d** trade. .... Eze 28:18
trustworthy and not lazy or **d**. .... Da 6:4
The merchants use **d** scales; .... Hos 12:7
praised the **d** manager for being. .... Lk 16:8
and whoever is **d** with a little .... Lk 16:10

with a little is **d** with a lot. .... Lk 16:10
kind, but also those who are **d**. 1Pe 2:18

DISHONOR
Do not **d** your daughter by .... Le 19:29
he must not **d** his father in this .... Dt 22:30
it is a **d** to his father." .... Dt 27:20
I will **d** those who ignore me. 1Sa 2:30
rulers down to the ground in **d**. .... La 2:2
as treasure, and they will **d** it. .... Eze 7:21
and they will **d** my treasured .... Eze 7:22
robbers will enter and **d** it. .... Eze 7:22
not continue to **d** my holy name .... Eze 20:39
holy things and **d** my Sabbaths. .... Eze 22:8
at that very time to **d** it. .... Eze 23:39
I am going to **d** my Temple. .... Eze 24:21
and they will **d** your greatness. .... Eze 28:7
I will not let them **d** me. .... Eze 39:25
to my Father, but you **d** me. .... Jn 8:49

DISHONORED
because he has **d** her, and he may .... Dt 22:29
mighty warrior's shield was **d**. 2Sa 1:21
we don't want to see the king **d**. .... Ezr 4:14
and their holy places will be **d**. .... Eze 7:24
you have **d** me among my people. .... Eze 13:19
it would not be **d** in full view .... Eze 20:9
They **d** my Sabbaths. .... Eze 20:13
it would not be **d** in full view .... Eze 20:14
They **d** my Sabbaths and wanted to .... Eze 20:16
They **d** my Sabbaths. .... Eze 20:21
it would not be **d** in full view .... Eze 20:22
my rules and **d** my Sabbaths .... Eze 20:24
will be **d** in the sight of the .... Eze 22:16
my Sabbaths, so I am **d** by them. .... Eze 22:26
same time they **d** my Sabbaths. .... Eze 23:38
were glad when my Temple was **d**, ... Eze 25:3
You **d** your places of worship .... Eze 28:18
They **d** my holy name in the .... Eze 36:20
Israel had **d** among the nations .... Eze 36:21
which you have **d** among the .... Eze 36:22
which has been **d** among the .... Eze 36:23
You have **d** it among these .... Eze 36:23
not let myself be **d** anymore. .... Eze 39:7
You **d** my Temple when you offered .... Eze 44:7

DISHONORS
will be cursed who **d** his father .... Dt 27:16

DISLIKES
breath, and my own family **d** me. .... Job 19:17

DISOBEDIENCE
D is as bad as the sin of 1Sa 15:23
a place where **d** has started. .... Ezr 4:15
a history of **d** to kings and has .... Ezr 4:19

DISOBEDIENT
If these **d** people are sorry for .... Le 26:41
know how stubborn and **d** you are. .... Dt 31:27
But they were **d** and turned .... Ne 9:26
were stubborn, unwilling, and **d**. .... Ne 9:29
who were stubborn and **d**. .... Ps 78:8
D people look only for trouble, ... Pr 17:11

DISOBEY
but I cannot **d** the Lord my God .... Nu 22:18
So do not **d** the commands I am .... Dt 11:28
Do not **d** anything I command you .... Dt 28:14
will **d** even more after I die! .... Dt 31:27
to the Lord and **d** my command?" 1Ki 2:43
'Why do you **d** the Lord's 2Ch 24:20
my demands and **d** my commands, ... Ps 89:31
Those who **d** what they have been .... Pr 28:4
to hurt others and to **d** God, ... Is 59:13
' you will **d** the Lord your God. .... Je 42:13
no law, there is nothing to **d**. .... Rm 4:15

people who **d** and are stubborn. .... Rm 10:21
not afraid to **d** the king's order .... Heb 11:23

DISPLAYED
death and his body **d** on a tree. .... Dt 21:22
whose body is **d** on a tree is .... Dt 21:23
whose body is **d** on a tree is .... Gal 3:13

DISPLEASE
do anything to **d** the Philistine 1Sa 29:7
chose to do things that **d** me." .... Is 65:12

DISPLEASED
The LORD was **d** by this wicked............... Ge 38:10
the king's officers **d** the king— .... Ge 40:1
He showed he was **d** with their .... Ps 107:40
The LORD will notice and be **d**. .... Pr 24:18
find any justice, and he was **d**. .... Is 59:15

DISQUALIFIED
myself will not be **d** after I 1Co 9:27

DISQUALIFY
not let anyone **d** you by making .... Col 2:18

DISRESPECT
they will not show **d** anymore. .... Dt 17:13
will be no end to **d** and anger. .... Est 1:18
foolish children **d** their mother. .... Pr 15:20
'How have we shown you **d**?' .... Mal 1:6

DISSOLVE
and stars will **d**, and the sky .... Is 34:4

DISTANCE
away a short **d** and sat down. .... Ge 21:16
up and saw the place in the **d**. .... Ge 22:4
stood a short **d** away to see what .... Ex 2:4
to me and worship me from a **d**............... Ex 24:1
scatter the coals a long **d** away. .... Nu 16:37
a heap a great **d** away at Adam, ... Jos 3:16
standing at a **d** from the cross, ... Mt 27:55
standing at a **d** from the cross, ... Mk 15:40
standing at a **d**, would not even .... Lk 18:13
stood at a **d** and watched. .... Lk 23:49
bridles for a **d** of about one .... Rev 14:20

DISTANT
tune of "The Dove in the **D** Oak." .... Ps 55:23

DISTRESS
them with all kinds of **d**........................ 2Ch 15:6
In my **d**, I said, "God cannot see............... Ps 31:22
In my **d** I said, "All people are .... Ps 116:11
d like a woman having her first .... Je 4:31
with fear. **D** has gripped him. .... Je 50:43
will hear Babylon's cry of **d**. .... Je 50:46
have come out of the great **d**. .... Rev 7:14

DISTRESSED
They are **d** over the land. .... Je 14:2

DISTRICT
to Ephrath, a **d** of Bethlehem,.................. Ge 35:19
powerful in the **d** of Ephrathah .... Ru 4:11
in charge of the **d** governors; 1Ki 4:5
was also over the **d** of Argob in 1Ki 4:13
the only governor over this **d**............... 1Ki 4:19
month one of the **d** governors.................. 1Ki 4:27
officers of the **d** governors will 1Ki 20:14
officers of the **d** governors, ... 1Ki 20:15
officers of the **d** governors 1Ki 20:17
officers of the **d** governors led 1Ki 20:19
we went to the **d** of Judah where .... Ezr 5:8
of half of the **d** of Jerusalem. .... Ne 3:9
of half of the **d** of Jerusalem, ... Ne 3:12
ruler of the **d** of Beth Hakkerem............... Ne 3:14
the ruler of the **d** of Mizpah, ... Ne 3:15
of half of the **d** of Beth Zur. .... Ne 3:16
of half of the **d** of Keilah, ... Ne 3:17

other half of the **d** of Keilah. .... Ne 3:18
of the **d** of Samgar; .... Je 39:3

DISTRICTS
governors over the **d** of Israel, ... 1Ki 4:7
food from their **d** for the king.................. 1Ki 4:7

DISTURBED
have you **d** me by bringing me up?............ 1Sa 28:15

DITCH
Then he dug a **d** around the altar 1Ki 18:32
off the altar and filled the **d**. 1Ki 18:35
dried up the water in the **d**...................... 1Ki 18:38
it falls into a **d** on the Sabbath .... Mt 12:11
you will help it out of the **d**. .... Mt 12:11
both will fall into a **d**." .... Mt 15:14
Both of them will fall into a **d**. .... Lk 6:39

DITCHES
I am not strong enough to dig **d**, ... Lk 16:3

DIVIDE
to **d** the water in two.".......................... Ge 1:6
will **d** them up among the tribes............... Ge 49:7
Throw lots to **d** it among the .... Nu 34:13
d the land the LORD is giving .... Dt 19:3
land when you **d** the land among .... Jos 13:6
you should **d** among yourselves............... Jos 22:8
you and Ziba will **d** the land." 2Sa 19:29
innocent will **d** up their silver.................. Job 27:17
Will they **d** it up among the .... Job 41:6
I will **d** Shechem and measure off .... Ps 60:6
In camp they **d** the wealth taken .... Ps 68:12
I will **d** Shechem and measure off .... Ps 108:7
We will **d** the land for ourselves .... Is 7:6
He will **d** it into seven small .... Is 11:15
land you will **d** among the tribes .... Eze 48:29
your land and **d** it among .... Am 7:17
to throw lots to **d** the land. .... Mic 2:5
No, I tell you, I came to **d** it. .... Lk 12:51
owned and then **d** the money and .... Ac 2:45
These are the people who **d** you, ... Jud 1:19

DIVIDED
d the light from the darkness.................. Ge 1:4
completely **d** and that chews .... Le 11:3
Then Joshua **d** the land among the............ Jos 11:23
the land and **d** it among the .... Jos 12:7
of each tribe **d** up the land by.................. Jos 19:51
Gideon **d** the three hundred men .... Jdg 7:16
next morning Saul **d** his soldiers 1Sa 11:11
Israel were **d** into two groups. 1Ki 16:21
The water **d** to the right and to 2Ki 2:8
The work was **d** by lots among the............ 1Ch 24:6
You **d** the sea in front of our .... Ne 9:11
They **d** my clothes among them,............... Ps 22:18
the country is **d** up among them............... Ec 5:9
Their land is **d** by rivers.......................... Is 18:2
who **d** the water before them to .... Is 63:12
holy area will be **d** among these............... Eze 48:10
kingdom will be a **d** kingdom. .... Da 2:41
kingdom is being **d** and will be .... Da 5:28
broken up and **d** out toward the .... Da 11:4
other nations. They **d** up my land .... Joe 3:2
from me and **d** our fields among .... Mic 2:4
have taken and will be **d** among you. .... Zch 14:1
kingdom that is **d** against itself .... Mt 12:25
Jesus **d** the bread and gave it to .... Mt 14:19
d the bread and gave it to his .... Mk 6:41
he **d** the two fish among them .... Mk 6:41
Jesus and **d** his clothes among .... Mk 15:24
Then he **d** the food and gave it .... Lk 9:16
kingdom that is **d** against itself .... Lk 11:17
family that is **d** against itself .... Lk 11:17
his clothes and **d** them into four............... Jn 19:23
They **d** my clothes among them,............... Jn 19:24

But the city was **d**. Some of the .... Ac 14:4
Sadducees, and the group was **d**. .... Ac 23:7
Christ has been **d** up into 1Co 1:13
together as a church you are **d**, ... 1Co 11:18

DIVIDES
the evening he **d** what he has .... Ge 49:27
where the road and one way .... Eze 21:19
has come to where the road **d**, ... Eze 21:21

DIVIDING
wings without **d** it into two .... Le 1:17
lands, **d** up the human race. .... Dt 32:8
leaders finished **d** the land and .... Jos 19:49
they were finished **d** the land.................. Jos 19:51
Surely they are **d** those things .... Jdg 5:30

DIVING
like an eagle **d** down from the .... Je 48:40

DIVISION
thousand men in his **d**. 1Ch 27:13
named one from each family **d**. .... Ezr 10:16

DIVISIONS
and list them by their **d**. .... Nu 1:3
of the **d** serving the king......................... 1Ch 28:1
other, causing **d** among people, ... Gal 5:20

DIVORCE
and he may not **d** her as long as.............. Dt 22:19
he may never **d** her for as long .... Dt 22:29
He writes out **d** papers for her, ... Dt 24:1
he writes out **d** papers for her, ... Dt 24:3
all promised to **d** their wives, ... Ezr 10:19
God of Israel says, "I hate **d**. .... Mal 2:16
so he planned to **d** her secretly. .... Mt 1:19
give her a written **d** paper.' .... Mt 5:31
for a man to **d** his wife is if.................... Mt 5:32
for a man to **d** his wife is if.................... Mt 19:9
reason a man can **d** his wife, ... Mt 19:10
again about the question of **d**. .... Mk 10:10
husband should not **d** his wife. 1Co 7:11
with him, he must not **d** her. 1Co 7:12
with her, she must not **d** him. 1Co 7:13

DIVORCED
unclean prostitute or a **d** woman, ... Le 21:7
not marry a widow, a **d** woman, or............ Le 21:14
daughter becomes widowed or **d**, ... Le 22:13
If a widow or **d** woman makes a.............. Nu 30:9
first husband who **d** her must not .... Dt 24:4
Israel, you say I **d** your mother. .... Is 50:1
Judah saw that I **d** unfaithful .... Je 3:8
not marry widows or **d** women. .... Eze 44:22
marries that **d** woman is guilty .... Mt 5:32
who marries a **d** woman is also .... Lk 16:18

DIVORCES
If a man **d** his wife and she.................... Je 3:1
'Anyone who **d** his wife must give .... Mt 5:31
anyone who **d** his wife forces .... Mt 5:32
you that anyone who **d** his wife .... Mt 19:9
Anyone who **d** his wife and .... Mk 10:11
And the woman who **d** her husband .... Mk 10:12
If a man **d** his wife and marries .... Lk 16:18

DIZAHAB
Tophel, Laban, Hazeroth, and **D**. .... Dt 1:1

DIZZY
You will feel **d** as if you're in .... Pr 23:34

DO-NOTHING
I call that country Rahab the **D**. .... Is 30:7

DOCTOR
Isn't there a **d** there? .... Je 8:22
the healthy people who need a **d**, ... Mt 9:12
the healthy people who need a **d**, ... Mk 2:17
old saying: 'D, heal yourself. .... Lk 4:23

the healthy people who need a **d**, ... Lk 5:31
friend Luke, the **d**, greet you. .... Col 4:14

DOCTORS
commanded the **d** who served him............ Ge 50:2
the **d** prepared Jacob's body to .... Ge 50:2
It took the **d** forty days to .... Ge 50:3
D prepared his body for burial, ... Ge 50:26
the LORD, but only from the **d**. 2Ch 16:12
You are worthless **d**, all of you! .... Job 13:4
much from many **d** and had spent .... Mk 5:26

DOE
To the tune of "The **D** of Dawn." .... Ps 21:13

DOG
not even a **d** will bark at the .... Ex 11:7
up like a **d** and those who bend .... Jdg 7:5
mouths, lapping it as a **d** does. .... Jdg 7:6
think I am a **d**, that you come.................. 1Sa 17:43
are chasing a dead **d** or a flea. 1Sa 24:14
I am no better than a dead **d**!" 2Sa 9:8
should this dead **d** curse you, ... 2Sa 16:9
said, "Am I a **d**? How could I do 2Ki 8:13
is like a **d** that goes back to .... Pr 26:11
like grabbing a **d** by the ears. .... Pr 26:17
even a live **d** is better off than .... Ec 9:4
A **d** goes back to what it has 2Pe 2:22

DOGS
Instead, give it to the **d**. .... Ex 22:31
in the city will be eaten by **d**, ... 1Ki 14:11
in the city will be eaten by **d**, ... 1Ki 16:4
same place the **d** licked up 1Ki 21:19
'D will eat the body of Jezebel 1Ki 21:23
in the city will be eaten by **d**, ... 1Ki 21:24
and the **d** licked his blood from 1Ki 22:38
The **d** will eat Jezebel at 2Ki 9:10
fathers sit with my sheep **d**. .... Job 30:1
like **d** they have trapped me. .... Ps 22:16
are like quiet **d** that don't know .... Is 56:10
are like hungry **d** that are never.............. Is 56:11
Don't give holy things to **d**,...................... Mt 7:6
bread and give it to the **d**." .... Mt 15:26
the **d** would come and lick his .... Lk 16:21
who are like **d**, who demand to .... Php 3:2

DOME
something like a **d** that sparkled .... Eze 1:22
And under the **d** the wings of the .... Eze 1:23
from above the **d** over the heads.............. Eze 1:25
Now above the **d** there was...................... Eze 1:26
and saw in the **d** above the heads .... Eze 10:1

DONATED
d about three hundred eighty 1Ch 29:7

DONKEY
the morning and saddled his **d**. .... Ge 22:3
is like a strong **d** who lies down .... Ge 49:14
them on a **d**, and started back .... Ex 4:20
every firstborn by offering a .... Ex 13:13
or his ox or his **d**, or anything .... Ex 20:17
man's ox or **d** comes and falls .... Ex 21:33
When the **d** saw the angel of the .... Nu 22:23
But the **d** said to Balaam, ... Nu 22:30
your ox, your **d**, or any of your .... Dt 5:14
When she got down from her **d**, ... Jos 15:18
found the jawbone of a dead **d**, ... Jdg 15:15
and a **d** knows where its owner .... Is 1:3
They will bury him like a **d**, ... Je 22:19
is like a wild **d** all by itself...................... Hos 8:9
He is gentle and riding on a **d**, ... Zch 9:9
quickly find a **d** tied there with .... Mt 21:2
He is gentle and riding on a **d**, ... Mt 21:5
But a **d**, which cannot talk, told 2Pe 2:16

DONKEYS

male and female **d,** male and .... Ge 12:16
make us slaves, and take our **d."** .... Ge 43:18
ride on white **d** and sit on .... Jdg 5:10
and food for our **d** and bread and .... Jdg 19:19
Now the **d** of Saul's father, ... 1Sa 9:3
plowing and the **d** were eating .... Job 1:14
become like wild **d** in the desert............. Job 24:5
the wild **d** come there to drink. .... Ps 104:11
the wild **d** and was fed grass .... Da 5:21
mules, camels, **d,** and all the .... Zch 14:15
you why you are taking the **d,** .... Mt 21:3

DOOMED

and it is **d** to destruction. .... Mic 2:10

DOOR

Put a **d** in the side of the boat. .... Ge 6:16
LORD closed the **d** behind them. .... Ge 7:16
them, closing the **d** behind him. .... Ge 19:6
were ready to break down the **d.** .... Ge 19:9
staying with Lot opened the **d,** .... Ge 19:10
outside the **d** with blindness, ... Ge 19:11
to him at the **d** of the house. .... Ge 43:19
to take him to a **d** or doorframe .... Ex 21:6
the meat at the **d** of the Meeting............. Le 8:31
awl through his ear into the **d;** .... Dt 15:17
brought to the **d** of her father's .... Dt 22:21
they locked the **d** behind them. .... Jdg 9:51
approached the **d** of the tower to .... Jdg 9:52
the house and beat on the **d.** .... Jdg 19:22
fell down at the **d** and lay there .... Jdg 19:26
he opened the **d** of the house and .... Jdg 19:27
outside the **d** of the palace as 2Sa 11:9
from me! Lock the **d** after her." 2Sa 13:17
room and bolted the **d** after her............... 2Sa 13:18
there was a square **d** frame made 1Ki 6:33
d had two parts so the doors 1Ki 6:34
heard her walking to the **d,** 1Ki 14:6
house and shut the **d** behind you 2Ki 4:4
and shut the **d** behind her and 2Ki 4:5
Then she shut the **d** and left. 2Ki 4:21
entered the room and shut the **d,** 2Ki 4:33
house and stood outside the **d.** 2Ki 5:9
arrives, shut the **d** and hold it; 2Ki 6:32
' Then open the **d** and run away............... 2Ki 9:3
opened the **d** and ran away. 2Ki 9:10
at the front **d** of the Temple 2Ki 23:11
at my neighbor's **d** for his wife, ... Job 31:9
even go near the **d** of her house,............. Pr 5:8
watching at my **d** every day, ... Pr 8:34
She sits at the **d** of her house .... Pr 9:14
bow down at the **d** of those who .... Pr 14:19
Like a **d** turning back and forth .... Pr 26:14
up to open the **d** for my lover.................. Sng 5:5
I opened the **d** for my lover, ... Sng 5:6
If she is a **d,** we will protect .... Sng 8:9
the frame around the **d** to shake, ... Is 6:4
If he opens a **d,** no one will be .... Is 22:22
if he closes a **d,** no one will be .... Is 22:22
the Temple where the **d** opened. .... Eze 9:3
stood over the **d** of the Temple. .... Eze 10:4
LORD left the **d** of the Temple .... Eze 10:18
from one **d** to the opposite door............... Eze 40:13
a room with a **d** that opened onto .... Eze 40:38
One **d** faced north, and the other .... Eze 41:11
me back to the **d** of the Temple, ... Eze 47:1
Valley of Trouble a **d** of hope.................. Hos 2:15
and close the **d** and pray to your .... Mt 6:6
and the **d** will open for you. .... Mt 7:7
knocks will have the **d** opened. .... Mt 7:8
You close the **d** for people to .... Mt 23:13
the **d** was closed and locked. .... Mt 25:10
Sir, sir, open the **d** to let us .... Mt 25:11

whole town gathered at the **d.** .... Mk 1:33
house, not even outside the **d**................... Mk 2:2
street near the **d** of a house, ... Mk 11:4
guarding the **d** always to be .... Mk 13:34
The **d** is already locked, and my .... Lk 11:7
and the **d** will open for you. .... Lk 11:9
knocks will have the **d** opened. .... Lk 11:10
immediately open the **d** for him............... Lk 12:36
to enter through the narrow **d,** .... Lk 13:24
house gets up and closes the **d,** .... Lk 13:25
enter the sheepfold by the **d,** .... Jn 10:1
enters by the **d** is the shepherd .... Jn 10:2
who guards the **d** opens it for .... Jn 10:3
truth, I am the **d** for the sheep. .... Jn 10:7
I am the **d,** and the person who .... Jn 10:9
Peter waited outside near the **d.** .... Jn 18:16
The girl at the **d** said to Peter, ... Jn 18:17
your husband are at the **d,** .... Ac 5:9
were guarding the **d** of the jail. .... Ac 12:6
Peter knocked on the outside **d,** .... Ac 12:13
happy she forgot to open the **d.** .... Ac 12:14
and when they opened the **d,** .... Ac 12:16
When he opens a **d,** no one can .... Rev 3:7
I have put an open **d** before you, ... Rev 3:8
I stand at the **d** and knock. .... Rev 3:20
hear my voice and open the **d,** .... Rev 3:20
me was an open **d** in heaven. .... Rev 4:1

DOORFRAME

to a door or **d** and punch a hole .... Ex 21:6

DOORKEEPER

rather be a **d** in the Temple...................... Ps 84:10
of Shallum, the **d** in the Temple.............. Je 35:4

DOORPOST

and their **d** next to my doorpost .... Eze 43:8

DOORSILL

house, with her hands on the **d.** .... Jdg 19:27
Ashdod refuse to step on the **d.** 1Sa 5:5

DOORWAY

was lying at the **d** of the house, ... Jdg 19:27
off and were lying in the **d**..................... 1Sa 5:4
called her, she stood in the **d.** 2Ki 4:15
guarding the **d** put all the money 2Ki 12:9
eunuchs who guarded the **d.** .... Est 2:21
in the hall, facing the **d.** .... Est 5:1
who guarded the **d** and who had .... Est 6:2
every day, waiting at my open **d.** .... Pr 8:34
The **d** was twenty-four and..................... Eze 40:48
the side walls of the next **d.** .... Eze 41:3
By the **d,** the Temple had wood .... Eze 41:16
by putting their **d** next to my .... Eze 43:8
from under the **d** and flowing................. Eze 47:1

DOR

king of Naphoth **D** in the west .... Jos 11:2
D (in Naphoth Dor), Goyim in .... Jos 12:23
who lived in **D** and its small .... Jos 17:11
safety), Hammoth **D,** and Kartan, ... Jos 21:32
Shan, Taanach, **D,** Ibleam, ... Jdg 1:27
was governor of Naphoth **D.** 1Ki 4:11
Megiddo, and **D,** and the villages 1Ch 7:29

DORCAS

(whose Greek name was **D**). .... Ac 9:36

DOTHAN

them say they were going to **D."**............... Ge 37:17
back and reported, "He is in **D."** 2Ki 6:13
chariots, and many troops to **D.** 2Ki 6:14

DOUBLE

sixth curtain **d** over the front .... Ex 26:9
and folded **d** to make a pocket. .... Ex 28:16
it was folded **d** to make a pocket .... Ex 39:9
me a **d** share of your spirit...................... 2Ki 2:9

or poke through its **d** armor. .... Job 41:13
will receive a **d** share of the .... Is 61:7
D shelves three inches wide were .... Eze 40:43
the Most Holy Place had **d** doors. .... Eze 41:23
be punished for their **d** sins. .... Hos 10:10
well should receive **d** honor, ... 1Ti 5:17

DOUBLE-EDGED
and is sharper than a **d** sword. .... Heb 4:12
and a sharp **d** sword came out of .... Rev 1:16
the sharp, **d** sword says this: .... Rev 2:12

DOUBLED
frames are to be **d** at the bottom............. Ex 26:24
two frames were **d** at the bottom .... Ex 36:29

DOUBT
faith is small. Why did you **d**?" .... Mt 14:31
if you have faith and do not **d,** .... Mt 21:21
Why do you **d** what you see? .... Lk 24:38
'Listen, you people who **d**! .... Ac 13:41
Without **d,** the secret of our 1Ti 3:16
you must believe and not **d**. .... Jam 1:6

DOUBTED
I smiled at them when they **d,**............... Job 29:24
trusted the LORD and never **d**. .... Ps 26:1
He never **d** that God would keep .... Rm 4:20

DOUBTING
them without **d,** because I have .... Ac 10:20
me to go with them without **d**. .... Ac 11:12

DOUBTS
if you have no **d** in your mind................ Mk 11:23
Anyone who **d** is like a wave in .... Jam 1:6
mercy to some people who have **d.**........... Jud 1:22

DOUGH
took their **d** before the yeast .... Ex 12:34
women make the **d** for cakes of .... Je 7:18

DOVE
sent out the **d** from the boat, ... Ge 8:10
I wish I had wings like a **d.**................... Ps 55:6
tune of "The **D** in the Distant .... Ps 55:23
darling, my **d,** my perfect one. .... Sng 5:2
like a bird and moaned like a **d.** .... Is 38:14
down on him in the form of a **d.**.............. Lk 3:22

DOVES
His eyes are like **d** by springs .... Sng 5:12
We call out sadly like the **d.** .... Is 59:11
as snakes and as innocent as **d.** .... Mt 10:16
of those who were selling **d.** .... Mt 21:12

DOWNSTAIRS
carried the boy **d** and gave him 1Ki 17:23
Get up and go **d.** Go with them .... Ac 10:20

DRAG
Don't **d** me away with the wicked, ... Ps 28:3
D the evil people away like..................... Je 12:3
dogs to **d** the bodies away, ... Je 15:3
He will surely **d** away the young .... Je 49:20
He will surely **d** away the young .... Je 50:45
the enemy will **d** Egypt and all .... Eze 32:20
I will **d** them off, and no one .... Hos 5:14

DRAGGED
at the body, he **d** it from the 2Sa 20:12
their tents and **d** off to Death,............... Job 18:14
at him and **d** him out of town, ... Ac 14:19
Paul and Silas and **d** them before .... Ac 16:19
they **d** Jason and some other .... Ac 17:6
and **d** him out of the Temple. .... Ac 21:30

DRAGON
was a giant red **d** with seven .... Rev 12:3
his angels fought against the **d,** .... Rev 12:7
But the **d** was not strong enough, ... Rev 12:8

The giant **d** was thrown down out .... Rev 12:9
the **d** saw he had been thrown .... Rev 12:13
came from the mouth of the **d.** .... Rev 12:16
Then the **d** was very angry at the .... Rev 12:17
And the **d** stood on the seashore. .... Rev 12:18

DRAGS
But God **d** away the strong by his .... Job 24:22
in his net and **d** them in his .... Hab 1:15

DRAINED
blood must be **d** out on the side .... Le 1:15

DRANK
When he **d** wine made from his .... Ge 9:21
' So I **d,** and she gave water to .... Ge 24:46
with him ate and **d** and spent the .... Ge 24:54
and he ate and **d,** and then left. .... Ge 25:34
them, and they all ate and **d.** .... Ge 26:30
Jacob gave him wine, and he **d.** .... Ge 27:25
because they **d** water from this .... Ge 29:2
ate and **d** freely with him .... Ge 43:34
Then they ate and **d** together. .... Ex 24:11
people and their animals **d** it. .... Nu 20:11
no bread and **d** no wine or beer .... Dt 29:6
You **d** the juice of grapes. .... Dt 32:14
who **d** the wine of their drink................. Dt 32:38
where they ate and **d** and cursed .... Jdg 9:27
When Samson **d,** he felt better; .... Jdg 15:19
and ate, **d,** and slept there. .... Jdg 19:4
so Uriah ate and **d** with David. 2Sa 11:13
his food and **d** from his cup 2Sa 12:3
people ate, **d,** and were happy. 1Ki 4:20
and he ate and **d** with him there. 1Ki 13:19
but you came back and ate and **d.** 1Ki 13:22
and he **d** water from the stream................ 1Ki 17:6
a jar of water, so he ate and **d.** 1Ki 19:6
So Elijah got up and ate and **d.** 1Ki 19:8
they ate and **d,** the king sent 2Ki 6:23
one of the tents and ate and **d.** 2Ki 7:8
into the house and ate and **d.** 2Ki 9:34
people ate and **d** with much joy, ... 1Ch 29:22
for rain and **d** in my words like .... Job 29:23
you **d** the whole cup until you................. Is 51:17
You **d** it and could not walk .... Is 51:22
The nations **d** Babylon's wine, ... Je 51:7
guests and **d** wine with them. .... Da 5:1
and his slave women **d** from them............. Da 5:3
slave women **d** wine from them................ Da 5:23
Because you **d** in my Temple, ... Ob 1:16
you ate and **d,** it was really..................... Zch 7:6
and they all **d** from the cup. .... Mk 14:23
say, 'We ate and **d** with you, and .... Lk 13:26
this well and **d** from it himself .... Jn 4:12
who ate and **d** with him after he.............. Ac 10:41
and all **d** the same spiritual 1Co 10:4
They **d** from that spiritual rock 1Co 10:4

DRAW
and did not **d** it back until all .... Jos 8:26
looks and **d** back in fear as it .... Job 41:25
The wicked **d** their swords and .... Ps 37:14
joy as you would **d** water from a .... Is 12:3
and a compass to **d** on the wood. .... Is 44:13
and **d** a map of Jerusalem on it. .... Eze 4:1
I will **d** all people toward me." .... Jn 12:32

DRAWING
Divide the land by **d** lots, ... Nu 26:55
and small groups by **d** lots." .... Nu 26:56

DRAWN
in the road with his sword **d.** .... Nu 22:31
his sword **d** and pointed at 1Ch 21:16
of Assyria with their swords **d.** .... Mic 5:6

DRAWS

d the horizon like a circle on .... Job 26:10
unless the Father d him to me, ... Jn 6:44

DREAD

diseases of Egypt that you d, ... Dt 28:60
I still d all my suffering. .... Job 9:28
do not d those things. .... Is 8:12
he is the one you should d. .... Is 8:13
do not d those things." 1Pe 3:14

DREADED

I feared and d has happened to .... Job 3:25

DREAM

to Abimelech in a d and said, ... Ge 20:3
God said to Abimelech in the d, ... Ge 20:6
that had happened in the d. .... Ge 20:8
I had a d during the season when .... Ge 31:10
to me in that d and said, ' .... Ge 31:11
the Aramean in a d and said, ... Ge 31:24
Joseph had a d, and when he told .... Ge 37:5
said, "Listen to the d I had...................... Ge 37:6
Then Joseph had another d, ... Ge 37:9
told his father about this d,.................... Ge 37:10
him wine and the baker had a d. .... Ge 40:5
to the king told Joseph his d. .... Ge 40:9
I will explain the d to you. .... Ge 40:12
explanation of the d was good, ... Ge 40:16
will tell you what the d means. .... Ge 40:18
In his d he saw seven full and................. Ge 41:5
and he realized it was only a d. .... Ge 41:7
we each had a d on the same .... Ge 41:11
each man the meaning of his d, ... Ge 41:12
I have had a d, but no one can .... Ge 41:15
In my d I was standing on the .... Ge 41:17
I had another d. I saw seven .... Ge 41:22
I told this d to the magicians, ... Ge 41:24
telling his friend about a d..................... Jdg 7:13
Your d is about the sword of .... Jdg 7:14
heard about the d and what it................ Jdg 7:15
to him in a d during the night. 1Ki 3:5
Solomon woke up from the d,................. 1Ki 3:15
fly away like a d and not be .... Job 20:8
He speaks in a d or a vision of .... Job 33:15
It will be like waking from a d. .... Ps 73:20
Jerusalem will be like a d; .... Is 29:7
lie down and d and love to sleep .... Is 56:10
They say, 'I have had a d! .... Je 23:25
I had a d that bothers me, ... Da 2:3
tell us, your servants, your d, ... Da 2:4
must tell me the d and what it .... Da 2:5
you tell me my d and its meaning .... Da 2:6
servants, the d, and we will .... Da 2:7
If you don't tell me my d, ... Da 2:9
tell the king what his d meant. .... Da 2:16
you told us about the king's d." .... Da 2:23
will tell him what his d means." .... Da 2:24
tell the king what his d means." .... Da 2:25
This is your d, the vision you .... Da 2:28
O king, in your d you saw a huge .... Da 2:31
That was your d. Now we will .... Da 2:36
The d is true, and you can trust .... Da 2:45
but I had a d that made me.................... Da 4:5
me and tell me what my d meant. .... Da 4:6
and I told them about the d. .... Da 4:7
is in him.) I told my d to him. .... Da 4:8
tell me what the d means. .... Da 4:18
of the d frightened me. .... Da 4:19
a tree in your d that grew large .... Da 4:20
This is the meaning of the d, ... Da 4:24
king of Babylon, Daniel had a d. .... Da 7:1
That was the end of the d. .... Da 7:28
of the Lord came to him in a d. .... Mt 1:20
wise men in a d not to go back .... Mt 2:12

came to Joseph in a d and said, ... Mt 2:13
to Joseph in a d while he was.................. Mt 2:19
After being warned in a d, ... Mt 2:22
Today I had a d about him, ... Mt 27:19
and your old men will d dreams. .... Ac 2:17

DREAMED

Jacob d that there was a ladder .... Ge 28:12
He said, "I d I saw a vine, and .... Ge 40:9
I d there were three bread .... Ge 40:16
later the king d he was standing.............. Ge 41:1
slept again and d a second time............... Ge 41:5
I d that a loaf of barley bread .... Jdg 7:13
them to tell him what he had d. .... Da 2:2
tell me what I d and what it .... Da 2:26
This was what I d; tell me what .... Da 4:9
what I, King Nebuchadnezzar, d. .... Da 4:18
and he wrote down what he had d........... Da 7:1

DREAMER

each other, "Here comes that d. .... Ge 37:19

DREAMERS

listen to those prophets or d. .... Dt 13:3
prophets or d must be killed, ... Dt 13:5

DREAMING

it seemed as if we were d. .... Ps 126:1

DREAMS

because of his d and what he had .... Ge 37:8
see what will become of his d." .... Ge 37:20
We both had d last night, ... Ge 40:8
told them his d, but no one .... Ge 41:8
we told him our d, he explained .... Ge 41:12
to explain the meaning of d, ... Ge 41:16
Both of these d mean the same .... Ge 41:25
Both d mean the same thing. .... Ge 41:26
had two d which mean the same .... Ge 41:32
remembered his d about his .... Ge 42:9
drinking and for explaining d. .... Ge 44:5
learn things by signs and d?" .... Ge 44:15
I will speak to them in d. .... Nu 12:6
the future with d might come to .... Dt 13:1
did not answer him through d, ... 1Sa 28:6
either by prophets or in d. 1Sa 28:15
by explaining signs and d, ... 2Ki 21:6
by explaining signs and d. 2Ch 33:6
frighten me with d and terrify .... Job 7:14
who chases empty d is not wise. .... Pr 12:11
who chase empty d instead will .... Pr 28:19
Bad d come from too much...................... Ec 5:3
promises are like so many d; .... Ec 5:7
a hungry man who d he is eating, ... Is 29:8
by telling each other these d. .... Je 23:27
wants to tell about his d,........................ Je 23:28
prophets who prophesy false d," .... Je 23:32
who explain d, the mediums, ... Je 27:9
Don't listen to their d............................. Je 29:8
also understand visions and d. .... Da 1:17
he had d that bothered him and .... Da 2:1
He could explain d and secrets .... Da 5:12
your old men will dream d,..................... Joe 2:28
visions and tell about false d. .... Zch 10:2
and your old men will dream d. .... Ac 2:17
They are guided by d and make .... Jud 1:8

DRENCH

I will d the land with your .... Eze 32:6

DREW

They d water from the ground and........... 1Sa 7:6
and the Israelites d back. 2Sa 23:9
Then Jehu d his bow and shot 2Ki 9:24

DRIED

water had d up from the earth. .... Ge 8:7
if the water had d up from the .... Ge 8:8

water was **d** up from the land. .... Ge 8:13
how the LORD **d** up the Red Sea .... Jos 2:10
that the LORD **d** up the Jordan .... Jos 5:1
bowstrings that have not been **d**. .... Jdg 16:7
bowstrings that had not been **d**, ... Jdg 16:8
the stream **d** up because there 1Ki 17:7
d up the water in the ditch. 1Ki 18:38
d up all the rivers of Egypt. 2Ki 19:24
They lived in **d** up streambeds, ... Job 30:6
My strength has **d** up like a clay. .... Ps 22:15
grass that has been cut and **d**. .... Ps 102:4
shadow; I am like **d** grass. .... Ps 102:11
the Red Sea, and it **d** up. .... Ps 106:9
the water of Nimrim has **d** up. .... Is 15:6
d up all the rivers of Egypt. .... Is 37:25
You **d** up the sea and the waters. .... Is 51:10
the land stay **d** up and the grass .... Je 12:4
and the pastures have **d** up. .... Je 23:10
the waters of Nimrim are **d** up. .... Je 48:34
her waters so they will be **d** up. .... Je 50:38
The east wind **d** it up. .... Eze 19:12
Our bones are **d** up, and our hope .... Eze 37:11
the ground is **d** up. The grain is .... Joe 1:10
and the fig trees are **d** up. .... Joe 1:12
because the grain has **d** up. .... Joe 1:17
The streams of water have **d** up, ... Joe 1:20
another field got none and **d** up. .... Am 4:7
the plants **d** up, because they .... Mt 13:6
The tree immediately **d** up. .... Mt 21:19
the plants **d** up because they did .... Mk 4:6
and she **d** them with her hair, ... Lk 7:38
her tears and **d** them with her .... Lk 7:44
in the river was **d** up to prepare .... Rev 16:12

DRIED-UP

from a vine or **d** figs from a fig .... Is 34:4
give them **d** breasts that cannot .... Hos 9:14

DRIES

river loses its water and **d** up. .... Job 14:11
the roof that **d** up before it has .... Ps 129:6
Because of this the land **d** up, ... Hos 4:3
he **d** up all the rivers. .... Nah 1:4
heat and **d** up the plants. .... Jam 1:11

DRINK

with water and gave the boy a **d**. .... Ge 21:19
put your jar down so I can **d**.' .... Ge 24:14
Rebekah said, "**D**, sir." .... Ge 24:18
all the camels enough to **d**. .... Ge 24:20
me water from your jar to **d**." .... Ge 24:43
let her say, "**D** this water, and .... Ge 24:44
to her, 'Please give me a **d**.' .... Ge 24:45
her shoulder and said, '**D** this. .... Ge 24:46
When the animals came to **d**, ... Ge 30:38
and he poured a **d** offering and .... Ge 35:14
will not be able to **d** the water .... Ex 7:18
could not **d** water from it. .... Ex 7:21
Egyptians could not **d** the water .... Ex 7:24
they could not **d** it because it .... Ex 15:23
and asked, "What will we **d**?" .... Ex 15:24
the water became good to **d**. .... Ex 15:25
water there for the people to **d**. .... Ex 17:1
and said, "Give us water to **d**." .... Ex 17:2
of it so that the people can **d**." .... Ex 17:6
for pouring out the **d** offerings. .... Ex 25:29
a quart of wine as a **d** offering. .... Ex 29:40
offering and **d** offering as you .... Ex 29:41
grain offering, or **d** offering. .... Ex 30:9
They sat down to eat and **d**, ... Ex 32:6
forced the Israelites to **d** it. .... Ex 32:20
he did not eat food or **d** water. .... Ex 34:28
for pouring the **d** offerings. .... Ex 37:16
sons must not **d** wine or beer .... Le 10:9
a quart of wine as a **d** offering. .... Le 23:13

grain offerings and **d** offerings, ... Le 23:18
sacrifices, and **d** offerings—each .... Le 23:37
and the jars for **d** offerings on .... Nu 4:7
the woman of the bitter water .... Nu 5:24
will make the woman **d** the water .... Nu 5:26
they must not **d** wine or beer, ... Nu 6:3
offerings and **d** offerings that .... Nu 6:15
offering, and the **d** offering. .... Nu 6:17
that, the Nazirites may **d** wine. .... Nu 6:20
a quart of wine as a **d** offering. .... Nu 15:5
quarts of wine as a **d** offering. .... Nu 15:7
quarts of wine as a **d** offering. .... Nu 15:10
and the **d** offering with it .... Nu 15:24
and there's no water to **d**!" .... Nu 20:5
and will not **d** water from the .... Nu 20:17
or our animals **d** any of your .... Nu 20:19
or **d** water from the wells. .... Nu 21:22
with each lamb as a **d** offering; .... Nu 28:7
grain offering and a **d** offering. .... Nu 28:8
Also give a **d** offering and a .... Nu 28:9
burnt offering and **d** offering. .... Nu 28:10
The **d** offering with each bull .... Nu 28:14
burnt offerings and **d** offerings, ... Nu 28:15
offering and its **d** offering. .... Nu 28:24
offerings and their **d** offerings .... Nu 28:31
offerings and **d** offerings must .... Nu 29:6
offering, and the **d** offerings. .... Nu 29:11
with its grain and **d** offerings. .... Nu 29:16
the grain and **d** offerings for .... Nu 29:18
with its grain and **d** offerings. .... Nu 29:19
the grain and **d** offerings for .... Nu 29:21
with its grain and **d** offerings. .... Nu 29:22
the grain and **d** offerings for .... Nu 29:24
with its grain and **d** offerings. .... Nu 29:25
the grain and **d** offerings for .... Nu 29:27
with its grain and **d** offerings. .... Nu 29:28
the grain and **d** offerings for .... Nu 29:30
with its grain and **d** offerings. .... Nu 29:31
the grain and **d** offerings for .... Nu 29:33
with its grain and **d** offerings. .... Nu 29:34
the grain and **d** offerings for .... Nu 29:37
with its grain and **d** offerings. .... Nu 29:38
d offerings and fellowship .... Nu 29:39
the people had no water to **d**. .... Nu 33:14
food you eat or water you **d**.'" .... Dt 2:6
any food we eat or water we **d**. .... Dt 2:28
I did not eat bread or **d** water. .... Dt 9:9
I did not eat bread or **d** water. .... Dt 9:18
pick the grapes or **d** the wine, ... Dt 28:39
the wine of their **d** offerings? .... Dt 32:38
Please give me some water to **d**." .... Jdg 4:19
bag of milk and gave him a **d**. .... Jdg 4:19
those who **d** water by lapping .... Jdg 7:5
got down on their knees to **d**. .... Jdg 7:6
Be careful not to **d** wine or beer .... Jdg 13:4
Don't **d** wine or beer or eat .... Jdg 13:7
a grapevine, or **d** any wine or .... Jdg 13:14
sat down to eat and **d** together. .... Jdg 19:6
and had something to eat and **d**. .... Jdg 19:21
you may go and **d** from the water .... Ru 2:9
water to **d** and some food to eat. 1Sa 30:11
to eat and **d** and have sexual 2Sa 11:11
for anyone to **d** who might become 2Sa 16:2
old to taste what I eat or **d**. 2Sa 19:35
David, but he refused to **d** it. 2Sa 23:16
So David refused to **d** it. 2Sa 23:17
will not eat or **d** anything in 1Ki 13:8
not to eat or **d** anything nor to 1Ki 13:9
I can't eat or **d** with you in 1Ki 13:16
'Don't eat or **d** anything there 1Ki 13:17
you should eat and **d** with me." 1Ki 13:18
not to eat or **d** anything in this 1Ki 13:22
You may **d** from the stream, ... 1Ki 17:4

in a cup so I may have a **d**?" 1Ki 17:10
go, eat, and **d,** because a heavy 1Ki 18:41
So King Ahab went to eat and **d.** 1Ki 18:42
and your other animals can **d.** 2Ki 3:17
them eat and **d** and then go home 2Ki 6:22
and poured out his **d** offering. 2Ki 16:13
and the **d** offering for all the 2Ki 16:15
own dung and **d** their own urine 2Ki 18:27
fig tree and to **d** water from his 2Ki 18:31
David, but he refused to **d** it. 1Ch 11:18
So David refused to **d** it. 1Ch 11:19
They also brought **d** offerings. 1Ch 29:21
sandals, food, **d,** and medicine. 2Ch 28:15
offerings and **d** offerings. 2Ch 29:35
offerings and **d** offerings that .... Ezr 7:17
did not eat or **d,** because he was............. Ezr 10:6
people went away to eat and **d,** .... Ne 8:12
permitted to **d** as much as they .... Est 1:8
king and Haman sat down to **d,** .... Est 3:15
do not eat or **d** for three days, ... Est 4:16
sisters to eat and **d** with them. .... Job 1:4
you let them **d** from your river .... Ps 36:8
meat of bulls or **d** the blood of .... Ps 50:13
food and gave me vinegar to **d,** .... Ps 69:21
drop, and the wicked **d** it all. .... Ps 75:8
so no one could **d** the water. .... Ps 78:44
you have made them **d** many tears. .... Ps 80:5
wild donkeys come there to **d.** .... Ps 104:11
The king will **d** from the brook .... Ps 110:7
just as you **d** water from your .... Pr 5:15
my food and **d** the wine I have .... Pr 9:5
you, "Eat and **d,**" but they don't .... Pr 23:7
Don't **d** too much wine or eat too .... Pr 23:20
Those who **d** and eat too much .... Pr 23:21
is people who **d** too much wine, ... Pr 23:30
Then I would get another **d.**" .... Pr 23:35
If he is thirsty, give him a **d.** .... Pr 25:21
is like a cool **d** when you are .... Pr 25:25
Kings should not **d** wine, Lemuel, ... Pr 31:4
If they **d,** they might forget the .... Pr 31:5
Let them **d** and forget their need .... Pr 31:7
do is eat, **d,** and enjoy their..................... Ec 2:24
people to eat and **d** and be happy .... Ec 3:13
should eat and **d** and enjoy their .... Ec 5:18
is to eat, **d,** and enjoy life .... Ec 8:15
d your wine and be happy, ... Ec 9:7
Eat, friends, and **d;** yes, drink.................. Sng 5:1
yes, **d** deeply, lovers. .... Sng 5:1
would give you a **d** of spiced .... Sng 8:2
morning to look for strong **d,** .... Is 5:11
they eat and **d.** Leaders, stand .... Is 21:5
eat the food and **d** the wine. .... Is 22:13
sing while they **d** their wine. .... Is 24:9
or let thirsty people **d** water. .... Is 32:6
own dung and **d** their own urine .... Is 36:12
fig tree and to **d** water from his .... Is 36:16
If he does not **d** water, he .... Is 44:12
The LORD made you **d** that wine; .... Is 51:17
you who are thirsty, come and **d.** .... Is 55:1
say, "Come, let's **d** some wine; .... Is 56:12
You pour **d** offerings on them to............. Is 57:6
let your enemies **d** the new wine .... Is 62:8
grapes will **d** the wine in the .... Is 62:9
My servants will **d,** but you evil .... Is 65:13
to Egypt and **d** from the Shihor .... Je 2:18
given us poisoned water to **d.** .... Je 8:14
food and **d** poisoned water..................... Je 9:15
one will offer a **d** to comfort .... Je 16:7
feast to sit down to eat and **d,**................. Je 16:8
and gave **d** offerings to gods. .... Je 19:13
satisfied to have food and **d.** .... Je 22:15
They will **d** my anger and stumble .... Je 25:16
nations and made them **d** from it. .... Je 25:17

these people **d** of the LORD's .... Je 25:19
kingdoms on earth **d** from the cup .... Je 25:26
of Babylon will **d** from this cup .... Je 25:26
D this cup of my anger. .... Je 25:27
the cup from your hand and **d,** .... Je 25:28
and poured out **d** offerings to .... Je 32:29
and offer them wine to **d.**" .... Je 35:2
I said to them, "**D** some wine." .... Je 35:5
men answered, "We never **d** wine. .... Je 35:6
sons, or daughters ever **d** wine. .... Je 35:8
his descendants not to **d** wine, ... Je 35:14
and pour out **d** offerings to .... Je 44:17
pouring out **d** offerings to her, ... Je 44:18
and to pour out **d** offerings to .... Je 44:19
to pour out **d** offerings to her................ Je 44:25
but they had to **d** from the cup .... Je 49:12
and bowls used for **d** offerings. .... Je 52:19
We have to buy the water we **d;** .... La 5:4
You will **d** about two-thirds of a .... Eze 4:11
They will **d** water that is .... Eze 4:16
with fear as you **d** your water. .... Eze 12:18
food with fear and **d** their water............. Eze 12:19
poured out their **d** offerings. .... Eze 20:28
like a bitter cup to **d.** .... Eze 23:31
You will **d** the same cup your .... Eze 23:32
You will **d** everything in it, ... Eze 23:34
eat your fruit and **d** your milk. .... Eze 25:4
enough for you to **d** clear water? .... Eze 34:18
and must they **d** what you make............. Eze 34:19
Israel. Eat flesh and **d** blood! .... Eze 39:17
of the mighty and **d** the blood of .... Eze 39:18
are to eat and **d** from my .... Eze 39:19
the priests may **d** wine when they .... Eze 44:21
offerings, and **d** offerings. .... Eze 45:17
food or **d** his wine because .... Da 1:8
me to give you this food and **d.** .... Da 1:10
to eat and water to **d.** .... Da 1:12
women could **d** from those cups. .... Da 5:2
or meat, or **d** any wine, or use .... Da 10:3
All you people who **d** wine, ... Joe 1:5
no more grain or **d** offerings to .... Joe 1:9
no more grain or **d** offerings to .... Joe 1:13
Grain and **d** offerings belong to .... Joe 2:14
sold girls to buy wine to **d.** .... Joe 3:3
they buy wine to **d** in the house .... Am 2:8
the Nazirites **d** wine and told .... Am 2:12
"Bring us something to **d!**" .... Am 4:1
they could not get enough to **d.** .... Am 4:8
but you will not **d** the wine from .... Am 5:11
d wine by the bowlful and use .... Am 6:6
vineyards and **d** the wine from .... Am 9:14
the nations will **d** on and on. .... Ob 1:16
let them eat food or **d** water. .... Jnh 3:7
but you will not **d** the new wine. .... Mic 6:15
that makes its neighbors **d,**.................... Hab 2:15
It's your turn to **d** and fall to .... Hab 2:16
they will not **d** any wine from................ Zph 1:13
d, but you are still thirsty. .... Hag 1:6
They will **d** and shout like .... Zch 9:15
the food or **d** you need to live .... Mt 6:25
' or 'What will we **d?**' .... Mt 6:31
did not eat or **d** like other .... Mt 11:18
you **d** the cup that I am about................. Mt 20:22
the cup that I am about to **d?**" .... Mt 20:22
them, "You will **d** from my cup. .... Mt 20:23
a fly out of a **d** and then .... Mt 23:24
and you gave me something to **d.** .... Mt 25:35
and give you something to **d?** .... Mt 25:37
and you gave me nothing to **d.** .... Mt 25:42
said, "Every one of you **d** this. .... Mt 26:27
will not **d** of this fruit of the .... Mt 26:29
Jesus wine mixed with gall to **d.**............. Mt 27:34
stick and gave it to Jesus to **d.** .... Mt 27:48

gives you a **d** of water because .... Mk 9:41
Can you **d** the cup that I must................ Mk 10:38
You will **d** the same cup that I .... Mk 10:39
will not **d** of this fruit of the .... Mk 14:25
wine mixed with myrrh to **d,** .... Mk 15:23
and gave it to Jesus to **d.**...................... Mk 15:36
up snakes and **d** poison without .... Mk 16:18
He will never **d** wine or beer, ... Lk 1:15
Why do you eat and **d** with tax .... Lk 5:30
eat and **d** all the time." .... Lk 5:33
Rest, eat, **d,** and enjoy life!"' .... Lk 12:19
and to eat and **d** and get drunk. .... Lk 12:45
lead them to **d** water every day— .... Lk 13:15
will not **d** again from the fruit .... Lk 22:18
you may eat and **d** at my table in .... Lk 22:30
to her, "Please give me a **d.**" .... Jn 4:7
that you ask me for a **d,** .... Jn 4:9
the Son of Man and **d** his blood............... Jn 6:53
eat my flesh and **d** my blood have .... Jn 6:54
food, and my blood is true **d.** .... Jn 6:55
eat my flesh and **d** my blood live .... Jn 6:56
who is thirsty come to me and **d.** .... Jn 7:37
Shouldn't I **d** the cup the Father .... Jn 18:11
not see and did not eat or **d.** .... Ac 9:9
not to eat or **d** anything until .... Ac 23:12
not to eat or **d** until we have .... Ac 23:14
not to eat or **d** until they have................ Ac 23:21
if he is thirsty, give him a **d.** .... Rm 12:20
not to eat meat or **d** wine or do .... Rm 14:21
enough to eat or **d** or to wear.................. 1Co 4:11
not have the right to eat and **d?** 1Co 9:4
all drank the same spiritual **d.** 1Co 10:4
They sat down to eat and **d,** 1Co 10:7
You cannot **d** the cup of the Lord 1Co 10:21
is, if you eat or **d,** or if you 1Co 10:31
while others have too much to **d.** 1Co 11:21
You can eat and **d** in your own 1Co 11:22
When you **d** this, do it to........................ 1Co 11:25
this bread and **d** this cup you 1Co 11:26
you eat the bread and **d** the cup,............. 1Co 11:28
the bread and **d** the cup without.............. 1Co 11:29
Let us eat and **d,** because 1Co 15:32
He must not **d** too much wine or 1Ti 3:3
They must not **d** too much wine or........... 1Ti 3:8
but **d** a little wine to help your 1Ti 5:23
They must not **d** too much wine, ... Tit 1:7
about food and **d** and special .... Heb 9:10
made all the nations **d** the wine .... Rev 14:8
one also will **d** the wine of .... Rev 14:10
blood to **d** as they deserve." .... Rev 16:6

DRINKING
After the camels had finished **d,**.............. Ge 24:22
because he had been **d** much wine. .... Est 1:10
are famous for **d** wine and are .... Is 5:22
eating and **d,** and people say .... Mt 11:19
were eating and **d,** marrying and .... Mt 24:38
eating and **d** are not important. .... Rm 14:17
people died from **d** the water .... Rev 8:11

DRINKS
a land that **d** rain from heaven. .... Dt 11:11
and enjoy good food and sweet **d.** .... Ne 8:10
my spirit **d** in their poison; .... Job 6:4
and rotten and **d** up evil as if .... Job 15:16
and my tears fall into my **d.** .... Ps 102:9
all different kinds of strong **d.** .... Pr 23:30
and are champions at mixing **d.** .... Is 5:22
too much and **d** too much wine, ... Mt 11:19
too much and **d** too much wine, ... Lk 7:34
Everyone who **d** this water will .... Jn 4:13
but whoever **d** the water I give .... Jn 4:14
eats the bread or **d** the cup of................. 1Co 11:27

DRIP
My bride, your lips **d** honey; .... Sng 4:11
day wine will **d** from the........................ Joe 3:18
Wine will **d** from the mountains .... Am 9:13

DRIPPING
quarreling wife is like **d** water. .... Pr 19:13
as a continual **d** on a rainy day. .... Pr 27:15
Myrrh was **d** from my hands and .... Sng 5:5

DRIVE
defeat them and **d** them away. .... Ge 49:19
it hard to **d** the chariots. .... Ex 14:25
desert wind, he will **d** it away. .... Is 27:8
Chariot drivers, **d** hard! .... Je 46:9
doing here that **d** me far away .... Eze 8:6
and thorns will **d** them out of .... Hos 9:6
authority to **d** out evil spirits .... Mt 10:1

DRIVEN
his house and **d** through his body .... Ezr 6:11
They will be **d** from light into .... Job 18:18
as smoke is **d** away by the wind .... Ps 68:2
that have been **d** in firmly. .... Ec 12:11
So we have **d** away justice, ... Is 59:14
d by the breath of the LORD. .... Is 59:19
'I was **d** out of your presence,................. Jnh 2:4
Too much study has **d** you crazy!" .... Ac 26:24

DRIVER
King Ahab said to his chariot **d,**............... 1Ki 22:34
King Ahab said to his chariot **d,**............... 2Ch 18:33
hear the shout of the slave **d.** .... Job 3:18

DRIVING
the chariot is **d** like Jehu son 2Ki 9:20

DROP
a person might **d** a rock on .... Nu 35:23
the olives will **d** off the trees. .... Dt 28:40
My teaching will **d** like rain; .... Dt 32:2
where the skies **d** their dew. .... Dt 33:28
d some full heads of grain for................. Ru 2:16
pours it out even to the last **d,** .... Ps 75:8
and the clouds **d** rain on the .... Pr 3:20
like one small **d** in a bucket; .... Is 40:15

DROPPED
rained, and the clouds **d** water. .... Jdg 5:4
woman **d** a grinding stone on his .... Jdg 9:53
to leave, she **d** him, and now he 2Sa 4:4

DROVE
night the LORD **d** back the sea .... Ex 14:21
his tent and **d** his spear through.............. Nu 25:8
They **d** over the people of Gilead .... Am 1:3

DROWN
let the flood **d** me or the deep................. Ps 69:15
floods cannot **d** love. If a man .... Sng 8:7
cross rivers, you will not **d.**..................... Is 43:2
Lord, save us! We will **d!**" .... Mt 8:25
Master! We will **d!**" Jesus got up .... Lk 8:24

DROWNED
officers are **d** in the Red Sea. .... Ex 15:4
when he **d** them in the Red Sea as .... Dt 11:4
but their enemies **d** in the sea. .... Ps 78:53
and his army **d** in the Red Sea. .... Ps 136:15
hill into the lake and were **d.** .... Mt 8:32
the neck and be **d** in the sea. .... Mt 18:6
hill into the lake and were **d.** .... Mk 5:13
his neck and be **d** in the sea. .... Mk 9:42
hill into the lake and was **d.** .... Lk 8:33
Egyptians tried it, they were **d.** .... Heb 11:29

DROWNING
have been like a flood **d** us; .... Ps 124:4
don't you care that we are **d!**" .... Mk 4:38

DRUNK

he became **d** and lay naked in his .... Ge 9:21
too much, and he is always **d.**" .... Dt 21:20
not heard. Eli thought she was **d** 1Sa 1:13
you who are **d** but not from wine. .... Is 51:21
and to eat and drink and get **d.** .... Lk 12:45
people are not **d**, as you think; .... Ac 2:15
not have wild parties or get **d.** .... Rm 13:13
envy, being **d**, having wild .... Gal 5:21
not be **d** with wine, which will .... Eph 5:18
Those who get **d**, get drunk at 1Th 5:7
the earth became **d** from the wine .... Rev 17:2
the woman was **d** with the blood .... Rev 17:6
of the earth drunk **d** the wine of .... Rev 18:3

DRUNKARDS

the **d** make up songs about me. .... Ps 69:12
a rich valley where **d** live. .... Is 28:1
and **d** were brought from the .... Eze 23:42

DRUNKEN

the pride of Israel's **d** people! .... Is 28:1
the pride of Israel's **d** people, ... Is 28:3
in this land like a **d** person— .... Je 13:13
wild and **d** parties, and hateful 1Pe 4:3

DRUNKENNESS

desires, **d**, wild and drunken 1Pe 4:3

DRY

so the **d** land will appear. .... Ge 1:9
God named the **d** land "earth" and .... Ge 1:10
and pour it on the **d** ground. .... Ex 4:9
people can cross it on **d** land. .... Ex 14:16
making the sea become **d** ground. .... Ex 14:21
and stood there on **d** ground. .... Jos 3:17
the wool was **d**, but the ground .... Jdg 6:40
for you like someone in a **d,** .... Ps 63:1
He turned the sea into **d** land. .... Ps 66:6
pools of water and **d** ground into .... Ps 107:35
As a **d** land needs rain, I thirst .... Ps 143:6
better to eat a **d** crust of bread .... Pr 17:1
tell the deep waters, 'Become **d!** .... Is 44:27
like a root growing in a **d** land. .... Is 53:2
She will be an empty, **d** desert. .... Je 50:12
I will **d** up Babylon's sea and .... Je 51:36
and make her springs become **d.** .... Je 51:36
It has become a **d**, desert land, ... Je 51:43
their bones; it is as **d** as wood. .... La 4:8
and say to them, 'D bones, hear .... Eze 37:4
The **d** measure and the liquid .... Eze 45:11
desert where it was hot and **d.** .... Hos 13:5
vines have become **d**, and the fig .... Joe 1:12
a roaring fire burning **d** stalks. .... Joe 2:5
it travels through **d** places, ... Lk 11:24
Red Sea as if it were **d** land. .... Heb 11:29

DRYING

be a place for **d** fishing nets. .... Eze 26:14
d them with the towel that was .... Jn 13:5

DRYNESS

As heat and **d** quickly melt the .... Job 24:19

DUE

the food that was **d** a governor, ... Ne 5:18

DUG

that you believe I **d** this well." .... Ge 21:30
of Isaac's father Abraham had **d.** .... Ge 26:15
time Abraham had **d** many wells, ... Ge 26:18
Isaac's servants **d** a well in the .... Ge 26:19
his servants **d** another well. .... Ge 26:21
from there and **d** another well. .... Ge 26:22
and his servants **d** a well. .... Ge 26:25
him about the well they had **d,** .... Ge 26:32
so all of them **d** along the bank .... Ex 7:24
Princes **d** this well. Important .... Nu 21:18

Then he **d** a ditch around the 1Ki 18:32
I have **d** wells in foreign 2Ki 19:24
in the desert and **d** many wells, ... 2Ch 26:10
wells that were already **d,** .... Ne 9:25
have fallen into the pit they **d.** .... Ps 9:15
no reason they **d** a pit for me. .... Ps 35:7
d a pit in my path, but they .... Ps 57:6
until a pit is **d** for the wicked. .... Ps 94:13
people have **d** pits to trap me. .... Ps 119:85
He **d** and cleared the field of .... Is 5:2
I have **d** wells in foreign .... Is 37:25
quarry from which you were **d.** .... Is 51:1
And they have **d** their own wells, ... Je 2:13
went to Perath and **d** up the belt .... Je 13:7
but they have **d** a pit in order .... Je 18:20
my enemies have **d** a pit to .... Je 18:22
So I **d** through the wall and saw .... Eze 8:8
the evening I **d** through the wall .... Eze 12:7
wall around it and **d** a hole for .... Mt 21:33
bag went out and **d** a hole in the .... Mt 25:18
they **d** a hole in the roof right .... Mk 2:4
wall around it and **d** a hole for .... Mk 12:1
a house who **d** deep and laid .... Lk 6:48

DULL

spots on the skin are **d** white, ... Le 13:39
A **d** ax means harder work. .... Ec 10:10
gave the people a **d** mind so they .... Rm 11:8

DUMB

the minds of these people **d.** .... Is 6:10
by feeling, as **d** animals know .... Jud 1:10

DUMP

be thrown on the garbage **d,**" .... Am 4:3

DUMPED

insides will be **d** like trash. .... Zph 1:17

DUNGEON

like prisoners thrown into a **d**; .... Is 24:22
put Jeremiah into a cell in a **d,** .... Je 37:16

DURA

up on the plain of **D** in the area .... Da 3:1

DUSK

d until dawn the cloud above .... Nu 9:15
stayed only from **d** until dawn; .... Nu 9:21

DUST

LORD God took **d** from the ground .... Ge 2:7
and you will eat **d** all the days .... Ge 3:14
You are **d**, and when you die, you .... Ge 3:19
you will return to the **d.**" .... Ge 3:19
as many as the **d** of the earth. .... Ge 13:16
could count the **d** on the earth, ... Ge 13:16
Though I am only **d** and ashes, ... Ge 18:27
and strike the **d** on the ground. .... Ex 8:16
a powder like **d** and threw the .... Dt 9:21
raises the poor up from the **d,** 1Sa 2:8
pieces, like **d** on the ground. 2Sa 22:43
pieces, then beat them into **d.** 2Ki 23:15
as many as the **d** of the earth. 2Ch 1:9
cloth and put **d** on their heads .... Ne 9:1
whose foundations are made of **d,** .... Job 4:19
soon lie down in the **d** of death. .... Job 7:21
you now turn me back into **d?** .... Job 10:9
have buried my face in the **d.** .... Job 16:15
we go down together into the **d?**" .... Job 17:16
lie with them in the **d** of death. .... Job 20:11
nuggets into the **d** and your fine .... Job 22:24
and gold **d** is also found there. .... Job 28:6
together and turn back into **d.** .... Job 34:15
when the **d** becomes hard and the .... Job 38:38
I will sit in the **d** and ashes." .... Job 42:6
trample me into the **d** and bury .... Ps 7:5
into pieces, like **d** in the wind. .... Ps 18:42

You laid me in the **d** of death. .... Ps 22:15
to the grave? **D** cannot praise .... Ps 30:9
and make his enemies lick the **d.** .... Ps 72:9
He rained meat on them like **d.** .... Ps 78:27
You turn people back into **d.** .... Ps 90:3
they even care about her **d.** .... Ps 102:14
he remembers that we are **d.** .... Ps 103:14
breath, they die and turn to **d.** .... Ps 104:29
even the first **d** of the earth. .... Pr 8:26
both came from **d** and both will .... Ec 3:20
back into the **d** of the earth .... Ec 12:7
dies and blows away like **d.** .... Is 5:24
because a cloud of **d** comes from .... Is 14:31
to the ground, even to the **d.** .... Is 25:12
and throw it down into the **d.** .... Is 26:5
the rocks of the altar to **d,** .... Is 27:9
enemies will become like fine **d;** .... Is 29:5
measure all the **d** of the earth .... Is 40:12
more than the **d** on his measuring .... Is 40:15
more than fine **d** on his scales. .... Is 40:15
sword, and kings become like **d.** .... Is 41:2
shake off the **d** and stand up. .... Is 52:2
and his armies with clouds of **d.** .... Is 66:15
be like a name written in the **d,** .... Je 17:13
Roll around in the **d,** leaders of .... Je 25:34
They throw **d** on their heads and .... La 2:10
ground where **d** would cover it. .... Eze 24:7
will cover you with their **d.** .... Eze 26:10
They throw **d** on their heads and .... Eze 27:30
Roll in the **d** at Beth Ophrah. .... Mic 1:10
crawl in the **d** like a snake, ... Mic 7:17
clouds are the **d** beneath his .... Nah 1:3
blood will be poured out like **d,** .... Zph 1:17
up silver like **d** and gold like .... Zch 9:3
little piece of **d** in your .... Mt 7:3
piece of **d** out of your eye .... Mt 7:4
clearly to take the **d** out of .... Mt 7:5
and shake its **d** off your feet. .... Mt 10:14
Shake its **d** off your feet as a .... Mk 6:11
little piece of **d** in your .... Lk 6:41
piece of **d** out of your eye .... Lk 6:42
shake the **d** off of your feet as .... Lk 9:5
back to the grave and became **d.** .... Ac 13:34
shook the **d** off their feet. .... Ac 13:51
shook off the **d** from his clothes .... Ac 18:6
coats, and threw **d** into the air. .... Ac 22:23
came from the **d** of the earth. 1Co 15:47
And they threw **d** on their heads .... Rev 18:19

DUTIES

the rights and **d** of the king and 1Sa 10:25
Each group had certain **d.** 1Ch 24:3
had given them **d** in the Temple 2Ch 23:18
and Levites for their special **d,** 2Ch 31:2
chose the priests to do their **d,** 2Ch 35:2
appointed **d** for the priests and .... Ne 13:30
complete all the **d** of a servant 2Ti 4:5

DUTY

It is your **d** to provide children .... Ge 38:8
have done your **d** to the LORD .... Nu 32:22
who has the **d** of punishing. .... Nu 35:12
judge who is on **d** at that time. .... Dt 17:9
who has the **d** of punishing. .... Dt 19:6
who has the **d** of punishing. .... Dt 19:12
priests and judges who are on **d.** .... Dt 19:17
to war or be given any other **d.** .... Dt 24:5
which is his **d** to her as a .... Dt 25:5
He refuses to do his **d** for me." .... Dt 25:7
to the priest on **d** at that time, ... Dt 26:3
who has the **d** of punishing. .... Jos 20:3
who had the **d** of punishing .... Jos 20:9
our **d** to hand David over to you. 1Sa 23:20
who has the **d** of punishing. 2Sa 14:11

you who go on **d** on the Sabbath 2Ki 11:5
who go off **d** on the Sabbath 2Ki 11:7
men who came on **d** on the Sabbath 2Ki 11:9
who went off **d** on the Sabbath, ... 2Ki 11:9
they were on **d** day and night, ... 1Ch 9:33
division was on **d** one month each 1Ch 27:1
Levites go on **d** on the Sabbath. 2Ch 23:4
men who came on **d** on the Sabbath 2Ch 23:8
the gatekeepers are still on **d,** .... Ne 7:3
and your **d** to buy that field. .... Je 32:7
your right and **d** to buy it and .... Je 32:8
His **d** was to arrange the king's .... Je 51:59
are given the holy **d** of serving .... Eze 48:11
because his group was on **d.** .... Lk 1:8
I have a **d** to all people—Greeks .... Rm 1:14
Telling the Good News is my **d—** 1Co 9:16
only doing the **d** that was given 1Co 9:17
learn to do their **d** to their own 1Ti 5:4

DWARFS

hunchbacks, **d,** men who have .... Le 21:20

DWELLING

left his **d** at Shiloh, the Tent .... Ps 78:60

DYED

sheepskins that are **d** red; .... Ex 25:5
is taking pieces of **d** cloth. .... Jdg 5:30
are even taking pieces of **d,** .... Jdg 5:30

DYING

As she lay **d,** she named the boy .... Ge 35:18
and again, "My daughter is **d.** .... Mk 5:23
about twelve years old, was **d.** .... Lk 8:42
he keep Lazarus from **d?"** .... Jn 11:37
So living or **d,** we belong to the .... Rm 14:8
We seem to be **d,** but we continue 2Co 6:9
Jacob, as he was **d,** blessed each .... Heb 11:21
while he was **d,** spoke about .... Heb 11:22

DYSENTERY

was sick with a fever and **d.** .... Ac 28:8

E

EAGER

because he was **e** to help the 2Sa 21:2
like an athlete **e** to run a race. .... Ps 19:5
They are **e** to do evil and are .... Pr 1:16
but those **e** to get rich will be .... Pr 28:20
But they were still **e** to do evil .... Zph 3:7
they were **e** to go through all .... Zch 6:7
The Bereans were **e** to hear what .... Ac 17:11
So be **e** to do right, and change .... Rev 3:19

EAGERLY

They **e** run to do evil, and they .... Is 59:7
Spirit we wait **e** for this hope. .... Gal 5:5
e for me until he found me. 2Ti 1:17

EAGLE

He was like an **e** building its .... Dt 32:11
commands the **e** to fly and build .... Job 39:27
something dead, the **e** is there." .... Job 39:30
me young again, like the **e.** .... Ps 103:5
the way an **e** flies in the sky, ... Pr 30:19
will rise up as an **e** in the sky; .... Is 40:31
like an **e** diving down from the .... Je 48:40
one also had the face of an **e.** .... Eze 1:10
Make yourself bald like the **e,** .... Mic 1:16
The fourth was like a flying **e.** .... Rev 4:7
of a great **e** so she could fly .... Rev 12:14

EAGLE'S

out of Egypt, as if on **e** wings. .... Ex 19:4
your home as high as an **e** nest, ... Je 49:16

EAGLES

must not eat e, vultures, black .... Le 11:13
e, vultures, black vultures, ... Dt 14:12
They were faster than e. 2Sa 1:23
attack like e swooping down to .... Job 9:26
His horses are faster than e. .... Je 4:13
were faster than e in the sky. .... La 4:19

EAR

the slave's e using a sharp tool .... Ex 21:6
the bottom of Aaron's right e, ... Le 8:23
of the right e of the person to .... Le 14:14
of the right e of the person to .... Le 14:17
of the right e of the person to .... Le 14:25
of the right e of the person to .... Le 14:28
awl through his e into the door; .... Dt 15:17
The e tests words as the tongue .... Job 12:11
The e tests words as the tongue .... Job 34:3
a hole in my e to show that my .... Ps 40:6
or a scrap of an e of his sheep. .... Am 3:12
in your e you should shout .... Mt 10:27
high priest and cut off his e. .... Mt 26:51
high priest and cut off his e. .... Mk 14:47
priest and cut off his right e. .... Lk 22:50
the servant's e and healed him. .... Lk 22:51
priest, cutting off his right e. .... Jn 18:10
of the man whose e Peter had cut .... Jn 18:26
The e might say, "Because I am 1Co 12:16
not stop the e from being a part 1Co 12:16
If the whole body were an e, ... 1Co 12:17

EARLY

E the next morning, Abraham got .... Ge 19:27
E the next morning Abraham took .... Ge 21:14
Abraham got up e in the morning .... Ge 22:3
you can get up e and go home." .... Jdg 19:9
E the next day the people built .... Jdg 21:4
E the next morning Elkanah's 1Sa 1:19
of Ashdod rose e the next 1Sa 5:3
E the next morning Samuel got up 1Sa 15:12
E in the morning David left the 1Sa 17:20
E in the morning you and your 1Sa 29:10
his men got up e in the morning. 1Sa 29:11
would get up e and stand near 2Sa 15:2
E in the morning Job would offer .... Job 1:5
I wake up e in the morning and .... Ps 119:147
you to get up e and stay up late .... Ps 127:2
your neighbor e in the morning, ... Pr 27:14
Plant e in the morning, and work .... Ec 11:6
Let's go e to the vineyards and .... Sng 7:12
people who rise e in the morning .... Is 5:11
people got up e the next morning .... Is 37:36
figs that ripen e in the season. .... Je 24:2
dew that goes away e in the day. .... Hos 6:4
none of the figs I love. .... Mic 7:1
he went out very e to hire some .... Mt 20:1
E the next morning, as Jesus was .... Mt 21:18
Very e on that day, the first .... Mk 16:2
from the dead e on the first day .... Mk 16:9
the people got up e to go to the .... Lk 21:38
Very e on the first day of the .... Lk 24:1
E this morning they went to the .... Lk 24:22
e in the morning he went back .... Jn 8:2
E in the morning they led Jesus .... Jn 18:28
E on the first day of the week, ... Jn 20:1
into the Temple e in the morning .... Ac 5:21
that in the e days God chose .... Ac 15:7
until it was e morning, and then .... Ac 20:11

EARN

the last six to e your flocks. .... Ge 31:41
hard-working people e a profit, ... Pr 21:5
and e your living there, ... Am 7:12
You e money, but then you lose .... Hag 1:6
of what you e so there will be .... Mal 3:10

one-tenth of everything you e— .... Mt 23:23
your five bags to e five more.' .... Mt 25:20
your two bags to e two more.' .... Mt 25:22
work a month to e enough money .... Mk 6:37
you didn't e and gather food .... Lk 19:21
that I didn't e and gathering .... Lk 19:22
who must work to e our living? 1Co 9:6
They should e an honest living .... Eph 4:28
quietly and e their own food. 2Th 3:12
and all those who e their living .... Rev 18:17

EARNED

I e ten coins with the one you .... Lk 19:16

EARNESTLY

church prayed e to God for him .... Ac 12:5

EARNS

An evil person really e nothing, ... Pr 11:18
the money she e but will give .... Is 23:18

EARRING

give me a gold e from the things .... Jdg 8:24
threw down an e from what he had .... Jdg 8:25

EARRINGS

and the e they were wearing, ... Ge 35:4
off the gold e that your wives, ... Ex 32:2
took their gold e and brought .... Ex 32:3
of all kinds—pins, e, rings, and .... Ex 35:22
signet rings, e, and necklaces. .... Nu 31:50
The Ishmaelites wore gold e. .... Jdg 8:24
The gold e weighed about .... Jdg 8:26
valuable as gold e or fine gold .... Pr 25:12
for you gold e with silver hooks .... Sng 1:11
their e, bracelets, and veils, ... Is 3:19
in your nose, e in your ears, ... Eze 16:12

EARS

of the right e of Aaron and his .... Ex 29:20
on the bottom of their right e, ... Le 8:24
your eyes or hear with your e. .... Dt 29:4
my call for help reached his e. 2Sa 22:7
and my e heard a whisper of it. .... Job 4:12
my e have heard and understood .... Job 13:1
let your e hear what I say. .... Job 13:17
Terrible sounds fill their e, ... Job 15:21
fell very gently on their e. .... Job 29:22
speaks in their e and frightens .... Job 33:16
My e had heard of you before, ... Job 42:5
my call for help reached his e. .... Ps 18:6
deaf cobras that stop up their e .... Ps 58:4
Can't the creator of e hear? .... Ps 94:9
They have e, but they cannot .... Ps 115:6
They have e, but they cannot .... Ps 135:17
e to hear and eyes to see. .... Pr 20:12
is like grabbing a dog by the e. .... Pr 26:17
come again and again to our e, ... Ec 1:8
Your e will be deaf to the noise .... Ec 12:4
dumb. Shut their e. Cover their .... Is 6:10
eyes and hear with their e. .... Is 6:10
those who have e but don't hear. .... Is 43:8
They have e, but they don't .... Je 5:21
people of Israel have closed e, ... Je 6:10
open your e to hear the words of .... Je 9:20
not close your e and ignore my .... La 3:56
Even if they shout in my e, ... Eze 8:18
with a loud voice in my e, ... Eze 9:1
and they have e to hear, but .... Eze 12:2
in your e, and a beautiful .... Eze 16:12
will cut off your noses and e. .... Eze 23:25
your eyes and hear with your e. .... Eze 40:4
eyes to see, and your e to hear. .... Eze 44:5
Let those with e use them and .... Mt 11:15
with e use them and listen. .... Mt 13:9
They do not hear with their e, ... Mt 13:15
eyes and hear with their e. .... Mt 13:15

E

your eyes and hear with your **e.** .... Mt 13:16
Let those with **e** use them and .... Mt 13:43
Let those with **e** use them and .... Mk 4:9
Let those with **e** use them and .... Mk 4:23
with **e** use them and listen. .... Mk 7:16
in the man's **e** and then spit .... Mk 7:33
You have **e,** but you don't really .... Mk 8:18
Let those with **e** use them and .... Lk 8:8
Let those with **e** use them and .... Lk 14:35
covered their **e** and all ran at .... Ac 7:57
They don't hear with their **e,** .... Ac 28:27
eyes and hear with their **e.** .... Ac 28:27
see and their **e** so they could .... Rm 11:8
person who has **e** should listen .... Rev 2:7
who has **e** should listen to .... Rev 2:11
who has **e** should listen to .... Rev 2:17
who has **e** should listen to .... Rev 2:29
who has **e** should listen to .... Rev 3:6
who has **e** should listen to .... Rev 3:13
who has **e** should listen to .... Rev 3:22
Anyone who has **e** should listen: .... Rev 13:9

EARTH

God created the sky and the **e.** .... Ge 1:1
The **e** was empty and had no form. .... Ge 1:2
the dry land "**e**" and the water .... Ge 1:10
Let the **e** be filled with .... Ge 1:24
Fill the **e** and be its master. .... Ge 1:28
were still no plants on the **e.** .... Ge 2:5
rise up from the **e** and water all .... Ge 2:6
will wander around on the **e.**" .... Ge 4:12
I must wander around on the **e,** .... Ge 4:14
were on the **e** in those days .... Ge 6:4
beings on the **e** were very wicked .... Ge 6:5
People on **e** did what God said .... Ge 6:11
of water on the **e** to destroy all .... Ge 6:17
now I will send rain on the **e.** .... Ge 7:4
flooded the **e** for forty days, ... Ge 7:17
to cover the **e** for one hundred .... Ge 7:24
He made a wind blow over the **e,** .... Ge 8:1
water had dried up from the **e.** .... Ge 8:7
As long as the **e** continues, ... Ge 8:22
grow in number and fill the **e.** .... Ge 9:1
clouds over the **e** and a rainbow............ Ge 9:14
every living thing on the **e.**" .... Ge 9:16
because the **e** was divided during .... Ge 10:25
be scattered over all the **e.**" .... Ge 11:4
them from there over all the **e,** .... Ge 11:8
the people on **e** will be blessed .... Ge 12:3
as many as the dust of the **e.** .... Ge 13:16
the God who made heaven and **e.** .... Ge 14:19
High, who made heaven and **e.** .... Ge 14:22
all nations on **e** will be blessed .... Ge 18:18
You are the judge of all the **e.** .... Ge 18:25
resting on the **e** and reaching up .... Ge 28:12
you and your people from the **e.** .... Ex 9:15
and the **e** swallowed our enemies. .... Ex 15:12
Even though the whole **e** is mine, ... Ex 19:5
sky above or on the **e** below or .... Ex 20:4
like iron and the **e** like bronze. .... Le 26:19
as my glory fills the whole **e,** .... Nu 14:21
The **e** opened and swallowed them........... Nu 16:32
Then the **e** covered them. .... Nu 16:33
saying, "The **e** will swallow us, ... Nu 16:34
animals on **e** or birds that fly .... Dt 4:17
ask heaven and **e** to speak .... Dt 4:26
than any other nation on **e.**.................... Dt 28:1
ask heaven and **e** to be witnesses .... Dt 30:19
Listen, **e,** to what I say. .... Dt 32:1
Let the full **e** give the best .... Dt 33:16
heavens above and the **e** below! .... Jos 2:11
of Edom, the **e** shook, the skies .... Jdg 5:4
of the **e** belong to the LORD 1Sa 2:8

The LORD will judge all the **e.** 1Sa 2:10
all your enemies from the **e.**" 1Sa 20:15
of the great people on the **e.** 2Sa 7:9
The **e** trembled and shook. 2Sa 22:8
foundations of the **e** were seen. 2Sa 22:16
in heaven above or on **e** below. 1Ki 8:23
the nations on **e** to be your very 1Ki 8:53
kingdoms of the **e** will know that 2Ki 19:19
Sing to the LORD, all the **e.** 1Ch 16:23
skies rejoice and the **e** be glad. 1Ch 16:31
me all the kingdoms of the **e,** 2Ch 36:23
of the God of heaven and **e.** .... Ezr 5:11
been wandering around the **e,** .... Job 1:7
No one else on **e** is like him. .... Job 1:8
wise men of the **e** who built .... Job 3:14
Our days on **e** are only a shadow. .... Job 8:9
E, please do not cover up my .... Job 16:18
Should the **e** be vacant just for .... Job 18:4
People on **e** will not remember .... Job 18:17
end he will stand upon the **e.** .... Job 19:25
and hangs the **e** on nothing. .... Job 26:7
to rule over the **e** or put him in .... Job 34:13
animals of the **e** and wiser than .... Job 35:11
At dawn the **e** changes like clay .... Job 38:14
else on **e** is equal to it; .... Job 41:33
kings of the **e** prepare to fight .... Ps 2:2
the people on **e** will be yours. .... Ps 2:8
wonderful name in all the **e!** .... Ps 8:1
wonderful name in all the **e!** .... Ps 8:9
no true believers are left on **e.** .... Ps 12:1
The **e** trembled and shook. .... Ps 18:7
foundations of the **e** were seen. .... Ps 18:15
their words go everywhere on **e.**............. Ps 19:4
their families from the **e;**...................... Ps 21:10
The **e** belongs to the LORD, ... Ps 24:1
the LORD's love fills the **e.** .... Ps 33:5
be afraid even if the **e** shakes, ... Ps 46:2
the great King over all the **e!** .... Ps 47:2
over the **e** people praise you. .... Ps 48:10
listen, all you who live on **e.** .... Ps 49:1
calls the **e** from the rising to .... Ps 50:1
because the **e** and everything in .... Ps 50:12
his majesty covers the **e.**...................... Ps 57:5
and to the ends of the **e.** .... Ps 59:13
You made the **e** shake and crack. .... Ps 60:2
the ends of the **e** when I am .... Ps 61:2
everywhere on the **e** and beyond .... Ps 65:5
Everything on **e,** shout with joy .... Ps 66:1
You guide all the nations on **e.** .... Ps 67:4
Kingdoms of the **e,** sing to God; .... Ps 68:32
Heaven and **e** should praise him, ... Ps 69:34
like showers that water the **e.**............... Ps 72:6
They say that they own the **e.** .... Ps 73:9
You bring salvation to the **e.** .... Ps 74:12
You set all the limits on the **e;** .... Ps 74:17
The **e** with all its people may .... Ps 75:3
and the **e** was afraid and silent. .... Ps 76:8
save the needy people of the **e.** .... Ps 76:9
the kings on **e** fear him. .... Ps 76:12
The **e** trembled and shook. .... Ps 77:18
Like the **e,** he built it to last .... Ps 78:69
and judge the **e,** because you own .... Ps 82:8
God Most High over all the **e.**............... Ps 83:18
e people will be loyal to God, ... Ps 85:11
skies and the **e** belong to you. .... Ps 89:11
son, the greatest king on **e.**................... Ps 89:27
you created the **e** and the world, ... Ps 90:2
up, Judge of the **e,** and give the .... Ps 94:2
The deepest places on **e** are his, ... Ps 95:4
sing to the LORD, all the **e.** .... Ps 96:1
the LORD, all nations on **e;** .... Ps 96:7
before him, everyone on **e.** .... Ps 96:9
The **e** is set, and it cannot be .... Ps 96:10

skies rejoice and the **e** be glad; .... Ps 96:11
king. Let the **e** rejoice; faraway .... Ps 97:1
ends of the **e** have seen God's................. Ps 98:3
with wings. Let the **e** shake. .... Ps 99:1
Shout to the LORD, all the **e**. .... Ps 100:1
the kings on **e** will honor you. .... Ps 102:15
high as the sky is above the **e**, ... Ps 103:11
You built the **e** on its .... Ps 104:5
and everything the **e** produced. .... Ps 105:35
your glory be over all the **e**. .... Ps 108:5
to look at the skies and the **e**.................. Ps 113:6
E, shake with fear before the .... Ps 114:7
the LORD, who made heaven and **e**. .... Ps 115:15
am a stranger on **e**. Do not hide.............. Ps 119:19
LORD, your love fills the **e**..................... Ps 119:64
you made the **e**, and it still .... Ps 119:90
the LORD, who made heaven and **e**. .... Ps 121:2
the LORD, who made heaven and **e**. .... Ps 124:8
Zion, he who made heaven and **e**. .... Ps 134:3
in heaven and on **e**, in the seas .... Ps 135:6
clouds from the ends of the **e**............... Ps 135:7
He spread out the **e** on the seas............. Ps 136:6
kings of the **e** praise you when .... Ps 138:4
made heaven and **e**, the sea and............. Ps 146:6
rain to the **e** and makes grass .... Ps 147:8
Praise him high above the **e**. .... Ps 148:1
LORD made the **e**, using his .... Pr 3:19
the clouds drop rain on the **e**.................. Pr 3:20
had not made the **e** or fields, ... Pr 8:26
people will be rewarded on **e**,................. Pr 11:31
the skies or the depth of the **e**. .... Pr 25:3
set in place the ends of the **e**?................ Pr 30:4
the hard work they do here on **e**? .... Ec 1:3
have seen real misery here on **e**:   .... Ec 5:13
into the dust of the **e** again, ... Ec 12:7
Heaven and **e**, listen, because................. Is 1:2
His glory fills the whole **e**." .... Is 6:3
because the **e** will be full of .... Is 11:9
Judah from all parts of the **e**. .... Is 11:12
The **e** will dry up and die; .... Is 24:4
The **e** and all the people in it .... Is 34:1
above the circle of the **e**,...................... Is 40:22
spread out the **e** and everything .... Is 42:5
who formed the **e** and made it. .... Is 45:18
I made the **e** with my own hands. .... Is 48:13
spread it everywhere on **e**. .... Is 48:20
Then everyone on **e** will see the .... Is 52:10
is called the God of all the **e**. .... Is 54:5
heavens are higher than the **e**, ... Is 55:9
They will receive the **e** forever. .... Is 60:21
make new heavens and a new **e**, ... Is 65:17
and the **e** is my footstool. .... Is 66:1
make new heavens and the new **e**, ... Is 66:22
I looked at the **e**, and it was .... Je 4:23
by everyone on **e** because of what .... Je 15:4
the secrets of the **e** below, ... Je 31:37
that made the whole **e** drunk.................. Je 51:7
of Israel from the sky to the **e**; .... La 2:1
city, the happiest place on **e**?" .... La 2:15
prisoner of the **e** is crushed .... La 3:34
Kings of the **e** and people of the............. La 4:12
me up between the **e** and the sky. .... Eze 8:3
Eden in the place below the **e**. .... Eze 31:18
people on **e** and were unclean, ... Eze 32:24
No one on **e** can do what the king .... Da 2:10
that filled the whole **e**. .... Da 2:35
part, will rule over the **e**....................... Da 2:39
to the far parts of the **e**. .... Da 4:22
miracles in heaven and on **e**. .... Da 6:27
that will come from the **e**. .... Da 7:17
kingdom that will come on the **e**. .... Da 7:23
since nations have been on **e**, ... Da 12:1
they will give rain to the **e**..................... Hos 2:21

the sky and the **e** will shake. .... Joe 3:16
of all the families of the **e**, ... Am 3:2
e and all you who live on it. .... Mic 1:2
to the Lord of all the **e**." .... Mic 4:13
The **e** will be ruined for the .... Mic 7:13
The **e** trembles when he comes; .... Nah 1:5
the **e** should be silent in his .... Hab 2:20
He stands and shakes the **e**. .... Hab 3:6
You split the **e** with rivers. .... Hab 3:9
destroy all the gods of the **e**. .... Zph 2:11
the plants which the **e** produces, ... Hag 1:11
shake the heavens and the **e**, ... Hag 2:6
to shake the heavens and the **e**. .... Hag 2:21
LORD sent through all the **e**."................... Zch 1:10
We have gone through all the **e**, ... Zch 1:11
to serve the Lord of all the **e**." .... Zch 4:14
River to the ends of the **e**. .... Zch 9:10
for the whole **e** will be theirs.................. Mt 5:5
You are the salt of the **e**........................ Mt 5:13
law until heaven and **e** are gone. .... Mt 5:18
an oath using the name of the **e**, ... Mt 5:35
because the **e** belongs to God. .... Mt 5:35
here on **e** as it is in heaven. .... Mt 6:10
yourselves here on **e** where moths .... Mt 6:19
authority on **e** to forgive sins................... Mt 9:6
I came to bring peace to the **e**. .... Mt 10:34
of heaven and **e**, because you .... Mt 11:25
don't allow on **e** will be the .... Mt 16:19
you allow on **e** will be the .... Mt 16:19
don't allow on **e** will be the .... Mt 18:18
you allow on **e** will be the .... Mt 18:18
if two of you on **e** agree about .... Mt 18:19
call any person on **e** 'Father,' .... Mt 23:9
who have been killed on **e**— .... Mt 23:35
his angels all around the **e**,..................... Mt 24:31
E and sky will be destroyed, ... Mt 24:35
e shook and rocks broke apart. .... Mt 27:51
heaven and on **e** is given to me. .... Mt 28:18
By itself the **e** produces grain. .... Mk 4:28
on **e** let there be peace among .... Lk 2:14
of heaven and **e**, because you .... Lk 10:21
find those on **e** who believe in .... Lk 18:8
one who is from the **e** belongs to .... Jn 3:31
If I am lifted up from the **e**,.................... Jn 12:32
to do, I brought you glory on **e**. .... Jn 17:4
in the sky and on the **e**: .... Ac 2:19
and the **e** is my footstool. .... Ac 7:49
His life on **e** has ended."......................... Ac 8:33
being lowered to **e** by its four .... Ac 10:11
be talked about in all the **e**." .... Rm 9:17
words go everywhere on **e**." .... Rm 10:18
because the **e** belongs to the 1Co 10:26
man came from the dust of the **e**. 1Co 15:47
will have a long life on the **e**." .... Eph 6:3
in heaven, on **e**, and under the .... Php 2:10
in heaven, not the things on **e**. .... Col 3:2
visitors and strangers on **e**...................... Heb 11:13
in caves and holes in the **e**. .... Heb 11:38
to him when he warned them on **e**, ... Heb 12:25
voice shook the **e**, but now he .... Heb 12:26
shake not only the **e** but also .... Heb 12:26
the **e** was made from water and 2Pe 3:5
and a new **e** where goodness 2Pe 3:13
Christ came to **e** as a human is 1Jn 4:2
Christ came to **e** as a human. 2Jn 1:7
the ruler of the kings of the **e**. .... Rev 1:5
peoples of the **e** will cry loudly .... Rev 1:7
to test those who live on **e**. .... Rev 3:10
and they will rule on the **e**." .... Rev 5:10
in heaven and on **e** and under the .... Rev 5:13
sky fell to the **e** like figs .... Rev 6:13
at the four corners of the **e**. .... Rev 7:1
angels was thrown down to the **e**. .... Rev 12:9

But the e helped the woman by .... Rev 12:16
beast coming up out of the e. .... Rev 13:11
who had been bought from the e. .... Rev 14:3
bowls of God's anger on the e." .... Rev 16:1
kings of the e sinned sexually .... Rev 17:2
AND OF THE EVIL THINGS OF THE E ...Rev 17:5
I saw a new heaven and a new e. .... Rev 21:1

EARTHLY

made to look like e people,..................... Rm 1:23
part of me that is e and sinful. .... Rm 7:18
and they are the e family into................. Rm 9:5
crown is an e thing that lasts 1Co 9:25
heavenly bodies and e bodies. 1Co 15:40
beauty of the e bodies is 1Co 15:40
the things we did in the e body. 2Co 5:10
a picture of the e city of .... Gal 4:25
they think only about e things. .... Php 3:19
rules refer to e things that are .... Col 2:22

EARTHQUAKE

there was an e, but the LORD was 1Ki 19:11
After the e, there was a fire, ... 1Ki 19:12
surely be a great e in Israel. .... Eze 38:19
Israel two years before the e. .... Am 1:1
ran from the e when Uzziah was .... Zch 14:5
Jesus saw this e and everything .... Mt 27:54
that time there was a strong e. .... Mt 28:2
there was a strong e that shook .... Ac 16:26
seal, and there was a great e. .... Rev 6:12
and loud noises, and an e. .... Rev 8:5
same hour there was a great e, ... Rev 11:13
thunder, an e, and a great .... Rev 11:19
thunder, and a big e—the worst .... Rev 16:18

EARTHQUAKES

and there will be e in different .... Mt 24:7

EASE

wicked, always at e, and getting.............. Ps 73:12
while other people are at e, ... 2Co 8:13

EASIER

That will make it e for you,..................... Ex 18:22
Now, make it e for us, and don't............. 1Ki 12:4
Now make our work e.' 1Ki 12:10
Now, make it e for us, and don't............. 2Ch 10:4
Now make our work e.' 2Ch 10:10
Make things e for me when I am .... Ps 4:1
of the innocent makes life e, ... Pr 11:5
Being wise will make it e. .... Ec 10:10
Which is e: to say, 'Your sins .... Mt 9:5
you that it is e for a camel to .... Mt 19:24
Which is e: to tell this .... Mk 2:9
is e for a camel to go through................. Mk 10:25
Which is e: to say, 'Your sins .... Lk 5:23
It would be e for heaven and .... Lk 16:17
is e for a camel to go through................. Lk 18:25

EASILY

future you can e see if I am .... Ge 30:33
the ropes as e as if they were .... Jdg 16:12
What they hope in is e broken; .... Job 8:14
evil person is e led to do wrong .... Pr 12:26
Money that comes e disappears .... Pr 13:11
knowledge comes e to those with .... Pr 14:6
who chases her will e catch her;.............. Je 2:24
do cruel things as e as they put .... Mal 2:16
will not e say evil things .... Mk 9:39
Do not become e upset in your 2Th 2:2
that are not e seen cannot stay 1Ti 5:25
the sin that so e holds us back. .... Heb 12:1
Do not become angry e, ... Jam 1:19

EAST

in the land of Nod, e of Eden.................. Ge 4:16
So Lot chose to move e and live .... Ge 13:11

They will spread west and e, ... Ge 28:14
the land of the people of the E. .... Ge 29:1
the sea with a strong e wind, ... Ex 14:21
peoples from the e were camped .... Jdg 7:12
by lot to guard the E Gate. 1Ch 26:14
his stomach with the hot e wind. .... Job 15:2
us as far as the e is from west. .... Ps 103:12
the one to come from the e? .... Is 41:2
a man from the e to carry out my .... Is 46:11
and destroy the people of the E. .... Je 49:28
they faced e and were worshiping .... Eze 8:16
worshiping the sun in the e. .... Eze 8:16
stood where the e gate of the .... Eze 10:19
the man went to the e gateway. .... Eze 40:6
border from the e side to .... Eze 48:1
miles on the e and three miles .... Eze 48:18
news from the e and the north .... Da 11:44
he chases the e wind all day. .... Hos 12:1
sent a very hot e wind to blow, ... Jnh 4:8
Mount of Olives, e of Jerusalem. .... Zch 14:4
men from the e came to Jerusalem........... Mt 2:1
his star in the e and have come .... Mt 2:2
come from the e and from the .... Mt 8:11
flashing from the e to the west. .... Mt 24:27
There were three gates on the e,.............. Rev 21:13

EASTERN

Your e border will begin at .... Nu 34:10
land along the e side of the..................... Jos 12:1
was the border on the e side. .... Jos 18:20
land will reach to the e border. .... Eze 45:7

EASTWARD

it turned e toward Taanath .... Jos 16:6
and continued e to Janoah...................... Jos 16:6
continued e to Gath Hepher and............. Jos 19:13

EASY

that I ask you to accept is e; .... Mt 11:30
gentle, and e to please. .... Jam 3:17

EAT

You may e the fruit from any .... Ge 2:16
you must not e the fruit from .... Ge 2:17
knows that if you e the fruit .... Ge 3:5
and you will e dust all the days .... Ge 3:14
which I commanded you not to e. .... Ge 3:17
you must not e meat that still .... Ge 9:4
bring it to me, and I will e. .... Ge 27:4
some tasty food for me to e. .... Ge 27:7
Israel do not e the muscle that .... Ge 32:32
the brothers sat down to e. .... Ge 37:25
the birds will e your flesh.".................... Ge 40:19
and they will e the best food we .... Ge 45:18
They will e anything that was.................. Ex 10:5
houses where they e the lambs. .... Ex 12:7
They must e it with bitter herbs .... Ex 12:8
Do not e the lamb raw or boiled.............. Ex 12:9
This is the way you must e it:.................. Ex 12:11
feast you must e bread made .... Ex 12:15
foreigner is to e the Passover.................. Ex 12:43
the LORD has given you to e,................... Ex 12:16
father-in-law to e the holy meal .... Ex 18:12
days you must e bread that is .... Ex 23:15
They sat down to e and drink, ... Ex 32:6
must not e any fat or blood.' .... Le 3:17
the priests may e what is left, ... Le 6:16
People must not e meat that .... Le 7:19
You must e it in a holy place, ... Le 10:13
and daughters may e the breast.............. Le 10:14
hoofs, and you must not e them. .... Le 11:4
must not e any of the animals .... Le 11:12
Don't e meat that still has .... Le 17:14
You may e it the same day you .... Le 19:6
you may e the fruit from the .... Le 19:25

E

he cannot **e** the holy offerings .... Le 22:4
person must not **e** the holy .... Le 22:6
he may **e** the holy offerings; .... Le 22:7
other animal, he must not **e** it. .... Le 22:8
priest's family may **e** this food. .... Le 22:13
not priests to **e** the holy .... Le 22:16
and you will **e** as much as you .... Le 25:19
You will **e** the bodies of your .... Le 26:29
juice or **e** grapes or raisins. .... Nu 6:3
they must not **e** anything that .... Nu 6:4
LORD will give you meat to **e**. .... Nu 11:18
for any food you **e** or water you .... Dt 2:6
When you have all you want to **e**, ... Dt 8:10
or unclean, may **e** this meat, ... Dt 12:15
but do not **e** the blood. Pour it .... Dt 12:16
Don't **e** the life with the meat. .... Dt 12:23
you may not **e** camels, rabbits .... Dt 14:7
You may **e** anything that has fins .... Dt 14:9
but do not **e** anything that does .... Dt 14:10
You may **e** any clean bird. .... Dt 14:11
for seven days **e** bread made .... Dt 16:3
E bread made without yeast for .... Dt 16:8
You can **e** the fruit from the .... Dt 20:19
you may **e** as many grapes as you .... Dt 23:24
because the worms will **e** them. .... Dt 28:39
They will **e** the calves from your .... Dt 28:51
she will plan to **e** the baby and .... Dt 28:57
and you **e** from vineyards and .... Jos 24:13
wine or beer or **e** anything that .... Jdg 13:4
the eater comes something to **e**. .... Jdg 14:14
E some of our bread and dip it .... Ru 2:14
would cry and not **e** anything. 1Sa 1:7
you will always **e** at my table." 2Sa 9:7
served him, but he refused to **e**. 2Sa 13:9
old to taste what I **e** or drink. 2Sa 19:35
allow them to **e** at your table. 1Ki 2:7
you not to **e** or drink anything 1Ki 13:22
who **e** at Jezebel's table." 1Ki 18:19
King Ahab went to **e** and drink. 1Ki 18:42
so upset that you refuse to **e**?" 1Ki 21:5
'Dogs will **e** the body of Jezebel 1Ki 21:23
your son so we can **e** him today. 2Ki 6:28
will have to **e** their own dung. 2Ki 18:27
be strong and **e** the good things .... Ezr 9:12
people went away to **e** and drink, ... Ne 8:12
will be left for them to **e**; .... Job 20:21
Poor people will **e** until they .... Ps 22:26
rained manna down on them to **e**; .... Ps 78:24
you sit down to **e** with a ruler, ... Pr 23:1
Don't **e** the food of selfish .... Pr 23:6
honey, don't **e** too much, or it .... Pr 25:16
person who has plenty to **e**, ... Pr 30:22
best that people can do is **e**, ... Ec 2:24
can do here on earth is to **e**, ... Ec 8:15
So go **e** your food and enjoy it; .... Ec 9:7
garden and **e** its best fruits. .... Sng 4:16
you will **e** good crops from the .... Is 1:19
for that person to **e** milk curds. .... Is 7:22
Lions will **e** hay as oxen do. .... Is 11:7
They say, "Let us **e** and drink, ... Is 22:13
old clothes; moths will **e** them. .... Is 50:9
not have money, come, buy and **e**! .... Is 55:1
They **e** the meat of pigs, and .... Is 65:4
Lions will **e** hay like oxen, ... Is 65:25
Women **e** their own babies, the .... La 2:20
what you find; **e** this scroll. .... Eze 3:1
tremble as you **e** your food, ... Eze 12:18
They will **e** their food with fear .... Eze 12:19
you are not to **e** the food people .... Eze 24:22
but vegetables to **e** and water to .... Da 1:12
of fruit for everyone to **e**. .... Da 4:21
and wild animals will **e** them. .... Hos 2:12
They will **e** but not have enough; .... Hos 4:10

You **e** tender lambs and fattened .... Am 6:4
plant gardens and **e** their fruit. .... Am 9:14
You will **e**, but you won't become .... Mic 6:14
there are no grapes left to **e**, ... Mic 7:1
will let their sheep **e** grass. .... Zph 2:7
They will **e** and lie down with no .... Zph 3:13
You **e**, but you do not become .... Hag 1:6
that are left **e** each other." .... Zch 11:9
But he will **e** the best sheep and .... Zch 11:16
so they won't **e** your crops. .... Mal 3:11
worry and say, 'What will we **e**?' .... Mt 6:31
does your teacher **e** with tax .... Mt 9:11
to pick the grain and **e** it. .... Mt 12:1
lawful only for priests to **e**. .... Mt 12:4
You give them something to **e**." .... Mt 14:16
even the dogs **e** the crumbs that .... Mt 15:27
for you to **e** the Passover meal? .... Mt 26:17
Take this bread and **e** it; .... Mt 26:26
the Jews never **e** before washing .... Mk 7:3
the table can **e** the children's .... Mk 7:28
May no one ever **e** fruit from you .... Mk 11:14
Why do you **e** and drink with tax .... Lk 5:30
your followers **e** and drink all .... Lk 5:33
is lawful only for priests to **e**. .... Lk 6:4
asked Jesus to **e** with him, ... Lk 7:36
Rest, **e**, drink, and enjoy life!" .... Lk 12:19
when Jesus went to **e** at the home .... Lk 14:1
I will not **e** another Passover .... Lk 22:16
so you may **e** and drink at my .... Lk 22:30
him, "Teacher, **e** something." .... Jn 4:31
for all these people to **e**?" .... Jn 6:5
them bread from heaven to **e**.'" .... Jn 6:31
man give us his flesh to **e**?" .... Jn 6:52
said to them, "Come and **e**." .... Jn 21:12
Get up, Peter; kill and **e**." .... Ac 10:13
an oath not to **e** or drink .... Ac 23:12
it is right to **e** all kinds of .... Rm 14:2
is right to **e** any kind of food .... Rm 14:3
is better not to **e** meat or drink .... Rm 14:21
those who **e** something without .... Rm 14:23
Do not even **e** with people like 1Co 5:11
encouraged to **e** meat sacrificed 1Co 8:10
if the food I **e** causes them to 1Co 8:13
They sat down to **e** and drink, ... 1Co 10:7
may invite you to **e** with them. 1Co 10:27
e anything that is put before 1Co 10:27
is, if you **e** or drink, or if...................... 1Co 10:31
This is because when you **e**, ... 1Co 11:21
Every time you **e** this bread and........... 1Co 11:26
hearts before you **e** the bread.............. 1Co 11:28
when you come together to **e**, ... 1Co 11:33
hungry should **e** at home so that 1Co 11:34
I have enough to **e** and when I go .... Php 4:12
refuses to work should not **e**." 2Th 3:10
tell them not to **e** certain foods 1Ti 4:3
people who do nothing but **e**." .... Tit 1:12
the Holy Tent cannot **e** from it. .... Heb 13:10
stay warm and get plenty to **e**," .... Jam 2:16
It will **e** your bodies like fire. .... Jam 5:3
lion looking for someone to **e**. 1Pe 5:8
e with you and have no fear, ... Jud 1:12
give the right to **e** the fruit .... Rev 2:7
sexual sins and to **e** food that .... Rev 2:20
I will come in and **e** with you, ... Rev 3:20
Take the scroll and **e** it. .... Rev 10:9
so he could **e** her baby as soon .... Rev 12:4
They will **e** her body and burn .... Rev 17:16
so that you can **e** the bodies of .... Rev 19:18
receive the right to **e** the fruit .... Rev 22:14

EATEN
family had **e** all the grain they .... Ge 43:2
meal must be **e** inside a house; .... Ex 12:46

EATER

It must not be **e**, because it is .... Ex 29:34
animals may be **e** and which ones .... Le 11:47
with half of its flesh **e** away. .... Nu 12:12
don't rest until they have **e**, ... Nu 23:24
have not **e** any of the holy part .... Dt 26:14
after they had **e** their meal in 1Sa 1:9
because he had **e** nothing all 1Sa 28:20
he had not **e** any food or drunk 1Sa 30:12
We have not **e** food at the king's............. 2Sa 19:42
lion had not **e** the body or hurt 1Ki 13:28
in the city will be **e** by dogs, ... 1Ki 14:11
in the city will be **e** by dogs, ... 1Ki 16:4
in the city will be **e** by dogs, ... 1Ki 21:24
food is not without salt, ... Job 6:6
like clothing **e** by moths................... Job 13:28
'All have **e** what they want of .... Job 31:31
like sheep to be **e** and have.................... Ps 44:11
as if I had **e** the best foods.................... Ps 63:5
with swords and **e** by wild dogs.............. Ps 63:10
food in secret tastes better. .... Pr 9:17
throw up the little you have **e**, ... Pr 23:8
as if she had **e** and washed her .... Pr 30:20
I have **e** my honeycomb and my .... Sng 5:1
gods have **e** up in sacrifice .... Je 3:24
They have **e** them up completely .... Je 10:25
'The parents have **e** sour grapes, ... Je 31:29
now I've never **e** anything that .... Eze 4:14
'The parents have **e** sour grapes, ... Eze 18:2
country to be **e** by wild animals .... Eze 33:27
caught and **e** by all the wild .... Eze 34:8
nations have **e** up his strength, ... Hos 7:9
you have **e** the fruit of your .... Hos 10:13
the swarming locusts have **e**; .... Joe 1:4
After they had **e**, Jesus sent .... Mk 8:9
the people had **e** the bread after............. Jn 6:23
I have never **e** food that is .... Ac 10:14
I have never **e** anything that is .... Ac 11:8
and he was **e** by worms and died. .... Ac 12:23
When they had **e** all they wanted, ... Ac 27:38
God created to be **e** with thanks.............. 1Ti 4:3
clothes have been **e** by moths. .... Jam 5:2

EATER

Out of the **e** comes something to .... Jdg 14:14
fall into the mouth of the **e**. .... Nah 3:12

EATING

keep them from **e** some of the .... Ge 3:22
animals that Isaac enjoyed **e**. .... Ge 25:28
they finished **e**, they spent .... Ge 31:54
the birds were **e** this food out .... Ge 40:17
they stood there, **e** the grass. .... Ge 41:2
will still be **e** from the old .... Le 25:22
around us like an ox **e** grass." .... Nu 22:4
its mouth to keep it from **e**...................... Dt 25:4
flesh of his children he is **e**, ... Dt 28:55
his hands and walked along **e** it. .... Jdg 14:9
Refresh yourself by **e** something. .... Jdg 19:5
will not begin **e** until the seer 1Sa 9:13
they finished **e**, they came down 1Sa 9:25
They're e meat without draining.............. 1Sa 14:33
the LORD by **e** meat without 1Sa 14:34
was in the house, **e** like a king. 1Sa 25:36
e and drinking and celebrating 1Sa 30:16
now they are **e** and drinking with 1Ki 1:25
of God finished **e** and drinking, ... 1Ki 13:23
with David, **e** and drinking, ... 1Ch 12:39
daughters were **e** and drinking .... Job 1:13
the donkeys were **e** grass nearby, ... Job 1:14
daughters were **e** and drinking .... Job 1:18
they worked for without **e** it; .... Job 20:18
people as if they were **e** bread. .... Ps 14:4
people as if they were **e** bread. .... Ps 53:4
they were still **e**, and while the .... Ps 78:30

as if they were **e** bread and..................... Pr 4:17
come true are like **e** fruit from .... Pr 13:12
trouble is like **e** with a broken .... Pr 25:19
will be **e** milk curds and honey .... Is 7:15
go back to **e** just milk curds .... Is 7:22
a hungry man who dreams he is **e**,........... Is 29:8
to give up **e** to honor the LORD................ Je 36:9
While they were **e** a meal with .... Je 41:1
e fat until you are full and .... Eze 39:19
and he began **e** grass like an ox. .... Da 4:33
like grasshoppers **e** crops, ... Nah 3:15
blood and from **e** forbidden food. .... Zch 9:7
Son of Man came, **e** and drinking, ... Mt 11:19
e with unwashed hands does not .... Mt 15:20
people were **e** and drinking, ... Mt 24:38
on Jesus' head while he was **e**. .... Mt 26:7
As they were **e**, Jesus said, "I................. Mt 26:21
While they were **e**, Jesus took .... Mt 26:26
sinners" were **e** there with Jesus .... Mk 2:15
saw Jesus **e** with the tax .... Mk 2:16
Herod and the people **e** with him. .... Mk 6:22
While Jesus was **e** there, a woman........... Mk 14:3
they were all **e**, Jesus said, "I .... Mk 14:18
While they were **e**, Jesus took .... Mk 14:22
apostles while they were **e**,.................... Mk 16:14
and other people were **e** there, ... Lk 5:29
Son of Man came **e** and drinking, ... Lk 7:34
that Jesus was **e** at the .... Lk 7:37
e and drinking what the people .... Lk 10:7
to eat the pods the pigs were **e**, ... Lk 15:16
After I finish **e** and drinking, ... Lk 17:8
People were **e**, drinking, ... Lk 17:27
People were **e**, drinking, buying, ... Lk 17:28
one of the people **e** with Jesus. .... Jn 12:2
they finished **e**, Jesus said to .... Jn 21:15
Once when he was **e** with them,............... Ac 1:4
e animals that have been .... Ac 15:20
e any animals that have been .... Ac 15:29
waiting and watching and not **e**.............. Ac 27:33
broke off a piece and began **e**. .... Ac 27:35
all felt better and started **e**,.................... Ac 27:36
faith by **e** food he thinks is .... Rm 14:15
e and drinking are not important. .... Rm 14:17
Do not let the **e** of food destroy .... Rm 14:20
I say about **e** meat sacrificed 1Co 8:4
and **e** does not make us better in 1Co 8:8
might see you **e** there and be 1Co 8:10
vineyard without **e** some of the 1Co 9:7
its mouth to keep it from **e**." 1Co 9:9
you and because **e** it might be 1Co 10:28
are not really **e** the Lord's 1Co 11:20
Peter stopped **e** with those who .... Gal 2:12
for you about **e** and drinking .... Col 2:16
its mouth to keep it from **e**," 1Ti 5:18
you while **e** meals with you. 2Pe 2:13
to sin by **e** food offered to .... Rev 2:14

EATS

Anybody who **e** yeast during this .... Ex 12:19
and anyone who **e** the meat will.............. Le 7:18
anyone is unclean and **e** the meat .... Le 7:20
If he then **e** meat from the .... Le 7:21
If someone **e** fat from an animal.............. Le 7:25
Anyone who **e** blood must be cut .... Le 7:27
Anyone who **e** meat from this.................. Le 11:40
Anyone who **e** in that house or .... Le 14:47
living with you who **e** blood. .... Le 17:10
who **e** blood must be cut off. .... Le 17:14
e an animal that died by itself .... Le 17:15
Anyone who **e** it then will be .... Le 19:8
If someone **e** some of the holy .... Le 22:14
He **e** too much, and he is always .... Dt 21:20
said any man who **e** today will be 1Sa 14:28

Disease e away parts of their .... Job 18:13
I made you. It e grass like an .... Job 40:15
e too much and drinks too much .... Mt 11:19
e too much and drinks too much .... Lk 7:34
sinners and even e with them." .... Lk 15:2
Anyone who e this bread will .... Jn 6:50
Anyone who e this bread will .... Jn 6:51
whoever e me will live because .... Jn 6:57
and whoever e this bread will............... Jn 6:58
the one who e only vegetables. .... Rm 14:3
the person who e only vegetables .... Rm 14:3
that the one who e all foods is .... Rm 14:3
who has knowledge e in an idol's 1Co 8:10
each person e without waiting 1Co 11:21
So a person who e the bread or 1Co 11:27

EBAL
and the curses from Mount E.................. Dt 11:29

EBED-MELECH
But E, a Cushite and a servant .... Je 38:7

EBENEZER
camped at E and the Philistines 1Sa 4:1

EBER
the father of all the sons of E.................. Ge 10:21

EBEZ
Rabbith, Kishion, E, ... Jos 19:20

EDEN
a place called E, and put the .... Ge 2:8
flowed through E and watered .... Ge 2:10
the garden of E to care for it .... Ge 2:15
of the garden of E to work the .... Ge 3:23
in the land of Nod, east of E. .... Ge 4:16
the people of E living in Tel 2Ki 19:12
son of Zimmah and E son of Joah........... 2Ch 29:12
E, Miniamin, Jeshua, Shemaiah,............... 2Ch 31:15
the people of E living in Tel .... Is 37:12
deserts into a garden like E; .... Is 51:3
Haran, Canneh, E, and the .... Eze 27:23
as if you were in E, the garden .... Eze 28:13
all the trees of E in the garden .... Eze 31:9
all the trees of E and the best .... Eze 31:16
So no tree in E is equal to you .... Eze 31:18
has become like the garden of E. .... Eze 36:35
of them is like the garden of E; .... Joe 2:3
as well as the leader of Beth E. .... Am 1:5

EDGE
from the e of the roof down. .... Ge 6:16
Machpelah at the e of his field. .... Ge 23:9
up a stone on e in that place .... Ge 35:14
at the e of the Nile River. .... Ex 2:3
meet him by the e of the river, ... Ex 7:15
Etham, on the e of the desert. .... Ex 13:20
the e of the land of Canaan. .... Ex 16:35
that stands up all around the e, ... Ex 25:25
blue cloth on the e of the end .... Ex 26:4
loops down the e of the end .... Ex 26:10
on the inside e next to the holy .... Ex 28:26
cloth along the e of the end .... Ex 36:11
loops along the e of the outside .... Ex 36:17
that stood up all around the e, ... Ex 37:12
on the inside e next to the holy .... Ex 39:19
the people at the e of the camp. .... Nu 11:1
a town on the e of your land. .... Nu 20:16
Arnon, at the e of his country. .... Nu 22:36
could see the e of the Israelite .... Nu 22:41
Etham, at the e of the desert. .... Nu 33:6
Aroer on the e of the Arnon .... Dt 2:36
on the e of the Arnon Ravine,............... Dt 4:48
wall around the e of the roof so .... Dt 22:8
to go to the e of the Jordan................. Jos 3:8
Ark came to the e of the river................ Jos 3:15

along the northern e of Jericho, ... Jos 18:12
down to the e of the enemy camp. .... Jdg 7:11
When I get to the e of the camp,............. Jdg 7:17
him came to the e of the enemy .... Jdg 7:19
getting near the e of the city, ... 1Sa 9:27
the outer e of the bowl was.................... 1Ki 7:24
came to the e of the camp, ... 2Ki 7:8
as far as the e of the desert, ... 1Ch 5:9
from the e of the horizon. .... Is 13:5
were along the e of the paved................. Eze 40:17
Its e was the foundation for the .... Eze 41:8
about nine inches around its e. .... Eze 43:13
and touched the e of his coat.................. Mt 9:20
touch just the e of his coat,.................... Mt 14:36
touch just the e of his coat,.................... Mk 6:56
took him to the e of the cliff .... Lk 4:29
and touched the e of his coat,................. Lk 8:44

EDGES
or cut the e of your beard. .... Le 19:27
earth by its e and shake evil .... Job 38:13

EDOM
the mountains of E to El Paran .... Ge 14:6
That is why people call him E. .... Ge 25:30
called Seir in the country of E. .... Ge 32:3
will meet you, my master, in E." .... Ge 33:14
history of Esau (also called E). .... Ge 36:1
of the tribes of E will be very .... Ex 15:15
messengers to the king of E. .... Nu 20:14
to go around the country of E. .... Nu 21:4
E will be conquered; his enemy .... Nu 24:18
Mount Hor, on the border of E. .... Nu 33:37
of Zin near the border of E. .... Nu 34:3
defeated you from E to Hormah. .... Dt 1:44
mountains of E for many days. .... Dt 2:1
and rose like the sun from E; .... Dt 33:2
Mount Halak near E to Baal Gad .... Jos 11:17
Lebanon and Mount Halak near E. .... Jos 12:7
far south, at the border of E. .... Jos 15:1
the mountains of E to Esau, ... Jos 24:4
you came from E, when you .... Jdg 5:4
messengers to the king of E, ... Jdg 11:17
the Ammonites, E, the king of 1Sa 14:47
nations were E, Moab, Ammon, ... 2Sa 8:12
the Red Sea, in the land of E. 1Ki 9:26
of the family of the king of E,............... 1Ki 11:14
time the land of E had no king; 1Ki 22:47
"Through the Desert of E." 2Ki 3:8
In Jehoram's time E broke away............... 2Ki 8:20
have defeated E, but you have 2Ki 14:10
kings ruled in E before there 1Ch 1:43
living in the mountains of E. 1Ch 4:42
E, Moab, the Ammonites, the 1Ch 18:11
the Red Sea in the land of E. 2Ch 8:17
is coming against you from E, ... 2Ch 20:2
are men from Ammon, Moab, and E. 2Ch 20:10
E broke away from Judah's rule 2Ch 21:8
the country of E has fought 2Ch 21:10
of Salt in the valley of E. 2Ch 25:11
I throw my sandals at E. .... Ps 60:8
the families of E and the...................... Ps 83:6
I throw my sandals at E. .... Ps 108:9
They will conquer E and Moab, ... Is 11:14
Someone calls to me from E, ... Is 21:11
will cut through E and destroy .... Is 34:5
smoke will rise from E forever. .... Is 34:10
Who is this coming from E, ... Is 63:1
of Egypt, Judah, E, Ammon, Moab, ... Je 9:26
people of E, Moab, and Ammon; .... Je 25:21
send messages to the kings of E, ... Je 27:3
in Moab, Ammon, E, and other .... Je 40:11
message is to E. This is what .... Je 49:7
glad, people of E, you who live .... La 4:21

E

EDOMITE

LORD will punish the sins of E; .... La 4:22
Moab and E say, "The people of .... Eze 25:8
E is there also, with its kings .... Eze 32:29
look toward E and prophesy .... Eze 35:2
I speak against the people of E, ... Eze 36:5
many countries, but E, Moab, and .... Da 11:41
empty, and E an empty desert, ... Joe 3:19
of one area as slaves to E. .... Am 1:6
of the king of E into lime. .... Am 2:1
what is left of E and the other .... Am 9:12
what the Lord GOD says about E: .... Ob 1:1
Attack! Let's go attack E!" .... Ob 1:1
The people of E might say, ... Mal 1:4

EDOMITE

These E leaders, listed by their .... Ge 36:40
He was Doeg the E, the chief of 1Sa 21:7
Doeg the E, who was standing 1Sa 22:9
So Doeg the E went and killed 1Sa 22:18
Doeg the E was there at Nob that 1Sa 22:22
The LORD caused Hadad the E, ... 1Ki 11:14
When Doeg the E came to Saul and .... Ps 51:19
And now the E women and their .... Eze 16:57

EDOMITES

He is the ancestor of the E, ... Ge 36:9
Esau was the father of the E. .... Ge 36:43
Then the E went out to meet them .... Nu 20:20
The E refused to let them pass .... Nu 20:21
E forced them out of the land .... Dt 2:22
hate E; they are your close .... Dt 23:7
and all the E became his 2Sa 8:14
Ammonites, E, Sidonians, ... 1Ki 11:1
The E surrounded him and his 2Ki 8:21
ten thousand E in the Valley 2Ki 14:7
E moved into Elath, and they 2Ki 16:6
eighteen thousand E in the 1Ch 18:12
and all the E became his 1Ch 18:13
and Moabites attacked the E, ... 2Ch 20:23
The E surrounded him and his 2Ch 21:9
army killed ten thousand E. 2Ch 25:11
came home after defeating the E, ... 2Ch 25:14
twelve thousand E at the Valley .... Ps 59:17
what the E did on the day .... Ps 137:7
and the E became guilty because .... Eze 25:12
is always angry with the E.' .... Mal 1:4

EDUCATED

were to be handsome and well e, ... Da 1:4
Where is the e person? 1Co 1:20

EDUCATION

had no special training or e. .... Ac 4:13

EFFORT

so make every e to continue .... Eph 4:3
Make every e to give yourself to 2Ti 2:15
make every e to come to me at .... Tit 3:12

EFFORTS

But e to clean the pot have .... Eze 24:12
break through all e to stop them .... Joe 2:8
not the result of your own e, ... Eph 2:9

EGG

no flavor in the white of an e. .... Job 6:6
hatching an e it did not lay, ... Je 17:11
if your children ask for an e, ... Lk 11:12

EGGS

sitting on the young birds or e, ... Dt 22:6
ostrich lays its e on the ground .... Job 39:14
nations, like a person taking e. .... Is 10:14
Owls will nest there and lay e. .... Is 34:15
hatch evil like e from poisonous .... Is 59:5
If you eat one of those e, ... Is 59:5

EGLON

of Lachish, and Debir king of E. .... Jos 10:3
Lachish, and E—gathered their .... Jos 10:5
Hebron, Jarmuth, Lachish, and E. .... Jos 10:23
went from Lachish to E. .... Jos 10:34
Israelites went from E to Hebron .... Jos 10:36
Just as they had done to E, ... Jos 10:37
E, Gezer, ... Jos 12:12
Lachish, Bozkath, E, ... Jos 15:39
So the LORD gave E king of Moab .... Jdg 3:12
E got the Ammonites and the .... Jdg 3:13
were ruled by E king of Moab for .... Jdg 3:14
sent Ehud to give E king of Moab .... Jdg 3:15
Ehud gave E king of Moab the .... Jdg 3:17
he had given E the payment, ... Jdg 3:18
he turned around and said to E, ... Jdg 3:19
Ehud went to King E, as he was .... Jdg 3:20
so Ehud left the sword in E. .... Jdg 3:22

EGYPT

went down to E to live because .... Ge 12:10
Abram came to E, the Egyptians .... Ge 12:14
the river of E and the great .... Ge 15:18
the Ishmaelites took him to E. .... Ge 37:28
the magicians and wise men of E. .... Ge 41:8
and set him over the land of E. .... Ge 41:33
he began serving the king of E. .... Ge 41:46
became terrible in all of E, ... Ge 41:55
sold grain to the people of E, ... Ge 41:56
has made me master over all E. .... Ge 45:9
the people in E and Canaan had .... Ge 47:15
me you will not bury me in E. .... Ge 47:29
carry me out of E, and bury me .... Ge 47:30
they put him in a coffin in E. .... Ge 50:26
son Joseph was already in E. .... Ex 1:5
Then a new king began to rule E, ... Ex 1:8
Then the king of E sent for the .... Ex 1:18
a long time, the king of E died. .... Ex 2:23
my people have suffered in E, ... Ex 3:7
am sending you to the king of E. .... Ex 3:10
you lead the people out of E, ... Ex 3:12
I will strike E with all the .... Ex 3:20
me go back to my people in E. .... Ex 4:18
the king of E that he must let .... Ex 6:11
then I will punish E terribly, ... Ex 7:4
I will punish E with my power, ... Ex 7:5
canals, ponds, and pools in E.' .... Ex 7:19
came up onto the land of E. .... Ex 8:7
All the farm animals in E died, ... Ex 9:6
dust through all the land of E. .... Ex 9:9
the worst in E since it became a .... Ex 9:18
falling in all the land of E. .... Ex 9:24
the land of E and will eat all .... Ex 10:12
stick over the land of E, ... Ex 10:13
all the land of E and settled .... Ex 10:14
will cover the land of E. .... Ex 10:21
everywhere in E for three days. .... Ex 10:22
the king and the people of E. .... Ex 11:1
and Aaron in the land of E: .... Ex 12:1
the land of E and kill all .... Ex 12:12
and people in the land of E. .... Ex 12:12
you when I punish the land of E. .... Ex 12:13
a loud outcry everywhere in E. .... Ex 12:30
power to bring you out of E. .... Ex 13:9
their minds and go back to E." .... Ex 13:17
all the other chariots of E, ... Ex 14:7
of the land of E where you were .... Ex 20:2
foreigners in the land of E. .... Ex 22:21
brought out of E with your great .... Ex 32:11
the fish we ate for free in E. .... Nu 11:5
We were better off in E!" .... Nu 11:18
seven years before Zoan in E. .... Nu 13:22
had died in E or in this desert. .... Nu 14:2

be better off going back to E." .... Nu 14:3
I did in E and in the desert .... Nu 14:22
went down into E and we lived .... Nu 20:15
it will go to the brook of E, ... Nu 34:5
fight for you as he did in E; .... Dt 1:30
the LORD brought you out of E, ... Dt 4:20
you out of E himself by his .... Dt 4:37
them when they came out of E. .... Dt 4:45
were slaves in E and that the .... Dt 5:15
We were slaves to the king of E, ... Dt 6:21
brought us out of E by his great .... Dt 6:21
brought out from E are ruining .... Dt 9:12
when they went down to E, ... Dt 10:22
brought you out of E at night. .... Dt 16:1
because you left E in a hurry. .... Dt 16:3
send people to E to get more .... Dt 17:16
diseases of E that you dread, ... Dt 28:60
send you back to E in ships, ... Dt 28:68
Red Sea when you came out of E. .... Jos 2:10
who had come out of E had been .... Jos 5:5
As slaves in E you were ashamed, ... Jos 5:9
I sent Moses and Aaron to E, ... Jos 24:5
of the Euphrates River and in E. .... Jos 24:14
people of Israel came out of E. .... Jdg 19:30
were slaves to the king of E. 1Sa 2:27
your people from slavery in E. 2Sa 7:23
the king of E by marrying his 1Ki 3:1
of the East, or any wisdom in E. 1Ki 4:30
imported horses from E and Kue. 1Ki 10:28
Shishak king of E, where he 1Ki 11:40
messengers to So, the king of E. 2Ki 17:4
king of E will hurt all those 2Ki 18:21
do you depend on E to give you 2Ki 18:24
Neco king of E went to help the 2Ki 23:29
chariots from E for about 2Ch 1:17
all the way to the border of E. 2Ch 26:8
Messengers will come from E; .... Ps 68:31
he did in E and his wonders .... Ps 78:43
brought us out of E as if we .... Ps 80:8
and worked wonders in E. .... Ps 105:27
who had done great things in E, ... Ps 106:21
the Israelites went out of E, ... Ps 114:1
sons in E the firstborn .... Ps 135:8
the people of Israel out of E. .... Ps 136:11
But the king of E and his army .... Ps 136:15
The idols of E will tremble .... Is 19:1
five cities in E will speak .... Is 19:18
and the Assyrians will go to E, ... Is 19:23
Assyria, and E will join .... Is 19:24
away prisoners from E and Cush. .... Is 20:4
River to the brook of E. .... Is 27:12
they want E to protect them. .... Is 30:2
I gave E to pay for you, and I .... Is 43:3
Then he will safely leave E. .... Je 43:12
and get some balm, people of E! .... Je 46:11
Announce this message in E, ... Je 46:14
messengers to E and asking them .... Eze 17:15
unclean with the idols of E. .... Eze 20:7
they went to E and became .... Eze 23:3
When the killing begins in E, ... Eze 30:4
I set fire to E and when all .... Eze 30:8
I will punish E, and they will .... Eze 30:19
the pride of E and all its .... Eze 32:12
song people will sing for E. .... Eze 32:16
First they call to E for help. .... Hos 7:11
and I called my son out of E. .... Hos 11:1
send a gift of olive oil to E. .... Hos 12:1
against you, as I did to E. .... Am 4:10
fall like the Nile River in E." .... Am 8:8
and falls like the river of E. .... Am 9:5
Cush and E gave her endless .... Nah 3:9
the land of E and gather them .... Zch 10:10
and his mother and escape to E, ... Mt 2:13

stayed in E until Herod died .... Mt 2:15
in a dream while he was in E. .... Mt 2:19
and sold him to be a slave in E. .... Ac 7:9
The king of E liked Joseph and .... Ac 7:10
went down to E, where he and his .... Ac 7:15
to have all the treasures of E, ... Heb 11:26
that Moses left E and was not .... Heb 11:27
them out of the land of E. .... Jud 1:5
This city is named Sodom and E, ... Rev 11:8

EGYPTIAN
The E officers saw her and told .... Ge 12:15
by Hagar, Sarah's E slave. .... Ge 21:9
Hagar, Sarah's E servant, was .... Ge 25:12
An E named Potiphar was an .... Ge 39:1
of his master, Potiphar the E, ... Ge 39:2
Every E sold Joseph his field, ... Ge 47:20
much stronger than the E women. .... Ex 1:19
saw an E beating a Hebrew man, ... Ex 2:11
he killed the E and hid his body .... Ex 2:12
to kill me as you killed the E?" .... Ex 2:14
us away, but an E defended us. .... Ex 2:19
cries when the E slave masters .... Ex 3:7
should ask her E neighbor and .... Ex 3:22
The E slave masters beat these .... Ex 5:14
their tricks the E magicians .... Ex 7:11
the same as the E people. .... Ex 8:22
officers and the E people .... Ex 11:3
and asked their E neighbors for .... Ex 12:35
and fire at the E army and made .... Ex 14:24
woman and an E father who was .... Le 24:10
see what he did to the E army, ... Dt 11:4
They found an E in a field and 1Sa 30:11
answered, "I'm an E, the slave 1Sa 30:13
So the E led David to the 1Sa 30:16
killed a large E who had a spear 2Sa 23:21
and E kings to attack us! 2Ki 7:6
Benaiah killed an E who was 1Ch 11:23
heard about the E army marching .... Je 37:5
bring back the E captives and .... Eze 29:14
Moses saw an E mistreating one .... Ac 7:24
as you killed the E yesterday?' .... Ac 7:28
you were the E who started some .... Ac 21:38

EGYPTIANS
When the E see you, they will .... Ge 12:12
said to all the E, "Go to Joseph .... Ge 41:55
and the E who ate with him at .... Ge 43:32
so loudly that the E heard him, ... Ge 45:2
away from the E, because they .... Ge 46:34
And the E had a time of sorrow .... Ge 50:3
E are showing great sorrow! .... Ge 50:11
So the E made life hard for the .... Ex 1:11
But the harder the E forced the .... Ex 1:12
The E were not merciful to them .... Ex 1:14
down to save them from the E. .... Ex 3:8
the way the E have made life .... Ex 3:9
I will cause the E to think well .... Ex 3:21
with you the riches of the E." .... Ex 3:22
whom the E are treating as .... Ex 6:5
hard work the E force you to do. .... Ex 6:6
hard work the E force you to do. .... Ex 6:7
The E will not be able to drink .... Ex 7:18
so the E could not drink water .... Ex 7:21
The E could not drink the water .... Ex 7:24
The E put them in piles, and the .... Ex 8:14
the E hate the sacrifices .... Ex 8:26
because all the E had boils, ... Ex 9:11
how I was hard on the E. .... Ex 10:2
well as the houses of all the E. .... Ex 10:6
LORD had caused the E to respect .... Ex 11:3
through Egypt to kill the E, ... Ex 12:23
he killed the E, he saved our .... Ex 12:27
and all the E got up during the .... Ex 12:30

The E also asked the Israelites .... Ex 12:33
LORD caused the E to think well .... Ex 12:36
the E will know that I am the .... Ex 14:4
E—with all the king's horses, ... Ex 14:9
we will stay and serve the E.' .... Ex 14:12
see these E again after today. .... Ex 14:13
I will make the E stubborn so .... Ex 14:17
E will know that I am the LORD. .... Ex 14:18
came between the E and the .... Ex 14:20
The E shouted, "Let's get away .... Ex 14:25
water will come back over the E, ... Ex 14:26
The E tried to run from it, ... Ex 14:27
saved the Israelites from the E, ... Ex 14:30
the LORD had used against the E, ... Ex 14:31
sicknesses I brought on the E. .... Ex 15:26
king and the E to help Israel. .... Ex 18:8
he had saved them from the E. .... Ex 18:9
you from the E and their king, ... Ex 18:10
children of the E and took all .... Nu 3:13
The E will hear about it! .... Nu 14:13
the E will tell this to those .... Nu 14:14
boldly in front of all the E. .... Nu 33:3
The E were burying their .... Nu 33:4
Don't hate E, because you were .... Dt 23:7
But the E were cruel to us, ... Dt 26:6
with boils like those the E had. .... Dt 28:27
brought many disasters on the E. .... Jos 24:5
and the E chased them with .... Jos 24:6
you and the E and made the sea............. Jos 24:7
you from the E and from all .... Jdg 6:9
When the E, Amorites, Ammonites .... Jdg 10:11
who struck the E with all kinds 1Sa 4:8
the king of Egypt and the E. 1Sa 6:6
Moabites, E, and Amorites did. .... Ezr 9:1
He caused the E to hate his .... Ps 105:25
signs among the E and worked .... Ps 105:27
but the E turned against what he .... Ps 105:28
The E were glad when they left, ... Ps 105:38
the firstborn sons of the E. .... Ps 136:10
the LORD will whistle for the E,.............. Is 7:18
will cause the E to fight .... Is 19:2
The E will be afraid, and I will .... Is 19:3
In that day the E will be like .... Is 19:16
LORD will show himself to the E, ... Is 19:21
So the E will be shamed........................ Is 20:4
E are only people and are not................ Is 31:3
had sexual relations with the E, ... Eze 16:26
will scatter the E among the .... Eze 29:12
will scatter the E among the .... Eze 30:23
will scatter the E among the .... Eze 30:26
I will let the E' water become .... Eze 32:14
The E will fall among those .... Eze 32:20
If the E do not go to Jerusalem, ... Zch 14:18
The E taught Moses everything .... Ac 7:22
But when the E tried it, they .... Heb 11:29

EHI
Gera, Naaman, E, Rosh, Muppim, ... Ge 46:21

EHUD
He was E, son of Gera from the .... Jdg 3:15
Israel sent E to give Eglon king .... Jdg 3:15
E made himself a sword with two .... Jdg 3:16
E gave Eglon king of Moab the .... Jdg 3:17
E sent away the people who had .... Jdg 3:18
E went to King Eglon, as he was .... Jdg 3:20
E said, "I have a message from .... Jdg 3:20
E reached with his left hand and .... Jdg 3:21
so E left the sword in Eglon. .... Jdg 3:22
returned just after E left,...................... Jdg 3:24
were waiting, E had escaped. .... Jdg 3:26
the hills with E leading them. .... Jdg 3:27
Israel followed E and captured .... Jdg 3:28
After E, Shamgar son of Anath .... Jdg 3:31

After E died, the Israelites .... Jdg 4:1
Jeush, Benjamin, E, Kenaanah, ... 1Ch 7:10
the descendants of E and leaders 1Ch 8:6

EHUD'S
E descendants were Naaman,.................. 1Ch 8:7

EIGHT
when a baby boy is e days old, ... Ge 17:12
when he was e days old as God .... Ge 21:4
Jesse had e sons. In Saul's 1Sa 17:12
Josiah was e years old when he 2Ki 22:1
and its stairway had e steps. .... Eze 40:31
up seven shepherds, e leaders of .... Mic 5:5
When the baby was e days old, ... Lk 2:21
a few people—e in all—were saved 1Pe 3:20

EIGHTEEN
there who, for e years, had an .... Lk 13:11
been held by Satan for e years. .... Lk 13:16

EIGHTEENTH
In Josiah's e year as king, ... 2Ki 22:3
in Nebuchadnezzar's e year, ... Je 52:29

EIGHTH
on the first day and the e day. .... Le 23:39
When you plant in the e year,................. Le 25:22
Then on the e day, they must .... Nu 6:10
king, in the e month, the month 1Ki 6:38
alive now, is also an e king. .... Rev 17:11
was chrysolite, the e was beryl, ... Rev 21:20

EIGHTY
Moses was e years old and Aaron .... Ex 7:7
peace in the land for e years. .... Jdg 3:30
or, if we are strong, e years. .... Ps 90:10
of about one hundred e miles. .... Rev 14:20

EIGHTY-EIGHT
were two hundred e of them. 1Ch 25:7

EIGHTY-FIVE
Now here I am, e years old. .... Jos 14:10
day he killed e men who wore 1Sa 22:18
killed one hundred e thousand 2Ki 19:35
killed one hundred e thousand .... Is 37:36

EIGHTY-FOUR
and she was a widow for e years. .... Lk 2:37

EIGHTY-SEVEN
show there were e thousand 1Ch 7:5
the gateway was e and one-half .... Eze 40:15
which was e and one-half feet .... Eze 40:36
long and e and one-half feet .... Eze 42:2
Temple that is e and one-half .... Eze 45:2

EIGHTY-SIX
Abram was e years old when Hagar .... Ge 16:16

EIGHTY-THREE
and Aaron was e when they spoke........... Ex 7:7

EKED
road to Beth E of the Shepherds. 2Ki 10:12
them at the well near Beth E— 2Ki 10:14

EKER
They were Maaz, Jamin, and E. 1Ch 2:27

EKRON
of Egypt to E in the north, ... Jos 13:3
sent the Ark of God to E. 1Sa 5:10
of Gath and to the gates of E.................. 1Sa 17:52
god of E, if I will recover 2Ki 1:2
Ashkelon, Gaza, E, and the..................... Je 25:20

EL
the mountains of Edom to E Paran........... Ge 14:6
to the Valley of Iphtah E. .... Jos 19:14
and the Valley of Iphtah E. .... Jos 19:27
Iron, Migdal E, Horem, Beth .... Jos 19:38
room of the temple of E Berith. .... Jdg 9:46

ELA

Shimei son of E was governor of 1Ki 4:18

ELAH

Oholibamah, E, Pinon, ... Ge 36:41
the Valley of E and camped there 1Sa 17:2
and the army in the Valley of E, ... 1Sa 17:19
you killed in the Valley of E, ... 1Sa 21:9
and his son E became king in his 1Ki 16:6
Hoshea son of E made plans 2Ki 15:30
Hoshea son of E became king over 2Ki 17:1
Hoshea son of E was king of 2Ki 18:1
Oholibamah, E, Pinon, ... 1Ch 1:52
sons were Iru, E, and Naam. 1Ch 4:15
of Jeroham and E son of Uzzi. 1Ch 9:8

ELAM

of Shem were E, Asshur, Arphaxad .... Ge 10:22
Kedorlaomer was king of E, ... Ge 14:1
Egypt, Cush, E, Babylonia, ... Is 11:11
city of Susa, in the area of E. .... Da 8:2

ELAMITE

Babylon, the E people of Susa, ... Ezr 4:9
of Jehiel the E said to Ezra, ... Ezr 10:2

ELASAH

Nethanel, Jozabad, and E. .... Ezr 10:22
of Judah sent E son of Shaphan .... Je 29:3

ELATH

the towns of E and Ezion Geber.............. Dt 2:8
town near E on the shore of the 1Ki 9:26
the town of E and made it part 2Ki 14:22
back the city of E for Aram, ... 2Ki 16:6
Then Edomites moved into E,................. 2Ki 16:6
Ezion Geber and E near the Red 2Ch 8:17
the town of E and made it part 2Ch 26:2

ELDAAH

Epher, Hanoch, Abida, and E.................. Ge 25:4
Epher, Hanoch, Abida, and E................. 1Ch 1:33

ELDAD

Two men named E and Medad were .... Nu 11:26
E and Medad are prophesying in .... Nu 11:27

ELDER

But an e must not be a new 1Ti 3:6
An e must also have the respect 1Ti 3:7
to someone who accuses an e, ... 1Ti 5:19
An e must not be guilty of doing .... Tit 1:6
I also am an e. I have seen 1Pe 5:1
From the E. To the chosen lady 2Jn 1:1
From the E. To my dear friend 3Jn 1:1
And the e said to me, "These .... Rev 7:14

ELDERS

officers, the e of his court, ... Ge 50:7
and gather the e and tell them .... Ex 3:16
seventy of the e of Israel must .... Ex 24:1
e of the group of people must .... Le 4:15
seventy of the e together and .... Nu 11:24
Your e and judges should go to .... Dt 21:2
of the e who lived after .... Jos 24:31
the e of Gilead went to Jephthah .... Jdg 11:5
gathered ten of the e of the................... Ru 4:2
all the people and e who were at .... Ru 4:11
watching over the e of the .... Ezr 5:5
and takes away the wisdom of e. .... Job 12:20
him in the meeting of the e. .... Ps 107:32
case against the e and other .... Is 3:14
My priests and my e have died in .... La 1:19
The e of Jerusalem sit on the .... La 2:10
they did not respect our e. .... La 5:12
advice from the e will be lost.................. Eze 7:26
house with the e of Judah in .... Eze 8:1
were seventy of the e of Israel .... Eze 8:11
where the Jewish e, the leading .... Mt 16:21

and the Jewish e of the people. .... Mt 26:47
the law and the e were gathered. .... Mt 26:57
priests and e of the people .... Mt 27:1
priests and e convinced the .... Mt 27:20
the Jewish e were also making .... Mt 27:41
the law, and the e came to him. .... Mk 11:27
sent some Jewish e to him to ask .... Lk 7:3
they were afraid of the e. .... Jn 7:13
the rulers, the e, and the...................... Ac 4:5
These e had trusted the Lord,................ Ac 14:23
this with the apostles and e. .... Ac 15:2
apostles and the e gathered to .... Ac 15:6
called for the e of the church................. Ac 20:17
whole council of the e and can tell you .... Ac 22:5
priests and the e and said, ... Ac 23:14
The e who lead the church well 1Ti 5:17
could appoint e in every town, ... Tit 1:5
sick should call the church's e. .... Jam 5:14
to say to the e in your group. 1Pe 5:1
twenty-four e sitting on them .... Rev 4:4

ELEAD

Ezer and E went to Gath to steal 1Ch 7:21

ELEADAH

Tahath's son was E. Eleadah's 1Ch 7:20

ELEALEH

rebuilt Heshbon, E, Kiriathaim, ... Nu 32:37
Heshbon and E cry out loud. .... Is 15:4
the people of Heshbon and E.................. Is 16:9
from Heshbon to E and Jahaz. .... Je 48:34

ELEASAH

Helez was the father of E. 1Ch 2:39
E was the father of Sismai..................... 1Ch 2:40
E was Raphah's son, and Azel was 1Ch 8:37
E was Rephaiah's son, and Azel.............. 1Ch 9:43

ELEAZAR

to Nadab, Abihu, E, and Ithamar. .... Ex 6:23
E son of Aaron married a .... Ex 6:25
his other sons, E and Ithamar, ... Le 10:6
very angry with E and Ithamar, ... Le 10:16
So E and Ithamar served as .... Nu 3:4
Phinehas son of E, the son of .... Nu 25:7
E became priest in his place. .... Dt 10:6
E the priest, Joshua son of Nun, ... Jos 14:1
And E son of Aaron died and was .... Jos 24:33
descendant of E, and Ahimelech, ... 1Ch 24:3

ELEVEN

two slave girls, and his e sons. .... Ge 32:22
and e stars bowing down to me." .... Ge 37:9
e curtains made from goat hair. .... Ex 26:7
another tent of e curtains made .... Ex 36:14
e curtains were the same size— .... Ex 36:15
On the third day offer e bulls, ... Nu 29:20
Mount Seir road takes e days. .... Dt 1:2
There were e towns and their................. Jos 15:51
it held about e thousand gallons............. 1Ki 7:26
king in Jerusalem for e years. 2Ki 23:36
king in Jerusalem for e years. 2Ki 24:18
king in Jerusalem for e years. 2Ch 36:5
king in Jerusalem for e years. 2Ch 36:11
and during the e years that................... Je 1:3
king in Jerusalem for e years. .... Je 52:1
The e followers went to Galilee .... Mt 28:16
himself to the e apostles while .... Mk 16:14
these things to the e apostles .... Lk 24:9
they found the e apostles and .... Lk 24:33
an apostle with the other e. .... Ac 1:26
stood up with the e apostles, ... Ac 2:14

ELEVENTH

on the first day of the e month, ... Dt 1:3
during the e year he was king, ... 1Ki 6:38

ELHANAN

Judah in the **e** year Joram son 2Ki 9:29
until Zedekiah's **e** year as king. 2Ki 25:2
and Macbannai was **e** in command. 1Ch 12:13
The **e** was Eliashib. 1Ch 24:12
E, twelve men were chosen from 1Ch 25:18
e commander, for the eleventh 1Ch 27:14
month in Zedekiah's **e** year. .... Je 39:2
until Zedekiah's **e** year as king. .... Je 52:5
It was the **e** year of our .... Eze 26:1
It was in the **e** year of our .... Eze 30:20
It was in the **e** year of our .... Eze 31:1
-fourth day of the **e** month, ... Zch 1:7
chrysoprase, the **e** was jacinth, ... Rev 21:20

ELHANAN

E son of Jaare-Oregim from 2Sa 21:19
E son of Dodo from Bethlehem; 2Sa 23:24
E son of Dodo from Bethlehem; 1Ch 11:26
E son of Jair killed Lahmi, ... 1Ch 20:5

ELI

the sons of **E**, served as priests 1Sa 1:3
Now **E** the priest was sitting on 1Sa 1:9
praying, **E** watched her mouth. 1Sa 1:12
was not heard. **E** thought she was 1Sa 1:13
E answered, "Go! I wish you well. 1Sa 1:17
Hannah brought Samuel to **E**. 1Sa 1:25
She said to **E**, "As surely as you 1Sa 1:26
the LORD under **E** the priest. 1Sa 2:11
When **E** blessed Elkanah and his 1Sa 2:20
Now **E** was very old. He heard 1Sa 2:22
E said to his sons, "Why do you 1Sa 2:23
A man of God came to **E** and said, ... 1Sa 2:27
Samuel served the LORD under **E**. 1Sa 3:1
ran to **E** and said, "I am here. 1Sa 3:5
Samuel again went to **E** and said, ... 1Sa 3:6
got up and went to **E** and said, ... 1Sa 3:8
I will do to **E** and his family 1Sa 3:12
I told **E** I would punish his 1Sa 3:13
to tell **E** about the vision, ... 1Sa 3:15
but **E** called to him, "Samuel, my 1Sa 3:16
E asked, "What did the LORD say 1Sa 3:17
So Samuel told **E** everything and 1Sa 3:18
E was by the side of the road. 1Sa 4:13
E heard the crying and asked, ... 1Sa 4:14
E was now ninety-eight years old, ... 1Sa 4:15
E asked, "What happened, my son? 1Sa 4:16
E fell backward off his chair. 1Sa 4:18
God had been taken and that **E**, ... 1Sa 4:19
the son of **E**, the LORD's priest 1Sa 14:3
about the priest **E** and his 1Ki 2:27
in a loud voice, "**E**, Eli, lama .... Mt 27:46

ELIAB

tribe of Zebulun—**E** son of Helon; .... Nu 1:9
of Zebulun is **E** son of Helon. .... Nu 2:7
E son of Helon was over the .... Nu 10:16
were brothers, the sons of **E**; .... Nu 16:1
the sons of **E**, but they said, ... Nu 16:12
The son of Pallu was **E**, ... Nu 26:8
the sons of **E** the Reubenite, ... Dt 11:6
Samuel saw **E**, and he thought, ... 1Sa 16:6
at how handsome **E** is or how tall 1Sa 16:7
first son was **E**, the second was 1Sa 17:13
oldest brother **E** heard David 1Sa 17:28
Jesse's first son was **E**. 1Ch 2:13
son was **E**. Eliab's son was 1Ch 6:27
second in command. **E** was third, ... 1Ch 12:9
Jehiel, Unni, **E**, Benaiah, ... 1Ch 15:18
Jehiel, Unni, **E**, Maaseiah, and 1Ch 15:20
Mattithiah, **E**, Benaiah, ... 1Ch 16:5
Abihail was the daughter of **E**, ... 2Ch 11:18

ELIADA

Elishama, **E**, and Eliphelet. 2Sa 5:16
Solomon's enemy—Rezon son of **E**. 1Ki 11:23
E, a brave soldier, had two 2Ch 17:17

ELIAHBA

E the Shaalbonite; the sons of 2Sa 23:32
Baharumite; **E** the Shaalbonite 1Ch 11:33

ELIAKIM

so the king sent **E**, Shebna, and 2Ki 18:18
Then **E** son of Hilkiah, Shebna, ... 2Ki 18:26
Then **E**, Shebna, and Joah tore 2Ki 18:37
Hezekiah sent **E**, the palace 2Ki 19:2
Josiah's son **E** the king in place 2Ki 23:34
brother **E** the king of Judah 2Ch 36:4
E, Maaseiah, Miniamin, Micaiah, ... Ne 12:41
for my servant **E** son of Hilkiah. .... Is 22:20
E, Shebna, and Joah went out to .... Is 36:3
Then **E**, Shebna, and Joah said to .... Is 36:11
Then **E**, Shebna, and Joah tore .... Is 36:22
Hezekiah sent **E**, the palace .... Is 37:2
Abiud was the father of **E**. .... Mt 1:13
Jonam was the son of **E**. .... Lk 3:30

ELIAM

is Bathsheba daughter of **E**. 2Sa 11:3
E son of Ahithophel the Gilonite; 2Sa 23:34

ELIASAPH

the tribe of Gad—**E** son of Deuel; .... Nu 1:14
people of Gad is **E** son of Deuel. .... Nu 2:14
of Gershon was **E** son of Lael. .... Nu 3:24
E son of Deuel was over the .... Nu 10:20

ELIASHIB

Hodaviah, **E**, Pelaiah, Akkub, ... 1Ch 3:24
The eleventh was **E**. 1Ch 24:12
the room of Jehohanan son of **E**. .... Ezr 10:6
Among the singers: **E**. Among the .... Ezr 10:24
E, Mattaniah, Jeremoth, ... Ezr 10:27
Vaniah, Meremoth, **E**, ... Ezr 10:36
E the high priest and his fellow .... Ne 3:1
the entrance to the house of **E**, ... Ne 3:20
Joiakim was the father of **E**. .... Ne 12:10
written down in the days of **E**, ... Ne 12:22
to the time of Johanan son of **E**. .... Ne 12:23
that happened, **E** the priest, who .... Ne 13:4
E let Tobiah use one of the .... Ne 13:5
found out the evil **E** had done by .... Ne 13:7
the son of **E** the high priest. .... Ne 13:28

ELIATHAH

Hananiah, Hanani, **E**, Giddalti, ... 1Ch 25:4
twelve men were chosen from **E**, ... 1Ch 25:27

ELIDAD

of Benjamin, **E** son of Kislon; .... Nu 34:21

ELIEHOENAI

was sixth, and **E** was seventh. 1Ch 26:3
E son of Zerahiah, with two .... Ezr 8:4

ELIEL

Ishi, **E**, Azriel, Jeremiah, ... 1Ch 5:24
Eliel's son. **E** was Toah's son. 1Ch 6:34
Elienai, Zillethai, **E**, ... 1Ch 8:20
sons were Ishpan, Eber, **E**, ... 1Ch 8:22
E the Mahavite; Jeribai and 1Ch 11:46
E, Obed, and Jaasiel the 1Ch 11:47
Attai was sixth, **E** was seventh, ... 1Ch 12:11
group, with **E** as their leader. 1Ch 15:9
Shemaiah, **E**, and Amminadab. 1Ch 15:11
Jozabad, **E**, Ismakiah, Mahath 2Ch 31:13

ELIENAI

E, Zillethai, Eliel, ... 1Ch 8:20

ELIEZER
so my slave E from Damascus will .... Ge 15:2
The other son was named E, ... Ex 18:4
Joash, E, Elioenai, Omri 1Ch 7:8
and E had the job of blowing 1Ch 15:24
Moses' sons were Gershom and E. 1Ch 23:15
E had no other sons, but 1Ch 23:17
were Shubael's relatives from E: 1Ch 26:25
E son of Zicri was over the 1Ch 27:16
Then E son of Dodavahu from the 2Ch 20:37
E, Ariel, Shemaiah, Elnathan,................. Ezr 8:16
E, Jarib, and Gedaliah. .... Ezr 10:18
), Pethahiah, Judah, and E. .... Ezr 10:23
E, Ishijah, Malkijah, Shemaiah, ... Ezr 10:31
Joshua was the son of E......................... Lk 3:29
E was the son of Jorim. .... Lk 3:29

ELIHOREPH
E and Ahijah, sons of Shisha,................. 1Ki 4:3

ELIHU
E was Tohu's son, and Tohu was 1Sa 1:1
Jozabad, E, and Zillethai. 1Ch 12:20
Obed, Elzabad, E, and Semakiah. 1Ch 26:7
E, and Semakiah were skilled 1Ch 26:7
E, one of David's brothers, was 1Ch 27:18
But E son of Barakel the Buzite,............. Job 32:2
E was also angry with Job's .... Job 32:3
E had waited before speaking to .... Job 32:4
when E saw that the three men .... Job 32:5
So E son of Barakel the Buzite .... Job 32:6
Then E said: .... Job 34:1
Then E said: .... Job 35:1
E continued: .... Job 36:1

ELIJAH
Now E the Tishbite was a prophet 1Ki 17:1
and did what E told her to do. 1Ki 17:15
E carried the boy downstairs and 1Ki 17:23
Ahab and told him where E was. 1Ki 18:16
Then E said to the prophets of 1Ki 18:25
The LORD gave his power to E, ... 1Ki 18:46
his oxen and ran to follow E. 1Ki 19:20
his knees before E and begged, ... 2Ki 1:13
The LORD's angel said to E, ... 2Ki 1:15
E told Ahaziah, "This is what 2Ki 1:16
the LORD, through E, had said he 2Ki 1:17
LORD to take E by a whirlwind 2Ki 2:1
E said to Elisha, "Please stay 2Ki 2:2
E took off his coat, rolled it 2Ki 2:8
and separated E from Elisha. 2Ki 2:11
is the LORD, the God of E?" 2Ki 2:14
now has the spirit E had." 2Ki 2:15
his servant E the Tishbite: '.................. 2Ki 9:36
I will send you E the prophet .... Mal 4:5
you will believe that John is E, ... Mt 11:14
say you are E, and still others................. Mt 16:14
Then Moses and E appeared to .... Mt 17:3
one for Moses, and one for E." .... Mt 17:4
law say that E must come first? .... Mt 17:10
I tell you that E has already .... Mt 17:12
this said, "He is calling E." .... Mt 27:47
say you are E, and others say .... Mk 8:28
Lord in spirit and power like E. .... Lk 1:17
in Israel during the time of E................. Lk 4:25
you? Are you E?" He answered, ... Jn 1:21
the Christ or E or the Prophet, ... Jn 1:25
what the Scripture says about E, ... Rm 11:2
E was a human being just like us. .... Jam 5:17

ELIKA
the Harodite; E the Harodite; 2Sa 23:25

ELIM
Then the people traveled to E, ... Ex 15:27
community left E and came to the .... Ex 16:1

which was between E and Sinai; .... Ex 16:1
They left Marah and went to E; .... Nu 33:9
They left E and camped near the .... Nu 33:10
is heard as far away as Beer E. .... Is 15:8

ELIMELECH
a man named E left the town of .... Ru 1:2
Naomi's husband, E, died, and .... Ru 1:3
that belonged to our relative E. .... Ru 4:3
that belonged to E and Kilion................. Ru 4:9

ELIOENAI
E, Hizkiah, and Azrikam. 1Ch 3:23
E had seven sons: Hodaviah, ... 1Ch 3:24
Eliezer, E, Omri, Jeremoth 1Ch 7:8
E, Maaseiah, Ishmael, Nethanel, ... Ezr 10:22
E, Eliashib, Mattaniah, Jeremoth, ... Ezr 10:27
Miniamin, Micaiah, E, Zechariah, ... Ne 12:41

ELIPHAL
Sacar the Hararite; E son of Ur; 1Ch 11:35

ELIPHAZ
Adah gave birth to E for Esau. .... Ge 36:4
Esau's sons were E, son of Adah .... Ge 36:10
E had five sons: Teman, Omar, ... Ge 36:11
E also had a slave woman named .... Ge 36:12
and Timna and E gave birth to .... Ge 36:12
Esau's first son was E. .... Ge 36:15
that came from E in the land of .... Ge 36:16
sons were E, Reuel, Jeush, ... 1Ch 1:35
E the Temanite, Bildad the .... Job 2:11
Then E the Temanite answered: .... Job 4:1
Then E the Temanite answered: .... Job 15:1
Then E the Temanite answered: .... Job 22:1
he said to E the Temanite, ... Job 42:7
So E the Temanite, Bildad the................. Job 42:9

ELIPHELEHU
Mattithiah, E, Mikneiah, ... 1Ch 15:18
Mattithiah, E, Mikneiah, ... 1Ch 15:21

ELIPHELET
Elishama, Eliada, and E........................ 2Sa 5:16
E son of Ahasbai the Maacathite; 2Sa 23:34
was Jeush, and E was his third. 1Ch 8:39
Elishama, Beeliada, and E. 1Ch 14:7
E, Jeuel, and Shemaiah, with .... Ezr 8:13
Mattattah, Zabad, E, Jeremai,................. Ezr 10:33

ELISHA
oil on E son of Shaphat from 1Ki 19:16
Elijah said to E, "Please stay 2Ki 2:2
E now has the spirit Elijah had. 2Ki 2:15
When E, the man of God, heard 2Ki 5:8
Then E prayed, "LORD, open my 2Ki 6:17
Then E went to Damascus, where 2Ki 8:7
At this time E became sick. 2Ki 13:14
Then E died and was buried. 2Ki 13:20
the time of the prophet E. .... Lk 4:27

ELISHAH
of Javan were E, Tarshish, ... Ge 10:4
sons were E, Tarshish, Kittim 1Ch 1:7

ELISHAMA
son of Joseph—E son of Ammihud; .... Nu 1:10
of Ephraim is E son of Ammihud. .... Nu 2:18
and E son of Ammihud was the .... Nu 10:22
E, Eliada, and Eliphelet. 2Sa 5:16
son of E from the king's family, ... 2Ki 25:25
Jekamiah was the father of E. 1Ch 2:41
E was Ammihud's son. 1Ch 7:26
E, Beeliada, and Eliphelet. 1Ch 14:7
sent the priests E and Jehoram. 2Ch 17:8
E the royal secretary; .... Je 36:12
in the room of E the royal .... Je 36:20
from the room of E the royal .... Je 36:21
Nethaniah was the son of E. .... Je 41:1

E

ELISHAPHAT
of Adaiah, and E son of Zicri.................2Ch 23:1

ELISHEBA
Aaron married E, the daughter of ....Ex 6:23
E gave birth to Nadab, Abihu, ...Ex 6:23

ELISHUA
Ibhar, E, Nepheg, Japhia, ...2Sa 5:15
Ibhar, E, Elpelet, ...1Ch 14:5

ELIUD
Akim was the father of E. ....Mt 1:14
E was the father of Eleazar. ....Mt 1:15

ELIZABETH
Zechariah's wife, E, came from ....Lk 1:5
Zechariah and E did what ....Lk 1:6
because E could not have a baby, ...Lk 1:7
Your wife, E, will give birth to ....Lk 1:13
wife, E, became pregnant ....Lk 1:24
house for five months. E said, ...Lk 1:24
Now E, your relative, is also ....Lk 1:36
Zechariah's house and greeted E. ....Lk 1:40
When E heard Mary's greeting, ...Lk 1:41
and E was filled with the Holy ....Lk 1:41
stayed with E for about three ....Lk 1:56
it was time for E to give birth, ...Lk 1:57
people said to E, "But no one ....Lk 1:61

ELIZAPHAN
families were E son of Uzziel. ....Nu 3:30
of Zebulun, E son of Parnach; ....Nu 34:25

ELIZUR
of Reuben—E son of Shedeur; ....Nu 1:5
of Reuben is E son of Shedeur. ....Nu 2:10
and E son of Shedeur was the ....Nu 10:18

ELKANAH
Then E and Hannah would go home. 1Sa 2:20

ELKOSH
who was from the town of E. ....Nah 1:1

ELLASAR
was king of E, Kedorlaomer was ....Ge 14:1
and Arioch king of E—four kings ....Ge 14:9

ELMADAM
Cosam was the son of E.......................Lk 3:28
E was the son of Er. ....Lk 3:28

ELOI
in a loud voice, "E, Eloi, lama ....Mk 15:34
voice, "Eloi, E, lama ....Mk 15:34

ELON
E from the tribe of Zebulun was.............Jdg 12:11

ELONITE
Elon came the E family group; ....Nu 26:26

ELPELET
Ibhar, Elishua, E,................................1Ch 14:5

ELTEKEH
E, Gibbethon, Baalath, ...Jos 19:44
The tribe of Dan gave them E, ...Jos 21:23

ELTEKON
Maarath, Beth Anoth, and E. ....Jos 15:59

ELTOLAD
E, Kesil, Hormah, ...Jos 15:30
E, Bethul, Hormah, ...Jos 19:4

ELUL
day of the month of E. ....Ne 6:15

ELUZAI
There were E, Jerimoth, Bealiah, ...1Ch 12:5

ELYMAS
But E, the magician, was against ....Ac 13:8
E is the name for Bar-Jesus in ....Ac 13:8

He looked straight at E ....Ac 13:9
everything became dark for E, ...Ac 13:11

ELZABAD
Johanan was eighth, E was ninth, ...1Ch 12:12
Rephael, Obed, E, Elihu, and 1Ch 26:7

ELZAPHAN
were Mishael, E, and Sithri. ....Ex 6:22
two sons named Mishael and E. ....Le 10:4
Mishael and E obeyed Moses and ....Le 10:5

EMBARRASS
and you e those who are poor. 1Co 11:22

EMBARRASSED
too ashamed and e to lift up my ....Ezr 9:6
because he was e and ashamed..............Est 6:12
Let them be ashamed and e, ...Ps 35:26
Don't let me be e because of my...........Ps 119:116
The moon will be e, and the sun...........Is 24:23
Don't be e, because you will not..............Is 54:4
ashamed and e and cover their ....Je 14:3
ashamed and e about your ways, ...Eze 36:32
who see the future will be e. ....Mic 3:7
you will be e and will have to.................Lk 14:9

EMBARRASSMENT
cause them only shame and e." ....Is 30:5

EMBROIDERED
e cloth for the necks of the ....Jdg 5:30

EMEK
Jericho, Beth Hoglah, E Keziz, ...Jos 18:21
went north of Beth E and Neiel ....Jos 19:27

EMERALD
turquoise, a sapphire, and an e; ....Ex 28:18
turquoise, a sapphire, and an e; ....Ex 39:11
topaz, and e, yellow quartz, ...Eze 28:13
was a rainbow the color of an e..............Rev 4:3
chalcedony, the fourth was e, ...Rev 21:19

EMITES
and the E in Shaveh Kiriathaim................Ge 14:5
The E, who lived in Ar before, ...Dt 2:10
The E were thought to be ....Dt 2:11
Moabite people called them E. ....Dt 2:11

EMMAUS
were going to a town named E, ...Lk 24:13
They came near the town of E, ...Lk 24:28

EMPEROR
He wants a decision from the e. ....Ac 25:21
to write the e about him........................Ac 25:26

EMPIRE
from all Xerxes' e were there. ....Est 1:3
in all the e of King Xerxes....................Est 1:16
a holiday for all the e and had ....Est 2:18
all the king's e ordering them................Est 3:13
this in all the e of King Xerxes ....Est 8:12
through all the e became Jews, ...Est 8:17
in all the e of King Xerxes ....Est 9:2
living in the e were afraid of ....Est 9:2
He was famous in all the e,...................Est 9:4
in the rest of the king's e! ....Est 9:12
in the king's e also met to ....Est 9:16
in all the e of King Xerxes,....................Est 9:20

EMPTIED
As the brothers e their sacks, ...Ge 42:35
person be shaken out and e!"..................Ne 5:13

EMPTY
It was e, and there was no water ....Ge 37:24
sky out over e space and hangs ....Job 26:7
to satisfy the e land so the ....Job 38:27
the earth and leave it e; ....Is 24:1
it finds the house still e, ...Mt 12:44

house will be left completely e. .... Mt 23:38
your house is left completely e. .... Lk 13:35
his place be e; leave no one to .... Ac 1:20
the doors, the jail was e!" .... Ac 5:23
you in this will not be e words. 2Co 9:3
with false and e teaching that................ Col 2:8

EMPTY-HANDED
But you sent widows away e, ... Job 22:9
beat him and sent him away e. .... Mk 12:3
the servant and sent him away e. .... Lk 20:10
for him, and sent him away e. .... Lk 20:11

ENAIM
by the gate of E on the road to .... Ge 38:14
of the people at the town of E, ... Ge 38:21

ENAM
Zanoah, En Gannim, Tappuah, E, ... Jos 15:34

ENAN
of Naphtali—Ahira son of E." .... Nu 1:15
of Naphtali is Ahira son of E. .... Nu 2:29
Ahira son of E was over the .... Nu 10:27
and it will end at Hazar E. .... Nu 34:9
at Hazar E and go to Shepham. .... Nu 34:10
Sea east to the town of Hazar E, ... Eze 47:17
way to Hazar E, where Damascus .... Eze 48:1

ENCLOSED
inner courtyard was e by walls, ... 1Ki 6:36

ENCOURAGE
E him, because he will lead .... Dt 1:38
E Joab with these words." 2Sa 11:25
strengthen and e you in your 1Th 3:2

ENCOURAGED
of the believers and e them. .... Ac 16:40
After he e them and then told................. Ac 20:1
the people can be taught and e. 1Co 14:31
we are e about you because of 1Th 3:7

ENCOURAGEMENT
us patience and e so that we can .... Rm 15:4
patience and e that come from .... Rm 15:5
them strength, e, and comfort. 1Co 14:3

ENCOURAGES
The craftsman e the goldsmith, ... Is 41:7
with a hammer e the one who .... Is 41:7
which means "one who e"). .... Ac 4:36
this mean that Christ e sin? .... Gal 2:17

ENCOURAGING
said kind and e words to me, ... Ru 2:13
happy because of the e message. .... Ac 15:31
has the gift of e others should .... Rm 12:8
forgotten the e words that call .... Heb 12:5

END
slept on and set it up on its e.................. Ge 28:18
set up on its e will be the .... Ge 28:22
you set up on e and where you .... Ge 31:13
rock and set it up on its e. .... Ge 31:45
here is the rock I set up on e. .... Ge 31:51
this rock set on e will remind .... Ge 31:52
Before the e of three days the................. Ge 40:13
Before the e of three days, ... Ge 40:19
crops came to an e in the land .... Ge 41:53
slaves from one e of Egypt to .... Ge 47:21
put one on each e of the lid. .... Ex 25:18
one creature on one e of the lid .... Ex 25:19
the edge of the e curtain of one .... Ex 26:4
fifty loops on the e curtain of .... Ex 26:5
the edge of the e curtain of one .... Ex 26:10
rear or west e of the Holy Tent .... Ex 26:22
frames together on the west e, ... Ex 26:27
The west e of the courtyard must .... Ex 27:12
The east e of the courtyard must .... Ex 27:13

camp from one e to the other.................. Ex 32:27
the edge of the e curtain on the .... Ex 36:11
rear or west e of the Holy Tent .... Ex 36:27
frames together on the west e, ... Ex 36:32
them to each e of the lid. .... Ex 37:7
one creature on one e of the lid .... Ex 37:8
other creature on the other e. .... Ex 37:8
and let me e up like them!" .... Nu 23:10
at the south e of the Dead Sea, ... Nu 34:3
and it will e at the .... Nu 34:5
and it will e at Hazar Enan. .... Nu 34:9
River and end at the Dead Sea .... Nu 34:12
and look from one e of heaven to .... Dt 4:32
would go well for you in the e. .... Dt 8:16
beginning of the year to the e. .... Dt 11:12
one e of the land to the other.................. Dt 13:7
At the e of every third year, ... Dt 14:28
At the e of every seven years,................. Dt 15:1
away, from the e of the world, ... Dt 28:49
from one e of the earth to the .... Dt 28:64
to the e of Lake Galilee. .... Jos 13:27
at the south e of the Dead Sea .... Jos 15:2
at the northern e of the Valley .... Jos 15:8
bread with the e of the stick .... Jdg 6:21
I promised, from beginning to e. 1Sa 3:12
so he dipped the e of his stick 1Sa 14:27
honey from the e of my stick................... 1Sa 14:43
using the back e of his spear, ... 2Sa 2:23
this will only e in sadness! 2Sa 2:26
At the e of every year, Absalom 2Sa 14:26
feet from the e of one wing to................ 1Ki 6:24
one wing to the e of the other. 1Ki 6:24
at each e faced each other. 1Ki 7:5
By the e of twenty years, King 1Ki 9:10
one lion at each e of each step. 1Ki 10:20
from one e to the other with 2Ki 21:16
from beginning to e, is recorded............. 1Ch 29:29
the e of twenty years, Solomon 2Ch 8:1
one lion at each e of each step. 2Ch 9:19
from the beginning to the e, ... 2Ch 9:29
from the beginning to the e, ... 2Ch 12:15
from the beginning to the e, ... 2Ch 16:11
find them at the e of the ravine 2Ch 20:16
from the beginning to the e, ... 2Ch 20:34
the e of the year, the Aramean 2Ch 24:23
from the beginning to the e, ... 2Ch 25:26
beginning to e, were written 2Ch 26:22
from beginning to e, are written............... 2Ch 28:26
from one e to the other. .... Ezr 9:11
house to the far e of it. .... Ne 3:21
there will be no e to disrespect .... Est 1:18
forward and touched the e of it. .... Est 5:2
the hair on my body stood on e................ Job 4:15
they come to an e without hope.............. Job 7:6
long-winded speeches never e? .... Job 16:3
and in the e he will stand upon .... Job 19:25
their lives have come to an e. .... Job 21:21
limits and your sins have no e. .... Job 22:5
and their lives e in disgrace. .... Job 36:14
and put an e to suffering so .... Ps 10:18
sun rises at one e of the sky .... Ps 19:6
in the e the wicked will die. .... Ps 37:38
tell me when the e will come and .... Ps 39:4
agreement with him will never e. .... Ps 89:28
Our years with a moan. .... Ps 90:9
and your life will never e. .... Ps 102:27
I will keep them until the e. .... Ps 119:33
you demand forever, until the e............... Ps 119:112
all of their plans come to an e. .... Ps 146:4
All greedy people e up this way;.............. Pr 1:19
But in the e she will bring you .... Pr 5:4
groan at the e of your life when .... Pr 5:11
that her guests e up deep in the .... Pr 9:18

A lazy person will **e** up poor, ... Pr 10:4
what they should and **e** up poor................ Pr 11:24
correction will **e** up poor and .... Pr 13:18
but in the **e** it leads to death. .... Pr 14:12
and joy may **e** in sadness. .... Pr 14:13
but in the **e** it leads to death. .... Pr 16:25
and in the **e** you will be wise. .... Pr 19:20
will do you no good in the **e**. .... Pr 20:21
good sense will **e** up among the .... Pr 21:16
cruel anger will come to an **e**................... Pr 22:8
too much and **e** up wearing rags. .... Pr 23:21
dreams instead will **e** up poor. .... Pr 28:19
foolish people **e** the same way. .... Ec 2:14
e up the same way; both came .... Ec 3:20
sorrow, and they **e** up sick, ... Ec 5:17
and bad people **e** up the same—.............. Ec 9:2
The **e** of Babylon is near; .... Is 13:22
have put an **e** to shouts of joy. .... Is 16:10
government in Damascus will **e**............... Is 17:3
will bring an **e** to the pain the .... Is 21:2
music of the tambourines will **e**............... Is 24:8
music from the harps will **e**. .... Is 24:8
without mercy will come to an **e;** .... Is 29:20
day you brought me to this **e**. .... Is 38:12
day you brought me to this **e**. .... Is 38:13
I am the beginning and the **e**................... Is 44:6
you what would happen in the **e**. .... Is 46:10
I am the beginning and the **e**.................. Is 48:12
and my goodness will never **e**. .... Is 51:6
and the hills may come to an **e**, ... Is 54:10
and your time of sadness will **e**. .... Is 60:20
There is no **e** to the evil things .... Je 5:28
will you do when the **e** comes? .... Je 5:31
I will **e** the happy sounds of the .... Je 7:34
land from one **e** to the other. .... Je 12:12
understand why my pain has no **e**............ Je 15:18
At the **e** of their lives, it will .... Je 17:11
and my life will **e** in shame. .... Je 20:18
I will bring an **e** to the sounds .... Je 25:10
reach from one **e** of the earth to .... Je 25:33
'At the **e** of every seven years, ... Je 34:14
let us put an **e** to that nation!'................ Je 48:2
The **e** of Moab is near, and she .... Je 48:16
but your **e** as a nation has come. .... Je 51:13
The words of Jeremiah **e** here. .... Je 51:64
the streets. Our **e** is near. Our................ La 4:18
Then my anger will come to an **e**. .... Eze 5:13
be broken and brought to an **e**. .... Eze 6:6
of Israel: An **e**! The end has .... Eze 7:2
The **e** has come on the four .... Eze 7:2
Now the **e** has come for you, ... Eze 7:3
e has come! The end has come! .... Eze 7:6
I will also **e** the pride of the .... Eze 7:24
I will put an **e** to your sexual .... Eze 16:41
them or put an **e** to them in the .... Eze 20:17
come to the **e** of your years. .... Eze 22:4
I will put an **e** to sexual sins .... Eze 23:48
and it will be the **e** of you. .... Eze 26:21
You have come to a terrible **e**, ... Eze 27:36
in the land's power will **e**. .... Eze 33:28
porch was at the inner **e**. .... Eze 40:22
Its porch was at the inner **e**, ... Eze 40:26
the room at the **e** of the Holy .... Eze 41:4
at the open **e** of a path beside................ Eze 42:12
I saw a place at the west **e**..................... Eze 46:19
the **e** of the time set for them .... Da 1:18
kingdoms and bring them to an **e**, ... Da 2:44
At the **e** of that time, I, ... Da 4:34
days until your kingdom will **e**. .... Da 5:26
and his rule will never **e**...................... Da 6:26
That was the **e** of the dream. .... Da 7:28
is about the time of the **e**." .... Da 8:17
was about the set time of the **e**. .... Da 8:19

When the **e** comes near for those .... Da 8:23
God; to put an **e** to sin; to take .... Da 9:24
The **e** of the city will come like .... Da 9:26
war will continue until the **e**. .... Da 9:26
until the ordered **e** comes to the .... Da 9:27
will put an **e** to the pride........................ Da 11:18
That will be the **e** of him. .... Da 11:19
set a time for their **e** to come.................. Da 11:27
until the time of the **e** comes. .... Da 11:35
At the time of the **e**, the king .... Da 11:40
finally, his **e** will come, and no .... Da 11:45
happen at the time of the **e**. .... Da 12:4
sealed until the time of the **e**. .... Da 12:9
who wait for the **e** of the 1,335 .... Da 12:12
Daniel, go your way until the **e**. .... Da 12:13
I will put an **e** to the kingdom .... Hos 1:4
I will put an **e** to all her .... Hos 2:11
So I will bring an **e** to the king .... Am 2:3
great houses will come to an **e**,".............. Am 3:15
lying around will come to an **e**. .... Am 6:7
An **e** has come for my people .... Am 8:2
and its **e** like the end of an .... Am 8:10
be defeated and brought to an **e**. .... Nah 1:12
There is no **e** to the treasure— .... Nah 2:9
suddenly he will bring an **e**, ... Zph 1:18
faith until the **e** will be saved.................. Mt 10:22
time is the **e** of the age, ... Mt 13:39
it will be at the **e** of the age. .... Mt 13:40
be this way at the **e** of the age. .... Mt 13:49
At the **e** of the day, the owner.................. Mt 20:8
again and for this age to **e**?" .... Mt 24:3
must happen before the **e** comes. .... Mt 24:6
faith until the **e** will be saved................. Mt 24:13
nation. Then the **e** will come. .... Mt 24:14
even until the **e** of this age." .... Mt 28:20
that is the **e** of Satan. .... Mk 3:26
must happen before the **e** comes. .... Mk 13:7
faith until the **e** will be saved................. Mk 13:13
and his kingdom will never **e**." .... Lk 1:33
but the **e** will come later." .... Lk 21:9
sickness will not **e** in death. .... Jn 11:4
loved them all the way to the **e**. .... Jn 13:1
a weight on the **e** of it into the .... Ac 27:28
and for life that has no **e**. .... Rm 2:7
wisdom and knowledge have no **e**!........... Rm 11:33
strong until the **e** so that there 1Co 1:8
but it will come to an **e**. 1Co 13:8
that are not perfect will **e**. 1Co 13:10
and then the **e** will come. 1Co 15:24
did not want them to see it **e**. 2Co 3:13
But in the **e** they will be 2Co 11:15
purpose to **e** the hatred between.............. Eph 2:16
angry before the **e** of the day.................. Eph 4:26
the **e**, they will be destroyed. .... Php 3:19
e this letter now in my own 2Th 3:17
and your life will never **e**." .... Heb 1:12
keep till the **e** the sure faith .... Heb 3:14
Lord's purpose for him in the **e**. .... Jam 5:11
shown to you at the **e** of time.................. 1Pe 1:5
is near when all things will **e**.................. 1Pe 4:7
be obedient to me until the **e**. .... Rev 2:26
Omega, the Beginning and the **E**. .... Rev 21:6
Last, the Beginning and the **E**. .... Rev 22:13

ENDED

When this time of sorrow had **e**,.............. Ge 50:4
the four hundred thirty years **e**, ... Ex 12:41
went to Gezer and **e** at the sea. .... Jos 16:3
Kanah Ravine and **e** at the sea. .... Jos 16:8
Beth Hoglah and **e** at the north .... Jos 18:19
as Lakkum, and **e** at the Jordan .... Jos 19:33
So he **e** their days without .... Ps 78:33
summer has **e**, and we have not .... Je 8:20

then the vision I had seen **e**.	Eze 11:24
and when those days were **e**,	Lk 4:2
His life on earth has **e**."	Ac 8:33
e the law so that everyone	Rm 10:4
of prophecy, but they will be **e**.	1Co 13:8
rules, but Christ with that law.	Eph 2:15
until the thousand years were **e**.	Rev 20:3
until the thousand years were **e**.	Rev 20:5

ENDING

on to Jabneel, **e** at the sea.	Jos 15:11
and Eth Kazin, **e** at Rimmon.	Jos 19:13
went toward Hosah, **e** at the sea.	Jos 19:29
My life is **e** in sadness, and my	Ps 31:10

ENDLESS

and Egypt gave her **e** strength;	Nah 3:9
has felt your **e** cruelty.	Nah 3:19

ENDOR

There is a medium in **E**."	1Sa 28:7
They died at **E**, and their bodies	Ps 83:10

ENDS

one piece with the lid at the **e**.	Ex 25:19
Attach the other **e** of the two	Ex 28:25
two rings at the **e** of the chest	Ex 39:17
the other two **e** of the chains to	Ex 39:18
send you to the **e** of the earth,	Dt 30:4
could see the **e** of the poles.	1Ki 8:8
could see the **e** of the poles.	2Ch 5:9
from the far **e** of the earth.	Ne 1:9
and to the **e** of the earth.	Ps 59:13
to you from the **e** of the earth	Ps 61:2
people at the **e** of the earth	Ps 65:8
River to the **e** of the earth.	Ps 72:8
This **e** the prayers of David son	Ps 72:20
All the **e** of the earth have seen	Ps 98:3
clouds from the **e** of the earth.	Ps 135:7
set in place the **e** of the earth?	Pr 30:4
things and **e** by saying crazy	Ec 10:13
people from the **e** of the earth.	Is 5:26
This **e** the judgment on Moab.	Je 48:47
The LORD's love never **e**;	La 3:22
burns up both **e** and starts to	Eze 15:4
River to the **e** of the earth.	Zch 9:10
that it begins and **e** with faith.	Rm 1:17
Love never **e**. There are gifts of	1Co 13:8
Christ with love that never **e**.	Eph 6:24
comes glory that never **e**.	2Ti 2:10
receiving the life that never **e**.	Tit 3:7
is true, and this **e** all arguing.	Heb 6:16
God the first system of	Heb 10:9

ENDURES

always hopes, and always **e**.	1Co 13:7

ENEMIES

helped you to defeat your **e**."	Ge 14:20
capture the cities of their **e**.	Ge 22:17
will defeat your **e** and kill them	Le 26:8
and your **e** will defeat you.	Le 26:17
and will save you from your **e**.	Nu 10:9
Scatter your **e**: make those who	Nu 10:35
brought you here to curse my **e**,	Nu 23:11
they have drunk their **e**' blood."	Nu 23:24
war against your **e** and you see	Dt 20:1
against your **e** and to save you.	Dt 20:4
rest from all the **e** around you	Dt 25:19
will serve the **e** the LORD sends	Dt 28:48
put all these curses on your **e**,	Dt 30:7
the people defeated their **e**.	Jos 10:13
None of their **e** defeated them;	Jos 21:44
Let all your **e** die this way,	Jdg 5:31
I can laugh at my **e**;	1Sa 2:1
God will save us from our **e**."	1Sa 4:3
give you peace from all your **e**.	2Sa 7:11

the Philistines and our other **e**,	2Sa 19:9
And our **e** said, "The Jews won't	Ne 4:11
lived near our **e** came and told	Ne 4:12
day to strike back at their **e**.	Est 8:13
people get rid of their **e**.	Est 9:22
God has made my brothers my **e**,	Job 19:13
have struck my **e** on the cheek;	Ps 3:7
are weak from crying about my **e**.	Ps 6:7
from my **e** who surround me.	Ps 17:9
and I will be saved from my **e**.	Ps 18:3
a meal for me in front of my **e**.	Ps 23:5
do not let my **e** laugh at me.	Ps 25:2
e and those who hate me attack	Ps 27:2
my troubles, my **e** hate me, and	Ps 31:11
Do not let my **e** laugh at me;	Ps 35:19
The LORD's **e** will be like the	Ps 37:20
My **e** are strong and healthy,	Ps 38:19
e are saying evil things about	Ps 41:5
My **e**' insults make me feel as if	Ps 42:10
Let my **e** be punished with their	Ps 54:5
and I have seen my **e** defeated.	Ps 54:7
My **e** have chased me all day;	Ps 56:2
He will help me defeat my **e**.	Ps 59:10
He will defeat our **e**.	Ps 60:12
My **e** make plans against me,	Ps 71:10
and make his **e** lick the dust.	Ps 72:9
but their **e** drowned in the sea.	Ps 78:53
struck down his **e** and disgraced	Ps 78:66
us, and our **e** make fun of us.	Ps 80:6
your power you scattered your **e**.	Ps 89:10
strength to his **e** and have made	Ps 89:42
LORD, surely your **e**, surely your	Ps 92:9
He saved them from their **e**,	Ps 106:10
until I put your **e** under your	Ps 110:1
and you will rule over your **e**.	Ps 110:2
Your **e** use your name	Ps 139:20
hate for them; they are my **e**.	Ps 139:22
their **e** will make peace with	Pr 16:7
You, my **e**, will not cause me any	Is 1:24
pay back his **e** for what they	Is 59:18
It is the LORD punishing his **e**,	Is 66:6
Judah I will hand over to the **e**,	Je 15:9
Elam in front of their **e**,	Je 49:37
against her and are now her **e**.	La 1:2
Those who are my **e** for no reason	La 3:52
thoughts of my **e** are against me	La 3:62
the dream were about your **e**,	Da 4:19
and taken away by their **e**,	Am 9:4
and he stays angry with his **e**.	Nah 1:2
come and go because of the **e**;	Zch 8:10
But I say to you, love your **e**.	Mt 5:44
until I put your **e** under your	Mk 12:36
save us from our **e** and from the	Lk 1:71
who are listening, love your **e**.	Lk 6:27
we were God's **e**, he made us his	Rm 5:10
Good News, so they are God's **e**.	Rm 11:28
he puts all **e** under his control	1Co 15:25
until I put your **e** under your	Heb 1:13
their mouths and kills their **e**.	Rev 11:5

ENEMY

hand broke the **e** to pieces.	Ex 15:6
I will be an **e** to your enemies.	Ex 23:22
so that your **e** will defeat you.	Le 26:25
fighting an **e** who attacks you	Nu 10:9
Your **e** will surround you.	Dt 28:53
I didn't want their **e** to brag;	Dt 32:27
heads of the **e** leaders will be	Dt 32:42
will force your **e** out ahead of	Dt 33:27
handed Samson our **e** over to us."	Jdg 16:23
he was David's **e** all his life.	1Sa 18:29
'I will give your **e** over to you.	1Sa 24:4
hear that your father is your **e**,	2Sa 16:21

cities by their e or will become 1Ki 8:37
So you have found me, my e!" 1Ki 21:20
to help the king against the e. 2Ch 26:13
e and foe is this wicked Haman!............... Est 7:6
the e of the Jewish people, ... Est 8:1
don't think of me as your e. .... Job 13:24
he considers me his e............................ Job 33:10
How long will my e win over me? .... Ps 13:2
Otherwise my e will say, "I have .... Ps 13:4
up, face the e, and throw them .... Ps 17:13
e is getting even with insults .... Ps 44:16
by what the e says and how the .... Ps 55:3
It was not an e insulting me. .... Ps 55:12
can stand up against the e...................... Ps 60:4
us fight the e. Human help is .... Ps 60:11
will bring the e back from .... Ps 68:22
the e wrecked everything in the .... Ps 74:3
will the e make fun of you .... Ps 74:10
time he saved them from the e. .... Ps 78:42
No e will make him give forced .... Ps 89:22
happy when your e is defeated; .... Pr 24:17
If your e is hungry, feed him. .... Pr 25:21
the kisses of an e are nothing................. Pr 27:6
gone away as captives of the e. .... La 1:5
The Lord was like an e; .... La 2:5
E, don't laugh at me. I have .... Mic 7:8
If your e is taking you to........................ Mt 5:25
his e came and planted weeds .... Mt 13:25
that is greater than the e has. .... Lk 10:19
You are an e of everything that .... Ac 13:10
If your e is hungry, feed him; .... Rm 12:20
The last e to be destroyed will 1Co 15:26
of the world becomes God's e. .... Jam 4:4

ENEMY'S
If you see your e ox or donkey .... Ex 23:4
Save me from the e power. .... Job 6:23

ENERGY
her work with e, and her arms .... Pr 31:17

ENGAGED
Is any man e to a woman and not .... Dt 20:7
but she is e to another man, ... Dt 22:23
But if a man meets an e girl out .... Dt 22:25
the man found the e girl in the .... Dt 22:27
who is not e to be married .... Dt 22:28
You will be e to a woman, but .... Dt 28:30
sister on the day she becomes e? .... Sng 8:8
Mary was e to marry Joseph .... Mt 1:18
She was e to marry a man named .... Lk 1:27
to whom he was e and who was now .... Lk 2:5
thing with the girl he is e to, ... 1Co 7:36
marry the one to whom he is e, ... 1Co 7:37

ENGRAVINGS
He must also know how to make e. 2Ch 2:7
in making e and can make any 2Ch 2:14

ENJOY
It will e its time of rest all .... Le 26:34
After I e being with you for a .... Rm 15:24
richly gives us everything to e. 1Ti 6:17
We do not e being disciplined. .... Heb 12:11

ENJOYED
animals that Isaac e eating. .... Ge 25:28
them in the special way Isaac e............... Ge 27:14
Jonathan and e them while they.............. 2Sa 1:23
I e your friendship so much. 2Sa 1:26
they e your great goodness. .... Ne 9:25
bothered him, he e listening to .... Mk 6:20
the truth, but e doing evil. 2Th 2:12
things our bodies wanted and e............... Tit 3:3
light, and e heaven's gift, ... Heb 6:4

ENJOYING
people were e the celebration .... Jdg 16:25
While they were e themselves, ... Jdg 19:22
e all the good things you had .... Ne 9:35
e the land that was fertile and .... Ne 9:35
heart, never e any happiness. .... Job 21:25
It paws wildly, e its strength, ... Job 39:21
e his presence all the time, ... Pr 8:30
e the whole world, and delighted .... Pr 8:31
kept you from e good things. .... Je 5:25
instead of e sin for a short .... Heb 11:25

ENJOYS
Naphtali e special kindnesses, ... Dt 33:23
A foolish person e doing wrong,.............. Pr 10:23
understanding e doing what is .... Pr 10:23
without wisdom e being foolish,.............. Pr 15:21
whoever e someone's trouble will .... Pr 17:5
a stranger e them instead. .... Ec 6:2

ENLARGE
The LORD will e your kingdom .... Ps 110:2
They e the little boxes holding .... Mt 23:5

ENLARGES
LORD your God e your country as .... Dt 12:20

ENLISTING
wants to please the e officer, ... 2Ti 2:4

ENOCH
one day **E** could not be found, ... Ge 5:24
E was the father of Methuselah. 1Ch 1:3
was by faith that **E** was taken to.............. Heb 11:5
E, the seventh descendant from .... Jud 1:14

ENORMOUS
them with an e army and three 2Ch 14:9
against this e army in your name 2Ch 14:11
everywhere in his e kingdom................... Est 1:20

ENOSH
Seth was the father of **E**........................ 1Ch 1:1

ENSLAVED
others or e to too much wine .... Tit 2:3

ENSURE
were to e that the governors .... Da 6:2

ENSURED
This e that no one would move .... Da 6:17

ENTER
Moses could not e the Meeting .... Ex 40:35
He will not e the land that I'm .... Nu 20:24
are all here to e into an .... Dt 29:12
sharp arrows will e the hearts .... Ps 45:5
they e the king's palace. .... Ps 45:15
'They will never e my rest.'" .... Ps 95:11
who are good may e through it. .... Ps 118:20
my lover e the garden and eat .... Sng 4:16
signal them to e through the .... Is 13:2
on a fast cloud to e Egypt. .... Is 19:1
and the good people will e,..................... Is 26:2
not pure will not e you again................... Is 52:1
is not allowed to e the city. .... Is 59:14
They will soon e it and start a .... Je 32:29
you will never e the kingdom of............... Mt 5:20
E through the narrow gate...................... Mt 7:13
are our Lord' will e the kingdom .... Mt 7:21
When you e a city or town,..................... Mt 10:11
you e that home, say, 'Peace .... Mt 10:12
anyone wants to e a strong..................... Mt 12:29
you will never e the kingdom of............... Mt 18:3
a rich person to e the kingdom .... Mt 19:23
When you e it, you will quickly .... Mt 21:2
prostitutes will e the kingdom .... Mt 21:31
door for people to e the kingdom .... Mt 23:13
stop others who are trying to e. .... Mt 23:13

ENTERED

Jesus could not e a town if .... Mk 1:45
No one can e a strong person's .... Mk 3:27
better for you to e the kingdom .... Mk 9:47
child, or you will never e it." .... Mk 10:15
When you e a house, stay there .... Lk 9:4
allow the thief to e his house. .... Lk 12:39
When you e it, you will find a .... Lk 19:30
He cannot e his mother's womb .... Jn 3:4
you cannot e God's kingdom. .... Jn 3:5
who does not e the sheepfold .... Jn 10:1
'They will never e my rest.'" .... Heb 3:11
not allowed to e and have God's .... Heb 3:19
the way to be saved did not e, ... Heb 4:6
free to e the Most Holy .... Heb 10:19
book of life will e the city. .... Rev 21:27

ENTERED

already come up when Lot e Zoar. .... Ge 19:23
him until he e the Meeting Tent. .... Ex 33:8
every time they e the Meeting. .... Ex 40:32
day, when Moses e the Tent, he .... Nu 17:8
came to you and e your house. .... Jos 2:3
Spirit of the LORD e Jephthah. .... Jdg 11:29
friend Hushai e Jerusalem just 2Sa 15:37
As soon as she e her home, ... 1Ki 14:17
It never e my mind that they .... Je 32:35
the Spirit e me and put me on my .... Eze 2:2
When Jesus e the city of .... Mt 8:5
until the day Noah e the boat. .... Mt 24:38
Jesus e the house and said to .... Mk 5:39
until the day Noah e the boat. .... Lk 17:27
Satan e Judas Iscariot, one of .... Lk 22:3
already left death and e life. .... Jn 5:24
took the bread, Satan e him. .... Jn 13:27
When they e the city, they went .... Ac 1:13
When Peter e, Cornelius met him, ... Ac 10:25
and we the house of Cornelius. .... Ac 11:12
e the greater and more perfect .... Heb 9:11
Christ e the Most Holy Place .... Heb 9:12
have secretly e your group. .... Jud 1:4
people who have e your group. .... Jud 1:8

ENTERING

land you are e to take as your .... Dt 23:20
land you are e to take as your .... Dt 28:63
land you are e to take as your .... Dt 30:16
gods of the land they are e. .... Dt 31:16
people from leaving or e Judah, ... 1Ki 15:17
people from leaving or e Judah, ... 2Ch 16:1
land you are e to own is ruined .... Ezr 9:11
e through windows like thieves. .... Joe 2:9

ENTERS

When Aaron e the Holy Place, ... Ex 28:29
heard when he e and leaves the .... Ex 28:35
Before he e, he must offer a .... Le 16:3
or anyone who e it will be .... Nu 19:14
the food that e the mouth goes .... Mt 15:17
know that nothing that e someone .... Mk 7:18
him into the house that he e, ... Lk 22:10
things before he e his glory." .... Lk 24:26
The one who e by the door is the .... Jn 10:2
the person who e through me will .... Jn 10:9
It e behind the curtain in the .... Heb 6:19
The high priest e the Most Holy .... Heb 9:25

ENTERTAINMENT

not have any e brought to him, ... Da 6:18

ENTHUSIASM

E without knowledge is not good. .... Pr 19:2
Do your work with e. .... Eph 6:7

ENTHUSIASTIC

I was so e I tried to hurt the .... Php 3:6

ENTIRE

run along the e length of each .... Ex 26:28
run along the e length of each .... Ex 36:33
have purified the e Temple of 2Ch 29:18
Babylon and his e nation for .... Je 25:12
but the e crowd rejoiced at all .... Lk 13:17
was worth an e year's wages. .... Jn 12:5
able to control their e selves, ... Jam 3:2

ENTRANCE

Moses stood at the e to the camp .... Ex 32:26
and stay at the e of the Tent .... Ex 33:9
and stood at the e to the Tent. .... Nu 12:5
the LORD at the e to the Meeting .... Jos 19:51
he must stop at the e gate, ... Jos 20:4
Go stand at the e to the tent. .... Jdg 4:20
standing at the e to the city .... Jdg 9:35
ran to the e gate to the city .... Jdg 9:44
Danites stood at the e gate, ... Jdg 18:16
for war stood by the e gate. .... Jdg 18:17
a chair near the e to the LORD's 1Sa 1:9
served at the e to the Meeting. 1Sa 2:22
all the way to the e of the city 1Sa 17:52
and stood at the e to the cave. 1Ki 19:13
near the e to the gate of 1Ki 22:10
standing by his pillar at the e. 2Ch 23:13
to block the e of the tomb. .... Mk 15:46
that covers the e of the tomb?" .... Mk 16:3
away from the e of the tomb, ... Lk 24:2
a large stone covering the e. .... Jn 11:38
moved the stone away from the e. .... Jn 11:41

ENTRANCES

stand at the e of their tents, ... Ex 33:8
stood in the e of their tents. .... Nu 11:10
gates, at the e into the city, ... Pr 8:3
Show them its exits and e, ... Eze 43:11

ENTRY

one side of the e, there is to .... Ex 27:14
On the other side of the e, ... Ex 27:15
The e to the courtyard is to be .... Ex 27:16
at the e to the courtyard; .... Ex 35:17
one side of the e there was a .... Ex 38:14
side of the e there was also .... Ex 38:15
curtain for the e of the .... Ex 38:18
curtains at the e to the .... Ex 38:31
covered the e to the courtyard .... Ex 39:40
curtain at the e to the .... Ex 40:8
curtain at the e to the .... Ex 40:33
at the e to the courtyard .... Nu 3:26
curtain for the e to the .... Nu 4:26
me to the e of the courtyard .... Eze 8:7

ENVIED

that the Philistines e him. .... Ge 26:14
Jacob, she e her sister Leah. .... Ge 30:1

ENVY

look with e on the mountain .... Ps 68:16
Don't e sinners, but always, ... Pr 23:17
Don't e evil people or try to be .... Pr 24:1
Don't e evil people, and don't .... Pr 24:19
can no longer love or hate or e. .... Ec 9:6
feeling e, being drunk, having .... Gal 5:21

EPAPHRAS

about God's grace from E, ... Col 1:7
E, a servant of Jesus Christ, ... Col 4:12
E, a prisoner with me for Christ .... Phm 1:23

EPAPHRODITUS

E, my brother in Christ, works .... Php 2:25
because E brought your gift to .... Php 4:18

EPENETUS

Greetings to my dear friend E, ... Rm 16:5

EPHAH

The sons of Midian were **E**, ... Ge 25:4
quarts, or one-tenth of an **e**. .... Ex 16:36
sons were **E**, Epher, Hanoch, ... 1Ch 1:33
Caleb's slave woman was named **E**, ... 1Ch 2:46
Geshan, Pelet, **E**, and Shaaph. 1Ch 2:47
young camels from Midian and **E**. .... Is 60:6
and the **e** will always be a tenth .... Eze 45:11
a sixth of an **e** from every homer .... Eze 45:13
a sixth of an **e** from every homer .... Eze 45:13

EPHAI

the sons of **E** the Netophathite, ... Je 40:8

EPHER

were Ephah, **E**, Hanoch, Abida, ... Ge 25:4
were Ephah, **E**, Hanoch, Abida, ... 1Ch 1:33
E, Ishi, Eliel, Azriel, Jeremiah, ... 1Ch 5:24

EPHES

and camped at **E** Dammim between 1Sa 17:1

EPHESUS

they went to **E**, where Paul left .... Ac 18:19
And so he sailed away from **E**. .... Ac 18:21
the people in **E**—Jews and Greeks— .... Ac 19:17
People of **E**, everyone knows .... Ac 19:35
animals in **E** only with human 1Co 15:32
will stay at **E** until Pentecost, ... 1Co 16:8
God's holy people living in **E**,................. Eph 1:1
to stay longer in **E** when I went 1Ti 1:3
how many ways he helped me in **E**. 2Ti 1:18
I sent Tychicus to **E**. 2Ti 4:12
E, Smyrna, Pergamum, Thyatira, ... Rev 1:11
to the angel of the church in **E**: .... Rev 2:1

EPHLAL

Zabad was the father of **E**. 1Ch 2:37
E was the father of Obed. 1Ch 2:37

EPHOD

son of Joseph, Hanniel son of **E**; .... Nu 34:23

EPHPHATHA

sighed and said to the man, "**E**!" .... Mk 7:34

EPHRAIM

named the second son **E** and said, ... Ge 41:52
of Manasseh and **E** by his wife .... Ge 48:20
The tribe of **E**, a son of Joseph, ... Nu 1:32
and the lands of **E** and Manasseh, ... Dt 34:2
country of **E** is too small for .... Jos 17:15
The men of **E** asked Gideon, ... Jdg 8:1
When the men of **E** heard Gideon's .... Jdg 8:3
they fought in the forest of **E**.................. 2Sa 18:6
from the Gate of **E** to the Corner 2Ki 14:13
Benjamin, **E**, and Manasseh. 2Ch 31:1
E is like my helmet............................... Ps 60:7
E is like my helmet............................... Ps 108:8
fight against the people of **E**, ... Is 9:21
and **E** will fight against .... Is 9:21
the mountains of **E** shout this................. Je 31:6
on the hills of **E** and Gilead." .... Je 50:19
it, 'The stick of **E**, for Joseph .... Eze 37:16
used to fear the tribe of **E**; .... Hos 13:1
the lands of **E** and Samaria, ... Ob 1:19
chariots from **E** and the horses .... Zch 9:10
a town called **E** and stayed there .... Jn 11:54

EPHRAIMITE

He was an **E** from the town of 1Ki 11:26

EPHRAIMITES

group in the tribe of the **E**. .... Jos 16:8
The **E** could not force the .... Jos 16:10
still live among the **E** today, ... Jos 16:10
but they became slaves of the **E**............. Jos 16:10
down because the **E** had said,................. Jdg 12:4

EPHRATH

they came to **E**, Rachel began................. Ge 35:16
was buried on the road to **E**, ... Ge 35:19
as we were traveling toward **E**. .... Ge 48:7
her there beside the road to **E**." .... Ge 48:7
Today **E** is Bethlehem............................ Ge 48:7
Azubah died, Caleb married **E**. 1Ch 2:19

EPHRATHAH

in the district of **E** and famous .... Ru 4:11
After Hezron died in Caleb **E**,................. 1Ch 2:24
you, Bethlehem **E**, though you are .... Mic 5:2

EPHRATHAHITES

They were **E** from Bethlehem in .... Ru 1:2

EPHRATHITE

an **E** from Bethlehem in Judah. 1Sa 17:12

EPHRON

here, speak to **E**, the son of .... Ge 23:8
E was sitting among the Hittites............. Ge 23:10
He said to **E** before all the .... Ge 23:13
E answered Abraham,........................... Ge 23:14
agreed and paid **E** in front of .... Ge 23:16
in the field of **E** east of Mamre. .... Ge 25:9
E was the son of Zohar the..................... Ge 25:9
in the field of **E** the Hittite................... Ge 49:29
and cave from **E** the Hittite for .... Ge 49:30
and field from **E** the Hittite to................ Ge 50:13
went to the cities near Mount **E**. .... Jos 15:9
Jeshanah, and, **E**, and the small 2Ch 13:19

EPICUREAN

Some of the **E** and Stoic .... Ac 17:18

EPILEPSY

He has **e** and is suffering very .... Mt 17:15

EPILEPTICS

some were **e**, and some were .... Mt 4:24

EQUAL

all will have an **e** share of the................. Dt 18:8
else on earth is **e** to it;........................... Job 41:33
Who in heaven is **e** to the LORD? .... Ps 89:6
you could want is **e** to it......................... Pr 3:15
to anyone? Is anyone **e** to me?" .... Is 40:25
No one is **e** to me or like me. .... Is 46:5
making himself **e** with God!" .... Jn 5:18
think that being **e** with God was............. Php 2:6
its length was **e** to its width. .... Rev 21:16

EQUALLY

You will divide the land **e**. .... Eze 47:14
he judges each person's work **e**............... 1Pe 1:17

EQUIPMENT

of war and **e** for his chariots. 1Sa 8:12
of clothes and **e** that the 2Ki 7:15
they threw out the ship's **e**..................... Ac 27:19

ER

But **E**, Judah's oldest son, did................. Ge 38:7
Judah's sons, **E** and Onan, died .... Nu 26:19

ERAN

E came the Eranite family group. .... Nu 26:36

ERANITE

Eran came the **E** family group. .... Nu 26:36

ERASE

then **e** my name from the book in .... Ex 32:32
I will **e** from my book the names .... Ex 32:33
their crimes or **e** their sins .... Je 18:23
I will not **e** their names from .... Rev 3:5

ERASED

them and **e** any memory of them .... Is 26:14
agreement with death will be **e**; .... Is 28:18

ERASES

am the One who **e** all your sins, ... Is 43:25

ERASTUS
sent Timothy and E, two of his .... Ac 19:22
to you, as do E, the city .... Rm 16:23
E stayed in Corinth, and I left................. 2Ti 4:20

ERECH
covered Babylon, E, Akkad, and............... Ge 10:10
Persia, E, and Babylon, ... Ezr 4:9

ERI
Shuni, Ezbon, E, Arodi, and .... Ge 46:16
E came the Erite family group; .... Nu 26:16

ERITE
Eri came the E family group; .... Nu 26:16

ERROR
from others who live in e. 2Pe 2:18

ESARHADDON
Sennacherib's son E became king 2Ki 19:37
the time of E king of Assyria,................. Ezr 4:2
Sennacherib's son E became king .... Is 37:38

ESAU
a hairy robe, he was named E. .... Ge 25:25
E became a skilled hunter. .... Ge 25:27
Isaac loved E because he hunted .... Ge 25:28
So E showed how little he cared.............. Ge 25:34
My brother E is a hairy man, ... Ge 27:11
of her older son E that were in .... Ge 27:15
are hairy like the hands of E." .... Ge 27:22
"Are you really my son E?" .... Ge 27:24
Then E began to cry out loud.................. Ge 27:38
After that E hated Jacob because .... Ge 27:41
E learned that Isaac had blessed .... Ge 28:6
This is the family history of E. .... Ge 36:1
of Edom. (E is also named Edom. .... Ge 36:8
two sons named Jacob and E................... Jos 24:4
the people of E will be like dry .... Ob 1:18
E and Jacob were brothers. .... Mal 1:2
but I hated E. I destroyed his .... Mal 1:3
I loved Jacob, but I hated E." .... Rm 9:13
the future of Jacob and E. .... Heb 11:20
or is like E and never thinks .... Heb 12:16

ESCAPE
into the boat to e the waters .... Ge 7:7
in the family of Judah will e. 2Ki 19:30
Jewish people you alone will e. .... Est 4:13
guilty person will e and be .... Job 22:30
I would hurry to my place of e, ... Ps 55:8
God, do not let them e; .... Ps 56:7
not go free; liars will never e.................. Pr 19:5
you going to e God's judgment? .... Mt 23:33
enough to e all these things .... Lk 21:36
of them could swim away and e. .... Ac 27:42
will be able to e the judgment .... Rm 2:3
you a way to e so that you will 1Co 10:13
Those people will not e. 1Th 5:3
may wake up and e from the trap 2Ti 2:26
on earth, and they did not e. .... Heb 12:25

ESCAPED
were waiting, Ehud had e. .... Jdg 3:26
But David e from him twice. 1Sa 18:11
the only one who e to tell you!" .... Job 1:15
have e by the skin of my teeth. .... Job 19:20
We e like a bird from the .... Ps 124:7
The trap broke, and we e. .... Ps 124:7
Then they e to the land of .... Is 37:38
people who have e from other .... Is 45:20
person who had e from Jerusalem .... Eze 33:21
Jesus again, but he e from them. .... Jn 10:39
the prisoners had already e, ... Ac 16:27
be as one who e from a fire. 1Co 3:15
So I e from the governor. 2Co 11:33

ESCAPES
a person who e will come to you .... Eze 24:26

ESCAPING
gave food to those who were e. .... Is 21:14
running away and the woman e. .... Je 48:19

ESH-BAAL
Malki-Shua, Abinadab, and E. 1Ch 8:33
Malki-Shua, Abinadab, and E. 1Ch 9:39

ESHAN
the mountains: Arab, Dumah, E, ... Jos 15:52

ESHBAN
were Hemdan, E, Ithran, and .... Ge 36:26
sons were Hemdan, E, Ithran, and 1Ch 1:41

ESHCOL
was a brother of E and Aner, ... Ge 14:13
give Aner, E, and Mamre their .... Ge 14:24
In the Valley of E, they cut off .... Nu 13:23
was called the Valley of E, ... Nu 13:24
went as far as the Valley of E, ... Nu 32:9
Valley of E they explored it. .... Dt 1:24

ESHEK
brother was E. Eshek's first son 1Ch 8:39

ESHEK'S
E first son was Ulam, his second 1Ch 8:39

ESHTAOL
the cities of Zorah and E. .... Jdg 13:25

ESHTAOLITES
The Zorathites and the E came 1Ch 2:53

ESHTARAH
safety, and Be E, and the .... Jos 21:27

ESHTEMOA
Jattir, E, ... Jos 21:14
Aroer, Siphmoth, E,............................. 1Sa 30:28
wife were E and the father 1Ch 4:19
and E was from the Maacathite 1Ch 4:19
pastures of Libnah, Jattir, E, ... 1Ch 6:57

ESHTEMOH
Anab, E, Anim, ... Jos 15:50

ESHTON
Mehir was the father of E. 1Ch 4:11
E was the father of Beth Rapha,............. 1Ch 4:12

ESLI
Nahum was the son of E. .... Lk 3:25
E was the son of Naggai. .... Lk 3:25

ESPECIALLY
And this is e true when the work 1Sa 21:5
Each one was e chosen to make............... 1Ch 12:31
all of you—e you, King Agrippa .... Ac 26:26
spiritual gifts, e the gift of 1Co 14:1
the world, and e with you, we................. 2Co 1:12
of all people, e of those who 1Ti 4:10
own relatives, e his own family 1Ti 5:8
e those who work hard by 1Ti 5:17
I e beg you to pray so that God .... Heb 13:19
punishment, and e is for those who 2Pe 2:10

ESTABLISHES
south pillar He E and the north 1Ki 7:21
south pillar He E and the north 2Ch 3:17

ESTHER
Hadassah was also called E, ... Est 2:7
asked, "What is it, Queen E? .... Est 5:3
E said, "Our enemy and foe is .... Est 7:6

ETAM
in a cave in the rock of E. .... Jdg 15:8
in the rock of E and said to.................... Jdg 15:11
near these cities were E,....................... 1Ch 4:32
cities of Bethlehem, E, Tekoa,................ 2Ch 11:6

ETERNAL

The LORD is the E One of Israel. 1Sa 15:29
and God, the E One, sat on his .... Da 7:9
to send them into e darkness. .... Lk 8:31
believes can have e life in him. .... Jn 3:15
not be lost, but have e life. .... Jn 3:16
believe in the Son have e life, ... Jn 3:36
that person, giving e life." .... Jn 4:14
is gathering crops for e life. .... Jn 4:36
the One who sent me has e life. .... Jn 5:24
you think they give you e life. .... Jn 5:39
good always and gives e life. .... Jn 6:27
and believe in him have e life, ... Jn 6:40
whoever believes has e life. .... Jn 6:47
and drink my blood have e life. .... Jn 6:54
have the words that give e life. .... Jn 6:68
give them e life, and they will. .... Jn 10:28
I know that e life comes from .... Jn 12:50
Son could give e life to all .... Jn 17:2
And this is e life: that people .... Jn 17:3
not worthy of having e life! .... Ac 13:46
his e power and all the things .... Rm 1:20
command of the e God it is made .... Rm 16:26
us gain an e glory that is much 2Co 4:17
they will receive e life from .... Gal 6:8
our harvest of e life at the .... Gal 6:9
able to give e salvation to all .... Heb 5:9
of the dead and e judgment. .... Heb 6:2
through the e Spirit as a .... Heb 9:14
welcome into the e kingdom of 2Pe 1:11
murderers have e life in them. 1Jn 3:15
has given us e life, and this 1Jn 5:11
you will know you have e life. 1Jn 5:13
that does not lead to e death 1Jn 5:16
sin does not lead to e death. 1Jn 5:16
that does not lead to e death. 1Jn 5:17
is the true God and the e life. 1Jn 5:20
suffer the punishment of e fire, ... Jud 1:7
He had the e Good News to preach .... Rev 14:6

ETH

to Gath Hepher and E Kazin, ... Jos 19:13

ETHAM

left Succoth and camped at E, ... Ex 13:20
left Succoth and camped at E, ... Nu 33:6
They left E and went back to Pi .... Nu 33:7
days through the Desert of E, ... Nu 33:8

ETHAN

even wiser than E the Ezrahite, ... 1Ki 4:31
Zimri, E, Heman, Calcol, and 1Ch 2:6
Ethan's son. E was Zimmah's son 1Ch 6:42
this group was E son of Kishi. 1Ch 6:44
and his relatives Asaph and E. 1Ch 15:17
And E, from the Merari family 1Ch 15:17
and E played bronze cymbals. 1Ch 15:19
A maskil of E the Ezrahite. .... Ps 88:18

ETHANIM

the festival in the month of E, ... 1Ki 8:2

ETHBAAL

married Jezebel daughter of E, ... 1Ki 16:31

ETHER

western hills: Libnah, E, Ashan, ... Jos 15:42
of Ain, Rimmon, E, and Ashan, ... Jos 19:7

ETHIOPIA

On the road he saw a man from E, ... Ac 8:27

ETHIOPIANS

of Candace, the queen of the E; .... Ac 8:27

ETHNAN

sons were Zereth, Zohar, E, ... 1Ch 4:7

ETHNI

Ethni's son. E was Zerah's son 1Ch 6:41

ETHNI'S

Malkijah was E son. Ethni was 1Ch 6:41

EUBULUS

E sends greetings to you. 2Ti 4:21

EUNICE

Lois and in your mother E, ... 2Ti 1:5

EUNUCH

the king's e in charge of the .... Est 2:3
the king's e in charge of the .... Est 2:14
was the king's e who was in .... Est 2:15
The e should not say, "Because .... Is 56:3
he saw a man from Ethiopia, a e. .... Ac 8:27

EUNUCHS

to the seven e who served him— .... Est 1:10
e told Queen Vashti about the .... Est 1:12
which the e took to her." .... Est 1:15
two of the king's e who guarded .... Est 2:21
servant girls and e came to her .... Est 4:4
of the king's e chosen by the .... Est 4:5
the king's e came to Haman's. .... Est 6:14
one of the e there serving the .... Est 7:9
The e should obey the law about .... Is 56:4

EUODIA

I ask E and Syntyche to agree in .... Php 4:2

EUPHRATES

The fourth river is the E. .... Ge 2:14
of Egypt and the great river E. .... Ge 15:18
brook of Egypt to the E River. 2Ki 24:7
a town on the E River. 2Ch 35:20
are tied at the great river E." .... Rev 9:14

EUTYCHUS

A young man named E was sitting .... Ac 20:9
E was falling into a deep sleep. .... Ac 20:9
Paul went down to E, knelt down, ... Ac 20:10

EVAPORATES

He e the drops of water from the .... Job 36:27

EVE

named his wife E, because she .... Ge 3:20
relations with his wife E, ... Ge 4:1
E said, "With the LORD's help, I .... Ge 4:1
E gave birth to Cain's brother. .... Ge 4:2
relations with his wife E again. .... Ge 4:25
of Christ just as E was tricked 2Co 11:3
was formed first and then E. 1Ti 2:13

EVENING

E passed, and morning came. .... Ge 1:5
to Sodom in the e as Lot was .... Ge 19:1
the e, when the women come out .... Ge 24:11
day until the e of the .... Ex 12:18
tree and left him there until e. .... Jos 8:29
morning and e and stood before 1Sa 17:16
it was time for the e sacrifice. 1Ki 18:29
but by e they dry up and die. .... Ps 90:6
go to work and work until e. .... Ps 104:23
It was the twilight of the e; .... Pr 7:9
and work until e, because you .... Ec 11:6
and my wife died in the e. .... Eze 24:18
the time of the e sacrifice, ... Da 9:21
That e, after the sun went down, ... Mk 1:32
be in the e, or at midnight .... Mk 13:35
When it was e on the first day .... Jn 20:19

EVENINGS

hundred e and mornings. .... Da 8:14
you about these e and mornings. .... Da 8:26

EVENLY

which was e spread over them. 1Ki 6:35

EVENTS

Fearful e and great signs will .... Lk 21:11

EVENTUALLY

You will e leave that place with .... Je 2:37

EVER

If you e eat fruit from that .... Ge 2:17
animal, tame or wild, will e be. .... Ge 3:14
the Israelites e had a king: .... Ge 36:31
e since that time he has made................. Ex 5:23
or ancestors have e seen— .... Ex 10:6
be with you if e I let you and .... Ex 10:10
locusts than e before or after, ... Ex 10:14
person cannot e buy it back. .... Le 27:20
"Why did we e leave Egypt?"'" .... Nu 11:20
E since he was a young boy, ... Nu 11:28
I e done this to you before? .... Nu 22:30
like this has e happened before!.............. Dt 4:32
like this has e been heard .... Dt 4:32
people have e heard God speak............... Dt 4:33
No other god has e taken for .... Dt 4:34
human being has e heard the .... Dt 5:26
nor your ancestors had e seen. .... Dt 8:3
you e forgive the LORD your God .... Dt 8:19
among you will e do such an evil .... Dt 13:11
among you will e do such an evil .... Dt 19:20
or woman must e become a temple .... Dt 23:17
no tool was e used on them. .... Jos 8:31
Did he e quarrel or fight with................ Jdg 11:25
like this has e happened before, ... Jdg 19:30
and no one will e cut his hair 1Sa 1:11
Did I e secretly accept money to 1Sa 12:3
to the kings of Judah e since. 1Sa 27:6
has planned this e since Amnon............. 2Sa 13:32
like this had e been made for 1Ki 10:20
keep me from e giving my land to 1Ki 21:3
We praise you forever and e. 1Ch 29:10
one had e given such spices as 2Ch 9:9
one in Judah had e seen such................. 2Ch 9:11
like this had e happened 2Ch 9:19
kings of Israel had e celebrated 2Ch 35:18
guards with me e took off our .... Ne 4:23
who lives forever and e." .... Ne 9:5
Moabite should e be allowed in .... Ne 13:1
are not the first man e born; .... Job 15:7
let my cry e stop being heard .... Job 16:18
e since people were first put on .... Job 20:4
where no one has e walked; .... Job 28:4
No stranger e had to spend the .... Job 31:32
Have you e ordered the morning .... Job 38:12
Have you e gone to where the sea .... Job 38:16
Have you e gone into the .... Job 38:22
No one has e given me anything .... Job 41:11
out their names forever and e. .... Ps 9:5
Nothing bad will e happen to me; .... Ps 10:6
The LORD is King forever and e. .... Ps 10:16
throne will last forever and e................. Ps 45:6
will praise you forever and e. .... Ps 45:17
God is our God forever and e. .... Ps 48:14
No payment is e enough. .... Ps 49:8
trust God's love forever and e. .... Ps 52:8
You will make me greater than e, ... Ps 71:21
and e we will praise you. .... Ps 79:13
Then no one will e remember the .... Ps 83:4
him continues forever and e, ... Ps 103:17
so please don't e leave me. .... Ps 119:8
your teachings forever and e................... Ps 119:44
on your throne forever and e." .... Ps 132:12
I will praise you forever and e. .... Ps 145:1
I will praise you forever and e. .... Ps 145:2
put them in place forever and e;............. Ps 148:6
Don't e forget kindness and .... Pr 3:3
Don't e forget my words; .... Pr 4:21

don't e say things that are not .... Pr 4:24
and you might not e be respected .... Pr 25:10
a foolish person e be honored. .... Pr 26:1
nor can we e really see all we................. Ec 1:8
in Jerusalem had e had before. .... Ec 2:7
the women a man could e want. .... Ec 2:8
and night and hardly e sleeping. .... Ec 8:16
No one will e live there or .... Is 13:20
no one will e cut us down again. .... Is 14:8
one will e travel through that .... Is 34:10
of happiness forever and e..................... Is 60:15
ago no one has e heard of a God .... Is 64:4
No one has e seen a God besides .... Is 64:4
No one has e heard of that .... Is 66:8
no one has e seen that happen. .... Is 66:8
same way no one e saw a country .... Is 66:8
no one has e heard of a new .... Is 66:8
See if there has e been anything .... Je 2:10
Has a nation e exchanged its .... Je 2:11
you e heard anything like this? .... Je 18:13
of Judah had e known before. .... Je 19:4
if these laws should e fail," .... Je 31:36
descendants e stop being a .... Je 31:36
sons, or daughters e drink wine. .... Je 35:8
you nor your ancestors e knew. .... Je 44:3
no people will e live there .... Je 50:39
and there is more pride than e. .... Eze 7:10
No one was e destroyed like .... Eze 27:32
powerful king has e asked the .... Da 2:10
Praise God forever and e, ... Da 2:20
Nothing has e been done on earth .... Da 9:12
of gods that no one has e heard............. Da 11:36
shine like stars forever and e................. Da 12:3
like this has e happened during .... Joe 1:2
the LORD our God forever and e. .... Mic 4:5
than any other person e born, ... Mt 11:11
than there has e been since .... Mt 24:21
as bad will e happen again. .... Mt 24:21
no one e pours new wine into old .... Mk 2:22
which no one has e ridden...................... Mk 11:2
May no one e eat fruit from you .... Mk 11:14
than there has e been since .... Mk 13:19
as bad will e happen again. .... Mk 13:19
mercy forever and e to those who .... Lk 1:50
no one e pours new wine into old .... Lk 5:37
than any other person e born, ... Lk 7:28
which no one has e ridden..................... Lk 19:30
No one has e seen God. But God .... Jn 1:18
only one who has e gone up to .... Jn 3:13
who told me everything I e did. .... Jn 4:29
"He told me everything I e did." .... Jn 4:39
other person who has e spoken!" .... Jn 7:46
Nobody has e heard of anyone .... Jn 9:32
that no one else has e done. .... Jn 15:24
hurt every prophet who e lived. .... Ac 7:52
of God will e see me again..................... Ac 20:25
whole world will e be able to .... Rm 8:39
No one has e given God anything .... Rm 11:35
No one has e seen this, and no 1Co 2:9
and no one has e heard about it. 1Co 2:9
No one has e imagined what God 1Co 2:9
No soldier e serves in the army 1Co 9:7
No one e plants a vineyard 1Co 9:7
If no one is e raised from the 1Co 15:13
in us brings e greater glory, ... 2Co 3:18
belongs to God forever and e................. Gal 1:5
greater than anyone can e know, ... Eph 3:19
for all time, forever and e. .... Eph 3:21
No one e hates his own body, ... Eph 5:29
God and Father forever and e! .... Php 4:20
honor and glory forever and e. 1Ti 1:17
one has e seen God, or can see 1Ti 6:16
forever and e be the Lord's. 2Ti 4:18

throne will last forever and **e**..................Heb 1:8
from that tribe **e** served as a ....Heb 7:13
belong to him forever and **e**. 1Pe 4:11
All power is his forever and **e**. 1Pe 5:11
in the Scriptures **e** comes from 2Pe 1:20
No prophecy **e** came from what a 2Pe 1:21
No one has **e** seen God, but if we 1Jn 4:12
glory and power forever and **e**! ....Rev 1:6
look, I am alive forever and **e**! ....Rev 1:18
throne, who lives forever and **e**. ....Rev 4:9
him who lives forever and **e**. ....Rev 4:10
glory and power forever and **e**." ....Rev 5:13
belong to our God forever and **e**. ....Rev 7:12
the One who lives forever and **e**. ....Rev 10:6
and he will rule forever and **e**." ....Rev 11:15
pain will rise forever and **e**. ....Rev 14:11
of God, who lives forever and **e**...............Rev 15:7
that has **e** happened since ....Rev 16:18
any job will **e** be found in you ....Rev 18:22
smoke will rise forever and **e**." ....Rev 19:3
day and night forever and **e**. ....Rev 20:10
or tells lies will **e** go into it. ....Rev 21:27
rule as kings forever and **e**. ....Rev 22:5

EVERLASTING
let the **e** hills give the best ....Dt 33:15
The **e** God is your place of ....Dt 33:27
was set up long ago; you are **e**. ....Ps 93:2
He made his agreement **e**. ....Ps 111:9
very much, and his truth is **e**. ....Ps 117:2
LORD, your word is **e**;..................Ps 119:89
LORD, your name is **e**; ....Ps 135:13
Lead me on the road to **e** life..................Ps 139:24
Jerusalem, your God is **e**. ....Ps 146:10
Then you will go to your **e** home, ...Ec 12:5
bound with **e** chains, to be ....Jud 1:6

EVERYDAY
army wastes time with **e** matters. 2Ti 2:4

EVI
Among those they killed were **E,** ....Nu 31:8
including **E,** Rekem, Zur, Hur, ...Jos 13:21

EVIL
the knowledge of good and **e**..................Ge 2:9
they thought about was **e**. ....Ge 6:5
thoughts are **e** even when they ....Ge 8:21
have you paid back **e** for good? ....Ge 44:4
God turned your **e** into good to ....Ge 50:20
relatives. It is **e** to do this. ....Le 18:17
will these **e** people complain ....Nu 14:27
to all these **e** people who have ....Nu 14:35
from the tents of these **e** men! ....Nu 16:26
don't do **e** things. ....Dt 4:25
the LORD your God says is **e**,..................Dt 4:25
must get rid of the **e** among you. ....Dt 17:7
you do what the LORD says is **e**, ...Dt 31:29
promised that **e** will come to you ....Jos 23:15
because of the **e** Israel did. ....Jdg 3:12
have not done **e** by turning from 2Sa 22:22
I have kept myself from doing **e**. 2Sa 22:24
you are against those who are **e**. 2Sa 22:27
Israel and speak **e** about them. 1Ki 9:7
Jeroboam did not stop doing **e**. 1Ki 13:33
have done more **e** than anyone who 1Ki 14:9
They had done many **e** things, ...1Ki 14:24
he did more **e** than all the kings..................1Ki 16:25
Stop your **e** ways and obey my 2Ki 17:13
to rebuild that **e** city that ....Ezr 4:12
We have done **e** things, and our ....Ezr 9:13
to stop the **e** plan that Haman ....Est 8:3
God and stayed away from **e**. ....Job 1:1
God and staying away from **e**. ....Job 2:3
stay away from **e** is ....Job 28:28

for good, only **e** came to me; ....Job 30:26
wicked actions done by **e** people, ...Ps 7:9
You must not say **e** things, ...Ps 34:13
Stop doing **e** and do good. ....Ps 34:14
Stop doing **e** and do good, so you ....Ps 37:27
repay me with **e** for the good I ....Ps 38:20
are saying **e** things about me..................Ps 41:5
I fear when **e** people surround me ....Ps 49:5
stop your mouth from speaking **e**, ...Ps 50:19
People who love the LORD hate **e**. ....Ps 97:10
avoided every **e** way so I could ....Ps 119:101
They say **e** things about you. ....Ps 139:20
are eager to do **e** and are quick ....Pr 1:16
make **e** plans in their hearts ....Pr 6:14
and bragging, **e** ways and lies. ....Pr 8:13
the wicked simply pour out **e**..................Pr 15:28
Good people stay away from **e**. ....Pr 16:17
person with an **e** heart will find ....Pr 17:20
Don't envy **e** people or try to be ....Pr 24:1
will be ruined by their own **e**,..................Pr 28:10
have planned **e,** shut your mouth ....Pr 30:32
do a hundred **e** things and might ....Ec 8:12
in secret, the good and the **e**. ....Ec 12:14
to choose good and reject **e,** ....Is 7:16
our God will punish **e** people..................Is 61:2
go from one **e** thing to another ....Je 9:3
you are accustomed to doing **e**. ....Je 13:23
should not be paid back with **e,** ....Je 18:20
They have done **e** things among..................Je 29:23
our sins and the **e** things done ....Da 9:16
to sin; to take away **e;** to bring ....Da 9:24
to do good, not **e,** so that you ....Am 5:14
Hate **e** and love good; be fair in ....Am 5:15
turn away from **e** living and stop ....Jnh 3:8
eyes are too good to look at **e;** ....Hab 1:13
all kinds of **e** things about you ....Mt 5:11
yes or no, it is from the **E** One. ....Mt 5:37
on good people and on **e** people, ...Mt 5:45
but save us from the **E** One.' ....Mt 6:13
Why are you thinking **e** thoughts? ....Mt 9:4
hearts, so they say **e** things. ....Mt 12:35
E and sinful people are the ones..................Mt 12:39
Out of the mind come **e** thoughts, ...Mt 15:19
suppose that **e** servant thinks ....Mt 24:48
good or to do **e,** to save a life ....Mk 3:4
All these **e** things begin inside ....Mk 7:21
greed, **e** actions, lying, doing ....Mk 7:22
of sicknesses and **e** spirits: ....Lk 8:2
had an **e** spirit in her that made ....Lk 13:11
they were doing **e** things. ....Jn 3:19
All who do **e** hate the light and ....Jn 3:20
believe and said **e** things about ....Ac 19:9
was afraid some **e** people would..................Ac 23:10
We should do **e** so that good will ....Rm 3:8
used to show that sin is very **e**. ....Rm 7:13
to do good, **e** is there with me. ....Rm 7:21
Hate what is **e,** and hold on to ....Rm 12:9
Do not let **e** defeat you, but..................Rm 12:21
from wanting **e** things as those 1Co 10:6
no pleasure in **e** but rejoices 1Co 13:6
people say **e** things about us 2Co 6:8
us from this **e** world we live ....Gal 1:4
others. Never do anything **e**. ....Eph 4:31
good, because these are **e** times..................Eph 5:16
on the day of **e** you will be able ....Eph 6:13
away from everything that is **e**. 1Th 5:22
of money causes all kinds of **e**. 1Ti 6:10
who are **e** and cheat others..................2Ti 3:13
to speak no **e** about anyone, ...Tit 3:2
that none of you has an **e,** ....Heb 3:12
difference between good and **e**. ....Heb 5:14
E cannot tempt God, and God ....Jam 1:13
It is wild and **e** and full of ....Jam 3:8

do not tell **e** lies about each .... Jam 4:11
He must not say **e** things, and he 1Pe 3:10
belonged to the E One and killed 1Jn 3:12
one who does **e** has never known 3Jn 1:11
the false teachings of **e** people. .... Rev 2:2

EVIL-MERODACH

thirty-seventh year E became 2Ki 25:27
E spoke kindly to Jehoiachin and 2Ki 25:28
year E became king of Babylon .... Je 52:31
E spoke kindly to Jehoiachin and .... Je 52:32

EVILS

My people have done two **e**: .... Je 2:13

EXACT

must decide the **e** price by .... Le 27:18
from them the **e** time they first .... Mt 2:7
o'clock was the **e** time that .... Jn 4:53

EXACTLY

things happened **e** as he said .... Ge 41:13
won't know **e** what we will need ...... Ex 10:26
E three months after the .... Ex 19:1
Moses did **e** what the LORD had .... Nu 1:19
Tell each man **e** what to carry. .... Nu 4:32
It was exactly the way the LORD .... Nu 8:4
you, and follow the commands **e**. .... Dt 5:32
they decide, **e** as they tell you. .... Dt 17:11
Do **e** what the priests, the .... Dt 24:8
Do **e** as I command, and do not .... Dt 28:14
you follow them **e**, you will be .... Jos 1:7
e as they were written in the .... Jos 8:34
It is **e** like the LORD's altar, ... Jos 22:28
was built **e** as it was planned................ 1Ki 6:38
will happen **e** as I planned them........... Is 14:24
will happen **e** as I set them up .... Is 14:24
the wood look like a person, ... Is 44:13
I do **e** what the Father told me .... Jn 14:31
decided **e** when and where they .... Ac 17:26
of Christ, who is **e** like God. 2Co 4:4
but Jesus Christ is **e** like him................ Col 1:15
God and shows **e** what God is like .... Heb 1:3

EXAMINE

e them every morning and test .... Job 7:18
E and see how good the LORD is. .... Ps 34:8
God, **e** me and know my heart; .... Ps 139:23
Let us **e** and see what we have .... La 3:40

EXAMINED

You have **e** my heart; .... Ps 17:3
you have **e** me and know all about .... Ps 139:1
you have already **e** and seen how 1Pe 2:3

EXAMINES

will not do well if he **e** you;..................... Job 13:9

EXAMPLE

said, "Explain the **e** to us." .... Mt 15:15
I did this as an **e** so that you .... Jn 13:15
try to follow my **e** and to copy .... Php 3:17
be an **e** to the believers with 1Ti 4:12
follow the **e** of the prophets who .... Jam 5:10
you and gave you an **e** to follow. 1Pe 2:21

EXAMPLES

are not good **e** for you to follow .... Mt 23:3
and myself as **e** so you could 1Co 4:6
things happened as **e** for us, ... 1Co 10:6
happened to those people are **e**. 1Co 10:11
Do I need to give more **e**? .... Heb 11:32
for, but be good **e** to them. 1Pe 5:3

EXCELLENT

The gold of that land is **e**. .... Ge 2:12
and you are an **e** speaker, so God .... Ps 45:2
She did an **e** thing for me. .... Mt 26:10
She did an **e** thing for me. .... Mk 14:6

beginning, most **e** Theophilus, it.............. Lk 1:3
king said to the servant, 'E!' .... Lk 19:17
To the Most E Governor Felix: .... Ac 23:26
him, saying, "Most E Felix!.................... Ac 24:2
said, "Most E Festus, I am not.................. Ac 26:25

EXCHANGE

them food in **e** for their horses ...... Ge 47:17
us and our land in **e** for food, ... Ge 47:19
animal in its place or **e** it, ... Le 27:10
from the bad or **e** one animal for .... Le 27:33
e your one-tenth for silver. .... Dt 14:25

EXCHANGED

They **e** their glorious God for a .... Ps 106:20
Has a nation ever **e** its gods? .... Je 2:11
my people have **e** their glorious .... Je 2:11

EXCHANGING

feasting and a day for **e** gifts. .... Est 9:19
those who were **e** different kinds .... Mt 21:12
those who were **e** different kinds .... Mk 11:15
e different kinds of money. .... Jn 2:14
money of those who were **e** it. .... Jn 2:15

EXCITE

not to awaken or **e** my feelings .... Sng 2:7
not to awaken or **e** my feelings .... Sng 3:5
because they **e** me too much. .... Sng 6:5
not to awaken or **e** my feelings .... Sng 8:4

EXCITED

all the people became very **e**. .... Ru 1:19
the whole city is **e**, and that is 1Ki 1:45
opening, and I felt **e** inside. .... Sng 5:4
the dead is **e** to meet you when .... Is 14:9
he will be **e** like a man ready to .... Is 42:13
you will be **e** and full of joy, ... Is 60:5
Babylon, you are **e** and happy, ... Je 50:11
to attack; their horses are **e**. .... Nah 2:3
who did not believe **e** the others .... Ac 14:2
was always very **e** when he spoke .... Ac 18:25

EXCITEMENT

I saw some great **e**, but I don't 2Sa 18:29
With great **e**, the horse races .... Job 39:24
all the city was filled with **e**. .... Mt 21:10
waiting with **e** for God to show .... Rm 8:19

EXCUSE

given them an **e** to kill us." .... Ex 5:21
He did not **e** anyone from the 2Ch 23:8
who sin without **e** will be .... Ps 25:3
a better **e** than wicked Judah................ Je 3:11
provided an **e** for your sisters................. Eze 16:52
go look at it. Please **e** me.' .... Lk 14:18
go and try them. Please **e** me.' .... Lk 14:19
they have no **e** for their sin. .... Jn 15:22
So people have no **e** for the bad .... Rm 1:20
freedom as an **e** to do what.................... Gal 5:13
your freedom as an **e** to do evil. 1Pe 2:16

EXCUSES

But all the guests made **e**. .... Lk 14:18
This stops all **e** and brings the .... Rm 3:19

EXECUTED

he **e** the officers who had 2Ki 14:5
he **e** the officers who had 2Ch 25:3

EXIST

power we live and move and **e**.' .... Ac 17:28

EXISTED

you now about what has always **e**,........... 1Jn 1:1
know the One who **e** from the 1Jn 2:13
know the One who **e** from the 1Jn 2:14
Everything **e** and was made, ... Rev 4:11

EXITS

Show them its e and entrances, ... Eze 43:11
and to all the e from the Temple.............. Eze 44:5

EXPAND

ahead of you and e the borders .... Ex 34:24

EXPECT

army when they did not e it. .... Jdg 8:11
call on God and e him to answer .... Job 12:4
an evil person can e nothing. .... Pr 10:28
the wicked can to be defeated .... Pr 11:23
they e a harvest, but there is .... Pr 20:4
amazing things we did not e. .... Is 64:3
There I will e your offerings, ... Eze 20:40
come at a time you don't e him. .... Mt 24:44
at a time when you don't e him!" .... Lk 12:40
they gave in a way we did not e:.............. 2Co 8:5
e and hope that I will not fail .... Php 1:20
but we really e better things .... Heb 6:9

EXPECTED

I e good grapes to grow, ... Is 5:4
with much, much more will be e. .... Lk 12:48

EXPECTING

The people are not e an attack. .... Jdg 18:10
a pile of grain e to find twenty .... Hag 2:16
is not ready and is not e him. .... Mt 24:50
is not ready and is not e him. .... Lk 12:46
I am e him to come with the 1Co 16:11

EXPECTS

one who made it e his own work .... Hab 2:18

EXPENSE

at the king's e or taken 2Sa 19:42
would not be an e to any of you. 2Th 3:8

EXPENSES

Pay their e so they can shave .... Ac 21:24

EXPENSIVE

He also gave e gifts to her .... Ge 24:53
gold, spices, e perfumes, his 2Ki 20:13
and red thread, and e linen. 2Ch 2:14
red thread, and e linen, and he 2Ch 3:14
of linen and other e material. .... Pr 31:22
name is pleasant like e perfume. .... Sng 1:3
gold, spices, e perfumes, his .... Is 39:2
cannot buy those e statues,.................... Is 40:20
and silver, e jewels and gifts. .... Da 11:38
jar filled with e perfume. .... Mt 26:7
jar filled with very e perfume, ... Mk 14:3
in a pint of very e perfume made .... Jn 12:3
or gold or pearls or e clothes................. 1Ti 2:9
made from ivory, e wood, bronze, ... Rev 18:12
was bright like a very e jewel, ... Rev 21:11

EXPERIENCE

who have understanding and e— .... Dt 1:13
full of shame and e only pain. .... Job 10:15
if they will e love or hate. .... Ec 9:1

EXPERIENCED

the wise and e leaders of your .... Dt 1:15
skilled and e in bronze work. 1Ki 7:14
servants are e at cutting down 2Ch 2:8

EXPERIENCES

Were all your e wasted? .... Gal 3:4
your e have been like those of 1Th 2:14

EXPERT

was an e on the law of Moses, ... Mt 22:35
Then an e on the law stood up to .... Lk 10:25
The e on the law answered, ... Lk 10:37
of that house like an e builder. 1Co 3:10

EXPERTS

to ask advice from e about law .... Est 1:13
to cruel men, e in destruction. .... Eze 21:31
the Pharisees and e on the law .... Lk 7:30
One of the e on the law said to .... Lk 11:45
for you, you e on the law! .... Lk 11:46
for you, you e on the law. .... Lk 11:52
the Pharisees and e on the law, ... Lk 14:3
priests, the e on the law, and .... Lk 19:47

EXPLAIN

one could e its meaning to me. .... Ge 41:24
Moses began to e what God had............. Dt 1:5
in my kingdom can e it to me, ... Da 4:18
E to us the meaning of the story............. Mt 13:36
it is hard to e because you are .... Heb 5:11

EXPLAINED

writings, he e the kingdom of................. Ac 28:23
with a joy that cannot be e, ... 1Pe 1:8

EXPLAINING

for drinking and for e dreams. .... Ge 44:5
the future by e signs and dreams 2Ki 21:6
the future by e signs and dreams 2Ch 33:6

EXPLAINS

in heaven who e secret things, ... Da 2:28
unless someone e it to me?" .... Ac 8:31

EXPLANATION

that Joseph's e of the dream was .... Ge 40:16
and you can trust this e." .... Da 2:45

EXPLANATIONS

spoke, and listened to your e................... Job 32:11

EXPLORE

Send men to e the land of .... Nu 13:2
men Moses sent to e the land. .... Nu 13:16
sent them to e Canaan and said,............. Nu 13:17
Moses had sent to e the land had .... Nu 14:36
to spy out and e the land. .... Jdg 18:2
were told, "Go, e the land." .... Jdg 18:2

EXPLORED

So they went up and e the land, ... Nu 13:21
report about the land they e, ... Nu 13:32
land that we e is too large to .... Nu 13:32
who had e the land, tore .... Nu 14:6
The land we e is very good. .... Nu 14:7
the forty days you e the land. .... Nu 14:34
the men who e the land did not .... Nu 14:38
the Valley of Eshcol they e it. .... Dt 1:24
men who had e the land around.............. Jdg 18:14

EXPLORING

After forty days of e the land,................... Nu 13:25

EXPOSED

and everything in it will be e................... 2Pe 3:10

EXTEND

Levites will e fifteen hundred.................. Nu 35:4
land will e east of the holy .... Eze 48:21

EXTENDS

tower that e from the palace. .... Ne 3:26
tower that e from the palace .... Ne 3:27

EXTRA

Let the half piece of cloth .... Ex 26:12
full price plus an e one-fifth .... Le 6:5
give back the e amount you .... Ne 5:11
carry a bag or e clothes or .... Mt 10:10
bag, bread, money, or e clothes. .... Lk 9:3

EXTRAORDINARY

This is e, Lord GOD. 2Sa 7:19
knowledge and e understanding. .... Da 5:14

EYE

e for eye, tooth for tooth, hand	Ex 21:24
eye for **e**, tooth for tooth, hand	Ex 21:24
male or female slave in the **e**,	Ex 21:26
the eye, and the **e** is blinded,	Ex 21:26
free the slave to pay for the **e**.	Ex 21:26
broken bone, **e** for eye, tooth	Le 24:20
eye for **e**, tooth for tooth.	Le 24:20
for a life, an **e** for an eye, a	Dt 19:21
an eye for an **e**, a tooth for	Dt 19:21
out the right **e** of each of you	1Sa 11:2
put on her **e** makeup and fixed	2Ki 9:30
do; he keeps his **e** on them	Ps 11:4
as you would protect your own **e**.	Ps 17:8
He keeps his **e** on the nations,	Ps 66:7
can vanish in the wink of an **e**.	Pr 23:5
strike his arm and his right **e**.	Zch 11:17
and his right **e** will go blind."	Zch 11:17
If your right eye causes you to	Mt 5:29
it was said, 'An **e** for an eye,	Mt 5:38
An eye for an **e**, and a tooth for	Mt 5:38
The **e** is a light for the body.	Mt 6:22
of dust in your friend's **e**,	Mt 7:3
big piece of wood in your own **e**?	Mt 7:3
piece of dust out of your **e**' ?	Mt 7:4
big piece of wood in your own **e**.	Mt 7:4
take the wood out of your own **e**.	Mt 7:5
the dust out of your friend's **e**.	Mt 7:5
If your **e** causes you to sin,	Mt 18:9
have only one **e** and live forever	Mt 18:9
go through the **e** of a needle	Mt 19:24
If your **e** causes you to sin,	Mk 9:47
with only one **e** than to have two	Mk 9:47
go through the **e** of a needle	Mk 10:25
of dust in your friend's **e**,	Lk 6:41
big piece of wood in your own **e**?	Lk 6:41
out of your **e**' when you cannot	Lk 6:42
big piece of wood in your own **e**!	Lk 6:42
take the wood out of your own **e**.	Lk 6:42
the dust out of your friend's **e**.	Lk 6:42
Your **e** is a light for the body.	Lk 11:34
go through the **e** of a needle	Lk 18:25
I am not an **e**, I am not part	1Co 12:16
If the whole body were an **e**,	1Co 12:17
The **e** cannot say to the hand,	1Co 12:21
as quickly as an **e** blinks—when	1Co 15:52

EYEBROWS

his beard, his **e**, and the rest	Le 14:9

EYELIDS

of water will flow from our **e**.	Je 9:18

EYES

was as if their **e** were opened.	Ge 3:7
Leah had weak **e**, but Rachel was	Ge 29:17
before their **e** so they would	Ge 30:41
will close your **e** when you die."	Ge 46:4
His **e** are dark like the color of	Ge 49:12
something wrong with their **e**,	Le 21:20
destroy your **e** and slowly kill	Le 26:16
what your bodies and **e** want.	Nu 15:39
you put out the **e** of these men?	Nu 16:14
and my **e** are open as I fall	Nu 24:4
and my **e** are open as I fall	Nu 24:16
hooks in your **e** and thorns in	Nu 33:55
Egypt, right before your own **e**.	Dt 4:34
you have seen with your own **e**.	Dt 10:21
His **e** are on it continually,	Dt 11:12
ox will be killed before your **e**,	Dt 28:31
before your own **e** to the king	Dt 29:2
your own **e** you saw the great	Dt 29:3
see with your **e** or hear with	Dt 29:4
His **e** were not weak, and he was	Dt 34:7
your back and thorns in your **e**,	Jos 23:13

Samson and tore out his **e**.	Jdg 16:21
back for putting out my two **e**!"	Jdg 16:28
seemed right in their own **e**.	Jdg 21:25
But your **e** will cry and your	1Sa 2:33
Eli's **e** were so weak he was	1Sa 3:2
the LORD did before your **e**.	1Sa 12:16
something with your own **e** today.	1Sa 24:10
come and seen it with my own **e**.	1Ki 10:7
boy's mouth, his **e** on the boy's	2Ki 4:34
on the boy's **e**, and his hands	2Ki 4:34
seven times and opened his **e**.	2Ki 4:35
my servant's **e**, and let him see.	2Ki 6:17
LORD opened the **e** of the young	2Ki 6:17
these men's **e** so they can see.	2Ki 6:20
So the LORD opened their **e**,	2Ki 6:20
You will see it with your **e**,	2Ki 7:2
You will see it with your **e**,	2Ki 7:19
Open your **e**, LORD, and see.	2Ki 19:16
put out his **e** and put bronze	2Ki 25:7
come and seen it with my own **e**.	2Ch 9:6
did not hide trouble from my **e**.	Job 3:10
A shape stood before my **e**,	Job 4:16
My **e** will never see happy times	Job 7:7
you have human **e** that see as we	Job 10:4
Now my **e** have seen all this;	Job 13:1
Why do your **e** flash with anger?	Job 15:12
heavens are not pure in his **e**.	Job 15:15
stares at me with his angry **e**.	Job 16:9
I have dark circles around my **e**.	Job 16:16
My **e** pour out tears to God.	Job 16:20
e of their children go blind.	Job 17:5
will see him with my very own **e**.	Job 19:27
Their **e** should see their own	Job 21:20
the stars are not pure in his **e**.	Job 25:5
they open their **e**, everything is	Job 27:19
from the **e** of every living	Job 28:21
I was **e** for the blind and feet	Job 29:15
with my **e** not to look with	Job 31:1
been led by my **e** to do wrong,	Job 31:7
its **e** can see it from far away.	Job 39:29
blind its **e** and capture it?	Job 40:24
and its **e** look like the light at	Job 41:18
but now my **e** have seen you.	Job 42:5
My **e** are weak from so much	Ps 6:7
your **e** can see what is true.	Ps 17:2
My **e** are always looking to the	Ps 25:15
with my own **e** at his Temple.	Ps 27:4
My **e** are weak from so much	Ps 31:9
My **e** are tired from waiting for	Ps 69:3
Let their **e** be closed so they	Ps 69:23
You keep my **e** from closing.	Ps 77:4
My **e** are weak from crying.	Ps 88:9
Can't the maker of **e** see?	Ps 94:9
have **e**, but they cannot see.	Ps 115:5
You stopped my **e** from crying;	Ps 116:8
Open my **e** to see the miracles in	Ps 119:18
My **e** are tired from looking for	Ps 119:82
My **e** are tired from looking for	Ps 119:123
stream from my **e**, because people	Ps 119:136
or close my **e**, or let myself	Ps 132:4
have **e**, but they cannot see.	Ps 135:16
Keep your **e** focused on what is	Pr 4:25
go to sleep or even rest your **e**.	Pr 6:4
with their **e**, tapping with	Pr 6:13
as you would your own **e**.	Pr 7:2
on the teeth or smoke in the **e**.	Pr 10:26
The LORD's **e** see everything;	Pr 15:3
happiness will show in your **e**.	Pr 15:30
ears to hear and **e** to see.	Pr 20:12
bruises? Who has bloodshot **e**?	Pr 23:29
Your **e** will see strange sights,	Pr 23:33
the LORD gave **e** to both of them.	Pr 29:13
the valley will peck out your **e**,	Pr 30:17

and your **e** will not see clearly. .... Ec 12:3
and your **e** are like doves. .... Sng 1:15
Your **e** behind your veil are like .... Sng 4:1
heart with a glance of your **e**, ... Sng 4:9
His **e** are like doves by springs .... Sng 5:12
your **e** from me, because they .... Sng 6:5
Your **e** are like the pools in .... Sng 7:4
and they flirt with their **e**. .... Is 3:16
Cover their **e**. Otherwise, they .... Is 6:10
see with their **e** and hear with .... Is 6:10
great things before you." .... Is 12:6
their **e** will see the Holy One of .... Is 17:7
has closed your **e**. (The prophets .... Is 29:10
The prophets are your **e**. .... Is 29:10
your teacher with your own **e**. .... Is 30:20
Your **e** will see the king in his .... Is 33:17
Open your **e**, LORD, and see. .... Is 37:17
My **e** became tired as I looked to .... Is 38:14
people who have **e** but don't see .... Is 43:8
is as if their **e** are covered so .... Is 44:18
with their own **e** when the LORD .... Is 52:8
feel our way as if we had no **e**. .... Is 59:10
do you put color around your **e**? .... Je 4:30
They have **e**, but they don't .... Je 5:21
water and my **e** like a fountain .... Je 9:1
Then our **e** will fill with tears, ... Je 9:18
and my **e** will overflow with .... Je 13:17
But their **e** go blind, because .... Je 14:6
'Let my **e** be filled with tears .... Je 14:17
sin is not hidden from my **e**. .... Je 16:17
let your **e** fill with tears. .... Je 31:16
face and see him with his own **e**. .... Je 32:4
king of Babylon with your own **e**, ... Je 34:3
Then he put out Zedekiah's **e**. .... Je 39:7
come true with your own **e**. .... Je 39:16
Then he put out Zedekiah's **e**, ... Je 52:11
my **e** overflow with tears. .... La 1:16
e have no more tears, and I am .... La 2:11
Do not stop or let your **e** rest. .... La 2:18
Streams of tears flow from my **e**, ... La 3:48
Also, our **e** grew tired, looking .... La 4:17
afraid, and now our **e** are dim. .... La 5:17
and were full of **e** all around. .... Eze 1:18
wheels were full of **e** all over. .... Eze 10:12
They have **e** to see, but they do .... Eze 12:2
painted their **e**, and put on .... Eze 23:40
myself holy before their **e**, ... Eze 36:23
look with your **e** and hear with .... Eze 40:4
Use your **e** to see, and your ears .... Eze 44:5
horn with **e** like a human's. .... Da 7:8
horn with eyes like a human's **e**. .... Da 7:8
It had **e** and a mouth that kept .... Da 7:20
between his **e** that was easy to .... Da 8:5
between its **e** is the first king. .... Da 8:21
Open your **e** and see all the .... Da 9:18
and his **e** were like fire. .... Da 10:6
Your **e** are too good to look at .... Hab 1:13
you will see with your own **e**," .... Zph 3:20
are the seven **e** of the LORD, ... Zch 4:10
Their **e** will rot in their .... Zch 14:12
these things with your own **e**. .... Mal 1:5
If your **e** are good, your whole .... Mt 6:22
But if your **e** are evil, your .... Mt 6:23
Jesus touched their **e** and said, ... Mt 9:29
and they have closed their **e**. .... Mt 13:15
see with their **e** and hear with .... Mt 13:15
see with your **e** and hear with .... Mt 13:16
than to have two **e** and be thrown .... Mt 18:9
blind men and touched their **e**, ... Mt 20:34
because their **e** were heavy. .... Mt 26:43
You have **e**, but you don't really .... Mk 8:18
on the man's **e** and put his hands .... Mk 8:23
put his hands on the man's **e**. .... Mk 8:25

man opened his **e** wide and they .... Mk 8:25
than to have two **e** and be thrown .... Mk 9:47
because their **e** were very heavy. .... Mk 14:40
With my own **e** I have seen your .... Lk 2:30
When your **e** are good, your whole .... Lk 11:34
But when your **e** are evil, your .... Lk 11:34
will be able to see with your **e**. .... Lk 17:20
open your **e** and look at the .... Jn 4:35
and put the mud on the man's **e**. .... Jn 9:6
some mud and put it on my **e**. .... Jn 9:11
and healed his **e** was a Sabbath .... Jn 9:14
put mud on my **e**, I washed, and............ Jn 9:15
since it was your **e** he opened?" .... Jn 9:17
We don't know who opened his **e**. .... Jn 9:21
from, and yet he opened my **e**. .... Jn 9:30
demon open the **e** of the blind?" .... Jn 10:21
opened the **e** of the blind man .... Jn 11:37
has blinded their **e**, and he has .... Jn 12:40
see with their **e** and understand .... Jn 12:40
the ground and opened his **e**, ... Ac 9:8
fish scales fell from Saul's **e**, ... Ac 9:18
She opened her **e**, and when she .... Ac 9:40
to open their **e** so that they may .... Ac 26:18
and they have closed their **e**. .... Ac 28:27
see with their **e** and hear with .... Ac 28:27
He closed their **e** so they could .... Rm 11:8
Let their **e** be closed so they .... Rm 11:10
We set our **e** not on what we see 2Co 4:18
taken out your **e** and given them .... Gal 4:15
of Jesus with our own **e**. 2Pe 1:16
we have seen with our own **e**,................ 1Jn 1:1
his **e** were like flames of fire. .... Rev 1:14
who has **e** that blaze like fire .... Rev 2:18
put on your **e** so you can truly .... Rev 3:18
creatures with **e** all over them, ... Rev 4:6
and was covered all over with **e**, ... Rev 4:8
He had seven horns and seven **e**, ... Rev 5:6
away every tear from their **e**." .... Rev 7:17
His **e** are like burning fire, ... Rev 19:12
away every tear from their **e**, ... Rev 21:4

EYESIGHT
was old, his **e** was poor, so he .... Ge 27:1
time Israel's **e** was bad because .... Ge 48:10

EZBAI
the Carmelite; Naarai son of **E**; 1Ch 11:37

EZBON
Haggi, Shuni, **E**, Eri, Arodi, ... Ge 46:16
E, Uzzi, Uzziel, Jerimoth, and................. 1Ch 7:7

EZEKIEL
spoke his word to **E** son of Buzi .... Eze 1:3
'The vision that **E** sees is for a .... Eze 12:27
E is to be an example for you. .... Eze 24:24
will let you, **E**, speak to them.................... Eze 29:21

EZEL
began. Wait by the rock **E**. 1Sa 20:19
The people in Beth **E** will cry,................... Mic 1:11

EZEM
Baalah, Iim, **E**,..................................... Jos 15:29
Hazar Shual, Balah, **E**, ... Jos 19:3
Bilhah, **E**, Tolad, ... 1Ch 4:29

EZER
Dishon, **E**, and Dishan. These .... Ge 36:21
The sons of **E** were Bilhan, ... Ge 36:27
Dishon, **E**, and Dishan. These men .... Ge 36:30
Anah, Dishon, **E**, and Dishan. 1Ch 1:38
E and Elead went to Gath to 1Ch 7:21
E was the leader of Gad's army, ... 1Ch 12:9
Next to them, **E** son of Jeshua, ... Ne 3:19
Malkijah, Elam, and **E**. .... Ne 12:42

EZION

Abronah and camped at E Geber.	Nu 33:35
They left E Geber and camped at	Nu 33:36
of Elath and E Geber and	Dt 2:8
also built ships at E Geber,	1Ki 9:26
ships were wrecked at E Geber,	1Ki 22:48
the towns of E Geber and Elath	2Ch 8:17
built in the town of E Geber.	2Ch 20:36

EZRA

This E came to Jerusalem from	Ezr 7:6
E arrived in Jerusalem in the	Ezr 7:8
king of kings, to E the priest,	Ezr 7:12
E opened the book in full view	Ne 8:5

EZRAHITE

was even wiser than Ethan the E,	1Ki 4:31
A maskil of Heman the E.	Ps 87:7
A maskil of Ethan the E.	Ps 88:18

EZRI

E son of Kelub was in charge of	1Ch 27:26

F

F

FACE

covered her f with her veil.	Ge 24:65
and he made them f the streaked	Ge 30:40
I have seen God f to face,	Ge 32:30
I have seen God face to f,	Ge 32:30
very happy to see your f again.	Ge 33:10
It is like seeing the f of God,	Ge 33:10
and covered her f with a veil to	Ge 38:14
had covered her f with a veil.	Ge 38:15
veil that covered her f and put	Ge 38:19
he washed his f and came out.	Ge 43:31
have seen your f and I know you	Ge 46:30
covered his f because he was	Ex 3:6
creatures are to f each other	Ex 25:20
spoke to Moses f to face as a	Ex 33:11
Moses face to f as a man speaks	Ex 33:11
cannot see my f, because no one	Ex 33:20
But my f must not be seen."	Ex 33:23
not know that his f was shining	Ex 34:29
saw that Moses' f was shining,	Ex 34:30
he put a covering over his f.	Ex 34:33
see that Moses' f was shining.	Ex 34:35
he would cover his f again until	Ex 34:35
I speak f to face with him—	Nu 12:8
I speak face to f with him—	Nu 12:8
If her father had spit in her f,	Nu 12:14
that you were seen f to face.	Nu 14:14
that you were seen face to f.	Nu 14:14
LORD spoke to you f to face from	Dt 5:4
to you face to f from the fire	Dt 5:4
and spit in his f and say,	Dt 25:9
The LORD knew Moses f to face	Dt 34:10
The LORD knew Moses face to f	Dt 34:10
too afraid to f the Israelites.	Jos 5:1
Why are you down on your f?	Jos 7:10
cannot f their enemies.	Jos 7:12
angel of the LORD f to face!"	Jdg 6:22
angel of the LORD face to f!"	Jdg 6:22
low with her f to the ground	Ru 2:10
fallen on his f for the creature	1Sa 5:3
up their men to f each other in	1Sa 17:21
won't be able to f your brother	2Sa 2:22
covered his f and cried loudly.	2Sa 19:4
he covered his f with his coat	1Ki 19:13
wrapped his f in a cloth so no	1Ki 20:38
took the cloth from his f.	1Ki 20:41
bed, turned his f to the wall,	1Ki 21:4
and slapped him in the f.	1Ki 22:24

walking stick on the boy's f."	2Ki 4:29
walking stick on the boy's f,	2Ki 4:31
he put it over Ben-Hadad's f,	2Ki 8:15
Come, let's meet f to face."	2Ki 14:8
Come, let's meet face to f."	2Ki 14:8
You have a proud look on your f,	2Ki 19:22
leave you to f Shishak alone.'	2Ch 12:5
and slapped him in the f.	2Ch 18:23
Come, let's meet f to face."	2Ch 25:17
Come, let's meet face to f."	2Ch 25:17
to lift up my f to you,	Ezr 9:6
Why does your f look sad even	Ne 2:2
My f is sad because the city	Ne 2:3
had a very pretty figure and f.	Est 2:7
came in and covered Haman's f.	Est 7:8
he will curse you to your f."	Job 1:11
he will curse you to your f."	Job 2:5
A spirit glided past my f,	Job 4:15
I would not lie to your f.	Job 6:28
the look on my f and smile,'	Job 9:27
lift up your f without shame,	Job 11:15
still defend my ways to his f.	Job 13:15
Don't hide your f from me;	Job 13:24
have buried my f in the dust.	Job 16:15
My f is red from crying;	Job 16:16
curse word; people spit in my f.	Job 17:6
thick darkness that covers my f.	Job 23:17
He covers the f of the moon,	Job 26:9
do not mind spitting in my f.	Job 30:10
will see God's f and will shout	Job 33:26
If he hides his f, who can see	Job 34:29
so honest people will see his f.	Ps 11:7
LORD, rise up, f the enemy, and	Ps 17:13
lived right, I will see your f.	Ps 17:15
Don't they all f death?	Ps 49:9
you and accuse you to your f.	Ps 50:21
your f from my sins and wipe	Ps 51:9
and my f is covered with	Ps 69:7
the poor will f no sudden danger.	Pr 13:8
reflects your f, so your mind	Pr 27:19
she had eaten and washed her f;	Pr 30:20
given us terrible things to f.	Ec 1:13
Show me your f, and let me hear	Sng 2:14
is sweet, and your f is lovely.	Sng 2:14
used two wings to cover its f,	Is 6:2
away every tear from every f.	Is 25:8
You have a proud look on your f,	Is 37:23
I won't hide my f from them when	Is 50:6
But your f still looks like the	Je 3:3
like the f of a prostitute.	Je 3:3
up over your f so everyone will	Je 13:26
is everyone's f turning white	Je 30:6
white like a dead man's f?	Je 30:6
king of Babylon f to face and	Je 32:4
Babylon face to f and see him.	Je 32:4
he will talk to you f to face.	Je 34:3
he will talk to you face to f.	Je 34:3
we f death in the desert.	La 5:9
had a human f and the face	Eze 1:10
a human face and the f of a lion	Eze 1:10
right side and the f of an ox on	Eze 1:10
one also had the f of an eagle.	Eze 1:10
Turn your f toward the city as	Eze 4:3
The first f was the face of a	Eze 10:14
face was the f of a creature	Eze 10:14
The second f was a human face,	Eze 10:14
The second face was a human f,	Eze 10:14
the third was the f of a lion,	Eze 10:14
fourth was the f of an eagle.	Eze 10:14
Cover your f so you cannot see	Eze 12:6
will cover his f so he cannot	Eze 12:12
I will judge you f to face.	Eze 20:35
I will judge you face to f.	Eze 20:35

Every **f** from south to north will .... Eze 20:47
not cover your **f**, and do not eat .... Eze 24:17
you are not to cover your **f**, ... Eze 24:22
all over the **f** of the earth, ... Eze 34:6
One was a human **f** looking toward .... Eze 41:19
was a lion's **f** looking toward .... Eze 41:19
' holy rooms that **f** north. .... Eze 46:19
His **f** turned white, his knees .... Da 5:6
and his **f** became even whiter.................. Da 5:9
or let your **f** be white with fear .... Da 5:10
My **f** became white from fear,................. Da 7:28
sleep with my **f** on the ground. .... Da 8:18
His **f** was bright like lightning, ... Da 10:6
my **f** turned white like a dead................. Da 10:8
sleep with my **f** on the ground. .... Da 10:9
and everyone's **f** becomes pale. .... Joe 2:6
he will hide his **f** from them, ... Mic 3:4
of Israel in the **f** with a club. .... Mic 5:1
and everyone's **f** grows pale. .... Nah 2:10
dress up over your **f** and show .... Nah 3:5
don't put on a sad **f** like the .... Mt 6:16
comb your hair and wash your **f**. .... Mt 6:17
f became bright like the sun, ... Mt 17:2
spat in Jesus' **f** and beat him .... Mt 26:67
the appearance of his **f** changed, ... Lk 9:29
cloth, and a cloth around his **f**. .... Jn 11:44
and hit him in the **f**. .... Jn 19:3
and saw that his **f** looked like .... Ac 6:15
looked like the **f** of an angel. .... Ac 6:15
been allowed to **f** his accusers .... Ac 25:16
made Moses' **f** so bright that 2Co 3:7
over his **f** so the Israelites 2Co 3:13
God that is in the **f** of Christ. 2Co 4:6
than you, or hit you in the **f**. 2Co 11:20
I challenged him to his **f**, ... Gal 2:11
that we must **f** these troubles................. 1Th 3:3
to you and talk **f** to face so we 2Jn 1:12
and talk face to **f** so we can be 2Jn 1:12
see you soon and talk **f** to face. 3Jn 1:14
see you soon and talk face to **f**. 3Jn 1:14
The third had a **f** like a man. .... Rev 4:7
Hide us from the **f** of the One .... Rev 6:16
His **f** was like the sun, and his .... Rev 10:1
will see his **f**, and his name................... Rev 22:4

FACED

the creatures **f** each other .... Ex 37:9
The Temple **f** east.) The water................. Eze 47:1

FACES

of the hill that **f** the city of .... Jdg 16:3
with their **f** to the ground. 2Ch 7:3
oil that makes our **f** shine. .... Ps 104:15
and grind the **f** of the poor .... Is 3:15
f will shine with happiness .... Je 31:12
them had four **f** and four wings. .... Eze 1:6
Their **f** looked the same as the .... Eze 10:22
They make their **f** look sad to .... Mt 6:16

FACT

In **f**, drop some full heads of .... Ru 2:16
In **f**, he was the leader of the 1Ch 12:4
' In **f**, on every high hill and .... Je 2:20
They are judged by this **f**: .... Jn 3:19
In **f**, the Father judges no one, ... Jn 5:22
They do in **f** tell about me, ... Jn 5:39
In **f**, they shared everything. .... Ac 4:32
The **f** that you have lawsuits 1Co 6:7

FACTS

must look at the **f** before you.................. 2Co 10:7

FADED

If the sore has **f** and has not .... Le 13:6
than the skin and it has **f**, ... Le 13:21
deeper than the skin and has **f**, ... Le 13:26

spread on the skin but has **f**, ... Le 13:28
might have **f** after the piece .... Le 13:56

FAIL

God so that you **f** to obey his .... Dt 8:11
You will **f** in everything you do. .... Dt 28:29
messages **f** to come true........................ 1Sa 3:19
bow did not **f** to kill many 2Sa 1:22
sword did not **f** to wound many 2Sa 1:22
He will not **f** you or leave you................. 1Ch 28:20
ask for every day without **f**. .... Ezr 6:9
Their bulls never **f** to mate;................... Job 21:10
so they do not **f** to keep them. .... Ps 37:31
Plans **f** without good advice, ... Pr 15:22
Don't **f** to punish children. .... Pr 23:13
if these laws should ever **f**," .... Je 31:36
to come true. But they will **f**. .... Da 11:14
But you **f** to be fair to others .... Lk 11:42
from human authority, it will **f**. .... Ac 5:38
is in you—unless you **f** the test. 2Co 13:5
that I will not **f** Christ in .... Php 1:20
so none of you will **f** to enter. .... Heb 4:1
that no one will **f** by following .... Heb 4:11

FAILED

that he has not **f** to keep any of .... Jos 23:14
more to say; words have **f** them............... Job 32:15
what you told me; I have not **f**. .... Ps 17:5
forgotten you or **f** to keep our................ Ps 44:17
be ashamed because they have **f**, ... Je 20:11
efforts to clean the pot have **f**. .... Eze 24:12
It is not that God **f** to keep his .... Rm 9:6
ourselves have not **f** the test. 2Co 13:6
even if it seems we have **f**. 2Co 13:7
all the rules we **f** to follow. .... Col 2:14
and they have **f** in trying to.................... 2Ti 3:8

FAILS

the first attack **f**, people will 2Sa 17:9
that no one **f** to receive God's .... Heb 12:15
God's law but **f** to obey even one .... Jam 2:10

FAILURE

But their **f** brought salvation to .... Rm 11:11
The Jews' **f** brought rich .... Rm 11:12
our visit to you was not a **f**. 1Th 2:1

FAINT

I am weak and **f**. I moan from the .... Ps 38:8
about to **f** before my murderers!............. Je 4:31
seven sons felt **f** because they............... Je 15:9
They **f** like wounded soldiers in .... La 2:12
They might **f** while going home." .... Mt 15:32
hungry, they will **f** on the way. .... Mk 8:3
will be so afraid they will **f**, ... Lk 21:26

FAINTING

and babies are **f** in the streets................ La 2:11
children who are **f** with hunger .... La 2:19

FAITH

And the LORD accepted Abram's **f**, ... Ge 15:6
and that **f** made him right with .... Ge 15:6
things God tested Abraham's **f**. .... Ge 22:1
because he had **f** and obeyed the .... Jos 14:14
and strengthened his **f** in God. 1Sa 23:16
them and have complete **f** in me, ... 1Ki 2:4
Have **f** in the LORD your God, ... 2Ch 20:20
Have **f** in his prophets, and you 2Ch 20:20
I had almost lost my **f** .... Ps 73:2
your **f** is not strong, you will .... Is 7:9
right with God will live by **f**. .... Hab 2:4
Don't have so little **f**! .... Mt 6:30
is the greatest **f** I have found, ... Mt 8:10
You don't have enough **f**." .... Mt 8:26
Jesus saw the **f** of these people, ... Mt 9:2
who keep their **f** until the end................ Mt 10:22

stumble in their f because of me.............. Mt 11:6
there because they had no f. .... Mt 13:58
Jesus said, "Your f is small. .... Mt 14:31
Woman, you have great f! .... Mt 15:28
having bread? Your f is small. .... Mt 16:8
people have no f, and your lives .... Mt 17:17
Because your f is too small. .... Mt 17:20
if your f is as big as a mustard .... Mt 17:20
if you have f and do not doubt, ... Mt 21:21
if you have f, it will happen. .... Mt 21:21
will lose their f, and they will .... Mt 24:10
who keep their f until the end .... Mt 24:13
stumble in your f on account of .... Mt 26:31
in their f because of you, ... Mt 26:33
Jesus saw the f of these people, ... Mk 2:5
Do you still have no f?" .... Mk 4:40
at how many people had no f................. Mk 6:6
answered, "You people have no f. .... Mk 9:19
Jesus answered, "Have f in God. .... Mk 11:22
who keep their f until the end .... Mk 13:13
You will all stumble in your f,................ Mk 14:27
else may stumble in their f,.................. Mk 14:29
them because they had no f. .... Mk 16:14
Seeing their f, Jesus said, ... Lk 5:20
is the greatest f I have found .... Lk 7:9
stumble in their f because of me.............. Lk 7:23
followers, "Where is your f?" .... Lk 8:25
people have no f, and your lives .... Lk 9:41
Don't have so little f! .... Lk 12:28
to the Lord, "Give us more f!" .... Lk 17:5
If your f were the size of a .... Lk 17:6
to have f you will save your .... Lk 21:19
that you will not lose your f! .... Lk 22:32
It was f in Jesus that made this .... Ac 3:16
a man with great f and full of .... Ac 6:5
and helping them stay in the f. .... Ac 14:22
stronger in the f and grew .... Ac 16:5
world are talking about your f. .... Rm 1:8
each other with the f we have. .... Rm 1:12
f will help me, and my faith .... Rm 1:12
help me, and my f will help you. .... Rm 1:12
that it begins and ends with f. .... Rm 1:17
right with God will live by f." .... Rm 1:17
through their f in Jesus Christ. .... Rm 3:22
through f in the blood .... Rm 3:25
any person who has f in Jesus. .... Rm 3:26
is the way of f that stops all .... Rm 3:27
made right with God through f, ... Rm 3:28
Jews right with him by their f, ... Rm 3:30
right with him through their f. .... Rm 3:30
law by following the way of f? .... Rm 3:31
F causes us to be what the law .... Rm 3:31
of our people, learned about f? .... Rm 4:1
and God accepted Abraham's f, ... Rm 4:3
that f made him right with God. .... Rm 4:3
accepts their f, and that makes .... Rm 4:5
Abraham's f and that faith .... Rm 4:9
faith and that f made him right .... Rm 4:9
with God through f before he was .... Rm 4:11
following the f that our father................ Rm 4:12
being right with God by his f................. Rm 4:13
the law, then f is worthless. .... Rm 4:14
God's promise by having f. .... Rm 4:16
who lives with f like that of .... Rm 4:16
f in God did not become weak. .... Rm 4:19
stronger in his f and gave .... Rm 4:20
God accepted Abraham's f,.................. Rm 4:22
that f made him right with God. .... Rm 4:22
"God accepted Abraham's f" .... Rm 4:23
made right with God by our f, ... Rm 5:1
who through our f has brought us .... Rm 5:2
with God because of their f. .... Rm 9:30
being made right through f: .... Rm 10:6

is the teaching of f that we are .... Rm 10:8
So f comes from hearing the Good........... Rm 10:17
amount of f God has given you. .... Rm 12:3
gift in agreement with the f. .... Rm 12:6
group someone who is weak in f, ... Rm 14:1
or sister's f because of .... Rm 14:15
someone's f by eating food he .... Rm 14:15
who are strong in f should help .... Rm 15:1
to help them be stronger in f, ... Rm 15:2
and who upset other people's f. .... Rm 16:17
you strong in f by the Good News .... Rm 16:25
was so that your f would be in 1Co 2:5
are weak in f to fall into sin. 1Co 8:9
who is weak in f might see you 1Co 8:10
Spirit gives f to one person. 1Co 12:9
and I may have f so great I can 1Co 13:2
forever: f, hope, and love. 1Co 13:13
and your f is worth nothing. 1Co 15:14
then your f has nothing to it; 1Co 15:17
Continue strong in the f. 1Co 16:13
not trying to control your f. 2Co 1:24
You are strong in f. But we are 2Co 1:24
Our f is like this, too. 2Co 4:13
making many people rich in f. 2Co 6:10
have not ruined the f of anyone,............. 2Co 7:2
in everything—in f, in speaking,............. 2Co 8:7
because he has much f in you. 2Co 8:22
It is a proof of your f. 2Co 9:13
that as your f continues to grow 2Co 10:15
see if you are living in the f. 2Co 13:5
the same f that he once tried .... Gal 1:23
have put our f in Christ Jesus, ... Gal 2:16
I live by f in the Son of God .... Gal 2:20
and God accepted Abraham's f, ... Gal 3:6
that f made him right with God. .... Gal 3:6
of Abraham are those who have f. .... Gal 3:7
people right through their f. .... Gal 3:8
right with God will live by f." .... Gal 3:11
The law is not based on f. .... Gal 3:12
be given through f to people who .... Gal 3:22
Before this f came, we were all .... Gal 3:23
us the way of f that was coming. .... Gal 3:23
made right with God through f. .... Gal 3:24
Now the way of f has come, ... Gal 3:25
thing is f—the kind of faith................. Gal 5:6
the kind of f that works through .... Gal 5:6
heard about your f in the Lord .... Eph 1:15
can do this through f in Christ. .... Eph 3:12
your hearts by f and that your .... Eph 3:17
one Lord, one f, and one baptism .... Eph 4:5
in the same f and in the same................ Eph 4:13
the shield of f with which you .... Eph 6:16
and love with f to you brothers .... Eph 6:23
you grow and have joy in your f. .... Php 1:25
one for the f of the Good News, ... Php 1:27
f makes you offer your lives .... Php 2:17
God uses my f to make me right.............. Php 3:9
heard about the f you have in .... Col 1:4
You have this f and love because .... Col 1:5
strong and sure in your f. .... Col 1:23
and your strong f in Christ. .... Col 2:5
Be strong in the f, just as you .... Col 2:7
through your f in God's power .... Col 2:12
because of your f and the work 1Th 1:3
but now your f in God has become........... 1Th 1:3
and encourage you in your f 1Th 3:2
so I could learn about your f. 1Th 3:5
good news about your f and love. 1Th 3:6
about you because of your f. 1Th 3:7
you need to make your f strong.............. 1Th 3:10
We should wear f and love to 1Th 5:8
because your f is growing more 2Th 1:3
strong and have f even though 2Th 1:4

F

the works that come from your **f**. 2Th 1:11
holy and by your **f** in the truth. 2Th 2:13
God's work, which is done in **f**. 1Ti 1:4
a good conscience and a true **f**. 1Ti 1:5
grace came the **f** and love that 1Ti 1:14
to have **f** and do what you 1Ti 1:19
their **f** has been shipwrecked.................1Ti 1:19
children if she continues in **f**, ...1Ti 2:15
secret of the **f** that God made 1Ti 3:9
bold in their **f** in Christ Jesus.................1Ti 3:13
will stop believing the **f**. 1Ti 4:1
the words of the **f** and the good 1Ti 4:6
your love, your **f**, and your pure 1Ti 4:12
against the **f** and is worse than 1Ti 5:8
Some people have left the **f**, ...1Ti 6:10
God, have **f**, love, patience 1Ti 6:11
Fight the good fight of **f**, ...1Ti 6:12
some have missed the true **f**. 1Ti 6:21
I remember your true **f**. 2Ti 1:5
That **f** first lived in your 2Ti 1:5
I know you now have that same **f**. 2Ti 1:5
you heard from me in **f** and love, ...2Ti 1:13
destroying the **f** of some people................2Ti 2:18
to live right and to have **f**, ...2Ti 2:22
in trying to follow the **f**. 2Ti 3:8
live, my goal, **f**, patience, and 2Ti 3:10
through **f** in Christ Jesus. 2Ti 3:15
the race, I have kept the **f**. 2Ti 4:7
to help the **f** of God's chosen ....Tit 1:1
That **f** and that knowledge come ....Tit 1:2
my true child in the **f** we share: ....Tit 1:4
they may become strong in the **f**, ...Tit 1:13
wise, strong in **f**, in love, ...Tit 2:2
those who love us in the **f**. ....Tit 3:15
holy people and the **f** you have ....Phm 1:5
I pray that the **f** you share may ....Phm 1:6
and is the high priest of our **f**. ....Heb 3:1
till the end the sure **f** we had ....Heb 3:14
it but did not accept it with **f**. ....Heb 4:2
let us hold on to the **f** we have. ....Heb 4:14
teaching about **f** in God and ....Heb 6:1
who through **f** and patience will ....Heb 6:12
a sincere heart and a sure **f**, ...Heb 10:22
right with me will live by **f**.....................Heb 10:38
people who have **f** and are saved. ....Heb 10:39
F means being sure of the things ....Heb 11:1
F is the reason we remember ....Heb 11:2
is by **f** we understand that the ....Heb 11:3
was by **f** that Abel offered God ....Heb 11:4
a good man because of his **f**. ....Heb 11:4
but through his **f** he is still ....Heb 11:4
It was by **f** that Enoch was taken ....Heb 11:5
Without **f** no one can please God. ....Heb 11:6
was by **f** that Noah heard God's ....Heb 11:7
By his **f**, Noah showed that the ....Heb 11:7
made right with God through **f**. ....Heb 11:7
It was by **f** Abraham obeyed God's...........Heb 11:8
It was by **f** that he lived like a ....Heb 11:9
was by **f** that Abraham was made ....Heb 11:11
these great people died in **f**. ....Heb 11:13
It was by **f** that Abraham, when ....Heb 11:17
It was by **f** that Isaac blessed ....Heb 11:20
was by **f** that Jacob, as he was ....Heb 11:21
was by **f** that Joseph, while he ....Heb 11:22
It was by **f** that Moses' parents ....Heb 11:23
It was by **f** that Moses, when he ....Heb 11:24
was by **f** that Moses left Egypt ....Heb 11:27
It was by **f** that Moses prepared ....Heb 11:28
It was by **f** that the people ....Heb 11:29
It was by **f** that the walls of.................Heb 11:30
It was by **f** that Rahab, the ....Heb 11:31
Through their **f** they defeated ....Heb 11:33
people are known for their **f**, ...Heb 11:39

lives tell us what **f** means. ....Heb 12:1
who began our **f** and who makes it ....Heb 12:2
and died, and copy their **f**. ....Heb 13:7
that these troubles test your **f**, ...Jam 1:3
After they have proved their **f**, ...Jam 1:12
to be rich with **f** and to receive ....Jam 2:5
if people say they have **f**, ...Jam 2:14
nothing, their **f** is worth ....Jam 2:14
Can **f** like that save them? ....Jam 2:14
the same way, **f** by itself—that ....Jam 2:17
say, "You have **f**, but I have...................Jam 2:18
Show me your **f** without doing ....Jam 2:18
will show you my **f** by what I do. ....Jam 2:18
be shown that **f** that does ....Jam 2:20
that Abraham's **f** and the things ....Jam 2:22
His **f** was made perfect by what ....Jam 2:22
and God accepted Abraham's **f**, ...Jam 2:23
that **f** made him right with God. ....Jam 2:23
by what they do, not by **f** only. ....Jam 2:24
so **f** that does nothing is dead! ....Jam 2:26
that is said with **f** will make ....Jam 5:15
through your **f** until salvation 1Pe 1:5
to prove that your **f** is pure. 1Pe 1:7
This purity of **f** is worth more................1Pe 1:7
purity of your **f** will bring you 1Pe 1:7
receiving the goal of your **f**— 1Pe 1:9
So your **f** and your hope are in 1Pe 1:21
by standing strong in your **f**. 1Pe 5:9
have received a **f** as valuable as 2Pe 1:1
to your **f**, add goodness; 2Pe 1:5
and weak in **f** explain these 2Pe 3:16
not fall from your strong **f**. 2Pe 3:17
anyone to stumble in his **f**. 1Jn 2:10
that conquers the world—our **f**. 1Jn 5:4
hard for the **f** that was given ....Jud 1:3
use your most holy **f** to build ....Jud 1:20
tell about your **f** in me even ....Rev 2:13
your love, your **f**, your service, ...Rev 2:19
about not giving up your **f**. ....Rev 3:10
strong in your **f** so no one will ....Rev 3:11
people must have patience and **f**. ....Rev 13:10
and keep their **f** in Jesus. ....Rev 14:12
because of their **f** in Jesus. ....Rev 17:6

FAITHFUL

LORD your God is God, the **f** God............Dt 7:9
He is a **f** God who does no wrong, ...Dt 32:4
They were not **f** to God but.....................Jdg 2:17
Abijam was not **f** to the LORD his 1Ki 15:3
was **f** to the LORD all his life. 1Ki 15:14
because they were not **f** to God. 1Ch 9:1
because he was not **f** to the LORD 1Ch 10:13
Even so, Asa was **f** all his life. 2Ch 15:17
had promised to be **f** to Tobiah, ...Ne 6:18
You found him **f** to you, so you ....Ne 9:8
Be **f** to your own wife, just as ....Pr 5:15
this **f** king will be from the ....Is 16:5
ask for them from the **f** God. ....Is 65:16
in the name of the **f** God, ...Is 65:16
'I remember how **f** you were to me...........Je 2:2
new rulers who will be **f** to me, ...Je 3:15
I want **f** love more than I want ....Hos 6:6
against God, the **f** Holy One. ....Hos 11:12
by others who are not **f** to me." ....Mic 1:7
All of the **f** people are gone; ....Mic 7:2
If some Jews were not **f** to him, ...Rm 3:3
Jesus Christ our Lord, is **f**. 1Co 1:9
I love Timothy, and he is **f**. 1Co 4:17
whom we love and a **f** servant of ....Eph 6:21
I ask you, my **f** friend, to help...............Php 4:3
To the holy and **f** brothers and ....Col 1:2
with us and is a **f** servant of ....Col 1:7
in Christ and a **f** minister and.................Col 4:7

a f and dear brother in Christ, ... Col 4:9
But the Lord is f and will give 2Th 3:3
must have been f to her husband. 1Ti 5:9
we are not f, he will still be..................... 2Ti 2:13
will still be f, because he must 2Ti 2:13
their merciful and f high priest .... Heb 2:17
Jesus was f to God as Moses was .... Heb 3:2
Moses was f in God's family as a .... Heb 3:5
But Christ is f as a Son over .... Heb 3:6
souls to the f Creator as they 1Pe 4:19
who I know is a f brother in 1Pe 5:12
is the f witness, the first .... Rev 1:5
But be f, even if you have to .... Rev 2:10
my f witness who was killed in .... Rev 2:13
The Amen, the f and true .... Rev 3:14
because they were f to the word .... Rev 6:9
chosen, and f followers.".......................... Rev 17:14
the horse is called F and True, ... Rev 19:11
they were f to the message .... Rev 20:4

FAITHFULLY
by my rules and obeys my laws f. .... Eze 18:9

FAITHFULNESS
who has great love and f........................ Ex 34:6
You have great love and f. .... Ps 86:15
Your f is like a morning mist, ... Hos 6:4
patience, kindness, goodness, f, ... Gal 5:22

FALCON
kites, any kind of f,............................. Le 11:14
the f has not seen it. .... Job 28:7

FALCONS
red kites, f, any kind of kite, ... Dt 14:13

FALL
and horror will f on them. .... Ex 15:16
of the city will f so the people.................. Jos 6:5
his head will f to the ground! 1Sa 14:45
they will f into their own evil .... Job 18:7
let my arm f off my shoulder .... Job 31:22
to the snow, 'F on the earth,' .... Job 37:6
will not f, because the LORD .... Ps 37:24
or the mountains f into the sea, ... Ps 46:2
Let burning coals f on them. .... Ps 140:10
Let the wicked f into their own .... Ps 141:10
who digs a pit might f into it; .... Ec 10:8
the captives or f down among the .... Is 10:4
They will f back and be .... Is 28:13
and young people trip and f. .... Is 40:30
Disaster will f on you, and you .... Is 47:11
When people f down, don't they .... Je 8:4
So they will f, along with .... Je 8:12
They stumble and f in the north, ... Je 46:6
the wall around the city will f. .... Je 51:44
and to the hills, "F on us!" .... Hos 10:8
A bird will not f into a trap .... Am 3:5
But it did not f, because it was .... Mt 7:25
both will f into a ditch." .... Mt 15:14
the crumbs that f from their .... Mt 15:27
The stars will f from the sky. .... Mt 24:29
to cause the f and rise of many .... Lk 2:34
I saw Satan f like lightning.................... Lk 10:18
say to the mountains, 'F on us!' .... Lk 23:30
his shadow might f on them. .... Ac 5:15
fell, did that f destroy them? .... Rm 11:11
you should be careful not to f. 1Co 10:12
thing to f into the hands .... Heb 10:31
grass dies and the flowers f, ... 1Pe 1:24
a rock that makes them f." 1Pe 2:8
these things, you will never f. 2Pe 1:10
so you will not f from your 2Pe 3:17
and can help you not to f. .... Jud 1:24
and the rocks, "F on us. .... Rev 6:16
I saw a star f from the sky to .... Rev 9:1

FALLEN
donkey has f because its load .... Ex 23:5
donkey or ox f on the road, ... Dt 22:4
that Dagon had f on his face 1Sa 5:3
found Dagon f on the ground 1Sa 5:4
of them have f and are dead. 2Sa 1:4
How the mighty have f in battle! 2Sa 1:19
How the mighty have f in battle! 2Sa 1:25
How the mighty have f! 2Sa 1:27
coat that had f from him. 2Ki 2:13
destroys my hope like a f tree. .... Job 19:10
The nations have f into the pit .... Ps 9:15
and the stone walls had f down. .... Pr 24:31
has stumbled, and Judah has f. .... Is 3:8
These bricks have f, but we will .... Is 9:10
The king has f, so no one will................. Is 14:8
star, you have f from heaven, ... Is 14:12
that have f from their nest .... Is 16:2
back the answer, "Babylon has f. .... Is 21:9
fallen. It has f! All the .... Is 21:9
crowns have f from your heads." .... Je 13:18
of them have f down together!" .... Je 46:12
her towers have f, and her walls............. Je 50:15
has suddenly f and been broken. .... Je 51:8
together they have f. .... La 2:8
gates have f to the ground; .... La 2:9
The crown has f from our head. .... La 5:16
the wall has f, people will ask .... Eze 13:12
tremble, now that you have f. .... Eze 26:18
of the sky live on the f tree. .... Eze 31:13
among the tree's f branches. .... Eze 31:13
You will lie f on the ground, ... Eze 39:5
The young girl Israel has f,..................... Am 5:2
of David is like a f tent, ... Am 9:11
I have f, but I will get up........................ Mic 7:8
cedar has f, because the tall .... Zch 11:2
Our friend Lazarus has f asleep,............ Jn 11:11
of David is like a f tent. .... Ac 15:16
has sinned and f short of God's .... Rm 3:23

FALLS
or donkey comes and f into it, ... Ex 21:33
animal dies and f on something............. Le 11:32
the animal f on must be washed............. Le 11:32
unclean animal f into a clay .... Le 11:33
unclean animal f on something, ... Le 11:35
unclean animal f on a seed to be .... Le 11:37
unclean animal f on them, they .... Le 11:38
If grain f onto the ground, ... Le 19:9
If grain f onto the ground, ... Le 23:22
if someone f off the roof......................... Dt 22:8
on him as dew f on the ground. 2Sa 17:12
When the land f into the hands .... Job 9:24
Without leadership a nation f, ... Pr 11:14
one f down, the other can help .... Ec 4:10
the person who is alone and f, ... Ec 4:10
evil when it suddenly f on them............. Ec 9:12
but it will stay where it f. .... Ec 11:3
of them becomes tired or f down. .... Is 5:27
them gets sleepy and f asleep. .... Is 5:27
cracks in it that f suddenly and .... Is 30:13
because no rain f on the land.................. Je 14:4
And when the wall f, you will be .... Eze 13:14
Nile River and f like the river................ Am 9:5
not even a tiny stone f through. .... Am 9:9
and it f into a ditch on the .... Mt 12:11
because he often f into the fire .... Mt 17:15
The person who f on this stone .... Mt 21:44
and on whomever that stone f, ... Mt 21:44
the teaching f on the road. .... Mk 4:15
your child or ox f into a well .... Lk 14:5
Everyone who f on that stone .... Lk 20:18

and the person on whom it **f**, ... Lk 20:18
The flower **f** off, and its beauty .... Jam 1:11

FALSE

prophets who prophesy **f** dreams," .... Je 23:32
and don't love **f** promises. .... Zch 8:17
Be careful of **f** prophets. .... Mt 7:15
Many **f** prophets will come and .... Mt 24:11
F Christs and false prophets .... Mt 24:24
in danger with **f** Christians. 2Co 11:26
you away with **f** and empty.................... Col 2:8
used to be **f** prophets among 2Pe 2:1
have some **f** teachers in your 2Pe 2:1
the beast and the **f** prophet. .... Rev 20:10

FALSELY

each other **f** and tell lies........................ Is 59:4
Will you **f** accuse other people? .... Je 7:9
lies, who speak **f**, and who do................. 1Ti 1:10
of what is **f** called "knowledge."............... 1Ti 6:20
in faith explain these things **f**. 2Pe 3:16
They also **f** explain the other 2Pe 3:16

FAME

give you praise, **f**, and honor, ... Dt 26:19
we heard of the **f** of the LORD .... Jos 9:9
Sheba heard about Solomon's **f**,............ 2Ch 9:1
his **f** is great in Israel. .... Ps 76:1
and your **f** goes on and on. .... Ps 102:12
So **f** and power are useless, ... Ec 4:16
won for yourself wonderful **f**. .... Is 63:14
would be my people and bring **f**, ... Je 13:11

FAMILIES

bird went out of the boat by **f**. .... Ge 8:19
the list of the **f** from the sons .... Ge 10:32
listed by their **f** and family .... Nu 1:18
the Levites by **f** and family .... Nu 3:15
the leaders of the **f** of Israel. .... Nu 36:1
all the **f** of Zerah presented .... Jos 7:17
the heads of the **f** of all the .... Jos 21:1
of the Levite **f** said to them, ... Jos 21:2
included the **f** who lived at 1Ch 2:55
in their **f** were Michael, ... 1Ch 5:13
I feared being hated by other **f**. .... Job 31:34
destroy their **f** from the earth;................. Ps 21:10
made their **f** grow like flocks .... Ps 107:41
I will help the **f** of Israel and .... Je 31:27
away from the two **f** of Israel .... Je 33:24
them to be from important **f**, ... Da 1:3
of you came from important **f**. 1Co 1:26
their children and their own **f**. 1Ti 3:12
upsetting whole **f** by teaching................. Tit 1:11

FAMILY

and your father's **f**, and go to .... Ge 12:1
my father's people and to my **f**. .... Ge 24:38
a member of the foreigner's **f**, ... Le 25:47
out by families and **f** groups. .... Nu 2:34
These were the **f** groups from .... Nu 26:40
These also were Levite **f** groups: .... Nu 26:58
belonged to the **f** groups of .... Nu 27:1
nearest relative in his **f** group. .... Nu 27:11
then that land will leave our **f**, ... Nu 36:3
their father's **f** group and tribe .... Nu 36:12
someone outside her husband's **f**. .... Dt 25:5
and his whole **f** went down to get .... Jdg 16:31
their own tribes and **f** groups,................. Jdg 21:24
named Boaz, from Elimelech's **f**. .... Ru 2:1
to Boaz, from Elimelech's **f**. .... Ru 2:3
And my **f** group is the smallest 1Sa 9:21
had them pass by in **f** groups,................. 1Sa 10:21
of Elisha from the king's **f**, ... 2Ki 25:25
anyone about her **f** or who her .... Est 2:10
city and two from every **f** group,.............. Je 3:14
of this evil **f** who are not dead .... Je 8:3

the whole **f** he brought out .... Am 3:1
land will cry, each **f** by itself: .... Zch 12:12
from the high priest's **f**. .... Ac 4:6
king learned about Joseph's **f**. .... Ac 7:13
sons of the **f** of Abraham, ... Ac 13:26
He and his **f** were very happy.................. Ac 16:34

FAMOUS

who became **f** and were the mighty .... Ge 6:4
We will become **f**. Then we will .... Ge 11:4
I will make you **f**, and you will .... Ge 12:2
and Joshua became **f** through all .... Jos 6:27
of Ephrathah and **f** in Bethlehem. .... Ru 4:11
May he become **f** in Israel. .... Ru 4:14
So this became a **f** saying: 1Sa 10:12
Saul's officers. So he became **f**. 1Sa 18:30
I will make you as **f** as any of................. 2Sa 7:9
David was **f** after he returned................. 2Sa 8:13
He became as **f** as the Three 2Sa 23:18
He was as **f** as the Three. 2Sa 23:22
Solomon even more **f** than you and 1Ki 1:47
King Solomon became **f** in all the 1Ki 4:31
brave, and **f** men, and leaders................. 1Ch 5:24
He became as **f** as the Three 1Ch 11:20
He was as **f** as the Three. 1Ch 11:24
and were **f** men in their own 1Ch 12:30
So David became **f** in all the 1Ch 14:17
I will make you as **f** as any of 1Ch 17:8
which will be **f** everywhere for 1Ch 22:5
his name became **f** all the way to 2Ch 26:8
So Uzziah became **f** in faraway 2Ch 26:15
became as **f** as you are today.................. Ne 9:10
He was **f** in all the empire, ... Est 9:4
I will make your name **f** from now .... Ps 45:17
Let the king be **f** forever; .... Ps 72:17
I became very **f**, even greater .... Ec 2:9
people who are **f** for drinking................. Is 5:22
them to make his name **f** forever, ... Is 63:12
people not left that **f** city yet? .... Je 49:25
Then you became **f** among the .... Eze 16:14
because you were so **f**. .... Eze 16:15
'Tyre, you **f** city, you have been .... Eze 26:17
give them a place **f** for its good .... Eze 34:29
they will be as **f** as the wine .... Hos 14:7

FANCY

their hair fixed in **f** ways, ... Is 3:24
did not eat any **f** food or meat, ... Da 10:3
You have built **f** houses of cut................. Am 5:11
to be living in **f** houses while .... Hag 1:4
walk around wearing **f** clothes, ... Mk 12:38
walk around wearing **f** clothes, ... Lk 20:46
They use **f** talk and fine words .... Rm 16:18
secret with **f** words or a show................. 1Co 2:1
It is not **f** hair, gold jewelry, ... 1Pe 3:3
All your rich and **f** things have .... Rev 18:14

FANGS

the snake's **f** will kill them...................... Job 20:16
I broke the **f** of evil people and .... Job 29:17
Tear out the **f** of those lions, ... Ps 58:6
a snake with poison in its **f**. .... Pr 23:32

FANNED

A fire not **f** by people will .... Job 20:26
The fire is **f** to make it hotter,.................. Je 6:29

FANS

He **f** the fire to make it hotter, ... Is 54:16

FARAWAY

well as foreigners from **f** lands, ... Dt 29:22
have traveled from a **f** country. .... Jos 9:6
who lived in the **f** mountains of .... Jdg 5:1
They came from a **f** country— 2Ki 20:14
became famous in **f** places,..................... 2Ch 26:15
and the **f** lands bring him .... Ps 72:10

f lands should be glad. .... Ps 97:1
Good news from a f place is like .... Pr 25:25
flies from Egypt's f streams. .... Is 7:18
Listen, all you f countries. .... Is 8:9
army is coming from a f land,.................. Is 13:5
and grapevines from f places.................. Is 17:10
You people in f lands, hear what .... Is 33:13
They came from a f country— .... Is 39:3
The LORD says, "F countries,.................. Is 41:1
All you f places, look and be .... Is 41:5
and called you from a f country............... Is 41:9
you people living in f places. .... Is 42:10
People in f lands should praise .... Is 42:12
and my daughters from f places. .... Is 43:6
All of you people in f places, ... Is 49:1
All the f places are waiting for .... Is 51:5
sent your messengers to f lands;.............. Is 57:9
the people in f places as they .... Is 59:18
People in f lands are waiting .... Is 60:9
your children from f lands,.................. Is 60:9
is speaking to all the f lands: .... Is 62:11
Greece, and all the f lands. .... Is 66:19
are coming from a f country .... Je 4:16
cane from a f land?............................ Je 6:20
They cry from a f land: .... Je 8:19
from the f places on earth. .... Je 25:32
you from that f place where you............... Je 30:10
them from the f places on earth.............. Je 31:8
message in the f lands by the .... Je 31:10
you from those f places and your .... Je 46:27
the LORD in the f land and think .... Je 51:50
sent my people to that f place, ... Joe 3:7
Then everyone in f places will .... Zph 2:11
but in those f places, they will .... Zch 10:9

FAREWELL
So you must give f gifts to .... Mic 1:14

FARM
They also took their f animals .... Ge 46:6
and take care of f animals, ... Ge 46:32
taken care of f animals all our .... Ge 46:34
give me your f animals, and I .... Ge 47:16
brought their f animals to .... Ge 47:17
food for their f animals that .... Ge 47:17
disease on your f animals that .... Ex 9:3
All the f animals in Egypt died, ... Ex 9:6
firstborn f animals will die..................... Ex 11:5
the firstborn f animals died. .... Ex 12:29
and our f animals with thirst?" .... Ex 17:3
If a man lets his f animal graze .... Ex 22:5
or an unclean f animal or an .... Le 5:2
your servants will f the land 2Sa 9:10
in their own land and f it."'" .... Je 27:11
become rich with f animals and .... Eze 38:12
and to take away f animals and .... Eze 38:13
of Israel will f this land. .... Eze 48:19
the people, the f animals, and.............. Hag 1:11
are like God's f, God's house. 1Co 3:9

FARMED
field workers who f the land. 1Ch 27:26

FARMER
of flocks, and Cain became a f. .... Ge 4:2
Noah became a f and planted a .... Ge 9:20
A f does not plow his field all .... Is 28:24
A f doesn't use heavy boards to .... Is 28:27
The f separates the wheat from .... Is 28:28
seeds for the f and bread for .... Is 55:10
will lie like grain a f has cut, ... Je 9:22
I am a f and have been a farmer............. Zch 13:5
been a f since I was young.' .... Zch 13:5
A f went out to plant his seed. .... Mt 13:3
of that story about the f. .... Mt 13:18

A f went out to plant his seed. .... Mk 4:3
f is like a person who plants .... Mk 4:14
is ready, the f cuts it, because.................. Mk 4:29
A f went out to plant his seed. .... Lk 8:5
of you as a f sifts his wheat. .... Lk 22:31
gives seed to the f and bread 2Co 9:10
The f who works hard should be 2Ti 2:6
A f patiently waits for his .... Jam 5:7

FARMERS
Like f plowing, they plowed over .... Ps 129:3
Lazy f don't plow when they .... Pr 20:4
The f are upset and sad, so they .... Je 14:4
The f will plant them and enjoy .... Je 31:5
F and those who move around with .... Je 31:24
I use you to smash f and oxen. .... Je 51:23
Be sad, f. Cry loudly, you who .... Joe 1:11
will call the f to come and weep .... Am 5:16
the land to some f and left for .... Mt 21:33
servants to the f to get his .... Mt 21:34
But the f grabbed the servants, ... Mt 21:35
some other servants to the f, ... Mt 21:36
But the f did the same thing to .... Mt 21:36
to send his son to the f. .... Mt 21:37
But when the f saw the son, ... Mt 21:38
Then the f grabbed the son, ... Mt 21:39
do to these f when he comes?" .... Mt 21:40
some other f who will give him .... Mt 21:41
the land to some f and left for .... Mk 12:1
servant to the f to get his .... Mk 12:2
the f grabbed the servant and.............. Mk 12:3
the f beat some of them and .... Mk 12:5
But the f said to each other, ... Mk 12:7
and kill those f and will give .... Mk 12:9
give the vineyard to other f. .... Mk 12:9
and leased it to some f. .... Lk 20:9
a servant to the f to get some .... Lk 20:10
f wounded him and threw him out. .... Lk 20:12
But when the f saw the son, ... Lk 20:14
the f threw the son out of the .... Lk 20:15
and kill those f and will give .... Lk 20:16
give the vineyard to other f." .... Lk 20:16

FARMLAND
Lebanon will become rich f, ... Is 29:17
and the rich will seem like a.................. Is 29:17

FARMLANDS
lived on the f near the towns or 2Ch 31:19
away the great trees and rich f, ... Is 10:18

FARMS
had gone back to their own f. .... Ne 13:10
or f to follow me will get much .... Mt 19:29
or f for me and for the Good .... Mk 10:29

FARTHEST
have gone to its f places and to 2Ki 19:23
he looks to the f parts of the .... Job 28:24
sends it to the f parts of the .... Job 37:3

FAST
run there f, because I cannot .... Ge 19:22
Now Asahel was a f runner, ... 2Sa 2:18
as f as a deer in the field. 2Sa 2:18
baby is dead, why should I f? 2Sa 12:23
which the people are to f. 1Ki 21:9
on which the people were to f. 1Ki 21:12
as lions and as f as gazelles 1Ch 12:8
in Judah should f during this 2Ch 20:3
hard and are building very f. .... Ezr 5:8
would all f and deny ourselves .... Ezr 8:21
For my sake, f; do not eat or .... Est 4:16
my servant girls will also f..................... Est 4:16
by messengers on f horses, ... Est 8:10
people should f and cry loudly. .... Est 9:31
it is so f that it laughs at the .... Job 39:18

When I cry and **f**, they make fun .... Ps 69:10
is coming on a **f** cloud to enter .... Is 19:1
"We will ride away on **f** horses." .... Is 30:16
those who chase you will be **f**. .... Is 30:16
these special days when you **f**, ... Is 58:4
on your special days when you **f**, ... Is 58:5
tell you the kind of **f** I want: .... Is 58:6
if they **f**, I will not listen .... Je 14:12
was king, a **f** was announced................. Je 36:9
The **f** runners cannot run away; .... Je 46:6
River, like strong, **f** rivers? .... Je 46:7
River, like strong, **f** rivers. .... Je 46:8
whole earth so **f** that his feet .... Da 8:5
all your heart. **F**, cry, and be .... Joe 2:12
and even **f** runners will not get .... Am 2:15
lie down, and he fell **f** asleep. .... Jnh 1:5
that they would **f** for a while, ... Jnh 3:5
it is near and coming **f**. .... Zph 1:14
days when you **f** in the fourth, ... Zch 8:19
When you **f**, don't put on a sad .... Mt 6:16
when you **f**, comb your hair and........... Mt 6:17
Pharisees often **f** for a certain................ Mt 9:14
from them, and then they will **f**. .... Mt 9:15
seed grew very **f**, because the................. Mt 13:5
of the Pharisees often **f**, ... Mk 2:18
bridegroom do not **f** while the .... Mk 2:19
is with them, they cannot **f**. .... Mk 2:19
from them, and then they will **f**. .... Mk 2:20
seed grew very **f**, because the................. Mk 4:5
followers often **f** for a certain .... Lk 5:33
the bridegroom **f** while he is .... Lk 5:34
them, and then they will **f**." .... Lk 5:35
I **f** twice a week, and I give .... Lk 18:12

FAST-FLOWING
come quickly like a **f** river, ... Is 59:19

FASTED
to the LORD and **f** all day until .... Jdg 20:26
before the LORD and **f** that day............... 1Sa 7:6
of Jabesh **f** for seven days 1Sa 31:13
and cried and **f** until evening................. 2Sa 1:12
David **f** and went into his house 2Sa 12:16
alive, you **f** and you cried. 2Sa 12:21
still alive, I **f**, and I cried. 2Sa 12:22
rough cloth, **f**, and even slept 1Ki 21:27
of Jabesh **f** for seven days. 1Ch 10:12
So we **f** and prayed to our God .... Ezr 8:23
I was sad and **f**. I prayed to................... Ne 1:4
f, and they wore rough cloth .... Ne 9:1
They **f** and cried out loud, ... Est 4:3
we had special days when we **f**, ... Is 58:3
my sadness, I **f**, put on rough .... Da 9:3
we have shown our sadness and **f**. .... Zch 7:3
seventy years you **f** and cried .... Zch 7:5
Jesus **f** for forty days and .... Mt 4:2
Pharisees often **f** for a certain................ Mk 2:18
So after they **f** and prayed, ... Ac 13:3

FASTEN
and nails they **f** them down so .... Je 10:4

FASTENED
curtains were **f** together to make .... Ex 36:10
other five were **f** together to .... Ex 36:10
and they **f** the other two ends of............. Ex 39:18
Then she **f** it with a pin. .... Jdg 16:14

FASTER
They were **f** than eagles......................... 2Sa 1:23
My days go by **f** than a weaver's .... Job 7:6
My days go by **f** than a runner; .... Job 9:25
them away alive **f** than burning .... Ps 58:9
His horses are **f** than eagles. .... Je 4:13
who chased us were **f** than eagles .... La 4:19

Their horses are **f** than leopards.............. Hab 1:8
other follower ran **f** than Peter .... Jn 20:4

FASTEST
The **f** runner does not always win .... Ec 9:11
escape, not even the **f** runner................... Am 2:14
harness the **f** horse to the .... Mic 1:13

FASTING
and showed my sorrow by **f**. .... Ps 35:13
weak from **f**, and I have grown .... Ps 109:24
on a day when the people are **f**. .... Je 36:6
sad to show people they are **f**. .... Mt 6:16
will not know that you are **f**, ... Mt 6:18
only if you use prayer and **f**. .... Mt 17:21
the Lord and **f** for a certain .... Ac 13:2
by praying and **f** for a certain................. Ac 14:23

FASTS
Call for a day when everyone **f**! .... Joe 1:14
call for a day when everyone **f**. .... Joe 2:15

FAT
saw seven **f** and beautiful cows .... Ge 41:2
Then take the **f** from the male .... Ex 29:22
male sheep, the **f** tail, and the .... Ex 29:22
All the **f** belongs to the LORD. .... Le 3:16
he will burn the **f** of the sin .... Le 16:25
as much as they want and get **f**.............. Dt 31:20
Now Eglon was a very **f** man.................. Jdg 3:17
The king's **f** covered the whole .... Jdg 3:22
Even before the **f** was burned, ... 1Sa 2:15
than to offer the **f** of sheep..................... 1Sa 15:22
until they were full and grew **f**; .... Ne 9:25
you offerings of **f** animals, ... Ps 66:15
sheep that are **f** and strong. .... Eze 34:16
judge between the **f** sheep and .... Eze 34:20
you kill the **f** calf for him!' .... Lk 15:30
yourselves **f**, like an animal .... Jam 5:5

FATE
religious feasts for the god **F**, ... Is 65:11
I decide your **f**, and I will .... Is 65:12

FATHER
will leave his **f** and mother and .... Ge 2:24
Ham was the **f** of Canaan. .... Ge 9:18
While his **f**, Terah, was still.................... Ge 11:28
making you a **f** of many nations. .... Ge 17:5
Let's get our **f** drunk and have .... Ge 19:32
the two girls got their **f** drunk, ... Ge 19:33
became pregnant by their **f**. .... Ge 19:36
She is the daughter of my **f**, ... Ge 20:12
Isaac said to his **f** Abraham, ... Ge 22:7
oath I made to Abraham your **f**. .... Ge 26:3
I am the God of your **f** Abraham. .... Ge 26:24
If my **f** touches me, he will know .... Ge 27:12
food and brought it to his **f**. .... Ge 27:31
He said, "**F**, rise and eat the .... Ge 27:31
Esau heard the words of his **f**, ... Ge 27:34
you have only one blessing, **F**? .... Ge 27:38
Esau saw that his **f** Isaac did .... Ge 28:8
seen that your **f** is not as..................... Ge 31:5
God whom his **f** Isaac worshiped. .... Ge 31:53
said, "God of my **f** Abraham! .... Ge 32:9
went to his **f** Isaac at Mamre .... Ge 35:27
Joseph gave his **f** bad reports .... Ge 37:2
saw that their **f** loved him more .... Ge 37:4
told his **f** about this dream, ... Ge 37:10
but his **f** thought about what all .... Ge 37:11
sons of the same **f**, and we live .... Ge 42:13
to their **f** Jacob in the land .... Ge 42:29
Then Reuben said to his **f**, ... Ge 42:37
Then Judah said to his **f** Jacob, ... Ge 43:8
How is your aged **f** you told me .... Ge 43:27
young boy cannot leave his **f**, ... Ge 44:22
he leaves him, his **f** would die.' .... Ge 44:22

went back to our **f** and told him .... Ge 44:24
when our **f** sees the young boy is .... Ge 44:31
Is my **f** still alive?" .... Ge 45:3
So leave quickly and go to my **f**............... Ge 45:9
to the God of his **f** Isaac......................... Ge 46:1
king and gave his **f** and brothers .... Ge 47:11
said to his **f**, "You are doing it .... Ge 48:18
But his **f** refused and said, ... Ge 48:19
hugged his **f** and cried over .... Ge 50:1
everyone who lived with his **f**. .... Ge 50:8
loudly and bitterly for his **f**. .... Ge 50:10
they went back to their **f** Reuel, ... Ex 2:18
Honor your **f** and your mother so .... Ex 20:12
who hits his **f** or mother .... Ex 21:15
things to his **f** or mother must .... Ex 21:17
shame your **f** by having sexual .... Le 18:7
a prostitute, she shames her **f**. .... Le 21:9
an Egyptian **f** who was walking .... Le 24:10
Our **f** died in the desert. .... Nu 27:3
And if his **f** had no brothers, ... Nu 27:11
Honor your **f** and your mother as .... Dt 5:16
My **f** was a wandering Aramean. .... Dt 26:5
He is your **F** and Maker, who made .... Dt 32:6
Allow my **f**, mother, brothers,.................. Jos 2:13
him to ask her **f** for a field.................... Jos 15:18
the **f** of Abraham and Nahor, ... Jos 24:2
him to ask her **f** for a field..................... Jdg 1:14
belongs to your **f** and a second .... Jdg 6:25
months she returned to her **f**, ... Jdg 11:39
His **f** and mother answered, ... Jdg 14:3
with us and be our **f** and priest. .... Jdg 18:19
Obed was the **f** of Jesse, and .... Ru 4:17
Now the donkeys of Saul's **f**, ... 1Sa 9:3
My **f** Saul is looking for a 1Sa 19:2
be empty, so my **f** will miss you. 1Sa 20:18
I will be his **f**, and he will be 2Sa 7:14
after David, his **f**, and he was 1Ki 2:12
commands his **f** David had given 1Ki 3:3
to your servant, my **f** David. 1Ki 3:6
as your **f** David did, I will 1Ki 3:14
to your servant David, my **f**. 1Ki 8:25
the city of David, his **f**. 1Ki 11:27
My **f** beat you with whips, but I 1Ki 12:11
same sins his **f** before him had 1Ki 15:3
the same way as his **f** Jeroboam. 1Ki 15:26
the cities my **f** took from your 1Ki 20:34
saw it and shouted, "My **f**! 2Ki 2:12
was not like his **f** and mother; 2Ki 3:2
Jehoash said, "My **f**, my father! 2Ki 13:14
Jehoash said, "My father, my **f**! 2Ki 13:14
everything his **f** Joash had done, ... 2Ki 14:3
in the same way his **f** had lived: 2Ki 21:21
be my son, and I will be his **f**................ 1Ch 22:10
be my son, and I will be his **f**.................. 1Ch 28:6
you, LORD, God of our **f** Israel. 1Ch 29:10
I made with your **f** David, ... 2Ch 7:18
who had no **f** or mother, so................... Est 2:7
You are my **f**,' and to the worm .... Job 17:14
I was like a **f** to needy people, ... Job 29:16
Does the rain have a **f**? .... Job 38:28
Who is **f** to the drops of dew?................. Job 38:28
And their **f** Job gave them land .... Job 42:15
He is a **f** to orphans, and he .... Ps 68:5
me, 'You are my **f**, my God, the .... Ps 89:26
a **f** has mercy on his children............. Ps 103:13
f taught me and said, "Hold on .... Pr 4:4
children make their **f** happy, ... Pr 10:1
make their **f** sad and cause their .... Pr 17:25
who curse their **f** or mother will............. Pr 20:20
Whoever robs **f** or mother and .... Pr 28:24
make fun of your **f** and refuse to .... Pr 30:17
to say 'my **f**' or 'my mother.' .... Is 8:4
Powerful God, **F** Who Lives .... Is 9:6

will be like a **f** to the people .... Is 22:21
Your first **f** sinned, and your .... Is 43:27
the child who says to his **f**, ' .... Is 45:10
You are our **f**. Abraham doesn't .... Is 63:16
you are our **f**. You are called .... Is 63:16
But LORD, you are our **f**. .... Is 64:8
You are my **f**,' and to idols .... Je 2:27
to me, 'My **f**, you have been my .... Je 3:4
would call me 'My **F**' and not .... Je 3:19
man who brought my **f** the news: .... Je 20:15
f was satisfied to have food.................. Je 22:15
am Israel's **f**, and Israel is my................. Je 31:9
We are like orphans with no **f**; .... La 5:3
Your **f** was an Amorite, and your .... Eze 16:3
and your **f** was an Amorite. .... Eze 16:45
But the **f** himself has not done .... Eze 18:11
But his **f** took other people's .... Eze 18:18
days of your **f**, this man showed.............. Da 5:11
A son will not honor his **f**, ... Mic 7:6
son honors his **f**, and a servant .... Mal 1:6
I am a **f**, so why don't you .... Mal 1:6
We all have the same **f**; .... Mal 2:10
since his **f** Herod had died. .... Mt 2:22
yourselves, 'Abraham is our **f**.' .... Mt 3:9
in a boat with their **f** Zebedee, ... Mt 4:21
will praise your **F** in heaven. .... Mt 5:16
Your **F** can see what is done in .... Mt 6:4
and pray to your **F** who cannot be .... Mt 6:6
'Our **F** in heaven, may your name .... Mt 6:9
but your heavenly **F** feeds them. .... Mt 6:26
do what my **F** in heaven wants. .... Mt 7:21
first let me go and bury my **f**." .... Mt 8:21
a son will be against his **f**, ... Mt 10:35
who love their **f** or mother more........... Mt 10:37
I praise you, **F**, Lord of heaven .... Mt 11:25
Yes, **F**, this is what you really .... Mt 11:26
My **F** has given me all things................. Mt 11:27
sun in the kingdom of their **F**................... Mt 13:43
'Honor your **f** and your mother,' .... Mt 15:4
things to his **f** or mother must .... Mt 15:4
F in heaven showed you who I am. .... Mt 16:17
will leave his **f** and mother and .... Mt 19:5
sisters, **f**, mother, children .... Mt 19:29
call any person on earth 'F,' .... Mt 23:9
have one **f**, who is in heaven. .... Mt 23:9
even the Son. Only the **F** knows. .... Mt 24:36
my **F** has given you his blessing. .... Mt 25:34
in the name of the **F** and the Son .... Mt 28:19
even the Son. Only the **F** knows. .... Mk 13:32
prayed, "Abba, **F**! You can do all .... Mk 14:36
Your **f** and I were very worried .... Lk 2:48
yourselves, 'Abraham is our **f**.' .... Lk 3:8
first let me go and bury my **f**." .... Lk 9:59
The younger son said to his **f**, ' .... Lk 15:12
return to my **f** and say to him, ... Lk 15:18
and your **f** killed the fat calf, ... Lk 15:27
called, 'F Abraham, have mercy .... Lk 16:24
Honor your **f** and mother.'" .... Lk 18:20
Jesus said, "**F**, forgive them, ... Lk 23:34
a loud voice, "**F**, I give you my .... Lk 23:46
send you what my **F** has promised, ... Lk 24:49
to the only Son of the **F**— .... Jn 1:14
only Son is very close to the **F**, ... Jn 1:18
F loves the Son and has given .... Jn 3:35
than Jacob, our **f**, who gave us .... Jn 4:12
will worship the **F** in spirit and .... Jn 4:23
My **F** never stops working,................. Jn 5:17
he says that God is his own **F**,................. Jn 5:18
Life comes from the **F** himself, ... Jn 5:26
the things my **F** gave me to do, ... Jn 5:36
to do, prove that the **F** sent me. .... Jn 5:36
before the **F** and say you are .... Jn 5:45
The **F** is the One who sent me. .... Jn 6:44

They asked, "Where is your f?" ....Jn 8:19
You don't know me or my F. ....Jn 8:19
only what the F has taught me. ....Jn 8:28
you what my F has shown me, ...Jn 8:38
do what your f has told you." ....Jn 8:38
answered, "Our f is Abraham." ....Jn 8:39
the things your own f did." ....Jn 8:41
You belong to your f the devil, ...Jn 8:44
he is a liar and the f of lies. ....Jn 8:44
are greater than our f Abraham,..............Jn 8:53
Your f Abraham was very happy ....Jn 8:56
just as the F knows me, and I..................Jn 10:15
The F and I are one." ....Jn 10:30
But if I do what my F does,..................Jn 10:38
and said, "F, I thank you that ....Jn 11:41
Should I say, 'F, save me from................Jn 12:27
this world and go back to the F. ....Jn 13:1
knew that the F had given him ....Jn 13:3
only way to the F is through me. ....Jn 14:6
to him, "Lord, show us the F. ....Jn 14:8
has seen me has seen the F. ....Jn 14:9
because I am going to the F. ....Jn 14:12
I will ask the F, and he will....................Jn 14:16
you will know that I am in my F, ...Jn 14:20
that I am going back to the F,.................Jn 14:28
must know that I love the F, ...Jn 14:31
what the F told me to do. ....Jn 14:31
true vine; my F is the gardener. ....Jn 15:1
which brings glory to my F. ....Jn 15:8
the F will give you anything ....Jn 15:16
hates me also hates my F. ....Jn 15:23
send you the Helper from the F; ....Jn 15:26
my F will give you anything you ....Jn 16:23
will ask the F for things in my ....Jn 16:26
came from the F into the world. ....Jn 16:28
and prayed, "F, the time has ....Jn 17:1
Holy F, keep them safe by the..................Jn 17:11
F, I pray that they can be one..................Jn 17:21
F, you are the One who is good. ....Jn 17:25
I drink the cup the F gave me?" ....Jn 18:11
I have not yet gone up to the F. ....Jn 20:17
the F sent me, I now send you." ....Jn 20:21
from the F which I told you ....Ac 1:4
The F has given the Holy Spirit ....Ac 2:33
you from God our F and the Lord ....Rm 1:7
Abraham is the f of all those ....Rm 4:11
is also the f of those who have ....Rm 4:12
Abraham, who is the f of us all. ....Rm 4:16
by the wonderful power of the F, ...Rm 6:4
that Spirit we cry out, "F." ....Rm 8:15
glory to God the F of our Lord ....Rm 15:6
us there is only one God—our F..............1Co 8:6
to the God and F of our Lord 2Co 1:3
I will be your f, and you will 2Co 6:18
and God the F who raised Jesus..............Gal 1:1
the glorious F, to give you ....Eph 1:17
to come to the F in one Spirit. ....Eph 2:18
is one God and F of everything. ....Eph 4:6
and bring glory to God the F. ....Php 2:11
to our God and F forever and ....Php 4:20
and peace to you from God our F. ....Col 1:2
the F of our Lord Jesus Christ, ...Col 1:3
to God the F through Jesus. ....Col 3:17
Today I have become your F."..................Heb 1:5
Melchizedek's f or mother was, ...Heb 7:3
from the F of our spirits so ....Heb 12:9
to praise our Lord and F,.........................Jam 3:9
to the God and F of our Lord 1Pe 1:3
honor and glory from God the F. 2Pe 1:17
with God the F and was shown to 1Jn 1:2
is with God the F and with his 1Jn 1:3
helper in the presence of the F— 1Jn 2:1
the love of the F is not in you. 1Jn 2:15

not accept the F and his Son. 1Jn 2:22
The F has loved us so much that 1Jn 3:1
that the F sent his Son to 1Jn 4:14
whoever loves the F also loves 1Jn 5:1
from God the F and his Son, ...2Jn 1:3
of priests who serve God his F. ....Rev 1:6
to me before my F and before his ....Rev 3:5

FATHER'S
and your f family, and go to ....Ge 12:1
Shechem to graze their f flocks. ....Ge 37:12
him to prepare his f body, ...Ge 50:2
married his f sister Jochebed,..................Ex 6:20
relations with your f wife; ....Le 18:8
should go to his f brothers......................Nu 27:10
A man must not marry his f wife; ....Dt 22:30
Pull down your f altar to Baal, ...Jdg 6:25
the death of all your f family. 1Sa 22:22
with my f slave woman?" 2Sa 3:7
comfort Hanun about his f death. 2Sa 10:2
blame be on me and my f family. 2Sa 14:9
with his f slave women. 2Sa 16:22
finger is bigger than my f legs. 1Ki 12:10
to make him king in his f place. 2Ki 23:30
in Jerusalem in his f place. 2Ch 36:1
you and your f family will all ....Est 4:14
your people and your f family. ....Ps 45:10
young boy in my f house and like ....Pr 4:3
son, keep your f commands, and ....Pr 6:20
to the people of your f family....................Is 7:17
die without your F knowing it. ....Mt 10:29
new with you in my F kingdom." ....Mt 26:29
that I must be in my F house?" ....Lk 2:49
'All of my f servants have ....Lk 15:17
Don't make my F house a place ....Jn 2:16
steal my sheep out of my F hand. ....Jn 10:29
are many rooms in my F house; ....Jn 14:2
you so that the F glory will be ....Jn 14:13
I have obeyed my F commands, ...Jn 15:10
A man there has his f wife......................1Co 5:1
his name and his F name written ....Rev 14:1

FATHER-IN-LAW
of Midian and also Moses' f. ....Ex 3:1
Jethro, Moses' f, was the priest ....Ex 18:1
the Midianite, who was Moses' f. ....Nu 10:29
to Annas, the f of Caiaphas, ...Jn 18:13

FATHERLESS
The f child is grabbed from its ....Job 24:9

FATHERS
you back to the land of your f. ....Ge 48:21
than your f or ancestors have ....Ex 10:6
and for f with daughters living ....Nu 30:16
land we received from our f." ....Nu 36:4
their f I would give them. ....Jos 1:6
their f or brothers come to us ....Jdg 21:22
land was given to their f only,..................Job 15:19
even let their f sit with my ....Job 30:1
have sons to replace your f. ....Ps 45:16
curse their f and do not bless ....Pr 30:11
F and sons will stumble over ....Je 6:21
and the f use the wood to make a ....Je 7:18
one another, f and sons alike,..................Je 13:14
land and their mothers and f: ....Je 16:3
place, the God their f trusted." ....Je 50:7
in you hate their f and mothers. ....Eze 22:7
with their f' wives and with ....Eze 22:10
leaders and our f are ashamed, ...Da 9:8
F and sons have sexual relations ....Am 2:7
and f will give their own ....Mt 10:21
without the ability to become f. ....Mt 19:12
and f will give their own ....Mk 13:12
Brothers and f, listen to me. ....Ac 7:2

Brothers and **f,** listen to my .... Ac 22:1
Christ, you do not have many **f.** 1Co 4:15
inherit their **f'** property are .... Gal 4:1
reach the age set by their **f,** .... Gal 4:2
F, do not make your children .... Eph 6:4
F, do not nag your children. .... Col 3:21
who kill their **f** and mothers, ... 1Ti 1:9
are disciplined by their **f.** .... Heb 12:7
We have all had **f** here on earth .... Heb 12:9
f on earth disciplined us for .... Heb 12:10
Our **f** have died, but the world 2Pe 3:4
I write to you, **f,** because you 1Jn 2:13
I write to you, **f,** because you 1Jn 2:14

FATTENED
kinds of deer, and **f** birds. 1Ki 4:23
offerings of **f** cattle,............................. Am 5:22
eat tender lambs and **f** calves. .... Am 6:4

FAULT
said to Abram, "This is your **f.** .... Ge 16:5
it will be our **f.** We will cause .... Ge 44:31
but it is your own people's **f.**" .... Ex 5:16
he saw no **f** in Israel. .... Nu 23:21
and is killed, it is his own **f.** .... Jos 2:19
The ways of God are without **f;** 2Sa 22:31
He makes my way free from **f.** 2Sa 22:33
and it will be your own **f.**" 1Ki 2:37
has happened to us is our own **f.** .... Ezr 9:13
But God has found **f** with me;................. Job 33:10
The ways of God are without **f.** .... Ps 18:30
He makes my way free from **f.** .... Ps 18:32
good sense find **f** with their **f** .... Pr 11:12
gave you, and it is your own **f.** .... Je 17:4
know it is my **f** that this great .... Jnh 1:12
were without **f** in keeping his .... Lk 1:6
saved, it will be your own **f!** .... Ac 18:6
people find **f** with us and say .... Rm 3:8
anyone to find **f** with our work, ... 2Co 6:3
could be pure and without **f,** .... Eph 5:27
be God's children without **f.** .... Php 2:15
one could find **f** with the way I .... Php 3:6
holy and honest way, without **f.** 1Th 2:10
holy and without **f** before our 1Th 3:13
safe and without **f** when our Lord 1Th 5:23
as pure and without **f** is this: .... Jam 1:27
to be without sin and without **f.** 2Pe 3:14
lies; they are without **f.** .... Rev 14:5

FAULTS
and without **f** until the time .... Da 11:35
for correcting **f,** and for 2Ti 3:16

FAVOR
'You must do a special **f** for me. .... Ge 20:13
show special **f** to poor people .... Le 19:15
answered, "Do me a special **f.** .... Jos 15:19
him, "Do me a special **f.** .... Jdg 1:15
But I pray to you, LORD, for **f.** .... Ps 69:13
Kind people do themselves a **f,** .... Pr 11:17
get wisdom do themselves a **f,** .... Pr 19:8
judged in **f** of the holy people .... Da 7:22
asked Festus to do them a **f.** .... Ac 25:3
to gain their **f,** but serve them................. Col 3:22
without showing **f** of any kind to 1Ti 5:21

FAVORITE
let him be his brothers' **f.** .... Dt 33:24

FAVORITES
brothers as **f** or give special .... Dt 33:9

FAVORS
give special **f** to his children .... Dt 33:9
people will want **f** from you. .... Job 11:19
not help you or show you any **f.**'.............. Je 16:13

FAWN
the deer gives birth to her **f?** .... Job 39:1
leaves her newborn **f** to die, ... Je 14:5

FAWNS
runs free, that has beautiful **f.**................. Ge 49:21
Your breasts are like two **f,** .... Sng 4:5
Your breasts are like two **f,** .... Sng 7:3

FEAR
the sea will respect and **f** you. .... Ge 9:2
do not yet **f** the LORD God." .... Ex 9:30
hear this and tremble with **f;** .... Ex 15:14
men of Moab will shake with **f;** .... Ex 15:15
they shook with **f** and stood far .... Ex 20:18
will shake with **f,** and they will .... Dt 2:25
to all the nations you now **f.** .... Dt 7:19
gods your ancestors did not **f.**................. Dt 32:17
in his army were shaking with **f.** 1Sa 13:7
of Bethlehem shook with **f.**.................... 1Sa 16:4
shook with **f** when he saw David, ... 1Sa 21:1
and his heart pounded with **f.**................. 1Sa 28:5
lightning confused them with **f.** 2Sa 22:15
Now let each of you **f** the LORD. 2Ch 19:7
completely, and you must **f** him. 2Ch 19:9
who trembled in **f** at the word of .... Ezr 9:4
right. Don't you **f** God? Don't .... Ne 5:9
up or tremble with **f** before him,............. Est 5:9
I was trembling with **f;** .... Job 4:14
you will not **f** the wild animals .... Job 5:22
Rahab lie at his feet in **f.**....................... Job 9:13
you can stand strong without **f.** .... Job 11:15
homes are safe and without **f;** .... Job 21:9
'The **f** of the Lord is wisdom; .... Job 28:28
I **f** destruction from God, and I .... Job 31:23
from God, and I **f** his majesty,................. Job 31:23
It laughs at and is afraid of .... Job 39:22
powerful **f** its terrible looks.................... Job 41:25
and draw back in **f** as it moves. .... Job 41:25
it is a creature without **f.**....................... Job 41:33
Obey the LORD with great **f.** .... Ps 2:11
Because I **f** and respect you, ... Ps 5:7
Teach them to **f** you, LORD. .... Ps 9:20
lightning confused them with **f.** .... Ps 18:14
f him, all you Israelites. .... Ps 22:23
So why should I **f** anyone? .... Ps 27:1
safe, I said, "I will never **f.**" .... Ps 30:6
stored up for those who **f** you, ... Ps 31:19
the whole world should **f** him. .... Ps 33:8
looks after those who **f** him, ... Ps 33:18
camps around those who **f** God, ... Ps 34:7
who belong to the LORD, **f** him! .... Ps 34:9
Those who **f** him will have .... Ps 34:9
hearts. They have no **f** of God. .... Ps 36:1
were amazed. They ran away in **f.** .... Ps 48:5
F took hold of them; they hurt .... Ps 48:6
Why should I **f** when evil people .... Ps 49:5
right will see this and **f** God. .... Ps 52:6
there had been nothing to **f.** .... Ps 53:5
not change; they do not **f** God. .... Ps 55:19
to gather those who **f** you. .... Ps 60:4
what belongs to those who **f** you. .... Ps 61:5
Then everyone will **f** God. .... Ps 64:9
of the earth **f** your miracles. .... Ps 65:8
All of you who **f** God, come and .... Ps 66:16
all over the earth will **f** him. .... Ps 67:7
the kings on earth **f** him........................ Ps 76:12
the deep waters shook with **f.** .... Ps 77:16
safety so they had nothing to **f,** .... Ps 78:53
ones meet, it is God they **f.** .... Ps 89:7
as great as our **f** of you should .... Ps 90:11
You will not **f** any danger by .... Ps 91:5
Let the peoples shake with **f.** .... Ps 99:1
Nations will **f** the name of the .... Ps 102:15

gives food to those who f him. .... Ps 111:5
shake with f before the Lord, ... Ps 114:7
and the f of the grave took hold .... Ps 116:3
away the shame I f, because your .... Ps 119:39
I shake in f of you; I respect .... Ps 119:120
but I f your law in my heart. .... Ps 119:161
at peace, without f of injury." .... Pr 1:33
you won't f the ruin that comes .... Pr 3:25
will get what they f most, ... Pr 10:24
You will f high places and will .... Ec 12:5
They shook with f like trees of .... Is 7:2
Don't be afraid of what they f; .... Is 8:12
He is the one you should f; .... Is 8:13
People will be weak with f, ... Is 13:7
will look at each other in f, ... Is 13:8
man who caused great f on earth, ... Is 14:16
they are shaking with f. .... Is 15:4
of Judah will bring f to Egypt. .... Is 19:17
I see causes me to shake with f. .... Is 21:3
and I am shaking with f. .... Is 21:4
evening has become a night of f. .... Is 21:4
from strong cities will f you. .... Is 25:3
but you should shake with f. .... Is 32:11
makes people run away in f; .... Is 33:3
separated from God shake with f. .... Is 33:14
away on the earth, shake with f. .... Is 41:5
Why should you f people who die .... Is 51:12
so you will have nothing to f. .... Is 54:14
from the west will f the LORD, ... Is 59:19
from the east will f his glory. .... Is 59:19
will shake with f when they see .... Is 64:2
or stubborn and who f my word. .... Is 66:2
them with what they f most. .... Is 66:4
and shake with great f!" .... Je 2:12
is wrong not to f me," says the .... Je 2:19
shake with f in my presence. .... Je 5:22
'We should f the LORD our God, ... Je 5:24
army and are helpless from f. .... Je 6:24
brought pain and f on the people .... Je 15:8
those people you f because they .... Je 22:25
We hear people crying from f. .... Je 30:5
handed over to the people you f. .... Je 39:17
Now you f the king of Babylon, ... Je 42:11
fill them with great f." .... Je 48:39
F, deep pits, and traps wait for .... Je 48:43
will run from f, but they will .... Je 48:44
go crazy with f over them. .... Je 50:38
and he became helpless with f. .... Je 50:43
hands will hang weakly with f, ... Eze 7:17
will tremble all over with f. .... Eze 7:18
who own land will shake with f. .... Eze 7:27
and shake with f as you drink .... Eze 12:18
food with f and drink their .... Eze 12:19
every heart will melt with f, ... Eze 21:7
Their hearts will melt with f, ... Eze 21:15
It is the cup of f and ruin. .... Eze 23:33
will shake with f when they hear .... Eze 26:15
shore shake with f when your .... Eze 27:28
and their faces show their f. .... Eze 27:35
and Cush will tremble with f. .... Eze 30:4
will tremble with f when Egypt .... Eze 30:9
I will spread f through the land .... Eze 30:13
nations shake with f at the .... Eze 31:16
tremble with f because of you................. Eze 32:10
will shake with f before me. .... Eze 38:20
let your face be white with f! .... Da 5:10
of you must f and respect the .... Da 6:26
My face became white from f, ... Da 7:28
God who causes f and wonder. .... Da 9:4
they will turn in f to the LORD, ... Hos 3:5
People used to f the tribe of .... Hos 13:1
live in the land shake with f, ... Joe 2:1
shake with f, and everyone's .... Joe 2:6

I f the LORD, the God of heaven, ... Jnh 1:9
they began to f the LORD very .... Jnh 1:16
and will turn in f before you. .... Mic 7:17
all who live in it shake with f................... Nah 1:5
and make you shake with f. .... Hab 2:7
and the nations shake with f. .... Hab 3:6
saw you and shook with f. .... Hab 3:10
of Gaza will shake with f, ... Zch 9:5
And they did honor me and f me. .... Mal 2:5
one you should f is the one who .... Mt 10:28
a ghost!" and cried out in f. .... Mt 14:26
the tomb shook with f because of .... Mt 28:4
Shaking with f, she told him the.............. Mk 5:33
confused and shaking with f, ... Mk 16:8
so we could serve him without f, ... Lk 1:74
I will show you the one to f. .... Lk 12:5
F the one who has the power to .... Lk 12:5
this is the one you should f. .... Lk 12:5
Don't f, little flock, because .... Lk 12:32
him and said, "You should f God! .... Lk 23:40
in him for f they would be put .... Jn 12:42
to speak your word without f.................. Ac 4:29
they spoke God's word without f. .... Ac 4:31
these things were filled with f. .... Ac 5:11
shake with f and was afraid to .... Ac 7:32
shaking with f, fell down before .... Ac 16:29
filled with f and gave great .... Ac 19:17
"They have no f of God." .... Rm 3:18
not make us slaves again to f;................. Rm 8:15
do not have to f the rulers; .... Rm 13:3
only those who do wrong f them. .... Rm 13:3
he has nothing to f with you, ... 1Co 16:10
what it means to f the Lord, ... 2Co 5:11
the outside and f on the inside. 2Co 7:5
welcomed him with respect and f. 2Co 7:15
God with freedom and without f. .... Eph 3:12
here on earth with f and respect.............. Eph 6:5
of the Good News without f. .... Eph 6:19
News I will speak without f, ... Eph 6:20
salvation with f and trembling, ... Php 2:12
because of their f of death. .... Heb 2:15
Holy Place without f because of .... Heb 10:19
is nothing but f in waiting for .... Heb 10:27
But if they turn back with f, ... Heb 10:38
said, "I am shaking with f." .... Heb 12:21
pleases him with respect and f, ... Heb 12:28
stand without f at the judgment .... Jam 2:13
too, and they tremble with f. .... Jam 2:19
Don't be afraid of what they f; 1Pe 3:14
we can be without f and not be 1Jn 2:28
can come without f into God's 1Jn 3:21
can be without f on the day God.............. 1Jn 4:17
is, there is no f, because God's 1Jn 4:18
God's perfect love drives out f. 1Jn 4:18
that makes a person f,........................... 1Jn 4:18
They eat with you and have no f, ... Jud 1:12
mercy mixed with f to others,.................. Jud 1:23
F God and give him praise,..................... Rev 14:7

FEARED

the nurses f God, so they did .... Ex 1:17
the nurses f God, he gave them .... Ex 1:21
Egyptians, they f the LORD, and .... Ex 14:31
We f that someday your people .... Jos 22:24
' So we f that your children .... Jos 22:25
he f David even more............................. 1Sa 18:15
Israel's enemies, they f God. 2Ch 20:29
not do that, because I f God. .... Ne 5:15
was honest and f God more than .... Ne 7:2
Everything I f and dreaded has .... Job 3:25
inside because I f being hated.................. Job 31:34
He saved me from all that I f. .... Ps 34:4
You are f; no one can stand .... Ps 76:7

it is great, holy and to be **f**..................... Ps 99:3
who are **f** everywhere........................... Is 18:2
who are **f** everywhere........................... Is 18:7
that Hezekiah **f** the LORD and .... Je 26:19
You have **f** the sword, but I will .... Eze 11:8
And the people **f** the LORD. .... Hag 1:12
and I am **f** by all the nations. .... Mal 1:14

FEARFUL
We have been frightened and **f**, ... La 3:47
F events and great signs will .... Lk 21:11
They were **f** and terrified and .... Lk 24:37
I was weak and **f** and trembling. 1Co 2:3

FEARING
if he stops **f** the Almighty.' .... Job 6:14

FEARS
F come over them like a flood, ... Job 27:20
Great **f** overwhelm me. They blow .... Job 30:15
a friend to everyone who **f** you, ... Ps 119:63
Who among you **f** the LORD and .... Is 50:10
perfect in the person who **f**. 1Jn 4:18

FEAST
so they may hold a **f** for me in   .... Ex 5:1
it with a **f** to the LORD. .... Ex 12:14
celebrate the **F** of Unleavened .... Ex 12:17
must celebrate the **F** of Weeks. .... Ex 23:16
must celebrate the **F** of Shelters .... Ex 23:16
the **F** of Unleavened Bread, ... Dt 16:16
And Samson gave a **f**, as was the .... Jdg 14:10
during the seven days of the **f**. .... Jdg 14:12
After a **f** was over, Job would .... Job 1:5
heart is like a continual **f**. .... Pr 15:15
celebrate the **F** of Passover. .... Eze 45:21
days of the **f** he must offer .... Eze 45:23
to celebrate the **F** of Shelters. .... Zch 14:16
not celebrate the **F** of Shelters. .... Zch 14:18
We must not do it during the **f**, ... Mt 26:5
Passover and the **F** of Unleavened .... Mk 14:1
to Jerusalem for the Passover **F**. .... Lk 2:41
invites you to a wedding **f**, ... Lk 14:8
Every year at the Passover **f**, ... Lk 23:17
give it to the master of the **f**.'' .... Jn 2:8
at the Passover **F** in Jerusalem, ... Jn 4:45
to Jerusalem for a special **f**. .... Jn 5:1
you go to the **f**. I will not go .... Jn 7:8
day of the **f** Jesus stood up .... Jn 7:37
almost time for the Passover **F**. .... Jn 13:1
after the **F** of Unleavened .... Ac 20:6
So let us celebrate this **f**, ... 1Co 5:8
drinking or about a religious **f**, ... Col 2:16
together for the great **f** of God   .... Rev 19:17

FEASTING
and made it a day of joyful **f**. .... Est 9:17
and made it a day of joyful **f**. .... Est 9:18
a day of joyful **f** and a day for .... Est 9:19
days of joyful **f** and as a time .... Est 9:22
f and lying around will come .... Am 6:7
not to spend your time **f**,....................... Lk 21:34

FEASTS
appointed **f** as holy meetings .... Le 23:2
These are my special **f**. .... Le 23:2
during your **f** and at New Moon .... Nu 10:10
and the three yearly **f**—the Feast 2Ch 8:13
your New Moon **f** and your other .... Is 1:14
because no one comes for the **f**. .... La 1:4
animal insides left from your **f**, ... Mal 2:3
important seats at **f** and in the   .... Mt 23:6
in the synagogues and at **f**..................... Mk 12:39
in the synagogues and at **f**..................... Lk 20:46
Let their own **f** trap them and................. Rm 11:9

FEATHERS
them and carries them on its **f**. .... Dt 32:11
are not like the **f** of the stork. .... Job 39:13
He will cover you with his **f**, ... Ps 91:4
wings and long **f** of many .... Eze 17:3
eagle with big wings and many **f**. .... Eze 17:7
long like the **f** of an eagle, ... Da 4:33

FED
and then he **f** you with manna, ... Dt 8:3
of the land and **f** them the fruit .... Dt 32:13
house, and he **f** their donkeys. .... Jdg 19:21
The poor man **f** the lamb, and it 2Sa 12:3
cows that were **f** on good grain, ... 1Ki 4:23
of the herds that **f** in the Plain 1Ch 27:29
I **f** one hundred fifty Jewish   .... Ne 5:17
body was well **f**, and his bones .... Job 21:24
You have **f** your people with .... Ps 80:5
my brother who **f** at my mother's   .... Sng 8:1
they **f** themselves instead of my .... Eze 34:8
and better **f** than all the young   .... Da 1:15
and will be **f** grass like an ox.................. Da 4:32
donkeys and was **f** grass like an .... Da 5:21
neck and bent down and **f** them. .... Hos 11:4
So I **f** the flock about to be .... Zch 11:7
other Union, and I **f** the flock. .... Zch 11:7
of bread that **f** the five   .... Mt 16:9
bread that **f** the four thousand   .... Mt 16:10

FEEBLE
is weak and **f**, like an old man, ... Hos 7:9

FEED
grain back to **f** your hungry   .... Ge 42:19
and take grain to **f** your hungry .... Ge 42:33
I'll **f** your body to the birds of................. 1Sa 17:44
Today I'll **f** the bodies of the 1Sa 17:46
man wanted to **f** the traveler, ... 2Sa 12:4
when I got up to **f** my baby, ... 1Ki 3:21
each day to **f** himself and all 1Ki 4:22
each year to **f** the people who................. 1Ki 5:11
How can I **f** a hundred people 2Ki 4:43
and my mother's breasts **f** me? .... Job 3:12
an ox is quiet when it has **f**. .... Job 6:5
like eagles swooping down to **f**. .... Job 9:26
Live in the land and **f** on truth. .... Ps 37:3
like wild animals they **f** on us. .... Ps 80:13
your mouth and I will **f** you. .... Ps 81:10
If your enemy is hungry, **f** him. .... Pr 25:21
of goat's milk to **f** you and your .... Pr 27:27
work just to **f** themselves, ... Ec 6:7
where do you **f** your sheep? .... Sng 1:7
the sheep and **f** your young goats .... Sng 1:8
f in the gardens and to gather................. Sng 6:2
lambs will **f** on the land that   .... Is 5:17
Birds will **f** on them all summer,............. Is 18:6
A fool does not **f** the hungry or .... Is 32:6
you **f** those who are hungry and............. Is 58:10
their milk to **f** their young, ... La 4:3
of Israel who **f** only themselves! .... Eze 34:2
don't the shepherds **f** the flock? .... Eze 34:2
but you do not **f** the flock. .... Eze 34:3
I will **f** them in a good pasture, ... Eze 34:14
I will **f** my flock and lead them .... Eze 34:15
He will **f** them and tend them and .... Eze 34:23
People will **f** you grass like an   .... Da 4:25
the LORD will **f** them like lambs   .... Hos 4:16
winepress will not **f** the people, ... Hos 9:2
that cannot **f** their babies. .... Hos 9:14
that still **f** at their mothers   .... Joe 2:16
Let them **f** in Bashan and Gilead   .... Mic 7:14
place where they **f** their young? .... Nah 2:11
F the flock that are about to be   .... Zch 11:4
injured ones, or **f** the healthy. .... Zch 11:16
enough bread to **f** all these .... Mt 15:33

enough bread to f all these .... Mk 8:4
son into the fields to f pigs....................... Lk 15:15
Jesus said, "F my lambs." .... Jn 21:15
He said to him, "F my sheep. .... Jn 21:17
If your enemy is hungry, f him; .... Rm 12:20

FEEDING

and stay by your f box at night? .... Job 39:9
a gazelle, f among the lilies. .... Sng 4:5
will stop f themselves,........................... Eze 34:10
f them vegetables instead. .... Da 1:16
was a large herd of pigs f. .... Mt 8:30
of pigs was f on a hill near .... Mk 5:11
and laid him in a f trough. .... Lk 2:7
of cloth and lying in a f box." .... Lk 2:12
who was lying in a f trough. .... Lk 2:16
herd of pigs was f on a hill, ... Lk 8:32

FEEDS

her family and f her servant .... Pr 31:15
I am his. He f among the lilies .... Sng 2:16
He f among the lilies. .... Sng 6:3
knows where its owner f it,................... Is 1:3
but your heavenly Father f them. .... Mt 6:26
or barns, but God f them. .... Lk 12:24
but f and takes care of it. .... Eph 5:29

FEEL

Let me f the pillars that hold .... Jdg 16:26
You will f dizzy as if you're in .... Pr 23:34
shepherds don't f sorry for .... Zch 11:5

FEELING

f completely safe and .... Job 21:23
like the blind f our way along................. Is 59:10
these people lived, f shocked. .... Eze 3:15
were crying and f sad because .... Lk 8:52
Again f very upset, Jesus came .... Jn 11:38
think is right without f guilty. .... Rm 14:22
f envy, being drunk, having wild .... Gal 5:21
They have lost all f of shame, ... Eph 4:19
do know, by f, as dumb animals .... Jud 1:10

FEELINGS

if her husband has f of jealousy .... Nu 5:14
how strong my f are for the LORD 2Ki 10:16
You know our thoughts and f. .... Ps 7:9
people have no f, but I love................... Ps 119:70
or excite my f of love until it .... Sng 2:7
or excite my f of love until it .... Sng 3:5
or excite my f of love until it .... Sng 8:4
without guilt f before God up to .... Ac 23:1
for us with deep f that words .... Rm 8:26
Our f of love for you have not................ 2Co 6:12
stopped your f of love for us. 2Co 6:12
their old selfish f and the evil .... Gal 5:24
thoughts and f in our hearts. .... Heb 4:12

FEELS

You know how it f to be a .... Ex 23:9
I will find out how my father f. 1Sa 20:12
If he f good toward you, I will 1Sa 20:12
birth before she f the pain; .... Is 66:7
soon as she f the birth pains. .... Is 66:8
know what my revenge f like,............... Eze 25:14
frighten Cush, which now f safe. .... Eze 30:9
marry and he f he should marry............. 1Co 7:36

FEET

so all of you can wash your f................. Ge 18:4
He put his f back on the bed, ... Ge 49:33
touched Moses' f with it and .... Ex 4:25
Under his f was a surface that .... Ex 24:10
the big toes of their right f................... Le 8:24
walk on four f you are to hate. .... Le 11:23
the soles of your f to the tops .... Dt 28:35
soon as their f touched dry land............. Jos 4:18

sandals on their f and wore old .... Jos 9:5
Put your f on the necks of these .... Jos 10:24
Jael's f he sank. He fell, and .... Jdg 5:27
was a woman lying near his f! .... Ru 3:8
His f were not in chains. 2Sa 3:34
who was crippled in both f. 2Sa 4:4
off the hands and f of Recab and 2Sa 4:12
had not cared for his f, ... 2Sa 19:24
with dark clouds under his f. 2Sa 22:10
They fell beneath my f. 2Sa 22:39
old, he got a disease in his f. 1Ki 15:23
came in and fell at Elisha's f, ... 2Ki 4:37
back to life and stood on his f. 2Ki 13:21
and their f did not swell. .... Ne 9:21
You put my f in chains and keep .... Job 13:27
the blind and f for the lame. .... Job 29:15
Their f are caught in the nets .... Ps 9:15
with dark clouds under his f. .... Ps 18:9
They fell beneath my f. .... Ps 18:38
on a rock and made my f steady. .... Ps 40:2
will wash their f in the blood .... Ps 58:10
can stick your f in their blood, ... Ps 68:23
around his f and an iron ring .... Ps 105:18
They have f, but they cannot .... Ps 115:7
a lamp for my f and a light for .... Ps 119:105
with their f, and making signs .... Pr 6:13
coals without burning your f. .... Pr 6:28
cutting off your f or drinking .... Pr 26:6
have washed my f and don't want .... Sng 5:3
to cover its f, and two wings .... Is 6:2
you and kiss the dirt at your f. .... Is 49:23
While your f were stuck in the .... Je 38:22
out a net for my f and turned me .... La 1:13
up on your f so I may speak .... Eze 2:1
hands, stamp your f, and groan .... Eze 6:11
while its f were made partly of .... Da 2:33
stood up on two f like a human, ... Da 7:4
are the dust beneath his f. .... Nah 1:3
f long and fifteen feet wide. .... Zch 5:2
feet long and fifteen f wide." .... Zch 5:2
ashes under your f on the day I .... Mal 4:3
and shake its dust off your f. .... Mt 10:14
They put them at Jesus' f, ... Mt 15:30
hands and two f and be thrown .... Mt 18:8
hold of his f, and worshiped .... Mt 28:9
came to Jesus and fell at his f. .... Mk 7:25
than to have two f and be thrown .... Mk 9:45
and stood behind Jesus at his f, ... Lk 7:38
to wash his f with her tears, ... Lk 7:38
the man sitting at Jesus' f, ... Lk 8:35
Look at my hands and my f. .... Lk 24:39
began to wash the followers' f, ... Jn 13:5
wash not only my f, but wash my .... Jn 13:9
washed your f, you also should .... Jn 13:14
at the head and one at the f. .... Jn 20:12
the man's f and ankles became .... Ac 3:7
up, stood on his f, and began to .... Ac 3:8
fell down by his f and died.................... Ac 5:10
him, fell at his f, and .... Ac 10:25
the dust off their f and went to .... Ac 13:51
cried out, "Stand up on your f!" .... Ac 14:10
and pinned their f down between .... Ac 16:24
it to tie his own hands and f. .... Ac 21:11
On your f wear the Good News of .... Eph 6:15
washing the f of God's people, ... 1Ti 5:10
"Sit on the floor by my f." .... Jam 2:3
f were like bronze that glows .... Rev 1:15
down at his f like a dead man .... Rev 1:17
stood on their f, and everyone .... Rev 11:11
and the moon was under her f, ... Rev 12:1
with f like a bear's feet and a .... Rev 13:2

FELIX

be taken to Governor F safely."	Ac 23:24
the Most Excellent Governor F:	Ac 23:26
him, saying, "Most Excellent F!	Ac 24:2
said, "Governor F, I know you	Ac 24:10
F already understood much about	Ac 24:22
F told the officer to keep Paul	Ac 24:23
After some days F came with his	Ac 24:24
But F became afraid when Paul	Ac 24:25
the same time F hoped that Paul	Ac 24:26
F was replaced by Porcius Festus	Ac 24:27
But F had left Paul in prison to	Ac 24:27
is a man that F left in prison.	Ac 25:14

FELL

brother's blood f and where your	Ge 4:11
rain f on the earth for forty	Ge 7:12
of the soldiers f into the tar	Ge 14:10
Abram f into a deep sleep.	Ge 15:12
Shechem f in love with Dinah,	Ge 34:3
When the dew f on the camp each	Nu 11:9
shout, the walls f, and everyone	Jos 6:20
eat scraps that f from my table.	Jdg 1:7
He f, and he lay there.	Jdg 5:27
feet he sank. He f. Where Sisera	Jdg 5:27
Sisera sank, there he f, dead!	Jdg 5:27
tent turned over and f flat!"	Jdg 7:13
strings and f off his hands!	Jdg 15:14
Samson f in love with a woman	Jdg 16:4
was staying and f down at the	Jdg 19:26
Eli f backward off his chair.	1Sa 4:18
He f beside the gate, broke his	1Sa 4:18
and Goliath f facedown on the	1Sa 17:49
place where Jonathan's arrow f,	1Sa 20:37
She f at David's feet and said,	1Sa 25:24
quickly f flat on the ground	1Sa 28:20
So the men f down together.	2Sa 2:16
He f at the hands of evil men."	2Sa 3:34
his sword f out of its case.	2Sa 20:8
until the rain f on her sons'	2Sa 21:10
They f beneath my feet.	2Sa 22:39
But Solomon f in love with	1Ki 11:2
and its ashes f to the ground.	1Ki 13:5
they f down to the ground,	1Ki 18:39
a city wall f on twenty-seven	1Ki 20:30
Ahaziah f down through the	2Ki 1:2
captain came and f down on his	2Ki 1:13
She came in and f at Elisha's	2Ki 4:37
head of his ax f into the water.	2Ki 6:5
and he f down in his chariot.	2Ki 9:24
First, the lot f to Joseph, from	1Ch 25:9
I f on my knees with my hands	Ezr 9:5
She f at the king's feet and	Est 8:3
from God f from the sky.	Job 1:16
The house f in on the young	Job 1:19
have comforted those who f,	Job 4:4
My words f very gently on their	Job 29:22
my enemies f or laughed when	Job 31:29
They f beneath my feet.	Ps 18:38
but they f into it themselves.	Ps 57:6
horses and riders f dead.	Ps 76:6
Their priests f by the sword,	Ps 78:64
as the sky f and f low to the	Ps 107:26
stumbled and f like people who	Ps 107:27
did on the day Jerusalem f.	Ps 137:7
They f together and will never	Is 43:17
and again and f over each other.	Je 46:16
who were in the city when it f.	Je 52:25
tree's branches f on the	Eze 31:12
King Nebuchadnezzar f facedown	Da 2:46
and Abednego f into the blazing	Da 3:23
I f into a deep sleep with my	Da 8:18
I f into a deep sleep with my	Da 10:9

Rain f on one field, but another	Am 4:7
lie down, and he f fast asleep.	Jnh 1:5
and it f with a big crash."	Mt 7:27
some seed f by the road,	Mt 13:4
Some seed f on rocky ground,	Mt 13:5
Some other seed f among thorny	Mt 13:7
Some other seed f on good ground	Mt 13:8
is the seed that f by the road?	Mt 13:19
the seed that f on rocky ground	Mt 13:20
the seed that f among the thorny	Mt 13:22
is the seed that f on the good	Mt 13:23
frightened they f to the ground.	Mt 17:6
But the servant f on his knees	Mt 18:26
The other servant f on his knees	Mt 18:29
f to the ground and prayed,	Mt 26:39
He f to his knees and begged	Mk 1:40
they f down before him and	Mk 3:11
some seed f by the road,	Mk 4:4
seed f on rocky ground where	Mk 4:5
Some other seed f among thorny	Mk 4:7
Some other seed f on good ground	Mk 4:8
to him, and f down before him	Mk 5:6
saw Jesus, and f at his feet.	Mk 5:22
came and f at Jesus' feet.	Mk 5:33
came to Jesus and f at his feet.	Mk 7:25
and he f down and rolled on the	Mk 9:20
ran to him and f on his knees	Mk 10:17
Jesus f to the ground and prayed	Mk 14:35
the house quickly f and was	Lk 6:49
some seed f by the road.	Lk 8:5
Some seed f on rock, and when it	Lk 8:6
Some seed f among thorny weeds,	Lk 8:7
And some seed f on good ground	Lk 8:8
The seed that f beside the road	Lk 8:12
The seed that f on rock is like	Lk 8:13
The seed that f among the thorny	Lk 8:14
And the seed that f on the good	Lk 8:15
were sailing, Jesus f asleep.	Lk 8:23
cried out and f down before him	Lk 8:28
came to Jesus and f at his feet,	Lk 8:41
and f down before Jesus.	Lk 8:47
the tower of Siloam f on them?	Lk 13:4
of food that f from the rich	Lk 16:21
she f at his feet and said,	Jn 11:32
moved back and f to the ground.	Jn 18:6
But he f to his death, his body	Ac 1:18
moment Sapphira f down by his	Ac 5:10
He f on his knees and cried in a	Ac 7:60
Saul f to the ground and heard a	Ac 9:4
fish scales f from Saul's eyes	Ac 9:18
met him, f at his feet,	Ac 10:25
And the chains f off Peter's.	Ac 12:7
f down before Paul and Silas.	Ac 16:29
holy stone that f from heaven.	Ac 19:35
sound asleep and f to the ground	Ac 20:9
I f to the ground and heard a	Ac 22:7
We all f to the ground.	Ac 26:14
When the Jews f, did that fall	Rm 11:11
But they f away from Christ.	Heb 6:6
of Jericho f after the people	Heb 11:30
I f down at his feet like a dead	Rev 1:17
where you were before you f.	Rev 2:5
stars in the sky f to the earth	Rev 6:13
like a torch, f from the sky.	Rev 8:10
f on a third of the rivers and	Rev 8:10
f from the sky upon people.	Rev 16:21

FELLOW

not hate your f citizen in your	Le 19:17
may help their f Levites with	Nu 16:9
and all your f Levites near to	Nu 16:10
you your f Levites from your	Nu 18:2
myself chose your f Levites from	Nu 18:6

who is not a f Israelite. .... Dt 17:15
is better than his f Israelites, ... Dt 17:20
will be like his f Levites who .... Dt 18:7
liar, lying about a f Israelite, ... Dt 19:18
If you see your f Israelite's ox................ Dt 22:1
If you see your f Israelite's .... Dt 22:4
you loan your f Israelites money .... Dt 23:19
but not f Israelites. .... Dt 23:20
someone kidnaps a f Israelite, ... Dt 24:7
whether they are f Israelites or .... Dt 24:14
listen to their f Israelites. .... Jdg 20:13
Let's tell our f Israelites in 1Ch 13:2
because their f Levites had 2Ch 35:15
Jozadak and his f priests joined .... Ezr 3:2
their f priests and Levites, ... Ezr 3:8
and their f workers—the judges .... Ezr 4:9
to all their f workers living in .... Ezr 4:17
and their f workers went to the .... Ezr 5:3
and their f workers carried out .... Ezr 6:13
and your f Jews may spend the .... Ezr 7:18
priest and his f priests went to .... Ne 3:1
loudly against their f Jews..................... Ne 5:1
We are just like our f Jews,..................... Ne 5:5
freedom for our f Jews who had............ Ne 5:8
are selling your f Jews to us!" .... Ne 5:8
and their f Levites: Shebaniah, ... Ne 10:10
They joined their f Israelites .... Ne 10:29
in charge over his f Levites. .... Ne 11:17
His f Jews respected him very .... Est 10:3
bring all your f Israelites from .... Is 66:20
Your f Israelites will come on .... Is 66:20
was to keep a f Jew as a slave. .... Je 34:9
a f Hebrew has sold himself to .... Je 34:14
freedom to his f Hebrews who .... Je 34:15
given freedom to your f Hebrews, ... Je 34:17
If your f believer sins against .... Mt 18:15
when my f believer sins against .... Mt 18:21
My f Jews, and all of you who .... Ac 2:14
he talked with his f Jews about .... Ac 17:2
to Herodion, my f citizen. .... Rm 16:11
Warn them as f believers. 2Th 3:15
against your f believers or .... Jam 4:11
still some of their f servants .... Rev 6:11

FELLOWSHIP
called you into f with his Son, ... 1Co 1:9
and the f of the Holy Spirit be 2Co 13:14
want you also to have f with us. 1Jn 1:3
Our f is with God the Father and 1Jn 1:3
So if we say we have f with God, ... 1Jn 1:6
we can share f with each other. 1Jn 1:7
enemies of Christ were in our f, ... 1Jn 2:19

FELT
him back to Egypt, he f better. .... Ge 45:27
so she f sorry for him and said, ... Ex 2:6
and she f in her body that she .... Mk 5:29
the pain they f was like the.................... Rev 9:5

FEMALE
He created them male and f. .... Ge 1:27
male with its f, of every kind .... Ge 7:2
donkeys, male and f servants, ... Ge 12:16
your male or f slaves, your .... Ex 20:10
bull kills a male or f slave, ... Ex 21:32
your male or f slaves, your ox, ... Dt 5:14
his male or f slaves, his ox .... Dt 5:21
your male and f servants, ... Dt 12:18
Also do this to a f slave. .... Dt 15:17
your male and f servants, the .... Dt 16:11
your male and f servants, the .... Dt 16:14
and five hundred f donkeys. .... Job 1:3
my male and f slaves when they .... Job 31:13
oxen, and a thousand f donkeys. .... Job 42:12
I had male and f singers and all .... Ec 2:8

Hebrew slaves, both male and f.............. Je 34:9
'he made them male and f.'..................... Mt 19:4
'he made them male and f.'..................... Mk 10:6
and free person, male and f. .... Gal 3:28

FENCE
wall, like a f ready to fall? .... Ps 62:3

FENCES
have gates or f to protect it. .... Je 49:31

FERTILIZER
around it and put on some f. .... Lk 13:8

FESTIVAL
a New Moon F, or a Sabbath day .... Col 2:16

FESTIVALS
your feasts and at New Moon f. .... Nu 10:10
At your f you should bring .... Nu 29:39
at the New Moon f, and at all 1Ch 23:31
New Moon and all the f commanded .... Ezr 3:5
Sabbaths, New Moon f, and .... Ne 10:33
Your f have continued year after .... Is 29:1
at Jerusalem, the city of our f. .... Is 33:20
her yearly f, her New Moon .... Hos 2:11
New Moon f, and her Sabbaths. .... Hos 2:11
will change your f into days of .... Am 8:10

FESTUS
by Porcius F as governor. .... Ac 24:27
and F told the king about Paul's............ Ac 25:14
Agrippa said to F, "I would also .... Ac 25:22

FEVER
with disease, f, swelling, heat .... Dt 28:22
off, as my body burns with f. .... Job 30:30
was sick in bed with a f. .... Mt 8:14
her hand, and the f left her. .... Mt 8:15
at one o'clock the f left him." .... Jn 4:52

FIELD
"Let's go out into the f." .... Ge 4:8
the cave in the f of Machpelah, ... Ge 23:19
Sarah in the same f that he had .... Ge 25:10
every tree growing in the f...................... Ex 10:5
graze in his f or vineyard, ... Ex 22:5
thornbushes to his neighbor's f. .... Ex 22:6
or sow your f with two different .... Le 19:19
seed in your f for six years, ... Le 25:3
person gives the f after the .... Le 27:18
person does not buy back the f, ... Le 27:20
the road and went into the f. .... Nu 22:23
lying in a f in the land the .... Dt 21:1
harvest in the f and leave .... Dt 24:19
him to ask her father for a f. .... Jos 15:18
him to ask her father for a f. .... Jdg 1:14
that the f belonged to Boaz.................... Ru 2:3
work in another f, someone might .... Ru 2:22
So David hid in the f. 1Sa 20:24
is called the F of Knives.......................... 2Sa 2:16
Look, Joab's f is next to mine, ... 2Sa 14:30
officer, and his f commander. 2Ki 18:17
with the stones in the f, ... Job 5:23
grow like the grass in a f .... Ps 72:16
we grow like a flower in the f. .... Ps 103:15
She inspects a f and buys it. .... Pr 31:16
I will ruin my f. It will not be .... Is 5:6
wheat as a border around the f. .... Is 28:25
They were like grass in the f, ... Is 37:27
is like the flowers of the f. .... Is 40:6
will be plowed like a f. .... Je 26:18
so buy my f near the town of .... Je 32:7
it in a good f near plenty of .... Eze 17:5
it in the f with the grass........................ Da 4:23
weeds growing in a plowed f. .... Hos 10:4
will be plowed like a f. .... Mic 3:12
at how the lilies in the f grow................ Mt 6:28

God clothes the grass in the **f**, ... Mt 6:30
who planted good seed in his **f**. .... Mt 13:24
story about the weeds in the **f**." .... Mt 13:36
The **f** is the world, and the good .... Mt 13:38
like a treasure hidden in a **f**. .... Mt 13:44
Two men will be in the **f**. .... Mt 24:40
to buy Potter's **F** as a place to .... Mt 27:7
is why that **f** is still called .... Mt 27:8
The older son was in the **f**, ... Lk 15:25
Akeldama means "F of Blood." .... Ac 1:19
Joseph owned a **f**, sold it, ... Ac 4:37
is like the flowers of the **f**. 1Pe 1:24

FIELDS
and fed them the fruit of the **f**. .... Dt 32:13
take your best **f**, vineyards,.................... 1Sa 8:14
may their **f** produce no grain, ... 2Sa 1:21
God had not made the earth or **f**, ... Pr 8:26
again buy houses and **f** for grain .... Je 32:15
will again buy **f** in this land. .... Je 32:43
were in the **f** nearby watching .... Lk 2:8
the son into the **f** to feed pigs. .... Lk 15:15
and look at the **f** ready for .... Jn 4:35
those who owned **f** or houses sold .... Ac 4:34
who mowed your **f** cries out .... Jam 5:4

FIERCE
They were as **f** as lions and as 1Ch 12:8
brought, because of his **f** anger. .... Je 25:38

FIERY
breastplates that were **f** red, ... Rev 9:17

FIFTEEN
I will add **f** years to your life. 2Ki 20:6
I will add **f** years to your life. .... Is 38:5
feet long and **f** feet wide." .... Zch 5:2
and stayed with him for **f** days. .... Gal 1:18

FIFTEENTH
there on the **f** day of the second .... Ex 16:1
'On the **f** day of the seventh .... Le 23:34
festival on the **f** day of the 1Ki 12:32
the **f** day of the eighth month. 1Ki 12:33
It was the **f** year of the rule of .... Lk 3:1

FIFTH
came. This was the **f** day. .... Ge 1:23
Then in the **f** year, you may eat .... Le 19:25
In the **f** month of his last year, ... Je 1:3
When the Lamb opened the **f** seal, ... Rev 6:9
Then the **f** angel blew his .... Rev 9:1

FIFTIES
hundreds, **f**, and tens. .... Ex 18:21
hundreds, **f**, and tens. .... Ex 18:25
over thousands or over **f**. 1Sa 8:12

FIFTIETH
the **f** day, the first day after.................... Le 23:16
Make the **f** year a special year, ... Le 25:10
f year will be a special time .... Le 25:11
during Uzziah's **f** year as king 2Ki 15:23

FIFTY
four hundred **f** feet long,...................... Ge 6:15
What if there are **f** good people .... Ge 18:24
men from thirty to **f** years old, ... Nu 4:3
for himself and **f** men to run 2Sa 15:1
with his **f** men to Elijah. 2Ki 1:9
seven hundred **f** thousand pounds .... Est 3:9
wine vat to take out **f** jarfuls, ... Hag 2:16
in groups of about **f** people." .... Lk 9:14
You are not even **f** years old.".................. Jn 8:57

FIFTY-FIVE
and he was king **f** years in 2Ki 21:1
he was king for **f** years in 2Ch 33:1

FIFTY-FOUR
was a total of **f** hundred pieces .... Ezr 1:11

FIFTY-SECOND
during Uzziah's **f** year as king 2Ki 15:27

FIFTY-SEVEN
and one hundred **f** and one-half .... Eze 41:12

FIFTY-SIX
nine hundred **f** people living 1Ch 9:9

FIFTY-THREE
were one hundred **f** thousand six 2Ch 2:17
one hundred **f** in all, but even................. Jn 21:11

FIFTY-TWO
and he ruled **f** years in 2Ki 15:2
They were about **f** feet tall,................... 2Ch 3:15
and he ruled **f** years in 2Ch 26:3
It took **f** days to rebuild. .... Ne 6:15
long and **f** and one-half feet .... Eze 46:22

FIG
so they sewed **f** leaves together .... Ge 3:7
and barley, vines, **f** trees, ... Dt 8:8
the trees said to the **f** tree, ' .... Jdg 9:10
are young figs on the **f** trees, ... Sng 2:13
under his own vine and **f** tree, ... Mic 4:4
F trees may not grow figs, ... Hab 3:17
Seeing a **f** tree beside the road, ... Mt 21:19
How did the **f** tree dry up so .... Mt 21:20
Learn a lesson from the **f** tree: .... Mt 24:32
The **f** tree you cursed is dry and............. Mk 11:21
A man had a **f** tree planted in................ Lk 13:6
you I saw you under the **f** tree? .... Jn 1:50
falling from a **f** tree when the .... Rev 6:13

FIGHT
our enemies and **f** us and escape .... Ex 1:10
the LORD will **f** for you." .... Ex 14:14
men and go and **f** the Amalekites. .... Ex 17:9
went out to **f** the Benjaminites .... Jdg 20:20
will go and **f** this Philistine!" 1Sa 17:32
remain brave and **f** the LORD's 1Sa 18:17
Israel, don't **f** against the LORD 2Ch 13:12
Our God will **f** for us." .... Ne 4:20
Help us the enemy. Human help .... Ps 60:11
come down to **f** on Mount Zion .... Is 31:4
will **f** against you, but they .... Je 1:19
will **f** against you, but they .... Je 15:20
'If you **f** against the............................. Je 32:5
Children will **f** against their .... Mt 10:21
Nations will **f** against other .... Mk 13:8
king is going to **f** another king, ... Lk 14:31
Nations will **f** against other .... Lk 21:10
kings of the earth prepare to **f**, ... Ac 4:26
I **f** like a boxer who is hitting 1Co 9:26
F the good fight of faith, ... 1Ti 6:12
fought the good **f**, I have 2Ti 4:7
you argue and **f**. You do not get .... Jam 4:2
you quickly and **f** against them .... Rev 2:16

FIGHTER
had a champion **f** from Gath named 1Sa 17:4
Your father is a skilled **f**....................... 2Sa 17:8
know your father is a **f**. 2Sa 17:10
was a brave **f** from Kabzeel who 2Sa 23:20
was a brave **f** from Kabzeel who 1Ch 11:22

FIGHTERS
and all its men were good **f**. .... Jos 10:2
They are skilled **f**. .... Jos 17:16
brave Benjaminite **f** were killed.............. Jdg 20:44

FIGHTING
saw two Hebrew men **f** each other............ Ex 2:13
All of them were brave **f** men. 2Ch 14:8
Moses saw two men of Israel **f**, ... Ac 7:26

FIGHTS

the LORD your God f for you, ... Jos 23:10
The army that f for us is larger 2Ki 6:16
evil plans, who always start f.................. Ps 140:2
has pain? Who f? Who complains?........... Pr 23:29
himself and f against his own .... Mk 3:26
in the same way the world f. 2Co 10:3
know where your f and arguments........... Jam 4:1

FIGS

said, "Make a paste from f." 2Ki 20:7
There are young f on the fig .... Sng 2:13
baskets had very good f in it, ... Je 24:2
as good, like these good f. .... Je 24:5
make them like bad f that are................. Je 29:17
and f don't come from thorny................. Mt 7:16
to see if it had any f on it. .... Mk 11:13
don't gather f from thornbushes, ... Lk 6:44
or can a grapevine make f?..................... Jam 3:12
to the earth like f falling from .... Rev 6:13

FIGURE

had a very pretty f and face. .... Est 2:7

FILL

F the water of the seas, and let .... Ge 1:22
F the earth and be its master. .... Ge 1:28
grow in number and f the earth................ Ge 9:1
his servants to f his brothers' .... Ge 42:25
F your container with olive oil 1Sa 16:1
Then he said, "F four jars with 1Ki 18:34
God will yet f your mouth with .... Job 8:21
before him and f my mouth with .... Job 23:4
The autumn rains f it with pools............. Ps 84:6
things and f our houses with .... Pr 1:13
"If all of heaven and earth," .... Je 23:24
I will surely f you with so many .... Je 51:14
and f your stomach with it." .... Eze 3:3
Egypt and will f the land with .... Eze 30:11
the servants, "F the jars with .... Jn 2:7
gives hope will f you with much.............. Rm 15:13
did that to f everything with .... Eph 4:10
which f them with foolish pride .... Col 2:18

FILLED

Let the water be f with living .... Ge 1:20
The sea is f with these living .... Ge 1:21
Let the earth be f with animals, ... Ge 1:24
all that f them were finished. .... Ge 2:1
and his heart was f with pain. .... Ge 6:6
to the well and f her bag with................. Ge 21:19
to the spring and f her jar, ... Ge 24:16
The Philistines f those wells .... Ge 26:15
Philistines f them with dirt. .... Ge 26:18
been short and f with trouble— .... Ge 47:9
of Egypt was f with them. .... Ex 1:7
Nile River will be f with frogs. .... Ex 8:3
it into the bowl f with blood, ... Ex 12:22
I have f Bezalel with the Spirit .... Ex 31:3
The LORD has f Bezalel with the .... Ex 35:31
of the LORD f the Holy Tent. .... Ex 40:34
of the LORD f the Holy Tent. .... Ex 40:35
country will be f with all kinds .... Le 19:29
gold dishes f with incense .... Nu 7:86
give me his palace f with silver .... Nu 24:13
of Nun was then f with wisdom,............. Dt 34:9
They were new and f with wine,............. Jos 9:13
jugs that the young men have f." .... Ru 2:9
and a leather bag f with wine. 1Sa 1:24
The LORD has f my heart with 1Sa 2:1
beginning where the land was f 2Sa 5:9
the forest and f the pit with 2Sa 18:17
cloud f the Temple of the LORD............. 1Ki 8:10
the Temple was f with the glory 1Ki 8:11
Solomon f in the surrounding................. 1Ki 9:24

off the altar and f the ditch. 1Ki 18:35
the valley will be f with water. 2Ki 3:17
of Edom and f the valley. 2Ki 3:20
the vine and f his robe with it................. 2Ki 4:39
the temple was f from one side 2Ki 10:21
people and had f Jerusalem with 2Ki 24:4
the land was f in and going to 1Ch 11:8
of the LORD was f with a cloud.............. 2Ch 5:13
the LORD's glory f the Temple of 2Ch 5:14
The LORD's glory f the Temple. 2Ch 7:1
because the LORD's glory f it. 2Ch 7:2
laid him on a bed f with spices 2Ch 16:14
area that was f in on the east 2Ch 32:5
Their evil f the land with .... Ezr 9:11
Then Haman was f with terror .... Est 7:6
with rulers who f their houses .... Job 3:15
it was God who f their houses .... Job 22:18
they are f with frightening .... Job 41:14
the wicked are f with terror, ... Ps 14:5
The wicked are f with terror .... Ps 53:5
are f with good things in your .... Ps 65:4
we took root and f the land. .... Ps 80:9
they are f with good food. .... Ps 104:28
their country was f with frogs, ... Ps 105:30
them quail and f them with bread .... Ps 105:40
Cursing others f his body and................. Ps 109:18
Then we were f with laughter, ... Ps 126:2
Let our barns be f with crops of .... Ps 144:13
the best fruit, f with flowers .... Sng 4:13
like gold fingers, f with jewels. .... Sng 5:14
drinking cup always f with wine. .... Sng 7:2
She used to be f with fairness; .... Is 1:21
have become f with wrong ideas .... Is 2:6
land has been f with silver .... Is 2:7
land has been f with horses; .... Is 2:7
His long robe f the Temple..................... Is 6:1
as the Temple f with smoke. .... Is 6:4
land will be f with weeds and................. Is 7:25
left, but they will not be f. .... Is 9:20
he lives will be f with glory. .... Is 11:10
It is f with the sound of wings. .... Is 18:1
valleys will be f with chariots. .... Is 22:7
the world will be f with their .... Is 27:6
with beer and are f with wine. .... Is 28:7
that city will be f with sadness .... Is 29:2
will have streams f with water. .... Is 30:25
His mouth is f with anger, ... Is 30:27
that once were f with joy. .... Is 32:13
land will be f with their blood .... Is 34:7
well-fed horses f with sexual .... Je 5:8
wine should be f with wine.' .... Je 13:12
bags should be f with wine.' .... Je 13:12
'Let my eyes be f with tears .... Je 14:17
and you f me with anger at the .... Je 15:17
have f my country with their .... Je 16:18
They f this place with the blood .... Je 19:4
people will be f with the good .... Je 31:14
Moab is f with shame, because .... Je 48:20
will never be f with people .... Je 50:39
He f his stomach with our best .... Je 51:34
The LORD f me with misery. .... La 3:15
he should be f with shame..................... La 3:30
They have f the land with .... Eze 8:17
The land is f with people who................. Eze 9:9
a cloud f the inner courtyard. .... Eze 10:3
The Temple was f with the cloud, ... Eze 10:4
cities will be f with flocks of .... Eze 36:38
mountain that f the whole earth. .... Da 2:35
and a trench f with water around .... Da 9:25
buildings are f with treasures................. Am 3:10
place will be f with many people .... Mic 2:12
But I am f with power, with the .... Mic 3:8
punishes and is f with anger. .... Nah 1:2

F

f his cave with the animals he .... Nah 2:12
he f his den with meat he had................. Nah 2:12
will be f with disgrace, ... Hab 2:16
streets will be f with boys and .... Zch 8:5
They will be f like a bowl used .... Zch 9:15
the star, they were f with joy. .... Mt 2:10
the followers f twelve baskets .... Mt 14:20
his followers f seven baskets .... Mt 15:37
that you f many baskets with .... Mt 16:9
many baskets you f then also? .... Mt 16:10
followers were f with sadness. .... Mt 17:23
the city was f with excitement .... Mt 21:10
wedding hall was f with guests. .... Mt 22:10
alabaster jar f with expensive................. Mt 26:7
a sponge and f it with vinegar .... Mt 27:48
The followers f twelve baskets .... Mk 6:43
his followers f seven baskets .... Mk 8:8
an alabaster jar f with very................... Mk 14:3
got a sponge, f it with vinegar .... Mk 15:36
will be f with the Holy Spirit. .... Lk 1:15
Elizabeth was f with the Holy................. Lk 1:41
He has f the hungry with good .... Lk 1:53
was f with the Holy Spirit and .... Lk 1:67
He was f with wisdom, and God's .... Lk 2:40
Every valley should be f in,.................... Lk 3:5
Jesus, f with the Holy Spirit, ... Lk 4:1
They came and f both boats so .... Lk 5:7
They were f with much respect .... Lk 5:26
So they f the jars to the top. .... Jn 2:7
the pieces and f twelve baskets .... Jn 6:13
the perfume f the whole house .... Jn 12:3
Your hearts are f with sadness .... Jn 16:6
heaven and f the whole house .... Ac 2:2
They were all f with the Holy .... Ac 2:4
Then Peter, f with the Holy .... Ac 4:8
They were all f with the Holy .... Ac 4:31
these things were f with fear. .... Ac 5:11
you have f Jerusalem with your .... Ac 5:28
see again and be f with the Holy .... Ac 9:17
was f with the Holy Spirit. .... Ac 13:9
followers were f with joy and .... Ac 13:52
this and were f with fear and .... Ac 19:17
minds were f with darkness. .... Rm 1:21
They are f with every kind of .... Rm 1:29
have been f with sadness so 1Co 5:2
but they have f your place. 1Co 16:17
The church is f with Christ, ... Eph 1:23
Then you can be f with the .... Eph 3:19
you, but be f with the Spirit. .... Eph 5:18
that you will be f with the good .... Php 1:11
see you so I can be f with joy................. 2Ti 1:4
So you are f with a joy that 1Pe 1:8
Then the angel f the incense pan .... Rev 8:5
He is f with anger, because he .... Rev 12:12
golden bowls f with the anger .... Rev 15:7
The temple was f with smoke from .... Rev 15:8
city the cup f with the wine .... Rev 16:19
a cup f with evil things and the .... Rev 17:4

FILLING
Solomon was f in the land and 1Ki 11:27
f Jerusalem from one end to............. 2Ki 21:16
those nations, f them with dead .... Ps 110:6
f their houses with treasures. .... Pr 8:21
f its streets with their bodies. .... Eze 11:6
the LORD's glory f the Temple. .... Eze 43:5
glory of the LORD f the Temple .... Eze 44:4
gathered up, f twelve baskets................. Lk 9:17
you food and f your hearts with .... Ac 14:17

FILLS
as my glory f the whole earth, ... Nu 14:21
God f his hands with lightning .... Job 36:32
He f the clouds with water and .... Job 37:11

the LORD's love f the earth. .... Ps 33:5
because violence f every dark. .... Ps 74:20
the thirsty and f up the hungry. .... Ps 107:9
LORD, your love f the earth. .... Ps 119:64
He f the sky with clouds and .... Ps 147:8
your country and f you with the .... Ps 147:14
His glory f the whole earth." .... Is 6:3
He f Jerusalem with fairness and .... Is 33:5
and his praise f the earth. .... Hab 3:3
and Christ f everything in every .... Eph 1:23

FILTH
wash away the f from the women .... Is 4:4
of the world—the f of the earth. 1Co 4:13

FILTHY
them away like f rags and say, ... Is 30:22
done are like f pieces of cloth. .... Is 64:6
will throw f garbage on you and.............. Nah 3:6
because of the f lives of evil 2Pe 2:7
and make themselves f with sin............. Jud 1:8

FINAL
heard, so I give my f advice: .... Ec 12:13
time of your f punishment has .... Eze 21:25
the time of f punishment has .... Eze 21:29
the time of their f punishment. .... Eze 35:5
you free when the f day comes. .... Eph 4:30

FINALLY
F, the woman died. .... Mt 22:27
F the woman died too. .... Mk 12:22
F, the woman died also. .... Lk 20:32
F, he went sound asleep and fell .... Ac 20:9
for a week. F, we came to Rome .... Ac 28:14
F, be strong in the Lord and in .... Eph 6:10
F, all of you should be in........................ 1Pe 3:8

FIND
If I f fifty good people in the .... Ge 18:26
and old, could not f the door. .... Ge 19:11
own straw wherever you can f it. .... Ex 5:11
and I will f out what more the .... Nu 22:19
and you will f him if you look................. Dt 4:29
F out what makes Samson so .... Jdg 16:5
You will f out that the city of .... Ezr 4:15
I knew where to f God so I could .... Job 23:3
They will not f joy in the........................ Job 27:10
until I f a place for the LORD. .... Ps 132:5
you will f that you know God. .... Pr 2:5
to life for those who f them; .... Pr 4:22
and those who seek me f me. .... Pr 8:17
look for it and do not f it, ... Pr 14:6
it is hard to f a trustworthy................... Pr 20:6
It is hard to f a good wife, ... Pr 31:10
and tried very hard to f wisdom, ... Ec 7:25
together to f some meaning for .... Ec 7:27
I did not f one man among the .... Ec 7:28
"I f no pleasure in them." .... Ec 12:1
for him, but I could not f him................. Sng 3:1
for him, but I could not f him. .... Sng 3:2
if you f my lover, tell .... Sng 5:8
but you will not f them. .... Is 41:12
all your heart, you will f me! .... Je 29:13
to me, "Human, eat what you f; .... Eze 3:3
tried to f reasons to accuse................... Da 6:4
they will not be able to f him,................. Hos 5:6
Search, and you will f. .... Mt 7:7
Everyone who searches will f. .... Mt 7:8
you will f rest for your lives. .... Mt 11:29
you will quickly f a donkey tied .... Mt 21:2
suddenly and f you sleeping. .... Mk 13:36
You will f a baby wrapped in .... Lk 2:12
they did not f him, they went .... Lk 2:45
three years, but I never f any................. Lk 13:7
will he f those on earth who .... Lk 18:8

"I f nothing against this man." .... Lk 23:4
they did not f his body there. .... Lk 24:23
for me, but you will not f me. .... Jn 7:34
but you will not f me,' and 'You .... Jn 7:36
in and go out and f pasture. .... Jn 10:9
the boat, and you will f some." .... Jn 21:6
could not f the apostles. .... Ac 5:22
could not f anything to eat...................... Ac 7:11
But when they did not f them, ... Ac 17:6
every day to f out if these .... Ac 17:11
all around for him and f him, ... Ac 17:27
We f nothing wrong with this .... Ac 23:9
Some people f fault with us and .... Rm 3:8
with me and f that you are not 2Co 9:4
teaching that will f many more 2Ti 4:3
those who truly want to f him. .... Heb 11:6
to die, but they will not f it..................... Rev 9:6

FINDING

to the city without f them. .... Jos 2:22
F a wild vine, he picked fruit 2Ki 4:39
go about their job of f food. .... Job 24:5
me without f anything wrong; .... Ps 17:3
are always f more friends, ... Pr 19:4
it was like f grapes in the .... Hos 9:10
were like f the first figs .... Hos 9:10

FINDS

Suppose a man f a woman who is .... Ex 22:16
If a priest f an animal that .... Le 22:8
the dead person f the killer.................... Nu 35:27
him before he f walled cities 2Sa 20:6
is the person who f wisdom, ... Pr 3:13
When a man f a wife, he finds .... Pr 18:22
a wife, he f something good. .... Pr 18:22
live upright and be loyal f life, ... Pr 21:21
it f more rest than that man. .... Ec 6:5
he f a tree that will not rot...................... Is 40:20
Then he f a skilled craftsman to .... Is 40:20
it f the house still empty,........................ Mt 12:44
if he f it he is happier about .... Mt 18:13
master comes and f the servant .... Mt 24:46
when it f no place, it says, '.................... Lk 11:24
it f that house swept clean and .... Lk 11:25
he comes in and f them still .... Lk 12:38
master comes and f the servant .... Lk 12:43
the lost sheep until he f it. .... Lk 15:4
when he f it, he happily puts .... Lk 15:5
for the coin until she f it. .... Lk 15:8
And when she f it, she will call .... Lk 15:9

FINE

twenty quarts of f flour, ... Ge 18:6
gave Joseph f linen clothes to .... Ge 41:42
it must be made from f flour. .... Le 2:1
about two quarts of f flour as .... Le 5:11
made with f flour mixed with .... Nu 6:15
four quarts of f flour mixed .... Nu 28:9
pounds and two f pieces of .... Ezr 8:27
courtyard had f white curtains .... Est 1:6
the dust and your f gold among .... Job 22:24
You have poured f oils on me.................... Ps 92:10
they all have f clothes to keep .... Pr 31:21
than there is f gold in Ophir. .... Is 13:12
and there your f chariots will .... Is 22:18
enemies will become like f dust;.............. Is 29:5
sewed on, f linen, coral, ... Eze 27:16
to make the f flour moist, ... Eze 46:14
with a belt of f gold wrapped .... Da 10:5
A man dressed in f clothes? .... Lk 7:25
people who have f clothes and .... Lk 7:25
anyone's money or f clothes. .... Ac 20:33
fancy talk and f words to fool .... Rm 16:18
f clothes that should make you 1Pe 3:3
jewels, pearls, f linen, purple .... Rev 18:12

F linen, bright and clean, was.................. Rev 19:8
heaven, dressed in f linen, ... Rev 19:14

FINEST

give you the f wheat and fill .... Ps 81:16
His head is like the f gold; .... Sng 5:11
You plant the f grapevines and .... Is 17:10
you put on your f dress and .... Je 4:30
dressed in the f clothes and .... Lk 16:19

FINGER

off from his own f his ring with .... Ge 41:42
and he put it on Joseph's f..................... Ge 41:42
Use your f to put some of the .... Ex 29:12
them, written by the f of God.................. Ex 31:18
is to dip his f into the blood .... Le 4:6
Dipping his f in the blood, ... Le 4:17
sin offering on his f and put it .... Le 4:25
goat's blood on his f and put it .... Le 4:30
sin offering on his f and put it .... Le 4:34
and with his f put some of it on .... Le 8:15
and he dipped his f in the blood .... Le 9:9
will dip a f of his right hand .... Le 14:16
and with his f he will sprinkle .... Le 14:16
Then with a f of his right hand, ... Le 14:27
it with his f on the front .... Le 16:14
with his f he will sprinkle the .... Le 16:14
Then, with his f, he will .... Le 16:19
blood on his f and sprinkle it .... Nu 19:4
had written on with his own f. .... Dt 9:10
'My little f is bigger than my 1Ki 12:10
'My little f is bigger than my 2Ch 10:10
and pointing your f at others,.................. Is 58:9
put a ring on his f and sandals .... Lk 15:22
to dip his f in water and cool .... Lk 16:24
on the ground with his f......................... Jn 8:6
and put my f where the nails .... Jn 20:25
Put your f here, and look at .... Jn 20:27

FINGERS

had six f on each hand and six 2Sa 21:20
twenty-four f and toes in all. 2Sa 21:20
had six f on each hand and six 1Ch 20:6
twenty-four f and toes in all. 1Ch 20:6
which you made with your f. .... Ps 8:3
and making signs with their f. .... Pr 6:13
my hands and flowing from my f, ... Sng 5:5
and shaped with their own f. .... Is 2:8
and with your f you have done .... Is 59:3
them and point f at them and .... Je 24:9
Suddenly the f of a person's .... Da 5:5
He put his f in the man's ears.................. Mk 7:33

FINISH

When the officers f speaking to .... Dt 20:9
and before I f defeating my..................... 1Sa 14:24
After you f, the king may be 2Sa 11:20
took him thirteen years to f it. 1Ki 7:1
the people, but he did not f. 1Ch 27:24
Be strong and f the job." 1Ch 28:10
Can they f it in one day?......................... Ne 4:2
before they f growing and will .... Job 15:32
f your outside work and prepare .... Pr 24:27
It is better to f something than .... Ec 7:8
He will f his job, his strange .... Is 28:21
After you f reading this scroll, ... Je 51:63
light the fire. F cooking the .... Eze 24:10
When you f making the altar pure .... Eze 43:23
When they f their drinking, ... Hos 4:18
you will not f going through all .... Mt 10:23
have enough money to f the job.............. Lk 14:28
but you would not be able to f. .... Lk 14:29
to build but was not able to f.' .... Lk 14:30
After I f eating and drinking, ... Lk 17:8
me to do and to f his work...................... Jn 4:34

and you get to f up their work." .... Jn 4:38
for God to f making us his own .... Rm 8:23
to help you f this special work 2Co 8:6
So now f the work you started. 2Co 8:11
They will f getting in order the 2Co 9:5
Be sure to f the work the Lord .... Col 4:17
so you could f doing the things .... Tit 1:5

FINISHED

and all that filled them were f. .... Ge 2:1
So Moses f the work. .... Ex 40:33
they have f my whole harvest. .... Ru 2:21
of the Lord had not yet been f, ... 1Ki 3:2
So Huram f all his work for King 1Ki 7:40
When he f praying, he got up. 1Ki 8:54
Solomon f building the Temple of 1Ki 9:1
going on, but it is not yet f." .... Ezr 5:16
they had f with all the men who .... Ezr 10:17
sword will kill until it is f, ... Je 46:10
After you have f these three .... Eze 4:6
After Jesus f telling these .... Mt 11:1
When Jesus f teaching with these .... Mt 13:53
After Jesus f saying all these .... Mt 26:1
Having f the work you gave me to .... Jn 17:4
the vinegar, he said, "It is f." .... Jn 19:30
fight, I have f the race, I have 2Ti 4:7
trumpet, God's secret will be f. .... Rev 10:7
the throne, saying, "It is f!" .... Rev 16:17
the throne said to me, "It is f. .... Rev 21:6

FINISHES

When the Lord f doing what he .... Is 10:12
stop until he f what he plans to .... Je 23:20
stay angry until he f punishing .... Je 30:24
angry until he f the punishment .... Je 30:24

FINISHING

with him were f their meal. 1Ki 1:41
he was f his work, he said, ' .... Ac 13:25

FINS

if the animal has f and scales, ... Le 11:9
and does not have f and scales— .... Le 11:10
that does not have f and scales. .... Le 11:12
anything that has f and scales, ... Dt 14:9
that does not have f and scales. .... Dt 14:10

FIR

stork's home is in the f trees. .... Ps 104:17
I will put pine, f, and cypress .... Is 41:19
its pine, f, and cypress trees .... Is 60:13
boards of f trees from Mount .... Eze 27:5

FIRE

and a sword of f that flashed .... Ge 3:24
took the knife and the f. .... Ge 22:6
We have the f and the wood, ... Ge 22:7
to him in flames of f coming out .... Ex 3:2
saw that the bush was on f, ... Ex 3:2
must roast the lamb over a f. .... Ex 12:8
Roast the whole lamb over a f— .... Ex 12:9
you must burn it with f. .... Ex 12:10
in a pillar of f to give them .... Ex 13:21
the pillar of f was always with .... Ex 13:22
of cloud and f at the Egyptian .... Ex 14:24
them, like f burning straw. .... Ex 15:7
the Lord came down on it in f. .... Ex 19:18
a man starts a f that spreads .... Ex 22:6
If the f burns his neighbor's .... Ex 22:6
who started the f must pay for .... Ex 22:6
looked like a f burning on top .... Ex 24:17
offering made by f to the Lord. .... Ex 29:18
offering made by f to the Lord; .... Ex 29:25
offering made by f to the Lord, ... Ex 29:41
a sacrifice to the Lord by f, ... Ex 30:20
had made and melted it in the f. .... Ex 32:20
it into the f and out came this .... Ex 32:24

not light a f in any of your .... Ex 35:3
and pans for carrying the f. .... Ex 38:3
and there was a f in the cloud .... Ex 40:38
put wood and f on the altar, ... Le 1:7
that is on the f of the altar. .... Le 1:8
offering made by f, and its .... Le 1:9
that is on the f of the altar. .... Le 1:12
offering made by f, and its .... Le 1:13
on the wood which is on the f. .... Le 1:17
offering made by f, and its .... Le 1:17
It is an offering made by f, ... Le 2:2
offerings made by f to the Lord. .... Le 2:3
altar, as an offering made by f. .... Le 2:9
offerings made to the Lord by f. .... Le 2:10
offering made by f to the Lord. .... Le 2:11
of new grain roasted in the f. .... Le 2:14
is an offering by f to the Lord. .... Le 2:16
a sacrifice by f to the Lord. .... Le 3:3
that is on the wood of the f. .... Le 3:5
It is an offering made by f, ... Le 3:5
a sacrifice by f to the Lord. .... Le 3:9
offering made by f to the Lord. .... Le 3:11
a sacrifice by f to the Lord. .... Le 3:14
It is an offering made by f, ... Le 3:16
burn it on a wood f on the pile .... Le 4:12
made by f for the Lord. .... Le 4:35
offerings made by f to the Lord; .... Le 5:12
and the altar's f must be kept .... Le 6:9
But the f must be kept burning .... Le 6:12
whole burnt offering on the f, ... Le 6:12
f must be kept burning on the .... Le 6:13
the offerings made to me by f; .... Le 6:17
offerings made to the Lord by f, ... Le 6:18
offering must be burned with f. .... Le 6:30
offering made by f to the Lord. .... Le 7:5
they must burn this meat with f. .... Le 7:19
offering made by f to the Lord, ... Le 7:25
offering made by f to the Lord. .... Le 7:30
offerings made by f to the Lord. .... Le 7:35
them in a f outside the camp .... Le 8:17
offering made by f to the Lord; .... Le 8:21
offering made by f to the Lord, ... Le 8:28
F came out from the Lord and .... Le 9:24
incense, put f in them, and .... Le 10:1
use the special f Moses had .... Le 10:1
So f came down from the Lord and .... Le 10:2
offered by f to the Lord, ... Le 10:12
offerings made by f to the Lord .... Le 10:13
part of the offering made by f, ... Le 10:15
must burn it in f; it does not .... Le 13:55
mildew must be burned with f. .... Le 13:57
incense on the f before the Lord .... Le 16:13
will be burned in the f. .... Le 16:27
the two women in f so that your .... Le 20:14
offerings made by f to the Lord, ... Le 21:6
She must be burned with f. .... Le 21:9
offerings made by f to the Lord. .... Le 21:21
as an offering by f to the Lord. .... Le 22:22
as a sacrifice by f to the Lord. .... Le 22:27
offering made by f to the Lord. .... Le 23:8
offering made by f to the Lord; .... Le 23:13
will be an offering made by f, ... Le 23:18
made by f to the Lord.'" .... Le 23:25
offering made by f to the Lord. .... Le 23:27
made by f to the Lord each .... Le 23:36
offering made by f to the Lord. .... Le 23:36
offerings made by f to the Lord. .... Le 23:37
offering made by f to the Lord. .... Le 24:7
offerings made by f to the Lord. .... Le 24:9
wrong kind of f before the Lord .... Nu 3:4
the pans for carrying the f, ... Nu 4:14
be put in the f that is under .... Nu 6:18
above the Tent looked like f. .... Nu 9:15

and at night it looked like f. .... Nu 9:16
f from the LORD burned among .... Nu 11:1
the LORD, the f stopped burning. .... Nu 11:2
the LORD's f had burned among .... Nu 11:3
the day and with f at night..................... Nu 14:14
the LORD offerings made by f. .... Nu 15:3
This offering is made by f, ... Nu 15:10
offerings by f will be pleasing................. Nu 15:13
offerings by f so the smell will .... Nu 15:14
by f and a sin offering. .... Nu 15:25
Tomorrow put f and incense in .... Nu 16:7
Then a f came down from the LORD .... Nu 16:35
the incense pans out of the f. .... Nu 16:37
and put f from the altar and .... Nu 16:46
fat as an offering made by f. .... Nu 18:17
f began in Heshbon; flames came .... Nu 21:28
same time the f burned up the .... Nu 26:10
LORD with the wrong kind of f. .... Nu 26:61
me food offerings made by f, ... Nu 28:2
This offering is made by f, ... Nu 28:8
the LORD an offering made by f, ... Nu 28:19
offering made by f each day for .... Nu 28:24
are made by f to the LORD, ... Nu 29:6
offerings, made by f, as a smell .... Nu 29:13
Bring an offering made by f, ... Nu 29:36
burn—into the f, and then it .... Nu 31:23
If something cannot stand the f, ... Nu 31:23
In a f at night and in a cloud .... Dt 1:33
it blazed with f that reached to .... Dt 4:11
LORD spoke to you from the f. .... Dt 4:12
you from the f at Mount Sinai, ... Dt 4:15
like a f that burns things up. .... Dt 4:24
speak from a f and have still .... Dt 4:33
showed you his great f on earth,............ Dt 4:36
you heard him speak from the f.............. Dt 4:36
face from the f on the mountain. .... Dt 5:4
afraid of the f, so you would .... Dt 5:5
in a loud voice out of the f, ... Dt 5:22
the mountain was blazing with f, ... Dt 5:23
have heard his voice from the f. .... Dt 5:24
This great f will burn us up, ... Dt 5:25
from a f and still lived........................... Dt 5:26
and burn their idols in the f. .... Dt 7:5
Burn up their idols in the f..................... Dt 7:25
them like a f that burns things .... Dt 9:3
on the mountain out of the f .... Dt 9:10
that was burning with f, ... Dt 9:15
had made and burned it in the f. .... Dt 9:21
you on the mountain from the f,............. Dt 10:4
their Asherah poles in the f .... Dt 12:3
offerings made to the LORD by f, ... Dt 18:1
as a sacrifice in the f. .... Dt 18:10
look at this terrible f anymore, ... Dt 18:16
like a burning f against those .... Dt 29:20
has started a f that burns down .... Dt 32:22
and it will set f to the base of .... Dt 32:22
will himself be destroyed by f. .... Jos 7:15
of it, and quickly set it on f. .... Jos 8:19
Then f jumped up from the rock.............. Jdg 6:21
let f come out of the thornbush .... Jdg 9:15
may f come out of Abimelech and .... Jdg 9:20
Also may f come out of the..................... Jdg 9:20
they set them on f and burned .... Jdg 9:49
of the tower to set it on f, ... Jdg 9:52
the f burned, the angel of the .... Jdg 13:20
is like the last spark of a f. 2Sa 14:7
servants set f to Joab's field. 2Sa 14:30
and burning f came out of his................ 2Sa 22:9
thrown in the f and burned where 2Sa 23:7
completely as f burns up manure. 1Ki 14:10
into the palace and set it on f, ... 1Ki 16:18
a widow gathering wood for a f............... 1Ki 17:10
but they are not to set f to it. 1Ki 18:23

wood but not setting f to it...................... 1Ki 18:23
by setting f to his wood is 1Ki 18:24
god, but don't start the f." 1Ki 18:25
Then f from the LORD came down............ 1Ki 18:38
there was a f, but the LORD was 1Ki 19:12
but the LORD was not in the f. 1Ki 19:12
After the f, there was a quiet,................ 1Ki 19:12
used their wooden yoke for a f. 1Ki 19:21
let f come down from heaven and 2Ki 1:10
Then f came down from heaven 2Ki 1:10
let f come down from heaven and 2Ki 1:12
Then f came down from heaven 2Ki 1:12
f came down from heaven and 2Ki 1:14
chariot and horses of f appeared 2Ki 2:11
Put the large pot on the f, ... 2Ki 4:38
and chariots of f all around 2Ki 6:17
cities with f and kill their 2Ki 8:12
made his son pass through f. 2Ki 16:3
pass through f and tried to find 2Ki 17:17
burned their children in the f,................ 2Ki 17:31
of these nations into the f, ... 2Ki 19:18
made his own son pass through f. 2Ki 21:6
against this place like a f, ... 2Ki 22:17
Nebuzaradan set f to the Temple 2Ki 25:9
by sending down f from heaven 1Ch 21:26
f came down from the sky and 2Ch 7:1
of Israel saw the f came down 2Ch 7:3
made a large f to honor him. 2Ch 16:14
not make a f to honor Jehoram 2Ch 21:19
his children pass through the f. 2Ch 28:3
and they let the f go out in the 2Ch 29:7
pass through f in the Valley of 2Ch 33:6
over the f as they were 2Ch 35:13
his army set f to God's Temple 2Ch 36:19
gates have been destroyed by f." .... Ne 2:3
that had been destroyed by f. .... Ne 2:13
and with a pillar of f at night................ Ne 9:12
the pillar of f led them at .... Ne 9:19
his anger was like a burning f. .... Est 1:12
F will destroy the tents of .... Job 15:34
tents are set on f, and sulfur .... Job 18:15
A f not fanned by people will .... Job 20:26
and f burns up their wealth.' .... Job 22:20
things are changed as if by f. .... Job 28:5
It is like a f that burns and .... Job 31:12
mouth; sparks of f shoot out. .... Job 41:19
from a large pot over a hot f. .... Job 41:20
Its breath sets coals on f, ... Job 41:21
like silver purified by f, ... Ps 12:6
and burning f came out of his................ Ps 18:8
up, and f will burn them up. .... Ps 21:9
burns up the chariots with f. .... Ps 46:9
A f burns in front of him, ... Ps 50:3
We went through f and flood, ... Ps 66:12
melts before a f, let the wicked .... Ps 68:2
by the light of a f by night.................... Ps 78:14
anger was like f to the people............... Ps 78:21
men died by f, and the young .... Ps 78:63
your jealousy burn like a f? .... Ps 79:5
is cut down and burned with f; .... Ps 80:16
Be like a f that burns a forest .... Ps 83:14
will your anger burn like a f? .... Ps 89:46
A f goes before him and burns up .... Ps 97:3
my bones are burned up with f. .... Ps 102:3
and flames of f are your .... Ps 104:4
and lit up the night with f. .... Ps 105:39
f burned among their followers, ... Ps 106:18
them into the f or into pits .... Ps 140:10
words are like a burning f. .... Pr 16:27
Without wood, a f will go out,................ Pr 26:20
and wood keep a f going, ... Pr 26:21
rain, and f that never says .... Pr 30:16
of thorns in a cooking f. .... Ec 7:6

flames and burns like a hot **f**. .... Sng 8:6
cities have been burned with **f**. .... Is 1:7
will be able to put out that **f**.'' .... Is 1:31
of fairness and the spirit of **f**. .... Is 4:4
a bright, flaming **f** at night. .... Is 4:5
destroyed just as **f** burns straw .... Is 5:24
creatures of **f** stood above him. .... Is 6:2
has been thrown into the **f**. .... Is 9:5
Evil is like a small **f**. .... Is 9:18
people are like fuel for the **f**; .... Is 9:19
burned up like a **f** burning until .... Is 10:16
of Israel, will be like a **f**; .... Is 10:17
will be like a **f** that suddenly .... Is 10:17
The **f** burns away the great trees .... Is 10:18
with their faces red like **f**. .... Is 13:8
Burn them in the **f** you have .... Is 26:11
winds, and a **f** that destroys. .... Is 29:6
coals from the **f** or to get water .... Is 30:14
anger is like a **f** with thick .... Is 30:27
his tongue is like a burning **f**. .... Is 30:27
like a great **f** that burns .... Is 30:30
and wide with much wood and **f**. .... Is 30:33
burning sulfur and set it on **f**. .... Is 30:33
f is in Jerusalem and whose .... Is 31:9
wind will burn you like **f**. .... Is 33:11
through this **f** that destroys? .... Is 33:14
can live near this **f** that burns .... Is 33:14
of these nations into the **f**, ... Is 37:19
of Israel had **f** all around them, ... Is 42:25
walk through **f**, you will not be .... Is 43:2
the wood for a **f** to keep himself .... Is 44:15
He also starts a **f** to bake his .... Is 44:15
burns half of the wood in the **f**. .... Is 44:16
He uses the **f** to cook his meat, ... Is 44:16
the wood in the **f** and used the .... Is 44:19
f will quickly burn them up. .... Is 47:14
from the power of the **f**. .... Is 47:14
nor like a **f** that you may sit .... Is 47:14
pure, but not by **f**, as silver is .... Is 48:10
He fans the **f** to make it hotter, ... Is 54:16
Like a **f** that burns twigs, ... Is 64:2
like a **f** that makes water boil, ... Is 64:2
now it has been burned with **f**, ... Is 64:11
a **f** that burns all the time, ... Is 65:5
is coming with **f** and his armies .... Is 66:15
punish them with flames of **f**. .... Is 66:15
will judge the people with **f**, ... Is 66:16
will spread among you like a **f**, ... Je 4:4
words I give you will be like **f**, ... Je 5:14
The **f** is fanned to make it .... Je 6:29
use the wood to make a **f**. .... Je 7:18
be like a hot **f** that no one can .... Je 7:20
as a person tests metal in a **f**. .... Je 9:7
he will set that tree on **f**, ... Je 11:16
like a hot **f**, and it will burn .... Je 15:14
made my anger burn like a hot **f**, ... Je 17:4
I will start a **f** at the gates of .... Je 17:27
their children in the **f** to Baal. .... Je 19:5
like a burning **f** inside me, ... Je 20:9
and he will burn it with **f**.' .... Je 21:10
will be like a **f** that no one can .... Je 21:12
I will start a **f** in your forests .... Je 21:14
beams and throw them into the **f**. .... Je 22:7
Isn't my message like a **f**?'' .... Je 23:29
of Babylon burned in the **f**.' .... Je 29:22
it and start a **f** to burn down .... Je 32:29
make a funeral **f** to honor you. .... Je 34:5
it, set it on **f**, and burn it .... Je 34:22
There was a **f** burning in a small .... Je 36:22
scroll was burned in the **f**. .... Je 36:23
of Judah had burned in the **f**. .... Je 36:32
Babylonians set **f** to the palace .... Je 39:8
will set **f** to the temples .... Je 43:12

But **f** started in Heshbon; .... Je 48:45
I will set **f** to the walls of .... Je 49:27
I will start a **f** in her towns,................. Je 50:32
Nebuzaradan set **f** to the Temple .... Je 52:13
He sent **f** from above that went .... La 1:13
like a flaming **f** that burns up .... La 2:3
his anger like **f** on the tents .... La 2:4
set **f** to Jerusalem, burning it .... La 4:11
around it and **f** flashing out of .... Eze 1:4
was in the center of the **f**. .... Eze 1:4
coals of **f** or like torches .... Eze 1:13
F went back and forth among the .... Eze 1:13
glowing metal with **f** inside. .... Eze 1:27
the waist down it looked like **f**, ... Eze 1:27
for your **f** to bake your bread. .... Eze 4:15
one-third with **f** in the middle................. Eze 5:2
into the **f** and burn them up. .... Eze 5:4
From there a **f** will spread to .... Eze 5:4
the waist down it looked like **f**, ... Eze 8:2
with coals of **f** from between .... Eze 10:2
Take **f** from between the wheels, ... Eze 10:6
his hand to the **f** that was among .... Eze 10:7
took some of the **f**, and put it .... Eze 10:7
the man took the **f** and went out. .... Eze 10:7
is thrown into the **f** for fuel, ... Eze 15:4
and the **f** burns up both ends and .... Eze 15:4
When the **f** has burned it .... Eze 15:5
wood of the vine as fuel for **f**. .... Eze 15:6
they came through one **f**, ... Eze 15:7
f will still destroy them. .... Eze 15:7
them up in **f** to the idols................. Eze 16:21
F spread from the vine's main .... Eze 19:14
their first children in the **f**. .... Eze 20:26
and sacrifice them in the **f**, ... Eze 20:31
to start a **f** in you that will .... Eze 20:47
I, the LORD, have started the **f**. .... Eze 20:48
you with the **f** of my anger. .... Eze 21:31
You will be like fuel for the **f**; .... Eze 21:32
melt them down in a blazing **f**. .... Eze 22:20
that was like **f** because of all .... Eze 22:31
in the **f** to be food for .... Eze 23:37
up the wood and light the **f**. .... Eze 24:10
be removed, even in the **f**. .... Eze 24:12
the gems that shined like **f**................. Eze 28:14
the gems that shined like **f**. .... Eze 28:16
I set on **f** the place where you................. Eze 28:18
lived, and the **f** burned you up. .... Eze 28:18
LORD when I set **f** to Egypt and................. Eze 30:8
empty and start a **f** in Zoan and .... Eze 30:14
I will set **f** to Egypt. Pelusium............. Eze 30:16
I will send **f** on Magog and those .... Eze 39:6
men and throw them into the **f**?'' .... Da 3:24
men walking around in the **f**. .... Da 3:25
and Abednego came out of the **f**. .... Da 3:26
saw that the **f** had not harmed .... Da 3:27
saved his servants from the **f**!................. Da 3:28
His throne was made from **f**, ... Da 7:9
his throne were blazing with **f**. .... Da 7:9
A river of **f** was flowing from in .... Da 7:10
was thrown into the burning **f**. .... Da 7:11
and his eyes were like **f**. .... Da 10:6
does not need to stir up the **f**. .... Hos 7:4
comes, it becomes a roaring **f**. .... Hos 7:6
I will send **f** on their cities .... Hos 8:14
because **f** has burned up the open .... Joe 1:19
and **f** has burned up the open .... Joe 1:20
In front of them a **f** destroys; .... Joe 2:3
of a roaring **f** burning dry .... Joe 2:5
blood, **f**, and thick smoke. .... Joe 2:30
So I will send **f** upon the house .... Am 1:4
So I will send a **f** on the walls................. Am 1:7
So I will send **f** on the walls of .... Am 1:10
So I will send **f** on the city of .... Am 1:12

I will send f on the city wall .... Am 1:14
So I will send f on Moab that .... Am 2:2
So I will send f on Judah, ... Am 2:5
a burning stick pulled from a f, ... Am 4:11
or he will move like f against .... Am 5:6
f will burn Bethel, and there .... Am 5:6
was calling for f to come down .... Am 7:4
will be like a f and the people................ Ob 1:18
set them on f and burn them up .... Ob 1:18
like wax near a f, like water .... Mic 1:4
her idols will be burned with f. .... Mic 1:7
His anger is poured out like f; .... Nah 1:6
flashes like f when they are .... Nah 2:3
f has burned the bars of your .... Nah 3:13
There the f will burn you up. .... Nah 3:15
will send f to destroy what .... Hab 2:13
will be like a f that will burn .... Zph 1:18
will be like f that will burn up .... Zph 3:8
will be a wall of f around it,' .... Zch 2:5
stick pulled from the f." .... Zch 3:2
her is like a f burning in me.".................. Zch 8:2
city will be destroyed by f. .... Zch 9:4
your gates so f may burn your .... Zch 11:1
Judah like a f burning a stack .... Zch 12:6
wood or like a f burning straw. .... Zch 12:6
that is left I will test with f,................. Zch 13:9
a purifying f and like laundry................ Mal 3:2
cut down and thrown into the f. .... Mt 3:10
you with the Holy Spirit and f. .... Mt 3:11
the chaff with a f that cannot .... Mt 3:12
be in danger of the f of hell. .... Mt 5:22
tomorrow is thrown into the f. .... Mt 6:30
cut down and thrown into the f. .... Mt 7:19
pulled up and burned in the f, ... Mt 13:40
into the f or into the water. .... Mt 17:15
thrown into the f that burns .... Mt 18:8
be thrown into the f of hell. .... Mt 18:9
Go into the f that burns forever .... Mt 25:41
him into a f or into water to .... Mk 9:22
where the f never goes out..................... Mk 9:43
not die; the f is never put out.................. Mk 9:44
not die; the f is never put out.................. Mk 9:46
not die; the f is never put out.................. Mk 9:48
person will be salted with f. .... Mk 9:49
warming himself by the f. .... Mk 14:54
himself at the f and looked .... Mk 14:67
cut down and thrown into the f." .... Lk 3:9
you with the Holy Spirit and f. .... Lk 3:16
the chaff with a f that cannot .... Lk 3:17
want us to call f down from .... Lk 9:54
tomorrow is thrown into the f. .... Lk 12:28
I came to set f to the world, ... Lk 12:49
I am suffering in this f!' .... Lk 16:24
f and sulfur rained down from .... Lk 17:29
started a f in the middle .... Lk 22:55
It felt like a f burning in us..................... Lk 24:32
them into the f, and burn them. .... Jn 15:6
had built a f and were standing .... Jn 18:18
they saw a f of hot coals. .... Jn 21:9
were fish on the f, and there .... Jn 21:9
like flames of f that were .... Ac 2:3
blood, f, and thick smoke. .... Ac 2:19
made a f and welcomed all of us. .... Ac 28:2
them on the f when a poisonous.............. Ac 28:3
off into the f and was not hurt. .... Ac 28:5
That Day will appear with f, ... 1Co 3:13
and the f will test everyone's 1Co 3:13
be as one who escaped from a f................ 1Co 3:15
with burning f from heaven with 2Th 1:7
as a small flame grows into a f. 2Ti 1:6
become like flames of f." .... Heb 1:7
God and will be destroyed by f. .... Heb 6:8
and the terrible f that will .... Heb 10:27

and that is burning with f. .... Heb 12:18
God is like a f that burns .... Heb 12:29
A big forest f can be started .... Jam 3:5
And the tongue is like a f. .... Jam 3:6
The tongue is set on f by hell,................. Jam 3:6
it starts a f that influences .... Jam 3:6
It will eat your bodies like f. .... Jam 5:3
to be pure by f but will ruin. 1Pe 1:7
in order to be destroyed by f. 2Pe 3:7
in them will be destroyed by f, ... 2Pe 3:10
skies will be destroyed with f, ... 2Pe 3:12
the punishment of eternal f, ... Jud 1:7
out of the f, and save them..................... Jud 1:23
his eyes were like flames of f.................. Rev 1:14
that blaze like f and feet like .... Rev 2:18
gold made pure in f so you can .... Rev 3:18
incense pan with f from the .... Rev 8:5
and hail and f mixed with blood.............. Rev 8:7
burning with f, was thrown..................... Rev 8:8
of lions, with f, smoke, and..................... Rev 9:17
f, the smoke, and the sulfur. .... Rev 9:18
his legs were like pillars of f. .... Rev 10:1
f comes from their mouths and .... Rev 11:5
that it even makes f come down .... Rev 13:13
has power over the f, came from .... Rev 14:18
a sea of glass mixed with f. .... Rev 15:2
power to burn the people with f............... Rev 16:8
her body and burn her with f.................. Rev 17:16
and she will be destroyed by f, ... Rev 18:8
His eyes are like burning f,.................... Rev 19:12
the lake of f that burns with .... Rev 19:20
But f came down from heaven and........... Rev 20:9
were thrown into the lake of f. .... Rev 20:14
lake of f is the second death. .... Rev 20:14
was thrown into the lake of f.................. Rev 20:15

FIRE'S

can see because of the f light." .... Is 44:16

FIRELIGHT

Peter sitting there in the f, ... Lk 22:56

FIREPOT

a smoking f and a blazing .... Ge 15:17
in a small f in front of him...................... Je 36:22
and threw them into the f. .... Je 36:23

FIRES

The f will burn night and day; .... Is 34:10
are not enough for the altar f,.................. Is 40:16
light your own f and make your .... Is 50:11
walk in the light of your f, ... Is 50:11
and the f that burn them will .... Is 66:24
made funeral f to honor your .... Je 34:5
out and make f with the enemy's .... Eze 39:9
burn in their f for seven years. .... Eze 39:9
they will make f with the .... Eze 39:10
not light useless f on my altar! .... Mal 1:10
stopped great f and were saved .... Heb 11:34

FIREWOOD

must put more f on the altar .... Le 6:12
so women will use them for f.................. Is 27:11
we must pay for the f............................. La 5:4
field or chop f from the forests .... Eze 39:10

FIRM

they were fat and full and f. .... Dt 32:15
and he was in f control of his 1Ki 2:12
He will take f hold of you .... Is 22:17
The mast is not held f. .... Is 33:23
leader will make f an agreement .... Da 9:27
Lebanon, their roots will be f.................. Hos 14:5
made between two persons is f. .... Gal 3:15

FIRMLY

that God has f decided that this .... Ge 41:32
that Ruth had f made up her mind .... Ru 1:18
that have been driven in f. .... Ec 12:11
F tied, Shadrach, Meshach, and .... Da 3:23
So f tell those people they are .... Tit 1:13
Let us hold f to the hope that .... Heb 10:23

FIRST

came. This was the f day. .... Ge 1:5
The f river, named Pishon, flows .... Ge 2:11
that by the f day of the tenth .... Ge 8:5
in the f day of the first month .... Ge 8:13
On the f day, you are to remove .... Ex 12:15
Offer to God the f things you .... Ex 23:16
stone tablets like the f two, ... Ex 34:1
during their f special time. .... Nu 6:12
The f one born to any family, ... Nu 18:15
fourteenth day of the f month. .... Nu 28:16
meeting on the f day of the .... Nu 29:1
fifteenth day of the f month, ... Nu 33:3
Give them the f of your grain, ... Dt 18:4
Who will be f to go and fight .... Jdg 1:1
death during the f days of the 2Sa 21:9
Give the baby to the f woman, ... 1Ki 3:27
on the first day of the f month, ... 2Ch 29:17
In the f year Cyrus was king of 2Ch 36:22
In the f year Cyrus was king of .... Ezr 1:1
who had seen the f Temple cried .... Ezr 3:12
is one of the f of God's works, ... Job 40:19
F we heard and now we have seen .... Ps 48:8
F, it burns weeds and thorns. .... Is 9:18
was the f one to tell Jerusalem .... Is 41:27
Your f father sinned, and your .... Is 43:27
F my people went down to Egypt .... Is 52:4
like a woman having her f child. .... Je 4:31
where I f made a place to be .... Je 7:12
f lion to eat them up was the .... Je 50:17
and was like the f pillar. .... Je 52:22
The f face was the face of a .... Eze 10:14
Belshazzar's f year as king of .... Da 7:1
The f animal looked like a lion, ... Da 7:4
which was like the f one. .... Da 8:1
between its eyes is the f king. .... Da 8:21
army, larger than the f one. .... Da 11:13
'I will go back to my f husband, ... Hos 2:7
finding the f figs on the fig .... Hos 9:10
Seek f God's kingdom and what .... Mt 6:33
F, take the wood out of your own .... Mt 7:5
f let me go and bury my father." .... Mt 8:21
he must f tie up the strong .... Mt 12:29
F gather the weeds and tie them .... Mt 13:30
say that Elijah must come f?" .... Mt 17:10
After you catch the f fish, ... Mt 17:27
Many who are f now will be last .... Mt 19:30
now will be f in the future. .... Mt 19:30
wants to become f among you must .... Mt 20:27
This is the f and most important .... Mt 22:38
F make the inside of the cup .... Mt 23:26
On the f day of the Feast of .... Mt 26:17
be even worse than the f one." .... Mt 27:64
day was the f day of the week. .... Mt 28:1
F the plant grows, then the head, ... Mk 4:28
say that Elijah must come f?" .... Mk 9:11
Elijah must come f and make .... Mk 9:12
The f brother married and died, ... Mk 12:20
things are like the f pains when .... Mk 13:8
was now the f day of the Feast .... Mk 14:12
that day, the f day of the week .... Mk 16:2
early on the f day of the week, ... Mk 16:9
This was the f registration; .... Lk 2:2
you f sit down and decide how .... Lk 14:28
these things must happen f, ... Lk 21:9

early on the f day of the week, ... Lk 24:1
The f thing Andrew did was to .... Jn 1:41
the f person to go into the pool .... Jn 5:4
can throw the f stone at her." .... Jn 8:7
place where John had f baptized. .... Jn 10:40
the legs of the f man on the .... Jn 19:32
Early on the f day of the week, ... Jn 20:1
Peter and reached the tomb f. .... Jn 20:4
who had reached the tomb f, ... Jn 20:8
on the f day of the week, ... Jn 20:19
Christians for the f time. .... Ac 11:26
the message of God to you f. .... Ac 13:46
F I want to say that I thank my .... Rm 1:8
to save the Jews f, and then to .... Rm 1:16
now than when we f believed. .... Rm 13:11
has given a place f to apostles, ... 1Co 12:28
is sitting, the f speaker should 1Co 14:30
The f man, Adam, became a living 1Co 15:45
On the f day of every week, ... 1Co 16:2
They f gave themselves to the 2Co 8:5
you were the f to want to give, ... 2Co 8:10
that I came to you the f time, ... Gal 4:13
We are the f people who hoped in .... Eph 1:12
It means that he f came down to .... Eph 4:9
This is the f command that has .... Eph 6:2
believing in Christ will rise f. 1Th 4:16
Adam was formed f and then Eve. 1Ti 2:13
That faith f lived in your 2Ti 1:5
should be the f person to get 2Ti 2:6
The f time I defended myself, ... 2Ti 4:16
Lord himself f told about this .... Heb 2:3
you again the f lessons of God's .... Heb 5:12
every day, f for their own sins, ... Heb 7:27
wrong with the f agreement, ... Heb 8:7
he has made the f agreement old. .... Heb 8:13
God ends the f system of .... Heb 10:9
comes from God is f of all pure, ... Jam 3:17
We love because God f loved us. 1Jn 4:19
f among those raised from the .... Rev 1:5
I am the F and the Last. .... Rev 1:17
hearts and do what you did at f. .... Rev 2:5
One who is the F and the Last, ... Rev 2:8
more now than you did at f. .... Rev 2:19
The f living creature was like a .... Rev 4:7
Lamb opened the f of the seven .... Rev 6:1
The f angel blew his trumpet, ... Rev 8:7
The f trouble is past; .... Rev 9:12
before the f beast and uses .... Rev 13:12
miracles to serve the f beast. .... Rev 13:14
to the idol of the f one so that .... Rev 13:15
followed the f angel and said, ... Rev 14:8
angel followed the f two angels, ... Rev 14:9
The f angel left and poured out .... Rev 16:2
He belongs to the f seven kings, ... Rev 17:11
is the f raising of the dead. .... Rev 20:5
who share in this f raising of .... Rev 20:6
The f heaven and the first earth .... Rev 21:1
The f foundation was jasper, ... Rev 21:19
the Omega, the F and the Last, ... Rev 22:13

FIRSTBORN

from some of the f of his flock. .... Ge 4:4
I am your son—your f son—Esau." .... Ge 27:32
the head of Manasseh, the f son. .... Ge 48:14
Israel is my f son. .... Ex 4:22
so I will kill your f son.' " .... Ex 4:23
Every f son in the land of Egypt .... Ex 11:5
Give every f male to me. .... Ex 13:12
Buy back every f donkey by .... Ex 13:13
place of all the f children of .... Nu 3:12
because the f are mine. .... Nu 3:13
for every f child and every .... Nu 18:15
has the majesty of a f bull; .... Dt 33:17

killed all the **f** sons in Egypt, ... Ps 78:51
father, and Israel is my **f** son. .... Je 31:9
as someone who has lost a **f** son. .... Zch 12:10
Every **f** male shall be given to .... Lk 2:23
would be the **f** of many brothers............. Rm 8:29
God brings his **f** Son into the .... Heb 1:6
meeting of God's **f** children .... Heb 12:23

FIRSTFRUITS
the best of the **f** of your land .... Ex 23:19
On the day of **f** when you bring .... Nu 28:26
wealth and the **f** from all your .... Pr 3:9

FISH
them rule over the **f** in the sea .... Ge 1:26
Rule over the **f** in the sea and................ Ge 1:28
Then the **f** in the Nile will die, ... Ex 7:18
remember the **f** we ate for free .... Nu 11:5
or of **f** in the water below. .... Dt 4:18
birds, crawling things, and **f.** 1Ki 4:33
entrance of the F Gate and 2Ch 33:14
in the sky, the **f** in the sea, ... Ps 8:8
into blood and made their **f** die. .... Ps 105:29
and their **f** rot because there is .... Is 50:2
caused a big **f** to swallow Jonah .... Jnh 1:17
was inside the **f** three days and .... Jnh 1:17
Or if your children ask for a **f,** .... Mt 7:10
of the big **f** for three days .... Mt 12:40
five loaves of bread and two **f.**" .... Mt 14:17
took the five loaves and two **f**................ Mk 6:41
leftover pieces of bread and **f.** .... Mk 6:43
also had a few small **f.** .... Mk 8:7
caught so many **f** that the nets .... Lk 5:6
If your children ask for a **f,**................ Lk 11:11
gave him a piece of broiled **f.** .... Lk 24:42
barley bread and two little **f,** .... Jn 6:9
was full of big **f,** one hundred............... Jn 21:11
another, and **f** have another. 1Co 15:39

FISHED
They **f** that night but caught .... Jn 21:3

FISHERMEN
the lake because they were **f.** .... Mt 4:18

FISHHOOKS
and what is left of you with **f.**................ Am 4:2

FISHING
or fill its head with **f** spears? .... Job 41:7
be a place for drying **f** nets. .... Eze 26:14
will be places to spread **f** nets. .... Eze 47:10

FISHNET
his net and drags them in his **f.** .... Hab 1:15

FIST
other with a rock or with his **f,** .... Ex 21:18
Balaam, and he pounded his **f.** .... Nu 24:10
the size of a human **f,** coming............... 1Ki 18:44
shake their **f** at Mount Zion, ... Is 10:32
I will shake my **f** at you for.................... Eze 22:13
raise your **f** in victory over .... Mic 5:9

FISTS
they shake their **f** at God and .... Job 15:25
and hit each other with your **f.** .... Is 58:4
will make fun and shake their **f.**............... Zph 2:15
face and beat him with their **f.** .... Mt 26:67
beat him with their **f** and said, ... Mk 14:65

FIT
he will grow food **f** for a king. .... Ge 49:20
In a bowl **f** for a ruler, she .... Jdg 5:25
make Babylon **f** only for owls................. Is 14:23
purple clothes **f** for a king and .... Da 5:7
you purple clothes **f** for a king .... Da 5:16
make him more **f** for hell than .... Mt 23:15

FITTING
it, a peg **f** into each base. .... Ex 26:19

FIVE
for the lack of **f** good people?" .... Ge 18:28
was given **f** times more food .... Ge 43:34
for a man **f** to twenty years................... Le 27:5
Then these **f** Amorite kings— .... Jos 10:5
f Philistine leaders at Gaza, ... Jos 13:3
Make **f** gold models of the 1Sa 6:4
also wrote one thousand **f** songs. 1Ki 4:32
At that time **f** cities in Egypt .... Is 19:18
F enemies will make threats, ... Is 30:17
we have lots of loaves of bread .... Mt 14:17
There were about **f** thousand men .... Mt 14:21
were foolish and **f** were wise.................. Mt 25:2
gave one servant **f** bags of gold,.............. Mt 25:15
out of her house for **f** months. .... Lk 1:24
F sparrows are sold for only two .... Lk 12:6
I earned **f** coins with your one.' .... Lk 19:18
'You can rule over **f** cities.' .... Lk 19:19
Really you have had **f** husbands, ... Jn 4:18
There were now about **f** thousand .... Ac 4:4
rather speak **f** words I........................... 1Co 14:19
was seen by more than **f** hundred 1Co 15:6
F times the Jews have given me 2Co 11:24
pain to the people for **f** months. .... Rev 9:5
to hurt people for **f** months. .... Rev 9:10
F of the kings have already been .... Rev 17:10

FIVE-SIDED
These doors had **f** frames. 1Ki 6:31

FIX
this Temple and **f** these walls?" .... Ezr 5:3
If he doesn't **f** it, the house .... Ec 10:18
of Israel, **f** the road signs. .... Je 31:21

FIXED
her eye makeup and **f** her hair. 2Ki 9:30
is built and its walls are **f,** .... Ezr 4:13
city is rebuilt and its walls **f,** .... Ezr 4:16
their hair **f** in fancy ways, ... Is 3:24

FIXING
They are **f** the walls and .... Ezr 4:12

FLAME
LORD went up to heaven in the **f.** .... Jdg 13:20
A **f** will dry up their branches; .... Job 15:30
and the **f** in their lamps will .... Job 18:5
wicked is like a **f** going out. .... Pr 13:9
die like a **f** that is put out .... Pr 24:20
cannot put out the **f** of love; .... Sng 8:7
the Holy One will be like a **f.** .... Is 10:17
grass or put out even a weak **f.** .... Is 42:3
destroyed as a **f** is put out. .... Is 43:17
salvation burns bright like a **f.** .... Is 62:1
in back of them a **f** burns. .... Joe 2:3
the people of Joseph like a **f.** .... Ob 1:18
out even a weak **f** until he makes .... Mt 12:20
as a small **f** grows into a fire. 2Ti 1:6
be started with only a little **f.** .... Jam 3:5

FLAMES
bursts into **f** and burns like..................... Sng 8:6

FLAMING
he has made his **f** arrows. .... Ps 7:13
There God broke the **f** arrows, ... Ps 76:3
with a bright, **f** fire at night. .... Is 4:5
Jacob like a **f** fire that burns .... La 2:3

FLAP
wings of the ostrich **f** happily, ... Job 39:13

FLASH
Why do your eyes **f** with anger? .... Job 15:12
and makes his lightning **f?** .... Job 37:15

s voice makes the lightning **f**. .... Ps 29:7
is polished to **f** like lightning. .... Eze 21:10
is made to **f** like lightning. .... Eze 21:15
destroy, to **f** like lightning! .... Eze 21:28
they saw the **f** of your flying .... Hab 3:11

FLASHED
Your lightning **f** back and forth .... Ps 77:17

FLASHES
presence came **f** of lightning. 2Sa 22:13
f of light are thrown out, ... Job 41:18
on the chariots **f** like fire when .... Nah 2:3
f across the sky and lights .... Lk 17:24
Lightning **f** and noises and .... Rev 4:5
and there were **f** of lightning, ... Rev 8:5
Then there were **f** of lightning, ... Rev 11:19
Then there were **f** of lightning, ... Rev 16:18

FLAT
and bowed down **f** on the ground .... Ge 33:3
they tied this **f** piece to the .... Ex 39:31
them into **f** sheets that will .... Nu 16:38
hammered into **f** sheets to put .... Nu 16:39
tent turned over and fell **f**!" .... Jdg 7:13
quickly fell **f** on the ground 1Sa 28:20
Let's fight them on the **f** land, ... 1Ki 20:23
fight the Israelites on **f** land, ... 1Ki 20:25
we are **f** on the ground. .... Ps 44:25
makes the ground **f** and smooth. .... Is 28:25
and hill should be made **f**. .... Is 40:4
you and make the mountains **f**. .... Is 45:2
you will become **f** land, ... Zch 4:7
and hill should be made **f**. .... Lk 3:5

FLATTER
to everyone and not **f** anyone. .... Job 32:21
know how to **f**, and if I did, my .... Job 32:22
and they **f** others to get what .... Jud 1:16

FLATTERING
will stop those **f** lips and cut .... Ps 12:3

FLAVOR
and there is no **f** in the white .... Job 6:6

FLAX
The **f** was in bloom, and the .... Ex 9:31
under stalks of **f** that she had .... Jos 2:6
for wool and **f** and likes to work .... Pr 31:13
make cloth from **f** will be sad, ... Is 19:9
water, wool and **f**, wine and .... Hos 2:5

FLEA
are chasing a dead dog or a **f**. 1Sa 24:14
has come out looking for a **f**! 1Sa 26:20

FLED
ancestor Jacob **f** to Northwest .... Hos 12:12

FLEEING
His hand stabs the **f** snake. .... Job 26:13

FLESH
forever, because they are **f**. .... Ge 6:3
"You are my own **f** and blood." .... Ge 29:14
brother, our own **f** and blood." .... Ge 37:27
and the birds will eat your **f**." .... Ge 40:19
with half of its **f** eaten away. .... Nu 12:12
any of the **f** of his children .... Dt 28:55
my sword will eat their **f**. .... Dt 32:42
and destroy his **f** and bones, ... Job 2:5
of stone; my **f** is not bronze. .... Job 6:12
You dressed me with skin and **f**; .... Job 10:11
their bellies are fat with **f**, ... Job 15:27
in my **f** I will see God. .... Job 19:26
trouble you to eat their own **f**. .... Is 49:26
are circumcised only in the **f**: .... Je 9:25
He wore out my **f** and skin and .... La 3:4
them an obedient heart of **f**. .... Eze 11:19

scatter your **f** on the mountains .... Eze 32:5
ravines will be full of your **f**. .... Eze 32:6
give you obedient hearts of **f**. .... Eze 36:26
on you and **f** on you and cover .... Eze 37:6
the bones, and **f** grew, and skin .... Eze 37:8
Israel. Eat **f** and drink blood! .... Eze 39:17
are to eat the **f** of the mighty .... Eze 39:18
The **f** for the offering was put .... Eze 40:43
in the **f** and had not given .... Eze 44:7
circumcised in **f** and who do not .... Eze 44:9
and tear the **f** off their bones. .... Mic 3:2
eat my people's **f** and skin them .... Mic 3:3
Their **f** will rot away while they .... Zch 14:12
This bread is my **f**, which I will .... Jn 6:51
this man give us his **f** to eat?" .... Jn 6:52
you must eat the **f** of the Son of .... Jn 6:53
Those who eat my **f** and drink my .... Jn 6:54
My **f** is true food, and my blood .... Jn 6:55
Those who eat my **f** and drink my .... Jn 6:56
The **f** doesn't give life. .... Jn 6:63
things made of **f** are not the 1Co 15:39
people have one kind of **f**, ... 1Co 15:39
F and blood cannot have a part 1Co 15:50

FLEW
It **f** here and there until the .... Ge 8:7
large birds **f** down to eat the .... Ge 15:11
a creature with wings and **f**. 2Sa 22:11
a creature with wings and **f**. .... Ps 18:10
he **f** to me with the hot coal .... Is 6:6
Then the living creatures **f** up. .... Eze 10:15
their wings and **f** up from the .... Eze 10:19

FLIES
He also made every bird that **f**, ... Ge 1:21
send swarms of **f** into your .... Ex 8:21
The **f** will be on you, your .... Ex 8:21
of Egypt will be full of **f**, ... Ex 8:21
will not be any **f** in the land of .... Ex 8:22
and great swarms of **f** came into .... Ex 8:24
over Egypt **f** were ruining the .... Ex 8:24
will take the **f** away from you, ... Ex 8:29
He removed the **f** from the king, ... Ex 8:31
If the ax head **f** off the handle, ... Dt 19:5
that the hawk **f** and spreads its .... Job 39:26
He sent **f** that bit the people. .... Ps 78:45
The LORD spoke and **f** came, ... Ps 105:31
the way an eagle **f** in the sky, ... Pr 30:19
Dead **f** can make even perfume .... Ec 10:1
will come like **f** from Egypt's .... Is 7:18
F are spread out like your bed .... Is 14:11
and its people will die like **f**. .... Is 51:6

FLINT
But Zipporah took a **f** knife and .... Ex 4:25
Make knives from **f** stones and .... Jos 5:2
made knives from **f** stones and .... Jos 5:3
the rocks of **f** and dig away at .... Job 28:9

FLIRT
and they **f** with their eyes. .... Is 3:16

FLOAT
it with tar so that it would **f**. .... Ex 2:3
them together and **f** them along 1Ki 5:9
and it made the iron head **f**. 2Ki 6:6
Tyre so they would **f** cedar logs .... Ezr 3:7

FLOATED
boat it on it above the earth. .... Ge 7:18

FLOATING
are like foam **f** on the water. .... Job 24:18
a chip of wood **f** on the water. .... Hos 10:7

FLOCK
some of the firstborn of his **f**. .... Ge 4:4
and dark animals in Laban's **f**. .... Ge 30:40

troughs for their father's f. .... Ex 2:16
was taking care of Jethro's f. .... Ex 3:1
priest a male sheep from the f, ... Le 5:18
them some of your f, your grain, ... Dt 15:14
out their children like a f; .... Job 21:11
sheep so he could lead the f, ... Ps 78:71
hair is like a f of goats .... Sng 4:1
hair is like a f of goats .... Sng 6:5
Where is the f God gave you to .... Je 13:20
like the goats that lead the f. .... Je 50:8
are like a f of sheep that are .... Je 50:17
the best of the f, and pile wood .... Eze 24:5
but you do not feed the f. .... Eze 34:3
not let them tend the f anymore. .... Eze 34:10
will feed my f and lead them to .... Eze 34:15
people grow in number like a f. .... Eze 36:37
tending the f and said to me, ... Am 7:15
animal, herd or f, will be......................... Jnh 3:7
a pen, like a f in its pasture; .... Mic 2:12
Feed the f that are about to be .... Zch 11:4
So I fed the f about to be .... Zch 11:7
fear, little f, because your .... Lk 12:32
sheep that are not in this f, ... Jn 10:16
shepherd God's f, for whom you............... 1Pe 5:2

FLOCKS
has given him many f of sheep, ... Ge 24:35
of all the f that were left.......................... Ge 30:36
so the f mated in front of the .... Ge 30:39
careful with my f and their .... Ge 33:13
where they are grazing the f?" .... Ge 37:16
will take one-tenth of your f, ... 1Sa 8:17
He had many f and herds, because........... 2Ch 32:29
they steal f and take them to .... Job 24:2
large herds and f, more than .... Ec 2:7
F will wander freely in those .... Is 17:2
of Sharon will be a field for f,................. Is 65:10
for—their f and herds, their .... Je 3:24
where they let their f rest. .... Je 33:12
be as many as the f brought to .... Eze 36:38
even the f of sheep suffer. .... Joe 1:18
watchtower of the f, hill of .... Mic 4:8
F and herds will lie down there, ... Zph 2:14
along with his sons and f?" .... Jn 4:12

FLOOD
Seven days later the f started.................. Ge 7:10
all living things by a f. .... Ge 9:11
the f Noah lived 350 years. .... Ge 9:28
Fears come over them like a f, ... Job 27:20
The LORD controls the f. .... Ps 29:10
They surround me daily like a f;............... Ps 88:17
like a sudden f of water pouring............... Is 28:2
I would never f the world again................ Is 54:9
of the city will come like a f, ... Da 9:26
In those days before the f, ... Mt 24:38
until the f came and destroyed .... Mt 24:39
the f came and killed them all. .... Lk 17:27
he brought a f to the world that 2Pe 2:5
woman so the f would carry her............... Rev 12:15

FLOODED
f the earth for forty days, ... Ge 7:17
the world was f and destroyed 2Pe 3:6

FLOODING
was like the noise of f water. .... Rev 1:15
the noise of f water and like .... Rev 14:2
like the noise of f water, ... Rev 19:6

FLOODS
F will never again destroy all .... Ge 9:15
when the Jordan f the valley. 1Ch 12:15
If the river f, it will not be .... Job 40:23
flame of love; f cannot drown .... Sng 8:7
rained hard, the f came, and the............... Mt 7:25

rained hard, the f came, and the............... Mt 7:27
When the f came, the water tried .... Lk 6:48
When the f came, the house .... Lk 6:49

FLOOR
dirt from the f of the Holy Tent .... Nu 5:17
offering from the threshing f. .... Nu 15:20
the threshing f and winepress. .... Dt 16:13
came here to the threshing f." .... Ru 3:14
by the threshing f of Araunah 2Sa 24:16
which reached from f to ceiling............... 1Ki 6:16
the threshing f of Araunah the 1Ch 21:15
of grain to the threshing f. .... Mic 4:12
to the ground from the third f. .... Ac 20:9
or, "Sit on the f by my feet." .... Jam 2:3

FLOORS
grain from the threshing f." 1Sa 23:1
The f of both rooms were covered 1Ki 6:30
And the threshing f will be full .... Joe 2:24

FLOUR
Use fine wheat f without yeast .... Ex 29:2
it must be made from fine f. .... Le 2:1
and with twenty quarts of f, ... Jdg 6:19
bushel of f, and a leather bag.................. 1Sa 1:24
a handful of f in a jar and only 1Ki 17:12
stones to grind grain into f. .... Is 47:2
a large tub of f until it made .... Mt 13:33
oil, fine f, wheat, cattle, ... Rev 18:13

FLOW
the breezes, and the waters f. .... Ps 147:18
That water will f into Judah and............. Is 8:8
He made water f from a rock for .... Is 48:21
water will f from our eyelids. .... Je 9:18
have stopped the f of wine from .... Je 48:33
My tears f continually, without .... La 3:49
milk will f from the hills, ... Joe 3:18
But let justice f like a river,.................... Am 5:24
water will f from Jerusalem. .... Zch 14:8
living water will f out from .... Jn 7:38
and bad water f from the same .... Jam 3:11

FLOWED
A river f through Eden and..................... Ge 2:10
from which a spring of water f. .... Ge 26:19
a stream that f down the .... Dt 9:21
and spears until their blood f,................. 1Ki 18:28
His blood f down to the bottom 1Ki 22:35
the stream that f through the 2Ch 32:4
poured out and rivers f down................... Ps 78:20
split the rock, and water f out; .... Ps 105:41
things would have f to you like .... Is 48:18
split the rock, and water f out. .... Is 48:21
Rivers f around the bottom of................. Eze 31:4
The water f down from the south .... Eze 47:1
your powerful waves f over me. .... Jnh 2:3
rushing water f. The sea made .... Hab 3:10
and blood f out of the winepress .... Rev 14:20

FLOWER
we grow like a f in the field. .... Ps 103:15
wind blows, the f is gone, and .... Ps 103:16
rot and whose f dies and blows .... Is 5:24
will produce flowers. Like a f, ... Is 35:1
die like a wild f in the grass. .... Jam 1:10
The f falls off, and its beauty .... Jam 1:11

FLOWER-LIKE
Its base, stand, f cups, buds, ... Ex 25:31
f cups, buds, and petals were .... Ex 37:17

FLOWERS
be like the f of the fields; .... Ps 37:20
will be like f in your hair .... Pr 1:9
like a bunch of f from the .... Sng 1:14
fruit, filled with f and nard, ... Sng 4:13

FLOWING

crown of f is just a dying .... Is 28:1
and the f of Lebanon dry up. .... Nah 1:4
beautifully as one of these f. .... Mt 6:29
some bulls and f to the city .... Ac 14:13
is like the f of the field. 1Pe 1:24

FLOWING

underground springs stopped f, ... Ge 8:2
or the rivers f with honey and .... Job 20:17
but wisdom is like a f stream. .... Pr 18:4
well of fresh water f down from .... Sng 4:15
of the river, f over the land. .... Is 8:7
Its cool, f streams do not dry .... Je 18:14
under the doorway and f east. .... Eze 47:1
of fire was f from in front .... Da 7:10
crystal and was f from the .... Rev 22:1

FLOWN

bird in the sky had f away. .... Je 4:25
The birds have f away, and the .... Je 9:10

FLOWS

f around the whole land of .... Ge 2:11
f around the whole land of Cush. .... Ge 2:13
f out of Assyria toward the east. .... Ge 2:14
if the fluid f freely or if it .... Le 15:3
the Jordan River f into the sea. .... Jos 18:19
the canal that f toward Ahava, ... Ezr 8:15
like water that f away. .... Ps 58:7
where the water f into the upper .... Is 7:3
the olive oil f to the lamps?" .... Zch 4:12

FLUTE

person to play the harp and f. .... Ge 4:21
sound of the f makes them happy .... Job 21:12
and my f is tuned to moaning. .... Job 30:31
for Moab like a f playing a .... Je 48:36
It cries like a f for the people .... Je 48:36
make sounds—like a f or a harp. 1Co 14:7

FLUTES

tambourines, f, and lyres, ... 1Sa 10:5
Playing f and shouting for joy, ... 1Ki 1:40
of music. For f. A psalm of .... Ps 4:8
with stringed instruments and f. .... Ps 150:4
harps, tambourines, f, and wine. .... Is 5:12
listening to f as they come to .... Is 30:29
of the horns, f, lyres, zithers, ... Da 3:5
of the horns, f, lyres, zithers, ... Da 3:7
of the horns, f, lyres, zithers, ... Da 3:15
instruments, f, and trumpets, ... Rev 18:22

FLUTTERS

its nest that f over its young. .... Dt 32:11

FLY

and let birds f in the air above .... Ge 1:20
so that not one f was left. .... Ex 8:31
or birds that f in the air, ... Dt 4:17
as surely as sparks f upward. .... Job 5:7
they f away without my seeing .... Job 9:25
They will f away like a dream. .... Job 20:8
eagle to f and build its nest. .... Job 39:27
F like a bird to your mountain. .... Ps 11:1
Then I would f away and rest. .... Ps 55:6
to grow wings and f away like an .... Pr 23:5
swallows that f around and never .... Pr 26:2
a bird might f and tell what you .... Ec 10:20
their wings to f up from the .... Eze 10:16
birds in their branches f away. .... Da 4:14
glory will f away like a bird; .... Hos 9:11
if you f high like the eagle .... Ob 1:4
strip the land and then f away. .... Nah 3:16
comes up, they f away, and no .... Nah 3:17
who picks a f out of a drink .... Mt 23:24
so she could f to the place .... Rev 12:14

FLYING

like a bird f away from a. .... Pr 6:5
Jerusalem, like an army f flags. .... Sng 6:4
as wonderful as an army f flags. .... Sng 6:10
its feet, and two wings for f. .... Is 6:2
like birds f over their nests. .... Is 31:5
like doves f to their nests. .... Is 60:8
came f quickly to me about the .... Da 9:21
the flash of your f arrows and .... Hab 3:11
up again and saw a f scroll. .... Zch 5:1
I see a f scroll, thirty .... Zch 5:2
The fourth was like a f eagle. .... Rev 4:7
eagle that was f high in the air .... Rev 8:13
another angel f high in the air .... Rev 14:6
to all the birds f in the sky: .... Rev 19:17

FOAM

They are like f floating on the .... Job 24:18
even if the oceans roar and f, ... Ps 46:3
of himself and f at the mouth. .... Lk 9:39
own shameful actions like f. .... Jud 1:13

FOAMING

on the ground, f at the mouth. .... Mk 9:20

FOAMS

Then my son f at the mouth, ... Mk 9:18

FOCUSED

Keep your eyes f on what is .... Pr 4:25

FOE

Our enemy and f is this wicked .... Est 7:6

FOES

my f like those who are wrong. .... Job 27:7
us from our f, and you made our .... Ps 44:7
turn my hand against their f. .... Ps 81:14
and the water covered their f. .... Ps 106:11
Her f are now her masters. .... La 1:5
that enemies and f could enter .... La 4:12

FOG

surrounded by f and clouds. 2Sa 22:12
surrounded by f and clouds. .... Ps 18:11

FOLD

F the sixth curtain double over .... Ex 26:9
You f your hands and lie down to .... Pr 6:10
You f your hands and lie down to .... Pr 24:33
is foolish to f your hands and .... Ec 4:5
carries in the f of his clothes .... Hag 2:12
If that f touches bread, cooked .... Hag 2:12
You will f them like a coat. .... Heb 1:12

FOLDED

and f double to make a pocket. .... Ex 28:16
was f double to make a pocket. .... Ex 39:9
had two parts so the doors f. 1Ki 6:34
which was f up and laid in a .... Jn 20:7

FOLDS

I shook out the f of my robe and .... Ne 5:13
stand out like f in a coat. .... Job 38:14
The f of its skin are tightly .... Job 41:23
the king is captured in its f. .... Sng 7:5
them in the f of your clothes. .... Eze 5:3

FOLLOW

I will f you slowly and let the .... Ge 33:14
LORD your God and f other gods .... Dt 8:19
over you must f the LORD your 1Sa 12:14
gave. Should we f it? If not, ... 2Sa 17:6
wrong and did not f the LORD 1Ki 11:6
the true God, f him, but if Baal 1Ki 18:21
F me and I'll take you to the 2Ki 6:19
F all the teachings that I 2Ki 17:13
of the LORD to f the LORD and 2Ki 23:3
They try to f God; they look to .... Ps 24:6
all who are honest will f it. .... Ps 94:15

and they f other gods to serve ....Je 13:10
said, "Come f me, and I will ....Mt 4:19
I will f you any place you go." ....Mt 8:19
Jesus told him, "F me, and let ....Mt 8:22
the cross and f me is not worthy.............Mt 10:38
people want to f me, they must ....Mt 16:24
in heaven. Then come and f me." ....Mt 19:21
to them, "Come f me, and I will ....Mk 1:17
"I will f you any place you go." ....Lk 9:57
Philip and said to him, "F me." ....Jn 1:43
and they f him because they know ....Jn 10:4
I know them, and they f me. ....Jn 10:27
I am going you cannot f now, ...Jn 13:36
"Put on your coat and f me." ....Ac 12:8
for those who refuse to f it......................1Ti 1:9
this so you can f them and fight 1Ti 1:18
that would f those sufferings 1Pe 1:11
and gave you an example to f. 1Pe 2:21
good for you to f closely what 2Pe 1:19
They f the Lamb every place he ....Rev 14:4

FOLLOWED
the elders of Israel f him. ....Nu 16:25
people have not f me completely. ....Nu 32:11
Agreement with the LORD f them............Jos 6:8
Elisha left and f Elijah and 1Ki 19:21
men f the Aramean army as far 2Ki 7:15
He f the ways of the kings of 2Ki 8:18
Ahaziah f the ways of Ahab's.................2Ki 8:27
they f the same gods as their ....Am 2:4
gods as their ancestors had f....................Am 2:4
left their nets and f him. ....Mt 4:20
their father, and they f Jesus. ....Mt 4:22
across the Jordan River f him. ....Mt 4:25
the hill, great crowds f him. ....Mt 8:1
there, two blind men f him......................Mt 9:27
have left everything and f you. ....Mt 19:27
Peter f far behind to the ....Mt 26:58
women who had f Jesus from ....Mt 27:55
Peter f far behind and entered ....Mk 14:54
left everything and f Jesus. ....Lk 5:11
to see, and he f Jesus, thanking ....Lk 18:43
the two men who f Jesus after ....Jn 1:40
to worship God f Paul and ....Ac 13:43
that spiritual rock that f them, ...1Co 10:4
But you have f what I teach, ...2Ti 3:10
to be f until the time of God's...............Heb 9:10
lived long ago and f God made 1Pe 3:5
They have f the way of Cain, ...Jud 1:11
Thyatira have not f her teaching............Rev 2:24
was amazed and f the beast. ....Rev 13:3
second angel f the first angel ....Rev 14:8
a third angel f the first two ....Rev 14:9

FOLLOWERS
called, chosen, and faithful f." ....Rev 17:14

FOLLOWING
who continued f the LORD your..............Dt 4:4
The Israelites quit f the LORD ....Jdg 2:13
to leave you or to stop f you. ....Ru 1:16
f the evil example of the other 2Ch 36:14
and we haven't stopped f you. ....Ps 44:18
Jesus turned and saw them f him, ...Jn 1:38
Then f him, Simon Peter arrived.............Jn 20:6
lost their way, f the way Balaam..............2Pe 2:15

FOLLOWS
hunger that f will be so great..................Ge 41:31
to anyone who f him in being.................Le 20:5
differently and f me completely...............Nu 14:24
is chasing him f him to that ....Jos 20:5
with a sword anyone who f her." 2Ki 11:15
with a sword anyone who f her." 2Ch 23:14
Everybody f after them, and many ....Job 21:33

end of the sky and f its path to ....Ps 19:6
Disaster f disaster; ....Je 4:20
One messenger f another; ....Je 51:31
messenger f messenger. ....Je 51:31
One murder f another..........................Hos 4:2
him, and disease f behind him. ....Hab 3:5
The person who f me will never ....Jn 8:12
a person changes and f the Lord, ...2Co 3:16
A person who f all of God's law ....Jam 2:10

FONDLE
Don't f a woman who is not your ....Pr 5:20

FOOD
in them. They will be f for you. ....Ge 1:29
green plants as f for every wild ....Ge 1:30
that was good for f to grow out ....Ge 2:9
Then Laban gave the servant f, ...Ge 24:33
the land of Canaan to buy f." ....Ge 42:7
wife from having f or clothing ....Ex 21:10
these parts on the altar as f; ....Le 3:11
these parts on the altar as f. ....Le 3:16
It will be f for your men and ....Le 25:6
bodies will be f for all the ....Dt 28:26
awhile, I would not eat your f. ....Jdg 13:16
It shared his f and drank from 2Sa 12:3
come in and give me f to eat. 2Sa 13:5
Bring the f into the bedroom so 2Sa 13:10
who gathered f from their 1Ki 4:7
The f made him strong enough to 1Ki 19:8
Give them f and water, and let 2Ki 6:22
Tasteless f is not eaten without ....Job 6:6
touch it; such f makes me sick. ....Job 6:7
words as the tongue tastes f. ....Job 34:3
is how he gives us enough f. ....Job 36:31
Who gives f to the birds when ....Job 38:41
night, my tears have been my f. ....Ps 42:3
They wander about looking for f, ...Ps 59:15
put poison in my f and gave me ....Ps 69:21
them all the f they could eat. ....Ps 78:25
You make f grow from the earth. ....Ps 104:14
They look to God for f. ....Ps 104:21
give them their f at the right ....Ps 104:27
He gives f to every living ....Ps 136:25
He gives f to the hungry.......................Ps 146:7
they store up f in the summer.................Pr 6:8
you will have plenty of f. ....Pr 20:13
Stolen f may taste sweet at ....Pr 20:17
share their f with the poor. ....Pr 22:9
notice the f that is in front of ....Pr 23:1
because that f might be a trick. ....Pr 23:3
ship, bringing f from far away. ....Pr 31:14
and prepares f for her family ....Pr 31:15
the trees will be used for f, ...Eze 47:12
me to give you this f and drink. ....Da 1:10
bringing unclean f to my altar. ....Mal 1:7
so there will be f in my house. ....Mal 3:10
For f, he ate locusts and wild ....Mt 3:4
worry about the f or drink you ....Mt 6:25
their f at the right time? ....Mt 24:45
I was hungry, and you gave me f. ....Mt 25:35
unless we go buy f for all these ....Lk 9:13
is more than f, and the body is ....Lk 12:23
them, "Do you have any f here?" ....Lk 24:41
were in town buying some f. ....Jn 4:8
I have f to eat that you know ....Jn 4:32
My f is to do what the One who ....Jn 4:34
work for the f that spoils. ....Jn 6:27
flesh is true f, and my blood is ....Jn 6:55
served the f, and Lazarus was ....Jn 12:2
gone without f for a long time ....Ac 27:21
faith by eating f he thinks is ....Rm 14:15
milk, not solid f, because you 1Co 3:2
But f will not bring us closer 1Co 8:8

So if the f I eat causes them to 1Co 8:13
all ate the same spiritual f, ... 1Co 10:3
"That f was offered to idols," 1Co 10:28
to the farmer and bread for f. 2Co 9:10
times I have been without f. 2Co 11:27
But solid f is for those who are .... Heb 5:14
were only about f and drink and .... Heb 9:10
Christ might need clothes or f. .... Jam 2:15
sin by eating f offered to idols .... Rev 2:14
and to eat f that is offered .... Rev 2:20

FOODS

some of the best f in our land .... Ge 43:11
as if I had eaten the best f. .... Ps 63:5
of the best f and olive oil, ... Pr 21:20
Don't be greedy for his fine f, ... Pr 23:3
be greedy for their fine f. .... Pr 23:6
once ate fine f are now starving .... La 4:5
If he touches any of these f, ... Hag 2:13
the one who eats all f is wrong, ... Rm 14:3
refuse to eat some f do that for .... Rm 14:6
All f are all right to eat, ... Rm 14:20
to eat certain f which God 1Ti 4:3
not by obeying rules about f, ... Heb 13:9

FOOL

Did Abner die like a f? 2Sa 3:33
Whoever tells lies is a f. .... Pr 10:18
A f will be a servant to the .... Pr 11:29
a warning than a f will learn .... Pr 17:10
A f should not live in luxury. .... Pr 19:10
spoken by a f is as useless as .... Pr 26:7
spoken by a f is like a thorn .... Pr 26:9
A f who repeats his foolishness .... Pr 26:11
the f only shouts or laughs, ... Pr 29:9
person and the f will both die, ... Ec 2:16
than to be praised by a f. .... Ec 7:5
A f talks too much. No one knows ...... Ec 10:14
You think the prophet is a f, ... Hos 9:7
And if you call someone a f, ... Mt 5:22
not f yourselves. If you think 1Co 3:18
and brag. (I am talking as a f.) 2Co 11:21
would not be a f, because I 2Co 12:6

FOOLISH

the LORD, you f and unwise .... Dt 32:6
You are talking like a f woman. .... Job 2:10
will not punish you for being f. .... Job 42:8
come from those f people all day .... Ps 74:22
Come in here, you f people! .... Pr 9:16
but f children make their mother .... Pr 10:1
A f child brings disaster to a .... Pr 19:13
a f person may gain some wisdom. .... Pr 21:11
be too wicked, and don't be f. .... Ec 7:17
A fool says f things, and in his .... Is 32:6
wise people are stupid and f. .... Je 10:8
will be for the f prophets who .... Eze 13:3
them is like a f man who built .... Mt 7:26
of them were f and five were .... Mt 25:2
You are f and slow to believe .... Lk 24:25
Their f minds were filled with .... Rm 1:21
made the wisdom of the world f. 1Co 1:20
God chose the f things of the 1Co 1:27
But you were f; you let someone .... Gal 3:1
Stay away from f and stupid 2Ti 2:23
In the past we also were f. .... Tit 3:3
You f person! Must you be shown .... Jam 2:20
you should stop f people from 1Pe 2:15

FOOLISHLY

Samuel said, "You acted f! 1Sa 13:13
answer fools when they speak f, ... Pr 26:4
Answer fools when they speak f, ... Pr 26:5
must not speak f or tell evil .... Eph 5:4

FOOLISHNESS

Don't let them go back to f. .... Ps 85:8
will be held captive by his f. .... Pr 5:23
F is like a loud woman; .... Pr 9:13
with nothing but more f, ... Pr 14:18
but fools only get more f. .... Pr 14:24
with quick tempers show their f. .... Pr 14:29
speak, but fools pour out f. .... Pr 15:2
but fools just want more f. .... Pr 15:14
f brings punishment to fools. .... Pr 16:22
own f ruins their lives, ... Pr 19:3
is full of f, but punishment .... Pr 22:15
who repeats his f is like a dog .... Pr 26:11
you couldn't remove the f. .... Pr 27:22
a little f can spoil wisdom. .... Ec 10:1
the cross is f to those who are 1Co 1:18
to stumble and is f to non-Jews. 1Co 1:23
Even the f of God is wiser than 1Co 1:25
of this world is f with God. 1Co 3:19

FOOLS

like the shameful f in Israel! 2Sa 13:13
f hate wisdom and discipline. .... Pr 1:7
You f, how long will you be .... Pr 1:22
f will die because they don't .... Pr 10:21
but f hate to stop doing evil. .... Pr 13:19
Stay away from f, because they .... Pr 14:7
F don't care if they sin, but .... Pr 14:9
but f only get more foolishness. .... Pr 14:24
brings punishment to f. .... Pr 16:22
Answer f when they speak .... Pr 26:5
not happy with f, so give God .... Ec 5:4
wise people are f if they let .... Ec 7:7
wears f out; they don't even .... Ec 10:15
You are blind f! Which is .... Mt 23:17
Be careful that no one f you. .... Mt 24:4
Be careful that no one f you. .... Mk 13:5
said, "No, he f the people." .... Jn 7:12
were wise, but they became f. .... Rm 1:22
We are f for Christ's sake, ... 1Co 4:10
will gladly be patient with f! 2Co 11:19
It f those who live on earth by .... Rev 13:14

FOOT

lift a hand or a f without your .... Ge 41:44
and not to touch the f of it. .... Ex 19:12
stood at the f of the mountain. .... Ex 19:17
hand for hand, f for foot, ... Ex 21:24
hand for hand, foot for f, ... Ex 21:24
on the big toe of his right f. .... Le 8:23
big toe of the person's right f. .... Le 14:14
big toe of the person's right f. .... Le 14:17
big toe of the person's right f. .... Le 14:25
big toe of the person's right f. .... Le 14:28
men with a crippled f or hand, ... Le 21:19
crushing Balaam's f against it. .... Nu 22:25
land—not even a f of it, because .... Dt 2:5
hand for a hand, a f for a foot. .... Dt 19:21
hand for a hand, a foot for a f. .... Dt 19:21
Soon their f will slip, because .... Dt 32:35
his chariot and ran away on f. .... Jdg 4:15
thousand f soldiers and ten. 1Sa 15:4
and twenty thousand f soldiers. 2Sa 8:4
thousand Aramean f soldiers from 2Sa 10:6
on him from his head to his f. 2Sa 14:25
hand and six toes on each f— 2Sa 21:20
and ten thousand f soldiers. 2Ki 13:7
and twenty thousand f soldiers. 1Ch 18:4
thousand Aramean f soldiers. 1Ch 19:18
hand and six toes on each f—. 1Ch 20:6
a seventy-five f platform built, ... Est 5:14
a seventy-five f platform stands .... Est 7:9
to think that a f might step on .... Job 39:15
people crossed the river on f. .... Ps 66:6

will not hit your **f** on a rock. .... Ps 91:12
or walking with a crippled **f**. .... Pr 25:19
princes walk like servants on **f**. .... Ec 10:7
bottom of your **f** to the top of .... Is 1:6
The **f** of a human will not stir .... Eze 32:13
not hit your **f** on a rock.'" .... Mt 4:6
him on **f** from the towns. .... Mt 14:13
hand or your **f** causes you to sin.............. Mt 18:8
If your **f** causes you to sin, ... Mk 9:45
not hit your **f** on a rock.'" .... Lk 4:11
guard and chained hand and **f**, ... Lk 8:29
this land, not even a **f** of it. .... Ac 7:5
The **f** might say, "Because I am 1Co 12:15
not stop the **f** from being a part 1Co 12:15
the head cannot say to the **f**, ... 1Co 12:21
put his right **f** on the sea and .... Rev 10:2
sea and his left **f** on the land. .... Rev 10:2

FOOTPRINTS
but your **f** were not seen. .... Ps 77:19
their **f** are bloody. .... Hos 6:8

FOOTSTOOL
I wanted it to be God's **f**........................ 1Ch 28:2
six steps on it and a gold **f**. 2Ch 9:18
worship at the Temple, his **f**. .... Ps 99:5
Let's worship at his **f**. .... Ps 132:7
throne, and the earth is my **f**. .... Is 66:1
the Temple, his **f**, on the day of .... La 2:1
throne, and the earth is my **f**. .... Ac 7:49

FORBID
They **f** people to marry and tell 1Ti 4:3

FORBIDDEN
who were **f** by law to marry .... Dt 23:2
blood and from eating **f** food. .... Zch 9:7

FORCE
was taken by **f** from the land of .... Ge 40:15
brother! Don't **f** me! This should 2Sa 13:12
was in charge of the labor **f**. 1Ki 4:6
been trying to take it by **f**. .... Mt 11:12
and take him by **f** and make him .... Jn 6:15

FORCES
until the LORD **f** out the enemy. .... Nu 32:21
LORD your God **f** those nations .... Dt 7:22
the country and **f** her to have .... Dt 22:25
to be married and **f** her to have .... Dt 22:28
angel of the LORD **f** them away................ Ps 35:5
They join **f** against people who .... Ps 94:21
And another **f** his half sister to .... Eze 22:11
his wife **f** her to be guilty .... Mt 5:32
If someone **f** you to go with him.............. Mt 5:41
And if Satan **f** out himself, ... Mt 12:26

FORCING
masters kept **f** the people to .... Ex 5:13
I am **f** nations out of their .... Le 18:24
I am **f** out ahead of you the.................... Le 20:23
f out the Amorites who lived .... Nu 21:32
with him, **f** him to take an oath .... Eze 17:13
Stop **f** my people out of their .... Eze 45:9
people's land, **f** them out of .... Eze 46:18
on poor people, **f** them to give .... Am 5:11
get rich by **f** others to pay them .... Hab 2:6
the synagogues and **f** out demons. .... Mk 1:39
and tomorrow I am **f** demons out .... Lk 13:32
f them to leave their babies................... Ac 7:19

FOREHEAD
on the **f** of the one who was .... Ge 49:26
hand or a reminder on your **f**. .... Ex 13:9
a reminder on your **f** to help you .... Ex 13:16
Aaron must wear this on his **f**. .... Ex 28:38
of his head and has a bald **f**, ... Le 13:41
sore on his bald head or **f**, ... Le 13:42

his bald head or **f** is red-white, ... Le 13:43
them on your **f** to remind you, ... Dt 6:8
on the **f** of the one who was .... Dt 33:16
and went deep into his **f**,...................... 1Sa 17:49
skin disease broke out on his **f**. 2Ch 26:19
saw the skin disease on his **f**. 2Ch 26:20
their right hand or on their **f**. .... Rev 13:16
mark on the **f** or on the hand,................ Rev 14:9
her **f** a title was written that .... Rev 17:5

FOREHEADS
them on your **f** to remind you. .... Dt 11:18
a mark on the **f** of the people .... Eze 9:4
with a sign the **f** of the people .... Rev 7:3
have the sign of God on their **f**. .... Rev 9:4
name written on their **f**. .... Rev 14:1
beast on their **f** or on their .... Rev 20:4
name will be written on their **f**. .... Rev 22:4

FOREIGN
Put away the **f** gods you have, ... Ge 35:2
there was no **f** god helping him .... Dt 32:12
away the **f** gods among them,................. Jdg 10:16
thing for all his **f** wives so 1Ki 11:8
You must not have **f** gods; .... Ps 81:9
while we are in this **f** country! .... Ps 137:4
LORD and served **f** idols in your .... Je 5:19
women who worship **f** gods. .... Mal 2:11
words and **f** languages I will 1Co 14:21

FOREIGNER
am only a stranger and a **f** here.............. Ge 23:4
No **f** is to eat the Passover. .... Ex 12:43
as your king a **f** who is not a .... Dt 17:15
Not even a **f** living among the................. Eze 44:9
he lived like a **f** in the country .... Heb 11:9

FOREIGNERS
and **f** living in your towns so .... Dt 31:12
F who have joined the LORD .... Is 56:3
and all the **f** there; .... Je 25:20
F in Babylon say, 'We tried to .... Je 51:9
our houses have been given to **f**. .... La 5:2
Jewish are not **f** or strangers .... Eph 2:19

FOREMEN
to the slave masters and **f**. .... Ex 5:6
the slave masters and **f** went to .... Ex 5:10
the Israelite **f** responsible for .... Ex 5:14
the Israelite **f** went to the king .... Ex 5:15
The Israelite **f** knew they were .... Ex 5:19

FORESKIN
Cut away your **f** to show that you .... Ge 17:11

FORESKINS
Philistine **f** to get even with 1Sa 18:25
brought all their **f** to Saul so 1Sa 18:27

FOREST
of cedars from the **F** of Lebanon, ... 1Ki 7:2
the Palace of the **F** of Lebanon. 1Ki 10:17
the keeper of the king's **f**, ... Ne 2:8
animal of the **f** is already mine. .... Ps 50:10
Sing, too, you trees in the **f**! .... Is 44:23
are just wood cut from the **f**, ... Je 10:3
against the **f** of the southern .... Eze 20:46
Say to that **f**: 'Hear the word of .... Eze 20:47
A lion in the **f** does not roar .... Am 3:4
the mighty **f** has been cut down .... Zch 11:2
A big **f** fire can be started with .... Jam 3:5

FORESTS
places and to its best **f**. 2Ki 19:23
cities and towers in the **f**. 2Ch 27:4
greatest heights and its best **f**. .... Is 37:24
a fire in your **f** that will burn .... Je 21:14
are tall like the **f** of Gilead, ... Je 22:6
or chop firewood from the **f**, ... Eze 39:10

FOREVER

of life, or they will live f." .... Ge 3:22
not remain in human beings f, ... Ge 6:3
to you and your descendants f. .... Ge 13:15
The Lord will be king f!" .... Ex 15:18
be rebuilt; let it be ruined f. .... Dt 13:16
and your children will own it f. .... Jos 14:9
a witness between you and me f." 1Sa 20:23
to Joab, "Must the sword kill f? 2Sa 2:26
Your throne will last f.'" 2Sa 7:16
Israel your very own people f, ... 2Sa 7:24
keep the promise f that you made 2Sa 7:25
a place for you to live f." 1Ki 8:13
worshiped there f and will watch 1Ki 9:3
on you and your children f." 2Ki 5:27
be worshiped f in this Temple 2Ki 21:7
He will keep his agreement f; 1Ch 16:15
His love continues f. 1Ch 16:34
from him, he will leave you f. 1Ch 28:9
the king, "May the king live f! .... Ne 2:3
I don't want to live f. .... Job 7:16
out their names f and ever. .... Ps 9:5
But the Lord rules f. .... Ps 9:7
The Lord is King f and ever. .... Ps 10:16
it will last f. The judgments .... Ps 19:9
live in the house of the Lord f. .... Ps 23:6
The Lord will be King f. .... Ps 29:10
my God, I will praise you f. .... Ps 30:12
the land and will live in it f. .... Ps 37:29
Get up! Don't reject us f. .... Ps 44:23
throne will last f and ever. .... Ps 45:6
will praise you f and ever. .... Ps 45:17
I trust God's love f and ever. .... Ps 52:8
Let me live in your Holy Tent f. .... Ps 61:4
Praise his glorious name f. .... Ps 72:19
is my strength. He is mine f. .... Ps 73:26
Will they insult you f? .... Ps 74:10
Will you be angry f? .... Ps 79:5
say, "Your love continues f; .... Ps 89:2
His family will go on f. .... Ps 89:36
will continue f, like the moon, ... Ps 89:37
Will you ignore us f? .... Ps 89:46
He will keep his agreement f; .... Ps 105:8
His love continues f. .... Ps 106:1
are a priest f, a priest like .... Ps 110:4
and his goodness continues f. .... Ps 111:3
their goodness will continue f. .... Ps 112:3
obey your teachings f and ever. .... Ps 119:44
it continues f in heaven. .... Ps 119:89
Zion, which sits unmoved f. .... Ps 125:1
surrounds his people now and f. .... Ps 125:2
your hope in the Lord now and f. .... Ps 131:3
Lord, you will be remembered f. .... Ps 135:13
His love continues f. .... Ps 136:1
I will praise you f and ever. .... Ps 145:1
I will praise you f and ever. .... Ps 145:2
The Lord will be King f. .... Ps 146:10
will not go on f, nor do .... Pr 27:24
but the earth continues f. .... Ec 1:4
and will continue to grow f. .... Is 9:7
he will destroy death f. .... Is 25:8
because he is our Rock f. .... Is 26:4
it will bring calm and safety f. .... Is 32:17
word of our God will live f." .... Is 40:8
my salvation will continue f, ... Is 51:6
But my goodness will continue f, ... Is 51:8
don't remember our sins f. .... Is 64:9
Will your anger last f?' .... Je 3:5
with them that will last f. .... Je 32:40
will not reject his people f. .... La 3:31
for so long? Have you left us f? .... La 5:20
will all live on the land f: .... Eze 37:25
Then I will live among them f. .... Eze 43:9

language, "O king, live f! .... Da 2:4
an end, but it will continue f. .... Da 2:44
and glory to him who lives f. .... Da 4:34
King Darius, live f! .... Da 6:6
shine like stars f and ever. .... Da 12:3
by the name of God who lives f, ... Da 12:7
make you my promised bride f. .... Hos 2:19
and the glory are yours f. .... Mt 6:13
Abraham and to his children f." .... Lk 1:55
eats this bread will live f." .... Jn 6:58
does not stay with a family f, ... Jn 8:35
a son belongs to the family f. .... Jn 8:35
world will keep true life f. .... Jn 12:25
law that the Christ will live f. .... Jn 12:34
another Helper to be with you f— .... Jn 14:16
things, who should be praised f. .... Rm 1:25
To him be the glory f. .... Rm 11:36
God be glory f through Jesus .... Rm 16:27
are right and will continue f." 2Co 9:9
and he is to be praised f. 2Co 11:31
glory belongs to God f and ever. .... Gal 1:5
Jesus for all time, f and ever. .... Eph 3:21
so you could have him back f— .... Phm 1:15
throne will last f and ever. .... Heb 1:8
are a priest f, a priest like .... Heb 5:6
But because Jesus lives f, ... Heb 7:24
for sins, f, he sat down at .... Heb 10:12
he made perfect f those who are .... Heb 10:14
same yesterday, today, and f. .... Heb 13:8
word of the Lord will live f." 1Pe 1:25
glory belong to him f and ever. 1Pe 4:11
Glory be to him now and f! 2Pe 3:18
who does what God wants lives f. 1Jn 2:17
in us and will be with us f. 2Jn 1:2
has been kept for them f. .... Jud 1:13
be glory and power f and ever! .... Rev 1:6
him who lives f and ever. .... Rev 4:10
and he will rule f and ever." .... Rev 11:15
pain will rise f and ever. .... Rev 14:11
her smoke will rise f and ever." .... Rev 19:3
day and night f and ever. .... Rev 20:10
will rule as kings f and ever. .... Rev 22:5

FOREVERMORE

Your Temple will be holy f. .... Ps 93:5

FORGAVE

the Lord," and you f my guilt. .... Ps 32:5
He f their sins and did not .... Ps 78:38
f the guilt of the people and .... Ps 85:2
to forgive—I f it for you, as if 2Co 2:10
just as God f you in Christ. .... Eph 4:32
Christ, and he f all our sins. .... Col 2:13
person because the Lord f you. .... Col 3:13

FORGET

God has made me f all the .... Ge 41:51
Don't f the Agreement of the .... Dt 4:23
Do not f the Lord, who brought .... Dt 6:12
will happen to those who f God; .... Job 8:13
I say, 'I will f my complaint; .... Job 9:27
and so will all those who f God. .... Ps 9:17
How long will you f me, Lord? .... Ps 13:1
Think about this, you who f God. .... Ps 50:22
Never f your poor people. .... Ps 74:19
Lord and do not f all his .... Ps 103:2
and I will not f your word. .... Ps 119:16
Jerusalem, if I f you, let my .... Ps 137:5
My child, do not f my teaching, ... Pr 3:1
Can a woman f the baby she .... Is 49:15
if she could f her children, ... Is 49:15
made Jerusalem f the set feasts .... La 2:6
Do not f to do good to others, ... Heb 13:16
But do not f this one thing, ... 2Pe 3:8
So do not f what you have .... Rev 3:3

FORGETFULNESS
be known in the land of f? .... Ps 88:12

FORGETS
Even if he f about it, when he .... Le 5:4
LORD never f to punish guilty .... Nu 14:18
is born, she f the pain, because .... Jn 16:21

FORGETTING
F the past and straining toward .... Php 3:13

FORGIVE
Tell Joseph to f you, his .... Ge 50:17
please f them of this sin. .... Ex 32:32
heaven, and when you hear, f us. 1Ki 8:30
F the sins of your people Israel, ... 1Ki 8:34
I will f their sin, and I will 2Ch 7:14
listen! Lord, f! Lord, hear us .... Da 9:19
F us for our sins, just as we .... Mt 6:12
if you f others for their sins, ... Mt 6:14
Only God can f sins." .... Lk 5:21
F, and you will be forgiven...................... Lk 6:37
If you f anyone his sins, they .... Jn 20:23
you don't f them, they are not.................. Jn 20:23
sins, he will f our sins, ... 1Jn 1:9

FORGIVEN
is the person whose sins are f, ... Ps 32:1
young man. Your sins are f." .... Mt 9:2
people can be f for every sin .... Mt 12:31
said, "Friend, your sins are f." .... Lk 5:20
said to her, "Your sins are f." .... Lk 7:48
anyone his sins, they are f. .... Jn 20:23
are they whose sins are f, ... Rm 4:7
your sins are f through Christ. 1Jn 2:12

FORGIVENESS
Love and truth bring f of sin. .... Pr 16:6
people and asked f for those who .... Is 53:12
and lives for the f of sins. .... Mk 1:4
and lives for the f of sins. .... Lk 3:3
and lives and f of sins would be .... Lk 24:47
Christ for the f of your sins. .... Ac 2:38
receive f through faith in the .... Rm 3:25
death, and so we have f of sins. .... Eph 1:7
our sins, and in him we have f. .... Col 1:14

FORGIVES
The LORD f people for evil, ... Ex 34:7
He f sin and law breaking. .... Nu 14:18
f all my sins and heals all my .... Ps 103:3
trouble, but love f all wrongs. .... Pr 10:12
Whoever f someone's sin makes a .... Pr 17:9
"Who is this who even f sins?" .... Lk 7:49

FORGIVING
But you are a f God. .... Ne 9:17
are kind and f and have great.................. Ps 86:5
them that you are a f God, ... Ps 99:8

FORGOT
Joseph. He f all about him. .... Ge 40:23
They f about the LORD their God .... Jdg 3:7
after her lovers, but she f me!" .... Hos 2:13

FORGOTTEN
song will not be f by their .... Dt 31:21
away, and my friends have f me. .... Job 19:14
my Rock, "Why have you f me? .... Ps 42:9
Has God f mercy? Is he too angry .... Ps 77:9
but I have not f your teachings. .... Ps 119:61
troubles of the past will be f. .... Is 65:16
Israel has f their Maker and has.............. Hos 8:14
blind and has f that he was made 2Pe 1:9
and God has not f the wrongs she .... Rev 18:5

FORK
come carrying a f that had three 1Sa 2:13
would plunge the f into the pot 1Sa 2:14
Whatever the f brought out of 1Sa 2:14

FORKS
blood, the meat f, and the pans .... Ex 27:3
blood, meat f, and pans for...................... Ex 38:3
fire, the meat f, the shovels, ... Nu 4:14
should be used to make the f,.................. 1Ch 28:17
pots, shovels, f, and all the 2Ch 4:16

FORM
earth was empty and had no f. .... Ge 1:2
of curtains to f a courtyard .... Ex 27:9
of curtains to f a courtyard .... Ex 38:9
has even seen the f of the LORD. .... Nu 12:8
Cedar trees f our roof;........................... Sng 1:17
his f was so changed they could.............. Is 52:14
beauty or f to make us notice .... Is 53:2
down on him in the f of a dove. .... Lk 3:22
in its present f will soon be..................... 1Co 7:31

FORMATION
but they all go forward in f. .... Pr 30:27

FORMED
the ground and f a man from it. .... Ge 2:7
put the man he had f into it. .... Ge 2:8
the ground God f every wild .... Ge 2:19
the people and f it with a tool.................. Ex 32:4
normal or is not perfectly f, ... Le 22:23
Maker, who made you and f you. .... Dt 32:6
wall that f the side of each 1Ki 6:6
You f me inside my mother like .... Job 10:10
mother like cheese f from milk. .... Job 10:10
the same God f both of us in our .... Job 31:15
You made me and f me with your .... Ps 119:73
you f me in my mother's body. .... Ps 139:13
my bones being f as I took shape .... Ps 139:15
you saw my body as it was f. .... Ps 139:16
An idol is f by a craftsman,.................... Is 40:19
he f you, people of Israel. .... Is 43:1
my glory, whom I f and made." .... Is 43:7
who f you in your mother's body, ... Is 44:2
who f you in your mother's body: .... Is 44:24
is the God who f the earth and .... Is 45:18
Your breasts f, and your hair .... Eze 16:7
the marketplace, f a mob, and .... Ac 17:5
because Adam was f first and.................. 1Ti 2:13

FORMING
He was f a swarm of locusts, ... Am 7:1
f a deep valley that runs east .... Zch 14:4

FORMS
on the lifeless f of your idols. .... Le 26:30
wisdom, which has so many f. .... Eph 3:10

FORTIETH
the f year after the Israelites .... Nu 33:38
In David's f year as king, ... 1Ch 26:31

FORTRESS
is my rock, my f, my Savior. 2Sa 22:2

FORTUNATUS
that Stephanas, F, and Achaicus.............. 1Co 16:17

FORTUNE-TELLER
a medium or a f must be put to .... Le 20:27
or f can explain to the king the .... Da 2:27

FORTUNE-TELLERS
go to mediums or f for advice, ... Le 19:31
to mediums and f for advice, ... Le 20:6
group coming from the f' tree!" .... Jdg 9:37
the mediums and f from the land. 1Sa 28:3
the mediums and f from the land. 1Sa 28:9
got advice from mediums and f. 2Ki 21:6

the mediums, **f,** house gods, and............ 2Ki 23:24
got advice from mediums and **f.** 2Ch 33:6
the mediums and **f,** who whisper .... Is 8:19
The mediums and **f** do not speak .... Is 8:20
from their mediums and **f.**".................... Is 19:3
than all the **f** and magicians .... Da 1:20
So the king called for his **f,**.................... Da 2:2
king has ever asked the **f,** .... Da 2:10
The **f,** magicians, and wise men .... Da 4:7
the most important of all the **f.** .... Da 4:9
all the wise men, **f,** magicians, ... Da 5:11
use so you will have no more **f.** .... Mic 5:12
f see false visions and tell .... Zch 10:2

FORTUNES
for his owners by telling **f.** .... Ac 16:16

FORTY
It will rain **f** days and forty.................... Ge 7:4
the earth for **f** days and forty .... Ge 7:12
said, "If I find **f,** I will not .... Ge 18:29
ate manna for **f** years,.......................... Ex 16:35
mountain for **f** days and forty................ Ex 24:18
for forty days and **f** nights. .... Ex 24:18
After **f** days of exploring the .... Nu 13:25
be shepherds here for **f** years. .... Nu 14:33
For **f** years you will suffer for .... Nu 14:34
During these **f** years, your .... Dt 8:4
hit a person more than **f** times, ... Dt 25:3
land was at peace for **f** years................ Jdg 3:11
He had led Israel for **f** years. 1Sa 4:18
over all Israel for **f** years. 1Ki 11:42
to walk for **f** days and nights to 1Ki 19:8
care of them for **f** years in the .... Ne 9:21
with those people for **f** years. .... Ps 95:10
saying, "After **f** days, Nineveh .... Jnh 3:4
fasted for **f** days and nights .... Mt 4:2
was in the desert **f** days and was .... Mk 1:13
devil tempted Jesus for **f** days. .... Lk 4:2
Jesus during the **f** days after he .... Ac 1:3
whom was God angry for **f** years? .... Heb 3:17

FORTY-EIGHT
a total of **f** cities and their .... Nu 35:7
A total of **f** towns with their .... Jos 21:41

FORTY-FIRST
died in the **f** year of his rule. 2Ch 16:13

FORTY-FIVE
if there are only **f** good people .... Ge 18:28

FORTY-FOUR
one hundred **f** thousand people .... Rev 14:1

FORTY-NINE
of seven years, or **f** years. .... Le 25:8
comes will be **f** years and four .... Da 9:25

FORTY-ONE
Rehoboam was **f** years old when 1Ki 14:21
ruled in Jerusalem for **f** years. 1Ki 15:10
Jeroboam ruled **f** years, ... 2Ki 14:23
was **f** years old when he became 2Ch 12:13

FORTY-SEVEN
to be one hundred **f** years old. .... Ge 47:28

FORTY-SIX
were **f** hundred men from Levi. 1Ch 12:26
with about **f** thousand pounds 2Ch 3:8
It took **f** years to build this .... Jn 2:20

FORTY-THREE
earrings weighed about **f** pounds. .... Jdg 8:26

FORTY-TWO
f feet long and six feet wide. .... Ex 26:2
f feet long and six feet wide. .... Ex 36:9
must also give **f** other cities to .... Nu 35:6
f thousand people from Ephraim .... Jdg 12:6

he was king over Israel **f** years. 1Sa 13:1
woods and tore **f** of the boys to 2Ki 2:24
well near Beth Eked—**f** of them. 2Ki 10:14
on the holy city for **f** months. .... Rev 11:2
to use its power for **f** months.................. Rev 13:5

FORWARD
Bringing Aaron and his sons **f,** .... Le 8:6
Moses brought Aaron's sons **f.** .... Le 8:13
Levi, should come **f,** because .... Dt 21:5
Joab stepped **f,** his sword fell 2Sa 20:8
the shadow to go **f** ten steps or 2Ki 20:9
the shadow to go **f** ten steps. 2Ki 20:10
so Esther went **f** and touched the .... Est 5:2
but we march **f** and win........................ Ps 20:8
person can look **f** to happiness, ... Pr 10:28
people can look **f** to a bright .... Pr 13:9
but they all go **f** in formation................. Pr 30:27
She looks **f** to the future with .... Pr 31:25
and marching **f** with his great................ Is 63:1
They went backward, not **f.** .... Je 7:24
with me came **f** and said to me, ... Zch 5:5
has been going **f** in strength, ... Mt 11:12
hide, she came **f,** shaking, and .... Lk 8:47
Pharisee group came **f** and said,............ Ac 15:5
for and look **f** to the coming 2Pe 3:12

FOUGHT
came and **f** the Israelites. .... Ex 17:8
The stars **f** from heaven:...................... Jdg 5:20
from their paths, they **f** Sisera. .... Jdg 5:20
When David **f** the Arameans of .... Ps 59:17
If I **f** wild animals in Ephesus 1Co 15:32
and his angels **f** against the .... Rev 12:7

FOUND
and onyx are also **f** there. .... Ge 2:12
one day Enoch could not be **f,** .... Ge 5:24
they **f** a plain in the land of.................... Ge 11:2
angel of the LORD **f** Hagar beside .... Ge 16:7
and his mother **f** a wife for him .... Ge 21:21
dug, saying, "We **f** water in that .... Ge 26:32
f a stone and laid his head on................ Ge 28:11
the field and **f** some mandrake .... Ge 30:14
seven days Laban **f** him in the .... Ge 31:23
but you have **f** nothing that.................... Ge 31:37
If you have **f** anything, show it .... Ge 31:37
is the man who **f** the hot springs .... Ge 36:24
a man **f** him wandering in the .... Ge 37:15
brothers and **f** them in Dothan. .... Ge 37:17
and said, "We **f** this robe. .... Ge 37:32
each of them **f** his money in his .... Ge 42:35
sacks each of us **f** all his money .... Ge 43:21
the money we **f** in our sacks. .... Ge 44:8
f the cup in Benjamin's sack. .... Ge 44:12
that was to be **f** in Egypt and .... Ge 47:14
and they **f** that not one of them .... Ex 9:7
in the desert but **f** no water. .... Ex 15:22
But if the thief is never **f,** .... Ex 22:8
back what he **f** and lied about .... Le 6:4
an animal he **f** dead or torn by .... Le 7:24
they **f** a man gathering wood on............ Nu 15:32
Those who **f** him gathering wood .... Nu 15:33
When they **f** Balaam, they told .... Nu 22:7
He has **f** no wrong in the people............ Nu 23:21
gold things that each of us **f:** .... Nu 31:50
of the things in that city, ... Dt 13:17
you might be **f** doing something............ Dt 17:2
Suppose someone is **f** murdered, ... Dt 21:1
go to where the body was **f,** .... Dt 21:2
If a man is **f** having sexual .... Dt 22:22
man **f** the engaged girl in the .... Dt 22:27
because he has **f** something bad............ Dt 24:1
He **f** them in a desert, a windy, ... Dt 32:10
to the tent and **f** the things .... Jos 7:22

but someone f them hiding in the ....Jos 10:17
everything they f in the cities,...............Jos 11:14
There they f Adoni-Bezek, the ....Jdg 1:5
they f the doors to the room ....Jdg 3:24
dead lion and f a swarm of bees..............Jdg 14:8
they had not f the answer. ....Jdg 14:14
Samson f the jawbone of a dead.............Jdg 15:15
they burned every city they f...................Jdg 20:48
They f that no one from the ....Jdg 21:8
soldiers f four hundred young ....Jdg 21:12
the Philistines f out that the 1Sa 4:6
they f that Dagon had fallen on 1Sa 5:3
they again f Dagon fallen on the 1Sa 5:4
ago, because they have been f. 1Sa 9:20
were looking for have been f. 1Sa 10:2
the donkeys had already been f." 1Sa 10:16
They f the Philistines confused, ...1Sa 14:20
But when they f an animal that 1Sa 15:9
they f just an idol on the bed 1Sa 19:16
When Saul f out that David had 1Sa 23:13
I have f nothing wrong in David............1Sa 29:3
to me, I have f no wrong in you..............1Sa 29:6
evil have you f in me from the 1Sa 29:8
he f that the Amalekites had 1Sa 30:1
they f the town had been burned 1Sa 30:3
but David f strength in the LORD 1Sa 30:6
They f an Egyptian in a field 1Sa 30:11
they f Saul and his three sons................1Sa 31:8
the king would have f out, ...2Sa 18:13
they f a girl named Abishag from 1Ki 1:3
man of God and f him sitting 1Ki 13:14
went out and f the body lying 1Ki 13:28
could not be f in his country. 1Ki 18:10
left that place and f Elisha son 1Ki 19:19
a lion f him and killed him....................1Ki 20:36
So you have f me, my enemy!" 1Ki 21:20
answered, "Yes, I have f you. 1Ki 21:20
They f only her skull, feet, and 2Ki 9:35
gold that was f in the 2Ki 12:18
of Assyria f out that Hoshea 2Ki 17:4
he f the king fighting against 2Ki 19:8
I've f the Book of the Teachings 2Ki 22:8
words in the book that was f. 2Ki 22:13
that was f in the Temple 2Ki 23:2
the priest had f in the Temple 2Ki 23:24
They f good pastures with plenty 1Ch 4:40
they f Saul and his sons dead on 1Ch 10:8
family were f living at Jazer 1Ch 26:31
and he also f wives for them. 2Ch 11:23
They looked for him and f him. 2Ch 15:4
They looked for God and f him. 2Ch 15:15
valuables, they f many supplies,.............2Ch 20:25
f the leaders of Judah and the 2Ch 22:8
things they f in the Temple 2Ch 29:16
Hilkiah the priest f the Book of 2Ch 34:14
I've f the Book of the Teachings 2Ch 34:15
words in the book that was f. 2Ch 34:21
that was f in the Temple 2Ch 34:30
f that Jerusalem has a history.................Ezr 4:19
A scroll was f in Ecbatana,....................Ezr 6:2
I f the family history of those ....Ne 7:5
This is what I f written there: ....Ne 7:5
This is what they f written in ....Ne 8:14
You f him faithful to you, ...Ne 9:8
and they f that it said no.........................Ne 13:1
I f out the evil Eliashib had ....Ne 13:7
Then I f out the people were not..............Ne 13:10
But Mordecai f out about their ....Est 2:22
it was f to be true, ...Est 2:23
It was f recorded that Mordecai ....Est 6:2
I have already been f guilty, ...Job 9:29
like a dream and not be f again;..............Job 20:8
Sapphires are f in rocks, and ....Job 28:6

and gold dust is also f there. ....Job 28:6
But where can wisdom be f, ...Job 28:12
it cannot be f among those who ....Job 28:13
Don't say, 'We have f wisdom; ....Job 32:13
But God has f fault with me; ....Job 33:10
f a way to pay for his life. ....Job 33:24
for him, but he couldn't be f. ....Ps 37:36
I f no one to comfort me. ....Ps 69:20
He f a way to show his anger...................Ps 78:50
The sparrows have f a home, ...Ps 84:3
I have f my servant David; ....Ps 89:20
they will not be f near me. ....Ps 101:3
They f no city in which to live. ....Ps 107:4
let him be f guilty, and let ....Ps 109:7
as if I had f a great treasure. ....Ps 119:162
We f it at Kiriath Jearim........................Ps 132:6
looking for you and have f you. ....Pr 7:15
but they are f even in kings' ....Pr 30:28
I f that this is also useless. ....Ec 2:1
I f that some women are worse ....Ec 7:26
one man among the thousands I f. ....Ec 7:28
they have f all kinds of ways ....Ec 7:29
The watchmen f me as they ....Sng 3:3
left them, I f the one I love......................Sng 3:4
The watchmen f me as they ....Sng 5:7
If I f you outside, I would kiss ....Sng 8:1
Justice will be f even in the....................Is 32:16
fairness will be f in the ....Is 32:16
They will not be f there. ....Is 35:9
he f the king fighting against ....Is 37:8
of Israel will be f to be good, ...Is 45:25
I came home and f no one there; ....Is 50:2
You f new strength, so you did ....Is 57:10
goodness is nowhere to be f. ....Is 59:9
Truth cannot be f anywhere, ...Is 59:15
I was f by those who were not ....Is 65:1
I have f them doing evil things ....Je 23:11
the enemy's sword f help in the ....Je 31:2
He had f Jeremiah in Ramah bound ....Je 40:1
Nebuzaradan f Jeremiah, ...Je 40:2
sins will be f, because I will ....Je 50:20
you were f and taken prisoner. ....Je 50:24
nations, but she has f no rest..................La 1:3
lovers with whom you f pleasure. ....Eze 16:37
into a land I had f for them, ...Eze 20:6
until evil was f in you............................Eze 28:15
scattered flock when it is f,....................Eze 34:12
measured it and f it was one ....Eze 40:23
I f the water coming out on the ....Eze 47:2
talked to them and f that none ....Da 1:19
I have f a man among the ....Da 2:25
The wild animals f shelter under ....Da 4:12
scales and f not good enough. ....Da 5:27
as a group and f Daniel praying..............Da 6:11
When I f Israel, it was like ....Hos 9:10
where he f a ship that was going ....Jnh 1:3
Israel's sins were f in you. ....Mic 1:13
is the greatest faith I have f, ...Mt 8:10
One day a man f the treasure, ...Mt 13:44
When he f a very valuable pearl, ...Mt 13:46
same servant f another servant ....Mt 18:28
his followers and f them asleep. ....Mt 26:40
and again he f them asleep, ...Mt 26:43
When they f him, they said, ...Mk 1:37
Jesus f many people there making...........Mk 5:38
When they f out, they said, ...Mk 6:38
went home and f her daughter ....Mk 7:30
f a colt tied in the street near ....Mk 11:4
But he f no figs, only leaves, ...Mk 11:13
his followers and f them asleep. ....Mk 14:37
and again he f them asleep, ...Mk 14:40
quickly and f Mary and Joseph ....Lk 2:16
three days they f Jesus sitting.................Lk 2:46

the book and f the place where .... Lk 4:17
When they f him, they tried to .... Lk 4:42
faith I have f anywhere, ... Lk 7:9
house where they f the servant .... Lk 7:10
they f the man sitting at Jesus' .... Lk 8:35
on the tree, but he f none. .... Lk 13:6
me because I f my lost sheep.'............... Lk 15:6
because I have f the coin that I .... Lk 15:9
He was lost, but now he is f!' .... Lk 15:24
He was lost, but now he is f.' " .... Lk 15:32
into town and f the colt just as .... Lk 19:32
and John left and f everything .... Lk 22:13
his followers and f them asleep .... Lk 22:45
and I have not f him guilty of .... Lk 23:14
Herod f nothing wrong with him; .... Lk 23:15
f the stone rolled away from .... Lk 24:2
f it just as the women said, ... Lk 24:24
There they f the eleven apostles .... Lk 24:33
to him, "We have f the Messiah." .... Jn 1:41
He f Philip and said to him, ... Jn 1:43
Philip f Nathanael and told him,............. Jn 1:45
We have f the man that Moses .... Jn 1:45
the Temple he f people selling .... Jn 2:14
Jesus f the man at the Temple................ Jn 5:14
When the people f Jesus on the .... Jn 6:25
him out, Jesus f him and said, ... Jn 9:35
Jesus f a colt and sat on it. .... Jn 12:14
Then if Saul f any followers of .... Ac 9:2
sent had f Simon's house .... Ac 10:17
and when he f Saul, he brought .... Ac 11:26
'I have f in David son of Jesse .... Ac 13:22
f an altar that had these words .... Ac 17:23
There he f some followers .... Ac 19:1
There we f a ship going to .... Ac 21:2
We f some followers in Tyre and.............. Ac 21:4
We have f this man to be a .... Ac 24:5
this when they f me in the .... Ac 24:18
here if they f any wrong in me .... Ac 24:20
f no reason to order his death. .... Ac 25:25
There the officer f a ship from .... Ac 27:6
They f that the water was one................ Ac 27:28
We f some believers there who .... Ac 28:14
And sin f a way to use that .... Rm 7:8
Sin f a way to fool me by using .... Rm 7:11
I was f by those who were not .... Rm 10:20
We f trouble all around us. 2Co 7:5
has come and is f in Christ. .... Col 2:17
eagerly for me until he f me. 2Ti 1:17
They f out how good God's word .... Heb 6:5
But God f something wrong with .... Heb 8:8
the law of Moses was f guilty .... Heb 10:28
He could not be f, because God .... Heb 11:5
royal law is f in the Scriptures .... Jam 2:8
not, and you f they are liars. .... Rev 2:2
I have f that what you are doing.............. Rev 3:2
and it will never be f again. .... Rev 18:21
job will ever be f in you again. .... Rev 18:22
whose name was not f written in .... Rev 20:15

FOUNDATION
one who lays the f of this city................ Jos 6:26
be used for the f of the Temple. 1Ki 5:17
On top of these f stones were 1Ki 7:11
from the day the f of the Temple............. 2Ch 8:16
of you will be the f of the. 2Ch 23:5
but the f of the LORD's Temple .... Ezr 3:6
laying the f of the Temple .... Ezr 3:10
f of his Temple has been laid." .... Ezr 3:11
they saw the f of this Temple................. Ezr 3:12
you when I made the earth's f? .... Job 38:4
when he laid the earth's f. .... Pr 8:29
to use for the f of a building, ... Je 51:26
people will see the wall's f..................... Eze 13:14

Its edge was the f for the side................ Eze 41:8
working on the f of the Temple .... Hag 2:18
has laid the f of this Temple, ... Zch 4:9
words when the f was laid for .... Zch 8:9
dug deep and laid the f on rock. .... Lk 6:48
house on the ground without a f. .... Lk 6:49
might lay the f, but you would .... Lk 14:29
that shook the f of the jail. .... Ac 16:26
I laid the f of that house like 1Co 3:10
Others are building on that f, ... 1Co 3:10
The f that has already been laid 1Co 3:11
no one can lay down any other f. 1Co 3:11
But if people build on that f, ... 1Co 3:12
been put on the f still stands, ... 1Co 3:14
built on the f of the apostles .... Eph 2:20
the support and f of the truth................ 1Ti 3:15
as a strong f for the future. 1Ti 6:19
But God's strong f continues to 2Ti 2:19
were built on twelve f stones, ... Rev 21:14
The f stones of the city walls .... Rev 21:19
The first f was jasper, the .... Rev 21:19

FOUNTAIN
rode on toward the F Gate and .... Ne 2:14
of Mizpah, repaired the F Gate. .... Ne 3:15
went from the F Gate straight up .... Ne 12:37
as your f gives you water. .... Pr 5:18
give life, like a f of water, ... Pr 10:11
It is like a f that can save .... Pr 13:14
It is like a f that can save .... Pr 14:27
is like a f which gives life to .... Pr 16:22
walled-in spring, a closed-up f. .... Sng 4:12
like a garden f—a well of fresh .... Sng 4:15
and my eyes like a f of tears! .... Je 9:1
A f will flow from the Temple of.............. Joe 3:18
At that time a f will be open .... Zch 13:1

FOUNTAINS
the dry land into f of water. .... Is 41:18

FOUR
branched out to become f rivers. .... Ge 2:10
f kings fighting against five. .... Ge 14:9
hitting all f corners of the .... Job 1:19
really f that never say, ' .... Pr 30:15
really f I don't understand: .... Pr 30:18
really f that walk as if they...................... Pr 30:29
had read three or f columns, ... Je 36:23
I will bring the f winds against .... Je 49:36
looked like f living creatures .... Eze 1:5
of them had f faces and four .... Eze 1:6
them had four faces and f wings. .... Eze 1:6
has come on the f corners of the .... Eze 7:2
I saw the f wheels by the living .... Eze 10:9
All f wheels looked alike: .... Eze 10:10
come from the f winds, and .... Eze 37:9
gave these f young men wisdom.............. Da 1:17
see f men walking around in the .... Da 3:25
a leopard with f wings on its .... Da 7:6
'The f great animals are four .... Da 7:17
up and saw f animal horns. .... Zch 1:18
There were about f thousand men .... Mt 15:38
bread that fed the f thousand .... Mt 16:10
F people came, carrying a .... Mk 2:3
'F more months till harvest.' .... Jn 4:35
to earth by its f corners. .... Ac 10:11
came f hundred thirty years .... Gal 3:17
voice to the f angels to whom.................. Rev 7:2
elders and the f living .... Rev 7:11

FOUR-FIFTHS
You may keep f for yourselves to .... Ge 47:24

FOURTEEN
the first f to get your two .... Ge 31:41
So there were f generations from .... Mt 1:17

there were f generations from................. Mt 1:17
there were f generations from................. Mt 1:17

FOURTEENTH
twilight on the f day of the .... Nu 9:5

FOURTH
came. This was the f day. .... Ge 1:19
The f river is the Euphrates. .... Ge 2:14
It came in the f year that....................... Je 25:1
and the f was the face of an .... Eze 10:14
Then there will be a f kingdom, ... Da 2:40
front of me a f animal that was .... Da 7:7
days when you fast in the f, ... Zch 8:19
The f was like a flying eagle. .... Rev 4:7
When the Lamb opened the f seal, ... Rev 6:7
voice of the f living creature .... Rev 6:7
power over a f of the earth to .... Rev 6:8
Then the f angel blew his .... Rev 8:12

FOX
If a f climbed up on the stone .... Ne 4:3
Go tell that f Herod, 'Today.................... Lk 13:32

FOXES
out and caught three hundred f. .... Jdg 15:4
He took two f at a time, tied .... Jdg 15:4
to the tails of each pair of f. .... Jdg 15:4
he let the f loose in the .... Jdg 15:5
Catch the f for us—the little .... Sng 2:15
the little f that ruin the .... Sng 2:15
The f have holes to live in, ... Mt 8:20
The f have holes to live in, ... Lk 9:58

FRAGILE
you, you who are f and gentle. .... Je 6:2

FRANKINCENSE
onycha, galbanum, and pure f. .... Ex 30:34
treasures of gold, f, and myrrh. .... Mt 2:11
incense, myrrh, f, wine, olive .... Rev 18:13

FREE
year you are to set him f, ... Ex 21:2
because the woman was not f. .... Le 19:20
the fish we ate for f in Egypt. .... Nu 11:5
nobody is left, slaves or f. .... Dt 32:36
did before and shake myself f." .... Jdg 16:20
ruler of the people set him f. .... Ps 105:20
and set my people f without any.............. Is 45:13
F the people you have put in .... Is 58:6
was supposed to f his Hebrew .... Je 34:9
and the truth will make you f." .... Jn 8:32
So if the Son makes you f, ... Jn 8:36
But God's f gift is not like .... Rm 5:15
were made f from sin, and now .... Rm 6:18
made you f from the law that .... Rm 8:2
called them are f persons who 1Co 7:22
I am a f man. I am an apostle. I 1Co 9:1
f from anything that makes body 2Co 7:1
Greek, slave and f person, male .... Gal 3:28
is above, is like the f woman. .... Gal 4:26
slave woman, but of the f woman. .... Gal 4:31
Live as f people, but do not use 1Pe 2:16

FREED
Barabbas to be f and for Jesus .... Mt 27:20
man who was f from the demons .... Mk 5:18
her to be f from her sickness .... Lk 13:16
prisoners were f from their.................... Ac 16:26
God has f us from the power of .... Col 1:13

FREEING
f the guilty and punishing the............ Pr 17:15
But today I am f you from................. Je 40:4

FREELY
leaving me and will love them f,.............. Hos 14:4
I give you these powers f, ... Mt 10:8

freely, so help other people f. .... Mt 10:8
but when they f do what the law .... Rm 2:14
giving to others should give f. .... Rm 12:8
because God f gave his blessings .... Gal 3:18
God gave that grace to us f, ... Eph 1:6

FREES
He f me from my enemies. 2Sa 22:49
who follow him and f them from .... Ps 97:10

FREQUENT
stomach and your f sicknesses. 1Ti 5:23

FRIEND
face as a man speaks with his f............... Ex 33:11
Come here, f, and sit down." .... Ru 4:1
had always been David's f. 1Ki 5:1
descendants of your f Abraham............. 2Ch 20:7
best and truest f, who ate at my .... Ps 41:9
A f loves you all the time, ... Pr 17:17
but a real f will be more loyal................. Pr 18:24
The slap of a f can be trusted .... Pr 27:6
this is my lover and my f. .... Sng 5:16
from the family of my f Abraham. .... Is 41:8
your neighbor or trust a f. .... Mic 7:5
and he is a f of tax collectors .... Mt 11:19
said to him, 'F, loan me three .... Lk 11:5
But the f who helps the .... Jn 3:29
Our f Lazarus has fallen asleep, ... Jn 11:11
man go, you are no f of Caesar." .... Jn 19:12
our dear f and worker with us; .... Phm 1:1
And Abraham was called God's f. .... Jam 2:23
who wants to be a f of the world .... Jam 4:4

FRIENDLY
Laban was not as f as he had .... Ge 31:2
father is not as f with me as he .... Ge 31:5
storerooms, was f with Tobiah. .... Ne 13:4
words are not f but are lies..................... Ps 35:20

FRIENDS
me and my f go and cry together. .... Jdg 11:37
Now Job had three f: .... Job 2:11
All my close f hate me; .... Job 19:19
angry with you and your two f, ... Job 42:7
After Job had prayed for his f, ... Job 42:10
but the rich have many f. .... Pr 14:20
are always finding more f, ... Pr 19:4
my milk. Eat, f, and drink; yes .... Sng 5:1
and your f who are sitting in .... Zch 3:8
when the officer sent f to say.................. Lk 7:6
He calls to his f and neighbors .... Lk 15:6
will call her f and neighbors .... Lk 15:9
but on that day they became f. .... Lk 23:12
can show is to die for his f..................... Jn 15:13
You are my f if you do what I .... Jn 15:14
But I call you f, because I have .... Jn 15:15

FRIENDSHIP
I enjoyed your f so much. 2Sa 1:26
God's close f blessed my house .... Job 29:4
We had a good f and walked .... Ps 55:14
few years, a new f will develop. .... Da 11:6
if f is not enough to make him .... Lk 11:8

FRIENDSHIPS
trouble, and a gossip ruins f. .... Pr 16:28
about the sin breaks up f. .... Pr 17:9

FRIGHTEN
You f us very much. .... Jos 2:9
and I'll f him so all his people................. 2Sa 17:2
paid him to f me so I would .... Ne 6:13
who have been trying to f me." .... Ne 6:14
So Tobiah sent letters to f me. .... Ne 6:19
Then you f me with dreams and............. Job 7:14
his terror would no longer f me.............. Job 9:34
and f them with your wind. .... Ps 83:15

FRIGHTENED

will amaze and f everyone who	Je 19:3
will be no enemy to f them.	Je 30:10
messengers in ships to f Cush,	Eze 30:9
used to f people when they	Eze 32:27
They scare and f people.	Hab 1:7
The LORD will f them, because he	Zph 2:11

FRIGHTENED

them, and they became very f.	Lk 2:9
But the people were f.	Lk 8:35

FROGS

I will punish Egypt with f.	Ex 8:2
that looked like f coming out of	Rev 16:13

FROST

thin flakes like f were on the	Ex 16:14
gives birth to the f from the	Job 38:29
and scatters the f like ashes.	Ps 147:16
and in the cold f of the night.	Je 36:30
will be no light, cold, or f.	Zch 14:6

FROZEN

and the wide waters become f.	Job 37:10
the surface of the ocean is f?	Job 38:30

FRUIT

All kinds of f trees will grow	Eze 47:12
It had plenty of good f on it,	Da 4:12
showed me: a basket of summer f.	Am 8:1
the summer f has been picked—	Mic 7:1
are like fig trees with ripe f.	Nah 3:12
trees have not given f yet.	Hag 2:19
their grapevines will have f,	Zch 8:12
every good tree produces good f,	Mt 7:17
but a bad tree produces bad f.	Mt 7:17
you want good f, you must make	Mt 12:33
"You will never again have f."	Mt 21:19
drink of this f of the vine	Mt 26:29
and producing f in their lives.	Mk 4:19
it and patiently produce good f.	Lk 8:15
of mine that does not produce f.	Jn 15:2
that produces f so that it will	Jn 15:2
it will produce even more f.	Jn 15:2
in them, they produce much f.	Jn 15:5
produce much f and show that you	Jn 15:8
go and produce f, fruit that	Jn 15:16
Spirit produces the f of love,	Gal 5:22
You will produce f in every good	Col 1:10
trees without f that are pulled	Jud 1:12
right to eat the f from the tree	Rev 2:7
and the f of the earth is ripe."	Rev 14:15
It produces f twelve times a	Rev 22:2
right to eat the f from the tree	Rev 22:14

FUEL

people are like f for the fire;	Is 9:19
only become f for the flames!	Je 51:58
is thrown into the fire for f,	Eze 15:4
wood of the vine as f for fire.	Eze 15:6
You will be like f for the fire;	Eze 21:32

FULL

ate the seven f and good heads.	Ge 41:7
He must pay the f price plus an	Le 6:5
houses of good things you did	Dt 6:11
got a f bowl of water from it.	Jdg 6:38
wages be paid in f by the LORD,	Ru 2:12
see that it was f of money.	2Ch 24:11
I am f of shame and experience	Job 10:15
I am f of words, and the spirit	Job 32:18
Their mouths are f of curses,	Ps 10:7
They will be f in times of	Ps 37:19
people ate and became very f.	Ps 78:29
the moon is f, when our feast	Ps 81:3
My life is f of troubles, and I	Ps 88:3
man who has his bag f of arrows.	Ps 127:5

FURIOUS

angry quickly but is f of love.	Ps 145:8
Then your barns will be f,	Pr 3:10
When you are f, not even honey	Pr 27:7
their jaws seem f of knives.	Pr 30:14
but the sea never becomes f.	Ec 1:7
If clouds are f of rain, they	Ec 11:3
your hands are f of blood.	Is 1:15
Their land is f of idols.	Is 2:8
earth will be f of the knowledge	Is 11:9
have felt the f anger of the	Is 51:20
Like cages f of birds, their	Je 5:27
land of Judah is f of people who	Je 23:10
Jerusalem once was f of people,	La 1:1
and were f of eyes all around.	Eze 1:18
the land is f of bloody crimes	Eze 7:23
f of wisdom and perfect in	Eze 28:12
of a valley. It was f of bones.	Eze 37:1
fat until you are f and drinking	Eze 39:19
whole body will be f of light.	Mt 6:22
When it was f, the fishermen	Mt 13:48
they are f of the bones of dead	Mt 23:27
inside you are f of hypocrisy	Mt 23:28
My heart is f of sorrow, to	Mt 26:38
that it was already f of water.	Mk 4:37
So, be f of salt, and have peace	Mk 9:50
those days will be f of trouble.	Mk 13:19
It was worth a f year's work.	Mk 14:5
My heart is f of sorrow, to	Mk 14:34
both boats so f that they were	Lk 5:7
f of joy at that time, because	Lk 6:23
will be for you who are f now,	Lk 6:25
who are ungrateful and f of sin.	Lk 6:35
Being f of pain, Jesus prayed	Lk 22:44
and he was f of grace and truth.	Jn 1:14
dragging the net f of fish.	Jn 21:8
was f of big fish, one hundred	Jn 21:11
f of the Spirit and full of	Ac 6:3
of the Spirit and f of wisdom.	Ac 6:3
faith and f of the Holy Spirit	Ac 6:5
Paul stayed two f years in his	Ac 28:30
they became f of sexual sin,	Rm 1:24
They are f of jealousy, murder,	Rm 1:29
Their mouths are f of cursing,	Rm 3:14
sure that you are f of goodness.	Rm 15:14
and evil and f of deadly poison.	Jam 3:8
be explained, a joy f of glory.	1Pe 1:8
world that was f of people who	2Pe 2:5
to you so we may be f of joy.	1Jn 1:4
and golden bowls f of incense,	Rev 5:8
the bodies until they were f.	Rev 19:21
the seven bowls f of the seven	Rev 21:9

FULL-FLOWING

have had peace like a f river.	Is 48:18

FULLEST

joy will be the f possible joy.	Jn 15:11
joy will be the f possible joy.	Jn 16:24

FULLNESS

to give life—life in all its f.	Jn 10:10
can be filled with the f of God.	Eph 3:19

FUR

I caught it by its f and hit it	1Sa 17:35

FURIOUS

became angry and f with them,	Dt 29:28
wall, he was very angry, even f.	Ne 4:1
Don't punish me when you are f.	Ps 38:1
because I was f and very angry	Je 32:37
was f with Shadrach,	Da 3:19
men had tricked him, he was f.	Mt 2:16
The king was f and sent his army	Mt 22:7
heard this, they became f.	Ac 7:54

F

FURNACE

the land, like smoke from a **f**. .... Ge 19:28
took ashes from a **f** and went and .... Ex 9:10
mountain like smoke from a **f,** .... Ex 19:18
you like a **f** for melting iron .... Dt 4:20
pulling them out of a blazing **f.** 1Ki 8:51
A hot **f** tests silver and gold, ... Pr 17:3
and whose **f** is in Jerusalem. .... Is 31:9
was like a **f** for melting iron! .... Je 11:4
be thrown into a blazing **f.**" .... Da 3:6
He ordered the **f** to be heated .... Da 3:19
throw them into the blazing **f,** .... Mt 13:42
evil people into the blazing **f,** .... Mt 13:50
bronze that glows hot in a **f,** .... Rev 1:15
hole like smoke from a big **f.** .... Rev 9:2

FURNISHED

upstairs that is **f** and ready..................... Mk 14:15
you a large, **f** room upstairs. .... Lk 22:12

FURNITURE

and all its **f,** hooks, frames,................... Ex 39:33
the holy **f** and all the holy .... Nu 4:15
take care of the **f** and utensils................. 1Ch 9:29

FURY

of the roar and **f** of the sea. .... Lk 21:25

FUTURE

will give you hope and a good **f.**............. Je 29:11
there is hope for you in the **f,**" .... Je 31:17
is about a time in the **f.**" .... Da 10:14

G

GABBATHA

Hebrew language the name is **G.** .... Jn 19:13

GABRIEL

G, explain the vision to this .... Da 8:16
G came to where I was standing. .... Da 8:17
But **G** said to me, "Human being, ... Da 8:17
While **G** was speaking, I fell .... Da 8:18
G came to me. (I had seen him in .... Da 9:21
The angel answered him, "I am **G.**......... Lk 1:19
sent the angel **G** to Nazareth, ... Lk 1:26

GAD

I am lucky," so she named him **G.** .... Ge 30:11
is the tribe of **G.** The leader .... Nu 2:14
Reuben, **G,** Asher, Zebulun, Dan, ... Dt 27:13
to the land of **G** and Gilead. 1Sa 13:7
But the prophet **G** said to David, ... 1Sa 22:5
and the records of **G** the seer................. 1Ch 29:29
the tribe of **G** twelve thousand, ... Rev 7:5

GADARENE

in the area of the **G** people, ... Mt 8:28

GADDAH

Hazar **G,** Heshmon, Beth Pelet, ... Jos 15:27

GADDI

tribe of Joseph), **G** son of Susi; .... Nu 13:11

GADDIEL

tribe of Zebulun, **G** son of Sodi; .... Nu 13:10

GADI

Menahem son of **G** came up from 2Ki 15:14
Menahem son of **G** became king 2Ki 15:17

GADITES

and the **G** the land that .... Dt 3:16
G lived in Gilead, Bashan and 1Ch 5:16

GAHAM

names were Tebah, **G,** Tahash, and .... Ge 22:24

GAHAR

Giddel, **G,** Reaiah, ... Ezr 2:47
Hanan, Giddel, **G,** .... Ne 7:49

GAIN

What will we **g** if we kill our .... Ge 37:26
of what you **g** and your special .... Dt 12:6
of a tenth of what you **g,**................... Dt 12:11
would we **g** by praying to him? .... Job 21:15
Does he **g** anything if you are................. Job 22:3
don't **g** anything by not sinning............... Job 35:3
Even if you **g** more riches, ... Ps 62:10
correction **g** understanding. .... Pr 15:32
people will **g** some wisdom. .... Pr 19:25
and they will **g** knowledge..................... Pr 19:25
person may **g** some wisdom. .... Pr 21:11
do people really **g** from all the .... Ec 1:3
is nothing to **g** from anything we .... Ec 2:11
Do people really **g** anything from .... Ec 3:9
So what do people really **g?** .... Ec 5:11
They **g** nothing except to look at .... Ec 5:11
So what do they **g** from chasing .... Ec 5:16
He will **g** power and control in .... Da 11:16
He will **g** much power, but only a .... Da 11:23
Evil people **g** while good people............. Hab 1:4
But I **g** nothing if I do not have 1Co 13:3
helping us **g** an eternal glory 2Co 4:17
watching you, to **g** their favor, ... Col 3:22

GAINED

or the riches my hands had **g.** .... Job 31:25
You have **g** gold and silver and .... Eze 28:4
and his army **g** nothing from .... Eze 29:18
human hopes, I have **g** nothing. 1Co 15:32

GAINS

the person who **g** more knowledge........... Ec 1:18
knowledge also **g** more sorrow. .... Ec 1:18

GAIUS

grabbed **G** and Aristarchus, ... Ac 19:29
of Thessalonica; **G,** from Derbe; .... Ac 20:4
G is letting me and the whole .... Rm 16:23
any of you except Crispus and **G** 1Co 1:14
To my dear friend **G,** whom I love 3Jn 1:1

GALAL

Heresh, **G,** and Mattaniah son 1Ch 9:15
son, and **G** was Jeduthun's 1Ch 9:16
was the son of **G,** the son of .... Ne 11:17

GALATIA

of Phrygia and **G** since the Holy............... Ac 16:6
the regions of **G** and Phrygia.................... Ac 18:23
To the churches in **G:** .... Gal 1:2
You people in **G** were told very .... Gal 3:1
went to **G,** and Titus went 2Ti 4:10
around Pontus, **G,** Cappadocia, ... 1Pe 1:1

GALATIAN

I told the **G** churches to do:..................... 1Co 16:1

GALBANUM

resin, onycha, **g,** and pure .... Ex 30:34

GALILEE

Kedesh in **G** in the mountains of .... Jos 20:7
twenty towns in **G** to Hiram king 1Ki 9:11
the Jordan River and north to **G,** .... Is 9:1
dream, he went to the area of **G,** .... Mt 2:22
This is **G** where the non-Jewish .... Mt 4:15
Jesus went everywhere in **G,** .... Mt 4:23
people from **G,** the Ten Towns, ... Mt 4:25
from the town of Nazareth in **G.**" .... Mt 21:11
tell my followers to go on to **G,** .... Mt 28:10
So he went everywhere in **G,** .... Mk 1:39
the most important people in **G.** .... Mk 6:21
to Nazareth, a town in **G,** .... Lk 1:26
Herod, the ruler of **G;** .... Lk 3:1

a city in **G**, and on the Sabbath .... Lk 4:31
in the town of Cana in **G**. .... Jn 2:1
Jesus had come from Judea to **G**, ... Jn 4:47
The Christ will not come from **G**. .... Jn 7:41
answered, "Are you from **G**, too? .... Jn 7:52
They said, "Men of **G**, why are .... Ac 1:11

GALL
wine mixed with **g** to drink. .... Mt 27:34

GALLIM
son of Laish, who was from **G**. 1Sa 25:44
out, Bath **G**! Laishah, listen! .... Is 10:30

GALLIO
When **G** was the governor of the .... Ac 18:12
something, but **G** spoke, saying, ... Ac 18:14
And **G** made them leave the court. .... Ac 18:16
But this did not bother **G**. .... Ac 18:17

GALLON
must give a **g** of olive oil for .... Eze 45:24
also give a **g** of olive oil for .... Eze 46:5
must give a **g** of olive oil for .... Eze 46:7
should give a **g** of olive oil for .... Eze 46:11

GALLONS
held about twenty or thirty **g**. .... Jn 2:6

GALLOPING
G, galloping go Sisera's mighty .... Jdg 5:22
g go Sisera's mighty horses. .... Jdg 5:22
Hear horses **g** and chariots .... Nah 3:2

GAMALIEL
But a Pharisee named **G** stood up .... Ac 5:34
a student of **G**, who carefully .... Ac 22:3

GAMBLE
You would even **g** for orphans and .... Job 6:27

GAMES
in the **g** use self-control 1Co 9:25

GAMMAD
of **G** were in your watchtowers .... Eze 27:11

GAMUL
The twenty-second was **G**. 1Ch 24:17
Beth **G**, and Beth Meon; .... Je 48:23

GANG
from that **g** who does evil. .... Ps 64:2
a **g** of cruel people is trying to .... Ps 86:14
in the middle of a **g** of thieves. .... Je 48:27

GANNIM
Zanoah, En **G**, Tappuah, Enam, ... Jos 15:34
Remeth, En **G**, En Haddan, and .... Jos 19:21
Jarmuth, and En **G**, and the .... Jos 21:29

GAP
that there was not one **g** in it. .... Ne 6:1

GARBAGE
lie in the streets like **g**. .... Is 5:25
will be thrown on the **g** dump," .... Am 4:3
throw filthy **g** on you and make .... Nah 3:6
we were the **g** of the world— 1Co 4:13

GARDEN
God planted a **g** in the east, ... Ge 2:8
the man in the **g** of Eden to care .... Ge 2:15
fruit from any tree in the **g**?" .... Ge 3:1
walking in the **g** during the cool .... Ge 3:8
out of the **g** of Eden to work .... Ge 3:23
like the LORD's **g**, like the land .... Ge 13:10
a vegetable **g**, by using your .... Dt 11:10
to the King's **G** all the way to .... Ne 3:15
you are like a **g** locked up, ... Sng 4:12
dying or like a **g** without water. .... Is 1:30
her deserts into a **g** like Eden; .... Is 51:3
lands like the **g** of the LORD. .... Is 51:3
He cut down his Temple like a **g**; .... La 2:6

you were in Eden, the **g** of God. .... Eze 28:13
seed that a man plants in his **g**. .... Lk 13:19
On the other side there was a **g**, ... Jn 18:1
was crucified, there was a **g**. .... Jn 19:41
In the **g** was a new tomb that had .... Jn 19:41
life, which is in the **g** of God. .... Rev 2:7

GARDENER
So the man said to his **g**, ' .... Lk 13:7
true vine; my Father is the **g**. .... Jn 15:1
he was the **g**, she said to him, ... Jn 20:15

GARDENS
made **g** and parks, and I planted .... Ec 2:5
to feed in the **g** and to gather .... Sng 6:2
to their gods in their **g**, ... Is 65:3
When your **g** and your vineyards .... Am 4:9

GAREB
Ira the Ithrite; **G** the Ithrite, ... 2Sa 23:38
Ira the Ithrite; **G** the Ithrite; 1Ch 11:40
Gate straight to the hill of **G**. .... Je 31:39

GARLIC
melons, leeks, onions, and **g**. .... Nu 11:5

GARMENT
on and puts a **g** on their bodies .... Job 12:18
taken off my **g** and don't want to .... Sng 5:3

GARMITE
Keilah was from the **G** people, ... 1Ch 4:19

GASPING
sound of Jerusalem **g** for breath. .... Je 4:31

GASPS
and ignore my **g** and shouts." .... La 3:56

GATAM
Omar, Zepho, **G**, and Kenaz. .... Ge 36:11
Korah, **G**, and Amalek. These were .... Ge 36:16
Omar, Zepho, **G**, Kenaz, Timna, ... 1Ch 1:36

GATE
Lot was sitting near the city **g**. .... Ge 19:1
to the elders at the city **g**. .... Dt 22:15
went to the city **g** and sat there .... Ru 4:1
for battle at the city **g**. 2Sa 10:8
So the king went to the city **g**. 2Sa 18:8
that the king was at the **g**, ... 2Sa 18:8
was close to him to guard the **g**, ... 2Ki 7:17
from the **G** of Ephraim to 2Ki 14:13
Gate of Ephraim to the Corner **G**, ... 2Ki 14:13
to the King's **G** on the east side 1Ch 9:18
each family chose a **g** to guard. 1Ch 26:13
by lot to guard the East **G**. 1Ch 26:14
guard every day at the East **G**; 1Ch 26:17
in Jerusalem at the Corner **G**, ... 2Ch 26:9
Gate, the Valley **G**, and where 2Ch 26:9
of the Fish **G** and around the 2Ch 33:14
at night through the Valley **G**. .... Ne 2:13
the Dragon Well and the Trash **G**. .... Ne 2:13
to work and rebuild the Sheep **G**. .... Ne 3:1
as a point opposite the Water **G**. .... Ne 3:26
square by the Water **G** Ezra read .... Ne 8:3
at the king's **g** and saw that .... Est 5:9
sitting at the king's **g**." .... Est 5:13
would go to the city **g** and sit .... Job 29:7
is the LORD's **g**; only those who .... Ps 118:20
near the Gate of Bath Rabbim. .... Sng 7:4
those who battle at the city **g**. .... Is 28:6
the front of the Potsherd **G**. .... Je 19:2
of the New **G** of the Temple. .... Je 36:10
through the **g** between the two .... Je 52:7
to the north **g** of the inner .... Eze 8:3
The width of the **g** was about .... Eze 40:11
man measured from **g** to gate on .... Eze 40:27
to me, "This **g** will stay shut; .... Eze 44:2

GATEKEEPER

the bar of the **g** to Damascus .... Am 1:5
Enter through the narrow **g.** .... Mt 7:13
The **g** is wide and the road is .... Mt 7:13
was laid at the rich man's **g.** .... Lk 16:20
This pool is near the Sheep **G.** .... Jn 5:2
to the iron **g** that separated..................... Ac 12:10
outside the city **g** to the river .... Ac 16:13
each **g** having been made from a .... Rev 21:21

GATEKEEPER

and he called to the **g,** "Look! 2Sa 18:26
was the **g** at the entrance to 1Ch 9:21

GATEKEEPERS

and called to the **g** of the city.............. 2Ki 7:10
These **g** from the tribe of Levi 1Ch 9:18
of Korah were **g** and were 1Ch 9:19
These are the groups of the **g.** 1Ch 26:1
as secretaries, officers, and **g.**.............. 2Ch 34:13
singers, **g,** Temple servants.................... Ezr 7:24

GATEPOST

the gateway and stand by the **g,** .... Eze 46:2

GATES

with high walls and **g** with bars. .... Dt 3:5
write them on your doors and **g.** .... Dt 6:9
closed the city **g** and guarded................ Jos 6:1
inner and outer **g** of the city. 2Sa 18:24
guards at the **g** of the Temple 2Ch 23:19
and its **g** have been burned." .... Ne 1:3
The **g** of Jerusalem should not be .... Ne 7:3
the storerooms next to the **g:** .... Ne 12:25
hope go down to the **g** of death?.............. Job 17:16
me go through the **g** of death.................. Ps 9:13
Then, at the **g** of Jerusalem, I .... Ps 9:14
Open up, you **g.** Open wide, you.............. Ps 24:7
Open up, you **g.** Open wide, you.............. Ps 24:9
He loves its **g** more than any .... Ps 87:2
we are standing at your **g.** .... Ps 122:2
Beside the city **g,** at the .... Pr 8:3
like the barred **g** of a palace. .... Pr 18:19
jewels for the **g** and precious .... Is 54:12
Salvation and your **g** Praise. .... Is 60:18
Go through, go through the **g!** .... Is 62:10
load through the **g** of Jerusalem............... Je 17:24
a fire at the **g** of Jerusalem, ... Je 17:27
It does not have **g** or fences to .... Je 49:31
down and her high **g** burned. .... Je 51:58
No one passes through her **g.**.................. La 1:4
logs to break down the city **g,**............... Eze 21:22
The river **g** are thrown open, ... Nah 2:6
the city **g** day and night, ... Ac 9:24
wall with twelve **g** with twelve .... Rev 21:12
The city's **g** will never be shut .... Rev 21:25

GATH

left in Gaza, **G,** and Ashdod. .... Jos 11:22
Gaza, Ashkelon, **G,** and Ekron. 1Sa 6:17
won them back, from Ekron to **G.** 1Sa 7:14
fighter from **G** named Goliath. 1Sa 17:4
the Philistine champion from **G,**............... 1Sa 17:23
and went to Achish king of **G.** 1Sa 21:10
that David had run away to **G,** 1Sa 27:4
tell it in **G.** Don't announce.................... 2Sa 1:20
then go down to **G** of the .... Am 6:2
Don't tell it in **G.** Don't cry in .... Mic 1:10

GATHER

g some of every kind of food .... Ge 6:21
all the flocks would **g** there, ... Ge 29:3
told his relatives to **g** rocks, ... Ge 31:46
They should **g** all the food that .... Ge 41:35
Go and **g** the elders and tell .... Ex 3:16
Let them **g** their own straw. .... Ex 5:7
must go out and **g** what they need .... Ex 16:4
they are to **g** twice as much as .... Ex 16:5

as much as they **g** on other days. .... Ex 16:5
one of you must **g** what he needs, ... Ex 16:16
You should **g** the food for six .... Ex 16:26
the people went out to **g** food, ... Ex 16:27
when you **g** all the crops from .... Ex 23:16
G from the people of Israel this .... Ex 30:16
Weeks when you **g** the first grain .... Ex 34:22
Then **g** the people together at .... Le 8:3
onto the ground, don't **g** it up. .... Le 19:9
will give you and **g** its harvest. .... Le 23:10
onto the ground, don't **g** it up. .... Le 23:22
or **g** the grapes from your vines .... Le 25:5
we don't plant seeds or **g** crops, ... Le 25:20
They must **g** all the things used .... Nu 4:12
They must **g** all the things used .... Nu 4:14
and **g** all the Israelites around. .... Nu 8:9
the people should **g** before you .... Nu 10:3
When you want to **g** the people, ... Nu 10:7
The people would go to **g** it, ... Nu 11:8
Aaron should **g** the people....................... Nu 20:8
G the people and I will give .... Nu 21:16
will be able to **g** your grain, ... Dt 11:14
G up everything those people .... Dt 13:16
but he will **g** you and bring you .... Dt 30:4
G all the people: the men, women, ... Dt 31:12
G all the older leaders of your .... Dt 31:28
'Go and **g** ten thousand men of .... Jdg 4:6
enough to let me **g** the grain he .... Ru 2:2
grain and **g** what they leave .... Ru 2:7
Don't go to **g** grain for yourself .... Ru 2:8
Let her **g** even around the piles .... Ru 2:15
your hands, and let her **g** them. .... Ru 2:16
Where did you **g** all this grain .... Ru 2:19
no one can **g** it back. 2Sa 14:14
G all the Israelites from Dan to 2Sa 17:11
I came here to **g** some wood so I 1Ki 17:12
G an army like the one that was.............. 1Ki 20:25
out into the field to **g** plants. 2Ki 4:39
living in Israel to **g** together. 1Ch 22:2
it took three days to **g** it all. 2Ch 20:25
of Judah and **g** the money all 2Ch 24:5
will **g** your people from the far .... Ne 1:9
God caused me to **g** the important .... Ne 7:5
have the right to **g** together to .... Est 8:11
His armies; they prepare to .... Job 19:12
They **g** hay and straw in the .... Job 24:6
in your grain and **g** it to your .... Job 39:12
G the nations around you and .... Ps 7:7
He says, "**G** around, you who .... Ps 50:5
a banner to **g** those who fear you .... Ps 60:4
give it to them, they **g** it up. .... Ps 104:28
the summer and **g** their supplies .... Pr 6:8
Those who **g** crops on time are .... Pr 10:5
G the grass from the hills. .... Pr 27:25
Who can **g** up the waters in his .... Pr 30:4
stones and a time to **g** them. .... Ec 3:5
in the gardens and to **g** lilies. .... Sng 6:2
I will **g** some men to be reliable .... Is 8:2
and he will **g** the people of .... Is 11:12
will **g** the scattered people of .... Is 11:12
the people **g** up what they have .... Is 15:7
from Elam will **g** their arrows................. Is 22:6
and no summer fruit to **g.** .... Is 32:10
owls will **g** their young under................. Is 34:15
will **g** with their own kind. .... Is 34:15
his Spirit will **g** them together. .... Is 34:16
the east and **g** you from the west .... Is 43:5
All the nations **g** together, ... Is 43:9
g together and come before me; .... Is 45:20
Those who **g** food will eat it, ... Is 62:9
who **g** the grapes will drink .... Is 62:9
I will **g** all nations and all .... Is 66:18
G the few people of Israel who .... Je 6:9

you would g the last grapes on .... Je 6:9
The children g wood, and the .... Je 7:18
No one will g up the bones and .... Je 8:2
will be no one to g them.'" .... Je 9:22
Go, g the wild animals. .... Je 12:9
but I will g those who are left .... Je 23:3
for them or g up their bodies .... Je 25:33
but I will g you from all the .... Je 29:14
and I will g them from the .... Je 31:8
But soon I will g them from all .... Je 32:37
no one will be able to g you. .... Je 49:5
G your armies to attack it! .... Je 49:14
their crops or g the harvest. .... Je 50:16
will g you from the nations and .... Eze 11:17
So I will g all your lovers with .... Eze 16:37
I will g all those who loved and .... Eze 16:37
I will g them against you from .... Eze 16:37
and anger I will g you from the .... Eze 20:34
nations and g you from the lands .... Eze 20:41
same way I will g you in my hot............. Eze 22:20
I will g the people of Israel .... Eze 28:25
forty years I will g Egypt from .... Eze 29:13
from the nations and g them from .... Eze 34:13
the nations and g you out of all .... Eze 36:24
will g them from all around and............. Eze 37:21
other lands and g them from the .... Eze 39:27
the North will g another army, ... Da 11:13
the South will g a large and .... Da 11:25
nations, I will g them together. .... Hos 8:10
will g all the nations together .... Joe 3:2
your soldiers to g the nations. .... Joe 3:11
time, I will g the crippled; .... Mic 4:6
So, strong city, g your soldiers .... Mic 5:1
road. Get ready. G all your .... Nah 2:1
They g other nations for .... Hab 2:5
G together, gather, you unwanted .... Zph 2:1
Gather together, g, you unwanted .... Zph 2:1
decided that I will g nations .... Zph 3:8
cannot walk and g my people who .... Zph 3:19
At that time I will g you;..................... Zph 3:20
my people and g them together. .... Zch 10:8
of Egypt and g them from Assyria .... Zch 10:10
more workers to g his harvest." .... Mt 9:38
First g the weeds and tie them .... Mt 13:30
Then g the wheat and bring it to .... Mt 13:30
the workers who g are God's .... Mt 13:39
and they will g out of his .... Mt 13:41
I wanted to g your people as .... Mt 23:37
there the vultures will g......................... Mt 24:28
they will g his chosen people .... Mt 24:31
g crops where you did not sow .... Mt 25:24
plant and that I g crops where I .... Mt 25:26
the earth to g his chosen people............. Mk 13:27
People don't g figs from .... Lk 6:44
workers to help g his harvest................. Lk 10:2
I wanted to g your people as .... Lk 13:34
there the vultures will g." .... Lk 17:37
didn't earn and g food that you .... Lk 19:21
G the leftover pieces of fish .... Jn 6:12
sharp sickle and g the bunches .... Rev 14:18
whole world to g them together .... Rev 16:14
Come and g together for the .... Rev 19:17
and Magog—to g them for battle .... Rev 20:8

GATHERED

under the sky be g together so .... Ge 1:9
that was g together "seas." .... Ge 1:10
Then Abraham g Ishmael, all the .... Ge 17:23
that year he g a great harvest................. Ge 26:12
He g more wealth until he became .... Ge 26:13
the sheep to be g for the night, ... Ge 29:7
that until all the flocks are g. .... Ge 29:8
so he g his relatives and began .... Ge 31:23

bundles of wheat g around it and .... Ge 37:7
And Joseph g all the food .... Ge 41:48
Moses and Aaron g all the elders .... Ex 4:29
some people g much, and some .... Ex 16:17
much, and some g little. .... Ex 16:17
The person who g more did not .... Ex 16:18
the person who g less have too .... Ex 16:18
Each person g just as much as he .... Ex 16:18
each person g as much food as he .... Ex 16:21
the people g twice as much food— .... Ex 16:22
Eat the food you g yesterday. .... Ex 16:25
So they g around Aaron and said, ... Ex 32:1
family of Levi g around Moses. .... Ex 32:26
Moses and g the Israelite .... Ex 35:1
after you have g in the crops of .... Le 23:39
He g seventy of the elders .... Nu 11:24
went out and g quail all that .... Nu 11:32
Everyone g at least sixty...................... Nu 11:32
of all the Israelites g there. .... Nu 14:5
These men g two hundred fifty .... Nu 16:2
Korah g all his followers who .... Nu 16:19
the priest g all the bronze .... Nu 16:39
When the people g to complain .... Nu 16:42
Moses and Aaron g the people in .... Nu 20:10
He g his whole army together, ... Nu 21:23
Israelites were g at the .... Nu 25:6
on the day you were g there. .... Dt 9:10
on the day you were g there. .... Dt 10:4
after you have g your harvest................. Dt 16:13
when you were g at Mount Sinai. .... Dt 18:16
the leaders of the people g,..................... Dt 33:5
the leaders of the people g,..................... Dt 33:21
morning Joshua g his men .... Jos 8:10
the Israelites were g together— .... Jos 8:35
these kings g to fight Joshua .... Jos 9:2
They g old sacks and old leather .... Jos 9:4
and Eglon—g their armies, went .... Jos 10:5
of the Israelites g together at .... Jos 18:1
g all the tribes of Israel .... Jos 24:1
he g ten thousand men to follow .... Jdg 4:10
Sisera g his nine hundred iron .... Jdg 4:13
Beth Millo g beside the great .... Jdg 9:6
they g in the safest room of the .... Jdg 9:46
Tower of Shechem had g there. .... Jdg 9:47
the fields and g the grain that................. Ru 2:3
So Ruth g grain in the field.................... Ru 2:17
saw how much she had g........................ Ru 2:18
Boaz g ten of the elders of the .... Ru 4:2
When Samuel g all the tribes of 1Sa 10:20
Saul g the people together at 1Sa 11:8
Philistines g to fight Israel 1Sa 13:5
Then Saul g his army and entered 1Sa 14:20
The Philistines g their armies................. 1Sa 17:1
the Israelites g in the Valley 1Sa 17:2
Everyone g here will know the 1Sa 17:47
was unsatisfied g around David,............. 1Sa 22:2
the Philistines g their armies 1Sa 28:1
Saul g all the Israelites and 1Sa 28:4
The Philistines g all their 1Sa 29:1
Joab came back and g the people 2Sa 2:30
David again g all the chosen men 2Sa 6:1
g all the Israelites together...................... 2Sa 10:5
So David g all the army and went 2Sa 12:29
and soldiers g all around David.............. 2Sa 16:6
armor also g around Absalom 2Sa 18:15
Then the people g the bodies of 2Sa 21:13
Philistines were g for battle, ... 2Sa 23:9
who g food from their districts 1Ki 4:7
the Israelites g before the Ark 1Ki 8:5
Rezon g some men and became the 1Ki 11:24
he g one hundred eighty thousand.......... 1Ki 12:21
So they g around him, and 1Ki 18:30
king of Aram g together all his 1Ki 20:1

G

So Ahab g the young officers of 1Ki 20:15
Ben-Hadad g the army of Aram 1Ki 20:26
Samaria and g Israel's army. 2Ki 3:6
So they g everyone old enough to 2Ki 3:21
king of Aram g his whole army 2Ki 6:24
Then Jehu g all the people 2Ki 10:18
have g from the people 2Ki 22:4
Then the king g all the elders 2Ki 23:1
So David g all the Israelites, ... 1Ch 13:5
about this, he g all the 1Ch 19:17
David g all the leaders of 1Ch 23:2
all the Israelites who were g, ... 1Ch 29:1
of all the people who were g. 1Ch 29:10
we have g all this to build your 1Ch 29:16
Your people g here are happy to.............. 1Ch 29:17
to all the people who were g, ... 1Ch 29:20
the Israelites g before the Ark 2Ch 5:6
the people of Israel g there, ... 2Ch 6:13
he g one hundred eighty thousand 2Ch 11:1
of Judah who had g in Jerusalem 2Ch 12:5
Then Asa g all the people from 2Ch 15:9
and these people g in Jerusalem.............. 2Ch 15:10
in Judah and g the Levites 2Ch 23:2
and they g the leaders of the 2Ch 23:2
did this often and g much money. 2Ch 24:11
Amaziah g the people of Judah 2Ch 25:5
g the things from the Temple 2Ch 28:24
and Levites and g them in the 2Ch 29:4
These Levites g their brothers 2Ch 29:15
King Hezekiah g the leaders 2Ch 29:20
had not yet g in Jerusalem.................... 2Ch 30:3
gatekeepers had g from the 2Ch 34:9
Then the king g all the elders 2Ch 34:29
and I g the leaders of Israel to .... Ezr 7:28
God of Israel g around me .... Ezr 9:4
and children g around him who .... Ezr 10:1
and Benjamin g in Jerusalem. .... Ezr 10:9
did all my men who were g there. .... Ne 5:16
the people of Israel g together .... Ne 8:1
listen and understand had g. .... Ne 8:2
They g to study the words of the .... Ne 8:13
the people g as the law said. .... Ne 8:18
month, the people of Israel g. .... Ne 9:1
Then I g the Levites and .... Ne 13:11
girls were g the second time. .... Est 2:19
bundles of grain g at the right .... Job 5:26
God's terrors are g against me. .... Job 6:4
wear what evil people have g,................ Job 27:17
They g desert plants among the .... Job 30:4
He g the water of the sea into a .... Ps 33:7
in trouble, they g and laughed; .... Ps 35:15
they g to attack before I knew .... Ps 35:15
and has g them from other lands, ... Ps 107:3
money that is g little by little .... Pr 13:11
I also g silver and gold for .... Ec 2:8
I have g my myrrh with my spice. .... Sng 5:1
They will be g together like .... Is 24:22
that Israel might be g to him. .... Is 49:5
join those who are already g." .... Is 56:8
the gods you have g help you. .... Is 57:13
and on the young men g together. .... Je 6:11
And I g all of Jaazaniah's .... Je 35:3
at Mizpah and g a large harvest.............. Je 40:12
all the Jews g around you would .... Je 40:15
Common people g, and drunkards .... Eze 23:42
will have been g from many .... Eze 38:8
have been g from the nations,................. Eze 38:12
He has g them like bundles of .... Mic 4:12
Large crowds g around him, ... Mt 13:2
the streets and g all the people .... Mt 22:10
the world will be g before him, ... Mt 25:32
the law and the elders were g. .... Mt 26:57
When the people g at Pilate's .... Mt 27:17

and they all g around him. .... Mt 27:27
The whole town g at the door. .... Mk 1:33
Many people g together so that .... Mk 2:2
went home, but again a crowd g. .... Mk 3:20
A great crowd g around him, ... Mk 4:1
large crowd g around him there. .... Mk 5:21
The apostles g around Jesus and .... Mk 6:30
Jerusalem, they g around Jesus. .... Mk 7:1
the teachers of the law were g. .... Mk 14:53
great crowd was g, and people .... Lk 8:4
and what was left over was g up, ... Lk 9:17
of people had g that they were .... Lk 12:1
younger son g up all that was.............. Lk 15:13
people who had g there to watch .... Lk 23:48
eleven apostles and others g. .... Lk 24:33
So they g up the pieces and .... Jn 6:13
Some people g around him and .... Jn 10:24
where he saw many people g.................. Ac 10:27
They g the money and gave it to.............. Ac 11:30
people were g there, praying. .... Ac 12:12
But the followers g around him, ... Ac 14:10
Paul and Barnabas g the church.............. Ac 14:27
the elders g to consider this .... Ac 15:6
Antioch where they g the church .... Ac 15:30
Some women had g there, so we .... Ac 16:13
the place where the crowd was g. .... Ac 21:32
and all who are g here with us, ... Ac 25:24
Paul g a pile of sticks and was .... Ac 28:3
The person who g more did not 2Co 8:15
the person who g less have too 2Co 8:15
alive will be g up with them 1Th 4:17
of angels g together with joy. .... Heb 12:22
g the earth's grapes and threw .... Rev 14:19
the evil spirits g the kings .... Rev 16:16
armies were g together to make .... Rev 19:19
the earth and g around the camp .... Rev 20:9

GATHERING

they found a man g wood on the .... Nu 15:32
who found him g wood brought him .... Nu 15:33
followers were g in Galilee, ... Mt 17:22
saw that a crowd was quickly g,.............. Mk 9:25
I didn't earn and g food that I................ Lk 19:22
paid and is g crops for eternal .... Jn 4:36
who was with the g of the .... Ac 7:38
no people were g around me. .... Ac 24:18

GATHERS

He g them like lambs in his arms .... Is 40:11
who g the Israelites that were.................. Is 56:8
like someone who g grapes." .... Je 6:9
people as a hen g her chicks .... Mt 23:37
people as a hen g her chicks .... Lk 13:34

GAVE

The man g names to all the tame .... Ge 2:20
She also g some of the fruit to .... Ge 3:6
You g this woman to me and she .... Ge 3:12
Then Abram g Melchizedek a.................. Ge 14:20
I g my slave girl to you, and .... Ge 16:5
water and g the boy a drink. .... Ge 21:19
she g water to my camels too.................. Ge 24:46
Then Jacob g Esau bread and................. Ge 25:34
Then she g Jacob the tasty food .... Ge 27:17
Laban g his slave girl Zilpah to .... Ge 29:24
she g her slave girl Zilpah to .... Ge 30:9
The same land I g to Abraham and .... Ge 35:12
Joseph g them wagons as the king........... Ge 45:21
and he g his daughter Zipporah .... Ex 2:21
for the Egyptians but g light to .... Ex 14:20
he g him the two stone tablets .... Ex 31:18
East Manasseh I g the rest of .... Dt 3:13
of Jephunneh and g him the city .... Jos 14:13
So the LORD g the people all the .... Jos 21:43
The LORD g them peace on all .... Jos 21:44

for water, but Jael g him milk. .... Jdg 5:25
And Samson g a feast, as was the .... Jdg 14:10
and she g birth to a son. .... Ru 4:13
neighbors g the boy his name, ... Ru 4:17
the Israelites g a great shout 1Sa 4:5
the meat I g you, the portion 1Sa 9:23
Then Saul g him his daughter. 1Sa 18:27
I g you his kingdom and his 2Sa 12:8
g birth to a baby while she was 1Ki 3:17
God g Solomon great wisdom so he 1Ki 4:29
of the land I g their ancestors. 2Ki 21:8
He g it to Shaphan, who read 2Ki 22:8
So the LORD g them peace in all 2Ch 15:15
prisoners and g those who were 2Ch 28:15
spoke to him and g him a sign. 2Ch 32:24
Then these men g help to the .... Ezr 8:36
took some and g it to the king. .... Ne 2:1
you g them bread from heaven. .... Ne 9:15
You g your good Spirit to teach .... Ne 9:20
g them manna to eat and water .... Ne 9:20
The LORD g these things to me, ... Job 1:21
the LORD g him success again. .... Job 42:10
The Lord g the command, and a .... Ps 68:11
in my food and g me vinegar to .... Ps 69:21
he g them grain from heaven. .... Ps 78:24
He g this rule to the people of .... Ps 81:5
the rules and laws he g them. .... Ps 99:7
will return to God who g it. .... Ec 12:7
of the one who g her birth. .... Sng 6:9
I g Egypt to pay for you, and I .... Is 43:3
The Lord GOD g me the ability to .... Is 50:4
to the land I g their ancestors, ... Je 30:3
Jehoiachin and g him a seat of .... Je 52:32
in the land I g to your .... Eze 36:28
chief officer, g them Babylonian .... Da 1:7
g these four young men wisdom .... Da 1:17
So King Darius g the order, ... Da 6:16
I g her much silver and gold, ... Hos 2:8
So I g you a king, but only in .... Hos 13:11
together and g them authority to .... Mt 10:1
the bread and g it to his .... Mt 14:19
the fish and g thanks to God. .... Mt 15:36
Who g you this authority?" .... Mt 21:23
He g one servant five bags of .... Mt 25:15
I was hungry, and you g me food. .... Mt 25:35
The soldiers g Jesus wine mixed .... Mt 27:34
g it to the girl, and the girl .... Mk 6:28
she g birth to her first son. .... Lk 2:7
Then Levi g a big dinner for .... Lk 5:29
out two coins, g them to the .... Lk 10:35
servants and g a coin to each .... Lk 19:13
took a cup, g thanks, and said .... Lk 22:17
some bread, g thanks, broke it .... Lk 22:19
g him a piece of broiled fish. .... Lk 24:42
believe in him he g the right to .... Jn 1:12
so much that he g his one and .... Jn 3:16
g us this well and drank from .... Jn 4:12
g them bread from heaven to eat. .... Jn 6:31
and g it to Judas Iscariot, ... Jn 13:26
of your name, the name you g me. .... Jn 17:12
glory that you g me so that they .... Jn 17:22
Pilate g his permission, so .... Jn 19:38
and he g those commands to us. .... Ac 7:38
which God g you through his .... Ac 7:53
He g her his hand and helped her .... Ac 9:41
they were happy and g honor to .... Ac 13:48
church and g them the letter. .... Ac 15:30
God g me the special work of an .... Rm 1:5
And God g Jesus to show today .... Rm 3:26
The teaching I g you was like 1Co 3:2
us did the work God g us to do. 1Co 3:5
And they g in a way we did not 2Co 8:5
Jesus g himself for our sins to .... Gal 1:4

loved me and g himself to save .... Gal 2:20
God g that grace to us freely, ... Eph 1:6
and he g gifts to people." .... Eph 4:8
And Christ g gifts to people— .... Eph 4:11
the church and g himself for it .... Eph 5:25
g himself as a payment to free 1Ti 2:6
and Abraham g him a tenth of .... Heb 7:2
leaving Egypt and g instructions .... Heb 11:22
because of the Spirit God g us. 1Jn 3:24
which God g to him, to show .... Rev 1:1
very afraid and g glory to the .... Rev 11:13
agreement God g to his people .... Rev 11:19
Then the woman g birth to a son .... Rev 12:5
And the dragon g the beast all .... Rev 13:2
living creatures g to the seven .... Rev 15:7
The sea g up the dead who were .... Rev 20:13

GAZA

The men of Judah captured G, ... Jdg 1:18
day Samson went to G and saw a .... Jdg 16:1
For the many crimes of G, ... Am 1:6
leads down to G from Jerusalem— .... Ac 8:26

GAZELLE

as if it were a deer or a g; .... Dt 12:15
as you would eat g or deer meat. .... Dt 12:22
deer, g, roe deer, wild goats, ... Dt 14:5
as they would eat a g or a deer. .... Dt 15:22
is like a g or a young deer .... Sng 2:9
Be like a g or a young deer on .... Sng 2:17
like twins of a g, feeding among .... Sng 4:5
two fawns, like twins of a g. .... Sng 7:3
be like a g or a young deer on .... Sng 8:14

GAZELLES

and as fast as g over the hills. 1Ch 12:8
me by the g and the deer not .... Sng 2:7
me by the g and the deer not .... Sng 3:5

GAZEZ

mother of Haran, Moza, and G. 1Ch 2:46
Haran was the father of G. 1Ch 2:46

GAZZAM

Rezin, Nekoda, G, ... Ezr 2:48
G, Uzza, Paseah, ... Ne 7:51

GEBA

incense, from G to Beersheba. 2Ki 23:8

GEBALITES

the G, and the area of Lebanon .... Jos 13:5

GEDALIAH

of Babylon had made G governor, ... 2Ki 25:23
so they came to G at Mizpah. 2Ki 25:23

GEDER

Debir, G, ... Jos 12:13
Baal-Hanan, from G, was in 1Ch 27:28

GEDERAH

Adithaim, and G (also called .... Jos 15:36
in Netaim and G and worked for 1Ch 4:23
Johanan, and Jozabad from G. 1Ch 12:4

GEDEROTH

G, Beth Dagon, Naamah, and .... Jos 15:41
Aijalon, G, Soco, Timnah, ... 2Ch 28:18

GEDEROTHAIM

and Gederah (also called G). .... Jos 15:36

GEHAZI

So G went after Naaman. 2Ki 5:21

GELILOTH

It continued to G near the .... Jos 18:17
and East Manasseh went to G, ... Jos 22:10
at the border of Canaan at G, ... Jos 22:11

GEM

It looked like a sapphire **g**. .... Eze 1:26
like a sapphire **g** which looked .... Eze 10:1
Every valuable **g** was on you: .... Eze 28:13

GEMALLI

tribe of Dan, Ammiel son of **G;** .... Nu 13:12

GEMARIAH

of Shaphan and **G** son of Hilkiah .... Je 29:3
in the room of **G** son of Shaphan, ... Je 36:10
Micaiah son of **G**, the son of .... Je 36:11
son of Acbor; **G** son of Shaphan; .... Je 36:12
and **G** even tried to talk King .... Je 36:25

GENERALS

the rulers, the **g**, the rich....................... Rev 6:15
of kings, **g**, mighty people, ... Rev 19:18

GENERATIONS

for ten **g** may not come .... Dt 23:2
descendants for ten **g** may come .... Dt 23:3
were fourteen **g** from Abraham to .... Mt 1:17
were fourteen **g** from David until .... Mt 1:17
were fourteen **g** from the .... Mt 1:17

GENEROUS

wine, because he was very **g**. .... Est 1:7
It is good to be merciful and **g**. .... Ps 112:5
G people will be blessed, ... Pr 22:9
in order the **g** gift you promised 2Co 9:5
And it will be a **g** gift—not one 2Co 9:5
of grace, showing how **g** he is. .... Eph 4:7
to be **g** and ready to share...................... 1Ti 6:18
is **g** to everyone and will give .... Jam 1:5

GENNESARET

lake, they came to shore at **G**. .... Mt 14:34
came to shore at **G** and tied the .... Mk 6:53

GENTLE

and a **g** word can get through to.............. Pr 25:15
because I am **g** and humble in .... Mt 11:29
But we were very **g** with you, ... 1Th 2:7
but rather be **g** and peaceable, ... 1Ti 3:3
and to be **g** and polite to all .... Tit 3:2
is able to be **g** with those who .... Heb 5:2
then peaceful, **g**, and easy to .... Jam 3:17

GENTLENESS

punishment or with love and **g**? 1Co 4:21
you with the **g** and the kindness.............. 2Co 10:1
g, self-control. There is no law .... Gal 5:23
humility, **g**, and patience. .... Col 3:12
faith, love, patience, and **g**. 1Ti 6:11
Then in **g** accept God's teaching.............. Jam 1:21
good things with a **g** that comes.............. Jam 3:13

GENTLY

He **g** leads the mothers of the.................. Is 40:11

GENUBATH

They had a son named **G**. 1Ki 11:20

GERA

Beker, Ashbel, **G**, Naaman, Ehi, ... Ge 46:21
son of **G** from the people of .... Jdg 3:15
his name was Shimei son of **G**. 2Sa 16:5
Shimei son of **G**, a Benjaminite 2Sa 19:16
Shimei son of **G** came to him and 2Sa 19:18
son of **G**, the Benjaminite, ... 1Ki 2:8
sons were Addar, **G**, Abihud, ... 1Ch 8:3
G, Shephuphan, and Huram. 1Ch 8:5
were Naaman, Ahijah, and **G**. 1Ch 8:7
G forced them to leave. 1Ch 8:7

GERAHS

shekel will be worth twenty **g**, ... Eze 45:12

GERAR

Abimelech king of **G** heard this,............... Ge 20:2
the town of **G** to see Abimelech .... Ge 26:1

GERASENE

to the area of the **G** people. .... Mk 5:1
to the area of the **G** people. .... Lk 8:26
people of the **G** country asked .... Lk 8:37

GERIZIM

from Mount **G** and the curses .... Dt 11:29
stand on Mount **G** to bless the .... Dt 27:12
half stood in front of Mount **G**. .... Jos 8:33
and stood on the top of Mount **G**. .... Jdg 9:7

GERSHOM

Moses named him **G**, because Moses .... Ex 2:22
The first son was named **G**, ... Ex 18:3
Jonathan son of **G**, Moses' son, ... Jdg 18:30
Moses' sons were **G** and Eliezer. 1Ch 23:15
descendant of **G**, who was Moses' 1Ch 26:24
of Phinehas: **G**. From the .... Ezr 8:2

GERSHON

Levi's sons were **G**, Kohath, and.............. Ge 46:11

GESHAN

Regem, Jotham, **G**, Pelet, Ephah, ... 1Ch 2:47

GESHEM

and **G** the Arab heard about it, ... Ne 2:19
Tobiah, **G** the Arab, and our .... Ne 6:1
So Sanballat and **G** sent me this............... Ne 6:2
Sanballat and **G** sent the same .... Ne 6:4
nations, and **G** says it is true .... Ne 6:6

GESHUR

After Absalom ran away to **G**, ... 2Sa 13:38
while I was living in **G** in Aram................ 2Sa 15:8

GESHURITES

border of the **G** and Maacathites .... Dt 3:14

GET

I want you to **g** her for me so I .... Jdg 14:2
G away from me, you who do evil, ... Ps 119:115
G wisdom and understanding. .... Pr 4:5
It is better to **g** wisdom than .... Pr 16:16
said to me, "**G** up, my darling; .... Sng 2:10
Don't let the belt **g** wet.".......................... Je 13:1
not let anyone go out to **g** food. .... Je 19:9
G rid of all the sins you have .... Eze 18:31
and **g** for yourselves a new heart .... Eze 18:31
love you, you will **g** no reward. .... Mt 5:46
Where did this man **g** this wisdom .... Mt 13:54
his followers to **g** into the boat .... Mt 14:22
How can we **g** enough bread to .... Mt 15:33
not go back to **g** their coats. .... Mt 24:18
not go back to **g** their coats. .... Mk 13:16
where will you **g** this living.................... Jn 4:11
said to Peter, "**G** up, Peter; .... Ac 10:13

GETHER

were Uz, Hul, **G**, and Meshech. .... Ge 10:23
were Uz, Hul, **G**, and Meshech. 1Ch 1:17

GETHSEMANE

followers to a place called **G**. .... Mt 26:36
went to a place called **G**......................... Mk 14:32

GETS

his idol and **g** the beast's mark .... Rev 14:9

GETTING

people from **g** what they want. .... Pr 10:3

GEUEL

the tribe of Gad, **G** son of Maki............... Nu 13:15

GEZER

force the Canaanites to leave **G**, ... Jos 16:10
of the Canaanites living in **G**. .... Jdg 1:29

cities of Hazor, Megiddo, and **G**.............. 1Ki 9:15
had attacked and captured **G**.................. 1Ki 9:16

GHOST
sound like the voice of a **g**; .... Is 29:4
They said, "It's a **g**!" .... Mt 14:26
he was a **g** and cried out. .... Mk 6:49
thought they were seeing a **g**............... Lk 24:37
because a **g** does not have a .... Lk 24:39

GHOSTS
g will not rise from death. .... Is 26:14

GIAH
near **G** on the way to the desert 2Sa 2:24

GIANT
He was like a **g** snake that .... Je 51:34
g eagle with big wings and long.............. Eze 17:3
was another **g** eagle with big .... Eze 17:7
There was a **g** red dragon with .... Rev 12:3
The **g** dragon was thrown down out .... Rev 12:9
G hailstones, each weighing .... Rev 16:21

GIANTS
northern end of the Valley of **G**. .... Jos 15:8

GIBBAR
the descendants of **G**—95. .... Ezr 2:20

GIBEA
the father of Macbenah and **G**. 1Ch 2:49

GIBEAH
and I came to **G** in Benjamin to .... Jdg 20:4
the men of **G** came after me. .... Jdg 20:5
Saul also went to his home in **G**. 1Sa 10:26
and went to **G** in Benjamin. 1Sa 13:15
the people at **G** of Saul will run .... Is 10:29
the horn in **G** and the trumpet .... Hos 5:8
have sinned since the time of **G**,............ Hos 10:9

GIBEATH
the Israelites at **G** Haaraloth. .... Jos 5:3

GIBEON
the people of **G** heard how Joshua .... Jos 9:3
G was not a little town like Ai; .... Jos 10:2
Sun, stand still over **G**. .... Jos 10:12
men at the pool of **G**. 2Sa 2:13
Solomon went to **G** to offer a 1Ki 3:4
at the place of worship in **G**. 1Ch 16:39
from the town of **G**, spoke to me .... Je 28:1
near the big pool of water at **G**. .... Je 41:12

GIBEONITES
David called the **G** together and.............. 2Sa 21:2

GIDDALTI
Eliathah, **G**, Romamti-Ezer, ... 1Ch 25:4
twelve men were chosen from **G**, ... 1Ch 25:29

GIDDEL
G, Gahar, Reaiah, ... Ezr 2:47
Jaala, Darkon, **G**, ... Ezr 2:56
Hanan, **G**, Gahar, ... Ne 7:49
Jaala, Darkon, **G**, ... Ne 7:58

GIDEON
G, Joash's son, was separating .... Jdg 6:11
So **G** built an altar there to .... Jdg 6:24
Spirit of the Lord entered **G**, ... Jdg 6:34
"A sword for the Lord and for **G**!" .... Jdg 7:20
G used the gold to make a holy .... Jdg 8:27
a trap for **G** and his family....................... Jdg 8:27
So **G** son of Joash died at a good .... Jdg 8:32
have time to tell you about **G**,................ Heb 11:32

GIDOM
as far as **G** and killed 2,000.................... Jdg 20:45

GIFT
must bring his **g** to make the .... Nu 7:11
and the king sent a **g** to him. 2Sa 11:8

A secret **g** will calm an angry .... Pr 21:14
you offer your **g** to God at the .... Mt 5:23
knew the free **g** of God and who .... Jn 4:10
will receive the **g** of the Holy .... Ac 2:38
some spiritual **g** to make you .... Rm 1:11
But God's free **g** is not like .... Rm 5:15
and the great **g** of being made .... Rm 5:17
us the free **g** of life forever .... Rm 6:23
person has his own **g** from God............. 1Co 7:7
I may have the **g** of prophecy. 1Co 13:2
to take your **g** to Jerusalem. 1Co 16:3
the generous **g** you promised so 2Co 9:5
And it will be a generous **g**— 2Co 9:5
be to God for his **g** that is too 2Co 9:15
yourselves; it was a **g** from God............. Eph 2:8
God's special **g** of grace given .... Eph 3:7
of us the special **g** of grace, ... Eph 4:7
brought your **g** to me. .... Php 4:18
Use the **g** you have, which was 1Ti 4:14
keep using the **g** God gave you 2Ti 1:6
enjoyed heaven's **g**, and shared .... Heb 6:4
and every perfect **g** is from God. .... Jam 1:17
has received a **g** to use to serve 1Pe 4:10
the water of life as a free **g**. .... Rev 22:17

GIFTED
positions while **g** people are .... Ec 10:6

GIFTS
You received **g** from the people, ... Ps 68:18
you with **g** and great honor .... Da 2:6
gave Daniel many **g** plus an .... Da 2:48
may keep your **g** for yourself,................ Da 5:17
They opened their **g** and gave him .... Mt 2:11
to give good **g** to your children .... Mt 7:11
putting their **g** into the Temple .... Lk 21:1
have different **g**, each of which .... Rm 12:6
to understand about spiritual **g**. 1Co 12:1
There are different kinds of **g**, ... 1Co 12:4
one Spirit gives **g** of healing. 1Co 12:9
want to have the greater **g**. 1Co 12:31
and he gave **g** to people." .... Eph 4:8
giving people **g** through the Holy .... Heb 2:4
them to offer **g** and sacrifices .... Heb 5:1
pleased with the **g** Abel offered .... Heb 11:4
They will send each other **g**, ... Rev 11:10

GIHON
river, named **G**, flows around .... Ge 2:13
him down to the spring called **G**. 1Ki 1:33
took him to the spring called **G**. 1Ki 1:38
on Solomon at **G** to make him king 1Ki 1:45
pool of the **G** spring and made 2Ch 32:30
side of the **G** spring and went.................. 2Ch 33:14

GILALAI
Milalai, **G**, Maai, Nethanel .... Ne 12:36

GILBOA
Israelites and made camp at **G**. 1Sa 28:4
were killed on Mount **G**. 1Sa 31:1
his three sons dead on Mount **G**. 1Sa 31:8
I happened to be on Mount **G**. 2Sa 1:6
or rain on the mountains of **G**, ... 2Sa 1:21
after they had killed Saul at **G**. 2Sa 21:12
were killed on Mount **G**. 1Ch 10:1
and his sons dead on Mount **G**. 1Ch 10:8

GILBOA'S
Jonathan is dead on **G** hills. 2Sa 1:25

GILEAD
Makir was the father of **G**);..................... Nu 26:29
the land of **G** for their own. .... Nu 32:29
son was Makir, the father of **G**. .... Jos 17:1
the priest to **G** to talk to the .... Jos 22:13
was a strong soldier from **G**. .... Jdg 11:1

River to the land of Gad and **G.** 1Sa 13:7
Jordan known as the land of **G.** 2Ki 10:33
G and Manasseh are mine. .... Ps 60:7
of goats streaming down Mount **G.** .... Sng 6:5
there balm in the land of **G**? .... Je 8:22
The people of **G** are evil, worth .... Hos 12:11
the people of **G** with threshing .... Am 1:3
pregnant women in **G** so they.................. Am 1:13
and Benjamin will take over **G.** .... Ob 1:19

GILEADITE
Gilead came the **G** family group. .... Nu 26:29

GILGAL
in the Jordan Valley opposite **G.** .... Dt 11:30
the first month and camped at **G,** .... Jos 4:19
and Joshua set them up at **G.** .... Jos 4:20
So Joshua named that place **G,** .... Jos 5:9
were camped at **G** on the plains .... Jos 5:10
to Joshua in the camp near **G.** .... Jos 9:6
to Joshua in his camp at **G:**................... Jos 10:6
marched out of **G** with his whole .... Jos 10:7
all night from **G** for a surprise .... Jos 10:9
army went back to the camp at **G.** .... Jos 10:15
returned to their camp at **G.** .... Jos 10:43
(in Naphoth Dor), Goyim in **G,** .... Jos 12:23
of Judah went to Joshua at **G,** .... Jos 14:6
toward the north and went to **G.**............. Jos 15:7
G is across from the road that .... Jos 15:7
went up from **G** to Bokim and said........... Jdg 2:1
he passed the statues near **G,** .... Jdg 3:19
went from Bethel to **G** to Mizpah 1Sa 7:16
Go ahead of me to **G.** 1Sa 10:8
people, "Come, let's go to **G.** 1Sa 11:14
So all the people went to **G,** 1Sa 11:15
were called to join Saul at **G.** 1Sa 13:4
Saul stayed at **G,** and all the 1Sa 13:7
But Samuel did not come to **G,** 1Sa 13:8
will come against me at **G,** 1Sa 13:12
Then Samuel left **G** and went to 1Sa 13:15
Now he has gone down to **G.**" 1Sa 15:12
to the LORD your God at **G.**" 1Sa 15:21
to pieces before the LORD at **G.** 1Sa 15:33
of Judah came to **G** to meet him.............. 2Sa 19:15
When the king crossed over to **G,** 2Sa 19:40
and Elisha were leaving **G,** 2Ki 2:1
When Elisha returned to **G,** 2Ki 4:38
from Beth **G** and the areas .... Ne 12:29
Don't go to **G** or go up to Beth .... Hos 4:15
were very wicked in **G,** .... Hos 9:15
people sacrifice bulls at **G,** .... Hos 12:11
come to **G** and sin even more. .... Am 4:4
not look in Bethel or go to **G,** .... Am 5:5
The people of **G** will be taken.................. Am 5:5
Acacia to **G** so that you will .... Mic 6:5

GILOH
Holon, and **G.** There were eleven .... Jos 15:51
to come from his hometown of **G.** 2Sa 15:12

GILONITE
Eliam son of Ahithophel the **G;** 2Sa 23:34

GIMZO
Timnah, and **G,** and the villages 2Ch 28:18

GINATH
Tibni son of **G** to be king, ... 1Ki 16:21
the followers of Tibni son of **G,** 1Ki 16:22

GINNETHON
Daniel, **G,** Baruch, ... Ne 10:6
Iddo, **G,** Abijah, ... Ne 12:4

GIRGASHITES
of the Jebusites, Amorites, **G,**............... Ge 10:16
Canaanites, **G,** and Jebusites." .... Ge 15:21
the Hittites, **G,** Amorites, ... Dt 7:1

Perizzites, **G,** Amorites, ... Jos 3:10
Hittites, **G,** Hivites, ... Jos 24:11
Jebusites, Amorites, **G,** 1Ch 1:14
Perizzites, Jebusites, and **G.** .... Ne 9:8

GIRL
soldier is given a **g** or two. .... Jdg 5:30
The young **g** Israel has fallen,.................. Am 5:2
The **g** is not dead, only asleep." .... Mt 9:24
a platter and gave it to the **g,** .... Mt 14:11
servant **g** came to him and said,.............. Mt 26:69
means, "Young **g,** I tell you to.................. Mk 5:41
and a servant **g** named Rhoda came .... Ac 12:13
for prayer, a servant **g** met us. .... Ac 16:16
This **g** followed Paul and us, ... Ac 16:17

GIRLS
filled with boys and **g** playing." .... Zch 8:5

GIRZI
people of Geshur, **G,** and Amalek. 1Sa 27:8

GISHPA
and Ziha and **G** were in charge of .... Ne 11:21

GITTAIM
people of Beeroth ran away to **G,** 2Sa 4:3
Hazor, Ramah, **G,** .... Ne 11:33

GITTITH
of music. On the **g.** A psalm of .... Ps 7:17
of music. By the **g.** A psalm of .... Ps 80:19
of music. On the **g.** A psalm of .... Ps 83:18

GIVE
be in the sky to **g** light to the .... Ge 1:15
I will **g** this land to your .... Ge 12:7
you see I will **g** to you and your .... Ge 13:15
Lord GOD, what can you **g** me? .... Ge 15:2
so that I could **g** you this land .... Ge 15:7
I will **g** you the land and the .... Ge 23:11
I will **g** this land to your .... Ge 24:7
and I will also **g** water to your .... Ge 24:14
Please **g** me a little water from .... Ge 24:17
G me Rachel so that I may marry .... Ge 29:21
and I will **g** you Rachel to marry .... Ge 29:27
said to Jacob, "**G** me children, ... Ge 30:1
G this message to my master .... Ge 32:4
First **g** me something to keep as .... Ge 38:17
because I did not **g** her to my .... Ge 38:26
were also to **g** them what they .... Ge 42:25
G them to the man as a gift: .... Ge 43:11
I will **g** them the best land in .... Ge 45:18
time you must **g** one-fifth to the .... Ge 47:24
They **g** birth to their babies .... Ex 1:19
will **g** gifts to your people. .... Ex 3:21
I will no longer **g** you straw. .... Ex 5:10
with them to **g** them the land .... Ex 6:4
and I will **g** you that land to .... Ex 6:8
pillar of fire to **g** them light. .... Ex 13:21
and said, "**G** us water to drink. .... Ex 17:2
and I will **g** you some advice. .... Ex 18:19
must **g** me your firstborn sons. .... Ex 22:29
day you must **g** them to me. .... Ex 22:30
and I will **g** you two stone .... Ex 24:12
There I will **g** you all my........................ Ex 25:22
or older must **g** this amount to .... Ex 30:14
person must not **g** more than .... Ex 30:15
a poor person must not **g** less. .... Ex 30:15
and I will **g** you victory."........................ Ex 33:14
Then he must **g** it all to the.................... Le 5:16
You must not **g** any of your.................... Le 18:21
I will **g** you rains at the right .... Le 26:4
I will **g** peace to your country; .... Le 26:6
and I didn't **g** birth to them. .... Nu 11:12
that the Israelites **g** to me, ... Nu 18:8
people and I will **g** them water."............... Nu 21:16

G this command to the people of .... Nu 34:2
to g the land to the Israelites .... Nu 36:2
I will g him and his descendants .... Dt 1:36
Jacob, and he will g it to you................. Dt 6:10
us here and to g us the land he .... Dt 6:23
G them the first of your grain, ... Dt 18:4
G the coat back at sunset, ... Dt 24:13
ancestors that he would g us." .... Dt 26:3
g me some water to drink.".................... Jdg 4:19
and you did not g the women to .... Jdg 21:22
may the LORD g you many children .... Ru 4:12
He will g power to his king and 1Sa 2:10
and g honor to Israel's God. 1Sa 6:5
G us a king to rule over us like 1Sa 8:5
saying, "G me my wife Michal. 2Sa 3:14
You g me a better way to live,............... 2Sa 22:37
whatever you want me to g you." 1Ki 3:5
I ask that you g me a heart that 1Ki 3:9
pieces, and g each woman half. 1Ki 3:25
kill him! G the baby to her!.................... 1Ki 3:26
from you and g it to one of your............. 1Ki 11:11
said to her, "G me your son." 1Ki 17:19
g you another vineyard for it. 1Ki 21:6
'G up your son so we can eat him 2Ki 6:28
G thanks to the LORD and pray to 1Ch 16:8
I will g the land of Canaan to 1Ch 16:18
and I will g Israel peace and 1Ch 22:9
May the LORD g you wisdom and 1Ch 22:12
Now g me wisdom and knowledge so 2Ch 1:10
The LORD can g you much more 2Ch 25:9
to g thanks and praise at the 2Ch 31:2
Carefully g him whatever the God .... Ezr 7:23
with him to g his descendants .... Ne 9:8
land you had promised to g them. .... Ne 9:15
A man will g all he has to save .... Job 2:4
You must g your whole heart to .... Job 11:13
me, I will g you the nations; .... Ps 2:8
"Who will g us anything good?"............... Ps 4:6
You g me a better way to live,................ Ps 18:36
they have done; g them their .... Ps 28:4
and he will g you what you want. .... Ps 37:4
sacrifices, or I would g them. .... Ps 51:16
I will g them a long, full life, ... Ps 91:16
G thanks to the LORD and pray to .... Ps 105:1
them g thanks to the LORD for .... Ps 107:31
please, LORD, g us success. .... Ps 118:25
G me life by your love so I can .... Ps 119:88
G thanks to the LORD because he .... Ps 136:1
G thanks to the Lord of lords................. Ps 136:3
you g it to them at the right .... Ps 145:15
wise and g knowledge and sense .... Pr 1:4
or you will g your riches to.................... Pr 5:9
g your mother a reason to be .... Pr 23:25
If he is thirsty, g him a drink. .... Pr 25:21
they will g you satisfaction. .... Pr 29:17
daughters named 'G' and 'Give.'............. Pr 30:15
G beer to people who are dying .... Pr 31:6
G her the reward she has earned; .... Pr 31:31
so g God what you promised. .... Ec 5:4
There I will g you my love. .... Sng 7:12
my own vineyard is mine to g. .... Sng 8:12
Lord himself will g you a sign: .... Is 7:14
king of Egypt g wrong advice. .... Is 19:11
I will g you two thousand horses .... Is 36:8
will not g my glory to another; .... Is 42:8
They should g glory to the LORD. .... Is 42:12
because I g you honor and love .... Is 43:4
the north: G my people to me .... Is 43:6
to the land and g the land that .... Is 49:8
I will g you the blessings I .... Is 55:3
I will g them a crown to replace .... Is 61:3
Israel does not g itself to...................... Je 9:26
ancestors to g them a fertile .... Je 11:5

g you hope and a good future. .... Je 29:11
of the guard saw me g the record .... Je 32:12
I will g the order, says the .... Je 34:22
will g them a desire to respect .... Eze 11:19
and I will g them an obedient .... Eze 11:19
and I will g you obedient hearts .... Eze 36:26
that time I will g Gog a burial................. Eze 39:11
Please g us this test for ten.................... Da 1:12
or you may g those rewards to .... Da 5:17
I have come to g you wisdom and .... Da 9:22
who g me my food and water,................ Hos 2:5
There I will g her back her .... Hos 2:15
g them what they should have. .... Hos 9:14
Israel, how can I g you up?................... Hos 11:8
Should I g my first child for .... Mic 6:7
the ground will g good crops, ... Zch 8:12
comfort they g is worth nothing .... Zch 10:2
She will g birth to a son,....................... Mt 1:21
I will g you all these things." .... Mt 4:9
his wife must g her a written .... Mt 5:31
you for something, g it to him. .... Mt 5:42
G us the food we need for each .... Mt 6:11
Don't g holy things to dogs, ... Mt 7:6
of you would g them a stone? .... Mt 7:9
you know how to g good gifts to .... Mt 7:11
I g you these powers freely, ... Mt 10:8
loads, and I will g you rest..................... Mt 11:28
G me the head of John the .... Mt 14:8
I will g you the keys of .... Mt 16:19
then did Moses g a command for .... Mt 19:7
serve others and to g his life .... Mt 20:28
the moon will not g its light. .... Mt 24:29
master trusts to g the other................... Mt 24:45
to the wise, 'G us some of your .... Mt 25:8
that servant and g it to the .... Mt 25:28
see you hungry and g you food, ... Mt 25:37
and g the money to the poor, ... Mk 10:21
and will g the vineyard to .... Mk 12:9
the moon will not g its light. .... Mk 13:24
He said he would g mercy to our .... Lk 1:72
I will g you all these kingdoms .... Lk 4:6
G to everyone who asks you, ... Lk 6:30
G, and you will receive. .... Lk 6:38
G us the food we need for each .... Lk 11:3
him get up to g you the bread, ... Lk 11:8
of you would g them a snake .... Lk 11:11
you know how to g good things to .... Lk 11:13
Father will g the Holy Spirit to .... Lk 11:13
wants to g you the kingdom. .... Lk 12:32
possessions and g to the poor. .... Lk 12:33
'G this person your seat.' .... Lk 14:9
When you g a lunch or a dinner, ... Lk 14:12
'G me my share of the property.'............ Lk 15:12
and I g one-tenth of everything .... Lk 18:12
I will g half of my possessions .... Lk 19:8
this servant and g it to the .... Lk 19:24
and will g the vineyard to .... Lk 20:16
to her, "Please g me a drink." .... Jn 4:7
the water I g will never be .... Jn 4:14
g me this water so I will never .... Jn 4:15
said, "Sir, g us this bread .... Jn 6:34
which I will g up so that the .... Jn 6:51
did not g you circumcision;.................... Jn 7:22
You should g God the glory by .... Jn 9:24
the feast or to g something to................ Jn 13:29
then God will g glory to the Son............. Jn 13:32
God will g him glory quickly. .... Jn 13:32
I g you a new command;........................ Jn 13:34
and he will g you another Helper .... Jn 14:16
peace; my peace I g you. I do .... Jn 14:27
do not g it to you as the world .... Jn 14:27
the Father will g you anything .... Jn 15:16
the Son could g eternal life to................ Jn 17:2

have something else I can g you. .... Ac 3:6
commands from God that g life. .... Ac 7:38
G me also this power so that .... Ac 8:19
did not g the glory to God, ... Ac 12:23
'I will g you the holy and sure .... Ac 13:34
blessed to g than to receive. .... Ac 20:35
God will surely g us all things. .... Rm 8:32
if he is thirsty, g him a drink. .... Rm 12:20
G my greetings to Priscilla and .... Rm 16:3
not refuse to g your bodies to 1Co 7:5
I may g away everything I have, ... 1Co 13:3
but we do not g up the hope of 2Co 4:8
We want God to g us our heavenly 2Co 5:2
you were the first to want to g, ... 2Co 8:10
Each of you should g as you have 2Co 9:7
to g you a spirit of wisdom and .... Eph 1:17
Do not g the devil a way to .... Eph 4:27
and g thanks whatever happens. 1Th 5:18
must not g people a reason 1Ti 3:2
g your life to doing them so 1Ti 4:15
After they g themselves to 1Ti 5:11
g the crown to me on that day— 2Ti 4:8
you do and will g glory to God 1Pe 2:12
and God will g the sinner life. 1Jn 5:16
victory I will g the right to .... Rev 2:7
and I will g you the crown of .... Rev 2:10
I will g some of the hidden .... Rev 2:17
also g him the morning star. .... Rev 2:28
These living creatures g glory, ... Rev 4:9
Fear God and g him praise, ... Rev 14:7
and lives and g glory to God. .... Rev 16:9
the Lord God will g them light. .... Rev 22:5

GIVEN

I have g all the green plants as .... Ge 1:30
fear you. I have g them to you. .... Ge 9:2
Look, you have g me no son, so a .... Ge 15:3
g them an excuse to kill us. .... Ex 5:21
and I have g you rules for .... Le 17:11
I have g the Levites to .... Nu 8:19
land the Lord our God has g us." .... Dt 2:29
your God has g them on the other .... Dt 3:20
sheep will be g to your enemies, ... Dt 28:31
The Lord has g you a place to .... Jos 1:15
Look, I have g you Jericho, its .... Jos 6:2
they were g all the burned .... Jos 13:14
You should be g more than one .... Jos 17:17
that your god Chemosh has g you. .... Jdg 11:24
wife was g to his best man. .... Jdg 14:20
the Lord had g him peace from 2Sa 7:1
his father David had g him, ... 1Ki 3:3
has g David a wise son to rule 1Ki 5:7
are these towns you have g me, ... 1Ki 9:13
the priest has g me a book." 2Ki 22:10
the towns that Hiram had g him, ... 2Ch 8:2
that had been g through Moses. 2Ch 34:14
has g me all the kingdoms of the 2Ch 36:23
has g all the kingdoms of the .... Ezr 1:2
beauty treatments be g to them. .... Est 2:3
asked for was g to her to take .... Est 2:13
Light is not g to evil people; .... Job 38:15
You have g your people trouble. .... Ps 60:3
God had g them what they wanted. .... Ps 78:29
They have g the bodies of your .... Ps 79:2
I have g strength to a warrior; .... Ps 89:19
the good things he has g to me? .... Ps 116:12
you have g me life by them .... Ps 119:93
God has g his people a king. .... Ps 148:14
wealth will be g to those who .... Pr 28:8
God has g us terrible things .... Ec 1:13
life God has g them on earth is .... Ec 5:18
God has g you here on earth, ... Ec 9:9
the children the Lord has g me. .... Is 8:18

God has g a son to us. .... Is 9:6
lives who has g us breath and .... Je 38:16
flesh and had not g themselves .... Eze 44:7
as the land g to each tribe. .... Eze 45:7
because you have g me wisdom and .... Da 2:23
kingdom will be g back to you .... Da 4:26
and will be g to the Medes .... Da 5:28
it was g the mind of a human. .... Da 7:4
He was g authority, glory, and .... Da 7:14
give to others will be g to you. .... Mt 7:2
But no sign will be g to them, ... Mt 12:39
understanding will be g more, ... Mt 13:12
from you and g to people who do .... Mt 21:43
nor will they be g to someone to .... Mt 22:30
and the money g to the poor." .... Mt 26:9
the one who had g Jesus to his .... Mt 27:3
heaven and on earth is g to me. .... Mt 28:18
the name g by the angel before .... Lk 2:21
You will be g much. Pressed down .... Lk 6:38
understanding will be g more. .... Lk 8:18
that she be g something to eat. .... Lk 8:55
but no sign will be g them, ... Lk 11:29
marry and are g to someone to .... Lk 20:34
as my Father has g me a kingdom, ... Lk 22:29
The law was g through Moses, ... Jn 1:17
the Son and has g him power over .... Jn 3:35
he would have g you living water .... Jn 4:10
And the Father has g the Son the .... Jn 5:27
sent me has g proof about me. .... Jn 5:37
after the Lord had g thanks. .... Jn 6:23
The Spirit had not yet been g, ... Jn 7:39
Pharisees had g orders that if .... Jn 11:57
and the money g to the poor?" .... Jn 12:5
the Father had g him power over .... Jn 13:3
want, and it will be g to you. .... Jn 15:7
I have g them your teaching. .... Jn 17:14
I have g these people the glory .... Jn 17:22
me from being g over to the .... Jn 18:36
me is the power g to you by God. .... Jn 19:11
the Spirit was g to people when .... Ac 8:18
Holy Spirit has g to you to .... Ac 20:28
offering would be g for each of .... Ac 21:26
Jerusalem and g to the Romans. .... Ac 28:17
Spirit, whom God has g to us. .... Rm 5:5
God has g all people over to .... Rm 11:32
Because God has g me a special .... Rm 12:3
unless God has g him the power. .... Rm 13:1
hair is g to her as a covering. 1Co 11:15
church God has g a place first 1Co 12:28
Then God has g a place to those 1Co 12:28
work has been g to me now. 1Co 16:9
that they have g themselves to 1Co 16:15
that is being g to more and more 2Co 4:15
and he has g us the Spirit to be 2Co 5:5
great grace that God has g you. 2Co 9:14
the work that was g us to do. 2Co 10:13
the Jews have g me their. 2Co 11:24
physical problem was g to me. 2Co 12:7
would be g through faith to .... Gal 3:22
out your eyes and g them to me .... Gal 4:15
gift of grace g to me through .... Eph 3:7
of our Lord was fully g to me, ... 1Ti 1:14
But I was g mercy so that in me, ... 1Ti 1:16
prophecies that were g about you 1Ti 1:18
That grace was g to us through 2Ti 1:9
life is being g as an offering 2Ti 4:6
are the children God has g me." .... Heb 2:13
He is the work of going before .... Heb 5:1
teaching that was g to them. 2Pe 2:21
God has g us eternal life, ... 1Jn 5:11
come and has g us understanding 1Jn 5:20
faith that was g the holy people .... Jud 1:3
money they have g themselves to .... Jud 1:11

GIVER

for my name and have not g up. .... Rev 2:3
I have g her time to change her .... Rev 2:21
bow, and he was g a crown, and .... Rev 6:2
to whom were g seven trumpets. .... Rev 8:2
The star was g the key to the .... Rev 9:1
and they were g the power to .... Rev 9:3
I was g a measuring stick like a .... Rev 11:1
and he was g power to burn the .... Rev 16:8

GIVER

You are the g of life. .... Ps 36:9

GIVES

and she g birth to sons or .... Ex 21:4
town the LORD your God g you, ... Dt 16:5
'Anyone who g a wife to a man of .... Jdg 21:18
He g rain to the earth and sends .... Job 5:10
Almighty, that g understanding. .... Job 32:8
who g us songs in the night, ... Job 35:10
this is how he g us enough food. .... Job 36:31
The God of Israel g his people .... Ps 68:35
Learning your words g wisdom and .... Ps 119:130
The LORD g sleep to those he .... Ps 127:2
He g food to every living. .... Ps 136:25
He g food to the hungry. .... Ps 146:7
g knowledge and understanding. .... Pr 2:6
but he g grace to those who are .... Pr 3:34
good person who g in to evil is .... Pr 25:26
Whoever g to the poor will have .... Pr 28:27
God g some people the ability to .... Ec 5:19
wealth and property he g them, ... Ec 5:19
who g us autumn and spring rains .... Je 5:24
He g them the full punishment .... Je 51:56
of kings and g their power to .... Da 2:21
he g those kingdoms to anyone .... Da 4:25
the light that g light to the .... Mt 5:14
whoever g you a drink of water .... Mk 9:41
true Light that g light to all. .... Jn 1:9
raises the dead and g them life, ... Jn 5:21
heaven and g life to the world. .... Jn 6:33
It is the Spirit that g life. .... Jn 6:63
The good shepherd g his life for .... Jn 10:11
This God is the One who g life, ... Ac 17:25
the God who g life to the dead .... Rm 4:17
calls and the things he g them. .... Rm 11:29
of the power that the Spirit g. 1Co 2:4
But God g it a body that he has 1Co 15:38
death, but the Spirit g life. 2Co 3:6
richly g us everything to enjoy. 1Ti 6:17
g us the strength to do that, ... 2Ti 1:9
But God g us even more grace, ... Jam 4:6
but he g grace to the humble." .... Jam 4:6
but he g grace to the humble." 1Pe 5:5
the spirit that g all prophecy." .... Rev 19:10

GIVING

of your ancestors, is g to you. .... Dt 4:1
your God is g you as your own .... Dt 21:23
the land I am g to the .... Jos 1:2
marrying and g their children to .... Mt 24:38
and g their children to be .... Lk 17:27
this to us by g them the Holy .... Ac 15:8
has the gift of g to others .... Rm 12:8
sadness and g up completely. 2Co 2:7
strong also in the grace of g, ... 2Co 8:7
And your g through us will cause 2Co 9:11
and g her life to do all kinds 1Ti 5:10
by g people gifts through the .... Heb 2:4
about not g up your faith. .... Rev 3:10

GIZONITE

the sons of Hashem the G; 1Ch 11:34

GLAD

I am g because you have helped 1Sa 2:1
Be g that you are his; let those 1Ch 16:10

rejoice and the earth be g. 1Ch 16:31
comfort and be g even in this .... Job 6:10
Good people can watch and be g; .... Job 22:19
let them sing g songs forever. .... Ps 5:11
the people of Israel will be g. .... Ps 14:7
I rejoice and am g. Even my body .... Ps 16:9
you made him g because you were .... Ps 21:6
I will be g and rejoice in your .... Ps 31:7
The poor will hear and be g. .... Ps 34:2
who follow you be happy and g. .... Ps 40:16
the people of Israel will be g. .... Ps 53:6
people will be g when they see .... Ps 58:10
should be g and sing because .... Ps 67:4
right should be g and should .... Ps 68:3
they should be happy and g. .... Ps 68:3
people will see this and be g. .... Ps 69:32
worship you rejoice and be g. .... Ps 70:4
rejoice and the earth be g; .... Ps 96:11
faraway lands should be g. .... Ps 97:1
this, she is g, and the towns .... Ps 97:8
Be g that you are his; let those .... Ps 105:3
Egyptians were g when they left, ... Ps 105:38
Then I, your servant, will be g. .... Ps 109:28
Let us rejoice and be g today! .... Ps 118:24
for us, and we are very g. .... Ps 126:3
children are g because of them. .... Pr 23:24
your mother a reason to be g. .... Pr 23:25
don't be g when he is .... Pr 24:17
king will be g to obey the LORD .... Is 11:3
rejoice and are g to do my will. .... Is 13:3
will be g and will produce .... Is 35:1
This made my father very g. .... Je 20:15
the army officers, they were g. .... Je 41:13
Be happy and g, people of Edom. .... La 4:21
You were g when my Temple was .... Eze 25:3
rulers are g with their lies .... Hos 7:3
at her and be g we have defeated .... Mic 4:11
I will still be g in the LORD; .... Hab 3:18
Shout and be g, Jerusalem. .... Zch 2:10
they will be g as when they have .... Zch 10:7
Rejoice and be g, because you .... Mt 5:12
he was very g, because he had .... Lk 23:8
they were g to take him into .... Jn 6:21
He saw that day and was g." .... Jn 8:56
And I am g for your sakes I was. .... Jn 11:15
So I am g, and I rejoice. .... Ac 2:26
the believers were g to see us. .... Ac 21:17
you sad, who will make me g? 2Co 2:2
you can make me g—particularly 2Co 2:2
far in the future and were g. .... Heb 11:13

GLADLY

will g give you what you want. .... Jdg 8:25
you and will g praise you." 1Ch 16:35
to see their leaders give so g, ... 1Ch 29:9
thank you and will g praise you. .... Ps 106:47
God's teaching and accept it g, ... Lk 8:13
down quickly and welcomed him g. .... Lk 19:6
will g be patient with fools! 2Co 11:19

GLADNESS

happiness, joy, g, and honor for .... Est 8:16
was joy and g among the Jewish .... Est 8:17
me hear sounds of joy and g; .... Ps 51:8
Their g and joy will fill them .... Is 35:10
have joy and g, and all sadness .... Is 51:11
the oil of g to replace their .... Is 61:3
sounds of joy and g and the .... Je 16:9
sounds of joy and g and the .... Je 33:11
He will bring you joy and g, ... Lk 1:14

GLANCE

my heart with a g of your eyes, ... Sng 4:9

GLANDS

or men who have damaged sex g. .... Le 21:20
torn, or cut sex g, you must not .... Le 22:24

GLASS

that looked like a sea of g, ... Rev 4:6
like a sea of g mixed with fire. .... Rev 15:2
were standing by the sea of g. .... Rev 15:2
made of pure gold, as pure as g. .... Rev 21:18
made of pure gold as clear as g. .... Rev 21:21

GLEAM

arrows and the g of your shining .... Hab 3:11

GLEAMING

are shining, spears are g! .... Nah 3:3

GLIDE

They g past like paper boats. .... Job 9:26

GLIDED

A spirit g past my face, and the .... Job 4:15

GLIDING

send them vicious animals and g, ... Dt 32:24
punish Leviathan, the g snake. .... Is 27:1

GLOOM

darkness and g have that day. .... Job 3:5
from the land of darkness and g, ... Job 10:21
the land of g and confusion, ... Job 10:22
Some sat in g and darkness; .... Ps 107:10
them out of their g and darkness .... Ps 107:14
trouble, darkness, and awful g. .... Is 8:22
will be no more g for the land .... Is 9:1
of having darkness and g, ... Is 29:18
he will change it into deep g. .... Je 13:16
of darkness and g, a day of .... Zph 1:15

GLOOMY

It will be a dark, g day, cloudy .... Joe 2:2

GLORIFIED

those he made right, he also g. .... Rm 8:30

GLORIFY

G the LORD with me, and let us .... Ps 34:3

GLORIOUS

must respect the g and wonderful .... Dt 28:58
shield and helper, your g sword. .... Dt 33:29
you and praise your g name. 1Ch 29:13
doors and the g King will come .... Ps 24:7
Who is this g King? .... Ps 24:8
doors and the g King will come .... Ps 24:9
Who is this g King? .... Ps 24:10
All-Powerful—he is the g King. .... Ps 24:10
The g God thunders; .... Ps 29:3
his glory! Make his praise g! .... Ps 66:2
Praise his g name forever. .... Ps 72:19
You are their g strength, and in .... Ps 89:17
exchanged their g God for a .... Ps 106:20
What he does is g and splendid, ... Ps 111:3
exchanged their g God for idols .... Je 2:11
the honor from your g throne. .... Je 14:21
honored as a g throne for God. .... Je 17:12
and g day of the Lord .... Ac 2:20
Our g God appeared to Abraham, ... Ac 7:2
short of God's g standard, ... Rm 3:23
Christ, the g Father, to give .... Eph 1:17
how rich and g are the blessings .... Eph 1:18
make them like his own g body. .... Php 3:21
this rich and g secret which he .... Col 1:27
who calls you to his g kingdom. 1Th 2:12
believers in our g Lord Jesus .... Jam 2:1
because the g Spirit, the Spirit 1Pe 4:14
you will get a g crown that will 1Pe 5:4

GLORY

you will see the g of the LORD, ... Ex 16:7
There the g of the LORD appeared .... Ex 16:10
The g of the LORD came down on .... Ex 24:16
Israelites the g of the LORD .... Ex 24:17
will be holy because of my g. .... Ex 29:43
Now, please show me your g." .... Ex 33:18
When my g passes that place, ... Ex 33:22
and the g of the LORD filled the. .... Ex 40:34
and the g of the LORD filled the .... Ex 40:35
so you will see the LORD's g." .... Le 9:6
and the LORD's g came to all the .... Le 9:23
But the g of the LORD appeared .... Nu 14:10
surely as my g fills the whole .... Nu 14:21
people saw my g and the miracles .... Nu 14:22
Then the g of the LORD appeared .... Nu 16:19
The g of the LORD appeared. .... Nu 16:42
and the g of the LORD appeared .... Nu 20:6
has shown us his g and majesty, ... Dt 5:24
saying, "Israel's g is gone." 1Sa 4:21
said, "Israel's g is gone, ... 1Sa 4:22
filled with the g of the LORD. 1Ki 8:11
Tell the nations about his g; 1Ch 16:24
He has g and majesty; he has 1Ch 16:27
Praise the LORD's g and power; 1Ch 16:28
praise the g of the LORD's name. 1Ch 16:29
You have g, victory, and honor. 1Ch 29:11
the LORD's g filled the Temple 2Ch 5:14
The LORD's g filled the Temple. 2Ch 7:1
because the LORD's g filled it. 2Ch 7:2
and the LORD's g on the Temple, ... 2Ch 7:3
and his own great riches and g. .... Est 1:4
His bright g would scare you, ... Job 13:11
nor admired the moon moving in g .... Job 31:26
yourself with g and beauty; .... Job 40:10
crowned them with g and honor. .... Ps 8:5
heavens declare the g of God, ... Ps 19:1
He has great g because you gave .... Ps 21:5
where you live, where your g is. .... Ps 26:8
praise the LORD's g and power. .... Ps 29:1
the LORD for the g of his name; .... Ps 29:2
everyone says, "G to God!" .... Ps 29:9
Show your g and majesty. .... Ps 45:3
your g be over all the earth. .... Ps 57:11
have seen your strength and g. .... Ps 63:2
about his g! Make his praise .... Ps 66:2
Let his g fill the whole world. .... Ps 72:19
he let the Ark, his g, be taken. .... Ps 78:61
and his g will be seen in our .... Ps 85:9
Tell the nations of his g; .... Ps 96:3
The LORD has g and majesty; .... Ps 96:6
praise the LORD's g and power. .... Ps 96:7
Praise the g of the LORD's name. .... Ps 96:8
and all the people see his g. .... Ps 97:6
there his g will be seen. .... Ps 102:16
are clothed with g and majesty; .... Ps 104:1
the g of the LORD be forever. .... Ps 104:31
your g be over all the earth. .... Ps 108:5
his g reaches to the skies. .... Ps 113:4
The g belongs to you because of. .... Ps 115:1
because the LORD's g is great. .... Ps 138:5
wonderful majesty, and g. .... Ps 145:5
tell about the g of your kingdom .... Ps 145:11
you do and the g and majesty of .... Ps 145:12
worship him rejoice in his g. .... Ps 149:5
The young in their strength, ... Pr 20:29
receive g by judging fairly; .... Is 5:16
His g fills the whole earth." .... Is 6:3
he lives will be filled with g. .... Is 11:10
will be like the g of Israel," .... Is 17:3
by Egypt's g will be shamed. .... Is 20:5
year all the g of the country .... Is 21:16
will see the g of the LORD .... Is 35:2
Then the g of the LORD will be .... Is 40:5
and all their g is like the .... Is 40:6
I will not give my g to another; .... Is 42:8

They should give **g** to the LORD. .... Is 42:12
I made for my **g**, whom I formed .... Is 43:7
He showed his **g** when he saved .... Is 44:23
and bring **g** to Israel." .... Is 46:13
will not let some god take my **g**............... Is 48:11
I will show my **g** through you." .... Is 49:3
and the **g** of the LORD will.................... Is 58:8
from the east will fear his **g**. .... Is 59:19
and the **g** of the LORD shines on .... Is 60:1
and people see his **g** around you. .... Is 60:2
and your God will be your **g**. .... Is 60:19
and all kings will see your **g**. .... Is 62:2
will come together and see my **g**. .... Is 66:18
what I have done nor seen my **g**. .... Is 66:19
tell the nations about my **g**. .... Is 66:19
Give **g** to the LORD your God................. Je 13:16
He missed his chance for **g**!'"................. Je 46:17
Moab's power and **g** are gone.' .... Je 48:11
to look like the **g** of the LORD. .... Eze 1:28
the **g** of the LORD in heaven." .... Eze 3:12
I saw the **g** of the LORD standing .... Eze 3:23
like the **g** I saw by the Kebar .... Eze 3:23
I saw the **g** of the God of Israel .... Eze 8:4
Then the **g** of the God of Israel .... Eze 9:3
Then the **g** of the LORD went up .... Eze 10:4
from the **g** of the LORD. .... Eze 10:4
Then the **g** of the LORD left the .... Eze 10:18
and the **g** of the God of Israel .... Eze 10:19
and the **g** of the God of Israel .... Eze 11:22
The **g** of the LORD went up from .... Eze 11:23
because of the **g** I gave you, ... Eze 16:14
and I will show my **g** among you. .... Eze 28:22
I will show my **g** among the .... Eze 39:21
and I saw the **g** of the God of .... Eze 43:2
The **g** of the LORD came into the .... Eze 43:4
I saw the LORD's **g** filling the................ Eze 43:5
I saw the **g** of the LORD filling .... Eze 44:4
kingdom, power, strength, and **g**. .... Da 2:37
to show my and my majesty. .... Da 4:30
gave honor and **g** to him who................. Da 4:34
returned the **g** to my kingdom. .... Da 4:36
and honor and **g** to the King .... Da 4:37
throne. His **g** was taken away. .... Da 5:20
given authority, **g**, and the .... Da 7:14
Israel's **g** will fly away like a .... Hos 9:11
to shout for joy about its **g**,................. Hos 10:5
The **g** of Israel will go in to................... Mic 1:15
you've taken my **g** from their .... Mic 2:9
will know the LORD's **g**....................... Hab 2:14
Selah His **g** covers the skies, ... Hab 3:3
I will fill this Temple with **g**,' .... Hag 2:7
'And I will be the **g** within it.' .... Zch 2:5
and the **g** are yours forever. .... Mt 6:13
with his Father's **g** and with his .... Mt 16:27
the sky with great power and **g**. .... Mt 24:30
will come again in his great **g**, ... Mt 25:31
his Father's **g** and with the holy .... Mk 8:38
side in your **g** in your kingdom. .... Mk 10:37
clouds with great power and **g**. .... Mk 13:26
The **g** of the Lord was shining .... Lk 2:9
Give **g** to God in heaven, and on .... Lk 2:14
and all their power and **g**. .... Lk 4:6
he comes in his **g** and with the .... Lk 9:26
and with the **g** of the Father .... Lk 9:26
They appeared in heavenly **g**, ... Lk 9:31
they saw the **g** of Jesus and the .... Lk 9:32
peace in heaven and **g** to God!" .... Lk 19:38
a cloud with power and great **g**. .... Lk 21:27
things before he enters his **g**." .... Lk 24:26
We saw his **g**—the glory that .... Jn 1:14
the **g** that belongs to the only .... Jn 1:14
he showed his **g**, and his....................... Jn 2:11
had not yet been raised to **g**. .... Jn 7:39

should give God the **g** by telling .... Jn 9:24
It is for the **g** of God, to bring................. Jn 11:4
to bring **g** to the Son of God.".................. Jn 11:4
you would see the **g** of God?"................. Jn 11:40
But after Jesus was raised to **g**, ... Jn 12:16
the Son of Man to receive his **g**. .... Jn 12:23
Father, bring **g** to your name!" .... Jn 12:28
I have brought **g** to it, and I .... Jn 12:28
he saw Jesus' **g** and spoke about .... Jn 12:41
the Son of Man receives his **g**, ... Jn 13:31
and God receives **g** through him. .... Jn 13:31
If God receives **g** through him, ... Jn 13:32
God will give **g** to the Son .... Jn 13:32
God will give him **g** quickly." .... Jn 13:32
the Father's **g** will be shown .... Jn 14:13
which brings **g** to my Father. .... Jn 15:8
of truth will bring **g** to me, ... Jn 16:14
Give **g** to your Son so that the .... Jn 17:1
that the Son can give **g** to you. .... Jn 17:1
to do, I brought you **g** on earth. .... Jn 17:4
now, Father, give me **g** with you; .... Jn 17:5
give me the **g** I had with you .... Jn 17:5
And my **g** is shown through them. .... Jn 17:10
people the **g** that you gave me .... Jn 17:22
them to see my **g**, which you gave .... Jn 17:24
would die to give **g** to God. .... Jn 21:19
ancestors, gave **g** to Jesus, his .... Ac 3:13
and saw the **g** of God and Jesus .... Ac 7:55
Herod did not give the **g** to God, ... Ac 12:23
did not give **g** to God or thank .... Rm 1:21
They traded the **g** of God who .... Rm 1:23
live for God's **g**, for honor, and .... Rm 2:7
But he will give **g**, honor, and................. Rm 2:10
gives him **g**, because my lie .... Rm 3:7
hope we have of sharing God's **g**. .... Rm 5:2
that we will have **g** as Christ .... Rm 8:17
will have glory as Christ has **g**. .... Rm 8:17
the great **g** that will be shown .... Rm 8:18
his children's **g** completely...................... Rm 8:19
the freedom and **g** that belong to .... Rm 8:21
They have seen the **g** of God, ... Rm 9:4
known his rich **g** to the people .... Rm 9:23
these people to have his **g**, ... Rm 9:23
To him be the **g** forever! .... Rm 11:36
you will give **g** to God the .... Rm 15:6
which will bring **g** to God. .... Rm 15:7
not Jews could give **g** to God for .... Rm 15:9
G to God who can make you strong .... Rm 16:25
wise God be **g** forever through .... Rm 16:27
planned this wisdom for our **g**. 1Co 2:7
have crucified the Lord of **g**. 1Co 2:8
do it all for the **g** of God. 1Co 10:31
he is the likeness and **g** of God. 1Co 11:7
of God. But woman is man's **g**. 1Co 11:7
But long hair is a woman's **g**. 1Co 11:15
honor, but it is raised in **g**. 1Co 15:43
we say yes to the **g** of God....................... 2Co 1:20
came with God's **g**, which made 2Co 3:7
But that **g** later disappeared. 2Co 3:7
the Spirit has even more **g**....................... 2Co 3:8
people guilty of sin had **g**, ... 2Co 3:9
with God has much greater **g**................. 2Co 3:9
old law had **g**, but it really 2Co 3:10
really loses its **g** when it is 2Co 3:10
much greater **g** of this new way. 2Co 3:10
which disappeared came with **g**, ... 2Co 3:11
forever has much greater **g**. 2Co 3:11
g was disappearing, and Moses 2Co 3:13
show the Lord's **g**, and we are 2Co 3:18
in us brings ever greater **g**,.................... 2Co 3:18
Good News about the **g** of Christ, ... 2Co 4:4
us know the **g** of God that is 2Co 4:6
thanks to God for his **g**. 2Co 4:15

gain an eternal g that is much 2Co 4:17
service to bring g to the Lord 2Co 8:19
and they bring g to Christ. 2Co 8:23
The g belongs to God forever and .... Gal 1:5
would bring praise to God's g. .... Eph 1:12
to bring praise to God's g. .... Eph 1:14
My sufferings are for your g. .... Eph 3:13
Father in his great g to give .... Eph 3:16
To him be g in the church and in .... Eph 3:21
Christ to bring g and praise to .... Php 1:11
both of which bring g to Christ. .... Php 1:29
Lord and bring g to God the .... Php 2:11
G to our God and Father forever .... Php 4:20
He is our only hope for g. .... Col 1:27
again, you will share in his g. .... Col 3:4
Truly you are our g and our joy. 1Th 2:20
comes to receive g because of................. 2Th 1:12
Jesus Christ will have g in you, ... 2Th 1:12
and you will have g in him..................... 2Th 1:12
That g comes from the grace of 2Th 1:12
him with the g of his coming. 2Th 2:8
can share in the g of our Lord 2Th 2:14
be honor and g forever and ever. 1Ti 1:17
by the world, and taken up in g. 1Ti 3:16
comes g that never ends 2Ti 2:10
G forever and ever be the Lord's. 2Ti 4:18
coming of the g of our great God .... Tit 2:13
reflects the g of God and shows .... Heb 1:3
crowned them with g and honor. .... Heb 2:7
a crown of g and honor because.............. Heb 2:9
and all things are for his g. .... Heb 2:10
have many children share his g, ... Heb 2:10
creatures that showed God's g, ... Heb 9:5
you praise and g and honor when 1Pe 1:7
be explained, a joy full of g. 1Pe 1:8
about the g that would follow 1Pe 1:11
from the dead and gave him g. 1Pe 1:21
and all their g is like the 1Pe 1:24
do and will give g to God on the............. 1Pe 2:12
and g belong to him forever 1Pe 4:11
when Christ comes again in g. 1Pe 4:13
will share in the g that will be 1Pe 5:1
you to share in his g in Christ, ... 1Pe 5:10
a g that will continue forever. 1Pe 5:10
called us by his g and goodness.............. 2Pe 1:3
the Greatest G, when he received 2Pe 1:17
received honor and g from God 2Pe 1:17
G be to him now and forever! 2Pe 3:18
you before his g without any .... Jud 1:24
To him be g, greatness, power, ... Jud 1:25
Jesus Christ be g and power .... Rev 1:6
These living creatures give g, ... Rev 4:9
receive g and honor and power, ... Rev 4:11
strength, honor, g, and praise!" .... Rev 5:12
honor and g and power forever .... Rev 5:13
g, wisdom, thanks, honor, ... Rev 7:12
afraid and gave g to the God of .... Rev 11:13
smoke from the g and the power .... Rev 15:8
and lives and give g to God. .... Rev 16:9
and his g made the earth bright.............. Rev 18:1
herself much g and rich living. .... Rev 18:7
Salvation, g, and power belong .... Rev 19:1
and be happy and give God g, ... Rev 19:7
shining with the g of God and .... Rev 21:11
because the g of God is its .... Rev 21:23
will bring their g into it. .... Rev 21:24
The g and the honor of the .... Rev 21:26

GLOW

surrounding g looked like the................. Eze 1:28
hot and its copper sides g. .... Eze 24:11

GLOWING

that looked like g metal was in .... Eze 1:4
looked like g metal with fire .... Eze 1:27
it looked like bright g metal. .... Eze 8:2

GLOWS

and as long as the moon g...................... Ps 72:5
bronze that g hot in a furnace .... Rev 1:15

GNATS

the dust will change into g." .... Ex 8:16
Egypt the dust changed into g. .... Ex 8:17
g got on the people and animals. .... Ex 8:17
not make the dust change into g. .... Ex 8:18
The g remained on the people and .... Ex 8:18
and g were everywhere in the................. Ps 105:31

GNAWED

People g their tongues because .... Rev 16:10

GNAWING

my bones ache; g pains never................. Job 30:17

GNAWS

death g at their arms and legs. .... Job 18:13

GOAH

will turn to the place named **G.** .... Je 31:39

GOAL

to be one people with one g. .... Je 32:39
third day, I will reach my g.' .... Lk 13:32
So I do not run without a g. 1Co 9:26
the past have reached their g.................. 1Co 10:11
Our only g is to please God 2Co 5:9
His g was to carry out his plan, ... Eph 1:10
I have not yet reached that g, ... Php 3:12
I have not yet reached that g, ... Php 3:13
to reach the g and get the prize .... Php 3:14
way I live, my g, faith,.......................... 2Ti 3:10
receiving the g of your faith— 1Pe 1:9
love has truly reached its g. 1Jn 2:5

GOAT

a three-year-old g, a .... Ge 15:9
cook a young g in its mother's .... Ex 23:19
he will offer the living g........................ Le 16:20
The person who led the g, ... Le 16:26
Bring one g as a sin offering, ... Nu 28:22
cook a baby g in its mother's .... Dt 14:21
went in and cooked a young g, ... Jdg 6:19
I saw a male g come from the................. Da 8:5
g had one large horn between .... Da 8:5
male g is the king of Greece, ... Da 8:21
me even a young g to have at a .... Lk 15:29

GOATS

the skins of the g and put them .... Ge 27:16
all the male g that had streaks .... Ge 30:35
there were fat sheep and g..................... Dt 32:14
near the Rocks of the Wild **G.**................ 1Sa 24:2
when the mountain g give birth? .... Job 39:1
bulls or drink the blood of g. .... Ps 50:13
mountains belong to the wild g. .... Ps 104:18
like a flock of g streaming down .... Sng 4:1
with the blood from lambs and g, ... Is 34:6
separates the sheep from the g. .... Mt 25:32
his right and the g on his left................... Mt 25:33
him the blood of g and calves. .... Heb 9:12
The blood of g and bulls and the .... Heb 9:13
of bulls and g to take away sins .... Heb 10:4

GOB

Later, at **G,** there was another 2Sa 21:18
another battle at **G** with the 2Sa 21:19

GOBBLE

People like to g them up......................... Pr 18:8
people like to g them up......................... Pr 26:22

GOBBLED

They have g up the people of .... Ps 79:7

GOD

the beginning G created the sky .... Ge 1:1
G said, "Let there be light, ... Ge 1:3
G saw that the light was good, ... Ge 1:4
G named the light "day" and the .... Ge 1:5
Then G said, "Let there be .... Ge 1:6
G made the air and placed some .... Ge 1:7
G named the air "sky." Evening .... Ge 1:8
G said, "Let the water under .... Ge 1:9
G named the dry land "earth" and .... Ge 1:10
G saw that this was good. .... Ge 1:10
Then G said, "Let the earth .... Ge 1:11
G saw that all this was good. .... Ge 1:12
G said, "Let there be lights.................... Ge 1:14
So G made the two large lights. .... Ge 1:16
G put all these in the sky to .... Ge 1:17
G saw that all these things were .... Ge 1:18
Then G said, "Let the water be .... Ge 1:20
So G created the large sea .... Ge 1:21
G saw that this was good. .... Ge 1:21
G blessed them and said, "Have .... Ge 1:22
Then G said, "Let the earth be .... Ge 1:24
So G made the wild animals, ... Ge 1:25
G saw that this was good. .... Ge 1:25
Then G said, "Let us make human .... Ge 1:26
So G created human beings in his .... Ge 1:27
the image of G he created them .... Ge 1:27
G blessed them and said, "Have .... Ge 1:28
G said, "Look, I have given you .... Ge 1:29
G looked at everything he had .... Ge 1:31
the seventh day G finished the .... Ge 2:2
G blessed the seventh day and .... Ge 2:3
When the LORD G first made the .... Ge 2:4
the LORD G had not yet made .... Ge 2:5
Then the LORD G took dust from .... Ge 2:7
Then the LORD G planted a garden .... Ge 2:8
LORD G caused every beautiful .... Ge 2:9
G put the tree that gives life .... Ge 2:9
The LORD G put the man in the.............. Ge 2:15
The LORD G commanded him, ... Ge 2:16
Then the LORD G said, "It is not .... Ge 2:18
From the ground G formed every .... Ge 2:19
So the LORD G caused the man to .... Ge 2:21
G removed one of the man's ribs. .... Ge 2:21
Then G closed up the man's skin .... Ge 2:21
The LORD G used the rib from the........... Ge 2:22
animals the LORD G had made. .... Ge 3:1
Did G really say that you must .... Ge 3:1
But G told us, 'You must not eat .... Ge 3:3
G knows that if you eat the.................... Ge 3:5
evil and you will be like G!" .... Ge 3:5
they heard the LORD G walking in .... Ge 3:8
from the LORD G among the trees........... Ge 3:8
But the LORD G called to the man .... Ge 3:9
G asked, "Who told you that you .... Ge 3:11
Then the LORD G said to the .... Ge 3:13
The LORD G said to the snake, ... Ge 3:14
Then G said to the woman,.................... Ge 3:16
Then G said to the man, "You............... Ge 3:17
The LORD G made clothes from.............. Ge 3:21
Then the LORD G said, "Humans .... Ge 3:22
So the LORD G forced Adam out of .... Ge 3:23
After G forced humans out of the .... Ge 3:24
from the ground as a gift to G. .... Ge 4:3
G has given me another child. .... Ge 4:25
When G created human beings, ... Ge 5:1
walked with G 300 years more .... Ge 5:22
walked with G; one day Enoch .... Ge 5:24
be found, because G took him. .... Ge 5:24
the sons of G saw that these .... Ge 6:2

when the sons of G had sexual .... Ge 6:4
his time, and he walked with G. .... Ge 6:9
earth did what G said was evil, ... Ge 6:11
When G saw that everyone on the .... Ge 6:12
everything that G commanded him. .... Ge 6:22
just as G had commanded Noah. .... Ge 7:9
just as G had commanded Noah. .... Ge 7:16
G destroyed from the earth every .... Ge 7:23
G remembered Noah and all the .... Ge 8:1
Then G said to Noah, ... Ge 8:15
on the altar as offerings to G. .... Ge 8:20
Then G blessed Noah and his sons........... Ge 9:1
because G made humans in his own .... Ge 9:6
G said to Noah and his sons, ... Ge 9:8
And G said, "This is the sign of .... Ge 9:12
So G said to Noah, "The rainbow .... Ge 9:17
May the LORD, the G of Shem, be .... Ge 9:26
May G give more land to Japheth. .... Ge 9:27
He was a priest for G Most High .... Ge 14:18
you be blessed by G Most High, ... Ge 14:19
the G who made heaven and earth. .... Ge 14:19
And we praise G Most High, ... Ge 14:20
the LORD, the G Most High, who .... Ge 14:22
Then G led Abram outside and .... Ge 15:5
faith made him right with G. .... Ge 15:6
G said to Abram, "I am the LORD .... Ge 15:7
Abram brought them all to G.................. Ge 15:10
"You are 'G who sees me,'" .... Ge 16:13
I really seen G who sees me?" .... Ge 16:13
him and said, "I am G Almighty. .... Ge 17:1
on the ground. G said to him, ... Ge 17:3
I will be your G and the God of .... Ge 17:7
your God and the G of all your .... Ge 17:7
And I will be the G of your .... Ge 17:8
Then G said to Abraham, "You and .... Ge 17:9
G said to Abraham, "I will .... Ge 17:15
Abraham said to G, "Please let .... Ge 17:18
G said, "No, Sarah your wife .... Ge 17:19
After G finished talking with .... Ge 17:22
with Abraham, G rose and left .... Ge 17:22
in his camp as G had told him to .... Ge 17:23
G destroyed the cities in the .... Ge 19:29
So G saved Lot's life, but he .... Ge 19:29
But one night G spoke to .... Ge 20:3
Then G said to Abimelech in the .... Ge 20:6
place respected G and that .... Ge 20:11
When G told me to leave my .... Ge 20:13
prayed to G, and God healed .... Ge 20:17
to God, and G healed Abimelech, ... Ge 20:17
at the time G had said it would. .... Ge 21:2
days old as G had commanded. .... Ge 21:4
And Sarah said, "G has made me .... Ge 21:6
But G said to Abraham, "Don't be .... Ge 21:12
G heard the boy crying, and .... Ge 21:17
G has heard the boy crying there. .... Ge 21:17
Then G showed Hagar a well of .... Ge 21:19
G was with the boy as he grew up........... Ge 21:20
G is with you in everything you .... Ge 21:22
me here before G that you will .... Ge 21:23
LORD, the G who lives forever. .... Ge 21:33
these things G tested Abraham's .... Ge 22:1
G said to him, "Abraham!" .... Ge 22:1
G said, "Take your only son, ... Ge 22:2
to the place G had told them to .... Ge 22:3
G will give us the lamb for the .... Ge 22:8
came to the place G had told him .... Ge 22:9
that you trust G and that you .... Ge 22:12
as a whole burnt offering to G, ... Ge 22:13
the G of heaven and earth. .... Ge 24:3
The LORD, the G of heaven, ... Ge 24:7
said, "LORD, G of my master .... Ge 24:12
the G of my master Abraham. .... Ge 24:27
I said, 'LORD, G of my master .... Ge 24:42

G

the **G** of my master Abraham, ... Ge 24:48
Abraham died, **G** blessed his son .... Ge 25:11
I am the **G** of your father .... Ge 26:24
Lord your **G** helped me to find .... Ge 27:20
G give you plenty of rain and .... Ge 27:28
G Almighty bless you and give .... Ge 28:3
the land **G** gave to Abraham." .... Ge 28:4
he saw angels of **G** going up and .... Ge 28:12
the **G** of Abraham your .... Ge 28:13
grandfather, and the **G** of Isaac. .... Ge 28:13
the house of **G** and the gate .... Ge 28:17
I want **G** to be with me and to .... Ge 28:20
these things, he will be my **G.** .... Ge 28:21
its end will be the house of **G.** .... Ge 28:22
And I will give **G** one-tenth of .... Ge 28:22
Can I do what only **G** can do? .... Ge 30:2
G has judged me innocent. .... Ge 30:6
Then **G** answered Leah's prayer, ... Ge 30:17
G has given me what I paid for, ... Ge 30:18
G has given me a fine gift. .... Ge 30:20
Then **G** remembered Rachel and .... Ge 30:22
"**G** has taken away my shame," .... Ge 30:23
but the **G** of my father has been .... Ge 31:5
G has not allowed your father .... Ge 31:7
So **G** has taken the animals away .... Ge 31:9
The angel of **G** spoke to me in .... Ge 31:11
am the **G** who appeared to you at .... Ge 31:13
G took all this wealth from our .... Ge 31:16
whatever **G** has told you to do. .... Ge 31:16
That night **G** came to Laban the .... Ge 31:24
last night the **G** of your father .... Ge 31:29
But the **G** of my father, the God .... Ge 31:42
the **G** of Abraham and the God of .... Ge 31:42
of Abraham and the **G** of Isaac, ... Ge 31:42
Remember that **G** is our witness............. Ge 31:50
Let the **G** of Abraham, who is the .... Ge 31:53
is the **G** of Nahor and the God .... Ge 31:53
of Nahor and the **G** of their .... Ge 31:53
name of the **G** whom his father .... Ge 31:53
way, the angels of **G** met him................ Ge 32:1
said, "This is the camp of **G!**"................. Ge 32:2
Then Jacob said, "**G** of my father .... Ge 32:9
father Abraham! **G** of my father............. Ge 32:9
wrestled with **G** and with people, ... Ge 32:28
I have seen **G** face to face, ... Ge 32:30
are the children **G** has given me. .... Ge 33:5
G has been good to me, your .... Ge 33:5
It is like seeing the face of **G,** .... Ge 33:10
G has been very good to me, ... Ge 33:11
there and named it after **G,**................... Ge 33:20
it after God, the **G** of Israel. .... Ge 33:20
G said to Jacob, "Go to the city .... Ge 35:1
altar to the **G** who appeared to .... Ge 35:1
I will build an altar to **G,**....................... Ge 35:3
But **G** caused the people in the .... Ge 35:5
Bethel, after **G,** because God had .... Ge 35:7
because **G** had appeared to him .... Ge 35:7
G appeared to him again and .... Ge 35:9
G said to him, "Your name is .... Ge 35:10
G said to him, "I am God .... Ge 35:11
said to him, "I am **G** Almighty. .... Ge 35:11
Then **G** left him. .... Ge 35:13
that place where **G** had talked to .... Ge 35:14
on it to make it special for **G.** .... Ge 35:14
thing? It is a sin against **G.**" .... Ge 39:9
G is the only One who can .... Ge 40:8
G will do this for the king." .... Ge 41:16
G is telling you what he is .... Ge 41:25
G is showing the king what he is .... Ge 41:28
This shows that **G** has firmly .... Ge 41:32
G has shown you all this. .... Ge 41:39
G has made me forget all the .... Ge 41:51
G has given me children in the .... Ge 41:52

other, "What has **G** done to us?" .... Ge 42:28
pray that **G** Almighty will cause .... Ge 43:14
Your **G,** the God of your father, ... Ge 43:23
Your God, the **G** of your father, ... Ge 43:23
to Benjamin, "**G** be good to you, ... Ge 43:29
G has uncovered our guilt, ... Ge 44:16
G sent me here ahead of you to .... Ge 45:5
G sent me here ahead of you to .... Ge 45:7
not you who sent me here, but **G.** .... Ge 45:8
G has made me the highest. .... Ge 45:8
G has made me master over all .... Ge 45:9
sacrifices to the **G** of his .... Ge 46:1
the night **G** spoke to Israel .... Ge 46:2
Then **G** said, "I am God, the God .... Ge 46:3
God said, "I am **G,** the God of .... Ge 46:3
I am God, the **G** of your father. .... Ge 46:3
G Almighty appeared to me at Luz .... Ge 48:3
are my sons that **G** has given me .... Ge 48:9
and now **G** has let me see you and .... Ge 48:11
Abraham and Isaac served our **G,** .... Ge 48:15
like a shepherd **G** has led me all............. Ge 48:15
'May **G** make you like Ephraim and .... Ge 48:20
But **G** will be with you and will .... Ge 48:21
from the Mighty **G** of Jacob and............. Ge 49:24
Your father's **G** helps you. .... Ge 49:25
helps you. **G** Almighty blesses .... Ge 49:25
of the **G** of your father. .... Ge 50:17
Can I do what only **G** can do? .... Ge 50:19
but **G** turned your evil into good .... Ge 50:20
but **G** will take care of you..................... Ge 50:24
nurses feared **G,** so they did not .... Ex 1:17
G was good to the nurses. .... Ex 1:20
Because the nurses feared **G,** .... Ex 1:21
cried for help, **G** heard them. .... Ex 2:23
G heard their cries, and he .... Ex 2:24
to Sinai, the mountain of **G.** .... Ex 3:1
G called to him from the bush, ... Ex 3:4
Then **G** said, "Do not come any .... Ex 3:5
I am the **G** of your ancestors— .... Ex 3:6
your ancestors—the **G** of Abraham, ... Ex 3:6
God of Abraham, the **G** of Isaac, ... Ex 3:6
of Isaac, and the **G** of Jacob." .... Ex 3:6
he was afraid to look at **G.** .... Ex 3:6
But Moses said to **G,** "I am not a .... Ex 3:11
G said, "I will be with you. .... Ex 3:12
Moses said to **G,** "When I go to .... Ex 3:13
'The **G** of your ancestors sent me .... Ex 3:13
Then **G** said to Moses, "I AM WHO .... Ex 3:14
G also said to Moses, "This is.................. Ex 3:15
Lord is the **G** of your ancestors— .... Ex 3:15
your ancestors—the **G** of Abraham, ... Ex 3:15
God of Abraham, the **G** of Isaac, ... Ex 3:15
of Isaac, and the **G** of Jacob. .... Ex 3:15
the **G** of your ancestors Abraham, ... Ex 3:16
The Lord, the **G** of the Hebrews, ... Ex 3:18
sacrifices to the Lord our **G.'** .... Ex 3:18
I am the **G** of their ancestors, ... Ex 4:5
ancestors, the **G** of Abraham, the .... Ex 4:5
God of Abraham, the **G** of Isaac, ... Ex 4:5
of Isaac, and the **G** of Jacob." .... Ex 4:5
You will tell him what **G** says, ... Ex 4:16
with him the walking stick of **G.** .... Ex 4:20
mountain of **G,** and kissed him. .... Ex 4:27
the Lord, the **G** of Israel, says: .... Ex 5:1
The **G** of the Hebrews has met .... Ex 5:3
sacrifices to the Lord our **G.**................... Ex 5:3
to offer sacrifices to our **G.** .... Ex 5:8
Then **G** said to Moses, "I am the .... Ex 6:2
Jacob by the name **G** Almighty, ... Ex 6:3
people, and I will be your **G.** .... Ex 6:7
know that I am the Lord your **G,** .... Ex 6:7
have made you like **G** to the king .... Ex 7:1
The Lord, the **G** of the Hebrews, ... Ex 7:16

is no one like the LORD our **G**. .... Ex 8:10
the power of **G** had done this................... Ex 8:19
sacrifices to your **G** here in.................... Ex 8:25
we offer to the LORD our **G**. .... Ex 8:26
to the LORD our **G** there, ... Ex 8:27
the LORD your **G** in the desert, ... Ex 8:28
the LORD, the **G** of the Hebrews, ... Ex 9:1
the LORD, the **G** of the Hebrews, ... Ex 9:13
do not yet fear the LORD **G**." .... Ex 9:30
the LORD, the **G** of the Hebrews, ... Ex 10:3
go to worship the LORD their **G**. .... Ex 10:7
Go and worship the LORD your **G**.......... Ex 10:8
the LORD your **G** and against you........... Ex 10:16
the LORD your **G**, and ask him to .... Ex 10:17
to offer them to the LORD our **G**. .... Ex 10:25
to worship the LORD our **G**. .... Ex 10:26
G did not lead them on the road .... Ex 13:17
G said, "If they have to fight, ... Ex 13:17
So **G** led them through the desert .... Ex 13:18
He had said, "When **G** saves you, ... Ex 13:19
Now the angel of **G** that usually .... Ex 14:19
He is my **G**, and I will praise .... Ex 15:2
He is the **G** of my ancestors, ... Ex 15:2
the LORD your **G** and do what he .... Ex 15:26
know I am the LORD your **G**.'" .... Ex 16:12
walking stick of **G** in my hands." .... Ex 17:9
everything that **G** had done for .... Ex 18:1
The **G** of my father is my help. .... Ex 18:4
desert near the mountain of **G**. .... Ex 18:5
and other sacrifices to **G**. .... Ex 18:12
the holy meal together before **G**. .... Ex 18:12
I want **G** to be with you. .... Ex 18:19
must speak to **G** for the people .... Ex 18:19
men who respect **G**, who can be............. Ex 18:21
you do this as **G** commands you, ... Ex 18:23
went up on the mountain to **G**. .... Ex 19:3
themselves for service to **G**, ... Ex 19:14
out of the camp to meet **G**, ... Ex 19:17
and the voice of **G** answered him. .... Ex 19:19
Then **G** spoke all these words: .... Ex 20:1
the LORD your **G**, who brought you .... Ex 20:2
I, the LORD your **G**, am a jealous .... Ex 20:5
LORD your God, am a jealous **G**. .... Ex 20:5
the LORD your **G** thoughtlessly;............. Ex 20:7
rest to honor the LORD your **G**. .... Ex 20:10
the LORD your **G** is going to give .... Ex 20:12
But don't let **G** speak to us,.................. Ex 20:19
because **G** has come to test you............. Ex 20:20
near the dark cloud where **G** was. .... Ex 20:21
Then **G** said to Moses, "These are .... Ex 21:1
master must take him to **G**................... Ex 21:6
accidentally, **G** allowed that to .... Ex 21:13
promise before **G** that he has not .... Ex 22:8
man must bring his case to **G**. .... Ex 22:9
his promise made before **G**. .... Ex 22:11
to any **g** except the LORD .... Ex 22:20
speak against **G** or curse a .... Ex 22:28
Offer to the **G** first things you.............. Ex 23:16
must come to worship the LORD **G**. .... Ex 23:17
Holy Tent of the LORD your **G**. .... Ex 23:19
If you worship the LORD your **G**, ... Ex 23:25
and saw the **G** of Israel. .... Ex 24:10
leaders of the Israelites saw **G**, ... Ex 24:11
but **G** did not destroy them. .... Ex 24:11
up to Sinai, the mountain of **G**. .... Ex 24:13
for service to **G** and making it .... Ex 29:37
people of Israel and be their **G**. .... Ex 29:45
the LORD their **G** who led them .... Ex 29:46
them. I am the LORD their **G**................. Ex 29:46
service to **G** by putting blood .... Ex 30:10
them ready for service to **G**. .... Ex 30:25
these things for service to **G**, ... Ex 30:29
them ready for service to **G**. .... Ex 30:31

the Spirit of **G** and have given .... Ex 31:3
written by the finger of **G**. .... Ex 31:18
begged the LORD his **G** and said, ... Ex 32:11
G himself had made the tablets,.............. Ex 32:16
and **G** himself had written the .... Ex 32:16
The LORD, the **G** of Israel, says .... Ex 32:27
and **G** has blessed you for this." .... Ex 32:29
The LORD is a **G** who shows mercy, ... Ex 34:6
Don't worship any other **g**,.................. Ex 34:14
the Jealous One, am a jealous **G**. .... Ex 34:14
the Lord GOD, the **G** of Israel. .... Ex 34:23
the LORD your **G** three times each........... Ex 34:24
to the Tent of the LORD your **G**. .... Ex 34:26
the Spirit of **G** and has given .... Ex 35:31
Give the altar for service to **G**, ... Ex 40:10
will be given for service to **G**................. Ex 40:11
for service to **G** so that he may .... Ex 40:13
sin so he will belong to **G**. .... Le 1:4
agreement with **G** that will last .... Le 2:13
LORD his **G** has commanded must........... Le 4:22
to give a gift to **G** or because .... Le 7:16
holy and ready for service to **G**. .... Le 8:15
sins so you will belong to **G**. .... Le 9:7
the LORD your **G**. Keep yourselves .... Le 11:44
you out of Egypt to be your **G**; .... Le 11:45
Israel: 'I am the LORD your **G**. .... Le 18:2
them. I am the LORD your **G**................. Le 18:4
that you do not respect your **G**. .... Le 18:21
I am the LORD your **G**.'" .... Le 18:30
am the LORD your **G**. You must be .... Le 19:2
Sabbaths. I am the LORD your **G**. .... Le 19:3
I am the LORD your **G**. .... Le 19:4
country. I am the LORD your **G**. .... Le 19:10
that you don't respect your **G**. .... Le 19:12
But you must respect your **G**. .... Le 19:14
for you. I am the LORD your **G**. .... Le 19:25
unclean. I am the LORD your **G**. .... Le 19:31
Show respect also to your **G**. .... Le 19:32
in Egypt. I am the LORD your **G**. .... Le 19:34
the LORD your **G**. I brought you .... Le 19:36
because I am the LORD your **G**............... Le 20:7
the LORD your **G**, and I have set .... Le 20:24
holy to their **G** and show respect .... Le 21:6
which is the food of their **G**. .... Le 21:6
because he is holy to his **G**. .... Le 21:7
he offers up the food of your **G**. .... Le 21:8
the special food of their **G**. .... Le 21:17
cannot offer the food of his **G**. .... Le 21:21
you out of Egypt to be your **G**. .... Le 22:33
bring your offering to your **G**, ... Le 23:14
I am the LORD your **G**.'" .... Le 23:22
the LORD your **G** for seven days. .... Le 23:40
I am the LORD your **G**.'" .... Le 23:43
curses his **G**, he is guilty...................... Le 24:15
I am the LORD your **G**.'" .... Le 24:22
but you must respect your **G**. .... Le 25:17
your God. I am the LORD your **G**. .... Le 25:17
loan to him, but respect your **G**;........... Le 25:36
the LORD your **G**, who brought you .... Le 25:38
to you and to become your **G**................ Le 25:38
but you must respect your **G**. .... Le 25:43
of Egypt. I am the LORD your **G**. .... Le 25:55
because I am the LORD your **G**............... Le 26:1
walk with you and be your **G**,............... Le 26:12
the LORD your **G**, who brought you .... Le 26:13
because I am the LORD their **G**.............. Le 26:44
Egypt so I could become their **G**; .... Le 26:45
to belong to **G** in a special way. .... Nu 6:7
The LORD your **G** will take notice .... Nu 10:9
will help you remember your **G**............... Nu 10:10
your God. I am the LORD your **G**." .... Nu 10:10
to the LORD, "**G**, please heal her .... Nu 12:13
the LORD your **G**, who brought you .... Nu 15:41

G

you out of Egypt to be your **G.** .... Nu 15:41
I am the LORD your **G.**'" .... Nu 15:41
G of Israel has separated you .... Nu 16:9
and cried out, "**G,** you are the .... Nu 16:22
you are the **G** over the spirits .... Nu 16:22
to me, you who turn against **G!** .... Nu 20:10
and grumbled at **G** and Moses. .... Nu 21:5
G came to Balaam and asked, ... Nu 22:9
Balaam said to **G,** "The king of .... Nu 22:10
But **G** said to Balaam, "Do not go .... Nu 22:12
the LORD my **G** in anything, ... Nu 22:18
That night **G** came to Balaam and .... Nu 22:20
G became angry because Balaam .... Nu 22:22
only say what **G** tells me to say. .... Nu 22:38
G came to Balaam there, and .... Nu 23:4
But **G** has not cursed them, ... Nu 23:8
I will meet with **G** over there." .... Nu 23:15
G is not a human being, and he .... Nu 23:19
The LORD their **G** is with them, ... Nu 23:21
G brought them out of Egypt; .... Nu 23:22
'Look what **G** has done for Israel! .... Nu 23:23
Maybe **G** will be pleased to let .... Nu 23:27
Spirit of **G** took control of him, ... Nu 24:2
a man who hears the words of **G.** .... Nu 24:4
G brought them out of Egypt; .... Nu 24:8
a man who hears the words of **G.** .... Nu 24:16
I know well the Most High **G.** .... Nu 24:16
one can live when **G** does this. .... Nu 24:23
concern for the honor of his **G.** .... Nu 25:13
so they would belong to **G.**" .... Nu 25:13
The LORD is the **G** of the spirits............. Nu 27:16
sins so you will belong to **G.** .... Nu 28:22
sins so you will belong to **G.** .... Nu 28:30
sins so you will belong to **G.** .... Nu 29:5
to explain what **G** had commanded. .... Dt 1:5
The LORD our **G** spoke to us at .... Dt 1:6
LORD your **G** has made you grow .... Dt 1:10
the LORD, the **G** of your .... Dt 1:11
your decision comes from **G.** .... Dt 1:17
as the LORD our **G** commanded us, ... Dt 1:19
the LORD our **G** will give us. .... Dt 1:20
The LORD, the **G** of your .... Dt 1:21
the LORD your **G** is giving us." .... Dt 1:25
the command of the LORD your **G,** .... Dt 1:26
The LORD your **G** will go ahead of .... Dt 1:30
how the LORD your **G** carried you, ... Dt 1:31
did not trust the LORD your **G,** .... Dt 1:32
as the LORD our **G** commanded us." .... Dt 1:41
The LORD your **G** has blessed .... Dt 2:7
LORD your **G** has been with you .... Dt 2:7
the LORD our **G** has given us." .... Dt 2:29
the LORD your **G** had made him .... Dt 2:30
the LORD our **G** gave Sihon to us .... Dt 2:33
LORD our **G** gave us all of them. .... Dt 2:36
as the LORD our **G** had commanded......... Dt 2:37
the LORD our **G** gave us Og king .... Dt 3:3
The LORD your **G** has given you .... Dt 3:18
the LORD your **G** has given them .... Dt 3:20
the LORD your **G** has done to................. Dt 3:21
LORD your **G** will fight for you. .... Dt 3:22
and no other **g** in heaven or on .... Dt 3:24
There is no other **g** like you. .... Dt 3:24
the LORD, the **G** of your .... Dt 4:1
the LORD your **G** that I give you .... Dt 4:2
how the LORD your **G** destroyed .... Dt 4:3
the LORD your **G** are still alive .... Dt 4:4
the LORD my **G** commanded me. .... Dt 4:5
the LORD our **G** comes near when .... Dt 4:7
the LORD your **G** at Mount Sinai. .... Dt 4:10
the LORD your **G** has made these .... Dt 4:19
the LORD your **G** is giving you as .... Dt 4:21
of the LORD your **G** that he made .... Dt 4:23
as the LORD your **G** has commanded ...... Dt 4:23

LORD your **G** is a jealous God, ... Dt 4:24
LORD your **G** is jealous as, ... Dt 4:24
the LORD your **G** says is evil,................. Dt 4:25
can look for the LORD your **G,** .... Dt 4:29
to the LORD your **G** and obey him, ... Dt 4:30
the LORD your **G** is a merciful .... Dt 4:31
LORD your **G** is a merciful **G.**.............. Dt 4:31
way back to when **G** made humans .... Dt 4:32
have ever heard **G** speak from a .... Dt 4:33
No other **g** has ever taken for .... Dt 4:34
the LORD your **G** did this for you .... Dt 4:34
would know that the LORD is **G,** .... Dt 4:35
there is no other **G** besides him. .... Dt 4:35
today that the LORD is **G.** .... Dt 4:39
He is **G** in heaven above and on .... Dt 4:39
below. There is no other **g!** .... Dt 4:39
The LORD your **G** is giving to you .... Dt 4:40
The LORD our **G** made an Agreement ...... Dt 5:2
the LORD your **G;** I brought you .... Dt 5:6
I, the LORD your **G,** am a jealous .... Dt 5:9
LORD your God, am a jealous **G.** .... Dt 5:9
the LORD your **G** thoughtlessly,............... Dt 5:11
LORD your **G** has commanded you. .... Dt 5:12
rest to honor the LORD your **G.** .... Dt 5:14
the LORD your **G** brought you out .... Dt 5:15
So the LORD your **G** has commanded ...... Dt 5:15
as the LORD your **G** has commanded ...... Dt 5:16
the LORD your **G** is going to give ...... Dt 5:16
The LORD our **G** has shown us his .... Dt 5:24
live even if **G** speaks to him. .... Dt 5:24
the LORD our **G** speak anymore. .... Dt 5:25
heard the living **G** speaking from .... Dt 5:26
everything the LORD our **G** says. .... Dt 5:27
what the LORD our **G** tells you, ... Dt 5:27
the LORD your **G** has commanded......... Dt 5:32
the LORD your **G** has commanded........... Dt 5:33
the LORD your **G** told me to teach .... Dt 6:1
the LORD your **G** as long as you .... Dt 6:2
as the LORD, the **G** of your..................... Dt 6:3
The LORD our **G** is the only LORD. .... Dt 6:4
the LORD your **G** with all your .... Dt 6:5
The LORD your **G** will bring you .... Dt 6:10
Respect the LORD your **G.** .... Dt 6:13
LORD your **G** is a jealous God. .... Dt 6:15
LORD your God is a jealous **G.** .... Dt 6:15
the LORD your **G** as you did at .... Dt 6:16
of the LORD your **G** and the rules .... Dt 6:17
rules the LORD our **G** gave us?"............... Dt 6:20
the LORD our **G** so that we will .... Dt 6:24
the presence of the LORD our **G,** .... Dt 6:25
The LORD your **G** will bring you .... Dt 7:1
The LORD your **G** will hand these .... Dt 7:2
who belong to the LORD your **G.** .... Dt 7:6
that the LORD your **G** is God,................. Dt 7:9
that the LORD your God is **G,**................... Dt 7:9
your God is God, the faithful **G.** .... Dt 7:9
the LORD your **G** will keep his .... Dt 7:12
the LORD your **G** hands over to .... Dt 7:16
what the LORD your **G** did to all .... Dt 7:18
The LORD your **G** will do the same .... Dt 7:19
The LORD your **G** will also send .... Dt 7:20
the LORD your **G** is with you;................... Dt 7:21
he is a great **G** and people are .... Dt 7:21
the LORD your **G** forces those .... Dt 7:22
the LORD your **G** will hand those .... Dt 7:23
The LORD your **G** hates it. .... Dt 7:25
how the LORD your **G** has led you .... Dt 8:2
the LORD your **G** corrects you as .... Dt 8:5
the commands of the LORD your **G,** .... Dt 8:6
The LORD your **G** is bringing you .... Dt 8:7
the LORD your **G** for giving you............... Dt 8:10
the LORD your **G** so that you fail .... Dt 8:11
You will forget the LORD your **G,** .... Dt 8:14

G

the Lord your **G** will choose to .... Dt 26:2
the Lord your **G** that I have come............ Dt 26:3
of the altar of the Lord your **G**. .... Dt 26:4
announce before the Lord your **G**: .... Dt 26:5
the Lord, the **G** of our ancestors .... Dt 26:7
the Lord your **G** and bow down .... Dt 26:10
the Lord your **G** has given good .... Dt 26:11
Then say to the Lord your **G**, ... Dt 26:13
of my harvest that belongs to **G**,.............. Dt 26:13
you, the Lord my **G**, and have .... Dt 26:14
the Lord your **G** commands you to .... Dt 26:16
said that the Lord is your **G**,................... Dt 26:17
holy people to the Lord your **G**, ... Dt 26:19
the Lord your **G** is giving you. .... Dt 27:2
the Lord your **G** is giving you, ... Dt 27:3
as the Lord, the **G** of your..................... Dt 27:3
stones there to the Lord your **G**, ... Dt 27:5
of the Lord your **G** with stones.............. Dt 27:6
on it to the Lord your **G**, ... Dt 27:6
rejoice before the Lord your **G**. .... Dt 27:7
the people of the Lord your **G**. .... Dt 27:9
the Lord your **G**, and keep his .... Dt 27:10
completely obey the Lord your **G**, ... Dt 28:1
the Lord your **G** will make you .... Dt 28:1
the Lord your **G** so that all .... Dt 28:2
The Lord your **G** will bless you .... Dt 28:8
the Lord your **G** that I am giving .... Dt 28:13
the Lord your **G** and carefully .... Dt 28:15
obey the Lord your **G** and keep .... Dt 28:45
the Lord your **G** with joy and a .... Dt 28:47
the Lord your **G** is giving you. .... Dt 28:52
the Lord your **G** gave you. .... Dt 28:53
name of the Lord your **G**, ... Dt 28:58
did not obey the Lord your **G**. .... Dt 28:62
that I am the Lord your **G**, ... Dt 29:6
here before the Lord your **G**— .... Dt 29:10
a promise with the Lord your **G**, ... Dt 29:12
the Lord your **G** is making with .... Dt 29:12
will be your **G**, as he told you................. Dt 29:13
before the Lord your **G** today, ... Dt 29:15
the Lord our **G** to go and serve .... Dt 29:18
of the Lord, the **G** of their..................... Dt 29:25
the Lord our **G** has kept secret, ... Dt 29:29
the Lord your **G** has sent you .... Dt 30:1
will return to the Lord your **G**,.............. Dt 30:2
the Lord your **G** will give you .... Dt 30:3
The Lord your **G** will prepare you .... Dt 30:6
The Lord your **G** will put all................. Dt 30:7
The Lord your **G** will make you .... Dt 30:9
the Lord your **G** by keeping all.............. Dt 30:10
the Lord your **G** with your whole .... Dt 30:10
today to love the Lord your **G**, ... Dt 30:16
the Lord your **G** will bless you .... Dt 30:16
life is to love the Lord your **G**, ... Dt 30:20
the Lord your **G** will lead you .... Dt 31:3
Lord your **G** will go with you. .... Dt 31:6
the Lord your **G** and carefully .... Dt 31:12
the Lord your **G** for as long as .... Dt 31:13
'It is because **G** is not with us .... Dt 31:17
Agreement with the Lord your **G**. .... Dt 31:26
Praise **G** because he is great! .... Dt 32:3
He is a faithful **G** who does no .... Dt 32:4
G Most High gave the nations .... Dt 32:8
was no foreign **g** helping him. .... Dt 32:12
They left the **G** who made them .... Dt 32:15
They made **G** jealous with foreign .... Dt 32:16
to demons, not **G**, to gods they .... Dt 32:17
You left **G** who is the Rock, ... Dt 32:18
you forgot the **G** who gave you .... Dt 32:18
will see that I am the one **G**! .... Dt 32:39
God! There is no **g** but me. I .... Dt 32:39
Moses, the man of **G**, gave this .... Dt 33:1
Praise **G** who gives Gad more................ Dt 33:20

is no one like the **G** of Israel, ... Dt 33:26
The everlasting **G** is your place .... Dt 33:27
the Lord your **G** will be with you .... Jos 1:9
the Lord your **G** is giving you.'............... Jos 1:11
the Lord your **G** would give you .... Jos 1:13
the Lord their **G** is giving them. .... Jos 1:15
the Lord your **G** be with you just .... Jos 1:17
Lord your **G** rules the heavens .... Jos 2:11
Agreement with the Lord your **G**, ... Jos 3:3
to the words of the Lord your **G**. .... Jos 3:9
that the living **G** is with you .... Jos 3:10
the Ark of the Lord your **G** is. .... Jos 4:5
The Lord your **G** caused the water .... Jos 4:23
respect the Lord your **G**.'" .... Jos 4:24
The Lord, the **G** of Israel, says .... Jos 7:13
to the Lord, the **G** of Israel. .... Jos 7:19
the Lord, the **G** of Israel. .... Jos 7:20
Lord your **G** will give you the .... Jos 8:7
for the Lord, the **G** of Israel,.................. Jos 8:30
of the fame of the Lord your **G**. .... Jos 9:9
the Lord, the **G** of Israel. .... Jos 9:18
the Lord, the **G** of Israel, so we .... Jos 9:19
water for the house of my **G**."................ Jos 9:23
the Lord your **G** commanded his .... Jos 9:24
the Lord your **G** will hand them .... Jos 10:19
The Lord, the **G** of Israel, had .... Jos 10:40
the Lord, the **G** of Israel, was .... Jos 10:42
the Lord, the **G** of Israel, as he .... Jos 13:14
the Lord, the **G** of Israel, ... Jos 13:33
believed in the Lord, my **G**.' .... Jos 14:9
the Lord, the **G** of Israel. .... Jos 14:14
got the land **G** had promised them .... Jos 15:20
The Lord, the **G** of your .... Jos 18:3
the presence of the Lord our **G**. .... Jos 18:6
the Lord your **G** gave you. .... Jos 22:3
The Lord your **G** promised to give .... Jos 22:4
love the Lord your **G** and obey............... Jos 22:5
you turn against the **G** of Israel .... Jos 22:16
for which **G** made many Israelites .... Jos 22:17
altar for the Lord our **G**. .... Jos 22:19
The Lord is **G** of gods! The Lord .... Jos 22:22
gods! The Lord is **G** of gods! God........... Jos 22:22
G knows, and we want you to know .... Jos 22:22
the Lord, the **G** of Israel. .... Jos 22:24
to the Lord our **G** is in front .... Jos 22:29
They were pleased and thanked **G**............ Jos 22:33
That We Believe the Lord Is **G**................ Jos 22:34
The Lord your **G** fought for you. .... Jos 23:3
The Lord your **G** will force out.............. Jos 23:5
to follow the Lord your **G**, ... Jos 23:8
the Lord your **G** fights for you,.............. Jos 23:10
careful to love the Lord your **G**. .... Jos 23:11
Lord your **G** will not help you .... Jos 23:13
the Lord your **G** has given you. .... Jos 23:13
the Lord your **G** made has come .... Jos 23:15
agreement with the Lord your **G**............. Jos 23:16
of Israel to stand before **G**. .... Jos 24:1
the Lord, the **G** of Israel, says .... Jos 24:2
the Lord our **G** who brought our .... Jos 24:17
the Lord, because he is our **G**." .... Jos 24:18
is a holy **G** and a jealous God. .... Jos 24:19
is a holy God and a jealous **G**. .... Jos 24:19
the Lord, the **G** of Israel, with .... Jos 24:23
We will serve the Lord our **G**, ... Jos 24:24
the Book of the Teachings of **G**. .... Jos 24:26
will not turn against your **G**." .... Jos 24:27
Now **G** has paid me back for what .... Jdg 1:7
the **G** of their ancestors who had .... Jdg 2:12
not faithful to **G** but worshiped .... Jdg 2:17
the Lord their **G** and served the .... Jdg 3:7
have a message from **G** for you." .... Jdg 3:20
The Lord, the **G** of Israel, ... Jdg 4:6
that day **G** defeated Jabin king .... Jdg 4:23

G

the LORD your **G** will keep you 1Sa 25:29
the LORD, the **G** of Israel, who 1Sa 25:32
the LORD, the **G** of Israel, lives 1Sa 25:34
Today **G** has handed your enemy 1Sa 26:8
against me, and **G** has left me. 1Sa 28:15
are as good as an angel from **G**. 1Sa 29:9
strength in the LORD his **G**. 1Sa 30:6
me before **G** that you won't 1Sa 30:15
As surely as **G** lives, if you had 2Sa 2:27
May **G** help me if I don't join 2Sa 3:9
May **G** punish me terribly if I 2Sa 3:35
the LORD **G** All-Powerful was 2Sa 5:10
to bring back the Ark of **G**. 2Sa 6:2
put the Ark of **G** on a new cart 2Sa 6:3
which had the Ark of **G** on it. 2Sa 6:4
out to steady the Ark of **G**. 2Sa 6:6
died there beside the Ark of **G**. 2Sa 6:7
because the Ark of **G** is there." 2Sa 6:12
but the Ark of **G** is in a tent!" 2Sa 7:2
everything **G** had said in this 2Sa 7:17
There is no **G** except you. 2Sa 7:22
on earth that **G** chose to be his 2Sa 7:23
and, LORD, you are their **G**. 2Sa 7:24
Now, LORD **G**, keep the promise 2Sa 7:25
All-Powerful is **G** over Israel!' 2Sa 7:26
the **G** of Israel, you 2Sa 7:27
GOD, you are **G**, and your words 2Sa 7:28
people and the cities of our **G**. 2Sa 10:12
the LORD, the **G** of Israel, says: 2Sa 12:7
David prayed to **G** for the baby. 2Sa 12:16
in the name of the LORD your **G**. 2Sa 14:11
way against the people of **G**? 2Sa 14:13
But **G** doesn't take away life. 2Sa 14:14
from getting what **G** says.' 2Sa 14:16
an angel of **G**, you know what 2Sa 14:17
the LORD your **G** be with you!'" 2Sa 14:17
like an angel of **G** who knows 2Sa 14:20
the Ark of the Agreement with **G**. 2Sa 15:24
Take the Ark of **G** back into the 2Sa 15:25
took the Ark of **G** back to 2Sa 15:29
where people used to worship **G**, ... 2Sa 15:32
said, "Praise the LORD your **G**!' 2Sa 18:28
May **G** punish me terribly if I 2Sa 19:13
king, are like an angel from **G**. 2Sa 19:27
Then **G** answered the prayers for 2Sa 21:14
G is my rock. I can run to him 2Sa 22:3
cried out to my **G**. From his 2Sa 22:7
done evil by turning from my **G**. 2Sa 22:22
The ways of **G** are without fault; 2Sa 22:31
Who is **G**? Only the LORD. Who is 2Sa 22:32
Who is the Rock? Only our **G**. 2Sa 22:32
G is my protection. He makes my 2Sa 22:33
G, the Rock, who saves me! 2Sa 22:47
G gives me victory over my 2Sa 22:48
great by the Most High **G** speaks. 2Sa 23:1
king of the **G** of Jacob; 2Sa 23:1
The **G** of Israel spoke; the Rock 2Sa 23:3
who rules with respect for **G**, ... 2Sa 23:3
This is how **G** has cared for my 2Sa 23:5
G made a lasting agreement with 2Sa 23:5
May the LORD your **G** give you a 2Sa 24:3
the LORD your **G** be pleased with 2Sa 24:23
to the LORD my **G** burnt offerings 2Sa 24:24
in the name of the LORD your **G**. 1Ki 1:17
of the LORD, the **G** of Israel. 1Ki 1:30
the LORD, the **G** of my master, ... 1Ki 1:36
'May your **G** make Solomon even 1Ki 1:47
down on his bed to worship **G**, ... 1Ki 1:47
Bless the LORD, the **G** of Israel. 1Ki 1:48
Obey the LORD your **G**. Follow him 1Ki 2:3
May **G** punish me terribly if this 1Ki 2:23
G said, "Ask for whatever you 1Ki 3:5
LORD my **G**, now you have made me, ... 1Ki 3:7

So **G** said to him, "You did not 1Ki 3:11
had wisdom from **G** to make the 1Ki 3:28
G gave Solomon great wisdom so 1Ki 4:29
for worshiping the LORD his **G**. 1Ki 5:3
now the LORD my **G** has given me 1Ki 5:4
for worshiping the LORD my **G**. 1Ki 5:5
the LORD, the **G** of Israel. 1Ki 8:15
for the LORD, the **G** of Israel. 1Ki 8:17
for the LORD, the **G** of Israel. 1Ki 8:20
LORD, **G** of Israel, there is no 1Ki 8:23
there is no **g** like you in heaven 1Ki 8:23
Now LORD, **G** of Israel, keep the 1Ki 8:25
Now, **G** of Israel, please 1Ki 8:26
But, **G**, can you really live here 1Ki 8:27
LORD my **G**, hear this prayer your........... 1Ki 8:28
the LORD our **G** be with us as he 1Ki 8:57
May the LORD our **G** remember this 1Ki 8:59
the LORD is the only true **G**. 1Ki 8:60
the LORD our **G** and follow all 1Ki 8:61
they left the LORD their **G**. 1Ki 9:9
This was the **G** who brought their 1Ki 9:9
the LORD your **G**, who was pleased 1Ki 10:9
to the wisdom **G** had given him. 1Ki 10:24
caused him to turn away from **G**. 1Ki 11:3
the hated **g** of the Ammonites. 1Ki 11:5
the hated **g** of the Moabites, ... 1Ki 11:7
the hated **g** of the Ammonites. 1Ki 11:7
the LORD, the **G** of Israel. 1Ki 11:9
G also caused another man to be 1Ki 11:23
LORD, the **G** of Israel, says: ' 1Ki 11:31
the Sidonian **g** Ashtoreth, ... 1Ki 11:33
the Moabite **g** Chemosh, ... 1Ki 11:33
and the Ammonite **g** Molech. 1Ki 11:33
G spoke his word to Shemaiah, ... 1Ki 12:22
to Shemaiah, a man of **G**, saying, ... 1Ki 12:22
a man of **G** from Judah to go 1Ki 13:1
the man of **G** to speak against 1Ki 13:2
day the man of **G** gave proof that 1Ki 13:3
what the man of **G** said about the 1Ki 13:4
had told the man of **G** to give. 1Ki 13:5
the king said to the man of **G**, ... 1Ki 13:6
pray to the LORD your **G** for me, ... 1Ki 13:6
So the man of **G** prayed to the 1Ki 13:6
the king said to the man of **G**, ... 1Ki 13:7
But the man of **G** answered the 1Ki 13:8
what the man of **G** had done there 1Ki 13:11
road the man of **G** from Judah had 1Ki 13:12
after the man of **G** and found him 1Ki 13:14
Are you the man of **G** who came 1Ki 13:14
you," the man of **G** answered. 1Ki 13:16
So the man of **G** went to the old............... 1Ki 13:19
out to the man of **G** from Judah, ... 1Ki 13:21
the LORD your **G** commanded you. 1Ki 13:21
the man of **G** finished eating 1Ki 13:23
back the man of **G** heard what had 1Ki 13:26
is the man of **G** who did not obey 1Ki 13:26
sad for the man of **G** and said, ... 1Ki 13:30
the LORD, the **G** of Israel, says: 1Ki 14:7
the LORD, the **G** of Israel. 1Ki 14:13
and **G** had taken the land away 1Ki 14:24
to the LORD his **G** as David, ... 1Ki 15:3
the LORD, the **G** of Israel, very 1Ki 15:30
the LORD, the **G** of Israel, angry 1Ki 16:13
the LORD, the **G** of Israel, very 1Ki 16:26
the LORD, the **G** of Israel, angry 1Ki 16:33
the LORD, the **G** of Israel," 1Ki 17:1
surely as the LORD your **G** lives, ... 1Ki 17:12
LORD, the **G** of Israel, says, ' 1Ki 17:14
Elijah, "Man of **G**, what have you 1Ki 17:18
LORD my **G**, this widow is letting 1Ki 17:20
LORD, "LORD my **G**, let this boy 1Ki 17:21
you really are a man from **G**," 1Ki 17:24
surely as the LORD your **G** lives, ... 1Ki 18:10

If the LORD is the true **G**, ... 1Ki 18:21
but if Baal is the true **G**, ... 1Ki 18:21
pray to your **g**, and I will pray 1Ki 18:24
g who answers by setting fire 1Ki 18:24
fire to his wood is the true **G**." 1Ki 18:24
Pray to your **g**, but don't start 1Ki 18:25
Baal really is a **g**, maybe he is 1Ki 18:27
you are the **G** of Abraham, Isaac 1Ki 18:36
that you are the **G** of Israel and 1Ki 18:36
are **G** and that you will change 1Ki 18:37
ground, crying, "The LORD is **G**! 1Ki 18:39
The LORD is God! The LORD is **G**!" 1Ki 18:39
Mount Sinai, the mountain of **G**. 1Ki 19:8
answered, "LORD **G** All-Powerful, ... 1Ki 19:10
answered, "LORD **G** All-Powerful, ... 1Ki 19:14
A man of **G** came to the king of 1Ki 20:28
the LORD, am a **g** of the 1Ki 20:28
not a **g** of the valleys. 1Ki 20:28
speak against **G** and the king. 1Ki 21:10
speak against **G** and the king. 1Ki 21:13
worshiped and served the Baal, ... 1Ki 22:53
the LORD, the **G** of Israel, very 1Ki 22:53
ask Baal-Zebub, **g** of Ekron, if I 2Ki 1:2
of Baal-Zebub, **g** of Ekron? 2Ki 1:3
think there is no **G** in Israel?" 2Ki 1:3
of Baal-Zebub, **g** of Ekron? 2Ki 1:6
think there is no **G** in Israel? 2Ki 1:6
him, "Man of **G**, the king says, ... 2Ki 1:9
I am a man of **G**, let fire come 2Ki 1:10
to him, "Man of **G**, this is what 2Ki 1:11
I am a man of **G**, let fire come 2Ki 1:12
begged, "Man of **G**, please 2Ki 1:13
of Baal-Zebub, **g** of Ekron. 2Ki 1:16
there is no **G** in Israel to ask 2Ki 1:16
is the LORD, the **G** of Elijah?" 2Ki 2:14
is a holy man of **G** who passes by 2Ki 4:9
master, man of **G**, let it to 2Ki 4:16
to the man of **G** and return." 2Ki 4:22
the man of **G**, at Mount Carmel................. 2Ki 4:25
shouted, "Man of **G**, there's 2Ki 4:40
said, "I'm not **G**! I can't kill 2Ki 5:7
Elisha, the man of **G**, heard that 2Ki 5:8
on the name of the LORD his **G**................. 2Ki 5:11
there is no **G** in all the earth 2Ki 5:15
servant of Elisha the man of **G**, ... 2Ki 5:20
the man of **G**, sent a message to............. 2Ki 6:9
May **G** punish me terribly if the 2Ki 6:31
did as the man of **G** had said................. 2Ki 8:2
the servant of the man of **G**. 2Ki 8:4
"The man of **G** has arrived." 2Ki 8:7
LORD, the **G** of Israel says: ' 2Ki 9:6
the LORD, the **G** of Israel, with 2Ki 10:31
The man of **G** was angry with him. 2Ki 13:19
the LORD, the **G** of Israel, had 2Ki 14:25
the LORD his **G** said was right. 2Ki 16:2
altar to ask questions of **G**." 2Ki 16:15
sinned against the LORD their **G**. 2Ki 17:7
against the LORD their **G**. 2Ki 17:9
not believe in the LORD their **G**. 2Ki 17:14
commands of the LORD their **G**. 2Ki 17:16
commands of the LORD their **G**. 2Ki 17:19
the law of the **g** of the land. 2Ki 17:26
don't know what the **g** wants." 2Ki 17:26
the people what the **g** wants."................. 2Ki 17:27
made Succoth Benoth their **g**, ... 2Ki 17:30
Instead worship the LORD your **G**, ... 2Ki 17:39
in the LORD, the **G** of Israel. 2Ki 18:5
did not obey the LORD their **G**. 2Ki 18:12
depending on the LORD our **G**,"............. 2Ki 18:22
a **g** of any other nation saved 2Ki 18:33
to make fun of the living **G**. 2Ki 19:4
the LORD your **G** will hear what 2Ki 19:4
be fooled by the **g** you trust. 2Ki 19:10

LORD, **G** of Israel, whose throne 2Ki 19:15
only you are **G** of all the 2Ki 19:15
has said to insult the living **G**. 2Ki 19:16
Now, LORD our **G**, save us from............. 2Ki 19:19
that you, LORD, are the only **G**." 2Ki 19:19
the LORD, the **G** of Israel, says: 2Ki 19:20
in the temple of his **g** Nisroch, ... 2Ki 19:37
the **G** of your ancestor David,................. 2Ki 20:5
the LORD, the **G** of Israel, says: 2Ki 21:12
LORD, the **G** of his ancestors,................. 2Ki 21:22
the LORD, the **G** of Israel, says: 2Ki 22:15
the LORD, the **G** of Israel, says 2Ki 22:18
Chemosh, the hated **g** of Moab. 2Ki 23:13
the hated **g** of the Ammonites. 2Ki 23:13
it would through the man of **G**. 2Ki 23:16
of the man of **G** who came from............. 2Ki 23:17
the LORD your **G** as it is written 2Ki 23:21
Jabez prayed to the **G** of Israel, ... 1Ch 4:10
And **G** did what Jabez had asked. 1Ch 4:10
Gad prayed to **G** during the war, ... 1Ch 5:20
killed because **G** helped the 1Ch 5:22
sinned against the **G** that their 1Ch 5:25
the people **G** was destroying. 1Ch 5:25
So the **G** of Israel made Pul king 1Ch 5:26
the Holy Tent, the house of **G**. 1Ch 6:48
sins so they could belong to **G**. 1Ch 6:49
they were not faithful to **G**..................... 1Ch 9:1
responsible for the Temple of **G**............... 1Ch 9:11
for serving in the Temple of **G**. 1Ch 9:13
treasures in the Temple of **G**. 1Ch 9:26
night guarding the Temple of **G**,............. 1Ch 9:27
The LORD your **G** said to you, ' 1Ch 11:2
May **G** keep me from drinking this........... 1Ch 11:19
the **G** of our ancestors will see 1Ch 12:17
because your **G** helps you." 1Ch 12:18
large, like the army of **G**. 1Ch 12:22
it is what the LORD our **G** wants, ... 1Ch 13:2
the Ark of our **G** back to us. 1Ch 13:3
use it to ask **G** for help while 1Ch 13:3
bring the Ark of **G** back from the 1Ch 13:5
to get the Ark of **G** the LORD. 1Ch 13:6
the Ark of **G** from Abinadab's 1Ch 13:7
in the presence of **G**. 1Ch 13:8
died there in the presence of **G**. 1Ch 13:10
was afraid of **G** that day and 1Ch 13:12
bring the Ark of **G** home to me?" 1Ch 13:12
The Ark of **G** stayed with 1Ch 13:14
David asked **G**, "Should I go and 1Ch 14:10
G has broken through my enemies........... 1Ch 14:11
David prayed to **G** again, and God 1Ch 14:14
God again, and **G** answered him, ... 1Ch 14:14
I, **G**, will have gone out before 1Ch 14:15
David did as **G** commanded, and he 1Ch 14:16
a place for the Ark of **G**......................... 1Ch 15:1
Levites may carry the Ark of **G**. 1Ch 15:2
of the LORD, the **G** of Israel, to 1Ch 15:12
so the LORD our **G** punished us." 1Ch 15:13
of the LORD, the **G** of Israel. 1Ch 15:14
carry the Ark of **G** on their...................... 1Ch 15:15
in front of the Ark of **G**. 1Ch 15:24
Because **G** helped the Levites who 1Ch 15:26
the Ark of **G** and put it inside.................. 1Ch 16:1
and fellowship offerings to **G**................... 1Ch 16:1
the LORD, the **G** of Israel. 1Ch 16:4
the Ark of the Agreement with **G**. 1Ch 16:6
is the LORD our **G**. His laws are............... 1Ch 16:14
to him, "Save us, **G** our Savior, ... 1Ch 16:35
the LORD, the **G** of Israel. 1Ch 16:36
when songs were sung to **G**. 1Ch 16:42
to do, because **G** is with you." 1Ch 17:2
But that night **G** spoke his word............. 1Ch 17:3
everything **G** had said in this 1Ch 17:15
David said, "LORD **G**, who am I? 1Ch 17:16

that was not enough for you, **G.** 1Ch 17:17
LORD **G,** you have treated me like 1Ch 17:17
There is no **G** except you. 1Ch 17:20
on earth that **G** chose to be his 1Ch 17:21
and, LORD, you are their **G.** 1Ch 17:22
the **G** over Israel, is 1Ch 17:24
God over Israel, is Israel's **G!'** 1Ch 17:24
My **G,** you have told me that you 1Ch 17:25
LORD, you are **G,** and you have 1Ch 17:26
people and the cities of our **G.** 1Ch 19:13
done something **G** had said was 1Ch 21:7
was wrong, so **G** punished Israel. 1Ch 21:7
David said to **G,** "I have sinned 1Ch 21:8
G sent an angel to destroy 1Ch 21:15
David said to **G,** "I am the one 1Ch 21:17
LORD my **G,** please punish me and 1Ch 21:17
the Holy Tent to speak with **G,** 1Ch 21:30
of the LORD **G** and the altar for 1Ch 22:1
in building the Temple of **G.** 1Ch 22:2
for the LORD, the **G** of Israel. 1Ch 22:6
for worshiping the LORD my **G.** 1Ch 22:7
a temple for the LORD your **G,** 1Ch 22:11
teachings of the LORD your **G.** 1Ch 22:12
The LORD your **G** is with you. 1Ch 22:18
to obeying the LORD your **G.** 1Ch 22:19
the holy place of the LORD **G;** 1Ch 22:19
belong to **G** into the Temple. 1Ch 22:19
was the man of **G,** and his sons 1Ch 23:14
The LORD, the **G** of Israel, has 1Ch 23:25
was to serve in the Temple of **G.** 1Ch 23:28
the LORD, the **G** of Israel, had 1Ch 24:19
G promised to make Heman strong, ... 1Ch 25:5
G gave him fourteen sons and 1Ch 25:5
of serving in the Temple of **G.** 1Ch 25:6
G blessed Obed-Edom with.................... 1Ch 26:5
of the Temple of **G** and for the 1Ch 26:20
G became angry with Israel for 1Ch 27:24
But **G** said to me, 'You must not 1Ch 28:3
the LORD, the **G** of Israel, chose 1Ch 28:4
From that family **G** was pleased 1Ch 28:4
the hearing of **G,** I tell you 1Ch 28:8
the commands of the LORD your **G.** 1Ch 28:8
accept the **G** of your father. 1Ch 28:9
the LORD **G,** my God, is with 1Ch 28:20
the LORD God, my **G,** is with you. 1Ch 28:20
all the work on the Temple of **G.** 1Ch 28:21
were gathered, "**G** chose my son 1Ch 29:1
people; it is for the LORD **G.** 1Ch 29:1
for building the Temple of **G.** 1Ch 29:2
the Temple of my **G** to be built. 1Ch 29:3
of iron to the Temple of **G.** 1Ch 29:7
you, LORD, **G** of our father..................... 1Ch 29:10
Now, our **G,** we thank you and 1Ch 29:13
LORD our **G,** we have gathered all........... 1Ch 29:16
I know, my **G,** that you test.................... 1Ch 29:17
you are the **G** of our ancestors, ... 1Ch 29:18
ancestors, the **G** of Abraham,................. 1Ch 29:18
Praise the LORD your **G.**" 1Ch 29:20
the LORD, the **G** of their........................ 1Ch 29:20
the LORD his **G** was with him and 2Ch 1:1
the Ark of **G** from Kiriath 2Ch 1:4
That night **G** appeared to Solomon 2Ch 1:7
Now, LORD **G,** may your promise to 2Ch 1:9
G said to Solomon, "You have not 2Ch 1:11
for worshiping the LORD my **G,**............... 2Ch 2:4
commanded by the LORD our **G.** 2Ch 2:4
because our **G** is greater than................. 2Ch 2:5
really build a house for our **G.** 2Ch 2:6
the LORD, the **G** of Israel, who 2Ch 2:12
for building the Temple of **G.** 2Ch 3:3
King Solomon on the Temple of **G:**........... 2Ch 4:11
s glory filled the Temple of **G.**................ 2Ch 5:14
the LORD, the **G** of Israel. 2Ch 6:4

for the LORD, the **G** of Israel................... 2Ch 6:7
for the LORD, the **G** of Israel................... 2Ch 6:10
He said, "LORD, **G** of Israel, ... 2Ch 6:14
there is no **g** like you in heaven 2Ch 6:14
Now, LORD, **G** of Israel, keep the 2Ch 6:16
Now, LORD, **G** of Israel, please 2Ch 6:17
But, **G,** can you really live here 2Ch 6:18
LORD my **G,** hear this prayer your........... 2Ch 6:19
Now, my **G,** look at us. Listen............... 2Ch 6:40
Now, rise, LORD **G,** and come to 2Ch 6:41
salvation, LORD **G,** and may your 2Ch 6:41
LORD **G,** do not reject your 2Ch 6:42
the people gave the Temple to **G.** 2Ch 7:5
the altar for the worship of **G.** 2Ch 7:9
the LORD, the **G** of their........................ 2Ch 7:22
the **G** who brought them out of 2Ch 7:22
the man of **G,** had commanded. 2Ch 8:14
the LORD your **G** who was pleased 2Ch 9:8
to rule for the LORD your **G,** 2Ch 9:8
because your **G** loves the people 2Ch 9:8
to the wisdom **G** had given him............... 2Ch 9:23
G caused this to happen so that 2Ch 10:15
to Shemaiah, a man of **G,** saying, ... 2Ch 11:2
obey the LORD, the **G** of Israel. 2Ch 11:16
to the LORD, the **G** of their.................... 2Ch 11:16
the LORD, the **G** of Israel, gave 2Ch 13:5
as for us, the LORD is our **G;** 2Ch 13:10
the command of the LORD our **G,** 2Ch 13:11
G himself is with us as our 2Ch 13:12
the LORD, the **G** of your 2Ch 13:12
G caused Jeroboam and the army 2Ch 13:15
G handed them over to Judah. 2Ch 13:16
on the LORD, the **G** of their 2Ch 13:18
the LORD his **G** said was good 2Ch 14:2
the LORD, the **G** of their........................ 2Ch 14:4
we have obeyed the LORD our **G.** 2Ch 14:7
called out to the LORD his **G,**................. 2Ch 14:11
Help us, LORD our **G,** because we 2Ch 14:11
you are our **G.** Don't let anyone 2Ch 14:11
The Spirit of **G** entered Azariah 2Ch 15:1
without the true **G** and without a 2Ch 15:3
to the LORD, the **G** of Israel. 2Ch 15:4
because **G** troubled them with all 2Ch 15:6
the LORD, Asa's **G,** was with him. 2Ch 15:9
the LORD, the **G** of their........................ 2Ch 15:12
the LORD, the **G** of Israel, was 2Ch 15:13
They looked for **G** and found him. 2Ch 15:15
into the Temple of **G** the gifts 2Ch 15:18
you and not on the LORD your **G.** 2Ch 16:7
but from the **G** of his father. 2Ch 17:4
G will hand them over to you. 2Ch 18:5
tell him only what my **G** says." 2Ch 18:13
G made the chariot commanders 2Ch 18:31
and you have tried to obey **G.**" 2Ch 19:3
to the LORD, the **G** of their.................... 2Ch 19:4
the LORD our **G** wants people to 2Ch 19:7
special time of prayer to **G.**..................... 2Ch 20:3
he said, "LORD, **G** of our 2Ch 20:6
you are the **G** in heaven......................... 2Ch 20:6
Our **G,** you forced out the people 2Ch 20:7
Our **G,** punish those people. 2Ch 20:12
the LORD, the **G** of Israel, with 2Ch 20:19
Have faith in the LORD your **G,** 2Ch 20:20
they began to sing and praise **G,** 2Ch 20:22
Israel's enemies, they feared **G.** 2Ch 20:29
G gave him peace from all the 2Ch 20:30
to follow the **G** of their 2Ch 20:33
the LORD, the **G** of his ancestors 2Ch 21:10
the **G** of your ancestor David,................. 2Ch 21:12
and Jerusalem to sin against **G,** 2Ch 21:13
G caused Ahaziah's death when he 2Ch 22:7
the Temple of **G** for six years.................. 2Ch 22:12
the king in the Temple of **G.** 2Ch 23:3

were kept in the Temple of **G**................. 2Ch 23:9
to repair the Temple of your **G**. 2Ch 24:5
the Temple of **G** and used its 2Ch 24:7
Moses, the servant of **G**, had 2Ch 24:9
the Temple of **G** to be as it was 2Ch 24:13
in Judah for **G** and his Temple. 2Ch 24:16
of the LORD, the **G** of their 2Ch 24:18
G was angry with the people of 2Ch 24:18
the Spirit of **G** entered 2Ch 24:20
and said, "This is what **G** says: 2Ch 24:20
the LORD, the **G** of their 2Ch 24:24
the Temple of **G** are written 2Ch 24:27
But a man of **G** came to Amaziah 2Ch 25:7
for war, but **G** will defeat you. 2Ch 25:8
Amaziah said to the man of **G**, ... 2Ch 25:9
The man of **G** answered, "The 2Ch 25:9
I know that **G** has decided to 2Ch 25:16
G caused this to happen so that 2Ch 25:20
the Temple of **G** that Obed-Edom 2Ch 25:24
Uzziah obeyed **G** while Zechariah 2Ch 26:5
how to respect and obey **G**. 2Ch 26:5
the LORD, **G** gave him success 2Ch 26:5
G helped Uzziah fight the 2Ch 26:7
unfaithful to the LORD his **G**;............... 2Ch 26:16
the LORD **G** will not honor you 2Ch 26:18
he always obeyed the LORD his **G**. 2Ch 27:6
So the LORD his **G** handed over.............. 2Ch 28:5
the LORD, the **G** of their 2Ch 28:6
The LORD, the **G** of your 2Ch 28:9
But **G** has seen the cruel way you 2Ch 28:9
sinned against the LORD your **G**. 2Ch 28:10
the Temple of **G** and broke them 2Ch 28:24
the LORD, the **G** of his ancestors 2Ch 28:25
of the LORD of your 2Ch 29:5
unfaithful to **G** and did what 2Ch 29:6
holy place to the **G** of Israel. 2Ch 29:7
the LORD, the **G** of Israel, so he 2Ch 29:10
unfaithful to **G** and removed some 2Ch 29:19
Temple ready for service to **G**. 2Ch 29:21
so they would belong to **G**. 2Ch 29:24
So they praised **G** with joy and 2Ch 29:30
very happy that **G** had made it 2Ch 29:36
for the LORD, the **G** of Israel. 2Ch 30:1
for the LORD, the **G** of Israel.................. 2Ch 30:5
to the LORD, the **G** of Abraham, ... 2Ch 30:6
Then **G** will return to you who 2Ch 30:6
the LORD, the **G** of their 2Ch 30:7
the LORD your **G** so he will not 2Ch 30:8
The LORD your **G** is kind and 2Ch 30:9
And **G** united all the people of 2Ch 30:12
Moses, the man of **G**, commanded............. 2Ch 30:16
the LORD, the **G** of their 2Ch 30:22
and **G** heard them because their............ 2Ch 30:27
were given to the LORD their **G**, ... 2Ch 31:6
the Temple of **G** had chosen them 2Ch 31:13
the people wanted to give to **G**. 2Ch 31:14
obedient before the LORD his **G**. 2Ch 31:20
tried to obey **G** in his service 2Ch 31:21
his service of the Temple of **G**, ... 2Ch 31:21
himself fully to his work for **G**. 2Ch 31:21
the LORD our **G** to help us and to 2Ch 32:8
'The LORD our **G** will save us 2Ch 32:11
your **g** cannot save you from my 2Ch 32:14
g of any nation or kingdom has 2Ch 32:15
Your **g** is even less able to save 2Ch 32:15
the LORD **G** and his servant 2Ch 32:16
the LORD, the **G** of Israel. 2Ch 32:17
way Hezekiah's **g** won't be able 2Ch 32:17
spoke about the **G** of Jerusalem 2Ch 32:19
went into the Temple of his **g**, ... 2Ch 32:21
not thank **G** for his kindness, ... 2Ch 32:25
because **G** had given Hezekiah 2Ch 32:29
G left Hezekiah alone to test 2Ch 32:31

love for **G** and the other 2Ch 32:32
and put it in the Temple of **G**. 2Ch 33:7
G had said to David and his son.............. 2Ch 33:7
begged the LORD his **G** for help.............. 2Ch 33:12
before the **G** of his ancestors. 2Ch 33:12
that the LORD is the true **G**. 2Ch 33:13
offerings to show thanks to **G**. 2Ch 33:16
serve the LORD, the **G** of Israel. 2Ch 33:16
were only to the LORD their **G**. 2Ch 33:17
prayer to his **G**, and what the 2Ch 33:18
of the LORD, the **G** of Israel—all 2Ch 33:18
to obey the **G** of his ancestor 2Ch 34:3
of the LORD, the **G** of Josiah. 2Ch 34:8
brought into the Temple of **G**................. 2Ch 34:9
the LORD, the **G** of Israel, says: 2Ch 34:23
the LORD, the **G** of Israel, says 2Ch 34:26
obeyed the agreement of **G**, ... 2Ch 34:32
God, the **G** of their ancestors. 2Ch 34:32
to serve the LORD their **G**. 2Ch 34:33
the LORD, the **G** of their 2Ch 34:33
the LORD your **G** and his people 2Ch 35:3
G told me to hurry, and he is on 2Ch 35:21
So don't fight **G**, or he will 2Ch 35:21
the LORD his **G** said was wrong. 2Ch 36:5
the LORD his **G** said was wrong. 2Ch 36:12
obey the LORD, the **G** of Israel. 2Ch 36:13
The LORD, the **G** of their 2Ch 36:15
So **G** brought the king of Babylon 2Ch 36:17
G handed all of them over to 2Ch 36:17
the things from the Temple of **G**, ... 2Ch 36:18
The LORD, the **G** of heaven, has.............. 2Ch 36:23
may the LORD your **G** be with all 2Ch 36:23
The LORD, the **G** of heaven, has.............. Ezr 1:2
May **G** be with all of you who are .... Ezr 1:3
the LORD, the **G** of Israel, who .... Ezr 1:3
the Temple of **G** in Jerusalem. .... Ezr 1:4
everyone **G** had caused to want to .... Ezr 1:5
put in the temple of his own **g**. .... Ezr 1:7
food offered to **G** until a priest .... Ezr 2:63
the Temple of **G** on the same site .... Ezr 2:68
altar of the **G** of Israel where .... Ezr 3:2
of Moses, the man of **G**. .... Ezr 3:2
at the Temple of **G** in Jerusalem, ... Ezr 3:8
of building the Temple of **G**: .... Ezr 3:9
for the LORD, the **G** of Israel,............... Ezr 4:1
you and want to worship your **G**. .... Ezr 4:2
help us build a Temple to our **G**............... Ezr 4:3
for the LORD, the **G** of Israel,............... Ezr 4:3
on the Temple of **G** in Jerusalem .... Ezr 4:24
in the name of the **G** of Israel, ... Ezr 5:1
the Temple of **G** in Jerusalem. .... Ezr 5:2
the prophets of **G** were there, ... Ezr 5:2
their **G** was watching over the .... Ezr 5:5
the Temple of the great **G** is. .... Ezr 5:8
servants of the **G** of heaven and .... Ezr 5:11
made the **G** of heaven angry, ... Ezr 5:12
that came from the Temple of **G**. .... Ezr 5:14
the Temple of **G** where it was.' .... Ezr 5:15
of the Temple of **G** in Jerusalem. .... Ezr 5:16
the Temple of **G** in Jerusalem .... Ezr 6:3
the Temple of **G** should be put .... Ezr 6:5
the Temple of **G** in Jerusalem." .... Ezr 6:5
the work on that Temple of **G**. .... Ezr 6:7
offerings to the **G** of heaven, ... Ezr 6:9
pleasing to the **G** of heaven, ... Ezr 6:10
G has chosen Jerusalem as the .... Ezr 6:12
Temple as the **G** of Israel had .... Ezr 6:14
the Temple to **G** to honor him. .... Ezr 6:16
gave the Temple to **G** by offering .... Ezr 6:17
time to serve **G** in the Temple at............ Ezr 6:18
the LORD, the **G** of Israel. .... Ezr 6:21
the Temple of the **G** of Israel. .... Ezr 6:22
by the LORD, the **G** of Israel. .... Ezr 7:6

G

G moves mountains without anyone .... Job 9:5
It is G who made the Bear, ... Job 9:9
G will not hold back his anger. .... Job 9:13
So how can I argue with G, ... Job 9:14
could only beg G, my Judge, for .... Job 9:15
to strength, G is stronger than .... Job 9:19
'G destroys both the innocent .... Job 9:22
G will laugh at the suffering of .... Job 9:23
If it is not G who does this, ... Job 9:24
G is not human like me, so I .... Job 9:32
I will say to G: Do not hold me .... Job 10:2
you when you make fun of G. .... Job 11:3
wish G would speak and open his .... Job 11:5
G has even forgotten some of .... Job 11:6
you understand the secrets of G? .... Job 11:7
If G comes along and puts you in .... Job 11:10
G knows who is evil, and when he .... Job 11:11
when I call on G and expect him .... Job 12:4
those who make G angry are safe. .... Job 12:6
have their g in their pocket .... Job 12:6
But only G has wisdom and power, ... Job 12:13
If G holds back the waters, ... Job 12:15
G leads the wise away as .... Job 12:17
and to argue my case with G. .... Job 13:3
not speak evil in the name of G; .... Job 13:7
should not argue the case for G. .... Job 13:8
you cannot fool G as you might .... Job 13:9
G would surely scold you if you .... Job 13:10
Even if G kills me, I have hope .... Job 13:15
G, please just give me these two .... Job 13:20
destroy respect for G and limit .... Job 15:4
Is the comfort G gives you not .... Job 15:11
heart carried you away from G? .... Job 15:12
speak out your anger against G? .... Job 15:13
G places no trust in his holy .... Job 15:15
their fists at G and try to get .... Job 15:25
charge at G with thick, ... Job 15:26
People without G can produce .... Job 15:34
G, you have surely taken away my .... Job 16:7
G attacks me and tears me with .... Job 16:9
G has turned me over to evil .... Job 16:11
but G broke me into pieces; .... Job 16:12
Again and again G attacks me; .... Job 16:14
My eyes pour out tears to G. .... Job 16:20
begs G on behalf of a human as .... Job 16:21
G, make me a promise. No one .... Job 17:3
G has made my name a curse word; ...... Job 17:6
of one who does not know G." .... Job 18:21
Then know that G has wronged me .... Job 19:6
G has blocked my way so I cannot .... Job 19:8
G has made my brothers my .... Job 19:13
the hand of G has hit me. .... Job 19:21
Why do you chase me as G does? .... Job 19:22
in my flesh I will see G. .... Job 19:26
G will make them vomit their .... Job 20:15
G will send his burning anger .... Job 20:23
This is what G plans for evil .... Job 20:29
without fear; G does not punish .... Job 21:9
They say to G, 'Leave us alone! .... Job 21:14
'G saves up a person's. .... Job 21:19
' But G should punish the wicked .... Job 21:19
No one can teach knowledge to G; .... Job 21:22
Can anyone be of real use to G? .... Job 22:2
Does G punish you for respecting .... Job 22:4
G is in the highest part of .... Job 22:12
But you ask, 'What does G know? .... Job 22:13
They said to G, 'Leave us alone! .... Job 22:17
But it was G who filled their .... Job 22:18
Obey G and be at peace with him; .... Job 22:21
where to find G so I could go to .... Job 23:3
could present his case to G, ... Job 23:7
go to the east, G is not there; .... Job 23:8
But G knows the way that I take, ... Job 23:10

he is the only G. Who can come .... Job 23:13
G has made me afraid; the .... Job 23:16
Those who know G do not see such .... Job 24:1
but G accuses no one of doing .... Job 24:12
But G drags away the strong by .... Job 24:22
G may let these evil people feel .... Job 24:23
G rules and he must be honored; .... Job 25:2
be good in the presence of G, ... Job 25:4
Death is naked before G; .... Job 26:6
G stretches the northern sky out .... Job 26:7
As surely as G lives, who has .... Job 27:2
when G takes their life away? .... Job 27:8
G will not listen to their cries .... Job 27:9
they call out to G all the time. .... Job 27:10
the power of G and will not hide .... Job 27:11
Here is what G has planned for .... Job 27:13
Only G understands the way to .... Job 28:23
When G gave power to the wind .... Job 28:25
the days when G watched over me .... Job 29:2
G has taken away my strength and .... Job 30:11
his great power G grabs hold of .... Job 30:18
out to you, G, but you do not .... Job 30:20
What has G above promised for .... Job 31:2
G sees my ways and counts every .... Job 31:4
then let G weigh me on honest .... Job 31:6
how could I tell G what I did? .... Job 31:14
G made me in my mother's womb, ... Job 31:15
the same G formed both of us in .... Job 31:15
I fear destruction from G, ... Job 31:23
my heart was pulled away from G. .... Job 31:27
would have been unfaithful to G. .... Job 31:28
would explain to G every step I .... Job 31:37
he was right instead of G. .... Job 32:2
G will show Job to be wrong, ... Job 32:13
The Spirit of G created me, ... Job 33:4
I am just like you before G; .... Job 33:6
But G has found fault with me; .... Job 33:10
G is greater than we are. .... Job 33:12
do you accuse G of not answering .... Job 33:13
G does speak—sometimes one way .... Job 33:14
G does this to save people from .... Job 33:18
That person will pray to G, ... Job 33:26
pray to God, and G will listen .... Job 33:26
And G will set things right for .... Job 33:26
G bought my life back from death, ... Job 33:28
G does all these things to a .... Job 33:29
and G has refused me a fair .... Job 34:5
is no use to try to please G.' .... Job 34:9
can understand. G can never do .... Job 34:10
G pays people back for what they .... Job 34:11
Truly G will never do wrong; .... Job 34:12
No one chose G to rule over the .... Job 34:13
If G should decide to take away .... Job 34:14
can you blame G who is both fair .... Job 34:17
G is the one who says to kings, ' .... Job 34:18
G watches where people go; .... Job 34:21
G breaks powerful people into .... Job 34:24
Because G knows what people do, ... Job 34:25
following G and did not care .... Job 34:27
The cry of the poor comes to G; .... Job 34:28
But if G keeps quiet, who can .... Job 34:29
G still rules over both nations .... Job 34:29
But suppose someone says to G, ... Job 34:31
should G reward you as you want .... Job 34:33
to his sin by turning against G. .... Job 34:37
more and more against G." .... Job 34:37
'G will show that I am right,' .... Job 35:2
you sin, it does nothing to G; .... Job 35:6
are good, you give nothing to G; .... Job 35:7
asks, 'Where is G, my Maker, who .... Job 35:10
G does not answer evil people .... Job 35:12
G does not listen to their .... Job 35:13
there is more to be said for G. .... Job 36:2

G is powerful, but he does not .... Job 36:5
G tells them what they have done, ... Job 36:9
G makes them listen to his .... Job 36:10
Even when G punishes them, ... Job 36:13
But G saves those who suffer .... Job 36:15
G is gently calling you from the .... Job 36:16
be led away from G by riches; .... Job 36:18
G is great and powerful; .... Job 36:22
one can say to G, 'You have done .... Job 36:23
G is so great, greater than we .... Job 36:26
understands how G spreads out .... Job 36:29
Watch how G scatters his .... Job 36:30
This is the way G governs the................. Job 36:31
G fills his hands with lightning .... Job 36:32
knows it is the work of G. .... Job 37:7
The breath of G makes ice,..................... Job 37:10
Do you know how G controls the .... Job 37:15
Do you know the miracles of G,............. Job 37:16
the sky like G and make it look .... Job 37:18
Should G be told that I want to .... Job 37:20
G comes out of the north in .... Job 37:22
cry out to G and wander about .... Job 38:41
because G did not give the .... Job 39:17
G did not give it a share of .... Job 39:17
who accuses G answer him." .... Job 40:2
as strong as G? Can your voice .... Job 40:9
about me, "G won't rescue him. .... Ps 3:2
my wonderful G who gives me .... Ps 3:3
rise up! My G, come save me!................. Ps 3:7
my G who does what is right. .... Ps 4:1
my King and my G, because I pray........... Ps 5:2
You are not a G who is pleased .... Ps 5:4
G, declare them guilty! Let them .... Ps 5:10
LORD my G, I trust in you for .... Ps 7:1
LORD my G, what have I done? .... Ps 7:3
have done no wrong, G Most High. .... Ps 7:8
G, you do what is right. .... Ps 7:9
G protects me like a shield;................... Ps 7:10
G judges by what is right, ... Ps 7:11
and G is always ready to punish............. Ps 7:11
their lives, G will sharpen his .... Ps 7:12
G Most High, I will sing praises .... Ps 9:2
so will all those who forget G. .... Ps 9:17
do not look for G; there is no .... Ps 10:4
is no room for G in their .... Ps 10:4
wicked think, "G has forgotten .... Ps 10:11
Why do wicked people hate G? .... Ps 10:13
themselves, "G won't punish us............. Ps 10:13
Answer me, my G; tell me, or I .... Ps 13:3
to themselves, "There is no G." .... Ps 14:1
was looking to G for help. .... Ps 14:2
because G is with those who do .... Ps 14:5
Protect me, G, because I trust................. Ps 16:1
I call to you, G, and you answer .... Ps 17:6
Savior. My G is my rock. I can .... Ps 18:2
I cried out to my G for help. .... Ps 18:6
evil by turning away from my G. .... Ps 18:21
My G brightens the darkness .... Ps 18:28
The ways of G are without fault. .... Ps 18:30
Who is G? Only the LORD. Who is........... Ps 18:31
Who is the Rock? Only our G. .... Ps 18:31
G is my protection. He makes my .... Ps 18:32
Praise the G who saves me! .... Ps 18:46
G gives me victory over my .... Ps 18:47
heavens declare the glory of G, ... Ps 19:1
May the G of Jacob protect you............... Ps 20:1
a flag in the name of our G. .... Ps 20:5
but we trust the LORD our G................... Ps 20:7
Because G Most High always loves .... Ps 21:7
My G, my God, why have you................. Ps 22:1
My God, my G, why have you................. Ps 22:1
My G, I call to you during the................. Ps 22:2
have been my G since my mother .... Ps 22:10

born will hear what G has done. .... Ps 22:31
in the name of a false g. .... Ps 24:4
G who saves them will declare .... Ps 24:5
try to follow G; they look to .... Ps 24:6
they look to the G of Jacob for .... Ps 24:6
my G, I trust you. Do not let me .... Ps 25:2
and teach me, my G, my Savior................ Ps 25:5
G, save Israel from all their .... Ps 25:22
or leave me alone, G, my Savior. .... Ps 27:9
The glorious G thunders; .... Ps 29:3
everyone says, "Glory to G!" .... Ps 29:9
LORD, my G, I prayed to you, and .... Ps 30:2
LORD, my G, I will praise you .... Ps 30:12
Save me, LORD, G of truth. .... Ps 31:5
I have said, "You are my G." .... Ps 31:14
I said, "G cannot see me!" .... Ps 31:22
the nation whose G is the LORD, ... Ps 33:12
camps around those who fear G, ... Ps 34:7
My G and Lord, fight for me! .... Ps 35:23
LORD my G, defend me with your .... Ps 35:24
hearts. They have no fear of G. .... Ps 36:1
G, your love is so precious!...................... Ps 36:7
G is pleased with their ways. .... Ps 37:23
of their G are in their heart .... Ps 37:31
You will answer, my Lord and G. .... Ps 38:15
leave me; my G, don't go away. .... Ps 38:21
a song of praise to our G. .... Ps 40:3
LORD my G, you have done many .... Ps 40:5
G, I want to do what you want. .... Ps 40:8
and savior. My G, do not wait. .... Ps 40:17
the LORD, the G of Israel. .... Ps 41:13
water, so I thirst for you, G. .... Ps 42:1
I thirst for the living G. .... Ps 42:2
saying, "Where is your G?" .... Ps 42:3
put my hope in G and keep .... Ps 42:5
my G. I am very sad. So I .... Ps 42:6
and I pray to my living G. .... Ps 42:8
I say to G, my Rock, "Why have.............. Ps 42:9
saying, "Where is your G?" .... Ps 42:10
put my hope in G and keep................... Ps 42:11
him, my Savior and my G. .... Ps 42:11
G, defend me. Argue my case................... Ps 43:1
G, you are my strength. Why have .... Ps 43:2
I will go to the altar of G, ... Ps 43:4
G who is my joy and happiness................ Ps 43:4
you with a harp, G, my God. .... Ps 43:4
you with a harp, God, my G. .... Ps 43:4
put my hope in G and keep .... Ps 43:5
him, my Savior and my G. .... Ps 43:5
G, we have heard about you. .... Ps 44:1
My G, you are my King. Your .... Ps 44:4
We will praise G every day; .... Ps 44:8
forgotten our G or lifted our .... Ps 44:20
G would have known, because he .... Ps 44:21
so G has blessed you forever. .... Ps 45:2
G, your throne will last forever .... Ps 45:6
so G has chosen you from among .... Ps 45:7
G is our protection and our................... Ps 46:1
brings joy to the city of G, ... Ps 46:4
place where G Most High lives .... Ps 46:4
G is in that city, and so it .... Ps 46:5
G will help her at dawn. .... Ps 46:5
G shouts and the earth crumbles. .... Ps 46:6
the G of Jacob is our defender. .... Ps 46:7
G says, "Be still and know that .... Ps 46:10
Be still and know that I am G. .... Ps 46:10
the G of Jacob is our defender. .... Ps 46:11
you people. Shout to G with joy............. Ps 47:1
G has risen with a shout of joy; .... Ps 47:5
Sing praises to G. Sing praises. .... Ps 47:6
G is King of all the earth, ... Ps 47:7
G is King over the nations. .... Ps 47:8
G sits on his holy throne. .... Ps 47:8

the people of the G of Abraham, ... Ps 47:9
of the earth belong to G. .... Ps 47:9
be praised in the city of our G, ... Ps 48:1
G is within its palaces; .... Ps 48:3
have seen that G will always .... Ps 48:8
-Powerful, the city of our G. .... Ps 48:8
G, we come into your Temple to .... Ps 48:9
G, your name is known everywhere; ..... Ps 48:10
This G is our God forever and .... Ps 48:14
This God is our G forever and .... Ps 48:14
No one can pay G for his own .... Ps 49:7
But G will save my life and will .... Ps 49:15
The G of gods, the LORD, speaks. .... Ps 50:1
G shines from Jerusalem, whose .... Ps 50:2
Our G comes, and he will not be .... Ps 50:3
G is the judge, and even the .... Ps 50:6
G says, "My people, listen to me; .... Ps 50:7
against you. I am G, your God. .... Ps 50:7
against you. I am God, your G. .... Ps 50:7
an offering to show thanks to G. .... Ps 50:14
Give G Most High what you have .... Ps 50:14
But G says to the wicked, ... Ps 50:16
about this, you who forget G. .... Ps 50:22
And I, G, will save those who do .... Ps 50:23
G, be merciful to me because you .... Ps 51:1
me a pure heart, G, and make my .... Ps 51:10
G, save me from the guilt of .... Ps 51:14
of murder, G of my salvation .... Ps 51:14
sacrifice G wants is a broken .... Ps 51:17
G, you will not reject a heart .... Ps 51:17
But G will ruin you forever. .... Ps 52:5
right will see this and fear G. .... Ps 52:6
did not depend on G but depended .... Ps 52:7
G, I will thank you forever for .... Ps 52:9
to themselves, "There is no G." .... Ps 53:1
G looked down from heaven on all .... Ps 53:2
was looking to G for help. .... Ps 53:2
They do not ask G for help. .... Ps 53:4
G will scatter the bones of your .... Ps 53:5
because G has rejected them. .... Ps 53:5
Zion! May G bring them back .... Ps 53:6
G, save me because of who you .... Ps 54:1
my prayer, G; listen to what .... Ps 54:2
They do not care about G. .... Ps 54:3
See, G will help me; the Lord .... Ps 54:4
G, listen to my prayer and do .... Ps 55:1
But I will call to G for help, ... Ps 55:16
G who lives forever will hear me .... Ps 55:19
not change; they do not fear G. .... Ps 55:19
But, G, you will bring down the .... Ps 55:23
G, be merciful to me because .... Ps 56:1
I praise G for his word. .... Ps 56:4
I trust G, so I am not afraid. .... Ps 56:4
G, do not let them escape; .... Ps 56:7
I know that G is on my side. .... Ps 56:9
I praise G for his word to me; .... Ps 56:10
I trust in G. I will not be .... Ps 56:11
G, I must keep my promises to .... Ps 56:12
will walk with G in light among .... Ps 56:13
merciful to me, G; be merciful .... Ps 57:1
I cry out to G Most High, to the .... Ps 57:2
to the G who does everything for .... Ps 57:2
Selah G sends me his love and .... Ps 57:3
G is supreme over the skies; .... Ps 57:5
heart is steady, G; my heart is .... Ps 57:7
G, you are supreme above the .... Ps 57:11
evil people turn away from G; .... Ps 58:3
G, break the teeth in their .... Ps 58:6
There really is a G who judges .... Ps 58:11
G, save me from my enemies. .... Ps 59:1
You are the LORD G All-Powerful, ... Ps 59:5
All-Powerful, the G of Israel. .... Ps 59:5
G, my strength, I am looking to .... Ps 59:9

you, because G is my defender. .... Ps 59:9
My G loves me, and he goes in .... Ps 59:10
will know that G rules over .... Ps 59:13
G, my strength, I will sing .... Ps 59:17
G, my defender, you are the God .... Ps 59:17
you are the G who loves me. .... Ps 59:17
G, you have rejected us and .... Ps 60:1
G has said from his Temple, ... Ps 60:6
G, surely you have rejected us; .... Ps 60:10
G, hear my cry; listen to my .... Ps 61:1
G, you have heard my promises. .... Ps 61:5
in the presence of G forever. .... Ps 61:7
I find rest in G; only he can .... Ps 62:1
I find rest in G; only he gives .... Ps 62:5
honor and salvation come from G. .... Ps 62:7
People, trust G all the time. .... Ps 62:8
because G is our protection. .... Ps 62:8
G has said this, and I have .... Ps 62:11
it over and over: G is strong. .... Ps 62:11
G, you are my God. I search for .... Ps 63:1
God, you are my G. I search for .... Ps 63:1
the king will rejoice in his G. .... Ps 63:11
G, listen to my complaint. .... Ps 64:1
But G will shoot them with .... Ps 64:7
Then everyone will fear G. .... Ps 64:9
They will tell what G has done, ... Ps 64:9
G, you will be praised in .... Ps 65:1
in amazing ways, G our Savior. .... Ps 65:5
The rivers of G are full of .... Ps 65:9
on earth, shout with joy to G! .... Ps 66:1
Say to G, "Your works are .... Ps 66:3
Come and see what G has done, ... Ps 66:5
You people, praise our G; .... Ps 66:8
G, you have tested us; you have .... Ps 66:10
of you who fear G, come and .... Ps 66:16
But G has listened; he has heard .... Ps 66:19
Praise G, who did not ignore my .... Ps 66:20
G, have mercy on us and bless us .... Ps 67:1
G, the people should praise you; .... Ps 67:3
G, the people should praise you; .... Ps 67:5
given its crops. G, our God, ... Ps 67:6
crops. God, our G, blesses us. .... Ps 67:6
G blesses us so people all over .... Ps 67:7
Let G rise up and scatter his .... Ps 68:1
wicked be destroyed before G. .... Ps 68:2
and should rejoice before G; .... Ps 68:3
Sing to G; sing praises to his .... Ps 68:4
G is in his holy Temple. .... Ps 68:5
G gives the lonely a home. .... Ps 68:6
who turn against G will live in .... Ps 68:6
G, you led your people out when .... Ps 68:7
sky poured down rain before G, ... Ps 68:8
God, the G of Mount Sinai, ... Ps 68:8
Sinai, before G, the God of .... Ps 68:8
before God, the G of Israel. .... Ps 68:8
G, you sent much rain; you .... Ps 68:9
G, in your goodness you took .... Ps 68:10
mountain that G chose for his .... Ps 68:16
G comes with millions of .... Ps 68:17
And the LORD G will live there. .... Ps 68:18
the Lord, G our Savior, who .... Ps 68:19
Our G is a God who saves us; .... Ps 68:20
Our God is a G who saves us; .... Ps 68:20
the LORD G saves us from death. .... Ps 68:20
G will crush his enemies' heads, ... Ps 68:21
G, people have seen your victory .... Ps 68:24
G my King marched into the holy .... Ps 68:24
Praise G in the meeting place; .... Ps 68:26
G, order up your power; show the .... Ps 68:28
people of Cush will pray to G. .... Ps 68:31
of the earth, sing to G; .... Ps 68:32
Announce that G is powerful. .... Ps 68:34
G, you are wonderful in your .... Ps 68:35

G

The **G** of Israel gives his people .... Ps 68:35
power. Praise **G**! For the .... Ps 68:35
G, save me, because the water .... Ps 69:1
from waiting for **G** to help me. .... Ps 69:3
G, you know what I have done .... Ps 69:5
G of Israel, do not let your .... Ps 69:6
G, because of your great love, ... Ps 69:13
G, save me and protect me..................... Ps 69:29
I will praise **G** in a song and .... Ps 69:30
encouraged, you who worship **G**. .... Ps 69:32
G will save Jerusalem and .... Ps 69:35
G, come quickly and save me. .... Ps 70:1
"Praise the greatness of **G**." .... Ps 70:4
and helpless; **G**, hurry to me. .... Ps 70:5
My **G**, save me from the power of .... Ps 71:4
They say, "**G** has left him. .... Ps 71:11
G, don't be far off. My God, ... Ps 71:12
be far off. My **G**, hurry to help .... Ps 71:12
G, you have taught me since I................ Ps 71:17
and gray, do not leave me, **G**. .... Ps 71:18
G, your justice reaches to the .... Ps 71:19
G, there is no one like you. .... Ps 71:19
trust you, my **G**. I will sing to .... Ps 71:22
G, give the king your good .... Ps 72:1
Praise the LORD **G**, the God of .... Ps 72:18
LORD God, the **G** of Israel, who............ Ps 72:18
G is truly good to Israel,....................... Ps 73:1
They say, "How can **G** know? .... Ps 73:11
What does **G** Most High know?" .... Ps 73:11
G, if I had decided to talk like .... Ps 73:15
until I went to the Temple of **G**. .... Ps 73:17
weak, but **G** is my strength. .... Ps 73:26
who are far from **G** will die; .... Ps 73:27
I am close to **G**, and that is .... Ps 73:28
G, why have you rejected us for .... Ps 74:1
place where **G** was worshiped .... Ps 74:8
G, how much longer will the .... Ps 74:10
G, you have been our king for a .... Ps 74:12
G, arise and defend yourself. .... Ps 74:22
G, we thank you; we thank you .... Ps 75:1
G is the judge; he judges one .... Ps 75:7
sing praise to the **G** of Jacob. .... Ps 75:9
in Judah know **G**; his fame is .... Ps 76:1
G broke the flaming arrows, ... Ps 76:3
G, how wonderful you are! .... Ps 76:4
G of Jacob, when you spoke .... Ps 76:6
G, you stood up to judge and to .... Ps 76:9
promises to the LORD your **G**. .... Ps 76:11
should come to the **G** we worship. .... Ps 76:11
G breaks the spirits of great .... Ps 76:12
I cry out to **G**; I call to God, ... Ps 77:1
call to **G**, and he will hear me. .... Ps 77:1
I remember **G**, I become upset .... Ps 77:3
Has **G** forgotten mercy? Is he too .... Ps 77:9
the power of **G** Most High was .... Ps 77:10
G, your ways are holy. No god is .... Ps 77:13
No **g** is as great as our God. .... Ps 77:13
No god is as great as our **G**. .... Ps 77:13
You are the **G** who does miracles; .... Ps 77:14
G, the waters saw you; they saw............ Ps 77:16
would all trust **G** and would not .... Ps 78:7
hearts were not loyal to **G**, ... Ps 78:8
agreement with **G** and refused to .... Ps 78:10
they turned against **G** Most High. .... Ps 78:17
decided to test **G** by asking for .... Ps 78:18
Then they spoke against **G**, ... Ps 78:19
Can **G** prepare food in the .... Ps 78:19
had not believed **G** and had not .... Ps 78:22
G had given them what they .... Ps 78:29
G became angry with them. .... Ps 78:31
come back to **G**, treat us well. .... Ps 78:34
remember that **G** was their Rock, ... Ps 78:35
that **G** Most High had saved them. .... Ps 78:35

were not really loyal to **G**; .... Ps 78:37
Still **G** was merciful. He forgave........... Ps 78:38
They turned against **G** so often .... Ps 78:40
they tested **G** and brought pain .... Ps 78:41
G killed all the firstborn sons .... Ps 78:51
But **G** led his people out like .... Ps 78:52
So **G** brought them to his holy .... Ps 78:54
But they tested **G** and turned .... Ps 78:56
and turned against **G** Most High; .... Ps 78:56
They made **G** angry by building .... Ps 78:58
G heard them, he became very .... Ps 78:59
But **G** rejected the family of .... Ps 78:67
G, nations have come against .... Ps 79:1
G our Savior, help us so people .... Ps 79:9
nations say, "Where is their **G**?"............ Ps 79:10
G, take us back. Show us your .... Ps 80:3
LORD **G** All-Powerful, how long............. Ps 80:4
G All-Powerful, take us back. .... Ps 80:7
G All-Powerful, come back. .... Ps 80:14
LORD **G** All-Powerful, take us .... Ps 80:19
Sing for joy to **G**, our strength; .... Ps 81:1
out loud to the **G** of Jacob. .... Ps 81:1
the command of the **G** of Jacob. .... Ps 81:4
must not worship any false **g**................. Ps 81:9
LORD, am your **G**, who brought you .... Ps 81:10
G is in charge of the great .... Ps 82:1
are all sons of **G** Most High.' .... Ps 82:6
G, come and judge the earth, ... Ps 82:8
G, do not keep quiet; God, do .... Ps 83:1
G, do not be silent or still. .... Ps 83:1
G, do to them what you did to .... Ps 83:9
pasturelands that belong to **G**." .... Ps 83:12
My **G**, make them like tumbleweed, ... Ps 83:13
only you are **G** Most High over .... Ps 83:18
wants to be with the living **G**. .... Ps 84:2
All-Powerful, my King and my **G**. .... Ps 84:3
meets with **G** in Jerusalem...................... Ps 84:7
LORD **G** All-Powerful, hear my .... Ps 84:8
G of Jacob, listen to me. .... Ps 84:8
G, look at our shield; be kind .... Ps 84:9
in the Temple of my **G** than live .... Ps 84:10
The LORD **G** is like a sun and .... Ps 84:11
G our Savior, bring us back .... Ps 85:4
I will listen to **G** the LORD..................... Ps 85:8
G will soon save those who................... Ps 85:9
earth people will be loyal to **G**, ... Ps 85:11
will go before **G** and prepare the .... Ps 85:13
My **G**, save me, your servant who .... Ps 86:2
there is no **g** like you and no .... Ps 86:8
you do miracles. Only you are **G**. .... Ps 86:10
Lord, my **G**, I will praise you .... Ps 86:12
G, proud people are attacking me; .... Ps 86:14
you are a **G** who shows mercy and........... Ps 86:15
City of **G**, wonderful things are .... Ps 87:3
G says, "I will put Egypt and .... Ps 87:4
G Most High will strengthen her." .... Ps 87:5
you are the **G** who saves me. .... Ps 88:1
ones meet, it is **G** they fear. .... Ps 89:7
LORD **G** All-Powerful, who is like .... Ps 89:8
are my father, my **G**, the Rock, ... Ps 89:26
A prayer of Moses, the man of **G**. .... Ps 89:52
earth and the world, you are **G**. .... Ps 90:2
Lord our **G**, treat us well. .... Ps 90:17
Those who go to **G** Most High for .... Ps 91:1
You are my **G** and I trust you." .... Ps 91:2
G will save you from hidden .... Ps 91:3
you have made **G** Most High your .... Ps 91:9
to sing praises to **G** Most High. .... Ps 92:1
in the courtyards of our **G**. .... Ps 92:13
The LORD is a **G** who punishes............... Ps 94:1
G, show your greatness and .... Ps 94:1
the **G** of Jacob doesn't notice." .... Ps 94:7
my **G** is the rock of my .... Ps 94:22

G will pay them back for their .... Ps 94:23
LORD our G will destroy them. .... Ps 94:23
because the LORD is the great G, ... Ps 95:3
because he is our G and we are .... Ps 95:7
the LORD our G, and worship at .... Ps 95:6
LORD our G, you answered them. .... Ps 99:8
them that you are a forgiving G,.......... Ps 99:8
the LORD our G, and worship at .... Ps 99:9
because the LORD our G is holy. .... Ps 99:9
Know that the LORD is G. .... Ps 100:3
G has made me tired of living; .... Ps 102:23
So I said, "My G, do not take me .... Ps 102:24
LORD my G, you are very great. .... Ps 104:1
They look to G for food. .... Ps 104:21
praises to my G as long as I .... Ps 104:33
is the LORD our G. His laws are............. Ps 105:7
G ordered a time of hunger in .... Ps 105:16
G split the rock, and water .... Ps 105:41
So G brought his people out with .... Ps 105:43
desert, and they tested G there. .... Ps 106:14
their glorious G for a statue of .... Ps 106:20
forgot the G who saved them,........... Ps 106:21
So G said he would destroy them. .... Ps 106:23
did not believe what G promised. .... Ps 106:24
turned against the Spirit of G, ... Ps 106:33
unfaithful to G in what they did .... Ps 106:39
But G saw their misery when he .... Ps 106:44
LORD our G, save us and bring us .... Ps 106:47
the LORD, the G of Israel. .... Ps 106:48
the words of G and had refused .... Ps 107:11
the advice of G Most High. .... Ps 107:11
turned against G and suffered .... Ps 107:17
G gave the command and healed .... Ps 107:20
and G guided them to the port .... Ps 107:30
G blessed them, and they grew in .... Ps 107:38
G, my heart is steady. I will .... Ps 108:1
G, you are supreme above the .... Ps 108:5
G has said from his Temple, ... Ps 108:7
G, surely you have rejected us; .... Ps 108:11
G, I praise you. Do not be .... Ps 109:1
LORD my G, help me; because you .... Ps 109:26
No one is like the LORD our G, ... Ps 113:5
the Lord, before the G of Jacob. .... Ps 114:7
nations ask, "Where is their G?" .... Ps 115:2
Our G is in heaven. He does what .... Ps 115:3
is right; our G is merciful. .... Ps 116:5
G bless the one who comes in the .... Ps 118:26
The LORD is G, and he has shown............ Ps 118:27
You are my G, and I will thank .... Ps 118:28
you are my G, and I will praise .... Ps 118:28
evil, what will G do to you? .... Ps 120:3
of the Temple of the LORD our G, ... Ps 122:9
we depend on the LORD our G; .... Ps 123:2
to the Mighty G of Jacob. .... Ps 132:2
home for the Mighty G of Jacob." .... Ps 132:5
Give thanks to the G of gods. .... Ps 136:2
Give thanks to the G of heaven. .... Ps 136:26
G, your thoughts are precious to .... Ps 139:17
G, I wish you would kill the .... Ps 139:19
G, examine me and know my heart; .... Ps 139:23
to the LORD, "You are my G." .... Ps 140:6
LORD G, my mighty savior, you.............. Ps 140:7
you want, because you are my G. .... Ps 143:10
G, I will sing a new song to you; .... Ps 144:9
the people whose G is the LORD. .... Ps 144:15
your greatness, my G the King; .... Ps 145:1
praises to my G as long as I .... Ps 146:2
are helped by the G of Jacob. .... Ps 146:5
hope is in the LORD their G. .... Ps 146:5
your G is everlasting. .... Ps 146:10
good to sing praises to our G; .... Ps 147:1
praise our G with harps. .... Ps 147:7
Jerusalem, praise your G. .... Ps 147:12

G has given his people a king. .... Ps 148:14
be happy because of G, ... Ps 149:2
punish them as G has written. .... Ps 149:9
G is honored by all who worship .... Ps 149:9
LORD! Praise G in his Temple; .... Ps 150:1
you will find that you know G. .... Pr 2:5
the promise she made before G. .... Pr 2:17
will please both G and people. .... Pr 3:4
G had not made the earth or .... Pr 8:26
I was there when G put the skies .... Pr 8:27
is kind to the needy honors G. .... Pr 14:31
king are like a message from G, ... Pr 16:10
something to G too quickly. .... Pr 20:25
G, who is always right, watches .... Pr 21:12
G, their defender, is strong; .... Pr 23:11
about this," G, who knows what's .... Pr 24:12
G is honored for what he keeps .... Pr 25:2
Where there is no word from G, ... Pr 29:18
and I don't know much about G, ... Pr 30:3
Every word of G is true. .... Pr 30:5
and disgrace the name of my G. .... Pr 30:9
I learned that G has given us .... Ec 1:13
saw that even this comes from G, ... Ec 2:24
people please G, God will give .... Ec 2:26
please God, G will give them .... Ec 2:26
give to the ones who please G. .... Ec 2:26
the hard work G has given people .... Ec 3:10
G has given them a desire to .... Ec 3:11
G wants all people to eat and .... Ec 3:13
work, which are gifts from G. .... Ec 3:13
that everything G does will .... Ec 3:14
add anything to what G has done, ... Ec 3:14
G does it this way to make .... Ec 3:14
G makes the same things happen .... Ec 3:15
G has planned a time for every .... Ec 3:17
I decided that G leaves it the .... Ec 3:18
spirit goes up to G and that the .... Ec 3:21
careful about what you say to G. .... Ec 5:2
G is in heaven, and you are on .... Ec 5:2
so say only a few words to G. .... Ec 5:2
If you make a promise to G, ... Ec 5:4
G is not happy with fools, ... Ec 5:4
so give G what you promised. .... Ec 5:4
G will become angry with your .... Ec 5:6
nothing. You should respect G. .... Ec 5:7
because the life G has given .... Ec 5:18
G gives some people the ability .... Ec 5:19
because G keeps them busy with .... Ec 5:20
G gives great wealth, riches, ... Ec 6:2
But G does not let them enjoy .... Ec 6:2
enjoy the good G gives him or .... Ec 6:3
enjoy the good G gives him. .... Ec 6:6
argue with G, who is stronger .... Ec 6:10
Look at what G has done: .... Ec 7:13
G gives good times and hard .... Ec 7:14
those who honor G will hold them .... Ec 7:18
man who pleases G will be saved .... Ec 7:26
G made people good, but they .... Ec 7:29
because you made a promise to G. .... Ec 8:2
be better for those who honor G. .... Ec 8:12
because they do not honor G. .... Ec 8:13
the hard work G gives them here .... Ec 8:15
I also saw all that G has done. .... Ec 8:17
understand what G does here on .... Ec 8:17
saw that G controls good people .... Ec 9:1
promises to G and to one who .... Ec 9:2
that is what G wants you to do. .... Ec 9:7
this useless life G has given .... Ec 9:9
you don't know what G is doing, ... Ec 11:5
remember that G will judge you .... Ec 11:9
will return to G who gave it. .... Ec 12:7
Honor G and obey his commands, ... Ec 12:13
G will judge everything, even .... Ec 12:14

G

they hate **G**, the Holy One of .... Is 1:4
listen to the teaching of our **G**! .... Is 1:10
there lived the way **G** wanted. .... Is 1:21
the City That Is Right with **G**, ... Is 1:26
to the Temple of the **G** of Jacob. .... Is 2:3
Then **G** will teach us his ways, ... Is 2:3
with shame. **G**, do not forgive .... Is 2:9
holy **G** will show himself holy .... Is 5:16
They say, "Let **G** hurry; let him .... Is 5:19
from the Holy **G** of Israel. .... Is 5:24
from the LORD your **G** to prove to .... Is 7:11
wear out the patience of my **G**? .... Is 7:13
useless, because **G** is with us. .... Is 8:10
should ask their **G** for help. .... Is 8:19
curse their king and their **G**. .... Is 8:21
In the past **G** made the lands of .... Is 9:1
G, you have caused the nation to .... Is 9:3
G has given a son to us. .... Is 9:6
Powerful **G**, Father Who Lives .... Is 9:6
says that **G** will judge Israel. .... Is 9:8
will know that **G** has sent it. .... Is 9:9
separated from **G** and are very .... Is 9:17
G says, "How terrible it will be .... Is 10:5
nation that is separated from **G**. .... Is 10:6
things, so **G** will punish him. .... Is 10:12
G, the Light of Israel, will be .... Is 10:17
again follow the powerful **G**. .... Is 10:21
G has announced that he will .... Is 10:22
G will raise a banner as a sign .... Is 11:12
G is the one who saves me; .... Is 12:2
G showed Isaiah son of Amoz this .... Is 13:1
But **G** will destroy it like Sodom. .... Is 13:19
I will be like **G** Most High." .... Is 14:14
says the LORD, the **G** of Israel. .... Is 17:6
that time people will look to **G**, ... Is 17:7
forgotten the **G** who saves you; .... Is 17:10
remembered that **G** is your place .... Is 17:10
but when **G** speaks harshly to .... Is 17:13
will worship **G** and offer many .... Is 19:21
will worship **G** together. .... Is 19:23
from the **G** of Israel. .... Is 21:10
The LORD, the **G** of Israel, has .... Is 21:17
not trust the **G** who made these .... Is 22:11
agreement with **G** that was to .... Is 24:5
of the LORD, the **G** of Israel. .... Is 24:15
part of the earth praising **G**, ... Is 24:16
LORD, you are my **G**. I honor you .... Is 25:1
But you, **G**, stop their violent .... Is 25:5
On this mountain **G** will destroy .... Is 25:7
will say, "Our **G** is doing this! .... Is 25:9
But **G** will bring down their .... Is 25:11
but **G** will destroy these walls. .... Is 25:12
G protects us with its strong .... Is 26:1
will enter, those who follow **G**. .... Is 26:2
for those who are right with **G**; .... Is 26:7
LORD, our **G**, other masters .... Is 26:13
so **G** will not comfort them; .... Is 27:11
G said to them, "Here is a place .... Is 28:12
His **G** teaches him and shows him .... Is 28:26
do not respect the **G** will disappear. .... Is 29:20
will respect the **G** of Israel. .... Is 29:23
telling us about **G**, the Holy One .... Is 30:11
LORD is a fair **G**, and everyone .... Is 30:18
they don't trust **G**, the Holy One .... Is 31:1
are only people and are not **G**. .... Is 31:3
come back to the **G** you fought .... Is 31:6
run away from the sword of **G**, ... Is 31:8
continue until **G** pours his .... Is 32:15
from **G** shake with fear. .... Is 33:14
G will make it an empty .... Is 34:11
G has given the command, so his .... Is 34:16
G has divided the land among .... Is 34:17
LORD and the splendor of our **G**. .... Is 35:2

Look, your **G** will come, and he .... Is 35:4
will be for the people **G** saves; .... Is 35:9
depending on the LORD our **G**," .... Is 36:7
' Has a **g** of any other nation .... Is 36:18
to make fun of the living **G**. .... Is 37:4
the LORD your **G** will hear what .... Is 37:4
be fooled by the **g** you trust. .... Is 37:10
you are the **G** of Israel, whose .... Is 37:16
only you are **G** of all the .... Is 37:16
has said to insult the living **G**. .... Is 37:17
Now, LORD our **G**, save us from .... Is 37:20
that you, LORD, are the only **G**." .... Is 37:20
the LORD, the **G** of Israel, says: .... Is 37:21
in the temple of his **g** Nisroch, ... Is 37:38
the **G** of your ancestor David, ... Is 38:5
Your **G** says, "Comfort, comfort .... Is 40:1
road in the dry lands for our **G**. .... Is 40:3
word of our **G** will live forever. .... Is 40:8
of Judah, "Here is your **G**." .... Is 40:9
Can you compare **G** to anything? .... Is 40:18
G sits on his throne above the .... Is 40:22
G, the Holy One, says, "Can you .... Is 40:25
The LORD is the **G** who lives .... Is 40:28
be afraid, because I am your **G**, ... Is 41:10
the LORD your **G**, who holds your .... Is 41:13
I, the **G** of Israel, will not .... Is 41:17
G, the Holy One, said these things. .... Is 42:5
LORD, am your **G**, the Holy One .... Is 43:3
understand that I am the true **G**. .... Is 43:10
There was no **G** before me, and .... Is 43:10
and there will be no **G** after me. .... Is 43:10
not some foreign **g** among you. .... Is 43:12
and I am **G**," says the LORD. .... Is 43:12
always been **G**. No one can save .... Is 43:13
and the end. I am the only **G**. .... Is 44:6
Who is a **g** like me? That god .... Is 44:7
That **g** should come and prove it. .... Is 44:7
There is no other **G** but me. .... Is 44:8
part of the wood to make a **g**, ... Is 44:15
that is left and calls it his **g**. .... Is 44:17
to it and says, "You are my **g**. .... Is 44:17
I am holding is a false **g**." .... Is 44:20
you mountains, with thanks to **G**. .... Is 44:23
the LORD, the **G** of Israel, who .... Is 45:3
is no other **G**; I am the only .... Is 45:5
I am the only **G**. I will make you .... Is 45:5
will know there is no other **G**. .... Is 45:6
argue with the **G** who made them. .... Is 45:9
to you, saying, '**G** is with you, ... Is 45:14
and there is no other **G**.'" .... Is 45:14
G and Savior of Israel, you are .... Is 45:15
you are a **G** that people cannot .... Is 45:15
He is the **G** who formed the earth .... Is 45:18
the LORD. There is no other **G**. .... Is 45:18
They pray to a **g** who cannot save .... Is 45:20
There is no other **G** besides me. .... Is 45:21
the only good **G**. I am the Savior .... Is 45:21
the LORD. There is no other **G**. .... Is 45:21
be saved. I am **G**. There is no .... Is 45:22
I am God. There is no other **G**. .... Is 45:22
and he makes it into a **g**. .... Is 46:6
things, you who turn against **G**. .... Is 46:8
that I am **G**, and there is no .... Is 46:9
am God, and there is no other **G**. .... Is 46:9
I am **G**, and there is no one like .... Is 46:9
yourself, 'I am **G**, and no one is .... Is 47:10
name and praise the **G** of Israel, ... Is 48:1
you depend on the **G** of Israel, ... Is 48:2
not let some **g** take my glory. .... Is 48:11
be my people. I am **G**; I am the .... Is 48:12
the LORD your **G**, who teaches you .... Is 48:17
G will decide my reward." .... Is 49:4
will get my strength from my **G**. .... Is 49:5

G who comforts them will lead .... Is 49:10
LORD and yet depend on his **G**. .... Is 50:10
the LORD your **G**, who stirs the .... Is 51:15
Your **G** will defend his people. .... Is 51:22
is what the LORD your **G** says: .... Is 51:22
do not worship **G** and who are not .... Is 52:1
to Jerusalem, "Your **G** is King." .... Is 52:7
will see the salvation of our **G**. .... Is 52:10
and the **G** of Israel will guard............... Is 52:12
and thought **G** was punishing him............ Is 53:4
make many people right with **G**; .... Is 53:11
The **G** who made you is like your .... Is 54:5
is called the **G** of all the earth................. Is 54:5
you to be his," says your **G**. .... Is 54:6
G says, "I left you for a short .... Is 54:7
you because of the LORD your **G**, ... Is 55:5
They should come to our **G**, ... Is 55:7
who are right with **G** may die, ... Is 57:1
who live as **G** wants find rest .... Is 57:2
You turn against **G**, and you are .... Is 57:4
G lives forever and is holy. .... Is 57:15
for evil people," says my **G**. .... Is 57:21
they have done against their **G**; .... Is 58:1
obeys the commands of its **G**................ Is 58:2
They want **G** to be near them. .... Is 58:2
Your **G** will walk before you, ... Is 58:8
has separated you from your **G**. .... Is 59:2
many wrong things against our **G**; .... Is 59:12
know we have turned against **G**; .... Is 59:12
from our **G**, planning to hurt .... Is 59:13
to hurt others and to disobey **G**,............. Is 59:13
This will honor the LORD your **G**, ... Is 60:9
and your **G** will be your glory. .... Is 60:19
time when our **G** will punish evil .... Is 61:2
be named the servants of our **G**. .... Is 61:6
all that I am rejoices in my **G**................. Is 61:10
called the People that **G** Left, ... Is 62:4
land the Land that **G** Destroyed............... Is 62:4
be called the People **G** Loves, ... Is 62:4
will be called the Bride of **G**, ... Is 62:4
so your **G** will rejoice over you. .... Is 62:5
will be called the City **G** Wants, ... Is 62:12
the City **G** Has Not Rejected. .... Is 62:12
has ever heard of a **G** like you. .... Is 64:4
has ever seen a **G** besides you, ... Is 64:4
who worship the **g** Luck, who hold .... Is 65:11
religious feasts for the **g** Fate,................. Is 65:11
for them from the faithful **G**. .... Is 65:16
in the name of the faithful **G**, ... Is 65:16
your new nation," says your **G**. .... Is 66:9
their glorious **G** for idols worth .... Je 2:11
from the LORD your **G** when he was .... Je 2:17
turn away from the LORD your **G**. .... Je 2:19
G is not angry with me.' .... Je 2:35
the LORD your **G** and worshiped .... Je 3:13
have forgotten the LORD their **G**, ... Je 3:21
because you are the LORD our **G**. .... Je 3:22
comes from the LORD our **G**. .... Je 3:23
sinned against the LORD our **G**,............... Je 3:25
have not obeyed the LORD our **G**." .... Je 3:25
they refused to turn back to **G**. .... Je 5:3
and what their **G** wants them to .... Je 5:4
know what **G** wants them to do. .... Je 5:5
the word of **G** is not in them. .... Je 5:13
is what the LORD **G** All-Powerful .... Je 5:14
the LORD our **G** done all these .... Je 5:19
'We should fear the LORD our **G**, ... Je 5:24
the **G** of Israel, says: .... Je 7:3
incense to the **g** Baal and follow............... Je 7:9
the **G** of Israel, says: .... Je 7:21
I will be your **G** and you will be .... Je 7:23
has not obeyed the LORD its **G**. .... Je 7:28
The LORD our **G** has decided that .... Je 8:14

G, you are my comfort when I am .... Je 8:18
But **G** says, "Why did the people .... Je 8:19
they are all unfaithful to **G**;................... Je 9:2
the **G** of Israel, says: .... Je 9:15
But the LORD is the only true **G**. .... Je 10:10
the only living **G**, the King .... Je 10:10
G made the earth by his power. .... Je 10:12
But **G**, who is Jacob's Portion, ... Je 10:16
the LORD, the **G** of Israel, says: .... Je 11:3
my people, and I will be your **G**............... Je 11:4
to that shameful **g** Baal as there .... Je 11:13
G does not see what happens to us. .... Je 12:4
the LORD, the **G** of Israel, says: .... Je 13:12
the LORD your **G** before he brings............ Je 13:16
is the flock **G** gave you to care .... Je 13:20
cry goes up to **G** from Jerusalem .... Je 14:2
G, the Hope of Israel, you have .... Je 14:8
No, it is you, LORD our **G**. .... Je 14:22
your name, LORD **G** All-Powerful. .... Je 15:16
the **G** of Israel, says: .... Je 16:9
we done against the LORD our **G**?' .... Je 16:10
the good things **G** can give. .... Je 16:19
as a glorious throne for **G**. .... Je 17:12
offerings to show thanks to **G**. .... Je 17:26
the **G** of Israel, says: .... Je 19:3
the **G** of Israel, says: .... Je 19:15
the LORD, the **G** of Israel, says: .... Je 21:4
agreement with the LORD their **G**............ Je 22:9
is what it means to know **G**," .... Je 22:16
the LORD, the **G** of Israel, says: .... Je 23:2
live as if there were no **G**. .... Je 23:11
"I am a **G** who is near," says the .... Je 23:23
"I am also a **G** who is far away." .... Je 23:23
have changed the words of our **G**, ... Je 23:36
our God, the living **G**, the LORD .... Je 23:36
the LORD, the **G** of Israel, says: .... Je 24:5
I will be their **G**, because they .... Je 24:7
The LORD, the **G** of Israel, said .... Je 25:15
the **G** of Israel, says: .... Je 25:27
good and obey the LORD your **G**. .... Je 26:13
us comes from the LORD our **G**." .... Je 26:16
the **G** of Israel, says: .... Je 27:4
the **G** of Israel, says............................ Je 27:21
the **G** of Israel, says: .... Je 28:2
the **G** of Israel, says: .... Je 28:14
the **G** of Israel, says: .... Je 29:4
the **G** of Israel, says: .... Je 29:8
the **G** of Israel, says: .... Je 29:21
the **G** of Israel, says: .... Je 29:25
The LORD, the **G** of Israel, said:........... Je 30:2
the LORD their **G** and David their .... Je 30:9
people, and I will be your **G**." .... Je 30:22
time I will be **G** of all Israel's .... Je 31:1
to worship the LORD our **G**!'" .... Je 31:6
You truly are the LORD my **G**. .... Je 31:18
the **G** of Israel, says: .... Je 31:23
I will be their **G**, and they will .... Je 31:33
the **G** of Israel, says: .... Je 32:14
the **G** of Israel, says: .... Je 32:15
and powerful **G**, your name is .... Je 32:18
the **G** of every person on the .... Je 32:27
the LORD, the **G** of Israel, says .... Je 32:36
people, and I will be their **G**. .... Je 32:38
the LORD, the **G** of Israel, says .... Je 33:4
the LORD, the **G** of Israel, said:........... Je 34:2
the LORD, the **G** of Israel, says: .... Je 34:13
of Igdaliah, who was a man of **G**. .... Je 35:4
the **G** of Israel, says: .... Je 35:13
So the LORD **G** All-Powerful, ... Je 35:17
the **G** of Israel, says: .... Je 35:17
the **G** of Israel, says: .... Je 35:18
the **G** of Israel, says: .... Je 35:19
pray to the LORD our **G** for us."............... Je 37:3

the LORD, the **G** of Israel, says: .... Je 37:7
is what the LORD **G** All-Powerful, ... Je 38:17
the **G** of Israel, says: .... Je 38:17
the **G** of Israel, says: .... Je 39:16
The LORD your **G** announced this .... Je 40:2
to the LORD your **G** for all the .... Je 42:2
the LORD your **G** will tell us .... Je 42:3
to the LORD your **G** as you have .... Je 42:4
your **G** sends you to tell us. .... Je 42:5
We will obey the LORD our **G,** .... Je 42:6
is what the **G** of Israel says: .... Je 42:9
will disobey the LORD your **G.** .... Je 42:13
the **G** of Israel, says: .... Je 42:15
the **G** of Israel, says: .... Je 42:18
You sent me to the LORD your **G,** .... Je 42:20
'Pray to the LORD our **G** for us. .... Je 42:20
everything the LORD our **G** says .... Je 42:20
the LORD your **G** in all that he .... Je 42:21
message from the LORD their **G;** .... Je 43:1
the LORD their **G** had sent him to .... Je 43:1
The LORD our **G** did not send you .... Je 43:2
the **G** of Israel, says: .... Je 43:10
temple of the sun **g** in Egypt, ... Je 43:13
the **G** of Israel, says: .... Je 44:2
the **G** of Israel, says: .... Je 44:7
the **G** of Israel, says: .... Je 44:11
the **G** of Israel, says: .... Je 44:25
the LORD, the **G** of Israel, says .... Je 45:2
the **G** of Israel, says: .... Je 46:25
the **g** of the city of Thebes. .... Je 46:25
the **G** of Israel, says: .... Je 48:1
The **g** Chemosh will go into .... Je 48:7
Israel trusted that **g** in the .... Je 48:13
be ashamed of their **g** Chemosh. .... Je 48:13
The **g** Bel will be put to shame, ... Je 50:2
and the **g** Marduk will be afraid. .... Je 50:2
and look for the LORD their **G.** .... Je 50:4
the **G** their fathers trusted.' .... Je 50:7
the **G** of Israel, says: .... Je 50:18
how the LORD our **G** is punishing .... Je 50:28
G is strong and will buy them .... Je 50:34
G completely destroyed the .... Je 50:40
what the LORD our **G** has done.' .... Je 51:10
But **G,** who is Jacob's Portion, ... Je 51:19
the **G** of Israel, says: .... Je 51:33
punish the **g** Bel in Babylon. .... Je 51:44
the LORD is a **G** who punishes .... Je 51:56
unfairly before the Most High **G;** .... La 3:35
the command of the Most High **G.** .... La 3:38
from our hearts to **G** in heaven: .... La 3:41
opened, and I saw visions of **G.** .... Eze 1:1
like the voice of **G** Almighty, ... Eze 1:24
teachings of **G** from the priest .... Eze 7:26
me in visions of **G** to Jerusalem, ... Eze 8:3
that caused **G** to be jealous. .... Eze 8:3
glory of the **G** of Israel there .... Eze 8:4
that caused **G** to be jealous. .... Eze 8:5
glory of the **G** of Israel went .... Eze 9:3
the voice of **G** Almighty when he .... Eze 10:5
the glory of the **G** of Israel was .... Eze 10:19
I had seen under the **G** of Israel .... Eze 10:20
people, and I will be their **G.** .... Eze 11:20
the glory of the **G** of Israel was .... Eze 11:24
vision given by the Spirit of **G,** .... Eze 11:24
I will be their **G,** says the LORD .... Eze 14:11
them, "I am the LORD your **G.**" .... Eze 20:5
of Egypt. I am the LORD your **G.**" .... Eze 20:7
am the LORD your **G.** Live by my .... Eze 20:19
know that I am the LORD your **G.**" .... Eze 20:20
or showers when **G** is angry.' .... Eze 22:24
are proud, you say, "I am a **g,** .... Eze 28:2
the throne of a **g** in the middle .... Eze 28:2
think you are as wise as a **g,** .... Eze 28:2

but you are a human, not a **g.** .... Eze 28:2
You think you are wise like a **g,** .... Eze 28:6
able to say anymore, "I am a **g.**" .... Eze 28:9
only a human, not a **g,** when your .... Eze 28:9
were in Eden, the garden of **G.** .... Eze 28:13
you on the holy mountain of **G.** .... Eze 28:14
disgrace from the mountain of **G.** .... Eze 28:16
that I am the LORD their **G.**'" .... Eze 28:26
in the garden of **G** were not as .... Eze 31:8
the garden of **G** was as beautiful .... Eze 31:8
in the garden of **G** wanted to be .... Eze 31:9
will be their **G,** and my servant .... Eze 34:24
the LORD their **G,** am with them. .... Eze 34:30
and I am your **G,** says the Lord .... Eze 34:31
my people, and I will be your **G.** .... Eze 36:28
people, and I will be their **G.** .... Eze 37:23
I will be their **G,** and they will .... Eze 37:27
know that I am the LORD their **G.** .... Eze 39:22
know that I am the LORD their **G,** .... Eze 39:28
the visions of **G** he brought me .... Eze 40:2
glory of the **G** of Israel coming .... Eze 43:2
they will give the altar to **G.** .... Eze 43:26
because the LORD **G** of Israel has .... Eze 44:2
sins so you will belong to **G,** .... Eze 45:15
the things from the Temple of **G,** .... Da 1:2
G made Ashpenaz, the chief .... Da 1:9
G gave these four young men .... Da 1:17
pray that the **G** of heaven would .... Da 2:18
During the night **G** explained the .... Da 2:19
Daniel praised the **G** of heaven. .... Da 2:19
Praise **G** forever and ever, ... Da 2:20
praise you, **G** of my ancestors .... Da 2:23
But there is a **G** in heaven who .... Da 2:28
G, who can tell people about .... Da 2:29
G also told this secret to me, ... Da 2:30
G of heaven has given you a .... Da 2:37
G made you ruler over them. .... Da 2:38
the **G** of heaven will set up .... Da 2:44
way the great **G** showed you what .... Da 2:45
I know your **G** is the greatest .... Da 2:47
What **g** will be able to save you .... Da 3:15
the **G** we serve is able to save .... Da 3:17
But even if **G** does not save us, ... Da 3:18
Servants of the Most High **G,** .... Da 3:26
Praise the **G** of Shadrach, ... Da 3:28
Their **G** has sent his angel and .... Da 3:28
trusted their **G** and refused to .... Da 3:28
worship any **g** other than their .... Da 3:28
against the **G** of Shadrach, ... Da 3:29
No other **g** can save his people .... Da 3:29
Most High **G** has done miracles .... Da 4:2
him Belteshazzar to honor my **g,** .... Da 4:8
the Most High **G** rules over every .... Da 4:17
G gives those kingdoms to anyone .... Da 4:17
The Most High **G** has commanded .... Da 4:24
The Most High **G** is ruler over .... Da 4:25
The Most High **G** rules over every .... Da 4:32
gave praise to the Most High **G;** .... Da 4:34
G does what he wants with the .... Da 4:35
and **G** gave back my great honor .... Da 4:36
the Temple of **G** in Jerusalem. .... Da 5:3
the Most High **G** made your father .... Da 5:18
Because **G** made him important, ... Da 5:19
The Most High **G** rules over every .... Da 5:21
did not honor **G,** who has power .... Da 5:23
So **G** sent the hand that wrote on .... Da 5:24
G has counted the days until .... Da 5:26
it is about the law of his **G.**" .... Da 6:5
pray to any **g** or human except to .... Da 6:7
kneel down to pray and thank **G,** .... Da 6:10
praying and asking **G** for help. .... Da 6:11
pray to any **g** or human except .... Da 6:12
prays to his **G** three times every .... Da 6:13

May the **G** you serve all the time .... Da 6:16
Daniel, servant of the living **G!** .... Da 6:20
Has your **G** that you always .... Da 6:20
My **G** sent his angel to close the............. Da 6:22
my **G** knows I am innocent. .... Da 6:22
Daniel had trusted in his **G**. .... Da 6:23
and respect the **G** of Daniel. .... Da 6:26
Daniel's **G** is the living God; .... Da 6:26
Daniel's God is the living **G**; .... Da 6:26
G rescues and saves people and .... Da 6:27
places, and **G**, the Eternal One .... Da 7:9
He came near **G**, who has been .... Da 7:13
forever, and he was led to **G**. .... Da 7:13
to the Most High **G** will receive .... Da 7:18
until **G**, who has been alive.................... Da 7:22
who belong to the Most High **G**;............. Da 7:22
speak against the Most High **G**, ... Da 7:25
that belong to **G** will be in that .... Da 7:25
to the Most High **G** will have the .... Da 7:27
set itself up as equal to **G**, ... Da 8:11
there was a turning away from **G**, ... Da 8:12
turning away from **G** that brings .... Da 8:13
people have turned against **G**. .... Da 8:23
turned to the Lord **G** and prayed .... Da 9:3
to the Lord my **G** and told him .... Da 9:4
are a great **G** who causes fear .... Da 9:4
But, Lord our **G**, you show us .... Da 9:9
the Lord our **G** or the teachings .... Da 9:10
the servant of **G**, because we .... Da 9:11
not pleaded with the Lord our **G**............ Da 9:13
because the Lord our **G** is right .... Da 9:14
Lord our **G**, you used your power .... Da 9:15
Now, our **G**, hear the prayers of .... Da 9:17
My **G**, pay attention and hear me. .... Da 9:18
to the Lord, my **G**, confessing my........... Da 9:20
because **G** loves you very much............... Da 9:23
G has ordered four hundred .... Da 9:24
people from turning against **G**; .... Da 9:24
G has ordered that place to be .... Da 9:26
to me, "Daniel, **G** loves you very .... Da 10:11
humble yourself before your **G**. .... Da 10:12
Since that time **G** has listened .... Da 10:12
don't be afraid. **G** loves you .... Da 10:19
because **G** has set a time for .... Da 11:27
have not obeyed **G** to be ruined. .... Da 11:32
those who know **G** and obey him .... Da 11:32
he is even better than a **g**. .... Da 11:36
against the **G** of gods that no .... Da 11:36
what **G** has planned to happen .... Da 11:36
worshiped or the **g** that women .... Da 11:37
He won't care about any **g**..................... Da 11:37
more important than any **g**. .... Da 11:37
will honor the **g** of power with .... Da 11:38
with the help of a foreign **g**. .... Da 11:39
by the name of **G** who lives .... Da 12:7
Lord their **G**, will save them. .... Hos 1:7
my people, and I am not your **G**. .... Hos 1:9
'children of the living **G**.' .... Hos 1:10
say to me, 'You are our **G**.'" .... Hos 2:23
the Lord their **G** and follow him .... Hos 3:5
not loyal to **G**, nor do those who .... Hos 4:1
the teachings of your **G**. .... Hos 4:6
gods and have left their own **G**. .... Hos 4:12
deeds and return to their **G**. .... Hos 5:4
who do not know the true **G**. .... Hos 5:5
the Lord their **G** or look to him .... Hos 7:10
did not turn to the Most High **G**. .... Hos 7:16
out to me, 'Our **G**, we in Israel .... Hos 8:2
made; it is not **G**. Israel's .... Hos 8:6
a prostitute against your **G**. .... Hos 9:1
G will reject them, because they............. Hos 9:17
they refuse to turn back to **G**................. Hos 11:5
again. I am **G** and not a human; I .... Hos 11:9

And Judah turns against **G**, ... Hos 11:12
to be a man, he wrestled with **G**. .... Hos 12:3
G met with him at Bethel and................ Hos 12:4
It was the Lord **G** All-Powerful; .... Hos 12:5
You must return to your **G**; .... Hos 12:6
always trust in him as your **G**. .... Hos 12:6
But I am the Lord your **G**, ... Hos 12:9
have been your **G** since you were .... Hos 13:4
have known no other **G** except me. .... Hos 13:4
because it fought against **G**. .... Hos 13:16
return to the Lord your **G**, ... Hos 14:1
who turn against **G** die because .... Hos 14:9
Servants of my **G**, keep your .... Joe 1:13
offer in the Temple of your **G**............... Joe 1:13
the Temple of the Lord your **G**, ... Joe 1:14
gone from the Temple of our **G**. .... Joe 1:16
Come back to the Lord your **G**, ... Joe 2:13
belong to the Lord your **G**. .... Joe 2:14
ask, 'Where is their **G**?'" .... Joe 2:17
be joyful in the Lord your **G**. .... Joe 2:23
the name of the Lord your **G**, ... Joe 2:26
that I am the Lord your **G**, ... Joe 2:27
God, and there is no other **G**. .... Joe 2:27
the Lord your **G**, live on my holy .... Joe 3:17
drink in the house of their **g**. .... Am 2:8
Lord God, the **G** All-Powerful. .... Am 3:13
Just as surely as I am a holy **G**, ... Am 4:2
ready to meet your **G**, Israel.'" .... Am 4:12
name is the Lord **G** All-Powerful............ Am 4:13
G is the one who made the star .... Am 5:8
and the Lord **G** All-Powerful will .... Am 5:14
Maybe the Lord **G** All-Powerful .... Am 5:15
Lord, the Lord **G** All-Powerful,............. Am 5:16
your king, the **G** Sakkuth, and .... Am 5:26
name is the **G** All-Powerful. .... Am 5:27
the Lord **G** All-Powerful says: .... Am 6:8
The Lord **G** All-Powerful says, ... Am 6:14
surely as the **g** of Dan lives . . . . Am 8:14
'As surely as the **g** of Beersheba .... Am 8:14
them," says the Lord your **G**. .... Am 9:15
and each man cried to his own **g**. .... Jnh 1:5
Get up and pray to your **g!** .... Jnh 1:6
Maybe your **g** will pay attention .... Jnh 1:6
the Lord, the **G** of heaven, who .... Jnh 1:9
to the Lord his **G** and said, ... Jnh 2:1
the pit of death, Lord my **G**. .... Jnh 2:6
people of Nineveh believed **G**. .... Jnh 3:5
people should cry loudly to **G**. .... Jnh 3:8
Maybe **G** will change his mind. .... Jnh 3:9
When **G** saw what the people did, ... Jnh 3:10
that you are a **G** who is kind .... Jnh 4:2
G sent a worm to attack the .... Jnh 4:7
G sent a very hot east wind to .... Jnh 4:8
But **G** said to Jonah, "Do you .... Jnh 4:9
there will be no answer from **G**." .... Mic 3:7
how they have turned against **G**, ... Mic 3:8
to the Temple of the **G** of Jacob,............ Mic 4:2
the Lord our **G** forever and ever. .... Mic 4:5
of the name of the Lord his **G**. .... Mic 5:4
when I bow before **G** on high? .... Mic 6:6
and live humbly, obeying your **G**. .... Mic 6:8
I will wait for **G** to save me; .... Mic 7:7
to save me; my **G** will hear me. .... Mic 7:7
'Where is the Lord your **G**?' .... Mic 7:10
to the Lord our **G** and will turn .... Mic 7:17
There is no **G** like you. You................... Mic 7:18
is a jealous **G** who punishes; .... Nah 1:2
your promised sacrifices to **G**. .... Nah 1:15
live forever, my **G**, my holy God. .... Hab 1:12
live forever, my God, my holy **G**. .... Hab 1:12
to learn how **G** will answer my .... Hab 2:1
are right with **G** will live by .... Hab 2:4
G is coming from Teman; the Holy........... Hab 3:3

G

fall down. **G** has always done .... Hab 3:6
I will rejoice in **G** my Savior. .... Hab 3:18
both the LORD and the g Molech, ... Zph 1:5
On the day that **G** will show his .... Zph 1:18
The LORD their **G** will pay .... Zph 2:7
the **G** of Israel, says, ... Zph 2:9
it doesn't worship its **G**. .... Zph 3:2
The LORD your **G** is with you; .... Zph 3:17
the LORD their **G** and the message .... Hag 1:12
the LORD their **G** had sent him. .... Hag 1:12
worked on the Temple of their **G**, ... Hag 1:14
obey the LORD your **G**." .... Zch 6:15
will be their good and loyal **G**." .... Zch 8:8
heard that **G** is with you.'" .... Zch 8:23
left alive will belong to **G**. .... Zch 9:7
the LORD their **G** will save them .... Zch 9:16
because I am the LORD their **G**, ... Zch 10:6
This is what the LORD my **G** says: .... Zch 11:4
the agreement **G** made with all .... Zch 11:10
LORD All-Powerful is their **G**.' .... Zch 12:5
family of David will be like **G**, ... Zch 12:8
will say, 'The LORD is our **G**.'" .... Zch 13:9
Then the LORD my **G** will come and .... Zch 14:5
Now ask **G** to be kind to you, ... Mal 1:9
the same **G** made us. So why .... Mal 2:10
our ancestors made with **G**? .... Mal 2:10
done something **G** hates in Israel .... Mal 2:11
G made husbands and wives to .... Mal 2:15
have children who are true to **G**. .... Mal 2:15
The LORD **G** of Israel says, ... Mal 2:16
"Where is the **G** who is fair?".................. Mal 2:17
a person rob **G**? But you are .... Mal 3:8
'It is useless to serve **G**. .... Mal 3:14
They challenge **G** and get away .... Mal 3:15
those who serve **G** and those who .... Mal 3:18
which means "**G** is with us." .... Mt 1:23
But **G** warned the wise men in a.............. Mt 2:12
So what **G** had said through the.............. Mt 2:17
And so what **G** had said through .... Mt 2:23
' I tell you that **G** could make .... Mt 3:9
are the Son of **G**, tell these .... Mt 4:3
but by everything **G** says.'"..................... Mt 4:4
you are the Son of **G**, jump down, ... Mt 4:6
'Do not test the Lord your **G**.'" .... Mt 4:7
Lord your **G** and serve only him. .... Mt 4:10
who grieve, for **G** will comfort .... Mt 5:4
for **G** will show mercy to them. .... Mt 5:7
are pure, for they will see **G**. .... Mt 5:8
your gift to **G** at the altar, ... Mt 5:23
because the earth belongs to **G**. .... Mt 5:35
who don't know **G** are nice to................. Mt 5:47
those people who don't know **G**. .... Mt 6:7
thinking that **G** will hear them .... Mt 6:7
cannot serve both **G** and worldly .... Mt 6:24
G clothes the grass in the field, ... Mt 6:30
sure that **G** will clothe you. .... Mt 6:30
who don't know **G** keep trying to .... Mt 6:32
God's kingdom and what **G** wants............ Mt 6:33
Ask, and **G** will give to you. .... Mt 7:7
do you want with us, Son of **G**? .... Mt 8:29
This man speaks as if he were **G**. .... Mt 9:3
and praised **G** for giving power .... Mt 9:8
G even knows how many hairs are .... Mt 10:30
kingdom of **G** has come to you. .... Mt 12:28
everything they say against **G**. .... Mt 12:31
he thanked **G** for the food. .... Mt 14:19
"Truly you are the Son of **G**!" .... Mt 14:33
G said, 'Honor your father and .... Mt 15:4
I have given it to **G** already.' .... Mt 15:5
rejected what **G** said for the .... Mt 15:6
G sent me only to the lost .... Mt 15:24
they praised the **G** of Israel for .... Mt 15:31
the fish and gave thanks to **G**. .... Mt 15:36

to show them a miracle from **G**. .... Mt 16:1
the Son of the living **G**." .... Mt 16:16
things that **G** does not allow, ... Mt 16:19
be the things that **G** allows." .... Mt 16:19
G save you from these things, ... Mt 16:22
care about the things of **G**, ... Mt 16:23
not believe in **G** or like a tax .... Mt 18:17
be the things **G** does not allow. .... Mt 18:18
be the things that **G** allows. .... Mt 18:18
When **G** made the world, 'he made .... Mt 19:4
And **G** said, 'So a man will leave .... Mt 19:5
G has joined the two together, ... Mt 19:6
but **G** has made some able to .... Mt 19:11
is good? Only **G** is good. But if .... Mt 19:17
to enter the kingdom of **G**." .... Mt 19:24
for **G** all things are possible. .... Mt 19:26
G bless the One who comes in the .... Mt 21:9
Lord! Praise to **G** in heaven!" .... Mt 21:9
that come from **G** or just from .... Mt 21:25
'John's baptism was from **G**,' .... Mt 21:25
the kingdom of **G** before you do. .... Mt 21:31
the kingdom of **G** will be taken .... Mt 21:43
who do the things **G** wants in his .... Mt 21:43
give to **G** the things that are .... Mt 22:21
don't know about the power of **G**. .... Mt 22:29
have read what **G** said to you .... Mt 22:31
G said, 'I am the God of Abraham,........... Mt 22:32
said, 'I am the **G** of Abraham,................... Mt 22:32
God of Abraham, the **G** of Isaac, ... Mt 22:32
of Isaac, and the **G** of Jacob.' .... Mt 22:32
' **G** is the God of the living,..................... Mt 22:32
' God is the **G** of the living,..................... Mt 22:32
the Lord your **G** with all your .... Mt 22:37
You give to **G** one-tenth of .... Mt 23:23
'**G** bless the One who comes in .... Mt 23:39
G has decided to make that .... Mt 24:22
But **G** will make that time short .... Mt 24:22
even the people **G** has chosen, ... Mt 24:24
the kingdom **G** has prepared for .... Mt 25:34
and thanked **G** for it and broke .... Mt 26:26
and thanked **G** for it and gave .... Mt 26:27
agreement that **G** makes with his .... Mt 26:28
the Temple of **G** and build it .... Mt 26:61
by the power of the living **G**: .... Mt 26:63
are the Christ, the Son of **G**." .... Mt 26:63
sitting at the right hand of **G**, ... Mt 26:64
said things that are against **G**! .... Mt 26:65
him say these things against **G**. .... Mt 26:65
if you are really the Son of **G**!" .... Mt 27:40
He trusts in **G**, so let God save .... Mt 27:43
God, so let **G** save him now, if .... Mt 27:43
him now, if **G** really wants him .... Mt 27:43
said, 'I am the Son of **G**.'" .... Mt 27:43
This means, "My **G**, my God, why .... Mt 27:46
My God, my **G**, why have you................... Mt 27:46
"He really was the Son of **G**!" .... Mt 27:54
Jesus Christ, the Son of **G**, ... Mk 1:1
preaching the Good News from **G**. .... Mk 1:14
The kingdom of **G** is near. .... Mk 1:15
He is speaking as if he were **G**. .... Mk 2:7
Only **G** can forgive sins." .... Mk 2:7
were amazed and praised **G**. .... Mk 2:12
shouted, "You are the Son of **G**!" .... Mk 3:11
say against **G** can be forgiven. .... Mk 3:28
are those who do what **G** wants." .... Mk 3:35
secret about the kingdom of **G**. .... Mk 4:11
who hear the teaching of **G**, ... Mk 4:15
is the way **G** will give to you .... Mk 4:24
but **G** will give you even more. .... Mk 4:24
The kingdom of **G** is like someone .... Mk 4:26
what the kingdom of **G** is like? .... Mk 4:30
The kingdom of **G** is like a .... Mk 4:31
Jesus, Son of the Most High **G**? .... Mk 5:7

he thanked **G** for the food. .... Mk 6:41
following the commands of **G**, ... Mk 7:8
the commands of **G** so you can .... Mk 7:9
but it is Corban—a gift to **G**.' .... Mk 7:11
you are rejecting what **G** said. .... Mk 7:13
gave thanks to **G**, and divided .... Mk 8:6
Jesus for a miracle from **G**. .... Mk 8:11
care about the things of **G**, ... Mk 8:33
the kingdom of **G** come with power .... Mk 9:1
the kingdom of **G** with only one .... Mk 9:47
But when **G** made the world, ' .... Mk 10:6
G has joined the two together, ... Mk 10:9
the kingdom of **G** belongs to .... Mk 10:14
the kingdom of **G** as if you were .... Mk 10:15
call me good? Only **G** is good. .... Mk 10:18
rich to enter the kingdom of **G**!" .... Mk 10:23
hard to enter the kingdom of **G**! .... Mk 10:24
to enter the kingdom of **G**." .... Mk 10:25
for **G** all things are possible. .... Mk 10:27
behind him, shouting, "Praise **G**! .... Mk 11:9
G bless the One who comes in the .... Mk 11:9
G bless the kingdom of our.................. Mk 11:10
coming! Praise to **G** in heaven!" .... Mk 11:10
answered, "Have faith in **G**, ... Mk 11:22
will happen, **G** will do it for .... Mk 11:23
and **G** will give them to you. .... Mk 11:24
authority from **G** or just from .... Mk 11:30
'John's baptism was from **G**,' .... Mk 11:31
give to **G** the things that are .... Mk 12:17
you know about the power of **G**? .... Mk 12:24
have read what **G** said about .... Mk 12:26
it says that **G** told Moses, ' .... Mk 12:26
Moses, 'I am the **G** of Abraham, ... Mk 12:26
God of Abraham, the **G** of Isaac, ... Mk 12:26
of Isaac, and the **G** of Jacob.' .... Mk 12:26
G is the God of the living, ... Mk 12:27
God is the **G** of the living, ... Mk 12:27
The Lord our **G** is the only Lord. .... Mk 12:29
the Lord your **G** with all your................ Mk 12:30
when you said **G** is the only Lord .... Mk 12:32
there is no other **G** besides him. .... Mk 12:32
One must love **G** with all his .... Mk 12:33
and sacrifices we offer to **G**." .... Mk 12:33
are close to the kingdom of **G**." .... Mk 12:34
when **G** made the world,...................... Mk 13:19
G has decided to make that .... Mk 13:20
But **G** will make that time short .... Mk 13:20
even the people **G** has chosen, ... Mk 13:22
and thanked **G** for it and broke .... Mk 14:22
and thanked **G** for it and gave .... Mk 14:23
agreement that **G** makes with his .... Mk 14:24
it new in the kingdom of **G**." .... Mk 14:25
the Son of the blessed **G**?" .... Mk 14:61
sitting at the right hand of **G**, ... Mk 14:62
him say these things against **G**. .... Mk 14:64
This means, "My **G**, my God, why .... Mk 15:34
My God, my **G**, why have you................ Mk 15:34
man really was the Son of **G**!" .... Mk 15:39
for the kingdom of **G** to come. .... Mk 15:43
he sat at the right side of **G**. .... Mk 16:19
and served **G** by telling people .... Lk 1:2
truly did what **G** said was good. .... Lk 1:6
serving as a priest before **G**, ... Lk 1:8
G has heard your prayer. .... Lk 1:13
return to the Lord their **G**. .... Lk 1:16
are not obeying **G** back to the .... Lk 1:17
I stand before **G**, who sent me to .... Lk 1:19
G sent the angel Gabriel to .... Lk 1:26
G has shown you his grace. .... Lk 1:30
The Lord **G** will give him the .... Lk 1:32
and will be called the Son of **G**. .... Lk 1:35
G can do anything!" .... Lk 1:37
G has blessed you more than any .... Lk 1:42

heart rejoices in **G** my Savior,.................. Lk 1:47
G will show his mercy forever .... Lk 1:50
again, and he began praising **G**.............. Lk 1:64
the Lord, the **G** of Israel,.................... Lk 1:68
G promised Abraham, our father, ... Lk 1:73
and good before **G** as long as we .... Lk 1:75
a prophet of the Most High **G**. .... Lk 1:76
With the loving mercy of our **G**, ... Lk 1:78
angel, praising **G** and saying: .... Lk 2:13
Give glory to **G** in heaven, ... Lk 2:14
among the people who please **G**." .... Lk 2:14
praising **G** and thanking him for .... Lk 2:20
the time when **G** would take away .... Lk 2:25
baby in his arms and thanked **G**: .... Lk 2:28
G has chosen this child to cause .... Lk 2:34
a sign from **G** that many people .... Lk 2:34
left the Temple but worshiped **G**, ... Lk 2:37
she thanked **G** and spoke about .... Lk 2:38
were waiting for **G** to free .... Lk 2:38
liked him, and he pleased **G**. .... Lk 2:52
the word of **G** came to John son .... Lk 3:2
about the salvation of **G**!' " .... Lk 3:6
' I tell you that **G** could make .... Lk 3:8
of Adam. Adam was the son of **G**. .... Lk 3:38
are the Son of **G**, tell this rock .... Lk 4:3
Lord your **G** and serve only him. .... Lk 4:8
you are the Son of **G**, jump down. .... Lk 4:9
'Do not test the Lord your **G**.' " .... Lk 4:12
G sent me to free those who have .... Lk 4:18
"You are the Son of **G**." .... Lk 4:41
him to hear the word of **G**. .... Lk 5:1
who is speaking as if he were **G**? .... Lk 5:21
Only **G** can forgive sins." .... Lk 5:21
mat, and went home, praising **G**. .... Lk 5:25
amazed and began to praise **G**. .... Lk 5:26
he spent the night praying to **G**. .... Lk 6:12
the kingdom of **G** belongs to you. .... Lk 6:20
be children of the Most High **G**, ... Lk 6:35
is the way **G** will give to you. .... Lk 6:38
amazed and began praising **G**, ... Lk 7:16
G has come to help his people." .... Lk 7:16
the kingdom of **G** is greater than .... Lk 7:28
secrets about the kingdom of **G**. .... Lk 8:10
Jesus, Son of the Most High **G**? .... Lk 8:28
how much **G** has done for you. .... Lk 8:39
he thanked **G** for the food. .... Lk 9:16
"You are the Christ from **G**." .... Lk 9:20
kingdom of **G** before they die. .... Lk 9:27
amazed at the great power of **G**............. Lk 9:43
tell about the kingdom of **G**." .... Lk 9:60
of no use in the kingdom of **G**." .... Lk 9:62
So pray to **G**, who owns the .... Lk 10:2
'The kingdom of **G** is near you.' .... Lk 10:9
that the kingdom of **G** is near.' .... Lk 10:11
the Lord your **G** with all your................ Lk 10:27
you, ask, and **G** will give to you .... Lk 11:9
use the power of **G** to force out .... Lk 11:20
kingdom of **G** has come to you. .... Lk 11:20
the teaching of **G** and obey it." .... Lk 11:28
give **G** one-tenth of even your................ Lk 11:42
be fair to others and to love **G**. .... Lk 11:42
is why in his wisdom **G** said, ' .... Lk 11:49
the key to learning about **G**. .... Lk 11:52
G does not forget any of them. .... Lk 12:6
But **G** even knows how many hairs .... Lk 12:7
the angels of **G** that they belong........... Lk 12:8
the angels of **G** that they do not .... Lk 12:9
But **G** said to him, 'Foolish man! .... Lk 12:20
and are not rich toward **G**." .... Lk 12:21
or barns, but **G** feeds them. .... Lk 12:24
G clothes the grass in the field, ... Lk 12:28
how much more will **G** clothe you? .... Lk 12:28
they were sacrificing to **G**. .... Lk 13:1

straight and began praising **G**. ....Lk 13:13
the table in the kingdom of **G**. ....Lk 13:29
'**G** bless the One who comes in ....Lk 13:35
the angels of **G** when one sinner ....Lk 15:10
against **G** and against you. ....Lk 15:18
against **G** and against you. ....Lk 15:21
cannot serve both **G** and worldly ....Lk 16:13
but **G** knows what is really in..................Lk 16:15
the kingdom of **G** is being told, ...Lk 16:16
praising **G** in a loud voice. ....Lk 17:15
one who came back to thank **G**?" ....Lk 17:18
will the kingdom of **G** come?" ....Lk 17:20
did not respect **G** or care about ....Lk 18:2
I don't respect **G** or care about ....Lk 18:4
G will always give what is right ....Lk 18:7
G will help his people quickly. ....Lk 18:8
and prayed, '**G**, I thank you that ....Lk 18:11
He said, '**G**, have mercy on me, a ....Lk 18:13
was right with **G**, but the ....Lk 18:14
the kingdom of **G** belongs to ....Lk 18:16
the kingdom of **G** as if you were ....Lk 18:17
call me good? Only **G** is good. ....Lk 18:19
to enter the kingdom of **G**. ....Lk 18:24
to enter the kingdom of **G**." ....Lk 18:25
for people are possible for **G**." ....Lk 18:27
or children for the kingdom of **G** ....Lk 18:29
he followed Jesus, thanking **G**. ....Lk 18:43
people who saw this praised **G**. ....Lk 18:43
shouting praise to **G** for all the ....Lk 19:37
G bless the king who comes in ....Lk 19:38
peace in heaven and glory to **G**!" ....Lk 19:38
time when **G** came to save you. ....Lk 19:44
authority from **G** or just from ....Lk 20:4
'John's baptism was from **G**,' ....Lk 20:5
give to **G** the things that are ....Lk 20:25
are children of **G**, because they ....Lk 20:36
the Lord is 'the **G** of Abraham, ...Lk 20:37
God of Abraham, the **G** of Isaac, ...Lk 20:37
of Isaac, and the **G** of Jacob.' ....Lk 20:37
G is the God of the living, ...Lk 20:38
God is the **G** of the living, ...Lk 20:38
stones and gifts offered to **G**. ....Lk 21:5
and **G** will be angry with these ....Lk 21:23
the time when **G** will free you is..............Lk 21:28
meaning in the kingdom of **G**." ....Lk 22:16
agreement that **G** makes with his ....Lk 22:20
What **G** has planned for the Son ....Lk 22:22
right hand of the powerful **G**." ....Lk 22:69
"Then are you the Son of **G**?" ....Lk 22:70
and said, "You should fear **G**! ....Lk 23:40
he praised **G**, saying, "Surely ....Lk 23:47
for the kingdom of **G** to come. ....Lk 23:51
before **G** and all the people. ....Lk 24:19
Temple all the time, praising **G**. ....Lk 24:53
Word was with **G**, and the Word ....Jn 1:1
with God, and the Word was **G**. ....Jn 1:1
He was with **G** in the beginning. ....Jn 1:2
named John who was sent by **G**. ....Jn 1:6
right to become children of **G**. ....Jn 1:12
desire. They were born of **G**. ....Jn 1:13
has ever seen **G**. But God the ....Jn 1:18
But **G** the only Son is very close..............Jn 1:18
he has shown us what **G** is like. ....Jn 1:18
the Lamb of **G**, who takes away ....Jn 1:29
This man is the Son of **G**." ....Jn 1:34
he said, "Look, the Lamb of **G**!" ....Jn 1:36
Teacher, you are the Son of **G**; ....Jn 1:49
and 'angels of **G** going up and ....Jn 1:51
you are a teacher sent from **G**, ...Jn 3:2
you do unless **G** is with him." ....Jn 3:2
G loved the world so much that ....Jn 3:16
G did not send his Son into the ....Jn 3:17
they do were done through **G**." ....Jn 3:21

can get only what **G** gives him. ....Jn 3:27
says has proven that **G** is true. ....Jn 3:33
The One whom **G** sent speaks the ....Jn 3:34
God sent speaks the words of **G**, ...Jn 3:34
G gives him the Spirit fully. ....Jn 3:34
the free gift of **G** and who it is ....Jn 4:10
G is spirit, and those who ....Jn 4:24
Now he says that **G** is his own ....Jn 5:18
making himself equal with **G**!" ....Jn 5:18
hear the voice of the Son of **G**, ...Jn 5:25
that comes from the only **G**. ....Jn 5:44
bread, thanked **G** for them, and ....Jn 6:11
because on him **G** the Father has ....Jn 6:27
the things **G** wants us to do?" ....Jn 6:28
The work **G** wants you to do is ....Jn 6:29
to do what **G** wants me to do,..................Jn 6:38
lose even one whom **G** gave me,..............Jn 6:39
'They will all be taught by **G**.' ....Jn 6:45
except the One who is from **G**; ....Jn 6:46
you are the Holy One from **G**." ....Jn 6:69
choose to do what **G** wants, ...Jn 7:17
comes from **G** and not from me..............Jn 7:17
the truth which I heard from **G**, ...Jn 8:40
father was. **G** is our Father; he ....Jn 8:41
If **G** were really your Father, ...Jn 8:42
I came from **G** and now I am here ....Jn 8:42
by my own authority; **G** sent me. ....Jn 8:42
belongs to **G** accepts what God ....Jn 8:47
to God accepts what **G** says. ....Jn 8:47
you don't accept what **G** says, ...Jn 8:47
because you don't belong to **G**." ....Jn 8:47
and you say he is your **G**. ....Jn 8:54
day, so he is not from **G**." ....Jn 9:16
You should give **G** the glory by ....Jn 9:24
We know that **G** spoke to Moses, ...Jn 9:29
all know that **G** does not listen ....Jn 9:31
If this man were not from **G**, ...Jn 9:33
but because you speak against **G**. ....Jn 10:33
you say you are the same as **G**!" ....Jn 10:33
in your law that **G** said, '......................Jn 10:34
speak against **G** because I said, ...Jn 10:36
I am the one **G** chose and sent ....Jn 10:36
the glory of **G**, to bring glory ....Jn 11:4
to bring glory to the Son of **G**." ....Jn 11:4
that even now **G** will give you ....Jn 11:22
the Son of **G**, the One coming to ....Jn 11:27
you would see the glory of **G**?" ....Jn 11:40
meet Jesus, shouting, "Praise **G**! ....Jn 12:13
G bless the One who comes in the ....Jn 12:13
G bless the King of Israel!" ....Jn 12:13
people more than praise from **G**. ....Jn 12:43
he had come from **G** and was going ....Jn 13:3
God and was going back to **G**. ....Jn 13:3
G receives glory through him. ....Jn 13:31
If **G** receives glory through him,..............Jn 13:32
then **G** will give glory to the ....Jn 13:32
G will give him glory quickly....................Jn 13:32
Trust in **G**, and trust in me......................Jn 14:1
they are offering service to **G**. ....Jn 16:2
being right with **G**, and about..................Jn 16:8
being right with **G** comes from my...........Jn 16:10
and believed that I came from **G**. ....Jn 16:27
us believe you came from **G**." ....Jn 16:30
the only true **G**, and that they..................Jn 17:3
he said he is the Son of **G**." ....Jn 19:7
is the power given to you by **G**. ....Jn 19:11
Father, to my **G** and your God.'" ....Jn 20:17
Father, to my God and your **G**.'" ....Jn 20:17
said to him, "My Lord and my **G**!"...........Jn 20:28
is the Christ, the Son of **G**. ....Jn 20:31
would die to give glory to **G**. ....Jn 21:19
to them about the kingdom of **G**. ....Ac 1:3
the great things **G** has done!"..................Ac 2:11

'G says: In the last days I will .... Ac 2:17
G clearly showed this to you by .... Ac 2:22
G raised Jesus from the dead and .... Ac 2:24
and knew G had promised him .... Ac 2:30
the One whom G raised from the .... Ac 2:32
G has made Jesus—the man you .... Ac 2:36
Lord our G calls to himself." .... Ac 2:39
felt great respect for G. .... Ac 2:43
They praised G and were liked by .... Ac 2:47
and jumping and praising G. .... Ac 3:8
The G of Abraham, Isaac, and .... Ac 3:13
and Jacob, the G of our .... Ac 3:13
but G raised him from the dead. .... Ac 3:15
G said through the prophets that .... Ac 3:18
And now G has made these things .... Ac 3:18
Come back to G, and he will .... Ac 3:19
G told about this time long ago .... Ac 3:21
'The Lord your G will give you a .... Ac 3:22
who spoke for G after Samuel, ... Ac 3:24
the agreement G made with your .... Ac 3:25
G has raised up his servant .... Ac 3:26
but G raised him from the dead. .... Ac 4:10
You decide what G would want. .... Ac 4:19
want. Should we obey you or G? .... Ac 4:19
praising G for what had been .... Ac 4:21
they prayed to G together, ... Ac 4:24
And G blessed all the believers .... Ac 4:33
You lied to G, not to us!" .... Ac 5:4
We must obey G, not human .... Ac 5:29
But G, the God of our ancestors, ... Ac 5:30
But God, the G of our ancestors, ... Ac 5:30
the One whom G raised to be on .... Ac 5:31
whom G has given to all who obey .... Ac 5:32
if it is from G, you will not be .... Ac 5:39
be fighting against G himself!" .... Ac 5:39
and to teach the word of G." .... Ac 6:4
The word of G was continuing to .... Ac 6:7
richly blessed by G who gave him .... Ac 6:8
against Moses and against G." .... Ac 6:11
Our glorious G appeared to .... Ac 7:2
G said to Abraham, 'Leave your .... Ac 7:3
G sent him to this place where .... Ac 7:4
G did not give Abraham any of .... Ac 7:5
G promised that he would give .... Ac 7:5
This is what G said to him: ' .... Ac 7:6
G made an agreement with Abraham, ... Ac 7:8
in Egypt. But G was with him .... Ac 7:9
of the wisdom G gave him. .... Ac 7:10
The promise G made to Abraham .... Ac 7:17
understand that G was using him .... Ac 7:25
'I am the G of your ancestors, ... Ac 7:32
ancestors, the G of Abraham, ... Ac 7:32
is the same man G sent to be a .... Ac 7:35
'G will give you a prophet like .... Ac 7:37
commands from G that give life, ... Ac 7:38
G turned against them and did .... Ac 7:42
G says, 'People of Israel, you .... Ac 7:42
of the star g Rephan that you .... Ac 7:43
Holy Tent where G spoke to our .... Ac 7:44
G told Moses how to make this .... Ac 7:44
it like the plan G showed him. .... Ac 7:44
and G forced the other people .... Ac 7:45
who pleased G and asked God to .... Ac 7:46
God and asked G to let him build .... Ac 7:46
a house for him, the G of Jacob. .... Ac 7:46
have not given your hearts to G, ... Ac 7:51
which G gave you through his .... Ac 7:53
saw the glory of G and Jesus .... Ac 7:55
This man has the power of G, ... Ac 8:10
the kingdom of G and the power .... Ac 8:12
had accepted the word of G, ... Ac 8:14
heart is not right before G. .... Ac 8:21
Jesus Christ is the Son of G." .... Ac 8:37

saying, "Jesus is the Son of G." .... Ac 9:20
his house worshiped the true G. .... Ac 10:2
the poor and prayed to G often. .... Ac 10:2
An angel of G came to him and .... Ac 10:3
G has heard your prayers. .... Ac 10:4
G has made these things clean, ... Ac 10:15
he worships G. All the people .... Ac 10:22
But G has shown me that I should .... Ac 10:28
G has heard your prayer and has .... Ac 10:31
all here before G to hear. .... Ac 10:33
now that to G every person is .... Ac 10:34
every country G accepts anyone .... Ac 10:35
the message that G has sent to .... Ac 10:36
that G gave him the Holy Spirit .... Ac 10:38
devil, because G was with him. .... Ac 10:38
G raised Jesus to life and .... Ac 10:40
by the witnesses G had already .... Ac 10:41
he is the one whom G chose to be .... Ac 10:42
languages and praising G. .... Ac 10:46
'G has made these things clean, ... Ac 11:9
Since G gave them the same gift .... Ac 11:17
how could I stop the work of G?" .... Ac 11:17
They praised G and said, "So God .... Ac 11:18
So G is allowing even other .... Ac 11:18
prayed earnestly to G for him. .... Ac 12:5
This is the voice of a g, ... Ac 12:22
did not give the glory to G, ... Ac 12:23
the Good News of G in the .... Ac 13:5
wanted to hear the message of G. .... Ac 13:7
and you who worship G, ... Ac 13:16
G of the Israelites chose our .... Ac 13:17
G destroyed seven nations in the .... Ac 13:19
G gave them judges until the .... Ac 13:20
so G gave them Saul son of Kish. .... Ac 13:21
After G took him away, God made .... Ac 13:22
him away, G made David their .... Ac 13:22
their king. G said about him: ' .... Ac 13:22
So G has brought Jesus, one of .... Ac 13:23
others who worship G, listen! .... Ac 13:26
G raised him up from the dead! .... Ac 13:30
about the promise G made to our .... Ac 13:32
G has made this promise come .... Ac 13:33
G raised Jesus from the dead, ... Ac 13:34
become dust. So G said: 'I will .... Ac 13:34
But in another place G says: ' .... Ac 13:35
But the One G raised from the .... Ac 13:37
to worship G followed Paul. .... Ac 13:43
the message of G to you first. .... Ac 13:46
he believed G could heal him. .... Ac 14:9
things and turn to the living G. .... Ac 14:15
G let all the nations do what .... Ac 14:16
all about what G had done with .... Ac 14:27
with them and how G had made it .... Ac 14:27
other nations had turned to G. .... Ac 15:3
about everything G had done with .... Ac 15:4
the early days G chose me from .... Ac 15:7
G, who knows the thoughts of .... Ac 15:8
To G, those people are not .... Ac 15:9
are you testing G by putting a .... Ac 15:10
signs that G did through them .... Ac 15:12
told us how G showed his love .... Ac 15:14
people who are turning to G. .... Ac 15:19
that G had called us to .... Ac 16:10
She worshiped G, and he opened .... Ac 16:14
are servants of the Most High G. .... Ac 16:17
singing songs to G as the other .... Ac 16:25
because they now believed in G. .... Ac 16:34
Greeks who worshiped G and many .... Ac 17:4
the word of G in Berea. .... Ac 17:13
and the Greeks who worshiped G. .... Ac 17:17
TO A G WHO IS NOT KNOWN. .... Ac 17:23
You worship a g that you don't .... Ac 17:23
and this is the G I am telling .... Ac 17:23

G

The G who made the whole world .... Ac 17:24
G is the One who gives life, ... Ac 17:25
G began by making one person, ... Ac 17:26
G decided exactly when and where .... Ac 17:26
G wanted them to look for him .... Ac 17:27
not think that G is like .... Ac 17:29
people did not understand G, ... Ac 17:30
G tells all people in the world................ Ac 17:30
G has set a day that he will................... Ac 17:31
G has proved this to everyone .... Ac 17:31
synagogue. This man worshiped G. .... Ac 18:7
to worship G in a way that is .... Ac 18:13
he had made a promise to G. .... Ac 18:18
to you again if G wants me to." .... Ac 18:21
better understand the way of G. .... Ac 18:26
he said about the kingdom of G.............. Ac 19:8
G used Paul to do some very .... Ac 19:11
lives and turn to G and believe .... Ac 20:21
the kingdom of G will ever see .... Ac 20:25
everything G wants you to know. .... Ac 20:27
shepherds to the church of G,................ Ac 20:28
in the care of G and the message .... Ac 20:32
the blessings G has for all his................ Ac 20:32
them everything G had done among .... Ac 21:19
they heard this, they praised G. .... Ac 21:20
men have made a promise to G. .... Ac 21:23
very serious about serving G, ... Ac 22:3
'The G of our ancestors chose .... Ac 22:14
before G up to this day." .... Ac 23:1
to Ananias, "G will hit you, too .... Ac 23:3
I worship the G of our ancestors .... Ac 24:14
same love in G that they have— .... Ac 24:15
is right before G and people. .... Ac 24:16
and the time when G will judge .... Ac 24:25
the promise that G made to our .... Ac 26:6
as they serve G day and night. .... Ac 26:7
impossible for G to raise people .... Ac 26:8
the power of Satan and to G. .... Ac 26:18
and turn to G and do things to .... Ac 26:20
But G has helped me, and so I .... Ac 26:22
pray to G that not only you but .... Ac 26:29
came to me from the G I belong .... Ac 27:23
And G has promised you that he .... Ac 27:24
trust in G that everything will................ Ac 27:25
and thanked G for it before all .... Ac 27:35
minds and said, "He is a g!" .... Ac 28:6
he was encouraged and thanked G. .... Ac 28:15
he explained the kingdom of G, ... Ac 28:23
you to know that G has also sent .... Ac 28:28
kingdom of G and taught about .... Ac 28:31
G called me to be an apostle and .... Rm 1:1
G promised this Good News long .... Rm 1:2
G gave me the special work of an .... Rm 1:5
you in Rome whom G loves and has .... Rm 1:7
peace to you from G our Father .... Rm 1:7
that I thank my G through Jesus .... Rm 1:8
G, whom I serve with my whole .... Rm 1:9
this will happen if G wants it................. Rm 1:10
it is the power G uses to save .... Rm 1:16
News shows how G makes people .... Rm 1:17
are right with G will live by .... Rm 1:17
G shows his anger because some .... Rm 1:19
G has shown himself to them. .... Rm 1:19
all the things that make him G. .... Rm 1:20
understand by what G has made. .... Rm 1:20
They knew G, but they did not .... Rm 1:21
give glory to G or thank him. .... Rm 1:21
the glory of G who lives forever .... Rm 1:23
G left them and let them go .... Rm 1:24
traded the truth of G for a lie............... Rm 1:25
instead of the G who created .... Rm 1:25
G left them and let them do the .... Rm 1:26
to have a true knowledge of G. .... Rm 1:28

So G left them and allowed them .... Rm 1:28
other. They hate G. They are .... Rm 1:30
G judges those who do wrong .... Rm 2:2
to escape the judgment of G? .... Rm 2:3
understand that G is kind to you .... Rm 2:4
G will reward or punish every .... Rm 2:6
G will give them life forever. .... Rm 2:7
G will give them his punishment .... Rm 2:8
For G judges all people in the .... Rm 2:11
not make people right with G. .... Rm 2:13
will happen on the day when G, ... Rm 2:16
brag that you are close to G. .... Rm 2:17
bring shame to G by breaking his .... Rm 2:23
gets praise from G rather than .... Rm 2:29
G trusted the Jews with his.................... Rm 3:2
will that stop G from doing what .... Rm 3:3
G will continue to be true even .... Rm 3:4
more clearly that G is right. .... Rm 3:5
can we say that G is wrong to................ Rm 3:5
If G could not punish us, he .... Rm 3:6
no one who looks to G for help. .... Rm 3:11
"They have no fear of G." .... Rm 3:18
made right with G by following .... Rm 3:20
But G has a way to make people .... Rm 3:21
G makes people right with .... Rm 3:22
made right with G by his grace, ... Rm 3:24
G sent him to die in our place................ Rm 3:25
showed that G always does what .... Rm 3:25
And G gave Jesus to show today .... Rm 3:26
G did this so he could judge .... Rm 3:26
made right with G through faith, ... Rm 3:28
Is G only the God of the Jews? .... Rm 3:29
Is God only the G of the Jews? .... Rm 3:29
he not also the G of those who .... Rm 3:29
because there is only one G. .... Rm 3:30
Abraham believed G, and God .... Rm 4:3
and G accepted Abraham's faith, ... Rm 4:3
faith made him right with G." .... Rm 4:3
will make them right with G. .... Rm 4:5
Then G accepts their faith, ... Rm 4:5
people are truly blessed when G, ... Rm 4:6
already said that G accepted .... Rm 4:9
faith made him right with G. .... Rm 4:9
Did G accept Abraham before or .... Rm 4:10
was right with G through faith .... Rm 4:11
accepted as being right with G. .... Rm 4:11
being right with G by his faith. .... Rm 4:13
could receive what G promised by .... Rm 4:14
true before G, the God Abraham .... Rm 4:17
before God, the G Abraham .... Rm 4:17
the G who gives life to the dead .... Rm 4:17
Abraham believed G and continued .... Rm 4:18
As G told him, "Your descendants .... Rm 4:18
his faith in G did not become .... Rm 4:19
doubted that G would keep his .... Rm 4:20
his faith and gave praise to G. .... Rm 4:20
felt sure that G was able to do .... Rm 4:21
G accepted Abraham's faith, ... Rm 4:22
faith made him right with G.".................. Rm 4:22
"G accepted Abraham's faith" .... Rm 4:23
G will accept us also because we .... Rm 4:24
dead to make us right with G. .... Rm 4:25
made right with G by our faith, ... Rm 5:1
our faith, we have peace with G. .... Rm 5:1
because G has poured out his................. Rm 5:5
Spirit, whom G has given to us. .... Rm 5:5
we were living against G. .... Rm 5:6
But G shows his great love for .... Rm 5:8
made right with G by the blood .... Rm 5:9
very happy with G through our Lord .... Rm 5:11
the grace from G was much .... Rm 5:15
But the gift of G is different. .... Rm 5:16
it makes people right with G. .... Rm 5:16

makes all people right with **G**. .... Rm 5:18
man disobeyed **G**, and many became .... Rm 5:18
one man obeyed **G**, and many will .... Rm 5:19
but **G** gave people more of his .... Rm 5:21
sinning so that **G** will give us .... Rm 6:1
and his new life is with **G**. .... Rm 6:10
and alive with **G** through Christ .... Rm 6:11
yourselves to **G** as people who .... Rm 6:13
of your body to be used in .... Rm 6:13
or you can obey **G**, which makes .... Rm 6:16
thank **G**, you fully obeyed the................. Rm 6:17
Then you will live only for **G**. .... Rm 6:19
sin and have become slaves of **G**. .... Rm 6:22
you a life that is only for **G**, ... Rm 6:22
But **G** gives us the free gift of .... Rm 6:23
might be used in service to **G**. .... Rm 7:4
So now we serve **G** in a new way .... Rm 7:6
I thank **G** for saving me through .... Rm 7:25
But **G** did what the law could not .... Rm 8:3
G used a human life to destroy .... Rm 8:3
they are against **G**, because they .... Rm 8:7
sinful selves cannot please **G**................. Rm 8:8
if that Spirit of **G** really lives .... Rm 8:9
Christ made you right with **G**. .... Rm 8:10
G raised Jesus from the dead,................. Rm 8:11
G is the One who raised Christ .... Rm 8:11
true children of **G** are those who .... Rm 8:14
it makes us children of **G**. .... Rm 8:15
blessings from **G** together with .... Rm 8:17
Everything **G** made is waiting .... Rm 8:19
with excitement for **G** to show .... Rm 8:19
Everything **G** made was changed to .... Rm 8:20
own wish but because **G** wanted it .... Rm 8:20
that everything **G** made would be .... Rm 8:21
that everything **G** made has been .... Rm 8:22
are waiting for **G** to finish .... Rm 8:23
himself speaks to **G** for us, ... Rm 8:26
even begs **G** for us with deep .... Rm 8:26
G can see what is in people's .... Rm 8:27
speaks to **G** for his people .... Rm 8:27
his people in the way **G** wants. .... Rm 8:27
in everything **G** works for the............... Rm 8:28
G knew them before he made the .... Rm 8:29
G planned for them to be like................ Rm 8:30
G is for us, no one can defeat .... Rm 8:31
G will surely give us all things. .... Rm 8:32
accuse the people **G** has chosen? .... Rm 8:33
because **G** is the One who makes .... Rm 8:33
side, appealing to **G** for us..................... Rm 8:34
through **G** who showed his .... Rm 8:37
from the love of **G** that is in .... Rm 8:39
They have seen the glory of **G**, ... Rm 9:4
agreements that **G** made between .... Rm 9:4
G gave them the law of Moses and........... Rm 9:4
was born, who is **G** over all. .... Rm 9:5
It is not that **G** failed to keep .... Rm 9:6
Abraham. But **G** said to Abraham .... Rm 9:7
the promise **G** made to Abraham. .... Rm 9:9
about this? Is **G** unfair? In no .... Rm 9:14
G said to Moses, "I will show .... Rm 9:15
So **G** will choose the one to whom .... Rm 9:16
So **G** shows mercy where he wants .... Rm 9:18
Then why does **G** blame us for our........... Rm 9:19
have no right to question **G**. .... Rm 9:20
It is the same way with **G**. .... Rm 9:22
are those people whom **G** called. .... Rm 9:24
children of the living **G**.'" .... Rm 9:26
to make themselves right with **G**, ... Rm 9:30
made right with **G** because of................. Rm 9:30
to make themselves right with **G**. .... Rm 9:31
of trusting in **G** to make them............... Rm 9:32
saved. That is my prayer to **G**. .... Rm 10:1
They really try to follow **G**,................... Rm 10:2

know the way that **G** makes people .... Rm 10:3
in him may be right with **G**. .... Rm 10:4
your heart that **G** raised Jesus .... Rm 10:9
and so we are made right with **G**. .... Rm 10:10
about Israel **G** says, "All day .... Rm 10:21
Did **G** throw out his people? .... Rm 11:1
G chose the Israelites to be his .... Rm 11:2
how he prayed to **G** against the .... Rm 11:2
what answer did **G** give Elijah? .... Rm 11:4
few people that **G** has chosen by .... Rm 11:5
tried to be right with **G**, ... Rm 11:7
but the ones **G** chose did become .... Rm 11:7
and refused to listen to **G**. .... Rm 11:7
G gave the people a dull mind so .... Rm 11:8
the kind of people **G** wants. .... Rm 11:12
G turned away from the Jews, ... Rm 11:15
So when **G** accepts the Jews, ... Rm 11:15
piece of bread is offered to **G**,............... Rm 11:16
If **G** did not let the natural .... Rm 11:21
So you see that **G** is kind and................. Rm 11:22
But **G** is kind to you, if you .... Rm 11:22
Jews will believe in **G** again, ... Rm 11:23
G is able to put them back where .... Rm 11:23
who are not Jews have come to **G**. .... Rm 11:25
G never changes his mind about .... Rm 11:29
one time you refused to obey **G**, ... Rm 11:30
because **G** showed mercy to you. .... Rm 11:31
G has given all people over to .... Rm 11:32
explain the things **G** decides or .... Rm 11:33
has ever given **G** anything that .... Rm 11:35
Yes, **G** made all things, and .... Rm 11:36
G has shown us great mercy, ... Rm 12:1
be only for **G** and pleasing to .... Rm 12:1
to decide what **G** wants for you;............ Rm 12:2
Because **G** has given me a special .... Rm 12:3
amount of faith **G** has given you. .... Rm 12:3
because of the grace **G** gave us. .... Rm 12:6
but wait for **G** to punish them............... Rm 12:19
one rules unless **G** has given him .... Rm 13:1
now without that power from **G**,........... Rm 13:1
against what **G** has commanded. .... Rm 13:2
are working for **G** and give their .... Rm 13:6
G has accepted that person. .... Rm 14:3
and they give thanks to **G**. .... Rm 14:6
Lord, and they give thanks to **G**. .... Rm 14:6
all stand before **G** to be judged, ... Rm 14:10
will say that I am **G**.'" .... Rm 14:11
of us will have to answer to **G**. .... Rm 14:12
In the kingdom of **G**, eating and............. Rm 14:17
things are living right with **G**,................ Rm 14:17
way is pleasing **G** and will be .... Rm 14:18
of food destroy the work of **G**. .... Rm 14:20
kept secret between you and **G**. .... Rm 14:22
that come from **G** allow you to .... Rm 15:5
give glory to **G** the Father of .... Rm 15:6
which will bring glory to **G**. .... Rm 15:7
give glory to **G** for the mercy he............. Rm 15:9
I pray that the **G** who gives hope .... Rm 15:13
did this because **G** gave me this .... Rm 15:15
I served **G** by teaching his Good............ Rm 15:16
an offering that **G** would accept— .... Rm 15:16
have done for **G** in Christ Jesus................ Rm 15:17
who are not Jews to obey **G**. .... Rm 15:18
have obeyed **G** because of what .... Rm 15:18
my work by praying to **G** for me. .... Rm 15:30
Then, if **G** wants me to, I will .... Rm 15:32
G who gives peace be with you .... Rm 15:33
The **G** who brings peace will soon .... Rm 16:20
Glory to **G** who can make you .... Rm 16:25
the eternal **G** it is made known .... Rm 16:26
the only wise **G** be glory forever .... Rm 16:27
G called me to be an apostle of 1Co 1:1
because that is what **G** wanted. 1Co 1:1

G once said, "Let the light 2Co 4:6
This is the same G who made his 2Co 4:6
know the glory of G that is in 2Co 4:6
We have this treasure from G, ... 2Co 4:7
that the great power is from G, ... 2Co 4:7
persecuted, but G does not leave 2Co 4:9
G raised the Lord Jesus from the 2Co 4:14
we know that G will also raise 2Co 4:14
G will bring us together with 2Co 4:14
so the grace of G that is being 2Co 4:15
thanks to G for his glory. 2Co 4:15
G will have a house for us. 2Co 5:1
want G to give us our heavenly 2Co 5:2
This is what G made us for, ... 2Co 5:5
is to please G whether we live 2Co 5:9
G knows what we really are, ... 2Co 5:11
out of our minds, it is for G. 2Co 5:13
this is from G. Through Christ 2Co 5:18
G made peace between us and 2Co 5:18
G gave us the work of telling 2Co 5:18
G was in Christ, making peace 2Co 5:19
G did not hold the world guilty 2Co 5:19
It is as if G is calling to you 2Co 5:20
beg you to be at peace with G. 2Co 5:20
G made him become sin so that 2Co 5:21
we could become right with G. 2Co 5:21
We are workers together with G, ... 2Co 6:1
received from G be for nothing. 2Co 6:1
G says, "At the right time I 2Co 6:2
we show we are servants of G: 2Co 6:4
are servants of G by our pure 2Co 6:6
The temple of G cannot have any 2Co 6:16
are the temple of the living G. 2Co 6:16
living God. As G said: "I will 2Co 6:16
I will be their G, and they will 2Co 6:16
we have these promises from G, ... 2Co 7:1
we live, because we respect G. 2Co 7:1
G, who comforts those who are 2Co 7:6
sad in the way G wanted you to, ... 2Co 7:9
kind of sorrow G wants makes 2Co 7:10
the sorrow G wanted you to have— 2Co 7:11
see, before G, the great care 2Co 7:12
about the grace G gave the 2Co 8:1
and to us. This is what G wants. 2Co 8:5
I thank G because he gave Titus 2Co 8:16
G loves the person who gives 2Co 9:7
G can give you more blessings 2Co 9:8
G is the One who gives seed to 2Co 9:10
cause many to give thanks to G. 2Co 9:11
brings many more thanks to G. 2Co 9:12
will praise G because you obey 2Co 9:13
grace that G has given you. 2Co 9:14
Thanks be to G for his gift that 2Co 9:15
have power from G that can 2Co 10:4
against the knowledge of G. 2Co 10:5
to the work that G gave us, ... 2Co 10:13
a jealousy that comes from G. 2Co 11:2
G knows that I love you. 2Co 11:11
G knows I am not lying. He is 2Co 11:31
He is the G and Father of the 2Co 11:31
or out of his body, but G knows. 2Co 12:2
speaking in Christ and before G. 2Co 12:19
my G will make me ashamed before 2Co 12:21
pray to G that you will not do 2Co 13:7
the G of love and peace will 2Co 13:11
the love of G, and the 2Co 13:14
Jesus Christ and G the Father .... Gal 1:1
peace to you from G our Father .... Gal 1:3
in, as G the Father planned. .... Gal 1:4
belongs to G forever and ever. .... Gal 1:5
G, by his grace through Christ, ... Gal 1:6
G is the One I am trying to .... Gal 1:10
the church of G and tried to .... Gal 1:13

But G had special plans for me .... Gal 1:15
When G called me, I did not get .... Gal 1:16
G knows that these things I .... Gal 1:20
praised G because of me. .... Gal 1:24
I went because G showed me I .... Gal 2:2
To G everyone is the same. .... Gal 2:6
G gave Peter the power to work .... Gal 2:8
understood that G had given me .... Gal 2:9
made right with G not by .... Gal 2:16
made right with G because we .... Gal 2:16
made right with G by following .... Gal 2:16
trying to be made right with G, ... Gal 2:17
so that I can now live for G. .... Gal 2:19
in the Son of G who loved me, ... Gal 2:20
law could make us right with G, ... Gal 2:21
Does G give you the Spirit and .... Gal 3:5
Abraham believed G, and God .... Gal 3:6
and G accepted Abraham's faith, ... Gal 3:6
faith made him right with G." .... Gal 3:6
said that G would make the .... Gal 3:8
be made right with G by the law, ... Gal 3:11
are right with G will live by .... Gal 3:11
the Spirit that G promised. .... Gal 3:14
G made promises both to Abraham .... Gal 3:16
G did not say, "and to your .... Gal 3:16
But G said, "and to your .... Gal 3:16
G had an agreement with Abraham .... Gal 3:17
because G freely gave his .... Gal 3:18
one side, and G is only one. .... Gal 3:20
law could make us right with G. .... Gal 3:21
G did not give a law that can .... Gal 3:21
no freedom until G showed us the .... Gal 3:23
made right with G through faith. .... Gal 3:24
the promise G made to Abraham. .... Gal 3:29
G sent his Son who was born of a .... Gal 4:4
G did this so he could buy .... Gal 4:5
G sent the Spirit of his Son .... Gal 4:6
and G will give you the blessing. .... Gal 4:7
In the past you did not know G. .... Gal 4:8
But now you know the true G. .... Gal 4:9
Really, it is G who knows you. .... Gal 4:9
welcomed me as an angel from G, ... Gal 4:14
the promise G made to Abraham. .... Gal 4:23
between G and his people. .... Gal 4:24
is the law that G made on Mount .... Gal 4:24
right with G through the law .... Gal 5:4
from being made right with G, ... Gal 5:5
and sisters, G called you to be .... Gal 5:13
the teaching of G should share .... Gal 6:6
cannot cheat G. People harvest .... Gal 6:7
being the new people G has made. .... Gal 6:15
because that is what G wanted. .... Eph 1:1
peace to you from G our Father .... Eph 1:2
Praise be to the G and Father of .... Eph 1:3
G has given us every spiritual. .... Eph 1:3
G had already decided to make us .... Eph 1:5
brings praise to G because of .... Eph 1:6
G gave that grace to us freely, ... Eph 1:6
G, with full wisdom and .... Eph 1:8
This was what G wanted, and he .... Eph 1:9
beginning G had decided this .... Eph 1:11
G put his special mark of .... Eph 1:13
receive what G promised for his .... Eph 1:14
his people until G gives full .... Eph 1:14
giving thanks to G for you. .... Eph 1:16
asking the G of our Lord Jesus .... Eph 1:17
the blessings G has promised his .... Eph 1:18
G used to raise Christ from the .... Eph 1:20
G has put Christ over all rulers, ... Eph 1:21
G put everything under his power .... Eph 1:22
the things you did against G. .... Eph 2:1
in those who refuse to obey G. .... Eph 2:2
of the things we did against G, ... Eph 2:5

G

you to the other churches of **G**. 2Th 1:4
is proof that **G** is right in his 2Th 1:5
G will do what is right. 2Th 1:6
who do not know **G** and who do not 2Th 1:8
asking our **G** to help you live 2Th 1:11
with his power **G** will help you 2Th 1:11
the grace of our **G** and the Lord 2Th 1:12
turning away from **G** happens and 2Th 2:3
any so-called **g** or anything that 2Th 2:4
sit there and say that he is **G**. 2Th 2:4
For this reason **G** sends them 2Th 2:11
G chose you from the beginning 2Th 2:13
we must always thank **G** for you. 2Th 2:13
G used the Good News that we 2Th 2:14
by the command of **G** our Savior 1Ti 1:1
and peace from **G** the Father and 1Ti 1:2
are against **G** and are sinful, ... 1Ti 1:9
against the true teaching of **G**. 1Ti 1:10
of the blessed **G** that he gave me 1Ti 1:11
But **G** showed me mercy, because I 1Ti 1:13
seen, the only **G**, be honor and 1Ti 1:17
learn not to speak against **G**. 1Ti 1:20
asking **G** for what they need and 1Ti 2:1
of worship and respect for **G**. 1Ti 2:2
and it pleases **G** our Savior, ... 1Ti 2:3
There is one **G** and one mediator 1Ti 2:5
that human beings can reach **G**. 1Ti 2:5
women who say they worship **G**. 1Ti 2:10
the faith that **G** made known to 1Ti 3:9
how to live in the family of **G**. 1Ti 3:15
is the church of the living **G**, ... 1Ti 3:15
foods which **G** created to be 1Ti 4:3
Everything **G** made is good, ... 1Ti 4:4
is made holy by what **G** has said 1Ti 4:5
but train yourself to serve **G**. 1Ti 4:7
but serving **G** helps you in every 1Ti 4:8
in the living **G** who is the 1Ti 4:10
or grandparents. That pleases **G**. 1Ti 5:4
her hope in **G** and continues to 1Ti 5:5
who does not believe in **G**. 1Ti 5:8
Before **G** and Christ Jesus and 1Ti 5:21
shows the true way to serve **G**. 1Ti 6:3
that serving **G** is a way to get 1Ti 6:5
G does make us very rich, ... 1Ti 6:6
But you, man of **G**, run away from 1Ti 6:11
right way, serve **G**, have faith, ... 1Ti 6:11
the sight of **G**, who gives life 1Ti 6:13
G will make that happen at his 1Ti 6:15
has ever seen **G**, or can see him 1Ti 6:16
and power belong to **G** forever. 1Ti 6:16
them to hope in **G**, not in their 1Ti 6:17
G richly gives us everything to 1Ti 6:17
guard what **G** has trusted to you. 1Ti 6:20
Christ Jesus by the will of **G**. 2Ti 1:1
G sent me to tell about the 2Ti 1:1
peace to you from **G** the Father 2Ti 1:2
thank **G** as I always mention you 2Ti 1:3
using the gift **G** gave you when I 2Ti 1:6
G did not give us a spirit that 2Ti 1:7
G, who gives us the strength to 2Ti 1:8
that those whom **G** has chosen can 2Ti 2:10
give yourself to **G** as the kind 2Ti 2:15
lead people further away from **G**. 2Ti 2:16
maybe **G** will let them change 2Ti 2:25
be the kind of people **G** wants. 2Ti 3:2
will love pleasure instead of **G**, ... 2Ti 3:4
as if they serve **G** but will not 2Ti 3:5
who wants to live as **G** desires, ... 2Ti 3:12
is inspired by **G** and is useful 2Ti 3:16
who serves **G** will be capable, ... 2Ti 3:17
the presence of **G** and Christ 2Ti 4:1
the duties of a servant of **G**. 2Ti 4:5
being given as an offering to **G**, ... 2Ti 4:6

a crown for being right with **G**. 2Ti 4:8
a servant of **G** and an apostle of .... Tit 1:1
shows people how to serve **G**. .... Tit 1:1
which **G** promised to us before .... Tit 1:2
time began. And **G** cannot lie. .... Tit 1:2
the right time **G** let the world .... Tit 1:3
by the command of **G** our Savior. .... Tit 1:3
and peace from **G** the Father .... Tit 1:4
say they know **G**, but their .... Tit 1:16
the teaching **G** gave us. .... Tit 2:5
the teaching of **G** our Savior .... Tit 2:10
to live against **G** nor to do the .... Tit 2:12
in a way that shows we serve **G**. .... Tit 2:12
of our great **G** and Savior Jesus .... Tit 2:13
and love of **G** our Savior was .... Tit 3:4
G poured out richly upon us that .... Tit 3:6
made right with **G** by his grace, ... Tit 3:7
who believe in **G** will be careful .... Tit 3:8
peace to you from **G** our Father .... Phm 1:3
always thank my **G** when I mention .... Phm 1:4
because I hope **G** will answer .... Phm 1:22
In the past **G** spoke to our .... Heb 1:1
these last days **G** has spoken to .... Heb 1:2
G has chosen his Son to own all .... Heb 1:2
the glory of **G** and shows exactly .... Heb 1:3
shows exactly what **G** is like. .... Heb 1:3
sat down at the right side of **G**, ... Heb 1:3
and **G** gave him a name that is .... Heb 1:4
This is because **G** never said to .... Heb 1:5
Nor did **G** say of any angel, ... Heb 1:5
And when **G** brings his firstborn .... Heb 1:6
This is what **G** said about the .... Heb 1:7
G makes his angels become like .... Heb 1:7
But **G** said this about his Son: .... Heb 1:8
G, your throne will last forever .... Heb 1:8
so **G** has chosen you from among .... Heb 1:9
G also says, "Lord, in the .... Heb 1:10
And **G** never said this to an .... Heb 1:13
who serve **G** and are sent to .... Heb 1:14
The teaching **G** spoke through .... Heb 2:2
G also testified to the truth of .... Heb 2:4
G did not choose angels to be .... Heb 2:5
When **G** put everything under .... Heb 2:8
G is the One who made all things, ... Heb 2:10
also says, "I will trust in **G**." .... Heb 2:13
the children **G** has given me." .... Heb 2:13
high priest in service to **G**. .... Heb 2:17
were called by **G**, think about .... Heb 3:1
was faithful to **G** as Moses was .... Heb 3:2
of everything is **G** himself. .... Heb 3:4
and he told what **G** would say in .... Heb 3:5
past when you turned against **G**, ... Heb 3:8
when you tested **G** in the desert. .... Heb 3:8
turn you away from the living **G**. .... Heb 3:12
when you turned against **G**." .... Heb 3:15
with whom was **G** angry for forty .... Heb 3:17
And to whom was **G** talking when .... Heb 3:18
since **G** has left us the promise .... Heb 4:1
As **G** has said, "I was angry and .... Heb 4:3
seventh day **G** rested from all .... Heb 4:4
again in the Scripture **G** said, ... Heb 4:5
So **G** planned another day, called .... Heb 4:7
because **G** spoke later about .... Heb 4:8
rest from his work as **G** did. .... Heb 4:10
the world can be hidden from **G**. .... Heb 4:13
Jesus the Son of **G**, who has gone .... Heb 4:14
of going before **G** for them to .... Heb 5:1
be called by **G** as Aaron was. .... Heb 5:4
a high priest, but **G** chose him. .... Heb 5:5
G said to him, "You are my Son. .... Heb 5:5
And in another Scripture **G** says, ... Heb 5:6
he prayed to **G** and asked God for .... Heb 5:7
to God and asked **G** for help. .... Heb 5:7

G

was heard because he trusted **G.** .... Heb 5:7
though Jesus was the Son of **G,** .... Heb 5:8
In this way **G** made Jesus a high .... Heb 5:10
about faith in **G** and about .... Heb 6:1
grown-up teaching if **G** allows. .... Heb 6:3
the Son of **G** to a cross again .... Heb 6:6
to be cursed by **G** and will be .... Heb 6:8
G is fair; he will not forget .... Heb 6:10
receive what **G** has promised................... Heb 6:12
G made a promise to Abraham. .... Heb 6:13
there is no one greater than **G,** .... Heb 6:13
and he received what **G** promised. .... Heb 6:15
G wanted to prove that his .... Heb 6:17
G cannot lie when he makes a .... Heb 6:18
us who came to **G** for safety. .... Heb 6:18
and a priest for **G** Most High. .... Heb 7:1
is like the Son of **G**; .... Heb 7:3
this hope we can come near to **G.** .... Heb 7:19
important that **G** did this with .... Heb 7:20
God's oath. **G** said: "The Lord .... Heb 7:21
agreement from **G** to his people. .... Heb 7:22
those who come to **G** through him .... Heb 7:25
lives, asking **G** to help them. .... Heb 7:25
of worship that was made by **G,** .... Heb 8:2
gifts and sacrifices to **G.** .... Heb 8:3
must also offer something to **G.** .... Heb 8:3
the law by offering gifts to **G.** .... Heb 8:4
This is why **G** warned Moses when .... Heb 8:5
brought from **G** to his people is .... Heb 8:6
But **G** found something wrong with .... Heb 8:8
I will be their **G,** and they will .... Heb 8:10
G called this a new agreement, ... Heb 8:13
bread that was made holy for **G.** .... Heb 9:2
he offered to **G** for himself and .... Heb 9:7
as a perfect sacrifice to **G.** .... Heb 9:14
so we may serve the living **G.** .... Heb 9:14
agreement from **G** to his people. .... Heb 9:15
are called by **G** can now receive .... Heb 9:15
Agreement that **G** commanded you .... Heb 9:20
there now before **G** to help us. .... Heb 9:24
who come near to worship **G.** .... Heb 10:1
G, I have come to do what you .... Heb 10:7
G ends the first system of .... Heb 10:9
sat down at the right side of **G.** .... Heb 10:12
us come near to **G** with a sincere .... Heb 10:22
we can trust **G** to do what he .... Heb 10:23
all those who live against **G.** .... Heb 10:27
who do not respect the Son of **G,** .... Heb 10:29
We know that **G** said, "I will .... Heb 10:30
into the hands of the living **G.** .... Heb 10:31
you can do what **G** wants and .... Heb 10:36
that Abel offered **G** a better .... Heb 11:4
G said he was pleased with the .... Heb 11:4
because **G** had taken him away. .... Heb 11:5
was a man who truly pleased **G.**............... Heb 11:5
faith no one can please **G.** .... Heb 11:6
who comes to **G** must believe that .... Heb 11:6
He obeyed **G** and built a large .... Heb 11:7
made right with **G** through faith. .... Heb 11:7
another place **G** promised to give .... Heb 11:8
the country **G** promised to give .... Heb 11:9
that same promise from **G.** .... Heb 11:9
the city planned and built by **G.** .... Heb 11:10
he trusted **G** to do what he had .... Heb 11:11
the things that **G** promised his .... Heb 11:13
So **G** is not ashamed to be called .... Heb 11:16
ashamed to be called their **G,** .... Heb 11:16
that Abraham, when **G** tested him,........... Heb 11:17
G made the promises to Abraham,............ Heb 11:17
G had said, "The descendants I .... Heb 11:18
believed that **G** could raise the .... Heb 11:19
could see the **G** that no one can .... Heb 11:27
those who refused to obey **G.** .... Heb 11:31

received what **G** had promised. .... Heb 11:39
G planned to give us something .... Heb 11:40
the joy that **G** put before him................... Heb 12:2
G is treating you as children. .... Heb 12:7
But **G** disciplines us to help us, ... Heb 12:10
Esau and never thinks about **G.** .... Heb 12:16
to the city of the living **G,** .... Heb 12:22
You have come to **G,** the judge of .... Heb 12:23
agreement from **G** to his people, ... Heb 12:24
refuse to listen when **G** speaks. .... Heb 12:25
to listen to **G** who warns us .... Heb 12:25
should worship **G** in a way that .... Heb 12:28
because our **G** is like a fire .... Heb 12:29
G will judge as guilty those who............... Heb 13:4
G has said, "I will never leave .... Heb 13:5
always offer to **G** our sacrifice .... Heb 13:15
such sacrifices please **G.**.......................... Heb 13:16
to pray so that **G** will send me .... Heb 13:19
a servant of **G** and of the Lord .... Jam 1:1
wisdom, you should ask **G** for it. .... Jam 1:5
But when you ask **G,** you must .... Jam 1:6
take pride that **G** has made them .... Jam 1:9
take pride that **G** has shown them .... Jam 1:10
G will reward them with life .... Jam 1:12
G promised to all those who .... Jam 1:12
not say, "**G** is tempting me...................... Jam 1:13
cannot tempt **G,** and God himself .... Jam 1:13
G himself does not tempt anyone. .... Jam 1:13
every perfect gift is from **G.** .... Jam 1:17
G decided to give us life .... Jam 1:18
the right kind of life **G** wants................... Jam 1:20
Religion that **G** accepts as pure .... Jam 1:27
G chose the poor in the world to .... Jam 2:5
the kingdom **G** promised to those .... Jam 2:5
The same **G** who said, "You must .... Jam 2:11
or **G** will not show mercy to you............... Jam 2:13
to that person, "**G** will be with you! .... Jam 2:16
You believe there is one **G.** .... Jam 2:19
made right with **G** by what he did .... Jam 2:21
Abraham believed **G,** and God .... Jam 2:23
and **G** accepted Abraham's faith, ... Jam 2:23
faith made him right with **G.**"................... Jam 2:23
right with **G** by what they do .... Jam 2:24
made right with **G** by something .... Jam 2:25
people, whom **G** made like himself............ Jam 3:9
not come from **G** but from the .... Jam 3:15
that comes from **G** is first of .... Jam 3:17
want, because you do not ask **G.** .... Jam 4:2
So, you are not loyal to **G!** .... Jam 4:4
world is the same as hating **G.** .... Jam 4:4
The Spirit that **G** made to live................... Jam 4:5
But **G** gives us even more grace,............... Jam 4:6
Scripture says, "**G** is against .... Jam 4:6
give yourselves completely to **G.** .... Jam 4:7
near to **G,** and God will come .... Jam 4:8
and **G** will come near to you. .... Jam 4:8
to follow **G** and the world at .... Jam 4:8
G is the only Lawmaker and Judge. .... Jam 4:12
each other so **G** can heal you.................... Jam 5:16
G planned long ago to choose you 1Pe 1:2
G wanted you to obey him and to 1Pe 1:2
Praise be to the **G** and Father of 1Pe 1:3
for the blessings **G** has for his 1Pe 1:4
children of **G** do not live as you 1Pe 1:14
you do, just as **G,** the One who 1Pe 1:15
You pray to **G** and call him 1Pe 1:17
should live with respect for **G.** 1Pe 1:17
Through Christ you believe in **G,** 1Pe 1:21
faith and your hope are in **G.** 1Pe 1:21
but he was the stone **G** chose, ... 1Pe 2:4
offer spiritual sacrifices to **G.** 1Pe 2:5
they do not obey what **G** says, ... 1Pe 2:8
is what **G** planned to happen 1Pe 2:8

G

desires which are against **G**." .... Jud 1:18
G is strong and can help you not .... Jud 1:24
He is the only **G**, the One who .... Jud 1:25
Christ, which **G** gave to him, to .... Rev 1:1
It is the word of **G**; it is the .... Rev 1:2
priests who serve **G** his Father. .... Rev 1:6
The Lord **G** says, "I am the Alpha .... Rev 1:8
the word of **G** and the message .... Rev 1:9
which is in the garden of **G**. .... Rev 2:7
The Son of **G**, who has eyes that .... Rev 2:18
is less than what my **G** wants. .... Rev 3:2
pillars in the temple of my **G**, ... Rev 3:12
the name of my **G** and the name .... Rev 3:12
the name of the city of my **G**, ... Rev 3:12
down out of heaven from my **G**. .... Rev 3:12
the ruler of all **G** has made, ... Rev 3:14
are the seven spirits of **G**. .... Rev 4:5
holy is the Lord **G** Almighty. .... Rev 4:8
our Lord and **G**, to receive glory .... Rev 4:11
seven spirits of **G** that were .... Rev 5:6
people for **G** from every tribe .... Rev 5:9
a kingdom of priests for our **G**, ... Rev 5:10
to the word of **G** and to the.................... Rev 6:9
had the seal of the living **G**. .... Rev 7:2
angels to whom **G** had given power .... Rev 7:2
of the people who serve our **G**." .... Rev 7:3
Salvation belongs to our **G**, ... Rev 7:10
the throne and worshiped **G**, ... Rev 7:11
to our **G** forever and ever. .... Rev 7:12
they are before the throne of **G**. .... Rev 7:15
And **G** will wipe away every tear .... Rev 7:17
stand before **G** and to whom were .... Rev 8:2
angel's hand to **G** with the .... Rev 8:4
have the sign of **G** on their .... Rev 9:4
golden altar that is before **G**. .... Rev 9:13
is the Good News **G** told to his .... Rev 10:7
the temple of **G** and the altar, ... Rev 11:1
G put the breath of life into .... Rev 11:11
gave glory to the **G** of heaven. .... Rev 11:13
sit on their thrones before **G**, ... Rev 11:16
on their faces and worshiped **G**. .... Rev 11:16
to you, Lord **G** Almighty, who is.............. Rev 11:17
the agreement **G** gave to his .... Rev 11:19
taken up to **G** and to his throne.............. Rev 12:5
to a place **G** prepared for her .... Rev 12:6
kingdom of our **G** and the .... Rev 12:10
them day and night before our **G**, ... Rev 12:10
A name against **G** was written on .... Rev 13:1
proud words and words against **G**,........... Rev 13:5
its mouth to speak against **G**, ... Rev 13:6
against the place where **G** lives, ... Rev 13:6
to be offered to **G** and the Lamb. .... Rev 14:4
Fear **G** and give him praise, ... Rev 14:7
time has come for **G** to judge all.............. Rev 14:7
So worship **G** who made the .... Rev 14:7
had harps that **G** had given them. .... Rev 15:2
the servant of **G**, and the song .... Rev 15:3
things, Lord **G** Almighty. .... Rev 15:3
filled with the anger of **G**, ... Rev 15:7
the glory and the power of **G**, ... Rev 15:8
Yes, Lord **G** Almighty, the way .... Rev 16:7
and they cursed the name of **G**, ... Rev 16:9
and lives and give glory to **G**.................. Rev 16:9
also cursed the **G** of heaven .... Rev 16:11
on the great day of **G** Almighty. .... Rev 16:14
And **G** remembered the sins of .... Rev 16:19
People cursed **G** for the disaster.............. Rev 16:21
names against **G** written on it, ... Rev 17:3
G made the ten horns want to .... Rev 17:17
what **G** has said comes about. .... Rev 17:17
and **G** has not forgotten the .... Rev 18:5
because the Lord **G** who judges .... Rev 18:8
G has punished her because of .... Rev 18:20

and power belong to our **G**, ... Rev 19:1
bowed down and worshiped **G**, ... Rev 19:4
Praise our **G**, all you who serve .... Rev 19:5
Our Lord **G**, the Almighty, rules. .... Rev 19:6
and be happy and give **G** glory, ... Rev 19:7
"These are the true words of **G**." .... Rev 19:9
Worship **G**, because the message .... Rev 19:10
and his name is the Word of **G**. .... Rev 19:13
anger of **G** the Almighty. .... Rev 19:15
for the great feast of **G** .... Rev 19:17
of Jesus and the message from **G**. .... Rev 20:4
be priests for **G** and for Christ .... Rev 20:6
people and the city **G** loves. .... Rev 20:9
down out of heaven from **G**. .... Rev 21:2
G himself will be with them and............. Rev 21:3
with them and will be their **G**. .... Rev 21:3
I will be their **G**, and they will .... Rev 21:7
down out of heaven from **G**. .... Rev 21:10
the glory of **G** and was bright.................. Rev 21:11
because the Lord **G** Almighty and .... Rev 21:22
the glory of **G** is its light, ... Rev 21:23
the throne of **G** and of the Lamb .... Rev 22:1
Nothing that **G** judges guilty .... Rev 22:3
The throne of **G** and of the Lamb .... Rev 22:3
because the Lord **G** will give .... Rev 22:5
the **G** of the spirits of the .... Rev 22:6
words in this book. Worship **G**!" .... Rev 22:9
G will add to that person the .... Rev 22:18
G will take away that one's..................... Rev 22:19

GOD'S

because heaven is **G** throne. .... Mt 5:34
to God the things that are **G**.".................. Mt 22:21
cannot insult **G** high priest like .... Ac 23:4
to put many of **G** people in jail, ... Ac 26:10
Who can say **G** people are guilty? .... Rm 8:34
did not accept **G** way of making............. Rm 10:3
The ruler is **G** servant to help.................. Rm 13:4
We are **G** workers, working 1Co 3:9
are like **G** farm, God's house. 1Co 3:9
because **G** temple is holy and you 1Co 3:17
thing is obeying **G** commands. 1Co 7:19

GOD-FEARING

said to them, "I am a **G** man. .... Ge 42:18

GODDESS

the **g** of the people of Sidon, ... 1Ki 11:5
the hated **g** of the Sidonians. 2Ki 23:13
they offer them to the Queen **G**. .... Je 7:18
make sacrifices to the Queen **G**, ... Je 44:17
to the Queen **G** and stopped .... Je 44:18
to the Queen **G** and to pour out .... Je 44:19
to the Queen **G** and to pour out .... Je 44:25
the temple of the **g** Artemis. .... Ac 19:24
of the great **g** Artemis is not .... Ac 19:27
Artemis is the **g** that everyone .... Ac 19:27
Artemis, the **g** of Ephesus, is .... Ac 19:28
of the great **g** Artemis and her .... Ac 19:35
evil against our **g** or stolen .... Ac 19:37

GODLY

for the **g** people in the world, ... Ps 16:3
Simeon who was a good man and **g**. .... Lk 2:25

GODS

Put away the foreign **g** you have, ... Ge 35:2
also punish all the **g** of Egypt. .... Ex 12:12
Are there any **g** like you, ... Ex 15:11
the LORD is greater than all **g**, ... Ex 18:11
not have any other **g** except me............... Ex 20:3
worship these **g** in addition to .... Ex 20:23
down to their **g** or worship them .... Ex 23:24
not have any other **g** except me............. Dt 5:7
worship other **g** as the people................. Dt 6:14
follow other **g** and worship them .... Dt 8:19

is God of all **g** and Lord of all.................. Dt 10:17
and have turned to other **g**..................... Dt 31:18
LORD is God of **g**! God knows, and .... Jos 22:22
Throw away the **g** that your .... Jos 24:14
their **g** will be a trap for you. .... Jdg 2:3
time they chose to follow new **g**. .... Jdg 5:8
to her own people and her own **g**. .... Ru 1:15
He used his **g'** names to curse 1Sa 17:43
here are your **g** who brought you 1Ki 12:28
The **g** of Israel are mountain 1Ki 20:23
have burned incense to other **g**. 2Ki 22:17
house **g**, and idols................................. 2Ki 23:24
our God is greater than all **g**. 2Ch 2:5
priest of idols that are not **g**. 2Ch 13:9
places where **g** were worshiped.............. 2Ch 14:3
The **g** of those nations could not.............. 2Ch 32:13
the great King over all the **g**. .... Ps 95:3
be honored more than all the **g**, ... Ps 96:4
they brag about their **g**. .... Ps 97:7
All the **g** should worship the .... Ps 97:7
you are supreme over all **g**...................... Ps 97:9
Give thanks to the God of **g**. .... Ps 136:2
'You are our **g'** will be rejected .... Is 42:17
green tree to worship your **g**. .... Is 57:5
a nation ever exchanged its **g**? .... Je 2:11
g are not really gods at all. .... Je 2:11
love those other **g**, and I must................ Je 2:25
'These **g** did not make heaven and .... Je 10:11
and worshiped other **g** instead. .... Je 11:10
people make **g** for themselves? .... Je 16:20
holy name with your gifts and **g**. .... Eze 20:39
Only the **g** could tell the king................. Da 2:11
God is the greatest of all **g**,................... Da 2:47
praised their **g**, which were made .... Da 5:4
has the spirit of the holy **g**. .... Da 5:11
You praised the **g** of silver, ... Da 5:23
God said, 'I said, you are **g**.' .... Jn 10:34
those people **g** who received .... Jn 10:35
'Make us **g** who will lead us. .... Ac 7:40
The **g** have become like humans.............. Ac 14:11
says the **g** made by human hands .... Ac 19:26
there are things called **g**, ... 1Co 8:5
were slaves to **g** that were not .... Gal 4:8

GOG

was Joel's son. **G** was Shemaiah's 1Ch 5:4
look toward **G** of the land of .... Eze 38:2
I am against you, **G**, chief ruler .... Eze 38:3
and say to **G**, 'This is what .... Eze 38:14
G, then the nations will know me .... Eze 38:16
On the day **G** attacks the land of .... Eze 38:18
for a war against **G** on all my .... Eze 38:21
I will punish **G** with disease and............. Eze 38:22
and burning sulfur on **G**, ... Eze 38:22
prophesy against **G** and say, ' .... Eze 39:1
I am against you, **G**, chief ruler .... Eze 39:1
I will give **G** a burial place .... Eze 39:11
G and all his army will be .... Eze 39:11
in all the earth—**G** and Magog—to .... Rev 20:8

GOIIM

Elam, and Tidal was king of **G**. .... Ge 14:1
Tidal king of **G**, Amraphel king .... Ge 14:9

GOLAN

and **G** in Bashan was for the .... Dt 4:43
and **G** in Bashan in the land of .... Jos 20:8
Manasseh gave them **G** in Bashan,........... Jos 21:27
and pastures of **G** in Bashan 1Ch 6:71

GOLD

The **g** of that land is excellent. .... Ge 2:12
rich in cattle, silver, and **g**. .... Ge 13:2
gave Rebekah a **g** ring weighing .... Ge 24:22
and he put a **g** chain around .... Ge 41:42

You must not use **g** or silver to .... Ex 20:23
Ark inside and out with pure **g**, ... Ex 25:11
made for themselves gods from **g**. .... Ex 32:31
They hammered the **g** into sheets .... Ex 39:3
was made from hammered **g**, ... Nu 8:4
his palace full of silver and **g**,................ Nu 22:18
not have too much silver and **g**. .... Dt 17:17
of wood, stone, silver, and **g**. .... Dt 29:17
one and one-fourth pounds of **g**.............. Jos 7:21
of you to give me a **g** earring .... Jdg 8:24
box with the **g** rats and models 1Sa 6:11
creatures were covered with **g**. 1Ki 6:28
cedar, pine, and **g** he wanted. 1Ki 9:11
about nine thousand pounds of **g**. 1Ki 9:14
ships brought **g** from Ophir, ... 1Ki 10:11
large shields of hammered **g**, ... 1Ki 10:16
smaller shields of hammered **g**, ... 1Ki 10:17
of Lebanon, were made of pure **g**. 1Ki 10:21
bringing back **g**, silver, ivory, ... 1Ki 10:22
made of pure **g** or silver.......................... 2Ki 25:15
one-half million pounds of **g**,.................. 1Ch 22:14
that were made of **g** or silver. 1Ch 28:14
own treasures of **g** and silver, ... 1Ch 29:3
eighty thousand pounds of **g**, ... 1Ch 29:7
is skilled in working with **g**, ... 2Ch 2:14
took silver and **g** from the 2Ch 16:2
1,100 pounds of **g**, about 6,000 .... Ezr 2:69
gave them twenty **g** bowls that .... Ezr 8:27
that were as valuable as **g**. .... Ezr 8:27
And there were **g** and silver .... Est 1:6
and white and a large **g** crown. .... Est 8:15
Throw your **g** nuggets into the .... Job 22:24
me, I will come out like **g**. .... Job 23:10
and places where **g** is made pure. .... Job 28:1
and **g** dust is also found there. .... Job 28:6
Wisdom cannot be bought with **g**, ... Job 28:15
my trust in **g** or said to pure .... Job 31:24
a piece of silver and a **g** ring. .... Job 42:11
They are worth more than **g**, ... Ps 19:10
him and placed a **g** crown on his .... Ps 21:3
Her gown is woven with **g**. .... Ps 45:13
Let him receive **g** from Sheba. .... Ps 72:15
idols are made of silver and **g**, ... Ps 115:4
is better than the finest **g**, ... Pr 8:19
is like a **g** ring in a pig's .... Pr 11:22
is better to get wisdom than **g**, ... Pr 16:16
hot furnace tests silver and **g**,................ Pr 17:3
hot furnace tests silver and **g**,................ Pr 27:21
His head is like the finest **g**; .... Sng 5:11
away their **g** and silver idols .... Is 2:20
from Tarshish and **g** from Uphaz, ... Je 10:9
how the **g** has lost its shine, ... La 4:1
and their **g** will be like trash. .... Eze 7:19
You have gained **g** and silver and .... Eze 28:4
Your jewelry was made of **g**, ... Eze 28:13
the statue was made of pure **g**. .... Da 2:32
g broke to pieces at the same .... Da 2:35
the head of **g** on that statue. .... Da 2:38
clay, silver, and **g** to pieces...................... Da 2:45
and worship the **g** statue that .... Da 3:5
or worship the **g** statue you have .... Da 3:18
they brought the **g** cups that had .... Da 5:3
made from **g**, silver, bronze, ... Da 5:4
a king and a **g** chain around his .... Da 5:7
their silver and **g** into idols, ... Hos 8:4
Take the **g**! There is no end.................... Nah 2:9
mine, and the **g** is mine,' says .... Hag 2:8
I see a solid **g** lampstand with a .... Zch 4:2
branches beside the two **g** pipes, ... Zch 4:12
silver, testing them like **g**. .... Zch 13:9
and gave him treasures of **g**, ... Mt 2:11
I don't have any silver or **g**, ... Ac 3:6
people imagine or make from **g**,.............. Ac 17:29

using *g*, silver, jewels, ... 1Co 3:12
braided hair or *g* or pearls 1Ti 2:9
things made of *g* and silver, ... 2Ti 2:20
Ark covered with *g* that held the .... Heb 9:4
nice clothes and a *g* ring. .... Jam 2:2
that ruins like *g* or silver, ... 1Pe 1:18
not fancy hair, *g* jewelry, or 1Pe 3:3
to buy from me *g* made pure in .... Rev 3:18
rod made of *g* to measure the .... Rev 21:15
and the city was made of pure *g*, ... Rev 21:18

GOLDEN

worshiping the *g* calves in 2Ki 10:29
chain or break like a *g* bowl. .... Ec 12:6
In it was a *g* altar for burning................. Heb 9:4
this Ark was a *g* jar of manna, ... Heb 9:4
turned, I saw seven *g* lampstands .... Rev 1:12
them had a harp and *g* bowls full .... Rev 5:8
offering on the *g* altar before .... Rev 8:3
She had a *g* cup in her hand, ... Rev 17:4

GOLDSMITH

of Harhaiah, a *g*, made repairs. .... Ne 3:8
and a *g* covers it with gold and .... Is 40:19
The craftsman encourages the *g*, ... Is 41:7
They hire a *g*, and he makes it .... Is 46:6

GOLDSMITHS

one of the *g*, made repairs. .... Ne 3:31
The *g* and the traders made .... Ne 3:32
are made by craftsmen and *g*.................. Je 10:9
G are made ashamed by their................. Je 10:14
G are made ashamed by their................. Je 51:17

GOLGOTHA

all came to the place called *G*, ... Mt 27:33
led Jesus to the place called *G*, ... Mk 15:22
the Hebrew language is called *G*. .... Jn 19:17

GOLIATH

fighter from Gath named *G*. 1Sa 17:4
G stood and shouted to the 1Sa 17:8
with them, *G*, the Philistine 1Sa 17:23
When the Israelites saw *G*,..................... 1Sa 17:24
for the man who would kill *G*. 1Sa 17:27
G has been a warrior since he 1Sa 17:33
When *G* looked at David and saw 1Sa 17:42
As *G* came near to attack him, ... 1Sa 17:48
and *G* fell facedown on the..................... 1Sa 17:49
Saul saw David go out to meet *G*, ... 1Sa 17:55
David came back from killing *G*, ... 1Sa 17:57
when he killed *G* the Philistine, ... 1Sa 19:5
The sword of *G* the Philistine, ... 1Sa 21:9
the sword of *G* the Philistine. 1Sa 22:10
Bethlehem killed *G* from Gath. 2Sa 21:19
Lahmi, the brother of *G*, who was 1Ch 20:5

GOMER

The sons of Japheth were *G*, ... Ge 10:2
The sons of *G* were Ashkenaz, ... Ge 10:3
sons were *G*, Magog, Madai, ... 1Ch 1:5
There will also be *G* with all .... Eze 38:6
So Hosea married *G* daughter of .... Hos 1:3
G became pregnant again and gave .... Hos 1:6
After *G* had stopped nursing .... Hos 1:8

GOMER'S

G sons were Ashkenaz, Riphath, ... 1Ch 1:6

GOMORRAH

and then to Sodom, *G*, Admah, and .... Ge 10:19
the LORD destroyed Sodom and *G*. .... Ge 13:10
Birsha king of *G*, Shinab king of .... Ge 14:2
of Sodom, *G*, Admah, Zeboiim .... Ge 14:8
of Sodom and *G* and their armies .... Ge 14:10
the people of Sodom and *G* owned, ... Ge 14:11
the people of Sodom and *G*. .... Ge 18:20
down from the sky on Sodom and *G* .... Ge 19:24

toward Sodom and *G* and all the .... Ge 19:28
is like Sodom and *G*, and Admah .... Dt 29:23
and their fields are like *G*. .... Dt 32:32
like the cities of Sodom and *G*. .... Is 1:9
your people are like those of *G*. .... Is 1:10
destroy it like Sodom and *G*. .... Is 13:19
are like the city of *G* to me!" .... Je 23:14
of Sodom and *G* and the towns .... Je 49:18
of Sodom and *G* and the towns .... Je 50:40
you as I destroyed Sodom and *G*. .... Am 4:11
Ammon will be destroyed like *G*— .... Zph 2:9
towns of Sodom and *G* than for .... Mt 10:15
the cities of Sodom and *G*." .... Rm 9:29
of Sodom and *G* by burning them 2Pe 2:6
of Sodom and *G* and the other .... Jud 1:7

GOOD

God saw that the light was *g*, ... Ge 1:4
God saw that this was *g*. .... Ge 1:10
he had made, and it was very *g*. .... Ge 1:31
tree that was *g* for food to grow .... Ge 2:9
It is not *g* for the man to be .... Ge 2:18
learn about *g* and evil and you .... Ge 3:5
that its fruit was *g* to eat, ... Ge 3:6
explanation of the dream was *g*,............. Ge 40:16
during the *g* years that are .... Ge 41:35
God be *g* to you, my son!" .... Ge 43:29
have you paid back evil for *g*? .... Ge 44:4
your evil into *g* to save the .... Ge 50:20
hear all the *g* things the LORD .... Ex 18:9
money makes *g* people tell lies .... Ex 23:8
exchange it, a *g* animal for a .... Le 27:10
or a bad animal for a *g* one. .... Le 27:10
to whether it is *g* or bad;....................... Le 27:12
whether the house is *g* or bad; .... Le 27:14
live in? Is it *g* or bad? What .... Nu 13:19
The land we explored is very *g*. .... Nu 14:7
I promised a *g* land to your..................... Dt 1:35
houses full of *g* things you did .... Dt 6:11
the LORD says is *g* and right so .... Dt 6:18
giving you today for your own *g*. .... Dt 10:13
your God says is *g* and right. .... Dt 12:28
and your land will give *g* crops. .... Dt 28:11
fields will produce *g* crops,..................... Dt 30:9
The LORD may have been *g* to you, ... Jos 24:20
my sweet and *g* fruit and go .... Jdg 9:11
have been *g* to me, but I have 1Sa 24:17
because you were *g* to me today. 1Sa 24:19
I did *g* to him, but he has paid 1Sa 25:21
know what is *g* and what is bad 2Sa 14:17
kept all the *g* promises he gave 1Ki 8:56
cut down every *g* tree and stop 2Ki 3:19
ruin every *g* field with rocks. 2Ki 3:19
Today we have *g* news, but we are 2Ki 7:9
Thank the LORD because he is *g*. 1Ch 16:34
this song: "He is *g*; his love, ... 2Ch 5:13
the LORD, saying, "He is *g*; 2Ch 7:3
his God said was *g* and right. 2Ch 14:2
prophesies anything *g* about me, ... 2Ch 18:7
and eat the *g* things of the land .... Ezr 9:12
for all the *g* I have done for .... Ne 5:19
me about the *g* things Tobiah was .... Ne 6:19
Go and enjoy *g* food and sweet .... Ne 8:10
true teachings, *g* orders and .... Ne 9:13
we take only *g* things from God .... Job 2:10
If you are *g* and honest, he will .... Job 8:6
I hoped for *g*, only evil came .... Job 30:26
is no one who does anything *g*. .... Ps 14:1
g thing I have comes from you. .... Ps 16:2
The LORD is *g* and right; .... Ps 25:8
and see how *g* the LORD is. .... Ps 34:8
Stop doing evil and do *g*. .... Ps 34:14
with evil for the *g* I have done, ... Ps 35:12

G

If you are trying hard to do g,.................. 1Pe 3:13
evil of your g life in Christ 1Pe 3:16
made to God from a g conscience. 1Pe 3:21
Be g servants of God's various 1Pe 4:10
very hard for a g person to be 1Pe 4:18
had the eternal G News to preach .... Rev 14:6
the g things you wanted are gone .... Rev 18:14
linen means the g things done by .... Rev 19:8

GOOD-BYE

and my daughters g. .... Ge 31:28
Then Joshua said g to them, ... Jos 22:6
When Naomi kissed the women g, ... Ru 1:9
her mother-in-law Naomi g, ... Ru 1:14
kiss my father and my mother g," 1Ki 19:20
me go and say g to my family." .... Lk 9:61
things, you will do well. G. .... Ac 15:29
them and then told them g,..................... Ac 20:1
After all said g to them,....................... Ac 21:1
we said g and got on the ship, ... Ac 21:6
So I said g to them at Troas and.............. 2Co 2:13
brothers and sisters, I say g. 2Co 13:11

GOOD-LOOKING

he killed all the g people; .... La 2:4

GOODS

all their flocks, herds, and g. .... Nu 31:9
the people and animals and g. .... Nu 31:11
and the g back to Moses and .... Nu 31:12
should take a count of the g, ... Nu 31:26
may bring g or grain to sell .... Ne 10:31
of Tobiah's g out of the room.................. Ne 13:8
all kinds of g spent the night .... Ne 13:20
fill our houses with stolen g, ... Pr 1:13
will share with you stolen g." .... Pr 1:14
The g made in Egypt and Cush and .... Is 45:14
enemies—its g, its valuables, ... Je 20:5
tents, all their g, and their .... Je 49:29
They traded your g for silver, ... Eze 27:12
They traded your g for slaves .... Eze 27:13
traded your g for work horses, ... Eze 27:14
selling your g on many .... Eze 27:15
traded your g for turquoise, ... Eze 27:16
traded your g for wheat from .... Eze 27:17
traded your g for all the best .... Eze 27:22
your trade, your g, your seamen, ... Eze 27:27
When the g you traded went out .... Eze 27:33
With your great wealth and g, ... Eze 27:33
Your g and all the people on .... Eze 27:34
full of lies and g stolen from .... Nah 3:1
anyone to carry g through the .... Mk 11:16
store all my grain and other g. .... Lk 12:18

GOSHEN

in the land of G where you will .... Ge 45:10
live in the land of G in Egypt................. Ge 47:27

GOSPEL

News of Christ—the g you say you........... 2Co 9:13
a spirit or g that is different 2Co 11:4

GOSSIP

to their neighbors and do not g. .... Ps 15:3
bad news. Then they go and g. .... Ps 41:6
and a g ruins friendships. .... Pr 16:28
The words of a g are like tasty .... Pr 18:8
telling g brings angry looks. .... Pr 25:23
and without g, quarreling will .... Pr 26:20
The words of a g are like tasty .... Pr 26:22
worst about each other. They g .... Rm 1:29
fighting, evil talk, g, pride, ... 2Co 12:20
but also begin to g and busy 1Ti 5:13
to forgive, will g, and will not................. 2Ti 3:3

GOSSIPING

but g about the sin breaks up .... Pr 17:9

GOSSIPS

G can't keep secrets, but a .... Pr 11:13
G can't keep secrets, so avoid................. Pr 20:19

GOVERN

Can anyone g who hates what is .... Job 34:17
I help kings to g and rulers to................. Pr 8:15
who are able to g, and those who 1Co 12:28

GOVERNED

and he g the people of the land. 2Ki 15:5
and he g the people of the land. 2Ch 26:21

GOVERNMENT

his soldiers, g leaders,........................... 1Ki 9:22
of money your g collects will be.............. Ezr 4:13
Since we must be loyal to the g,............. Ezr 4:14
continue, it will hurt the g. .... Ezr 4:22
and had the g give away gifts. .... Est 2:18
then his g will be honest and .... Pr 25:5
his g will continue forever. .... Pr 29:14
military leaders and g leaders, ... Is 3:3
The g in Damascus will end. .... Is 17:3
Daniel about his work in the g. .... Da 6:4
the most important g leaders,................. Mk 6:21
against the g not long ago .... Ac 21:38
you must yield to the g rulers. .... Rm 13:1
are against the g are really..................... Rm 13:2
So you must yield to the g, ... Rm 13:5
of rulers and g leaders, ... Tit 3:1

GOVERNMENTS

because g only continue if they .... Pr 16:12
forever, nor do g go on forever. .... Pr 27:24

GOVERNOR

Now Joseph was g over Egypt. .... Ge 42:6
Try giving them to your g. .... Mal 1:8
Jesus stood before Pilate the g, ... Mt 27:11
king made him g of Egypt and put .... Ac 7:10
To the Most Excellent G Felix: .... Ac 23:26

GOVERNOR'S

Shimshai the g secretary wrote .... Ezr 4:8
The g soldiers took Jesus into.................. Mt 27:27
took Jesus into the g palace, ... Mt 27:27
took Jesus into the g palace .... Mk 15:16
house to the Roman g palace................... Jn 18:28

GOVERNORS

and to the g of Trans-Euphrates .... Ezr 8:36
to stand before g and kings. .... Mt 10:18
to stand before kings and g, ... Mk 13:9
you to stand before kings and g, ... Lk 21:12

GOVERNS

is the way God g the nations; .... Job 36:31
Every morning he g the people .... Zph 3:5

GOWN

Her g is woven with gold. .... Ps 45:13

GOYIM

in Naphoth Dor), G in Gilgal, ... Jos 12:23

GRACE

but he gives g to those who are .... Pr 3:34
God has shown you his g. .... Lk 1:30
at the words of g he spoke....................... Lk 4:22
and he was full of g and truth. .... Jn 1:14
he was full of g and truth, ... Jn 1:16
but g and truth came through................. Jn 1:17
to continue trusting in God's g. .... Ac 13:43
message about his g was true by .... Ac 14:3
by the g of the Lord Jesus. .... Ac 15:11
in Jesus because of God's g, ... Ac 18:27
the Good News about God's g. .... Ac 20:24
God and the message about his g. .... Ac 20:32
G and peace to you from God our .... Rm 1:7
be made right with God by his g, ... Rm 3:24

of God's g that we now enjoy .... Rm 5:2
But the g from God was much .... Rm 5:15
of life by the g of the one man, ... Rm 5:15
accept God's full g and the .... Rm 5:17
grew worse, God's g increased. .... Rm 5:20
more of his g so that grace .... Rm 5:21
his grace so that g could rule .... Rm 5:21
God will give us even more g? .... Rm 6:1
not under law but under God's g. .... Rm 6:14
are under g and not under law? .... Rm 6:15
that God has chosen by his g. .... Rm 11:5
And if he chose them by g, ... Rm 11:6
God's gift of g would not really .... Rm 11:6
because of the g God gave us.................. Rm 12:6
The g of our Lord Jesus be with .... Rm 16:20
The g of our Lord Jesus Christ .... Rm 16:24
G and peace to you from God our 1Co 1:3
because of the g God has given 1Co 1:4
But God's g has made me what I 1Co 15:10
and his g to me was not wasted. 1Co 15:10
it was God's g that was with me. 1Co 15:10
The g of the Lord Jesus be with 1Co 16:23
G and peace to you from God our 2Co 1:2
this by God's g, not by the kind 2Co 1:12
so the g of God that is being 2Co 4:15
Do not let the g that you 2Co 6:1
to know about the g God gave the 2Co 8:1
special work of g since he is 2Co 8:6
strong also in the g of giving. 2Co 8:7
You know the g of our Lord Jesus 2Co 8:9
the great g that God has given 2Co 9:14
said to me, "My g is enough for 2Co 12:9
The g of the Lord Jesus Christ, ... 2Co 13:14
G and peace to you from God our .... Gal 1:3
God, by his g through Christ, ... Gal 1:6
He called me through his g .... Gal 1:15
God had given me this special g, ... Gal 2:9
I am not going against God's g. .... Gal 2:21
is over—you have left God's g. .... Gal 5:4
the g of our Lord Jesus Christ .... Gal 6:18
G and peace to you from God our .... Eph 1:2
God because of his wonderful g. .... Eph 1:6
God gave that g to us freely, ... Eph 1:6
of sins. How rich is God's g, ... Eph 1:7
You have been saved by God's g. .... Eph 2:5
riches of his g by being kind to .... Eph 2:7
been saved by g through .... Eph 2:8
work to tell you about his g. .... Eph 3:2
special gift of g given to me .... Eph 3:7
one of us the special gift of g,................ Eph 4:7
G to all of you who love our .... Eph 6:24
G and peace to you from God our .... Php 1:2
share in God's g with me while I .... Php 1:7
The g of the Lord Jesus Christ .... Php 4:23
G and peace to you from God our .... Col 1:2
the truth about the g of God. .... Col 1:6
about God's g from Epaphras, ... Col 1:7
me in prison. G be with you. .... Col 4:18
Jesus Christ: G and peace to you 1Th 1:1
The g of our Lord Jesus Christ 1Th 5:28
G and peace to you from God the 2Th 1:2
glory comes from the g of our 2Th 1:12
The g of our Lord Jesus Christ 2Th 3:18
G, mercy, and peace from God the 1Ti 1:2
But the g of our Lord was fully 1Ti 1:14
and with that g came the faith 1Ti 1:14
the true faith. G be with you. 1Ti 6:21
G, mercy, and peace to you from 2Ti 1:2
because of God's purpose and g. 2Ti 1:9
That g was given to us through 2Ti 1:9
be strong in the g we have in 2Ti 2:1
with your spirit. G be with you. 2Ti 4:22
G and peace from God the Father .... Tit 1:4

because God's g that can save .... Tit 2:11
that g teaches us to live in the .... Tit 2:12
made right with God by his g, ... Tit 3:7
in the faith. G be with you all .... Tit 3:15
G and peace to you from God our .... Phm 1:3
The g of our Lord Jesus Christ .... Phm 1:25
And by God's g, he died for .... Heb 2:9
God's throne where there is g. .... Heb 4:16
mercy and g to help us when .... Heb 4:16
insult the Spirit of God's g? .... Heb 10:29
to receive God's g and begins to............ Heb 12:15
be strengthened by God's g, ... Heb 13:9
G be with you all. .... Heb 13:25
But God gives us even more g, ... Jam 4:6
but he gives g to the humble." .... Jam 4:6
G and peace be yours more and 1Pe 1:2
about the g that was coming to 1Pe 1:10
for the gift of g that will be.................... 1Pe 1:13
the g that gives true life. 1Pe 3:7
of God's various gifts of g. 1Pe 4:10
but he gives g to the humble." 1Pe 5:5
God, who gives all g, will make 1Pe 5:10
that this is the true g of God. 1Pe 5:12
Stand strong in that g. 1Pe 5:12
G and peace be given to you more 2Pe 1:2
But grow in the g and knowledge 2Pe 3:18
G, mercy, and peace from God the 2Jn 1:3
have changed the g of our God .... Jud 1:4
G and peace to you from the One .... Rev 1:4
The g of the Lord Jesus be with .... Rev 22:21

GRACEFUL
is as lovely and g as a deer. .... Pr 5:19

GRAIN
good heads of g growing on one.............. Ge 41:5
Joseph stored much g, as much as .... Ge 41:49
in Egypt to buy g because the.................. Ge 41:57
brothers' bags with g and to put.............. Ge 42:25
growing g or grain that has .... Ex 22:6
with the same g offering and .... Ex 29:41
or any kind of g offering, ... Ex 30:9
continual g offering, and the .... Nu 4:16
good crops and will give you g, ... Dt 7:13
of your g, new wine, or oil .... Dt 12:17
time you begin to harvest the g, ... Dt 16:9
Give them the first of your g, ... Dt 18:4
When an ox is working in the g,............. Dt 25:4
without yeast and roasted g. .... Jos 5:11
me gather the g he leaves behind .... Ru 2:2
lying beside the pile of g. .... Ru 3:7
built storage buildings for g, ... 2Ch 32:28
may bring goods or g to sell on .... Ne 10:31
like bundles of g gathered in .... Job 5:26
the valleys are covered with g. .... Ps 65:13
grow plenty of g and the hills .... Ps 72:16
curse those who keep all the g, ... Pr 11:26
will be like the g harvest in..................... Is 17:5
"Where is the g and wine?" .... La 2:12
I was the one who gave her g, ... Hos 2:8
take away my g at harvest time .... Hos 2:9
will produce g, new wine, and .... Hos 2:22
cow that likes to thresh g. .... Hos 10:11
storerooms for g have been .... Joe 1:17
be over so we can sell g?....................... Am 8:5
someone shaking g through a................. Am 9:9
some fields of g on a Sabbath................. Mt 12:1
and the heads of g,................................ Mt 13:26
a g of wheat must fall to the .... Jn 12:24
heard there was g in Egypt, ... Ac 7:12
When an ox is working in the g,.............. 1Co 9:9
When an ox is working in the g,.............. 1Ti 5:18

GRAINFIELD
you go into your neighbor's g, ... Dt 23:25

GRAINFIELDS
loose in the **g** of the.............................Jdg 15:5

GRAINS
as many as the **g** of sand. ....Is 48:19

GRANDCHILDREN
them to your children and **g**. ....Dt 4:9
see his children, **g**, ...Job 42:16

GRANDDAUGHTER
a **g** of Omri king of Israel. 2Ki 8:26
name was Athaliah, a **g** of Omri. 2Ch 22:2

GRANDDAUGHTERS
grandsons, his daughters and **g**...............Ge 46:7

GRANDFATHER
the God of Abraham your **g**, ...Ge 28:13
all the land of your **g** Saul, ...2Sa 9:7
Josiah was the **g** of Jehoiachin ....Mt 1:11
was the **g** of Zerubbabel. ....Mt 1:12

GRANDFATHER'S
have killed all my **g** family....................2Sa 19:28

GRANDMOTHER
His **g** Maacah had made a terrible 1Ki 15:13
Maacah, his **g**, from being queen 2Ch 15:16
lived in your **g** Lois and in your 2Ti 1:5

GRANDMOTHER'S
His **g** name was Maacah, the 1Ki 15:10

GRANDPARENTS
and to repay their parents or **g**. 1Ti 5:4

GRANDSON
Abram, his **g** Lot (Haran's son) ....Ge 11:31
Do you know Laban, **g** of Nahor?"............Ge 29:5
the son of Carmi and **g** of Zabdi, ...Jos 7:1
son and your **g** to rule over us. ....Jdg 8:22
the LORD who gave you this **g**, ...Ru 4:14
she has given birth to your **g**," ....Ru 4:15
your master's **g** everything that 2Sa 9:9
your master's **g**, will always eat 2Sa 9:10
Saul's **g**, also went down to 2Sa 19:24
and his son and **g**. ....Je 27:7
was the **g** of Shealtiel............................Lk 3:27

GRAPE
continue until the **g** harvest, ...Le 26:5
and your **g** harvest will continue ....Le 26:5
not even drink **g** juice or eat ....Nu 6:3
There will be no **g** harvest and ....Is 32:10

GRAPES
grape juice or eat **g** or raisins. ....Nu 6:3
had one bunch of **g** on it and ....Nu 13:23
not put any **g** into your basket. ....Dt 23:24
You drank the juice of **g**........................Dt 32:14
breasts are like bunches of **g**, ...Sng 7:8
hoped good **g** would grow there, ...Is 5:2
There will be no **g** on the vine ....Je 8:13
who walk on **g** to make wine;..............Je 25:30
'The parents have eaten sour **g**, ...Eze 18:2
the juice from **g** when it's time ....Am 9:13

GRAPEVINE
He ties his donkey to a **g**, ...Ge 49:11
Joseph is like a **g** that produces ....Ge 49:22
anything that comes from the **g**,............Nu 6:4
off a branch of a **g** that had one ....Nu 13:23
eat anything that grows on a **g**, ...Jdg 13:14
fruit from his own **g** and fig 2Ki 18:31
fruit from his own **g** and fig ....Is 36:16
gather the last grapes on a **g**................Je 6:9
has made my **g** a waste and made ....Joe 1:7
under your own **g** and under your ....Zch 3:10
olives, or can a **g** make figs? ....Jam 3:12

GRAPEVINES
no grain, figs, **g**, or ....Nu 20:5
under their own fig trees and **g**. 1Ki 4:25
down their **g** and fig trees, ...Ps 105:33
and planted the best **g** there. ....Is 5:2
that have a thousand **g**, ...Is 7:23
rulers have destroyed the **g**. ....Is 16:8
The **g** once spread as far as the ....Is 16:8
of Jazer for the **g** of Sibmah. ....Is 16:9
the finest **g** and grapevines...................Is 17:10
grapevines and **g** from faraway ....Is 17:10
You plant your **g** one day and try ....Is 17:11
will be bad, and the **g** will die. ....Is 24:7
the **g** of the town of Sibmah. ....Je 48:32
trees and their **g** have grown much ....Joe 2:22
peace, their **g** will have fruit ....Zch 8:12

GRASS
a rain that makes the **g** sprout 2Sa 23:4
made you. It eats **g** like an ox. ....Job 40:15
like the **g**, they will soon.......................Ps 37:2
Let him be like rain on the **g**, ...Ps 72:6
grow like the **g** in a field. ....Ps 72:16
They are like **g** that grows up in ....Ps 90:5
Wicked people grow like the **g**. ....Ps 92:7
life is like **g**; we grow like ....Ps 103:15
is like the dew on the **g**. ....Pr 19:12
hay, and let the new **g** appear. ....Pr 27:25
The **g** has dried up, and all the ....Is 15:6
Say all people are like the **g**, ...Is 40:6
The **g** dies and the flowers fall ....Is 40:7
Surely the people are like **g**. ....Is 40:7
will feed you **g** like an ox, ...Da 4:25
and will be fed **g** like an ox. ....Da 4:32
God clothes the **g** in the field,................Mt 6:30
sit in groups on the green **g**. ....Mk 6:39
There was plenty of **g** there, ...Jn 6:10
die like a wild flower in the **g**. ....Jam 1:10
All people are like the **g**,........................1Pe 1:24
not to harm the **g** on the earth ....Rev 9:4

GRASSHOPPER
along like a **g** when you walk. ....Ec 12:5

GRASSHOPPERS
We felt like **g**, and we looked ....Nu 13:33
to him, people are like **g**. ....Is 40:22

GRASSLAND
eat in rich **g** on the mountains ....Eze 34:14

GRATEFUL
in, and he will be **g** to you. ....Dt 24:13

GRAVE
no one knows where his **g** is. ....Dt 34:6
people to the **g**, and he raises 1Sa 2:6
own city near the **g** of my father 2Sa 19:37
will come to the **g** with all your ....Job 5:26
go to the **g** and never return ....Job 7:9
straight from birth to the **g**. ....Job 10:19
and then go peacefully to the **g**. ....Job 21:13
You lifted me out of the **g**; ....Ps 30:3
and lie silent in the **g**. ....Ps 31:17
body lying in a **g** whom you don't ....Ps 88:5
have been scattered at the **g**."................Ps 141:7
because you are going to the **g**, ...Ec 9:10
jealousy is as strong as the **g**..................Sng 8:6
you are thrown out of your **g**,.................Is 14:19

GRAVEDIGGERS
there until the **g** bury the bone ....Eze 39:15

GRAVEL
feel like a mouth full of **g**. ....Pr 20:17
my teeth with **g** and trampled me ....La 3:16

GRAVES

the dust on the g of the common 2Ki 23:6
will open your g and cause you .... Eze 37:12
The g opened, and many of God's .... Mt 27:52
came out of the g after Jesus .... Mt 27:53
dead and in their g will hear .... Jn 5:28

GRAVEYARD

ancestors in a g that belonged 2Ch 26:23

GRAY

I am old and g, and my sons are.............. 1Sa 12:2
people with g hair are on our .... Job 15:10
Even though I am old and g, ... Ps 71:18
G hair is like a crown of honor; .... Pr 16:31
are honored for their g hair. .... Pr 20:29
when your hair has turned g, ... Is 46:4

GRAY-HAIRED

and so will babies and g men. .... Dt 32:25

GRAZE

to Shechem to g their father's................ Ge 37:12
his farm animal g in his field .... Ex 22:5

GRAZING

your brothers are g the flocks." .... Ge 37:13
me where they are g the flocks?" .... Ge 37:16

GREAT

children, you will have g pain. .... Ge 3:16
He was a g hunter before the .... Ge 10:9
a g hunter before the LORD." .... Ge 10:9
the g city between Nineveh and .... Ge 10:12
I will make you a g nation, ... Ge 12:2
as far as the g tree of Moreh at .... Ge 12:6
live near the g trees of Mamre .... Ge 13:18
camped near the g trees of Mamre........... Ge 14:13
and I will give you a g reward." .... Ge 15:1
land, taking g wealth with them. .... Ge 15:14
Egypt and the g river Euphrates. .... Ge 15:18
the father of twelve g leaders,................ Ge 17:20
I will make him into a g nation. .... Ge 17:20
near the g trees of Mamre. .... Ge 18:1
certainly become a g and .... Ge 18:18
food, Abraham gave a g feast. .... Ge 21:8
Ishmael into a g nation because .... Ge 21:13
descendants into a g nation." .... Ge 21:18
you are a g leader among us. .... Ge 23:6
have been guilty of a g sin." .... Ge 26:10
year he gathered a g harvest. .... Ge 26:12
them under the g tree near the .... Ge 35:4
that follows will be so g. .... Ge 41:31
will cause the g sorrow that .... Ge 44:31
descendants a g nation there. .... Ge 46:3
because the hunger was very g. .... Ge 47:20
Manasseh will be g and have many ...... Ge 48:19
Egyptians are showing g sorrow!" .... Ge 50:11
said to God, "I am not a g man! .... Ex 3:11
Only a g power will force him to .... Ex 3:19
so I will use my g power against .... Ex 3:20
I will use my g power against.................. Ex 6:1
I will free you by my g power, ... Ex 6:6
and g swarms of flies came into .... Ex 8:24
considered Moses to be a g man. .... Ex 11:3
all these g miracles in front .... Ex 11:10
LORD with his g power brought.............. Ex 13:3
LORD used his g power to bring .... Ex 13:9
With his g power, the LORD .... Ex 13:14
out of Egypt with his g power." .... Ex 13:16
saw the power the LORD had .... Ex 14:31
because he is worthy of g honor. .... Ex 15:1
In your g victory you destroyed .... Ex 15:7
because he is worthy of g honor; .... Ex 15:21
your descendants a g nation.".................. Ex 32:10
Egypt with your g power and .... Ex 32:11
who has g love and faithfulness .... Ex 34:6

little owls, cormorants, g owls, ... Le 11:17
rats, all kinds of g lizards, ... Le 11:29
to poor people or g people,..................... Le 19:15
you such a g blessing during .... Le 25:21
I will break your g pride, ... Le 26:19
I will show my g anger; .... Le 26:28
make you into a g nation that................ Nu 14:12
from there by your g power, ... Nu 14:13
quickly, but he has g love. .... Nu 14:18
By your g love, forgive these .... Nu 14:19
my God in anything, g or small. .... Nu 22:18
their kingdom will be very g. .... Nu 24:7
because he had g concern for the .... Nu 25:13
After the g sickness, the LORD .... Nu 26:1
Go as far as the g river, the.................... Dt 1:7
traveled through this g desert. .... Dt 2:7
me, your servant, how g you are. .... Dt 3:24
have g strength, and no other .... Dt 3:24
This g nation of Israel is wise. .... Dt 4:6
other nation is as g as we are. .... Dt 4:7
war, and g sights, by his .... Dt 4:34
by his g power and strength. .... Dt 4:34
showed you his g fire on earth, ... Dt 4:36
Egypt himself by his g strength............... Dt 4:37
of there by his g power and .... Dt 5:15
This g fire will burn us up, ... Dt 5:25
you will become a g nation in a .... Dt 6:3
us out of Egypt by his g power. .... Dt 6:21
LORD showed us g and terrible .... Dt 6:22
Egypt by his g power and freed .... Dt 7:8
how the LORD's g power and................... Dt 7:19
he is a g God and people are .... Dt 7:21
of Egypt by your g power and .... Dt 9:26
Egypt with your g power and .... Dt 9:29
He is the g God, who is strong .... Dt 10:17
who has done g and wonderful .... Dt 10:21
saw all these g things the LORD.............. Dt 11:7
are near the g trees of Moreh .... Dt 11:30
little owls, g owls, white owls, ... Dt 14:16
but they became g, powerful, ... Dt 26:5
of Egypt with his g power and .... Dt 26:8
using g terrors, signs, ... Dt 26:8
own eyes you saw the g troubles, ... Dt 29:3
Praise God because he is g! .... Dt 32:3
Moses had g power, and he did .... Dt 34:12
he did g and wonderful things .... Dt 34:12
All the land from the g river, ... Jos 1:4
to make you g in the opinion .... Jos 3:7
in a heap a g distance away at .... Jos 3:16
made Joshua g in the opinion .... Jos 4:14
know he has g power and so you .... Jos 4:24
you do for your own g name?" .... Jos 7:9
them in a g victory at Gibeon .... Jos 10:10
Makir was a g soldier, so the .... Jos 17:1
of you, and you have g power. .... Jos 17:17
down to the g Stone of Bohan .... Jos 18:17
has forced many a g and powerful .... Jos 23:9
LORD has done g things for you. .... Jos 23:14
but the LORD did g things for us .... Jos 24:17
he will send you g trouble. .... Jos 24:20
had seen what g things the LORD .... Jdg 2:7
his tent by the g tree in .... Jdg 4:11
beside the g tree standing .... Jdg 9:6
In a g defeat Jephthah struck .... Jdg 11:33
and I fought a g battle against .... Jdg 12:2
entered Samson with g power, ... Jdg 14:6
Samson and gave him g power. .... Jdg 14:19
Samson and gave him g power. .... Jdg 15:14
your servant, this g victory. .... Jdg 15:18
the secret of your g strength." .... Jdg 16:15
and to offer a g sacrifice to.................... Jdg 16:23
May your family be g like his." .... Ru 4:12
humble, and others he makes g.............. 1Sa 2:7

G

was very g because they did 1Sa 2:17
gave a g shout of joy that 1Sa 4:5
It was a g defeat for Israel, ... 1Sa 4:10
his head to show his g sadness. 1Sa 4:12
it to Gath, there was a g panic. 1Sa 5:9
has given us this g sickness. 1Sa 6:9
Israelites had a g celebration. 1Sa 11:15
and see the g thing the LORD................. 1Sa 12:16
had g success in everything he 1Sa 18:14
the LORD won a g victory for all 1Sa 19:5
do anything g or small without 1Sa 20:2
will do g things and succeed. 1Sa 26:25
You know that a g man died today 2Sa 3:38
his kingdom because the LORD 2Sa 5:12
as any of the g people on the 2Sa 7:9
have done this g thing because 2Sa 7:21
This is why you are g, Lord GOD! 2Sa 7:22
You did g and wonderful miracles 2Sa 7:23
'I will make your family g.' 2Sa 7:27
me, I saw some g excitement, but 2Sa 18:29
came to the g rock at Gibeon,................. 2Sa 20:8
You have stooped to make me g. 2Sa 22:36
LORD gives g victories to his 2Sa 22:51
The man made g by the Most High 2Sa 23:1
LORD gave a g victory for the 2Sa 23:10
And the LORD gave a g victory. 2Sa 23:12
said to Gad, "I am in g trouble. 2Sa 24:14
showed g kindness to him when............... 1Ki 3:6
to rule this g people of yours." 1Ki 3:9
other king will be as g as you. 1Ki 3:13
God gave Solomon g wisdom so he 1Ki 4:29
everything from the g cedar 1Ki 4:33
son to rule over this g nation!" 1Ki 5:7
a g sickness will spread among 1Ki 8:37
g many people celebrated before 1Ki 8:65
became a very g sin, because 1Ki 12:30
So there was g anger against the 2Ki 3:27
had told you to do some g thing, ... 2Ki 5:13
So he prepared a g feast for the 2Ki 6:23
tell me all the g things Elisha 2Ki 8:4
because I have a g sacrifice for 2Ki 10:19
of Egypt with g power and 2Ki 17:36
The g king, the king of 2Ki 18:19
Listen to what the g king, ... 2Ki 18:28
The LORD gave them a g victory. 1Ch 11:14
that he had made his kingdom g. 1Ch 14:2
Obed-Edom's house with g joy. 1Ch 15:25
The LORD is g; he should be 1Ch 16:25
as any of the g people on the 1Ch 17:8
made known all these g things. 1Ch 17:19
known by the g and wonderful 1Ch 17:21
that you would make my family g. 1Ch 17:25
said to Gad, "I am in g trouble. 1Ch 21:13
We should build a g Temple for 1Ch 22:5
LORD, you are g and powerful. 1Ch 29:11
to make anyone g and strong.................. 1Ch 29:12
LORD made Solomon g before all 1Ch 29:25
with him and made him very g. 2Ch 1:1
The temple I build will be g, ... 2Ch 2:5
a g sickness will spread among 2Ch 6:28
told even half of your g wisdom! 2Ch 9:6
and cattle as a g feast to honor 2Ch 18:2
the g prophecies against him, ... 2Ch 24:27
who fought with g power to help 2Ch 26:13
is already so g that he is angry 2Ch 28:13
days with g joy to the LORD 2Ch 30:21
those whom the g and honorable .... Ezr 4:10
the Temple of the g God is. .... Ezr 5:8
Temple that a g king of Israel .... Ezr 5:11
until now, our guilt has been g. .... Ezr 9:7
evil things, and our guilt is g. .... Ezr 9:13
you are the g God who is to be .... Ne 1:5
with your g strength and power................ Ne 1:10

the wall from the g tower that .... Ne 3:27
the Lord, who is g and powerful. .... Ne 4:14
I am doing a g work, and I can't................. Ne 6:3
the LORD, the g God, and all .... Ne 8:6
and to celebrate with g joy. .... Ne 8:12
quickly, and you have g love. .... Ne 9:17
You have g mercy, so you did not .... Ne 9:19
they enjoyed your g goodness. .... Ne 9:25
You had g mercy and gave them............... Ne 9:27
But because your mercy is g, ... Ne 9:31
you are the g and mighty and................. Ne 9:32
The land's g harvest belongs to .... Ne 9:37
God had given them g joy. .... Ne 12:43
on me because of your g love. .... Ne 13:22
showing off the g wealth of his .... Est 1:4
and his own g riches and glory. .... Est 1:4
the king gave a g banquet for .... Est 2:18
there was g sadness and loud .... Est 4:3
And all the g things Xerxes did .... Est 10:2
Mordecai, whom the king made g. .... Est 10:2
Suddenly a g wind came from the .... Job 1:19
People g and small are in the .... Job 3:19
is deep, and his power is g; .... Job 9:4
He makes nations g and then .... Job 12:23
I could make g speeches against .... Job 16:4
and g misery will come down on .... Job 20:22
'Where is this g man's house?' .... Job 21:28
I will always have g strength.' .... Job 29:20
G fears overwhelm me. They blow .... Job 30:15
my honor away as if by a g wind, ... Job 30:15
In his g power God grabs hold of .... Job 30:18
celebrated my g wealth or the .... Job 31:25
while in bed in g pain; .... Job 33:19
nor all your g strength will .... Job 36:19
God is g and powerful; .... Job 36:22
God is so g, greater than we can .... Job 36:26
when he thunders with a g sound. .... Job 37:4
he does g things we cannot.................... Job 37:5
reach. He has g strength; he is .... Job 37:23
wild ox for its g strength and .... Job 39:11
With g excitement, the horse .... Job 39:24
Let your g anger punish;....................... Job 40:11
its g strength and well-formed .... Job 41:12
one can force open its g jaws;................. Job 41:14
There is g strength in its neck. .... Job 41:22
Obey the LORD with g fear. .... Ps 2:11
Because of your g love, I can .... Ps 5:7
You have stooped to make me g. .... Ps 18:35
LORD gives g victories to his .... Ps 18:50
Keeping them brings g reward. .... Ps 19:11
He has g glory because you gave .... Ps 21:5
you in the g meeting of your .... Ps 22:25
I praise you in the g meeting. .... Ps 26:12
How g is your goodness that you .... Ps 31:19
He made the g ocean stay in its .... Ps 33:7
No king is saved by his g army. .... Ps 33:16
escapes by g strength. .... Ps 33:16
praise you in the g meeting. .... Ps 35:18
is as deep as the g ocean. .... Ps 36:6
goodness in the g meeting of .... Ps 40:9
the people in the g meeting. .... Ps 40:10
But it was your g power and .... Ps 44:3
He is the g King over all the .... Ps 47:2
The LORD is g; he should be .... Ps 48:1
it is the city of the G King. .... Ps 48:2
Listen, both g and small, rich .... Ps 49:2
g love reaches to the skies, ... Ps 57:10
your power is g, your enemies .... Ps 66:3
and a g army told the news: .... Ps 68:11
of your g love, answer me .... Ps 69:13
Because of your g kindness, ... Ps 69:16
You have done g things; .... Ps 71:19
his fame is g in Israel............................. Ps 76:1

G

breaks the spirits of g leaders; .... Ps 76:12
No god is as g as our God. .... Ps 77:13
Use your g power to save those .... Ps 79:11
is in charge of the g meeting; .... Ps 82:1
and have g love for those who .... Ps 86:5
You are g and you do miracles. .... Ps 86:10
You have g love for me. .... Ps 86:13
have g love and faithfulness. .... Ps 86:15
Your arm has g power. Your hand .... Ps 89:13
Your anger is as g as our fear .... Ps 90:11
you have done such g things! .... Ps 92:5
because the LORD is the g God, ... Ps 95:3
great God, the g King over all .... Ps 95:3
because the LORD is g; .... Ps 96:4
The LORD in Jerusalem is g; .... Ps 99:2
it is g, holy and to be feared. .... Ps 99:3
Because of your g anger, you .... Ps 102:10
quickly, and he has g love. .... Ps 103:8
so g is his love for those who .... Ps 103:11
LORD my God, you are very g. .... Ps 104:1
own sake, to show his g power. .... Ps 106:8
who had done g things in Egypt, ... Ps 106:21
for them because of his g love. .... Ps 106:45
did business on the g oceans. .... Ps 107:23
g love reaches to the skies, ... Ps 108:4
The LORD does g things; .... Ps 111:2
They will be given g honor. .... Ps 112:9
rules as people enjoy g riches. .... Ps 119:14
as if I had found a g treasure. .... Ps 119:162
LORD has done g things for them. .... Ps 126:2
LORD has done g things for us, ... Ps 126:3
LORD, I am in g trouble, so I .... Ps 130:1
I don't do g things, and I can't .... Ps 131:1
I know that the LORD is g. .... Ps 135:5
Only he can do g miracles. .... Ps 136:4
did it with his g power and .... Ps 136:12
He defeated g kings. His love .... Ps 136:17
because the LORD's glory is g. .... Ps 138:5
The LORD is g and worthy of our .... Ps 145:3
one can understand how g he is. .... Ps 145:3
and I will tell how g you are. .... Ps 145:6
remember your g goodness and .... Ps 145:7
Our Lord is g and very powerful. .... Ps 147:5
the LORD, because he alone is g. .... Ps 148:13
wisdom, and it will make you g; .... Pr 4:8
hard worker will have g wealth. .... Pr 12:27
people have g understanding, ... Pr 14:29
what is right makes a nation g, ... Pr 14:34
and cause their mother g sorrow. .... Pr 17:25
in secrecy will quiet g anger. .... Pr 21:14
important than having g riches. .... Pr 22:1
people have g power, and those .... Pr 24:5
with knowledge have g strength. .... Pr 24:5
Those two can cause g disaster! .... Pr 24:22
king and act as if you are g. .... Pr 25:6
triumph, there is g happiness, ... Pr 28:12
Then I did g things: I built .... Ec 2:4
God gives g wealth, riches, and .... Ec 6:2
A g king fought against it and .... Ec 9:14
calm solves g problems. .... Ec 10:4
there are a g many treasures .... Is 2:7
the LORD and from his g power! .... Is 2:10
Lebanon and the g oak trees of .... Is 2:13
of the LORD and his g power, ... Is 2:19
of the LORD and his g power, ... Is 2:21
the heroes and g soldiers, ... Is 3:2
will be very beautiful and g. .... Is 4:2
All the g people will die of .... Is 5:13
people and the g people will be .... Is 5:15
me with his g power and warned .... Is 8:11
those lands will be made g. .... Is 9:1
now they have seen a g light. .... Is 9:2
but we will put g cedars there." .... Is 9:10

burns away the g trees and rich .... Is 10:18
with his g power will chop them .... Is 10:33
chop them down like a g tree. .... Is 10:33
who are g will be cut down; .... Is 10:33
And the g trees of Lebanon will .... Is 10:34
he has done and how g he is. .... Is 12:4
because he has done g things. .... Is 12:5
of Israel does g things before .... Is 12:6
man who caused g fear on earth, ... Is 14:16
is like the crashing of g waves. .... Is 17:12
the g leaders in this land will .... Is 24:4
with his g and hard and powerful .... Is 27:1
at that time a g trumpet will be .... Is 27:13
earthquakes, and g noises, with .... Is 29:6
The harvest will be rich and g, ... Is 30:23
to hear his g voice and to see .... Is 30:30
like a g fire that burns .... Is 30:30
like a g storm with much rain. .... Is 30:30
Fools will not be called g, ... Is 32:5
The LORD is very g, and he lives .... Is 33:5
Then your g wealth will be .... Is 33:23
The g king, the king of .... Is 36:4
Listen to what the g king, ... Is 36:13
understand how g his wisdom is. .... Is 40:28
because the LORD did g things! .... Is 44:23
idols will be put to g shame; .... Is 45:16
g leaders will bow down before .... Is 49:7
ruin and disaster, g hunger and .... Is 51:19
will make him a g man among .... Is 53:12
but with g kindness I will bring .... Is 54:7
The g trading ships will come. .... Is 60:9
The g trees of Lebanon will be .... Is 60:13
But I will make you g from now .... Is 60:15
forward with his g power? .... Is 63:1
He has shown g mercy to us and .... Is 63:7
happened and shake with g fear!" .... Je 2:12
by the LORD and his g anger. .... Je 4:26
g nation is coming from the far .... Je 6:22
are g, and your name is great .... Je 10:6
and your name is g and powerful. .... Je 10:6
of Judah and the g pride of .... Je 13:9
anger, my very g anger, I myself .... Je 21:5
you with my g power and strength .... Je 21:5
to Jerusalem, this g city?' .... Je 22:8
'I will build a g palace for .... Je 22:14
in your house make you a g king? .... Je 22:15
many nations and many g kings. .... Je 25:14
animals with my g power and .... Je 27:5
nations and g kings will make .... Je 27:7
many countries and g kingdoms. .... Je 28:8
This is a time of g trouble for .... Je 30:7
guilt was so g and your sins .... Je 30:14
to you because of your g guilt, ... Je 30:15
A g many people will come back. .... Je 31:8
earth with your very g power. .... Je 32:17
G and powerful God, your name is .... Je 32:18
You plan and do g things. .... Je 32:19
miracles and your g power and .... Je 32:21
brought g terror on everyone. .... Je 32:21
have brought this g disaster to .... Je 32:42
them enjoy g peace and safety. .... Je 33:6
So I showed my g anger against .... Je 44:6
you doing such g harm to .... Je 44:7
to her, we have had g problems. .... Je 44:18
'I have sworn by my g name: .... Je 44:26
are looking for g things for .... Je 45:5
army as if it were a g forest," .... Je 46:23
I know Moab's g pride, but it is .... Je 48:30
happened fill them with g fear." .... Je 48:39
against Babylon many g nations. .... Je 50:9
Run from the LORD's g anger. .... Je 51:45
Jerusalem once was a g city .... La 1:1
me on the day of his g anger. .... La 1:12

and the priest in his g anger. ....La 2:6
LORD, your loyalty is g. ....La 3:23
he also has mercy and g love. ....La 3:32
was a g cloud with a bright ....Eze 1:4
I felt the g power of the LORD. ....Eze 3:14
when I punish you in my g anger. ....Eze 5:15
of Israel and Judah is very g. ....Eze 9:9
Even if three g men like Noah, ...Eze 14:14
of food and lived in g comfort, ...Eze 16:49
fruit and become a g cedar tree. ....Eze 17:23
I will use my g power and ....Eze 20:33
With my g power and strength and ....Eze 20:34
breaking heart and g sadness. ....Eze 21:6
She had g sexual desire for her ....Eze 23:5
attack with g armies and with ....Eze 23:24
anger and do g acts of revenge ....Eze 25:17
horsemen, and a g army. ....Eze 26:7
your people had g power on the ....Eze 26:17
you because of your g wealth. ....Eze 27:12
With your g wealth and goods, ...Eze 27:33
Through your g skill in trading, ...Eze 28:5
You are like a g crocodile that ....Eze 29:3
I will destroy g numbers of ....Eze 30:10
I will destroy g numbers of ....Eze 30:15
Pelusium will be in g pain. ....Eze 30:16
g nations lived in the tree's ....Eze 31:6
So the tree was g and beautiful, ...Eze 31:7
of God were not as g as it was. ....Eze 31:8
trees did not have such g limbs. ....Eze 31:8
the g waters stopped flowing. ....Eze 31:15
her sadness about the g tree, ...Eze 31:15
down with the g tree to the ....Eze 31:17
lived under the g tree's shade. ....Eze 31:17
prove the holiness of my g name, ...Eze 36:23
jealousy and g anger I tell you ....Eze 38:19
will surely be a g earthquake in ....Eze 38:19
Then I will show how g I am. ....Eze 38:23
a g sacrifice which I will ....Eze 39:17
you with gifts and g honor. ....Da 2:6
No g and powerful king has ever ....Da 2:10
it will not be as g as yours. ....Da 2:39
In this way the g God showed you ....Da 2:45
I wish you peace and g wealth! ....Da 4:1
acts are g, and his miracles ....Da 4:3
You have become g and powerful, ...Da 4:22
have built this g Babylon as my ....Da 4:30
gave back my g honor and power ....Da 4:36
your father Nebuchadnezzar a g, ...Da 5:18
I wish you g peace and wealth. ....Da 6:25
'The four g animals are four ....Da 7:17
so the male goat became very g. ....Da 8:8
you are a g God who causes fear ....Da 9:4
you brought on us a g disaster. ....Da 9:12
received a vision about a g war. ....Da 10:1
beside the g Tigris River. ....Da 10:4
alone, watching this g vision. ....Da 10:8
will rule with g power and will ....Da 11:3
his own kingdom with g power. ....Da 11:5
the g prince who protects your ....Da 12:1
day of Jezreel will be truly g. ....Hos 1:11
sent to the g king of Assyria ....Hos 5:13
under the g king of Assyria ....Hos 8:10
very much, and your hatred is g. ....Hos 9:7
Assyria as a gift to the g king. ....Hos 10:6
the LORD is his g name. ....Hos 12:5
I took him away in my g anger. ....Hos 13:11
g and powerful army will spread ....Joe 2:2
quickly, and he has g love. ....Joe 2:13
I sent my g army against you ....Joe 2:25
of Moab will die in a g noise, ...Am 2:2
where you will see g confusion ....Am 3:9
g houses will come to an end, ...Am 3:15
there go to the g city Hamath; ....Am 6:2

go to the g city of Nineveh, ...Jnh 1:2
LORD sent a g wind on the sea ....Jnh 1:4
fault that this g storm has come ....Jnh 1:12
up, go to the g city Nineveh, ...Jnh 3:2
quickly, and you have g love. ....Jnh 4:2
concern for the g city Nineveh, ...Jnh 4:11
quickly, and his power is g. ....Nah 1:3
do g things once again in our ....Hab 3:2
horses, stirring the g waters. ....Hab 3:15
remember how g the Temple was ....Hag 2:3
say, 'The LORD is g, even ....Mal 1:5
I am a g king," says the LORD ....Mal 1:14
before that g and terrifying day ....Mal 4:5
in darkness will see a g light. ....Mt 4:16
Some were in g pain, some had ....Mt 4:24
you have a g reward waiting for ....Mt 5:12
them will be g in the kingdom ....Mt 5:19
that is the city of the g King. ....Mt 5:35
from the hill, g crowds followed ....Mt 8:1
A g storm arose on the lake so ....Mt 8:24
he saw a g crowd waiting. ....Mt 14:14
Woman, you have g faith! ....Mt 15:28
G crowds came to Jesus, bringing ....Mt 15:30
of Man will sit on his g throne. ....Mt 19:28
wants to become g among you must ....Mt 20:26
a g many people followed him. ....Mt 20:29
makes himself g will be made ....Mt 23:12
himself humble will be made g. ....Mt 23:12
come and perform g wonders and ....Mt 24:24
the sky with g power and glory. ....Mt 24:30
will come again in his g glory, ...Mt 25:31
be King and sit on his g throne. ....Mt 25:31
been sold for a g deal of money ....Mt 26:9
A g crowd gathered around him, ...Mk 4:1
he saw a g crowd waiting. ....Mk 6:34
there was a g crowd with Jesus ....Mk 8:1
they saw a g crowd around them ....Mk 9:14
wants to become g among you must ....Mk 10:43
followers and a g many people, ...Mk 10:46
you see all these g buildings? ....Mk 13:2
come and perform g wonders and ....Mk 13:22
clouds with g power and glory. ....Mk 13:26
There were a g many people ....Lk 1:10
John will be a g man for the ....Lk 1:15
He will be g and will be called ....Lk 1:32
One has done g things for me. ....Lk 1:49
proud and think g things about ....Lk 1:51
news that will be a g joy to all ....Lk 2:10
you have a g reward in heaven. ....Lk 6:23
Then you will have a g reward, ...Lk 6:35
A g prophet has come to us! ....Lk 7:16
forgiven, so she showed g love. ....Lk 7:47
When a g crowd was gathered, ...Lk 8:4
amazed at the g power of God. ....Lk 9:43
There are a g many people to ....Lk 10:2
make themselves g will be made ....Lk 14:11
humble will be made g." ....Lk 14:11
make themselves g will be made ....Lk 18:14
humble will be made g." ....Lk 18:14
there will be g earthquakes, ...Lk 21:11
events and g signs will come ....Lk 21:11
G trouble will come upon this ....Lk 21:23
a cloud with power and g glory. ....Lk 21:27
The next day a g crowd who had ....Jn 12:12
about the g things God has done ....Ac 2:11
everyone felt g respect for God. ....Ac 2:43
they have done a g miracle, ...Ac 4:16
With g power the apostles were ....Ac 4:33
said he was a g man, and about ....Ac 5:36
a man with g faith and full of ....Ac 6:5
and a g number of the Jewish ....Ac 6:7
the power to do g miracles and ....Ac 6:8
and called himself a g man. ....Ac 8:9

of God, called 'the **G** Power'!" .... Ac 8:10
the people g during the time .... Ac 13:17
of that country with g power. .... Ac 13:17
so well that a g many Jews and .... Ac 14:1
fear and gave g honor to the .... Ac 19:17
temple of the g goddess Artemis .... Ac 19:27
the goddess of Ephesus, is g!" .... Ac 19:28
"**G** is Artemis of Ephesus!" .... Ac 19:34
temple of the g goddess Artemis .... Ac 19:35
So there was a g uproar. .... Ac 23:9
Bernice appeared with g show, ... Ac 25:23
small and g, what I have seen. .... Ac 26:22
But God shows his g love for us .... Rm 5:8
grace and the g gift of being .... Rm 5:17
compared to the g glory that .... Rm 8:18
I have g sorrow and always feel .... Rm 9:2
descendants of our g ancestors, ... Rm 9:5
are very g, and his wisdom .... Rm 11:33
since God has shown us g mercy, ... Rm 12:1
and the g things they saw .... Rm 15:19
Not many of you had g influence. 1Co 1:26
all were bought at a g price, ... 1Co 7:23
I may have faith so g I can move 1Co 13:2
for a g and growing work 1Co 16:9
We had g burdens there that were 2Co 1:8
from these g dangers of death, ... 2Co 1:10
shows that the g power is from 2Co 4:7
difficulties, and in g problems. 2Co 6:4
of our troubles I have g joy. 2Co 7:4
me about your g care for me, ... 2Co 7:7
the g care you have for us. 2Co 7:12
have been tested by g troubles, ... 2Co 8:2
much because of their g joy. 2Co 8:2
there will be a g harvest from 2Co 9:10
because of the g grace that God 2Co 9:14
that those "g apostles" are any 2Co 11:5
but those "g apostles" are not 2Co 12:11
power is very g for us who .... Eph 1:19
is the same as the g strength .... Eph 1:19
God's mercy is g, and he loved .... Eph 2:4
show the very g riches of his .... Eph 2:7
are too g to understand fully. .... Eph 3:8
Father in his g glory to give .... Eph 3:16
in the Lord and in his g power. .... Eph 6:10
which is so g we cannot .... Php 4:7
that you will also have g wisdom .... Col 1:9
you with his own g power so that .... Col 1:11
using Christ's g strength that .... Col 1:29
the Lord and from his g power. 2Th 1:9
will have g power, and he will 2Th 2:9
of our life of worship is g: 1Ti 3:16
Encourage them with g patience 2Ti 4:2
we wait for our g hope and the .... Tit 2:13
glory of our g God and Savior .... Tit 2:13
I have g joy and comfort, my .... Phm 1:7
of God, the **G** One in heaven. .... Heb 1:3
if we ignore this g salvation. .... Heb 2:3
using wonders, g signs, many .... Heb 2:4
Since we have a g high priest, ... Heb 4:14
can see how g Melchizedek was .... Heb 7:4
Abraham, the g father, gave him .... Heb 7:4
since we have a g priest over .... Heb 10:21
the past, which has a g reward. .... Heb 10:35
we remember g people who lived .... Heb 11:2
these g people died in faith. .... Heb 11:13
They stopped g fires and were .... Heb 11:34
surrounded by a g cloud of .... Heb 12:1
but it brags about g things. .... Jam 3:5
person prays, g things happen. .... Jam 5:16
God's g mercy he has caused us 1Pe 1:3
gave us the very g and precious 2Pe 1:4
will be given a very g welcome 2Pe 1:11
to be judged on the g day. .... Jud 1:6

in you and can give you g joy. .... Jud 1:24
and there was a g earthquake. .... Rev 6:12
The g day for their anger has .... Rev 6:17
and there was a g number of .... Rev 7:9
have come out of the g distress. .... Rev 7:14
tied at the g river Euphrates." .... Rev 9:14
the street of the g city where .... Rev 11:8
hour there was a g earthquake, ... Rev 11:13
have used your g power and have .... Rev 11:17
who respect you, g and small. .... Rev 11:18
earthquake, and a g hailstorm. .... Rev 11:19
And then a g wonder appeared in .... Rev 12:1
two wings of a g eagle so she .... Rev 12:14
and his throne and g authority. .... Rev 13:2
beast does g miracles so that .... Rev 13:13
small and g, rich and poor, ... Rev 13:16
ruined is the g city of Babylon! .... Rev 14:8
them into the g winepress of .... Rev 14:19
heaven that was g and amazing. .... Rev 15:1
You do g and wonderful things, ... Rev 15:3
They were burned by the g heat, ... Rev 16:9
bowl on the g river Euphrates .... Rev 16:12
the battle on the g day of God .... Rev 16:14
The g city split into three .... Rev 16:19
the sins of Babylon the **G**, ... Rev 16:19
be given to the g prostitute, ... Rev 17:1
THE **G** BABYLON MOTHER OF .... Rev 17:5
you saw is the g city that rules .... Rev 17:18
This angel had g power, and his .... Rev 18:1
ruined is the g city of Babylon! .... Rev 18:2
rich from the g wealth of her .... Rev 18:3
crying, and g hunger, and she .... Rev 18:8
for you, g city, powerful .... Rev 18:10
How terrible for the g city! .... Rev 18:16
never a city like this g city!" .... Rev 18:18
How terrible for the g city! .... Rev 18:19
the g city of Babylon will be .... Rev 18:21
were the world's g people, ... Rev 18:23
sounded like a g many people .... Rev 19:1
honor him, both small and g!" .... Rev 19:5
sounded like a g many people, ... Rev 19:6
together for the g feast of God .... Rev 19:17
free, slave, small, and g." .... Rev 19:18
Then I saw a g white throne and .... Rev 20:11
I saw the dead, g and small, ... Rev 20:12
The city had a g high wall with .... Rev 21:12

GREAT-GRANDCHILDREN
even your grandchildren and g. .... Ex 20:5
grandchildren, their g, and .... Ex 34:7
grandchildren, their g, and .... Nu 14:18
even their grandchildren and g. .... Dt 5:9
The g of these two peoples may .... Dt 23:8
his children, grandchildren, g, ... Job 42:16

GREAT-GRANDFATHER
God as David, his g, had been. 1Ki 15:3

GREAT-GREAT-GRANDCHILDREN
After your g are born, your .... Ge 15:16
and their g." .... Ex 34:7
-grandchildren, and their g.' .... Nu 14:18
far as your g will be kings of 2Ki 10:30
down to your g will be kings 2Ki 15:12
great-grandchildren, and g. .... Job 42:16

GREATLY
You will g desire your husband, ... Ge 3:16
cause their numbers to grow g. .... Ge 17:20
The Lord has g blessed my master .... Ge 24:35
Then Isaac trembled and said, ... Ge 27:33
and their number grew g. .... Ex 1:7
he has done has helped you g. 1Sa 9:4
Saul said, "I am g troubled. 1Sa 28:15
stones, which g upset David. 1Sa 30:6

G

death, he missed Absalom g. 2Sa 13:39
Absalom was g praised for his 2Sa 14:25
I have sinned g by what I have 2Sa 24:10
the LORD and led them to sin g. 2Ki 17:21
I have sinned g by what I have 1Ch 21:8
he added g to the wall at Ophel. 2Ch 27:3
its traders were g respected. .... Is 23:8
those who were g respected. .... Is 23:9
People will g honor and respect .... Is 52:13
people of Judah have sinned g. .... Je 5:6
and you will be g hated by .... Je 49:15
I am upset and g troubled. .... La 1:20
When the people are suffering g, ... Eze 7:25
king will cry g, the prince will .... Eze 7:27
You will be g hated by everyone. .... Ob 1:2
Rejoice g, people of Jerusalem! .... Zch 9:9
The followers were g amazed. .... Mk 6:51
home alive and were g comforted. .... Ac 20:12
her will suffer g if they do not .... Rev 2:22

GREECE
The male goat is the king of G, ... Da 8:21
Macedonia. Then he went to G, ... Ac 20:2

GREED
g kills selfish people. .... Pr 1:19
G has two daughters named 'Give' .... Pr 30:15
g, evil actions, lying, doing .... Mk 7:22
you are full of g and evil. .... Lk 11:39
guard against all kinds of g. .... Lk 12:15
you, or any kind of evil or g. .... Eph 5:3
things that are evil, and g. .... Col 3:5

GREEDY
All g people end up this way; .... Pr 1:19
or does evil things, or is g. .... Eph 5:5

GREEK
She was G, born in Phoenicia, in .... Mk 7:26
he go to the G cities where our .... Jn 7:35
and teach the G people there? .... Jn 7:35
There were some G people, too, ... Jn 12:20
in Hebrew, in Latin, and in G. .... Jn 19:20
the Jewish people who spoke G, ... Ac 9:29
(whose G name was Dorcas) .... Ac 9:36
for Bar-Jesus in the G language. .... Ac 13:8
but his father was a G. .... Ac 16:1
that Timothy's father was G. .... Ac 16:3
many important G women and men. .... Ac 17:12
every Jew and G in Asia heard .... Ac 19:10
commander said, "Do you speak G? .... Ac 21:37
even though he was a G. .... Gal 2:3
no difference between Jew and G, ... Gal 3:28
Abaddon and in the G language is .... Rev 9:11

GREEK-SPEAKING
the G followers had an argument .... Ac 6:1
The G widows were not getting .... Ac 6:1

GREEKS
Jerusalem to the G so that you .... Joe 3:6
spoke also to G, telling them .... Ac 11:20
great many Jews and G believed. .... Ac 14:1
with many of the G who worshiped .... Ac 17:4
the Jews and the G who worshiped .... Ac 17:17
the Jews and the G in the synagogue .... Ac 18:4
Ephesus—Jews and G—learned about ...... Ac 19:17
both Jews and G to change their .... Ac 20:21
brought some G into the Temple. .... Ac 21:28
G and those who are not Greeks, ... Rm 1:14
Greeks and those who are not G, ... Rm 1:14
miracles, and the G want wisdom. 1Co 1:22
God has called—Jews and G. 1Co 1:24
others—Jews, G, or God's church— 1Co 10:32
of us are Jews, and some are G. 1Co 12:13
difference between G and Jews, ... Col 3:11

GREEN
given all the g plants as food .... Ge 1:30
Earlier I gave you the g plants, ... Ge 9:3
He lets me rest in g pastures. .... Ps 23:2
Like g plants, they will soon .... Ps 37:2
will be healthy like a g leaf. .... Pr 11:28
its leaves are always g. .... Je 17:8
sit in groups on the g grass. .... Mk 6:39
and all the g grass, and a third .... Rev 8:7

GREET
They will g you and offer you 1Sa 10:4
arrived, and Saul went to g him. 1Sa 13:10
at Carmel, and g him for me. 1Sa 25:5
from the desert to g our master, ... 1Sa 25:14
son Joram to g and congratulate 2Sa 8:10
Hadoram to g and congratulate 1Ch 18:10
If you loudly g your neighbor .... Pr 27:14
up from their thrones to g you. .... Is 14:9
love people to g them with .... Mt 23:7
for people to g them with .... Mk 12:38
for people to g them with .... Lk 20:46
g for me the church that meets .... Rm 16:5
G each other with a holy kiss. .... Rm 16:16
and Priscilla g you in the Lord, ... 1Co 16:19
G each other with a holy kiss. 2Co 13:12
G each of God's people in Christ .... Php 4:21
All of God's people g you, ... Php 4:22
the cousin of Barnabas, g you. .... Col 4:10
friend Luke, the doctor, g you. .... Col 4:14
G the brothers and sisters in .... Col 4:15
And g Nympha and the church that .... Col 4:15
g you and write this with my own .... Col 4:18
G Priscilla and Aquila and the 2Ti 4:19
and sisters in Christ g you. 2Ti 4:21
All who are with me g you. .... Tit 3:15
G those who love us in the faith. .... Tit 3:15
G all your leaders and all of .... Heb 13:24
of your chosen sister g you. 2Jn 1:13
The friends here g you. 3Jn 1:15
Please g each friend there by 3Jn 1:15

GREETED
Micah's house, and g the Levite. .... Jdg 18:15
Bethlehem and g his workers, ... Ru 2:4
David g the men at the ravine. 1Sa 30:21
Jehu g him and said, "Are you as 2Ki 10:15
house and g Elizabeth. .... Lk 1:40
you love to be g with respect .... Lk 11:43
where we g the believers and .... Ac 21:7
Paul g them and told them .... Ac 21:19

GREETING
Ahimaaz called a g to the king. 2Sa 18:28
wondered what this g might mean. .... Lk 1:29
When Elizabeth heard Mary's g, ... Lk 1:41
me no kiss of g, but she has .... Lk 7:45
am writing this g with my own 1Co 16:21

GREETINGS
to Jesus and said, "G, Teacher!" .... Mt 26:49
Jesus met them and said, "G." .... Mt 28:9
Antioch, Syria, and Cilicia: G! .... Ac 15:23
he went and gave g to the church .... Ac 18:22

GREETS
If anyone g you, don't respond. 2Ki 4:29
is called Justus, also g you. .... Col 4:11
from your group, also g you. .... Col 4:12
my son in Christ, also g you. 1Pe 5:13

GREW
Isaac g, and when he became old .... Ge 21:8
and their number g greatly. .... Ex 1:7
more the Israelites g in number .... Ex 1:12
the child g older, the woman .... Ex 2:10
and it g up with him and his 2Sa 12:3

The tree g large and strong. .... Da 4:11
off and four horns g in place of .... Da 8:8
little horn g until it reached .... Da 8:10
which g and choked the good .... Mk 4:7
And so the child g up and became .... Lk 1:80
The little child g and became .... Lk 2:40
the faith and g larger every day .... Ac 16:5
Cilicia, but I g up in this city .... Ac 22:3
Moses, when he g up, refused to.............. Heb 11:24

GRIDDLE
grain offering is cooked on a g, ... Le 2:5
with oil and cooked on a g,.................... Le 6:21
oven, cooked on a g, or baked in .... Le 7:9

GRIEF
words, he tore his clothes in g. 2Ki 6:30
rough cloth to show their g. 1Ch 21:16
my whole being is tired from g. .... Ps 31:9
Because of my g, my skin hangs .... Ps 102:5
they will bring you g later on. .... Pr 29:21
your breasts in g, because the .... Is 32:12
sadness and attacked me with g. .... La 3:5

GRIEVE
are blessed who g, for God will .... Mt 5:4

GRIEVED
in the desert and g him there.................. Ps 78:40

GRIND
large stones to g grain into .... Is 47:2
will cry and g their teeth with .... Mt 22:13
will cry and g your teeth with................ Lk 13:28

GRINDING
hear the millstone g grain. .... Ec 12:4
women will be g grain with a .... Mt 24:41
The sound of g grain will never .... Rev 18:22

GRINDS
he g his teeth at me; .... Job 16:9
foams at the mouth, g his teeth, ... Mk 9:18

GRINS
and the one who g is planning .... Pr 16:30

GRIPPED
We are g by our pain, like a .... Je 6:24
Distress has g him. His pain is .... Je 50:43

GRIPS
and shaking, and terror g me. .... Ps 55:5

GROAN
I g because God's heavy hand is.............. Job 23:2
Dying people g in the city, ... Job 24:12
You will g at the end of your .... Pr 5:11
will moan and g for the raisin .... Is 16:7
from the Nile, will g and cry; .... Is 19:8
how you will g like a woman .... Je 22:23
Her priests g, her young women.............. La 1:4
All of Jerusalem's people g, ... La 1:11
g over and over again, and I am .... La 1:22
g because of all the hateful, ... Eze 6:11
the people who g and cry about .... Eze 9:4
g with breaking heart and great .... Eze 21:6
G in front of the people. .... Eze 21:6
G silently; do not cry loudly .... Eze 24:17
your sins and g to each other.................. Eze 24:23
are injured and dying will g. .... Eze 26:15
But now we g in this tent. 2Co 5:2
body, we have burdens, and we g. 2Co 5:4

GROANED
people of Israel g, because they .... Ex 2:23

GROANING
have heard my g, and there is no .... La 1:21
more moaning and g for Judah. .... La 2:5

they ask you, 'Why are you g?' .... Eze 21:7
The animals are g! The herds of .... Joe 1:18

GROANS
my g pour out like water. .... Job 3:24
saving me, far away from my g, ... Ps 22:1
evil people rule, everyone g. .... Pr 29:2
She g and turns away.......................... La 1:8

GROUND
was no person to care for the g, ... Ge 2:5
dust from the g and formed a man .... Ge 2:7
for food to grow out of the g. .... Ge 2:9
So I will put a curse on the g,.................. Ge 3:17
Later you will return to the g, ... Ge 3:19
Eden to work the g from which he .... Ge 3:23
from the g as a gift to God..................... Ge 4:3
is crying out to me from the g. .... Ge 4:10
cursed in your work with the g, ... Ge 4:11
again curse the g because of .... Ge 8:21
facedown on the g before them .... Ge 18:2
you are standing on holy g. .... Ex 3:5
LORD said, "Throw it on the g."............... Ex 4:3
making the sea become dry g. .... Ex 14:21
the fire. He g it into powder. .... Ex 32:20
about three feet deep on the g, ... Nu 11:31
the g under the men split open. .... Nu 16:31
but the g around it was wet with .... Jdg 6:40
He made them lie on the g,.................... 2Sa 8:2
on him as dew falls on the g. 2Sa 17:12
Elisha crossed over on dry g. 2Ki 2:8
down to the g to worship God. .... Job 1:20
they sat on the g with Job seven .... Job 2:13
times do not come up from the g, ... Job 5:6
if its roots grow old in the g, ... Job 14:8
its eggs on the g and lets them .... Job 39:14
down and will speak from the g; .... Is 29:4
and the dry g will have springs. .... Is 35:7
The young men g grain at the.............. La 5:13
his feet hardly touched the g. .... Da 8:5
sheep to the g and then walked .... Da 8:7
plow the new g of knowledge. .... Hos 10:12
rain and the g holds back its .... Hag 1:10
fell on good g where it grew .... Mt 13:8
told the people to sit on the g. .... Mt 15:35
and hid your money in the g. .... Mt 25:25
fell on good g and began to grow .... Mk 4:8
drops of blood falling to the g. .... Lk 22:44
on the g with his finger. .... Jn 8:6
he spit on the g and made some .... Jn 9:6
fall to the g and die to make .... Jn 12:24
you are standing on holy g. .... Ac 7:33
got up from the g and opened his .... Ac 9:8
fell to the g and heard a voice .... Ac 22:7
We all fell to the g. .... Ac 26:14
must die in the g before it can 1Co 15:36
a stone in the g in Jerusalem. 1Pe 2:6
that are pulled out of the g.................... Jud 1:12

GROUP
Saul met a g of prophets. 1Sa 10:10

GROUPED
He g all the people of Judah and 2Ch 25:5

GROUPS
the people sit in g on the green .... Mk 6:39
people to sit in g of about .... Lk 9:14

GROVES
and olive g and give them to his.............. 1Sa 8:14

GROW
good for food to g out of the .... Ge 2:9
They must let their hair g long. .... Nu 6:5
But his hair began to g again.................. Jdg 16:22
moon, and stars will g dark; .... Ec 12:2

A new branch will **g** from a stump .... Is 11:1
Cry loudly, you who **g** grapes. .... Joe 1:11
you did nothing to make it **g**. .... Jnh 4:10
how the lilies in the field **g**..................... Mt 6:28
and the wheat **g** together until .... Mt 13:30
the sun will **g** dark, and the .... Mt 24:29
Consider how the lilies **g**; .... Lk 12:27
we will **g** up in every way into .... Eph 4:15
make your love **g** more and 1Th 3:12
you know they **g** into quarrels. 2Ti 2:23
valuable crop to **g** from the.................... Jam 5:7
But **g** in the grace and knowledge 2Pe 3:18

GROWL

Lions may roar and **g**, but when.............. Job 4:10
Like dogs they **g** and roam around........... Ps 59:6
Like dogs they **g** and roam around........... Ps 59:14
They **g** as they grab their .... Is 5:29
All of us **g** like the bears. .... Is 59:11
they **g** like baby lions............................ Je 51:38
it does not **g** in its den when it .... Am 3:4

GROWLED

they have **g** at Israel. .... Je 2:15

GROWN

your flocks have **g** while I cared.............. Ge 30:29
younger son Shelah had **g** up, ... Ge 38:14
food that is **g** during the seven .... Ge 41:34
that had been **g** in the fields .... Ge 41:48
food has **g** on the land for two .... Ge 45:6
family of Levi) had **g** leaves. .... Nu 17:8
people ate food **g** on that land: .... Jos 5:11
They ate the food **g** in the land .... Jos 5:12
Joshua, you have **g** old, but.................... Jos 13:1
wait until they were **g** into men? .... Ru 1:13
until your beards have **g** back. 2Sa 10:5
young men who had **g** up with him 1Ki 12:8
young men who had **g** up with him 1Ki 12:10
until your beards have **g** back. 1Ch 19:5
young men who had **g** up with him 2Ch 10:8
young men who had **g** up with him 2Ch 10:10
sight has **g** weak because of my .... Job 17:7
My troubles have **g** larger; .... Ps 25:17
from fasting, and I have **g** thin. .... Ps 109:24
that dries up before it has **g**. .... Ps 129:6
strong ox, much grain can be **g**.............. Pr 14:4
Thorns had **g** up everywhere. .... Pr 24:31
and her breasts are not yet **g**.................. Sng 8:8
They have **g** big and fat. .... Je 5:28
have **g** strong in the land. .... Je 9:3
violence has **g**, and there is .... Eze 7:10
Violence has **g** into a weapon for .... Eze 7:11
the open pastures have **g** grass. .... Joe 2:22
grapevines have **g** much fruit.................. Joe 2:22
to Nazareth, where he had **g** up.............. Lk 4:16
Manaen (who had **g** up with Herod, ... Ac 13:1
get some of the food that was **g**.............. 2Ti 2:6
food is for those who are **g** up. .... Heb 5:14
the earth have **g** rich from the .... Rev 18:3

GROWN-UP

So let us go on to **g** teaching. .... Heb 6:1
will go on to **g** teaching if God .... Heb 6:3

GROWS

until my young son Shelah **g** up." .... Ge 38:11
everything that **g** in the fields................. Ex 9:22
If any food **g** there, allow the .... Ex 23:11
you like a plant that **g** bitter, ... Dt 29:18
planted, nothing **g**, and nothing .... Dt 29:23
anything that **g** on a grapevine, ... Jdg 13:14
will eat the grain that **g** wild, ... 2Ki 19:29
will eat what **g** wild from that. 2Ki 19:29
Food **g** on top of the earth, ... Job 28:5
g because you make it grow. .... Ps 65:9

like grass that **g** up in the .... Ps 90:5
know how a baby **g** inside the .... Ec 11:5
be proud of what the land **g**. .... Is 4:2
will eat the grain that **g** wild, ... Is 37:30
will eat what **g** wild from that. .... Is 37:30
a wild vine that **g** bad fruit? .... Je 2:21
a desert that **g** in a land where .... Je 17:6
Even if Babylon **g** until she.................... Je 51:53
and everyone's face **g** pale..................... Nah 2:10
person **g** and produces fruit, ... Mt 13:23
seeds, but when it **g**, it is one .... Mt 13:32
the seed still **g**, but the person .... Mk 4:27
person does not know how it **g**. .... Mk 4:27
the plant **g**, then the head, ... Mk 4:28
this seed **g** and becomes the .... Mk 4:32
The seed **g** and becomes a tree, ... Lk 13:19
So it **g** in the way God wants it .... Col 2:19
as a small flame **g** into a fire. 2Ti 1:6
land that **g** thorns and weeds .... Heb 6:8
then the sin **g** and brings death .... Jam 1:15

GROWTHS

You will have bad **g**, sores, and .... Dt 28:27
and gave them **g** on their skin. 1Sa 5:6
people in Gath **g** on their skin. 1Sa 5:9
troubled with **g** on their skin. 1Sa 5:12
models of the **g** on your skin 1Sa 6:4
models of the **g** and the rats 1Sa 6:5
and models of **g** on the cart. 1Sa 6:11
gold models of the **g** as penalty 1Sa 6:17

GRUMBLE

he has heard you **g** against him................ Ex 16:7
he has heard you **g** against him................ Ex 16:8

GRUMBLED

The people **g** to Moses and asked, ... Ex 15:24
community **g** to Moses and Aaron .... Ex 16:2
water, so they **g** against Moses. .... Ex 17:3
and **g** at God and Moses. .... Nu 21:5
We sinned when we **g** at you and .... Nu 21:7
g in your tents, saying, "The .... Dt 1:27
All the Israelites **g** against the .... Jos 9:18
They **g** in their tents and did .... Ps 106:25

GRUMBLING

so you are not **g** against us, ... Ex 16:7
You are not **g** against Aaron and .... Ex 16:8
you are **g** against the LORD." .... Ex 16:8
have heard the **g** and complaining .... Nu 14:27

GRUMBLINGS

because he has heard your **g**.'" .... Ex 16:9
I have heard the **g** of the people .... Ex 16:12

GUARANTEE

I will **g** you that he will be .... Ge 43:9
my father a **g** that the young .... Ge 44:32
about giving a **g** for somebody .... Pr 6:1
and don't **g** anyone's loan. .... Pr 22:26
hearts to be a **g** for all he has 2Co 1:22
Spirit to be a **g** for this new 2Co 5:5
Spirit is the **g** that we will .... Eph 1:14
that Jesus is the **g** of a better .... Heb 7:22

GUARANTEED

about Christ has been a **g** to you, ... 1Co 1:6

GUARANTEES

Whoever **g** to pay somebody else's........... Pr 11:15

GUARD

and captain of the palace **g**. .... Ge 37:36
were the rear **g** for all the .... Nu 10:25
So why have you set a **g** over me? .... Job 7:12
g me from the power of wicked .... Ps 140:4
you, Nineveh. **G** the defenses................... Nah 2:1
will stand like a **g** to watch and .... Hab 2:1
putting soldiers there to **g** it. .... Mt 27:66

GUARDED

Arrest him and g him while you .... Mk 14:44
been kept under g and chained .... Lk 8:29
Be careful and g against all .... Lk 12:15
The g said, "Is that the way you .... Jn 18:22
was ordered to g them carefully. .... Ac 16:23
to be kept under g in Herod's .... Ac 23:35
g what God has trusted to you. 1Ti 6:20

GUARDED

with the soldier who g him. .... Ac 28:16

GUARDIAN

the law was our g leading us to .... Gal 3:24
and we no longer live under a g. .... Gal 3:25

GUARDIANS

Jezreel and to the g of the sons 2Ki 10:1
the g sent a message to Jehu. 2Ki 10:5
of the city who were their g. 2Ki 10:6

GUARDING

the soldiers g Jesus saw this .... Mt 27:54

GUARDROOM

would put them back in the g. 1Ki 14:28
would put them back in the g. 2Ch 12:11

GUARDS

the g are watching for nothing. .... Ps 127:1
The LORD g knowledge, but he .... Pr 22:12
He g those who come to him for.............. Pr 30:5
down with the g to see what .... Mt 26:58
first and second g and came to .... Ac 12:10
questioned the g and ordered .... Ac 12:19
so he put g around the city.................... 2Co 11:32
All the palace g and everyone................. Php 1:13

GUDGODAH

From Moserah they went to G, ... Dt 10:7
and from G they went to .... Dt 10:7

GUEST

This man is a g in my house. .... Jdg 19:23
me to be her g with the king. .... Est 5:12
Where is my g room in which I .... Mk 14:14
Where is the g room in which I .... Lk 22:11

GUESTS

after the g have been drinking .... Jn 2:10

GUIDANCE

and understanding, g and power. .... Is 11:2

GUIDE

of your name, lead me and g me. .... Ps 31:3
I will g you and watch over you.............. Ps 32:8
He will g us from now on. .... Ps 48:14
They will g you when you walk.............. Pr 6:22
g us into the path of peace. .... Lk 1:79
think you are a g for the blind .... Rm 2:19
selfishness or pride be your g. .... Php 2:3

GUIDED

cart, and Uzzah and Ahio g it. 1Ch 13:7
pillar of cloud g them by day, ... Ne 9:19
From my birth I g the widows. .... Job 31:18
sheep and he g them like a flock .... Ps 78:52
heart and g them with skillful .... Ps 78:72
and God g them to the port they.............. Ps 107:30
people will be g by honesty; .... Pr 11:3
They are g by dreams and make.............. Jud 1:8

GUIDES

your g lead you in the wrong way .... Is 3:12

GUIDING

were written with the LORD g me............. 1Ch 28:19
I am g you in the way of wisdom, ... Pr 4:11

GUILT

that he brings g on the people, ... Le 4:3
from Israel the g of murdering .... Dt 19:13
make our sin and g even worse. 2Ch 28:13

evil things, and our g is great. .... Ezr 9:13
will be responsible for their g. .... Eze 14:10
saying you see, your g remains." .... Jn 9:41
life without g feelings before .... Ac 23:1

GUILTY

not forget to punish g people.................. Ex 34:7
of these things, he is g of sin. .... Le 6:4
forgets to punish g people. .... Nu 14:18
person and not be g of murder. .... Nu 35:27
declare them g! Let them fall .... Ps 5:10
let him be found g, and let even .... Ps 109:7
G people live dishonest lives, ... Pr 21:8
are not Jews are all g of sin. .... Rm 3:9
the Lord does not consider g." .... Rm 4:8
of it will be g of sinning 1Co 11:27
one command is g of breaking all .... Jam 2:10

GULLS

owls, sea g, any kind of hawk................. Le 11:16
owls, sea g, any kind of hawk................. Dt 14:15

GUNI

sons were Jahziel, G, Jezer, and .... Ge 46:24
G came the Gunite family group; .... Nu 26:48
sons were Jahziel, G, Jezer, and 1Ch 7:13

GUNI'S

son, and Abdiel was G son. 1Ch 5:15

GUNITE

Guni came the G family group; .... Nu 26:48

GUR

on the way up to G near Ibleam. 2Ki 9:27
the Arabs living in G Baal, ... 2Ch 26:7

GUSHING

spring of water g up inside that .... Jn 4:14

GUTTER

The altar's g is twenty-one .... Eze 43:13
and its g is twenty-one inches................. Eze 43:17

H

HAAHASHTARI

Ahuzzam, Hepher, Temeni, and H............. 1Ch 4:6

HAARALOTH

the Israelites at Gibeath H. .... Jos 5:3

HABAKKUK

is the message H the prophet .... Hab 1:1
is the prayer of H the prophet, ... Hab 3:1

HABAZZINIAH

son of Jeremiah, the son of H. .... Je 35:3

HABITS

"Bad friends will ruin good h." 1Co 15:33

HABOR

Halah, in Gozan on the H River,............. 2Ki 17:6
Halah, in Gozan on the H River,............. 2Ki 18:11
away to Halah, H, Hara, and near 1Ch 5:26

HACALIAH

the words of Nehemiah son of H. .... Ne 1:1
Nehemiah the governor, son of H. .... Ne 10:1

HACKING

and they began h at the walls to.............. 2Sa 20:15

HACMONI

Jehiel son of H took care of the 1Ch 27:32

HACMONITE

Jashobeam was from the H people. 1Ch 11:11

HADAD

H, Tema, Jetur, Naphish, and .... Ge 25:15
Husham died, H son of Bedad, who .... Ge 36:35
H was from the city of Avith. .... Ge 36:35

When **H** died, Samlah became king. .... Ge 36:36
of Acbor died, **H** became king. .... Ge 36:39
The LORD caused **H** the Edomite, ... 1Ki 11:14
At that time **H** was only a young 1Ki 11:17
king, who gave **H** a house, some 1Ki 11:18
The king liked **H** so much he gave 1Ki 11:19
Hadad so much he gave **H** a wife— 1Ki 11:19
H heard that David had died and 1Ki 11:21
So **H** said to the king, "Let me 1Ki 11:21
"Nothing," **H** answered, "but 1Ki 11:22
Both Rezon and **H** made trouble 1Ki 11:25
Mishma, Dumah, Massa, **H**, Tema, ... 1Ch 1:30
H son of Bedad became king, ... 1Ch 1:46
H defeated Midian in the country 1Ch 1:46
When **H** died, Samlah became king. 1Ch 1:47
Baal-Hanan died, **H** became king, ... 1Ch 1:50
Then **H** died. The leaders of the 1Ch 1:51
the crying for **H** Rimmon in the .... Zch 12:11

HADAD'S
H wife was named Mehetabel, ... 1Ch 1:50

HADADEZER
also defeated **H** son of Rehob, ... 2Sa 8:3
came to help **H** king of Zobah, ... 2Sa 8:5
had defeated all the army of **H**. 2Sa 8:9
King David for defeating **H**. 2Sa 8:10
H had been at war with Toi. 2Sa 8:10
had taken from **H** son of Rehob, ... 2Sa 8:12
H sent messengers to bring the 2Sa 10:16
the kings who served **H** saw that 2Sa 10:19
his master, **H** king of Zobah. 1Ki 11:23
also defeated **H** king of Zobah 1Ch 18:3
came to help **H** king of Zobah, ... 1Ch 18:5
all the army of **H** king of Zobah. 1Ch 18:9
King David for defeating **H**. 1Ch 18:10
H had been at war with Toi. 1Ch 18:10
When those who served **H** saw that 1Ch 19:19

HADADEZER'S
had belonged to **H** officers and 2Sa 8:7
had been cities under **H** control. 2Sa 8:8
the commander of **H** army. 2Sa 10:16
had belonged to **H** officers and 1Ch 18:7
had been cities under **H** control. 1Ch 18:8
the commander of **H** army. 1Ch 19:16

HADASHAH
Zenan, **H**, Migdal Gad, ... Jos 15:37

HADASSAH
Mordecai had a cousin named **H**, ... Est 2:7
H was also called Esther, and .... Est 2:7

HADATTAH
Hazor **H**, Kerioth Hezron (also .... Jos 15:25

HADDAH
Gannim, En **H**, and Beth Pazzez. .... Jos 19:21

HADES
and **H** was following close behind .... Rev 6:8
and Death and **H** gave up the dead .... Rev 20:13
And Death and **H** were thrown into .... Rev 20:14

HADID
of Lod, **H** and Ono—725; .... Ezr 2:33
of Lod, **H**, and Ono—721; .... Ne 7:37
H, Zeboim, Neballat, ... Ne 11:34

HADLAI
and Amasa son of **H**—met the 2Ch 28:12

HADORAM
H, Uzal, Diklah, ... Ge 10:27
H, Uzal, Diklah, ... 1Ch 1:21
So Toi sent his son **H** to greet 1Ch 18:10
H brought items made of gold, ... 1Ch 18:10

HADRACH
the land of **H** and the city .... Zch 9:1

HAELEPH
Zelah, **H**, the Jebusite city .... Jos 18:28

HAGAB
H, Shalmai, Hanan, ... Ezr 2:46

HAGABA
Lebana, **H**, Shalmai, ... Ne 7:48

HAGABAH
Lebanah, **H**, Akkub, ... Ezr 2:45

HAGAR
a slave girl from Egypt named **H**. .... Ge 16:1
that Sarai gave **H** to her husband .... Ge 16:3
H was her slave girl from Egypt. .... Ge 16:3
had sexual relations with **H**, ... Ge 16:4
When **H** learned she was pregnant, ... Ge 16:4
Then Sarai was hard on **H**, ... Ge 16:6
hard on Hagar, and **H** ran away. .... Ge 16:6
the LORD found **H** beside a spring. .... Ge 16:7
angel said, "**H**, Sarai's slave .... Ge 16:8
H answered, "I am running away .... Ge 16:8
H gave birth to a son for Abram, ... Ge 16:15
years old when **H** gave birth to .... Ge 16:16
was the son of Abraham by **H**, ... Ge 21:9
He gave them to **H** and sent her .... Ge 21:14
H went and wandered in the .... Ge 21:14
H put her son under a bush. .... Ge 21:15
angel called to **H** from heaven. .... Ge 21:17
He said, "What is wrong, **H**? .... Ge 21:17
God showed **H** a well of water .... Ge 21:19
H, Sarah's Egyptian servant, was .... Ge 25:12
The mother named **H** is like that .... Gal 4:24

HAGAR'S
to Sarai, "You are **H** mistress. .... Ge 16:6

HAGGAI
The prophets **H** and Zechariah, ... Ezr 5:1
the preaching of **H** the prophet .... Ezr 6:14
The prophet **H** spoke the word of .... Hag 1:1
H the prophet spoke the word .... Hag 1:3
the message from the prophet, ... Hag 1:12
H, the LORD's messenger, gave .... Hag 1:13
his word through **H** the prophet, ... Hag 2:1
spoke his word to **H** the prophet, ... Hag 2:10
Then **H** said, "A person who .... Hag 2:13
Then **H** answered, "The LORD says, ... Hag 2:14
a second time to **H** on the .... Hag 2:20

HAGGAN
he ran away toward Beth **H**. 2Ki 9:27

HAGGEDOLIM
Zabdiel son of **H** was appointed .... Ne 11:14

HAGGI
were Zephon, **H**, Shuni, Ezbon, ... Ge 46:16
from **H** came the Haggite family .... Nu 26:15

HAGGIAH
son was **H**, and Haggiah's 1Ch 6:30

HAGGIAH'S
Haggiah, and **H** son was Asaiah. 1Ch 6:30

HAGGIDGAD
Bene Jaakan and camped at Hor **H**. .... Nu 33:32
They left Hor **H** and camped at .... Nu 33:33

HAGGITE
Haggi came the **H** family group; .... Nu 26:15

HAGGITH
Adonijah, whose mother was **H**. 2Sa 3:4
was the son of King David and **H**, ... 1Ki 1:5
Adonijah son of **H** went to 1Ki 2:13
Adonijah, whose mother was **H**. 1Ch 3:2

HAGGITH'S
that Adonijah, **H** son, has made 1Ki 1:11

H

HAGGOYIM

in Harosheth **H**, was the .... Jdg 4:2
from Harosheth **H** to the Kishon .... Jdg 4:13
and army to Harosheth **H.** .... Jdg 4:16

HAGRI

Nathan of Zobah; the son of **H**; 2Sa 23:36
of Nathan; Mibhar son of **H**; 1Ch 11:38

HAGRITE

a war against the **H** people and 1Ch 5:10

HAGRITES

belonged to the **H** in all the 1Ch 5:10
war against the **H** and the people 1Ch 5:19
over to them the **H** and all those 1Ch 5:20
animals that belonged to the **H**; 1Ch 5:21
Many **H** were killed because God 1Ch 5:22
Jaziz, from the **H**, was in charge 1Ch 27:31
the Ishmaelites, Moab and the **H**, ... Ps 83:6

HAHIROTH

to turn back to Pi **H** and to camp .... Ex 14:2
near Pi **H** and Baal Zephon. .... Ex 14:9
Etham and went back to Pi **H**, ... Nu 33:7
left Pi **H** and walked through .... Nu 33:8

HAIL

The **h** will fall on every person .... Ex 9:19
Then the **h** will start falling in .... Ex 9:22
the LORD sent thunder and **h**, ... Ex 9:23
So he caused **h** to fall upon the .... Ex 9:23
There was **h**, and lightning .... Ex 9:24
The **h** destroyed all the people .... Ex 9:25
it did not **h** was in the land .... Ex 9:26
enough of God's thunder and **h**. .... Ex 9:28
and the thunder and **h** will stop. .... Ex 9:29
and the thunder and **h** stopped. .... Ex 9:33
that the rain, **h**, and thunder .... Ex 9:34
plants the **h** did not destroy. .... Ex 10:12
that was left after the **h**— .... Ex 10:15
or seen the storehouses for **h**, ... Job 38:22
clouds with **h** and lightning. .... Ps 18:12
and there was **h** and lightning. .... Ps 18:13
their vines with **h** and their .... Ps 78:47
animals with **h** and their cattle .... Ps 78:48
made **h** fall like rain and sent .... Ps 105:32
He throws down **h** like rocks. .... Ps 147:17
lightning and **h**, snow and mist, ... Ps 148:8
a storm of **h** and strong wind .... Is 28:2
will be destroyed as if by **h**. .... Is 28:17
storm with much rain and **h**. .... Is 30:30
H will destroy the forest, ... Is 32:19
mildew, and **h**, but you still did .... Hag 2:17
of him, saying, "**H**, King of the .... Mt 27:29
out to him, "**H**, King of the Jews .... Mk 15:18
times and said, "**H**, King of the .... Jn 19:3
and **h** and fire mixed with blood .... Rev 8:7
God for the disaster of the **h**, ... Rev 16:21

HAILED

and lightning flashed as it **h**— .... Ex 9:24

HAILSTONES

LORD threw large **h** on them from .... Jos 10:11
were killed by the **h** than by the .... Jos 10:11
will pour down, **h** will fall, ... Eze 13:11
and **h** will destroy the wall. .... Eze 13:13
a heavy rain with **h** and burning .... Eze 38:22
Giant **h**, each weighing about a .... Rev 16:21

HAILSTORM

send a terrible **h**, the worst in .... Ex 9:18
worst **h** in Egypt since it had .... Ex 9:24
left from the **h** and the leaves .... Ex 10:5
an earthquake, and a great **h**. .... Rev 11:19

HAIR

red thread; fine linen, goat **h**, ... Ex 25:4
and if the **h** from the spot has .... Le 13:4
day he must shave off all his **h**— .... Le 14:9
They must let their **h** grow long. .... Nu 6:5
the Nazirites cut off their **h**, ... Nu 6:19
But his **h** began to grow again. .... Jdg 16:22
not even a **h** of his head will 1Sa 14:45
would cut his **h**, because it 2Sa 14:26
of them, and pulled out their **h**. .... Ne 13:25
and the **h** on my body stood on .... Job 4:15
Your **h** is like a flock of goats .... Sng 4:1
is shaving the **h** from Judah's .... Is 7:20
and weigh and divide the **h**. .... Eze 5:1
Their **h** was not burned, their .... Da 3:27
h grew long like the feathers .... Da 4:33
and the **h** on his head was white .... Da 7:9
made of **h** to trick people. .... Zch 13:4
were made from camel's **h**. .... Mt 3:4
and she dried them with her **h**, ... Lk 7:38
and wiped his feet with her **h**. .... Jn 11:2
At Cenchrea Paul cut off his **h**, ... Ac 18:18
lose even one **h** off your heads." .... Ac 27:34
wearing long **h** is shameful for 1Co 11:14
But long **h** is a woman's glory. 1Co 11:15
h is given to her as a covering. 1Co 11:15
using braided **h** or gold or 1Ti 2:9
It is not fancy **h**, gold jewelry, ... 1Pe 3:3
His head and **h** were white like .... Rev 1:14
Their **h** was like women's hair, ... Rev 9:8
Their hair was like women's **h**, ... Rev 9:8

HAIRS

are no white **h** in it and the .... Le 13:21
are no yellow **h** growing in it, ... Le 13:32
more sins than **h** on my head, ... Ps 40:12
for no reason than **h** on my head; .... Ps 69:4
a few of these **h** and tie them .... Eze 5:3
how many **h** are on your head. .... Mt 10:30
knows how many **h** you have on .... Lk 12:7

HAIRY

his skin was like a **h** robe, ... Ge 25:25
My brother Esau is a **h** man, ... Ge 27:11
your hands are **h** like the hands .... Ge 27:22
his hands were **h** like Esau's .... Ge 27:23
He was a **h** man and wore a 2Ki 1:8
the **h** skulls of those who .... Ps 68:21

HAKILAH

on the hill of **H**, south of 1Sa 23:19
the hill of **H** opposite Jeshimon. 1Sa 26:1
on the hill of **H** opposite 1Sa 26:3
certain that Saul had come to **H**. 1Sa 26:4

HAKKATAN

Johanan son of **H**, with one .... Ezr 8:12

HAKKEREM

ruler of the district of Beth **H**, ... Ne 3:14
flag over the town of Beth **H**! .... Je 6:1

HAKKOZ

seventh was **H**. The eighth was 1Ch 24:10
Hobaiah, **H**, and Barzillai, who .... Ezr 2:61
Uriah, the son of **H**, made .... Ne 3:4
Uriah, the son of **H**, repaired .... Ne 3:21
of Hobaiah, **H**, and Barzillai. .... Ne 7:63

HAKUPHA

Bakbuk, **H**, Harhur, ... Ezr 2:51
Bakbuk, **H**, Harhur, ... Ne 7:53

HALAH

settled them in **H**, in Gozan on 2Ki 17:6
Assyria and settled them in **H**, ... 2Ki 18:11
and he took them away to **H**, ... 1Ch 5:26

HALAK

land from Mount H near Edom to .... Jos 11:17
Lebanon and Mount H near Edom. .... Jos 12:7

HALF

laying each **h** opposite the other.............. Ge 15:10
each half opposite the other **h.** .... Ge 15:10
he did not cut the birds in **h.** .... Ge 15:10
Both men will get **h** of the money .... Ex 21:35
the money and **h** of the bull that.............. Ex 21:35
put **h** of the blood of these .... Ex 24:6
the other **h** of the blood .... Ex 24:6
Let the extra **h** piece of cloth .... Ex 26:12
of liquid myrrh, **h** that amount .... Ex 30:23
h of it in the morning and half .... Le 6:20
morning and **h** in the evening. .... Le 6:20
baby is born with **h** of its flesh .... Nu 12:12
Take it from the soldiers' **h,** .... Nu 31:29
the people's **h,** take one item .... Nu 31:30
people's **h** from the soldiers' .... Nu 31:42
half from the soldiers' **h.**...................... Nu 31:42
the people's **h** Moses took one .... Nu 31:47
as well as **h** of the mountain .... Dt 3:12
H of the people stood in front................ Jos 8:33
and **h** stood in front of Mount................ Jos 8:33
Sihon ruled over **h** the land of .... Jos 12:2
Og also ruled **h** the land of .... Jos 12:5
h the land of the Ammonites that .... Jos 13:25
H of all the family groups in .... Jos 13:29
h of Gilead, Ashtaroth, and................ Jos 13:31
and **h** of all his sons were given .... Jos 13:31
over a **h** acre of ground. 1Sa 14:14
Take this **h** bushel of cooked 1Sa 17:17
he shaved off **h** their beards 2Sa 10:4
Even if **h** of us are killed, ... 2Sa 18:3
troops of Judah and **h** the troops 2Sa 19:40
pieces, and give each woman **h.**" 1Ki 3:25
I was not told even **h** of it! 1Ki 10:7
you gave me **h** of your kingdom, ... 1Ki 13:8
commanded **h** of Elah's chariots. 1Ki 16:9
H of the people wanted Tibni son 1Ki 16:21
while the other **h** wanted Omri. 1Ki 16:21
and **h** of a pint of dove's dung 2Ki 6:25
were Haroeh, **h** the Manahathites, ... 1Ch 2:52
Beth Joab, **h** the Manahathites 1Ch 2:54
not told even **h** of your great 2Ch 9:6
h my people worked on the wall. .... Ne 4:16
The other **h** was ready with .... Ne 4:16
to work with **h** the men holding .... Ne 4:21
went Hoshaiah and **h** the leaders .... Ne 12:32
of the wall with **h** the people. .... Ne 12:38
H of the leaders and I did also. .... Ne 12:40
H their children were speaking .... Ne 13:24
grow only **h** a bushel of grain. .... Is 5:10
The man burns **h** of the wood in.............. Is 44:16
I burned **h** of the wood in the .... Is 44:19
When their lives are **h** finished, ... Je 17:11
did not do **h** the sins you do; .... Eze 16:51
forces his **h** sister to have .... Eze 22:11
H the mountain will move toward .... Zch 14:4
h will move toward the south................ Zch 14:4
H of it will flow east to the .... Zch 14:8
and **h** will flow west to the .... Zch 14:8
to you—up to **h** of my kingdom." .... Mk 6:23
I will give **h** of my possessions .... Lk 19:8
When the feast was about **h** over, ... Jn 7:14
mountain is about **h** a mile from .... Ac 1:12
stayed there for a year and a **h,** .... Ac 18:11
were cut in **h,** and they were .... Heb 11:37
land for three and a **h** years! .... Jam 5:17
in heaven for about **h** an hour. .... Rev 8:1

HALF-BROTHER

the sister of my **h** Absalom." 2Sa 13:4
He is your **h.** Don't let this 2Sa 13:20

HALF-BUSHEL

He must give a **h** grain offering .... Eze 46:5
must give a **h** grain offering .... Eze 46:7

HALFWAY

is to be set **h** up the frames, ... Ex 26:28
under its rim, **h** up from the .... Ex 27:5
It was set **h** up the frames. .... Ex 36:33
its rim, **h** up from the bottom.................. Ex 38:4

HALHUL

the mountains: **H,** Beth Zur, ... Jos 15:58

HALI

Helkath, **H,** Beten, Acshaph, ... Jos 19:25

HALL

people, called the **H** of Justice. 1Ki 7:7
was built like the **H** of Justice, ... 1Ki 7:8
and it was behind this **h.**...................... 1Ki 7:8
palace, facing the king's **h.**.................. Est 5:1
on his royal throne in the **h,** .... Est 5:1
palace garden to the banquet **h,** .... Est 7:8
the wedding **h** was filled with.................. Mt 22:10

HALLELUJAH

heaven saying: "**H!** Salvation,.................. Rev 19:1
they said: "**H!** She is burning,.................. Rev 19:3
throne. They said: "Amen, **H!**" .... Rev 19:4
were saying: "**H!** Our Lord God,.............. Rev 19:6

HALLOHESH

Next to them Shallum son of **H,**.............. Ne 3:12
H, Pilha, Shobek, ... Ne 10:24

HALVES

passed between the **h** of the dead .... Ge 15:17

HAM

father of Shem, **H,** and Japheth. .... Ge 5:32
sons: Shem, **H,** and Japheth. .... Ge 6:10
his sons Shem, **H,** and Japheth, ... Ge 7:13
him were Shem, **H,** and Japheth. .... Ge 9:18
H was the father of Canaan. .... Ge 9:18
H, the father of Canaan, looked .... Ge 9:22
youngest son, **H,** had done to him .... Ge 9:24
history of Shem, **H,** and Japheth, ... Ge 10:1
sons of **H** were Cush, Mizraim, ... Ge 10:6
these people were the sons of **H,** .... Ge 10:20
the Zuzites in **H,** and the Emites .... Ge 14:5
Noah were Shem, **H,** and Japheth. 1Ch 1:4
oldest son of each family of **H.** .... Ps 78:51

HAM'S

H sons were Cush, Mizraim, Put, ... 1Ch 1:8
H descendants had lived there in 1Ch 4:40

HAMAN

Xerxes honored **H** son of .... Est 3:1
but **H** hurried home with his head .... Est 6:12
enemy and foe is this wicked **H!**" .... Est 7:6
So they hanged **H** on the platform .... Est 7:10
the ten sons of **H,** son of .... Est 9:10

HAMAN'S

let the bodies of **H** ten sons be .... Est 9:13

HAMATH

Mount Hor it will go to Lebo **H,** .... Nu 34:8
of Damascus and **H** for Israel. 2Ki 14:28
are the gods of **H** and Arpad?.................. 2Ki 18:34
are the kings of **H** and Arpad? 2Ki 19:13
there go to the great city **H;** .... Am 6:2

HAMATHITES

Arvadites, Zemarites, and **H.** .... Ge 10:18
Arvadites, Zemarites, and **H.** 1Ch 1:16

HAMITES
They fought against the **H,** 1Ch 4:41

HAMMATH
Ziddim, Zer, **H,** Rakkath, ... Jos 19:35
family group who came from **H.** 1Ch 2:55

HAMMEDATHA
Haman son of **H** the Agagite. .... Est 3:1
and gave it to Haman son of **H,** .... Est 3:10
of Haman, son of **H,** the enemy .... Est 9:10
Haman son of **H,** the Agagite, was .... Est 9:24

HAMMER
tent peg and a **h** and quietly .... Jdg 4:21
reached for the workman's **h.** .... Jdg 5:26
Isn't it like a **h** that smashes a .... Je 23:29
Babylon was the **h** of the whole .... Je 50:23

HAMMERED
of one piece, **h** out of pure gold .... Ex 25:36
lampstand was made from **h** gold, ... Nu 8:4
smaller shields of **h** gold, ... 1Ki 10:17
and one-half pounds of **h** gold. 2Ch 9:15

HAMMERING
of pure gold, **h** out its base and .... Ex 37:17

HAMMERS
was no noise of **h,** axes, or any 1Ki 6:7
h and nails they fasten them .... Je 10:4

HAMMOLEKETH
Makir's sister **H** gave birth to 1Ch 7:18

HAMMON
to Abdon, Rehob, **H,** and Kanah............... Jos 19:28
in Galilee, **H,** and Kiriathaim. 1Ch 6:76

HAMMOTH
of safety), **H** Dor, and Kartan .... Jos 21:32

HAMMUEL
Mishma's son was **H.** Hammuel's 1Ch 4:26

HAMMUEL'S
was Hammuel. **H** son was Zaccur. 1Ch 4:26

HAMON
had a vineyard at Baal **H.** .... Sng 8:11

HAMONAH
A city will be there named **H.** .... Eze 39:16

HAMOR
told his father, **H,** "Please get .... Ge 34:4
killed **H** and his son Shechem .... Ge 34:26

HAMUL
Perez's sons were Hezron and **H.** .... Ge 46:12
from **H** came the Hamulite family .... Nu 26:21
Perez's sons were Hezron and **H.** 1Ch 2:5

HAMULITE
Hamul came the **H** family group. .... Nu 26:21

HAMUTAL
mother's name was **H,** who was the 2Ki 23:31
mother's name was **H** daughter of 2Ki 24:18
mother's name was **H** daughter of .... Je 52:1

HANAMEL
Your cousin **H,** son of your uncle .... Je 32:7
H will say to you, 'Jeremiah, ... Je 32:7
My cousin **H** came to me in the .... Je 32:8
at Anathoth from my cousin **H,** .... Je 32:9
My cousin **H,** the other witnesses .... Je 32:12

HANANEL
they went on to the Tower of **H.** .... Ne 3:1
to the Tower of **H** and the Tower .... Ne 12:39
the Tower of **H** to the Corner .... Je 31:38
the Tower of **H** to the king's .... Zch 14:10

HANANIAH
spoke to the prophet **H** in front .... Je 28:5
H died in the seventh month of .... Je 28:17
men were Daniel, **H,** Mishael, and .... Da 1:6
to watch Daniel, **H,** Mishael, and .... Da 1:11

HAND
reached out his **h** and took the .... Ge 8:9
him up and take him by the **h.** .... Ge 21:18
owned, "Put your **h** under my leg. .... Ge 24:2
servant put his **h** under his .... Ge 24:9
birth, one baby put his **h** out. .... Ge 38:28
a red string on his **h** and said, ... Ge 38:28
But he pulled his **h** back in, ... Ge 38:29
red string on his **h** was born, ... Ge 38:30
his coat in her **h** and ran out .... Ge 39:12
cup of wine into the king's **h.** .... Ge 40:21
Egypt may lift a **h** or a foot................... Ge 41:44
me, put your **h** under my leg. .... Ge 47:29
was near Israel's left **h,** .... Ge 48:13
was near Israel's right **h.**...................... Ge 48:13
and put his right **h** on the head .... Ge 48:14
He put his left **h** on the head of .... Ge 48:14
put his right **h** on Ephraim's .... Ge 48:17
he took hold of his father's **h,**............... Ge 48:17
Put your right **h** on his head." .... Ge 48:18
him, "What is that in your **h?**" .... Ex 4:2
again became a stick in his **h.**............... Ex 4:4
"Put your **h** inside your coat." .... Ex 4:6
Moses put his **h** inside his coat .... Ex 4:6
Now put your **h** inside your coat .... Ex 4:7
Moses put his **h** inside his coat .... Ex 4:7
took it out, his **h** was healthy .... Ex 4:7
River with this stick in my **h,** .... Ex 7:17
stick in your **h** and stretch your .... Ex 7:19
stretch your **h** over the rivers .... Ex 7:19
stick in his **h** over the rivers, ... Ex 8:5
So Aaron held his **h** over all the .... Ex 8:6
that was in his **h** and struck the .... Ex 8:17
Raise your **h** toward the sky. .... Ex 9:22
Raise your **h** over the land of .... Ex 10:12
Raise your **h** toward the sky, ... Ex 10:21
raised his **h** toward the sky, ... Ex 10:22
your walking stick in your **h.** .... Ex 12:11
a mark on your **h** or a reminder .... Ex 13:9
a mark on your **h** and a reminder .... Ex 13:16
Moses held his **h** over the sea. .... Ex 14:21
Hold your **h** over the sea so that........... Ex 14:26
Moses raised his **h** over the sea, ... Ex 14:27
Your right **h,** LORD, is amazingly .... Ex 15:6
your right **h** broke the enemy to............. Ex 15:6
and my **h** will destroy them.' .... Ex 15:9
reached out with your right **h,** .... Ex 15:12
took a tambourine in her **h.** .... Ex 15:20
tooth for tooth, **h** for hand,................... Ex 21:24
hand for **h,** foot for foot,....................... Ex 21:24
cover you with my **h** until I have .... Ex 33:22
Then I will take away my **h,** .... Ex 33:23
must put his **h** on the animal's .... Le 1:4
must put his **h** on the animal's .... Le 3:2
and put his **h** on its head. .... Le 3:8
and put his **h** on its head. .... Le 3:13
the LORD, put his **h** on its head,............. Le 4:4
must put his **h** on the goat's .... Le 4:24
must put his **h** on the animal's .... Le 4:29
must put his **h** on the animal's .... Le 4:33
on the thumb of Aaron's right **h,** .... Le 8:23
person's right **h** and on the big .... Le 14:14
and pour it into his own left **h.** .... Le 14:15
of his right **h** into the oil that .... Le 14:16
the oil that is in his left **h,** .... Le 14:16
oil from his **h** on the bottom .... Le 14:17
thumb of the person's right **h,** .... Le 14:17

is in his left **h** on the head ....Le 14:18
the person's right **h** and some on ....Le 14:25
of the oil into his own left **h**. ....Le 14:26
with a finger of his right **h**,......................Le 14:27
oil from his left **h** seven times..................Le 14:27
of the oil from his **h** and put it ....Le 14:28
the person's right **h** and some on ....Le 14:28
oil that is in his **h** on the head ....Le 14:29
men with a crippled foot or **h**, ...Le 21:19
He will **h** her the offering of ....Nu 5:18
lifted his **h** and hit the rock.....................Nu 20:11
will **h** him, his whole army, and ....Nu 21:34
the road with a sword in his **h**, ...Nu 22:23
I wish I had a sword in my **h**! ....Nu 22:29
is in him. Put your **h** on him, ...Nu 27:18
with his **h** and cause death ....Nu 35:21
because I will **h** him, his whole ....Dt 3:2
your God will **h** these nations..................Dt 7:2
your God will **h** those nations..................Dt 7:23
city of safety and **h** him over to ....Dt 19:12
for a tooth, a **h** for a hand, a ....Dt 19:21
a hand for a **h**, a foot for a ....Dt 19:21
do not **h** over the slave to his ....Dt 23:15
you must cut off her **h**. ....Dt 25:12
I raise my **h** toward heaven and ....Dt 32:40
I will take it in my **h** to judge...................Dt 32:41
of him with a sword in his **h**. ....Jos 5:13
because I will **h** them over to ....Jos 10:8
God will **h** them over to you. ....Jos 10:19
city must not **h** over the killer..................Jos 20:5
with his left **h** and took out....................Jdg 3:21
I will **h** Sisera over to you.'" ....Jdg 4:7
day the LORD will **h** over Sisera. ....Jdg 4:14
Her right **h** reached for the ....Jdg 5:26
of the stick that was in his **h**. ....Jdg 6:21
save you and **h** Midian over to ....Jdg 7:7
God will **h** Midian and the whole ....Jdg 7:14
If you will **h** over the Ammonites ....Jdg 11:30
tie you up and to **h** you over to ....Jdg 15:12
to the servant holding his **h**, ...Jdg 16:26
with his right **h** on one and his ....Jdg 16:29
one and his left **h** on the other. ....Jdg 16:29
H over the wicked men in Gibeah ....Jdg 20:13
I will **h** them over to you. ....Jdg 20:28
to Ahijah, "Put your **h** down!" 1Sa 14:19
stick in his **h** and chose five 1Sa 17:40
the LORD will **h** you over to me, ...1Sa 17:46
and he will **h** you over to us." 1Sa 17:47
not even have a sword in his **h**. 1Sa 17:50
but Saul had a spear in his **h**. 1Sa 18:10
house with his spear in his **h**. 1Sa 19:9
Why is **h** me over to your father?" 1Sa 20:8
He had a spear in his **h**. 1Sa 22:6
of Keilah **h** me over to Saul? 1Sa 23:11
leaders of Keilah **h** me and my 1Sa 23:12
our duty to **h** David over to you...............1Sa 23:20
this piece of your robe in my **h**! 1Sa 24:11
The LORD will **h** over both Israel 1Sa 28:19
The LORD will **h** over the army of 1Sa 28:19
I didn't **h** you over to David. 2Sa 3:8
Will you **h** them over to me?" 2Sa 5:19
certainly **h** them over to you. 2Sa 5:19
watch and eat it from her **h**.'"..................2Sa 13:5
so I may eat from your **h**." 2Sa 13:10
robe and put her **h** on her head................2Sa 13:19
reach out his **h** and take hold 2Sa 15:5
with his right **h** he took Amasa 2Sa 20:9
watching the sword in Joab's **h**. 2Sa 20:10
fingers on each **h** and six toes 2Sa 21:20
that cannot be held in a **h**. 2Sa 23:6
was so tired his **h** stuck to his..................2Sa 23:10
who had a spear in his **h**. 2Sa 23:21
the Egyptian's **h** and killed him 2Sa 23:21

with them and **h** them over to..................1Ki 8:46
king raised his **h** from the altar 1Ki 13:4
for you to **h** me over to Ahab 1Ki 18:9
I will **h** it over to you today so 1Ki 20:13
Lord will **h** them over to you. 1Ki 22:6
LORD will **h** the Arameans over..............1Ki 22:12
LORD will **h** them over to you. 1Ki 22:15
kings together to **h** us over to 2Ki 3:10
kings together to **h** us over to 2Ki 3:13
he will also **h** Moab over to you...............2Ki 3:18
stick in your **h** and go quickly. 2Ki 4:29
would wave his **h** over the place..............2Ki 5:11
gift in your **h** and go meet him. 2Ki 8:8
bottle of olive oil in your **h**.....................2Ki 9:1
you are, then give me your **h**." 2Ki 10:15
So Jehonadab gave him his **h**, ...2Ki 10:15
the king, with weapons in **h**. 2Ki 11:8
place with his weapons in his **h**..............2Ki 11:11
but **h** over the money for the 2Ki 12:7
to him, "Put your **h** on the bow." 2Ki 13:16
So Jehoash put his **h** on the bow. 2Ki 13:16
will stab your **h** and hurt you. 2Ki 18:21
the Egyptian's **h** and killed him 1Ch 11:23
out his **h** to steady the Ark. 1Ch 13:9
Will you **h** them over to me?" 1Ch 14:10
I will **h** them over to you." 1Ch 14:10
fingers on each **h** and six toes 1Ch 20:6
them and will **h** them over to 2Ch 6:36
God will **h** them over to you. 2Ch 18:5
LORD will **h** the Arameans over 2Ch 18:11
man with his weapon in his **h**. 2Ch 23:7
where to stand with weapon in **h**. 2Ch 23:10
and in his **h** was a pan for 2Ch 26:19
work with one **h** and carried ....Ne 4:17
in his **h** was an unsealed letter. ....Ne 6:5
gold scepter that was in his **h**, ...Est 5:2
But reach out your **h** and destroy ....Job 1:11
reach out your **h** and destroy his ....Job 2:5
reach out his **h** to destroy me. ....Job 6:9
away the sin that is in your **h**;..................Job 11:14
knows that the **h** of the LORD has ....Job 12:9
of all people are in God's **h**. ....Job 12:10
because the **h** of God has hit me. ....Job 19:21
put your **h** over your mouth in ....Job 21:5
because God's heavy **h** is on me. ....Job 23:2
His **h** stabs the fleeing snake......................Job 26:13
your powerful **h** you attacked me. ....Job 30:21
My **h** has never offered the sun ....Job 31:27
he receives nothing from your **h**. ....Job 35:7
I will put my **h** over my mouth. ....Job 40:4
If you put one **h** on it, you will ....Job 41:8
at your right **h** I will find ....Ps 16:11
support me with your right **h**....................Ps 18:35
him with his strong right **h**. ....Ps 20:6
Your **h** is against all your ....Ps 21:8
Do not **h** me over to my enemies, ...Ps 27:12
because the LORD holds their **h**. ....Ps 37:24
and your **h** has come down on me..............Ps 38:2
right **h** is full of goodness. ....Ps 48:10
support me with your right **h**...................Ps 63:8
with you; you have held my **h**. ....Ps 73:23
holds a cup of anger in his **h**; ....Ps 75:8
With your **h**, strengthen the one ....Ps 80:17
and turn my **h** against their foes..............Ps 81:14
power. Your **h** is strong; your ....Ps 89:13
your right **h** is lifted up. ....Ps 89:13
him with my **h** and strengthen him ....Ps 89:21
By his right **h** and holy arm he ....Ps 98:1
you open your **h**, they are filled ....Ps 104:28
your helping **h**, because I have ....Ps 119:173
arrows in the **h** of a warrior. ....Ps 127:4
of it to fill a **h** or to make ....Ps 129:7
let my right **h** lose its skill. ....Ps 137:5

to the man, "Hold out your **h**." ....Lk 6:10
man held out his **h**, and it was ....Lk 6:10
guard and chained **h** and foot, ...Lk 8:29
took hold of her **h** and called to ....Lk 8:54
wrong so they could **h** him over ....Lk 20:20
about a way to **h** Jesus over to ....Lk 22:4
the best time to **h** Jesus over to ....Lk 22:6
his **h** is with mine on the table. ....Lk 22:21
at the right **h** of the powerful ....Lk 22:69
one can steal them out of my **h**. ....Jn 10:28
my sheep out of my Father's **h**. ....Jn 10:29
and put my **h** into his side." ....Jn 20:25
Put your **h** here in my side. ....Jn 20:27
the man's right **h** and lifted him ....Ac 3:7
my **h** made all these things!'" ....Ac 7:50
with Saul took his **h** and led him ....Ac 9:8
He gave her his **h** and helped her ....Ac 9:41
sign with his **h** to tell them to ....Ac 12:17
someone to lead him by the **h**. ....Ac 13:11
up, raised his **h**, and said, "You ....Ac 13:16
waved his **h** so he could explain ....Ac 19:33
and waved his **h** to quiet the ....Ac 21:40
the young man's **h** and led him to ....Ac 23:19
Romans do not **h** him over until ....Ac 25:16
raised his **h** and began to speak. ....Ac 26:1
the heat and bit him on the **h**. ....Ac 28:3
from Paul's **h** and said to each ....Ac 28:4
then **h** this man over to Satan. 1Co 5:5
I am not a **h**, I am not part 1Co 12:15
The eye cannot say to the **h**, ...1Co 12:21
and he will **h** over the kingdom 1Co 15:24
this greeting with my own **h**. 1Co 16:21
sitting at the right **h** of God. ....Col 3:1
and write this with my own **h**. ....Col 4:18
am writing this with my own **h**. ....Phm 1:19
took them by the **h** to bring them ....Heb 8:9
God's powerful **h** so he will lift 1Pe 5:6
held seven stars in his right **h**, ...Rev 1:16
put his right **h** on me and said, ...Rev 1:17
saw in my right **h** and the seven ....Rev 1:20
in his right **h** and walks among ....Rev 2:1
in the right **h** of the One ....Rev 5:1
from the right **h** of the One ....Rev 5:7
held a pair of scales in his **h**. ....Rev 6:5
from the angel's **h** to God with ....Rev 8:4
a small scroll open in his **h**. ....Rev 10:2
raised his right **h** to heaven, ...Rev 10:5
that is in the **h** of the angel ....Rev 10:8
from the angel's **h** and ate it. ....Rev 10:10
on their right **h** or on their ....Rev 13:16
on the forehead or on the **h**, ...Rev 14:9
and a sharp sickle in his **h**. ....Rev 14:14
She had a golden cup in her **h**, ...Rev 17:4
pit and a large chain in his **h**. ....Rev 20:1

HANDED
which have been **h** down to us? ....Mk 7:5
he **h** Jesus over to the soldiers ....Mk 15:15

HANDFUL
must take a **h** of the fine flour ....Le 2:2
will take a **h** of the flour as ....Le 5:12
must take a **h** of fine flour, ...Le 6:15
He took a **h** of the grain and ....Le 9:17
He will take a **h** of the grain, ...Nu 5:26
have only a **h** of flour in a jar 1Ki 17:12
of my men to get a **h** of dust!" 1Ki 20:10

HANDFULS
LORD and two **h** of sweet incense ....Le 16:12
For **h** of barley and pieces of ....Eze 13:19

HANDKERCHIEFS
people took **h** and clothes that ....Ac 19:12

HANDLE
many and too strong for us to **h**! ....Ex 1:9
If the ax head flies off the **h**, ...Dt 19:5
the **h** sank in, and the blade ....Jdg 3:22
each one as much as he could **h**. ....Mt 25:15
"Don't **h** this," "Don't taste that, ...Col 2:21

HANDLES
fingers, onto the **h** of the lock. ....Sng 5:5

HANDLING
way we are **h** this large gift. 2Co 8:20

HANDMILLS
then grind it in **h**, or crush it ....Nu 11:8

HANDS
and where your **h** killed him. ....Ge 4:11
the two men took the **h** of Lot, ...Ge 19:16
put them on Jacob's **h** and neck. ....Ge 27:16
but your **h** are hairy like the ....Ge 27:22
are hairy like the **h** of Esau." ....Ge 27:22
because his **h** were hairy like ....Ge 27:23
hands were hairy like Esau's **h**, ...Ge 27:23
his coat in her **h** and had run ....Ge 39:13
Joseph's own **h** will close your ....Ge 46:4
Fill your **h** with ashes from a ....Ex 9:8
I will raise my **h** to the LORD in ....Ex 9:29
He raised his **h** to the LORD, ...Ex 9:33
Lord, that your **h** have made. ....Ex 15:17
walking stick of God in my **h**." ....Ex 17:9
As long as Moses held his **h** up, ...Ex 17:11
but when Moses put his **h** down, ...Ex 17:11
Aaron and Hur held up Moses' **h**— ....Ex 17:12
They kept his **h** steady until the ....Ex 17:12
I lifted my **h** toward the LORD's ....Ex 17:16
must put their **h** on the bull's ....Ex 29:10
sons put their **h** on its head. ....Ex 29:15
sons put their **h** on its head. ....Ex 29:19
of their right **h** and on the big ....Ex 29:20
of these in the **h** of Aaron and ....Ex 29:24
them from their **h** and burn them ....Ex 29:25
must wash their **h** and feet with ....Ex 30:19
must wash their **h** and their feet. ....Ex 30:21
in his **h** he had the two stone ....Ex 32:15
of the Agreement in his **h**. ....Ex 34:29
woman used her **h** to make the ....Ex 35:25
water to wash their **h** and feet. ....Ex 40:31
must put their **h** on the bull's ....Le 4:15
gift in his own **h** as an offering ....Le 7:30
sons put their **h** on its head. ....Le 8:14
sons put their **h** on its head. ....Le 8:18
sons put their **h** on its head. ....Le 8:22
on the thumbs of their right **h**, ...Le 8:24
he put in the **h** of Aaron and his ....Le 8:27
from their **h** and burned them ....Le 8:28
Aaron lifted his **h** toward the ....Le 9:22
not washed his **h** in water and ....Le 15:11
will put both his **h** on the head ....Le 16:21
must put their **h** on his head, ...Le 24:14
should put their **h** on them. ....Nu 8:10
will put their **h** on the bulls' ....Nu 8:12
went with payment in their **h**. ....Nu 22:7
and he put his **h** on him and gave ....Nu 27:23
tie them to your **h** as a sign. ....Dt 6:8
the LORD your God **h** over to you. ....Dt 7:16
with the Agreement were in my **h**. ....Dt 9:15
with the two tablets in my **h**. ....Dt 10:3
tie them to your **h** as a sign; ....Dt 11:18
wash their **h** over the young ....Dt 21:6
you may pick grain with your **h**, ...Dt 23:25
defend themselves with their **h**. ....Dt 33:7
Moses had put his **h** on him. ....Dt 34:9
who used their **h** to bring water ....Jdg 7:6
in their left **h** and the trumpets ....Jdg 7:20

the trumpets in their right **h**. .... Jdg 7:20
the lion apart with his bare **h**. .... Jdg 14:6
with his **h** and walked along .... Jdg 14:9
strings and fell off his **h**! .... Jdg 15:14
with her **h** on the doorsill. .... Jdg 19:27
from what you have in your **h**, ... Ru 2:16
head and **h** had broken off and 1Sa 5:4
up, using his **h** and feet, and 1Sa 14:13
out of your **h** and given it to 1Sa 28:17
and mixed dough with her **h**. 1Sa 28:24
His **h** were not tied. His feet 2Sa 3:34
He fell at the **h** of evil men." 2Sa 3:34
They cut off the **h** and feet of 2Sa 4:12
I will eat them from her **h**." 2Sa 13:6
pressed it together with her **h**. 2Sa 13:8
him so he could eat from her **h**, ... 2Sa 13:11
He trains my **h** for battle so my 2Sa 22:35
spread out his **h** toward the sky 1Ki 8:22
finished it with your **h** today. 1Ki 8:24
spread their **h** in prayer toward 1Ki 8:38
and his **h** on the boy's hands. 2Ki 4:34
and his hands on the boy's **h**. 2Ki 4:34
feet, and the palms of her **h**. 2Ki 9:35
they clapped their **h** and said, ... 2Ki 11:12
Elisha put his **h** on the king's 2Ki 13:16
put his hands on the king's **h**. 2Ki 13:16
right or left **h** to shoot arrows. 1Ch 12:2
behind him. He spread out his **h**. 2Ch 6:12
spread out his **h** toward the sky. 2Ch 6:13
finished it with your **h** today. 2Ch 6:15
spread their **h** in prayer toward 2Ch 6:29
people put their **h** on the goats, ... 2Ch 29:23
which are made by human **h**. 2Ch 32:19
placed bronze chains on his **h**, ... 2Ch 33:11
my knees with my **h** spread out to .... Ezr 9:5
people held up their **h** and said, ... Ne 8:6
and the weak **h** you have made .... Job 4:3
he injures, but his **h** also heal. .... Job 5:18
falls into the **h** of evil people, ... Job 9:24
and scrub my **h** with strong soap .... Job 9:30
about me, the work of your **h**? .... Job 10:3
Your **h** shaped and made me. .... Job 10:8
hold out your **h** to him for help .... Job 11:13
and take my life in my own **h**? .... Job 13:14
the creature your **h** have made. .... Job 14:15
my **h** have never done anything .... Job 16:17
and those whose **h** are not dirty .... Job 17:9
saved because your **h** are clean." .... Job 22:30
if the wind is clapping its **h**; .... Job 27:23
their mouths with their **h**. .... Job 29:9
or my **h** have been made unclean, ... Job 31:7
or the riches my **h** had gained. .... Job 31:25
he made them all with his own **h**. .... Job 34:19
He claps his **h** in protest, ... Job 34:37
God fills his **h** with lightning .... Job 36:32
Have my **h** done something wrong? .... Ps 7:3
He trains my **h** for battle so my .... Ps 18:34
announce what his **h** have made. .... Ps 19:1
with clean **h** and pure hearts .... Ps 24:4
I wash my **h** to show I am .... Ps 26:6
Evil is in their **h**, and they do .... Ps 26:10
I raise my **h** toward your Most .... Ps 28:2
life is in your **h**. Save me from .... Ps 31:15
God or lifted our **h** in prayer to .... Ps 44:20
Clap your **h**, all you people. .... Ps 47:1
will lift up my **h** in prayer to .... Ps 63:4
have I kept my **h** from doing .... Ps 73:13
All night long I reach out my **h**, ... Ps 77:2
and guided them with skillful **h**. .... Ps 78:72
with your own **h** and strengthened .... Ps 80:15
have lifted my **h** in prayer to .... Ps 88:9
you in their **h** so that you will................. Ps 91:12
joy about what your **h** have done. .... Ps 92:4

created the land with his own **h**.............. Ps 95:5
Let the rivers clap their **h**; .... Ps 98:8
and your **h** made the skies...................... Ps 102:25
and gold, the work of human **h**. .... Ps 115:4
They have **h**, but they cannot .... Ps 115:7
in your **h**, join the feast .... Ps 118:27
me and formed me with your **h**. .... Ps 119:73
Raise your **h** in the Temple and .... Ps 134:2
and gold, the work of human **h**. .... Ps 135:15
I lift my **h** to you in prayer. .... Ps 143:6
two-edged swords in their **h**. .... Ps 149:6
You fold your **h** and lie down to .... Pr 6:10
h that kill innocent people,.................... Pr 6:17
You fold your **h** and lie down to .... Pr 24:33
may put their **h** in the dish. .... Pr 26:15
and likes to work with her **h**. .... Pr 31:13
thread with her **h** and weaves her .... Pr 31:19
to fold your **h** and do nothing, ... Ec 4:5
dripping from my **h** and flowing............. Sng 5:5
His **h** are like gold hinges, ... Sng 5:14
your **h** are full of blood. .... Is 1:15
with their own **h** and shaped with .... Is 2:8
or notice the work of his **h**..................... Is 5:12
trust what their **h** have made, ... Is 17:8
the children I made with my **h**, ... Is 29:23
Make the weak **h** strong and the .... Is 35:3
to its maker, 'You have no **h**.' .... Is 45:9
With my own **h** I stretched out .... Is 45:12
I made the earth with my own **h**. .... Is 48:13
you with my **h** and protect you. .... Is 51:16
in the fields will clap their **h**. .... Is 55:12
With your **h** you have killed .... Is 59:3
they use their **h** to hurt others. .... Is 59:6
the work of my own **h** to show my .... Is 60:21
the potter; your **h** made us all. .... Is 64:8
they had made with their own **h**. .... Je 1:16
place with your **h** on your head,............. Je 2:37
She lifts her **h** in prayer and .... Je 4:31
take power into their own **h**, ... Je 5:31
He was using his **h** to make a pot .... Je 18:4
You are in my **h** like the clay in .... Je 18:6
like the clay in the potter's **h**. .... Je 18:6
Jeremiah's **h** and feet between .... Je 20:2
of war in your **h** to defend .... Je 21:4
that are the work of your own **h**, ... Je 25:6
were the work of your own **h**,................. Je 25:7
for all their own **h** have done." .... Je 25:14
Lock his **h** and feet between .... Je 29:26
idols made with their own **h**,"................. Je 32:30
Everyone's **h** are cut, and .... Je 48:37
return from war with empty **h**. .... Je 50:9
they are tied together by his **h**; .... La 1:14
Jerusalem reaches out her **h**, ... La 1:17
on the road clap their **h** at you; .... La 2:15
Lift up your **h** in prayer to him .... La 2:19
us lift up our **h** and pray from................. La 3:41
jars made by the **h** of a potter. .... La 4:2
no **h** reached out to help her. .... La 4:6
With their own **h** kind women cook .... La 4:10
Princes were hung by the **h**; .... La 5:12
had human **h** under their wings .... Eze 1:8
Clap your **h**, stamp your feet,................. Eze 6:11
h will hang weakly with fear, ... Eze 7:17
and the **h** of the people who own .... Eze 7:27
fill your **h** with coals of fire .... Eze 10:2
and put it in the **h** of the man .... Eze 10:7
backs, their **h**, their wings, ... Eze 10:12
things that looked like human **h**. .... Eze 10:21
dug through the wall with my **h**............. Eze 12:7
and save my people from your **h**. .... Eze 13:21
and all **h** will become weak. .... Eze 21:7
human, prophesy and clap your **h**........... Eze 21:14
will also clap my **h** and use up .... Eze 21:17

clapped your h and stamped your .... Eze 25:6
When their h grabbed you, you .... Eze 29:7
me and set me on my h and knees. .... Da 10:10
raised his h toward heaven. .... Da 12:7
' to the things our h have made. .... Hos 14:3
worship what your h have made. .... Mic 5:13
With both h they are doing evil. .... Mic 7:3
will put their h over their .... Mic 7:16
and all the work of your h." .... Hag 1:11
do with their h is unclean to me .... Hag 2:14
you in their h so that you will .... Mt 4:6
wash their h before they eat. .... Mt 15:2
with unwashed h does not make .... Mt 15:20
than to have two h and two feet .... Mt 18:8
could put his h on them and pray .... Mt 19:13
Jesus put his h on the children, ... Mt 19:15
'Tie this man's h and feet. .... Mt 22:13
the person who h the Son of Man .... Mt 26:24
water and washed his h in front .... Mt 27:24
to tie the man's h and feet. .... Mk 5:4
come and put your h on her so .... Mk 5:23
people by putting his h on them. .... Mk 6:5
ate food with h that were not .... Mk 7:2
washing their h in the way .... Mk 7:3
their food with h that are not .... Mk 7:5
eyes and put his h on the man .... Mk 8:23
Jesus put his h on the man's .... Mk 8:25
to have two h and go to hell, ... Mk 9:43
his arms, put his h on them, and .... Mk 10:16
the person who h the Son of Man .... Mk 14:21
you in their h so that you will .... Lk 4:11
Putting his h on each sick .... Lk 4:40
them in their h, and ate them .... Lk 6:1
not wash his h before the meal. .... Lk 11:38
Jesus put his h on her, and .... Lk 13:13
Look at my h and my feet. .... Lk 24:39
he showed them his h and feet. .... Lk 24:40
he raised his h and blessed them .... Lk 24:50
his h and feet wrapped with .... Jn 11:44
but wash my h and my head, ... Jn 13:9
showed them his h and his side .... Jn 20:20
marks in his h and put my finger .... Jn 20:25
finger here, and look at my h. .... Jn 20:27
put out your h and someone else .... Jn 21:18
prayed and laid their h on them. .... Ac 6:6
they had made with their own h. .... Ac 7:41
that people build with their h. .... Ac 7:48
laying their h on the people, ... Ac 8:17
apostles laid their h on them. .... Ac 8:18
on whom I lay my h will receive .... Ac 8:19
to him and lays his h on him. .... Ac 9:12
He laid his h on Saul and said, ... Ac 9:17
the chains fell off Peter's h. .... Ac 12:7
they laid their h on Barnabas .... Ac 13:3
in temples built by human h. .... Ac 17:24
Then Paul laid his h on them, ... Ac 19:6
made by human h are not real. .... Ac 19:26
it to tie his own h and feet. .... Ac 21:11
with their own h they threw out .... Ac 27:19
and put his h on the man and .... Ac 28:8
with our own h for our food. 1Co 4:12
not be a house made by human h; 2Co 5:1
a circumcision not done by h. .... Col 2:11
up their h in a holy manner 1Ti 2:8
of elders laid their h on you. 1Ti 4:14
before you lay your h on anyone, ... 1Ti 5:22
you when I laid my h on you. 2Ti 1:6
and your h made the skies .... Heb 1:10
laying on of h, about the .... Heb 6:2
to fall into the h of the living .... Heb 10:31
and we have touched with our h. 1Jn 1:1
palm branches in their h. .... Rev 7:9

they had made with their own h. .... Rev 9:20
their foreheads or on their h. .... Rev 20:4

HANDSOME
Now Joseph was well built and h. .... Ge 39:6
He is a good speaker and h, ... 1Sa 16:18
They were to be h and well .... Da 1:4

HANDWRITING
end this letter now in my own h. 2Th 3:17

HANES
your messengers have gone to H, ... Is 30:4

HANNAH
two wives named H and Peninnah 1Sa 1:2
special share of the meat to H, ... 1Sa 1:5
relations with his wife H, ... 1Sa 1:19

HANNATHON
to the north to H and continued .... Jos 19:14

HANNIEL
son of Joseph, H son of Ephod; .... Nu 34:23
sons were Arah, H, and Rizia. 1Ch 7:39

HANOCH
Ephah, Epher, H, Abida, and .... Ge 25:4
sons were H, Pallu, Hezron, ... Ge 46:9
H, Pallu, Hezron, and Carmi. .... Ex 6:14
From H came the Hanochite family .... Nu 26:5
Ephah, Epher, H, Abida, and 1Ch 1:33
sons were H, Pallu, Hezron, ... 1Ch 5:3

HANOCHITE
Hanoch came the H family group; .... Nu 26:5

HANUN
his son H became king after him. 2Sa 10:1
I will be loyal to his son H." 2Sa 10:2
to comfort H about his father's 2Sa 10:2
the Ammonite leaders said to H, ... 2Sa 10:3
So H arrested David's officers. 2Sa 10:4
I will be loyal to his son H." 1Ch 19:2
to comfort H about his father's 1Ch 19:2
of the Ammonites to comfort H. 1Ch 19:2
the Ammonite leaders said to H, ... 1Ch 19:3
So H arrested David's officers. 1Ch 19:4
H and the Ammonites sent about 1Ch 19:6
H and the people of Zanoah .... Ne 3:13
Shelemiah, and H, the sixth son .... Ne 3:30

HAPHARAIM
H, Shion, Anaharath, ... Jos 19:19

HAPPIZZEZ
The eighteenth was H. 1Ch 24:15

HAPPY
H is the man who has his bag .... Ps 127:5
what you did to us will be h. .... Ps 137:8
H are those who are like this; .... Ps 144:15
People are h if they can do what .... Rm 14:22

HARA
to Halah, Habor, H, and near the 1Ch 5:26

HARADAH
Mount Shepher and camped at H. .... Nu 33:24
They left H and camped at .... Nu 33:25

HARAM
the valley, Beth H, Beth Nimrah, ... Jos 13:27

HARAN
Abram, Nahor, and H were born. .... Ge 11:26
father of Abram, Nahor, and H. .... Ge 11:27
old, and then he died in H. .... Ge 11:32
before he lived in H. .... Ac 7:2
Chaldea and went to live in H. .... Ac 7:4

HARARITE
was Shammah son of Agee the H. 2Sa 23:11
son of Shammah the H; 2Sa 23:33

Ahiam son of Sharar the H; 2Sa 23:33
Jonathan son of Shagee the H; 1Ch 11:34
Ahiam son of Sacar the H; 1Ch 11:35

HARBONA
Biztha, H, Bigtha, Abagtha .... Est 1:10
H, one of the eunuchs there .... Est 7:9

HARBOR
The houses and h of Tyre are .... Is 23:1
There is no h for you now! .... Is 23:10
that h was not a good place .... Ac 27:12
a h which faced southwest and .... Ac 27:12

HARBORS
the seashore, at their safe h. .... Jdg 5:17

HARD
Is anything too h for the LORD?............... Ge 18:14
to work h to make bricks .... Ex 1:14
brought the h cases to Moses,................. Ex 18:26
to test him with h questions. 1Ki 10:1
You have asked a h thing. 2Ki 2:10
father forced us to work very h. 2Ch 10:4
Its chest is as h as a rock, ... Job 41:24
is nothing too h for you to do. .... Je 32:17
will be h for a rich person to .... Mt 19:23
I knew that you were a h man. .... Mt 25:24
but it is h to explain because .... Heb 5:11
letters are h to understand,.................... 2Pe 3:16

HARD-HEADED
word can get through to the h. .... Pr 25:15

HARD-WORKING
The plans of h people earn a .... Pr 21:5

HARDENED
will become h because sin has .... Heb 3:13

HARDER
hard as a diamond, h than stone. .... Eze 3:9
I worked h than all the other 1Co 15:10
I have worked much h than they. 2Co 11:23
I tried h than anyone else to .... Gal 1:14

HARDLY
and kind she would h even walk .... Dt 28:56
and night and h ever sleeping. .... Ec 8:16
that his feet h touched the .... Da 8:5

HARESETH
Kir H was the only city with its 2Ki 3:25
raisin cakes they had in Kir H. .... Is 16:7
I am very sad for Kir H. .... Is 16:11
people from the town of Kir H. .... Je 48:31
flute for the people from Kir H. .... Je 48:36

HARHAIAH
Uzziel son of H, a goldsmith, ... Ne 3:8

HARHAS
the son of H, who took care 2Ki 22:14
the son of H, who took care 2Ch 34:22

HARHUR
Bakbuk, Hakupha, H, ... Ezr 2:51
Bakbuk, Hakupha, H, ... Ne 7:53

HARIM
The third was H. The fourth was 1Ch 24:8
of H—320; .... Ezr 2:32
the descendants of H—1,017. .... Ezr 2:39
From the descendants of H: .... Ezr 10:21
From the descendants of H: .... Ezr 10:31
Malkijah son of H and Hasshub .... Ne 3:11
of H—320; .... Ne 7:35
the descendants of H—1,017. .... Ne 7:42
H, Meremoth, Obadiah, ... Ne 10:5
Malluch, H, and Baanah. .... Ne 10:27

HARIM'S
Adna, from H family; .... Ne 12:15

HARIPH
the descendants of H—112;.................... Ne 7:24
H, Anathoth, Nebai, ... Ne 10:19

HARM
a curse on those who h you. .... Ge 12:3
not allowed your father to h me.............. Ge 31:7
I have the power to h you, ... Ge 31:29
will know if you h my daughters .... Ge 31:50
I told you not to h the boy, ... Ge 42:22
that he did not h or kill the .... Ex 22:11
I might h what I can pass on to .... Ru 4:6
say, 'David wants to h you'? 1Sa 24:9
I said, 'I won't h my master, ... 1Sa 24:10
were with us, we did not h them. 1Sa 25:7
us. They did not h us. They.................... 1Sa 25:15
one can h the LORD's appointed 1Sa 26:9
but I wouldn't h the LORD's 1Sa 26:23
make up for the h done so you 2Sa 21:3
me from those who want to h me. 2Sa 22:3
he warned kings not to h them. 1Ch 16:21
and don't h my prophets." 1Ch 16:22
But they were planning to h me.............. Ne 9:2
those who wanted to h them. .... Est 9:2
and from the h done by powerful .... Job 5:15
seven troubles will not h you. .... Job 5:19
their arm is raised to do h, ... Job 38:15
those who plan to h me turn back .... Ps 35:4
he warned kings not to h them. .... Ps 105:14
and don't h my prophets." .... Ps 105:15
rest until they h someone. .... Pr 4:16
No h comes to a good person, ... Pr 12:21
people only want to h others. .... Pr 21:10
Curses will not h someone who is .... Pr 26:2
him good and not h for as long .... Pr 31:12
Sometimes people h those they .... Ec 8:9
such great h to yourselves?................... Je 44:7
change his mind about doing h. .... Joe 2:13
and stop doing h all the time. .... Jnh 3:8
you would choose not to cause h. .... Jnh 4:2
in a safe place and escape h. .... Hab 2:9
these things can really h you. .... Lk 21:18
Wish good for those who h you;.............. Rm 12:14
you do more h than good. 1Co 11:17
had given power to h the earth .... Rev 7:2
Do not h the land or the sea or .... Rev 7:3
were told not to h the grass .... Rev 9:4
They could h only the people who .... Rev 9:4

HARMED
someone who has not h you. .... Pr 3:30
cuts logs might be h by them.................. Ec 10:9
the fire had not h their bodies. .... Da 3:27
again be afraid of being h. .... Zph 3:15
will punish all those who h you............... Zph 3:19

HARMFUL
do not say h things, but say .... Eph 4:29
foolish and h things that ruin 1Ti 6:9
did many h things against me. 2Ti 4:14

HARMING
keep me from h his appointed 1Sa 26:11

HARMLESS
the disease is only a h rash. .... Le 13:39

HARMONY
you to live in h with each other .... Rm 15:5
Live in h. Do what I have 2Co 13:11

HARNEPHER
sons were Suah, H, Shual, Beri, ... 1Ch 7:36

HARNESS
row with a h so it will plow .... Job 39:10
H the horses and get on them! .... Je 46:4
h the fastest horse to the...................... Mic 1:13

H

HARNESSES
horses, and **h** are for donkeys .... Pr 26:3

HAROD
their camp at the spring of H................... Jdg 7:1

HARODITE
Shammah the **H**; Elika the 2Sa 23:25
the Harodite; Elika the **H**; 2Sa 23:25

HAROEH
Shobal's descendants were **H**, ... 1Ch 2:52

HARORITE
Shammoth the **H**; Helez the 1Ch 11:27

HAROSHETH
who lived in **H** Haggoyim, was .... Jdg 4:2
from **H** Haggoyim to the Kishon............... Jdg 4:13
chariots and army to **H** Haggoyim. .... Jdg 4:16

HARP
person to play the **h** and flute. .... Ge 4:21
for someone who can play the **h**. 1Sa 16:16
Jesse of Bethlehem play the **h**. 1Sa 16:18
David would take his **h** and play. 1Sa 16:23
was playing the **h** as he usually 1Sa 18:10
David was playing the **h**....................... 1Sa 19:9
me someone who plays the **h**." 2Ki 3:15
While the **h** was being played, ... 2Ki 3:15
and used a **h** to give thanks 1Ch 25:3
h is tuned to sing a sad song, ... Job 30:31
Praise the Lord on the **h**; .... Ps 33:2
I will praise you with a **h**, ... Ps 43:4
will explain my riddle on the **h**. .... Ps 49:4
soul. Wake up, **h** and lyre! I .... Ps 57:8
I will praise you with the **h**. .... Ps 71:22
and with the soft-sounding **h**. .... Ps 92:3
Wake up, **h** and lyre! I will wake .... Ps 108:2
to you on the ten-stringed **h**. .... Ps 144:9
for Moab like a **h** playing a................... Is 16:11
Take your **h** and walk through the .... Is 23:16
city. Play your **h** well. Sing .... Is 23:16
make sounds—like a flute or a **h**. 1Co 14:7
of them had a **h** and golden bowls .... Rev 5:8

HARPS
playing lyres, **h**, tambourines,.................. 1Ch 13:8
played cymbals, lyres, and **h**. 1Ch 15:28
Jeduthun to preach and play **h**, ... 1Ch 25:1
trees nearby we hung our **h**. .... Ps 137:2
had **h** that God had given them. .... Rev 15:2

HARSH
will not have to be **h** in my use 2Co 13:10

HARSHA
Bazluth, Mehida, **H**, ... Ezr 2:52
Tel Melah, Tel **H**, Kerub, Addon,............... Ezr 2:59
Bazluth, Mehida, **H**, ... Ne 7:54
Tel Melah, Tel **H**, Kerub, Addon,............... Ne 7:61

HARSHLY
but when God speaks **h** to them, ... Is 17:13

HARUM
Aharhel was the son of H. 1Ch 4:8

HARUMAPH
Jedaiah son of **H** made repairs .... Ne 3:10

HARUPH
There was Shephatiah from H. 1Ch 12:5

HARUZ
was Meshullemeth daughter of **H**, ... 2Ki 21:19

HARVEST
planting and **h**, cold and hot, ... Ge 8:22
During the wheat **h** Reuben went .... Ge 30:14
things you **h** from the crops .... Ex 23:16
season and the **h** season. .... Ex 34:21
the first grain of the wheat **h**. .... Ex 34:22
do not **h** all the way to the .... Le 19:9
crop until the **h** of the ninth .... Le 25:22
the beginning of the barley **h**................... Ru 1:22
until the barley **h** and the wheat............... Ru 2:23
and they had a good **h**. .... Ps 107:37
they expect a **h**, but there is .... Pr 20:4
snow in summer or rain at **h**. .... Pr 26:1
we have the **h** at the right time. .... Je 5:24
the people say, "**H** time is over; .... Je 8:20
their crops or gather the **h**. .... Je 50:16
crush the grain at **h** time. .... Je 51:33
you three months before **h** time............... Am 4:7
a few workers to help **h** them. .... Mt 9:37
who owns the **h**, that he will .... Mt 9:38
more workers to gather his **h**." .... Mt 9:38
grow together until the **h** time. .... Mt 13:30
At **h** time I will tell the .... Mt 13:30
h time is the end of the age, ... Mt 13:39
are a great many people to **h**, ... Lk 10:2
God, who owns the **h**, that he .... Lk 10:2
'Four more months till **h**.' .... Jn 4:35
at the fields ready for **h** now. .... Jn 4:35

HARVESTED
but they have **h** only thorns. .... Je 12:13
have plowed evil and **h** trouble; .... Hos 10:13
the earth, and the earth was **h**. .... Rev 14:16

HARVESTERS
who was with the grain **h**. 2Ki 4:18

HARVESTING
of years left for **h** crops, ... Le 25:15
Beth Shemesh were **h** their wheat 1Sa 6:13
will still be **h** crops when it's .... Am 9:13

HARVESTS
of all the first **h** and all the .... Eze 44:30
the one who **h** is being paid and............... Jn 4:36
and the one who **h** celebrate at .... Jn 4:36
person plants, and another **h**.' .... Jn 4:37

HASADIAH
Ohel, Berekiah, **H**, and 1Ch 3:20

HASHABIAH
H was Amaziah's son........................... 1Ch 6:45
H was from the family of Merari. 1Ch 9:14
Shimei, **H**, and Mattithiah. 1Ch 25:3
twelve men were chosen from **H**, ... 1Ch 25:19
H was from the Hebron family. 1Ch 26:30
H son of Kemuel was over the 1Ch 27:17
and Nethanel, and **H**, Jeiel, and 2Ch 35:9
brought to us **H** and Jeshaiah................. Ezr 8:19
Sherebiah, **H**, and ten of their .... Ezr 8:24
to him, **H**, the ruler of half .... Ne 3:17
Mica, Rehob, **H**, ... Ne 10:11
son of Azrikam, the son of **H**................... Ne 11:15
H was the son of Bunni. .... Ne 11:15
Bani was the son of **H**, the son .... Ne 11:22
H, from Hilkiah's family; .... Ne 12:21
leaders of the Levites were **H**, ... Ne 12:24

HASHABIAH'S
Malluch was **H** son............................. 1Ch 6:45
son, and Azrikam was **H** son................... 1Ch 9:14
hundred skilled men in **H** group. 1Ch 26:30

HASHABNAH
Rehum, **H**, Maaseiah, ... Ne 10:25

HASHABNEIAH
Hattush son of **H** made repairs. .... Ne 3:10
Kadmiel, Bani, **H**, Sherebiah, ... Ne 9:5

HASHBADDANAH
Malkijah, Hashum, **H**, Zechariah, ... Ne 8:4

HASHEM
the sons of **H** the Gizonite; 1Ch 11:34

HASHMONAH
left Mithcah and camped at **H.** .... Nu 33:29
They left **H** and camped at .... Nu 33:30

HASHUBAH
H, Ohel, Berekiah, Hasadiah, and 1Ch 3:20

HASHUM
the descendants of **H**—223;................ Ezr 2:19
From the descendants of **H:** .... Ezr 10:33
the descendants of **H**—328;................ Ne 7:22
Malkijah, **H,** Hashbaddanah, ... Ne 8:4
Hodiah, **H,** Bezai, ... Ne 10:18

HASSENAAH
The sons of **H** rebuilt the Fish................. Ne 3:3

HASSENUAH
and Judah son of **H** was second in .... Ne 11:9

HASSENUAH'S
son, and Hodaviah was **H** son. 1Ch 9:7

HASSHUB
there was Shemaiah son of **H.** 1Ch 9:14
H was Azrikam's son, and Azrikam 1Ch 9:14
son of Harim and **H** son of .... Ne 3:11
Benjamin and **H** made repairs in .... Ne 3:23
Hoshea, Hananiah, **H,**......................... Ne 10:23
There was Shemaiah son of **H.** .... Ne 11:15
H was the son of Azrikam, the .... Ne 11:15

HASSOPHERETH
descendants of Sotai, **H,** Peruda, ... Ezr 2:55

HASUPHA
of Ziha, **H,** Tabbaoth, ... Ezr 2:43
of Ziha, **H,** Tabbaoth, ... Ne 7:46

HATCH
When they **h** open, the owls will .... Is 34:15
They **h** evil like eggs from .... Is 59:5

HATCHETS
panels with their axes and **h.** .... Ps 74:6

HATCHING
Like a bird **h** an egg it did not .... Je 17:11

HATE
If you **h** me, I will punish your .... Ex 20:5
You must not **h** your fellow..................... Le 19:17
and pay back those who **h** me. .... Dt 32:41
crying, and said, "You **h** me! .... Jdg 14:16
You **h** all those who do evil. .... Ps 5:5
See how much they **h** me! .... Ps 25:19
they **h** me for no reason........................ Ps 35:19
and many **h** me for no reason. .... Ps 38:19
You love right and **h** evil, ... Ps 45:7
You **h** my teachings and turn your .... Ps 50:17
People who love the LORD **h** evil. .... Ps 97:10
so I **h** lying ways. .... Ps 119:104
I **h** disloyal people, but I love .... Ps 119:113
I **h** and despise lies, but I love.............. Ps 119:163
I feel only **h** for them; .... Ps 139:22
fun of wisdom and **h** knowledge? .... Pr 1:22
the LORD, you will also **h** evil. .... Pr 8:13
Those who **h** me love death." .... Pr 8:36
a time to love and a time to **h.** .... Ec 3:8
this terrible thing that I **h.'** .... Je 44:4
H evil and love good; be fair in .... Am 5:15
but you **h** good and love evil. .... Mic 3:2
neighbor and **h** your enemies.' .... Mt 5:43
The person will **h** one master and .... Mt 6:24
People will **h** you, shut you out, ... Lk 6:22
Do good to those who **h** you, ... Lk 6:27
The world cannot **h** you, but it .... Jn 7:7
to do, and I do the things I **h.** .... Rm 7:15
You **h** what the Nicolaitans do, ... Rev 2:6

HATED
After that Esau **h** Jacob because.............. Ge 27:41
they **h** their brother and could .... Ge 37:4
After that, Amnon **h** Tamar. 2Sa 13:15
defeated those who **h** them. .... Est 9:1
So I **h** life. It made me sad to .... Ec 2:17
but I **h** Esau. I destroyed his .... Mal 1:3
remember that it **h** me first. .... Jn 15:18
the world has **h** them, because .... Jn 17:14
I loved Jacob, but I **h** Esau." .... Rm 9:13
People **h** us, and we hated each .... Tit 3:3
hated us, and we **h** each other. .... Tit 3:3

HATHACH
Esther called for **H,** one of the .... Est 4:5
H went to Mordecai, who was in .... Est 4:6
Mordecai told **H** everything that............. Est 4:7
and he told **H** about the amount............. Est 4:7
He wanted **H** to show it to Esther .... Est 4:8
H went back and reported to .... Est 4:9
Esther told **H** to tell Mordecai, ... Est 4:10

HATHATH
sons were **H** and Meonothai. 1Ch 4:13

HATING
king of Judah for **h** my promise .... Eze 17:19
witchcraft, **h,** making trouble,............... Gal 5:20
the world is the same as **h** God. .... Jam 4:4
h even their clothes which are .... Jud 1:23

HATIPHA
Neziah, and **H.** .... Ezr 2:54
Neziah, and **H.** .... Ne 7:56

HATITA
Akkub, **H,** and Shobai—139. .... Ezr 2:42
Akkub, **H,** and Shobai—138. .... Ne 7:45

HATRED
shove someone, and not from **h.**............... Nu 35:22
anyone and no **h** for the one who .... Nu 35:23
was not killed because of **h,** .... Dt 4:42
meaning to, not out of **h.**....................... Dt 19:4
With pride and **h** they speak .... Ps 31:18
H stirs up trouble, but love .... Pr 10:12
Because of their strong **h,** .... Eze 25:15
very much, and your **h** is great. .... Hos 9:7
sin, evil, selfishness, and **h.**................... Rm 1:29
to end the **h** between the two .... Eph 2:16

HATTAAVAH
named that place Kibroth **H,** .... Nu 11:34
From Kibroth **H** the people went .... Nu 11:35
Sinai and camped at Kibroth **H.** .... Nu 33:16
They left Kibroth **H** and camped .... Nu 33:17
Taberah, Massah, and Kibroth **H.** .... Dt 9:22

HATTICON
town of Hazer **H** on the border .... Eze 47:16

HATTIL
Shephatiah, **H,**............................... Ezr 2:57
Shephatiah, **H,**............................... Ne 7:59

HATTUSH
sons were **H,** Igal, Bariah, ... 1Ch 3:22
From the descendants of David: **H** .... Ezr 8:2
H son of Hashabneiah made repairs. .... Ne 3:10
H, Shebaniah, Malluch, ... Ne 10:4
Amariah, Malluch, **H,** .... Ne 12:2

HAURAN
the border of the country of **H.** .... Eze 47:16
a point between **H** and Damascus. .... Eze 47:18

HAVENS
came to a place called Fair **H,**................ Ac 27:8

HAVILAH
around the whole land of **H,** ....Ge 2:11
were Seba, **H,** Sabtah, Raamah ....Ge 10:7
Ophir, **H,** and Jobab. ....Ge 10:29
lived from **H** to Shur, ...Ge 25:18
them all the way from **H** to Shur, ...1Sa 15:7
were Seba, **H,** Sabta, Raamah, ...1Ch 1:9
Ophir, **H,** and Jobab. 1Ch 1:23

HAWK
owls, sea gulls, any kind of **h,**..................Le 11:16
owls, sea gulls, any kind of **h,**..................Dt 14:15
No **h** knows that path; the falcon ....Job 28:7
wisdom that the **h** flies and.....................Job 39:26
come like a **h** from a country ....Is 46:11

HAWKS
H will gather with their own ....Is 34:15
bird attacked on all sides by **h.** ....Je 12:9

HAY
They gather **h** and straw in the ....Job 24:6
Bring in the **h,** and let the new ....Pr 27:25
Lions will eat **h** as oxen do. ....Is 11:7
that are like **h** and straw. ....Is 33:11
Lions will eat **h** like oxen, ...Is 65:25

HAZAEL
olive oil on **H** to make him king 1Ki 19:15
The king said to **H,** "Take a gift 2Ki 8:8
So **H** went to meet Elisha, taking 2Ki 8:9
Elisha said to **H,** "Go and tell 2Ki 8:10
H stared at Elisha until he felt 2Ki 8:11
H asked, "Why are you crying, ...2Ki 8:12
H said, "Am I a dog? How could I 2Ki 8:13
Then **H** left Elisha and came to 2Ki 8:14
H answered, "He told me that 2Ki 8:14
the next day **H** took a blanket 2Ki 8:15
So **H** became king in Ben-Hadad's 2Ki 8:15
fought against **H** king of Aram. 2Ki 8:28
when he fought **H** king of Aram. 2Ki 8:29
in Gilead from **H** king of Aram. 2Ki 9:14
fought against **H** king of Aram. 2Ki 9:15
H defeated the Israelites in all 2Ki 10:32
About this time **H** king of Aram 2Ki 12:17
this treasure to **H** king of Aram,..............2Ki 12:18
them over to **H** king of Aram 2Ki 13:3
H king of Aram troubled Israel. 2Ki 13:22
When **H** king of Aram died, his 2Ki 13:24
During a war **H** had taken some..............2Ki 13:25
fought against **H** king of Aram. 2Ch 22:5
when he fought **H** king of Aram. 2Ch 22:6
the house of **H** that will destroy ....Am 1:4

HAZAEL'S
anyone who escapes from **H** sword, ...1Ki 19:17
cities from **H** son Ben-Hadad..................2Ki 13:25

HAZAIAH
son of Col-Hozeh, the son of **H.** ....Ne 11:5
H was the son of Adaiah, the son ....Ne 11:5

HAZAR
it will go to **H** Addar and over ....Nu 34:4
and it will end at **H** Enan. ....Nu 34:9
will begin at **H** Enan and go to ....Nu 34:10
H Gaddah, Heshmon, Beth Pelet, ...Jos 15:27
H Shual, Beersheba, Biziothiah, ...Jos 15:28
H Shual, Balah, Ezem, ...Jos 19:3
Ziklag, Beth Marcaboth, **H** Susah, ...Jos 19:5
in Beersheba, Moladah, **H** Shual, ...1Ch 4:28
Beth Marcaboth, **H** Susim, Beth 1Ch 4:31
H Shual, Beersheba and its.....................Ne 11:27
Sea east to the town of **H** Enan, ...Eze 47:17
all the way to **H** Enan, where ....Eze 48:1

HAZARMAVETH
of Almodad, Sheleph, **H,** Jerah, ...Ge 10:26
of Almodad, Sheleph, **H,** Jerah, ...1Ch 1:20

HAZAZON
Amorites who lived in **H** Tamar...............Ge 14:7
They are already in **H** Tamar!" 2Ch 20:2
H Tamar is also called En Gedi. 2Ch 20:2

HAZER
go on to the town of **H** Hatticon ....Eze 47:16

HAZEROTH
the people went to stay at **H.** ....Nu 11:35
the people left **H** and camped in..............Nu 12:16
Hattaavah and camped at **H.** ....Nu 33:17
They left **H** and camped at ....Nu 33:18
Tophel, Laban, **H,** and Dizahab. ....Dt 1:1

HAZIEL
were Shelomoth, **H,** and Haran. 1Ch 23:9

HAZO
there are Kesed, **H,** Pildash, ...Ge 22:22

HAZOR
Jabin king of **H** heard about all ....Jos 11:1
the city of **H** and killed its ....Jos 11:10
H had been the leader of all the ....Jos 11:10
Israel killed everyone in **H,**.....................Jos 11:11
Then they burned **H** itself. ....Jos 11:11
built on their mounds, except **H;** ....Jos 11:13
Madon, **H,** ....Jos 12:19
Kedesh, **H,** Ithnan, ...Jos 15:23
H Hadattah, Kerioth Hezron (also ....Jos 15:25
Kerioth Hezron (also called **H**), ...Jos 15:25
Adamah, Ramah, **H,** ....Jos 19:36
Kedesh, Edrei, En **H,** ....Jos 19:37
who ruled in the city of **H,** ....Jdg 4:2
at peace with Jabin king of **H.** ....Jdg 4:17
the commander of the army of **H,** 1Sa 12:9
had some men come to Baal **H,** 2Sa 13:23
them rebuild the cities of **H,** 1Ki 9:15
Maacah, Janoah, Kedesh, and **H.** 2Ki 15:29
H, Ramah, Gittaim, ...Ne 11:33
of Kedar and the kingdoms of **H,** ....Je 49:28
People in **H,** find a good place ....Je 49:30
The city of **H** will become a home ....Je 49:33

HAZZOBEBAH
father of Anub, **H,** and the 1Ch 4:8

HE'S
women answered, "Yes, **h** here. 1Sa 9:12
Yes, he's here. **H** ahead of you. 1Sa 9:12
H hiding behind the baggage." 1Sa 10:22
against David? **H** innocent......................1Sa 19:5
H the man they dance and sing 1Sa 21:11
Look at the man! **H** crazy! Why do 1Sa 21:14
H at the hideouts of Horesh, ...1Sa 23:19
did you let him go? Now **h** gone. 2Sa 3:24
H just the prophet for you. ....Mic 2:11

HEAD
descendants will crush your **h,** ....Ge 3:15
and I bowed my **h** and thanked the ....Ge 24:48
and laid his **h** on it to go to....................Ge 28:11
three bread baskets on my **h.** ....Ge 40:16
food out of the basket on my **h.**" ....Ge 40:17
the king will cut off your **h!** ....Ge 40:19
right hand on the **h** of Ephraim,..............Ge 48:14
left hand on the **h** of Manasseh's ....Ge 48:14
his right hand on Ephraim's **h,** ....Ge 48:17
from Ephraim's **h** to Manasseh's ....Ge 48:17
Ephraim's head to Manasseh's **h.** ....Ge 48:17
Put your right hand on his **h.**" ....Ge 48:18
rest on the **h** of Joseph, ...Ge 49:26
a fire—with its **h,** legs, and ....Ex 12:9
on a person's **h** to make him a ....Ex 25:6

in the center for Aaron's **h**,...................... Ex 28:32
this on his **h** so the LORD will .... Ex 28:38
turban on his **h**, and put the .... Ex 29:6
and pour it on his **h** to make him .... Ex 29:7
put their hands on the bull's **h**. .... Ex 29:10
sons put their hands on its **h**. .... Ex 29:15
them with its **h** and its other .... Ex 29:17
sons put their hands on its **h**. .... Ex 29:19
put his hand on the animal's **h**, ... Le 1:4
are to lay the **h**, the fat, and .... Le 1:8
lay them, with the **h** and fat, on .... Le 1:12
to the altar and pull off its **h**, ... Le 1:15
on the animal's **h** and kill it at .... Le 3:2
and put his hand on its **h**. .... Le 3:8
and put his hand on its **h**. .... Le 3:13
his hand on its **h**, and kill it .... Le 4:4
of the bull—its **h**, legs, ... Le 4:11
on the bull's **h** before the LORD, ... Le 4:15
hand on the goat's **h** and kill it .... Le 4:24
on the animal's **h** and kill it at .... Le 4:29
on the animal's **h** and kill it as .... Le 4:33
pull the bird's **h** from its neck, ... Le 5:8
put the turban on Aaron's **h**. .... Le 8:9
oil on Aaron's **h** to make Aaron .... Le 8:12
sons put their hands on its **h**. .... Le 8:14
sons put their hands on its **h**. .... Le 8:18
into pieces and burned the **h**, ... Le 8:20
sons put their hands on its **h**. .... Le 8:22
the pieces and the **h** of the burnt .... Le 9:13
his skin from his **h** to his feet, ... Le 13:12
skin disease of the **h** or chin. .... Le 13:30
hair from his **h** and is bald, ... Le 13:40
front of his **h** and has a bald .... Le 13:41
sore on his bald **h** or forehead, ... Le 13:42
sore on his bald **h** or forehead .... Le 13:43
because of the sore on his **h**. .... Le 13:44
hair from his **h**, his beard, his............... Le 14:9
hand on the **h** of the person to .... Le 14:18
his hand on the **h** of the person .... Le 14:29
his hands on the **h** of the living .... Le 16:21
people's sins on the goat's **h**. .... Le 16:21
olive oil poured on his **h**. .... Le 21:10
poured on his **h** to separate him .... Le 21:12
must put their hands on his **h**, ... Le 24:14
shave their **h** seven days later .... Nu 6:9
stick for the **h** of each tribe. .... Nu 17:3
the ax **h** flies off the handle, ... Dt 19:5
must shave her **h** and cut her .... Dt 21:12
make you like the **h** and not like .... Dt 28:13
be like the **h**, and you will be .... Dt 28:44
rest on the **h** of Joseph, ... Dt 33:16
side of Sisera's **h** and into the................ Jdg 4:21
with the tent peg in his **h**. .... Jdg 4:22
She smashed his **h**! She crushed .... Jdg 5:26
and pierced the side of his **h**! .... Jdg 5:26
a grinding stone on his **h**, ... Jdg 9:53
will become the **h** of all those .... Jdg 10:18
shaved my **h**, I would lose my............... Jdg 16:17
put it on her **h** and went back to .... Ru 3:15
put dust on his **h** to show his 1Sa 4:12
His **h** and hands had broken off 1Sa 5:4
Saul stood a **h** taller than any............... 1Sa 9:2
oil and poured it on Saul's **h**. 1Sa 10:1
was a **h** taller than anyone else. 1Sa 10:23
even a hair of his **h** will fall 1Sa 14:45
helmet on his **h** and a coat of 1Sa 17:5
helmet on his **h** and dressed him 1Sa 17:38
kill you and cut off your **h**.................... 1Sa 17:46
killed him by cutting off his **h**. 1Sa 17:51
took Goliath's **h** to Jerusalem 1Sa 17:54
was still holding Goliath's **h**. 1Sa 17:57
and put goats' hair at its **h**.................... 1Sa 19:13
bed with goats' hair on its **h**. 1Sa 19:16

stuck in the ground near his **h**. 1Sa 26:7
jug that are near Saul's **h**. 1Sa 26:11
jug that were near Saul's **h**, ... 1Sa 26:12
water jug that were near his **h?**".............. 1Sa 26:16
off Saul's **h** and took off his 1Sa 31:9
torn and he had dirt on his **h**................ 2Sa 1:2
from his **h** and the bracelet.................... 2Sa 1:10
him by the **h** and stabbed him 2Sa 2:16
gave his **h** to David and said 2Sa 4:8
Here is the **h** of Ish-Bosheth son.............. 2Sa 4:8
Ish-Bosheth's **h** and buried it 2Sa 4:12
off their king's **h** and had it 2Sa 12:30
and had it placed on his own **h**. 2Sa 12:30
put ashes on her **h** and tore her 2Sa 13:19
robe and put her hand on her **h**.............. 2Sa 13:19
one hair from his **h** will fall to 2Sa 14:11
on him from his **h** to his foot. 2Sa 14:25
He covered his **h** and went 2Sa 15:30
dirt on his **h** to show how sad................ 2Sa 15:32
me go over and cut off his **h**!" 2Sa 16:9
Absalom's **h** got caught in the 2Sa 18:9
His **h** will be thrown over the 2Sa 20:21
They cut off the **h** of Sheba son 2Sa 20:22
Tahkemonite, was **h** of the Three. 2Sa 23:8
on Solomon's **h** to show he was 1Ki 1:39
even a single hair from his **h**. 1Ki 1:52
ground with his **h** between his 1Ki 18:42
saw near his **h** a loaf baked over 1Ki 19:6
boy said to his father, "My **h**! 2Ki 4:19
My head! My **h**!" The father said 2Ki 4:19
the **h** of his ax fell into the 2Ki 6:5
and it made the iron **h** float. 2Ki 6:6
that a donkey's **h** sold for about 2Ki 6:25
terribly if the **h** of Elisha son 2Ki 6:31
is sending men to cut off my **h**. 2Ki 6:32
the oil on Jehu's **h** and say, ' 2Ki 9:3
oil on Jehu's **h** and said to him, ... 2Ki 9:6
and took his **h** and his armor.................. 1Ch 10:9
and hung his **h** in the temple 1Ch 10:10
He was the **h** of the Three, ... 1Ch 11:11
crown off the **h** of their king, ... 1Ch 20:2
and had it placed on his own **h**. 1Ch 20:2
pulled hair from my **h** and beard, ... Ezr 9:3
crown on her **h** and made her.................. Est 2:17
with a royal crown on its **h**, ... Est 6:8
hurried home with his **h** covered, ... Est 6:12
and shaved his **h** to show how sad .... Job 1:20
the top of his **h** to the soles of .... Job 2:7
I am right, I cannot lift my **h**. .... Job 10:15
If I hold up my **h**, you hunt me .... Job 10:16
you and shake my **h** at you. .... Job 16:4
and removed the crown from my **h**. .... Job 19:9
God's lamp shined on my **h**, ... Job 29:3
skin or fill its **h** with fishing .... Job 41:7
placed a gold crown on his **h**................. Ps 21:3
pour oil of blessing on my **h**; .... Ps 23:5
My **h** is higher than my enemies .... Ps 27:6
more sins than hairs on my **h**, ... Ps 40:12
no reason than hairs on my **h**; .... Ps 69:4
on the priest's **h** and running .... Ps 133:2
be like perfumed oil on my **h**................. Ps 141:5
a beautiful crown on your **h**." .... Pr 4:9
pouring burning coals on his **h**, ... Pr 25:22
lover's left hand is under my **h**, ... Sng 2:6
put on his **h** on his wedding .... Sng 3:11
h is wet with dew, and my hair .... Sng 5:2
His **h** is like the finest gold; .... Sng 5:11
Your **h** is like Mount Carmel, ... Sng 7:5
lover's left hand is under my **h**, ... Sng 8:3
Your whole **h** is hurt, and your .... Is 1:5
your foot to the top of your **h**;............... Is 1:6
hair from Judah's **h** and legs and .... Is 7:20
cut off Israel's **h** and tail, ... Is 9:14

and important men were the **h**, ... Is 9:15
h and beard has been shaved .... Is 15:2
and your **h** was like bronze. .... Is 48:4
helmet of salvation on his **h**. .... Is 59:17
by shaving the top of your **h**. .... Je 2:16
place with your hands on your **h**, ... Je 2:37
wish my **h** were like a spring of .... Je 9:1
shave his **h** to show sorrow for .... Je 16:6
you shook your **h** and acted as if .... Je 48:27
h has been shaved and every .... Je 48:37
up over my **h**, and I said, "I .... La 3:54
The crown has fallen from our **h**. .... La 5:16
razor to shave your **h** and beard. .... Eze 5:1
caught me by the hair on my **h**. .... Eze 8:3
and a beautiful crown on your **h**. .... Eze 16:12
soldier's **h** was rubbed bare .... Eze 29:18
cut off my **h** because of you. .... Da 1:10
The **h** of the statue was made of.............. Da 2:32
you are the **h** of gold on that .... Da 2:38
the hair on his **h** was white like .... Da 7:9
ten horns on its **h** and about the............. Da 7:20
Like a stalk with no **h** of grain, ... Hos 8:7
will come back upon your own **h**. .... Ob 1:15
seaweed was wrapped around my **h**. .... Jnh 2:5
hot on Jonah's **h** that he became .... Jnh 4:8
he had, from **h** to toe. .... Hab 3:13
no one could even lift up his **h**. .... Zch 1:21
"Put a clean turban on his **h**." .... Zch 3:5
turban on his **h** and dressed him .... Zch 3:5
put it on the **h** of Joshua son .... Zch 6:11
Don't even swear by your own **h**, ... Mt 5:36
one hair on your **h** become white .... Mt 5:36
Man has no place to rest his **h**." .... Mt 8:20
If the **h** of the family is called............... Mt 10:25
how many hairs are on your **h**. .... Mt 10:30
Give me the **h** of John the .... Mt 14:8
the prison to cut off John's **h**................... Mt 14:10
perfume on Jesus' **h** while he was .... Mt 26:7
put it on his **h**, and put a stick .... Mt 27:29
and began to beat him on the **h**.............. Mt 27:30
above Jesus' **h** with a charge .... Mt 27:37
grows, then the **h**, and then all .... Mk 4:28
and then all the grain in the **h**. .... Mk 4:28
with his **h** on a cushion. .... Mk 4:38
John by cutting off his **h**. .... Mk 6:16
for the **h** of John the Baptist. .... Mk 6:24
I want the **h** of John the Baptist .... Mk 6:25
a soldier to bring John's **h**. .... Mk 6:27
cut off John's **h** in the prison .... Mk 6:27
hit him on the **h** and showed no .... Mk 12:4
poured the perfume on Jesus' **h**.............. Mk 14:3
to make a crown for his **h**. .... Mk 15:17
Jesus on the **h** many times with .... Mk 15:19
You did not put oil on my **h**, ... Lk 7:46
cut off John's **h**, so who is this .... Lk 9:9
Man has no place to rest his **h**." .... Lk 9:58
many hairs you have on your **h**. .... Lk 12:7
but wash my hands and my **h**, ... Jn 13:9
it on Jesus' **h** and put a purple .... Jn 19:2
Then he bowed his **h** and died. .... Jn 19:30
that had been around Jesus' **h**, ... Jn 20:7
at the **h** and one at the feet. .... Jn 20:12
burning coals on his **h**." .... Rm 12:20
The **h** of every man is Christ, ... 1Co 11:3
the **h** of a woman is the man, ... 1Co 11:3
and the **h** of Christ is God. 1Co 11:3
with his **h** covered brings 1Co 11:4
covered brings shame to his **h**. 1Co 11:4
with her **h** uncovered brings 1Co 11:5
uncovered brings shame to her **h**. 1Co 11:5
as a woman who has her **h** shaved. 1Co 11:5
If a woman does not cover her **h**, ... 1Co 11:6
off her hair or to shave her **h**,.................. 1Co 11:6

head, she should cover her **h**. 1Co 11:6
a man should not cover his **h**,.................. 1Co 11:7
a symbol of authority on her **h**, ... 1Co 11:10
to God with her **h** uncovered?.................. 1Co 11:13
And the **h** cannot say to the 1Co 12:21
together in Christ as the **h**. .... Eph 1:10
made him the **h** over everything.............. Eph 1:22
way into Christ, who is the **h**. .... Eph 4:15
husband is the **h** of the wife, ... Eph 5:23
Christ is the **h** of the church. .... Eph 5:23
is the **h** of the body, which is .... Col 1:18
hold tightly to Christ, the **h**. .... Col 2:19
His **h** and hair were white like .... Rev 1:14
cloud with a rainbow over his **h**. .... Rev 10:1
of twelve stars was on her **h**. .... Rev 12:1
and seven crowns on each **h**. .... Rev 12:3
God was written on each **h**. .... Rev 13:1
gold crown on his **h** and a sharp .... Rev 14:14
and on his **h** are many crowns. .... Rev 19:12

HEADBANDS

belts, and **h** for Aaron's sons .... Ex 28:40
the **h** on their heads, and tie .... Ex 29:9
made turbans, **h**, and .... Ex 39:28
them, and put **h** on them, as the .... Le 8:13
their **h**, their necklaces .... Is 3:18

HEADED

her steps are **h** straight to the.................. Pr 5:5
walls and then **h** toward the .... Je 39:4
and his men **h** toward the Jordan .... Je 52:7
So Saul **h** toward Damascus. .... Ac 9:3

HEADS

full and good **h** of grain growing .... Ge 41:5
seven more **h** of grain sprang up, ... Ge 41:6
thin **h** of grain ate the seven .... Ge 41:7
ate the seven full and good **h**.................. Ge 41:7
full and good **h** of grain growing .... Ge 41:22
seven more **h** of grain sprang .... Ge 41:23
but these **h** were thin and ugly .... Ge 41:23
Then the thin **h** ate the seven .... Ge 41:24
thin heads ate the seven good **h**.............. Ge 41:24
the seven good **h** of grain stand .... Ge 41:26
the seven thin **h** of grain burned.............. Ge 41:27
oil on their **h** to appoint them.................. Ex 28:41
Put the headbands on their **h**,................. Ex 29:9
bring crushed **h** of new grain .... Le 2:14
sides of your **h** or cut the edges .... Le 19:27
Priests must not shave their **h**, ... Le 21:5
the **h** of Israel's family groups. .... Nu 1:16
were the **h** of the families, ... Nu 7:2
put their hands on the bulls' **h**—.............. Nu 8:12
the **h** of the family groups of .... Nu 10:4
will crush the **h** of the Moabites .... Nu 24:17
your **h** to show your sadness. .... Dt 14:1
your feet to the tops of your **h**. .... Dt 28:35
The **h** of the enemy leaders will .... Dt 32:42
lion, who tears off arms and **h**. .... Dt 33:20
dirt on their **h** to show their .... Jos 7:6
h of the Levite families went .... Jos 21:1
and to the **h** of the families of.................. Jos 21:1
h of the Levite families said .... Jos 21:2
all the elders, **h** of families,..................... Jos 23:2
the elders, **h** of families, ... Jos 24:1
brought the **h** of Oreb and Zeeb .... Jdg 7:25
drop some full **h** of grain for .... Ru 2:16
covered their **h** also and cried 2Sa 15:30
of Israel, the **h** of the tribes, ... 1Ki 8:1
and wear ropes on our **h**. 1Ki 20:31
wore ropes on their **h** and went 1Ki 20:32
cut off the **h** of your master's 2Ki 10:6
They put their **h** in baskets and 2Ki 10:7
have brought the **h** of the king's.............. 2Ki 10:8
Lay the **h** in two piles at the 2Ki 10:8

David, by the **h** of families, ... 1Ch 26:26
of Israel, the **h** of the tribes, ... 2Ch 5:2
They are higher than our **h.** .... Ezr 9:6
and Tobiah back on their own **h.** .... Ne 4:4
dust on their **h** to show their .... Ne 9:1
there were family **h** with him................. Ne 11:13
dirt on their **h** to show how sad .... Job 2:12
their **h** may touch the clouds, ... Job 20:6
are cut off like the **h** of grain............... Job 24:24
their tongues and shake their **h.** .... Ps 22:7
nations; people shake their **h.** .... Ps 44:14
who see them will shake their **h.** .... Ps 64:8
let our enemies walk on our **h.** .... Ps 66:12
God will crush his enemies' **h,** .... Ps 68:21
and broke the **h** of the sea .... Ps 74:13
You smashed the **h** of the monster .... Ps 74:14
look at me and shake their **h.** .... Ps 109:25
around with their **h** held high, ... Is 3:16
sores on the **h** of those women .... Is 3:17
Naphtali hang their **h** in shame, ... Is 9:1
they cut the **h** of grain from .... Is 17:5
to shave their **h** and wear rough............. Is 22:12
He has covered your **h.** .... Is 29:10
heads. (The seers are your **h.**)................ Is 29:10
just to bow their **h** like a plant .... Is 58:5
crowns have fallen from your **h.**" .... Je 13:18
appoint as your **h** those you had .... Je 13:21
and cover their **h** in shame. .... Je 14:3
so they cover their **h** in shame. .... Je 14:4
will shake their **h** as they pass .... Je 18:16
and shake their **h** when they pass .... Je 19:8
down on the **h** of those wicked .... Je 23:19
will be sad and shave their **h.** .... Je 47:5
will shake their **h** when they see .... Je 50:13
dust on their **h** and put on rough .... La 2:10
bow their **h** to the ground .... La 2:10
of Jerusalem and shake their **h.** .... La 2:15
over the **h** of the living .... Eze 1:22
dome over the **h** of the living .... Eze 1:25
and all their **h** will be shaved................ Eze 7:18
their evil back on their **h.**" .... Eze 9:10
dome above the **h** of the living .... Eze 10:1
waists and turbans on their **h.** .... Eze 23:15
and beautiful crowns on their **h.** .... Eze 23:42
turbans must stay on your **h,** .... Eze 24:23
on their **h** and roll in ashes .... Eze 27:30
They shave their **h** for you,................... Eze 27:31
laid under their **h** and their................... Eze 32:27
turbans on their **h** and linen .... Eze 44:18
not shave their **h** or let their .... Eze 44:20
the hair of their **h** trimmed. .... Eze 44:20
animal had four **h** and was given .... Da 7:6
make you shave your **h** as well. .... Am 8:10
pillars fall on the people's **h;** .... Am 9:1
and the **h** of grain grew, ... Mt 13:26
Jesus and shook their **h,** .... Mt 27:39
Jesus and shook their **h,** .... Mk 15:29
followers picked the **h** of grain, ... Lk 6:1
look up and hold your **h** high, ... Lk 21:28
and bowed their **h** to the ground. .... Lk 24:5
so they can shave their **h** .... Ac 21:24
lose even one hair off your **h.**" .... Ac 27:34
had golden crowns on their **h.** .... Rev 4:4
On their **h** they wore what looked .... Rev 9:7
The **h** of the horses looked like .... Rev 9:17
horses looked like **h** of lions, ... Rev 9:17
tails were like snakes with **h,** .... Rev 9:19
with seven **h** and seven crowns .... Rev 12:3
It had ten horns and seven **h,** .... Rev 13:1
One of the **h** of the beast looked........... Rev 13:3
it had seven **h** and ten horns. .... Rev 17:3
one with seven **h** and ten horns............. Rev 17:7

The seven **h** on the beast are .... Rev 17:9
dust on their **h** and cried out, ... Rev 18:19

HEAL
the LORD, "God, please **h** her!" .... Nu 12:13
I can hurt, and I can **h.** .... Dt 32:39
me, and ask him to **h** my arm." 1Ki 13:6
you so you can **h** him of his skin 2Ki 5:6
with a skin disease for me to **h?** 2Ki 5:7
the place and the disease. 2Ki 5:11
Jezreel to **h** from the wound he 2Ki 8:29
Jezreel to **h** from the injuries 2Ki 9:15
your tears, so I will **h** you. 2Ki 20:5
the LORD will **h** me and that I 2Ki 20:8
sin, and I will **h** their land. 2Ch 7:14
to Jezreel to **h** from the wounds 2Ch 22:6
injures, but his hands also **h.** .... Job 5:18
H me, LORD, because my bones.............. Ps 6:2
H me, because I have sinned .... Ps 41:4
H its breaks because it is .... Ps 60:2
a time to kill and a time to **h.** .... Ec 3:3
but then he will **h** them. .... Is 19:22
to their prayers and **h** them. .... Is 19:22
have done, but I will **h** them. .... Is 57:18
near, and I will **h** them," says .... Is 57:19
and your wounds will quickly **h.** .... Is 58:8
They tried to **h** my people's .... Je 6:14
They tried to **h** my people's .... Je 8:11
for a time when he would **h** us, ... Je 8:15
LORD, **h** me, and I will truly be .... Je 17:14
your injury will not **h.** .... Je 30:12
health and **h** your injuries," .... Je 30:17
I will **h** them and let them enjoy............ Je 33:6
We tried to **h** Babylon, but she .... Je 51:9
as the sea. No one can **h** you. .... La 2:13
But he cannot **h** you or cure your .... Hos 5:13
has hurt us, but he will **h** us. .... Hos 6:1
When I **h** Israel, Israel's sin .... Hos 7:1
Nothing can **h** your wound; .... Nah 3:19
your injury will not **h.** .... Nah 3:19
young ones, or **h** the injured .... Zch 11:16
you can **h** me if you will." .... Mt 8:2
officer, "I will go and **h** him." .... Mt 8:7
evil spirits and to **h** every kind .... Mt 10:1
H the sick, raise the dead to .... Mt 10:8
h those who have skin diseases,............ Mt 10:8
right to **h** on the Sabbath day? .... Mt 12:10
"You can **h** me if you will." .... Mk 1:40
to see if he would **h** the man on .... Mk 3:2
there except to **h** a few sick .... Mk 6:5
his hand on the man to **h** him. .... Mk 7:32
saying: 'Doctor, **h** yourself.' .... Lk 4:23
you can **h** me if you will." .... Lk 5:12
Jesus the power to **h** people. .... Lk 5:17
if Jesus would **h** on the Sabbath .... Lk 6:7
Jesus to come and **h** his servant. .... Lk 7:3
but no one was able to **h** her. .... Lk 8:43
and the ability to **h** sicknesses. .... Lk 9:1
God's kingdom and to **h** the sick. .... Lk 9:2
H the sick who live there, ... Lk 10:9
or wrong to **h** on the Sabbath................ Lk 14:3
come to Capernaum and **h** his son, ... Jn 4:47
miracles he did to **h** the sick. .... Jn 6:2
Show us your power to **h.** .... Ac 4:30
he believed God could **h** him. .... Ac 14:9
the Lord will **h** that person. .... Jam 5:15
for each other so God can **h** you. .... Jam 5:16

HEALED
to God, and God **h** Abimelech, his .... Ge 20:17
man until he is completely **h.** .... Ex 21:19
a boil on his skin that is **h.** .... Le 13:18
growing in it, the sore has **h.** .... Le 13:37
If the skin disease is **h,** .... Le 14:3

in camp until they were **h**. ....Jos 5:8
If you are then **h**, you will know..............1Sa 6:3
king's arm was **h**, becoming as it 1Ki 13:6
'I have **h** this water.................................2Ki 2:21
water has been **h** to this day 2Ki 2:22
skin will be **h**, and you will be 2Ki 5:10
prayer, and he **h** the people. 2Ch 30:20
I prayed to you, and you **h** me. ....Ps 30:2
God gave the command and **h** them, ...Ps 107:20
and come back to me and be **h**." ....Is 6:10
and we are **h** because of his ....Is 53:5
aren't the hurts of my people **h**? ....Je 8:22
My wound cannot be **h**. ....Je 10:19
why my injury is not cured or **h**..............Je 15:18
mind is evil and cannot be **h**. ....Je 17:9
heal me, and I will truly be **h**................Je 17:14
So you will not be **h**. ....Je 30:13
not work; you will not be **h**. ....Je 46:11
pain, and maybe she can be **h**. ....Je 51:8
Babylon, but she cannot be **h**................Je 51:9
You have not **h** the sick or put ....Eze 34:4
understand that I had **h** them. ....Hos 11:3
Samaria's wound cannot be **h**. ....Mic 1:9
paralyzed. Jesus **h** all of them. ....Mt 4:24
I will. Be **h**!" And immediately ....Mt 8:3
the man was **h** from his disease..............Mt 8:3
it, and my servant will be **h**. ....Mt 8:8
servant will be **h** just as you ....Mt 8:13
servant was **h** that same hour. ....Mt 8:13
them, and he **h** all the sick.....................Mt 8:16
touch his clothes, I will be **h**.".................Mt 9:21
the woman was **h** from that moment ....Mt 9:22
people with skin diseases are **h**................Mt 11:5
and he **h** all who were sick. ....Mt 12:15
Jesus **h** the man so that he could ....Mt 12:22
and come back to me and be **h**.' ....Mt 13:15
for them and **h** those who were ....Mt 14:14
and all who touched it were **h**. ....Mt 14:36
the woman's daughter was **h**...................Mt 15:28
at Jesus' feet, and he **h** them. ....Mt 15:30
and the boy was **h** from that time ....Mt 17:18
him, and he **h** them there. ....Mt 19:2
in the Temple, and he **h** them................Mt 21:14
Jesus **h** many who had different...............Mk 1:34
him and said, "I will. Be **h**!" ....Mk 1:41
left the man, and he was **h**.....................Mk 1:42
everyone that Jesus had **h** him, ...Mk 1:45
held out his hand and it was **h**. ....Mk 3:5
He had **h** many people, so all the ....Mk 3:10
so she will be **h** and will live." ....Mk 5:23
touch his clothes, I will be **h**.".................Mk 5:28
that she was **h** from her disease ....Mk 5:29
that she was **h**, came and fell at ....Mk 5:33
be **h** of your disease." ....Mk 5:34
on many sick people and **h** them. ....Mk 6:13
and all who touched it were **h**. ....Mk 6:56
his eyes wide and they were **h**, ...Mk 8:25
you are **h** because you believed." ....Mk 10:52
sick, and the sick will be **h**." ....Mk 16:18
of them were **h**, only Naaman, who ....Lk 4:27
person, he **h** every one of them. ....Lk 4:40
said, "I will. Be **h**!" ....Lk 5:13
Jesus and to be **h** of their ....Lk 5:15
held out his hand, and it was **h**. ....Lk 6:10
teach and to be **h** of their ....Lk 6:18
and he **h** those who were troubled ....Lk 6:18
it, and my servant will be **h**. ....Lk 7:7
Jesus **h** many people of their ....Lk 7:21
people with skin diseases are **h**................Lk 7:22
who had been **h** of sicknesses...............Lk 8:2
whom Jesus had **h** begged to go..............Lk 8:38
how she had been instantly **h**. ....Lk 8:47
kingdom and **h** those who needed ....Lk 9:11

healed those who needed to be **h**. ....Lk 9:11
evil spirit and **h** the boy and ....Lk 9:42
because Jesus **h** on the Sabbath ....Lk 13:14
So come to be **h** on one of those...........Lk 13:14
This woman that I **h**, a daughter..............Lk 13:16
took the man, **h** him, and sent ....Lk 14:4
ten men were going, they were **h**. ....Lk 17:14
one of them saw that he was **h**, ...Lk 17:15
Jesus said, "Weren't ten men **h**? ....Lk 17:17
were **h** because you believed." ....Lk 17:19
You are **h** because you believed." ....Lk 18:42
the servant's ear and **h** him. ....Lk 22:51
the pool was **h** from any sickness ....Jn 5:4
said to the man who had been **h**, ...Jn 5:10
who had been **h** did not know who ....Jn 5:13
had made mud and his eyes was...........Jn 9:14
and come back to me and be **h**." ....Jn 12:40
saw the **h** man standing there..................Ac 4:14
spirits, and all of them were **h**. ....Ac 5:16
Philip also **h** many weak and ....Ac 8:7
the sick were **h** and evil spirits ....Ac 19:12
his hands on the man and **h** him. ....Ac 28:8
to Paul, and he **h** them, too. ....Ac 28:9
and come back to me and be **h**.' ....Ac 28:27
you are **h** because of his wounds. 1Pe 2:24
but this death wound was **h**. ....Rev 13:3
had the death wound that was **h**. ....Rev 13:12

HEALING
a sword, but wise words bring **h**. ....Pr 12:18
gives fruit, **h** words give life, ...Pr 15:4
We looked for a time of **h**, ...Je 14:19
bring health and **h** to the people..............Je 33:6
the sun, with **h** in its rays. ....Mal 4:2
and **h** all the people's diseases ....Mt 4:23
and **h** all kinds of diseases and ....Mt 9:35
and offer a gift for your **h**, ...Lk 5:14
coming from him and **h** them all. ....Lk 6:19
Good News and **h** people ....Lk 9:6
forcing demons out and **h** people. ....Lk 13:32
angry at me for **h** a person's ....Jn 7:23
the miracle of **h** was more than ....Ac 4:22
doing good and **h** those who were ....Ac 10:38
one Spirit gives gifts of **h**. 1Co 12:9
those who have gifts of **h**, ...1Co 12:28
Not all have gifts of **h**............................1Co 12:30
tree are for the **h** of all the ....Rev 22:2

HEALS
I am the LORD who **h** you." ....Ex 15:26
my sins and **h** all my diseases ....Ps 103:3
He **h** the brokenhearted and ....Ps 147:3
people and **h** the hurts he gave ....Is 30:26
"Aeneas, Jesus Christ **h** you. ....Ac 9:34

HEALTH
men asked about each other's **h**, ...Ex 18:7
who belong to you have good **h**!..............1Sa 25:6
they bring **h** to the whole body. ....Pr 4:22
your life when your **h** is gone. ....Pr 5:11
bring back your **h** and heal your ....Je 30:17
I will bring **h** and healing to ....Je 33:6
found the servant in good **h**. ....Lk 7:10
way and that your **h** is good. 3Jn 1:2

HEALTHIER
days they looked **h** and better..................Da 1:15

HEALTHIEST
He killed some of the **h** of them;..............Ps 78:31

HEALTHY
a **h** vine watered by a spring, ...Ge 49:22
out, his hand was **h** again, like ....Ex 4:7
But it must be **h**, with nothing ....Le 22:21
their cows have **h** calves. ....Job 21:10
and his bones were strong and **h**. ....Job 21:24

strong like a **h** tree in good .... Ps 37:35
my bones are not **h** because of my .... Ps 38:3
My enemies are strong and **h**, ... Ps 38:19
they are **h** and strong. .... Ps 73:4
they will be **h** and fresh. .... Ps 92:14
body will be **h**, and your bones .... Pr 3:8
person will be **h** like a green .... Pr 11:28
Peace of mind means a **h** body, ... Pr 14:30
making people happy and **h**. .... Pr 16:24
to make your servant girls **h**. .... Pr 27:27
My lover is **h** and tan, the best .... Sng 5:10
There is no **h** spot from the .... Is 1:6
the injured ones, or feed the **h**. .... Zch 11:16
It is not the **h** people who need .... Mt 9:12
It is not the **h** people who need .... Mk 2:17
It is not the **h** people who need .... Lk 5:31

HEAP

and will stand up in a **h**.'' .... Jos 3:13
stood up in a **h** a great distance .... Jos 3:16
The wicked may **h** up silver like .... Job 27:16
the water of the sea into a **h**. .... Ps 33:7
city of Jerusalem a **h** of ruins, ... Je 9:11
Gomorrah—a **h** of weeds, a pit .... Zph 2:9

HEAPS

her dead bodies like **h** of grain. .... Je 50:26

HEAR

Adah and Zillah, **h** my voice! .... Ge 4:23
nations will **h** this and tremble .... Ex 15:14
was very happy to **h** all the good .... Ex 18:9
The people will **h** me speaking .... Ex 19:9
I certainly will **h** their cry. .... Ex 22:23
it so the people could **h** him. .... Ex 24:7
the sound of singing that I **h**.'' .... Ex 32:18
name, the LORD, so you can **h** it. .... Ex 33:19
The Egyptians will **h** about it! .... Nu 14:13
and listen. **H** me, son of Zippor .... Nu 23:18
When they **h** reports about you, ... Dt 2:25
When they **h** about these laws, ... Dt 4:6
cannot see, **h**, eat, or smell. .... Dt 4:28
will die if we **h** the LORD our .... Dt 5:25
in Israel will **h** about this and .... Dt 13:11
and you might **h** something about .... Dt 13:12
Then everyone will **h** about this .... Dt 17:13
the people will **h** about this and .... Dt 19:20
of Israel will **h** about this and .... Dt 21:21
your eyes or **h** with your ears. .... Dt 29:4
of people who **h** these curses .... Dt 29:19
know this law, they must **h** it. .... Dt 31:13
say these things for them to **h**, ... Dt 31:28
all the people of Israel to **h**: .... Dt 31:30
H, heavens, and I will speak. .... Dt 32:1
this song for the people to **h**. .... Dt 32:44
When you **h** that sound, have all .... Jos 6:5
this country will **h** about this .... Jos 7:9
Was it to **h** the music played for .... Jdg 5:16
you will **h** what they are saying. .... Jdg 7:11
us your riddle so we can **h** it.'' .... Jdg 14:13
will shock those who **h** about it. 1Sa 3:11
Let the Hebrews **h** what happened. 1Sa 13:3
Then why do I **h** cattle mooing 1Sa 15:14
Saul will **h** the news and will 1Sa 16:2
When you **h** the sound of marching 2Sa 5:24
When you **h** the trumpets, say 2Sa 15:10
the desert until I **h** from you.'' 2Sa 15:28
everything you **h** in the royal 2Sa 15:35
to tell me everything you **h**.'' 2Sa 15:36
all Israel will **h** that your 2Sa 16:21
so I can **h** what he says.'' 2Sa 17:5
will **h** the news and think, ... 2Sa 17:9
and king, **h** the good news! 2Sa 18:31
I am too old to **h** the voices of 2Sa 19:35
As soon as they **h** me, they obey 2Sa 22:45

and that is the noise you **h**. 1Ki 1:45
h this prayer your servant prays 1Ki 8:28
' **H** the prayer I pray facing 1Ki 8:29
H my prayers and the prayers of 1Ki 8:30
H from your home in heaven, ... 1Ki 8:30
and when you **h**, forgive us. 1Ki 8:30
h in heaven. Judge the case, ... 1Ki 8:32
then **h** them in heaven. Forgive 1Ki 8:34
please **h** their prayer in heaven, ... 1Ki 8:36
then **h** their prayers from your 1Ki 8:39
Then **h** from your home in heaven, ... 1Ki 8:43
Then **h** in heaven their prayers, ... 1Ki 8:45
Then **h** their prayers from your 1Ki 8:49
they are able to **h** your wisdom. 1Ki 10:8
H the message from the LORD: 1Ki 22:19
the Aramean army to **h** the sound 2Ki 7:6
there; we didn't **h** anyone. The 2Ki 7:10
on the city wall can **h** you.'' 2Ki 18:26
your God will **h** what the 2Ki 19:4
will **h** a report that will make 2Ki 19:7
H, LORD, and listen. Open your 2Ki 19:16
When you **h** the sound of marching 1Ch 14:15
h this prayer your servant prays 2Ch 6:19
H the prayer I pray facing this 2Ch 6:20
H my prayers and the prayers of 2Ch 6:21
H from your home in heaven, ... 2Ch 6:21
and when you **h**, forgive us. 2Ch 6:21
h in heaven. Judge the case, ... 2Ch 6:23
this happens, **h** their prayer 2Ch 6:27
then **h** their prayers from your 2Ch 6:30
will **h** about your greatness and 2Ch 6:32
Then **h** from your home in heaven, ... 2Ch 6:33
Then **h** in heaven their prayers, ... 2Ch 6:35
Then **h** their prayers from your 2Ch 6:39
I will **h** them from heaven. 2Ch 7:14
they are able to **h** your wisdom. 2Ch 9:7
H the message from the LORD: 2Ch 18:18
Then you will **h** and save us.' 2Ch 20:9
H the prayer that I, your .... Ne 1:6
I prayed, ''**H** us, our God. .... Ne 4:4
Wherever you **h** the sound of the .... Ne 4:20
The king will **h** about this. .... Ne 6:7
and Media will **h** about the .... Est 1:17
who no longer **h** the shout of the .... Job 3:18
so **h** it and decide what it means .... Job 5:27
and **h** the pleading of my lips. .... Job 13:6
let your ears **h** what I say. .... Job 13:17
him, and he will **h** you, and you .... Job 22:27
only **h** a small whisper of him. .... Job 26:14
I wish a court would **h** my case! .... Job 31:35
H my words, you wise men; .... Job 34:2
If you can understand, **h** this; .... Job 34:16
and the wise who **h** me say, ... Job 34:34
that you can **h** the roar when he .... Job 37:4
and it does not **h** the drivers .... Job 39:7
mercy on me and **h** my prayer. .... Ps 4:1
every morning you **h** my voice. .... Ps 5:3
h me begging for fairness; .... Ps 17:1
to me now, and **h** what I say. .... Ps 17:6
As soon as they **h** me, they obey .... Ps 18:44
yet born will **h** what God has .... Ps 22:31
LORD, **h** me when I call; .... Ps 27:7
H the sound of my prayer, when I .... Ps 28:2
h me and have mercy on me. .... Ps 30:10
The poor will **h** and be glad. .... Ps 34:2
deaf; I cannot **h**. Like the mute, ... Ps 38:13
I am like those who do not **h**, ... Ps 38:14
LORD, **h** my prayer, and listen to .... Ps 39:12
Make me **h** sounds of joy and .... Ps 51:8
H my prayer, God; listen to what .... Ps 54:2
forever will **h** me and punish .... Ps 55:19
they cannot **h** the music of the .... Ps 58:5
God, **h** my cry; listen to my .... Ps 61:1

You **h** our prayers. All people .... Ps 65:2
I call to God, and he will **h** me. .... Ps 77:1
H the moans of the prisoners. .... Ps 79:11
God All-Powerful, **h** my prayer; .... Ps 84:8
LORD, **h** my prayer, and listen .... Ps 86:6
Can't the creator of ears **h**?.................... Ps 94:9
have ears, but they cannot **h.** .... Ps 115:6
H my cry to you, LORD. Let your .... Ps 119:169
Lord, **h** my voice; listen to my .... Ps 130:2
have ears, but they cannot **h.** .... Ps 135:17
you when they **h** the words you .... Ps 138:4
LORD, **h** my prayer; listen to my .... Ps 143:1
ears to **h** and eyes to see. .... Pr 20:12
but we never **h** enough, nor can .... Ec 1:8
or you might **h** your servant .... Ec 7:21
you will barely **h** the millstone .... Ec 12:4
but you will barely **h** singing. .... Ec 12:4
I **h** my lover's voice. Here he .... Sng 2:8
face, and let me **h** your voice................... Sng 2:14
I **h** my lover knocking. .... Sng 5:2
for your voice; let me **h** it. .... Sng 8:13
H the word of the LORD; .... Is 1:10
eyes and **h** with their ears. .... Is 6:10
You can **h** their voices far away .... Is 15:4
You will **h** a trumpet sound. .... Is 18:3
What I **h** makes me very afraid; .... Is 21:3
will **h** the news about Tyre, ... Is 23:5
h songs from every part of the .... Is 24:16
I will **h** your voice rising from .... Is 29:4
time the deaf will **h** the words .... Is 29:18
The LORD will **h** your crying, ... Is 30:19
you will **h** a voice behind you .... Is 30:21
all people to **h** his great voice .... Is 30:30
who feel safe now, **h** what I say. .... Is 32:9
faraway lands, **h** what I have .... Is 33:13
You sailors from other lands, **h:** .... Is 33:23
see again, and the deaf will **h.** .... Is 35:5
on the city wall can **h** you." .... Is 36:11
your God will **h** what the .... Is 37:4
will **h** a report that will make .... Is 37:7
H, LORD, and listen. Open your .... Is 37:17
You who are deaf, **h** me. .... Is 42:18
h, but you refuse to listen." .... Is 42:20
those who have ears but don't **h.** .... Is 43:8
time I will **h** your prayers. .... Is 49:8
teachings should **h** what I say. .... Is 51:7
can **h** you when you ask him for .... Is 59:1
from you, so he does not **h** you. .... Is 59:2
to them, but they did not **h** me. .... Is 66:4
h the noise from the Temple. .... Is 66:6
H the word of the LORD, family .... Je 2:4
You can **h** crying on the bare .... Je 3:21
I **h** a cry like a woman having a .... Je 4:31
H this message, you foolish .... Je 5:21
so they cannot **h** my warnings. .... Je 6:10
H this, people of the earth: .... Je 6:19
H the word of the LORD, ... Je 7:2
your ears to **h** the words of his .... Je 9:20
'H the word of the LORD, kings .... Je 17:20
I **h** many people whispering about .... Je 20:10
Let him **h** loud crying in the .... Je 20:16
'H the word of the LORD. .... Je 21:11
'H the word of the LORD, king of .... Je 22:2
land of Judah, **h** the word of the .... Je 22:29
angels to see or **h** the message .... Je 23:18
I **h** the sound of the leaders .... Je 25:36
I **h** the leaders of the people .... Je 25:36
We **h** people crying from fear................ Je 30:5
it when they **h** about the good .... Je 33:9
of Judah will **h** what disasters I .... Je 36:3
but which they refused to **h.**' " .... Je 36:31
not see war, or **h** the trumpets .... Je 42:14
are now in Egypt, **h** the word of .... Je 44:24

But **h** the word of the LORD. .... Je 44:26
They will **h** the sound of the .... Je 47:3
the Ammonites, **h** the battle cry. .... Je 49:2
all nations will **h** Babylon's cry .... Je 50:46
so all the people can **h** you. .... Je 51:61
Any time you **h** a word from my.............. Eze 3:17
have ears to **h,** but they do not .... Eze 12:2
but they do not **h,** because they .... Eze 12:2
So, prostitute, **h** the word of .... Eze 16:35
'H the word of the LORD. .... Eze 20:47
with information for you to **h.** .... Eze 24:26
'H the word of the Lord GOD. .... Eze 25:3
fear when they **h** about your .... Eze 26:15
If they **h** the sound of the .... Eze 33:4
If you **h** a word from my mouth,.............. Eze 33:7
h the message from the LORD.' .... Eze 33:30
were my people and **h** your words,.......... Eze 33:31
They **h** your words, but they will .... Eze 33:32
So, you shepherds, **h** the word of .... Eze 34:7
So, you shepherds, **h** the word of .... Eze 34:9
of Israel, **h** the word of the .... Eze 36:1
h the word of the Lord GOD. .... Eze 36:4
them, 'Dry bones, **h** the word of .... Eze 37:4
your eyes and **h** with your ears. .... Eze 40:4
eyes to see, and your ears to **h.** .... Eze 44:5
See and **h** everything I tell you .... Eze 44:5
When you **h** the sound of the .... Da 3:5
moment you will again **h** the .... Da 3:15
cannot see or **h** or understand .... Da 5:23
h the prayers of your servant................. Da 9:17
My God, pay attention and **h** me. .... Da 9:18
Lord, **h** us and do something! .... Da 9:19
the North will **h** news from the .... Da 11:44
your people will **h** the noise of .... Hos 10:14
H this, all you nations; .... Mic 1:2
Now **h** what the LORD says: .... Mic 6:1
let the hills **h** your story. .... Mic 6:1
to save me; my God will **h** me. .... Mic 7:7
H the sound of whips and the................. Nah 3:2
H horses galloping and chariots .... Nah 3:2
I **h** these things, and my body................. Hab 3:16
lips tremble when I **h** the sound. .... Hab 3:16
they would not **h** the words he .... Zch 7:12
the Jordan River to **h** John. .... Mt 3:5
that God will **h** them because of .... Mt 6:7
What you **h** whispered in your ear .... Mt 10:27
Go tell John what you **h** and see: .... Mt 11:4
The deaf can **h,** the dead are .... Mt 11:5
no one will **h** his voice in the .... Mt 12:19
They **h,** but they don't really .... Mt 13:13
don't really **h** or understand. .... Mt 13:13
They do not **h** with their ears,................. Mt 13:15
eyes and **h** with their ears. .... Mt 13:15
your eyes and **h** with your ears. .... Mt 13:16
they wanted to **h** the things that .... Mt 13:17
hear the things that you now **h,** .... Mt 13:17
hear, but they did not **h** them,................ Mt 13:17
Do you **h** the things these .... Mt 21:16
will **h** about wars and stories .... Mt 24:6
Don't you **h** them accusing you of .... Mt 27:13
the people who **h** the teaching of .... Mk 4:15
They **h** the teaching and quickly .... Mk 4:16
weeds. They **h** the teaching, ... Mk 4:18
They **h** the teaching and accept .... Mk 4:20
carefully about what you **h.** .... Mk 4:24
man was able to **h** and to use his .... Mk 7:35
makes the deaf **h!** And those who .... Mk 7:37
people unable to **h** or speak, ... Mk 9:25
very sad to **h** Jesus say this, ... Mk 10:22
you **h** about wars and stories .... Mk 13:7
were very sad to **h** this. .... Mk 14:19
around him to **h** the word of God. .... Lk 5:1
people came to **h** Jesus and to be .... Lk 5:15

They all came to **h** Jesus teach .... Lk 6:18
The deaf came to **h,** the dead are .... Lk 7:22
the people who **h** God's teaching, ... Lk 8:12
like those who **h** God's teaching............. Lk 8:13
like those who **h** God's teaching, ... Lk 8:14
like those who **h** God's teaching............. Lk 8:15
is this man I **h** such things .... Lk 9:9
they wanted to **h** what you now .... Lk 10:24
wanted to hear what you now **h,** .... Lk 10:24
are those who **h** the teaching of .... Lk 11:28
'What is this I **h** about you? .... Lk 16:2
When you **h** about wars and riots, ... Lk 21:9
people could **h** about the Light .... Jn 1:7
to and you **h** the sound of it .... Jn 3:8
that he gets to **h** the .... Jn 3:29
when the dead will **h** the voice .... Jn 5:25
and those who **h** will have life. .... Jn 5:25
their graves will **h** his voice. .... Jn 5:28
everyone can see and **h** him, ... Jn 7:26
Why do you want to **h** it again? .... Jn 9:27
I know that you always **h** me, ... Jn 11:42
teaching that you **h** is not .... Jn 14:24
these people that we **h** speaking............. Ac 2:7
that we each **h** them in our own .... Ac 2:8
But we **h** them telling in our own .... Ac 2:11
this is what you now see and **h.** .... Ac 2:33
that he can **h** what you have to .... Ac 10:22
here before God to **h** everything. .... Ac 10:33
wanted to **h** the message of God. .... Ac 13:7
the city came to **h** the word of .... Ac 13:44
were eager to **h** what Paul and .... Ac 17:11
We will **h** more about this from .... Ac 17:32
One, and to **h** words from him. .... Ac 22:14
I will **h** your case when those .... Ac 23:35
I want Caesar to **h** my case!" .... Ac 25:11
also like to **h** this man myself. .... Ac 25:22
"Tomorrow you will **h** him." .... Ac 25:22
has asked Caesar to **h** his case."............... Ac 26:32
But we want to **h** your ideas, ... Ac 28:22
They don't **h** with their ears, ... Ac 28:27
eyes and **h** with their ears. .... Ac 28:27
in him, they must **h** about him; .... Rm 10:14
for them to **h** about the Lord, ... Rm 10:14
and people **h** the Good News when .... Rm 10:17
Didn't people **h** the Good News? .... Rm 10:18
their ears so they could not **h.** .... Rm 11:8
I **h** that when you meet together.............. 1Co 11:18
it would not be able to **h.** 1Co 12:17
be judged by all that they **h.** 1Co 14:24
what they see me do or **h** me say. 2Co 12:6
teaching we **h** from people who .... Eph 4:14
I will **h** that you are standing .... Php 1:27
and you **h** about the struggles I .... Php 1:30
or afraid if you **h** that the day................ 2Th 2:2
We **h** that some people in your 2Th 3:11
the things they want to **h.** 2Ti 4:3
because I **h** about the love you .... Phm 1:5
begged not to **h** another word. .... Heb 12:19
did not want to **h** the command:............ Heb 12:20
Those who **h** God's teaching and .... Jam 1:23
joy than to **h** that my children 3Jn 1:4
the people who **h** this message .... Rev 1:3
If you **h** my voice and open the .... Rev 3:20
that cannot see or **h** or walk. .... Rev 9:20

HEARD

Then they **h** the Lᴏʀᴅ God walking .... Ge 3:8
I **h** you walking in the garden, ... Ge 3:10
the Lᴏʀᴅ has **h** your cries...................... Ge 16:11
As for Ishmael, I have **h** you. .... Ge 17:20
I have **h** many complaints against .... Ge 18:20
if they are as bad as I have **h.**................ Ge 18:21
The Lᴏʀᴅ has **h** of all the evil .... Ge 19:13

Abimelech king of Gerar **h** this, ... Ge 20:2
God **h** the boy crying, and God's .... Ge 21:17
God has **h** the boy crying there. .... Ge 21:17
Laban had **h** what she had said .... Ge 24:30
Abraham's servant **h** these words, ... Ge 24:52
The Lᴏʀᴅ **h** Isaac's prayer, ... Ge 25:21
I **h** your father saying to your.................. Ge 27:6
When Esau **h** the words of his .... Ge 27:34
Rebekah **h** about Esau's plan to .... Ge 27:42
When Laban **h** the news about his .... Ge 29:13
The Lᴏʀᴅ has **h** that I am not .... Ge 29:33
One day Jacob **h** Laban's sons .... Ge 31:1
Jacob's sons **h** what had happened........... Ge 34:7
come to the city gate **h** this. .... Ge 34:24
Bilhah, and Israel **h** about it. .... Ge 35:22
I **h** them say they were going to .... Ge 37:17
Reuben **h** their plan and saved .... Ge 37:21
Joseph's master **h** what his wife.............. Ge 39:19
I have **h** that you can explain a .... Ge 41:15
I have **h** that there is grain in .... Ge 42:2
they had **h** they were going .... Ge 43:25
loudly that the Egyptians **h** him,.............. Ge 45:2
in the king's palace **h** about it. .... Ge 45:2
When the king **h** what Moses had .... Ex 2:15
they cried for help, God **h** them............... Ex 2:23
God **h** their cries, and he .... Ex 2:24
I have **h** their cries when the .... Ex 3:7
I have **h** the cries of the people .... Ex 3:9
When they **h** that the Lᴏʀᴅ was .... Ex 4:31
Now I have **h** the cries of the .... Ex 6:5
because he has **h** you grumble .... Ex 16:7
because he has **h** you grumble .... Ex 16:8
he has **h** your grumblings. .... Ex 16:9
I have **h** the grumblings of the .... Ex 16:12
He **h** about everything that God .... Ex 18:1
When the people **h** the thunder .... Ex 20:18
bells will be **h** when he enters .... Ex 28:35
When Joshua **h** the sound of the .... Ex 32:17
When the people **h** this bad news, ... Ex 33:4
When Moses **h** this, he was .... Le 10:20
the people who **h** him must put .... Le 24:14
he **h** the Lᴏʀᴅ speaking to him. .... Nu 7:89
and when he **h** them, he became .... Nu 11:1
Moses **h** every family crying as .... Nu 11:10
And the Lᴏʀᴅ **h** this. .... Nu 11:2
They have already **h** about you, ... Nu 14:14
who have **h** about your power .... Nu 14:15
I have **h** the grumbling and.................... Nu 14:27
I **h** what you said, and as surely .... Nu 14:28
When Moses **h** this, he bowed .... Nu 16:4
around them **h** their screams .... Nu 16:34
he **h** us and sent us an angel to .... Nu 20:16
When he **h** that the Israelites .... Nu 21:1
When Balak **h** that Balaam was .... Nu 22:36
them long after he **h** about them, ... Nu 30:15
h that the Israelites were........................ Nu 33:40
When the Lᴏʀᴅ **h** what you said, ... Dt 1:34
h the sound of words, but you .... Dt 4:12
like this has ever been **h** .... Dt 4:32
people have ever **h** God speak .... Dt 4:33
you **h** him speak from the fire. .... Dt 4:36
When you **h** the voice from the .... Dt 5:23
and we have **h** his voice from the .... Dt 5:24
being has ever **h** the living God .... Dt 5:26
The Lᴏʀᴅ **h** what you said to me, ... Dt 5:28
I have **h** what the people said to .... Dt 5:28
them, and you have **h** it said: .... Dt 9:2
of our ancestors, and he **h** us................. Dt 26:7
because we have **h** how the Lᴏʀᴅ .... Jos 2:10
have **h** how you destroyed Sihon .... Jos 2:10
When we **h** this, we were very .... Jos 2:11
Mediterranean Sea **h** that the .... Jos 5:1
the Jordan River **h** about these .... Jos 9:1

people of Gibeon **h** how Joshua .... Jos 9:3
because we **h** of the fame of the .... Jos 9:9
We **h** about what he has done and .... Jos 9:9
We **h** that he defeated the two .... Jos 9:10
We **h** that the LORD your God .... Jos 9:24
of Jerusalem **h** that Joshua had .... Jos 10:1
king of Hazor **h** about all that .... Jos 11:1
Back then you **h** that the Anakite .... Jos 14:12
at Shiloh **h** about the altar .... Jos 22:11
and the ten leaders **h** the people........... Jos 22:30
of Israel **h** it and went down .... Jdg 3:27
he **h** a man telling his friend .... Jdg 7:13
When Gideon **h** about the dream .... Jdg 7:15
of Ephraim **h** Gideon's answer, ... Jdg 8:3
When Jotham **h** this, he went and .... Jdg 9:7
h what Gaal son of Ebed said, ... Jdg 9:30
Tower of Shechem **h** what had .... Jdg 9:46
Abimelech **h** that all the leaders.............. Jdg 9:47
God **h** Manoah's prayer, and the........... Jdg 13:9
When the people of Gaza **h,** .... Jdg 16:2
I **h** you speak a curse about the .... Jdg 17:2
people of Benjamin **h** that the.................. Jdg 20:3
she **h** that the LORD had come to .... Ru 1:6
moved, but her voice was not **h.** 1Sa 1:13
He **h** about everything his sons 1Sa 2:22
Philistines **h** Israel's shout, ... 1Sa 4:6
Eli **h** the crying and asked, ... 1Sa 4:14
When she **h** the news that the Ark 1Sa 4:19
The Philistines **h** the Israelites 1Sa 7:7
the Israelites **h** they were 1Sa 7:7
After Samuel **h** all that the 1Sa 8:21
his oxen when he **h** the people 1Sa 11:5
When Saul **h** their words, God's.............. 1Sa 11:6
other Philistines **h** about it...................... 1Sa 13:3
All the Israelites **h** the news. 1Sa 13:4
of Ephraim **h** that the Philistine 1Sa 14:22
Jonathan had not **h** the oath Saul 1Sa 14:27
Israelites **h** the Philistine's 1Sa 17:11
as usual, and David **h** him. 1Sa 17:23
brother Eliab **h** David talking 1Sa 17:28
Saul **h** that David was in Naioth.............. 1Sa 19:19
When Saul **h** the news, he sent 1Sa 19:21
other relatives **h** that he was 1Sa 22:1
Saul **h** that David and his men 1Sa 22:6
I have **h** that Saul plans to come.............. 1Sa 23:10
come down to Keilah, as I **h?** 1Sa 23:11
I have **h** that he is clever. 1Sa 23:22
but David **h** about it and went 1Sa 23:25
When Saul **h** that, he followed 1Sa 23:25
he **h** that Nabal was cutting the 1Sa 25:4
have **h** that you are cutting the 1Sa 25:7
I have **h** your words, and I will 1Sa 25:35
David **h** that Nabal was dead,.................. 1Sa 25:39
When he **h** Saul had followed him,........... 1Sa 26:3
When Saul **h** that David had run 1Sa 27:4
in Jabesh Gilead **h** what the 1Sa 31:11
Later when David **h** the news, ... 2Sa 3:28
of Saul **h** that Abner had died 2Sa 4:1
the Philistines **h** that David had 2Sa 5:17
But when David **h** the news, ... 2Sa 5:17
We have **h** all this ourselves! 2Sa 7:22
king of Hamath **h** that David had 2Sa 8:9
When David **h** about this, he sent 2Sa 10:7
When David **h** about this, he 2Sa 10:17
Bathsheba **h** that her husband 2Sa 11:26
When King David **h** the news, ... 2Sa 13:21
Everyone **h** the king's orders to 2Sa 18:5
We **h** the king command you, ... 2Sa 18:12
because they **h** that the king was 2Sa 19:2
my house I have **h** what all the 2Sa 19:11
From his temple he **h** my voice; 2Sa 22:7
Nathan **h** about this, he went 1Ki 1:11
Have you **h** that Adonijah, ... 1Ki 1:11

When he **h** the sound from the 1Ki 1:41
When Joab **h** about what had.................. 1Ki 2:28
Shimei **h** that his slaves were in 1Ki 2:39
people of Israel **h** about King 1Ki 3:28
because they had **h** of Solomon's. 1Ki 4:34
When Hiram **h** that Solomon had 1Ki 5:1
When Hiram **h** what Solomon asked,......... 1Ki 5:7
I have **h** your prayer and what 1Ki 9:3
queen of Sheba **h** about Solomon, ... 1Ki 10:1
What I **h** in my own country about............ 1Ki 10:6
are much greater than I had **h.** 1Ki 10:7
Hadad **h** that David had died and 1Ki 11:21
When Jeroboam **h** about Rehoboam 1Ki 12:2
the Israelites **h** that Jeroboam................ 1Ki 12:20
When King Jeroboam **h** what the 1Ki 13:4
the man of God **h** what had 1Ki 13:26
When Ahijah **h** her walking to the 1Ki 14:6
When Baasha **h** about these 1Ki 15:21
men in the camp **h** that Zimri had 1Ki 16:16
But no voice was **h;** Baal did not 1Ki 18:29
Elijah **h** this, he was afraid 1Ki 19:3
When Elijah **h** it, he covered his.............. 1Ki 19:13
We have **h** that the kings of 1Ki 20:31
them say they **h** Naboth speak 1Ki 21:10
they had **h** him speak against.................. 1Ki 21:13
When Jezebel **h** that Naboth had 1Ki 21:15
When Ahab **h** that Naboth of 1Ki 21:16
the Moabites **h** that the kings 2Ki 3:21
h that the king of Israel had 2Ki 5:8
When the king **h** the woman's 2Ki 6:30
to Jezreel, Jezebel **h** about it. 2Ki 9:30
When Athaliah **h** the noise of the 2Ki 11:13
King Hezekiah **h** the message, ... 2Ki 19:1
be afraid of what you have **h.** 2Ki 19:6
field commander **h** that the king 2Ki 19:8
When the king of Assyria **h** this, ... 2Ki 19:9
You have **h** what the kings of 2Ki 19:11
I have **h** your prayer to me about 2Ki 19:20
of Assyria, surely you have **h.**.................. 2Ki 19:25
because I have **h** your proud 2Ki 19:28
I have **h** your prayer and seen 2Ki 20:5
because he had **h** that Hezekiah.............. 2Ki 20:12
When the king **h** the words of the 2Ki 22:11
says about the words you **h:** 2Ki 22:18
When you **h** my words against this 2Ki 22:19
is why I have **h** you, says the 2Ki 22:19
and their men **h** that the king.................. 2Ki 25:23
in Jabesh Gilead **h** what the 1Ch 10:11
the Philistines **h** that David had 1Ch 14:8
David **h** about it and went out 1Ch 14:8
We have **h** all this ourselves! 1Ch 17:20
king of Hamath **h** that David had 1Ch 18:9
When David **h** about this, he sent 1Ch 19:8
When David **h** about this, he 1Ch 19:17
I have **h** your prayer and have 2Ch 7:12
queen of Sheba **h** about Solomon's 2Ch 9:1
What I **h** in my own country about........... 2Ch 9:5
are much greater than I had **h.** 2Ch 9:6
When Jeroboam **h** about Rehoboam 2Ch 10:2
felt brave when he **h** these words 2Ch 15:8
When Baasha **h** about this, he 2Ch 16:5
around them **h** how the LORD had........... 2Ch 20:29
When Athaliah **h** the noise of the 2Ch 23:12
and God **h** them because their 2Ch 30:27
the LORD **h** him and had pity on 2Ch 33:13
When the king **h** the words of the 2Ch 34:19
says about the words you **h:** 2Ch 34:26
When you **h** my words against this 2Ch 34:27
is why I have **h** you, says the 2Ch 34:27
noise it could be **h** far away, ... Ezr 3:13
and Benjamin **h** that the returned .... Ezr 4:1
When I **h** this, I angrily tore my .... Ezr 9:3
I **h** these things, I sat down..................... Ne 1:4

Ammonite officer **h** about this, ... Ne 2:10
and Geshem the Arab **h** about it, ... Ne 2:19
When Sanballat **h** we were .... Ne 4:1
angry when they **h** that the .... Ne 4:7
Then our enemies **h** that we knew .... Ne 4:15
When I **h** their complaints about .... Ne 5:6
our other enemies **h** that I had .... Ne 6:1
all our enemies **h** about it and .... Ne 6:16
in Egypt and **h** them cry out at .... Ne 9:9
to you, and you **h** from heaven. .... Ne 9:27
to you again, you **h** from heaven. .... Ne 9:28
Jerusalem could be **h** far away. .... Ne 12:43
When the people **h** this teaching, ... Ne 13:3
and Media have **h** about the .... Est 1:18
command and order had been **h**, ... Est 2:8
When Mordecai **h** about all that .... Est 4:1
When Job **h** this, he got up and .... Job 1:20
When these friends **h** about Job's .... Job 2:11
with no shout of joy to be **h**. .... Job 3:7
and my ears **h** a whisper of it. .... Job 4:12
my eyes, and I **h** a quiet voice. .... Job 4:16
ears have **h** and understood it. .... Job 13:1
I have **h** many things like these. .... Job 16:2
let my cry ever stop being **h**! .... Job 16:18
'We have **h** reports about it.' .... Job 28:22
who **h** me spoke well of me, ... Job 29:11
But I **h** what you have said;.................... Job 33:8
you have said; I **h** every word. .... Job 33:8
flashing when his voice is **h**. .... Job 37:4
My ears had **h** of you before, ... Job 42:5
the LORD has **h** my crying. .... Ps 6:8
The LORD has **h** my cry for help; .... Ps 6:9
You have **h** my complaint; .... Ps 9:4
you have **h** what the poor people .... Ps 10:17
From his temple he **h** my voice; .... Ps 18:6
they have no voice to be **h**. .... Ps 19:3
because he **h** my prayer for help. .... Ps 28:6
LORD's voice is **h** over the sea. .... Ps 29:3
I have **h** many insults........................... Ps 31:13
But you **h** my prayer when I .... Ps 31:22
and the LORD **h** him and saved him .... Ps 34:6
He turned to me and **h** my cry. .... Ps 40:1
God, we have **h** about you. .... Ps 44:1
First we **h** and now we have seen .... Ps 48:8
God, you have **h** my promises. .... Ps 61:5
and I have **h** it over and over:................ Ps 62:11
listened; he has **h** my prayer. .... Ps 66:19
We have **h** them and known them by .... Ps 78:3
the LORD **h** them, he was very .... Ps 78:21
When God **h** them, he became very .... Ps 78:59
I **h** a language I did not know, ... Ps 81:5
I **h** the cries of those who are .... Ps 92:11
He **h** the moans of the prisoners, ... Ps 102:20
the LORD will be **h** in Jerusalem; .... Ps 102:21
his praise will be **h** there. .... Ps 102:21
misery when he **h** their cry. .... Ps 106:44
We **h** about the Ark in Bethlehem. .... Ps 132:6
your prayers will not be **h**, ... Pr 28:9
has been **h**, so I give my final .... Ec 12:13
of doves is **h** in our land....................... Sng 2:12
Then I **h** the Lord's voice, ... Is 6:8
When Ahaz **h** this, he and the .... Is 7:2
Crying is **h** everywhere in Moab. .... Is 15:8
Their crying is **h** as far away as .... Is 15:8
is **h** as far away as Beer Elim................. Is 15:8
have **h** that the people of Moab .... Is 16:6
you what I have **h** from the LORD .... Is 21:10
King Hezekiah **h** the message, ... Is 37:1
be afraid of what you have **h**. .... Is 37:6
field commander **h** that the king .... Is 37:8
When the king of Assyria **h** this, ... Is 37:9
You have **h** what the kings of .... Is 37:11
of Assyria, surely you have **h**................. Is 37:26

because I have **h** your proud .... Is 37:29
I have **h** your prayer and seen .... Is 38:5
because he had **h** that Hezekiah .... Is 39:1
know. Surely you have **h**. Surely .... Is 40:21
Surely you have **h**. The LORD is............. Is 40:28
no one **h** you tell about it. .... Is 41:26
You **h** and saw everything that .... Is 48:6
you have not **h** about them before .... Is 48:7
But you have not **h** me; .... Is 48:8
LORD and have **h** God's angry .... Is 51:20
things they had not **h**." .... Is 52:15
would have believed what we **h**?........... Is 53:1
your prayers are **h** in heaven. .... Is 58:4
no one has ever **h** of a God like .... Is 64:4
never again be **h** in that city .... Is 65:19
No one has ever **h** of that .... Is 66:8
one has ever **h** of a new nation .... Is 66:8
have never **h** about what I have .... Is 66:19
because I have **h** the sound of................ Je 4:19
I have **h** the shouts of war. .... Je 4:19
destruction are **h** within her. .... Je 6:7
We have **h** the news about that .... Je 6:24
of the enemy's horses is **h**. .... Je 8:16
mooing of cattle cannot be **h**. .... Je 9:10
loud crying is **h** from Jerusalem: .... Je 9:19
you ever **h** anything like this?............... Je 18:13
When he **h** Jeremiah prophesying .... Je 20:1
Let your voice be **h** in Bashan. .... Je 22:20
I have **h** the prophets who .... Je 23:25
all the people **h** Jeremiah .... Je 26:7
of Judah **h** about what was .... Je 26:10
and you **h** him yourselves.".................. Je 26:11
you have **h** about this Temple .... Je 26:12
leaders of Judah **h** Uriah preach, ... Je 26:21
But Uriah **h** about it and was .... Je 26:21
A voice was **h** in Ramah of .... Je 31:15
I have **h** Israel moaning: .... Je 31:18
you have never **h** before.' .... Je 33:3
have you **h** what the people are .... Je 33:24
h all the messages from the LORD........... Je 36:11
he had **h** Baruch read to .... Je 36:13
the officers **h** all the words, ... Je 36:16
his servants **h** everything that.............. Je 36:24
When they **h** about the Egyptian .... Je 37:5
son of Malkijah **h** what Jeremiah .... Je 38:1
h that the officers had put .... Je 38:7
no one had **h** what Jeremiah .... Je 38:27
They **h** that the king of Babylon .... Je 40:7
countries also **h** that the king .... Je 40:11
And they **h** the king of Babylon .... Je 40:11
the people of Judah **h** this news,............ Je 40:12
officers with him **h** about all .... Je 41:11
nations have **h** of your shame, ... Je 46:12
of pain and suffering can be **h**. .... Je 48:5
We have **h** that the people of .... Je 48:29
crying can be **h** from Moabite................ Je 48:34
can be **h** from Zoar as far away .... Je 48:34
have **h** a message from the LORD. .... Je 49:14
cry will be **h** all the way to .... Je 49:21
because they have **h** bad news. .... Je 49:23
of battle can be **h** all over the .... Je 50:22
king of Babylon **h** about those .... Je 50:43
people crying are **h** in Babylon. .... Je 51:54
things are **h** in the land .... Je 51:54
of their voices is **h** all around. .... Je 51:55
People have **h** my groaning, ... La 1:21
my enemies have **h** of my trouble, ... La 1:21
You **h** me calling, "Do not close .... La 3:56
you have **h** their insults and all .... La 3:61
I **h** the sound of their wings, ... Eze 1:24
the ground and **h** a voice .... Eze 1:28
I **h** the LORD speaking to me. .... Eze 2:2
and I **h** a loud rumbling sound .... Eze 3:12

I **h** the wings of the living .... Eze 3:13
creatures was **h** all the way to .... Eze 10:5
I **h** the wheels being called .... Eze 10:13
The nations **h** about him. .... Eze 19:4
his roar could not be **h** again on.............. Eze 19:9
of what I have **h** is going to .... Eze 21:7
harps will not be **h** anymore. .... Eze 26:13
They **h** the sound of the trumpet .... Eze 33:5
have **h** all your insults against .... Eze 35:12
talk against me. I have **h** you................... Eze 35:13
I **h** someone speaking to me from .... Eze 43:6
When the king **h** their answer, ... Da 2:12
When they **h** the sound of the............... Da 3:7
that everyone who **h** the horns, ... Da 3:10
who had **h** the voices of the king .... Da 5:10
I have **h** that the spirit of the .... Da 5:14
I have **h** that you are able to .... Da 5:16
very upset when he **h** this. .... Da 6:14
Then I **h** a holy angel speaking. .... Da 8:13
And I **h** a man's voice calling .... Da 8:16
Then I **h** the man in the vision .... Da 10:9
of gods that no one has ever **h**. .... Da 11:36
And I **h** him swear by the name of .... Da 12:7
I **h** the answer, but I did not .... Da 12:8
We have **h** a message from the .... Ob 1:1
to you, and you **h** my voice. .... Jnh 2:2
you **h** my prayers in your Holy .... Jnh 2:7
the king of Nineveh **h** this news, ... Jnh 3:6
voices will no longer be **h**."..................... Nah 2:13
I have **h** the news about you; .... Hab 3:2
a cry will be **h** at the Fish .... Zph 1:10
I have **h** the insults of the .... Zph 2:8
because we have **h** that God is .... Zch 8:23
the Lᴏʀᴅ listened and **h** them. .... Mal 3:16
When King Herod **h** this, he was .... Mt 2:3
After the wise men **h** the king, ... Mt 2:9
A voice was **h** in Ramah of .... Mt 2:18
But he **h** that Archelaus was now .... Mt 2:22
When Jesus **h** that John had been .... Mt 4:12
You have **h** that it was said to................. Mt 5:21
You have **h** that it was said, ... Mt 5:27
You have **h** that it was said to .... Mt 5:33
You have **h** that it was said, ... Mt 5:38
You have **h** that it was said, ... Mt 5:43
Jesus **h** this, he was amazed. .... Mt 8:10
When Jesus **h** them, he said, "It .... Mt 9:12
but he **h** about what the Christ .... Mt 11:2
When the Pharisees **h** this, ... Mt 12:24
of Galilee, **h** the reports about .... Mt 14:1
and his dinner guests had **h** him. .... Mt 14:9
When Jesus **h** what had happened .... Mt 14:13
But the crowds **h** about it and............... Mt 14:13
When his followers **h** the voice, ... Mt 17:6
But when the young man **h** this,............... Mt 19:22
When Jesus' followers **h** this, ... Mt 19:25
the other ten followers **h** this,................. Mt 20:24
by the road **h** that Jesus was .... Mt 20:30
the Pharisees **h** these stories, ... Mt 21:45
When the men **h** what Jesus said, ... Mt 22:22
the people **h** this, they were .... Mt 22:33
When the high priest **h** this, ... Mt 26:65
you all **h** him say these things .... Mt 26:65
standing there who **h** this said, ... Mt 27:47
Jesus **h** this and said to them,................. Mk 2:17
they **h** what Jesus was doing, ... Mk 3:8
his family **h** this, they went..................... Mk 3:21
When the woman **h** about Jesus, ... Mk 5:27
Many people **h** him and were .... Mk 6:2
Herod **h** about Jesus, because................. Mk 6:14
When Herod **h** this, he said, "I .... Mk 6:16
and his dinner guests had **h** it. .... Mk 6:26
When John's followers **h** this,................. Mk 6:29
on mats wherever they **h** he was. .... Mk 6:55

spirit in her **h** that he was .... Mk 7:25
the other ten followers **h** this,................. Mk 10:41
When he **h** that Jesus from .... Mk 10:47
Jesus' followers **h** him say this. .... Mk 11:14
of the law **h** all this and began .... Mk 11:18
the law came and **h** Jesus arguing .... Mk 12:28
We **h** this man say, 'I will .... Mk 14:58
When the high priest **h** this, ... Mk 14:63
You all **h** him say these things .... Mk 14:64
people standing there **h** this, ... Mk 15:35
God has **h** your prayer. .... Lk 1:13
Elizabeth **h** Mary's greeting, ... Lk 1:41
When I **h** your voice, the baby .... Lk 1:44
relatives **h** how good the Lord .... Lk 1:58
The people who **h** about them .... Lk 1:66
everything they had seen and **h**............... Lk 2:20
All who **h** him were amazed at his .... Lk 2:47
While you **h** these words just .... Lk 4:21
'We **h** about the things you did .... Lk 4:23
in the synagogue **h** these things, ... Lk 4:28
When the officer **h** about Jesus, ... Lk 7:3
Jesus **h** this, he was amazed. .... Lk 7:9
John what you saw and **h** here. .... Lk 7:22
tax collectors, **h** this, they all .... Lk 7:29
When Jesus **h** this, he said to .... Lk 8:50
h about all the things that were .... Lk 9:7
the dark will be **h** in the light, ... Lk 12:3
table with Jesus **h** these things .... Lk 14:15
h the sound of music and dancing............ Lk 15:25
When Jesus **h** this, he said to .... Lk 18:22
when the man **h** this, he became .... Lk 18:23
When the people **h** this, they .... Lk 18:26
When he **h** the people coming down .... Lk 18:36
When the people **h** this story, ... Lk 20:16
We ourselves **h** him say this." .... Lk 22:71
Pilate **h** this and asked if Jesus .... Lk 23:6
because he had **h** about Jesus and .... Lk 23:8
two followers **h** John say this, ... Jn 1:37
after they **h** John speak about .... Jn 1:40
You yourselves **h** me say, 'I am .... Jn 3:28
He tells what he has seen and **h**, ... Jn 3:32
The Pharisees **h** that Jesus was .... Jn 4:1
the Pharisees had **h** about him, ... Jn 4:3
because we **h** him ourselves. .... Jn 4:42
When he **h** that Jesus had come .... Jn 4:47
You have never **h** his voice or .... Jn 5:37
the followers of Jesus **h** this, ... Jn 6:60
The Pharisees **h** the crowd .... Jn 7:32
When the people **h** Jesus' words, ... Jn 7:40
Those who **h** Jesus began to leave .... Jn 8:9
things I have **h** from the One who .... Jn 8:26
the truth which I **h** from God,.................. Jn 8:40
Nobody has ever **h** of anyone .... Jn 9:32
Jesus **h** that they had thrown .... Jn 9:35
who were nearby **h** Jesus say this .... Jn 9:40
Jesus **h** this, he said, "This .... Jn 11:4
But when he **h** that Lazarus was .... Jn 11:6
When Martha **h** that Jesus was .... Jn 11:20
When Mary **h** this, she got up .... Jn 11:29
I thank you that you **h** me. .... Jn 11:41
crowd of people **h** that Jesus was .... Jn 12:9
Passover Feast **h** that Jesus was .... Jn 12:12
because they had **h** about this .... Jn 12:18
there, who **h** the voice, said it .... Jn 12:29
We have **h** from the law that the.............. Jn 12:34
h me say to you, 'I am going, ... Jn 14:28
everything I **h** from my Father. .... Jn 15:15
the people who **h** my teaching. .... Jn 18:21
When Pilate **h** this, he was even .... Jn 19:8
When Pilate **h** what they were .... Jn 19:13
When Peter **h** him say this,..................... Jn 21:7
When they **h** this noise, a crowd.............. Ac 2:6
because each one **h** them speaking .... Ac 2:6

the people **h** this, they felt .... Ac 2:37
those who had **h** Peter and John.............. Ac 4:4
about what we have seen and **h**." .... Ac 4:20
When the believers **h** this, ... Ac 4:24
the others who **h** about these .... Ac 5:11
the apostles **h** this, they obeyed .... Ac 5:21
When the leaders **h** this, they .... Ac 5:33
We **h** Stephen speak against Moses .... Ac 6:11
We **h** him say that Jesus from................. Ac 6:14
But when Jacob **h** there was grain .... Ac 7:12
When Moses **h** him say this, ... Ac 7:29
Moses **h** the Lord's voice say, ... Ac 7:31
I have **h** their cries and have .... Ac 7:34
When the leaders **h** this, they .... Ac 7:54
people there **h** Philip and saw .... Ac 8:6
in Jerusalem **h** that the people .... Ac 8:14
he **h** the man reading from Isaiah .... Ac 8:30
the ground and **h** a voice saying............... Ac 9:4
They **h** the voice, but they saw .... Ac 9:7
people who **h** him were amazed. .... Ac 9:21
in Joppa that Peter was .... Ac 9:38
said, "God has **h** your prayers. .... Ac 10:4
God has **h** your prayer and has .... Ac 10:31
These believers **h** them speaking .... Ac 10:46
in Judea **h** that some who were .... Ac 11:1
I **h** a voice say to me, 'Get up,................. Ac 11:7
When the believers **h** this, ... Ac 11:18
in Jerusalem **h** about all of this .... Ac 11:22
were not Jewish **h** Paul say this,.............. Ac 13:48
and Paul, **h** about it, they .... Ac 14:14
They **h** the Good News from me, ... Ac 15:7
We have **h** that some of our group .... Ac 15:24
he **h** this order, he put them .... Ac 16:24
When the officers **h** that Paul .... Ac 16:38
of the city **h** these things, ... Ac 17:8
When the people **h** about Jesus .... Ac 17:32
when Priscilla and Aquila **h** him, ... Ac 18:26
never even **h** of a Holy Spirit.................. Ac 19:2
When they **h** this, they were .... Ac 19:5
and Greek in Asia **h** the word of .... Ac 19:10
When the others **h** this, they .... Ac 19:28
When we all **h** this, we and the .... Ac 21:12
When they **h** this, they praised .... Ac 21:20
They have **h** about your teaching, ... Ac 21:21
They have **h** that you tell them .... Ac 21:21
what they have **h** about you is .... Ac 21:24
When they **h** him speaking the .... Ac 22:2
the ground and **h** a voice saying, ... Ac 22:7
about what you have seen and **h**. .... Ac 22:15
the officer **h** this, he went to .... Ac 22:26
h this and told the men who were .... Ac 23:2
Paul's nephew **h** about this plan .... Ac 23:16
Then I **h** a voice speaking to me.............. Ac 26:14
I know he has **h** about all of .... Ac 26:26
believers in Rome **h** that we were .... Ac 28:15
Yes, they **h**—as the Scripture .... Rm 10:18
people have never **h** of Christ, ... Rm 15:20
who have not **h** about him will .... Rm 15:21
believers have **h** that you obey, ... Rm 16:19
and no one has ever **h** about it. 1Co 2:9
the right time I **h** your prayers. 2Co 6:2
me, and when I **h** this, I was 2Co 7:7
You have **h** about my past life in .... Gal 1:13
They had only **h** it said, "This................. Gal 1:23
because you **h** the Good News .... Gal 3:2
because you **h** the Good News .... Gal 3:5
When you **h** the true teaching— .... Eph 1:13
why since I **h** about your faith .... Eph 1:15
Surely you have **h** that God gave .... Eph 3:2
I know that you **h** about him, ... Eph 4:21
because you **h** that he was sick. .... Php 2:26
because we have **h** about the .... Col 1:4
hope when you **h** the message .... Col 1:5

since you **h** the Good News and .... Col 1:6
since the day we **h** about you,................. Col 1:9
you by the Good News that you **h**. .... Col 1:23
because when you **h** his message 1Th 2:13
that you **h** from me in faith..................... 2Ti 1:13
and many others have **h** me say............... 2Ti 2:2
and those who **h** him testified it .... Heb 2:3
h God's voice and was against .... Heb 3:16
teaching they **h** did not help .... Heb 4:2
because they **h** it but did not .... Heb 4:2
those who first **h** the way to be .... Heb 4:6
his prayer was **h** because he .... Heb 5:7
faith that Noah **h** God's warnings .... Heb 11:7
people of Israel **h** and begged................. Heb 12:19
They do not forget what they **h**, ... Jam 1:25
workers have been **h** by the Lord .... Jam 5:4
You have **h** about Job's patience, ... Jam 5:11
about the truths you have now **h**. 1Pe 1:12
Jesus **h** the voice of God, the 2Pe 1:17
h that voice from heaven while 2Pe 1:18
by the evil things he saw and **h**. 2Pe 2:8
which we have **h**, we have seen 1Jn 1:1
to you what we have seen and **h**, ... 1Jn 1:3
message we have **h** from Christ 1Jn 1:5
the teaching you have already **h**. 1Jn 2:7
You have **h** that the enemy of 1Jn 2:18
the teaching you **h** from the 1Jn 2:24
follow what you **h** from the..................... 1Jn 2:24
teaching you have **h** from the 1Jn 3:11
which you have **h** is coming, ... 1Jn 4:3
you have **h** from the beginning, ... 2Jn 1:6
and I **h** a loud voice behind me .... Rev 1:10
what you have received and **h**. .... Rev 3:3
I **h** the voices of many angels .... Rev 5:11
Then I **h** all creatures in heaven .... Rev 5:13
I **h** one of the four living .... Rev 6:1
I **h** the second living creature .... Rev 6:3
I **h** the third living creature..................... Rev 6:5
Then I **h** something that sounded .... Rev 6:6
I **h** the voice of the fourth .... Rev 6:7
Then I **h** how many people were .... Rev 7:4
h an eagle that was flying high .... Rev 8:13
and I **h** a voice coming from the.............. Rev 9:13
I **h** how many troops on horses .... Rev 9:16
But I **h** a voice from heaven say,.............. Rev 10:4
Then I **h** the same voice from .... Rev 10:8
the two prophets **h** a loud voice .... Rev 11:12
Then I **h** a loud voice in heaven .... Rev 12:10
And I **h** a sound from heaven like .... Rev 14:2
The sound I **h** was like people .... Rev 14:2
Then I **h** a voice from heaven .... Rev 14:13
Then I **h** a loud voice from the .... Rev 16:1
Then I **h** the angel of the waters............. Rev 16:5
And I **h** a voice coming from the .... Rev 16:7
Then I **h** another voice from .... Rev 18:4
will never be **h** in you again. .... Rev 18:22
will never be **h** in you again. .... Rev 18:22
will never be **h** in you again. .... Rev 18:23
announcement **h** what sounded .... Rev 19:1
Then I **h** what sounded like a .... Rev 19:6
And I **h** a loud voice from the................. Rev 21:3
am the one who **h** and saw these .... Rev 22:8
When I **h** and saw them, I bowed .... Rev 22:8

HEARING

Lord, and in the **h** of God, I 1Ch 28:8
After **h** that, I, Jeremiah, woke .... Je 31:26
you who are **h** these words today. .... Zch 8:9
person without **h** him and knowing .... Jn 7:51
H this, the captain of the......................... Ac 5:24
H the law does not make people............... Rm 2:13
comes from **h** the Good News, ... Rm 10:17

HEARS

Everyone who **h** about this will .... Ge 21:6
of a man who **h** the words of God. .... Nu 24:4
of a man who **h** the words of God. .... Nu 24:16
if her father **h** about the .... Nu 30:4
if her father **h** about the .... Nu 30:5
if her husband **h** about it and .... Nu 30:7
if her husband **h** about it and .... Nu 30:8
if her husband **h** about it but .... Nu 30:11
if her husband **h** about it and .... Nu 30:12
If he **h** about them and says .... Nu 30:14
that anyone who **h** about it will 2Ki 21:12
he **h** the cry of the needy. .... Job 34:28
still when it **h** the trumpet. .... Job 39:24
h the shouts of commanders and .... Job 39:25
The LORD **h** good people when they .... Ps 34:17
When Jerusalem **h** this, she is .... Ps 97:8
he **h** the prayers of those who................. Pr 15:29
Whoever **h** it might shame you, ... Pr 25:10
look or decide by what he **h**. .... Is 11:3
Anyone there who **h** the name .... Is 19:17
When he **h** you, he will help you. .... Is 30:19
be afraid when it **h** the voice of .... Is 30:31
everyone who **h** about it........................ Je 19:3
person who **h** my message speak .... Je 23:28
Everyone who **h** about you .... Nah 3:19
Everyone who **h** my words and .... Mt 7:24
Everyone who **h** my words and does .... Mt 7:26
the person who **h** the message .... Mt 13:19
the person who **h** the teaching .... Mt 13:20
the person who **h** the teaching .... Mt 13:22
the person who **h** the teaching .... Mt 13:23
If the governor **h** about this, ... Mt 28:14
comes to me and **h** my words and .... Lk 6:47
But the one who **h** my words and .... Lk 6:49
h what I say and believes .... Jn 5:24
Anyone who **h** my words and does........... Jn 12:47
he will speak only what he **h**, ... Jn 16:13
with what he wants, he **h** us. 1Jn 5:14
If we know he **h** us every time we 1Jn 5:15
Let the one who **h** this say, ... Rev 22:17
I warn everyone who **h** the words .... Rev 22:18

HEART

and his **h** was filled with pain. .... Ge 6:6
the sons of Israel over his **h**, ... Ex 28:29
be on Aaron's **h** when he goes .... Ex 28:30
your fellow citizen in your **h**. .... Le 19:17
LORD your God with all your **h**,............... Dt 6:5
to know what was in your **h**. .... Dt 8:2
in your **h** that the LORD your .... Dt 8:5
then your **h** will become proud. .... Dt 8:14
or his **h** will be led away from .... Dt 17:17
your God with joy and a pure **h**,.............. Dt 28:47
Terror will be in your **h**, ... Dt 28:67
and in your **h** so you may obey .... Dt 30:14
God of Israel, with all your **h**." .... Jos 24:23
My **h** is with the commanders of .... Jdg 5:9
praying in her **h** so her lips 1Sa 1:13
LORD has filled my **h** with joy; 1Sa 2:1
eyes will cry and your **h** be sad, ... 1Sa 2:33
Samuel, God changed Saul's **h**. 1Sa 10:9
Serve the LORD with all your **h**............... 1Sa 12:20
truly serve him with all your **h**. 1Sa 12:24
but the LORD looks at the **h**.".................. 1Sa 16:7
you are proud and wicked at **h**. 1Sa 17:28
h stopped, and he became like 1Sa 25:37
and his **h** pounded with fear. 2Sa 28:5
spears and stabbed him in the **h**. 2Sa 18:14
you give me a **h** that understands 1Ki 3:9
know what is in a person's **h**. 1Ki 8:39
know what is in everyone's **h**.................. 1Ki 8:39
and followed me with all his **h**. 1Ki 14:8

arrow went through Joram's **h**, ... 2Ki 9:24
God of Israel, with all his **h**. 2Ki 10:31
obeyed the LORD with all his **h**,............... 2Ki 23:25
and I gave with an honest **h**. 1Ch 29:17
know what is in a person's **h**. 2Ch 6:30
had promised with all their **h**................. 2Ch 15:15
obeyed the LORD with all his **h**." 2Ch 22:9
that was in Hezekiah's **h**. 2Ch 32:31
not sick? Your **h** must be sad." .... Ne 2:2
But in your **h** you hid other .... Job 10:13
your whole **h** to him and hold............... Job 11:13
Has your **h** carried you away from .... Job 15:12
along with the desires of my **h**. .... Job 17:11
How my **h** wants that to happen! .... Job 19:27
person dies with an unhappy **h**, ... Job 21:25
and keep his words in your **h**................. Job 22:22
and I made the widow's **h** sing. .... Job 29:13
or my **h** has been led by my eyes .... Job 31:7
That person's **h** blessed me, ... Job 31:20
that my **h** was pulled away from............. Job 31:27
My words come from an honest **h**, ... Job 33:3
my **h** pounds as if it will jump .... Job 37:1
mind or understanding in the **h**? .... Job 38:36
I will change my **h** and life. .... Job 42:6
praise you, LORD, with all my **h**. .... Ps 9:1
and feel sad in my **h** all day? .... Ps 13:2
My **h** is happy because you saved .... Ps 13:5
You have examined my **h**; .... Ps 17:3
of joint. My **h** is like wax; it .... Ps 22:14
look closely into my **h** and mind. .... Ps 26:2
My **h** said of you, "Go, worship .... Ps 27:8
of their God are in their **h**, ... Ps 37:31
My **h** pounds, and my strength is .... Ps 38:10
Your teachings are in my **h**." .... Ps 40:8
not hide your goodness in my **h**;............. Ps 40:10
things, I speak with a broken **h**. .... Ps 42:4
and my **h** speaks with .... Ps 49:3
in me a pure **h**, God, and make my .... Ps 51:10
not reject a **h** that is broken .... Ps 51:17
butter, but war is in his **h**. .... Ps 55:21
My **h** is steady, God; my heart is............... Ps 57:7
steady, God; my **h** is steady. I .... Ps 57:7
No, in your **h** you plan evil; .... Ps 58:2
I had known of any sin in my **h**,............... Ps 66:18
have broken my **h** and left me .... Ps 69:20
So why have I kept my **h** pure? .... Ps 73:13
When my **h** was sad and I was .... Ps 73:21
an innocent **h** and guided them .... Ps 78:72
I will praise you with all my **h**, ... Ps 86:12
My **h** is like grass that has been .... Ps 102:4
God, my **h** is steady. I will sing .... Ps 108:1
with all my **h** in the meeting .... Ps 111:1
to obey him with their whole **h**. .... Ps 119:2
I praised you with an honest **h**. .... Ps 119:7
With all my **h** I try to obey you. .... Ps 119:10
your words to **h** so I would not .... Ps 119:11
obeying them with all my **h**. .... Ps 119:34
I prayed to you with all my **h**. .... Ps 119:58
your orders with all my **h**. .... Ps 119:69
I call to you with all my **h**. .... Ps 119:145
but I fear your law in my **h**. .... Ps 119:161
LORD, my **h** is not proud; .... Ps 131:1
I will thank you with all my **h**; .... Ps 138:1
God, examine me and know my **h**;........... Ps 139:23
the people closest to his **h**. .... Ps 148:14
have told you what's in my **h**;................. Pr 1:23
them on your **h** as if on a tablet .... Pr 3:3
Trust the LORD with all your **h**, ... Pr 3:5
on to my words with all your **h**. .... Pr 4:4
them on your **h** as if on a tablet .... Pr 7:3
a happy **h** is like a continual .... Pr 15:15
with an evil **h** will find no .... Pr 17:20
A happy **h** is like good medicine, ... Pr 17:22

whippings can change an evil **h**.............. Pr 20:30
h of the wise leads to right, ... Ec 10:2
but the **h** of a fool leads to .... Ec 10:2
Do whatever your **h** desires, ... Ec 11:9
day, when his **h** was happy! .... Sng 3:11
bride, you have thrilled my **h**;............... Sng 4:9
have thrilled my **h** with a glance .... Sng 4:9
I sleep, but my **h** is awake. .... Sng 5:2
Put me like a seal on your **h**, ... Sng 8:6
hurt, and your whole **h** is sick. .... Is 1:5
My **h** cries with sorrow for Moab. .... Is 15:5
My **h** cries for Moab like a harp .... Is 16:11
back to me with her whole **h**, ... Je 3:10
The pain stabs your **h**!” .... Je 4:18
Oh, the torture in my **h**! .... Je 4:19
My **h** is pounding inside me. .... Je 4:19
But you know my **h**, LORD. .... Je 12:3
you change your **h** and return to .... Je 15:19
into a person's **h** and test the .... Je 17:10
his stubborn, evil **h** wants!'” .... Je 18:12
deeply into the **h** and mind of a .... Je 20:12
prophets: My **h** is broken. All .... Je 23:9
search for me with all your **h**,............... Je 29:13
you, I changed my **h** and life. .... Je 31:19
My **h** cries sadly for Moab like a .... Je 48:36
My **h** is troubled, because I have .... La 1:20
Pour out your **h** like water in .... La 2:19
out the stubborn **h** of stone from .... Eze 11:19
them an obedient **h** of flesh. .... Eze 11:19
yourselves a new **h** and a new way .... Eze 18:31
with breaking **h** and great .... Eze 21:6
every **h** will melt with fear, ... Eze 21:7
Their **h** was false, and now they .... Hos 10:2
My **h** beats for you, and my love .... Hos 11:8
person will take them to **h**. .... Hos 14:9
come back to me with all your **h**. .... Joe 2:12
sad; tear your **h** be broken. Come .... Joe 2:13
and rejoice with all your **h**. .... Zph 3:14
Your **h** will be where your .... Mt 6:21
the things that are in the **h**...................... Mt 12:34
was planted in that person's **h**. .... Mt 13:19
brother or sister from your **h**.” .... Mt 18:35
Lord your God with all your **h**, ... Mt 22:37
to them, “My **h** is full of sorrow .... Mt 26:38
Lord your God with all your **h**, ... Mk 12:30
must love God with all his **h**, ... Mk 12:33
to them, “My **h** is full of sorrow .... Mk 14:34
my **h** rejoices in God my Savior, ... Lk 1:47
happen will make your **h** sad,................. Lk 2:35
Lord your God with all your **h**, ... Lk 10:27
Your **h** will be where your .... Lk 12:34
who changes his **h** and life, ... Lk 15:7
sinner changes his **h** and life.” .... Lk 15:10
flow out from that person's **h**,................. Jn 7:38
work since your **h** is not right................. Ac 8:21
Change your **h**! Turn away from .... Ac 8:22
If you believe with all your **h**, ... Ac 8:37
with my whole **h** by telling the .... Rm 1:9
is done in the **h** by the Spirit, ... Rm 2:29
is in your mouth and in your **h**.”............. Rm 10:8
believe in your **h** that God .... Rm 10:9
the Lord with all your **h**........................... Rm 12:11
honest and sincere **h** from God. 2Co 1:12
troubled and unhappy in my **h**, ... 2Co 2:4
rather than what is in the **h**. 2Co 5:12
have decided in your **h** to give. 2Co 9:7
in your **h** so you will know .... Eph 1:18
respect and from a sincere **h**, ... Eph 6:5
With all your **h** you must do what .... Eph 6:6
because I have you in my **h**. .... Php 1:7
my body, my **h** is with you, and .... Col 2:5
with all our **h** that we can see................. 1Th 3:10
comes from a pure **h** and a good 1Ti 1:5

with him I am sending my own **h**. .... Phm 1:12
Refresh my **h** in Christ. .... Phm 1:20
unbelieving **h** that will turn you .... Heb 3:12
with a sincere **h** and a sure.................... Heb 10:22
other deeply with all your **h**. 1Pe 1:22
his good **h** was hurt by the evil 2Pe 2:8
to change her **h** and turn away .... Rev 2:21

HEARTS
I wish their **h** would always .... Dt 5:29
to the LORD with all your **h**, ... 1Sa 7:3
God touched the **h** of certain 1Sa 10:26
stole the **h** of all Israel. 2Sa 15:6
touched the **h** of all the people 2Sa 19:14
God, that you test people's **h**. 1Ch 29:17
you know what is in people's **h**. 2Ch 6:30
and cursed God in their **h**.”..................... Job 1:5
h plan ways to trick others. .... Job 15:35
who have wicked **h** hold on to .... Job 36:13
in their **h** they want to destroy .... Ps 5:9
saves those whose **h** are right. .... Ps 7:10
speak the truth from their **h** .... Ps 15:2
May your **h** live forever! .... Ps 22:26
with clean hands and pure **h**, ... Ps 24:4
but evil is in their **h**. .... Ps 28:3
Sing all you whose **h** are right. .... Ps 32:11
He made their **h** and understands .... Ps 33:15
speaks to the wicked in their **h**. .... Ps 36:1
swords will stab their own **h**, ... Ps 37:15
Our **h** haven't turned away from.............. Ps 44:18
he knows what is in our **h**. .... Ps 44:21
will enter the **h** of the king's .... Ps 45:5
but in their **h** they curse......................... Ps 62:4
to those who have pure **h**. .... Ps 73:1
Their **h** were not loyal to God, ... Ps 78:8
Their **h** were not really loyal to .... Ps 78:37
that makes happy **h** and olive oil .... Ps 104:15
their **h** are steady because they .... Ps 112:7
are good, whose **h** are honest. .... Ps 125:4
plans in their **h** and are always .... Pr 6:14
those with evil **h** but is pleased .... Pr 11:20
and gold, but the LORD tests **h**. .... Pr 17:3
but their **h** are far from me. .... Is 29:13
and to those whose **h** are broken. .... Is 57:15
those whose **h** are broken, ... Is 61:1
of the goodness of their **h**, ... Is 65:14
their stubborn, evil **h** anymore. .... Je 3:17
evil from your **h** so that you can.............. Je 4:14
whatever their evil **h** wanted. .... Je 7:24
what their own evil **h** wanted. .... Je 11:8
to test peoples' **h** and minds. .... Je 11:20
but their **h** are really far away .... Je 12:2
into the stone that is their **h**. .... Je 17:1
return to me with their whole **h**............... Je 24:7
minds and write them on their **h**. .... Je 31:33
you changed your **h** and did what .... Je 34:15
and in their **h** they think they................. Je 48:29
pray from our **h** to God in heaven .... La 3:41
We have no more joy in our **h**; .... La 5:15
Change your **h** and lives, and.................. Eze 14:6
Change your **h** and stop all your .... Eze 18:30
change your **h** and lives so you .... Eze 18:32
Their **h** will melt with fear, ... Eze 21:15
taken revenge with hateful **h**. .... Eze 25:15
but their **h** desire their selfish................. Eze 33:31
joy and with hate in their **h**. .... Eze 36:5
out the stubborn **h** of stone from .... Eze 36:26
give you obedient **h** of flesh. .... Eze 36:26
their **h** burn inside them. .... Hos 7:6
do not call to me from their **h**. .... Hos 7:14
made their **h** as hard as rock .... Zch 7:12
Change your **h** and lives because .... Mt 3:2
have changed your **h** and lives. .... Mt 3:8

show that your **h** and lives have .... Mt 3:11
Change your **h** and lives, because .... Mt 4:17
have good things in their **h**, ... Mt 12:35
people have evil in their **h**, ... Mt 12:35
but their **h** are far from me.   .... Mt 15:8
of changed **h** and lives for .... Mk 1:4
Change your **h** and lives and .... Mk 1:15
should change their **h** and lives. .... Mk 6:12
but their **h** are far from me.   .... Mk 7:6
of changed **h** and lives for .... Lk 3:3
have changed your **h** and lives. .... Lk 3:8
to change their **h** and lives." .... Lk 5:32
the good they stored in their **h**. .... Lk 6:45
the evil they stored in their **h**................... Lk 6:45
the things that are in their **h**. .... Lk 6:45
honest **h** and obey it and....................... Lk 8:15
you change your **h** and lives, ... Lk 13:3
you change your **h** and lives, ... Lk 13:5
knows what is really in your **h**. .... Lk 16:15
and change their **h** and lives.' .... Lk 16:30
and that a change of **h** and lives............... Lk 24:47
Don't let your **h** be troubled. .... Jn 14:1
So don't let your **h** be troubled .... Jn 14:27
Your **h** are filled with sadness .... Jn 16:6
Change your **h** and lives and be .... Ac 2:38
share their food with joyful **h**. .... Ac 2:46
must change your **h** and lives! .... Ac 3:19
united in their **h** and spirit..................... Ac 4:32
change their **h** and lives and .... Ac 5:31
have not given your **h** to God,................. Ac 7:51
baptism of changed **h** and lives. .... Ac 13:24
and filling your **h** with joy." .... Ac 14:17
believed, he made their **h** pure. .... Ac 15:9
to change their **h** and lives..................... Ac 17:30
baptism of changed **h** and lives. .... Ac 19:4
change their **h** and lives and .... Ac 26:20
will change your **h** and lives. .... Rm 2:4
that in their **h** they know what .... Rm 2:15
out his love to fill our **h**. .... Rm 5:5
can see what is in people's **h**. .... Rm 8:27
believe with our **h**, and so we .... Rm 10:10
secret purposes of people's **h**................... 1Co 4:5
into your own **h** before you eat 1Co 11:28
things in their **h** will be made................. 1Co 14:25
our own **h** we believed we would 2Co 1:9
Spirit in our **h** to be a 2Co 1:22
written on our **h**, known and read 2Co 3:2
on stone tablets but on human **h**. 2Co 3:3
can know in their **h** what kind of 2Co 4:2
shine in our **h** by letting us 2Co 4:6
I hope that in your **h** you know, ... 2Co 5:11
and have opened our **h** to you. 2Co 6:11
we have done—open your **h** to us. 2Co 6:13
Open your **h** to us. We have not 2Co 7:2
people change their **h** and lives. 2Co 7:10
not changed their **h** or turned................. 2Co 12:21
Spirit of his Son into your **h**, ... Gal 4:6
live in your **h** by faith and that .... Eph 3:17
taught to be made new in your **h**, ... Eph 4:23
music in your **h** to the Lord. .... Eph 5:19
will keep your **h** and minds in .... Php 4:7
thankfulness in your **h** to God. .... Col 3:16
but God, who tests our **h**. 1Th 2:4
your **h** be made strong so that 1Th 3:13
Lord lead your **h** into God's love 2Th 3:5
trust in the Lord from pure **h**................... 2Ti 2:22
thoughts and feelings in our **h**. .... Heb 4:12
minds and write them on their **h**. .... Heb 8:10
in their **h** and write them .... Heb 10:16
Your **h** should be strengthened by .... Heb 13:9
that is planted in your **h**,....................... Jam 1:21
have bitter jealousy in your **h**, ... Jam 3:14
as the holy Lord in your **h**. 1Pe 3:15

morning star rises in your **h**. 2Pe 1:19
taught their **h** to be greedy..................... 2Pe 2:14
to change their **h** and lives...................... 2Pe 3:9
if our **h** do not make us feel 1Jn 3:21
Change your **h** and do what you............. Rev 2:5
So change your **h** and lives. .... Rev 2:16
One who searches **h** and minds, ... Rev 2:23
and change your **h** and lives. .... Rev 3:3
and change your **h** and lives. .... Rev 3:19
not change their **h** and turn away .... Rev 9:20
not change their **h** and turn away .... Rev 9:21
to change their **h** and lives and .... Rev 16:9
to change their **h** and turn away.............. Rev 16:11

HEAT

swelling, **h**, lack of rain, ... Dt 28:22
them before the **h** of the day. 1Sa 11:11
h and dryness quickly melt the .... Job 24:19
Nothing hides from its **h**. .... Ps 19:6
was gone as in the summer **h**. .... Ps 32:4
than burning thorns can **h** a pot. .... Ps 58:9
people from the **h** of the sun and .... Is 4:6
I live, like **h** in the sunshine, ... Is 18:4
dew in the **h** of harvest time. .... Is 18:4
that protects them from the **h**. .... Is 25:4
like the **h** in the desert. .... Is 25:5
workman uses tools to **h** iron, ... Is 44:12
be left out in the **h** of the day .... Je 36:30
to north will feel their **h**........................ Eze 20:47
make you feel the **h** of my anger. .... Eze 22:21
out because of the **h** and bit him .... Ac 28:3
rises with burning **h** and dries .... Jam 1:11
in them will melt with **h**........................ 2Pe 3:12
them, and no **h** will burn them, ... Rev 7:16
They were burned by the great **h**, ... Rev 16:9

HEATED

the furnace to be **h** seven times .... Da 3:19
are like an oven **h** by a baker................... Hos 7:4

HEATS

Like someone who **h** and purifies .... Mal 3:3

HEAVEN

the God who made **h** and earth. .... Ge 14:19
Most High, who made **h** and earth. .... Ge 14:22
angel called to Hagar from **h**. .... Ge 21:17
called to him from **h** and said, ... Ge 22:11
to Abraham from **h** a second time .... Ge 22:15
LORD, the God of **h** and earth. .... Ge 24:3
LORD, the God of **h**, brought me .... Ge 24:7
earth and reaching up into **h**, ... Ge 28:12
house of God and the gate of **h**." .... Ge 28:17
that I talked with you from **h**. .... Ex 20:22
other god in **h** or on earth can .... Dt 3:24
I ask **h** and earth to speak .... Dt 4:26
from one end of **h** to the other. .... Dt 4:32
to you from **h** to teach you...................... Dt 4:36
He is God in **h** above and on the .... Dt 4:39
a land that drinks rain from **h**. .... Dt 11:11
look down from **h**, your holy home .... Dt 26:15
It is not up in **h**. You do not .... Dt 30:12
will go up to **h** and get it for .... Dt 30:12
Today I ask **h** and earth to be .... Dt 30:19
so that I may ask **h** and earth to .... Dt 31:28
my hand toward **h** and make this .... Dt 32:40
land with wonderful dew from **h**, ... Dt 33:13
no longer got the manna from **h**. .... Jos 5:12
The stars fought from **h**; .... Jdg 5:20
LORD went up to **h** in the flame. .... Jdg 13:20
will thunder in **h** against them. 1Sa 2:10
of Ekron cried loudly to **h**. 1Sa 5:12
foundations of **h** began to shake. 2Sa 22:8
The LORD thundered from **h**; 2Sa 22:14
god like you in **h** above or on 1Ki 8:23

place in **h** cannot contain	1Ki 8:27
from your home in **h,** and when	1Ki 8:30
then hear in **h.** Judge the case,	1Ki 8:32
hear them in **h.** Forgive the sins	1Ki 8:34
please hear their prayer in **h,**	1Ki 8:36
prayers from your home in **h.**	1Ki 8:39
Then hear from your home in **h,**	1Ki 8:43
Then hear in **h** their prayers,	1Ki 8:45
prayers from your home in **h,**	1Ki 8:49
with his arms raised toward **h.**	1Ki 8:54
come down from **h** and burn up you	2Ki 1:10
came down from **h** and burned up	2Ki 1:10
come down from **h** and burn up you	2Ki 1:12
came down from **h** and burned up	2Ki 1:12
came down from **h** and burned up	2Ki 1:14
Elijah by a whirlwind up into **h.**	2Ki 2:1
went up to **h** in a whirlwind.	2Ki 2:11
down fire from **h** on the altar of	1Ch 21:26
Everything in **h** cannot contain	1Ch 29:11
of Israel, who made **h** and earth!	2Ch 2:12
god like you in **h** or on earth.	2Ch 6:14
place in **h** cannot contain	2Ch 6:18
from your home in **h,** and when	2Ch 6:21
then hear in **h.** Judge the case,	2Ch 6:23
listen from **h.** Forgive the sin	2Ch 6:25
their prayer in **h,** and forgive	2Ch 6:27
prayers from your home in **h.**	2Ch 6:30
Then hear from your home in **h,**	2Ch 6:33
Then hear in **h** their prayers,	2Ch 6:35
your home in **h** and do what is	2Ch 6:39
come down from **h** and the LORD's	2Ch 7:3
ways, I will hear them from **h.**	2Ch 7:14
ancestors, you are the God in **h.**	2Ch 20:6
because their prayer reached **h,**	2Ch 30:27
of Amoz prayed to **h** about this.	2Ch 32:20
LORD, the God of **h,** has given me	2Ch 36:23
LORD, the God of **h,** has given	Ezr 1:2
of the God of **h** and earth.	Ezr 5:11
made the God of **h** angry,	Ezr 5:12
burnt offerings to the God of **h,**	Ezr 6:9
pleasing to the God of **h,**	Ezr 6:10
of the Law of the God of **h.**	Ezr 7:12
of the Law of the God of **h,**	Ezr 7:21
whatever the God of **h** wants for	Ezr 7:23
for the Temple of the God of **h.**	Ezr 7:23
I prayed to the God of **h,**	Ne 1:4
LORD, the God of **h,** you are the	Ne 1:5
First I prayed to the God of **h.**	Ne 2:4
The God of **h** will give us	Ne 2:20
and spoke from **h** to our	Ne 9:13
you gave them bread from **h.**	Ne 9:15
to you, and you heard from **h.**	Ne 9:27
to you again, you heard from **h.**	Ne 9:28
have one who speaks for me in **h;**	Job 16:19
God is in the highest part of **h.**	Job 22:12
he set up order in his high **h.**	Job 25:2
the one who sits in **h** laughs;	Ps 2:4
It brings you praise in **h** above.	Ps 8:1
LORD sits on his throne in **h.**	Ps 11:4
down from **h** on all people to	Ps 14:2
The LORD thundered from **h;**	Ps 18:13
from his holy **h** and saves him	Ps 20:6
looks down from **h** and sees every	Ps 33:13
down from **h** on all people to	Ps 53:2
sends help from **h** and saves me.	Ps 57:3
H and earth should praise him,	Ps 69:34
I have no one in **h** but you;	Ps 73:25
try to use your power against **h.**	Ps 75:5
From **h** you gave the decision,	Ps 76:8
above and opened the doors of **h.**	Ps 78:23
he gave them grain from **h.**	Ps 78:24
east wind from **h** and led the	Ps 78:26
Look down from **h** and see.	Ps 80:14
goodness will shine down from **h.**	Ps 85:11
Who in **h** is equal to the LORD?	Ps 89:6
from **h** he looked down at the	Ps 102:19
LORD has set his throne in **h,**	Ps 103:19
filled them with bread from **h.**	Ps 105:40
LORD our God, who rules from **h,**	Ps 113:5
Our God is in **h.** He does what he	Ps 115:3
the LORD, who made **h** and earth.	Ps 115:15
H belongs to the LORD, but he	Ps 115:16
it continues forever in **h.**	Ps 119:89
the LORD, who made **h** and earth.	Ps 121:2
to you, you who live in **h.**	Ps 123:1
the LORD, who made **h** and earth.	Ps 124:8
Zion, he who made **h** and earth.	Ps 134:3
he pleases, in **h** and on earth,	Ps 135:6
Give thanks to the God of **h.**	Ps 136:26
He made **h** and earth, the sea and	Ps 146:6
Praise him, all you armies of **h.**	Ps 148:2
more wonderful than **h** and earth.	Ps 148:13
praise him in his mighty **h.**	Ps 150:1
has gone up to **h** and come back	Pr 30:4
God is in **h,** and you are on the	Ec 5:2
H and earth, listen, because the	Is 1:2
fallen from **h,** even though you	Is 14:12
yourself, "I will go up to **h.**	Is 14:13
out the army of **h** one by one and	Is 40:26
your prayers are heard in **h.**	Is 58:4
wonderful and holy home in **h.**	Is 63:15
H is my throne, and the earth is	Is 66:1
gods did not make **h** and earth;	Je 10:11
disappear from **h** and earth.'"	Je 10:11
"I fill all of **h** and earth,"	Je 23:24
will roar from **h** and will shout	Je 25:30
Then **h** and earth and all that is	Je 51:48
from our hearts to God in **h:**	La 3:41
LORD looks down and sees from **h.**	La 3:50
the glory of the LORD in **h.**	Eze 3:12
the God of **h** would show them	Da 2:18
Daniel praised the God of **h.**	Da 2:19
there is a God in **h** who explains	Da 2:28
of **h** has given you a kingdom,	Da 2:37
the God of **h** will set up another	Da 2:44
a holy angel coming down from **h.**	Da 4:13
coming down from **h** who said, '	Da 4:23
learn that one in **h** rules your	Da 4:26
mouth when a voice from **h** said,	Da 4:31
looked up toward **h,** and I could	Da 4:34
the powers of **h** and the people	Da 4:35
and glory to the King of **h.**	Da 4:37
yourself against the Lord of **h.**	Da 5:23
miracles in **h** and on earth.	Da 6:27
the kingdoms under **h** with power	Da 7:27
of the army of **h** to the ground	Da 8:10
the army of **h** being walked on?	Da 8:13
raised his hands toward **h.**	Da 12:7
climb up into **h,** I will bring	Am 9:2
LORD, the God of **h,** who made the	Jnh 1:9
you like the four winds of **h,"**	Zch 2:6
These are the four spirits of **h.**	Zch 6:5
windows of **h** for you and pour	Mal 3:10
the kingdom of **h** is near."	Mt 3:2
Then **h** opened, and he saw God's	Mt 3:16
And a voice from **h** said, "This	Mt 3:17
the kingdom of **h** is near."	Mt 4:17
News about the kingdom of **h,**	Mt 4:23
kingdom of **h** belongs to them.	Mt 5:3
kingdom of **h** belongs to them.	Mt 5:10
reward waiting for you in **h.**	Mt 5:12
will praise your Father in **h.**	Mt 5:16
the law until **h** and earth are	Mt 5:18
important in the kingdom of **h.**	Mt 5:19
be great in the kingdom of **h.**	Mt 5:19
never enter the kingdom of **h.**	Mt 5:20

H

Master and their Master is in **h,** .... Eph 6:9
Jesus—everyone in **h,** on earth, ... Php 2:10
our homeland is in **h,** and we are .... Php 3:20
Jesus Christ, to come from **h.** .... Php 3:20
for is kept safe for you in **h.** .... Col 1:5
made—things in **h** and on earth, ... Col 1:16
things on earth and things in **h,** .... Col 1:20
at what is in **h,** where Christ is .... Col 3:1
only about the things in **h,** .... Col 3:2
that you have a Master in **h.** .... Col 4:1
from the dead, to come from **h.** 1Th 1:10
come down from **h** with a loud 1Th 4:16
fire from **h** with his powerful 2Th 1:7
side of the Great One in **h.** .... Heb 1:3
who has gone into **h,** let us hold .... Heb 4:14
in the Most Holy Place in **h,** .... Heb 6:19
right side of God's throne in **h.** .... Heb 8:1
and a shadow of what is in **h.** .... Heb 8:5
real things in **h** had to be made .... Heb 9:23
things in **h** need much better .... Heb 9:23
He went into **h** itself and is .... Heb 9:24
was taken to **h** so he would not .... Heb 11:5
whose names are written in **h.** .... Heb 12:23
to God who warns us from **h.** .... Heb 12:25
use the name of **h,** earth, or .... Jam 5:12
beauty, are kept in **h** for you. 1Pe 1:4
Holy Spirit who was sent from **h**— 1Pe 1:12
has gone into **h** and is at God's 1Pe 3:22
that voice from **h** while we were 2Pe 1:18
By the word of God **h** was made, ... 2Pe 3:5
God is keeping **h** and earth that 2Pe 3:7
for a new **h** and a new earth 2Pe 3:13
comes down out of **h** from my God. .... Rev 3:12
before me was an open door in **h.** .... Rev 4:1
and before me was a throne in **h,** .... Rev 4:2
was no one in **h** or on earth .... Rev 5:3
all creatures in **h** and on earth .... Rev 5:13
was silence in **h** for about half .... Rev 8:1
coming down from **h** dressed in a .... Rev 10:1
But I heard a voice from **h** say, ... Rev 10:4
land raised his right hand to **h,** .... Rev 10:5
the same voice from **h** again, ... Rev 10:8
a loud voice from **h** saying, ... Rev 11:12
they went up into **h** in a cloud .... Rev 11:12
and gave glory to the God of **h.** .... Rev 11:13
And there were loud voices in **h,** .... Rev 11:15
God's temple in **h** was opened. .... Rev 11:19
a great wonder appeared in **h:** .... Rev 12:1
another wonder appeared in **h:** .... Rev 12:3
Then there was a war in **h.** .... Rev 12:7
angels lost their place in **h.** .... Rev 12:8
dragon was thrown down out of **h.** .... Rev 12:9
heard a loud voice in **h** saying: .... Rev 12:10
against all those who live in **h.** .... Rev 13:6
come down from **h** to earth while .... Rev 13:13
a sound from **h** like the noise .... Rev 14:2
I heard a voice from **h** saying, ... Rev 14:13
came out of the temple in **h,** .... Rev 14:17
wonder in **h** that was great .... Rev 15:1
the Agreement) in **h** was opened. .... Rev 15:5
the God of **h** because of their .... Rev 16:11
angel coming down from **h.** .... Rev 18:1
another voice from **h** saying: .... Rev 18:4
Be happy because of this, **h!** .... Rev 18:20
a great many people in **h** saying: .... Rev 19:1
Then I saw **h** opened, and there .... Rev 19:11
The armies of **h,** dressed in fine .... Rev 19:14
saw an angel coming down from **h.** .... Rev 20:1
came down from **h** and burned them .... Rev 20:9
I saw a new **h** and a new earth .... Rev 21:1
The first **h** and the first earth .... Rev 21:1
coming down out of **h** from God. .... Rev 21:2
coming down out of **h** from God. .... Rev 21:10

HEAVEN'S

H foundations shake when he .... Job 26:11
the Commander of **h** armies. .... Da 8:11
and enjoyed **h** gift, and shared .... Heb 6:4

HEAVENLY

will open up his **h** storehouse so .... Dt 28:12
throne with his **h** army standing 1Ki 22:19
throne with his **h** army standing 2Ch 18:18
The **h** army worships you. .... Ne 9:6
H creatures of fire stood above .... Is 6:2
One of the **h** creatures used a .... Is 6:6
but your **h** Father feeds them. .... Mt 6:26
more your **h** Father will give .... Mt 7:11
king did what my **h** Father will .... Mt 18:35
appeared in **h** glory, talking .... Lk 9:31
more your **h** Father will give .... Lk 11:13
Also there are **h** bodies and 1Co 15:40
beauty of the **h** bodies is one 1Co 15:40
want God to give us our **h** home, ... 2Co 5:2
to be clothed with our **h** home. 2Co 5:4
But the **h** Jerusalem, which is .... Gal 4:26
blessing in the **h** world. .... Eph 1:3
his right side in the **h** world. .... Eph 1:20
powers in the **h** world will now .... Eph 3:10
powers of evil in the **h** world. .... Eph 6:12
me safely to his **h** kingdom. 2Ti 4:18
a better country—a **h** country. .... Heb 11:16
the living God, the **h** Jerusalem. .... Heb 12:22

HEAVENS

in it—the **h,** even the highest .... Dt 10:14
even the highest **h,** are his. .... Dt 10:14
will shut the **h** so it will not .... Dt 11:17
Hear, **h,** and I will speak. .... Dt 32:1
your God rules the **h** above and .... Jos 2:11
You made the **h** and the earth. 2Ki 19:15
the highest of **h** can hold him. 2Ch 2:6
You made the **h,** even the highest .... Ne 9:6
even the highest **h,** with all the .... Ne 9:6
limits are higher than the **h;** .... Job 11:8
awakened until the **h** disappear. .... Job 14:12
and even the **h** is not pure in .... Job 15:15
pride may be as high as the **h,** .... Job 20:6
The **h** will show their guilt, ... Job 20:27
I look at your **h,** which you made .... Ps 8:3
The **h** declare the glory of God, ... Ps 19:1
your love reaches to the **h,** .... Ps 36:5
the **h** praise you for your .... Ps 89:5
idols, but the LORD made the **h.** .... Ps 96:5
The **h** tell about his goodness, ... Ps 97:6
the skies, your truth to the **h.** .... Ps 108:4
I go up to the **h,** you are there. .... Ps 139:8
highest **h** and you waters above .... Ps 148:4
the dead or as high as the **h.**" .... Is 7:11
You made the **h** and the earth. .... Is 37:16
tired as I looked to the **h.** .... Is 38:14
The LORD created the **h.** .... Is 45:18
H and earth, be happy. .... Is 49:13
Look up to the **h.** Look around .... Is 51:6
I made the **h** and the earth, ... Is 51:16
Just as the **h** are higher than .... Is 55:9
look down from the **h** and see; .... Is 63:15
will make new **h** and a new earth .... Is 65:17
I will make new **h** and the new .... Is 66:22
destroy them from under your **h.** .... La 3:66
again shake the **h** and the earth, ... Hag 2:6
to shake the **h** and the earth. .... Hag 2:21
powers of the **h** will be shaken. .... Mt 24:29
powers of the **h** will be shaken. .... Mk 13:25
powers of the **h** will be shaken. .... Lk 21:26
us a seat with him in the **h.** .... Eph 2:6
and he is raised above the **h.** .... Heb 7:26
only the earth but also the **h.**" .... Heb 12:26

H

you **h** and all who live there! .... Rev 12:12
So worship God who made the **h,** .... Rev 14:7

HEAVIER

sadness would be **h** than the sand .... Job 6:3

HEAVY

because its load is too **h,** .... Ex 23:5
I broke the **h** weights that were .... Le 26:13
with you, one **h** and one light. .... Dt 25:13
The fighting was **h** around Saul. 1Sa 31:3
hair, because it became too **h.** 2Sa 14:26
because a **h** rain is coming." 1Ki 18:41
and soon a **h** rain began to fall. 1Ki 18:45
The fighting was **h** around Saul, ... 1Ch 10:3
me had placed a **h** load on the .... Ne 5:15
Have I become a **h** load for you? .... Job 7:20
because God's **h** hand is on me. .... Job 23:2
to the shower, 'Be a **h** rain.' .... Job 37:6
waterway for the **h** rains and .... Job 38:25
and leave your **h** work for it to .... Job 39:11
trapped and put a **h** load on us. .... Ps 66:11
Worry is a **h** load, but a kind .... Pr 12:25
Stone is **h,** and sand is weighty, ... Pr 27:3
have become a **h** weight on me, ... Is 1:14
taken away their **h** load and the .... Is 9:4
load and the **h** pole from their .... Is 9:4
He placed a **h** load on my people, ... Is 14:25
sin is like a **h** weight on its .... Is 24:20
doesn't use **h** boards to crush .... Is 28:27
are only **h** loads that must .... Is 46:1
'You are a **h** load to the LORD, ... Je 23:33
he put **h** chains on me. .... La 3:7
and put **h** logs in place to break .... Eze 4:2
Its **h** rust cannot be removed, ... Eze 24:12
a ship full of **h** cargo in the .... Eze 27:25
I will send a **h** rain with .... Eze 38:22
I will make it like a **h** rock; .... Zch 12:3
who are tired and have **h** loads, ... Mt 11:28
because their eyes were **h.** .... Mt 26:43
because their eyes were very **h.** .... Mk 14:40
God by putting a **h** load around .... Ac 15:10
not have a **h** load to carry, ... Ac 15:28

HEBER

sons were **H** and Malkiel. .... Ge 46:17
From **H** came the Heberite family .... Nu 26:45
Now **H** the Kenite had left the .... Jdg 4:11
H had put up his tent by the .... Jdg 4:11
was the wife of **H,** one of the .... Jdg 4:17
the wife of **H,** took a tent peg .... Jdg 4:21
the wife of **H** the Kenite, be .... Jdg 5:24
sons were **H** and Malkiel. 1Ch 7:31
H was the father of Japhlet, ... 1Ch 7:32
Zebadiah, Meshullam, Hizki, **H,** 1Ch 8:17

HEBER'S

H family was at peace with Jabin .... Jdg 4:17

HEBERITE

Heber came the **H** family group; .... Nu 26:45

HEBREW

to Abram, the **H,** and told him .... Ge 14:13
the place the same name in **H.** .... Ge 31:47
This **H** slave was brought here to .... Ge 39:14
This **H** slave was brought here to .... Ge 39:17
A young **H** man, a servant of the .... Ge 41:12
Two **H** nurses, named Shiphrah and ..... Ex 1:15
are helping the **H** women give .... Ex 1:16
The **H** women are much stronger .... Ex 1:19
And the **H** people continued to .... Ex 1:20
"This is one of the **H** babies." .... Ex 2:6
go and find a **H** woman to nurse .... Ex 2:7
saw an Egyptian beating a **H** man, ... Ex 2:11
and saw two **H** men fighting each .... Ex 2:13
If you buy a **H** slave, he will .... Ex 21:2

whether it is a **H** man or woman, ... Dt 15:12
this shouting in the **H** camp?" 1Sa 4:6
LORD had come into the **H** camp. 1Sa 4:6
A god has come into the **H** camp! 1Sa 4:7
speak to us in **H,** because the 2Ki 18:26
loudly in the **H** language, ... 2Ki 18:28
king's officers shouted in **H,** 2Ch 32:18
cities in Egypt will speak **H,** .... Is 19:18
speak to us in **H,** because the .... Is 36:11
loudly in the **H** language, ... Is 36:13
to free all the **H** slaves. .... Je 34:8
supposed to free his **H** slaves, ... Je 34:9
you must set his **H** slaves free. .... Je 34:14
a fellow **H** has sold himself to .... Je 34:14
Jonah said to them, "I am a **H.** .... Jnh 1:9
Bethesda in the **H** language. .... Jn 5:2
In the **H** language the name is .... Jn 19:13
in the **H** language is called .... Jn 19:17
The sign was written in **H,** .... Jn 19:20
and said in the **H** language, ... Jn 20:16
spoke to them in the **H** language. .... Ac 21:40
him speaking the **H** language, ... Ac 22:2
to me in the **H** language, ... Ac 26:14
I am a **H,** and my parents were .... Php 3:5
His name in the **H** language is .... Rev 9:11
Armageddon in the **H** language. .... Rev 16:16

HEBREWS

by force from the land of the **H,** .... Ge 40:15
not like **H** and never ate with .... Ge 43:32
time a boy is born to the **H,** .... Ex 1:22
God of the **H,** appeared to us. .... Ex 3:18
The God of the **H** has met with us .... Ex 5:3
very many **H,** and now you want .... Ex 5:5
God of the **H,** sent me to you. .... Ex 7:16
LORD, the God of the **H,** says: .... Ex 9:1
LORD, the God of the **H,** says: .... Ex 9:13
LORD, the God of the **H,** says: ' .... Ex 10:3
"Let the **H** hear what happened." 1Sa 13:3
Some **H** even went across the 1Sa 13:7
H might make swords and spears." 1Sa 13:19
The **H** are crawling out of the 1Sa 14:11
there were **H** who had served the 1Sa 14:21
"What are these **H** doing here?" 1Sa 29:3
to his fellow **H** who were slaves. .... Je 34:15
given freedom to your fellow **H,** .... Je 34:17
Are they **H?** So am I. Are they 2Co 11:22
a Hebrew, and my parents were **H.** .... Php 3:5

HEBRON

trees of Mamre at the city of **H.** .... Ge 13:18
Abraham left **H** and traveled to .... Ge 20:1
Arba (that is, **H**) in the land of .... Ge 23:2
was later called **H** in the land .... Ge 23:19
father Isaac at Mamre near **H,** .... Ge 35:27
sent him from the Valley of **H.** .... Ge 37:14
Amram, Izhar, **H,** and Uzziel. .... Ex 6:18
Amram, Izhar, **H,** and Uzziel. .... Nu 3:19
of Amram, Izhar, **H,** and Uzziel .... Nu 3:27
through the southern area to **H,** .... Nu 13:22
The city of **H** had been built .... Nu 13:22
a message to Hoham king of **H,** .... Jos 10:3
of Jerusalem, **H,** Jarmuth, ... Jos 10:5
of Jerusalem, **H,** Jarmuth, ... Jos 10:23
from Eglon to **H** and attacked it, ... Jos 10:36
Israelites inside everyone in **H;** .... Jos 10:37
just as they had done to **H.** .... Jos 10:39
who lived in the mountains of **H,** .... Jos 11:21
Jerusalem, **H,** .... Jos 12:10
him the city of **H** as his own. .... Jos 14:13
H still belongs to the family of .... Jos 14:14
of Kiriath Arba, also called **H.** .... Jos 15:13
Anakite families living in **H:** .... Jos 15:14
Arba (also called **H**), and Zior. .... Jos 15:54

also called **H**) in the mountains .... Jos 20:7
Arba, also called **H**, and all its .... Jos 21:11
gave the city of **H** to the .... Jos 21:13
of Aaron (**H** was a city of safety .... Jos 21:13
the Canaanites in the city of **H** .... Jdg 1:10
had promised, **H** was given to .... Jdg 1:20
hill that faces the city of **H**. .... Jdg 16:3
H, and to the people in all the 1Sa 30:31
The LORD answered, "To **H**." 2Sa 2:1
David went up to **H** with his two 2Sa 2:2
their homes in the cities of **H**. 2Sa 2:3
of Judah came to **H** and appointed 2Sa 2:4
was king in **H** for seven years 2Sa 2:11
sun came up as they reached **H**. 2Sa 2:32
Sons were born to David at **H**. 2Sa 3:2
sons were born to David at **H**. 2Sa 3:5
He then went to **H** to tell David 2Sa 3:19
with twenty men to David at **H**. 2Sa 3:20
so he was not with David at **H**. 2Sa 3:22
and all his army arrived at **H**, ... 2Sa 3:23
Abner arrived at **H**, Joab took 2Sa 3:27
buried Abner in **H**, and David and 2Sa 3:32
heard that Abner had died at **H**, ... 2Sa 4:1
they arrived at **H**, they gave his 2Sa 4:8
hung them over the pool of **H**. 2Sa 4:12
buried it in Abner's tomb at **H**. 2Sa 4:12
to David at **H** and said to him 2Sa 5:1
Israel came to King David at **H**, ... 2Sa 5:3
with them in **H** in the presence 2Sa 5:3
over Judah in **H** for seven years 2Sa 5:5
he came from **H**, David took for 2Sa 5:13
David, "Please let me go to **H**. 2Sa 15:7
I will worship him in **H**.'" 2Sa 15:8
So Absalom went to **H**. 2Sa 15:9
'Absalom is the king at **H**!'" 2Sa 15:10
years in **H** and thirty-three 1Ki 2:11
Mareshah was the father of **H**. 1Ch 2:42
David's sons who were born in **H**. 1Ch 3:1
of David were born to him in **H**, ... 1Ch 3:4
Amram, Izhar, **H**, and Uzziel. 1Ch 6:2
Amram, Izhar, **H**, and Uzziel. 1Ch 6:18
given the city of **H** in Judah 1Ch 6:55
the villages near **H** were given 1Ch 6:56
of Aaron were given **H**, ... 1Ch 6:57
David at the town of **H** and said, ... 1Ch 11:1
Israel came to King David at **H**. 1Ch 11:3
with them in **H** in the presence 1Ch 11:3
battle who joined David at **H**. 1Ch 12:23
They came to **H** fully agreed to 1Ch 12:38
Amram, Izhar, **H**, and Uzziel. 1Ch 23:12
of Amram, Izhar, **H**, and Uzziel. 1Ch 23:12
Hashabiah was from the **H** family. 1Ch 26:30
history of the **H** family shows 1Ch 26:31
men of the **H** family were found 1Ch 26:31
years in **H** and thirty-three 1Ch 29:27
Zorah, Aijalon, and **H**. 2Ch 11:10

HEBRON'S
H sons were Korah, Tappuah, ... 1Ch 2:43
people from **H** family group, ... 1Ch 15:9
H first son was Jeriah, his 1Ch 23:19
H first son was Jeriah, Amariah 1Ch 24:23

HEBRONITE
group, the **H** family group, ... Nu 26:58

HEDGE
will remove the **h**, and it will .... Is 5:5

HEEL
head, and you will bite his **h**." .... Ge 3:15
he was holding on to Esau's **h**, ... Ge 25:26
catch them by the **h** and hold .... Job 18:9
to his brother's **h** while the two .... Hos 12:3

HEGAI
and put under the care of **H**, ... Est 2:3
and put under the care of **H**. .... Est 2:8
and put under the care of **H**, ... Est 2:8
Esther pleased **H**, and he liked .... Est 2:9
So **H** quickly began giving Esther .... Est 2:9
for only what **H** suggested she .... Est 2:15
H was the king's eunuch who was .... Est 2:15

HEIGHT
same **h** as the curtains around .... Ex 38:18
rebuilt the wall to half its **h**, ... Ne 4:6
can measure the **h** of the skies .... Pr 25:3
and it became proud of its **h**. .... Eze 31:10

HEIGHTS
them to the **h** of the land and .... Dt 32:13
When you went up to the **h**, ... Ps 68:18
to its greatest **h** and its best .... Is 37:24
When he went up to the **h**, ... Eph 4:8

HELAH
two wives named **H** and Naarah. 1Ch 4:5

HELAH'S
H sons were Zereth, Zohar, Ethnan, ... 1Ch 4:7

HELAM
River, and they went to **H**. 2Sa 10:16
the Jordan River and went to **H**. 2Sa 10:17

HELBAH
Aczib, **H**, Aphek, and Rehob. .... Jdg 1:31

HELD
So Aaron **h** his hand over all the .... Ex 8:6
Then Moses **h** his hand over the .... Ex 14:21
As long as Moses **h** his hands up, ... Ex 17:11
Aaron and Hur **h** up Moses' hands— .... Ex 17:12
h up by three posts on three .... Ex 27:14
h up by three posts on three .... Ex 27:15
is to be **h** up by four posts on .... Ex 27:16
Five crossbars **h** the frames .... Ex 36:31
and five **h** the frames together .... Ex 36:32
five crossbars **h** the frames .... Ex 36:32
because they **h** the poles for .... Ex 37:14
these rings **h** the poles for .... Ex 37:27
It was **h** up by silver hooks and .... Ex 38:12
h up by three posts and three .... Ex 38:14
h up by three posts and three .... Ex 38:15
It was **h** up by four posts and .... Ex 38:19
The people **h** him as a prisoner .... Le 24:12
They **h** the man under guard, ... Nu 15:34
So Joshua **h** his spear toward .... Jos 8:18
had **h** his spear toward Ai, ... Jos 8:26
They **h** the torches in their left .... Jdg 7:20
but Ruth **h** on to her tightly. .... Ru 1:14
So Ruth **h** her shawl open, ... Ru 3:15
took the boy, **h** him in her arms, ... Ru 4:16
The man who **h** his shield walked 1Sa 17:41
He had been **h** there before the 1Sa 21:7
a belt that **h** his sword in its 2Sa 20:8
that cannot be **h** in a hand. 2Sa 23:6
and it **h** about eleven thousand 1Ki 7:26
table which **h** the bread that 1Ki 7:48
when they are **h** as prisoners 1Ki 8:47
where they are **h** as prisoners, ... 1Ki 8:47
Ahab was **h** up in his chariot 1Ki 22:35
the bronze bulls that **h** it up, ... 2Ki 16:17
of Judah was **h** in Babylon for 2Ki 25:27
each table that **h** the holy bread 1Ch 28:16
it **h** about seventeen thousand 2Ch 4:5
tables which **h** the bread that 2Ch 4:19
when they are **h** as prisoners 2Ch 6:37
where they are **h** as prisoners, ... 2Ch 6:37
LORD **h** his anger back and did 2Ch 12:12
King Ahab **h** himself up in his 2Ch 18:34

H

all the people **h** up their hands .... Ne 8:6
It was **h** in the courtyard of the .... Est 1:5
He **h** out to her the gold scepter .... Est 5:2
The king held out the gold scepter .... Est 8:4
he **h** me by the neck and crushed .... Job 16:12
with you; you have **h** my hand. .... Ps 73:23
Many times he **h** back his anger............... Ps 78:38
by those who **h** them captive. .... Ps 106:46
I **h** out my hand, but you paid no .... Pr 1:24
don't be **h** captive by a woman .... Pr 5:20
and he will be **h** captive by his .... Pr 5:23
little as if you had been **h** up. .... Pr 6:11
little as if you had been **h** up. .... Pr 24:34
I **h** him and would not let him go .... Sng 3:4
around with their heads **h** high, ... Is 3:16
The mast is not **h** firm. .... Is 33:23
been quiet and **h** myself back. .... Is 42:14
will be nursed and **h** in my arms .... Is 66:12
But I **h** back my anger. I acted .... Eze 20:22
It is meant to be **h** in the hand. .... Eze 21:11
It is **h**, ready for killing. .... Eze 21:15
men touched and **h** back their young .... Eze 23:21
covered them and **h** back their .... Eze 31:15
ancestor Jacob **h** on to his .... Hos 12:3
I **h** back the rain from you three............... Am 4:7
city where they were **h** captive. .... Mic 2:13
The man **h** out his hand, and it .... Mt 12:13
The man **h** out his hand and it .... Mk 3:5
The man **h** out his hand, and it .... Lk 6:10
has been **h** by Satan for eighteen .... Lk 13:16
jar **h** about twenty or thirty .... Jn 2:6
that he be **h** until I could send .... Ac 25:21
the law **h** us like prisoners,..................... Rm 7:6
we were all **h** prisoners by the .... Gal 3:23
body are joined and **h** together. .... Eph 4:16
are cared for and **h** together. .... Col 2:19
crown is being **h** for me—a crown 2Ti 4:8
with gold that **h** the old .... Heb 9:4
He **h** on while wicked people were............ Heb 12:3
they are being **h** for judgment. 2Pe 2:4
He **h** seven stars in his right .... Rev 1:16
The rider on the horse **h** a bow, ... Rev 6:2
and its rider **h** a pair of scales .... Rev 6:5

HELDAI
for the twelfth month, was **H**. 1Ch 27:15
Take silver and gold from **H**, ... Zch 6:10
Temple of the LORD to remind **H**, ... Zch 6:14

HELED
H son of Baanah the Netophathite; 2Sa 23:29
H son of Baanah the Netophathite; 1Ch 11:30

HELEK
from **H** came the Helekite family .... Nu 26:30
Abiezer, **H**, Asriel, Shechem .... Jos 17:2

HELEKITE
Helek came the **H** family group;............... Nu 26:30

HELEPH
in Zaanannim, which is near **H**. .... Jos 19:33

HELEZ
H the Paltite; Ira son of Ikkesh 2Sa 23:26
Azariah was the father of **H**. 1Ch 2:39
H was the father of Eleasah. 1Ch 2:39
the Harorite; **H** the Pelonite; 1Ch 11:27
for the seventh month, was **H**. 1Ch 27:10

HELI
Joseph was the son of **H**. .... Lk 3:23
H was the son of Matthat. .... Lk 3:24

HELIOPOLIS
The young men of **H** and Bubastis .... Eze 30:17

HELKAI
H, from Meremoth's family; .... Ne 12:15

HELKATH
land included **H**, Hali, Beten, ... Jos 19:25
H, and Rehob, and the pastures .... Jos 21:31

HELL
be in danger of the fire of **h**. .... Mt 5:22
your whole body thrown into **h**. .... Mt 5:29
your whole body to go into **h**.................... Mt 5:30
road is wide that leads to **h**, ... Mt 7:13
the soul and the body in **h**. .... Mt 10:28
be thrown into the fire of **h**. .... Mt 18:9
him more fit for **h** than you are. .... Mt 23:15
to have two hands and go to **h**, ... Mk 9:43
In **h** the worm does not die; .... Mk 9:44
two feet and be thrown into **h**. .... Mk 9:45
In **h** the worm does not die; .... Mk 9:46
two eyes and be thrown into **h**. .... Mk 9:47
In **h** the worm does not die; .... Mk 9:48
and also to throw you into **h**. .... Lk 12:5
who is on his way to **h**, appears............... 2Th 2:3
The tongue is set on fire by **h**, ... Jam 3:6
sent them to **h** and put them in 2Pe 2:4

HELLO
If you meet anyone, don't say **h**............... 2Ki 4:29

HELMET
with a bronze **h** on his head and 1Sa 17:5
put a bronze **h** on his head and 1Sa 17:38
Ephraim is like my **h**. .... Ps 60:7
Ephraim is like my **h**. .... Ps 108:8
He put the **h** of salvation on his .... Is 59:17
God's salvation as your **h**, ... Eph 6:17
of salvation should be our **h**. 1Th 5:8

HELMETS
shields, spears, **h**, armor, bows, ... 2Ch 26:14
for battle and put on your **h**! .... Je 46:4
and small shields and with **h**. .... Eze 23:24
shields and **h** on your sides. .... Eze 27:10
of them having shields and **h**.................... Eze 38:5

HELON
tribe of Zebulun—Eliab son of **H**; .... Nu 1:9
of Zebulun is Eliab son of **H**. .... Nu 2:7
Eliab son of **H** was over the .... Nu 10:16

HELP
With the LORD's **h**, I have given .... Ge 4:1
made an agreement to **h** Abram. .... Ge 14:13
H him up and take him by the .... Ge 21:18
truly want to **h** me bury my dead .... Ge 23:8
before you to **h** you get a wife .... Ge 24:7
angel with you and will **h** you. .... Ge 24:40
father's wealth will not **h** me." .... Ge 25:32
cried for **h**, God heard them. .... Ex 2:23
I will **h** you speak, and I will .... Ex 4:12
will **h** both of you to speak and .... Ex 4:15
This feast will **h** you remember, ... Ex 13:9
your forehead to **h** you remember .... Ex 13:16
and cried to the LORD for **h**. .... Ex 14:10
The God of my father is my **h**. .... Ex 18:4
and the Egyptians to **h** Israel.................... Ex 18:8
to me for God's **h** in solving .... Ex 18:15
and they cry out to me for **h**, ... Ex 22:23
If he cries out to me for **h**, ... Ex 22:27
don't **h** a wicked person by..................... Ex 23:1
You must **h** your enemy get the .... Ex 23:5
chest covering to **h** in making.................... Ex 28:15
They will **h** in making decisions .... Ex 28:30
and wanted to **h** made thread................. Ex 35:26
who wanted to **h** brought gifts to .... Ex 35:29
they wanted to **h** with the work............... Ex 36:2
These teachings **h** people know .... Le 11:47
they **h** people know which animals .... Le 11:47
they **h** people decide when things .... Le 14:57
h him to live among you as you .... Le 25:35

work hard, but it will not **h**. .... Le 26:20
of his family, will **h** you. .... Nu 1:4
names of the men who will **h** you: .... Nu 1:5
to Aaron the priest to **h** him. .... Nu 3:6
They will **h** him and all the..................... Nu 3:7
They will **h** remove the .... Nu 8:19
They may **h** their fellow Levites .... Nu 8:26
they will **h** you remember your .... Nu 10:10
They will **h** you care for the .... Nu 11:17
they will **h** you and your sons................. Nu 18:2
If you will **h** us defeat these .... Nu 21:2
We will **h** the other Israelites .... Nu 32:17
the LORD and **h** you take the land .... Nu 32:29
each tribe to **h** divide the land. .... Nu 34:18
Appoint Joshua and **h** him be................ Dt 3:28
The LORD will **h** you defeat their .... Dt 7:24
the LORD will **h** you defeat them .... Dt 21:10
ignore it. **H** the owner get it .... Dt 22:4
a city and did not scream for **h**. .... Dt 22:24
The LORD will **h** you defeat the .... Dt 28:7
The LORD will **h** your enemies .... Dt 28:25
and **h** them take it as their own. .... Dt 31:7
Let those gods come to **h** you! .... Dt 32:38
H them fight their enemies!" .... Dt 33:7
through the skies to **h** you, ... Dt 33:26
of your brothers to **h** them..................... Jos 1:14
But you must **h** them until they .... Jos 1:15
I will not **h** you anymore unless .... Jos 7:12
I will **h** you defeat the king of .... Jos 8:1
of the city to **h** with the fight. .... Jos 8:22
with me and **h** me attack Gibeon .... Jos 10:4
quickly and **h** us! Save us! All .... Jos 10:6
king of Gezer came to **h** Lachish, ... Jos 10:33
has done to our enemies to **h** us. .... Jos 23:3
With his **h**, one Israelite could .... Jos 23:10
God will not **h** you defeat your .... Jos 23:13
Come and **h** us fight the .... Jdg 1:3
we will go and **h** you fight for............... Jdg 1:3
the Israelites cried for **h**....................... Jdg 2:18
force them out or **h** Joshua's .... Jdg 2:23
they cried to the LORD for **h**. .... Jdg 4:3
they did not come to **h** the LORD. .... Jdg 5:23
said you would **h** me save Israel. .... Jdg 6:36
So go call to them for **h**. .... Jdg 10:14
didn't you call us to **h** you .... Jdg 12:1
but you didn't come to **h** me. .... Jdg 12:2
I saw that you would not **h** me, ... Jdg 12:3
LORD had come to **h** his people .... Ru 1:6
about all the **h** you have given .... Ru 2:11
against someone, God can **h** you. 1Sa 2:25
LORD himself, no one can **h** you!" 1Sa 2:25
to do, because God will **h** you. 1Sa 10:7
no one comes to **h** us, we will.............. 1Sa 11:3
cried to the LORD for **h**. 1Sa 12:8
They can't **h** you or save you. 1Sa 12:21
Maybe the LORD will **h** us...................... 1Sa 14:6
the Philistines with God's **h**!" 1Sa 14:45
me if I did not **h** him escape, ... 1Sa 19:17
h you defeat the Philistines." 1Sa 23:4
May God **h** me if I don't join 2Sa 3:9
I will **h** you unite all Israel..................... 2Sa 3:12
Damascus came to **h** Hadadezer.............. 2Sa 8:5
strong for me, you must **h** me. 2Sa 10:11
strong for you, I will **h** you. 2Sa 10:11
were afraid to **h** the Ammonites.............. 2Sa 10:19
and said, "My king, **h** me!".................... 2Sa 14:4
and I could **h** them get justice." 2Sa 15:4
You can **h** us most by staying in 2Sa 18:3
the Jordan to **h** bring the king's 2Sa 19:18
he was eager to **h** the people of 2Sa 21:2
my call for **h** reached his ears. 2Sa 22:7
your **h** I can attack an army. 2Sa 22:30
With God's **h** I can jump over a 2Sa 22:30

They called for **h**, but no one 2Sa 22:42
and they agreed to **h** him. 1Ki 1:7
May he also **h** Solomon and make 1Ki 1:37
men of Israel to **h** in this work. 1Ki 5:13
them anytime they ask you for **h**. 1Ki 8:52
everyone had to **h**. They carried 1Ki 15:22
of Ahab went to **h** Jehoshaphat, ... 1Ki 22:49
answered, "How can I **h** you? 2Ki 4:2
out to him, "**H** me, my master 2Ki 6:26
If the LORD doesn't **h** you, ... 2Ki 6:27
Can I get **h** from the threshing 2Ki 6:27
king chose an officer to **h** her. 2Ki 8:6
one was left who could **h** Israel. 2Ki 14:26
trusting for **h** so that you turn 2Ki 18:20
are depending on Egypt to **h** you, ... 2Ki 18:21
lean on it for **h**, it will stab 2Ki 18:21
of Egypt went to **h** the king of 2Ki 23:29
the war, asking them to **h** them. 1Ch 5:20
had to come and **h** them at times. 1Ch 9:25
have come peacefully to **h** me, ... 1Ch 12:17
Success to those who **h** you, ... 1Ch 12:18
not really the Philistines......................... 1Ch 12:19
They came to **h** turn the kingdom 1Ch 12:23
to ask God for **h** while Saul was............. 1Ch 13:3
always go to him for **h**. 1Ch 16:11
Damascus came to **h** Hadadezer............. 1Ch 18:5
had come to **h** were out in this 1Ch 19:9
strong for me, you must **h** me. 1Ch 19:12
strong for you, I will **h** you. 1Ch 19:12
refused to **h** the Ammonites again 1Ch 19:19
of Israel to **h** his son Solomon. 1Ch 22:17
David, with the **h** of Zadok, and 1Ch 24:3
go to him for **h**, you will get 1Ch 28:9
worker is ready to **h** you with................. 1Ch 28:21
H him always obey your commands, ... 1Ch 29:19
H him build the Temple for which 1Ch 29:19
can rule them without your **h**." 2Ch 1:10
H me as you helped my father 2Ch 2:3
and my servants will **h** them. 2Ch 2:8
He will **h** your craftsmen and the 2Ch 2:14
praise and to **h** the priests do 2Ch 8:14
sons, and the Levites **h** them. 2Ch 13:10
only you can **h** weak people 2Ch 14:11
H us, LORD our God, because we 2Ch 14:11
king of Aram to **h** you and not 2Ch 16:7
depended on the LORD to **h** you, ... 2Ch 16:8
did not ask for **h** from the LORD, ... 2Ch 16:12
did not ask for **h** from the Baal 2Ch 17:3
Why did you **h** evil people?..................... 2Ch 19:2
together to ask the LORD for **h**; 2Ch 20:4
to do, so we look to you for **h**." 2Ch 20:12
the power to **h** you or to defeat 2Ch 25:8
have you asked their gods for **h**? 2Ch 25:15
Judah asked for **h** from the gods 2Ch 25:20
power to **h** the king against 2Ch 26:13
he had much **h** until he became 2Ch 26:15
gave Ahaz trouble instead of **h**. 2Ch 28:20
of Assyria, but it did not **h**. 2Ch 28:21
to them, they will **h** me also." 2Ch 28:23
our God to **h** us and to fight 2Ch 32:8
nothing to trust in to **h** you. 2Ch 32:10
LORD his God for **h** and humbled 2Ch 33:12
said, "Let us **h** you build, ... Ezr 4:2
You will not **h** us build a Temple .... Ezr 4:3
had set up to **h** the Levites. .... Ezr 8:20
these men gave **h** to the people .... Ezr 8:36
had come to **h** the Israelites. .... Ne 2:20
been done with the **h** of our God. .... Ne 6:16
someone else will **h** and save the .... Est 4:14
I have no power to **h** myself, ... Job 6:13
You also have been no **h**. .... Job 6:21
should ask God for **h** and pray to .... Job 8:5
out your hands to him for **h**. .... Job 11:13

I scream for **h** but I get no .... Job 19:7
Does it **h** the Almighty for you .... Job 22:3
and the injured cry out for **h,** .... Job 24:12
You are no **h** to the helpless! .... Job 26:2
the orphan who had no one to **h.** .... Job 29:12
they cry for **h** in their time .... Job 30:24
up in public and cry for **h.** .... Job 30:28
up hope while looking for **h.** .... Job 31:16
powerful people die without **h.** .... Job 34:20
them, they do not cry for **h.** .... Job 36:13
to my cry for **h,** my King and my .... Ps 5:2
The LORD has heard my cry for **h;**............ Ps 6:9
h those who do what is right. .... Ps 7:9
Don't forget those who need **h.** .... Ps 10:12
in trouble look to you for **h.** .... Ps 10:14
Our tongues will **h** us win. .... Ps 12:4
will give them the **h** they want." .... Ps 12:5
anyone was looking to God for **h.** .... Ps 14:2
They do not ask the LORD for **h.** .... Ps 14:4
listen to my cry for **h.** .... Ps 17:1
I cried out to my God for **h.** .... Ps 18:6
my call for **h** reached his ears. .... Ps 18:6
your **h** I can attack an army. .... Ps 18:29
With God's **h** I can jump over a .... Ps 18:29
They called for **h,** but no one .... Ps 18:41
he send you **h** from his Temple .... Ps 20:2
Answer us when we call for **h.** .... Ps 20:9
to you for **h** and were rescued .... Ps 22:5
say, "Turn to the LORD for **h.** .... Ps 22:8
near, and there is no one to **h.** .... Ps 22:11
are my strength; hurry to **h** me. .... Ps 22:19
look to the God of Jacob for **h.** .... Ps 24:6
looking to the LORD for **h.** .... Ps 25:15
Wait for the LORD's **h.** Be strong .... Ps 27:14
and wait for the LORD's **h.** .... Ps 27:14
Rock, I call out to you for **h.** .... Ps 28:1
when I cry out to you for **h.** .... Ps 28:2
he heard my prayer for **h.** .... Ps 28:6
have mercy on me. LORD, **h** me." .... Ps 30:10
when I cried out to you for **h.** .... Ps 31:22
He is our **h,** our shield to .... Ps 33:20
the LORD for **h,** and he answered .... Ps 34:4
who go to him for **h** are happy, ... Ps 34:5
and armor. Rise up and **h** me.................... Ps 35:2
for the LORD's **h** and follow him. .... Ps 37:34
Quickly come and **h** me, my Lord .... Ps 38:22
save me. Hurry, LORD, **h** me. .... Ps 40:13
With your **h** we pushed back our .... Ps 44:5
I don't trust my bow to **h** me, ... Ps 44:6
Get up and **h** us. Because of your .... Ps 44:26
God will **h** her at dawn. .... Ps 46:5
anyone was looking to God for **h.** .... Ps 53:2
They do not ask God for **h.** .... Ps 53:4
See, God will **h** me; the Lord .... Ps 54:4
and do not ignore my cry for **h.** .... Ps 55:1
But I will call to God for **h,** .... Ps 55:16
I call for **h,** my enemies will .... Ps 56:9
He sends **h** from heaven and saves............ Ps 57:3
Wake up to **h** me, and look. .... Ps 59:4
He will **h** me defeat my enemies. .... Ps 59:10
H us fight the enemy. Human help .... Ps 60:11
the enemy. Human **h** is useless, ... Ps 60:11
but we can win with God's **h.** .... Ps 60:12
You are my **h.** Because of your .... Ps 63:7
I am tired from calling for **h;** .... Ps 69:3
from waiting for God to **h** me. .... Ps 69:3
I am in trouble. Hurry to **h** me! .... Ps 69:17
of David. To **h** people remember. .... Ps 69:36
save me. LORD, hurry to **h** me. .... Ps 70:1
to me. You **h** me and save me. .... Ps 70:5
far off. My God, hurry to **h** me. .... Ps 71:12
H him judge your people fairly .... Ps 72:2
H him be fair to the poor and .... Ps 72:4

He will **h** the poor when they cry .... Ps 72:12
needy when no one else will **h.** .... Ps 72:12
they would look to him for **h;** .... Ps 78:34
h us so people will praise you. .... Ps 79:9
and we will call to you for **h.** .... Ps 80:18
joined them to **h** Ammon and Moab, ... Ps 83:8
I have called out to you for **h;** .... Ps 88:13
you did not **h** him stand in .... Ps 89:43
Who will **h** me fight against the .... Ps 94:16
let my cry for **h** come to you. .... Ps 102:1
When I cry for **h,** answer me .... Ps 102:2
always go to him for **h.** .... Ps 105:4
h me when you save them. .... Ps 106:4
H us fight the enemy. Human help .... Ps 108:12
the enemy. Human **h** is useless, ... Ps 108:12
but we can win with God's **h.** .... Ps 108:13
LORD my God, **h** me; because you .... Ps 109:26
The Lord is beside you to **h** you............... Ps 110:5
he listens to my prayers for **h.** .... Ps 116:1
call to him for **h** as long as I .... Ps 116:2
The LORD is with me to **h** me, ... Ps 118:7
H me understand your orders. .... Ps 119:27
H me understand, so I can keep .... Ps 119:34
Liars are hurting me. **H** me! .... Ps 119:86
H me, and I will be saved. .... Ps 119:117
Promise that you will **h** me, ... Ps 119:122
H me understand so I can live. .... Ps 119:144
Let your word **h** me understand. .... Ps 119:169
you, and let your laws **h** me. .... Ps 119:175
but where does my **h** come from? .... Ps 121:1
My **h** comes from the LORD, who .... Ps 121:2
To **h** my relatives and friends,.................. Ps 122:8
Our **h** comes from the LORD, ... Ps 124:8
listen to my prayer for **h.** .... Ps 130:2
I wait for the LORD to **h** me, ... Ps 130:5
for the Lord to **h** me more than .... Ps 130:6
listen to my prayer for **h.** .... Ps 140:6
LORD, **h** me control my tongue;................ Ps 141:3
h me be careful about what I say. .... Ps 141:3
GOD, I look to you for **h.** .... Ps 141:8
they will **h** you understand wise................ Pr 1:2
wisdom will **h** you be good and .... Pr 2:20
do good to people who need **h.** .... Pr 3:27
be so hurt no one can **h** them. .... Pr 6:15
from them will **h** you have life. .... Pr 6:23
h kings to govern and rulers to .... Pr 8:15
words will **h** many others, ... Pr 10:21
Riches will not **h** when it's time .... Pr 11:4
those who **h** others will .... Pr 11:25
people will **h** get you in to see .... Pr 18:16
If you **h** them out once, you will .... Pr 19:19
they cry for **h** will also cry for .... Pr 21:13
will also cry for **h** and not be .... Pr 21:13
friend can be trusted to **h** you, ... Pr 27:6
your family for **h** when trouble .... Pr 27:10
Don't **h** those who are guilty of .... Pr 28:17
No one can **h** another person see .... Ec 3:22
down, the other can **h** him up. .... Ec 4:10
because no one is there to **h.** .... Ec 4:10
friends they have to **h** spend it. .... Ec 5:11
They both **h** those who are alive. .... Ec 7:11
money: they both **h.** But wisdom .... Ec 7:12
these joys will **h** them do the .... Ec 8:15
who hurt others. **H** the orphans................ Is 1:17
they aren't able to **h** you. .... Is 2:22
say, "I cannot **h** you, because I .... Is 3:7
will wait for the LORD to **h** us, ... Is 8:17
should ask their God for **h.** .... Is 8:19
Where will you run for **h?** .... Is 10:3
They say: "**H** us. Tell us what to .... Is 16:3
can do; no one there can **h.**..................... Is 19:15
people cry to the LORD for **h,**.................. Is 19:20
to Cush for **h** will be afraid, ... Is 20:5

We trusted them to **h** us. .... Is 20:6
with death will not **h** you. .... Is 28:18
but they don't ask me to **h** them. .... Is 30:1
to Egypt for **h** without asking me ..... Is 30:2
It will give no **h** and will be of .... Is 30:5
to a nation that cannot **h** them, ... Is 30:6
to Egypt whose **h** is useless. .... Is 30:7
on cruelty and lies to **h** you. .... Is 30:12
waits for his **h** will be happy. .... Is 30:18
he hears you, he will **h** you. .... Is 30:19
who go down to Egypt for **h**. .... Is 31:1
Israel, or ask the LORD for **h**. .... Is 31:1
those who try to **h** evil people. .... Is 31:2
people who wanted **h** will fall. .... Is 31:3
will look to the king for **h,** .... Is 32:3
We have waited for your **h.** .... Is 33:2
trusting for **h** so that you turn .... Is 36:5
are depending on Egypt to **h** you, ... Is 36:6
lean on it for **h,** it will stab .... Is 36:6
I have troubles. Please **h** me." .... Is 38:14
die don't trust you to **h** them. .... Is 38:18
his children that you provide **h.** .... Is 38:19
did he ask for **h**? Who taught him .... Is 40:14
The workers **h** each other and say .... Is 41:6
make you strong and will **h** you; .... Is 41:10
Don't be afraid. I will **h** you.' .... Is 41:13
I myself will **h** you," says the .... Is 41:14
You will **h** the blind to see. .... Is 42:7
mother's body, who will **h** you: .... Is 44:2
hand and will **h** you defeat .... Is 45:1
with the LORD's **h,** the people .... Is 45:25
Maybe they will **h** you; maybe you .... Is 47:12
they will not be able to **h** you. .... Is 47:15
day of salvation I will **h** you. .... Is 49:8
wait for my power to **h** them. .... Is 51:5
you cry out for **h,** let the gods .... Is 57:13
gods you have gathered **h** you. .... Is 57:13
don't refuse to **h** your own .... Is 58:7
hear you when you ask him for **h.** .... Is 59:1
not find anyone to **h** the people, ... Is 59:16
that there was no one to **h.** .... Is 59:16
and to **h** the sorrowing people of .... Is 61:3
but I saw no one to **h** me. .... Is 63:5
h those who enjoy doing good, ... Is 64:5
you or even asks you to **h** us. .... Is 64:7
who were not asking me for **h.** .... Is 65:1
and I will **h** them while they are .... Is 65:24
they are still asking for **h.** .... Is 65:24
It did not **h** to go to Egypt and .... Je 2:18
did not **h** to go to Assyria and .... Je 2:18
your people, but it did not **h.** .... Je 2:30
of the orphan or **h** the poor be .... Je 5:28
for them or beg me to **h** them, ... Je 7:16
and they can't **h** you either." .... Je 10:5
They will cry to me for **h,** .... Je 11:11
not be able to **h** when disaster .... Je 11:12
something to **h** us for the good .... Je 14:7
so don't leave us without **h!** .... Je 14:9
I will not **h** you or show you .... Je 16:13
idols that didn't **h** them. .... Je 16:19
not see me coming to **h** them; .... Je 18:17
for this city and not to **h** it, ... Je 21:10
They can't **h** the people of Judah .... Je 23:32
sword found **h** in the desert. .... Je 31:2
when I will **h** the families .... Je 31:27
will ask the LORD to **h** them. .... Je 36:7
of Judah sent you to seek my **h.** .... Je 37:7
of Egypt came here to **h** you, ... Je 37:7
in that country will cry for **h;** .... Je 47:2
will not **h** their children .... Je 47:3
they will be too weak to **h.** .... Je 47:3
alive who could **h** the cities of .... Je 47:4
little children will cry for **h.** .... Je 48:4

ashamed when there was no **h.** .... Je 48:13
and no one will **h** her get up. .... Je 50:32
will work hard, but it won't **h;** .... Je 51:58
and there was no one to **h** her. .... La 1:7
and beg for **h,** but he ignores .... La 3:8
me stray and left me without **h.** .... La 3:11
no hands reached out to **h** her. .... La 4:6
looking for **h** that never came. .... La 4:17
I allow them to ask me for **h?** .... Eze 14:3
as the one who asks him for **h;** .... Eze 14:10
did not **h** the poor and needy. .... Eze 16:49
people will not **h** the king of .... Eze 17:17
to the idols of Israel for **h.** .... Eze 18:6
He looks to idols for **h.** .... Eze 18:12
to the idols of Israel for **h.** .... Eze 18:15
other nations to **h** them fight .... Eze 21:23
tried to lean on you for **h,** .... Eze 29:6
sin in turning to Egypt for **h.** .... Eze 29:16
and the nations which **h** him: ' .... Eze 32:21
your idols for **h,** and you murder .... Eze 33:25
do something to **h** my holy name, ... Eze 36:22
inside you and **h** you live by my .... Eze 36:27
They must **h** my people know what .... Eze 44:23
them mercy and **h** them understand .... Da 2:18
family came to me for **h** again. .... Da 4:36
praying and asking God for **h.** .... Da 6:11
and prayed and asked him for **h.** .... Da 9:3
Listen to my prayer for **h,** .... Da 9:17
wisdom and to **h** you understand. .... Da 9:22
angels, came to **h** me, because I .... Da 10:13
plans will not succeed or **h** him. .... Da 11:17
who are wise will **h** the others .... Da 11:33
will get a little **h,** but many .... Da 11:34
ones will not **h** them in their .... Da 11:34
cities with the **h** of a foreign .... Da 11:39
come, and no one will **h** him. .... Da 11:45
went to Assyria for **h** and sent .... Hos 5:13
look to him for **h** in all this. .... Hos 7:10
First they call to Egypt for **h.** .... Hos 7:11
I am calling to you for **h,** .... Joe 1:19
Wild animals also need your **h.** .... Joe 1:20
there is no one to **h** her up." .... Am 5:2
Israelites come to you for **h.** .... Am 6:1
will be false to the kings .... Mic 1:14
I will look to the LORD for **h.** .... Mic 7:7
must I ask for **h** and you ignore .... Hab 1:2
expects his own work to **h** him, ... Hab 2:18
'The LORD won't **h** us or punish us. .... Zph 1:12
ask the LORD All-Powerful for **h.** .... Zch 8:21
and to pray to the LORD for **h.**" .... Zch 8:22
Elijah will **h** parents love their .... Mal 4:6
came to him, begging for **h.** .... Mt 8:5
a few workers to **h** harvest them. .... Mt 9:37
powers freely, so **h** other people .... Mt 10:8
you will **h** it out of the ditch. .... Mt 12:11
something I could use to **h** you, ... Mt 15:5
him and said, "Lord, **h** me!" .... Mt 15:25
are unwilling to **h** those who .... Mt 23:4
time short to **h** the people he .... Mt 24:22
see these things and not **h** you?' .... Mt 25:44
from Galilee to **h** him were .... Mt 27:55
day was made to **h** people; .... Mk 2:27
something I could use to **h** you, ... Mk 7:11
have pity on us and **h** us." .... Mk 9:22
I do believe! **H** me to believe .... Mk 9:24
time short to **h** the people he .... Mk 13:20
and you can **h** them anytime you .... Mk 14:7
to **h** you know that what you have .... Lk 1:4
He will **h** many people of Israel .... Lk 1:16
he has come to **h** his people and .... Lk 1:68
and they asked Jesus to **h** her. .... Lk 4:38
other boat to come and **h** them. .... Lk 5:7
officer is worthy of your **h.** .... Lk 7:4

God has come to **h** his people." .... Lk 7:16
own money to **h** Jesus and his .... Lk 8:3
workers to **h** gather his harvest. .... Lk 10:2
all the work? Tell her to **h** me." .... Lk 10:40
the judge refused to **h** her. .... Lk 18:4
God will **h** his people quickly. .... Lk 18:8
H your brothers be stronger when .... Lk 22:32
there is no one to **h** me get into .... Jn 5:7
there is no light to **h** him see." .... Jn 11:10
with the **h** of the Holy Spirit, ... Ac 1:2
with the **h** of those who don't .... Ac 2:23
Lord, **h** us, your servants, to .... Ac 4:29
with the **h** of the angel that .... Ac 7:35
spoke with the **h** of the Holy .... Ac 11:28
all decided to **h** the believers .... Ac 11:29
John Mark was with them to **h**. .... Ac 13:5
alive may ask the Lord for **h,** .... Ac 15:17
"Come over to Macedonia and **h** us." .... Ac 16:9
does not need any **h** from them; .... Ac 17:25
back anything that would **h** you. .... Ac 20:20
work as I did and **h** the weak. .... Ac 20:35
"People of Israel, **h** us! .... Ac 21:28
made right through your wise **h.** .... Ac 24:2
I want us to **h** each other with .... Rm 1:12
Your faith will **h** me, and my .... Rm 1:12
me, and my faith will **h** you. .... Rm 1:12
so that I could **h** you grow .... Rm 1:13
no one who looks to God for **h.** .... Rm 3:11
we were unable to **h** ourselves, ... Rm 5:6
use the Spirit's **h** to stop doing .... Rm 8:13
I wish I could **h** my Jewish .... Rm 9:3
Christ if that would **h** them. .... Rm 9:3
people can ask the Lord for **h,** .... Rm 10:14
who were not asking me for **h.** .... Rm 10:20
h some of them to be saved. .... Rm 11:14
happened to **h** you who are not .... Rm 11:28
with God's people who need **h.** .... Rm 12:13
ruler is God's servant to **h** you. .... Rm 13:4
in faith should **h** the weak with .... Rm 15:1
to **h** them be stronger in faith. .... Rm 15:2
I hope you can **h** me on my trip. .... Rm 15:24
to Jerusalem to **h** God's people. .... Rm 15:25
their money to **h** the poor among .... Rm 15:26
possessions to **h** the Jews. .... Rm 15:27
I beg you to **h** me in my work by .... Rm 15:30
Judea and that this **h** I bring to .... Rm 15:31
H her with anything she needs, ... Rm 16:2
He will **h** you remember my way of 1Co 4:17
I am saying this to **h** you, ... 1Co 7:35
but not all things **h** others grow 1Co 10:23
with the **h** of God's Spirit 1Co 12:3
without the **h** of the Holy 1Co 12:3
those who can **h** others, those 1Co 12:28
will it **h** you if I come to you 1Co 14:6
will **h** you only if I bring you 1Co 14:6
the gifts that **h** the church grow 1Co 14:12
should be to **h** the church grow 1Co 14:26
Then you can **h** me on my trip, ... 1Co 16:6
but **h** him on his trip in peace 1Co 16:11
And you can **h** us with your 2Co 1:11
wanted to get **h** from you for my 2Co 1:16
we try to **h** people accept the 2Co 5:11
asked Titus to **h** you finish this 2Co 8:6
wanting to **h,** and in the love 2Co 8:7
others that really want to **h.** 2Co 8:8
you have can **h** others who are 2Co 8:14
they can **h** you when you are in 2Co 8:14
show that we really want to **h.** 2Co 8:19
who is always ready to **h.** 2Co 8:22
and he wants to **h** even more now, ... 2Co 8:22
who is working with me to **h** you. 2Co 8:23
about this **h** for God's people. 2Co 9:1
know you want to **h.** I have been 2Co 9:2

you will **h** our work to grow much 2Co 10:15
get advice or **h** from any person. .... Gal 1:16
was to remember to **h** the poor— .... Gal 2:10
and gently **h** make him right .... Gal 6:1
the opportunity to **h** anyone, ... Gal 6:10
words that will **h** others become .... Eph 4:29
of peace to **h** you stand strong. .... Eph 6:15
God for the **h** you gave me while .... Php 1:5
h you gave from the first day .... Php 1:5
Christ because they want to **h.** .... Php 1:15
stay with you to **h** you grow and .... Php 1:25
in you to **h** you want to do .... Php 2:13
the Lord will **h** me to come to .... Php 2:24
When I needed **h,** you sent him to .... Php 2:25
to give me the **h** you could not .... Php 2:30
it will **h** you to be more ready. .... Php 3:1
friend, to **h** these women. .... Php 4:3
the only church that gave me **h.** .... Php 4:15
h in preaching that Good News. .... Col 1:23
were with you in order to **h** you. 1Th 1:5
who are afraid. **h** those who are 1Th 5:14
our God to **h** you live the kind 2Th 1:11
power God will **h** you do the good 2Th 1:11
the right to ask you to **h** us, ... 2Th 3:9
they do not **h** God's work, which 1Ti 1:4
pray night and day for God's **h.** 1Ti 5:5
a little wine to **h** your stomach 1Ti 5:23
it with the **h** of the Holy Spirit 2Ti 1:14
It does not **h** anyone, and it 2Ti 2:14
he can **h** me in my work here. 2Ti 4:11
I was sent to **h** the faith of .... Tit 1:1
people and to **h** them know the .... Tit 1:1
overseers can **h** people by using .... Tit 1:9
are good and will **h** everyone. .... Tit 3:8
nothing and will not **h** anyone. .... Tit 3:9
all you can to **h** Zenas the .... Tit 3:13
place he might **h** me while I am .... Phm 1:13
and are sent to **h** those who will .... Heb 1:14
And now he can **h** those who are .... Heb 2:18
H each other so none of you .... Heb 3:13
they heard did not **h** them, ... Heb 4:2
and grace to **h** us when we need .... Heb 4:16
to God and asked God for **h.** .... Heb 5:7
lives, asking God to **h** them. .... Heb 7:25
is there now before God to **h** us. .... Heb 9:24
each other and **h** each other to .... Heb 10:24
But God disciplines us to **h** us, ... Heb 12:10
which do not **h** those who obey .... Heb 13:9
It will not **h** you to make their .... Heb 13:17
anger will not **h** you live the .... Jam 1:20
orphans or widows who need **h,** .... Jam 1:27
always ready to **h** those who are .... Jam 3:17
things with the **h** of the Holy 1Pe 1:12
letter with the **h** of Silas, ... 1Pe 5:12
they will **h** you to be useful and 2Pe 1:8
I will always **h** you remember. 2Pe 1:12
right for me to **h** you remember 2Pe 1:13
written you to **h** your honest 2Pe 3:1
sister in need, but does not **h.** 1Jn 3:17
is good that you **h** the brothers 3Jn 1:5
Please **h** them to continue their 3Jn 1:6
So we should **h** such people; 3Jn 1:8
strong and can **h** you not to fall .... Jud 1:24

HELPED

h you to defeat your enemies. .... Ge 14:20
LORD your God **h** me to find it." .... Ge 27:20
who has **h** me during my time of .... Ge 35:3
h the Israelite women give birth .... Ex 1:15
of the tribe of Dan **h** him. .... Ex 38:23
Rahab had **h** the men he had .... Jos 6:25
LORD has **h** you to defeat your .... Jdg 3:28
leaders of Shechem had **h** him. .... Jdg 9:24

the LORD **h** you defeat your .... Jdg 11:36
I am glad because you have **h** me! 1Sa 2:1
the women who **h** her said,...................... 1Sa 4:20
"The LORD has **h** us to this point." 1Sa 7:12
he has done has **h** you greatly. 1Sa 19:4
The LORD has always **h** you, ... 1Ki 1:37
because you **h** carry the Ark of 1Ki 2:26
because Hiram had **h** with the 1Ki 9:11
No one who had **h** Ahab was left 2Ki 10:11
mercy on them and **h** them because 2Ki 13:23
he **h** them because they trusted 1Ch 5:20
killed because God **h** the people 1Ch 5:22
they came they **h** the gatekeepers 1Ch 9:25
warriors who **h** make David's................. 1Ch 11:10
warriors who **h** David in battle. 1Ch 12:1
and they **h** David fight against 1Ch 12:21
Because God **h** the Levites who 1Ch 15:26
And they **h** their relatives, ... 1Ch 23:32
He **h** me understand everything in 1Ch 28:19
Help me as you **h** my father David 2Ch 2:3
shouting, and the LORD **h** him. 2Ch 18:31
God **h** Uzziah fight the 2Ch 26:7
of the kings of Aram **h** them. 2Ch 28:23
Levites **h** them until the work................ 2Ch 29:34
Shecaniah **h** Kore in the towns 2Ch 31:15
and commanders **h** Hezekiah. 2Ch 32:3
All their neighbors **h** them,..................... Ezr 1:6
so that he **h** them in the work................. Ezr 6:22
Our God **h** us and protected us .... Ezr 8:31
The Levites **h** calm the people, ... Ne 8:11
king's officers **h** the Jewish .... Est 9:3
Who has **h** you say these words? .... Job 26:4
anger; you have **h** me. Do not .... Ps 27:9
you **h** me even on the day of my............. Ps 71:6
have **h** me and comforted me................. Ps 86:17
LORD had not **h** me, I would have .... Ps 94:17
They stumbled, and no one **h**................. Ps 107:12
defeated, but the LORD **h** me................. Ps 118:13
are those who are **h** by the God .... Ps 146:5
others will themselves be **h**. .... Pr 11:25
My wisdom **h** me in all this. .... Ec 2:9
my children and **h** them grow up, ... Is 1:2
no one among the nations **h** me............... Is 63:3
but you will not be **h** by them, ... Je 2:37
He **h** those who were poor and .... Je 22:16
But these Levites **h** the people .... Eze 44:12
him shade and **h** him to be more .... Jnh 4:6
have **h** that person to be your .... Mt 18:15
would not have **h** them kill the .... Mt 23:30
took her hand, and **h** her up. .... Mk 1:31
hand and **h** him to stand up. .... Mk 9:27
Jesus in Galilee and **h** him...................... Mk 15:41
to people, and the Lord **h** them. .... Mk 16:20
He has **h** his servant, the people............. Lk 1:54
followers of Saul **h** him leave .... Ac 9:25
gave her his hand and **h** her up. .... Ac 9:41
But Peter **h** him up, saying,..................... Ac 10:26
The church **h** them leave on the .... Ac 15:3
to their home and **h** him better .... Ac 18:26
So the believers **h** him and wrote .... Ac 18:27
arrived, he **h** them very much. .... Ac 18:27
But God has **h** me, and so I stand .... Ac 26:22
as I have **h** the other non-Jewish .... Rm 1:13
because she has **h** me and many .... Rm 16:2
of God who **h** you believe. 1Co 3:5
that the whole church can be **h**. 1Co 14:5
but the other person is not **h**. 1Co 14:17
the day of salvation I **h** you." 2Co 6:2
to me has **h** to spread the Good .... Php 1:12
good that you **h** me when I needed.......... Php 4:14
But our God **h** us to be brave and 1Th 2:2
who has often **h** me and was not 2Ti 1:16
many ways he **h** me in Ephesus............... 2Ti 1:18

I defended myself, no one **h** me;............. 2Ti 4:16
h the prisoners. You even had................. Heb 10:34
into her home and **h** them escape .... Jam 2:25
But the earth **h** the woman by .... Rev 12:16

HELPER
make a **h** who is right for him. .... Ge 2:18
did not find a **h** that was right .... Ge 2:20
Moses and his **h** Joshua set out, ... Ex 24:13
but Moses' young **h**, Joshua son .... Ex 33:11
your shield and **h**, your glorious.............. Dt 33:29
Elijah and became his **h**....................... 1Ki 19:21
There was Heman's **h** Asaph, ... 1Ch 6:39
every man and his **h** stay inside .... Ne 4:22
Sanballat sent his **h** to me with .... Ne 6:5
the son of Mattaniah, their **h**. .... Ne 13:13
You are my **h** and savior. .... Ps 40:17
is your **h** and your protection. .... Ps 115:9
is your **h** and your protection. .... Ps 115:10
is your **h** and your protection. .... Ps 115:11
as a hired **h** would count time. .... Is 16:14
a year as a hired **h** counts time. .... Is 21:16
Who will be your **h** then? .... Hos 13:9
you lost your **h**, so that you are .... Mic 4:9
give you another **H** to be with .... Jn 14:16
But the **H** will teach you .... Jn 14:26
This **H** is the Holy Spirit whom .... Jn 14:26
send you the **H** from the Father;............. Jn 15:26
away, I will send the **H** to you. .... Jn 16:7
go away, the **H** will not come................. Jn 16:7
When the **H** comes, he will prove .... Jn 16:8
the **H** will prove to them that .... Jn 16:11
a **h** in the church in Cenchrea. .... Rm 16:1
because the Lord is my **h**. .... Heb 13:6
we have a **h** in the presence of 1Jn 2:1

HELPERS
family were the **h** of Heman and 1Ch 6:44
The governors' **h** before me also .... Ne 5:15
Even the **h** of the monster Rahab .... Job 9:13
the king—his **h** and all his army— .... Eze 12:14
two of his **h**, ahead to Macedonia .... Ac 19:22
of the seven **h**, and stayed with .... Ac 21:8

HELPING
When you are **h** the Hebrew women .... Ex 1:16
there was no foreign god **h** him............... Dt 32:12
But now with the LORD **h** me, ... Jos 14:12
The LORD bless you for **h** me. 1Sa 23:21
rulers **h** him were getting 1Ki 20:16
had the job of **h** Aaron's 1Ch 23:28
of God were there, **h** them. .... Ezr 5:2
the LORD his God was **h** him. .... Ezr 7:6
month, because God was **h** him............... Ezr 7:9
the LORD my God was **h** me, ... Ezr 7:28
Our God was **h** us, so Iddo's .... Ezr 8:18
mercy on me by **h** me obey your............. Ps 119:29
Give me your **h** hand, because I .... Ps 119:173
hold yourself back from **h** us,................. Is 64:12
aside without **h** while strangers .... Ob 1:11
You are not **h** me! You don't care .... Mt 16:23
the Spirit was **h** him to speak................. Ac 6:10
The Lord was **h** the believers,................. Ac 11:21
Jesus stronger and **h** them stay .... Ac 14:22
languages are **h** only themselves, ... 1Co 14:4
prophesy are **h** the whole church. 1Co 14:4
they are **h** us gain an eternal 2Co 4:17
By **h** each other with your .... Gal 6:2
Spirit of Jesus Christ is **h** me,................. Php 1:19
God's people, **h** those in trouble 1Ti 5:10
because they are **h** believers 1Ti 6:2
showed for him by **h** his people............... Heb 6:10
that you are still **h** them......................... Heb 6:10

H

HELPLESS

You are no help to the **h**!	Job 26:2
they watch in secret for the **h**.	Ps 10:8
Because of the moans of the **h**,	Ps 12:5
bows to kill the poor and **h**,	Ps 37:14
good people left **h** or their	Ps 37:25
I am poor and **h**, please remember	Ps 40:17
I am poor and **h**; God, hurry to	Ps 70:5
Let the poor and **h** praise you.	Ps 74:21
to us soon, because we are **h**!	Ps 79:8
Save the weak and **h**;	Ps 82:4
and answer me. I am poor and **h**.	Ps 86:1
from your terrors, and I am **h**.	Ps 88:15
I am poor and **h** and very sad.	Ps 109:22
He defends the **h** and saves them	Ps 109:31
and takes the **h** from the ashes.	Ps 113:7
when I was **h**, he saved me.	Ps 116:6
to my cry, because I am **h**.	Ps 142:6
you protect the **h** when they are	Is 25:4
that army and are **h** from fear.	Je 6:24
and he became **h** with fear.	Je 50:43
like a dead person, and I was **h**.	Da 10:8
I saw in the vision. I feel **h**.	Da 10:16
who walk on **h** people, you who	Am 8:4
because they were hurting and **h**,	Mt 9:36

HELPS

Your father's God **h** you.	Ge 49:25
covering that **h** in making	Ex 28:29
After the Lord **h** us take the	Nu 32:22
He **h** orphans and widows, and he	Dt 10:18
Ammonites and the Lord **h** me win,	Jdg 11:9
he **h** me stand on the steep	2Sa 22:34
you, because your God **h** you."	1Ch 12:18
Our God **h** everyone who obeys	Ezr 8:22
to destroy me, and no one **h** me.	Job 30:13
good you do only **h** other human	Job 35:8
are the one who **h** the orphans.	Ps 10:14
he **h** me stand on the steep	Ps 18:33
I know the Lord **h** his appointed	Ps 20:6
I trust him, and he **h** me.	Ps 28:7
The Lord **h** them and saves them;	Ps 37:40
He always **h** in times of trouble.	Ps 46:1
our Savior, who **h** us every day.	Ps 68:19
He **h** me keep my people under	Ps 144:2
The Lord **h** those who have been	Ps 145:14
and that **h** them be better	Pr 16:23
The workers' hunger **h** them,	Pr 16:26
and a brother **h** in time of	Pr 17:17
the poor and **h** the needy.	Pr 31:20
and the one who **h** will stumble,	Is 31:3
The Lord God **h** me learn, and I	Is 50:5
The Lord God **h** me, so I will not	Is 50:7
It is the Lord God who **h** me.	Is 50:9
who **h** the people who trust you.	Is 64:4
the friend who **h** the bridegroom	Jn 3:29
the Spirit **h** us with our	Rm 8:26
because the Lord **h** him do well.	Rm 14:4
makes peace and **h** one another.	Rm 14:19
This **h** you to accept patiently	2Co 1:6
you do not only **h** the needs of	2Co 9:12
a special work to do that **h** you,	Col 1:25
us for God and **h** us tell people	1Th 3:2
your body **h** you in some ways,	1Ti 4:8
but serving God **h** you in every	1Ti 4:8
it is not angels that Jesus **h**,	Heb 2:16
someone **h** that person come back,	Jam 5:19

HEMAN

as well as **H**, Calcol, and Darda—	1Ki 4:31
Zimri, Ethan, **H**, Calcol, and	1Ch 2:6
family there was **H** the singer.	1Ch 6:33
the singer. **H** was Joel's son.	1Ch 6:33
were the helpers of **H** and Asaph,	1Ch 6:44

appointed **H** and his relatives	1Ch 15:17
and Ethan. **H** was Joel's son.	1Ch 15:17
The singers **H**, Asaph, and Ethan	1Ch 15:19
With them were **H** and Jeduthun	1Ch 16:41
H and Jeduthun also had the job	1Ch 16:42
sons of Asaph, **H**, and Jeduthun	1Ch 25:1
were sons of **H**, David's seer.	1Ch 25:5
God promised to make **H** strong,	1Ch 25:5
strong, so **H** had many sons.	1Ch 25:5
H directed all his sons in	1Ch 25:6
of Asaph, Jeduthun, and **H**.	1Ch 25:6
musicians—Asaph, **H**, Jeduthun,	2Ch 5:12
David, Asaph, **H**, and Jeduthun,	2Ch 35:15
A maskil of **H** the Ezrahite.	Ps 87:7

HEMAN'S

There was **H** helper Asaph, whose	1Ch 6:39
group stood by **H** right side.	1Ch 6:39
and they stood by **H** left side.	1Ch 6:44
H sons who served were Bukkiah,	1Ch 25:4
From **H** family there were Jehiel	2Ch 29:14

HEMDAN

The sons of Dishon were **H**,	Ge 36:26
sons were **H**, Eshban, Ithran,	1Ch 1:41

HEN

your people as a **h** gathers her	Mt 23:37
your people as a **h** gathers her	Lk 13:34

HENA

of Sepharvaim, **H**, and Ivvah?	2Ki 18:34
of Sepharvaim, **H**, and Ivvah?"	2Ki 19:13
of Sepharvaim, **H**, and Ivvah?"	Is 37:13

HENADAD

and the sons of **H** and their sons	Ezr 3:9
son of **H** and his relatives	Ne 3:18
Binnui son of **H** repaired the	Ne 3:24
of the sons of **H**, Kadmiel,	Ne 10:9

HEPHER

from **H** came the Hepherite family	Nu 26:32
Zelophehad son of **H** had no sons;	Nu 26:33
Zelophehad was the son of **H**,	Nu 27:1
Tappuah, **H**,	Jos 12:17
Asriel, Shechem, **H**, and Shemida.	Jos 17:2
Zelophehad was the son of **H**,	Jos 17:3
to Gath and Eth Kazin,	Jos 19:13
Socoh, and all the land of **H**.	1Ki 4:10
the prophet from Gath **H**.	2Ki 14:25
Naarah were Ahuzzam, **H**, Temeni,	1Ch 4:6
H the Mekerathite; Ahijah the	1Ch 11:36

HEPHERITE

Hepher came the **H** family group.	Nu 26:32

HEPHZIBAH

His mother's name was **H**.	2Ki 21:1

HERBS

it with bitter **h** and bread made	Ex 12:8
with bitter **h** and bread made	Nu 9:11

HERD

Abraham ran to his **h** and took	Ge 18:7
keep some space between each **h**."	Ge 32:16
an animal from the **h** or flock.	Le 1:2
whole burnt offering from the **h**,	Le 1:3
to the Lord is from the **h**,	Le 3:1
be from the **h** or from the flock	Le 22:21
from a person's **h** or flock,	Le 27:32
your flock or **h** at the place	Dt 16:2
or animal, **h** or flock, will be	Jnh 3:7
was a large **h** of pigs feeding.	Mt 8:30
send us into that **h** of pigs."	Mt 8:31
Then the whole **h** rushed down the	Mt 8:32
A large **h** of pigs was feeding on	Mk 5:11
Then the **h** of pigs—about two	Mk 5:13

A large **h** of pigs was feeding on .... Lk 8:32
and the **h** ran down the hill into .... Lk 8:33

HERDS

also had flocks, **h**, and tents. .... Ge 13:5
flocks of sheep, **h** of cattle, ... Ge 24:35
and flocks and **h** that the .... Ge 26:14
all the flocks, **h**, and camels .... Ge 32:7
I saw many **h** as I was coming .... Ge 33:8
took the flocks, **h**, and donkeys, ... Ge 34:28
with him, his **h** and other .... Ge 36:6
because they had too many **h**. .... Ge 36:7
your flocks and **h**, and all that .... Ge 45:10
and their **h** and everything .... Ge 46:32
flocks and **h** and everything .... Ge 47:1
their **h** in the land of Goshen.................. Ge 50:8
our flocks and **h**, because we are .... Ex 10:9
leave your flocks and **h** here." .... Ex 10:24
your flocks and **h** as you leave .... Ex 12:32
the flocks or **h** may eat grass .... Ex 34:3
is born in your flocks and **h**. .... Ex 34:19
we killed all the flocks and **h**,.............. Nu 11:22
may be from your **h** or flocks, ... Nu 15:3
all their flocks, **h**, and goods. .... Nu 31:9
and Gad had large flocks and **h**............ Nu 32:1
He will bless your **h** with calves .... Dt 7:13
your **h** and flocks grow large .... Dt 8:13
born to your **h** and flocks. .... Dt 12:6
born to your **h** or flocks; .... Dt 12:17
animals from your **h** and flocks,............. Dt 12:21
born first to your **h** and flocks. .... Dt 14:23
born to your **h** and flocks. .... Dt 15:19
your **h** will be blessed with .... Dt 28:4
calves of your **h** and the lambs .... Dt 28:18
from your **h** and the harvest .... Dt 28:51
calves from your **h** or lambs from .... Dt 28:51
was in charge of the **h** that fed 1Ch 27:29
charge of the **h** in the valleys............... 1Ch 27:29
many flocks and **h**, because God 2Ch 32:29
firstborn of our **h** and flocks, ... Ne 10:36
His flocks and **h** are so large .... Job 1:10
I had large **h** and flocks, more .... Ec 2:7
H of camels will cover your land, ... Is 60:6
will be a place for **h** to rest. .... Is 65:10
their flocks and **h**, their sons .... Je 3:24
They will eat your flocks and **h**. .... Je 5:17
and their large **h** of cattle as .... Je 49:32
bringing their flocks and **h**, ... Hos 5:6
The **h** of cattle wander around .... Joe 1:18
and **h** will lie down there, ... Zph 2:14

HERDSMEN

so Abram's **h** and Lot's herdsmen .... Ge 13:7
and Lot's **h** began to argue. .... Ge 13:7
or between your **h** and mine, ... Ge 13:8
But the **h** of Gerar argued with .... Ge 26:20
The **h** ran away and went into .... Mt 8:33
The **h** ran away and went to the .... Mk 5:14
the **h** saw what had happened, ... Lk 8:34

HERE'S

the people, "**H** what the LORD, ... Jos 24:2

HERES

determined to stay in Mount **H**, ... Jdg 1:35
the battle by the Pass of **H**.................... Jdg 8:13

HERESH

were also Bakbakkar, **H**, Galal, ... 1Ch 9:15

HERETH

and went to the forest of **H**. 1Sa 22:5

HERMAS

Hermes, Patrobas, **H**, and all the .... Rm 16:14

HERMES

Barnabas "Zeus" and Paul "**H**," .... Ac 14:12
Phlegon, **H**, Patrobas, Hermas, ... Rm 16:14

HERMOGENES

left me, even Phygelus and **H**.................. 2Ti 1:15

HERMON

the Arnon Ravine to Mount **H**, ... Dt 3:8
H is called Sirion by the .... Dt 3:9
of the Arnon Ravine, to Mount **H**. .... Dt 4:48
lived below Mount **H** in the area .... Jos 11:3
of Lebanon, below Mount **H**. .... Jos 11:17
Ravine to Mount **H** and all the .... Jos 12:1
ruled over Mount **H**, Salecah, and .... Jos 12:5
below Mount **H** to Lebo Hamath. .... Jos 13:5
and all of Mount **H** and Bashan as .... Jos 13:11
Mount Baal **H** to Lebo Hamath. .... Jdg 3:3
of Bashan all the way to Baal **H**, ... 1Ch 5:23
Baal Hermon, Senir, and Mount **H**. 1Ch 5:23
calf and Mount **H** jump like a .... Ps 29:6
the peaks of Mount and Mount Mizar. .... Ps 42:6
Tabor and Mount **H** sing for joy .... Ps 89:12
dew of Mount **H** falling on the .... Ps 133:3
tops of Mount Senir and Mount **H**............ Sng 4:8
of fir trees from Mount **H**. .... Eze 27:5

HEROD

during the time when **H** was king. .... Mt 2:1
When King **H** heard this, he was .... Mt 2:3
H called a meeting of all the .... Mt 2:4
Then **H** had a secret meeting with .... Mt 2:7
in a dream not to go back to **H**, ... Mt 2:12
because **H** is starting to look .... Mt 2:13
stayed in Egypt until **H** died. .... Mt 2:15
When **H** saw that the wise men had .... Mt 2:16
After **H** died, an angel of the .... Mt 2:19
since his father **H** had died. .... Mt 2:22
At that time **H**, the ruler of .... Mt 14:1
this, **H** had arrested John, ... Mt 14:3
H did this because of Herodias, ... Mt 14:3
had been telling **H**, "It is not .... Mt 14:4
H wanted to kill John, but he .... Mt 14:5
danced for **H** and his guests, ... Mt 14:6
so she said to **H**, "Give me the .... Mt 14:8
Although King **H** was very sad, ... Mt 14:9
So **H** ordered that what she asked .... Mt 14:9
H heard about Jesus, because .... Mk 6:14
When **H** heard this, he said, "I .... Mk 6:16
H himself had ordered his .... Mk 6:17
but then **H** had married her. .... Mk 6:17
had been telling **H**, "It is not .... Mk 6:18
because **H** was afraid of John and .... Mk 6:20
she pleased **H** and the people .... Mk 6:22
So King **H** said to the girl, ... Mk 6:22
Pharisees and the yeast of **H**." .... Mk 8:15
During the time **H** ruled Judea, ... Lk 1:5
H, the ruler of Galilee; .... Lk 3:1
spoke against **H**, the governor, ... Lk 3:19
many other evil things **H** did. .... Lk 3:19
So **H** did something even worse: .... Lk 3:20
H, the governor, heard about all .... Lk 9:7
H said, "I cut off John's head, ... Lk 9:9
And **H** kept trying to see Jesus. .... Lk 9:9
away from here! **H** wants to kill .... Lk 13:31
Go tell that fox **H**, 'Today and................ Lk 13:32
Pilate sent Jesus to **H**, who was .... Lk 23:7
When **H** saw Jesus, he was very.............. Lk 23:8
H asked Jesus many questions, ... Lk 23:9
After **H** and his soldiers had .... Lk 23:11
Pilate and **H** had always been.................. Lk 23:12
H found nothing wrong with him; .... Lk 23:15
things really happened when **H**,.............. Ac 4:27
same time King **H** began to .... Ac 12:1
H saw that some of the people .... Ac 12:3

After H arrested Peter, he put .... Ac 12:4
H planned to bring Peter before .... Ac 12:4
night before H was to bring him.............. Ac 12:6
rescued me from H and from all............... Ac 12:11
H looked everywhere for him but .... Ac 12:19
Later H moved from Judea and .... Ac 12:19
H was very angry with the people .... Ac 12:20
side, they asked H for peace, ... Ac 12:20
On a chosen day H put on his.................. Ac 12:21
Because H did not give the glory .... Ac 12:23
had grown up with H, the ruler), ... Ac 13:1

HEROD'S
the wife of Philip, H brother. .... Mt 14:3
On H birthday, the daughter of .... Mt 14:6
wife of Philip, H brother, but .... Mk 6:17
On H birthday, he gave a dinner.............. Mk 6:21
Philip, H brother, the ruler of .... Lk 3:1
the wife of H brother, and .... Lk 3:19
Cuza (the manager of H house); .... Lk 8:3
Jesus was under H authority, ... Lk 23:7
be kept under guard in H palace. .... Ac 23:35

HERODIANS
people from the group called H. .... Mt 22:16
plans with the H about a way to.............. Mk 3:6
Pharisees and H to Jesus to trap .... Mk 12:13

HERODIAS
Herod did this because of H, ... Mt 14:3
for you to be married to H." .... Mt 14:4
the daughter of H danced for .... Mt 14:6
H told her daughter what to ask.............. Mt 14:8
in order to please his wife, H.............. Mk 6:17
So H hated John and wanted to .... Mk 6:19
time came for H to cause John's.............. Mk 6:21
the daughter of H came in and .... Mk 6:22
because of his sin with H, ... Lk 3:19

HERODION
Greetings to H, my fellow .... Rm 16:11

HEROES
These h and all the people of 1Ch 11:10
pool and the House of the H. .... Ne 3:16
the h and great soldiers, the .... Is 3:2
and your h will die in war. .... Is 3:25

HERON
any kind of h, hoopoes, or bats .... Le 11:19
any kind of h, the hoopoes,.................... Dt 14:18

HESHBON
H and all the towns around it. .... Nu 21:25
H was the city where Sihon, ... Nu 21:26
Come to H and rebuild it; .... Nu 21:27
A fire began in H; flames came .... Nu 21:28
their towns from H to Dibon, ... Nu 21:30
Amorite king who lived in H." .... Nu 21:34
Reubenites rebuilt H, Elealeh, ... Nu 32:37
Amorite people and lived in H. .... Dt 1:4
king of H, and I am giving .... Dt 2:24
of Kedemoth to Sihon king of H. .... Dt 2:26
Sihon king of H would not let us .... Dt 2:30
the Amorites, who ruled in H." .... Dt 3:2
the cities of Sihon king of H. .... Dt 3:6
ruled in H and was defeated .... Dt 4:46
Sihon king of H and Og king of .... Dt 29:7
Sihon king of H and Og king of .... Jos 9:10
in the city of H and ruled the .... Jos 12:2
the border of Sihon king of H. .... Jos 12:5
who ruled in the city of H, ... Jos 13:10
H and all the towns on the plain: .... Jos 13:17
had ruled from the town of H. .... Jos 13:21
the area from H to Ramath Mizpah .... Jos 13:26
Sihon king of H had ruled east .... Jos 13:27
H, and Jazer, and the pastures .... Jos 21:39

of the city of H, asking, 'Let .... Jdg 11:19
have lived in H and Aroer and .... Jdg 11:26
Sihon king of H and the country .... Ne 9:22
the pools in H near the gate .... Sng 7:4
in the cities H and Elealeh cry .... Is 15:4
the fields of H and the vines .... Is 16:8
the people of H and Elealeh. .... Is 16:9
in the town of H plan Moab's .... Je 48:2
from H to Elealeh and Jahaz. .... Je 48:34
and have gone to H for safety. .... Je 48:45
But fire started in H; .... Je 48:45
in the town of H, cry sadly .... Je 49:3

HESHMON
Hazar Gaddah, H, Beth Pelet, ... Jos 15:27

HETH
Sidon, his first son, and of H. .... Ge 10:15

HETHLON
will go through H, toward Lebo .... Eze 47:15
sea through H to Lebo Hamath, ... Eze 48:1

HEZEKIAH
and Ahaz's son H became king in 2Ki 16:20
H son of Ahaz king of Judah 2Ki 18:1
H was twenty-five years old when 2Ki 18:2
H did what the LORD said was 2Ki 18:3
But H broke it into pieces. 2Ki 18:4
H trusted in the LORD, the God 2Ki 18:5
H was loyal to the LORD and did 2Ki 18:6
the LORD was with H, so he had 2Ki 18:7
H defeated the Philistines all 2Ki 18:8
in the fourth year H was king. 2Ki 18:9
in the sixth year H was king, ... 2Ki 18:10
Then H king of Judah sent a 2Ki 18:14
of Assyria made H pay about 2Ki 18:14
H gave him all the silver that 2Ki 18:15
H stripped all the gold that.................... 2Ki 18:16
H had put gold on these doors 2Ki 18:16
Lachish to King H in Jerusalem. 2Ki 18:17
said to them, "Tell H this: 2Ki 18:19
but H destroyed the LORD's 2Ki 18:22
H told Judah and Jerusalem, ... 2Ki 18:22
you should not let H fool you,.................. 2Ki 18:29
Don't let H talk you into 2Ki 18:30
Don't listen to H.............................. 2Ki 18:31
Don't listen to H................................ 2Ki 18:32
because King H had ordered, ... 2Ki 18:36
men went to H and told him what 2Ki 18:37
When King H heard the message, ... 2Ki 19:1
H sent Eliakim, the palace 2Ki 19:2
Isaiah, "This is what H says: 2Ki 19:3
he sent messengers to H, saying, ... 2Ki 19:9
Tell H king of Judah: 2Ki 19:10
When H received the letter from 2Ki 19:14
sent a message to H that said, ... 2Ki 19:20
the LORD said, 'H, I will give 2Ki 19:29
At that time H became so sick he 2Ki 20:1
H turned toward the wall and.................. 2Ki 20:2
Then H cried loudly. 2Ki 20:3
back and tell H, the leader of 2Ki 20:5
H had asked Isaiah, "What will 2Ki 20:8
H answered, "It's easy for the 2Ki 20:10
He sent letters and a gift to H, ... 2Ki 20:12
he had heard that H was sick. 2Ki 20:12
H listened to the messengers, ... 2Ki 20:13
went to King H and asked him, ... 2Ki 20:14
H said, "They came from a 2Ki 20:14
H said, "They saw everything in.............. 2Ki 20:15
Then Isaiah said to H, "Listen 2Ki 20:16
H told Isaiah, "These words from 2Ki 20:19
Everything else H did—all his 2Ki 20:20
H died, and his son Manasseh 2Ki 20:21
father, H, had destroyed 2Ki 21:3

Ahaz's son was **H**. Hezekiah's son 1Ch 3:13
to Gedor while **H** was king of 1Ch 4:41
Ahaz's son **H** became king in his 2Ch 28:27
H was twenty-five years old when 2Ch 29:1
H did what the LORD said was 2Ch 29:2
H opened the doors of the Temple 2Ch 29:3
H brought in the priests and 2Ch 29:4
H said, "Listen to me, Levites. 2Ch 29:5
Now I, **H**, have decided to make 2Ch 29:10
they went to King **H** and said, ... 2Ch 29:18
next morning King **H** gathered the 2Ch 29:20
King **H** commanded the priests, ... 2Ch 29:21
King **H** put the Levites in the 2Ch 29:25
Then **H** gave the order to 2Ch 29:27
King **H** and everyone with him 2Ch 29:29
King **H** and his officers ordered 2Ch 29:30
H said, "Now that you people 2Ch 29:31
And **H** and the people were very 2Ch 29:36
King **H** sent messages to all the 2Ch 30:1
H invited all these people to 2Ch 30:1
King **H**, his officers, and all 2Ch 30:2
satisfied King **H** and all the 2Ch 30:4
in obeying King **H** and his 2Ch 30:12
H encouraged all the Levites who 2Ch 30:22
H king of Judah gave one 2Ch 30:24
King **H** appointed groups of 2Ch 31:2
H gave some of his own animals 2Ch 31:3
H commanded the people living in 2Ch 31:4
When **H** and his officers came and 2Ch 31:8
H asked the priests and Levites 2Ch 31:9
family, answered **H**, "Since the 2Ch 31:10
Then **H** commanded the priests to 2Ch 31:11
King **H** and Azariah the officer 2Ch 31:13
is what King **H** did in Judah. 2Ch 31:20
H tried to obey God in his 2Ch 31:21
After **H** did all these things to 2Ch 32:1
H knew that Sennacherib had come 2Ch 32:2
So **H** and his officers and army 2Ch 32:3
and commanders helped **H**. 2Ch 32:3
Then **H** made Jerusalem stronger. 2Ch 32:5
H put army commanders over the 2Ch 32:6
H encouraged them, saying, ... 2Ch 32:6
by the words of **H** king of Judah. 2Ch 32:8
for King **H** of Judah and all 2Ch 32:9
H says to you, 'The LORD our God 2Ch 32:11
H himself removed your LORD's 2Ch 32:12
Do not let **H** fool you or trick 2Ch 32:15
the LORD God and his servant **H**. 2Ch 32:16
King **H** and the prophet Isaiah 2Ch 32:20
the LORD saved **H** and the people 2Ch 32:22
gifts to King **H** of Judah. 2Ch 32:23
on all the nations respected **H**. 2Ch 32:23
At that time **H** became so sick he 2Ch 32:24
But **H** did not thank God for his 2Ch 32:25
But later **H** and the people of 2Ch 32:26
punish them while **H** was alive. 2Ch 32:26
H had many riches and much honor. 2Ch 32:27
God had given **H** much wealth. 2Ch 32:29
It was **H** who cut off the upper 2Ch 32:30
And **H** was successful in 2Ch 32:30
of Babylon sent messengers to **H**, ... 2Ch 32:31
God left **H** alone to test him so 2Ch 32:31
H died and was buried on a hill, ... 2Ch 32:33
honored **H** when he died, ... 2Ch 32:33
father, **H**, had torn down 2Ch 33:3
(through the family of **H**)—98; .... Ezr 2:16
of Ater (through **H**)—98; .... Ne 7:21
Ater, **H**, Azzur, ... Ne 10:17
by the men of **H** king of Judah. .... Pr 25:1
and **H** were kings of Judah. .... Is 1:1
Lachish to King **H** in Jerusalem. .... Is 36:2
said to them, "Tell **H** this: .... Is 36:4
but **H** destroyed the LORD's .... Is 36:7

H told Judah and Jerusalem, ... Is 36:7
you should not let **H** fool you, ... Is 36:14
Don't let **H** talk you into .... Is 36:15
Don't listen to **H**. .... Is 36:16
Don't let **H** fool you, saying, ... Is 36:18
because King **H** had ordered, ... Is 36:21
men went to **H** and told him what .... Is 36:22
When King **H** heard the message, ... Is 37:1
H sent Eliakim, the palace .... Is 37:2
Isaiah, "This is what **H** says: .... Is 37:3
he sent messengers to **H**, saying, ... Is 37:9
Tell **H** king of Judah: .... Is 37:10
When **H** received the letter from .... Is 37:14
sent a message to **H** that said, ... Is 37:21
the LORD said, '**H**, I will give .... Is 37:30
At that time **H** became very sick; .... Is 38:1
H turned toward the wall and .... Is 38:2
Then **H** cried loudly. .... Is 38:3
Go to **H** and tell him: .... Is 38:5
After **H** king of Judah got well, ... Is 38:9
H then asked Isaiah, "What will .... Is 38:22
He sent a message to **H**, ... Is 39:1
had heard that **H** had been sick .... Is 39:1
H was pleased and showed the .... Is 39:2
went to King **H** and asked him, ... Is 39:3
H said, "They came from a .... Is 39:3
H said, "They saw everything in .... Is 39:4
Then Isaiah said to **H**: .... Is 39:5
H told Isaiah, "These words from .... Is 39:8
Manasseh son of **H** was king of .... Je 15:4
during the time **H** was king of .... Je 26:18
H king of Judah and the people .... Je 26:19
You know that **H** feared the LORD .... Je 26:19
and **H** were kings of Judah and .... Hos 1:1
and **H** were kings of Judah, ... Mic 1:1
Amariah, who was the son of **H**. .... Zph 1:1
Ahaz was the father of **H**. .... Mt 1:9
H was the father of Manasseh. .... Mt 1:10

HEZEKIAH'S
H fourteenth year as king, ... 2Ki 18:13
When **H** officers came to Isaiah, ... 2Ki 19:5
made it and put it on **H** boil, ... 2Ki 20:7
H son was Manasseh. 1Ch 3:13
The LORD listened to **H** prayer, ... 2Ch 30:20
In the same way **H** god won't be 2Ch 32:17
everything that was in **H** heart. 2Ch 32:31
H love for God and the other 2Ch 32:32
H fourteenth year as king, ... Is 36:1
When **H** officers came to Isaiah, ... Is 37:5
from figs and put it on **H** boil. .... Is 38:21

HEZION
Tabrimmon, who was the son of **H**. 1Ki 15:18

HEZIR
The seventeenth was **H**. 1Ch 24:15
Magpiash, Meshullam, **H**, ... Ne 10:20

HEZRO
H the Carmelite; Paarai the 2Sa 23:35
H the Carmelite; Naarai son of 1Ch 11:37

HEZRON
Hanoch, Pallu, **H**, and Carmi. .... Ge 46:9
Perez's sons were **H** and Hamul. .... Ge 46:12
Hanoch, Pallu, **H**, and Carmi. .... Ex 6:14
from **H** came the Hezronite family .... Nu 26:6
From **H** came the Hezronite family. .... Nu 26:21
and continued past **H** to Addar. .... Jos 15:3
Hadattah, Kerioth **H** (also called .... Jos 15:25
of Perez, the father of **H**. .... Ru 4:18
H was the father of Ram, who was .... Ru 4:19
Perez's sons were **H** and Hamul. 1Ch 2:5
Caleb son of **H** had children by 1Ch 2:18
when **H** was sixty years old, ... 1Ch 2:21

H had sexual relations with 1Ch 2:21
After H died in Caleb Ephrathah, ... 1Ch 2:24
were Perez, H, Carmi, Hur, and 1Ch 4:1
Hanoch, Pallu, H, and Carmi. 1Ch 5:3
Perez was the father of H. .... Mt 1:3
H was the father of Ram. .... Mt 1:3
Arni was the son of H. .... Lk 3:33
H was the son of Perez. .... Lk 3:33

HEZRON'S

H sons were Jerahmeel, Ram, and 1Ch 2:9
H first son was Jerahmeel. 1Ch 2:25

HEZRONITE

Hezron came the H family group; .... Nu 26:6
Hezron came the H family group; .... Nu 26:21

HID

man and his wife h from the LORD .... Ge 3:8
because I was naked, so I h." .... Ge 3:10
and he h them under the great .... Ge 35:4
she h him for three months. .... Ex 2:2
the Egyptian and h his body in .... Ex 2:12
because Rahab h the two spies we .... Jos 6:17
ran away and h in a cave near .... Jos 10:16
h from Abimelech and escaped. .... Jdg 9:5
the night and h near Shechem in .... Jdg 9:34
three groups and h them in the .... Jdg 9:43
place where you h when this 1Sa 20:19
So David h in the field. 1Sa 20:24
Obadiah h a hundred of them in............ 1Ki 18:4
s prophets, I h a hundred of 1Ki 18:13
to the city and h in a room................... 1Ki 20:30
out of the camp and h them. 2Ki 7:8
from this tent and h them, ... 2Ki 7:8
He h with her in the Temple of 2Ki 11:3
four sons who were with him h. 1Ch 21:20
h Joash so Athaliah could not 2Ch 22:11
He h with them in the Temple of 2Ch 22:12
in your heart you h other plans. .... Job 10:13
The proud h a trap for me. .... Ps 140:5
He h me in the shadow of his .... Is 49:2
He h me in the holder for his .... Is 49:2
very angry and h from you for a............. Is 54:8
to Perath and h the belt there, ... Je 13:5
that they ran away and h. .... Da 10:7
woman took and h in a large tub .... Mt 13:33
and then he h it in the field.................. Mt 13:44
in the ground and h the master's .... Mt 25:18
afraid and went and h your money......... Mt 25:25
woman took and h in a large tub .... Lk 13:21
in a piece of cloth and h...................... Lk 19:20
But Jesus h himself, and then he .... Jn 8:59
he left and h himself from them. .... Jn 12:36
a cloud h him from their sight. .... Ac 1:9
Moses' parents h him for three .... Heb 11:23
the free people h themselves in .... Rev 6:15

HIDDAI

H from the ravines of Gaash; 2Sa 23:30

HIDDEN

Rachel had h the idols inside .... Ge 31:34
might be kept h from her husband .... Nu 5:13
clearly, not with h meanings. .... Nu 12:8
from the treasures h in the sand............ Dt 33:19
But the woman had h the two men. .... Jos 2:4
roof and had h them there under .... Jos 2:6
and found the things h there, ... Jos 7:22
Israelites in the mountains 1Sa 14:22
He has h it from me." 2Ki 4:27
But she had h him." 2Ki 6:29
death more than for h treasure. .... Job 3:21
God has h the road ahead. .... Job 3:23
them, and they have h nothing. .... Job 15:18
for them is h on the ground, ... Job 18:10

But I am not h by the darkness, ... Job 23:17
and bring things h out into the .... Job 28:11
It is h from the eyes of every .... Job 28:21
have not h my sin as others do, ... Job 31:33
bones that were h now stick out. .... Job 33:21
h by the tall grass in the swamp. .... Job 40:21
my cries are not h from you. .... Ps 38:9
will save you from h traps and .... Ps 91:3
I walk, a trap is h for me. .... Ps 142:3
and hunt for it like h treasure. .... Pr 2:4
away and the h riches so you .... Is 45:3
h things that you don't know yet. .... Is 48:6
have h your idols behind your .... Is 57:8
took it from where I had h it. .... Je 13:7
their sin is not h from my eyes. .... Je 16:17
me and have h traps for my feet............. Je 18:22
But the LORD had h them. .... Je 36:26
that we have h in a field." .... Je 41:8
secrets that are deep and h; .... Da 2:22
he knows what is h in darkness,............. Da 2:22
they have done is not h from me. .... Hos 5:3
will find all your h treasures! .... Ob 1:6
is built on a hill cannot be h. .... Mt 5:14
that is h will be shown. .... Mt 10:26
because you have h these things. .... Mt 11:25
is like a treasure h in a field. .... Mt 13:44
that is h will be made clear.................. Mk 4:22
there, but he could not stay h. .... Mk 7:24
that is h will become clear .... Lk 8:17
the meaning was h from them so .... Lk 9:45
because you have h these things............. Lk 10:21
because you are like h graves, ... Lk 11:44
that is h will be shown, ... Lk 12:2
the meaning was h from them, ... Lk 18:34
But now it is h from you. .... Lk 19:42
secret that was h for long ages .... Rm 16:25
wisdom, which he has kept h.................. 1Co 2:7
that are now h in darkness, ... 1Co 4:5
Good News that we preach is h, ... 2Co 4:3
is h only to those who are lost. 2Co 4:3
which has been h in him since .... Eph 3:9
secret that was h from everyone............. Col 1:26
not easily seen cannot stay h................. 1Ti 5:25
all the world can be h from God. .... Heb 4:13
give some of the h manna to .... Rev 2:17
Keep h what the seven thunders............. Rev 10:4

HIDE

and now I must h from you. .... Ge 4:14
our brother and h his death? .... Ge 37:26
with a veil to h who she was. .... Ge 38:14
was not able to h the baby any .... Ex 2:3
H there for three days. .... Jos 2:16
don't try to h anything from me............. Jos 7:19
may go to a city of safety to h. .... Jos 20:3
the night and h in the fields .... Jdg 9:32
Go and h in the vineyards. .... Jdg 21:20
to you? Don't h it from me. May............. 1Sa 3:17
terribly if you h from me 1Sa 3:17
and did not h anything from him. 1Sa 3:18
they went to h in caves and 1Sa 13:6
morning. H in a secret place. 1Sa 19:2
but let me h in the field until 1Sa 20:5
David said, "Do not h the truth. 2Sa 14:18
and go east and h near Kerith 1Ki 17:3
day you go to h in an inside 1Ki 22:25
of the camp to h in the field. 2Ki 7:12
in a bedroom to h him from 2Ki 11:2
day you go to h in an inside 2Ch 18:24
not h their guilt or take away .... Ne 4:5
day. Let a cloud h it. Let thick .... Job 3:5
and did not h trouble from my .... Job 3:10
and then I will not h from you: .... Job 13:20

Don't **h** your face from me;.........................Job 13:24
wish you would **h** me in the grave ....Job 14:13
h me until your anger is gone. ....Job 14:13
and they may **h** it under their ....Job 20:12
poor of the land **h** from them. ....Job 24:4
God and will not **h** the ways of ....Job 27:11
who do evil can **h** from him. ....Job 34:22
in their dens or **h** in the bushes ....Job 38:40
The lotus plants **h** it in their ....Job 40:22
off its outer **h** or poke through ....Job 41:13
Why do you **h** when there is ....Ps 10:1
They **h** near the villages.........................Ps 10:8
How long will you **h** from me? ....Ps 13:1
H me under the shadow of your ....Ps 17:8
He doesn't **h** from them but ....Ps 22:24
with those who **h** their sin. ....Ps 26:4
He will **h** me in his Holy Tent, ...Ps 27:5
to you and didn't **h** my guilt. ....Ps 32:5
I do not **h** your goodness in my ....Ps 40:10
I do not **h** your love and truth.................Ps 40:10
Why do you **h** from us? Have you ....Ps 44:24
hated me. I could **h** from him.................Ps 55:12
They wait. They **h**. They watch my...........Ps 56:6
me **h** under the shadow of your ....Ps 57:1
H me from those who plan wicked............Ps 64:2
I cannot **h** my guilt from you...................Ps 69:5
Do not **h** from me, your servant..............Ps 69:17
reject me? Why do you **h** from me? ....Ps 88:14
and under his wings you can **h**. ....Ps 91:4
Do not **h** from me in my time of ....Ps 102:2
Do not **h** your commands from me. ....Ps 119:19
say, "The darkness will **h** me...................Ps 139:11
me from my enemies; I **h** in you. ....Ps 143:9
Lies can **h** hate, but the evil ....Pr 26:26
If you **h** your sins, you will not ....Pr 28:13
dig holes and **h** in the ground..................Is 2:10
dig holes and **h** in the ground..................Is 2:19
the people will **h** in caves and..................Is 2:21
a safe place to **h** from the storm..............Is 4:6
Where will you **h** your riches ....Is 10:3
H us, because we are running for ....Is 16:3
H us from our enemies." ....Is 16:4
and people will **h** behind closed ....Is 24:10
H in your rooms for a short time ....Is 26:20
and our tricks will **h** us." ....Is 28:15
The lies you **h** behind will be ....Is 28:17
those who try to **h** things from ....Is 29:15
will not continue to **h** from you, ...Is 30:20
in secret or **h** my words in some..............Is 45:19
I won't **h** my face from them when............Is 50:6
They **h** in the thick bushes and ....Je 4:29
H the belt there in a crack in ....Je 13:4
the belt I told you to **h** there.".................Je 13:6
They cannot **h** from me the things ....Je 16:17
can **h** where I cannot see him, ...Je 23:24
no place for the leaders to **h**; ....Je 25:35
You and Jeremiah must go and **h**, ...Je 36:19
Do not **h** anything from me, ...Je 38:14
and not **h** anything from you..................Je 42:4
run away and **h** in deep caves................Je 49:8
will not be able to **h** from me.................Je 49:10
Hazor, find a good place to **h**!" ....Je 49:30
If they **h** at the top of Mount ....Am 9:3
If they try to **h** from me at the ....Am 9:3
time he will **h** his face from ....Mic 3:4
too. You will **h**; you will look ....Nah 3:11
And people don't **h** a light under ....Mt 5:15
Do you **h** a lamp under a bowl or ....Mk 4:21
the woman saw she could not **h**,.............Lk 8:47
known does not **h** what he does. ....Jn 7:4
own evil lives they **h** the truth. ....Rm 1:18
to the parts we want to **h**. 1Co 12:23

no selfishness to **h** from you. 1Th 2:5
H us from the face of the One................Rev 6:16

HIDEOUT
and his men went up to their **h**. 1Sa 24:22
came down toward the mountain **h**. 1Sa 25:20
to you than a **h** for robbers. ....Je 7:11
it into a '**h** for robbers.'" ....Mt 21:13
house into a '**h** for robbers.'" ....Mk 11:17
it into a '**h** for robbers'!" ....Lk 19:46

HIDEOUTS
in the desert **h** and in the hills 1Sa 23:14
He's at the **h** of Horesh, on the 1Sa 23:19
and stayed in the **h** of En Gedi. 1Sa 23:29

HIDES
If he **h** his face, who can see ....Job 34:29
Nothing **h** from its heat. ....Ps 19:6
Whoever **h** hate is a liar. ....Pr 10:18
wicked get control, everybody **h**. ....Pr 28:12
everybody **h**, but when they die ....Pr 28:28
hand, and there he **h** his power. ....Hab 3:4
with a bowl or **h** it under a bed. ....Lk 8:16
same covering **h** the meaning when 2Co 3:14
is a lie that **h** the truth. ....Jam 3:14

HIDING
are alive and **h** from you will ....Dt 7:20
and, after **h** and waiting,......................Dt 19:11
other men were **h** to the west. ....Jos 8:13
out of their **h** place and hurried ....Jos 8:19
found them **h** in the cave at ....Jos 10:17
they had been **h** and covered ....Jos 10:27
the Israelites made **h** places in ....Jdg 6:2
came out of their **h** places. ....Jdg 9:35
Some men were **h** in another room. ....Jdg 16:9
Some men were **h** in another room. ....Jdg 16:12
ran out from their **h** places went............Jdg 20:33
The men in **h** rushed into Gibeah, ...Jdg 20:37
up a signal with the men in **h**. ....Jdg 20:38
He's behind the baggage." 1Sa 10:22
out of the holes they were **h** 1Sa 14:11
in the field where you are **h**, ...1Sa 19:3
here,' you may come out of **h**.................1Sa 20:21
as David was **h** in the stronghold 1Sa 22:4
him, "David is **h** in our land. 1Sa 23:19
Find all the **h** places he uses, ...1Sa 23:23
and his men were **h** far back in 1Sa 24:3
David is **h** on the hill of 1Sa 26:1
probably already **h** in a cave or 2Sa 17:9
go to David wherever he is **h**..................2Sa 17:12
tell that anyone was **h** there...................2Sa 17:19
and tremble in their **h** places..................2Sa 22:46
when David was **h** from Saul son 1Ch 12:1
men caught him **h** in Samaria,................2Ch 22:9
They wait in **h** like a lion. ....Ps 10:9
like lions, they sit in **h**. ....Ps 17:12
and tremble in their **h** places..................Ps 18:45
You are my **h** place. You protect ....Ps 32:7
think David is **h** among our ....Ps 53:6
From their **h** places they shoot ....Ps 64:4
The rocks are **h** places for the ....Ps 104:18
are my **h** place and my shield; ....Ps 119:114
is like a dove **h** in the cracks ....Sng 2:14
the people of Gebim are **h**. ....Is 10:31
But **h** in Egypt will bring you ....Is 30:3
I will find all their **h** places, ...Je 49:10
to attack me, like a lion in **h**. ....La 3:10
People **h** in the strongholds and ....Eze 33:27
forty men are **h** and waiting to ....Ac 23:21

HIEL
H from Bethel rebuilt the city.................1Ki 16:34
It cost **H** the life of Abiram, ...1Ki 16:34

HIERAPOLIS
the people in Laodicea and in **H**. .... Col 4:13

HIGGAION
by what they do. **H**. Selah .... Ps 9:16

HIGHER
and went **h** up the mountain. .... Ex 24:18
Then Balaam went to a **h** place. .... Nu 23:3
wall of Jerusalem and made it **h**. 2Ch 33:14
They are **h** than our heads....................... Ezr 9:6
a new rank that was **h** than all .... Est 3:1
had placed him **h** than his .... Est 5:11
His limits are **h** than the .... Job 11:8
My head is **h** than my enemies .... Ps 27:6
to give you a **h** position than to .... Pr 25:7
is cheated by a **h** officer who in .... Ec 5:8
is cheated by even **h** officers. .... Ec 5:8
heavens are **h** than the earth, ... Is 55:9
so are my ways **h** than your ways .... Is 55:9
and my thoughts **h** than your .... Is 55:9
were wider on each **h** story, ... Eze 41:7
As the sun rose **h** in the sky, ... Jnh 4:8
He ranks **h** than everything that.............. Col 1:15

HIGHEST
that even the **h** mountains under .... Ge 7:19
has made me the **h** officer of the .... Ge 45:8
You have the **h** position among my........... Ge 49:3
even the **h** heavens, are his. .... Dt 10:14
sky and the **h** place in heaven 1Ki 8:27
to the **h** mountains of Lebanon. 2Ki 19:23
Not even the **h** of heavens can 2Ch 2:6
sky and the **h** place in heaven 2Ch 6:18
even the **h** heavens, with all .... Ne 9:6
steps to the **h** part of the wall .... Ne 12:37
king and had the **h** rank in the .... Est 1:14
God is in the **h** part of heaven. .... Job 22:12
See how high the **h** stars are! .... Job 22:12
and the **h** mountains belong to .... Ps 95:4
h heavens and you waters above .... Ps 148:4
out from the **h** place in the city .... Pr 9:3
her house at the **h** place in the .... Pr 9:14
to the **h** mountains of Lebanon. .... Is 37:24
was a priest and the **h** officer .... Je 20:1
she makes her **h** cities strong, ... Je 51:53
story to the **h** through the .... Eze 41:7
person the third **h** ruler in the .... Da 5:7
become the third **h** ruler in the .... Da 5:16
was the third **h** ruler in the .... Da 5:29
and led Jesus to their **h** court.................... Lk 22:66
God raised him to the **h** place. .... Php 2:9
king, who is the **h** authority, ... 1Pe 2:13

HIGHLANDS
and it burned the Arnon **h**. .... Nu 21:28

HIGHWAY
life is like a smooth **h**............................. Pr 15:19
there will be a **h** from Egypt to .... Is 19:23
this **h** will be called "The Road .... Is 35:8

HIGHWAYS
along back roads and on poor **h**. .... Je 18:15

HILEN
H, Debir, ... 1Ch 6:58

HILKIAH
Eliakim son of **H** was the palace 2Ki 18:18
Eliakim son of **H**, Shebna, and 2Ki 18:26
Eliakim son of **H** was the palace 2Ki 18:37
Go up to **H** the high priest, ... 2Ki 22:4
H the high priest said to 2Ki 22:8
H the priest has given me a book. 2Ki 22:10
He gave orders to **H** the priest, ... 2Ki 22:12
So **H** the priest, Ahikam, Acbor,.............. 2Ki 22:14
king commanded **H** the high priest 2Ki 23:4

in the book **H** the priest had 2Ki 23:24
Shallum was the father of **H**. 1Ch 6:13
H was the father of Azariah. 1Ch 6:13
H was Amzi's son. Amzi was 1Ch 6:46
Azariah son of **H**. (Hilkiah was 1Ch 9:11
H was Meshullam's son. 1Ch 9:11
H was his second son, Tabaliah 1Ch 26:11
men went to **H** the high priest 2Ch 34:9
H the priest found the Book of 2Ch 34:14
H said to Shaphan the royal 2Ch 34:15
H the priest has given me a book. 2Ch 34:18
He gave orders to **H**, Ahikam son 2Ch 34:20
H and those the king sent with 2Ch 34:22
H, Zechariah, and Jehiel, the 2Ch 35:8
son of Azariah, the son of **H**, ... Ezr 7:1
Anaiah, Uriah, **H**, and Maaseiah. .... Ne 8:4
Seraiah son of **H**, the supervisor .... Ne 11:11
H was the son of Meshullam, ... Ne 11:11
Sallu, Amok, **H**, and Jedaiah. .... Ne 12:7
for my servant Eliakim son of **H**. .... Is 22:20
Eliakim son of **H** was the palace .... Is 36:3
Eliakim son of **H** was the palace .... Is 36:22
the words of Jeremiah son of **H**.............. Je 1:1
Gemariah son of **H** to Babylon to .... Je 29:3

HILKIAH'S
son. Amaziah was **H** son. 1Ch 6:45
Hashabiah, from **H** family; .... Ne 12:21

HILL
and Sephar in the **h** country in .... Ge 10:30
will stand on the top of the **h**,.............. Ex 17:9
Hur went to the top of the **h**. .... Ex 17:10
them as they went down the **h**. .... Jos 7:5
are living in the **h** country from .... Jos 13:6
Shahar on the **h** in the valley,................. Jos 13:19
the top of the **h** on the west .... Jos 15:8
to the **h** north of Ekron. .... Jos 15:11
which is on the **h** south of Lower .... Jos 18:13
At the **h** to the south of Beth .... Jos 18:14
near the western side of the **h**. .... Jos 18:14
down to the bottom of the **h**, ... Jos 18:16
bottom of the **h** called Moreh.................. Jdg 7:1
to the top of the **h** that faces .... Jdg 16:3
LORD to Abinadab's house on a **h**. 1Sa 7:1
were going up the **h** to the town, ... 1Sa 9:11
controlled one **h** while the 1Sa 17:3
tree on the **h** at Gibeah, ... 1Sa 22:6
Horesh, on the **h** of Hakilah, ... 1Sa 23:19
is hiding on the **h** of Hakilah 1Sa 26:1
the road on the **h** of Hakilah 1Sa 26:3
side of the **h** and stood on top 1Sa 26:13
they arrived at the **h** of Ammah,.............. 2Sa 2:24
together at the top of the **h**. 2Sa 2:25
of Abinadab's house on the **h**. 2Sa 6:3
from the other side of the **h**. 2Sa 13:34
on stakes on a **h** in the presence.............. 2Sa 21:9
men to work in the **h** country,................. 1Ki 5:15
a **h** east of Jerusalem, Solomon 1Ki 11:7
on every high **h** and under every 1Ki 14:23
He bought the **h** of Samaria from 1Ki 16:24
a city on that **h** and called it 1Ki 16:24
who was sitting on top of the **h**, ... 2Ki 1:9
Elisha at the **h** and grabbed his 2Ki 4:27
they came to the **h**, Gehazi took 2Ki 5:24
on every high **h** and under every 2Ki 17:10
to cut stone in the **h** country, ... 2Ch 2:2
towns in the **h** country of Judah 2Ch 27:4
died and was buried on a **h**, ... 2Ch 32:33
Gate and around the **h** of Ophel. 2Ch 33:14
on the Temple **h** and in Jerusalem 2Ch 33:15
who lived on the **h** of Ophel made .... Ne 3:26
lived on the **h** of Ophel, ... Ne 11:21
myrrh and to that **h** of incense. .... Sng 4:6

a vineyard on a **h** with very rich .... Is 5:1
Zion, at the **h** of Jerusalem. .... Is 10:32
plant set on a **h** above a rich .... Is 28:1
plant set on a **h** above a rich .... Is 28:4
a hilltop, like a banner on a **h**. .... Is 30:17
mountain and **h** will have streams .... Is 30:25
on Mount Zion and on its **h**. .... Is 31:4
as beautiful as the **h** of Carmel .... Is 35:2
mountain and **h** should be made .... Is 40:4
bed on every **h** and mountain, ... Is 57:7
on every high **h** and under every .... Je 2:20
idols on every **h** and under every .... Je 3:6
mountain and **h** and in the cracks .... Je 16:16
the **h** where the Temple stands .... Je 26:18
be rebuilt on its **h** of ruins, ... Je 30:18
Gate straight to the **h** of Gareb. .... Je 31:39
It will become a **h** covered with .... Je 49:2
on every high **h**, on all the .... Eze 6:13
saw every high **h** and every leafy .... Eze 20:28
mountains and on every high **h**. .... Eze 34:6
and let them live around my **h**. .... Eze 34:26
your city on your holy **h**. .... Da 9:16
and praying for God's holy **h**, ... Da 9:20
and the **h** on which the Temple .... Mic 3:12
the flocks, **h** of Jerusalem, to .... Mic 4:8
he went up on a **h** and sat down. .... Mt 5:1
built on a **h** cannot be hidden. .... Mt 5:14
When Jesus came down from the **h**, ... Mt 8:1
rushed down the **h** into the lake .... Mt 8:32
He went up on a **h** and sat there. .... Mt 15:29
on the **h** and go to look for .... Mt 18:12
at the **h** called the Mount .... Mt 21:1
was feeding on a **h** near there. .... Mk 5:11
rushed down the **h** into the lake .... Mk 5:13
mountain and **h** should be made .... Lk 3:5
herd of pigs was feeding on a **h**, ... Lk 8:32
ran down the **h** into the lake .... Lk 8:33
near the **h** called the Mount .... Lk 19:29
went up on a **h** and sat down .... Jn 6:3

HILLEL

Abdon son of **H** from the city of .... Jdg 12:13
Then Abdon son of **H** died and was .... Jdg 12:15

HILLS

things of the long-lasting **h**. .... Ge 49:26
I see them from the the **h**. .... Nu 23:9
and along the **h** east of Lake .... Nu 34:11
western **h**, the southern area, ... Dt 1:7
that flow in the valleys and **h**, ... Dt 8:7
you can dig copper out of the **h**. .... Dt 8:9
take is a land of **h** and valleys, ... Dt 11:11
mountains and **h** and under every .... Dt 12:2
the everlasting **h** give the best .... Dt 33:15
Go into the **h** so the king's men .... Jos 2:16
went into the **h** where they .... Jos 2:22
They left the **h** and crossed the .... Jos 2:23
and on the western **h** and along .... Jos 9:1
the western **h**, and the slopes. .... Jos 10:40
Galilee and in the western **h**. .... Jos 11:2
the western **h**, and the Jordan .... Jos 11:16
Israel and all the **h** near them. .... Jos 11:16
western **h**, the Jordan Valley, ... Jos 12:8
Beth Peor, the **h** of Pisgah, and .... Jos 13:20
these towns in the western **h:** .... Jos 15:33
these towns in the western **h:** .... Jos 15:37
these towns in the western **h:** .... Jos 15:42
the south, and in the western **h**. .... Jdg 1:9
down from the **h** with Ehud .... Jdg 3:27
and in the **h** of the Desert 1Sa 23:14
have been killed on the **h**. 2Sa 1:15
Jonathan is dead on Gilboa's **h**. 2Sa 1:25
the fig trees on the western **h**. 1Ki 10:27
over the **h** like sheep without 1Ki 22:17

on the **h**, and under every 2Ki 16:4
as fast as gazelles over the **h**. 1Ch 12:8
sycamore trees in the western **h**. 1Ch 27:28
the fig trees on the western **h**. 2Ch 1:15
the fig trees on the western **h**. 2Ch 9:27
captured in the **h** of Ephraim. 2Ch 15:8
over the **h** like sheep without 2Ch 18:16
worship gods on the **h** in Judah. 2Ch 21:11
on the western **h** and in the 2Ch 26:10
vineyards in the **h** and in the 2Ch 26:10
and on the **h**, and under every 2Ch 28:4
in the western **h** and in southern 2Ch 28:18
you are not older than the **h**. .... Job 15:7
the **h** and valleys stand out like .... Job 38:14
It roams the **h** looking for .... Job 39:8
The **h**, where the wild animals .... Job 40:20
cattle on a thousand **h** are mine. .... Ps 50:10
grass and the **h** with happiness. .... Ps 65:12
on the **h** for the people. .... Ps 72:3
grain and the **h** be covered with .... Ps 72:16
than the **h** full of animals. .... Ps 76:4
flames that blaze through the **h**. .... Ps 83:14
sheep and the **h** like little .... Ps 114:4
H, why did you skip like little .... Ps 114:6
look up to the **h**, but where does .... Ps 121:1
falling on the **h** of Jerusalem. .... Ps 133:3
and makes grass grow on the **h**. .... Ps 147:8
mountains and all **h**, fruit trees .... Ps 148:9
before the **h** were there, before .... Pr 8:25
Gather the grass from the **h**. .... Pr 27:25
mountains, skipping over the **h**. .... Sng 2:8
dens and from the leopards' **h**. .... Sng 4:8
It will be raised above the **h**, ... Is 2:2
tall mountains and the high **h**, ... Is 2:14
worked and grew food on these **h**, ... Is 7:25
like chaff on the **h** being blown .... Is 17:13
to weigh the mountains and **h?** .... Is 40:12
you will make the **h** like chaff. .... Is 41:15
flow on the dry **h** and springs .... Is 41:18
will destroy the **h** and mountains .... Is 42:15
will find food even on bare **h**. .... Is 49:9
and the **h** may come to an end, ... Is 54:10
The mountains and **h** will burst .... Is 55:12
and shamed me on those **h**. .... Is 65:7
idols on the **h** and on the .... Je 3:23
All the **h** were trembling. .... Je 4:24
marched over those barren **h**. .... Je 12:12
you slip and fall on the dark **h**. .... Je 13:16
acts on the **h** and in the fields .... Je 13:27
stand on the bare **h** and sniff .... Je 14:6
green trees and on the high **h**. .... Je 17:2
from the western **h**, from the .... Je 17:26
again on the **h** around Samaria. .... Je 31:5
the western **h**, and in southern .... Je 32:44
mountains and in the western **h**, ... Je 33:13
the high places of the **h**. .... Je 49:16
around in the mountains and **h**. .... Je 50:6
and be full on the **h** of Ephraim .... Je 50:19
mountains, the **h**, the ravines, ... Eze 6:3
in war will fall on your **h**, ... Eze 35:8
the mountains, **h**, ravines, and .... Eze 36:4
the mountains, **h**, ravines, and .... Eze 36:6
They burn offerings on the **h**, ... Hos 4:13
and to the **h**, "Fall on us!" .... Hos 10:8
milk will flow from the **h**, ... Joe 3:18
mountains and pour from the **h**. .... Am 9:13
back the western **h** from the .... Ob 1:19
It will be raised above the **h**, ... Mic 4:1
let the **h** hear your story. .... Mic 6:1
in front of him, and the **h** melt. .... Nah 1:5
Look, there on the **h**, someone is .... Nah 1:15
pieces; the old **h** fall down. God .... Hab 3:6
loud crash will echo from the **h**. .... Zph 1:10

area and the western **h.**'" .... Zch 7:7
himself up into the **h** to pray. .... Mt 14:23
the burial caves and on the **h,**.................. Mk 5:5
he went into the **h** to pray. .... Mk 6:46
to a town in the **h** of Judea. .... Lk 1:39
' And they will say to the **h,** ' .... Lk 23:30
left and went into the **h** alone. .... Jn 6:15

HILLSIDE

Shimei followed on the nearby **h.** 2Sa 16:13
like water running down a **h.** .... Mic 1:4

HILLTOP

alone like a flagpole on a **h,** .... Is 30:17
Go up to the bare **h** and cry out,............... Je 7:29

HILLTOPS

put men on the **h** in ambush who .... Jdg 9:25
On the **h** along the road and at .... Pr 8:2
Look up to the bare **h,** Judah. .... Je 3:2
can hear crying on the bare **h.** .... Je 3:21
from the bare **h** of the desert .... Je 4:11
places on **h** to worship Baal .... Je 19:5

HINGES

the gold **h** for the doors of the 1Ki 7:50
making nails and **h** for the gate 1Ch 22:3
turning back and forth on its **h,** .... Pr 26:14
His hands are like gold **h,** .... Sng 5:14

HINNOM

through the Valley of Ben **H,** .... Jos 15:8
on the west side of **H** Valley, ... Jos 15:8
was near the Valley of Ben **H,**................. Jos 18:16
down the **H** Valley just south .... Jos 18:16
Valley of Ben **H,** so no one could 2Ki 23:10
the Valley of Ben **H** and made his 2Ch 28:3
fire in the Valley of Ben **H.** 2Ch 33:6
all the way to the Valley of **H.**................. Ne 11:30
Topheth in the Valley of Ben **H.** .... Je 7:31
or the Valley of Ben **H** anymore................ Je 7:32
go out to the Valley of Ben **H,**................. Je 19:2
the Valley of Ben **H** or Topheth, ... Je 19:6
Valley of Ben **H** they built .... Je 32:35

HIP

struck Jacob's **h** and put it out .... Ge 32:25
that is on the **h** joint of .... Ge 32:32
his right **h** under his clothes. .... Jdg 3:16
that was tied to his right **h.**..................... Jdg 3:21

HIPS

cut off their clothes at the **h.** 2Sa 10:4
cut off their clothes at the **h.** 1Ch 19:4

HIRAH

with a man named **H** in the town .... Ge 38:1
His friend **H** from Adullam went .... Ge 38:12
sent his friend **H** with the young .... Ge 38:20
given her, but **H** could not find .... Ge 38:20

HIRAM

H king of the city of Tyre sent 2Sa 5:11
H, the king of Tyre, had always 1Ki 5:1
When **H** heard that Solomon had 1Ki 5:1
this message back to King **H:** 1Ki 5:2
When **H** heard what Solomon asked, ... 1Ki 5:7
Then **H** sent back this message to 1Ki 5:8
So **H** gave Solomon as much cedar 1Ki 5:10
And Solomon gave **H** about one 1Ki 5:11
was peace between **H** and Solomon; 1Ki 5:12
in Galilee to **H** king of Tyre, ... 1Ki 9:11
because **H** had helped with the 1Ki 9:11
H had given Solomon all the 1Ki 9:11
So **H** traveled from Tyre to see 1Ki 9:12
H had sent Solomon about nine 1Ki 9:14
H had skilled sailors, so he..................... 1Ki 9:27
H king of the city of Tyre sent 1Ch 14:1
this message to **H** king of the 2Ch 2:3

Then **H** king of Tyre answered 2Ch 2:11
H also said: "Praise the LORD, ... 2Ch 2:12
the towns that **H** had given him,............... 2Ch 8:2
H sent ships to Solomon that 2Ch 8:18

HIRAM'S

Solomon's and **H** builders and the 1Ki 5:18
H ships brought gold from Ophir, ... 1Ki 10:11
at sea, along with **H** ships. 1Ki 10:22
H men went with Solomon's men to 2Ch 8:18
H men and Solomon's men brought 2Ch 9:10
to trade, with **H** men as the 2Ch 9:21

HIRE

the silver to **h** some worthless, ... Jdg 9:4
pounds of silver to **h** chariots 1Ch 19:6
The Lord will **h** Assyria and use............... Is 7:20
They h a goldsmith, and he makes............ Is 46:6
was no money to **h** people or .... Zch 8:10
very early to **h** some people to .... Mt 20:1

HIRED

country nor a **h** worker may eat .... Ex 12:45
not keep a **h** worker's salary .... Le 19:13
priest or a **h** worker must not .... Le 22:10
for your **h** workers, and for .... Le 25:6
He will be like a **h** worker and a .... Le 25:40
really only **h** himself out for .... Le 25:50
will live like a **h** person with .... Le 25:53
twice the work of a **h** person................. Dt 15:18
And they **h** Balaam son of Beor,............... Dt 23:4
Don't cheat **h** servants who are .... Dt 24:14
done for him, saying, "He **h** me................. Jdg 18:4
they **h** twenty thousand Aramean 2Sa 10:6
They also **h** the king of Maacah 2Sa 10:6
king of Israel has **h** the Hittite 2Ki 7:6
The Ammonites **h** thirty-two 1Ch 19:7
And they **h** stoneworkers and.................. 2Ch 24:12
They also **h** people to work with 2Ch 24:12
Amaziah also **h** one hundred 2Ch 25:6
Their enemies **h** others to delay .... Ezr 4:5
they had **h** Balaam to put a curse .... Ne 13:2
three years as a **h** helper would .... Is 16:14
is a year as a **h** helper counts .... Is 21:16
The **h** soldiers in Egypt's army .... Je 46:21
all the soldiers **h** from other .... Je 50:37
They have **h** other nations to .... Hos 8:9
the last people I **h** and end with .... Mt 20:8
and end with those I **h** first.' .... Mt 20:8
who were **h** at five o'clock .... Mt 20:9
workers who were **h** first came to .... Mt 20:10
people were **h** last and worked .... Mt 20:12
the man who was **h** last the same .... Mt 20:14
the boat with the **h** workers and............... Mk 1:20

HIRING

H a foolish person or anyone .... Pr 26:10

HISS

among the nations **h** at you. .... Eze 27:36

HISSING

Egypt is like a **h** snake that is.................. Je 46:22

HISTORIES

are written in their family **h:** 1Ch 5:7
The family **h** show that all these............... 1Ch 8:28
were listed in their family **h,** 1Ch 9:1
and those family **h** were put in 1Ch 9:1
in their family **h** in their 1Ch 9:22
were listed in their family **h,** 1Ch 9:34
Iddo the seer, in the family **h.** 2Ch 12:15
names in the Levite family **h.** 2Ch 31:16
as listed in the family **h.** 2Ch 31:17
who were listed in the family **h,** 2Ch 31:18
in the family **h** of the Levites 2Ch 31:19

long lists of names in family **h.** 1Ti 1:4
about useless family **h** and argue .... Tit 3:9

HISTORY

This is the family **h** of Adam. .... Ge 5:1
This is the family **h** of Noah. .... Ge 6:9
This is the family **h** of Shem, ... Ge 10:1
This is the family **h** of Shem, ... Ge 11:10
This is the family **h** of Terah. .... Ge 11:27
This is the family **h** of Ishmael, ... Ge 25:12
This is the family **h** of Isaac. .... Ge 25:19
This is the family **h** of Esau .... Ge 36:1
This is the family **h** of Esau. .... Ge 36:9
This is the family **h** of Jacob: .... Ge 37:2
according to their family **h:** .... Ex 6:16
according to their family **h.** .... Ex 6:19
is the family **h** of Aaron and .... Nu 3:1
This is the family **h** of Perez, ... Ru 4:18
recorded the **h** of the people; 1Ki 4:3
in the book of the **h** of Solomon. 1Ki 11:41
the book of the **h** of the kings 1Ki 14:19
the book of the **h** of the kings 1Ki 14:29
the book of the **h** of the kings 1Ki 15:7
the book of the **h** of the kings 1Ki 15:23
the book of the **h** of the kings 1Ki 15:31
the book of the **h** of the kings 1Ki 16:5
the book of the **h** of the kings 1Ki 16:14
the book of the **h** of the kings 1Ki 16:20
the book of the **h** of the kings 1Ki 16:27
the book of the **h** of the kings 1Ki 22:39
the book of the **h** of the kings 1Ki 22:45
the book of the **h** of the kings 2Ki 1:18
the book of the **h** of the kings 2Ki 8:23
the book of the **h** of the kings 2Ki 10:34
the book of the **h** of the kings 2Ki 12:19
the book of the **h** of the kings 2Ki 13:8
the book of the **h** of the kings 2Ki 13:12
the book of the **h** of the kings 2Ki 14:15
the book of the **h** of the kings 2Ki 14:18
the book of the **h** of the kings 2Ki 14:28
the book of the **h** of the kings 2Ki 15:6
the book of the **h** of the kings 2Ki 15:11
the book of the **h** of the kings 2Ki 15:15
the book of the **h** of the kings 2Ki 15:21
the book of the **h** of the kings 2Ki 15:26
the book of the **h** of the kings 2Ki 15:31
the book of the **h** of the kings 2Ki 15:36
the book of the **h** of the kings 2Ki 16:19
the book of the **h** of the kings 2Ki 20:20
the book of the **h** of the kings 2Ki 21:17
the book of the **h** of the kings 2Ki 21:25
the book of the **h** of the kings 2Ki 23:28
the book of the **h** of the kings 2Ki 24:5
wrote the **h** of their family. 1Ch 4:33
In the family **h** Reuben's name is 1Ch 5:1
in the family **h** of Gad during 1Ch 5:17
In the family **h** of Tola's 1Ch 7:2
Their family **h** shows they had 1Ch 7:4
Their family **h** shows they had 1Ch 7:7
Their family **h** listed the family 1Ch 7:9
Their family **h** lists that they 1Ch 7:40
The family **h** of Benjamin lists 1Ch 9:9
The **h** of the Hebron family shows 1Ch 26:31
not put in the **h** book about King 1Ch 27:24
the book of the **h** of 2Ch 33:18
has a **h** of disobedience .... Ezr 4:19
the family **h** of those who had .... Ne 7:5
were written down in the **h** book, ... Ne 12:23
Who has controlled **h** since the .... Is 41:4
is the family **h** of Jesus Christ. .... Mt 1:1

HIT

H that rock with the stick, ... Ex 17:6
the one who **h** him is not to be .... Ex 21:19

fighting and **h** a pregnant woman .... Ex 21:22
his hand and **h** the rock twice .... Nu 20:11
Balaam **h** the donkey to force her .... Nu 22:23
against it. So he **h** her again. .... Nu 22:25
so angry that he **h** her with his .... Nu 22:27
to make you **h** me three times? .... Nu 22:28
Why have you **h** your donkey three .... Nu 22:32
a person might **h** someone with .... Nu 35:21
throw something and **h** someone. .... Nu 35:22
But don't **h** a person more than .... Dt 25:3
hammer. She **h** Sisera! She .... Jdg 5:26
It **h** the tent so hard that the .... Jdg 7:13
by its fur and **h** it and killed 1Sa 17:35
The stone **h** the Philistine and 1Sa 17:49
He **h** him and killed him. 1Sa 17:50
I won't need to **h** him twice." 1Sa 26:8
prophets told another, "**H** me!" 1Ki 20:35
man and said, "**H** me, please!" 1Ki 20:37
So the man **h** him and hurt him. 1Ki 20:37
but he **h** Ahab king of Israel 1Ki 22:34
rolled it up, and **h** the water. 2Ki 2:8
Elisha **h** the water with Elijah's 2Ki 2:14
When he **h** the water, it divided 2Ki 2:14
an arrow which **h** Ahab king of 2Ch 18:33
curses on them, **h** some of them, ... Ne 13:25
make fun of me and **h** my cheeks .... Job 16:10
the hand of God has **h** me. .... Job 19:21
The wind will **h** them without .... Job 27:22
Miners **h** the rocks of flint and .... Job 28:9
When he **h** the rock, water poured .... Ps 78:20
that you will not **h** your foot on .... Ps 91:12
think, "They **h** me, but I'm not .... Pr 23:35
the city. They **h** me and hurt me; .... Sng 5:7
and fight and **h** each other with .... Is 58:4
It **h** the statue on its feet of .... Da 2:34
the rock that **h** the statue .... Da 2:35
them before they **h** the floor of .... Da 6:24
They will **h** the leader of Israel .... Mic 5:1
Sword, **h** the shepherd. Attack .... Zch 13:7
that you will not **h** your foot on .... Mt 4:6
the winds blew and **h** that house. .... Mt 7:25
the winds blew and **h** that house, ... Mt 7:27
It was being **h** by waves, because .... Mt 14:24
you Christ! Tell us who **h** you!" .... Mt 26:68
h him on the head and showed .... Mk 12:4
that you will not **h** your foot on .... Lk 4:11
prophet, and tell us who **h** you." .... Lk 22:64
the guards standing there **h** him. .... Jn 18:22
said is true, why do you **h** me?" .... Jn 18:23
and **h** him in the face. .... Jn 19:3
near Paul to **h** him on the mouth. .... Ac 23:2
Ananias, "God will **h** you, too! .... Ac 23:3
you are telling them to **h** me, ... Ac 23:3
the ship would **h** the sandbanks .... Ac 27:17
that we would **h** the rocks. .... Ac 27:29
But the ship **h** a sandbank. .... Ac 27:41
than you, or **h** you in the face. 2Co 11:20

HITCH

H the cows to the cart, and take 1Sa 6:7

HITCHED

had calves and **h** them to the 1Sa 6:10

HITS

Anyone who **h** a person and kills .... Ex 21:12
Anyone who **h** his father or his .... Ex 21:15
and one **h** the other with a rock .... Ex 21:18
If a man **h** his male or female .... Ex 21:26
trouble **h** you, and you are .... Job 4:5
sword that **h** it does not hurt .... Job 41:26
the east wind **h** it in the area .... Eze 17:10

HITTING

me, a young man for **h** me......................... Ge 4:23
Why are you **h** one of your own .... Ex 2:13
h and killing the neighbor, ... Dt 19:5
h all four corners of the house .... Job 1:19
like a boxer who is **h** something— 1Co 9:26

HITTITE

in front of the **H** witnesses...................... Ge 23:16
was the son of Zohar the **H**. .... Ge 25:9
he married two **H** women—Judith .... Ge 26:34
Isaac, "I am tired of **H** women. .... Ge 27:46
of these **H** women here in this .... Ge 27:46
Adah daughter of Elon the **H;**.................. Ge 36:2
in the field of Ephron the **H**. .... Ge 49:29
from Ephron the **H** for a burying .... Ge 49:30
were bought from the **H** people." .... Ge 49:32
from Ephron the **H** to use as a .... Ge 50:13
Ahimelech the **H** and Abishai son 1Sa 26:6
She is the wife of Uriah the **H**." 2Sa 11:3
"Send Uriah the **H** to me." 2Sa 11:6
And Uriah the **H** was one of them. 2Sa 11:17
Uriah the **H** also died.'" 2Sa 11:21
servant Uriah the **H** also died." 2Sa 11:24
killed Uriah the **H** with the 2Sa 12:9
of Uriah the **H** for yourself!' 2Sa 12:10
and Uriah the **H**. There were 2Sa 23:39
sinned against Uriah the **H**. 1Ki 15:5
has hired the **H** and Egyptian 2Ki 7:6
Uriah the **H;** Zabad son of Ahlai; 1Ch 11:41
and your mother was a **H**. .... Eze 16:3
mother was a **H**, and your father .... Eze 16:45

HITTITES

H, Perizzites, Rephaites, ... Ge 15:20
body and went to talk to the **H**. .... Ge 23:3
The **H** answered Abraham,...................... Ge 23:5
the people of the land, the **H**. .... Ge 23:7
among the **H** at the city gate .... Ge 23:10
Abraham bowed down before the **H**. .... Ge 23:12
in it from the **H** to use as a .... Ge 23:20
that he had bought from the **H**. .... Ge 25:10
of the Canaanites, **H**, Amorites, ... Ex 3:8
of the Canaanites, **H**, Amorites, ... Ex 3:17
the Canaanites, **H**, Amorites, ... Ex 13:5
of the Amorites, **H**, Perizzites, ... Ex 23:23
and **H** out of your way. .... Ex 23:28
Amorites, **H**, Perizzites, Hivites .... Ex 33:2
Canaanites, **H**, Perizzites, ... Ex 34:11
the **H**, Jebusites, and Amorites .... Nu 13:29
the **H**, Girgashites, Amorites, ... Dt 7:1
the **H**, Amorites, Canaanites, ... Dt 20:17
including the land of the **H**. .... Jos 1:4
out the Canaanites, **H**, Hivites, ... Jos 3:10
the kings of the **H**, Amorites, ... Jos 9:1
to the Amorites, **H**, Perizzites, ... Jos 11:3
This was the land where the **H**, ... Jos 12:8
Canaanites, **H**, Girgashites, ... Jos 24:11
land where the **H** lived and built .... Jdg 1:26
the Canaanites, **H**, Amorites, ... Jdg 3:5
Amorites, **H**, Perizzites, Hivites 1Ki 9:20
kings of the **H** and the Arameans 1Ki 10:29
Edomites, Sidonians, and **H**. 1Ki 11:1
He was also the father of the **H**, ... 1Ch 1:13
kings of the **H** and the Arameans 2Ch 1:17
not Israelites—the **H**, Amorites, ... 2Ch 8:7
the Canaanites, **H**, Perizzites, ... Ezr 9:1
of the Canaanites, **H**, Amorites, ... Ne 9:8

HIVITE

When Shechem son of Hamor the **H**, ... Ge 34:2
Anah, the son of Zibeon the **H;** .... Ge 36:2

HIVITES

H, Arkites, Sinites, ... Ge 10:17
Perizzites, **H**, and Jebusites. .... Ex 3:8
Perizzites, **H**, and Jebusites— .... Ex 3:17
Amorites, **H**, and Jebusites. .... Ex 13:5
Canaanites, **H**, and Jebusites, ... Ex 23:23
of you that will force the **H**, ... Ex 23:28
Perizzites, **H**, and Jebusites. .... Ex 33:2
Perizzites, **H**, and Jebusites, ... Ex 34:11
Perizzites, **H**, and Jebusites— .... Dt 7:1
Perizzites, **H**, and Jebusites, as .... Dt 20:17
Hittites, **H**, Perizzites, ... Jos 3:10
Perizzites, **H**, and Jebusites. .... Jos 9:1
The Israelites said to these **H**,............... Jos 9:7
The **H** said to Joshua, "We are .... Jos 9:8
Jabin also sent one to the **H**, ... Jos 11:3
with Israel—the **H** living in .... Jos 11:19
Perizzites, **H**, and the **H** living had .... Jos 12:8
Girgashites, **H**, and Jebusites .... Jos 24:11
and the **H** who lived in the .... Jdg 3:3
Perizzites, **H**, and Jebusites. .... Jdg 3:5
cities of the **H** and Canaanites. 2Sa 24:7
Perizzites, **H**, and Jebusites. 1Ki 9:20
H, Arkites, Sinites, ... 1Ch 1:15
Perizzites, **H**, and Jebusites. 2Ch 8:7
cities the **H** and the Amorites .... Is 17:9

HIZKI

Zebadiah, Meshullam, **H**, Heber, ... 1Ch 8:17

HIZKIAH

Elioenai, **H**, and Azrikam. 1Ch 3:23

HOBAB

H was the son of Reuel the .... Nu 10:29
Moses said to **H**, "We are moving .... Nu 10:29
But **H** answered, "No, I will not .... Nu 10:30
the descendants of **H**, Moses' .... Jdg 4:11

HOBAH

chased them all the way to **H**,............... Ge 14:15

HOBAIAH

descendants of **H**, Hakkoz, and .... Ezr 2:61
descendants of **H**, Hakkoz, and .... Ne 7:63

HOD

Bezer, **H**, Shamma, Shilshah, ... 1Ch 7:37

HODAVIAH

H, Eliashib, Pelaiah, Akkub, ... 1Ch 3:24
Jeremiah, **H**, and Jahdiel. 1Ch 5:24
son, and **H** was Hassenuah's son 1Ch 9:7
through the family of **H**)—74. .... Ezr 2:40
who were the descendants of **H;** .... Ezr 3:9
Kadmiel through the family of **H** .... Ne 7:43

HODAVIAH'S

Meshullam was **H** son, and..................... 1Ch 9:7

HODIAH

Shabbethai, **H**, Maaseiah, Kelita............... Ne 8:7
Sherebiah, **H**, Shebaniah, ... Ne 9:5
Shebaniah, **H**, Kelita, Pelaiah, ... Ne 10:10
H, Bani, and Beninu. .... Ne 10:13
H, Hashum, Bezai, ... Ne 10:18

HODIAH'S

H wife was Naham's sister...................... 1Ch 4:19
The sons of **H** wife were Eshtemoa 1Ch 4:19

HODSHI

land of Tahtim **H** and to Dan Jaan 2Sa 24:6

HOED

It will not be trimmed or **h**,................... Is 5:6

HOES

have their plows, **h**, axes, and................. 1Sa 13:20
for sharpening plows and **h**. 1Sa 13:21

HOGLAH

were Mahlah, Noah, **H,** Milcah, ... Nu 26:33
were Mahlah, Noah, **H,** Milcah, ... Nu 27:1
Mahlah, Tirzah, **H,** Milcah, and .... Nu 36:11
it went to Beth **H** and continued .... Jos 15:6
Mahlah, Noah, **H,** Milcah, and .... Jos 17:3
part of Beth **H** and ended at .... Jos 18:19
Jericho, Beth **H,** Emek Keziz, ... Jos 18:21

HOHAM

a message to **H** king of Hebron, ... Jos 10:3

HOLD

he had to **h** back the tears .... Ge 43:30
So he took **h** of his father's................... Ge 48:17
out and took **h** of the snake, ... Ex 4:4
go so they may **h** a feast for me .... Ex 5:1
Tell Aaron to **h** his walking................... Ex 8:5
them go and continue to **h** them, ... Ex 9:2
stick and **h** it over the sea .... Ex 14:16
H your hand over the sea so that .... Ex 14:26
terror will take **h** of the .... Ex 15:14
Do not **h** back your offering from .... Ex 22:29
year you must **h** a feast to honor .... Ex 23:14
because they will **h** the poles .... Ex 25:27
five crossbars to **h** the frames................. Ex 26:26
five to **h** the frames together .... Ex 26:27
five crossbars to **h** the frames................. Ex 26:27
the frames to **h** the crossbars,................. Ex 26:29
screen to **h** the burning wood .... Ex 27:4
the stones to **h** them on the holy .... Ex 28:11
two gold pieces to **h** the stones .... Ex 28:13
gold pieces that **h** the stones.................. Ex 28:14
the frames to **h** the crossbars,................. Ex 36:34
screen to **h** the burning wood .... Ex 38:4
bronze rings to **h** the poles for .... Ex 38:5
he will **h** the bitter water that .... Nu 5:18
his arms will **h** you up forever. .... Dt 33:27
said to Joshua, "**H** your spear.................. Jos 8:18
got up and took **h** of the doors .... Jdg 16:3
pillars that **h** up the temple so .... Jdg 16:26
me your shawl and **h** it open." .... Ru 3:15
May the LORD **h** David's enemies 1Sa 20:16
hand and take **h** of them and kiss 2Sa 15:5
My master, don't **h** me guilty. 2Sa 19:19
Don't **h** it against me. 2Sa 19:19
went and took **h** of the corners 1Ki 1:50
LORD and took **h** of the corners............... 1Ki 2:28
across and could **h** about two 1Ki 7:38
was too small to **h** all the burnt 1Ki 8:64
big enough to **h** about thirteen 1Ki 18:32
you will **h** a son in your arms." 2Ki 4:16
arrives, shut the door and **h** it; 2Ki 6:32
and make his **h** on the kingdom 2Ki 15:19
highest of heavens can **h** him. 2Ch 2:6
had made could not **h** the burnt 2Ch 7:7
they agreed to **h** the celebration .... Est 9:23
grab it, but it does not **h** up.................... Job 8:15
God will not **h** back his anger. .... Job 9:13
I know you will **h** me guilty. .... Job 9:28
Do not **h** me guilty, but tell me .... Job 10:2
If I **h** up my head, you hunt me .... Job 10:16
to him and **h** out your hands .... Job 11:13
by the heel and **h** them tight. .... Job 18:9
power God grabs **h** of my clothing .... Job 30:18
wicked hearts to **h** on to anger. .... Job 36:13
He does not **h** back the flashing .... Job 37:4
in order to take **h** of the earth................. Job 38:13
Can you hold it to the plowed row .... Job 39:10
they **h** on to each other and .... Job 41:17
the chains that **h** us back and .... Ps 2:3
not **h** back your mercy from me; .... Ps 40:11
Fear took **h** of them; they hurt .... Ps 48:6
my prayer or **h** back his love .... Ps 66:20

and from the **h** of evil and cruel .... Ps 71:4
Why do you **h** back your power? .... Ps 74:11
He does not **h** back anything good .... Ps 84:11
But I will not **h** back my love .... Ps 89:33
fear of the grave took **h** of me. .... Ps 116:3
I **h** on to your rules. LORD, do .... Ps 119:31
your right hand you would **h** me. .... Ps 139:10
h on to wisdom and good sense................. Pr 3:21
H on to my words with all your .... Pr 4:4
H on to wisdom, and it will take............... Pr 4:6
h on to it, and it will bring .... Pr 4:8
Nothing will **h** you back;....................... Pr 4:12
her love always **h** you captive. .... Pr 5:19
Who can **h** the wind in his hand? .... Pr 30:4
who honor God will **h** them both. .... Ec 7:18
their arms **h** men like chains. .... Ec 7:26
tree and take **h** of its fruit.".................... Sng 7:8
He will take firm **h** of you .... Is 22:17
pegs that **h** her in place will .... Is 33:20
and I will **h** your hand and .... Is 42:6
I **h** your right hand and will .... Is 45:1
more people than the land can **h,** .... Is 49:19
wider. Do not **h** back. Make the .... Is 54:2
loud. Don't **h** back. Shout out.................. Is 58:1
will you **h** yourself back from .... Is 64:12
who **h** religious feasts for the .... Is 65:11
wells that cannot **h** water. .... Je 2:13
I used to **h** you and said, ' .... Je 2:20
At that time who can **h** her back? .... Je 2:24
so I have taken **h** of you and .... Je 15:6
of trying to **h** it inside of me, ... Je 20:9
me, and finally, I cannot **h** it .... Je 20:9
tear off the ropes that **h** them. .... Je 30:8
But I will **h** you responsible for .... Eze 3:18
But I will **h** you responsible for .... Eze 3:20
will not **h** back punishment from .... Eze 7:4
I will not **h** back punishment. .... Eze 7:9
how can Israel **h** back the enemy .... Eze 13:5
to Lebanon and took **h** of the top .... Eze 17:3
men touch and **h** their breasts. .... Eze 23:3
I will not **h** back punishment or .... Eze 24:14
enough to **h** a sword in war. .... Eze 30:21
H the sticks on which you wrote .... Eze 37:20
iron and clay do not **h** together. .... Da 2:43
this land can't **h** all his words. .... Am 7:10
come and take **h** of a Judean by .... Zch 8:23
room and took **h** of her hand,................. Mt 9:25
Those who try to **h** on to their .... Mt 10:39
for me will **h** on to true life. .... Mt 10:39
hand, "**H** out your hand." .... Mt 12:13
up to him, took **h** of his feet, ... Mt 28:9
to the man, "**H** out your hand." .... Mk 3:5
Taking **h** of the girl's hand, ... Mk 5:41
But Jesus took **h** of the boy's .... Mk 9:27
to the man, "**H** out your hand." .... Lk 6:10
times it had taken **h** of him. .... Lk 8:29
But Jesus took **h** of her hand and .... Lk 8:54
you and will **h** you in on all .... Lk 19:43
look up and **h** your heads high, ... Lk 21:28
to her, "Don't **h** on to me, ... Jn 20:17
because death could not **h** him. .... Ac 2:24
do not **h** this sin against them." .... Ac 7:60
you and did not **h** back anything .... Ac 20:20
the ship to **h** it together. .... Ac 27:17
what is sin, and **h** on to what................. Rm 12:9
clay jars that **h** the treasure. 2Co 4:7
God did not **h** the world guilty 2Co 5:19
They do not **h** tightly to Christ, ... Col 2:19
Do not **h** back the work of the 1Th 5:19
grabbing **h** of the life that 1Ti 6:12
us **h** on to the faith we have. .... Heb 4:14
us strength to **h** on to the hope .... Heb 6:18
Let us **h** firmly to the hope that .... Heb 10:23

HOLDER

must **h** on, so you can do what .... Heb 10:36
So **h** on through your sufferings, ... Heb 12:7
He will **h** evil people and punish 2Pe 2:9
And I **h** the keys to death and to .... Rev 1:18

HOLDER

sword out of its **h** and killed 1Sa 17:51
put his sword back into its **h**. 1Ch 21:27
hid me in the **h** for his arrows. .... Is 49:2
Return to your **h**. Stop and be .... Je 47:6
will pull my sword out of its **h**, ... Eze 21:3
out from its **h** and attack all .... Eze 21:4
pulled my sword out from its **h**. .... Eze 21:5
a sword is pulled out of its **h**. .... Eze 21:28
Put the sword back in its **h**. .... Eze 21:30

HOLDING

he was **h** on to Esau's heel, ... Ge 25:26
he saw Isaac **h** his wife Rebekah .... Ge 26:8
was **h** the king's cup, so I took .... Ge 40:11
h the walking stick of God in my .... Ex 17:9
and your jars **h** the right amount .... Le 19:36
said to the servant **h** his hand, ... Jdg 16:26
was still **h** Goliath's head. 1Sa 17:57
is at the altar, **h** on to its 1Ki 1:51
h his sword drawn and pointed at 1Ch 21:16
with half the men **h** spears from.............. Ne 4:21
took turns **h** feasts in their .... Job 1:4
I will complain without **h** back; .... Job 10:1
good people give without **h** back. .... Pr 21:26
statue I am **h** is a false god. .... Is 44:20
and I am tired of **h** it in. .... Je 6:11
leather bags for **h** wine should .... Je 13:12
I was tired of **h** back my anger. .... Je 15:6
every strong man **h** his stomach.............. Je 30:6
up and saw a man **h** a line for .... Zch 2:1
little boxes **h** Scriptures that .... Mt 23:5
While the man was **h** on to Peter .... Ac 3:11
agreeing and the coats of..................... Ac 22:20
ropes that were **h** the rudders. .... Ac 27:40
By **h** on to the trustworthy word.............. Tit 1:9
h on as he did when we are .... Heb 13:13
The angels were **h** the four winds .... Rev 7:1
white robes and **h** palm branches .... Rev 7:9
h a golden pan for incense...................... Rev 8:3
The angel was **h** a small scroll .... Rev 10:2

HOLDS

unless the king **h** out his gold................. Est 4:11
If God **h** back the waters, there .... Job 12:15
because the LORD **h** their hand............... Ps 37:24
Judah **h** my royal scepter. .... Ps 60:7
I am the one who **h** it steady. .... Ps 75:3
The LORD **h** a cup of anger in his .... Ps 75:8
Judah **h** my royal scepter. .... Ps 108:8
do not know what the future **h**, ... Ec 8:7
and his right arm **h** me tight. .... Sng 2:6
and his right arm **h** me tight. .... Sng 8:3
your God, who **h** your right hand, ... Is 41:13
on anyone who **h** back his sword .... Je 48:10
the sky **h** back its rain and the .... Hag 1:10
and the ground **h** back its crops. .... Hag 1:10
Love is what **h** you all together .... Col 3:14
h everything together with his .... Heb 1:3
sin that so easily **h** us back. .... Heb 12:1
The One who **h** the seven stars in .... Rev 2:1
and true, who **h** the key of David .... Rev 3:7
The Ark that **h** the agreement God........... Rev 11:19

HOLE

punch a **h** through the slave's................. Ex 21:6
Make a **h** in the center for .... Ex 28:32
around the **h** so it will not .... Ex 28:32
They made a **h** in the center of .... Ex 39:23
dig a **h** and cover up your dung............... Dt 23:13

God opened up a **h** in the ground .... Jdg 15:19
box and made a **h** in the top of 2Ki 12:9
as if through a **h** in the wall, ... Job 30:14
They dig a **h** to trap others,..................... Ps 7:15
you have made a **h** in my ear to .... Ps 40:6
able to play near a cobra's **h**, ... Is 11:8
of terror will fall into a **h**. .... Is 24:18
out of the **h** will be caught .... Is 24:18
I looked, I saw a **h** in the wall. .... Eze 8:7
Dig a **h** through the wall while .... Eze 12:5
will dig a **h** through the wall .... Eze 12:12
cloth over a **h** in an old coat. .... Mt 9:16
the coat, making the **h** worse.................. Mt 9:16
it and dug a **h** for a winepress .... Mt 21:33
out and dug a **h** in the ground .... Mt 25:18
they dug a **h** in the roof right .... Mk 2:4
cloth over a **h** in an old coat. .... Mk 2:21
Then the **h** will be worse. .... Mk 2:21
it and dug a **h** for a winepress .... Mk 12:1
to cover a **h** in an old coat. .... Lk 5:36
through a **h** in the city wall.................... 2Co 11:33
key to the deep **h** that leads to .... Rev 9:1
it opened up the **h** that leads to .... Rev 9:2
came up from the **h** like smoke .... Rev 9:2
because of the smoke from the **h**. .... Rev 9:2

HOLES

the singers at the watering **h**. .... Jdg 5:11
out of the **h** they were hiding 1Sa 14:11
says to dig **h** in the valley. 2Ki 3:16
and that the **h** in the wall were .... Ne 4:7
h and hide in the ground from .... Is 2:10
cliffs and will dig **h** and hide .... Is 2:19
the thornbushes and watering **h**. .... Is 7:19
are terrors, **h**, and traps for .... Is 24:17
the city through **h** in the walls, ... Am 4:3
from their **h** to the LORD our God .... Mic 7:17
put it into a purse full of **h**." .... Hag 1:6
The foxes have **h** to live in,..................... Mt 8:20
The foxes have **h** to live in, ... Lk 9:58
in caves and **h** in the earth...................... Heb 11:38

HOLIDAY

He announced a **h** for all the .... Est 2:18

HOLIEST

the best and **h** part from what .... Nu 18:29

HOLINESS

promised by my **h**, I will not lie .... Ps 89:35
been dressed in **h** from birth; .... Ps 110:3
I will show my **h** by defeating................. Eze 28:22
will show my **h** when the nations .... Eze 28:25
will prove the **h** of my great .... Eze 36:23
will show my **h**, and I will make.............. Eze 38:23
faith, love, and **h**, with 1Ti 2:15

HOLLOW

boards and leave the inside **h**. .... Ex 27:8
of boards and left the inside **h**. .... Ex 38:7
You live in the **h** places of the................. Je 49:16
feet around, and **h** inside. .... Je 52:21
who live in the **h** places of the .... Ob 1:3

HOLON

Goshen, **H**, and Giloh. There were .... Jos 15:51
H, Debir, ... Jos 21:15
H, Jahzah, and Mephaath; .... Je 48:21

HOLY

you are standing on **h** ground. .... Ex 3:5
will guide them to your **h** place. .... Ex 15:13
the LORD's **h** day of rest. .... Ex 16:23
of priests and a **h** nation.' .... Ex 19:6
You are to be my **h** people. .... Ex 22:31
will separate the **H** Place from .... Ex 26:33
put the **h** crown on the turban. .... Ex 29:6

service to God and making it **h**. .... Ex 29:37
a perfume to make a **h** olive oil. .... Ex 30:25
to it to keep it pure and **h**. .... Ex 30:35
of rest, a day **h** for the LORD. .... Ex 31:15
the seventh day will be a **h** day, ... Ex 35:2
it is a most **h** part of the .... Le 2:3
the **h** things of the LORD, ... Le 5:15
without yeast in a **h** place. .... Le 6:16
be respected as **h** by those who .... Le 10:3
keep what is **h** separate from .... Le 10:10
Keep yourselves **h** for me because .... Le 11:44
into the Most **H** Place where the............... Le 16:2
may enter the Most **H** Place: .... Le 16:3
must put on the **h** linen inner .... Le 16:4
makes the Most **H** Place ready for .... Le 16:17
he did not respect my **h** name, ... Le 20:3
him as **h**, because he offers............... Le 21:8
offerings are **h**, and they are .... Le 22:2
family may eat the **h** offering............... Le 22:10
give their **h** offerings to the .... Le 22:15
appointed feasts as **h** meetings. .... Le 23:2
gives a house as **h** to the LORD,............... Le 27:14
have covered the **h** furniture and .... Nu 4:15
go near the Most **H** Place and not .... Nu 4:19
to carry the **h** things on their .... Nu 7:9
the one who is **h** near to him;............... Nu 16:5
took with him the **h** things and .... Nu 31:6
had the **h** oil poured on him .... Nu 35:25
Keep the Sabbath as a **h** day, ... Dt 5:12
You are **h** people who belong to .... Dt 7:6
for you, so the camp must be **h**. .... Dt 23:14
down from heaven, your **h** home. .... Dt 26:15
where you are standing is **h**." .... Jos 5:15
because he is a **h** God and a .... Jos 24:19
There is no one **h** like the LORD. 1Sa 2:2
priest gave David the **h** bread............... 1Sa 21:6
doors of the Most **H** Place and 1Ki 7:50
Tent, and the **h** utensils; 1Ki 8:4
that this is a **h** man of God who 2Ki 4:9
against me, the **H** One of Israel. 2Ki 19:22
Then he made the Most **H** Place. 2Ch 3:8
reached heaven, his **h** home. 2Ch 30:27
Put the **H** Ark in the Temple that 2Ch 35:3
live in safety in his **h** place. .... Ezr 9:8
This is a **h** day to the LORD your .... Ne 8:9
them about your **h** Sabbath and .... Ne 9:14
buy on the Sabbath or any **h** day. .... Ne 10:31
live in Jerusalem, the **h** city. .... Ne 11:1
in Jerusalem on my **h** mountain, ... Ps 2:6
answer me from his **h** mountain. .... Ps 3:4
The LORD is in his **h** temple; .... Ps 11:4
who may enter your **H** Tent? .... Ps 15:1
You will not let your **h** one rot. .... Ps 16:10
him from his **h** heaven and saves .... Ps 20:6
Who may stand in his **h** Temple? .... Ps 24:3
hands toward your Most **H** Place. .... Ps 28:2
because we trust his **h** name. .... Ps 33:21
the **h** place where God Most High .... Ps 46:4
God sits on his **h** throne............... Ps 47:8
of our God, on his **h** mountain. .... Ps 48:1
you or take your **H** Spirit away .... Ps 51:11
God is in his **h** Temple. .... Ps 68:5
from Mount Sinai to his **h** place. .... Ps 68:17
with the lyre, **H** One of Israel. .... Ps 71:22
God brought them to his **h** land,............... Ps 78:54
it is great, **h** and to be feared............... Ps 99:3
in me, praise his **h** name. .... Ps 103:1
remembered his **h** promise to his .... Ps 105:42
He is **h** and wonderful. .... Ps 111:9
praise his **h** name forever. .... Ps 145:21
begins with knowing the **H** One. .... Pr 9:10
know much about God, the **H** One. .... Pr 30:3
hate God, the **H** One of Israel, ... Is 1:4

in Jerusalem will be called **h**; .... Is 4:3
H, holy, holy is the LORD .... Is 6:3
the **H** One will be like a flame. .... Is 10:17
each other on all my **h** mountain, ... Is 11:9
because the **H** One of Israel does .... Is 12:6
beautiful again, **h** city of............... Is 52:1
LORD will show his **h** power to .... Is 52:10
God lives forever and is **h**. .... Is 57:15
I live in a high and **h** place, ... Is 57:15
yourselves on that **h** day. .... Is 58:13
will be called the **H** People,............... Is 62:12
and made his **H** Spirit very sad .... Is 63:10
one who put his **H** Spirit among............... Is 63:11
other on all my **h** mountain," .... Is 65:25
presence of the **H** One of Israel. .... Je 51:5
to dishonor my **h** name with your .... Eze 20:39
They dishonored my **h** name in the .... Eze 36:20
the LORD, the **H** One in Israel. .... Eze 39:7
what was **h** from that which .... Eze 42:20
between what is **h** and what is .... Eze 44:23
spirit of the **h** gods is in you, ... Da 4:9
h angel coming down from heaven. .... Da 4:13
h ones declared the sentence. .... Da 4:17
spirit of the **h** gods is in you. .... Da 4:18
and to appoint a most **h** place. .... Da 9:24
to go against the **h** agreement. .... Da 11:28
I am the **H** One, and I am among .... Hos 11:9
God, live on my **h** Mount Zion. .... Joe 3:17
Jerusalem will be a **h** place, ... Joe 3:17
and so they ruin my **h** name. .... Am 2:7
to see your **H** Temple again.' .... Jnh 2:4
the Lord from his **H** Temple. .... Mic 1:2
live forever, my God, my **h** God. .... Hab 1:12
The LORD is in his **H** Temple; .... Hab 2:20
H One comes from Mount Paran. .... Hab 3:3
as his own part of the **h** land, ... Zch 2:12
by the power of the **H** Spirit. .... Mt 1:18
you with the **H** Spirit and fire. .... Mt 3:11
led Jesus to the **h** city of .... Mt 4:5
Don't give **h** things to dogs, ... Mt 7:6
against the **H** Spirit will not be .... Mt 12:32
this standing in the **h** place." .... Mt 24:15
dead and went into the **h** city,............... Mt 27:53
and the Son and the **H** Spirit. .... Mt 28:19
I know who you are—God's **H** One!" .... Mk 1:24
it will be the **H** Spirit. .... Mk 13:11
be filled with the **H** Spirit. .... Lk 1:15
The **H** Spirit will come upon you, ... Lk 1:35
the baby will be **h** and will be............... Lk 1:35
things for me. His name is **h**. .... Lk 1:49
this through his **h** prophets who .... Lk 1:70
he would remember his **h** promise. .... Lk 1:72
and the **H** Spirit was in him. .... Lk 2:25
been told by the **H** Spirit that .... Lk 2:26
you with the **H** Spirit and fire. .... Lk 3:16
the **H** Spirit came down on him .... Lk 3:22
filled with the **H** Spirit, ... Lk 4:1
was talking about the **H** Spirit. .... Jn 7:39
This Helper is the **H** Spirit whom .... Jn 14:26
H Father, keep them safe by the .... Jn 17:11
and said, "Receive the **H** Spirit. .... Jn 20:22
with the help of the **H** Spirit, ... Ac 1:2
be baptized with the **H** Spirit." .... Ac 1:5
But when the **H** Spirit comes to .... Ac 1:8
all filled with the **H** Spirit, ... Ac 2:4
by the power the **H** Spirit was .... Ac 2:4
You will not let your **H** One rot. .... Ac 2:27
has given the **H** Spirit to Jesus .... Ac 2:33
the gift of the **H** Spirit. .... Ac 2:38
the One who is **h** and good but .... Ac 3:14
Jesus is your **h** servant, the One............... Ac 4:27
to lie to the **H** Spirit and to .... Ac 5:3
faith and full of the **H** Spirit .... Ac 6:5

you are standing on **h** ground. .... Ac 7:33
what the **H** Spirit is trying .... Ac 7:51
might receive the **H** Spirit. .... Ac 8:15
will receive the **H** Spirit." .... Ac 8:19
be filled with the **H** Spirit.". .... Ac 9:17
encouraged by the **H** Spirit, ... Ac 9:31
be baptized with the **H** Spirit.' .... Ac 11:16
sent out by the **H** Spirit, went .... Ac 13:4
will not let your **H** One rot.' .... Ac 13:35
with joy and the **H** Spirit. .... Ac 13:52
pleased the **H** Spirit that you .... Ac 15:28
receive the **H** Spirit when you .... Ac 19:2
is written in the **H** Scriptures................. Rm 1:2
his love through the **H** Spirit, ... Rm 5:5
So the law is **h,** and the command .... Rm 7:12
is ruled by the **H** Spirit, ... Rm 9:1
peace, and joy in the **H** Spirit. .... Rm 14:17
by the power of the **H** Spirit. .... Rm 15:13
an offering made **h** by the Holy .... Rm 15:16
Greet each other with a **h** kiss. .... Rm 16:16
God's temple is **h** and you are 1Co 3:17
a temple for the **H** Spirit who is 1Co 6:19
a believer is made **h** through his.......... 1Co 7:14
the help of the **H** Spirit. 1Co 12:3
of the **H** Spirit be with 2Co 13:14
giving you the **H** Spirit that he .... Eph 1:13
grow and become a **h** temple in .... Eph 2:21
do not make the **H** Spirit sad. .... Eph 4:30
presence as people who are **h,** .... Col 1:22
you and made you his **h** people. .... Col 3:12
power, with the **H** Spirit, and 1Th 1:5
that comes from the **H** Spirit. 1Th 1:6
One who gives us his **H** Spirit. 1Th 4:8
up their hands in a **h** manner,................ 1Ti 2:8
the help of the **H** Spirit who 2Ti 1:14
known the **H** Scriptures which 2Ti 3:15
and be **h** and self-controlled. .... Tit 1:8
new people through the **H** Spirit. .... Tit 3:5
and shared in the **H** Spirit. .... Heb 6:4
the Most **H** Place only once—............. Heb 9:7
go into the Most **H** Place made by .... Heb 9:24
enters the Most **H** Place once .... Heb 9:25
The **H** Spirit also tells us about .... Heb 10:15
you by making you his **h** people, ... 1Pe 1:2
But be **h** in all you do, just as 1Pe 1:15
must be **h,** because I am holy. 1Pe 1:16
to be **h** priests who offer 1Pe 2:5
priests, a **h** nation, a people 1Pe 2:9
people led by the **H** Spirit spoke............ 2Pe 1:21
gift that the **H** One gave you, ... 1Jn 2:20
use your most **h** faith to build........... Jud 1:20
what the One who is **h** and true,............. Rev 3:7
H, holy, holy is the Lord God .... Rev 4:8
a loud voice, "**H** and true Lord, ... Rev 6:10
trample on the **h** city for .... Rev 11:2
sulfur before the **h** angels and .... Rev 14:10
Only you are **h.** All the nations .... Rev 15:4
God's **h** people and apostles and .... Rev 18:20
Blessed and **h** are those who .... Rev 20:6
showed me the **h** city, Jerusalem .... Rev 21:10
is **h** continue to be holy. .... Rev 22:11

HOMAM
sons of Lotan were Hori and **H.** .... Ge 36:22
Lotan's sons were Hori and **H,** 1Ch 1:39

HOME
has brought me **h** with nothing. .... Ru 1:21
"Please come **h** and eat with me." 1Ki 13:15
The sparrows have found a **h,**............... Ps 84:3
the stork's **h** is in the fir .... Ps 104:17
I will not go **h** to my house, ... Ps 132:3
will bless the **h** of those who do .... Pr 3:33
stubborn and never stayed at **h.** .... Pr 7:11

My husband is not **h;** he has gone .... Pr 7:19
will go to your everlasting **h,** .... Ec 12:5
It was a **h** for the wild animals, ... Da 4:21
great Babylon as my royal **h.** .... Da 4:30
my servant is at **h** in bed. .... Mt 8:6
Go **h** to your family and tell .... Mk 5:19
and goes **h.** He calls to his .... Lk 15:6
them and make our **h** with them. .... Jn 14:23
took her to live in his **h.** .... Jn 19:27
should eat at **h** so that in..................... 1Co 11:34
ask their own husbands at **h.** 1Co 14:35
body and be at **h** with the Lord. 2Co 5:8
good workers at **h,** to be kind, ... Tit 2:5
the church that meets in your **h:**............. Phm 1:2
spies into her **h** and helped them .... Jam 2:25
power but left their proper **h.** .... Jud 1:6
has become a **h** for demons and............. Rev 18:2

HOMELAND
son with me back to your **h?**"................ Ge 24:5
a foreigner. This is not your **h.** 2Sa 15:19
and destroyed their **h.** .... Je 10:25
never return or see his **h** again. .... Je 22:10
you to be taken far from your **h.**............. Je 27:10
to our own people and our **h.** .... Je 46:16
But our **h** is in heaven, and we .... Php 3:20

HOMELANDS
In their **h** those soldiers called .... Je 46:17

HOMELESS
h people into your own homes. .... Is 58:7
Jerusalem is suffering and **h.** .... La 1:7

HOMER
will always be a tenth of a **h,** .... Eze 45:11
will always be a tenth of a **h.** .... Eze 45:11
they follow will be the **h.** .... Eze 45:11
an ephah from every **h** of wheat, ... Eze 45:13
an ephah from every **h** of barley. .... Eze 45:13
Ten baths make a **h** and also make........... Eze 45:14

HOMES
have a hundred times more **h,** .... Mk 10:30
will welcome me into their **h.'**................ Lk 16:4
They ate together in their **h,** .... Ac 2:46
and in people's **h** they continued .... Ac 5:42
went into the **h** of people who .... Ac 11:3
you in public and in your **h.** .... Ac 20:20
strangers in need into your **h.**................ Rm 12:13
we have no **h** in which to live. 1Co 4:11
can eat and drink in your own **h!** 1Co 11:22
children, and manage their **h.**............... 1Ti 5:14
them go into **h** and get control 2Ti 3:6
away from their **h** and are 1Pe 1:1
Open your **h** to each other, ... 1Pe 4:9

HOMETOWN
which he put in his **h** of Ophrah. .... Jdg 8:27
to Ophrah, the **h** of his father,................ Jdg 9:5
from his family and his **h.** .... Ru 4:10
him go to his **h** of Bethlehem.................. 1Sa 20:6
buried Samuel in his **h** of Ramah. 1Sa 28:3
to come from his **h** of Giloh. 2Sa 15:12
his donkey and went to his **h.**................. 2Sa 17:23
at Gibeah, the **h** of Saul, the 2Sa 21:6
spread from the **h** of Sihon king............. Je 48:45
He went to his **h** and taught the .... Mt 13:54
in his **h** and in his own home................. Mt 13:57
left there and went to his **h,** .... Mk 6:1
except in his **h** and with his own .... Mk 6:4
is not accepted in his **h.** .... Lk 4:24

HOMETOWNS
Israelites settled in their **h.** .... Ezr 2:70
were settled in their **h,** .... Ezr 3:1

HONEST

Their **h** will surely be shocked .... Je 49:20
Their **h** will surely be shocked .... Je 50:45

HONEST

you can easily see if I am **h**. .... Ge 30:33
We are **h** men, not spies." .... Ge 42:11
you are **h** men, let one of your .... Ge 42:19
we told him that we were **h** men, ... Ge 42:31
a way I can know you are **h** men: .... Ge 42:33
you are not spies but **h** men. .... Ge 42:34
innocent or **h** person to be put .... Ex 23:7
not because you are good and **h**, ... Dt 9:5
must have true and **h** weights and .... Dt 25:15
completely **h** and sincere when .... Jdg 9:16
you have been **h** and sincere to .... Jdg 9:19
and he was **h** and lived right. 1Ki 3:6
because the workers were **h**. 2Ki 12:15
and I gave with an **h** heart. 1Ch 29:17
Hananiah was **h** and feared God .... Ne 7:2
Everyone knew they were **h**. .... Ne 13:13
He was an **h** and innocent man; .... Job 1:1
He is an **h** and innocent man, ... Job 1:8
He is an **h** and innocent man, ... Job 2:3
h people will never be destroyed. .... Job 4:7
H words are painful, but your .... Job 6:25
are good and **h**, he will stand .... Job 8:6
H people are upset about this; .... Job 17:8
Then an **h** person could present .... Job 23:7
let God weigh me on **h** scales. .... Job 31:6
My words come from an **h** heart, ... Job 33:3
dark places at those who are **h**. .... Ps 11:2
so **h** people will see his face. .... Ps 11:7
h people should praise him. .... Ps 33:1
to kill those who are **h**. .... Ps 37:14
person, and watch the **h** one. .... Ps 37:37
H people will rule over them in .... Ps 49:14
who is **h** praise the LORD .... Ps 64:10
all who are **h** will follow it. .... Ps 94:15
joy belongs to those who are **h**. .... Ps 97:11
the children of **h** people will be .... Ps 112:2
shines in the dark for **h** people, ... Ps 112:4
I praised you with an **h** heart. .... Ps 119:7
are good, whose hearts are **h**. .... Ps 125:4
h people will live in his .... Ps 140:13
you to do what is **h** and fair and .... Pr 1:3
up wisdom for those who are **h**. .... Pr 2:7
what is **h** and fair and what .... Pr 2:9
Those who are **h** will live in the .... Pr 2:21
is a friend to those who are **h**. .... Pr 3:32
Everything I say is **h**; .... Pr 8:8
h person will live in safety, ... Pr 10:9
he is pleased with **h** weights. .... Pr 11:1
brings freedom to **h** people, ... Pr 11:6
An **h** witness tells the truth, ... Pr 12:17
is right protects the **h** person, ... Pr 13:6
h people work at being right. .... Pr 14:9
likes the prayers of **h** people. .... Pr 15:8
but an **h** person's life is like a .... Pr 15:19
The LORD wants **h** balances and .... Pr 16:11
Kings like **h** people; they value .... Pr 16:13
or to beat leaders for being **h**. .... Pr 17:26
to be poor and **h** than to be .... Pr 19:1
people who live **h** lives will be .... Pr 20:7
lives, but **h** people do right. .... Pr 21:8
An **h** answer is as pleasing as a .... Pr 24:26
will be **h** and last a long .... Pr 25:5
hate an **h** person and try to .... Pr 29:10
the wicked hate those who are **h**. .... Pr 29:27
but you are not **h** or sincere. .... Is 48:1
is **h** is not allowed to enter .... Is 59:14
in a truthful, **h**, and right way, ... Je 4:2
one person who does **h** things, ... Je 5:1
and do what is right and **h**. .... Eze 33:14

must have **h** scales, an honest .... Eze 45:10
an **h** dry measurement and an .... Eze 45:10
and an **h** liquid measurement .... Eze 45:10
the most **h** of them is worse than .... Mic 7:4
that you are an **h** man and that .... Mt 22:16
we know that you are an **h** man. .... Mk 12:14
h hearts and obey it and .... Lk 8:15
we have had an **h** and sincere 2Co 1:12
They should earn an **h** living for .... Eph 4:28
we lived in a holy and **h** way, ... 1Th 2:10
It is always fair and **h**. .... Jam 3:17
to help your **h** minds remember. 2Pe 3:1

HONESTLY

because they are working **h**." 2Ki 22:7
But he will judge the poor **h**; .... Is 11:4
but tell me everything **h**." .... Je 38:14
but serve them **h**, because you .... Col 3:22

HONESTY

so may goodness and **h** guard me. .... Ps 25:21
Good people will be guided by **h**; .... Pr 11:3
With peace and **h** they did what I .... Mal 2:6
do it with **h** and seriousness. .... Tit 2:7

HONEY

balm, some **h**, spices, myrrh, ... Ge 43:11
tasted like wafers made with **h**. .... Ex 16:31
any yeast or **h** in an offering .... Le 2:11
bring yeast and **h** to the LORD as .... Le 2:12
pomegranates, olive oil, and **h**. .... Dt 8:8
He gave them **h** from the rocks. .... Dt 32:13
a swarm of bees and **h** in it. .... Jdg 14:8
got some of the **h** with his hands .... Jdg 14:9
he had taken the **h** from the body .... Jdg 14:9
said, "What is sweeter than **h**? .... Jdg 14:18
there was some **h** on the ground. 1Sa 14:25
upon some **h**, but no one took 1Sa 14:26
stick into the **h** and lifted some 1Sa 14:27
just tasting a little of this **h**! 1Sa 14:29
tasted a little **h** from the end 1Sa 14:43
h, milk curds, sheep, and cheese 2Sa 17:29
some cakes, and a jar of **h**. 1Ki 14:3
and vineyards, olives, and **h**. 2Ki 18:32
new wine, oil, **h**, and everything 2Ch 31:5
rivers flowing with **h** and cream. .... Job 20:17
sweeter than **h**, even the finest .... Ps 19:10
than honey, even the finest **h**. .... Ps 19:10
fill you with **h** from the rocks. .... Ps 81:16
sweeter than **h** in my mouth! .... Ps 119:103
man's wife may seem sweet as **h**; .... Pr 5:3
My child, eat **h** because it is .... Pr 24:13
H from the honeycomb tastes .... Pr 24:13
If you find **h**, don't eat too .... Pr 25:16
is not good to eat too much **h**, ... Pr 25:27
full, not even **h** tastes good, ... Pr 27:7
My bride, your lips drip **h**; .... Sng 4:11
h and milk are under your tongue. .... Sng 4:11
eaten my honeycomb and my **h**. .... Sng 5:1
milk curds and **h** when he learns .... Is 7:15
to eating just milk curds and **h**. .... Is 7:22
barley and oil and **h** that we .... Je 41:8
was as sweet as **h** in my mouth. .... Eze 3:3
fine flour, **h**, and olive oil. .... Eze 16:13
flour, oil, and **h** I gave you to .... Eze 16:19
Minnith, and for **h**, olive oil, ... Eze 27:17
food, he ate locusts and wild **h**. .... Mt 3:4
and ate locusts and wild **h**. .... Mk 1:6
mouth it will be sweet as **h**." .... Rev 10:9
my mouth it tasted sweet as **h**, ... Rev 10:10

HONEYCOMB

Pleasant words are like a **h**, ... Pr 16:24
Honey from the **h** tastes sweet. .... Pr 24:13
I have eaten my **h** and my honey. .... Sng 5:1

HONOR

This will bring **h** to me, and the .... Ex 14:4
H your father and your mother so .... Ex 20:12
H your father and your mother as .... Dt 5:16
for: riches and **h.** During your 1Ki 3:13
will no longer **h** their husbands. .... Est 1:17
not bow down or show him **h.** .... Est 3:2
king want to **h** more than me?" .... Est 6:6
They blow my **h** away as if by a .... Job 30:15
crowned them with glory and **h.** .... Ps 8:5
you gave him **h** and praise. .... Ps 21:5
the kings on earth will **h** you. .... Ps 102:15
H the LORD with your wealth and .... Pr 3:9
hand she gives you riches and **h.** .... Pr 3:16
finds life, success, and **h.** .... Pr 21:21
Giving **h** to a foolish person is .... Pr 26:8
H God and obey his commands, ... Ec 12:13
mouths, and **h** me with their .... Is 29:13
give praise and **h** and glory to .... Da 4:37
You did not **h** God, who has power. .... Da 5:23
a father, so why don't you **h** me? .... Mal 1:6
'**H** your father and your mother,' .... Mt 15:4
person not to **h** his father or .... Mt 15:6
people show **h** to me with words .... Mt 15:8
people will **h** the Son as much .... Jn 5:23
I give **h** to my Father, but you .... Jn 8:49
If I give **h** to myself, that .... Jn 8:54
My Father will **h** anyone who .... Jn 12:26
each other more **h** than you want .... Rm 12:10
Show respect and **h** to them all. .... Rm 13:7
to which we give the most **h.** 1Co 12:23
be **h** and glory forever and ever. 1Ti 1:17
well should receive double **h,** 1Ti 5:17
crowned them with glory and **h.** .... Heb 2:7
glory and **h** when Jesus Christ 1Pe 1:7
family, respect God, **h** the king. 1Pe 2:17
serve him and all you who **h** him, ... Rev 19:5
glory and the **h** of the nations .... Rev 21:26

HONORABLE

the great and **h** Ashurbanipal .... Ezr 4:10
that are true and **h** and right .... Php 4:8
in a way that is holy and **h.** 1Th 4:4
are making an **h** place for 1Ti 3:13

HONORED

and was more **h** than the Three. 2Sa 23:19
and Jerusalem **h** Hezekiah when he 2Ch 32:33
All the **h** and important things .... Is 22:24
of sheep nor **h** me with your .... Is 43:23
Those who **h** her now hate her, ... La 1:8
king **h** him and commanded that .... Da 2:46
A prophet is **h** everywhere except .... Mt 13:57
A prophet is **h** everywhere except .... Mk 6:4
Or if one part of our body is **h,** 1Co 12:26
should be **h** by everyone, ... Heb 13:4

HONORING

more can I say to you for **h** me, ... 1Ch 17:18
h God and staying away from evil. .... Job 1:8
h God and staying away from evil. .... Job 2:3

HONORS

had received many riches and **h.** 1Ch 29:28
Job **h** God for a good reason. .... Job 1:9
New **h** will come to me .... Job 29:20
is kind to the needy **h** God. .... Pr 14:31
Holy One of Israel with **h** in you." .... Is 55:5
the priests or **h** the elders. .... La 4:16
but none of them **h** me at all. .... Hos 11:7
and the wise person **h** him. .... Mic 6:9
says, "A son **h** his father, and a .... Mal 1:6
and a servant **h** his master." .... Mal 1:6
kind of life that **h** and pleases. .... Col 1:10

HOOF

not a **h** will be left behind. .... Ex 10:26
cud but does not have a split **h;** .... Le 11:4
cud but does not have a split **h;** .... Le 11:5
cud but does not have a split **h;** .... Le 11:6
pig has a split **h** that is .... Le 11:7
has a split **h** and chews the cud, ... Dt 14:6

HOOFS

that has split **h** completely .... Le 11:3
the cud or only have split **h,** .... Le 11:4
Some animals have split **h,** .... Le 11:26
but the **h** are not completely .... Le 11:26
but they do not have split **h,** .... Dt 14:7
they have split **h,** but they do .... Dt 14:8
the horses' **h** beat the ground .... Jdg 5:22
a bull with horns and **h.** .... Ps 69:31
The horses' **h** are hard as rocks, ... Is 5:28
like a calf's **h** and sparkled. .... Eze 1:7
h of his horses will run over .... Eze 26:11
and the **h** of cattle will not .... Eze 32:13
horns of iron and **h** of bronze. .... Mic 4:13
best sheep and tear off their **h.** .... Zch 11:16

HOOK

I will put my **h** in your nose and 2Ki 19:28
on a fish **h** or tie its tongue .... Job 41:1
its nose or a **h** in its jaw? .... Job 41:2
I will put my **h** in your nose and .... Is 37:29

HOOKS

make fifty gold **h** to join the .... Ex 26:6
make fifty bronze **h** and put them .... Ex 26:11
curtain by gold **h** on four posts .... Ex 26:32
curtain from the **h** in the roof, ... Ex 26:33
Make gold **h** for them on which to .... Ex 26:37
with silver **h** and bands on .... Ex 27:10
curtains on silver **h** and bands .... Ex 27:11
bands and **h** and bronze bases. .... Ex 27:17
its covering, the **h,** frames, ... Ex 35:11
made fifty gold **h** to join the .... Ex 36:13
they made gold **h** for the posts, ... Ex 36:36
made five posts and **h** for it. .... Ex 36:38
hung on silver **h** and bands, ... Ex 38:10
it hung on silver **h** and bands on .... Ex 38:11
up by silver **h** and bands on ten .... Ex 38:12
The **h** and the bands on the posts .... Ex 38:17
h and bands on the posts were .... Ex 38:19
to make the **h** for the posts .... Ex 38:28
its furniture, **h,** frames, ... Ex 39:33
be like sharp **h** in your eyes .... Nu 33:55
Manasseh, put **h** in him, placed 2Ch 33:11
Can anyone put **h** in its nose? .... Job 40:24
you gold earrings with silver **h.** .... Sng 1:11
their spears into **h** for trimming .... Is 2:4
brought him with **h** to the land .... Eze 19:4
But I will put **h** in your jaws, ... Eze 29:4
around and put **h** in your jaws. .... Eze 38:4
spears from your **h** for trimming .... Joe 3:10
you will be taken away by **h,** .... Am 4:2
their spears into **h** for trimming .... Mic 4:3
The enemy brings them in with **h.** .... Hab 1:15

HOOPOES

any kind of heron, **h,** or bats. .... Le 11:19
kind of heron, the **h,** or bats. .... Dt 14:18

HOOT

The owl will **h** through the .... Zph 2:14

HOPE

'I still have **h'** and had another .... Ru 1:12
I **h** I can continue to please .... Ru 2:13
I **h** I will always be able to 2Sa 16:4
is like a shadow. There is no **h.** 1Ch 29:15
our God gives us **h** and a little .... Ezr 9:8
there is still **h** for Israel. .... Ezr 10:2

should have **h** because you are .... Job 4:6
the poor have **h,** while those who .... Job 5:16
God would give me what I **h** for............... Job 6:8
There is nothing to **h** for, ... Job 6:11
they come to an end without **h.** .... Job 7:6
h of the wicked will be gone. .... Job 8:13
What they **h** in is easily broken; .... Job 8:14
feel safe because there is **h;** .... Job 11:18
Their only **h** will be to die." .... Job 11:20
God kills me, I have **h** in him; .... Job 13:15
there is **h** that it will grow .... Job 14:7
In the same way, you destroy **h.** .... Job 14:19
the only home I **h** for is the .... Job 17:13
then, is my **h?** Who can see any .... Job 17:15
Who can see any **h** for me?................... Job 17:15
Will **h** go down to the gates of .... Job 17:16
he destroys my **h** like a fallen................. Job 19:10
What **h** do the wicked have when .... Job 27:8
widows give up **h** while looking .... Job 31:16
There is no **h** of defeating it; .... Job 41:9
and am glad. Even my body has **h,**........... Ps 16:9
I **h** my words and thoughts please .... Ps 19:14
My **h** is in you, so may goodness .... Ps 25:21
you who put your **h** in the LORD .... Ps 31:24
who put their **h** in his love. .... Ps 33:18
So our **h** is in the LORD......................... Ps 33:20
to us as we put our **h** in you. .... Ps 33:22
So, Lord, what **h** do I have? .... Ps 39:7
hope do I have? You are my **h.** .... Ps 39:7
should put my **h** in God and keep .... Ps 42:5
should put my **h** in God and keep .... Ps 42:11
should put my **h** in God and keep .... Ps 43:5
rest in God; only he gives me **h.** .... Ps 62:5
let those who **h** in you be .... Ps 69:6
LORD, you are my **h.** LORD, I have .... Ps 71:5
always have **h** and will praise................. Ps 71:14
me, your servant; it gives me **h.** .... Ps 119:49
because I put my **h** in your word. .... Ps 119:74
save me, but I **h** in your word. .... Ps 119:81
and my shield; I **h** in your word............... Ps 119:114
and cry out. I **h** in your word.................. Ps 119:147
put your **h** in the LORD because............... Ps 130:7
put your **h** in the LORD now and .... Ps 131:3
h is in the LORD their God. .... Ps 146:5
wicked die, **h** dies with them; .... Pr 11:7
their **h** in riches will come to .... Pr 11:7
children while there is still **h;** .... Pr 19:18
you will have **h** for the future, ... Pr 23:18
you have **h** for the future, ... Pr 24:14
person has nothing to **h** for; .... Pr 24:20
There is more **h** for a foolish .... Pr 26:12
There is more **h** for a foolish .... Pr 29:20
But anyone still alive has **h;** .... Ec 9:4
who weave linen will lose **h.** .... Is 19:9
They **h** they will be saved by the .... Is 30:2
will not lose **h** or give up until .... Is 42:4
We **h** for a bright light, but all .... Is 59:9
h for light, but he will turn .... Je 13:16
God, the **H** of Israel, you have .... Je 14:8
are our only **h,** because you are .... Je 14:22
LORD, **h** of Israel, those who .... Je 17:13
give you **h** and a good future. .... Je 29:11
is **h** for you in the future, ... Je 31:17
and I have no **h** in the LORD." .... La 3:18
But I have **h** when I think of .... La 3:21
LORD is mine, so I **h** in him." .... La 3:24
is good to those who **h** in him, ... La 3:25
maybe there is still **h.** .... La 3:29
the prince will give up **h,** .... Eze 7:27
they still **h** their words will .... Eze 13:6
that there was no **h** for her cub. .... Eze 19:5
dried up, and our **h** has gone.................. Eze 37:11
Valley of Trouble a door of **h.** .... Hos 2:15

but I **h** to see your Holy Temple .... Jnh 2:4
the people of Ekron will lose **h.** .... Zch 9:5
who have **h,** return to your .... Zch 9:12
the non-Jewish people find **h.**" .... Mt 12:21
always pray and never lose **h.**................. Lk 18:1
I rejoice. Even my body has **h,** .... Ac 2:26
I have the same **h** in God that .... Ac 24:15
they have—the **h** that all people,............ Ac 24:15
h you can question him and give .... Ac 25:26
because I **h** for the promise .... Ac 26:6
of our people **h** to receive as .... Ac 26:7
me because I **h** for this same .... Ac 26:7
we lost all **h** of being saved. .... Ac 27:20
I believe in the **h** of Israel."................... Ac 28:20
was no **h** that Abraham would .... Rm 4:18
because of the **h** we have of .... Rm 5:2
and character produces **h.** .... Rm 5:4
And this **h** will never disappoint............. Rm 5:5
all along there was this **h:** .... Rm 8:20
were saved, and we have this **h.** .... Rm 8:24
for, that is not really **h.** .... Rm 8:24
People do not **h** for something .... Rm 8:24
I **h** I can make my own people .... Rm 11:14
Be joyful because you have **h.**............... Rm 12:12
so that we can have **h.**............................ Rm 15:4
they will have **h** because of him............. Rm 15:12
God who gives **h** will fill you .... Rm 15:13
Then your **h** will overflow by the .... Rm 15:13
I **h** to visit you on my way to .... Rm 15:24
I **h** you can help me on my trip. .... Rm 15:24
the grain should **h** to get some 1Co 9:10
forever: faith, **h,** and love. 1Co 13:13
If our **h** in Christ is for this.................... 1Co 15:19
I **h** to stay a longer time with 1Co 16:7
Our **h** for you is strong, knowing 2Co 1:7
We even gave up **h** of living. 2Co 1:8
We have put our **h** in him, and he 2Co 1:10
We have this **h,** so we are very 2Co 3:12
do not give up the **h** of living................. 2Co 4:8
and I **h** that in your hearts you 2Co 5:11
h that as your faith continues 2Co 10:15
But I **h** you will see that we 2Co 13:6
experiences wasted? I **h** not! .... Gal 3:4
we have the true **h** that comes .... Gal 5:5
we wait eagerly for this **h.** .... Gal 5:5
I **h** I will never brag about .... Gal 6:14
will know the **h** to which he has............. Eph 1:18
You had no **h,** and you did not .... Eph 2:12
God called you to have one **h.**................ Eph 4:4
I expect and **h** that I will not .... Php 1:20
I **h** in the Lord Jesus to send .... Php 2:19
Then I have that I myself will .... Php 3:11
and love because of your **h,** .... Col 1:5
and what you **h** for is kept safe .... Col 1:5
about this **h** when you heard .... Col 1:5
away from the **h** brought to you .... Col 1:23
He is our only **h** for glory....................... Col 1:27
because of your **h** in our Lord 1Th 1:3
You are our **h,** our joy, and the 1Th 2:19
be sad, as others who have no **h.** 1Th 4:13
and the **h** of salvation should be 1Th 5:8
Savior and Christ Jesus our **h.** 1Ti 1:1
Although I **h** I can come to you 1Ti 3:14
h in the living God who is the................. 1Ti 4:10
puts her **h** in God and continues............ 1Ti 5:5
Tell them to **h** in God, not in 1Ti 6:17
from the **h** for life forever, ... Tit 1:2
for our great **h** and the coming .... Tit 2:13
we could have the **h** of receiving .... Tit 3:7
because I **h** God will answer your .... Phm 1:22
we confidently maintain our **h.** .... Heb 3:6
will surely get what you **h** for. .... Heb 6:11
to hold on to the **h** we have been .... Heb 6:18

H

HOPED (continued)

We have this **h** as an anchor for .... Heb 6:19
now a better **h** has been given .... Heb 7:19
and with this **h** we can come near .... Heb 7:19
firmly to the **h** that we have .... Heb 10:23
the things we **h** for and knowing .... Heb 11:1
I **h** you stay warm and get plenty .... Jam 2:16
Do not give up **h**, because the................. Jam 5:8
be born again into a living **h**, ... 1Pe 1:3
Now we **h** for the blessings God.............. 1Pe 1:4
your **h** should be for the gift 1Pe 1:13
faith and your **h** are in God. 1Pe 1:21
to explain about the **h** you have,............. 1Pe 3:15
who have their **h** in Christ keep 1Jn 3:3
I **h** to come to you and talk face 2Jn 1:12
h to see you soon and talk face 3Jn 1:14

HOPED

people had **h** to defeat them, ... Est 9:1
But when I **h** for good, only evil .... Job 30:26
sad not to get what you **h** for. .... Pr 13:12
He **h** good grapes would grow .... Is 5:2
He **h** for right living, but there .... Is 5:7
We **h** to have peace, but nothing.............. Je 8:15
We **h** for a time when he would .... Je 8:15
We **h** for peace, but nothing good .... Je 14:19
the one you **h** would save you. .... Jn 5:45
time Felix **h** that Paul would .... Ac 24:26
They **h** we could go to Phoenix .... Ac 27:12
first people who **h** in Christ, ... Eph 1:12

HOPEFULLY

and the traders of Sheba look **h**. .... Job 6:19

HOPES

h of the poor will never die. .... Ps 9:18
be embarrassed because of my **h**. .... Ps 119:116
trusts, always **h**, and always 1Co 13:7
in Ephesus only with human **h**, ... 1Co 15:32

HOPHNI

Shiloh was where **H** and Phinehas, ... 1Sa 1:3
Both your sons, **H** and Phinehas, ... 1Sa 2:34
Eli's two sons, **H** and Phinehas, ... 1Sa 4:4
Eli's two sons, **H** and Phinehas, ... 1Sa 4:11

HOPHRA

'H king of Egypt has enemies who .... Je 44:30

HOPING

h to take them for himself. 2Ch 32:1
watch my steps, **h** to kill me. .... Ps 56:6
wicked things, **h** things will .... Da 2:9
H to trap him, they asked Jesus .... Mk 8:11
the people were **h** for the Christ .... Lk 3:15
always **h** to get something back,.............. Lk 6:34
them without **h** to get anything .... Lk 6:35
h to see Jesus work a miracle. .... Lk 23:8
But we were **h** that he would free .... Lk 24:21
h that when Peter passed by at .... Ac 5:15
believed God and continued **h**, ... Rm 4:18
But we are **h** for something we do .... Rm 8:25

HOPPING

have left, the **h** locusts have .... Joe 1:4
what the **h** locusts have left, ... Joe 1:4
swarming locusts and **h** locusts, ... Joe 2:25
Grow in number like **h** locusts; .... Nah 3:15

HOR

moved from Kadesh to Mount **H**, ... Nu 20:22
his son Eleazar up on Mount **H**, ... Nu 20:25
climbed up Mount **H**, and all the .... Nu 20:27
left Mount **H** and went on the................. Nu 21:4
and camped at **H** Haggidgad. .... Nu 33:32
They left **H** Haggidgad and camped .... Nu 33:33
Kadesh and camped at Mount **H**, ... Nu 33:37
the LORD and went up Mount **H**. .... Nu 33:38
old when he died on Mount **H**. .... Nu 33:39

people left Mount **H** and camped .... Nu 33:41
Sea and go to Mount **H**. .... Nu 34:7
From Mount **H** it will go to Lebo .... Nu 34:8
died on Mount **H** and joined his .... Dt 32:50

HORAM

this same time **H** king of Gezer .... Jos 10:33

HOREM

Iron, Migdal El, **H**, Beth Anath, ... Jos 19:38

HORESH

David was at **H** in the Desert 1Sa 23:15
to David at **H** and strengthened 1Sa 23:16
home, but David stayed at **H**. 1Sa 23:18
He's at the hideouts of **H**, ... 1Sa 23:19

HORI

sons of Lotan were **H** and Homam. .... Ge 36:22
of Simeon, Shaphat son of **H**; .... Nu 13:5
Lotan's sons were **H** and Homam, ... 1Ch 1:39

HORITE

were the sons of Seir the **H**, ... Ge 36:20
were the names of the **H** leaders: .... Ge 36:29
leaders of the **H** families who .... Ge 36:30

HORITES

defeated the **H** in the mountains.............. Ge 14:6
the leaders of the **H** in Edom. .... Ge 36:21
The **H** also lived in Edom before, ... Dt 2:12
Edom, when he destroyed the **H**. .... Dt 2:22

HORIZON

He draws the **h** like a circle on .... Job 26:10
stretched the **h** over the oceans .... Pr 8:27
land, from the edge of the **h**. .... Is 13:5

HORMAH

beat them back all the way to **H**. .... Nu 14:45
so the place was named **H**. .... Nu 21:3
and defeated you from Edom to **H**............ Dt 1:44
H, Arad, ... Jos 12:14
Eltolad, Kesil, **H**,................................. Jos 15:30
Eltolad, Bethul, **H**, ... Jos 19:4
the city, so they called it **H**.................... Jdg 1:17
H, Bor Ashan, Athach, ... 1Sa 30:30
Bethuel, **H**, Ziklag, ... 1Ch 4:30

HORN

of the altar stick out like a **h**, ... Ex 27:2
stuck out like a **h** was joined .... Ex 37:25
stick out like a **h** so the .... Ex 38:2
must blow the **h** of a male sheep .... Le 25:9
must blow the **h** through the .... Le 25:9
another **h** grew up among them............... Da 7:8
It was a little **h** with eyes like .... Da 7:8
The little **h** pulled out three of .... Da 7:8
the little **h** was bragging. .... Da 7:11
the little **h** that grew there .... Da 7:20
the little **h** began making war................. Da 7:21
but one **h** was longer and newer............. Da 8:3
had one large **h** between his eyes .... Da 8:5
his big **h** broke off and four .... Da 8:8
grew in place of the one big **h**. .... Da 8:8
Then a little **h** grew from one of.............. Da 8:9
That little **h** grew until it .... Da 8:10
That little **h** set itself up as .... Da 8:11
and the **h** was successful in .... Da 8:12
and the big **h** between its eyes .... Da 8:21
of the broken **h** are four .... Da 8:22
Blow the **h** in Gibeah and the................. Hos 5:8
and there was a crown on each **h**. .... Rev 13:1

HORNED

h owls, screech owls, sea gulls, ... Le 11:16
h owls, screech owls, sea gulls, ... Dt 14:15

HORNS

sheep caught in a bush by its **h**. .... Ge 22:13
with their **h** are all one piece .... Ex 27:2
stick out like **h** must be one .... Ex 30:2
horn so that the **h** and the altar .... Ex 38:2
made from **h** of male sheep .... Jos 6:4
Kenaanah had made some iron **h**. 1Ki 22:11
'You will use these **h** to fight 1Ki 22:11
shouted, blew **h** and trumpets, ... 1Ch 15:28
blowing trumpets and sheep's **h**. 2Ch 15:14
Kenaanah had made some iron **h**. 2Ch 18:10
'You will use these **h** to fight 2Ch 18:10
save me from the **h** of the bulls. .... Ps 22:21
a bull with **h** and hoofs. .... Ps 69:31
the trumpets and the sheep's **h;** .... Ps 98:6
sheep with your **h** until you have .... Eze 34:21
shaped like **h** and reaching up .... Eze 43:15
you hear the sound of the **h,** .... Da 3:5
they heard the sound of the **h,** .... Da 3:7
that everyone who heard the **h,** .... Da 3:10
again hear the sound of the **h,** .... Da 3:15
seen before, and it had ten **h**. .... Da 7:7
I was thinking about the **h,** .... Da 7:8
pulled out three of the other **h**. .... Da 7:8
know about the ten **h** on its head .... Da 7:20
of the other ten **h** and looked .... Da 7:20
The ten **h** are ten kings who will .... Da 7:24
It had two long **h,** but one horn .... Da 8:3
with the two **h** that I had seen .... Da 8:6
and break the sheep's two **h**. .... Da 8:7
off and four **h** grew in place .... Da 8:8
Those four **h** pointed in four .... Da 8:8
grew from one of those four **h,** .... Da 8:9
You saw a male sheep with two **h,** .... Da 8:20
four **h** that grew in the place .... Da 8:22
if you had **h** of iron and hoofs .... Mic 4:13
looked up and saw four animal **h**. .... Zch 1:18
These are the **h** that scattered................ Zch 1:19
to scare and throw down the **h**. .... Zch 1:21
These **h** scattered the people of .... Zch 1:21
These **h** stand for the nations .... Zch 1:21
He had seven **h** and seven eyes, ... Rev 5:6
coming from the **h** on the golden .... Rev 9:13
on each head. He also had ten **h**. .... Rev 12:3
It had ten **h** and seven heads, ... Rev 13:1
It had two **h** like a lamb, but it .... Rev 13:11
it had seven heads and ten **h**. .... Rev 17:3
one with seven heads and ten **h**............... Rev 17:7
The ten **h** you saw are ten kings............. Rev 17:12
The ten **h** and the beast you saw .... Rev 17:16
God made the ten **h** want to carry .... Rev 17:17

HORON

going up to Beth **H** and killed................ Jos 10:10
down the Beth **H** Pass to Azekah, ... Jos 10:11
to the area of the Lower Beth **H**. .... Jos 16:3
the east, went to Upper Beth **H,** .... Jos 16:5
the hill south of Lower Beth **H**. .... Jos 18:13
the hill to the south of Beth **H,** .... Jos 18:14
and Beth **H**. There were four .... Jos 21:22
group went on the Beth **H** road. 1Sa 13:18
built the cities of Lower Beth **H** 1Ki 9:17
Jokmeam, Beth **H,** 1Ch 6:68
built Lower Beth **H,** Upper Beth 1Ch 7:24
Horon, Upper Beth **H,** and Uzzen 1Ch 7:24
of Upper Beth **H** and Lower Beth 2Ch 8:5
Beth Horon and Lower Beth **H,** 2Ch 8:5
Samaria to Beth **H** they killed 2Ch 25:13

HORONAIM

are going on the road to **H,**................... Is 15:5
to the cries from the town of **H,** .... Je 48:3
road down to **H,** cries of pain .... Je 48:5
Zoar as far away as **H** and Eglath .... Je 48:34

HORONITE

When Sanballat the **H** and Tobiah .... Ne 2:10
when Sanballat the **H,** Tobiah the .... Ne 2:19
a daughter of Sanballat the **H,** .... Ne 13:28

HORRIBLE

of Israel have done a **h** thing. .... Je 18:13
happy about this **h** punishment .... Eze 21:10
I have seen **h** things in Israel................... Hos 6:10

HORROR

Terror and **h** will fall on them. .... Ex 15:16
become a thing of **h** among all .... Dt 28:25

HORSE

has thrown the **h** and its rider .... Ex 15:1
has thrown the **h** and its rider .... Ex 15:21
and a **h** cost nearly four pounds............. 1Ki 10:29
escaped on a **h** with some of his............. 1Ki 20:20
the entrance of the **H** Gate near 2Ch 23:15
made repairs above the **H** Gate, ... Ne 3:28
And also bring a **h** with a royal .... Est 6:8
h that the king himself has .... Est 6:8
robe and the **h** be given to one .... Est 6:9
lead him on the **h** through the .... Est 6:9
robe and the **h** just as you have .... Est 6:10
Haman took the robe and the **h,**............. Est 6:11
laughs at the **h** and its rider. .... Job 39:18
one who gives the **h** its strength............. Job 39:19
Do you make the **h** jump like a .... Job 39:20
the **h** races over the ground; .... Job 39:24
blows, the **h** snorts, 'Aha!' .... Job 39:25
So don't be like a **h** or donkey, ... Ps 32:9
strength of a **h** or with human .... Ps 147:10
Like a **h** walking through a..................... Is 63:13
like a **h** charging into a battle. .... Je 8:6
far as the corner of the **H** Gate— .... Je 31:40
the fastest **h** to the chariot....................... Mic 1:13
Their **h** soldiers attack quickly; .... Hab 1:8
I saw a man riding a red **h**....................... Zch 1:8
confuse every **h** and cause its .... Zch 12:4
there before me was a white **h**. .... Rev 6:2
The rider on the **h** held a bow, ... Rev 6:2
Then another **h** came out, a red .... Rev 6:4
there before me was a black **h,** .... Rev 6:5
there before me was a pale **h**. .... Rev 6:8
there before me was a white **h**. .... Rev 19:11
The rider on the **h** is called..................... Rev 19:11
the rider on the **h** and his army. .... Rev 19:19
the mouth of the rider on the **h,** .... Rev 19:21

HORSE'S

snake bites a **h** leg, and the .... Ge 49:17
rattles against the **h** side, ... Job 39:23

HORSEBACK

he led him on **h** through the city .... Est 6:11
and lieutenants riding on **h**. .... Eze 23:6

HORSEFLY

but a **h** is coming from the north .... Je 46:20

HORSEMAN

Take a **h** and send him to meet 2Ki 9:17
The **h** rode out to meet Jehu, ... 2Ki 9:18
Then Joram sent out a second **h**. 2Ki 9:19

HORSEMEN

and forty thousand Aramean **h**. 2Sa 10:18
on a horse with some of his **h**. 1Ki 20:20
chariots of Israel and their **h!"** 2Ki 2:12
Jehoahaz's army except fifty **h,** 2Ki 13:7
chariots of Israel and their **h!"** 2Ki 13:14
to give you chariots and **h?**..................... 2Ki 18:24
chariots and sixty thousand **h**. 2Ch 12:3
army and many chariots and **h**. 2Ch 16:8
for soldiers and **h** to protect us .... Ezr 8:22
H will be ordered to guard the .... Is 22:7

and strong **h** will save them. .... Is 31:1
to give you chariots and **h**? .... Is 36:9
sound of the **h** and the archers .... Je 4:29
H, charge into battle! .... Je 46:9
chariots, **h**, and a great army .... Eze 26:7
will shake at the noise of **h**, ... Eze 26:10
horses, and **h**, all of whom will .... Eze 38:4
swords, horses or **h**, or weapons .... Hos 1:7
will fight and defeat the **h**. .... Zch 10:5
seventy **h**, and two hundred .... Ac 23:23
next day the **h** went with Paul .... Ac 23:32
When the **h** came to Caesarea and .... Ac 23:33

HORSES
all the king's **h**, chariot .... Ex 14:9
Then all the king's **h**, chariots, ... Ex 14:23
not have too many **h** for himself, ... Dt 17:16
with their **h** and chariots. .... Jos 11:4
cripple their **h** and burn all.................... Jos 11:6
but a hundred of the chariot **h**. 2Sa 8:4
imported **h** from Egypt and Kue. 1Ki 10:28
a chariot and **h** of fire appeared 2Ki 2:11
orders by messengers on fast **h**, ... Est 8:10
we need **h** to run away on." .... Is 30:16
They think **h** will save them. .... Is 31:1
Their **h** are only animals and are .... Is 31:3
His **h** are faster than eagles. .... Je 4:13
how can you race against **h**? .... Je 12:5
important men and all riding **h**. .... Eze 23:23
bows or swords, **h** or horsemen, ... Hos 1:7
They look like **h**, and they run .... Joe 2:4
H do not run on rocks, and..................... Am 6:12
Hear **h** galloping and chariots .... Nah 3:2
Their **h** are faster than leopards .... Hab 1:8
Red **h** pulled the first chariot.................. Zch 6:2
h pulled the third chariot, ... Zch 6:3
h pulled the fourth chariot..................... Zch 6:3
that time the **h**' bells will have .... Zch 14:20
were following him on white **h**. .... Rev 19:14

HOSAH
it turned and went toward **H**, ... Jos 19:29
H and Obed-Edom son of Jeduthun 1Ch 16:38
the Merari family, **H** had sons. 1Ch 26:10
H had thirteen sons and 1Ch 26:11
Shuppim and **H** were chosen for 1Ch 26:16

HOSEA
spoke his word to **H** son of Beeri .... Hos 1:1
Lord began speaking through **H**, ... Hos 1:2
So **H** married Gomer daughter of .... Hos 1:3
The Lord said to **H**, "Name him .... Hos 1:4
The Lord said to **H**, "Name her .... Hos 1:6
As the Scripture says in **H**: .... Rm 9:25

HOSEA'S
and gave birth to **H** son. .... Hos 1:3

HOSHAIAH
Behind them went **H** and half the .... Ne 12:32
Jezaniah son of **H** went to .... Je 42:1
Azariah son of **H**, Johanan son of .... Je 43:2

HOSHAMA
Jekamiah, **H**, and Nedabiah. 1Ch 3:18

HOSHEA
tribe of Ephraim, **H** son of Nun; .... Nu 13:8
Moses gave **H** son of Nun the new .... Nu 13:16
Then **H** son of Elah made plans 2Ki 15:30
Then **H** became king in Pekah's 2Ki 15:30
H son of Elah became king over............... 2Ki 17:1
H ruled in Samaria nine years. 2Ki 17:1
of Assyria came to attack **H**. 2Ki 17:3
H had been Shalmaneser's servant 2Ki 17:3
found out that **H** had made plans 2Ki 17:4
H had also stopped giving 2Ki 17:4

that, the king put **H** in prison................... 2Ki 17:4
in the ninth year **H** was king, ... 2Ki 17:6
the third year **H** son of Elah was 2Ki 18:1
seventh year **H** son of Elah was 2Ki 18:9
H son of Azaziah was over the 1Ch 27:20
H, Hananiah, Hasshub, ... Ne 10:23

HOSHEA'S
which was **H** ninth year as king 2Ki 18:10

HOST
The **h**, who invited both of you, ... Lk 14:9
When the **h** comes to you, he may .... Lk 14:10

HOSTAGES
of the palace and some **h**. 2Ki 14:14
from the palace and some **h**. 2Ch 25:24

HOT
but when the sun became **h**, ... Ex 16:21
bread was replaced with **h** bread. 1Sa 21:6
from a large pot over a **h** fire.................... Job 41:20
He will send **h** coals and burning .... Ps 11:6
He showed them his **h** anger. .... Ps 78:49
cannot walk on **h** coals without .... Pr 6:28
Our skin is **h** like an oven; .... La 5:10
was made so **h** that the flames .... Da 3:22
people are as **h** as an oven;..................... Hos 7:7
say, 'It will be a **h** day,' and .... Lk 12:55
are destroyed as if by a **h** iron. 1Ti 4:2
that you are not **h** or cold. .... Rev 3:15

HOTHAM
Japhlet, Shomer, **H**, and their 1Ch 7:32
Shomer's brother was **H**. 1Ch 7:35
Jeiel sons of **H** the Aroerite; 1Ch 11:44

HOTHAM'S
H sons were Zophah, Imna, ... 1Ch 7:35

HOTHIR
Mallothi, **H**, and Mahazioth. 1Ch 25:4
twelve men were chosen from **H**, ... 1Ch 25:28

HOTTER
He fans the fire to make it **h**, ... Is 54:16
The fire is fanned to make it **h**, ... Je 6:29
heated seven times **h** than usual. .... Da 3:19

HOTTEST
during the **h** part of the day. .... Ge 18:1

HOUR
servant was healed that same **h**................ Mt 8:13
last and worked only one **h**. .... Mt 20:12
the day or the **h** the Son of Man .... Mt 25:13
stay awake with me for one **h**? .... Mt 26:40
stay awake with me for one **h**? .... Mk 14:37
About an **h** later, another man .... Lk 22:59
that **h** of the night the jailer .... Ac 16:33
to this very **h** we do not have 1Co 4:11
put ourselves in danger every **h**? 1Co 15:30
in heaven for about half an **h**. .... Rev 8:1
ready for this **h** and day and .... Rev 9:15
In the same **h** there was a great .... Rev 11:13
rule with the beast for one **h**. .... Rev 17:12
punishment has come in one **h**!" .... Rev 18:10
have been destroyed in one **h**!" .... Rev 18:17
she has been destroyed in one **h**! .... Rev 18:19

HOURS
or like a few **h** in the night..................... Ps 90:4
the darkness lasted for three **h**. .... Mt 27:45
the darkness lasted for three **h**. .... Mk 15:33
there not twelve **h** in the day?................. Jn 11:9
About three **h** later his wife .... Ac 5:7
the same thing for two **h**: .... Ac 19:34

HOUSE
the people in his **h** because of................. Ge 12:17
slave born in my **h** will inherit .... Ge 15:3

the door of the **h** and went .... Jdg 19:27
lying at the doorway of the **h,** .... Jdg 19:27
surrounded the **h** and wanted to .... Jdg 20:5
one of us will go back to his **h!** .... Jdg 20:8
of you to your own mother's **h.** .... Ru 1:8
went up to the **h** of the LORD at 1Sa 1:7
the entrance to the LORD's **h.** 1Sa 1:9
took him to the **h** of the LORD at 1Sa 1:24
You will see trouble in my **h.** 1Sa 2:32
was also in bed in the LORD's **h,** 1Sa 3:3
the doors of the **h** of the LORD. 1Sa 3:15
LORD to Abinadab's **h** on a hill. 1Sa 7:1
tell me where the seer's **h** is." 1Sa 9:18
with Saul on the roof of his **h.** 1Sa 9:25
went out of the **h** with Samuel. 1Sa 9:26
him go home to his father's **h.** 1Sa 18:2
and he prophesied in his **h.** 1Sa 18:10
sitting in his **h** with his spear 1Sa 19:9
to David's **h** to watch it and to 1Sa 19:11
messengers entered David's **h,** 1Sa 19:16
Don't let him in my **h!**" 1Sa 21:15
Everyone in your **h** respects him. 1Sa 22:14
he was in the **h,** eating like a 1Sa 25:36
At the **h** the woman had a fat 1Sa 28:24
Ish-Bosheth's **h** in the afternoon 2Sa 4:5
on his own bed in his own **h!**" 2Sa 4:11
out of Abinadab's **h** on the hill. 2Sa 6:3
took it to the **h** of Obed-Edom, ... 2Sa 6:10
in Obed-Edom's **h** for three 2Sa 6:11
from Obed-Edom's **h** to Jerusalem 2Sa 6:12
you build a **h** for me to live 2Sa 7:5
now I have not lived in a **h.** 2Sa 7:6
you built me a **h** of cedar?"' 2Sa 7:7
He will build a **h** for me, and I 2Sa 7:13
He is at the **h** of Makir son of 2Sa 9:4
son from the **h** of Makir son of 2Sa 9:5
Then she went back to her **h.** 2Sa 11:4
servants to bring her to his **h.** 2Sa 11:27
went into his **h** and stayed there 2Sa 12:16
into the LORD's **h** to worship. 2Sa 12:20
brother Amnon's **h** and make some 2Sa 13:7
went to her brother Amnon's **h,** 2Sa 13:8
brother Absalom's **h** and was sad 2Sa 13:20
Absalom must go to his own **h.** 2Sa 14:24
went to his own **h** and did not go 2Sa 14:24
to Absalom's **h** and said to him, ... 2Sa 14:31
set out with everyone in his **h,** 2Sa 15:16
they stopped at a **h** far away. 2Sa 15:17
went to a man's **h** in Bahurim. 2Sa 17:18
to the woman at the **h** and asked, ... 2Sa 17:20
went into the king's **h** and said, ... 2Sa 19:5
'Even in my **h** I have heard what 2Sa 19:11
Now he put them in a locked **h.** 2Sa 20:3
Build a **h** for yourself in 1Ki 2:36
woman and I live in the same **h.** 1Ki 3:17
one else was in the **h** with us; 1Ki 3:18
Surely this **h** which I have built 1Ki 8:27
who gave Hadad a **h,** some food, ... 1Ki 11:18
God went to the old prophet's **h,** 1Ki 13:19
into Arza's **h** and killed Elah 1Ki 16:10
who owned the **h** became sick. 1Ki 17:17
is letting me stay in her **h.** 1Ki 17:20
what do you have in your **h?**" 2Ki 4:2
go into your **h** and shut the door 2Ki 4:4
passes by our **h** all the time. 2Ki 4:9
Elisha came to the woman's **h.** 2Ki 4:11
When Elisha came into the **h,** 2Ki 4:32
to Elisha's **h** and stood outside 2Ki 5:9
servants and put them in the **h.** 2Ki 5:24
in his **h** with the elders. 2Ki 6:32
when the king came to his **h.** 2Ki 7:17
beg the king for her **h** and land. 2Ki 8:3
the king for her **h** and land. 2Ki 8:5

Jehu got up and went into the **h.** 2Ki 9:6
went into the **h** and ate and 2Ki 9:34
he had to live in a separate **h.** 2Ki 15:5
h gods, and idols 2Ki 23:24
the music in the **h** of the LORD. 1Ch 6:31
in the Holy Tent, the **h** of God. 1Ch 6:48
from Abinadab's **h** on a new cart, ... 1Ch 13:7
took it to the **h** of Obed-Edom 1Ch 13:13
in his **h** for three months, ... 1Ch 13:14
Obed-Edom's **h** with great joy. 1Ch 15:25
to build a **h** for me to live 1Ch 17:4
now I have not lived in a **h.** 1Ch 17:5
you built me a **h** of cedar?"' 1Ch 17:6
He will build a **h** for me, and I 1Ch 17:12
in charge of my **h** and kingdom 1Ch 17:14
really build a **h** for our God. 2Ch 2:6
Surely this **h** which I have built 2Ch 6:18
in a separate **h** and could not 2Ch 26:21
at the gates of the LORD's **h.** 2Ch 31:2
pulled from his **h** and driven .... Ezr 6:11
make his **h** a pile of ruins. .... Ezr 6:11
for the **h** in which I will live. .... Ne 2:8
made repairs opposite his own **h.** .... Ne 3:10
pool and the **H** of the Heroes. .... Ne 3:16
entrance to the **h** of Eliashib, ... Ne 3:20
Eliashib's **h** to the far end of .... Ne 3:21
repairs in front of their own **h.** .... Ne 3:23
made repairs beside his own **h.** .... Ne 3:23
from Azariah's **h** to the bend .... Ne 3:24
working in front of his own **h.** .... Ne 3:28
repairs across from his own **h.** .... Ne 3:29
as far as the **h** of the Temple .... Ne 3:31
shake him out of his **h** and out .... Ne 5:13
I went to the **h** of Shemaiah son .... Ne 6:10
went on above the **h** of David to .... Ne 12:37
came to Haman's **h** and made him .... Est 6:14
the queen while I am in the **h?**" .... Est 7:8
platform stands near Haman's **h.** .... Est 7:9
at the oldest brother's **h.** .... Job 1:13
at the oldest brother's **h.** .... Job 1:18
four corners of the **h** at once. .... Job 1:19
The **h** fell in on the young .... Job 1:19
'Where is this great man's **h?** .... Job 21:28
So remove evil from your **h.** .... Job 22:23
close friendship blessed my **h.** .... Job 29:4
and I will die in my own **h.** .... Job 29:18
servants of my **h** have always .... Job 31:31
and sisters came to his **h,** .... Job 42:11
I will live in the **h** of the LORD .... Ps 23:6
in the LORD's **h** all my life. .... Ps 27:4
eat the rich food in your **h,** .... Ps 36:8
"David is in Ahimelech's **h.**" .... Ps 51:19
to watch David's **h** to kill him. .... Ps 58:11
with good things in your **h,** .... Ps 65:4
live an innocent life in my **h.** .... Ps 101:2
is dishonest will live in my **h;** .... Ps 101:7
He made him the master of his **h;** .... Ps 105:21
If the LORD doesn't build the **h,** .... Ps 127:1
I will not go home to my **h,** .... Ps 132:3
Let's go to the LORD's **h.** .... Ps 132:7
Her **h** is on the way to death; .... Pr 2:18
will curse the evil person's **h,** .... Pr 3:33
my father's **h** and like an only .... Pr 4:3
even go near the door of her **h,** .... Pr 5:8
the window of my **h** I looked out .... Pr 7:6
on the road leading to her **h.** .... Pr 7:8
Her **h** is on the road to death, ... Pr 7:27
Wisdom has built her **h;** .... Pr 9:1
the door of her **h** at the highest .... Pr 9:14
wicked person's **h** will be .... Pr 14:11
tear down the proud person's **h,** .... Pr 15:25
than inside the **h** with a .... Pr 21:9
watches the **h** of the wicked and .... Pr 21:12

and attack a good family's **h**; .... Pr 24:15
that, you can build your **h**. .... Pr 24:27
to your neighbor's **h** too often; .... Pr 25:17
than inside the **h** with a .... Pr 25:24
slaves were also born in my **h**. .... Ec 2:7
doesn't fix it, the **h** will leak. .... Ec 10:18
I brought him to my mother's **h**, ... Sng 3:4
and bring you to my mother's **h**; .... Sng 8:2
everything in his **h** for love, ... Sng 8:7
have food or clothes in my **h**. .... Is 3:7
a disgrace to your master's **h**. .... Is 22:18
the key to the **h** of David around .... Is 22:22
honored chair in his father's **h**. .... Is 22:23
of a person sits in the **h**. .... Is 44:13
give them joy in my **h** of prayer. .... Is 56:7
will be called a **h** for prayer .... Is 56:7
person build a **h** and someone .... Is 65:22
think you can build a **h** for me? .... Is 66:1
a **h** where travelers spend the .... Je 9:2
not go into a **h** where there is .... Je 16:5
not go into a **h** where the people .... Je 16:8
Go down to the potter's **h**, ... Je 18:2
to the potter's **h** and saw him .... Je 18:3
everyone in your **h** will be taken .... Je 20:6
cedar in your **h** make you a great .... Je 22:15
him in jail in the **h** of Jonathan .... Je 37:15
me back to the **h** of Jonathan .... Je 37:20
back to Jonathan's **h** to die.'" .... Je 38:26
shut yourself up in your **h**. .... Eze 3:24
sitting in my **h** with the elders .... Eze 8:1
Israel is like a **h** in ruins, ... Eze 13:5
went to his **h** and explained .... Da 2:17
and have his **h** turned into a .... Da 3:29
in an upstairs room in his **h**, ... Da 6:10
He is an enemy in God's **h**. .... Hos 9:8
fire upon the **h** of Hazael that .... Am 1:4
to drink in the **h** of their god. .... Am 2:8
I will tear down the winter **h**, ... Am 3:15
together with the summer **h**. .... Am 3:15
goes into his **h** and puts his .... Am 5:19
people left alive in just one **h**, ... Am 6:9
the large **h** will be broken into .... Am 6:11
and the small **h** into bits. .... Am 6:11
in the wicked **h** wicked treasures .... Mic 6:10
while my **h** is still in ruins! .... Hag 1:9
that person's **h** and destroy it .... Zch 5:4
same day to the **h** of Josiah son .... Zch 6:10
was laid for the **h** of the LORD .... Zch 8:9
'I was hurt at my friend's **h**.' .... Zch 13:6
so there will be food in my **h**. .... Mal 3:10
came to the **h** where the child .... Mt 2:11
for all the people in the **h**. .... Mt 5:15
man who built his **h** on rock. .... Mt 7:24
the winds blew and hit that **h**. .... Mt 7:25
man who built his **h** on sand. .... Mt 7:26
the winds blew and hit that **h**, ... Mt 7:27
for you to come into my **h**. .... Mt 8:8
When Jesus went to Peter's **h**, ... Mt 8:14
having dinner at Matthew's **h**, ... Mt 9:10
the leader and went into his **h**. .... Mt 9:23
had been thrown out of the **h**, ... Mt 9:25
went into God's **h**, and he and .... Mt 12:4
strong person's **h** and steal his .... Mt 12:29
can steal the things from the **h**. .... Mt 12:29
'I will go back to the **h** I left.' .... Mt 12:44
it finds the **h** still empty, ... Mt 12:44
went out of the **h** and sat by the .... Mt 13:1
the crowd and went into the **h**. .... Mt 13:36
heaven is like the owner of a **h**. .... Mt 13:52
went into the **h**, but before he .... Mt 17:25
will be called a **h** for prayer.' .... Mt 21:13
Now your **h** will be left .... Mt 23:38
owner of the **h** knew what time .... Mt 24:43

and you invited me into your **h**. .... Mt 25:35
home and invite you into our **h**? .... Mt 25:38
did not invite me into your **h**. .... Mt 25:43
in Bethany at the **h** of Simon, ... Mt 26:6
my followers at your **h**."'" .... Mt 26:18
led him to the **h** of Caiaphas, ... Mt 26:57
of the high priest's **h**, ... Mt 26:58
people gathered at Pilate's **h**, ... Mt 27:17
Jesus woke and left the **h**. .... Mk 1:35
that there was no room in the **h**, ... Mk 2:2
was having dinner at Levi's **h**, ... Mk 2:15
went into God's **h** and ate the .... Mk 2:26
strong person's **h** and steal his .... Mk 3:27
he can steal things from the **h**. .... Mk 3:27
came from the **h** of the synagogue .... Mk 5:35
came to the **h** of the synagogue .... Mk 5:38
entered the **h** and said to them .... Mk 5:39
throwing them out of the **h**, ... Mk 5:40
When you enter a **h**, stay there .... Mk 6:10
the people and went into the **h**, ... Mk 7:17
went into a **h**, he did not want .... Mk 7:24
When Jesus went into the **h**, ... Mk 9:28
When they went into a **h** there, ... Mk 9:33
Later, in the **h**, his followers .... Mk 10:10
the street near the door of a **h**, ... Mk 11:4
will be called a **h** for prayer .... Mk 11:17
changing God's **h** into a 'hideout .... Mk 11:17
He leaves his **h** and lets his .... Mk 13:34
owner of the **h** will come back. .... Mk 13:35
in Bethany at the **h** of Simon, ... Mk 14:3
he goes into a **h**, tell the owner .... Mk 14:14
the owner of the **h**, 'The Teacher .... Mk 14:14
went to that **h** with the twelve. .... Mk 14:17
led him to the **h** of the high .... Mk 14:53
of the high priest's **h**. .... Mk 14:54
go out of her **h** for five months .... Lk 1:24
to Zechariah's **h** and greeted .... Lk 1:40
I must be in my Father's **h**?" .... Lk 2:49
a big dinner for Jesus at his **h**. .... Lk 5:29
went into God's **h** and took and .... Lk 6:4
a man building a **h** who dug deep .... Lk 6:48
water tried to wash the **h** away, ... Lk 6:48
because the **h** was built well. .... Lk 6:48
who built his **h** on the ground. .... Lk 6:49
the **h** quickly fell and was .... Lk 6:49
the officer's **h** when the officer .... Lk 7:6
to have you come into my **h**. .... Lk 7:6
back to the **h** where they found .... Lk 7:10
into the Pharisee's **h** and sat at .... Lk 7:36
was eating at the Pharisee's **h**. .... Lk 7:37
Jesus to come to his **h** saw this, ... Lk 7:39
came into your **h**, you gave me no ...... Lk 7:44
Cuza (the manager of Herod's **h**); ...... Lk 8:3
in the burial caves, not in a **h**. .... Lk 8:27
begging him to come to his **h**. .... Lk 8:41
was on his way to Jairus' **h**, ... Lk 8:42
came from the **h** of the synagogue ..... Lk 8:49
Jesus went to the **h**, he let only .... Lk 8:51
When you enter a **h**, stay there .... Lk 9:4
you go into a **h**, say, 'Peace be .... Lk 10:5
say, 'Peace be with this **h**.' .... Lk 10:5
Stay in the same **h**, eating and .... Lk 10:7
Don't move from **h** to house. .... Lk 10:7
Don't move from house to **h**. .... Lk 10:7
Martha let Jesus stay at her **h**. .... Lk 10:38
to your friend's **h** at midnight .... Lk 11:5
friend inside the **h** answers, ' .... Lk 11:7
many weapons guards his own **h**, ... Lk 11:21
'I will go back to the **h** I left.' .... Lk 11:24
it finds that **h** swept clean and .... Lk 11:25
owner of the **h** knew what time .... Lk 12:39
allow the thief to enter his **h**. .... Lk 12:39
the owner of the **h** gets up and ...... Lk 13:25

Now your **h** is left completely .... Lk 13:35
to come so my **h** will be full. .... Lk 14:23
a lamp, sweep the **h,** and look .... Lk 15:8
and as he came closer to the **h,** .... Lk 15:25
send Lazarus to my father's **h.** .... Lk 16:27
are in the **h** should not go .... Lk 17:31
I must stay at your **h** today." .... Lk 19:5
has come to this **h** today, ... Lk 19:9
Temple will be a **h** for prayer.' .... Lk 19:46
him into the **h** that he enters, ... Lk 22:10
and tell the owner of the **h,** ' .... Lk 22:11
him into the **h** of the high .... Lk 22:54
make my Father's **h** a place for .... Jn 2:16
who lived in his **h** believed in .... Jn 4:53
Jews were with Mary in the **h,** .... Jn 11:31
the perfume filled the whole **h.** .... Jn 12:3
are many rooms in my Father's **h;** .... Jn 14:2
from Caiaphas's **h** to the Roman .... Jn 18:28
followers were in the **h** again, ... Jn 20:26
the whole **h** where they were .... Ac 2:2
was cared for in his father's **h.** .... Ac 7:20
to let him build a **h** for him, ... Ac 7:46
think you can build a **h** for me? .... Ac 7:49
going from **h** to house, dragging .... Ac 8:3
from house to **h,** dragging out .... Ac 8:3
Find the **h** of Judas, and ask for .... Ac 9:11
Ananias went to the **h** of Judas. .... Ac 9:17
who lived in his **h** worshiped the .... Ac 10:2
and has a **h** beside the sea." .... Ac 10:6
found Simon's **h** and were .... Ac 10:17
to come to his **h** so that he can .... Ac 10:22
praying in my **h** at this same .... Ac 10:30
is staying in the **h** of a man, ... Ac 10:32
and has a **h** beside the sea.' .... Ac 10:32
came to the **h** where I was .... Ac 11:11
we entered the **h** of Cornelius. .... Ac 11:12
angel he saw standing in his **h.** .... Ac 11:13
people in her **h** were baptized. .... Ac 16:15
Lord, then come stay in my **h."** .... Ac 16:15
and all the people in your **h."** .... Ac 16:31
and all the people in his **h.** .... Ac 16:32
went to Lydia's **h** where they saw .... Ac 16:40
ran to Jason's **h,** looking for .... Ac 17:5
Jason is keeping them in his **h.** .... Ac 17:7
living in his **h** believed in the .... Ac 18:8
away from the **h** naked and hurt. .... Ac 19:16
his own rented **h** and welcomed .... Ac 28:30
church that meets at their **h.** .... Rm 16:5
are like God's farm, God's **h.** 1Co 3:9
of that **h** like an expert 1Co 3:10
church that meets in their **h.** 1Co 16:19
God will have a **h** for us. 2Co 5:1
It will not be a **h** made by human 2Co 5:1
the church that meets in her **h.** .... Col 4:15
time, going from **h** to house. 1Ti 5:13
time, going from house to **h.** 1Ti 5:13
In a large **h** there are not only 2Ti 2:20
builder of a **h** has more honor .... Heb 3:3
more honor than the **h** itself. .... Heb 3:3
Every **h** is built by someone, ... Heb 3:4
faithful as a Son over God's **h.** .... Heb 3:6
And we are God's **h** if we .... Heb 3:6
a great priest over God's **h,** .... Heb 10:21
accept that person into your **h.** 2Jn 1:10

HOUSEHOLD

a holy vest and some **h** idols. .... Jdg 17:5
a holy vest, **h** gods, an idol, ... Jdg 18:14
the holy vest, the **h** idols, and .... Jdg 18:17
the holy vest, the **h** idols, and .... Jdg 18:18
the holy vest, the **h** idols, and .... Jdg 18:20

HOUSES

of the **h** where they eat .... Ex 12:7
all the yeast from your **h.** .... Ex 12:15
passed over the **h** of Israel, ... Ex 12:27
build nice **h** and live in them, ... Dt 8:12
David built **h** for himself in 1Ch 15:1
olive trees, and **h** right now. .... Ne 5:11
filled their **h** with good things .... Job 22:18
I built **h** and planted vineyards .... Ec 2:4
The fine **h** will be destroyed; .... Is 5:9
and for all the **h** that once were .... Is 32:13
Build **h** and settle in the land. .... Je 29:5
The **h** decorated with ivory will .... Am 3:15
be stolen and their **h** destroyed. .... Zph 1:13
living in fancy **h** while the .... Hag 1:4
away widows' **h,** and you say long .... Mt 23:14
all those who have left **h,** .... Mk 10:29
who owned fields or **h** sold them, ... Ac 4:34

HOUSETOP

grass on the **h** that is burned 2Ki 19:26
I am like a lonely bird on a **h.** .... Ps 102:7
grass on the **h** that is burned .... Is 37:27

HOUSETOPS

ear you should shout from the **h.** .... Mt 10:27
room will be shouted from the **h.** .... Lk 12:3

HOUSING

king's food and **h** on the trip. .... Je 51:59

HOWEVER

H, suppose the bull has hurt .... Ex 21:29
H, I speak a wisdom to those who 1Co 2:6

HOWL

and they **h** if they do not find .... Ps 59:15
Wolves will **h** within the strong .... Is 13:22

HOWLED

They **h** like animals among the .... Job 30:7

HUBBAH

sons were Rohgah, **H,** and Aram. 1Ch 7:34

HUBS

rims, spokes, and **h**—were made of 1Ki 7:33

HUDDLED

among the bushes and **h** together .... Job 30:7

HUG

is a time to **h** and a time not to .... Ec 3:5
time to hug and a time not to **h.** .... Ec 3:5

HUGE

took place. A **h** man was there; 2Sa 21:20
allow you to defeat this **h** army, ... 1Ki 20:28
took place. A **h** man was there; 1Ch 20:6
in your dream you saw a **h,** .... Da 2:31
saw four **h** animals come up from .... Da 7:3
There are **h** numbers of people in .... Joe 3:14

HUGGED

Laban **h** him and kissed him and .... Ge 29:13
his arms around him and **h** him. .... Ge 33:4
Then Joseph **h** his brother .... Ge 45:14
brothers and cried as he **h** them. .... Ge 45:15
his father, he **h** him, and cried .... Ge 46:29
Joseph **h** his father and cried .... Ge 50:1
ran to him and **h** and kissed him. .... Lk 15:20

HUKKOK

Aznoth Tabor and stopped at **H.** .... Jos 19:34

HUL

of Aram were Uz, **H,** Gether, and .... Ge 10:23
sons were Uz, **H,** Gether, and 1Ch 1:17

HULDAH

to talk to **H** the prophetess. 2Ki 22:14
H lived in Jerusalem, in the new 2Ki 22:14

to talk to **H** the prophetess...................... 2Ch 34:22
H lived in Jerusalem, in the new 2Ch 34:22

HUMAN
might touch **h** uncleanness— .... Le 5:3
destroyed, and not by **h** power. .... Da 8:25
You judge by **h** standards. .... Jn 8:15
are only a **h**, but you say you .... Jn 10:33
with the same **h** life that others .... Rm 8:3
You are only **h**, and human beings .... Rm 9:20
not with words of **h** wisdom that 1Co 2:4
judged by you or by any **h** court. 1Co 4:3
do you take care of **h** beings? .... Heb 2:6
a priest by **h** rules and laws .... Heb 7:16
feet high, by **h** measurements, ... Rev 21:17

HUMBLE
Now Moses was very **h**. .... Nu 12:3
some people **h**, and others he 1Sa 2:7
You save the **h**, but you bring 2Sa 22:28
my name, will **h** themselves, if 2Ch 7:14
Amon did not **h** himself before 2Ch 33:23
He makes the **h** person important .... Job 5:11
people are made **h** and you say, ' .... Job 22:29
' then the **h** will be saved. .... Job 22:29
at the proud and make them **h**. .... Job 40:12
You save the **h**, but you bring .... Ps 18:27
those who are **h** how to do right, ... Ps 25:9
takes care of those who are **h**, ... Ps 138:6
defends the **h**, but he throws .... Ps 147:6
with his people; he saves the **h**. .... Ps 149:4
to shame; it is wise to be **h**................... Pr 11:2
to be honored, you must be **h**. .... Pr 15:33
is better to be **h** and be with .... Pr 16:19
but the **h** will be honored. .... Pr 18:12
those who are **h** will be honored .... Pr 29:23
Proud people will be made **h**, ... Is 2:11
proud people will be made **h**, ... Is 2:17
so now I will be **h** all my life. .... Is 38:15
with people who are sad and **h**. .... Is 57:15
to those who are **h** and to those .... Is 57:15
is able to make proud people **h**. .... Da 4:37
and to **h** yourself before your .... Da 10:12
Learn to be **h**. Maybe you will .... Zph 2:3
in the city the **h** and those who .... Zph 3:12
They are blessed who are **h**, ... Mt 5:5
I am gentle and **h** in spirit, ... Mt 11:29
makes himself **h** like this child .... Mt 18:4
himself great will be made **h**. .... Mt 23:12
makes himself **h** will be made .... Mt 23:12
concern for his **h** servant girl................. Lk 1:48
thrones and raised up the **h**. .... Lk 1:52
themselves great will be made **h**, ... Lk 14:11
make themselves **h** will be made .... Lk 14:11
themselves great will be made **h**, ... Lk 18:14
make themselves **h** will be made .... Lk 18:14
be **h**, gentle, and patient,...................... Eph 4:2
be **h** and give more honor to .... Php 2:3
change our **h** bodies and make .... Php 3:21
but he gives grace to the **h**." .... Jam 4:6
H yourself in the Lord's .... Jam 4:10
as family, being kind and **h**. 1Pe 3:8
be very **h** with each other. 1Pe 5:5
but he gives grace to the **h**." 1Pe 5:5
h under God's powerful hand so.............. 1Pe 5:6

HUMBLED
had done and **h** yourself before 2Ki 22:19
for help and **h** himself before 2Ch 33:12
idols before he **h** himself—................... 2Ch 33:19
done and you **h** yourself before 2Ch 34:27
those who are proud will be **h**. .... Is 5:15
We **h** ourselves to honor you, ... Is 58:3
he **h** himself and was fully .... Php 2:8

HUMBLY
others, and live **h**, obeying your .... Mic 6:8

HUMILIATE
women and their neighbors **h** you. .... Eze 16:57
Even the Philistine women **h** you. .... Eze 16:57
you by making you **h** yourself and .... Col 2:18

HUMILIATED
You **h** your sister Sodom when you   .... Eze 16:56

HUMILITY
mercy, kindness, **h**, gentleness, ... Col 3:12

HUMTAH
H, Kiriath Arba (also called .... Jos 15:54

HUNCHBACKS
h, dwarfs, men who have .... Le 21:20

HUNDREDS
of thousands, **h**, fifties, and..................... Ex 18:21
of thousands, **h**, fifties, and..................... Ex 18:25
thousands of men or **h** of men? 1Sa 22:7
thousands and commanders of **h**. 2Sa 18:1

HUNDREDTH
you charged—the **h** part of the .... Ne 5:11

HUNG
The curtains **h** on silver hooks .... Ex 38:10
and it **h** on silver hooks and .... Ex 38:11
and fine linen and **h** them around .... Ex 39:24
of pure gold and **h** them over the .... Ex 39:25
the Tent and **h** the curtain to .... Ex 40:21
Then he **h** the curtain at the .... Ex 40:28
five kings and **h** their bodies .... Jos 10:26
the Ashtoreths and **h** his body on 1Sa 31:10
and Baanah and **h** them over the 2Sa 4:12
killed them and **h** them on stakes 2Sa 21:9
Philistines had **h** the bodies of 2Sa 21:12
of their idols and **h** his head in 1Ch 10:10
trees nearby we **h** our harps. .... Ps 137:2
Princes were **h** by the hands; .... La 5:12
in your navy and **h** their shields .... Eze 27:10
watchtowers and **h** their shields.............. Eze 27:11

HUNGER
in the fields, weak from **h**. .... Ge 25:29
because I am weak with **h**." .... Ge 25:30
said, "I am almost dead from **h**. .... Ge 25:32
They will be full in times of **h**. .... Ps 37:19
disaster, great **h** and fighting. .... Is 51:19
off than those killed by **h**. .... La 4:9
food will only satisfy their **h**; .... Hos 9:4
cause a time of **h** in the land. .... Am 8:11
are blessed who **h** and thirst .... Mt 5:6
I am here, almost dying with **h**. .... Lk 15:17
or sufferings or **h** or nakedness .... Rm 8:35
and great **h**, and she will be .... Rev 18:8

HUNGRY
people who were **h** are hungry no 1Sa 2:5
and you kept food from the **h**. .... Job 22:7
were **h** and thirsty, and they .... Ps 107:5
the thirsty and fills up the **h**. .... Ps 107:9
He gives food to the **h**. .... Ps 146:7
If your enemy is **h**, feed him. .... Pr 25:21
when you are **h**, even something .... Pr 27:7
will be like a **h** man who dreams .... Is 29:8
not feed the **h** or let thirsty.................... Is 32:6
food with the **h** and bring poor, ... Is 58:7
but you evil people will be **h**. .... Is 65:13
bread to the **h** and clothes to .... Eze 18:7
After this, he was very **h**. .... Mt 4:2
followers were **h**, so they began .... Mt 12:1
and the people with him were **h**? .... Mt 12:3
don't want to send them away **h**. .... Mt 15:32
I was **h**, and you gave me food. .... Mt 25:35

leaving Bethany, he became **h**. .... Mk 11:12
He was **h** and wanted to eat, ... Ac 10:10
If your enemy is **h**, feed him; .... Rm 12:20
Anyone who is too **h** should eat 1Co 11:34
enough to eat and when I go **h**, ... Php 4:12
people will never be **h** again, ... Rev 7:16

HUNT

Esau went out in the field to **h**. .... Ge 27:5
you **h** me like a lion and again .... Job 10:16
Do you **h** food for the female .... Job 38:39
Let evil quickly **h** down cruel .... Ps 140:11
and **h** for it like hidden .... Pr 2:4
And they will **h** the people of .... Je 16:16

HUNTED

Esau because he **h** the wild.................... Ge 25:28
meat of the animal I **h** for you. .... Ge 27:19
who was it that **h** the animals................ Ge 27:33
run away like **h** deer or like .... Is 13:14
for no reason **h** me like a bird. .... La 3:52
enemies **h** us, so we could not .... La 4:18
to tear the animals he **h**, ... Eze 19:3
to tear the animals he **h**, ... Eze 19:6
They **h** down their relatives, ... Am 1:11
he **h** for the woman who had given .... Rev 12:13

HUNTER

was a great **h** before the LORD, ... Ge 10:9
a great **h** before the LORD." .... Ge 10:9
up, Esau became a skilled **h**. .... Ge 25:27
like a deer running from a **h**, ... Pr 6:5

HUNTER'S

like a bird from the **h** trap. .... Ps 124:7

HUNTERS

Like **h**, the wicked string their .... Ps 11:2
send for many **h** to come to this .... Je 16:16
are weak and run from the **h**.................. La 1:6

HUNTING

came in from **h** in the fields, ... Ge 25:29
arrows and go **h** in the field for .... Ge 27:3
Isaac, Esau came in from **h**. .... Ge 27:30
but you are **h** me to kill me. 1Sa 24:11
You're just **h** a bird in the 1Sa 26:20
and useful only as a **h** ground. .... Is 7:24
like wild dogs **h** to kill and eat .... Eze 13:4
will stop you from **h** down others .... Nah 2:13

HUPHAM

from **h** came the Huphamite family .... Nu 26:39

HUPHAMITE

Hupham came the **H** family group............. Nu 26:39

HUPPAH

The thirteenth was **H**............................ 1Ch 24:13

HUPPIM

Ehi, Rosh, Muppim, **H**, and Ard................ Ge 46:21

HUPPITES

Shuppites and **H** were descendants 1Ch 7:12
a wife from the **H** and Shuppites. 1Ch 7:15

HUR

H went to the top of the hill. .... Ex 17:10
Then Aaron and **H** held up Moses'............ Ex 17:12
on one side and **H** on the other. .... Ex 17:12
Aaron and **H** are with you, and .... Ex 24:14
Judah. (Uri was the son of **H**.) .... Ex 31:2
Bezalel son of Uri the son of **H**, ... Ex 35:30
the son of **H** of the tribe of .... Ex 38:22
Evi, Rekem, Zur, **H**, and Reba, ... Nu 31:8
Evi, Rekem, Zur, **H**, and Reba. .... Jos 13:21
Ephrath. They had a son named **H**, ... 1Ch 2:19
Hezron, Carmi, **H**, and Shobal. 1Ch 4:1
was the son of **H**, had made was 2Ch 1:5
repaired by Rephaiah son of **H**, ... Ne 3:9

HURAI

H from the ravines of Gaash; 1Ch 11:32

HURAM

Tyre and had **H** brought to him. 1Ki 7:13
H was also very skilled and 1Ki 7:14
H put these two bronze pillars 1Ki 7:21
Then **H** made from bronze a large 1Ki 7:23
Then **H** made ten bronze stands, ... 1Ki 7:27
This is the way **H** made the ten 1Ki 7:37
H also made ten bronze bowls, ... 1Ki 7:38
H put five stands on the south 1Ki 7:39
H also made bowls, shovels, and 1Ki 7:40
So **H** finished all his work for.................. 1Ki 7:40
H made everything King Solomon 1Ki 7:45
Gera, Shephuphan, and **H**. 1Ch 8:5
H also made bowls, shovels, and 2Ch 4:11

HURAM'S

H mother was a widow from the 1Ki 7:14

HURAM-ABI

a skilled and wise man named **H**. 2Ch 2:13
H is skilled in working with 2Ch 2:14
the things that **H** made for King.............. 2Ch 4:16

HURI

was Huri's son. **H** was Jaroah's 1Ch 5:14

HURI'S

Abihail was **H** son. Huri was 1Ch 5:14

HURRICANE

His anger will be like a **h**. .... Je 23:19
them like a **h** to other countries .... Zch 7:14

HURRIED

Abraham **h** to the tent where .... Ge 18:6
who **h** to kill it and to prepare .... Ge 18:7
They **h** down to Egypt and stood .... Ge 43:15
Then Joseph **h** off because he had .... Ge 43:30
of the LORD and **h** to bring their .... Ex 9:20
The people **h** across the river.................... Jos 4:10
next morning and **h** out to fight .... Jos 8:14
place and **h** toward the city.................... Jos 8:19
Abigail **h**. She took two hundred 1Sa 25:18
But as she **h** to leave, she 2Sa 4:4
h down with the men of Judah to 2Sa 19:16
They all **h** to the Jordan River 2Sa 19:17
Then the officers **h**, and each 2Ki 9:13
So they **h** him out of the Temple. 2Ch 26:20
set out, **h** by the king's .... Est 3:15
but Haman in home with his head .... Est 6:12
The messengers **h** out, riding on.............. Est 8:14
your orders, it **h** away. .... Ps 104:7
h and did not wait to obey your .... Ps 119:60
up at dawn and **h** to the lions' .... Da 6:19

HURRIEDLY

thrown away as they had **h** left. 2Ki 7:15

HURRIES

and then it **h** back to where it.................. Ec 1:5

HURRY

the angels begged Lot to **h**...................... Ge 19:15
Now **h** and bring him back to me." .... Ge 45:13

HURRYING

They were **h** to get away from 1Sa 23:26
He was **h** to be in Jerusalem on .... Ac 20:16
and chariots **h** into battle. .... Rev 9:9

HURT

the one who is **h** but not killed .... Ex 21:18
take money to **h** innocent people .... Ps 15:5
they were happy when I **h**. .... Ps 35:26
who want to **h** me plan trouble; .... Ps 38:12
LORD did not let anyone **h** them; .... Ps 105:14
They hit me, but I'm not **h**. .... Pr 23:35
boulders might be **h** by them; .... Ec 10:9

HURTING (continued)

They will not **h** or destroy each .... Is 11:9
on the ground will not **h** anyone. .... Is 65:25
They have not **h** me, because my .... Da 6:22
he will **h** and kill God's holy .... Da 7:25
will not be **h** by the second .... Rev 2:11

HURTING

blame me for **h** you Philistines!" .... Jdg 15:3
he has kept me from **h** you. 1Sa 25:34
because I am lonely and **h**. .... Ps 25:16
I am sad and **h**. God, save me and .... Ps 69:29
proudly they speak of **h** others. .... Ps 73:8
you judge those who are **h** me? .... Ps 119:84
Liars are **h** me. Help me! .... Ps 119:86
people of Judah are really **h**, ... Je 7:19
They are only **h** themselves and .... Je 7:19
for me those who are **h** me. .... Je 15:15
those who are **h** me be ashamed, ... Je 17:18
law-breaking and sins are **h** us. .... Eze 33:10
Stop being cruel and **h** people, ... Eze 45:9
confusion and people **h** others." .... Am 3:9
things and **h** others in front of .... Hab 1:3
they were **h** and helpless, ... Mt 9:36
then left the man without **h** him. .... Lk 4:35
spirit keeps on **h** him and almost .... Lk 9:39
Why are you **h** each other?' .... Ac 7:26
The man who was **h** the other .... Ac 7:27
You are only **h** yourself by .... Ac 26:14
If you go on **h** each other and............... Gal 5:15

HURTS

God **h**, but he also bandages up;........... Job 5:18
their neighbors, even when it **h**. .... Ps 15:4
When people insult you, it **h** me. .... Ps 69:9
it **h** them as much as a club, ... Pr 25:18
with wounds, **h**, and open sores .... Is 1:6
and heals the **h** he gave them. .... Is 30:26
the sickness and **h** of Jerusalem. .... Je 6:7
So why aren't the **h** of my people .... Je 8:22
which **h** its own people. .... Zph 3:1
touches your **h** what is precious .... Zch 2:8
Love never **h** a neighbor, so .... Rm 13:10
people insult you, it **h** me." .... Rm 15:3

HUSBAND

fruit to her **h** who was with her .... Ge 3:6
You will greatly desire your **h**, ... Ge 3:16
Sarai gave Hagar to her **h** Abram. .... Ge 16:3
My **h** and I are too old to have a............. Ge 18:12
Surely now my **h** will love me." .... Ge 29:32
surely my **h** will be close to me, ... Ge 29:34
have already taken away my **h**, ... Ge 30:15
I gave my slave girl to my **h**." .... Ge 30:18
his coat until her **h** came home, ... Ge 39:16
the woman's **h** says and the court .... Ex 21:22
to him because she has no **h**. .... Le 21:3
hidden from her **h** so that he .... Nu 5:13
But if her **h** has feelings of .... Nu 5:14
The **h** must also take an offering .... Nu 5:15
you been unfaithful to your **h**? .... Nu 5:19
unfaithful to your **h** and have .... Nu 5:20
if she has sinned against her **h**. .... Nu 5:27
while she is married to her **h**. .... Nu 5:29
In this way the **h** can be proven .... Nu 5:31
and if her **h** hears about it and .... Nu 30:7
But if her **h** hears about it and .... Nu 30:8
and if her **h** hears about it but .... Nu 30:11
But if her **h** has canceled it, so .... Nu 30:12
Her **h** has canceled it, so .... Nu 30:12
A woman's **h** may make her keep or .... Nu 30:13
Every **h** and wife will have .... Dt 7:14
You will be her **h**, and she will .... Dt 21:13
the things the **h** said about his .... Dt 22:20
but her second **h** does not like .... Dt 24:3
Or the second **h** might die. .... Dt 24:3

HUSBAND (continued)

first **h** who divorced her must.................. Dt 24:4
to save her **h** from his attacker .... Dt 25:11
be cruel to her **h** whom she loves .... Dt 28:56
daughter never had a **h**. .... Jdg 11:39
her **h** Manoah was not with her................ Jdg 13:9
Trick your **h** into telling us the .... Jdg 14:15
Then her **h** went to ask her to................. Jdg 19:3
So the **h** of the murdered woman .... Jdg 20:4
Then Naomi's **h**, Elimelech, died, ... Ru 1:3
without her **h** or her two sons. .... Ru 1:5
another happy home and a new **h**." .... Ru 1:9
I am too old to have another **h**. .... Ru 1:12
hope' and had another **h** tonight, ... Ru 1:12
mother-in-law after your **h** died.......... Ru 2:11
Her **h** Elkanah would say to her, ... 1Sa 1:8
Hannah's **h**, said to her, "Do 1Sa 1:23
went with her **h** to Shiloh for 1Sa 2:19
Phinehas, her **h**, were both dead 1Sa 4:19
father-in-law and **h** were dead. 1Sa 4:21
But she did not tell her **h**. 1Sa 25:19
Michal from her **h** Paltiel son of 2Sa 3:15
Michal's **h** went with her, crying 2Sa 3:16
heard that her **h** was dead, ... 2Sa 11:26
"I am a widow; my **h** is dead. 2Sa 14:5
Your servant, my **h**, is dead. 2Ki 4:1
woman said to her **h**, "I know 2Ki 4:9
has no son, and her **h** is old." 2Ki 4:14
called to her **h**, "Send me one................ 2Ki 4:22
The **h** said, "Why do you want to 2Ki 4:23
Is your **h** all right? 2Ki 4:26
leaves the **h** she married when .... Pr 2:17
Jealousy makes a **h** very angry, ... Pr 6:34
My **h** is not home; he has gone on .... Pr 7:19
wife is like a crown for her **h**,................ Pr 12:4
Her **h** trusts her completely. .... Pr 31:11
Her **h** is known at the city .... Pr 31:23
Her **h** also praises her, ... Pr 31:28
lose your children and your **h**. .... Is 47:9
than the woman who has a **h**. .... Is 54:1
you felt when you lost your **h**. .... Is 54:4
God who made you is like your **h**. .... Is 54:5
like a woman whose **h** left her, ... Is 54:6
young and then her **h** left her. .... Is 54:6
him as a bride belongs to her **h**. .... Is 62:4
her first **h** come back to her .... Je 3:1
who is unfaithful to her **h**, ... Je 3:20
A **h** and his wife will both be .... Je 6:11
was a **h** to them, but they broke .... Je 31:32
strangers instead of your **h**. .... Eze 16:32
who hated her **h** and children. .... Eze 16:45
She, her **h**, her child, and those .... Da 11:6
wife, and I am no longer her **h**. .... Hos 2:2
'I will go back to my first **h**, ... Hos 2:7
future she will call me 'my **h**;'................ Hos 2:16
Joseph was the **h** of Mary, and .... Mt 1:16
Because Mary's **h**, Joseph, was a .... Mt 1:19
who divorces her **h** and marries .... Mk 10:12
Then her **h** died, and she was a .... Lk 2:37
get your **h** and come back here. .... Jn 4:16
woman answered, "I have no **h**." .... Jn 4:17
are right to say you have no **h**. .... Jn 4:17
you live with now is not your **h**. .... Jn 4:18
with a man who is not her **h**. .... Jn 8:4
did you and your **h** agree to test .... Ac 5:9
buried your **h** are at the door .... Ac 5:9
out and buried her beside her **h**............... Ac 5:10
married to her **h** as long as he .... Rm 7:2
But if her **h** dies, she is free .... Rm 7:2
man while her **h** is still alive, ... Rm 7:3
But if her **h** dies, she is free .... Rm 7:3
woman should have her own **h**. 1Co 7:2
The **h** should give his wife all.................. 1Co 7:3
should give her **h** all that she 1Co 7:3

H

all that she owes him as her **h**. 1Co 7:3
her own body; her **h** shares them. 1Co 7:4
And the **h** does not have full 1Co 7:4
A wife should not leave her **h**. 1Co 7:10
she should make up with her **h**. 1Co 7:11
Also the **h** should not divorce 1Co 7:11
woman has a **h** who is not a 1Co 7:13
The **h** who is not a believer is 1Co 7:14
holy through her believing **h**. 1Co 7:14
maybe you will save your **h**. 1Co 7:16
And **h**, you don't know; 1Co 7:16
as to how she can please her **h**. 1Co 7:34
stay with her **h** as long as he 1Co 7:39
But if her **h** dies, she is free 1Co 7:39
you to Christ, as your only **h**. 2Co 11:2
than the woman who has a **h**." .... Gal 4:27
because the **h** is the head of the .... Eph 5:23
and a wife must respect her **h**. .... Eph 5:33
have been faithful to her **h**. 1Ti 5:9
and **h** and wife should keep their .... Heb 13:4
Abraham, her **h**, and called him 1Pe 3:6
like a bride dressed for her **h**. .... Rev 21:2

HUSBANDS

gave to Moses for **h** and wives, ... Nu 30:16
Their **h** were from the tribe of .... Nu 36:12
to more sons to give you new **h**; .... Ru 1:11
for so many years without **h**? .... Ru 1:13
will no longer honor their **h**. .... Est 1:17
in the same way to their **h**, ... Est 1:18
the women will respect their **h**, ... Est 1:20
wives lose their children and **h**. .... Je 18:21
other gods, and have I known it. .... Je 44:15
Our **h** knew what we were doing. .... Je 44:19
Our **h** knew we were making cakes .... Je 44:19
who hated their **h** and children. .... Eze 16:45
you command your **h**, "Bring us .... Am 4:1
God made **h** and wives to become .... Mal 2:15
Really you have had five **h**, ... Jn 4:18
should ask their own **h** at home 1Co 14:35
yield to your **h**, as you do to .... Eph 5:22
yield to your **h** in everything. .... Eph 5:24
H, love your wives as Christ .... Eph 5:25
h should love their wives as .... Eph 5:28
to the authority of your **h**, ... Col 3:18
H, love your wives and be gentle .... Col 3:19
the young women to love their **h**, ... Tit 2:4
kind, and to yield to their **h**. .... Tit 2:5
wives should yield to your **h**. 1Pe 3:1
if some **h** do not obey God's 1Pe 3:1
Your **h** will see the pure lives 1Pe 3:2
yielding to their own **h**. 1Pe 3:5
h should live with your wives 1Pe 3:7

HUSH

the one who asked will say, "**H**! .... Am 6:10

HUSHAH

He was from **H** and was from 1Ch 27:11

HUSHAI

H the Arkite came to meet him. 2Sa 15:32
David said to **H**, "If you go with 2Sa 15:33
David's friend **H** entered 2Sa 15:37
David's friend **H** the Arkite came 2Sa 16:16
H said, "I belong to the one 2Sa 16:18
said, "Now call **H** the Arkite, so 2Sa 17:5
When **H** came to Absalom, Absalom 2Sa 17:6
H said to Absalom, "Ahithophel's 2Sa 17:7
H added, "You know your father 2Sa 17:8
The advice of **H** the Arkite is 2Sa 17:14
H told Zadok and Abiathar, ... 2Sa 17:15
himself had suggested. **H** said, ... 2Sa 17:15
Baana son of **H** was governor of 1Ki 4:16
H, from the Arkite people, was 1Ch 27:33

HUSHAI'S

H coat was torn, and there was 2Sa 15:32

HUSHAM

When Jobab died, **H** became king. .... Ge 36:34
When **H** died, Hadad son of Bedad, ... Ge 36:35
When Jobab died, **H** became king. 1Ch 1:45
When **H** died, Hadad son of Bedad 1Ch 1:46

HUSHATHITE

Sibbecai the **H** killed Saph, ... 2Sa 21:18
the Anathothite; Mebunnai the **H**; 2Sa 23:27
the **H**; Ilai the Ahohite; 1Ch 11:29
Sibbecai the **H** killed Sippai, ... 1Ch 20:4

HUSHIM

Dan's son was **H**. .... Ge 46:23

HUSHITES

and the **H** were descendants of 1Ch 7:12

HUT

like a **h** that a guard builds. .... Job 27:18
like a **h** left in a field of .... Is 1:8
will shake like a **h** in a storm. .... Is 24:20

HUZOTH

went with Balak to Kiriath **H**. .... Nu 22:39

HYENAS

animals will live with the **h**, ... Is 34:14
animals and **h** will live there, ... Je 50:39

HYMENAEUS

H and Alexander have done that, ... 1Ti 1:20
H and Philetus are like that. 2Ti 2:17

HYMN

After singing a **h**, they went out .... Mt 26:30
After singing a **h**, they went out .... Mk 14:26

HYMNS

with psalms, **h**, and spiritual .... Eph 5:19
singing psalms, **h**, and spiritual .... Col 3:16

HYPOCRISY

you are full of **h** and evil. .... Mt 23:28
evil, all lying, **h**, jealousy, ... 1Pe 2:1

HYPOCRITE

You **h**! First, take the wood out .... Mt 7:5
your own eye! You **h**! First, take .... Lk 6:42
So Peter was a **h**, as were the .... Gal 2:13

HYPOCRITES

the poor, don't be like the **h**. .... Mt 6:2
those **h** already have their full .... Mt 6:2
you pray, don't be like the **h**. .... Mt 6:5
put on a sad face like the **h**. .... Mt 6:16
those **h** already have their full .... Mt 6:16
You are **h**! Isaiah was right when .... Mt 15:7
trick him, Jesus said, "You **h**! .... Mt 22:18
Pharisees! You are **h**! You close .... Mt 23:13
You are **h**. You take away .... Mt 23:14
You are **h**! You travel across .... Mt 23:15
You are **h**! You give to God .... Mt 23:23
Pharisees! You are **h**! You wash .... Mt 23:25
You are **h**! You are like .... Mt 23:27
You are **h**! You build tombs. .... Mt 23:29
send him away to be with the **h**, ... Mt 24:51
right when he spoke about you **h**. .... Mk 7:6
Pharisees, because they are **h**. .... Lk 12:1
H! You know how to understand .... Lk 12:56
The Lord answered, "You **h**! .... Lk 13:15

HYSSOP

Take a branch of the **h** plant, ... Ex 12:22
and a **h** plant be brought for .... Le 14:4
wood, the red string, and the **h**; .... Le 14:6
of red string, and a **h** plant. .... Le 14:49
cedar wood, the **h**, and the red .... Le 14:51
cedar wood, the **h**, and the red .... Le 14:52

a cedar stick, a **h** branch, and a .... Nu 19:6
must take a **h** branch and dip it .... Nu 19:18
sponge on a branch of a **h** plant, ... Jn 19:29
a branch of the **h** plant to .... Heb 9:19

I

IBEX
deer, wild goats, **i,** antelope, ... Dt 14:5

IBHAR
I, Elishua, Nepheg, Japhia, ... 2Sa 5:15
I, Elishua, Elpelet, ... 1Ch 14:5

IBLEAM
I and its small towns; .... Jos 17:11
Shan, Taanach, Dor, **I,** Megiddo,.............. Jdg 1:27
on the way up to Gur near **I.** 2Ki 9:27

IBNEIAH
There was also **I** son of Jeroham 1Ch 9:8

IBNIJAH'S
son, and Reuel was **I** son. 1Ch 9:8

IBRI
named Shoham, Zaccur, and **I.** 1Ch 24:27

IBSAM
Jeriel, Jahmai, **I,** and Samuel,................. 1Ch 7:2

IBZAN
I from Bethlehem was a judge for .... Jdg 12:8
I judged Israel for seven years. .... Jdg 12:9
I died, Elon from the tribe .... Jdg 12:11

ICE
dark by melting **i** and rise with .... Job 6:16
The breath of God makes **i,**................... Job 37:10
Who is the mother of the **i?** .... Job 38:29
that sparkled like **i** and was .... Eze 1:22

ICHABOD
named the baby **I,** saying, ... 1Sa 4:21
I was the son of Phinehas, ... 1Sa 14:3

ICHABOD'S
was a son of **I** brother Ahitub. 1Sa 14:3

ICONIUM
off their feet and went to **I.**..................... Ac 13:51
In **I,** Paul and Barnabas went as .... Ac 14:1
Barnabas stayed in **I** a long time .... Ac 14:3
from Antioch and **I** and persuaded............ Ac 14:19
to Lystra, **I,** and Antioch, ... Ac 14:21
Lystra and **I** respected Timothy .... Ac 16:2
as in Antioch, **I,** and Lystra. 2Ti 3:11

IDALAH
Shimron, **I,** and Bethlehem. .... Jos 19:15

IDDO
Ahinadab son of **I** was governor.............. 1Ki 4:14
Joah's son was **I.** Iddo's son was 1Ch 6:21
I son of Zechariah was over East 1Ch 27:21
in the visions of **I** the seer, ... 2Ch 9:29
the prophet and **I** the seer, ... 2Ch 12:15
the writings of the prophet **I.** 2Ch 13:22
a descendant of **I,** prophesied to.............. Ezr 5:1
Zechariah, a descendant of **I.** .... Ezr 6:14
these men to **I,** the leader at .... Ezr 8:17
what to say to **I** and his .... Ezr 8:17
I, Ginnethon, Abijah, ... Ne 12:4
Berekiah, who was the son of **I.** .... Zch 1:1
Berekiah, who was the son of **I.** .... Zch 1:7

IDDO'S
son was Iddo. **I** son was Zerah. 1Ch 6:21
I relatives gave us Sherebiah,................. Ezr 8:18
Zechariah, from **I** family; .... Ne 12:16

IDLE
and **i** people will go hungry. .... Pr 19:15

IDOL
Manasseh carved an **i** and put it.............. 2Ch 33:7
people made an **i** that looked .... Ac 7:41
We know that an **i** is really 1Co 8:4
it as being sacrificed to an **i.** 1Co 8:7
sacrificed to an **i** is important. 1Co 10:19

IDOLATRIES
false visions, **i,** worthless .... Je 14:14

IDOLS
stole the **i** that belonged to .... Ge 31:19
on the lifeless forms of your **i.** .... Le 26:30
holy vest and some household **i.**.............. Jdg 17:5
because of their worthless **i.** 1Ki 16:13
gods and Asherah **i** on every high 2Ki 17:10
They served **i** when the LORD had........... 2Ki 17:12
gods of the nations are only **i,** 1Ch 16:26
the goat and calf **i** he had made.............. 2Ch 11:15
the Asherah idols and other **i.** 2Ch 24:18
back the **i** they worshiped 2Ch 25:14
Their **i** are made of silver and................. Ps 115:4
those kingdoms that worship **i,** .... Is 10:10
The **i** of Egypt will tremble .... Is 19:1
advice from their **i** and spirits................. Is 19:3
make me angry by worshiping **i,** .... Je 8:19
i will be broken and brought .... Eze 6:6
to worship **i** and put up evil .... Eze 14:4
them myself for worshiping **i.**................. Eze 14:4
left me because of all their **i.'** .... Eze 14:5
with all the **i** of everyone she .... Eze 23:7
part in adultery with their **i.** .... Eze 23:37
people ask wooden **i** for advice; .... Hos 4:12
worship useless **i** give up their .... Jnh 2:8
I tell lies; fortune-tellers see .... Zch 10:2
food that has been offered to **i** .... Ac 15:20
food that has been offered to **i,** .... Ac 15:29
saw that the city was full of **i.**................ Ac 17:16
You hate **i,** but you steal from................. Rm 2:22
eating meat sacrificed to **i:** 1Co 8:4
and led away to worship **i—** 1Co 12:2
worshiping **i** and began serving 1Th 1:9
food offered to **i** and by taking .... Rev 2:14
demons and **i** made of gold, ... Rev 9:20

IDUMEA
Jerusalem, from **I,** from the .... Mk 3:8

IEZER
From **I** came the Iezerite family .... Nu 26:30

IEZERITE
Iezer came the **I** family group; .... Nu 26:30

IGAL
of Issachar, **I** son of Joseph; .... Nu 13:7
I son of Nathan of Zobah; 2Sa 23:36
were Hattush, **I,** Bariah, Neariah 1Ch 3:22

IGDALIAH
of the sons of Hanan son of **I,**................. Je 35:4

IGNORANT
people who are **i** and weak in................. 2Pe 3:16

IIM
Baalah, **I,** Ezem, ... Jos 15:29

IJON
They defeated the towns of **I,** 1Ki 15:20
capturing the cities of **I,** 2Ki 15:29
They defeated the towns of **I,** 2Ch 16:4

IKKESH
Ira son of **I** from Tekoa; 2Sa 23:26
Ira son of **I** from Tekoa; 1Ch 11:28
was Ira son of **I** from the town 1Ch 27:9

ILAI
the Hushathite; I the Ahohite;................. 1Ch 11:29

ILLNESS
Israel saw its i and Judah saw .... Hos 5:13
because of an i that I came to................. Gal 4:13

ILLYRICUM
all the way around to I, ... Rm 15:19

IMAGE
beings in our i and likeness. .... Ge 1:26
created human beings in his i. .... Ge 1:27
In the i of God he created them. .... Ge 1:27
son in his likeness and i,........................ Ge 5:3
God made humans in his own i. .... Ge 9:6
Micah's house and took the i,................. Jdg 18:18
compare him to an i of anything? .... Is 40:18
i and name are on the coin? .... Mt 22:20
i and name are on the coin? .... Mk 12:16
Whose i and name are on it?" .... Lk 20:24
not worship the i of the beast .... Rev 13:15

IMAGES
idols and all the hateful i. .... Eze 11:18
the idols and metal i that are .... Nah 1:14

IMAGINE
that people i or make from gold, ... Ac 17:29
than anything we can ask or i. .... Eph 3:20

IMAGINED
No one has ever i what God has.............. 1Co 2:9

IMLAH
He is Micaiah son of I." 1Ki 22:8
He is Micaiah son of I." 2Ch 18:7

IMMANUEL
a son, and she will name him I. .... Is 7:14
I, this army will spread its .... Is 8:8
and they will name him I," .... Mt 1:23

IMMEDIATELY
but I cursed his home i. .... Job 5:3
and worship will i be thrown .... Da 3:6
you will i be thrown into the .... Da 3:15
I the words came true. .... Da 4:33
and Andrew i left their nets .... Mt 4:20
I they left the boat and their .... Mt 4:22
And i the man was healed from .... Mt 8:3
I Jesus told his followers to .... Mt 14:22
I Jesus reached out his hand and .... Mt 14:31
The tree i dried up. .... Mt 21:19
i, as Jesus was coming up out of .... Mk 1:10
and Andrew i left their nets .... Mk 1:18
Jesus i called them, and they .... Mk 1:20
I the disease left the man, ... Mk 1:42
Jesus knew i what these teachers .... Mk 2:8
I the paralyzed man stood up, ... Mk 2:12
I the king sent a soldier to .... Mk 6:27
I Jesus told his followers to .... Mk 6:45
boat, people i recognized Jesus. .... Mk 6:54
I the father cried out, "I do .... Mk 9:24
I Zechariah could talk again, ... Lk 1:64
and i she got up and began.................... Lk 4:39
I the disease disappeared. .... Lk 5:13
i open the door for him. .... Lk 12:36
and i she was able to stand up .... Lk 13:13
God's kingdom would appear i. .... Lk 19:11
And i the man was well; .... Jn 5:9
Jesus gave him and i went out. .... Jn 13:30
I the man's feet and ankles.................... Ac 3:7
I, something that looked like .... Ac 9:18
Aeneas stood up i. .... Ac 9:34
I sent for you, and it was .... Ac 10:33
angel of the Lord i caused him .... Ac 12:23
we i prepared to leave for .... Ac 16:10
I, the spirit came out. .... Ac 16:18

all his people were baptized i. .... Ac 16:33
The Temple doors were closed i............... Ac 21:30
I he took some officers and .... Ac 21:32
' I I was able to see him. .... Ac 22:13
Paul moved away from him i. .... Ac 22:29
I I was in the Spirit, and .... Rev 4:2

IMMER
was Bilgah. The sixteenth was I. 1Ch 24:14
the descendants of I—1,052; .... Ezr 2:37
Addon, and I, but they could .... Ezr 2:59
From the descendants of I: .... Ezr 10:20
Zadok son of I made repairs .... Ne 3:29
the descendants of I—1,052; .... Ne 7:40
Addon, and I, but they could .... Ne 7:61
Meshillemoth was the son of I. .... Ne 11:13
Pashhur son of I was a priest .... Je 20:1

IMNAH
sons were I, Ishvah, Ishvi, ... Ge 46:17
From I came the Imnite family .... Nu 26:44
sons were I, Ishvah, Ishvi, ... 1Ch 7:30
Kore son of I the Levite was in 2Ch 31:14

IMNITE
Imnah came the I family group; .... Nu 26:44

IMPATIENT
the people became i on the way .... Nu 21:4
I have reason to be i. .... Job 21:4
to me, and I got i with them. .... Zch 11:8

IMPORTANCE
was second in i to King Xerxes, ... Est 10:3
to show the i of his question, ... Lk 10:29

IMPORTED
He i horses from Egypt and Kue. 1Ki 10:28
He i horses from Egypt and Kue; 2Ch 1:16
They i chariots from Egypt for 2Ch 1:17
Solomon i horses from Egypt and 2Ch 9:28

IMPOSSIBLE
This made it i for Tamar to .... Ge 38:9
is i to rule this great people 1Ki 3:9
It is i for the Almighty to do .... Job 34:10
Nothing is i for me.............................. Je 32:27
people this is i, but for God .... Mt 19:26
people this is i, but for God .... Mk 10:27
The things i for people are .... Lk 18:27
think it is i for God to raise.................... Ac 26:8
It is i to bring them back to a .... Heb 6:6
because it is i for the blood of .... Heb 10:4

IMPRESSED
He is not i with the strength of .... Ps 147:10
wise here on earth that i me. .... Ec 9:13

IMPROVE
to correction to i your life, ... Pr 15:31
so people can i each other. .... Pr 27:17

IMPROVING
instead of i, she was getting .... Mk 5:26

IMPURE
everything that makes it i. 2Ch 29:5

IMRAH
Suah, Harnepher, Shual, Beri, I,............. 1Ch 7:36

IMRI
Imri's son. I was Bani's son. 1Ch 9:4
and Zaccur son of I built next .... Ne 3:2

IMRI'S
son. Omri was I son. Imri was 1Ch 9:4

INCENSE
of acacia wood for burning i. .... Ex 30:1
sweet-smelling i on the altar .... Ex 30:7
He must burn i again in the .... Ex 30:8
altar for offering any other i, ... Ex 30:9

its tools, and on the **i** altar. .... Ex 30:27
the same way you make this **i**. .... Ex 30:37
and the pure, sweet-smelling **i**. .... Ex 37:29
He must put the **i** on the fire .... Le 16:13
prayer be like **i** placed before .... Ps 141:2
I hate the **i** you burn. .... Is 1:13
make you tired with **i** to burn. .... Is 43:23
So you did not buy **i** for me; .... Is 43:24
from Sheba bringing gold and **i**, ... Is 60:6
permission to burn **i** to the .... Je 44:19
Your **i** altars will be cut down, ... Eze 6:6
pan for burning **i** in his hand, ... Eze 8:11
gave my oil and **i** as an offering .... Eze 16:18
offering and **i** be presented to .... Da 2:46
Baals and burned **i** to the idols. .... Hos 11:2
net and burns **i** to worship it, ... Hab 1:16
Temple of the Lord and burn **i**. .... Lk 1:9
at the time the **i** was offered. .... Lk 1:10
the right side of the **i** table. .... Lk 1:11
harp and golden bowls full of **i**, ... Rev 5:8
cinnamon, spice, **i**, myrrh, ... Rev 18:13

INCIDENT
After this **i** King Jeroboam did 1Ki 13:33

INCREASE
and your silver and gold **i**, ... Dt 8:13
against me and **i** your anger .... Job 10:17
will **i** the number of people who .... Eze 36:10
will **i** the number of people and .... Eze 36:11
will **i** the harvest of the field .... Eze 36:30

INCREASED
of followers in Jerusalem **i**, ... Ac 6:7
sin grew worse, God's grace **i**. .... Rm 5:20

INCREASING
will bring **i** thanks to God for 2Co 4:15
they are **i** their sins to the 1Th 2:16
of you has for each other is **i**. 2Th 1:3

INDEPENDENT
the Lord women are not **i** of men, ... 1Co 11:11
and men are not **i** of women. 1Co 11:11

INDIA
states from **I** to Cush. .... Est 1:1
that reached from **I** to Cush. .... Est 8:9

INDIRECTLY
you these things **i** in stories. .... Jn 16:25

INFECTED
stink and become **i** because I was .... Ps 38:5

INFLUENCE
and sadness has a good **i** on you. .... Ec 7:3
Not many of you had great **i**. 1Co 1:26
never tried to **i** you by saying 1Th 2:5
free from the world's evil **i**. .... Jam 1:27

INFLUENCED
wife Jezebel **i** him to do evil. 1Ki 21:25
want decisions **i** by money." 2Ch 19:7
yourselves be **i** and led away to 1Co 12:2
Barnabas was **i** by what these .... Gal 2:13
We will not be **i** by every new .... Eph 4:14
pure, not **i** by sinners, and he .... Heb 7:26

INFLUENCES
a fire that **i** all of life. .... Jam 3:6

INFORM
your elders and they will **i** you. .... Dt 32:7

INFORMATION
to you with **i** for you to hear. .... Eze 24:26

INHERIT
house will **i** everything I have. .... Ge 15:3
be the one to **i** what you have. .... Ge 15:4
own who will **i** what you have." .... Ge 15:4

Her son should not **i** anything; .... Ge 21:10
You will not **i** any of the land, ... Nu 18:20
Israelites, only you will **i** me. .... Nu 18:20
Levites will not **i** any land .... Nu 18:23
'They will not **i** any land among .... Nu 18:24
the land that they are to **i**, ... Dt 3:28
When you **i** the lands of these .... Dt 12:2
They will not **i** any of the land .... Dt 18:2
they will **i** the LORD himself, ... Dt 18:2
It marks what you **i** in the land .... Dt 19:14
their children will **i** the land. .... Ps 25:13
trust the LORD will **i** the land. .... Ps 37:9
not proud will **i** the land and .... Ps 37:11
LORD blesses will **i** the land, ... Ps 37:22
Good people will **i** the land and .... Ps 37:29
He chose the land we would **i**. .... Ps 47:4
his servants will **i** that land, ... Ps 69:36
he had his people **i** the land. .... Ps 78:55
and will even **i** a share of what .... Pr 17:2
'This son will **i** the vineyard. .... Mt 21:38
'This son will **i** the vineyard. .... Mk 12:7
'This son will **i** the vineyard. .... Lk 20:14
will **i** all of God's blessings .... Gal 3:29
those who will **i** their fathers' .... Gal 4:1
woman should not **i** anything. .... Gal 4:30
things will not **i** God's kingdom. .... Gal 5:21

INHERITED
and wealth are **i** from parents, ... Pr 19:14
i quickly in the beginning .... Pr 20:21

INHERITS
A woman who **i** her father's land .... Nu 36:8

INJURED
he must pay the **i** man for the .... Ex 21:19
support the **i** man until he is .... Ex 21:19
person must be **i** in the same way .... Le 24:20
and the **i** cry out for help, ... Job 24:12
were only a few **i** men left in .... Je 37:10
of you who are **i** and dying will .... Eze 26:15
ones, or heal the **i** ones, or .... Zch 11:16

INJURES
Anyone who **i** another person must .... Le 24:20
he **i**, but his hands also heal. .... Job 5:18

INJURIES
if I will recover from my **i**." 2Ki 1:2
heal from the **i** the Arameans had 2Ki 9:15
serious **i** as if they were .... Je 6:14
serious **i** as if they were .... Je 8:11
your health and heal your **i**," .... Je 30:17
will be amazed at all her **i**. .... Je 49:17
heads when they see all her **i**. .... Je 50:13

INJURY
is no further **i**, the man who .... Ex 21:22
But if there is further **i**, ... Ex 21:23
causes an **i** to a neighbor .... Le 24:19
the same kind of **i** in return: .... Le 24:19
be at peace, without fear of **i**." .... Pr 1:33
will be for me because of my **i**. .... Je 10:19
understand why my **i** is not cured .... Je 15:18
your **i** will not heal. .... Je 30:12
are you crying out about your **i**? .... Je 30:15
and did not find any **i** on him, ... Da 6:23
your **i** will not heal. .... Nah 3:19

INK
down with **i** on this scroll." .... Je 36:18
not written with **i** but with the 2Co 3:3
do not want to use paper and **i**. 2Jn 1:12
I do not want to use pen and **i**. 3Jn 1:13

INN
were no rooms left in the **i**, ... Lk 2:7
took him to an **i** where he cared .... Lk 10:34

INNER

main room and the i room of the	.... 1Ki 6:5
The i courtyard was enclosed by	.... 1Ki 6:36
'The Christ is in the i room,'	.... Mt 24:26
whispered in an i room will be	.... Lk 12:3
never enter the i room without	.... Heb 9:7

INNKEEPER

them to the i, and said, 'Take .... Lk 10:35

INNOCENCE

my i is being questioned.	.... Job 6:29
way you have regained your i.	.... 2Co 7:11

INNOCENT

allow an i or honest person	.... Ex 23:7
so that i people will not be	.... Dt 19:10
money to murder an i person."	.... Dt 27:25
that the i will not die;	.... Job 4:7
laugh at the suffering of the i.	.... Job 9:23
I am i and free from guilt.	.... Job 33:9
not take money to hurt i people.	.... Ps 15:5
be pure and i of the greatest	.... Ps 19:13
and sentence to death the i.	.... Ps 94:21
They killed i people, their own	.... Ps 106:38
attack some i people just for	.... Pr 1:11
hands that kill i people,	.... Pr 6:17
No one can say, "I am i;	.... Pr 20:9
always ready to kill i people.	.... Is 59:7
but you say, 'I am i.	.... Je 2:35
because my God knows I am i.	.... Da 6:22
guilty of killing an i person.	.... Jnh 1:14
I handed over to you an i man."	.... Mt 27:4
to that man, because he is i.	.... Mt 27:19
is good and i in what is evil	.... Rm 16:19
you will be i and without any	.... Php 2:15
and then murdered i people,	.... Jam 5:6

INNS

and the Three I to meet us. .... Ac 28:15

INSIGNIFICANT

are not just an i village in .... Mt 2:6

INSIST

I will i that I am right;	.... Job 27:6
those who i on circumcision	.... Tit 1:10

INSISTED

But Peter i, "I will never say	.... Mk 14:31
another man i, "Certainly this	.... Lk 22:59
we i that you live good lives	.... 1Th 2:12

INSISTING

They were i, saying, "But Jesus .... Lk 23:5

INSPECTING

i the walls of Jerusalem that	.... Ne 2:13
the valley at night, i the wall.	.... Ne 2:15

INSPECTION

which is across from the I Gate, ... Ne 3:31

INSPECTS

She i a field and buys it. .... Pr 31:16

INSPIRED

All Scripture is i by God and is 2Ti 3:16

INSTANT

will strike them in an i;	.... Pr 6:15
kingdoms of the world in an i.	.... Lk 4:5

INSTANTLY

i a man with an evil spirit came	.... Mk 5:2
I her bleeding stopped, and she	.... Mk 5:29
I the man was able to hear and	.... Mk 7:35
and i her bleeding stopped.	.... Lk 8:44
and how she had been i healed.	.... Lk 8:47

INSTRUCT

I have written to i the people."	.... Ex 24:12
wisdom to teach and i each other	.... Col 3:16

INSTRUCTED

Then Absalom i his servants, ... 2Sa 13:28

INSTRUCTIONS

David's last i were to count the	.... 1Ch 23:27
his father David's i and chose.	.... 2Ch 8:14
Egypt and gave i about what to	.... Heb 11:22

INSTRUCTORS

or pay attention to my i. .... Pr 5:13

INSTRUMENT

and plays a musical i well. .... Eze 33:32

INSTRUMENTS

tambourines and stringed i.	.... 1Sa 18:6
They were playing wooden i:	.... 2Sa 6:5
and the musical i of David king	.... 2Ch 29:27
him with stringed i and flutes.	.... Ps 150:4
you compose songs on musical i.	.... Am 6:5
On my stringed i.	.... Hab 3:19
playing harps and other i,	.... Rev 18:22

INTENT

there was no i to kill his .... Dt 19:6

INTEREST

charge him any i on money you	.... Le 25:36
Don't lend him money for i,	.... Le 25:37
your own brothers too much i."	.... Ne 5:7
do not charge i on money they	.... Ps 15:5
to get too much i or profit.	.... Eze 18:8
money for too much i and profit.	.... Eze 18:13
take too much i or profit when	.... Eze 18:17
take unfair i and profits and	.... Eze 22:12
received my gold back with i.'	.... Mt 25:27
money would have earned some i.'	.... Lk 19:23
for people to show i in you,	.... Gal 4:18

INTERESTED

Do not be i only in your own	.... Php 2:4
but be i in the lives of others.	.... Php 2:4
Other people are i only in their	.... Php 2:21

INTERFERED

David had never i with Adonijah 1Ki 1:6

INTERFERING

I in someone else's quarrel as .... Pr 26:17

INTERPRET

ability to i those languages.	.... 1Co 12:10
Not all i those languages.	.... 1Co 12:30
the gift to i what is spoken.	.... 1Co 14:13
the other, and someone should i.	.... 1Co 14:27

INTERPRETATION

comes from the prophet's own i. 2Pe 1:20

INTERPRETER

he used an i, so they did not	.... Ge 42:23
if there is no i, then those who	.... 1Co 14:28

INTERPRETS

another person i that language. 1Co 14:26

INTESTINES

meat, skin, and i, and burn them	.... Ex 29:14
its head, legs, i, and other	.... Le 4:11
and its i and burned them in a	.... Le 8:17
i will be burned in the fire.	.... Le 16:27
and the i must all be burned.	.... Nu 19:5
disease in your i that will	.... 2Ch 21:15
will cause your i to come out."	.... 2Ch 21:15
disease in his i that could not	.... 2Ch 21:18
Jehoram's i came out because of	.... 2Ch 21:19
open, and all his i poured out.	.... Ac 1:18

INTRODUCE

his brothers to i to the king. .... Ge 47:2

INTRODUCED

Jacob and i him to the king .... Ge 47:7

INTRODUCTION
send them with letters of i, ... 1Co 16:3
need letters of i to you or from 2Co 3:1

INVADE
He will i many countries and .... Da 11:40

INVADERS
'I are coming from a faraway .... Je 4:16

INVENT
They i ways of doing evil. .... Rm 1:30

INVENTED
clever stories that someone i. 2Pe 1:16

INVEST
I what you have, because after a .... Ec 11:1
I what you have in several .... Ec 11:2
went quickly to i the money and .... Mt 25:16

INVESTED
had two bags i them and earned............ Mt 25:17

INVESTIGATED
the report was i, it was found .... Est 2:23

INVITE
I Jesse to the sacrifice. 1Sa 16:3
corners and i everyone you find .... Mt 22:9
give a feast, i the poor, the .... Lk 14:13

INVITED
and he i them to come to the 1Sa 16:5
Queen Esther i to come with .... Est 5:12
The king i some people to the .... Mt 22:3
than you may have been i. .... Lk 14:8
So when you are i, go sit in a .... Lk 14:10
were also i to the wedding..................... Jn 2:2

INVITES
When someone i you to a wedding........... Lk 14:8

INVITING
if you were i them to a feast. .... La 2:22

INWARDLY
to be strong i through his .... Eph 3:16

IPHDEIAH
I, and Penuel. 1Ch 8:25

IPHTAH
I, Ashnah, Nezib, ... Jos 15:43
continued to the Valley of I El. .... Jos 19:14
Zebulun and the Valley of I El. .... Jos 19:27

IR
Nineveh, Rehoboth I, and Calah. .... Ge 10:11
Zorah, Eshtaol, I Shemesh,..................... Jos 19:41
Huppites were descendants of I,............. 1Ch 7:12

IRA
and I the Jairite was David's 2Sa 20:26
I son of Ikkesh from Tekoa; 2Sa 23:26
I the Ithrite; Gareb the Ithrite, ... 2Sa 23:38
I son of Ikkesh from Tekoa; 1Ch 11:28
I the Ithrite; Gareb the Ithrite; 1Ch 11:40
I son of Ikkesh from the town................ 1Ch 27:9

IRAD
a son named I, Irad had a son .... Ge 4:18
I had a son named Mehujael, ... Ge 4:18

IRAM
Magdiel, and I. They were the .... Ge 36:43
Magdiel, and I. These were the 1Ch 1:54

IRI
Jerimoth, and I, and they were 1Ch 7:7

IRIJAH
name was I son of Shelemiah .... Je 37:13
I said, "You are leaving us to .... Je 37:13
Jeremiah said to I, "That's not .... Je 37:14
I refused to listen to .... Je 37:14

IRON
made tools out of bronze and i. .... Ge 4:22
the sky like i and the earth .... Le 26:19
silver, bronze, i, tin, or lead— .... Nu 31:22
who uses an i weapon to kill .... Nu 35:16
bed was made of i, and it was................. Dt 3:11
like a furnace for melting i, ... Dt 4:20
the rocks are i, and where you .... Dt 8:9
but don't use any i tool to cut .... Dt 27:5
the ground below will be like i. .... Dt 28:23
will have locks of i and bronze, ... Dt 33:25
from bronze and i belong to the .... Jos 6:19
silver, gold, bronze, and i. .... Jos 6:24
I, Migdal El, Horem, Beth Anath, ... Jos 19:38
gold, bronze, and i, and many .... Jos 22:8
because they had i chariots. .... Jdg 1:19
nine hundred i chariots and was .... Jdg 4:3
nine hundred i chariots and all .... Jdg 4:13
with saws, i picks, and axes 2Sa 12:31
except with a tool of i or wood. 2Sa 23:7
or any other i tools at the 1Ki 6:7
Kenaanah had made some i horns............ 1Ki 22:11
and it made the i head float. 2Ki 6:6
with saws, i picks, and axes 1Ch 20:3
large amount of i to be used for 1Ch 22:3
much bronze and i it cannot be 1Ch 22:14
gold, silver, bronze, and i, ... 1Ch 22:16
of bronze and i for the things 1Ch 29:2
iron for the things made of i. 1Ch 29:2
pounds of i to the Temple 1Ch 29:7
bronze, and i, and with purple, ... 2Ch 2:7
silver, bronze, i, stone, and 2Ch 2:14
Kenaanah had made some i horns............ 2Ch 18:10
to work with i and bronze to 2Ch 24:12
carved with an i pen into lead, ... Job 19:24
may run away from an i weapon, ... Job 20:24
I is taken from the ground, ... Job 28:2
its legs are like bars of i....................... Job 40:18
It treats i as if it were straw .... Job 41:27
rule over them with an i rod. .... Ps 2:9
feet and an i ring around his .... Ps 105:18
gates and cuts apart i bars..................... Ps 107:16
those important men in i bands............... Ps 149:8
i sharpens iron, so people can .... Pr 27:17
iron sharpens i, so people can .... Pr 27:17
workman uses tools to heat i,................. Is 44:12
and cut through their i bars. .... Is 45:2
your neck was like an i muscle, ... Is 48:4
in place of i, bronze in place .... Is 60:17
place of wood, i in place of..................... Is 60:17
strong city, an i pillar, a .... Je 1:18
like bronze and i that became................ Je 6:28
like a furnace for melting i!' .... Je 11:4
smash a piece of i or bronze .... Je 15:12
Judah is written with an i tool. .... Je 17:1
make a yoke of i in its place! .... Je 28:13
put a yoke of i on the necks .... Je 28:14
and put i rings around his neck............. Je 29:26
get yourself an i plate and set................ Eze 4:3
it up like an i wall between you .... Eze 4:3
copper, tin, i, and lead left .... Eze 22:18
silver, copper, i, lead, and tin .... Eze 22:20
your towers with his i bars. .... Eze 26:9
for silver, i, tin, and lead. .... Eze 27:12
part of the legs made of i, ... Da 2:33
made partly of i and partly of................ Da 2:33
on its feet of i and clay and................... Da 2:34
the i, clay, bronze, silver,....................... Da 2:35
a fourth kingdom, strong as i................. Da 2:40
the same way that i crushes and............. Da 2:40
partly baked clay and partly i. .... Da 2:41
some of the strength of i in it,................. Da 2:41
just as you saw i was mixed with .... Da 2:41

were partly i and partly clay. .... Da 2:42
partly strong like i and partly .... Da 2:42
You saw the i mixed with clay, ... Da 2:43
but i and clay do not hold .... Da 2:43
rock broke the i, bronze, clay, ... Da 2:45
with a band of i and bronze .... Da 4:15
with a band of i and bronze .... Da 4:23
silver, bronze, i, wood, and .... Da 5:4
gold, bronze, i, wood, and stone .... Da 5:23
It had large i teeth. It crushed.................. Da 7:7
and had i teeth and bronze .... Da 7:19
boards that had i teeth. .... Am 1:3
you had horns of i and hoofs of .... Mic 4:13
and came to the i gate that .... Ac 12:10
are destroyed as if by a hot i. 1Ti 4:2
rule over them with an i rod, ... Rev 2:27
looked like i breastplates, ... Rev 9:9
all the nations with an i rod. .... Rev 12:5
wood, bronze, i, and marble; .... Rev 18:12
will rule them with a rod of i. .... Rev 19:15

IRPEEL
Rekem, I, Taralah, ... Jos 18:27

IRU
sons were I, Elah, and Naam. 1Ch 4:15

ISAAC
a son, and you will name him I. .... Ge 17:19
named his son I, the son Sarah .... Ge 21:3
He circumcised I when he was .... Ge 21:4
I promised you will be from I. .... Ge 21:12
your only son, I, the son you .... Ge 22:2
I said, "We have the fire and .... Ge 22:7
tied up his son I and laid him .... Ge 22:9
and get a wife for my son I." .... Ge 24:4
Then I brought Rebekah into the .... Ge 24:67
sons I and Ishmael buried him .... Ge 25:9
I loved Esau because he hunted .... Ge 25:28
So I dug those wells again and .... Ge 26:18
When I was old, his eyesight was .... Ge 27:1
I trembled greatly and said, ... Ge 27:33
grandfather, and the God of I. .... Ge 28:13
God of Abraham and the God of I, ... Ge 31:42
of my father I! LORD, you told .... Ge 32:9
Abraham and I be known through .... Ge 48:16
made with Abraham, I, and Jacob. .... Ex 2:24
the God of I, and the God .... Ex 3:6
to Abraham, I, and Jacob, and I .... Ex 6:8
ancestors—Abraham, I, and Jacob .... Dt 1:8
servants Abraham, I, and Jacob. .... Dt 9:27
gave I two sons named Jacob and .... Jos 24:4
God of Abraham, I, and Israel," 1Ki 18:36
with Abraham, I, and Jacob. 2Ki 13:23
and the promise he made to I. 1Ch 16:16
of Abraham, I, and Jacob. .... Je 33:26
against the descendants of I.' .... Am 7:16
eat with Abraham, I, and Jacob .... Mt 8:11
the God of I, and the God .... Mt 22:32
see Abraham, I, Jacob, and all .... Lk 13:28
I promised you will be from I." .... Rm 9:7
of his promise, as I was then. .... Gal 4:28
was by faith that I blessed the .... Heb 11:20
offered his son I on the altar. .... Jam 2:21

ISAAC'S
I wife could not have children, ... Ge 25:21
The LORD heard I prayer, and .... Ge 25:21
the servants of I father Abraham .... Ge 26:15
I servants dug a well in the...................... Ge 26:19
day I servants came and told .... Ge 26:32
and I sons were Esau and Israel. 1Ch 1:34
The places where I descendants .... Am 7:9

ISAIAH
and the older priests to I. 2Ki 19:2
Hezekiah's officers came to I,.................. 2Ki 19:5
and the prophet I son of Amoz 2Ch 32:20
of the prophet I son of Amoz.................. 2Ch 32:32
is the vision I son of Amoz saw .... Is 1:1
I my servant has walked around.............. Is 20:3
what the prophet I had said: .... Mt 4:14
the things I said about them .... Mt 13:14
I was right when he said about .... Mt 15:7
The book of I the prophet was .... Lk 4:17
I said this because he saw Jesus' .... Jn 12:41
reading from the Book of I, ... Ac 8:28
ancestors through I the prophet,.............. Ac 28:25
I said, "Lord, who believed what .... Rm 10:16
Then I is bold enough to say: .... Rm 10:20

ISCAH
the father of both Milcah and I. .... Ge 11:29

ISCARIOT
apostles, Judas I, went to talk.................. Mt 26:14
had already persuaded Judas I, ... Jn 13:2
Judas (not Judas I) said, "But, ... Jn 14:22

ISH-BOSHETH
took Saul's son I to Mahanaim 2Sa 2:8
Saul's son I was forty years old 2Sa 2:10
the servants of I son of Saul 2Sa 2:12
of Benjamin for I son of Saul,.................. 2Sa 2:15
I said to Abner, "Why did you 2Sa 3:7
angry because of what I said, ... 2Sa 3:8
I couldn't say anything to Abner, ... 2Sa 3:11
sent messengers to Saul's son I, ... 2Sa 3:14
I sent men to take Michal from 2Sa 3:15
When I son of Saul heard that 2Sa 4:1
in Saul's army came to I. 2Sa 4:2
is the head of I son of Saul, ... 2Sa 4:8

ISH-BOSHETH'S
met Abner and I men at the pool 2Sa 2:13
went to I house in the afternoon.............. 2Sa 4:5
Then they took I head and buried 2Sa 4:12

ISHBAK
Medan, Midian, I, and Shuah.................. Ge 25:2
Medan, Midian, I, and Shuah.................. 1Ch 1:32

ISHBI-BENOB
I, one of the sons of Rapha, had 2Sa 21:16

ISHHOD
Hammoleketh gave birth to I, ... 1Ch 7:18

ISHI
Appaim's son was I, who became 1Ch 2:31
Epher, I, Eliel, Azriel, ... 1Ch 5:24

ISHI'S
I sons were Zoheth and 1Ch 4:20
I sons, Pelatiah, Neariah, ... 1Ch 4:42

ISHIJAH
Eliezer, I, Malkijah, Shemaiah, ... Ezr 10:31

ISHMAEL
old when Hagar gave birth to I. .... Ge 16:16
And I, his son, was thirteen .... Ge 17:25
His sons Isaac and I buried him .... Ge 25:9
me go and kill I son of .... Je 40:15
I also killed all the Jews and .... Je 41:3
I captured all the other people .... Je 41:10

ISHMAELITE
son of a man named Jether the I. 2Sa 17:25
and his father was Jether, an I. 1Ch 2:17
Obil, an I, was in charge of the 1Ch 27:30

ISHMAELITES
they saw a group of I traveling .... Ge 37:25
Let's sell him to these I. .... Ge 37:27

ISHMAIAH

sold him to the I for eight .... Ge 37:28
And the I took him to Egypt. .... Ge 37:28
from the I who had brought .... Ge 39:1
The I wore gold earrings. .... Jdg 8:24
the families of Edom and the I, ... Ps 83:6

ISHMAIAH

And there was I from the town of 1Ch 12:4
I son of Obadiah was over the 1Ch 27:19

ISHMERAI

I, Izliah, and Jobab............................... 1Ch 8:18

ISHPAH

Michael, I, and Joha. 1Ch 8:16

ISHPAN

sons were I, Eber, Eliel, ... 1Ch 8:22

ISHVAH

sons were Imnah, I, Ishvi, and .... Ge 46:17
sons were Imnah, I, Ishvi, and 1Ch 7:30

ISHVI

Imnah, Ishvah, I, and Beriah, ... Ge 46:17
from I came the Ishvite family .... Nu 26:44
Jonathan, I, and Malki-Shua. 1Sa 14:49
Imnah, Ishvah, I, and Beriah. 1Ch 7:30

ISHVITE

Ishvi came the I family group; .... Nu 26:44

ISLAND

But we will crash on an i." .... Ac 27:26
was on the i of Patmos, because .... Rev 1:9
Then every i ran away, and................... Rev 16:20

ISLANDS

and all the i of the sea. .... Is 11:11
People in the i of the sea, ... Is 24:15
To him the i are no more than .... Is 40:15
The i of the sea are afraid .... Eze 26:18

ISMAKIAH

Jozabad, Eliel, I, Mahath, and 2Ch 31:13

ISRAEL

name will now be I, because you .... Ge 32:28
today the people of I do not eat .... Ge 32:32
Your new name will be I." .... Ge 35:10
born when his father I was old, ... Ge 37:3
the sons of I went to Egypt to................ Ge 42:5
of the children of I who went .... Ge 46:8
to meet his father I in Goshen. .... Ge 46:29
Then I said to Joseph, "Now I am .... Ge 46:30
When I knew he soon would die, ... Ge 47:29
Then I saw Joseph's sons and............... Ge 48:8
I kissed the boys and put his .... Ge 48:10
Listen to I, your father." .... Ge 49:2
through all the tribes of I. .... Ge 49:7
the Shepherd, the Rock of I. .... Ge 49:24
are the twelve tribes of I, ... Ge 49:28
are the names of the sons of I: .... Ex 1:1
the people of I had many .... Ex 1:7
When you go to the people of I, ... Ex 3:14
and the elders of I will go to .... Ex 3:18
I is my firstborn son. .... Ex 4:22
the LORD, the God of I, says: ' .... Ex 5:1
should I obey him and let I go? .... Ex 5:2
leaders of the families of I: .... Ex 6:14
the LORD treats I differently .... Ex 11:7
community of I that on the tenth .... Ex 12:3
person will be cut off from I. .... Ex 12:15
The people of I had lived in .... Ex 12:40
community of I must take part .... Ex 12:47
The people of I called the food .... Ex 16:31
Jacob, and tell the people of I: .... Ex 19:3
the elders of I must come up to .... Ex 24:1
of the elders of I went up the .... Ex 24:9
and saw the God of I. .... Ex 24:10

of the twelve sons of I on them, ... Ex 28:9
people said, "I, these are your .... Ex 32:4
you—Abraham, Isaac, and I. .... Ex 32:13
an agreement with you and I." .... Ex 34:27
of the twelve sons of I. .... Ex 39:7
whole nation of I sins .... Le 4:13
the people of I, your relatives .... Le 10:6
the people of I these things: ' .... Le 20:2
Mount Sinai for the people of I. .... Le 27:34
who will serve in the army of I, ... Nu 1:3
all the people of I together on................ Nu 1:18
and the twelve leaders of I,................... Nu 1:44
Every man of I twenty years old............. Nu 1:45
among the other people of I. .... Nu 2:33
the firstborn of I to be mine, ... Nu 3:13
firstborn sons in I one month .... Nu 3:40
and the leaders of I counted all .... Nu 4:46
the firstborn in I—people or .... Nu 8:17
of all the firstborn in I. .... Nu 8:18
heads of the family groups of I, ... Nu 10:4
has promised good things to I." .... Nu 10:29
the thousands of people of I." .... Nu 10:36
the elders of I followed him. .... Nu 16:25
people of I around them heard .... Nu 16:34
the people of I give me a tenth .... Nu 18:21
they must be cut off from I. .... Nu 19:13
out to meet I in the desert. .... Nu 21:23
I captured all the Amorite .... Nu 21:25
he saw no fault in I. .... Nu 23:21
a ruler will rise from I. .... Nu 24:17
conquered, but I will grow .... Nu 24:18
be angry with the people of I." .... Nu 25:4
all the people of I by families. .... Nu 26:2
from each of the tribes of I." .... Nu 31:4
the LORD even more angry with I........... Nu 32:14
of safety for citizens of I, ... Nu 35:15
he will lead I to take the land .... Dt 1:38
their place as I did in the land .... Dt 2:12
Moses gave to the people of I. .... Dt 4:44
the people of I together and .... Dt 5:1
people of I! The LORD our God .... Dt 6:4
Listen, I. You will soon cross .... Dt 9:1
Now, I, this is what the LORD .... Dt 10:12
everyone in I will hear about .... Dt 13:11
this sin from your people I,................... Dt 21:8
the people of I will hear about .... Dt 21:21
name will not be forgotten in I. .... Dt 25:6
on his brother's name in I. .... Dt 25:7
teachings to the people of I. .... Dt 33:10
another prophet in I like Moses............... Dt 34:10
the people of I walked across .... Jos 3:17
'I crossed the Jordan River on .... Jos 4:22
The people of I were camped at .... Jos 5:10
Then I burned the whole city and .... Jos 6:24
thing among the people of I!' " .... Jos 7:15
to the LORD, the God of I. .... Jos 7:19
king of Ai saw the army of I, ... Jos 8:14
The people of I kept for .... Jos 8:27
the God of I, on Mount Ebal, ... Jos 8:30
before the LORD, the God of I. .... Jos 9:18
agreement with I and that they .... Jos 10:1
those armies when I attacked, ... Jos 10:10
the LORD was fighting for I! .... Jos 10:14
LORD, the God of I, was fighting .... Jos 10:42
The people of I kept for .... Jos 11:14
the mountains of I and all the................ Jos 11:16
made a peace agreement with I— .... Jos 11:19
the tribes of I decided what .... Jos 14:1
to the different tribes of I. .... Jos 19:51
all the tribes of I together at .... Jos 24:1
LORD, the God of I, with all .... Jos 24:23
what the LORD had done for I. .... Jos 24:31
was angry with the people of I, ... Jdg 2:14

I will use them to test I, ... Jdg 2:22
Shamgar son of Anath saved I. .... Jdg 3:31
was judge of I at that time. .... Jdg 4:4
music to the LORD, the God of I. .... Jdg 5:3
were no warriors in I until I, ... Jdg 5:7
powerful and were cruel to I, ... Jdg 6:2
I became very poor because of .... Jdg 6:6
strength and save I from the .... Jdg 6:14
Midian was under the rule of I; .... Jdg 8:28
ruled I for three years. .... Jdg 9:22
the Ammonites fought against I. .... Jdg 11:4
this came a custom in I that .... Jdg 11:39
young women of I would go out .... Jdg 11:40
At that time I did not have a .... Jdg 17:6
At that time I did not have a .... Jdg 18:1
to each area of I because the .... Jdg 20:6
must remove this evil from I." .... Jdg 20:13
The men of I went out to fight .... Jdg 20:20
from all of I attacked Gibeah. .... Jdg 20:34
LORD, God of I, why has this .... Jdg 21:3
The people of I felt sorry for .... Jdg 21:15
In those days I did not have a .... Jdg 21:25
Long ago in I when people traded .... Ru 4:7
and built up the people of I. .... Ru 4:11
May he become famous in I. .... Ru 4:14
May the God of I give you what 1Sa 1:17
Then all I, from Dan to 1Sa 3:20
Samuel spread through all of I. 1Sa 4:1
the elders of I asked, "Why did 1Sa 4:3
He had led I for forty years. 1Sa 4:18
of the God of I can't stay with 1Sa 5:7
back the Ark of the God of I, ... 1Sa 6:3
the people of I began to follow 1Sa 7:2
spoke to the whole group of I, ... 1Sa 7:3
All I must meet at Mizpah, ... 1Sa 7:5
served as judge of I at Mizpah. 1Sa 7:6
came near to attack I. 1Sa 7:10
as judge of I all his life. 1Sa 7:15
he made his sons judges for I. 1Sa 8:1
Samuel told the people of I, ... 1Sa 8:22
if someone in I wanted to ask 1Sa 9:9
the smallest tribe in I. 1Sa 9:21
kingdom continue in I always, ... 1Sa 13:13
The men of I were miserable that 1Sa 14:24
the leader of the tribes of I. 1Sa 15:17
he rejects you as king of I." 1Sa 15:26
LORD is the Eternal One of I. 1Sa 15:29
I stand and dare the army of I! 1Sa 17:10
the God of the armies of I! 1Sa 17:45
will know there is a God in I! 1Sa 17:46
will be king of I, and I will be 1Sa 23:17
men from all I and began looking 1Sa 24:2
He will make you leader over I. 1Sa 25:30
the God of I, who sent you to 1Sa 25:32
Philistines fought against I, ... 1Sa 31:1
I, your leaders have been killed 2Sa 1:19
daughters of I, cry for Saul. 2Sa 1:24
make David king of I and Judah, ... 2Sa 3:10
a great man died today in I. 2Sa 3:38
the one who led I in battle. 2Sa 5:2
all the elders of I came to King 2Sa 5:3
to take care of my people I, ... 2Sa 7:7
made you leader of my people I. 2Sa 7:8
I chose judges for my people I. 2Sa 7:11
the people of I your very own 2Sa 7:24
All-Powerful is God over I!' 2Sa 7:26
the God of I, you have said to 2Sa 7:27
best soldiers of I and sent them 2Sa 10:9
saw that I had defeated them 2Sa 10:15
the soldiers of I and Judah are 2Sa 11:11
the LORD, the God of I, says: ' 2Sa 12:7
I made you king of I and Judah. 2Sa 12:8
be like the shameful fools in I! 2Sa 13:13

No man in I was as handsome as 2Sa 14:25
stole the hearts of all I. 2Sa 15:6
to Absalom and the elders of I. 2Sa 17:15
will be put to death in I today. 2Sa 19:22
the peaceful, loyal people of I. 2Sa 20:19
who are left in the land of I. 2Sa 21:5
and the disease in I stopped. 2Sa 24:25
be king over the people of I.' 1Ki 2:4
He had ruled over I forty years— 1Ki 2:11
King Solomon ruled over all I. 1Ki 4:1
over the districts of I, ... 1Ki 4:7
Solomon's life Judah and I, ... 1Ki 4:25
I will never leave my people I." 1Ki 6:13
my people I out of Egypt, ... 1Ki 8:16
Now I rule I as the LORD 1Ki 8:20
LORD, God of I, there is no god 1Ki 8:23
the sins of your people I, ... 1Ki 8:34
the prayers of your people I. 1Ki 8:52
his family would always rule I. 1Ki 9:5
I will force I to leave the land 1Ki 9:7
ruled Aram, and he hated I. 1Ki 11:25
over all I for forty years. 1Ki 11:42
People of I, let's go to our own 1Ki 12:16
I has been against the family of 1Ki 12:19
I, here are your gods who 1Ki 12:28
the LORD, the God of I, says: ' 1Ki 14:7
Then the LORD will punish I, ... 1Ki 14:15
he made the people of I sin. 1Ki 14:16
the history of the kings of I. 1Ki 14:19
had led the people of I to sin, ... 1Ki 15:30
the history of the kings of I. 1Ki 15:31
became king of I during Asa's 1Ki 15:33
and led the people of I to sin, ... 1Ki 16:13
had led the people of I to sin, ... 1Ki 16:19
the God of I, angry than all 1Ki 16:33
the God of I," Elijah said to 1Ki 17:1
the biggest troublemaker in I?" 1Ki 18:17
Now tell all I to meet me at 1Ki 18:19
Isaac, and I," he prayed. 1Ki 18:36
people left in I who have never 1Ki 19:18
led the people of I to sin.' 1Ki 21:22
was peace between I and Aram. 1Ki 22:1
saw the army of I scattered over 1Ki 22:17
—except the king of I." 1Ki 22:31
the people of I into more sin. 1Ki 22:52
you think there is no God in I?' 2Ki 1:3
of I and their horsemen! 2Ki 2:12
became king over I at Samaria 2Ki 3:1
Elisha said to the king of I, ... 2Ki 3:13
Moabites came to the camp of I, ... 2Ki 3:24
that the king of I had torn his 2Ki 5:8
better than all the waters of I. 2Ki 5:12
destroyed Baal worship in I, ... 2Ki 10:28
LORD, the God of I, with all his 2Ki 10:31
Jehoash king of I went to Elisha 2Ki 13:14
one was left who could help I. 2Ki 14:26
destroy I from the world, ... 2Ki 14:27
will be kings of I," 2Ki 15:12
things the kings of I had done. 2Ki 16:3
and attacked all the land of I. 2Ki 17:5
and seer to warn I and Judah. 2Ki 17:13
very angry with the people of I, ... 2Ki 17:18
rejected all the people of I. 2Ki 17:20
of Jacob, whom he had named I. 2Ki 17:34
against me, the Holy One of I. 2Ki 19:22
all the people of I were listed 1Ch 9:1
praising the LORD, the God of I. 1Ch 16:4
Praise the LORD, the God of I. 1Ch 16:36
David was king over all of I, ... 1Ch 18:14
was against I, and he caused 1Ch 21:1
sent a terrible disease on I, ... 1Ch 21:14
for the LORD, the God of I. 1Ch 22:6
family will rule I forever.' " 1Ch 22:10

the leaders of the tribes of I. 1Ch 27:22
became angry with I for counting 1Ch 27:24
you, LORD, God of our father I. 1Ch 29:10
live as the people of I lived. 2Ch 17:4
saw the army of I scattered over 2Ch 18:16
Ahab king of I and Jehoshaphat................ 2Ch 18:28
—except the king of I." 2Ch 18:30
hit Ahab king of I between the 2Ch 18:33
in the ways of the kings of I, ... 2Ch 21:6
the people of I used for the.................... 2Ch 24:6
soldiers from I for about 2Ch 25:6
let the army of I go with you. 2Ch 25:7
in the graves of the kings of I 2Ch 28:27
the holy place to the God of I 2Ch 29:7
should be made for all I. 2Ch 29:24
an announcement everywhere in I,............ 2Ch 30:5
all through I and Judah. 2Ch 30:6
chosen from all the tribes of I. 2Ch 33:7
the incense altars in all of I. 2Ch 34:7
LORD your God and his people I. 2Ch 35:3
like this in I since the prophet 2Ch 35:18
a custom in I to sing these 2Ch 35:25
LORD, the God of I, who is in................ Ezr 1:3
of the God of I where they could .... Ezr 3:2
David king of I had said to do. .... Ezr 3:10
for the LORD, the God of I,.................... Ezr 4:1
on the Temple of the God of I. .... Ezr 6:22
and laws the LORD gave I. .... Ezr 7:11
all the people of I promise to .... Ezr 10:5
You have made I more guilty. .... Ezr 10:10
The people of I and the Levites .... Ne 10:39
separated all foreigners from I. .... Ne 13:3
made King Solomon of I sin. .... Ne 13:26
will come to I from Mount Zion! .... Ps 14:7
praises of I are your throne. .... Ps 22:3
save I from all their troubles! .... Ps 25:22
Praise the LORD, the God of I. .... Ps 41:13
God All-Powerful, the God of I. .... Ps 59:5
God rules over I and to the ends, ... Ps 59:13
the LORD in the gathering of I. .... Ps 68:26
rules over I, and his power is .... Ps 68:34
with the lyre, Holy One of I. .... Ps 71:22
is truly good to I, to those who .... Ps 73:1
his fame is great in I. .... Ps 76:1
and gave the teachings to I, ... Ps 78:5
pain to the Holy One of I. .... Ps 78:41
his own people, the people of I. .... Ps 78:71
Shepherd of I, listen to us. .... Ps 80:1
This is the law for I; .... Ps 81:4
listen to me; I did not want me .... Ps 81:11
I wish I would live my way. .... Ps 81:13
his deeds to the people of I. .... Ps 103:7
agreement with I to last forever .... Ps 105:10
Praise the LORD, the God of I. .... Ps 106:48
I became the land he ruled. .... Ps 114:2
Family of I, trust the LORD; .... Ps 115:9
the people of I say, "His love .... Ps 118:2
He who guards I never rests or .... Ps 121:4
is the rule in I to praise the.................... Ps 122:4
our side? (Let I repeat this.) .... Ps 124:1
Let there be peace in I. .... Ps 125:5
He will save I from all their .... Ps 130:8
people of I for his very own. .... Ps 135:4
Solomon son of David, king of I. .... Pr 1:1
was king over I in Jerusalem................... Ec 1:12
it, the finest soldiers of I. .... Sng 3:7
the people of I do not know me;............ Is 1:3
I is a nation of sin, a people .... Is 1:4
the Mighty One of I, says: .... Is 1:24
All-Powerful is the nation of I; .... Is 5:7
and they ate up I with their .... Is 9:12
God, the Light of I, will be .... Is 10:17
left alive in I from the family .... Is 10:20

the Holy One of I does great .... Is 12:6
I made you. I, I own you. You .... Is 19:25
I will grow like a plant .... Is 27:6
they will respect the God of I................ Is 29:23
of I, why do you say, "The .... Is 40:27
few people of I who are left, ... Is 41:14
he formed you, people of I. .... Is 43:1
the Creator of I, your King." .... Is 43:15
people of I, you have become .... Is 43:22
People of I, I chose you." .... Is 44:1
his glory when he saved I. .... Is 44:23
LORD, the God of I, who calls .... Is 45:3
you people from I who are still .... Is 46:3
Jerusalem and bring glory to I.".............. Is 46:13
and you depend on the God of I, ... Is 48:2
He told me, "I, you are my .... Is 49:3
The people of I were holy to the.............. Je 2:3
the people of I become slaves? .... Je 2:14
you see what unfaithful I did? .... Je 3:6
salvation of I comes from the .... Je 3:23
will return, I, then return to .... Je 4:1
family of I," says the LORD, ... Je 5:15
the few people of I who are left .... Je 6:9
the Hope of I, you have saved.................. Je 14:8
the people of I out of Egypt . . .' .... Je 16:14
' The people of I have done a .... Je 18:13
the God of I, says to them: .... Je 23:2
and I will live in safety. .... Je 23:6
things among the people of I. .... Je 29:23
People of I, I will build you up .... Je 31:4
and I is my firstborn son. .... Je 31:9
the people of I and Judah have .... Je 32:32
bring Judah and I back from .... Je 33:7
the throne of the family of I. .... Je 33:17
don't be frightened, I. .... Je 46:27
I was caught in the middle of a .... Je 48:27
you think that I has no children .... Je 49:1
The people of I are like a flock .... Je 50:17
did not leave I and Judah, ... Je 51:5
and he chose I to be his special .... Je 51:19
greatness of I from the sky to .... La 2:1
he swallowed up I. He swallowed .... La 2:5
to the people of I, and speak my .... Eze 3:4
But the people of I will not be .... Eze 3:7
I now make you a watchman for I............ Eze 3:17
attack. This is a sign to I. .... Eze 4:3
look toward the mountains of I, ... Eze 6:2
of the elders of I and Jaazaniah .... Eze 8:11
left alive in I when you turn .... Eze 9:8
under the God of I by the Kebar.............. Eze 10:20
of the God of I was above them. .... Eze 11:22
and nobody in I will use this .... Eze 12:23
against the prophets of I. .... Eze 13:2
the elders of I came to me and .... Eze 14:1
him from among my people I. .... Eze 14:9
tell a story to the people of I. .... Eze 17:2
use this saying in I anymore. .... Eze 18:3
' Listen, people of I. .... Eze 18:25
do you want to die, people of I? .... Eze 18:31
When I chose I, I made a promise .... Eze 20:5
mountain of I, all Israel will .... Eze 20:40
people, for all the rulers of I. .... Eze 21:12
unclean and evil leader of I, ... Eze 21:25
I have made a watchman for I. .... Eze 33:7
to die, do you, people of I?".................... Eze 33:11
' I, I will judge all of you by .... Eze 33:20
against the leaders of I, ... Eze 34:2
and the tribes of I with him, ... Eze 37:16
I, the LORD, make I holy.'".................... Eze 37:28
prophets of I, who prophesied .... Eze 38:17
be a great earthquake in I. .... Eze 38:19
fall dead on the mountains of I. .... Eze 39:4
give Gog a burial place in I, ... Eze 39:11

my Spirit into the people of I,.................. Eze 39:29
glory of the God of I coming .... Eze 43:2
far enough, you rulers of I! .... Eze 45:9
at all the other feasts of I. .... Eze 45:17
among the twelve tribes of I. .... Eze 47:13
named for the tribes of I. .... Eze 48:31
the people of I have disobeyed .... Da 9:11
the people of I and praying for .... Da 9:20
put an end to the kingdom of I .... Hos 1:4
I will not pity I anymore, ... Hos 1:6
the people of I will return to .... Hos 3:5
people of I are stubborn like .... Hos 4:16
Pay attention, people of I. .... Hos 5:1
know all about the people of I; .... Hos 5:3
The people of I will stumble .... Hos 5:5
When I heal I, Israel's sin will .... Hos 7:1
I is eaten up; the people are .... Hos 8:8
I has forgotten their Maker and .... Hos 8:14
When I found I, it was like .... Hos 9:10
up, the king of I will die. .... Hos 10:15
When I was a child, I loved him, ... Hos 11:1
I, how can I give you up? .... Hos 11:8
they were important people in I............... Hos 13:1
I, I will destroy you. .... Hos 13:9
I will be like the dew to I, ... Hos 14:5
my own people I and forced them .... Joe 3:2
For the many crimes of I, ... Am 2:6
The young girl I has fallen,.................... Am 5:2
LORD says to the nation of I: .... Am 5:4
among my people I to show how .... Am 7:8
message to Jeroboam king of I: .... Am 7:10
the people of I will be taken as .... Am 7:11
'Go, prophesy to my people I.' .... Am 7:15
'Don't prophesy against I, ... Am 7:16
The people of I will definitely .... Am 7:17
An end has come for my people I, ... Am 8:2
bring my people I back from .... Am 9:14
all those left alive in I. .... Mic 2:12
the people of I how they have................. Mic 3:8
come who will rule I for me. .... Mic 5:2
The King of I, the LORD, is with .... Zph 3:15
a shepherd for my people I.'" .... Mt 2:6
faith I have found, even in I. .... Mt 8:10
But go to the people of I, ... Mt 10:6
the cities of I before the Son .... Mt 10:23
lost sheep, the people of I."................... Mt 15:24
judging the twelve tribes of I. .... Mt 19:28
He says he is the king of I! .... Mt 27:42
'Listen, people of I! .... Mk 12:29
the king of I, let him come down .... Mk 15:32
the people of I, remembering to .... Lk 1:54
the God of I, because he has .... Lk 1:68
when he came out to preach to I. .... Lk 1:80
the fall and rise of many in I. .... Lk 2:34
hoping that he would free I. .... Lk 24:21
the people of I would know who .... Jn 1:31
you are the King of I." .... Jn 1:49
are an important teacher in I,................. Jn 3:10
God bless the King of I!" .... Jn 12:13
to give the kingdom back to I?" .... Ac 1:6
People of I, listen to these .... Ac 2:22
them, "People of I, why are you .... Ac 3:12
People of I, be careful what .... Ac 5:35
descendants, to I to be its .... Ac 13:23
the people of I are truly God's .... Rm 9:6
And Isaiah cries out about I: .... Rm 9:27
But about I God says, "All day .... Rm 10:21
of I has been made stubborn, ... Rm 11:25
that is how all I will be saved. .... Rm 11:26
You were not citizens of I, ... Eph 2:12
the people of I and the tribe .... Php 3:5
the people of I and the people .... Heb 8:8
the people of I at that time,.................. Heb 8:10

kill the firstborn sons of I. .... Heb 11:28
the people of I heard and begged .... Heb 12:19
the people of I to sin by eating .... Rev 2:14
every tribe of the people of I. .... Rev 7:4
one of the twelve tribes of I. .... Rev 21:12

ISRAEL'S
near the Jordan River on I side. .... Jos 22:11
the God over Israel, is I God!' 1Ch 17:24

ISRAELITE
he said, "Here is truly an I.................... Jn 1:47
he defended the I and punished .... Ac 7:24
I myself am an I from the family .... Rm 11:1

ISRAELITE'S
see your fellow I ox or sheep .... Dt 22:1
see your fellow I donkey or ox .... Dt 22:4

ISRAELITES
God chose the I to be his people............. Rm 11:2
am I. Are they I? So am I. Are 2Co 11:22
spoke about the I leaving Egypt .... Heb 11:22

ISSACHAR
Levi, Judah, I, and Zebulun. .... Ge 35:23
I is like a strong donkey who .... Ge 49:14
The princes of I were with .... Jdg 5:15
from the people of I and lived................. Jdg 10:1
the tribe of I twelve thousand, ... Rev 7:7

ISSHIAH
Michael, Obadiah, Joel, and I. 1Ch 7:3
were Elkanah, I, Azarel, Joezer,............... 1Ch 12:6
was Micah and his second was I. 1Ch 23:20
I was the first son of Rehabiah. 1Ch 24:21
brother was I, and Isshiah's son 1Ch 24:25

ITALIAN
an officer in the I group of the .... Ac 10:1

ITALY
moved to Corinth from I, ... Ac 18:2
that we would sail for I. .... Ac 27:1
Alexandria that was going to I, ... Ac 27:6
Those from I send greetings to .... Heb 13:24

ITCH
It is an i, a harmful skin .... Le 13:30

ITCHES
sores, and i that can't be cured .... Dt 28:27

ITCHING
men who have an i disease or a .... Le 21:20

ITHAI
I son of Ribai from Gibeah in 2Sa 23:29
I son of Ribai from Gibeah in 1Ch 11:31

ITHAMAR
to Nadab, Abihu, Eleazar, and I............... Ex 6:23
Nadab, Abihu, Eleazar, and I................... Ex 28:1
and I son of Aaron was in charge .... Ex 38:21
sons, Eleazar and I, "Don't show .... Le 10:6
Eleazar, and I obeyed Moses. .... Le 10:7
Eleazar and I, "Eat the part .... Le 10:12
very angry with Eleazar and I, ... Le 10:16
oldest, Abihu, Eleazar, and I. .... Nu 3:2
So Eleazar and I served as .... Nu 3:4
I son of Aaron, the priest, will .... Nu 4:28
I son of Aaron, the priest, will .... Nu 4:33
I son of Aaron, the priest, ... Nu 7:8
of Nadab, Abihu, Eleazar, and I............... Nu 26:60
Nadab, Abihu, Eleazar, and I................... 1Ch 6:3
Nadab, Abihu, Eleazar, and I................... 1Ch 24:1
So Eleazar and I served as the 1Ch 24:2
a descendant of I, separated 1Ch 24:3
the families of Eleazar and I. 1Ch 24:6
From the descendants of I: .... Ezr 8:2

ITHAMAR'S
Eleazar's family than from I— 1Ch 24:4
and eight leaders from I family. 1Ch 24:4
from Eleazar's and I families by 1Ch 24:5

ITHIEL
Maaseiah was the son of I, ... Ne 11:7
is his message to I and Ucal: .... Pr 30:1

ITHLAH
Shaalabbin, Aijalon, I, ... Jos 19:42

ITHMAH
Elnaam's sons; I the Moabite; 1Ch 11:46

ITHNAN
Kedesh, Hazor, I, ... Jos 15:23

ITHRAN
Hemdan, Eshban, I, and Keran. .... Ge 36:26
Hemdan, Eshban, I, and Keran. 1Ch 1:41
Shamma, Shilshah, I, and Beera. 1Ch 7:37

ITHREAM
sixth son was I, whose mother 2Sa 3:5
sixth son was I, whose mother 1Ch 3:3

ITHRITE
Ira the ruler of the I; Gareb the Ithrite, ... 2Sa 23:38
Ira the Ithrite; Gareb the I, ... 2Sa 23:38
Ira the I; Gareb the Ithrite; 1Ch 11:40
Ira the Ithrite; Gareb the I; 1Ch 11:40

ITHRITES
I, Puthites, Shumathites, and 1Ch 2:53

ITTAI
king said to I, a man from Gath 2Sa 15:19
But I said to the king, "As 2Sa 15:21
David said to I, "Go, march on." 2Sa 15:22
So I from Gath and all his 2Sa 15:22
And I from Gath commanded the 2Sa 18:2
Abishai, and I, "Be gentle with 2Sa 18:5
Abishai, and I, 'Be careful not 2Sa 18:12

ITUREA
the ruler of I and Traconitis; .... Lk 3:1

IVORY
large throne of i and covered it 1Ki 10:18
gold, silver, i, apes, and 1Ki 10:22
decorated with i and the cities 1Ki 22:39
large throne of i and covered it 2Ch 9:17
gold, silver, i, apes, and 2Ch 9:21
From palaces of i music comes to .... Ps 45:8
is like shiny i covered with .... Sng 5:14
Your neck is like an i tower. .... Sng 7:4
of Cyprus and set i into it. .... Eze 27:6
They brought back i tusks and .... Eze 27:15
decorated with i will be .... Am 3:15
decorated with i and stretch out .... Am 6:4
all kinds of things made from i, ... Rev 18:12

IVVAH
gods of Sepharvaim, Hena, and I? 2Ki 18:34
of Sepharvaim, Hena, and I?" 2Ki 19:13
of Sepharvaim, Hena, and I?" .... Is 37:13

IYE
went from Oboth to I Abarim, ... Nu 21:11
Oboth and camped at I Abarim, ... Nu 33:44
They left I Abarim and camped at .... Nu 33:45

IZHAR
Kohath were Amram, I, Hebron, ... Ex 6:18
groups were Amram, I, Hebron, ... Nu 3:19
groups of Amram, I, Hebron, and .... Nu 3:27
was the son of I, the son of .... Nu 16:1
sons were Amram, I, Hebron, and 1Ch 6:2
sons were Amram, I, Hebron, and 1Ch 6:18
Izhar's son. I was Kohath's son 1Ch 6:38
Amram, I, Hebron, and Uzziel. 1Ch 23:12

From the I family group, there 1Ch 24:22
groups of Amram, I, Hebron, and 1Ch 26:23
Kenaniah was from the I family. 1Ch 26:29

IZHAR'S
I sons were Korah, Nepheg, and .... Ex 6:21
Korah was I son. Izhar was 1Ch 6:38
I first son was Shelomith. 1Ch 23:18

IZLIAH
Ishmerai, I, and Jobab. 1Ch 8:18

IZRAH'S
was Shamhuth, from I family. 1Ch 27:8

IZRAHIAH
Uzzi's son was I. Izrahiah's 1Ch 7:3

IZRAHIAH'S
I sons were Michael, Obadiah, ... 1Ch 7:3

IZRI
twelve men were chosen from I, ... 1Ch 25:11

IZZIAH
Ramiah, I, Malkijah, Mijamin, ... Ezr 10:25

J

JAAKAN
Moseroth and camped at Bene J. .... Nu 33:31
They left Bene J and camped at .... Nu 33:32

JAAKANITES
the wells of the J to Moserah. .... Dt 10:6

JAALA
J, Darkon, Giddel, ... Ezr 2:56
J, Darkon, Giddel, ... Ne 7:58

JAAN
Hodshi and to Dan J and around 2Sa 24:6

JAARE-OREGIM
Elhanan son of J from Bethlehem 2Sa 21:19

JAARESHIAH
J, Elijah, and Zicri. 1Ch 8:27

JAASIEL
Obed, and J the Mezobaites. 1Ch 11:47
J son of Abner was over the 1Ch 27:21

JAASU
Mattaniah, Mattenai, and J. .... Ezr 10:37

JAAZANIAH
the Netophathite, J son of the 2Ki 25:23
I went to get J son of Jeremiah .... Je 35:3
the Netophathite, J son of the .... Je 40:8
of Israel and J son of Shaphan. .... Eze 8:11
among them J son of Azzur and .... Eze 11:1

JAAZANIAH'S
gathered all of J brothers and .... Je 35:3

JAAZIAH
and Mushi. Merari's son was J. 1Ch 24:26
J son of Merari had sons named 1Ch 24:27

JAAZIEL
Zechariah, J, Shemiramoth, ... 1Ch 15:18
Zechariah, J, Shemiramoth, ... 1Ch 15:20
Levites were J, Shemiramoth, ... 1Ch 16:5

JABAL
Adah gave birth to J, who became .... Ge 4:20

JABAL'S
J brother was Jubal, the first .... Ge 4:21

JABBOK
rose and crossed the J River at .... Ge 32:22
the Arnon River to the J River. .... Nu 21:24
on the shores of the J River, ... Dt 2:37
border) to the J River, which is .... Dt 3:16

the Arnon Ravine to the **J** River. .... Jos 12:2
Arnon River to the **J** River to .... Jdg 11:13
the Arnon River to the **J** River, ... Jdg 11:22

JABESH

the city of **J** in Gilead. 1Sa 11:1
the brave men of **J** marched all 1Sa 31:12

JABEZ

the families who lived at **J**, ... 1Ch 2:55
was a man named **J**, who was 1Ch 4:9
named him **J** because she said 1Ch 4:9
J prayed to the God of Israel, ... 1Ch 4:10
And God did what **J** had asked. 1Ch 4:10

JABIN

When **J** king of Hazor heard about .... Jos 11:1
J also sent one to the Hivites, ... Jos 11:3
he let **J**, a king of Canaan who .... Jdg 4:2
at peace with **J** king of Hazor. .... Jdg 4:17
God defeated **J** king of Canaan .... Jdg 4:23
stronger against **J** king of .... Jdg 4:24
to Sisera and **J** at the Kishon .... Ps 83:9

JABIN'S

was the commander of **J** army. .... Jdg 4:2
the commander of **J** army, and his .... Jdg 4:7

JABNEEL

Baalah and continued on to **J**, ... Jos 15:11
went through Adami Nekeb and **J**, ... Jos 19:33

JABNEH

towns of Gath, **J**, and Ashdod 2Ch 26:6

JACAN

Sheba, Jorai, **J**, Zia, and Eber. 1Ch 5:13

JACINTH

third must have a **j**, an agate, ... Ex 28:19
in the third there was a **j**, ... Ex 39:12
eleventh was **j**, and the twelfth .... Rev 21:20

JACOB

But **J** was a quiet man and stayed .... Ge 25:27
eating. But Rebekah loved **J**. .... Ge 25:28
One day **J** was boiling a pot of .... Ge 25:29
But **J** said, "First, promise me .... Ge 25:33
Then **J** gave Esau bread and .... Ge 25:34
Isaac finished blessing **J**. .... Ge 27:30
J is the right name for him. .... Ge 27:36
After that Esau hated **J** because .... Ge 27:41
Then **J** woke from his sleep and .... Ge 28:16
Then **J** made a promise. .... Ge 28:20
Then **J** kissed Rachel and cried. .... Ge 29:11
Then Laban said to **J**, "You are .... Ge 29:15
J loved Rachel, so he said to .... Ge 29:18
J worked for Laban seven years .... Ge 29:20
J separated the young animals .... Ge 30:40
J put the branches before their .... Ge 30:41
One day **J** heard Laban's sons .... Ge 31:1
So Laban caught up with **J**. .... Ge 31:25
and **J** gave the place the same .... Ge 31:47
So **J** made a promise in the name .... Ge 31:53
Then **J** was very afraid and .... Ge 32:7
So **J** was alone, and a man came .... Ge 32:24
Your name will no longer be **J**. .... Ge 32:28
Then **J** asked him, "Please tell .... Ge 32:29
So they gave **J** all the foreign .... Ge 35:4
Your name is **J**, but you will not .... Ge 35:10
J set up a stone on edge in that .... Ge 35:14
and **J** set up a rock on her grave .... Ge 35:20
about it. **J** had twelve sons .... Ge 35:22
This is the family history of **J**: .... Ge 37:2
Then **J** tore his clothes and put .... Ge 37:34
Then **J** left Beersheba. .... Ge 46:5
in the family of **J** in Egypt was .... Ge 46:27
in his father **J** and introduced .... Ge 47:7
the king said to **J**, "How old are .... Ge 47:8

together and listen, sons of **J**. .... Ge 49:2
to Abraham, Isaac, and **J**." .... Ge 50:24
God of Isaac, and the God of **J**." .... Ex 3:6
Isaac, and **J**, has appeared to me .... Ex 3:16
remember my agreement with **J**, ... Le 26:42
curse on the people of **J** for me. .... Nu 23:7
are beautiful, people of **J**! .... Nu 24:5
A star will come from **J**; .... Nu 24:17
that belong to the people of **J**. .... Dt 33:4
Isaac two sons named **J** and Esau. .... Jos 24:4
appointed king of the God of **J**; 2Sa 23:1
the people of **J** will rejoice, ... Ps 14:7
May the God of **J** protect you. .... Ps 20:1
look to the God of **J** for help. .... Ps 24:6
the God of **J** is our defender. .... Ps 46:7
the God of **J** is our defender. .... Ps 46:11
the children of **J**, whom he loved .... Ps 47:4
sing praise to the God of **J**. .... Ps 75:9
God of **J**, when you spoke .... Ps 76:6
descendants of **J** and Joseph. .... Ps 77:15
an agreement with **J** and gave the .... Ps 78:5
like fire to the people of **J**; .... Ps 78:21
the people of **J**, his own people, ... Ps 78:71
shout out loud to the God of **J**. .... Ps 81:1
God of **J**, listen to me. .... Ps 84:8
brought back the people of **J**. .... Ps 85:1
the God of **J** doesn't notice." .... Ps 94:7
it a law for the people of **J**; .... Ps 105:10
came to Egypt; **J** lived in Egypt. .... Ps 105:23
the Lord, before the God of **J**. .... Ps 114:7
promise to the Mighty God of **J**. .... Ps 132:2
the people of **J** for himself; .... Ps 135:4
He gave his word to **J**, his laws .... Ps 147:19
to the Temple of the God of **J**. .... Is 2:3
in Israel from the family of **J**. .... Is 10:20
that the Holy One of **J** is holy, ... Is 29:23
People of **J**, I chose you. .... Is 41:8
The King of **J** says, "Tell me .... Is 41:21
He created you, people of **J**; .... Is 43:1
says, "People of **J**, you are my .... Is 44:1
the family of **J** to look for me .... Is 45:19
Family of **J**, listen to me! .... Is 46:3
the people of **J** back to him so .... Is 49:5
One of **J** who saves you." .... Is 49:26
the family of **J** about their sins .... Is 58:1
the land your ancestor **J** had." .... Is 58:14
have destroyed the people of **J**. .... Je 10:25
and sing for the people of **J**. .... Je 31:7
the people of **J** and will buy .... Je 31:11
the people of **J** like a flaming .... La 2:3
the people of **J** back from .... Eze 39:25
Their ancestor **J** held on to his .... Hos 12:3
When **J** wrestled with the angel .... Hos 12:4
against the family of **J**," .... Am 3:13
the Pride of **J**, "I will never .... Am 8:7
The people of **J** will take back .... Ob 1:17
The people of **J** will be like a .... Ob 1:18
leaders of the people of **J**; .... Mic 3:1
the people of **J** how they have .... Mic 3:8
Esau and **J** were brothers. .... Mal 1:2
descendants of **J** have not been .... Mal 3:6
and **J** in the kingdom of heaven. .... Mt 8:11
God of Isaac, and the God of **J**.' .... Mt 22:32
over the people of **J** forever, ... Lk 1:33
see Abraham, Isaac, **J**, and all .... Lk 13:28
God of Isaac, and the God of **J**.' .... Lk 20:37
greater than **J**, our father, who .... Jn 4:12
Isaac, and **J**, the God of our .... Ac 3:13
also circumcised his son **J**, ... Ac 7:8
says, "I loved **J**, but I hated .... Rm 9:13
all evil from the family of **J**. .... Rm 11:26
lived in tents with Isaac and **J**, ... Heb 11:9
the future of **J** and Esau. .... Heb 11:20

JACOB'S

Your voice sounds like **J** voice, ... Ge 27:22
So Laban looked in **J** tent, ... Ge 31:33
struck **J** hip and put it out of .... Ge 32:25
Reuben was **J** first son. .... Ge 46:8
the tents of **J** people as they .... Je 30:18
J well was there. Jesus was .... Jn 4:6
J sons became jealous of Joseph .... Ac 7:9
J sons, our ancestors, could not .... Ac 7:11

JADA

Onam's sons were Shammai and **J**. 1Ch 2:28
J was Shammai's brother, and 1Ch 2:32

JADA'S

and **J** sons were Jether and 1Ch 2:32

JADAH

J was the father of Alemeth, ... 1Ch 9:42

JADAH'S

Ahaz was **J** father. Jadah was the 1Ch 9:42

JADDAI

Zabad, Zebina, **J**, Joel, and .... Ezr 10:43

JADDUA

Meshezabel, Zadok, **J**, ... Ne 10:21
Jonathan was the father of **J**. .... Ne 12:11
Johanan, and **J**, while Darius .... Ne 12:22

JADON

J from Meronoth made repairs. .... Ne 3:7

JAEL

away to the tent where **J** lived. .... Jdg 4:17
May **J**, the wife of Heber the .... Jdg 5:24
for water, but **J** gave him milk. .... Jdg 5:25
J reached out and took the tent .... Jdg 5:26

JAGUR

of Edom: Kabzeel, Eder, **J**, ... Jos 15:21

JAHATH

Reaiah was the father of **J**, ... 1Ch 4:2
and **J** was the father of Ahumai 1Ch 4:2
J was Gershon's son, and Gershon 1Ch 6:43
J, Ziza, Jeush, and Beriah. 1Ch 23:10
J was the first son, and Ziza 1Ch 23:11
and **J** was a descendant of 1Ch 24:22
supervisors were **J** and Obadiah, ... 2Ch 34:12

JAHATH'S

Shimei was **J** son. Jahath was 1Ch 6:43

JAHAZ

At **J** they fought the Israelites. .... Nu 21:23
came out and fought us at **J**, ... Dt 2:32
J, Kedemoth, Mephaath, ... Jos 13:18
of Reuben gave them Bezer, **J**, ... Jos 21:36
and camped at **J** and fought with .... Jdg 11:20
voices far away in the city **J**. .... Is 15:4
from Heshbon to Elealeh and **J**. .... Je 48:34

JAHAZIEL

There were Jeremiah, **J**, Johanan, ... 1Ch 12:4
Benaiah and **J** were priests who 1Ch 16:6
his third was **J**, and his fourth 1Ch 23:19
was his second, **J** was his third, ... 1Ch 24:23
Spirit of the LORD entered **J**. 2Ch 20:14
J was Zechariah's son. 2Ch 20:14
J, a Levite and a descendant of 2Ch 20:14
Shecaniah son of **J**, with three .... Ezr 8:5

JAHDAI'S

J sons were Regem, Jotham, ... 1Ch 2:47

JAHDIEL

Jeremiah, Hodaviah, and **J**. 1Ch 5:24

JAHDO

Jahdo's son, and **J** was the son 1Ch 5:14

JAHDO'S

Jeshishai was **J** son, and Jahdo 1Ch 5:14

JAHLEEL

sons were Sered, Elon, and **J**. .... Ge 46:14
J came the Jahleelite family .... Nu 26:26

JAHLEELITE

Jahleel came the **J** family group. .... Nu 26:26

JAHMAI

Rephaiah, Jeriel, **J**, Ibsam, and 1Ch 7:2

JAHZAH

Holon, **J**, and Mephaath; .... Je 48:21

JAHZEEL

J came the Jahzeelite family .... Nu 26:48

JAHZEELITE

Jahzeel came the **J** family group; .... Nu 26:48

JAHZEIAH

son of Asahel, **J** son of Tikvah, ... Ezr 10:15

JAHZERAH

J was Meshullam's son. 1Ch 9:12

JAHZERAH'S

Adiel was **J** son. 1Ch 9:12

JAHZIEL

sons were **J**, Guni, Jezer, ... Ge 46:24
sons were **J**, Guni, Jezer, ... 1Ch 7:13

JAIR

J son of Manasseh went out and .... Nu 32:41
all the towns of **J** in Bashan, ... Jos 13:30
J from the region of Gilead .... Jdg 10:3

JAIRITE

Ira the **J** was David's priest. 2Sa 20:26

JAIRUS

named **J**, came there, saw .... Mk 5:22
A man named **J**, a leader of the .... Lk 8:41
J' only daughter, about twelve .... Lk 8:42
was on his way to **J'** house, ... Lk 8:42
this, he said to **J**, "Don't be .... Lk 8:50

JAKEH

are the words of Agur son of **J**. .... Pr 30:1

JAKIM

sons were **J**, Zicri, Zabdi, ... 1Ch 8:19
was Eliashib. The twelfth was **J**. 1Ch 24:12

JAKIN

Jamin, Ohad, **J**, Zohar, and Shaul .... Ge 46:10
Ohad, **J**, Zohar, and Shaul, ... Ex 6:15
from **J** came the Jakinite family .... Nu 26:12
were Jedaiah, Jehoiarib, **J**, ... 1Ch 9:10
The twenty-first was **J**. 1Ch 24:17
was Jedaiah son of Joiarib, **J**, ... Ne 11:10

JAKINITE

Jakin came the **J** family group; .... Nu 26:12

JALAM

gave him Jeush, **J**, and Korah. .... Ge 36:5
birth to Jeush, **J**, and Korah. .... Ge 36:14
leaders: Jeush, **J**, and Korah. .... Ge 36:18
Reuel, Jeush, **J**, and Korah. 1Ch 1:35

JAMBRES

as Jannes and **J** were against 2Ti 3:8
because as with Jannes and **J**, ... 2Ti 3:9

JAMES

other brothers, **J** and John, the .... Mt 4:21
J son of Alphaeus, and Thaddaeus; .... Mt 10:3
brothers are **J**, Joseph, Simon, ... Mt 13:55
Jesus took Peter, **J**, and John, ... Mt 17:1
Mary the mother of **J** and Joseph, ... Mt 27:56
they went with **J** and John to the .... Mk 1:29
took Peter, **J**, and John with .... Mk 14:33

was seen by **J** and later by all 1Co 15:7
apostles, except **J**, the brother .... Gal 1:19
Jesus Christ and a brother of **J**. .... Jud 1:1

JAMIN
were Jemuel, **J**, Ohad, Jakin, ... Ge 46:10
were Jemuel, **J**, Ohad, Jakin, ... Ex 6:15
from **J** came the Jaminite family .... Nu 26:12
They were Maaz, **J**, and Eker. 1Ch 2:27
were Nemuel, **J**, Jarib, Zerah, ... 1Ch 4:24
Bani, Sherebiah, **J**, Akkub, ... Ne 8:7

JAMINITE
Jamin came the **J** family group; .... Nu 26:12

JANAI
and then **J** and Shaphat were 1Ch 5:12

JANIM
J, Beth Tappuah, Aphekah, ... Jos 15:53

JANNAI
Melki was the son of **J**. .... Lk 3:24
J was the son of Joseph. .... Lk 3:24

JANNES
Just as **J** and Jambres were 2Ti 3:8
because as with **J** and Jambres, ... 2Ti 3:9

JANOAH
and continued eastward to **J**. .... Jos 16:6
went down from **J** to Ataroth and .... Jos 16:7
Abel Beth Maacah, **J**, Kedesh, and 2Ki 15:29

JAPHETH
Shem, Ham, and **J**, and their .... Ge 7:13
May God give more land to **J**. .... Ge 9:27

JAPHIA
of Jarmuth, **J** king of Lachish .... Jos 10:3
and on to Daberath and to **J**. .... Jos 19:12
Ibhar, Elishua, Nepheg, **J**, ... 2Sa 5:15
Nogah, Nepheg, **J**, ... 1Ch 14:6

JAPHLET
Heber was the father of **J**, ... 1Ch 7:32

JAPHLETITES
border of the **J** and continued to .... Jos 16:3

JAR
some cakes, and a **j** of honey. 1Ki 14:3
j of flour and the jug of oil 1Ki 17:16

JARED
So **J** lived a total of 962 years, ... Ge 5:20

JARFULS
wine vat to take out fifty **j**, ... Hag 2:16

JARHA
a servant from Egypt named **J**. 1Ch 2:34
daughter marry his servant **J**, ... 1Ch 2:35

JARIB
Nemuel, Jamin, **J**, Zerah, and 1Ch 4:24
Elnathan, **J**, Elnathan, Nathan, ... Ezr 8:16
Eliezer, **J**, and Gedaliah. .... Ezr 10:18

JARKON
Me **J**, Rakkon, and the area near .... Jos 19:46

JARMUTH
Jerusalem, Hebron, **J**, Lachish, ... Jos 10:5
J, and En Gannim, and the .... Jos 21:29

JAROAH
Jaroah's son. **J** was Gilead's son 1Ch 5:14

JASHAR
are written in the Book of **J**. .... Jos 10:13
it is written in the Book of **J**: 2Sa 1:18

JASHEN
the sons of **J**; Jonathan 2Sa 23:32

JASHOBEAM
J was from the Hacmonite people. 1Ch 11:11
J from the family group of Korah. 1Ch 12:6
J son of Zabdiel was in charge 1Ch 27:2
J, one of the descendants of 1Ch 27:3

JASHUB
were Tola, Puah, **J**, and Shimron. .... Ge 46:13
from **J** came the Jashubite family .... Nu 26:24
Tola, Puah, **J**, and Shimron. 1Ch 7:1
Malluch, Adaiah, **J**, Sheal, and .... Ezr 10:29

JASHUBITE
Jashub came the **J** family group; .... Nu 26:24

JASON
they dragged **J** and some other .... Ac 17:6
J is keeping them in his house. .... Ac 17:7
They made **J** and the others put .... Ac 17:9
as Lucius, **J**, and Sosipater, ... Rm 16:21

JASON'S
They ran to **J** house, looking for .... Ac 17:5

JASPER
a chrysolite, an onyx, and a **j**. .... Ex 28:20
stones, like **j** and carnelian. .... Rev 4:3
wall was made of **j**, and the city .... Rev 21:18

JATHNIEL
was third, **J** was fourth, ... 1Ch 26:2

JATTIR
the mountains: Shamir, **J**, Socoh, ... Jos 15:48
J, Eshtemoa, ... Jos 21:14
the southern part of Judah, **J**, ... 1Sa 30:27
pastures of Libnah, **J**, Eshtemoa, ... 1Ch 6:57

JAVAN
Magog, Madai, **J**, Tubal, Meshech, ... Ge 10:2
The sons of **J** were Elishah, ... Ge 10:4
Magog, Madai, **J**, Tubal, Meshech, ... 1Ch 1:5

JAVAN'S
J sons were Elishah, Tarshish, ... 1Ch 1:7

JAW
its nose or a hook in its **j**? .... Job 41:2

JAWBONE
found the **j** of a dead donkey .... Jdg 15:15
With a donkey's **j** I made donkeys .... Jdg 15:16
With a donkey's **j** I killed a .... Jdg 15:16
speaking, he threw away the **j**. .... Jdg 15:17

JAWS
you from the **j** of trouble to .... Job 36:16
one can force open its great **j**; .... Job 41:14
their **j** seem full of knives. .... Pr 30:14
But I will put hooks in your **j**, ... Eze 29:4
around and put hooks in your **j**. .... Eze 38:4
like a lion, **j** like a female .... Joe 1:6

JAZIZ
J, from the Hagrites, was in 1Ch 27:31

JEALOUS
the LORD your God, am a **j** God. .... Ex 20:5
I, the LORD, the **J** One, am a .... Ex 34:14
if the man gets **j** because he .... Nu 5:30
the LORD your God, am a **j** God. .... Dt 5:9
I speak in my **j** anger, because .... Eze 36:6
I am **j** over you with a jealousy 2Co 11:2

JEALOUSY
has feelings of **j** and suspects .... Nu 5:14
this is a grain offering for **j**, ... Nu 5:15
long will your **j** burn like a .... Ps 79:5
J makes a husband very angry, ... Pr 6:34
j is as strong as the grave. .... Sng 8:6
With **j** and great anger I tell .... Eze 38:19
sinful things, **j**, speaking evil .... Mk 7:22
of bitter **j** and ruled by sin. .... Ac 8:23

They are full of j, murder, ... Rm 1:29
of any kind, no fighting or j. .... Rm 13:13
there is j and quarreling 1Co 3:3
you with a j that comes from 2Co 11:2
hypocrisy, j, and evil speech. 1Pe 2:1

JEATHERAI
And Zerah's son was J. 1Ch 6:21

JEBEREKIAH
priest and Zechariah son of J." .... Is 8:2

JEBUS
traveled toward the city of J .... Jdg 19:10
almost over, they came near J. .... Jdg 19:11
time Jerusalem was called J, ... 1Ch 11:4

JEBUSITE
the southern side of the J city................. Jos 15:8
south of the J city to En Rogel. .... Jos 18:16
Haeleph, the J city (Jerusalem), ... Jos 18:28
not make the J people leave .... Jdg 1:21
floor of Araunah the J. 2Sa 24:16
floor of Araunah the J." 2Sa 24:18
floor of Araunah the J. 1Ch 21:15
floor of Araunah the J. 1Ch 21:18
floor of Araunah the J. 2Ch 3:1

JEBUSITES
Canaanites, Girgashites, and J."............... Ge 15:21
that time the J have lived with .... Jdg 1:21
To defeat the J you must go 2Sa 5:8

JECOLIAH
mother was named J, and she was 2Ki 15:2
mother's name was J, and she was............ 2Ch 26:3

JEDIAEL
three sons: Bela, Beker, and J. 1Ch 7:6
All these sons of J were leaders 1Ch 7:11
J son of Shimri; Joha, Jediael's 1Ch 11:45
Adnah, Jozabad, J, Michael, ... 1Ch 12:20
was his first son, J was second, ... 1Ch 26:2

JEDIDAH
mother's name was J daughter of 2Ki 22:1

JEDIDIAH
the prophet to name the baby J, ... 2Sa 12:25

JEDUTHUN
and J to preach and play harps, ... 1Ch 25:1
of them, and J directed them. 1Ch 25:3
Heman, and J, the king's seer................. 2Ch 35:15

JEHALLELEL
of Abdi and Azariah son of J................. 2Ch 29:12

JEHATH
Libni's son was J. Jehath's son 1Ch 6:20

JEHDEIAH
and J was a descendant of 1Ch 24:20
J, from Meronoth, was in charge 1Ch 27:30

JEHEZKEL
The twentieth was J. 1Ch 24:16

JEHIAH
Obed-Edom and J were also guards 1Ch 15:24

JEHIZKIAH
Meshillemoth, J son of Shallum,............... 2Ch 28:12

JEHOADDAH
Ahaz was the father of J. 1Ch 8:36
J was the father of Alemeth, ... 1Ch 8:36

JEHOADDIN
mother was named J, and she was 2Ki 14:2
mother's name was J, and she was............ 2Ch 25:1

JEHOAHAZ
J son of Jehu became king over 2Ki 13:1
Then J begged the LORD, and the 2Ki 13:4
Everything else J did and all 2Ki 13:8

J died and was buried in Samaria, ... 2Ki 13:9
Jehoash son of J was king of 2Ki 14:1
Josiah's son J and poured olive 2Ki 23:30
But Neco took J to Egypt, where 2Ki 23:34
took his brother J to Egypt. 2Ch 36:4
of Egypt made J brother Eliakim 2Ch 36:4

JEHOASH
and his son J became king in his 2Ki 13:9
J son of Jehoahaz became king of 2Ki 13:10
Then J king of Israel answered 2Ki 14:9
other acts of J and his......................... 2Ki 14:15
J died and was buried in Samaria 2Ki 14:16

JEHOHANAN
Elam was fifth, J was sixth, and 1Ch 26:3
J was the commander of two 2Ch 17:15
Ishmael son of J, Azariah son of 2Ch 23:1
Azariah son of J, Berekiah son 2Ch 28:12
the room of J son of Eliashib. .... Ezr 10:6
J, Hananiah, Zabbai, and Athlai. .... Ezr 10:28
And Tobiah's son J had married .... Ne 6:18
J, from Amariah's family; .... Ne 12:13
Uzzi, J, Malkijah, Elam, ... Ne 12:42

JEHOIACHIN
J was eighteen years old when he 2Ki 24:8
carried away J to Babylon, ... 2Ki 24:15
J king of Judah was held in 2Ki 25:27
J was eighteen years old when he 2Ch 36:9

JEHOIACHIN'S
along with J mother, servants, ... 2Ki 24:12
he made Mattaniah, J uncle, king 2Ki 24:17
uncle, king in J place............................. 2Ki 24:17
made J uncle Zedekiah 2Ch 36:10

JEHOIADA
Benaiah son of J led the 2Sa 20:23
everything J the priest had 2Ki 11:9
Then J made an agreement between 2Ki 11:17
right as long as J the priest.................... 2Ki 12:2
Joash called for J the priest 2Ki 12:7
J and his sons brought out the 2Ch 23:11
Joash called for J the leading 2Ch 24:6

JEHOIAKIM
changed Eliakim's name to J. 2Ki 23:34
While J was king, Nebuchadnezzar 2Ki 24:1
happened while J was king and 2Ki 24:5
J died, and his son Jehoiachin 2Ki 24:6
son of J and king of Judah .... Je 24:1
Then they took him to King J, ... Je 26:23
third year that J was king of .... Da 1:1

JEHOIARIB
there were Jedaiah, J, Jakin, ... 1Ch 9:10
The first one chosen was J..................... 1Ch 24:7

JEHONADAB
there, he met J son of Recab, ... 2Ki 10:15
J answered, "Yes, I am." 2Ki 10:15
So J gave him his hand, and 2Ki 10:15
So Jehu had J ride in his...................... 2Ki 10:16
and J son of Recab went into 2Ki 10:23

JEHONATHAN
Shemiramoth, J, Adonijah, ... 2Ch 17:8
J, from Shemaiah's family; .... Ne 12:18

JEHORAM
Then his son J became king in 1Ki 22:50
J son of Jehoshaphat became king............ 2Ki 8:16
Ahaziah son of J became king of 2Ki 8:25
Ahaziah son of J and king of 2Ch 22:6
Jehoshaphat was the father of J. .... Mt 1:8

JEHOSHAPHAT
J son of Ahilud was the recorder. 2Sa 8:16
Then J, Asa's son, became king 1Ki 15:24

J

the third year **J** king of Judah.................. 1Ki 22:2
J son of Asa became king of 1Ki 22:41
J fought many wars, and these 1Ki 22:45
J died and was buried with his 1Ki 22:50
find Jehu son of **J**, the son of 2Ki 9:2
J had much wealth and honor, ... 2Ch 18:1
Then King Ahab said to **J**, ... 2Ch 18:7
J lived in Jerusalem. 2Ch 19:4
came to start a war with **J**. 2Ch 20:1
J was afraid, so he decided to................ 2Ch 20:3
J bowed facedown on the ground. 2Ch 20:18
J ruled over the country of 2Ch 20:31
The other things **J** did as king, ... 2Ch 20:34
of Mareshah spoke against **J**. 2Ch 20:37
your father **J** lived and as Asa 2Ch 21:12
Asa was the father of **J**. .... Mt 1:8

JEHOSHEBA
But **J**, King Jehoram's daughter 2Ki 11:2
But **J**, King Jehoram's daughter,.............. 2Ch 22:11
So **J**, who was King Jehoram's 2Ch 22:11

JEHOZABAD
of Shimeath and **J** son of Shomer. 2Ki 12:21
first son, **J** was second, Joah 1Ch 26:4
And **J** had one hundred eighty 2Ch 17:18
Joash were Jozabad and **J**. 2Ch 24:26
And **J** was the son of Shimrith, ... 2Ch 24:26

JEHOZADAK
and Seraiah was the father of **J**. 1Ch 6:14
J was forced to leave his home 1Ch 6:15
Joshua son of **J**, the high priest .... Hag 1:1
Shealtiel and Joshua son of **J**,.................. Hag 1:12
Joshua son of **J**, the high priest .... Hag 1:14
Joshua son of **J**, the high priest .... Hag 2:2
son of **J**, the high priest, ... Hag 2:4
on the head of Joshua son of **J**, ... Zch 6:11

JEHU
J son of Hanani spoke the word 1Ki 16:1
the prophet **J** son of Hanani. 1Ki 16:7
J will kill anyone who escapes 1Ki 19:17
So **J** son of Jehoshaphat, the son 2Ki 9:14
is driving like **J** son of Nimshi. 2Ki 9:20
When Joram saw **J**, he said, "Is 2Ki 9:22
he said, "Is all in order, **J**?".................... 2Ki 9:22
J chased him, saying, "Shoot 2Ki 9:27
When **J** came to Jezreel, Jezebel 2Ki 9:30
J wrote letters and sent them to 2Ki 10:1
So **J** killed everyone of Ahab's 2Ki 10:11
But **J** was tricking them so he 2Ki 10:19
So **J** destroyed Baal worship in 2Ki 10:28
But **J** was not careful to follow 2Ki 10:31
other things **J** did—everything 2Ki 10:34
J died and was buried in Samaria, ... 2Ki 10:35
Jehoahaz son of **J** became king 2Ki 13:1
While **J** was punishing Ahab's 2Ch 22:8
the family of **J** for the people .... Hos 1:4

JEHUCAL
Zedekiah sent **J** son of Shelemiah .... Je 37:3
J and Zephaniah, I know Zedekiah .... Je 37:7
son of Pashhur, **J** son of .... Je 38:1

JEHUD
J, Bene Berak, Gath Rimmon,.................. Jos 19:45

JEHUDI
a man named **J** son of Nethaniah .... Je 36:14
J said to Baruch, "Bring the .... Je 36:14
and went with **J** to the officers. .... Je 36:14
Jehoiakim sent **J** to get the .... Je 36:21
J brought the scroll from the .... Je 36:21
After **J** had read three or four .... Je 36:23

JEKABZEEL
surroundings, in **J** and its .... Ne 11:25

JEKAMEAM
Jahaziel, and his fourth was **J**. 1Ch 23:19
his third, and **J** was his fourth. 1Ch 24:23

JEKAMIAH
Shallum was the father of **J**, ... 1Ch 2:41
J was the father of Elishama. 1Ch 2:41
Pedaiah, Shenazzar, **J**, Hoshama, ... 1Ch 3:18

JEMIMAH
He named the first daughter **J**, ... Job 42:14

JEMUEL
sons were **J**, Jamin, Ohad, ... Ge 46:10
sons were **J**, Jamin, Ohad, ... Ex 6:15

JEPHTHAH
J was a strong soldier from..................... Jdg 11:1
So **J** ran away from his brothers............... Jdg 11:3
The elders of Gilead said to **J**, ... Jdg 11:8
J sent messengers to the king of.............. Jdg 11:12
Spirit of the LORD entered **J**. .... Jdg 11:29
J made a promise to the LORD, ... Jdg 11:30
When **J** returned to his home in .... Jdg 11:34
the daughter of **J** from Gilead. .... Jdg 11:40
J was a judge for Israel for six .... Jdg 12:7
Gideon, Barak, **J**, and Samuel. 1Sa 12:11
Barak, Samson, **J**, David, Samuel, ... Heb 11:32

JEPHUNNEH
Caleb son of **J** and Joshua son .... Nu 14:30
Caleb son of **J** and gave him .... Jos 14:13
been given to Caleb son of **J**. .... Jos 21:12

JERAH
Sheleph, Hazarmaveth, **J**, ... Ge 10:26
Sheleph, Hazarmaveth, **J**, ... 1Ch 1:20

JERAHMEEL
of Judah, or **J**, or to the land 1Sa 27:10
sons were **J**, Ram, and Caleb. 1Ch 2:9
Hezron's first son was **J**......................... 1Ch 2:25
J had another wife, named Atarah. 1Ch 2:26
Kish's son was **J**................................... 1Ch 24:29
king ordered **J** son of the king .... Je 36:26

JERAHMEEL'S
J sons were Ram, Bunah, Oren, ... 1Ch 2:25
Ram was **J** first son. 1Ch 2:25
J first son, Ram, had sons. 1Ch 2:27
These were **J** descendants. 1Ch 2:33
Caleb was **J** brother. 1Ch 2:42

JERAHMEELITES
cities of the **J** and the Kenites, ... 1Sa 30:29

JEREMAI
Zabad, Eliphelet, **J**, Manasseh, ... Ezr 10:33

JEREMIAH
J wrote some sad songs about 2Ch 35:25
prophet **J** spoke messages from 2Ch 36:12
spoken by **J** would come true. 2Ch 36:22
spoken by **J** would come true. .... Ezr 1:1
the words of **J** son of Hilkiah.................. Je 1:1
"**J**, what do you see?" .... Je 1:11
word that the LORD spoke to **J**: .... Je 7:1
words that the LORD spoke to **J**: .... Je 11:1
let's make plans against **J**. .... Je 18:18
he had **J** the prophet beaten. .... Je 20:2
Pashhur took **J** out of the blocks .... Je 20:3
crowded around **J** in the Temple.............. Je 26:9
the LORD spoke his word to **J**: .... Je 29:30
While **J** was still locked up in................ Je 33:1
So **J** called for Baruch son of .... Je 36:4
Then **J** commanded Baruch, "I .... Je 36:5
You and I must go and hide, ... Je 36:19
all the words I had spoken to .... Je 36:27
the LORD spoke his word to **J**: .... Je 36:27
J took another scroll and gave .... Je 36:32

As J spoke, Baruch wrote on the .... Je 36:32
Now J tried to travel from .... Je 37:12
When J got to the Benjamin Gate .... Je 37:13
very angry with J and beat him. .... Je 37:15
those people put J into a cell .... Je 37:16
orders for J to be put under .... Je 37:21
the officers took J and put him .... Je 38:6
ropes to lower J into the well, ... Je 38:6
palace and lift J the prophet .... Je 38:10
some ropes to J in the well. .... Je 38:11
the Cushite said to J, ... Je 38:12
J said to Zedekiah, "If I give .... Je 38:15
made a secret promise to J, ... Je 38:16
Then King Zedekiah said to J, ... Je 38:19
They had J taken out of the .... Je 39:14
commander Nebuzaradan found J,........... Je 40:2
So J went to Gedaliah son of .... Je 40:6
the LORD spoke his word to J: .... Je 43:8
J the prophet told these things .... Je 45:1
J had written on a scroll all .... Je 51:60
The words of J end here......................... Je 51:64
the LORD told J that Jerusalem .... Da 9:2
through the prophet J came true: .... Mt 2:17
others say you are J or one of .... Mt 16:14
So what J the prophet had said .... Mt 27:9

JEREMIAH'S
the yoke off J neck and broke it .... Je 28:10

JEREMOTH
Elioenai, Omri, J, Abijah, ... 1Ch 7:8
sons were Ahio, Shashak, J, ... 1Ch 8:14
Jehiel, Abdi, J, and Elijah. .... Ezr 10:26
Mattaniah, J, Zabad, and Aziza............... Ezr 10:27
Adaiah, Jashub, Sheal, and J................... Ezr 10:29

JERIAH
first son was J, his second was 1Ch 23:19
first son was J, Amariah was his 1Ch 24:23
shows that J was their leader 1Ch 26:31
J had twenty-seven hundred 1Ch 26:32

JERIBAI
J and Joshaviah, Elnaam's sons;............. 1Ch 11:46

JERICHO
the Jordan River across from J. .... Nu 22:1
Jordan River, across from J." .... Nu 34:15
country of Moab, across from J. .... Dt 32:49
whole Valley of J up to Zoar. .... Dt 34:3
the men went to J and stayed at .... Jos 2:1
So the king of J sent this .... Jos 2:3
going toward the plains of J. .... Jos 4:13
The people of J were afraid .... Jos 6:1
have given you J, its king, and .... Jos 6:2
Stay in J until your beards have 2Sa 10:5
Bethel rebuilt the city of J. 1Ki 16:34
of prophets at J came to Elisha 2Ki 2:5
his followers were leaving J, ... Mt 20:29
going down from Jerusalem to J, ... Lk 10:30
was going through the city of J. .... Lk 19:1
that the walls of J fell after.................... Heb 11:30

JERIEL
Rephaiah, J, Jahmai, Ibsam, ... 1Ch 7:2

JERIOTH
by his wife Azubah and by J. 1Ch 2:18

JEROBOAM
J son of Nebat was one of 1Ki 11:26
J was a capable man, and Solomon 1Ki 11:28
J son of Nebat was still in 1Ki 12:2
Then J made Shechem in the 1Ki 12:25
J was standing by the altar to................ 1Ki 13:1
When King J heard what the man 1Ki 13:4
this way the family of J sinned, ... 1Ki 13:34
J sinned, and then he made the 1Ki 14:16

Everything else J did is written 1Ki 14:19
Nadab son of J became king of 1Ki 15:25
J son of Nebat had led the 1Ki 16:26
family of King J son of Nebat................. 1Ki 21:22
Everything else J did is written 2Ki 14:28
J died and was buried with his 2Ki 14:29
was war between Abijah and J. 2Ch 13:2
God caused J and the army of 2Ch 13:15
J never became strong again 2Ch 13:20
of Judah and J son of Jehoash .... Hos 1:1
message to J king of Israel: .... Am 7:10
'J will die by the sword, and .... Am 7:11

JERUB-BAAL
that day Gideon got the name J,.............. Jdg 6:32
in the morning J (also called .... Jdg 7:1
not kind to the family of J, ... Jdg 8:35

JERUB-BESHETH
who killed Abimelech son of J? 2Sa 11:21

JERUEL
that leads to the Desert of J. 2Ch 20:16

JERUSALEM
king of J heard that Joshua .... Jos 10:1
city (which is called J). .... Jos 15:8
the Jebusite city (J), Gibeah, ... Jos 18:28
lived in J, because he always 2Sa 9:13
But David stayed in J............................. 2Sa 11:1
and brought Absalom back to J............... 2Sa 14:23
of God back to J and stayed 2Sa 15:29
came back to his palace in J. 2Sa 20:3
his arm toward J to destroy it, ... 2Sa 24:16
yourself in J and live there. 1Ki 2:36
families to come to him in J. 1Ki 8:1
and build the wall around J. 1Ki 9:15
In J Solomon made silver as 1Ki 10:27
a hill east of J, Solomon built.................. 1Ki 11:7
my servant, in J, the city where 1Ki 11:36
of the LORD in J to offer 1Ki 12:27
king of Egypt attacked J. 1Ki 14:25
Then he went to attack J. 2Ki 12:17
went up to J and broke down 2Ki 14:13
of Israel, came up to attack J.................. 2Ki 16:5
Lachish to King Hezekiah in J. 2Ki 18:17
Hezekiah told Judah and J,.................... 2Ki 18:22
the LORD save J from my power." 2Ki 18:35
"I will be worshiped in J," 2Ki 21:4
much trouble on J and Judah that 2Ki 21:12
line of Samaria over J, ... 2Ki 21:13
them outside J in the open 2Ki 23:4
took it outside J to the Kidron 2Ki 23:6
serve at the LORD's altar in J. 2Ki 23:9
I will reject J, which I chose. 2Ki 23:27
king of Babylon came up to J. 2Ki 24:10
taken captive from J to Babylon. 2Ki 24:15
fifty-six people living in J, ... 1Ch 9:9
God sent an angel to destroy J, ... 1Ch 21:15
J Solomon made silver and gold............. 2Ch 1:15
Then you may carry it to J." 2Ch 2:16
the LORD in J on Mount Moriah. 2Ch 3:1
lived in J and built strong 2Ch 11:5
king of Egypt attacked J, ... 2Ch 12:2
of Judah and J met in front.................... 2Ch 20:5
people living in Judah and J. 2Ch 20:15
from Judah and J back to 2Ch 20:20
He led the people of J to sin, ... 2Ch 21:11
with the people of Judah and J. 2Ch 24:18
Then Jehoash brought him to J. 2Ch 25:23
the people in J made plans 2Ch 25:27
built towers in J at the Corner 2Ch 26:9
on every street corner in J. 2Ch 28:24
and was buried in the city of J, ... 2Ch 28:27
with the people of Judah and J, ... 2Ch 29:8

had not yet gathered in **J**. 2Ch 30:3
people to come to **J** to celebrate 2Ch 30:5
was much joy in **J**, because there 2Ch 30:26
you to stay in **J** under attack. 2Ch 32:10
to the people of **J** who were on 2Ch 32:18
will be worshiped in **J** forever," 2Ch 33:4
from Judah and **J** the gods,......................2Ch 34:3
the Passover to the LORD in **J**. 2Ch 35:1
were there, and the people of **J**. 2Ch 35:18
chariot and carried him to **J**. 2Ch 35:24
every valuable thing in **J**. 2Ch 36:19
a Temple for him at **J** in Judah. 2Ch 36:23
a Temple for him at **J** in Judah. ....Ezr 1:2
are free to go to **J** in Judah and ....Ezr 1:3
for the Temple of God in **J**. ....Ezr 1:4
captives went from Babylon to **J**. ....Ezr 1:11
at the Temple of God in **J**, ...Ezr 3:8
the people of Judah and **J**. ....Ezr 4:6
a letter against **J** to Artaxerxes ....Ezr 4:8
J has had powerful kings who ....Ezr 4:20
people in **J** and forced them ....Ezr 4:23
in the Temple in **J** and rebuild ....Ezr 5:15
to rebuild this Temple in **J**. ....Ezr 5:17
the priests in **J** anything they ....Ezr 6:9
the Temple at **J** as it is written ....Ezr 6:18
he arrived in **J** on the first day ....Ezr 7:9
to protect us in Judah and **J**. ....Ezr 9:9
wall around **J** is broken down, ...Ne 1:3
God had caused me to do for **J**. ....Ne 2:12
the walls of **J** that had been ....Ne 2:13
J is a pile of ruins, and its ....Ne 2:17
the wall of **J** so we won't be ....Ne 2:17
leaders of Israel lived in **J**. ....Ne 11:1
When the wall of **J** was offered ....Ne 12:27
of happiness in **J** could be heard ....Ne 12:43
Do whatever good you wish for **J**. ....Ps 51:18
They have turned **J** into ruins. ....Ps 79:1
blood like water all around **J**. ....Ps 79:3
of the LORD will be heard in **J**; ....Ps 102:21
in the Temple courtyards in **J**. ....Ps 116:19
J, we are standing at your gates. ....Ps 122:2
J is built as a city with the ....Ps 122:3
Pray for peace in **J**: ....Ps 122:6
As the mountains surround **J**,..................Ps 125:2
good things of **J** all your life. ....Ps 128:5
You people of **J**, praise the LORD ....Ps 135:21
J, if I forget you, let my right ....Ps 137:5
not think about **J** as my greatest ....Ps 137:6
The LORD rebuilds **J**; ....Ps 147:2
J, praise the LORD; ....Ps 147:12
a son of David, king in **J**. ....Ec 1:1
was king over Israel in **J**. ....Ec 1:12
anyone who ruled **J** before me. ....Ec 1:16
me, women of **J**, if you find my ....Sng 5:8
as lovely as the city of **J**,.......................Sng 6:4
would happen to Judah and **J**. ....Is 1:1
happen because **J** has stumbled,................Is 3:8
the filth from the women of **J**. ....Is 4:4
he planned to Mount Zion and **J**, ...Is 10:12
at Mount Zion, the hill of **J**. ....Is 10:32
LORD on that holy mountain in **J**. ....Is 27:13
to the people of **J** and tell them ....Is 40:2
I say to **J**, 'People will live in ....Is 44:26
Awake! Get up, **J**. The LORD was ....Is 51:17
Wake up, wake up, **J**! ....Is 52:1
J, your buildings are destroyed ....Is 52:9
J, I have put guards on the ....Is 62:6
until he builds up **J** and makes ....Is 62:7
J is like a desert; ....Is 64:10
I will make a **J** that is full of ....Is 65:18
the people of **J** were taken away ....Je 1:3
the entrance of the gates of **J**..................Je 1:15
Go and speak to the people of **J**,...............Je 2:2

people of Judah and people of **J**. ....Je 4:4
Spread this news in **J**: ' ....Je 4:16
up and down the streets of **J**. ....Je 5:1
Run away from **J**! Blow the war ....Je 6:1
Cut down the trees around **J**, ...Je 6:6
of Judah or in the streets of **J**, ...Je 7:34
prophets, and the people of **J**..................Je 8:1
the city of **J** a heap of ruins ....Je 9:11
Judah and in the streets of **J**: ' ....Je 11:6
Judah and the great pride of **J**. ....Je 13:9
be thrown into the streets of **J**. ....Je 14:16
Who will feel sorry for you, **J**? ....Je 15:5
any loads into **J** on the Sabbath. ....Je 17:27
start a fire at the gates of **J**, ...Je 17:27
of the people of Judah and **J**. ....Je 19:7
the prophets of **J** do terrible ....Je 23:14
the people from **J** who are left ....Je 24:8
from Judah and **J** to Babylon.................Je 27:20
as captives from **J** to Babylon. ....Je 29:1
of Babylon was surrounding **J**. ....Je 32:2
and the people of **J** will live in ....Je 33:16
and to everyone living in **J**.....................Je 35:17
army left **J** to fight the army ....Je 37:11
until the day **J** was captured. ....Je 38:28
broke down the walls around **J**. ....Je 39:8
captives from **J** and Judah who ....Je 40:1
streets of **J** so they are only ....Je 44:6
Judah and in the streets of **J**. ....Je 44:9
as I punished **J**, using swords, ...Je 44:13
year, 832 people from **J**; ....Je 52:29
J sinned terribly, so she has ....La 1:8
J reaches out her hands, but ....La 1:17
elders of **J** sit on the ground ....La 2:10
What can I say about you, **J**? ....La 2:13
foes could enter the gates of **J**. ....La 4:12
you, and draw a map of **J** on it. ....Eze 4:1
Then you will look toward **J**, ...Eze 4:7
off the supply of bread to **J**. ....Eze 4:16
took me in visions of God to **J**, ...Eze 8:3
you turn loose your anger on **J**?" ....Eze 9:8
about the king in **J** and all the ....Eze 12:10
who prophesy to **J** and who see ....Eze 13:16
My plans for **J** are much worse! ....Eze 14:21
Babylon came to **J** and took the ....Eze 17:12
look toward **J** and speak against ....Eze 21:2
is Samaria, and Oholibah is **J**. ....Eze 23:4
has surrounded **J** this very day. ....Eze 24:2
and said. "**J** has been captured. ....Eze 33:21
Babylon came to **J** and surrounded ....Da 1:1
had taken from the Temple in **J**. ....Da 5:2
windows that opened toward **J**. ....Da 6:10
Jeremiah that **J** would be empty..............Da 9:2
command will come to rebuild **J**. ....Da 9:25
will roar like a lion from **J**;.....................Joe 3:16
J will be a holy place, and ....Joe 3:17
The LORD will roar from **J**; ....Am 1:2
forced to leave **J** and live in ....Ob 1:20
visions about Samaria and **J**. ....Mic 1:1
flocks, hill of **J**, to you will ....Mic 4:8
LORD, will search **J** with lamps..............Zph 1:12
show mercy to **J** and the cities ....Zch 1:12
'I have a strong love for **J**. ....Zch 1:14
to measure **J**, to see how wide ....Zch 2:2
when **J** and the surrounding towns ....Zch 7:7
will return to **J** and live in it ....Zch 8:3
Rejoice greatly, people of **J**! ....Zch 9:9
I will make **J** like a cup of ....Zch 12:2
there will be much crying in **J**, ...Zch 12:11
the Mount of Olives, east of **J**. ....Zch 14:4
fresh water will flow from **J**. ....Zch 14:8
Every pot in **J** and Judah will be ....Zch 14:21
God hates in Israel and **J**: ....Mal 2:11
as were all the people in **J**. ....Mt 2:3

the Ten Towns, J, Judea, and the .... Mt 4:25
an oath using the name of J, ... Mt 5:35
followers that he must go to J, ... Mt 16:21
While Jesus was going to J, ... Mt 20:17
J, Jerusalem! You kill the .... Mt 23:37
from Judea, from J, from Idumea, ... Mk 3:8
J lived a man named Simeon who .... Lk 2:25
were waiting for God to free J. .... Lk 2:38
parents took J for the .... Lk 2:41
boy Jesus stayed behind in J, ... Lk 2:43
went back to J to look for him .... Lk 2:45
devil led Jesus to J and put him .... Lk 4:9
he would soon bring about in J. .... Lk 9:31
he was determined to go to J. .... Lk 9:51
going down from J to Jericho, ... Lk 10:30
be killed anywhere except in J. .... Lk 13:33
you see armies all around J, ... Lk 21:20
J will be crushed by non-Jewish............. Lk 21:24
only visitor in J who does not .... Lk 24:18
to all nations, starting at J. .... Lk 24:47
must stay in J until you have .... Lk 24:49
and returned to J very happy. .... Lk 24:52
the leaders in J sent priests .... Jn 1:19
Jesus went to J for the Passover .... Jn 2:23
but you say that J is the place................ Jn 4:20
when neither in J nor on this .... Jn 4:21
Jesus went to J for a special .... Jn 5:1
the Feast of Dedication at J. .... Jn 10:22
was about two miles from J. .... Jn 11:18
he told them not to leave J..................... Ac 1:4
my witnesses—in J, in all of .... Ac 1:8
went back to J from the Mount .... Ac 1:12
Jews staying in J who were from .... Ac 2:5
you have filled J with your .... Ac 5:28
of followers in J increased,..................... Ac 6:7
day the church of J began to be .... Ac 8:1
that leads down to Gaza from J— .... Ac 8:26
He had gone to J to worship. .... Ac 8:27
them and bring them back to J. .... Ac 9:2
he did to your holy people in J. .... Ac 9:13
man who was in J trying to .... Ac 9:21
prophets came from J to Antioch. .... Ac 11:27
hurrying to be in J on the day .... Ac 20:16
the Holy Spirit and go to J. .... Ac 20:22
they warned Paul not to go to J. .... Ac 21:4
only ready to be tied up in J, ... Ac 21:13
the Roman army in J learned that .... Ac 21:31
to worship in J only twelve days .... Ac 24:11
he went from Caesarea to J, ... Ac 25:1
Damascus, then in J, and in .... Ac 26:20
I was arrested in J and given to .... Ac 28:17
I am going to J to help God's .... Rm 15:25
poor among God's people at J. .... Rm 15:26
I did not go to J to see those .... Gal 1:17
years I went to J to meet Peter .... Gal 1:18
years I went to J again, ... Gal 2:1
of the earthly city of J. .... Gal 4:25
the heavenly J, which is above .... Gal 4:26
the living God, the heavenly J. .... Heb 12:22
put a stone in the ground in J. 1Pe 2:6
my God, the new J, that comes .... Rev 3:12
city, the new J, coming down out .... Rev 21:2
the holy city, J, coming down .... Rev 21:10

JERUSHA
name was J daughter of Zadok 2Ki 15:33
name was J daughter of Zadok 2Ch 27:1

JESARELAH
twelve men were chosen from J,............. 1Ch 25:14

JESHAIAH
descendants were Pelatiah and J, ... 1Ch 3:21
Gedaliah, Zeri, J, Shimei, ... 1Ch 25:3
twelve men were chosen from J,............. 1Ch 25:15

Rehabiah's son J, Jeshaiah's son 1Ch 26:25
J son of Athaliah, with seventy .... Ezr 8:7
to us Hashabiah and J from the .... Ezr 8:19
the son of Ithiel, the son of J. .... Ne 11:7

JESHAIAH'S
son Jeshaiah, J son Joram, ... 1Ch 26:25

JESHANAH
towns of Bethel, J, and Ephron, ... 2Ch 13:19

JESHEBEAB
The fourteenth was J. 1Ch 24:13

JESHER
Caleb and Azubah's sons were J, ... 1Ch 2:18

JESHIMON
the hill of Hakilah, south of J. 1Sa 23:19
in the desert area south of J. 1Sa 23:24
the hill of Hakilah opposite J." 1Sa 26:1
the hill of Hakilah opposite J,................. 1Sa 26:3

JESHIMOTH
went from Beth J to Abel Acacia. .... Nu 33:49
ruled from Beth J south to the .... Jos 12:3
the hills of Pisgah, and Beth J. .... Jos 13:20
J, Baal Meon, and Kiriathaim. .... Eze 25:9

JESHISHAI
J was Jahdo's son, and Jahdo was 1Ch 5:14

JESHISHAI'S
Michael was J son. 1Ch 5:14

JESHUA
with Zerubbabel, J, Nehemiah, ... Ezr 2:2
Then J son of Jozadak and his .... Ezr 3:2
Shealtiel and J son of Jozadak .... Ezr 5:2

JESSE
the father of J, and Jesse was .... Ru 4:22
and J was the father of David. .... Ru 4:22
I am sending you to J who lives 1Sa 16:1
J had seven of his sons pass by 1Sa 16:10
J said to his son David, "Take................. 1Sa 17:17
an agreement with the son of J! 1Sa 22:8
We have no part in the son of J! 2Sa 20:1
the prayers of David son of J. .... Ps 72:20
will come from the family of J. .... Is 11:1
the family of J will stand as .... Is 11:10
J was the father of King David. .... Mt 1:6
David son of J the kind of man .... Ac 13:22
will come from the family of J. .... Rm 15:12

JESUS
the family history of J Christ................... Mt 1:1
and Mary was the mother of J. .... Mt 1:16
how the birth of J Christ came .... Mt 1:18
will name him J, because he will .... Mt 1:21
J was born in the town of .... Mt 2:1
At that time J came from Galilee .... Mt 3:13
the Spirit led J into the desert .... Mt 4:1
When J heard that John had been .... Mt 4:12
When J finished saying these .... Mt 7:28
J reached out his hand and..................... Mt 8:3
Then J said to the officer, ... Mt 8:13
But J told him, "Follow me, and .... Mt 8:22
When J arrived at the other side .... Mt 8:28
whole town went out to see J..................... Mt 8:34
people brought to J a man who .... Mt 9:2
J sent out these twelve men with .... Mt 10:5
After J finished telling these .... Mt 11:1
J knew what the Pharisees were............... Mt 12:25
Then J left the crowd and went .... Mt 13:36
When J finished teaching with .... Mt 13:53
So the people were upset with J. .... Mt 13:57
Then they went and told J. .... Mt 14:12
J said, "Come." And Peter left .... Mt 14:29
Immediately J reached out his .... Mt 14:31

J called his followers to him .... Mt 15:32
Then **J** warned his followers not.............. Mt 16:20
that time on **J** began telling his .... Mt 16:21
Six days later, **J** took Peter,.................... Mt 17:1
up, they saw **J** was now alone. .... Mt 17:8
J commanded the demon inside the ...... Mt 17:18
came to **J** when he was alone .... Mt 17:19
J called a little child to him.................... Mt 18:2
After **J** said all these things, ... Mt 19:1
but **J** said, "Let the little .... Mt 19:14
J felt sorry for the blind men .... Mt 20:34
As **J** and his followers were .... Mt 21:1
said, "This man is **J**, the .... Mt 21:11
J went into the Temple and threw .... Mt 21:12
J finished saying all these .... Mt 26:1
a trap to arrest **J** and kill him. .... Mt 26:4
J was in Bethany at the house of .... Mt 26:6
J took some bread and thanked .... Mt 26:26
J answered, "Friend, do what you .... Mt 26:50
and grabbed **J** and arrested him. .... Mt 26:50
also were with **J** of Galilee." .... Mt 26:69
man was with **J** of Nazareth." .... Mt 26:71
Barabbas or **J** who is called the .... Mt 27:17
be freed and for **J** to be killed. .... Mt 27:20
But **J** was beaten with whips and .... Mt 27:26
soldiers took **J** into the .... Mt 27:27
put a sign above **J'** head with a .... Mt 27:37
three o'clock **J** cried out in a .... Mt 27:46
a follower of **J** from the town of .... Mt 27:57
and asked to have **J'** body. .... Mt 27:58
know that you are looking for **J**,............. Mt 28:5
Suddenly, **J** met them and said, ... Mt 28:9
mountain where **J** had told them .... Mt 28:16
of the Good News about **J** Christ, ... Mk 1:1
that time **J** came from the town .... Mk 1:9
put in prison, **J** went into .... Mk 1:14
J of Nazareth! What do you want .... Mk 1:24
While **J** was still far away, ... Mk 5:6
want with me, **J**, Son of the Most .... Mk 5:7
When the woman heard about **J**, ... Mk 5:27
gathered around **J** and told him .... Mk 6:30
crowd with **J** that had nothing .... Mk 8:1
Six days later, **J** took Peter,.................... Mk 9:2
to them, talking with **J**. .... Mk 9:4
But **J** said, "Don't stop him, ... Mk 9:39
J called them together and said,............. Mk 10:42
he heard that **J** from Nazareth .... Mk 10:47
to shout, "**J**, Son of David, ... Mk 10:47
the colt to **J** and put their .... Mk 11:7
When **J** returned to Jerusalem, ... Mk 11:15
J said, "Leave her alone. .... Mk 14:6
J answered, "It is one of the .... Mk 14:20
people who arrested **J** led him to .... Mk 14:53
something that **J** had done wrong .... Mk 14:55
J answered, "I am. And in the .... Mk 14:62
decided what to do with **J**. .... Mk 15:1
But **J** still said nothing, so .... Mk 15:5
three o'clock **J** cried in a loud................ Mk 15:34
Then **J** cried in a loud voice and.............. Mk 15:37
to Pilate and ask for **J'** body. .... Mk 15:43
are looking for **J** from Nazareth, ... Mk 16:6
a son, and you will name him **J**.............. Lk 1:31
was circumcised and was named **J**, ... Lk 2:21
The boy **J** stayed behind in .... Lk 2:43
J became wiser and grew .... Lk 2:52
J returned to Galilee in the .... Lk 4:14
J traveled to Nazareth, where he .... Lk 4:16
J of Nazareth! What do you want .... Lk 4:34
J said to Simon, "Don't be .... Lk 5:10
When **J** was in one of the towns, ... Lk 5:12
When they came to **J**, they found .... Lk 8:35
Then **J** said, "Who touched me?" .... Lk 8:45
But **J** gave a strong command to .... Lk 9:42

J said to them, "The foxes have .... Lk 9:58
But **J** said to him, "Let the .... Lk 9:60
Then **J** rejoiced in the Holy..................... Lk 10:21
angry because **J** healed on the .... Lk 13:14
but called to him, "**J**! .... Lk 17:13
man cried out, "**J**, Son of David,.............. Lk 18:38
J said to him, "Salvation has .... Lk 19:9
brought it to **J**, threw their .... Lk 19:35
While **J** was speaking, a crowd .... Lk 22:47
to arrest **J** were the leading .... Lk 22:52
were guarding **J** began making fun .... Lk 22:63
When Herod saw **J**, he was very............... Lk 23:8
wanted to let **J** go free and told .... Lk 23:20
and he handed **J** over to them to .... Lk 23:25
As they led **J** away, Simon, a man .... Lk 23:26
J said, "Father, forgive them, ... Lk 23:34
J cried out in a loud voice, ... Lk 23:46
Pilate to ask for the body of **J**. .... Lk 23:52
J said to them, "What are you .... Lk 24:19
J himself stood right in the .... Lk 24:36
and truth came through **J** Christ. .... Jn 1:17
say this, so they followed **J**. .... Jn 1:37
He is **J**, the son of Joseph, from .... Jn 1:45
As **J** saw Nathanael coming toward .... Jn 1:47
J and his followers were also .... Jn 2:2
J answered, "Dear woman, why .... Jn 2:4
J said to the servants, "Fill .... Jn 2:7
Cana of Galilee **J** did his first .... Jn 2:11
Feast, **J** went to Jerusalem. .... Jn 2:13
Nicodemus came to **J** and said, ... Jn 3:2
Then **J** said, "I am he—I, the one .... Jn 4:26
J said, "My food is to do what .... Jn 4:34
J went again to visit Cana in .... Jn 4:46
J answered, "Go. Your son will .... Jn 4:50
miracle **J** did after coming .... Jn 4:54
When **J** saw the man and knew that .... Jn 5:6
Because **J** was doing this on the.............. Jn 5:16
J went up on a hill and sat down .... Jn 6:3
When **J** looked up and saw a large........... Jn 6:5
Then **J** took the loaves of bread,.............. Jn 6:11
saw this miracle that **J** did,.................... Jn 6:14
people saw that **J** and his .... Jn 6:24
said, "This is **J**, the son of .... Jn 6:42
J asked the twelve followers,................. Jn 6:67
J traveled around Galilee. .... Jn 7:1
J went to the Temple and began .... Jn 7:14
J was talking about the Holy .... Jn 7:39
who had gone to see **J** before, ... Jn 7:50
J went to the Mount of Olives. .... Jn 8:1
this to trick **J** so that they .... Jn 8:6
When **J** said this, the people .... Jn 8:59
The man named **J** made some mud .... Jn 9:11
day **J** had made mud and healed .... Jn 9:14
J heard that they had thrown .... Jn 9:35
J said, "I came into this world .... Jn 9:39
J told the people this story,.................... Jn 10:6
because of these words of **J**. .... Jn 10:19
J loved Martha and her sister................. Jn 11:5
J meant that Lazarus was dead, ... Jn 11:13
Martha said to **J**, "Lord, if you .... Jn 11:21
J said, "Your brother will rise................. Jn 11:23
J said to her, "I am the .... Jn 11:25
When **J** saw Mary crying and the .... Jn 11:33
J cried.. Jn 11:35
J said, "Move the stone away." .... Jn 11:39
J said to them, "Take the cloth .... Jn 11:44
prophesying that **J** would die for .... Jn 11:51
Feast, **J** went to Bethany .... Jn 12:1
poured the perfume on **J'** feet, ... Jn 12:3
J answered, "Leave her alone. .... Jn 12:7
leaving them and believing in **J**.............. Jn 12:11
The followers of **J** did not .... Jn 12:16
Sir, we would like to see **J**." .... Jn 12:21

then Andrew and Philip told **J**. .... Jn 12:22
J knew that it was time for him .... Jn 13:1
sitting next to **J** was the .... Jn 13:23
and that they know **J** Christ, ... Jn 17:3
answered, "**J** from Nazareth." .... Jn 18:5
J said to Peter, "Put your sword .... Jn 18:11
and the guards arrested **J**. .... Jn 18:12
another one of **J**' followers went .... Jn 18:15
When **J** said this, one of the .... Jn 18:22
so that what **J** said about how he .... Jn 18:32
J answered, "My kingdom does not .... Jn 18:36
ordered that **J** be taken away .... Jn 19:1
So **J** came out, wearing the crown .... Jn 19:5
But **J** did not answer him. .... Jn 19:9
There they crucified **J**. .... Jn 19:18
J OF NAZARETH, THE KING OF THE ..... Jn 19:19
After the soldiers crucified **J**, ... Jn 19:23
near his cross were **J**' mother, ... Jn 19:25
if he could take the body of **J**.................. Jn 19:38
was a secret follower of **J**, ... Jn 19:38
earlier had come to **J** at night, ... Jn 19:39
two men took **J**' body and wrapped .... Jn 19:40
The men laid **J** in that tomb .... Jn 19:42
and the follower whom **J** loved. .... Jn 20:2
around and saw **J** standing there, ... Jn 20:14
J asked her, "Woman, why are you .... Jn 20:15
J said to her, "Mary." .... Jn 20:16
J said to her, "Don't hold on to .... Jn 20:17
J' followers were together. .... Jn 20:19
but **J** came in and stood right in .... Jn 20:26
Then **J** told him, "You believe................. Jn 20:29
J did many other miracles in the .... Jn 20:30
believe that **J** is the Christ, ... Jn 20:31
the next morning **J** stood on the............... Jn 21:4
The follower whom **J** loved said .... Jn 21:7
the third time **J** showed himself .... Jn 21:14
was hurt because **J** asked him the .... Jn 21:17
the follower **J** loved was walking .... Jn 21:20
are many other things **J** did. .... Jn 21:25
about everything **J** began to do .... Ac 1:1
J, whom you saw taken up from............... Ac 1:11
including Mary the mother of **J**, ... Ac 1:14
J from Nazareth was a very .... Ac 2:22
So **J** is the One whom God raised .... Ac 2:32
God has made **J**—the man you .... Ac 2:36
in the name of **J** Christ for the .... Ac 2:38
gave glory to **J**, his servant. .... Ac 3:13
up his servant **J** and sent him to............... Ac 3:26
by the power of **J** Christ from............... Ac 4:10
Peter and John had been with **J**................ Ac 4:13
teach at all in the name of **J**. .... Ac 4:18
together against **J** here in .... Ac 4:27
that the Lord **J** was truly raised .... Ac 4:33
You killed **J** by hanging him on a .... Ac 5:30
to speak in the name of **J** again............... Ac 5:40
Good News—that **J** is the Christ. .... Ac 5:42
glory of God and **J** standing at .... Ac 7:55
the man the Good News about **J**. .... Ac 8:35
I believe that **J** Christ is the .... Ac 8:37
answered, "I am **J**, whom you are .... Ac 9:5
Saul, the Lord **J** sent me. .... Ac 9:17
in the name of **J** in Damascus. .... Ac 9:27
him, "Aeneas, **J** Christ heals you .... Ac 9:34
peace has come through **J** Christ. .... Ac 10:36
You know about **J** from Nazareth, ... Ac 10:38
believed in the Lord **J** Christ, ... Ac 11:17
the Good News about the Lord **J**. .... Ac 11:20
has brought **J**, one of David's .... Ac 13:23
by the grace of the Lord **J**." .... Ac 15:11
to serve our Lord **J** Christ. .... Ac 15:26
By the power of **J** Christ, ... Ac 16:18
in the Lord **J** and you will be .... Ac 16:31
is another king, called **J**." .... Ac 17:7

name of the Lord **J** to force the .... Ac 19:13
to them, "I know **J**, and I know .... Ac 19:15
work that the Lord **J** gave me— .... Ac 20:24
'I am **J** from Nazareth whom you .... Ac 22:8
said, 'I am **J**, the one you are .... Ac 26:15
to believe these things about **J**. .... Ac 28:23
Paul, a servant of Christ **J**. .... Rm 1:1
called to belong to **J** Christ. .... Rm 1:6
Father and the Lord **J** Christ. .... Rm 1:7
God, through Christ **J**, will .... Rm 2:16
through their faith in **J** Christ. .... Rm 3:22
God gave **J** to show today that .... Rm 3:26
any person who has faith in **J**. .... Rm 3:26
in the One who raised **J** our Lord .... Rm 4:24
forever in Christ **J** our Lord. .... Rm 6:23
are in Christ **J** are not judged .... Rm 8:1
Through Christ **J** the law of the .... Rm 8:2
God raised **J** from the dead, ... Rm 8:11
that is in Christ **J** our Lord. .... Rm 8:39
your mouth, "**J** is Lord," and if .... Rm 10:9
the Lord **J** Christ and forget .... Rm 13:14
of Christ **J** to those who are .... Rm 15:16
I have done for God in Christ **J**. .... Rm 15:17
together with me in Christ **J** .... Rm 16:3
of Christ **J** because that is 1Co 1:1
have been made holy in Christ **J**. 1Co 1:2
J will keep you strong until the 1Co 1:8
except **J** Christ and his 1Co 2:2
in the name of our Lord **J**, ... 1Co 5:4
there is only one Lord—**J** Christ. 1Co 8:6
I have seen **J** our Lord. 1Co 9:1
when the Lord **J** was handed over 1Co 11:23
Spirit says, "**J** be cursed." 1Co 12:3
no one can say, "**J** is Lord," 1Co 12:3
through our Lord **J** Christ. 1Co 15:57
Father and the Lord **J** Christ. 2Co 1:2
we preach that **J** Christ is Lord 2Co 4:5
that we are your servants for **J**. 2Co 4:5
the death of **J** in our own bodies 2Co 4:10
the life of **J** can also be seen 2Co 4:10
raised the Lord **J** from the dead,............... 2Co 4:14
but **J** Christ showed it to me. .... Gal 1:12
but by trusting in **J** Christ. .... Gal 2:16
come through **J** Christ to those .... Gal 3:14
are all the same in Christ **J**. .... Gal 3:28
we are in Christ **J**, it is not .... Gal 5:6
of our Lord **J** Christ is my only .... Gal 6:14
that show I belong to Christ **J**. .... Gal 6:17
Paul, an apostle of Christ **J**. .... Eph 1:1
did this for those in Christ **J** .... Eph 2:6
In Christ **J**, God made us to do .... Eph 2:10
Christ **J** himself is the most .... Eph 2:20
of Christ **J** for you who are .... Eph 3:1
taught the truth that is in **J**. .... Eph 4:21
love our Lord **J** Christ with love .... Eph 6:24
Timothy, servants of Christ **J**. .... Php 1:1
you with the love of Christ **J**. .... Php 1:8
the Spirit of **J** Christ is .... Php 1:19
think and act like Christ **J**. .... Php 2:5
knee will bow to the name of **J**— .... Php 2:10
confess that **J** Christ is Lord .... Php 2:11
in the Lord **J** to send Timothy................. Php 2:19
of knowing Christ **J** my Lord. .... Php 3:8
hearts and minds in Christ **J**. .... Php 4:7
riches in Christ **J** to give you .... Php 4:19
of God's people in Christ **J**...................... Php 4:21
J, who is called Justus, also .... Col 4:11
He is **J**, who saves us from God's 1Th 1:10
when our Lord **J** comes with all 1Th 3:13
We believe that **J** died and that 1Th 4:14
will raise with **J** those who have............... 1Th 4:14
when our Lord **J** Christ comes. 1Th 5:23
News about our Lord **J** Christ. 2Th 1:8

coming of our Lord **J** Christ and 2Th 2:1
the glory of our Lord **J** Christ. 2Th 2:14
I thank Christ **J** our Lord, ...1Ti 1:12
Christ **J** came into the world to 1Ti 1:15
That way is through Christ **J**, ...1Ti 2:5
be a good servant of Christ **J**..................1Ti 4:6
our Lord **J** Christ comes again. 1Ti 6:14
apostle of Christ **J** by the will.................2Ti 1:1
and love, which are in Christ **J**. 2Ti 1:13
like a good soldier of Christ **J**. 2Ti 2:3
desires, in Christ **J**, will be 2Ti 3:12
Father and Christ **J** our Savior. ....Tit 1:4
great God and Savior **J** Christ. ....Tit 2:13
of Christ **J**, and from Timothy................Phm 1:1
also a prisoner for Christ **J**, ...Phm 1:9
a prisoner with me for Christ **J**, ...Phm 1:23
But we see **J**, who for a short ....Heb 2:9
think about **J**, who was sent to ....Heb 3:1
high priest, **J** the Son of God,................Heb 4:14
where **J** has gone ahead of us and ....Heb 6:20
This means that **J** is the ....Heb 7:22
of the blood of **J'** death. ....Heb 10:19
us look only to **J**, the One who ....Heb 12:2
You have come to **J**, the One who ....Heb 12:24
J Christ is the same yesterday, ...Heb 13:8
Peter, an apostle of **J** Christ. 1Pe 1:1
and honor when **J** Christ is shown 1Pe 1:7
servant and apostle of **J** Christ. 2Pe 1:1
Then the blood of **J**, God's Son, ...1Jn 1:7
of the Father—**J** Christ, the One 1Jn 2:1
does not accept **J** as the Christ. 1Jn 2:22
confesses that **J** Christ came to 1Jn 4:2
confesses that **J** is the Son of 1Jn 4:15
believes that **J** is the Son of 1Jn 5:5
J Christ is the One who came by 1Jn 5:6
a servant of **J** Christ and a ....Jud 1:1
is the revelation of **J** Christ, ...Rev 1:1
it is the message from **J** Christ. ....Rev 1:2
of God and the message about **J**. ....Rev 1:9
because of their faith in **J**. ....Rev 17:6
grace of the Lord **J** be with all. ....Rev 22:21

JETHER

said to **J**, his oldest son, ...Jdg 8:20
But **J** was only a boy and was ....Jdg 8:20
of a man named **J** the Ishmaelite. 2Sa 17:25
son of Ner and Amasa son of **J**. 1Ki 2:5
Amasa son of **J**, the commander..............1Ki 2:32
his father was **J**, an Ishmaelite. 1Ch 2:17
Jada's sons were **J** and Jonathan. 1Ch 2:32
J died without having children. 1Ch 2:32

JETHETH

names were Timna, Alvah, **J**, ...Ge 36:40
of Edom were Timna, Alvah, **J**, ...1Ch 1:51

JETHRO

J was the priest of Midian and ....Ex 3:1
J had sent a message ahead to ....Ex 18:6

JETUR

Hadad, Tema, **J**, Naphish, and ....Ge 25:15
J, Naphish, and Kedemah. 1Ch 1:31
Hagrites and the people of **J**, ...1Ch 5:19

JEUEL

people there were **J** and other 1Ch 9:6
Eliphelet, **J**, and Shemaiah, with ....Ezr 8:13

JEUSH

and Oholibamah gave him **J**, ...Ge 36:5
and Oholibamah gave birth to **J**,..............Ge 36:14
these leaders: **J**, Jalam, and ....Ge 36:18
Eliphaz, Reuel, **J**, Jalam, and 1Ch 1:35
sons were **J**, Benjamin, Ehud,..................1Ch 7:10
his second was **J**, and Eliphelet 1Ch 8:39
Jahath, Ziza, **J**, and Beriah. 1Ch 23:10

But **J** and Beriah did not have 1Ch 23:11
J, Shemariah, and Zaham. 2Ch 11:19

JEW

Queen Esther and Mordecai the **J**, ...Est 8:7
with a **J** about religious ....Jn 3:25
Here he met a **J** named Aquila who ....Ac 18:2
A **J** named Apollos came to ....Ac 18:24
every **J** and Greek in Asia heard ....Ac 19:10
they saw that Alexander was a **J**, ...Ac 19:34
I am a **J** from Tarsus in the ....Ac 21:39
I am a **J**, born in Tarsus in the ....Ac 22:3
You call yourself a **J**. You trust ....Rm 2:17
is not a true **J** if he is only a ....Rm 2:28
he is only a **J** in his physical ....Rm 2:28
A person is a **J** only if he is a ....Rm 2:29
a Jew only if he is a **J** inside; ....Rm 2:29
became like a **J** to win the Jews 1Co 9:20
you are a **J**, but you are not ....Gal 2:14
but you are not living like a **J**. ....Gal 2:14
difference between **J** and Greek, ...Gal 3:28

JEWEL

one **j** for each of the names of ....Ex 28:21
Each **j** had the name of one of ....Ex 39:14
and became like a beautiful **j**..................Eze 16:7
bright like a very expensive **j**,................Rev 21:11
decorated with every kind of **j**. ....Rev 21:19

JEWELRY

gold and silver **j** and clothes. ....Ge 24:53
people, 'Take off your gold **j**,' ....Ex 32:24
sad, and none of them put on **j**. ....Ex 33:4
take off all your **j**, and I will ....Ex 33:5
took off their **j** at Mount Sinai. ....Ex 33:6
brought gold **j** of all kinds— ....Ex 35:22
as gold earrings or fine gold **j**. ....Pr 25:12
woman does not forget her **j**, ...Je 2:32
decorate yourself with gold **j**?................Je 4:30
their beautiful **j** and used it to................Eze 7:20
put **j** on you: bracelets on your ....Eze 16:11
You also took your beautiful **j**, ...Eze 16:17
clothes and take away your **j**, ...Eze 16:39
your clothes and steal your **j**. ....Eze 23:26
their eyes, and put on **j**. ....Eze 23:40
Your **j** was made of gold. ....Eze 28:13
her rings and **j** and went chasing ....Hos 2:13
hair, gold **j**, or fine clothes 1Pe 3:3

JEWELS

thighs are like **j** shaped by an..................Sng 7:1
be like **j** that a bride wears ....Is 49:18
and shining **j** for the gates ....Is 54:12
and precious **j** for all your ....Is 54:12
like a bride dressed in **j**. ....Is 61:10
silver, expensive **j** and gifts. ....Da 11:38
in his land like **j** in a crown. ....Zch 9:16
gold, silver, **j**, wood, grass, ...1Co 3:12
gold, precious **j**, and pearls she ....Rev 17:4
of gold, silver, **j**, pearls, fine ....Rev 18:12
gold, precious **j**, and pearls! ....Rev 18:16

JEWISH

will help and save the **J** people, ...Est 4:14
where the **J** elders, the leading ....Mt 16:21
be rejected by the **J** elders ....Mk 8:31
he sent some **J** elders to him to ....Lk 7:3
be rejected by the **J** elders, ...Lk 9:22
time for the **J** Passover Feast, ...Jn 2:13
given over to the **J** leaders.....................Jn 18:36
a follower of the **J** religion ....Ac 6:5
our law for **J** people to ....Ac 10:28
mother was **J** and a believer, ...Ac 16:1
who was **J**, and asked for ....Ac 24:24
None of our **J** brothers who have ....Ac 28:21
accepting **J** false stories and ....Tit 1:14

JEWS

You and your fellow **J** may spend .... Ezr 7:18
What are these weak **J** doing? .... Ne 4:2
The **J** won't know or see anything .... Ne 4:11
loudly against their fellow **J**. .... Ne 5:1
We are just like our fellow **J**, ... Ne 5:5
for our fellow **J** who had been .... Ne 5:8
selling your fellow **J** to us!" .... Ne 5:8
people, the **J**, in all of Xerxes'................. Est 3:6
had planned against the **J**. .... Est 8:3
of Mordecai's orders to the **J**, ... Est 8:9
through all the empire became **J**, ... Est 8:17
The **J** met in their cities in all .... Est 9:2
His fellow **J** respected him very .... Est 10:3
and many **J** sitting in the .... Je 32:12
of some **J** who have already .... Je 38:19
will not hand you over to the **J**, ... Je 38:20
The **J** in Moab, Ammon, Edom, and .... Je 40:11
had left a few **J** alive in the.................... Je 40:11
Then all the **J** gathered around .... Je 40:15
killed all the **J** and the .... Je 41:3
this while the **J** are watching .... Je 43:9
for all the **J** living in Egypt— .... Je 44:1
all you **J** living in Egypt. .... Je 44:26
The **J** who live in Egypt will die .... Je 44:27
in the seventh year, 3,023 **J**; .... Je 52:28
guards, took 745 **J** as captives. .... Je 52:30
born to be the king of the **J**? .... Mt 2:2
"Are you the king of the **J**?" .... Mt 27:11
saying, "Hail, King of the **J**!" .... Mt 27:29
IS JESUS, THE KING OF THE **J**. .... Mt 27:37
and all the **J** never eat before .... Mk 7:3
"Are you the king of the **J**?" .... Mk 15:2
me to free the king of the **J**?" .... Mk 15:9
man you call the king of the **J**?"........... Mk 15:12
to him, "Hail, King of the **J**!" .... Mk 15:18
on it: THE KING OF THE **J**. .... Mk 15:26
"Are you the king of the **J**?" .... Lk 23:3
If you are the king of the **J**,.................. Lk 23:37
THIS IS THE KING OF THE **J**. .... Lk 23:38
jars that the **J** used in their .... Jn 2:6
salvation comes from the **J**. .... Jn 4:22
So the **J** said to the man who had .... Jn 5:10
So the **J** asked, "Will he kill .... Jn 8:22
Jesus said to the **J** who believed .... Jn 8:31
Many of the **J** had come there to .... Jn 11:19
The **J** were with Mary in the .... Jn 11:31
crying and the **J** who came with............. Jn 11:33
So the **J** said, "See how much he .... Jn 11:36
many of the **J** were leaving them .... Jn 12:11
I told the **J**, I tell you now .... Jn 13:33
who told the **J** that it would be .... Jn 18:14
where all the **J** come together. .... Jn 18:20
to death," the **J** answered. .... Jn 18:31
"Are you the king of the **J**?" .... Jn 18:33
me to free the 'king of the **J**'?" .... Jn 18:39
and said, "Hail, King of the **J**!" .... Jn 19:3
OF NAZARETH, THE KING OF THE **J**....... Jn 19:19
write, 'The King of the **J**.' .... Jn 19:21
"I am the King of the **J**.'" ".................. Jn 19:21
were some religious **J** staying in.............. Ac 2:5
J and those who had become Jews........... Ac 2:11
Jews and those who had become **J**........... Ac 2:11
My fellow **J**, and all of you who .... Ac 2:14
and some **J** and non-Jews all came .... Ac 4:27
about me to those who are not **J**, ... Ac 9:15
the **J** in Jerusalem killed him .... Ac 10:39
to others, but only to **J**. .... Ac 11:19
that a great many **J** and Greeks .... Ac 14:1
of the people agreed with the **J**, ... Ac 14:4
Some who were not **J**, some Jews, ... Ac 14:5
not Jews, some **J**, and some of .... Ac 14:5
These men are **J** and are making .... Ac 16:20

with his fellow **J** about the .... Ac 17:2
talked with the **J** and the Greeks .... Ac 17:17
that all **J** must leave Rome...................... Ac 18:2
he talked with the **J** and Greeks .... Ac 18:4
strongly with the **J** before all .... Ac 18:28
people in Ephesus—**J** and Greeks— .... Ac 19:17
I warned both **J** and Greeks to .... Ac 20:21
and all the **J** who lived there .... Ac 22:12
to learn why the **J** were accusing .... Ac 22:30
The **J** have decided to ask you to .... Ac 23:20
Some of the **J** had taken this man .... Ac 23:27
Paul in prison to please the **J**................... Ac 24:27
This is why the **J** took me and .... Ac 26:21
more of the **J** met with Paul at .... Ac 28:23
Paul said this, the **J** left. .... Ac 28:29
to save the **J** first, and then to................ Rm 1:16
to the **J** first and also to those .... Rm 2:9
and also to those who are not **J**. .... Rm 2:9
to the **J** first and also to those .... Rm 2:10
and also to those who are not **J**. .... Rm 2:10
Those who are not **J** do not have .... Rm 2:14
who are not **J** speak against .... Rm 2:24
People who are not **J** are not .... Rm 2:26
You **J** have the written law and .... Rm 2:27
do **J** have anything that other.................. Rm 3:1
the **J** with his teachings. .... Rm 3:2
If some **J** were not faithful to .... Rm 3:3
So are we **J** better than others? .... Rm 3:9
said that **J** and those who are .... Rm 3:9
who are not **J** are all guilty. .... Rm 3:9
Is God only the God of the **J**? .... Rm 3:29
the God of those who are not **J**? .... Rm 3:29
He will make **J** right with him by .... Rm 3:30
who are not **J** right with him .... Rm 3:30
us not from the **J** only but also .... Rm 9:24
also from those who are not **J**. .... Rm 9:24
who are not **J** were not trying................. Rm 9:30
is for all the **J** to be saved. .... Rm 10:1
those who are **J** and those who .... Rm 10:12
But not all the **J** accepted the .... Rm 10:16
When the **J** fell, did that fall .... Rm 11:11
to those who are not **J**, ... Rm 11:11
in order to make the **J** jealous. .... Rm 11:11
The **J**' failure brought rich .... Rm 11:12
and the **J**' loss brought rich .... Rm 11:12
when enough **J** become the kind .... Rm 11:12
speaking to you who are not **J**, ... Rm 11:13
apostle to those who are not **J**, ... Rm 11:13
When God turned away from the **J**, ... Rm 11:15
So when God accepts the **J**, ... Rm 11:15
life of the first tree, the **J**. .... Rm 11:17
And if the **J** will believe in God .... Rm 11:23
you who are not **J** are like a .... Rm 11:24
But since those **J** are like a .... Rm 11:24
who are not **J** have come to God. .... Rm 11:25
The **J** refuse to accept the Good .... Rm 11:28
to help you who are not **J**. .... Rm 11:28
But the **J** are still God's chosen .... Rm 11:28
And now the **J** refuse to obey, ... Rm 11:31
a servant of the **J** to show that .... Rm 15:8
who are not **J** could give glory .... Rm 15:9
you who are not **J**, together with .... Rm 15:10
you who are not **J**, praise the .... Rm 15:11
Jesus to those who are not **J**. .... Rm 15:16
those who are not **J** to obey God. .... Rm 15:18
These who are not **J** have shared .... Rm 15:27
have shared in the **J**' spiritual................ Rm 15:27
possessions to help the **J**. .... Rm 15:27
The **J** ask for miracles, and the 1Co 1:22
This causes the **J** to stumble and 1Co 1:23
God has called—**J** and Greeks. 1Co 1:24
To the **J** I became like a Jew to 1Co 9:20
became like a Jew to win the **J**. 1Co 9:20

J

hurt others—J, Greeks, or God's 1Co 10:32
Some of us are J, and some are 1Co 12:13
Five times the J have given me 2Co 11:24
own people, the J, and those who 2Co 11:26
Jews, and those who are not J. 2Co 11:26
than most other J of my age. .... Gal 1:14
had the work of telling the J. .... Gal 2:7
apostle for those who are not J. .... Gal 2:8
them. He was afraid of the J. .... Gal 2:12
are not Jewish to live like J?" .... Gal 2:14
non-Jewish "sinners," but as J. .... Gal 2:15
J came to Christ, trying to be .... Gal 2:17
Christ to those who are not J. .... Gal 3:14
so the J will accept them. .... Gal 6:12
are the people the J call .... Eph 2:11
those who are not J one people. .... Eph 2:14
together with the J into a place .... Eph 2:22
Jesus for you who are not J. .... Eph 3:1
who are not J will share with .... Eph 3:6
share with the J in God's .... Eph 3:6
those who are not J the Good .... Eph 3:8
difference between Greeks and J, ... Col 3:11
as they suffered from the J 1Th 2:14
who are not J so they may be 1Th 2:16
who are not J to believe and to 1Ti 2:7
News to all those who are not J. 2Ti 4:17
say they are J, but they are not .... Rev 2:9
Jews, but they are not true J. .... Rev 2:9
belongs to Satan say they are J, ... Rev 3:9
Jews, but they are not true J; .... Rev 3:9

JEZANIAH
of Kareah and J son of Hoshaiah .... Je 42:1

JEZEBEL
married J daughter of Ethbaal, ... 1Ki 16:31
J was killing all the LORD's 1Ki 18:4
King Ahab told J every thing 1Ki 19:1
J heard that Naboth had been 1Ki 21:15
eat the body of J in the city 1Ki 21:23
let that woman J spread false .... Rev 2:20

JEZER
Jahziel, Guni, J, and Shillem. .... Ge 46:24
from J came the Jezerite family .... Nu 26:49
Jahziel, Guni, J, and Shillem. 1Ch 7:13

JEZERITE
Jezer came the J family group; .... Nu 26:49

JEZIEL
There were also J and Pelet, ... 1Ch 12:3

JEZRAHIAH
The choruses sang, led by J. .... Ne 12:42

JEZREEL
are also in the Valley of J." .... Jos 17:16
Naboth owned a vineyard in J, ... 1Ki 21:1
of Jezebel in the city of J.' 1Ki 21:23
Jehu came to J, Jezebel heard 2Ki 9:30
Name him J, because soon I .... Hos 1:4
army in the Valley of J." .... Hos 1:5
the day of J will be truly .... Hos 1:11
because my people are called J. .... Hos 2:22

JEZREELITE
at the property of Naboth the J. 2Ki 9:21
into the field of Naboth the J. 2Ki 9:25

JIDLAPH
Hazo, Pildash, J, and Bethuel." .... Ge 22:22

JOAB
Abner said to J, "Let the young 2Sa 2:14
three sons, J, Abishai, and 2Sa 2:18
Just then J and David's men came 2Sa 3:22
J and his family are responsible 2Sa 3:29
So David sent a message to J: 2Sa 11:6

wrote a letter to J and sent it 2Sa 11:14
So J sent messengers to Tekoa to 2Sa 14:2
Did J tell you to say all these 2Sa 14:19
sent for J so he could send 2Sa 14:29
Then J blew the trumpet, so the 2Sa 18:16
As J stepped forward, his sword 2Sa 20:8
J asked Amasa, "Brother, is 2Sa 20:9
Listen! Tell J to come here. I 2Sa 20:16
So J came near her. She asked 2Sa 20:17
Asahel brother of J; Elhanan son 2Sa 23:24
When J heard about what had 1Ki 2:28
will be free of the guilt of J, ... 1Ki 2:31
brother of J was the captain 1Ch 11:20

JOAB'S
Look, J field is next to 2Sa 14:30

JOAHAZ
and Joah son of J the recorder 2Ch 34:8

JOANAN
Joda was the son of J. .... Lk 3:27
J was the son of Rhesa. .... Lk 3:27

JOANNA
J, the wife of Cuza (the manager .... Lk 8:3
Mary Magdalene, J, Mary the .... Lk 24:10

JOASH
the sword of Gideon son of J, ... Jdg 7:14
Gideon son of J went to his home .... Jdg 8:29
Everything else J did is written 2Ki 12:19
Amaziah son of J became king of 2Ki 14:1
Amaziah son of J, the king of 2Ki 14:17
J was seven years old when he 2Ch 24:1
J did what the LORD said was 2Ch 24:2

JOB
A man named J lived in the land .... Job 1:1
J would send and have them made .... Job 1:5
in the morning J would offer a .... Job 1:5
Have you noticed my servant J? .... Job 1:8
J honors God for a good reason. .... Job 1:9
When J heard this, he got up and .... Job 1:20
In all this J did not sin or .... Job 1:22
J took a piece of broken pottery .... Job 2:8
After seven days J cried out and .... Job 3:1
The words of J are finished. .... Job 31:40
men stopped trying to answer J, ... Job 32:1
one of you has proved J wrong; .... Job 32:12
There is no other man like J; .... Job 34:7
'J speaks without knowing what .... Job 34:35
I wish J would be tested .... Job 34:36
J, listen to this: Stop and .... Job 37:14
Then J answered the LORD: .... Job 40:3
LORD had said these things to J, ... Job 42:7
go to my servant J, and offer a .... Job 42:8
After J had prayed for his .... Job 42:10
their father J gave them land .... Job 42:15
Then J died; he was old and had .... Job 42:17
and J were in that country, ... Eze 14:14
Daniel, and J were in the land .... Eze 14:20
is your J? Where do you come .... Jnh 1:8
answered, 'No one gave us a j.' .... Mt 20:7
each one a special j to do. .... Mk 13:34
enough money to finish the j. .... Lk 14:28
So he got a j with one of the .... Lk 15:15
is taking my j away from me? .... Lk 16:3
when I lose my j people will .... Lk 16:4
of Thyatira whose j was selling .... Ac 16:14
workman doing any j will ever be .... Rev 18:22

JOB'S
friends heard about J troubles, ... Job 2:11
the LORD listened to J prayer. .... Job 42:9
J brothers and sisters came to .... Job 42:11

JOCHEBED
married his father's sister J, ... Ex 6:20
whose wife was named J. .... Nu 26:59

JODA
Josech was the son of J. .... Lk 3:26
J was the son of Joanan. .... Lk 3:27

JOED
Meshullam was the son of J, ... Ne 11:7

JOELAH
And there were J and Zebadiah, ... 1Ch 12:7

JOEZER
Isshiah, Azarel, J, and 1Ch 12:6

JOGBEHAH
Atroth Shophan, Jazer, J, ... Nu 32:35
in tents east of Nobah and J, ... Jdg 8:11

JOGLI
tribe of Dan, Bukki son of J; .... Nu 34:22

JOHA
Michael, Ishpah, and J. 1Ch 8:16
J, Jediael's brother, the Tizite; 1Ch 11:45

JOHANAN
J son of Kareah and all the army .... Je 40:13

JOHN
About that time J the Baptist .... Mt 3:1
and wanted J to baptize him. .... Mt 3:13
brothers, James and J, the sons .... Mt 4:21
the followers of J came to Jesus .... Mt 9:14
J the Baptist is greater than .... Mt 11:11
Since the time J the Baptist .... Mt 11:12
happen until the time J came. .... Mt 11:13
J came and did not eat or drink .... Mt 11:18
had arrested J, tied him up, ... Mt 14:3
the head of J the Baptist here .... Mt 14:8
Some say you are J the Baptist. .... Mt 16:14
When J baptized people, did that .... Mt 21:25
was baptized by J in the Jordan .... Mk 1:9
brothers, James and J, the sons .... Mk 1:19
James and J, the sons of Zebedee .... Mk 3:17
said, "He is J the Baptist, who .... Mk 6:14
want the head of J the Baptist .... Mk 6:25
and J up on a high mountain by .... Mk 9:2
a son, and you will name him J. .... Lk 1:13
talking to the people about J: .... Lk 7:24
were preached until J came. .... Lk 16:16
they believe J was a prophet." .... Lk 20:6
Jesus said to Peter and J, ... Lk 22:8
was a man named J who was sent .... Jn 1:6
J tells the truth about him and .... Jn 1:15
Here is the truth J told when .... Jn 1:19
This was before J was put into .... Jn 3:24
baptizing more followers than J, ... Jn 4:1
You have sent people to J, ... Jn 5:33
to him and said, "J never did a .... Jn 10:41
J baptized people with water, ... Ac 1:5
Peter, J, James, Andrew, Philip, ... Ac 1:13
was holding on to Peter and J, ... Ac 3:11
of Mary, the mother of J Mark. .... Ac 12:12
taking J Mark with them. .... Ac 12:25
wanted to take J Mark with them, ... Ac 15:37
was the baptism that J taught. .... Ac 18:25
Peter, and J, who seemed to be .... Gal 2:9
to show it to his servant J, ... Rev 1:1

JOHN'S
Some of J followers had an .... Jn 3:25
J baptism was a baptism of .... Ac 19:4

JOIADA
J son of Paseah and Meshullam .... Ne 3:6
Eliashib was the father of J. .... Ne 12:10
J was the father of Jonathan, ... Ne 12:11

days of Eliashib, J, Johanan, ... Ne 12:22
J was the son of Eliashib the .... Ne 13:28

JOIADA'S
One of J sons married a daughter .... Ne 13:28

JOIAKIM
Jeshua was the father of J. .... Ne 12:10
J was the father of Eliashib. .... Ne 12:10
In the days of J, these priests .... Ne 12:12
in the days of J son of Jeshua, ... Ne 12:26

JOIARIB
And I called J and Elnathan, ... Ezr 8:16
the son of Adaiah, the son of J. .... Ne 11:5
J was the son of Zechariah, ... Ne 11:5
There was Jedaiah son of J, ... Ne 11:10
Shemaiah, J, Jedaiah, ... Ne 12:6

JOIARIB'S
Mattenai, from J family; .... Ne 12:19

JOIN
they might j our enemies and .... Ex 1:10
Foreigners will j the LORD to .... Is 56:6
Then j them together into one .... Eze 37:17
of the others dared to j them, ... Ac 5:13
he tried to j the group of .... Ac 9:26

JOINED
must all be j together in one .... Ex 25:31
the bottom and j at the top with .... Ex 26:24
Holy Tent was j together as one .... Ex 36:13
the bottom and j at the top with .... Ex 36:29
petals were j together in one .... Ex 37:17
like a horn was j into one piece .... Ex 37:25
the altar were j together in one .... Ex 38:2
it was j to the holy vest as one .... Ex 39:5
followers have j together. .... Nu 16:11
Mount Hor and j his ancestors. .... Dt 32:50
mountains have j their armies .... Jos 10:6
j their armies together into one .... Jos 11:5
the east j together and came .... Jdg 6:33
j together before the LORD in .... Jdg 20:1
but now they j the Israelites 1Sa 14:21
also j the battle and chased 1Sa 14:22
He ran away and j David. 1Sa 22:20
His servants j the woman in 1Sa 28:23
You j me only a short time ago. 2Sa 15:20
where they were j by other men. 1Ki 11:18
the people of Gad j David at his 1Ch 12:8
Manasseh also j David when he 1Ch 12:19
from Manasseh who j David when 1Ch 12:20
Every day more men j David, ... 1Ch 12:22
battle who j David at Hebron. 1Ch 12:23
from all over Israel j Rehoboam. 2Ch 11:13
evil men j Jeroboam against 2Ch 13:7
because you j with Ahaziah, ... 2Ch 20:37
fellow priests j Zerubbabel son .... Ezr 3:2
They j their fellow Israelites .... Ne 10:29
They are j strongly to one .... Job 41:17
folds of its skin are tightly j; .... Job 41:23
Kings j together and came to .... Ps 48:4
Even Assyria has j them to help .... Ps 83:8
j in worshiping Baal at Peor .... Ps 106:28
and Israel have j together." .... Is 7:2
who have j the LORD should not .... Is 56:3
leaders had all j together to .... Je 5:5
They j those who were killed in .... Eze 31:17
God has j the two together, ... Mt 19:6
God has j the two together, ... Mk 10:9
from heaven j the first angel, ... Lk 2:13
about four hundred men j him. .... Ac 5:36
the followers from Joppa j him. .... Ac 10:23
The crowd j the attack against .... Ac 16:22
convinced and j Paul and Silas, ... Ac 17:4
people believed Paul and j him. .... Ac 17:34

Macedonia and j Paul in Corinth. .... Ac 18:5
and we have been j with him by .... Rm 6:5
we will also be j with him by .... Rm 6:5
that has been j to that first .... Rm 11:17
I could be j to their tree." .... Rm 11:19
olive tree and j to a good olive .... Rm 11:24
they can be j to their own tree .... Rm 11:24
Then you will all be j together, ... Rm 15:6
you be completely j together by 1Co 1:10
Jewish believers who j with him. .... Gal 2:13
on earth would be j together in .... Eph 1:10
whole building is j together in .... Eph 2:21
You are j together with peace .... Eph 4:3
until we are all j together in .... Eph 4:13
of the body are j and held .... Eph 4:16
strengthened and j together with .... Col 2:2
the soul and the spirit are j, ... Heb 4:12

JOINS
himself j with our spirits .... Rm 8:16
that anyone who j with a 1Co 6:16
But the one who j with the Lord 1Co 6:17

JOINT
Jacob's hip and put it out of j. .... Ge 32:25
that is on the hip j of animals, ... Ge 32:32
shoulder and be broken at the j. .... Job 31:22
and my bones are out of j. .... Ps 22:14

JOINTS
legs with j above their feet .... Le 11:21
the center of our j and bones. .... Heb 4:12

JOKDEAM
Jezreel, J, Zanoah, ... Jos 15:56

JOKE
my name is a j among them. .... Job 30:9
made us a j to our neighbors; .... Ps 44:13
You made us a j to the other .... Ps 44:14
of sadness, they j about me. .... Ps 69:11
We are a j to the other nations; .... Ps 79:4
have become a j; everyone makes .... Je 20:7
I was a j to all my people, ... La 3:14

JOKES
them and tell j about them and .... Je 24:9
speak foolishly or tell evil j. .... Eph 5:4

JOKING
But they thought Lot was j. .... Ge 19:14
and then says, "I was just j." .... Pr 26:19

JOKMEAM
to Abel Meholah across from J. 1Ki 4:12
J, Beth Horon, ... 1Ch 6:68

JOKNEAM
Kedesh, J in Carmel, ... Jos 12:22
near Dabbesheth and then near J. .... Jos 19:11
tribe of Zebulun gave them J, ... Jos 21:34
the towns and pastures of J, ... 1Ch 6:77

JOKSHAN
to Zimran, J, Medan, Midian, ... Ge 25:2
J was the father of Sheba and .... Ge 25:3
to Zimran, J, Medan, Midian, ... 1Ch 1:32

JOKTAN
and the other was named J. .... Ge 10:25
J was the father of Almodad, ... Ge 10:26
these people were the sons of J. .... Ge 10:29
Peleg's brother was named J. 1Ch 1:19
J was the father of Almodad, ... 1Ch 1:20

JOKTHEEL
Dilean, Mizpah, J, ... Jos 15:38
He called it J, as it is still 2Ki 14:7

JONADAB
a friend named J son of Shimeah, ... 2Sa 13:3
Our ancestor J son of Recab gave .... Je 35:6
our ancestor J commanded us. .... Je 35:10

JONAH
his servant J son of Amittai, ... 2Ki 14:25
his word to J son of Amittai: .... Jnh 1:1
J got up to run away from the .... Jnh 1:3
had happened because of J. .... Jnh 1:7
caused a big fish to swallow J, ... Jnh 1:17
and J was inside the fish three .... Jnh 1:17
While J was inside the fish, ... Jnh 2:1
fish threw up J onto the dry .... Jnh 2:10
his word to J again and said, ... Jnh 3:1
So J obeyed the LORD and got up .... Jnh 3:3
But this made J very unhappy, ... Jnh 4:1
J went out and sat down east of .... Jnh 4:5
the sign of the prophet J. .... Mt 12:39
J was in the stomach of the big .... Mt 12:40
When J preached to them, they .... Mt 12:41
As J was a sign for those people .... Lk 11:30
When J preached to them, they .... Lk 11:32
someone greater than J is here. .... Lk 11:32

JONAM
Joseph was the son of J. .... Lk 3:30
J was the son of Eliakim. .... Lk 3:30

JONATHAN
with Saul and J had no swords 1Sa 13:22
shouted to J and his officer.................... 1Sa 14:12
is I or J my son who is guilty. 1Sa 14:42
J felt very close to David. 1Sa 18:1
J made an agreement with David, ... 1Sa 18:3
J talked to Saul his father, ... 1Sa 19:4
So J made an agreement with 1Sa 20:16
Then J gave his weapons to the 1Sa 20:40
killing his sons J, Abinadab, ... 1Sa 31:2
Saul and his son J are dead?".................. 2Sa 1:5
song about Saul and his son J, ... 2Sa 1:17
I cry for you, my brother J. 2Sa 1:26
J has a son still living who is 2Sa 9:3
bones of Saul and J from the men 2Sa 21:12
and Saul was the father of J, ... 1Ch 8:33

JONATHAN'S
who carried J armor said to him 1Sa 14:7
to the place where J arrow fell, ... 1Sa 20:37
J bow did not fail to kill many 2Sa 1:22
to that person for J sake!" 2Sa 9:1
servants bring J son from the 2Sa 9:5
Mephibosheth, J son, came before 2Sa 9:6
to you for your father J sake. 2Sa 9:7
J sons were Peleth and Zaza. 1Ch 2:33
J son was Merib-Baal, who was 1Ch 8:34
J son was Merib-Baal, who was 1Ch 9:40
send me back to J house to die.' .... Je 38:26

JOPPA
bring it on rafts by sea to J. 2Ch 2:16
to the seacoast town of J. .... Ezr 3:7
to the city of J, where he found .... Jnh 1:3
is near J and the followers .... Ac 9:38
Peter stayed in J for many days .... Ac 9:43
the city of J, and while I was .... Ac 11:5
some men to J and invite Simon.............. Ac 11:13

JORAH
the descendants of J—112; .... Ezr 2:18

JORAI
Meshullam, Sheba, J, Jacan, Zia, ... 1Ch 5:13

JORAM
the fifth year J son of Ahab was 2Ki 8:16
twelfth year J son of Ahab was 2Ki 8:25
J said, "Get my chariot ready." 2Ki 9:21

J

JOSHAPHAT

During **J** life Ephraim had .... Ge 50:23
But **J** family received the 1Ch 5:2
They asked, "Isn't this **J** son?" .... Lk 4:22
the king learned about **J** family. .... Ac 7:13
blessed each one of **J** sons. .... Heb 11:21

JOSHAPHAT

son of Maacah; **J** the Mithnite; 1Ch 11:43
Shebaniah, **J**, Nethanel, Amasai 1Ch 15:24

JOSHAVIAH

Jeribai and **J**, Elnaam's sons; 1Ch 11:46

JOSHBEKASHAH

Romamti-Ezer, **J**, Mallothi, ... 1Ch 25:4
twelve men were chosen from **J**,............... 1Ch 25:24

JOSHEB-BASSHEBETH

J, the Tahkemonite, was head of............... 2Sa 23:8

JOSHUA

J obeyed Moses and went to fight .... Ex 17:10
So **J** defeated the Amalekites in .... Ex 17:13
Moses and his helper **J** set out, ... Ex 24:13
young helper, **J** son of Nun, did .... Ex 33:11
J son of Nun said, "Moses, my .... Nu 11:28
son of Nun the new name **J**. .... Nu 13:16
this command to **J** son of Nun: .... Dt 31:23
So **J** chose one man from each .... Jos 4:4
J also put twelve rocks in the .... Jos 4:9
and **J** set them up at Gilgal. .... Jos 4:20
So **J** made knives from flint .... Jos 5:3
so **J** circumcised them. .... Jos 5:7
are standing is holy." So **J** did. .... Jos 5:15
J saved Rahab the prostitute, ... Jos 6:25
Then **J** tore his clothes in .... Jos 7:6
Then **J** said to Achan, "My son, ... Jos 7:19
Then **J** burned the city of Ai and .... Jos 8:28
J built an altar for the LORD, ... Jos 8:30
Gibeon heard how **J** had defeated .... Jos 9:3
So **J** agreed to make peace with .... Jos 9:15
this message to **J** in his camp at .... Jos 10:6
the cave at Makkedah and told **J**. .... Jos 10:17
brought the five kings out to **J**, ... Jos 10:24
At sunset **J** told his men to take .... Jos 10:27
So **J** defeated all the kings of .... Jos 10:40
only that city was burned by **J**. .... Jos 11:13
J also captured all the kings in .... Jos 11:17
Now **J** fought the Anakites who .... Jos 11:21
J and the Israelites also .... Jos 12:7
When **J** was very old, the LORD............... Jos 13:1
J blessed Caleb son of Jephunneh .... Jos 14:13
There **J** threw lots in the......................... Jos 18:10
passed, and **J** grew very old. .... Jos 23:1
day at Shechem **J** made an .... Jos 24:25
J wrote these things in the Book .... Jos 24:26
the lifetime of **J** and during .... Jos 24:31
After **J** died, the Israelites .... Jdg 1:1
who were left when **J** died...................... Jdg 2:21
and to **J** son of Jehozadak, ... Hag 1:1
he showed me **J**, the high priest .... Zch 3:1
J was wearing dirty clothes and .... Zch 3:3
Listen, **J** the high priest,....................... Zch 3:8
Er was the son of **J**. Joshua was .... Lk 3:29
J led our ancestors to capture................. Ac 7:45
We know that **J** did not lead the .... Heb 4:8

JOSIAH

family will have a son named **J**. 1Ki 13:2
J was eight years old when he 2Ki 22:1
was the royal secretary. **J** said, ... 2Ki 22:3
Everything else **J** did is written 2Ki 23:28
king in place of **J** his father. 2Ki 23:34
was Amon, and Amon's son was **J**. 1Ch 3:14
J was eight years old when he 2Ch 34:1
J gave the Israelites thirty 2Ch 35:7
In the battle King **J** was shot by 2Ch 35:23

wrote some sad songs about **J**. 2Ch 35:25
and honor **J** with these songs. 2Ch 35:25
year that **J** son of Amon was king .... Je 1:2
When King **J** was ruling Judah, ... Je 3:6
Jehoahaz son of **J** who became .... Je 22:11
son of **J** king of Judah: .... Je 22:18
Zedekiah son of **J** to be king of .... Je 37:1
Zephaniah while **J** son of Amon............... Zph 1:1
Amon was the father of **J**. .... Mt 1:10
J was the grandfather of .... Mt 1:11

JOSIPHIAH

Shelomith son of **J**, with one .... Ezr 8:10

JOTBAH

of Haruz, who was from **J**. 2Ki 21:19

JOTBATHAH

Hor Haggidgad and camped at **J**. .... Nu 33:33
They left **J** and camped at .... Nu 33:34
from Gudgodah they went to **J**, ... Dt 10:7

JOTHAM

youngest son, **J**, hid from .... Jdg 9:5
Then **J** ran away and escaped to............... Jdg 9:21
curse spoken by **J**, the youngest .... Jdg 9:57
other things **J** did while he was 2Ki 15:36
J died and was buried with his 2Ki 15:38
was the son of **J** king of Judah. 2Ki 16:1
while Uzziah, **J**, Ahaz, and .... Is 1:1
Now Ahaz was the son of **J**, ... Is 7:1
time that Uzziah, **J**, Ahaz, and .... Hos 1:1
the time that **J**, Ahaz, and .... Mic 1:1
Uzziah was the father of **J**. .... Mt 1:9

JOURNEY

Then you may continue your **j**." .... Ge 18:5
you may continue your **j**." .... Ge 19:2
me and to protect me on this **j**. .... Ge 28:20
Jacob continued his **j** and came .... Ge 29:1
three days' **j** away from Jacob .... Ge 30:36
began their **j** back to Isaac,..................... Ge 31:18
continued his **j** and camped just .... Ge 35:21
a three-day **j** into the desert .... Ex 8:27
food for your **j** and go and meet .... Jos 9:11
are worn out from the long **j**." .... Jos 9:13
God if our **j** will be successful. .... Jdg 18:5
LORD is pleased with your **j**." .... Jdg 18:6
about the **j** we have taken."..................... 1Sa 9:6
he will tell us about our **j**. 1Sa 9:8
is too long a **j** for you to go to................. 1Ki 12:28
the **j** will be too hard for you." 1Ki 19:7
I go on the **j** of no return. .... Job 16:22
Apollos on their **j** so that they .... Tit 3:13

JOY

sent you away with **j** and singing .... Ge 31:27
They sang songs of **j**, danced,................... 1Sa 18:6
flutes and shouting for **j**,....................... 1Ki 1:40
because the **j** of the LORD will .... Ne 8:10
there was **j** and gladness among............... Est 8:17
and the **j** of the wicked lasts .... Job 20:5
all the angels shouted with **j**? .... Job 38:7
with you will fill me with **j**; .... Ps 16:11
but **j** comes in the morning. .... Ps 30:5
God who is my **j** and happiness................. Ps 43:4
and brings **j** to the whole world .... Ps 48:2
hear sounds of **j** and gladness; .... Ps 51:8
Give me back the **j** of your .... Ps 51:12
Jerusalem as my greatest **j**...................... Ps 137:6
strangers cannot share your **j**. .... Pr 14:10
is no **j** in being the parent .... Pr 17:21
them wisdom, knowledge, and **j**. .... Ec 2:26
salvation with **j** as you would .... Is 12:3
but **j** will have turned to .... Is 24:11
will enter Jerusalem with **j**,................... Is 35:10
and enter Jerusalem with **j**..................... Is 51:11

They are all shouting for J! .... Is 52:8
will go out with j and be led .... Is 55:12
will be excited and full of j, ... Is 60:5
them comfort and j instead of................ Je 31:13
J and happiness are gone from .... Je 48:33
Damascus was a city of my j. .... Je 49:25
We have no more j in our hearts; .... La 5:15
themselves with j and with hate .... Eze 36:5
J and happiness are gone from .... Joe 1:16
for j, people of Jerusalem! .... Zch 9:9
star, they were filled with j. .... Mt 2:10
and quickly accepts it with j. .... Mt 13:20
Come and share my j with me.' .... Mt 25:21
will bring you j and gladness,.................. Lk 1:14
baby inside me jumped with j. .... Lk 1:44
be a great j to all the people. .... Lk 2:10
Be full of j at that time, ... Lk 6:23
there is more j in heaven over .... Lk 15:7
there is j in the presence of..................... Lk 15:10
can have the same j I have and .... Jn 15:11
but your sadness will become j. .... Jn 16:20
no one will take away your j. .... Jn 16:22
so that your j will be the......................... Jn 16:24
can have all of my j in them. .... Jn 17:13
with you will fill me with j.' .... Ac 2:28
on his way home, full of j. .... Ac 8:39
were filled with j and the Holy .... Ac 13:52
and filling your hearts with j." .... Ac 14:17
also have j with our troubles, ... Rm 5:3
to others should do so with j. .... Rm 12:8
peace, and j in the Holy Spirit. .... Rm 14:17
you with much j and peace while .... Rm 15:13
I will come to you with j, ... Rm 15:32
workers with you for your own j. 2Co 1:24
you, that you would share my j. 2Co 2:3
of our troubles I have great j. 2Co 7:4
much because of their great j,................. 2Co 8:2
then, but where is that j now?................. Gal 4:15
Start singing and shout for j. .... Gal 4:27
fruit of love, j, peace, ... Gal 5:22
praying with j for all of you. .... Php 1:4
grow and have j in your faith.................. Php 1:25
You bring me j and make me proud .... Php 4:1
teaching with the j that comes 1Th 1:6
our hope, our j, and the crown 1Th 2:19
you are our glory and our j. 1Th 2:20
because of the j that God put .... Heb 12:2
you should be full of j, ... Jam 1:2
filled with a j that cannot be 1Pe 1:8
and full of j when Christ comes 1Pe 4:13
to you so we may be full of j. 1Jn 1:4
gives me greater j than to hear 3Jn 1:4
in you and can give you great j. .... Jud 1:24

JOYFUL
between the j shouting and the .... Ezr 3:13
Bread in a very j way. .... Ezr 6:22
and made it a day of j feasting. .... Est 9:17
and made it a day of j feasting. .... Est 9:18
It is a day of j feasting and a .... Est 9:19
days as days of j feasting and.................. Est 9:22
I will offer j sacrifices in his .... Ps 27:6
The j music from the harps will .... Is 24:8
the Sabbath a j day and honor it .... Is 58:13
and dance with those who are j............... Je 31:4
be j in the LORD your God. .... Joe 2:23
will sing and be j about you." .... Zph 3:17
become glad, happy feasts .... Zch 8:19
share their food with j hearts.................. Ac 2:46
Be j because you have hope. .... Rm 12:12
Always be j.. 1Th 5:16

JOYFULLY
song to him; play well and j. .... Ps 33:3
followers began j shouting .... Lk 19:37
you will j give thanks to the .... Col 1:12

JOYS
because these j will help them .... Ec 8:15

JOZADAK
Jeshua son of J and his fellow .... Ezr 3:2
Jeshua son of J, their fellow .... Ezr 3:8
Jeshua son of J started working............... Ezr 5:2
of Jeshua son of J and Jeshua's .... Ezr 10:18
son of Jeshua, the son of J...................... Ne 12:26

JUBAL
brother was J, the first person .... Ge 4:21

JUBILEE
This time will be called J. .... Le 25:10
keep it until the year of J. .... Le 25:28
with you until the year of J. .... Le 25:40
gives a field at the year of J, ... Le 27:17

JUDAH
then Simeon, Levi, J, Issachar, ... Ge 35:23
Then J said to his brothers, ... Ge 37:26
J chose a girl named Tamar to be .... Ge 38:6
Then J said to his .... Ge 38:11
J is like a young lion. .... Ge 49:9
someone from J will always be on .... Ge 49:10
Reuben, Simeon, Levi, J,....................... Ex 1:2
son of Uri from the tribe of J.................. Ex 31:2
The tribe of J totaled 74,600 .... Nu 1:27
all the land of J as far as the .... Dt 34:2
Debir, Anab, J, and Israel, and .... Jos 11:21
the west, and J, at the Jordan .... Jos 19:34
pastures in the mountains of J. .... Jos 21:11
them, "The tribe of J will go. .... Jdg 1:2
with the men of J to the Desert .... Jdg 1:16
city of Bethlehem in J who was .... Jdg 17:7
answered, "J shall go first. .... Jdg 20:18
town of Bethlehem in J to live .... Ru 1:2
started back to the land of J. .... Ru 1:7
to the kings of J ever since. 1Sa 27:6
up to any of the cities of J?" 2Sa 2:1
Then the men of J came to Hebron 2Sa 2:4
make David king of Israel and J, ... 2Sa 3:10
He was king over J in Hebron for 2Sa 5:5
the men of J to meet King David. 2Sa 19:16
the people of Israel and J." 2Sa 24:1
to southern J, to Beersheba. 2Sa 24:7
many people in J and Israel as 1Ki 4:20
Solomon's life J and Israel,..................... 1Ki 4:25
the tribes of J and Benjamin. 1Ki 12:21
the king of J, and to all 1Ki 12:23
and follow Rehoboam king of J." 1Ki 12:27
people of J did what the LORD 1Ki 14:22
the history of the kings of J. 1Ki 14:29
an order to all the people of J; 1Ki 15:22
they came to Beersheba in J, ... 1Ki 19:3
not destroy J because of his 2Ki 8:19
Israel defeated J, and every man 2Ki 14:12
made it part of J again after 2Ki 14:22
how he won back from J the towns 2Ki 14:28
forced out all the people of J. 2Ki 16:6
Only the tribe of J was left..................... 2Ki 17:18
But even J did not obey the 2Ki 17:19
cities of J and captured them................... 2Ki 18:13
in the family of J will escape. 2Ki 19:30
Jerusalem and J that anyone who 2Ki 21:12
the elders of J and Jerusalem 2Ki 23:1
priests from the cities of J. 2Ki 23:8
burned against J because of all 2Ki 23:26
I will send J out of my sight, ... 2Ki 23:27
against Jehoiakim to destroy J. 2Ki 24:2

J

So the people of **J** were led away 2Ki 25:21
Jehoiachin king of **J** was held in 2Ki 25:27
made the kingdom of **J** strong, ... 2Ch 11:17
There was some good in **J**. 2Ch 12:12
Then the men of **J** gave a battle 2Ch 13:15
idols from all of **J** and Benjamin 2Ch 15:8
of the kings of **J** and Israel. 2Ch 16:11
that everyone in **J** should fast 2Ch 20:3
J and Jerusalem, don't be afraid............. 2Ch 20:17
people of **J** and Jerusalem. 2Ch 20:20
the people of **J** together. 2Ch 25:5
of the kings of **J** and Israel. 2Ch 25:26
western hills and in southern **J**. 2Ch 28:18
trouble us because Ahaz their 2Ch 28:19
of Assyria came and attacked **J**............... 2Ch 32:1
the people of **J** and Jerusalem. 2Ch 32:25
the people of **J** and Jerusalem to 2Ch 33:9
to remove from **J** and Jerusalem 2Ch 34:3
also from all the people of **J**, ... 2Ch 34:9
for him at Jerusalem in **J**. 2Ch 36:23
for him at Jerusalem in **J**. .... Ezr 1:2
Sheshbazzar, the prince of **J**. .... Ezr 1:8
returned to Jerusalem and **J**, ... Ezr 2:1
of the people of **J** and Benjamin .... Ezr 4:1
protect us in **J** and Jerusalem. .... Ezr 9:9
me to the city in **J** where my .... Ne 2:5
the land of **J** in the twentieth .... Ne 5:14
the people of **J** then brought to .... Ne 13:12
speak the language of **J**. .... Ne 13:24
and all the towns of **J** rejoice,................ Ps 48:11
J holds my royal scepter. .... Ps 60:7
and rebuild the cities of **J**. .... Ps 69:35
People in **J** know God; his fame .... Ps 76:1
and the towns of **J** rejoice. .... Ps 97:8
Then **J** became God's holy place; .... Ps 114:2
the men of Hezekiah king of **J**. .... Pr 25:1
would happen to **J** and Jerusalem. .... Is 1:1
message about **J** and Jerusalem: .... Is 2:1
he loves is the people of **J**. .... Is 5:7
since Israel separated from **J**. .... Is 7:17
and **J** will have no more enemies. .... Is 11:13
people will sing this song in **J**: .... Is 26:1
cities of **J** and captured them................. Is 36:1
to the towns of **J**, "Here is your .... Is 40:9
you come from the family of **J**. .... Is 48:1
Josiah was king of **J** and during............. Je 1:3
and all the cities in **J**. .... Je 1:15
People of **J**, you have as many .... Je 2:28
sister **J** saw what she did. .... Je 3:7
this message in **J** and say it in .... Je 4:5
the people of **J** to leave their .... Je 8:3
the cities of **J** so no one can .... Je 9:11
the towns of **J** an empty desert .... Je 10:22
Look, people of **J**, you have as .... Je 11:13
of the people of **J** and the great .... Je 13:9
of southern **J** are locked up, ... Je 13:19
The nation of **J** cries as if .... Je 14:2
rejected the nation of **J**? .... Je 14:19
the people of **J** is written with .... Je 17:1
the people of **J** and Jerusalem. .... Je 19:7
In his time **J** will be saved, ... Je 23:6
king of **J** and all the other .... Je 28:4
and leaders of **J** and Jerusalem; .... Je 29:2
captives from **J** in Babylon will .... Je 29:22
bring Israel and **J** back from .... Je 30:3
such a thing and cause **J** to sin. .... Je 32:35
I will bring **J** and Israel back .... Je 33:7
At that time **J** will be saved, ... Je 33:16
the cities of **J** that had not yet .... Je 34:7
the people in Jerusalem and **J**— .... Je 36:31
of **J** as Zedekiah watched. .... Je 39:6
the poorest people of **J** behind. .... Je 39:10
be governor over the towns of **J**.............. Je 40:5

the towns of **J** and the streets................. Je 44:6
the kings and queens of **J** did? .... Je 44:9
The people of **J** now living in .... Je 44:26
did not leave Israel and **J**, ... Je 51:5
Zedekiah king of **J** in the fourth.............. Je 51:59
J has gone into captivity where .... La 1:3
crushed the capital city of **J**. .... La 1:15
the elders of **J** in front of me. .... Eze 8:1
will put it with the stick of **J**. .... Eze 37:19
to capture Jehoiakim king of **J**. .... Da 1:2
Azariah from the people of **J**. .... Da 1:6
father the king brought from **J**? .... Da 5:13
were kings of **J** and Jeroboam son .... Hos 1:1
show pity to the people of **J**. .... Hos 1:7
the people of **J** will stumble .... Hos 5:5
like a rot to the people of **J**. .... Hos 5:12
illness and **J** saw its wounds, ... Hos 5:13
Israel, like a young lion to **J**. .... Hos 5:14
J, what should I do with you? .... Hos 6:4
And **J** turns against God, the .... Hos 11:12
also has some things against **J**. .... Hos 12:2
better for **J** and Jerusalem, ... Joe 3:1
always be people living in **J**, ... Joe 3:20
was king of **J** and Jeroboam son .... Am 1:1
For the many crimes of **J**, ... Am 2:4
will send fire on **J**, and it will .... Am 2:5
Seer, go back right now to **J**. .... Am 7:12
and Hezekiah were kings of **J**, ... Mic 1:1
will spread to **J**; it will reach .... Mic 1:9
be among the army groups from **J**,.......... Mic 5:2
son of Amon was king of **J**. .... Zph 1:1
descendants of **J** who are left .... Zph 2:7
the governor of **J**, and to Joshua.............. Hag 1:1
the governor of **J**, 'I am going................. Hag 2:21
that scattered the people of **J**,............... Zch 1:19
good, joyful, happy feasts in **J**. .... Zch 8:19
I will use **J** like a bow and .... Zch 9:13
come and attack Jerusalem and **J**. .... Zch 12:2
Then the leaders of **J** will say .... Zch 12:5
Jerusalem and **J** will be holy to .... Zch 14:21
people of **J** have broken their .... Mal 2:11
The people of **J** did not respect .... Mal 2:11
offerings from **J** and Jerusalem, ... Mal 3:4
the father of **J** and his brothers .... Mt 1:2
in the land of **J**, are not just .... Mt 2:6
an insignificant village in **J**. .... Mt 2:6
Lord came from the tribe of **J**, ... Heb 7:14
of Israel and the people of **J**. .... Heb 8:8
The Lion from the tribe of **J**, ... Rev 5:5
the tribe of **J** twelve thousand................. Rev 7:5

JUDAH'S

But Er, **J** oldest son, did what .... Ge 38:7
Say to **J** royal family: .... Je 21:11
People will try to find **J** sins, ... Je 50:20

JUDAS

Simon the Zealot and **J** Iscariot,............... Mt 10:4
still speaking, **J**, one of the .... Mt 26:47
Satan entered **J** Iscariot, one of .... Lk 22:3
J Iscariot, one of Jesus' .... Jn 12:4
already persuaded **J** Iscariot, ... Jn 13:2
why Jesus said this to **J**. .... Jn 13:28
J took the bread Jesus gave him............... Jn 13:30
J (not Judas Iscariot) said, ... Jn 14:22
and **J** son of James were there. .... Ac 1:13
a man named **J** came from Galilee .... Ac 5:37
chose **J** Barsabbas and Silas, ... Ac 15:22

JUDE

J, a servant of Jesus Christ .... Jud 1:1

JUDEA

Bethlehem in **J** during the time .... Mt 2:1
in the desert area of **J**. .... Mt 3:1

Towns, Jerusalem, **J**, and the .... Mt 4:25
into the area of **J** on the other .... Mt 19:1
the people from **J** and Jerusalem .... Mk 1:5
mountains of **J** people continued .... Lk 1:65
to the town of Bethlehem in **J**, ... Lk 2:4
Pontius Pilate, the ruler of **J**; .... Lk 3:1
had come from **J** to Galilee, ... Jn 4:47
in all of **J**, in Samaria, ... Ac 1:8
Mesopotamia, **J**, Cappadocia, ... Ac 2:9
nonbelievers in **J** and that this .... Rm 15:31
help from you for my trip to **J**. 2Co 1:16
In **J** the churches in Christ had .... Gal 1:22
in Christ that are in **J**. 1Th 2:14

JUDEAN

take hold of a **J** by his coat. .... Zch 8:23

JUDGE

You are the **j** of all the earth. .... Ge 18:25
Who made you our ruler and **j**? .... Ex 2:14
J fairly between two Israelites .... Dt 1:16
may be too difficult to **j**. .... Dt 17:8
respect for the **j** or priest who .... Dt 17:12
the **j** will make that person lie .... Dt 25:2
I will take it in my hand to **j**. .... Dt 32:41
the LORD, the **J**, decide whether .... Jdg 11:27
The LORD will **j** all the earth. 1Sa 2:10
Our king will **j** for us and go 1Sa 8:20
May the LORD **j** between us, ... 1Sa 24:12
would make me **j** in this land! 2Sa 15:4
J the case, punish the guilty, ... 1Ki 8:32
he is coming to **j** the world. 1Ch 16:33
only beg God my, **J**, for mercy. .... Job 9:15
would be saved forever by my **J**. .... Job 23:7
LORD, **j** the people. LORD, defend .... Ps 7:8
and he will **j** the world in .... Ps 9:8
God is the **j**, and even the skies .... Ps 50:6
you speak and fair when you **j**. .... Ps 51:4
Do you **j** people fairly? .... Ps 58:1
Help him **j** your people fairly .... Ps 72:2
for trial, and I will **j** fairly. .... Ps 75:2
God, come and **j** the earth, ... Ps 82:8
He is coming to **j** the world; .... Ps 96:13
up and **j** fairly, and defend .... Pr 31:9
he will **j** both good people and .... Ec 3:17
and stands to **j** the people. .... Is 3:13
He will not **j** by the way things .... Is 11:3
is because the LORD is our **j**. .... Is 33:22
All-Powerful, you are a fair **j**. .... Je 11:20
wronged. Now **j** my case for me. .... La 3:59
Will you **j** them? Will you judge .... Eze 20:4
I will **j** between one sheep and .... Eze 34:17
will **j** between the fat sheep and .... Eze 34:20
The Lord will **j** many nations; .... Mic 4:3
might turn you over to the **j**, ... Mt 5:25
Don't **j** others, or you will be .... Mt 7:1
the same way that you **j** others, ... Mt 7:2
said I should **j** or decide .... Lk 12:14
enemy might take you to the **j**, ... Lk 12:58
to what the unfair **j** said. .... Lk 18:6
They will **j** you in their .... Lk 21:12
I **j** only the way I am told, ... Jn 5:30
but **j** by what is really right." .... Jn 7:24
law does not **j** a person without .... Jn 7:51
You **j** by human standards. .... Jn 8:15
But when I do **j**, I judge .... Jn 8:16
I did not come to **j** the world, ... Jn 12:47
is a **j** for those who refuse .... Jn 12:48
yourselves and **j** him by your own .... Jn 18:31
'Who made you our ruler and **j**? .... Ac 7:27
chose to be the **j** of the living .... Ac 10:42
day that he will **j** all the world .... Ac 17:31
want to be a **j** of these things." .... Ac 18:15
sit there and **j** me, using the .... Ac 23:3

If you think you can **j** others, ... Rm 2:1
When you **j** them, you are really .... Rm 2:1
will **j** people's secret thoughts. .... Rm 2:16
us, he could not **j** the world. .... Rm 3:6
You cannot **j** another person's .... Rm 14:4
So why do you **j** your brothers or .... Rm 14:10
God's people will **j** the world. 1Co 6:2
in the future we will **j** angels, ... 1Co 6:3
j for yourselves what I say. 1Co 10:15
right way, God would not **j** us. 1Co 11:31
of which God can **j** you guilty. .... Col 1:22
One who will **j** the living and 2Ti 4:1
The Lord, the **j** who judges 2Ti 4:8
"The Lord will **j** his people." .... Heb 10:30
to God, the **j** of all people, ... Heb 12:23
God will **j** as guilty those who .... Heb 13:4
your fellow believers or **j** them, ... Jam 4:11
God is the only Lawmaker and **J**. .... Jam 4:12
And the **J** is ready to come! .... Jam 5:9
who is ready to **j** the living and 1Pe 4:5
how long until you **j** the people .... Rev 6:10

JUDGED

said, "God has **j** me innocent. .... Ge 30:6
and they **j** Israel fairly." .... Dt 33:21
before he was **j**, by the relative .... Jos 20:9
Ibzan **j** Israel for seven years. .... Jdg 12:9
He **j** Israel for ten years. .... Jdg 12:11
He **j** Israel for eight years. .... Jdg 12:14
Samson **j** Israel for twenty years .... Jdg 15:20
to Mizpah and **j** the Israelites 1Sa 7:16
There he **j** Israel and built an 1Sa 7:17
a throne room where he **j** people, ... 1Ki 7:7
you bring me before you to be **j**? .... Job 14:3
your throne and **j** by what was .... Ps 9:4
good people will be **j** guilty. .... Ps 34:21
who trusts him will be **j** guilty. .... Ps 34:22
or let good people be **j** guilty. .... Ps 37:33
When he is **j**, let him be found .... Ps 109:7
good people to be **j** fairly. .... Is 5:23
to hurt Israel were **j** guilty. .... Je 2:3
or help the poor be **j** fairly. .... Je 5:28
When they are **j**, they will be .... Je 10:15
When they are **j**, they will be .... Je 51:18
way they have **j** others is the .... Eze 7:27
the same way I **j** your ancestors .... Eze 20:36
time when the nations will be **j**. .... Eze 30:3
He **j** in favor of the holy people .... Da 7:22
because you will all be **j**. .... Hos 5:1
who murders another will be **j**.' .... Mt 5:21
or sister, you will be **j**. .... Mt 5:22
you will be **j** by the council. .... Mt 5:22
judge others, or you will be **j**. .... Mt 7:1
You will be **j** in the same way .... Mt 7:2
When you are arrested and **j**, ... Mk 13:11
others, and you will not be **j**. .... Lk 6:37
in God's Son are not **j** guilty. .... Jn 3:18
have already been **j** guilty, ... Jn 3:18
They are **j** by this fact: .... Jn 3:19
will not be **j** guilty but has .... Jn 5:24
evil will rise to be **j** guilty. .... Jn 5:29
Has no one **j** you guilty?" .... Jn 8:10
so that the world could be **j**. .... Jn 9:39
the time for the world to be **j**; .... Jn 12:31
the ruler of this world was **j**. .... Jn 16:11
seat now, where I should be **j**. .... Ac 25:10
go to Jerusalem and be **j** there?' ...... Ac 25:20
When I **j** him, I found no reason .... Ac 25:25
he asked to be **j** by Caesar, ... Ac 25:25
sinners will be **j** by the law. .... Rm 2:12
So why am I **j** a sinner?" .... Rm 3:7
sinned once, he was **j** guilty. .... Rm 5:16
Christ Jesus are not **j** guilty. .... Rm 8:1

J

all stand before God to be j, ... Rm 14:10
they can only be j to be true by 1Co 2:14
care if I am j by you or by any 1Co 4:3
I have already j the man who did 1Co 5:3
ordinary cases that must be j, ... 1Co 6:4
freedom is j by someone else's 1Co 10:29
But if we j ourselves in the 1Co 11:31
they will be j by all that they 1Co 14:24
If the law that j people guilty 2Co 3:9
all stand before Christ to be j. 2Co 5:10
It will be j by what you have, ... 2Co 8:12
we should be j guilty! .... Gal 1:8
let that person be j guilty! .... Gal 1:9
those will be j guilty who did 2Th 2:12
himself and be j guilty just as 1Ti 3:6
will be j for not doing what................... 1Ti 5:12
to see even before they are j, ... 1Ti 5:24
must die once and then be j, ... Heb 9:27
you will be j by the law that .... Jam 2:12
teach will be j more strictly. .... Jam 3:1
You have j guilty and then .... Jam 5:6
other or you will be j guilty. .... Jam 5:9
no so you will not be j guilty. .... Jam 5:12
they were j like all people 1Pe 4:6
people who will be j guilty. .... Jud 1:4
to be j on the great day. .... Jud 1:6
The dead were j by what they had .... Rev 20:12
Each person was j by what he had .... Rev 20:13

JUDGES
God's j will decide who is .... Ex 22:9
So Moses said to Israel's j, ... Nu 25:5
Appoint j and officers for your .... Dt 16:18
priests and j who are on duty................ Dt 19:17
The j must check the matter .... Dt 19:18
Your elders and j should go to .... Dt 21:2
the j will decide the case. .... Dt 25:1
The elders, officers, j, and all .... Jos 8:33
of families, j, and officers .... Jos 23:2
of families, j, and officers .... Jos 24:1
the LORD chose leaders called j, ... Jdg 2:16
did not listen to their j. .... Jdg 2:17
for them and sent j to save them .... Jdg 2:18
with those j all their lives. .... Jdg 2:18
But when the j died, the .... Jdg 2:19
ago when the j ruled Israel, ... Ru 1:1
and he j what people do....................... 1Sa 2:3
he made his sons j for Israel. 1Sa 8:1
and Abijah were j in Beersheba............. 1Sa 8:2
when I chose j for my people 2Sa 7:11
this since the j led Israel. 2Ki 23:22
when I chose j for my people 1Ch 17:10
Levites will be officers and j, ... 1Ch 23:4
as officers and j in different 1Ch 26:29
thousand men, the j, every 2Ch 1:2
appointed j in all the land, ... 2Ch 19:5
of Israelite families to be j. 2Ch 19:8
j and important officers over .... Ezr 4:9
God to choose j and lawmakers to .... Ezr 7:25
the elders and j of each town at .... Ezr 10:14
he covers the j' faces so they .... Job 9:24
captives and turns j into fools. .... Job 12:17
is the one who j even the most .... Job 21:22
God j by what is right, and God .... Ps 7:11
is a God who j the world." .... Ps 58:11
he j one person as guilty and .... Ps 75:7
he j among the "gods." .... Ps 82:1
but the LORD j your reasons. .... Pr 21:2
If a king j poor people fairly, ... Pr 29:14
bring back j as you had long .... Is 1:26
soldiers, the j and prophets, ... Is 3:2
wisdom to the j who must decide .... Is 28:6
the j stumble when they make .... Is 28:7

and the j of this world worth .... Is 40:23
He j fairly between one person .... Eze 18:8
In court they will act as j. .... Eze 44:24
the treasury, j, rulers, and all .... Da 3:2
the Valley Where the LORD J. .... Joe 3:2
in the Valley Where the LORD J. .... Joe 3:12
Its j take money to decide who .... Mic 3:11
and j' decisions are bought for .... Mic 7:3
the j no longer hear fair .... Hab 1:4
So they will be your j............................ Mt 12:27
So they will be your j........................... Lk 11:19
fact, the Father j no one, but .... Jn 5:22
God gave them j until the time .... Ac 13:20
the courts and j where they can .... Ac 19:38
God j those who do wrong things, ... Rm 2:2
For God j all people in the same .... Rm 2:11
in the way the world j wisdom. 1Co 1:26
The Lord is the One who j me. 1Co 4:4
to go before j who are not right 1Co 6:1
people as j who mean nothing 1Co 6:4
But when the Lord j us, he 1Co 11:32
the judge who j rightly, will 2Ti 4:8
And it j the thoughts and .... Heb 4:12
show mercy to you when he j you. .... Jam 2:13
and he j each person's work 1Pe 1:17
God, the One who j rightly, take........... 1Pe 2:23
fear on the day God j us,...................... 1Jn 4:17
Lord God who j her is powerful............ Rev 18:8
right when he j and makes war. .... Rev 19:11
Nothing that God j guilty will............... Rev 22:3

JUDGING
j the twelve tribes of Israel.................... Mt 19:28
And if that j begins with us, ... 1Pe 4:17

JUDGMENT
Then you will know there is j." .... Job 19:29
king your good j and the king's .... Ps 72:1
J will again be fair, and all .... Ps 94:15
I am wisdom, and I have good j............. Pr 8:12
J has come to these towns: .... Je 48:21
J has come to all the towns of .... Je 48:24
This ends the j on Moab....................... Je 48:47
Zion some will escape the j, ... Ob 1:17
on the J Day it will be better .... Mt 10:15
on the J Day it will be fair. .... Mt 11:22
on the J Day it will be better .... Mt 11:24
that on the J Day people will .... Mt 12:36
On the J Day the people from............... Mt 12:41
On the J Day, the Queen of the .... Mt 12:42
are you going to escape God's j? .... Mt 23:33
on the J Day it will be better .... Lk 10:12
But on the J Day it will be .... Lk 10:14
On the J Day the Queen of the .... Lk 11:31
On the J Day the people of .... Lk 11:32
way I am told, so my j is fair. .... Jn 5:30
right with God, and about j. .... Jn 16:8
to them that j happened when .... Jn 16:11
standing at Caesar's j seat now, ... Ac 25:10
went into the j room with the .... Ac 25:23
be able to escape the j of God? .... Rm 2:3
the whole world under God's j, ... Rm 3:19
because the Day of J will make 1Co 3:13
eat and drink j against 1Co 11:29
not bring God's j on yourselves............. 1Co 11:34
God's angry j that is sure to 1Th 1:10
that God is right in his j....................... 2Th 1:5
of the dead and eternal j. .... Heb 6:2
waiting for the j and the .... Heb 10:27
can stand without fear at the j. .... Jam 2:13
It is time for j to begin with 1Pe 4:17
Their j spoken against them long 2Pe 2:3
where they are being held for j. 2Pe 2:4

JUDGMENTS

while waiting for the **J** Day. 2Pe 2:9
are being kept for the **J** Day and 2Pe 3:7

JUDGMENTS

money secretly to make wrong **j.** 1Sa 8:3
The **j** of the LORD are true; .... Ps 19:9
are happy because of your **j,** .... Ps 97:8
will announce my **j** against my .... Je 1:16
I will announce **j** against the .... Je 4:12
everyone will see God's right **j.** .... Rm 2:5
his **j** are true and right. .... Rev 19:2

JUDITH

J daughter of Beeri and Basemath .... Ge 26:34

JUG

spear and water **j** that are near 1Sa 26:11
spear and water **j** that were near 1Sa 26:12
spear and water **j** that were near 1Sa 26:16
only a little olive oil in a **j.** 1Ki 17:12
and the **j** will always have oil 1Ki 17:14
of flour and the **j** of oil were 1Ki 17:16
pouring from the **j** of wine until .... Hab 2:15

JUGS

from the water **j** that the young .... Ru 2:9
Moab's jars and smash her **j.** .... Je 48:12

JUICE

and squeezed the **j** into the cup. .... Ge 40:11
even drink grape **j** or eat grapes .... Nu 6:3
You drank the **j** of grapes. .... Dt 32:14
When there is **j** left in the .... Is 65:8
walk on grapes to get their **j,** .... Joe 3:13
be taking the **j** from grapes when .... Am 9:13

JULIA

Greetings to Philologus and **J,** .... Rm 16:15

JULIUS

officer named **J,** who served in .... Ac 27:1
J was very good to Paul and gave .... Ac 27:3
J, the officer, wanted to let .... Ac 27:43

JUNIA

Greetings to Andronicus and **J,** .... Rm 16:7

JUNIPER

well as much **j** wood and jewels. 1Ki 10:11
Solomon used the **j** wood to build 1Ki 10:12
Such fine **j** wood has not been 1Ki 10:12
cedar, pine, and **j** logs from 2Ch 2:8
from Ophir, **j** wood, and jewels 2Ch 9:10
Solomon used the **j** wood to build 2Ch 9:11
our ceiling is made of **j** wood. .... Sng 1:17

JUSHAB-HESED

Ohel, Berekiah, Hasadiah, and **J.** 1Ch 3:20

JUST

the blame. **J** do what I said. .... Ge 27:13
j as Jacob left his father Isaac, ... Ge 27:30
and Aaron did **j** as the LORD had .... Ex 7:6
to him if I ask **j** one more thing. .... Jdg 6:39
told him to do, **j** as the LORD 2Sa 24:19
You are **j** making it up in your .... Ne 6:8
They **j** come to get bad news. .... Ps 41:6
are **j** like animals that .... Ps 49:20
j as parents correct the child .... Pr 3:12
but fools **j** want more .... Pr 15:14
work hard is **j** like someone who .... Pr 18:9
work **j** to feed themselves, ... Ec 6:7
leave your job **j** because your .... Ec 10:4
flowers is **j** a dying plant set .... Is 28:1
flowers is **j** a dying plant set .... Is 28:4
a puff of wind will take them .... Is 57:13
will treat you **j** as you treated .... Eze 35:11
be with you **j** as you say he is .... Am 5:14
J as wine can trick a person, ... Hab 2:5

j as you ran from the earthquake .... Zch 14:5
j as your Father in heaven is .... Mt 5:48
J as the weeds are pulled up and .... Mt 13:40
of Man will die, **j** as the .... Mt 26:24
let them touch **j** the edge of his .... Mk 6:56
of Man will die, **j** as the .... Mk 14:21
It had been **j** as the angel had .... Lk 2:20
j as your Father shows mercy. .... Lk 6:36
found the colt **j** as Jesus had .... Lk 19:32
J as the Father raises the dead .... Jn 5:21
came on them **j** as he came on us .... Ac 11:15
j as are all of you here today. .... Ac 22:3
J before dawn Paul began .... Ac 27:33
right and wrong, **j** as the law .... Rm 2:15
j as the Scriptures say: .... Rm 2:24
J as our witness about Christ 1Co 1:6
as I, also, try to please 1Co 10:33
the teachings **j** as I gave them. 1Co 11:2
are blessed **j** as Abraham was. .... Gal 3:9
each other **j** as God forgave you .... Eph 4:32
Do not obey **j** when they are .... Col 3:22
want to see us **j** as much as we 1Th 3:6
J as Jannes and Jambres were 2Ti 3:8
preached to us **j** as it was to .... Heb 4:2
for all time at **j** the right time .... Heb 9:26
J as everyone must die once and .... Heb 9:27
was a human being **j** like us. .... Jam 5:17
j as you will have some false 2Pe 2:1
people who are **j** beginning to 2Pe 2:18
each other, **j** as he commanded. 1Jn 3:23

JUSTICE

and I could help them get **j.**" 2Sa 15:4
people, called the Hall of **J.** 1Ki 7:7
was built like the Hall of **J,** 1Ki 7:8
you king to keep **j** and to rule 1Ki 10:9
over them to keep **j** and to rule 2Ch 9:8
God does not twist **j;** .... Job 8:3
when it comes to **j,** no one can .... Job 9:19
scream for help but I get no **j.** .... Job 19:7
the wicked; you are getting **j.** .... Job 36:17
and he loves **j,** so honest people .... Ps 11:7
my God, defend me with your **j.** .... Ps 35:24
Your **j** is as deep as the great .... Ps 36:6
The LORD loves **j** and will not .... Ps 37:28
your **j** reaches to the skies. .... Ps 71:19
tell about your **j** all day long. .... Ps 71:24
King is powerful and loves **j.** .... Ps 99:4
the LORD will get **j** for the poor .... Ps 140:12
He makes sure that **j** is done, ... Pr 2:8
right and follow the path of **j.** .... Pr 8:20
to do wrong there can be no **j.** .... Pr 17:23
When **j** is done, good people are .... Pr 21:15
Evil people do not understand **j,** .... Pr 28:5
care about **j** for the poor, ... Pr 29:7
but **j** comes only from the LORD. ...... Pr 29:26
Where there should have been **j,** ...... Ec 3:16
to do good. Seek **j.** Punish those ...... Is 1:17
don't seek **j** for the orphans .... Is 1:23
He looked for **j,** but there was .... Is 5:7
by ruling with **j** and goodness. .... Is 9:7
are waiting for your way of **j.** .... Is 26:8
When your way of **j** comes to the ...... Is 26:9
I will use **j** as a measuring line ...... Is 28:17
who lie and take **j** from innocent ...... Is 29:21
rule in a way that brings **j,** .... Is 32:1
J will be found even in the .... Is 32:16
Jerusalem with fairness and **j.** .... Is 33:5
he will bring **j** to all nations. .... Is 42:1
He will truly bring **j**; .... Is 42:3
until he brings **j** to the world. ...... Is 42:4
Give **j** to all people, and do .... Is 56:1
We look for **j,** but there isn't .... Is 59:11

JUSTLY

have driven away **j,** and we have .... Is 59:14
looked and could not find any **j,** .... Is 59:15
I, the LORD, love **j.** .... Is 61:8
to ask you about the **j** you give. .... Je 12:1
j comes out like bright light. .... Hos 6:5
You turn **j** upside down, and you .... Am 5:7
poor from getting **j** in court. .... Am 5:12
But let **j** flow like a river, ... Am 5:24
LORD, and with **j** and strength, ... Mic 3:8
are weak, and **j** never comes. .... Hab 1:4
who hunger and thirst after **j,** .... Mt 5:6
will tell of my **j** to all people. .... Mt 12:18
he makes **j** win the victory. .... Mt 12:20
of the law—**j,** mercy, and being .... Mt 23:23
J does not want him to live." .... Ac 28:4

JUSTLY

We are punished **j,** getting what .... Lk 23:41

JUSTUS

who was also called **J.** .... Ac 1:23
moved into the home of Titius **J,** .... Ac 18:7
is called **J,** also greets you. .... Col 4:11

JUTTAH

Maon, Carmel, Ziph, **J,** .... Jos 15:55
Ain, **J,** and Beth Shemesh, and .... Jos 21:16
Ashan, **J,** and Beth Shemesh. 1Ch 6:59

K

KABZEEL

border of Edom: **K,** Eder, Jagur, ... Jos 15:21
fighter from **K** who did mighty 2Sa 23:20
fighter from **K** who did mighty 1Ch 11:22
and all the Israelites at **K,** .... Nu 13:26
of Zin, and they stayed at **K,** .... Nu 20:1
the LORD shakes the Desert of **K.** .... Ps 29:8

KADMONITES

of the Kenites, Kenizzites, **K,** .... Ge 15:19

KAIN

K, Gibeah, and Timnah. There .... Jos 15:57

KAIWAN

god Sakkuth, and **K** your idol, ... Am 5:26

KALLAI

K, from Sallu's family; .... Ne 12:20

KAMON

and was buried in the city of **K.** .... Jdg 10:5

KANAH

Tappuah west to **K** Ravine and .... Jos 16:8
continued south to **K** Ravine. .... Jos 17:9
K and continued to Greater Sidon. .... Jos 19:28

KARKA

Addar it turned and went to **K.** .... Jos 15:3

KARKOR

army were in the city of **K.** .... Jdg 8:10

KARNAIM

the Rephaites in Ashteroth **K,** .... Ge 14:5
taken **K** by our own strength. .... Am 6:13

KARTAH

of Zebulun gave them Jokneam, **K,** .... Jos 21:34
of Jokneam, **K,** Rimmono, and 1Ch 6:77

KARTAN

Hammoth Dor, and **K,** and the .... Jos 21:32

KATTATH

border were the cities of **K,** .... Jos 19:15

KAZIN

to Gath Hepher and Eth **K,** .... Jos 19:13

KEDAR

son, then **K,** Adbeel, Mibsam, ... Ge 25:13
sons were **K,** Adbeel, Mibsam, ... 1Ch 1:29
to live among the people of **K.** .... Ps 120:5
like the tents of **K,** like the .... Sng 1:5
the country of **K** will be gone. .... Is 21:16
the soldiers of **K,** will be left .... Is 21:17
settlements of **K** should praise .... Is 42:11
the sheep from **K** will be given .... Is 60:7
the land of **K** to look closely. .... Je 2:10
to the tribe of **K** and the .... Je 49:28
Go and attack the people of **K,** .... Je 49:28
the rulers of **K** became traders .... Eze 27:21

KEDEMAH

Tema, Jetur, Naphish, and **K.** .... Ge 25:15
Jetur, Naphish, and **K.** 1Ch 1:31

KEDEMOTH

the desert of **K** to Sihon king .... Dt 2:26
Jahaz, **K,** Mephaath, ... Jos 13:18
K, and Mephaath, along with the .... Jos 21:37

KEDESH

K in Galilee in the mountains of .... Jos 20:7
Barak lived in the city of **K,** .... Jdg 4:6

KEEP

and female. **K** them alive with .... Ge 6:19
descendants must **k** this .... Ge 17:9
king answered, "**K** your promise. .... Ge 50:6
are to **k** watch to honor .... Ex 12:42
his commands and **k** his rules, ... Ex 15:26
of the Agreement to **k** it safe. .... Ex 16:34
you obey me and **k** my agreement, ... Ex 19:5
Remember to **k** the Sabbath holy. .... Ex 20:8
'You must **k** the rules about my .... Ex 31:13
K my command not to do these .... Le 18:30
the LORD bless you and **k** you. .... Nu 6:24
she must **k** her promises. .... Nu 30:14
K the Sabbath as a holy day, ... Dt 5:12
He will **k** his agreement of love .... Dt 7:9
k away from unclean things. .... Dt 23:9
loan back, don't **k** it overnight. .... Dt 24:12
see if Israel will **k** the LORD's .... Jdg 2:22
Why would he **k** this from me? 1Sa 20:2
have no son to **k** my name alive. 2Sa 18:18
k the promise you made to your 1Ki 8:25
and it won't **k** the land from 2Ki 2:21
k the promise forever that you 1Ch 17:23
to build a place to **k** the Ark of 1Ch 28:2
If you **k** quiet at this time, ... Est 4:14
and **k** his words in your heart. .... Job 22:22
K me from the wicked who attack .... Ps 17:9
K me from the sins of pride; .... Ps 19:13
He will **k** me from any traps. .... Ps 25:15
K me strong by giving me a .... Ps 51:12
They didn't **k** their agreement .... Ps 78:10
they did not **k** his rules. .... Ps 78:56
and to those who **k** his agreement .... Ps 103:18
hated because I **k** your rules. .... Ps 119:113
and I will **k** them until the end. .... Ps 119:33
so I can **k** your teachings, ... Ps 119:34
who do not **k** your teachings. .... Ps 119:53
and I will **k** your demands. .... Ps 119:145
He helps me **k** my people under .... Ps 144:2
LORD will **k** all his promises; .... Ps 145:13
the LORD will **k** you safe. .... Pr 3:26
K my commands and you will live. .... Pr 4:4
K all that you have learned; .... Pr 4:13
K your eyes focused on what is .... Pr 4:25
will **k** you from sinful women .... Pr 6:24
will be good to **k** these things .... Pr 22:18
is a time to **k** things and a time .... Ec 3:6
to God, don't be slow to **k** it. .... Ec 5:4

will be able to **k** only one young............Is 7:21
to the LORD and will **k** them.................Is 19:21
Tyre will not **k** the money she...............Is 23:18
Don't **k** my people in prison. ....Is 43:6
I cannot **k** quiet, because I have ....Je 4:19
No one was to **k** a fellow Jew as.............Je 34:9
and obey my laws and **k** them. ....Eze 11:20
k your agreement of love with ....Da 9:4
the wise person will **k** quiet, ...Am 5:13
Will he **k** on taking riches with ....Hab 1:17
they must **k** that promise.' ....Mt 23:16
allow us to **k** this money with................Mt 27:6
tried to **k** him from leaving. ....Lk 4:42
no place to **k** all my crops.'....................Lk 12:17
who try to **k** their lives will..................Lk 17:33
man does not **k** the Sabbath day, ...Jn 9:16
this world will **k** true life ....Jn 12:25
k them safe by the power of your ....Jn 17:11
Spirit and **k** for yourself ....Ac 5:3
Can anyone **k** these people from ....Ac 10:47
were barely able to **k** the crowd ....Ac 14:18
Jesus will **k** you strong until 1Co 1:8
its mouth to **k** it from eating."................1Co 9:9
that we will not **k** anyone from 1Co 9:12
women should **k** quiet in the 1Co 14:34
Abraham and promised to **k** it. ....Gal 3:17
K on working to complete your ....Php 2:12
I **k** trying to reach the goal and ....Php 3:14
will **k** your hearts and minds in ....Php 4:7
K your roots deep in him and................Col 2:7
test everything. **K** what is good, ...1Th 5:21
its mouth to **k** it from eating,".............1Ti 5:18
sins of others. **K** yourself pure. 1Ti 5:22
I remind you to **k** using the gift 2Ti 1:6
wanted to **k** him with me so that ....Phm 1:13
K a clear conscience so that 1Pe 3:16
support you and **k** you from 1Pe 5:10
hope in Christ **k** themselves pure 1Jn 3:3
k yourselves away from false 1Jn 5:21
angels who did not **k** their place.............Jud 1:6
K yourselves in God's love as ....Jud 1:21
So I will **k** you from the time of ....Rev 3:10
of the earth to **k** them from...................Rev 7:1
K hidden what the seven thunders ....Rev 10:4
God's commands and **k** their faith ....Rev 14:12
stay awake and **k** their clothes ....Rev 16:15
Do not **k** secret the words of ....Rev 22:10

KEEPER
the **k** of the king's forest, ...Ne 2:8

KEEPERS
the king, **k** of the treasury, ...Da 3:2

KEEPING
of Aaron was in charge of **k** it. ....Ex 38:21
k the agreement he promised to ....Dt 8:18
K them brings great reward. ....Ps 19:11
are you **k** your love and mercy ....Is 63:15
continue only by **k** its agreement ....Eze 17:14
were without fault in **k** his law. ....Lk 1:6
Jason is **k** them in his house. ....Ac 17:7
decided this in **k** with his plan. ....Eph 1:11
praying, **k** alert, and always ....Col 4:2
and **k** yourself free from the ....Jam 1:27
of God is heaven and earth 2Pe 3:7

KEEPS
He **k** coming out to challenge................1Sa 17:25
and someone **k** watch over their............Job 21:32
He **k** company with those who do ....Job 34:8
if God **k** quiet, who can blame ....Job 34:29
He **k** the wicked from ruling and ....Job 34:30
people do; he **k** his eye on them. ....Ps 11:4
but he **k** me safe in battle. ....Ps 55:18

He **k** his eye on the nations, ...Ps 66:7
he **k** evil people from getting ....Pr 10:3
is honored for what he **k** secret..............Pr 25:2
person **k** an argument going ....Pr 26:21
because God **k** them busy with ....Ec 5:20
He **k** his hand from doing wrong. ....Eze 18:8
He **k** his hand from doing wrong. ....Eze 18:17
so he **k** it only a short time. ....Mt 13:21
The evil spirit **k** on hurting him ....Lk 9:39
a field but **k** looking back is ....Lk 9:62
is the city that **k** the temple of ....Ac 19:35
The Son of God **k** them safe, ...1Jn 5:18

KEHELATHAH
left Rissah and camped at **K**. ....Nu 33:22
They left **K** and camped at Mount ....Nu 33:23

KEILAH
Attack them, and save **K**." 1Sa 23:2
and his men went to **K** and fought 1Sa 23:5

KELAIAH
Jozabad, Shimei, **K** (also called ....Ezr 10:23

KELAL
Adna, **K**, Benaiah, Maaseiah, ...Ezr 10:30

KELITA
also called **K**), Pethahiah, Judah..............Ezr 10:23
Maaseiah, **K**, Azariah, Jozabad ....Ne 8:7
Hodiah, **K**, Pelaiah, Hanan, ...Ne 10:10

KELUB
K, Shuhah's brother, was the 1Ch 4:11
Ezri son of **K** was in charge of 1Ch 27:26

KELUHI
Benaiah, Bedeiah, **K**, ...Ezr 10:35

KEMUEL
The third son is **K** (the father ....Ge 22:21
of Joseph, **K** son of Shiphtan;.................Nu 34:24
Hashabiah son of **K** was over the 1Ch 27:17

KENAANAH
Zedekiah son of **K** had made some 1Ki 22:11
Zedekiah son of **K** went up to................1Ki 22:24
Benjamin, Ehud, **K**, Zethan, ...1Ch 7:10
Zedekiah son of **K** had made some 2Ch 18:10
Zedekiah son of **K** went up to................2Ch 18:23

KENANI
Bunni, Sherebiah, Bani, and **K**. ....Ne 9:4

KENANIAH
Levite leader **K** was in charge 1Ch 15:22
Ark, and **K**, the man in charge 1Ch 15:27
K was from the Izhar family. 1Ch 26:29

KENATH
and captured **K** and the small................Nu 32:42
as well as **K** and the small towns 1Ch 2:23

KENITE
one of the **K** family groups. ....Jdg 4:17

KENITES
He said to the **K**, "Go away. 1Sa 15:6
or to the land of the **K**. 1Sa 27:10

KENIZZITE
Jephunneh the **K** and Joshua son ....Nu 32:12
Caleb son of Jephunneh the **K**. ....Jos 14:6
Jephunneh the **K** because he had ....Jos 14:14

KENIZZITES
of the Kenites, **K**, Kadmonites, ...Ge 15:19

KEPHAR
K Ammoni, Ophni, and Geba..................Jos 18:24

KEPHIRAH
Gibeon, **K**, Beeroth, and Kiriath ....Jos 9:17
Mizpah, **K**, Mozah, ...Jos 18:26

KEPHIRIM

Kiriath Jearim, **K**, and Beeroth— .... Ezr 2:25
Kiriath Jearim, **K**, and Beeroth— .... Ne 7:29

KEPHIRIM

meet together in **K** on the plain .... Ne 6:2

KEPT

why should we be **k** from offering .... Nu 9:7
the LORD our God has **k** secret, ... Dt 29:29
the LORD has **k** his promise. .... Jos 14:10
rest that the people had not **k**. 2Ch 36:21
I would have **k** quiet, because .... Est 7:4
and you **k** food from the hungry. .... Job 22:7
I have not **k** my food to myself .... Job 31:17
I have **k** myself from doing evil. .... Ps 18:23
When I **k** things to myself, ... Ps 32:3
So I **k** very quiet. I didn't even .... Ps 39:2
I have **k** quiet while you did .... Ps 50:21
bothered him and **k** him awake at .... Da 2:1
I **k** on looking because the .... Da 7:11
all the time and have not **k** them. .... Am 1:11
my rules and have not **k** them. .... Mal 3:7
may your name always be **k** holy. .... Mt 6:9
So the soldiers **k** the money and .... Mt 28:15
But his mother **k** in her mind all .... Lk 2:51
Then he **k** on preaching in the .... Lk 4:44
was a widow who **k** coming to this........... Lk 18:3
were **k** from recognizing him................... Lk 24:16
near where the money is **k**.................... Jn 8:20
was the one who **k** the money box, ... Jn 12:6
was the one who **k** the money box, ... Jn 13:29
I **k** them safe by the power of .... Jn 17:12
followers **k** telling Thomas,.................... Jn 20:25
He **k** back part of the money for .... Ac 5:2
So Peter was **k** in jail, but the................. Ac 12:5
that Paul would be **k** in Caesarea .... Ac 25:4
he asked to be **k** in Caesarea................... Ac 25:21
should be **k** secret between................... Rm 14:22
the race, I have **k** the faith. 2Ti 4:7
beauty, are **k** in heaven for you 1Pe 1:4
Sardis who have **k** their clothes .... Rev 3:4
sides and was **k** closed with .... Rev 5:1
who had been **k** ready for this .... Rev 9:15
because they **k** themselves pure. .... Rev 14:4

KERAMIM

as far as the city of Abel **K**. .... Jdg 11:33

KERAN

Hemdan, Eshban, Ithran, and **K**. .... Ge 36:26
Hemdan, Eshban, Ithran, and **K**. 1Ch 1:41

KEREN-HAPPUCH

and the third daughter **K**. .... Job 42:14

KERETHITES

the southern area of the **K**, ... 1Sa 30:14
was over the **K** and Pelethites. 2Sa 8:18
by him—the **K** and Pelethites,................... 2Sa 15:18
Joab's men, the **K** and the 2Sa 20:7
led the **K** and Pelethites. 2Sa 20:23
left with the **K** and Pelethites................... 1Ki 1:38
was over the **K** and Pelethites. 1Ch 18:17
I will kill the **K**, and I will .... Eze 25:16

KERIOTH

Hazor Hadattah, **K** Hezron (also .... Jos 15:25
K and Bozrah. Judgment has come .... Je 48:24
buildings of the city of **K**. .... Am 2:2

KERITH

east and hide near **K** Ravine east 1Ki 17:3
he went to **K** Ravine, east of the............... 1Ki 17:5

KEROS

K, Siaha, Padon, ... Ezr 2:44
K, Sia, Padon, ... Ne 7:47

KERUB

Tel Harsha, **K**, Addon, and Immer .... Ezr 2:59
Tel Harsha, **K**, Addon, and Immer .... Ne 7:61

KESALON

also called **K**) and came to Beth .... Jos 15:10

KESED

Then there are **K**, Hazo, Pildash, ... Ge 22:22

KESIL

Eltolad, **K**, Hormah, ... Jos 15:30

KESULLOTH

included Jezreel, **K**, Shunem, ... Jos 19:18

KETTLE

the fork into the pot or the **k**. 1Sa 2:14

KETTLES

offerings in pots, **k**, and pans. 2Ch 35:13

KETURAH

again, and his new wife was **K**. .... Ge 25:1
All these were descendants of **K**. .... Ge 25:4
K, Abraham's slave woman, gave 1Ch 1:32
All these were descendants of **K**. 1Ch 1:33

KEY

So they got the **k** and unlocked .... Jdg 3:25
Power is not the **k** to success. 1Sa 2:9
They are the **k** to life for those .... Pr 4:22
I will put the **k** to the house of .... Is 22:22
taken away the **k** to learning .... Lk 11:52
who holds the **k** of David, says. .... Rev 3:7
was given the **k** to the deep hole .... Rev 9:1
He had the **k** to the bottomless .... Rev 20:1

KEYS

give you the **k** of the kingdom .... Mt 16:19
And I hold the **k** to death and to............. Rev 1:18

KEZIAH

second daughter **K**, and the third .... Job 42:14

KEZIB

She was at **K** when this third son .... Ge 38:5

KEZIZ

Jericho, Beth Hoglah, Emek **K**, ... Jos 18:21

KIBROTH

named that place **K** Hattaavah, ... Nu 11:34
From **K** Hattaavah the people went .... Nu 11:35
Sinai and camped at **K** Hattaavah. .... Nu 33:16
They left **K** Hattaavah and camped .... Nu 33:17
Massah, and **K** Hattaavah. .... Dt 9:22

KIBZAIM

K, and Beth Horon. There were .... Jos 21:22

KICKED

Israel grew fat and **k**; .... Dt 32:15

KICKING

by and saw you **k** about in your .... Eze 16:6

KIDNAPPER

sell him, the **k** must be killed................... Dt 24:7

KIDNAPS

Anyone who **k** someone and either .... Ex 21:16
If someone **k** a fellow Israelite, ... Dt 24:7

KIDNEYS

the liver, both **k**, and the fat .... Ex 29:13
the fat from the **k** of sheep..................... Is 34:6

KIDON

to the threshing floor of **K**, ... 1Ch 13:9

KIDRON

King David crossed the **K** Valley, ... 2Sa 15:23
followers across the **K** Valley.................. Jn 18:1

KIDS

of the lambs and **k** died during .... Ge 31:38

KILEAB

second son was **K,** whose mother 2Sa 3:3

KILION

sons were named Mahlon and **K.** .... Ru 1:2
when Mahlon and **K** also died. .... Ru 1:5
to Elimelech and **K** and Mahlon. .... Ru 4:9

KILL

anyone who meets me can **k** me." .... Ge 4:14
' Then they will **k** me but let .... Ge 12:12
them, they made a plan to **k** him. .... Ge 37:18
but if it is a boy, **k** him!" .... Ex 1:16
you going to **k** me as you killed .... Ex 2:14
had done, he tried to **k** him. .... Ex 2:15
him there and tried to **k** him. .... Ex 4:24
of Israel will **k** them in the .... Ex 12:6
your families and **k** the lamb for .... Ex 12:21
it to **k** us, our children, and.................... Ex 17:3
Then **k** the bull before the LORD .... Ex 29:11
He must **k** the young bull before .... Le 1:5
goat's head and **k** it in the .... Le 4:24
he will **k** the bull for the sin .... Le 16:11
Then Aaron must **k** the goat of .... Le 16:15
you must **k** the woman and the .... Le 20:16
doing this to me, then **k** me now. .... Nu 11:15
K all the Midianite boys, and .... Nu 31:17
k all the Midianite women who .... Nu 31:17
In the streets the sword will **k;** .... Dt 32:25
Take out your sword and **k** me. .... Jdg 9:54
dawn comes, we will **k** Samson!" .... Jdg 16:2
want to **k** us and our people?" 1Sa 5:10
the news and will try to **k** me." 1Sa 16:2
can fight and **k** me, we will be 1Sa 17:9
your robe, but I didn't **k** you. 1Sa 24:11
I will tell you, '**K** Amnon.' 2Sa 13:28
Please, my master, don't **k** him! 1Ki 3:26
I can't **k** and make alive again! 2Ki 5:7
is a time to **k** and a time to .... Ec 3:3
he did not **k** me before I was .... Je 20:17
Let me go and **k** Ishmael son of .... Je 40:15
who can **k** the body but cannot .... Mt 10:28
and they will **k** him. But on the .... Mt 17:23
If we **k** him, it will be ours!' .... Mt 21:38
you over to be hurt, and **k** you. .... Mt 24:9
evil, to save a life or to **k**?" .... Mk 3:4
to people, and they will **k** him. .... Mk 9:31
here! Herod wants to **k** you!" .... Lk 13:31
our fat calf and **k** it so we can .... Lk 15:23
trying to find a way to **k** Jesus, ... Lk 22:2
I can find no reason to **k** him. .... Lk 23:22
them try still harder to **k** him.................. Jn 5:18
people there wanted to **k** him. .... Jn 7:1
to steal and **k** and destroy, ... Jn 10:10
angry and wanted to **k** them. .... Ac 5:33
days, they made plans to **k** Saul. .... Ac 9:23
Get up, Peter; **k** and eat." .... Ac 10:13
decided to **k** the prisoners so .... Ac 27:42
I will also **k** her followers. .... Rev 2:23

KILLED

his brother Abel and **k** him. .... Ge 4:8
I **k** a man for wounding me, ... Ge 4:23
They **k** Hamor and his son Shechem .... Ge 34:26
The brothers **k** a goat and dipped .... Ge 37:31
was evil, so the LORD **k** him. .... Ge 38:7
so he **k** the Egyptian and hid his .... Ex 2:12
offering must be **k** in front of .... Le 6:25
I would have **k** you by now, ... Nu 22:33
no one knows who **k** the person. .... Dt 21:1
Beth Horon and **k** men all the way............ Jos 10:10
on them from the sky and **k** them. .... Jos 10:11
The Israelites **k** many people .... Jos 13:22
He **k** them all on one stone. .... Jdg 9:5
to say, 'A woman **k** Abimelech.' " .... Jdg 9:54

So Samson **k** more of the .... Jdg 16:30
have **k** both a lion and a bear! 1Sa 17:36
He hit him and **k** him.............................. 1Sa 17:50
that Saul had **k** the LORD's 1Sa 22:21
were **k** on Mount Gilboa. 1Sa 31:1
'I have **k** the LORD's appointed 2Sa 1:16
You **k** Uriah the Hittite with the 2Sa 12:9
Kishon Valley, where he **k** them. 1Ki 18:40
and **k** your prophets with swords. 1Ki 19:10
So Jehu **k** everyone of Ahab's 2Ki 10:11
he **k** all of Ahab's family in 2Ki 10:17
Neco faced him and **k** him. 2Ki 23:29
with ten men and **k** Gedaliah.................. 2Ki 25:25
They **k** the servants with swords, ... Job 1:15
your camels and **k** the servants. .... Job 1:17
no more than sheep to be **k.** .... Ps 44:22
of Babylon **k** Zedekiah's sons.................. Je 39:6
that the flames **k** the strong .... Da 3:22
I **k** your young men with swords, ... Am 4:10
them he must be **k** and then be .... Mt 16:21
of Man must be **k** and then rise .... Mk 8:31
beat some of them and **k** others.............. Mk 12:5
will be **k** and after three days .... Lk 9:22
They **k** the prophets, and you .... Lk 11:48
and your father the fat calf,.................... Lk 15:27
They will be **k** by the sword and.............. Lk 21:24
And so you **k** the One who gives .... Ac 3:15
in Jerusalem **k** him by hanging .... Ac 10:39
of John, to be **k** by the sword.................. Ac 12:2
no more than sheep to be **k.**" .... Rm 8:36
they have **k** your prophets, ... Rm 11:3
k both the Lord Jesus and the 1Th 2:15
witness who was **k** in your city, ... Rev 2:13
the image of the beast to be **k.** .... Rev 13:15
armies were **k** with the sword................ Rev 19:21

KILLING

to his father by **k** his seventy .... Jdg 9:56
Cursing, lying, **k,** stealing and .... Hos 4:2
of Abel to the **k** of Zechariah,.................. Lk 11:51
good works are you **k** me for?" .... Jn 10:32
punished the Egyptian by **k** him. .... Ac 7:24
coats of those who were **k** him!' .... Ac 22:20
earth and punish them for **k** us?" .... Rev 6:10

KILLINGS

The blood from her **k** is still in .... Eze 24:7

KILLS

If anyone **k** you, I will punish .... Ge 4:15
If an Israelite **k** an ox, a lamb, ... Le 17:3
Whoever **k** another person must .... Le 24:17
for someone who **k** another person .... Dt 19:4
before it **k** us and our people!.................. 1Sa 5:11
the man who **k** this Philistine 1Sa 17:26
mouths and **k** their enemies. .... Rev 11:5

KILMAD

and **K** became merchants for you. .... Eze 27:23

KIMHAM

But here is **K,** your servant. 2Sa 19:37
answered, "**K** will go with me................ 2Sa 19:38
over to Gilgal, **K** went with him................ 2Sa 19:40

KINAH

K, Dimonah, Adadah, ... Jos 15:22

KIND

more of its own **k** of plant." .... Ge 1:11
Two of every **k** of bird, animal, ... Ge 6:20
'Be **k** to the men of Benjamin. .... Jdg 21:22
is known by the **k** of fruit it .... Mt 12:33
That **k** of spirit comes out only .... Mt 17:21
don't know what **k** of spirit you .... Lk 9:55
with their own **k** than spiritual .... Lk 16:8
is patient and **k.** Love is not 1Co 13:4

People have one **k** of flesh, ... 1Co 15:39
Be **k** and loving to each other, ... Eph 4:32
you live the **k** of life he called................... 2Th 1:11
live the right **k** of life God .... Jam 1:20
as family, being **k** and humble. 1Pe 3:8
So what **k** of people should you 2Pe 3:11
to send every **k** of trouble to .... Rev 11:6

KINDER
nor **k** to rich people than poor .... Job 34:19

KINDEST
even the **k** acts of the wicked .... Pr 12:10

KINDLY
Dinah, and he spoke **k** to her.................... Ge 34:3
spoke **k** to Jehoiachin 2Ki 25:28
Speak **k** to the people of .... Is 40:2
spoke **k** to Jehoiachin .... Je 52:32
all our sin and **k** receive us, ... Hos 14:2

KINDNESS
Please show this **k** to my master .... Ge 24:12
you will show **k** to my family .... Jos 2:12
This act of **k** is greater than .... Ru 3:10
But show me the **k** of the LORD as 1Sa 20:14
I want to show **k** to that person 2Sa 9:1
to show God's **k** to that person." 2Sa 9:3
because God was showing **k** to me. .... Ne 2:8
God, and he has shown **k** to us. .... Ps 118:27
but his **k** is like the dew on the .... Pr 19:12
show you mercy with **k** forever," .... Is 54:8
will show his **k** and the time .... Is 61:2
led them with cords of human **k,** .... Hos 11:4
a spirit of **k** and mercy. .... Zch 12:10
peace, patience, **k,** goodness, ... Gal 5:22
with mercy, **k,** humility, ... Col 3:12
But when the **k** and love of God .... Tit 3:4
add **k** for your brothers and 2Pe 1:7

KINDNESSES
Naphtali enjoys special **k,** .... Dt 33:23
and do not forget all his **k.** .... Ps 103:2
did not remember all your **k,** .... Ps 106:7

KINDS
rats, all **k** of great lizards, ... Le 11:29
will plant many **k** of trees for .... Le 19:23
two different **k** of seeds in your .... Dt 22:9
I planted all **k** of fruit trees .... Ec 2:5
men and all **k** of soldiers,' .... Eze 39:20
There will be many **k** of fish in .... Eze 47:10
All **k** of fruit trees will grow .... Eze 47:12
from different **k** of diseases. .... Mt 4:24
in different **k** of languages 1Co 12:10
that there are all **k** of sounds 1Co 14:10
of money causes all **k** of evil. 1Ti 6:10
wood and all **k** of things made .... Rev 18:12

KING
Now Amraphel was **k** of Babylonia, ... Ge 14:1
against Kedorlaomer **k** of Elam,.............. Ge 14:9
Melchizedek **k** of Salem brought .... Ge 14:18
Abimelech **k** of Gerar heard this, ... Ge 20:2
officers displeased the **k**— .... Ge 40:1
he began serving the **k** of Egypt. .... Ge 41:46
a new **k** began to rule Egypt, ... Ex 1:8
long time, the **k** of Egypt died. .... Ex 2:23
Go tell the **k** of Egypt that he .... Ex 6:11
to Sihon, **k** of the Amorites, ... Nu 21:21
Sihon, the Amorite **k,** lived. .... Nu 21:26
k of Bashan and his whole army .... Nu 21:33
k of Moab brought me from the .... Nu 23:7
appoint as your **k** a foreigner .... Dt 17:15
you and your **k** away to a nation .... Dt 28:36
Someone told the **k** of Jericho, ... Jos 2:2
to Ai and its **k** what you did to .... Jos 8:2

time Adoni-Zedek **k** of Jerusalem .... Jos 10:1
Ehud to give Eglon **k** of Moab the .... Jdg 3:15
a **k** of Canaan who ruled in the .... Jdg 4:2
they made Abimelech their **k.**.................. Jdg 9:6
appoint a **k** to rule over them. .... Jdg 9:8
to the **k** of the Ammonites .... Jdg 11:12
The **k** of the Ammonites answered........... Jdg 11:13
to the Ammonite **k** again. .... Jdg 11:14
time Israel did not have a **k,** .... Jdg 17:6
time Israel did not have a **k.** .... Jdg 18:1
give power to his **k** and make his 1Sa 2:10
Give us a **k** to rule over us like 1Sa 8:5
asked him for a **k** what the LORD 1Sa 8:10
shouted, "Long live the **k!**".................... 1Sa 10:24
LORD, the people made Saul **k.** 1Sa 11:15
saw Nahash **k** of the Ammonites 1Sa 12:12
me to appoint you **k** over Israel.............. 1Sa 15:1
Now he rejects you as **k.**" 1Sa 15:23
towns of Israel to meet **K** Saul. 1Sa 18:6
and went to Achish **k** of Gath. 1Sa 21:10
to Saul, "My master and **k!**" 1Sa 24:8
you guard your master the **k?** 1Sa 26:15
appointed David **k** over Judah. 2Sa 2:4
have appointed me their **k.**" 2Sa 2:7
K David sang this funeral song 2Sa 3:33
Israel came to **K** David at Hebron 2Sa 5:3
David to make him **k** over Israel. 2Sa 5:3
what honor the **k** of Israel acted........... 2Sa 6:20
'I appointed you **k** of Israel and 2Sa 12:7
Absalom went to the **k** and said, ... 2Sa 13:24
When **K** David got over Amnon's 2Sa 13:39
k said to Joab, "Look, I will 2Sa 14:21
Joab went to the **k** and told him 2Sa 14:33
Then the **k** called for Absalom. 2Sa 14:33
problem for the **k** to settle 2Sa 15:2
The **k** set out with everyone in 2Sa 15:16
The **k** said to Ittai, a man from 2Sa 15:19
said to the **k,** "As surely as 2Sa 15:21
The **k** said to Zadok, "Take the 2Sa 15:25
son of Zeruiah said to the **k,** 2Sa 16:9
said to him, "Long live the **k!**" 2Sa 16:16
the **k** would have found out, ... 2Sa 18:13
The **k** said, "Ahimaaz is a good 2Sa 18:27
Master and **k,** hear the good 2Sa 18:31
The **k** asked the Cushite, "Is 2Sa 18:32
Then the **k** was very upset,................... 2Sa 18:33
the **k** is sad and crying because 2Sa 19:1
heard that the **k** was very sad............... 2Sa 19:2
The **k** covered his face and cried 2Sa 19:4
last tribe to bring back the **k?'** 2Sa 19:12
I know I am **k** over Israel!"................... 2Sa 19:22
Then the **k** promised Shimei, ... 2Sa 19:23
Mephibosheth said to the **k,** 2Sa 19:30
my master the **k** has arrived 2Sa 19:30
go with you, my master and **k.** 2Sa 19:37
talk about bringing our **k** back!" 2Sa 19:43
stayed with their **k** all the way 2Sa 20:2
The **k** said to Amasa, "Tell the 2Sa 20:4
more time than the **k** had said. 2Sa 20:5
At this time **K** David was very 1Ki 1:1
cared for the **k** and served him. 1Ki 1:4
was the son of **K** David and 1Ki 1:5
Go to **K** David and tell him, ' 1Ki 1:13
you are still talking to the **k,** 1Ki 1:14
see the aged **k** in his bedroom, ... 1Ki 1:15
bowed and knelt before the **k.** 1Ki 1:16
to you, Adonijah has become **k.** 1Ki 1:18
saying, 'Long live **K** Adonijah!' 1Ki 1:25
Then the **k** made this promise, ... 1Ki 1:29
Solomon would be **k** after me and 1Ki 1:30
and knelt before the **k** and said, ... 1Ki 1:31
him and make him **k** over Israel. 1Ki 1:34
shout, 'Long live **K** Solomon!'................. 1Ki 1:34

K

the book to the k and reported 2Ch 34:16
the royal secretary told the k, ... 2Ch 34:18
read from the book to the k. 2Ch 34:18
When the k heard the words of 2Ch 34:19
The k stood by his pillar and 2Ch 34:31
Neco k of Egypt led an army to 2Ch 35:20
In the battle K Josiah was shot 2Ch 35:23
Then K Neco of Egypt removed 2Ch 36:3
The k of Egypt made Jehoahaz's 2Ch 36:4
God brought the k of Babylon to 2Ch 36:17
and from the k and his officers. 2Ch 36:18
year Cyrus was k of Persia, ... 2Ch 36:22
is what Cyrus k of Persia says: .... Ezr 1:2
time of Esarhaddon k of Assyria, ... Ezr 4:2
the time Cyrus was k of Persia. .... Ezr 4:5
Artaxerxes became k of Persia, ... Ezr 4:7
K Artaxerxes, you should know .... Ezr 4:12
K Artaxerxes sent this answer: .... Ezr 4:17
year Cyrus was k of Babylon, ... Ezr 5:13
Now, if the k wishes, let a .... Ezr 5:17
See if K Cyrus gave an order to .... Ezr 5:17
the life of the k and his sons. .... Ezr 6:10
K Artaxerxes had given a letter .... Ezr 7:11
From Artaxerxes, k of kings, to .... Ezr 7:12
God or of the k must be punished .... Ezr 7:26
I said to the k, "May the king .... Ne 2:3
So the k gave me the letters, ... Ne 2:8
"There is a k of Judah!" .... Ne 6:7
The k will hear about this. .... Ne 6:7
back to Artaxerxes k of Babylon .... Ne 13:6
the thirty-second year he was k. .... Ne 13:6
the k gave another banquet. .... Est 1:5
The k commanded that the guests .... Est 1:8
the banquet, K Xerxes was very .... Est 1:10
Then the k became very angry; .... Est 1:12
beautiful young girls for the k. .... Est 2:2
she was ready to go to the k. .... Est 2:13
the k was pleased with Esther .... Est 2:17
to make plans to kill K Xerxes. .... Est 2:21
Then Haman said to K Xerxes, ... Est 3:8
the k took his signet ring off .... Est 3:10
chosen by the k to serve her. .... Est 4:5
may go to the k in the inner .... Est 4:11
When the k saw Queen Esther .... Est 5:2
My k, if you are pleased with me .... Est 5:8
night the k could not sleep. .... Est 6:1
had warned the k about Bigthana .... Est 6:2
The k asked, "What honor and .... Est 6:3
the k asked him, "What should .... Est 6:6
The k was very angry, so he got .... Est 7:7
the eunuchs there serving the k, ... Est 7:9
Then the k took off his signet .... Est 8:2
The k held out the gold scepter .... Est 8:4
all the empire of K Xerxes was .... Est 8:12
because the k commanded those .... Est 8:14
K Xerxes demanded taxes .... Est 10:1
in importance to K Xerxes, ... Est 10:3
off to Death, the K of Terrors. .... Job 18:14
appointed my own k to rule in .... Ps 2:6
cry for help, my K and my God, ... Ps 5:2
The LORD is K forever and ever. .... Ps 10:16
gives great victories to his k. .... Ps 18:50
LORD, save the k! Answer us when .... Ps 20:9
The k truly trusts the LORD. .... Ps 21:7
and the glorious K will come .... Ps 24:7
Who is this glorious K? .... Ps 24:8
Who is this glorious K? .... Ps 24:10
The LORD will be K forever. .... Ps 29:10
No k is saved by his great army. .... Ps 33:16
God, you are my K. Your commands .... Ps 44:4
The k loves your beauty. .... Ps 45:11
clothes she is brought to the k. .... Ps 45:14
He is the great K over all the .... Ps 47:2

praises to our K. Sing praises. .... Ps 47:6
God is K of all the earth, ... Ps 47:7
it is the city of the Great K. .... Ps 48:2
But the k will rejoice in his .... Ps 63:11
God my K marched into the holy .... Ps 68:24
have been our k for a long time .... Ps 74:12
All-Powerful, my K and my God. .... Ps 84:3
the great K over all gods. .... Ps 95:3
shout for joy to the LORD the K. .... Ps 98:6
your greatness, my God the K; .... Ps 145:1
rejoice because of their K. .... Ps 149:2
son of David, k of Israel. .... Pr 1:1
An angry k is like a roaring .... Pr 20:2
A wise k sorts out the evil .... Pr 20:26
and truth keep a k in power; .... Pr 20:28
have even the k as a friend. .... Pr 22:11
respect the LORD and the k. .... Pr 24:21
The LORD and the k will quickly .... Pr 24:22
the men of Hezekiah k of Judah. .... Pr 25:1
If a k is fair, he makes his .... Pr 29:4
a k judges poor people fairly, ... Pr 29:14
Locusts have no k, but they all .... Pr 30:27
and a k when his army is around .... Pr 30:31
These are the words of K Lemuel, ... Pr 31:1
a son of David, k in Jerusalem. .... Ec 1:1
was k over Israel in Jerusalem. .... Ec 1:12
a foolish but old k who doesn't .... Ec 4:13
A boy became k. He had been born .... Ec 4:14
to prison before becoming k. .... Ec 4:14
for a country whose k is a child .... Ec 10:16
fun of the k, and don't make .... Ec 10:20
The k takes me into his rooms. .... Sng 1:4
K Solomon had a couch made for .... Sng 3:9
go out and see K Solomon. .... Sng 3:11
In the year that K Uzziah died, ... Is 6:1
but I have seen the K, the LORD .... Is 6:5
of Tabeel the new k of Judah." .... Is 7:6
will bring the k of Assyria to .... Is 7:17
Sargon k of Assyria sent a .... Is 20:1
A k will rule in a way that .... Is 32:1
will see the k in his beauty. .... Is 33:17
The LORD is our k. He will save .... Is 33:22
prophet went to K Hezekiah and .... Is 39:3
The K of Jacob says, "Tell me .... Is 41:21
the Creator of Israel, your K." .... Is 43:15
LORD, the k of Israel, is the .... Is 44:6
Jerusalem's k still there?" .... Je 8:19
respect you, K of the nations; .... Je 10:7
only living God, the K forever. .... Je 10:10
Nebuchadnezzar k of Babylon. .... Je 25:9
but the k of Babylon will drink .... Je 25:26
to see Zedekiah k of Judah. .... Je 27:3
Nebuchadnezzar k of Babylon .... Je 27:8
their God and David their k, ... Je 30:9
the army of the k of Babylon was .... Je 34:7
K Jehoiakim sent Jehudi to get .... Je 36:21
K Jehoiakim was sitting in the .... Je 36:22
the k cut those columns off of .... Je 36:23
So K Jehoiakim burned the scroll .... Je 36:27
Jeremiah said to K Zedekiah, ... Je 37:18
now, my master, k of Judah, ... Je 37:20
Riblah the k of Babylon killed .... Je 39:6
'Hophra k of Egypt has enemies. .... Je 44:30
'The k of Egypt is only a lot of .... Je 46:17
them up was the k of Assyria. .... Je 50:17
Nebuchadnezzar k of Babylon." .... Je 50:17
Riblah the k of Babylon killed .... Je 52:10
Hamath, the k had them killed. .... Je 52:27
I will bring a k from the north .... Eze 26:7
funeral song for the k of Tyre. .... Eze 28:12
look toward the k of Egypt, ... Eze 29:2
One k will rule all of them. .... Eze 37:22
that Jehoiakim was k of Judah, ... Da 1:1

Nebuchadnezzar **k** of Babylon came .... Da 1:1
The **k** gave the young men a .... Da 1:5
servants of the **k** of Babylon. .... Da 1:5
The **k** talked to them and found .... Da 1:19
time the **k** asked them about .... Da 1:20
the first year Cyrus was **k.** .... Da 1:21
So the **k** called for his .... Da 2:2
in and stood in front of the **k.** .... Da 2:2
answered the **k** in the Aramaic .... Da 2:4
language, "O **k,** live forever! .... Da 2:4
When the **k** heard their answer, ... Da 2:12
Why did the **k** order such a .... Da 2:15
Daniel went to **K** Nebuchadnezzar .... Da 2:16
took Daniel to the **k** and said,................ Da 2:25
can tell the **k** what his dream .... Da 2:25
he has shown **K** Nebuchadnezzar .... Da 2:28
k, as you were lying there, you .... Da 2:29
O **k,** you are the greatest king. .... Da 2:37
K Nebuchadnezzar, you saw a rock .... Da 2:45
the **k** gave Daniel many gifts .... Da 2:48
K Nebuchadnezzar made a gold............. Da 3:1
who advised the **k,** keepers.................. Da 3:2
the gold statue **K** Nebuchadnezzar .... Da 3:7
save us from your power, O **k.** .... Da 3:17
we want you, O **k,** to know this: .... Da 3:18
Then the **k** promoted Shadrach, ... Da 3:30
and glory to the **K** of heaven. .... Da 4:37
K Belshazzar gave a big banquet .... Da 5:1
or tell the **k** what it meant. .... Da 5:8
K Belshazzar became even more .... Da 5:9
Your father, **K** Nebuchadnezzar,............. Da 5:11
Then Daniel answered the **k,** .... Da 5:17
k of the Babylonian people, ... Da 5:30
as a group to the **k** and said: .... Da 6:6
god or human except to you, O **k.** .... Da 6:7
So **K** Darius signed the law. .... Da 6:9
Then the **k** used his signet ring .... Da 6:17
next morning **K** Darius got up at .... Da 6:19
answered, "O **k,** live forever! .... Da 6:21
bold and cruel **k** who tells lies .... Da 8:23
Then a mighty **k** will come, ... Da 11:3
The **k** of the South will become .... Da 11:5
daughter of the **k** of the South .... Da 11:6
son of Jehoash was **k** of Israel. .... Hos 1:1
many days without a **k** or leader, ... Hos 3:4
him and the **k** from David's .... Hos 3:5
say, "We have no **k,** because we .... Hos 10:3
So I gave you a **k,** but only in .... Hos 13:11
the time Uzziah was **k** of Judah .... Am 1:1
son of Jehoash was **k** of Israel. .... Am 1:1
the bones of the **k** of Edom into .... Am 2:1
message to Jeroboam **k** of Israel: .... Am 7:10
When the **k** of Nineveh heard this .... Jnh 3:6
plans of Balak **k** of Moab and................ Mic 6:5
The **K** of Israel, the LORD, is .... Zph 3:15
second year that Darius was **k,** .... Hag 1:1
Your **k** is coming to you......................... Zch 9:9
when Uzziah was **k** of Judah.................. Zch 14:5
LORD will be **k** over the whole .... Zch 14:9
to Jerusalem to worship the **K,** .... Zch 14:17
I am a great **k,**" says the LORD .... Mal 1:14
the time when Herod was **k.** .... Mt 2:1
born to the **k** of the Jews? .... Mt 2:2
that is the city of the great **K.** .... Mt 5:35
Your **k** is coming to you .... Mt 21:5
Then the **K** will say to the .... Mt 25:34
"Are you the **k** of the Jews?" .... Mt 27:11
saying, "Hail, **K** of the Jews!" .... Mt 27:29
IS JESUS, THE **K** OF THE JEWS. .... Mt 27:37
He says he is the **k** of Israel! .... Mt 27:42
the Christ, the **k** of Israel, let .... Mk 15:32
If a **k** is going to fight another .... Lk 14:31
God bless the **k** who comes in the .... Lk 19:38

calls himself the Christ, a **k.**" .... Lk 23:2
you are the **K** of Israel." .... Jn 1:49
by force and make him their **k,** .... Jn 6:15
Your **k** is coming, sitting on the .... Jn 12:15
Pilate said, "So you are a **k!**" .... Jn 18:37
makes himself **k** is against .... Jn 19:12
to the crowd, "Here is your **k!**" .... Jn 19:14
you want me to crucify your **k?**" .... Jn 19:15
"The only **k** we have is Caesar." .... Jn 19:15
OF NAZARETH, THE **K** OF THE JEWS. ... Jn 19:19
write, 'The **K** of the Jews.' .... Jn 19:21
away, God made David their **k.** .... Ac 13:22
A few days later **K** Agrippa and .... Ac 25:13
My **k,** they have accused me .... Ac 26:7
K Agrippa, after I had this .... Ac 26:19
K Agrippa knows about these .... Ac 26:26
K Agrippa, do you believe what .... Ac 26:27
To the **K** that rules forever, ... 1Ti 1:17
the **K** of all kings and the Lord 1Ti 6:15
Melchizedek was the **k** of Salem .... Heb 7:1
name means "**k** of goodness," .... Heb 7:2
and he is **k** of Salem, which .... Heb 7:2
Salem, which means "**k** of peace." .... Heb 7:2
the son of the **k** of Egypt's .... Heb 11:24
the **k,** who is the highest 1Pe 2:13
respect God, honor the **k.** 1Pe 2:17
and true, **K** of the nations. .... Rev 15:3
alive now, is also an eighth **k.**................ Rev 17:11
is Lord of lords and **K** of kings. .... Rev 17:14
K OF KINGS AND LORD OF LORDS. ...... Rev 19:16

KING'S

They took her to the **k** palace, ... Ge 12:15
of Shaveh (now called **K** Valley). .... Ge 14:17
prison where the **k** prisoners .... Ge 39:20
two of the **k** officers displeased .... Ge 40:1
to the king and the **k** baker. .... Ge 40:1
night both the **k** officer who .... Ge 40:5
He asked the **k** officers who were .... Ge 40:7
was holding the **k** cup, so I took............. Ge 40:11
again he put the **k** cup of wine .... Ge 40:21
cup of wine into the **k** hand. .... Ge 40:21
and under the **k** authority they .... Ge 41:35
And he left the **k** court and.................... Ge 41:46
the people in the **k** palace heard............. Ge 45:2
that money to the **k** palace.................... Ge 47:14
So the land became the **k,** .... Ge 47:20
spoke to the **k** officers and said .... Ge 50:4
All the **k** officers, the elders .... Ge 50:7
The **k** daughter opened the basket .... Ex 2:6
sister asked the **k** daughter, ... Ex 2:7
The **k** daughter said, "Go!".................... Ex 2:8
k daughter said to the woman, ... Ex 2:9
took him to the **k** daughter, ... Ex 2:10
The **k** daughter named him Moses, ... Ex 2:10
The **k** slave masters had made the .... Ex 5:14
came into the **k** palace and his .... Ex 8:24
Some of the **k** officers respected .... Ex 9:20
The **k** officers asked him, ... Ex 10:7
and both the **k** officers and the .... Ex 11:3
with all the **k** horses, chariot .... Ex 14:9
Then all the **k** horses, chariots, ... Ex 14:23
and all the **k** army that had .... Ex 14:28
The **k** best officers are drowned .... Ex 15:4
travel only along the **k** road, ... Nu 20:17
only along the **k** road until we .... Nu 21:22
Egypt and to the **k** leaders and .... Dt 29:2
the **k** men went out looking for .... Jos 2:7
just after the **k** men left the .... Jos 2:7
the hills so the **k** men will not .... Jos 2:16
After the **k** men return, you may .... Jos 2:16
The **k** men looked for them all .... Jos 2:22
his men to take the **k** body down .... Jos 8:29

K

She fell at the **k** feet and cried .... Est 8:3
Now, in the **k** name, write .... Est 8:8
order with the **k** signet ring, ... Est 8:8
written in the **k** name and sealed .... Est 8:8
that time the **k** secretaries were .... Est 8:9
letters with the **k** signet ring. .... Est 8:10
Then he sent the **k** orders by .... Est 8:10
These were the **k** orders:........................ Est 8:11
A copy of the **k** order was to be .... Est 8:13
left the **k** presence wearing. .... Est 8:15
As the **k** order went to every .... Est 8:17
city to which the **k** order went, ... Est 8:17
and the **k** officers helped the .... Est 9:3
very important in the **k** palace. .... Est 9:4
in the rest of the **k** empire! .... Est 9:12
people in the **k** empire also met .... Est 9:16
the hearts of the **k** enemies. .... Ps 45:5
they enter the **k** palace. .... Ps 45:15
judgment and his **k** son your .... Ps 72:1
LORD can control a **k** mind as he .... Pr 21:1
people from the **k** presence; .... Pr 25:5
Obey the **k** command, because you .... Ec 8:2
obeys the **k** command will be .... Ec 8:5
a mare among the **k** stallions................. Sng 1:9
which is the length of a **k** life. .... Is 23:15
save us from the **k** power so that .... Is 37:20
like a **k** crown in your God's .... Is 62:3
Jerusalem and the **k** palaces will .... Je 19:13
name that this **k** palace will .... Je 22:5
out of the **k** palace and went .... Je 26:10
of the LORD and in the **k** palace .... Je 27:18
of the LORD and in the **k** palace .... Je 27:21
and the **k** palace will stand in .... Je 30:18
room in the **k** palace where all .... Je 36:12
Malkijah, the **k** son, which was .... Je 38:6
and went out from the **k** garden. .... Je 39:4
of the **k** special guards, ... Je 39:9
a member of the **k** family and had .... Je 41:1
k daughters and all the other .... Je 41:10
children, and the **k** daughters. .... Je 43:6
The **K** name is the LORD .... Je 46:18
arrange the **k** food and housing .... Je 51:59
the two walls by the **k** garden. .... Je 52:7
commander of the **k** special .... Je 52:12
of the **k** special guards, ... Je 52:14
of the **k** special guards, ... Je 52:15
commander of the **k** special .... Je 52:19
commander of the **k** special .... Je 52:24
of the **k** special guards, ... Je 52:30
his life, he ate at the **k** table. .... Je 52:33
good enough for a **k** scepter. .... Eze 19:11
not to eat the **k** food or drink .... Da 1:8
men look who eat the **k** food. .... Da 1:13
young men who ate the **k** food. .... Da 1:15
took away the **k** special food .... Da 1:16
young men became the **k** servants.......... Da 1:19
to be the **k** servant until .... Da 1:21
the commander of the **k** guards,............ Da 2:14
you told us about the **k** dream." .... Da 2:23
The **k** command was very strict,............. Da 3:22
Then all the **k** wise men came in,.......... Da 5:8
Then the **k** mother, who had heard.......... Da 5:10
be in that **k** power for three .... Da 7:25
He will go into that **k** strong, ... Da 11:7
honor of being from a **k** family. .... Da 11:21
This is the **k** holy place, and it .... Am 7:13
princes and the **k** sons and all .... Zph 1:8
of Hananel to the **k** winepresses. .... Zch 14:10
the **k** children or others?" .... Mt 17:25
One of the **k** important officers .... Jn 4:46
the **k** daughter adopted him and.............. Ac 7:21
Blastus, the **k** personal servant, ... Ac 12:20

afraid to disobey the **k** order. .... Heb 11:23
was not afraid of the **k** anger................. Heb 11:27

KINGDOM

first Nimrod's **k** covered Babylon .... Ge 10:10
you bring this trouble to my **k**? .... Ge 20:9
you will be my **k** of priests and .... Ex 19:6
their **k** will be very great. .... Nu 24:7
land had been the **k** of Sihon,................. Nu 32:33
Amorites, and the **k** of Og, king............. Nu 32:33
area of Argob, Og's **k** in Bashan. .... Dt 3:4
towns in Og's **k** of Bashan. .... Dt 3:10
and all of Bashan, the **k** of Og. .... Dt 3:13
may rule the **k** for a long time. .... Dt 17:20
All the **k** of Og king of Bashan .... Jos 13:12
have made your **k** continue in 1Sa 13:13
now your **k** will not continue.................. 1Sa 13:14
LORD has torn the **k** of Israel................. 1Sa 15:28
left for him to have is the **k**!" 1Sa 18:8
will never be king or have a **k**. 1Sa 20:31
you will rule the **k** of Israel. 1Sa 24:20
He has torn the **k** out of your 1Sa 28:17
will take the **k** from the family 2Sa 3:10
My **k** and I are innocent forever 2Sa 3:28
had made his **k** great because................ 2Sa 5:12
king, and I will set up his **k**. 2Sa 7:12
I will let his **k** rule always. 2Sa 7:13
family and your **k** will continue 2Sa 7:16
I gave you his **k** and his wives. 2Sa 12:8
my father's **k** back to me!'" 2Sa 16:3
LORD has given the **k** to your son 2Sa 16:8
We have ten tribes in the **k**, ... 2Sa 19:43
he was in firm control of his **k**. 1Ki 2:12
at one time the **k** was mine," 1Ki 2:15
and given the **k** to me and my 1Ki 2:24
was in full control of his **k**. 1Ki 2:46
had peace on all sides of his **k**. 1Ki 4:24
I will make your **k** strong. 1Ki 9:5
ever been made for any other **k**........... 1Ki 10:20
I will tear your **k** away from you 1Ki 11:11
tear away all the **k** from him, ... 1Ki 11:13
'I will tear the **k** away from................... 1Ki 11:31
not take all the **k** away from 1Ki 11:34
I will take the **k** away from his 1Ki 11:35
of Israel to take back his **k**................... 1Ki 12:21
The **k** will probably go back to 1Ki 12:26
if you gave me half of your **k**,............... 1Ki 13:8
I tore the **k** away from David's 1Ki 14:8
LORD gave him a **k** in Jerusalem 1Ki 15:4
Amaziah took control of the **k**, ... 2Ki 14:5
make his hold on the **k** stronger. 2Ki 15:19
in his palace and his **k**. 2Ki 20:13
and gave the **k** to Jesse's son 1Ch 10:14
helped make David's **k** strong. 1Ch 11:10
Israel also supported David's **k**. 1Ch 11:10
help turn the **k** of Saul over to 1Ch 12:23
that he had made his **k** great. 1Ch 14:2
another, from one **k** to another. 1Ch 16:20
king, and I will set up his **k**. 1Ch 17:11
I will let his **k** rule always. 1Ch 17:12
of my house and **k** forever. 1Ch 17:14
to spread his **k** to the Euphrates.............. 1Ch 18:3
I will make his **k** strong; 1Ch 22:10
Israel is the LORD's **k**. 1Ch 28:5
will make his **k** strong forever. 1Ch 28:7
The **k** belongs to you, LORD; 1Ch 29:11
I will make your **k** strong. 2Ch 7:18
ever been made for any other **k**. 2Ch 9:19
fight Israel to take back his **k**. 2Ch 11:1
made the **k** of Judah strong 2Ch 11:17
After Rehoboam's **k** was set up 2Ch 12:1
plans against the LORD's **k**, ... 2Ch 13:8
So the **k** had peace while Asa was 2Ch 14:5

Jehoshaphat's **k** was not at war.	2Ch 20:30
gave the **k** to Jehoram,	2Ch 21:3
took control of his father's **k**,	2Ch 21:4
take control of the **k** of Judah.	2Ch 22:9
took strong control of the **k**,	2Ch 25:3
people and the **k** of Judah and to	2Ch 29:21
any nation or **k** has been able to	2Ch 32:15
to Jerusalem and to his **k**.	2Ch 33:13
the Persian **k** defeated Babylon.	2Ch 36:20
an announcement to his whole **k**.	2Ch 36:22
to his whole **k** and to put it in	Ezr 1:1
Israelite in my **k** who wishes may	Ezr 7:13
were living in their **k**,	Ne 9:35
wealth of his **k** and his own	Est 1:4
had the highest rank in the **k**.	Est 1:14
everywhere in his enormous **k**.	Est 1:20
states of the **k** in the writing	Est 1:22
state of his **k** to bring every	Est 2:3
the Jews, in all of Xerxes' **k**.	Est 3:6
in all the states of your **k**.	Est 3:8
to continue living in your **k**.	Est 3:8
you as much as half of my **k**."	Est 5:3
you as much as half of my **k**."	Est 5:6
you as much as half of my **k**."	Est 7:2
Jewish people in all of your **k**.	Est 8:5
living in the **k** so the Jewish	Est 8:13
states of the **k** of Xerxes,	Est 9:30
will rule your **k** with fairness.	Ps 45:6
Let his **k** go from sea to sea,	Ps 72:8
Your **k** will go on and on.'"	Ps 89:4
Your **k** is built on what is right	Ps 89:14
and his **k** will last as long as	Ps 89:29
His **k** will last before me like	Ps 89:36
your **k** was set up long ago;	Ps 93:2
His **k** is built on what is right	Ps 97:2
and his **k** rules over everything.	Ps 103:19
another, from one **k** to another.	Ps 105:13
enlarge your **k** beyond Jerusalem	Ps 110:2
glory of your **k** and will speak	Ps 145:11
the glory and majesty of your **k**.	Ps 145:12
Your **k** will go on and on, and	Ps 145:13
born poor in the **k** and had even	Ec 4:14
will be in his **k** and will	Is 9:7
throne and over David's **k**.	Is 9:7
in his palace and in his **k**.	Is 39:2
The nation or **k** that doesn't	Is 60:12
a nation or a **k** that I will pull	Je 18:7
He threw her **k** and its rulers	La 2:2
to make the **k** weak so it would	Eze 17:14
Then the **k** of Judah could	Eze 17:14
They will become a weak **k** there.	Eze 29:14
be the weakest **k**, and it will	Eze 29:15
and magicians in his **k**!	Da 1:20
God of heaven has given you a **k**,	Da 2:37
Another **k** will come after you,	Da 2:39
Next a third **k**, the bronze part,	Da 2:39
Then there will be a fourth **k**,	Da 2:40
fourth **k** will smash and crush	Da 2:40
means the fourth **k** will be a	Da 2:41
kingdom will be a divided **k**.	Da 2:41
So the fourth **k** will be partly	Da 2:42
of the fourth **k** will be a	Da 2:43
set up another **k** that will never	Da 2:44
This **k** will crush all the other	Da 2:44
an important position in his **k**.	Da 2:48
and all other officers in his **k**.	Da 3:2
His **k** goes on forever, and his	Da 4:3
God rules over every **k** on earth.	Da 4:17
wise men in my **k** can explain it	Da 4:18
is ruler over every **k** on earth,	Da 4:25
your **k** will be given back to you	Da 4:26
that one in heaven rules your **k**.	Da 4:26
rules over every **k** on earth and	Da 4:32
his **k** continues for all time.	Da 4:34
and returned the glory to my **k**.	Da 4:36
third highest ruler in the **k**."	Da 5:7
is a man in your **k** who has the	Da 5:11
third highest ruler in the **k**."	Da 5:16
God rules over every **k** on earth,	Da 5:21
the days until your **k** will end.	Da 5:26
Your **k** is being divided and will	Da 5:28
third highest ruler in the **k**,	Da 5:29
governors who would rule his **k**.	Da 6:1
Daniel in charge of the whole **k**.	Da 6:3
people in every part of my **k**.	Da 6:26
His **k** will never be destroyed,	Da 6:26
and his **k** will never be	Da 7:14
is a fourth **k** that will come	Da 7:23
will come from this fourth **k**.	Da 7:24
and his **k** will be completely	Da 7:26
against the **k** of Greece.	Da 11:2
his **k** will be broken up and	Da 11:4
His **k** will not go to his	Da 11:4
because his **k** will be pulled up	Da 11:4
rule his own **k** with great power.	Da 11:5
attack the **k** when the people	Da 11:21
put an end to the **k** of Israel	Hos 1:4
am watching the sinful **k** Israel.	Am 9:8
The **k** of David is like a fallen	Am 9:11
And the **k** will belong to the	Ob 1:21
will come the **k** as in the past.	Mic 4:8
His **k** will go from sea to sea,	Zch 9:10
because the **k** of heaven is near	Mt 3:2
the **k** of heaven is near."	Mt 4:17
Good News about the **k** of heaven,	Mt 4:23
for the **k** of heaven belongs to	Mt 5:3
for the **k** of heaven belongs to	Mt 5:10
important in the **k** of heaven.	Mt 5:19
be great in the **k** of heaven.	Mt 5:19
never enter the **k** of heaven.	Mt 5:20
your **k** come and what you want	Mt 6:10
The **k**, the power, and the	Mt 6:13
Seek first God's **k** and what God	Mt 6:33
' will enter the **k** of heaven.	Mt 7:21
will enter the **k** of heaven are	Mt 7:21
and Jacob in the **k** of heaven.	Mt 8:11
be in the **k** will be thrown	Mt 8:12
the Good News about the **k**,	Mt 9:35
'The **k** of heaven is near.'	Mt 10:7
person in the **k** of heaven is	Mt 11:11
the **k** of heaven has been going	Mt 11:12
Every **k** that is divided against	Mt 12:25
and his **k** will not continue.	Mt 12:26
then the **k** of God has come to	Mt 12:28
secrets about the **k** of heaven,	Mt 13:11
message about the **k** but does not	Mt 13:19
The **k** of heaven is like a man	Mt 13:24
The **k** of heaven is like a	Mt 13:31
The **k** of heaven is like yeast	Mt 13:33
children who belong to the **k**.	Mt 13:38
out of his **k** all who cause sin	Mt 13:41
sun in the **k** of their Father.	Mt 13:43
The **k** of heaven is like a	Mt 13:44
the **k** of heaven is like a man	Mt 13:45
the **k** of heaven is like a net	Mt 13:47
taught about the **k** of heaven is	Mt 13:52
you the keys of the **k** of heaven;	Mt 16:19
with his **k** before they die.	Mt 16:28
is greatest in the **k** of heaven?"	Mt 18:1
never enter the **k** of heaven.	Mt 18:3
person in the **k** of heaven is the	Mt 18:4
The **k** of heaven is like a king	Mt 18:23
because of the **k** of heaven.	Mt 19:12
because the **k** of heaven belongs	Mt 19:14
person to enter the **k** of heaven.	Mt 19:23
person to enter the **k** of God."	Mt 19:24

The **k** of heaven is like a person .... Mt 20:1
at your left side in your **k**." .... Mt 20:21
will enter the **k** of God before .... Mt 21:31
you that the **k** of God will be .... Mt 21:43
the things God wants in his **k**. .... Mt 21:43
The **k** of heaven is like a king. .... Mt 22:2
people to enter the **k** of heaven. .... Mt 23:13
about God's **k** will be preached .... Mt 24:14
that time the **k** of heaven will .... Mt 25:1
The **k** of heaven is like a man. .... Mt 25:14
Receive the **k** God has prepared .... Mt 25:34
new with you in my Father's **k**." .... Mt 26:29
The **k** of God is near. .... Mk 1:15
k that is divided cannot continue, ... Mk 3:24
the secret about the **k** of God. .... Mk 4:11
The **k** of God is like someone who .... Mk 4:26
you what the **k** of God is like? .... Mk 4:30
The **k** of God is like a mustard .... Mk 4:31
give to you—up to half of my **k**." .... Mk 6:23
will see the **k** of God come with .... Mk 9:1
to enter the **k** of God with only .... Mk 9:47
because the **k** of God belongs to .... Mk 10:14
must accept the **k** of God as if .... Mk 10:15
the rich to enter the **k** of God!" .... Mk 10:23
very hard to enter the **k** of God! .... Mk 10:24
person to enter the **k** of God." .... Mk 10:25
side in your glory in your **k**." .... Mk 10:37
God bless the **k** of our father .... Mk 11:10
David! That **k** is coming! Praise .... Mk 11:10
"You are close to the **k** of God." .... Mk 12:34
I drink it new in the **k** of God." .... Mk 14:25
for the **k** of God to come. .... Mk 15:43
and his **k** will never end." .... Lk 1:33
about God's **k** to other towns, ... Lk 4:43
because the **k** of God belongs to .... Lk 6:20
in the **k** of God is greater .... Lk 7:28
the Good News about God's **k**. .... Lk 8:1
the secrets about the **k** of God. .... Lk 8:10
tell about God's **k** and to heal .... Lk 9:2
about God's **k** and healed those .... Lk 9:11
will see the **k** of God before .... Lk 9:27
go and tell about the **k** of God." .... Lk 9:60
is of no use in the **k** of God." .... Lk 9:62
'The **k** of God is near you.' .... Lk 10:9
that the **k** of God is near.' .... Lk 10:11
be kept holy. May your **k** come. .... Lk 11:2
Every **k** that is divided against .... Lk 11:17
his **k** will not continue. .... Lk 11:18
then the **k** of God has come to .... Lk 11:20
But seek God's **k**, and all your .... Lk 12:31
Father wants to give you the **k**. .... Lk 12:32
said, "What is God's **k** like? .... Lk 13:18
What can I compare God's **k** with? .... Lk 13:20
and all the prophets in God's **k**, ... Lk 13:28
at the table in the **k** of God. .... Lk 13:29
share in the meal in God's **k**." .... Lk 14:15
News about the **k** of God is being .... Lk 16:16
"When will the **k** of God come?" .... Lk 17:20
answered, "God's **k** is coming, ... Lk 17:20
because God's **k** is within you." .... Lk 17:21
because the **k** of God belongs to .... Lk 18:16
must accept the **k** of God as if .... Lk 18:17
people to enter the **k** of God. .... Lk 18:24
person to enter the **k** of God." .... Lk 18:25
or children for the **k** of God .... Lk 18:29
thought God's **k** would appear .... Lk 19:11
people in the **k** hated the man. .... Lk 19:14
will know that God's **k** is near. .... Lk 21:31
true meaning in the **k** of God." .... Lk 22:16
the vine until God's **k** comes." .... Lk 22:18
as my Father has given me a **k**, ... Lk 22:29
a kingdom, I also give you a **k** .... Lk 22:29
and drink at my table in my **k**. .... Lk 22:30

me when you come into your **k**." .... Lk 23:42
for the **k** of God to come. .... Lk 23:51
you cannot be in God's **k**." .... Jn 3:3
you cannot enter God's **k**. .... Jn 3:5
My **k** does not belong to this .... Jn 18:36
But my **k** is from another place." .... Jn 18:36
to them about the **k** of God. .... Ac 1:3
to give the **k** back to Israel?" .... Ac 1:6
Good News about the **k** of God and .... Ac 8:12
many things to enter God's **k**." .... Ac 14:22
The **k** of David is like a fallen .... Ac 15:16
he said about the **k** of God. .... Ac 19:8
preaching the **k** of God will ever .... Ac 20:25
he explained the **k** of God, ... Ac 28:23
about the **k** of God and taught .... Ac 28:31
In the **k** of God, eating and .... Rm 14:17
because the **k** of God is present 1Co 4:20
hand over the **k** to God the 1Co 15:24
have a part in the **k** of 1Co 15:50
things will not inherit God's **k**. .... Gal 5:21
have a place in the **k** of Christ .... Eph 5:5
his people in the **k** of light. .... Col 1:12
us into the **k** of his dear Son. .... Col 1:13
work with me for the **k** of God, ... Col 4:11
who calls you to his glorious **k**. 1Th 2:12
worthy of his **k** for which you 2Th 1:5
and by his coming and his **k**: 2Ti 4:1
me safely to his heavenly **k**. 2Ti 4:18
will rule your **k** with fairness. .... Heb 1:8
we have a **k** that cannot be .... Heb 12:28
to receive the **k** God promised to .... Jam 2:5
into the eternal **k** of our Lord 2Pe 1:11
made us to be a **k** of priests who .... Rev 1:6
in the **k**, and in patience .... Rev 1:9
them to be a **k** of priests for .... Rev 5:10
the power and the **k** of our God .... Rev 12:10
and darkness covered its **k**. .... Rev 16:10

KINGDOMS

thing to all the **k** where you are .... Dt 3:21
leader of all the **k** that fought .... Jos 11:10
over all the **k** from the 1Ki 4:21
God of all the **k** of the earth. 2Ki 19:15
given me all the **k** of the earth, ... 2Ch 36:23
given all the **k** of the earth to .... Ezr 1:2
Nations tremble and **k** shake. .... Ps 46:6
K of the earth, sing to God; .... Ps 68:32
you and with the **k** that do not .... Ps 79:6
and **k** will serve the LORD. .... Ps 102:22
I defeated those **k** that worship .... Is 10:10
Listen to the noise among the **k**, ... Is 13:4
is the most beautiful of all **k**, ... Is 13:19
fear on earth, who shook the **k**, ... Is 14:16
the sea and made its **k** tremble. .... Is 23:11
you in charge of nations and **k**. .... Je 1:10
I use you to destroy **k**. .... Je 51:20
be divided into two **k** anymore. .... Eze 37:22
all the other **k** and bring them .... Da 2:44
of the broken horn are four **k**. .... Da 8:22
You are no better than these **k**. .... Am 6:2
the foreign **k** and take away .... Hag 2:22
showed him all the **k** of the .... Lk 4:5
their faith they defeated **k**. .... Heb 11:33

KINGLY

dressed him in a **k** robe and sent .... Lk 23:11

KINGS

four **k** fighting against five. .... Ge 14:9
When the **k** of Sodom and Gomorrah ...... Ge 14:10
and Og, the **k** of the Amorites, ... Dt 31:4
these five Amorite **k**—the kings .... Jos 10:5
the five **k** out to Joshua, ... Jos 10:24
Seventy **k** whose thumbs and big .... Jdg 1:7
k. Pay attention, rulers! .... Jdg 5:3

The **k** came, and they fought. .... Jdg 5:19
when the **k** normally went out to 2Sa 11:1
The **k** of all nations sent them 1Ki 4:34
the history of the **k** of Israel. 1Ki 14:19
that the **k** of Assyria have 2Ki 19:17
in the book of the **k** of Israel. 1Ch 9:1
in the ways of the **k** of Israel, ... 2Ch 21:6
but not in the graves for the **k.** 2Ch 21:20
written in the book of the **k.** 2Ch 24:27
king of **k,** to Ezra the priest .... Ezr 7:12
books of the **k** of Media and .... Est 10:2
with **k** and wise men of the earth .... Job 3:14
chains that **k** put on and puts .... Job 12:18
The **k** of the earth prepare to .... Ps 2:2
So, **k,** be wise; rulers, learn.................... Ps 2:10
K joined together and came to .... Ps 48:4
K and their armies run away. .... Ps 68:12
K will bring their wealth to you,.............. Ps 68:29
all **k** bow down to him and all .... Ps 72:11
he warned **k** not to harm them. .... Ps 105:14
becomes angry, he will crush **k.** .... Ps 110:5
your rules with **k** and will not .... Ps 119:46
nations and killed powerful **k:** .... Ps 135:10
He defeated great **k.** His love .... Ps 136:17
He killed powerful **k.** His love .... Ps 136:18
all the **k** of the earth praise.................... Ps 138:4
I help **k** to govern and rulers to .... Pr 8:15
will work for **k,** not for .... Pr 22:29
K are honored for what they can .... Pr 25:2
K should not drink wine, Lemuel, ... Pr 31:4
and Hezekiah were **k** of Judah. .... Is 1:1
from the old family of the **k**'? .... Is 19:11
K will be amazed and shut their.............. Is 52:15
and their **k** will be led to you.................. Is 60:11
Judah's **k,** officers, priests, ... Je 1:18
the **k** who sit on David's throne,.............. Je 13:13
k who sit on David's throne will .... Je 22:4
all the **k** of Tyre and Sidon;.................... Je 25:22
all the **k** of Zimri, Elam, and .... Je 25:25
and all the **k** of the north, ... Je 25:26
the evil the **k** and queens of .... Je 44:9
K of the earth and people of the.............. La 4:12
the power of **k** and gives their .... Da 2:21
all gods, the Lord of all the **k.**.............. Da 2:47
are the **k** of Media and Persia. .... Da 8:20
more **k** will rule in Persia, ... Da 11:2
All their **k** fall, and no one .... Hos 7:7
chose their own **k** without asking .... Hos 8:4
to stand before governors and **k,** .... Mt 10:18
many prophets and **k** wanted to .... Lk 10:24
to stand before **k** and governors, ... Lk 21:12
The **k** of the non-Jewish people .... Lk 22:25
the King of all **k** and the Lord 1Ti 6:15
back after defeating the **k.** .... Heb 7:1
the ruler of the **k** of the earth. .... Rev 1:5
nations, languages, and **k.**"...................... Rev 10:11
the way for the **k** from the east .... Rev 16:12
they are seven **k.** Five of the .... Rev 17:10
you saw are ten **k** who have not .... Rev 17:12
is Lord of lords and King of **k.** .... Rev 17:14
KING OF **K** AND LORD OF LORDS.......... Rev 19:16

KINNERETH
Zer, Hammath, Rakkath, **K,** .... Jos 19:35

KIOS
next day came to a place near **K.** .... Ac 20:15

KIR
K Hareseth was the only city 2Ki 3:25
sent all its people away to **K.** 2Ki 16:9
took the wealth from **K** in Moab, ... Is 15:1
cakes they had in **K** Hareseth. .... Is 16:7
I am very sad for **K** Hareseth.................. Is 16:11
K will prepare their shields. .... Is 22:6

from the town of **K** Hareseth. .... Je 48:31
for the people from **K** Hareseth. .... Je 48:36
captive to the country of **K,**" .... Am 1:5
Crete, and the Arameans from **K.** .... Am 9:7

KISH
of Saul's father, **K,** were lost. 1Sa 9:3
K said to Saul, his son, "Take 1Sa 9:3
and Saul son of **K** was picked. 1Sa 10:21
in the tomb of Saul's father **K.** 2Sa 21:14
so God gave them Saul son of **K.** .... Ac 13:21

KISHI
this group was Ethan son of **K.** 1Ch 6:44
son of Kishi. **K** was Abdi's son. 1Ch 6:44

KISHION
Rabbith, **K,** Ebez, ... Jos 19:20
tribe of Issachar gave them **K,** .... Jos 21:28

KISHON
army meet you at the **K** River. .... Jdg 4:7
Haggoyim to the **K** River. .... Jdg 4:13
The **K** River swept Sisera's men .... Jdg 5:21
that old river, the **K** River. .... Jdg 5:21
led them down to the **K** Valley. 1Ki 18:40
Sisera and Jabin at the **K** River. .... Ps 83:9

KISLEV
In the month of **K** in the .... Ne 1:1
is called **K,** the LORD spoke .... Zch 7:1

KISLON
of Benjamin, Elidad son of **K;**.................. Nu 34:21

KISLOTH
to the area of **K** Tabor and on to.............. Jos 19:12

KISS
"My son, come near and **k** me." .... Ge 27:26
not even let me **k** my .... Ge 31:28
take hold of them and **k** them. 2Sa 15:5
Amasa by the beard to **k** him.................... 2Sa 20:9
Let me **k** my father and my mother 1Ki 19:20
the sun and moon a **k** of worship. .... Job 31:27
as pleasing as a **k** on the lips.................... Pr 24:26
K me with the kisses of your .... Sng 1:2
is sweet to **k,** and I desire him .... Sng 5:16
I would **k** you, and no one .... Sng 8:1
before you and **k** the dirt at .... Is 49:23
K those calf idols and sacrifice .... Hos 13:2
saying, "The man I **k** is Jesus. .... Mt 26:48
saying, "The man I **k** is Jesus. .... Mk 14:44
You gave me no **k** of greeting, ... Lk 7:45
to Jesus so he could **k** him.................... Lk 22:47
you using the **k** to give the Son .... Lk 22:48
Greet each other with a holy **k.** .... Rm 16:16
other a holy **k** when you meet. 1Co 16:20
Greet each other with a holy **k.** 2Co 13:12
other a holy **k** when you meet. 1Th 5:26
each other a **k** of Christian love 1Pe 5:14

KISSED
went to his father and **k** him. .... Ge 27:27
Then Jacob **k** Rachel and cried. .... Ge 29:11
hugged him and **k** him and brought .... Ge 29:13
morning Laban **k** his .... Ge 31:55
Then Esau **k** him, and they both.............. Ge 33:4
Joseph **k** all his brothers and .... Ge 45:15
Israel **k** the boys and put his .... Ge 48:10
and cried over him and **k** him. .... Ge 50:1
the mountain of God, and **k** him. .... Ex 4:27
and bowed down and **k** him. .... Ex 18:7
When Naomi **k** the women .... Ru 1:9
Then Orpah **k** her mother-in-law .... Ru 1:14
k Saul and said, "The LORD has 1Sa 10:1
David and Jonathan **k** each other 1Sa 20:41
the king, and the king **k** him. 2Sa 14:33
The king **k** Barzillai and blessed 2Sa 19:39

KISSES

mouths have never **k** his idol." 1Ki 19:18
She grabbed him and **k** him. .... Pr 7:13
Greetings, Teacher!" and **k** him. .... Mt 26:49
and said, "Teacher!" and **k** him. .... Mk 14:45
ran to him and hugged and **k** him. .... Lk 15:20

KISSES

the **k** of an enemy are nothing .... Pr 27:6
me with the **k** of your mouth, ... Sng 1:2

KISSING

k them many times and rubbing.............. Lk 7:38
she has been **k** my feet since I .... Lk 7:45

KITCHEN

and your **k** will be blessed .... Dt 28:5
and your **k** will be cursed. .... Dt 28:17

KITCHENS

These are the **k** where those who .... Eze 46:24

KITE

kites, falcons, any kind of **k,** .... Dt 14:13

KITES

k, any kind of falcon, ... Le 11:14
k, falcons, any kind of kite, ... Dt 14:13

KITLISH

Cabbon, Lahmas, **K,** .... Jos 15:40

KITRON

in the cities of **K** and Nahalol. .... Jdg 1:30

KITTIM

Tarshish, **K,** and Rodanim. .... Ge 10:4
Tarshish, **K,** and Rodanim. 1Ch 1:7

KNEE

so that every **k** will bow to the .... Php 2:10

KNEEL

made the camels **k** down at the .... Ge 24:11
bow down and **k** before Haman,............... Est 3:2
Let's **k** before the LORD who made .... Ps 95:6
day Daniel would **k** down to pray .... Da 6:10
enough even to **k** down and untie .... Mk 1:7

KNEELED

Then he **k** in front of all the 2Ch 6:13
He **k** down and prayed, ... Lk 22:41
of the room and **k** and prayed. .... Ac 9:40

KNEELING

k in front of the altar with his 1Ki 8:54

KNEES

boils on your **k** and legs that .... Dt 28:35
got down on their **k** to drink. .... Jdg 7:6
with his head between his **k.** 1Ki 18:42
fell down on his **k** before Elijah 2Ki 1:13
and I fell on my **k** with my hands .... Ezr 9:5
did my mother's **k** receive me, ... Job 3:12
My **k** are weak from fasting, ... Ps 109:24
strong and the weak **k** steady. .... Is 35:3
in my arms and bounced on my **k.** .... Is 66:12
all **k** will become weak as water. .... Eze 7:17
all **k** will become weak as water. .... Eze 21:7
water that came up to my **k.** .... Eze 47:4
white, his **k** knocked together................ Da 5:6
me and set me on my hands and **k.** .... Da 10:10
courage, and their **k** knock. .... Nah 2:10
fell on his **k** and begged, ' .... Mt 18:26
fell on his **k** and begged him, ' .... Mt 18:29
He fell on his **k** and begged .... Mk 1:40
and fell on his **k** before Jesus. .... Mk 10:17
bowing on their **k** and worshiping .... Mk 15:19
He fell on his **k** and cried in a .... Ac 7:60

KNELT

bowed and **k** before the king. 1Ki 1:16
the ground and **k** before the king 1Ki 1:31
to Eutychus, **k** down, and put his .... Ac 20:10

he **k** down with all of them and .... Ac 20:36
After we all **k** on the beach and .... Ac 21:5

KNEW

The LORD **k** Moses face to face .... Dt 34:10
wish I **k** where to find God so I .... Job 23:3
you already **k** these things, ... Da 5:22
though Daniel **k** that the new law .... Da 6:10
you who do evil. I never **k** you.' .... Mt 7:23
Jesus **k** what the Pharisees were .... Mt 12:25
I **k** that you were a hard man.................. Mt 25:24
You say you **k** that I harvest .... Mt 25:26
You **k** that I am a hard man, ... Lk 19:22
who had brought the water **k.**................. Jn 2:9
he **k** what was in people's .... Jn 2:25
If you only **k** the free gift of .... Jn 4:10
Jesus **k** that it was time for him .... Jn 13:1
Jesus **k** who would turn against .... Jn 13:11
only baptism Apollos **k** about was .... Ac 18:25
k God, but they did not give .... Rm 1:21
because you **k** you had something .... Heb 10:34

KNIFE

himself took the **k** and the fire. .... Ge 22:6
took his **k** and was about to .... Ge 22:10
took a flint **k** and circumcised .... Ex 4:25
he took a **k** and cut his slave .... Jdg 19:29
him in the side with a **k.** 2Sa 2:16
cut it up with the **k** all around .... Eze 5:2

KNIVES

Make **k** from flint stones and .... Jos 5:2

KNOCK

K, and the door will open for you. .... Mt 7:7
K, and the door will open for you. .... Lk 11:9
stand outside and **k** on the door .... Lk 13:25
continued to **k,** and when they .... Ac 12:16
I stand at the door and **k.** .... Rev 3:20

KNOCKED

The city walls will be **k** down, ... Is 22:5
his knees **k** together, and he .... Da 5:6
The goat **k** the sheep to the.................... Da 8:7
Peter **k** on the outside door, ... Ac 12:13

KNOCKING

I hear my lover **k.** .... Sng 5:2

KNOCKS

If a master **k** out a tooth of his .... Ex 21:27
anyone who **k** down a wall might .... Ec 10:8
And everyone who **k** will have the .... Mt 7:8
And everyone who **k** will have the .... Lk 11:10
he comes and **k,** the servants .... Lk 12:36

KNOW

one of us; they **k** good and evil. .... Ge 3:22
Cain answered, "I don't **k.** .... Ge 4:9
But Lot did not **k** when she lay .... Ge 19:33
and don't **k** when I might die.................. Ge 27:2
this place, but I did not **k** it." .... Ge 28:16
Jacob did not **k** that Rachel had .... Ge 31:32
We don't **k** who put that money in .... Ge 43:22
who did not **k** who Joseph was. .... Ex 1:8
I do not **k** the LORD, and I will .... Ex 5:2
but we don't **k** what has happened........... Ex 32:1
You **k** that these people are.................... Ex 32:22
said to me, 'I **k** you very well, ... Ex 33:12
You will **k** me as your enemy.' .... Nu 14:34
You **k** about all the troubles we .... Nu 20:14
K and believe today that .... Dt 4:39
he wanted to **k** what was in your .... Dt 8:2
He wanted to **k** if you would obey .... Dt 8:2
to gods they did not even **k.** .... Dt 29:26
I **k** what they plan to do, even............... Dt 31:21
I **k** how stubborn and disobedient .... Dt 31:27
I don't **k** where they went, ... Jos 2:5

K

You **k** and fully believe that the .... Jos 23:14
in our town **k** you are a good .... Ru 3:11
Samuel did not yet **k** the LORD, ... 1Sa 3:7
the world will **k** there is a God 1Sa 17:46
You **k** Abner son of Ner! 2Sa 3:25
Today I **k** you are pleased with 2Sa 14:22
I don't even **k** where I'm going? 2Sa 15:20
I will **k** how many there are. 2Sa 24:2
You **k** the many wrong things you 1Ki 2:44
treated because you **k** what is in 1Ki 8:39
Only you **k** what is in everyone's 1Ki 8:39
everywhere will **k** you and 1Ki 8:43
Now I **k** you really are a man 1Ki 17:24
I **k** that this is a holy man of 2Ki 4:9
I **k** that God has decided to 2Ch 25:16
They **k** the laws of your God, ... Ezr 7:25
anyone who does not **k** them. .... Ezr 7:25
The Jews won't **k** or see anything .... Ne 4:11
places will not **k** them anymore .... Job 7:10
has two sides. **K** this: God has .... Job 11:6
What you **k,** I also know. .... Job 13:2
and I **k** I will be proved right. .... Job 13:18
of one who does not **k** God." .... Job 18:21
I **k** that my Defender lives, ... Job 19:25
I **k** very well your thoughts and .... Job 21:27
But you ask, 'What does God **k**? .... Job 22:13
Then he will **k** I have done .... Job 31:6
Do you **k** how God controls the .... Job 37:15
Do you **k** how the clouds hang in .... Job 37:16
be? Surely you **k**! Who stretched .... Job 38:5
you **k,** if you were already .... Job 38:21
Do you **k** the laws of the sky and .... Job 38:33
Do you **k** when the mountain goats .... Job 39:1
I **k** that you can do all things .... Job 42:2
You **k** that the LORD has chosen .... Ps 4:3
Those who **k** the LORD trust him, ... Ps 9:10
Now I **k** the LORD helps his .... Ps 20:6
They ask me things I do not **k.** .... Ps 35:11
Let me **k** how long I have. .... Ps 39:4
Be still and **k** that I am God. .... Ps 46:10
I **k** about my wrongs, and I can't .... Ps 51:3
Then they will **k** that God rules .... Ps 59:13
you **k** what I have done wrong; .... Ps 69:5
You **k** all my enemies and what .... Ps 69:19
They say, "How can God **k**? .... Ps 73:11
that do not **k** you and with .... Ps 79:6
Then they will **k** that you are .... Ps 83:18
the people who **k** how to praise .... Ps 89:15
people don't **k** these things, ... Ps 92:6
teacher of people **k** everything? .... Ps 94:10
K that the LORD is God. .... Ps 100:3
to me, those who **k** your rules. .... Ps 119:79
You **k** when I sit down and when I .... Ps 139:2
I say a word, you already **k** it. .... Ps 139:4
examine me and **k** my heart; .... Ps 139:23
test me and **k** my anxious .... Ps 139:23
he didn't **k** what he did would .... Pr 7:23
"We don't **k** anything about this," .... Pr 24:12
don't **k** what may happen then. .... Pr 27:1
son's name? Tell me, if you **k**! .... Pr 30:4
I **k** what wisdom and knowledge .... Ec 1:16
You **k** that many times you have .... Ec 7:22
They do not **k** what the future .... Ec 8:7
The living **k** they will die, ... Ec 9:5
don't even **k** how to get home .... Ec 10:15
you don't **k** if this or that .... Ec 11:6
people of Israel do not **k** me; .... Is 1:3
will **k** that God has sent it. .... Is 9:9
then they will **k** he is the LORD. .... Is 19:21
and we will **k** how they will turn .... Is 41:22
They **k** nothing, so they will be .... Is 44:9
things that you don't **k** yet. .... Is 48:6
everyone will **k** I, the LORD, am .... Is 49:26

You people who **k** what is right .... Is 51:7
so my people will **k** who I am, ... Is 52:6
nations that you don't yet **k.** .... Is 55:5
speak a language you do not **k;** .... Je 5:15
They do not **k** who I am," says .... Je 9:3
I **k** that our lives don't really .... Je 10:23
that do not **k** you and do not .... Je 10:25
and relatives to **k** the LORD, ... Je 31:34
because all people will **k** me, ... Je 31:34
all you who **k** her, cry for her .... Je 48:17
But they will **k** that a prophet .... Eze 2:5
Then you will **k** that I am the .... Eze 6:7
Then all people will **k** that I, ... Eze 21:5
Edomites will **k** what my revenge .... Eze 25:14
"Lord GOD, only you **k.**" .... Eze 37:3
the nations will **k** that I, ... Eze 37:28
nations will **k** me when they see .... Eze 38:16
nations will **k** Israel was taken .... Eze 39:23
and I want to **k** what it means." .... Da 2:3
I **k** that the spirit of the holy .... Da 4:9
I wanted to **k** what the fourth .... Da 7:19
she does not **k** that I was the .... Hos 2:8
bride, and you will **k** the LORD. .... Hos 2:20
and **k** him. Let's try to learn .... Hos 6:3
strength, but he doesn't **k** it. .... Hos 7:9
wise person will **k** these things, ... Hos 14:9
I **k** it is my fault that this .... Jnh 1:12
who do not **k** right from wrong .... Jnh 4:11
Then you will **k** that the LORD .... Zch 2:9
don't let anyone **k** what you are .... Mt 6:3
you **k** how to give good gifts to .... Mt 7:11
You will **k** these people by what .... Mt 7:16
you will **k** these false prophets .... Mt 7:20
been chosen to **k** the secrets .... Mt 13:11
in the sky and **k** what they mean. .... Mt 16:3
appear, you **k** summer is near. .... Mt 24:32
you don't **k** the day your Lord .... Mt 24:42
truth, I don't want to **k** you.' .... Mt 25:12
because you don't **k** the day or .... Mt 25:13
swear I don't **k** this man Jesus! .... Mt 26:72
I **k** that you are looking for .... Mt 28:5
I **k** who you are—God's Holy One!" .... Mk 1:24
You can **k** the secret about the .... Mk 4:11
k the commands: 'You must not .... Mk 10:19
we **k** that you are an honest man. .... Mk 12:14
And they did not **k** what to say .... Mk 14:40
to help you **k** that what you have .... Lk 1:4
How can I **k** that what you say is .... Lk 1:18
Didn't you **k** that I must be in .... Lk 2:49
You don't **k** what kind of spirit .... Lk 9:55
k it will soon be destroyed. .... Lk 21:20
you will **k** that God's kingdom is .... Lk 21:31
times that you don't **k** me." .... Lk 22:34
he said, "Woman, I don't **k** him." .... Lk 22:57
they don't **k** what they are .... Lk 23:34
does not **k** what just happened .... Lk 24:18
but the world did not **k** him. .... Jn 1:10
He did not **k** where the wine came .... Jn 2:9
we **k** you are a teacher sent from .... Jn 3:2
but you don't **k** where the wind .... Jn 3:8
about what we **k,** and we tell .... Jn 3:11
"I **k** that the Messiah is coming." .... Jn 4:25
eat that you **k** nothing about." .... Jn 4:32
We **k** that this man really is the .... Jn 4:42
We **k** his father and mother. .... Jn 6:42
believe and **k** that you are the .... Jn 6:69
they will **k** that my teaching .... Jn 7:17
out, "Yes, you **k** me, and you .... Jn 7:28
and you **k** where I am from. .... Jn 7:28
who is true, whom you don't **k.** .... Jn 7:28
of Man, you will **k** that I am he. .... Jn 8:28
Then you will **k** the truth, ... Jn 8:32
I **k** you are Abraham's children, ... Jn 8:37

rejected **k** and did not choose.................. Pr 1:29
he gives **k** and understanding. .... Pr 2:6
and **k** will be pleasing to you.................. Pr 2:10
With his **k**, he made springs flow .... Pr 3:20
and those with **k** know my words .... Pr 8:9
and **k** rather than the finest .... Pr 8:10
I also have **k** and good sense. .... Pr 8:12
she does not have wisdom or **k**. .... Pr 9:13
but **k** comes easily to those with.............. Pr 14:6
the wise are rewarded with **k**.................. Pr 14:18
people use **k** when they speak .... Pr 15:2
use their words to spread **k**, ... Pr 15:7
there is no **k** in the thoughts .... Pr 15:7
with understanding want more **k**, ... Pr 15:14
with understanding gets **k**; .... Pr 18:15
without **k** is not good. .... Pr 19:2
and they will gain **k**. .... Pr 19:25
only a few people speak with **k**. .... Pr 20:15
teach the wise, they will get **k**. .... Pr 21:11
The LORD guards **k**, but he .... Pr 22:12
which give **k** and good advice. .... Pr 22:20
listen carefully to words of **k**. .... Pr 23:12
It takes **k** to fill a home with .... Pr 24:4
and those with **k** have great .... Pr 24:5
leader with understanding and **k**, ... Pr 28:2
what wisdom and **k** really are." .... Ec 1:16
wisdom and **k** and also about................. Ec 1:17
who gains more **k** also gains more.......... Ec 1:18
all their wisdom, **k**, and skill, ... Ec 2:21
give them wisdom, **k**, and joy. .... Ec 2:26
planning, no **k**, and no wisdom. .... Ec 9:10
be full of the **k** of the LORD, ... Is 11:9
of salvation, wisdom, and **k**. .... Is 33:6
Who taught him **k** and showed him .... Is 40:14
wisdom and **k** have fooled you .... Is 47:10
lead you with **k** and .... Je 3:15
who are wise and **k** to those who .... Da 2:21
understanding, **k**, and wisdom .... Da 5:11
wise and had **k** and understanding.......... Da 5:12
wise and have **k** and .... Da 5:14
here and there to find true **k**." .... Da 12:4
because they have no **k**. .... Hos 4:6
plow the new ground of **k**. .... Hos 10:12
because some **k** of him has been .... Rm 1:19
to have a true **k** of God. .... Rm 1:28
his wisdom and the **k** have no end! .... Rm 11:33
you have all the **k** you need and .... Rm 15:14
your speaking and in all your **k**.............. 1Co 1:5
We know that "we all have **k**." 1Co 8:1
K puffs you up with pride, ... 1Co 8:1
of you who has **k** eats in an 1Co 8:10
is ruined because of your "**k**." 1Co 8:11
the ability to speak with **k**. 1Co 12:8
things of God and have all **k**, ... 1Co 13:2
is the gift of **k**, but it will 1Co 13:8
is that our **k** and our ability to 1Co 13:9
you a new truth or some new **k**, ... 1Co 14:6
to spread his **k** everywhere like 2Co 2:14
in speaking, in **k**, in truly 2Co 8:7
itself against the **k** of God. 2Co 10:5
speaker, but I do have **k**....................... 2Co 11:6
and in the same **k** of the Son of .... Eph 4:13
you will have **k** and.............................. Php 1:9
work and grow in the **k** of God. .... Col 1:10
of wisdom and **k** are safely kept. .... Col 2:3
brings you the true **k** of God. .... Col 3:10
and with sure **k** that it is true................. 1Th 1:5
of what is falsely called "**k**." 1Ti 6:20
By saying that "**k**," 1Ti 6:21
faith and that **k** come from the .... Tit 1:2
and to your goodness, add **k**; 2Pe 1:5
and to your **k**, add self-control; 2Pe 1:6

in your **k** of our Lord Jesus...................... 2Pe 1:8
in the grace and **k** of our Lord 2Pe 3:18

KNOWN

May my name be **k** through these .... Ge 48:16
and Isaac be **k** through them. .... Ge 48:16
LORD as long as I have **k** you. .... Dt 9:24
gods you have not **k**) "and let's .... Dt 13:2
you nor your ancestors have **k**, ... Dt 13:6
These are gods you have not **k**. .... Dt 13:13
family shall be **k** in Israel as .... Dt 25:10
you nor your ancestors have **k**. .... Dt 28:64
gods they had never **k**, new gods .... Dt 32:17
people who had **k** Saul before saw........... 1Sa 10:11
You made your name well **k**. 2Sa 7:23
of all the bronze was never **k**................... 1Ki 7:47
land of the Jordan **k** as the land.............. 2Ki 10:33
You have made **k** all these great 1Ch 17:19
your name well **k** by the great 1Ch 17:21
of all the bronze was never **k**................... 2Ch 4:18
was to be made **k** to the people .... Est 8:13
everyone who had **k** him before, ... Job 42:11
has made himself **k** by his fair .... Ps 9:16
God would have **k**, because he .... Ps 44:21
he is **k** as its defender. .... Ps 48:3
your name is **k** everywhere; .... Ps 48:10
If I had **k** of any sin in my .... Ps 66:18
heard them and **k** them by what.............. Ps 78:3
your miracles be **k** in the dark .... Ps 88:12
your goodness be **k** in the land .... Ps 88:12
LORD has made **k** his power to .... Ps 98:2
The wise are **k** for their .... Pr 16:21
children are **k** by their behavior .... Pr 20:11
plans will be **k** as a .... Pr 24:8
Her husband is **k** at the city .... Pr 31:23
Who has **k** the mind of the LORD .... Is 40:13
along paths they have not **k**. .... Is 42:16
these things and made them **k**; .... Is 48:3
You will be **k** for repairing the .... Is 58:12
children will be **k** among the .... Is 61:9
I made myself **k** to people who .... Is 65:1
other gods you have not **k**?..................... Je 7:9
in a land you have never **k**...................... Je 15:14
to a land you have never **k**...................... Je 17:4
of Judah had ever **k** before. .... Je 19:4
All I have **k** is trouble and .... Je 20:18
So you have become well **k**. .... Je 32:20
of Moab have never **k** trouble. .... Je 48:11
made myself **k** to them in Egypt, ... Eze 20:9
made myself **k** to the Israelites .... Eze 20:9
to lands you have not **k**. .... Eze 32:9
I will make myself **k** to the many .... Eze 38:23
make myself **k** among my people .... Eze 39:7
He makes **k** secrets that are deep .... Da 2:22
your name is **k** even today. .... Da 9:15
You should have **k** no other God .... Hos 13:4
makes his thoughts **k** to people................ Am 4:13
that is secret will be made **k**................... Mt 10:26
A tree is **k** by the kind of fruit .... Mt 12:33
who was **k** to be very bad. .... Mt 27:16
secret thing will be made **k**. .... Mk 4:22
because he was now well **k**. .... Mk 6:14
Bethlehem in Judea, **k** as the .... Lk 2:4
thoughts of many will be made **k**. .... Lk 2:35
Each tree is **k** by its own fruit. .... Lk 6:44
secret thing will be made **k**. .... Lk 8:17
that is secret will be made **k**. .... Lk 12:2
wants to be well **k** does not hide .... Jn 7:4
I have made **k** to you everything .... Jn 15:15
they have not **k** the Father and .... Jn 16:3
Father and they have not **k** me. .... Jn 16:3
Simon (**k** as the Zealot), ... Ac 1:13
have been **k** for a long time. .... Ac 15:18

TO A GOD WHO IS NOT **K.** .... Ac 17:23
They have **k** me for a long time. .... Ac 26:5
never have **k** what it means to   .... Rm 7:7
he could make **k** his rich glory   .... Rm 9:23
I made myself **k** to people who   .... Rm 10:20
Who has the mind of the Lord, ... Rm 11:34
ages past but is now made **k.**   .... Rm 16:25
God it is made **k** to all nations   .... Rm 16:26
Who has the mind of the Lord? 1Co 2:16
and will make the secret 1Co 4:5
God, that person is **k** by God. 1Co 8:3
know fully, as God has **k** me. 1Co 13:12
in their hearts will be made **k.** 1Co 14:25
on our hearts, **k** and read by 2Co 3:2
We are not **k,** but we are well 2Co 6:9
not known, but we are well **k.** 2Co 6:9
now it is made **k** to God's holy   .... Col 1:26
God has made **k** about Christ.   .... Col 4:3
in God has become **k** everywhere. 1Th 1:8
the faith that God made **k** to us. 1Ti 3:9
must be **k** for her good works— 1Ti 5:10
a child you have **k** the Holy 2Ti 3:15
must not be **k** as children who   .... Tit 1:6
people are **k** for their faith .... Heb 11:39
to have never **k** the right way 2Pe 2:21
us is that they have not **k** him. 1Jn 3:1
Christ and has never **k** him. 1Jn 3:6
who does evil has never **k** God. 3Jn 1:11
you have done are now made **k.''**   .... Rev 15:4

KNOWS

God **k** that if you eat the fruit .... Ge 3:5
today no one **k** where his grave .... Dt 34:6
And who **k,** you may have been .... Est 4:14
God **k** who is evil, and when he .... Job 11:11
But God **k** the way that I take, ... Job 23:10
No hawk **k** that path; the falcon   .... Job 28:7
because he **k** what is in our   .... Ps 44:21
and no one **k** how long this will .... Ps 74:9
Who **k** the full power of your .... Ps 90:11
The LORD **k** what people think. .... Ps 94:11
He **k** how we were made;   .... Ps 103:14
the sun always **k** when to set. .... Ps 104:19
She **k** that she makes is .... Pr 31:18
No one **k** the future, and no one .... Ec 10:14
and a donkey **k** where its owner. .... Is 1:3
he **k** what is hidden in darkness, ... Da 2:22
your Father **k** the things you   .... Mt 6:8
in heaven **k** you need them.   .... Mt 6:32
No one **k** the Son, except the .... Mt 11:27
No one **k** when that day or time .... Mt 24:36
but God **k** what is really in your .... Lk 16:15
as the Father **k** me, and I know   .... Jn 10:15
who **k** the thoughts of everyone, ... Ac 15:8
And he **k** what is in the mind of .... Rm 8:27
Who **k** the thoughts that another 1Co 2:11
The Lord **k** what wise people 1Co 3:20
or out of his body, but God **k.** 2Co 12:2
Lord **k** those who belong to him, ... 2Ti 2:19
Anyone who **k** the right thing to .... Jam 4:17
So the Lord **k** how to save those 2Pe 2:9
become God's child and **k** God. 1Jn 4:7
one **k** this new name except the .... Rev 2:17

KOA

Shoa, and **K** will attack you   .... Eze 23:23

KOHATH

were Gershon, **K,** and Merari.   .... Ge 46:11
K lived one hundred thirty-three   .... Ex 6:18
the son of **K,** the son of Levi   .... Nu 16:1
from **K** came the Kohathite family .... Nu 26:57

KOHATHITES

Then came the **K,** who carried the .... Nu 10:21

KOLAIAH

was the son of **K,** the son of   .... Ne 11:7
Ahab son of **K** and Zedekiah son   .... Je 29:21

KORAH

Izhar's sons were **K,** Nepheg, and   .... Ex 6:21
So **K,** you and all your followers   .... Nu 16:6
did, and like **K,** they surely .... Jud 1:11

KORAH'S

All **K** men and everything they   .... Nu 16:32
was not one of **K** followers who .... Nu 27:3
son was Korah. **K** son was Assir. 1Ch 6:22
son. Ebiasaph was **K** son. 1Ch 6:37
son, and Ebiasaph was **K** son. 1Ch 9:19

KORAHITE

group, and the **K** family group.   .... Nu 26:58
Kohathite and **K** people stood up 2Ch 20:19

KORAHITES

are the family groups of the **K.**   .... Ex 6:24

KORAZIN

said, "How terrible for you, **K!**   .... Mt 11:21
How terrible for you, **K!** .... Lk 10:13

KORE

K was Ebiasaph's son, and 1Ch 9:19
there was Meshelemiah son of **K,** 1Ch 26:1
K son of Imnah the Levite was in 2Ch 31:14
K was the guard at the East Gate. 2Ch 31:14
Shecaniah helped **K** in the towns 2Ch 31:15

KORE'S

Shallum was **K** son. Kore was 1Ch 9:19

KOUM

he said to her, "Talitha, **k!''** .... Mk 5:41

KOZ

and **K.** Koz was the father of 1Ch 4:8
K was the father of Anub, ... 1Ch 4:8

KUE

horses from Egypt and **K.** 1Ki 10:28
His traders bought them in **K.** 1Ki 10:28
horses from Egypt and **K;** 2Ch 1:16
his traders bought them in **K.** 2Ch 1:16

KUSHAIAH'S

Merari family group, was **K** son. 1Ch 15:17

L

LABAN

She had a brother named **L,**   .... Ge 24:29
and the sister of **L** the Aramean.   .... Ge 25:20
to **L** the brother of Rebekah.   .... Ge 28:5
Then **L** said to Jacob, "You are   .... Ge 29:15
While I was gone to cut the wool .... Ge 31:19
So **L** caught up with Jacob. .... Ge 31:25
So **L** looked through the camp, ... Ge 31:35
L named that place in his   .... Ge 31:47
L said to Jacob, "This pile of   .... Ge 31:48
slave girl whom **L** gave to his .... Ge 46:18
slave girl whom **L** gave to his .... Ge 46:25
towns of Tophel, **L,** Hazeroth, ... Dt 1:1

LABAN'S

When Jacob saw **L** daughter Rachel .... Ge 29:10
daughter Rachel and **L** sheep, ... Ge 29:10
its mouth and watered **L** sheep. .... Ge 29:10
and dark animals in **L** flock.   .... Ge 30:40
his animals separate from **L.**   .... Ge 30:40
from the weaker animals were **L,**   .... Ge 30:42
day Jacob heard **L** sons talking. .... Ge 31:1
that Rachel had stolen **L** idols.   .... Ge 31:32

LABOR
was in charge of the l force. 1Ki 4:6
of the forced l Solomon used to 1Ki 9:15
was in charge of the forced l. 1Ki 12:18
was in charge of the forced l. 2Ch 10:18
unfair and stop their hard l. .... Is 58:6

LABORER
days are like those of a l. .... Job 7:1
like a l waiting to be paid. .... Job 7:2
we put in our time like a l. .... Job 14:6

LACHISH
army surrounded and attacked L. 2Ch 32:9
large army from L to King .... Is 36:2
not yet been taken—L and Azekah. .... Je 34:7

LACK
whole city for the l of five .... Ge 18:28
swelling, heat, l of rain, plant .... Dt 28:22
Evil people never l an appetite, ... Job 20:20
anyone die for l of clothes or .... Job 31:19
sicknesses, and a l of food. .... Lk 21:11
because of a l of self-control. 1Co 7:5

LACKS
Your advice l wisdom! You have .... Job 26:3

LADAN
L was Tahan's son. Ammihud was 1Ch 7:26
there were L and Shimei. 1Ch 23:7
L had three sons. His first son 1Ch 23:8
L was Gershon's son and the 1Ch 26:21

LADAN'S
son. Ammihud was L son. Elishama 1Ch 7:26
sons were leaders of L families. 1Ch 23:9

LADDER
that there was a l resting on .... Ge 28:12
going up and coming down the l. .... Ge 28:12
the LORD standing above the l, ... Ge 28:13

LADIES
of her servant l answer her, ... Jdg 5:29

LADY
the chosen l and her children: 2Jn 1:1
And now, dear l, this is not a 2Jn 1:5

LAEL
Gershon was Eliasaph son of L. .... Nu 3:24

LAGGING
and attacked all those l behind. .... Dt 25:18

LAHAD
was the father of Ahumai and L. 1Ch 4:2

LAHAI
Bered, was called Beer L Roi. .... Ge 16:14
had left Beer L Roi and was .... Ge 24:62
was now living at Beer L Roi. .... Ge 25:11

LAHMAS
Cabbon, L, Kitlish, ... Jos 15:40

LAHMI
Elhanan son of Jair killed L, ... 1Ch 20:5

LAID
l the wood on it and then tied .... Ge 22:9
son Isaac and l him on the wood .... Ge 22:9
a stone and l his head on it to .... Ge 28:11
took an idol, l it on the bed, ... 1Sa 19:13
from the road, l it in a field, ... 2Sa 20:12
and l him on the bed in the room 1Ki 17:19
and l the pieces on the wood. 1Ki 18:33
him up and l him on Elisha's 2Ki 4:21
on ahead and l the walking stick 2Ki 4:31
They l him on a bed filled with 2Ch 16:14
's Temple had not yet been l. .... Ezr 3:6
of his Temple has been l." .... Ezr 3:11
came and l the foundations. .... Ezr 5:16

Let its foundations be l; .... Ezr 6:3
They l its boards and set its .... Ne 3:6
our bodies are l in the ground; .... Job 14:10
they are l low and buried like .... Job 24:24
are caught in the nets they l. .... Ps 9:15
You l me in the dust of death. .... Ps 22:15
was there when he l the earth's .... Pr 8:29
had their swords l under their .... Eze 32:27
Zerubbabel has l the foundation. .... Zch 4:9
foundation was l for the house .... Zch 8:9
and l the foundations of the .... Zch 12:1
colt to Jesus and l their coats .... Mt 21:7
saw the place where Jesus was l. .... Mk 15:47
here is the place they l him. .... Mk 16:6
of cloth and l him in a feeding .... Lk 2:7
dug deep and l the foundation .... Lk 6:48
was l at the rich man's gate. .... Lk 16:20
tomb and how Jesus' body was l. .... Lk 23:55
The men l Jesus in that tomb .... Jn 19:42
folded up and l in a different .... Jn 20:7
who prayed and l their hands on .... Ac 6:6
when the apostles l their hands .... Ac 8:18
He l his hands on Saul and said, ... Ac 9:17
they l their hands on Barnabas .... Ac 13:3
the cross and l him in a tomb. .... Ac 13:29
Then Paul l his hands on them, ... Ac 19:6
l l the foundation of that house 1Co 3:10
already been l is Jesus Christ 1Co 3:11
group of elders l their hands on 1Ti 4:14
you when l l my hands on you 2Ti 1:6

LAISH
When they came to the city of L, ... Jdg 18:7
the land around L said to their .... Jdg 18:14
and his priest and went on to L. .... Jdg 18:27
no one to save the people of L. .... Jdg 18:28
L was in a valley near Beth .... Jdg 18:28
changed the name of L to Dan, ... Jdg 18:29
given her to Paltiel son of L, ... 1Sa 25:44
her husband Paltiel son of L. .... ♠ 2Sa 3:15

LAISHAH
out, Bath Gallim! L, listen! .... Is 10:30

LAKE
was standing beside L Galilee, ... Lk 5:1
them, "Let's go across the l." .... Lk 8:22
strong wind blew up on the l, ... Lk 8:23
hill into the l and was drowned .... Lk 8:33
thrown into the l of burning .... Rev 20:10
was thrown into the l of fire. .... Rev 20:15

LAKKUM
as far as L, and ended at. .... Jos 19:33

LAMA
"Eli, Eli, l sabachthani?". .... Mt 27:46
Eloi, Eloi, l sabachthani." .... Mk 15:34

LAMB
where is the l we will burn as. .... Ge 22:7
will give us the l for the .... Ge 22:8
every black l, and every spotted .... Ge 30:32
spotted or any l that isn't .... Ge 30:33
must get one l for the people .... Ex 12:3
in his house to eat a whole l, ... Ex 12:4
must be enough l for everyone to .... Ex 12:4
l must be a one-year-old male. .... Ex 12:5
must roast the l over a fire. .... Ex 12:8
not eat the l raw or boiled in .... Ex 12:9
Roast the whole l over a fire— .... Ex 12:9
and kill the l for the Passover. .... Ex 12:21
donkey by offering a l. .... Ex 13:13
Offer one l in the morning and .... Ex 29:39
when you offer the first l, ... Ex 29:40
the second l in the evening .... Ex 29:41
by paying for it with a l, ... Ex 34:20

to the LORD is a l or a goat, ... Le 3:6
If he offers a l, he must bring .... Le 3:7
brings a l as his offering .... Le 4:32
it must be a female l or goat .... Le 5:6
if the person cannot afford a l, ... Le 5:7
and a calf and a l for a whole .... Le 9:3
entrance a year-old l for a .... Le 12:6
If she cannot afford a l, ... Le 12:8
year-old female l that has .... Le 14:10
kill the male l in the holy .... Le 14:13
take one male l for a penalty .... Le 14:21
will take the l for the penalty .... Le 14:24
will kill the l of the penalty................... Le 14:25
kills an ox, a l, or a goat .... Le 17:3
If an ox or l is smaller than .... Le 22:23
offer a male l, one year old, ... Le 23:12
must bring a male l a year old .... Nu 6:12
a year-old male l that has .... Nu 6:14
year-old female l that has .... Nu 6:14
Eat the l with bitter herbs and .... Nu 9:11
time you offer a l as a burnt .... Nu 15:5
or male sheep, l or young goat .... Nu 15:11
Offer one l in the morning and .... Nu 28:4
and the other l at twilight. .... Nu 28:4
of wine with each l as a drink .... Nu 28:7
Offer the second l at twilight. .... Nu 28:8
with each l of two quarts .... Nu 28:13
and with each l it will be one .... Nu 28:14
from the first l born to your .... Dt 15:19
took a baby l and offered it to 1Sa 7:9
little female l he had bought. 2Sa 12:3
man fed the l, and it grew up 2Sa 12:3
l was like a daughter to him. 2Sa 12:3
he took the l from the poor man........... 2Sa 12:4
must pay for the l four times 2Sa 12:6
the Passover l on the fourteenth 2Ch 30:15
made each l holy for the LORD 2Ch 30:17
The Passover l was killed on the 2Ch 35:1
captivity ate the Passover l. .... Ezr 6:21
Send a l from Sela through the .... Is 16:1
He was like a l being led to be .... Is 53:7
was like a gentle l waiting to .... Je 11:19
give a year-old l that has....................... Eze 46:13
with the l every morning. .... Eze 46:14
So you must always give the l, ... Eze 46:15
the Passover l was sacrificed. .... Mk 14:12
said, "Look, the L of God, who .... Jn 1:29
he said, "Look, the L of God!" .... Jn 1:36
a l is quiet while its wool is..................... Ac 8:32
our Passover l, has been 1Co 5:7
was like a pure and perfect l. 1Pe 1:19
Then l saw a L standing in the .... Rev 5:6
The L looked as if he had been .... Rev 5:6
The L came and took the scroll .... Rev 5:7
elders bowed down before the L. .... Rev 5:8
all sang a new song to the L: .... Rev 5:9
The L who was killed is worthy .... Rev 5:12
throne and to the L be praise .... Rev 5:13
while the L opened the first .... Rev 6:1
When the L opened the second .... Rev 6:3
the L opened the third seal, ... Rev 6:5
When the L opened the fourth .... Rev 6:7
the L opened the fifth seal, ... Rev 6:9
while the L opened the sixth .... Rev 6:12
and from the anger of the L! .... Rev 6:16
the throne and before the L, ... Rev 7:9
on the throne, and to the L." .... Rev 7:10
white in the blood of the L....................... Rev 7:14
because the L at the center of................. Rev 7:17
When the L opened the seventh .... Rev 8:1
The L is the One who was killed. .... Rev 13:8
It had two horns like a l,....................... Rev 13:11
me was the L standing on Mount .... Rev 14:1

They follow the L every place he .... Rev 14:4
to be offered to God and the L. .... Rev 14:4
the holy angels and the L. .... Rev 14:10
of God, and the song of the L: .... Rev 15:3
will make war against the L, ... Rev 17:14
but the L will defeat them, ... Rev 17:14
the wedding of the L has come, ... Rev 19:7
to the wedding meal of the L!" .... Rev 19:9
the bride, the wife of the L." .... Rev 21:9
of the twelve apostles of the L. .... Rev 21:14
Almighty and the L are the..................... Rev 21:22
and the L is the city's lamp. .... Rev 21:23
the throne of God and of the L .... Rev 22:1
God and of the L will be there, ... Rev 22:3

LAMB'S
and the L bride has made herself .... Rev 19:7
written in the L book of life .... Rev 21:27

LAMBS
on the altar two l that are one .... Ex 29:38
take two male l that have .... Le 14:10
the Passover l for all the .... Ezr 6:20
and the hills like little l. .... Ps 114:4
with the blood from l and goats,............. Is 34:6
gathers them l in his arms .... Is 40:11
You eat tender l and fattened .... Am 6:4
when the Passover l had to be .... Lk 22:7
Jesus said, "Feed my l." .... Jn 21:15

LAME
dropped him, and now he was l................ 2Sa 4:4
the blind and feet for the l. .... Job 29:15
with them the l, the blind, ... Mt 15:30
The l could walk, and the blind .... Mt 15:31
crippled, the l, and the blind. .... Lk 14:13
crippled, the blind, and the l.' .... Lk 14:21

LAMECH
L said to his wives: .... Ge 4:23
L lived 595 years and had other .... Ge 5:30

LAMP
the oil for the l, the .... Nu 4:16
God's l was still burning. 1Sa 3:3
LORD, you give light to my l. 2Sa 22:29
The l of the wicked will be put .... Job 18:5
God's l shined on my head,..................... Job 29:3
LORD, you give light to my l. .... Ps 18:28
word is like a l for my feet .... Ps 119:105
These commands are like a l; .... Pr 6:23
Her l burns late into the night. .... Pr 31:18
take away the light of the l. .... Je 25:10
Do you hide a l under a bowl or .... Mk 4:21
You put the l on a lampstand................... Mk 4:21
after lighting a l covers it .... Lk 8:16
No one lights a l and puts it in .... Lk 11:33
as when a l shines on you." .... Lk 11:36
will light a l, sweep the house.............. Lk 15:8
like a burning and shining l, ... Jn 5:35
In it were the l and the table .... Heb 9:2
light of a l will never shine .... Rev 18:23
and the Lamb is the city's l. .... Rev 21:23
the light of a l or the light .... Rev 22:5

LAMPS
seven small oil l and put them .... Ex 25:37
evening when he lights the l, ... Ex 30:8
the lampstand and set up its l. .... Ex 40:4
will search Jerusalem with l. .... Zph 1:12
there are seven l and also seven .... Zch 4:2
took their l and went to wait .... Mt 25:1
because our l are going out.' .... Mt 25:8
the throne seven l were burning, ... Rev 4:5

LAMPSTAND

Hammer pure gold to make a l. .... Ex 25:31
out from the l was the same. .... Ex 37:19
the area in front of the l.'" .... Nu 8:2
near the l in the royal palace. .... Da 5:5
They put it on a l so the light .... Mt 5:15
You put the lamp on a l. .... Mk 4:21
puts it on a l so those who come.............. Lk 8:16
take away your l from its place. .... Rev 2:5

LAMPSTANDS

the l of pure gold (five on the 1Ki 7:49
I turned, I saw seven golden l.................. Rev 1:12
among the l who was "like .... Rev 1:13
and the two l that stand before .... Rev 11:4

LAND

so the dry l will appear." .... Ge 1:9
God named the dry l "earth" and .... Ge 1:10
a plain in the l of Babylonia .... Ge 11:2
and go to the l I will show you. .... Ge 12:1
through that l as far as the .... Ge 12:6
I will give this l to your .... Ge 12:7
was not much food in the l, ... Ge 12:10
The whole l is there in front of .... Ge 13:9
like the l of Egypt in the .... Ge 13:10
all this l because I am now .... Ge 13:17
I could give you this l to own." .... Ge 15:7
travel in a l they don't own. .... Ge 15:13
me and to this l where you have.............. Ge 21:23
went back to the l of the .... Ge 21:32
and go to the l of Moriah. .... Ge 22:2
father and the l of my relatives .... Ge 24:7
I will give this l to your .... Ge 24:7
was a time of hunger in the l, ... Ge 26:1
Hittite women here in this l, ... Ge 27:46
you may own the l where you are .... Ge 28:4
descendants the l on which you .... Ge 28:13
will bring you back to this l. .... Ge 28:15
of Shechem in the l of Canaan. .... Ge 33:18
The same l I gave to Abraham and........... Ge 35:12
Jacob lived in the l of Canaan, ... Ge 37:1
force from the l of the Hebrews,.............. Ge 40:15
to eat in all the l of Egypt. .... Ge 41:29
grew in the l of Egypt will be .... Ge 41:30
and set him over the l of Egypt. .... Ge 41:33
in the l of my troubles. .... Ge 41:52
people in the l of Canaan were .... Ge 42:5
come from the l of Canaan to buy .... Ge 42:7
master of that l spoke unkindly .... Ge 42:30
Live in the l of Goshen where .... Ge 45:10
give them the best l in Egypt, ... Ge 45:18
and your brothers the best l; .... Ge 47:6
brothers the best l in Egypt, ... Ge 47:11
was no food anywhere in the l, ... Ge 47:13
except our bodies and our l. .... Ge 47:18
bought all the l in Egypt for .... Ge 47:20
only l he did not buy was the .... Ge 47:22
to live in the l of Goshen in.................... Ge 47:27
back to the l of your fathers. .... Ge 48:21
good and how pleasant his l is, ... Ge 49:15
you out of this l to the land he .... Ge 50:24
this land to the l he promised .... Ge 50:24
went to live in the l of Midian. .... Ex 2:15
a stranger in a l that was not .... Ex 2:22
out of that l and lead them to .... Ex 3:8
to a good l with lots of room— .... Ex 3:8
lead you to the l of the .... Ex 3:17
to give them the l of Canaan. .... Ex 6:4
you to the l that I promised.................... Ex 6:8
let the Israelites leave his l." .... Ex 6:11
the Israelites, out of that l. .... Ex 7:4
came up onto the l of Egypt. .... Ex 8:7
be any flies in the l of Goshen, ... Ex 8:22

Egypt flies were ruining the l.................. Ex 8:24
to fall upon the l of Egypt. .... Ex 9:23
stick over the l of Egypt,........................ Ex 10:13
the whole l so that it was .... Ex 10:15
go through the l of Egypt and................ Ex 12:12
when I punish the l of Egypt. .... Ex 12:13
sons in the l of Egypt— .... Ex 12:29
lead you to the l of the .... Ex 13:5
went through the sea on dry l, ... Ex 14:22
crossed the sea on dry l, ... Ex 14:29
walked through the sea on dry l. .... Ex 15:19
had killed us in the l of Egypt. .... Ex 16:3
they came to the l where they................ Ex 16:35
you out of the l of Egypt where .... Ex 20:2
long time in the l that the LORD .... Ex 20:12
foreigners in the l of Egypt. .... Ex 22:21
of you to take over the l. .... Ex 23:30
you out of the l of Egypt!" .... Ex 32:4
all this l that I have promised .... Ex 32:13
the people who live in that l. .... Ex 34:15
expand the borders of your l. .... Ex 34:24
The l has become unclean, and I .... Le 18:25
harvest your crops on your l, ... Le 19:9
you enter the l I will give you, ... Le 25:2
year, you must let the l rest. .... Le 25:4
you will live safely in the l. .... Le 25:18
The l will give good crops to .... Le 25:19
The l really belongs to me, ... Le 25:23
living for a while on my l. .... Le 25:23
People might sell their l, ... Le 25:24
l will produce crops, and the .... Le 26:4
eat and live safely in your l. .... Le 26:5
men to explore the l of Canaan, ... Nu 13:2
some of the fruit from that l." .... Nu 13:20
us to this l to be killed with .... Nu 14:3
The l we explored is very good. .... Nu 14:7
to explore the l had returned .... Nu 14:36
'You are going to another l, ... Nu 15:18
will not inherit any of the l, ... Nu 18:20
a town on the edge of your l. .... Nu 20:16
not enter the l that I'm giving............... Nu 20:24
Kadesh Barnea to look at the l. .... Nu 32:8
the LORD helps us take the l,................. Nu 32:22
over the l and settle there, ... Nu 33:53
divide up the l by family groups .... Nu 33:54
Don't let murder spoil your l. .... Nu 35:33
given you this l, so go in and .... Dt 1:8
men before us to spy out the l. .... Dt 1:22
fruit from that l and brought it .... Dt 1:25
That l was also thought to be a .... Dt 2:20
Edom let us go through their l, ... Dt 2:29
given you this l as your own. .... Dt 3:18
see the good l by the Jordan. .... Dt 3:25
die here in this l and not cross .... Dt 4:22
long time in the l that the LORD............. Dt 4:40
for you in the l that the LORD .... Dt 5:16
take the good l the LORD .... Dt 6:18
to give us the l he promised our .... Dt 6:23
is bringing you into a good l, ... Dt 8:7
a l with rivers and pools of .... Dt 8:7
a l that has wheat and barley,................ Dt 8:8
It is a l where you will have .... Dt 8:9
people into the l he promised .... Dt 9:28
not receive any l of their own; .... Dt 10:9
But the l that you will soon................... Dt 11:11
rain on your l at the right time .... Dt 11:14
Your l will go from the desert .... Dt 11:24
obey in the l the LORD, ... Dt 12:1
you in the l he is giving you .... Dt 15:4
always have the l the LORD your .... Dt 16:20
you do in the l you are entering .... Dt 23:20
sin into the l the LORD your God .... Dt 24:4
and bless the l you have given .... Dt 26:15

destroyed the l and everything .... Je 8:16
We must leave our l, because our .... Je 9:19
longer will the l stay dried up .... Je 12:4
who take the l I gave my people .... Je 12:14
because no rain falls on the l .... Je 14:4
you like a stranger in the l, ... Je 14:8
from the northern l and from all .... Je 16:15
that grows in a l where no one .... Je 17:6
he will not see this l again." .... Je 22:12
The l of Judah is full of people .... Je 23:10
longer be in the l I gave to .... Je 24:10
and you will die in another l, ... Je 27:10
save your family from that l. .... Je 30:10
return from their enemy's l. .... Je 31:16
things in the l of Egypt. .... Je 32:20
them in this l and make them .... Je 32:41
people who were left in the l: .... Je 40:7
Stay in the l and serve the king .... Je 40:9
and let you stay in your l.' .... Je 42:12
people of the l burned incense .... Je 44:21
sacrifice in the l of the north, ... Je 46:10
happy, because you took my l. .... Je 50:11
Attack the l of Merathaim. .... Je 50:21
Lift up a banner in the l! .... Je 51:27
The l shakes and moves in pain, ... Je 51:29
a dry, desert l, a land where no .... Je 51:43
will spread through the l, ... Je 51:46
and the whole l will be .... Je 51:47
people of the l to take care .... Je 52:16
at Riblah, in the l of Hamath, ... Je 52:27
says this to the l of Israel: .... Eze 7:2
on the four corners of the l. .... Eze 7:2
The LORD has left the l.'" .... Eze 8:12
have filled the l with violence .... Eze 8:17
The l is filled with people who .... Eze 9:9
say to the people of the l: ' .... Eze 12:19
'Let a war be fought in that l,' .... Eze 14:17
were in the l, they could not .... Eze 14:20
the l of the king who made him .... Eze 17:16
desert, in a dry and thirsty l. .... Eze 19:13
them into the l I promised to .... Eze 20:28
in the l where you were born. .... Eze 21:30
an end to sexual sins in the l. .... Eze 23:48
Egypt, to the l they came .... Eze 29:14
will bring darkness over your l, ... Eze 32:8
everything that is in the l, ... Eze 32:15
I bring a war against a l. .... Eze 33:2
the ruins in the l of Israel are .... Eze 33:24
and the l will give its harvest. .... Eze 34:27
murdered in the l and because .... Eze 36:18
I will put you in your own l. .... Eze 37:14
toward Gog of the l of Magog, ... Eze 38:2
be like a cloud covering the l. .... Eze 38:9
like a cloud that covers the l. .... Eze 38:16
day Gog attacks the l of Israel, ... Eze 38:18
to make the l clean again. .... Eze 39:12
you divide the l for the .... Eze 45:1
to sell or trade any of this l. .... Eze 48:14
toward the beautiful l of Judah. .... Da 8:9
pay him for the l they rule. .... Da 11:39
attack the beautiful l of Judah. .... Da 11:41
They will come up from the l, ... Hos 1:11
desert, like a l without water, ... Hos 2:3
against you who live in the l: .... Hos 4:1
Because of this the l dries up, ... Hos 4:3
will not stay in the LORD's l. .... Hos 9:3
you were in the l of Egypt. .... Hos 13:4
about his l and felt sorry for .... Joe 2:18
innocent people in that l. .... Joe 3:19
and was going to burn up the l. .... Am 7:4
much that this l can't hold all .... Am 7:10
will measure your l and divide .... Am 7:17
The whole l will shake because .... Am 8:8

who made the sea and the l." .... Jnh 1:9
to row the ship back to the l, ... Jnh 1:13
threw up Jonah onto the dry l. .... Jnh 2:10
conquer the l of Assyria with .... Mic 5:6
when they come into our l, ... Mic 5:6
of what you did to that l, ... Hab 2:17
a time without rain on the l, ... Hag 1:11
earth, the sea and the dry l. .... Hag 2:6
as his own part of the holy l, ... Zch 2:12
take away the sin of this l.' .... Zch 3:9
This good l was left so ruined .... Zch 7:14
will shine in his l like jewels .... Zch 9:16
The l will cry, each family by .... Zch 12:12
in the l of Judah, are not .... Mt 2:6
L of Zebulun and land of .... Mt 4:15
of Zebulun and l of Naphtali .... Mt 4:15
was already far away from l. .... Mt 14:24
travel across l and sea to find .... Mt 23:15
to push off a little from the l. .... Lk 5:3
When Jesus got out on the l, ... Lk 8:27
was a rich man who had some l, ... Lk 12:16
trouble will come upon this l, ... Lk 21:23
the whole l became dark until .... Lk 23:44
the boat came to l at the place .... Jn 6:21
our people went into this new l, ... Ac 7:45
the people made it safely to l. .... Ac 27:44
the Red Sea as if it were dry l. .... Heb 11:29
did not rain on the l for three .... Jam 5:17
them out of the l of Egypt. .... Jud 1:5
sea and his left foot on the l. .... Rev 10:2

LANDED

Tiberias and l near the place .... Jn 6:23
When Paul l at Caesarea, he went .... Ac 18:22
and Pamphylia and l at the city .... Ac 27:5

LANDS

their own l, and their own .... Ge 10:20
In all the l people had nothing .... Ge 41:54
their l on my way to Judah. .... Ne 2:7
He gave them l of other nations, ... Ps 105:44
has gathered them from other l, ... Ps 107:3
given all these l to .... Je 27:6
will become captives in other l. .... Je 30:16
from the l across the Jordan .... Mk 3:8
to capture the l of the other .... Ac 7:45

LANES

out to the roads and country l, ... Lk 14:23

LANGUAGE

with its own land and its own l. .... Ge 10:5
the whole world spoke one l, ... Ge 11:1
confuse their l so they will not .... Ge 11:7
in the Aramaic l and translated. .... Ezr 4:7
state and in the l of each group .... Est 1:22
and in the l of each people. .... Est 8:9
I heard a l I did not know, ... Ps 81:5
speak Hebrew, the l of Canaan, ... Is 19:18
to teach them the l and writings .... Da 1:4
called Bethesda in the Hebrew l. .... Jn 5:2
Hebrew the name is Gabbatha. .... Jn 19:13
in the Hebrew l is called .... Jn 19:17
In their l Akeldama means "Field .... Ac 1:19
them speaking in his own l. .... Ac 2:6
spoke to them in the Hebrew l. .... Ac 21:40
in a different l I should pray for 1Co 14:13
people, and l of the earth. .... Rev 7:9
name in the Hebrew l is Abaddon .... Rev 9:11

LANGUAGES

these families had their own l, ... Ge 10:20
by families, l, countries, ... Ge 10:31
different l during his life. 1Ch 1:19
and foreign l to speak to these .... Is 28:11
kinds of l more than all 1Co 14:18

and foreign I I will speak to 1Co 14:21
peoples, races, nations, and I. .... Rev 17:15
LANTERNS
torches, I, and weapons. .... Jn 18:3
LAODICEA
you, those in L, and others who .... Col 2:1
the people in L and in .... Col 4:13
the brothers and sisters in L. .... Col 4:15
is also read to the church in L. .... Col 4:16
the letter that I wrote to L. .... Col 4:16
Sardis, Philadelphia, and L." .... Rev 1:11
to the angel of the church in L: .... Rev 3:14
LAP
sons off Israel's I and bowed .... Ge 48:12
Samson to sleep, lying in her I. .... Jdg 16:19
on his mother's I until noon. 2Ki 4:20
it will spill into your I........................... Lk 6:38
LAPPED
hundred men who I the water, ... Jdg 7:7
LAPPIDOTH
the wife of L, was judge of .... Jdg 4:4
LAPPING
drink water by I it up like a .... Jdg 7:5
their mouths, I it as a dog does .... Jdg 7:6
LASEA
Fair Havens, near the city of L. .... Ac 27:8
LASHA
Admah, and Zeboiim, as far as L. .... Ge 10:19
LASHARON
Aphek, L,... Jos 12:18
LASHES
The number of I should match the .... Dt 25:2
of thirty-nine I with a whip. 2Co 11:24
LASHINGS
will learn from a hundred I. .... Pr 17:10
LAST
L night I had sexual relations................. Ge 19:34
breathed his I breath and died .... Ge 25:8
them, and Rachel and Joseph I. .... Ge 33:2
bed, took his I breath, and died .... Ge 49:33
These are the I words of David. 2Sa 23:1
David's I instructions were to 1Ch 23:27
from the first day to the I. .... Ne 8:18
they are rich for the I time;.................... Job 27:19
be honest and I a long time. .... Pr 25:5
with God that was to I forever. .... Is 24:5
jar so they will I a long time. .... Je 32:14
the things in this vision I— .... Da 8:13
In the I days they will turn in .... Hos 3:5
the I day many people will say .... Mt 7:22
now will be I in the future. .... Mt 19:30
And many who are I now will be .... Mt 19:30
were hired I and worked only .... Mt 20:12
He sent him I of all, saying, ' .... Mk 12:6
stored to I for many years. .... Lk 12:19
raise them all on the I day. .... Jn 6:39
I will raise them on the I day. .... Jn 6:40
On the I and most important day .... Jn 7:37
the resurrection on the I day." .... Jn 11:24
be their judge on the I day. .... Jn 12:48
In the I days I will pour out my .... Ac 2:17
the I day an offering would be .... Ac 21:26
has put us apostles in I place,................. 1Co 4:9
L of all he was seen by me— 1Co 15:8
The I enemy to be destroyed will 1Co 15:26
But the I Adam became a spirit 1Co 15:45
when the I trumpet sounds. 1Co 15:52
In the I days there will be many 2Ti 3:1
But now in these I days God has .... Heb 1:2

your treasure for the I days. .... Jam 5:3
world in these I times for your 1Pe 1:20
what will happen in the I days. 2Pe 3:3
children, these are the I days.................. 1Jn 2:18
know that these are the I days. 1Jn 2:18
In the I times there will be .... Jud 1:18
I am the First and the L. .... Rev 1:17
One who is the First and the L, ... Rev 2:8
These are the I disasters, ... Rev 15:1
of the seven I troubles came to .... Rev 21:9
First and the L, the Beginning .... Rev 22:13
LATE
to get up early and stay up I, ... Ps 127:2
this place, and it is already I. .... Mt 14:15
Stay with us, because it is I; .... Lk 24:29
LATER
A short time I, some people were .... Mk 14:70
About three hours I his wife .... Ac 5:7
sins of others are seen only I. 1Ti 5:24
LATIN
in Hebrew, in L, and in Greek. .... Jn 19:20
LAUGH
to Abraham, "Why did Sarah I? .... Ge 18:13
she lied and said, "I didn't I." .... Ge 18:15
Sarah said, "God has made me I. .... Ge 21:6
hears about this will I with me. .... Ge 21:6
You will I at destruction and .... Job 5:22
But, LORD, you I at them; .... Ps 59:8
they I and make fun of us. .... Ps 79:4
a time to cry and a time to I. .... Ec 3:4
because you will I with joy..................... Lk 6:21
LAUGHED
facedown on the ground and I. .... Ge 17:17
I to herself, "My husband and .... Ge 18:12
LAUGHING
Someone who is I may be sad................. Pr 14:13
will be for you who are I now, ... Lk 6:25
LAUGHS
and it I when they shake a spear .... Job 41:29
But the Lord I at the wicked, ... Ps 37:13
LAUGHTER
your mouth with I and your lips .... Job 8:21
Then we were filled with I, ... Ps 126:2
better than I, and sadness has .... Ec 7:3
The I of fools is like the .... Ec 7:6
There will be the sound of I. .... Je 30:19
Your I is like the neighing of .... Je 50:11
Change your I into crying and .... Jam 4:9
LAUNDRY
road where people do their I, ... 2Ki 18:17
road where people do their I. .... Is 7:3
road where people do their I, ... Is 36:2
purifying fire and like I soap. .... Mal 3:2
LAW
What have I broken to cause .... Ge 31:36
So Joseph made a I in Egypt, ... Ge 47:26
This is a I that will last from .... Ex 12:17
command as a I for you and your .... Ex 12:24
people a rule and a I to live .... Ex 15:25
this same I if the bull kills .... Ex 21:31
This will be a I that will last .... Ex 28:43
This I will continue for .... Le 3:17
burnt offering, as the I says. .... Le 5:10
I will continue from now on. .... Le 10:9
This I will always continue for .... Le 16:29
This I will continue forever. .... Le 16:31
That I for removing the sins of .... Le 16:34
This I will always continue for .... Le 23:14
I will continue for you from .... Le 23:21

L

this I will continue for people .... Le 23:31
I will continue from now on; .... Le 23:41
I will continue from now on. .... Le 24:3
The I will be the same for the .... Le 24:22
This is a I for you and your..................... Nu 10:8
He forgives sin and I breaking. .... Nu 14:18
I is the same for you and for .... Nu 15:15
I you must also give the grain................ Nu 15:24
stop obeying the I in any way so .... Dt 17:20
forbidden by I to marry may come .... Dt 23:2
obey everything in this I.................... Dt 31:12
children do not know this I, ... Dt 31:13
that this is against God's I................ Jos 22:16
That one man broke God's I, ... Jos 22:20
we broke God's I, we ask the .... Jos 22:23
who do not know the I of the god 2Ki 17:26
He made it a I for the people of 1Ch 16:17
wise man and a teacher of the I............... 1Ch 27:32
cases about the I of the LORD 2Ch 19:8
rules, or some other I..................... 2Ch 19:10
the Passover as the I commanded. 2Ch 30:5
a teacher of the L of the God of .... Ezr 7:12
are obeying the L of your God, ... Ezr 7:14
a teacher of the L of the God of .... Ezr 7:21
does not obey the I of your God .... Ezr 7:26
people gathered as the I said. .... Ne 8:18
from experts about I and order. .... Est 1:13
What does the I say must be done .... Est 1:15
The I should say Vashti is never .... Est 1:19
given out as a I in every state .... Est 3:14
There is only one I about this: .... Est 4:11
even though it is against the I, ... Est 4:16
sent out as a I in every state. .... Est 8:13
A I was given in Susa, and the .... Est 9:14
This is the I for Israel;........................... Ps 81:4
you teach them from your I. .... Ps 94:12
They use the I to cause .... Ps 94:20
He made it a I for the people of .... Ps 105:10
but I fear your I in my heart. .... Ps 119:161
he made a I that will never .... Ps 148:6
might forget the I and keep the .... Pr 31:5
What the king says is I; .... Ec 8:4
obeys the I about the Sabbath .... Is 56:2
should obey the I about the..................... Is 56:4
to obey the I about the Sabbath,.............. Is 56:6
must obey God's I about the .... Is 58:13
teaching of the I by the priest .... Je 18:18
it is about the I of his God." .... Da 6:5
make a new I for everyone to .... Da 6:7
make the I and sign your name to .... Da 6:8
then it will be a I of the Medes .... Da 6:8
So King Darius signed the I. .... Da 6:9
that the new I had been written .... Da 6:10
to him about the I he had made............... Da 6:12
you sign a I that says no one .... Da 6:12
Yes, that is the I, and the laws .... Da 6:12
O king, or to the I you signed. .... Da 6:13
the I of the Medes and Persians .... Da 6:15
says that no I or command given .... Da 6:15
am making a new I for people in .... Da 6:26
teachers of the I and asked them .... Mt 2:4
come to destroy the I of Moses .... Mt 5:17
disappear from the I until .... Mt 5:18
teachers of the I and the .... Mt 5:20
is the meaning of the I of Moses.............. Mt 7:12
like their teachers of the I. .... Mt 7:29
a teacher of the I came to Jesus .... Mt 8:19
teachers of the I said to .... Mt 9:3
prophets and the I of Moses told .... Mt 11:13
not read in the I of Moses that .... Mt 12:5
break this I about the Sabbath .... Mt 12:5
of the I answered Jesus, ... Mt 12:38
teacher of the I who has been.................. Mt 13:52

teachers of the I came to Jesus .... Mt 15:1
teachers of the I would make him .... Mt 16:21
teachers of the I say that....................... Mt 17:10
and the teachers of the I, ... Mt 20:18
teachers of the I saw that Jesus .... Mt 21:15
teachers of the I very angry. .... Mt 21:15
was an expert on the I of Moses, ... Mt 22:35
command in the I is the most .... Mt 22:36
the I and the writings of the .... Mt 22:40
teachers of the I and the .... Mt 23:2
you what the I of Moses says. .... Mt 23:2
teachers of the I love to have .... Mt 23:6
teachers of the I and Pharisees! .... Mt 23:13
teachers of the I and Pharisees. .... Mt 23:14
teachers of the I and Pharisees! .... Mt 23:15
teachers of the I and Pharisees! .... Mt 23:23
important teachings of the I— .... Mt 23:23
teachers of the I and Pharisees! .... Mt 23:25
teachers of the I and Pharisees! .... Mt 23:27
teachers of the I and Pharisees! .... Mt 23:29
teachers of the I and the elders .... Mt 26:57
Our I does not allow us to keep .... Mt 27:6
teachers of the I, and the .... Mt 27:41
like their teachers of the I. .... Mk 1:22
teachers of the I were sitting .... Mk 2:6
teachers of the I were thinking. .... Mk 2:8
teachers of the I who were .... Mk 2:16
teachers of the I from Jerusalem .... Mk 3:22
teachers of the I said that he .... Mk 3:30
teachers of the I came from .... Mk 7:1
teachers of the I said to Jesus, ... Mk 7:5
and the teachers of the I. .... Mk 8:31
teachers of the I say that........................ Mk 9:11
of the I arguing with them. .... Mk 9:14
and the teachers of the I. .... Mk 10:33
teachers of the I heard all this .... Mk 11:18
teachers of the I, and the .... Mk 11:27
teachers of the I came and heard .... Mk 12:28
teachers of the I say that the .... Mk 12:35
Beware of the teachers of the I. .... Mk 12:38
teachers of the I were trying to .... Mk 14:1
teachers of the I, and the .... Mk 14:43
teachers of the I were gathered. .... Mk 14:53
teachers of the I, and all the .... Mk 15:1
teachers of the I were also .... Mk 15:31
without fault in keeping his I. .... Lk 1:6
to do what the I of Moses taught .... Lk 2:22
is written in the I of the Lord:.................. Lk 2:23
as the I of the Lord says:....................... Lk 2:24
do what the I said they must do, ... Lk 2:27
everything the I of the Lord .... Lk 2:39
teachers of the I from every .... Lk 5:17
teachers of the I and the .... Lk 5:21
who taught the I for the .... Lk 5:30
teachers of the I and the .... Lk 6:7
teachers of the I were very .... Lk 6:11
experts on the I refused to .... Lk 7:30
and the teachers of the I. .... Lk 9:22
expert on the I stood up to test .... Lk 10:25
What is written in the I? .... Lk 10:26
The expert on the I answered, ... Lk 10:37
experts on the I said to Jesus,.................. Lk 11:45
for you, you experts on the I! .... Lk 11:46
for you, you experts on the I. .... Lk 11:52
teachers of the I and the .... Lk 11:53
Pharisees and experts on the I, ... Lk 14:3
Pharisees and teachers of the I, ... Lk 14:5
teachers of the I began to .... Lk 15:2
The I of Moses and the writings .... Lk 16:16
a letter in the I to be changed. .... Lk 16:17
'They have the I of Moses and .... Lk 16:29
the experts on the I, and some .... Lk 19:47
teachers of the I, and elders .... Lk 20:1

L

and the power of sin is the l. 1Co 15:56
agreement is not a written l, ... 2Co 3:6
The written l brings death, ... 2Co 3:6
The l that brought death was 2Co 3:7
If the l that judged people 2Co 3:9
That old l had glory, but it 2Co 3:10
If that l which disappeared came 2Co 3:11
when they read the l of Moses, ... 2Co 3:15
with God not by following the l, ... Gal 2:16
not because we followed the l, ... Gal 2:16
with God by following the l. .... Gal 2:16
It was the l that put me to .... Gal 2:19
I died to the l so that I can .... Gal 2:19
the l could make us right with .... Gal 2:21
the Spirit by following the l? .... Gal 3:2
you because you follow the l? .... Gal 3:5
on following the l to make them .... Gal 3:10
written in the Book of the **L**." .... Gal 3:10
be made right with God by the l, ... Gal 3:11
The l is not based on faith. .... Gal 3:12
away the curse the l put on us. .... Gal 3:13
The l, which came four hundred .... Gal 3:17
If the l could give us Abraham's .... Gal 3:18
So what was the l for? It was .... Gal 3:19
The l was given through angels .... Gal 3:19
to give the l to people. .... Gal 3:19
mean that the l is against God's .... Gal 3:21
true only if the l could make us .... Gal 3:21
did not give a l that can bring .... Gal 3:21
all held prisoners by the l. .... Gal 3:23
the l was our guardian leading .... Gal 3:24
a woman and lived under the l. .... Gal 4:4
were under the l and so we could .... Gal 4:5
still want to be under the l. .... Gal 4:21
do you know what the l says? .... Gal 4:21
agreement is the l that God made .... Gal 4:24
its people are slaves to the l. .... Gal 4:25
back into the slavery of the l. .... Gal 5:1
you go back to the l by being .... Gal 5:2
you must follow all the l. .... Gal 5:3
right with God through the l, ... Gal 5:4
The whole l is made complete in .... Gal 5:14
you, you are not under the l. .... Gal 5:18
There is no l that says these .... Gal 5:23
you truly obey the l of Christ. .... Gal 6:2
do not obey the l themselves, ... Gal 6:13
The Jewish l had many commands .... Eph 2:15
rules, but Christ ended that l. .... Eph 2:15
I had a strict view of the l, ... Php 3:5
the way I obeyed the l of Moses. .... Php 3:6
not because I followed the l, ... Php 3:9
want to be teachers of the l, ... 1Ti 1:7
we know that the l is good if 1Ti 1:8
know that the l is not made for 1Ti 1:9
are against the l and for those 1Ti 1:9
argue and quarrel about the l. .... Tit 3:9
Now the l says that those in the .... Heb 7:5
were given the l concerning the .... Heb 7:11
comes, the l must be changed, ... Heb 7:12
The l of Moses could not make .... Heb 7:19
The l chooses high priests who .... Heb 7:28
oath came later than the l. .... Heb 7:28
who follow the l by offering .... Heb 8:4
people every command in the l. .... Heb 9:19
on the book of the l and on all .... Heb 9:19
I says that almost everything .... Heb 9:22
The l is only an unclear picture .... Heb 10:1
people under the l offer the .... Heb 10:1
the l could make them perfect, ... Heb 10:2
sacrifices that the l commands. .... Heb 10:8
to obey the l of Moses was found .... Heb 10:28
perfect l that makes people .... Jam 1:25
This royal l is found in the .... Jam 2:8

you obey this l, you are doing .... Jam 2:8
are guilty of breaking God's l. .... Jam 2:9
all of God's l but fails to obey .... Jam 2:10
all the commands in that l. .... Jam 2:10
of breaking all of God's l. .... Jam 2:11
be judged by the l that makes .... Jam 2:12
against the l they follow. .... Jam 4:11
And when you are judging the l, ... Jam 4:11
no longer a follower of the l. .... Jam 4:11
person who sins breaks God's l. 1Jn 3:4
sin is living against God's l. 1Jn 3:4

LAW'S
know that the l commands are for .... Rm 3:19
But when the l command came to .... Rm 7:9

LAW-BREAKING
our l and sins are hurting .... Eze 33:10

LAWFUL
was l only for priests to eat. .... Mt 12:4
So it is l to do good things on .... Mt 12:12
It is not l for you to be .... Mt 14:4
what is not l on the Sabbath .... Mk 2:24
which is l only for priests to .... Mk 2:26
Which is l on the Sabbath day: .... Mk 3:4
It is not l for you to be .... Mk 6:18
do what is not l on the Sabbath .... Lk 6:2
which is l only for priests to .... Lk 6:4
which is l on the Sabbath day: .... Lk 6:9

LAWFULLY
is good if someone uses it l. 1Ti 1:8

LAWLESS
a country is l, it has one ruler .... Pr 28:2

LAWMAKER
God is the only **L** and Judge. .... Jam 4:12

LAWMAKERS
choose judges and l to rule the .... Ezr 7:25

LAWS
obeys your l, he will live, ... Ne 9:29
they do not obey the king's l. .... Est 3:8
His l are for all the world. .... Ps 105:7
or obey God's l or keep their .... Is 24:5
you, your commands, and your l. .... Da 9:5
required by their unwritten l. .... Mk 7:3
follow many other unwritten l, ... Mk 7:4
the unwritten l which have been .... Mk 7:5
things against the l of Caesar. .... Ac 17:7
that were wrong by their own l, ... Ac 23:29
obey the l of my tradition .... Ac 26:5
by human rules and l but through .... Heb 7:16

LAWSUITS
that you have l against each 1Co 6:7

LAWYER
elders and a l named Tertullus .... Ac 24:1
to help Zenas the l and Apollos .... Tit 3:13

LAY
drunk and l naked in his tent. .... Ge 9:21
know when she l down or when she .... Ge 19:33
know when she l down or when she .... Ge 19:35
she l dying, she named the boy .... Ge 35:18
talking to his sons, he l down. .... Ge 49:33
morning dew l around the camp. .... Ex 16:13
are to l the head, the fat, and .... Le 1:8
and the priest must l them, ... Le 1:12
of the LORD, she l down under .... Nu 22:27
there Sisera l dead, with the .... Jdg 4:22
He fell, and he l there. .... Jdg 5:27
at the door and l there until .... Jdg 19:26
cover from his feet and l down. .... Ru 3:7
Samuel went and l down in bed. 1Sa 3:9
Samuel l down until morning. 1Sa 3:15

bodies I on the Shaaraim 1Sa 17:52
He I that way all day and all 1Sa 19:24
the place where Asahel's body I. 2Sa 2:23
his clothes and I on the ground 2Sa 13:31
Amasa I in the middle of the 2Sa 20:12
His body I on the road, with the 1Ki 13:24
Then Elijah I on top of the boy 1Ki 17:21
Then he I down under the tree 1Ki 19:5
Ahab I down on his bed, turned 1Ki 21:4
and he I on his mother's lap 2Ki 4:20
L my walking stick on the boy's.............. 2Ki 4:29
to the bed and I on the boy, ... 2Ki 4:34
L the heads in two piles at the 2Ki 10:8
and many of them I down on rough .... Est 4:3
They I traps for my feet and .... Job 30:12
as they I asleep in death .... Ps 76:5
Owls will nest there and I eggs. .... Is 34:15
green tree you I down as a .... Je 2:20
hatching an egg it did not I, ... Je 17:11
I will I the dead bodies of the .... Eze 6:5
I down among the young lions. .... Eze 19:2
if you come and I your hand on .... Mt 9:18
you might I the foundation,.................... Lk 14:29
anyone on whom I I my hands will.......... Ac 8:19
and no one can I down any other 1Co 3:11
before you I your hands on.................... 1Ti 5:22

LAYER
and then one I of timbers. .... Ezr 6:4

LAYERS
have three I of large stones.................... Ezr 6:4

LAYING
I each half opposite the other .... Ge 15:10
finished I the foundation....................... Ezr 3:10
I its boards and setting its .... Ne 3:3
you started I stones on top .... Hag 2:15
two apostles began I their hands .... Ac 8:17
baptisms, about I on of hands, ... Heb 6:2

LAYS
The one who I the foundation of.............. Jos 6:26
The ostrich I its eggs on the .... Job 39:14
to him and I his hands on him .... Ac 9:12

LAZARUS
And a very poor man named L, ... Lk 16:20
far away with L at his side..................... Lk 16:23
A man named L was sick. .... Jn 11:1
brother was L, the man who was .... Jn 11:2
Martha and her sister and L. .... Jn 11:5
Jesus said plainly, "L is dead.................. Jn 11:14
in a loud voice, "L, come out!" .... Jn 11:43

LAZY
Though the I person puts his .... Pr 19:24
the I person turns over and over............. Pr 26:14
The I person thinks he is wiser .... Pr 26:16
'You are a wicked and I person!' .... Mt 25:26
I people who do nothing but eat." .... Tit 1:12
We do not want you to become I. .... Heb 6:12

LEAD
God did not I them on the road .... Ex 13:17
They sank like I in the raging................. Ex 15:10
carved with an iron pen into I, ... Job 19:24
of your name, I me and guide me. .... Ps 31:3
the crowd and I them to God's .... Ps 42:4
Let them I me to your holy .... Ps 43:3
city? Who will I me to Edom? .... Ps 60:9
You I the people of Joseph like .... Ps 80:1
L me on the road to everlasting .... Ps 139:24
your good Spirit I me on level................. Ps 143:10
sinners try to I you into sin, ... Pr 1:10
who tries to I you into adultery .... Pr 2:16
use me to I, and so do all .... Pr 8:16

talk will I to your ruin. .... Pr 10:10
correction will I others away .... Pr 10:17
and I them to do wrong. .... Pr 16:29
Those who I good people to do .... Pr 28:10
and a little child will I them. .... Is 11:6
and you will I those who live in .... Is 42:7
Then I will I the blind along a................ Is 42:16
I will I those people by streams .... Je 31:9
guard him while you I him away." .... Mk 14:44
a blind person I another blind .... Lk 6:39
work animals and I them to drink .... Lk 13:15
someone to I him by the hand. .... Ac 13:11
I you in the Lord and teach you............. 1Th 5:12
that does not I to eternal death 1Jn 5:16
He will I them to springs of .... Rev 7:17

LEADER
Let's choose a I and go back to .... Nu 14:4
Maaseiah the city I, and Joah 2Ch 34:8
another man replace him as I. .... Ps 109:8
good things make him a good I. .... Is 32:8
along with the I and went into .... Mt 9:23
named Jairus, a I of the .... Lk 8:41
the synagogue I and said to him.............. Lk 8:49
and an important Jewish I. .... Jn 3:1
another man replace him as I.' .... Ac 1:20
to be their I, will not listen 3Jn 1:9

LEADERS
people to be I of their tribes .... Nu 1:16
and the twelve I of Israel, ... Nu 1:44
and the I of Israel counted the .... Nu 4:34
well-known I chosen by the .... Nu 16:2
Get all the I of the people and.................. Nu 25:4
experienced I of your tribes, ... Dt 1:15
The I led Israel. The people................... Jdg 5:2
Then the I sent a message to 1Ki 21:14
Asher and I of their families. 1Ch 7:40
You are the I of the families of 1Ch 15:12
There were more I from Eleazar's 1Ch 24:4
All the I and soldiers and King 1Ch 29:24
Then the I of Judah and King 2Ch 12:6
gathered the I of the city and 2Ch 29:20
the soldiers, I, and officers 2Ch 32:21
one time the I of Babylon sent 2Ch 32:31
These men were I of the Levites. 2Ch 35:9
Cry, you I! Cry out loud! Roll .... Je 25:34
they are blind I. And if a blind .... Mt 15:14
and some of the I of the people .... Lk 19:47
later Paul sent for the I there.................. Ac 28:17

LEADERSHIP
Without I a nation falls, but .... Pr 11:14

LEADING
colony and the I city in that .... Ac 16:12
The people I Paul went with him .... Ac 17:15
One time the I priests gave me .... Ac 26:12
through me in I those who are .... Rm 15:18
to follow the I of people like 1Co 16:16
our guardian I us to Christ so .... Gal 3:24
But if the Spirit is I you, ... Gal 5:18

LEADS
He I me to calm water. .... Ps 23:2
He I me on paths that are right .... Ps 23:3
don't go where she I you. .... Pr 7:25
Pride I only to shame;.......................... Pr 11:2
like a mist and I to death. .... Pr 21:6
the road is wide that I to hell,................. Mt 7:13
is narrow that I to true life..................... Mt 7:14
a blind person I a blind person, ... Mt 15:14
sheep by name and I them out. .... Jn 10:3
should try hard when he I. .... Rm 12:8
who always I us as captives in 2Co 2:14

LEAF
a fresh olive l in its mouth. .... Ge 8:11
by the sound of a l being blown .... Le 26:36
Don't punish a l that is blown................. Job 13:25
will be healthy like a green l. .... Pr 11:28
a fig tree in l from far away, ... Mk 11:13

LEAFY
poplars, and other l trees. .... Le 23:40
LORD called you "a l olive tree, ... Je 11:16
every green tree and l oak— .... Eze 6:13
high hill and every l tree. .... Eze 20:28

LEAH
The older was L, and the younger .... Ge 29:16
brought his daughter L to Jacob, ... Ge 29:23
Jacob loved Rachel more than L. .... Ge 29:30
the daughter of L and Jacob, ... Ge 34:1
like Rachel and L, who had many .... Ru 4:11

LEAH'S
Then God answered L prayer, ... Ge 30:17
in Jacob's tent, in L tent, and .... Ge 31:33
he left L tent, he went into .... Ge 31:33
had two sons by L slave girl .... Ge 35:26

LEAK
a quarrel is like a l in a dam, ... Pr 17:14
fix it, the house will l. .... Ec 10:18

LEAN
temple so I can l against them." .... Jdg 16:26
someone who must l on a crutch. 2Sa 3:29
If you l on it for help, it will 2Ki 18:21
They l on the spider's web, ... Job 8:15
If you l on it for help, it will .... Is 36:6
tried to l on you for help .... Eze 29:6
But they l on the LORD and say, ... Mic 3:11

LEANED
worshiped as he l on the top of .... Ge 47:31
I have l on you since the day I .... Ps 22:10
When they l on you, you broke .... Eze 29:7
That follower l closer to Jesus .... Jn 13:25
who had l against Jesus at .... Jn 21:20
worshiped as he l on the top of .... Heb 11:21

LEANING
There I saw Saul l on his spear. 2Sa 1:6
Who is like a l wall, like a .... Ps 62:3
of the desert, l on her lover? .... Sng 8:5

LEANNOTH
By the mahalath l. A maskil of .... Ps 87:7

LEANS
to worship, he l on my arm. 2Ki 5:18

LEAP
wild goats will l about in the .... Is 13:21

LEARN
L them and obey them carefully. .... Dt 5:1
so I would l your demands..................... Ps 119:71
A wise person will l more from a .... Pr 17:10
L to do good. Seek justice. .... Is 1:17
are near me, l about my power. .... Is 33:13
Go and l what this means: ' .... Mt 9:13
my teachings and l from me, ... Mt 11:29
L a lesson from the fig tree: .... Mt 24:32
If they want to l something, ... 1Co 14:35
so they will l not to speak 1Ti 1:20
Let a woman l by listening 1Ti 2:11
them first l to do their duty................... 1Ti 5:4
they l to waste their time, ... 1Ti 5:13
No one could l the new song .... Rev 14:3

LEARNED
he l that Lazarus had already................. Jn 11:17
in Thessalonica l that Paul was .... Ac 17:13
But I l that he is a Roman .... Ac 23:27

against the true teaching you l, ... Rm 16:17
But what you l in Christ was not .... Eph 4:20
Do what you l and received from .... Php 4:9
have l to be satisfied with the .... Php 4:11
I have l the secret of being .... Php 4:12
You l about this hope when you .... Col 1:5
You l about God's grace from .... Col 1:7
following the teachings you l................... 2Ti 3:14
l obedience by what he suffered. .... Heb 5:8

LEARNING
L your words gives wisdom and .... Ps 119:130
Anyone who loves l accepts .... Pr 12:1
those who love l will succeed................... Pr 19:8
capable of l and understanding, ... Da 1:4
away the key to l about God. .... Lk 11:52
and you stopped others from l, ... Lk 11:52
spent their time l the apostles' .... Ac 2:42
Anyone who is l the teaching of .... Gal 6:6
are always l new teachings, ... 2Ti 3:7

LEARNS
When he l about his sin, he must .... Le 4:23
When the person l about his sin, ... Le 4:28
But when he l about it, he will .... Le 5:3
honey when he l to reject what .... Is 7:15
before the child l to choose..................... Is 7:16
before the boy l to say 'my .... Is 8:4
the Father and l from him comes .... Jn 6:45

LEASE
Then he will l the vineyard to................. Mt 21:41

LEASED
Then he l the land to some .... Mt 21:33
Then he l the land to some .... Mk 12:1
a vineyard and l it to some .... Lk 20:9

LEASH
or put it on a l for your girls? .... Job 41:5

LEATHER
knitted), or of l, or something................. Le 13:48
or something made from l. .... Le 13:48
in the clothing, l, or woven or............... Le 13:49
man and wore a l belt around his 2Ki 1:8

LEAVES
they sewed fig l together and .... Ge 3:7
their l will not dry and die. .... Eze 47:12
and their l for medicine." .... Eze 47:12
l of the tree were beautiful..................... Da 4:12
no figs on the tree, only l. .... Mt 21:19
green and soft and new l appear, ... Mt 24:32
no figs, only l, because it was .... Mk 11:13
The l of the tree are for the..................... Rev 22:2

LEBANA
L, Hagaba, Shalmai, ... Ne 7:48

LEBANAH
L, Hagabah, Akkub, ... Ezr 2:45

LEBANON
to Baal Gad in the Valley of L, ... Jos 11:17
down cedar trees for me from L. 1Ki 5:6
them down from L to the sea................... 1Ki 5:9
of cedars from the Forest of L, ... 1Ki 7:2
logs from L to the seacoast..................... Ezr 3:7
the LORD breaks the cedars of L. .... Ps 29:5
the land of L dance like a calf .... Ps 29:6
smell like the cedars of L. .... Sng 4:11
down from the mountains of L. .... Sng 4:15
mountain of L that looks down .... Sng 7:4
cedar trees from L and the great .... Is 2:13
beautiful like the forest of L, ... Is 35:2
the mountains of L never melts .... Je 18:14
cedar tree from L to make a .... Eze 27:5

a cedar tree in L with beautiful .... Eze 31:3
be as famous as the wine of L. .... Hos 14:7

LEBAOTH
L, Shilhim, Ain, and Rimmon. .... Jos 15:32
Beth L, and Sharuhen. .... Jos 19:6

LEBONAH
and south of the city of L." .... Jdg 21:19

LED
because he l me on the right .... Ge 24:48
When Moses l the flock to the .... Ex 3:1
So God l them through the desert .... Ex 13:18
Moses l the Israelites away from .... Ex 15:22
your God has l you in the desert.............. Dt 8:2
He l you through the large and .... Dt 8:15
I l you through the desert for .... Dt 29:5
from Egypt and l you to the land .... Jdg 2:1
Jeroboam had l the people of 1Ki 15:26
of Nebat had l Israel to sin,.................... 2Ki 15:28
He l the people of Jerusalem to 2Ch 21:11
a hundred men, who l the army.............. 2Ch 23:14
you l a parade of captives. .... Ps 68:18
You l your people like a flock .... Ps 77:20
l them with a cloud by day and .... Ps 78:14
He l them on a straight road to .... Ps 107:7
He l his people through the.................... Ps 136:16
who are being l to their death; .... Pr 24:11
thirsty when he l them through .... Is 48:21
a lamb being l to be killed. .... Is 53:7
with joy and be l out in peace. .... Is 55:12
who l Moses by the right hand .... Is 63:12
Then the man l me south where I .... Eze 40:24
Then the Spirit l Jesus into the .... Mt 4:1
arrested Jesus l him to the .... Mt 26:57
Then they l him away to be.................... Mt 27:31
blind man's hand and l him out .... Mk 8:23
arrested Jesus l him to the .... Mk 14:53
Then the devil l Jesus to .... Lk 4:9
stood up and l Jesus to Pilate................. Lk 23:1
Jesus l his followers as far as .... Lk 24:50
and l him first to Annas, the .... Jn 18:13
a sheep being l to be killed. .... Ac 8:32
his hand and l him into Damascus .... Ac 9:8
minds will be l away from your 2Co 11:3
time someone l into sin. 2Co 11:29
he l a parade of captives, ... Eph 4:8
of sin and are l by many evil 2Ti 3:6
people Moses l out of Egypt. .... Heb 3:16
but people l by the Holy Spirit 2Pe 1:21

LEDGE
the ground up to the lower l, ... Eze 43:14
from the smaller l to the larger .... Eze 43:14
the larger l and is twenty-one................. Eze 43:14
The upper l is also square, ... Eze 43:17
on the four corners of the l, ... Eze 43:20
corners of the l of the altar, ... Eze 45:19

LEDGES
walls there were l for the side................. Eze 41:6
rested on the l but were not .... Eze 41:6

LEEKS
cucumbers, melons, l, onions,................. Nu 11:5

LEFT
If you go to the l, I will go to .... Ge 13:9
side and Manasseh on his l. .... Ge 48:13
on their right and on their l. .... Ex 14:22
reached with his l hand and took .... Jdg 3:21
the torches in their l hands and .... Jdg 7:20
one and his l hand on the other. .... Jdg 16:29
Then Solomon l the place of 2Ch 1:13
the priests l the Holy Place. 2Ch 5:11
with her l hand she gives you................. Pr 3:16

family will be l with nothing .... Pr 11:29
My lover's l hand is under my .... Sng 2:6
the face of an ox on the l side. .... Eze 1:10
Then lie down on your l side, ... Eze 4:4
Immediately they l the boat and.............. Mt 4:22
her hand, and the fever l her. .... Mt 8:15
will sit at your l side in your .... Mt 20:21
will sit at my right or my l; .... Mt 20:23
right and the goats on his l. .... Mt 25:33
will say to those on his l, ' .... Mt 25:41
right and the other on the l. .... Mt 27:38
The first angel l and poured out .... Rev 16:2

LEFT-HANDED
people of Benjamin, who was l. .... Jdg 3:15
these trained soldiers were l, ... Jdg 20:16

LEFTOVER
the fields and pick up l grapes .... Job 24:6
with the l pieces of food.......................... Mt 14:20
with the l pieces of food.......................... Mt 15:37
with the l pieces of bread .... Mk 6:43
with the l pieces of food.......................... Mk 8:8
you fill with l pieces of food? .... Mk 8:19
you fill with l pieces of food? .... Mk 8:20
Gather the l pieces of fish and .... Jn 6:12

LEFTOVERS
filled many baskets with the l? .... Mt 16:9

LEG
Put your hand under my l. .... Ge 24:2
his master's l and made a .... Ge 24:9
was limping because of his l. .... Ge 32:31
me, put your hand under my l. .... Ge 47:29
That snake bites a horse's l, ... Ge 49:17
only two l bones or a scrap.................... Am 3:12
on his upper l was written this .... Rev 19:16

LEGAL
listen to the LORD's l case.................... Mic 6:2
LORD has l a case against his .... Mic 6:2

LEGION
My name is L, because we are .... Mk 5:9
He answered, "L," because many .... Lk 8:30

LEGS
with its head, l, and inner .... Ex 12:9
They have bitten my arms and l. .... Ps 22:16
useless as the l of a crippled .... Pr 26:7
Judah's head and l and removing .... Is 7:20
part of the l were made of iron .... Da 2:33
dead, they did not break his l. .... Jn 19:33
his l were like pillars of fire. .... Rev 10:1

LEHABITES
Anamites, L, Naphtuhites, ... Ge 10:13
Anamites, L, and Naphtuhites, ... 1Ch 1:11

LEHI
of Judah, near a place named L.............. Jdg 15:9
came to the place named L, ... Jdg 15:14
that place was named Ramath L. .... Jdg 15:17
up a hole in the ground at L, ... Jdg 15:19
Spring, which is still in L. .... Jdg 15:19

LEMUEL
These are the words of King L, ... Pr 31:1
not drink wine, L, and rulers .... Pr 31:4

LEND
If you l money to one of my .... Ex 22:25
Don't l him money for interest, ... Le 25:37
and you will l to other nations, ... Dt 15:6
l them whatever they need...................... Dt 15:8
You will l to other nations, ... Dt 28:12
Foreigners will l money to you, ... Dt 28:44
will not be able to l to them. .... Dt 28:44
on money they l and do not take .... Ps 15:5

L

LENDERS

people always l freely to others ....Ps 37:26
who borrow and those who l, ...Is 24:2
He does not l money to get too ....Eze 18:8
If you l things to people, ...Lk 6:34
Even sinners l to other sinners ....Lk 6:34
and l to them without hoping to ....Lk 6:35

LENDERS

and borrowers are servants to l. ....Pr 22:7

LENDING

men are also l money and grain ....Ne 5:10
the poor is like l to the LORD; ....Pr 19:17

LENDS

He l money for too much interest ....Eze 18:13
or profit when he l money. ....Eze 18:17

LENGTH

along the entire l of each side..................Ex 26:28
along the entire l of each side..................Ex 36:33
you measure the l or weight or ....Le 19:35
the next rope l were allowed to 2Sa 8:2
which is the l of a king's life. ....Is 23:15
veils of every l to trap people!.................Eze 13:18
The man measured the l and width ....Eze 40:20
measured the l of the building ....Eze 41:15
north with the same l and width.............Eze 42:11
its full l will be about seven ....Eze 48:13
areas run the l of the lands.....................Eze 48:21
its l was equal to its width. ....Rev 21:16

LENGTHS

within one rope l were killed, ...2Sa 8:2

LEOPARD

A l is waiting for them near ....Je 5:6
Can a l change his spots? ....Je 13:23
looked like a l with four wings ....Da 7:6
like a l waiting by the road. ....Hos 13:7
This beast looked like a l, ...Rev 13:2

LEOPARDS

dens and from the l' hills. ....Sng 4:8
and I will lie down to rest with ....Is 11:6
are faster than l and quicker ....Hab 1:8

LESHEM

They went and fought against L, ...Jos 19:47
the town of L and changed its ....Jos 19:47

LETTER

David wrote a l to Joab and sent 2Sa 11:14
had given a l to Ezra, ...Ezr 7:11
in his hand was an unsealed l. ....Ne 6:5
wrote this second l about Purim. ....Est 9:29
This is the l that Jeremiah the ....Je 29:1
priest read the l to Jeremiah ....Je 29:29
and gave the l to the governor, ...Ac 23:33
I am writing this l from Paul. ....Rm 16:22
This l is not written with ink 2Co 3:3
Even if my l made you sad,.......................2Co 7:8
message or in a l as if it came 2Th 2:2

LETTERS

wrote some l, signed Ahab's 1Ki 21:8
give me l for the governors of.................Ne 2:7
and gave them the king's l.......................Ne 2:9
Then he sent l to all the Jewish ....Est 9:30
him to write l to the synagogues ....Ac 9:2
Do we need l of introduction to 2Co 3:1
See what large l l use to write ....Gal 6:11

LETUSH

people of Assyria, L, and Leum...............Ge 25:3

LEUM

of Assyria, Letush, and L. ....Ge 25:3

LEVEL

good Spirit lead me on l ground. ....Ps 143:10
path of life is l for those who ....Is 26:7
rough ground should be made l, ...Is 40:4
will l it to the ground so that ....Eze 13:14
and he stood on l ground. ....Lk 6:17

LEVI

She named him L and said, ...Ge 29:34
sons, Simeon and L (Dinah's ....Ge 34:25
then Simeon, L, Judah, Issachar..............Ge 35:23
Simeon and L are brothers who ....Ge 49:5
the family of L married a woman ....Ex 2:1
was also from the family of L. ....Ex 2:1
which stood for the family of L ....Nu 17:8
the tribe of L to carry the Ark ....Dt 10:8
the tribes of L and Benjamin, ...1Ch 21:6
Family of L, praise the LORD. ....Ps 135:20
descendants of L who can come ....Eze 40:46
agreement with L will continue," ....Mal 2:4
a man named L son of Alphaeus ....Mk 2:14
collector named L sitting in the ....Lk 5:27
Then L gave a big dinner for ....Lk 5:29
in the tribe of L who become ....Heb 7:5
was not from the tribe of L, ...Heb 7:6
even say that L, who receives.................Heb 7:9
L was not yet born, but he was ....Heb 7:10
of priests from the tribe of L, ...Heb 7:11
the tribe of L twelve thousand, ...Rev 7:7

LEVI'S

was having dinner at L house, ...Mk 2:15

LEVIATHAN

to wake up the sea monster L. ....Job 3:8
Can you catch L on a fish hook ....Job 41:1
you make a pet of L as you would ....Job 41:5
of the monster L and gave it to ....Ps 74:14
and there is the sea monster L, ...Ps 104:26
time the LORD will punish L, ...Is 27:1
He will punish L, the coiled ....Is 27:1

LEVIATHAN'S

speak about L arms and legs, ...Job 41:12

LEVITE

man who was a L from the city ....Jdg 17:7
I'm a L from Bethlehem in Judah. ....Jdg 17:9
I have a L as my priest." ....Jdg 17:13
Next, a L came there, and after ....Lk 10:32
Joseph, a L born in Cyprus. ....Ac 4:36

LEVITE'S

So they stopped at the L house, ...Jdg 18:15

LEVITES

of the family groups of the L. ....Ex 6:25
ordered the L to make this list ....Ex 38:21
The L may always buy back ....Le 25:32
Instead put the L in charge of................Nu 1:50
is moved, the L must take it ....Nu 1:51
But the L must make their camp ....Nu 1:53
leader of the L was Eleazar son ....Nu 3:32
the people the L could not ....Nu 3:49
be cut off from the L. ....Nu 4:18
you bring the L before the LORD, ...Nu 8:10
present the L before the LORD ....Nu 8:11
The L will put their hands on ....Nu 8:12
some of its cities to the L, ...Nu 35:8
priests who are L and to the ....Dt 17:9
of Israel were given to the L. ....Jos 21:41
The L took down the Ark of the 1Sa 6:15
Some of the L were musicians in 1Ch 9:33
the priests and L prepared 1Ch 15:14
God helped the L who carried the 1Ch 15:26
separated the L into three 1Ch 23:6
and the L brought them up. 2Ch 5:5

service and the **L** to lead the	2Ch 8:14
sons, and the **L** help them.	2Ch 13:10
The **L** must stay near the king,	2Ch 23:7
Hezekiah said, "Listen to me, **L**.	2Ch 29:5
relatives the **L** helped them.	2Ch 29:34
The **L** had been more careful to	2Ch 29:34
priests and the **L** were ashamed,	2Ch 30:15
The **L** twenty years old and older	2Ch 31:17
histories of the **L** received part	2Ch 31:19
Some **L** worked as secretaries,	2Ch 34:13
the priests and **L** went to their	2Ch 35:10
Then the **L** skinned the animals	2Ch 35:11
the **L** prepared meat for	2Ch 35:14
The priests and **L** had made	Ezr 6:20
the priests and **L** accepted the	Ezr 8:30
and the **L** who were teaching said	Ne 8:9
The **L** helped calm the people,	Ne 8:11
These **L** were standing on the	Ne 9:4
a tenth of our crops to the **L**,	Ne 10:37
must be with the **L** when they	Ne 10:38
over the **L** in Jerusalem.	Ne 11:22
priests and **L** from the fields	Ne 12:44
also set aside part for the **L**.	Ne 12:47
of the priests and **L** unclean.	Ne 13:29
the **L** will have a share about	Eze 48:13
sent priests and **L** to ask him,	Jn 1:19

LIAR

witness who is a **l**, lying about	Dt 19:18
a fair trial, I am called a **l**.	Job 34:6
Whoever hides hate is a **l**.	Pr 10:18
to be poor than to be a **l**.	Pr 19:22
you and prove you are a **l**.	Pr 30:6
while that I was still alive	Mt 27:63
because he is a **l** and the father	Jn 8:44
him, I would be a **l** like you.	Jn 8:55
we make God a **l**, and we do not	1Jn 1:10
not obey God's commands is a **l**,	1Jn 2:4
Who is the **l**? It is the person	1Jn 2:22
does not believe makes God a **l**,	1Jn 5:10

LIAR'S

but a **l** tongue will be stopped.	Pr 10:31

LIARS

I said, "All people are **l**."	Ps 116:11
are always **l**, evil animals,	Tit 1:12
not, and you found they are **l**.	Rev 2:2
Jews; they are **l**. I will make	Rev 3:9

LIBYA

to Tarshish, **L**, Lud (the land of	Is 66:19
Lydia, Arabia, **L**, and some of my	Eze 30:5
Put and **L** supported her.	Nah 3:9
the areas of **L** near Cyrene,	Ac 2:10

LIBYAN

L and Nubian people will obey	Da 11:43

LIBYANS

brought troops of **L**, Sukkites,	2Ch 12:3
The Cushites and **L** had a large	2Ch 16:8

LICK

they will also **l** up your blood!'	1Ki 21:19
your dogs can **l** their share."	Ps 68:23
and make his enemies **l** the dust.	Ps 72:9
dogs would come and **l** his sores.	Lk 16:21

LICKED

place the dogs **l** up Naboth's	1Ki 21:19
the dogs **l** his blood from the	1Ki 22:38

LIE

You must not **l** when you accuse	Ex 23:7
who wants you to **l** in court,	Ex 23:8
might **l** about what happened to	Le 6:2
or he might **l** about a promise he	Le 6:2
been lost and then **l** about it.	Le 6:3

you must not **l** to each other.	Le 19:11
you will **l** down in peace, and no	Le 26:6
suffer until you **l** dead in the	Nu 14:33
human being, and he will not **l**.	Nu 23:19
a lion, they **l** waiting to attack	Nu 24:9
you **l** down and when you get up.	Dt 6:7
you **l** down and when you get up.	Dt 11:19
make that person **l** down and be	Dt 25:2
ones will **l** down in safety,	Dt 33:12
of Israel will **l** down in safety.	Dt 33:28
and asked, "Why did you **l** to us?	Jos 9:22
cover off his feet and **l** down.	Ru 3:4
does not **l** or change his mind.	1Sa 15:29
He made them **l** on the ground,	2Sa 8:2
fire and burned where they **l**."	2Sa 23:7
She will **l** close to you and keep	1Ki 1:2
Then he told a **l**. He said, "An	1Ki 13:18
has made your prophets **l** to you,	1Ki 22:23
man of God, don't **l** to me, your	2Ki 4:16
I tell you not to **l** to me?"	2Ki 4:28
has made your prophets **l** to you,	2Ch 18:22
I would not **l** to your face.	Job 6:28
I **l** down, I think, 'How long	Job 7:4
will soon **l** down in the dust of	Job 7:21
the monster Rahab **l** at his feet	Job 9:13
You will **l** down, and no one will	Job 11:19
we **l** down and do not rise again;	Job 14:12
but it will **l** with them in the	Job 20:11
and my tongue will not tell a **l**.	Job 27:4
The dew will **l** on the branches	Job 29:19
while they **l** in their dens or	Job 38:40
They **l** down, their young are	Job 39:3
I can **l** down and go to sleep,	Ps 3:5
be disgraced and silent in the	Ps 31:17
They **l** about me because I try to	Ps 38:20
come to see me, but they **l**.	Ps 41:6
your brother and about your	Ps 50:20
that bite and tongues that **l**.	Ps 52:4
I must **l** down among them.	Ps 57:4
even the greatest are just a **l**.	Ps 62:9
holiness, I will not **l** to David.	Ps 89:35
I **l** awake. I am like a lonely	Ps 102:7
go back to their dens to **l** down.	Ps 104:22
my house, or **l** down on my bed,	Ps 132:3
where I go and where I **l** down.	Ps 139:3
I **l** down in the grave, you are	Ps 139:8
When you **l** down, you won't be	Pr 3:24
when you **l** down, you will sleep	Pr 3:24
How long will you **l** there,	Pr 6:9
your hands and **l** down to rest.	Pr 6:10
A truthful witness does not **l**,	Pr 14:5
your hands and **l** down to rest.	Pr 24:33
When you **l** about your neighbors,	Pr 25:18
two **l** down together, they will	Ec 4:11
bodies **l** in the streets like	Is 5:25
leopards will **l** down to rest	Is 11:6
Their young will **l** down to rest	Is 11:7
be able to **l** down in safety.	Is 14:30
statues for your gods **l** broken on	Is 21:9
You who **l** in the ground, wake up	Is 26:19
They will **l** down there and eat	Is 27:10
those who **l** about others in	Is 29:21
those who **l** and take justice	Is 29:21
like children who **l** and refuse	Is 30:9
You will **l** down in a place of	Is 50:11
fall down and **l** on every street	Is 51:20
They **l** down and dream and love	Is 56:10
rough cloth and **l** in ashes to	Is 58:5
my children will not **l** to me."	Is 63:8
The cities of Israel **l** in ruins,	Je 2:15
Let us **l** down in our shame,	Je 3:25
have taught their tongues to **l**.	Je 9:5
of people will **l** in the open	Je 9:22

They will I like grain a farmer .... Je 9:22
bodies will I on the ground .... Je 16:4
He has made you believe a l. .... Je 29:31
People young and old I outside .... La 2:21
Then I down on your left side, ... Eze 4:4
of days you I on your left side. .... Eze 4:4
ninety days, you I on a second .... Eze 4:6
ninety days you I on your side. .... Eze 4:9
people will I dead among their .... Eze 6:13
worst of cities that I in ruins. .... Eze 30:7
You will I among unclean people, ... Eze 31:18
I down in death with those who .... Eze 32:19
have come down here and I dead.' .... Eze 32:21
and all its army I dead there. .... Eze 32:22
be broken and I among those who .... Eze 32:28
but now they I in death with .... Eze 32:29
people will I among those who .... Eze 32:32
They will I down on good ground .... Eze 34:14
You will I fallen on the ground, ... Eze 39:5
ruler, but he will I to them. .... Da 11:23
same table and I to each other, ... Da 11:27
They just I on their beds and .... Hos 7:14
they I dry and dead in the dirt. .... Joe 1:17
I down on clothes taken from .... Am 2:8
You I on beds decorated with .... Am 6:4
far inside the ship to I down, ... Jnh 1:5
I on their beds and make evil .... Mic 2:1
important men I down to rest. .... Nah 3:18
and herds will I down there, ... Zph 2:14
will eat and I down with no one .... Zph 3:13
They will I and say all kinds of .... Mt 5:11
That I would be even worse than .... Mt 27:64
money, and don't I about them. .... Lk 3:14
When he tells a I, he shows what .... Jn 8:44
your thoughts to I to the Holy .... Ac 5:3
traded the truth of God for a l. .... Rm 1:25
say, "When I I, it really gives .... Rm 3:7
because my I shows God's truth. .... Rm 3:7
truth; I do not I. My conscience .... Rm 9:1
apostles but are workers who l. 2Co 11:13
Do not I to each other. You have............. Col 3:9
truth so they will believe a l. 2Th 2:11
spirits that I and teachings 1Ti 4:1
time began. And God cannot l. .... Tit 1:2
God cannot I when he makes a .... Heb 6:18
and he cannot I when he makes an .... Heb 6:18
Your bragging is a I that hides .... Jam 3:14
know that no I comes from the 1Jn 2:21
witnesses will I in the street .... Rev 11:8

LIED

afraid, so she I and said, "I..................... Ge 18:15
back what he found and I about .... Le 6:4
have stolen and I and have taken .... Jos 7:11
We I to you because we were .... Jos 9:24
of me. You I to me. Now tell .... Jdg 16:10
fool of me. You I to me. Tell me .... Jdg 16:13
But he I about me to you. 2Sa 19:27
been dishonest or I to others, ... Job 31:5
and their tongues I to him. .... Ps 78:36
ashamed because they I about me............. Ps 119:78
wrong, and he had never I. .... Is 53:9
so afraid of that you I to me? .... Is 57:11
With your lips you have l, ... Is 59:3
people have I about the LORD .... Je 5:12
That person has I, so I will .... Je 23:34
stood up and I about Jesus,..................... Mk 14:57
You I to God, not to us!" .... Ac 5:4
I was tricky and I to catch you. 2Co 12:16
sinned, and he had never l." 1Pe 2:22

LIES

Anything she I on during this................. Le 15:20
every bed he I on will be........................ Le 15:24

man has told I about my daughter .... Dt 22:17
know where he I down to sleep. .... Ru 3:4
speak God's truth by telling l................... Job 13:7
full of curses, I, and threats; .... Ps 10:7
enjoy telling l. With their .... Ps 62:4
witness who l, and someone who .... Pr 6:19
witness who I will not go free, ... Pr 19:9
If a ruler pays attention to l, ... Pr 29:12
who speak I were the tail. .... Is 9:15
each other falsely and tell l. .... Is 59:4
shooting I from their mouths .... Je 9:3
are prophesying I in my name. .... Je 14:14
of adultery and live by l. .... Je 23:14
crocodile that I in the Nile .... Eze 29:3
will tell I and cause those .... Da 11:32
have eaten the fruit of your l. .... Hos 10:13
is only a statue that teaches l................... Hab 2:18
came and told I about him, ... Mt 26:60
slaves, who tell l, who speak 1Ti 1:10
is clear and I open before him, ... Heb 4:13
and who love lies and tell l. .... Rev 22:15

LIEUTENANTS

young captains and I riding on .... Eze 23:6
captains and I riding horses. .... Eze 23:12
handsome young captains and l, ... Eze 23:23

LIFE

the breath of I into the man's .... Ge 2:7
tree that gives I and also the .... Ge 2:9
eat dust all the days of your l................... Ge 3:14
its food all the days of your l. .... Ge 3:17
of the fruit from the tree of l, ... Ge 3:22
from getting to the tree of l. .... Ge 3:24
that has the breath of l. .... Ge 6:17
had the breath of I came to Noah .... Ge 7:15
had the breath of I in it died. .... Ge 7:22
in it, because blood gives l....................... Ge 9:4
I will demand blood for l. .... Ge 9:5
will demand the I of any animal............... Ge 9:5
will demand the I of anyone who .... Ge 9:5
who takes another person's l................... Ge 9:5
destroy all I on the earth. .... Ge 9:15
earth was divided during his l, ... Ge 10:25
kind to me and have saved my l. .... Ge 19:19
God saved Lot's l, but he........................ Ge 19:29
after a long and satisfying l. .... Ge 25:8
happened during Abraham's l. .... Ge 26:1
to face, but my I was saved." .... Ge 32:30
you, you can blame me all my l. .... Ge 43:9
important in our father's I that .... Ge 44:30
you can blame me all my l.' .... Ge 44:32
My I has been spent wandering .... Ge 47:9
God has led me all my l........................... Ge 48:15
During Joseph's I Ephraim had .... Ge 50:23
So the Egyptians made I hard for .... Ex 1:11
have made I hard for them....................... Ex 3:9
serve that master all his l. .... Ex 21:6
that must be paid is I for life, ... Ex 21:23
that must be paid is life for l, ... Ex 21:23
the bull may buy back his l, ... Ex 21:30
buy back his I from the LORD so .... Ex 30:12
is because the I of the body is................. Le 17:11
the sins, because it is l. .... Le 17:11
the animal's I is still in it. .... Le 17:14
the animal's I is in its blood. .... Le 17:14
put your neighbor's I in danger. .... Le 19:16
to spare the I of a murderer who .... Nu 35:31
the murderer's I could be saved .... Dt 4:42
have a long I in the land you .... Dt 5:33
because the I is in the blood. .... Dt 12:23
Don't eat the I with the meat. .... Dt 12:23
and has a good I with you, ... Dt 15:16
he will be your slave for l. .... Dt 15:17

So all your l you will remember .... Dt 16:3
read from it every day of his l. .... Dt 17:19
cities in order to save his l. .... Dt 19:4
of these cities to save his l. .... Dt 19:5
A l must be paid for a life, ... Dt 19:21
A life must be paid for a l, ... Dt 19:21
and abused all your l. .... Dt 28:33
today l offer you l and success, ... Dt 30:15
I am offering you l or death, ... Dt 30:19
Now, choose l! Then you and your .... Dt 30:19
To choose l is to love the LORD .... Dt 30:20
is your l, and he will let you .... Dt 30:20
me. I send l and death; I can .... Dt 32:39
but rather they mean l for you! .... Dt 32:47
able to defeat you all your l. .... Jos 1:5
They respected Joshua all his l, ... Jos 4:14
you and risked his l to save you .... Jdg 9:17
I risked my own l and went .... Jdg 12:3
what kind of l should the boy .... Jdg 13:12
My l is much too sad for you to .... Ru 1:13
Almighty has made my l very sad. .... Ru 1:20
give you new l and will take .... Ru 4:15
give him back to you all his l, ... 1Sa 1:11
belong to the LORD all his l." 1Sa 1:28
sends death, and he brings to l. 1Sa 2:6
and he raises them to l again. 1Sa 2:6
the Philistines all Samuel's l. 1Sa 7:13
as judge of Israel all his l. 1Sa 7:15
All Saul's l he fought hard 1Sa 14:52
Saul again the rest of his l, ... 1Sa 15:35
he was David's enemy all his l. 1Sa 18:29
risked his l when he killed 1Sa 19:5
Tonight you must run for your l. 1Sa 19:11
respected my l, so I will not 1Sa 26:21
As I respected your l today, ... 1Sa 26:24
also respect my l and save me 1Sa 26:24
I have risked my l and done what 1Sa 28:21
I can't bring him back to l. 2Sa 12:23
But God doesn't take away l. 2Sa 14:14
whether it means l or death." 2Sa 15:21
They saved your l and the lives 2Sa 19:5
Philistine and saved David's l. 2Sa 21:17
doesn't cost Adonijah his l! 1Ki 2:23
You did not ask for a long l, ... 1Ki 3:11
During your l no other king will 1Ki 3:13
I will also give you a long l." 1Ki 3:14
under his control all his l. 1Ki 4:21
Solomon's l Judah and Israel 1Ki 4:25
During his l he spoke three. 1Ki 4:32
him rule all his l because of my 1Ki 11:34
obeyed his commands all his l, ... 1Ki 15:5
faithful to the LORD all his l. 1Ki 15:14
It cost Hiel the l of Abiram, ... 1Ki 16:34
and it cost the l of Segub, ... 1Ki 16:34
he was afraid and ran for his l, ... 1Ki 19:3
to give your l in his place. 1Ki 20:39
so your l will be taken instead 1Ki 20:42
to come to him during his l, ... 1Ki 21:29
please respect my l and the 2Ki 1:13
But now, respect my l." 2Ki 1:14
son he had brought back to l. 2Ki 8:1
brought a dead boy back to l. 2Ki 8:5
brought back to l came and 2Ki 8:5
son Elisha brought back to l." 2Ki 8:5
you must pay with your own l." 2Ki 10:24
came back to l and stood on his 2Ki 13:21
add fifteen years to your l. 2Ki 20:6
For the rest of his l, he ate at 2Ki 25:29
languages during his l. 1Ch 1:19
long l and had received many. 1Ch 29:28
your enemies, or for a long l. 2Ch 1:11
Asa was faithful all his l. 2Ch 15:17
may pray for the l of the king .... Ezr 6:10

to us and has given us new l. .... Ezr 9:9
stones back to l from piles of .... Ne 4:2
I run for my l into the Temple? .... Ne 6:11
you give l to everything. .... Ne 9:6
beg Queen Esther to save his l. .... Est 7:7
all he has to save his own l. .... Job 2:4
but you may not take his l." .... Job 2:6
Why is l given to those who are .... Job 3:20
that my l is only a breath. .... Job 7:7
hate my l; I don't want to live .... Job 7:16
about myself. I hate my own l. .... Job 9:21
I hate my l, so I will complain .... Job 10:1
You gave me l and showed me .... Job 10:12
your care you watched over my l. .... Job 10:12
days of my l are almost over. .... Job 10:20
Your l will be as bright as the .... Job 11:17
The l of every creature and the .... Job 12:10
and long l brings understanding. .... Job 12:12
and take my l in my own hands? .... Job 13:14
days of my l are almost gone. .... Job 17:1
God's breath of l is in my nose, ... Job 27:3
when God takes their l away? .... Job 27:8
Now my l is almost over; .... Job 30:16
sin by cursing my enemies' l. .... Job 31:30
of the Almighty gave me l. .... Job 33:4
and their l is almost over. .... Job 33:22
found a way to pay for his l.' .... Job 33:24
God bought my l back from death, ... Job 33:28
and I will continue to enjoy l.' .... Job 33:28
and so he may still enjoy l. .... Job 33:30
to take away l and breath, ... Job 34:14
you take it as your slave for l? .... Job 41:4
I will change my heart and l. .... Job 42:6
part of Job's l even more than .... Job 42:12
My share in l has been pleasant; .... Ps 16:6
teach me how to live a holy l. .... Ps 16:11
those whose reward is in this l. .... Ps 17:14
asked you for l, and you gave it .... Ps 21:4
save my l from the dogs. .... Ps 22:20
love will be with me all my l, ... Ps 23:6
will enjoy a good l, and their .... Ps 25:13
I have lived an innocent l. .... Ps 26:1
sinners or take my l with those .... Ps 26:9
But I have lived an innocent l, ... Ps 26:11
The LORD protects my l. .... Ps 27:1
in the LORD's house all my l. .... Ps 27:4
I give you my l. Save me, LORD, ... Ps 31:5
My l is ending in sadness, ... Ps 31:10
My l is in your hands. Save me .... Ps 31:15
things to enjoy l and have many. .... Ps 34:12
Save my l from their attacks; .... Ps 35:17
You are the giver of l. .... Ps 36:9
Your light lets us enjoy l. .... Ps 36:9
have given me only a short l; .... Ps 39:5
Everyone's l is only a breath. .... Ps 39:5
Everyone's l is only a breath. .... Ps 39:11
that my body and l are yours. .... Ps 40:6
and spare their l and will bless .... Ps 41:2
can buy back the l of another. .... Ps 49:7
one can pay God for his own l, ... Ps 49:7
the price of a l is high. .... Ps 49:8
will save my l and will take me .... Ps 49:15
Give the king a long l; .... Ps 61:6
your love is better than l, ... Ps 63:3
protect my l from them. .... Ps 64:1
their names from the book of l, ... Ps 69:28
but you will give me l again. .... Ps 71:20
us l again, and we will call .... Ps 80:18
Won't you give us l again? .... Ps 85:6
because I give my l to you, ... Ps 86:4
My l is full of troubles, and I .... Ps 88:3
You have cut his l short and .... Ps 89:45
Remember how short my l is. .... Ps 89:47

L

a long, full l, and they will .... Ps 91:16
careful to live an innocent l. .... Ps 101:2
live an innocent l in my house. .... Ps 101:2
My l is passing away like smoke, ... Ps 102:3
living; he has cut short my l. .... Ps 102:23
take me in the middle of my l. .... Ps 102:24
and your l will never end. .... Ps 102:27
He saves my l from the grave and .... Ps 103:4
Human l is like grass; we grow .... Ps 103:15
will sing to the LORD all my l; .... Ps 104:33
Let his l be cut short, and let .... Ps 109:8
filled his body and his l, ... Ps 109:18
a young person live a pure l? .... Ps 119:9
Give me l, as you have promised. .... Ps 119:25
you about my l, and you answered........... Ps 119:26
Give me l because of your .... Ps 119:40
Your promise gives me l........................ Ps 119:50
LORD, you are my share in l; .... Ps 119:57
about my l, and I decided .... Ps 119:59
Give me l by your love so I can .... Ps 119:88
you have given me l by them. .... Ps 119:93
LORD, give me l by your word. .... Ps 119:107
My l is always in danger, but I .... Ps 119:109
LORD, give me l by your laws. .... Ps 119:149
give me l by your laws. .... Ps 119:156
LORD, give me l by your love. .... Ps 119:159
dangers; he will guard your l.................. Ps 121:7
things of Jerusalem all your l. .... Ps 128:5
have treated me badly all my l. .... Ps 129:1
have treated me badly all my l, ... Ps 129:2
gives his blessing of l forever................. Ps 133:3
me on the road to everlasting l. .... Ps 139:24
You are all I want in this l." .... Ps 142:5
I will praise the LORD all my l; .... Ps 146:2
or walks the path of l again. .... Pr 2:19
and your l will be successful. .... Pr 3:2
hand wisdom offers you a long l, ... Pr 3:16
will make your l pleasant and.................. Pr 3:17
wisdom gives l to those who use .... Pr 3:18
will give you l and beauty like .... Pr 3:22
Then you will have a long l. .... Pr 4:10
the most important thing in l..................... Pr 4:13
are the key to l for those who .... Pr 4:22
your thoughts run your l. .... Pr 4:23
She gives little thought to l. .... Pr 5:6
years of your l will be given to .... Pr 5:9
the end of your l when your .... Pr 5:11
from them will help you have l. .... Pr 6:23
in adultery may cost you your l. .... Pr 6:26
who find me find l, and the LORD .... Pr 8:35
wisdom will add years to your l............... Pr 9:11
words of a good person give l, ... Pr 10:11
Good people are rewarded with l, ... Pr 10:16
correction is on the way to l, ... Pr 10:17
will lead others away from l. .... Pr 10:17
the LORD will have a long l, ... Pr 10:27
but the l of an evil person will .... Pr 10:27
of the innocent makes l easier, ... Pr 11:5
A good person gives l to others; .... Pr 11:30
an evil person's l is full of .... Pr 12:21
what is right is the way to l, ... Pr 12:28
eating fruit from the tree of l. .... Pr 13:12
of a wise person gives l. .... Pr 13:14
Respect for the LORD gives l................... Pr 14:27
words give l, but dishonest .... Pr 15:4
lazy person's l is like a patch .... Pr 15:19
honest person's l is like a .... Pr 15:19
to correction to improve your l. .... Pr 15:31
smiling king can give people l; .... Pr 16:15
which gives l to those who use .... Pr 16:22
it is earned by living a good l. .... Pr 16:31
you say can mean l or death. .... Pr 18:21
him angry may cost you your l. .... Pr 20:2

what his l is all about............................. Pr 20:24
live right and be loyal finds l, ... Pr 21:21
bring you wealth, honor, and l. .... Pr 22:4
will take the l of those who.................... Pr 22:23
gave you l, and do not forget .... Pr 23:22
do during their few days of l. .... Ec 2:3
So I hated l. It made me sad to .... Ec 2:17
can eat or enjoy l without him. .... Ec 2:25
Why don't I let myself enjoy l?" .... Ec 4:8
because the l God has given them .... Ec 5:18
their state in l and enjoy their................. Ec 5:19
not worry about how short l is, ... Ec 5:20
to know how to get along in l. .... Ec 6:8
useless days of l on the earth;............... Ec 6:12
their short l passes like a .... Ec 6:12
Why was I better in the 'good .... Ec 7:10
When I is good, enjoy it. .... Ec 7:14
But when l is hard, remember: .... Ec 7:14
In my useless l I have seen both .... Ec 7:15
was more important to enjoy l. .... Ec 8:15
drink, and enjoy l, because .... Ec 8:15
Enjoy l with the wife you love. .... Ec 9:9
of this useless l God has given .... Ec 9:9
Soon your l will snap like a .... Ec 12:6
that make l hard for people. .... Is 10:1
is the length of a king's l. .... Is 23:15
The path of l is level for those .... Is 26:7
make the way of l smooth for .... Is 26:7
add fifteen years to your l. .... Is 38:5
I am in the middle of my l. .... Is 38:10
the rest of my l taken away from .... Is 38:10
now I will be humble all my l. .... Is 38:15
He gives l to all people on .... Is 42:5
other nations to save your l. .... Is 43:4
'Why are you giving me l?' .... Is 45:10
but he wanted l on the earth. .... Is 45:18
The LORD made his l a penalty .... Is 53:10
descendants and live a long l................. Is 53:10
he will see l and be satisfied. .... Is 53:11
gave his l and was treated .... Is 53:12
I give new l to those who are .... Is 57:15
then human l would grow weak. .... Is 57:16
who doesn't have a long l. .... Is 65:20
He saves the l of the poor from .... Je 20:13
and my l will end in shame. .... Je 20:18
will save his l as if it were .... Je 21:9
you, I changed my heart and l. .... Je 31:19
who has given us breath and l, ... Je 38:16
Babylon, your l will be saved................. Je 38:17
you, and your l will be saved. .... Je 38:20
and for the rest of his l, ... Je 52:33
him for the l of your children .... La 2:19
my case and given me back my l. .... La 3:58
But you will have saved your l. .... Eze 3:19
And you will have saved your l." .... Eze 3:21
The l of the parent is mine, ... Eze 18:4
and the l of the child is mine. .... Eze 18:4
to the sinful l you began when .... Eze 23:27
a wonderful l, as if you were .... Eze 28:13
Your l was right and good from .... Eze 28:15
will be afraid for his own l..................... Eze 32:10
But you have saved your l. .... Eze 33:9
that give l and do not sin, ... Eze 33:15
enter you so you will come to l. .... Eze 37:5
in you so you will come to l. .... Eze 37:6
so they can come back to l.'" .... Eze 37:9
and they came to l and stood on............. Eze 37:10
you, and you will come to l. .... Eze 37:14
power over your l and everything .... Da 5:23
will wake up to have l forever, ... Da 12:2
because I was better then for me .... Hos 2:7
days he will put new l in us; .... Hos 6:2
who have an easy l in Jerusalem, ... Am 6:1

L

will also give l to your bodies .... Rm 8:11
and he will give l through his .... Rm 8:11
your body, you will have true l. .... Rm 8:13
death, nor l, nor angels, nor .... Rm 8:38
will bring them l after death. .... Rm 11:15
the strength and l of the first .... Rm 11:17
their own lives to save my l. .... Rm 16:4
world, l, death, the present, ... 1Co 3:22
my way of l in Christ Jesus, ... 1Co 4:17
the ordinary things of this l. 1Co 6:3
will have trouble in this l, ... 1Co 7:28
was raised to l on the third day 1Co 15:4
in Christ is for this l only, ... 1Co 15:19
will be raised to l in the right 1Co 15:23
to him will be raised to l, ... 1Co 15:23
the dead who are raised to l. 1Co 15:42
is raised to a l that cannot be 1Co 15:42
became a spirit that gives l. 1Co 15:45
the smell of l that brings life 2Co 2:16
the smell of life that brings l. 2Co 2:16
death, but the Spirit gives l. 2Co 3:6
so that the l of Jesus can also 2Co 4:10
so that the l of Jesus can be 2Co 4:11
in us, but l is working in you 2Co 4:12
will be fully covered with l. 2Co 5:4
be a guarantee for this new l. 2Co 5:5
about my past l in the Jewish .... Gal 1:13
began your l in Christ by the .... Gal 3:3
not give a law that can bring l. .... Gal 3:21
your l with Christ is over— .... Gal 5:4
get our new l from the Spirit, ... Gal 5:25
eternal l from the Spirit. .... Gal 6:8
of eternal l at the right time .... Gal 6:9
he gave us new l with Christ. .... Eph 2:5
and that your l will be strong .... Eph 3:17
to live up to the l to which God .... Eph 4:1
have the l that God gives. .... Eph 4:18
Live a l of love just as Christ .... Eph 5:2
have a long l on the earth." .... Eph 6:3
produced in your l by Christ to .... Php 1:11
of Christ in my l here on earth, ... Php 1:20
to leave this l and be with .... Php 1:23
Does your l in Christ give you .... Php 2:1
interested only in your own l, ... Php 2:4
offer the teaching that gives l. .... Php 2:16
He risked his l to give me the .... Php 2:30
through Christ to the l above. .... Php 3:14
are written in the book of l. .... Php 4:3
live the kind of l that honors .... Col 1:10
a full and true l in Christ, ... Col 2:10
and your new l is kept with .... Col 3:3
Christ is your l, and when he .... Col 3:4
all evil things out of your l: .... Col 3:5
l you also did these things. .... Col 3:7
put these things out of your l: .... Col 3:8
your old sinful l and the things .... Col 3:9
have begun to live the new l, ... Col 3:10
This new l brings you the true .... Col 3:10
In the new l there is no .... Col 3:11
l is really full if you stand 1Th 3:8
you can to live a peaceful l. 1Th 4:11
the kind of l he called you to 2Th 1:11
in him and have l forever. 1Ti 1:16
the secret of our l of worship 1Ti 3:16
in this l and in the future 1Ti 4:8
this life and in the future l, ... 1Ti 4:8
your faith, and your pure l. 1Ti 4:12
your l to doing them so your 1Ti 4:15
Be careful in your l and in your 1Ti 4:16
who uses her l to please herself 1Ti 5:6
and giving her l to do all kinds 1Ti 5:10
hold of the l that continues 1Ti 6:12
to have that l when you 1Ti 6:12

who gives l to everything, ... 1Ti 6:13
able to have the l that is true 1Ti 6:19
to have the life that is true l. 1Ti 6:19
the promise of l that is in 2Ti 1:1
the way to have l that cannot be 2Ti 1:10
My l is being given as an 2Ti 4:6
has come for me to leave this l. 2Ti 4:6
from the hope for l forever, ... Tit 1:2
know about that l through .... Tit 1:3
receiving the l that never ends .... Tit 3:7
what you owe me for your own l. .... Phm 1:19
and your l will never end." .... Heb 1:12
back again to a changed l. .... Heb 6:4
them back to a changed l again, ... Heb 6:6
but through the power of his l, ... Heb 7:16
dead relatives raised back to l. .... Heb 11:35
from the dead to a better l. .... Heb 11:35
our spirits so we will have l. .... Heb 12:9
Anyone whose l is not holy will .... Heb 12:14
will reward them with l forever. .... Jam 1:12
to give us l through the word .... Jam 1:18
the right kind of l God wants. .... Jam 1:20
put out of your l every evil .... Jam 1:21
a fire that influences all of l. .... Jam 3:6
tomorrow! Your l is like a mist. .... Jam 4:14
Your l on earth was full of rich .... Jam 5:5
were saved from that useless l. 1Pe 1:18
and this new l did not come from 1Pe 1:23
the grace that gives true l. 1Pe 3:7
things to enjoy l and have many 1Pe 3:10
of your good l in Christ will be 1Pe 3:16
you about the Word that gives l. 1Jn 1:1
He who gives l was shown to us. 1Jn 1:2
you that he has l that continues 1Jn 1:2
Son promised to us—l forever. 1Jn 2:25
because the new l from God 1Jn 3:9
have come into l because we love 1Jn 3:14
have eternal l in them. 1Jn 3:15
Jesus gave his l for us. 1Jn 3:16
we could have l through him. 1Jn 4:9
God has given us eternal l, ... 1Jn 5:11
life, and this l is in his Son. 1Jn 5:11
Whoever has the Son has l, ... 1Jn 5:12
the Son of God does not have l. 1Jn 5:12
will know you have eternal l. 1Jn 5:13
and God will give the sinner l. 1Jn 5:16
the true God and the eternal l. 1Jn 5:20
is this: Live a l of love. 2Jn 1:6
truth in your l and how you are 3Jn 1:3
his mercy to give you l forever. .... Jud 1:21
the fruit from the tree of l, ... Rev 2:7
who died and came to l again, ... Rev 2:8
I will give you the crown of l. .... Rev 2:10
their names from the book of l, ... Rev 3:5
to springs of water that give l. .... Rev 7:17
put the breath of l into the two .... Rev 11:11
written in the Lamb's book of l. .... Rev 13:8
sword but sprang to l again. .... Rev 13:14
given power to give l to the .... Rev 13:15
in the book of l since the .... Rev 17:8
came back to l and ruled with .... Rev 20:4
and the book of l was opened. .... Rev 20:12
in the book of l was thrown .... Rev 20:15
of the water of l to anyone who .... Rev 21:6
the Lamb's book of l will enter .... Rev 21:27
me the river of the water of l. .... Rev 22:1
The tree of l was on each side .... Rev 22:2
from the tree of l and may go .... Rev 22:14
the water of l as a free gift. .... Rev 22:17
of the tree of l and of the holy .... Rev 22:19

LIFEBOAT

barely able to bring in the l. .... Ac 27:16
After the men took the l in,.................... Ac 27:17
lowered the l, pretending they .... Ac 27:30
ropes and let the l fall into .... Ac 27:32

LIFELESS

bodies on the l forms of your .... Le 26:30
been sacrificed to l statues..................... Ps 106:28
same as with l things that make 1Co 14:7

LIFETIME

during the l of their father .... Nu 3:4
the LORD during the l of Joshua .... Jos 24:31
the LORD during the l of Joshua .... Jdg 2:7
advised Solomon during his l, ... 1Ki 12:6
and Jeroboam during Abijam's l. 1Ki 15:6
be peace and security in my l." 2Ki 20:19
advised Solomon during his l, ... 2Ch 10:6
but his kindness lasts for a l. .... Ps 30:5
my l is like nothing to you. .... Ps 39:5
liars will live only half a l. .... Ps 55:23
Our l is seventy years or, ... Ps 90:10
be peace and security in my l." .... Is 39:8
This will happen during your l. .... Je 16:9
will not be successful in his l.................. Je 22:30
during your l or during your .... Joe 1:2
in your l that you won't .... Hab 1:5
did God's will during his l. .... Ac 13:36
in your l that you won't .... Ac 13:41

LIFETIMES

for a thousand l to those who .... Dt 5:10
for a thousand l for people who .... Dt 7:9
and during the l of the elders .... Jos 24:31
and during the l of the elders .... Jdg 2:7
or during your ancestors' l..................... Joe 1:2

LIFT

of Egypt may l a hand or a foot .... Ge 41:44
go and l the cover off his feet .... Ru 3:4
embarrassed to l up my face to .... Ezr 9:6
I am right, I cannot l my head. .... Job 10:15
Then you can l up your face .... Job 11:15
them down and not l them up. .... Ps 28:5
L up your spears, both large and .... Ps 35:3
will l up my hands in prayer to .... Ps 63:4
will l up the cup of salvation, ... Ps 116:13
I l my hands to you in prayer. .... Ps 143:6
won't l the food to his mouth.................. Pr 19:24
are too tired to l the food to .... Pr 26:15
I will l my hand to signal the .... Is 49:22
from the palace and l Jeremiah .... Je 38:10
L up a banner and tell them. .... Je 50:2
L up a banner against the walls .... Je 51:12
L up a banner in the land! .... Je 51:27
L up your hands in prayer to him .... La 2:19
Let us l up our hands and pray .... La 3:41
L them onto your shoulders with .... Eze 12:6
told his servants to l Daniel .... Da 6:23
no one could even l up his head. .... Zch 1:21
When you l up the Son of Man, ... Jn 8:28
hand so he will l you up when 1Pe 5:6

LIFTED

and as it rose it l the boat off .... Ge 7:17
I l my hands toward the LORD's.............. Ex 17:16
Then Aaron l his hands toward .... Le 9:22
when the cloud l the next .... Nu 9:21
When the cloud l, day or night, ... Nu 9:21
but when it l, they moved. .... Nu 9:22
The cloud l from the Tent of the .... Nu 10:11
When the cloud l from the Tent .... Nu 12:10
Then Moses l his hand and hit .... Nu 20:11
So the priests l the Ark and .... Jos 3:6
him quietly and l the cover from .... Ru 3:7

the honey and l some out and ate 1Sa 14:27
the priests l up the Ark. 1Ki 8:3
the Levites l up the Ark. 2Ch 5:4
You l me out of the grave; .... Ps 30:3
He l me out of the pit of .... Ps 40:2
our God or l our hands in prayer .... Ps 44:20
I have l my hands in prayer to .... Ps 88:9
your right hand is l up. .... Ps 89:13
But he l the poor out of their .... Ps 107:41
He is high and l up. He says, "I .... Is 57:15
with the ropes and l him out of .... Je 38:13
creatures were l up from the .... Eze 1:19
the wheels also were l up. .... Eze 1:19
wheels were l up beside them, ... Eze 1:20
were l from the ground, ... Eze 1:21
the wheels were l beside them, ... Eze 1:21
Then the Spirit l me up, and I .... Eze 3:12
the Spirit l me up and took me .... Eze 3:14
The Spirit l me up between the .... Eze 8:3
living creatures l their wings .... Eze 10:16
The Spirit l me up and brought .... Eze 11:1
creatures l their wings with .... Eze 11:22
The Spirit l me up and brought .... Eze 11:24
So they l him out and did not .... Da 6:23
It was l from the ground so that .... Da 7:4
touched me and l me to my feet.............. Da 8:18
I l the yoke from their neck and .... Hos 11:4
and they l the basket between .... Zch 5:9
will you be l up to heaven? .... Mt 11:23
will you be l up to heaven? .... Lk 10:15
Just as Moses l up the snake in .... Jn 3:14
Son of Man must also be l up. .... Jn 3:14
If I am l up from the earth, ... Jn 12:32
'The Son of Man must be l up'? .... Jn 12:34
hyssop plant, and to Jesus' .... Jn 19:29
he was l up, and a cloud .... Ac 1:9
Jesus was l to heaven and is .... Ac 2:33
the one who was l up to heaven, ... Ac 2:34
man's right hand and l him up. .... Ac 3:7

LIFTING

l up their hands in a holy 1Ti 2:8

LIFTS

and he l the needy from the 1Sa 2:8
important and l the sad to .... Job 5:11
LORD l the poor from the dirt .... Ps 113:7
The LORD l up people who are in .... Ps 146:8
She l her hands in prayer and .... Je 4:31

LIGHT

Let there be l," and there was................. Ge 1:3
be light," and there was l. .... Ge 1:3
God saw that the l was good, ... Ge 1:4
he divided the l from the....................... Ge 1:4
God named the l "day" and the .... Ge 1:5
the sky to give l to the earth.".............. Ge 1:15
the brighter l to rule the day .... Ge 1:16
made the smaller l to rule the................ Ge 1:16
to separate the l from the .... Ge 1:18
Israelites had l where they .... Ex 10:23
a pillar of fire to give them l. .... Ex 13:21
but gave l to the Israelites .... Ex 14:20
so that they give l to the area .... Ex 25:37
day you must not l a fire in any .... Ex 35:3
lampstand for the l and all the .... Ex 35:14
lamps, and olive oil for the l; .... Ex 35:14
and the olive oil for the l; .... Ex 39:37
where they can l the area in .... Nu 8:2
with you, one heavy and one l. .... Dt 25:13
up as soon as it is l and go." 1Sa 29:10
LORD, you give l my lamp...................... 2Sa 22:29
is like the morning l at dawn, ... 2Sa 23:4
And they l the lamps on the gold 2Ch 13:11
Don't let l shine on it. .... Job 3:4

Believe in the l while you still................. Jn 12:36
you will become children of l." .... Jn 12:36
I have come as l into the world .... Jn 12:46
a bright l from heaven suddenly.............. Ac 9:3
and a l shined in the cell. .... Ac 12:7
not even the l from the sun." .... Ac 13:11
made you a l for the nations .... Ac 13:47
told someone to bring a l. .... Ac 16:29
a bright l from heaven suddenly.............. Ac 22:6
the voice, but they saw the l. .... Ac 22:9
the bright l had made me blind .... Ac 22:11
at noon, I saw a l from heaven. .... Ac 26:13
away from darkness to the l, ... Ac 26:18
he would bring l to all people." .... Ac 26:23
the blind and a l for those who .... Rm 2:19
used for fighting in the l. .... Rm 13:12
will bring to l things that are 1Co 4:5
see the l of the Good News— 2Co 4:4
the l shine out of the darkness! 2Co 4:6
God who made his l shine in our 2Co 4:6
L and darkness cannot share 2Co 6:14
to look like an angel of l. 2Co 11:14
you are full of l in the Lord. .... Eph 5:8
children who belong to the l, ... Eph 5:8
L brings every kind of goodness, ... Eph 5:9
But the l makes all things easy .... Eph 5:13
made easy to see can become l. .... Eph 5:14
his people in the kingdom of l. .... Col 1:12
belong to the l and to the day. 1Th 5:5
He lives in l so bright no one 1Ti 6:16
They were once in God's l, ... Heb 6:4
darkness into his wonderful l. 1Pe 2:9
would follow a l shining in a 2Pe 1:19
God is l, and in him there is no 1Jn 1:5
if we live in the l, as God is................. 1Jn 1:7
as God is in the l, we can share 1Jn 1:7
and the true l is already 1Jn 2:8
says, "I am in the l," but hates 1Jn 2:9
lives in the l and will not 1Jn 2:10
third of the day was without l, ... Rev 8:12
The l of a lamp will never shine .... Rev 18:23
the glory of God is its l, ... Rev 21:23
By its l the people of the world .... Rev 21:24
will not need the l of a lamp or .... Rev 22:5
of a lamp or the l of the sun, ... Rev 22:5
the Lord God will give them l. .... Rev 22:5

LIGHT'S
What is the path to l home,.................. Job 38:19

LIGHTED
lamps so they l the area in .... Nu 8:3

LIGHTER
into the sea to make the ship l. .... Jnh 1:5
making the ship l by throwing .... Ac 27:38

LIGHTING
l the way they were to go. .... Ne 9:19
l up the deepest parts of the .... Job 36:30
No one after l a lamp covers it .... Lk 8:16

LIGHTNING
they saw the l and the smoke .... Ex 20:18
He turns his l loose under the............... Job 37:3
He sends the l with the rain. .... Ps 135:7
Send the l and scatter my .... Ps 144:6
His face was bright like l, ... Da 10:6
like l flashing from the east to .... Mt 24:27
He was shining as bright as l,............... Mt 28:3
Satan fall like l from heaven. .... Lk 10:18

LIGHTS
Let there be l in the sky to .... Ge 1:14
These l will be used for signs,............... Ge 1:14
So God made the two large l. .... Ge 1:16
the evening when he l the lamps, ... Ex 30:8

Miners bring l and search deep .... Job 28:3
His lightning l up the world; .... Ps 97:4
all the shining l in the sky .... Eze 32:8
No one l a lamp and puts it in a .... Lk 11:33
the sky and l it up from one .... Lk 17:24

LIKENESS
human beings in our image and l. .... Ge 1:26
he made them in his own l,................... Ge 5:1
another son in his l and image, ... Ge 5:3
I will see your l and be .... Ps 17:15
he is the l and glory of God 1Co 11:7

LIKHI
Ahian, Shechem, L, and Aniam............... 1Ch 7:19

LILIES
I am his. He feeds among the l .... Sng 2:16
Look at how the l in the field .... Mt 6:28

LILY
of a cup or like a l blossom. 1Ki 7:26
of a cup or like a l blossom. 2Ch 4:5
the tune of "L of the Agreement. .... Ps 59:17
of Sharon, a l in the valleys. .... Sng 2:1
is like a l among thorns! .... Sng 2:2
and they will blossom like a l. .... Hos 14:5

LIMB
into twelve parts, l by limb. .... Jdg 19:29
into twelve parts, limb by l. .... Jdg 19:29

LIMBS
We had l like the mighty cedar .... Ps 80:10
Your l are like an orchard of .... Sng 4:13
The l will become dry and break .... Is 27:11
I became long and big because .... Eze 31:5
their nests in the tree's l,................... Eze 31:6
trees did not have such great l. .... Eze 31:8
and its broken l were in all the .... Eze 31:12

LIME
until their bones become like l; .... Is 33:12
of the king of Edom into l. .... Am 2:1

LIMIT
But you l wisdom to yourself................. Job 15:8
There is no l to what he knows. .... Ps 147:5
this to help you, not to l you. 1Co 7:35
We will l our bragging to the 2Co 10:13
We l our bragging to the work 2Co 10:15
increasing their sins to the l. 1Th 2:16
that he has patience without l. 1Ti 1:16

LIMITED
Our time is l. You have given us .... Job 14:5

LIMITS
search the l of the Almighty? .... Job 11:7

LIMP
You will l along like a .... Ec 12:5

LIMPING
Jacob was l because of his leg. .... Ge 32:31

LINE
to the battle l to talk to his 1Sa 17:22
the measuring l of Samaria over 2Ki 21:13
and the plumb l used against 2Ki 21:13
The family l included Shem, ... 1Ch 1:24
as a measuring l and goodness as .... Is 28:17
workman uses a l and a compass .... Is 44:13
measuring l will stretch from .... Je 31:39
you into l with my agreement. .... Eze 20:37
the east with a l in his hand .... Eze 47:3
be the border l of the land: .... Eze 47:15
So the border l will go from the .... Eze 47:17
side the border l will go east .... Eze 47:19
be the border l up to a place .... Eze 47:20
other, because each walks in l. .... Joe 2:8

LINED

with a plumb l in his hand................... Am 7:7
said, "A plumb l." Then the Lord .... Am 7:8
put a plumb l among my people .... Am 7:8
the measuring l will be used to .... Zch 1:16
a man holding a l for measuring .... Zch 2:1

LINED

army is coming l up for battle, ... Je 6:23
a powerful army l up for battle. .... Joe 2:5

LINEN

Joseph fine l clothes to wear .... Ge 41:42
Make for them l underclothes to.............. Ex 28:42
made the cloth belt of fine l, ... Ex 39:29
must put on his l robe and linen.............. Le 6:10
be clothing made of l or wool .... Le 13:47
put on the holy l inner robe, ... Le 16:4
must put on the holy l clothes................ Le 16:32
of wool and l woven together................. Dt 22:11
As a boy he wore a l holy vest. 1Sa 2:18
are made of l and other .... Pr 31:22
She makes l clothes and sells .... Pr 31:24
their mirrors, l dresses, ... Is 3:23
Go and buy a l belt and put it................. Je 13:1
you in fine l and covered you .... Eze 16:10
sail of l with designs sewed .... Eze 27:7
man dressed in l clothes with a .... Da 10:5
my wool and l that covered her .... Hos 2:9
wrapped it in a clean l cloth. .... Mt 27:59
man, wearing only a l cloth, was .... Mk 14:51
the spices in pieces of l cloth, ... Jn 19:40
shining l and wore golden bands .... Rev 15:6
pearls, fine l, purple cloth, ... Rev 18:12

LINES

on the front l where the 2Sa 11:15

LINING

were l up their men to......................... 1Sa 17:21

LINUS

Also Pudens, L, Claudia, and all.............. 2Ti 4:21

LION

Judah is like a young l. .... Ge 49:9
Like a l, he stretches out and .... Ge 49:9
get up like a l. Lions don't .... Nu 23:24
Like a l, they lie waiting to .... Nu 24:9
there like a l, who tears off.................... Dt 33:20
I came roaring toward Samson! .... Jdg 14:5
and he tore the l apart with his .... Jdg 14:6
body of the dead l and found a .... Jdg 14:8
from the body of the dead l." .... Jdg 14:9
What is stronger than a l?"................... Jdg 14:18
When a l or bear came and took a 1Sa 17:34
have killed both a l and a bear! 1Sa 17:36
saved me from a l and a bear 1Sa 17:37
and killed a l on a snowy day. 2Sa 23:20
each armrest had a l beside it. 1Ki 10:19
one l at each end of each step. 1Ki 10:20
a l attacked and killed him. 1Ki 13:24
and the l standing nearby. 1Ki 13:24
body and the l standing nearby 1Ki 13:25
the LORD sent a l to kill him,................. 1Ki 13:26
donkey and the l still standing 1Ki 13:28
The l had not eaten the body or 1Ki 13:28
so a l will kill you as soon as 1Ki 20:36
a l found him and killed him. 1Ki 20:36
and killed a l on a snowy day. 1Ch 11:22
each armrest had a l beside it. 2Ch 9:18
one l at each end of each step. 2Ch 9:19
teeth of a strong l are broken, ... Job 4:10
that l dies of hunger. The cubs .... Job 4:11
of the mother l are scattered. .... Job 4:11
hunt me like a l and again show............ Job 10:16
food for the female l to satisfy .... Job 38:39
a l they will tear me apart. .... Ps 7:2

They wait in hiding like a l. .... Ps 10:9
angry king is like a roaring l, ... Pr 19:12
angry king is like a roaring l. .... Pr 20:2
says, "There's a l outside! .... Pr 22:13
says, "There's a l in the road! .... Pr 26:13
There's a l in the streets!" .... Pr 26:13
good people are as brave as a l. .... Pr 28:1
as a roaring l or a charging .... Pr 28:15
a l, the proudest animal, which .... Pr 30:30
dog is better off than a dead l! .... Ec 9:4
shout is like the roar of a l;.................... Is 5:29
it is loud like a young l. .... Is 5:29
When a l or a lion's cub kills .... Is 31:4
but the l will not be afraid of .... Is 31:4
Like a l, he crushed all my .... Is 38:13
your prophets like a hungry l. .... Je 2:30
A l has come out of his den; .... Je 4:7
So a l from the forest will .... Je 5:6
to me like a l in the forest. .... Je 12:8
Like a l, he has left his den. .... Je 25:38
Like a l coming up from the .... Je 49:19
The first l to eat them up was .... Je 50:17
The last l to crush their bones .... Je 50:17
Like a l coming up from the .... Je 50:44
attack me, like a l in hiding. .... La 3:10
the face of a l on the right .... Eze 1:10
the third was the face of a l, ... Eze 10:14
'Your mother was like a female l. .... Eze 19:2
her cubs, he became a strong l. .... Eze 19:3
The mother l waited and saw .... Eze 19:5
cubs and made him a strong l. .... Eze 19:5
was now a strong l. He learned .... Eze 19:6
Like a roaring l that tears the .... Eze 22:25
are like a young l among the .... Eze 32:2
first animal looked like a l, ... Da 7:4
I will be like a l to Israel, ... Hos 5:14
Israel, like a young l to Judah. .... Hos 5:14
and he will roar like a l. .... Hos 11:10
why I will be like a l to them, ... Hos 13:7
them like a l and tear them................... Hos 13:8
has teeth like a l, jaws like a .... Joe 1:6
a lion, jaws like a female l. .... Joe 1:6
roar like a l from Jerusalem; .... Joe 3:16
A l in the forest does not roar.............. Am 3:4
The l has roared! Who wouldn't .... Am 3:8
who runs from a l and meets a .... Am 5:19
will be like a l among the .... Mic 5:8
like a young l in a flock of .... Mic 5:8
Where did the l, lioness, and .... Nah 2:11
I killed enough for his cubs, ... Nah 2:12
like a roaring l looking for 1Pe 5:8
living creature was like a l.................... Rev 4:7
The L from the tribe of Judah, ... Rev 5:5
loudly like the roaring of a l. .... Rev 10:3

LION'S

Dan is like a l cub, who jumps .... Dt 33:22
Rescue me from the l mouth; .... Ps 22:21
When a lion or a l cub kills an .... Is 31:4
The other was a l face looking .... Eze 41:19
save from a l mouth only two .... Am 3:12
So I was saved from the l mouth. 2Ti 4:17
feet and a mouth like a l mouth.............. Rev 13:2

LIONESS

The people rise up like a l; .... Nu 23:24
like a l, no one would be brave .... Nu 24:9
did the lion, l, and cubs go .... Nah 2:11

LIONESSES

place full of lions and l, ... Is 30:6

LIONS

They were stronger than l. 2Sa 1:23
wings, as well as l, palm trees, ... 1Ki 7:36

so he sent I among them which 2Ki 17:25
Even I may get weak and hungry, ... Ps 34:10
these people who are like I. .... Ps 35:17
Tear out the fangs of those I, ... Ps 58:6
will be thrown into the I' den. .... Da 6:7
over the opening of the I' den. .... Da 6:17
Daniel be brought to the I' den. .... Da 6:24
and shut the mouths of I. .... Heb 11:33
their teeth were like I' teeth. .... Rev 9:8
horses looked like heads of I, ... Rev 9:17

LIPS

in her heart so her I moved, ... 1Sa 1:13
laughter and your I with shouts .... Job 8:21
speak and open his I against you .... Job 11:5
and hear the pleading of my I. .... Job 13:6
your own I testify against you. .... Job 15:6
my I will not speak evil, and my .... Job 27:4
those flattering I and cut off .... Ps 12:3
So silence their lying I. .... Ps 31:18
his praise is always on my I. .... Ps 34:1
you know my I are not silent. .... Ps 40:9
Insults come from their I, ... Ps 59:7
I will sing, and my mouth will .... Ps 63:5
I will tell about all the laws .... Ps 119:13
as pleasing as a kiss on the I. .... Pr 24:26
Your I are like red silk thread, ... Sng 4:3
My bride, your I drip honey; .... Sng 4:11
His I are like lilies flowing .... Sng 5:13
gently past the I and teeth. .... Sng 7:9
hot coal has touched your I. .... Is 6:7
and honor me with their I, ... Is 29:13
With your I you have lied, ... Is 59:3
it has disappeared from their I. .... Je 7:28
looked like a man touched my I, ... Da 10:16
the trumpet to your I and give .... Hos 8:1
my I tremble when I hear the .... Hab 3:16
from I that speak his name. .... Heb 13:15

LIQUID

pounds of I myrrh, half that .... Ex 30:23
holding the right amount of I. .... Le 19:36
and an honest I measurement. .... Eze 45:10
measure and the I measure will .... Eze 45:11
The I measure will always be a .... Eze 45:11

LISTEN

of Lamech, I to what I say. .... Ge 4:23
do not believe me or I to me? .... Ex 4:1
I told you, but you would not I. .... Dt 1:43
but the LORD did not I to you; .... Dt 1:45
quiet, Israel. L! Today you have .... Dt 27:9
did not I to their judges. .... Jdg 2:17
said to Ruth, "L, my daughter. .... Ru 2:8
But please I to my prayer and my 1Ki 8:28
Don't I to Hezekiah. 2Ki 18:31
L carefully to my words; .... Job 33:1
pay attention and I to me; .... Job 33:31
God does not I to the useless .... Job 35:13
You said, 'L now, and I will .... Job 42:4
Children, come and I to me. .... Ps 34:11
L to me, daughter; look and pay .... Ps 45:10
My people, I. I am warning you. .... Ps 81:8
Now, my sons, I to me; .... Pr 7:24
of wisdom won't I to correction. ...... Pr 13:1
L to advice and accept .... Pr 19:20
L to your father, who gave you .... Pr 23:22
Family of Jacob, I to me! .... Is 46:3
L closely to me, and you will .... Is 55:2
Don't I to their dreams. .... Je 29:8
will not be willing to I to you, ... Eze 3:7
Lord, I! Lord, forgive! Lord, ... Da 9:19
L! A farmer went out to plant .... Mk 4:3
told you, and you didn't I. .... Jn 9:27
made him crazy. Why I to him?" .... Jn 10:20

Brothers and fathers, I to me. .... Ac 7:2
you who worship God, please I! .... Ac 13:16
L, my dear brothers and sisters! .... Jam 2:5

LISTENED

and I to your explanations. .... Job 32:11
you have not I to my messages, ... Je 25:8
Men, you should have I to me. .... Ac 27:21

LISTENERS

One of the I was a woman named .... Ac 16:14

LISTENING

Sarah was I at the entrance of .... Ge 18:10
Rebekah was I as Isaac said this .... Ge 27:5
But I say to you who are I, ... Lk 6:27
but every person I to me today .... Ac 26:29
a woman learn by I quietly and 1Ti 2:11
They will stop I to the truth 2Ti 4:4

LISTENS

The LORD I when I pray to him. .... Ps 4:3
from them but I when they call .... Ps 22:24
good people and I to their .... Ps 34:15
The LORD I to those in need and ...... Ps 69:33
because he I to my prayers for .... Ps 116:1
He I when they cry, and he saves ...... Ps 145:19
Whoever I to what is taught will .... Pr 16:20
the wise person I to learn more. .... Pr 18:15
If he I to you, you have helped .... Mt 18:15
Whoever I to you listens to me, ... Lk 10:16
Whoever listens to you I to me, ... Lk 10:16
stands by and I to him. .... Jn 3:29
' Everyone who I to the Father .... Jn 6:45
but he I to anyone who worships ...... Jn 9:31
belongs to the truth I to me." .... Jn 18:37
good people and I to their 1Pe 3:12
world, and the world I to them. 1Jn 4:5

LISTING

family groups, I the name of .... Nu 1:2

LISTS

family history I that they had 1Ch 7:40
of Benjamin I nine hundred 1Ch 9:9
true and on long I of names in 1Ti 1:4

LIT

After he I the torches, he let .... Jdg 15:5
It I the way they were supposed .... Ne 9:12
Lightning I up the world. .... Ps 77:18
with a cloud and I up the night .... Ps 105:39

LITTLE

because there was so I food. .... Ge 12:10
that I town over there is not .... Ge 19:20
It's really just a I town, ... Ge 19:20
is named Zoar, because it is I. .... Ge 19:22
give me a I water from your .... Ge 24:17
Esau showed how I he cared about ... Ge 25:34
I came, you had I, but now you .... Ge 30:30
again and buy a I more grain for ..... Ge 43:2
again and buy us a I more food.' ..... Ge 44:25
much, and some gathered I. .... Ex 16:17
who gathered less have too I. .... Ex 16:18
I owls, cormorants, great owls, ... Le 11:17
will be very I bread to eat; .... Le 26:26
wives, children, and I babies. .... Nu 16:27
Your I children that you said .... Dt 1:39
he will do it I by little ahead .... Dt 7:22
do it little by I ahead of you. .... Dt 7:22
I owls, great owls, white owls, ... Dt 14:16
Gibeon was not a I town like Ai; ..... Jos 10:2
it and all the I towns near it. .... Jos 10:37
and all the I towns near it, ... Jos 10:39
putting their I children, their ...... Jdg 18:21
they had gone a I way from .... Jdg 18:22
mother made a I coat for him and .. 1Sa 2:19

L

will beg for a l money or a 1Sa 2:36
money or a l food and say, ... 1Sa 2:36
just tasting a l of this honey! 1Sa 14:29
I only tasted a l honey from the 1Sa 14:43
except one l female lamb he had 2Sa 12:3
But I am like a l child;........................... 1Ki 3:7
'My l finger is bigger than my 1Ki 12:10
you bring me a l water in a cup 1Ki 17:10
jar and only a l olive oil in a 1Ki 17:12
a hundred people with so l?" 2Ki 4:43
and had taken a l girl as a 2Ki 5:2
l girl served Naaman's wife. 2Ki 5:2
served Baal a l, but Jehu will 2Ki 10:18
'My l finger is bigger than my 2Ch 10:10
us hope and a l relief from our .... Ezr 9:8
old, women and l children, too. .... Est 3:13
Even the l boys hate me and talk .... Job 19:18
their l ones dance about......................... Job 21:11
a l while they are important, ... Job 24:24
You have shown l understanding! .... Job 26:3
Listen to me a l longer, and I .... Job 36:2
You made them a l lower than the .... Ps 8:5
In a l while the wicked will be .... Ps 37:10
better to have l and be right .... Ps 37:16
and the hills like l lambs. .... Ps 114:4
why did you dance like l lambs?.............. Ps 114:6
and to the l birds that call. .... Ps 147:9
She gives l thought to life. .... Pr 5:6
You sleep a l; you take a nap. .... Pr 6:10
you will have as l as if you had .... Pr 6:11
thoughts are worth very l. .... Pr 10:20
is gathered l by little will .... Pr 13:11
gathered little by l will grow. .... Pr 13:11
wise say very l, and those with .... Pr 17:27
throw up the l you have eaten, ... Pr 23:8
You sleep a l; you take a nap. .... Pr 24:33
you will have as l as if you had .... Pr 24:34
be content with what l you have. .... Ec 4:6
important if they eat l or much. .... Ec 5:12
a poor person l good to know how........... Ec 6:8
l foolishness can spoil wisdom. .... Ec 10:1
A l bird might carry your words; .... Ec 10:20
the l foxes that ruin the .... Sng 2:15
We have a l sister, and her .... Sng 8:8
and a l child will lead them. .... Is 11:6
Their l children will be beaten .... Is 13:16
will they feel sorry for l ones.................. Is 13:18
Arnon like l birds that have .... Is 16:2
the adults and l children will .... Is 22:24
A l lesson here, a little lesson .... Is 28:10
lesson here, a l lesson there." .... Is 28:10
A l lesson here, a little lesson .... Is 28:13
lesson here, a l lesson there." .... Is 28:13
are so stupid and know so l. .... Je 10:14
l children will cry for help. .... Je 48:4
are so stupid and know so l. .... Je 51:17
men and women, l children, and .... Eze 9:6
But for a l while I have become .... Eze 11:16
It was a l horn with eyes like a .... Da 7:8
The l horn pulled out three of................. Da 7:8
because the l horn was bragging .... Da 7:11
and about the l horn that grew .... Da 7:20
the l horn began making war .... Da 7:21
Then a l horn grew from one of .... Da 8:9
l horn grew until it reached .... Da 8:10
That l horn set itself up as .... Da 8:11
they will get a l help, but many .... Da 11:34
planted much, but you harvest l. .... Hag 1:6
look for much, but you find l. .... Hag 1:9
I was only a l angry at them, ... Zch 1:15
That is how l they thought I .... Zch 11:13
and I will punish the l ones." .... Zch 13:7
Don't have so l faith! .... Mt 6:30

you notice the l piece of dust .... Mt 7:3
Let me take that l piece of dust .... Mt 7:4
give one of these l ones a cup................. Mt 10:42
those who are like l children. .... Mt 11:25
Jesus called a l child to him .... Mt 18:2
and become like l children....................... Mt 18:3
If one of these l children .... Mt 18:6
Don't think these l children are .... Mt 18:10
any of these l children to be .... Mt 18:14
brought their l children to .... Mt 19:13
Let the l children come to me. .... Mt 19:14
They enlarge the l boxes holding .... Mt 23:5
After walking a l farther away .... Mt 26:39
That is how l the Israelites .... Mt 27:9
Going a l farther, Jesus saw two............. Mk 1:19
If one of these l children .... Mk 9:42
brought their l children to .... Mk 10:13
Let the l children come to me. .... Mk 10:14
of God as if you were a l child, ... Mk 10:15
After walking a l farther away .... Mk 14:35
The l child grew and became .... Lk 2:40
to push off a l from the land. .... Lk 5:3
you notice the l piece of dust .... Lk 6:41
let me take that l piece of dust .... Lk 6:42
forgiven only a l will love only .... Lk 7:47
a little will love only a l." .... Lk 7:47
so he took a l child and stood................. Lk 9:47
accepts this l child in my name .... Lk 9:48
those who are like l children. .... Lk 10:21
you cannot do even the l things,............. Lk 12:26
Don't have so l faith! .... Lk 12:28
Don't fear, l flock, because .... Lk 12:32
be trusted with a l can also be .... Lk 16:10
dishonest with a l is dishonest .... Lk 16:10
one of these l ones to sin. .... Lk 17:2
Let the l children come to me. .... Lk 18:16
person to have only a l piece." .... Jn 6:7
of barley bread and two l fish, ... Jn 6:9
be with you a l while longer. .... Jn 7:33
will be with you for a l longer, ... Jn 12:35
be with you only a l longer. .... Jn 13:33
In a l while the world will not................. Jn 14:19
After a l while you will not see .... Jn 16:16
then after a l while you will .... Jn 16:16
'After a l while you will not.................... Jn 16:17
then after a l while you will .... Jn 16:17
does he mean by 'a l while'? .... Jn 16:18
'After a l while you will not.................... Jn 16:19
then after a l while you will .... Jn 16:19
leave the meeting for a l while. .... Ac 5:34
made l silver models that looked .... Ac 19:24
went a l farther and lowered .... Ac 27:28
Just a l yeast makes the whole 1Co 5:6
who gathered less have too l." 2Co 8:15
who plants a l will have a small 2Co 9:6
me even when I am a l foolish, ... 2Co 11:1
Then I can brag a l, too. 2Co 11:16
My l children, again I feel the................. Gal 4:19
Just a l yeast makes the whole .... Gal 5:9
already written a l about this.................. Eph 3:3
caring for her l children.......................... 1Th 2:7
but drink a l wine to help your 1Ti 5:23
You made them a l lower than the .... Heb 2:7
be started with only a l flame. .... Jam 3:5
I know you have l strength, ... Rev 3:8

LIVE

life, or they will l forever." .... Ge 3:22
they will kill me but let you l.................. Ge 12:12
You l in the land of Canaan now .... Ge 17:8
Do this and I will let you l: .... Ge 42:18
our children may l and not die. .... Ge 43:8
L in the land of Goshen where .... Ge 45:10

a girl, let her l, but if it is .... Ex 1:16
king and went to l in the land .... Ex 2:15
or an animal, he will not l. .... Ex 19:13
because no one can see me and l. .... Ex 33:20
them will l because of them .... Le 18:5
at it, that person will l." .... Nu 21:8
L the way the LORD your God has .... Dt 5:33
does not l on bread alone, ... Dt 8:3
them out and l in their cities .... Dt 19:1
As surely as I l forever, ... Dt 32:40
Hivites, "Maybe you l near us. .... Jos 9:7
shouted, "Long l the king!" 1Sa 10:24
for me and let the baby l.' 2Sa 12:22
because you are not going to l, ... 2Ki 20:1
king, "May the king l forever! .... Ne 2:3
I don't want to l forever. .... Job 7:16
Will the dead l again? All my .... Job 14:14
do evil people l a long time? .... Job 21:7
and liars will l only half a .... Ps 55:23
will praise you as long as l l. .... Ps 63:4
Then people will l there and own .... Ps 69:35
to my God as long as I l. .... Ps 104:33
to him for help as long as I l. .... Ps 116:2
so I can l, so I can obey .... Ps 119:17
to my God as long as I l. .... Ps 146:2
Keep my commands and you will l. .... Pr 4:4
and I l among people who are not .... Is 6:5
died, but they will l again; .... Is 26:19
Lord, because of you, people l. .... Is 38:16
listen to me so you may l. .... Is 55:3
to stop their bad ways and l. .... Eze 18:23
people will l if they obey them .... Eze 20:11
What can we do so we will l?' .... Eze 33:10
As surely as I l, I do not want .... Eze 33:11
You will surely l,' they might .... Eze 33:13
me, "Human, can these bones l?" .... Eze 37:3
language, "O king, l forever! .... Da 2:4
King Darius, l forever! .... Da 6:6
so that we may l in his presence .... Hos 6:2
of Israel: "Come to me and l. .... Am 5:4
to the LORD and l, or he will .... Am 5:6
so that you will l, and the LORD .... Am 5:14
better for me to die than to l." .... Jnh 4:3
right with God will l by faith. .... Hab 2:4
hand on her, she will l again." .... Mt 9:18
Do this and you will l." .... Lk 10:28
the dead and I again will not .... Lk 20:35
His teaching does not l in you, ... Jn 5:38
eats this bread will l forever. .... Jn 6:51
and I l because of the Father. .... Jn 6:57
eats me will l because of me. .... Jn 6:57
that he will rise and l again in .... Jn 11:24
Because I l, you will live, too. .... Jn 14:19
Because I live, you will l, too. .... Jn 14:19
'By his power we l and move and .... Ac 17:28
He doesn't deserve to l!" .... Ac 22:22
right with God will l by faith." .... Rm 1:17
we also can l a new life. .... Rm 6:4
we know we will also l with him. .... Rm 6:8
Those who l following their .... Rm 8:5
sinful selves or l the way our .... Rm 8:12
Do your best to l in peace with .... Rm 12:18
If we l, we are living for the .... Rm 14:8
the dead to l again was so he .... Rm 14:9
and she is happy to l with him, ... 1Co 7:12
and he is happy to l with her, ... 1Co 7:13
came from him, and we l for him. 1Co 8:6
so that those who l would not 2Co 5:15
be dying, but we continue to l. 2Co 6:9
much we would l or die with you. 2Co 7:3
are not Jewish to l like Jews?" .... Gal 2:14
law so that I can now l for God. .... Gal 2:19
and I do not l anymore—it is .... Gal 2:20

I still l in my body, but I live .... Gal 2:20
but I l by faith in the Son of .... Gal 2:20
right with God will l by faith." .... Gal 3:11
things will l because of them. .... Gal 3:12
we no longer l under a guardian .... Gal 3:25
who are not wise, but l wisely. .... Eph 5:15
on earth, whether I l or die. .... Php 1:20
Be sure that you l in a way that .... Php 1:27
so that we can l together with 1Th 5:10
him, we will also l with him. 2Ti 2:11
who wants to l as God desires, ... 2Ti 3:12
anyone, to l in peace, and to .... Tit 3:2
right with me will l by faith. .... Heb 10:38
by the way their wives l. 1Pe 3:1
we need to l and to serve God. 2Pe 1:3
those who l by doing the evil 2Pe 2:10
from others who l in error. 2Pe 2:18
We know that we l in God and he 1Jn 4:13
were dead did not l again until .... Rev 20:5
and he will l with them, and .... Rev 21:3

LIVED

Adam l 800 years and had other .... Ge 5:4
the flood Noah l 350 years. .... Ge 9:28
Abraham l to be one hundred .... Ge 25:7
The people that l in Canaan saw .... Ge 50:11
Israel had l in Egypt for four .... Ex 12:40
at the bronze snake and l. .... Nu 21:9
from a fire and still l, ... Dt 5:26
l fifteen years after the death 2Ki 14:17
Job l one hundred forty years. .... Job 42:16
Jerusalem l a man named Simeon .... Lk 2:25
know the way I l all the time I .... Ac 20:18
and evil; you l only for evil. .... Rm 6:19
Remember how they l and died, ... Heb 13:7
the people who l before you. 1Pe 1:18
holy women who l long ago and 1Pe 3:5
because he l with evil people 2Pe 2:8
in God must live as Jesus l. 1Jn 2:6

LIVER

well as the best part of the l, ... Ex 29:13
through the l with an arrow. .... Pr 7:23
looks at the l of a sacrificed .... Eze 21:21

LIVERS

pull the points out of their l. .... Job 20:25

LIVES

ahead of you to save people's l. .... Ge 45:5
They made their l bitter. .... Ex 1:14
everyone who l in that city. .... Dt 13:15
It will be our l for your lives .... Jos 2:14
of Zebulun risked their l, ... Jdg 5:18
as the LORD, l, I would not kill .... Jdg 8:19
myself, as surely as the LORD l. .... Ru 3:13
as the LORD l and as surely as 1Sa 25:26
your enemies' l as he would 1Sa 25:29
God of Israel, l, he has kept me 1Sa 25:34
The LORD l! May my Rock be 2Sa 22:47
of the men who risked their l!" 2Sa 23:17
surely as the LORD your God l, ... 1Ki 17:12
standing and ran for their l. 2Ki 7:7
I know that my Defender l, ... Job 19:25
The LORD l! May my Rock be .... Ps 18:46
us how short our l really are so .... Ps 90:12
Even if he l two thousand years, ... Ec 6:6
Run for your l! Go like a bush .... Je 48:6
We risk our l to get our food; .... La 5:9
would have saved their own l. .... Eze 33:5
and glory to him who l forever. .... Da 4:34
the name of God who l forever, ... Da 12:7
surely as the god of Dan l . . . ' .... Am 8:14
as the god of Beersheba l, ... Am 8:14
faith, and your l are all wrong. .... Lk 9:41

everyone who l in sin is a slave .... Jn 8:34
And everyone who l and believes .... Jn 11:26
We died to our old sinful l, ... Rm 6:2
know that nothing good l in me— .... Rm 7:18
their own l to save my life .... Rm 16:4
her husband as long as he l. 1Co 7:39
but he l now by God's power. 2Co 13:4
—it is Christ who l in me. ....,............ Gal 2:20
with you, but even our own l. 1Th 2:8
with other people's l, ... 1Ti 5:13
But because Jesus l forever, ... Heb 7:24
through him because he always l, ... Heb 7:25
of people whose l tell us what................. Heb 12:1
Lord Jesus, the "stone" that l. 1Pe 2:4
should give our l for our 1Jn 3:16
I am the One who l; I was dead, ... Rev 1:18
throne, who l forever and ever. .... Rev 4:9
worship him who l forever and .... Rev 4:10
not love their l so much that .... Rev 12:11

LIVING

water be filled with l things, ... Ge 1:20
and every l thing that moves .... Ge 1:21
and the man became a l person. .... Ge 2:7
the man called each l thing, ... Ge 2:19
she was the mother of all the l. .... Ge 3:20
the boat two of every l thing, ... Ge 6:19
the earth every l thing that was .... Ge 7:23
destroy every l thing on the .... Ge 8:21
and every l thing on the earth. .... Ge 9:16
Then he will take the l bird, ... Le 14:6
between the dead and the l, ... Nu 16:48
to us—both the l and the dead!" .... Ru 2:20
the armies of the l God?" 1Sa 17:26
Cut the l baby into two pieces, ... 1Ki 3:25
to make fun of the l God. 2Ki 19:4
from the eyes of every l thing, ... Job 28:21
where all l people must go........................ Job 30:23
I thirst for the l God. .... Ps 42:2
wants to be with the l God........................ Ps 84:2
like an owl l among the ruins. .... Ps 102:6
God has made me tired of l; .... Ps 102:23
and you satisfy all l things...................... Ps 145:16
dead are better off than the l. .... Ec 4:2
I know they will die, but the .... Ec 9:5
are still l in Jerusalem will .... Is 4:3
My people l in Jerusalem, ... Is 10:24
and all the people l on it. .... Is 45:12
from me, the spring of l water. .... Je 2:13
He is the only l God, the King .... Je 10:10
the LORD, the spring of l water. .... Je 17:13
of our God, the l God, the LORD .... Je 23:36
looked like four l creatures, ... Eze 1:5
would go, the l creatures would .... Eze 1:20
Then the l creatures flew up. .... Eze 10:15
in the world of the l again. .... Eze 26:20
wisdom than any other l person, ... Da 2:30
Daniel, servant of the l God! .... Da 6:20
called 'children of the l God.' .... Hos 1:10
Christ, the Son of the l God." .... Mt 16:16
' God is the God of the l, ... Mt 22:32
you by the power of the l God: .... Mt 26:63
skin diseases l in Israel during .... Lk 4:27
wasted his money in foolish l. .... Lk 15:13
looking for a l person in this .... Lk 24:5
would have given you l water." .... Jn 4:10
I am the l bread that came down .... Jn 6:51
The l Father sent me, and I live .... Jn 6:57
rivers of l water will flow out .... Jn 7:38
the judge of the l and the dead. .... Ac 10:42
children of the l God.'" .... Rm 9:26
your lives as a l sacrifice to .... Rm 12:1
over both the dead and the l. .... Rm 14:9

man, Adam, became a l person." 1Co 15:45
with the Spirit of the l God. 2Co 3:3
we are the temple of the l God. 2Co 6:16
serving the l and true God. 1Th 1:9
is the church of the l God, ... 1Ti 3:15
We hope in the l God who is the 1Ti 4:10
will judge the l and the dead, ... 2Ti 4:1
turn you away from the l God. .... Heb 3:12
acts so we may serve the l God. .... Heb 9:14
a new and l way that Jesus .... Heb 10:20
into the hands of the l God. .... Heb 10:31
the city of the l God, the .... Heb 12:22
to be born again into a l hope, ... 1Pe 1:3
You also are like l stones, ... 1Pe 2:5
to judge the l and the dead. 1Pe 4:5
throne were four l creatures .... Rev 4:6
who had the seal of the l God. .... Rev 7:2
elders and the four l creatures. .... Rev 7:11

LIZARDS

rats, all kinds of great l, ... Le 11:29
crocodiles, l, sand reptiles, ... Le 11:30
L can be caught in the hand, ... Pr 30:28

LO

Makir son of Ammiel in L Debar." 2Sa 9:4
Makir son of Ammiel in L Debar. 2Sa 9:5
son of Ammiel was from L Debar, ... 2Sa 17:27
that the town of L Debar was .... Am 6:13

LO-AMMI

said, "Name him L, because you .... Hos 1:9

LO-RUHAMAH

Name her L, because I will .... Hos 1:6
Gomer had stopped nursing L, ... Hos 1:8

LOAD

your brothers to l their animals .... Ge 45:17
lies down while carrying his l. .... Ge 49:14
his back to the l and become a .... Ge 49:15
because its l is too heavy, ... Ex 23:5
LORD will put a l on you until .... Dt 28:48
placed a heavy l on the people. .... Ne 5:15
at the gates so no l could come .... Ne 13:19
Have I become a heavy l for you? .... Job 7:20
like a l it weighs me down. .... Ps 38:4
and you l the wagons with many .... Ps 65:11
trapped and put a heavy l on us. .... Ps 66:11
I took the l off their............................... Ps 81:6
is a heavy l, but a kind word .... Pr 12:25
away their heavy l and the heavy .... Is 9:4
and the l they make you carry .... Is 10:27
placed a heavy l on my people, ... Is 14:25
not to carry a l on the Sabbath .... Je 17:21
take a l out of your houses .... Je 17:22
must not bring a l through the .... Je 17:24
'You are a heavy l to the LORD, ... Je 23:33
I l give you to carry is light. .... Mt 11:30
putting a heavy l around the .... Ac 15:10
is a l that neither we nor our .... Ac 15:10
not have a heavy l to carry,.................... Ac 15:28
me every day the l of my concern 2Co 11:28
will not put any other l on you. .... Rev 2:24

LOADED

ten donkeys l with the best .... Ge 45:23
ten female donkeys l with grain, ... Ge 45:23
sons of Israel l their father,................... Ge 46:5
So Jesse l a donkey with bread, ... 1Sa 16:20
row of donkeys l with two 2Sa 16:1
forty camels l with every good 2Ki 8:9
a people l down with guilt, ... Is 1:4
as a wagon l with grain gets .... Am 2:13

LOADING

in grain and l it on donkeys. .... Ne 13:15

LOADS

seventy thousand men to carry l, ...2Ch 2:2
thousand of them to carry l, ...2Ch 2:18
who carried l and all the other 2Ch 34:13
they were bringing l of wine, ...Ne 13:15
the grave and l me with love ....Ps 103:4
are only heavy l that must be ....Is 46:1
not carry any l into Jerusalem ....Je 17:27
boys stumbled under l of wood. ....La 5:13
who are tired and have heavy l, ...Mt 11:28

LOAF

dreamed that a l of barley bread ....Jdg 7:13
only one l of bread with them.................Mk 8:14

LOAVES

grain and ten l of bread to your 1Sa 17:17
the five l of bread that fed ....Mt 16:9
Or the seven l of bread that fed ....Mt 16:10
took the five l and two fish ....Mk 6:41
boy with five l of barley bread ....Jn 6:9
Then Jesus took the l of bread, ...Jn 6:11

LOCK

away from me! L the door after 2Sa 13:17
onto the handles of the l. ....Sng 5:5
L his hands and feet between ....Je 29:26

LOCKED

closed and l the doors behind................Jdg 3:23

LOCKS

gates will have l of iron and ....Dt 33:25
He l my feet in chains and ....Job 33:11

LOCUST

l was left anywhere in Egypt. ....Ex 10:19
make the horse jump like a l?................Job 39:20
I am shaken off like a l. ....Ps 109:23

LOCUSTS

the l were too many to count. ....Ps 105:34
L have no king, but they all go ....Pr 30:27
food, he ate l and wild honey.................Mt 3:4
waist, and ate l and wild honey. ....Mk 1:6
Then l came down to the earth ....Rev 9:3

LOD

of L, Hadid and Ono—725; ....Ezr 2:33
of L, Hadid, and Ono—721; ....Ne 7:37
L, Ono, and in the Valley of the ....Ne 11:35

LOG

There everyone can get a l,....................2Ki 6:2

LOGS

I will separate the l there, ...1Ki 5:9

LOIS

your grandmother L and in your 2Ti 1:5

LONELY

people's sins to a l place in ....Le 16:22
house and was sad and l. 2Sa 13:20
because I am l and hurting. ....Ps 25:16
God gives me a home. ....Ps 68:6
am like a l bird on a housetop. ....Ps 102:7
I was sad and l, defeated and ....Is 49:21
me so sad and l that I am weak ....La 1:13
My children are left sad and l, ...La 1:16
your altars will become l ruins. ....Eze 6:6
and went to a l place by himself.............Mt 14:13
He went to a l place, where he ....Mk 1:35
we will go to a l place to get ....Mk 6:31
boat by themselves to a l place. ....Mk 6:32
Jesus went to a l place, but the ....Lk 4:42
by the demon out into a l place. ....Lk 8:29

LONG

the mighty warriors of l ago. ....Ge 6:4
four hundred fifty feet l, ...Ge 6:15

As l as the earth continues,.....................Ge 8:22
will take that l, because I am ....Ge 15:16
of the Philistines for a l time. ....Ge 21:34
after a l and satisfying life......................Ge 25:8
Isaac lived there a l time. ....Ge 26:8
L before this time Abraham had..............Ge 26:18
a special robe with l sleeves. ....Ge 37:3
off his robe with l sleeves ....Ge 37:23
sad about his son for a l time.................Ge 37:34
After a l time Judah's wife,....................Ge 38:12
and cried there for a l time. ....Ge 46:29
a l time, the king of Egypt ....Ex 2:23
'How l will you refuse to be ....Ex 10:3
How l will this man make trouble ....Ex 10:7
How l will you people refuse to ....Ex 16:28
As l as Moses held his hands up, ...Ex 17:11
the trumpet will make a l blast, ...Ex 19:13
you will live a l time in the ....Ex 20:12
will allow you to live l lives. ....Ex 23:26
an Ark forty-five inches l, ...Ex 25:10
inches l and twenty-seven ....Ex 25:17
inches l, eighteen inches ....Ex 25:23
feet l and six feet wide. ....Ex 26:2
feet l and six feet wide. ....Ex 26:8
be fifteen feet l and ....Ex 26:16
one-half feet l and seven and ....Ex 27:1
one hundred fifty feet l. ....Ex 27:9
be one hundred fifty feet l. ....Ex 27:11
of curtains seventy-five feet l,................Ex 27:12
also be seventy-five feet l. ....Ex 27:13
twenty-two and one-half feet l, ...Ex 27:14
twenty-two and one-half feet l, ...Ex 27:15
fifty feet l and seventy-five ....Ex 27:18
inches l and nine inches wide— ....Ex 28:16
eighteen inches l and eighteen ....Ex 30:2
saw that a l time had passed ....Ex 32:1
set it up a l way outside the ....Ex 33:7
feet l and six feet wide. ....Ex 36:9
feet l and six feet wide. ....Ex 36:15
it was forty-five inches l,.......................Ex 37:1
inches l and twenty-seven ....Ex 37:6
it was thirty-six inches l,.......................Ex 37:10
eighteen inches l and eighteen ....Ex 37:25
one-half feet l and seven and ....Ex 38:1
fifty feet l and were made ....Ex 38:9
also one hundred fifty feet l, ...Ex 38:11
was seventy-five feet l. ....Ex 38:12
was also seventy-five feet l. ....Ex 38:13
twenty-two and one-half feet l, ...Ex 38:14
twenty-two and one-half feet l, ...Ex 38:15
was thirty feet l and seven and ....Ex 38:18
sheets and then cut it into l, ...Ex 39:3
inches l and nine inches wide— ....Ex 39:9
but as l as the cloud stayed on ....Ex 40:37
is one he has had for a l time.................Le 13:11
unclean for as l as she ....Le 15:25
They must let their hair grow l. ....Nu 6:5
over the Tent for a l time, ...Nu 9:19
As l as it stayed, the people ....Nu 9:22
How l will these people ignore ....Nu 14:11
How l will they not believe me ....Nu 14:11
How l will these evil people ....Nu 14:27
the coals a l distance away....................Nu 16:37
he cancels them l after he heard..............Nu 30:15
as l as the person is from your ....Nu 36:6
You have stayed l enough at this ....Dt 1:6
you stayed in Kadesh a l time. ....Dt 1:46
these mountains l enough. ....Dt 2:3
thirteen feet l and six feet ....Dt 3:11
forget them as l as you live, ...Dt 4:9
respect me as l as they live. ....Dt 4:10
the land a l time and have had ....Dt 4:25
not live there l after that, ...Dt 4:26

peace continue as I as there is .... Ps 72:7
L live the king! Let him receive .... Ps 72:15
for him and bless him all day I. .... Ps 72:15
be remembered as I as the sun .... Ps 72:17
I have suffered all day I; .... Ps 73:14
have you rejected us for so I? .... Ps 74:1
the people you bought I ago. .... Ps 74:2
one knows how I this will last. .... Ps 74:9
have been our king for a I time. .... Ps 74:12
those foolish people all day I. .... Ps 74:22
night I I reach out my hands, ... Ps 77:2
old days, the years of I ago. .... Ps 77:5
the miracles you did I ago. .... Ps 77:11
tell secret things from I ago. .... Ps 78:2
LORD, how I will this last? .... Ps 79:5
How I will your jealousy burn .... Ps 79:5
how I will you be angry at the .... Ps 80:4
How I will you defend evil .... Ps 82:2
How I will you show greater .... Ps 82:2
will last as I as the skies. .... Ps 89:29
LORD, how I will this go on? .... Ps 89:46
How I will your anger burn like .... Ps 89:46
how I before you return and show .... Ps 90:13
I will give them a I, full life, ... Ps 91:16
your kingdom was set up I ago; .... Ps 93:2
How I will the wicked be happy? .... Ps 94:3
wicked be happy? How I, LORD? .... Ps 94:3
All day I enemies insult me; .... Ps 102:8
to my God as I as I live. .... Ps 104:33
to him for help as I as I live. .... Ps 116:2
I remember your laws from I ago, ... Ps 119:52
How I will I live? When will you .... Ps 119:84
I think about them all day I. .... Ps 119:97
I have suffered for a I time.................... Ps 119:107
L ago I learned from your rules .... Ps 119:152
have lived too I with people who .... Ps 120:6
over my back, making I wounds. .... Ps 129:3
in darkness like those I dead. .... Ps 143:3
I remember what happened I ago; .... Ps 143:5
to my God as I as I live. .... Ps 146:2
how I will you be foolish? .... Pr 1:22
I will you make fun of wisdom .... Pr 1:22
Then you will live a I time, ... Pr 3:2
hand wisdom offers you a I life, ... Pr 3:16
Then you will have a I life. .... Pr 4:10
How I will you lie there, you .... Pr 6:9
he has gone on a I trip. .... Pr 7:19
I before he made anything else. .... Pr 8:22
wisely, you will live a I time; .... Pr 9:11
the LORD will have a I life,.................... Pr 10:27
All day I they wish for more, ... Pr 21:26
be honest and last a I time..................... Pr 25:5
money will rule a I time........................ Pr 28:16
not harm for as I as she lives.................. Pr 31:12
remember what happened I ago, ... Ec 1:11
will remember either one for I. .... Ec 2:16
themselves as I as they live. .... Ec 3:12
children and live a I time, ... Ec 6:3
happens was planned I ago. .... Ec 6:10
people live a I time in spite .... Ec 7:15
things and might live a I time, ... Ec 8:12
no matter how I they live. .... Ec 11:8
You will be dead a I time. .... Ec 11:8
back judges as you had I ago;................. Is 1:26
dresses, turbans, and I shawls. .... Is 3:23
His I robe filled the Temple. .... Is 6:1
Lord, how I should I do this? .... Is 6:11
the One who planned them I ago. .... Is 22:11
done what you planned I ago. .... Is 25:1
been made ready for a I time;................ Is 30:33
L ago I, the LORD, planned these .... Is 37:26
L ago I designed them, and now I .... Is 37:26
For a I time I have said .... Is 42:14

Who told you I ago that this .... Is 45:21
Who told about it I ago? .... Is 45:21
Remember what happened I ago. .... Is 46:9
A I time ago I told you things .... Is 46:10
L ago I told you what would .... Is 48:3
So a I time ago I told you about .... Is 48:5
are happening now, not I ago;............... Is 48:7
Even I ago you did not listen to .... Is 48:8
times, as you did a I time ago. .... Is 51:9
All day I they speak against me.............. Is 52:5
descendants and live a I life. .... Is 53:10
I have been quiet for a I time. .... Is 57:11
the places destroyed I ago. .... Is 61:4
that were destroyed for so I. .... Is 61:4
Since I ago he has picked them .... Is 63:9
remembered what happened I ago,........... Is 63:11
From I ago no one has ever heard .... Is 64:4
For a I time we disobeyed, ... Is 64:5
day I I stood ready to accept .... Is 65:2
who doesn't have a I life. .... Is 65:20
My people will live a I time, ... Is 65:22
a long time, as trees live I. .... Is 65:22
L ago you refused to obey me as .... Je 2:20
How I must I look at the war .... Je 4:21
How I must I listen to the war .... Je 4:21
nation that has lasted a I time. .... Je 5:15
evening shadows are growing I. .... Je 6:4
How I will you continue being .... Je 13:27
makes fun of me all day I. .... Je 20:7
people make fun of me all day I............... Je 20:8
How I will this continue in the .... Je 23:26
were prophets I before we became .... Je 28:8
You will be there for a I time, ... Je 29:28
How I will you wander before you .... Je 31:22
jar so they will last a I time. .... Je 32:14
to their ancestors I ago, ... Je 32:22
you will live a I time in the .... Je 35:7
Jeremiah was there for a I time. .... Je 37:16
how I will you cut yourselves? .... Je 47:5
how I will you keep fighting? .... Je 47:6
This lasted as I as he lived, ... Je 52:34
word that he commanded I ago. .... La 2:17
me again and again, all day I................... La 3:3
who have been dead a I time. .... La 3:6
fun of me with songs all day I. .... La 3:14
have you forgotten us for so I? .... La 5:20
have such as I as they live, ... Eze 7:13
big wings and I feathers of many .... Eze 17:3
to join those who died I ago. .... Eze 26:20
limbs became I and big because .... Eze 31:5
with its I branches, because .... Eze 31:7
who were killed in battle I ago, ... Eze 32:27
a I time you will be called .... Eze 38:8
which were empty for a I time. .... Eze 38:8
was ten and one-half feet I.................... Eze 40:5
and one-half feet I and ten and .... Eze 40:7
one-half feet I and forty-four .... Eze 40:21
one-half feet I and forty-four .... Eze 40:25
one-half feet I and forty-four .... Eze 40:29
forty-four feet I and about nine .... Eze 40:30
one-half feet I and forty-four .... Eze 40:33
one-half feet I and forty-four .... Eze 40:36
tables about three feet I,...................... Eze 40:42
feet I and one hundred .... Eze 40:47
thirty-five feet I and .... Eze 40:49
seventy feet I and thirty-five .... Eze 41:2
feet I and thirty-five .... Eze 41:4
fifty-seven and one-half feet I................. Eze 41:12
one hundred seventy-five feet I. .... Eze 41:13
one hundred seventy-five feet I. .... Eze 41:13
feet I and eighty-seven .... Eze 42:2
one hundred seventy-five feet I. .... Eze 42:4
-seven and one-half feet I, ... Eze 42:8

L

one hundred seventy-five feet l. .... Eze 42:8
feet l and eight hundred .... Eze 42:20
twenty-one feet l and twenty-one .... Eze 43:16
one-half feet l and twenty-four .... Eze 43:17
their hair grow l but must keep .... Eze 44:20
about seven miles l and about .... Eze 45:1
seven miles l and three miles .... Eze 45:3
about seven miles l and more .... Eze 45:5
wide and about seven miles l, ... Eze 45:6
will be as l as the land given .... Eze 45:7
seventy feet l and fifty-two and .... Eze 46:22
wide and as l and wide as one .... Eze 48:8
seven miles l and three miles .... Eze 48:9
about seven miles l on the north............. Eze 48:10
seven miles l and three miles .... Eze 48:13
miles wide and seven miles l. .... Eze 48:15
Along the l side of the holy.................... Eze 48:18
hair grew l like the feathers .... Da 4:33
It had two l horns, but one horn .... Da 8:3
How l will the things in this .... Da 8:13
won't happen for a l time." .... Da 8:26
How l will it be before these .... Da 12:6
All night l their anger is low, ... Hos 7:6
How l will they remain unclean? .... Hos 8:5
old times, from days l ago." .... Mic 5:2
and Gilead as in days l ago. .... Mic 7:14
to our ancestors l ago. .... Mic 7:20
water before the l war begins. .... Nah 3:14
I must l ask for help and you .... Hab 1:2
It may seem like a l time, ... Hab 2:3
How l will that nation get rich .... Hab 2:6
how l will it be before you show........... Zch 1:12
see how wide and how l it is." .... Zch 2:2
feet l and fifteen feet wide. .... Zch 5:2
was said to our people l ago, ' .... Mt 5:21
was said to our people l ago, ' .... Mt 5:33
their lives a l time ago. .... Mt 11:21
How l must l put up with you? .... Mt 17:17
How l must l continue to be .... Mt 17:17
special prayer clothes very l. .... Mt 23:5
and you say l prayers so that .... Mt 23:14
After a l time the master came .... Mt 25:19
As l as the bridegroom is with .... Mk 2:19
the prophets who lived l ago." .... Mk 6:15
of them live a l way from here." .... Mk 8:3
How l must l stay with you? .... Mk 9:19
How l must l put up with you? .... Mk 9:19
"How l has this been happening?" .... Mk 9:21
look good by saying l prayers. .... Mk 12:40
was staying so l in the Temple. .... Lk 1:21
holy prophets who lived l ago: .... Lk 1:70
good before God as we live. .... Lk 1:75
For a l time he had worn no .... Lk 8:27
who lived l ago has risen .... Lk 9:8
prophets from l ago who has come .... Lk 9:19
How l must l stay with you and .... Lk 9:41
have changed their lives l ago. .... Lk 10:13
the son was still a l way off, ... Lk 15:20
Then he went away for a l time. .... Lk 20:9
look good by saying l prayers. .... Lk 20:47
wanted to meet him for a l time............. Lk 23:8
Jesus was tired from his l trip, ... Jn 4:6
had been sick for such a l time, ... Jn 5:6
How l will you make us wonder .... Jn 10:24
have been with you a l time now. .... Jn 14:9
They also took his l shirt, ... Jn 19:23
plan which he had made l ago; .... Ac 2:23
about this time l ago when he............... Ac 3:21
prophets said l ago that the One............. Ac 7:52
his magic so l that the people .... Ac 8:11
in Iconium a l time and spoke .... Ac 14:3
they stayed there a l time with .... Ac 14:28
After a l debate, Peter stood up .... Ac 15:7

have been known for a l time.' .... Ac 15:18
because for a l time in every .... Ac 15:21
by the man he chose l ago. .... Ac 17:31
He spoke to them a l time, ... Ac 20:11
not want to stay too l in Asia................. Ac 20:16
government not l ago and led .... Ac 21:38
chose you l ago to know his .... Ac 22:14
over this nation for a l time. .... Ac 24:10
They have known me for a l time. .... Ac 26:5
it is a short or a l time, ... Ac 26:29
gone without food for a l time, ... Ac 27:21
and watched him for a l time, ... Ac 28:6
He spoke to them all day l. .... Ac 28:23
this Good News l ago through his .... Rm 1:2
her husband as l as he is alive. .... Rm 7:2
All day l I stood ready to .... Rm 10:21
was hidden for l ages past but .... Rm 16:25
her husband as l as he lives. 1Co 7:39
that wearing l hair is shameful 1Co 11:14
But l hair is a woman's glory. 1Co 11:15
L hair is given to her as a 1Co 11:15
how wide and how l and how high........... Eph 3:18
will have a l life on the earth. .... Eph 6:3
not true and on l lists of names 1Ti 1:4
day through David a l time later............. Heb 4:7
you, because it is not very l. .... Heb 13:22
God planned l ago to choose you 1Pe 1:2
women who lived l ago and 1Pe 3:5
to obey God l ago in the time 1Pe 3:20
remember as l as I am in this 2Pe 1:13
against them l ago is still 2Pe 2:3
punished the world l ago when he 2Pe 2:5
to remember what happened l ago. 2Pe 3:5
L ago the prophets wrote about .... Jud 1:4
was dressed in a l robe and had .... Rev 1:13
how l until you judge the people............. Rev 6:10
The city was 1,500 miles l, ... Rev 21:16

LONG-LASTING
the good things of the l hills. .... Ge 49:26

LONG-SLEEVED
they brought the l robe to their .... Ge 37:32

LONG-WINDED
Will your l speeches never end? .... Job 16:3

LONGER
Your name will no l be Jacob.................... Ge 32:28
will not be called Jacob any l.................. Ge 35:10
in front of his servants any l, ... Ge 45:1
ancestors lived much l than I." .... Ge 47:9
so you will no l lead your .... Ge 49:4
not able to hide the baby any l, ... Ex 2:3
I will no l give you straw. .... Ex 5:10
do not have to stay here any l." .... Ex 9:28
and do not be stubborn any l................... Dt 10:16
they are no l his children; .... Dt 32:5
Israelites no l got the manna .... Jos 5:12
this the LORD was no l angry. .... Jos 7:26
I will no l defeat the nations .... Jdg 2:21
shield will no l be rubbed with 2Sa 1:21
people will no l bother them as 2Sa 7:10
I wait for the LORD any l?" 2Ki 6:33
people will no l hurt them as 1Ch 17:9
and would no l be a member .... Ezr 10:8
won't be full of shame any l." .... Ne 2:17
Then they will no l honor their .... Est 1:17
captives who no l hear the shout .... Job 3:18
terror would no l frighten me. .... Job 9:34
His limits are l than the earth. .... Job 11:9
The wicked will no l get rich, ... Job 15:29
they own will no l spread over .... Job 15:29
me a little l, and I will show .... Job 36:2
so they will no l be afraid of .... Ps 10:18

they are no l wise or good. .... Ps 36:3
they cannot do evil any l. .... Ps 36:12
how much l will the enemy make .... Ps 74:10
and let the wicked live no l. .... Ps 104:35
they can no l love or hate or .... Ec 9:6
but she is no l loyal to him. .... Is 1:21
Nations will no l fight other .... Is 2:4
be proud any l but will bow low .... Is 2:9
and they will no l be important. .... Is 2:12
Israel will no l be a nation. .... Is 7:8
They will no l have to work hard .... Is 14:3
how much l will it be night?" .... Is 21:11
you will not rejoice any l, ... Is 23:12
People will no l sing while they .... Is 24:9
will not cover the dead any l. .... Is 26:21
those who no l nurse at their .... Is 28:9
be ashamed or disgraced any l. .... Is 29:22
No l will you see those proud .... Is 33:19
You are no l the ruler. .... Is 47:1
You will no l be called tender .... Is 47:1
will no l be called the queen .... Is 47:5
Make the ropes l and its stakes .... Is 54:2
The sun will no l be your light .... Is 60:19
time people will no l say, ' .... Je 3:16
How much l will the land stay .... Je 12:4
they will no l be in the land l .... Je 24:10
time people will no l say: ' .... Je 31:29
People will no l have to teach .... Je 31:34
slaves and no l keep them as .... Je 34:10
not be patient with you any l. .... Je 44:22
men of Edom no l give good .... Je 49:7
will no l come to Babylon .... Je 51:44
The elders no l sit at the city .... La 5:14
the young men no l sing......................... La 5:14
will no l be trapped by your .... Eze 13:21
you will no l pay your lovers. .... Eze 16:41
so you will no l be a nation, ... Eze 25:7
There will no l be a leader in .... Eze 30:13
she will no l be proud of her .... Eze 30:18
so they will no l be their food. .... Eze 34:10
so they will no l suffer from .... Eze 34:29
so it will no l be a ruin for .... Eze 36:34
not think like a human any l, ... Da 4:16
one horn no l and newer than .... Da 8:3
because she is no l my wife, ... Hos 2:2
and I am no l her husband..................... Hos 2:2
' no l will she call me 'my baal. .... Hos 2:16
I will no l love them; .... Hos 9:15
not look the other way any l. .... Am 7:8
You will no l walk proudly,................... Mic 2:3
Nations will no l raise swords................ Mic 4:3
that you will no l worship what .... Mic 5:13
they will no l brag about their .... Mic 7:16
voices will no l be heard." .... Nah 2:13
the judges no l make fair .... Hab 1:4
I will no l take care of you .... Zch 11:9
no l let that person use that .... Mk 7:12
he meant that no l was any food............. Mk 7:19
I am no l worthy to be called .... Lk 15:19
I am no l worthy to be called .... Lk 15:21
you can't be my manager any l.' .... Lk 16:2
be with you a little while l. .... Jn 7:33
So Jesus no l traveled openly .... Jn 11:54
will be with you for a little l, ... Jn 12:35
be with you only a little l. .... Jn 13:33
I will not talk with you much l, ... Jn 14:30
no l call you servants, because .... Jn 15:15
not stay in the world any l. .... Jn 17:11
asked him to stay with them l, ... Ac 18:20
Now, why wait any l? Get up, be............. Ac 22:16
that he should not live any l. .... Ac 25:24
hope to stay a l time with you............... 1Co 16:7
no l think of him in that way. 2Co 5:16

and we no l live under a .... Gal 3:25
foreigners or strangers any l, ... Eph 2:19
Then we will no l be babies. .... Eph 4:14
When we could not wait any l, ... 1Th 3:1
could wait no l, I sent Timothy 1Th 3:5
you to stay l in Ephesus when I 1Ti 1:3
no l as a slave, but better than .... Phm 1:16
People will no l have to teach .... Heb 8:11
and they would no l have a sense .... Heb 10:2
is no l any sacrifice for sins. .... Heb 10:26
you are no l a follower of the .... Jam 4:11
was told to wait a short time l. .... Rev 6:11

LOOK

God said, "L, I have given you .... Ge 1:29
Why do you l so unhappy? .... Ge 4:6
to Abram, "L all around you— .... Ge 13:14
Abram said, "L, you have given .... Ge 15:3
outside and said, "L at the sky. .... Ge 15:5
said to Abram, "L, the LORD has .... Ge 16:2
L! I have two daughters who have .... Ge 19:8
Don't l back or stop anywhere in .... Ge 19:17
L, that little town over there .... Ge 19:20
and said, "L around you at my .... Ge 20:15
L, his daughter Rachel is coming .... Ge 29:6
Jacob said, "But l, it is still .... Ge 29:7
When you come to l at my flocks, ... Ge 30:33
The angel said, 'L! Only the .... Ge 31:12
You may l for anything that .... Ge 31:32
Joseph went to l for his .... Ge 37:17
L it over carefully and see if .... Ge 37:32
L at this seal and its cord and................ Ge 38:25
in her house and said, "L! .... Ge 39:14
"Why do you l so unhappy today?" .... Ge 40:7
the king said to Joseph, "L! .... Ge 41:41
Israel said to Joseph, "L at me; .... Ge 48:21
king said to his people, "L! .... Ex 1:9
was coming to l at the bush, ... Ex 3:4
he was afraid to l at God. .... Ex 3:6
L, the LORD has made the Sabbath .... Ex 16:29
the Israelites, "L, the LORD has............... Ex 35:30
The priest must l at the sore on .... Le 13:3
the priest must l at the person .... Le 13:5
the priest must l at the person .... Le 13:6
The priest must l at him, and if .... Le 13:8
and the priest must l at him. .... Le 13:10
priest must l at the person's .... Le 13:12
The priest must l at him, and if .... Le 13:17
And the priest must l at it. .... Le 13:20
the priest must l at it. .... Le 13:25
the priest must l at him again. .... Le 13:27
a priest must l at the sore. .... Le 13:30
the priest must l at the sore. .... Le 13:32
the priest must l at him. .... Le 13:34
the priest must l at him again. .... Le 13:36
doesn't need to l for the .... Le 13:36
a priest must l at them. .... Le 13:39
A priest must l at that person. .... Le 13:43
The priest must l at the mildew, ... Le 13:50
day he must l at the mildew .... Le 13:51
the priest must l at it again. .... Le 13:55
camp and l at the one who had .... Le 14:3
he goes in to l at the mildew. .... Le 14:36
priest will go in to l at it..................... Le 14:36
He will l at the mildew, and if................ Le 14:37
not enter and l at the holy .... Nu 4:20
tassels to l at to remind you .... Nu 15:39
You have made me l foolish! .... Nu 22:29
'L what God has done for Israel!' .... Nu 23:23
and l at the land I have given .... Nu 27:12
Kadesh Barnea to l at the land. .... Nu 32:8
L, here it is! Go up and take it. .... Dt 1:21
top of Mount Pisgah and l west,............. Dt 3:27

L

You can I at the land, but you .... Dt 3:27
but you can only I at it." .... Dt 3:28
L, I have taught you the laws .... Dt 4:5
When you I up at the sky, you .... Dt 4:19
there you can I for the LORD .... Dt 4:29
find him if you I for him with .... Dt 4:29
L at the past, long before you .... Dt 4:32
and I from one end of heaven to .... Dt 4:32
Don't I at how stubborn these................. Dt 9:27
don't I at their sin and evil..................... Dt 9:27
I for the place the LORD your............... Dt 12:5
you must I into the matter .... Dt 17:4
don't make us I at this terrible .... Dt 18:16
So I down from heaven, your holy .... Dt 26:15
and they will I mean. They will .... Dt 28:50
L, today I offer you life and .... Dt 30:15
L at the land of Canaan that I.................. Dt 32:49
now you will only I at the land .... Dt 32:52
' I have let you I at it, Moses, ... Dt 34:4
to them, "Go and I at the land, ... Jos 2:1
said to Joshua, "**L**, I have given .... Jos 6:2
L at our bread. On the day we .... Jos 9:12
L at our leather wine bags....................... Jos 9:13
sent me to I at the land where .... Jos 14:7
soldiers, he said to Zebul, "**L**!................. Jdg 9:36
The shadows just I like people." .... Jdg 9:36
Gaal said, "**L**, there are people .... Jdg 9:37
he went over to I at the body .... Jdg 14:8
Bethlehem to I for another place .... Jdg 17:8
L, here are my daughter, who has .... Jdg 19:24
Naomi said to Ruth, "**L**, your .... Ru 1:15
You didn't I for a young man to .... Ru 3:10
and go and I for the donkeys." 1Sa 9:3
L, I have one-tenth of an ounce 1Sa 9:8
them, the Philistines said, "**L**!............... 1Sa 14:11
Someone said to Saul, "**L**! 1Sa 14:33
Don't I at how handsome Eliab is 1Sa 16:7
People I at the outside of a 1Sa 16:7
the command to I for someone who 1Sa 16:16
They said, "**L** at this man! 1Sa 17:25
and say, "**L**, the king likes 1Sa 18:22
So David said, "**L**, tomorrow is 1Sa 20:5
to the boy, '**L**, the arrows are 1Sa 20:22
to his servants, "**L** at the man! 1Sa 21:14
told David, "**L**, the Philistines............. 1Sa 23:1
and his men went to I for David, ... 1Sa 23:25
I at this piece of your robe in 1Sa 24:11
of Israel to I for David there. 1Sa 26:2
s appointed king. **L**! Where are 1Sa 26:16
asked, "What does he I like?" 1Sa 28:14
She said, "**L**, I, your servant, ... 1Sa 28:21
said to him, "**L**, we are your own 2Sa 5:1
Philistines went to I for him. 2Sa 5:17
the prophet, "**L**, I am living 2Sa 7:2
They said, "**L**, we tried to talk 2Sa 12:18
why do you I so sad day after 2Sa 13:4
to King David, "**L**, I was right! 2Sa 13:35
said to Joab, "**L**, I will do what 2Sa 14:21
his servants, "**L**, Joab's field 2Sa 14:30
would say, "**L**, your claims are 2Sa 15:3
then went to I for Jonathan................... 2Sa 17:20
he called to the gatekeeper, "**L**! 2Sa 18:26
told Joab, "**L**, the king is sad 2Sa 19:1
was stopping to I at the body, ... 2Sa 20:12
We will I for a young woman to 1Ki 1:2
"Go and I toward the sea." 1Ki 18:43
told him to go and I again. 1Ki 18:43
did the man I like who met you 2Ki 1:7
them go and I for your master 2Ki 2:16
said to Elisha, "**L**, master, this 2Ki 2:19
I wouldn't even I at you or 2Ki 3:14
his servant Gehazi, "**L**, there's 2Ki 4:25
and said, "**L**, I now know there 2Ki 5:15

L, I made plans against my..................... 2Ki 10:9
of Baal, "**L** around, and make................. 2Ki 10:23
L, you are depending on Egypt to 2Ki 18:21
You have a proud I on your face, ... 2Ki 19:22
the valley to I for pasture for 1Ch 4:39
and said, "**L**, we are your own 1Ch 11:1
Israel, they went to I for him. 1Ch 14:8
the prophet, "**L**, I am living 1Ch 17:1
L, I will also give you oxen for 1Ch 21:23
Now, my God, I at us. Listen to 2Ch 6:40
to do, so we I to you for help. 2Ch 20:12
L and listen carefully. .... Ne 1:6
does your face I sad even though .... Ne 2:2
L, we are slaves today in the .... Ne 9:36
things, but I, we are slaves .... Ne 9:36
king, said, "**L**, a seventy-five .... Est 7:9
travelers from Tema I for water, ... Job 6:19
traders of Sheba I hopefully. .... Job 6:19
But now please I at me. .... Job 6:28
you will I for me, but I will be................. Job 7:8
Will you never I away from me or .... Job 7:19
of rocks and I for a place among .... Job 8:17
I will change the I on my face................. Job 9:27
You I for the evil I have done .... Job 10:6
you will I around and rest in .... Job 11:18
So I away from us and leave us .... Job 14:6
make yourselves I better than I, ... Job 19:5
they I at me as if I were a .... Job 19:15
L at me and be shocked;........................ Job 21:5
and you will I up to him......................... Job 22:26
stand up, but you just I at me................. Job 30:20
my eyes not to I with desire at .... Job 31:1
L up at the sky and see the..................... Job 35:5
people I at it from far off. .... Job 36:25
God and make it I as hard as .... Job 37:18
No one can I at the sun when it .... Job 37:21
me to make yourself I right? .... Job 40:8
I at the proud and bring them................. Job 40:11
L at the proud and make them .... Job 40:12
L at Behemoth, which I made just .... Job 40:15
L at the strength it has in its .... Job 40:16
and its eyes I like the light at .... Job 41:18
makes the sea I as if it had .... Job 41:32
is false and I for new lies? .... Ps 4:2
I I at your heavens, which you .... Ps 8:3
They do not I for God; there is .... Ps 10:4
They I for innocent people to .... Ps 10:8
I at them and do something. .... Ps 10:14
in trouble I to you for help. .... Ps 10:14
I at me. Answer me, my God; .... Ps 13:3
Those who I at me laugh. .... Ps 22:7
people I and stare at me......................... Ps 22:17
those who I to the LORD will .... Ps 22:26
they I to the God of Jacob for .... Ps 24:6
L at my suffering and troubles, ... Ps 25:18
L at how many enemies I have! .... Ps 25:19
I closely into my heart and mind. .... Ps 26:2
s beauty and I with my own eyes .... Ps 27:4
even my neighbors I down on me. .... Ps 31:11
but those who I to the LORD will .... Ps 34:10
L for peace and work for it. .... Ps 34:14
may I for them, but they will .... Ps 37:10
Then I said, "**L**, I have come. .... Ps 40:7
to me, daughter; I and pay .... Ps 45:10
they are. **L** at the palaces. .... Ps 48:13
L what happened to the man who .... Ps 52:7
says and how the wicked I at me. .... Ps 55:3
L, they are waiting to ambush me. .... Ps 59:3
Wake up to help me, and I. .... Ps 59:4
with many peaks I with envy on............... Ps 68:16
and does not I down on captives............... Ps 69:33
I I for the Lord on the day of .... Ps 77:2
they would I to him for help; .... Ps 78:34

L

L down from heaven and see.................. Ps 80:14
Then people will l for you, ... Ps 83:16
God, l at our shield; be kind to .... Ps 84:9
When my enemies l, they will be .... Ps 86:17
I will not l at anything wicked. .... Ps 101:3
be proud and l down on others. .... Ps 101:5
I will l for trustworthy people................. Ps 101:6
They l to God for food. .... Ps 104:21
L at the sea, so big and wide, ... Ps 104:25
they l at me and shake their .... Ps 109:25
they will l down on their....................... Ps 112:8
who bends down to l at the skies .... Ps 113:6
L at me and have mercy on me as .... Ps 119:132
L for your servant, because I .... Ps 119:176
I l up to the hills, but where .... Ps 121:1
LORD, I l upward to you, you who .... Ps 123:1
I don't l down on others. .... Ps 131:1
GOD, I l to you for help. .... Ps 141:8
L around me and see. No one .... Ps 142:4
living things l to you for food .... Ps 145:15
You will l for me, but you will .... Pr 1:28
and l straight ahead to what is .... Pr 4:25
a proud l, a lying tongue, ... Pr 6:17
A good person can l forward to .... Pr 10:28
Good people can l forward to a .... Pr 13:9
fun of wisdom l for it and do .... Pr 14:6
people l only for trouble;................... Pr 17:11
Some people have such a proud l! .... Pr 30:13
look! They l down on others. .... Pr 30:13
might say, "L, this is new," .... Ec 1:10
is a time to l for something............... Ec 3:6
except to l at their riches. .... Ec 5:11
L at what God has done:....................... Ec 7:13
and make yourself l good. .... Ec 9:8
those who l at every cloud will .... Ec 11:4
Don't l at how dark I am, at how ...... Sng 1:6
Why should I l for you near your .... Sng 1:7
L, he stands behind our wall .... Sng 2:9
L, the winter is past; the rains .... Sng 2:11
L, it's Solomon's couch with .... Sng 3:7
We will l for him with you. .... Sng 6:1
to l for buds on the vines, ... Sng 6:11
come back, so we may l at you! .... Sng 6:13
do you want to l at the woman .... Sng 6:13
and no one would l down on me. .... Sng 8:1
I will refuse to l at you. .... Is 1:15
The l on their faces shows they .... Is 3:9
the morning to l for strong .... Is 5:11
of the earth. L! The enemy comes .... Is 5:26
And when people l at the land, ... Is 5:30
coal and said, "L, your guilt is .... Is 6:7
will l and look, but you will .... Is 6:9
will look and l, but you will .... Is 6:9
angry and will l up and curse .... Is 8:21
They will l around them at their.............. Is 8:22
the way things l or decide by .... Is 11:3
They will l at each other in .... Is 13:8
L, the LORD's day of judging is .... Is 13:9
L, I will cause the armies of .... Is 13:17
that time people will l to God, ... Is 17:7
All you people of the world, l! .... Is 18:3
who lives in that country, l!................. Is 18:3
L, the LORD is coming on a fast.............. Is 19:1
sea will say, 'L at those .... Is 20:6
L, I see a man coming in a .... Is 21:9
So I say, "Don't l at me. .... Is 22:4
But l, the people are happy and .... Is 22:13
L, mighty one! The LORD will .... Is 22:17
L at your once happy city! .... Is 23:7
L at your old, old city!......................... Is 23:7
L at the land of the Babylonians; .... Is 23:13
L! The LORD will destroy the................. Is 24:1
L, the Lord has someone who is .... Is 28:2

L! The LORD comes from far away. .... Is 30:27
People will l to the king for.................... Is 32:3
L at Jerusalem, the city of our .... Is 33:20
L at Jerusalem, that beautiful .... Is 33:20
L at the LORD's scroll and read .... Is 34:16
L, your God will come, and he .... Is 35:4
L, you are depending on Egypt to .... Is 36:6
You have a proud l on your face, ... Is 37:23
L, the Lord GOD is coming with............... Is 40:10
L, he will bring reward for his .... Is 40:10
L up to the skies. Who created .... Is 40:26
faraway places, l and be afraid;............. Is 41:5
You will l for your enemies, ... Is 41:12
L, I have made you like a new .... Is 41:15
and needy people l for water, ... Is 41:17
I l at the idols, but there is .... Is 41:28
L, all these idols are false. .... Is 41:29
You who are blind, l and see. .... Is 42:18
L at the new thing I am going to .... Is 43:19
makes the wood l exactly like a .... Is 44:13
but I make them l foolish. .... Is 44:25
of Jacob to l for me in empty .... Is 45:19
L, people are coming to me from .... Is 49:12
L up and look around you. .... Is 49:18
Look up and l around you. .... Is 49:18
L, I need only to shout and the .... Is 50:2
L! It is the Lord GOD who helps............... Is 50:9
prove me guilty? L! All those .... Is 50:9
L at the rock from which you .... Is 51:1
l at the stone quarry from which .... Is 51:1
L at Abraham, your ancestor, and .... Is 51:2
L up to the heavens. Look around .... Is 51:6
L around you at the earth below. .... Is 51:6
damaged he did not l like a man; .... Is 52:14
People would not even l at him. .... Is 53:3
So you should l for the LORD................. Is 55:6
perfumes to l nice for Molech................. Is 57:9
l for justice, but there isn't .... Is 59:11
L around you. People are .... Is 60:4
of Jerusalem, 'L, your Savior is .... Is 62:11
l down from the heavens and see; .... Is 63:15
L at us from your wonderful and............... Is 63:15
Please, l at us, because we are .... Is 64:9
L, it is written here before me. .... Is 65:6
L, I will make new heavens and a .... Is 65:17
L, the LORD is coming with fire............... Is 66:15
the land of Kedar to l closely. .... Je 2:10
L at the things you did in the .... Je 2:23
' Those people won't l at me; .... Je 2:27
L up to the bare hilltops,................... Je 3:2
L! The enemy rises up like a .... Je 4:13
long must I l at the war flag .... Je 4:21
L around and discover these .... Je 5:1
don't you l for truth in people? .... Je 5:3
where the roads cross and l. .... Je 6:16
L, an army is coming from the .... Je 6:22
But l, you are trusting lies, ... Je 7:8
L! I am sending poisonous snakes .... Je 8:17
L, people of Judah, you have as .... Je 11:13
l up and see the people coming .... Je 13:20
l into a person's heart and test .... Je 17:10
you l deeply into the heart and .... Je 20:12
But you only l for and think .... Je 22:17
L, the punishment from the LORD .... Je 23:19
I will l after them and bring .... Je 24:6
L! I am already bringing........................ Je 25:29
so no one will l down on them. .... Je 30:19
L! It is a storm from the LORD! .... Je 30:23
L, I will soon bring Israel from .... Je 31:8
"L, the time is coming," says .... Je 31:31
L! The enemy has surrounded the .... Je 32:24
L, the whole country is open to .... Je 40:4
Don't l for them, because I will .... Je 45:5

the LORD says: "L! Someone is .... Je 48:40
They will cry and I for the LORD .... Je 50:4
L! An army is coming from the .... Je 50:41
city says, "L, LORD, and see. .... La 1:11
to care. Come, l at me and see: .... La 1:12
you people, and l at my pain. .... La 1:18
L at me, LORD. I am upset and .... La 1:20
L at all their evil. Do to them .... La 1:22
L how the Lord in his anger has............. La 2:1
L, LORD, and see to whom you .... La 2:20
L! In everything they do they .... La 3:63
them and did not l after them .... La 4:16
L and see our disgrace. .... La 5:1
It seemed to l like the glory of .... Eze 1:28
you will l toward Jerusalem. .... Eze 4:7
l toward the mountains of Israel, ... Eze 6:2
up against you! L! It has come! .... Eze 7:6
L, the day is here. It has come. .... Eze 7:10
greatly, they will l for peace, ... Eze 7:25
Human, now l toward the north............. Eze 8:5
L, they are insulting me every .... Eze 8:17
whitewash to make it l strong. .... Eze 13:10
l toward the women among your .... Eze 13:17
make your sisters l good because .... Eze 16:51
you made your sisters l good................ Eze 16:52
He does not l to the idols of .... Eze 18:6
He does not l to the idols of .... Eze 18:15
Human, l toward the south. .... Eze 20:46
l toward Jerusalem and speak .... Eze 21:2
L, it is coming, and it will .... Eze 21:7
the woman you l at with love............... Eze 24:16
and you l at it with love and .... Eze 24:21
They l at it with love, and it .... Eze 24:25
l toward the people of Ammon and .... Eze 25:2
People will l for you, but they .... Eze 26:21
They made you l beautiful. .... Eze 27:10
l toward the city of Sidon .... Eze 28:21
l toward the king of Egypt, ... Eze 29:2
l toward Edom and prophesy .... Eze 35:2
l toward Gog of the land of.................. Eze 38:2
l with your eyes and hear with .... Eze 40:4
If you begin to l worse than .... Da 1:10
compare how we l with how the............. Da 1:13
other young men l who eat the .... Da 1:13
were sent to l for Daniel and .... Da 2:13
king said, "L! I see four men .... Da 3:25
She will l for them, but she.................. Hos 2:7
trouble they will l for me." .... Hos 5:15
L at Israel's prostitution;...................... Hos 6:10
their God or l to him for help .... Hos 7:10
L for the LORD until he comes .... Hos 10:12
They l like horses, and they run .... Joe 2:4
But do not l in Bethel or go to .... Am 5:5
Go l at the city of Calneh, ... Am 6:2
I will not l the other way any .... Am 7:8
L, I am planning trouble against .... Mic 2:3
prophets into l into the future .... Mic 3:11
We will l at her and be glad we .... Mic 4:11
I will l to the LORD for help. .... Mic 7:7
' I will l down on them. .... Mic 7:10
you don't l at the sins of your .... Mic 7:18
L, there on the hills, someone............... Nah 1:15
squares. They l like torches; .... Nah 2:4
you will l for a place safe from .... Nah 3:11
L at your soldiers. They are all .... Nah 3:13
things and make me l at trouble? .... Hab 1:3
L at the nations! Watch them and .... Hab 1:5
eyes are too good to l at evil; .... Hab 1:13
so that it can l at their naked .... Hab 2:15
You l for much, but you find .... Hag 1:9
What does it l like now? .... Hag 2:3
said to Joshua, "L, I have taken .... Zch 3:4
L, I put this stone in front of .... Zch 3:9

which l back and forth across................. Zch 4:10
"L up and see what is going out." .... Zch 5:5
called to me, "L, the horses .... Zch 6:8
dying sheep, or l for the young .... Zch 11:16
They will l at me, the one they .... Zch 12:10
L carefully for the child. .... Mt 2:8
starting to l for the child so .... Mt 2:13
make their faces l sad to show .... Mt 6:16
L at the birds in the air. .... Mt 6:26
L at how the lilies in the field .... Mt 6:28
your eye' ? L at yourself! You .... Mt 7:4
and people say, 'L at him! .... Mt 11:19
this, they said to Jesus, "L!................... Mt 12:2
will l look and, but you will .... Mt 13:14
will look and l, but you will .... Mt 13:14
hill and go to l for the lost .... Mt 18:12
said to Jesus, "L, we have left............... Mt 19:27
L, we are going to Jerusalem................. Mt 20:18
those tombs l fine, but inside, ... Mt 23:27
People l at you and think you .... Mt 23:28
might say to you, 'L, there is .... Mt 24:23
L, here comes the man who has .... Mt 26:46
Mary went to l at the tomb. .... Mt 28:1
his friends went to l for Jesus. .... Mk 1:36
'They will l and look, but they .... Mk 4:12
will look and l, but they will .... Mk 4:12
L at how many people are pushing .... Mk 5:31
l like trees walking around. .... Mk 8:24
said to Jesus, "L, we have left............... Mk 10:28
He said, "L, we are going to .... Mk 10:33
and said to Jesus, "Teacher, l!............... Mk 11:21
Bring me a coin to l at." .... Mk 12:15
make themselves l good by saying .... Mk 12:40
said to him, "L, Teacher!..................... Mk 13:1
might say to you, 'L, there is .... Mk 13:21
L, here comes the man who has .... Mk 14:42
L, here is the place they laid .... Mk 16:6
he did not l the same as before. .... Mk 16:12
L what the Lord has done for me! .... Lk 1:25
they began to l for him among .... Lk 2:44
to Jerusalem to l for him there. .... Lk 2:45
and you say, 'L at him! .... Lk 7:34
'They will l, but they may not .... Lk 8:10
please come and l at my son, ... Lk 9:38
L at the birds. They don't plant .... Lk 12:24
a field, and I must go l at it. .... Lk 14:18
L, this man welcomes sinners and .... Lk 15:2
and go out and l for the lost .... Lk 15:4
and l carefully for the coin .... Lk 15:8
make yourselves l good in front .... Lk 16:15
will not say, 'L, here it is!' .... Lk 17:21
say to you, 'L, there he is!' .... Lk 17:23
he is!' or, 'L, here he is!' .... Lk 17:23
would not even l up to heaven. .... Lk 18:13
Peter said, "L, we have left................... Lk 18:28
make themselves l good by saying .... Lk 20:47
l up and hold your heads high, ... Lk 21:28
L at the fig tree and all the .... Lk 21:29
said, "L, Lord, here are .... Lk 22:38
L, he has done nothing for which .... Lk 23:15
L at my hands and my feet. .... Lk 24:39
John said, "L, the Lamb of God,............. Jn 1:29
he said, "L, the Lamb of God! .... Jn 1:36
your eyes and l at the fields .... Jn 4:35
judging by the way things l, ... Jn 7:24
You will l for me, but you will .... Jn 7:34
said, 'You will l for me, but .... Jn 7:36
and you will l for me, but you................ Jn 8:21
right for us. L! The whole world............. Jn 12:19
You will l for me, and what I .... Jn 13:33
said to them, "L, I am bringing .... Jn 19:4
will l at the one they stabbed................. Jn 19:37
finger here, and l at my hands. .... Jn 20:27

They said, "**L!** Aren't all these .... Ac 2:7
at him and said, "**L** at us!" .... Ac 3:4
of the Lord? **L!** The men who .... Ac 5:9
But **l**, you have filled Jerusalem .... Ac 5:28
and went near to **l** closer. .... Ac 7:31
with fear and was afraid to **l**. .... Ac 7:32
He said, "**L!** I see heaven open .... Ac 7:56
officer said, "**L**, here is water. .... Ac 8:36
city of Tarsus to **l** for Saul, ... Ac 11:25
God wanted them to **l** for him and .... Ac 17:27
But **l** at what this man Paul is .... Ac 19:26
will **l** and look, but you will .... Ac 28:26
will look and **l**, but you will .... Ac 28:26
of idols made to **l** like earthly .... Rm 1:23
I ask you to **l** out for those who .... Rm 16:17
I at what you were when God 1Co 1:26
not **l** out only for yourselves. 1Co 10:24
L out for the good of others 1Co 10:24
L into your own hearts before 1Co 11:28
But **l!** I tell you this secret: 1Co 15:51
could not continue to **l** at it. 2Co 3:7
You must **l** at the facts before 2Co 10:7
themselves to **l** like apostles 2Co 11:13
himself to **l** like an angel....................... 2Co 11:14
make themselves **l** like servants 2Co 11:15
L closely at yourselves. 2Co 13:5
L, the time is coming, says the .... Heb 8:8
Then I said, '**L**, I have come. .... Heb 10:7
Then he said, "**L**, I have come to .... Heb 10:9
who **l** at the blood of the .... Heb 10:29
Let us **l** only to Jesus, the One .... Heb 12:2
like people who **l** at themselves .... Jam 1:23
into which angels desire to **l**. 1Pe 1:12
He must **l** for peace and work for 1Pe 3:11
Every time they **l** at a woman 2Pe 2:14
as you wait for and **l** forward to 2Pe 3:12
L, the Lord is coming with many .... Jud 1:14
L, Jesus is coming with the.................... Rev 1:7
I was dead, but **l**, I am alive .... Rev 1:18
open the scroll or **l** inside it. .... Rev 5:3
to open the scroll or **l** inside. .... Rev 5:4
people will **l** for a way to die .... Rev 9:6
and nation will **l** at the bodies .... Rev 11:9
sitting on the throne said, "**L!**............... Rev 21:5

LOOKED

God **l** at everything he had made, ... Ge 1:31
l at his naked father and told .... Ge 9:22
Lot **l** all around and saw the .... Ge 13:10
He **l** up and saw three men .... Ge 18:2
At that point Lot's wife **l** back. .... Ge 19:26
He **l** down toward Sodom and .... Ge 19:28
third day Abraham **l** up and saw .... Ge 22:4
Then Abraham **l** up and saw a male .... Ge 22:13
he **l** up and saw camels coming. .... Ge 24:63
Rebekah also **l** and saw Isaac. .... Ge 24:64
Philistines **l** out his window, ... Ge 26:8
He **l** and saw a well in the field .... Ge 29:2
So Laban **l** in Jacob's tent, ... Ge 31:33
Although Laban **l** through the .... Ge 31:34
So Laban **l** through the camp,................ Ge 31:35
You have **l** through everything I .... Ge 31:37
Jacob **l** up and saw Esau coming, ... Ge 33:1
When Esau **l** up and saw the women .... Ge 33:5
When they **l** up, they saw a group .... Ge 37:25
Jacob **l** it over and said, ... Ge 37:33
They **l** just as thin and ugly as .... Ge 41:21
l at each other because they .... Ge 43:33
Moses **l** all around and saw that.............. Ex 2:12
the Lord **l** down from the pillar .... Ex 14:24
Israelites, they **l** toward the................... Ex 16:10
to those who **l** down on Israel." .... Ex 18:11
a surface that **l** as if it were .... Ex 24:10

glory of the Lord **l** like a fire .... Ex 24:17
Moses **l** closely at all the work .... Ex 39:43
Moses **l** for the goat of the sin .... Le 10:16
above the Tent **l** like fire. .... Nu 9:15
and at night it **l** like fire. .... Nu 9:16
as they **l** for a place to camp. .... Nu 10:33
we **l** like grasshoppers to them. .... Nu 13:33
They all **l**, and each man took .... Nu 17:9
person **l** at the bronze snake .... Nu 21:9
any magic but **l** toward the .... Nu 24:1
When I **l**, I saw you had sinned .... Dt 9:16
The king's men **l** for them all .... Jos 2:22
Jericho when he **l** up and saw a .... Jos 5:13
When the men of Ai **l** back, ... Jos 8:20
Sisera's mother **l** out through .... Jdg 5:28
She **l** through the curtains and .... Jdg 5:28
one of them **l** like a prince." .... Jdg 8:18
He **l** like an angel from God; .... Jdg 13:6
When they **l** up and saw the Ark 1Sa 6:13
of Beth Shemesh **l** into the Ark 1Sa 6:19
But when they **l** for Saul, they 1Sa 10:21
The Lord has **l** for the kind of 1Sa 13:14
When Goliath **l** at David and saw 1Sa 17:42
he **l** down on David with disgust. 1Sa 17:42
Every day Saul **l** for David,.................... 1Sa 23:14
Saul **l** back, and David bowed 1Sa 24:8
When he **l** back and saw me, ... 2Sa 1:7
Abner **l** back and asked, "Is that 2Sa 2:20
Michal **l** out the window........................ 2Sa 6:16
and as he **l** up, he saw a man 2Sa 18:24
Araunah **l** and saw the king and 2Sa 24:20
When I **l** at him more closely, ... 1Ki 18:43
The servant went and **l**. 1Ki 18:43
The Israelites **l** like two small 1Ki 20:27
fifty men who **l** for three days, ... 2Ki 2:17
turned around, **l** at them, and 2Ki 2:24
them, and it **l** as red as blood................. 2Ki 3:22
the people and saw he had on 2Ki 6:30
Then she **l** out the window. 2Ki 9:30
l up at the window and said, ... 2Ki 9:32
three servants **l** out the window 2Ki 9:32
She **l**, and there was the king, ... 2Ki 11:14
David **l** up and saw the angel of 1Ch 21:16
They **l** for him and found him. 2Ch 15:4
They **l** for God and found him. 2Ch 15:15
l at the enemy's large army. 2Ch 20:24
Then Jehu **l** for Ahaziah. 2Ch 22:9
She **l**, and there was the king 2Ch 23:13
other priests **l** at him and saw 2Ch 26:20
Then I **l** around and stood up and .... Ne 4:14
so he **l** for a way to destroy all .... Est 3:6
he **l** so different they almost .... Job 2:12
then he **l** at wisdom and decided .... Job 28:27
when I **l** for light, darkness.................... Job 30:26
While you **l** for words to use, ... Job 32:11
The Lord **l** down from heaven on .... Ps 14:2
and cruel man who **l** strong like .... Ps 37:35
I **l** for him, but he couldn't be .... Ps 37:36
God **l** down from heaven on all .... Ps 53:2
I **l** for sympathy, but there was .... Ps 69:20
When I **l**, I saw my enemies; .... Ps 92:11
The Lord **l** down from his holy .... Ps 102:19
from heaven he **l** down at the .... Ps 102:19
The Red Sea **l** and ran away; .... Ps 114:3
of my house I **l** out through .... Pr 7:6
I **l** at everything done on earth .... Ec 1:14
But then I **l** at what I had done, ... Ec 2:11
The Teacher **l** for just the right .... Ec 12:10
on my bed, I **l** for the one I .... Sng 3:1
I **l** for him, but I could not find .... Sng 3:1
I **l** for him, but I could not find .... Sng 3:2
I **l** for him, but I could not find .... Sng 5:6
He **l** for justice, but there was................ Is 5:7

People who I to Cush for help.................Is 20:5
tired as I I to the heavens. ....Is 38:14
and you have I at their ....Is 57:8
LORD I and could not find any ....Is 59:15
I I around, but I saw no one to ....Is 63:5
I I at the earth, and it was ....Je 4:23
I at the sky, and its light was ....Je 4:23
I I at the mountains, and they.................Je 4:24
I I, and there were no people. ....Je 4:25
I I, and the good, rich land had ....Je 4:26
We I for a time of healing, ...Je 14:19
Jeremiah, woke up and I around. ....Je 31:26
afraid and I at each other. ....Je 36:16
cakes that I like her and were.................Je 44:19
they I like sapphires. ....La 4:7
When I I, I saw a stormy wind ....Eze 1:4
Something that I like glowing..................Eze 1:4
was what I like four living ....Eze 1:5
Their faces I like this:.............................Eze 1:10
was what their faces I like. ....Eze 1:11
living creatures I like burning..................Eze 1:13
Now as I I at the living ....Eze 1:15
I like sparkling chrysolite. ....Eze 1:16
All four of them I the same, ...Eze 1:16
something that I like a throne. ....Eze 1:26
It I like a sapphire gem. ....Eze 1:26
up the shape I like glowing......................Eze 1:27
the waist down it I like fire, ...Eze 1:27
glow I like the rainbow ....Eze 1:28
I I and saw a hand stretched ....Eze 2:9
I and saw something that looked ....Eze 8:2
something that I like a human. ....Eze 8:2
the waist down it I like fire, ...Eze 8:2
the waist up it I like bright ....Eze 8:2
So I I up toward the north, ...Eze 8:5
When I I, I saw a hole in the ....Eze 8:7
I entered and I, and I saw every ....Eze 8:10
Then I I and saw in the dome ....Eze 10:1
gem which I like a throne. ....Eze 10:1
Something that I like a human ....Eze 10:8
I like shining chrysolite. ....Eze 10:9
All four wheels I alike: ....Eze 10:10
Each I like a wheel crossways...................Eze 10:10
things that I like human hands. ....Eze 10:21
Their faces I the same as the ....Eze 10:22
I passed by you and I at you, ...Eze 16:8
I I for someone to build up the ....Eze 22:30
They all I like chariot officers.................Eze 23:15
no one searched or I for them. ....Eze 34:6
I I and saw muscles come on the ....Eze 37:8
buildings that I like a city. ....Eze 40:2
I saw a man who I as if he were ....Eze 40:3
Place was something that I like ....Eze 41:21
As I I, I saw the glory of the ....Eze 44:4
After ten days they I healthier ....Da 1:15
I, and there in front of me was ....Da 4:10
Nebuchadnezzar, I up toward ....Da 4:34
The first animal I like a lion, ...Da 7:4
before me that I like a bear. ....Da 7:5
After that, I I, and there ....Da 7:6
animal I like a leopard with ....Da 7:6
on its back that I like a bird's ....Da 7:6
As I I, thrones were put in ....Da 7:9
of me someone who I like a human ....Da 7:13
ten horns and I greater than ....Da 7:20
when I I up and saw a male sheep ....Da 8:3
I saw someone who I like a man...............Da 8:15
I I up and saw a man dressed in ....Da 10:5
one who I like a man touched..................Da 10:16
The one who I like a man touched ....Da 10:18
Then I, Daniel, I, and saw two ....Da 12:5
Then I I up and saw four animal..............Zch 1:18
I I up and saw a man holding ....Zch 2:1

I I up again and saw a flying ....Zch 5:1
Then I I up and saw two women..............Zch 5:9
I I up again and saw four ....Zch 6:1
When they I up, they saw Jesus ....Mt 17:8
Jesus I at them and said,.........................Mt 19:26
was angry as he I at the people, ...Mk 3:5
he I at those sitting around ....Mk 3:34
The man I up and said, "Yes, I ....Mk 8:24
turned and I at his followers ....Mk 8:33
James, and John I around, but ....Mk 9:8
The boy I as if he were dead, ...Mk 9:26
Then Jesus I at his followers ....Mk 10:23
Jesus I at them and said,.........................Mk 10:27
After he had I at everything, ...Mk 11:11
the fire and I closely at him. ....Mk 14:67
Then the women I and saw that ....Mk 16:4
place, but the people I for him. ....Lk 4:42
Jesus I around at all of them ....Lk 6:10
Jesus I at his followers and....................Lk 6:20
he went over and I at the man, ...Lk 10:32
very good and I down on everyone.........Lk 18:9
Jesus I at him and said, "It is ....Lk 18:24
that place, he I up and said to................Lk 19:5
But Jesus I at them and said, ...Lk 20:17
As Jesus I up, he saw some rich ....Lk 21:1
Lord turned and I straight at ....Lk 22:61
Jesus I at him and said, "You ....Jn 1:42
When Jesus I up and saw a large ....Jn 6:5
Then Jesus I up and said, ...Jn 11:41
The people I for Jesus and stood ....Jn 11:56
followers all I at each other, ...Jn 13:22
he I toward heaven and prayed, ...Jn 17:1
bent down and I in and saw the ....Jn 20:5
bent down and I inside the tomb. ....Jn 20:11
Peter and John I straight at him ....Ac 3:4
The man I at them, thinking they ....Ac 3:5
that his face I like the face ....Ac 6:15
made an idol that I like a calf. ....Ac 7:41
He I up to heaven and saw the ....Ac 7:55
something that I like fish ....Ac 9:18
down that I like a big sheet.....................Ac 10:11
something that I heard the big ....Ac 11:5
I I inside it and saw animals, ...Ac 11:6
Herod I everywhere for him but ....Ac 12:19
He I straight at Elymas ....Ac 13:9
Paul I straight at him and saw ....Ac 14:9
models that I like the temple ....Ac 19:24
Paul I at the council and said,................Ac 23:1
he I eagerly for me until he.....................2Ti 1:17
quickly forget what they I like. ....Jam 1:24
eyes, we have I at, and we have 1Jn 1:1
He I like the sun shining at its ....Rev 1:16
the vision of these things I I, ...Rev 4:1
on the throne I like precious ....Rev 4:3
was something that I like a sea ....Rev 4:6
The Lamb I as if he had been ....Rev 5:6
Then I I, and I heard the voices ....Rev 5:11
I I, and there before me was a ....Rev 6:2
I I, and there before me was a ....Rev 6:5
I I, and there before me was a ....Rev 6:8
the vision of these things I I, ...Rev 7:9
and something that I like a big ....Rev 8:8
The locusts I like horses ....Rev 9:7
they wore what I like crowns of ....Rev 9:7
their faces I like human faces. ....Rev 9:7
Their chests I like iron ....Rev 9:9
I saw in the vision I like this: ....Rev 9:17
of the horses I like heads of ....Rev 9:17
This beast I like a leopard, ...Rev 13:2
of the beast I as if it had been................Rev 13:3
Then I I, and there before me ....Rev 14:1
Then I I, and there before me ....Rev 14:14
was One who I like a Son of Man ....Rev 14:14

I saw what I like a sea of glass .... Rev 15:2
spirits that I like frogs coming .... Rev 16:13

LOOKING
the worst I cows I have seen in .... Ge 41:19
Keep me from I at worthless .... Ps 119:37
the windows, I through the .... Sng 2:9
While you were I at the statue, ... Da 2:34
I know that you are I for Jesus, ... Mt 28:5
said, "Everyone is I for you!" .... Mk 1:37
Jesus, I at the man, loved him................. Mk 10:21
field but keeps I back is of no................. Lk 9:62
dry places, I for a place to .... Lk 11:24
he asked, "What are you I for?" .... Jn 1:38
Whom are you I for?" .... Jn 20:15
people who were not I for me." .... Rm 10:20
show they are I for a country .... Heb 11:14
he was I for God's reward. .... Heb 11:26
but we are I for the city that .... Heb 13:14
a roaring lion I for someone to 1Pe 5:8

LOOKOUT
The I was standing on the 2Ki 9:17
The I reported, "The messenger 2Ki 9:18
The I reported, "The second man 2Ki 9:20
place a I for the city and have................. Is 21:6
Then the I called out, "My .... Is 21:8

LOOKS
but the LORD I at the heart." 1Sa 16:7
The LORD I down from heaven and .... Ps 33:13
your face still I like the face .... Je 3:3
until the LORD I down and sees .... La 3:50
you that if anyone I at a woman .... Mt 5:28
what the world I down on and 1Co 1:28

LOOSE
the goat will let it I there. .... Le 16:22
he let the foxes I in the .... Jdg 15:5
the city gate and tore them I, ... Jdg 16:3
his lightning I under the whole .... Job 37:3
The ropes on your boats hang I. .... Is 33:23
The LORD turned I all of his .... La 4:11
Israel when you turn I your .... Eze 9:8
They are like a I bow that can't .... Hos 7:16
And they let I the four angels .... Rev 9:15

LOOSEN
LORD, and he will I her hair. .... Nu 5:18
the Pleiades or I the ropes of .... Job 38:31

LOOT
foreigners as I from war and to .... Eze 7:21
capture treasures and take I. .... Eze 38:12
your troops together to take I? .... Eze 38:13
will take the I of those who.................... Eze 39:10
loot of those who took their I,................. Eze 39:10

LORD
But Abram said, "L GOD, what can .... Ge 15:2
But Abram said, "L GOD, how can........... Ge 15:8
been brave to speak to the L. .... Ge 18:27
Abraham said, "L, please don't .... Ge 18:30
been brave to speak to the L. .... Ge 18:31
Abraham said, "L, please don't .... Ge 18:32
so he said, "L, would you .... Ge 20:4
LORD, "Please, L, I have never .... Ex 4:10
said, "Please, L, send someone .... Ex 4:13
LORD and said, "L, why have you .... Ex 5:22
the temple, L, that your hands .... Ex 15:17
He said, "L, if you are pleased .... Ex 34:9
must come before the L GOD, ... Ex 34:23
So show your strength now, L. .... Nu 14:17
L GOD, you have begun to show .... Dt 3:24
LORD and said, "L GOD, do not.............. Dt 9:26
of all gods and L of all lords. .... Dt 10:17
with the L of the whole world................. Jos 3:11

Joshua said, "L GOD, you brought .... Jos 7:7
L, there is nothing I can say .... Jos 7:8
answered, "L, how can I save .... Jdg 6:15
So Gideon cried out, "L GOD! .... Jdg 6:22
L, I beg you to let the man of .... Jdg 13:8
the LORD, "L GOD, remember me. .... Jdg 16:28
your enemies, my I and king?" 1Sa 29:8
David said, "L GOD, who am I? 2Sa 7:18
is not enough for you, L GOD. 2Sa 7:19
This is extraordinary, L GOD................... 2Sa 7:19
I say to you, L GOD, since you 2Sa 7:20
is why you are great, L GOD! 2Sa 7:22
L GOD, you are God, and your 2Sa 7:28
L GOD, you have said so. 2Sa 7:29
I promised him before the L, ' 1Ki 2:8
the Ark of the L GOD while 1Ki 2:26
The L was pleased that Solomon 1Ki 3:10
ancestors out of Egypt, L GOD.".............. 1Ki 8:53
because the L will hand them................. 1Ki 22:6
L had caused the Aramean army 2Ki 7:6
your messengers to insult the L........... 2Ki 19:23
L, listen carefully to the .... Ne 1:11
Remember the L, who is great and........... Ne 4:14
today is a holy day to the L. .... Ne 8:10
L, do you need to watch me like.............. Job 14:3
'The fear of the L is wisdom; .... Job 28:28
the L makes fun of them. .... Ps 2:4
our L, your name is the most .... Ps 8:1
our L, your name is the most .... Ps 8:9
said to the LORD, "You are my L. .... Ps 16:2
will always be told about the L. .... Ps 22:30
L, how long will you watch this .... Ps 35:17
L, do not leave me alone. .... Ps 35:22
My God and L, fight for me! .... Ps 35:23
But the L laughs at the wicked; .... Ps 37:13
L, you know everything I want; .... Ps 38:9
You will answer, my L and God. .... Ps 38:15
and help me, my L and Savior. .... Ps 38:22
So, L, what hope do I have? .... Ps 39:7
L, because I am poor and .... Ps 40:17
up, L! Why are you sleeping? .... Ps 44:23
L, let me speak so I may praise .... Ps 51:15
help me; the L will support me. .... Ps 54:4
L, destroy and confuse their .... Ps 55:9
L, I will praise you among the .... Ps 57:9
L, our protector, do not kill................. Ps 59:11
The L is loving. You reward .... Ps 62:12
the L would not have listened to.............. Ps 66:18
The L gave the command, and a............. Ps 68:11
the L comes from Mount Sinai to .... Ps 68:17
Praise the L, God our Savior, ... Ps 68:19
The L said, "I will bring the .... Ps 68:22
sing praises to the L. .... Ps 68:32
L GOD All-Powerful, do not let .... Ps 69:6
your powerful works, L GOD................... Ps 71:16
L, when you rise up, they will.............. Ps 73:20
The L GOD is my protection. .... Ps 73:28
I look for the L on the day of .... Ps 77:2
Will the L reject us forever? .... Ps 77:7
Then the L got up as if he had .... Ps 78:65
for their insults to you, L. .... Ps 79:12
L, have mercy on me, because I .... Ps 86:3
I give my life to you, L. .... Ps 86:4
L, you are kind and forgiving................. Ps 86:5
L, there is no god like you and .... Ps 86:8
L, all the nations you have made .... Ps 86:9
L, my God, I will praise you .... Ps 86:12
But, L, you are a God who shows .... Ps 86:15
L, where is your love from times .... Ps 89:49
L, remember how they insulted .... Ps 89:50
L, you have been our home since .... Ps 90:1
L our God, treat us well......................... Ps 90:17
before the L of all the earth. .... Ps 97:5

L

But you, L GOD, be kind to me so	Ps 109:21
LORD said to my L, "Sit by me at	Ps 110:1
The L is beside you to help you.	Ps 110:5
shake with fear before the L,	Ps 114:7
L, hear my voice; listen to my	Ps 130:2
sins, no one would be left, L.	Ps 130:3
I wait for the L to help me more	Ps 130:6
Our L is greater than all the	Ps 135:5
Give thanks to the L of lords.	Ps 136:3
L is great and very powerful.	Ps 147:5
So the L GOD All-Powerful,	Is 1:24
The L GOD All-Powerful will take	Is 3:1
The L GOD All-Powerful says	Is 3:15
So the L will put sores on the	Is 3:17
that time the L will take away	Is 3:18
The L will wash away the filth	Is 4:4
I saw the L sitting on a very	Is 6:1
Then the L said, "Go and tell	Is 6:9
I asked, "L, how long should	Is 6:11
But I, the L GOD, say, " 'Their	Is 7:7
The L himself will give you a	Is 7:14
The L will hire Assyria and use	Is 7:20
will be as if the L is shaving	Is 7:20
So I, the L, will bring the king	Is 8:7
The L sent a message against the	Is 9:8
So the L is not happy with the	Is 9:17
When the L finishes doing what	Is 10:12
So the L GOD All-Powerful will	Is 10:16
The L GOD All-Powerful will	Is 10:23
is what the L GOD All-Powerful	Is 10:24
The L GOD All-Powerful with his	Is 10:33
that time the L will again reach	Is 11:11
The L GOD All-Powerful says,	Is 19:4
The L said to me, "Go, place a	Is 21:6
This is what the L said to me:	Is 21:16
L GOD All-Powerful has chosen	Is 22:5
The L GOD All-Powerful told the	Is 22:12
The L GOD All-Powerful said	Is 22:14
is what the L GOD All-Powerful	Is 22:15
The L GOD will wipe away every	Is 25:8
the L has someone who is strong	Is 28:2
this is what the L GOD says:	Is 28:16
The L GOD All-Powerful has told	Is 28:22
L says: "These people worship	Is 29:13
This is what the L GOD, the Holy	Is 30:15
The L has given you sorrow and	Is 30:20
your messengers to insult the L.	Is 37:24
to the heavens. L, I have	Is 38:14
The L told me what would happen	Is 38:15
L, because of you, people live.	Is 38:16
the L GOD is coming with power	Is 40:10
the L GOD has sent me with his	Is 48:16
the L has forgotten me."	Is 49:14
This is what the L GOD says:	Is 49:22
The L GOD gave me the ability to	Is 50:4
The L GOD helps me learn, and I	Is 50:5
L GOD helps me, so I will not	Is 50:7
It is the L GOD who helps me.	Is 50:9
This is what the L GOD says:	Is 52:4
The L GOD says—he who gathers	Is 56:8
The L GOD has put his Spirit in	Is 61:1
the same way the L GOD will make	Is 61:11
So this is what the L GOD says:	Is 65:13
and the L GOD will put you to	Is 65:15
I said, "But L GOD, I don't know	Je 1:6
says the L GOD All-Powerful.	Je 2:19
of your guilt," says the L GOD.	Je 2:22
but only pretended," says the L.	Je 3:10
Then I said, "L GOD, you have	Je 4:10
So this is what the L GOD says:	Je 7:20
But I said, "Oh, L GOD, the	Je 14:13
Oh, L GOD, you made the skies	Je 32:17
now, L GOD, you tell me, 'Buy	Je 32:25
"As surely as the L GOD lives . . ."	Je 44:26
belongs to the L GOD	Je 46:10
L GOD All-Powerful will offer	Je 46:10
says the L GOD All-Powerful.	Je 49:5
because the L GOD All-Powerful	Je 50:25
says the L GOD All-Powerful.	Je 50:31
The L GOD All-Powerful did not	Je 51:5
L has handed me over to those	La 1:14
The L has rejected all my mighty	La 1:15
the L has crushed the capital	La 1:15
Look how the L in his anger has	La 2:1
The L swallowed up without mercy	La 2:2
The L was like an enemy;	La 2:5
The L has rejected his altar and	La 2:7
The people cry out to the L.	La 2:18
like water in prayer to the L.	La 2:19
killed in the Temple of the L.	La 2:20
The L will not reject his people	La 3:31
the L sees if someone is cheated	La 3:36
happen unless the L commands it.	La 3:37
L, you have taken my case and	La 3:58
'This is what the L GOD says.'	Eze 2:4
to them, 'The L GOD says this.'	Eze 3:11
to them, 'The L GOD says this.'	Eze 3:27
But I said, "No, L GOD!	Eze 4:14
This is what the L GOD says:	Eze 5:5
So this is what the L GOD says:	Eze 5:7
So this is what the L GOD says:	Eze 5:8
So the L GOD says: You have made	Eze 5:11
listen to the word of the L GOD.	Eze 6:3
The L GOD says this to the	Eze 6:3
This is what the L GOD says:	Eze 6:11
the L GOD says this to the land	Eze 7:2
This is what the L GOD says:	Eze 7:5
I felt the power of the L GOD.	Eze 8:1
and I cried out, "Oh, L GOD!	Eze 9:8
So this is what the L GOD says:	Eze 11:7
against you, says the L GOD.	Eze 11:8
a loud voice, "Oh no, L GOD!	Eze 11:13
'This is what the L GOD says:	Eze 11:16
'This is what the L GOD says:	Eze 11:17
evil ways, says the L GOD."	Eze 11:21
'This is what the L GOD says:	Eze 12:10
is what the L GOD says about	Eze 12:19
'This is what the L GOD says:	Eze 12:23
and do it, says the L GOD.' "	Eze 12:25
to them: 'The L GOD says this:	Eze 12:28
will be done, says the L GOD.' "	Eze 12:28
This is what the L GOD says:	Eze 13:3
So this is what the L GOD says:	Eze 13:8
am against you, says the L GOD.	Eze 13:8
will know that I am the L GOD.	Eze 13:9
So this is what the L GOD says:	Eze 13:13
will be gone, says the L GOD." '	Eze 13:16
'This is what the L GOD says:	Eze 13:18
So this is what the L GOD says:	Eze 13:20
'This is what the L GOD says:	Eze 14:4
'This is what the L GOD says:	Eze 14:6
be their God, says the L GOD.' "	Eze 14:11
only themselves, says the L GOD.	Eze 14:14
I live, says the L GOD, even if	Eze 14:16
I live, says the L GOD, even if	Eze 14:18
I live, says the L GOD, even if	Eze 14:20
This is what the L GOD says:	Eze 14:21
to Jerusalem, says the L GOD."	Eze 14:23
So this is what the L GOD says:	Eze 15:6
not been loyal, says the L GOD."	Eze 15:8
'This is what the L GOD says to	Eze 16:3
you became mine, says the L GOD.	Eze 16:8
I gave you, says the L GOD.	Eze 16:14
what happened, says the L GOD.	Eze 16:19
will be for you, says the L GOD.	Eze 16:23
will is weak, says the L GOD.	Eze 16:30

took their loot, says the L God. .... Eze 39:10
of my victory, says the L God. .... Eze 39:13
this is what the L God says: .... Eze 39:17
of soldiers,' says the L God. .... Eze 39:20
So this is what the L God says: .... Eze 39:25
of Israel, says the L God." .... Eze 39:29
this is what the L God says: .... Eze 43:18
me to serve me, says the L God. .... Eze 43:19
accept you, says the L God." .... Eze 43:27
'This is what the L God says: .... Eze 44:6
This is what the L God says: .... Eze 44:9
for their sin, says the L God. .... Eze 44:12
they sacrifice, says the L God. .... Eze 44:15
for himself, says the L God. .... Eze 44:27
This is what the L God says: .... Eze 45:9
of their homes, says the L God. .... Eze 45:9
belong to God, says the L God. .... Eze 45:15
This is what the L God says: .... Eze 45:18
This is what the L God says: .... Eze 46:1
This is what the L God says: .... Eze 46:16
This is what the L God says: .... Eze 47:13
him some land," says the L God. .... Eze 47:23
their shares," says the L God. .... Eze 48:29
The L allowed Nebuchadnezzar to .... Da 1:2
all gods, the L of all the kings .... Da 2:47
against the L of heaven. .... Da 5:23
Temple of the L to be brought to .... Da 5:23
I turned to the L God and prayed .... Da 9:3
I said, "L, you are a great God .... Da 9:4
L, you are good and right, but .... Da 9:7
But, L our God, you show us .... Da 9:9
L our God, you used your power .... Da 9:15
L, you do what is right, but.................... Da 9:16
L, listen! Lord, forgive! Lord, ... Da 9:19
Lord, listen! L, forgive! Lord, ... Da 9:19
L, hear us and do something! .... Da 9:19
The L will remember the evil .... Hos 9:9
made the L angry when they .... Hos 12:14
The L will make them pay for the .... Hos 12:14
will die," says the L God. .... Am 1:8
Before the L God does anything, ... Am 3:7
be afraid? The L God has spoken............. Am 3:8
So this is what the L God says: .... Am 3:11
Jacob," says the L God, the God .... Am 3:13
The L God has promised this: .... Am 4:2
do, Israelites," says the L God. .... Am 4:5
This is what the L God says: .... Am 5:3
This is what the L, the Lord God .... Am 5:16
The L God made this promise: .... Am 6:8
is what the L God showed me: .... Am 7:1
I said, "L God, forgive us. .... Am 7:2
is what the L God showed me: .... Am 7:4
The L God was calling for fire .... Am 7:4
Then I cried out, "L God, stop! .... Am 7:5
not happen," said the L God................... Am 7:6
The L stood by a straight wall, ... Am 7:7
Then the L said, "See, I will .... Am 7:8
is what the L God showed me: .... Am 8:1
funeral songs," says the L God. .... Am 8:3
The L God says: "At that time I .... Am 8:9
The L God says: "The days are .... Am 8:11
I saw the L standing by the.................... Am 9:1
The L God All-Powerful touches .... Am 9:5
I, the L God, am watching the .... Am 9:8
is what the L God says about .... Ob 1:1
The L God will be a witness .... Mic 1:2
the L from his Holy Temple. .... Mic 1:2
The L will judge many nations; .... Mic 4:3
to the L of all the earth. .... Mic 4:13
The L God is my strength....................... Hab 3:19
Be silent before the L God, ... Zph 1:7
serve the L of all the earth." .... Zch 4:14
presence of the L of the whole .... Zch 6:5

But the L will take away all she .... Zch 9:4
The L God will blow the trumpet, ... Zch 9:14
the Temple of the L will be like .... Zch 14:20
offers to the L an animal that .... Mal 1:14
the L you are looking for will .... Mal 3:1
an angel of the L came to him in .... Mt 1:20
what the L had said through .... Mt 1:22
'Prepare the way for the L. .... Mt 3:3
'Do not test the L your God.'" .... Mt 4:7
must worship the L your God and .... Mt 4:10
him and said, "L, you can heal .... Mt 8:2
answered, "L, I am not worthy .... Mt 8:8
said to him, "L, first let me go .... Mt 8:21
woke him, saying, "L, save us! .... Mt 8:25
you, Father, L of heaven and .... Mt 11:25
Son of Man is L of the Sabbath .... Mt 12:8
Peter said, "L, if it is really .... Mt 14:28
woman said, "Yes, L, but even .... Mt 15:27
save you from those things, L! .... Mt 16:22
said to Jesus, "L, it is good .... Mt 17:4
and asked, "L, when my fellow .... Mt 18:21
they shouted, "L, Son of David, ... Mt 20:30
even more, "L, Son of David, ... Mt 20:31
answered, "L, we want to see. .... Mt 20:33
who comes in the name of the L! .... Mt 21:9
Love the L your God with all .... Mt 22:37
The L said to my Lord, "Sit by .... Mt 22:44
David calls the Christ 'L,' .... Mt 22:45
know the day your L will come. .... Mt 24:42
will answer, 'L, when did we see .... Mt 25:37
will answer, 'L, when did we see .... Mt 25:44
Jesus, "Surely, L, I am not the .... Mt 26:22
field, as the L commanded me." .... Mt 27:10
An angel of the L came down from .... Mt 28:2
comes in the name of the L! .... Mk 11:9
The L our God is the only Lord. .... Mk 12:29
the L your God with all your .... Mk 12:30
everything the L commanded and .... Lk 1:6
Temple of the L and burn incense .... Lk 1:9
will be a great man for the L................... Lk 1:15
L has blessed you and is with................. Lk 1:28
The L God will give him the .... Lk 1:32
I am the servant of the L. .... Lk 1:38
the mother of my L comes to me? .... Lk 1:43
what the L said to you would .... Lk 1:45
said, "My soul praises the L; .... Lk 1:46
heard how good the L was to her, ... Lk 1:58
an angel of the L stood before .... Lk 2:9
of David. He is Christ, the L. .... Lk 2:11
which the L has told us about. .... Lk 2:15
to present him to the L. .... Lk 2:22
The L has put his Spirit in me, ... Lk 4:18
time when the L will show his .... Lk 4:19
begged him, "L, you can heal me .... Lk 5:12
The L was giving Jesus the power .... Lk 5:17
to say, "L, don't trouble .... Lk 7:6
But he said, "L, first let me..................... Lk 9:59
Love the L your God with all .... Lk 10:27
Peter said, "L, did you tell .... Lk 12:41
stood and said to the L, ... Lk 19:8
said to Jesus, "L, I am ready to .... Lk 22:33
Then the L turned and looked .... Lk 22:61
remembered what the L had said: .... Lk 22:61
The L really has risen from the .... Lk 24:34
after the L had given thanks. .... Jn 6:23
answered him, "L, who would we .... Jn 6:68
He said, "L, I believe!" .... Jn 9:38
said to Jesus, "L, if you had .... Jn 11:21
Martha answered, "Yes, L. .... Jn 11:27
feet and said, "L, if you had .... Jn 11:32
L, who believed what we told .... Jn 12:38
said to him, "L, are you going .... Jn 13:6
You call me 'Teacher' and 'L,' .... Jn 13:13

If I, your **L** and Teacher, have .... Jn 13:14
asked Jesus, "**L**, where are you .... Jn 13:36
said to Jesus, "**L**, we don't know .... Jn 14:5
said to him, "**L**, show us the .... Jn 14:8
taken the **L** out of the tomb, ... Jn 20:2
to the followers, "I saw the **L**!" .... Jn 20:18
thrilled when they saw the **L**. .... Jn 20:20
said to him, "My **L** and my God!" .... Jn 20:28
said to Peter, "It is the **L**!" .... Jn 21:7
answered, "Yes, **L**, you know that .... Jn 21:15
and had said, "**L**, who will turn .... Jn 21:20
glorious day of the **L** will come. .... Ac 2:20
calls on the **L** will be saved. .... Ac 2:21
'I keep the **L** before me always. .... Ac 2:25
The **L** said to my Lord, "Sit by .... Ac 2:34
Lord said to my **L**, "Sit by me at.............. Ac 2:34
to the cross—both **L** and Christ." .... Ac 2:36
everyone the **L** our God calls to .... Ac 2:39
Every day the **L** added those who .... Ac 2:47
Then the **L** will send the time of............. Ac 3:19
'The **L** your God will give you a .... Ac 3:22
God together, "**L**, you are the .... Ac 4:24
against the **L** and his Christ.' .... Ac 4:26
And now, **L**, listen to their .... Ac 4:29
L, help us, your servants, to .... Ac 4:29
people that the **L** Jesus was .... Ac 4:33
to test the Spirit of the **L**? .... Ac 5:9
believed in the **L** and were added .... Ac 5:14
an angel of the **L** opened the .... Ac 5:19
L said to him, 'Take off your .... Ac 7:33
for me? says the **L**. Do I need a .... Ac 7:49
prayed, "I Jesus, receive .... Ac 7:59
a loud voice, "**L**, do not hold .... Ac 7:60
in the name of the **L** Jesus, ... Ac 8:16
have done, and pray to the **L**. .... Ac 8:22
for me to the **L** so the things .... Ac 8:24
had spoken the message of the **L**, ... Ac 8:25
angel of the **L** said to Philip, ... Ac 8:26
Spirit of the **L** took Philip away .... Ac 8:39
followers of the **L** by saying he .... Ac 9:1
Saul said, "Who are you, **L**?" .... Ac 9:5
The **L** spoke to Ananias in a .... Ac 9:10
answered, "Here I am, **L**." .... Ac 9:10
The **L** said to him, "Get up and .... Ac 9:11
answered, "**L**, many people have .... Ac 9:13
But the **L** said to Ananias, ... Ac 9:15
Saul, the **L** Jesus sent me. .... Ac 9:17
Saul had seen the **L** on the road .... Ac 9:27
the road and the **L** had spoken to .... Ac 9:27
boldly in the name of the **L**. .... Ac 9:28
Respecting the **L** by the way they .... Ac 9:31
saw him and turned to the **L**. .... Ac 9:35
and many believed in the **L**. .... Ac 9:42
and said, "What do you want, **L**?" .... Ac 10:4
But Peter said, "No, **L**! .... Ac 10:14
everything the **L** has commanded .... Ac 10:33
Jesus is the **L** of all people!.................... Ac 10:36
But I said, 'No, **L**! I have never .... Ac 11:8
I remembered the words of the **L**. .... Ac 11:16
believed in the **L** Jesus Christ, ... Ac 11:17
the Good News about the **L** Jesus. .... Ac 11:20
The **L** was helping the believers, ... Ac 11:21
believed and turned to the **L**. .... Ac 11:21
an angel of the **L** stood there,............... Ac 12:7
know that the **L** really sent his .... Ac 12:11
explained how the **L** led him out .... Ac 12:17
an angel of the **L** immediately .... Ac 12:23
worshiping the **L** and fasting for .... Ac 13:2
the **L** will touch you, and you .... Ac 13:11
at the teaching about the **L**. .... Ac 13:12
came to hear the word of the **L**. .... Ac 13:44
is what the **L** told us to do, ... Ac 13:47
honor to the message of the **L**. .... Ac 13:48

message of the **L** was spreading.............. Ac 13:49
and spoke bravely for the **L**. .... Ac 14:3
These elders had trusted the **L**, ... Ac 14:23
by the grace of the **L** Jesus." .... Ac 15:11
alive may ask the **L** for help, ... Ac 15:17
to me, says the **L**, who will make .... Ac 15:17
to serve our **L** Jesus Christ. .... Ac 15:26
the people the message of the **L**. .... Ac 15:35
preached the message of the **L**. .... Ac 15:36
I am truly a believer in the **L**, ... Ac 16:15
Believe in the **L** Jesus and you .... Ac 16:31
message of the **L** to the jailer .... Ac 16:32
in it is the **L** of the land and .... Ac 17:24
in his house believed in the **L**. .... Ac 18:8
the **L** told Paul in a vision: .... Ac 18:9
the way of the **L** and was always .... Ac 18:25
in the name of the **L** Jesus. .... Ac 19:5
in Asia heard the word of the **L**............. Ac 19:10
the name of the **L** Jesus to force........... Ac 19:13
gave great honor to the **L** Jesus. .... Ac 19:17
the word of the **L** kept spreading .... Ac 19:20
always served the **L** unselfishly, ... Ac 20:19
God and believe in our **L** Jesus. .... Ac 20:21
work that the **L** Jesus gave me— .... Ac 20:24
ready to die for the **L** Jesus!" .... Ac 21:13
that what the **L** wants will be .... Ac 21:14
I asked, 'Who are you, **L**?' .... Ac 22:8
I said, 'What shall I do, **L**?' .... Ac 22:10
' The **L** answered, 'Get up and go .... Ac 22:10
I saw the **L** saying to me, ' .... Ac 22:18
But I said, '**L**, they know that .... Ac 22:19
the **L** said to me, 'Leave now. .... Ac 22:21
next night the **L** came and stood .... Ac 23:11
I said, 'Who are you, **L**?' .... Ac 26:15
' The **L** said, 'I am Jesus, the .... Ac 26:15
taught about the **L** Jesus Christ,............. Ac 28:31
Father and the **L** Jesus Christ. .... Rm 1:7
person whom the **L** does not .... Rm 4:8
Jesus our **L** from the dead. .... Rm 4:24
through our **L** Jesus Christ, ... Rm 5:1
God through our **L** Jesus Christ............... Rm 5:11
through Jesus Christ our **L**. .... Rm 5:21
forever in Christ Jesus our **L**. .... Rm 6:23
me through Jesus Christ our **L**! .... Rm 7:25
that is in Christ Jesus our **L**. .... Rm 8:39
because the **L** will quickly and .... Rm 9:28
The **L** All-Powerful allowed a few .... Rm 9:29
mouth, "Jesus is **L**," and if you .... Rm 10:9
same **L** is the Lord of all and .... Rm 10:12
Lord is the **L** of all and gives .... Rm 10:12
calls on the **L** will be saved." .... Rm 10:13
people can ask the **L** for help,............... Rm 10:14
for them to hear about the **L**, ... Rm 10:14
Isaiah said, "**L**, who believed .... Rm 10:16
"**L**," he said, "they have killed .... Rm 11:3
Who has known the mind of the **L**, ... Rm 11:34
the **L** with all your heart. .... Rm 12:11
I will repay them," says the **L**. .... Rm 12:19
with the **L** Jesus Christ .... Rm 13:14
well because the **L** helps him do............. Rm 14:4
days are doing that for the **L**. .... Rm 14:6
food are doing that for the **L**, ... Rm 14:6
some foods do that for the **L**, ... Rm 14:6
living for the **L**, and if we die,............... Rm 14:8
we die, we are dying for the **L**. .... Rm 14:8
or dying, we belong to the **L**. .... Rm 14:8
so he would be **L** over both the .... Rm 14:9
live,' says the **L**, 'Everyone .... Rm 14:11
I am in the **L** Jesus, and I know .... Rm 14:14
Father of our **L** Jesus Christ. .... Rm 15:6
who are not Jews, praise the **L**. .... Rm 15:11
because of our **L** Jesus and the .... Rm 15:30
her in the **L** in the way God's .... Rm 16:2

my dear friend in the **L**. .... Rm 16:8
Narcissus who belong to the **L**. .... Rm 16:11
who work very hard for the **L**. .... Rm 16:12
has worked very hard for the **L**. .... Rm 16:12
is a special person in the **L**, ... Rm 16:13
not serving our **L** Christ but are .... Rm 16:18
The grace of our **L** Jesus be with .... Rm 16:20
send greetings to you in the **L**. .... Rm 16:22
grace of our **L** Jesus Christ be .... Rm 16:24
the name of the **L** Jesus Christ— 1Co 1:2
Jesus Christ—their **L** and ours: 1Co 1:2
Father and the **L** Jesus Christ. 1Co 1:3
wait for our **L** Jesus Christ to 1Co 1:7
on the day our **L** Jesus Christ 1Co 1:8
Jesus Christ our **L**, is faithful. 1Co 1:9
the name of our **L** Jesus Christ 1Co 1:10
should brag only about the **L**." 1Co 1:31
have crucified the **L** of glory. 1Co 2:8
Who has known the mind of the **L**? 1Co 2:16
The **L** knows what wise people 1Co 3:20
not make me right before the **L**. 1Co 4:4
The **L** is the One who judges me. 1Co 4:4
wait until the **L** comes. 1Co 4:5
to you Timothy, my son in the **L**. 1Co 4:17
you very soon if the **L** wishes. 1Co 4:19
in the name of our **L** Jesus,.................... 1Co 5:4
with the power of our **L** Jesus, ... 1Co 5:4
be saved on the day of the **L**. 1Co 5:5
the name of the **L** Jesus Christ 1Co 6:11
for sexual sin but for the **L**, ... 1Co 6:13
Lord, and the **L** is for the body. 1Co 6:13
has raised the **L** from the dead 1Co 6:14
joins with the **L** is one spirit 1Co 6:17
Lord is one spirit with the **L**. 1Co 6:17
it is from the **L**.) A wife should 1Co 7:10
I am saying this, not the **L**): 1Co 7:12
slaves when the **L** called them 1Co 7:22
persons who belong to the **L**. 1Co 7:22
command from the **L** about this; 1Co 7:25
the **L** has shown me mercy.................... 1Co 7:25
work, trying to please the **L**. 1Co 7:32
his wife and pleasing the **L**. 1Co 7:34
fully to the **L** without concern 1Co 7:35
is only one **L**—Jesus Christ. 1Co 8:6
I have seen Jesus our **L**. 1Co 9:1
an example of my work in the **L**. 1Co 9:1
that I am an apostle in the **L**. 1Co 9:2
the **L** has commanded that those 1Co 9:14
the cup of the **L** and the cup 1Co 10:21
we trying to make the **L** jealous? 1Co 10:22
the earth belongs to the **L**, ... 1Co 10:26
But in the **L** women are not 1Co 11:11
teaching I received from the **L**: 1Co 11:23
when the **L** Jesus was handed 1Co 11:23
the cup of the **L** in a way that 1Co 11:27
the body and the blood of the **L**............... 1Co 11:27
But when the **L** judges us, he 1Co 11:32
say, "Jesus is **L**," without the 1Co 12:3
serve but the same **L** to serve. 1Co 12:5
not listen to me," says the **L**. 1Co 14:21
about us in Christ Jesus our **L**.............. 1Co 15:31
through our **L** Jesus Christ. 1Co 15:57
fully to the work of the **L**, ... 1Co 15:58
work in the **L** is never wasted.................. 1Co 15:58
with you if he **L** allows it. 1Co 16:7
working for the **L** just as I am. 1Co 16:10
Priscilla greet you in the **L**,................. 1Co 16:19
If anyone does not love the **L**,............... 1Co 16:22
God—lost forever! Come, O **L**! 1Co 16:22
The grace of the **L** Jesus be with 1Co 16:23
Father and the **L** Jesus Christ. 2Co 1:2
Father of our **L** Jesus Christ. 2Co 1:3
the **L** gave me a good opportunity 2Co 2:12

changes and follows the **L**, ... 2Co 3:16
The **L** is the Spirit, and where 2Co 3:17
where the Spirit of the **L** is, ... 2Co 3:17
comes from the **L**, who is the 2Co 3:18
Jesus Christ is **L** and that we 2Co 4:5
God raised the **L** Jesus from the 2Co 4:14
body, we are away from the **L**. 2Co 5:6
body and be at home with the **L**. 2Co 5:8
what it means to fear the **L**, ... 2Co 5:11
and be separate, says the **L**. 2Co 6:17
says the **L** Almighty." 2Co 6:18
themselves to the **L** and to us. 2Co 8:5
the grace of our **L** Jesus Christ. 2Co 8:9
glory to the **L** and to show that 2Co 8:19
do what the **L** accepts as right 2Co 8:21
the authority the **L** gave us. 2Co 10:8
should brag only about the **L**." 2Co 10:17
but those the **L** thinks are good. 2Co 10:18
talking as the **L** would talk but 2Co 11:17
Father of the **L** Jesus Christ, ... 2Co 11:31
and revelations from the **L**..................... 2Co 12:1
I begged the **L** three times to 2Co 12:8
The **L** gave me this authority to 2Co 13:10
The grace of the **L** Jesus Christ, ... 2Co 13:14
Father and the **L** Jesus Christ. .... Gal 1:3
James, the brother of the **L**. .... Gal 1:19
I trust in the **L** that you will .... Gal 5:10
cross of our **L** Jesus Christ is .... Gal 6:14
grace of our **L** Jesus Christ be .... Gal 6:18
Father and the **L** Jesus Christ. .... Eph 1:2
Father of our **L** Jesus Christ. .... Eph 1:3
faith in the **L** Jesus and your .... Eph 1:15
the God of our **L** Jesus Christ, ... Eph 1:17
become a holy temple in the **L**. .... Eph 2:21
plan through Christ Jesus our **L**. .... Eph 3:11
because I belong to the **L**. .... Eph 4:1
There is one **L**, one faith, and.................. Eph 4:5
you are full of light in the **L**. .... Eph 5:8
Try to learn what pleases the **L**. .... Eph 5:10
what the **L** wants you to do. .... Eph 5:17
music in your hearts to the **L**................... Eph 5:19
the name of our **L** Jesus Christ. .... Eph 5:20
husbands, as you do to the **L**,............... Eph 5:22
your parents as the **L** wants, ... Eph 6:1
training and teaching of the **L**. .... Eph 6:4
as if you were serving the **L**, ... Eph 6:7
Remember that the **L** will give a............ Eph 6:8
strong in the **L** and in his great .... Eph 6:10
Father and the **L** Jesus Christ. .... Eph 6:23
you who love our **L** Jesus Christ............... Eph 6:24
Father and the **L** Jesus Christ. .... Php 1:2
will be able to work for the **L**. .... Php 1:22
Christ is **L** and bring glory .... Php 2:11
I hope in the **L** Jesus to send .... Php 2:19
sure that the **L** will help me to .... Php 2:24
him in the **L** with much joy. .... Php 2:29
be full of joy in the **L**. .... Php 3:1
of knowing Christ Jesus my **L**. .... Php 3:8
our Savior, the **L** Jesus Christ, ... Php 3:20
strong in the **L** as I have told .... Php 4:1
and Syntyche to agree in the **L**. .... Php 4:2
Be full of joy in the **L** always.................... Php 4:4
and kind. The **L** is coming soon................ Php 4:5
happy in the **L** that you have .... Php 4:10
grace of our **L** Jesus Christ be................. Php 4:23
Father of our **L** Jesus Christ, ... Col 1:3
and pleases the **L** in every way. .... Col 1:10
you received Christ Jesus the **L**,............... Col 2:6
because the **L** forgave you. .... Col 3:13
to be done to obey Jesus your **L**. .... Col 3:17
the right thing to do in the **L**. .... Col 3:18
because this pleases the **L**. .... Col 3:20
because you respect the **L**. .... Col 3:22

if you were doing it for the **L**, ... Col 3:23
receive your reward from the **L**, ... Col 3:24
You are serving the **L** Christ. .... Col 3:24
and the **L** treats everyone the .... Col 3:25
and servant with me in the **L**. .... Col 4:7
finish the work the **L** gave you." .... Col 4:17
Father and the **L** Jesus Christ: 1Th 1:1
your hope in our **L** Jesus Christ 1Th 1:3
became like us and like the **L**. 1Th 1:6
who killed both the **L** Jesus and 1Th 2:15
pride in when our **L** Jesus Christ 1Th 2:19
if you stand strong in the **L**. 1Th 3:8
himself and our **L** Jesus prepare 1Th 3:11
May the **L** make your love grow 1Th 3:12
Father when our **L** Jesus comes 1Th 3:13
you in the **L** Jesus to live that 1Th 4:1
by the authority of the **L** Jesus. 1Th 4:2
The **L** will punish people who do 1Th 4:6
living when the **L** comes again 1Th 4:15
L himself will come down from 1Th 4:16
clouds to meet the **L** in the air. 1Th 4:17
we will be with the **L** forever. 1Th 4:17
the day the **L** comes again will 1Th 5:2
through our **L** Jesus Christ. 1Th 5:9
lead you in the **L** and teach you. 1Th 5:12
when our **L** Jesus Christ comes. 1Th 5:23
authority of the **L** to read this 1Th 5:27
grace of our **L** Jesus Christ be 1Th 5:28
Father and the **L** Jesus Christ: 2Th 1:1
Father and the **L** Jesus Christ. 2Th 1:2
us also when the **L** Jesus appears 2Th 1:7
News about our **L** Jesus Christ. 2Th 1:8
away from the **L** and from his 2Th 1:9
the day when the **L** Jesus comes........... 2Th 1:10
the name of our **L** Jesus Christ. 2Th 1:12
our God and the **L** Jesus Christ. 2Th 1:12
the coming of our **L** Jesus Christ 2Th 2:1
the day of the **L** has already 2Th 2:2
That day of the **L** will not come 2Th 2:3
and the **L** Jesus will kill him 2Th 2:8
whom the **L** loves, God chose 2Th 2:13
the glory of our **L** Jesus Christ. 2Th 2:14
But the **L** is faithful and will 2Th 3:3
L makes us feel sure that you 2Th 3:4
May the **L** lead your hearts into 2Th 3:5
of our **L** Jesus Christ we 2Th 3:6
beg them in the **L** Jesus Christ 2Th 3:12
Now may the **L** of peace give you 2Th 3:16
The **L** be with all of you. 2Th 3:16
grace of our **L** Jesus Christ be 2Th 3:18
Father and Christ Jesus our **L**. 1Ti 1:2
I thank Christ Jesus our **L**, ... 1Ti 1:12
grace of our **L** was fully given 1Ti 1:14
teaching of our **L** Jesus Christ 1Ti 6:3
blame until our **L** Jesus Christ 1Ti 6:14
kings and the **L** of all lords. 1Ti 6:15
Father and Christ Jesus our **L**. 2Ti 1:2
tell people about our **L** Jesus, ... 2Ti 1:8
of me, in prison for the **L**. 2Ti 1:8
May the **L** show mercy to the 2Ti 1:16
the **L** allow him to find mercy............... 2Ti 1:18
mercy from the **L** on that day................ 2Ti 1:18
because the **L** will give you the 2Ti 2:7
L knows those who belong to him,........... 2Ti 2:19
belong to the **L** must stop doing 2Ti 2:19
trust in the **L** from pure hearts. 2Ti 2:22
servant of the **L** must not 2Ti 2:24
the **L** saved me from all those 2Ti 3:11
The **L**, the judge who judges 2Ti 4:8
The **L** will punish him for what 2Ti 4:14
the **L** stayed with me and gave 2Ti 4:17
The **L** will save me when anyone 2Ti 4:18
The **L** be with your spirit. 2Ti 4:22

Father and the **L** Jesus Christ. .... Phm 1:3
faith you have in the **L** Jesus. .... Phm 1:5
and as a believer in the **L**. .... Phm 1:16
you do this for me in the **L**: .... Phm 1:20
grace of our **L** Jesus Christ be .... Phm 1:25
God also says, "**L**, in the .... Heb 1:10
The **L** himself first told about .... Heb 2:3
clear that our **L** came from the .... Heb 7:14
The **L** has made a promise and .... Heb 7:21
coming, says the **L**, when I will .... Heb 8:8
away from them, says the **L**. .... Heb 8:9
Israel at that time, says the **L**............... Heb 8:10
and relatives to know the **L**, ... Heb 8:11
them at that time, says the **L**. .... Heb 10:16
"The **L** will judge his people." .... Heb 10:30
L disciplines those he loves, ... Heb 12:6
not holy will never see the **L**. .... Heb 12:14
because the **L** is my helper...................... Heb 13:6
God and of the **L** Jesus Christ. .... Jam 1:1
in our glorious **L** Jesus Christ, ... Jam 2:1
to praise our **L** and Father, ... Jam 3:9
say, "If the **L** wants, we will .... Jam 4:15
heard by the **L** All-Powerful. .... Jam 5:4
patient until the **L** comes again. .... Jam 5:7
because the **L** is coming soon. .... Jam 5:8
prophets who spoke for the **L**. .... Jam 5:10
You know the **L** is full of mercy .... Jam 5:11
the person in the name of the **L**........... Jam 5:14
the **L** will heal that person. .... Jam 5:15
Father of our **L** Jesus Christ. 1Pe 1:3
word of the **L** will live forever. 1Pe 1:25
and seen how good the **L** is. 1Pe 2:3
Come to the **L** Jesus, the "stone" 1Pe 2:4
The **L** sees the good people and 1Pe 3:12
But the **L** is against those who 1Pe 3:12
as the holy **L** in your hearts. 1Pe 3:15
truly know God and Jesus our **L**. 2Pe 1:2
knowledge of our **L** Jesus Christ. 2Pe 1:8
kingdom of our **L** and Savior 2Pe 1:11
our **L** Jesus Christ has shown me. 2Pe 1:14
coming of our **L** Jesus Christ,............... 2Pe 1:16
So the **L** knows how to save those 2Pe 2:9
them with insults before the **L**. 2Pe 2:11
knowing our **L** and Savior Jesus 2Pe 2:20
command our **L** and Savior gave 2Pe 3:2
the **L** one day is as a thousand 2Pe 3:8
The **L** is not slow in doing what 2Pe 3:9
the day of the **L** will come like 2Pe 3:10
saved because our **L** is patient. 2Pe 3:15
of our **L** and Savior Jesus 2Pe 3:18
Christ, our only Master and **L**. .... Jud 1:4
that the **L** saved his people .... Jud 1:5
The **L** has kept these angels in .... Jud 1:6
he said, "The **L** punish you." .... Jud 1:9
the **L** is coming with many .... Jud 1:14
apostles of our **L** Jesus Christ................. Jud 1:17
you wait for the **L** Jesus Christ .... Jud 1:21
Jesus Christ our **L** for all time .... Jud 1:25
The **L** God says, "I am the Alpha .... Rev 1:8
holy is the **L** God Almighty. .... Rev 4:8
are worthy, our **L** and God, to................. Rev 4:11
Holy and true **L**, how long until .... Rev 6:10
stand before the **L** of the earth. .... Rev 11:4
city where the **L** was killed. .... Rev 11:8
belongs to our **L** and his Christ, ... Rev 11:15
thanks to you, **L** God Almighty, ... Rev 11:17
who die from now on in the **L**." .... Rev 14:13
things, **L** God Almighty. .... Rev 15:3
Everything the **L** does is right .... Rev 15:3
respect you, **L**, and will honor .... Rev 15:4
Yes, **L** God Almighty, the way you .... Rev 16:7
because he is **L** of lords and .... Rev 17:14
because the **L** God who judges her........... Rev 18:8

L

Our L God, the Almighty, rules. .... Rev 19:6
KING OF KINGS AND L OF LORDS. ...... Rev 19:16
because the L God Almighty and .... Rev 21:22
because the L God will give them .... Rev 22:5
The L, the God of the spirits .... Rev 22:6
soon." Amen. Come, L Jesus! .... Rev 22:20
The grace of the L Jesus be with .... Rev 22:21

LORD'S

gave it to the L service and set .... Ne 3:1
and gave it to the L service. .... Ne 3:1
I heard the L voice, saying,..................... Is 6:8
You say about the L altar, ' .... Mal 1:12
he did what the L angel had told .... Mt 1:24
Who saw the L power in this?" .... Jn 12:38
Moses heard the L voice say, ... Ac 7:31
change the L truths into lies. .... Ac 13:10
Barnabas put them in the L care. .... Ac 14:23
put Paul into the L care, ... Ac 15:40
And the L servant will do well .... Rm 14:4
married is busy with the L work, ... 1Co 7:32
married is busy with the L work. 1Co 7:34
apostles and the L brothers and 1Co 9:5
share in the L table and the 1Co 10:21
not really eating the L Supper. 1Co 11:20
others about the L death until 1Co 11:26
writing to you is the L command. 1Co 14:37
We all show the L glory, and we............... 2Co 3:18
In the L name, I tell you this. .... Eph 4:17
faithful servant of the L work. .... Eph 6:21
And the L teaching spread from.............. 1Th 1:8
you now is the L own message. 1Th 4:15
for us that the L teaching will.................. 2Th 3:1
The L servant must gently teach 2Ti 2:25
Glory forever and ever be the L............... 2Ti 4:18
don't think the L discipline is .... Heb 12:5
yourself in the L presence, ... Jam 4:10
you know the L purpose for him .... Jam 5:11
For the L sake, yield to the 1Pe 2:13
the L day I was in the Spirit, ... Rev 1:10

LORD (YHWH)

When the L God first made the .... Ge 2:4
Then the L God took dust from .... Ge 2:7
Then the L God planted a garden .... Ge 2:8
The L God caused every beautiful .... Ge 2:9
The L God put the man in the.................. Ge 2:15
So the L God caused the man to.............. Ge 2:21
The L God used the rib from the .... Ge 2:22
they heard the L God walking .... Ge 3:8
But the L God called to the man.............. Ge 3:9
the L God said to the woman,.................. Ge 3:13
The L God made clothes from .... Ge 3:21
So the L God forced Adam out of .... Ge 3:23
said, "With the L's help, I have .... Ge 4:1
L accepted Abel and his gift, ... Ge 4:4
The L asked Cain, "Why are you .... Ge 4:6
The L said to Cain, "No! .... Ge 4:15
went away from the L and lived .... Ge 4:16
people began to pray to the L. .... Ge 4:26
the ground the L has cursed."................... Ge 5:29
The L said, "My Spirit will not .... Ge 6:3
The L saw that the human beings .... Ge 6:5
But Noah pleased the L. .... Ge 6:8
the L closed the door behind .... Ge 7:16
Noah built an altar to the L. .... Ge 8:20
The L was pleased with these.................. Ge 8:21
said, "May the L, the God of .... Ge 9:26
was a great hunter before the L,............... Ge 10:9
The L came down to see the city .... Ge 11:5
The L said, "Now, these people .... Ge 11:6
So the L scattered them from .... Ge 11:8
that is where the L confused the............... Ge 11:9
The L said to Abram, "Leave your .... Ge 12:1

L appeared to Abram and said, ... Ge 12:7
But the L sent terrible diseases .... Ge 12:17
It was like the L's garden, ... Ge 13:10
I make a promise to the L, ... Ge 14:22
the L spoke his word to Abram in .... Ge 15:1
believed the L. And the LORD .... Ge 15:6
I am the L who led you out of Ur .... Ge 15:7
on that day the L made an .... Ge 15:18
the L has not allowed me to have .... Ge 16:2
Let the L decide who is right— .... Ge 16:5
The angel of the L found Hagar .... Ge 16:7
Then the L said to Abraham, ... Ge 18:13
Is anything too hard for the L? .... Ge 18:14
The L said, "Should I tell .... Ge 18:17
stood there before the L.......................... Ge 18:22
The L said, "If I find .... Ge 18:28
The L said, "If I find forty, I .... Ge 18:29
When the L finished speaking to .... Ge 18:33
The L has heard of all the evil .... Ge 19:13
So the L was merciful to Lot and .... Ge 19:16
The L sent a rain of burning .... Ge 19:24
The L had kept all the women in .... Ge 20:18
The L cared for Sarah as he had .... Ge 21:1
named that place The L Provides. .... Ge 22:14
L, the God of heaven, brought .... Ge 24:7
servant said, "L, God of my .... Ge 24:12
bowed and worshiped the L .... Ge 24:26
Isaac prayed to the L for her. .... Ge 25:21
Jacob saw the L standing above .... Ge 28:13
Surely the L is in this place, ... Ge 28:16
If the L does these things, ... Ge 28:21
Let the L watch over us while we .... Ge 31:49
did what the L said was evil, ... Ge 38:7
The L was with Joseph, and he .... Ge 39:2
because the L was with Joseph .... Ge 39:23
L, I wait for your salvation. .... Ge 49:18
angel of the L appeared to him .... Ex 3:2
L is the God of your ancestors— .... Ex 3:15
and tell him, 'The L, the God of .... Ex 3:18
the L said to him, "Reach out .... Ex 4:4
Then the L said to Moses, ... Ex 4:6
said to the L, "Please, Lord, I .... Ex 4:10
Meanwhile the L said to Aaron, ... Ex 4:27
everything the L had said to him .... Ex 4:28
of Egypt said, "Who is the L? .... Ex 5:2
returned to the L and said, ... Ex 5:22
God said to Moses, "I am the L, ... Ex 6:2
not know me by my name, the L. .... Ex 6:3
that I say to them, 'I am the L. .... Ex 6:6
know that I am the L your God, ... Ex 6:7
that land to own. I am the L.' " .... Ex 6:8
The L, the God of the Hebrews, ... Ex 7:16
Pray to the L to take the frogs .... Ex 8:8
is no one like the L our God. .... Ex 8:10
the L will punish you. He will.................. Ex 9:3
the L made the king stubborn, ... Ex 9:12
the L sent thunder and hail, ... Ex 9:23
my hands to the L in prayer, ... Ex 9:29
that the earth belongs to the L. .... Ex 9:29
do not yet fear the L God." .... Ex 9:30
go to worship the L their God. .... Ex 10:7
to have a feast to honor the L." .... Ex 10:9
and the L caused a strong wind .... Ex 10:13
sinned against the L your God .... Ex 10:16
When the L goes through Egypt to........... Ex 12:23
sacrifice to honor the L. .... Ex 12:27
At midnight the L killed all the .... Ex 12:29
That night the L kept watch to .... Ex 12:42
animal must be given to the L. .... Ex 13:12
the L brought us out from Egypt, ... Ex 13:14
The L showed them the way; .... Ex 13:21
will see the L save you today. .... Ex 14:13
the L will fight for you." .... Ex 14:14

that night the L drove back the .... Ex 14:21
but the L swept them away into .... Ex 14:27
So that day the L saved the.................... Ex 14:30
great power the L had used .... Ex 14:31
they feared the L, and they..................... Ex 14:31
sang this song to the L: .... Ex 15:1
will sing to the L, because he .... Ex 15:1
L gives me strength and makes .... Ex 15:2
The L is a warrior; the L .... Ex 15:3
is a warrior; the L is his name. .... Ex 15:3
Your right hand, L, is amazingly .... Ex 15:6
Are there any gods like you, L? .... Ex 15:11
until your people pass by, L. .... Ex 15:16
The L will be king forever!" .... Ex 15:18
the L covered them with water .... Ex 15:19
must obey the L your God and do .... Ex 15:26
you will see the glory of the L, ... Ex 16:7
against us, but against the L." .... Ex 16:7
Each evening the L will give you .... Ex 16:8
are grumbling against the L.".................. Ex 16:8
in the presence of the L, ... Ex 16:9
the glory of the L appeared in a .... Ex 16:10
The L said to Moses, ... Ex 16:11
know I am the L your God.'" .... Ex 16:12
the bread the L has given you to .... Ex 16:15
The L has commanded, 'Each one .... Ex 16:16
This is what the L commanded, ... Ex 16:23
Then place it before the L, ... Ex 16:33
Why are you testing the L?" .... Ex 17:2
cried to the L, "What can I do .... Ex 17:4
good things the L had done for .... Ex 18:9
He said, "Praise the L. .... Ex 18:10
because the L came down on it in .... Ex 19:18
When the L came down on top of .... Ex 19:20
L said to Moses, "Go down and .... Ex 19:21
don't, I, the L, will punish .... Ex 19:22
because I, the L your God, am .... Ex 20:5
use the name of the L your God .... Ex 20:7
of rest to honor the L your God............... Ex 20:10
six days the L made everything— .... Ex 20:11
So the L blessed the Sabbath day .... Ex 20:11
before the L that he did not .... Ex 22:11
to any god except the L......................... Ex 22:20
The L told Moses, "You, Aaron, ... Ex 24:1
people all the L's words and .... Ex 24:3
fellowship offerings to the L. .... Ex 24:5
everything that the L has said; .... Ex 24:7
which the L has made with you .... Ex 24:8
The glory of the L came down on .... Ex 24:16
the glory of the L looked like a .... Ex 24:17
before the L from evening till .... Ex 27:21
presence of the L as reminders .... Ex 28:12
continual reminder before the L. .... Ex 28:29
heart when he goes before the L. .... Ex 28:30
Place before the L so that Aaron .... Ex 28:35
carve a seal: 'Holy to the L.' .... Ex 28:36
on his head so the L will accept .... Ex 28:38
before the L at the entrance .... Ex 29:11
offering made by fire to the L. .... Ex 29:18
Its smell is pleasing to the L. .... Ex 29:18
which you put before the L. .... Ex 29:23
them as an offering to the L. .... Ex 29:24
offering made by fire to the L; .... Ex 29:25
must give to the L from their .... Ex 29:28
burn before the L every day from .... Ex 30:8
completely to the L's service." .... Ex 30:10
his life from the L so that no .... Ex 30:12
that I, the L, make you holy. .... Ex 31:13
of rest, a day holy for the L. .... Ex 31:15
six days I, the L, made the sky .... Ex 31:17
a special feast to honor the L." .... Ex 32:5
the L changed his mind and did .... Ex 32:14
So the L caused terrible things .... Ex 32:35

to ask the L about something .... Ex 33:7
while the L spoke with Moses. .... Ex 33:9
L spoke to Moses face to face................ Ex 33:11
the L came down in the cloud................ Ex 34:5
The L passed in front of Moses .... Ex 34:6
of Moses and said, "I am the L. .... Ex 34:6
because I, the L, the Jealous .... Ex 34:14
go before the L your God three .... Ex 34:24
there with the L forty days and .... Ex 34:28
Sabbath of rest to honor the L. .... Ex 35:2
presented their gold to the L. .... Ex 35:22
gifts to the L for all the work .... Ex 35:29
do the work the L has commanded, ... Ex 36:1
for Aaron as the L had commanded .... Ex 39:1
on the lampstand before the L, ... Ex 40:25
glory of the L filled the Holy .... Ex 40:34
the cloud of the L was over the .... Ex 40:38
you bring an offering to the L, ... Le 1:2
the young bull before the L, ... Le 1:5
its smell is pleasing to the L. .... Le 1:9
side of the altar before the L, ... Le 1:11
from the first harvest to the L, ... Le 2:14
offering to the L is from the .... Le 3:1
times before the L in front .... Le 4:6
the holy things of the L. .... Le 5:15
his penalty offering to the L. .... Le 5:15
as a memorial offering to the L. .... Le 6:15
be completely burned to the L. .... Le 6:22
in front of the L in the same .... Le 6:25
offering that belongs to the L, ... Le 7:20
offerings made by fire to the L. .... Le 7:35
is put before the L each day, ... Le 8:26
you don't obey the L's commands, ... Le 8:35
Offer all these things to the L, ... Le 9:4
and they stood before the L. .... Le 9:5
to use in the presence of the L. .... Le 10:1
down from the L and destroyed .... Le 10:2
because the L has appointed you .... Le 10:7
and burnt offering before the L, ... Le 10:19
so he can belong to the L again;............... Le 14:31
will be for the L and the other .... Le 16:8
be brought alive before the L.................. Le 16:10
you will belong to the L again. .... Le 16:30
as a gift to the L in front of..................... Le 17:4
of Israel: 'I am the L your God. .... Le 18:2
because of them. I am the L. .... Le 18:5
close relatives. I am the L. .... Le 18:6
respect your God. I am the L. .... Le 18:21
things that belong to the L...................... Le 19:8
from the tree will be the L's, ... Le 19:24
I am the L, and I have made you .... Le 20:8
you must not offer it to the L................... Le 22:24
offering of thanks to the L, ... Le 22:29
will announce the L's appointed .... Le 23:2
'These are the L's appointed .... Le 23:4
The L's Passover is on the .... Le 23:5
as an offering before the L, ... Le 23:20
those for the L's Sabbath days, ... Le 23:38
until morning before the L; .... Le 24:3
of pure gold before the L. .... Le 24:4
the golden table before the L, ... Le 24:6
L said to Moses at Mount Sinai, ... Le 25:1
time of rest, to honor the L. .... Le 25:2
and teachings the L made between .... Le 26:46
a servant to the L by paying a .... Le 27:2
be used as sacrifices to the L................... Le 27:9
presence of the L when they .... Nu 3:4
counted as the L had commanded .... Nu 4:49
is really sinning against the L. .... Nu 5:6
wrong owes the L and must pay............... Nu 5:8
and make her stand before the L. .... Nu 5:16
the L will make the people curse .... Nu 5:21
belong to the L in a special way............... Nu 6:2

Then Samuel prayed to the L,................. 1Sa 12:18
that same day the L sent thunder 1Sa 12:18
must honor the L and truly serve 1Sa 12:24
asked for the L's approval.' 1Sa 13:12
Maybe the L will help us. 1Sa 14:6
Saul built an altar to the L.................... 1Sa 14:35
The L sent me to appoint you 1Sa 15:1
the L spoke his word to Samuel: 1Sa 15:10
as sacrifices to the L your God, ... 1Sa 15:15
Why didn't you obey the L? 1Sa 15:19
What pleases the L more: 1Sa 15:22
have rejected the L's command. 1Sa 15:23
You rejected the L's command, ... 1Sa 15:26
The L has torn the kingdom of 1Sa 15:28
pieces before the L at Gilgal. 1Sa 15:33
And the L was very sorry he had 1Sa 15:35
But the L said to Samuel, ... 1Sa 16:7
but the L looks at the heart." 1Sa 16:7
The L has not chosen this man 1Sa 16:8
the L's Spirit worked in David. 1Sa 16:13
the L's Spirit had left Saul, ... 1Sa 16:14
and the L is with him." 1Sa 16:18
prayed to the L for David and............... 1Sa 22:10
and kill the priests of the L, ... 1Sa 22:17
May the L judge between us, ... 1Sa 24:12
The L will certainly let your 1Sa 25:28
days later the L struck Nabal 1Sa 25:38
If the L made you angry with me, ... 1Sa 26:19
The L rewards us for the things 1Sa 26:23
He prayed to the L, but the LORD 1Sa 28:6
but the L did not answer him 1Sa 28:6
You did not obey the L; 1Sa 28:18
May the L give them the 2Sa 3:39
Today the L has paid back Saul 2Sa 4:8
the name of the L All-Powerful, ... 2Sa 6:2
in the presence of the L......................... 2Sa 6:5
was afraid of the L that day, ... 2Sa 6:9
The Ark of the L stayed in 2Sa 6:11
with all his might before the L. 2Sa 6:14
in and sat in front of the L.................... 2Sa 7:18
The L gave David victory 2Sa 8:6
The L sent Nathan to David. 2Sa 12:1
"I have sinned against the L."................. 2Sa 12:13
did caused the L's enemies to 2Sa 12:14
the L caused the son of David 2Sa 12:15
in the name of the L your God. 2Sa 14:11
my promise that I made to the L............. 2Sa 15:7
me because the L told him to,................. 2Sa 16:10
Maybe the L will see my misery 2Sa 16:12
I swear by the L that if you 2Sa 19:7
this song to the L when the LORD 2Sa 22:1
The L is my rock, my fortress, ... 2Sa 22:2
call to the L, who is worthy 2Sa 22:4
In my trouble I called to the L; 2Sa 22:7
The L thundered from heaven; 2Sa 22:14
trouble, but the L supported me. 2Sa 22:19
The L spared me because I did 2Sa 22:21
have followed the ways of the L; 2Sa 22:22
L, you give light to my lamp. 2Sa 22:29
God? Only the L. Who is the Rock 2Sa 22:32
will praise you, L, among the 2Sa 22:50
The L's Spirit spoke through me, ... 2Sa 23:2
He poured it out before the L, ... 2Sa 23:16
The L was angry with Israel 2Sa 24:1
Let the L punish us, because the 2Sa 24:14
So the L sent a terrible disease 2Sa 24:15
the L felt very sorry about the 2Sa 24:16
The angel of the L was then by 2Sa 24:16
an altar to the L on the 2Sa 24:18
an altar to the L there and 2Sa 24:25
you in the name of the L, ... 1Ki 1:30
The L has always helped you,................ 1Ki 1:37
swore by the name of the L, ... 1Ki 2:23

from being the L's priest. 1Ki 2:27
be peace from the L for David, ... 1Ki 2:33
he loved the L by following 1Ki 3:3
the L appeared to him in a dream 1Ki 3:5
Ark of the Agreement with the L, ... 1Ki 3:15
for worshiping the L his God.................. 1Ki 5:3
The L gave Solomon wisdom as he 1Ki 5:12
Temple of the L was finished.................. 1Ki 7:51
filled with the glory of the L. 1Ki 8:11
The L has kept all the good 1Ki 8:56
May the L our God be with us as 1Ki 8:57
fully obey the L our God and 1Ki 8:61
Temple of the L and the palace, ... 1Ki 10:12
not follow the L completely as 1Ki 11:4
did what the L said was wrong 1Ki 11:6
The L had appeared to Solomon 1Ki 11:9
pray to the L your God for me, ... 1Ki 13:6
The L said you did not obey him! 1Ki 13:21
The L said to him, "Jeroboam's 1Ki 14:5
Then the L will punish Israel,................ 1Ki 14:15
The L will pull up Israel from................. 1Ki 14:15
faithful to the L his God as 1Ki 15:3
Because the L loved David,.................... 1Ki 15:4
did what the L said was right 1Ki 15:5
faithful to the L all his life..................... 1Ki 15:14
did what the L said was wrong. 1Ki 15:26
the L spoke his word to Elijah: 1Ki 18:1
Spirit of the L may carry you to 1Ki 18:12
was killing the L's prophets, ... 1Ki 18:13
If the L is the true God, follow 1Ki 18:21
the only prophet of the L here, ... 1Ki 18:22
L, you are the God of Abraham,............. 1Ki 18:36
Then fire from the L came down 1Ki 18:38
ground, crying, "The L is God! 1Ki 18:39
have had enough, L," he prayed. 1Ki 19:4
Later the L's angel came to him 1Ki 19:7
The L said to Elijah, "Go, stand 1Ki 19:11
to break in front of the L 1Ki 19:11
But the L was not in the wind. 1Ki 19:11
the L was not in the earthquake. 1Ki 19:11
The L says, 'The people of Aram 1Ki 20:28
there a prophet of the L here? 1Ki 22:7
Hear the message from the L:................ 1Ki 22:19
the L has not spoken through me. 1Ki 22:28
The L's angel said to Elijah, ... 2Ki 1:15
Where is the L, the God of 2Ki 2:14
Spirit of the L has taken Elijah 2Ki 2:16
played, the L gave Elisha power............. 2Ki 3:15
You know he honored the L. 2Ki 4:1
let the L pardon me for this: 2Ki 5:18
he prayed to the L, "Make these............. 2Ki 6:18
trouble has come from the L. 2Ki 6:33
my feelings are for the L." 2Ki 10:16
The L said to Jehu, "You have 2Ki 10:30
follow the teachings of the L,................. 2Ki 10:31
death in the Temple of the L.".............. 2Ki 11:15
between the L and the king 2Ki 11:17
But the L was kind to the 2Ki 13:23
did what the L said was right, ... 2Ki 15:3
The L struck Uzziah with a skin............. 2Ki 15:5
sinning against the L their God............... 2Ki 17:9
whom the L had forced out of the 2Ki 17:11
so the L rejected all the people 2Ki 17:20
until the L removed the 2Ki 17:23
they did not worship the L,................... 2Ki 17:25
honored the L but also worshiped 2Ki 17:41
loyal to the L and did not stop 2Ki 18:6
are depending on the L our God," 2Ki 18:22
went up to the Temple of the L. 2Ki 19:14
and prayed to the L: "LORD, God 2Ki 19:15
Hear, L, and listen. Open your 2Ki 19:16
Open your eyes, L, and see. 2Ki 19:16
Now, L our God, save us from the 2Ki 19:19

love of the **L** All-Powerful will 2Ki 19:31
the wall and prayed to the **L**, ... 2Ki 20:2
L, please remember that I have 2Ki 20:3
rejected the **L**, the God of his 2Ki 21:22
in the Temple of the **L**," 2Ki 22:8
that was in the Temple of the **L**. 2Ki 22:9
Go and ask the **L** about the words 2Ki 22:13
presence of the **L** to follow the 2Ki 23:3
Passover to the **L** your God as it 2Ki 23:21
the **L** would not forgive these 2Ki 24:4
Temple of the **L** and the palace 2Ki 25:9
with the **L** entered Jerusalem 1Ch 15:29
thanks to the **L** and pray to him. 1Ch 16:8
on the **L** and his strength; 1Ch 16:11
Sing to the **L**, all the earth. 1Ch 16:23
The **L** is great; he should be 1Ch 16:25
idols, but the **L** made the skies. 1Ch 16:26
Praise the **L**, all nations on 1Ch 16:28
the glory of the **L**'s name. 1Ch 16:29
the **L** because he is holy. 1Ch 16:29
everywhere say, "The **L** is king!" 1Ch 16:31
This is what the **L** All-Powerful 1Ch 17:7
So the **L** gave David victory 1Ch 18:6
The **L** will do what he thinks is 1Ch 19:13
days of punishment from the **L**, ... 1Ch 21:12
So the **L** sent a terrible disease 1Ch 21:14
the **L** saw it and felt very sorry 1Ch 21:15
The angel of the **L** was then 1Ch 21:15
angel of the **L** told Gad to tell 1Ch 21:18
will praise the **L** with musical 1Ch 23:5
holy things for the **L**'s service, ... 1Ch 23:13
Temple of the **L** with cymbals, ... 1Ch 25:6
in making music for the **L**. 1Ch 25:7
repairing the Temple of the **L**. 1Ch 26:27
because the **L** knows what is in 1Ch 28:9
for people; it is for the **L** God. 1Ch 29:1
and completely to the **L**. 1Ch 29:9
praised the **L** in front of all 1Ch 29:10
L, you are great and powerful. 1Ch 29:11
joy, and the **L** was with them. 1Ch 29:22
The **L** made Solomon great before 1Ch 29:25
because the **L** his God was with 2Ch 1:1
presence of the **L** at the Meeting 2Ch 1:6
Temple of the **L** was finished. 2Ch 5:1
they praised and thanked the **L**. 2Ch 5:13
praised the **L** with this song: 2Ch 5:13
because the **L**'s glory filled the 2Ch 5:14
Now, rise, **L** God, and come to 2Ch 6:41
L God, do not reject your 2Ch 6:42
the Temple of the **L** was begun, ... 2Ch 8:16
Israel who wanted to obey the **L**, ... 2Ch 11:16
obeying the teachings of the **L**. 2Ch 12:1
he did not want to obey the **L**. 2Ch 12:14
the Levites and the **L**'s priests, ... 2Ch 13:9
The **L** struck Jeroboam, and he 2Ch 13:20
Asa called out to the **L** his God, ... 2Ch 14:11
towns were afraid of the **L**. 2Ch 14:14
The **L** searches all the earth for 2Ch 16:9
there a prophet of the **L** here? 2Ch 18:6
Hear the message from the **L**: 2Ch 18:18
the **L** has made your prophets lie 2Ch 18:22
always serve the **L** completely, ... 2Ch 19:9
people not to sin against the **L**. 2Ch 19:10
and you will see the **L** save you. 2Ch 20:17
Have faith in the **L** your God, ... 2Ch 20:20
But the **L** would not destroy 2Ch 21:7
whom the **L** had appointed to 2Ch 22:7
the **L** with all his heart." 2Ch 22:9
worked on the Temple of the **L**. 2Ch 24:12
May the **L** see what you are doing 2Ch 24:22
was unfaithful to the **L** his God; 2Ch 26:16
right to burn incense to the **L**. 2Ch 26:18
because the **L** was punishing him. 2Ch 26:20

prophet of the **L** named Oded was 2Ch 28:9
sinned against the **L** your God. 2Ch 28:10
The **L** brought trouble on Judah 2Ch 28:19
and he was unfaithful to the **L**. 2Ch 28:19
The **L** chose you to stand before 2Ch 29:11
Temple of the **L** to purify it. 2Ch 29:15
Temple of the **L** with cymbals, ... 2Ch 29:25
the Levites to praise the **L**, ... 2Ch 29:30
were, but obey the **L** willingly. 2Ch 30:8
back to the **L**. Then the people 2Ch 30:9
made each lamb holy for the **L**. 2Ch 30:17
commanded in the **L**'s Teachings. 2Ch 31:3
obedient before the **L** his God. 2Ch 31:20
we have the **L** our God to help 2Ch 32:8
So the **L** saved Hezekiah and the 2Ch 32:22
gifts for the **L** to Jerusalem, ... 2Ch 32:23
prayed to the **L**, the LORD spoke 2Ch 32:24
The **L** spoke to Manasseh and his 2Ch 33:10
Then he set up the **L**'s altar and 2Ch 33:16
before the **L** as his father 2Ch 33:23
things from the Temple of the **L**, ... 2Ch 36:7
so what the **L** had told Israel 2Ch 36:21
the **L** had Cyrus send an 2Ch 36:22
the **L** caused Cyrus to send an .... Ezr 1:1
and build the Temple of the **L**, ... Ezr 1:3
Temple of the **L** in Jerusalem, ... Ezr 2:68
festivals commanded by the **L**. .... Ezr 3:5
in order to worship the **L**, ... Ezr 6:21
The **L** had made them happy by .... Ezr 6:22
L, God of heaven, you are the .... Ne 1:5
is a holy day to the **L** your God. .... Ne 8:9
the joy of the **L** will make you .... Ne 8:10
Teachings of the **L** their God. .... Ne 9:3
You are the only **L**. You made the .... Ne 9:6
The **L** said to Satan, "Where have .... Job 1:7
The **L** gave these things to me, ... Job 1:21
Praise the name of the **L**." .... Job 1:21
Then the **L** answered Job from the .... Job 38:1
Naamathite did as the **L** said, ... Job 42:9
the **L** gave him success again. .... Job 42:10
The **L** blessed the last part of .... Job 42:12
They love the **L**'s teachings, ... Ps 1:2
is because the **L** takes care of .... Ps 1:6
against the **L** and his appointed .... Ps 2:2
you what the **L** has declared: .... Ps 2:7
Obey the **L** with great fear. .... Ps 2:11
The **L** can save his people. .... Ps 3:8
know that the **L** has chosen for .... Ps 4:3
L listens when I pray to him. .... Ps 4:3
the **L** hates those who kill and .... Ps 5:6
L, since I have many enemies, ... Ps 5:8
L, have mercy on me because I am .... Ps 6:2
L, how long will it be? .... Ps 6:3
will praise you, **L**, with all my .... Ps 9:1
praises to the **L** who is king .... Ps 9:11
L, have mercy on me. See how my .... Ps 9:13
L, why are you so far away? .... Ps 10:1
The **L** is King forever and ever. .... Ps 10:16
The **L** is in his holy temple; .... Ps 11:4
The **L** tests those who do right, ... Ps 11:5
The **L**'s words are pure, like .... Ps 12:6
I sing to the **L** because he has .... Ps 13:6
The **L** looked down from heaven on .... Ps 14:2
May the **L** bring them back. .... Ps 14:7
praise the **L** because he advises .... Ps 16:7
I keep the **L** before me always. .... Ps 16:8
I love you, **L**. You are my .... Ps 18:1
The **L** is my rock, my protection, ... Ps 18:2
L, you give light to my lamp. .... Ps 18:28
The **L** lives! May my Rock be .... Ps 18:46
teachings of the **L** are perfect; .... Ps 19:7
rules of the **L** can be trusted; .... Ps 19:7
The orders of the **L** are right; .... Ps 19:8

The commands of the **L** are pure; .... Ps 19:8
Respect for the **L** is good; .... Ps 19:9
The judgments of the **L** are true; .... Ps 19:9
L, you are my Rock, the one who .... Ps 19:14
The king truly trusts the **L.** .... Ps 21:7
say, "Turn to the **L** for help. .... Ps 22:8
remember and will turn to the **L.** .... Ps 22:27
The **L** is my shepherd; I have .... Ps 23:1
in the house of the **L** forever. .... Ps 23:6
go up on the mountain of the **L?** .... Ps 24:3
receive a blessing from the **L;** .... Ps 24:5
The **L**, strong and mighty. .... Ps 24:8
The **L**, the powerful warrior. .... Ps 24:8
The **L** All-Powerful—he is the .... Ps 24:10
L, tell me your ways. Show me .... Ps 25:4
there those who respect the **L?** .... Ps 25:12
L, defend me because I have .... Ps 26:1
L, try me and test me; look .... Ps 26:2
and I come to your altar, **L**....................... Ps 26:6
L is my light and the one who .... Ps 27:1
The **L** protects my life. .... Ps 27:1
I ask only one thing from the **L.** .... Ps 27:4
me live in the **L**'s house all my .... Ps 27:4
So I come to worship you, **L.** .... Ps 27:8
L, teach me your ways, and guide .... Ps 27:11
live to see the **L**'s goodness. .... Ps 27:13
The **L** is my strength and shield. .... Ps 28:7
Praise the **L** for the glory of .... Ps 29:2
the **L** because he is holy.......................... Ps 29:2
The **L**'s voice is heard over the .... Ps 29:3
The **L** controls the flood.......................... Ps 29:10
The **L** will be King forever. .... Ps 29:10
The **L** gives strength to his .... Ps 29:11
will praise you, **L**, because you .... Ps 30:1
L, hear me and have mercy on me. .... Ps 30:10
have mercy on me. **L**, help me." .... Ps 30:10
your hope in the **L** be strong and .... Ps 31:24
person whom the **L** does not .... Ps 32:2
will confess my sins to the **L**," .... Ps 32:5
Praise the **L** on the harp; .... Ps 33:2
the **L**'s love fills the earth. .... Ps 33:5
the nation whose God is the **L**, ... Ps 33:12
The **L** looks down from heaven and .... Ps 33:13
But the **L** looks after those who .... Ps 33:18
So our hope is in the **L.** .... Ps 33:20
will praise the **L** at all times; .... Ps 34:1
My whole being praises the **L.** .... Ps 34:2
Glorify the **L** with me, and let.................. Ps 34:3
I asked the **L** for help, and he.................. Ps 34:4
the **L** heard him and saved him .... Ps 34:6
The angel of the **L** camps around .... Ps 34:7
and see how good the **L** is. .... Ps 34:8
L hears good people when they .... Ps 34:17
The **L** is close to the .... Ps 34:18
will say, "**L**, who is like you .... Ps 35:10
Trust the **L** and do good......................... Ps 37:3
serving the **L**, and he will give .... Ps 37:4
Depend on the **L**; trust him, and............. Ps 37:5
and trust the **L**. Don't be upset .... Ps 37:7
people's steps follow the **L**,.................... Ps 37:23
L, don't leave me; my God, don't .... Ps 38:21
I waited patiently for the **L.** .... Ps 40:1
The **L** All-Powerful is with us; .... Ps 46:7
The **L** is great; he should be .... Ps 48:1
The God of gods, the **L**, speaks. .... Ps 50:1
Give your worries to the **L**,...................... Ps 55:22
The **L** listens to those in need.................. Ps 69:33
me and save me. **L**, do not wait. .... Ps 70:5
your promises to the **L** your God. .... Ps 76:11
I remember what the **L** did; .... Ps 77:11
L God All-Powerful, make us back. .... Ps 80:19
courtyards of the **L**'s Temple. .... Ps 84:2
your altars, **L** All-Powerful, my .... Ps 84:3

The **L** God is like a sun and .... Ps 84:11
the **L** gives us kindness and .... Ps 84:11
L, listen to me and answer me. .... Ps 86:1
L, teach me what you want me to .... Ps 86:11
always sing about the **L**'s love; .... Ps 89:1
Who in heaven is equal to the **L?** .... Ps 89:6
L God All-Powerful, who is like .... Ps 89:8
L, how long before you return .... Ps 90:13
L, surely your enemies, surely .... Ps 92:9
The **L** is king. He is clothed in .... Ps 93:1
The **L** is a God who punishes.................... Ps 94:1
If the **L** had not helped me,..................... Ps 94:17
But the **L** is my defender; .... Ps 94:22
let's sing for joy to the **L.** .... Ps 95:1
because the **L** is the great God, ... Ps 95:3
kneel before the **L** who made us, ... Ps 95:6
Sing to the **L** a new song; .... Ps 96:1
sing to the **L**, all the earth. .... Ps 96:1
because the **L** is great; .... Ps 96:4
but the **L** made the heavens. .... Ps 96:5
Praise the **L**, all nations on .... Ps 96:7
the **L** because he is holy. .... Ps 96:9
the nations, "The **L** is king." .... Ps 96:10
to the **L** a new song, because .... Ps 98:1
joy to the **L**, all the earth; .... Ps 98:4
Shout to the **L**, all the earth. .... Ps 100:1
the **L** with joy; come before .... Ps 100:2
Know that the **L** is God. .... Ps 100:3
The **L** is good. His love is .... Ps 100:5
The **L** looked down from his holy .... Ps 102:19
All that I am, praise the **L;** .... Ps 103:1
The **L** has mercy on those who .... Ps 103:13
But the **L**'s love for those who .... Ps 103:17
My whole being, praise the **L**................... Ps 104:1
thanks to the **L** and pray to him. .... Ps 105:1
his teachings. Praise the **L!** .... Ps 105:45
Praise the **L!** Thank the LORD .... Ps 106:1
Thank the **L** because he is good. .... Ps 106:1
mighty things the **L** has done; .... Ps 106:2
whom the **L** has saved should.................. Ps 107:2
misery they cried out to the **L**, ... Ps 107:6
thanks to the **L** for his love.................... Ps 107:8
know that you have done it, **L.** .... Ps 109:27
The **L** said to my Lord, "Sit by .... Ps 110:1
The **L** will enlarge your kingdom .... Ps 110:2
L has made a promise and will .... Ps 110:4
The **L** is kind and merciful....................... Ps 111:4
begins with respect for the **L;** .... Ps 111:10
The **L**'s name should be praised .... Ps 113:2
The **L** is supreme over all the .... Ps 113:4
It does not belong to us, **L.** .... Ps 115:1
Family of Israel, trust the **L;** .... Ps 115:9
Dead people do not praise the **L;** .... Ps 115:17
praise the **L** now and forever .... Ps 115:18
I love the **L**, because he listens .... Ps 116:1
The **L** is kind and does what is .... Ps 116:5
The **L** watches over the foolish; .... Ps 116:6
will walk with the **L** in the land .... Ps 116:9
I give the **L** for all the good .... Ps 116:12
will give the **L** what I promised .... Ps 116:14
All you nations, praise the **L.** .... Ps 117:1
trouble, so I called to the **L.** .... Ps 118:5
to trust the **L** to trust .... Ps 118:8
The **L** gives me strength and a .... Ps 118:14
"The **L** has done powerful things."........... Ps 118:15
The **L** has taught me a hard .... Ps 118:18
is the day that the **L** has made. .... Ps 118:24
who comes in the name of the **L**. .... Ps 118:26
of you from the Temple of the **L**. .... Ps 118:26
L, teach me your demands, and I .... Ps 119:33
L, your word is everlasting; .... Ps 119:89
L, give me life by your word. .... Ps 119:107
L, you are very kind; give me .... Ps 119:156

I called to the **L**, and he .... Ps 120:1
from the **L**, who made heaven .... Ps 121:2
L guards you. The LORD is the .... Ps 121:5
The **L** is the shade that protects .... Ps 121:5
The **L** will protect you from all .... Ps 121:7
go to the Temple of the **L**." .... Ps 122:1
What if the **L** had not been on .... Ps 124:1
who trust the **L** are like Mount .... Ps 125:1
the **L** surrounds his people now .... Ps 125:2
L, be good to those who are good, ... Ps 125:4
When the **L** brought the prisoners .... Ps 126:1
The **L** has done great things for .... Ps 126:2
the **L** doesn't build the house,................ Ps 127:1
If the **L** doesn't guard the city, ... Ps 127:1
Children are a gift from the **L**; .... Ps 127:3
L, if you punished people for .... Ps 130:3
I wait for the **L** to help me, ... Ps 130:5
your hope in the **L** because he is .... Ps 130:7
Praise the **L**! Praise the name of............ Ps 135:1
Praise the name of the **L**; .... Ps 135:1
I know that the **L** is great. .... Ps 135:5
The **L** does what he pleases, ... Ps 135:6
Family of Israel, praise the **L**. .... Ps 135:19
thanks to the **L** because he is .... Ps 136:1
L, remember what the Edomites.............. Ps 137:7
sing about what the **L** has done,............. Ps 138:5
L, even before I say a word, you............. Ps 139:4
L, I hate those who hate you; .... Ps 139:21
L, help me control my tongue; .... Ps 141:3
the **L**, my Rock, who trains.................... Ps 144:1
L, tear open the sky and come .... Ps 144:5
the people whose God is the **L**. .... Ps 144:15
The **L** is great and worthy of our .... Ps 145:3
The **L** is good to everyone; .... Ps 145:9
L, everything you have made will .... Ps 145:10
Everything the **L** does is right. .... Ps 145:17
The **L** sets the prisoners free. .... Ps 146:7
The **L** gives sight to the blind. .... Ps 146:8
The **L** rebuilds Jerusalem; .... Ps 147:2
begins with respect for the **L**, ... Pr 1:7
Only the **L** gives wisdom; .... Pr 2:6
Trust the **L** with all your heart, ... Pr 3:5
Honor the **L** with your wealth and .... Pr 3:9
not reject the **L**'s discipline, ... Pr 3:11
The **L** corrects those he loves, ... Pr 3:12
The **L** made the earth, using his .... Pr 3:19
The **L** hates those who do wrong, ... Pr 3:32
are six things the **L** hates. .... Pr 6:16
you respect the **L**, you will also .... Pr 8:13
was with the **L** when he began his .... Pr 8:22
and the **L** will be pleased with .... Pr 8:35
begins with respect for the **L**, ... Pr 9:10
The **L**'s eyes see everything; .... Pr 15:3
and respect the **L** than to be .... Pr 15:16
but the **L** will judge your..................... Pr 16:2
live so that they please the **L**, ... Pr 16:7
but the **L** decides what they will............ Pr 16:9
but the answer comes from the **L**. .... Pr 16:33
gold, but the **L** tests hearts.................... Pr 17:3
wise wife is a gift from the **L**, ... Pr 19:14
who respect the **L** will live and .... Pr 19:23
L has made both these things: .... Pr 20:12
The **L** decides what a person will .... Pr 20:24
but the **L** judges your reasons. .... Pr 21:2
The **L** will defend them in court .... Pr 22:23
in that the **L** gave eyes to both .... Pr 29:13
who respects the **L** should be .... Pr 31:30
because the **L** is speaking: .... Is 1:2
have left the **L**; they hate God, ... Is 1:4
The **L** All-Powerful allowed a few .... Is 1:9
The **L** himself said these .... Is 1:20
go up to the mountain of the **L**, ... Is 2:3
the message of the **L** will go out............. Is 2:3

let us follow the way of the **L**................. Is 2:5
time only the **L** will still be .... Is 2:11
The **L** takes his place in court................ Is 3:13
to the **L** All-Powerful is .... Is 5:7
holy is the **L** All-Powerful. .... Is 6:3
ask for a sign or test the **L**." .... Is 7:12
The **L** will bring troubled times .... Is 7:17
the children the **L** has given me. .... Is 8:18
Israel from the **L** All-Powerful, ... Is 8:18
The **L** All-Powerful will do this .... Is 9:7
The Spirit of the **L** will rest.................... Is 11:2
him to know and respect the **L**. .... Is 11:2
full of the knowledge of the **L**, ... Is 11:9
L, the LORD gives me strength .... Is 12:2
praise to the **L**, because he has .... Is 12:5
The **L** has broken the scepter of .... Is 14:5
the **L** is coming on a fast cloud .... Is 19:1
an altar for the **L** in the middle .... Is 19:19
monument to the **L** at the border .... Is 19:19
years the **L** will deal with .... Is 23:17
The **L** will destroy the earth and............ Is 24:1
praise the greatness of the **L**. .... Is 24:14
the earth. The **L** has spoken. .... Is 25:8
So, trust the **L** always, because .... Is 26:4
L, you multiplied the number of .... Is 26:15
things from the **L** and who do .... Is 29:15
The **L** will make the poor people .... Is 29:19
L is a fair God, and everyone .... Is 30:18
come to the mountain of the **L**, ... Is 30:29
The **L** will cause all people to .... Is 30:30
the **L**'s breath will come like .... Is 30:33
The **L** will stretch out his arm, ... Is 31:3
says wrong things about the **L**. .... Is 32:6
for the **L** is the greatest .... Is 33:6
There the **L** will be our Mighty .... Is 33:21
is because the **L** is our judge. .... Is 33:22
our judge. The **L** makes our laws. .... Is 33:22
The **L**'s sword will be covered................ Is 34:6
the angel of the **L** went out and .... Is 37:36
the wall and prayed to the **L**, ... Is 38:2
in the desert the way for the **L**. .... Is 40:3
glory of the **L** will be shown, ... Is 40:5
breath of the **L** blows on them. .... Is 40:7
the mind of the **L** or been able .... Is 40:13
The **L** does not see what happens .... Is 40:27
The **L** is the God who lives .... Is 40:28
who trust the **L** will become .... Is 40:31
I, the **L**, am the one. I .... Is 41:4
I am the **L**. That is my name. I .... Is 42:8
Sing a new song to the **L**; .... Is 42:10
I myself am the **L**; I am the only............. Is 43:11
joy because the **L** did great.................... Is 44:23
The **L** saved the people of Jacob! .... Is 44:23
they will know I alone am the **L**. .... Is 45:6
I, the **L**, have created it. .... Is 45:8
The **L** says, "Family of Jacob, ... Is 48:1
The **L** has saved his servants, ... Is 48:20
for evil people," says the **L**.................... Is 48:22
the **L** called me to serve him. .... Is 49:1
because the **L** comforts his .... Is 49:13
said, "The **L** has left me; .... Is 49:14
So the **L** will comfort Jerusalem; .... Is 51:3
lands like the garden of the **L**. .... Is 51:3
forgotten the **L** who made you, ... Is 51:13
The **L** was very angry with you; .... Is 51:17
own eyes when the **L** returns to .... Is 52:8
because the **L** has comforted his .... Is 52:9
The **L** will show his holy power .... Is 52:10
Who saw the **L**'s power in this? .... Is 53:1
But the **L** has put on him the .... Is 53:6
But it was the **L** who decided to .... Is 53:10
The **L** made his life a penalty .... Is 53:10
look for the **L** before it is too .... Is 55:6

L

return to the L so he may have .... Is 55:7
think this is what the L wants? .... Is 58:5
call out, and the L will answer. .... Is 58:9
honor it as the L's holy day. .... Is 58:13
Then you will find joy in the L, ... Is 58:14
from the west will fear the L, ... Is 59:19
glory of the L shines on you. .... Is 60:1
will call you The City of the L, ... Is 60:14
because the L has appointed me .... Is 61:1
time when the L will show his .... Is 61:2
planted by the L to show his .... Is 61:3
will be called priests of the L .... Is 61:6
The L has made a promise, and by .... Is 62:8
the Saved People of the L, ... Is 62:12
will tell about the L's kindness .... Is 63:7
recognize us. L, you are our .... Is 63:16
who obey the words of the L, ... Is 66:5
L is coming with fire and his .... Is 66:15
The L will judge the people with .... Is 66:16
The L spoke his word to me, ... Je 1:4
the L said to me, "Don't say, ... Je 1:7
you to protect you," says the L. .... Je 1:8
Then the L reached out his hand .... Je 1:9
you to protect you!" says the L. .... Je 1:19
of Israel were holy to the L, ... Je 2:3
turn away from the L your God. .... Je 2:19
to come back to me?" says the L. .... Je 3:1
Jerusalem The Throne of the L, ... Je 3:17
sinned against the L our God, ... Je 3:25
anger of the L has not turned .... Je 4:8
happens," says the L, "the king .... Je 4:9
have lied about the L and said, ... Je 5:12
are afraid of me," says the L. .... Je 5:22
I am full of the anger of the L, ... Je 6:11
This is the Temple of the L. .... Je 7:4
because the L has rejected these .... Je 7:29
coming, says the L, when people .... Je 7:32
when I punish them, says the L. .... Je 8:12
We have sinned against the L, ... Je 8:14
not know who I am," says the L. .... Je 9:3
Let them brag that I am the L, ... Je 9:24
pleases me," says the L. .... Je 9:24
But the L is the only true God. .... Je 10:10
The L showed me that people were .... Je 11:18
But, L All-Powerful, you are a .... Je 11:20
L, when I bring my case to you, ... Je 12:1
days later the L said to me, ... Je 13:6
I, the L, will give you peace in .... Je 14:13
you and save you," says the L. .... Je 15:20
This is what the L says: .... Je 17:5
trusts in the L will be blessed .... Je 17:7
The L will show him that he can .... Je 17:7
L, heal me, and I will truly be .... Je 17:14
you?" says the L. "You are in my .... Je 18:6
L All-Powerful, you test good .... Je 20:12
the towns the L destroyed .... Je 20:16
says the L, I swear by my own .... Je 22:5
agreement with the L their God. .... Je 22:9
means to know God," says the L. .... Je 22:16
Judah, hear the word of the L! .... Je 22:29
my people," says the L. .... Je 23:1
The L Does What Is Right. .... Je 23:6
or hear the message of the L .... Je 23:18
from the L will come like .... Je 23:19
wheat?" says the L. "If a .... Je 23:28
false dreams," says the L. .... Je 23:32
'This is a message from the L.' .... Je 23:34
'The L will roar from heaven and .... Je 25:30
because the L will accuse all .... Je 25:31
killed by the L will reach from .... Je 25:33
because the L is destroying. .... Je 25:36
because the L is very angry. .... Je 25:37
The L sent me to say everything .... Je 26:12

good and obey the L your God. .... Je 26:13
Let the L really do that! .... Je 28:6
May the L make the message you .... Je 28:6
as one truly sent by the L," .... Je 28:9
The L did not send you, and you .... Je 28:15
did not send them," says the L. .... Je 29:9
let you find me," says the L. .... Je 29:14
The L has given us prophets here .... Je 29:15
'May the L treat you like .... Je 29:22
'The L has made you priest in .... Je 29:26
the L says, I will soon punish .... Je 29:32
will serve the L their God and .... Je 30:9
be frightened," says the L. .... Je 30:10
It is a storm from the L! .... Je 30:23
far away the L appeared to his .... Je 31:3
This is what the L says: .... Je 31:15
coming," says the L, "when I .... Je 31:31
that agreement," says the L. .... Je 31:32
at that time," says the L: .... Je 31:33
and relatives to know the L, ... Je 31:34
These are the words of the L, ... Je 33:2
it order, whose name is the L: .... Je 33:2
The L Does What Is Right." .... Je 33:16
So this is what the L says: .... Je 34:17
give you eating to honor the L .... Je 36:9
messages from the L that were .... Je 36:11
there any message from the L?" .... Je 37:17
Obey the L by doing what I tell .... Je 38:20
Pray to the L your God for all .... Je 42:2
May the L be a true and loyal .... Je 42:5
You sent me to the L your God, ... Je 42:20
You sinned against the L. .... Je 44:23
here in Egypt,' says the L. ' .... Je 44:29
on all the people, says the L. .... Je 45:5
Sword of the L, how long will .... Je 47:6
and its arm broken!" says the L. .... Je 48:25
again to Moab," says the L. .... Je 48:47
one will defeat it," says the L. .... Je 49:31
and join themselves to the L. .... Je 50:5
people sinned against the L, ... Je 50:7
Because of the L's anger, no one .... Je 50:13
I commanded you!" says the L. .... Je 50:21
L has opened up his storeroom .... Je 50:25
Jerusalem how the L our God is .... Je 50:28
L says, "Let a sword kill .... Je 50:35
and never wake up!" says the L. .... Je 51:39
Run from the L's great anger. .... Je 51:45
to destroy Babylon," says the L. .... Je 51:48
set fire to the Temple of the L, ... Je 52:13
were in the Temple of the L. .... Je 52:17
She says, "L, see how I suffer, ... La 1:9
uproar in the L's Temple was .... La 2:7
teaching of the L has stopped, ... La 2:9
and I have no hope in the L." .... La 3:18
The L is good to those who hope .... La 3:25
done and then return to the L. .... La 3:40
until the L looks down and sees .... La 3:50
The L turned loose all of his .... La 4:11
But the L will punish the sins .... La 4:22
The L spoke his word to Ezekiel. .... Eze 1:3
to look like the glory of the L. .... Eze 1:28
I felt the great power of the L. .... Eze 3:14
you will know that I am the L. .... Eze 6:7
they will know that I am the L. .... Eze 6:10
that I am the L who punishes. .... Eze 7:9
save them from the L's anger. .... Eze 7:19
They say, 'The L doesn't see us. .... Eze 8:12
The L has left the land.' " .... Eze 8:12
entrance to the Temple of the L, ... Eze 8:16
people say, 'The L has left the .... Eze 9:9
Then the glory of the L went up .... Eze 10:4
the Spirit of the L entered me .... Eze 11:5
The glory of the L went up from .... Eze 11:23

battle on the L's day of judging .... Eze 13:5
actions that I hate, says the L. .... Eze 16:58
The L spoke his word to me, ... Eze 18:1
that I am the L who made them .... Eze 20:12
you will know that I am the L. .... Eze 20:42
Then you will know I am the L, ... Eze 20:44
see that I, the L, have started .... Eze 20:48
you will know that I am the L. .... Eze 25:5
the L's day of judging is near. .... Eze 30:3
the power of the L on me the .... Eze 33:22
I felt the power of the L on me, ... Eze 37:1
Spirit of the L and put me down .... Eze 37:1
bones, hear the word of the L. .... Eze 37:4
know that I, the L, have spoken .... Eze 37:14
they will know that I am the L.' .... Eze 38:23
they will know that I am the L. .... Eze 39:6
will know that I am the L, ... Eze 39:7
know that I am the L their God. .... Eze 39:22
I saw the L's glory filling. .... Eze 43:5
them in the presence of the L, ... Eze 43:24
the glory of the L filling the .... Eze 44:4
of the L on the Sabbaths. .... Eze 46:3
offer to the L on the Sabbath .... Eze 46:4
come into the L's presence at .... Eze 46:9
as a grain offering to the L. .... Eze 46:14
because it belongs to the L. .... Eze 48:14
city will be The L Is There." .... Eze 48:35
I saw that the L told Jeremiah .... Da 9:2
prayed to the L my God and told .... Da 9:4
things in my prayer to the L, ... Da 9:20
the L began speaking through .... Hos 1:2
I, the L their God, will save .... Hos 1:7
but she forgot me!" says the L. .... Hos 2:13
bride, and you will know the L. .... Hos 2:20
will speak to you," says the L. .... Hos 2:21
L said to me again, "Go, show .... Hos 3:1
will return to the L their God .... Hos 3:5
they will turn in fear to the L, ... Hos 3:5
listen to the L's message. .... Hos 4:1
The L has this against you who .... Hos 4:1
they do not know the L. .... Hos 5:4
Come, let's go back to the L. .... Hos 6:1
Let's try to learn about the L; .... Hos 6:3
L, give them what they should .... Hos 9:14
because we didn't honor the L. .... Hos 10:3
Look for the L until he comes .... Hos 10:12
It was the L God All-Powerful; .... Hos 12:5
But I am the L your God, who .... Hos 12:9
Later the L used a prophet to .... Hos 12:13
I, the L, have been your God .... Hos 13:4
to the L your God, because .... Hos 14:1
The L's ways are right. .... Hos 14:9
The L's day of judging is near, ... Joe 1:15
because the L's day of judging .... Joe 2:1
The priests, the L's servants, ... Joe 2:17
They should say, "L, have mercy .... Joe 2:17
because the L has done a .... Joe 2:21
and terrible day of the L comes. .... Joe 2:31
calls on the L will be saved, ... Joe 2:32
saved, just as the L has said. .... Joe 2:32
The L will roar like a lion from .... Joe 3:16
But the L will be a safe place .... Joe 3:16
Temple of the L and give water .... Joe 3:18
The L will roar from Jerusalem; .... Am 1:2
This is what the L says: .... Am 1:3
to a city, the L has caused it. .... Am 3:6
do what is right," says the L. .... Am 3:10
the garbage dump," says the L. .... Am 4:3
come back to me," says the L. .... Am 4:6
Come to the L and live, or he .... Am 5:6
Maybe the L God All-Powerful .... Am 5:15
who want the L's day of judging .... Am 5:18
So the L's day of judging will .... Am 5:20

says the L, whose name is .... Am 5:27
must not say the name of the L." .... Am 6:10
So the L changed his mind about .... Am 7:3
"It will not happen," said the L. .... Am 7:3
So the L changed his mind about .... Am 7:6
The L said to me, "Amos, what do .... Am 7:8
The L has sworn by his name, ... Am 8:7
run away from the L by going to .... Jnh 1:3
Tarshish to run away from the L. .... Jnh 1:3
But the L sent a great wind on .... Jnh 1:4
I fear the L, the God of heaven, ... Jnh 1:9
began to fear the L very much; .... Jnh 1:16
sacrifice to the L and made .... Jnh 1:16
The L caused a big fish to .... Jnh 1:17
prayed to the L his God and said .... Jnh 2:1
from the pit of death, L my God. .... Jnh 2:6
Salvation comes from the L!" .... Jnh 2:9
Then the L spoke to the fish, ... Jnh 2:10
The L made a plant grow quickly .... Jnh 4:6
L is coming out of his place; .... Mic 1:3
The L is becoming angry about .... Mic 2:7
Spirit of the L, and with .... Mic 3:8
But they lean on the L and say, ... Mic 3:11
go up to the mountain of the L, ... Mic 4:2
word of the L from that city. .... Mic 4:2
L will be their king in Mount .... Mic 4:7
know what the L is thinking; .... Mic 4:12
and give their wealth to the L, ... Mic 4:13
listen to the L's legal case. .... Mic 6:2
me when I come before the L, ... Mic 6:6
Will the L be pleased with a .... Mic 6:7
The L has told you, human, what .... Mic 6:8
the L will be a light for me. .... Mic 7:8
The L is a jealous God who .... Nah 1:2
The L does not become angry .... Nah 1:3
L, you live forever, my God, my .... Hab 1:12
The L is in his Holy Temple; .... Hab 2:20
I will still be glad in the L; .... Hab 3:18
that time I, the L, will search .... Zph 1:12
The L's day of judging is coming .... Zph 1:14
be very sad on the day of the L; .... Zph 1:14
Come to the L, all you who are .... Zph 2:3
The L your God is with you; .... Zph 3:17
The L stirred up Zerubbabel son .... Hag 1:14
The L was very angry with your .... Zch 1:2
Then the L's angel asked, ... Zch 1:12
So the L answered the angel who .... Zch 1:13
This is what the L All-Powerful .... Zch 1:17
the L showed me four craftsmen. .... Zch 1:20
join with the L and will become .... Zch 2:11
in the presence of the L. .... Zch 2:13
The L said to Satan, "The LORD .... Zch 3:2
to Satan, "The L says no to you, ... Zch 3:2
are the seven eyes of the L, ... Zch 4:10
this is what the L All-Powerful .... Zch 6:12
all these things," says the L. .... Zch 8:17
message is the word of the L. .... Zch 9:1
Ask the L for rain during the .... Zch 10:1
because I am the L their God, ... Zch 10:6
they will be happy in the L. .... Zch 10:7
will live as I say," says the L. .... Zch 10:12
The L said to me, "Throw the .... Zch 11:13
At that time the L will protect .... Zch 12:8
angel of the L in front of them. .... Zch 12:8
The L's day of judging is coming .... Zch 14:1
and the L knows when it will .... Zch 14:7
Then the L will be king over the .... Zch 14:9
time there will be only one L, ... Zch 14:9
HOLY TO THE L. The cooking pots .... Zch 14:20
The L said, "I have loved you." .... Mal 1:2
The L said, "Esau and Jacob .... Mal 1:2
respect the altar of the L. .... Mal 1:7
messenger of the L All-Powerful. .... Mal 2:7

L

tired the **L** with your words. .... Mal 2:17
The **L** All-Powerful says, "I will .... Mal 3:1
And the **L** will accept the .... Mal 3:4

LORDS
of all gods and Lord of all **l**. .... Dt 10:17
Give thanks to the Lord of **l**. .... Ps 136:3
there are many "gods" and "**l**" 1Co 8:5
authorities, **l**, and rulers. .... Col 1:16
all kings and the Lord of all **l**. 1Ti 6:15
he is Lord of **l** and King of .... Rev 17:14
KING OF KINGS AND LORD OF **L**. .... Rev 19:16

LOSE
don't want to **l** both of my sons .... Ge 27:45
of Canaan will **l** all their .... Ex 15:15
left alive will **l** their courage .... Le 26:36
has made you **l** your reward." .... Nu 24:11
So we will **l** some of our land. .... Nu 36:3
Don't **l** your courage or be .... Dt 20:3
cause others to **l** their courage, ... Dt 20:8
this city will **l** his oldest son, ... Jos 6:26
the gates will **l** his youngest .... Jos 6:26
I would **l** my strength and be as .... Jdg 16:17
other mothers **l** their children. 1Sa 15:33
Maybe I will **l** even more honor, ... 2Sa 6:22
s enemies to **l** all respect for 2Sa 12:14
would **l** his greatest leader. 2Sa 21:17
he will not **l** even a single hair 1Ki 1:52
three days would **l** his property .... Ezr 10:8
are starting to **l** power to .... Est 6:13
let my right hand **l** its skill. .... Ps 137:5
but the poor **l** all theirs. .... Pr 19:4
Foolish people **l** their tempers, ... Pr 29:11
They **l** it all in a bad deal and .... Ec 5:14
he will make them **l** their hair. .... Is 3:17
proud people to **l** their pride, ... Is 13:11
who weave linen will **l** hope. .... Is 19:9
wise men will **l** their wisdom; .... Is 29:14
he will not **l** hope or give up .... Is 42:4
be a widow or **l** my children.' .... Is 47:8
will **l** your children and your .... Is 47:9
officers will **l** their courage. .... Je 4:9
You will **l** the land I gave you, ... Je 17:4
they will **l** their riches. .... Je 17:11
Let their wives **l** their children .... Je 18:21
Don't **l** courage; rumors will .... Je 51:46
army, but he will **l** the battle, ... Da 11:11
but he will **l** his power. .... Da 11:19
Edom, will really **l** everything! .... Ob 1:6
The people **l** their courage, ... Nah 2:10
people gain while good people **l**; .... Hab 1:4
of it, you will **l** your lives. .... Hab 2:10
but then you **l** it all as if you .... Hag 1:6
the people of Ekron will **l** hope. .... Zch 9:5
His arm will **l** all its strength, ... Zch 11:17
It is better to **l** one part of .... Mt 5:29
It is better to **l** one part of .... Mt 5:30
world if they **l** their souls. .... Mt 16:26
for you to **l** part of your body .... Mt 18:8
time, many will **l** their faith, ... Mt 24:10
world if they **l** their souls. .... Mk 8:36
it made the boy **l** control of. .... Mk 9:20
for you to **l** part of your body .... Mk 9:43
for you to **l** part of your body .... Mk 9:45
It causes him to **l** control of .... Lk 9:39
and made him **l** control of .... Lk 9:42
so that when I **l** my job people .... Lk 16:4
to keep their lives will **l** them, ... Lk 17:33
always pray and never **l** hope. .... Lk 18:1
that you will not **l** your faith! .... Lk 22:32
I must not **l** even one whom God .... Jn 6:39
love their lives will **l** them, ... Jn 12:25
business will **l** its good name, ... Ac 19:27

None of you will **l** even one hair .... Ac 27:34
of Christ would not **l** its power. 1Co 1:17
the wise to **l** their wisdom; 1Co 1:19
So do not **l** the courage you had .... Heb 10:35
or be spoiled or **l** their beauty, ... 1Pe 1:4
that will never **l** its beauty. 1Pe 5:4
that you do not **l** everything you 2Jn 1:8

LOSES
When anyone **l** hair from his head .... Le 13:40
If he **l** hair from the front of .... Le 13:41
a river **l** its water and dries .... Job 14:11
olive tree that **l** its blossoms. .... Job 15:33
becomes hungry, he **l** his power. .... Is 44:12
if the salt **l** its salty taste .... Mt 5:13
if the salt **l** its salty taste .... Mk 9:50
but if it **l** its salty taste, ... Lk 14:34
hundred sheep but **l** one of them. .... Lk 15:4
has ten silver coins, but **l** one. .... Lk 15:8
but it really **l** its glory when 2Co 3:10

LOSING
'Absalom's followers are **l**!' 2Sa 17:9
is gone. I am **l** my sight. .... Ps 38:10
world, who are **l** their power. 1Co 2:6

LOSS
but made up for the **l** myself. .... Ge 31:39
man for the **l** of his time, ... Ex 21:19
owner of the animal for the **l**. .... Ex 21:34
pay back the **l** from the best .... Ex 22:5
the rental price covers the **l**. .... Ex 22:15
clean from her **l** of blood. .... Le 12:4
clean from her **l** of blood. .... Le 12:5
be clean from her **l** of blood. .... Le 12:7
If a woman has a **l** of blood for .... Le 15:25
to have a **l** of blood after her .... Le 15:25
not have all this trouble and **l**. .... Ac 27:21
and the Jews' **l** brought rich .... Rm 11:12
the builder will suffer **l**. 1Co 3:15

LOST
that had been **l** and then lie .... Le 6:3
But now we have **l** our appetite; .... Nu 11:6
head, and I have **l** my courage. .... Ps 40:12
I have wandered like a **l** sheep. .... Ps 119:176
felt when you **l** your husband. .... Is 54:4
people have been like **l** sheep. .... Je 50:6
search for the **l**, bring back .... Eze 34:16
of Israel, who are like **l** sheep. .... Mt 10:6
God sent me only to the **l** sheep, ... Mt 15:24
of Man came to save **l** people. .... Mt 18:11
and look for the **l** sheep until .... Lk 15:4
me because I found my **l** sheep.' .... Lk 15:6
I have found the coin that I **l**.' .... Lk 15:9
He was **l**, but now he is found!" .... Lk 15:24
was **l**, but now he is found.'" .... Lk 15:32
came to find **l** people and save .... Lk 19:10
believes in him may not be **l**, ... Jn 3:16
l so that the Scripture would .... Jn 17:12
I have not **l** any of the ones you .... Jn 18:9

LOT
for the LORD by throwing the **l**, ... Le 16:9
Pur (that is, the **l**) was thrown .... Est 3:7
that is, the **l**) to choose a day .... Est 9:24
from the word "Pur" (the **l**). .... Est 9:26
listen to me, you who know a **l**. .... Job 34:2
and Moab, the descendants of **L**. .... Ps 83:8
took a **l** of money with him and .... Pr 7:20
If you talk a **l**, you are sure to .... Pr 10:19
Whoever brags a **l** is asking for .... Pr 17:19
sleep a **l**, and idle people. .... Pr 19:15
with a quick temper sins a **l**. .... Pr 29:22
Does having a **l** of cedar in your .... Je 22:15
of Egypt is only a **l** of noise. .... Je 46:17

LOT'S (continued)

I in his right hand tells him..................... Eze 21:22
They cheat a l! Thieves break.................. Hos 7:1
I showed that the trouble had .... Jnh 1:7
was chosen by I to go into the .... Lk 1:9
can also be trusted with a l, ... Lk 16:10
a little is dishonest with a l. .... Lk 16:10
same as during the time of L. .... Lk 17:28
But the day L left Sodom, fire................. Lk 17:29
she earned a I of money for her .... Ac 16:16
that we make a I of money from............. Ac 19:25
I paid a I of money to become a .... Ac 22:28
there will be a I of trouble on .... Ac 27:10
who plants a I will have a big 2Co 9:6
he saved L from those cities. 2Pe 2:7
L, a good man, was troubled 2Pe 2:7
L was a good man, but because he........... 2Pe 2:8

LOT'S

herdsmen and L herdsmen began to .... Ge 13:7
of Sodom surrounded L house. .... Ge 19:4
that point L wife looked back. .... Ge 19:26
So God saved L life, but he.................... Ge 19:29
So both of L daughters became .... Ge 19:36
Remember L wife. .... Lk 17:32

LOTAN

L, Shobal, Zibeon, Anah, ... Ge 36:20
The sons of L were Hori and .... Ge 36:22
L, Shobal, Zibeon, Anah, ... Ge 36:29
sons were L, Shobal, Zibeon 1Ch 1:38

LOTAN'S

and Homam. (Timna was L sister.) .... Ge 36:22
L sons were Hori and Homam, ... 1Ch 1:39

LOTION

and don't put I on yourself..................... 2Sa 14:2

LOTIONS

himself, put I on, and changed 2Sa 12:20
and use the best perfumed I. .... Am 6:6

LOTS

will throw I for the two goats— .... Le 16:8
Joshua threw I in the presence .... Jos 18:10
they threw I for my clothing. .... Ps 22:18
Let's throw I to see who caused .... Jnh 1:7
they threw I to decide who would .... Mt 27:35
Then they used I to choose .... Ac 1:26
and the I showed that Matthias .... Ac 1:26

LOTUS

It lies under the I plants, ... Job 40:21
The I plants hide it in their .... Job 40:22

LOUD

he let out a I and bitter cry.................... Ge 27:34
Then Esau began to cry out I. .... Ge 27:38
There will be I outcries .... Ex 11:6
So there was a I outcry .... Ex 12:30
There was a very I blast from a .... Ex 19:16
people answered out I together, ... Ex 24:3
I sound will tell them to move. .... Nu 10:6
on the mountain in a I voice out .... Dt 5:22
people of Israel in a I voice: .... Dt 27:14
all the people give a I shout. .... Jos 6:5
-bye, they began to cry out I. .... Ru 1:9
cried together out I again. .... Ru 1:14
against them with I thunder. 1Sa 7:10
Then, in a I voice, he stood and 1Ki 8:55
shouting with a I voice and.................... 2Ch 15:14
of Israel, with very I voices. 2Ch 20:19
the LORD every day with I music. 2Ch 30:21
answered Ezra with a I voice, ... Ezr 10:12
the Teachings out I from early .... Ne 8:3
LORD their God with I voices. .... Ne 9:4
great sadness and I crying among .... Est 4:3
They fasted and cried out I, ... Est 4:3

LOUD (continued)

shout out I to the God of Jacob. .... Ps 81:1
The sound of the water is l;.................... Ps 93:4
Praise him with I cymbals; .... Ps 150:5
She was I and stubborn and never .... Pr 7:11
Foolishness is like a I woman; .... Pr 9:13
make people I and uncontrolled .... Pr 20:1
it is I like a young lion. .... Is 5:29
Listen to the I noise in the .... Is 13:4
Heshbon and Elealeh cry out I. .... Is 15:4
Shout out I the good news. .... Is 40:9
The LORD says, "Shout out I..................... Is 58:1
Shout out I like a trumpet. .... Is 58:1
Listen to the I noise coming .... Is 66:6
' Shout out I and say, 'Come .... Je 4:5
The sound of I crying is heard .... Je 9:19
I noise comes from the north to .... Je 10:22
Let him hear I crying in the .... Je 20:16
leaders! Cry out I! Roll around .... Je 25:34
the sound is I like the roaring .... Je 50:42
and making the I sounds of the .... Je 51:55
and I heard a I rumbling sound .... Eze 3:12
It was a I rumbling sound. .... Eze 3:13
shouted with a I voice in my .... Eze 9:1
and shouted with a I voice, ... Eze 11:13
And in their I crying they sing .... Eze 27:32
for the king said in a I voice, ... Da 3:4
of the altar, cry out I. .... Joe 1:13
his I voice will thunder from .... Joe 3:16
people to cry out I for them. .... Am 5:16
The sea made a I noise, and its .... Hab 3:10
and a I crash will echo from the .... Zph 1:10
He will use a I trumpet to send .... Mt 24:31
Jesus cried out in a I voice, ... Mt 27:46
out again in a I voice and died. .... Mt 27:50
violently, gave a I cry, and .... Mk 1:26
The man shouted in a I voice, ... Mk 5:7
Jesus cried in a I voice, ... Mk 15:34
cried in a I voice and died. .... Mk 15:37
She cried out in a I voice, ... Lk 1:42
spirit shouted in a I voice, ... Lk 4:33
He said with a I voice, "What do .... Lk 8:28
praising God in a I voice. .... Lk 17:15
Their yelling became so I that.................. Lk 23:23
Jesus cried out in a I voice, ... Lk 23:46
stood up and said in a I voice, ... Jn 7:37
he cried out in a I voice, ... Jn 11:43
and in a I voice he spoke to the .... Ac 2:14
knees and cried in a I voice, ... Ac 7:60
spirits made a I noise when they .... Ac 8:7
from heaven with a I command, ... 1Th 4:16
He prayed with I cries and tears.............. Heb 5:7
will disappear with a I noise. 2Pe 3:10
and I heard a I voice behind me .... Rev 1:10
angel calling in a I voice, ... Rev 5:2
saying in a I voice: "The Lamb .... Rev 5:12
souls shouted in a I voice, ... Rev 6:10
called out in a I voice to the .... Rev 7:2
They were shouting in a I voice, ... Rev 7:10
lightning, thunder and I noises, ... Rev 8:5
in the air cry out in a I voice, ... Rev 8:13
prophets heard a I voice from .... Rev 11:12
And there were I voices in .... Rev 11:15
Then I heard a I voice in heaven.............. Rev 12:10
Rev and like the sound of I thunder. .... Rev 14:2
He preached in a I voice, ... Rev 14:7
two angels, saying in a I voice: .... Rev 14:9
called out in a I voice to the .... Rev 14:15
Then I heard a I voice from the .... Rev 16:1
Then a I voice came out of the .... Rev 16:17
and like the noise of I thunder. .... Rev 19:6
he called with a I voice to all .... Rev 19:17
And I heard a I voice from the .... Rev 21:3

L

LOUDER

sound from the trumpet became l. .... Ex 19:19
of them. "Pray l!" he said. "If 1Ki 18:27
prophets prayed l, cutting 1Ki 18:28
they shouted l, "Crucify him!" .... Mt 27:23
But they shouted even l, ... Mk 15:14

LOUDLY

Joseph cried so l that the .... Ge 45:2
they cried l and bitterly for..................... Ge 50:10
may cry l about the LORD burning .... Le 10:6
When you l blow the trumpets, ... Nu 10:5
When you l blow them again, ... Nu 10:6
but don't blow them as l. .... Nu 10:7
own land, blow the trumpets l. .... Nu 10:9
in the camp began crying l. .... Nu 14:1
from the LORD, they cried l. .... Jdg 2:4
God until evening, crying l. .... Jdg 21:2
all the people in town cried l. 1Sa 4:13
of Ekron cried l to heaven. 1Sa 5:12
people the news, they cried l. 1Sa 11:4
David my son?" And he cried l. 1Sa 24:16
his army cried l until they were 1Sa 30:4
Then she went away, crying l. 2Sa 13:19
king's sons arrived, crying l. 2Sa 13:36
the people cried l as everyone 2Sa 15:23
covered his face and cried l, ... 2Sa 19:4
and shouted l in the Hebrew 2Ki 18:28
Then Hezekiah cried l. 2Ki 20:3
then all the people shouted l, ... Ezr 3:11
him who were also crying l. .... Ezr 10:1
wives complained l against their .... Ne 5:1
the city crying l and painfully. .... Est 4:1
people should fast and cry l. .... Est 9:31
began to cry l and tore their .... Job 2:12
our God; I sing his praise .... Ps 66:8
If you l greet your neighbor .... Pr 27:14
squares, they are crying l. .... Is 15:3
me. Let me cry l. Don't hurry to .... Is 22:4
to bring peace are weeping l. .... Is 33:7
and shouted l in the Hebrew .... Is 36:13
Then Hezekiah cried l. .... Is 38:3
night l cried l. Like a lion, he .... Is 38:13
yell or speak l in the streets. .... Is 42:2
You will cry l, because your .... Is 65:14
show how sad you are, and cry l. .... Je 4:8
people in the land will cry l, ... Je 4:28
Cry l for those who are dead, ... Je 6:26
I cry l and am afraid for them. .... Je 8:21
will cry l for the mountains and .... Je 9:10
come quickly and cry l for us. .... Je 9:18
your daughters how to cry l. .... Je 9:20
He will roar l against his land. .... Je 25:30
leaders of the people crying l, ... Je 25:36
of Luhith, crying l as they go. .... Je 48:5
to show your sadness, and cry l............. Je 49:3
She cries l at night, and tears .... La 1:2
be sad or cry l for her or shed .... Eze 24:16
do not cry l for the dead. .... Eze 24:17
You must not cry l, but you must .... Eze 24:23
They cry l about you; .... Eze 27:30
cry and sob for you; they cry l. .... Eze 27:31
I made the deep springs cry l. .... Eze 31:15
He spoke very l and said, ' .... Da 4:14
Cry l, you who grow grapes. .... Joe 1:11
and people should cry l to God. .... Jnh 3:8
I will cry l like the wild dogs .... Mic 1:8
Now, why do you cry so l? .... Mic 4:9
lots of noise and crying l. .... Mk 5:38
they shouted l and covered their .... Ac 7:57
Stephen and cried l for him. .... Ac 8:2
Festus said l, "Paul, you are .... Ac 26:24
earth will cry l because of him. .... Rev 1:7

Then he shouted l like the .... Rev 10:3
they cried out l, "There was .... Rev 18:18

LOVE

Isaac, the son you l, and go to .... Ge 22:2
prepare the tasty food that I l, ... Ge 27:4
now my husband will l me." .... Ge 29:32
Shechem fell in l with Dinah, ... Ge 34:3
is deeply in l with Dinah. .... Ge 34:8
to him, "If you l me, put your .... Ge 47:29
thousands who l me and obey my .... Ex 20:6
slave says, 'I l my master, my .... Ex 21:5
who has great l and faithfulness............. Ex 34:6
L your neighbor as you love .... Le 19:18
your neighbor as you l yourself.............. Le 19:18
L foreigners as you love .... Le 19:34
foreigners as you l yourselves, ... Le 19:34
quickly, but he has great l. .... Nu 14:18
By your great l, forgive these .... Nu 14:19
to those who l me and obey my .... Dt 5:10
L the LORD your God with all .... Dt 6:5
agreement of l for a thousand................ Dt 7:9
people who l him and obey his .... Dt 7:9
agreement and show his l to you, ... Dt 7:12
He will l and bless you. .... Dt 7:13
told you to do. L him. Serve the .... Dt 10:12
You also must l foreigners, ... Dt 10:19
L the LORD your God and always .... Dt 11:1
today and l the LORD your God .... Dt 11:13
to follow, and l the LORD your .... Dt 11:22
find out if you l him with your .... Dt 13:3
the wife you l, or a close .... Dt 13:6
to the wife he does not l,........................ Dt 21:15
son of the wife he does not l. .... Dt 21:16
is from the wife he does not l. .... Dt 21:17
descendants to l him with your .... Dt 30:6
today to l the LORD your God, ... Dt 30:16
life is to l the LORD your God .... Dt 30:20
Urim belong to Levi, whom you l. .... Dt 33:8
to l the LORD your God and obey .... Jos 22:5
be careful to l the LORD your................ Jos 23:11
L the LORD, the God of Israel, ... Jos 24:23
people who l you be as strong .... Jdg 5:31
don't really l me! You told my .... Jdg 14:16
Samson fell in l with a woman .... Jdg 16:4
can you say, 'I l you,' when you .... Jdg 16:15
His servants l you. You should 1Sa 18:22
repeat this promise of l for him, ... 1Sa 20:17
Your l to me was wonderful, ... 2Sa 1:26
better than the l of women. 2Sa 1:26
I took away my l from Saul, ... 2Sa 7:15
told him, "I l Tamar, the sister 2Sa 13:4
because you l those who hate 2Sa 19:6
and you hate those who l you. 2Sa 19:6
child was full of l for her son................. 1Ki 3:26
your agreement of l with your 1Ki 8:23
LORD has constant l for Israel, ... 1Ki 10:9
fell in l with these women. 1Ki 11:2
because of my l for your father 1Ki 11:12
The strong l of the LORD 2Ki 19:31
His l continues forever. 1Ch 16:34
because his l continues forever. 1Ch 16:41
I took away my l from Saul, ... 1Ch 17:13
his l continues forever." 2Ch 5:13
your agreement of l with your 2Ch 6:14
Remember your l for your servant 2Ch 6:42
his l continues forever." 2Ch 7:3
"His l continues forever." 2Ch 7:6
always watch over it and l it. 2Ch 7:16
Why do you l those who hate the 2Ch 19:2
his l continues forever." 2Ch 20:21
Hezekiah's l for God and the 2Ch 32:32
l for Israel continues forever. .... Ezr 3:11

his I in the presence of the .... Ezr 7:28
with those who I you and obey .... Ne 1:5
servants who I to honor you. .... Ne 1:11
quickly, and you have great I. .... Ne 9:17
You keep your agreement of I. .... Ne 9:32
not ignore my I for the Temple .... Ne 13:14
on me because of your great I. .... Ne 13:22
even those I I have turned .... Job 19:19
water his earth and show his I. .... Job 37:13
They I the LORD's teachings, ... Ps 1:2
long will you I what is false .... Ps 4:2
of your great I, I can come into .... Ps 5:7
those who I you and who are .... Ps 5:11
and those who I to hurt others. .... Ps 11:5
I trust in your I. My heart is .... Ps 13:5
Your I is wonderful. By your .... Ps 17:7
I I you, LORD. You are my .... Ps 18:1
goodness and I will be with me .... Ps 23:6
your mercy and I that you have .... Ps 25:6
But remember to I me always .... Ps 25:7
I see your I, and I live by your .... Ps 26:3
I I the Temple where you live, ... Ps 26:8
be glad and rejoice in your I, ... Ps 31:7
Save me because of your I. .... Ps 31:16
His I to me was wonderful when .... Ps 31:21
L the LORD, all you who belong .... Ps 31:23
but the LORD's I surrounds those .... Ps 32:10
the LORD's I fills the earth. .... Ps 33:5
who put their hope in his I. .... Ps 33:18
show your I to us as we put our .... Ps 33:22
your I reaches to the heavens, ... Ps 36:5
God, your I is so precious! .... Ps 36:7
Continue to I those who know you .... Ps 36:10
a moth, you destroy what they I. .... Ps 39:11
I do not hide your I and truth .... Ps 40:10
let your I and truth always .... Ps 40:11
They I you for saving them. .... Ps 40:16
LORD shows his true I every day. .... Ps 42:8
Because of your I, save us. .... Ps 44:26
A I song of the sons of Korah. .... Ps 44:26
You I right and hate evil, ... Ps 45:7
Temple think about your I. .... Ps 48:9
God's I will continue forever. .... Ps 52:1
You I wrong more than right and .... Ps 52:3
I words that bite and tongues .... Ps 52:4
trust God's I forever and ever. .... Ps 52:8
God sends me his I and truth. .... Ps 57:3
Your great I reaches to the .... Ps 57:10
I will sing about your I. .... Ps 59:16
the people you I will be rescued .... Ps 60:5
him with your I and truth. .... Ps 61:7
Because your I is better than .... Ps 63:3
or hold back his I from me. .... Ps 66:20
those nations that I war. .... Ps 68:30
My strong I for your Temple .... Ps 69:9
of your great I, answer me. .... Ps 69:13
me because your I is so good. .... Ps 69:16
and those who I him will live .... Ps 69:36
Let those who I your salvation .... Ps 70:4
Is his I gone forever? Has he .... Ps 77:8
they plot against those you I. .... Ps 83:3
show us your I, and save us. .... Ps 85:7
L and truth belong to God's .... Ps 85:10
and have great I for those who .... Ps 86:5
You have great I for me. .... Ps 86:13
You have great I and .... Ps 86:15
your I be told in the grave? .... Ps 88:11
always sing about the LORD's I; .... Ps 89:1
Your I continues forever; .... Ps 89:2
L and truth are in all you do. .... Ps 89:14
My loyalty and I will be with .... Ps 89:24
I will watch over him forever, ... Ps 89:28
not hold back my I from David, ... Ps 89:33

where is your I from times past, ... Ps 89:49
us with your I every morning. .... Ps 90:14
to tell of your I in the morning .... Ps 92:2
but, LORD, your I kept me safe. .... Ps 94:18
People who I the LORD hate evil. .... Ps 97:10
remembered his I and his loyalty .... Ps 98:3
I is forever, and his loyalty .... Ps 100:5
sing of your I and fairness; .... Ps 101:1
Your servants I even her stones; .... Ps 102:14
and loads me with I and mercy. .... Ps 103:4
quickly, and he has great I. .... Ps 103:8
so great is his I for those who .... Ps 103:11
But the LORD's I for those who .... Ps 103:17
His I continues forever. .... Ps 106:1
for them because of his great I. .... Ps 106:45
His I continues forever. .... Ps 107:1
the LORD for his I and for the .... Ps 107:8
the LORD for his I and for the .... Ps 107:15
the LORD for his I and for the .... Ps 107:21
the LORD for his I and for the .... Ps 107:31
think about the I of the LORD. .... Ps 107:43
Your great I reaches to the .... Ps 108:4
the people you I will be rescued .... Ps 108:6
no one show him I or have mercy .... Ps 109:12
Because your I is good, save me. .... Ps 109:21
because of your I and loyalty. .... Ps 115:1
I I the LORD, because he listens .... Ps 116:1
His I continues forever. .... Ps 118:1
"His I continues forever." .... Ps 118:2
"His I continues forever." .... Ps 118:3
"His I continues forever." .... Ps 118:4
His I continues forever. .... Ps 118:29
show me your I, and save me as .... Ps 119:41
your commands, which I I. .... Ps 119:47
commands, which I I, and I think .... Ps 119:48
LORD, your I fills the earth. .... Ps 119:64
but I I your teachings. .... Ps 119:70
me with your I, as you promised. .... Ps 119:76
I may live. I I your teachings. .... Ps 119:77
me life by your I so I can obey .... Ps 119:88
How I I your teachings! .... Ps 119:97
people, but I I your teachings. .... Ps 119:113
So I will I your rules. .... Ps 119:119
Show your I to me, your servant, ... Ps 119:124
I I your commands more than the .... Ps 119:127
as you do for those who I you. .... Ps 119:132
so I, your servant, I them. .... Ps 119:143
misery, but I I your commands. .... Ps 119:143
Listen to me because of your I; .... Ps 119:149
Those who I evil are near, ... Ps 119:150
See how I I your orders. .... Ps 119:159
LORD, give me life by your I. .... Ps 119:159
lies, but I I your teachings. .... Ps 119:163
Those who I your teachings will .... Ps 119:165
rules, and I I them very much. .... Ps 119:167
me, LORD. I I your teachings. .... Ps 119:174
May those who I her be safe. .... Ps 122:6
His I continues forever. .... Ps 136:1
His I continues forever. .... Ps 136:2
His I continues forever. .... Ps 136:3
His I continues forever. .... Ps 136:4
His I continues forever. .... Ps 136:5
His I continues forever. .... Ps 136:6
His I continues forever. .... Ps 136:7
His I continues forever. .... Ps 136:8
His I continues forever. .... Ps 136:9
His I continues forever. .... Ps 136:10
His I continues forever. .... Ps 136:11
His I continues forever. .... Ps 136:12
His I continues forever. .... Ps 136:13
His I continues forever. .... Ps 136:14
His I continues forever. .... Ps 136:15
His I continues forever. .... Ps 136:16

L

His l continues forever. .... Ps 136:17
His l continues forever. .... Ps 136:18
His l continues forever. .... Ps 136:19
His l continues forever. .... Ps 136:20
His l continues forever. .... Ps 136:21
His l continues forever. .... Ps 136:22
His l continues forever. .... Ps 136:23
His l continues forever. .... Ps 136:24
His l continues forever. .... Ps 136:25
His l continues forever. .... Ps 136:26
you for your l and loyalty. .... Ps 138:2
LORD, your l continues forever. .... Ps 138:8
me in the morning about your l, ... Ps 143:8
In your l defeat my enemies. .... Ps 143:12
angry quickly but is full of l. .... Ps 145:8
with those who trust his l. .... Ps 147:11
L it, and it will keep you safe. .... Pr 4:6
don't give your l to just any .... Pr 5:16
Let her l always make you happy; .... Pr 5:19
let her l always hold you........................ Pr 5:19
let's make l until morning. .... Pr 7:18
Let's enjoy each other's l. .... Pr 7:18
I l those who love me, and those .... Pr 8:17
I love those who l me, and those .... Pr 8:17
I give wealth to those who l me, ... Pr 8:21
Those who hate me l death." .... Pr 8:36
the wise, and they will l you. .... Pr 9:8
but l forgives all wrongs. .... Pr 10:12
you don't l them, but if you.................... Pr 13:24
but if you l your children, ... Pr 13:24
with those who l you than to eat .... Pr 15:17
L and truth bring forgiveness of.............. Pr 16:6
and those who l learning will .... Pr 19:8
wicked people l what is evil. .... Pr 19:28
If you l to sleep, you will be .... Pr 20:13
than to have l and not show it. .... Pr 27:5
Those who l wisdom make their............. Pr 29:3
way a man and a woman fall in l. .... Pr 30:19
is a time to l and a time to .... Ec 3:8
busy with what they l to do. .... Ec 5:20
Their l is like a net, and their .... Ec 7:26
they will experience l or hate.................. Ec 9:1
can no longer l or hate or envy. .... Ec 9:6
Enjoy life with the wife you l.................. Ec 9:9
because your l is better than .... Sng 1:2
why the young women l you. .... Sng 1:3
we praise your l more than wine. .... Sng 1:4
reason, the young women l you............... Sng 1:4
me, you whom I l, where do you.............. Sng 1:7
and his banner over me is l. .... Sng 2:4
because I am weak with l. .... Sng 2:5
my feelings of l until it is .... Sng 2:7
bed, I looked for the one I l; .... Sng 3:1
looking for the one I l. .... Sng 3:2
"Have you seen the one I l?" .... Sng 3:3
left them, I found the one I l. .... Sng 3:4
my feelings of l until it is .... Sng 3:5
women of Jerusalem wove with l. .... Sng 3:10
Your l is so sweet, my sister, ... Sng 4:10
Your l is better than wine, ... Sng 4:10
tell him I am weak with l. .... Sng 5:8
my l, you are full of delights. .... Sng 7:6
There I will give you my l. .... Sng 7:12
my feelings of l until it is .... Sng 8:4
L is as strong as death; .... Sng 8:6
L bursts into flames and burns .... Sng 8:6
cannot put out the flame of l; .... Sng 8:7
cannot drown l. If a man offered .... Sng 8:7
everything in his house for l, ... Sng 8:7
of his strong l for his people. .... Is 9:7
your strong l for your people .... Is 26:11
donkeys will l to live there,.................... Is 32:14
The strong l of the LORD .... Is 37:32

Because you l me very much, ... Is 38:17
I give you honor and I you, ... Is 43:4
but my l will never disappear; .... Is 54:10
LORD to worship him and l him, ... Is 56:6
down and dream and l to sleep. .... Is 56:10
with those whose beds you l, ... Is 57:8
in the coat of his strong l. .... Is 59:17
I, the LORD, l justice. .... Is 61:8
Because I l Jerusalem, I will .... Is 62:1
Because of his l and kindness, ... Is 63:9
is your strong l and power? .... Is 63:15
keeping your l and mercy from .... Is 63:15
and they l the terrible things .... Is 66:3
All you people who l Jerusalem,.............. Is 66:10
I l those other gods, and I must .... Je 2:25
know how to chase after l. .... Je 2:33
and my people l it this way. .... Je 5:31
the people I l over to their .... Je 12:7
They really l to wander from me; .... Je 14:10
my blessing, my l, and my pity .... Je 16:5
I l you people with a love that .... Je 31:3
people with a l that will last .... Je 31:3
is my dear son, The child I l. .... Je 31:20
I l him very much, and I want to .... Je 31:20
You show l and kindness to .... Je 32:18
His l continues forever!' .... Je 33:11
The LORD's l never ends; .... La 3:22
he also has mercy and great l. .... La 3:32
that you were old enough for l. .... Eze 16:8
the woman you look at with l. .... Eze 24:16
at it with l and tenderness. .... Eze 24:21
look at it with l, and it makes .... Eze 24:25
mouths they tell me they l me, ... Eze 33:31
singer who sings l songs and has .... Eze 33:32
agreement of l with all who love .... Da 9:4
with all who l you and obey your .... Da 9:4
own people who l to fight will .... Da 11:14
I will show you my l and mercy............... Hos 2:19
show your l to a woman loved by .... Hos 3:1
other gods and l to eat the .... Hos 3:1
they l these disgraceful ways.................... Hos 4:18
I want faithful l more than l .... Hos 6:6
You l the pay of prostitutes on .... Hos 9:1
I will no longer l them; .... Hos 9:15
will kill the children they l." .... Hos 9:16
human kindness, with ropes of l. .... Hos 11:4
and my l for you stirs up my .... Hos 11:8
l him, do what is just, and .... Hos 12:6
me and will l them freely, ... Hos 14:4
quickly, and he has great l....................... Joe 2:13
this is what you l to do, ... Am 4:5
Hate evil and l good; be fair in .... Am 5:15
quickly, and you have great l.................. Jnh 4:2
are sad for the children you l.................... Mic 1:16
but you hate good and l evil. .... Mic 3:2
to other people, l being kind to .... Mic 6:8
none of the early figs I l......................... Mic 7:1
You will rest in his l; .... Zph 3:17
'I have a strong l for Jerusalem. .... Zch 1:14
a very strong l for Jerusalem. .... Zch 8:2
My strong l for her is like a .... Zch 8:2
and don't l false promises. .... Zch 8:17
But you must l truth and peace." .... Zch 8:19
help parents l their children .... Mal 4:6
and children l their parents. .... Mal 4:6
my Son, whom I l, and I am very .... Mt 3:17
'L your neighbor and hate your .... Mt 5:43
I say to you, l your enemies. .... Mt 5:44
you l only the people who love .... Mt 5:46
love only the people who l you, ... Mt 5:46
l to stand in the synagogues .... Mt 6:5
hate one master and l the other,.............. Mt 6:24
Those who l their father or .... Mt 10:37

more than they l me are not .... Mt 10:37
who l their son or daughter .... Mt 10:37
more than they l me are not .... Mt 10:37
I l him, and I am pleased with .... Mt 12:18
my Son, whom I l, and I am very .... Mt 17:5
and l your neighbor as you love .... Mt 19:19
neighbor as you l yourself.'" .... Mt 19:19
non-Jewish people l to show .... Mt 20:25
leaders l to use all their .... Mt 20:25
L the Lord your God with all .... Mt 22:37
'L your neighbor as you love .... Mt 22:39
neighbor as you l yourself.' .... Mt 22:39
of the law l to have the most .... Mt 23:6
They l people to greet them with .... Mt 23:7
l to have people call them ' .... Mt 23:7
showing their l for each other. .... Mt 24:12
my Son, whom I l, and I am very .... Mk 1:11
This is my Son, whom I l. .... Mk 9:7
those rulers l to show their .... Mk 10:42
leaders l to use all their .... Mk 10:42
L the Lord your God with all .... Mk 12:30
'L your neighbor as you love .... Mk 12:31
neighbor as you l yourself.' .... Mk 12:31
One must l God with all his .... Mk 12:33
And one must l his neighbor as .... Mk 12:33
and they l for people to greet .... Mk 12:38
l to have the most important .... Mk 12:39
my Son, whom I l, and I am very .... Lk 3:22
are listening, l your enemies. .... Lk 6:27
you l only the people who love .... Lk 6:32
love only the people who l you, ... Lk 6:32
Even sinners l the people who .... Lk 6:32
love the people who l them. .... Lk 6:32
But l your enemies, do good to .... Lk 6:35
person will l the banker more? .... Lk 7:42
forgiven, so she showed great l. .... Lk 7:47
a little will l only a little." .... Lk 7:47
L the Lord your God with all .... Lk 10:27
L your neighbor as you love .... Lk 10:27
neighbor as you l yourself." .... Lk 10:27
be fair to others and to l God. .... Lk 11:42
because you l to have the most .... Lk 11:43
and you l to be greeted with .... Lk 11:43
hate one master and l the other, ... Lk 16:13
I will send my son whom I l. .... Lk 20:13
and they l for people to greet .... Lk 20:46
l to have the most important .... Lk 20:46
My strong l for your Temple .... Jn 2:17
you don't have God's l in you. .... Jn 5:42
Father, you would l me, because .... Jn 8:42
Lord, the one you l is sick." .... Jn 11:3
Those who l their lives will.................... Jn 12:25
a new command: L each other. You .... Jn 13:34
You must l each other as I have .... Jn 13:34
followers if you l each other." .... Jn 13:35
If you l me, you will obey my .... Jn 14:15
obey them are the ones who l me, ... Jn 14:21
my Father will l those who love .... Jn 14:21
Father will love those who l me. .... Jn 14:21
I will l them and will show .... Jn 14:21
If people l me, they will obey .... Jn 14:23
My Father will l them, and we .... Jn 14:23
Those who do not l me do not .... Jn 14:24
must know that I l the Father, ... Jn 14:31
loved me. Now remain in my l. .... Jn 15:9
commands, and I remain in his l. .... Jn 15:10
you will remain in my l. .... Jn 15:10
L each other as I have loved you. .... Jn 15:12
The greatest l a person can show .... Jn 15:13
is my command: L each other. .... Jn 15:17
it would l you as it loves its .... Jn 15:19
have the same l that you have................. Jn 17:26
do you l me more than these?" .... Jn 21:15

Lord, you know that I l you." .... Jn 21:15
Simon son of John, do you l me?" .... Jn 21:16
Lord, you know that I l you." .... Jn 21:16
Simon son of John, do you l me?" .... Jn 21:17
the third time, "Do you l me?" .... Jn 21:17
you know that I l you!" .... Jn 21:17
God showed his l for those .... Ac 15:14
poured out his l to fill our .... Rm 5:5
gave us his l through the Holy .... Rm 5:5
shows his great l for us in this .... Rm 5:8
for the good of those who l him. .... Rm 8:28
us from the l Christ has for us? .... Rm 8:35
God who showed his l for us. .... Rm 8:37
us from the l of God that is .... Rm 8:39
I will show my l to those people .... Rm 9:25
to those people I did not l." .... Rm 9:25
Your l must be real. Hate what .... Rm 12:9
L each other like brothers and .... Rm 12:10
always owe l to each other, ... Rm 13:8
L your neighbor as you love .... Rm 13:9
neighbor as you l yourself." .... Rm 13:9
L never hurts a neighbor, so .... Rm 13:10
really following the way of l. .... Rm 14:15
Jesus and the l that the Holy .... Rm 15:30
prepared for those who l him." 1Co 2:9
I l Timothy, and he is faithful. 1Co 4:17
or with l and gentleness? 1Co 4:21
up with pride, but l builds up. 1Co 8:1
if I do not have l, I am only a 1Co 13:1
if I do not have l, then I am 1Co 13:2
gain nothing if I do not have l. 1Co 13:3
L is patient and kind. Love is 1Co 13:4
L is not jealous, it does not 1Co 13:4
L is not rude, is not selfish, ... 1Co 13:5
L does not count up wrongs that 1Co 13:5
L takes no pleasure in evil but 1Co 13:6
L patiently accepts all things. 1Co 13:7
L never ends. There are gifts of 1Co 13:8
faith, hope, and l. And the 1Co 13:13
And the greatest of these is l. 1Co 13:13
seek after l, and you should 1Co 14:1
Do everything in l. 1Co 16:14
If anyone does not l the Lord, ... 1Co 16:22
l be with all of you in Christ 1Co 16:24
let you know how much I l you. 2Co 2:4
beg you to show that you l him. 2Co 2:8
The l of Christ controls us, ... 2Co 5:14
by the Holy Spirit, by true l, ... 2Co 6:6
Our feelings of l for you have 2Co 6:12
your feelings of l for us. 2Co 6:12
before that we l you so much we 2Co 7:3
And his l for you is stronger 2Co 7:15
in the l you learned from us. 2Co 8:7
want to see if your l is true by 2Co 8:8
Titus the same l for you that I 2Co 8:16
proof of your l and the reason 2Co 8:24
it is because I do not l you? 2Co 11:11
God knows that I l you. 2Co 11:11
I l you more, will you love me 2Co 12:15
you more, will you l me less? 2Co 12:15
Then the God of l and peace will 2Co 13:11
Lord Jesus Christ, the l of God, ... 2Co 13:14
of faith that works through l. .... Gal 5:6
Serve each other with l. .... Gal 5:13
L your neighbor as you love .... Gal 5:14
neighbor as you l yourself." .... Gal 5:14
Spirit produces the fruit of l, ... Gal 5:22
of his l, God had already. .... Eph 1:5
Jesus and your l for all God's .... Eph 1:15
will be strong in l and be built .... Eph 3:17
in love and be built on l. .... Eph 3:17
the greatness of Christ's l— .... Eph 3:18
how high and how deep that l is. .... Eph 3:18

Christ's l is greater than .... Eph 3:19
you will be able to know that l. .... Eph 3:19
accepting each other in l. .... Eph 4:2
Speaking the truth with l, ... Eph 4:15
body grow and be strong with l. .... Eph 4:16
Live a life of l just as Christ .... Eph 5:2
l your wives as Christ loved the .... Eph 5:25
husbands should l their wives as .... Eph 5:28
as they l their own bodies. .... Eph 5:28
one of you must l his wife as he .... Eph 5:33
brother whom we l and a faithful .... Eph 6:21
Peace and l with faith to you .... Eph 6:23
all of you who l our Lord Jesus .... Eph 6:24
Christ with l that never ends .... Eph 6:24
because I l all of you with the .... Php 1:8
you with the l of Christ Jesus .... Php 1:8
that your l will grow more and .... Php 1:9
and understanding with your l; .... Php 1:9
They preach because they have l, ... Php 1:16
Does his l comfort you? .... Php 2:1
the same l, and having one .... Php 2:2
I l you and want to see you. .... Php 4:1
Jesus and the l you have for all .... Col 1:4
this faith and l because of your .... Col 1:5
grace from Epaphras, whom we l. .... Col 1:7
us about the l you have from .... Col 1:8
together with l so that they may .... Col 2:2
all this, clothe yourself in l. .... Col 3:14
L is what holds you all together .... Col 3:14
l your wives and be gentle with .... Col 3:19
you have done because of your l. 1Th 1:3
news about your faith and l. 1Th 3:6
the Lord make your l grow more 1Th 3:12
so that you will l others as we 1Th 3:12
will love others as we l you. 1Th 3:12
you about having l for your 1Th 4:9
taught you to l each other. 1Th 4:9
truly you do l the Christians 1Th 4:10
you to l them even more. 1Th 4:10
wear faith and l to protect us,.............. 1Th 5:8
a very special l because of the 1Th 5:13
and the l that every one of you 2Th 1:3
they refused to l the truth. 2Th 2:10
hearts into God's l and Christ's 2Th 3:5
command is for people to have l, ... 1Ti 1:5
a l that comes from a pure heart 1Ti 1:5
the faith and l that are in 1Ti 1:14
in faith, l, and holiness, with 1Ti 2:15
actions, your l, your faith, ... 1Ti 4:12
are helping believers they l. 1Ti 6:2
but is sick with a l for arguing 1Ti 6:4
The l of money causes all kinds 1Ti 6:10
God, have faith, l, patience, ... 1Ti 6:11
of power and l and self-control. 2Ti 1:7
heard from me in faith and l, ... 2Ti 1:13
and to have faith, l, and peace, ... 2Ti 2:22
people will l themselves,....................... 2Ti 3:2
love themselves, l money, brag, ... 2Ti 3:2
They will not l others, will 2Ti 3:3
will l pleasure instead of God, ... 2Ti 3:4
my goal, faith, patience, and l. 2Ti 3:10
waited with l for him to come................ 2Ti 4:8
welcome guests, l what is good, ... Tit 1:8
in faith, in l, and in patience. .... Tit 2:2
young women to l their husbands, ... Tit 2:4
husbands, to l their children, ... Tit 2:4
the kindness and l of God our .... Tit 3:4
those who l us in the faith .... Tit 3:15
hear about the l you have for .... Phm 1:5
because the l you have shown to .... Phm 1:7
But because I l you, I am .... Phm 1:9
I l him very much, but you will .... Phm 1:16
but you will l him even more,................ Phm 1:16

You l right and hate evil,....................... Heb 1:9
you did and the l you showed for .... Heb 6:10
other to show l and do good .... Heb 10:24
lives free from the l of money, ... Heb 13:5
this to all those who l him. .... Jam 1:12
God promised to those who l him. .... Jam 2:5
L your neighbor as you love .... Jam 2:8
neighbor as you l yourself." .... Jam 2:8
Christ, but still you l him. 1Pe 1:8
you can have true l for your 1Pe 1:22
So l each other deeply with all 1Pe 1:22
L the brothers and sisters of 1Pe 2:17
importantly, l each other deeply............ 1Pe 4:8
because l will cause people to................ 1Pe 4:8
of Christian l when you meet.................. 1Pe 5:14
and to this kindness, add l...................... 2Pe 1:7
my Son, whom I l, and I am very 2Pe 1:17
person God's l has truly reached 1Jn 2:5
Do not l the world or the things 1Jn 2:15
If you l the world, the love of 1Jn 2:15
l of the Father is not in you. 1Jn 2:15
who do not l their brothers 1Jn 3:10
beginning: We must l each other. 1Jn 3:11
life because we l each other. 1Jn 3:14
does not l is still dead. 1Jn 3:14
is how we know what real l is: 1Jn 3:16
Then God's l is not living in 1Jn 3:17
we should l people not only with 1Jn 3:18
and that we l each other, just 1Jn 3:23
friends, we should l each other, ... 1Jn 4:7
other, because l comes from God. 1Jn 4:7
Whoever does not l does not know........... 1Jn 4:8
not know God, because God is l. 1Jn 4:8
is how God showed his l to us: 1Jn 4:9
This is what real l is: 1Jn 4:10
It is not our l for God;.......................... 1Jn 4:10
it is God's l for us. He sent 1Jn 4:10
we also should l each other. 1Jn 4:11
God, but if we l each other, God 1Jn 4:12
and his l is made perfect in us. 1Jn 4:12
we know the l that God has for 1Jn 4:16
has for us, and we trust that l. 1Jn 4:16
love. God is l. Those who live 1Jn 4:16
Those who live in l live in God, ... 1Jn 4:16
This is how l is made perfect in 1Jn 4:17
Where God's l is, there is no 1Jn 4:18
God's perfect l drives out fear. 1Jn 4:18
so l is not made perfect in the.............. 1Jn 4:18
We l because God first loved us............. 1Jn 4:19
people say, "I l God," but hate 1Jn 4:20
who do not l their brothers 1Jn 4:20
seen, cannot l God, whom they 1Jn 4:20
Those who l God must also love 1Jn 4:21
God must also l their brothers 1Jn 4:21
how we know we l God's children:........... 1Jn 5:2
we l God and obey his commands............ 1Jn 5:2
I l all of you in the truth,....................... 2Jn 1:1
those who know the truth l you. 2Jn 1:1
We l you because of the truth 2Jn 1:2
will be with us in truth and l. 2Jn 1:3
you that we all l each other. 2Jn 1:5
And l means living the way God.............. 2Jn 1:6
is this: Live a life of l. 2Jn 1:6
Gaius, whom I l in the truth: 3Jn 1:1
told the church about your l. 3Jn 1:6
peace, and l be yours richly. .... Jud 1:2
in God's l as you wait for .... Jud 1:21
You have left the l you had in .... Rev 2:4
know about your l, your faith, ... Rev 2:19
and punish those whom I l..................... Rev 3:19
They did not l their lives so .... Rev 12:11
and who l lies and tell lies. .... Rev 22:15

LOVED

Isaac I her very much, and so he .... Ge 24:67
He I to be out in the fields. .... Ge 25:27
Isaac I Esau because he hunted .... Ge 25:28
eating. But Rebekah I Jacob. .... Ge 25:28
Jacob I Rachel, so he said to .... Ge 29:18
him because he I Rachel very .... Ge 29:20
and Jacob I Rachel more than .... Ge 29:30
that Jacob I Rachel more than .... Ge 29:31
LORD has heard that I am not I, ... Ge 29:33
because he I Jacob's daughter. .... Ge 34:19
Israel I him more than his other .... Ge 37:3
their father I him more than he .... Ge 37:4
loved him more than he I them, ... Ge 37:4
the LORD I your ancestors, ... Dt 4:37
LORD chose you because he I you, ... Dt 7:8
cared for and I your ancestors, ... Dt 10:15
them as those he I very much. .... Dt 32:10
The LORD'S I ones will lie down .... Dt 33:12
because he I Hannah and because 1Sa 1:5
He I David as much as he loved 1Sa 18:1
David as much as he I himself. 1Sa 18:1
because he I David as much as 1Sa 18:3
and Judah I David because he 1Sa 18:16
other daughter, Michal, I David. 1Sa 18:20
his daughter Michal I David. 1Sa 18:28
because he I David as much as he 1Sa 20:17
David as much as he I himself. 1Sa 20:17
We I Saul and Jonathan and 2Sa 1:23
because the LORD I his people 2Sa 5:12
Solomon. The LORD I Solomon. 2Sa 12:24
because the LORD I the child. 2Sa 12:25
named Tamar, and Amnon I her. 2Sa 13:1
more than he had I her before. 2Sa 13:15
Solomon showed he I the LORD by 1Ki 3:3
King Solomon I many women who 1Ki 11:1
He I the daughter of the king of 1Ki 11:1
the LORD I David, the LORD 1Ki 15:4
this because he I his people 1Ch 14:2
Rehoboam I Maacah more than his 2Ch 11:21
lands, because he I the land. 2Ch 26:10
God I Solomon and made him king .... Ne 13:26
with them because you I them. .... Ps 44:3
children of Jacob, whom he I, ... Ps 47:4
taken away my I ones and friends .... Ps 88:18
even though I I them and prayed .... Ps 109:4
I I them, but they hate me in .... Ps 109:5
He I to put curses on others, ... Ps 109:17
If I had not I your teachings, ... Ps 119:92
do good will be I and trusted. .... Pr 14:22
You I me like a young bride. .... Je 2:2
that the people I and served and .... Je 8:2
all who I her are gone. .... La 1:2
all those you I and those you .... Eze 16:37
to a woman I by someone else .... Hos 3:1
was a child, I I him, and I .... Hos 11:1
The LORD said, "I have I you." .... Mal 1:2
you ask, "How have you I us?" .... Mal 1:2
Jacob were brothers. I I Jacob, ... Mal 1:2
at the man, I him and said, ... Mk 10:21
left to send, his son whom he I. .... Mk 12:6
The Pharisees, who I money, were .... Lk 16:14
God I the world so much that he .... Jn 3:16
Jesus I Martha and her sister .... Jn 11:5
said, "See how much he I him." .... Jn 11:36
They I praise from people more .... Jn 12:43
He had always I those who were .... Jn 13:1
and he I them all the way to the .... Jn 13:1
Jesus was the follower Jesus I. .... Jn 13:23
love each other as I have I you. .... Jn 13:34
' If you I me, you should be................. Jn 14:28
I I you as the Father loved me. .... Jn 15:9
I loved you as the Father I me. .... Jn 15:9

Love each other as I have I you. .... Jn 15:12
because you I me and believed .... Jn 16:27
me and that you I them just as .... Jn 17:23
them just as much as you I me. .... Jn 17:23
me because you I me before the .... Jn 17:24
follower he I standing nearby .... Jn 19:26
and the follower whom Jesus I. .... Jn 20:2
whom Jesus I said to Peter, ... Jn 21:7
follower Jesus I was walking .... Jn 21:20
says, "I I Jacob, but I hated .... Rm 9:13
the Son of God who I me and gave .... Gal 2:20
is great, and he I us very much. .... Eph 2:4
just as Christ I us and gave .... Eph 5:2
wives as Christ I the church and............. Eph 5:25
Because we I you, we were happy 1Th 2:8
If they I the truth, they would 2Th 2:10
Demas, who I this world, left 2Ti 4:10
than a slave, as a I brother. .... Phm 1:16
I being paid for doing wrong. 2Pe 2:15
The Father has I us so much that 1Jn 3:1
if God I us that much we also 1Jn 4:11
We love because God first I us. 1Jn 4:19
will know that I have I you. .... Rev 3:9

LOVELY

how I is your Temple! .... Ps 84:1
She is as I and graceful as a .... Pr 5:19
I'm dark but I, women of .... Sng 1:5
is sweet, and your face is I. .... Sng 2:14
thread, and your mouth is I. .... Sng 4:3
as I as the city of Jerusalem, ... Sng 6:4
because the I land of the Jordan.............. Zch 11:3

LOVER

My I is like a bag of myrrh that .... Sng 1:13
My I is like a bunch of flowers .... Sng 1:14
so handsome, my I, and so .... Sng 1:16
I is like an apple tree in the .... Sng 2:3
I is like a gazelle or a young .... Sng 2:9
My I spoke and said to me, ... Sng 2:10
My I is mine, and I am his. .... Sng 2:16
Turn, my I. Be like a gazelle .... Sng 2:17
my I enter the garden and eat .... Sng 4:16
I hear my I knocking. .... Sng 5:2
My I put his hand through the .... Sng 5:4
up to open the door for my I. .... Sng 5:5
I opened the door for my I, ... Sng 5:6
but my I had left and was gone. .... Sng 5:6
if you find my I, tell him I am .... Sng 5:8
How is your I better than other .... Sng 5:9
How is your I better than other .... Sng 5:9
I is healthy and tan, the best .... Sng 5:10
this is my I and my friend. .... Sng 5:16
Where has your I gone, most .... Sng 6:1
Which way did your I turn? .... Sng 6:1
I has gone down to his garden, ... Sng 6:2
I belong to my I, and my lover .... Sng 6:3
lover, and my I belongs to me. .... Sng 6:3
wine go down sweetly for my I; .... Sng 7:9
I belong to my I, and he desires .... Sng 7:10
Come, my I, let's go out into .... Sng 7:11
them for you, my I, the old .... Sng 7:13
of the desert, leaning on her I? .... Sng 8:5
Hurry, my I, be like a gazelle .... Sng 8:14
Now, listen, you I of pleasure. .... Is 47:8
was charming and a I of magic. .... Nah 3:4

LOVER'S

My I left hand is under my head, ... Sng 2:6
I hear my I voice. Here he comes .... Sng 2:8
My I left hand is under my head, ... Sng 8:3

LOVERS

yes, drink deeply, I. .... Sng 5:1
your lover better than other I, ... Sng 5:9

your lover better than other l? .... Sng 5:9
like a prostitute with many l, ... Je 3:1
sat by the road waiting for l, ... Je 3:2
useless. Your l hate you; they .... Je 4:30
pay all your l to come to you. .... Eze 16:33
them as your l and with all your............ Eze 16:36
gather all your l with whom you............ Eze 16:37
also hand you over to your l. .... Eze 16:39
you will no longer pay your l............... Eze 16:41
great sexual desire for her l, ... Eze 23:5
So I handed her over to her l, ... Eze 23:9
You are tired of your l. .... Eze 23:22
You became tired of your l,............... Eze 23:28
chase after my l, who give me my .... Hos 2:5
run after her l, but she won't .... Hos 2:7
show her nakedness to her l, ... Hos 2:10
said were her pay from her l. .... Hos 2:12
and went chasing after her l, ... Hos 2:13

LOVES

and our father l him very much.' .... Ge 44:20
and he l foreigners and gives .... Dt 10:18
because he l you and your .... Dt 15:16
one he l and one he doesn't. .... Dt 21:15
of the wife he l what belongs to .... Dt 21:16
because the LORD your God l you. .... Dt 23:5
his wife whom he l, and his .... Dt 28:54
husband whom she l and to her .... Dt 28:56
The LORD surely l his people and .... Dt 33:3
The ones he l rest with him." .... Dt 33:12
your daughter-in-law who l you............... Ru 4:15
because the LORD l his people, ... 2Ch 2:11
because your God l the people of 2Ch 9:8
is right, and he l justice, so .... Ps 11:7
everyone l what is wrong. .... Ps 12:8
God Most High always l him, ... Ps 21:7
He l what is right and fair; .... Ps 33:5
l to see his servants do well. .... Ps 35:27
The LORD l justice and will not .... Ps 37:28
The king l your beauty. .... Ps 45:11
God l me, and he goes in front .... Ps 59:10
you are the God who l me. .... Ps 59:17
and Mount Zion, which he l. .... Ps 78:68
He l its gates more than any .... Ps 87:2
"Whoever l me, I will save. .... Ps 91:14
King is powerful and l justice. .... Ps 99:4
because the LORD l us very much,........... Ps 117:2
LORD gives sleep to those he l. .... Ps 127:2
walled city, and l me. .... Ps 144:2
protects everyone who l him, ... Ps 145:20
The LORD l those who do right............... Ps 146:8
The LORD corrects those he l, ... Pr 3:12
Anyone who l learning accepts .... Pr 12:1
but he l those who do what is .... Pr 15:9
A friend l you all the time, ... Pr 17:17
Whoever l to argue loves to sin. .... Pr 17:19
Whoever loves to argue l sin. .... Pr 17:19
Whoever l pleasure will become .... Pr 21:17
whoever l wine and perfume will .... Pr 21:17
Whoever l pure thoughts and kind .... Pr 22:11
Whoever l money will never have .... Ec 5:10
Whoever l wealth will not be .... Ec 5:10
garden that he l is the people .... Is 5:7
will be called the People God L, ... Is 62:4
of God, because the LORD l you. .... Is 62:4
because God l you very much. .... Da 9:23
"Daniel, God l you very much. .... Da 10:11
be afraid. God l you very much. .... Da 10:19
same way the LORD l the people .... Hos 3:1
the Temple that the LORD l, ... Mal 2:11
his neighbor as he l himself. .... Mk 12:33
He l our people, and he built us .... Lk 7:5
comes to me but l his father, ... Lk 14:26

The Father l the Son and has .... Jn 3:35
The Father l the Son and shows .... Jn 5:20
The Father l me because I give .... Jn 10:17
would love you as it l its own............... Jn 15:19
The Father himself l you. .... Jn 16:27
l you because you loved me and............. Jn 16:27
Rome whom God l and has called .... Rm 1:7
and he l them very much because .... Rm 11:28
the person who l others has .... Rm 13:8
proved that he truly l Christ. .... Rm 16:10
if any person l God, that person 1Co 8:3
l the person God gives happily. 2Co 9:7
freely, in Christ, the One he l................ Eph 1:6
are God's children whom he l, ... Eph 5:1
who l his wife loves himself. .... Eph 5:28
who loves his wife l himself. .... Eph 5:28
love his wife as he l himself, ... Eph 5:33
holy people. He l you. So you .... Col 3:12
sisters, God l you, and we know............. 1Th 1:4
whom the Lord l, God chose you 2Th 2:13
The Lord disciplines those he l, ... Heb 12:6
Whoever l a brother or sister 1Jn 2:10
Everyone who l has become God's 1Jn 4:7
and whoever l the Father also................ 1Jn 5:1
the Father also l the Father's 1Jn 5:1
Diotrephes, who l to be their 3Jn 1:9
God the Father l you, and you .... Jud 1:1
is the One who l us, who made us .... Rev 1:5
God's people and the city God l............... Rev 20:9

LOVING

You keep your l promise and lead .... Ex 15:13
I will never stop l your son. 2Sa 7:15
I will never stop l your son. 1Ch 17:13
LORD's ways are l and true for .... Ps 25:10
to me because you are l. .... Ps 51:1
The Lord is l. You reward people .... Ps 62:12
He did not remember to be l. .... Ps 109:16
because you are l, save me.................... Ps 109:26
because he is l and able to save .... Ps 130:7
With the l mercy of our God, ... Lk 1:78
so l is obeying all the law. .... Rm 13:10
Be kind and l to each other, ... Eph 4:32
and peaceable, not l money. 1Ti 3:3
Keep on l each other as brothers .... Heb 13:1
should know that l the world is .... Jam 4:4
each other, l each other as 1Pe 3:8
L God means obeying his commands. 1Jn 5:3

LOWERED

She quickly l the jar from her................ Ge 24:18
She quickly l the jar from her................ Ge 24:46
brother quickly l his sack to .... Ge 44:11
stopped, they l their wings.................... Eze 1:24
stopped, they l their wings.................... Eze 1:25
l the mat with the paralyzed .... Mk 2:4
on the roof and l the man on his .... Lk 5:19
sheet being l to earth by its.................... Ac 10:11
a big sheet being l from heaven .... Ac 11:5
so they l the sail and let the .... Ac 27:17
they l a rope with a weight on .... Ac 27:28
farther and l the rope again. .... Ac 27:28
ship, and they l the lifeboat, ... Ac 27:30
But my friends l me in a basket 2Co 11:33

LOWERING

the city by l him in a basket .... Ac 9:25

LOYAL

you were not l, they will suffer .... Nu 14:33
Be l to him and make your .... Dt 10:20
you to do, and are l to him,................... Dt 11:22
Serve him and be l to him. .... Dt 13:4
will not be l to me but will .... Dt 31:16
of Issachar were l to Barak and .... Jdg 5:15

protects those who are I to him, ... 1Sa 2:9
I will choose a I priest for 1Sa 2:35
Jonathan, be I to me, your 1Sa 20:8
servant who is as I as David, ... 1Sa 22:14
as the LORD lives, you are I. 1Sa 29:6
LORD now be I and true to you 2Sa 2:6
I have been I to Saul and his 2Sa 3:8
Nahash was I to me, so I will 2Sa 10:2
I will be I to his son Hanun." 2Sa 10:2
Why are you not I to your friend 2Sa 16:17
the peaceful, I people of Israel 2Sa 20:19
are I to those who are loyal, ... 2Sa 22:26
are loyal to those who are I, ... 2Sa 22:26
He is I to his appointed King, ... 2Sa 22:51
Hezekiah was I to the LORD and 2Ki 18:6
had remained I to Saul's family 1Ch 12:29
Nahash was I to me, so I will 1Ch 19:2
I will be I to his son Hanun." 1Ch 19:2
in God's name to be I to him. 2Ch 36:13
Since we must be I to the .... Ezr 4:14
You are I, and you keep your .... Ne 1:5
have been I, but we have been .... Ne 9:33
Show that you are I to his son, ... Ps 2:12
himself those who are I to him. .... Ps 4:3
are I to those who are loyal, ... Ps 18:25
are loyal to those who are I, ... Ps 18:25
He is I to his appointed King, ... Ps 18:50
them because you are I to me. .... Ps 54:5
Their hearts were not I to God, ... Ps 78:8
hearts were not really I to God; .... Ps 78:37
earth people will be I to God, ... Ps 85:11
David, nor will I stop being I. .... Ps 89:33
'They are not I to me and have .... Ps 95:10
I were more I in obeying your............... Ps 119:5
me because you are I and good. .... Ps 143:1
he is I to all he has made. .... Ps 145:13
He is I to all he has made. .... Ps 145:17
in it. He remains I forever. .... Ps 146:6
protects those who are I to him. .... Pr 2:8
will be more I than a brother. .... Pr 18:24
People want others to be I, ... Pr 19:22
Many people claim to be I, ... Pr 20:6
he continues to rule if he is I. .... Pr 20:28
live right and be I finds life, ... Pr 21:21
but she is no longer I to him. .... Is 1:21
Is Right with God, the L City." .... Is 1:26
Then a new I king will come; .... Is 16:5
will promise to be I to the LORD .... Is 19:18
be a true and I witness against .... Je 42:5
sin against me by not being I, ... Eze 14:13
the people have not been I, ... Eze 15:8
because they were not I to you. .... Da 9:7
not true, not I to God, nor do .... Hos 4:1
I will be their good and I God." .... Zch 8:8
law—justice, mercy, and being I............. Mt 23:23
is the wise and I servant that .... Mt 24:45
You are a good and I servant. .... Mt 25:21
Because you were I with small .... Mt 25:21
You are a good and I servant. .... Mt 25:23
Because you were I with small .... Mt 25:23
'They are not I to me and have .... Heb 3:10
So, you are not I to God!....................... Jam 4:4

LOYALTY

there he tested their I to him. .... Ex 15:25
do right and for our I to him. 1Sa 26:23
You have shown I to your master 2Sa 2:5
are giving their I to Absalom." 2Sa 15:13
kindness and I be shown to you............... 2Sa 15:20
made them promise I, and then he 2Ki 11:4
heavens, your I to the skies. .... Ps 36:5
about your I and salvation. .... Ps 40:10
Will your I be told in the place .... Ps 88:11

will tell of his I from now on. .... Ps 89:1
I goes on and on like the sky. .... Ps 89:2
and for your I in the meeting .... Ps 89:5
My I and love will be with him. .... Ps 89:24
which in your I you promised to .... Ps 89:49
morning and of your I at night. .... Ps 92:2
his love and his I to the people .... Ps 98:3
love is forever, and his I goes .... Ps 100:5
you because of your love and I. .... Ps 115:1
Your I will go on and on;....................... Ps 119:90
thank you for your love and I. .... Ps 138:2
L and truth keep a king in power; .... Pr 20:28
LORD, your I is great. .... La 3:23
the fruit of I, plow the new .... Hos 10:12
idols give up their I to you. .... Jnh 2:8
continue in your I until I come. .... Rev 2:25

LUCIUS

called Niger), L (from the city................. Ac 13:1
as well as L, Jason, and .... Rm 16:21

LUCK

worship the god L, who hold .... Is 65:11

LUCKY

said, "I am I," so she named .... Ge 30:11
men and officers are very I, ... 1Ki 10:8
people and officials are very I, ... 2Ch 9:7
How I a country is whose king .... Ec 10:17

LUD

Asshur, Arphaxad, L, and Aram. .... Ge 10:22
Asshur, Arphaxad, L, and Aram. 1Ch 1:17
to Tarshish, Libya, L (the land .... Is 66:19

LUDITES

Mizraim was the father of the L, ... Ge 10:13
Mizraim was the father of the L, ... 1Ch 1:11

LUHITH

going up the mountain road to L, ... Is 15:5
go up the path to the town of L, ... Je 48:5

LUKE

Demas and our dear friend L,................. Col 4:14
L is the only one still with me. 2Ti 4:11
Demas, and L, workers together.............. Phm 1:24

LUKEWARM

because you are I—neither hot, ... Rev 3:16

LUNCH

left over from I and gave it to .... Ru 2:18
When you give a I or a dinner, ... Lk 14:12

LUXURY

A fool should not live in I. .... Pr 19:10
and lived in I every day. .... Lk 16:19
from the great wealth of her I." .... Rev 18:3

LUZ

the name of that city was L, ... Ge 28:19
who were with him went to L, ... Ge 35:6
appeared to me at L in the land .... Ge 48:3
also called L) to the Arkite .... Jos 16:2
From there it went south to L .... Jos 18:13
which used to be called L). .... Jdg 1:23
named it L, which it is called .... Jdg 1:26

LYCAONIA

Derbe, cities in L, and to the .... Ac 14:6

LYCAONIAN

they shouted in the L language, ... Ac 14:11

LYCIA

at the city of Myra, in L. .... Ac 27:5

LYDDA

God's people who lived in L. .... Ac 9:32
living in L and on the Plain .... Ac 9:35
Peter was in L, Tabitha became .... Ac 9:37

L

LYDIA

Since **L** is near Joppa and the .... Ac 9:38
Joppa heard that Peter was in **L,** .... Ac 9:38

LYDIA

soldiers from **L** who use bows. .... Je 46:9
Men of Persia, **L,** and Put were .... Eze 27:10
Cush, Put, **L,** Arabia, Libya, and.............. Eze 30:5
a woman named **L** from the city.............. Ac 16:14

LYDIA'S

they went to **L** house where they .... Ac 16:40

LYING

three flocks of sheep **l** nearby, ... Ge 29:2
dangerous snake **l** near the path. .... Ge 49:17
saw the Egyptians **l** dead on the.............. Ex 14:30
l about a fellow Israelite,..................... Dt 19:18
l in a field in the land the .... Dt 21:1
they are an evil and **l** people. .... Dt 32:5
saw their king **l** dead on the .... Jdg 3:25
Samson to sleep, **l** in her lap. .... Jdg 16:19
slave woman was **l** at the doorway .... Jdg 19:27
went to sleep **l** beside the pile.................. Ru 3:7
was a woman **l** near his feet! .... Ru 3:8
One night he was **l** in bed. 1Sa 3:2
off and were **l** in the doorway. 1Sa 5:4
were **l** around on the ground, ... 1Sa 30:16
stayed there, **l** on the ground 2Sa 12:16
found the body **l** on the road,.................. 1Ki 13:28
get up from the bed you are **l** 2Ki 1:4
get up from the bed you are **l** 2Ki 1:6
the boy was **l** dead on his bed. 2Ki 4:32
saw dead bodies **l** on the ground; 2Ch 20:24
on the couch where Esther was **l.** .... Est 7:8
I would be **l** dead in peace;.................. Job 3:13
a deep sleep, **l** on their beds. .... Job 33:15
So silence my **l** lips. .... Ps 31:18
trouble and **l** never leave its .... Ps 55:11
remember you while I'm **l** in bed; .... Ps 63:6
like a body **l** in a grave whom................. Ps 88:5
understanding, so I hate **l** ways. .... Ps 119:104
your orders, so I hate **l** ways. .... Ps 119:128
proud look, a **l** tongue, hands .... Pr 6:17
A **l** witness will be forgotten, ... Pr 21:28
Keep me from **l** and being .... Pr 30:8
the signs of the **l** prophets are .... Is 44:25
I will judge you guilty of **l,** .... Je 2:35
the minds of these **l** prophets? .... Je 23:26
will be left **l** on the ground .... Je 25:33
said to Jeremiah, "You are **l!** .... Je 43:2
many dead people **l** all around. .... Je 51:47
By **l** to my people, who listen to .... Eze 13:19
false visions and by **l** messages............... Eze 22:28
l with those killed in war. .... Eze 32:30
soldiers still **l** dead on the .... Eze 39:14
you saw while **l** on your bed: .... Da 2:28
king, as you were **l** there, you................. Da 2:29
As I was **l** on my bed, I saw .... Da 4:5
I saw while I was **l** in my bed: .... Da 4:10
in the vision while **l** on my bed, ... Da 4:13
visions as he was **l** on his bed, ... Da 7:1
take power by **l** to the people.................. Da 11:21
Cursing, **l,** killing, stealing .... Hos 4:2
feasting and **l** around will come .... Am 6:7
adultery, and **l** under oath, ... Mal 3:5
was paralyzed and **l** on a mat. .... Mt 9:2
sins, stealing, **l,** and speaking................. Mt 15:19
evil actions, **l,** doing sinful .... Mk 7:22
and found her daughter **l** in bed; .... Mk 7:30
of cloth and **l** in a feeding box. .... Lk 2:12
who was **l** in a feeding trough. .... Lk 2:16
him, and left him **l** there, ... Lk 10:30
people were **l** on the porches .... Jn 5:3
A man was **l** there who had been .... Jn 5:5

strips of linen cloth **l** there,..................... Jn 20:5
saw the strips of linen **l** there. .... Jn 20:6
murder, fighting, **l,** and .... Rm 1:29
and it tells me I am not **l.** .... Rm 9:1
we are guilty of **l** about God, ... 1Co 15:15
knows I am not **l.** He is the God 2Co 11:31
truth; I am not **l.**) I was chosen 1Ti 2:7
of all evil, all **l,** hypocrisy, ... 1Pe 2:1

LYRE

for him on a ten-stringed **l.** .... Ps 33:2
up, harp and **l!** I will wake up.................. Ps 57:8
I will sing to you with the **l,** .... Ps 71:22
with the ten-stringed **l** and with .... Ps 92:3
up, harp and **l!** I will wake up.................. Ps 108:2

LYRES

flutes, and **l,** and they will be 1Sa 10:5
l, harps, tambourines, rattles,............... 2Sa 6:5
make harps and **l** for the....................... 1Ki 10:12
they were singing and playing **l,**............... 1Ch 13:8
as singers to play their **l,**....................... 1Ch 15:16
and Benaiah played the **l.** 1Ch 15:20
played cymbals, **l,** and harps. 1Ch 15:28
They played the **l** and harps. 1Ch 16:5
and play harps, **l,** and cymbals. 1Ch 25:1
LORD with cymbals, **l,** and harps; 1Ch 25:6
played cymbals, harps, and **l.** 2Ch 5:12
and to make **l** and harps for 2Ch 9:11
with harps, **l,** and trumpets.................... 2Ch 20:28
harps, and **l,** as David, Gad, ... 2Ch 29:25
music of cymbals, harps, and **l.** .... Ne 12:27
music on the harps and **l.** .... Ps 81:2
praise him with harps and **l.** .... Ps 150:3
At their parties they have **l,** .... Is 5:12
flutes, **l,** zithers, harps, ... Da 3:5
flutes, **l,** zithers, pipes, ... Da 3:7
the horns, **l,** zithers, harps .... Da 3:10
flutes, **l,** zithers, harps, ... Da 3:15

LYSANIAS

and **L,** the ruler of Abilene..................... Lk 3:1

LYSIAS

From Claudius **L.** To the Most.................. Ac 23:26
But the officer **L** came and used.............. Ac 24:7
And **L** commanded those who wanted ...... Ac 24:8
When commander **L** comes here, ... Ac 24:22

LYSTRA

they ran away to **L** and Derbe, ... Ac 14:6
L there sat a man who had been .... Ac 14:8
Paul and Barnabas returned to **L,** .... Ac 14:21
to Derbe and **L,** where a follower .... Ac 16:1
The believers in **L** and Iconium .... Ac 16:2
as in Antioch, Iconium, and **L.** 2Ti 3:11

M

MAADAI

of Bani: **M,** Amram, Uel,........................ Ezr 10:34

MAAI

Gilalai, **M,** Nethanel, Judah .... Ne 12:36

MAARATH

M, Beth Anoth, and Eltekon. .... Jos 15:59

MAASAI

And there was **M** son of Adiel. 1Ch 9:12

MAATH

Naggai was the son of **M.** .... Lk 3:26
M was the son of Mattathias. .... Lk 3:26

MAAZ

They were **M,** Jamin, and Eker. 1Ch 2:27

MAAZIAH
The twenty-fourth was **M**. 1Ch 24:18
M, Bilgai, and Shemaiah. .... Ne 10:8

MACBANNAI
and **M** was eleventh in command. 1Ch 12:13

MACBENAH
was the father of **M** and Gibea. 1Ch 2:49

MACEDONIA
saw in a vision a man from **M**. .... Ac 16:9
"Come over to **M** and help us." .... Ac 16:9
God gave the churches in **M**. 2Co 8:1
the believers in **M** and Southern.............. 1Th 1:7
when I went into **M** so you could 1Ti 1:3

MACHPELAH
me the cave of **M** at the edge of .... Ge 23:9
in the cave in the field of **M**, ... Ge 23:19
in the cave of **M** in the field .... Ge 25:9
in the field of **M** east of Mamre.............. Ge 49:30
in the field of **M** near Mamre.................. Ge 50:13

MACNADEBAI
M, Shashai, Sharai,............................. Ezr 10:40

MAD
you see will cause you to go **m**. .... Dt 28:34
were so **m** they were grinding .... Ac 7:54
Do not be bitter or angry or **m**. .... Eph 4:31

MADAI
Gomer, Magog, **M**, Javan, Tubal,.............. Ge 10:2
Gomer, Magog, **M**, Javan, Tubal,.............. 1Ch 1:5

MADE
So God **m** the air and placed some............ Ge 1:7
So God **m** the two large lights. .... Ge 1:16
He **m** the brighter light to rule .... Ge 1:16
looked at everything he had **m**, ... Ge 1:31
seventh day and **m** it a holy day, ... Ge 2:3
together and **m** something to .... Ge 3:7
he **m** them in his own likeness. .... Ge 5:1
beings that I **m** on the earth. .... Ge 6:7
He **m** a wind blow over the earth, ... Ge 8:1
because God **m** humans in his own .... Ge 9:6
cannot say, 'I **m** Abram rich.' .... Ge 14:23
day the LORD **m** an agreement with .... Ge 15:18
Sarah said, "God has **m** me laugh. .... Ge 21:6
the LORD has **m** my trip........................ Ge 24:56
Now the LORD has **m** room for us, ... Ge 26:22
food and the bread she had **m**. .... Ge 27:17
Then Jacob **m** a promise. .... Ge 28:20
and he **m** them face the streaked .... Ge 30:40
He **m** Joseph a special robe with .... Ge 37:3
that the LORD **m** Joseph........................ Ge 39:3
God has **m** me forget all the .... Ge 41:51
God has **m** me the highest officer .... Ge 45:8
God has **m** me master over all .... Ge 45:9
So Joseph **m** a law in Egypt, ... Ge 47:26
m a promise to him that I would.............. Ge 50:5
They **m** their lives bitter. .... Ex 1:14
Who **m** you our ruler and judge? .... Ex 2:14
to him, "Who **m** a person's mouth .... Ex 4:11
I have **m** you like God to the .... Ex 7:1
that you, LORD, **m** for yourself .... Ex 15:17
Lord, that your hands have **m**. .... Ex 15:17
Israelites and **m** them leaders................. Ex 18:25
six days the LORD **m** everything—.......... Ex 20:11
burnt offering **m** by fire to the .... Ex 29:18
days I, the LORD, **m** the sky and .... Ex 31:17
with a tool and **m** a statue of a .... Ex 32:4
They have **m** for themselves gods .... Ex 32:31
did with the calf Aaron had **m**. .... Ex 32:35
m the Ark of acacia wood; .... Ex 37:1
m the holy clothes for Aaron .... Ex 39:1
an offering **m** by fire, and its .... Le 1:9

LORD must be **m** without yeast,.............. Le 2:11
be clothing **m** of linen or wool .... Le 13:47
or something **m** from leather. .... Le 13:48
matter what **m** the person unclean .... Le 22:5
or vinegar **m** from wine or beer............... Nu 6:3
The Levites **m** themselves clean .... Nu 8:21
the Israelites **m** this promise to .... Nu 21:2
Moses **m** a bronze snake and put .... Nu 21:9
any promise or pledge she has **m**. .... Nu 30:13
he **m** them wander in the desert .... Nu 32:13
and I **m** them your leaders...................... Dt 1:15
your God had **m** him stubborn. .... Dt 2:30
The LORD our God **m** an Agreement .... Dt 5:2
calf idol you had **m** and burned .... Dt 9:21
agreement he had **m** with them at .... Dt 29:1
left the God who **m** them and .... Dt 32:15
from the oath you **m** us swear." .... Jos 2:20
So Joshua **m** knives from flint .... Jos 5:3
city of Ai and **m** it a pile of.................... Jos 8:28
after they had **m** the agreement,.............. Jos 9:16
all the land had **m** a peace .... Jos 11:19
Shechem Joshua **m** an agreement .... Jos 24:25
He **m** rules and laws for them to .... Jos 24:25
Ehud **m** himself a sword with two .... Jdg 3:16
There they **m** Abimelech their .... Jdg 9:6
If you **m** me commander of these .... Jdg 9:29
m a promise to the LORD,...................... Jdg 11:30
With it he **m** an idol and a .... Jdg 17:4
She **m** a promise, saying, "LORD 1Sa 1:11
he **m** his sons judges for Israel. 1Sa 8:1
LORD, the people **m** Saul king. 1Sa 11:15
very sorry he had **m** Saul king of 1Sa 15:35
David and **m** him the officer 1Sa 16:21
Jonathan **m** an agreement with 1Sa 18:3
So Jonathan **m** an agreement with 1Sa 20:16
and he **m** an agreement with them........... 2Sa 5:3
King David has **m** Solomon the new 1Ki 1:43
Solomon **m** an agreement with the........... 1Ki 3:1
now you have **m** me, your servant 1Ki 3:7
these two kings **m** a treaty 1Ki 5:12
so he **m** you king to keep justice 1Ki 10:9
about Rehoboam being **m** king, ... 1Ki 12:2
to a meeting and **m** him king over 1Ki 12:20
Then he **m** two golden calves.................. 1Ki 12:28
the calves in Bethel he had **m**. 1Ki 12:32
the places of worship he had **m**. 1Ki 12:32
the people and **m** you the leader 1Ki 14:7
me and have **m** other gods and 1Ki 14:9
and then he **m** the people of 1Ki 14:16
the gold shields Solomon had **m**. 1Ki 14:26
of Issachar, **m** plans to kill 1Ki 15:27
sin, so he **m** Israel sin, and the 1Ki 16:19
the LORD has **m** your prophets lie 1Ki 22:23
and it **m** the iron head float. 2Ki 6:6
Then Jehoiada **m** an agreement 2Ki 11:17
people of Judah **m** Uzziah king 2Ki 14:21
He even **m** his son pass through 2Ki 16:3
the Israelites **m** Jeroboam son of 2Ki 17:21
from Babylon **m** Succoth Benoth 2Ki 17:30
the bronze snake Moses had **m**. 2Ki 18:4
You **m** the heavens and the earth. 2Ki 19:15
So they **m** it and put it on 2Ki 20:7
wrong, which **m** the LORD angry. 2Ki 21:6
those who had **m** plans to kill.................. 2Ki 21:24
by the pillar and **m** an agreement 2Ki 23:3
King Neco **m** Josiah's son Eliakim 2Ki 23:34
So I **m** plans to build a temple. 1Ch 28:2
the gold shields Solomon had **m**. 2Ch 12:9
King Rehoboam **m** bronze shields 2Ch 12:10
in Jerusalem **m** plans against him 2Ch 25:27
the Ammonites **m** the payments 2Ch 26:8
those who had **m** plans to kill.................. 2Ch 33:25
by his pillar and **m** an agreement 2Ch 34:31

and were **m** holy for service to 2Ch 35:3
But they **m** fun of God's prophets 2Ch 36:16
them things **m** of silver and gold .... Ezr 1:6
our ancestors **m** the God of .... Ezr 5:12
let a search be **m** in the royal .... Ezr 5:17
a perfume maker, **m** repairs. .... Ne 3:8
So they all **m** plans to come to .... Ne 4:8
you **m** an agreement with him to .... Ne 9:8
Let a search be **m** for beautiful .... Est 2:2
on her head and **m** her queen in.............. Est 2:17
Haman's house and **m** him hurry to .... Est 6:14
they rested and **m** it a day of .... Est 9:17
fifteenth day and **m** it a day of .... Est 9:18
send and have them **m** clean. .... Job 1:5
weak hands you have **m** strong. .... Job 4:3
Your hands shaped and **m** me. .... Job 10:8
God has **m** my name a curse word; .... Job 17:6
has **m** me afraid; the Almighty .... Job 23:16
Almighty, who has **m** me unhappy,........... Job 27:2
when he **m** rules for the rain and .... Job 28:26
But I **m** an agreement with my .... Job 31:1
God **m** me in my mother's womb, ... Job 31:15
I too am **m** out of clay. .... Job 33:6
You **m** them a little lower than .... Ps 8:5
in charge of everything you **m**. .... Ps 8:6
He **m** darkness his covering, ... Ps 18:11
You **m** my enemies bow before me. .... Ps 18:39
You **m** me the leader of nations. .... Ps 18:43
You **m** me trust you while I was .... Ps 22:9
The sky was **m** at the LORD's................... Ps 33:6
and streams and **m** the flowing .... Ps 74:15
He **m** the water stand up like a .... Ps 78:13
have **m** them drink many tears. .... Ps 80:5
You **m** those around us fight over .... Ps 80:6
I **m** an agreement with the man of .... Ps 89:3
you have **m** me happy by what you .... Ps 92:4
The sea is his because he **m** it, ... Ps 95:5
The LORD has **m** known his power .... Ps 98:2
He **m** us, and we belong to him; .... Ps 100:3
He knows how we were **m**;....................... Ps 103:14
LORD, you have **m** many things; .... Ps 104:24
with your wisdom you **m** them all. .... Ps 104:24
which you **m** to play there. .... Ps 104:26
people **m** a gold calf at Mount .... Ps 106:19
the LORD, who **m** heaven and earth .... Ps 115:15
is the day that the LORD has **m**............... Ps 118:24
With his wisdom he **m** the skies. .... Ps 136:5
He **m** the sun and the moon. .... Ps 136:7
you because you **m** me in an .... Ps 139:14
LORD has **m** both these things: .... Pr 20:12
I **m** gardens and parks, and I .... Ec 2:5
m pools of water for myself and .... Ec 2:6
God **m** people good, but they have .... Ec 7:29
these idols they **m** with their .... Is 2:8
which they **m** for themselves to .... Is 2:20
You **m** a pool between the two .... Is 22:11
We have **m** an agreement with .... Is 28:15
can tell the one who **m** it, ... Is 29:16
men will be caught and **m** slaves. .... Is 31:8
and hill should be **m** flat. .... Is 40:4
are mine, whom I **m** for my glory, ... Is 43:7
who formed the earth and **m** it. .... Is 45:18
He **m** my tongue like a sharp .... Is 49:2
forgotten the LORD who **m** you,............... Is 51:13
The LORD **m** his life a penalty .... Is 53:10
against him and **m** his Holy .... Is 63:10
My hand **m** all things. All things .... Is 66:2
idols they had **m** with their own .... Je 1:16
you came and **m** my land unclean .... Je 2:7
God **m** the earth by his power. .... Je 10:12
because you have **m** my anger burn .... Je 17:4
They have **m** this a place for .... Je 19:4
those nations and **m** them drink.............. Je 25:17

'The LORD has **m** you priest in .... Je 29:26
He has **m** you believe a lie....................... Je 29:31
the agreement I **m** with their .... Je 31:32
you **m** the skies and the earth................... Je 32:17
had set free and **m** them slaves .... Je 34:11
were slaves and **m** an agreement .... Je 34:13
He **m** me so sad and lonely that I .... La 1:13
He **m** me sit in the dark, like .... La 3:6
he **m** me drunk with suffering. .... La 3:15
entered me and **m** me stand on my .... Eze 3:24
because I have **m** you a sign to .... Eze 12:6
You **m** your beauty hateful,..................... Eze 16:25
I **m** a promise to the descendants .... Eze 20:5
another has shamefully **m** his................... Eze 22:11
They **m** your beauty perfect. .... Eze 27:11
River is mine, and I have **m** it," .... Eze 29:9
I **m** it beautiful with many .... Eze 31:9
the one I have **m** a watchman for .... Eze 33:7
the statue was **m** of pure gold. .... Da 2:32
chest and arms were **m** of silver. .... Da 2:32
Nebuchadnezzar **m** a gold statue .... Da 3:1
I had a dream that **m** me afraid................ Da 4:5
gods, which were **m** from gold, ... Da 5:4
leaders, and you **m** them happen; .... Da 9:12
valuable things **m** of silver and .... Da 11:8
m their silver and gold into..................... Hos 8:4
idol is something a craftsman **m**; .... Hos 8:6
is the one who **m** the star groups .... Am 5:8
who **m** the sea and the land." .... Jnh 1:9
There he **m** a shelter for himself............... Jnh 4:5
The LORD **m** a plant grow quickly........... Jnh 4:6
insulted and **m** fun of the people .... Zph 2:10
the same God **m** us. So why do .... Mal 2:10
are **m** well because you believed. .... Mt 9:22
The crippled were **m** strong. .... Mt 15:31
Others were **m** that way later in .... Mt 19:12
All these things **m** the priests .... Mt 21:15
for you since the world was **m**. .... Mt 25:34
This **m** the followers very sad. .... Mt 26:22
to the tomb and **m** it safe from .... Mt 27:66
day was **m** to help people; .... Mk 2:27
But when God **m** the world, ' .... Mk 10:6
this Temple that people **m**. .... Mk 14:58
Then they **m** signs to his father .... Lk 1:62
and hill should be **m** flat. .... Lk 3:5
the ground and **m** him lose .... Lk 9:42
that is secret will be **m** known. .... Lk 12:2
his soldiers had **m** fun of Jesus. .... Lk 23:11
All things were **m** by him, and .... Jn 1:3
and nothing was **m** without him. .... Jn 1:3
and the world was **m** by him, ... Jn 1:10
Jesus **m** a whip out of cords and .... Jn 2:15
the ground and **m** some mud with .... Jn 9:6
man named Jesus **m** some mud and .... Jn 9:11
because I have **m** known to you .... Jn 15:15
loved me before the world was **m**. .... Jn 17:24
The soldiers **m** a crown from some........... Jn 19:2
God has **m** Jesus—the man you .... Ac 2:36
goodness that **m** this man walk. .... Ac 3:12
God **m** an agreement with Abraham, ... Ac 7:8
my hand **m** all these things!'" .... Ac 7:50
but Philip **m** the evil spirits..................... Ac 8:7
believed, he **m** their hearts pure .... Ac 15:9
the decisions **m** by the apostles .... Ac 16:4
God who **m** the whole world and .... Ac 17:24
says the gods **m** by human hands .... Ac 19:26
to understand by what God has **m**........... Rm 1:20
worship of idols **m** to look like .... Rm 1:23
God, and many will be **m** right. .... Rm 5:19
not ask the person who **m** it, ... Rm 9:20
but they were **m** right with God .... Rm 9:30
and so we are **m** right with God. .... Rm 10:10
an offering **m** holy by the Holy .... Rm 15:16

It has been **m** clear through the .... Rm 16:26
eternal God it is **m** known to all .... Rm 16:26
has **m** the wisdom of the world 1Co 1:20
And man was not **m** for woman, ... 1Co 11:9
we were all **m** to share in the 1Co 12:13
all of us will be **m** alive again. 1Co 15:22
things **m** of flesh are not the 1Co 15:39
Just as we were **m** like the man 1Co 15:49
not be a house **m** by human hands; 2Co 5:1
but God **m** him become sin so that 2Co 5:21
my power is **m** perfect in you." 2Co 12:9
like a fool, but you **m** me do it. 2Co 12:11
that faith **m** him right with God............... Gal 3:6
through the promise he had **m**. .... Gal 3:18
now, because Christ **m** us free. .... Gal 5:1
the world was **m** so that we would .... Eph 1:4
God has **m** us what we are................. Eph 2:10
God **m** us to do good works, ... Eph 2:10
m both Jewish people and those............ Eph 2:14
with God and **m** himself nothing. .... Php 2:7
m his name greater than every .... Php 2:9
which is the reason he **m** me his. .... Php 3:12
God **m** peace through the blood of .... Col 1:20
that you were **m** free from the .... Col 2:11
God **m** you alive with Christ, ... Col 2:13
Christ and were **m** free from the .... Col 2:20
and through him he **m** the world. .... Heb 2:7
You **m** them a little lower than .... Heb 2:7
God **m** a promise to Abraham. .... Heb 6:13
The Lord has **m** a promise and .... Heb 7:21
the agreement I **m** with their .... Heb 8:9
so he has **m** the first agreement .... Heb 8:13
It is not **m** by humans and does .... Heb 9:11
had to be **m** clean by animal .... Heb 9:23
sacrifice he **m** perfect forever .... Heb 10:14
whole world was **m** by God's .... Heb 11:3
God **m** the promises to Abraham, ... Heb 11:17
weak, and yet were **m** strong.................. Heb 11:34
people who have been **m** perfect. .... Heb 12:23
us that everything that was **m**— .... Heb 12:27
His faith was **m** perfect by what .... Jam 2:22
he was **m** alive in the spirit. 1Pe 3:18
but the promise to God from a 1Pe 3:21
he was **m** clean from his past 2Pe 1:9
so love is not **m** perfect in the................. 1Jn 4:18
who **m** us free from our sins with .... Rev 1:5
He **m** us to be a kingdom of .... Rev 1:6

MADMAN
he acted like a **m** and clawed on.............. 1Sa 21:13
a **m** shooting deadly, burning .... Pr 26:18
should arrest any **m** who acts................. Je 29:26

MADMANNAH
Ziklag, **M**, Sansannah, ... Jos 15:31
Shaaph was the father of **M**. 1Ch 2:49

MADMEN
have enough **m**. I don't need you 1Sa 21:15
and act like **m** because of the .... Je 25:16
' Town of **M**, you will also be .... Je 48:2

MADMENAH
people of **M** are running away; .... Is 10:31

MADNESS
Lᴏʀᴅ will give you **m**, blindness, ... Dt 28:28

MADON
messages to Jobab king of **M**,................ Jos 11:1
M, Hazor,... Jos 12:19

MAGADAN
boat and went to the area of **M**. .... Mt 15:39

MAGBISH
of **M**—156; .... Ezr 2:30

MAGDALENE
Mary **M**, and Mary the mother of .... Mt 27:56
Mary **M** and the other woman named ...... Mt 27:61
Mary **M** and another woman named .... Mt 28:1
them were Mary **M**, Salome, and .... Mk 15:40
And Mary **M** and Mary the mother .... Mk 15:47
day, Mary **M**, Mary the mother .... Mk 16:1
showed himself first to Mary **M**............... Mk 16:9
Mary, called **M**, from whom seven .... Lk 8:2
It was Mary **M**, Joanna, Mary the .... Lk 24:10
the wife of Clopas, and Mary **M**. .... Jn 19:25
Mary **M** went to the tomb while it .... Jn 20:1
Mary **M** went and said to the .... Jn 20:18

MAGDIEL
M, and Iram. They were the .... Ge 36:43
M, and Iram. These were the 1Ch 1:54

MAGIC
who had used **m** brought their .... Ac 19:19

MAGICIAN
wise man, **m**, or fortune-teller .... Da 2:27
they met a **m** named Bar-Jesus .... Ac 13:6
But Elymas, the **m**, was against .... Ac 13:8

MAGICIANS
sent for all the **m** and wise men .... Ge 41:8
the **m** of Egypt did the same .... Ex 7:22
fortune-tellers, **m**, wizards, and .... Da 2:2

MAGOG
were Gomer, **M**, Madai, Javan, ... Ge 10:2
were Gomer, **M**, Madai, Javan, ... 1Ch 1:5
toward Gog of the land of **M**, ... Eze 38:2
will send fire on **M** and those................. Eze 39:6
earth—Gog and **M**—to gather them .... Rev 20:8

MAGPIASH
M, Meshullam, Hezir, ... Ne 10:20

MAHALATH
and he married **M**, Ishmael's .... Ge 28:9
M was the sister of Nebaioth.................. Ge 28:9
Rehoboam married **M**, the daughter 2Ch 11:18
M gave Rehoboam these sons: 2Ch 11:19
of music. By **m**. A maskil of .... Ps 52:9
of music. By the **m** leannoth. A .... Ps 87:7

MAHANAIM
David arrived at **M**................................. 2Sa 17:24

MAHANEH
he was in the city of **M** Dan, ... Jdg 13:25
is named **M** Dan to this day. .... Jdg 18:12

MAHARAI
the Ahohite; **M** the Netophathite; 2Sa 23:28
M the Netophathite; Heled son of 1Ch 11:30
for the tenth month, was **M**. 1Ch 27:13

MAHATH
Mahath's son. **M** was Amasai's son 1Ch 6:35
there were **M** son of Amasai 2Ch 29:12
Eliel, Ismakiah, **M**, and Benaiah. 2Ch 31:13

MAHATH'S
Elkanah was **M** son. Mahath was 1Ch 6:35

MAHAVITE
Eliel the **M**; Jeribai and 1Ch 11:46

MAHAZIOTH
Mallothi, Hothir, and **M**. 1Ch 25:4
twelve men were chosen from **M**, ... 1Ch 25:30

MAHER-SHALAL-HASH-BAZ
on it with an ordinary pen: 'M.' .... Is 8:1
Lᴏʀᴅ told me, "Name the boy **M**, ... Is 8:3

MAHLAH
names were **M**, Noah, Hoglah, ... Nu 26:33
The daughters' names were **M**, ... Nu 27:1
daughters—**M**, Tirzah, Hoglah, ... Nu 36:11

M

named **M**, Noah, Hoglah, ... Jos 17:3
birth to Ishhod, Abiezer, and **M**. 1Ch 7:18

MAHLI

sons of Merari were **M** and Mushi. .... Ex 6:19
family groups were **M** and Mushi. .... Nu 3:20
family groups of **M** and Mushi .... Nu 3:33
Merari's sons were **M** and Mushi. 1Ch 6:19
son was **M**. Mahli's son was 1Ch 6:29
Mahli's son. **M** was Mushi's son 1Ch 6:47
Merari's sons were **M** and Mushi. 1Ch 23:21
Mushi's three sons were **M**, ... 1Ch 23:23
descendants were **M** and Mushi. 1Ch 24:26
Mushi's sons were **M**, Eder, and 1Ch 24:30
descendants of **M** son of Levi, ... Ezr 8:18

MAHLI'S

son was Mahli. **M** son was Libni. 1Ch 6:29
Shemer was **M** son. Mahli was 1Ch 6:47
M sons were Eleazar and Kish. 1Ch 23:21
M son was Eleazar, but Eleazar 1Ch 24:28

MAHLITE

group, the **M** family group, ... Nu 26:58

MAHLON

sons were named **M** and Kilion. .... Ru 1:2
when **M** and Kilion also died. .... Ru 1:5
to Elimelech and Kilion and **M**. .... Ru 4:9
Moabite who was the wife of **M**, ... Ru 4:10

MAHOL

and Darda—the three sons of **M**. 1Ki 4:31

MAHSEIAH

son of Neriah, the son of **M**. .... Je 32:12
of Neriah, who was the son of **M**. .... Je 51:59

MAID

and a **m** who replaces her .... Pr 30:23

MAIDS

with her five **m** following her. 1Sa 25:42

MAIM

Misrephoth **M**, and the Valley .... Jos 11:8
from Lebanon to Misrephoth **M**, ... Jos 13:6

MAIN

Place and the **m** room of the 1Ki 7:50
because he was the **m** speaker. .... Ac 14:12

MAINLY

m those who insist on .... Tit 1:10

MAINTAIN

if we confidently **m** our hope. .... Heb 3:6

MAJESTIC

the LORD's voice is **m**. .... Ps 29:4

MAJESTY

has shown us his glory and **m**, ... Dt 5:24
not see his **m**, his power, his .... Dt 11:2
Joseph has the **m** of a firstborn .... Dt 33:17
rides on the clouds in his **m**. .... Dt 33:26
He has glory and **m**; he has power 1Ch 16:27
and I fear his **m**, so I could not .... Job 31:23
Show your glory and **m**. .... Ps 45:3
In your **m** win the victory for .... Ps 45:4
his **m** covers the earth. .... Ps 57:5
He is clothed in **m**. The LORD is .... Ps 93:1
is clothed in **m** and armed with .... Ps 93:1
The LORD has glory and **m**; .... Ps 96:6
are clothed with glory and **m**; .... Ps 104:1
wonderful **m**, and glory. .... Ps 145:5
the glory and **m** of your kingdom .... Ps 145:12
to show my glory and my **m**." .... Da 4:30

MAKAZ

Ben-Deker was governor of **M**, ... 1Ki 4:9

MAKE

Let us **m** human beings in our .... Ge 1:26
I will **m** a helper who is right .... Ge 2:18
and that it would **m** her wise. .... Ge 3:6
M rooms in it and cover it .... Ge 6:14
I **m** this agreement with you: .... Ge 9:11
Let's **m** bricks and bake them to .... Ge 11:3
and bake them to **m** them hard." .... Ge 11:3
I will **m** you a great nation, ... Ge 12:2
will **m** you famous, and you will .... Ge 12:2
will **m** your descendants as many .... Ge 13:16
will **m** an agreement between us, ... Ge 17:2
I will **m** an agreement between .... Ge 17:7
M an altar to the God who .... Ge 35:1
people straw to **m** bricks as you .... Ex 5:7
You must not **m** for yourselves an .... Ex 20:4
gold or silver to **m** idols for .... Ex 20:23
the house must **m** a promise .... Ex 22:8
You must not **m** an agreement with .... Ex 23:32
M four gold rings for the Ark .... Ex 25:12
M holy clothes for your brother .... Ex 28:2
M the altar ready for service to .... Ex 29:36
M us gods who will lead us." .... Ex 32:1
M us gods who will lead us.' .... Ex 32:23
of flour to **m** those loaves .... Le 23:17
Don't **m** idols for yourselves .... Le 26:1
and no one will **m** you afraid. .... Le 26:6
They will **m** you so few in number .... Le 26:22
the LORD will **m** the people curse .... Nu 5:21
inside you and **m** your body .... Nu 5:22
and **m** the woman drink the bitter .... Nu 5:24
the Nazirites who **m** a promise. .... Nu 6:21
'M yourselves holy for tomorrow, ... Nu 11:18
you want to **m** offerings by fire .... Nu 15:14
to Moses, "M a bronze snake, ... Nu 21:8
Don't **m** any kind of idol, and .... Dt 4:25
and will **m** the people afraid .... Dt 11:25
if they do not **m** peace with you .... Dt 20:12
They must **m** him pay about two .... Dt 22:19
If you **m** a promise to give .... Dt 23:21
heaven and **m** this promise: .... Dt 32:40
How can we **m** a peace agreement .... Jos 9:7
used the gold to **m** a holy vest, ... Jdg 8:27
evil spirit to **m** trouble between .... Jdg 9:23
May the LORD **m** this woman, ... Ru 4:11
to his king and **m** his appointed 1Sa 2:10
M models of the growths and the 1Sa 6:5
secretly to **m** wrong judgments. 1Sa 8:3
Hebrews might **m** swords and 1Sa 13:19
Will David **m** you commanders over 1Sa 22:7
you that I will **m** your 2Sa 7:11
Solomon and **m** King Solomon's 1Ki 1:37
sinning when you **m** them suffer. 1Ki 8:35
Now **m** our work easier.' 1Ki 12:10
Let's **m** a small room on the roof 2Ki 4:10
would support him and **m** his hold 2Ki 15:19
Assyria says, 'M peace with me, ... 2Ki 18:31
chosen to **m** David king. 1Ch 12:31
I will **m** you as famous as any of 1Ch 17:8
He wants to **m** them strong. 2Ch 16:9
prophets and **m** them tell lies.' 2Ch 18:21
our officers **m** a decision for .... Ezr 10:14
I will need it to **m** boards for .... Ne 2:8
M shelters with them, as it is .... Ne 8:15
Why do you **m** people so important .... Job 7:17
Almighty does not **m** wrong what .... Job 8:3
you when you **m** fun of God. .... Job 11:3
against me and **m** me suffer for .... Job 13:26
evil people who **m** friends with .... Job 24:17
like God and **m** it look as hard .... Job 37:18
M things easier for me when I am .... Ps 4:1
Those people who **m** fun of you .... Ps 5:5
You have stooped to **m** me great. .... Ps 18:35

They **m** plans against me and want .... Ps 31:13
m music for him on a .... Ps 33:2
M those who want to kill me be .... Ps 35:4
let wicked fools **m** fun of me. .... Ps 39:8
M me hear sounds of joy and .... Ps 51:8
about his glory! **M** his praise .... Ps 66:2
M and keep your promises to the .... Ps 76:11
'I will **m** your family continue................ Ps 89:4
The birds **m** their nests there;............... Ps 104:17
people and to **m** plans against .... Ps 105:25
Then **m** people forget about them .... Ps 109:15
People who **m** idols will be like .... Ps 115:8
M me strong again as you have .... Ps 119:28
People who **m** idols will be like .... Ps 135:18
who **m** evil plans, who always .... Ps 140:2
long will you **m** fun of wisdom .... Pr 1:22
wise, my child, and **m** me happy. .... Pr 27:11
things that **m** the earth tremble .... Pr 30:21
If you **m** a promise to God,.................... Ec 5:4
nice clothes and **m** yourself look .... Ec 9:8
We will **m** for you gold earrings .... Sng 1:11
yourselves and **m** yourselves .... Is 1:16
M the minds of these people dumb. .... Is 6:10
ourselves and **m** the son of .... Is 7:6
one day and try to **m** them grow, ... Is 17:11
He decided to **m** these proud .... Is 23:9
you must not **m** fun of these .... Is 28:22
M the weak hands strong and the .... Is 35:3
M a straight road in the dry .... Is 40:3
you will **m** the hills like chaff. .... Is 41:15
I will **m** rivers flow on the dry .... Is 41:18
I will **m** the darkness become................ Is 42:16
Cush and Seba to **m** you mine. .... Is 43:3
Some people **m** idols, but they .... Is 44:9
before you and **m** the mountains .... Is 45:2
Sky above, **m** victory fall like .... Is 45:8
they only **m** people tired. .... Is 46:1
to crush him and **m** him suffer. .... Is 53:10
I will **m** an agreement with you .... Is 55:3
The webs they **m** cannot be used .... Is 59:6
will use them to **m** my Temple .... Is 60:13
to do things that **m** me angry............... Is 65:3
use the wood to **m** a fire. .... Je 7:18
The women **m** the dough for cakes........... Je 7:18
will **m** the city of Jerusalem a................ Je 9:11
people **m** gods for themselves? .... Je 16:20
I will teach those who **m** idols. .... Je 16:21
M those who are hurting me be .... Je 17:18
his hands to **m** a pot from clay, ... Je 18:4
I will **m** this city like Topheth. .... Je 19:12
The people **m** fun of me all day .... Je 20:8
for me to **m** some mistake. .... Je 20:10
when I will **m** a new agreement .... Je 31:31
I will **m** an agreement with them .... Je 32:40
and no one will **m** them afraid. .... Je 46:27
will **m** your tongue stick to the .... Eze 3:26
from the vine to **m** anything? .... Eze 15:3
I will **m** the streams of the Nile .... Eze 30:12
will **m** southern Egypt empty and .... Eze 30:14
I will **m** an agreement of peace .... Eze 34:25
I will **m** you a ruin forever;.................. Eze 35:9
I will **m** them into one stick, ... Eze 37:19
I will **m** them one nation in the .... Eze 37:22
I will **m** an agreement of peace .... Eze 37:26
baths in a homer and also make............... Eze 45:14
dew from the sky will **m** you wet. .... Da 4:25
And I will **m** that person the .... Da 5:7
that you should **m** a new law for .... Da 6:7
That leader will **m** firm an .... Da 9:27
he will **m** himself more important .... Da 11:37
time I will **m** an agreement for .... Hos 2:18
I don't want to **m** you like Admah .... Hos 11:8
at noon and **m** the earth dark................. Am 8:9

M yourself bald like the eagle, ... Mic 1:16
and no one will **m** him afraid,.................... Mic 4:3
at kings and **m** fun of rulers. .... Hab 1:10
They will **m** fun of the............................ Hab 2:6
m those things happen again in .... Hab 3:2
with no one to **m** them afraid." .... Zph 3:13
'and I will **m** you important like .... Hag 2:23
the Levites and **m** them pure like .... Mal 3:3
M the road straight for him.'" .... Mt 3:3
I will **m** you fish for people." .... Mt 4:19
you cannot **m** one hair on your .... Mt 5:36
If you **m** us leave these men, ... Mt 8:31
fruit, you must **m** the tree good. .... Mt 12:33
and they **m** their special prayer .... Mt 23:5
you **m** him more fit for hell than ....Mt 23:15
Temple when they **m** a promise,.............. Mt 23:16
But God will **m** that time short .... Mt 24:22
So go and **m** followers of all .... Mt 28:19
happened to the Scriptures................... Mk 14:49
He will **m** peace between parents .... Lk 1:17
us **m** three tents—one for you, ... Lk 9:33
You **m** strict rules that are very ....Lk 11:46
those who **m** themselves humble .... Lk 14:11
would see it would **m** fun of you, ... Lk 14:29
m friends for yourselves using .... Lk 16:9
but all who **m** themselves humble .... Lk 18:14
then try to **m** themselves look................ Lk 20:47
M up your minds not to worry .... Lk 21:14
m my Father's house a place .... Jn 2:16
by force and **m** him their king, ...Jn 6:15
and the truth will **m** you free." .... Jn 8:32
long will you **m** us wonder about .... Jn 10:24
come to them and **m** our home with .... Jn 14:23
M them ready for your service .... Jn 17:17
that he would **m** a person from .... Ac 2:30
spiritual gift to **m** you strong. .... Rm 1:11
the law does not **m** people right .... Rm 2:13
and he will also **m** those who are .... Rm 3:30
The potter can **m** anything he................... Rm 9:21
the same clay to **m** one thing for .... Rm 9:21
We must **m** up our minds not to do .... Rm 14:13
that will **m** another Christian .... Rm 14:13
to God who can **m** you strong in .... Rm 16:25
eating does not **m** us better in 1Co 8:8
we trying to **m** the Lord jealous 1Co 10:22
lifeless things that **m** sounds— 1Co 14:7
If they do not **m** clear musical 1Co 14:7
you need and **m** it grow so there 2Co 9:10
He will **m** you rich in every way............. 2Co 9:11
if the law could **m** us right with .... Gal 2:21
if the law could **m** us right with .... Gal 3:21
gently help **m** him right again .... Gal 6:1
do not **m** your children angry, ... Eph 6:4
May the Lord **m** your love grow 1Th 3:12
which are able to **m** you wise. 2Ti 3:15
Moses could not **m** anything .... Heb 7:19
when I will **m** a new agreement .... Heb 8:8
I will **m** with the people .... Heb 8:10
help you to **m** their work hard .... Heb 13:17
or can a grapevine **m** figs? .... Jam 3:12
the same time, **m** your thinking .... Jam 4:8
year, do business, and **m** money." .... Jam 4:13
not sinned, we **m** God a liar, and 1Jn 1:10
have power to **m** the waters .... Rev 11:6
given power to **m** war against................. Rev 13:7
together to **m** war against .... Rev 19:19

MAKER
your Father and **M,** who made you............ Dt 32:6
a perfume **m,** made repairs. .... Ne 3:8
a person be pure before his **m?** .... Job 4:17
my **M** would quickly take me away. .... Job 32:22
Where is God, my **M,** who gives us .... Job 35:10

I will show that my **M** is right. ....Job 36:3
works, but its **M** can destroy it. ....Job 40:19
Can't the **m** of eyes see? ....Ps 94:9
happy because of God, their **M**. ....Ps 149:2
the poor insults their **M,** ....Pr 14:31
the poor insults their **M;** ....Pr 17:5
will look to God, their **M;** ....Is 17:7
M will not be kind to them.....................Is 27:11
is like a pot telling its **m,**.....................Is 29:16
is made doesn't say to its **m,** ' ....Is 45:9
One of Israel, and its **M,** says:..................Is 45:11
forgotten their **M** and has built ....Hos 8:14

MAKES

If a man **m** a promise to the Lᴏʀᴅ............Nu 30:2
The Lᴏʀᴅ **m** some people poor,..............1Sa 2:7
m me like a deer that does not 2Sa 22:34
He **m** my way free from fault..................Ps 18:32
m me like a deer that does not ....Ps 18:33
He **m** the land of Lebanon dance ....Ps 29:6
give us wine that **m** happy hearts ....Ps 104:15
to the earth and **m** grass grow ....Ps 147:8
He **m** your city gates strong and.............Ps 147:13
Happiness **m** a person smile, ...Pr 15:13
She **m** linen clothes and sells ....Pr 31:24
A party **m** you feel good, wine ....Ec 10:19
He **m** the idol and bows down to ....Is 44:15
But he **m** a statue from the wood ....Is 44:17
He **m** clouds rise in the sky all ....Je 10:13
He **m** known secrets that are deep ....Da 2:22
weak flame until he **m** justice.................Mt 12:20
well. He **m** the deaf hear! ....Mk 7:37
So if the Son **m** you free, you ....Jn 8:36
God is the One who **m** them right. ....Rm 8:33
Only God, who **m** things grow, is 1Co 3:7
a little yeast **m** the whole batch 1Co 5:6
God **m** his angels become like ....Heb 1:7
by the law that **m** people free. ....Jam 2:12
right when he judges and **m** war. ....Rev 19:11

MAKEUP

put on her eye **m** and fixed her 2Ki 9:30

MAKHELOTH

left Haradah and camped at **M.** ....Nu 33:25
left **M** and camped at Tahath. ....Nu 33:26

MAKI

tribe of Gad, Geuel son of **M.** ....Nu 13:15

MAKING

Now I am **m** my agreement with you ....Ge 9:9
I am **m** my agreement with you:............Ge 17:4
because I am **m** you a father of ....Ge 17:5
saw Ishmael **m** fun of Isaac. ....Ge 21:9
m it possible for her to have ....Ge 30:22
Why aren't you **m** as many bricks ....Ex 5:14
bowls for **m** dough in clothing ....Ex 12:34
m the sea become dry ground. ....Ex 14:21
m it hard to drive the chariots. ....Ex 14:25
covering to help in **m** decisions. ....Ex 28:15
that helps in **m** decisions. ....Ex 28:29
They will help in **m** decisions ....Ex 28:30
seven days **m** the altar ready ....Ex 29:37
service to God and **m** it holy. ....Ex 29:37
I am **m** this agreement with you. ....Ex 34:10
to the Lᴏʀᴅ for **m** the Meeting ....Ex 35:21
everything in it, **m** things holy ....Le 8:10
teachings for **m** a person clean ....Le 14:32
has finished **m** the Most Holy.................Le 16:20
the acts for **m** things ready for ....Le 16:32
your daughter by **m** her become a ....Le 19:29
money the person **m** the vow can ....Le 27:8
that I am **m** my peace agreement ....Nu 25:12
sinful people are **m** the Lᴏʀᴅ ....Nu 32:14
sin by **m** idols of any kind, ...Dt 4:16

m us suffer and work very hard. ....Dt 26:6
your God is **m** with you today. ....Dt 29:12
I am not just **m** this agreement ....Dt 29:14
Should I stop **m** it and go and..................Jdg 9:9
'Should I stop **m** my sweet and ....Jdg 9:11
Should I stop **m** it and go and..................Jdg 9:13
against me by **m** war on me. ....Jdg 11:27
learned Saul was **m** evil plans 1Sa 23:9
been skilled in **m** things from 1Ki 7:14
They served by **m** music at the 1Ch 6:32
be used for **m** nails and hinges 1Ch 22:3
all his sons in **m** music for the 1Ch 25:6
and skilled in **m** music for the 1Ch 25:7
is skilled in **m** engravings and 2Ch 2:14
you people are **m** plans against 2Ch 13:8
of Judah by **m** them afraid to ....Ezr 4:4
You are just **m** it up in your own ....Ne 6:8
are **m** an agreement in writing, ...Ne 9:38
of their God in **m** things pure. ....Ne 12:45
you are **m** him even more angry ....Ne 13:18
grave the wicked stop **m** trouble, ...Job 3:17
are the people **m** useless plans? ....Ps 2:1
People are **m** fun of me. ....Ps 40:15
like a sharp razor, **m** up lies. ....Ps 52:2
Your enemies are **m** noises; ....Ps 83:2
They are **m** secret plans against ....Ps 83:3
over my back, **m** long wounds. ....Ps 129:3
and **m** signs with their fingers. ....Pr 6:13
m people happy and healthy. ....Pr 16:24
M him angry may cost you your..............Pr 20:2
always talk about **m** trouble. ....Pr 24:2
M foolish plans is sinful,........................Pr 24:9
and **m** fun of wisdom is hateful. ....Pr 24:9
m noise with their ankle ....Is 3:16
silver, which you sinned by **m.** ....Is 31:7
m seeds for the farmer and bread ....Is 55:10
Of whom are you **m** fun? ....Is 57:4
If you stop **m** trouble for ....Is 58:9
are you **m** us wander from your ....Is 63:17
Don't continue **m** evil plans. ....Je 4:14
people were **m** plans against me..............Je 11:18
own family are **m** plans against ....Je 12:6
for you and **m** plans against you. ....Je 18:11
will not stop **m** fun of it. ....Je 18:16
that you are **m** a mistake that ....Je 42:20
to make me angry by **m** idols? ....Je 44:8
since we stopped **m** sacrifices to..............Je 44:18
knew we were **m** cakes that looked ....Je 44:19
stop Moab from **m** burnt offerings ....Je 48:35
Babylon and **m** the loud sounds ....Je 51:55
I am **m** you as hard as a diamond, ...Eze 3:9
are **m** yourselves unclean with ....Eze 20:31
yourself unclean by **m** idols. ....Eze 22:3
with your feet, **m** the rivers.....................Eze 32:2
When you finish **m** the altar pure ....Eze 43:23
a dead person, **m** themselves ....Eze 44:25
I am **m** a new law for people in ....Da 6:21
horn began **m** war against God's ....Da 7:21
m them rulers in charge of many ....Da 11:39
Amos is **m** evil plans against you ....Am 7:10
destroy anyone **m** plans against ....Nah 1:9
from the coat, **m** the hole worse. ....Mt 9:16
elders were also **m** fun of Jesus..............Mt 27:41
left and began **m** plans with the ....Mk 3:6
people there **m** lots of noise ....Mk 5:38
you crying and **m** so much noise? ....Mk 5:39
law were also **m** fun of Jesus..................Mk 15:31
guarding Jesus began **m** fun of ....Lk 22:63
that Jesus was **m** and baptizing ....Jn 4:1
m himself equal with God!" ....Jn 5:18
I am **m** myself ready to serve so ....Jn 17:19
But others were **m** fun of them, ...Ac 2:13
are the people **m** useless plans? ....Ac 4:25

m the followers of Jesus .... Ac 14:22
Jews and are m trouble in our .... Ac 16:20
the people and m trouble. .... Ac 17:13
God began by m one person, ... Ac 17:26
around and m evil spirits go out .... Ac 19:13
are you crying and m me so sad? .... Ac 21:13
m serious charges against him, ... Ac 25:7
they began m the ship lighter by .... Ac 27:38
so you are m your own punishment .... Rm 2:5
m you a father of many nations................ Rm 4:17
could rule by m people right .... Rm 5:21
for God to finish m us his own .... Rm 8:23
God's way of m people right. .... Rm 10:3
m peace between the world and 2Co 5:19
but we are m many people rich in 2Co 6:10
hating, m trouble, being .... Gal 5:20
m people angry with each other, ... Gal 5:20
singing and m music in your .... Eph 5:19
disqualify you by m you .... Col 2:18
m the most of every opportunity. .... Col 4:5
as deacons are m an honorable 1Ti 3:13
You are m some people more .... Jam 2:4
m it go wherever the pilot wants. .... Jam 3:4
to choose you by m you his holy 1Pe 1:2
I am m everything new!" .... Rev 21:5

MAKKEDAH
men all the way to Azekah and M. .... Jos 10:10
away and hid in a cave near M, ... Jos 10:16
the cave at M and told Joshua. .... Jos 10:17
came back safely to him at M. .... Jos 10:21
That day Joshua defeated M. .... Jos 10:28
the king of M that he had done .... Jos 10:28
traveled from M to Libnah and .... Jos 10:29
M, Bethel, ... Jos 12:16
Beth Dagon, Naamah, and M. .... Jos 15:41

MALACHI
LORD given to Israel through M. .... Mal 1:1

MALCAM

MALCHUS
The servant's name was M...................... Jn 18:10

MALE
He created them m and female. .... Ge 1:27
He created them m and female, ... Ge 5:2
living thing, m and female. .... Ge 6:19
pairs, each m with its female, ... Ge 7:2
Every m among you must be .... Ge 17:10
m who is not circumcised will .... Ge 17:14
donkeys, and ten m donkeys. .... Ge 32:15
a one-year-old m that has .... Ex 12:5
daughter, your m or female .... Ex 20:10
every firstborn m animal that is .... Ex 34:19
it may be a m or female, but it .... Le 3:1
must blow the horn of a m sheep; .... Le 25:9
every m one month old or older............... Nu 3:15
sacrifice a m sheep to remove .... Nu 5:8
Do not bring a m or female .... Dt 23:18
from horns of m sheep and have .... Jos 6:4
He will take your m and female 1Sa 8:16
and killed every m in Edom. 1Ki 11:16
unfair to my m and female slaves .... Job 31:13
Any m who chases her will easily .... Je 2:24
slaves, both m and female. .... Je 34:9
I saw a m goat come from the .... Da 8:5
m goat is the king of Greece, ... Da 8:21
'he made them m and female.' .... Mt 19:4
'he made them m and female.' .... Mk 10:6
Every firstborn m shall be given. .... Lk 2:23
also on my m slaves and female .... Ac 2:18
and free person, m and female. .... Gal 3:28

MALES
all the m born in his camp, ... Ge 17:23
if all the m in his house become .... Ex 12:48
the firstborn m stay with their .... Ex 22:30
year all your m must come to .... Ex 23:17
year all your m must come before .... Ex 34:23
counted was 7,500 m one month............. Nu 3:22
They had 8,600 m one month old .... Nu 3:28
counted was 6,200 m one month............. Nu 3:34
there were 22,000 m one month .... Nu 3:39
the dead, he killed all the m. 1Ki 11:15
gave to the m three years old 2Ch 31:16
All the m and those named in the 2Ch 31:19

MALKI-SHUA
were Jonathan, Ishvi, and M. 1Sa 14:49
sons Jonathan, Abinadab, and M. 1Sa 31:2
father of Jonathan, M, Abinadab, ... 1Ch 8:33
father of Jonathan, M, Abinadab, ... 1Ch 9:39
sons Jonathan, Abinadab, and M. 1Ch 10:2

MALKIRAM
M, Pedaiah, Shenazzar, Jekamiah, ... 1Ch 3:18

MALLOTHI
Joshbekashah, M, Hothir, and 1Ch 25:4
twelve men were chosen from M, ... 1Ch 25:26

MALLUCH
M was Hashabiah's son. 1Ch 6:45
Meshullam, M, Adaiah, Jashub, ... Ezr 10:29
Benjamin, M, and Shemariah. .... Ezr 10:32
Hattush, Shebaniah, M, ... Ne 10:4
M, Harim, and Baanah. .... Ne 10:27
Amariah, M, Hattush, ... Ne 12:2

MALLUCH'S
was Abdi's son. Abdi was M son. 1Ch 6:44
Jonathan, from M family; .... Ne 12:14

MALTA
that the island was called M. .... Ac 28:1

MAMRE
the field of Machpelah, near M. .... Ge 23:19

MAN
ground and formed a m from it. .... Ge 2:7
the m became a living person. .... Ge 2:7
put the m he had formed into it. .... Ge 2:8
not good for the m to be alone. .... Ge 2:18
rib from the m to make a woman .... Ge 2:22
he brought the woman to the m.............. Ge 2:22
And the m said, "Now, this is .... Ge 2:23
So a m will leave his father and .... Ge 2:24
The m and his wife were naked,............. Ge 2:25
skins for the m and his wife .... Ge 3:21
I have given birth to a m." .... Ge 4:1
I killed a m for wounding me,................. Ge 4:23
Noah was a good m, the most................. Ge 6:9
who have never slept with a m. .... Ge 19:8
was a quiet m and stayed among .... Ge 25:27
My brother Esau is a hairy m, ... Ge 27:11
and a m came and wrestled with .... Ge 32:24
A young Hebrew m, a servant of .... Ge 41:12
find a better m than Joseph to .... Ge 41:38
Moses to be a great m. .... Ex 11:3
If a m beats his male or female .... Ex 21:20
If a m hits his male or female .... Ex 21:26
a man's guilt kills a m or woman, ... Ex 21:28
If a m borrows an animal from .... Ex 22:14
Suppose a m finds a woman who is .... Ex 22:16
to face as a m speaks with his .... Ex 33:11
and a m who has been appointed .... Le 16:21
If a m has sexual relations .... Le 20:10
If a m has sexual relations .... Le 20:13
If a m has sexual relations .... Le 20:15
The m has shamed his sister, ... Le 20:17

sexual relations with another **m.** .... Nu 5:13
they found a **m** gathering wood on............ Nu 15:32
'If a **m** dies and has no son, ... Nu 27:8
If a **m** makes a promise to the .... Nu 30:2
it is a Hebrew **m** or woman, ... Dt 15:12
No **m** should come before the LORD .... Dt 16:16
A **m** might have two wives, one he............ Dt 21:15
If a **m** marries a girl and has .... Dt 22:13
to this **m** to be his wife, ... Dt 22:16
But if a **m** meets an engaged girl .... Dt 22:25
only the **m** who had sexual.................... Dt 22:25
m who has just married must not .... Dt 24:5
Moses, the **m** of God, gave this .... Dt 33:1
up and saw a **m** standing in front .... Jos 5:13
not a **m** stayed to protect it. .... Jos 8:17
Now Eglon was a very fat **m**. .... Jdg 3:17
She said, "A **m** from God came to .... Jdg 13:6
be as weak as any other **m**." .... Jdg 16:7
was a young **m** who was a Levite .... Jdg 17:7
shouted to the old **m** who owned .... Jdg 19:22
a terrible thing to this **m**." .... Jdg 19:24
Kill every **m** in Jabesh Gilead .... Jdg 21:11
So a **m** named Elimelech left the .... Ru 1:2
The **m** I worked with today is .... Ru 2:19
look for a young **m** to marry, ... Ru 3:10
So the **m** came over and sat down. .... Ru 4:1
A **m** of God came to Eli and said, ... 1Sa 2:27
of Benjamin, was an important **m**. 1Sa 9:1
A **m** of God is in this town...................... 1Sa 9:6
Give it to the **m** of God. 1Sa 9:8
the town where the **m** of God was. 1Sa 9:10
be changed into a different **m**. 1Sa 10:6
for the kind of **m** he wants...................... 1Sa 13:14
One **m** was Ahijah who was wearing 1Sa 14:3
has not chosen this **m** either."................... 1Sa 16:8
to reward the **m** who kills this 1Sa 17:26
asked him, "Young **m**, who is your 1Sa 17:58
to his servants, "Look at the **m**! 1Sa 21:14
never brought a **m** or woman alive............ 1Sa 27:11
An old **m** wearing a coat is...................... 1Sa 28:14
know that a great **m** died today 2Sa 3:38
m had many sheep and cattle. 2Sa 12:2
the poor **m** had nothing except 2Sa 12:3
said to David, "You are the **m**! 2Sa 12:7
Bring back the young **m** Absalom." 2Sa 14:21
a **m** came out and cursed him. 2Sa 16:5
m answered, "I wouldn't touch 2Sa 18:12
place. A huge **m** was there; he 2Sa 21:20
an important **m**, so you must be 1Ki 1:42
show that he is a **m** of honor. 1Ki 1:52
LORD commanded a **m** of God from 1Ki 13:1
sad for the **m** of God and said 1Ki 13:30
said to Elijah, "**M** of God, what 1Ki 17:18
Each **m** go back to his own city 1Ki 22:36
He was a hairy **m** and wore a 2Ki 1:8
said to him, "**M** of God, the king 2Ki 1:9
this is a holy **m** of God who 2Ki 4:9
A **m** from Baal Shalishah came to 2Ki 4:42
When Elisha, the **m** of God, heard 2Ki 5:8
The **m** of God was angry with him. 2Ki 13:19
Israelites were burying a **m**, ... 2Ki 13:21
and every **m** of Judah ran away to 2Ki 14:12
gate, as David, the **m** of God, ... 2Ch 8:14
of Moses, the **m** of God, ... 2Ch 30:16
Tell the **m** who sent you to me, ... 2Ch 34:23
of Moses, the **m** of God. .... Ezr 3:2
Should a **m** like me run away? .... Ne 6:11
A **m** named Job lived in the land .... Job 1:1
He is an honest and innocent **m**, ... Job 1:8
A **m** will give all he has to save .... Job 2:4
are not the first **m** ever born; .... Job 15:7
There is no other **m** like Job; .... Job 34:7
strong like a **m**! I will ask you .... Job 38:3

I am like a worm instead of a **m**. .... Ps 22:6
This poor **m** called, and the LORD .... Ps 34:6
The **m** who has peace will have .... Ps 37:37
happened to the **m** who did not .... Ps 52:7
This is how the **m** who respects .... Ps 128:4
A **m** who takes part in adultery .... Pr 6:32
When a **m** finds a wife, he finds............... Pr 18:22
and the way a **m** and a woman fall............ Pr 30:19
the women a **m** could ever want. .... Ec 2:8
I saw a **m** who had no family,.................... Ec 4:8
m might have a hundred children .... Ec 6:3
it finds more rest than that **m**. .... Ec 6:5
m who pleases God will be saved .... Ec 7:26
I did not find one **m** among the .... Ec 7:28
poor but wise **m** in the town who .... Ec 9:15
If a **m** offered everything in his .... Sng 8:7
I see a **m** coming in a chariot .... Is 21:9
The **m** burns half of the wood in .... Is 44:16
he did not look like a **m**; .... Is 52:14
make him a great **m** among people, ... Is 53:12
If a **m** divorces his wife and she .... Je 3:1
a curse on the **m** who brought my .... Je 20:15
He is a **m** without children,.................... Je 22:30
was another **m** who prophesied .... Je 26:20
consider it: A **m** cannot have a .... Je 30:6
A woman will go seeking a **m**." .... Je 31:22
See the **m** running away and the .... Je 48:19
I am a **m** who has seen the .... La 3:1
One **m** in you does a hateful act .... Eze 22:11
and I saw a **m** who looked as if .... Eze 40:3
Let the **m** become wet with dew, ... Da 4:15
There is a **m** in your kingdom who........... Da 5:11
explain the vision to this **m**." .... Da 8:16
up and saw a **m** dressed in linen .... Da 10:5
The **m** in the vision said to me, ... Da 10:11
he grew to be a **m**, he wrestled .... Hos 12:3
cries when the **m** she was going............... Joe 1:8
and each **m** cried to his own god. .... Jnh 1:5
am like a hungry **m**, and all the .... Mic 7:1
up and saw a **m** holding a line .... Zch 2:1
This **m** was like a burning stick .... Zch 3:2
was a good **m**, he did not want .... Mt 1:19
like a foolish **m** who built his .... Mt 7:26
am a **m** under the authority of .... Mt 8:9
but the Son of **M** has no place to .... Mt 8:20
that the Son of **M** has authority .... Mt 9:6
The Son of **M** came, eating and .... Mt 11:19
So the Son of **M** is Lord of the .... Mt 12:8
the Son of **M** can be forgiven,.................... Mt 12:32
Son of **M** will be in the grave .... Mt 12:40
seed that a **m** planted in his .... Mt 13:31
do people say the Son of **M** is?" .... Mt 16:13
If a **m** has a hundred sheep but .... Mt 18:12
a command for a **m** to divorce his .... Mt 19:7
The young **m** said, "I have obeyed .... Mt 19:20
But when the young **m** heard this, ... Mt 19:22
The Son of **M** will be turned over .... Mt 20:18
sign of the Son of **M** will appear .... Mt 24:30
the Son of **M** coming on clouds .... Mt 24:30
When the Son of **M** comes, it will .... Mt 24:37
is like a **m** who was going to .... Mt 25:14
I knew that you were a hard **m**. .... Mt 25:24
I don't know this **m** Jesus!" .... Mt 26:72
evening a rich **m** named Joseph, ... Mt 27:57
Why does this **m** say things like .... Mk 2:7
instantly a **m** with an evil .... Mk 5:2
brought a blind **m** to Jesus and .... Mk 8:22
said, "A **m** planted a vineyard. .... Mk 12:1
A young **m**, wearing only a linen .... Mk 14:51
m really was the Son of God! .... Mk 15:39
I am an old **m**, and my wife is .... Lk 1:18
engaged to marry a **m** named.................... Lk 1:27
lived a **m** named Simeon who.................... Lk 2:25

who was a good **m** and godly.................... Lk 2:25
there was a **m** covered with a .... Lk 5:12
on a mat a **m** who was paralyzed. .... Lk 5:18
is like a **m** building a house .... Lk 6:48
am a **m** under the authority of .... Lk 7:8
said, "Young **m**, I tell you, get.............. Lk 7:14
the demons came out of the **m**, ... Lk 8:33
m named Jairus, a leader of the .... Lk 8:41
A **m** had a fig tree planted in .... Lk 13:6
seed that a **m** plants in his .... Lk 13:19
this **m** welcomes sinners and even .... Lk 15:2
Jesus said, "A **m** had two sons. .... Lk 15:11
The rich **m** died, too, and was................. Lk 16:22
But when the **m** heard this,.................... Lk 18:23
A **m** was there named Zacchaeus, ... Lk 19:2
you, because you are a hard **m**. .... Lk 19:21
the Son of **M** to his enemies? .... Lk 22:48
But Peter said, "**M**, I am not!" .... Lk 22:58
"I find nothing against this **m**." .... Lk 23:4
together, "Take this **m** away! .... Lk 23:18
this **m** has done nothing wrong." .... Lk 23:41
"Surely this was a good **m**!" .... Lk 23:47
There was a **m** named John who was .... Jn 1:6
I said, 'A **m** will come after .... Jn 1:30
coming down' on the Son of **M**." .... Jn 1:51
There was a **m** named Nicodemus .... Jn 3:1
Son of **M** must also be lifted up............... Jn 3:14
m can get only what God gives him. .... Jn 3:27
of the Son of **M** and drink his.................. Jn 6:53
This **m** has never studied in .... Jn 7:15
"This **m** really is the Prophet." .... Jn 7:40
caused this **m** to be born blind— .... Jn 9:2
The **m** named Jesus made some mud .... Jn 9:11
for the Son of **M** to receive his .... Jn 12:23
'The Son of **M** must be lifted up'? .... Jn 12:34
I find nothing against this **m**. .... Jn 18:38
said to them, "Here is the **m**!" .... Jn 19:5
a **m** with great faith and full of .... Ac 6:5
and the Son of **M** standing at .... Ac 7:56
an army officer and a good **m**; .... Ac 10:22
of Jesse the kind of **m** I want................. Ac 13:22
in a vision a **m** from Macedonia. .... Ac 16:9
by the **m** he chose long ago. .... Ac 17:31
This **m** is a Roman citizen." .... Ac 22:26
find nothing wrong with this **m**. .... Ac 23:9
world because of what one **m** did, ... Rm 5:12
of the sin of that one **m**. .... Rm 5:15
What a miserable **m** I am! .... Rm 7:24
It is good for a **m** not to have 1Co 7:1
am a free **m**. I am an apostle. I 1Co 9:1
The head of every **m** is Christ, ... 1Co 11:3
the head of a woman is the **m**, ... 1Co 11:3
But a **m** should not cover his 1Co 11:7
M did not come from woman,.................. 1Co 11:8
When I became a **m**, I stopped 1Co 13:11
come because of what one **m** did, ... 1Co 15:21
The first **m**, Adam, became a 1Co 15:45
The first **m** came from the dust 1Co 15:47
I know a **m** in Christ who was 2Co 12:2
This **m** who was attacking us is .... Gal 1:23
So a **m** will leave his father and .... Eph 5:31
And when he was living as a **m**,............. Php 2:8
God happens and the **M** of Evil, ... 2Th 2:3
or to have authority over a **m**, ... 1Ti 2:12
not speak angrily to an older **m**,........... 1Ti 5:1
But you, **m** of God, run away from 1Ti 6:11
the **m** who had God's promises. .... Heb 7:6
This **m** was so old he was almost .... Heb 11:12
Lot, a good **m**, was troubled 2Pe 2:7
Lot was a good **m**, but because he 2Pe 2:8
who was "like a Son of **M**." .... Rev 1:13
down at his feet like a dead **m**. .... Rev 1:17
The third had a face like a **m**................. Rev 4:7

One who looked like a Son of **M**. .... Rev 14:14
blood like that of a dead **m**, ... Rev 16:3

MAN-MADE
and as far as the **m** pool and the .... Ne 3:16

MANAEN
of Cyrene), **M** (who had grown .... Ac 13:1

MANAGE
children, and **m** their homes. 1Ti 5:14

MANAGERS
God's **m**, overseers must not be .... Tit 1:7

MANAHATH
were Alvan, **M**, Ebal, Shepho,................. Ge 36:23
were Alvan, **M**, Ebal, Shepho,................. 1Ch 1:40
They were forced to move to **M**. 1Ch 8:6

MANAHATHITES
were Haroeh, half the **M**, ... 1Ch 2:52
half the **M**, and the Zorites. 1Ch 2:54

MANASSEH
named the first son **M** and said, ... Ge 41:51
Ephraim and **M** will be my sons .... Ge 48:5
people of East **M** I gave the rest .... Dt 3:13
region of Gad, Reuben, and **M**. 2Ki 10:33
and his son **M** became king in his 2Ki 20:21
M led them to do more evil than.............. 2Ki 21:9
M king of Judah has done these............... 2Ki 21:11
because of all the sins of **M**. 2Ki 24:3
Hezekiah's son was **M**. 1Ch 3:13
They captured **M**, put hooks in 2Ch 33:11
Hezekiah was the father of **M**. .... Mt 1:10
the tribe of **M** twelve thousand, ... Rev 7:6

MANASSEH'S
from Ephraim's head to **M** head. .... Ge 48:17

MANASSITES
Golan in Bashan was for the **M**............... Dt 4:43

MANDRAKE
and found some **m** plants and................. Ge 30:14
The **m** flowers give their sweet .... Sng 7:13

MANDRAKES
give me some of your son's **m**." .... Ge 30:14
trying to take away my son's **m**." .... Ge 30:15
you will give me your son's **m**, ... Ge 30:15
paid for you with my son's **m**." .... Ge 30:16

MANE
or puts a flowing **m** on its neck?.............. Job 39:19

MANNA
of Israel called the food **m**. .... Ex 16:31
fill it with two quarts of **m**. .... Ex 16:33
He put the jar of **m** in front of .... Ex 16:34
ate **m** for forty years, ... Ex 16:35
used for the **m** was two quarts, ... Ex 16:36
never see anything but this **m**!" .... Nu 11:6
m was like small white seeds.................. Nu 11:7
camp each night, so did the **m**. .... Nu 11:9
and then he fed you with **m**, ... Dt 8:3
and **m** to eat in the desert. .... Dt 8:16
M was something your ancestors .... Dt 8:16
this food, the **m** stopped coming. .... Jos 5:12
no longer got the **m** from heaven. .... Jos 5:12
You gave them **m** to eat and water .... Ne 9:20
He rained **m** down on them to eat; .... Ps 78:24
ate the **m** in the desert. .... Jn 6:31
ate the **m** in the desert, ... Jn 6:49
this Ark was a golden jar of **m**, ... Heb 9:4
of the hidden **m** to everyone who .... Rev 2:17

MANNER
up their hands in a holy **m**,.................... 1Ti 2:8

M

MANOAH

was a man named **M** from the tribe .... Jdg 13:2
Then **M** prayed to the LORD: .... Jdg 13:8
her husband **M** was not with her. .... Jdg 13:9
M got up and followed his wife. .... Jdg 13:11
So **M** asked, "When what you say .... Jdg 13:12
M said to the angel of the LORD, ... Jdg 13:15
M did not understand that the .... Jdg 13:16
Then **M** asked the angel of the .... Jdg 13:17
So **M** sacrificed a young goat on .... Jdg 13:19
thing happened as **M** and his wife .... Jdg 13:19
When **M** and his wife saw that, ... Jdg 13:20
Then **M** understood that the man .... Jdg 13:21
M said, "We have seen God, so we .... Jdg 13:22
and buried him in the tomb of **M,** .... Jdg 16:31

MANOAH'S

appeared to **M** wife and said, ... Jdg 13:3
Then **M** wife went to him and told .... Jdg 13:6
heard **M** prayer, and the angel .... Jdg 13:9
God came to **M** wife again while .... Jdg 13:9

MANURE

completely as fire burns up **m.** 1Ki 14:10
body will be like **m** on the field 2Ki 9:37
that is trampled down in the **m.** .... Is 25:10
no good for the soil or for **m;** .... Lk 14:35

MAOCH

and went to Achish son of **M,** 1Sa 27:2

MAON

M, Carmel, Ziph, Juttah, ... Jos 15:55
in the Desert of **M** in the desert 1Sa 23:24
and stayed in the Desert of **M.** 1Sa 23:25
David into the Desert of **M.** 1Sa 23:25
left the Desert of **M** and stayed 1Sa 23:29
David moved to the Desert of **M.** 1Sa 25:1
man in **M** who had land at Carmel 1Sa 25:2
Shammai was the father of **M,** 1Ch 2:45
M was the father of Beth Zur. 1Ch 2:45

MAONITES

Amalekites, and **M** were cruel to .... Jdg 10:12

MAP

chosen to **m** the land started .... Jos 18:8
and draw a **m** of Jerusalem on it. .... Eze 4:1

MARA

Call me **M,** because the Almighty .... Ru 1:20

MARAH

they came to **M,** where there was .... Ex 15:23
is why the place was named **M.** .... Ex 15:23
of Etham, they camped at **M.** .... Nu 33:8
They left **M** and went to Elim; .... Nu 33:9

MARALAH

it went west to **M** and came near .... Jos 19:11

MARBLE

valuable stones, and white **m.** 1Ch 29:2
silver rings on **m** pillars by .... Est 1:6
floor set with tiles of white **m,** .... Est 1:6
His legs are like large **m** posts, ... Sng 5:15
wood, bronze, iron, and **m;** .... Rev 18:12

MARCABOTH

Ziklag, Beth **M,** Hazar Susah, ... Jos 19:5
Beth **M,** Hazar Susim, Beth Biri, ... 1Ch 4:31

MARCH

together and to **m** out of camp. .... Nu 10:2
M around the city with your army .... Jos 6:3

MARCHED

flags and **m** out by families .... Nu 2:34
at dawn and **m** around the city, ... Jos 6:15

MARCHING

hear the sound of **m** in the tops 2Sa 5:24

MARDUK

and the god **M** will be afraid. .... Je 50:2

MARE

are like a **m** among the king's .... Sng 1:9

MARESHAH

Keilah, Aczib, and **M.** .... Jos 15:44
and his son **M** was the father of 1Ch 2:42
Gath, **M,** Ziph, ... 2Ch 11:8
came as far as the town of **M.** 2Ch 14:9
in the Valley of Zephathah at **M.** 2Ch 14:10
from the town of **M** spoke against 2Ch 20:37
your land, you who live in **M.** .... Mic 1:15

MARK

the LORD put a **m** on Cain warning .... Ge 4:15
You even **m** the soles of my feet. .... Job 13:27
made the moon to **m** the seasons, ... Ps 104:19
and put a **m** on the foreheads .... Eze 9:4
to have a **m** on their right hand .... Rev 13:16
those who had the **m** of the beast .... Rev 16:2

MARKED

bodies will be **m** to show that .... Ge 17:13
Who **m** off how big it should be? .... Job 38:5
people were **m** with the sign. .... Rev 7:4
thousand were **m** with the sign, ... Rev 7:5
thousand were **m** with the sign. .... Rev 7:8

MARKER

human bone is to put a **m** by it. .... Eze 39:15

MARKET

you people living in the **m** area, ... Zph 1:11
they buy something in the **m,** .... Mk 7:4
out as far as the **M** of Appius .... Ac 28:15
meat that is sold in the meat **m.** 1Co 10:25

MARKETPLACE

like children sitting in the **m,** .... Mt 11:16
man went to the **m** and saw some .... Mt 20:3
man went to the **m** again and saw .... Mt 20:6
like children sitting in the **m,** .... Lk 7:32
before the city rulers in the **m.** .... Ac 16:19
got some evil men from the **m,** .... Ac 17:5
every day with people in the **m.** .... Ac 17:17

MARKETPLACES

them with respect in the **m,** .... Mt 23:7
brought the sick to the **m.** .... Mk 6:56
them with respect in the **m.** .... Mk 12:38
greeted with respect in the **m.** .... Lk 11:43
them with respect in the **m.** .... Lk 20:46

MARKS

or put tattoo **m** on yourselves. .... Le 19:28
the stone that **m** the border of .... Dt 19:14
m what you inherit in the land .... Dt 19:14
the stone that **m** a neighbor's .... Dt 27:17
an old stone that **m** a border, ... Pr 22:28
an old stone that **m** a border, ... Pr 23:10
see the nail **m** in his hands and .... Jn 20:25

MAROTH

who live in **M** will be anxious .... Mic 1:12

MARRIAGE

full week of the **m** ceremony with .... Ge 29:27
was only related to him by **m.** .... Le 21:4
with King Ahab through **m.** 2Ch 18:1
men have given up **m** because of .... Mt 19:12
accept this teaching about **m.**" .... Mt 19:12
she is free from the law of **m.** .... Rm 7:2
she is free from the law of **m.** .... Rm 7:3
that there is no need for **m,** 1Co 7:37
M should be honored by everyone, ... Heb 13:4
wife should keep their **m** pure. .... Heb 13:4

MARRIAGES

by allowing **m** with these wicked .... Ezr 9:14

MARRIED

The woman you took is **m.**" .... Ge 20:3
wife (he had **m** a Cushite). .... Nu 12:1
He was **m** to Taphath, Solomon's 1Ki 4:11
like a wife who **m** young and then .... Is 54:6
The first one **m** and died. .... Mt 22:25
person said, 'I just got **m;** .... Lk 14:20
woman must stay **m** to her husband .... Rm 7:2
this command for the **m** people. 1Co 7:10
But a man who is **m** is busy with 1Co 7:33

MARRIES

And anyone who **m** that divorced .... Mt 5:32
his wife and **m** another woman is .... Mt 19:9
his wife and **m** another woman is .... Mk 10:11
her husband and **m** another man is .... Mk 10:12
his wife and **m** another woman, ... Lk 16:18
and the man who **m** a divorced .... Lk 16:18
But if she **m** another man while .... Rm 7:3
Then if she **m** another man, ... Rm 7:3
So the man who **m** his girl does 1Co 7:38

MARRY

and someone else would **m** her." .... Dt 20:7
your children will **m** your land. .... Is 62:5
wife, it is better not to **m.**" .... Mt 19:10
his brother must **m** the widow and .... Mt 22:24
they will not **m,** nor will they .... Mt 22:30
m and are given to someone .... Lk 20:34
themselves, they should **m.** 1Co 7:9
It is better to **m** than to burn 1Co 7:9
the best age to **m** and he feels 1Co 7:36
forbid people to **m** and tell them 1Ti 4:3
I want the younger widows to **m,** 1Ti 5:14

MARRYING

king of Egypt by **m** his daughter 1Ki 3:1
to our God by **m** women from the .... Ezr 10:2
m and giving their children to .... Mt 24:38
drinking, **m,** and giving their .... Lk 17:27

MARSENA

Tarshish, Meres, **M,** and Memucan, ... Est 1:14

MARSHES

its swamps and **m** will not become .... Eze 47:11

MARTHA

But **M** was busy with all the work .... Lk 10:40
answered her, "**M,** Martha, you .... Lk 10:41
her, "Martha, **M,** you are worried .... Lk 10:41
Mary and her sister **M** lived. .... Jn 11:1
So Mary and **M** sent someone to .... Jn 11:3
Jesus loved **M** and her sister and .... Jn 11:5
to comfort **M** and Mary about.................. Jn 11:19
When **M** heard that Jesus was .... Jn 11:20
M said to Jesus, "Lord, if you .... Jn 11:21
M answered, "I know that he will .... Jn 11:24
M, do you believe this?" .... Jn 11:26
M answered, "Yes, Lord......................... Jn 11:27
After **M** said this, she went back .... Jn 11:28
M said, "The Teacher is here and .... Jn 11:28
the place where **M** had met him. .... Jn 11:30
M, the sister of the dead man, ... Jn 11:39
M served the food, and Lazarus .... Jn 12:2

MARY

Joseph was the husband of **M,** .... Mt 1:16
mother **M** was engaged to marry .... Mt 1:18
his mother, **M,** and they bowed .... Mt 2:11
M Magdalene, and Mary the mother .... Mt 27:56
and **M** the mother of James and .... Mt 27:56
the son of **M** and the brother of .... Mk 6:3
himself first to **M** Magdalene. .... Mk 16:9
family of David. Her name was **M.** .... Lk 1:27
to her, "Don't be afraid, **M;** .... Lk 1:30
registered with **M,** to whom he .... Lk 2:5

But **M** treasured these things and .... Lk 2:19
M was the woman who later put .... Jn 11:2
comfort Martha and **M** about their........... Jn 11:19
M brought in a pint of very..................... Jn 12:3
mother's sister, **M** the wife of .... Jn 19:25
Jesus said to her, "**M.**" .... Jn 20:16
including **M** the mother of Jesus, ... Ac 1:14

MARY'S

Because **M** husband, Joseph, was a .... Mt 1:19
When Elizabeth heard **M** greeting,.......... Lk 1:41
M brother was Lazarus, the man .... Jn 11:2

MASKIL

strong and brave. A **m** of David............... Ps 31:24
A **m** of the sons of Korah. .... Ps 41:13
A **m** of the sons of Korah. .... Ps 43:5
of "Lilies." A **m.** A love song .... Ps 44:26
of music. A **m** of David. When .... Ps 51:19
By mahalath. A **m** of David. .... Ps 52:9
A **m** of David when the Ziphites.............. Ps 53:6
instruments. A **m** of David...................... Ps 54:7
you have done. A **m** of Asaph. .... Ps 73:28
Moses and Aaron. A **m** of Asaph. .... Ps 77:20
A **m** of Heman the Ezrahite. .... Ps 87:7
A **m** of Ethan the Ezrahite. .... Ps 88:18
A **m** of David when he was in the .... Ps 141:10

MASREKAH

became king. He was from **M.** .... Ge 36:36
became king. He was from **M.** 1Ch 1:47

MASSA

Mishma, Dumah, **M,** .... Ge 25:14
Mishma, Dumah, **M,** Hadad, Tema, ... 1Ch 1:30

MASSAH

He named that place **M,** because .... Ex 17:7
LORD your God as you did at **M.** .... Dt 6:16
angry at Taberah, **M,** and Kibroth .... Dt 9:22
tested him at **M** and argued with .... Dt 33:8
that day at **M** in the desert..................... Ps 95:8

MASSEIAH

There was also **M** son of Baruch. .... Ne 11:5

MAST

The **m** is not held firm. .... Is 33:23
to make a ship's **m** for you...................... Eze 27:5

MASTER

Fill the earth and be its **m.** .... Ge 1:28
LORD, God of my **m** Abraham, allow......... Ge 24:12
this kindness to my **m** Abraham. .... Ge 24:12
have shown kindness to my **m.**" .... Ge 24:14
LORD, the God of my **m** Abraham. .... Ge 24:27
blessed my **m** in everything, ... Ge 24:35
and my **m** has given everything he........... Ge 24:36
m had me make a promise to him .... Ge 24:37
I said to my **m,** 'What if the .... Ge 24:39
LORD, God of my **m** Abraham, ... Ge 24:42
the God of my **m** Abraham, because .... Ge 24:48
be kind and truthful to my **m?** .... Ge 24:49
"Now let me go back to my **m.**" .... Ge 24:54
Now let me go back to my **m.**" .... Ge 24:56
answered, "That is my **m.**" .... Ge 24:65
May you be **m** over your brothers, ... Ge 27:29
the power to be **m** over you, ... Ge 27:37
Give this message to my **m** Esau: .... Ge 32:4
gift to you, my **m** Esau, and he .... Ge 32:18
They were to please you, my **m.**" .... Ge 33:8
to him, "My **m,** you know that .... Ge 33:13
So, my **m,** you go on ahead of me, ... Ge 33:14
I will meet you, my **m,** in Edom." .... Ge 33:14
"I only want to please you, my **m.**" .... Ge 33:15
He lived in the house of his **m,** .... Ge 39:2
of Joseph's **m** began to desire................ Ge 39:7
My **m** trusts me with everything............... Ge 39:8

M

When Joseph's **m** heard what his .... Ge 39:19
brothers said to him, "No, my **m.** .... Ge 42:10
The **m** of that land spoke .... Ge 42:30
Then the **m** of the land said to .... Ge 42:33
They said, "**M**, we came here once............ Ge 43:20
the one my **m** uses for drinking .... Ge 44:5
Judah said, "**M**, what can we say? .... Ge 44:16
and said, "**M**, please let me...................... Ge 44:18
and I am the **m** of all the land .... Ge 45:8
has made me **m** over all Egypt. .... Ge 45:9
If the slave's eyes give him a.................. Ex 21:4
children will belong to the **m.**.............. Ex 21:4
I love my **m,** my wife and my .... Ex 21:5
the slave's **m** must take him to .... Ex 21:6
The **m** is to take him to a door .... Ex 21:6
will serve that **m** all his life. .... Ex 21:6
If the **m** wanted to marry her but .... Ex 21:8
If a **m** knocks out a tooth of his .... Ex 21:27
must pay the **m** the price for .... Ex 21:32
answered, "Don't be angry, **m.** .... Ex 32:22
said, "Moses, my **m,** stop them!" .... Nu 11:28
Please, my **m,** forgive us for .... Nu 12:11
do what you, our **m,** command. .... Nu 32:25
LORD, as you, our **m,** have said." .... Nu 32:27
you, our **m,** to give the land .... Nu 36:2
hand over the slave to his **m.** .... Dt 23:15
of the LORD, the **M** of the whole .... Jos 3:13
Does my **m** have a command for me, ... Jos 5:14
to him, "Come into my tent, **m!** .... Jdg 4:18
So the servant said to his **m,** .... Jdg 19:11
But his **m** said, "No. We won't go .... Jdg 19:12
house where her **m** was staying .... Jdg 19:26
and brought it back to his **m.** 1Sa 20:38
Ahimelech answered, "Yes, **m.**" 1Sa 22:12
from doing such a thing to my **m!** 1Sa 24:6
to Saul, "My **m** and king!" 1Sa 24:8
I won't harm my **m,** because he is 1Sa 24:10
from the desert to greet our **m,** 1Sa 25:14
is coming to our **m** and all his 1Sa 25:17
and said, "My **m,** let the blame 1Sa 25:24
m, don't pay attention to this 1Sa 25:25
you guard your **m** the king? 1Sa 26:15
camp to kill your **m** the king! 1Sa 26:15
You haven't guarded your **m,** 1Sa 26:16
Yes, it is, my **m** and king." 1Sa 26:17
Why are you chasing me, my **m?** 1Sa 26:18
My **m** and king, listen to me. 1Sa 26:19
David asked him, "Who is your **m?** 1Sa 30:13
Three days ago my **m** left me,............... 1Sa 30:13
kill me or give me back to my **m.** 1Sa 30:15
brought them here to you, my **m.**" 2Sa 1:10
to your **m** Saul by burying 2Sa 2:5
Saul your **m** is dead, and the 2Sa 2:7
to David, "My **m** and king, I will 2Sa 3:21
do everything my **m,** the king, ... 2Sa 9:11
to Hanun, their **m,** "Do you think 2Sa 10:3
My **m** Joab and his officers are 2Sa 11:11
My **m** and king, don't think that............ 2Sa 13:33
My **m** and king, you and your 2Sa 14:9
to you, my **m** and king." 2Sa 14:12
m and king, I came to say this 2Sa 14:15
the words of my **m** the king give 2Sa 14:17
woman said, "My **m** the king,............... 2Sa 14:18
As you live, my **m** the king, no 2Sa 14:19
My **m,** you are wise like an angel 2Sa 14:20
He said, "**M** and king, hear the 2Sa 18:31
the king, "My **m,** don't hold me 2Sa 19:19
meet you today, my **m** and king!" 2Sa 19:20
answered, "My **m,** my servant Ziba 2Sa 19:26
You, my **m** and king, are like an 2Sa 19:27
land now that my **m** the king has 2Sa 19:30
him go with you, my **m** and king. 2Sa 19:37
may my **m** the king live to see 2Sa 24:3

has my **m** the king come to me? 2Sa 24:21
to David, "My **m** and king, you 2Sa 24:22
tell him, 'My **m** and king, you.................. 1Ki 1:13
She answered, "My **m,** you made a 1Ki 1:17
m and king, all the Israelites 1Ki 1:20
Nathan said, "My **m** and king, ... 1Ki 1:24
"Long live my **m** King David!" 1Ki 1:31
the God of my **m,** has declared! 1Ki 1:36
m King David has made Solomon 1Ki 1:43
do what you say, my **m** and king." 1Ki 2:38
women said, "My **m,** this woman 1Ki 3:17
Please, my **m,** don't kill him! 1Ki 3:26
Rezon had run away from his **m,** 1Ki 11:23
Is it really you, **m?**"............................ 1Ki 18:7
"Go tell your **m** that I am here." 1Ki 18:8
me to go to my **m** and tell him, '............... 1Ki 18:11
go and tell my **m** you are here? 1Ki 18:14
answered, "My **m** and king, I 1Ki 20:4
messengers, "Tell my **m** the king: 1Ki 20:9
will take your **m** away from you 2Ki 2:3
will take your **m** away from you 2Ki 2:5
let them go and look for your **m.** 2Ki 2:16
Elisha, "Look, **m,** this city is 2Ki 2:19
woman said, "No, **m,** man of God, ... 2Ki 4:16
She said, "**M,** did I ask you for 2Ki 4:28
honored by his **m,** and he had 2Ki 5:1
I wish my **m** would meet the 2Ki 5:3
When my **m** goes into the temple 2Ki 5:18
My **m** has not accepted what 2Ki 5:20
all right. My **m** has sent me. He 2Ki 5:22
came in and stood before his **m,**............ 2Ki 5:25
He yelled, "Oh, my **m!**............................ 2Ki 6:5
said, "None, my **m** and king. 2Ki 6:12
"Oh, my **m,** what can we do? 2Ki 6:15
and then go home to their **m.**" 2Ki 6:22
and they went home to their **m.** 2Ki 6:23
him, "Help me, my **m** and king!" 2Ki 6:26
Gehazi said, "My **m** and king, ... 2Ki 8:5
asked, "Why are you crying, **m?**" 2Ki 8:12
left Elisha and came to his **m.**.................. 2Ki 8:14
the family of Ahab your **m.**...................... 2Ki 9:7
Zimri, you who killed your **m?**" 2Ki 9:31
against my **m** and killed him. 2Ki 10:9
Now make an agreement with my **m,**........ 2Ki 18:23
my **m** did not send me to tell 2Ki 18:27
said to them, "Tell your **m** this: 2Ki 19:6
David goes back to his **m** Saul, ... 1Ch 12:19
m the king, all the Israelites 1Ch 21:3
do you want to do this, my **m?** 1Ch 21:3
My **m** the king, do anything you............ 1Ch 21:23
son, turned against his **m.** 2Ch 13:6
the slave is freed from his **m.** .... Job 3:19
what we wish; no one is our **m.**"............... Ps 12:4
he is your **m,** you should obey .... Ps 45:11
He made him the **m** of his house; .... Ps 105:21
share of what the **m** leaves his .... Pr 17:2
takes care of his **m** will receive .... Pr 27:18
An ox knows its **m,** and a donkey .... Is 1:3
hand Egypt over to a hard **m,** .... Is 19:4
called out, "My **m,** each day I .... Is 21:8
Now make an agreement with my **m,**........ Is 36:8
My **m** did not send me to tell .... Is 36:12
said to them, "Tell your **m** this: .... Is 37:6
the LORD, "because I am your **m.** .... Je 3:14
'Oh, **m,**' or 'Oh, my king.' .... Je 22:18
for you and sadly say, "Ah, **m!**" .... Je 34:5
But now, my **m,** king of Judah, ... Je 37:20
My **m** and king, these rulers have .... Je 38:9
I am afraid of my **m,** the king. .... Da 1:10
answered, "My **m,** I wish the .... Da 4:19
to happen to my **m** the king: .... Da 4:24
in front of me, "**M,** I am upset .... Da 10:16
M, how can I, your servant, talk .... Da 10:17

and said, "**M**, speak, since you .... Da 10:19
so I asked, "**M**, what will happen .... Da 12:8
and a servant honors his **m**." .... Mal 1:6
I am a **m**, so why don't you .... Mal 1:6
will hate one **m** and love the .... Mt 6:24
will follow one **m** and refuse to .... Mt 6:24
is not better than his **m**. .... Mt 10:24
satisfied to become like his **m**. .... Mt 10:25
have enough money to pay his **m,** .... Mt 18:25
So the **m** ordered that everything .... Mt 18:25
The **m** felt sorry for his servant .... Mt 18:27
and told their **m** all that had .... Mt 18:31
Then the **m** called his servant in............. Mt 18:32
The **m** was very angry and put the........... Mt 18:34
say that the **M** needs them,..................... Mt 21:3
you should not be called '**M**,' .... Mt 23:10
' because you have only one **M**, ... Mt 23:10
servant that the **m** trusts to..................... Mt 24:45
When the **m** comes and finds the .... Mt 24:46
the **m** will choose that servant .... Mt 24:47
'My **m** will not come back soon,' .... Mt 24:48
m will come when that servant .... Mt 24:50
the **m** will cut him in pieces .... Mt 24:51
a long time the **m** came home and .... Mt 25:19
more bags to the **m** and said, ' .... Mt 25:20
and said, '**M**, you trusted me .... Mt 25:20
The **m** answered, 'You did well. .... Mt 25:21
gold came to the **m** and said, ' .... Mt 25:22
and said, '**M**, you gave me two .... Mt 25:22
The **m** answered, 'You did well. .... Mt 25:23
gold came to the **m** and said, ' .... Mt 25:24
and said, '**M**, I knew that you .... Mt 25:24
m answered, 'You are a wicked .... Mt 25:26
So the **m** told his other .... Mt 25:28
Then the **m** said, 'Throw that .... Mt 25:30
tell him its **M** needs the colt, ... Mk 11:3
answered, "**M**, we worked hard .... Lk 5:5
Jesus and woke him, saying, "**M!** .... Lk 8:24
"Master! **M!** We will drown! .... Lk 8:24
Peter said, "**M**, the people are................. Lk 8:45
said to Jesus, "**M**, it is good .... Lk 9:33
answered, "**M**, we saw someone............... Lk 9:49
waiting for their **m** to come home .... Lk 12:36
blessed when their **m** comes home, ... Lk 12:37
m will dress himself to serve .... Lk 12:37
servant that the **m** trusts to..................... Lk 12:42
When the **m** comes and finds the .... Lk 12:43
the **m** will choose that servant .... Lk 12:44
'My **m** will not come back soon,' .... Lk 12:45
m will come when that servant .... Lk 12:46
the **m** will cut him in pieces .... Lk 12:46
knows what his **m** wants but is .... Lk 12:47
does not do what the **m** wants, ... Lk 12:47
know what his **m** wants and does .... Lk 12:48
answered, '**M**, let the tree have .... Lk 13:8
told him **m** what had happened. .... Lk 14:21
the **m** became angry and said, ... Lk 14:21
said to him, '**M**, I did what you .... Lk 14:22
The **m** said to the servant, '................... Lk 14:23
I do since my **m** is taking my job .... Lk 16:3
who owed the **m** any money. .... Lk 16:5
the **m** praised the dishonest .... Lk 16:8
will hate one **m** and love the .... Lk 16:13
will follow one **m** and refuse to .... Lk 16:13
for doing what his **m** commanded. .... Lk 17:9
to him, "Jesus! **M!** Have mercy on .... Lk 17:13
it, say that the **M** needs it." .... Lk 19:31
answered, "The **M** needs it." .... Lk 19:34
give it to the **m** of the feast." .... Jn 2:8
So they took the water to the **m**............... Jn 2:8
The **m** of the wedding called the............. Jn 2:9
is not greater than his **m**. .... Jn 13:16
not know what his **m** is doing. .... Jn 15:15

is not greater than his **m**. .... Jn 15:20
not be your **m**, because you are .... Rm 6:14
The person you obey is your **m**. .... Rm 6:16
The **m** decides if the servant is .... Rm 14:4
One who is your **M** and their .... Eph 6:9
Master and their **M** is in heaven, ... Eph 6:9
that you have a **M** in heaven. .... Col 4:1
useful to the **M**, ready to do any............. 2Ti 2:21
husband, and called him her **m**. 1Pe 3:6
even refuse to accept the **M**, ... 2Pe 2:1
Christ, our only **M** and Lord. .... Jud 1:4

MASTER'S

has chosen her for my **m** son.' .... Ge 24:44
I have given your **m** grandson 2Sa 9:9
your **m** grandson, will........................... 2Sa 9:10
are a disgrace to your **m** house. .... Is 22:18
one of my **m** least important .... Is 36:9
the ground and hid the **m** money. .... Mt 25:18

MASTERS

They put slave **m** over them, ... Ex 1:11
the Egyptian slave **m** hurt them............... Ex 3:7
to the slave **m** and foremen. .... Ex 5:6
So the slave **m** and foremen went .... Ex 5:10
The slave **m** kept forcing the .... Ex 5:13
The king's slave **m** had made the .... Ex 5:14
Egyptian slave **m** beat these men .... Ex 5:14
Our slave **m** beat us, but it is .... Ex 5:16
running away from their **m** today! 1Sa 25:10
depend on their **m**, and a female .... Ps 123:2
about servants to their **m**, ... Pr 30:10
to slaves and **m**, to women slaves .... Is 24:2
women slaves and their women **m**,........... Is 24:2
other **m** besides you have ruled .... Is 26:13
Those **m** are now dead; .... Is 26:14
give this message to their **m**: ' .... Je 27:4
of Israel, says: "Tell your **m**: .... Je 27:4
Her foes are now her **m**. .... La 1:5
No one can serve two **m**......................... Mt 6:24
that fall from their **m**' table." .... Mt 15:27
No servant can serve two **m**. .... Lk 16:13
obey your **m** here on earth with .... Eph 6:5
M, in the same way, be good to .... Eph 6:9
obey your **m** in all things. .... Col 3:22
M, give what is good and fair to .... Col 4:1
respect to their **m** so no one 1Ti 6:1
The slaves whose **m** are believers 1Ti 6:2
show their **m** any less respect................. 1Ti 6:2
serve their **m** even better, ... 1Ti 6:2
to their own **m** at all times,..................... Tit 2:9
show their **m** they can be fully .... Tit 2:10
of your **m** with all respect 1Pe 2:18

MATCH

of lashes should **m** the crime................... Dt 25:2
of models must **m** the number 1Sa 6:4

MATCHED

The number of rats **m** the number 1Sa 6:18

MATCHING

four hundred ten **m** silver bowls, ... Ezr 1:10

MATE

so they would **m** near the .... Ge 30:41
You must not two different .... Le 19:19
Their bulls never fail to **m**; .... Job 21:10
none will be without its **m**. .... Is 34:16
for his cubs, enough for his **m**. .... Nah 2:12

MATED

to drink, they also **m** there,................... Ge 30:38
so the flocks **m** in front of the................. Ge 30:39
But when the weaker animals **m**, ... Ge 30:42

M

MATERIAL

or knitted **m** is green or red .... Le 13:49
kinds of **m** mixed together. .... Le 19:19
of linen and other expensive **m**. .... Pr 31:22
should use their **m** possessions .... Rm 15:27
if we should harvest **m** things? 1Co 9:11

MATERIALS

that is made with the same **m**— .... Ex 28:8
is a list of the **m** used to make .... Ex 38:21
got many of the **m** ready before 1Ch 22:5
many of the **m** for building 1Ch 22:14
who carried **m** did their work .... Ne 4:17

MATING

animals in the flock were **m**, ... Ge 30:41
season when the flocks were **m**. .... Ge 31:10
goats who were **m** were streaked, ... Ge 31:10
or spotted male goats are **m**. .... Ge 31:12
she-camel in **m** season that runs .... Je 2:23
and sniffs the wind at **m** time. .... Je 2:24
at **m** time, it is easy to find .... Je 2:24

MATRED

was Mehetabel daughter of **M**, ... Ge 36:39
and she was the daughter of **M**, ... 1Ch 1:50

MATRI'S

groups, and **M** family was picked 1Sa 10:21
he had each man of **M** family pass 1Sa 10:21

MATS

sick people on **m** wherever they .... Mk 6:55
on beds and **m** in the streets, ... Ac 5:15

MATTAN

They also killed **M**, the priest 2Ki 11:18
They killed **M**, the priest of 2Ch 23:17
Shephatiah son of **M**, Gedaliah .... Je 38:1

MATTANAH

went from the desert to **M**. .... Nu 21:18
From **M** they went to Nahaliel and .... Nu 21:19

MATTANIAH

Then he made **M**, Jehoiachin's 2Ki 24:17
Galal, and **M** son of Mica. 1Ch 9:15
Bukkiah, **M**, Uzziel, Shubael, ... 1Ch 25:4
twelve men were chosen from **M**, ... 1Ch 25:16
there were Zechariah and **M**. 2Ch 29:13
M, Zechariah, Jehiel, Abdi, ... Ezr 10:26
Eliashib, **M**, Jeremoth, Zabad, ... Ezr 10:27
Maaseiah, **M**, Bezalel, Binnui, ... Ezr 10:30
M, Mattenai, and Jaasu. .... Ezr 10:37
There was **M** son of Mica. .... Ne 11:17
M was the director who led the .... Ne 11:17
son of Hashabiah, the son of **M**. .... Ne 11:22
M was the son of Mica. .... Ne 11:22
Sherebiah, Judah, and **M**. .... Ne 12:8
M and his relatives were in .... Ne 12:8
M, Bakbukiah, Obadiah, Meshullam, ... Ne 12:25
son of Shemaiah, the son of **M**. .... Ne 12:35
M was the son of Micaiah, the .... Ne 12:35
the son of **M**, their helper. .... Ne 13:13

MATTANIAH'S

He also changed **M** name to 2Ki 24:17
son, and Jeiel was **M** son. 2Ch 20:14

MATTATHA

Menna was the son of **M**. .... Lk 3:31
M was the son of Nathan. .... Lk 3:31

MATTATHIAS

Joseph was the son of **M**. .... Lk 3:25
M was the son of Amos. .... Lk 3:25
Maath was the son of **M**. .... Lk 3:26
M was the son of Semein. .... Lk 3:26

MATTATTAH

Mattenai, **M**, Zabad, Eliphelet, ... Ezr 10:33

MATTENAI

M, Mattattah, Zabad, Eliphelet, ... Ezr 10:33
Mattaniah, **M**, and Jaasu. .... Ezr 10:37
M, from Joiarib's family; .... Ne 12:19

MATTHAN

Eleazar was the father of **M**. .... Mt 1:15
M was the father of Jacob. .... Mt 1:15

MATTHAT

Heli was the son of **M**. .... Lk 3:24
M was the son of Levi. .... Lk 3:24
Jorim was the son of **M**. .... Lk 3:29
M was the son of Levi. .... Lk 3:29

MATTHEW

saw a man named **M** sitting in the .... Mt 9:9
Thomas and **M**, the tax collector; .... Mt 10:3
Bartholomew, **M**, Thomas, James .... Mk 3:18
M, Thomas, James son of Alphaeus, ... Lk 6:15
Thomas, Bartholomew, **M**, James .... Ac 1:13

MATTHEW'S

was having dinner at **M** house, ... Mt 9:10

MATTHIAS

called Justus. The other was **M**. .... Ac 1:23
lots showed that **M** was the one. .... Ac 1:26

MATTITHIAH

a Levite named **M** who was 1Ch 9:31
Maaseiah, **M**, Eliphelehu, ... 1Ch 15:18
M, Eliphelehu, Mikneiah, ... 1Ch 15:21
Jehiel, **M**, Eliab, Benaiah, ... 1Ch 16:5
Shimei, Hashabiah, and **M**. 1Ch 25:3
twelve men were chosen from **M**, ... 1Ch 25:21
Jeiel, **M**, Zabad, Zebina, Jaddai, ... Ezr 10:43
his right were **M**, Shema, Anaiah, ... Ne 8:4

MATURE

a wisdom to those who are **m**. 1Co 2:6
We must become like a **m** person, ... Eph 4:13
are spiritually **m** should think .... Php 3:15
as a **m** person in Christ. .... Col 1:28
to be spiritually **m** and have .... Col 4:12
They are **m** enough to know the .... Heb 5:14
it you can **m** in your salvation, ... 1Pe 2:2

ME-ZAHAB

who was the daughter of **M**. .... Ge 36:39
who was the daughter of **M**. 1Ch 1:50

MEAL

Then Lot prepared a **m** for them. .... Ge 19:3
his relatives to share in the **m**. .... Ge 31:54
Kill an animal and prepare a **m**. .... Ge 43:16
himself and said, "Serve the **m**." .... Ge 43:31
The **m** must be eaten inside a .... Ex 12:46
Israel, he may share in the **m**. .... Ex 12:48
may not eat the Passover **m**. .... Ex 12:48
eat the holy **m** together before .... Ex 18:12
his evening **m**, Boaz felt good .... Ru 3:7
had eaten their **m** in Shiloh, ... 1Sa 1:9
with him were finishing their **m**. 1Ki 1:41
go home and cook our last **m**. 1Ki 17:12
the first of our ground **m**, ... Ne 10:37
hate food, even the very best **m**. .... Job 33:20
You prepare a **m** for me in front .... Ps 23:5
where there is a funeral **m**. .... Je 16:5
the sound of people grinding **m**. .... Je 25:10
were eating a **m** with Gedaliah at .... Je 41:1
to eat a **m** in the presence .... Eze 44:3
for you to eat the Passover **m**?" .... Mt 26:17
they prepared the Passover **m**. .... Mt 26:19
for you to eat the Passover **m**?" .... Mk 14:12
Passover **m** with my followers? .... Mk 14:14
so they prepared the Passover **m**. .... Mk 14:16
not wash his hands before the **m**. .... Lk 11:38
share in the **m** in God's kingdom. .... Lk 14:15

the Passover **m** for us to eat." .... Lk 22:8
Passover **m** with my followers? .... Lk 22:11
Prepare the Passover **m** there." .... Lk 22:12
they prepared the Passover **m**. .... Lk 22:13
this Passover **m** with you before .... Lk 22:15
another Passover **m** until it is .... Lk 22:16
followers were at the evening **m**. .... Jn 13:2
So during the **m** Jesus stood up .... Jn 13:4
wanted to eat the Passover **m**. .... Jn 18:28
I eat the **m** with thankfulness, ... 1Co 10:30
he sold all that for a single **m**. .... Heb 12:16
to the wedding **m** of the Lamb!" .... Rev 19:9

MEALS

you may do is to prepare your **m**. .... Ex 12:16
you while eating **m** with you. 2Pe 2:13
special Christian **m** you share. .... Jud 1:12

MEALTIME

At **m** Boaz told Ruth, "Come here. .... Ru 2:14
eat only at **m** and for strength, ... Ec 10:17

MEAN

you, 'What do these rocks **m**?' .... Jos 4:6
each other, "What does this **m**? .... Lk 4:36
each other, "What does this **m**?" .... Ac 2:12
He went up," what does it **m**? .... Eph 4:9
with crooked and **m** people all .... Php 2:15

MEANING

This is the **m** of the dream, ... Da 4:24
understand the **m** of what someone 1Co 14:11

MEANINGS

he explained their **m** to us. .... Ge 41:12
him—clearly, not with hidden **m**. .... Nu 12:8

MEANS

will tell you what the dream **m**. .... Ge 40:18
which **m** "let Baal fight against .... Jdg 6:32
His name **m** 'fool,' and he is 1Sa 25:25
whether it **m** life or death." 2Sa 15:21
it and decide what it **m** to you." .... Job 5:27
all this talk that **m** nothing? .... Job 27:12
Peace of mind **m** a healthy body, ... Pr 14:30
A dull ax **m** harder work. .... Ec 10:10
but their bragging **m** nothing. .... Is 16:6
That is what it **m** to know God," .... Je 22:16
and I want to know what it **m**." .... Da 2:3
we will tell you what it **m**." .... Da 2:4
tell me the dream and what it **m**. .... Da 2:5
me the dream and what it **m**." .... Da 2:6
and we will tell you what it **m**." .... Da 2:7
can tell me what it really **m**!" .... Da 2:9
will tell him what his dream **m**." .... Da 2:24
tell the king what his dream **m**." .... Da 2:25
what I dreamed and what it **m**?" .... Da 2:26
so that you may know what it **m**. .... Da 2:30
we will tell the king what it **m**. .... Da 2:36
That **m** the fourth kingdom will .... Da 2:41
I dreamed; tell me what it **m**. .... Da 4:9
tell me what the dream **m**. .... Da 4:18
what the writing on the wall **m**." .... Da 5:12
and to explain what it **m**, ... Da 5:15
will explain to you what it **m**. .... Da 5:17
which **m** "God is with us." .... Mt 1:23
Go and learn what this **m**: ' .... Mt 9:13
make a promise, that **m** nothing. .... Mt 23:16
make a promise, that **m** nothing. .... Mt 23:18
should understand what it **m**. .... Mt 24:15
which **m** the Place of the Skull. .... Mt 27:33
This **m**, "My God, my God, why .... Mt 27:46
which **m** "Sons of Thunder .... Mk 3:17
This **m**, "Young girl, I tell .... Mk 5:41
This **m**, "Be opened." .... Mk 7:34
should understand what it **m**. .... Mk 13:14
which **m** the Place of the Skull. .... Mk 15:22

This **m**, "My God, my God, why .... Mk 15:34
m the day before the Sabbath .... Mk 15:42
This is what the story **m**: .... Lk 8:11
"Rabbi" **m** "Teacher." .... Jn 1:38
"Messiah" **m** "Christ." .... Jn 1:41
"Cephas" **m** "Peter." .... Jn 1:42
Siloam." (Siloam **m** Sent.) So the .... Jn 9:7
Rabboni." (This **m** "Teacher.") .... Jn 20:16
Akeldama ("Field of Blood." .... Ac 1:19
which **m** "one who encourages" .... Ac 4:36
to know what this teaching **m**." .... Ac 17:20
known what it **m** to want to take .... Rm 7:7
m I agree that the law is good. .... Rm 7:16
our bodies will be made free. .... Rm 8:23
This **m** that not all of Abraham's .... Rm 9:8
That **m**, "Who will go up to .... Rm 10:6
That **m**, "Who will go down .... Rm 10:7
we know what it **m** to fear the 2Co 5:11
That **m** only one person; .... Gal 3:16
It **m** that he first came down to .... Eph 4:9
name **m** "king of goodness, ... Heb 7:2
Salem, which **m** "king of peace." .... Heb 7:2
This **m** that Jesus is the .... Heb 7:22
will **m** nothing while the person .... Heb 9:17
Faith **m** being sure of the things .... Heb 11:1
lives tell us what faith **m**. .... Heb 12:1
the Scripture **m** nothing that .... Jam 4:5
Loving God **m** obeying his 1Jn 5:3
And love **m** living the way God 2Jn 1:6
This **m** that God's holy people .... Rev 13:10
This **m** God's holy people must be .... Rev 14:12
The fine linen **m** the good things .... Rev 19:8

MEANT

You **m** to hurt me, but God turned .... Ge 50:20

MEANTIME

In the **m** Absalom had run away. 2Sa 13:34

MEANWHILE

M the Midianites who had bought .... Ge 37:36
M the LORD said to Aaron, ... Ex 4:27
M, Absalom, Ahithophel, and all 2Sa 16:15
M the officers of Ben-Hadad king 1Ki 20:23
M, his followers were begging .... Jn 4:31

MEASURE

so much that he could not **m** it. .... Ge 41:49
m they used for the manna was .... Ex 16:36
one-half of the Holy Place **m**, ... Ex 30:13
all these by the Holy Place **m**. .... Ex 30:24
as set by the Holy Place **m**. .... Ex 38:24
as set by the Holy Place **m**. .... Ex 38:25
as set by the Holy Place **m**. .... Ex 38:26
as set by the Holy Place **m**. .... Le 5:15
not cheat when you **m** the length .... Le 19:35
They will **m** each piece of bread, ... Le 26:26
You must use the **m** as set by the .... Le 27:3
You must use the **m** as set by the .... Le 27:25
Use the **m** as set by the Holy .... Nu 3:47
the **m** set by the Holy Place. .... Nu 3:50
weight set by the Holy Place **m**. .... Nu 7:85
weight set by the Holy Place **m**. .... Nu 7:86
as set by the Holy Place **m**. .... Nu 18:16
Also **m** three thousand feet in .... Nu 35:5
and they should **m** how far it is .... Dt 21:2
then he used a rope to **m** them. 2Sa 8:2
five pounds by the royal **m**. 2Sa 14:26
was as hard to **m** as the grains 1Ki 4:29
Shechem and **m** off the Valley .... Ps 60:6
Shechem and **m** off the Valley .... Ps 108:7
No one can **m** the height of the .... Pr 25:3
has used his hand to **m** the sky? .... Is 40:12
used a bowl to **m** all the dust .... Is 40:12
his calipers to **m** the statue. .... Is 44:13

if people can **m** the sky above .... Je 31:37
the seashore that no one can **m**." .... Je 33:22
area you will **m** a part about .... Eze 45:3
The dry **m** and the liquid measure .... Eze 45:11
and the liquid **m** will be the .... Eze 45:11
The liquid **m** will always be a .... Eze 45:11
north side will **m** more than one................. Eze 48:30
east side will **m** more than one .... Eze 48:32
south side will **m** more than one .... Eze 48:33
west side will **m** more than one .... Eze 48:34
The city will **m** about six miles .... Eze 48:35
which no one can **m** or count. .... Hos 1:10
Other people will **m** your land .... Am 7:17
and the cursed false **m?** .... Mic 6:10
I am going to **m** Jerusalem,.................... Zch 2:2
use themselves to **m** themselves, ... 2Co 10:12
Go and **m** the temple of God and .... Rev 11:1
do not **m** the yard outside the.................. Rev 11:2
rod made of gold to **m** the city, ... Rev 21:15

MEASURED

Then they **m** it. The person who .... Ex 16:18
Those who were **m** within two rope 2Sa 8:2
to the wind and **m** the water, ... Job 28:25
Who has **m** the oceans in the palm............ Is 40:12
He **m** the wall and did not stop .... La 2:8
the bread that is **m** out to them, ... Eze 4:16
water that is **m** out to them, ... Eze 4:16
So the man **m** the wall, which was .... Eze 40:5
up its steps and the opening .... Eze 40:6
Then the man **m** the porch of the .... Eze 40:8
which **m** the same on each side............... Eze 40:10
The man **m** the width of the .... Eze 40:11
The man **m** the gateway from the .... Eze 40:13
The man also **m** the porch, which .... Eze 40:14
Then the man **m** from the outer .... Eze 40:19
The man **m** the length and width .... Eze 40:20
and its porch **m** the same as the .... Eze 40:21
of palm trees **m** the same as the .... Eze 40:22
man **m** it and found it was one .... Eze 40:23
He **m** its inner walls and its .... Eze 40:24
and they **m** the same as the other .... Eze 40:24
The man **m** from gate to gate on............. Eze 40:27
inner south gateway **m** the same .... Eze 40:28
and porch **m** the same as the .... Eze 40:29
He **m** the inner east gateway, ... Eze 40:32
porch **m** the same as the other .... Eze 40:33
He **m** it, and it was the same as .... Eze 40:35
porch **m** the same as the other .... Eze 40:36
The man **m** the inner courtyard................ Eze 40:47
the Temple and **m** each side wall .... Eze 40:48
Holy Place and **m** its side walls,.............. Eze 41:1
The man **m** the Holy Place, which .... Eze 41:2
went inside and **m** the side walls .... Eze 41:3
Then the man **m** the room at the .... Eze 41:4
Then the man **m** the wall of the .... Eze 41:5
Then the man **m** the Temple. .... Eze 41:13
The man **m** the length of the .... Eze 41:15
He **m** the area all around. .... Eze 42:15
The man **m** the east side with the .... Eze 42:16
He **m** the north side; .... Eze 42:17
He **m** the south side; .... Eze 42:18
it **m** eight hundred seventy-five .... Eze 42:19
So he **m** the Temple area on all .... Eze 42:20
his hand and **m** about one-third .... Eze 47:3
The man **m** about one-third of a .... Eze 47:4
Then he **m** about one-third of a .... Eze 47:4
The man **m** about one-third of a .... Eze 47:5
is not **m** by how much one owns. .... Lk 12:15
The angel **m** the city with the .... Rev 21:16
The angel also **m** the wall. .... Rev 21:17

MEASUREMENT

feet wide, using the old **m.** 2Ch 3:3
an honest dry **m** and an honest .... Eze 45:10
and an honest liquid **m.** .... Eze 45:10
m they follow will be the homer. .... Eze 45:11

MEASUREMENTS

used these **m** for building 2Ch 3:3
These are the **m** of the altar, ... Eze 43:13
These are the city's **m:** .... Eze 48:16
high, by human **m,** which the .... Rev 21:17

MEASURES

sets of **m** in your house, ... Dt 25:14
weights and **m** so that you will .... Dt 25:15
dishonest and uses dishonest **m.**............. Dt 25:16
weights and dishonest **m.** .... Pr 20:10
it **m** three and one-half feet. .... Eze 43:14
It **m** seven feet from the smaller .... Eze 43:14

MEASURING

stretch the **m** line of Samaria 2Ki 21:13
and mixing, and for the **m.** 1Ch 23:29
use justice as a **m** line and .... Is 28:17
than the dust on his **m** scales.................. Is 40:15
The **m** line will stretch from the .... Je 31:39
a stick in his hand, both for **m.** .... Eze 40:3
'and the **m** line will be used to .... Zch 1:16
man holding a line for **m** things. .... Zch 2:1
"It is a **m** basket going out." .... Zch 5:6
was given a **m** stick like a rod, ... Rev 11:1
with me had a **m** rod made of gold........... Rev 21:15

MEAT

the LORD will give you **m** to eat, ... Ex 16:8
Where can I get **m** for all these .... Nu 11:13
tomorrow, and you will eat **m.** .... Nu 11:18
he provide his people with **m?**" .... Ps 78:20
He rained **m** on them like dust. .... Ps 78:27
He uses the fire to cook his **m,** .... Is 44:16
did not eat any fancy food or **m,**............. Da 10:3
better not to eat **m** or drink .... Rm 14:21
will never eat **m** again so that I 1Co 8:13
Eat any **m** that is sold in the 1Co 10:25

MEBUNNAI

Anathothite; **M** the Hushathite; 2Sa 23:27

MECONAH

and **M** and its surroundings, ... Ne 11:28

MEDAD

named Eldad and **M** were also .... Nu 11:26
Eldad and **M** are prophesying in .... Nu 11:27

MEDAN

Jokshan, **M,** Midian, Ishbak .... Ge 25:2
Jokshan, **M,** Midian, Ishbak 1Ch 1:32

MEDE

So Darius the **M** became the new .... Da 5:31
year that Darius the **M** was king, ... Da 11:1

MEDEBA

them as far as Nophah, near **M.**" .... Nu 21:30
the whole plain from **M** to Dibon. .... Jos 13:9
Arnon Ravine to the town of **M,**.............. Jos 13:16
set up camp near the town of **M.** 1Ch 19:7
for the cities of Nebo and **M.** .... Is 15:2

MEDES

and in the cities of the **M.** 2Ki 17:6
and in the cities of the **M.** 2Ki 18:11
stirred up the kings of the **M,** .... Je 51:11
kings of the **M,** their governors .... Je 51:28
given to the **M** and the Persians................ Da 5:28
be a law of the **M** and Persians .... Da 6:8
the laws of the **M** and Persians .... Da 6:12
the law of the **M** and Persians .... Da 6:15
He was a descendant of the **M.** .... Da 9:1

MEDIA

Ecbatana, the capital city of **M**. .... Ezr 6:2
Persia and **M** and the important .... Est 1:3
important men of Persia and **M**. .... Est 1:14
of Persia and **M** will hear about .... Est 1:17
of Persia and **M** have heard about .... Est 1:18
in the laws of Persia and **M**, ... Est 1:19
of the kings of **M** and Persia. .... Est 10:2
the armies of **M** to attack .... Is 13:17
M, surround the city and attack .... Is 21:2
the kings of Zimri, Elam, and **M**; .... Je 25:25
are the kings of **M** and Persia. .... Da 8:20
Parthia, **M**, Elam, Mesopotamia,.............. Ac 2:9

MEDIATOR

Moses for a **m** to give the law................ Gal 3:19
But a **m** is not needed when there .... Gal 3:20
one God and one **m** so that human........... 1Ti 2:5

MEDICINE

sandals, food, drink, and **m**. 2Ch 28:15
A happy heart is like good **m**,.................. Pr 17:22
and no **m** takes away the pain. .... Is 1:6
food, and their leaves for **m**." .... Eze 47:12
from me **m** to put on your eyes .... Rev 3:18

MEDICINES

prepared many **m**, but they will .... Je 46:11

MEDIUM

or woman who is a **m** or a .... Le 20:27
a woman who is a **m** so I may go 1Sa 28:7
There is a **m** in Endor." 1Sa 28:7
even went to a **m** and asked her.............. 1Ch 10:13

MEDIUMS

Do not go to **m** or .... Le 19:31
anyone who goes to **m** and .... Le 20:6
let them be **m** or try to talk..................... Dt 18:11
had forced out the **m** and 1Sa 28:3
He has forced the **m** and...................... 1Sa 28:9
he got advice from **m** and 2Ki 21:6
the **m**, fortune-tellers, ... 2Ki 23:24
He got advice from **m** and 2Ch 33:6
Ask the **m** and fortune-tellers, ... Is 8:19
The **m** and fortune-tellers do not .... Is 8:20
their **m** and fortune-tellers..................... Is 19:3
dreams, the **m**, or magicians. .... Je 27:9

MEET

he ran from his tent to **m** them. .... Ge 18:2
So Moses went out to **m** his .... Ex 18:7
I will **m** with you there, above .... Ex 25:22
I will **m** with God over there. .... Nu 23:15
my house to **m** me when I return .... Jdg 11:31
first one to come out to **m** him, ... Jdg 11:34
let's **m** together in Kephirim on .... Ne 6:2
and they **m** together to kill me. .... Ps 71:10
the holy ones **m**, it is God they .... Ps 89:7
should go and **m** Ahaz at the .... Is 7:3
get ready to **m** your God, Israel.............. Am 4:12
is coming! Come and **m** him!'.................. Mt 25:6
a jar of water will **m** you. .... Mk 14:13
Many people went out to **m** Jesus, ... Jn 12:18
And they would all **m** together on .... Ac 5:12
but you should **m** together and .... Heb 10:25
of Christian love when you **m**. 1Pe 5:14

MEETING

This will be in the **M** Tent, ... Ex 27:21
all the things in the **M** Tent. .... Ex 39:40
Holy Tent, which is the **M** Tent. .... Ex 40:2
shouted in your **m** place and .... Ps 74:4
stood in the **m** of angels to see .... Je 23:18
into your church **m** wearing nice .... Jam 2:2

MEETS

anyone who **m** me can kill me." .... Ge 4:14
a man **m** a virgin in a city and .... Dt 22:23
But if a man **m** an engaged girl .... Dt 22:25
If a man **m** a virgin who is not .... Dt 22:28
and everyone **m** with God in .... Ps 84:7
runs from a lion and **m** a bear, ... Am 5:19
Whoever **m** a prophet and accepts .... Mt 10:41
church that **m** at their house. .... Rm 16:5
the whole church **m** together and 1Co 14:23
church that **m** in their house. 1Co 16:19
the church that **m** in her house. .... Col 4:15
the church that **m** in your home: .... Phm 1:2

MEGIDDO

Taanach, **M**,.. Jos 12:21
people in **M** and its small towns. .... Jos 17:11
Dor, Ibleam, **M**, and the small .... Jdg 1:27
at Taanach, by the waters of **M**. .... Jdg 5:19
of Taanach, **M**, and all of Beth 1Ki 4:12
cities of Hazor, **M**, and Gezer.................. 1Ki 9:15
got as far as **M** but died there. 2Ki 9:27
Neco, but at **M**, Neco faced him 2Ki 23:29
in a chariot from **M** to Jerusalem 2Ki 23:30
Beth Shan, Taanach, **M**, and Dor, ... 1Ch 7:29
went to fight on the plain of **M**. 2Ch 35:22
Hadad Rimmon in the plain of **M**. .... Zch 12:11

MEHETABEL

wife's name was **M** daughter of .... Ge 36:39
wife was named **M**, and she was 1Ch 1:50
son of Delaiah, the son of **M**. .... Ne 6:10

MEHIDA

Bazluth, **M**, Harsha, ... Ezr 2:52
Bazluth, **M**, Harsha, ... Ne 7:54

MEHIR

brother, was the father of **M**. 1Ch 4:11
M was the father of Eshton. 1Ch 4:11

MEHOLAH

as far as the border of Abel **M**, ... Jdg 7:22
gave her instead to Adriel of **M**. 1Sa 18:19
Beth Shan to Abel **M** across from 1Ki 4:12
Shaphat from Abel **M** to make him 1Ki 19:16

MEHOLATHITE

Barzillai the **M** was the father 2Sa 21:8

MEHUJAEL

had a son named **M**, Mehujael had........... Ge 4:18
M had a son named Methushael, ... Ge 4:18

MEHUMAN

who served him—**M**, Biztha, ... Est 1:10

MEKERATHITE

Hepher the **M**; Ahijah the 1Ch 11:36

MELAH

from the towns of Tel **M**,....................... Ezr 2:59
from the towns of Tel **M**,....................... Ne 7:61

MELATIAH

Next to them, **M** from Gibeon, ... Ne 3:7

MELCHIZEDEK

M king of Salem brought out .... Ge 14:18
Then Abram gave **M** a tenth of .... Ge 14:20
forever, a priest like **M**." .... Ps 110:4
forever, a priest like **M**." .... Heb 5:6
a high priest, a priest like **M**. .... Heb 5:10
priest forever, a priest like **M**.................. Heb 6:20
M was the king of Salem and a .... Heb 7:1
they met, **M** blessed Abraham, ... Heb 7:1
M is like the Son of God; .... Heb 7:3
You can see how great **M** was. .... Heb 7:4
M was not from the tribe of Levi, ... Heb 7:6
But **M**, who received a tenth from .... Heb 7:8
it when Abraham paid **M** a tenth. .... Heb 7:9

M

MELCHIZEDEK'S

his ancestor when **M** met Abraham. .... Heb 7:10
a priest like **M**, not Aaron. .... Heb 7:11
priest comes who is like **M**. .... Heb 7:15
forever, a priest like **M**." .... Heb 7:17

MELCHIZEDEK'S

M name means "king of goodness," .... Heb 7:2
one knows who **M** father or mother .... Heb 7:3

MELEA

Eliakim was the son of **M**. .... Lk 3:31
M was the son of Menna. .... Lk 3:31

MELECH

were Pithon, **M**, Tarea, and Ahaz. 1Ch 8:35
were Pithon, **M**, Tahrea, and Ahaz 1Ch 9:41

MELKI

Levi was the son of **M**. .... Lk 3:24
M was the son of Jannai. .... Lk 3:24
Neri was the son of **M**. .... Lk 3:28
M was the son of Addi. .... Lk 3:28

MELON

are like scarecrows in **m** fields; .... Je 10:5

MELONS

had cucumbers, **m**, leeks, onions, ... Nu 11:5
like a hut left in a field of **m**, ... Is 1:8

MELT

and dryness quickly **m** the snow, ... Job 24:19
like snails that **m** as they move. .... Ps 58:8
The mountains **m** like wax before .... Ps 97:5
and their courage will **m** away. .... Is 13:7
and Egypt's courage will **m** away. .... Is 19:1
hotter, but the lead does not **m**. .... Je 6:29
every heart will **m** with fear, ... Eze 21:7
Their hearts will **m** with fear, ... Eze 21:15
inside a furnace to **m** them down .... Eze 22:20
in Jerusalem and **m** you down. .... Eze 22:20
it may then **m** and its rust burn .... Eze 24:11
The mountains will **m** under him, ... Mic 1:4
front of him, and the hills **m**. .... Nah 1:5
in them will **m** with heat. 2Pe 3:12

MELTED

the sun became hot, it **m** away. .... Ex 16:21
had made and **m** it in the fire. .... Ex 32:20
Do not make gods of **m** metal. .... Ex 34:17
for each stand was **m** and poured 1Ki 7:37
and copper is **m** out of rocks. .... Job 28:2
is like wax; it has **m** inside me. .... Ps 22:14
will be **m** down inside Jerusalem. .... Eze 22:21
As silver is **m** in a furnace, ... Eze 22:22
you will be **m** inside the city. .... Eze 22:22

MELTING

you like a furnace for **m** iron, ... Dt 4:20
are made dark by **m** ice and rise .... Job 6:16
ice and rise with **m** snow. .... Job 6:16
was like a furnace for **m** iron!' .... Je 11:4

MELTS

As wax **m** before a fire, let the .... Ps 68:2
he gives a command, and it **m**. .... Ps 147:18
Lebanon never **m** from the rocks. .... Je 18:14

MEMBER

among you or to a **m** of the .... Le 25:47
least important of my family." .... Jdg 6:15
did not become a **m** of the Three. 2Sa 23:23
a **m** of the family of the king of 1Ki 11:14
did not become a **m** of the Three. 1Ch 11:25
longer be a **m** of the community .... Ezr 10:8
Ishmael was a **m** of the king's .... Je 41:1
Then he took a **m** of the family .... Eze 17:13
nor am I a **m** of a group of .... Am 7:14
an important **m** of the Jewish .... Mk 15:43

who was a **m** of the council. .... Lk 23:50
Dionysius, a **m** of the Areopagus .... Ac 17:34

MEMBERS

given by the **m** of the community .... Ex 38:25
own brothers and **m** of your own .... Je 12:6
enemies will be **m** of his own .... Mic 7:6
then the other **m** of the family .... Mt 10:25
will be **m** of his own family. .... Mt 10:36
especially his own family **m**, ... 1Ti 5:8

MEMORIAL

it on the altar as a **m** portion. .... Le 2:2
He will take out the **m** portion .... Le 2:9
priest will burn the **m** portion. .... Le 2:16
the flour as a **m** offering and .... Le 5:12
on the altar as a **m** offering to .... Le 6:15
row as the **m** portion to take .... Le 24:7
grain, which is a **m** offering, ... Nu 5:26
Tent as a **m** before the LORD .... Nu 31:54
claim, or **m** in Jerusalem." .... Ne 2:20

MEMORIALS

or set up statues or **m**........................... Le 26:1

MEMORY

destroy any **m** of the Amalekites .... Dt 25:19
will destroy any **m** of them on .... Dt 29:20
them and erased any **m** of them. .... Is 26:14

MEMPHIS

the leaders of **M** have believed .... Is 19:13
the cities of **M** and Tahpanhes .... Je 2:16
Tahpanhes, **M**, and in southern .... Je 44:1
the cities of **M** and Tahpanhes: ' .... Je 46:14
because **M** will be destroyed. .... Je 46:19
of gods from the city of **M**. .... Eze 30:13
and **M** will have troubles every .... Eze 30:16
capture them; **M** will bury them. .... Hos 9:6

MEMUCAN

Meres, Marsena, and **M**, seven of .... Est 1:14
Then **M** said to the king and the.............. Est 1:16
King Xerxes did as **M** suggested. .... Est 1:21

MEN

up and saw three **m** standing near .... Ge 18:2
has four hundred **m** with him." .... Ge 32:6
magicians and wise **m** of Egypt............... Ge 41:8
We are honest **m**, not spies." .... Ge 42:11
and brought the **m** to Joseph's .... Ge 43:17
saw two Hebrew **m** fighting each .... Ex 2:13
because the **m** who wanted to kill .... Ex 4:19
beat these **m** and asked them,............... Ex 5:14
in his wise **m** and his magicians............. Ex 7:11
Only the **m** may go and worship............. Ex 10:11
He chose capable **m** from all the .... Ex 18:25
Suppose two **m** are fighting and.............. Ex 21:22
m that you know are leaders .... Nu 11:16
Send **m** to explore the land of .... Nu 13:2
you put out the eyes of these **m**?........... Nu 16:14
If these **m** die a normal death— .... Nu 16:29
commanded these **m** to divide the .... Nu 34:29
daughters marry **m** from other .... Nu 36:3
choose some **m** from each tribe— .... Dt 1:13
as well as the **m**, women, and................. Dt 2:34
your fighting **m** must take their .... Dt 3:18
your fighting **m** must dress for .... Jos 1:14
the woman had hidden the two **m**. .... Jos 2:4
including his best fighting **m**. .... Jos 10:7
family and the **m** of the city .... Jdg 6:27
three hundred **m** who used their............... Jdg 7:6
three hundred **m** into three................... Jdg 7:16
reckless **m**, who followed him .... Jdg 9:4
'**M** and gods are honored by my .... Jdg 9:9
new wine makes **m** and gods happy. .... Jdg 9:13
punished the **m** of Shechem for .... Jdg 9:57

jawbone I killed a thousand **m**!"................Jdg 15:16
temple was full of **m** and women. ....Jdg 16:27
the night the **m** of Gibeah came ....Jdg 20:5
over the wicked **m** in Gibeah so ....Jdg 20:13
had 700 chosen **m** from Gibeah. ....Jdg 20:15
The **m** in hiding rushed into ....Jdg 20:37
m in the surprise attack were ....Jdg 20:38
warned the young **m** not to bother ....Ru 2:9
The **m** said to David, "Today is 1Sa 24:4
But the evil **m** and troublemakers 1Sa 30:22
uncircumcised **m** won't make fun 1Sa 31:4
He fell at the hands of evil **m**."...............2Sa 3:34
and Rehob and the **m** from Tob and 2Sa 10:8
When the **m** of the city came out 2Sa 11:17
eight hundred **m** at one time. 2Sa 23:8
blood of the **m** who risked their 2Sa 23:17
and fifty **m** for his personal 1Ki 1:5
in these ships with Solomon's **m**. 1Ki 9:27
Your **m** and officers are very 1Ki 10:8
The **m** cleaned Ahab's chariot at 1Ki 22:38
the brave **m** of Jabesh went and 1Ch 10:12
three hundred **m** at one time, ...1Ch 11:11
fifty thousand **m** from Zebulun. 1Ch 12:33
and some capable **m** of the Hebron 1Ch 26:31
who were skilled **m** and leaders 1Ch 26:32
eighty thousand **m** from Benjamin. 2Ch 14:8
These **m** were leaders of the 2Ch 35:9
names of the **m** working on this ....Ezr 5:4
I started out with a few **m**. ....Ne 2:12
with half the **m** holding spears ....Ne 4:21
morning until noon to the **m**, ...Ne 8:3
with the wise **m** who would know ....Est 1:13
kings and wise **m** of the earth ....Job 3:14
and spends time with wicked **m**, ...Job 34:8
M without mercy stand up to ....Ps 35:11
Saul sent **m** to watch David's ....Ps 58:11
taught the older **m** to be wise. ....Ps 105:22
young **m** and women, old people ....Ps 148:12
those important **m** in iron bands. ....Ps 149:8
but cruel **m** get only wealth. ....Pr 11:16
cause many **m** to be unfaithful ....Pr 23:28
copied by the **m** of Hezekiah king ....Pr 25:1
their arms hold **m** like chains. ....Ec 7:26
and important **m** were the head,..............Is 9:15
Egypt, where are your wise **m**? ....Is 19:12
Their wise **m** will lose their ....Is 29:14
but its young **m** will be caught ....Is 31:8
him, "What did these **m** say? ....Is 39:3
m who carry the LORD's things ....Is 52:11
The **m** from the cities of Memphis ....Je 2:16
and the young **m** who meet in the ....Je 9:21
soon punish the **m** from Anathoth............Je 11:22
Their young **m** will die in war. ....Je 11:22
Can the wise **m** of Edom no longer ....Je 49:7
Zedekiah and his **m** headed toward ......Je 52:7
all my mighty **m** inside my walls. ....La 1:15
women and young **m** have been ....La 2:21
said to the other **m**, "Go through ....Eze 9:5
Even if three great **m** like Noah,.............Eze 14:14
his **m** will take away your riches ....Eze 26:12
M from Sidon and Arvad used oars ....Eze 27:8
one of their **m** and make him ....Eze 33:2
all the young **m** who ate the ....Da 1:15
gave these four young **m** wisdom ....Da 1:17
that all the wise **m** of Babylon ....Da 2:12
He asked the **m** who advised him, ...Da 3:24
up only three **m** and throw them ....Da 3:24
I see four **m** walking around in ....Da 3:25
None of the wise **m** in my kingdom ....Da 4:18
Then all the king's wise **m** came ....Da 5:8
because the **m** have sexual ....Hos 4:14
your old **m** will dream dreams, ...Joe 2:28
and your young **m** will see ....Joe 2:28

killed your young **m** with swords, ...Am 4:10
and the young **m** will become weak ....Am 8:13
the **m** tried to row the ship back ....Jnh 1:13
So the **m** cried to the LORD, ...Jnh 1:14
and the **m** of Judah married women ....Mal 2:11
some wise **m** from the east came ....Mt 2:1
two **m** who had demons in them met ....Mt 8:28
out these twelve **m** with the ....Mt 10:5
five thousand **m** there who ate, ...Mt 14:21
four thousand **m** there who ate, ...Mt 15:38
the **m** who collected the Temple ....Mt 17:24
some **m** have given up marriage...............Mt 19:12
will surely kill those evil **m**. ....Mt 21:41
Two **m** will be in the field. ....Mt 24:40
and they became like dead **m**. ....Mt 28:4
The **m** were amazed at what Jesus ....Mk 12:17
ten **m** who had a skin disease met ....Lk 17:12
king said to the **m** who were ....Lk 19:24
five thousand **m** sat down there................Jn 6:10
m wearing white clothes stood ....Ac 1:10
They said, "**M** of Galilee, why................Ac 1:11
Your young **m** will see visions, ...Ac 2:17
your old **m** will dream dreams. ....Ac 2:17
that these **m** had no special ....Ac 4:13
of your own **m** who are good,................Ac 6:3
then three **m** who were sent to ....Ac 11:11
send some of their **m** with Paul ....Ac 15:22
they got some evil **m** from the ....Ac 17:5
important Greek women and **m**................Ac 17:12
m stopped having natural sex and ....Rm 1:27
were serving only **m** and women. ....Eph 6:7
I want the **m** everywhere to pray, ...1Ti 2:8
Treat younger **m** like brothers, ...1Ti 5:1
Teach older **m** to be......................Tit 2:2
encourage young **m** to be wise. ....Tit 2:6
are only **m** who live and then ....Heb 7:8

MEN'S
Fill the **m** sacks with as much..................Ge 44:1
A woman must not wear **m** clothes, ...Dt 22:5
these **m** eyes so they can see. 2Ki 6:20

MENAHEM
Then **M** son of Gadi came up from 2Ki 15:14
M started out from Tirzah and 2Ki 15:16
M son of Gadi became king over 2Ki 15:17
M ruled ten years in Samaria, ...2Ki 15:17
and all the time **M** was king, ...2Ki 15:18
M gave him about seventy-four 2Ki 15:19
M taxed Israel to pay about one 2Ki 15:20
Everything else **M** did is written.........2Ki 15:21
M died, and his son Pekahiah.................2Ki 15:22
Pekahiah son of **M** became king.............2Ki 15:23

MEND
it up again and **m** its broken ....Am 9:11

MENDED
bags that were cracked and **m**, ...Jos 9:4

MENDING
father Zebedee, **m** their nets. ....Mt 4:21
were in a boat, **m** their nets. ....Mk 1:19

MENE
'**M**, mene, tekel, and parsin.' ....Da 5:25
'Mene, **m**, tekel, and parsin.' ....Da 5:25
the words mean: **M**: God has ....Da 5:26

MENNA
Melea was the son of **M**.........................Lk 3:31
M was the son of Mattatha. ....Lk 3:31

MENTION
Why do you **m** my agreement? ....Ps 50:16
Son, knows that I always **m** you..............Rm 1:9
of you and **m** you when we pray. 1Th 1:2

M

God as I always **m** you in my 2Ti 1:3
God when I **m** you in my prayers, ... Phm 1:4

MENTIONED

close relative he had **m** passed .... Ru 4:1
When he **m** the Ark of God, Eli 1Sa 4:18
people will never be **m** again.................. Is 14:20

MEON

Nebo, Baal **M**, and Sibmah. .... Nu 32:38
and Baal **M** when they rebuilt .... Nu 32:38
Bamoth Baal, and Beth Baal **M**, ... Jos 13:17
all the way to Nebo and Baal **M**. 1Ch 5:8
Beth Gamul, and Beth **M**; .... Je 48:23
Baal **M**, and Kiriathaim. .... Eze 25:9

MEONOTHAI

sons were Hathath and **M**. 1Ch 4:13
M was the father of Ophrah. 1Ch 4:14

MEPHAATH

Jahaz, Kedemoth, **M**, ... Jos 13:18
Kedemoth, and **M**, along with the .... Jos 21:37
Holon, Jahzah, and **M**; .... Je 48:21

MEPHIBOSHETH

M, Jonathan's son, came before 2Sa 9:6
M, Saul's grandson, also went 2Sa 19:24
the king protected **M**, the son of............... 2Sa 21:7

MERAB

His older daughter was named **M**, ... 1Sa 14:49
Here is my older daughter **M**.................. 1Sa 18:17
daughter **M** to marry David, ... 1Sa 18:19
five sons of Saul's daughter **M**. 2Sa 21:8

MERAB'S

was the father of **M** five sons.................. 2Sa 21:8

MERAIAH

M, from Seraiah's family; .... Ne 12:12

MERAIOTH

Zerahiah was the father of **M**. 1Ch 6:6
M was the father of Amariah.................. 1Ch 6:7
M was Zerahiah's son. 1Ch 6:52
M was Ahitub's son. 1Ch 9:11
son of Azariah, the son of **M**, ... Ezr 7:3
was the son of **M**, the son of .... Ne 11:11

MERAIOTH'S

Amariah was **M** son. 1Ch 6:52
son. Zadok was **M** son. Meraioth 1Ch 9:11

MERARI

were Gershon, Kohath, and **M**. .... Ge 46:11

MERATHAIM

Attack the land of **M**. .... Je 50:21

MERCHANTS

gold from the traders and **m**, ... 1Ki 10:15
gold from traders and **m**. 2Ch 9:14
they divide it up among the **m**? .... Job 41:6
and provides belts to the **m**. .... Pr 31:24
you **m** of Sidon, be silent. .... Is 23:2
Its **m** were treated like princes, ... Is 23:8
and Meshech became **m** for you. .... Eze 27:13
of Rhodes became **m** for you, ... Eze 27:15
and Israel became **m** for you. .... Eze 27:17
of Dedan became **m** for you, ... Eze 27:20
The **m** of Sheba and Raamah .... Eze 27:22
and Raamah became **m** for you............... Eze 27:22
and Kilmad became **m** for you. .... Eze 27:23
The **m** use dishonest scales; .... Hos 12:7
because all the **m** will be dead; .... Zph 1:11
the **m** of the earth have grown .... Rev 18:3
And the **m** of the earth will cry .... Rev 18:11
The **m** will say, "Babylon, the .... Rev 18:14
The **m** who became rich from.................. Rev 18:15
Your **m** were the world's great .... Rev 18:23

MERCIES

never ends; his **m** never stop. .... La 3:22

MERCIFUL

So the LORD was **m** to Lot and his .... Ge 19:16
You have been **m** and kind to me .... Ge 19:19
governor to be **m** to you and that .... Ge 43:14
were not **m** to them in all .... Ex 1:14
I will listen, because I am **m**. .... Ex 22:27
the LORD your God is a **m** God............... Dt 4:31
I should kill you, but I was **m**. 1Sa 24:10
because the LORD is very **m**. 2Sa 24:14
because the LORD is very **m**. 1Ch 21:13
The LORD your God is kind and **m**. 2Ch 30:9
You are a kind and **m** God...................... Ne 9:31
be **m** to me because you are .... Ps 51:1
you are always ready to be **m**, ... Ps 51:1
be **m** to me because people are .... Ps 56:1
Be **m** to me, God; be merciful to .... Ps 57:1
be **m** to me because I come to you .... Ps 57:1
God was **m**. He forgave their .... Ps 78:38
The LORD is kind and **m**. .... Ps 111:4
those who are **m** and kind and .... Ps 112:4
It is good to be **m** and generous................ Ps 112:5
what is right; our God is **m**. .... Ps 116:5
he is **m** to all he has made. .... Ps 145:9
want to be kind and **m** to Daniel, ... Da 1:9
Be kind and **m** to each other. .... Zch 7:9
could be their **m** and faithful .... Heb 2:17

MERCY

Ark; this is the **m** seat. Make it .... Ex 25:17
and I will show **m** to anyone to .... Ex 33:19
anyone to whom I want to show **m**. .... Ex 33:19
The LORD is a God who shows **m**,........... Ex 34:6
his kindness and have **m** on you. .... Nu 6:25
with them or show them any **m**. .... Dt 7:2
will give you **m** and feel sorry .... Dt 13:17
Show no **m**. You must remove from .... Dt 19:13
Show no **m**. A life must be paid .... Dt 19:21
cut off her hand. Show her no **m**. .... Dt 25:12
and have **m** on his servants .... Dt 32:36
destroy them without **m**....................... Jos 11:20
such a thing. He had no **m**!" 2Sa 12:6
have captured them show them **m**........... 1Ki 8:50
he had **m** on them and helped them 2Ki 13:23
He had no **m** on the young men or........... 2Ch 36:17
You are kind and full of **m**..................... Ne 9:17
You have great **m**, so you did not .... Ne 9:19
You had great **m** and gave them .... Ne 9:28
Because of your **m**, you saved................. Ne 9:31
But because your **m** is great, ... Ne 9:31
Have **m** on me because of your .... Ne 13:22
to beg for **m** and to plead with .... Est 4:8
and pray to the Almighty for **m**. .... Job 8:5
only beg God, my Judge, for **m**. .... Job 9:15
He stabs my kidneys without **m**;............... Job 16:13
hit them without **m** as they try .... Job 27:22
You have turned on me without **m**;........... Job 30:21
angel will beg for **m** and say: ' .... Job 33:24
begging you for **m** and speak to .... Job 41:3
Have **m** on me and hear my prayer. .... Ps 4:1
have **m** on me because I am weak............. Ps 6:2
LORD, have **m** on me. See how my .... Ps 9:13
remember your **m** and love that .... Ps 25:6
Turn to me and have **m** on me, ... Ps 25:16
so save me and have **m** on me. .... Ps 26:11
I call; have **m** and answer me. .... Ps 27:7
and asked you to have **m** on me. .... Ps 30:8
LORD, hear me and have **m** on me. .... Ps 30:10
LORD, have **m**, because I am in .... Ps 31:9
Men without **m** stand up to...................... Ps 35:11
do not hold back your **m** from me; .... Ps 40:11
I said, "LORD, have **m** on me. .... Ps 41:4

M

MEREMOTH

to the priest **M** son of Uriah. .... Ezr 8:33
Vaniah, **M,** Eliashib, ... Ezr 10:36
M son of Uriah, the son of .... Ne 3:4
made repairs next to **M.** .... Ne 3:4
Next to him, **M** son of Uriah, the .... Ne 3:21
Harim, **M,** Obadiah, ... Ne 10:5
Shecaniah, Rehum, **M,** .... Ne 12:3

MEREMOTH'S

Helkai, from **M** family; .... Ne 12:15

MERES

Admatha, Tarshish, **M,** Marsena, ... Est 1:14

MERIB-BAAL

Jonathan's son was **M,** who was.............. 1Ch 8:34
Jonathan's son was **M,** who was.............. 1Ch 9:40

MERIBAH

He also named it **M,** because they .... Ex 17:7
These are the waters of **M,** .... Nu 20:13
my command at the waters of **M.** .... Nu 20:24
the people at the waters of **M.**" .... Nu 27:14
This was at **M** in Kadesh in .... Nu 27:14
me at the waters of **M** Kadesh in .... Dt 32:51
with him at the waters of **M.** .... Dt 33:8
tested you at the waters of **M.**................ Ps 81:7
as your ancestors were at **M,** .... Ps 95:8
also made the LORD angry at **M,** .... Ps 106:32
way to the waters of **M** Kadesh. .... Eze 47:19
Sea to the waters of **M** Kadesh. .... Eze 48:28

MERODACH-BALADAN

that time **M** son of Baladan was 2Ki 20:12
that time **M** son of Baladan was .... Is 39:1

MEROM

met together at the waters of **M,**.............. Jos 11:5
them at the waters of **M.** .... Jos 11:7

MERON

Shimron **M,** Acshaph, ... Jos 12:20

MERONOTH

Jehdeiah, from **M,** was in charge 1Ch 27:30
and Jadon from **M** made repairs. .... Ne 3:7

MEROZ

'May the town of **M** be cursed,' .... Jdg 5:23

MESHA

in the area between **M** and Sephar........... Ge 10:30
M king of Moab raised sheep.................. 2Ki 3:4
Caleb's first son was **M.** 1Ch 2:42
M was the father of Ziph, and 1Ch 2:42

MESHACH

Mishael's was **M,** and Azariah's .... Da 1:7
are Shadrach, **M,** and Abednego. ....Da 3:12

MESHECH

M and Tubal are there with the .... Eze 32:26
chief ruler of **M** and Tubal. .... Eze 38:3

MESHELEMIAH

Zechariah son of **M** was the 1Ch 9:21
there was **M** son of Kore, who 1Ch 26:1
M had sons. Zechariah was his 1Ch 26:2
M had sons and relatives who 1Ch 26:9
M was chosen by lot to guard the 1Ch 26:14

MESHELEMIAH'S

were thrown for **M** son Zechariah............. 1Ch 26:14

MESHEZABEL

the son of **M,** made repairs next.............. Ne 3:4
M, Zadok, Jaddua, ... Ne 10:21
Pethahiah son of **M** was the .... Ne 11:24
M was a descendant of Zerah, ... Ne 11:24

MESHILLEMITH

son, and **M** was Immer's son. 1Ch 9:12

MESHILLEMITH'S

Meshullam was **M** son, and 1Ch 9:12

MESHILLEMOTH

Berekiah son of **M,** Jehizkiah son 2Ch 28:12
the son of Ahzai, the son of **M.** .... Ne 11:13
M was the son of Immer......................... Ne 11:13

MESHULLEMETH

name was **M** daughter of Haruz 2Ki 21:19

MESOPOTAMIA

to Northwest **M** to Nahor's city. .... Ge 24:10
king of Northwest **M** to rule over .... Jdg 3:8
Media, Elam, **M,** Judea, ... Ac 2:9
in **M** before he lived in Haran. .... Ac 7:2

MESSAGE

I have a secret **m** for you, ... Jdg 3:19
chose to use the **m** that sounds 1Co 1:21
truth of the **m** by using wonders.............. Heb 2:4
Here is the **m** we have heard from 1Jn 1:5
it is the **m** from Jesus Christ. .... Rev 1:2

MESSENGER

a cruel **m** will be sent against .... Pr 17:11
or more deaf than the **m** I send. .... Is 42:19
because he is the **m** of the LORD .... Mal 2:7
I will send my **m,** who will .... Mal 3:1
the **m** of the agreement, whom you .... Mal 3:1
'I will send my **m** ahead of you, ... Mt 11:10
I will send my **m** ahead of you, ... Mk 1:2
'I will send my **m** ahead of you, ... Lk 7:27
A **m** is not greater than the one .... Jn 13:16
This problem was a **m** from Satan,........... 2Co 12:7

MESSENGERS

So David sent **m** to bring 2Sa 11:4
land sends **m** across the sea; .... Is 18:2
He sent some **m** ahead of him, ... Lk 9:52
truth before God, as **m** of God. 2Co 2:17
any of the **m** I sent to you? 2Co 12:17

MESSIAH

to him, "We have found the **M.**" .... Jn 1:41
"**M**" means "Christ." .... Jn 1:41
"I know that the **M** is coming." .... Jn 4:25
M is the One called Christ..................... Jn 4:25
When the **M** comes, he will..................... Jn 4:25

MET

who had demons in them **m** him. .... Mt 8:28
had a skin disease **m** him there. .... Lk 17:12
place where Martha had **m** him................ Jn 11:30
because Jesus **m** there often with .... Jn 18:2
Cornelius **m** him, fell at his.................... Ac 10:25
He **m** Abraham when Abraham was .... Heb 7:1
when Melchizedek **m** Abraham............... Heb 7:10

METHEG

and took the city of **M** Ammah. 2Sa 8:1

METHUSELAH

So **M** lived a total of 969 years, ... Ge 5:27

METHUSHAEL

Mehujael had a son named **M,** .... Ge 4:18
and **M** had a son named Lamech. .... Ge 4:18

MEUNIM

Asnah, **M,** Nephussim, ... Ezr 2:50
Besai, **M,** Nephussim, ... Ne 7:52

MEUNITES

against the **M** who lived there 1Ch 4:41
So there are no **M** there even 1Ch 4:41
and some **M** came to start a war 2Ch 20:1
living in Gur Baal, and the **M.** 2Ch 26:7

MEZOBAITES

Eliel, Obed, and Jaasiel the **M.** 1Ch 11:47

MIBHAR
of Nathan; M son of Hagri; 1Ch 11:38

MIBSAM
son, then Kedar, Adbeel, M, ... Ge 25:13
sons were Kedar, Adbeel, M, ... 1Ch 1:29
son was M. Mibsam's son was 1Ch 4:25

MIBSAM'S
was Mibsam. M son was Mishma. 1Ch 4:25

MIBZAR
Kenaz, Teman, M, ... Ge 36:42
Kenaz, Teman, M, ... 1Ch 1:53

MICA
had a young son named M.................... 2Sa 9:12
Galal, and Mattaniah son of M. 1Ch 9:15
M was Zicri's son, and Zicri was 1Ch 9:15
M, Rehob, Hashabiah, ... Ne 10:11
There was Mattaniah son of M. .... Ne 11:17
M was the son of Zabdi, the son.............. Ne 11:17
Mattaniah was the son of M. .... Ne 11:22

MICAH
was a man named M who lived .... Jdg 17:1
M made him a priest, and he .... Jdg 17:12
M, from the city of Moresheth, ... Je 26:18
the word of the LORD came to M, ... Mic 1:1

MICAIAH
He is M son of Imlah." 1Ki 22:8

MICHAEL
against these enemies except M, ... Da 10:21
At that time M, the great prince .... Da 12:1
the archangel M, when he argued .... Jud 1:9
M and his angels fought against.............. Rev 12:7

MICHAEL'S
son. Gilead was M son. Michael 1Ch 5:14
Shimea was M son. Michael was 1Ch 6:40

MICHAL
younger daughter was named M. 1Sa 14:49
other daughter, M, loved David. 1Sa 18:20
him his daughter M for his wife. 1Sa 18:27
that his daughter M loved David. 1Sa 18:28
But M, David's wife, warned him, ... 1Sa 19:11
Then M took an idol, laid it on 1Sa 19:13
but M said, "He is sick. 1Sa 19:14
Saul said to M, "Why did you............... 1Sa 19:17
M answered Saul, "David told me 1Sa 19:17
Saul's daughter M was also 1Sa 25:44
bring Saul's daughter M to me.".............. 2Sa 3:13
saying, "Give me my wife M. 2Sa 3:14
men to take M from her husband 2Sa 3:15
Saul's daughter M looked out the 2Sa 6:16
Saul's daughter M came out to 2Sa 6:20
Then David said to M, "I did it 2Sa 6:21
daughter M had no children 2Sa 6:23
Saul's daughter M watched from a........... 1Ch 15:29

MICHAL'S
M husband went with her, crying 2Sa 3:16

MICMASH
with him at M in the mountains 1Sa 13:2
went and camped at M, ... 1Sa 13:5
Philistines were gathering at M. 1Sa 13:11
made their camp at M. 1Sa 13:16
had gone out to the pass at M. 1Sa 13:23
One cliff faced north toward M. 1Sa 14:5
Philistines from M to Aijalon.................. 1Sa 14:31
of M—122; .... Ezr 2:27
of M—122; .... Ne 7:31
from Geba lived in M,........................ Ne 11:31
They will store their food in M. .... Is 10:28

MICMETHATH
From M it turned eastward toward .... Jos 16:6
in the area between Asher and M, ... Jos 17:7

MICRI'S
Uzzi. (Uzzi was M son.) And 1Ch 9:8

MIDDIN
Beth Arabah, M, Secacah, ... Jos 15:61

MIDDLE
In the m of the garden, God put .... Ge 2:9
that is in the m of the garden.................. Ge 3:3
Make an upper, m, and lower deck........... Ge 6:16
it is still the m of the day. .... Ge 29:7
solid in the m of the sea...................... Ex 15:8
The m crossbar is to be set .... Ex 26:28
They made the m crossbar run .... Ex 36:33
in the m of unclean people.................... Le 16:16
will be in the m of the other .... Nu 2:17
He ran to the m of the people, ... Nu 16:47
the m of the Arnon is the border .... Dt 3:16
and put it in the m of the city .... Dt 13:16
three cities in the m of the .... Dt 19:2
the LORD to the m of the river .... Jos 3:17
rocks from the m of the river,................. Jos 4:3
rocks from the m of the Jordan .... Jos 4:8
rocks in the m of the Jordan .... Jos 4:9
standing in the m of the river .... Jos 4:10
sun stopped in the m of the sky .... Jos 10:13
started in the m of the ravine,................ Jos 12:2
the town in the m of the ravine, ... Jos 13:9
the town in the m of the ravine; .... Jos 13:16
It was during the m watch of the .... Jdg 7:19
sleeping in the m of the camp................. 1Sa 26:5
asleep in the m of the camp with 1Sa 26:7
Amasa lay in the m of the road, ... 2Sa 20:12
stood in the m of the field 2Sa 23:12
Those on the m floor were nine 1Ki 6:6
each other in the m of the room. 1Ki 6:27
made holy the m part of the 1Ki 8:64
Isaiah had left the m courtyard, ... 2Ki 20:4
stopped in the m of that field 1Ch 11:14
placed it in the m of the outer................. 2Ch 6:13
made holy the m part of the 2Ch 7:7
a moment, in the m of the night. .... Job 34:20
In the m are the girls with the .... Ps 68:25
not take me in the m of my life. .... Ps 102:24
In the m of the night, I get up .... Ps 119:62
Israelites through the m of it. .... Ps 136:14
a tower in the m of it and cut .... Is 5:2
for the LORD in the m of Egypt .... Is 19:19
I am in the m of my life. .... Is 38:10
you live in the m of lies. .... Je 9:6
and sat down at the M Gate: .... Je 39:3
was caught in the m of a gang of .... Je 48:27
fire in the m of the city when .... Eze 5:2
left in the m of the city are .... Eze 11:7
be the best meat in the m of it. .... Eze 11:11
ends and starts to burn the m, ... Eze 15:4
heavy cargo in the m of the sea.............. Eze 27:25
to pieces in the m of the sea. .... Eze 27:26
of a god in the m of the seas." .... Eze 28:2
me down in the m of a valley.................. Eze 37:1
the highest through the m story.............. Eze 41:7
will be in the m of this area. .... Eze 48:8
the LORD will be in the m of it. .... Eze 48:10
The city will be in the m of it................. Eze 48:15
of the Temple will be in the m. .... Eze 48:21
will be in the m of the lands .... Eze 48:22
standing in the m of the earth. .... Da 4:10
the m of the sounds around and .... Am 2:2
forest in the m of a garden land .... Mic 7:14
up here in the m of everyone." .... Mk 3:3
boat was in the m of the lake,................. Mk 6:47

M

ceiling into the **m** of the crowd .... Lk 5:19
up here in the **m** of everyone." .... Lk 6:8
a fire in the **m** of the courtyard .... Lk 22:55
right in the **m** of them and said .... Lk 24:36
each side, with Jesus in the **m.** .... Jn 19:18
right in the **m** of them and said .... Jn 20:19
stood right in the **m** of them. .... Jn 20:26
throne and in the **m** of the four .... Rev 5:6
coming from the **m** of the four .... Rev 6:6
down the **m** of the street of the .... Rev 22:2

MIDIAN
went to live in the land of **M.** .... Ex 2:15
was the priest of **M.** .... Ex 18:1
Now the camp of **M** was in the .... Jdg 7:8
the kings of **M,** ran away, but .... Jdg 8:12
Like the time you defeated **M,** .... Is 9:4

MIDIAN'S
M sons were Ephah, Epher, Hanoch, ... 1Ch 1:33

MIDIANITE
So when the **M** traders came by, ... Ge 37:28
killed with the **M** woman was .... Nu 25:14

MIDIANITES
Meanwhile the **M** who had bought .... Ge 37:36
and save Israel from the **M.** .... Jdg 6:14
All the **M,** the Amalekites, and .... Jdg 6:33

MIDNIGHT
'About **m** tonight I will go .... Ex 11:4
At **m** the LORD killed all the .... Ex 12:29
with the prostitute until **m.** .... Jdg 16:3
About **m** Boaz was startled and .... Ru 3:8
At **m** someone cried out, 'The .... Mt 25:6
evening, or at **m,** or in the .... Mk 13:35
house at **m** and said to him, ... Lk 11:5
even if it is **m** or later. .... Lk 12:38
About **m** Paul and Silas were .... Ac 16:25
he kept on talking until **m.** .... Ac 20:7
About **m** the sailors thought we .... Ac 27:27

MIGDAL
and camped just south of **M** Eder. .... Ge 35:21
Zenan, Hadashah, **M** Gad, ... Jos 15:37
Iron, **M** El, Horem, Beth Anath, ... Jos 19:38

MIGDOL
camp between **M** and the Red Sea .... Ex 14:2
Baal Zephon, and camped near **M.** .... Nu 33:7
in the cities of **M,** Tahpanhes, ... Je 44:1
in Egypt, and preach it in **M.** .... Je 46:14
desert from **M** in the north to .... Eze 29:10
in war from **M** in the north to .... Eze 30:6

MIGHT
terrible **m** happen to him, ... Ge 44:29
who digs a pit **m** fall into it; .... Ec 10:8
You **m** say, "We are depending on .... Is 36:7
so that Israel **m** be gathered to .... Is 49:5
m ask yourself, "Why has this .... Je 13:22
you **m** continue to be successful. .... Da 4:27
Someone may say, "You have faith, ... Jam 2:18
A person **m** have to suffer even 1Pe 2:19
this so that you **m** receive a 1Pe 3:9

MIGHTY
and were the **m** warriors of long .... Ge 6:4
power from the **M** God of Jacob .... Ge 49:24
galloping go Sisera's **m** horses. .... Jdg 5:22
LORD is with you, **m** warrior!" .... Jdg 6:12
How the **m** have fallen in battle! 2Sa 1:19
there the **m** warrior's shield 2Sa 1:21
How the **m** have fallen in battle! 2Sa 1:25
How the **m** have fallen! 2Sa 1:27
from Kabzeel who did **m** things 2Sa 23:20
He was a **m** and brave man, but he 2Ki 5:1
grew up to become a **m** warrior on 1Ch 1:10

Ulam's sons were **m** warriors and 1Ch 8:40
from Kabzeel who did **m** things 1Ch 11:22
These were also **m** warriors: 1Ch 11:26
a stone thrown into **m** waters. .... Ne 9:11
the great and **m** and wonderful .... Ne 9:32
The LORD, strong and **m.** .... Ps 24:8
M warrior, why do you brag about .... Ps 52:1
He is my **m** rock and my .... Ps 62:7
show the **m** power you have used .... Ps 68:28
had limbs like the **m** cedar tree. .... Ps 80:10
You rule the **m** sea and calm the .... Ps 89:9
You are the **m** warriors who do .... Ps 103:20
tell all the **m** things the LORD .... Ps 106:2
the LORD has done **m** things. .... Ps 118:16
swept us away like a **m** stream. .... Ps 124:5
a promise to the **M** God of Jacob. .... Ps 132:2
a home for the **M** God of Jacob." .... Ps 132:5
LORD God, my **m** savior, you .... Ps 140:7
They will retell your **m** acts, ... Ps 145:4
will know the **m** things you do .... Ps 145:12
praise him in his **m** heaven. .... Ps 150:1
the **M** One of Israel, ... Is 1:24
and, like a **m** one, I have taken .... Is 10:13
fall by the power of the **M** One. .... Is 10:34
Look, **m** one! The LORD will throw .... Is 22:17
against them with his **m** weapons. .... Is 30:32
the LORD will be our **M** One. .... Is 33:21
and horses and the **m** armies. .... Is 43:17
rejected all my **m** men inside my .... La 1:15
Egypt with his **m** army and many .... Eze 17:17
handed it over to a **m** ruler of .... Eze 31:11
by the swords of **m** soldiers, ... Eze 32:12
leaders of the **m** ones will speak .... Eze 32:21
m soldiers used to frighten .... Eze 32:27
They were **m,** but now they lie in .... Eze 32:29
with you, a **m** army, all riding. .... Eze 38:15
the flesh of the **m** and drink the .... Eze 39:18
m men and all kinds of soldiers,' .... Eze 39:20
great, and his miracles are **m.** .... Da 4:3
people and does **m** miracles in .... Da 6:27
a **m** king will come, who will .... Da 11:3
the **m** One will save you. .... Zph 3:17
because the **m** forest has been .... Zch 11:2
has done **m** deeds by his power. .... Lk 1:51
kings, generals, **m** people, ... Rev 19:18

MIGRATE
know when it is time to **m.** .... Je 8:7

MIGRON
soldiers will walk through **M.** .... Is 10:28

MIJAMIN
was Malkijah. The sixth was **M.** 1Ch 24:9
Izziah, Malkijah, **M,** Eleazar, ... Ezr 10:25
Meshullam, Abijah, **M,** .... Ne 10:7
M, Moadiah, Bilgah, ... Ne 12:5

MIKLOTH
and **M.** Mikloth was the father of 1Ch 8:32
M was the father of Shimeah. 1Ch 8:32
Gedor, Ahio, Zechariah, and **M.** 1Ch 9:37
M was Shimeam's father. 1Ch 9:38
M was a leader in the division. 1Ch 27:4

MIKNEIAH
Eliphelehu, **M,** Obed-Edom, and 1Ch 15:18
Eliphelehu, **M,** Obed-Edom, Jeiel, ... 1Ch 15:21

MIKTAM
be destroyed. A **m** of David. .... Ps 15:5
A **m** of David when the .... Ps 55:23
A **m** of David when he escaped .... Ps 56:13
Do Not Destroy." A **m** of David. .... Ps 57:11
A **m** of David when Saul sent men .... Ps 58:11
Agreement." A **m** of David. For .... Ps 59:17

MILALAI
Azarel, **M**, Gilalai, Maai,...................... Ne 12:36

MILCAH
and Nahor's wife was named **M**.   .... Ge 11:29
the father of both **M** and Iscah. .... Ge 11:29
and his wife **M** have children now .... Ge 22:20
M was the mother of these eight   .... Ge 22:23
was the son of **M** and Nahor, ... Ge 24:15
the son of **M** and Nahor.'' .... Ge 24:24
is Bethuel son of **M** and Nahor.' .... Ge 24:47
Noah, Hoglah, **M**, and Tirzah.................. Nu 26:33
Noah, Hoglah, **M**, and Tirzah. .... Nu 27:1
Tirzah, Hoglah, **M**, and Noah— .... Nu 36:11
Noah, Hoglah, **M**, and Tirzah.................. Jos 17:3

MILDEW
diseases, and **m** until you die.................. Dt 28:22
crops die from disease and **m**.   .... Am 4:9
with diseases, **m**, and hail, but   .... Hag 2:17

MILE
forces you to go with him one **m**, ... Mt 5:41
about half a **m** from Jerusalem. .... Ac 1:12

MILES
about seven **m** from Jerusalem. .... Lk 24:13
was about two **m** from Jerusalem. .... Jn 11:18
miles wide, and 1,500 **m** high.................. Rev 21:16

MILETUS
and the next day we reached **M**. .... Ac 20:15
Now from **M** Paul sent to Ephesus .... Ac 20:17
and I left Trophimus sick in **M**. 2Ti 4:20

MILITARY
the **m** leaders and government   .... Is 3:3
of Assyria sent a **m** commander to........... Is 20:1

MILK
a young goat in its mother's **m**. .... Ex 23:19
for water, but Jael gave him **m**. .... Jdg 5:25
buy wine and **m** without money .... Is 55:1
teaching I gave you was like **m**, ... 1Co 3:2
without drinking some of the **m**. 1Co 9:7
the teaching that is like **m**. .... Heb 5:12
who lives on **m** is still a baby .... Heb 5:13
babies want **m**, you should want 1Pe 2:2

MILL
young men ground grain at the **m**, ... La 5:13
will be grinding grain with a **m**. .... Mt 24:41

MILLET
small peas, and **m** seeds, and put   .... Eze 4:9

MILLO
and Beth **M** gathered beside   .... Jdg 9:6
leaders of Shechem and Beth **M**!   .... Jdg 9:20
Shechem and Beth **M** and burn up .... Jdg 9:20
him at Beth **M** on the road down 2Ki 12:20

MILLSTONE
hear the **m** grinding grain. .... Ec 12:4

MINA
and a **m** will be worth sixty   .... Eze 45:12

MIND
LORD changed his **m** and did not   .... Ex 32:14
and he does not change his **m**. .... Nu 23:19
blindness, and a confused **m**. .... Dt 28:28
LORD will make your **m** worried, ... Dt 28:65
not given you a **m** that   .... Dt 29:4
made up her **m** to go with her, ... Ru 1:18
He does not lie or change his **m**. 1Sa 15:29
so he does not change his **m**. 1Sa 15:29
with him about all she had in **m**, ... 1Ki 10:2
knows what is in everyone's **m**, ... 1Ch 28:9
for everything he had in **m**: 1Ch 28:12
with him about all she had in **m**, ... 2Ch 9:1

by changing the **m** of the king   .... Ezr 6:22
making it up in your own **m**.''................... Ne 6:8
Change your **m**; do not be unfair;   .... Job 6:29
I know this was in your **m**. .... Job 10:13
But my **m** is as good as yours;   .... Job 12:3
but they do not **m** spitting in my   .... Job 30:10
inside the **m** or understanding. .... Job 38:36
closely into my heart and **m**. .... Ps 26:2
Beautiful words fill my **m**. .... Ps 45:1
The **m** of human beings is hard .... Ps 64:6
body and my **m** may become weak, ... Ps 73:26
and will not change his **m**. .... Ps 110:4
set your **m** on understanding.................... Pr 2:2
Wisdom will come into your **m**, ... Pr 2:10
but keep my commands in **m**. .... Pr 3:1
my words; keep them always in **m**............. Pr 4:21
a **m** that thinks up evil plans, ... Pr 6:18
their words in **m** forever as..................... Pr 6:21
Peace of **m** means a healthy body, ... Pr 14:30
but the **m** of a fool wanders   .... Pr 17:24
The **m** of a person with   .... Pr 18:15
a king's **m** as he controls   .... Pr 21:1
these things in **m** so that you .... Pr 22:18
Keep your **m** on what is right.   .... Pr 23:19
and your **m** will be confused.   .... Pr 23:33
who knows what's in your **m**,................... Pr 24:12
can understand the **m** of a king. .... Pr 25:3
from a wicked **m** are like a shiny   .... Pr 26:23
so your **m** shows what kind of   .... Pr 27:19
wine while my **m** was still   .... Ec 2:3
and in his **m** he plans evil. .... Ec 10:2
Who has known the **m** of the LORD .... Is 40:13
his confused **m** leads him the .... Is 44:20
easy for you to change your **m**. .... Je 3:19
spoken and will not change my **m**. .... Je 4:28
It never even entered my **m**.   .... Je 7:31
a person's **m** is evil and cannot   .... Je 17:9
a person's heart and test the **m**. .... Je 17:10
I will change my **m** and not carry .... Je 18:8
I will change my **m** and not carry   .... Je 18:10
or erase their sins from your **m**. .... Je 18:23
it never even entered my **m**.   .... Je 19:5
the heart and **m** of a person. .... Je 20:12
will change my **m** about bringing .... Je 26:3
will change his **m** and not bring   .... Je 26:13
LORD changed his **m** and did not   .... Je 26:19
entered my **m** that they would   .... Je 32:35
make up your **m** to go and live   .... Je 42:15
or feel pity or change my **m**. .... Eze 24:14
ideas will come into your **m**, ... Eze 38:10
what went through your **m**..................... Da 2:30
Abednego, and he changed his **m**.   .... Da 3:19
visions in my **m** that alarmed me. .... Da 4:5
him have the **m** of an animal for   .... Da 4:16
and his **m** became like the mind   .... Da 5:21
became like the **m** of an animal............... Da 5:21
it was given the **m** of a human. .... Da 7:4
went through my **m** frightened me. .... Da 7:15
can change his **m** about doing   .... Joe 2:13
LORD changed his **m** about this.   .... Am 7:3
changed his **m** about this too.................. Am 7:6
Maybe God will change his **m**.   .... Jnh 3:9
he changed his **m** and did not do   .... Jnh 3:10
not change my **m**,'' says the LORD........... Zch 8:14
his **m** he has already done that   .... Mt 5:28
Out of the **m** come evil thoughts, ... Mt 15:19
the son changed his **m** and went. .... Mt 21:29
all your soul, and all your **m**.'   .... Mt 22:37
thought he was out of his **m**. .... Mk 3:21
clothed, and in his right **m**..................... Mk 5:15
It does not go into the **m**, ... Mk 7:19
begin inside people, in the **m**:................. Mk 7:21
doubts in your **m** and believe .... Mk 11:23

soul, all your **m**, and all your .... Mk 12:30
heart, all his **m**, and all his .... Mk 12:33
mother kept in her **m** all that .... Lk 2:51
clothed and in his right **m**, ... Lk 8:35
your strength, and all your **m**." .... Lk 10:27
he opened her **m** to pay attention .... Ac 16:14
Paul, you are out of your **m**! .... Ac 26:24
In my **m**, I am happy with God's .... Rm 7:22
the law that my **m** accepts. .... Rm 7:23
So in my **m** I am a slave to God's .... Rm 7:25
what is in the **m** of the Spirit, ... Rm 8:27
people a dull **m** so they could .... Rm 11:8
changes his **m** about the people .... Rm 11:29
Who has known the **m** of the Lord, ... Rm 11:34
Let all be sure in their own **m**. .... Rm 14:5
Who has known the **m** of the Lord? 1Co 2:16
But we have the **m** of Christ. 1Co 2:16
sure in his **m** that there is no 1Co 7:37
praying, but my **m** does nothing. 1Co 14:14
but I will also pray with my **m**. 1Co 14:15
but I will also sing with my **m**. 1Co 14:15
and having one **m** and purpose. .... Php 2:2
and will not change his **m**. ' .... Heb 7:21
You need a wise **m** to understand .... Rev 17:9

MINDING
are going along, **m** their own .... Pr 9:15

MINDS
in their **m** and write them .... Je 31:33
who had slaves changed their **m**. .... Je 34:11
must make up our **m** not to do .... Rm 14:13
to fool the **m** of those who do .... Rm 16:18
their **m** were closed, and even 2Co 3:14
is a covering over their **m**. 2Co 3:15
has blinded the **m** of those who 2Co 4:4
that your **m** will be led away 2Co 11:3
hearts and **m** in Christ Jesus .... Php 4:7
who have evil **m** and have lost 1Ti 6:5
and write them on their **m**." .... Heb 10:16
One who searches hearts and **m**, ... Rev 2:23

MINERS
M bring lights and search deep .... Job 28:3
M dig a tunnel far from where .... Job 28:4
M hit the rocks of flint and dig .... Job 28:9

MINES
There are **m** where people dig .... Job 28:1
deep into the **m** for ore in thick .... Job 28:3

MINIAMIN
Eden, **M**, Jeshua, Shemaiah, ... 2Ch 31:15
Maaseiah, **M**, Micaiah, Elioenai .... Ne 12:41

MINIAMIN'S
from **M** and Moadiah's families; .... Ne 12:17

MINISTER
to be a **m** of Christ Jesus to .... Rm 15:16
a faithful **m** and servant with .... Col 4:7

MINISTRY
Jesus began his **m**, he was about .... Lk 3:23

MINNI
of Ararat, **M**, and Ashkenaz to .... Je 51:27

MINNITH
city of Aroer to the area of **M**, ... Jdg 11:33
your goods for wheat from **M**, ... Eze 27:17

MINT
earn—even your **m**, dill, and .... Mt 23:23
God one-tenth of even your **m**, ... Lk 11:42

MINUTE
me, I would have died in a **m**. .... Ps 94:17
those false believers for a **m**. .... Gal 2:5

MIRACLE
the king asks you to do a **m**, ... Ex 7:9
people ask for a **m** as a sign? .... Mk 8:12
hoping to see Jesus work a **m**. .... Lk 23:8
received the **m** of healing was .... Ac 4:22

MIRACLES
Where are the **m** our ancestors .... Jdg 6:13
showed this to you by the **m**, ... Ac 2:22
Paul to do some very special **m**. .... Ac 19:11
person the power to do **m**, ... 1Co 12:10
given a place to those who do **m**, ... 1Co 12:28
all are teachers. Not all do **m**. 1Co 12:29
many kinds of **m**, and by giving .... Heb 2:4

MIRIAM
Aaron's sister **M**, a prophetess, ... Ex 15:20
Tent and Aaron turned toward **M**, ... Nu 12:10
and Moses, and their sister **M**. .... Nu 26:59

MIRROR
as if we were looking into a **m**, ... 1Co 13:12
who look at themselves in a **m**. .... Jam 1:23

MIRRORS
the bronze from **m** that belonged .... Ex 38:8
their **m**, linen dresses, turbans, ... Is 3:23

MISERABLE
would be **m** until the day I die. .... Ge 44:29
and long and **m** sicknesses. .... Dt 28:59
Israel were **m** that day because 1Sa 14:24
It will make you **m** and drunk. .... Eze 23:33
What a **m** man I am! .... Rm 7:24
not know that you are really **m**, ... Rev 3:17

MISERY
weighed and my **m** put on scales. .... Job 6:2
they go they cause ruin and **m**. .... Rm 3:16

MISHAEL
Uzziel's sons were **M**, Elzaphan, ... Ex 6:22
two sons named **M** and Elzaphan. .... Le 10:4
So **M** and Elzaphan obeyed Moses .... Le 10:5
were Pedaiah, **M**, Malkijah, ... Ne 8:4
Daniel, Hananiah, **M**, and Azariah .... Da 1:6
Hananiah, **M**, and Azariah .... Da 1:11
Hananiah, **M**, and Azariah .... Da 1:19
Hananiah, **M**, and Azariah .... Da 2:17

MISHAEL'S
was Shadrach, **M** was Meshach, ... Da 1:7

MISHAL
Allammelech, Amad, and **M**. .... Jos 19:26
The tribe of Asher gave them **M**, ... Jos 21:30

MISHMA
M, Dumah, Massa, ... Ge 25:14
M, Dumah, Massa, Hadad, Tema, ... 1Ch 1:30
was Mibsam. Mibsam's son was **M**. 1Ch 4:25

MISHMA'S
M son was Hammuel. Hammuel's son 1Ch 4:26

MISHMANNAH
M was fourth, Jeremiah was fifth, ... 1Ch 12:10

MISHPAT
turned back and went to En **M** .... Ge 14:7

MISHRAITE
came from the **M** people. 1Ch 2:53

MISHRAITES
Puthites, Shumathites, and **M**. 1Ch 2:53

MISLEAD
because their lies **m** them. .... Ps 119:118
They **m** my people with their lies .... Je 23:32
things that **m** our people. .... Lk 23:2

MISLED
'Your good friends **m** you and .... Je 38:22

MISPAR
Bilshan, **M,** Bigvai, Rehum,..................... Ezr 2:2

MISPERETH
Bilshan, **M,** Bigvai, Nehum, ... Ne 7:7

MISREPHOTH
Greater Sidon, **M** Maim, and the .... Jos 11:8
country from Lebanon to **M** Maim, ... Jos 13:6

MISS
a stone at a hair and not **m!** .... Jdg 20:16
empty, so my father will **m** you. 1Sa 20:18
Don't let anyone **m** this meeting, ... 2Ki 10:19
I did not **m** any pleasure I .... Ec 2:10
or remember it or **m** it or make .... Je 3:16

MISSED
death, he **m** Absalom greatly. 2Sa 13:39
King David **m** Absalom very much. 2Sa 14:1
He **m** his chance for glory!'" .... Je 46:17
Some people have **m** these things 1Ti 1:6
some have **m** the true faith. 1Ti 6:21

MISSING
and not one of them is **m.** .... Nu 31:49

MISSION
And he sent you on a **m.**....................... 1Sa 15:18
thing is that I complete my **m,** .... Ac 20:24

MIST
but a **m** would rise up from the .... Ge 2:6
hail, snow and **m,** and stormy................. Ps 148:8
vanishes like a **m** and leads to .... Pr 21:6
is like a morning **m,** .... Hos 6:4
will be like the morning **m;**..................... Hos 13:3
life is like a **m.** You can see it .... Jam 4:14

MISTAKE
last time. Maybe it was a **m.** .... Ge 43:12
some of the holy offering by **m,** .... Le 22:14
too quickly, you might make a **m.** .... Pr 19:2
It is the kind of **m** rulers make: .... Ec 10:5
waiting for me to make some **m.** .... Je 20:10
are making a **m** that will cause .... Je 42:20

MISTAKES
he blames them for **m.** .... Job 4:18
People cannot see their own **m.** .... Ps 19:12
We all make many **m.** .... Jam 3:2

MISTREAT
You must not **m** a foreigner. .... Ex 23:9

MISTREATED
will be **m** and abused all your................. Dt 28:33
empty-handed, and you **m** orphans. .... Job 22:9
people who were **m** here on earth. .... Ec 4:1
you will see poor people **m.** .... Ec 5:8

MISTREATING
Whoever gets rich by **m** the poor, ... Pr 22:16
make profits by **m** your neighbor. .... Eze 22:29
saw an Egyptian **m** one of his................. Ac 7:24

MISTREATS
Whoever **m** the poor insults their .... Pr 14:31
Whoever **m** the poor insults their .... Pr 17:5
He **m** the poor and needy. .... Eze 18:12

MISTRESS
to treat her **m** Sarai badly. .... Ge 16:4
to Sarai, "You are Hagar's **m.**.................. Ge 16:6
running away from my **m** Sarai." .... Ge 16:8
"Go home to your **m** and obey her." .... Ge 16:9
She said to her **m,** "I wish my 2Ki 5:3
female servant depends on her **m.** .... Ps 123:2
and a maid who replaces her **m.**............... Pr 30:23

MISTRUST
speaking against others, evil **m,** 1Ti 6:4

MISUNDERSTAND
their enemy might **m** and say, ' .... Dt 32:27

MISUSES
punish anyone who **m** his name. .... Ex 20:7

MITHCAH
They left Terah and camped at **M.** .... Nu 33:28
They left **M** and camped at .... Nu 33:29

MITHNITE
son of Maacah; Joshaphat the **M;** 1Ch 11:43

MITHREDATH
of Persia had **M** the treasurer .... Ezr 1:8
Persia, Bishlam, **M,** Tabeel, and .... Ezr 4:7

MITYLENE
took him aboard and went to **M.** .... Ac 20:14
sailed from **M** and the next day .... Ac 20:15

MIX
and **m** it with the special oil .... Ex 29:21
and **m** all these things like a .... Ex 30:25
M in the spices, and let the..................... Eze 24:10
Get mud, **m** clay, make bricks! .... Nah 3:14

MIXED
bread, cakes **m** with olive oil, ... Ex 29:2
kinds of material **m** together. .... Le 19:19
as you saw iron was **m** with clay. .... Da 2:41
the people are **m** among the other .... Hos 8:8
of calves and **m** it with water. .... Heb 9:19
mercy **m** with fear to others, ... Jud 1:23
hail and fire **m** with blood were .... Rev 8:7
like a sea of glass **m** with fire. .... Rev 15:2

MIXES
like a person who **m** perfumes. .... Ex 37:29
While he **m** the dough, he does .... Hos 7:4
Israel **m** with other nations; .... Hos 7:8

MIXING
took care of **m** the spices. 1Ch 9:30
the baking and **m,** and for the 1Ch 23:29
and are champions at **m** drinks............... Is 5:22

MIXTURE
the fourth kingdom will be a **m,** .... Da 2:43

MIZAR
the peaks of Hermon and Mount **M.** .... Ps 42:6

MIZPAH
was also called **M,** because Laban .... Ge 31:49
and the city of **M** in Gilead to .... Jdg 11:29
All Israel must meet at **M,** 1Sa 7:5
Bethel to Gilgal to **M** and judged 1Sa 7:16
soldiers came to Gedaliah at **M:** .... Je 40:8

MIZRAIM
Ham were Cush, **M,** Put, and .... Ge 10:6
M was the father of the Ludites,............... Ge 10:13
sons were Cush, **M,** Put, and 1Ch 1:8
M was the father of the Ludites,............... 1Ch 1:11

MIZZAH
Nahath, Zerah, Shammah, and **M.** .... Ge 36:13
Nahath, Zerah, Shammah, and **M.** .... Ge 36:17
Nahath, Zerah, Shammah, and **M.** 1Ch 1:37

MNASON
us and took us to the home of **M,** .... Ac 21:16

MOAB
birth to a son and named him **M.** .... Ge 19:37
powerful men of **M** will shake .... Ex 15:15
And **M** was scared of so many .... Nu 22:3
king of **M** brought me from the .... Nu 23:7
on the plains of **M** across the .... Nu 26:63
the plains of **M** near the Jordan .... Nu 31:12
along the desert road to **M.**..................... Dt 2:8
died there in **M,** as the LORD had .... Dt 34:5
Eglon king of **M** the payment he .... Jdg 3:15

the country of **M** with his wife .... Ru 1:2
they came to **M,** they settled .... Ru 1:2
These sons married women from **M.** .... Ru 1:4
M broke away from Israel's rule. 2Ki 1:1
Mesha king of **M** raised sheep. 2Ki 3:4
M is like my washbowl. I throw .... Ps 60:8
This is a message about **M:** .... Is 15:1
message is to the country of **M.** .... Je 48:1
The nation of **M** will be .... Je 48:42
For the many crimes of **M,** .... Am 2:1
M will be destroyed like Sodom,.............. Zph 2:9

MOABITE

No Ammonite or **M** may come into .... Dt 23:3
is the young **M** woman who came .... Ru 2:6

MOABITES

between the **M** and the Amorites. .... Nu 21:13
The **M** said to the elders of .... Nu 22:4
the heads of the **M** and smash the .... Nu 24:17
land, and so did the **M** in Ar. .... Dt 2:29
Ammonites and **M** did not give you .... Dt 23:4
to defeat your enemies, the **M.**" .... Jdg 3:28
did not allow the **M** to cross the .... Jdg 3:28
as well as women of the **M,** 1Ki 11:1
god of the **M,** and the other 1Ki 11:7
to hand us over to the **M!**" 2Ki 3:10
to hand us over to the **M.**" 2Ki 3:13
All the **M** heard that the kings 2Ki 3:21
But when the **M** got up early in 2Ki 3:22
Come, **M,** let's take the 2Ki 3:23
When the **M** came to the camp of 2Ki 3:24
on into the land, killing the **M.** 2Ki 3:24
time groups of **M** would rob the 2Ki 13:20
they saw a group of **M** coming. 2Ki 13:21
Later the **M,** Ammonites, and some 2Ch 20:1
The Ammonites and **M** attacked the 2Ch 20:23
Ammonites, **M,** Egyptians, ... Ezr 9:1
Ammonites and **M** had not welcomed ...... Ne 13:2

MOADIAH

Mijamin, **M,** Bilgah, ... Ne 12:5

MOADIAH'S

from Miniamin's and **M** families; .... Ne 12:17

MOAN

I **m** from the pain I feel. .... Ps 38:8
Our years end with a **m.** .... Ps 90:9
They will **m** and groan for the .... Is 16:7
I **m** for the people from the town .... Je 48:31
I will **m** and cry because of this .... Mic 1:8
The slave girls **m** like doves and.............. Nah 2:7
You cry and **m,** because he does.............. Mal 2:13

MOANED

inside me. I **m** all day long..................... Ps 32:3
like a bird and **m** like a dove. .... Is 38:14

MOANING

and my flute is tuned to **m.**..................... Job 30:31
I have heard Israel **m:** .... Je 31:18
has caused more **m** and groaning .... La 2:5
m like doves of the valleys .... Eze 7:16

MOANS

of the **m** of the helpless, ... Ps 12:5
Hear the **m** of the prisoners. .... Ps 79:11
He heard the **m** of the prisoners, ... Ps 102:20

MOB

side they rise up like a **m.** .... Job 30:12
together a **m** against Samaria................. Eze 23:46
Let the **m** kill them by throwing.............. Eze 23:47
formed a **m,** and started a riot. .... Ac 17:5
The whole **m** was following them, ... Ac 21:36

MOCKER

proud," "bragger," and "**m.**" .... Pr 21:24

MOIST

the fine flour **m,** as a grain .... Eze 46:14

MOLADAH

Amam, Shema, **M,** .... Jos 15:26
(also called Sheba), **M,** .... Jos 19:2
in Beersheba, **M,** Hazar Shual, ... 1Ch 4:28
in Jeshua, **M,** Beth Pelet,...................... Ne 11:26

MOLD

was melted and poured into a **m,** 1Ki 7:37

MOLDED

They **m** statues of two calves, ... 2Ki 17:16
that you **m** me like a piece .... Job 10:9

MOLDS

poured into clay **m** that were 1Ki 7:46
poured into clay **m** that were 2Ch 4:17

MOLDY

and they took some dry, **m** bread. .... Jos 9:5
fresh, but now it is dry and **m.** .... Jos 9:12

MOLECH

children to be sacrificed to **M,** .... Le 18:21
other was a place to worship **M,**.............. 1Ki 11:7

MOLES

m, rats, all kinds of great .... Le 11:29
them away to the bats and **m.**................. Is 2:20

MOLID

and their sons were Ahban and **M.**........... 1Ch 2:29

MOMENT

to go with you even for a **m,** .... Ex 33:5
At that very **m** Barak came by .... Jdg 4:22
morning and test them every **m.**............. Job 7:18
alone so I can have a **m** of joy. .... Job 10:20
of the wicked lasts only a **m.** .... Job 20:5
can die in a **m,** in the middle .... Job 34:20
lasts only a **m,** but his kindness .... Ps 30:5
They are destroyed in a **m;** .... Ps 73:19
but lies are only for a **m.**....................... Pr 12:19
a new nation beginning in one **m.** .... Is 66:8
tents are destroyed in only a **m.** .... Je 4:20
will shake every **m** on the day .... Eze 32:10
In a **m** you will again hear the .... Da 3:15
the woman was healed from that **m** .... Mt 9:22
And at that **m** the woman's..................... Mt 15:28
At that **m** Sapphira fell down by.............. Ac 5:10

MOMENTS

stopped only a few **m** to rest in .... Ru 2:7

MONEY

Accept my **m,** and I will bury my .... Ge 23:13
all of the **m** you paid for us. .... Ge 31:15
to put the **m** the brothers had .... Ge 42:25
Then he saw his **m** in the top of .... Ge 42:27
The **m** I paid for the grain has .... Ge 42:28
of them found his **m** in his sack.............. Ge 42:35
twice as much **m** with you this .... Ge 43:12
take back the **m** that was .... Ge 43:12
twice as much **m** as they had .... Ge 43:15
because of the **m** that was put in .... Ge 43:18
us found all his **m** in his sack. .... Ge 43:21
brought that **m** with us to give .... Ge 43:21
have brought more **m** to pay for .... Ge 43:22
who put that **m** in our sacks."................. Ge 43:22
have put the **m** in your sacks................. Ge 43:23
I got the **m** you paid me for the .... Ge 43:23
put each man's **m** into his sack .... Ge 44:1
along with his **m** for the grain." .... Ge 44:2
of Canaan the **m** we found in our .... Ge 44:8
all the **m** that was to be .... Ge 47:14
he brought that **m** to the king's .... Ge 47:14
Egypt and Canaan had no **m** left, ... Ge 47:15
Our **m** is gone, and if we don't .... Ge 47:15

and with that **m** they buy wine to .... Am 2:8
right, you take **m** to do wrong, ... Am 5:12
Samaria earned her **m** by being .... Mic 1:7
this **m** will be carried off by .... Mic 1:7
Its judges take **m** to decide who .... Mic 3:11
Rulers ask for **m**, and judges' .... Mic 7:3
you have taken **m** will turn .... Hab 2:7
You earn **m**, but then you lose it .... Hag 1:6
there was no **m** to give people .... Zch 8:10
"Throw the **m** to the potter." .... Zch 11:13
Don't carry any **m** with you—.................. Mt 10:9
to collect the **m** his servants .... Mt 18:23
the king began to collect his **m**, ... Mt 18:24
not have enough **m** to pay his .... Mt 18:25
Then the **m** would be used to pay .... Mt 18:25
'Pay me the **m** you owe me!' .... Mt 18:28
and give the **m** to the poor. .... Mt 19:21
do what I want with my own **m**. .... Mt 20:15
exchanging different kinds of **m**, ... Mt 21:12
to invest the **m** and earned five .... Mt 25:16
ground and hid the master's **m**. .... Mt 25:18
what they did with his **m**. .... Mt 25:19
and hid your **m** in the ground. .... Mt 25:25
a great deal of **m** and the money .... Mt 26:9
and the **m** given to the poor. .... Mt 26:9
threw the **m** into the Temple .... Mt 27:5
to keep this **m** with the Temple .... Mt 27:6
this money with the Temple **m**, ... Mt 27:6
the soldiers a large amount of **m** .... Mt 28:12
kept the **m** and did as they .... Mt 28:15
and had spent all the **m** she had, ... Mk 5:26
bag, and no **m** in your pockets. .... Mk 6:8
earn enough **m** to buy that much .... Mk 6:37
person use that **m** for his father .... Mk 7:12
and give the **m** to the poor, ... Mk 10:21
exchanging different kinds of **m**, ... Mk 11:15
the Temple **m** box and watched .... Mk 12:41
the people put in their **m**. .... Mk 12:41
people gave large sums of **m**. .... Mk 12:41
sold and the **m** given to the poor .... Mk 14:5
and promised to pay Judas **m**. .... Mk 14:11
force people to give you **m**,.................... Lk 3:14
Two people owed **m** to the same .... Lk 7:41
They had no **m** to pay what they .... Lk 7:42
one who owed him the most **m**." .... Lk 7:43
used their own **m** to help Jesus .... Lk 8:3
bag, bread, **m**, or extra clothes. .... Lk 9:3
If you spend more **m** on him, ... Lk 10:35
you have enough **m** to finish the.............. Lk 14:28
wasted his **m** in foolish living. .... Lk 15:13
all your **m** on prostitutes, ... Lk 15:30
of what you have done with my **m**,........... Lk 16:2
who owed the master any **m**. .... Lk 16:5
who loved **m**, were listening to .... Lk 16:14
with this **m** until I get back.' .... Lk 19:13
who have my **m** so I can know how .... Lk 19:15
You even take **m** that you didn't .... Lk 19:21
taking **m** that I didn't earn and .... Lk 19:22
didn't you put my **m** in the bank? .... Lk 19:23
m would have earned some interest. .... Lk 19:23
gifts into the Temple **m** box. .... Lk 21:1
and agreed to give Judas **m**. .... Lk 22:5
exchanging different kinds of **m**. .... Jn 2:14
scattered the **m** of those who .... Jn 2:15
near where the **m** is kept. .... Jn 8:20
and the **m** given to the poor?" .... Jn 12:5
was the one who kept the **m** box, ... Jn 12:6
was the one who kept the **m** box, ... Jn 13:29
field with the **m** he got for his .... Ac 1:18
then divide the **m** and give it to .... Ac 2:45
to beg for **m** from the people .... Ac 3:2
the Temple and asked them for **m**. .... Ac 3:3
were going to give him some **m**................ Ac 3:5

houses sold them, brought the **m**, ... Ac 4:34
Then the **m** was given to anyone .... Ac 4:35
it, brought the **m**, and gave it .... Ac 4:37
back part of the **m** himself; .... Ac 5:2
the rest of the **m** and gave it to .... Ac 5:2
part of the **m** you received for .... Ac 5:3
have used the **m** any way you.................... Ac 5:4
was the **m** you got for your field............... Ac 5:8
for a sum of **m** from the sons .... Ac 7:16
So he offered the apostles **m**, ... Ac 8:18
You and your **m** should both be .... Ac 8:20
you could buy God's gift with **m**. .... Ac 8:20
for taking care of all her **m**. .... Ac 8:27
gave much of his **m** to the poor .... Ac 10:2
gathered the **m** and gave it to .... Ac 11:30
earned a lot of **m** for her owners .... Ac 16:16
could not use her to make **m**. .... Ac 16:19
the others put up a sum of **m**.................... Ac 17:9
who did this work made much **m**. .... Ac 19:24
a lot of **m** from our business. .... Ac 19:25
anyone's **m** or fine clothes. .... Ac 20:33
I paid a lot of **m** to become a .... Ac 22:28
back to bring **m** to my people.................. Ac 24:17
that Paul would give him some **m**, ... Ac 24:26
to give their **m** to help the poor .... Rm 15:26
Jerusalem get the **m** that has .... Rm 15:28
collection of **m** for God's people............... 1Co 16:1
put aside **m** as you have been 1Co 16:2
have to collect **m** after I come. 1Co 16:2
when we deliver this gift of **m**. 2Co 8:19
their **m** so I could serve you. 2Co 11:8
were not trying to get your **m**; 1Th 2:5
and peaceable, not loving **m**. 1Ti 3:3
The love of **m** causes all kinds 1Ti 6:10
they wanted to get more **m**, ... 1Ti 6:10
themselves, love **m**, brag, and be 2Ti 3:2
lives free from the love of **m**, ... Heb 13:5
year, do business, and make **m**." .... Jam 4:13
serve, not because you want **m**. 1Pe 5:2
false teachers only want your **m**, ... 2Pe 2:3
and for **m** they have given .... Jud 1:11

MONEYLENDER
do not treat him as a **m** would. .... Ex 22:25

MONSTER
to wake up the sea **m** Leviathan. .... Job 3:8
I am not the sea or the sea **m**............... Job 7:12
helpers of the **m** Rahab lie at .... Job 9:13
he destroys Rahab, the sea **m**. .... Job 26:12
broke the heads of the sea **m**.................... Ps 74:13
the heads of the **m** Leviathan and .... Ps 74:14
You crushed the sea **m** Rahab; .... Ps 89:10
there is the sea **m** Leviathan, ... Ps 104:26
He will kill the **m** in the sea. .... Is 27:1
pieces and killed that sea **m**. .... Is 51:9

MONTH
day of the first **m** of that year, ... Ge 8:13
This **m** will be the beginning of .... Ex 12:2
the fourteenth day of the **m**. .... Ex 12:6
Today, in the **m** of Abib, you are.............. Ex 13:4
a baby boy one **m** to five years .... Le 27:6
enough meat to eat for a **m**!' .... Nu 11:21
was the second **m**, the month of 1Ki 6:1
in the eighth **m**, the month of 1Ki 6:38
festival in the **m** of Ethanim, ... 1Ki 8:2
was on duty one **m** each year. 1Ch 27:1
first division for the first **m**. 1Ch 27:2
third day of the **m** of Adar in .... Ezr 6:15
In the **m** of Kislev in .... Ne 1:1
the royal palace in the tenth **m**, ... Est 2:16
twenty-third day of the third **m**, ... Est 8:9
In the fifth **m** of his last year, ... Je 1:3
-fourth day of the first **m**, ... Da 10:4

day of the eleventh **m**,........................... Zch 1:7
In one **m** I got rid of three .... Zch 11:8
sixth **m** of pregnancy, ... Lk 1:26
and day and **m** and year so they.............. Rev 9:15
times a year, once each **m**. .... Rev 22:2

MONTHLY

I am having my **m** period." .... Ge 31:35
is unclean during her **m** period. .... Le 12:2
is unclean during her **m** period. .... Le 12:5
When a woman has her **m** period, ... Le 15:19
a woman and her **m** period touches .... Le 15:24
not during her regular **m** period, ... Le 15:25
as she is during her **m** period. .... Le 15:25
bed during her regular **m** period. .... Le 15:26
as during her regular **m** period. .... Le 15:26
unclean from her **m** period, ... Le 15:33
with her during her **m** period, ... Le 18:19
a woman during her **m** period, ... Le 20:18
addition to the **m** and daily.................... Nu 29:6
herself from her **m** period. 2Sa 11:4
during her time of **m** bleeding. .... Eze 18:6
during their time of **m** bleeding............... Eze 22:10
in her time of **m** bleeding. .... Eze 36:17

MONTHS

About three **m** later someone told .... Ge 38:24
was, she hid him for three **m**. .... Ex 2:2
But after three **m** she was not................. Ex 2:3
will be the beginning of your........................ Ex 12:2
Exactly three **m** after the .... Ex 19:1
me be alone for two **m** to go to .... Jdg 11:37
So he sent her away for two **m**. .... Jdg 11:38
After two **m** she returned to her .... Jdg 11:39
and stayed there for four **m**. .... Jdg 19:2
where they stayed for four **m**................... Jdg 20:47
of God in their land seven **m**. 1Sa 6:1
land a year and four **m**. 1Sa 27:7
for seven years and six **m**. 2Sa 2:11
for seven years and six **m**, ... 2Sa 5:5
Obed-Edom's house for three **m**, ... 2Sa 6:11
After nine **m** and twenty days, ... 2Sa 24:8
enemies chase you for three **m**? 2Sa 24:13
month, then went home for two **m**. 1Ki 5:14
in Edom for six **m** and killed 1Ki 11:16
ruled for six **m** during Uzziah's 2Ki 15:8
king in Jerusalem for three **m**. 2Ki 23:31
was king three **m** in Jerusalem. 2Ki 24:8
family in his house for three **m**, ... 1Ch 13:14
choose three **m** of running from 1Ch 21:12
king in Jerusalem for three **m**. 2Ch 36:2
for three **m** and ten days. 2Ch 36:9
to complete twelve **m** of beauty .... Est 2:12
For six **m** she was treated with .... Est 2:12
and for six **m** with perfumes .... Est 2:12
year or put it in any of the **m**.................. Job 3:6
But I am given **m** that are empty, ... Job 7:3
us only so many **m** to live and .... Job 14:5
wish for the **m** that have passed.............. Job 29:2
you count the **m** until they give .... Job 39:2
for seven **m** to make the land .... Eze 39:12
After the seven **m** are finished, ... Eze 39:14
Twelve **m** later as he was walking .... Da 4:29
from you three **m** before harvest .... Am 4:7
in the fifth and seventh **m**, ... Zch 7:5
and tenth **m** will become good, ... Zch 8:19
go out of her house for five **m**. .... Lk 1:24
she has been pregnant for six **m**. .... Lk 1:36
for about three **m** and then .... Lk 1:56
'Four more **m** till harvest.' .... Jn 4:35
For three **m** Moses was cared for .... Ac 7:20
spoke out boldly for three **m**. .... Ac 19:8
where he stayed for three **m**. .... Ac 20:3
special days, **m**, seasons, and .... Gal 4:10

him for three **m** after he was .... Heb 11:23
pain to the people for five **m**. .... Rev 9:5
power to hurt people for five **m**............... Rev 9:10
the holy city for forty-two **m**. .... Rev 11:2
use its power for forty-two **m**................... Rev 13:5

MONUMENT

he has put up a **m** in his own 1Sa 15:12
called Absalom's **M** even today. 2Sa 18:18
asked, "What is that **m** I see?" 2Ki 23:17
of Egypt and a **m** to the LORD at .... Is 19:19

MOOD

was very drunk and in a good **m**. 1Sa 25:36

MOOING

on the road, **m** all the way, ... 1Sa 6:12
do I hear cattle **m** and sheep 1Sa 15:14
The **m** of cattle cannot be heard. .... Je 9:10

MOON

I saw the sun, **m**, and eleven .... Ge 37:9
feasts and at New **M** festivals. .... Nu 10:10
you see the sun, **m**, and stars,................. Dt 4:19
or to the sun or **m** or stars of .... Dt 17:3
best fruits that the **m** brings. .... Dt 33:14
M, stand still over the Valley .... Jos 10:12
and the **m** stopped until the .... Jos 10:13
tomorrow is the New **M** festival................ 1Sa 20:5
Tomorrow is the New **M** festival. 1Sa 20:18
When the New **M** festival came,............... 1Sa 20:24
isn't the New **M** or the Sabbath 2Ki 4:23
the sun, the **m**, the planets,...................... 2Ki 23:5
rest, at the New **M** festivals, ... 1Ch 23:31
for the New **M** and all the .... Ezr 3:5
the Sabbaths, New **M** festivals, ... Ne 10:33
Even the **m** is not bright and the .... Job 25:5
He covers the face of the **m**, ... Job 26:9
admired the **m** moving in glory .... Job 31:26
the sun and **m** a kiss of worship............. Job 31:27
I see the **m** and stars, which you .... Ps 8:3
and as long as the **m** glows. .... Ps 72:5
as long as there is a **m**. .... Ps 72:7
you made the sun and the **m**. .... Ps 74:16
at the time of the New **M**, ... Ps 81:3
Moon, when the **m** is full, when .... Ps 81:3
forever, like the **m**, like a .... Ps 89:37
You made the **m** to mark the .... Ps 104:19
and the **m** cannot hurt you at .... Ps 121:6
He made the sun and the **m**. .... Ps 136:7
He made the **m** and stars to rule .... Ps 136:9
him, sun and **m**. Praise him, all .... Ps 148:3
from the sun, **m**, and stars will .... Ec 12:2
She is as pretty as the **m**, ... Sng 6:10
hate your New **M** feasts and your .... Is 1:14
necklaces shaped like the **m**, ... Is 3:18
and the **m** will not give its .... Is 13:10
The **m** will be embarrassed, ... Is 24:23
light from the **m** will be bright .... Is 30:26
The sun, **m**, and stars will .... Is 34:4
from the **m** for your light, ... Is 60:19
and your **m** will never be dark, ... Is 60:20
every Sabbath and every New **M**," .... Is 66:23
under the sun, **m**, and stars that.............. Je 8:2
the day and the **m** and stars to .... Je 31:35
cloud, and the **m** will not shine .... Eze 32:7
day and on the day of the New **M**. .... Eze 46:1
day of the New **M** he must offer.............. Eze 46:6
her New **M** festivals, and her .... Hos 2:11
The sun and the **m** become dark, ... Joe 2:10
become dark, the **m** red as blood, ... Joe 2:31
The sun and the **m** will become .... Joe 3:15
will the New **M** festival be over .... Am 8:5
The sun and **m** stood still in the .... Hab 3:11
and the **m** will not give its .... Mt 24:29

M

and the **m** will not give its .... Mk 13:24
signs in the sun, **m**, and stars. .... Lk 21:25
become dark, the **m** red as blood, ... Ac 2:20
the sun, **m**, and stars. .... Ac 7:42
of beauty, the **m** has another 1Co 15:41
feast, a New **M** Festival, or a .... Col 2:16
of the sun, **m**, and stars, who .... Jam 1:17
and the whole **m** became red like .... Rev 6:12
a third of the **m**, and a third .... Rev 8:12
and the **m** was under her feet, ... Rev 12:1
the sun or the **m** to shine on it, ... Rev 21:23

MOONS

on Sabbath days and New **M,** 2Ch 2:4
days, New **M,** and the three 2Ch 8:13
days, during New **M,** and at other 2Ch 31:3
stand your New **M,** Sabbaths, and .... Is 1:13
at the stars and the new **m**— .... Is 47:13
at the New **M,** on the Sabbaths, ... Eze 45:17
LORD on the Sabbaths and New **M.** .... Eze 46:3

MORDECAI

whose name was **M** son of Jair. .... Est 2:5
M had a cousin named Hadassah, ... Est 2:7
when I see that Jew **M** sitting at .... Est 5:13
are all the things done by **M,** .... Est 10:2
M the Jew was second in .... Est 10:3

MORDECAI'S

of Abihail, **M** uncle, who had .... Est 2:15
would accept **M** behavior because .... Est 3:4
way to destroy all of **M** people, ... Est 3:6
wrote out all of **M** orders to the .... Est 8:9

MOREH

the great tree of **M** at Shechem. .... Ge 12:6
the great trees of **M** in the land .... Dt 11:30
the bottom of the hill called **M.** .... Jdg 7:1

MORESHETH

the city of **M,** was a prophet .... Je 26:18
came to Micah, who was from **M.** .... Mic 1:1
farewell gifts to **M** in Gath. .... Mic 1:14

MORIAH

love, and go to the land of **M.** .... Ge 22:2
LORD in Jerusalem on Mount **M.** 2Ch 3:1

MORNING

Evening passed, and **m** came................... Ge 1:5
Evening passed, and **m** came................... Ge 1:8
Evening passed, and **m** came................... Ge 1:13
Evening passed, and **m** came................... Ge 1:19
Evening passed, and **m** came................... Ge 1:23
Evening passed, and **m** came................... Ge 1:31
At dawn the next **m,** the angels .... Ge 19:15
Early the next **m,** Abraham got up .... Ge 19:27
early the next **m,** Abimelech .... Ge 20:8
Early the next **m** Abraham took .... Ge 21:14
early in the **m** and saddled his .... Ge 22:3
When they got up the next **m,** .... Ge 24:54
Early the next **m** the men swore.............. Ge 26:31
rose early in the **m** and took the.............. Ge 28:18
In the **m** when Jacob saw that he .... Ge 29:25
Early the next **m** Laban kissed .... Ge 31:55
Joseph came to them the next **m,** .... Ge 40:6
The next **m** the king was troubled .... Ge 41:8
In the **m** he eats what he has .... Ge 49:27
In the **m** the king will go out to .... Ex 7:15
up early in the **m,** and meet the .... Ex 8:20
up early in the **m** and go to the .... Ex 9:13
night, and when **m** came, the east .... Ex 10:13
not leave any of it until **m,** .... Ex 12:10
any of it is left over until **m,** .... Ex 12:10
may leave that house until **m.** .... Ex 12:22
m came, the LORD looked down .... Ex 14:24
Tomorrow **m** you will see the .... Ex 16:7

and every **m** he will give you all............... Ex 16:8
and every **m** you will eat all the .... Ex 16:12
the **m** dew lay around the camp............... Ex 16:13
part of it to eat the next **m.**..................... Ex 16:20
Every **m** each person gathered as .... Ex 16:21
of the food until tomorrow **m.**" .... Ex 16:23
saved it until the next **m,**....................... Ex 16:24
around him from **m** until night. .... Ex 18:13
around you from **m** until night!" .... Ex 18:14
On the **m** of the third day, ... Ex 19:16
up early the next **m** and built an .... Ex 24:4
the LORD from evening till **m.** .... Ex 27:21
of the bread is left the next **m,** .... Ex 29:34
one lamb in the **m** and the other .... Ex 29:39
In the **m,** when you offer the .... Ex 29:40
offering as you did in the **m.** .... Ex 29:41
the altar every **m** when he comes .... Ex 30:7
early the next **m** and offered .... Ex 32:6
ready tomorrow **m,** and then come........... Ex 34:2
the next **m** he went up Mount................. Ex 34:4
of Passover until the next **m.** .... Ex 34:25
bring gifts each **m** because they .... Ex 36:3
on the altar all night until **m,** .... Le 6:9
firewood on the altar every **m,** .... Le 6:12
half of it in the **m** and half in .... Le 6:20
none of it must be left until **m.** .... Le 7:15
salary all night until **m.** .... Le 19:13
any of the meat for the next **m.** .... Le 22:30
weeks from the **m** after the .... Le 23:15
evening until **m** before the LORD; .... Le 24:3
it until the next **m** or break any .... Nu 9:12
the cloud lifted the next **m,** .... Nu 9:21
Early the next **m** they started to .... Nu 14:40
Tomorrow **m** the LORD will show .... Nu 16:5
The next **m** Balaam awoke and said .... Nu 22:13
got up the next **m** and put a .... Nu 22:21
The next **m** Balak took Balaam to .... Nu 22:41
one lamb in the **m** and the other .... Nu 28:4
As in the **m,** also give a grain .... Nu 28:8
offerings you give every **m.**.................... Nu 28:23
and eat all the meat before **m;** .... Dt 16:4
next **m** go back to your tents. .... Dt 16:7
the **m** you will say, "I wish it .... Dt 28:67
will say, "I wish it were **m.**" .... Dt 28:67
Early the next **m** Joshua and all .... Jos 3:1
Early the next **m** Joshua got up, ... Jos 6:12
Tomorrow **m** you must be present .... Jos 7:14
Early the next **m** Joshua led all .... Jos 7:16
Early the next **m** Joshua gathered .... Jos 8:10
early the next **m** and hurried out .... Jos 8:14
of the city got up the next **m,** .... Jdg 6:28
Baal's side will be killed by **m!** .... Jdg 6:31
up early the next **m** and squeezed .... Jdg 6:38
Early in the **m** Jerub-Baal .... Jdg 7:1
as the sun comes up in the **m,**............... Jdg 9:33
day they got up early in the **m.** .... Jdg 19:5
got up early in the **m** to leave. .... Jdg 19:8
Tomorrow **m** you can get up early .... Jdg 19:9
In the **m** when the Levite got up, ... Jdg 19:27
The next **m** the Israelites got up .... Jdg 20:19
here, from **m** until just now. .... Ru 2:7
and in the **m** we will see if he .... Ru 3:13
So stay here until **m.**" .... Ru 3:13
feet until **m** but got up while .... Ru 3:14
the next **m** Elkanah's family 1Sa 1:19
Samuel lay down until **m.** 1Sa 3:15
of Ashdod rose early the next **m,** 1Sa 5:3
The next **m** when they rose, ... 1Sa 5:4
Tomorrow **m** I will answer all................. 1Sa 9:19
The next **m** Saul divided his 1Sa 11:11
Early the next **m** Samuel got up 1Sa 15:12
came out every **m** and evening and 1Sa 17:16
Early in the **m** David left the 1Sa 17:20

Watch out in the **m**. Hide in a 1Sa 19:2
it and to kill him in the **m**. 1Sa 19:11
you will be dead in the **m**." 1Sa 19:11
The next **m** Jonathan went out to 1Sa 20:35
of Nabal's men alive until **m**." 1Sa 25:22
men would have lived until **m**." 1Sa 25:34
him nothing until the next **m**. 1Sa 25:36
In the **m** when he was not drunk, ... 1Sa 25:37
Early in the **m** you and your 1Sa 29:10
up early in the **m** and went back 1Sa 29:11
chased their brothers until **m**." 2Sa 2:27
The next **m** David wrote a letter........... 2Sa 11:14
is like the **m** light at dawn, ... 2Sa 23:4
dawn, like a **m** without clouds. 2Sa 23:4
When David got up in the **m**, ... 2Sa 24:11
It began in the **m** and continued 2Sa 24:15
The next **m** when I got up to feed 1Ki 3:21
and meat every **m** and evening, ... 1Ki 17:6
to Baal from until noon, ... 1Ki 18:26
The next **m**, about the time the 2Ki 3:20
Moabites got up early in the **m**, ... 2Ki 3:22
piles at the city gate until **m**." 2Ki 10:8
the **m**, Jehu went out and stood 2Ki 10:9
altar burn the **m** burnt offering, ... 2Ki 16:15
people got up early the next **m**, ... 2Ki 19:35
and they opened it every **m**. 1Ch 9:27
Every **m** and evening they offered 1Ch 16:40
stood every **m** and gave thanks 1Ch 23:30
sacrifices every **m** and evening, ... 2Ch 2:4
to the LORD every **m** and evening.......... 2Ch 13:11
Desert of Tekoa early in the **m**.............. 2Ch 20:20
Early the next **m** King Hezekiah 2Ch 29:20
were given every **m** and evening, ... 2Ch 31:3
on it to the LORD **m** and evening. .... Ezr 3:3
loud from early **m** until noon to .... Ne 8:3
and in the **m** she would return to .... Est 2:14
in the **m** ask the king to have .... Est 5:14
Early in the **m** Job would offer a .... Job 1:5
Let that day's **m** stars never .... Job 3:9
them every **m** and test them .... Job 7:18
and darkness will seem like **m**. .... Job 11:17
Darkness is like **m** to all these .... Job 24:17
while the **m** stars sang together .... Job 38:7
you ever ordered the **m** to begin, ... Job 38:12
every **m** you hear my voice. .... Ps 5:3
Every **m**, I tell you what I need, ... Ps 5:3
a night, but joy comes in the **m**. .... Ps 30:5
will rule over them in the **m**, ... Ps 49:14
M, noon, and night I am troubled .... Ps 55:17
In the **m** I will sing about your .... Ps 59:16
I have been punished every **m**. .... Ps 73:14
every **m** I pray to you........................ Ps 88:13
grass that grows up in the **m**. .... Ps 90:5
In the **m** they are fresh and new, ... Ps 90:6
Fill us with your love every **m**. .... Ps 90:14
your love in the **m** and of your .... Ps 92:2
m I will destroy the wicked................ Ps 101:8
up early in the **m** and cry out. .... Ps 119:147
me in the **m** about your love, ... Ps 143:8
Come, let's make love until **m**. .... Pr 7:18
your neighbor early in the **m**, ... Pr 27:14
and whose leaders eat all **m**. .... Ec 10:16
early in the **m**, and work until .... Ec 11:6
rise early in the **m** to look for .... Is 5:11
of Babylon, **m** star, you have .... Is 14:12
Before **m**, no one will be left. .... Is 17:14
watchman answers, "**M** is coming,........ Is 21:12
It will come **m** after morning; .... Is 28:19
It will come morning after **m**; .... Is 28:19
Give us strength every **m**. .... Is 33:2
people got up early the next **m**, ... Is 37:36
Every **m** he wakes me. .... Is 50:4
crying in the **m** and battle cries .... Je 20:16

judge people fairly every **m**. .... Je 21:12
They are new every **m**; .... La 3:23
Then in the **m** the LORD spoke his........... Eze 12:8
I spoke to the people in the **m**, ... Eze 24:18
The next **m** I did as I had been .... Eze 24:18
to the LORD. Do it every **m**. .... Eze 46:13
offering with the lamb every **m**. .... Eze 46:14
every **m** as a burnt offering. .... Eze 46:15
The next **m** King Darius got up at .... Da 6:19
faithfulness is like a **m** mist, ... Hos 6:4
is low, but when **m** comes, it .... Hos 7:6
people will be like the **m** mist; .... Hos 13:3
will disappear like the **m** dew. .... Hos 13:3
Offer your sacrifices every **m**,............... Am 4:4
darkness into the **m** light, ... Am 5:8
When the **m** light comes, they do .... Mic 2:1
and in the **m** nothing is left of .... Zph 3:3
Every **m** he governs the people .... Zph 3:5
three and six o'clock in the **m**, ... Mt 14:25
in the **m** you say that it will .... Mt 16:3
One **m**, he went out very early to .... Mt 20:1
Early the next **m**, as Jesus was .... Mt 21:18
the next **m**, all the leading .... Mt 27:1
Early the next **m**, while it was .... Mk 1:35
three and six o'clock in the **m**, ... Mk 6:48
The next **m** as Jesus was passing .... Mk 11:20
or in the **m** while it is still .... Mk 13:35
Very early in the **m**, the leading .... Mk 15:1
o'clock in the **m** when they .... Mk 15:25
The next **m**, Jesus called his .... Lk 6:13
Every **m** all the people got up .... Lk 21:38
this **m** they went to the tomb, ... Lk 24:22
early in the **m** he went back to .... Jn 8:2
Early in the **m** they led Jesus .... Jn 18:28
Early the next **m** Jesus stood on .... Jn 21:4
is only nine o'clock in the **m**! .... Ac 2:15
early in the **m** and continued .... Ac 5:21
The next **m**, the Roman officers .... Ac 16:35
it was early **m**, and then he left .... Ac 20:11
In the **m** some evil people made a .... Ac 23:12
begins and the **m** star rises in.............. 2Pe 1:19
I will also give him the **m** star. .... Rev 2:28
and I am the bright **m** star." .... Rev 22:16

MORNING'S
to the **m** burnt offering. .... Le 9:17

MORNINGS
hundred evenings and **m**. .... Da 8:14
these evenings and **m** is true. .... Da 8:26

MORTAR
of stones, and tar instead of **m**. .... Ge 11:3
make bricks and **m** and to do all .... Ex 1:14

MOSERAH
wells of the Jaakanites to **M**. .... Dt 10:6
From **M** they went to Gudgodah, ... Dt 10:7

MOSEROTH
left Hashmonah and camped at **M**........... Nu 33:30
They left **M** and camped at Bene .... Nu 33:31

MOSES
The king's daughter named him **M**, ... Ex 2:10
M grew and became a man. .... Ex 2:11
man, one of **M**' own people. .... Ex 2:11
M looked all around and saw that .... Ex 2:12
The next day **M** returned and saw .... Ex 2:13
M was afraid and thought, ... Ex 2:14
the king heard what **M** had done, ... Ex 2:15
But **M** ran away from the king and........ Ex 2:15
but **M** defended the girls and .... Ex 2:17
M agreed to stay with Jethro, ... Ex 2:21
Zipporah to **M** to be his wife. .... Ex 2:21
M named him Gershom, because .... Ex 2:22
because **M** was a stranger in a .... Ex 2:22

One day **M** was taking care of .... Ex 3:1
the priest of Midian and also **M'**............... Ex 3:1
When **M** led the flock to the west .... Ex 3:1
M saw that the bush was on fire, ... Ex 3:2
When the LORD saw **M** was coming .... Ex 3:4
him from the bush, "**M,** Moses!" .... Ex 3:4
him from the bush, "Moses, **M!**" .... Ex 3:4
And **M** said, "Here I am." .... Ex 3:4
M covered his face because he .... Ex 3:6
But **M** said to God, "I am not a .... Ex 3:11
M said to God, "When I go to the .... Ex 3:13
God said to **M**, "I AM WHO I AM .... Ex 3:14
also said to **M**, "This is what .... Ex 3:15
Then **M** answered, "What if the .... Ex 4:1
M answered, "It is my walking .... Ex 4:2
So **M** threw it on the ground, ... Ex 4:3
became a snake. **M** ran from the .... Ex 4:3
When **M** reached out and took .... Ex 4:4
LORD said to **M**, "Put your hand .... Ex 4:6
So **M** put his hand inside his .... Ex 4:6
So **M** put his hand inside his .... Ex 4:7
But **M** said to the LORD, "Please, ... Ex 4:10
But **M** said, "Please, Lord, send .... Ex 4:13
became angry with **M** and said, ... Ex 4:14
M went back to Jethro, his .... Ex 4:18
Jethro said to **M**, "Go!........................... Ex 4:18
While **M** was still in Midian, ... Ex 4:19
So **M** took his wife and his sons, ... Ex 4:20
LORD said to **M**, "When you get .... Ex 4:21
As **M** was on his way to Egypt, ... Ex 4:24
she touched **M'** feet with it and .... Ex 4:25
So the LORD let **M** alone. .... Ex 4:26
out into the desert to meet **M**." .... Ex 4:27
Aaron went, he met **M** at Sinai, ... Ex 4:27
M told Aaron everything the LORD .... Ex 4:28
M and Aaron gathered all the................. Ex 4:29
that the LORD had told **M**. .... Ex 4:30
Then **M** did the miracles for all .... Ex 4:30
After **M** and Aaron talked to the .... Ex 5:1
Then Aaron and **M** said, "The God .... Ex 5:3
said to them, "**M** and Aaron, why .... Ex 5:4
to listen to the lies of **M**." .... Ex 5:9
king, they met **M** and Aaron, who .... Ex 5:20
So they said to **M** and Aaron, ... Ex 5:21
Then **M** returned to the LORD and........... Ex 5:22
LORD said to **M**, "Now you will............... Ex 6:1
God said to **M**, "I am the LORD................ Ex 6:2
M told this to the Israelites, ... Ex 6:9
Then the LORD said to **M**, ... Ex 6:10
But **M** answered, "The Israelites.............. Ex 6:12
LORD spoke to **M** and Aaron and .... Ex 6:13
who gave birth to Aaron and **M**............... Ex 6:20
the Aaron and **M** to whom the LORD........ Ex 6:26
Aaron and **M** are the ones who .... Ex 6:27
The LORD spoke to **M** in the land .... Ex 6:28
But **M** answered, "I am not a good........... Ex 6:30
The LORD said to **M**, "I have made .... Ex 7:1
M and Aaron did just as the LORD .... Ex 7:6
M was eighty years old and Aaron........... Ex 7:7
The LORD said to **M** and Aaron, ... Ex 7:8
M, when the king asks you to do .... Ex 7:9
So **M** and Aaron went to the king .... Ex 7:10
to listen to **M** and Aaron, ... Ex 7:13
the LORD said to **M**, "The king is .... Ex 7:14
The LORD said to **M**, "Tell Aaron: .... Ex 7:19
So **M** and Aaron did just as the .... Ex 7:20
to listen to **M** and Aaron, ... Ex 7:22
and ignored what **M** and Aaron had .... Ex 7:23
the LORD told **M**, "Go to the king .... Ex 8:1
LORD said to **M**, "Tell Aaron to .... Ex 8:5
king called for **M** and Aaron and .... Ex 8:8
M said to the king, "Please set .... Ex 8:9
M said, "What you want will .... Ex 8:10

After **M** and Aaron left the king, ... Ex 8:12
M asked the LORD about the frogs .... Ex 8:12
And the LORD did as **M** asked. .... Ex 8:13
did not listen to **M** and Aaron, ... Ex 8:15
LORD said to **M**, "Tell Aaron to .... Ex 8:16
The LORD told **M**, "Get up early .... Ex 8:20
king called for **M** and Aaron and .... Ex 8:25
M said, "It wouldn't be right .... Ex 8:26
M said, "I will leave and pray .... Ex 8:29
So **M** left the king and prayed to .... Ex 8:30
the LORD told **M**, "Go to the king .... Ex 9:1
The LORD said to **M** and Aaron, ... Ex 9:8
M, throw the ashes into the air .... Ex 9:8
So **M** and Aaron took ashes from a .... Ex 9:10
M threw ashes into the air, ... Ex 9:10
could not stand before **M,** .... Ex 9:11
to listen to **M** and Aaron, ... Ex 9:12
LORD said to **M**, "Get up early .... Ex 9:13
LORD told **M**, "Raise your hand.............. Ex 9:22
When **M** raised his walking stick .... Ex 9:23
king sent for **M** and Aaron and .... Ex 9:27
M told the king, "When I leave .... Ex 9:29
M left the king and went outside .... Ex 9:33
as the LORD had said through **M**. .... Ex 9:35
LORD said to **M**, "Go to the king .... Ex 10:1
So **M** and Aaron went to the king .... Ex 10:3
Then **M** turned and walked away .... Ex 10:6
So **M** and Aaron were brought back .... Ex 10:8
M answered, "We will go with our .... Ex 10:9
the king forced **M** and Aaron out .... Ex 10:11
LORD told **M**, "Raise your hand.............. Ex 10:12
So **M** raised his walking stick.................. Ex 10:13
quickly called for **M** and Aaron............... Ex 10:16
M left the king and prayed to .... Ex 10:18
the LORD told **M**, "Raise your .... Ex 10:21
M raised his hand toward the sky, ... Ex 10:22
the king of Egypt called for **M**. .... Ex 10:24
M said, "You must let us have .... Ex 10:25
he told **M**, "Get out of here, ... Ex 10:28
Then **M** told the king, "I'll do .... Ex 10:29
LORD had told **M**, "I have one .... Ex 11:1
considered **M** to be a great man .... Ex 11:3
So **M** said to the king, "This is .... Ex 11:4
Then **M** very angrily left the .... Ex 11:8
LORD had told **M**, "The king will .... Ex 11:9
M and Aaron did all these great .... Ex 11:10
The LORD spoke to **M** and Aaron in .... Ex 12:1
Then **M** called all the elders of .... Ex 12:21
the LORD commanded **M** and Aaron. .... Ex 12:28
king called for **M** and Aaron and .... Ex 12:31
did what **M** told them to do.................... Ex 12:35
The LORD told **M** and Aaron, ... Ex 12:43
LORD had commanded **M** and Aaron. .... Ex 12:50
Then the LORD said to **M**, ... Ex 13:1
M said to the people, "Remember .... Ex 13:3
M carried the bones of Joseph .... Ex 13:19
Then the LORD said to **M**, ... Ex 14:1
They said to **M**, "What have you .... Ex 14:11
M answered, "Don't be afraid! .... Ex 14:13
the LORD said to **M**, "Why are you .... Ex 14:15
Then **M** held his hand over the .... Ex 14:21
the LORD told **M**, "Hold your hand .... Ex 14:26
So **M** raised his hand over the .... Ex 14:27
trusted him and his servant **M**. .... Ex 14:31
Then **M** and the Israelites sang .... Ex 15:1
M led the Israelites away from .... Ex 15:22
people grumbled to **M** and asked, ... Ex 15:24
So **M** cried out to the LORD, ... Ex 15:25
When **M** threw the tree into the .... Ex 15:25
community grumbled to **M** and .... Ex 16:2
LORD said to **M**, "I will cause .... Ex 16:4
So **M** and Aaron said to all the .... Ex 16:6
And **M** said, "Each evening the .... Ex 16:8

Then **M** said to Aaron, "Speak to .... Ex 16:9
The LORD said to **M**, ... Ex 16:11
So **M** told them, "This is the .... Ex 16:15
M said to them, "Don't keep any .... Ex 16:19
not listen to **M** and kept part .... Ex 16:20
M was angry with those people. .... Ex 16:20
came and told this to **M**, ... Ex 16:22
morning, as **M** had commanded, ... Ex 16:24
M told the people, "Eat the food .... Ex 16:25
LORD said to **M**, "How long will .... Ex 16:28
Then **M** said, "The LORD said, ... Ex 16:32
M told Aaron, "Take a jar and .... Ex 16:33
what the LORD had commanded **M**. .... Ex 16:34
they quarreled with **M** and said, ... Ex 17:2
M said to them, "Why do you .... Ex 17:2
so they grumbled against **M**. .... Ex 17:3
M cried to the LORD, "What can .... Ex 17:4
The LORD said to **M**, "Go ahead of .... Ex 17:5
M did these things as the .... Ex 17:6
M said to Joshua, "Choose some .... Ex 17:9
Joshua obeyed **M** and went to .... Ex 17:10
while **M**, Aaron, and Hur .... Ex 17:10
As long as **M** held his hands up, ... Ex 17:11
but when **M** put his hands down, ... Ex 17:11
when **M'** arms became tired, ... Ex 17:12
Aaron and Hur held up **M'** hands— .... Ex 17:12
the LORD said to **M**, "Write about .... Ex 17:14
Then **M** built an altar and named .... Ex 17:15
M said, "I lifted my hands .... Ex 17:16
Jethro, **M'** father-in-law, was .... Ex 18:1
had done for **M** and his people, ... Ex 18:1
Now **M** had sent his wife Zipporah .... Ex 18:2
when he was born, **M** said, "I am .... Ex 18:3
he was born, **M** said, "The God .... Ex 18:4
Jethro, **M'** father-in-law, took .... Ex 18:5
took **M'** wife and his two sons .... Ex 18:5
and his two sons and went to **M**. .... Ex 18:5
a message ahead to **M** that said, ... Ex 18:6
So **M** went out to meet his .... Ex 18:7
health, they went into **M'** tent. .... Ex 18:7
M told his father-in-law .... Ex 18:8
Then Jethro, **M'** father-in-law, ... Ex 18:12
Israel came to **M'** father-in-law .... Ex 18:12
The next day **M** solved .... Ex 18:13
When **M'** father-in-law saw all .... Ex 18:14
saw all that **M** was doing for the .... Ex 18:14
M said to his father-in-law, ... Ex 18:15
M' father-in-law said to him, ... Ex 18:17
So **M** listened to his .... Ex 18:24
brought the hard cases to **M**, ... Ex 18:26
So **M** sent his father-in-law on .... Ex 18:27
Then **M** went up on the mountain .... Ex 19:3
So **M** went down and called the .... Ex 19:7
Then **M** took their answer back .... Ex 19:8
LORD said to **M**, "I will come to .... Ex 19:9
Then **M** told the LORD what the .... Ex 19:9
The LORD said to **M**, "Go to the .... Ex 19:10
After **M** went down from the .... Ex 19:14
Then **M** said to the people, ... Ex 19:15
Then **M** led the people out of the .... Ex 19:17
Then **M** spoke, and the voice of .... Ex 19:19
called **M** to come up to the top .... Ex 19:20
of the mountain, and **M** went up. .... Ex 19:20
The LORD said to **M**, "Go down and .... Ex 19:21
M told the LORD, "The people .... Ex 19:23
So **M** went down to the people and .... Ex 19:25
Then they said to **M**, "Speak to .... Ex 20:19
Then **M** said to the people, ... Ex 20:20
mountain while **M** went near the .... Ex 20:21
the LORD told **M** to say these .... Ex 20:22
Then God said to **M**, "These are .... Ex 21:1
The LORD told **M**, "You, Aaron, ... Ex 24:1
Then **M** alone must come near me; .... Ex 24:2

come up the mountain with **M**." .... Ex 24:2
M told the people all the LORD's .... Ex 24:3
So **M** wrote down all the words of .... Ex 24:4
Then **M** sent young Israelite men .... Ex 24:5
M put half of the blood of these .... Ex 24:6
Then **M** took the blood from the .... Ex 24:8
M, Aaron, Nadab, Abihu, and .... Ex 24:9
The LORD said to **M**, "Come up the .... Ex 24:12
So **M** and his helper Joshua set .... Ex 24:13
set out, and **M** went up to Sinai, ... Ex 24:13
M said to the elders, "Wait here .... Ex 24:14
When **M** went up on the mountain, ... Ex 24:15
the LORD called to **M** from inside .... Ex 24:16
Then **M** went into the cloud and .... Ex 24:18
The LORD said to **M**, ... Ex 25:1
The LORD said to **M**, ... Ex 30:11
The LORD said to **M**, ... Ex 30:17
Then the LORD said to **M**, ... Ex 30:22
the LORD said to **M**, "Take these .... Ex 30:34
Then the LORD said to **M**, ... Ex 31:1
Then the LORD said to **M**, ... Ex 31:12
speaking to **M** on Mount Sinai, ... Ex 31:18
had passed and **M** had not come .... Ex 32:1
Aaron and said, "**M** led us out of .... Ex 32:1
LORD said to **M**, "Go down from .... Ex 32:7
The LORD said to **M**, "I have seen .... Ex 32:9
M begged the LORD his God and .... Ex 32:11
Then **M** went down the mountain, ... Ex 32:15
he said to **M**, "It sounds like .... Ex 32:17
M answered: "It is not a shout .... Ex 32:18
When **M** came close to the camp, ... Ex 32:19
M said to Aaron, "What did these .... Ex 32:21
said to me, '**M** led us out of .... Ex 32:23
M saw that the people were .... Ex 32:25
M stood at the entrance to the .... Ex 32:26
of Levi gathered around **M**. .... Ex 32:26
Then **M** said to them, "The LORD, ... Ex 32:27
the family of Levi obeyed **M**, ... Ex 32:28
M said, "Today you have been .... Ex 32:29
The next day **M** told the people, ... Ex 32:30
So **M** went back to the LORD and .... Ex 32:31
the LORD told **M**, "I will erase .... Ex 32:33
the LORD said to **M**, "You and the .... Ex 33:1
because the LORD had said to **M**, ... Ex 33:5
M used to take a tent and set it .... Ex 33:7
Whenever **M** went out to the Tent, ... Ex 33:8
When **M** went into the Tent, ... Ex 33:9
while the LORD spoke with **M**. .... Ex 33:9
LORD spoke to **M** face to face as .... Ex 33:11
Then **M** would return to the camp, ... Ex 33:11
the camp, but **M'** young helper, ... Ex 33:11
M said to the LORD, "You have .... Ex 33:12
Then **M** said to him, "If you .... Ex 33:15
LORD said to **M**, "I will do what .... Ex 33:17
Then **M** said, "Now, please show .... Ex 33:18
LORD said to **M**, "Cut two more .... Ex 34:1
So **M** cut two stone tablets like .... Ex 34:4
cloud and stood there with **M**, ... Ex 34:5
passed in front of **M** and said, ... Ex 34:6
Then **M** quickly bowed to the .... Ex 34:8
the LORD said to **M**, "Write down .... Ex 34:27
M stayed there with the LORD .... Ex 34:28
And **M** wrote the words of the .... Ex 34:28
Then **M** came down from Mount .... Ex 34:29
Israel saw that **M'** face was .... Ex 34:30
But **M** called to them, so Aaron .... Ex 34:31
of the people returned to **M**, ... Ex 34:31
When **M** finished speaking to the .... Ex 34:33
Anytime **M** went before the LORD .... Ex 34:34
M took off the covering until he .... Ex 34:34
Then **M** would come out and tell .... Ex 34:34
would see that **M'** face was .... Ex 34:35
M gathered all the Israelite .... Ex 35:1

M

The LORD said to **M,** .... Nu 4:21
M, Aaron, and the leaders of .... Nu 4:34
whom **M** and Aaron counted as the .... Nu 4:37
as the LORD had commanded **M.** .... Nu 4:37
whom **M** and Aaron counted as the .... Nu 4:41
whom **M** and Aaron counted as the .... Nu 4:45
as the LORD had commanded **M.** .... Nu 4:45
So **M,** Aaron, and the leaders of .... Nu 4:46
as the LORD had commanded **M;** .... Nu 4:49
as the LORD had commanded **M.** .... Nu 4:49
The LORD said to **M,** .... Nu 5:1
did just as the LORD had told **M.** .... Nu 5:4
The LORD said to **M,** .... Nu 5:5
Then the LORD said to **M,** .... Nu 5:11
The LORD said to **M,** .... Nu 6:1
The LORD said to **M,** .... Nu 6:22
When **M** finished setting up the .... Nu 7:1
The LORD said to **M,** .... Nu 7:4
So **M** accepted the carts and the .... Nu 7:6
Then **M** gave four carts and eight .... Nu 7:8
M did not give any oxen or carts .... Nu 7:9
The LORD told **M,** "Each day one .... Nu 7:11
M went into the Meeting Tent .... Nu 7:89
The LORD said to **M,** .... Nu 8:1
the command the LORD gave **M.** .... Nu 8:3
the way the LORD had showed **M.** .... Nu 8:4
The LORD said to **M,** .... Nu 8:5
So **M,** Aaron, and all the .... Nu 8:20
what the LORD commanded **M.** .... Nu 8:20
what the LORD commanded **M.** .... Nu 8:22
The LORD said to **M,** .... Nu 8:23
LORD spoke to **M** in the Desert .... Nu 9:1
So **M** told the Israelites to .... Nu 9:4
just as the LORD commanded **M.** .... Nu 9:5
So they went to **M** and Aaron that .... Nu 9:6
said to **M,** "We are unclean .... Nu 9:7
M said to them, "Wait, and I .... Nu 9:8
Then the LORD said to **M,** .... Nu 9:9
that he commanded through **M.** .... Nu 9:23
The LORD said to **M,** .... Nu 10:1
it as the LORD had commanded **M.** .... Nu 10:13
Reuel the Midianite, who was **M'** .... Nu 10:29
M said to Hobab, "We are moving .... Nu 10:29
But **M** said, "Please don't leave .... Nu 10:31
left the camp, **M** said, "Rise up, ... Nu 10:35
was set down, **M** said, "Return, ... Nu 10:36
The people cried out to **M,** .... Nu 11:2
M heard every family crying as .... Nu 11:10
very angry, and **M** got upset. .... Nu 11:10
The LORD said to **M,** "Bring me .... Nu 11:16
M said, "LORD, here are six .... Nu 11:21
LORD said to **M,** "Do you think .... Nu 11:23
So **M** went out to the people and .... Nu 11:24
in the cloud and spoke to **M.** .... Nu 11:25
took some of the Spirit **M** had, ... Nu 11:25
A young man ran to **M** and said, ... Nu 11:27
of Nun said, "**M,** my master, stop .... Nu 11:28
Joshua had been **M'** assistant. .... Nu 11:28
But **M** answered, "Are you jealous .... Nu 11:29
Then **M** and the leaders of Israel .... Nu 11:30
to talk against **M** because of his .... Nu 12:1
Is **M** the only one the LORD .... Nu 12:2
Now **M** was very humble. .... Nu 12:3
So the LORD suddenly spoke to **M,** .... Nu 12:4
is not true with my servant **M.** .... Nu 12:7
to speak against my servant **M.''** .... Nu 12:8
Aaron said to **M,** "Please, my .... Nu 12:11
So **M** cried out to the LORD, ... Nu 12:13
LORD answered **M,** "If her father .... Nu 12:14
The LORD said to **M,** .... Nu 13:1
So **M** obeyed the LORD's command .... Nu 13:3
of the men **M** sent to explore .... Nu 13:16
M gave Hoshea son of Nun the new .... Nu 13:16

M sent them to explore Canaan .... Nu 13:17
came back to **M** and Aaron and all .... Nu 13:26
told **M,** "We went to the land .... Nu 13:27
the people near **M** to be quiet, ... Nu 13:30
complained against **M** and Aaron, ... Nu 14:2
Then **M** and Aaron bowed facedown .... Nu 14:5
LORD said to **M,** "How long will .... Nu 14:11
Then **M** said to the LORD, "The .... Nu 14:13
The LORD said to **M** and Aaron, ... Nu 14:26
men **M** had sent to explore the .... Nu 14:36
When **M** told these things to all .... Nu 14:39
But **M** said, "Why are you .... Nu 14:41
but **M** and the Ark of the .... Nu 14:44
The LORD said to **M,** .... Nu 15:1
The LORD said to **M,** .... Nu 15:17
these commands the LORD gave **M?** .... Nu 15:22
commands given to you through **M,** .... Nu 15:23
brought him to **M** and Aaron and .... Nu 15:33
LORD said to **M,** "The man must .... Nu 15:35
death, as the LORD commanded **M.** .... Nu 15:36
The LORD said to **M,** .... Nu 15:37
Abiram, and On turned against **M.** .... Nu 16:1
the community, and challenged **M.** .... Nu 16:2
group to speak to **M** and Aaron .... Nu 16:3
When **M** heard this, he bowed .... Nu 16:4
M also said to Korah, "Listen, ... Nu 16:8
Then **M** called Dathan and Abiram, ... Nu 16:12
M became very angry and said .... Nu 16:15
Then **M** said to Korah, "You and .... Nu 16:16
it and stood with **M** and Aaron at .... Nu 16:18
who were against **M** and Aaron, ... Nu 16:19
The LORD said to **M** and Aaron, ... Nu 16:20
But **M** and Aaron bowed facedown .... Nu 16:22
Then the LORD said to **M,** .... Nu 16:23
M stood and went to Dathan and .... Nu 16:25
M warned the people, "Move away .... Nu 16:26
Then **M** said, "Now you will know .... Nu 16:28
When **M** finished saying these .... Nu 16:31
The LORD said to **M,** .... Nu 16:36
had commanded him through **M.** .... Nu 16:40
against **M** and Aaron and said .... Nu 16:41
to complain against **M** and Aaron, ... Nu 16:42
Then **M** and Aaron went in front .... Nu 16:43
The LORD said to **M,** .... Nu 16:44
So **M** and Aaron bowed facedown .... Nu 16:45
Then **M** said to Aaron, "Get your .... Nu 16:46
So Aaron did as **M** said .... Nu 16:47
went back to **M** at the entrance .... Nu 16:50
The LORD said to **M,** .... Nu 17:1
So **M** spoke to the Israelites. .... Nu 17:6
M put them before the LORD in .... Nu 17:7
next day, when **M** entered the .... Nu 17:8
So **M** brought out to the .... Nu 17:9
the LORD said to **M,** "Put Aaron's .... Nu 17:10
So **M** obeyed what the LORD .... Nu 17:11
The people of Israel said to **M,** .... Nu 17:12
The LORD said to **M,** .... Nu 18:25
The LORD said to **M** and Aaron, ... Nu 19:1
together against **M** and Aaron. .... Nu 20:2
They argued with **M** and said, ... Nu 20:3
So **M** and Aaron left the people .... Nu 20:6
The LORD said to **M,** .... Nu 20:7
M took the stick from front .... Nu 20:9
M and Aaron gathered the people .... Nu 20:10
of the rock, and **M** said, "Now .... Nu 20:10
Then **M** lifted his hand and hit .... Nu 20:11
the LORD said to **M** and Aaron, ... Nu 20:12
M sent messengers to the king of .... Nu 20:14
the LORD said to **M** and Aaron, ... Nu 20:23
M obeyed the LORD's command. .... Nu 20:27
M took off Aaron's clothes and .... Nu 20:28
M and Eleazar came back down the .... Nu 20:28
and grumbled at God and **M.** .... Nu 21:5

M

the LORD had commanded M to do. .... Jos 11:20
LORD had told M to do long ago. .... Jos 11:23
LORD's servant M and the .... Jos 12:6
and M gave that land to the .... Jos 12:6
LORD's servant M had given them............ Jos 13:8
M had defeated them and had .... Jos 13:12
M had given each family group .... Jos 13:15
M had defeated him along with .... Jos 13:21
This is the land M gave to the.................. Jos 13:24
This is the land M had given to .... Jos 13:29
M had given this land to these .... Jos 13:32
But M had given no land to the .... Jos 13:33
had commanded M long ago how he .... Jos 14:2
M had already given the .... Jos 14:3
The LORD had told M how to give .... Jos 14:5
the prophet M about you and me. .... Jos 14:6
M, the LORD's servant, sent me .... Jos 14:7
told M what I thought about the.............. Jos 14:7
So that day M promised me, ' .... Jos 14:9
said this to M during the time.................. Jos 14:10
as I was the day M sent me out, ... Jos 14:11
The LORD told M to give us land .... Jos 17:4
M, the servant of the LORD, gave .... Jos 18:7
as I had M command you to do. .... Jos 20:2
LORD commanded M that you give .... Jos 21:2
as the LORD had commanded M. .... Jos 21:8
You have done everything M, ... Jos 22:2
to the land that M, the LORD's .... Jos 22:4
obey the teachings and laws M, ... Jos 22:5
M had given the land of Bashan............... Jos 22:7
to them by M as the LORD had .... Jos 22:9
the Book of the Teachings of M.............. Jos 23:6
I sent M and Aaron to Egypt, ... Jos 24:5
who were from the family of M' .... Jdg 1:16
As M had promised, Hebron was .... Jdg 1:20
given to their ancestors by M. .... Jdg 3:4
the descendants of Hobab, M' .... Jdg 4:11
son of Gershom, M' son, and his .... Jdg 18:30
the LORD who chose M and Aaron 1Sa 12:6
So the LORD sent M and Aaron, ... 1Sa 12:8
written in the teachings of M.................. 1Ki 2:3
tablets that M had put in the 1Ki 8:9
promised through M your servant 1Ki 8:53
he gave through his servant M. 1Ki 8:56
the Book of the Teachings of M. 2Ki 14:6
the bronze snake M had made. 2Ki 18:4
commands the LORD had given M. 2Ki 18:6
and did not obey all that M, ... 2Ki 18:12
my servant M gave them." 2Ki 21:8
all the Teachings of M. 2Ki 23:25
were Aaron, M, and Miriam. 1Ch 6:3
followed all the laws that M, ... 1Ch 6:49
shoulders, as M had commanded, ... 1Ch 15:15
The Holy Tent that M made while 1Ch 21:29
laws the LORD gave M for Israel. 1Ch 22:13
Amram's sons were Aaron and M. 1Ch 23:13
M was the man of God, and his 1Ch 23:14
M' sons were Gershom and Eliezer. 1Ch 23:15
of Gershom, who was M' son, was 1Ch 26:24
which M the LORD's servant had 2Ch 1:3
tablets that M had put in the 2Ch 5:10
every day as M had commanded. 2Ch 8:13
as the Teachings of M commanded, ... 2Ch 23:18
Jerusalem the tax money that M, ... 2Ch 24:6
to the LORD the tax money M, ... 2Ch 24:9
was written in the Book of M, ... 2Ch 25:4
Temple as the Teachings of M, ... 2Ch 30:16
commands I gave them through M." 2Ch 33:8
that had been given through M. 2Ch 34:14
LORD through M commanded us to 2Ch 35:6
as was written in the book of M. 2Ch 35:12
written in the Teachings of M, ... Ezr 3:2
it is written in the Book of M.................. Ezr 6:18

the Teachings of M that had been .... Ezr 7:6
laws you gave your servant M. .... Ne 1:7
what you taught your servant M, ... Ne 1:8
the Book of the Teachings of M, ... Ne 8:1
through M that the people .... Ne 8:14
through your servant M. .... Ne 9:14
given through M the servant of .... Ne 10:29
the Book of M to the people, ... Ne 13:1
a flock by using M and Aaron. .... Ps 77:20
A prayer of M, the man of God. .... Ps 89:52
M and Aaron were among his .... Ps 99:6
his ways to M and his deeds to .... Ps 103:7
Then he sent his servant M, ... Ps 105:26
were jealous of M and of Aaron, ... Ps 106:16
But M, his chosen one, stood .... Ps 106:23
and M was in trouble because of .... Ps 106:32
so M spoke without stopping to .... Ps 106:33
in the days of M and the......................... Is 63:11
who led M by the right hand with .... Is 63:12
of Judah even if M and Samuel .... Je 15:1
into the desert with M. .... Eze 20:35
written in the Teachings of M, ... Da 9:11
written in the Teachings of M. .... Da 9:13
I sent M, Aaron, and Miriam to .... Mic 6:4
the teaching of M my servant, ... Mal 4:4
the law of M or the teaching .... Mt 5:17
of the law of M and the teaching .... Mt 7:12
offer the gift M commanded for .... Mt 8:4
and the law of M told about what .... Mt 11:13
in the law of M that on every .... Mt 12:5
Then M and Elijah appeared to .... Mt 17:3
for you, one for M, and one for .... Mt 17:4
Why then did M give a command .... Mt 19:7
M allowed you to divorce your .... Mt 19:8
M said if a married man dies .... Mt 22:24
was an expert on the law of M, ... Mt 22:35
tell you what the law of M says. .... Mt 23:2
offer the gift M commanded for .... Mk 1:44
M said, 'Honor your father and .... Mk 7:10
Then Elijah and M appeared to .... Mk 9:4
for you, one for M, and one for .... Mk 9:5
"What did M command you to do?" .... Mk 10:3
M allowed a man to write out.................. Mk 10:4
M wrote that command for you .... Mk 10:5
M wrote that if a man's brother .... Mk 12:19
the book in which M wrote about .... Mk 12:26
that God told M, 'I am the God .... Mk 12:26
what the law of M taught about .... Lk 2:22
your healing, as M commanded............... Lk 5:14
Then two men, M and Elijah, were........... Lk 9:30
When M and Elijah were about to .... Lk 9:33
for you, one for M, and one for .... Lk 9:33
The law of M and the writings of .... Lk 16:16
have the law of M and the .... Lk 16:29
not listen to M and the prophets .... Lk 16:31
M wrote that if a man's brother .... Lk 20:28
Even M clearly showed that the .... Lk 20:37
as the law of M commanded. .... Lk 23:56
starting with what M and all the .... Lk 24:27
everything in the law of M,...................... Lk 24:44
The law was given through M, ... Jn 1:17
found the man that M wrote about .... Jn 1:45
Just as M lifted up the snake in .... Jn 3:14
one who says you are wrong is M, ... Jn 5:45
really believed M, you would .... Jn 5:46
me, because M wrote about me. .... Jn 5:46
you don't believe what M wrote,.............. Jn 5:47
it was not M who gave you bread .... Jn 6:32
M gave you the law, but none of............. Jn 7:19
M gave you the law about .... Jn 7:22
But really M did not give you .... Jn 7:22
day to obey the law of M, ... Jn 7:23
The law of M commands that we .... Jn 8:5

M

MOTH

but we are followers of **M**. .... Jn 9:28
We know that God spoke to **M**, ... Jn 9:29
M said, 'The Lord your God will............... Ac 3:22
against **M** and against God." .... Ac 6:11
holy place and the law of **M**. .... Ac 6:13
change the customs **M** gave us." .... Ac 6:14
At this time **M** was born, and he .... Ac 7:20
For three months **M** was cared for .... Ac 7:20
When they put **M** outside, the.................... Ac 7:21
taught **M** everything they .... Ac 7:22
When **M** was about forty years .... Ac 7:23
M saw an Egyptian mistreating .... Ac 7:24
M thought his own people would .... Ac 7:25
The next day when **M** saw two men .... Ac 7:26
other pushed **M** away and said, ' ....Ac 7:27
When **M** heard him say this, ... Ac 7:29
While he lived in Midian, he had .... Ac 7:29
appeared to **M** in the flames .... Ac 7:30
When **M** saw this, he was amazed .... Ac 7:31
M heard the Lord's voice say, ... Ac 7:31
' **M** began to shake with fear and .... Ac 7:32
now, **M**, I am sending you back .... Ac 7:34
This **M** was the same man the two .... Ac 7:35
' **M** is the same man God sent to .... Ac 7:35
of the angel that **M** saw in the .... Ac 7:35
M led the people out of Egypt. .... Ac 7:36
This is the same **M** that said to .... Ac 7:37
This is the **M** who was with the .... Ac 7:38
did not want to obey **M**. .... Ac 7:39
M led us out of Egypt, but we .... Ac 7:40
told **M** how to make this Tent, ... Ac 7:44
You received the law of **M**, ... Ac 7:53
the law of **M** and the writings.................. Ac 13:15
not circumcised as **M** taught us." .... Ac 15:1
be told to obey the law of **M**."............... Ac 15:5
the law of **M** has been taught .... Ac 15:21
important to obey the law of **M**. .... Ac 21:20
nations to leave the law of **M**. .... Ac 21:21
the law of **M** in your own life.................. Ac 21:24
teaching against the law of **M**, ... Ac 21:28
the law of **M**, and all the Jews .... Ac 22:12
using the law of **M**, but you are .... Ac 23:3
in the law of **M** and that is .... Ac 24:14
only what **M** and the prophets .... Ac 26:22
the law of **M** and the prophets .... Ac 28:23
the law of **M** and brag that you .... Rm 2:17
the law of **M** but for anyone .... Rm 4:16
the world before the law of **M**, ... Rm 5:13
time of Adam to the time of **M**, ... Rm 5:14
of you understand the law of **M**............... Rm 7:1
them the law of **M** and the right............... Rm 9:4
God said to **M**, "I will show .... Rm 9:15
M writes about being made right .... Rm 10:5
First, **M** says: "I will use .... Rm 10:19
It is written in the law of **M**: 1Co 9:9
to our ancestors who followed **M**. 1Co 10:1
as followers of **M** in the cloud 1Co 10:2
which made **M'** face so bright.................. 2Co 3:7
We are not like **M**, who put a 2Co 3:13
and **M** did not want them to see 2Co 3:13
when they read the law of **M**, ... 2Co 3:15
angels who used **M** for a mediator .... Gal 3:19
the way I obeyed the law of **M**. .... Php 3:6
and Jambres were against **M**, ... 2Ti 3:8
faithful to God as **M** was in .... Heb 3:2
Jesus has more honor than **M**, ... Heb 3:3
M was faithful in God's family .... Heb 3:5
those people **M** led out of Egypt. .... Heb 3:16
and **M** said nothing about priests .... Heb 7:14
The law of **M** could not make .... Heb 7:19
why God warned **M** when he was .... Heb 8:5
M told all the people every .... Heb 9:19
M sprinkled the blood on the .... Heb 9:21

obey the law of **M** was found .... Heb 10:28
by faith that **M'** parents hid him .... Heb 11:23
They saw that **M** was a beautiful .... Heb 11:23
by faith that **M**, when he grew up .... Heb 11:24
was by faith that **M** left Egypt .... Heb 11:27
M continued strong as if he .... Heb 11:27
It was by faith that **M** prepared .... Heb 11:28
saw was so terrible that **M** said, ... Heb 12:21
who would have the body of **M**, ... Jud 1:9
sang the song of **M**, the servant .... Rev 15:3

MOTH

who can be crushed like a **m**. .... Job 4:19
like a **m**, you destroy what they .... Ps 39:11
I am like a **m** to Israel, like a .... Hos 5:12

MOTHER

his father and **m** and be united .... Ge 2:24
she was the **m** of all the living .... Ge 3:20
will be the **m** of many nations .... Ge 17:16
she is not the daughter of my **m**. .... Ge 20:12
and his **m** found a wife for him .... Ge 21:21
Milcah was the **m** of these eight............... Ge 22:23
gifts to her brother and **m**. .... Ge 24:53
m and her brother said, ... Ge 24:55
Rebekah's brother and **m** said, ... Ge 24:57
may you be the **m** of thousands of .... Ge 24:60
of Sarah, his **m**, and she became .... Ge 24:67
servant, was Ishmael's **m**. .... Ge 25:12
But Jacob said to his **m** Rebekah, ... Ge 27:11
goats and brought them to his **m**, ... Ge 27:14
Rebekah was the **m** of Jacob and .... Ge 28:5
his father and **m** and had gone to .... Ge 28:7
brother of Rebekah, Jacob's **m**. .... Ge 29:10
and brought them to his **m** Leah. .... Ge 30:14
you really believe that your **m**, ... Ge 37:10
who had the same **m** as he, Joseph .... Ge 43:29
went and got the baby's own **m**............... Ex 2:8
father and your **m** so that you .... Ex 20:12
father or his **m** must be put to .... Ex 21:15
his father or **m** must be put to .... Ex 21:17
of every **m** belongs to me, ... Ex 34:19
the **m** will be unclean for two .... Le 12:5
the new **m** must bring certain.................. Le 12:6
sexual relations with your **m**. .... Le 18:7
She is your **m**; do not have .... Le 18:7
of your father or your **m**. .... Le 18:9
must respect your **m** and father, ... Le 19:3
his father or **m** must be put to .... Le 20:9
He has cursed his father or **m**, ... Le 20:9
with both a woman and her **m**, ... Le 20:14
of either his father or his **m**, ... Le 20:17
dead person is his **m** or father, ... Le 21:2
it is for his own father or **m**. .... Le 21:11
must stay seven days with its **m**. .... Le 22:27
and its **m** on the same day, ... Le 22:28
their own father, **m**, brother, or .... Nu 6:7
father and your **m** as the LORD .... Dt 5:16
father and **m** and doesn't obey .... Dt 21:18
and the **m** bird is sitting on the .... Dt 22:6
do not take the **m** bird with the .... Dt 22:6
you must let the **m** bird go free. .... Dt 22:7
who dishonors his father or **m**." .... Dt 27:16
said about his father and **m**, ' .... Dt 33:9
Allow my father, **m**, brothers, ... Jos 2:13
your father, **m**, brothers, and .... Jos 2:18
her father, **m**, brothers, and all .... Jos 6:23
I arose to be a **m** to Israel. .... Jdg 5:7
Sisera's **m** looked out through .... Jdg 5:28
and Sisera's **m** says to herself, ... Jdg 5:29
and his **m** was a prostitute...................... Jdg 11:1
he said to his father and **m**, ... Jdg 14:2
His father and **m** answered, ... Jdg 14:3
with his father and **m** to Timnah, ... Jdg 14:5

father or **m** what he had done. .... Jdg 14:6
even told my father or **m**. .... Jdg 14:16
He said to his **m**, "I heard you .... Jdg 17:2
His **m** said, "The LORD bless .... Jdg 17:2
pounds of silver to his **m**. .... Jdg 17:3
gave the silver back to his **m**, ... Jdg 17:4
your father and **m** and your own .... Ru 2:11
year Samuel's **m** made a little................ 1Sa 2:19
she became the **m** of three sons 1Sa 2:21
but the **m** had much trouble in 1Sa 4:19
your **m** will have no children. 1Sa 15:33
and on your **m** who gave birth to 1Sa 20:30
my father and **m** come and stay 1Sa 22:3
m was Ahinoam from Jezreel. 2Sa 3:2
was Kileab, whose **m** was Abigail, ... 2Sa 3:3
whose **m** was Maacah daughter of 2Sa 3:3
Adonijah, whose **m** was Haggith. 2Sa 3:4
Shephatiah, whose **m** was Abital. 2Sa 3:4
Ithream, whose **m** was Eglah, ... 2Sa 3:5
Amasa's **m** was Abigail daughter 2Sa 17:25
and sister of Zeruiah, Joab's **m**. 2Sa 17:25
the grave of my father and **m**................. 2Sa 19:37
went to Bathsheba, Solomon's **m**. 1Ki 1:11
went to Bathsheba, Solomon's **m**. 1Ki 2:13
bring another throne for his **m**. 1Ki 2:19
"Ask, **m**," the king answered. 1Ki 2:20
King Solomon answered his **m**, ... 1Ki 2:22
The real **m** of the living child 1Ki 3:26
because she is the real **m**." 1Ki 3:27
Huram's **m** was a widow from the 1Ki 7:14
His **m** was Naamah from Ammon. 1Ki 14:21
His **m** was Maacah daughter of 1Ki 15:2
removed her from being queen **m**. 1Ki 15:13
and gave him to his **m** and said,.............. 1Ki 17:23
my father and my **m** good-bye," 1Ki 19:20
his father Ahab, his **m** Jezebel, ... 1Ki 22:52
Then two **m** bears came out of the 2Ki 2:24
was not like his father and **m**; 2Ki 3:2
and to the prophets of your **m**!" 2Ki 3:13
servant, "Take him to his **m**!"................... 2Ki 4:19
The servant took him to his **m**, ... 2Ki 4:20
The boy's **m** said, "As surely as 2Ki 4:30
as long as your **m** Jezebel 2Ki 9:22
of the king and the king's **m**." 2Ki 10:13
When Ahaziah's **m**, Athaliah, saw 2Ki 11:1
His **m** was named Jehoaddin, ... 2Ki 14:2
m was named Jecoliah, and she 2Ki 15:2
but the **m** is not strong enough 2Ki 19:3
along with Jehoiachin's **m**, ... 2Ki 24:12
as the king's **m** and his wives, ... 2Ki 24:15
daughter of Shua, was their **m**. 1Ch 2:3
Abigail was the **m** of Amasa, ... 1Ch 2:17
She was the **m** of Onam........................ 1Ch 2:26
and she was the **m** of Haran, ... 1Ch 2:46
was the **m** of Sheber, Tirhanah, ... 1Ch 2:48
m was Ahinoam from Jezreel. 1Ch 3:1
whose **m** was Abigail from Carmel. 1Ch 3:1
whose **m** was Maacah daughter of 1Ch 3:2
Adonijah, whose **m** was Haggith. 1Ch 3:2
Shephatiah, whose **m** was Abital. 1Ch 3:3
was Ithream, whose **m** was Eglah. 1Ch 3:3
m named him Jabez because she 1Ch 4:9
who was the **m** of Asriel and 1Ch 7:14
m was from the people of Dan, ... 2Ch 2:14
Rehoboam's **m** was Naamah from the 2Ch 12:13
His **m** was Maacah daughter of 2Ch 13:2
being queen **m**, because she had 2Ch 15:16
because his **m** encouraged him to 2Ch 22:3
When Ahaziah's **m**, Athaliah, saw 2Ch 22:10
had no father or **m**, so Mordecai .... Est 2:7
when her father and **m** died. .... Est 2:7
The cubs of the **m** lion are .... Job 4:11
me inside my **m** like cheese .... Job 10:10

'You are my **m**' or 'You are my .... Job 17:14
Who is the **m** of the ice? .... Job 38:29
You had my **m** give birth to me. .... Ps 22:9
my God since my **m** gave me birth. .... Ps 22:10
If my father and **m** leave me, ... Ps 27:10
as if I were crying for my **m**. .... Ps 35:14
In sin my **m** gave birth to me.................. Ps 51:5
the sins of his **m** be wiped out. .... Ps 109:14
none and makes her a happy **m**.............. Ps 113:9
quiet, like a baby with its **m**. .... Ps 131:2
peace, like a baby with its **m**. .... Ps 131:2
and like an only child to my **m**, ... Pr 4:3
children make their **m** sad. .... Pr 10:1
children disrespect their **m**. .... Pr 15:20
and cause their **m** great sorrow. .... Pr 17:25
sends away his **m** brings shame .... Pr 19:26
their father or **m** will be like a .... Pr 20:20
forget your **m** when she is old .... Pr 23:22
Make your father and **m** happy; .... Pr 23:25
give your **m** a reason to be glad............... Pr 23:25
robs father or **m** and says, ... Pr 28:24
alone will disgrace their **m**..................... Pr 29:15
the childless **m**, the land that .... Pr 30:16
and refuse to obey your **m**,..................... Pr 30:17
the message his **m** taught him: .... Pr 31:1
how a baby grows inside the **m**. .... Ec 11:5
the crown his **m** put on his head............ Sng 3:11
there your **m** gave birth to you. .... Sng 8:5
to say 'my father' or 'my **m**.'".................. Is 8:4
but the **m** is not strong enough .... Is 37:3
the child who says to his **m**, ' .... Is 45:10
the body of my **m** to be his .... Is 49:5
you say I divorced your **m**...................... Is 50:1
me, your **m** was sent away. .... Is 50:1
child drinking milk from its **m**. .... Is 60:16
as a child is nursed by its **m**. .... Is 66:11
comfort you as a **m** comforts her .... Is 66:13
to the king and the queen **m**: .... Je 13:18
Even the **m** deer in the field .... Je 14:5
M, I am sorry that you gave .... Je 15:10
someone whose **m** or father has .... Je 16:7
the day when my **m** gave birth to .... Je 20:14
Then my **m** would have been my .... Je 20:17
you and your **m** into another .... Je 22:26
the king and the queen **m**; .... Je 29:2
Your **m** will be very ashamed; .... Je 50:12
and your **m** was a Hittite. .... Eze 16:3
"The daughter is like her **m**." .... Eze 16:44
are like your **m**, who hated her .... Eze 16:45
Your **m** was a Hittite, and your .... Eze 16:45
'Your **m** was like a female lion. .... Eze 19:2
The **m** lion waited and saw that .... Eze 19:5
Your **m** was like a vine in your .... Eze 19:10
their father, **m**, son, daughter,................. Eze 44:25
Then the king's **m**, who had heard .... Da 5:10
Plead with your **m**. Accuse her, ... Hos 2:2
Their **m** has acted like a .... Hos 2:5
I will also destroy your **m**. .... Hos 4:5
will turn against her **m**, ... Mic 7:6
own father and **m**, the ones who .... Zch 13:3
own father and **m** who gave birth .... Zch 13:3
Zerah. (Their **m** was Tamar.) .... Mt 1:3
Boaz. (Boaz's **m** was Rahab.) Boaz......... Mt 1:5
Obed. (Obed's **m** was Ruth.) Obed .... Mt 1:5
m had been Uriah's wife. .... Mt 1:6
and Mary was the **m** of Jesus. .... Mt 1:16
His **m** Mary was engaged to marry .... Mt 1:18
was and saw him with his **m**, ... Mt 2:11
the child and his **m** and escape .... Mt 2:13
night with the child and his **m**. .... Mt 2:14
child and his **m** and go to the .... Mt 2:20
the child and his **m** and went to .... Mt 2:21
daughter will be against her **m**, ... Mt 10:35

their father or **m** more than they .... Mt 10:37
m and brothers stood outside, ... Mt 12:46
Your **m** and brothers are standing .... Mt 12:47
He answered, "Who is my **m**?.................. Mt 12:48
Here are my **m** and my brothers. .... Mt 12:49
and sister and **m** are those who .... Mt 12:50
His **m** is Mary, and his brothers .... Mt 13:55
girl, and she took it to her **m.** .... Mt 14:11
'Honor your father and your **m**,' .... Mt 15:4
his father or **m** must be put to .... Mt 15:4
can tell his father or **m,** '...................... Mt 15:5
to honor his father or his **m.** .... Mt 15:6
his father and **m** and be united .... Mt 19:5
honor your father and **m;** .... Mt 19:19
sisters, father, **m,** children, or .... Mt 19:29
and Mary the **m** of James and .... Mt 27:56
and the **m** of James and John were .... Mt 27:56
Then Jesus' **m** and brothers .... Mk 3:31
Your **m** and brothers are waiting .... Mk 3:32
"Who are my **m** and my brothers?" .... Mk 3:33
Here are my **m** and my brothers! .... Mk 3:34
and sister and **m** are those who .... Mk 3:35
father and **m** and his three .... Mk 5:40
girl went to her **m** and asked, ... Mk 6:24
Her **m** answered, "Ask for the .... Mk 6:24
and the girl gave it to her **m.** .... Mk 6:28
'Honor your father and your **m**,' .... Mk 7:10
his father or **m** must be put to .... Mk 7:10
can tell his father or **m,** '...................... Mk 7:11
money for his father or his **m.** .... Mk 7:12
his father and **m** and be united .... Mk 10:7
Honor your father and **m.'** " .... Mk 10:19
sisters, **m,** father, children .... Mk 10:29
and Mary the **m** of James and .... Mk 15:40
and Mary the **m** of Joseph saw .... Mk 15:47
Magdalene, Mary the **m** of James, ... Mk 16:1
the **m** of my Lord comes to me? .... Lk 1:43
but his **m** said, "No! He will be .... Lk 1:60
father and **m** were amazed at .... Lk 2:33
His **m** said to him, "Son, why did .... Lk 2:48
But his **m** kept in her mind all .... Lk 2:51
A **m,** who was a widow, had lost .... Lk 7:12
was with the **m** while her son was .... Lk 7:12
Jesus gave him back to his **m.** .... Lk 7:15
Jesus' **m** and brothers came to .... Lk 8:19
Your **m** and your brothers are .... Lk 8:20
My **m** and my brothers are those .... Lk 8:21
father and **m** and go inside with .... Lk 8:51
Blessed is the **m** who gave birth .... Lk 11:27
m against daughter and daughter .... Lk 12:53
daughter and daughter against **m,** .... Lk 12:53
his father, **m,** wife, children, ... Lk 14:26
Honor your father and **m.'** " .... Lk 18:20
Joanna, Mary the **m** of James, and .... Lk 24:10
in Galilee. Jesus' **m** was there, ... Jn 2:1
was gone, Jesus' **m** said to him, ... Jn 2:3
His **m** said to the servants, ... Jn 2:5
town of Capernaum with his **m,** .... Jn 2:12
We know his father and **m.** .... Jn 6:42
near his cross were Jesus', ... Jn 19:25
Jesus saw his **m** and the follower .... Jn 19:26
he said to his **m,** "Dear woman, ... Jn 19:26
the follower, "Here is your **m.**" .... Jn 19:27
including Mary the **m** of Jesus, ... Ac 1:14
of Mary, the **m** of John Mark. .... Ac 12:12
Timothy's **m** was Jewish and a .... Ac 16:1
Lord, and to his **m,** who has been .... Rm 16:13
has been like a **m** to me also. .... Rm 16:13
The **m** of one son was a slave .... Gal 4:22
and the **m** of the other son was a .... Gal 4:22
The **m** named Hagar is like that .... Gal 4:24
the free woman. She is our **m.** .... Gal 4:26
his father and **m** and be united .... Eph 5:31

"Honor your father and **m.**" .... Eph 6:2
like a **m** caring for her little 1Th 2:7
Lois and in your **m** Eunice, ... 2Ti 1:5
Melchizedek's father or **m** was, ... Heb 7:3
GREAT BABYLON **M** OF PROSTITUTES ... Rev 17:5

MOTHER'S
and told her **m** family about all .... Ge 24:28
was comforted after his **m** death. .... Ge 24:67
and may your **m** sons bow down to .... Ge 27:29
of Bethuel, your **m** father, in .... Ge 28:2
Laban, your **m** brother, lives .... Ge 28:2
only one of his **m** children left .... Ge 44:20
cook a young goat in its **m** milk. .... Ex 23:19
a young goat in its **m** milk." .... Ex 34:26
relations with your **m** sister; .... Le 18:13
she is your **m** close relative. .... Le 18:13
with your **m** sister or your .... Le 20:19
The **m** name was Shelomith, the .... Le 24:11
cook a baby goat in its **m** milk. .... Dt 14:21
daughter or his **m** daughter." .... Dt 27:22
were my brothers, my **m** sons. .... Jdg 8:19
and all of his **m** family group, ... Jdg 9:1
each of you to your own **m** house. .... Ru 1:8
His **m** name was Azubah daughter 1Ki 22:42
he lay on his **m** lap until noon. 2Ki 4:20
Why did my **m** knees receive me, ... Job 3:12
me, and my **m** breasts feed me? .... Job 3:12
is grabbed from its **m** breast; .... Job 24:9
take a poor **m** baby to pay for .... Job 24:9
made me in my **m** womb, and he .... Job 31:15
and lie about your **m** son. .... Ps 50:20
a foreigner to my **m** children. .... Ps 69:8
you formed me in my **m** body. .... Ps 139:13
as I took shape in my **m** body. .... Ps 139:15
and do not forget your **m** advice. .... Pr 1:8
don't forget your **m** teaching. .... Pr 6:20
I brought him to my **m** house, ... Sng 3:4
She is her **m** only daughter, ... Sng 6:9
brother who fed at my **m** breasts. .... Sng 8:1
you and bring you to my **m** house; .... Sng 8:2
longer nurse at their **m** breast. .... Is 28:9
who formed you in your **m** body, ... Is 44:2
who formed you in your **m** body: .... Is 44:24
while I was still in my **m** womb. .... Is 49:1
I made you in your **m** womb, ... Je 1:5
I have to come out of my **m** body? .... Je 20:18
His **m** name was Hamutal daughter .... Je 52:1
won't come out of its **m** womb. .... Hos 13:13
cannot enter his **m** womb again. .... Jn 3:4
Jesus' mother, his **m** sister, ... Jn 19:25
Timothy to please his **m** people. .... Ac 16:3

MOTHER-IN-LAW
sexual relations with his **m.**" .... Dt 27:23
kissed her **m** Naomi good-bye, ... Ru 1:14
have given your **m** after your .... Ru 2:11
and her **m** saw how much she had .... Ru 2:18
Ruth told her **m** whose field she .... Ru 2:19
to live with Naomi, her **m.** .... Ru 2:23
Naomi, Ruth's **m,** said to her, ... Ru 3:1
did all her **m** told her to do. .... Ru 3:6
When Ruth went back to her **m,** .... Ru 3:16
without a gift for your **m.**'" .... Ru 3:17
will be against her **m;** .... Mic 7:6
that Peter's **m** was sick in bed .... Mt 8:14
will be against her **m.** .... Mt 10:35
Simon's **m** was sick in bed with a .... Mk 1:30
Simon's **m** was sick with a high .... Lk 4:38
m against daughter-in-law and .... Lk 12:53
and daughter-in-law against **m.**" .... Lk 12:53

MOTHERS
even the **m** with the children. .... Ge 32:11
with their **m** for seven days, ... Ex 22:30

calves home, away from their **m.** 1Sa 6:7
sword made other **m** lose their 1Sa 15:33
Their **m** forget them, and worms .... Job 24:20
both of us in our **m'** wombs. .... Job 31:15
and do not bless their **m.** .... Pr 30:11
gently leads the **m** of the lambs. .... Is 40:11
against the **m** of the young men .... Je 15:8
land and their **m** and fathers: .... Je 16:3
They ask their **m,** "Where is the .... La 2:12
city and die in their **m'** arms. .... La 2:12
our **m** are like widows. .... La 5:3
in you hate their fathers and **m.** .... Eze 22:7
when **m** and their children were .... Hos 10:14
still feed as their **m'** breasts. .... Joe 2:16
brothers, sisters, **m,** children, ... Mk 10:30
who kill their fathers and **m,** 1Ti 1:9
older women like **m,** and younger 1Ti 5:2

MOTHS

like clothing eaten by **m.** .... Job 13:28
old clothes; **m** will eat them. .... Is 50:9
M will eat those people as if .... Is 51:8
on earth where **m** and rust will .... Mt 6:19
be destroyed by **m** or rust and .... Mt 6:20
can't steal and **m** can't destroy. .... Lk 12:33
clothes have been eaten by **m.** .... Jam 5:2

MOTIONED

Peter **m** to him to ask Jesus .... Jn 13:24

MOUNDS

that were built on their **m,** .... Jos 11:13
they smell like **m** of perfume. .... Sng 5:13

MOUNT

M Sinai was covered with smoke, ... Ex 19:18
came down on top of **M** Sinai, ... Ex 19:20
cannot come up on **M** Sinai, ... Ex 19:23
the LORD came down on **M** Sinai, ... Ex 24:16
speaking to Moses on **M** Sinai, ... Ex 31:18
off their jewelry at **M** Sinai. .... Ex 33:6
and then come up on **M** Sinai. .... Ex 34:2
next morning he went up **M** Sinai, ... Ex 34:4
Moses came down from **M** Sinai, ... Ex 34:29
LORD had given him on **M** Sinai. .... Ex 34:32
Moses on **M** Sinai on the day he .... Le 7:38
LORD said to Moses at **M** Sinai, ... Le 25:1
through Moses at **M** Sinai. .... Le 26:46
gave to Moses at **M** Sinai for the .... Le 27:34
LORD talked to Moses on **M** Sinai. .... Nu 3:1
moved from Kadesh to **M** Hor, ... Nu 20:22
and his son Eleazar up on **M** Hor, ... Nu 20:25
They climbed up **M** Hor, and all .... Nu 20:27
Israelites left **M** Hor and went .... Nu 21:4
where the top of **M** Pisgah looks .... Nu 21:20
of Zophim, on top of **M** Pisgah. .... Nu 23:14
offering which began at **M** Sinai; .... Nu 28:6
and camped at **M** Shepher. .... Nu 33:23
They left **M** Shepher and camped .... Nu 33:24
left Kadesh and camped at **M** Hor, ... Nu 33:37
the LORD and went up **M** Hor. .... Nu 33:38
years old when he died on **M** Hor. .... Nu 33:39
The people left **M** Hor and camped .... Nu 33:41
Sea and go to **M** Hor. .... Nu 34:7
From **M** Hor it will go to Lebo .... Nu 34:8
The trip from **M** Sinai to Kadesh .... Dt 1:2
Barnea on the **M** Seir road takes .... Dt 1:2
spoke to us at **M** Sinai and said, ... Dt 1:6
we left **M** Sinai and went toward .... Dt 1:19
the Arnon Ravine to **M** Hermon, ... Dt 3:8
the Dead Sea west of **M** Pisgah. .... Dt 3:17
to the top of **M** Pisgah and look .... Dt 3:27
the LORD your God at **M** Sinai. .... Dt 4:10
to you from the fire at **M** Sinai, ... Dt 4:15
the Arnon Ravine, to **M** Hermon. .... Dt 4:48

as the Dead Sea below **M** Pisgah. .... Dt 4:49
an Agreement with us at **M** Sinai. .... Dt 5:2
M Sinai you made the LORD angry— ...... Dt 9:8
the blessings from **M** Gerizim and .... Dt 11:29
and the curses from **M** Ebal. .... Dt 11:29
you were gathered at **M** Sinai. .... Dt 18:16
set up these stones on **M** Ebal, ... Dt 27:4
must stand on **M** Gerizim to bless .... Dt 27:12
must stand on **M** Ebal to announce .... Dt 27:13
had made with them at **M** Sinai. .... Dt 29:1
M Nebo in the country of Moab, ... Dt 32:49
Aaron died on **M** Hor and joined .... Dt 32:50
LORD came from **M** Sinai and rose .... Dt 33:2
his greatness from **M** Paran. .... Dt 33:2
Then Moses climbed **M** Nebo from .... Dt 34:1
of Moab to the top of **M** Pisgah, ... Dt 34:1
the God of Israel, on **M** Ebal, as .... Jos 8:30
people stood in front of **M** Ebal, ... Jos 8:33
stood in front of **M** Gerizim. .... Jos 8:33
who lived below **M** Hermon in the .... Jos 11:3
the land from **M** Halak near Edom .... Jos 11:17
of Lebanon, below **M** Hermon. .... Jos 11:17
Arnon Ravine to **M** Hermon and all .... Jos 12:1
He ruled over **M** Hermon, Salecah, ... Jos 12:5
Lebanon and **M** Halak near Edom. .... Jos 12:7
Baal Gad below **M** Hermon to Lebo .... Jos 13:5
and all of **M** Hermon and Bashan .... Jos 13:11
to the cities near **M** Ephron. .... Jos 15:9
west and went toward **M** Seir. .... Jos 15:10
along the north side of **M** Jearim .... Jos 15:10
and went past **M** Baalah and .... Jos 15:11
border touched **M** Carmel and .... Jos 19:26
of Ephraim, north of **M** Gaash. .... Jos 24:30
determined to stay in **M** Heres, ... Jdg 1:35
of Ephraim, north of **M** Gaash. .... Jdg 2:9
mountains from **M** Baal Hermon to .... Jdg 3:3
and lead them to **M** Tabor. .... Jdg 4:6
of Abinoam had gone to **M** Tabor. .... Jdg 4:12
ten thousand men down **M** Tabor. .... Jdg 4:14
LORD, the God of Sinai, before .... Jdg 5:5
afraid may leave **M** Gilead and go .... Jdg 7:3
that you killed on **M** Tabor?" .... Jdg 8:18
stood on the top of **M** Gerizim. .... Jdg 9:7
all his men went up **M** Zalmon, ... Jdg 9:48
were killed on **M** Gilboa. 1Sa 31:1
his three sons dead on **M** Gilboa. 1Sa 31:8
David went up the **M** of Olives, ... 2Sa 15:30
over the top of the **M** of Olives, ... 2Sa 16:1
had put in the Ark at **M** Sinai. 1Ki 8:9
Israel to meet me at **M** Carmel. 1Ki 18:19
and those prophets to **M** Carmel. 1Ki 18:20
climbed to the top of **M** Carmel, ... 1Ki 18:42
days and nights to **M** Sinai, ... 1Ki 19:8
Elisha went to **M** Carmel and from 2Ki 2:25
the man of God, at **M** Carmel. 2Ki 4:25
a few from **M** Zion will live. 2Ki 19:31
south of the **M** of Olives. 2Ki 23:13
Hermon, Senir, and **M** Hermon. 1Ch 5:23
were killed on **M** Gilboa. 1Ch 10:1
and his sons dead on **M** Gilboa. 1Ch 10:8
LORD in Jerusalem on **M** Moriah. 2Ch 3:1
had put in the Ark at **M** Sinai. 2Ch 5:10
Abijah stood on **M** Zemaraim in 2Ch 13:4
came down to **M** Sinai and spoke .... Ne 9:13
the LORD who is king on **M** Zion. .... Ps 9:11
will come to Israel from **M** Zion! .... Ps 14:7
and support you from **M** Zion. .... Ps 20:2
like a calf and **M** Hermon jump .... Ps 29:6
the peaks of Hermon and **M** Mizar. .... Ps 42:6
M Zion is like the high .... Ps 48:2
M Zion is happy and all the .... Ps 48:11
will come to Israel from **M** Zion! .... Ps 53:6

M

God, the God of **M** Sinai, before .... Ps 68:8
kings like snow on **M** Zalmon. .... Ps 68:14
Lord comes from **M** Sinai to his .... Ps 68:17
After all, you live on **M** Zion. .... Ps 74:2
his home is on **M** Zion. .... Ps 76:2
the tribe of Judah and **M** Zion, ... Ps 78:68
M Tabor and Mount Hermon sing .... Ps 89:12
Mount Tabor and **M** Hermon sing .... Ps 89:12
a gold calf at **M** Sinai and .... Ps 106:19
trust the LORD are like **M** Zion, ... Ps 125:1
the LORD bless you from **M** Zion; .... Ps 128:5
like the dew of **M** Hermon falling .... Ps 133:3
the LORD bless you from **M** Zion, ... Ps 134:3
praise the LORD on **M** Zion. .... Ps 135:21
goats streaming down **M** Gilead. .... Sng 4:1
from the top of **M** Amana, from .... Sng 4:8
the tops of **M** Senir and Mount .... Sng 4:8
of Mount Senir and **M** Hermon. .... Sng 4:8
goats streaming down **M** Gilead. .... Sng 6:5
Your head is like **M** Carmel, ... Sng 7:5
LORD will cover **M** Zion and the .... Is 4:5
who lives on **M** Zion. .... Is 8:18
he planned to **M** Zion and .... Is 10:12
will shake their fist at **M** Zion, ... Is 10:32
LORD All-Powerful, to **M** Zion. .... Is 18:7
rule as king on **M** Zion in .... Is 24:23
fight as he did at **M** Perazim. .... Is 28:21
who fight against **M** Zion. .... Is 29:8
who live on **M** Zion in Jerusalem .... Is 30:19
to fight on **M** Zion and on its .... Is 31:4
a few from **M** Zion will live. .... Is 37:32
will be like **M** Tabor among the .... Je 46:18
mountains, like **M** Carmel by the .... Je 46:18
They will eat on **M** Carmel and in .... Je 50:19
M Zion is empty, and wild dogs .... La 5:18
of fir trees from **M** Hermon. .... Eze 27:5
M Seir and all Edom, you will .... Eze 35:15
a net spread out at **M** Tabor. .... Hos 5:1
because on **M** Zion and in .... Joe 2:32
God, live on my holy **M** Zion. .... Joe 3:17
even the top of **M** Carmel will .... Am 1:2
feel safe living on **M** Samaria. .... Am 6:1
hide at the top of **M** Carmel, ... Am 9:3
But on **M** Zion some will escape .... Ob 1:17
warriors will go up on **M** Zion, ... Ob 1:21
be their king in **M** Zion from now .... Mic 4:7
the Holy One comes from **M** Paran. .... Hab 3:3
will stand on the **M** of Olives, ... Zch 14:4
The **M** of Olives will split in .... Zch 14:4
I gave to him on **M** Sinai for all .... Mal 4:4
the hill called the **M** of Olives. .... Mt 21:1
was sitting on the **M** of Olives, ... Mt 24:3
went out to the **M** of Olives. .... Mt 26:30
Bethany near the **M** of Olives. .... Mk 11:1
was sitting on the **M** of Olives, ... Mk 13:3
went out to the **M** of Olives. .... Mk 14:26
the hill called the **M** of Olives, ... Lk 19:29
on the way down the **M** of Olives, ... Lk 19:37
and stayed on the **M** of Olives. .... Lk 21:37
and went to the **M** of Olives, ... Lk 22:39
Jesus went to the **M** of Olives. .... Jn 8:1
Jerusalem from the **M** of Olives. .... Ac 1:12
was in the desert near **M** Sinai. .... Ac 7:30
that spoke to him at **M** Sinai. .... Ac 7:38
law that God made on **M** Sinai, ... Gal 4:24
is like **M** Sinai in Arabia and .... Gal 4:25
But you have come to **M** Zion, ... Heb 12:22
was the Lamb standing on **M** Zion. .... Rev 14:1

MOUNTAIN

Shechem to the **m** east of Bethel .... Ge 12:8
On the **m** of the LORD it will be .... Ge 22:14
it as a sacrifice on the **m**, ... Ge 31:54

they spent the night on the **m**. .... Ge 31:54
he came to Sinai, the **m** of God. .... Ex 3:1
you will worship me on this **m**." .... Ex 3:12
at Sinai, the **m** of God, and .... Ex 4:27
place them on your very own **m**, ... Ex 15:17
in the desert near the **m** of God. .... Ex 18:5
in the desert in front of the **m**. .... Ex 19:2
Moses went up on the **m** to God. .... Ex 19:3
to him from the **m** and said, ... Ex 19:3
around the **m** that the people .... Ex 19:12
to go up on the **m** and not to .... Ex 19:12
who touches the **m** must be put to .... Ex 19:12
may the people go up on the **m**." .... Ex 19:13
down from the **m** to the people, ... Ex 19:14
with a thick cloud on the **m**. .... Ex 19:16
they stood at the foot of the **m**. .... Ex 19:17
smoke rose from the **m** like smoke .... Ex 19:18
and the whole **m** shook wildly. .... Ex 19:18
to come up to the top of the **m**, ... Ex 19:20
'Set a limit around the **m**, ... Ex 19:23
and the smoke rising from the **m**, ... Ex 20:18
and stood far away from the **m**. .... Ex 20:18
away from the **m** while Moses went .... Ex 20:21
not come up the **m** with Moses." .... Ex 24:2
altar near the bottom of the **m**. .... Ex 24:4
elders of Israel went up the **m** .... Ex 24:9
to Moses, "Come up the **m** to me. .... Ex 24:12
went up to Sinai, the **m** of God. .... Ex 24:13
When Moses went up on the **m**, ... Ex 24:15
a fire burning on top of the **m**. .... Ex 24:17
cloud and went higher up the **m**. .... Ex 24:18
He was on the **m** for forty days .... Ex 24:18
the plan I showed you on the **m**. .... Ex 25:40
the plan shown to you on the **m**. .... Ex 26:30
it as you were shown on the **m**. .... Ex 27:8
had not come down from the **m**. .... Ex 32:1
down from this **m**, because your .... Ex 32:7
Then Moses went down the **m**, ... Ex 32:15
them at the bottom of the **m**. .... Ex 32:19
me there on the top of the **m**. .... Ex 34:2
even be seen any place on the **m**. .... Ex 34:3
may eat grass near that **m**." .... Ex 34:3
So they left the **m** of the LORD .... Nu 10:33
died there on top of the **m**. .... Nu 20:28
Eleazar came back down the **m**, ... Nu 20:28
m that looks over the desert. .... Nu 23:28
Climb this **m** in the Abarim .... Nu 27:12
stayed long enough at this **m**. .... Dt 1:6
and go to the **m** country of the .... Dt 1:7
and went toward the **m** country of .... Dt 1:19
have now come to the **m** country .... Dt 1:20
as half of the **m** country of .... Dt 3:12
stood at the bottom of the **m**, ... Dt 4:11
to face from the fire on the **m**. .... Dt 5:4
so you would not go up on the **m**. .... Dt 5:5
of you on the **m** in a loud voice .... Dt 5:22
as the **m** was blazing with fire, ... Dt 5:23
went up on the **m** to receive the .... Dt 9:9
I stayed on the **m** for forty days .... Dt 9:9
to you on the **m** out of the fire, ... Dt 9:10
came down the **m** that was burning .... Dt 9:15
a stream that flowed down the **m**. .... Dt 9:21
ones and come up to me on the **m**. .... Dt 10:1
I went up on the **m** with the two .... Dt 10:3
told you on the **m** from the fire, ... Dt 10:4
I turned and came down the **m**; .... Dt 10:5
I stayed on the **m** forty days and .... Dt 10:10
ibex, antelope, and **m** sheep. .... Dt 14:5
On that **m** that you climb, you .... Dt 32:50
will call the people to the **m**, ... Dt 33:19
give me the **m** country the LORD .... Jos 14:12
The **m** country of Ephraim is too .... Jos 17:15
The **m** country of Ephraim is not .... Jos 17:16

also will have the **m** country. .... Jos 17:18
going along one side of the **m**, ... 1Sa 23:26
came down toward the **m** hideout. 1Sa 25:20
on top of the **m** far from Saul's 1Sa 26:13
the top of the **m** where people 2Sa 15:32
governor of the **m** country of 1Ki 4:8
to Mount Sinai, the **m** of God. 1Ki 19:8
stand in front of me on the **m**, ... 1Ki 19:11
The gods of Israel are **m** gods. 1Ki 20:23
Since we fought in a **m** area, ... 1Ki 20:23
on some **m** or in some valley. 2Ki 2:16
he saw that the **m** was full of 2Ki 6:17
he saw the graves on the **m**. 2Ki 23:16
A **m** washes away and crumbles; .... Job 14:18
are soaked from **m** rains and stay .... Job 24:8
know when the **m** goats give birth .... Job 39:1
rule in Jerusalem on my holy **m**, ... Ps 2:6
will answer me from his holy **m**. .... Ps 3:4
Fly like a bird to your **m**. .... Ps 11:1
Who may live on your holy **m**? .... Ps 15:1
may go up on the **m** of the LORD? .... Ps 24:3
will keep me safe on a high **m**. .... Ps 27:5
kindness made my **m** safe. .... Ps 30:7
Let them lead me to your holy **m**, ... Ps 43:3
city of our God, on his holy **m**. .... Ps 48:1
Carry me away to a high **m**. .... Ps 61:2
envy on the **m** that God chose .... Ps 68:16
the **m** country he took with his .... Ps 78:54
built Jerusalem on the holy **m**. .... Ps 87:1
and worship at his holy **m**, ... Ps 99:9
a young deer on the **m** valleys. .... Sng 2:17
will go to that **m** of myrrh and .... Sng 4:6
is like the **m** of Lebanon that .... Sng 7:4
last days the **m** on which the .... Is 2:2
us go up to the **m** of the LORD, ... Is 2:3
each other on all my holy **m**, ... Is 11:9
Raise a flag on the bare **m**. .... Is 13:2
I will sit on the **m** of the gods, ... Is 14:13
on the slopes of the sacred **m**. .... Is 14:13
going up the **m** road to Luhith, ... Is 15:5
desert to the **m** of Jerusalem. .... Is 16:1
will see a banner raised on a **m**............. Is 18:3
people will cry out to the **m**. .... Is 22:5
feast on this **m** for all people. .... Is 25:6
On this **m** God will destroy the .... Is 25:7
on that holy **m** in Jerusalem. .... Is 27:13
Every **m** and hill will have .... Is 30:25
they come to the **m** of the LORD, ... Is 30:29
and every **m** and hill should be .... Is 40:4
up on a high **m**. Jerusalem, you .... Is 40:9
to my holy **m** and give them joy .... Is 56:7
your bed on every hill and **m**,................. Is 57:7
the land and own my holy **m**." .... Is 57:13
of Judah will receive my **m**. .... Is 65:9
who forgot about my holy **m**, ... Is 65:11
each other on all my holy **m**,"................. Is 65:25
to my holy **m** in Jerusalem................. Is 66:20
of Judah on every **m** and hill .... Je 16:16
m in the open country and your .... Je 17:3
on top of the **m** over this valley .... Je 21:13
home of what is good, holy **m**.' .... Je 31:23
are a destroying **m**, and I am .... Je 51:25
I will make you a burned-out **m**............. Je 51:25
on all the **m** tops, and under .... Eze 6:13
stopped on the **m** on the east .... Eze 11:23
will plant it on a very high **m**................. Eze 17:22
it on the high **m** of Israel. .... Eze 17:23
not eat at the **m** places of .... Eze 18:6
son eats at the **m** places of .... Eze 18:11
not eat at the **m** places of .... Eze 18:15
On my holy **m**, the high mountain .... Eze 20:40
the high **m** of Israel, all .... Eze 20:40
to idols at the **m** places of .... Eze 22:9

I put you on the holy **m** of God. .... Eze 28:14
in disgrace from the **m** of God. .... Eze 28:16
put me down on a very high **m**. .... Eze 40:2
south of the **m** there were some .... Eze 40:2
the top of the **m** is most holy. .... Eze 43:12
a very large **m** that filled..................... Da 2:35
you saw a rock cut from a **m**, ... Da 2:45
the beautiful **m** where the holy .... Da 11:45
shout a warning on my holy **m**. .... Joe 2:1
of Bashan on the **M** of Samaria................ Am 4:1
last days the **m** on which the .... Mic 4:1
us go up to the **m** of the LORD, ... Mic 4:2
sea to sea and **m** to mountain. .... Mic 7:12
sea to sea and mountain to **m**. .... Mic 7:12
on my holy **m** in Jerusalem. .... Zph 3:11
Who are you, big **m**? .... Zch 4:7
and the **m** of the LORD .... Zch 8:3
will be called the Holy **M**." .... Zch 8:3
Half the **m** will move toward the .... Zch 14:4
run through this **m** valley to the .... Zch 14:5
I destroyed his **m** country and .... Mal 1:3
of a very high **m** and showed him .... Mt 4:8
up on a high **m** by themselves. .... Mt 17:1
As they were coming down the **m**, ... Mt 17:9
can say to this **m**, 'Move from .... Mt 17:20
will be able to say to this **m**, ' .... Mt 21:21
Galilee to the **m** where Jesus had .... Mt 28:16
On the **m** they saw Jesus and .... Mt 28:17
went up on a **m** and called to him .... Mk 3:13
up on a high **m** by themselves. .... Mk 9:2
As they were coming down the **m**, ... Mk 9:9
you can say to this **m**, 'Go, fall .... Mk 11:23
and every **m** and hill should be .... Lk 3:5
Jesus went off to a **m** to pray, ... Lk 6:12
apostles came down from the **m**, ... Lk 6:17
and went up on a **m** to pray. .... Lk 9:28
when they came down from the **m**, ... Lk 9:37
ancestors worshiped on this **m**, ... Jn 4:20
nor on this **m** will you actually .... Jn 4:21
This **m** is about half a mile from............. Ac 1:12
the plan I showed you on the **m**." .... Heb 8:5
have not come to a **m** that can be .... Heb 12:18
touches the **m**, it must be put to .... Heb 12:20
were with Jesus on the holy **m**. 2Pe 1:18
and every **m** and island was moved .... Rev 6:14
that looked like a big **m**, ... Rev 8:8
to a very large and high **m**..................... Rev 21:10

MOUNTAINS

even the highest **m** under the sky .... Ge 7:19
than twenty feet above the **m**................. Ge 7:20
the tops of the **m** could be seen. .... Ge 8:5
Horites in the **m** of Edom to El .... Ge 14:6
the others ran away to the **m**. .... Ge 14:10
Run to the **m**, or you will be .... Ge 19:17
But I can't run to the **m**. .... Ge 19:19
went to live in the **m** in a cave. .... Ge 19:30
on one of the **m** I will tell you.................. Ge 22:2
traveled toward the **m** of Gilead. .... Ge 31:21
found him in the **m** of Gilead. .... Ge 31:23
had made his camp in the **m**, ... Ge 31:25
their camp in the **m** of Gilead. .... Ge 31:25
So Esau lived in the **m** of Edom............... Ge 36:8
who live in the **m** of Edom. .... Ge 36:9
the blessings of the oldest **m**, ... Ge 49:26
them in the **m** and destroy them............. Ex 32:12
Canaan and then into the **m**. .... Nu 13:17
and Amorites live in the **m**;................. Nu 13:29
to go toward the top of the **m**, ... Nu 14:40
went toward the top of the **m**,................. Nu 14:44
who lived in those **m** came down .... Nu 14:45
brought me from the eastern **m**. .... Nu 23:7
see them from the top of the **m**; .... Nu 23:9

this mountain in the Abarim **M**, ... Nu 27:12
and camped in the **m** of Abarim, ... Nu 33:47
They left the **m** of Abarim and .... Nu 33:48
Valley, in the **m**, the western hills .... Dt 1:7
They left and went up to the **m**, ... Dt 1:24
would be easy to go into the **m**. .... Dt 1:41
so you went on up into the **m**, ... Dt 1:43
lived in those **m** came out and .... Dt 1:44
through the **m** of Edom for many .... Dt 2:1
through these **m** long enough. .... Dt 2:3
have given the **m** of Edom to Esau .... Dt 2:5
towns in the **m**, as the LORD our .... Dt 2:37
the beautiful **m** and Lebanon." .... Dt 3:25
These **m** are on the other side of .... Dt 11:30
on high **m** and hills and under .... Dt 12:2
set fire to the base of the **m**. .... Dt 32:22
up the Abarim **M**, to Mount Nebo .... Dt 32:49
of angels from the southern **m**. .... Dt 33:2
Let the old **m** give the finest .... Dt 33:15
They lived in the **m** and on the .... Jos 9:1
kings from the **m** have joined .... Jos 10:6
the **m**, southern Canaan, the .... Jos 10:40
the northern **m** and also to the .... Jos 11:2
and Jebusites in the **m**. .... Jos 11:3
control of the **m** and the area .... Jos 11:16
controlled the **m** of Israel and.................. Jos 11:16
who lived in the **m** of Hebron, ... Jos 11:21
This included the **m**, the western .... Jos 12:8
also given these towns in the **m**: .... Jos 15:48
also given these towns in the **m**: .... Jos 15:52
also given these towns in the **m**: .... Jos 15:55
also given these towns in the **m**: .... Jos 15:58
from Jericho to the **m** of Bethel. .... Jos 16:1
then it went west into the **m**. .... Jos 18:12
Serah in the **m** of Ephraim,.................. Jos 19:50
in Galilee in the **m** of Naphtali; .... Jos 20:7
Shechem in the **m** of Ephraim; .... Jos 20:7
Hebron) in the **m** of Judah;.................. Jos 20:7
its pastures in the **m** of Judah. .... Jos 21:11
Shechem in the **m** of Ephraim .... Jos 21:21
around the **m** of Edom to Esau .... Jos 24:4
Serah, in the **m** of Ephraim, ... Jos 24:30
at Gibeah in the **m** of Ephraim, ... Jos 24:33
Canaanites who lived in the **m**, ... Jdg 1:9
They took the land in the **m**, ... Jdg 1:19
back into the **m** and would not .... Jdg 1:34
Serah in the **m** of Ephraim, ... Jdg 2:9
in the Lebanon **m** from Mount Baal .... Jdg 3:3
he reached the **m** of Ephraim he .... Jdg 3:27
and Bethel, in the **m** of Ephraim. .... Jdg 4:5
The **m** shook before the LORD, ... Jdg 5:5
from Ephraim in the **m** of Amalek.............. Jdg 5:14
made hiding places in the **m**, ... Jdg 6:2
through all the **m** of Ephraim, ... Jdg 7:24
people coming down from the **m**!" .... Jdg 9:36
are seeing the shadows of the **m**. .... Jdg 9:36
of Shamir in the **m** of Ephraim. .... Jdg 10:1
for two months to go to the **m**. .... Jdg 11:37
stayed in the **m** and cried for .... Jdg 11:38
in the **m** where the Amalekites .... Jdg 12:15
who lived in the **m** of Ephraim. .... Jdg 17:1
house in the **m** of Ephraim.................... Jdg 17:8
They came to the **m** of Ephraim, ... Jdg 18:2
traveled on to the **m** of Ephraim. .... Jdg 18:13
in the faraway **m** of Ephraim. .... Jdg 19:1
home was in the **m** of Ephraim. .... Jdg 19:16
to my home in the **m** of Ephraim. .... Jdg 19:18
Ramathaim in the **m** of Ephraim. 1Sa 1:1
went through the **m** of Ephraim 1Sa 9:4
at Micmash in the **m** of Bethel, ... 1Sa 13:2
hidden in the **m** of Ephraim heard 1Sa 14:22
just hunting a bird in the **m**!" 1Sa 26:20
dew or rain on the **m** of Gilboa, ... 2Sa 1:21

man here from the **m** of Ephraim, ... 2Sa 20:21
helps me stand on the steep **m**. 2Sa 22:34
Shechem in the **m** of Ephraim a 1Ki 12:25
it caused the **m** to fall apart 1Ki 19:11
am a god of the **m**, not a god 1Ki 20:28
prophets in the **m** of Ephraim.................. 2Ki 5:22
have gone to the tops of the **m**, ... 2Ki 19:23
to the highest **m** of Lebanon. 2Ki 19:23
people living in the **m** of Edom. 1Ch 4:42
pastures in the **m** of Ephraim. 1Ch 6:67
of them to cut stone in the **m**,.................. 2Ch 2:18
Zemaraim in the **m** of Ephraim and 2Ch 13:4
Beersheba to the **m** of Ephraim, ... 2Ch 19:4
out into the **m**, and bring back .... Ne 8:15
God moves **m** without anyone .... Job 9:5
dig away at the bottom of the **m**. .... Job 28:9
of the **m** began to shake........................ Ps 18:7
helps me stand on the steep **m**. .... Ps 18:33
goodness is as high as the **m**. .... Ps 36:6
or the **m** fall into the sea, ... Ps 46:2
or the **m** shake at the raging sea .... Ps 46:3
is like the high **m** of the north; .... Ps 48:2
I know every bird on the **m**, ... Ps 50:11
You made the **m** by your strength; .... Ps 65:6
The **m** of Bashan are high; .... Ps 68:15
the **m** of Bashan have many peaks. .... Ps 68:15
do you **m** with many peaks look.............. Ps 68:16
be peace on the **m** and goodness .... Ps 72:3
his Temple high like the **m**...................... Ps 78:69
We covered the **m** with our shade. .... Ps 80:10
the **m** were born and before .... Ps 90:2
and the highest **m** belong to him. .... Ps 95:4
The **m** melt like wax before the .... Ps 97:5
let the **m** sing together for joy. .... Ps 98:8
the water was above the **m**. .... Ps 104:6
m rose; the valleys sank. The .... Ps 104:8
they flow between the **m**. .... Ps 104:10
You water the **m** from above. .... Ps 104:13
The high **m** belong to the wild .... Ps 104:18
touches the **m**, and they smoke. .... Ps 104:32
The **m** danced like sheep and the .... Ps 114:4
M, why did you dance like sheep? .... Ps 114:6
As the **m** surround Jerusalem, ... Ps 125:2
Touch the **m** so they will smoke.............. Ps 144:5
m and all hills, fruit trees and.................. Ps 148:9
before the **m** were put in place. .... Pr 8:25
he comes jumping across the **m**,.............. Sng 2:8
down from the **m** of Lebanon. .... Sng 4:15
deer on the **m** where spices grow .... Sng 8:14
the most important of all **m**. .... Is 2:2
all the tall **m** and the high .... Is 2:14
Even the **m** are frightened. .... Is 5:25
to the loud noise in the **m**, ... Is 13:4
I will trample him on my **m**. .... Is 14:25
birds of the **m** and for the wild .... Is 18:6
the blood will flow down the **m**. .... Is 34:3
have gone to the tops of the **m**, ... Is 37:24
to the highest **m** of Lebanon. .... Is 37:24
scales to weigh the **m** and hills? .... Is 40:12
will walk on **m** and crush them; .... Is 41:15
the hills and **m** and dry up all.................. Is 42:15
Sing, you **m**, with thanks to God. .... Is 44:23
before you and make the **m** flat. .... Is 45:2
I will make my **m** into roads, ... Is 49:11
M, shout with joy, because the .... Is 49:13
comes over the **m** to bring good .... Is 52:7
The **m** may disappear, and the .... Is 54:10
The **m** and hills will burst into .... Is 55:12
earth so that the **m** will tremble .... Is 64:1
and the **m** trembled before you. .... Is 64:3
gods on the **m** and shamed me on .... Is 65:7
idols on the hills and on the **m**. .... Je 3:23
bad news from the **m** of Ephraim. .... Je 4:15

I looked at the **m**, and they were .... Je 4:24
loudly for the **m** and sing a..................... Je 9:10
hills, from the **m**, and from..................... Je 17:26
The snow on the **m** of Lebanon .... Je 18:14
watchmen in the **m** of Ephraim .... Je 31:6
the towns of Judah and in the **m**, ... Je 32:44
count them on the **m** and in the .... Je 33:13
be like Mount Tabor among the **m**,........... Je 46:18
around us in the **m** and hills. .... Je 50:6
ran us into the **m** and ambushed .... La 4:19
look toward the **m** of Israel, ... Eze 6:2
Say, 'M of Israel, listen to the .... Eze 6:3
The Lord GOD says this to the **m**, ... Eze 6:3
be no happy shouting on the **m**. .... Eze 7:7
and who escape will be on the **m**, ... Eze 7:16
heard again on the **m** of Israel. .... Eze 19:9
branches fell on the **m** and in .... Eze 31:12
your flesh on the **m** and fill the .... Eze 32:5
flowing blood as far as the **m**, ... Eze 32:6
m of Israel will become empty .... Eze 33:28
over all the **m** and on every high .... Eze 34:6
pasture them on the **m** of Israel,........... Eze 34:13
grass on the high **m** of Israel. .... Eze 34:14
grassland on the **m** of Israel. .... Eze 34:14
I will fill its **m** with those who .... Eze 35:8
insults against the **m** of Israel. .... Eze 35:12
prophesy to the **m** of Israel and .... Eze 36:1
'M of Israel, hear the word of .... Eze 36:1
So, **m** of Israel, hear the word................ Eze 36:4
The Lord GOD speaks to the **m**,............ Eze 36:4
land of Israel and say to the **m**, ... Eze 36:6
But you, **m** of Israel, will....................... Eze 36:8
in the land, on the **m** of Israel. .... Eze 37:22
many nations to the **m** of Israel, ... Eze 38:8
Also the **m** will be thrown down, ... Eze 38:20
a war against Gog on all my **m**, ... Eze 38:21
you to attack the **m** of Israel. .... Eze 39:2
fall dead on the **m** of Israel. .... Eze 39:4
for you on the **m** of Israel. .... Eze 39:17
sacrifices on the tops of the **m**. .... Hos 4:13
Then they will say to the **m**, ... Hos 10:8
army will spread over the **m**. .... Joe 2:2
rumbling over the tops of the **m**, ... Joe 2:5
day wine will drip from the **m**, ... Joe 3:18
Come to the **m** of Samaria,..................... Am 3:9
one who makes the **m** and creates .... Am 4:13
walks over the **m** of the earth. .... Am 4:13
will drip from the **m** and pour .... Am 9:13
from the **m** of Edom. .... Ob 1:8
from the **m** of Edom will be .... Ob 1:9
will take back the **m** of Edom. .... Ob 1:19
the people living on Edom's **m**. .... Ob 1:21
to where the **m** of the sea start .... Jnh 2:6
to walk on the tops of the **m**. .... Mic 1:3
The **m** will melt under him,.................... Mic 1:4
the most important of all **m**. .... Mic 4:1
your case in front of the **m**;..................... Mic 6:1
M, listen to the LORD's legal .... Mic 6:2
The **m** shake in front of him, ... Nah 1:5
have been scattered on the **m**, ... Nah 3:18
The **m**, which stood for ages, ... Hab 3:6
The **m** saw you and shook with .... Hab 3:10
so I can walk on the steep **m**................... Hab 3:19
Go up to the **m**, bring back wood, ... Hag 1:8
land, and on the **m**, and on the .... Hag 1:11
going out between two **m**, ... Zch 6:1
two mountains, **m** of bronze. .... Zch 6:1
Judea should run away to the **m**. .... Mt 24:16
Judea should run away to the **m**. .... Mk 13:14
and in all the **m** of Judea people.............. Lk 1:65
Judea should run away to the **m**. .... Lk 21:21
Then people will say to the **m**, ' .... Lk 23:30
faith so great I can move **m**. 1Co 13:2

They wandered in deserts and **m**, ... Heb 11:38
caves and in the rocks on the **m**. .... Rev 6:15
called to the **m** and the rocks,................ Rev 6:16
ran away, and **m** disappeared. .... Rev 16:20
are seven **m** where the woman .... Rev 17:9

MOUNTAINTOPS
they should shout from the **m**. .... Is 42:11
Gilead, like the **m** of Lebanon. .... Je 22:6

MOUTH
a fresh olive leaf in its **m**. .... Ge 8:11
stone covered the **m** of the well............. Ge 29:2
the stone from the **m** of the well.............. Ge 29:8
the stone from its **m** and watered .... Ge 29:10
to him, "Who made a person's **m**? .... Ex 4:11
must not come out of your **m**................... Ex 23:13
and he must cover his **m**. .... Le 13:45
do not cover its **m** to keep it .... Dt 25:4
is in your **m** and in your heart .... Dt 30:14
as far as the **m** of the Jordan .... Jos 15:5
the sea at the **m** of the Jordan .... Jos 15:5
kept praying, Eli watched her **m**. 1Sa 1:12
and save the sheep from its **m**. 1Sa 17:35
burning fire came out of his **m**. 2Sa 22:9
with your own **m** and finished it.............. 1Ki 8:24
his **m** on the boy's mouth, ... 2Ki 4:34
his mouth on the boy's **m**, ... 2Ki 4:34
your nose and my bit in your **m**............... 2Ki 19:28
with your own **m** and finished it.............. 2Ch 6:15
yet fill your **m** with laughter .... Job 8:21
my own **m** would say I was wrong; .... Job 9:20
my **m** would say I was guilty. .... Job 9:20
sin teaches your **m** what to say; .... Job 15:5
It is your own **m**, not mine, that .... Job 15:6
these words pour out of your **m**? .... Job 15:13
when I beg him with my own **m**. .... Job 19:16
your hand over your **m** in shock. .... Job 21:5
Accept teaching from his **m**, ... Job 22:22
and fill my **m** with arguments. .... Job 23:4
have not let my **m** sin by cursing .... Job 31:30
I must open my **m** and answer................ Job 32:20
I open my **m** and ready to.................... Job 33:2
rumbling that comes from his **m**. .... Job 37:2
so I will put my hand over my **m**. .... Job 40:4
Jordan River rushes to its **m**. .... Job 40:23
Flames blaze from its **m**;....................... Job 41:19
and flames come out of its **m**.................. Job 41:21
I have not sinned with my **m**. .... Ps 17:3
burning fire came out of his **m**. .... Ps 18:8
sticks to the top of my **m**. .... Ps 22:15
Rescue me from the lion's **m**; .... Ps 22:21
breath from his **m**, he made all .... Ps 33:6
do not open my **m**, because you .... Ps 39:9
He put a new song in my **m**, ... Ps 40:3
don't stop your **m** from speaking .... Ps 50:19
sing, and my **m** will praise you. .... Ps 63:5
to him with my **m** and praised him........... Ps 66:17
the grave close its **m** over me................. Ps 69:15
Open your **m** and I will feed you. .... Ps 81:10
sweeter than honey in my **m**! .... Ps 119:103
to the roof of my **m** if I do not .... Ps 137:6
Don't use your **m** to tell lies; .... Pr 4:24
he won't lift the food to his **m**. .... Pr 19:24
feel like a **m** full of gravel. .... Pr 20:17
and not from your own **m**. .... Pr 27:2
have planned evil, shut your **m**. .... Pr 30:32
me with the kisses of your **m**,.................. Sng 1:2
thread, and your **m** is lovely. .... Sng 4:3
His **m** is sweet to kiss, and I .... Sng 5:16
and your **m** like the best wine. .... Sng 7:9
people, and it opens wide its **m**. .... Is 5:14
touched my **m** with the hot coal .... Is 6:7
or opened its **m** to stop me." .... Is 10:14

His **m** is filled with anger, ... Is 30:27
your nose and my hit in your **m**............... Is 37:29
he never opened his **m**. .... Is 53:7
out his hand and touched my **m**. .... Je 1:9
I am putting my words in your **m**. .... Je 1:9
ears to hear the words of his **m**. .... Je 9:20
Open your **m** and eat what I am .... Eze 2:8
So I opened my **m**, and he gave me .... Eze 3:2
was as sweet as honey in my **m**............... Eze 3:3
time you hear a word from my **m**, ... Eze 3:17
the roof of your **m** so you will .... Eze 3:26
I will open your **m**, and you will........... Eze 3:27
meat has never entered my **m**." .... Eze 4:14
not open your **m** again because .... Eze 16:63
very time your **m** will be opened. .... Eze 24:27
If you hear a word from my **m**, ... Eze 33:7
were still in his **m** when a voice .... Da 4:31
ribs in its **m** between its teeth.................. Da 7:5
It also had a **m**, and the mouth .... Da 7:8
a mouth, and the **m** was bragging. .... Da 7:8
It had eyes and a **m** that kept .... Da 7:20
so I opened my **m** and started to .... Da 10:16
from a lion's **m** only one leg .... Am 3:12
fall into the **m** of the eater. .... Nah 3:12
The **m** speaks the things that are .... Mt 12:34
food that enters the **m** goes into .... Mt 15:17
open its **m** and you will find a .... Mt 17:27
Then my son foams at the **m**, ... Mk 9:18
on the ground, foaming at the **m**. .... Mk 9:20
of himself and foam at the **m**.................. Lk 9:39
and lifted it to Jesus' **m**. .... Jn 19:29
he never opened his **m**. .... Ac 8:32
near Paul to hit him on the **m**. .... Ac 23:2
is in your **m** and in your heart. .... Rm 10:8
If you declare with your **m**,................... Rm 10:9
do not cover its **m** to keep it 1Co 9:9
from his **m** and will destroy 2Th 2:8
do not cover its **m** to keep it 1Ti 5:18
I was saved from the lion's **m**. 2Ti 4:17
and curses come from the same **m**! .... Jam 3:10
sword came out of his **m**. .... Rev 1:16
sword that comes out of my **m**. .... Rev 2:16
ready to spit you out of my **m**. .... Rev 3:16
but in your **m** it will be sweet .... Rev 10:9
my **m** it tasted sweet as honey, ... Rev 10:10
water out of its **m** like a river .... Rev 12:15
by opening its **m** and swallowing .... Rev 12:16
came from the **m** of the dragon. .... Rev 12:16
feet and a **m** like a lion's........................ Rev 13:2
and a mouth like a lion's **m**. .... Rev 13:2
It used its **m** to speak against .... Rev 13:6
out of the **m** of the dragon, ... Rev 16:13
out of the **m** of the beast, ... Rev 16:13
and out of the **m** of the false .... Rev 16:13
of the rider's **m** comes a sharp .... Rev 19:15
came out of the **m** of the rider .... Rev 19:21

MOUTHS

lions they open their **m** at me. .... Ps 22:13
They have **m**, but they cannot................. Ps 115:5
They have no breath in their **m**. .... Ps 135:17
people worship me with their **m**, ... Is 29:13
will be amazed and shut their **m**. .... Is 52:15
his angel to close the lions' **m**. .... Da 6:22
and shut the **m** of lions. .... Heb 11:33

MOVABLE

bowl and the **m** stands which 2Ki 25:16
it, and the **m** stands, which .... Je 52:20

MOVE

those who **m** around with their .... Je 31:24
here to there,' and it will **m**. .... Mt 17:20

MOVED

So Abram **m** his tents and went to .... Ge 13:18
the Israelites **m** from Kadesh to .... Nu 20:22
evil people have **m** in among you. .... Dt 13:13
in her heart so her lips **m**, ... 1Sa 1:13
As I have **m** with the Israelites, ... 2Sa 7:7
so it can never be **m**. .... Ps 104:5
earth will be **m** from its place.................. Is 13:13
they **m** the stone away from the .... Jn 11:41
You must not be **m** away from the .... Col 1:23
and island was **m** from its place. .... Rev 6:14

MOVES

living thing that **m** in the sea.................... Ge 1:21
thing that **m** on the earth." .... Ge 1:28
Everything that **m**, everything .... Ge 9:3
If a Levite **m** from one of your .... Dt 18:6
LORD your God **m** around through .... Dt 23:14
be cursed who **m** the stone that .... Dt 27:17
God **m** mountains without anyone .... Job 9:5
and draw back in fear as it **m**. .... Job 41:25
anyone who **m** boulders might be .... Ec 10:9
The land shakes and **m** in pain, ... Je 51:29

MOVING

Spirit was **m** over the water. .... Ge 1:2
the Israelites to start **m**. .... Ex 14:15
The **m** water stood like a wall; .... Ex 15:8
We are **m** to the land the LORD .... Nu 10:29
Keilah and kept **m** from place to 1Sa 23:13
I have been **m** around all this 2Sa 7:6
nor admired the moon **m** in glory .... Job 31:26
People are like shadows **m** about. .... Ps 39:6
pool when the water starts **m**.................... Jn 5:7

MOWED

the workers who **m** your fields .... Jam 5:4

MOZA

mother of Haran, **M**, and Gazez. 1Ch 2:46
Zimri was the father of **M**. 1Ch 8:36
M was the father of Binea. 1Ch 8:37
M was Binea's father. Rephaiah 1Ch 9:43

MOZA'S

and Zimri. Zimri was **M** father. 1Ch 9:42

MOZAH

Mizpah, Kephirah, **M**, ... Jos 18:26

MULBERRY

you could say to this **m** tree, '.................. Lk 17:6

MULE

As Absalom was riding his **m**, ... 2Sa 18:9
his **m** ran out from under him. 2Sa 18:9
put my son Solomon on my own **m**. 1Ki 1:33
King David's **m** and took him to............... 1Ki 1:38
put Solomon on the king's own **m**........... 1Ki 1:44

MULES

sons got on their **m** and escaped. 2Sa 13:29
weapons, spices, horses, and **m**............... 1Ki 10:25
our horses and **m** alive and not 1Ki 18:5
much as two of my **m** can carry................ 2Ki 5:17
on donkeys, camels, **m**, and oxen. 1Ch 12:40
weapons, spices, horses, and **m**. 2Ch 9:24
They had 736 horses, 245 **m**, ... Ezr 2:66
They had 736 horses, 245 **m**, ... Ne 7:68
work horses, war horses, and **m**. .... Eze 27:14
the horses, **m**, camels, donkeys, ... Zch 14:15

MULTIPLIED

you **m** the number of your people; .... Is 26:15
you **m** them and brought honor to .... Is 26:15

MULTIPLY

a storm and **m** my wounds for no .... Job 9:17
grow more and **m** for each other 1Th 3:12

MUPPIM
Ehi, Rosh, **M**, Huppim, and Ard............... Ge 46:21

MURDER
You must not **m** anyone. .... Dt 5:17
you steal and **m** and be guilty................. Je 7:9
ago, 'You must not **m** anyone.................. Mt 5:21
was in jail for rioting and **m**, ... Lk 23:25
of jealousy, **m**, fighting, lying .... Rm 1:29
You must not **m** anyone. .... Rm 13:9

MURDERED
of those who **m** the prophets. .... Mt 23:31
whom you **m** between the Temple .... Mt 23:35
and then **m** innocent people .... Jam 5:6

MURDERER
weapon to kill someone is a **m**. .... Nu 35:16
this **m** is sending men to cut off 2Ki 6:32
was a **m** from the beginning and .... Jn 8:44
Pilate to give you a **m** instead. .... Ac 3:14
other, "This man must be a **m**! .... Ac 28:4
a brother or sister is a **m**, ... 1Jn 3:15

MURDERER'S
the **m** life could be saved by .... Dt 4:42

MURDERERS
to kill the **m** and burn their.................... Mt 22:7
you know that no **m** have eternal 1Jn 3:15

MURDERING
the guilt of **m** innocent people .... Dt 19:13
the guilt of **m** an innocent .... Dt 21:9
stealing money and for **m** people. .... Eze 22:13
Since you did not hate **m** people, ... Eze 35:6
You build Jerusalem by **m** people; .... Mic 3:10

MURDERS
plans and **m** another person .... Ex 21:14
who attacks and **m** a neighbor; .... Dt 22:26
a wild son who **m** people and who .... Eze 18:10
who **m** another will be judged.' .... Mt 5:21

MUSCLE
do not eat the **m** that is on the .... Ge 32:32
on them near the lower back **m**, ... Le 3:4
the lower back **m**, and the best .... Le 3:10
on them near the lower back **m**, ... Le 3:15
on them near the lower back **m**, ... Le 4:9
on them near the lower back **m**, ... Le 7:4
your neck was like an iron **m**, ... Is 48:4

MUSCLES
me together with bones and **m**. .... Job 10:11
the **m** of its stomach are .... Job 40:16
the **m** of its thighs are woven .... Job 40:17
I will put **m** on you and flesh on.............. Eze 37:6
I looked and saw **m** come on the .... Eze 37:8

MUSHI
sons of Merari were Mahli and **M**. .... Ex 6:19
family groups were Mahli and **M**. .... Nu 3:20
of Mahli and **M** belonged to .... Nu 3:33
Merari's sons were Mahli and **M**. 1Ch 6:19
M was Merari's son, and Merari............... 1Ch 6:47
Merari's sons were Mahli and **M**. 1Ch 23:21
descendants were Mahli and **M**............... 1Ch 24:26

MUSHI'S
son. Mahli was **M** son. Mushi was 1Ch 6:47
M three sons were Mahli, Eder, ... 1Ch 23:23
M sons were Mahli, Eder, and 1Ch 24:30

MUSHITE
group, the **M** family group, ... Nu 26:58

MUSIC
sons in making **m** for the Temple 1Ch 25:6
in making **m** for the LORD. 1Ch 25:7
of the LORD's **m** that King David 2Ch 7:6

with David's instruments of **m**, ... 2Ch 29:26
The happy **m** of the tambourines .... Is 24:8
The joyful **m** from the harps will .... Is 24:8
them to the **m** of tambourines................. Is 30:32
the **m** of your harps will not be .... Eze 26:13
listen to the **m** of your harps. .... Am 5:23
For the director of **m**. .... Hab 3:19
'We played **m** for you, but you .... Mt 11:17
We played **m** for you, but you................. Lk 7:32
the sound of **m** and dancing. .... Lk 15:25
and making **m** in your hearts to .... Eph 5:19
m of people playing harps and .... Rev 18:22

MUSICAL
and other **m** instruments when 1Ch 16:42
the LORD with **m** instruments I 1Ch 23:5
were playing **m** instruments 2Ch 23:13
and the **m** instruments of David 2Ch 29:27
men played the **m** instruments of .... Ne 12:36
and plays a **m** instrument well. .... Eze 33:32
and all the other **m** instruments...............Da 3:5
and all the other **m** instruments,...............Da 3:7
all the other **m** instruments.....................Da 3:10
and all the other **m** instruments..............Da 3:15
compose songs on **m** instruments. .... Am 6:5
they do not make clear **m** notes,.............. 1Co 14:7

MUSICIANS
make harps and lyres for the **m**............... 1Ki 10:12
These are the **m** and their sons: 1Ch 6:33
Levites were **m** in the Temple. 1Ch 9:33
All the Levite **m**—Asaph, Heman, ... 2Ch 5:12
make lyres and harps for the **m**............... 2Ch 9:11
Levites were all skilled **m**. 2Ch 34:12
the funeral **m** and many people .... Mt 9:23

MUST
Naomi, you **m** also marry Ruth .... Ru 4:5
I **m** suffer through it." .... Je 10:19
that he **m** go to Jerusalem, ... Mt 16:21
say that Elijah **m** come first?"................. Mt 17:10
These things **m** happen before the .... Mt 24:6
the Son of Man **m** suffer many .... Mk 8:31
the Good News **m** be told to all .... Mk 13:10
up, we **m** go. Look, here comes .... Mk 14:42
you know that I **m** be in my .... Lk 2:49
I **m** stay at your house today." .... Lk 19:5
you, 'You **m** all be born again. .... Jn 3:7
Son of Man **m** also be lifted up. .... Jn 3:14
He **m** become greater, and I must .... Jn 3:30
and I **m** become less important. .... Jn 3:30
we **m** continue doing the work of .... Jn 9:4
flock, and I **m** bring them also. .... Jn 10:16
But Jesus **m** stay in heaven until .... Ac 3:21
we **m** warn them not to talk to .... Ac 4:17
will tell you what you **m** do." .... Ac 9:6
Men, what **m** I do to be saved? .... Ac 16:30
You **m** do the same in Rome."................. Ac 23:11
you **m** yield to the government, ... Rm 13:5
Christ **m** rule until he puts all................. 1Co 15:25
can be destroyed **m** clothe itself 1Co 15:53
because we **m** all stand before 2Co 5:10
An overseer **m** not give people a 1Ti 3:2
m be respected by others, ... 1Ti 3:8
women **m** be respected by others. 1Ti 3:11
and to him we **m** explain the way .... Heb 4:13
comes to God **m** believe that he .... Heb 11:6
his servants what **m** soon happen. .... Rev 1:1

MUSTARD
is like a **m** seed that a man .... Mt 13:31
faith is as big as a **m** seed, ... Mt 17:20
kingdom of God is like a **m** seed, ... Mk 4:31
It is like a **m** seed that a man .... Lk 13:19
faith were the size of a **m** seed, ... Lk 17:6

M

MUTE
Like the **m,** I cannot speak.....................Ps 38:13

MUTTER
who whisper and **m,** what to do." ....Is 8:19

MYRA
and landed at the city of **M,** ....Ac 27:5

MYRRH
carrying spices, balm, and **m.**.................Ge 37:25
made my bed smell sweet with **m,** ....Pr 7:17
is like a bag of **m** that lies all ....Sng 1:13
of gold, frankincense, and **m.** ....Mt 2:11
wine mixed with **m** to drink, ...Mk 15:23

MYRTLE
olive trees, **m** trees, palms, ...Ne 8:15
cedars, acacia, **m,** and olive ....Is 41:19
M trees will grow where weeds ....Is 55:13
among some **m** trees in a ravine, ...Zch 1:8
among the **m** trees explained,.................Zch 1:10
was standing among the **m** trees. ....Zch 1:11

MYSIA
they came near the country of **M,** ....Ac 16:7
they passed by **M** and went to ....Ac 16:8

N

N
n the fortieth year after the....................Nu 33:38

NAAM
sons were Iru, Elah, and **N.**....................1Ch 4:15

NAAMAH
The sister of Tubal-Cain was **N.** ....Ge 4:22
Beth Dagon, **N,** and Makkedah. ....Jos 15:41
His mother was **N** from Ammon. 1Ki 14:21
son of **N** from Ammon, died 1Ki 14:31
mother was **N** from the country 2Ch 12:13

NAAMAN
not accepted what **N** the Aramean 2Ki 5:20
them were healed, only **N,** who ....Lk 4:27

NAAMATHITE
the Shuhite, and Zophar the **N.** ....Job 2:11
Then Zophar the **N** answered: ....Job 11:1
Then Zophar the **N** answered: ....Job 20:1
and Zophar the **N** did as the LORD ....Job 42:9

NAAMITE
Naaman came the **N** family group............Nu 26:40

NAARAH
from Janoah to Ataroth and to **N.** ....Jos 16:7
had two wives named Helah and **N.** 1Ch 4:5
of Ashhur and **N** were Ahuzzam, ...1Ch 4:6
These were the descendants of **N.** 1Ch 4:6

NAARAI
the Carmelite; **N** son of Ezbai; 1Ch 11:37

NAARAN
villages near it, **N** on the east, ...1Ch 7:28

NABAL
he heard that **N** was cutting the 1Sa 25:4
to this worthless man **N.**.......................1Sa 25:25
may your enemies become like **N!** 1Sa 25:26
When Abigail went back to **N,** 1Sa 25:36

NABAL'S
One of **N** servants said to 1Sa 25:14

NABOTH
Ahab said to **N,** "Give me your 1Ki 21:2
for it.' But **N** refused."...........................1Ki 21:6
saying, "**N** has been killed.....................1Ki 21:14

NACON
to the threshing floor of **N,** 2Sa 6:6

NADAB
Moses, Aaron, **N,** Abihu, and ....Ex 24:9
with his sons **N,** Abihu, Eleazar,..............Ex 28:1
But **N** and Abihu died in the ....Nu 3:4
N was king of Israel for two 1Ki 15:25

NAG
Fathers, do not **n** your children. ....Col 3:21

NAGGAI
Esli was the son of **N.** ....Lk 3:25
N was the son of Maath. ....Lk 3:26

NAHALAL
of Kattath, **N,** Shimron, Idalah, ...Jos 19:15
Dimnah, and **N,** and the pastures ....Jos 21:35

NAHALIEL
they went to **N** and on to Bamoth. ....Nu 21:19

NAHALOL
in the cities of Kitron and **N.** ....Jdg 1:30

NAHAM'S
Hodiah's wife was **N** sister......................1Ch 4:19

NAHAMANI
Azariah, Raamiah, **N,** Mordecai, ...Ne 7:7

NAHARAI
N the Beerothite, who carried..................2Sa 23:37
N the Berothite, the officer who 1Ch 11:39

NAHASH
a month later **N** the Ammonite 1Sa 11:1

NAHATH
N, Zerah, Shammah, and Mizzah. ....Ge 36:13
N, Zerah, Shammah, and Mizzah. ....Ge 36:17
sons were **N,** Zerah, Shammah, ...1Ch 1:37
was Zophai. Zophai's son was **N.** 1Ch 6:26
Jehiel, Azaziah, **N,** Asahel,....................2Ch 31:13

NAHATH'S
N son was Eliab. Eliab's son was 1Ch 6:27

NAHBI
of Naphtali, **N** son of Vophsi; ....Nu 13:14

NAHOR
father of Abram, **N,** and Haran. ....Ge 11:27
Abram and **N** both married. ....Ge 11:29
Also **N** had other sons by ....Ge 22:24
you know Laban, grandson of **N?**"...........Ge 29:5
who is the God of **N** and the God ....Ge 31:53

NAHSHON
tribe of Judah—**N** son of......................Nu 1:7
Amminadab was the father of **N.** ....Mt 1:4

NAHSHON'S
and Amminadab was **N** father. 1Ch 2:10

NAHUM
is the book of the vision of **N,**.................Nah 1:1
Amos was the son of **N.** ....Lk 3:25
N was the son of Esli. ....Lk 3:25

NAIL
until I see the **n** marks in his ....Jn 20:25

NAILED
the man you **n** to the cross— ....Ac 2:36
its rules and **n** it to the cross. ....Col 2:14

NAILING
to death by **n** him to a cross. ....Ac 2:23
because they are **n** the Son of.................Heb 6:6

NAILS
shave her head and cut her **n** ....Dt 21:12
used for making **n** and hinges for 1Ch 22:3
The gold **n** weighed over a pound. 2Ch 3:9
They are like **n** that have been ....Ec 12:11

He **n** the statue to a base so it .... Is 41:7
hammers and **n** they fasten them .... Je 10:4
and his **n** grew like the claws of .... Da 4:33
where the **n** were and put my .... Jn 20:25

NAIN

Jesus went to a town called **N**, ... Lk 7:11

NAIOTH

went to **N** and stayed there. 1Sa 19:18
that David was in **N** at Ramah. 1Sa 19:19
answered, "In **N** at Ramah." 1Sa 19:22
When Saul went to **N** at Ramah, ... 1Sa 19:23
until he came to **N** at Ramah. 1Sa 19:23
David ran away from **N** in Ramah............ 1Sa 20:1

NAKED

The man and his wife were **n**,.............. Ge 2:25
They realized they were **n**, ... Ge 3:7
I was afraid because I was **n**, ... Ge 3:10
I was **n** when I was born, and I .... Job 1:21
Death is **n** before God; .... Job 26:6
walked around **n** and barefoot for .... Is 20:3
will be led away **n** and barefoot,............. Is 20:4
going around barefoot and **n**. .... Mic 1:8
came off, and he ran away **n**. .... Mk 14:52
away from the house **n** and hurt. .... Ac 19:16
clothe us so we will not be **n**. 2Co 5:3
not want to be **n**, but we want to 2Co 5:4
pitiful, poor, blind, and **n**. .... Rev 3:17
walk around **n** and have people .... Rev 16:15

NAKEDNESS

did not see their father's **n**. .... Ge 9:23
People will see your **n**; .... Is 47:3
and you have looked at their **n**. .... Is 57:8
because they have seen her **n**. .... La 1:8
over you and covered your **n**. .... Eze 16:8
You showed your **n** to other .... Eze 16:36
of them so they can see your **n**. .... Eze 16:37
and linen that covered her **n**. .... Hos 2:9
I will show her **n** to her lovers, ... Hos 2:10
nations your **n** and the kingdoms .... Nah 3:5
or hunger or **n** or danger or .... Rm 8:35
you can cover your shameful **n**. .... Rev 3:18

NAME

the man so the man could **n** them. .... Ge 2:19
am changing your **n** from Abram to .... Ge 17:5
I will change the **n** of Sarai, ... Ge 17:15
said to him, "What is your **n**?" .... Ge 32:27
to him, "Your **n** is Jacob, but .... Ge 35:10
Your new **n** will be Israel." .... Ge 35:10
gave Joseph the **n** .... Ge 41:45
the people say, 'What is his **n**?" .... Ex 3:13
' This will always be my **n**, ... Ex 3:15
and Jacob by the **n** God Almighty, ... Ex 6:3
is a warrior; the LORD is his **n**. .... Ex 15:3
not use the **n** of the LORD your .... Ex 20:7
will announce my **n**, the LORD, so .... Ex 33:19
and the LORD called out his **n**: .... Ex 34:5
Each jewel had the **n** of one of .... Ex 39:14
make a false promise by my **n**, ... Le 19:12
The mother's **n** was Shelomith, ... Le 24:11
not use the **n** of the LORD your .... Dt 5:11
who uses his **n** in this way. .... Dt 5:11
to bless the people in his **n**, ... Dt 10:8
says in the **n** of the LORD does .... Dt 18:22
brother so that his **n** will not .... Dt 25:6
n of the LORD your God, ... Dt 28:58
you do for your own great **n**?" .... Jos 7:9
LORD said, "Why do you ask my **n**? .... Jdg 13:18
will stay in the dead man's **n**." .... Ru 4:5
neighbors gave the boy his **n**, ... Ru 4:17
come to you in the **n** of the LORD 1Sa 17:45
is like his **n**. His name means ' 1Sa 25:25

His **n** means 'fool,' and he is 1Sa 25:25
the people in the **n** of the LORD. 2Sa 6:18
You made your **n** well known. 2Sa 7:23
the prophet to **n** the baby 2Sa 12:25
have no son to keep my **n** alive." 2Sa 18:18
I will sing praises to your **n**. 2Sa 22:50
changed Jacob's **n** to Israel. 1Ki 18:31
His mother's **n** was Jerusha 2Ki 15:33
listed by the **n** of the father of 1Ch 6:19
the glory of the LORD's **n**. 1Ch 16:29
were chosen by **n** to sing praises 1Ch 16:41
are called by my **n**, will humble 2Ch 7:14
swear in God's **n** to be loyal to 2Ch 36:13
Blessed be your wonderful **n**. .... Ne 9:5
Praise the **n** of the LORD." .... Job 1:21
n is the most wonderful name .... Ps 8:1
I will sing praises to your **n**. .... Ps 9:2
a flag in the **n** of our God. .... Ps 20:5
the LORD for the glory of his **n**; .... Ps 29:2
let us praise his **n** together. .... Ps 34:3
we will praise your **n** forever. .... Ps 44:8
up my hands in prayer to your **n**. .... Ps 63:4
praises to his **n**. Prepare the .... Ps 68:4
ever remember the **n** 'Israel.'" .... Ps 83:4
and I will honor your **n** forever. .... Ps 86:12
to the LORD and praise his **n**; .... Ps 96:2
Let them praise your **n**; .... Ps 99:3
Thank him and praise his **n**. .... Ps 100:4
in me, praise his holy **n**. .... Ps 103:1
The LORD's **n** should be praised .... Ps 113:2
them in the **n** of the LORD. .... Ps 118:10
who comes in the **n** of the LORD. .... Ps 118:26
have made your **n** and your word .... Ps 138:2
use your **n** thoughtlessly. .... Ps 139:20
praise his holy **n** forever. .... Ps 145:21
What is his **n** or his son's name? .... Pr 30:4
What is his name or his son's **n**? .... Pr 30:4
and disgrace the **n** of my God. .... Pr 30:9
and she will **n** him Immanuel. .... Is 7:14
N the boy Maher-Shalal-Hash-Baz, ... Is 8:3
His **n** will be Wonderful .... Is 9:6
want to remember you and your **n**. .... Is 26:8
and calls all the stars by **n**. .... Is 40:26
That is my **n**. I will not give .... Is 42:8
called you by **n**, and you are .... Is 43:1
Then you will have a new **n**, ... Is 62:2
to make his **n** famous forever,.............. Is 63:12
who have never worn your **n**. .... Is 63:19
called by your **n** so don't leave .... Je 14:9
are prophesying lies in my **n**. .... Je 14:14
not speak anymore in his **n**." .... Je 20:9
laugh at you with your bad **n**,.............. Eze 22:5
my holy **n** in the nations .... Eze 36:20
Daniel's new **n** was Belteshazzar, ... Da 1:7
your **n** is known even today. .... Da 9:15
said to Hosea, "**N** him Jezreel, ... Hos 1:4
to Hosea, "**N** her Lo-Ruhamah, ... Hos 1:6
The LORD said, "**N** him Lo-Ammi,........... Hos 1:9
will praise the **n** of the LORD .... Joe 2:26
and so they ruin my holy **n**. .... Am 2:7
and his **n** will be the only name .... Zch 14:9
Honor my **n**," says the LORD .... Mal 2:2
and they will **n** him Immanuel," .... Mt 1:23
may your **n** always be kept holy. .... Mt 6:9
a child in my **n** accepts me. .... Mt 18:5
who comes in the **n** of the Lord! .... Mt 21:9
comes in the **n** of the Lord.'" .... Mt 23:39
them in the **n** of the Father .... Mt 28:19
in God's **n** not to torture me!"............... Mk 5:7
a son, and you will **n** him John. .... Lk 1:13
family of David. Her **n** was Mary. .... Lk 1:27
things for me. His **n** is holy. .... Lk 1:49
obeyed us when we used your **n**!" .... Lk 10:17

N

in his **n** to all nations, ...Lk 24:47
own sheep by **n** and leads them ....Jn 10:3
Father, bring glory to your **n!**" ....Jn 12:28
if you ask for anything in my **n,** ....Jn 14:13
safe by the power of your **n,** ....Jn 17:12
you may have life through his **n.** ....Jn 20:31
in the **n** of Jesus Christ for the ....Ac 2:38
to people anymore using that **n.**" ....Ac 4:17
teach at all in the **n** of Jesus. ....Ac 4:18
speak in the **n** of Jesus again.................Ac 5:40
much he must suffer for my **n.**" ....Ac 9:16
in the **n** of Jesus Christ ....Ac 10:48
in the **n** of the Lord Jesus. ....Ac 19:5
against God's **n** because of you." ....Rm 2:24
you so that my **n** will be talked ....Rm 9:17
you baptized in the **n** of Paul? 1Co 1:13
and on earth gets its true **n.** ....Eph 3:15
made his **n** greater than every ....Php 2:9
name greater than every other **n** ....Php 2:9
knee will bow to the **n** of Jesus— ....Php 2:10
God gave him a **n** that is much ....Heb 1:4
always use the **n** of someone ....Heb 6:16
Melchizedek's **n** means "king of...............Heb 7:2
the person in the **n** of the Lord. ....Jam 5:14
God because you wear that **n.**...............1Pe 4:16
greet each friend there by **n.** 3Jn 1:15
troubles for my **n** and not ....Rev 2:3
with a new **n** written on it. ....Rev 2:17
knows this new **n** except the one ....Rev 2:17
were not afraid to speak my **n.** ....Rev 3:8
write on them the **n** of my God ....Rev 3:12
my God and the **n** of the city of ....Rev 3:12
also write on them my new **n.** ....Rev 3:12
The **n** of the star is Wormwood. ....Rev 8:11
His **n** in the Hebrew language is...............Rev 9:11
A **n** against God was written on ....Rev 13:1
against God's **n,** against the ....Rev 13:6
which is the **n** of the beast or ....Rev 13:17
beast or the number of its **n.** ....Rev 13:17
who had his **n** and his Father's ....Rev 14:1
his Father's **n** written on their.................Rev 14:1
or who get the mark of his **n.**" ....Rev 14:11
number of his **n** were standing ....Rev 15:2
and they cursed the **n** of God,................Rev 16:9
He has a **n** written on him, ...Rev 19:12
and his **n** is the Word of God. ....Rev 19:13
upper leg was written this **n:** ....Rev 19:16
And anyone whose **n** was not found ....Rev 20:15
was written the **n** of one of the ....Rev 21:12
and his **n** will be written on ....Rev 22:4

NAMED
was Luz, but Jacob **n** it Bethel. ....Ge 28:19
of Jacob, whom he had **n** Israel................2Ki 17:34
saw a man **n** Matthew sitting in ....Mt 9:9
a tax collector **n** Levi sitting ....Lk 5:27
Simon (Jesus **n** him Peter), his ....Lk 6:14
There was a man **n** Nicodemus who ....Jn 3:1
strong wind in the "northeaster ....Ac 27:14
below a small island **n** Cauda, ...Ac 27:16
The mother **n** Hagar is like that ....Gal 4:24
Its rider has **n** death, and Hades ....Rev 6:8
This city is **n** Sodom and Egypt,...............Rev 11:8

NAMES
The man gave **n** to all the tame ....Ge 2:20
Write the **n** in order, from the..................Ex 28:10
idols or even speak their **n.**....................Ps 16:4
officer, gave them Babylonian **n.** ....Da 1:7
These are the **n** of the twelve ....Mt 10:2
but because your **n** are written ....Lk 10:20
whose **n** are written in the book...............Php 4:3
on long lists of **n** in family 1Ti 1:4
children whose **n** are written in ....Heb 12:23

not erase their **n** from the book ....Rev 3:5
on earth whose **n** have not been ....Rev 17:8

NAMING
n it for their ancestor Dan, ...Jdg 18:29

NAOMI
wife was named **N,** and his two ....Ru 1:2
So **N** and her daughter-in-law.................Ru 1:22
Then **N,** Ruth's mother-in-law, ...Ru 3:1

NAOMI'S
Then **N** husband, Elimelech, died, ...Ru 1:3

NAP
while he was taking a **n.** 2Sa 4:5
you take a **n.** You fold your....................Pr 6:10
you take a **n.** You fold your....................Pr 24:33

NAPHISH
Tema, Jetur, **N,** and Kedemah. ....Ge 25:15
Jetur, **N,** and Kedemah. 1Ch 1:31
people of Jetur, **N,** and Nodab. 1Ch 5:19

NAPHOTH
to the king of **N** Dor in the west...............Jos 11:2
Dor (in **N** Dor), Goyim in Gilgal, ...Jos 12:23
people in **N** Dor and its small..................Jos 17:11
was governor of **N** Dor. 1Ki 4:11

NAPHTALI
slave girl Bilhah: Dan and **N.** ....Ge 35:25
all the land of **N** and carried 2Ki 15:29
Zebulun and **N** hang their heads ....Is 9:1
and land of **N** along the sea, ...Mt 4:15
the tribe of **N** twelve thousand, ...Rev 7:6

NAPHTALI'S
N sons were Jahziel, Guni, Jezer, ...Ge 46:24
N sons were Jahziel, Guni, Jezer, ...1Ch 7:13
South of **N** border, Manasseh will ....Eze 48:4
Gate, Asher's Gate, and **N** Gate...............Eze 48:34

NAPHTUHITES
Ludites, Anamites, Lehabites, **N,** ....Ge 10:13
Anamites, Lehabites, and **N,** 1Ch 1:11

NARCISSUS
in the family of **N** who belong to ....Rm 16:11

NARD
filled with flowers and **n,** ....Sng 4:13
n and saffron, calamus, and ....Sng 4:14
perfume, made of pure **n.** ....Mk 14:3
perfume made from pure **n.** ....Jn 12:3

NARROW
LORD stood on a **n** path between ....Nu 22:24
again and stood at a **n** place, ...Nu 22:26
too n to turn left or right. ....Nu 22:26
wife is like a **n** well. ....Pr 23:27
that was too **n** to wrap around ....Is 28:20
Enter through the **n** gate. ....Mt 7:13
and the road is **n** that leads to ....Mt 7:14
to enter through the **n** door, ...Lk 13:24

NARROWER
The windows were **n** on the side ....Eze 40:16
top rooms were **n,** because the ....Eze 42:5

NATHAN
David said to **N** the prophet, ...2Sa 7:2
When **N** heard about this, he went 1Ki 1:11
in the records of **N** the prophet, ...2Ch 9:29

NATHAN-MELECH
courtyard near the room of **N,** 2Ki 23:11

NATHANAEL
Philip found **N** and told him, ...Jn 1:45
called Didymus), **N** from Cana in ....Jn 21:2

NATION

I will make you a great **n**, ... Ge 12:2
will punish the **n** where they are .... Ge 15:14
of priests and a holy **n**.' .... Ex 19:6
and your descendants a great **n**." .... Ex 32:10
that this **n** is your people." .... Ex 33:13
other **n** is as great as we are. .... Dt 4:7
And no other **n** has such good .... Dt 4:8
will be given to another **n**, ... Dt 28:32
LORD will bring a **n** against you .... Dt 28:49
who are not a **n** to make them .... Dt 32:21
There is no **n** like your people 2Sa 7:23
Happy is the **n** whose God is the .... Ps 33:12
let's destroy them as a **n**. .... Ps 83:4
didn't do this for any other **n**. .... Ps 147:20
what is right makes a **n** great, ... Pr 14:34
Israel is a **n** of sin, a people .... Is 1:4
have caused the **n** to grow and .... Is 9:3
are a powerful **n** that defeats .... Is 18:2
of any other **n** saved his people .... Is 36:18
Has a **n** ever exchanged its gods? .... Je 2:11
But if a **n** will not listen to my .... Je 12:17
speak about a **n** or a kingdom .... Je 18:7
the people of that **n** stop doing .... Je 18:8
the **n** that is comfortable, ... Je 49:31
A powerful **n** and many kings are .... Je 50:41
our towers for a **n** to save us. .... La 4:17
That **n** has turned against me and .... Eze 2:3
Anyone from any **n** or language .... Da 3:29
of every tribe, **n**, and language .... Da 7:14
come from the **n** of the first .... Da 8:22
of the best **n** in the world; .... Am 6:1
make a strong **n** of those who................ Mic 4:7
How long will that **n** get rich by .... Hab 2:6
the whole **n** has robbed me. .... Mal 3:9
in all the world, to every **n**..................... Mt 24:14
take away our Temple and our **n**." .... Jn 11:48
for the whole **n** to be destroyed............. Jn 11:50
that Jesus would die for their **n** .... Jn 11:51
will punish the **n** where they are .... Ac 7:7
over this **n** for a long time .... Ac 24:10
who are not a **n** to make you .... Rm 10:19
I will use a **n** that does not .... Rm 10:19
priests, a holy **n**, a people for 1Pe 2:9
tribe, language, people, and **n**. .... Rev 5:9
from every **n**, tribe, people,.................... Rev 7:9
and **n** will look at the bodies of .... Rev 11:9
tribe, people, language, and **n**. .... Rev 13:7
earth—to every **n**, tribe, ... Rev 14:6

NATION'S

place, and it is the **n** temple." .... Am 7:13

NATIONS

grew and became different **n**, ... Ge 10:5
languages, countries, and **n**. .... Ge 10:31
make you the father of many **n**. .... Ge 17:4
will be the mother of many **n**................... Ge 17:16
and all **n** on earth will be .... Ge 18:18
to her, "Two **n** are in your body .... Ge 25:23
the other **n** saw these things. .... Le 26:45
they are different from other **n**. .... Nu 23:9
he will force out these **n**:...................... Dt 7:1
forces those **n** out of the land .... Dt 7:22
hateful things the other **n** do. .... Dt 18:9
thing to the **n** where the LORD .... Dt 28:37
over us like all the other **n**." 1Sa 8:5
be the same as all the other **n**. 1Sa 8:20
lived like the **n** the LORD had 2Ki 17:8
gods of these **n** into the fire, ... 2Ki 19:18
Tell the **n** about his glory; 1Ch 16:24
of the other **n** could not save 2Ch 32:17
I will scatter you among the **n**. .... Ne 1:8
who came from the **n** around us. .... Ne 5:17

Why are the **n** so angry?........................ Ps 2:1
ask me, I will give you the **n**; .... Ps 2:8
the foreign **n** and destroyed .... Ps 9:5
You made me the leader of **n**. .... Ps 18:43
families of the **n** will worship .... Ps 22:27
is King, and he rules the **n**.................... Ps 22:28
I will be praised in all the **n**; .... Ps 46:10
defeated **n** for us and put them .... Ps 47:3
God is King over the **n**. .... Ps 47:8
all **n** will learn that you can .... Ps 67:2
The **n** should be glad and sing .... Ps 67:4
down to him and all **n** serve him. .... Ps 72:11
Let the **n** be blessed because of .... Ps 72:17
Why should the **n** say, "Where is .... Ps 79:10
Tell the **n** of his glory; .... Ps 96:3
Tell the **n**, "The LORD is king." .... Ps 96:10
will judge those **n**, filling them .... Ps 110:6
LORD is supreme over all the **n**;............. Ps 113:4
idols of other **n** are made of .... Ps 135:15
will punish the **n** and defeat .... Ps 149:7
people from all **n** will come .... Is 2:2
among the **n** and will make .... Is 2:4
a banner for the **n** far away. .... Is 5:26
past all the **n** on earth bowed .... Is 14:12
He will judge the **n** as if he is .... Is 30:28
The **n** are like one small drop in............. Is 40:15
help you defeat **n** and take away .... Is 45:1
But now he will surprise many **n**. .... Is 52:15
prayer for people from all **n**." .... Is 56:7
Then all **n** will shake with fear .... Is 64:2
you as a prophet to the **n**." .... Je 1:5
you in charge of **n** and kingdoms. .... Je 1:10
a destroyer of **n** has begun to .... Je 4:7
respect you, King of the **n**; .... Je 10:7
went to those **n** and made them .... Je 25:17
the LORD will accuse all the **n**. .... Je 25:31
of all these **n** to make them .... Je 28:14
all those **n** where I scattered .... Je 30:11
the prophet about the **n**: .... Je 46:1
the most ruined of all the **n**. .... Je 50:23
Blow the trumpet among the **n**! .... Je 51:27
was a great city among the **n**,............... La 1:1
center of the **n** with countries............... Eze 5:5
a shame among the **n** around you, ... Eze 5:14
Then the **n** around you will shame .... Eze 5:15
give you to the **n** as if you were .... Eze 25:7
to insults from the **n** anymore; .... Eze 36:15
has been dishonored among the **n**........... Eze 36:23
dishonored it among these **n**, ... Eze 36:23
They will never again be two **n**; .... Eze 37:22
will show my glory among the **n**. .... Eze 39:21
them into captivity among the **n**, ... Eze 39:28
to the people, **n**, and those who .... Da 4:1
they will wander among the **n**. .... Hos 9:17
Many **n** will come and say, ... Mic 4:2
The Lord will judge many **n**; .... Mic 4:3
Look at the **n**! Watch them and be .... Hab 1:5
shake all the **n**, and they will .... Hag 2:7
will talk to the **n** about peace................ Zch 9:10
I will be honored among the **n**. .... Mal 1:11
and I am feared by all the **n**. .... Mal 1:14
All the **n** will call you blessed, ... Mal 3:12
N will fight against other .... Mt 24:7
will fight against other **n**; .... Mt 24:7
All the **n** of the world will be .... Mt 25:32
prayer for people from all **n**.' .... Mk 11:17
N will fight against other .... Mk 13:8
will fight against other **n**, ... Mk 13:8
N will fight against other .... Lk 21:10
'Why are the **n** so angry? .... Ac 4:25
destroyed seven **n** in the land .... Ac 13:19
n will be blessed through you. .... Gal 3:8
rule all the **n** with an iron rod................ Rev 12:5

N

races, **n**, and languages. .... Rev 17:15
and all the **n** were tricked by .... Rev 18:23

NATIVE
Euphrates River in his **n** land. .... Nu 22:5

NATURAL
with an animal; it is not **n**. .... Le 18:23
What they have done is not **n**. .... Le 20:12
a sword or who died a **n** death, ... Nu 19:16
that died a **n** death or one that .... Eze 44:31
stopped having **n** sex and started .... Rm 1:26
stopped having **n** sex and began .... Rm 1:27
did not let the **n** branches of .... Rm 11:21
It is not **n** for a wild branch to .... Rm 11:24

NATURALLY
will die **n**, or maybe he will 1Sa 26:10

NATURE
Even **n** itself teaches you that 1Co 11:14
because we were sinful by **n**. .... Eph 2:3
gifts you can share in God's **n**, ... 2Pe 1:4

NAVEL
Your **n** is like a round drinking .... Sng 7:2

NAVY
warriors in your **n** and hung .... Eze 27:10

NAZARENE
"He will be called a **N**." .... Mt 2:23
He is a leader of the **N** group. .... Ac 24:5

NAZARETH
a town called **N**, and lived there .... Mt 2:23
from the town of **N** in Galilee." .... Mt 21:11
"This man was with Jesus of **N**." .... Mt 26:71
"Can anything good come from **N**?" .... Jn 1:46
OF **N**, THE KING OF THE JEWS. .... Jn 19:19
power of Jesus Christ from **N**, ... Ac 3:6

NAZIRITE
makes the **N** promise must give .... Nu 6:21
he will be a **N**, given to God .... Jdg 13:5
boy will be a **N** to God from his .... Jdg 13:7
to God as a **N** since I was born .... Jdg 16:17

NAZIRITES
But you made the **N** drink wine .... Am 2:12

NEAH
border turned and went toward **N**. .... Jos 19:13
At **N** it turned again and went to .... Jos 19:14

NEAPOLIS
The next day we sailed to **N**. .... Ac 16:11

NEARIAH
Igal, Bariah, **N**, and Shaphat. 1Ch 3:22
N had three sons: Elioenai,...................... 1Ch 3:23
sons, Pelatiah, **N**, Rephaiah, and 1Ch 4:42

NEAT
empty, swept clean, and made **n**. .... Mt 12:44
house swept clean and made **n**. .... Lk 11:25

NEBAI
Hariph, Anathoth, **N**, ... Ne 10:19

NEBAIOTH
N, the first son, then Kedar, ... Ge 25:13
Mahalath was the sister of **N**. .... Ge 28:9
daughter, the sister of **N**. .... Ge 36:3
Ishmael's first son was **N**. 1Ch 1:29
the sheep from **N** will be brought .... Is 60:7

NEBALLAT
Hadid, Zeboim, **N**, ... Ne 11:34

NEBAT
son of **N** was king of Israel. 1Ki 15:1

NEBAT'S
who wrote about Jeroboam, **N** son. 2Ch 9:29

NEBO
climbed Mount **N** from the plains .... Dt 34:1
Bel and **N** bow down. Their idols .... Is 46:1

NEBO-SARSEKIM
N, a chief officer;................................... Je 39:3

NEBUCHADNEZZAR
officers of **N** king of Babylon 2Ki 24:10
King **N** said to them, "I meant .... Da 2:5
Then King **N** fell facedown on the .... Da 2:46
King **N** made a gold statue ninety .... Da 3:1
N was furious with Shadrach, ... Da 3:19
these things happened to King **N**. .... Da 4:28
that his ancestor **N** had taken.................. Da 5:2

NEBUSHAZBAN
N, a chief officer;................................... Je 39:13

NEBUZARADAN
N was the commander of the 2Ki 25:8
orders about Jeremiah through **N**, ... Je 39:11

NECESSARY
is **n** to have differences among 1Co 11:19
to be the weaker are really **n**................... 1Co 12:22
then the promise would not be **n**. .... Gal 3:18
provide what is **n** so that their .... Tit 3:14

NECK
a gold chain around Joseph's **n**. .... Ge 41:42
donkey back, then break its **n**. .... Ex 13:13
the young cow whose **n** was broken .... Dt 21:6
gate, broke his **n**, and died,.................... 1Sa 4:18
the water has risen to my **n**. .... Ps 69:1
like a necklace around your **n**. .... Pr 3:22
you had them tied around your **n**. .... Pr 6:21
Your **n** is like an ivory tower. .... Sng 7:4
the house of David around his **n**. .... Is 22:22
put it on the back of your **n**. .... Je 27:2
off Jeremiah's **n** and broke it.................. Je 28:10
off of the prophet Jeremiah's **n**. .... Je 28:12
and put iron rings around his **n**............... Je 29:26
and a gold chain around his **n**. .... Da 5:7
tied around the **n** and be drowned .... Mt 18:6
around your **n** than to cause one .... Lk 17:2

NECKLACE
wear pride like a **n** and put on .... Ps 73:6
your hair or a **n** around your .... Pr 1:9
Wear them like a **n**............................... Pr 3:3
beauty like a **n** around your neck .... Pr 3:22
with one sparkle from your **n**. .... Sng 4:9
your arms, a **n** around your neck, ... Eze 16:11

NECKLACES
signet rings, earrings, and **n**. .... Nu 31:50
the decorations, **n**, and purple .... Jdg 8:26
their **n** shaped like the moon,.................. Is 3:18

NECKS
feet on the **n** of these kings. .... Jos 10:24
and put their feet on their **n**. .... Jos 10:24
cloth for the **n** of the victors!' .... Jdg 5:30
decorations off their camels' **n**. .... Jdg 8:21
the chains from the camels' **n**. .... Jdg 8:26
have never had yokes on their **n**. 1Sa 6:7
those who break the **n** of dogs. .... Is 66:3
of iron on the **n** of all these...................... Je 28:14
yoke from their **n** and tear off .... Je 30:8
be put on the **n** of these unclean.............. Eze 21:29
load around the **n** of the .... Ac 15:10
the army of **N** king of Egypt, ... Je 46:2

NEDABIAH
Jekamiah, Hoshama, and **N**. 1Ch 3:18

NEED
those people anything they **n**— .... Ezr 6:9
do good to people who **n** help. .... Pr 3:27

we do not **n** to defend ourselves .... Da 3:16
I **n** to be baptized by you!" .... Mt 3:14
things you **n** before you ask him. .... Mt 6:8
in heaven knows you **n** them. .... Mt 6:32
healthy people who **n** a doctor, ... Mt 9:12
will have much more than they **n**. .... Mt 25:29
We don't **n** any more witnesses; .... Mt 26:65
healthy people who **n** a doctor, ... Mk 2:17
people who don't **n** to change. .... Lk 15:7
or sandals, did you **n** anything?" .... Lk 22:35
Do I **n** a place to rest? .... Ac 7:49
to the hand, "I don't **n** you!" 1Co 12:21
to the foot, "I don't **n** you!" 1Co 12:21
what people **n**—words that will .... Eph 4:29
you this because I **n** anything. .... Php 4:11
have more than I **n** and when I do .... Php 4:12
to give you everything you **n**. .... Php 4:19
So we do not **n** to say anything 1Th 1:8
tell people what they **n** to do. 2Ti 4:2
grace to help us when we **n** it. .... Heb 4:16
but you **n** someone to teach you .... Heb 5:12
sees a brother or sister in **n**, ... 1Jn 3:17
But I felt the **n** to write you .... Jud 1:3
wealthy and do not **n** anything.' .... Rev 3:17
The city does not **n** the sun or .... Rev 21:23
They will not **n** the light of a .... Rev 22:5

NEEDED
healed those who **n** to be healed. .... Lk 9:11
to buy what was **n** for the feast .... Jn 13:29
let his friends bring what he **n**. .... Ac 24:23
all that is **n** to do every good 2Ti 3:17
that still **n** to be done and so .... Tit 1:5

NEEDLE
the eye of a **n** than for a rich .... Mt 19:24
the eye of a **n** than for a rich .... Mk 10:25
the eye of a **n** than for a rich .... Lk 18:25

NEEDLEWORK
made with **n** on you and put .... Eze 16:10
linen, silk, and beautiful **n**. .... Eze 16:13
with beautiful **n** and covered the .... Eze 16:18
off their beautiful **n** clothes, ... Eze 26:16

NEEDS
all your other **n** will be met as .... Lk 12:31
He **n** only to wash his feet. .... Jn 13:10
Help her with anything she **n**, ... Rm 16:2
do not give what that person **n**, ... Jam 2:16

NEEDY
to the poor and **n** in your land. .... Dt 15:11
will save the **n** when no one else .... Ps 72:12
The poor and **n** people look for .... Is 41:17
He mistreats the poor and **n**. .... Eze 18:12
hurt people who are poor and **n**. .... Eze 22:29
and **n** people for the price of a .... Am 8:6
There were no **n** people among .... Ac 4:34

NEHELAMITE
to Shemaiah from the N family. .... Je 29:24
Lord says about Shemaiah the N: .... Je 29:31
Shemaiah the N and his family. .... Je 29:32

NEHEMIAH
Jeshua, N, Seraiah, Reelaiah .... Ezr 2:2

NEHUM
Bigvai, N, and Baanah. .... Ne 7:7

NEHUSHTA
mother's name was N daughter of 2Ki 24:8

NEHUSHTAN
had been burning incense to N, ... 2Ki 18:4

NEIEL
Beth Emek and N and passed north .... Jos 19:27

NEIGHBOR
her Egyptian **n** and any Egyptian .... Ex 3:22
must not tell lies about your **n**. .... Ex 20:16
borrows an animal from his **n**, ... Ex 22:14
not cheat your **n** or rob him. .... Le 19:13
your **n** as you love yourself. .... Le 19:18
must not tell lies about your **n**. .... Dt 5:20
says things against his **n**, ... Ps 101:5
It is a sin to hate your **n**, ... Pr 14:21
against your **n** for no good .... Pr 24:28
A **n** close by is better than a .... Pr 27:10
Everyone speaks nicely to his **n**, ... Je 9:8
Everybody will grab his **n**, ... Zch 14:13
your **n** and hate your enemies.' .... Mt 5:43
to Jesus, "And who is my **n**?" .... Lk 10:29
your **n** as you love yourself. .... Rm 13:9
your **n** as you love yourself. .... Gal 5:14
your **n** as you love yourself. .... Jam 2:8
right for you to judge your **n**. .... Jam 4:12

NEIGHBOR'S
not want to take your **n** house. .... Ex 20:17
the thornbushes to his **n** field. .... Ex 22:6
fire burns his **n** growing grain .... Ex 22:6
relations with his **n** wife, ... Le 20:10
not want to take your **n** wife. .... Dt 5:21
to take your **n** house or land, ... Dt 5:21
marks the border of your **n** land, ... Dt 19:14
relations with his **n** wife .... Eze 33:26
not want to take your **n** things." .... Rm 7:7

NEIGHBORING
No more will **n** nations be like .... Eze 28:24

NEIGHBORS
They say "Peace" to their **n**, ... Ps 28:3
You made us a joke to our **n**; .... Ps 44:13
to all my wicked **n** who take the .... Je 12:14
relatives, and your rich **n**. .... Lk 14:12
to his friends and **n** and says, ' .... Lk 15:6
The **n** and some people who had .... Jn 9:8

NEIGHING
shakes from the **n** of their large .... Je 8:16
is like the **n** of male horses. .... Je 50:11

NEKEB
through Adami N and Jabneel, ... Jos 19:33

NEKODA
Rezin, N, Gazzam, ... Ezr 2:48
of Delaiah, Tobiah, and N—652. .... Ezr 2:60
Reaiah, Rezin, N, ... Ne 7:50
of Delaiah, Tobiah, and N—642. .... Ne 7:62

NEMUEL
Eliab's sons were N, Dathan, and .... Nu 26:9
From N came the Nemuelite family .... Nu 26:12
sons were N, Jamin, Jarib, ... 1Ch 4:24

NEMUELITE
Nemuel came the N family group; .... Nu 26:12

NEPHEG
sons were Korah, N, and Zicri. .... Ex 6:21
Ibhar, Elishua, N, Japhia, ... 2Sa 5:15
Nogah, N, Japhia, ... 1Ch 14:6

NEPHEW
wife Sarai, his **n** Lot, and .... Ge 12:5
Abram's **n** who was living in .... Ge 14:12
But Paul's **n** heard about this .... Ac 23:16
Paul's **n** to the commander .... Ac 23:18

NEPHEWS
Merari, and his brothers and **n**. .... Ezr 8:19

NEPHILIM
The N were on the earth in those .... Ge 6:4
We saw the N people there. .... Nu 13:33
Anakites come from the N people. .... Nu 13:33

N

NEPHTOAH
the waters of **N** and then it went .... Jos 15:9
went west to the waters of **N**. .... Jos 18:15

NEPHUSSIM
Asnah, Meunim, **N**, ... Ezr 2:50
Besai, Meunim, **N**, ... Ne 7:52

NER
of his army was Abner son of **N**, ... 1Sa 14:50
the killing of Abner son of **N**. 2Sa 3:37

NEREUS
and Julia, **N** and his sister, ... Rm 16:15

NERGAL
people from Cuthah worshiped **N**. 2Ki 17:30

NERGAL-SHAREZER
N of the district of Samgar; .... Je 39:3
N, an important leader; .... Je 39:3
N, an important leader; .... Je 39:13

NERI
Shealtiel was the son of **N**. .... Lk 3:27
N was the son of Melki. .... Lk 3:28

NERIAH
and gave it to Baruch son of **N**, ... Je 36:32
to the officer Seraiah son of **N**, ... Je 51:59

NEST
building its **n** that flutters .... Dt 32:11
that makes its **n** at the entrance .... Je 48:28
home as high as an eagle's **n**, ... Je 49:16
and make your **n** among the stars, ... Ob 1:4

NESTING
its branches were **n** places for .... Da 4:21

NESTS
The birds make their **n** there; .... Ps 104:17
the birds have **n**, but the Son .... Mt 8:20
birds build **n** in its branches. .... Lk 13:19

NET
Then he made a **n** of seven chains 1Ki 7:17
me and pulled his **n** around me. .... Job 19:6
spread out their **n** to trap me; .... Ps 35:7
spread out a **n** right where the .... Pr 1:17
Like a fish caught in a **n**, ... Ec 9:12
He stretched out a **n** for my feet .... La 1:13
to his **n** and burns incense .... Hab 1:16
were throwing a **n** into the lake .... Mt 4:18
Andrew throwing a **n** into the................. Mk 1:16
Throw your **n** on the right side .... Jn 21:6
and pulled the **n** to the shore.................. Jn 21:11

NETAIM
They lived in **N** and Gederah and 1Ch 4:23

NETHANIAH
They were Ishmael son of **N**, ... 2Ki 25:23

NETOPHAH
He was from **N** and was from................. 1Ch 27:13
He was from **N** and was from................. 1Ch 27:15
of **N**—56; .... Ezr 2:22
the towns of Bethlehem and **N**— .... Ne 7:26

NETOPHATHITE
the Ahohite; Maharai the **N**; 2Sa 23:28
Heled son of Baanah the **N**; 2Sa 23:29
Seraiah son of Tanhumeth the **N**, ... 2Ki 25:23
Maharai the **N**; Heled son of 1Ch 11:30
Heled son of Baanah the **N**; 1Ch 11:30
Jerusalem, from the **N** villages, ... Ne 12:28
of Ephai the **N**, Jaazaniah son .... Je 40:8

NETOPHATHITES
Bethlehem, the **N**, Atroth Beth 1Ch 2:54
lived in the villages of the **N**. 1Ch 9:16

NETS
wicked fall into their own **n**, ... Ps 141:10
be a place for drying fishing **n**. .... Eze 26:14
left their **n** and followed him. .... Mt 4:20
father Zebedee, mending their **n**. .... Mt 4:21
them and were washing their **n**. .... Lk 5:2
and put your **n** in the water to .... Lk 5:4

NEVER-ENDING
goodness flow like a **n** stream. .... Am 5:24

NEW
Then a **n** king began to rule .... Ex 1:8
all the best **n** wine and grain. .... Nu 18:12
When you build a **n** house, build .... Dt 22:8
they chose to follow **n** gods. .... Jdg 5:8
So Delilah took **n** ropes and tied .... Jdg 16:12
must build a **n** cart and get two 1Sa 6:7
a land with grain and **n** wine,................. 2Ki 18:32
to burst like a **n** leather wine .... Job 32:19
Sing a **n** song to him; play well .... Ps 33:3
He put a **n** song in my mouth, ... Ps 40:3
Sing to the LORD a **n** song; .... Ps 96:1
is nothing **n** here on earth. .... Ec 1:9
I can't stand your **N** Moons, ... Is 1:13
now I tell you about **n** things. .... Is 42:9
Sing a **n** song to the LORD; .... Is 42:10
Look at the **n** thing I am going .... Is 43:19
I will make **n** heavens and a new .... Is 65:17
entrance of the **N** Gate of the .... Je 36:10
They are **n** every morning; .... La 3:23
inside them a **n** way of thinking .... Eze 11:19
yourselves a **n** heart and a new .... Eze 18:31
heart and a **n** way of thinking .... Eze 18:31
gave her grain, **n** wine, and oil. .... Hos 2:8
overflow with **n** wine and olive .... Joe 2:24
When will the **N** Moon festival be .... Am 8:5
people never pour **n** wine into .... Mt 9:17
brings out both **n** things and old .... Mt 13:52
which is the **n** agreement that .... Mt 26:28
when I drink it **n** with you in my .... Mt 26:29
body in a **n** tomb that he had .... Mt 27:60
man is teaching something **n**,................. Mk 1:27
the **n** patch will pull away from .... Mk 2:21
They will speak in **n** languages. .... Mk 16:17
I give you a **n** command:...................... Jn 13:34
the garden was a **n** tomb that had .... Jn 19:41
to us this **n** idea you have been .... Ac 17:19
you are saying are **n** to us, ... Ac 17:20
you will be a **n** batch of dough 1Co 5:7
This cup is the **n** agreement that 1Co 11:25
to be servants of a **n** agreement 2Co 3:6
Christ, there is a **n** creation. 2Co 5:17
have gone; everything is made **n**! 2Co 5:17
is being the **n** people God has................. Gal 6:15
people become one **n** people in .... Eph 2:15
to become a **n** person. That new............. Eph 4:24
have begun to live the **n** life, ... Col 3:10
I will make a **n** agreement with .... Heb 8:8
Christ brings a **n** agreement from .... Heb 9:15
enter through a **n** and living way .... Heb 10:20
a new heaven and a **n** earth where........... 2Pe 3:13
not writing a **n** command to you 1Jn 2:7
stone with a **n** name written on .... Rev 2:17
of my God, the **n** Jerusalem, that .... Rev 3:12
they all sang a **n** song to the .... Rev 5:9
Then I saw a **n** heaven and a new .... Rev 21:1
holy city, the **n** Jerusalem, ... Rev 21:2
I am making everything **n**!" .... Rev 21:5

NEWBORN
field leaves her **n** fawn to die,................. Je 14:5
n babies want milk, you should 1Pe 2:2

NEWER
was longer and **n** than the other. .... Da 8:3

NEWEST
time to talk about the **n** ideas. .... Ac 17:21

NEWLY
are white like **n** sheared sheep .... Sng 4:2

NEWS
He must be bringing good **n**!" 2Sa 18:27
else? I have bad **n** for you. 1Ki 14:6
Good **n** from a faraway place is .... Pr 25:25
the mountains to bring good **n**, ... Is 52:7
man who brought my father the **n**: .... Je 20:15
brought us good **n** about your 1Th 3:6

NEZIAH
N, and Hatipha. .... Ezr 2:54
N, and Hatipha. .... Ne 7:56

NEZIB
Iphtah, Ashnah, **N**, ... Jos 15:43

NIBHAZ
Avvites worshiped **N** and Tartak. 2Ki 17:31

NIBSHAN
N, the City of Salt, and En Gedi. .... Jos 15:62

NICANOR
Procorus, **N**, Timon, Parmenas .... Ac 6:5

NICER
is not **n** to princes than other .... Job 34:19

NICEST
Your **n** valleys will be filled .... Is 22:7

NICODEMUS
was a man named **N** who was one .... Jn 3:1
One night **N** came to Jesus and .... Jn 3:2
N said, "But if a person is .... Jn 3:4
N asked, "How can this happen?" .... Jn 3:9
N, who had gone to see Jesus .... Jn 7:50
N, who earlier had come to Jesus .... Jn 19:39

NICOLAITANS
hate what the **N** do, as much as I .... Rev 2:6
follow the teaching of the **N**. .... Rev 2:15

NICOLAS
Parmenas, and **N** (a man from .... Ac 6:5

NICOPOLIS
every effort to come to me at **N**, ... Tit 3:12

NIGER
Simeon (also called **N**), Lucius .... Ac 13:1

NIGHT
"day" and the darkness "**n**." .... Ge 1:5
the sky to separate day from **n**. .... Ge 1:14
the smaller light to rule the **n**. .... Ge 1:16
That **n** the two girls got their .... Ge 19:33
Study it day and **n** to be sure to .... Jos 1:8
Spend the **n** here and enjoy .... Jdg 19:9
and at **n** he and two of his men 1Sa 34:8
to you day and **n** for your .... Ne 1:6
That same **n** the king could not .... Est 6:1
and the **n** it was said, ' .... Job 3:3
vision of the **n** when people are .... Job 33:15
who gives us songs in the **n**, ... Job 35:10
about those teachings day and **n**. .... Ps 1:2
n my bed is wet with tears; .... Ps 6:6
Even at **n**, I feel his leading. .... Ps 16:7
n after night they tell it again. .... Ps 19:2
I call at **n**; I am not silent .... Ps 22:2
may last for a **n**, but joy comes .... Ps 30:5
Day and **n** you punished me. .... Ps 32:4
Day and **n**, my tears have been my .... Ps 42:3
I think about you through the **n**. .... Ps 63:6
the day and the **n** are yours; .... Ps 74:16
At **n** I remember my songs. .... Ps 77:6

or like a few hours in the **n**. .... Ps 90:4
any danger by **n** or an arrow .... Ps 91:5
and of your loyalty at **n**. .... Ps 92:2
the moon cannot hurt you at **n**. .... Ps 121:6
light around me turn into **n**." .... Ps 139:11
The **n** is as light as the day; .... Ps 139:12
Her lamp burns late into the **n**. .... Pr 31:18
At **n** on my bed, I looked for the .... Sng 3:1
how much of the **n** is left? .... Is 21:11
soul wants to be with you at **n**, ... Is 26:9
N animals will live there and .... Is 34:14
cry day and **n** for my people who .... Je 9:1
with day and **n** that they will .... Je 33:20
During the **n** God explained the .... Da 2:19
That very same **n** Belshazzar, ... Da 5:30
I saw my vision at **n**. .... Da 7:2
light, and the day into dark **n**. .... Am 5:8
There will be no day or **n**; .... Zch 14:7
during the **n** with the child .... Mt 2:14
came during the **n** and stole the .... Mt 28:13
That **n**, some shepherds were in .... Lk 2:8
worked hard all **n** trying to .... Lk 5:5
he spent the **n** praying to God. .... Lk 6:12
n Nicodemus came to Jesus and .... Jn 3:2
N is coming, when no one can work. .... Jn 9:4
immediately went out. It was **n**. .... Jn 13:30
They fished that **n** but caught .... Jn 21:3
during the **n**, an angel of the .... Ac 5:19
The **n** before Herod was to bring .... Ac 12:6
years, day and **n**, I never .... Ac 20:31
The "**n**" is almost finished, ... Rm 13:12
On the **n** when the Lord Jesus was 1Co 11:23
a thief that comes in the **n**. 1Th 5:2
belong to the **n** or to darkness. 1Th 5:5
Those who sleep, sleep at **n**. 1Th 5:7
you in my prayers, day and **n**. 2Ti 1:3
no rest, day or **n**, for those who .... Rev 14:11
day and **n** forever and ever .... Rev 20:10
because there is no **n** there. .... Rev 21:25

NIGHTMARE
was during a **n** when people are .... Job 4:13

NIGHTS
rain forty days and forty **n**, ... Ge 7:4
for forty days and forty **n**. .... Ex 24:18
forty days and **n** to Mount Sinai, ... 1Ki 19:8
with Job seven days and seven **n**. .... Job 2:13
the fish three days and three **n**. .... Jnh 1:17
fasted for forty days and **n**. .... Mt 4:2
fish for three days and three **n**. .... Mt 12:40

NILE
on the bank of the **N** River .... Ge 41:1
cows on the bank of the **N**. .... Ge 41:3
on the bank of the **N** River .... Ge 41:17
must throw him into the **N** River, ... Ex 1:22
at the edge of the **N** River. .... Ex 2:3
water from the **N** River and pour .... Ex 4:9
king will go out to the **N** River. .... Ex 7:15
The **N** River will be filled with .... Ex 8:3
and will remain only in the **N**." .... Ex 8:9
They will remain only in the **N**." .... Ex 8:11
you used to strike the **N** River. .... Ex 17:5
will disappear from the **N** River. .... Is 19:5
grain from the **N** Valley and sold .... Is 23:3
like the **N** goes through Egypt. .... Is 23:10
rising up like the **N** River, ... Je 46:7
Egypt rises up like the **N** River, ... Je 46:8
that lies in the **N** River. .... Eze 29:3
streams of the **N** River become .... Eze 30:12
whole land will rise like the **N**; .... Am 8:8
fall like the **N** River in Egypt." .... Am 8:8
rises like the **N** River and falls .... Am 9:5
who sits by the **N** River with .... Nah 3:8

N

from where the N River begins; .... Zph 3:10
and the N River will dry up. .... Zch 10:11

NIMRAH

Beth N, and Beth Haran......................... Nu 32:36
Beth Haram, Beth N, Succoth, and............ Jos 13:27

NIMRIM

But the water of N has dried up................ Is 15:6
the waters of N are dried up. .... Je 48:34

NIMROD

also had a descendant named N, ... Ge 10:8
people say someone is "like N, ... Ge 10:9
the father of N, who grew up to 1Ch 1:10

NIMROD'S

At first N kingdom covered .... Ge 10:10

NIMSHI

Jehu son of N to make him king.............. 1Ki 19:16
of Jehoshaphat, the son of N. 2Ki 9:2
the son of N, made plans against 2Ki 9:14
is driving like Jehu son of N. 2Ki 9:20
Joram to meet Jehu son of N, ... 2Ch 22:7

NINE

land among the n tribes and West .... Jos 13:7
healed? Where are the other n? .... Lk 17:17

NINE-AND-A-HALF

people of the n tribes threw .... Jos 14:2

NINETEEN

There were n towns and all their .... Jos 19:38
Asahel and n of David's men were.......... 2Sa 2:30
weighed about n pounds and two .... Ezr 8:27

NINETEENTH

Nebuchadnezzar's n year as king 2Ki 25:8
The n was Pethahiah. 1Ch 24:16
N, twelve men were chosen from 1Ch 25:26
Nebuchadnezzar's n year as king .... Je 52:12

NINETY

birth to a child when she is n?" .... Ge 17:17
hundred n bushels of grain, ... 1Ki 4:22
The Temple was n feet long, ... 1Ki 6:2
six hundred n of them in all. 1Ch 9:6
It was n feet long and thirty 2Ch 3:3
it should be n feet high and .... Ezr 6:3
feet high and n feet wide. .... Ezr 6:3
on you for three hundred n days. .... Eze 4:5
these three hundred n days, ... Eze 4:6
the three hundred n days you lie .... Eze 4:9
a gold statue n feet high and .... Da 3:1
four hundred n years for your .... Da 9:24
rope again. It was n feet deep. .... Ac 27:28

NINETY-EIGHT

Eli was now n years old, and he.............. 1Sa 4:15

NINETY-FIVE

one hundred n bushels of fine 1Ki 4:22

NINETY-NINE

When Abram was n years old, ... Ge 17:1
Abraham was n years old when he .... Ge 17:24
leave the other n on the hill .... Mt 18:12
than about the n that were never .... Mt 18:13
leave the other n sheep in the................. Lk 15:4
over n good people who don't.................. Lk 15:7

NINETY-SIX

for all Israel, n male sheep,.................... Ezr 8:35
There were n pomegranates on the .... Je 52:23

NINEVEH

where he built the cities of N,................. Ge 10:11
go to the great city of N,......................... Jnh 1:2
the great city N, and preach to .... Jnh 3:2
forty days, N will be destroyed .... Jnh 3:4
concern for the great city N, ... Jnh 4:11

away and say, 'N is in ruins. .... Nah 3:7
Day the people of N will stand .... Lk 11:32

NINTH

after the n day of the month .... Le 23:32
until the harvest of the n year. .... Le 25:22
Samaria in the n year Hoshea was 2Ki 17:6
which was Hoshea's n year as 2Ki 18:10
Zedekiah's n year as king, ... 2Ki 25:1
the n day of the fourth month, ... 2Ki 25:3
was eighth, Elzabad was n,.................... 1Ch 12:12
The n was Jeshua. The tenth was 1Ch 24:11
N, twelve men were chosen from 1Ch 25:16
The n commander, for the ninth.............. 1Ch 27:12
for the n month, was Abiezer 1Ch 27:12
twentieth day of the n month.................. Ezr 10:9
In the n month of the fifth year .... Je 36:9
It was the n month of the year, ... Je 36:22
month of the n year Zedekiah was........... Je 39:1
lasted until the n day of the .... Je 39:2
happened on Zedekiah's n year, ... Je 52:4
the n day of the fourth month, ... Je 52:6
word to me in the n year of our .... Eze 24:1
day of the n month in the second .... Hag 2:10
-fourth day of the n month,.................... Hag 2:18
the fourth day of the n month, ... Zch 7:1
was beryl, the n was topaz, the .... Rev 21:20

NISAN

the month of N in the twentieth .... Ne 2:1
Xerxes' rule—the month of N. .... Est 3:7

NISROCH

in the temple of his god N, ... 2Ki 19:37
in the temple of his god N, ... Is 37:38

NOADIAH

of Jeshua and N son of Binnui. .... Ezr 8:33
the prophetess N and the other .... Ne 6:14

NOAH

After N was 500 years old, ... Ge 5:32
But N pleased the LORD. .... Ge 6:8
This is the family history of N. .... Ge 6:9
N was a good man, the most .... Ge 6:9
remembered N and all the wild .... Ge 8:1
Then N built an altar to the .... Ge 8:20
Then God blessed N and his sons .... Ge 9:1
day is like the time of N to me. .... Is 54:9
GOD, even if N, Daniel, and Job.............. Eze 14:20
will be as it was when N lived. .... Lk 17:26
was by faith that N heard God's .... Heb 11:7
God long ago in the time of N. 1Pe 3:20
But God saved N, who preached.............. 2Pe 2:5

NOAH'S

These three men were N sons, ... Ge 9:19
what happened during N time. .... Mt 24:37

NOB

David went to N to see Ahimelech 1Sa 21:1
Ahimelech son of Ahitub at N. 1Sa 22:9
relatives who were priests at N. 1Sa 22:11
He also killed the people of N, ... 1Sa 22:19
Edomite was there at N that day. 1Sa 22:22
in Anathoth, N, Ananiah, ... Ne 11:32
day the army will stop at N. .... Is 10:32

NOBAH

N went and captured Kenath and .... Nu 32:42
he named it N after himself. .... Nu 32:42
in tents east of N and Jogbehah, ... Jdg 8:11

NOBLES

servants, n, and officers.......................... 2Ki 24:12

NOBODY

is gone, that n is left, slaves .... Dt 32:36
N can understand what God does .... Ec 8:17

N can speak and have it happen............. La 3:37
and n in Israel will use this..................... Eze 12:23
stayed in places where n lived, ... Mk 1:45
N has ever heard of anyone .... Jn 9:32

NOD
LORD and lived in the land of N, ... Ge 4:16

NODAB
people of Jetur, Naphish, and N. 1Ch 5:19

NOGAH
N, Nepheg, Japhia, ... 1Ch 14:6

NOHAH
N was his fourth, and Rapha was 1Ch 8:2

NOISE
and asked, "What's all this n?" 1Sa 4:14
made so much n the ground shook........... 1Ki 1:40
does all that n from the city 1Ki 1:41
and that is the n you hear. 1Ki 1:45
there was no n of hammers, ... 1Ki 6:7
heard the n of the guards 2Ki 11:13
heard the n of the people 2Ch 23:12
made so much n it could be heard .... Ezr 3:13
be deaf to the n in the streets, ... Ec 12:4
n with their ankle bracelets. .... Is 3:16
to the loud n in the mountains, ... Is 13:4
Listen to the n among the .... Is 13:4
is like the n from the sea. .... Is 17:12
full of n and wild parties. .... Is 22:2
yelling or upset by their n. .... Is 31:4
Listen to the loud n coming from .... Is 66:6
hear the n from the Temple. .... Is 66:6
A loud n comes from the north to .... Je 10:22
The n will spread all over the .... Je 25:31
of Egypt is only a lot of n. .... Je 46:17
The n of battle can be heard all .... Je 50:22
it is the n of much destruction. .... Je 50:22
There was the n of a reckless .... Eze 23:42
will shake at the n of horsemen,............ Eze 26:10
there was a n and a rattling. .... Eze 37:7
will hear the n of battle, ... Hos 10:14
It is like the n of chariots .... Joe 2:5
like the n of a roaring fire .... Joe 2:5
of Moab will die in a great n, ... Am 2:2
Take the n of your songs away .... Am 5:23
whips and the n of the wheels. .... Nah 3:2
sea made a loud n, and its waves .... Hab 3:10
lots of n and crying loudly..................... Mk 5:38
you crying and making so much n? .... Mk 5:39
Suddenly a n like a strong,.................... Ac 2:2
they heard this n, a crowd came............. Ac 2:6
made a loud n when they came out .... Ac 8:7
not come to the n of a trumpet .... Heb 12:19
will disappear with a loud n. 2Pe 3:10
was like the n of flooding water .... Rev 1:15
was like the n of many horses .... Rev 9:9
heaven like the n of flooding .... Rev 14:2
like the n of flooding water, ... Rev 19:6
and like the n of loud thunder. .... Rev 19:6

NOISES
Your enemies are making n; .... Ps 83:2
and great n, with storms, strong............. Is 29:6
flashes and n and thunder came............. Rev 4:5
thunder and loud n, and an .... Rev 8:5
of lightning, n, thunder, ... Rev 11:19
of lightning, n, thunder, and a .... Rev 16:18

NOISY
cries out in the n street and .... Pr 1:21
with their happy and n ones. .... Is 5:14
people will leave the n city. .... Is 32:14
but it will be n there soon! .... Je 33:10
horses and the n chariots .... Je 47:3

a roaring sound like a n army. .... Eze 1:24
I am only a n bell or a crashing 1Co 13:1

NON-ISRAELITE
an Israelite or n, must be cut .... Ex 12:19
Then n people will join the .... Is 14:1

NONBELIEVER
believer have together with a n?............. 2Co 6:15

NONBELIEVERS
saved from the n in Judea and .... Rm 15:31
much time doing what n enjoy. 1Pe 4:3
N think it is strange that you 1Pe 4:4
been accepting nothing from n. 3Jn 1:7

NONSENSE
can you comfort me with this n? .... Job 21:34
So Job is only speaking n, ... Job 35:16
because it sounded like n. .... Lk 24:11

NOON
to Baal from morning until n, ... 1Ki 18:26
Morning, n, and night I am................... Ps 55:17
morning and battle cries at n,............... Je 20:16
sun to go down at n and make the .... Am 8:9
About n when I came near .... Ac 22:6

NOONDAY
will be as bright as the n sun,............... Job 11:17
your fairness like the n sun. .... Ps 37:6

NOONTIME
a destroyer at n against the .... Je 15:8

NOPHAH
we destroyed them as far as N, ... Nu 21:30

NORTH
When he is at work in the n, ... Job 23:9
out of the n in golden light .... Job 37:22
the high mountains of the n; .... Ps 48:2
You created the n and the south. .... Ps 89:12
from east and west, n and south. .... Ps 107:3
it blows to the n. It blows from .... Ec 1:6
cloud of dust comes from the n. .... Is 14:31
water, tipping over from the n." .... Je 1:13
come from the n and strike all .... Je 1:14
sacrifice in the land of the n, ... Je 46:10
a king from the n against Tyre. .... Eze 26:7
the armies of the king of the N. .... Da 11:7
horses that went n have caused .... Zch 6:8
the east, west, n, and south and .... Lk 13:29

NORTHEASTER
wind named the "n" came from the .... Ac 27:14

NORTHERN
Your n border will begin at.................... Nu 34:7
This will be your n border. .... Nu 34:9
the kings in the n mountains and .... Jos 11:2
The n border started at the bay .... Jos 15:5
Then the n border went through............. Jos 15:7
n end of the Valley of Giants. .... Jos 15:8
The n border started at the.................... Jos 18:12
along the n edge of Jericho, ... Jos 18:12
continued to the n part of Beth .... Jos 18:18
it went to the n part of Beth .... Jos 18:19
God stretches the n sky out over .... Job 26:7
the people in the n kingdoms," .... Je 1:15
from the n land and from all .... Je 16:15
across from the n gateway like .... Eze 40:23
have one share at the n border. .... Eze 48:1
This will be Dan's n border from .... Eze 48:1
of soldiers from the n army, ... Da 11:12
enough to stop the n army. .... Da 11:15

NORTHWEST
He went to N Mesopotamia to .... Ge 24:10
who came from N Mesopotamia. .... Ge 25:20
father, in N Mesopotamia. .... Ge 28:2

NOSE

sent Jacob to N Mesopotamia, ... Ge 28:5
and sent him to N Mesopotamia to............ Ge 28:6
and had gone to N Mesopotamia. .... Ge 28:7
while he lived in N Mesopotamia. .... Ge 31:18
Jacob left N Mesopotamia and .... Ge 33:18
came back from N Mesopotamia, ... Ge 35:9
who were born in N Mesopotamia............ Ge 35:26
and Jacob born in N Mesopotamia, ... Ge 46:15
When I came from N Mesopotamia, ... Ge 48:7
from Pethor in N Mesopotamia, ... Dt 23:4
king of N Mesopotamia to rule .... Jdg 3:8
king of N Mesopotamia. .... Jdg 3:10
drivers from N Mesopotamia,.................. 1Ch 19:6
Arameans of N Mesopotamia and .... Ps 59:17
fled to N Mesopotamia where.................. Hos 12:12
which faced southwest and n................... Ac 27:12

NOSE

breath of life into the man's n, ... Ge 2:7
the ring in her n and the .... Ge 24:47
it until it comes out your n,..................... Nu 11:20
came out of his n, and burning 2Sa 22:9
The wind blew from his n. 2Sa 22:16
my hook in your n and my bit in 2Ki 19:28
God's breath of life is in my n, ... Job 27:3
Can anyone put hooks in its n? .... Job 40:24
through its n or a hook in its .... Job 41:2
pours out of its n, as if coming .... Job 41:20
came out of his n, and burning .... Ps 18:8
The wind blew from your n. .... Ps 18:15
Your n is like the mountain of .... Sng 7:4
their signet rings, n rings, ... Is 3:21
my hook in your n and my bit in .... Is 37:29
people are like smoke in my n. .... Is 65:5
a ring in your n, earrings in .... Eze 16:12

NOSES

They have n, but they cannot .... Ps 115:6
and twisting n makes them bleed, ... Pr 30:33
will cut off your n and ears. .... Eze 23:25

NOTE

is what was written on it: N: .... Ezr 6:2
he sees evil, he takes n of it. .... Job 11:11
He will n, "This person was born .... Ps 87:6
letter, then take n of them. 2Th 3:14

NOTES

do not make clear musical n, ... 1Co 14:7

NOTICE

God will take n of you and will .... Nu 10:9
have you been so kind to n me?" .... Ru 2:10
look at you or n you if............................ 2Ki 3:14
and that he doesn't n evil. .... Job 35:15
Stop and n God's miracles....................... Job 37:14
N how strong they are. .... Ps 48:13
N what comes from their mouths. .... Ps 59:7
the God of Jacob doesn't n." .... Ps 94:7
n the food that is in front of .... Pr 23:1
what's in your mind, will n. .... Pr 24:12
The LORD will n and be .... Pr 24:18
has done or n the work of his .... Is 5:12
beauty or form to make us n him; .... Is 53:2
hated, and we didn't even n him. .... Is 53:3
honor you, but you didn't n.'" .... Is 58:3
for you, and you will not n it." .... Ob 1:7
Why do you n the little piece of .... Mt 7:3
but you don't n the big piece of .... Mt 7:3
so that people will n you. .... Mt 23:14
Why do you n the little piece of .... Lk 6:41
but you don't n the big piece of .... Lk 6:41

NOTICED

Then Jacob n that Laban was not .... Ge 31:2
Blessed be whoever n you!" .... Ru 2:19
Have you n my servant Job? .... Job 1:8

Have you n my servant Job? .... Job 2:3
I have n that people who plow .... Job 4:8
without being n, they die and .... Job 4:20
I n one of them had no wisdom. .... Pr 7:7
He has n my sins; they are tied .... La 1:14
Then I n that from the waist up .... Eze 1:27
When Jesus n that some of the .... Lk 14:7

NOTICES

If your father n I am gone, ... 1Sa 20:6

NOWHERE

the same pattern, going n. .... Ec 1:6
goodness is n to be found. .... Is 59:9

NUBIAN

Libyan and N people will obey .... Da 11:43

NUGGETS

Throw your gold n into the dust .... Job 22:24

NUMBER

ones so that you may grow in n............... Ge 1:22
birds grow in n on the earth.".................. Ge 1:22
many children and grow in n................... Ge 1:28
The n of people on earth began .... Ge 6:1
so that they might grow in n." .... Ge 8:17
grow in n and fill the earth. .... Ge 9:1
to grow in n on the earth, ... Ge 9:7
and grow in n as a nation. .... Ge 35:11
So the total n of Jacob's direct .... Ge 46:26
so the total n in the family of .... Ge 46:27
had many children and grew in n. .... Ge 47:27
and their n grew greatly.......................... Ex 1:7
the n of their people will grow .... Ex 1:10
grew in n and spread out. .... Ex 1:12
people continued to grow in n, ... Ex 1:20
the same n of bricks as they .... Ex 5:8
considering the n of people. .... Ex 12:4
as well as a large n of sheep, ... Ex 12:38
to the people when you n them. .... Ex 30:12
count the n of years since the .... Le 25:15
and use that n to decide the .... Le 25:15
count the n of years left for .... Le 25:15
and use that n to decide the .... Le 25:15
That n must be used to decide .... Le 25:27
Use that n to decide the price, ... Le 25:50
out for a certain n of years. .... Le 25:50
you so few in n the roads will.................. Le 26:22
counting the n of years to the.................. Le 27:18
subtract that n from its value.................. Le 27:18
The total n of men was 603,550. .... Nu 1:46
The total n of Israelites in the .... Nu 2:32
The n that was counted was 7,500 .... Nu 3:22
The n that was counted was 6,200 .... Nu 3:34
total n of these men was 8,580. .... Nu 4:48
The total n of animals for the .... Nu 7:87
The total n of animals for the .... Nu 7:88
No one can n the many people of .... Nu 23:10
and the total n of men was .... Nu 26:7
and the total n of men was .... Nu 26:14
and the total n of men was .... Nu 26:18
and the total n of men was .... Nu 26:22
and the total n of men was .... Nu 26:25
and the total n of men was .... Nu 26:27
and the total n of men was .... Nu 26:34
and the total n of men was .... Nu 26:37
and the total n of men was .... Nu 26:41
and the total n of men in the .... Nu 26:43
and the total n of men was .... Nu 26:47
and the total n of men was .... Nu 26:50
So the total n of the men of .... Nu 26:51
these people by the n of names. .... Nu 26:53
depend on the n of its people.................. Nu 26:54
The total n of male Levites one .... Nu 26:62
according to the n required. .... Nu 29:18

according to the **n** required. .... Nu 29:21
according to the **n** required. .... Nu 29:24
according to the **n** required. .... Nu 29:27
according to the **n** required. .... Nu 29:30
according to the **n** required. .... Nu 29:33
according to the **n** required. .... Nu 29:37
but the **n** of cities they give .... Nu 35:8
made you grow in **n** so that there .... Dt 1:10
will make the **n** of your people .... Dt 7:13
animals will grow too many in **n**. .... Dt 7:22
you will live and grow in **n**, ... Dt 8:1
The **n** of lashes should match the .... Dt 25:2
things and made you grow in **n**, ... Dt 28:63
you will live and grow in **n**, ... Dt 30:16
The total **n** of kings was .... Jos 12:24
So the total **n** of towns given to .... Jos 21:40
The **n** of models must match the 1Sa 6:4
must match the **n** of Philistine 1Sa 6:4
The **n** of rats matched the number 1Sa 6:18
rats matched the **n** of towns 1Sa 6:18
tribes, the **n** of Jacob's sons. 1Ki 18:31
Then God's people were few in **n**, ... 1Ch 16:19
so the **n** of the people was not 1Ch 27:24
total **n** of those who returned .... Ezr 2:64
the right **n** of sacrifices for .... Ezr 3:4
everything by **n** and by weight, ... Ezr 8:34
are their names and their **n**: .... Ne 7:61
total **n** of those who returned .... Ne 7:66
On that day the **n** killed in the .... Est 9:11
also had a large **n** of servants. .... Job 1:3
Then God's people were few in **n**, ... Ps 105:12
LORD made his people grow in **n**, ... Ps 105:24
them, and they grew in **n**. .... Ps 107:38
multiplied the **n** of your people; .... Is 26:15
many children and grow in **n**. .... Je 23:3
don't become fewer in **n**. .... Je 29:6
so their **n** will not be small .... Je 30:19
This is the **n** of the people .... Je 52:28
on you for the **n** of days you lie .... Eze 4:4
given you the same **n** of days as .... Eze 4:5
will increase the **n** of people .... Eze 36:10
I will increase the **n** of people .... Eze 36:11
people grow in **n** like a flock. .... Eze 36:37
land and make them grow in **n**. .... Eze 37:26
But the **n** of the Israelites will .... Hos 1:10
Grow in **n** like hopping locusts; .... Nah 3:15
grow in **n** like swarming locusts! .... Nah 3:15
they will grow in **n** as they grew .... Zch 10:8
number as they grew in **n** before. .... Zch 10:8
added to the **n** of believers that .... Ac 2:41
The **n** of followers was growing. .... Ac 6:1
and a great **n** of the Jewish .... Ac 6:7
the **n** of people in Egypt grew .... Ac 7:17
there was a great **n** of people, ... Rev 7:9
the beast or the **n** of its name. .... Rev 13:17
find the meaning of the **n**, ... Rev 13:18
which is the **n** of a person. .... Rev 13:18
of a person. Its **n** is 666. .... Rev 13:18
and over the **n** of his name were .... Rev 15:2

NUMBERED
and even **n** the Israelites. .... Dt 32:8
the servants of Solomon **n** 392. .... Ezr 2:58

NUMBERS
cause their **n** to grow greatly .... Ge 17:20
These are the **n** of the soldiers 1Ch 12:23
destroy great **n** of people in .... Eze 30:10
will destroy great **n** of people .... Eze 30:15
There are huge **n** of people in .... Joe 3:14

NUN
Joshua son of **N**, did not leave .... Ex 33:11
Joshua son of **N** said, "Moses, my .... Nu 11:28

of Ephraim, Hoshea son of **N**; .... Nu 13:8
Hoshea son of **N** the new name .... Nu 13:16
Joshua son of **N** and Caleb son of .... Nu 14:6
and Joshua son of **N** will go .... Nu 14:30
Joshua son of **N** and Caleb son of .... Nu 14:38
Jephunneh and Joshua son of **N**. .... Nu 26:65
Joshua son of **N**, because my .... Nu 27:18
Joshua son of **N** followed the .... Nu 32:12
to Joshua son of **N**, and to the .... Nu 32:28
the priest and Joshua son of **N**. .... Nu 34:17
Joshua son of **N**, will enter it. .... Dt 1:38
this command to Joshua son of **N**: .... Dt 31:23
Moses came with Joshua son of **N**, ... Dt 32:44
Joshua son of **N** was then filled .... Dt 34:9
LORD spoke to Joshua son of **N**, ... Jos 1:1
Joshua son of **N** secretly sent .... Jos 2:1
to Joshua son of **N** and told him .... Jos 2:23
So Joshua son of **N** called the .... Jos 6:6
Joshua son of **N**, and the leaders .... Jos 14:1
to Joshua son of **N** and all the .... Jos 17:4
Joshua son of **N** his land also. .... Jos 19:49
Joshua son of **N**, and the leaders .... Jos 19:51
to Joshua son of **N**, and to the .... Jos 21:1
Joshua son of **N** died at the age .... Jos 24:29
Joshua son of **N**, the servant of .... Jdg 2:8
through Joshua son of **N**, ... 1Ki 16:34
N was Elishama's son, and Joshua 1Ch 7:27
and Joshua was the son of **N**. 1Ch 7:27
the time of Joshua son of **N**. .... Ne 8:17

NURSE
Rebekah and her **n** to go with .... Ge 24:59
Rebekah's **n**, died and was .... Ge 35:8
When Rachel's **n** saw this, she .... Ge 35:17
The **n** tied a red string on his .... Ge 38:28
The **n** said, "So you are able to .... Ge 38:29
Hebrew woman to **n** the baby for .... Ex 2:7
Take this baby and **n** him for me, ... Ex 2:9
my arms as a **n** carries a baby? .... Nu 11:12
at home to **n** her son until he 1Sa 1:23
Mephibosheth's **n** had picked him 2Sa 4:4
Joash and his **n** in a bedroom to 2Ki 11:2
put him and his **n** in a bedroom 2Ch 22:11
no longer **n** at their mother's .... Is 28:9
and who have no babies to **n**.' .... Lk 23:29

NURSED
woman took her baby and **n** him. .... Ex 2:9
as a child is **n** by its mother. .... Is 66:11
you will be **n** and held in my .... Is 66:12
gave birth to you and **n** you." .... Lk 11:27

NURSES
Two Hebrew **n**, named Shiphrah and .... Ex 1:15
The king of Egypt said to the **n**, ... Ex 1:15
the **n** feared God, so they did .... Ex 1:17
Egypt sent for the **n** and said, ... Ex 1:18
The **n** said to him, "The Hebrew .... Ex 1:19
God was good to the **n**. .... Ex 1:20
Because the **n** feared God, he .... Ex 1:21
a woman forget the baby she **n**? .... Is 49:15

NURSING
Gomer had stopped **n** Lo-Ruhamah, ... Hos 1:8
are pregnant or have **n** babies! .... Mt 24:19
are pregnant or have **n** babies! .... Mk 13:17
are pregnant or have **n** babies! .... Lk 21:23

NUT
the orchard of **n** trees to see .... Sng 6:11

NUTS
myrrh, pistachio **n**, and almonds. .... Ge 43:11

NYMPHA
And greet **N** and the church that .... Col 4:15

N

O

OAK
it up under the **o** tree near the ....Jos 24:26
will be like an **o** tree whose ....Is 6:13

OAKS
s voice shakes the **o** and strips ....Ps 29:9
the hills, under **o**, poplars, and ....Hos 4:13
cedar trees and as strong as **o**—..............Am 2:9
Cry, **o** in Bashan, because the.................Zch 11:2

OARS
They made your **o** from oak trees ....Eze 27:6
and Arvad used **o** to row you.................Eze 27:8

OATH
I will keep the **o** I made to ....Ge 26:3
Let us swear an **o** to each other...............Ge 26:28
men swore an **o** to each other. ....Ge 26:31
with an **o** to them and said ....Ex 32:13
promised with an **o** to give to ....Ex 33:1
make her take an **o** and ask her,..............Nu 5:19
the curse that the **o** will bring—...............Nu 5:21
he was angry and made an **o**,.................Dt 1:34
keeping this **o** you have made us ....Jos 2:17
from the **o** you made us swear. ....Jos 2:20
Then Joshua made this **o**: ....Jos 6:26
Israelites swore an **o** to keep ....Jos 9:15
breaking the **o** we swore to them. ....Jos 9:20
had made an **o** for all of them 1Sa 14:24
they were afraid of the **o**. 1Sa 14:26
had not heard the **o** Saul had put 1Sa 14:27
Your father made an **o** for all 1Sa 14:28
David took an **o**, saying, "Your 1Sa 20:3
If he swears an **o** that he is not 1Ki 8:31
If he swears an **o** that he is not 2Ch 6:22
leaders take an **o** to do what ....Ne 5:12
rest of the people took an **o**. ....Ne 10:28
leading men in taking an **o**, ...Ne 10:29
curse in case they broke the **o**. ....Ne 10:29
He made an **o** to the LORD, a ....Ps 132:2
him, forcing him to take an **o**.................Eze 17:13
and lying under **o**, those who ....Mal 3:5
I tell you, never swear an **o**. ....Mt 5:34
Don't swear an **o** using the name ....Mt 5:34
Don't swear an **o** using the name ....Mt 5:35
Don't swear an **o** using the name ....Mt 5:35
promised with an **o** to give her ....Mt 14:7
and they took an **o** not to eat or ....Ac 23:12
We have taken an **o** not to eat or ....Ac 23:14
have all taken an **o** not to eat ....Ac 23:21
The **o** proves that what they say ....Heb 6:16
never change, so he made an **o**. ....Heb 6:17
cannot lie when he makes an **o**. ....Heb 6:18
that God did this with an **o**. ....Heb 7:20
became priests without an **o**, ...Heb 7:20
became a priest with God's **o**................Heb 7:21
word of God's **o** came later than...............Heb 7:28
do not use an **o** when you make a ....Jam 5:12

OBADIAH
Ahab sent for **O**, who was in 1Ki 18:3
O hid a hundred of them in two 1Ki 18:4
This is the vision of **O**. ....Ob 1:1

OBAL
O, Abimael, Sheba, ...Ge 10:28
O, Abimael, Sheba, ...1Ch 1:22

OBED
Boaz, who was the father of **O**. ....Ru 4:21
Boaz was the father of **O**. ....Mt 1:5

OBED'S
of Obed. (**O** mother was Ruth. ....Mt 1:5

OBED-EDOM
he took it to the house of **O**, ...2Sa 6:10
the LORD blessed **O** and all his 2Sa 6:11

OBEDIENCE
sacrifices or **o** to his voice?....................1Sa 15:22
learned **o** by what he suffered. ....Heb 5:8
And because his **o** was perfect, ...Heb 5:9
Now that your **o** to the truth has 1Pe 1:22

OBEDIENT
and right and **o** before the LORD 2Ch 31:20
now you are not **o** when you do ....Ne 13:27
give them an **o** heart of flesh. ....Eze 11:19
will give you **o** hearts of flesh. ....Eze 36:26
you are no more **o** than the....................Mt 5:20
to Nazareth and was **o** to them. ....Lk 2:51
himself and was fully **o** to God, ...Php 2:8
that you are **o** children of God 1Pe 1:14
continues to be **o** to me until ....Rev 2:26

OBEY
So **o** me, my son, and do what I ....Ge 27:8
should I **o** him and let Israel ....Ex 5:2
So now if you **o** me and keep my ....Ex 19:5
to the LORD your God and **o** him, ...Dt 4:30
If you carefully **o** the commands ....Dt 11:13
bless you if you **o** the LORD your ....Dt 15:5
our God, and we will **o** him." ....Jos 24:24
You must **o** his word and not turn 1Sa 12:14
It is better to **o** than to 1Sa 15:22
O me, and I will be your God and ....Je 7:23
them to **o** the agreement, ...Je 11:8
If you don't **o** me, I will start ....Je 17:27
love you and **o** your commands. ....Da 9:4
the wind and the waves **o** him!" ....Mt 8:27
evil spirits, and they **o** him." ....Mk 1:27
We must **o** God, not human ....Ac 5:29
God has given to all who **o** him, ...Ac 5:32
did not want to **o** Moses.......................Ac 7:39
It is those who **o** the law who ....Rm 2:13
like slaves to **o** someone, ...Rm 6:16
The person you **o** is your master. ....Rm 6:16
o your parents as the Lord wants, ...Eph 6:1
o your parents in all things, ...Col 3:20
o your masters in all things. ....Col 3:22
and who do not **o** the Good News 2Th 1:8
people who do not **o** what we tell you 2Th 3:14
leaders, to **o** them, to be ready ....Tit 3:1
to those who did not **o** him. ....Heb 3:18
salvation to all who **o** him. ....Heb 5:9
O your leaders and act under ....Heb 13:17
do not **o** God's teaching,......................1Pe 3:1
people who do not **o** the Good 1Pe 4:17

OBEYED
be blessed, because you **o** me.'" ....Ge 22:18
your father Abraham **o** me. ....Ge 26:5
have not **o** the LORD our God or ....Da 9:10
who have not **o** God to be ruined ....Da 11:32
you fully **o** the things that you ....Rm 6:17
faith Abraham **o** God's call to go ....Heb 11:8
Sarah **o** Abraham, her husband,..............1Pe 3:6

OBEYING
must not stop **o** the law in any ....Dt 17:20
Follow him by **o** his demands, ...1Ki 2:3
said is right and **o** my laws and 1Ki 11:33
trouble by not **o** the LORD's 1Ki 18:18
done well in **o** what I said was 2Ki 10:30
completely to **o** the LORD your 1Ch 22:19
is **o** my laws and commands now. 1Ch 28:7
of Judah stopped the teachings 2Ch 12:1
When Amaziah stopped **o** the LORD,........2Ch 25:27
of Judah in **o** King Hezekiah 2Ch 30:12
Jerusalem are **o** the Law of your ....Ezr 7:14

more loyal in o your demands. .... Ps 119:5
a pure life? By o your word. .... Ps 119:9
I enjoy o your demands, and I .... Ps 119:16
your teachings, o them with all .... Ps 119:34
I enjoy o your commands, which I .... Ps 119:47
left me and quit o my teaching. .... Je 16:11
I see it doing evil by not o me, ... Je 18:10
who stopped o me when Israel .... Eze 44:10
who have stopped o the holy .... Da 11:30
will be ashamed for not o. .... Hos 10:6
and live humbly, o your God. .... Mic 6:8
you priests have stopped o me. .... Mal 2:8
those who are not o God back to .... Lk 1:17
faith, not through o the law. .... Rm 3:28
so loving is o all the law. .... Rm 13:10
thing is o God's commands. 1Co 7:19
as people who are o Christ. .... Eph 6:6
not by o rules about foods, ... Heb 13:9
Loving God means o his commands. 1Jn 5:3

OBIL

O, an Ishmaelite, was in charge 1Ch 27:30

OBJECT

twice as much as the o is worth. .... Ex 22:9
think that an o can tell the one .... Is 29:16
up a blasphemous o that brings .... Da 11:31
a blasphemous o that brings .... Da 12:11
a blasphemous o that brings .... Mt 24:15
see 'a blasphemous o that brings .... Mk 13:14
An o should not ask the person .... Rm 9:20

OBJECTS

it over the tent and all its o. .... Nu 19:18
been made into all kinds of o. .... Nu 31:51
up all the gold o Solomon king 2Ki 24:13
all the bronze o used to serve 2Ki 25:14
hundred pounds of silver o, ... Ezr 8:26
all the bronze o used to serve .... Je 52:18
city, I saw the o you worship. .... Ac 17:23

OBOTH

Israelites went and camped at O. .... Nu 21:10
They went from O to Iye Abarim, ... Nu 21:11
They left Punon and camped at O. .... Nu 33:43
They left O and camped at Iye .... Nu 33:44

OBSERVE

You must o their ways and test .... Je 6:27

OBSERVER

my bed, I saw an o, a holy angel .... Da 4:13
you saw an o, a holy angel, ... Da 4:23

OBSERVERS

The o gave this command; .... Da 4:17

OCCUR

not happen; they should never o. .... Eze 16:16

OCRAN

tribe of Asher—Pagiel son of O; .... Nu 1:13
of Asher is Pagiel son of O. .... Nu 2:27
Pagiel son of O was over the .... Nu 10:26

ODED

of God entered Azariah son of O. 2Ch 15:1
Azariah son of O the prophet. 2Ch 15:8
of the LORD named O was there. 2Ch 28:9

OFFER

him there and o him as a whole .... Ge 22:2
You must not o animal blood .... Ex 23:18
you are to o a bull to remove .... Ex 29:36
O one lamb in the morning and .... Ex 29:39
Then he will o the bull for the .... Le 1:6
to the priest and o them as .... Le 17:5
You must not o to the LORD any .... Le 22:22
You must not o any animals like............. Le 22:22
you must not o it to the LORD. .... Le 22:24

must also o one male goat for................. Le 23:19
time you o a lamb as a burnt .... Nu 15:5
the people must o a young bull .... Nu 15:24
O one lamb in the morning and .... Nu 28:4
When you o a bull or sheep as a............... Dt 18:3
o a burnt offering to the LORD." .... Jdg 13:16
to Shiloh to o sacrifices and to 1Sa 1:21
I o you three choices. 2Sa 24:12
to him and o sacrifices to him. 2Ki 17:36
to o sacrifices before the LORD,.............. 1Ch 23:13
Job would o a burnt offering .... Job 1:5
and o a burnt offering for .... Job 42:8
will not o blood to those idols. .... Ps 16:4
will o a sacrifice as a special .... Ps 54:6
before me to o burnt offerings .... Je 33:18
the second day o a male goat .... Eze 43:22
but he must o a sin offering for .... Eze 44:27
The Israelites o sacrifices to .... Hos 8:13
O bread made with yeast as a.................. Am 4:5
If you o me burnt offerings and .... Am 5:22
Whatever they o at the altar is .... Hag 2:14
his flock and promises to o it,................. Mal 1:14
the priest and o a gift for your .... Lk 5:14
on one cheek, o him the other .... Lk 6:29
God for them to o gifts and.................... Heb 5:1
high priest must o sacrifices .... Heb 5:3
who had to o sacrifices every .... Heb 7:27
must also o something to God. .... Heb 8:3
Christ did not o himself many .... Heb 9:25
time, not to o himself for sin, ... Heb 9:28
under the law o the same .... Heb 10:1
was ready to o his own son as .... Heb 11:17
Jesus let us always o to God our.............. Heb 13:15
be holy priests who o spiritual 1Pe 2:5
much incense to o with the.................... Rev 8:3

OFFERED

o it as a whole burnt offering .... Ge 22:13
animal and o it as a sacrifice .... Ge 31:54
be eaten the same day it is o; .... Le 7:15
the sacrifices o by fire to the .... Le 10:12
that must be o each month .... Nu 28:14
on a rock and o some grain as .... Jdg 13:19
of Beth Shemesh o whole burnt 1Sa 6:15
David o whole burnt offerings 2Sa 6:17
He o a thousand burnt offerings............... 1Ki 3:4
people o many sacrifices that .... Ne 12:43
o my cheeks to those who pulled .... Is 50:6
of Jerusalem o sacrifices to.................... Je 32:29
where they o sweet-smelling .... Eze 6:13
children and o them up in fire .... Eze 16:21
they o a sacrifice to the LORD .... Jnh 1:16
So he o the apostles money, ... Ac 8:18
food that has been o to idols, ... Ac 15:20
food that has been o to idols, ... Ac 15:29
food that has been o to idols, ... Ac 21:25
part of what is o at the altar. 1Co 9:13
to idols is o to demons, ... 1Co 10:20
Christ o his sacrifice only once .... Heb 7:27
for all time when he o himself. .... Heb 7:27
which he o to God for himself .... Heb 9:7
and sacrifices o cannot make .... Heb 9:9
He o himself through the eternal .... Heb 9:14
so Christ was o as a sacrifice .... Heb 9:28
But after Christ o one sacrifice .... Heb 10:12
faith Abel o God a better................. Heb 11:4
the gifts Abel o and called Abel .... Heb 11:4
o his son Isaac as a sacrifice. .... Heb 11:17

OFFERING

him as a whole burnt o on one of .... Ge 22:2
it as a whole burnt o to God, ... Ge 22:13
poured a drink o and olive oil................. Ge 35:14
This is an o to take away sin. .... Ex 29:14

O

it is a burnt **o** made by fire to .... Ex 29:18
them as an **o** to the LORD. .... Ex 29:24
it before the LORD as an **o**. .... Ex 29:26
a quart of wine as a drink **o**. .... Ex 29:40
the same grain **o** and drink.................... Ex 29:41
things as an **o** to the LORD every .... Ex 29:42
this altar for **o** any other..................... Ex 30:9
of grain offering, or drink **o**. .... Ex 30:9
altar of burnt **o** and its bronze .... Ex 35:16
'When you bring an **o** to the LORD, ... Le 1:2
the whole burnt **o** for the LORD .... Le 1:14
offers a grain **o** to the LORD, ... Le 2:1
the fellowship **o** he must make .... Le 3:3
If a person's **o** is a goat, ... Le 3:12
a sin **o** for the sin he has done. .... Le 4:3
fat from the bull of the sin **o—** .... Le 4:8
blood of the sin **o** on his finger .... Le 4:25
corners of the altar of burnt **o**. .... Le 4:25
must bring an **o** to the LORD as .... Le 5:6
second bird as a whole burnt **o**, ... Le 5:10
be his penalty **o** to the LORD.................. Le 5:15
from the burnt **o** on the altar .... Le 6:10
the teachings about the grain **o:** .... Le 6:14
along with his fellowship **o**, ... Le 7:13
a fellowship **o** just to give a .... Le 7:16
the fellowship **o** that belongs to .... Le 7:20
Aaron brought the **o** that was for .... Le 9:15
of the fellowship **o** that was .... Le 10:14
was part of the **o** made by fire, ... Le 10:15
oil for a grain **o** and two-thirds .... Le 14:10
blood of the penalty **o** and put .... Le 14:14
bull for a sin **o** and a male .... Le 16:3
male sheep for a whole burnt **o**. .... Le 16:3
goats for a sin **o** and one male .... Le 16:5
goat of the sin **o** for the people .... Le 16:15
a fellowship **o** to the LORD, ... Le 19:5
family may eat the holy **o**. .... Le 22:10
You must also offer a grain **o—** .... Le 23:13
an **o** made by fire to the LORD. .... Le 24:7
also take an **o** for her of two .... Nu 5:15
this is a grain **o** for jealousy, ... Nu 5:15
it, as a burnt **o**, a year-old .... Nu 6:14
sacrifice of the fellowship **o**. .... Nu 6:18
the fellowship **o** was twenty-four .... Nu 7:88
is the burnt **o** for every Sabbath .... Nu 28:10
give a grain **o** with each lamb................. Nu 28:13
food for the **o** made by fire each.......... Nu 28:24
the daily burnt **o** and its drink .... Nu 28:24
Bring this burnt **o** to the LORD: .... Nu 28:27
goat for a sin **o** to remove your .... Nu 29:5
Offer one male goat as a sin **o**. .... Nu 29:11
I am **o** you life or death, ... Dt 30:19
you as a burnt **o** the first thing .... Jdg 11:31
to the person **o** sacrifices and................. 1Sa 2:15
be removed by sacrifice or **o**.'" 1Sa 3:14
the penalty **o** in a box beside 1Sa 6:8
people continued **o** sacrifices 1Ki 22:43
him as a burnt **o** on the wall. 2Ki 3:27
For a sin **o** there were twelve .... Ezr 8:35
offer a burnt **o** for yourselves. .... Job 42:8
Give an **o** to show thanks to God. .... Ps 50:14
the LORD more than **o** him cattle, ... Ps 69:31
Bring an **o** and come into his .... Ps 96:8
give you an **o** to show thanks .... Ps 116:17
people as an **o** to the LORD. .... Is 34:5
LORD made his life a penalty **o**,............. Is 53:10
of cut stone for the burnt **o**. .... Eze 40:42
wrong with it for a sin **o**. .... Eze 43:22
give this special **o** to the ruler............. Eze 45:16
blood from this sin **o** and put it .... Eze 45:19
male goat every day as a sin **o**. .... Eze 45:23
offer a grain **o** with the lamb .... Eze 46:14
that an **o** and incense be...................... Da 2:46

the people from **o** the daily...................... Da 11:31
to Jesus and **o** him some vinegar. .... Lk 23:36
think they are **o** service to God. .... Jn 16:2
the crowd from **o** sacrifices to .... Ac 14:18
the last day an **o** would be given .... Ac 21:26
his Son to be an **o** for sin, ... Rm 8:3
Your **o** must be only for God and .... Rm 12:1
could be an **o** that God would................. Rm 15:16
an **o** made holy by the Holy .... Rm 15:16
my body as an **o** to be burned. 1Co 13:3
Our **o** to God is this: 2Co 2:15
sweet-smelling **o** and sacrifice .... Eph 5:2
is being given as an **o** to God,............... 2Ti 4:6
has the work of **o** gifts and .... Heb 8:3
the law by **o** gifts to God. .... Heb 8:4
often **o** the same sacrifices..................... Heb 10:11
angel put this **o** on the golden .... Rev 8:3

OFFERINGS

them on the altar as **o** to God. .... Ge 8:20
whole burnt **o** and fellowship .... Ex 20:24
whole burnt **o** and to sacrifice .... Ex 24:5
part of the **o** made by fire to .... Le 2:3
the fat of the fellowship **o**. .... Le 6:12
to bring their **o** to the LORD in .... Le 7:38
share of the **o** for you and your .... Le 10:15
with their grain **o** and drink .... Le 23:18
when you bring **o** made by fire to .... Le 23:37
over your burnt **o** and fellowship .... Nu 10:10
for the **o** given to me. .... Nu 18:8
give you the **o** the Israelites .... Nu 18:11
your burnt **o**, grain offerings, ... Nu 29:39
grain **o**, drink offerings .... Nu 29:39
your burnt **o** and sacrifices, ... Dt 12:11
whole burnt **o** and made 1Sa 6:15
burnt **o** and sacrifices or 1Sa 15:22
from the penalty **o** and sin 2Ki 12:16
a thousand burnt **o** on it........................ 2Ch 1:6
all the animals for the burnt **o**. 2Ch 29:34
his own animals for the burnt **o**,............. 2Ch 31:3
offered burnt **o** on it to the .... Ezr 3:3
returned made burnt **o** to the God .... Ezr 8:35
all your **o** and accept all .... Ps 20:3
to your Temple with burnt **o**. .... Ps 66:13
will bring you **o** of fat animals .... Ps 66:15
pour out drink **o** to other gods .... Je 7:18
and gave drink **o** to gods.'"................... Je 19:13
me to offer burnt **o** and grain .... Je 33:18
bringing grain **o** and incense to .... Je 41:5
brought **o** that made me angry .... Eze 20:28
LORD will eat the most holy **o**. .... Eze 42:13
to supply the burnt **o**, ... Eze 45:17
me more than I want burnt **o**.................. Hos 6:6
you offer me burnt **o** and grain .... Am 5:22
me sacrifices and **o** while you................. Am 5:25
I come before him with burnt **o**, ... Mic 6:6
robbed me in your **o** and the .... Mal 3:8
me sacrifices and **o** while you................. Ac 7:42
do not want sacrifices and **o**, ... Heb 10:5
ask for burnt **o** and offerings to .... Heb 10:6
do not want sacrifices and **o**. .... Heb 10:8

OFFERS

When anyone **o** a grain offering............... Le 2:1
If he **o** a lamb, he must bring it .... Le 3:7
priest who **o** the sin offering .... Le 6:26
The priest who **o** the sacrifice................. Le 7:7
The priest who **o** the burnt .... Le 7:8
belongs to the priest who **o** it................... Le 7:9
be eaten the same day he **o** it................. Le 7:16
the priest who **o** the blood and .... Le 7:33
living with you **o** a burnt .... Le 17:8
because he **o** up the food of your .... Le 21:8
his family group **o** a sacrifice.' 1Sa 20:6

OFFICER

hand wisdom o you a long life, ... Pr 3:16
enemy o sacrifices to his net .... Hab 1:16
everyone who o sacrifices will .... Zch 14:21
but then he o to the Lord an .... Mal 1:14
Place where he o this blood for .... Heb 13:11

OFFICER

an o to the king of Egypt and .... Ge 37:36
king chose the o who was close 2Ki 7:17
Ahitub was the o responsible for 1Ch 9:11
leading priest's o would come 2Ch 24:11
the o might throw you into jail. .... Lk 12:58

OFFICER'S

getting near the o house when .... Lk 7:6

OFFICERS

also appoint o over the land, ... Ge 41:34
Moses was angry with the army o, ... Nu 31:14
made them o over your tribes. .... Dt 1:15
judges, and o for your tribes .... Dt 16:18
orders to the o of the people: .... Jos 1:10
The elders, o, judges, and all .... Jos 8:33
judges, and o of Israel. .... Jos 23:2
and o of Israel to stand before .... Jos 24:1
The o and trumpeters were 2Ki 11:14
as secretaries, o, and 2Ch 34:13
their kings and o, their priests .... Je 32:32
the Roman o sent the police to .... Ac 16:35

OFFICIALS

people and o are very lucky, ... 2Ch 9:7

OG

O king of Bashan and his whole .... Nu 21:33
Only O king of Bashan was left .... Dt 3:11
what he did to Sihon and O, ... Dt 31:4
the Amorites, O king of Bashan, ... Ps 135:11
He defeated O king of Bashan. .... Ps 136:20

OG'S

we captured all of O cities, ... Dt 3:4
of Argob, O kingdom in Bashan. .... Dt 3:4
towns in O kingdom of Bashan. .... Dt 3:10

OHAD

Jemuel, Jamin, O, Jakin, Zohar, ... Ge 46:10
Jemuel, Jamin, O, Jakin, Zohar, ... Ex 6:15

OHEL

Hashubah, O, Berekiah, Hasadiah, ... 1Ch 3:20

OHOLAH

The older girl was named O, ... Eze 23:4
O is Samaria, and Oholibah is .... Eze 23:4

OHOLIAB

also chosen O son of Ahisamach .... Ex 31:6
LORD has given Bezalel and O, ... Ex 35:34
So Bezalel, O, and every skilled .... Ex 36:1
called Bezalel, O, and all the .... Ex 36:2
O son of Ahisamach of the tribe .... Ex 38:23

OHOLIBAH

and her sister was named O. .... Eze 23:4
is Samaria, and O is Jerusalem. .... Eze 23:4

OHOLIBAMAH

and O daughter of Anah, the son .... Ge 36:2
and O gave him Jeush, Jalam, and .... Ge 36:5
third wife was O the daughter of .... Ge 36:14
Esau and O gave birth to Jeush, ... Ge 36:14
Esau's wife O gave birth to .... Ge 36:18
from Esau's wife O the daughter .... Ge 36:18
were Dishon and O daughter of .... Ge 36:25
O, Elah, Pinon, ... Ge 36:41
O, Elah, Pinon, ... 1Ch 1:52

OIL

poured olive o on the top of it. .... Ge 28:18
olive o to burn in the lamps; .... Ex 25:6
the special olive o poured on a .... Ex 25:6
mixed with olive o, and wafers .... Ex 29:2
take four quarts of olive o, ... Ex 30:24
the holy olive o for appointing .... Ex 37:29
must be mixed with o and cooked .... Le 6:21
hand into the o that is in his .... Le 14:16
for the o used in the lamps. .... Nu 4:9
like bread baked with olive o, ... Nu 11:8
had the holy o poured on him. .... Nu 35:25
give you grain, new wine, and o. .... Dt 7:13
bringing o from the solid rock. .... Dt 32:13
him bathe his feet in olive o. .... Dt 33:24
and gods are honored by my o. .... Jdg 9:9
a jar of olive o and poured it 1Sa 10:1
container with olive o and go. 1Sa 16:1
will no longer be rubbed with o. 2Sa 1:21
only a little olive o in a jug. 1Ki 17:12
Then the o stopped flowing. 2Ki 4:6
sell the o and pay what you owe. 2Ki 4:7
poured the olive o on Jehu's 2Ki 9:6
wheat, barley, o, and wine you 2Ch 2:15
and o to the cities of Sidon and .... Ezr 3:7
money, grain, new wine, and o." .... Ne 5:11
trees, and our new wine and o. .... Ne 10:37
was treated with o and myrrh and .... Est 2:12
rocks poured out olive o for me. .... Job 29:6
You pour o of blessing on my .... Ps 23:5
His words are smoother than o, ... Ps 55:21
hearts and olive o that makes .... Ps 104:15
water and using olive o. .... Ps 109:18
It is like perfumed o poured on .... Ps 133:2
trying to grab o in your hand. .... Pr 27:16
and the o of gladness to replace .... Is 61:3
grain, new wine, o, young sheep, ... Je 31:12
to run as smoothly as olive o, ... Eze 32:14
offerings, and the olive o. .... Eze 45:25
and flax, wine and olive o.' .... Hos 2:5
gave her grain, new wine, and o. .... Hos 2:8
send a gift of olive o to Egypt. .... Hos 12:1
up, and the olive o runs out. .... Joe 1:10
with ten thousand rivers of o? .... Mic 6:7
the olive o flows to the lamps? .... Zch 4:12
their lamps and more o in jars. .... Mt 25:4
out and put olive o on many sick .... Mk 6:13
You did not put o on my head, ... Lk 7:46
poured olive o and wine on his .... Lk 10:34
hundred gallons of olive o.' .... Lk 16:6
for and pour o on the person .... Jam 5:14
damage the olive o and wine!" .... Rev 6:6
olive o, fine flour, wheat, ... Rev 18:13

OILS

You have poured fine o on me. .... Ps 92:10
of perfume and o is pleasant, ... Pr 27:9
You use your o and perfumes to .... Is 57:9

OLD

and will be buried at an o age. .... Ge 15:15
Abram was ninety-nine years o, ... Ge 17:1
Abraham and Sarah were very o. .... Ge 18:11
the younger, "Our father is o. .... Ge 19:31
a son for Abraham in his o age. .... Ge 21:2
he was eight days o as God had .... Ge 21:4
breath and died at an o age, ... Ge 25:8
a young man, seventeen years o. .... Ge 37:2
he was one hundred ten years o. .... Ge 50:26
was eighty years o and Aaron was .... Ex 7:7
is twenty years o or older must .... Ex 30:14
to sixty years o is about one .... Le 27:3
to twenty years o is about eight .... Le 27:5
to five years o is about two .... Le 27:6
male one month o or older." .... Nu 3:15
from thirty to fifty years o, ... Nu 4:3
twenty-five years o or older .... Nu 8:24

Remember the o days. Think of .... Dt 32:7
twenty years o when he died. .... Dt 34:7
They put o sandals on their feet .... Jos 9:5
their feet and wore o clothes, ... Jos 9:5
He said, "I am now very o. .... Jos 23:2
I am too o to have another .... Ru 1:12
of you in your o age because of .... Ru 4:15
Eli was very o. He heard about 1Sa 2:22
to him, "You're o, and your sons 1Sa 8:5
An o man wearing a coat is 1Sa 28:14
was forty years o when he became......... 2Sa 2:10
this time King David was very o, ... 1Ki 1:1
As Solomon grew o, his wives 1Ki 11:4
Now an o prophet was living in 1Ki 13:11
David had lived long and was o,.............. 1Ch 23:1
David died when he was o...................... 1Ch 29:28
twenty years o and older were 2Ch 31:17
its roots grow o in the ground, ... Job 14:8
to stay on the o path where evil .... Job 22:15
he was o and had lived many .... Job 42:17
and now I am o, but I have never .... Ps 37:25
Even though I am o and gray,................. Ps 71:18
your way through these o ruins; .... Ps 74:3
keep thinking about the o days, ... Ps 77:5
When they are o, they will still .... Ps 92:14
book before I was one day o. .... Ps 139:16
men and women, o people and .... Ps 148:12
O people are proud of their.................... Pr 17:6
when they are o, they will not .... Pr 22:6
your mother when she is o..................... Pr 23:22
O people and young people will .... Is 20:4
Even when you are o, I will be .... Is 46:4
become useless like o clothes; .... Is 50:9
will rebuild the o ruins and.................... Is 61:4
the young men and o men also. .... Je 31:13
People young and o lie outside .... La 2:21
your o men will dream dreams, ... Joe 2:28
He comes from very o times, ... Mic 5:2
who were two years o or younger. .... Mt 2:16
cloth over a hole in an o coat................. Mt 9:16
new wine into o leather bags................. Mt 9:17
new things and o things he has .... Mt 13:52
I am an o man, and my wife is .... Lk 1:18
with a son though she is very o. .... Lk 1:36
When he was twelve years o, ... Lk 2:42
about twelve years o, was dying. .... Lk 8:42
But if a person is already o, ... Jn 3:4
You are not even fifty years o." .... Jn 8:57
But when you are o, you will put .... Jn 21:18
your o men will dream dreams. .... Ac 2:17
know that our o life died with .... Rm 6:6
Take out all the o yeast so that 1Co 5:7
when they read the o agreement. 2Co 3:14
creation. The o things have gone 2Co 5:17
taught to leave your o self— .... Eph 4:22
Your o sinful self has died, ... Col 3:3
must be at least sixty years o................. 1Ti 5:9
has made the first agreement o. .... Heb 8:13
poor person comes in wearing o, ... Jam 2:2
to you but an o command you have 1Jn 2:7
He is that o snake called the .... Rev 12:9
that o snake who is the devil .... Rev 20:2

OLDER

the o will serve the younger. .... Ge 25:23
the o son said to his father,.................... Lk 15:25
not speak angrily to an o man, ... 1Ti 5:1
o women like mothers, and..................... 1Ti 5:2
Teach o men to be .... Tit 2:2

OLDEST

Abraham said to his o servant, ... Ge 24:2
going from the o brother to the .... Ge 44:12
Nadab, the o, Abihu, Eleazar, ... Nu 3:2

His three o sons followed Saul 1Sa 17:13
at the o brother's house. .... Job 1:13

OLIVE

him with a fresh o leaf in its .... Ge 8:11
and your orchards of o trees. .... Ex 23:11
vineyards and o trees you did................ Dt 6:11
you beat your o trees to knock .... Dt 24:20
They said to the o tree, 'You be .... Jdg 9:8
creatures from o wood and placed 1Ki 6:23
branches from o and wild olive .... Ne 8:15
But I am like an o tree growing .... Ps 52:8
will also be like the o harvest, ... Is 17:6
will be like an o tree after .... Is 24:13
are the two o branches beside .... Zch 4:12
branches from an o tree have .... Rm 11:17
from a wild o tree and joined .... Rm 11:24
are the two o trees and the two .... Rev 11:4

OLIVES

made from pressed o, to keep the .... Ex 27:20
David went up the Mount of O, ... 2Sa 15:30
step on your o, but you won't .... Mic 6:15
he will stand on the Mount of O, ... Zch 14:4
the hill called the Mount of O. .... Mt 21:1
they went out to the Mount of O. .... Mt 26:30
was sitting on the Mount of O, ... Mk 13:3
a fig tree make o, or can a .... Jam 3:12

OLYMPAS

his sister, and O, and to all .... Rm 16:15

OMAR

O, Zepho, Gatam, and Kenaz.................. Ge 36:11
leaders: Teman, O, Zepho, Kenaz, ... Ge 36:15
were Teman, O, Zepho, Gatam, ... 1Ch 1:36

OMEGA

I am the Alpha and the O. .... Rev 1:8
Alpha and the O, the Beginning .... Rev 21:6
the Alpha and the O, the First .... Rev 22:13

OMRI

day in the camp they made O, ... 1Ki 16:16
So O and all the Israelite army 1Ki 16:17
while the other half wanted O. 1Ki 16:21
Tibni died, and O became king. 1Ki 16:22
O became king of Israel during 1Ki 16:23
O ruled Israel for twelve years, ... 1Ki 16:23
O built a city on that hill and 1Ki 16:24
But O did what the LORD said was 1Ki 16:25
and O sinned in the same way as 1Ki 16:26
Everything else O did and all 1Ki 16:27
So O died and was buried in 1Ki 16:28
Ahab son of O became king of 1Ki 16:29
Ahab son of O did many things 1Ki 16:30
of O king of Israel. 2Ki 8:26
Elioenai, O, Jeremoth, Abijah................. 1Ch 7:8
Omri's son. O was Imri's son. 1Ch 9:4
O son of Michael was over the 1Ch 27:18
Athaliah, a granddaughter of O............... 2Ch 22:2
laws of King O and do all the .... Mic 6:16

OMRI'S

O followers were stronger than 1Ki 16:22
Ammihud was O son. Omri was............... 1Ch 9:4

ONAM

Manahath, Ebal, Shepho, and O. .... Ge 36:23
Manahath, Ebal, Shepho, and O. 1Ch 1:40
She was the mother of O. 1Ch 2:26

ONAM'S

O sons were Shammai and Jada. 1Ch 2:28

ONAN

to another son and named him O. .... Ge 38:4
Judah said to Er's brother O, ... Ge 38:8
But O knew that the children .... Ge 38:9

by this wicked thing O had done, ... Ge 38:10
done, so the LORD killed O also. .... Ge 38:10
sons were Er, O, Shelah, Perez, ... Ge 46:12
Er and O had died in the land .... Ge 46:12
sons, Er and O, died in Canaan. .... Nu 26:19
sons were Er, O, and Shelah. 1Ch 2:3

ONCE
will do these things o a year." .... Le 16:34
with your army o a day for six .... Jos 6:3
four corners of the house at o. .... Job 1:19
left alive where they o lived. .... Job 18:19
Sin o used death to rule us, ... Rm 5:21
God o said, "Let the light shine 2Co 4:6
that he o tried to destroy. .... Gal 1:23
We were o like children, slaves .... Gal 4:3
tried to come more than o, ... 1Th 2:18
They were o in God's light, ... Heb 6:4
sacrifice only o and for all .... Heb 7:27
Aaron's rod that o grew leaves, ... Heb 9:4
and he did that only o a year. .... Heb 9:7
the Most Holy Place only o— .... Heb 9:12
Holy Place o every year with .... Heb 9:25
came only o and for all time .... Heb 9:26
everyone must die o and then be .... Heb 9:27
in his body o and for all time .... Heb 10:10
O again I will shake not only .... Heb 12:26
The words "o again" clearly show .... Heb 12:27
himself suffered for sins o. 1Pe 3:18
of God o and for all time. .... Jud 1:3
you saw was o alive but is not .... Rev 17:8
because he was o alive, is not .... Rev 17:8
The beast that was o alive, ... Rev 17:11
times a year, o each month. .... Rev 22:2

ONE-EIGHTH
And they charged o of an ounce 1Sa 13:21

ONE-FIFTH
gold ring weighing o of an ounce .... Ge 24:22
should take o of all the food .... Ge 41:34
you must give o to the king. .... Ge 47:24
O of everything from the land .... Ge 47:26
counted must pay o of an ounce .... Ex 30:13
give more than o of an ounce, ... Ex 30:15
man had to pay o of an ounce .... Ex 38:26
thing, adding o to its value. .... Le 5:16
plus an extra o of the value .... Le 6:5
adding another o of the price of .... Le 22:14
an additional o must be added to .... Le 27:13
an additional o must be added to .... Le 27:15
o must be added to that price, ... Le 27:19
person must add o to that price. .... Le 27:27
o must be added to its price. .... Le 27:31
done, adding o to it, and giving .... Nu 5:7

ONE-FOURTH
about one and o pounds of silver .... Le 27:3
about one and o pounds of silver .... Le 27:16
about three and o pounds, ... Nu 7:85
with one and o quarts of olive .... Nu 15:6
prepare one and o quarts of wine .... Nu 15:7
one and o pounds of silver. .... Dt 22:29
than one and o pounds of gold. .... Jos 7:21
charged about o of an ounce of 1Sa 13:21
for one and o pounds of silver. 2Sa 24:24
about one and o pounds of silver 2Ki 15:20

ONE-HALF
seven and o pounds of silver. .... Ge 45:22
wood, four and o feet high. .... Ex 27:1
seven and o feet long and seven .... Ex 27:1
long and seven and o feet wide. .... Ex 27:1
twenty-two and o feet long, ... Ex 27:14
twenty-two and o feet long, ... Ex 27:15
around it seven and o feet high, ... Ex 27:18

is set by using o of the Holy .... Ex 30:13
seven and o feet long and seven .... Ex 38:1
long and seven and o feet wide— .... Ex 38:1
and it was four and o feet high. .... Ex 38:1
twenty-two and o feet long, ... Ex 38:14
twenty-two and o feet long, ... Ex 38:15
long and seven and o feet high, ... Ex 38:18
one and o ounces of silver. .... Le 27:6
it among the nine and o tribes, ... Nu 34:13
These two and o tribes received .... Nu 34:15
about two and o pounds of silver .... Dt 22:19
was about o bushel of barley. .... Ru 2:17
bull, o bushel of flour, ... 1Sa 1:24
about seven and o pounds and a 2Sa 21:16
were seven and o feet wide. 1Ki 6:6
them were ten and o feet wide. 1Ki 6:6
seven and o feet high and was 1Ki 6:10
wing was seven and o feet long, ... 1Ki 6:24
that were seven and o feet tall, ... 1Ki 7:16
and seven and o feet deep. 1Ki 7:23
wide, and four and o feet high. 1Ki 7:27
seven and o pounds of gold. 1Ki 10:16
was about four and o feet high. 2Ki 25:17
ruled for seven and o years. 1Ch 3:4
about seven and o feet tall and 1Ch 11:23
about seven and o million pounds 1Ch 22:14
was seven and o feet long and 2Ch 3:11
was also seven and o feet long, ... 2Ch 3:11
was also seven and o feet long. 2Ch 3:12
was also seven and o feet long. 2Ch 3:12
and seven and o feet deep. 2Ch 4:2
platform seven and o feet long, ... 2Ch 6:13
long, seven and o feet wide, and 2Ch 6:13
and seven and o feet high, ... 2Ch 6:13
about seven and o pounds of 2Ch 9:15
was about seven and o feet high. .... Je 52:22
hand was ten and o feet long. .... Eze 40:5
which was ten and o feet thick .... Eze 40:5
thick and ten and o feet high. .... Eze 40:5
It was ten and o feet deep. .... Eze 40:6
were ten and o feet long and ten .... Eze 40:7
long and ten and o feet wide. .... Eze 40:7
Temple was ten and o feet deep. .... Eze 40:7
were three and o feet thick. .... Eze 40:9
was seventeen and o feet wide. .... Eze 40:11
were ten and o feet on each side .... Eze 40:12
was eighty-seven and o feet. .... Eze 40:15
was eighty-seven and o feet long .... Eze 40:21
was eighty-seven and o feet long .... Eze 40:25
was eighty-seven and o feet long .... Eze 40:29
was eighty-seven and o feet long .... Eze 40:33
was eighty-seven and o feet long .... Eze 40:36
was twenty-four and o feet wide. .... Eze 40:48
were each ten and o feet thick. .... Eze 41:1
was seventeen and o feet wide. .... Eze 41:2
Each was three and o feet thick. .... Eze 41:3
doorway was ten and o feet wide, ... Eze 41:3
which was ten and o feet thick. .... Eze 41:5
and it was ten and o feet thick. .... Eze 41:8
twenty-two and o feet wide. .... Eze 41:12
fifty-seven and o feet long. .... Eze 41:12
eighty-seven and o feet wide. .... Eze 42:2
seventeen and o feet wide and .... Eze 42:7
for eighty-seven and o feet. .... Eze 42:7
eighty-seven and o feet long, ... Eze 42:8
it measures three and o feet. .... Eze 43:14
twenty-four and o feet long and .... Eze 43:17
and twenty-four and o feet wide. .... Eze 43:17
altar is ten and o inches wide, ... Eze 43:17
is eighty-seven and o feet wide. .... Eze 45:2
about one and o miles wide and .... Eze 45:6
grain offering o bushel for each .... Eze 45:24
each bull and o bushel for each .... Eze 45:24

with the bull and o bushel with .... Eze 46:7
of worship o bushel of grain .... Eze 46:11
and o bushel of grain must be .... Eze 46:11
and fifty-two and o feet wide. .... Eze 46:22
about one and o miles wide and .... Eze 48:15
power for three and o years. .... Da 7:25
after three and o years. .... Da 9:27
will be for three and o years. .... Da 12:7
in Israel for three and o years, ... Lk 4:25
witnesses for three and o days, ... Rev 11:9
But after three and o days, ... Rev 11:11
care of for three and o years, ... Rev 12:14

ONE-TENTH

will give God o of all he gives................ Ge 28:22
two quarts, or o of an ephah. .... Ex 16:36
O of all crops belongs to the .... Le 27:30
That o is holy to the LORD. .... Le 27:30
o of your grain, new wine, or .... Dt 12:17
Be sure to save o of all your .... Dt 14:22
exchange your o for silver. .... Dt 14:25
should bring o of that year's .... Dt 14:28
He will take o of your grain and............... 1Sa 8:15
He will take o of your flocks, ... 1Sa 8:17
I have o of an ounce of silver................ 1Sa 9:8
a large amount, o of everything................ 2Ch 31:5
also brought o of their cattle 2Ch 31:6
and sheep and o of the holy 2Ch 31:6
to the LORD and o of everything 2Ch 31:12
O of the people will be left in .... Is 6:13
and bring o of your crops every .... Am 4:4
You give to God o of everything .... Mt 23:23
give God o of even your mint,................ Lk 11:42
I give o of everything I get!...................... Lk 18:12

ONE-THIRD

it will be one and o quarts, ... Nu 28:14
Joab commanded o of the men. 2Sa 18:2
Burn o with fire in the middle .... Eze 5:2
Then take o and cut it up with .... Eze 5:2
And scatter o to the wind. .... Eze 5:2
give three and o quarts of grain .... Eze 46:14
and one and o quarts of olive .... Eze 46:14
and measured about o of a mile. .... Eze 47:3
measured about o of a mile again .... Eze 47:4
measured about o of a mile again .... Eze 47:4
about o of a mile again, ... Eze 47:5
be gone, and o will be left. .... Zch 13:8

ONE-YEAR-OLD

lamb must be a o male that has .... Ex 12:5
o lambs as a fellowship offering. .... Le 23:19

ONESIMUS

send him with O, a faithful and .... Col 4:9
with you for my child O,........................ Phm 1:10
Maybe O was separated from you .... Phm 1:15
O as you would welcome me. .... Phm 1:17

ONESIPHORUS

show mercy to the family of O, ... 2Ti 1:16
and Aquila and the family of O. 2Ti 4:19

ONIONS

melons, leeks, o, and garlic. .... Nu 11:5

ONO

of Lod, Hadid and O—725; .... Ezr 2:33
in Kephirim on the plain of O." .... Ne 6:2
of Lod, Hadid, and O—721;..................... Ne 7:37
Lod, O, and in the Valley of the .... Ne 11:35

ONTO

officers, and o your people. .... Ex 8:3
the water o the land of Egypt. .... Ex 8:5
frogs came up o the land of .... Ex 8:7
and designs were sewn o it, ... Ex 39:29
If grain falls o the ground, ... Le 19:9

If grain falls o the ground, ... Le 23:22
throw them o the burning cow. .... Nu 19:6
their city and o the roads." .... Jdg 20:32
insides to spill o the ground. 2Sa 20:10
water poured out o the ground, ... Ps 22:14
o the handles of the lock. .... Sng 5:5
Lift them o your shoulders with .... Eze 12:6
You will fall o the ground; .... Eze 29:5
land dropping you o the ground. .... Eze 32:4
door that opened o the porch of .... Eze 40:38
threw up Jonah o the dry land. .... Jnh 2:10
out of the boat and o the shore, ... Jn 21:9

ONWARD

From that time o the people of .... Eze 39:22

ONYCHA

resin, o, galbanum, and pure .... Ex 30:34

ONYX

and o are also found there...................... Ge 2:12
o stones, and other jewels to be .... Ex 25:7
Take two o stones and write the .... Ex 28:9
chrysolite, an o, and a jasper................... Ex 28:20
o stones, and other jewels to be .... Ex 35:9
leaders brought o stones and .... Ex 35:27
around the o stones and then .... Ex 39:6
chrysolite, an o, and a jasper. .... Ex 39:13
of wood and o for the settings 1Ch 29:2
with valuable o or sapphire gems .... Job 28:16
yellow quartz, o, and jasper, ... Eze 28:13
the fifth was o, the sixth was .... Rev 21:20

OPEN

the underground springs split o,............... Ge 7:11
tear the bird o by its wings...................... Le 1:17
and split o their pregnant 2Ki 8:12
the wall—the o places—and I put .... Ne 4:13
Their throats are like o graves; .... Ps 5:9
O wide, your aged doors and the .... Ps 24:9
I do not o my mouth, because you .... Ps 39:9
When you o your hand, they are .... Ps 104:28
O for me the Temple gates...................... Ps 118:19
O my eyes to see the miracles in .... Ps 119:18
O to me, my sister, my darling, ... Sng 5:2
no one will be able to o it. .... Is 22:22
O your eyes, LORD, and see. .... Is 37:17
I will o doors for you so city .... Is 45:1
up, and no one can o them...................... Je 13:19
O your mouth and eat what I am .... Eze 2:8
to you, I will o your mouth, and .... Eze 3:27
I will o your graves and cause .... Eze 37:12
O your eyes and see all the...................... Da 9:18
They ripped o the pregnant women .... Am 1:13
o its mouth and you will find a .... Mt 17:27
Sir, sir, o the door to let .... Mt 25:11
immediately o the door for him................ Lk 12:36
all see heaven o and 'angels of .... Jn 1:51
o your eyes and look at the...................... Jn 4:35
a demon o the eyes of the blind? .... Jn 10:21
his body burst o, and all his .... Ac 1:18
saw that the jail doors were o. .... Ac 16:27
Their throats are like o graves; .... Rm 3:13
O your hearts to us. We have not 2Co 7:2
is clear and lies o before him,.................. Heb 4:13
Place was not o while the system .... Heb 9:8
O your homes to each other, ... 1Pe 4:9
I have put an o door before you,............... Rev 3:8
the seals and o the scroll?" .... Rev 5:2
a small scroll o in his hand. .... Rev 10:2

OPENED

it was as if their eyes were o. .... Ge 3:7
days later Noah o the window he .... Ge 8:6
men staying with Lot o the door, ... Ge 19:10
And Joseph o the storehouses and .... Ge 41:56

The earth o and swallowed them .... Nu 16:32
seven times and o his eyes...................... 2Ki 4:35
clouds above and o the doors of .... Ps 78:23
Then the ground o up and .... Ps 106:17
he never o his mouth. .... Is 53:7
The sky o, and I saw visions of .... Eze 1:1
So I o my mouth, and he gave me .... Eze 3:2
a door that o onto the porch .... Eze 40:38
to begin, and the books were o. .... Da 7:10
Then heaven o, and he saw God's .... Mt 3:16
who knocks will have the door o. .... Mt 7:8
The graves o, and many of God's .... Mt 27:52
This means, "Be o."............................. Mk 7:34
o the book and found the place .... Lk 4:17
Then Jesus o their minds so they .... Lk 24:45
since it was your eyes he o?" .... Jn 9:17
an angel of the Lord o the doors .... Ac 5:19
he never o his mouth. .... Ac 8:32
and have o our hearts to you. 2Co 6:11
while the Lamb o the first of .... Rev 6:1
Then it o up the hole that leads .... Rev 9:2
I saw heaven o, and there before .... Rev 19:11
Then books were o, and the book .... Rev 20:12

OPENING
Make an o around the top of the .... Ge 6:16
Cover the o of the cave with .... Jos 10:18
are covering the o of the cave................ Jos 10:22
and covered the o of the cave .... Jos 10:27
a sheet over the o of the well 2Sa 17:19
The o of the bowl was round, ... 1Ki 7:31
put his hand through the o,.................... Sng 5:4
measured the o of the gateway. .... Eze 40:6
The o of the gateway next to the .... Eze 40:7
went to the o of the blazing .... Da 3:26
placed over the o of the lions'............... Da 6:17
through an o in the city wall .... Ac 9:25
helped the woman by o its mouth .... Rev 12:16

OPENLY
correct someone o than to have .... Pr 27:5
the beginning I have spoken o. .... Is 48:16
prostitution so o that everyone .... Eze 23:18
enough to talk about Jesus o, ... Jn 7:13
longer traveled o among the .... Jn 11:54
said o, "I tell you the truth,.................... Jn 13:21
I have spoken o to everyone. .... Jn 18:20
began to confess o and tell all .... Ac 19:18
to you very o about some things.............. Rm 15:15
take pleasure in o doing evil, ... 2Pe 2:13

OPENS
people, and it o wide its mouth. .... Is 5:14
If he o a door, no one will be .... Is 22:22
and with a stick he o the cumin. .... Is 28:27
-five men where the gate o,.................... Eze 11:1
guards the door o it for him. .... Jn 10:3
When he o a door, no one can .... Rev 3:7

OPHEL
added greatly to the wall at O. 2Ch 27:3
Gate and around the hill of O. 2Ch 33:14
on the hill of O made repairs as .... Ne 3:26
the palace to the wall of O...................... Ne 3:27
servants lived on the hill of O, ... Ne 11:21

OPHIR
O, Havilah, and Jobab. .... Ge 10:29
ships sailed to O and brought.................. 1Ki 9:28
ships brought gold from O,...................... 1Ki 10:11
ships to sail to O for gold. 1Ki 22:48
O, Havilah, and Jobab. 1Ch 1:23
pure gold from O and about five 1Ch 29:4
men to O and brought back 2Ch 8:18
men brought gold from O, ... 2Ch 9:10

right side wearing gold from O. .... Ps 45:9
than there is fine gold in O. .... Is 13:12

OPHNI
Kephar Ammoni, O, and Geba. .... Jos 18:24

OPHRAH
Avvim, Parah, O, ... Jos 18:23
the oak tree at O that belonged .... Jdg 6:11
It still stands at O, where the .... Jdg 6:24
he put in his hometown of O. .... Jdg 8:27
his father, in O, where the .... Jdg 8:32
went to O, the hometown of his .... Jdg 9:5
went on the O road in the land 1Sa 13:17
Meonothai was the father of O. 1Ch 4:14
Roll in the dust at Beth O. .... Mic 1:10

OPINION
you great in the o of all the.................... Jos 3:7
Joshua great in the o of all the .... Jos 4:14
be brought down in my own o, ... 2Sa 6:22
this; I give my o. But I can be 1Co 7:25
This is my o, but I believe I.................... 1Co 7:40

OPINIONS
faith, and do not argue about o. .... Rm 14:1

OPPORTUNITY
give you an o to tell about me. .... Lk 21:13
because a good o for a great and 1Co 16:9
he will come when he has the o.............. 1Co 16:12
the Lord gave me a good o there. 2Co 2:12
we have the o to help anyone, ... Gal 6:10
will give us an o to tell people .... Col 4:3
making the most of every o. .... Col 4:5

OPPOSITE
Mount of Olives, o the Temple, ... Mk 13:3
the o, if the law could make .... Gal 2:21

ORCHARD
are like an o of pomegranates .... Sng 4:13
down into the o of nut trees to .... Sng 6:11

ORCHARDS
and your o of olive trees. .... Ex 23:11
happiness in the o and no songs.............. Is 16:10

ORDER
sons in the o they were born: .... Ge 25:13
This was the o the Israelite.................... Nu 10:28
without an o from the LORD. 2Ki 18:25
He could o the princes as he .... Ps 105:22
set in o many wise teachings. .... Ec 12:9
without an o from the LORD. .... Is 36:10
So give the o for the tomb to be .... Mt 27:64
out for you. I arranged it in o, ... Lk 1:3
understand in o to teach others 1Co 14:19
raised to life in the right o. 1Co 15:23
be bold and o you to do what is .... Phm 1:8
afraid to disobey the king's o.................. Heb 11:23
we now have in o to be destroyed 2Pe 3:7

ORDERED
as the king had o and food for .... Ge 45:21
He has o peace for those who.................. Ps 85:8
God o a time of hunger in the.................. Ps 105:16

ORDERING
king's empire o them to destroy .... Est 3:13
young man away, o him, "Don't .... Ac 23:22

ORDERLY
be done in a right and o way. 1Co 14:40

ORDERS
He left o for his family and.................... 2Sa 17:23
heard the king's o to the 2Sa 18:5
and who remember to obey his o. .... Ps 103:18
had given o that if anyone knew.............. Jn 11:57

O

you strict o not to continue .... Ac 5:28
second beast o people to make .... Rev 13:14

ORDINARY
it on the bodies of o people, ... Ex 30:32
holy, even when we do o work. 1Sa 21:5
for kings, not for o people. .... Pr 22:29
and write on it with an o pen: ' .... Is 8:1
can judge the o things of this 1Co 6:3
If you have o cases that must be.............. 1Co 6:4
and others are made for o jobs. 2Ti 2:20

ORE
the mines for o in thick .... Job 28:3
and my people are like the o. .... Je 6:27

OREB
of Midian named O and Zeeb. .... Jdg 7:25
killed O at the rock of Oreb .... Jdg 7:25
Oreb at the rock of O and Zeeb .... Jdg 7:25
the heads of O and Zeeb to..................... Jdg 7:25
God let you capture O and Zeeb, ... Jdg 8:3
what you did to O and Zeeb. .... Ps 83:11
Midian at the rock of O. .... Is 10:26

OREN
were Ram, Bunah, O, Ozem, and 1Ch 2:25

ORGAN
part of his sex o cut off may .... Dt 23:1

ORGANIZE
He will o my people." 1Sa 9:17

ORGANS
its head, legs, and inner o. .... Ex 12:9
the fat that covers the inner o, ... Ex 29:13
wash its inner o and its legs, ... Ex 29:17
the fat that covers the inner o. .... Ex 29:22
animal's inner o and legs must .... Le 1:9
animal's inner o and legs with .... Le 1:13
the fat of the animal's inner o................. Le 3:3
fat of the inner o (both the fat.................. Le 3:9
the fat of the goat's inner o .... Le 3:14
fat on and around the inner o, ... Le 4:8
intestines, and other inner o. .... Le 4:11
the fat that covers the inner o, ... Le 7:3
from the inner o of the bull, ... Le 8:16
washed the inner o and legs with .... Le 8:21
all the fat on the inner o, ... Le 8:25
washed the inner o and the legs .... Le 9:14
the fat covering the inner o, ... Le 9:19
the cheeks, and the inner o. .... Dt 18:3
the attacker by his sex o, ... Dt 25:11

ORIGINAL
back to the o city of safety,..................... Nu 35:25

ORION
made the Bear, O, and the .... Job 9:9
the ropes of the stars in O?..................... Job 38:31
the star groups Pleiades and O; .... Am 5:8

ORNAMENTS
cheeks are beautiful with o, ... Sng 1:10

ORPAH
One was named O, and the other .... Ru 1:4
Then O kissed her mother-in-law .... Ru 1:14

ORPHAN
Do not cheat a widow or an o. .... Ex 22:22
unfair to a foreigner or an o. .... Dt 24:17
out and those who had no one to .... Job 29:12
never hurt an o even when I knew .... Job 31:21
the case of the o or help the .... Je 5:28

ORPHAN'S
chase away the o donkey and take............ Job 24:3

ORPHANED
or have mercy on his o children. .... Ps 109:12

ORPHANS
We are like o with no father; .... La 5:3
not leave you all alone like o; .... Jn 14:18
caring for o or widows who need .... Jam 1:27

OSPREYS
white owls, desert owls, o, ... Le 11:18
desert owls, o, cormorants, ... Dt 14:17

OSTRICH
The wings of the o flap happily, ... Job 39:13
o lays its eggs on the ground .... Job 39:14
The o is cruel to its young, ... Job 39:16
God did not give the o wisdom; .... Job 39:17
But when the o gets up to run, ... Job 39:18

OSTRICHES
to wild dogs and a friend to o. .... Job 30:29
are cruel like o in the desert. .... La 4:3

OTHER'S
men asked about each o health, ... Ex 18:7
Let's enjoy each o love. .... Pr 7:18
also should wash each o feet. .... Jn 13:14

OTHNI
sons were O, Rephael, Obed, ... 1Ch 26:7

OTHNIEL
O son of Kenaz, Caleb's younger .... Jdg 3:9

OUTCRIES
There will be loud o everywhere .... Ex 11:6

OUTCRY
there was a loud o everywhere in .... Ex 12:30

OUTER
can tear off its o hide or poke.................. Job 41:13
up and took off his o clothing. .... Jn 13:4

OUTNUMBERED
You people may have o the stars, ... Dt 28:62

OUTSTANDING
powerful warriors and o leaders. 1Ch 7:40

OUTWARD
that faced o from the center 1Ki 7:25
that faced o from the center 2Ch 4:4

OVEN
that was baked in the o, ... Le 2:4
offering that is baked in an o,.................. Le 7:9
If it is a clay o or a clay .... Le 11:35
to cook all your bread in one o. .... Le 26:26
Our skin is hot like an o;....................... La 5:10
They are like an o heated by a .... Hos 7:4
burn like an o; their hearts .... Hos 7:6
these people are as hot as an o; .... Hos 7:7

OVENS
come into your o and into your .... Ex 8:3
the wall and the Tower of the O............... Ne 3:11
of the O to the Broad Wall, ... Ne 12:38

OVERCHARGING
people get rich by o others,..................... Pr 28:8

OVERCOME
who has been o with wine. .... Je 23:9

OVERFLOW
barrels will o with new wine. .... Pr 3:10
and my eyes will o with tears, ... Je 13:17
my eyes will o with tears. .... La 1:16
the barrels will o with new wine .... Joe 2:24
your hope will o by the power .... Rm 15:13

OVERFLOWED
The river will o its banks, ... Jos 4:18

OVERFLOWING
you fill my cup to o. .... Ps 23:5
oceans, or springs o with water, ... Pr 8:24

OVERFLOWS (cont.)
to her like a river o its banks.................... Is 66:12
become like an o stream and will ....Je 47:2

OVERFLOWS
harvest the Jordan o its banks. ....Jos 3:15

OVERLOOK
I will not o their sins anymore ....Am 8:2

OVERLOOKS
border road that o the Valley of 1Sa 13:18

OVERNIGHT
do not leave it o. .... Dt 16:4
his body hanging on the tree o; .... Dt 21:23
the loan back, don't keep it o.................. Dt 24:12

OVERPOWER
you how we can o him and capture ....Jdg 16:5

OVERPOWERED
and the darkness has not o it................... Jn 1:5

OVERSEE
Spirit has given to you to o. ....Ac 20:28

OVERSEER
to become an o desires a good 1Ti 3:1
An o must not give people a 1Ti 3:2
Shepherd and O of your souls. 1Pe 2:25

OVERSEERS
including your o and deacons: ....Php 1:1
o must not be guilty of doing ....Tit 1:7
O must be ready to welcome ....Tit 1:8
o can help people by using true ....Tit 1:9

OVERTHROW
down, destroy and o, build up ....Je 1:10

OVERTURN
like spies to o the freedom we ....Gal 2:4

OVERWHELM
but would o me with misery. ....Job 9:18
they o them, like a king ready ....Job 15:24
Great fears o me. They blow my..............Job 30:15
when pain and trouble o you. ....Pr 1:27
will surely o them in Gibeah, ...Hos 10:9

OVERWHELMED
the deadly rivers o me. 2Sa 22:5
they are o and die because of ....Ps 9:3
the deadly rivers o me. ....Ps 18:4
They are o and defeated, but we..............Ps 20:8
loves him, he will not be o. ....Ps 21:7
but they are o and defeated. ....Ps 27:2
They are o; they cannot do ....Ps 36:12
My guilt has o me; ....Ps 38:4
you will not be o...................................Pr 4:12
wicked will be o by violence. ....Pr 10:6
but the wicked are o by trouble. ....Pr 24:16
don't be glad when he is o. ....Pr 24:17

OVERWHELMING
in golden light, in o greatness. ....Job 37:22
judging is an o and terrible day ....Joe 2:11
before the o and terrible day of ....Joe 2:31
before the o and glorious day of..............Ac 2:20

OVERWHELMS
just seeing it o people. ....Job 41:9
Our guilt o us, but you forgive ....Ps 65:3

OWE
'Pay me the money you o me!' ....Mt 18:28
you have paid everything you o." ....Lk 12:59
first one, 'How much do you o?' ....Lk 16:5
Do not o people anything, except ....Rm 13:8
about what you o me for your own..........Phm 1:19

OWED
foreigner pay what is o to you, ...Dt 15:3
a servant who o him several ....Mt 18:24

OWES
to you or if he o you anything, ...Phm 1:18

OWL
am like a desert o, like an owl ....Ps 102:6
an o living among the ruins. ....Ps 102:6
The o will hoot through the ....Zph 2:14

OWN
to produce more of their o kind..............Ge 1:25
he made them in his o likeness. ....Ge 5:1
a son of your o who will inherit ....Ge 15:4
kill your o sons and brothers,..................Ex 32:29
must not do this in your o land, ...Le 22:24
each go back to your o property, ...Le 25:10
God will give you as your o. ....Dt 12:9
person must die for his o sin. ....Dt 24:16
that you will eat your o babies, ...Dt 28:53
is killed, it is his o fault. ....Jos 2:19
him in his o land at Timnath ....Jos 24:30
He had seventy sons of his o, ...Jdg 8:30
like one of Micah's o sons. ....Jdg 17:11
what I can pass on to my o sons. ....Ru 4:6
Goliath's weapons in his o tent. 1Sa 17:54
your o son-in-law and captain of 1Sa 22:14
your very o people forever, ...2Sa 7:24
who comes from your o body,..................1Ki 8:19
come and seen it with my o eyes. 1Ki 10:7
Israel, let's go to our o homes! 1Ki 12:16
fruit from his o grapevine and 2Ki 18:31
your very o people forever, ...1Ch 17:22
Each must die for his o sins." 2Ch 25:4
each going back to his o town. ....Ezr 2:1
her as his o daughter when her ....Est 2:7
o mouth would say I was wrong; ....Job 9:20
about myself. I hate my o life..................Job 9:21
them land to o along with their ....Job 42:15
them fall into their o traps. ....Ps 5:10
them be caught in their o nets; ....Ps 35:8
swords will stab their o hearts, ...Ps 37:15
one can pay God for his o life, ...Ps 49:7
be punished with their o evil. ....Ps 54:5
their o sons and daughters,....................Ps 106:38
people and hated his o children..............Ps 106:40
wicked fall into their o nets, ...Ps 141:10
will fall into their o traps; ....Pr 1:18
depend on your o understanding. ....Pr 3:5
Don't depend on your o wisdom. ....Pr 3:7
Be faithful to your o wife, ...Pr 5:15
drink water from your o well...................Pr 5:15
might be caught by your o words. ....Pr 6:2
are ruined by their o evil, ...Pr 14:32
their o words will trap them. ....Pr 18:7
and not from your o mouth. ....Pr 27:2
hands and weaves her o cloth. ....Pr 31:19
made with their o hands and ....Is 2:8
your teacher with your o eyes. ....Is 30:20
him return to his o country, ...Is 37:7
and trust your o light to guide ....Is 50:11
So he used his o power to save ....Is 59:16
people choose their o ways, ...Is 66:3
had made with their o hands...................Je 1:16
don't trust your o relatives,....................Je 9:4
person will die for his o sin; ....Je 31:30
With their o hands kind women ....La 4:10
follow their o ideas and have ....Eze 13:3
bring them into their o land. ....Eze 37:21
any god other than their o. ....Da 3:28
scattered my o people Israel ....Joe 3:2
was still in my o country this ....Jnh 4:2
returned to their o country by a ....Mt 2:12
will have no o worries. ....Mt 6:34
big piece of wood in your o eye? ....Mt 7:3
who are dead bury their o dead." ....Mt 8:22

be members of his **o** family.' .... Mt 10:36
for the sake of your **o** rules. .... Mt 15:6
robe and put his **o** clothes on .... Mt 27:31
and with his **o** people and in his .... Mk 6:4
all went to their **o** towns to be .... Lk 2:3
With my **o** eyes I have seen your .... Lk 2:30
their **o** town in Galilee. .... Lk 2:39
to the world that was his **o,** .... Jn 1:11
his **o** people did not accept him. .... Jn 1:11
Jesus meant was his **o** body. .... Jn 2:21
not respected in his **o** country. .... Jn 4:44
says that God is his **o** Father, ... Jn 5:18
The things I teach are not my **o,** .... Jn 7:16
who teach their **o** ideas are.................... Jn 7:18
He calls his **o** sheep by name and .... Jn 10:3
I give my **o** life freely. .... Jn 10:18
who were his **o** in the world, ... Jn 13:1
Carrying his **o** cross, Jesus went .... Jn 19:17
hear them in our **o** languages? .... Ac 2:8
went to their **o** group and told .... Ac 4:23
strong that his **o** people in .... Ac 9:22
' Some of your **o** poets have said: .... Ac 17:28
with the death of his **o** son. .... Ac 20:28
full years in his **o** rented house .... Ac 28:30
He sent his **o** Son to earth with .... Rm 8:3
not spare his **o** Son but gave him .... Rm 8:32
themselves right in their **o** way. .... Rm 10:3
be joined to their **o** tree again. .... Rm 11:24
risked their **o** lives to save my .... Rm 16:4
will be rewarded for his **o** work............... 1Co 3:8
wise in their **o** clever traps." 1Co 3:19
hard with our **o** hands for our 1Co 4:12
a warning as my **o** dear children. 1Co 4:14
sin against their **o** bodies. 1Co 6:18
each man should have his **o** wife, ... 1Co 7:2
woman should have her **o** husband. 1Co 7:2
eat and drink in your **o** homes! 1Co 11:22
Look into your **o** hearts before 1Co 11:28
ask their **o** husbands at home................ 1Co 14:35
each kind of seed its **o** body. 1Co 15:38
this greeting with my **o** hand................... 1Co 16:21
judge his **o** actions and not .... Gal 6:4
as they love their **o** bodies..................... Eph 5:28
No one ever hates his **o** body, ... Eph 5:29
to be used for his **o** benefit. .... Php 2:6
to offer my **o** blood with your................ Php 2:17
only in their **o** lives. .... Php 2:21
and write this with my **o** hand. .... Col 4:18
Take care of your **o** business, ... 1Th 4:11
quietly and earn their **o** food. 2Th 3:12
letter now in my **o** handwriting. 2Th 3:17
children and their **o** families. 1Ti 3:12
not care for his **o** relatives, ... 1Ti 5:8
yield to their **o** masters at all .... Tit 2:9
for his **o** sins and also for .... Heb 5:3
first for their **o** sins, and then .... Heb 7:27
His sacrifice was his **o** blood, ... Heb 9:12
when their **o** evil desire leads .... Jam 1:14
use them for your **o** pleasures. .... Jam 4:3
the prophet's **o** interpretation. 2Pe 1:20
up their **o** shameful actions .... Jud 1:13
following their **o** evil desires .... Jud 1:18
had made with their **o** hands. .... Rev 9:20

OWNED

everything they **o,** as well as .... Ge 12:5
left with everything they **o.**..................... Ge 12:20
everything they **o,** and traveled .... Ge 13:1
people of Sodom and Gomorrah **o,**........... Ge 14:11
in Sodom, and everything he **o.** .... Ge 14:12
and Lot, and everything Lot **o.** .... Ge 14:16
in charge of everything he **o,** .... Ge 24:2
left everything he **o** to Isaac. .... Ge 25:5

taken everything our father **o,** .... Ge 31:1
animals that Jacob **o** walked .... Ge 31:18
valuable thing the people **o,** .... Ge 34:29
him with everything he **o.** .... Ge 39:4
house and everything Potiphar **o,** .... Ge 39:5
of everything he **o** and was not .... Ge 39:6
buy was the land the priests **o.** .... Ge 47:22
the one who **o** the bull may buy .... Ex 21:30
and everything they **o** went down. .... Nu 16:32
they **o** went with them. .... Nu 16:33
get what their father **o.** .... Nu 27:7
everything he **o** should go to his............... Nu 27:8
everything he **o** should go to his .... Nu 27:9
everything he **o** should go to his .... Nu 27:10
then everything he **o** should go .... Nu 27:11
up everything those people **o,** .... Dt 13:16
everything they **o** as a burnt .... Dt 13:16
tent, and everything he **o.** .... Jos 7:24
things the people of Ai had **o,**................ Jos 8:27
of Manasseh **o** these towns: .... Jos 17:11
everything they **o** in front of .... Jdg 18:21
to the old man who **o** the house,............. Jdg 19:22
the woman who **o** the house became 1Ki 17:17
o twelve teams of oxen and was.............. 1Ki 19:19
A man named Naboth **o** a vineyard 1Ki 21:1
family and everything he **o.** 1Ch 13:14
everything the Jewish people **o.** .... Est 3:13
He **o** seven thousand sheep, ... Job 1:3
were a powerful man who **o** land; .... Job 22:8
as much as he had **o** before. .... Job 42:10
land that rich people once **o.** .... Is 5:17
They **o** nothing, but that day he .... Je 39:10
everything he **o** to buy that..................... Mt 13:44
the servant **o** should be sold, ... Mt 18:25
like a person who **o** some land. .... Mt 20:1
to the man who **o** the land...................... Mt 20:11
But the man who **o** the vineyard............. Mt 20:13
was a man who **o** a vineyard................... Mt 21:33
things they **o** and then divide .... Ac 2:45
time those who **o** fields or .... Ac 4:34
Joseph **o** a field, sold it, ... Ac 4:37
around there **o** by Publius, ... Ac 28:7
when all that you **o** was taken .... Heb 10:34

OWNER

the **o** of the bull is not guilty. .... Ex 21:28
knows where its **o** feeds it, ... Is 1:3
heaven is like the **o** of a house. .... Mt 13:52
o of the vineyard said to the .... Mt 20:8

OWNER'S

go back to the first **o** family. .... Le 25:28

OWNERS

Money saved is a curse to its **o.** .... Ec 5:13
is now ruined back to its **o.**..................... Is 49:8
men and their fields to new **o.** .... Je 8:10
its **o** came out and asked the .... Lk 19:33
of money for her **o** by telling .... Ac 16:16
When the **o** of the servant girl .... Ac 16:19

OWNERSHIP

was the proof of **o** in Israel. .... Ru 4:7
both copies of the record of **o—** .... Je 32:11
had the demands and limits of **o,** .... Je 32:11
who signed the record of **o,** .... Je 32:12
give the record of **o** to Baruch. .... Je 32:12
both copies of the record of **o—** .... Je 32:14
the record of **o** to Baruch son .... Je 32:16
special mark of **o** on you by .... Eph 1:13

OWNS

everything he **o** to that son. .... Ge 24:36
The man who **o** these things has .... Ge 38:25
me in charge of everything he **o.** .... Ge 39:8
disagree about who **o** something—........... Ex 22:9

The LORD o the world and .... Dt 10:14
two shares of everything he o, ... Dt 21:17
Everything he o will be .... Jos 7:15
his family, and everything he o. .... Job 1:10
owes money take everything he o. .... Ps 109:11
it may cost him everything he o............. Pr 6:31
to the Lord, who o the harvest, ... Mt 9:38
to take care of everything he o. .... Mt 24:47
pray to God, who o the harvest, ... Lk 10:2
not measured by how much one o." .... Lk 12:15
to take care of everything he o. .... Lk 12:44
from the shepherd who o them. .... Jn 10:12
speak against Jesus, who o you............. Jam 2:7

OX

slaves, or his o or his donkey,.................. Ex 20:17
another man's o or donkey comes .... Ex 21:33
whether o, donkey, sheep, ... Ex 22:9
his donkey, o, sheep, or some .... Ex 22:10
see your enemy's o or donkey .... Ex 23:4
This lets your o and your donkey .... Ex 23:12
If an Israelite kills an o, ... Le 17:3
If an o or lamb is smaller .... Le 22:23
When an o, a sheep, or a goat is............. Le 22:27
day, either an o or a sheep. .... Le 22:28
leader giving an o, and every .... Nu 7:3
the firstborn o or sheep or goat .... Nu 18:17
us like an o eating grass." .... Nu 22:4
they are as strong as a wild o. .... Nu 23:22
they are as strong as a wild o. .... Nu 24:8
slaves, your o, your donkey, ... Dt 5:14
slaves, his o or his donkey, ... Dt 5:21
If an o or sheep has something .... Dt 17:1
Israelite's o or sheep wandering.............. Dt 22:1
donkey or o fallen on the road, ... Dt 22:4
plow with an o and a donkey tied .... Dt 22:10
When an o is working in the .... Dt 25:4
o will be killed before your.................... Dt 28:31
he is as strong as a wild o. .... Dt 33:17
I steal anyone's o or donkey? 1Sa 12:3
must bring his o and sheep to me 1Sa 14:34
o, six good sheep, and birds. .... Ne 5:18
and an o is quiet when it has .... Job 6:5
the widow's o when she has no .... Job 24:3
Will the wild o agree to serve .... Job 39:9
on the wild o for its great .... Job 39:11
you trust the o to bring in your .... Job 39:12
you. It eats grass like an o. .... Job 40:15
have made me as strong as an o. .... Ps 92:10
like an o led to the butcher, ... Pr 7:22
with a strong o, much grain can............. Pr 14:4
An o knows its master, and a .... Is 1:3
obey me as an o breaks its yoke............. Je 2:20
the face of an o on the left .... Eze 1:10
will feed you grass like an o, ... Da 4:25
and will be fed grass like an o. .... Da 4:32
he began eating grass like an o. .... Da 4:33
grass like an o and became wet .... Da 5:21
If your child or o falls into a .... Lk 14:5
When an o is working in the 1Co 9:9
When an o is working in the 1Ti 5:18

OXEN

they crippled o just for fun. .... Ge 49:6
six covered carts and twelve o— .... Nu 7:3
carts and one and gave them to .... Nu 7:6
carts and four o to the .... Nu 7:7
carts and eight o to the .... Nu 7:8
did not give any o or carts to .... Nu 7:9
you may eat: o, sheep, goats, ... Dt 14:4
the first calf born to your o, ... Dt 15:19
a sharp stick used to guide o. .... Jdg 3:31
fields with his o when he heard 1Sa 11:5
he took a pair of o and cut them 1Sa 11:7

pieces of the o to messengers 1Sa 11:7
happen to the o of anyone who 1Sa 11:7
and the sticks used to guide o. 1Sa 13:21
floor of Nacon, the o stumbled. 2Sa 6:6
Here are some o for the whole 2Sa 24:22
floor and the o for one and.................... 2Sa 24:24
a field with a team of o. 1Ki 19:19
teams of o and was plowing 1Ki 19:19
Elisha left his o and ran to 1Ki 19:20
his pair of o and killed them 1Ki 19:21
grapes, sheep, o, male servants, ... 2Ki 5:26
donkeys, camels, mules, and o. 1Ch 12:40
of Kidon, the o stumbled, and............... 1Ch 13:9
also give you o for the whole 1Ch 21:23
hundred teams of o, and five .... Job 1:3
The o were plowing and the .... Job 1:14
teams of o, and a thousand.................... Job 42:12
When there are no o, no food is .... Pr 14:4
Lions will eat hay as o do. .... Is 11:7
Your o and donkeys that work the .... Is 30:24
The o will be killed, and the .... Is 34:7
Lions will eat hay like o,....................... Is 65:25
use you to smash farmers and o. .... Je 51:23
people do not plow rocks with o. .... Am 6:12
just bought five pairs of o; .... Lk 14:19
was he thinking only about o? 1Co 9:9

OZEM

his sixth was O, and his seventh............. 1Ch 2:15
Ram, Bunah, Oren, O, and Ahijah............ 1Ch 2:25

OZNI

from O came the Oznite family .... Nu 26:16

OZNITE

Ozni came the O family group; .... Nu 26:16

P

PAARAI

the Carmelite; P the Arbite; 2Sa 23:35

PACK

p your things to be taken away .... Je 46:19
p your things as if you will be .... Eze 12:3
things you would p as captive. .... Eze 12:4

PACKED

what I had p as if I were being .... Eze 12:7

PACKS

foods in our land in your p. .... Ge 43:11

PADDLES

for donkeys, so p are good for .... Pr 26:3

PADON

Keros, Siaha, P, ... Ezr 2:44
Keros, Sia, P, ... Ne 7:47

PADS

arms to be p for the ropes." .... Je 38:12

PAGIEL

tribe of Asher—P son of Ocran; .... Nu 1:13
of Asher is P son of Ocran...................... Nu 2:27
P son of Ocran was over the .... Nu 10:26

PAHATH-MOAB

descendants of P (through the .... Ezr 2:6
From the descendants of P:................. Ezr 8:4
From the descendants of P:..................... Ezr 10:30
son of P repaired another .... Ne 3:11
descendants of P (through the .... Ne 7:11
Parosh, P, Elam, Zattu, Bani, ... Ne 10:14

PAID

answer, and no one p attention. 1Ki 18:29
people are p with punishment .... Pr 10:16

Jonah **p** for the trip and went .... Jnh 1:3
until you have **p** everything you .... Mt 5:26
also **p** it when Abraham paid .... Heb 7:9

PAIN
children, you will have great **p**. .... Ge 3:16
I moan from the **p** I feel. .... Ps 38:8
cries and has **p** from the birth. .... Is 26:17
gripped by our **p**, like a woman .... Je 6:24
understand why my **p** has no end. .... Je 15:18
crying, or **p**, because all .... Rev 21:4

PAINFUL
He put **p** sores on Job's body, ... Job 2:7
in Ramah of **p** crying and deep .... Mt 2:18
for this **p** thing to be taken .... Mt 26:42
p physical problem was given to 2Co 12:7
It is **p** at the time, but later, ... Heb 12:11
Then ugly and **p** sores came upon .... Rev 16:2

PAINFULLY
the city crying loudly and **p**. .... Est 4:1
I will cry **p**, and my eyes will .... Je 13:17
But cry **p** for the king who is .... Je 22:10
the people will cry **p**. .... Je 47:2
Peter went outside and cried **p**. .... Mt 26:75
Peter went outside and cried **p**. .... Lk 22:62

PAINS
ache; gnawing **p** never stop. .... Job 30:17
p are like the pains of giving .... Is 21:3
are like the **p** of giving birth. .... Is 21:3
soon as she feels the birth **p**. .... Is 66:8
like the first **p** when something .... Mt 24:8
like the first **p** when something .... Mk 13:8
is like **p** that come quickly to 1Th 5:3

PAINTED
for them, **p** their eyes, and put .... Eze 23:40
are like tombs that are **p** white. .... Mt 23:27
a wall that has been **p** white. .... Ac 23:3

PAINTS
for the walls, which he **p** red. .... Je 22:14

PAIR
to the tails of each **p** of foxes. .... Jdg 15:4
the poor to buy a **p** of sandals. .... Am 2:6
for the price of a **p** of sandals. .... Am 8:6
rider held a **p** of scales in his .... Rev 6:5

PAIRS
with you seven **p**, each male with .... Ge 7:2
Take seven **p** of all the birds of .... Ge 7:3
Three **p** of branches went out .... Ex 37:21
sent them out in **p** ahead of him .... Lk 10:1
have just bought five **p** of oxen; .... Lk 14:19

PALACE
the **p** of Ahab king of Israel. 1Ki 21:1
they enter the king's **p**. .... Ps 45:15
and able to serve in his **p**. .... Da 1:4
the lampstand in the royal **p**. .... Da 5:5
a meeting at the **p** of the high .... Mt 26:3
All the **p** guards and everyone .... Php 1:13

PALACES
From **p** of ivory music comes to .... Ps 45:8
God is within its **p**; .... Ps 48:3
are. Look at the **p**. Then you can .... Ps 48:13
they are found even in kings' **p**. .... Pr 30:28
and the king's **p** will become as .... Je 19:13
and the royal **p** of Judah that .... Je 33:4
up all her **p** and destroyed all .... La 2:5
the walls of Jerusalem's **p**. .... La 2:7
their Maker and has built **p**; .... Hos 8:14
fine clothes live in kings' **p**. .... Mt 11:8
much wealth live in kings' **p**. .... Lk 7:25

PALAL
P son of Uzai worked across from .... Ne 3:25
Next to **P**, Pedaiah son of Parosh .... Ne 3:25

PALE
and everyone's face becomes **p**. .... Joe 2:6
and everyone's face grows **p**. .... Nah 2:10
there before me was a **p** horse. .... Rev 6:8

PALLU
sons were Hanoch, **P**, Hezron, and .... Ge 46:9
Hanoch, **P**, Hezron, and Carmi. .... Ex 6:14
from **P** came the Palluite family .... Nu 26:5
The son of **P** was Eliab, ... Nu 26:8
sons were Hanoch, **P**, Hezron, and 1Ch 5:3

PALLUITE
Pallu came the **P** family group; .... Nu 26:5

PALM
of water and seventy **p** trees. .... Ex 15:27
is called the city of **p** trees. .... Dt 34:3
sit under the **P** Tree of Deborah, ... Jdg 4:5
people will grow like **p** trees; .... Ps 92:12
You are tall like a **p** tree, ... Sng 7:7
the oceans in the **p** of his hand? .... Is 40:12
branches of **p** trees and went .... Jn 12:13
and holding **p** branches in their .... Rev 7:9

PALMS
feet, and the **p** of her hands. 2Ki 9:35
trees, **p**, and shade trees. .... Ne 8:15

PALTI
of Benjamin, **P** son of Raphu; .... Nu 13:9

PALTIEL
of Issachar, **P** son of Azzan; .... Nu 34:26
had given her to **P** son of Laish, ... 1Sa 25:44
from her husband **P** son of Laish. 2Sa 3:15
Abner said to **P**, "Go back home. 2Sa 3:16

PALTITE
Helez the **P**; Ira son of Ikkesh 2Sa 23:26

PAMPHYLIA
Phrygia, **P**, Egypt, the areas of .... Ac 2:10
Paphos and came to Perga, in **P**. .... Ac 13:13
through Pisidia and came to **P**. .... Ac 14:24
but he had left them at **P**; .... Ac 15:38
by Cilicia and **P** and landed at .... Ac 27:5

PAN
grain offering is cooked in a **p**, ... Le 2:7
she took the **P** and served him, ... 2Sa 13:9
in his hand was a **p** for burning 2Ch 26:19
Each man had his **p** for burning .... Eze 8:11
pot, like meat in a cooking **p**. .... Mic 3:3
holding a golden **p** for incense. .... Rev 8:3
filled the incense **p** with fire .... Rev 8:5

PANCAKE
is like a **p** cooked only on one .... Hos 7:8

PANELS
off the side **p** from the bases 2Ki 16:17
He put **p** of pine on the walls of 2Ch 3:5
the carved **p** with their axes .... Ps 74:6
had wood **p** on the walls. .... Eze 41:16
Temple had wood **p** on the walls. .... Eze 41:16

PANIC
Egyptian army and made them **p**. .... Ex 14:24
Don't **p** or be frightened, ... Dt 20:3
it to Gath, there was a great **p**. 1Sa 5:9
shook! God had caused the **p**. 1Sa 14:15
will **p**, and their protection .... Is 31:9
are ready to **p**. The people feel .... Je 49:24
that time the LORD will cause **p**. .... Zch 14:13

PANICKED
All the Philistine soldiers **p**— 1Sa 14:15

PAPER

They glide past like **p** boats. .... Job 9:26
where is the **p** that proves it? .... Is 50:1
give her a written divorce **p**.' .... Mt 5:31
I do not want to use **p** and ink. 2Jn 1:12

PAPERS

He writes out divorce **p** for her, ... Dt 24:1
he writes out divorce **p** for her, ... Dt 24:3
wrote and copied important **p**. 1Ch 2:55
wife by giving her divorce **p**?" .... Mt 19:7
out divorce **p** and send her away .... Mk 10:4

PAPHOS

whole island to **P** where they met .... Ac 13:6
him sailed from **P** and came to .... Ac 13:13

PAPYRUS

P plants cannot grow where there .... Job 8:11

PARADE

you led a **p** of captives. .... Ps 68:18
captives in Christ's victory **p**. 2Co 2:14
heights, he led a **p** of captives, ... Eph 4:8

PARADISE

today you will be with me in **p**." .... Lk 23:43

PARAH

Avvim, **P**, Ophrah, ... Jos 18:23

PARALLEL

a wall outside **p** to the rooms .... Eze 42:7

PARALYZED

epileptics, and some were **p**. .... Mt 4:24
a man who was **p** and lying on a .... Mt 9:2
and some were **p** [, and they .... Jn 5:3
who was **p** and had not been able .... Ac 9:33

PARAN

He lived in the Desert of **P**, ... Ge 21:21
the Holy One comes from Mount **P**. .... Hab 3:3

PARCHMENT

the ones written on **p**. 2Ti 4:13

PARDON

But let the LORD **p** me for this: 2Ki 5:18
the LORD **p** me when I do that. 2Ki 5:18
Why don't you **p** my wrongs and .... Job 7:21

PARDONED

forgiven, whose wrongs are **p**. .... Ps 32:1
forgiven, whose wrongs are **p**. .... Rm 4:7

PARENT

is the first one born to its **p**, ... Le 27:26
you as a **p** corrects a child .... Dt 8:5
no joy in being the **p** of a fool. .... Pr 17:21
The life of the **p** is mine, ... Eze 18:4
and a **p** will not be punished for .... Eze 18:20
As a **p** shows mercy to his child .... Mal 3:17

PARENT'S

your friend or your **p** friend. .... Pr 27:10
not be punished for a **p** sin, ... Eze 18:20

PARENTS

their own **p** and have them put .... Mt 10:21
year Jesus' **p** went to Jerusalem .... Lk 2:41
brothers, **p**, or children for .... Lk 18:29
his own sin or his **p**' sin?" .... Jn 9:2
They do not obey their **p**. .... Rm 1:30
to save up to give to their **p**. 2Co 12:14
P should save to give to their 2Co 12:14
obey your **p** as the Lord wants, ... Eph 6:1
not obey their **p** or be thankful 2Ti 3:2
that Moses' **p** hid him for three .... Heb 11:23

PARKS

gardens and **p**, and I planted .... Ec 2:5

PARMASHTA

P, Arisai, Aridai, and Vaizatha, ... Est 9:9

PARMENAS

Nicanor, Timon, **P**, and Nicolas (a .... Ac 6:5

PARNACH

of Zebulun, Elizaphan son of **P**; .... Nu 34:25

PAROSH

the descendants of **P**—2,172; .... Ezr 2:3
From the descendants of **P**: .... Ezr 8:3
From the descendants of **P**: .... Ezr 10:25
Pedaiah son of **P** made repairs. .... Ne 3:25
the descendants of **P**—2,172; .... Ne 7:8
P, Pahath-Moab, Elam, Zattu, Bani, ... Ne 10:14

PARSHANDATHA

P, Dalphon, Aspatha, ... Est 9:7

PARSIN

'Mene, mene, tekel, and **p**.' .... Da 5:25
P: Your kingdom is being divided .... Da 5:28

PARTED

He **p** the water of the Red Sea. .... Ps 136:13

PARTHIA

P, Media, Elam, Mesopotamia, ... Ac 2:9

PARTING

call this place Rock of **P**. 1Sa 23:28

PARTNER

though she was your **p** and you .... Mal 2:14
is my **p** who is working with me 2Co 8:23
So if you consider me your **p**, ... Phm 1:17

PARTNERS

P of thieves are their own worst .... Pr 29:24
neighbors and **p** in sexual sin. .... Eze 16:26
called to their **p** in the other .... Lk 5:7
the sons of Zebedee, Simon's **p**. .... Lk 5:10

PARTY

camp and those in the raiding **p**. 1Sa 14:15
to go to a funeral than to a **p**. .... Ec 7:2
A **p** makes you feel good, wine .... Ec 10:19
he gave a dinner **p** for the most .... Mk 6:21
to come home from a wedding **p**. .... Lk 12:36

PARUAH

Jehoshaphat son of **P** was 1Ki 4:17

PARVAIM

with gems and gold from **P**. 2Ch 3:6

PAS

was with David at **P** Dammim when 1Ch 11:13

PASACH

Japhlet's sons were **P**, Bimhal, ... 1Ch 7:33

PASEAH

of Beth Rapha, **P**, and Tehinnah 1Ch 4:12
Uzza, **P**, Besai, ... Ezr 2:49
Joiada son of **P** and Meshullam .... Ne 3:6
Gazzam, Uzza, **P**, ... Ne 7:51

PASHHUR

P son of Immer was a priest and .... Je 20:1
next day when **P** took Jeremiah .... Je 20:3

PASHHUR'S

Jeroham was **P** son, and Pashhur 1Ch 9:12

PASS

the blood, I will **p** over you. .... Ex 12:13
be still until your people **p** .... Ex 15:16
goodness to **p** in front of you, ... Ex 33:19
Please let us **p** through your .... Nu 20:17
of Heshbon would not let us **p**, ... Dt 2:30
gone out to the **p** at Micmash. 1Sa 13:23
seven of his sons **p** by Samuel. 1Sa 16:10
As they **p** through the Valley of .... Ps 84:6
All our days **p** while you are .... Ps 90:9

P

They **p** quickly, and then we are .... Ps 90:10
Let those who **p** by them not say, ... Ps 129:8
nets, but let me **p** by safely .... Ps 141:10
quarrel as you **p** by is like .... Pr 26:17
into Judah and **p** through it, ... Is 8:8
When you **p** through the waters, ... Is 43:2
You who **p** by on the road don't .... La 1:12
All who **p** by on the road clap .... La 2:15
to be seen by all who **p** by. .... Eze 5:14
Seven years will **p**, and then you .... Da 4:25
because I will **p** among you to .... Am 5:17
P on your way, naked and ashamed, ... Mic 1:11
take the coats from people who **p** .... Mic 2:8
All those who **p** by will make fun .... Zph 2:15
and earth to **p** away than for .... Lk 16:17

PASSED
a blazing torch **p** between the .... Ge 15:17
the LORD **p** over the houses of .... Ex 12:27
The LORD **p** in front of Moses and .... Ex 34:6
until we have **p** through your .... Nu 20:17
afternoon **p**, and the prophets 1Ki 18:29
As Ahab king of Israel **p** by, ... 1Ki 20:39
months that have **p** and the days .... Job 29:2
wings until the trouble has **p**. .... Ps 57:1
their property **p** down from their .... Eze 46:16
that when Peter **p** by at least .... Ac 5:15
p by Mysia and went to Troas. .... Ac 16:8
I **p** on to you what I received, ... 1Co 15:3
to see that we have **p** the test, ... 2Co 13:7
a way **p** down from the people who 1Pe 1:18

PASSENGER
captain, every **p**, the sailors, ... Rev 18:17

PASSES
When my glory **p** that place, ... Ex 33:22
everyone who **p** by will be 1Ki 9:8
of God who **p** by our house all 2Ki 4:9
everyone who **p** by will be 2Ch 7:21
When he **p** me, I cannot see him; .... Job 9:11
everyone who **p** by steals from .... Ps 80:12
Everyone who **p** by steals from .... Ps 89:41
short life **p** like a shadow. .... Ec 6:12
When terrible punishment **p** by, ... Is 28:15
are empty, and no one **p** through. .... Je 9:10
Everyone who **p** by Babylon will .... Je 50:13
No one **p** through her gates. .... La 1:4
for everyone who **p** by to see. .... Eze 36:34

PASSING
of Israel was **p** by on the wall, ... 2Ki 6:26
We are like a **p** shadow that does .... Job 14:2
years are like the **p** of a day, ... Ps 90:4
My life is **p** away like smoke, ... Ps 102:3
My days are like a **p** shadow; .... Ps 102:11
their lives are like **p** shadows. .... Ps 144:4
She calls out to those who are **p** .... Pr 9:15
or anyone just **p** by is like an .... Pr 26:10
empty with no one **p** through .... Is 60:15
as Jesus was **p** by with his .... Mk 11:20
want to see you now just in **p**. 1Co 16:7
because the darkness is **p** away, ... 1Jn 2:8
people want in it are **p** away, ... 1Jn 2:17

PASSOVER
this is the LORD's **P**. .... Ex 12:11
and kill the lamb for the **P**. .... Ex 12:21
'This is the **P** sacrifice to .... Ex 12:27
of the Feast of **P** until the next .... Ex 34:25
they celebrated the **P** Feast. .... Jos 5:10
The **P** had not been celebrated 2Ki 23:22
for you to eat the **P** meal?'" .... Mt 26:17
Bread when the **P** lamb was .... Mk 14:12
I can eat the **P** meal with my .... Mk 14:14
much to eat this **P** meal with you .... Lk 22:15

time for the Jewish **P** Feast, ... Jn 2:13
Six days before the **P** Feast, ... Jn 12:1
on Preparation Day of **P** week. .... Jn 19:14
For Christ, our **P** lamb, has been 1Co 5:7
Moses prepared the **P** and spread .... Heb 11:28

PAST
A spirit glided **p** my face, ... Job 4:15
They glide **p** like paper boats .... Job 9:26
the winter is **p**; the rains are .... Sng 2:11
border the water can never go **p**. .... Je 5:22
the **p** they taught my people to .... Je 12:16
are left what I did in the **p**," .... Zch 8:11
Jerusalem, as it was in the **p**. .... Mal 3:4
written in the **p** was written to .... Rm 15:4
she is almost **p** the best age to 1Co 7:36
were given about you in the **p**. 1Ti 1:18
In the **p** we also were foolish. .... Tit 3:3
In the **p** he was useless to you, ... Phm 1:11
In the **p** God spoke to our .... Heb 1:1
great people who lived in the **p**. .... Heb 11:2
The first trouble is **p**; .... Rev 9:12

PASTE
said, "Make a **p** from figs." 2Ki 20:7
Make a **p** from figs and put it on .... Is 38:21

PASTURE
with us, the sheep of your **p**? .... Ps 74:1
of Israel back to their own **p**. .... Je 50:19
city of Rabbah a **p** for camels .... Eze 25:5
their own land and **p** them on the .... Eze 34:13
I will feed them in a good **p**, ... Eze 34:14
in a pen, like a flock in its **p**; .... Mic 2:12
come in and go out and find **p**. .... Jn 10:9

PASTURELAND
the Levites the **p** around these .... Nu 35:2
may live and **p** for their cattle .... Nu 35:3
The **p** you give the Levites will .... Nu 35:4
This will be **p** for the Levites' .... Nu 35:5
the people and took their **p**.' .... Eze 36:5

PASTURELANDS
and on all the **p** in the Plain of 1Ch 5:16
even left their **p** and property 2Ch 11:14
ourselves the **p** that belong to .... Ps 83:12

PASTURES
He lets me rest in green **p**. .... Ps 23:2
and be used for homes and **p** .... Eze 48:15
city's land for **p** will be about .... Eze 48:17
fire has burned up the open **p**. .... Joe 1:20
The **p** of the shepherds will .... Am 1:2

PATARA
and from there we went to **P**. .... Ac 21:1

PATCH
No one sews a **p** of unshrunk .... Mt 9:16

PATH
snake lying near the **p**. .... Ge 49:17
stood on a narrow **p** between two .... Nu 22:24
on the ground, right in their **p**. .... Job 18:10
stay on the old **p** where evil .... Job 22:15
push needy people off the **p**; .... Job 24:4
hawk knows that **p**; the falcon .... Job 28:7
rain and set a **p** for a .... Job 28:26
It was as if my **p** were covered .... Job 29:6
What is the **p** to light's home, ... Job 38:19
rains and sets a **p** for the .... Job 38:25
leaves a shining **p** in the water .... Job 41:32
and follows its **p** to the other .... Ps 19:6
dug a pit in my **p**, but they fell .... Ps 57:6
Lead me in the **p** of your .... Ps 119:35
my feet and a light for my **p**. .... Ps 119:105
In the **p** where I walk, a trap is .... Ps 142:3
took that **p** are now all dead. .... Pr 2:18

or walks the **p** of life again. .... Pr 2:19
I am leading you on the right **p**. .... Pr 4:11
and follow the **p** of justice. .... Pr 8:20
The **p** of life is level for those .... Is 26:7
blocking our **p**. Get out of our .... Is 30:11
the sea and a **p** through rough .... Is 43:16
people go up the **p** to the town .... Je 48:5
There was a **p** on the north side .... Eze 42:4
led into the rooms from this **p**. .... Eze 42:4
rooms had a **p** in front of them .... Eze 42:11
open end of a **p** beside the wall .... Eze 42:12
and do not move off their **p**. .... Joe 2:7
guide us into the **p** of peace." .... Lk 1:79
into following the wrong **p**..................... Eph 4:14
on the right **p**, so the weak will .... Heb 12:13

PATHLESS
them wander through a **p** desert. .... Job 12:24
made them wander in a **p** desert. .... Ps 107:40

PATHRUSITES
P, Casluhites, and the people of .... Ge 10:14
P, Casluhites, and Caphtorites. 1Ch 1:12

PATHS
their **p**, they fought Sisera. .... Jdg 5:20
turn away from their **p** and go .... Job 6:18
has covered my **p** with darkness. .... Job 19:8
God's ways or stay in his **p**. .... Job 24:13
He leads me on **p** that are right .... Ps 23:3
the sea and **p** through the deep .... Ps 77:19
keep away from evil **p**. .... Pr 4:27
lives are like **p** covered with .... Pr 22:5
roads, no one walking in the **p**. .... Is 33:8
guide them along **p** they have not .... Is 42:16

PATIENCE
P is better than strength........................ Pr 16:32
With **p** you can convince a ruler, ... Pr 25:15
you wear out the **p** of people?................ Is 7:13
to wear out the **p** of my God? .... Is 7:13
that these troubles produce **p**.............. Rm 5:3
And **p** produces character, and .... Rm 5:4
waited with **p** so that he could .... Rm 9:23
give us **p** and encouragement .... Rm 15:4
May the **p** and encouragement that .... Rm 15:5
understanding, **p**, and kindness,.............. 2Co 6:6
love, joy, peace, **p**, kindness, ... Gal 5:22
humility, gentleness, and **p**. .... Col 3:12
into God's love and Christ's **p**. 2Th 3:5
that he has **p** without limit..................... 1Ti 1:16
His **p** with me made me an example 1Ti 1:16
faith, love, **p**, and gentleness. 1Ti 6:11
my goal, faith, **p**, and love. 2Ti 3:10
them with great **p** and careful.................. 2Ti 4:2
in faith, in love, and in **p**. .... Tit 2:2
faith and **p** will receive what .... Heb 6:12
faith, and this will give you **p**. .... Jam 1:3
Let your **p** show itself perfectly .... Jam 1:4
You have heard about Job's **p**, ... Jam 5:11
and to your self-control, add **p**; 2Pe 1:6
and to your **p**, add service for.................. 2Pe 1:6
kingdom, and in **p** to continue. .... Rev 1:9
You have **p** and have suffered.................. Rev 2:3
faith, your service, and your **p**. .... Rev 2:19
people must have **p** and faith.................. Rev 13:10

PATIENT
He has been very kind and **p**, ... Rm 2:4
past when he was **p** and did not .... Rm 3:25
p when trouble comes, and pray.............. Rm 12:12
are weak. Be **p** with everyone. 1Th 5:14
everyone, a good teacher, and **p**. 2Ti 2:24
be **p** until the Lord comes again. .... Jam 5:7

PATIENTLY
I waited **p** for the LORD........................ Ps 40:1
Abraham waited **p** for this to .... Heb 6:15
you to listen **p** to this message .... Heb 13:22
farmer **p** waits for his valuable .... Jam 5:7
God was waiting **p** for them while 1Pe 3:20

PATMOS
the island of **P**, because I had .... Rev 1:9

PATROBAS
Hermes, **P**, Hermas, and all..................... Rm 16:14

PATROLLED
found me as they **p** the city, ... Sng 3:3
found me as they **p** the city. .... Sng 5:7

PATTERN
plans and a **p** of this altar to 2Ki 16:10
around and repeats the same **p**, ... Ec 1:6
Follow the **p** of true teachings.................. 2Ti 1:13

PAU
He was from the city of **P**. .... Ge 36:39
king, and his city was named **P**. 1Ch 1:50

PAUL
was also called **P**, was filled .... Ac 13:9
But **P** and Barnabas spoke very .... Ac 13:46
the people to turn against **P**. .... Ac 14:19
P and Barnabas gathered the .... Ac 14:27
About midnight **P** and Silas were .... Ac 16:25
learned that **P** was preaching the .... Ac 17:13
people leading **P** went with him .... Ac 17:15
the Lord told **P** in a vision: .... Ac 18:9
P was visiting some places on .... Ac 19:1
Then **P** laid his hands on them, ... Ac 19:6
God used **P** to do some very .... Ac 19:11
same Jesus that **P** talks about, ... Ac 19:13
I know about **P**, but who are you .... Ac 19:15
charges against **P** before the .... Ac 24:1
answered that **P** would be kept .... Ac 25:4
Agrippa said to **P**, "You may now .... Ac 26:1
P stayed two full years in his .... Ac 28:30
From **P**. God called me to be an 1Co 1:1
One of you says, "I follow **P**";.................. 1Co 1:12
Did **P** die on the cross for you? 1Co 1:13
you baptized in the name of **P**? 1Co 1:13
P, Apollos, and Peter; the world,.............. 1Co 3:22
From **P** and Timothy, servants of .... Php 1:1
Our dear brother **P** told you the 2Pe 3:15

PAUL'S
would not accept **P** teaching and .... Ac 18:6
us and borrowed **P** belt and used .... Ac 21:11
The commander took **P** chains off............. Ac 22:30
But **P** nephew heard about this .... Ac 23:16
the officer brought **P** nephew to .... Ac 23:18
told the king about **P** case. .... Ac 25:14
hanging from **P** hand and said to .... Ac 28:4
P letters are powerful and sound 2Co 10:10
things in **P** letters are hard 2Pe 3:16

PAULUS
stayed close to Sergius **P**, ... Ac 13:7

PAUSE
it does not **p** for any person. .... Mic 5:7

PAVED
as if it were **p** with blue .... Ex 24:10
along the edge of the **p** walkway. .... Eze 40:17

PAVEMENT
down on the **p** with their faces 2Ch 7:3
clay in the brick **p** in front of .... Je 43:9
saw rooms and a **p** of stones all .... Eze 40:17
p ran alongside the gates and.................. Eze 40:18
This was the lower **p**. .... Eze 40:18

P

PAWS

faced the stone **p** of the outer .... Eze 42:3
at the place called The Stone **P**. .... Jn 19:13

PAWS

walk on their **p** are unclean for .... Le 11:27
It **p** wildly, enjoying its .... Job 39:21

PAY

he must **p** the injured man for ...... Ex 21:19
he must **p** back twice as much as .... Ex 22:7
sell the oil and **p** what you owe. 2Ki 4:7
will not **p** taxes of any kind .... Ezr 4:13
I will **p** seven hundred fifty .... Est 3:9
P attention to my prayer,...................... Ps 17:1
P them back for what they have .... Ps 28:4
son, **p** attention to my wisdom; .... Pr 5:1
your god will **p** attention to us, ... Jnh 1:16
Its priests only teach for **p**, ... Mic 3:11
your teacher the Temple tax?" ..... Mt 17:24
he could **p** everything he owed. .... Mt 18:30
Is it right to **p** taxes to Caesar .... Mt 22:17
What will you **p** me for giving .... Mt 26:15
This is also why you **p** taxes. .... Rm 13:6
The **p** you did not give the .... Jam 5:4

PAZZEZ

Gannim, En Haddah, and Beth **P**. .... Jos 19:21

PEACE

will die in **p** and will be buried .... Ge 15:15
to you and sent you away in **p**. .... Ge 26:29
them away, and they left in **p**................ Ge 26:31
to return in **p** to my father's .... Ge 28:21
I will give **p** to your country; .... Le 26:6
lie down in **p**, and no one will .... Le 26:6
over you and give you **p**."' .... Nu 6:26
I am making my **p** agreement with........... Nu 25:12
They offered him **p**, saying, ... Dt 2:26
Do not make a **p** treaty with them .... Dt 7:2
first make them an offer of **p**. .... Dt 20:10
they do not make **p** with you and .... Dt 20:12
wish for their **p** or success as .... Dt 23:6
Make a **p** agreement with us." .... Jos 9:6
can we make a **p** agreement with .... Jos 9:7
Make a **p** agreement with us."' .... Jos 9:11
agreed to make **p** with the .... Jos 9:15
had made a **p** agreement with .... Jos 10:1
which has made a **p** agreement .... Jos 10:4
land had made a **p** agreement with .... Jos 11:19
and there was **p** in the land. .... Jos 11:23
this there was **p** in the land for .... Jos 14:15
LORD gave them **p** on all sides, ... Jos 21:44
to give the Israelites **p**, ... Jos 22:4
LORD gave Israel **p** from their .... Jos 23:1
land was at **p** for forty years .... Jdg 3:11
and there was **p** in the land for .... Jdg 3:30
family was at **p** with Jabin king .... Jdg 4:17
Then there was **p** in the land for .... Jdg 5:31
LORD and named it The LORD Is **P**. .... Jdg 6:24
the land had **p** for forty years .... Jdg 8:28
priest said to them, "Go in **p**. .... Jdg 18:6
offering to make **p** with them. .... Jdg 21:13
There was **p** also between Israel.............. 1Sa 7:14
asked, "Are you coming in **p**?" 1Sa 16:4
answered, "Yes, I come in **p**. 1Sa 16:5
said to David, "Go in **p**. 1Sa 20:42
He told her, "Go home in **p**. 1Sa 25:35
Go back in **p**. Don't do anything............. 1Sa 29:7
let Abner go, and he left in **p**. 2Sa 3:21
David had let Abner leave in **p**, ... 2Sa 3:22
and David let him leave in **p**."................. 2Sa 3:23
LORD had given him **p** from all 2Sa 7:1
I will give you **p** from all your 2Sa 7:11
they made **p** with the Israelites 2Sa 10:19
The king said, "Go in **p**." 2Sa 15:9

to the city in **p** and take your 2Sa 15:27
although it was a time of **p**. 1Ki 2:5
Do you come in **p**?" Bathsheba 1Ki 2:13
there will be **p** from the LORD 1Ki 2:33
And he had **p** on all sides of his 1Ki 4:24
to Beersheba, also lived in **p**; 1Ki 4:25
God has given me **p** on all sides 1Ki 5:4
there was **p** between Hiram and 1Ki 5:12
they may be coming to ask for **p**. 1Ki 20:18
two kings made a **p** agreement. 1Ki 20:34
years there was **p** between Israel 1Ki 22:1
was at **p** with the king.......................... 1Ki 22:44
Elisha said to him, "Go in **p**." 2Ki 5:19
you come in **p**, you Zimri, you 2Ki 9:31
Jerusalem had **p**, because 2Ki 11:20
says, 'Make **p** with me, and come 2Ki 18:31
There will be **p** and security in 2Ki 20:19
and you will be buried in **p**. 2Ki 22:20
made **p** with David and served 1Ch 19:19
have a son, a man of **p** and rest.............. 1Ch 22:9
give Israel **p** and quiet while 1Ch 22:9
and there was **p** in the country 2Ch 14:1
the kingdom had **p** while Asa was 2Ch 14:5
in Judah during the time of **p**................. 2Ch 14:6
because the LORD gave him **p**. 2Ch 14:6
he has given us **p** all around." 2Ch 14:7
LORD gave them **p** in all the 2Ch 15:15
His God gave him **p** from all the............. 2Ch 20:30
Jerusalem had **p**, because 2Ch 23:21
let you die and be buried in **p**. 2Ch 34:28
Greetings. May you have **p**. .... Ezr 5:7
not wish for their **p** or success. .... Ezr 9:12
them a message of **p** and truth. .... Est 9:30
I would be lying dead in **p**; .... Job 3:13
I have no **p** or quietness......................... Job 3:26
animals will be at **p** with you................... Job 5:23
someone to make **p** between us,............... Job 9:33
Obey God and be at **p** with him; .... Job 22:21
I go to bed and sleep in **p**, ... Ps 4:8
They say "**P**" to their neighbors, ... Ps 28:3
LORD blesses his people with **p**. .... Ps 29:11
Look for **p** and work for it....................... Ps 34:14
land and will enjoy complete **p**. .... Ps 37:11
The man who has **p** will have .... Ps 37:37
Let there be **p** on the mountains .... Ps 72:3
Let **p** continue as long as there .... Ps 72:7
He has ordered **p** for those who .... Ps 85:8
goodness and **p** will be theirs. .... Ps 85:10
your teachings will find true **p**, ... Ps 119:165
too long with people who hate **p**. .... Ps 120:6
When I talk **p**, they want war................... Ps 120:7
Pray for **p** in Jerusalem: .... Ps 122:6
May there be **p** within her walls .... Ps 122:7
I say, "Let Jerusalem have **p**.".................. Ps 122:8
Let there be **p** in Israel. .... Ps 125:5
Let there be **p** in Israel. .... Ps 128:6
I am at **p**, like a baby with its .... Ps 131:2
God's people live together in **p**! .... Ps 133:1
He brings **p** to your country and............. Ps 147:14
will live in safety and be at **p**, ... Pr 1:33
pleasant and will bring you **p**. .... Pr 3:17
lie down, you will sleep in **p**. .... Pr 3:24
but those who plan **p** are happy. .... Pr 12:20
P of mind means a healthy body, ... Pr 14:30
enemies will make **p** with them. .... Pr 16:7
crust of bread in **p** than to have .... Pr 17:1
or laughs, and there is no **p**. .... Pr 29:9
a time for war and a time for **p**. .... Ec 3:8
Those who work hard sleep in **p**; .... Ec 5:12
Who Lives Forever, Prince of **P**. .... Is 9:6
Power and **p** will be in his .... Is 9:7
will live in **p** with lambs,........................ Is 11:6
bears will eat together in **p**. .... Is 11:7

give true **p** to those who depend .... Is 26:3
you have done, so give us **p.** .... Is 26:12
and wants to make **p** with me, ... Is 27:5
should come and make **p** with me." ...... Is 27:5
This is the place of **p.**" .... Is 28:12
That fairness will bring **p,** .... Is 32:17
tried to bring **p** are weeping .... Is 33:7
says, 'Make **p** with me, and come .... Is 36:16
There will be **p** and security in .... Is 39:8
I bring **p,** and I cause troubles. .... Is 45:7
you would have had **p** like a .... Is 48:18
"There is no **p** for evil people," .... Is 48:22
who announces **p** and brings good........... Is 52:7
my promise of **p** will not come to .... Is 54:10
and they will have much **p.** .... Is 54:13
with joy and be led out in **p.** .... Is 55:12
and are given **p.** Those who live .... Is 57:2
I will give **p,** real peace, to .... Is 57:19
give peace, real **p,** to those far .... Is 57:19
"There is no **p** for evil people," .... Is 57:21
don't know how to live in **p,** .... Is 59:8
as they live will never have **p.** .... Is 59:8
change your punishment into **p,** .... Is 60:17
lambs will eat together in **p.** .... Is 65:25
I will give her **p** that will flow............... Is 66:12
You will have **p,**' but now the .... Je 4:10
We hoped to have **p,** but nothing .... Je 8:15
will give you **p** in this land.'" .... Je 14:13
We hoped for **p,** but nothing good .... Je 14:19
will have **p.**' They say to all.................... Je 23:17
we will have **p** and that message .... Je 28:9
They are afraid; there is no **p.**.............. Je 30:5
will be safe and have **p** again;............... Je 30:10
Judah will live together in **p.** .... Je 31:24
flocks will live together in **p.** .... Je 31:24
them enjoy great **p** and safety. .... Je 33:6
things and the **p** I will bring to .... Je 33:9
will live in **p** as it once did," .... Je 46:26
Jacob will have **p** and safety .... Je 46:27
I have no more **p.** I have .... La 3:17
will look for **p,** but there will .... Eze 7:25
the wrong way by saying, "**P**!" .... Eze 13:10
there is no **p.** When the people .... Eze 13:10
see visions of **p** for the city, ... Eze 13:16
there is no **p,** will be peace, ... Eze 13:16
an agreement of **p** with my sheep .... Eze 34:25
an agreement of **p** with them,................ Eze 37:26
I wish you **p** and great wealth! .... Da 4:1
I wish you great **p** and wealth. .... Da 6:25
you very much. **P** be with you. Be .... Da 10:19
the North in order to bring **p.** .... Da 11:6
he will make a **p** agreement with .... Da 11:17
people who are at **p** with you .... Ob 1:7
food to eat, they shout, '**P**!' .... Mic 3:5
He will bring **p.** Assyria will .... Mic 5:5
is announcing **p**! Celebrate your.............. Nah 1:15
in this place I will give **p,**' .... Hag 2:9
men will work together in **p.**' .... Zch 6:13
towns were at **p** and wealthy, ... Zch 7:7
will plant their seeds in **p,** .... Zch 8:12
But you must love truth and **p.**" .... Zch 8:19
talk to the nations about **p.**.................... Zch 9:10
them life and **p** so they would............... Mal 2:5
With **p** and honesty they did what .... Mal 2:6
They are blessed who work for **p,** .... Mt 5:9
Go and make **p** with that person, ... Mt 5:24
that home, say, '**P** be with you.' .... Mt 10:12
you, let your **p** stay there. .... Mt 10:13
back the **p** you wished for them. .... Mt 10:13
I came to bring **p** to the earth. .... Mt 10:34
I did not come to bring **p,** .... Mt 10:34
believed. Go in **p**; be healed of .... Mk 5:34
and have **p** with each other." .... Mk 9:50

He will make **p** between parents .... Lk 1:17
guide us into the path of **p.**" .... Lk 1:79
let there be **p** among the people .... Lk 2:14
servant, die in **p** as you said. .... Lk 2:29
saved from your sins. Go in **p.**" .... Lk 7:50
because you believed. Go in **p.**" .... Lk 8:48
a house, say, '**P** be with this .... Lk 10:5
blessing of **p** will stay with .... Lk 10:6
I came to give **p** to the earth? .... Lk 12:51
to speak to him and ask for **p.** .... Lk 14:32
There is **p** in heaven and glory .... Lk 19:38
today what would bring you **p.** .... Lk 19:42
them and said, "**P** be with you." .... Lk 24:36
I leave you **p**; my peace I give................ Jn 14:27
you peace; my **p** I give you. I do .... Jn 14:27
so that you can have **p** in me. .... Jn 16:33
them and said, "**P** be with you." .... Jn 20:19
said again, "**P** be with you. .... Jn 20:21
He said, "**P** be with you." .... Jn 20:26
he tried to make **p** between them. .... Ac 7:26
had a time of **p** and became .... Ac 9:31
News that **p** has come through .... Ac 10:36
asked Herod for **p,** because their .... Ac 12:20
sent off in **p** by the believers .... Ac 15:33
You can leave now. Go in **p.**" .... Ac 16:36
enjoy much **p** because of you,................ Ac 24:2
Grace and **p** to you from God our .... Rm 1:3
and **p** to everyone who does good— .... Rm 2:10
don't know how to live in **p.**" .... Rm 3:17
our faith, we have **p** with God. .... Rm 5:1
the Spirit, there is life and **p.** .... Rm 8:6
Live in **p** with each other. .... Rm 12:16
best to live in **p** with everyone. .... Rm 12:18
right with God, **p,** and joy in .... Rm 14:17
to do what makes **p** and helps one .... Rm 14:19
much joy and **p** while you trust .... Rm 15:13
God who gives **p** be with you all............. Rm 15:33
who brings **p** will soon defeat................ Rm 16:20
Grace and **p** to you from God our 1Co 1:3
But God called us to live in **p.**.................. 1Co 7:15
God of confusion but a God of **p.** 1Co 14:33
on his trip in **p** so that he can................. 1Co 16:11
Grace and **p** to you from God our 2Co 1:2
I had no **p,** because I did not 2Co 2:13
God made **p** between us and 2Co 5:18
about the **p** we can have with 2Co 5:18
making **p** between the world and 2Co 5:19
he gave us this message of **p.** 2Co 5:19
we beg you to be at **p** with God. 2Co 5:20
with each other, and live in **p.**.................. 2Co 13:11
God of love and **p** will be with 2Co 13:11
Grace and **p** to you from God our .... Gal 1:3
of love, joy, **p,** patience, ... Gal 5:22
P and mercy to those who follow .... Gal 6:16
Grace and **p** to you from God our .... Eph 1:2
Christ himself is our **p.** .... Eph 2:14
in him and in this way make **p.** .... Eph 2:15
and preached **p** to you who were .... Eph 2:17
together with **p** through the .... Eph 4:3
the Good News of **p** to help you .... Eph 6:15
P and love with faith to you .... Eph 6:23
Grace and **p** to you from God our .... Php 1:2
And God's **p,** which is so great .... Php 4:7
God who gives **p** will be with you .... Php 4:9
Grace and **p** to you from God our .... Col 1:2
God made **p** through the blood of .... Col 1:20
Let the **p** that Christ gives .... Col 3:15
together in one body to have **p.** .... Col 3:15
Christ: Grace and **p** to you. 1Th 1:1
"We have **p** and we are safe," 1Th 5:3
Live in **p** with each other. 1Th 5:13
the God of **p,** make you pure, ... 1Th 5:23
Grace and **p** to you from God the 2Th 1:2

may the Lord of **p** give you peace 2Th 3:16
of peace give you **p** at all times 2Th 3:16
and **p** from God the Father and 1Ti 1:2
and **p** to you from God the Father 2Ti 1:2
faith, love, and **p,** together 2Ti 2:22
Grace and **p** from God the Father .... Tit 1:4
to live in **p,** and to be gentle .... Tit 3:2
Grace and **p** to you from God our .... Phm 1:3
Salem, which means "king of **p.**" .... Heb 7:2
from it, we have **p,** because we .... Heb 12:11
to live in **p** with all people, ... Heb 12:14
who work for **p** in a peaceful way .... Jam 3:18
Grace and **p** be yours more and 1Pe 1:2
must look for **p** and work for it 1Pe 3:11
P to all of you who are in 1Pe 5:14
Grace and **p** be given to you more 2Pe 1:2
Try to be at **p** with God. 2Pe 3:14
p from God the Father and his 2Jn 1:3
P to you. The friends here greet 3Jn 1:15
Mercy, **p,** and love be yours .... Jud 1:2
Grace and **p** to you from the One .... Rev 1:4
to take away **p** from the earth................. Rev 6:4

PEACE-LOVING
but are lies about **p** people...................... Ps 35:20
If **p** people live there, your .... Lk 10:6

PEACEABLE
but rather be gentle and **p,** 1Ti 3:3

PEAK
the rocky **p** is its protected .... Job 39:28

PEAKS
near the **p** of Hermon and Mount .... Ps 42:6
mountains of Bashan have many **p.** .... Ps 68:15
with many **p** look with envy .... Ps 68:16

PEARL
When he found a very valuable **p,** .... Mt 13:46
been made from a single **p.**..................... Rev 21:21

PEARLS
don't throw your **p** before pigs. .... Mt 7:6
like a man looking for fine **p.** .... Mt 13:45
hair or gold or **p** or expensive 1Ti 2:9
jewels, and **p** she was wearing. .... Rev 17:4
silver, jewels, **p,** fine linen, ... Rev 18:12
gold, precious jewels, and **p!** .... Rev 18:16
The twelve gates were twelve **p,** .... Rev 21:21

PEAS
roasted grain, beans, small **p,**.................. 2Sa 17:28
small **p,** and millet seeds, ... Eze 4:9

PECK
the valley will **p** out your eyes, ... Pr 30:17

PEDAHEL
of Naphtali, **P** son of Ammihud." .... Nu 34:28

PEDAHZUR
son of Joseph—Gamaliel son of **P;** .... Nu 1:10
Manasseh is Gamaliel son of **P.** .... Nu 2:20
Gamaliel son of **P** was over the .... Nu 10:23

PEDAIAH
name was Zebidah daughter of **P,** 2Ki 23:36
P, Shenazzar, Jekamiah, ... 1Ch 3:18
son of **P** was over West Manasseh............ 1Ch 27:20
P son of Parosh made repairs. .... Ne 3:25
on his left were **P,** Mishael, ... Ne 8:4
the son of Joed, the son of **P.** .... Ne 11:7
P was the son of Kolaiah, the................. Ne 11:7
the teacher, and **P** a Levite...................... Ne 13:13

PEDAIAH'S
P sons were Zerubbabel and 1Ch 3:19

PEEKING
behind our wall **p** through the .... Sng 2:9

PEELED
and plane trees and **p** off some .... Ge 30:37

PEELS
skin has become black and **p** off, ... Job 30:30

PEG
took a tent **p** and a hammer and .... Jdg 4:21
reached out and took the tent **p.**............... Jdg 5:26
strong like a **p** that is hammered .... Is 22:23
it to make a **p** on which to hang............... Eze 15:3

PEGS
with two **p** side by side. .... Ex 26:17
and all the tent **p** for the Holy .... Ex 27:19
p of the Holy Tent and of the .... Ex 35:18
there were two **p** side by side .... Ex 36:22
All the tent **p** for the Holy Tent .... Ex 38:20
to make the tent **p** for the Holy .... Ex 38:31
the cords, **p,** and all the things .... Ex 39:40
their bases, tent **p,** and ropes.................. Nu 3:37
their bases, tent **p,** ropes, and................. Nu 4:32
p that hold her in place will .... Is 33:20

PEKAH
He attacked while **P** was king of 2Ki 15:29
of Aram and **P** son of Remaliah .... Is 7:1

PEKAH'S
became king in **P** place during 2Ki 15:30
and **P** army killed many soldiers 2Ch 28:5

PEKAHIAH
and his son **P** became king in his 2Ki 15:22

PEKAHIAH'S
Remaliah was one of **P** captains, ... 2Ki 15:25
Pekah became king in **P** place. 2Ki 15:25

PEKOD
Attack the people who live in **P.** .... Je 50:21
all Babylonia and men from **P,** .... Eze 23:23

PELAIAH
Eliashib, **P,** Akkub, Johanan, ... 1Ch 3:24
Azariah, Jozabad, Hanan, and **P.** .... Ne 8:7
Hodiah, Kelita, **P,** Hanan, ... Ne 10:10

PELALIAH
was the son of **P,** the son of .... Ne 11:12

PELATIAH
descendants were **P** and Jeshaiah, ... 1Ch 3:21
Ishi's sons, **P,** Neariah, ... 1Ch 4:42
P, Hanan, Anaiah, ... Ne 10:22
of Azzur and **P** son of Benaiah, ... Eze 11:1
I prophesied, **P** son of Benaiah .... Eze 11:13

PELEG
sons—one named **P,** because the .... Ge 10:25

PELEG'S
P brother was named Joktan. 1Ch 1:19

PELET
Hazar Gaddah, Heshmon, Beth **P,** .... Jos 15:27
Jotham, Geshan, **P,** Ephah, and 1Ch 2:47
There were also Jeziel and **P,** 1Ch 12:3
in Jeshua, Moladah, Beth **P,** .... Ne 11:26

PELETH
and On was the son of **P;** .... Nu 16:1
Jonathan's sons were **P** and Zaza. 1Ch 2:33

PELETHITES
was over the Kerethites and **P.** 2Sa 8:18
the Kerethites and **P,** all those................. 2Sa 15:18
Kerethites and the **P,** and all 2Sa 20:7
led the Kerethites and **P.**....................... 2Sa 20:23
left with the Kerethites and **P.**................. 1Ki 1:38
was over the Kerethites and **P.** 1Ch 18:17

PELONITE
the Harorite; Helez the P; 1Ch 11:27
the Mekerathite; Ahijah the P; 1Ch 11:36

PELONITES
He was from the P and a........................ 1Ch 27:10

PELUSIUM
pour out my anger against P, ... Eze 30:15
P will be in great pain. .... Eze 30:16

PEN
warned, did not keep it in a p. .... Ex 21:29
owner did not keep it in a p, ... Ex 21:36
carved with an iron p into lead, ... Job 19:24
is like the p of a skilled .... Ps 45:1
on it with an ordinary p: ' .... Is 8:1
to attack a strong p for sheep, ... Je 49:19
to attack a strong p for sheep, ... Je 50:44
them together like sheep in a p, ... Mic 2:12
I do not want to use p and ink. 3Jn 1:13

PENALTY
to the LORD as a p for sin; .... Le 5:6
the LORD as the p for his sin.................. Le 5:7
This will be his p offering to .... Le 5:15
measure. It is a p offering. .... Le 5:15
male sheep as the p offering. .... Le 5:16
It will be a p offering. .... Le 5:18
he must give the p offering to................ Le 5:19
day he brings his p offering. .... Le 6:5
must bring his p to the priest— .... Le 6:6
be a p offering to the LORD. .... Le 6:6
sin offering and the p offering. .... Le 6:17
teachings about the p offering, ... Le 7:1
The p offering must be killed .... Le 7:2
all the fat from the p offering— .... Le 7:3
to the LORD. It is a p offering. .... Le 7:5
The p offering is like the sin .... Le 7:7
sin offering, the p offering, ... Le 7:37
the olive oil as a p offering; .... Le 14:12
The p offering is like the sin .... Le 14:13
blood of the p offering and put .... Le 14:14
of the blood for the p offering. .... Le 14:17
one male lamb for a p offering. .... Le 14:21
the lamb for the p offering and .... Le 14:24
kill the lamb of the p offering, ... Le 14:25
the blood from the p offering.................. Le 14:28
male sheep as his p offering to .... Le 19:21
the sheep as a p offering before .... Le 19:22
lamb a year old as a p offering. .... Nu 6:12
are grain or sin or p offerings, ... Nu 6:14
You must give a p offering..................... 1Sa 6:3
What kind of p offering should 1Sa 6:4
models for the p offering in a 1Sa 6:8
of the growths as p offerings to 1Sa 6:17
money from the p offerings and 2Ki 12:16
from the flock as a p offering. .... Ezr 10:19
LORD made his life a p offering, ... Is 53:10
and p offerings were killed. .... Eze 40:39
and the p offerings, because .... Eze 42:13
sin offerings, and p offerings.................. Eze 44:29
the meat of the p offering and .... Eze 46:20

PENIEL
So Jacob named that place P, ... Ge 32:30
to the city of P and asked them .... Jdg 8:8
the people of P gave him the .... Jdg 8:8
So Gideon said to the men of P, ... Jdg 8:9
down the tower of P and killed .... Jdg 8:17
went to the city of P and made 1Ki 12:25

PENINNAH
two wives named Hannah and P. 1Sa 1:2
P had children, but Hannah had.............. 1Sa 1:2
to his wife P and to her sons 1Sa 1:4

P would tease Hannah and upset 1Sa 1:6
P would upset Hannah until 1Sa 1:7

PENKNIFE
scroll with a p and threw them .... Je 36:23

PENNIES
are sold for only two p, ... Lk 12:6

PENNY
Two sparrows cost only a p, ... Mt 10:29

PENTECOST
the day of P came, they were .... Ac 2:1
be in Jerusalem on the day of P,.............. Ac 20:16
I will stay at Ephesus until P, ... 1Co 16:8

PENUEL
Iphdeiah, and P. 1Ch 8:25

PEOPLE
Now, these p are united, all .... Ge 11:6
will be cut off from his p, ... Ge 17:14
were the p of Assyria,........................... Ge 25:3
two groups of p will be taken .... Ge 25:23
rule his own p like the other .... Ge 49:16
to save the lives of many p,.................... Ge 50:20
And the Hebrew p continued to .... Ex 1:20
and he will not let the p go. .... Ex 4:21
miracles for all the p to see, ... Ex 4:30
Moses and Aaron talked to the p, ... Ex 5:1
and refuses to let the p go. .... Ex 7:14
I will treat my p differently.................... Ex 8:23
king sent the p out of Egypt, ... Ex 13:17
in front of the p and stood .... Ex 14:19
will be still until your p pass .... Ex 15:16
The p grumbled to Moses and .... Ex 15:24
water there for the p to drink. .... Ex 17:1
What can I do with these p? .... Ex 17:4
disagreements among the p, ... Ex 18:13
what I did to the p of Egypt. .... Ex 19:4
the elders of the p together. .... Ex 19:7
Go to the p and have them spend .... Ex 19:10
and warn the p that they must .... Ex 19:21
bowls and sprinkled it on the p, ... Ex 24:8
must be cut off from his p.'" .... Ex 30:33
The p got up early the next.................... Ex 32:6
have seen these p, and I know .... Ex 32:9
terribly these p have sinned! .... Ex 32:31
happen to the p because of what .... Ex 32:35
that he brings guilt on the p, ... Le 4:3
the sins of the p so they will .... Le 4:20
he must be cut off from his p.................. Le 7:20
the offering that was for the p. .... Le 9:15
they came out and blessed the p, ... Le 9:23
will be angry with all the p. .... Le 10:6
false stories against other p, ... Le 19:16
your God, and you will be my p.............. Le 26:12
Now the p complained to the LORD .... Nu 11:1
The p cried out to Moses, and............... Nu 11:2
all the LORD's p could prophesy. .... Nu 11:29
and the p did not move on until .... Nu 12:15
All the p we saw are very tall. .... Nu 13:32
night all the p in the camp .... Nu 14:1
and all the p said to them, ... Nu 14:2
forgets to punish guilty p. .... Nu 14:18
He ran to the middle of the p,................. Nu 16:47
all the p of Israel arrived .... Nu 20:1
they bit the p, and many of the .... Nu 21:6
These p will take everything .... Nu 22:4
spoke to the p on the plains .... Nu 26:3
where the p had no water to .... Nu 33:14
'The p there are stronger and .... Dt 1:28
Bring the p together so I can .... Dt 4:10
No other p have ever heard God .... Dt 4:33
You are holy p who belong to the .... Dt 7:6
you from all the p on earth to................. Dt 7:6

lifetimes for **p** who love him and .... Dt 7:9
destroy your **p,** your own people .... Dt 9:26
are holy **p,** who belong to the .... Dt 14:2
all the **p** of that city will .... Dt 20:11
Bless your **p** Israel and bless .... Dt 26:15
on Mount Gerizim to bless the **p:** .... Dt 27:12
Then all the **p** will say, ... Dt 27:16
LORD will make you his holy **p,**.............. Dt 28:9
will defend his **p** and have mercy .... Dt 32:36
you are a **p** saved by the LORD .... Dt 33:29
The **p** of Israel were camped at .... Jos 5:10
the trumpets, the **p** shouted. .... Jos 6:20
The **p** of Ai killed about .... Jos 7:5
stayed the night with his **p.**.................... Jos 8:9
So the **p** took their positions; .... Jos 8:13
The **p** of Israel kept for .... Jos 11:14
Joshua said to the **p** of Joseph—.............. Jos 17:17
So the **p** called out to the LORD. .... Jos 24:7
The **p** served the LORD during the............ Jdg 2:7
announce to the **p,** 'Anyone who.............. Jdg 7:3
the same year those **p** destroyed.............. Jdg 10:8
and the **p** made him their leader.............. Jdg 11:11
You told my **p** a riddle, but you .... Jdg 14:16
The **p** are not expecting an .... Jdg 18:10
The **p** of Israel felt sorry for .... Jdg 21:15
come to help his **p** and had given .... Ru 1:6
Your **p** will be my people, and .... Ru 1:16
front of the **p** who are sitting .... Ru 4:4
was hard on the **p** of Ashdod and 1Sa 5:6
P respect his because everything 1Sa 9:6
He will organize my **p.**" 1Sa 9:17
has appointed him to rule his **p,** 1Sa 13:14
But the **p** told Samuel, "Saul has 1Sa 15:12
I will save my **p** Israel from the 2Sa 3:18
All the **p** saw what happened,.................. 2Sa 3:36
be a shepherd for my **p** Israel. 2Sa 5:2
any of the great **p** on the earth. 2Sa 7:9
is no nation like your **p** Israel. 2Sa 7:23
You made the **p** of Israel your.................. 2Sa 7:24
this way against the **p** of God? 2Sa 14:13
p will hear the news and think, ' 2Sa 17:9
cows' milk for David and his **p.** 2Sa 17:29
said to his **p,** "I will do what 2Sa 18:4
relatives, the **p** of Judah, steal 2Sa 19:41
saved me when my **p** attacked me............. 2Sa 22:44
to Beersheba, and count the **p.** 2Sa 24:2
seventy thousand **p** died. 2Sa 24:15
saw the angel that killed the **p,** 2Sa 24:17
am here among your chosen **p,** 1Ki 3:8
I can rule the **p** in the first 1Ki 3:9
as well as the **p** of Sidon." 1Ki 5:6
the prayers of your **p** Israel. 1Ki 8:52
would give rest to his **p** Israel, ... 1Ki 8:56
and his **p** Israel day by day. 1Ki 8:59
over the **p** who did the work 1Ki 9:23
and all the **p** returned to 1Ki 12:12
the young men and said to the **p,** 1Ki 12:14
chose priests from all the **p,** 1Ki 12:31
you a leader over my **p** Israel. 1Ki 16:2
during which the **p** are to fast. 1Ki 21:9
I live among my own **p.**" 2Ki 4:13
but the **p** trampled the officer.................. 2Ki 7:17
king and the **p** that they would 2Ki 11:17
money from the **p** and not to 2Ki 12:8
away all the **p** of Jerusalem, ... 2Ki 24:14
really come from me and my **p** 1Ch 29:14
Then if my **p,** who are called by 2Ch 7:14
prayer, and he healed the **p.** 2Ch 30:20
like the gods the **p** of the world 2Ch 32:19
relatives, the **p** of Israel, as 2Ch 35:6
also gave willingly to the **p,** 2Ch 35:8
with all of you who are his **p.** 2Ch 36:23
with all of you who are his **p.** .... Ezr 1:3

p made so much noise it could .... Ezr 3:13
Then the **p** around them tried to.............. Ezr 4:4
from the **p** living around you .... Ezr 10:11
because the **p** were willing to .... Ne 4:6
placed a heavy load on the **p.** .... Ne 5:15
and the common **p** so I could .... Ne 7:5
opened it, all the **p** stood up. .... Ne 8:5
all the **p** held up their hands .... Ne 8:6
Teachings to the **p** as they stood.............. Ne 8:7
were teaching said to all the **p,** .... Ne 8:9
the rest of the **p** threw lots to .... Ne 11:1
The **p** blessed those who........................ Ne 11:2
group of **p** scattered among .... Est 3:8
among the other **p** in all the .... Est 3:8
the order to kill the Jewish **p,** .... Est 4:8
all the other **p** living in the .... Est 9:2
house fell in on the young **p,** .... Job 1:19
the only wise **p** and that when .... Job 12:2
a curse word; **p** spit in my face. .... Job 17:6
Why are the **p** making useless .... Ps 2:1
Wicked **p** will go to the grave, ... Ps 9:17
destroy my **p** as if they were .... Ps 14:4
the **p** of Jacob will rejoice, ... Ps 14:7
P make fun of me and hate me. .... Ps 22:6
LORD gives strength to his **p;**.................. Ps 29:11
LORD blesses his **p** with peace. .... Ps 29:11
meet with the **p** of the God of .... Ps 47:9
P, trust God all the time. .... Ps 62:8
him judge your **p** fairly and .... Ps 72:2
power you have saved your **p,**.................. Ps 77:15
You led your **p** like a flock by .... Ps 77:20
But God led his **p** out like sheep.............. Ps 78:52
We are your **p,** the sheep of your .... Ps 79:13
Your **p** would rejoice in you. .... Ps 85:6
and truth belong to God's **p,** .... Ps 85:10
and we are the **p** he takes care .... Ps 95:7
are his **p,** the sheep he tends. .... Ps 100:3
Let all the **p** say, "Amen!" .... Ps 106:48
the **p** of Jacob left that foreign .... Ps 114:1
a gift to his **p,** the Israelites. .... Ps 135:12
He led his **p** through the desert. .... Ps 136:16
happy are the **p** whose God is the .... Ps 144:15
God has given his **p** a king. .... Ps 148:14
will bring disgrace to any **p.** .... Pr 14:34
When good **p** do well, everyone is .... Pr 29:2
word from God, **p** are .... Pr 29:18
Some **p** have teeth like swords; .... Pr 30:14
and taught the **p** what he knew. .... Ec 12:9
but the **p** of Israel do not know .... Is 1:3
a **p** loaded down with guilt, ... Is 1:4
I live among **p** who are not pure.............. Is 6:5
Go and tell this to the **p:** .... Is 6:9
Make the minds of these **p** dumb. .... Is 6:10
Some **p** say, "Ask the mediums and .... Is 8:19
those **p** lived in darkness, ... Is 9:2
My **p** living in Jerusalem, ... Is 10:24
out and take his **p** who are left .... Is 11:11
Babylon struck **p** in anger again.............. Is 14:6
from the **p** who are tall .... Is 18:7
saying, "Egypt, you are my **p**.................. Is 19:25
The **p** of the earth have ruined .... Is 24:5
on this mountain for all **p.** .... Is 25:6
shame of his **p** from the earth. .... Is 25:8
flowers for his **p** who are left .... Is 28:5
These **p** worship me with their .... Is 29:13
his broken **p** and heals the hurts .... Is 30:26
will be happy like **p** listening .... Is 30:29
you see those proud **p** from other .... Is 33:19
says, "Comfort, comfort my **p.** .... Is 40:1
Surely the **p** are like grass. .... Is 40:7
sign of my agreement with the **p,** .... Is 42:6
sign of my agreement with the **p.** .... Is 49:8
has taken away my **p** for nothing. .... Is 52:5

punished for the sins of my **p.** .... Is 53:8
the banner as a sign for the **p.** .... Is 62:10
ready to accept **p** who turned .... Is 65:2
' These **p** are like smoke in my .... Is 65:5
' The **p** who know the teachings .... Je 2:8
But my **p** have exchanged their .... Je 2:11
But my **p** have forgotten me for .... Je 2:32
the desert toward the LORD's **p.** .... Je 4:11
and my **p** love it this way. .... Je 5:31
hand and punish the **p** of Judah," .... Je 6:12
disaster to the **p** of Judah .... Je 6:19
p, put on rough cloth and roll .... Je 6:26
don't pray for these **p.** .... Je 7:16
your God and you will be my **p.** .... Je 7:23
my **p** don't know what the LORD .... Je 8:7
Listen to the sound of my **p.** .... Je 8:19
and all the **p** grabbed Jeremiah. .... Je 26:8
place where poor **p** are buried. .... Je 26:23
make with the **p** of Israel at .... Je 31:33
The **p** of Israel and Judah will .... Je 32:38
with all the **p** in Jerusalem to .... Je 34:8
and all the **p,** by what he is .... Je 38:4
captive some of the poorest **p,** .... Je 52:15
Jerusalem once was full of **p.** .... La 1:1
the sword is meant for my **p,** .... Eze 21:12
blow the trumpet and warn the **p.** .... Eze 33:3
p, you will know that I am the .... Eze 37:13
they will be my **p,** and I will be .... Eze 37:23
Now that my **p** Israel are living .... Eze 38:14
god can save his **p** like this." .... Da 3:29
fun of Jerusalem and your **p.** .... Da 9:16
city and your **p** are called by .... Da 9:19
The **p** of the leader who is to .... Da 9:26
you what will happen to your **p,** .... Da 10:14
you are not my **p,** and I am not .... Hos 1:9
brothers, 'my **p,'** and your .... Hos 2:1
p won't use their names anymore. .... Hos 2:17
My **p** will be destroyed, because .... Hos 4:6
priests are as wrong as the **p,** .... Hos 4:9
'Go, prophesy to my **p** Israel.' .... Am 7:15
The **p** of Nineveh believed God. .... Jnh 3:5
You skin my **p** alive and tear the .... Mic 3:2
who teach his **p** the wrong way .... Mic 3:5
shepherd your **p** with your stick. .... Mic 7:14
be any more proud **p** on my holy .... Zph 3:11
won't trick **p** with their words .... Zph 3:13
'The **p** say the right time has .... Hag 1:2
will save his **p** from their sins. .... Mt 1:21
a shepherd for my **p** Israel.'" .... Mt 2:6
These **p** who live in darkness .... Mt 4:16
some **p** brought another man to .... Mt 9:32
There are many **p** to harvest but .... Mt 9:37
the minds of these **p** have become .... Mt 13:15
heal a few sick **p** by putting his .... Mk 6:5
preached that **p** should change .... Mk 6:12
'These **p** show honor to me with .... Mk 7:6
they love for **p** to greet them .... Mk 12:38
to make a **p** ready for the coming .... Lk 1:17
My **p** are ashamed of me, but now .... Lk 1:25
be a great joy to all the **p.** .... Lk 2:10
for the non-Jewish **p** to see and .... Lk 2:32
When all the **p** were being .... Lk 3:21
we go buy food for all these **p.**" .... Lk 9:13
Jesus makes trouble with the **p,** .... Lk 23:5
But many of the **p** believed in .... Jn 7:31
to die for the **p** than for the .... Jn 11:50
I will draw all **p** toward me." .... Jn 12:32
if one man died for all the **p.** .... Jn 18:14
God and were liked by all the **p.** .... Ac 2:47
Why are the **p** making useless .... Ac 4:25
The **p** placed their sick on beds .... Ac 5:15
were afraid the **p** would stone .... Ac 5:26
Then he said, "**P** of Israel, be .... Ac 5:35

teaching the **p** and telling the .... Ac 5:42
miracles and signs among the **p.** .... Ac 6:8
all the other **p** who lived in his .... Ac 10:2
God showed his love for those **p.** .... Ac 15:14
many of my **p** are in this city." .... Ac 18:10
Please, let me speak to the **p.**" .... Ac 21:39
he would bring light to all **p.**" .... Ac 26:23
because these **p** have become .... Ac 28:27
'You are my **p**' to those I had .... Rm 9:25
ready to accept **p** who disobey .... Rm 10:21
Did God throw out his **p?** .... Rm 11:1
to be his **p** before they were .... Rm 11:2
evil things as those **p** did. 1Co 10:6
God, and they will be my **p.**" 2Co 6:16
make us pure **p** who belong only .... Tit 2:14
but the **p** who are from Abraham. .... Heb 2:16
for God's **p** is still coming. .... Heb 4:9
make with the **p** of Israel at .... Heb 8:10
told all the **p** every command .... Heb 9:19
"The Lord will judge his **p.**" .... Heb 10:30
suffer with God's **p** instead of .... Heb 11:25
city to make his **p** holy with his .... Heb 13:12
are a chosen **p,** royal priests, ... 1Pe 2:9
At one time you were not a **p,** 1Pe 2:10
They lead weak **p** into the trap 2Pe 2:14
tribe, language, **p,** and nation. .... Rev 5:9
nation, tribe, language, and **p.** .... Rev 14:6

PEOR
took Balaam to the top of **P,** .... Nu 23:28
began to worship Baal of **P,** .... Nu 25:3
become worshipers of Baal of **P.**" .... Nu 25:5
tricked you at **P** and because .... Nu 25:18
because the people sinned at **P.**" .... Nu 25:18
Israelites from the LORD at **P.** .... Nu 31:16
in the valley opposite Beth **P.** .... Dt 3:29
what the LORD did at Baal **P,** .... Dt 4:3
you who followed Baal in **P.** .... Dt 4:3
were in the valley near Beth **P,** .... Dt 4:46
in the valley opposite Beth **P,** .... Dt 34:6
Beth **P,** the hills of Pisgah, and .... Jos 13:20
Remember what happened at **P?** .... Jos 22:17
Baal at **P** and ate meat that .... Ps 106:28
But when they came to Baal **P,** .... Hos 9:10

PERATH
and are wearing, and go to **P.** .... Je 13:4
So I went to **P** and hid the belt .... Je 13:5
Now go to **P** and get the belt I .... Je 13:6
So I went to **P** and dug up the .... Je 13:7

PERAZIM
went to Baal **P** and defeated 2Sa 5:20
So David named the place Baal **P.** 2Sa 5:20
their idols behind at Baal **P,** 2Sa 5:21
the town of Baal **P** and defeated 1Ch 14:11
So that place was named Baal **P.** 1Ch 14:11
will fight as he did at Mount **P.** .... Is 28:21

PERCENT
and the ten **p** that the people .... Ne 12:44

PERESH
had a son whom she named **P.** 1Ch 7:16

PERESH'S
P brother was named Sheresh. 1Ch 7:16

PEREZ
first," and they named him **P.** .... Ge 38:29
Er, Onan, Shelah, **P,** and Zerah .... Ge 46:12
from **P** came the Perezite family .... Nu 26:20
were the family groups from **P:** .... Nu 26:21
Rithmah and camped at Rimmon **P.** .... Nu 33:19
They left Rimmon **P** and camped at .... Nu 33:20
gave birth to Judah's son **P,** .... Ru 4:12
This is the family history of **P,** .... Ru 4:18

P

Tamar gave birth to **P** and Zerah. 1Ch 2:4
Judah's descendants were **P**, ... 1Ch 4:1
Bani was a descendant of **P**, ... 1Ch 9:4
of Perez, and **P** was Judah's son. 1Ch 9:4
one of the descendants of **P**, ... 1Ch 27:3
Mahalalel was a descendant of **P**. .... Ne 11:4
the descendants of **P** who lived .... Ne 11:6
was the father of **P** and Zerah. .... Mt 1:3
P was the father of Hezron. .... Mt 1:3
Hezron was the son of **P**. .... Lk 3:33
P was the son of Judah. .... Lk 3:33

PEREZ'S
P sons were Hezron and Hamul. .... Ge 46:12
P sons were Hezron and Hamul. 1Ch 2:5

PEREZITE
Perez came the **P** family group; .... Nu 26:20

PERFECT
what he does is **p**, and he is .... Dt 32:4
The teachings of the LORD are **p**; .... Ps 19:7
Jerusalem, whose beauty is **p**. .... Ps 50:2
and say, "We have a **p** plan." .... Ps 64:6
who wait for **p** weather will .... Ec 11:4
my darling, my dove, my **p** one. .... Sng 5:2
only one like my dove, my **p** one. .... Sng 6:9
Your beauty was **p**, because of .... Eze 16:14
builders made your beauty **p**. .... Eze 27:4
They made your beauty **p**. .... Eze 27:11
were an example of what was **p**, ... Eze 28:12
full of wisdom and **p** in beauty. .... Eze 28:12
So you must be **p**, just as your .... Mt 5:48
as your Father in heaven is **p**. .... Mt 5:48
you want to be **p**, then go and .... Mt 19:21
the **p** time came for Herodias .... Mk 6:21
pleasing to him and what is **p**. .... Rm 12:2
ability to prophesy are not **p**. 1Co 13:9
things that are not **p** will end. 1Co 13:10
my power is made **p** in you." 2Co 12:9
you all together in **p** unity. .... Col 3:14
to salvation **p** through suffering .... Heb 2:10
And because his obedience was **p**, ... Heb 5:9
could not be made **p** through that .... Heb 7:11
Moses could not make anything **p**. .... Heb 7:19
Son has been made **p** forever. .... Heb 7:28
conscience of the worshiper **p**. .... Heb 9:9
the greater and more **p** tent. .... Heb 9:11
Spirit as a **p** sacrifice to God. .... Heb 9:14
can never make **p** those who come .... Heb 10:1
If the law could make them **p**, ... Heb 10:2
he made **p** forever those who .... Heb 10:14
so that they would be made **p**, ... Heb 11:40
our faith and who makes it **p**. .... Heb 12:2
people who have been made **p**. .... Heb 12:23
Then you will be **p** and complete .... Jam 1:4
and every **p** gift is from God .... Jam 1:17
study God's **p** law that makes .... Jam 1:25
faith was made **p** by what he did. .... Jam 2:22
they would be **p** and able to .... Jam 3:2
who was like a pure and **p** lamb. 1Pe 1:19
and his love is made **p** in us. 1Jn 4:12
is how love is made **p** in us: 1Jn 4:17
because God's **p** love drives out 1Jn 4:18
love is not made **p** in the person 1Jn 4:18

PERFECTION
when **p** comes, the things that 1Co 13:10
like Christ and have his **p**. .... Eph 4:13

PERFECTLY
than normal or is not **p** formed, ... Le 22:23
your demands **p** so I will not be .... Ps 119:80
show itself **p** in what you do. .... Jam 1:4

PERFORM
The priest will **p** the acts to .... Le 5:6
the priest will **p** the acts to .... Le 6:7
the people and **p** the acts to .... Le 9:7
will use it to **p** the acts that .... Le 16:10
Aaron will **p** the acts to make .... Le 16:16
So Aaron will **p** the acts to .... Le 16:17
p the acts for making things .... Le 16:32
the LORD and **p** the acts to make .... Le 23:28
"Bring Samson out to **p** for us." .... Jdg 16:25
on the roof watching Samson **p**. .... Jdg 16:27
will come and **p** great wonders .... Mt 24:24
will come and **p** great wonders .... Mk 13:22
you want and **p** the works that 2Th 1:11

PERFORMED
the prison, and he **p** for them. .... Jdg 16:25
They **p** the service of their God .... Ne 12:45

PERFUME
things like a **p** to make a holy .... Ex 30:25
and do not make **p** the same way .... Ex 30:32
anyone makes **p** like it or puts .... Ex 30:33
a person who makes **p** would do. .... Ex 30:35
this to use as **p** must be cut off .... Ex 30:38
yourself, put on **p**, change your .... Ru 3:3
to make **p** and cook and bake 1Sa 8:13
him, Hananiah, a **p** maker, made .... Ne 3:8
loves wine and **p** will never be .... Pr 21:17
The sweet smell of **p** and oils is .... Pr 27:9
to have respect than good **p**. .... Ec 7:1
flies can make even **p** stink. .... Ec 10:1
The smell of your **p** is pleasant, ... Sng 1:3
is pleasant like expensive **p**. .... Sng 1:3
The smell of my **p** spreads out to .... Sng 1:12
your **p** smells better than any .... Sng 4:10
they smell like mounds of **p**. .... Sng 5:13
their bottles of **p**, and charms, ... Is 3:20
of wearing sweet-smelling **p**, ... Is 3:24
jar filled with expensive **p**. .... Mt 26:7
She poured this **p** on Jesus' head .... Mt 26:7
They asked, "Why waste that **p**? .... Mt 26:8
This woman poured on my body .... Mt 26:12
filled with very expensive **p**, ... Mk 14:3
and poured the **p** on Jesus' head. .... Mk 14:3
each other, "Why waste that **p**? .... Mk 14:4
she poured **p** on my body to .... Mk 14:8
brought an alabaster jar of **p** .... Lk 7:37
and rubbing them with the **p**. .... Lk 7:38
but she poured **p** on my feet. .... Lk 7:46
woman who later put **p** on the .... Jn 11:2
very expensive **p** made from pure .... Jn 12:3
She poured the **p** on Jesus' feet, ... Jn 12:3
from the **p** filled the whole .... Jn 12:3
This **p** was worth an entire .... Jn 12:5
her to save this **p** for today, ... Jn 12:7
like a sweet-smelling **p**. 2Co 2:14

PERFUMED
It is like **p** oil poured on the .... Ps 133:2
would be like **p** oil on my head. .... Ps 141:5
use any **p** oil for three weeks. .... Da 10:3
and use the best **p** lotions. .... Am 6:6

PERFUMES
them like a person who mixes **p**. .... Ex 37:29
spices, expensive **p**, his swords 2Ki 20:13
and different kinds of mixed **p**, ... 2Ch 16:14
six months with **p** and cosmetics. .... Est 2:12
spices, expensive **p**, his swords .... Is 39:2
your oils and **p** to look nice for .... Is 57:9
left to prepare spices and **p**. .... Lk 23:56

PERGA

from Paphos and came to P, ... Ac 13:13
their trip from **P** and went to .... Ac 13:14
had preached the message in **P**, ... Ac 14:25

PERGAMUM

Ephesus, Smyrna, **P**, Thyatira, ... Rev 1:11
to the angel of the church in **P**: .... Rev 2:12

PERIDA

of Sotai, Sophereth, **P**, ... Ne 7:57

PERIOD

I am having my monthly **p**." .... Ge 31:35
is unclean during her monthly **p**. .... Le 12:2
is unclean during her monthly **p**. .... Le 12:5
When a woman has her monthly **p**, ... Le 15:19
and her monthly **p** touches him, ... Le 15:24
during her regular monthly **p**, ... Le 15:25
of blood after her regular **p**, ... Le 15:25
as she is during her monthly **p**. .... Le 15:25
during her regular monthly **p**. .... Le 15:26
as during her regular monthly **p**. .... Le 15:26
unclean from her monthly **p**, ... Le 15:33
with her during her monthly **p**, ... Le 18:19
a woman during her monthly **p**, ... Le 20:18
herself from her monthly **p**, ... 2Sa 11:4
to live for a certain **p** of time. .... Da 7:12

PERIZZITES

Canaanites and the **P** were living .... Ge 13:7
Hittites, **P**, Rephaites, ... Ge 15:20
Canaanites and the **P** who live in .... Ge 34:30
Hittites, Amorites, **P**, Hivites, ... Ex 3:8
Hittites, Amorites, **P**, Hivites, ... Ex 3:17
Hittites, **P**, Canaanites, ... Ex 23:23
Amorites, Hittites, **P**, Hivites, ... Ex 33:2
Hittites, **P**, Hivites, ... Ex 34:11
Canaanites, **P**, Hivites, ... Dt 7:1
Canaanites, **P**, Hivites, ... Dt 20:17
Hivites, **P**, Girgashites, ... Jos 3:10
Canaanites, **P**, Hivites, ... Jos 9:1
Hittites, **P**, and Jebusites .... Jos 11:3
Canaanites, **P**, Hivites, ... Jos 12:8
the land of the **P** and the .... Jos 17:15
the Amorites, **P**, Canaanites, ... Jos 24:11
Canaanites and the **P** to them, ... Jdg 1:4
the Canaanites and the **P**, ... Jdg 1:5
Hittites, Amorites, **P**, Hivites, ... Jdg 3:5
Amorites, Hittites, **P**, Hivites, ... 1Ki 9:20
Hittites, Amorites, **P**, Hivites, ... 2Ch 8:7
Hittites, **P**, Jebusites, ... Ezr 9:1
Amorites, **P**, Jebusites, ... Ne 9:8

PERMANENT

I'll make you my **p** bodyguard." 1Sa 28:2

PERMISSION

hand or a foot without your **p**." .... Ge 41:44
of Persia had given **p** for this. .... Ezr 3:7
Who gave you **p** to rebuild this .... Ezr 5:3
Who gave you **p** to rebuild this .... Ezr 5:9
who are in Susa **p** to do again .... Est 9:13
had their **p** to burn incense to .... Je 44:19
asked Ashpenaz for **p** not to make .... Da 1:8
own kings without asking my **p** .... Hos 8:4
Pilate gave his **p**, so Joseph .... Jn 19:38
commander gave **p**, so Paul stood .... Ac 21:40
priests gave me **p** and the power .... Ac 26:12
this to give you **p** to stay away 1Co 7:6

PERMIT

who will not **p** you to be tempted 1Co 10:13

PERMITTED

the LORD had **p** those nations to .... Jdg 2:23
the guests be **p** to drink as much .... Est 1:8
but they were **p** to live for a .... Da 7:12

PERSECUTE

some evil people began to **p** him. .... Jn 5:16

PERSECUTED

who are **p** for doing good, ... Mt 5:10
of Jerusalem began to be **p**, ... Ac 8:1
when they were **p** after Stephen .... Ac 11:19
I **p** the people who followed the .... Ac 22:4
because I **p** the church of God. 1Co 15:9
We are **p**, but God does not leave 2Co 4:9
Christ and **p** him and did all 1Ti 1:13
in Christ Jesus, will be **p**. 2Ti 3:12

PERSECUTING

Why are you **p** me?" .... Ac 9:4
I am Jesus, whom you are **p**. .... Ac 9:5
Saul, Saul, why are you **p** me?' .... Ac 22:7
from Nazareth whom you are **p**.' .... Ac 22:8
Saul, Saul, why are you **p** me? .... Ac 26:14
I am Jesus, the one you are **p**. .... Ac 26:15

PERSECUTION

When trouble or **p** comes because .... Mt 13:21
When trouble or **p** comes because .... Mk 4:17

PERSIA

first year Cyrus was king of **P**, ... 2Ch 36:22
is what Cyrus king of **P** says: 2Ch 36:23
first year Cyrus was king of **P**, ... Ezr 1:1
is what Cyrus king of **P** says: .... Ezr 1:2
Cyrus king of **P** had Mithredath .... Ezr 1:8
Cyrus king of **P** had given .... Ezr 3:7
the king of **P**, commanded us to .... Ezr 4:3
the time Cyrus was king of **P**. .... Ezr 4:5
the time Darius was king of **P**. .... Ezr 4:5
Artaxerxes became king of **P**, ... Ezr 4:7
from Tripolis, **P**, Erech, and .... Ezr 4:9
kings and areas controlled by **P**. .... Ezr 4:15
year Darius was king of **P**. .... Ezr 4:24
and Artaxerxes of **P** had ordered. .... Ezr 6:14
rule of Artaxerxes king of **P**, ... Ezr 7:1
the kings of **P** to be kind to us .... Ezr 9:9
the countries of **P** and Media .... Est 1:3
important men of **P** and Media. .... Est 1:14
important men of **P** and Media .... Est 1:17
important men of **P** and Media .... Est 1:18
in the laws of **P** and Media, ... Est 1:19
of the kings of Media and **P**. .... Est 10:2
Men of **P**, Lydia, and Put were .... Eze 27:10
P, Cush, and Put will be with .... Eze 38:5
are the kings of Media and **P** .... Da 8:20
Cyrus' third year as king of **P**, ... Da 10:1
the prince of **P** has been .... Da 10:13
left there with the king of **P**. .... Da 10:13
fight against the prince of **P**. .... Da 10:20
fight against the prince of **P**. .... Da 11:1
Three more kings will rule in **P**, ... Da 11:2
the kings of **P** before him and .... Da 11:2

PERSIAN

until the **P** kingdom defeated 2Ch 36:20
while Darius the **P** was king. .... Ne 12:22
and when Cyrus the **P** was king. .... Da 6:28

PERSIANS

given to the Medes and the **P**." .... Da 5:28
of the Medes and **P** and cannot be .... Da 6:8
of the Medes and **P** cannot be .... Da 6:12
the Medes and **P** says that no law .... Da 6:15

PERSIS

Greetings to my dear friend **P**, ... Rm 16:12

PERSON

and the man became a living **p**. .... Ge 2:7
because that **p** is being .... Le 20:6
daughter marries a **p** who is not .... Le 22:12
something wrong to another **p**, ... Nu 5:6

the sin of the **p** who sinned...................... Nu 15:28
to make that **p** clean again...................... Nu 19:17
money to murder an innocent **p**." .... Dt 27:25
We call the **p** a prophet today,.................. 1Sa 9:9
and treat each **p** as he should be 1Ki 8:39
a **p** be pure before his maker? .... Job 4:17
They must not go near a dead **p**, ... Eze 44:25
But a **p** from her family will .... Da 11:7
stand up against an evil **p**. .... Mt 5:39
call any **p** on earth 'Father,...................... Mt 23:9
will be for the **p** who hands the .... Mt 26:24
because God has accepted that **p**. .... Rm 14:3
can that **p** take care of God's 1Ti 3:5
important **p** blesses the less .... Heb 7:7
nothing while the **p** is alive; .... Heb 9:17
p like that can ruin many of you. .... Heb 12:15
A **p** must do these things to 1Pe 3:10
The **p** who has suffered in the 1Pe 4:1

PERSONAL
allowed him to be his **p** servant............... Ge 39:4
fifty men for his **p** bodyguard. 1Ki 1:5
Then the king's **p** servants .... Est 2:2
The king's **p** servants answered,.............. Est 6:3
The king's **p** servants said, ... Est 6:5
the king's **p** servant, to be .... Ac 12:20

PERSONALLY
and I will be **p** responsible for .... Ge 43:9

PERSONS
were thirty-three **p** in this part .... Ge 46:15
There were sixteen **p** in this .... Ge 46:18
were fourteen **p** in this part .... Ge 46:22
There were seven **p** in this part .... Ge 46:25
over both nations and **p** alike. .... Job 34:29
seventy-five **p** altogether)...................... Ac 7:14
them are free **p** who belong to 1Co 7:22
those **p** there without 1Co 14:16
or spiritual **p** should understand............ 1Co 14:37
made between two **p** is firm. .... Gal 3:15

PERSPIRE
wear anything that makes them **p**. .... Eze 44:18

PERSUADE
trying to **p** them to believe in .... Ac 18:4
We could not **p** him to stay away .... Ac 21:14
you think you can **p** me to become........... Ac 26:28
he tried to **p** them to believe .... Ac 28:23
wisdom that **p** people but with 1Co 2:4
are working hard to **p** you, ... Gal 4:17
They want to **p** you to turn .... Gal 4:17

PERSUADED
priests had **p** the people to ask .... Mk 15:11
had already **p** Judas Iscariot, ... Jn 13:2
and Iconium and **p** the people to .... Ac 14:19
And she **p** us to stay with her. .... Ac 16:15
the people and **p** them to accept............. Ac 19:8
will be **p** to believe without..................... 1Pe 3:1
They will be **p** by the way their 1Pe 3:1

PERSUADING
Barnabas were **p** them to continue........... Ac 13:43
dawn Paul began **p** all the people .... Ac 27:33

PERUDA
of Sotai, Hassophereth, **P**, ... Ezr 2:55

PET
Can you make a **p** of Leviathan as .... Job 41:5

PETAL
cup must have a bud and a **p**.................. Ex 25:33
and each cup had a bud and a **p**. .... Ex 37:19

PETALS
p must all be joined together .... Ex 25:31
cups must also have buds and **p**. .... Ex 25:34

p were joined together in one .... Ex 37:17
each with its buds and **p**. .... Ex 37:20

PETER
Simon (called **P**) and his brother .... Mt 4:18
as **P** was sitting in the .... Mt 26:69
And **P** remembered what Jesus had .... Mt 26:75
Simon (Jesus named him **P**), ... Mk 3:16
Then he told **P** not to talk that .... Mk 8:33
Jesus took **P**, James, and John .... Mk 14:33
She saw **P** warming himself at the .... Mk 14:67
and tell his followers and **P**, ' .... Mk 16:7
But Jesus said, "**P**, before the .... Lk 22:34
another person saw **P** and said, ... Lk 22:58
turned and looked straight at **P**. .... Lk 22:61
Then **P** went outside and cried .... Lk 22:62
where Andrew and **P** lived...................... Jn 1:44
Simon **P**, who had a sword, pulled .... Jn 18:10
P also was standing with them, ... Jn 18:18
the man whose ear **P** had cut off. .... Jn 18:26
Again **P** said it wasn't true...................... Jn 18:27
faster than **P** and reached the .... Jn 20:4
P, John, James, Andrew, Philip, ... Ac 1:13
of them). **P** stood up and said, ... Ac 1:15
P said to them, "Change your................. Ac 2:38
One day **P** and John went to the.............. Ac 3:1
But **P** said, "I don't have any .... Ac 3:6
Then **P** took the man's right hand .... Ac 3:7
was holding on to **P** and John, ... Ac 3:11
P saw this, he said to them, ... Ac 3:12
While **P** and John were speaking .... Ac 4:1
leaders grabbed **P** and John and .... Ac 4:3
who had heard **P** and John preach........... Ac 4:4
made **P** and John stand before .... Ac 4:7
Then **P**, filled with the Holy .... Ac 4:8
leaders saw that **P** and John were .... Ac 4:13
P and the other apostles .... Ac 5:29
Simon who is also called **P**...................... Ac 10:5
voice said to Peter, "Get up, **P**; .... Ac 10:13
But **P** said, "No, Lord!............................ Ac 10:14
When **P** entered, Cornelius met .... Ac 10:25
P was sleeping between two .... Ac 12:6
The angel struck **P** on the side .... Ac 12:7
P knocked on the outside door, ... Ac 12:13
to meet **P** and stayed with .... Gal 1:18
From **P**, an apostle of Jesus..................... 1Pe 1:1
From Simon **P**, a servant and 2Pe 1:1

PETER'S
When Jesus went to **P** house, ... Mt 8:14
he saw that **P** mother-in-law was .... Mt 8:14
him was Andrew, Simon **P** brother. .... Jn 1:40
Andrew, Simon **P** brother, said, ... Jn 6:8
And the chains fell off **P** hands. .... Ac 12:7
When she recognized **P** voice, ... Ac 12:14
they said, "It must be **P** angel." .... Ac 12:15

PETHAHIAH
The nineteenth was **P**. 1Ch 24:16
called (Kelita) **P**, Judah, and .... Ezr 10:23
Hodiah, Shebaniah, and **P**. .... Ne 9:5
P son of Meshezabel was the .... Ne 11:24

PETHOR
to Balaam son of Beor at **P**,...................... Nu 22:5
from **P** in Northwest Mesopotamia, ... Dt 23:4

PETHUEL
spoke his word to Joel son of **P**; .... Joe 1:1

PEULLETHAI
was seventh, and **P** was eighth. 1Ch 26:5

PHANUEL
the family of **P** in the tribe .... Lk 2:36

617

PHARISEE

One **P**, who was an expert on the .... Mt 22:35
When the **P** who asked Jesus to .... Lk 7:39
said to the **P**, "Simon, I have .... Lk 7:40
Simon, the **P**, answered, "I think .... Lk 7:43
a **P** asked Jesus to eat with him................ Lk 11:37
But the **P** was surprised when he .... Lk 11:38
eat at the home of a leading **P**, ... Lk 14:1
A **P** and a tax collector both .... Lk 18:10
The **P** stood alone and prayed, ' .... Lk 18:11
with God, but the **P** was not. .... Lk 18:14
But a **P** named Gamaliel stood up .... Ac 5:34
belonged to the **P** group came .... Ac 15:5
brothers, I am a **P**, and my .... Ac 23:6
Pharisee, and my father was a **P**. .... Ac 23:6
tell you that I was a good **P**. .... Ac 26:5
law, which is why I became a **P**. .... Php 3:5

PHARISEE'S

went into the **P** house and sat at.............. Lk 7:36
Jesus was eating at the **P** house............... Lk 7:37

PHARISEES

teachers of the law and the **P**,................. Mt 5:20
do we and the **P** often fast for................. Mt 9:14
The **P** and Sadducees came to .... Mt 16:1
of the **P** and the Sadducees. .... Mt 16:6
teaching of the **P** and the .... Mt 16:12
priests and the **P** heard these .... Mt 21:45
Then the **P** left that place and................. Mt 22:15
the law and the **P** have the .... Mt 23:2
teachers of the law and **P**. .... Mt 23:14
of John and the **P** often fasted .... Mk 2:18
But the **P** and the men who taught .... Lk 5:30
the law and the **P** were watching .... Lk 6:7
But the **P** and experts on the law .... Lk 7:30
The **P**, who loved money, were .... Lk 16:14
one of the **P** and an important .... Jn 3:1
the leading priests and the **P**, ... Jn 7:45
took to the **P** the man who had .... Jn 9:13
priests and **P** called a meeting .... Jn 11:47
between the **P** and the Sadducees, ... Ac 23:7

PHARPAR

The Abana and the **P**, the rivers 2Ki 5:12

PHICOL

Then Abimelech came with **P**,................. Ge 21:22
Abimelech and **P**, the commander .... Ge 21:32
him, and **P**, the commander .... Ge 26:26

PHILADELPHIA

Sardis, **P**, and Laodicea." .... Rev 1:11
to the angel of the church in **P**: .... Rev 3:7

PHILEMON

To **P**, our dear friend and worker .... Phm 1:1

PHILETUS

Hymenaeus and **P** are like that. 2Ti 2:17

PHILIP

Andrew, **P**, Bartholomew, Matthew, ... Mk 3:18
P, Herod's brother, the ruler of .... Lk 3:1
P found Nathanael and told him, ... Jn 1:45
said to **P**, "Can anything .... Jn 1:46
P told Andrew, and then Andrew .... Jn 12:22
the Holy Spirit), Procorus, ... Ac 6:5
An angel of the Lord said to **P**, ... Ac 8:26
Spirit said to **P**, "Go to that.................. Ac 8:29
Both **P** and the officer went down .... Ac 8:38
into the home of **P** the preacher,.............. Ac 21:8

PHILIPPI

came to the area of Caesarea **P**,............. Mt 16:13
to the towns around Caesarea **P**.............. Mk 8:27
Then we went by land to **P**,.................... Ac 16:12
We sailed from **P** after the Feast.............. Ac 20:6

in Christ Jesus who live in **P**, ... Php 1:1
came to you, we suffered in **P**. 1Th 2:2

PHILIPPIANS

You **P** remember when I first .... Php 4:15

PHILISTIA

Moab, Ammon, **P**, and Amalek. 2Sa 8:12
sandals at Edom. I shout at **P**." .... Ps 60:8
Ammon, Amalek, **P**, and Tyre. .... Ps 83:7
People from **P**, Tyre, and Cush .... Ps 87:4
sandals at Edom. I shout at **P**." .... Ps 108:9
Country of **P**, don't be happy .... Is 14:29
we tell the messengers from **P**? .... Is 14:32
and all of you regions of **P**!................... Joe 3:4
says the LORD. The People of **P** .... Am 1:5

PHILISTINE

I am a **P**, and you are Saul's 1Sa 17:8
Goliath, the **P** champion from................ 1Sa 17:23
who kills this **P** and takes away 1Sa 17:26
the bodies of the **P** soldiers to................ 1Sa 17:46
stone hit the **P** and went deep................ 1Sa 17:49
defeated the **P** with only a sling 1Sa 17:50
The sword of Goliath the **P**,.................... 1Sa 21:9

PHILISTINE'S

Israelites heard the **P** words, ... 1Sa 17:11

PHILISTINES

went back to the land of the **P**. .... Ge 21:32
to see Abimelech king of the **P**. .... Ge 26:1
terror will take hold of the **P**. .... Ex 15:14
regions of Geshur and of the **P**; .... Jos 13:2
six hundred **P** with a sharp stick .... Jdg 3:31
Ammon, and the gods of the **P**. .... Jdg 10:6
over to the **P** for forty years .... Jdg 13:1
to marry a woman from the **P**, ... Jdg 14:3
for a way to challenge the **P**, ... Jdg 14:4
of the **P** so that he burned .... Jdg 15:5
him, "Samson, the **P** are here!" .... Jdg 16:9
I can pay these **P** back for .... Jdg 16:28
"Let me die with these **P**!" .... Jdg 16:30
P went to meet the Israelites 1Sa 4:2
After the **P** had captured the Ark 1Sa 5:1
Now the **P** will really hate us!" 1Sa 13:4
planned to let the **P** kill David. 1Sa 18:25
daughters of the **P** will rejoice. 2Sa 1:20
killed a hundred **P** to get her." 2Sa 3:14
defeated the **P** and chased them 2Sa 5:25
defeated the **P**, conquered them,.............. 2Sa 8:1
River to the land of the **P**, ... 1Ki 4:21
fought a war against the **P**. 2Ch 26:6
will attack the **P** on the west. .... Is 11:14
and the last of the **P** will die,".................. Am 1:8
then go down to Gath of the **P**. .... Am 6:2
of Egypt, and the **P** from Crete. .... Am 9:7
by the Mediterranean Sea, you **P**! .... Zph 2:5
will destroy the pride of the **P**. .... Zch 9:6

PHILOLOGUS

Greetings to **P** and Julia, Nereus .... Rm 16:15

PHILOSOPHERS

and Stoic **p** argued with him, ... Ac 17:18

PHINEHAS

P son of Eleazar, the son of .... Nu 25:7
When the priest and the ten .... Jos 22:30
Shiloh was where Hophni and **P**, ... 1Sa 1:3
P prayed to the LORD, and the .... Ps 106:30
P did what was right, and it .... Ps 106:31

PHLEGON

to Asyncritus, **P**, Hermes, ... Rm 16:14

PHOEBE

I recommend to you our sister **P**, ... Rm 16:1

PHOENICIA

the Lord GOD. The People of **P** ....Am 1:8
was Greek, born in **P**, in Syria. ....Mk 7:26
Some of them went as far as **P**, ...Ac 11:19
the countries of **P** and Samaria, ...Ac 15:3
we found a ship going to **P**,....................Ac 21:2

PHOENIX

we could go to **P** and stay there ....Ac 27:12
P, a city on the island of Crete, ...Ac 27:12

PHRYGIA

P, Pamphylia, Egypt, the areas ....Ac 2:10
the areas of **P** and Galatia since ....Ac 16:6
the regions of Galatia and **P**. ....Ac 18:23

PHYGELUS

left me, even **P** and Hermogenes. 2Ti 1:15

PHYSICAL

he is only a Jew in his **p** body; ....Rm 2:28
that is "planted" is a **p** body. 1Co 15:44
There is a **p** body, and there is 1Co 15:44
the **p** and then the spiritual. 1Co 15:46
Our **p** body is becoming older and 2Co 4:16
a painful **p** problem was given to 2Co 12:7
from him by their **p** desires, ...1Ti 5:11
are people with **p** bodies, ...Heb 2:14

PHYSICALLY

The boy Samuel grew **p**.........................1Sa 2:26
Jesus became wiser and grew **p**...............Lk 2:52

PI

turn back to **P** Hahiroth and to ....Ex 14:2
near **P** Hahiroth and Baal Zephon...........Ex 14:9
and went back to **P** Hahiroth,..................Nu 33:7
They left **P** Hahiroth and walked ....Nu 33:8

PICK

Elisha said, "**P** up your son." 2Ki 4:36
to them, "**P** me up, and throw.................Jnh 1:12

PICKED

Then she **p** up her son and went...............2Ki 4:37
So they **p** up Jonah and threw him............Jnh 1:15

PICTURE

Arabia and is a **p** of the earthly ....Gal 4:25
only an unclear **p** of the good.................Heb 10:1

PICTURES

was carved with **p** of flowers and 1Ki 6:18
were carved with **p** of creatures 1Ki 6:29
covered with **p** of creatures with 1Ki 6:35
I saw **p** and visions in my mind ....Da 4:5

PIECE

wants to sell the **p** of land that ....Ru 4:3
each one gave Job a **p** of silver ....Job 42:11
the little **p** of dust in your ....Mt 7:3
notice the big **p** of wood in your..............Mt 7:3
take that little **p** of dust out...................Mt 7:4
have that big **p** of wood in your ....Mt 7:4
wrapped in a **p** of cloth and hid...............Lk 19:20
gave him a **p** of broiled fish. ....Lk 24:42
So Jesus took a **p** of bread,....................Jn 13:26
which was all one **p** of cloth, ...Jn 19:23

PIECES

and cut each of them into two **p**, ...Ge 15:10
bought for a hundred **p** of silver..............Jos 24:32
bowstrings like **p** of burned ....Jdg 16:9
of oxen and cut them into **p**. 1Sa 11:7
cut Agag to **p** before the LORD at 1Sa 15:33
coat and tore it into twelve **p**....................1Ki 11:30
break them into **p** like pottery." ....Ps 2:9
my enemies into **p**, like dust ....Ps 18:42
than thousands of **p** of gold and ....Ps 119:72
for battle and be smashed to **p**! ....Is 8:9
its gates will be smashed to **p**. ....Is 24:12

and breaks into small **p**. ....Is 30:13
like **p** of a broken jar ....Je 25:34
broke into **p** the bronze pillars, ...Je 52:17
all the bronze **p** to Babylon. ....Je 52:17
Put in the **p** of meat, the best ....Eze 24:4
gold broke to **p** at the same time ....Da 2:35
crushes and smashes things to **p**, ...Da 2:40
clay, silver, and gold to **p**. ....Da 2:45
children will be torn to **p**, ...Hos 13:16
house will be broken into **p**, ...Am 6:11
they paid me thirty **p** of silver. ....Zch 11:12
will cut him in **p** and send him ....Mt 24:51
the Temple was torn into two **p**, ...Mt 27:51
when pottery is broken into **p**.' ....Rev 2:27

PIERCED

crushed and **p** the side of his ....Jdg 5:26

PIG

Now the **p** has a split hoof that ....Le 11:7
and, "After a **p** is washed, it 2Pe 2:22

PIG'S

like a gold ring in a **p** snout. ....Pr 11:22

PIGEON

sheep, a dove, and a young **p**." ....Ge 15:9
it must be a dove or a young **p**. ....Le 1:14
a dove or young **p** for a sin....................Le 12:6
Israel has become like a **p**— ....Hos 7:11

PIGEONS

or two young **p** to the LORD as ....Le 5:7
afford two doves or two **p**, ...Le 5:11
bring two doves or two young **p**, ...Le 12:8
and two doves or two young **p**, ...Le 14:22
one of the doves or young **p**, ...Le 14:30
or two young **p** before the LORD ....Le 15:14
or two young **p** and bring them to ....Le 15:29
or two young **p** to the priest at ....Nu 6:10
two doves or two young **p**." ....Lk 2:24
to those who were selling **p**, ...Jn 2:16

PIGS

P are also unclean for you; ....Dt 14:8
Like wild **p** they walk over us; ....Ps 80:13
the meat of **p**, and their pots ....Is 65:4
who offer me the blood of **p**. ....Is 66:3
eat the meat of **p** and rats and ....Is 66:17
throw your pearls before **p**. ....Mt 7:6
P will only trample on them, ...Mt 7:6
was a large herd of **p** feeding. ....Mt 8:30
send us into that herd of **p**." ....Mt 8:31
the men and went into the **p**. ....Mt 8:32
A large herd of **p** was feeding on ....Mk 5:11
Jesus, "Send us into the **p**; ....Mk 5:12
the man and went into the **p**. ....Mk 5:13
Then the herd of **p**—about two ....Mk 5:13
him, and they told about the **p**. ....Mk 5:16
A large herd of **p** was feeding on ....Lk 8:32
to allow them to go into the **p**. ....Lk 8:32
went into the **p**, and the herd ....Lk 8:33
son into the fields to feed **p**. ....Lk 15:15
eat the pods the **p** were eating, ...Lk 15:16

PILATE

him over to **P**, the governor. ....Mt 27:2
Pontius **P**, the ruler of Judea; ....Lk 3:1
Jesus that **P** had killed some ....Lk 13:1
stood up and led Jesus to **P**. ....Lk 23:1
P and Herod had always been ....Lk 23:12
Then **P** went back inside the ....Jn 18:33
when he stood before Pontius **P**...............1Ti 6:13

PILATE'S

the people gathered at **P** house, ...Mt 27:17

PILDASH

are Kesed, Hazo, **P**, Jidlaph, and..............Ge 22:22

PILHA

Hallohesh, **P**, Shobek, ... Ne 10:24

PILLAR

she did, she became a **p** of salt. .... Ge 19:26
ahead of them in a **p** of cloud, ... Ex 13:21
he had set up a **p** for himself in 2Sa 18:18
named the south **p** He Establishes 1Ki 7:21
king stood by the **p** and made an 2Ki 23:3
city, an iron **p**, a bronze wall. .... Je 1:18

PILLARS

pieces the stone **p** they use in .... Ex 23:24
break their stone **p**, and cut .... Ex 34:13
Let me feel the **p** that hold up .... Jdg 16:26
the stone **p** used to worship 2Ch 31:1
rings on marble **p** by white and .... Est 1:6
the **p**, the large bronze bowl, ... Je 27:19
the top of the **p** so that even .... Am 9:1
Make the **p** fall on the people's .... Am 9:1
and the stone **p** you worship so .... Mic 5:13
crows will sit on the stone **p**. .... Zph 2:14
win the victory **p** in the temple .... Rev 3:12
his legs were like **p** of fire. .... Rev 10:1

PILOT

it go wherever the **p** wants. .... Jam 3:4

PILTAI

P, from Miniamin's and Moadiah's .... Ne 12:17

PIN

cloth, and tighten it with a **p**. .... Jdg 16:13
Then she fastened it with a **p**. .... Jdg 16:14
pulled out the **p** and the loom .... Jdg 16:14
"I'll **p** David to the wall." 1Sa 18:11
tried to **p** David to the wall 1Sa 19:10
Let me **p** Saul to the ground with 1Sa 26:8

PINE

the cedar and **p** trees you want. 1Ki 5:8
much cedar and **p** as he wanted. 1Ki 5:10
floor was made from **p** boards. 1Ki 6:15
Two doors were made from **p**. 1Ki 6:34
all the cedar, **p**, and gold he 1Ki 9:11
cedars and its best **p** trees. 2Ki 19:23
send me cedar, **p**, and juniper. 2Ch 2:8
He put panels of **p** on the walls 2Ch 3:5
Even the **p** trees are happy, ... Is 14:8
cedars and its best **p** trees. .... Is 37:24
I will put **p**, fir, and cypress .... Is 41:19
Or he plants a **p** tree, and the .... Is 44:14
its **p**, fir, and cypress trees .... Is 60:13
The **p** trees did not have such .... Eze 31:8
I am like a green **p** tree; .... Hos 14:8
Cry, **p** trees, because the cedar .... Zch 11:2

PINNED

the jail and **p** their feet down .... Ac 16:24

PINON

Oholibamah, Elah, **P**, ... Ge 36:41
Oholibamah, Elah, **P**, ... 1Ch 1:52

PINS

of all kinds—**p**, earrings, rings, ... Ex 35:22

PINT

two-thirds of a **p** of olive oil. .... Le 14:10
two-thirds of a **p** of olive oil .... Le 14:21
and half of a **p** of dove's dung 2Ki 6:25
brought in a **p** of very expensive .... Jn 12:3

PIPES

zithers, harps, **p**, and all the .... Da 3:5
lyres, zithers, harps, **p**, and the. .... Da 3:7
zithers, harps, **p**, and all the .... Da 3:10
zithers, harps, **p**, and all the .... Da 3:15
branches beside the two gold **p**, ... Zch 4:12

PIRAM

of Hebron, **P** king of Jarmuth .... Jos 10:3

PIRATHON

the city of **P** was a judge for .... Jdg 12:13
and was buried in **P** in the land .... Jdg 12:15
He was from **P** in Ephraim. 1Ch 27:14

PIRATHONITE

Benaiah the **P**; Hiddai from the 2Sa 23:30
in Benjamin; Benaiah the **P**; 1Ch 11:31

PISGAH

top of Mount **P** looks over the .... Nu 21:20
of Zophim, on top of Mount **P**. .... Nu 23:14
to the Dead Sea west of Mount **P**. .... Dt 3:17
top of Mount **P** and look west, ... Dt 3:27
as the Dead Sea below Mount **P**. .... Dt 4:49
of Moab to the top of Mount **P**, ... Dt 34:1
south to the slopes of **P**. .... Jos 12:3
Peor, the hills of **P**, and Beth .... Jos 13:20

PISHON

river, named **P**, flows around .... Ge 2:11

PISIDIA

went to Antioch, a city in **P**. .... Ac 13:14
they went through **P** and came to .... Ac 14:24

PISPAH

sons were Jephunneh, **P**, and Ara. 1Ch 7:38

PISTACHIO

spices, myrrh, **p** nuts, and .... Ge 43:11

PIT

a man takes the cover off a **p**, ... Ex 21:33
or digs a **p** and does not cover .... Ex 21:33
the owner of the **p** must pay the .... Ex 21:34
it into a large **p** in the forest 2Sa 18:17
and filled the **p** with many 2Sa 18:17
went down into a **p** and killed a 2Sa 23:20
they made it into a sewage **p**, ... 2Ki 10:27
went down into a **p** and killed a 1Ch 11:22
would push me into a dirty **p**, ... Job 9:31
have fallen into the **p** they dug. .... Ps 9:15
no reason they dug a **p** for me. .... Ps 35:7
them fall into the **p** and die. .... Ps 35:8
me out of the **p** of destruction, ... Ps 40:2
dug a **p** in my path, but they .... Ps 57:6
of trouble until a **p** is dug for .... Ps 94:13
is as dangerous as a deep **p**, ... Pr 23:27
Whoever digs a **p** for others will .... Pr 26:27
Anyone who digs a **p** might fall .... Ec 10:8
to be buried in a rocky **p**. .... Is 14:19
they have dug a **p** in order to .... Je 18:20
have dug a **p** to capture me. .... Je 18:22
They tried to kill me in a **p**; .... La 3:53
LORD, from the bottom of the **p**. .... La 3:55
He was trapped in their **p**, ... Eze 19:4
He was trapped in their **p**. .... Eze 19:8
saved me from the **p** of death, ... Jnh 2:6
heap of weeds, a **p** of salt, and .... Zph 2:9
free from the waterless **p**. .... Zch 9:11
there is a big **p** between you and .... Lk 16:26
that leads to the bottomless **p**. .... Rev 9:1
that leads to the bottomless **p**, ... Rev 9:2
the angel of the bottomless **p**. .... Rev 9:11
bottomless **p** will fight a war .... Rev 11:7
the bottomless **p** and go away to .... Rev 17:8
the bottomless **p** and a large .... Rev 20:1
threw him into the bottomless **p**, ... Rev 20:3

PITCHER

be like a broken **p** at a spring, ... Ec 12:6

PITCHERS

and **p** and how much gold should 1Ch 28:17
washing of cups, **p**, and pots. .... Mk 7:4

PITCHFORK
of Judah with my **p** and scattered .... Je 15:7

PITCHFORKS
use shovels and **p** to spread all .... Is 30:24

PITHOM
build the cities **P** and Rameses .... Ex 1:11

PITHON
sons were **P**, Melech, Tarea, ... 1Ch 8:35
sons were **P**, Melech, Tahrea, ... 1Ch 9:41

PITIED
them to be **p** by those who held .... Ps 106:46
we should be **p** more than anyone 1Co 15:19

PITIFUL
miserable, **p**, poor, blind,....................... Rev 3:17

PITS
were many tar **p** in the Valley .... Ge 14:10
soldiers fell into the tar **p**, ... Ge 14:10
the rocks, and in **p** and wells. 1Sa 13:6
people have dug **p** to trap me.................. Ps 119:85
fire or into **p** from which they.................. Ps 140:10
are trapped in **p** or locked up .... Is 42:22
Fear, deep **p**, and traps wait for .... Je 48:43
but they will fall into the **p**..................... Je 48:44
out of the **p** will be caught .... Je 48:44

PITY
LORD heard him and had **p** on him. 2Ch 33:13
prayer and God's **p** for him, ... 2Ch 33:19
because he had **p** on them and 2Ch 36:15
P me, my friends, pity me, ... Job 19:21
me, my friends, **p** me, because .... Job 19:21
Is he too angry to **p** us?"........................ Ps 77:9
he will have no **p** when he gets .... Pr 6:34
and will have **p** on those who .... Is 49:13
sorry or have **p** on them or show .... Je 13:14
and my **p** from these people," .... Je 16:5
the LORD destroyed without **p**. .... Je 20:16
any mercy or **p** or feel sorry for .... Je 21:7
and I will have **p** on Israel's .... Je 30:18
will have no **p**, and I will show .... Eze 5:11
I will have no **p** on you; .... Eze 7:4
I will show no **p**, and I will not .... Eze 7:9
will have no **p**, nor will I show .... Eze 8:18
Don't **p** anyone, and don't show .... Eze 9:5
will have no **p**, nor will I show .... Eze 9:10
But I had **p** on them. I did not................ Eze 20:17
or feel **p** or change my mind .... Eze 24:14
I will not **p** Israel anymore,..................... Hos 1:6
But I will show **p** to the people .... Hos 1:7
'you have been shown **p**.' .... Hos 2:1
will not take **p** on her children .... Hos 2:4
and I will show **p** to the one I .... Hos 2:23
one I had called 'not shown **p**.' .... Hos 2:23
my love for you stirs up my **p**. .... Hos 11:8
have **p** on us and help us." .... Mk 9:22

PLAIN
they found a **p** in the land of .... Ge 11:2
his brothers in **p** sight of Moses .... Nu 25:6
on the high **p** and all of Gilead .... Dt 3:10
in the desert high **p** was for the .... Dt 4:43
the whole **p** from Medeba to .... Jos 13:9
the whole **p** and the town .... Jos 13:16
and all the towns on the **p**: .... Jos 13:17
towns on the **p** and all the area .... Jos 13:21
out the people living on the **p**, ... Jdg 1:19
them come down to live in the **p**. .... Jdg 1:34
I don't have any **p** bread here, ... 1Sa 21:4
were made in the **p** of the Jordan 1Ki 7:46
in the **P** of Sharon all 1Ch 5:16
that fed in the **P** of Sharon...................... 1Ch 27:29
were made in the **p** of the Jordan 2Ch 4:17

to fight on the **p** of Megiddo. 2Ch 35:22
in Kephirim on the **p** of Ono." .... Ne 6:2
they make **p** people wise. .... Ps 19:7
the evil will be **p** to everyone.................. Pr 26:26
I am a rose in the **P** of Sharon, ... Sng 2:1
The **P** of Sharon is dry like the .... Is 33:9
of Carmel and the **P** of Sharon. .... Is 35:2
Then the **P** of Sharon will be a .... Is 65:10
the high **p** will be destroyed, ... Je 48:8
on the high **p** have been punished .... Je 48:21
Get up and go out to the **p**. .... Eze 3:22
I got up and went out to the **p**. .... Eze 3:23
there, as I had seen on the **p**. .... Eze 8:4
it up on the **p** of Dura in the .... Da 3:1
Rimmon in the **p** of Megiddo. .... Zch 12:11
Rimmon will be turned into a **p**............... Zch 14:10
speak to you in **p** words about .... Jn 16:25
Lydda and on the **P** of Sharon saw .... Ac 9:35

PLAINLY
please let me speak **p** to you, ... Ge 44:18
was deaf and could not talk **p**. .... Mk 7:32
Jesus told them **p** what would................. Mk 8:32
you are the Christ, tell us **p**." .... Jn 10:24
then Jesus said **p**, "Lazarus is .... Jn 11:14
told me quite **p** that there are 1Co 1:11
teach the truth **p**, showing 2Co 4:2

PLAINS
of Israel went to the **p** of Moab, ... Nu 22:1
the people on the **p** of Moab near .... Nu 26:3
on the **p** of Moab across .... Nu 26:63
counted on the **p** of Moab was .... Nu 26:64
camp was on the **p** of Moab near .... Nu 31:12
and camped on the **p** of Moab near .... Nu 33:48
the Jordan on the **p** of Moab, ... Nu 33:49
On the **p** of Moab by the Jordan .... Nu 33:50
to Moses on the **p** of Moab across .... Nu 35:1
through Moses on the **p** of Moab .... Nu 36:13
Nebo from the **p** of Moab to the .... Dt 34:1
staying in the **p** of Moab until................. Dt 34:8
going toward the **p** of Jericho. .... Jos 4:13
at Gilgal on the **p** of Jericho. .... Jos 5:10
tribes on the **p** of Moab across .... Jos 13:32
up with him in the **p** of Jericho. 2Ki 25:5
the western hills and in the **p**................... 2Ch 26:10
Zedekiah in the **p** of Jericho. .... Je 39:5
caught him in the **p** of Jericho. .... Je 52:8

PLAN
people who **p** to trip me up. .... Ps 140:4
If their **p** comes from human .... Ac 5:38

PLANE
and **p** trees and peeled off some .... Ge 30:37
The **p** trees did not have such .... Eze 31:8

PLANETS
the moon, the **p**, and all the 2Ki 23:5

PLANNED
to know that I **p** many times to .... Rm 1:13

PLANS
a mind that thinks up evil **p**, ... Pr 6:18
may make **p** in their minds, ... Pr 16:9
let's make **p** against Jeremiah. .... Je 18:18

PLANT
more of its own kind of **p**." .... Ge 1:11
seed grew its own kind of **p**. .... Ge 1:12
cry as they **p** crops will sing .... Ps 126:5
is a time to **p** and a time to .... Ec 3:2
weather will never **p** seeds;..................... Ec 11:4
P early in the morning, and work .... Ec 11:6
like a **p** whose roots rot .... Is 5:24
You **p** the finest grapevines and .... Is 17:10
that I will build up and **p**. .... Je 18:9

Every **p** that my Father in heaven .... Mt 15:13
harvest things you did not **p**. .... Mt 25:24
things I did not **p** and that I .... Mt 25:26
A farmer went out to **p** his seed............. Lk 8:5
every other **p** in your garden. .... Lk 11:42
They don't **p** or harvest, they .... Lk 12:24
yourself and **p** yourself in .... Lk 17:6
But if they **p** to please the .... Gal 6:8
of the hyssop to **p** to sprinkle it .... Heb 9:19
in a peaceful way **p** a good crop .... Jam 3:18
on the earth or any **p** or tree. .... Rev 9:4

PLANTED
Then the LORD God **p** a garden in .... Ge 2:8
a farmer and **p** a vineyard. .... Ge 9:20
Abraham **p** a tamarisk tree at .... Ge 21:33
Isaac **p** seed in that land, ... Ge 26:12
the crops you **p** in your fields. .... Ex 23:16
animal falls on a seed to be **p**, ... Le 11:37
are like spices **p** by the LORD, ... Nu 24:6
Has anyone **p** a vineyard and not .... Dt 20:6
that has never been plowed or **p**, ... Dt 21:4
Nothing is **p**, nothing grows, and .... Dt 29:23
Whenever the Israelites **p** crops, ... Jdg 6:3
Israelites had **p** as far away as .... Jdg 6:4
other people eat what I have **p**, ... Job 31:8
like a tree **p** by a river. .... Ps 1:3
nations and **p** us in the land. .... Ps 80:8
You **p** this shoot with your own .... Ps 80:15
Like trees **p** in the Temple of .... Ps 92:13
cedars of Lebanon, which he **p**. .... Ps 104:16
They **p** seeds in the fields and .... Ps 107:37
built houses and **p** vineyards for............. Ec 2:4
and I **p** all kinds of fruit trees .... Ec 2:5
of stones and **p** the best .... Is 5:2
Even the **p** fields by the Nile .... Is 19:7
ground, like seeds that are **p**. .... Is 40:24
They are the plant I have **p**, ... Is 60:21
trees by the LORD to show his .... Is 61:3
the seeds **p** in it to grow. .... Is 61:11
a land that had never been **p**. .... Je 2:2
But I **p** you as a special vine, ... Je 2:21
All-Powerful, who **p** you, has .... Je 11:17
people like wheat, but they .... Je 12:13
like a tree **p** near water that .... Je 17:8
up what I have **p** everywhere in .... Je 45:4
where he **p** it in a city of .... Eze 17:4
from the land and **p** it in a good .... Eze 17:5
p it to grow like a willow tree. .... Eze 17:5
where it was **p** toward the eagle .... Eze 17:7
It had been **p** in a good field by .... Eze 17:8
Even if it is **p** again, it will .... Eze 17:10
your vineyard, **p** beside the................. Eze 19:10
Now the vine is **p** in the desert, ... Eze 19:13
and seed will be **p** in you. .... Eze 36:9
and have **p** what was empty. .... Eze 36:36
Though we **p** fig seeds, they lie .... Joe 1:17
You have **p** beautiful vineyards, ... Am 5:11
You have **p** much, but you harvest .... Hag 1:6
away what was **p** in that person's .... Mt 13:19
like a man who **p** good seed in .... Mt 13:24
his enemy came and **p** weeds among .... Mt 13:25
'You **p** good seed in your field. .... Mt 13:27
answered, 'An enemy **p** weeds.' .... Mt 13:28
seed that a man **p** in his field............. Mt 13:31
The man who **p** the good seed in .... Mt 13:37
the enemy who **p** the bad seed is .... Mt 13:39
heaven has not **p** himself will be .... Mt 15:13
the teaching that was **p** in them. .... Mk 4:15
like the seed **p** on rocky ground .... Mk 4:16
like the seed **p** among the thorny .... Mk 4:18
are like the seed **p** in the good .... Mk 4:20
But when **p**, this seed grows and .... Mk 4:32

He said, "A man **p** a vineyard. .... Mk 12:1
a fig tree **p** in his vineyard. .... Lk 13:6
A man **p** a vineyard and leased it .... Lk 20:9
p the seed, and Apollos watered............. 1Co 3:6
Since we **p** spiritual seed among 1Co 9:11
The body that is "**p**" will ruin 1Co 15:42
the body is "**p**," it is without 1Co 15:43
the body is "**p**," it is weak, ... 1Co 15:43
body that is "**p**" is a physical 1Co 15:44
that is **p** in your hearts, ... Jam 1:21

PLANTING
earth continues, **p** and harvest, ... Ge 8:22
more years without **p** or harvest. .... Ge 45:6
even during the **p** season and the .... Ex 34:21
After **p** a tree, wait three years .... Le 19:23
plans are like the wind, ... Hos 8:7
a place for **p** vineyards. .... Mic 1:6
While he was **p**, some seed fell .... Mt 13:4
While he was **p**, some seed fell .... Mk 4:4
While he was **p**, some seed fell .... Lk 8:5
selling, **p**, and building. .... Lk 17:28

PLANTS
she earned, she **p** a vineyard. .... Pr 31:16
So the one who **p** is not 1Co 3:7

PLASTER
throw away the **p** they scraped .... Le 14:41
cover the walls with new clay **p**. .... Le 14:42
old stones and **p** and put in new............. Le 14:43
and put in new stones and **p**. .... Le 14:43
all its stones, **p**, and wood, and .... Le 14:45
new stones and **p** have been put............. Le 14:48
stones and cover them with **p**. .... Dt 27:2
today, and cover them with **p**............. Dt 27:4
writing on the **p** of the wall, ... Da 5:5

PLATE
silver **p** weighed about three .... Nu 7:85
yourself an iron **p** and set it up .... Eze 4:3

PLATES
Make the **p** and bowls for the................. Ex 25:29
p, bowls, cups, and jars used .... Ex 37:16
must put the **p**, pans, bowls, ... Nu 4:7
twelve silver **p**, twelve silver .... Nu 7:84
the silver **p** and silver bowls .... Nu 7:85

PLATFORM
took away the **p** for the royal 2Ki 16:18
had made a bronze **p** seven and 2Ch 6:13
Solomon stood on the **p**. 2Ch 6:13
on a high wooden **p** that had been .... Ne 8:4
a seventy-five foot **p** built, ... Est 5:14
so he ordered the **p** to be built. .... Est 5:14
on the **p** he had prepared .... Est 6:4
seventy-five foot **p** stands near .... Est 7:9
Haman on the **p** he had prepared .... Est 7:10
ten sons be hanged on the **p**."............. Est 9:13
sons should be hanged on the **p**. .... Est 9:25

PLATTER
John the Baptist here on a **p**." .... Mt 14:8
brought it on a **p** and gave it to .... Mt 14:11
the Baptist right now on a **p**."............. Mk 6:25
and brought it back on a **p**...................... Mk 6:28

PLAY
first person to the harp and .... Ge 4:21
for someone who can **p** the harp. 1Sa 16:16
you, he will **p**, and you will...................... 1Sa 16:16
someone who can **p** well and bring 1Sa 16:18
Jesse of Bethlehem the harp. 1Sa 16:18
David would take his harp and **p**. 1Sa 16:23
as singers to **p** their lyres, ... 1Ch 15:16
Jeduthun to preach and **p** harps, ... 1Ch 25:1
the wild animals **p**, provide food .... Job 40:20

P

new song to him; **p** well and .... Ps 33:3
the music. **P** the tambourines .... Ps 81:2
P pleasant music on the harps .... Ps 81:2
which you made to **p** there. .... Ps 104:26
I will **p** to you on the .... Ps 144:9
will be able to **p** near a cobra's .... Is 11:8
the city. **P** your harp well. .... Is 21:4
so we will **p** songs on stringed .... Is 38:20
the children who **p** in the street .... Je 6:11
children who **p** in the streets .... Je 9:21

PLAYED

hear the music **p** for your sheep? .... Jdg 5:16
and **p** tambourines and stringed.............. 1Sa 18:6
As they **p**, they sang, "Saul has 1Sa 18:7
While the harp was being **p**, ... 2Ki 3:15
and Ethan **p** bronze cymbals. 1Ch 15:19
and Benaiah **p** the lyres. 1Ch 15:20
Jeiel, and Azaziah **p** the harps. 1Ch 15:21
trumpets, and **p** cymbals, lyres, ... 1Ch 15:28
Asaph, who **p** the cymbals, was 1Ch 16:5
They **p** the lyres and harps. 1Ch 16:5
in white linen and **p** cymbals,................ 2Ch 5:12
sang as others **p** their trumpets, ... 2Ch 5:13
of David king of Israel were **p**. 2Ch 29:27
These men **p** the musical .... Ne 12:36
'We **p** music for you, but you did .... Mt 11:17
and saying, 'We **p** music for you, ... Lk 7:32
will not know what is being **p**. 1Co 14:7

PLAYING

followed her, **p** tambourines .... Ex 15:20
p a tambourine and dancing. .... Jdg 11:34
They will be **p** harps, ... 1Sa 10:5
David was **p** the harp as he 1Sa 18:10
David was **p** the harp. 1Sa 19:9
They were **p** wooden instruments: 2Sa 6:5
P flutes and shouting for joy, ... 1Ki 1:40
they were singing and **p** lyres, ... 1Ch 13:8
had the job of **p** the trumpets 1Ch 16:42
The singers were **p** musical 2Ch 23:13
like a harp **p** a funeral song; .... Is 16:11
like a flute **p** a funeral song. .... Je 48:36
filled with boys and girls **p**." .... Zch 8:5
I heard was like people **p** harps.............. Rev 14:2
of people **p** harps and other .... Rev 18:22

PLAYS

me someone who **p** the harp." 2Ki 3:15
charmer no matter how well he **p**. .... Ps 58:5
beautiful voice and **p** a musical .... Eze 33:32

PLEAD

mercy and to **p** with him for her............... Est 4:8
They won't **p** the case of the .... Je 5:28
P with your mother. Accuse her,.............. Hos 2:2
p your case in front of the .... Mic 6:1
p with him as if he were your................. 1Ti 5:1

PLEADED

But we have not **p** with the LORD .... Da 9:13
they begged and **p** with us to let.............. 2Co 8:4

PLEADING

and hear the **p** of my lips. .... Job 13:6
love you, I am **p** with you .... Phm 1:9
am **p** with you for my child.................... Phm 1:10

PLEASANT

is good and how **p** his land is, ... Ge 49:15
My share in life has been **p**; .... Ps 16:6
Play **p** music on the harps and .... Ps 81:2
It is good and **p** when God's .... Ps 133:1
praises to him, because it is **p**. .... Ps 135:3
it is good and **p** to praise him. .... Ps 147:1
make your life **p** and will bring .... Pr 3:17
Their **p** words make them better.............. Pr 16:21

P words are like a honeycomb, ... Pr 16:24
smell of perfume and oils is **p**, ... Pr 27:9
The smell of your perfume is **p**, ... Sng 1:3
your name is **p** like expensive .... Sng 1:3
so handsome, my lover, and so **p**! .... Sng 1:16
You are beautiful and **p**; .... Sng 7:6
My **p** evening has become a night .... Is 21:4
will sing about the **p** vineyard. .... Is 27:2
that were **p** are now empty..................... Is 32:12
children and give you a **p** land, ... Is 3:19
My sleep had been very **p**. .... Je 31:26
like Tyre, given a **p** place. .... Hos 9:13
I called one **P** and the other .... Zch 11:7
broke the stick named **P** to break .... Zch 11:10
you will have a **p** country," .... Mal 3:12
be kind and **p** so you will be .... Col 4:6

PLEASE

to her, 'P give me a drink.' .... Ge 24:45
P give me some of your son's .... Ge 30:14
If I have pleased you, **p** stay. .... Ge 30:27
'P let me follow the workers .... Ru 2:7
I hope I can continue to **p** you, ... Ru 2:13
P let me talk to you. 1Sa 25:24
live so that they **p** the LORD, ... Pr 16:7
place on my altar will **p** me, ... Is 56:7
doing whatever you **p** nor saying .... Is 58:13
now I ask you, LORD, **p** kill me................. Jnh 4:3
to Philip, "P tell me, who is .... Ac 8:34
sinful selves cannot **p** God...................... Rm 8:8
Let each of us **p** our neighbors .... Rm 15:2
did not live to **p** himself....................... Rm 15:3
work, trying to **p** the Lord. 1Co 7:32
the world, trying to **p** his wife. 1Co 7:33
as to how she can **p** her husband. 1Co 7:34
God is the One I am trying to **p**. .... Gal 1:10
live in a way that will **p** God, ... 1Th 4:1
soldier wants to **p** the enlisting 2Ti 2:4
Without faith no one can **p** God.............. Heb 11:6

PLEASED

But Noah **p** the LORD. .... Ge 6:8
The LORD was **p** with these .... Ge 8:21
him, "If I have **p** you, please .... Ge 30:27
If I have **p** you, then accept the .... Ge 33:10
decided he was not **p** with her, ... Ex 21:8
very well, and I am **p** with you.' .... Ex 33:12
If I have truly **p** you, show me .... Ex 33:13
that you are **p** with me and with............ Ex 33:16
very well, and I am **p** with you."............... Ex 33:17
if you are **p** with me, please .... Ex 34:9
the LORD is **p** with us, he will .... Nu 14:8
God will be **p** to let you curse................. Nu 23:27
But if you are not **p** with her, ... Dt 21:14
be **p** with the work they do. .... Dt 33:11
lived in the burning bush be **p**. .... Dt 33:16
and East Manasseh, they were **p**. .... Jos 22:30
They were **p** and thanked God. .... Jos 22:33
If you are **p** with me, give me .... Jdg 6:17
LORD is **p** with your journey." .... Jdg 18:6
He **p** the LORD, and the people. 1Sa 2:26
said that, Samuel was not **p**. 1Sa 8:6
p to make you his own people. 1Sa 12:22
which **p** Saul's officers and all 1Sa 18:5
When they told Saul, he was **p**. 1Sa 18:20
he was **p** to become the king's 1Sa 18:26
If you are **p** with me, give me 1Sa 27:5
would be **p** to have you serve in 1Sa 29:6
Today I know you are **p** with me, ... 2Sa 14:22
the LORD is **p** with me, he will 2Sa 15:25
LORD says he is not **p** with me, ... 2Sa 15:26
I can see you would be **p**. 2Sa 19:6
LORD your God be **p** with you."............... 2Sa 24:23
The Lord was **p** that Solomon had 1Ki 3:10

PLEASES

when he saw them, he was not **p.** 1Ki 9:12
who was **p** to make you king of 1Ki 10:9
king's family who **p** the LORD, ... 1Ki 14:13
family God was **p** to make me king 1Ch 28:4
God who was **p** to make you king 2Ch 9:8
are willing and if I have **p** you, ... Ne 2:5
It **p** the king to send me, ... Ne 2:6
p Hegai, and he liked her. .... Est 2:9
unless he was **p** with her and .... Est 2:14
the king was **p** with Esther more .... Est 2:17
in the courtyard, he was **p.** .... Est 5:2
if you are **p** with me and if it .... Est 5:8
if you are **p** with me, and if.................... Est 7:3
if you are **p** with me, and if.................... Est 8:5
a God who is **p** with the wicked .... Ps 5:4
LORD, God is **p** with their ways .... Ps 37:23
me, I know you are **p** with me. .... Ps 41:11
You are not **p** by sacrifices, ... Ps 51:16
Then you will be **p** with right .... Ps 51:19
The LORD is **p** with those who .... Ps 147:11
The LORD is **p** with his people; .... Ps 149:4
the LORD will be **p** with them. .... Pr 8:35
but he is **p** with honest weights. .... Pr 11:1
hearts but is **p** with those who .... Pr 11:20
LORD is **p** with a good person, ... Pr 12:2
tell lies but is **p** with those .... Pr 12:22
A king is **p** with a wise servant, ... Pr 14:35
but is **p** with kind words .... Pr 15:26
that the LORD is **p** with him. .... Pr 18:22
I will be so **p** if you speak what .... Pr 23:16
I was **p** with everything I did, ... Ec 2:10
am not **p** by the blood of bulls, ... Is 1:11
Hezekiah was **p** and showed the .... Is 39:2
I chose, and I am **p** with him. .... Is 42:1
are the people I am **p** with: .... Is 66:2
but the LORD is not **p** with them. .... Hos 8:13
was very **p** to have the plant. .... Jnh 4:6
the LORD be **p** with a thousand .... Mic 6:7
Will he be **p** with ten thousand .... Mic 6:7
Then I will be **p** with it and be .... Hag 1:8
Would he be **p** with you?...................... Mal 1:8
I am not **p** with you and will not .... Mal 1:10
and is not **p** with what you bring .... Mal 2:13
is good, and he is **p** with them." .... Mal 2:17
and I am very **p** with him." .... Mt 3:17
I love him, and I am **p** with him............. Mt 12:18
and his guests, and she **p** him. .... Mt 14:6
love, and I am very **p** with him. .... Mt 17:5
and I am very **p** with you." .... Mk 1:11
p Herod and the people eating .... Mk 6:22
These priests were **p** about this .... Mk 14:11
People liked him, and he **p** God............... Lk 2:52
and I am very **p** with you." .... Lk 3:22
They were **p** and agreed to give .... Lk 22:5
who **p** God and asked God to let .... Ac 7:46
has **p** the Holy Spirit that you.................. Ac 15:28
But God was not **p** with most of us.......... 1Co 10:5
what he wanted and what **p** him, ... Eph 1:5
that sacrifice and is **p** with it. .... Php 4:18
God was **p** for all of himself to .... Col 1:19
I will not be **p** with them." .... Heb 10:38
God said he was **p** with the gifts............. Heb 11:4
he was a man who truly **p** God. .... Heb 11:5
can stand the pain, God is **p.** 1Pe 2:19
you are patient, then God is **p.** 1Pe 2:20
love, and I am very **p** with him.".............. 2Pe 1:17

PLEASES

must do it in a way that **p** him. .... Le 22:29
If it **p** you, we would like this .... Nu 32:5
answered, "That the LORD more: 1Sa 14:7
our king, if it **p** you, give a .... Est 1:19
girl who most **p** the king become .... Est 2:4

it **p** the king, let an order be .... Est 3:9
My king, if it **p** you, come today.............. Est 5:4
pleased with me and if it **p** you, ... Est 5:8
me, and if it **p** you, let me live .... Est 7:3
and if it **p** you to do this,....................... Est 8:5
answered, "If it **p** the king, ... Est 9:13
is in heaven. He does what he **p.** .... Ps 115:3
LORD does what he **p,** in heaven .... Ps 135:6
makes everything go as he **p.** .... Pr 16:4
he can direct it as he **p.** .... Pr 21:1
A man who **p** God will be saved.............. Ec 7:26
the king does whatever he **p.** .... Ec 8:3
You do what **p** yourselves on .... Is 58:3
and not do what **p** yourselves on .... Is 58:13
This kind of bragging **p** me," .... Je 9:24
offering with the lambs as he **p.** .... Eze 46:5
may give as much grain as he **p.** .... Eze 46:7
may give as much grain as he **p.** .... Eze 46:11
only doing what **p** themselves. .... Rm 16:18
to do what **p** your sinful self .... Gal 5:13
Try to learn what **p** the Lord. .... Eph 5:10
do and be able to do what **p** him. .... Php 2:13
that honors and **p** the Lord in.................. Col 1:10
things, because this **p** the Lord. .... Col 3:20
good, and it **p** God our Savior, ... 1Ti 2:3
or grandparents. That **p** God. 1Ti 5:4
in a way that **p** him with respect .... Heb 12:28
commands and do what **p** him. 1Jn 3:22

PLEASING

Its smell is **p** to the LORD. .... Ex 29:18
its smell is **p** to the LORD. .... Ex 29:25
and its smell is **p** to him........................ Ex 29:41
and its smell is **p** to the LORD. .... Le 1:9
and its smell is **p** to the LORD. .... Le 1:13
and its smell is **p** to the LORD. .... Le 1:17
and its smell is **p** to the LORD. .... Le 2:2
Its smell is **p** to the LORD. .... Le 2:9
on the altar as a **p** smell........................ Le 2:12
and its smell is **p** to the LORD. .... Le 3:5
and its smell is **p** to the LORD. .... Le 3:16
altar as a smell **p** to the LORD. .... Le 4:31
Its smell is **p** to him. .... Le 6:15
a smell that is **p** to the LORD................... Le 6:21
its smell was **p** to the LORD. .... Le 8:21
and its smell was **p** to him. .... Le 8:28
altar, as a smell **p** to the LORD. .... Le 17:6
its smell will be **p** to him. .... Le 23:13
the smell will be **p** to the LORD............... Le 23:18
not smell the **p** smell of your .... Le 26:31
as a smell **p** to the LORD. .... Nu 15:3
Its smell will be **p** to the LORD. .... Nu 15:7
its smell will be **p** to the LORD. .... Nu 15:10
by fire will be **p** to the LORD. .... Nu 15:13
the smell will be **p** to the LORD, ... Nu 15:14
offering, a smell **p** to the LORD. .... Nu 15:24
The smell is **p** to the LORD. .... Nu 18:17
for a smell that is **p** to me, ... Nu 28:2
its smell is **p** to the LORD. .... Nu 28:6
and its smell is **p** to the LORD. .... Nu 28:8
and its smell is **p** to the LORD. .... Nu 28:13
a smell that is **p** to the LORD................... Nu 28:24
This smell will be **p** to the LORD. .... Nu 28:27
as a smell **p** to the LORD: .... Nu 29:2
and their smell is **p** to him. .... Nu 29:6
as a smell **p** to the LORD: .... Nu 29:8
as a smell **p** to the LORD : .... Nu 29:13
as a smell **p** to the LORD. .... Nu 29:36
offer sacrifices **p** to the God of .... Ezr 6:10
and knowledge will be **p** to you............... Pr 2:10
you into adultery with **p** words. .... Pr 2:16
and from the **p** words of another .... Pr 6:24
unfaithful wife and her **p** words. .... Pr 7:5

P

by her **p** words she led him into .... Pr 7:21
word at the right time is so **p**. .... Pr 15:23
same way, wisdom is **p** to you. .... Pr 24:14
honest answer is as **p** as a kiss .... Pr 24:26
They will be **p** sacrifices on my .... Is 60:7
false visions or **p** prophecies .... Eze 12:24
before the gods as a **p** smell. .... Eze 16:19
you like the **p** smell of.......................... Eze 20:41
others and by **p** only yourselves. .... Mt 23:25
I always do what is **p** to him, ... Jn 8:29
be only for God and **p** to him, ... Rm 12:1
is good and **p** to him and what .... Rm 12:2
this way is **p** God and will be .... Rm 14:18
p his wife and pleasing the Lord. 1Co 7:34
his wife and **p** the Lord. 1Co 7:34
does not make us less **p** to God, ... 1Co 8:8
living and **p** yourselves with .... Jam 5:5

PLEASURE
You will find **p** in the Almighty, ... Job 22:26
hand I will find **p** forever. .... Ps 16:11
them drink from your river of **p**. .... Ps 36:8
Your rules give me **p**; .... Ps 119:24
loves **p** will become poor; .... Pr 21:17
I did not miss any **p** I desired. .... Ec 2:10
this **p** was the reward for all .... Ec 2:10
you say, "I find no **p** in them." .... Ec 12:1
Now, listen, you lover of **p**. .... Is 47:8
lovers with whom you found **p**. .... Eze 16:37
crowd listened to Jesus with **p**. .... Mk 12:37
Love takes no **p** in evil but 1Co 13:6
will love **p** instead of God, ... 2Ti 3:4
take **p** in openly doing evil, ... 2Pe 2:13

PLEASURES
p of this life keep them from .... Lk 8:14
you can use them for your own **p**. .... Jam 4:3

PLEDGE
the promise or **p** and says .... Nu 30:4
promised. She must keep her **p**. .... Nu 30:4
the promise or **p** and does not .... Nu 30:5
the promise or **p** does not have .... Nu 30:5
a woman makes a **p** or a careless .... Nu 30:6
her promise or the **p** she made. .... Nu 30:7
he cancels her **p** or the careless .... Nu 30:8
makes a promise or **p** while she .... Nu 30:10
she must keep her promise or **p**. .... Nu 30:11
any promise or **p** she has made. .... Nu 30:13
No one will make a **p** for me. .... Job 17:3

PLEDGED
who were **p** to marry his........................ Ge 19:14
woman who is not **p** to be married .... Ex 22:16

PLEDGES
to the LORD or **p** to do something .... Nu 30:3

PLEIADES
the **P** and the groups of stars .... Job 9:9
the stars of the **P** or loosen the .... Job 38:31
the star groups **P** and Orion; .... Am 5:8

PLENTIFUL
silver and gold as **p** as stones 2Ch 1:15
trees as **p** as the fig trees 2Ch 1:15
trees as **p** as the fig trees 2Ch 9:27
goodness be **p** while he lives. .... Ps 72:7

PLENTY
God give you **p** of rain and good .... Ge 27:28
you will have **p** of grain and new .... Ge 27:28
good crops and **p** to eat in all .... Ge 41:29
it was like to have **p** of food, ... Ge 41:31
There were **p** of graves for us in .... Ex 14:11
you will have **p** to eat and live .... Le 26:5
crops will have **p** of water. .... Nu 24:7
where you will have **p** of food, ... Dt 8:9

and you will have **p** to eat. .... Dt 11:15
You had **p** of everything, but you .... Dt 28:47
safe and had **p** of everything. .... Jdg 18:7
you will see there is **p** of land— .... Jdg 18:10
plenty of land—**p** of everything! .... Jdg 18:10
who once had **p** of food now must 1Sa 2:5
good pastures with **p** of grass, ... 1Ch 4:40
He gave **p** of supplies to his 2Ch 11:23
we have had **p** to eat and plenty 2Ch 31:10
plenty to eat and **p** left over, ... 2Ch 31:10
And there was **p** of the king's .... Est 1:7
they still have **p**, trouble will .... Job 20:22
life. They have **p** of food. They .... Ps 17:14
Let the fields grow **p** of grain .... Ps 72:16
LORD's trees have **p** of water; .... Ps 104:16
I will bless her with **p**; .... Ps 132:15
their land will have **p** of food, ... Pr 12:11
field might produce **p** of food, ... Pr 13:23
awake, you will have **p** of food. .... Pr 20:13
There is gold and **p** of rubies, ... Pr 20:15
There will be **p** of goat's milk .... Pr 27:27
their land will have **p** of food, ... Pr 28:19
foolish person who has **p** to eat, ... Pr 30:22
they will have **p** of food and .... Is 23:18
and you will have **p** of food in .... Is 30:23
a garden that has **p** of water, ... Je 31:12
time we had **p** of food and were .... Je 44:17
proud and had **p** of food and .... Eze 16:49
in a good field near **p** of water. .... Eze 17:5
a good field by **p** of water so it .... Eze 17:8
because there was **p** of water. .... Eze 19:10
It had **p** of good fruit on it, ... Da 4:12
and it had **p** of fruit for .... Da 4:21
so he will have **p** of money...................... Da 11:20
vine that produced **p** of fruit. .... Hos 10:1
oil, so that you will have **p**. .... Joe 2:19
you will have **p** to eat and be .... Joe 2:26
servants have **p** of food. .... Lk 15:17
there was **p** of water there. .... Jn 3:23
There was **p** of grass there, ... Jn 6:10
At this time you have **p**. 2Co 8:14
when they have **p**, they can help 2Co 8:14
always have **p** of everything— 2Co 9:8
know how to live when I have **p**. .... Php 4:12
like land that gets **p** of rain. .... Heb 6:7
you stay warm and get **p** to eat," .... Jam 2:16

PLOT
they **p** against those you love.................... Ps 83:3

PLOW
do not **p** or plant your land. .... Ex 23:11
Don't **p** with an ox and a donkey .... Dt 22:10
of your other sons **p** his ground 1Sa 8:12
that people who **p** evil and plant .... Job 4:8
so it will **p** the valleys for .... Job 39:10
farmers don't **p** when they should .... Pr 20:4
farmer does not **p** his field all.................. Is 28:24
P your unplowed fields, and .... Je 4:3
Israel will **p**, and Judah will .... Hos 10:11
p the new ground of knowledge. .... Hos 10:12
people do not **p** rocks with oxen............... Am 6:12
crops when it's time to **p** again. .... Am 9:13
swords into **p** blades and their .... Mic 4:3
begins to **p** a field but keeps .... Lk 9:62

PLOWED
has never been **p** or planted, ... Dt 21:4
If you had not **p** with my young .... Jdg 14:18
and let my crops be **p** up. .... Job 31:8
all I have done would be **p** up. .... Job 31:12
me and its **p** rows are not wet.................. Job 31:38
hold it to the **p** row with a .... Job 39:10
You send rain to the **p** fields; .... Ps 65:10
plowing, they **p** over my back, ... Ps 129:3

PLOWING

The ground is **p** and broken up.	Ps 141:7
will be **p** like a field.	Je 26:18
You will be **p**, and seed will be	Eze 36:9
land will be **p** so it will no	Eze 36:34
weeds growing in a **p** field.	Hos 10:4
you have **p** evil and harvested	Hos 10:13
piles of stone in a **p** field.	Hos 12:11
will be **p** like a field.	Mic 3:12

PLOWING

home from **p** the fields with	1Sa 11:5
son of Shaphat **p** a field with a	1Ki 19:19
of oxen and was **p** with the	1Ki 19:19
The oxen were **p** and the donkeys	Job 1:14
Like farmers **p**, they plowed over	Ps 129:3
who has been **p** the ground or	Lk 17:7

PLOWS

the Philistines to have their **p**,	1Sa 13:20
for sharpening **p** and hoes.	1Sa 13:21
swords into **p** and their spears	Is 2:4
from your **p**, and make spears	Joe 3:10
The one who **p** and the one who	1Co 9:10

PLUMB

and the **p** line used against	2Ki 21:13
wall, with a **p** line in his hand.	Am 7:7
see?" I said, "A **p** line." Then	Am 7:8
I will put a **p** line among my	Am 7:8

PLUNGE

He would **p** the fork into the pot	1Sa 2:14

PLUS

the full price **p** an extra	Le 6:5
Daniel many gifts **p** an important	Da 2:48

POCKET

and folded double to make a **p**.	Ex 28:16
was folded double to make a **p**.	Ex 39:9
They have their god in their **p**.	Job 12:6

POCKETS

no bag, and no money in your **p**.	Mk 6:8

PODS

wanted to eat the **p** the pigs	Lk 15:16

POETS

That is why the **p** say:	Nu 21:27
' Some of your own **p** have said: '	Ac 17:28

POINT

that **p** Lot's wife looked back.	Ge 19:26
LORD has helped us to this **p**."	1Sa 7:12
Why did you bring me to this **p**?	2Sa 7:18
Why did you bring me to this **p**?	1Ch 17:16
as far as a **p** opposite the Water	Ne 3:26
He will **p** them to the best way.	Ps 25:12
cut with a hard **p** into the stone	Je 17:1
about them and **p** fingers at them	Je 24:9
They did not **p** out your sins to	La 2:14
south from a **p** between Hauran	Eze 47:18
of sorrow, to the **p** of death.	Mt 26:38
of sorrow, to the **p** of death.	Mk 14:34
of it to the **p** of being bound	2Ti 2:9
Here is the **p** of what we are	Heb 8:1

POINTED

from the altar and **p** at the man.	1Ki 13:4
sword drawn and **p** at Jerusalem.	1Ch 21:16
Those four horns **p** in four	Da 8:8
Then he **p** to his followers and	Mt 12:49

POINTING

cruel words and **p** your finger at	Is 58:9
the sword is **p** at our throats!	Je 4:10

POINTS

with whips that have sharp **p**.'"	1Ki 12:11
with whips that have sharp **p**."	1Ki 12:14

with whips that have sharp **p**.'"	2Ch 10:11
with whips that have sharp **p**."	2Ch 10:14
and pull the **p** out of their	Job 20:25
he **p** sinners to the right way.	Ps 25:8
come to the high **p** of Jerusalem	Je 31:12

POISON

Their grapes are full of **p**;	Dt 32:32
Their wine is like snake **p**,	Dt 32:33
like the deadly **p** of cobras.	Dt 32:33
my spirit drinks in their **p**;	Job 6:4
like the **p** of a snake inside	Job 20:14
They will suck the **p** of snakes,	Job 20:16
They put **p** in my food and gave	Ps 69:21
their words are like snake **p**.	Ps 140:3
a snake with **p** in its fangs.	Pr 23:32
off your feet or drinking **p**.	Pr 26:6
have changed fairness into **p**;	Am 6:12
like a cup of **p** to the nations	Zch 12:2
snakes and drink **p** without being	Mk 16:18
Their words are like snake **p**."	Rm 3:13
and evil and full of deadly **p**.	Jam 3:8

POISONED

has given us **p** water to drink.	Je 8:14
bitter food and drink **p** water.	Je 9:15
bitter food and drink **p** water,	Je 23:15

POISONOUS

So the LORD sent them **p** snakes;	Nu 21:6
and that had **p** snakes and	Dt 8:15
that grows bitter, **p** fruit.	Dt 29:18
animals and gliding, **p** snakes.	Dt 32:24
are like **p** snakes, like deaf	Ps 58:4
hand into the nest of a **p** snake.	Is 11:8
p snakes and darting snakes.	Is 30:6
evil like eggs from **p** snakes.	Is 59:5
one open, a **p** snake comes out.	Is 59:5
I am sending **p** snakes to attack	Je 8:17
like you live with **p** insects,	Eze 2:6
they are like **p** weeds growing in	Hos 10:4
A family of **p** snakes!	Mt 23:33
the fire when a **p** snake came out	Ac 28:3

POKE

I'm allowed to **p** out the right	1Sa 11:2
its outer hide or **p** through its	Job 41:13

POKERETH-HAZZEBAIM

Shephatiah, Hattil, **P**, and Ami.	Ezr 2:57
Shephatiah, Hattil, **P**, and Amon.	Ne 7:59

POLE

He will hang your body on a **p**,	Ge 40:19
king hanged the baker on a **p**.	Ge 40:22
that branch on a **p** between two	Nu 13:23
bronze snake, and put it on a **p**.	Nu 21:8
bronze snake and put it on a **p**.	Nu 21:9
and the heavy **p** from their backs	Is 9:4

POLES

Then make **p** from acacia wood and	Ex 25:13
Put the **p** through the rings on	Ex 25:14
and use these **p** to carry it.	Ex 25:14
These **p** must always stay in the	Ex 25:15
will hold the **p** for carrying it.	Ex 25:27
Make the **p** out of acacia wood,	Ex 25:28
carry the table with these **p**.	Ex 25:28
Make **p** of acacia wood for the	Ex 27:6
Put the **p** through the rings on	Ex 27:7
slide **p** through them to carry	Ex 30:4
Make the **p** from acacia wood and	Ex 30:5
the Agreement, its **p**, lid, and	Ex 35:12
table, and its **p**, all the things	Ex 35:13
the altar of incense and its **p**,	Ex 35:15
screen, its **p** and all its tools	Ex 35:16
Then he made **p** of acacia wood	Ex 37:4

put the **p** through the rings on .... Ex 37:5
they held the **p** for carrying it. .... Ex 37:14
p for carrying the table were .... Ex 37:15
held the **p** for carrying it. .... Ex 37:27
He made the **p** of acacia wood and........... Ex 37:28
rings to hold the **p** for carrying .... Ex 38:5
Then he made **p** of acacia wood .... Ex 38:6
put the **p** through the rings on .... Ex 38:7
of the Agreement, its **p** and lid; .... Ex 39:35
its screen, its **p** and all its .... Ex 39:39
put the **p** through the rings of.............. Ex 40:20
that, and put the **p** in place. .... Nu 4:6
leather, and put the **p** in place. .... Nu 4:8
leather, and put the **p** in place. .... Nu 4:11
over it and put the **p** in place.................. Nu 4:14
is used with the **p** around the .... Nu 4:32
With their scepters and **p,** .... Nu 21:18
covering it and its carrying **p.**................. 1Ki 8:7
The carrying **p** were so long that 1Ki 8:8
could see the ends of the **p,**................. 1Ki 8:8
The **p** are still there today. 1Ki 8:8
used special **p** to carry the Ark 1Ch 15:15
covering it and its carrying **p.**............... 2Ch 5:8
The carrying **p** were so long that 2Ch 5:9
could see the ends of the **p.**................. 2Ch 5:9
The **p** are still there today. 2Ch 5:9
Make a yoke out of straps and **p,** .... Je 27:2

POLICE

officers sent the **p** to tell the .... Ac 16:35
Paul said to the **p,** "They beat............... Ac 16:37
The **p** told the Roman officers .... Ac 16:38

POLISH

your helmets! **P** your spears. Put .... Je 46:4

POLISHED

Solomon wanted from **p** bronze.............. 1Ki 7:45
the LORD were made of **p** bronze. 2Ch 4:16
pieces of **p** bronze that were .... Ezr 8:27
it look as hard as **p** bronze. .... Job 37:18
and sparkled like **p** bronze. .... Eze 1:7
a sword, made sharp and **p.** .... Eze 21:9
It is **p** to flash like lightning. .... Eze 21:10
The sword should be **p.** .... Eze 21:11
is made sharp and **p,** ready for .... Eze 21:11
It is **p** to kill and destroy, ... Eze 21:28
legs were shiny like **p** bronze, ... Da 10:6

POLITE

be gentle and **p** to all people. .... Tit 3:2

POLITELY

and could not speak to him **p.** .... Ge 37:4

POMEGRANATE

be a gold bell and a **p** ball, ... Ex 28:34
ball, a gold bell and a **p** ball. .... Ex 28:34
there was a bell and a **p** ball, ... Ex 39:26
ball, a bell and a **p** ball. .... Ex 39:26
sitting under a **p** tree at the.................. 1Sa 14:2
veil are like slices of a **p.**..................... Sng 4:3
veil are like slices of a **p.**..................... Sng 6:7
to see if the **p** trees had .... Sng 6:11
p trees, the date palm trees, ... Joe 1:12

POMEGRANATES

Make balls like **p** of blue, ... Ex 28:33
they made balls like **p** of blue, ... Ex 39:24
They also got some **p** and figs. .... Nu 13:23
grapevines, or **p,** and there's no .... Nu 20:5
vines, fig trees, **p,** olive oil, ... Dt 8:8
rows of bronze **p** to go on the................. 1Ki 7:18
were two hundred **p** in rows all 1Ki 7:20
four hundred **p** for the two nets 1Ki 7:42
were two rows of **p** for each net 1Ki 7:42
and bronze **p** all around it. 2Ki 25:17

He made a hundred **p** and put them 2Ch 3:16
four hundred **p** for the two nets 2Ch 4:13
were two rows of **p** for each net 2Ch 4:13
an orchard of **p** with all the .... Sng 4:13
and if the **p** have bloomed. .... Sng 7:12
drink of spiced wine from my **p.**........... Sng 8:2
and bronze **p** all around it. .... Je 52:22
pillar also had **p** and was like................ Je 52:22
were ninety-six **p** on the sides .... Je 52:23
of a hundred **p** above the net .... Je 52:23
fig trees, **p,** and olive trees .... Hag 2:19

PONDS

rivers, canals, **p,** and pools in .... Ex 7:19
over the rivers, canals, and **p.**................. Ex 8:5

PONTIUS

P Pilate, the ruler of Judea;................... Lk 3:1
when Herod, **P** Pilate, and some .... Ac 4:27
when he stood before **P** Pilate. 1Ti 6:13

PONTUS

Judea, Cappadocia, **P,** Asia, ... Ac 2:9
been born in the country of **P.**............. Ac 18:2
and are scattered all around **P,** 1Pe 1:1

POOL

men at the **p** of Gibeon. 2Sa 2:13
group sat on one side of the **p;** 2Sa 2:13
hung them over the **p** of Hebron. 2Sa 4:12
chariot at a **p** in Samaria where 1Ki 22:38
from the upper **p** on the road 2Ki 18:17
his work on the **p,** his work on 2Ki 20:20
cut off the upper **p** of the Gihon 2Ch 32:30
Fountain Gate and the King's **P,** .... Ne 2:14
the wall of the **P** of Siloam next .... Ne 3:15
as the man-made **p** and the House .... Ne 3:16
turned a rock into a **p** of water, ... Ps 114:8
water flows into the upper **p,** .... Is 7:3
waters of the **p** of Shiloah and .... Is 8:6
stored up water in the lower **p.** .... Is 22:9
You made a **p** between the two .... Is 22:11
to save water from the old **p,** .... Is 22:11
from the upper **p** on the road .... Is 36:2
him near the big **p** of water at .... Je 41:12
Nineveh is like a **p,** and now its .... Nah 2:8
there is a **p** with five covered .... Jn 5:2
This **p** is near the Sheep Gate. .... Jn 5:2
on the porches beside the **p.** .... Jn 5:3
came down to the **p** and stirred .... Jn 5:4
to go into the **p** was healed from .... Jn 5:4
me get into the **p** when the water .... Jn 5:7
"Go and wash in the **P** of Siloam."........... Jn 9:7

POOLS

canals, ponds, and **p** in Egypt.' .... Ex 7:19
land with rivers and **p** of water, ... Dt 8:7
rains fill it with **p** of water. .... Ps 84:6
the desert into **p** of water and.................. Ps 107:35
I made **p** of water for myself and .... Ec 2:6
are like the **p** in Heshbon near .... Sng 7:4
desert will have **p** of water, ... Is 35:7
land and dry up the **p** of water. .... Is 42:15

POOR

eyesight was **p,** so he could not .... Ge 27:1
Egypt and Canaan became very **p.**........... Ge 47:13
to one of my people who is **p,**................. Ex 22:25
If a **p** person is in court, ... Ex 23:3
his side just because he is **p.** .... Ex 23:3
be unfair to a **p** person when he .... Ex 23:6
allow the **p** people to have it, ... Ex 23:11
and a **p** person must not give .... Ex 30:15
if the person is **p** and unable to .... Le 14:21
those things for **p** people and .... Le 19:10
favor to **p** people or great .... Le 19:15
Leave it for **p** people and .... Le 23:22

becomes very **p** and sells some .... Le 25:25
becomes too **p** to support himself .... Le 25:35
let the **p** live among you......................... Le 25:36
becomes very **p** and indebted .... Le 25:39
becomes so **p** that he has to .... Le 25:47
the **p** person has the right to be .... Le 25:48
anyone is too **p** to pay the price .... Le 27:8
it fertile or **p**? Are there trees .... Nu 13:20
should be no **p** people among you .... Dt 15:4
If there are **p** among you, in one .... Dt 15:7
Give freely to the **p** person,.................... Dt 15:10
will always be **p** people in the................ Dt 15:11
and to the **p** and needy in your .... Dt 15:11
a **p** person gives you a coat to .... Dt 24:12
servants who are **p** and needy, ... Dt 24:14
because they are **p** and need the .... Dt 24:15
naked, and **p,** and the LORD will .... Dt 28:48
Israel became very **p** because of.............. Jdg 6:6
you invite us here to make us **p**? .... Jdg 14:15
man to marry, either rich or **p.** .... Ru 3:10
The LORD makes some people **p,** 1Sa 2:7
LORD raises the **p** up from the 1Sa 2:8
He lets the **p** sit with princes 1Sa 2:8
I am **p** and unimportant." 1Sa 18:23
was rich, but the other was **p.**............... 2Sa 12:1
But the **p** man had nothing except 2Sa 12:3
The **p** man fed the lamb, and it 2Sa 12:3
lamb from the **p** man and cooked 2Sa 12:4
other and presents to the **p.** .... Est 9:22
So the **p** have hope, while those .... Job 5:16
will have to pay back the **p,** .... Job 20:10
troubled the **p** and left them .... Job 20:19
all the **p** of the land hide from .... Job 24:4
The **p** become like wild donkeys.............. Job 24:5
they take a **p** mother's baby to .... Job 24:9
So the **p** go around naked without .... Job 24:10
get up to kill the **p** and needy............... Job 24:14
I saved the **p** who called out .... Job 29:12
have been very sad for **p** people. .... Job 30:25
appeals of the **p** or let widows .... Job 31:16
to rich people than **p** people, ... Job 34:19
The cry of the **p** comes to God; .... Job 34:28
but he gives the **p** their rights. .... Job 36:6
hopes of the **p** will never die. .... Ps 9:18
They wait to catch **p** people; .... Ps 10:9
they catch the **p** in nets. .... Ps 10:9
The **p** are thrown down and .... Ps 10:10
heard what the **p** people want. .... Ps 10:17
because the **p** are being hurt. .... Ps 12:5
wicked upset the plans of the **p,** .... Ps 14:6
P people will eat until they are .... Ps 22:26
The **p** will hear and be glad. .... Ps 34:2
This **p** man called, and the LORD .... Ps 34:6
the weak and **p** from robbers." .... Ps 35:10
bows to kill the **p** and helpless, ... Ps 37:14
because I am **p** and helpless, ... Ps 40:17
are those who think about the **p.** .... Ps 41:1
and small, rich and **p** together. .... Ps 49:2
goodness you took care of the **p.** .... Ps 68:10
P people will see this and be .... Ps 69:32
I am **p** and helpless; God, hurry .... Ps 70:5
decide what is right for the **p.**................ Ps 72:2
be fair to the **p** and save the .... Ps 72:4
He will help the **p** when they cry .... Ps 72:12
will be kind to the weak and **p,** .... Ps 72:13
Never forget your **p** people. .... Ps 74:19
Let the **p** and helpless praise .... Ps 74:21
rights of the **p** and suffering. .... Ps 82:3
answer me. I am **p** and helpless.............. Ps 86:1
But he lifted the **p** out of their .... Ps 107:41
He hurt the **p,** the needy, and .... Ps 109:16
am **p** and helpless and very sad.............. Ps 109:22
They give freely to the **p.** .... Ps 112:9

LORD lifts the **p** from the dirt.................. Ps 113:7
I will fill her **p** with food. .... Ps 132:15
justice for the **p** and will .... Ps 140:12
you will be as **p** as if you had .... Pr 6:11
A lazy person will end up **p,** .... Pr 10:4
having no money destroys the **p.** .... Pr 10:15
what they should and end up **p.** .... Pr 11:24
pretend to be **p** but really are .... Pr 13:7
but the **p** will face no such .... Pr 13:8
will end up **p** and disgraced, ... Pr 13:18
A **p** person's field might produce .... Pr 13:23
p are rejected, even by their .... Pr 14:20
those who only talk will be **p.**................ Pr 14:23
mistreats the **p** insults their .... Pr 14:31
It is better to be **p** and respect .... Pr 15:16
is better to be **p** and right than .... Pr 16:8
mistreats the **p** insults their .... Pr 17:5
p beg for mercy, but the rich .... Pr 18:23
better to be **p** and honest than .... Pr 19:1
but the **p** lose all theirs. .... Pr 19:4
P people's relatives avoid them; .... Pr 19:7
kind to the **p** is like lending .... Pr 19:17
is better to be **p** than to be a .... Pr 19:22
love to sleep, you will be **p.**................... Pr 20:13
who act too quickly become **p.** .... Pr 21:5
ignores the **p** when they cry for .... Pr 21:13
loves pleasure will become **p;** .... Pr 21:17
The rich and the **p** are alike in .... Pr 22:2
rule over the **p,** and borrowers .... Pr 22:7
share their food with the **p.**................... Pr 22:9
gets rich by mistreating the **p,** .... Pr 22:16
to the wealthy, will become **p.**............... Pr 22:16
Do not abuse **p** people because .... Pr 22:22
poor people because they are **p,** .... Pr 22:22
drink and eat too much become **p.** .... Pr 23:21
you will be as **p** as if you had .... Pr 24:34
mistreat the **p** are like a hard .... Pr 28:3
is better to be **p** and innocent .... Pr 28:6
to those who are kind to the **p.** .... Pr 28:8
the **p** with understanding will .... Pr 28:11
is as dangerous to **p** people as a.............. Pr 28:15
dreams instead will end up **p.** .... Pr 28:19
not realize they soon will be **p.** .... Pr 28:22
gives to the **p** will have .... Pr 28:27
who ignores the **p** will receive .... Pr 28:27
care about justice for the **p,** .... Pr 29:7
p person and the cruel person .... Pr 29:13
a king judges **p** people fairly, ... Pr 29:14
don't make me either rich or **p;** .... Pr 30:8
' If I am **p,** I might steal and .... Pr 30:9
to remove the **p** from the earth .... Pr 30:14
the rights of the **p** and needy." .... Pr 31:9
She welcomes the **p** and helps the .... Pr 31:20
p but wise boy is better than a .... Ec 4:13
had been born **p** in the kingdom .... Ec 4:14
you will see **p** people mistreated.............. Ec 5:8
does a **p** person little good to .... Ec 6:8
Now there was a **p** but wise man .... Ec 9:15
forgot about the **p** man's wisdom .... Ec 9:16
of what you took from the **p.** .... Is 3:14
faces of the **p** into the dirt?" .... Is 3:15
They are not fair to the **p,** .... Is 10:2
Laishah, listen! **P** Anathoth! .... Is 10:30
he will judge the **p** honestly; .... Is 11:4
decisions for the **p** people of .... Is 11:4
and that his **p** people will go .... Is 14:32
You protect the **p;** you protect................ Is 25:4
who were made **p** by the city will .... Is 26:6
will make the **p** people happy; .... Is 29:19
to take everything from the **p.** .... Is 32:7
He destroys the **p** with lies,.................... Is 32:7
even when the **p** person is in the .... Is 32:7
A **p** person cannot buy those .... Is 40:20

The p and needy people look for .... Is 41:17
listen to me, p Jerusalem, you .... Is 51:21
You p city. Storms have hurt .... Is 54:11
with the hungry and bring p, ... Is 58:7
to tell the good news to the p. .... Is 61:1
have the blood of p and innocent .... Je 2:34
are only the p, foolish people. .... Je 5:4
or help the p be judged fairly. .... Je 5:28
are ashamed of their p harvest, ... Je 12:13
back roads and on p highways. .... Je 18:15
the life of the p from the power .... Je 20:13
those who were p and needy, ... Je 22:16
place where p people are buried. .... Je 26:23
did not help the p and needy. .... Eze 16:49
He mistreats the p and needy. .... Eze 18:12
hurt people who are p and needy. .... Eze 22:29
things and be kind to the p. .... Da 4:27
they sell the p to buy a pair of .... Am 2:6
They walk on p people as if they .... Am 2:7
on clothes taken from the p. .... Am 2:8
things from the p and crush .... Am 4:1
You walk on p people, forcing .... Am 5:11
and you keep the p from getting. .... Am 5:12
to destroy the p people of this .... Am 8:4
We will buy p people for silver, ... Am 8:6
P me! I am like a hungry man, ... Mic 7:1
robbing the p people in secret .... Hab 3:14
orphans, foreigners or the p; .... Zch 7:10
you give to the p, don't be like .... Mt 6:2
So when you give to the p, ... Mt 6:3
Good News is preached to the p. .... Mt 11:5
and give the money to the p. .... Mt 19:21
and the money given to the p." .... Mt 26:9
will always have the p with you, ... Mt 26:11
and give the money to the p, ... Mk 10:21
Then a p widow came and put in .... Mk 12:42
this p widow gave more than all .... Mk 12:43
woman is very p, but she gave .... Mk 12:44
and the money given to the p." .... Mk 14:5
will always have the p with you, ... Mk 14:7
to tell the Good News to the p. .... Lk 4:18
people who are p are blessed, ... Lk 6:20
Good News is preached to the p. .... Lk 7:22
what is in your dishes to the p, ... Lk 11:41
possessions and give to the p. .... Lk 12:33
invite the p, the crippled, ... Lk 14:13
bring in the p, the crippled, ... Lk 14:21
and the son was p and hungry. .... Lk 15:14
And a very p man named Lazarus, ... Lk 16:20
you have and give it to the p, ... Lk 18:22
half of my possessions to the p. .... Lk 19:8
Then he saw a p widow putting .... Lk 21:2
this p widow gave more than all .... Lk 21:3
woman is very p, but she gave .... Lk 21:4
and the money given to the p?" .... Jn 12:5
did not really care about the p; .... Jn 12:6
will always have the p with you, ... Jn 12:8
or to give something to the p. .... Jn 13:29
his money to the p and prayed to .... Ac 10:2
has seen that you give to the p, ... Ac 10:4
give to the p and remembers you. .... Ac 10:31
money to the p among God's .... Rm 15:26
I am sure the p in Jerusalem get .... Rm 15:28
you embarrass those who are p. 1Co 11:22
We are p, but we are making many 2Co 6:10
troubles, and they are very p. 2Co 8:2
you he became p so that by his 2Co 8:9
by his becoming p you might 2Co 8:9
He gives freely to the p. 2Co 9:9
was to remember to help the p— .... Gal 2:10
to share with those who are p. .... Eph 4:28
I know how to live when I am p, ... Php 4:12
They were p, abused, and treated .... Heb 11:37

who are p should take pride .... Jam 1:9
that they are spiritually p. .... Jam 1:10
the same time a p person comes. .... Jam 2:2
But you say to the p person, ... Jam 2:3
God chose the p in the world to .... Jam 2:5
you show no respect to the p. .... Jam 2:6
troubles and that you are p, ... Rev 2:9
pitiful, p, blind, and naked. .... Rev 3:17
rich and p, free and slave .... Rev 13:16

POOREST
Only the p people in the land 2Ki 24:14
some of the p people of the land. 2Ki 25:12
Even the p of my people will be .... Is 14:30
some of the p people of Judah .... Je 39:10
and children who were the p. .... Je 40:7
captive some of the p people, ... Je 52:15
some of the p people of the land. .... Je 52:16

POPLAR
Jacob cut green branches from p, ... Ge 30:37
the p trees by the streams .... Job 40:22
the p trees nearby we hung our .... Ps 137:2
like p trees growing beside .... Is 44:4

POPLARS
palm trees, p, and other leafy .... Le 23:40
it across the Ravine of the P. .... Is 15:7
under oaks, p, and other trees, ... Hos 4:13

PORATHA
P, Adalia, Aridatha, ... Est 9:8

PORCH
The p in front of the main room 1Ki 6:3
also built the p that had 1Ki 7:6
p was seventy-five feet long 1Ki 7:6
the front of the p was a roof 1Ki 7:6
and the p of the Temple were 1Ki 7:12
pillars in the p were shaped 1Ki 7:19
pillars at the p of the Temple. 1Ki 7:21
The p in front of the main room 2Ch 3:4
inside of the p with pure gold. 2Ch 3:4
LORD in front of the Temple p. 2Ch 8:12
in front of the p of the Temple 2Ch 15:8
doors of the p of the Temple, ... 2Ch 29:7
came to the p of the Temple, ... 2Ch 29:17
between the p and the altar. .... Eze 8:16
gateway next to the p that faced. .... Eze 40:7
measured the p of the gateway. .... Eze 40:8
The p of the gateway faced the .... Eze 40:9
The man also measured the p, ... Eze 40:14
The courtyard was around the p. .... Eze 40:14
the front of the p of the inner .... Eze 40:15
rooms and p had small windows .... Eze 40:16
and its p measured the same as .... Eze 40:21
Its windows, p, and carvings of .... Eze 40:22
the gateway's p was at the inner. .... Eze 40:22
its inner walls and its p, ... Eze 40:24
gateway and its p had windows .... Eze 40:25
Its p was at the inner end, ... Eze 40:26
and p measured the same as the. .... Eze 40:29
around the gateway and its p. .... Eze 40:29
Each p of each inner gateway was .... Eze 40:30
gateway's p faced the outer .... Eze 40:31
and p measured the same as the. .... Eze 40:33
around the gateway and its p. .... Eze 40:33
Its p faced the outer courtyard. .... Eze 40:34
and p measured the same as the. .... Eze 40:36
Its p faced the outer courtyard. .... Eze 40:37
opened onto the p of the inner .... Eze 40:38
tables on each side of the p, ... Eze 40:39
by each side wall of the p, ... Eze 40:40
brought me to the p of the .... Eze 40:48
each side wall of the p. .... Eze 40:48
The p was thirty-five feet long .... Eze 40:49

Most Holy Place, and the outer **p** .... Eze 41:15
and on the outside, in the **p,** .... Eze 41:17
roof over the front Temple **p.** .... Eze 41:25
on both side walls of the **p.** .... Eze 41:26
through the **p** of the gateway .... Eze 44:3
through the **p** of the gateway .... Eze 46:2
in through the **p** of the gateway, ... Eze 46:8
in the Temple in Solomon's **P.** .... Jn 10:23
and ran to them at Solomon's **P.** .... Ac 3:11
meet together on Solomon's **P.** .... Ac 5:12

PORCHES
is a pool with five covered **p,** .... Jn 5:2
lying on the **p** beside the pool. .... Jn 5:3

PORCIUS
was replaced by **P** Festus as .... Ac 24:27

PORT
them to the **p** they wanted. .... Ps 107:30

PORTION
it on the altar as a memorial **p.** .... Le 2:2
the memorial **p** from the grain .... Le 2:9
the memorial **p** of the crushed .... Le 2:16
This is the **p** that belongs to .... Le 7:35
as the memorial **p** to take the .... Le 24:7
as your share, your continual **p.** .... Nu 18:8
daughters as your continual **p.** .... Nu 18:19
given as the **p** you must give to .... Nu 18:29
the **p** I told you to set aside." 1Sa 9:23
and Levites the **p** that belonged 2Ch 31:4
of the first **p** of their grain, ... 2Ch 31:5
he has given them each their **p.** .... Is 34:17
from the ravines as your **p.** .... Is 57:6
who is Jacob's **P,** is not like..................... Je 10:16
who is Jacob's **P,** is not like..................... Je 51:19
part of the holy **p** of the land.................. Eze 48:12
p of Scripture he was reading................ Ac 8:32

PORTIONS
giving larger **p** to larger family .... Nu 33:54
and smaller **p** to smaller family .... Nu 33:54
Boaz poured six **p** of barley into............. Ru 3:15
gave me these six **p** of barley,................. Ru 3:17
They gave out the **p** that went to .... Ne 13:13

PORTS
has **p** for the Mediterranean .... Eze 27:3
to sail to different **p** in Asia. .... Ac 27:2

POSITION
who served wine his old **p,** .... Ge 40:21
I was given back my old **p,** .... Ge 41:13
the highest **p** among my sons, ... Ge 49:3
took their battle **p** at Gibeah. .... Jdg 20:20
getting into **p** for battle as .... Jdg 20:30
you a higher **p** than to bring you .... Pr 25:7
an important **p** in his kingdom. .... Da 2:48

POSITIONS
So the people took their **p;** .... Jos 8:13
got into battle **p** at a place .... Jdg 20:33
there and took their **p** to fight 1Sa 17:2
Why have you taken **p** for battle? 1Sa 17:8
was going out to their battle **p,** 1Sa 17:20
given important **p** while gifted .... Ec 10:6
Take your **p** for war against .... Je 50:14

POSSESSION
will be my own **p,** chosen from .... Ex 19:5
people of the East as their **p.** .... Eze 25:10
So you became a **p** of the other .... Eze 36:3
a people for God's own **p.** 1Pe 2:9

POSSESSIONS
There they got **p** and had many .... Ge 47:27
Then divide those **p** between the .... Nu 31:27
from the sale of family **p.** .... Dt 18:8

to robbers who took their **p.** .... Jdg 2:14
away no silver or **p** of Israel. .... Jdg 5:19
our children, and all our **p.** .... Ezr 8:21
all the wealth and **p** of Damascus .... Is 8:4
or robbed of their homes and **p.** .... Da 11:33
the nations who took your **p**— .... Zch 2:8
go and sell your **p** and give the .... Mt 19:21
his own house, his **p** are safe................. Lk 11:21
and will give away the **p.** .... Lk 11:22
your **p** and give to the poor. .... Lk 12:33
give half of my **p** to the poor. .... Lk 19:8
material **p** to help the Jews. .... Rm 15:27

POSSIBLE
he made it **p** for Leah to have................. Ge 29:31
it **p** for her to have children. .... Ge 30:22
must always be **p** for the family .... Le 25:24
As much as **p,** we have bought .... Ne 5:8
All things will be **p** for you. .... Mt 17:20
but for God all things are **p.**" .... Mt 19:26
God has chosen, if that is **p.** .... Mt 24:24
if it is **p,** do not give me .... Mt 26:39
if it is not **p** for this painful.................... Mt 26:42
All things are **p** for the one who............. Mk 9:23
but for God all things are **p.**" .... Mk 10:27
God has chosen, if that is **p.** .... Mk 13:22
prayed that, if **p,** he would not .... Mk 14:35
for people are **p** for God." .... Lk 18:27
joy will be the fullest **p** joy.................... Jn 15:11
joy will be the fullest **p** joy. .... Jn 16:24
Then how is it **p** that we each.............. Ac 2:8
God had made it **p** for those who .... Ac 14:27
of Pentecost, if that were **p.**................... Ac 20:16
to you, but this has not been **p.** .... Rm 11:13
save some of them in any way **p.** 1Co 9:22
But that is not **p,** because God .... Gal 3:18
given them to me if that were **p.**............. Gal 4:15

POSSIBLY
good person someone might **p** die............ Rm 5:7

POSTS
hooks on four **p** of acacia wood .... Ex 26:32
Make five **p** of acacia wood .... Ex 26:37
on twenty bronze **p** with twenty .... Ex 27:10
on twenty bronze **p** with twenty .... Ex 27:11
with ten **p** and ten bases on that............ Ex 27:12
up by three **p** on three bases. .... Ex 27:14
up by three **p** on three bases. .... Ex 27:15
held up by four **p** on four bases. .... Ex 27:16
All the **p** around the courtyard .... Ex 27:17
in which the **p** are set must be .... Ex 27:18
frames, crossbars, **p,** and bases; .... Ex 35:11
courtyard, their **p** and bases, ... Ex 35:17
They made four **p** of acacia wood .... Ex 36:36
they made gold hooks for the **p,**............. Ex 36:36
bases in which to set the **p.**................... Ex 36:36
they made five **p** and hooks for .... Ex 36:38
tops of the **p** and their bands .... Ex 36:38
five bronze bases for the **p.**.................... Ex 36:38
on twenty bronze **p** with twenty .... Ex 38:10
bands on twenty **p** with twenty .... Ex 38:11
bands on ten **p** with ten bases. .... Ex 38:12
up by three **p** and three bases. .... Ex 38:14
up by three **p** and three bases. .... Ex 38:15
The bases for the **p** were made of .... Ex 38:17
the bands on the **p** were made of .... Ex 38:17
the tops of the **p** were covered .... Ex 38:17
All the **p** in the courtyard had................ Ex 38:17
up by four **p** and four bronze .... Ex 38:19
and bands on the **p** were made of .... Ex 38:19
the tops on the **p** were covered .... Ex 38:19
the hooks for the **p** and to cover............ Ex 38:28
tops of the **p** and to make the .... Ex 38:28
frames, crossbars, **p,** and bases; .... Ex 39:33

with their **p** and bases, ... Ex 39:40
of the frames and set up the **p**. .... Ex 40:18
braces, the **p**, the bases, and .... Nu 3:36
for the **p** in the courtyard .... Nu 3:37
the crossbars, the **p**, and bases, ... Nu 4:31
addition to the **p** that go around .... Nu 4:32
and the two **p** of the city gate .... Jdg 16:3
some at guard **p** and some near .... Ne 7:3
He made its **p** of silver and its .... Sng 3:10
legs are like large marble **p**, ... Sng 5:15
and on the **p** of the gate to the .... Eze 45:19

POT

was boiling a **p** of vegetable .... Ge 25:29
The clay **p** the meat is cooked in .... Le 6:28
if a bronze **p** is used, it must .... Le 6:28
cooked it in a **p** or made cakes .... Nu 11:8
open jar or **p** without a cover .... Nu 19:15
a basket and the broth into a **p**. .... Jdg 6:19
the meat would be cooked in a **p**. 1Sa 2:13
fork into the **p** or the kettle. 1Sa 2:14
brought out of the **p** belonged to 1Sa 2:14
there except a **p** of oil." 2Ki 4:2
Put the large **p** on the fire, ... 2Ki 4:38
and cut up the fruit into the **p**. 2Ki 4:39
of God, there's death in the **p**!" 2Ki 4:40
He threw it into the **p** and said, ... 2Ki 4:41
was nothing harmful in the **p**. 2Ki 4:41
from a large **p** over a hot fire. .... Job 41:20
sea bubble like a boiling **p**; .... Job 41:31
up the sea like a **p** of oil. .... Job 41:31
has dried up like a clay **p**, ... Ps 22:15
I am like a piece of a broken **p**. .... Ps 31:12
burning thorns can heat a **p**. .... Ps 58:9
a shiny coating on a clay **p**. .... Pr 26:23
This is like a **p** telling its .... Is 29:16
I see a **p** of boiling water, ... Je 1:13
his hands to make a **p** from clay, ... Je 18:4
to make another **p** the way he .... Je 18:4
is like a broken **p** someone threw .... Je 22:28
This city is like a cooking **p**, ... Eze 11:3
this city is like the cooking **p**. .... Eze 11:7
city will not be your cooking **p**, ... Eze 11:11
says: Put on the **p**; put it on .... Eze 24:3
and pile wood under the **p**. .... Eze 24:5
for the rusty **p** whose rust will .... Eze 24:6
set the empty **p** on the coals so .... Eze 24:11
to clean the **p** have failed. .... Eze 24:12
them up like meat for the **p**, ... Mic 3:3
Every **p** in Jerusalem and Judah .... Zch 14:21

POTIPHAR

they sold him to **P**, an officer .... Ge 37:36
Egyptian named **P** was an officer .... Ge 39:1
of his master, **P** the Egyptian. .... Ge 39:2
P saw that the LORD was with .... Ge 39:3
So **P** was very happy with Joseph .... Ge 39:4
house and everything **P** owned, ... Ge 39:5
everything that belonged to **P**, ... Ge 39:5
So **P** left Joseph in charge of .... Ge 39:6
So **P** arrested Joseph and put him .... Ge 39:20

POTIPHAR'S

the people in **P** house because .... Ge 39:5

POTIPHERA

who was the daughter of **P**, ... Ge 41:45
wife was Asenath daughter of **P**, ... Ge 41:50
the daughter of **P**, priest .... Ge 46:20

POTS

the **p** to remove the ashes, ... Ex 27:3
the **p**, shovels, bowls for .... Ex 38:3
bowls, clay **p**, wheat, barley, ... 2Sa 17:28
the **p**, shovels, small bowls, and 1Ki 7:45
also took the **p**, shovels, wick 2Ki 25:14

the **p**, shovels, forks, and all 2Ch 4:16
boiled the holy offerings in **p**, ... 2Ch 35:13
their **p** are full of soup made .... Is 65:4
also took the **p**, shovels, wick .... Je 52:18
large bowls, **p**, lampstands, pans .... Je 52:19
The cooking **p** in the Temple of .... Zch 14:20
of cups, pitchers, and **p**. .... Mk 7:4

POTSHERD

near the front of the **P** Gate. .... Je 19:2

POTTER

the clay is equal to the **p**. .... Is 29:16
just as a **p** walks on the clay. .... Is 41:25
The clay does not ask the **p**, ' .... Is 45:9
like clay, and you are the **p**; .... Is 64:8
Go and buy a clay jar from a **p**. .... Je 19:1
jars made by the hands of a **p**. .... La 4:2
"Throw the money to the **p**." .... Zch 11:13
them to the **p** in the Temple .... Zch 11:13
The **p** can make anything he wants .... Rm 9:21

POTTER'S

Go down to the **p** house, and I .... Je 18:2
went down to the **p** house and saw .... Je 18:3
saw him working at the **p** wheel. .... Je 18:3
like the clay in the **p** hands. .... Je 18:6
coins to buy **P** Field as a place .... Mt 27:7
silver coins to buy the **p** field, ... Mt 27:10

POTTERS

These sons of Shelah were **p**. 1Ch 4:23

POTTERY

piece of broken **p** to scrape .... Job 2:8
body is like broken pieces of **p**. .... Job 41:30
break them into pieces like **p**." .... Ps 2:9
piece of broken **p** among many .... Is 45:9
as when **p** is broken into pieces. .... Rev 2:27

POUND

The gold nails weighed over a **p**. 2Ch 3:9
took about one **p** of silver from .... Ne 5:15
The waves may **p** the beach, ... Je 5:22
bring logs to **p** through your .... Eze 26:9

POUNDED

with Balaam, and he **p** his fist. .... Nu 24:10
and his heart **p** with fear. 1Sa 28:5

POUNDING

The seas raise up their **p** waves. .... Ps 93:3
My heart is **p** inside me. .... Je 4:19

POUNDS

seventy-five **p** of myrrh and .... Jn 19:39
each weighing about a hundred **p**, ... Rev 16:21

POUR

I will also **p** some water for .... Ge 24:19
Nile River and **p** it on the dry .... Ex 4:9
and **p** olive oil on their heads .... Ex 28:41
olive oil and **p** it on his head .... Ex 29:7
then **p** the blood that is left .... Ex 29:12
and **p** oil on it to make it holy. .... Ex 29:36
P out a quart of wine as a drink .... Ex 29:40
Do not **p** it on the bodies of .... Ex 30:32
olive oil and **p** it on the Holy .... Ex 40:9
P the special oil on the altar .... Ex 40:10
Then **p** the special olive oil on .... Ex 40:11
P the special oil on him, and .... Ex 40:13
P the special oil on them in the .... Ex 40:15
The person must **p** oil on it, ... Le 2:1
Crumble it and **p** oil over it; .... Le 2:6
blood he must **p** out at the .... Le 4:7
The priest must **p** out the rest .... Le 4:18
He must **p** out the rest of the .... Le 4:25
He must **p** out the rest of the .... Le 4:30
He must **p** out the rest of the .... Le 4:34

and then he must **p** the rest of .... Le 5:9
of the oil and **p** it into his own .... Le 14:15
He will also **p** some of the oil .... Le 14:26
that person must **p** the blood on .... Le 17:13
He must not **p** oil or incense on .... Nu 5:15
P fresh water over the ashes .... Nu 19:17
this song: "**P** out water, well .... Nu 21:17
p it out to the LORD at the Holy .... Nu 28:7
P it out on the ground like water. .... Dt 12:16
but **p** it out on the ground like .... Dt 12:24
p it out on the ground like .... Dt 15:23
they will **p** down like rain on .... Dt 32:2
Then **p** the broth on them." .... Jdg 6:20
prophet should **p** olive oil on 1Ki 1:34
p it on the meat and on the wood. 1Ki 18:34
p olive oil on Hazael to make 1Ki 19:15
Then **p** oil on Jehu son of Nimshi 1Ki 19:16
p oil on Elisha son of Shaphat 1Ki 19:16
P oil into all the jars, and set 2Ki 4:4
"**P** it out for the people to eat." 2Ki 4:41
the bottle and **p** the oil on 2Ki 9:3
my groans **p** out like water. .... Job 3:24
do these words **p** out of your .... Job 15:13
My eyes **p** out tears to God. .... Job 16:20
Who can **p** water from the jars of .... Job 38:37
p oil of blessing on my head; .... Ps 23:5
P your anger out on them; .... Ps 69:24
make springs **p** into the ravines .... Ps 104:10
I **p** out my problems to him; .... Ps 142:2
Don't **p** your water in the .... Pr 5:16
but fools **p** out foolishness. .... Pr 15:2
the wicked simply **p** out evil. .... Pr 15:28
in the sky will **p** out rain, ... Is 24:18
I will **p** out water for the .... Is 44:3
I will **p** out my Spirit into your .... Is 44:3
clouds, **p** down victory. .... Is 45:8
You **p** drink offerings on them to .... Is 57:6
P out my anger on the children .... Je 6:11
They **p** out drink offerings to .... Je 7:18
I will **p** out my anger on this .... Je 7:20
P out your anger on other .... Je 10:25
burn incense and **p** out drink .... Je 44:17
Goddess and to **p** out drink .... Je 44:19
Goddess and to **p** out drink .... Je 44:25
send people to **p** you from your .... Je 48:12
P out your heart like water in .... La 2:19
Soon I will **p** out my anger .... Eze 7:8
will **p** down, hailstones will .... Eze 13:11
In my anger rain will **p** down, ... Eze 13:13
I might **p** out my anger against .... Eze 14:19
Then I decided to **p** out my anger .... Eze 20:8
Then I decided to **p** out my anger .... Eze 20:13
So I decided to **p** out my anger .... Eze 20:21
will **p** out my anger against you .... Eze 21:31
put it on and **p** water in it. .... Eze 24:3
She did not **p** it on the ground .... Eze 24:7
I will **p** out my anger against .... Eze 30:15
I will **p** my punishment over them .... Hos 5:10
I will **p** out my Spirit on all .... Joe 2:28
that time I will **p** out my Spirit .... Joe 2:29
the sea to **p** out on the earth. .... Am 5:8
mountains and **p** from the hills. .... Am 9:13
will **p** her stones down into the .... Mic 1:6
I will **p** out my anger on them, ... Zph 3:8
I will **p** out on David's family .... Zch 12:10
heaven for you and **p** out all the .... Mal 3:10
people never **p** new wine into old .... Mt 9:17
people always **p** new wine into .... Mt 9:17
last days I will **p** out my Spirit .... Ac 2:17
that time I will **p** out my Spirit .... Ac 2:18
pray for and **p** oil on the person .... Jam 5:14
Go and **p** out the seven bowls of .... Rev 16:1

POURED

clouds in the sky **p** out rain. .... Ge 7:11
So she quickly **p** all the water .... Ge 24:20
he **p** olive oil on the top of it. .... Ge 28:18
where you **p** olive oil on the .... Ge 31:13
and he **p** a drink offering and .... Ge 35:14
olive oil **p** on a person's .... Ex 25:6
yeast that have oil **p** over them. .... Le 2:4
place where the ashes are **p** out .... Le 4:12
yeast that have oil **p** over them, ... Le 7:12
He **p** some of the special oil on .... Le 8:12
Then he **p** out the rest of the .... Le 8:15
p out the rest of the blood at .... Le 9:9
whom the oil was **p**, will perform .... Le 16:32
special olive oil **p** on his head. .... Le 21:10
priests was **p** on his head to .... Le 21:12
He also **p** oil on the altar and .... Nu 7:1
When the oil was **p** on the altar, ... Nu 7:10
when oil was **p** on the altar and .... Nu 7:84
after the oil had been **p** on it. .... Nu 7:88
priest had the holy oil **p** on him .... Nu 35:25
should be **p** beside the altar .... Dt 12:27
Boaz **p** six portions of barley .... Ru 3:15
the ground and **p** it out before 1Sa 7:6
of olive oil and **p** it on Saul's 1Sa 10:1
of olive oil and **p** it on Jesse's 1Sa 16:13
Then they **p** oil on David to make 2Sa 5:3
I **p** them out and walked on them 2Sa 22:43
He **p** it out before the LORD, ... 2Sa 23:16
the Holy Tent and **p** the oil on 1Ki 1:39
Nathan the prophet **p** olive oil 1Ki 1:45
was melted and **p** into a mold, ... 1Ki 7:37
these things **p** into clay molds 1Ki 7:46
jars to her, she **p** out the oil. 2Ki 4:5
They **p** out the stew for the 2Ki 4:40
young prophet **p** the olive oil 2Ki 9:6
him king and **p** olive oil on him. 2Ki 11:12
offerings and **p** out his drink 2Ki 16:13
Jehoahaz and **p** olive oil on him. 2Ki 23:30
Then they **p** oil on David to make 1Ch 11:3
He **p** it out before the LORD, ... 1Ch 11:18
They **p** olive oil on Solomon to 1Ch 29:22
And they **p** oil on Zadok to 1Ch 29:22
these things **p** into clay molds 2Ch 4:17
him king and **p** olive oil on him 2Ch 23:11
the rocks **p** out olive oil for .... Job 29:6
I **p** them out like mud in the .... Ps 18:42
water **p** out onto the ground, ... Ps 22:14
and the sky **p** down rain before .... Ps 68:8
The clouds **p** down their rain. .... Ps 77:17
water **p** out and rivers flowed .... Ps 78:20
You have **p** fine oils on me. .... Ps 92:10
they would have **p** over us like a .... Ps 124:4
perfumed oil **p** on the priest's .... Ps 133:2
punished them and **p** their blood .... Is 63:6
same houses and **p** out drink .... Je 32:29
I **p** out my anger in the towns of .... Je 44:6
have never been **p** from one jar .... Je 48:11
he **p** out his anger like fire on .... La 2:4
he **p** out his strong anger. .... La 4:11
incense and **p** out their drink .... Eze 20:28
have **p** out my anger on you.'" .... Eze 22:22
p the blood on the bare rock. .... Eze 24:7
I **p** out my anger against them, ... Eze 36:18
His anger is **p** out like fire; .... Nah 1:6
blood will be **p** out like dust, ... Zph 1:17
p this perfume on Jesus' head .... Mt 26:7
This woman **p** perfume on my body .... Mt 26:12
This blood is **p** out for many to .... Mt 26:28
opened the jar and **p** the perfume .... Mk 14:3
she **p** perfume on my body to .... Mk 14:8
This blood is **p** out for many. .... Mk 14:24
but she **p** perfume on my feet. .... Lk 7:46

P

p olive oil and wine on his ....Lk 10:34
my blood which is p out for you. ....Lk 22:20
p the perfume on Jesus' feet, ...Jn 12:3
Then he p water into a bowl and ....Jn 13:5
and all his intestines p out......................Ac 1:18
So Jesus has p out that Spirit, ...Ac 2:33
because God has p out his love ....Rm 5:5
God p out richly upon us that.................Tit 3:6
with blood were p down on the ....Rev 8:7
Then the snake p water out of ....Rev 12:15
angel left and p out his bowl ....Rev 16:2
The second angel p out his bowl ....Rev 16:3
The third angel p out his bowl ....Rev 16:4
have p out the blood of your ....Rev 16:6
The fourth angel p out his bowl ....Rev 16:8
The fifth angel p out his bowl................Rev 16:10
The sixth angel p out his bowl ....Rev 16:12
The seventh angel p out his bowl ....Rev 16:17

POURING
in the sky stopped p down rain. ....Ge 8:2
will be used for p out the drink ....Ex 25:29
and jars used for p the drink ....Ex 37:16
P oil on them will make them a ....Ex 40:15
given you rules for p that blood ....Le 17:11
the LORD by p olive oil on the ....Nu 7:1
began p out, and the people ....Nu 20:11
him by p holy oil on him........................Ps 89:20
a cold day or p vinegar on soda ....Pr 25:20
will be like p burning coals.....................Pr 25:22
flood of water p over the.........................Is 28:2
and stopped p out drink ....Je 44:18
like her and were p out drink ....Je 44:19
p from the jug of wine until ....Hab 2:15
will be like p burning coals.....................Rm 12:20

POURS
The rain then p down from the ....Job 36:28
Smoke p out of its nose, as if ....Job 41:20
He p it out even to the last ....Ps 75:8
continue until God p his Spirit ....Is 32:15
Jerusalem p out her evil as a ....Je 6:7
evil as a well p out its water. ....Je 6:7
he comes and p goodness on you ....Hos 10:12
of the sea and p them out on the ....Am 9:6
no one ever p new wine into old............Mk 2:22
no one ever p new wine into old.............Lk 5:37

POVERTY
who realize their spiritual p, ...Mt 5:3

POWDER
of the incense into a fine p,....................Ex 30:36
use this incense p only for its ....Ex 30:36
ground it into p. Then he threw ....Ex 32:20
he threw the p into the water ....Ex 32:20
that has been ground into p. ....Le 16:12
crushed it into a p like dust ....Dt 9:21
idols and beat them into p. 2Ch 34:4
he sprinkled the p on the graves..............2Ch 34:4
idols and beat the idols into p. 2Ch 34:7

POWER
I have the p to harm you, but ....Ge 31:29
to show you my p so that my name ....Ex 9:16
You have the p and strength to 1Ch 29:12
Be supreme, LORD, in your p. ....Ps 21:13
praise the LORD's glory and p. ....Ps 29:1
With your p scatter them and ....Ps 59:11
strength; you are dressed in p. ....Ps 65:6
Because your p is great, your ....Ps 66:3
gives his people strength and p. ....Ps 68:35
not remember his p or the time ....Ps 78:42
I will give him p over the sea ....Ps 89:25
knows the full p of your anger? ....Ps 90:11
and I have understanding and p. ....Pr 8:14

tired and more p to those who ....Is 40:29
God made the earth by his p. ....Je 10:12
you a kingdom, p, strength, and.............Da 2:37
He will save us from your p, ...Da 3:17
built it by my p to show my ....Da 4:30
Daniel from the p of the lions. ....Da 6:27
they have the p to do so. ....Mic 2:1
am filled with p, with the ....Mic 3:8
quickly, and his p is great. ....Nah 1:3
own strength or by your own p, ...Zch 4:6
kingdom, the p, and the glory.................Mt 6:13
God for giving p like this to ....Mt 9:8
don't know about the p of God. ....Mt 22:29
the sky with great p and glory. ....Mt 24:30
you by the p of the living God ....Mt 26:63
He uses p from the ruler of....................Mk 3:22
Jesus felt p go out from him ....Mk 5:30
God come with p before they die. ....Mk 9:1
in spirit and p like Elijah. ....Lk 1:17
and the p of the Most High will ....Lk 1:35
to Galilee in the p of the Holy................Lk 4:14
because p was coming from him ....Lk 6:19
I felt p go out from me." ....Lk 8:46
one who has the p to kill you ....Lk 12:5
a cloud with p and great glory. ....Lk 21:27
received that p from heaven."..................Lk 24:49
know I have p to set you free ....Jn 10:18
The only p you have over me is ....Jn 19:11
to you, you will receive p. ....Ac 1:8
By what p or authority did you ....Ac 4:7
who gave him the p to do great ....Ac 6:8
gave him the Holy Spirit and p. ....Ac 10:38
away from the p of Satan and to ....Ac 26:18
it is the p God uses to save ....Rm 1:16
his eternal p and all the things ....Rm 1:20
to show my p in you so that my ....Rm 9:17
and to let people see his p. ....Rm 9:22
overflow by the p of the Holy ....Rm 15:13
being saved it is the p of God. 1Co 1:18
But Christ is the p of God and 1Co 1:24
is present not in talk but in p.................1Co 4:20
Death's p to hurt is sin, and 1Co 15:56
that the great p is from God, ...2Co 4:7
my p is made perfect in you." 2Co 12:9
know that God's p is very great ....Eph 1:19
under his p and made him ....Eph 1:22
grace given to me through his p, ...Eph 3:7
With God's p working in us, ...Eph 3:20
in the Lord and in his great p. ....Eph 6:10
Christ and the p that raised him............Php 3:10
his own great p so that you will ....Col 1:11
freed us from the p of darkness,............Col 1:13
free from the p of your sinful ....Col 2:11
words, but with p, with the Holy 1Th 1:5
the Lord and from his great p. 2Th 1:9
afraid but a spirit of p and 2Ti 1:7
God but will not have his p. 2Ti 3:5
the one who has the p of death— ....Heb 2:14
but through the p of his life, ...Heb 7:16
God's p protects you through 1Pe 1:5
greatness, p, and authority ....Jud 1:25
receive glory and honor and p, ...Rev 4:11
were given the p to sting like ....Rev 9:3
horses' p was in their mouths.................Rev 9:19
and the p and the kingdom.....................Rev 12:10
second death has no p over them. ....Rev 20:6

POWERFUL
became a very p man on earth. ....Ge 10:8
become a great and p nation, ...Ge 18:18
become much more p than we are." ....Ge 26:16
that you are as p as the king of ....Ge 44:18
father about how p I have become ....Ge 45:13

my sons, and you are the most **p**. .... Ge 49:3
I could show them my **p** miracles. .... Ex 10:1
holy, amazingly **p**, a worker of .... Ex 15:11
p men of Moab will shake with .... Ex 15:15
with a large and **p** army. .... Nu 20:20
and they are too **p** for me. .... Nu 22:6
can do the **p** things you do. .... Dt 3:24
became a great, **p**, and large .... Dt 26:5
They have **p** weapons in Beth Shan .... Jos 17:16
they have **p** weapons and are .... Jos 17:18
great and **p** nations to leave .... Jos 23:9
were very **p** and were cruel to .... Jdg 6:2
May you become **p** in the district .... Ru 4:11
can save us from these **p** gods? 1Sa 4:8
He saved me from my **p** enemies, ... 2Sa 22:18
They were **p** warriors and 1Ch 7:40
Three, David's most **p** soldiers. 1Ch 11:11
the palace, the **p** men, and all 1Ch 28:1
LORD, you are great and **p**. 1Ch 29:11
son, became a **p** king, because 2Ch 1:1
had a large and **p** army and many 2Ch 16:8
grew more and more **p**. 2Ch 17:12
was very **p**, so his name became 2Ch 26:8
had much help until he became **p**. 2Ch 26:15
Uzziah became **p**, his pride led 2Ch 26:16
Jotham became **p**, because he 2Ch 27:6
has had **p** kings who have .... Ezr 4:20
the Lord, who is great and **p**. .... Ne 4:14
from the harm done by **p** people. .... Job 5:15
away naked and destroys the **p**. .... Job 12:19
They grow old and become more **p**. .... Job 21:7
You were a **p** man who owned land; .... Job 22:8
your **p** hand you attacked me. .... Job 30:21
God who is both fair and **p**? .... Job 34:17
p people die without help. .... Job 34:20
God breaks **p** people into pieces .... Job 34:24
beg for relief from **p** people. .... Job 35:9
God is **p**, but he does not hate .... Job 36:5
is **p** and sure of what he wants .... Job 36:5
God is great and **p**; .... Job 36:22
muscles of its stomach are **p**. .... Job 40:16
p fear its terrible looks and .... Job 41:25
He saved me from my **p** enemies, ... Ps 18:17
All the **p** people on earth will .... Ps 22:29
The LORD, the **p** warrior. .... Ps 24:8
The LORD is **p**; he gives victory .... Ps 28:8
The LORD's voice is **p**; .... Ps 29:4
Put on your sword, **p** warrior. .... Ps 45:3
and a **p** storm surrounds him. .... Ps 50:3
Announce that God is **p**. .... Ps 68:34
p enemies want to destroy me for .... Ps 69:4
and tell about your **p** works, ... Ps 71:16
you are **p** and completely .... Ps 89:8
ocean waves are **p**, but the LORD .... Ps 93:4
The King is **p** and loves justice. .... Ps 99:4
will be **p** in the land; .... Ps 112:2
"The LORD has done **p** things." .... Ps 118:15
many nations and killed **p** kings; .... Ps 135:10
He killed **p** kings. His love .... Ps 136:18
Our Lord is great and very **p**. .... Ps 147:5
Rock badgers are not very **p**, ... Pr 30:26
P people will be like small, ... Is 1:31
like a **p** flood of water from the .... Is 8:7
Counselor, **P** God, Father Who .... Is 9:6
will again follow the **p** God. .... Is 10:21
They are a **p** nation that defeats .... Is 18:2
They are a **p** nation that defeats .... Is 18:7
a **p** king will rule over them. .... Is 19:4
People from **p** nations will honor .... Is 25:3
his great and hard and **p** sword. .... Is 27:1
has someone who is strong and **p**. .... Is 28:2
and to see his **p** arm come down .... Is 30:30
Your **p** voice makes people run .... Is 33:3

no **p** ship will sail on them. .... Is 33:21
Because he is strong and **p**, ... Is 40:26
a statue, using his **p** arms. .... Is 44:12
in spite of your **p** tricks. .... Is 47:9
be freed from a **p** soldier? .... Is 49:24
am the **P** One of Jacob who saves .... Is 49:26
and use your strength, **p** LORD. .... Is 51:9
know that the **P** One of Jacob. .... Is 60:16
of you will become a **p** nation. .... Is 60:22
They have become rich and **p**, ... Je 5:27
and your name is great and **p**. .... Je 10:6
They will come like a **p** storm. .... Je 25:32
Babylon will be **p** for seventy .... Je 29:10
Great and **p** God, your name is .... Je 32:18
as I live, a **p** leader will come. .... Je 46:18
run from the **p** enemy and have .... Je 48:45
A **p** nation and many kings are .... Je 50:41
each with his **p** weapon in his .... Eze 9:2
broken the **p** arm of the king .... Eze 30:21
with the women of the **p** nations; .... Eze 32:18
No great and **p** king has ever .... Da 2:10
You have become great and **p**, ... Da 4:22
can stop his **p** hand or question .... Da 4:35
greater and more **p** than before. .... Da 4:36
a great, important, and **p** king. .... Da 5:18
he wanted and became very **p**. .... Da 8:4
will be very **p**, but his power .... Da 8:24
will destroy **p** people and even .... Da 8:24
very quickly, like a **p** flood. .... Da 11:10
large and **p** armies and even .... Da 11:22
large and very **p** army and .... Da 11:25
A **p** nation has come into my land .... Joe 1:6
a great and **p** army will spread .... Joe 2:2
They are like a **p** army lined up .... Joe 2:5
P warriors will go up on Mount .... Ob 1:21
and your **p** waves flowed over me. .... Jnh 2:3
When the **p** horses went out, ... Zch 6:7
Many people and **p** nations will .... Zch 8:22
of God, the **P** One, and coming .... Mt 26:64
my name to do **p** things will not .... Mk 9:39
of God, the **P** One, and coming .... Mk 14:62
because the **P** One has done great .... Lk 1:49
He has given us a **p** Savior from .... Lk 1:69
the leaders and other **p** people, ... Lk 12:11
at the right hand of the **p** God." .... Lk 22:69
and did many **p** things before God .... Lk 24:19
and he was a **p** man in what he .... Ac 7:22
miracles and the **p** things Philip .... Ac 8:13
But Saul grew more **p**. .... Ac 9:22
So in a **p** way the word of the .... Ac 19:20
but when it is raised, it is **p**. 1Co 15:43
Paul's letters are **p** and sound. 2Co 10:10
not weak among you, but he is **p**. 2Co 13:3
from heaven with his **p** angels. 2Th 1:7
them something **p** that leads them 2Th 2:11
together with his **p** word. .... Heb 1:3
They were **p** in battle and .... Heb 11:34
under God's **p** hand so he will 1Pe 5:6
you about the **p** coming of our 2Pe 1:16
stronger and more **p** than false 2Pe 2:11
And I saw a **p** angel calling in a .... Rev 5:2
rich people, the **p** people, the .... Rev 6:15
I saw another **p** angel coming. .... Rev 10:1
He shouted in a **p** voice: .... Rev 18:2
Lord God who judges her is **p**." .... Rev 18:8
great city, **p** city of Babylon .... Rev 18:10
Then a **p** angel picked up a large .... Rev 18:21

POWERFULLY
strength that works so **p** in me. .... Col 1:29

POWERLESS
the world that they were **p**. .... Col 2:15

POWERS

will punish the **p** in the sky	Is 24:21
he wants with the **p** of heaven	Da 4:35
I give you these **p** freely,	Mt 10:8
And the **p** of the heavens will be	Mt 24:29
And the **p** of the heavens will be	Mk 13:25
because the **p** of the heavens	Lk 21:26
nothing in the future, no **p,**	Rm 8:38
authorities, and **p,** and he will	1Co 15:24
authorities, **p,** and kings, not	Eph 1:21
of the evil **p** that are above	Eph 2:2
the rulers and **p** in the heavenly	Eph 3:10
and the **p** of this world's	Eph 6:12
against the spiritual **p** of evil	Eph 6:12
and unseen, all **p,** authorities,	Col 1:16
is ruler over all rulers and **p.**	Col 2:10
rulers and **p** of their authority	Col 2:15
received the **p** of his new world.	Heb 6:5
over angels, authorities, and **p.**	1Pe 3:22

PRACTICE

of God have any other **p.**	1Co 11:16

PRACTICED

p magic and told the future by	2Ki 21:6
He **p** magic and witchcraft and	2Ch 33:6
Simon had **p** magic and amazed all	Ac 8:9

PRAETORIUM

called the **P**) and called all	Mk 15:16

PRAISE

He is my God, and I will **p** him.	Ex 15:2
to **p** him because he is holy and	2Ch 20:21
Stand up and **p** the LORD your	Ne 9:5
I will **p** you, LORD, with all my	Ps 9:1
P the LORD, all you who respect	Ps 22:23
P the LORD on the harp;	Ps 33:2
I will **p** the LORD at all times;	Ps 34:1
his glory! Make his **p** glorious!	Ps 66:2
God, the people should **p** you;	Ps 67:3
Heaven and earth should **p** him,	Ps 69:34
spirits rise up and **p** you?	Ps 88:10
his courtyards with songs of **p.**	Ps 100:4
My whole being, **p** the LORD.	Ps 104:35
praise the LORD. **P** the LORD.	Ps 104:35
times a day I **p** you for your	Ps 119:164
p him, you servants of the LORD,	Ps 135:1
I will **p** you every day;	Ps 145:2
is great and worthy of our **p;**	Ps 145:3
don't know his laws. **P** the LORD!	Ps 147:20
P the LORD! Praise God in his	Ps 150:1
P him for his strength;	Ps 150:2
who give false **p** to their	Pr 29:5
place of the dead cannot **p** you;	Is 38:18
I will **p** the LORD for the many	Is 63:7
Sing to the LORD! **P** the LORD! He	Je 20:13
They will say, 'P the LORD	Je 33:11
Then I praise **p** to the Most High	Da 4:34
Temple, saying, "P to the Son of	Mt 21:15
They loved **p** from people more	Jn 12:43
people more than **p** from God.	Jn 12:43
a person sees **p** from God rather	Rm 2:29
in his faith and gave **p** to God.	Rm 4:20
you? Should I **p** you? I do not	1Co 11:22
nd it brings **p** to God because	Eph 1:6
to bring glory and **p** to God.	Php 1:11
p you in the public meeting.	Heb 2:12
offer to God our sacrifice of **p,**	Heb 13:15
will bring you **p** and glory and	1Pe 1:7
P our God, all you who serve him	Rev 19:5

PRAISED

the LORD, the God of Shem, be **p!**	Ge 9:26
I **p** the LORD, the God of my	Ge 24:48
saw him, they **p** their god,	Jdg 16:24

was greatly **p** for his handsome	2Sa 14:25
my Rock be **p!** Praise God, the	2Sa 22:47
he should be **p.** He should be	1Ch 16:25
said "Amen" and **p** the LORD.	1Ch 16:36
David **p** the LORD in front of all	1Ch 29:10
So they all **p** the LORD, the God	1Ch 29:20
one person as they **p** and thanked	2Ch 5:13
They **p** the LORD with this song:	2Ch 5:13
people stood up and **p** the LORD,	2Ch 20:19
of Beracah and **p** the LORD.	2Ch 20:26
So they **p** God with joy and bowed	2Ch 29:30
and priests **p** the LORD every day	2Ch 30:21
offerings, and **p** the LORD, the	2Ch 30:22
they **p** the LORD and his people,	2Ch 31:8
places and **p** the LORD just as	Ezr 3:10
Amen," and they **p** the LORD.	Ne 5:13
Ezra **p** the LORD, the great God,	Ne 8:6
and those who saw me **p** me,	Job 29:11
May my Rock be **p.** Praise the God	Ps 18:46
I will be **p** in all the nations;	Ps 46:10
will be **p** throughout the earth.	Ps 46:10
should be **p** in the city of our	Ps 48:1
though they were **p** when they	Ps 49:18
you will be **p** in Jerusalem.	Ps 65:1
You are **p** from where the sun	Ps 65:8
with my mouth and **p** him with my	Ps 66:17
he should be **p** at all times.	Ps 96:4
He should be **p** forever.	Ps 111:10
name should be **p** now and forever	Ps 113:2
name should be **p** from where the	Ps 113:3
I **p** you with an honest heart.	Ps 119:7
LORD, you should be **p.**	Ps 119:12
He should be **p** by all who belong	Ps 148:14
should be **p** by the Israelites,	Ps 148:14
respects the LORD should be **p.**	Pr 31:30
she should be **p** in public for	Pr 31:31
person than to be **p** by a fool.	Ec 7:5
and the slave women also **p** her.	Sng 6:9
only the LORD will still be **p.**	Is 2:11
time only the LORD will be **p,**	Is 2:17
Moab will not be **p** again.	Je 48:2
Then Daniel **p** the God of heaven.	Da 2:19
drinking, they **p** their gods,	Da 5:4
You **p** the gods of silver, gold,	Da 5:23
were amazed and **p** God for giving	Mt 9:8
And they **p** the God of Israel for	Mt 15:31
people were amazed and **p** God	Mk 2:12
synagogues, and everyone **p** him.	Lk 4:15
the master **p** the dishonest	Lk 16:8
the people who saw this **p** God.	Lk 18:43
what happened, he **p** God, saying,	Lk 23:47
They **p** God and were liked by all	Ac 2:47
They **p** God and said, "So God is	Ac 11:18
they heard this, they **p** God.	Ac 21:20
things, who should be **p** forever.	Rm 1:25
the brother who is **p** by all the	2Co 8:18
and he is to be **p** forever.	2Co 11:31
these believers **p** God because of	Gal 1:24
God will be **p** through Jesus	1Pe 4:11

PRAISES

I will sing **p** to your name.	2Sa 22:50
job of singing **p** to the LORD.	1Ch 16:7
Sing to him; sing **p** to him. Tell	1Ch 16:9
by name to sing **p** to the LORD	1Ch 16:41
instruments and leading **p.**	2Ch 23:13
I sing **p** to the LORD Most High.	Ps 7:17
babies to sing **p** to you because	Ps 8:2
I will sing **p** to your name.	Ps 9:2
Sing **p** to the LORD who is king	Ps 9:11
I will sing **p** to your name.	Ps 18:49
The **p** of Israel are your throne.	Ps 22:3
Sing **p** to the LORD, you who	Ps 30:4

PRAISING

My whole being **p** the LORD. .... Ps 34:2
p to God. Sing praises. Sing .... Ps 47:6
to God. Sing **p**. Sing praises to .... Ps 47:6
praises. Sing **p** to our King. .... Ps 47:6
praises to our King. Sing **p**. .... Ps 47:6
strength, I will sing **p** to you. .... Ps 59:17
worships you and sings **p** to you. .... Ps 66:4
They sing **p** to your name." .... Ps 66:4
Sing to God; sing **p** to his name. .... Ps 68:4
sing **p** to the Lord. .... Ps 68:32
for joy when I sing **p** to you. .... Ps 71:23
later about the **p** of the LORD. .... Ps 78:4
to sing **p** to God Most High. .... Ps 92:1
Let's shout **p** to the Rock who .... Ps 95:1
LORD, I will sing **p** to you. .... Ps 101:1
I will sing **p** to my God as long .... Ps 104:33
Sing to him; sing **p** to him. Tell .... Ps 105:2
said, and they sang **p** to him. .... Ps 106:12
sing **p** to him, because it is .... Ps 135:3
I will sing **p** to my God as long .... Ps 146:2
It is good to sing **p** to our God; .... Ps 147:1
Sing to the LORD; praise our .... Ps 147:7
They should sing **p** to him with .... Ps 149:3
Her husband also **p** her, ... Pr 31:28
have died cannot sing **p** to you; .... Is 38:18
they will sing **p** to the Lord. ' .... Is 60:6
Sing your **p** and shout this: ' .... Je 31:7
children and babies to sing **p**'?" .... Mt 21:16
Mary said, "My soul **p** the Lord; .... Lk 1:46
I will sing **p** to your name." .... Rm 15:9
All you people, sing **p** to him." .... Rm 15:11
P and curses come from the same .... Jam 3:10
who is happy should sing **p**. .... Jam 5:13

PRAISING

facing this place and **p** you; 1Ki 8:35
giving thanks and **p** the LORD, ... 1Ch 16:4
facing this place and **p** you; 2Ch 6:26
David had made for **p** the LORD. 2Ch 7:6
people running and **p** the king, ... 2Ch 23:12
my hope in God and keep **p** him, ... Ps 42:5
my hope in God and keep **p** him, ... Ps 42:11
my hope in God and keep **p** him, ... Ps 43:5
am always **p** you; all day long I .... Ps 71:8
they are always **p** you. .... Ps 84:4
join your own people in **p** you. .... Ps 106:5
every part of the earth **p** God, ... Is 24:16
children were **p** him in the .... Mt 21:15
talk again, and he began **p** God. .... Lk 1:64
first angel, **p** God and saying: .... Lk 2:13
p God and thanking him for .... Lk 2:20
his mat, and went home, **p** God. .... Lk 5:25
were amazed and began **p** God, ... Lk 7:16
up straight and began **p** God. .... Lk 13:13
back to Jesus, **p** God in a loud .... Lk 17:15
the Temple all the time, **p** God. .... Lk 24:53
walking and jumping and **p** God. .... Ac 3:8
the people were **p** God for what .... Ac 4:21
different languages and **p** God. .... Ac 10:46

PRAY

people began to **p** to the LORD. .... Ge 4:26
He will **p** for you, and you will .... Ge 20:7
I **p** that God Almighty will cause .... Ge 43:14
Now I **p** that he will bless these .... Ge 48:16
P to the LORD to take the frogs .... Ex 8:8
time when I should **p** for you, ... Ex 8:9
far away. Now go and **p** for me." .... Ex 8:28
I will leave and **p** to the LORD, ... Ex 8:29
P to the LORD. We have had .... Ex 9:28
P to the LORD your God, and ask .... Ex 10:17
P that the LORD will take away .... Nu 21:7
I **p** that the LORD, the God of .... Dt 1:11
God comes near when we **p** to him. .... Dt 4:7

I will **p** to the LORD for you." 1Sa 7:5
I will **p** for the LORD to send 1Sa 12:17
P to the LORD your God for us, ... 1Sa 12:19
am brave enough to **p** to you. 2Sa 7:27
Hear the prayer I **p** facing this 1Ki 8:29
Israel when we **p** facing this 1Ki 8:30
praise you and **p** to you in this 1Ki 8:33
Then they will **p**, facing this 1Ki 8:35
your people will **p** to you, ... 1Ki 8:44
will be sorry and **p** to you in 1Ki 8:47
They will **p** to you, facing this 1Ki 8:48
Please to the LORD your God 1Ki 13:6
prophets of Baal, **p** to your god, ... 1Ki 18:24
god, and I will **p** to the LORD. 1Ki 18:24
P to your god, but don't start 1Ki 18:25
fun of them. "**P** louder!" he said 1Ki 18:27
So **p** for the few of us who are 2Ki 19:4
thanks to the LORD and **p** to him. 1Ch 16:8
am brave enough to **p** to you. 1Ch 17:25
Hear the prayer I **p** facing this 2Ch 6:20
Israel when we **p** facing this 2Ch 6:21
praise you and **p** to you in this 2Ch 6:24
Then they will **p**, facing this 2Ch 6:26
far away to **p** at this Temple. 2Ch 6:32
your people will **p** to you, ... 2Ch 6:34
will be sorry and **p** to you in 2Ch 6:37
They will **p**, facing this land 2Ch 6:38
the prayers we **p** in this place. 2Ch 6:40
if they will **p** and seek me and 2Ch 7:14
and they may **p** for the life of .... Ezr 6:10
for help and **p** to the Almighty .... Job 8:5
You will **p** to him, and he will .... Job 22:27
That person will **p** to God, ... Job 33:26
My servant Job will **p** for you, ... Job 42:8
will **p** to the LORD, and he will .... Ps 3:4
Answer me when I **p** to you, ... Ps 4:1
LORD listens when I **p** to him. .... Ps 4:3
and my God, because I **p** to you. .... Ps 5:2
I **p** that victory will come to .... Ps 14:7
obey you through **p** to you while .... Ps 32:6
a song, and I **p** to my living God .... Ps 42:8
I **p** that victory will come to .... Ps 53:6
people of Cush will **p** to God. .... Ps 68:31
But I **p** to you, LORD, for favor. .... Ps 69:13
people always **p** for him and .... Ps 72:15
every morning I **p** to you. .... Ps 88:13
thanks to the LORD and **p** to him. .... Ps 105:1
and I will **p** to the LORD. .... Ps 116:13
you, and I will **p** to the LORD. .... Ps 116:17
P for peace in Jerusalem: .... Ps 122:6
But I **p** against those who do .... Ps 141:5
I **p** to the LORD for mercy. .... Ps 142:1
to all who truly **p** to him. .... Ps 145:18
of worship and will try to **p**, ... Is 16:12
they go to their temple to **p**, ... Is 16:12
So **p** for the few of us who are .... Is 37:4
down before you and **p** to you, ... Is 45:14
They **p** to a god who cannot save .... Is 45:20
Jeremiah, don't **p** for these .... Je 7:16
know you and do not **p** to you. .... Je 10:25
Jerusalem will **p** to their idols. .... Je 11:12
don't **p** for these people or cry .... Je 11:14
Don't **p** for good things to .... Je 14:11
let them **p** to the LORD .... Je 27:18
P to the LORD for the city where .... Je 29:7
You will come to me and **p** to me, ... Je 29:12
but they will **p** as I bring them .... Je 31:9
'Judah, to me, and I will .... Je 33:3
p to the LORD our God for us. .... Je 37:3
P to the LORD your God for all .... Je 42:2
So **p** that the LORD your God will .... Je 42:3
I will **p** to the LORD your God as .... Je 42:4
'**P** to the LORD our God for us. .... Je 42:20

our hands and **p** from our hearts .... La 3:41
his friends to **p** that the God .... Da 2:18
days no one should **p** to any god .... Da 6:7
he went to **p** in an upstairs room .... Da 6:10
kneel down to **p** and thank God, ... Da 6:10
says no one may **p** to any god or .... Da 6:12
Get up and **p** to your god! .... Jnh 1:6
'We are going to **p** to the LORD .... Zch 8:21
and to **p** to the LORD for .... Zch 8:22
P for those who hurt you. .... Mt 5:44
When you **p**, don't be like the .... Mt 6:5
corners and **p** so people will see .... Mt 6:5
When you **p**, you should go into .... Mt 6:6
the door and **p** to your Father .... Mt 6:6
And when you **p**, don't be like .... Mt 6:7
So when you **p**, you should pray .... Mt 6:9
pray, you should **p** like this: ' .... Mt 6:9
P to the Lord, who owns the .... Mt 9:38
himself up into the hills to **p**. .... Mt 14:23
about something and **p** for it, ... Mt 18:19
hands on them and **p** for them. .... Mt 19:13
P that it will not be winter or .... Mt 24:20
while I go over there and **p**." .... Mt 26:36
Stay awake and **p** for strength .... Mt 26:41
p that what you want will be done .... Mt 26:42
he went into the hills to **p**. .... Mk 6:46
P that these things will not .... Mk 13:18
to them, "Sit here while I **p**." .... Mk 14:32
Stay awake and **p** for strength .... Mk 14:38
away to be alone so he could **p**. .... Lk 5:16
fast for a certain time and **p**, ... Lk 5:33
went off to a mountain to **p**, ... Lk 6:12
p for those who are cruel to you. .... Lk 6:28
and went up on a mountain to **p**. .... Lk 9:28
So **p** to God, who owns the .... Lk 10:2
teach us to **p** as John taught his .... Lk 11:1
said to them, "When you **p**, say: .... Lk 11:2
should always **p** and never lose .... Lk 18:1
both went to the Temple to **p**. .... Lk 18:10
P that you will be strong enough .... Lk 21:36
P for strength against temptation. .... Lk 22:40
up and **p** for strength against .... Lk 22:46
But I **p** these things while I am .... Jn 17:13
I **p** for these followers, but I .... Jn 17:20
I **p** that they can be one. .... Jn 17:21
I **p** that they can also be one in .... Jn 17:21
can continue to **p** and to teach .... Ac 6:4
have done, and **p** to the Lord. .... Ac 8:22
Both of you **p** for me to the Lord .... Ac 8:24
was going up to the roof to **p**. .... Ac 10:9
We **p** that what the Lord wants .... Ac 21:14
I **p** to God that not only you but .... Ac 26:29
every time I **p**, I pray that I .... Rm 1:10
I **p** that I will be allowed to .... Rm 1:10
not know how to **p** as we should. .... Rm 8:26
comes, and **p** at all times. .... Rm 12:12
I **p** that the God who gives hope .... Rm 15:13
P that I will be saved from the .... Rm 15:31
everywhere who **p** in the name 1Co 1:2
for a woman to **p** to God with her 1Co 11:13
language should **p** for the gift 1Co 14:13
If I **p** in a different language, ... 1Co 14:14
I will **p** with my spirit, but I 1Co 14:15
but I will also **p** with my mind. 1Co 14:15
And when they **p**, they will wish 2Co 9:14
We **p** to God that you will not do 2Co 13:7
and we **p** that you will become 2Co 13:9
I **p** also that you will have .... Eph 1:18
p that Christ will live in your .... Eph 3:17
And I **p** that you and all God's .... Eph 3:18
but I **p** that you will be able to .... Eph 3:19
P in the Spirit at all times .... Eph 6:18
Always **p** for all God's people. .... Eph 6:18

Also **p** for me that when I speak, ... Eph 6:19
P that when I preach the Good .... Eph 6:20
but **p** and ask God for everything .... Php 4:6
We **p** that you will also have .... Col 1:9
Also **p** for us that God will give .... Col 4:3
P that we can preach the secret .... Col 4:3
P that I can speak in a way that .... Col 4:4
you and mention you when we **p**. 1Th 1:2
P continually, ... 1Th 5:17
Brothers and sisters, **p** for us. 1Th 5:25
That is why we always **p** for you, ... 2Th 1:11
p that with his power God will 2Th 1:11
p all this so that the name of 2Th 1:12
p for us that the Lord's 2Th 3:1
And **p** that we will be protected 2Th 3:2
I tell you to **p** for all people, ... 1Ti 2:1
P for rulers and for all who 1Ti 2:2
I want the men everywhere to **p**, ... 1Ti 2:8
and continues to **p** night and day 1Ti 5:5
I **p** that the faith you share may .... Phm 1:6
P for us. We are sure that we .... Heb 13:18
beg you to **p** so that God will .... Heb 13:19
who is having troubles should **p**. .... Jam 5:13
They should **p** for and pour oil .... Jam 5:14
each other and **p** for each other .... Jam 5:16
p to God and call him Father, ... 1Pe 1:17
so you will be able to **p**. 1Pe 4:7
person should **p**, and God will 1Jn 5:16
person should **p** about that sin. 1Jn 5:16
and I **p** that you are doing well 3Jn 1:2

PRAYED

Then Abraham **p** to God, and God .... Ge 20:17
at Beersheba and **p** to the LORD, ... Ge 21:33
so Isaac **p** to the LORD for her. .... Ge 25:21
left the king and **p** to the LORD, ... Ex 8:30
left the king and **p** to the LORD. .... Ex 10:18
and when he **p** to the LORD, ... Nu 11:2
So Moses **p** for the people. .... Nu 21:7
but then I **p** for Aaron, too. .... Dt 9:20
I **p** to the LORD and said, ... Dt 9:26
So we **p** to the LORD, the God of .... Dt 26:7
Then Manoah **p** to the LORD: .... Jdg 13:8
Then Samson **p** to the LORD, ... Jdg 16:28
she cried and **p** to the LORD. 1Sa 1:10
I **p** for this child, and the LORD 1Sa 1:27
Hannah **p**: "The LORD has filled 1Sa 2:1
the boy Hannah **p** for and gave 1Sa 2:20
not pleased. He **p** to the LORD, ... 1Sa 8:6
Then Samuel **p** to the LORD, ... 1Sa 12:18
Then Saul **p** to the LORD, the God 1Sa 14:41
Ahimelech **p** to the LORD for 1Sa 22:10
You **p** to God for him. 1Sa 22:13
first time I **p** to God for David 1Sa 22:15
David **p**, "LORD, God of Israel, I 1Sa 23:10
He **p** to the LORD, but the LORD 1Sa 28:6
Later, David **p** to the LORD, ... 2Sa 2:1
When David **p** to the LORD, he 2Sa 5:23
David **p** to God for the baby. 2Sa 12:16
So David **p**, "LORD, please make 2Sa 15:31
So David **p** to the LORD. 2Sa 21:1
Solomon **p** this prayer to the 1Ki 8:54
So the man of God **p** to the LORD, ... 1Ki 13:6
Then he **p** to the LORD: 1Ki 17:20
He **p** to the LORD, "LORD my God, ... 1Ki 17:21
p to Baal from morning until 1Ki 18:26
The prophets **p** louder, cutting 1Ki 18:28
Isaac, and Israel," he **p**. 1Ki 18:36
"I have had enough, LORD," he **p**. 1Ki 19:4
Then he **p** to the LORD. 2Ki 4:33
Then Elisha **p**, "LORD, open my 2Ki 6:17
toward Elisha, he **p** to the LORD, ... 2Ki 6:18
and **p** to the LORD: "LORD, God of 2Ki 19:15

the wall and **p** to the LORD, ... 2Ki 20:2
Jabez **p** to the God of Israel, ... 1Ch 4:10
and Gad **p** to God during the war, ... 1Ch 5:20
David **p** to God again, and God 1Ch 14:14
David **p** to the LORD, and he 1Ch 21:26
to the prayers **p** in this place. 2Ch 7:15
son of Amoz **p** to heaven about 2Ch 32:20
When he **p** to the LORD, the LORD 2Ch 32:24
When Manasseh **p**, the LORD heard 2Ch 33:13
we fasted and **p** to our God about .... Ezr 8:23
I **p**, "My God, I am too ashamed............ Ezr 9:6
I **p** to the God of heaven,.................... Ne 1:4
First I **p** to the God of heaven. .... Ne 2:4
I **p**, "Hear us, our God. .... Ne 4:4
we **p** to our God and appointed .... Ne 4:9
But I **p**, "God, make me strong.".......... Ne 6:9
p, "My God, remember Tobiah and .... Ne 6:14
After Job had **p** for his friends, ... Job 42:10
LORD, my God, I **p** to you, and .... Ps 30:2
I have **p** to you every day; .... Ps 88:9
But Phinehas **p** to the LORD, ... Ps 106:30
I loved them and **p** for them. .... Ps 109:4
I **p** to you with all my heart. .... Ps 119:58
You are the son I **p** for. .... Pr 31:2
and **p** to the LORD: .... Is 37:15
'You **p** to me about Sennacherib............ Is 37:21
the wall and **p** to the LORD, ... Is 38:2
if Moses and Samuel **p** for them. .... Je 15:1
son of Neriah, I **p** to the LORD, ... Je 32:16
the Lord God and **p** and asked him .... Da 9:3
I **p** to the LORD my God and told .... Da 9:4
he **p** to the LORD his God and .... Jnh 2:1
I **p** to you, and you heard my .... Jnh 2:7
He **p** to the LORD, "When I was............ Jnh 4:2
Jesus fell to the ground and **p**, ... Mt 26:39
went away a second time and **p**,............ Mt 26:42
went away a third time, ... Mt 26:44
to a lonely place, where he **p**. .... Mk 1:35
fell to the ground and **p** that, ... Mk 14:35
He **p**, "Abba, Father! You can do.......... Mk 14:36
went away and **p** the same thing. .... Mk 14:39
After Jesus **p** a third time, ... Mk 14:41
Pharisee stood alone and **p**, ' .... Lk 18:11
I have **p** that you will not lose .... Lk 22:32
He kneeled down and **p**, ... Lk 22:41
of pain, Jesus **p** even harder. .... Lk 22:44
he looked toward heaven and **p**,............ Jn 17:1
this, they **p** to God together .... Ac 4:24
they had **p**, the place where .... Ac 4:31
who **p** and laid their hands on .... Ac 6:6
stones, Stephen, **p**, "Lord Jesus, ... Ac 7:59
they **p** that the Samaritan .... Ac 8:15
of the room and kneeled and **p**. .... Ac 9:40
to the poor and **p** to God often. .... Ac 10:2
the church **p** earnestly to God .... Ac 12:5
So after they fasted and **p**, ... Ac 13:3
down with all of them and **p**. .... Ac 20:36
we all knelt on the beach and **p**,.......... Ac 21:5
the water and **p** for daylight to .... Ac 27:29
Paul went to him, **p**, and put his .... Ac 28:8
how he **p** to God against the .... Rm 11:2
he **p** to God and asked God for .... Heb 5:7
p with loud cries and tears to .... Heb 5:7
He **p** that it would not rain,................ Jam 5:17
Elijah **p** again, and the rain .... Jam 5:18

PRAYER

Before I finished my silent **p**, ... Ge 24:45
heard Isaac's **p**, and Rebekah .... Ge 25:21
listened to my **p** and has given .... Ge 30:6
Then God answered Leah's **p**,................ Ge 30:17
Rachel and answered her **p**, ... Ge 30:22
raise my hands to the LORD in **p**, ... Ex 9:29

LORD, listen to Judah's **p**; .... Dt 33:7
heard Manoah's **p**, and the angel .... Jdg 13:9
answered my **p** and gave him to 1Sa 1:27
answered his **p** for the country, ... 2Sa 24:25
listen to my **p** and my request, ... 1Ki 8:28
hear this **p** your servant prays 1Ki 8:28
' Hear the **p** I pray facing this.............. 1Ki 8:29
please hear their **p** in heaven,.................. 1Ki 8:36
hands in **p** toward this Temple, ... 1Ki 8:38
prayed this **p** to the LORD, ... 1Ki 8:54
remember this **p** day and night 1Ki 8:59
have heard your **p** and what you 1Ki 9:3
The LORD answered Elijah's **p**; 1Ki 17:22
answer my **p** so these people will 1Ki 18:37
I have heard your **p** to me about.............. 2Ki 19:20
have heard your **p** and seen your 2Ki 20:5
listen to my **p** and my request, ... 2Ch 6:19
hear this **p** your servant prays 2Ch 6:19
the **p** I pray facing this Temple. 2Ch 6:20
happens, hear their **p** in heaven,.............. 2Ch 6:27
hands in **p** toward this Temple, ... 2Ch 6:29
heard your **p** and have chosen 2Ch 7:12
this special time of **p** to God. 2Ch 20:3
LORD listened to Hezekiah's **p**, ... 2Ch 30:20
because their **p** reached heaven,.............. 2Ch 30:27
did as king, his **p** to his God, ... 2Ch 33:18
Manasseh's **p** and God's pity for 2Ch 33:19
Hear the **p** that I, your servant, ... Ne 1:6
to the **p** of your servant .... Ne 1:11
people in thanksgiving and **p**.................. Ne 11:17
cruel, and my **p** is pure. .... Job 16:17
and I will listen to his **p**. .... Job 42:8
the LORD listened to Job's **p**. .... Job 42:9
Have mercy on me and hear my **p**............ Ps 4:1
the LORD will answer my **p**. .... Ps 6:9
pleasure forever. A **p** of David. .... Ps 16:11
attention to my **p**, because I .... Ps 17:1
sound of my **p**, when I cry out .... Ps 28:2
because he heard my **p** for help................ Ps 28:6
you heard my **p** when I cried out .... Ps 31:22
LORD, hear my **p**, and listen to .... Ps 39:12
our hands in **p** to foreign gods, ... Ps 44:20
Hear my **p**, God; listen to what I............ Ps 54:2
listen to my **p** and do not ignore.............. Ps 55:1
hear my cry; listen to my **p**. .... Ps 61:1
up my hands in **p** to your name................ Ps 63:4
has listened; he has heard my **p**............... Ps 66:19
not ignore my **p** or hold back his .... Ps 66:20
God All-Powerful, hear my **p**; .... Ps 84:8
the way for him. A **p** of David. .... Ps 85:13
LORD, hear my **p**, and listen when........... Ps 86:6
Receive my **p**, and listen to my .... Ps 88:2
lifted my hands in **p** to you. .... Ps 88:9
A **p** of Moses, the man of God. .... Ps 89:52
A **p** of a person who is suffering .... Ps 101:8
LORD, listen to my **p**; .... Ps 102:1
Listen to my **p**; save me as you .... Ps 119:170
listen to my **p** for help. .... Ps 130:2
LORD, listen to my **p** for help. .... Ps 140:6
Let my **p** be like incense placed .... Ps 141:2
when he was in the cave. A **p**. .... Ps 141:10
LORD, hear my **p**; listen to my .... Ps 143:1
I lift my hands to you in **p**. .... Ps 143:6
you raise your arms to me in **p**, ... Is 1:15
have heard your **p** and seen your .... Is 38:5
give them joy in my house of **p**. .... Is 56:7
called a house for **p** for people .... Is 56:7
your needs in **p** should never be .... Is 62:6
lifts her hands in **p** and says, ... Je 4:31
like water in **p** to the Lord. .... La 2:19
your hands in **p** to him for the .... La 2:19
for help, but he ignores my **p**.................. La 3:8
and no **p** could get through. .... La 3:44

Listen to my **p** for help, and for .... Da 9:17
things in my **p** to the LORD, ... Da 9:20
This is the **p** of Habakkuk the .... Hab 3:1
only if you use **p** and fasting. .... Mt 17:21
will be called a house for **p**.' .... Mt 21:13
get anything you ask for in **p**." .... Mt 21:22
their special **p** clothes very .... Mt 23:5
can only be forced out by **p**." .... Mk 9:29
called a house for **p** for people .... Mk 11:17
the things you ask for in **p**, ... Mk 11:24
God has heard your **p**. .... Lk 1:13
Temple will be a house for **p**.' .... Lk 19:46
day for the afternoon **p** service. .... Ac 3:1
has heard your **p** and has seen .... Ac 10:31
find a special place for **p**. .... Ac 16:13
were going to the place for **p**, ... Ac 16:16
be saved. That is my **p** to God. .... Rm 10:1
so you can give your time to **p**. 1Co 7:5
say amen to your **p** of thanks, ... 1Co 14:16
So I bow in **p** before the Father .... Eph 3:14
This is my **p** for you: .... Php 1:9
by what God has said and by **p**. 1Ti 4:5
and his **p** was heard because he .... Heb 5:7
the **p** that is said with faith .... Jam 5:15

PRAYERS

God answered the **p** for the land. 2Sa 21:14
my **p** and the prayers of your 1Ki 8:30
prayers and the **p** of your people 1Ki 8:30
then hear their **p** from your home 1Ki 8:39
Then hear in heaven their **p**, ... 1Ki 8:45
Then hear their **p** from your home 1Ki 8:49
attention to my **p** and the 1Ki 8:52
prayers and the **p** of your people 1Ki 8:52
my **p** and the prayers of your 2Ch 6:21
prayers and the **p** of your people 2Ch 6:21
then hear their **p** from your home 2Ch 6:30
Then hear in heaven their **p**, ... 2Ch 6:35
Then hear their **p** from your home 2Ch 6:39
Listen to the **p** we pray in this 2Ch 6:40
listen to the **p** prayed in this 2Ch 7:15
our trip, and he answered our **p**. .... Ezr 8:23
servant and the **p** of your .... Ne 1:11
people and listens to their **p**. .... Ps 34:15
But my **p** were not answered. .... Ps 35:13
You hear our **p**. All people will .... Ps 65:2
This ends the **p** of David son of .... Ps 72:20
angry at the **p** of your people? .... Ps 80:4
will answer the **p** of the needy; .... Ps 102:17
he will not reject their **p**. .... Ps 102:17
let even his **p** show his guilt. .... Ps 109:7
he listens to my **p** for help. .... Ps 116:1
because my **p** go up to you. .... Ps 143:8
he likes the **p** of honest people .... Pr 15:8
he hears the **p** of those who do .... Pr 15:29
taught, your **p** will not be heard .... Pr 28:9
if you say many **p**, I will not .... Is 1:15
listen to their **p** and heal them. .... Is 19:22
they say quiet **p** to you when you .... Is 26:16
the LORD, will answer their **p**; .... Is 41:17
right time I will hear your **p**. .... Is 49:8
and believe your **p** are heard in .... Is 58:4
I will not listen to their **p**. .... Je 14:12
hear the **p** of your servant. .... Da 9:17
I have come because of your **p**. .... Da 10:12
answers your **p** and watches over .... Hos 14:8
and you heard my **p** in your Holy .... Jnh 2:7
you say long **p** so that people .... Mt 23:14
look good by saying long **p**. .... Mk 12:40
look good by saying long **p**. .... Lk 20:47
said, "God has heard your **p**. .... Ac 10:4
And you can help us with your **p**. 2Co 1:11
us because of their many **p**. 2Co 1:11

the right time I heard your **p**. 2Co 6:2
I always remember you in my **p**, ... Eph 1:16
all times with all kinds of **p**, ... Eph 6:18
In our **p** for you we always thank .... Col 1:3
as I always mention you in my **p**, ... 2Ti 1:3
God when I mention you in my **p**, ... Phm 1:4
will answer your **p** and I will be .... Phm 1:22
that nothing will stop your **p**. 1Pe 3:7
people and listens to their **p**. 1Pe 3:12
which are the **p** of God's holy .... Rev 5:8
offer with the **p** of all God's .... Rev 8:3
God with the **p** of God's people. .... Rev 8:4

PRAYING

the servant had finished **p**, ... Ge 24:15
Hannah kept **p**, Eli watched her 1Sa 1:12
She was **p** in her heart so her 1Sa 1:13
have been **p** because I have many 1Sa 1:16
stood near you **p** to the LORD. 1Sa 1:26
Don't stop **p** to the LORD our God 1Sa 7:8
will surely not stop **p** for you, ... 1Sa 12:23
When he finished **p**, he got up. 1Ki 8:54
finished **p**, fire came down 2Ch 7:1
As Ezra was **p** and confessing and .... Ezr 10:1
am **p** to you day and night for .... Ne 1:6
What would we gain by **p** to him?' .... Job 21:15
should not stop **p** to him until .... Is 62:7
a nation that was not **p** to me. .... Is 65:1
Israel crying and **p** for mercy. .... Je 3:21
found Daniel **p** and asking God .... Da 6:11
of Israel and **p** for God's holy .... Da 9:20
sacrifice, while I was still **p**. .... Da 9:21
first started **p**, an answer was .... Da 9:23
the LORD and **p** to him for .... Zph 1:6
When you are **p**, if you are angry .... Mk 11:25
people outside **p** at the time .... Lk 1:10
food and **p** day and night. .... Lk 2:37
While Jesus was **p**, heaven opened .... Lk 3:21
and he spent the night **p** to God. .... Lk 6:12
One time when Jesus was **p** alone, ... Lk 9:18
Jesus was **p**, the appearance .... Lk 9:29
time Jesus was **p** in a certain .... Lk 11:1
he finished **p**, he went to his .... Lk 22:45
am **p** for them. I am not **p**raying .... Jn 17:9
I am not **p** for people in the .... Jn 17:9
I am also **p** for all those who .... Jn 17:20
Jesus finished **p**, he went with .... Jn 18:1
all continued **p** together with .... Ac 1:14
breaking bread, and **p** together. .... Ac 2:42
of Tarsus. He is there now, **p**. .... Ac 9:11
I was **p** in my house at this same .... Ac 10:30
while I was **p**, I had a vision .... Ac 11:5
people were gathered there, **p**. .... Ac 12:12
by **p** and fasting for a certain .... Ac 14:23
and Silas were **p** and singing .... Ac 16:25
I was **p** in the Temple, ... Ac 22:17
in my work by **p** to God for me. .... Rm 1:9
my spirit is **p**, but my mind does 1Co 14:14
p with joy for all of you. .... Php 1:4
Because you are **p** for me and the .... Php 1:19
we have continued **p** for you, ... Col 1:9
Continue, keeping alert, and .... Col 4:2
day we continue **p** with all our 1Th 3:10
up, **p** in the Holy Spirit. .... Jud 1:20

PRAYS

your servant **p** to you today. 1Ki 8:28
prayer your servant **p** to you. 2Ch 6:19
close to everyone who **p** to him, ... Ps 145:18
He **p** to it and says, "You are my .... Is 44:17
Daniel still **p** to his God three .... Da 6:13
Every man who **p** or prophesies 1Co 11:4
every woman who **p** or prophesies 1Co 11:5

always **p** for you that you will .... Col 4:12
When a believing person **p,** .... Jam 5:16

PREACH

Jeduthun to **p** and play harps, ... 1Ch 25:1
King David chose Asaph to **p,** 1Ch 25:2
were supposed to **p** this message .... Ne 8:15
of the Temple and **p** this message .... Je 7:2
leaders of Judah heard Uriah **p,** .... Je 26:21
in Egypt, and **p** it in Migdol. .... Je 46:14
P it also in the cities of .... Je 46:14
of Nineveh, and **p** against it, ... Jnh 1:2
p to it what I tell you to say. .... Jnh 3:2
From that time Jesus began to **p,** .... Mt 4:17
When you go, **p** this: ' .... Mt 10:7
towns in Galilee to teach and **p.** .... Mt 11:1
here so I can **p** there too. .... Mk 1:38
he wanted to send them out to **p** .... Mk 3:14
when he came out to **p** to Israel............. Lk 1:80
continued to **p** the Good News, ... Lk 3:18
I must **p** about God's kingdom to .... Lk 4:43
Peter and John **p** believed the............... Ac 4:4
Soon he began to **p** about Jesus .... Ac 9:20
told us to **p** to the people and .... Ac 10:42
among you to **p** the Good News to .... Ac 15:7
did not let them **p** the Good News .... Ac 16:6
want so much to **p** the Good News........... Rm 1:15
Good News that I **p** says this. .... Rm 2:16
I always want to **p** the Good News .... Rm 15:20
people but to **p** the Good News. 1Co 1:17
he sent me to **p** the Good News 1Co 1:17
But we **p** a crucified Christ. 1Co 1:23
If I **p** because it is my own 1Co 9:17
But if I **p** and it is not my 1Co 9:17
to you, we all **p** the same thing, ... 1Co 15:11
came to Troas to **p** the Good News.......... 2Co 2:12
Good News that we **p** is hidden, ... 2Co 4:3
We do not **p** about ourselves, ... 2Co 4:5
but we **p** that Jesus Christ is 2Co 4:5
should **p** to you something .... Gal 1:8
Good News that I **p** to the .... Gal 2:2
change the Good News that I **p.** .... Gal 2:6
been sent to **p** this Good News, ... Eph 6:20
that when I **p** the Good News I .... Eph 6:20
is true that some **p** about Christ .... Php 1:15
others **p** about Christ because .... Php 1:15
They **p** because they have love, ... Php 1:16
the others **p** about Christ for .... Php 1:17
we continue to **p** Christ to each .... Col 1:28
that we can **p** the secret that .... Col 4:3
must teach and **p** these things. 1Ti 6:2
This is the Good News I **p,** 2Ti 2:8
P the Good News. Be ready at all 2Ti 4:2
Good News to **p** to those who live .... Rev 14:6

PREACHED

He **p** and used a harp to give 1Ch 25:3
He **p** the same things against .... Je 26:20
They **p** what was false and led .... La 2:14
for one day, he **p** to the people, ... Jnh 3:4
and they **p** to your ancestors, ... Zch 1:6
the Good News is **p** to the poor. .... Mt 11:5
When Jonah **p** to them, they were .... Mt 12:41
kingdom will be **p** in all the .... Mt 24:14
Good News is **p** in all the world .... Mt 26:13
is what John **p** to the people: .... Mk 1:7
out and **p** that people should .... Mk 6:12
Good News is **p** in all the world .... Mk 14:9
the Good News is **p** to the poor. .... Lk 7:22
p and told the Good News about .... Lk 8:1
When Jonah **p** to them, they were .... Lk 11:32
prophets were **p** until John came .... Lk 16:16
sins would be **p** in his name to .... Lk 24:47
Samaria and **p** about the Christ............. Ac 8:5

towns and **p** the Good News to .... Ac 8:25
called Azotus and **p** the Good............... Ac 8:40
boldly Saul had **p** in the name .... Ac 9:27
after John **p** to the people .... Ac 10:37
they **p** the Good News of God in............. Ac 13:5
John **p** to all the people of .... Ac 13:24
When they had **p** the message in .... Ac 14:25
p the Good News and taught the .... Ac 15:35
towns where we **p** the message .... Ac 15:36
You know I **p** to you and did not .... Ac 20:20
He boldly **p** about the kingdom of .... Ac 28:31
I **p** the Good News from Jerusalem .... Rm 15:19
after I have **p** to others. 1Co 9:27
So if I **p** to you or the other 1Co 15:11
or the other apostles **p** to you, ... 1Co 15:11
Now since we **p** that Christ was 1Co 15:12
and Timothy and I **p** to you, ... 2Co 1:19
Jesus from the one we **p**...................... 2Co 11:4
I **p** God's Good News to you 2Co 11:7
We **p** to you the Good News. .... Gal 1:8
the Good News I **p** to you was not .... Gal 1:11
Christ came and **p** peace to you .... Eph 2:17
gave me while I **p** the Good News— .... Php 1:5
when I first **p** the Good News .... Php 4:15
you while we **p** God's Good News 1Th 2:9
News that we **p** to call you to be............ 2Th 2:14
I **p** by the command of God our .... Tit 1:3
Good News was **p** to us just as it .... Heb 4:2
Those who **p** the Good News to you 1Pe 1:12
is the word that was **p** to you. 1Pe 1:25
he went and **p** to the spirits 1Pe 3:19
Good News was **p** to those who are 1Pe 4:6
Good News was **p** to them so they 1Pe 4:6
p about being right with God,................ 2Pe 2:5
because I had **p** the word of God .... Rev 1:9
death and by the message they **p.** .... Rev 12:11
He **p** in a loud voice, "Fear God .... Rev 14:7

PREACHER

into the home of Philip the **p,** .... Ac 21:8

PREACHES

comes to you and **p** a different 2Co 11:4

PREACHING

because of the **p** of Haggai the .... Ezr 6:14
Baptist began **p** in the desert .... Mt 3:1
p the Good News about the .... Mt 4:23
p the Good News about the .... Mt 9:35
in the desert and **p** a baptism of .... Mk 1:4
into Galilee, **p** the Good News .... Mk 1:14
p in the synagogues and forcing............. Mk 1:39
though John **p** always bothered .... Mk 6:20
the Jordan River **p** a baptism of .... Lk 3:3
Then he kept on **p** in the...................... Lk 4:44
p the Good News and healing................. Lk 9:6
people and were **p** that people .... Ac 4:2
p boldly in the name of the Lord. .... Ac 9:28
that Paul was **p** the word of God .... Ac 17:13
among whom I was **p** the kingdom .... Ac 20:25
I did not come **p** God's secret 1Co 2:1
My teaching and **p** were not with 1Co 2:4
in my work of **p** the Good News. 1Co 9:18
then our **p** is worth nothing, ... 1Co 15:14
his service in **p** the Good News. 2Co 8:18
If anyone is **p** something....................... Gal 1:9
us is now **p** the same faith that .... Gal 1:23
the first time, **p** the Good News .... Gal 4:13
p about the cross would not be .... Gal 5:11
they are **p** about Christ. .... Php 1:18
Paul, help in **p** that Good News. .... Col 1:23
know about that life through **p.** .... Tit 1:3

P

PRECIOUS

God, your love is so **p**! ....Ps 36:7
their lives are **p** to him. ....Ps 72:14
to the LORD is **p** in his sight. ....Ps 116:15
your thoughts are **p** to me. ....Ps 139:17
Wisdom is more **p** than rubies; ....Pr 3:15
Wisdom is more **p** than rubies. ....Pr 8:11
on this important and **p** rock. ....Is 28:16
Because you are **p** to me, because ....Is 43:4
the gates and **p** jewels for all ....Is 54:12
and all our **p** things have been ....Is 64:11
out and took all her **p** things. ....La 1:10
trading their **p** things for food ....La 1:11
The **p** people of Jerusalem were ....La 4:2
and you put my **p** treasures in ....Joe 3:5
you hurts what is **p** to me— ....Zch 2:8
but with the **p** blood of Christ, ...1Pe 1:19
stone God chose, and he was **p**. 1Pe 2:4
on this important and **p** rock. 1Pe 2:6
destroyed and is very **p** to God. 1Pe 3:4
the very great and **p** promises. 2Pe 1:4
the throne looked like **p** stones, ...Rev 4:3
with the gold, **p** jewels, and ....Rev 17:4
with gold, **p** jewels, and pearls ....Rev 18:16

PREDICTION

they will think this **p** is wrong, ...Eze 21:23

PREFER

I would **p** not to destroy or ruin 2Sa 20:20
or, if you **p**, I will pay you 1Ki 21:2
or, if you **p**, I will give you 1Ki 21:6

PREFERS

My throat **p** to be choked; ....Job 7:15

PREGNANCY

be no more **p**, no more births ....Hos 9:11
Elizabeth's sixth month of **p**, ...Lk 1:26

PREGNANT

much trouble when you are **p**, ...Ge 3:16
and she became **p** and gave birth ....Ge 4:1
and she became **p** and gave birth ....Ge 4:17
with Hagar, and she became **p**. ....Ge 16:4
When Hagar learned she was **p**, ...Ge 16:4
when she became **p**, she began to ....Ge 16:5
You are now **p**, and you will have ....Ge 16:11
became **p** by their father. ....Ge 19:36
Sarah became **p** and gave birth to ....Ge 21:2
prayer, and Rebekah became **p**. ....Ge 25:21
While she was **p**, the babies ....Ge 25:22
Leah became **p** and gave birth to ....Ge 29:32
Leah became **p** again and gave ....Ge 29:33
Leah became **p** again and gave ....Ge 29:34
became **p** and gave Jacob a son. ....Ge 30:5
Bilhah became **p** again and gave ....Ge 30:7
prayer, and she became **p** again. ....Ge 30:17
Leah became **p** again and gave ....Ge 30:19
When she became **p** and gave birth ....Ge 30:23
and she became **p** and gave birth ....Ge 38:3
Tamar to become **p** and for Er to ....Ge 38:9
relations, and Tamar became **p**. ....Ge 38:18
a prostitute, and now she is **p**." ....Ge 38:24
owns these things has made me **p**. ....Ge 38:25
She became **p** and gave birth to a ....Ex 2:2
are fighting and hit a **p** woman, ...Ex 21:22
you will become **p** and give birth ....Jdg 13:3
will become **p** and have a son. ....Jdg 13:5
'You will become **p** and will have ....Jdg 13:7
The LORD let her become **p**, ...Ru 4:13
Hannah became **p**, and in time she 1Sa 1:20
was **p** and was about to give 1Sa 4:19
became **p** and sent word to 2Sa 11:5
word to David, saying, "I am **p**." 2Sa 11:5
She became **p** again and had 2Sa 12:24

woman became **p** and gave birth 2Ki 4:17
and split open their **p** women." 2Ki 8:12
ripped open all their **p** women. 2Ki 15:16
She became **p** and gave birth to a 1Ch 7:23
The virgin will be **p**. ....Is 7:14
and she became **p** and had a son. ....Is 8:3
she would have stayed **p** forever. ....Je 20:17
of the women are **p**, and some are ....Je 31:8
and she became **p** and gave birth ....Hos 1:3
Gomer became **p** again and gave ....Hos 1:6
became **p** again and gave birth ....Hos 1:8
one who became **p** with them has ....Hos 2:5
more births, no more getting **p**. ....Hos 9:11
and their **p** women will be ripped ....Hos 13:16
open the **p** women in Gilead ....Am 1:13
learned she was **p** by the power ....Mt 1:18
The virgin will be **p**. ....Mt 1:23
women who are **p** or have nursing ....Mt 24:19
women who are **p** or have nursing ....Mk 13:17
became **p** and did not go out of ....Lk 1:24
You will become **p** and give birth ....Lk 1:31
is also **p** with a son though she ....Lk 1:36
she has been **p** for six months. ....Lk 1:36
was engaged and who was now **p**. ....Lk 2:5
women who are **p** or have nursing ....Lk 21:23
She was **p** and cried out with ....Rev 12:2

PREPARATION

the day after **P** Day, the leading ....Mt 27:62
This was **P** Day. (That means the ....Mk 15:42
This was late on **P** Day, and when ....Lk 23:54
about noon on **P** Day of Passover ....Jn 19:14
This day was **P** Day, and the next ....Jn 19:31

PREPARE

p twenty quarts of fine flour, ...Ge 18:6
to kill it and to **p** it for food. ....Ge 18:7
When you **p** the tasty food that I ....Ge 27:4
an animal and **p** some tasty food ....Ge 27:7
I will **p** them just the way your ....Ge 27:9
Kill an animal and **p** a meal. ....Ge 43:16
served him to **p** his father's. ....Ge 50:2
doctors forty days to **p** his body ....Ge 50:3
you may do is to **p** your meals. ....Ex 12:16
Then they are to **p** it." ....Ex 16:5
he made them **p** themselves for ....Ex 19:14
me, must first **p** themselves. ....Ex 19:22
You will **p** all these things for ....Ex 30:29
its tools to **p** them for service ....Nu 7:1
p a quart of wine as a drink ....Nu 15:5
also **p** a grain offering of four ....Nu 15:6
Also **p** one and one-fourth quarts ....Nu 15:7
If you **p** a young bull as a ....Nu 15:8
P each bull or male sheep, ...Nu 15:11
and **p** seven bulls and seven male ....Nu 23:1
altars here and **p** for me seven ....Nu 23:29
Then we will **p** for war. ....Nu 32:17
servants, will **p** for battle. ....Nu 32:27
and Reubenites **p** for battle and ....Nu 32:29
your God will **p** you and your ....Dt 30:6
But if you want to **p** something, ...Jdg 13:16
I will **p** the other bull, putting................1Ki 18:23
Choose a bull and **p** it. 1Ki 18:25
his men to **p** to attack the city 1Ki 20:12
"**P** a holy meeting for Baal." 2Ki 10:20
I will **p** for the building of it. 1Ch 22:5
were chosen to **p** the holy things 1Ch 23:13
done my best to **p** for building 1Ch 29:2
the priests to **p** the storerooms 2Ch 31:11
P yourselves by your family 2Ch 35:4
P the lambs for your relatives, ...2Ch 35:6
to the banquet I will **p** for you. ....Est 5:8
Let them **p** to wake up the sea ....Job 3:8
they **p** to attack me..............................Job 19:12

for my feet and **p** to attack me. .... Job 30:12
kings of the earth **p** to fight, ... Ps 2:2
You **p** a meal for me in front of .... Ps 23:5
P the way for him who rides .... Ps 68:4
Can God **p** food in the desert? .... Ps 78:19
before God and **p** the way for him .... Ps 85:13
outside work and **p** of your fields. .... Pr 24:27
P for battle and be smashed to .... Is 8:9
P for battle and be smashed to .... Is 8:9
P to kill his children, because .... Is 14:21
P the shields for battle! .... Is 21:5
Kir will **p** their shields. .... Is 22:6
will **p** a feast on this .... Is 25:6
P in the desert the way for the .... Is 40:3
Build a road! **P** the way! Make .... Is 57:14
you own and **p** to leave, ... Je 10:17
P your shields, large and small, ... Je 46:3
soldiers **p** their bows to shoot .... Je 51:3
sacrifice which I will **p** for you .... Eze 39:17
You must **p** a goat every day for .... Eze 43:25
the priests must **p** a young bull .... Eze 43:25
of the North will **p** for war. .... Da 11:10
powerful army and **p** for war. .... Da 11:25
the nations: **P** for war! Wake up .... Joe 3:9
who will **p** the way for me. .... Mal 3:1
'**P** the way for the Lord. .... Mt 3:3
who will **p** the way for you.' .... Mt 11:10
on my body to **p** me for burial. .... Mt 26:12
you want us to **p** for you to eat .... Mt 26:17
of you, who will **p** your way." .... Mk 1:2
'**P** the way for the Lord. .... Mk 1:3
on my body to **p** me for burial. .... Mk 14:8
us to go and **p** for you to eat .... Mk 14:12
P the food for us there." .... Mk 14:15
go before the Lord to **p** his way. .... Lk 1:76
'**P** the way for the Lord. .... Lk 3:4
who will **p** the way for you.' .... Lk 7:27
'**P** something for me to eat. .... Lk 17:8
Go and **p** the Passover meal for .... Lk 22:8
"Where do you want us to **p** it?" .... Lk 22:9
P the Passover meal there." .... Lk 22:12
the women left to **p** spices and .... Lk 23:56
one sent to **p** a place for him.' .... Jn 3:28
there to **p** a place for you. .... Jn 14:2
I go and **p** a place for you, ... Jn 14:3
kings of the earth **p** to fight, ... Ac 4:26
sound, who will **p** for battle? 1Co 14:8
those gifts to **p** God's holy .... Eph 4:12
our Lord Jesus the way for us 1Th 3:11
p a room for me in which to stay, ... Phm 1:22
So **p** your minds for service and 1Pe 1:13
dried up to **p** the way for the .... Rev 16:12
P wine for her that is twice as .... Rev 18:6

PREPARED

to show that you are **p** to follow .... Ge 17:11
Then Lot **p** a meal for them. .... Ge 19:3
I have **p** the house for you and .... Ge 24:31
So Isaac **p** food for them, and .... Ge 26:30
He also **p** some tasty food you .... Ge 27:31
the night and **p** a gift for Esau .... Ge 32:13
The men **p** their gift to give to .... Ge 43:25
Joseph **p** his chariot and went to .... Ge 46:29
so the doctors **p** Jacob's body to .... Ge 50:2
Doctors **p** his body for burial, ... Ge 50:26
the king **p** his war chariot and .... Ex 14:6
lead you to the place I have **p**. .... Ex 23:20
to him, "I have **p** seven altars, ... Nu 23:4
soldiers **p** for war passed .... Jos 4:13
p to fight against the .... Jos 24:9
and they **p** to go down to Keilah. 1Sa 23:8
There David **p** a feast for them. 2Sa 3:20
came out and **p** for battle at the 2Sa 10:8

There the Arameans **p** for battle 2Sa 10:17
the stones and **p** the stones 1Ki 5:18
The stones were **p** at the same 1Ki 6:7
Solomon **p** the inner room at the 1Ki 6:19
that was given to them and **p** it. 1Ki 18:26
Israelites also had **p** for war. 1Ki 20:27
So he **p** a great feast for the 2Ki 6:23
relatives had **p** food for them. 1Ch 12:39
Then he **p** a place for the Ark of 1Ch 15:1
and Levites **p** themselves for 1Ch 15:14
came out and **p** for battle at the 1Ch 19:9
He **p** them for battle, facing the 1Ch 19:17
the Temple for which I have **p**." 1Ch 29:19
place David had **p** on the 2Ch 3:1
and Jeroboam **p** to fight him with 2Ch 13:3
to fight Zerah and **p** for battle 2Ch 14:10
Levites **p** meat for themselves 2Ch 35:14
Levites had **p** everything for 2Ch 35:15
This is what was **p** every day: .... Ne 5:18
banquet that I have **p** for you." .... Est 5:4
banquet Esther had **p** for them. .... Est 5:5
on the platform he had **p**. .... Est 6:4
to the banquet Esther had **p**. .... Est 6:14
one Haman had **p** for Mordecai, ... Est 7:9
platform he had **p** for Mordecai. .... Est 7:10
See, I have **p** my case, and I .... Job 13:18
He has **p** his deadly weapons; .... Ps 7:13
She has **p** her food and wine; .... Pr 9:2
and drink the wine I have **p**. .... Pr 9:5
He has even **p** a day of disaster .... Pr 16:4
fire you have **p** for your enemies .... Is 26:11
You have **p** many medicines, ... Je 46:11
an enemy, he **p** to shoot his bow .... La 2:4
p to shoot his bow and made me .... La 3:12
It was **p** on the day you were .... Eze 28:13
Be **p**. Be prepared, you and all .... Eze 38:7
p, you and all the armies that .... Eze 38:7
which I have **p** for you, ... Eze 39:19
The LORD has **p** a sacrifice; .... Zph 1:7
for whom my Father has **p** them." .... Mt 20:23
a king who **p** a wedding feast .... Mt 22:2
kingdom God has **p** for you since .... Mt 25:34
forever that was **p** for the devil .... Mt 25:41
and they **p** the Passover meal. .... Mt 26:19
for whom they have been **p**." .... Mk 10:40
so they **p** the Passover meal. .... Mk 14:16
which you **p** before all people. .... Lk 2:31
things you have **p** for yourself?' .... Lk 12:20
And they **p** the Passover meal. .... Lk 22:13
bringing the spices they had **p**. .... Lk 24:1
day for me to be **p** for burial. .... Jn 12:7
but while the food was being **p**, ... Ac 10:10
we immediately **p** to leave for .... Ac 16:10
has **p** these people to have his .... Rm 9:23
God has **p** for those who love 1Co 2:9
all that he has **p** for his people .... Col 1:12
but you have **p** a body for me. .... Heb 10:5
he has **p** a city for them. .... Heb 11:16
faith that Moses **p** the Passover .... Heb 11:28
seven trumpets to blow them. .... Rev 8:6
looked like horses **p** for battle. .... Rev 9:7
to a place God **p** for her where .... Rev 12:6
to the place **p** for her in the .... Rev 12:14
which is **p** with all its strength .... Rev 14:14
as the wine she **p** for others. .... Rev 18:6
was **p** like a bride dressed for .... Rev 21:2

PREPARES

is still dark and **p** food for her .... Pr 31:15

PREPARING

today and tomorrow **p** themselves. .... Ex 19:10
had the job of **p** the special 1Ch 9:32
are you **p** your tomb in a high .... Is 22:16

I am **p** disaster for you and.....................Je 18:11
and they were **p** to start their ....Jn 19:42
tying him up, **p** to beat him, ...Ac 22:25
men who were **p** to question Paul ....Ac 22:29

PRESENCE

bless you in the **p** of the LORD ....Ge 27:7
together in the **p** of the LORD, ...Ex 16:9
you are in my **p** so that it is ....Ex 25:30
shoulders in the **p** of the LORD ....Ex 28:12
that shows we are in God's **p**;................Ex 35:13
showed they were in God's **p**;................Ex 39:36
to use in the **p** of the LORD. ....Le 10:1
stand up in their **p**. ....Le 19:32
died in the **p** of the LORD when..............Nu 3:4
shows a person is in God's **p**. ....Nu 4:7
sticks from the LORD's **p**. ....Nu 17:9
daylight in the **p** of the LORD. ....Nu 25:4
rules in the **p** of the LORD our ....Dt 6:25
LORD your God's **p** about the.................Dt 12:18
animals in the **p** of the LORD ....Dt 15:20
innocent in the **p** of the LORD ....Dt 18:13
must stand in the **p** of the LORD ....Dt 19:17
lots in the **p** of the LORD our ....Jos 18:6
lots in the **p** of the LORD here ....Jos 18:8
lots in the **p** of the LORD to ....Jos 18:10
They met in the **p** of the LORD at ....Jos 19:51
with us in the **p** of the LORD?" ....Jdg 21:5
bread from the **p** of God because 1Sa 21:6
die far away from the LORD's **p**. 1Sa 26:20
in Hebron in the **p** of the LORD..............2Sa 5:3
in the **p** of the LORD. 2Sa 6:5
dancing in the **p** of the LORD, ...2Sa 6:16
I did it in the **p** of the LORD. 2Sa 6:21
celebrate in the **p** of the LORD. 2Sa 6:21
stakes in the **p** of the LORD at 2Sa 21:6
on a hill in the **p** of the LORD. 2Sa 21:9
brightness of his **p** came flashes.............2Sa 22:13
shows God's people are in his **p**; 1Ki 7:48
he removed them from his **p**. 2Ki 17:18
he threw them out of his **p**...................2Ki 17:20
the Israelites from his **p**,...................2Ki 17:23
you were, and you cried in my **p**. 2Ki 22:19
agreement in the **p** of the LORD..............2Ki 23:3
to remove them from his **p**,..................2Ki 24:3
he threw them out of his **p**...................2Ki 24:20
in Hebron in the **p** of the LORD..............1Ch 11:3
celebrating in the **p** of God. 1Ch 13:8
died there in the **p** of God. 1Ch 13:10
him king in the **p** of the LORD. 1Ch 29:22
altar in the **p** of the LORD at 2Ch 1:6
sweet-smelling spices in his **p**. 2Ch 2:4
out the holy bread in God's **p**. 2Ch 2:4
shows God's people are in his **p**; 2Ch 4:19
you were, and you cried in my **p**. 2Ch 34:27
agreement in the **p** of the LORD..............2Ch 34:31
his love in the **p** of the king, ...Ezr 7:28
not been sad in his **p** before. ....Ne 2:1
to enter the **p** of King Xerxes.................Est 1:19
court record in the king's **p**. ....Est 2:23
into the king's **p** to beg for ....Est 4:8
left the king's **p** wearing royal ....Est 8:15
Then Satan left the LORD's **p**. ....Job 1:12
So Satan left the LORD's **p**. ....Job 2:7
anyone will rest in the **p** of God? ....Job 9:2
one can be good in the **p** of God, ...Job 25:4
of his **p** came clouds with ....Ps 18:12
them by your **p** from what people ....Ps 31:20
rule in the **p** of God forever. ....Ps 61:7
nations in our **p** that you punish.............Ps 79:10
live in the light of your **p**. ....Ps 89:15
children will live in your **p**,..................Ps 102:28
people will live in his **p**. ....Ps 140:13

enjoying his **p** all the time, ...Pr 8:30
wicked people from the king's **p**; ....Pr 25:5
should shake with fear in my **p**. ....Je 5:22
guilty in the **p** of the Holy One ....Je 51:5
he threw them out of his **p**....................Je 52:3
that is in the **p** of the LORD." ....Eze 41:22
offer them in the **p** of the LORD, ...Eze 43:24
eat a meal in the **p** of the LORD. ....Eze 44:3
stand in my **p** to offer me the ....Eze 44:15
gateway in the **p** of the LORD.................Eze 46:3
into the LORD's **p** at the special ....Eze 46:9
up so that we may live in his **p** ....Hos 6:2
'I was driven out of your **p**,....................Jnh 2:4
should be silent in his **p**." ....Hab 2:20
everyone, in the **p** of the LORD. ....Zch 2:13
just come from the **p** of the Lord ....Zch 6:5
written in his **p** in a book to be ....Mal 3:16
is joy in the **p** of the angels....................Lk 15:10
he said in the **p** of the people.................Lk 20:26
miracles in the **p** of his ....Jn 20:30
that no one can brag in his **p**. 1Co 1:29
to fill everything with his **p**. ....Eph 4:10
you into God's **p** as people who ....Col 1:22
one into God's **p** as a mature ....Col 1:28
people in God's **p** not to argue 2Ti 2:14
a command in the **p** of God and 2Ti 4:1
Humble yourself in the Lord's **p**, ...Jam 4:10
a helper in the **p** of the Father—..............1Jn 2:1
and not be ashamed in his **p**. 1Jn 2:28
come without fear into God's **p**; 1Jn 3:21
the boldness we have in God's **p**: 1Jn 5:14
Now God's **p** is with people, ...Rev 21:3

PRESENT

and tell them to **p** them as an ....Ex 29:24
and **p** it before the LORD as an ....Ex 29:26
P the grain offering that is ....Le 6:21
and they must **p** it to the LORD ....Le 10:15
will **p** them before the LORD as ....Le 14:12
he will **p** them as an offering ....Le 14:24
because they **p** the offerings ....Le 21:6
The priest will **p** the bundle ....Le 23:11
he will **p** the bundle on the day ....Le 23:11
the day when you **p** the bundle of ....Le 23:12
of grain to **p** as an offering. ....Le 23:15
The priest will **p** the two lambs ....Le 23:20
of Levi and **p** them to Aaron ....Nu 3:6
He will **p** it before the LORD and ....Nu 5:25
he will **p** the basket of bread ....Nu 6:17
the priest will **p** them to the ....Nu 6:20
he is to **p** the breast and the ....Nu 6:20
Aaron with the Levites before ....Nu 8:11
and his sons and **p** the Levites ....Nu 8:13
p them as an offering so that ....Nu 8:15
p these two hundred fifty pans ....Nu 16:17
Aaron must also **p** your pans." ....Nu 16:17
the Israelites **p** to me. ....Nu 18:11
Israelites **p** as holy gifts I, ...Nu 18:19
way you will **p** an offering to ....Nu 18:28
'When you **p** the best, it will be ....Nu 18:30
He is **p** with you, and if you ....Dt 6:15
P your burnt offerings on the ....Dt 12:27
you must be **p** with your tribes. ....Jos 7:14
all of Israel to **p** themselves in ....Jos 7:16
in that family to **p** themselves. ....Jos 7:18
Here is a **p** for you from the 1Sa 30:26
as a wedding **p** to his daughter 1Ki 9:16
as a place to **p** sacrifices. ....Ezr 6:3
I would **p** my case before him and ....Job 23:4
person could **p** his case to God, ...Job 23:7
a **p** given in secrecy will quiet ....Pr 21:14
The LORD says, "**P** your case." ....Is 41:21
food and a **p** let him go. ....Je 40:5

Jerusalem to **p** him to the Lord. .... Lk 2:22
death, the **p**, and the future— 1Co 3:22
kingdom of God is **p** not in talk 1Co 4:20
The **p** time is a time of trouble, ... 1Co 7:26
world in its **p** form will soon be 1Co 7:31
to live in the **p** age in a wise .... Tit 2:12
is an example for the **p** time. .... Heb 9:9
the throne will be **p** with them. .... Rev 7:15

PRESENTED

all **p** their gold to the LORD. .... Ex 35:22
the Holy Tent was **p** to the LORD. .... Ex 38:24
bronze which was **p** to the LORD .... Ex 38:29
to be **p** to the LORD as the .... Le 7:30
day they were **p** to the LORD as .... Le 7:35
and his sons and **p** them as an .... Le 8:27
the breast and **p** it as an .... Le 8:29
He **p** the breasts and the right .... Le 9:21
offering that was **p** to the LORD. .... Le 10:14
It will be **p** to the LORD to make .... Le 14:21
homes to be **p** as an offering. .... Le 23:17
p them in front of the altar. .... Nu 7:10
as an offering **p** from the .... Nu 8:11
Then Aaron **p** them as an offering .... Nu 8:21
fifty men who had **p** the incense. .... Nu 16:35
because they were **p** to the LORD, ... Nu 16:38
breast that is **p** and the right .... Nu 18:18
groups of Judah **p** themselves, ... Jos 7:17
families of Zerah **p** themselves, ... Jos 7:17
and incense be **p** to him. .... Da 2:46

PRESENTS

to each other and **p** to the poor. .... Est 9:22
and Seba bring their **p** to him. .... Ps 72:10
and gives **p** to the wealthy, ... Pr 22:16
The LORD **p** his case against the .... Is 3:14

PRESSED

oil, made from **p** olives, to keep .... Ex 27:20
one quart of oil from **p** olives. .... Ex 29:40
one quart of oil from **p** olives. .... Nu 28:5
cakes of **p** figs and put all 1Sa 25:18
dough and **p** it together with 2Sa 13:8
like clay being **p** by a seal; .... Job 38:14
battle has **p** me all day long. .... Ps 56:1
P down, shaken together, and .... Lk 6:38

PRESSING

many people were **p** all around .... Lk 5:1

PRETEND

accept money to **p** not to see 1Sa 12:3
said to her, "**P** to be very sad. 2Sa 14:2
she will **p** to be someone else." 1Ki 14:5
Some people **p** to be rich but .... Pr 13:7
Others **p** to be poor but really .... Pr 13:7
own words and **p** it is a message .... Je 23:31
make people **p** not to be proud .... Col 2:23

PRETENDED

So he **p** to be crazy in front of 1Sa 21:13
but only **p**," says the Lord .... Je 3:10

PRETENDING

are you **p** to be someone else? 1Ki 14:6
p they were throwing more .... Ac 27:30

PRETTY

She was very **p**, a virgin; .... Ge 24:16
had a very **p** figure and face. .... Est 2:7
She is as **p** as the moon, as .... Sng 6:10
They will be so **p** and beautiful. .... Zch 9:17

PRICE

I will pay him the full **p**. .... Ge 23:9
you the full **p** for the field. .... Ge 23:13
won't argue with you over the **p**. .... Ge 23:15
He weighed out the full **p**, ... Ge 23:16
master the **p** for a new slave, ... Ex 21:32

the rental **p** covers the loss. .... Ex 22:15
pay the full **p** plus an extra .... Le 6:5
one-fifth of the **p** of that food. .... Le 22:14
number to decide the right **p**. .... Le 25:15
number to decide the right **p**. .... Le 25:15
many years, the **p** will be high. .... Le 25:16
years, lower the **p**, because your .... Le 25:16
Use that number to decide the **p**, ... Le 25:50
pay back a large part of the **p**. .... Le 25:51
pay a small part of the first **p**. .... Le 25:52
by paying a **p** that is the same .... Le 27:2
the **p** for a man twenty to sixty .... Le 27:3
p for a woman twenty to sixty .... Le 27:4
The **p** for a man five to twenty .... Le 27:5
The **p** for a baby boy one month .... Le 27:6
a baby girl the **p** is about one .... Le 27:6
The **p** for a man sixty years old .... Le 27:7
anyone is too poor to pay the **p**, ... Le 27:8
and the priest will set the **p**. .... Le 27:8
will decide a **p** for the animal, ... Le 27:12
that is the **p** for the animal. .... Le 27:12
-fifth must be added to the **p**. .... Le 27:13
that is the **p** for the house. .... Le 27:14
-fifth must be added to the **p**. .... Le 27:15
decide the exact **p** by counting .... Le 27:18
must be added to that **p**, ... Le 27:19
must decide the **p** for the land, ... Le 27:23
and the **p** must be paid on that .... Le 27:23
it back for the **p** set by the .... Le 27:27
must add one-fifth to that **p**. .... Le 27:27
it for the **p** he had decided. .... Le 27:27
-fifth must be added to its **p**. .... Le 27:31
Sell it to me for the full **p**." 1Ch 21:22
pay the full **p** for the land. 1Ch 21:24
and the **p** of wisdom is much .... Job 28:18
because the **p** of a life is high. .... Ps 49:8
You were not sold for a **p**, ... Is 52:3
people for the **p** of a pair of .... Am 8:6
decisions are bought for a **p**. .... Mic 7:3
answered, "Yes, that was the **p**." .... Ac 5:8
you were bought by God for a **p**. 1Co 6:20
all were bought at a great **p**, ... 1Co 7:23
he might pay the **p** to free us .... Tit 2:14

PRICES

Holy Place in paying these **p**; .... Le 27:25

PRICKLY

of them is worse than a **p** plant. .... Mic 7:4

PRIDE

I will break your great **p**, ... Le 26:19
away your **p** and testing you .... Dt 8:2
took away your **p** when he let you .... Dt 8:3
take away your **p** and to test you .... Dt 8:16
P is as bad as the sin of 1Sa 15:23
powerful, his **p** led to his ruin. 2Ch 26:16
Their **p** may be as high as the .... Job 20:6
they have sinned in their **p**. .... Job 36:9
Keep me from the sins of **p**; .... Ps 19:13
With **p** and hatred they speak. .... Ps 31:18
lies, so let their **p** trap them. .... Ps 59:12
They wear **p** like a necklace and .... Ps 73:6
he broke their **p** by hard work. .... Ps 107:12
I hate **p** and bragging, evil ways .... Pr 8:13
P leads only to shame; .... Pr 11:2
P only leads to arguments, ... Pr 13:10
P leads to destruction; .... Pr 16:18
with stubborn **p** are called .... Pr 21:24
P will ruin people, but those .... Pr 29:23
and his **p** has made him do these .... Is 10:12
proud people to lose their **p**, ... Is 13:11
destroy the **p** of those who are .... Is 13:11
Your **p** has been sent down to the .... Is 14:11
what they take **p** in will be .... Is 16:14

P

But God will bring down their **p**, ... Is 25:11
p of Israel's drunken people! .... Is 28:1
p of Israel's drunken people, ... Is 28:3
and you will take **p** in them. .... Is 61:6
I will ruin the **p** of the people ....Je 13:9
and the great **p** of Jerusalem. .... Je 13:9
cry secretly because of your **p.** ....Je 13:17
know Moab's great **p,** but it is ....Je 48:30
but your **p** has fooled you. ....Je 49:16
acted with **p** against the LORD, ...Je 50:29
p of the whole earth has been.................Je 51:41
and there is more **p** than ever. ....Eze 7:10
also end the **p** of the strong, ...Eze 7:24
destroy the **p** of Egypt and all.................Eze 32:12
The people's **p** in the land's ....Eze 33:28
put an end to the **p** of the king ....Da 11:18
turning his **p** back on him. ....Da 11:18
Israel's **p** testifies against ....Hos 5:5
Israel's **p** will cause their ....Hos 7:10
I hate the **p** of the Israelites, ...Am 6:8
by his name, the **P** of Jacob, "I ....Am 8:7
Your **p** has fooled you, you who ....Ob 1:3
will destroy the **p** of the ....Zch 9:6
defeat Assyria's **p** and destroy ....Zch 10:11
evil of others, **p,** and foolish ....Mk 7:22
Knowledge puffs you up with **p,**.............1Co 8:1
talk, gossip, **p,** and confusion..............2Co 12:20
selfishness or **p** be your guide. ....Php 2:3
and our **p** is in Christ Jesus. ....Php 3:3
with foolish **p** because of their ....Col 2:18
we will take **p** in when our Lord...........1Th 2:19
is full of **p** and understands 1Ti 6:4
poor should take **p** that God has...............Jam 1:9
rich should take **p** that God has ....Jam 1:10

PRIEST

He was a **p** for God Most High ....Ge 14:18
was the **p** of Midian. ....Ex 18:1
it on someone who is not a **p,**...............Ex 30:33
clothes that the **p** will wear in ....Ex 35:19
Then the **p** must burn all the ....Le 1:9
The **p** is to dip his finger into ....Le 4:6
the appointed **p** must bring some ....Le 4:16
must bring his penalty to the **p—** ....Le 6:6
The **p** must look at the sore on ....Le 13:3
seventh day the **p** must look at ....Le 13:6
The **p** will take some of the oil ....Le 14:28
A **p** must not marry an unclean ....Le 21:7
The high **p,** who was chosen ....Le 21:10
high **p** must not go out of the ....Le 21:12
him to the **p,** and the priest...................Le 27:8
The **p** will bring in the woman ....Nu 5:16
The **p** will make the woman stand ....Nu 5:18
The **p** should write these......................Nu 5:23
Eleazar the **p** gathered all the................Nu 16:39
of safety until the high **p** dies. ....Nu 35:28
When Phinehas the **p** and the ten ....Jos 22:30
I have a Levite as my **p.**".....................Jdg 17:13
with us and be our father and **p**............Jdg 18:19
Now Eli the **p** was sitting on a 1Sa 1:9
choose a loyal **p** for myself who 1Sa 2:35
So the **p** gave David the holy 1Sa 21:6
David said to Abiathar the **p,** 1Sa 30:7
king also said to Zadok the **p,** 2Sa 15:27
Jehoiada the **p** had commanded. 2Ki 11:9
and without a **p** to teach them 2Ch 15:3
the leading **p,** will be over you 2Ch 19:11
Hilkiah the **p** found the Book of 2Ch 34:14
God until a **p** had settled this ....Ezr 2:63
a **p** and teacher who taught about ....Ezr 7:11
Ezra the **p** stood up and said to ....Ezr 10:10
Ezra the **p** brought out the ....Ne 8:2
Ezra the **p** and teacher, ...Ne 8:9

said, "You are a **p** forever, a ....Ps 110:4
Uriah the **p** and Zechariah son of ....Is 8:2
a prophet, or a **p** asks you: ' ....Je 23:33
of God from the **p** and the advice ....Eze 7:26
Amaziah, a **p** at Bethel, sent ....Am 7:10
A **p** should teach what he knows, ...Mal 2:7
yourself to the **p** and offer the ....Mt 8:4
at the palace of the high **p,** ....Mt 26:3
of the high **p** and cut off his ....Mt 26:51
Caiaphas, the high **p,** where the ....Mt 26:57
the time of Abiathar the high **p,** ....Mk 2:26
there was a **p** named Zechariah ....Lk 1:5
happened that a **p** was going down ....Lk 10:31
Caiaphas, the high **p** that year. ....Jn 11:49
the high **p,** Caiaphas, John, ...Ac 4:6
The **p** in the temple of Zeus, ...Ac 14:13
insult God's high **p** like that!"................Ac 23:4
faithful high **p** in service to....................Heb 2:17
and is the high **p** of our faith. ....Heb 3:1
Since we have a great high **p,** ....Heb 4:14
says, "You are a **p** forever, a ....Heb 5:6
of Salem and a **p** for God Most ....Heb 7:1
he continues being a **p** forever. ....Heb 7:3
became a **p** with God's oath ....Heb 7:21
We have a high **p** who sits on the ....Heb 8:1
only the high **p** could go into ....Heb 9:7
came as the high **p** of the good ....Heb 9:11
The high **p** enters the Most Holy ....Heb 9:25

PRIEST'S

Any male in a **p** family may eat ....Le 6:29
Any male in a **p** family may eat ....Le 7:6
in the special **p** inner robes, ...Le 10:5
If a **p** daughter makes herself.................Le 21:9
Only people in a **p** family may ....Le 22:10
If a **p** daughter marries a person ....Le 22:12
But if the **p** daughter becomes ....Le 22:13
people from a **p** family may eat ....Le 22:13
The **p** servant would then come 1Sa 2:13
the **p** servant would come to the.............1Sa 2:15
the **p** servant would answer, ...1Sa 2:16
and the leading **p** officer would 2Ch 24:11
poured on the **p** head and running...........Ps 133:2
courtyard of the high **p** house, ...Mt 26:58
courtyard of the high **p** house. ....Mk 14:54
Jesus into the high **p** courtyard. ....Jn 18:15
everyone from the high **p** family. ....Ac 4:6

PRIESTHOOD

because they made the **p** unclean ....Ne 13:29

PRIESTLY

appointed to wear the **p** clothes...............Le 21:10
But the **p** work that has been ....Heb 8:6

PRIESTS

kingdom of **p** and a holy nation................Ex 19:6
heads to appoint them as **p.** ....Ex 28:41
the sins of the **p** and all the ....Le 16:33
were appointed to serve as **p.** ....Nu 3:3
The **p** will carry the Ark of the ....Jos 3:13
Have seven **p** carry trumpets made ....Jos 6:4
relatives who were **p** at Nob. 1Sa 22:11
The **p** Zadok and Abiathar will be 2Sa 15:35
He also chose **p** from all the 1Ki 12:31
He also chose **p** in Bethel to 1Ki 12:32
priest and the **p** of the next...................2Ki 23:4
had chosen **p** for these gods. 2Ki 23:5
killed all the **p** of those places 2Ki 23:20
families of the **p** and Levites. 1Ch 24:6
groups of the **p** and Levites are 1Ch 28:21
also made the **p'** courtyard and 2Ch 4:9
chose his own **p** for the places 2Ch 11:15
of the sacrifices to the **p,**.....................2Ch 30:16
to give the **p** and Levites.......................2Ch 31:4

and his fellow **p** joined .... Ezr 3:2
they put the **p** and the Levites .... Ezr 6:18
of the **p** who were leaders, ... Ezr 8:24
The **p** made repairs above the................. Ne 3:28
We, the **p**, the Levites, and the .... Ne 10:34
and Aaron were among his **p**,................. Ps 99:6
will cover her **p** with salvation .... Ps 132:16
will be called **p** of the LORD; .... Is 61:6
to the family of **p** who lived in .... Je 1:1
officers, **p**, and the people .... Je 1:18
said to the **p** and the prophets, ... Je 26:16
captive and his **p** and officers................. Je 49:3
Israel's **p** do cruel things to my .... Eze 22:26
while the **p** offer the ruler's .... Eze 46:2
Listen, you **p**. Pay attention, ... Hos 5:1
p only teach for pay, and its .... Mic 3:11
Baal, the false **p**, and the other .... Zph 1:4
You **p** do not respect me....................... Mal 1:6
the leading **p**, and the teachers .... Mt 16:21
the leading **p** and the teachers .... Mt 20:18
the leading **p** and the elders .... Mt 26:3
back to the **p** and the leaders,................. Mt 27:3
is lawful only for **p** to eat. .... Mk 2:26
The leading **p** accused Jesus of .... Mk 15:3
is lawful only for **p** to eat. .... Lk 6:4
and show yourselves to the **p**." .... Lk 17:14
to the leading **p** and the people, ... Lk 23:4
them back to the leading **p**." .... Ac 9:21
The leading **p** gave me the power .... Ac 26:10
be a kingdom of **p** who serve God .... Rev 1:6
be a kingdom of **p** for our God, ... Rev 5:10

PRINCE
one of them looked like a **p**." .... Jdg 8:18
for Sheshbazzar, the **p** of Judah. .... Ezr 1:8
would come near to him like a **p**. .... Job 31:37
a **p** is ruined if he has none. .... Pr 14:28
you down in front of the **p**. .... Pr 25:7
me feel like a **p** in a chariot. .... Sng 6:12
in sandals, you daughter of a **p**. .... Sng 7:1
Who Lives Forever, **P** of Peace. .... Is 9:6
cry greatly, the **p** will give up .... Eze 7:27
to fight even the **P** of princes! .... Da 8:25
But the **p** of Persia has been .... Da 10:13
fight against the **p** of Persia. .... Da 10:20
I go, the **p** of Greece will come, ... Da 10:20
fight against the **p** of Persia. .... Da 11:1
armies and even a **p** who made an .... Da 11:22
the great **p** who protects your................. Da 12:1
The **p** of demons is the one that .... Mt 9:34

PRINCES
P dug this well. Important men .... Nu 21:18
The **p** of Issachar were with .... Jdg 5:15
captured two **p** of Midian named .... Jdg 7:25
Oreb and Zeeb, the **p** of Midian................. Jdg 8:3
the poor sit with **p** and receive 1Sa 2:8
and from the **p**, and he gave them 2Ch 28:21
is not nicer to **p** than other .... Job 34:19
Do to their **p** what you did to .... Ps 83:11
could order the **p** as he wished. .... Ps 105:22
seats them with **p**, the princes .... Ps 113:8
princes, the **p** of his people. .... Ps 113:8
trust the LORD than to trust **p**. .... Ps 118:9
Even if **p** speak against me, ... Ps 119:23
your trust in **p** or other people .... Ps 146:3
p and all rulers of the earth, ... Ps 148:11
P use me to lead, and so do all .... Pr 8:16
A slave should not rule over **p**. .... Pr 19:10
ride horses while **p** walk like .... Ec 10:7
merchants were treated like **p**, ... Is 23:8
Her king and her **p** are among the .... La 2:9
Our **p** were purer than snow, ... La 4:7
P were hung by the hands; .... La 5:12

to fight even the Prince of **p**! .... Da 8:25
will punish the **p** and the king's .... Zph 1:8

PRINCESS
The **p** is very beautiful. .... Ps 45:13

PRISCILLA
and his wife, **P**, had recently .... Ac 18:2
Paul went to visit Aquila and **P**. .... Ac 18:2
for Syria, with **P** and Aquila. .... Ac 18:18
where Paul left **P** and Aquila. .... Ac 18:19
and when **P** and Aquila heard him, ... Ac 18:26
my greetings to **P** and Aquila, ... Rm 16:3
Aquila and **P** greet you in the 1Co 16:19
P and Aquila and the family 2Ti 4:19

PRISON
him into the **p** where the king's .... Ge 39:20
Joseph stayed there in the **p**. .... Ge 39:20
and caused the **p** warden to like .... Ge 39:21
p warden chose Joseph to take .... Ge 39:22
for whatever was done in the **p**. .... Ge 39:22
put them in the **p** of the captain .... Ge 40:3
same **p** where Joseph was kept. .... Ge 40:3
they stayed in **p** for some time. .... Ge 40:4
me so I can get out of this **p**. .... Ge 40:14
here to deserve being put in **p**." .... Ge 40:15
he released from **p** the chief .... Ge 40:20
and you put us in **p** in the house............. Ge 41:10
In **p** we each had a dream on the .... Ge 41:11
the guard, was in the **p** with us. .... Ge 41:12
brought him out of the **p**, ... Ge 41:14
rest of you will stay here in **p**. .... Ge 42:16
them all in **p** for three days. .... Ge 42:17
stay here in **p** while the rest of .... Ge 42:19
made him grind grain in the **p**. .... Jdg 16:21
they brought Samson from the **p**, ... Jdg 16:25
put this man in **p** and give him 1Ki 22:27
that, the king put Hoshea in **p**. 2Ki 17:4
Jehoiachin out of **p** on the 2Ki 25:27
put away his **p** clothes. 2Ki 25:29
angry that he put Hanani in **p** 2Ch 16:10
put this man in **p** and give him 2Ch 18:26
and puts you in **p** or calls you................. Job 11:10
he puts in **p** cannot be let out .... Job 12:14
Free me from my **p**, and then I .... Ps 142:7
even gone to **p** before becoming............. Ec 4:14
they will be shut up in **p**. .... Is 24:22
will free those who are in **p**, ... Is 42:7
live in darkness out of their **p**. .... Is 42:7
in pits or locked up in **p**......................... Is 42:22
Don't keep my people in **p**..................... Is 43:6
prisoners, 'Come out of your **p**.' .... Is 49:9
People in **p** will soon be set .... Is 51:14
will not die in **p**, and they will .... Is 51:14
you have put in **p** unfairly and .... Is 58:6
had put Jeremiah in **p** there. .... Je 32:3
Jeremiah was in **p**, he said, "The .... Je 32:5
had not yet been put into **p**. .... Je 37:4
which had been made into a **p**. .... Je 37:15
Why have you thrown me into **p**? .... Je 37:18
kept Zedekiah in **p** there until .... Je 52:11
of Judah was in **p** in Babylon for .... Je 52:31
king of Judah out of **p**. .... Je 52:31
put away his **p** clothes, ... Je 52:33
put him into **p** so his roar could .... Eze 19:9
I was locked in this **p** forever,................. Jnh 2:6
that John had been put in **p**, ... Mt 4:12
John the Baptist was in **p**, ... Mt 11:2
tied him up, and put him into **p**. .... Mt 14:3
soldiers to the **p** to cut off .... Mt 14:10
servant into **p** until he could .... Mt 18:30
the servant in **p** to be punished .... Mt 18:34
I was in **p**, and you visited me.' .... Mt 25:36
sick or in **p** and care for you? .... Mt 25:39

was sick and in **p**, and you did .... Mt 25:43
without clothes or sick or in **p**? .... Mt 25:44
that time there was a man in **p**, ... Mt 27:16
John was put in **p**, Jesus went .... Mk 1:14
and put him in **p** in order to .... Mk 6:17
and cut off John's head in the **p** .... Mk 6:27
Barabbas in **p** who was a rebel .... Mk 15:7
even worse: He put John in **p**. .... Lk 3:20
go with you to **p** and even to die .... Lk 22:33
a man who was in **p** for his part .... Lk 23:19
was before John was put into **p**. .... Jn 3:24
had left Paul in **p** to please the .... Ac 24:27
is a man that Felix left in **p**. .... Ac 25:14
who were in **p** with me. .... Rm 16:7
We are beaten and thrown into **p**. 2Co 6:5
I have been in **p** more often. 2Co 11:23
am in **p** because I belong to the .... Eph 4:1
I am doing that now, here in **p**. .... Eph 6:20
while I am in **p** and while I am .... Php 1:7
knows that I am in **p** because I .... Php 1:13
Because I am in **p**, most of the .... Php 1:14
to make trouble for me in **p**. .... Php 1:17
This is why I am in **p**. .... Col 4:3
Remember me in **p**. Grace be with .... Col 4:18
of me, in **p** for the Lord. 2Ti 1:8
was not ashamed that I was in **p**. 2Ti 1:16
my child while I was in **p**. .... Phm 1:10
I am in **p** for the Good News. .... Phm 1:13
put in chains and thrown into **p**. .... Heb 11:36
those who are in **p** as if you .... Heb 13:3
as if you were in **p** with them. .... Heb 13:3
Timothy has been let out of **p**. .... Heb 13:23
and preached to the spirits in **p** 1Pe 3:19
some of you in **p** to test you, ... Rev 2:10
demons and a **p** for every evil .... Rev 18:2
and a **p** for every unclean bird .... Rev 18:2
will be set free from his **p**. .... Rev 20:7

PRISONER

the firstborn of the **p** in jail. .... Ex 12:29
him as a **p** while they waited .... Le 24:12
have come to make Samson our **p**, ... Jdg 15:10
sent messengers to take David **p**, ... 1Sa 19:14
Neco took Jehoahaz **p** at Riblah 2Ki 23:33
Jehoiachin a **p** in the eighth 2Ki 24:12
Jehoiachin was taken as a **p**. 1Ch 3:17
Can a **p** be freed from a powerful .... Is 49:24
Jerusalem, you once were a **p**. .... Is 52:2
Jerusalem, you once were a **p**. .... Is 52:2
You will be taken **p** by the king .... Je 38:23
so you were found and taken **p**. .... Je 50:24
He sees if any **p** of the earth is .... La 3:34
King Jehoiachin had been a **p**. .... Eze 1:2
would free one **p** whom the people .... Mt 27:15
would free one **p** whom the people .... Mk 15:6
him to free a **p** as he always did .... Mk 15:8
to release one **p** to the people. .... Lk 23:17
that I free one **p** to you at .... Jn 18:39
and said, "The **p**, Paul, asked me .... Ac 23:18
to send a **p** to Caesar without .... Ac 25:27
of sin, and it makes me its **p**. .... Rm 7:23
am a **p** of Christ Jesus for you .... Eph 3:1
Aristarchus, a **p** with me, and .... Col 4:10
From Paul, a **p** of Christ Jesus, ... Phm 1:1
and also a **p** for Christ Jesus, ... Phm 1:9
a **p** with me for Christ Jesus, ... Phm 1:23
you are to be a **p**, then you will .... Rev 13:10
prisoner, then you will be a **p**. .... Rev 13:10

PRISONERS

where the king's **p** were put. .... Ge 39:20
to take care of all the **p**, ... Ge 39:22
put the two **p** in Joseph's care .... Ge 40:4
daughters had been taken as **p**. 1Sa 30:3

they are held as **p** in another 1Ki 8:47
land where they are held as **p**, ... 1Ki 8:47
were ten thousand **p** in all. 2Ki 24:14
took them as **p** to Babylon. 2Ki 24:16
of the guards took some **p**— 2Ki 25:18
they are held as **p** in another 2Ch 6:37
land where they are held as **p**, ... 2Ch 6:37
of Judah as **p** to Damascus. 2Ch 28:5
bring the **p** from Judah here 2Ch 28:13
soldiers left the **p** and valuable 2Ch 28:14
named took the **p** and gave those 2Ch 28:15
gave the **p** clothes, sandals, ... 2Ch 28:15
They put the weak **p** on donkeys 2Ch 28:15
He leads **p** out with joy, but .... Ps 68:6
Hear the moans of the **p**. .... Ps 79:11
He heard the moans of the **p**, ... Ps 102:20
they were **p** suffering in chains. .... Ps 107:10
LORD brought the **p** back to .... Ps 126:1
LORD, return our **p** again, as you .... Ps 126:4
The LORD sets the **p** free. .... Ps 146:7
will carry away **p** from Egypt and .... Is 20:4
together like **p** thrown into a .... Is 24:22
will all be carried away like **p**. .... Is 46:2
You will tell the **p**, 'Come out .... Is 49:9
The **p** will be taken from the .... Is 49:25
and to tell the **p** they are .... Is 61:1
He will make **p** of those who are .... Je 43:11
took them as **p** and won't let .... Je 50:33
guards took as **p** Seraiah the .... Je 52:24
p are as many as the grains .... Hab 1:9
you I will set your **p** free from .... Zch 9:11
You **p** who have hope, return to .... Zch 9:12
and taken as **p** to all nations. .... Lk 21:24
to God as the other **p** listened. .... Ac 16:25
and all the **p** were freed from .... Ac 16:26
Thinking that the **p** had already .... Ac 16:27
guarded Paul and some other **p**. .... Ac 27:1
to kill the **p** so none of them .... Ac 27:42
the soldiers to kill the **p**. .... Ac 27:43
law held us like **p**, but our old .... Rm 7:6
we were all held **p** by the law. .... Gal 3:23
You helped the **p**. You even had .... Heb 10:34

PRIVATE

to talk with David in **p** and say, ... 1Sa 18:22
wanted to talk with Abner in **p**, ... 2Sa 3:27
asked him in **p**, "Is there any .... Je 37:17
to Gedaliah in **p** at Mizpah. .... Je 40:15
facing the **p** area at the west .... Eze 41:12
The **p** area, including the .... Eze 41:13
Temple and the **p** area on its .... Eze 41:14
facing the **p** area on the west .... Eze 41:15
across from the **p** area and the .... Eze 42:1
were across from the **p** area and .... Eze 42:10
across from the **p** area are holy .... Eze 42:13
and tell him in **p** what he did .... Mt 18:15
as though their **p** property .... Ac 4:32
in **p** I told their leaders the .... Gal 2:2

PRIVATELY

aside **p** and said to them, ... Mt 20:17
followers began asking him **p**, ... Mk 9:28
to his followers and said **p**, ... Lk 10:23

PRIVILEGES

the special **p** of the oldest son, ... 1Ch 5:1
So those special **p** were given to 1Ch 5:1
received the **p** that belonged to 1Ch 5:2
had special **p** to see the king .... Est 1:14

PRIZE

saying, "They are David's **p**." 1Sa 30:20
as if it were a **p** won in war. .... Je 21:9
run, but only one gets the **p**. 1Co 9:24
goal and get the **p** for which God .... Php 3:14

PRIZES

large herds of cattle as war p. .... Je 49:32

PROBABLY

He is p already hiding in a cave 2Sa 17:9
The kingdom will p go back to 1Ki 12:26

PROBLEM

who had a p for the king to 2Sa 15:2
' and the p would be solved. 2Sa 20:18
and this p can't be solved in a .... Ezr 10:13
be enough of a p to bother the .... Est 7:4
God and bring my p before him. .... Job 5:8
because the p lies with him,' .... Job 19:28
That's your p, not ours." .... Mt 27:4
gathered to consider this p. .... Ac 15:6
must solve this p yourselves. .... Ac 18:15
we do will be a p for anyone. 2Co 6:3
physical p was given to me 2Co 12:7
This p was a messenger from 2Co 12:7
to take this p away from me. 2Co 12:8
talked about this p because some .... Gal 2:4
the cross would not be a p. .... Gal 5:11

PROBLEMS

about all the p they had faced .... Ex 18:8
I cannot take care of your p, ... Dt 1:12
telling the Lord about all my p. 1Sa 1:15
from all your troubles and p, ... 1Sa 10:19
people with p could come to me 2Sa 15:4
Lord and settle p between the 2Ch 19:8
been a place of p and trouble. .... Ezr 4:19
grown larger; free me from my p. .... Ps 25:17
what is right may have many p, ... Ps 34:19
him all your p, because God is .... Ps 62:8
they don't have p like other .... Ps 73:5
I pour out my p to him; .... Ps 142:2
themselves don't have such p. .... Pr 22:5
causes serious p for people. .... Ec 6:1
Remaining calm solves great p. .... Ec 10:4
I will put p in front of Judah. .... Je 6:21
to her, we have had great p. .... Je 44:18
and could answer very hard p. .... Da 5:12
can find the answers to hard p. .... Da 5:16
laugh at their p in their time .... Ob 1:13
Can troubles or p or sufferings .... Rm 8:35
in difficulties, and in great p. 2Co 6:4

PROCLAIMED

was p to the nations, believed 1Ti 3:16

PROCORUS

Philip, P, Nicanor, Timon. .... Ac 6:5

PRODUCE

Let the earth p plants—some to .... Ge 1:11
Every seed will p more of its .... Ge 1:11
let each p more of its kind." .... Ge 1:24
animals to p more of their own .... Ge 1:25
The ground will p thorns and .... Ge 3:18
tree will then p more fruit for .... Le 19:25
the land will p enough crops for .... Le 25:21
the land will p crops, and the .... Le 26:4
of the field will p their fruit. .... Le 26:4
your fields will p good crops, ... Dt 30:9
and may their fields p no grain, ... 2Sa 1:21
People p trouble as surely as .... Job 5:7
without God can p nothing. .... Job 15:34
old, they will still p fruit; .... Ps 92:14
branches that p many olives. .... Ps 128:3
field might p plenty of food, ... Pr 13:23
will be glad and will p flowers. .... Is 35:1
you could eat its fruit and p. .... Je 2:7
They grow and p fruit. .... Je 12:2
earth will p grain, new wine, ... Hos 2:22
that does not p good fruit will .... Mt 3:10
A good tree cannot p bad fruit, ... Mt 7:18

a bad tree cannot p good fruit. .... Mt 7:18
that does not p good fruit is .... Mt 7:19
teaching does not p fruit in .... Mt 13:22
those plants did not p a crop. .... Mk 4:7
Then they grow and p fruit— .... Mk 4:20
that does not p good fruit will .... Lk 3:9
good tree does not p bad fruit, ... Lk 6:43
does a bad tree p good fruit. .... Lk 6:43
it and patiently p good fruit. .... Lk 8:15
have one more year to p fruit. .... Lk 13:8
of mine that does not p fruit. .... Jn 15:2
that it will p even more fruit. .... Jn 15:2
branch cannot p fruit alone but .... Jn 15:4
cannot p fruit alone but must .... Jn 15:4
in them, they p much fruit. .... Jn 15:5
You should p much fruit and show .... Jn 15:8
to go and p fruit, fruit that .... Jn 15:16
that these troubles p patience. .... Rm 5:3
You will p fruit in every good .... Col 1:10

PRODUCED

earth p plants with grain for .... Ge 1:12
and each bird p more of its own .... Ge 1:21
food that is p during the good .... Ge 41:35
all the food p in Egypt during .... Ge 41:48
blossomed, and p almonds. .... Nu 17:8
your land and hard work have p. .... Dt 28:33
land and everything the earth p. .... Ps 105:35
Even if it p something, other .... Hos 8:7
vine that p plenty of fruit .... Hos 10:1
where it grew and p a crop. .... Mt 13:8
It got taller and p a crop. .... Mk 4:8
the good things p in your life .... Php 1:11
and the land p crops again. .... Jam 5:18

PRODUCES

a grapevine that p much fruit, ... Ge 49:22
the land p during that year .... Le 25:6
the land p may be eaten. .... Le 25:7
The tree p fruit in season, ... Ps 1:3
like a vine that p much fruit. .... Ps 128:3
As a tree p fruit, wisdom gives .... Pr 3:18
rain comes; it always p fruit. .... Je 17:8
no head of grain, it p nothing. .... Hos 8:7
the plants which the earth p, ... Hag 1:11
every good tree p good fruit, ... Mt 7:17
but a bad tree p bad fruit. .... Mt 7:17
known by the kind of fruit it p. .... Mt 12:33
That person grows and p fruit, ... Mt 13:23
By itself the earth p grain. .... Mk 4:28
p large branches, and the wild .... Mk 4:32
If the tree p fruit next year, ... Lk 13:9
branch that p fruit so that it .... Jn 15:2
And patience p character, and .... Rm 5:4
character, and character p hope. .... Rm 5:4
But the Spirit p the fruit of .... Gal 5:22
The Land p a good crop for those .... Heb 6:7
It p fruit twelve times a year, ... Rev 22:2

PRODUCING

with each one p more of its own .... Ge 1:21
each p more of its own kind. .... Ge 1:24
growing and p fruit in their .... Mk 4:19
from growing and p good fruit. .... Lk 8:14

PRODUCTIVE

to be useful and p in your 2Pe 1:8

PROFIT

try to make a p from the food he .... Le 25:37
and made no p on the sale. .... Ps 44:12
it brings more p than gold. .... Pr 3:14
Those who work hard make a p, ... Pr 14:23
of hard-working people earn a p, ... Pr 21:5
to get too much interest or p. .... Eze 18:8
for too much interest and p. .... Eze 18:13

P

much interest or **p** when he lends .... Eze 18:17
have killed people for **p.** .... Eze 22:27
of God for a **p** as many other 2Co 2:17
and dying would be **p** for me. .... Php 1:21

PROFITS

are looking for **p** and do not .... Ps 73:7
sure he gets his share of the **p.** .... Ec 5:9
p will be saved for the LORD. .... Is 23:18
interest and **p** and make profits .... Eze 22:12
and make **p** by mistreating .... Eze 22:12
hearts desire their selfish **p.** .... Eze 33:31

PROGRESS

doing them so your **p** may be seen 1Ti 4:15

PROJECTS

who did the work on Solomon's **p.** 1Ki 9:23

PROMISE

Sodom, "I make a **p** to the LORD, ... Ge 14:22
p that I will not keep anything .... Ge 14:23
make a **p** to me here before God .... Ge 21:23
And Abraham said, "I **p.**" .... Ge 21:24
they made a **p** to each other .... Ge 21:31
make you this **p** by my own name: .... Ge 22:16
Make a **p** me before the LORD, ... Ge 24:3
you will be free from this **p.** .... Ge 24:8
and made a **p** to Abraham about .... Ge 24:9
me make a **p** to him and said, ' .... Ge 24:37
you will be free from the **p.** .... Ge 24:41
you will be free from this **p.'** .... Ge 24:41
p me that you will give it to me. .... Ge 25:33
So Esau made a **p** to Jacob and .... Ge 25:33
Then Jacob made a **p.** .... Ge 28:20
and where you made a **p** to me. .... Ge 31:13
So Jacob made a **p** in the name .... Ge 31:53
P me you will not bury me in .... Ge 47:29
Then Jacob said, "**P** me." .... Ge 47:31
I made a **p** to him that I would .... Ge 50:5
The king answered, "Keep your **p.** .... Ge 50:6
had the sons of Israel make a **p.** .... Ge 50:25
P me that you will carry my .... Ge 50:25
the Israelites **p** to do this. .... Ex 13:19
keep your loving **p** and lead the .... Ex 15:13
must make a **p** before God that .... Ex 22:8
neighbor must **p** before the LORD .... Ex 22:11
accept his **p** made before God .... Ex 22:11
his coat as a **p** for the money he .... Ex 22:26
might make a **p** before the LORD .... Le 5:4
It might be a **p** to do something .... Le 5:4
he might lie about a **p** he made. .... Le 6:2
might make a **p** before the LORD .... Le 6:3
or what he made a false **p** about. .... Le 6:5
because of a special **p** to him, ... Le 7:16
not make a false **p** by my name, ... Le 19:12
for some special **p** he has made .... Le 22:18
for a special **p** the person has .... Le 22:21
for a special **p** you have made. .... Le 22:23
makes a special **p** to give a .... Le 27:2
or women want to **p** to belong to .... Nu 6:2
keep their **p** to belong to God .... Nu 6:7
which was part of their **p,** .... Nu 6:9
they will again **p** to let their .... Nu 6:11
hair that they grew for their **p.** .... Nu 6:18
for the Nazirites who make a **p.** .... Nu 6:21
the Nazirite **p** must give all .... Nu 6:21
must keep their **p,** according to .... Nu 6:21
the whole earth, I make this **p:** .... Nu 14:21
for a special **p** or a fellowship .... Nu 15:8
made this **p** to the LORD: .... Nu 21:2
If a man makes a **p** to the LORD .... Nu 30:2
special, he must keep his **p.** .... Nu 30:2
at home makes a **p** to the LORD or .... Nu 30:3
hears about the **p** or pledge and .... Nu 30:4

hears about the **p** or pledge and .... Nu 30:5
then the **p** or pledge does not .... Nu 30:5
LORD will free her from her **p.** .... Nu 30:5
or a careless **p** and then gets .... Nu 30:6
must keep her **p** or the pledge .... Nu 30:7
or the careless **p** she made. .... Nu 30:8
or divorced woman makes a **p,** .... Nu 30:9
woman makes a **p** or pledge while .... Nu 30:10
she must keep her **p** or pledge. .... Nu 30:11
or cancel any **p** or pledge she .... Nu 30:13
if she breaks her **p.**" .... Nu 30:15
angry that day and made this **p:** .... Nu 32:10
and he kept his **p** to your .... Dt 7:8
to keep his **p** to your ancestors, ... Dt 9:5
you make a **p** to give something .... Dt 23:21
But if you do not make the **p,** .... Dt 23:22
to make the **p** to the LORD your .... Dt 23:23
agreement and a **p** with the LORD .... Dt 29:12
toward heaven and make this **p:** .... Dt 32:40
p me before the LORD that you .... Jos 2:12
of the **p** you made to her." .... Jos 6:22
they had made a **p** to them before .... Jos 9:18
have given our **p** before the LORD .... Jos 9:19
leaders kept their **p** to them. .... Jos 9:21
then, the LORD has kept his **p.** .... Jos 14:10
He kept every **p** he had made to .... Jos 21:45
peace, and he has kept his **p.** .... Jos 22:4
Every good **p** that the LORD your .... Jos 23:15
We **p** to do all that you tell us .... Jdg 11:10
Jephthah made a **p** to the LORD, ... Jdg 11:30
because I made a **p** to the LORD, ... Jdg 11:35
you made a **p** to the LORD. .... Jdg 11:36
P me you will not hurt me .... Jdg 15:12
if I do not keep this **p:** .... Ru 1:17
She made a **p,** saying, "LORD 1Sa 1:11
keep the **p** he had made to God. 1Sa 1:21
will again **p** to obey the king." 1Sa 11:14
Jonathan and then made this **p:** 1Sa 19:6
I **p** this before the LORD, ... 1Sa 20:12
to repeat his **p** of love for him, ... 1Sa 20:17
So David made the **p** to Saul. 1Sa 24:22
Saul made a **p** to the woman in 1Sa 28:10
if you **p** me before God that you 1Sa 30:15
he made a **p,** saying, "May God 2Sa 3:35
keep the **p** forever that you made 2Sa 7:25
Please **p** in the name of the LORD 2Sa 14:11
to carry out my **p** that I made to 2Sa 15:7
because of the **p** he had made to 2Sa 21:7
David's men made a **p** to him, ... 2Sa 21:17
you made a **p** to me in the name 1Ki 1:17
Then the king made this **p,** 1Ki 1:29
King Solomon to **p** me today that 1Ki 1:51
I **p** he will not lose even a 1Ki 1:52
will keep the **p** he made to me. 1Ki 2:4
and who has kept his **p** and given 1Ki 2:24
I made you **p** in the name of the 1Ki 2:42
did you break your **p** to the LORD 1Ki 2:43
Now the LORD has kept his **p.** 1Ki 8:20
have kept the **p** you made to your 1Ki 8:24
keep the **p** you made to your 1Ki 8:25
to keep that **p** you made to your 1Ki 8:26
This is the **p** I made to your 1Ki 9:5
to keep the **p** he had made to 1Ki 12:15
he made them **p** loyalty, and then 2Ki 11:4
Abraham and the **p** he made to 1Ch 16:16
keep the **p** forever that you made 1Ch 17:23
may your **p** to my father David 2Ch 1:9
Now the LORD has kept his **p.** 2Ch 6:10
have kept the **p** you made to your 2Ch 6:15
keep the **p** you made to your 2Ch 6:16
to keep that **p** you made to your 2Ch 6:17
could keep the **p** he had made to 2Ch 10:15
people made a **p** before the LORD 2Ch 15:14

of Judah were happy about the **p,** 2Ch 15:15
and Benjamin **p** to accept 2Ch 34:32
people of Israel **p** to do what .... Ezr 10:5
who does not keep his **p.**........................ Ne 5:13
have kept your **p,** because you do .... Ne 9:8
We **p** not to let our daughters .... Ne 10:30
forced them to make a **p** to God, ... Ne 13:25
God, make me a **p.** No one will .... Job 17:3
I made a **p** to my servant David............... Ps 89:3
I was angry and made a **p,** ' .... Ps 95:11
Abraham and the **p** he made to .... Ps 105:9
his holy **p** to his servant .... Ps 105:42
LORD has made a **p** and will not .... Ps 110:4
Keep your **p** to me, your servant, ... Ps 119:38
Remember your **p** to me, your .... Ps 119:49
Your **p** gives me life. .... Ps 119:50
tired from looking for your **p.**................... Ps 119:82
P that you will help me, your .... Ps 119:122
salvation and for your good **p.** .... Ps 119:123
a **p** to the Mighty God of Jacob. .... Ps 132:2
The LORD made a **p** to David, ... Ps 132:11
a sure **p** that he will not take .... Ps 132:11
ignores the **p** she made before .... Pr 2:17
and beg to be free from your **p.** .... Pr 6:3
is not wise to **p** to pay what .... Pr 17:18
dangerous to **p** something to God .... Pr 20:25
Don't **p** to pay what someone else .... Pr 22:26
If you make a **p** to God, don't be .... Ec 5:4
better not to **p** anything than to .... Ec 5:5
anything than to **p** something and .... Ec 5:5
because you made a **p** to God. .... Ec 8:2
p me by the gazelles and the .... Sng 2:7
p me by the gazelles and the .... Sng 3:5
P me, women of Jerusalem, if you .... Sng 5:8
Why do you want us to **p** this? .... Sng 5:9
p not to awaken or excite my .... Sng 8:4
All-Powerful has made this **p:**................. Is 14:24
and they will **p** to be loyal to .... Is 19:18
I will make a **p** by my own power, ... Is 45:23
my own power, and my **p** is true; .... Is 45:23
p that everyone will bow before .... Is 45:23
me and will **p** to follow me. .... Is 45:23
I **p** I will not be angry with you .... Is 54:9
p of peace will not come to an .... Is 54:10
be a reminder of the LORD's **p,** .... Is 55:13
LORD has made a **p,** and by his .... Is 62:8
by his power he will keep his **p.** .... Is 62:8
land who make a **p** will promise............... Is 65:16
a promise will **p** in the name .... Is 65:16
If you say when you make a **p,** ' .... Je 4:2
I will keep the **p** I made to your .... Je 11:5
I will keep my **p** to bring you .... Je 29:10
things that I **p** to do for them. .... Je 32:42
listen to the **p** of the LORD. .... Je 34:4
I myself make this **p** to you, ... Je 34:5
made a secret **p** to Jeremiah, ... Je 38:16
And I **p** not to hand you over to .... Je 38:16
made a **p** to them, saying .... Je 40:9
I also made a **p** to you and .... Eze 16:8
of Judah hated his **p** to the king .... Eze 17:16
that he hated the **p** by breaking .... Eze 17:18
for hating my **p** and breaking my .... Eze 17:19
was given as a **p** for a loan. .... Eze 18:7
I made a **p** to the descendants of .... Eze 20:5
with a **p** to bring them out .... Eze 20:9
them as a **p** to repay a loan, ... Eze 33:15
I **p** that the nations around you .... Eze 36:7
to fall, so I make this **p:** .... Eze 44:12
The Lord GOD made this **p;** .... Am 6:8
we **p** . . . ' So they will fall and .... Am 8:14
'I made a **p** to you when you came .... Hag 2:5
You broke your **p** to her, even.................. Mal 2:14
not break your **p** to the wife you .... Mal 2:15

he had made a **p,** and his dinner .... Mt 14:9
P that one of my sons will sit .... Mt 20:21
the Temple when they make a **p,** .... Mt 23:16
Temple, they must keep that **p.'** .... Mt 23:16
by the altar when they make a **p,** .... Mt 23:18
altar, they must keep that **p.'** .... Mt 23:18
he had made a **p,** and his dinner .... Mk 6:26
he would remember his holy **p.** .... Lk 1:72
to receive the **p** from the Father .... Ac 1:4
This **p** is for you, for your .... Ac 2:39
The **p** God made to Abraham was .... Ac 7:17
News about the **p** God made to our .... Ac 13:32
has made this **p** come true for us .... Ac 13:33
because he had made a **p** to God. .... Ac 18:18
of our men have made a **p** to God. .... Ac 21:23
hope for the **p** that God made to............. Ac 26:6
This is the **p** that the twelve .... Ac 26:7
because I hope for this same **p!** .... Ac 26:7
received the **p** that they would .... Rm 4:13
receive that **p** through the law .... Rm 4:13
God's **p** to Abraham is worthless,............. Rm 4:14
receive God's **p** by having faith. .... Rm 4:16
happens so the **p** can be a free .... Rm 4:16
children can have that **p.** .... Rm 4:16
that God would keep his **p,**.................... Rm 4:20
as the first part of God's **p.** .... Rm 8:23
failed to keep his **p** to them. .... Rm 9:6
of the **p** God made to Abraham. .... Rm 9:8
God's **p** to Abraham was this:................. Rm 9:9
so destroy God's **p** to Abraham. .... Gal 3:17
then the **p** would not be .... Gal 3:18
through the **p** he had made. .... Gal 3:18
This was so the **p** would be given .... Gal 3:22
because of the **p** God made to .... Gal 3:29
because of the **p** God made to .... Gal 4:23
God's children because of his **p,**............. Gal 4:28
with the **p** that God made to .... Eph 2:12
together in the **p** that God made............. Eph 3:6
command that has a **p** with it— .... Eph 6:2
tell about the **p** of life that is 2Ti 1:1
I was angry and made a **p,** ' .... Heb 3:11
has left us the **p** that we may .... Heb 4:1
I was angry and made a **p,** .... Heb 4:3
God made a **p** to Abraham..................... Heb 6:13
prove that his **p** was true to .... Heb 6:17
cannot lie when he makes a **p,** .... Heb 6:18
Lord has made a **p** and will not .... Heb 7:21
received that same **p** from God. .... Heb 11:9
use an oath when you make a **p.** .... Jam 5:12
the **p** made to God from a good 1Pe 3:21
They **p** them freedom, but they 2Pe 2:19
But God made a **p** to us, and we............. 2Pe 3:13
and he made a **p** by the power of .... Rev 10:6

PROMISED

let Ishmael be the son you **p.**"................. Ge 17:18
will give Abraham what I **p** him." .... Ge 21:1
and did for her what he had **p.** .... Ge 21:1
The descendants I **p** you will be .... Ge 21:12
And I **p** me, "I will give this .... Ge 24:7
I have done what I have **p** you." .... Ge 28:15
I **p** to work for you is over. .... Ge 29:21
I sent her the goat as I **p,** .... Ge 38:23
her to my son Shelah as I **p.**" .... Ge 38:26
I remember something I **p** to do, ... Ge 41:9
And Joseph **p** him that he would .... Ge 47:31
to the land he **p** to Abraham, ... Ge 50:24
I **p** I would take you out of your .... Ex 3:17
to the land that I **p** to Abraham, ... Ex 6:8
next day the LORD did as he **p.** .... Ex 9:6
land the LORD has **p** to give you. .... Ex 12:25
is the land he **p** your ancestors .... Ex 13:5
the land he **p** to give you and .... Ex 13:11

You **p** with an oath to them and .... Ex 32:13
this land that I have **p** them, ... Ex 32:13
the land that I **p** with an oath .... Ex 33:1
the time they have **p** to belong .... Nu 6:5
When the **p** time is over, they .... Nu 6:13
If they **p** to do more, they must .... Nu 6:21
the land the LORD **p** to give us. .... Nu 10:29
the LORD has **p** good things to .... Nu 10:29
to the land you **p** to our .... Nu 11:12
them into the land he **p** them................... Nu 14:16
see the land I **p** to their .... Nu 14:23
land where I **p** you would live; .... Nu 14:30
in addition to other **p** offerings .... Nu 29:39
nothing, she must do what she **p**. .... Nu 30:4
she must do whatever she **p**. .... Nu 30:9
the land that I **p** to Abraham, ... Nu 32:11
then you must do what you **p**." .... Nu 32:24
The LORD **p** it to your ancestors—........... Dt 1:8
all the wonderful things he **p**.................. Dt 1:11
I **p** a good land to your .... Dt 1:35
as the LORD had **p** would happen............. Dt 2:14
of your ancestors, has **p** you. .... Dt 6:3
into the land he **p** to your .... Dt 6:10
land the LORD **p** to your........................ Dt 6:18
us the land he **p** our ancestors. .... Dt 6:23
to you, as he **p** your ancestors. .... Dt 7:12
in the land he **p** your ancestors .... Dt 7:13
land the LORD **p** your ancestors. .... Dt 8:1
the agreement he **p** to your.................... Dt 8:18
people into the land he **p** them, ... Dt 9:28
the land I **p** their ancestors. .... Dt 10:11
that the LORD **p** to give to your .... Dt 11:9
land the LORD **p** your ancestors, ... Dt 11:21
will do what he **p** and will make.............. Dt 11:25
what you have **p** and the special............. Dt 12:6
best things you **p** to the LORD. .... Dt 12:11
whatever you have **p** to give; .... Dt 12:17
your country as he has **p**, ... Dt 12:20
the things you have **p** to give, ... Dt 12:26
larger, as he **p** to your .... Dt 13:17
your God will bless you as he **p**,.............. Dt 15:6
LORD himself, as he has **p** them. .... Dt 18:2
pay what you have **p** to the LORD,............ Dt 23:18
go in and get what they **p** you. .... Dt 24:11
land the LORD **p** our ancestors .... Dt 26:3
which you **p** to our ancestors— .... Dt 26:15
and you have **p** to do what he................. Dt 26:17
own people, as he has **p** you. .... Dt 26:18
the God of your ancestors, **p**. .... Dt 27:3
you his holy people, as he **p**. .... Dt 28:9
that the LORD **p** your ancestors .... Dt 28:11
you and as he **p** your ancestors .... Dt 29:13
the land he **p** to give your .... Dt 30:20
land the LORD **p** to give their................. Dt 31:7
into the land I **p** to their .... Dt 31:20
them into the land I **p** them." .... Dt 31:21
of Israel to the land I **p** them, ... Dt 31:23
This is the land I **p** to Abraham, ... Dt 34:4
I **p** Moses I would give you this .... Jos 1:3
the land that I **p** their fathers .... Jos 1:6
land he had **p** their ancestors .... Jos 5:6
because he had **p** it to them. .... Jos 11:23
God of Israel, as he had **p** them. .... Jos 13:14
p that he himself would be the .... Jos 13:33
that day Moses **p** me, 'The land .... Jos 14:9
the LORD **p** me that day long.................. Jos 14:12
got the land God had **p** them. .... Jos 15:20
received the land **p** to them, ... Jos 18:7
land he had **p** their ancestors .... Jos 21:43
as he had **p** their ancestors. .... Jos 21:44
The LORD your God **p** to give the .... Jos 22:4
west, the land I **p** to give you................. Jos 23:4
own the land, as he has **p** you. .... Jos 23:5

fights for you, as he **p** to do. .... Jos 23:10
He **p** that evil will come to you .... Jos 23:15
As Moses had **p**, Hebron was given .... Jdg 1:20
you to the land I **p** to give your .... Jdg 2:1
So do to me just what you **p**, ... Jdg 11:36
did to her what he had **p**. .... Jdg 11:39
'I **p** that your family and your.................. 1Sa 2:30
and his family everything I **p**,.................. 1Sa 3:12
We have **p** by the LORD that we............... 1Sa 20:42
what the LORD **p** does happen! 2Sa 3:9
She was **p** to me, and I killed a 2Sa 3:14
And you have **p** these good things 2Sa 7:28
Joab, "Look, I will do what I **p**. 2Sa 14:21
Then the king **p** Shimei, "You................. 2Sa 19:23
The Israelites had **p** not to hurt 2Sa 21:2
you **p** that my son Solomon would 1Ki 1:13
what I have **p** you in the name 1Ki 1:30
I **p** that your son Solomon would 1Ki 1:30
Jordan River, I **p** him before the 1Ki 2:8
The LORD **p** my father David, ... 1Ki 5:5
gave Solomon wisdom as he had **p**. 1Ki 5:12
for you what I **p** your father 1Ki 6:12
has done what he **p** to my father 1Ki 8:15
Now I rule Israel as the LORD **p**, ... 1Ki 8:20
This is what you **p** through Moses 1Ki 8:53
He **p** he would give rest to his 1Ki 8:56
the LORD, through Elijah, had **p**. 1Ki 17:16
The LORD had **p** that one of 2Ki 8:19
Then all the people **p** to obey 2Ki 23:3
Then Gedaliah **p** these army 2Ki 25:24
The LORD had **p** through Samuel 1Ch 11:3
king, just as the LORD had **p**.................. 1Ch 11:10
and you have **p** these good things 1Ch 17:26
God **p** to make Heman strong, ... 1Ch 25:5
The LORD had **p** to make the 1Ch 27:23
as king and **p** to obey him. 1Ch 29:24
barley, oil, and wine you **p**...................... 2Ch 2:15
has done what he **p** to my father 2Ch 6:4
Now I rule Israel as the LORD **p**, ... 2Ch 6:10
because they had **p** with all 2Ch 15:15
He had **p** that one of David's 2Ch 21:7
as the LORD **p** about David's 2Ch 23:3
what was suggested; and they **p**. .... Ezr 10:5
They all **p** to divorce their .... Ezr 10:19
the people did what they had **p**. .... Ne 5:13
people had **p** to be faithful to .... Ne 6:18
the land you had **p** to give them. .... Ne 9:15
They **p** to follow the Teachings .... Ne 10:29
of money Haman had **p** to pay into .... Est 4:7
What has God above **p** for people?........... Job 31:2
will see me do what I **p**. .... Ps 22:25
God Most High what you have **p**. .... Ps 50:14
I will give you what I **p**,......................... Ps 66:13
I **p** when I was in trouble. .... Ps 66:14
I have **p** by my holiness, I will .... Ps 89:35
in your loyalty you **p** to David? .... Ps 89:49
they did not believe what God **p**. .... Ps 106:24
LORD what I **p** in front of all .... Ps 116:14
LORD what I **p** in front of all .... Ps 116:18
Give me life, as you have **p**. .... Ps 119:25
me strong again as you have **p**. .... Ps 119:28
and save me as you have **p**. .... Ps 119:41
I have **p** to obey your words. .... Ps 119:57
Have mercy on me as you have **p**. .... Ps 119:58
servant, as you have **p**, LORD. .... Ps 119:65
love, as you **p** me, your servant .... Ps 119:76
do what I have **p** and obey your .... Ps 119:106
me as you **p** so I can live. .... Ps 119:116
Guide my steps as you **p**; .... Ps 119:133
to my prayer, save me as you **p**. .... Ps 119:170
He **p**, "I will make one of your .... Ps 132:11
fools, so give God what you **p**. .... Ec 5:4
"I didn't mean what I **p**." .... Ec 5:6

PROMISES

p then that I would never flood .... Is 54:9
you the blessings I p to David. .... Is 55:3
on Judah the disaster he had p. .... Je 26:19
land that you p to their .... Je 32:22
the good thing I p to the people .... Je 33:14
everything I p but which they .... Je 36:31
We p to make sacrifices to the .... Je 44:17
certainly do everything we p. .... Je 44:17
We p to make sacrifices to the .... Je 44:25
the things you p, and keep your .... Je 44:25
has p in his own name .... Je 51:14
the agreement you p to keep. .... Eze 16:59
He p to support Babylon, but he .... Eze 17:18
to return what was p for a loan. .... Eze 18:12
keep something p for a loan or .... Eze 18:16
Egypt, and I p them, "I am the .... Eze 20:5
At that time I p them I would .... Eze 20:6
into the land I p to give them, ... Eze 20:28
the land I p your ancestors, ... Eze 20:42
p to give it to your ancestors, ... Eze 47:14
make you my p bride forever. .... Hos 2:19
be true to you as my p bride, ... Hos 2:20
The Lord GOD has p this: .... Am 4:2
Abraham as you p to our .... Mic 7:20
and give your p sacrifices to .... Nah 1:15
I p them life and peace so they .... Mal 2:5
So he p with an oath to give her .... Mt 14:7
He p her, "Anything you ask for .... Mk 6:23
about this and p to pay Judas .... Mk 14:11
as he p to our ancestors, to .... Lk 1:55
He p he would save us from our .... Lk 1:71
God p Abraham, our father, ... Lk 1:73
he saw the Christ p by the Lord .... Lk 2:26
send you what my Father has p, ... Lk 24:49
and knew God had p him that he .... Ac 2:30
Holy Spirit to Jesus as he p. .... Ac 2:33
God p that he would give this .... Ac 7:5
to be its Savior, as he p. .... Ac 13:23
blessings that I p to David.' .... Ac 13:34
And God has p you that he will .... Ac 27:24
God p this Good News long ago .... Rm 1:2
stop God from doing what he p? .... Rm 3:3
receive what God p by following .... Rm 4:14
was able to do what he had p. .... Rm 4:21
The descendants p for all he has p, ... Rm 9:7
be a guarantee for all he has p. 2Co 1:22
generous gift you p so it will 2Co 9:5
I p to give you to Christ, ... 2Co 11:2
blessing p to Abraham might .... Gal 3:14
receive the Spirit that God p. .... Gal 3:14
with Abraham and p to keep it. .... Gal 3:17
who had been p, came. .... Gal 3:19
will give you the blessing he p, ... Gal 4:7
the Holy Spirit that he had p. .... Eph 1:13
receive what God p for his .... Eph 1:14
God has p his holy people. .... Eph 1:18
Lord, which he p to his people. .... Col 3:24
doing what they first p to do. 1Ti 5:12
which God p to us before time .... Tit 1:2
talking when he p that they .... Heb 3:18
will receive what God has p. .... Heb 6:12
and he received what God p. .... Heb 6:15
those who would get what he p, ... Heb 6:17
receive the blessings he has p, ... Heb 9:15
can trust God to do what he p. .... Heb 10:23
wants and receive what he has p. .... Heb 10:36
another place God p to give him. .... Heb 11:8
the country God p to give him. .... Heb 11:9
trusted God to do what he had p. .... Heb 11:11
things that God p his people, ... Heb 11:13
The descendants I p you will be .... Heb 11:18
of them received what God had p. .... Heb 11:39
but now he has p, "Once again I .... Heb 12:26

p this to all those who love him. .... Jam 1:12
the kingdom God p to those who .... Jam 2:5
say, "Jesus p to come again. 2Pe 3:4
is not slow in doing what he p— 2Pe 3:9
this is what the Son p to us— 1Jn 2:25
The angel p, "There will be no .... Rev 10:6

PROMISES

bought her p to let the woman .... Ex 21:9
give as payment for special p, ... Le 23:38
If someone p to bring one of .... Le 27:9
or sacrifices for special p, ... Nu 15:3
What he p, he makes come true. .... Nu 23:19
days, she must keep her p. .... Nu 30:14
nothing, she must keep her p. .... Nu 30:14
and make your p only in his name .... Dt 6:13
him and make your p in his name. .... Dt 10:20
agreement and its p with you .... Dt 29:14
not failed to keep any of his p. .... Jos 23:14
his other p will come true. .... Jos 23:15
keep all his p of good things 1Sa 25:30
have also made p about my future 2Sa 7:19
all the good p he gave through 1Ki 8:56
each person p or brings freely 2Ki 12:4
he will keep his p always. 1Ch 16:15
have also made p about my future 1Ch 17:17
and you will keep your p to him. .... Job 22:27
They keep their p to their .... Ps 15:4
who have not made p in the name .... Ps 24:4
his friends and breaks his p. .... Ps 55:20
God, I must keep my p to you. .... Ps 56:12
God, you have heard my p. .... Ps 61:5
and every day I will keep my p. .... Ps 61:8
All who make p in his name will .... Ps 63:11
We will keep our p to you. .... Ps 65:1
and keep your p to the LORD your .... Ps 76:11
he will keep his p always. .... Ps 105:8
Your p are sweet to me, sweeter .... Ps 119:103
Your p are proven, so I, your .... Ps 119:140
so I can think about your p. .... Ps 119:148
Let me live by your p. .... Ps 119:154
happy over your p as if I had .... Ps 119:162
sing about your p, because all .... Ps 119:172
The LORD will keep all his p; .... Ps 145:13
Today I have kept my special p. .... Pr 7:14
It is safer to avoid such p. .... Pr 11:15
with those who keep their p. .... Pr 12:22
of someone who p to pay a .... Pr 20:16
of someone who p to pay a .... Pr 27:13
Many useless p are like so many .... Ec 5:7
person who makes p to God and to .... Ec 9:2
They will make p to the LORD and .... Is 19:21
me and have made p to idols that .... Je 5:7
not kept the p they made before .... Je 34:18
certainly keep the p we made. .... Je 44:25
you promised, and keep your p. .... Je 44:25
again use my name to make p. .... Je 44:26
know that my p to hurt you will .... Je 44:29
the curses and p of punishment .... Da 9:11
time for God's p to come true. .... Da 11:14
Don't make p, saying, 'As surely .... Hos 4:15
make many false p and agreements .... Hos 10:4
will keep the p we made to you. .... Hos 14:2
They make p by the idol in .... Am 8:14
to the LORD and made p to him. .... Jnh 1:16
and I will keep my p to you. .... Jnh 2:9
want one who p to prophesy good .... Mic 2:11
and make p by both the LORD .... Zph 1:5
false p will be taken away. .... Zch 5:3
who use my name to make false p, ... Zch 5:4
and don't love false p. .... Zch 8:17
in his flock and p to offer it, ... Mal 1:14
break their p to each other .... Mal 2:10

of Judah have broken their **p**. .... Mal 2:11
Don't break your **p**, but keep the .... Mt 5:33
keep the **p** you make to the Lord. .... Mt 5:33
not keep their **p**, and they show .... Rm 1:31
right way of worship and his **p**. .... Rm 9:4
because of the **p** he made to .... Rm 11:28
show that God's **p** to the Jewish .... Rm 15:8
to all of God's **p** is in Christ, ... 2Co 1:20
we have these **p** from God, so we 2Co 7:1
God made **p** both to Abraham and .... Gal 3:16
that the law is against God's **p**? .... Gal 3:21
the man who had God's **p**. .... Heb 7:6
is based on **p** of better things................. Heb 8:6
God made the **p** to Abraham, ... Heb 11:17
received God's **p**, and shut the .... Heb 11:33
the very great and precious **p**. 2Pe 1:4

PROMISING
about **p** to pay what someone else .... Pr 6:1

PROMOTE
he wanted to **p**, he promoted. .... Da 5:19

PROMOTED
Then the king **p** Shadrach, ... Da 3:30
he wanted to promote, he **p**. .... Da 5:19

PRONGS
a fork that had three **p**. 1Sa 2:13

PROOF
This will be the **p** that I am.................... Ex 3:12
must bring the body as **p**, ... Ex 22:13
parents must bring **p** that she................. Dt 22:15
but here is the **p** that my .... Dt 22:17
and there is no **p** that she was a .... Dt 22:20
me some **p** that you will do this............... Jos 2:12
Here is the **p** that the living God is .... Jos 3:10
This altar is **p** to you and us .... Jos 22:27
the altar **P** That We Believe.................... Jos 22:34
give me **p** that it is really you .... Jdg 6:17
This was the **p** of ownership in .... Ru 4:7
bring back some **p** to show me 1Sa 17:18
man of God gave **p** that these 1Ki 13:3
to believe the **p** from witnesses. .... Is 33:8
but it is really **p** of their sin, ... Eze 21:23
Because of this **p** against you, ... Eze 21:24
But you give **p** that you are.................... Mt 23:31
could find no **p** of anything. .... Mk 14:55
be able to do these things as **p**: .... Mk 16:17
But I have a **p** about myself that............. Jn 5:36
sent me has given **p** about me. .... Jn 5:37
people but with **p** of the power 1Co 2:4
because you are **p** that I am an 1Co 9:2
first one and **p** that those who 1Co 15:20
these men the **p** of your love 2Co 8:24
It is a **p** of your faith. 2Co 9:13
You want **p** that Christ is 2Co 13:3
p is that he is not weak among 2Co 13:3
is God's **p** that you belong .... Eph 4:30
All of this is **p** that your .... Php 1:28
This is **p** that God is right in 2Th 1:5
p that came at the right time. 1Ti 2:6
guilty from the **p** given by two .... Heb 10:28
rust will be a **p** that you were .... Jam 5:3
saw him and can give **p** about it. 1Jn 1:2

PROOFS
are signs and **p** for the people .... Is 8:18
Give **p** and make miracles happen .... Ac 4:30
His **p** that Jesus is the Christ .... Ac 9:22

PROPER
gives him or have a **p** burial? .... Ec 6:3
will stand in its **p** place. .... Je 30:18
burn it in the **p** place in the .... Eze 43:21

should wear **p** clothes that show 1Ti 2:9
of power but left their **p** home. .... Jud 1:6

PROPERTY
will each go back to your own **p**, ... Le 25:10
each must go back to your own **p**. .... Le 25:13
gives some family **p** to the LORD, ... Le 27:16
become the **p** of the priests. .... Le 27:21
or field from the family **p**. .... Le 27:28
Give us **p** among our father's .... Nu 27:4
Give them **p** among their father's .... Nu 27:7
man wills his **p** to his sons he................ Dt 21:16
not get any of our father's **p**, ... Jdg 11:2
Amorites became the **p** of Israel. .... Jdg 11:21
dead husband's **p** will stay in .... Ru 4:10
over Nabal's **p** in the desert. 1Sa 25:21
husband's name and **p** will be 2Sa 14:7
orders for his family and **p**, ... 2Sa 17:23
to meet Jehu at the **p** of Naboth 2Ki 9:21
who took care of King David's **p**. 1Ch 27:31
care of the **p** and animals that 1Ch 28:1
pasturelands and **p** and came to 2Ch 11:14
or have his **p** taken away, or be .... Ezr 7:26
would lose his **p** and would no .... Ezr 10:8
by force the **p** of their enemies. .... Est 8:11
he will protect the widow's **p**................ Pr 15:25
share stolen **p** with the proud. .... Pr 16:19
the wealth and **p** he gives them, ... Ec 5:19
back to his own **p** and to his own .... Je 12:15
share of the **p** that belonged to .... Je 37:12
has been given to us as our **p**.' .... Eze 11:15
rich with farm animals and **p**, ... Eze 38:12
take away farm animals and **p**?''' .... Eze 38:13
about the priests and their **p**: .... Eze 44:28
They will have me instead of **p**. .... Eze 44:28
will be the ruler's **p** in Israel. .... Eze 45:8
It is their **p** passed down from .... Eze 46:16
will belong to you as family **p**. .... Eze 47:14
it as family **p** for yourselves .... Eze 47:22
share along with the city **p**. .... Eze 48:20
area and city **p** will belong to .... Eze 48:21
land and the city **p** will be in .... Eze 48:22
they rob them even of their **p**................ Mic 2:2
with me the **p** our father left us .... Lk 12:13
'Give me my share of the **p**.' .... Lk 15:12
divided the **p** between his two .... Lk 15:12
their private **p** belonged to .... Ac 4:32
their fathers' **p** are still .... Gal 4:1

PROPHECIES
sons, the great **p** against him,................ 2Ch 24:27
or pleasing **p** inside the nation .... Eze 12:24
those who make up their own **p**: ' .... Eze 13:2
Your **p** are lies, because I have .... Eze 13:7
people who make up their own **p**. .... Eze 13:17
ashamed of their visions and **p**. .... Zch 13:4
agrees with the **p** that were 1Ti 1:18

PROPHECY
LORD made this **p** against him: 2Ki 9:25
and in the **p** of Ahijah the 2Ch 9:29
is tricked into giving a **p**, ... Eze 14:9
to bring about the vision and **p**; .... Da 9:24
the gift of **p** should use that .... Rm 12:6
I may have the gift of **p**. 1Co 13:2
are gifts of **p**, but they will be................ 1Co 13:8
gifts, especially the gift of **p**. 1Co 14:1
knowledge, or **p**, or teaching. 1Co 14:6
And **p** is for those who believe, ... 1Co 14:22
Do not treat **p** as if it were 1Th 5:20
said this in a **p** or in a message 2Th 2:2
to you through **p** when the group 1Ti 4:14
p in the Scriptures ever comes 2Pe 1:20
p ever came from what a person 2Pe 1:21
is the spirit that gives all **p**." .... Rev 19:10

the words of **p** in this book." .... Rev 22:7
the words of **p** in this book, ... Rev 22:10
the words of the **p** of this book: .... Rev 22:18
the words of this book of **p,** .... Rev 22:19

PROPHESIED

in them, they **p,** but just that .... Nu 11:25
to them, and they **p** in the camp. .... Nu 11:26
and he **p** with the prophets. 1Sa 10:10
Saul, and he **p** in his house. 1Sa 10:10
Saul's men, and they also **p.** 1Sa 19:20
messengers, but they also **p.** 1Sa 19:21
a third time, but they also **p.** 1Sa 19:21
off his robes and **p** in front of 1Sa 19:24
p to the Jewish people in Judah .... Ezr 5:1
The prophets **p** in the name of .... Je 2:8
to whom you have **p** lies.'" .... Je 20:6
Those prophets **p** by Baal and led .... Je 23:13
to them, but they **p** anyway. .... Je 23:21
Jeremiah **p** about all those .... Je 25:13
He **p** against Jerusalem, and you .... Je 26:11
another man who **p** in the name .... Je 26:20
They **p** that war, hunger, and .... Je 28:8
Shemaiah has **p** to you, but I did .... Je 29:31
have you **p** the things you have? .... Je 32:3
prophets that **p** this message to .... Je 37:19
As I **p,** Pelatiah son of Benaiah .... Eze 11:13
So I **p** as I was commanded. .... Eze 37:7
While I **p,** there was a noise and .... Eze 37:7
So I **p** as the LORD commanded me. .... Eze 37:10
p for many years that I would. .... Eze 38:17
with the Holy Spirit and **p:** .... Lk 1:67
They **p** about the grace that was 1Pe 1:10

PROPHESIES

He never **p** anything good about 1Ki 22:8
He never **p** anything good about 1Ki 22:18
He never **p** anything good about 2Ch 18:7
He never **p** anything good about 2Ch 18:17
But if a prophet **p** that we will .... Je 28:9
' When he **p,** his own father and .... Zch 13:3
man who prays or **p** with his head 1Co 11:4
who prays or **p** with her head 1Co 11:5

PROPHESY

all the LORD's people could **p.** .... Nu 11:29
You will **p** with these prophets, ... 1Sa 10:6
had paid him to **p** against me. .... Ne 6:12
Don't **p** in the name of the LORD, ... Je 11:21
the LORD had sent him to **p,** .... Je 19:14
king of Judah and **p** this message .... Je 22:1
prophets who **p** lies in my name .... Je 23:25
They **p** from their own wishful .... Je 23:26
prophets who **p** false dreams," .... Je 23:32
will **p** against them with all .... Je 25:30
dare you **p** in the name of the .... Je 26:9
prophets who **p** to you will die. .... Je 27:15
the message you **p** come true. .... Je 28:6
you will **p** against Jerusalem. .... Eze 4:7
of Israel, and **p** against them. .... Eze 6:2
So **p** against them, prophesy, ... Eze 11:4
against them, **p,** human. .... Eze 11:4
p against the prophets of Israel. .... Eze 13:2
see false visions and **p** lies. .... Eze 13:6
see false visions and **p** lies. .... Eze 13:9
of Israel who **p** to foolish prophets .... Eze 13:16
own prophecies. **P** against them. .... Eze 13:17
see false visions or **p** anymore, ... Eze 13:23
P against the south and against .... Eze 20:46
P against the land of Israel. .... Eze 21:2
Human, **p** and say, 'This is what .... Eze 21:9
So, human, **p** and clap your .... Eze 21:14
And you, human, **p** and say: .... Eze 21:28
about you and **p** lies about you. .... Eze 21:29
of Ammon and **p** against them. .... Eze 25:2

city of Sidon and **p** against her. .... Eze 28:21
and **p** against him and all Egypt. .... Eze 29:2
Human, **p** and say, 'This is what .... Eze 30:2
p against the leaders of Israel, ... Eze 34:2
P and say to them: '........................ Eze 34:2
toward Edom and **p** against it. .... Eze 35:2
p to the mountains of Israel and .... Eze 36:1
So **p** and say: 'This is what the .... Eze 36:3
p about the land of Israel and .... Eze 36:6
P to these bones and say to .... Eze 37:4
he said to me, "**P** to the wind." .... Eze 37:9
P, human, and say to the wind, ' .... Eze 37:9
So, **p** and say to them, 'This is .... Eze 37:12
Meshech and Tubal. **P** against him .... Eze 38:2
So **p,** human, and say to Gog, ... Eze 38:14
Human, **p** against Gog and say, ... Eze 39:1
Your sons and daughters will **p,** .... Joe 2:28
and told the prophets not to **p.** .... Am 2:12
GOD has spoken. Who will not **p?** .... Am 3:8
but don't **p** anymore here at .... Am 7:13
said to me, 'Go, **p** to my people .... Am 7:15
me, 'Don't **p** against Israel, ... Am 7:16
prophets say, "Don't **p** to us!' .... Mic 2:6
Don't **p** about these things!' .... Mic 2:6
promises to **p** good things for .... Mic 2:11
If a person continues to **p,** .... Zch 13:3
Your sons and daughters will **p.** .... Ac 2:17
female slaves, and they will **p.** .... Ac 2:18
to another the ability to **p.** 1Co 12:10
ability to **p** are not perfect. 1Co 13:9
But those who **p** are speaking to 1Co 14:3
but those who **p** are helping the 1Co 14:4
but more, I wish you would **p.** 1Co 14:5
Those who **p** are greater than 1Co 14:5
You can all **p** one after the 1Co 14:31
you should truly want to **p.** 1Co 14:39
You must **p** again about many .... Rev 10:11
witnesses to **p** for one thousand .... Rev 11:3

PROPHESYING

and Medad are **p** in the camp." .... Nu 11:27
and lyres, and they will be **p.** 1Sa 10:5
before saw him **p** with the 1Sa 10:11
When Saul finished **p,** he entered 1Sa 10:13
they met a group of prophets **p,** 1Sa 19:20
p until he came to Naioth at 1Sa 19:23
prophets are **p** lies in my name. .... Je 14:14
They have been **p** false visions, ... Je 14:14
prophets who are **p** in my name. .... Je 14:15
heard Jeremiah **p** in the Temple .... Je 20:1
because they are **p** lies to you! .... Je 27:14
'They are **p** lies and saying the .... Je 27:15
They are **p** lies to you. .... Je 27:16
They are **p** lies to you, saying .... Je 29:9
two men have been **p** lies to you, ... Je 29:21
He is **p** about times far away.' .... Eze 12:27
p and earn your living there, ... Am 7:12
and stop **p** against the .... Am 7:16
he was really **p** that Jesus would .... Jn 11:51
different languages and **p.** .... Ac 19:6
daughters who had the gift of **p.** .... Ac 21:9
everyone is **p** and some people 1Co 14:24
If everyone is **p,** their sin will 1Co 14:24
during the time they are **p.** .... Rev 11:6

PROPHET

back. He is a **p.** He will pray .... Ge 20:7
Aaron will be like a **p** for you. .... Ex 7:1
God will give you a **p** like me, ... Dt 18:15
I will give them a **p** like you, ... Dt 18:18
But if a **p** says something I did .... Dt 18:20
or if a **p** speaks in the name of .... Dt 18:20
gods, that **p** must be killed. .... Dt 18:20
been another **p** in Israel like .... Dt 34:10

We call the person a **p** today, ... 1Sa 9:9
But the **p** Gad said to David, ... 1Sa 22:5
Then David said to Nathan the **p,** 2Sa 7:2
Now an old **p** was living in 1Ki 13:11
I am the only **p** of the LORD 1Ki 18:22
p Elijah went near the altar. 1Ki 18:36
I am the only **p** left, and now 1Ki 19:10
would meet the **p** who lives in 2Ki 5:3
know there is a **p** in Israel." 2Ki 5:8
Elisha the **p** called a man from 2Ki 9:1
when they came to Isaiah the **p,** 2Ki 19:2
down by the **p** Isaiah son of Amoz 2Ch 26:22
king's seer, and Nathan was a **p.** 2Ch 29:25
the vision of the **p** Isaiah son 2Ch 32:32
The **p** Jeremiah spoke messages.............. 2Ch 36:12
of Haggai the **p** and Zechariah, ... Ezr 6:14
David when the **p** Nathan came to .... Ps 50:23
fun of the LORD's **p** and say: .... Is 28:10
when they came to Isaiah the **p,** .... Is 37:2
you as a **p** to the nations." .... Je 1:5
he had Jeremiah the **p** beaten. .... Je 20:2
If a **p** wants to tell about his .... Je 23:28
the **p** Hananiah took the yoke .... Je 28:10
know that a **p** has been among .... Eze 2:5
try to get a vision from a **p;** .... Eze 7:26
they come to the **p** to ask me .... Eze 14:7
You think the **p** is a fool,...................... Hos 9:7
the LORD used a **p** to bring .... Hos 12:13
he used a **p** to take care of the .... Hos 12:13
I do not make my living as a **p,** .... Am 7:14
message Habakkuk the **p** received. ...... Hab 1:1
is the prayer of Habakkuk the **p,** .... Hab 3:1
The **p** Haggai spoke the word of............. Hag 1:1
Then Haggai the **p** spoke the word.......... Hag 1:3
you Elijah the **p** before that .... Mal 4:5
the Lord had said through the **p:** .... Mt 1:22
The **p** wrote about this in the .... Mt 2:5
said through the **p** Jeremiah came .... Mt 2:17
one Isaiah the **p** was talking .... Mt 3:3
Whoever meets a **p** and accepts .... Mt 10:41
out? To see a **p?** Yes, and I tell .... Mt 11:9
tell you, John is more than a **p.** .... Mt 11:9
except the sign of the **p** Jonah. .... Mt 12:39
A **p** is honored everywhere except .... Mt 13:57
the **p** from the town of Nazareth .... Mt 21:11
all believe that John was a **p."** .... Mt 21:26
Daniel the **p** spoke about 'a .... Mt 24:15
said. "Jesus is a **p,** like the .... Mk 6:15
be called a **p** of the Most High .... Lk 1:76
of Isaiah the **p** was given to him............. Lk 4:17
p is not accepted in his hometown. .... Lk 4:24
during the time of the **p** Elisha. .... Lk 4:27
He was a **p** who said and did many .... Lk 24:19
truly be the **P** who is coming .... Jn 6:14
But Joel the **p** wrote about what.............. Ac 2:16
God will give you a **p** like me, ... Ac 3:22
'God will give you a **p** like me, ... Ac 7:37
from the Book of Isaiah, the **p.** .... Ac 8:28
who is the **p** talking about— .... Ac 8:34
Bar-Jesus. He was a false **p**................... Ac 13:6
until the time of Samuel the **p.** .... Ac 13:20
with the beast and the false **p.** .... Rev 20:10

PROPHET'S

of God went to the old **p** house, ... 1Ki 13:19
won't wear the **p** clothes made .... Zch 13:4
comes from the **p** own........................... 2Pe 1:20
stopped the **p** crazy thinking. 2Pe 2:16

PROPHETESS

sister Miriam, a **p,** took a .... Ex 15:20
A **p** named Deborah, the wife of.............. Jdg 4:4
went to talk to Huldah the **p.** 2Ki 22:14
went to talk to Huldah the **p.** 2Ch 34:22

Also remember the **p** Noadiah and............ Ne 6:14
I went to the **p,** and she became .... Is 8:3
There was a **p,** Anna, from the .... Lk 2:36
She says she is a **p,** but by her .... Rev 2:20

PROPHETS

When **p** are among you, I, the .... Nu 12:6
a group of **p** will come down from 1Sa 10:5
saw him prophesying with the **p,** 1Sa 10:11
"Who is the father of these **p?"** 1Sa 10:12
was killing all the LORD's **p,** 1Ki 18:4
four hundred fifty **p** of Baal and.............. 1Ki 18:19
and killed your **p** with swords. 1Ki 19:14
The groups of **p** at Bethel came 2Ki 2:3
The groups of **p** at Jericho came............. 2Ki 2:5
The groups of **p** said to Elisha, ... 2Ki 6:1
you through my servants the **p."**.............. 2Ki 17:13
people, and don't harm my **p."** 1Ch 16:22
by your Spirit through the **p,** .... Ne 9:30
people, and don't harm my **p."** .... Ps 105:15
The **p** are your eyes. .... Is 29:10
The **p** prophesied in the name of .... Je 2:8
I saw the **p** of Samaria do .... Je 23:13
I am against the false **p,"** .... Je 23:31
and the **p** do not have visions .... La 2:9
because her **p** sinned and her .... La 4:13
for the foolish **p** who follow .... Eze 13:3
your **p** have been like wild dogs .... Eze 13:4
servants, the **p,** who spoke for .... Da 9:6
us through his servants, the **p.** .... Da 9:10
you by my **p** that I will kill .... Hos 6:5
his plans to his servants the **p.** .... Am 3:7
and its **p** only look into the.................... Mic 3:11
Its **p** are proud; they are people .... Zph 3:4
Spirit through the earlier **p.** .... Zch 7:12
said through the **p** came true:............... Mt 2:23
Moses or the teaching of the **p.** .... Mt 5:17
Be careful of false **p.** .... Mt 7:15
All the **p** and the law of Moses .... Mt 11:13
are Jeremiah or one of the **p."** .... Mt 16:14
have helped them kill the **p.'** .... Mt 23:30
of those who murdered the **p.**................. Mt 23:31
like the **p** who lived long ago." .... Mk 6:15
through his holy **p** who lived .... Lk 1:70
of all the **p** who were killed .... Lk 11:50
writings of the **p** were preached .... Lk 16:16
Moses and the writings of the **p;**.............. Lk 16:29
books of the **p,** and the Psalms. .... Lk 24:44
he spoke through his holy **p.** .... Ac 3:21
You are descendants of the **p.**................. Ac 3:25
the **p** say it is true that all .... Ac 10:43
the words that the **p** wrote,.................... Ac 13:27
words of the **p** agree with this .... Ac 15:15
News long ago through his **p,**................. Rm 1:2
killed your **p,** and they have .... Rm 11:3
second to **p,** and third to 1Co 12:28
Not all are **p.** Not all are 1Co 12:29
two or three **p** should speak, ... 1Co 14:29
The spirits of **p** are under the 1Co 14:32
the control of the **p** themselves. 1Co 14:32
of the apostles and **p.** .... Eph 2:20
some to be **p,** some to go and .... Eph 4:11
through the **p** many times .... Heb 1:1
David, Samuel, and the **p.** .... Heb 11:32
The **p** searched carefully and 1Pe 1:10
used to be false **p** among God's 2Pe 2:1
many false **p** have gone out into.............. 1Jn 4:1
told to his servants, the **p."** .... Rev 10:7

PROSTITUTE

sister to be treated like a **p."** .... Ge 34:31
she was a **p,** because she had .... Ge 38:15
Where is the **p** who was here by.............. Ge 38:21
"There has never been a **p** here." .... Ge 38:21

has never been a **p** here.' " .... Ge 38:22
is guilty of acting like a **p,** .... Ge 38:24
by making her become a **p.** .... Le 19:29
marry an unclean **p** or a divorced .... Le 21:7
herself unclean by becoming a **p,** .... Le 21:9
widow, a divorced woman, or a **p.** .... Le 21:14
must ever become a temple **p.** .... Dt 23:17
at the house of a **p** named Rahab. .... Jos 2:1
Only Rahab the **p** and everyone in .... Jos 6:17
saved Rahab the **p,** her family, ... Jos 6:25
Gilead, and his mother was a **p.** .... Jdg 11:1
went to Gaza and saw a **p** there. .... Jdg 16:1
with the **p** until midnight. .... Jdg 16:3
p will treat you like a loaf of .... Pr 6:26
dressed like a **p** and planning to .... Pr 7:10
A **p** is as dangerous as a deep .... Pr 23:27
will be like the **p** in this song: .... Is 23:15
It will be like a **p** for all the .... Is 23:17
green tree you lay down as a **p.** .... Je 2:20
acted like a **p** with many lovers .... Je 3:1
where you have not been a **p?** .... Je 3:2
you did evil and were like a **p.** .... Je 3:2
looks like the face of a **p.** .... Je 3:3
She was like a **p** with her idols .... Je 3:6
went out and acted like a **p!** .... Je 3:8
that she was acting like a **p.** .... Je 3:9
You became a **p,** because you were .... Eze 16:15
so you could be a **p** with them. .... Eze 16:17
the things a stubborn **p** does. .... Eze 16:30
were not like a **p** when you .... Eze 16:31
No man asks you to be a **p,** .... Eze 16:34
So, **p,** hear the word of the .... Eze 16:35
Samaria became a **p** for all the .... Eze 23:7
how she was a young **p** in Egypt, ... Eze 23:19
She is nothing but a **p.'** .... Eze 23:43
to her as they would go to a **p.** .... Eze 23:44
her to stop acting like a **p,** .... Hos 2:2
they are the children of a **p.** .... Hos 2:4
Their mother has acted like a **p;** .... Hos 2:5
must not be a **p,** and you must .... Hos 3:3
you act like a **p,** but do not be .... Hos 4:15
Now that Israel acts like a **p,** .... Hos 5:3
been like a **p** against your God .... Hos 9:1
will become a **p** in the city, ... Am 7:17
The city was like a **p;** .... Nah 3:4
of Christ and join them to a **p!** 1Co 6:15
joins with a **p** becomes one body 1Co 6:16
becomes one body with the **p.** 1Co 6:16
that Rahab, the **p,** welcomed the .... Heb 11:31
is Rahab, a **p,** who was made .... Jam 2:25
will be given to the great **p,** .... Rev 17:1
saw, where the **p** sits, are .... Rev 17:15
beast you saw will hate the **p.** .... Rev 17:16
has punished the **p** who made the .... Rev 19:2

PROSTITUTE'S

a male or female **p** pay to the .... Dt 23:18
the land, "Go into the **p** house. .... Jos 6:22

PROSTITUTES

which they have chased like **p.** .... Le 17:7
who were **p** came to Solomon. 1Ki 3:16
were even male **p** in the land. 1Ki 14:24
forced the male **p** at the worship 1Ki 15:12
pool in Samaria where **p** bathed, ... 1Ki 22:38
There were male **p** still in the 1Ki 22:46
houses of the male **p** who were in 2Ki 23:7
but friends of **p** waste their .... Pr 29:3
you children of **p** and those who .... Is 57:3
spent much time in houses of **p.** .... Je 5:7
Men pay **p,** but you pay all your .... Eze 16:33
you are different from other **p.** .... Eze 16:34
they went to Egypt and became **p.** .... Eze 23:3
girls were alike; both were **p.** .... Eze 23:13

sexual relations with the **p,** .... Hos 4:10
Like **p,** they have chased after .... Hos 4:12
So your daughters become **p,** .... Hos 4:13
your daughters for becoming **p,** .... Hos 4:14
relations with **p** and offer .... Hos 4:14
sacrifices with the temple **p.** .... Hos 4:14
give themselves to being **p;** .... Hos 4:18
love the pay of **p** on every .... Hos 9:1
traded boys for **p,** and they sold .... Joe 3:3
collectors and the **p** will enter .... Mt 21:31
collectors and **p** believed him. .... Mt 21:32
who wasted all your money on **p,** .... Lk 15:30
MOTHER OF **P** AND OF THE EVIL .... Rev 17:5

PROSTITUTION

the LORD your God hates **p.** .... Dt 23:18
snorting, your **p,** your hateful .... Je 13:27
There you carried on your **p.** .... Eze 16:16
She continued the **p** she began in .... Eze 23:8
in her sexual desire and **p.** .... Eze 23:11
continued her **p** so openly that .... Eze 23:18
so she took part in even more **p.** .... Eze 23:19
p, to old and new wine, which .... Hos 4:11
Look at Israel's **p;** .... Hos 6:10
slaves with her **p** and her .... Nah 3:4

PROTECT

to my house, and I must **p** them." .... Ge 19:8
you and will **p** you everywhere .... Ge 28:15
be with me and to **p** me on this .... Ge 28:20
who will **p** you as you travel. .... Ex 23:20
sides of the Holy Tent, to **p** it. .... Ex 26:13
They must **p** the killer from the .... Nu 35:25
not let them go free or **p** them. .... Dt 13:8
your camp to **p** you and to defeat .... Dt 23:14
to help you! Let them **p** you! .... Dt 32:38
not a man stayed to **p** it. .... Jos 8:17
they could not **p** themselves. .... Jdg 2:14
p me with your saving shield. 2Sa 22:36
watch over it and **p** it always. 1Ki 9:3
on the Sabbath must **p** the Temple 2Ki 11:7
will **p** the city for my sake and 2Ki 20:6
horsemen to **p** us from enemies .... Ezr 8:22
given us a wall to **p** us in Judah .... Ezr 9:9
gather together to **p** themselves. .... Est 8:11
also met to **p** themselves and get .... Est 9:16
P those who love you and who are .... Ps 5:11
you **p** them like a soldier's .... Ps 5:12
P the orphans and put an end to .... Ps 10:18
you will always **p** us from such .... Ps 12:7
poor, but the LORD will **p** them. .... Ps 14:6
P me, God, because I trust in .... Ps 16:1
P me as you would protect your .... Ps 17:8
me as you would **p** your own eye. .... Ps 17:8
p me with your saving shield. .... Ps 18:35
May the God of Jacob **p** you. .... Ps 20:1
P me and save me. I trust you, ... Ps 25:20
You **p** them by your presence from .... Ps 31:20
You **p** me from my troubles and .... Ps 32:7
is our help, our shield to **p** us. .... Ps 33:20
He will **p** their very bones; .... Ps 34:20
you **p** both people and animals. .... Ps 36:6
You **p** people in the shadow of .... Ps 36:7
He will always **p** them, but the .... Ps 37:28
your love and truth will always **p** me. ..... Ps 40:11
The LORD will **p** them and spare .... Ps 41:2
P me from those who come against .... Ps 59:1
P him with your love and truth. .... Ps 61:7
p my life from them. .... Ps 64:1
God, save me and **p** me. .... Ps 69:29
P me, because I worship you. .... Ps 86:2
I will **p** those who know me. .... Ps 91:14
The LORD will **p** you from all .... Ps 121:7
p me from cruel people .... Ps 140:1

p me from cruel people who plan .... Ps 140:4
savior, you **p** me in battle. .... Ps 140:7
P me from the traps they set for .... Ps 141:9
Good sense will **p** you; .... Pr 2:11
The LORD will **p** good people but .... Pr 10:29
what they say **p** their lives, ... Pr 13:3
words of the wise will **p** them. .... Pr 14:3
but he will **p** the widow's .... Pr 15:25
they do, they **p** their lives. .... Pr 16:17
trust their wealth to **p** them. .... Pr 18:11
obey the commands **p** themselves, ... Pr 19:16
we will **p** her with cedar boards. .... Sng 8:9
This covering will **p** the people .... Is 4:6
P us from our enemies as shade .... Is 16:3
You **p** the poor; you protect the .... Is 25:4
you **p** the helpless when they are .... Is 25:4
The LORD will **p** Jerusalem, ... Is 25:10
Moab's high walls **p** them, but .... Is 25:12
they want Egypt to **p** them..................... Is 30:2
I will hold your hand and **p** you. .... Is 42:6
will **p** you, and you will be the .... Is 49:8
you with my hands and **p** you. .... Is 51:16
the LORD will **p** you from behind .... Is 58:8
because I am with you to **p** you," .... Je 1:8
because I am with you to **p** you!" .... Je 1:19
have gates or fences to **p** it. .... Je 49:31
cities that **p** Moab's borders, ... Eze 25:9
hired other nations to **p** them. .... Hos 8:9
I will **p** my Temple from armies .... Zch 9:8
LORD All-Powerful will **p** them;............. Zch 9:15
time the LORD will **p** the people .... Zch 12:8
wear faith and love to **p** us,.................... 1Th 5:8
and will **p** you from the Evil 2Th 3:3
sure he is able to **p** what he has 2Ti 1:12
P the truth that you were given; 2Ti 1:14
p it with the help of the Holy 2Ti 1:14

PROTECTED

he has **p** you while you traveled .... Dt 2:7
but he **p** your word and guarded .... Dt 33:9
cities were large and well **p**. .... Jos 14:12
brought us out and **p** us while we .... Jos 24:17
Night and day they **p** us......................... 1Sa 25:16
He has **p** us and given us the 1Sa 30:23
and you would not have **p** me!" 2Sa 18:13
But the king **p** Mephibosheth,.................. 2Sa 21:7
so the king **p** himself there. 2Ki 6:10
helped us and **p** us from enemies .... Ezr 8:31
You will be **p** from the tongue................ Job 5:21
the rocky peak is its **p** place. .... Job 39:28
will be **p** by the Almighty. .... Ps 91:1
and their children will be **p**. .... Pr 14:26
do right are **p** even in death. .... Pr 14:32
He will be **p** as he would be in a.............. Is 33:16
They stay in their **p** cities. .... Je 60:16
We will be **p** by him among the .... La 4:20
which is **p** with strong walls. .... Eze 21:20
now they are **p** and have people .... Eze 36:35
He destroys the **p** city; .... Am 5:9
was afraid of John and **p** him. .... Mk 6:20
I **p** them, and only one of them, ... Jn 17:12
that we will be **p** from stubborn 2Th 3:2

PROTECTING

Beth Horon, **p** them with strong.............. 2Ch 8:5
The walls **p** Judah will fall...................... Is 22:8

PROTECTION

They have no **p**, but the LORD is .... Nu 14:9
is my **p**. He makes my way free 2Sa 22:33
are those who trust him for **p**. .... Ps 2:12
my God, I trust in you for **p**. .... Ps 7:1
I trust in the LORD for **p**. .... Ps 11:1
is my rock, my **p**, my Savior. .... Ps 18:2
is my **p**. He makes my way free .... Ps 18:32

my rock of **p**, a strong city to .... Ps 31:2
You are my rock and my **p**...................... Ps 31:3
for me, because you are my **p**. .... Ps 31:4
not take away his **p** or let good .... Ps 37:33
because they trust in him for **p**. .... Ps 37:40
God is our **p** and our strength. .... Ps 46:1
me because I come to you for **p**. .... Ps 57:1
have been my **p**, like a strong................. Ps 61:3
He is my mighty rock and my **p**.............. Ps 62:7
problems, because God is our **p**.............. Ps 62:8
Because of your **p**, I sing. .... Ps 63:7
the LORD and will find **p** in him. .... Ps 64:10
In you, LORD, is my **p**. .... Ps 71:1
because you are my strong **p**. .... Ps 71:7
The Lord GOD is my **p**. .... Ps 73:28
are my place of safety and **p**. .... Ps 91:2
truth will be your shield and **p**. .... Ps 91:4
The LORD is your **p**; .... Ps 91:9
my God is the rock of my **p**. .... Ps 94:22
he is your helper and your **p**. .... Ps 115:9
he is your helper and your **p**. .... Ps 115:10
he is your helper and your **p**. .... Ps 115:11
I say, "You are my **p**. .... Ps 142:5
my Savior, my shield and my **p**. .... Ps 144:2
Egypt's **p** will only disappoint .... Is 30:3
and their **p** will be destroyed. .... Is 31:9
you are my strength and my **p**, ... Je 16:19
will again live under my **p**. .... Hos 14:7
giving **p** in times of trouble. .... Nah 1:7
waist and the **p** of right living................. Eph 6:14

PROTECTOR

Lord, our **p**, do not kill them, ... Ps 59:11

PROTECTORS

He wore bronze **p** on his legs, ... 1Sa 17:6

PROTECTS

because he **p** them all day long. .... Dt 33:12
He **p** those who are loyal to him, ... 1Sa 2:9
God **p** me like a shield; .... Ps 7:10
The LORD **p** my life. .... Ps 27:1
The LORD **p** those who truly .... Ps 31:23
He **p** our lives and does not let .... Ps 66:9
the shade that **p** you from the................. Ps 121:5
He **p** me like a strong, walled .... Ps 144:2
The LORD **p** everyone who loves .... Ps 145:20
The LORD **p** the foreigners. .... Ps 146:9
Like a shield he **p** the innocent. .... Pr 2:7
and he **p** those who are loyal to .... Pr 2:8
Having lots of money **p** the rich,............ Pr 10:15
what is right **p** the honest .... Pr 13:6
as shade **p** us from the noon .... Is 16:3
like shade that **p** them from the .... Is 25:4
God **p** us with its strong walls .... Is 26:1
the Powerful One of Jacob **p** you. .... Is 60:16
great prince who **p** your people, ... Da 12:1
God's power **p** you through your 1Pe 1:5

PROTEST

his hands in **p**, speaking more .... Job 34:37

PROUD

was the least **p** person on earth............... Nu 12:3
they were **p**. They went toward .... Nu 14:44
You were **p**, so you went on up .... Dt 1:43
then your heart will become **p**. .... Dt 8:14
bragging, don't speak **p** words. 1Sa 2:3
I know you are **p** and wicked at 1Sa 17:28
you bring down those who are **p**. 2Sa 22:28
and Haggith, and he was very **p**. 1Ki 1:5
Edom, but you have become **p**. 2Ki 14:10
You have a **p** look on your face, ... 2Ki 19:22
I have heard your **p** words,..................... 2Ki 19:28
you have become **p**, and you brag. 2Ch 25:19
kindness, because he was so **p**. 2Ch 32:25

were sorry and stopped being **p**,.............. 2Ch 32:26
you knew how **p** they were. .... Ne 9:10
ancestors were **p** and stubborn .... Ne 9:16
but they were **p** and did not obey .... Ne 9:29
P animals have not walked there, ... Job 28:8
and to keep them from being **p**. .... Job 33:17
out, because the wicked are **p**. .... Job 35:12
is where your **p** waves must stop' .... Job 38:11
people with its **p** snorting. .... Job 39:20
look at the **p** and bring them .... Job 40:11
Look at the **p** and make them .... Job 40:12
down on all those who are too **p**; .... Job 41:34
is king over all **p** creatures." .... Job 41:34
The wicked people are too **p**. .... Ps 10:4
you bring down those who are **p**. .... Ps 18:27
punishes the **p** as much as they .... Ps 31:23
Don't let **p** people attack me and .... Ps 36:11
who are not **p** will inherit .... Ps 37:11
those who are **p** or to those who.............. Ps 40:4
there are many **p** people fighting .... Ps 56:2
I was jealous of **p** people. .... Ps 73:3
I say to those who are **p**, ' .... Ps 75:4
p people are attacking me; .... Ps 86:14
give the **p** what they deserve. .... Ps 94:2
They are full of **p** words;...................... Ps 94:4
people to be **p** and look down.................. Ps 101:5
You scold **p** people; those who .... Ps 119:21
P people always make fun of me, ... Ps 119:51
P people have made up lies about .... Ps 119:69
Make **p** people ashamed because .... Ps 119:78
P people have dug pits to trap .... Ps 119:85
Don't let **p** people wrong me. .... Ps 119:122
and much cruelty from the **p**. .... Ps 123:4
LORD, my heart is not **p**; .... Ps 131:1
but he stays away from the **p**.................. Ps 138:6
The **p** hid a trap for me. .... Ps 140:5
succeed, or they will become **p**. .... Ps 140:8
grace to those who are not **p**. .... Pr 3:34
get free. Don't be **p**. Go to your .... Pr 6:3
p look, a lying tongue, hands .... Pr 6:17
be punished for their **p** words, ... Pr 14:3
tear down the **p** person's house, ... Pr 15:25
The LORD hates those who are **p**. .... Pr 16:5
a **p** attitude brings ruin. .... Pr 16:18
stolen property with the **p**. .... Pr 16:19
Old people are **p** of their...................... Pr 17:6
children are **p** of their parents .... Pr 17:6
should not be **p**, and rulers .... Pr 17:7
P people will be ruined, but the .... Pr 18:12
P looks, proud thoughts, and .... Pr 21:4
Proud looks, **p** thoughts, and .... Pr 21:4
stubborn pride are called "**p**," .... Pr 21:24
and not being **p** will bring you .... Pr 22:4
children, and you will be **p**; .... Pr 29:17
Some people have such a **p** look! .... Pr 30:13
If you have been foolish and **p**, ... Pr 30:32
to be patient than to be **p**. .... Ec 7:8
People will not be **p** any longer .... Is 2:9
P people will be made humble, ... Is 2:11
will punish the **p** and those who.............. Is 2:12
At that time **p** people will be .... Is 2:17
Sodom, they are **p** of their sin. .... Is 3:9
The women of Jerusalem are **p**. .... Is 3:16
everything that makes them **p**; .... Is 3:18
Israel will be **p** of what the .... Is 4:2
those who are **p** will be humbled. .... Is 5:15
Those people are **p** and brag by .... Is 9:9
The king of Assyria is very **p**,................ Is 10:12
I will cause **p** people to lose .... Is 13:11
Babylonians are very **p** of it. .... Is 13:19
of Moab are **p** and very conceited .... Is 16:6
They are very **p** and angry,..................... Is 16:6
to make these **p** people .... Is 23:9

He will destroy the **p** city, ... Is 26:5
you see those **p** people from .... Is 33:19
You have a **p** look on your face, ... Is 37:23
I have heard your **p** words,..................... Is 37:29
you will be **p** of the Holy One of.............. Is 41:16
those who are not **p** or stubborn............. Is 66:2
Don't be too **p**, because the LORD .... Je 13:15
and some other men were too **p**. .... Je 43:2
people of Judah are still too **p**. .... Je 44:10
that the people of Moab are **p**, ... Je 48:29
of Moab are proud, very **p**. .... Je 48:29
They are **p**, very proud, and in .... Je 48:29
are proud, very **p**, and in their .... Je 48:29
and destroyed those **p** people. .... Je 48:45
you are too **p**, and I am against .... Je 50:31
P Babylon will stumble and fall,............. Je 50:32
They were **p** of their beautiful .... Eze 7:20
daughters were **p** and had plenty .... Eze 16:49
daughters were **p** and did things .... Eze 16:56
sister Sodom when you were **p**, ... Eze 16:56
You are **p** of it, and you look at .... Eze 24:21
and joy, that makes them **p**. .... Eze 24:25
Because you are **p**, you say, "I .... Eze 28:2
You are too **p** because of your .... Eze 28:5
You became too **p** because of your .... Eze 28:17
power she is **p** of will be lost .... Eze 30:6
no longer be **p** of her power. .... Eze 30:18
and it became **p** of its height. .... Eze 31:10
water will not be **p** to be tall; .... Eze 31:14
stopped your **p** talk against me .... Eze 35:13
to rule them who are not **p**.' .... Da 4:17
is able to make **p** people humble. .... Da 4:37
became too **p** and stubborn, ... Da 5:20
then be very **p** and will kill................... Da 11:12
they became too **p** and forgot me. .... Hos 13:6
evil nation is very **p** of itself; .... Hab 2:4
who are too **p** will not last, ... Hab 2:5
you who are not **p**, who obey his .... Zph 2:3
Moab and Ammon get for being **p**,........... Zph 2:10
prophets are **p**; they are people .... Zph 3:4
be any more **p** people on my holy .... Zph 3:11
humble and those who are not **p**, ... Zph 3:12
make them like my **p** war horses. .... Zch 10:3
So we say that **p** people are .... Mal 3:15
and all the **p** and evil people .... Mal 4:1
people who are **p** and think great .... Lk 1:51
it and were **p** of what they had .... Ac 7:41
Do not be **p**, but be afraid. .... Rm 11:20
Do not be **p**, but make friends .... Rm 12:16
I am **p** of what I have done for .... Rm 15:17
will not be more **p** of one person 1Co 4:6
Some of you have become **p**, ... 1Co 4:18
I will know what the **p** ones do, ... 1Co 4:19
And you are **p**! You should have.............. 1Co 5:2
does not brag, and it is not **p**. 1Co 13:4
is what we are **p** of, and I can............... 2Co 1:12
so you will be **p** of us. 2Co 5:12
those who are **p** about things 2Co 5:12
of you and am very **p** of you. 2Co 7:4
and the reason we are **p** of you. 2Co 8:24
and every **p** thing that raises 2Co 10:5
become too **p** of the wonderful 2Co 12:7
me and keep me from being too **p**. 2Co 12:7
We must not be **p** or make trouble .... Gal 5:26
Then he can be **p** for what he .... Gal 6:4
they are **p** of their shameful .... Php 3:19
me joy and make me **p** of you, ... Php 4:1
pretend not to be **p** and make................. Col 2:23
he might be too **p** of himself and 1Ti 3:6
of this world not to be **p**........................ 1Ti 6:17
love money, brag, and be **p**. 2Ti 3:2
is against the **p**, but he gives .... Jam 4:6
But now you are **p** and you brag. .... Jam 4:16

is against the **p**, but he gives 1Pe 5:5
and being too **p** of what we have. 1Jn 2:16
allowed to say **p** words and words .... Rev 13:5
PROUDEST
a lion, the **p** animal, which is .... Pr 30:30
PROUDLY
and let you walk **p** again. .... Le 26:13
P the wicked chase down those .... Ps 10:2
p they speak of hurting others. .... Ps 73:8
are three things that strut **p**, ... Pr 30:29
jewels that a bride wears **p**. .... Is 49:18
You will no longer walk **p**, ... Mic 2:3
PROVE
from me to **p** that you believe .... Ge 21:30
you a way to **p** that you are telling .... Ge 42:15
the first to **p** his father could .... Dt 21:17
P that you are the God of Israel 1Ki 18:36
but they could not **p** that their .... Ezr 2:59
but they could not **p** that their .... Ne 7:61
priests could not **p** that their .... Ne 7:63
they wrote to **p** the first letter .... Est 9:29
but your arguments **p** nothing. .... Job 6:25
not true, who can **p** I am wrong? .... Job 24:25
because I want to **p** you right. .... Job 33:32
understanding will **p** them wrong. .... Pr 28:11
you and **p** you are a liar. .... Pr 30:6
your God to **p** to yourself that................ Is 7:11
witnesses to **p** they were right. .... Is 43:9
That god should come and **p** it. .... Is 44:7
someone wants to **p** I have done............. Is 50:8
So who can **p** me guilty?....................... Is 50:9
will **p** the holiness of my great .... Eze 36:23
the LORD when I **p** myself holy .... Eze 36:23
when they see me **p** how holy I am .... Eze 38:16
But I will **p** to you that the Son .... Mt 9:6
of your words will **p** you right, ... Mt 12:37
your words will **p** you guilty.".............. Mt 12:37
P to us that you are a prophet, ... Mt 26:68
But I will **p** to you that the Son .... Mk 2:10
and said, "**P** you are a prophet! .... Mk 14:65
But I will **p** to you that the Son .... Lk 5:24
to stand against or **p** wrong. .... Lk 21:15
P that you are a prophet, ... Lk 22:64
us a miracle to **p** you have the .... Jn 2:18
gave me to do, **p** that the Father .... Jn 5:36
any of you **p** that I am guilty .... Jn 8:46
he will **p** to the people of the .... Jn 16:8
will **p** to them that sin is not .... Jn 16:9
He will **p** to them that being .... Jn 16:10
the Helper will **p** to them that.............. Jn 16:11
Then it will **p** to everyone that .... Ac 21:24
They cannot **p** the things they .... Ac 24:13
him, which they could not **p**. .... Ac 25:7
not trying to **p** ourselves to you 2Co 5:12
things that **p** I am an apostle— 2Co 12:12
their own sins **p** them wrong................. Tit 3:11
God wanted to **p** that his promise .... Heb 6:17
anything else to **p** what you say.............. Jam 5:12
come to **p** that your faith 1Pe 1:7
PROVED
If it is **p** that a hateful thing .... Dt 13:14
A case must be **p** by two or three .... Dt 19:15
and I know I will be **p** right. .... Job 13:18
not one of you has **p** Job wrong;............ Job 32:12
LORD's words that Joseph was .... Ps 105:19
' But wisdom is **p** to be right by .... Mt 11:19
case may be **p** by two or three .... Mt 18:16
The Lord that the Good News .... Mk 16:20
But wisdom is **p** to be right by .... Lk 7:35
to them and **p** in many ways that .... Ac 1:3
Yet he **p** he is real by showing .... Ac 14:17

explained and **p** that the Christ .... Ac 17:3
And God has **p** this to everyone .... Ac 17:31
was tested and **p** that he truly................ Rm 16:10
and you have **p** that what we 2Co 7:14
has **p** this to us in many ways, ... 2Co 8:22
case must be **p** by two or three 2Co 13:1
a human body, **p** right in spirit 1Ti 3:16
After they have **p** their faith, ... Jam 1:12
which can be **p** to be pure by 1Pe 1:7
PROVEN
the husband can be **p** correct,................ Nu 5:31
Your promises are **p**, so I, your .... Ps 119:140
he says has **p** that God is true. .... Jn 3:33
who has not been **p** guilty?" .... Ac 22:25
it must be **p** that the one who .... Heb 9:16
PROVES
when your neighbor **p** you wrong?........... Pr 25:8
where is the paper that **p** it? .... Is 50:1
also **p** these things are true." .... Ac 5:32
The oath **p** that what they say.............. Heb 6:16
PROVIDE
is your duty to **p** children for .... Ge 38:8
animals play, **p** food for it. .... Job 40:20
Will he **p** his people with meat?" .... Ps 78:20
want to **p** a home for the Mighty .... Ps 132:5
I will **p** my appointed one .... Ps 132:17
sun and will **p** a safe place to .... Is 4:6
his children that you **p** help. .... Is 38:19
I will **p** for their needs before .... Is 65:24
deeds to **p** what is necessary .... Tit 3:14
PROVIDED
of the LORD it will be **p**." .... Ge 22:14
because you have **p** an excuse for .... Eze 16:52
PROVIDES
named that place The LORD **P**. .... Ge 22:14
sells them and **p** belts to the .... Pr 31:24
PROVING
clearly **p** with the Scriptures .... Ac 18:28
am defending and **p** the truth of.............. Php 1:7
PSALM
instruments. A **p** of David. .... Ps 3:8
music. For flutes. A **p** of David. .... Ps 4:8
the sheminith. A **p** of David. .... Ps 5:12
On the gittith. A **p** of David. .... Ps 7:17
Death of the Son." A **p** of David. .... Ps 8:9
the sheminith. A **p** of David. .... Ps 11:7
director of music. A **p** of David. .... Ps 12:8
will be glad. A **p** of David. .... Ps 14:7
director of music. A **p** of David. .... Ps 18:50
director of music. A **p** of David. .... Ps 19:14
director of music. A **p** of David. .... Ps 20:9
The Doe of Dawn." A **p** of David. .... Ps 21:13
what God has done. A **p** of David. .... Ps 22:31
the LORD forever. A **p** of David............... Ps 23:6
them forever. A **p** of David....................... Ps 28:9
with peace. A **p** of David. A song .... Ps 29:11
director of music. A **p** of David. .... Ps 30:12
A **p** of David to remember. .... Ps 37:40
For Jeduthun. A **p** of David. .... Ps 38:22
director of music. A **p** of David. .... Ps 39:13
director of music. A **p** of David. .... Ps 40:17
A **p** of the sons of Korah. .... Ps 45:17
A **p** of the sons of Korah. .... Ps 46:11
A **p** of the sons of Korah. .... Ps 47:9
A **p** of the sons of Korah. .... Ps 48:14
animals that die. A **p** of Asaph. .... Ps 49:20
A **p** of David when the prophet .... Ps 50:23
For Jeduthun. A **p** of David. .... Ps 61:8
A **p** of David when he was in the .... Ps 62:12
director of music. A **p** of David. .... Ps 63:11

of music. A **p** of David. A song. .... Ps 64:10
director of music. A song. A **p.** .... Ps 65:13
instruments. A **p.** A song. .... Ps 66:20
of music. A **p** of David. A song. .... Ps 67:7
tune of "Lilies." A **p** of David. .... Ps 68:35
of music. A **p** of David. To help .... Ps 69:36
son of Jesse. A **p** of Asaph. .... Ps 72:20
Not Destroy." A **p** of Asaph. A .... Ps 74:23
instruments. A **p** of Asaph. A .... Ps 75:10
For Jeduthun. A **p** of Asaph. .... Ps 76:12
skillful hands. A **p** of Asaph. .... Ps 78:72
of the Agreement." A **p** of Asaph. .... Ps 79:13
By the gittith. A **p** of Asaph. .... Ps 80:19
from the rocks." A **p** of Asaph. .... Ps 81:16
nations. A song. A **p** of Asaph. .... Ps 82:8
A **p** of the sons of Korah. .... Ps 83:18
A **p** of the sons of Korah. .... Ps 84:12
A **p** of the sons of Korah. .... Ps 86:17
A **p** of the sons of Korah. .... Ps 87:7
how I can save." A **p.** A song for .... Ps 91:16
Praise his holy name. A **p.** .... Ps 97:12
our God is holy. A **p** of thanks. .... Ps 99:9
goes on and on. A **p** of David. .... Ps 100:5
the LORD. A song. A **p** of David. .... Ps 107:43
director of music. A **p** of David. .... Ps 108:13
who accuse them. A **p** of David. .... Ps 109:31
A **p** for going up to worship. .... Ps 119:176
against the rocks. A **p** of David. .... Ps 137:9
director of music. A **p** of David. .... Ps 138:8
director of music. A **p** of David. .... Ps 139:24
in his presence. A **p** of David. .... Ps 140:13
taken care of me. A **p** of David. .... Ps 142:7
God is the LORD. A **p** of praise. .... Ps 144:15
read about this also in **P** 2: ' .... Ac 13:33

PSALMS
In the book of **P**, David himself .... Lk 20:42
of the prophets, and the **P**." .... Lk 24:44
"In the Book of **P**," Peter said, ... Ac 1:20
Speak to each other with **p,** .... Eph 5:19
each other by singing **p,** .... Col 3:16

PTOLEMAIS
trip from Tyre and arrived at **P**, ... Ac 21:7
next day we left **P** and went to .... Ac 21:8

PUAH
sons were Tola, **P**, Jashub, and .... Ge 46:13
named Shiphrah and **P**, helped the .... Ex 1:15
P came the Puite family group; .... Nu 26:23
was Tola son of **P**, the son of .... Jdg 10:1
Tola, **P**, Jashub, and Shimron. 1Ch 7:1

PUBLIC
night in the city's **p** square." .... Ge 19:2
They came to the **p** square of the .... Jdg 19:15
traveler in the **p** square and .... Jdg 19:17
the night in the **p** square." .... Jdg 19:20
Jonathan in the **p** square of Beth 2Sa 21:12
gate and sit in the **p** square. .... Job 29:7
stand up in **p** and cry for help. .... Job 30:28
praise you in the **p** meeting. .... Ps 22:22
They make fun of me in **p** places, ... Ps 69:12
be praised in **p** for what she has .... Pr 31:31
the roofs and in the **p** squares, ... Is 15:3
the **p** squares of the city. .... Je 5:1
in Moab and in every **p** square. .... Je 48:38
Oh, no!' in the **p** places. They .... Am 5:16
not want to disgrace her in **p,** .... Mt 1:19
beat us in **p** without a trial .... Ac 16:37
you in **p** and in your homes. .... Ac 20:20
praise you in the **p** meeting." .... Heb 2:12

PUBLIUS
fields around there owned by **P**, ... Ac 28:7
P' father was sick with a fever .... Ac 28:8

PUDENS
Also **P**, Linus, Claudia, and all 2Ti 4:21

PUFF
thoughts are just a **p** of wind. .... Ps 94:11
just a **p** of wind will take them .... Is 57:13
thoughts are just a **p** of wind." 1Co 3:20

PUFFS
Knowledge **p** you up with pride, ... 1Co 8:1

PUITE
Puah came the **P** family group; .... Nu 26:23

PUL
P king of Assyria came to attack 2Ki 15:19
of silver so **P** would support him 2Ki 15:19
of Israel made **P** king of Assyria 1Ch 5:26
P was also called Tiglath-Pileser. 1Ch 5:26

PULL
I'll **p** out my sword, and my hand .... Ex 15:9
to the altar and **p** off its head, ... Le 1:15
He will **p** the bird's head from .... Le 5:8
he will not **p** it completely off. .... Le 5:8
and I will **p** out my sword and .... Le 26:33
P down your father's altar to .... Jdg 6:25
return and **p** down this tower. .... Jdg 8:9
P out your sword and kill me. 1Sa 31:4
him and tried to **p** him up from 2Sa 12:17
to that city and **p** it into the 2Sa 17:13
The LORD will **p** up Israel from 1Ki 14:15
Gehazi came near to **p** her away, ... 2Ki 4:27
P out your sword and stab me. 1Ch 10:4
They will **p** the arrows out of .... Job 20:25
their backs and **p** the points out .... Job 20:25
P me from the mud, and do not .... Ps 69:14
So why did you **p** down our walls? .... Ps 80:12
plant and a time to **p** up plants. .... Ec 3:2
They **p** their guilt and sins .... Is 5:18
them as people **p** wagons with .... Is 5:18
You will **p** up and tear down, ... Je 1:10
I will **p** them up and throw them .... Je 12:14
And I will **p** up the people of .... Je 12:14
But after I **p** them up, I will .... Je 12:15
I will **p** it up completely and .... Je 12:17
will **p** your skirts up over your .... Je 13:26
that I will **p** up by its roots .... Je 18:7
I will **p** down to destroy it. .... Je 18:7
hand, I would still **p** you off. .... Je 22:24
I will not **p** them up, but I will .... Je 24:6
to **p** them up and tear them down, ... Je 31:28
will plant you and not **p** you up, ... Je 42:10
and I will **p** up what I have .... Je 45:4
first eagle will **p** up the vine's .... Eze 17:9
or many people to **p** the vine up .... Eze 17:9
I will **p** my sword out of its .... Eze 21:3
of Tyre and **p** down her towers. .... Eze 26:4
They will **p** out their swords and .... Eze 28:7
I will **p** you up out of your .... Eze 29:4
They will **p** out their swords .... Eze 30:11
of people to **p** you up in my net .... Eze 32:3
over the land and **p** down your .... Am 3:11
I will **p** them up from there. .... Am 9:2
I will **p** your dress up over your .... Nah 3:5
will shrink and **p** away from the .... Mt 9:16
you want us to **p** up the weeds?' .... Mt 13:28
because when you **p** up the weeds, ... Mt 13:29
you might also **p** up the wheat. .... Mt 13:29
patch will shrink and **p** away— .... Mk 2:21
new patch will **p** away from the .... Mk 2:21
will you not **p** him out quickly?" .... Lk 14:5
they could not **p** the net back .... Jn 21:6

PULLED
p him back inside the house, ... Ge 19:10
they **p** off his robe with long .... Ge 37:23

P

But he **p** his hand back in, ... Ge 38:29
because she had **p** him out of the .... Ex 2:10
He has **p** down the altar of Baal .... Jdg 6:30
his altar that has been **p** down." .... Jdg 6:31
because Gideon **p** down Baal's .... Jdg 6:32
He also **p** down the tower of .... Jdg 8:17
Samson woke up and **p** out the pin .... Jdg 16:14
he **p** me from the deep water. 2Sa 22:17
and Jehu **p** him into the chariot. 2Ki 10:15
beam is to be **p** from his house .... Ezr 6:11
p hair from my head and beard, ... Ezr 9:3
of them, and **p** out their hair. .... Ne 13:25
ropes of their tents are **p** up, ... Job 4:21
grapes are **p** off before they .... Job 15:33
wronged me and **p** his net around .... Job 19:6
my heart was **p** away from God. .... Job 31:27
he **p** me from the deep water. .... Ps 18:16
will be **p** down and will speak .... Is 29:4
and the towers are **p** down. .... Is 30:25
her in place will never be **p** up, ... Is 33:20
home has been **p** down and taken .... Is 38:12
cheeks to those who **p** my beard. .... Is 50:6
You have **p** back the covers and .... Is 57:8
The men **p** Jeremiah up with the .... Je 38:13
be completely **p** down and her .... Je 51:58
his anger he **p** down the strong .... La 2:2
He **p** off the top branch and .... Eze 17:4
But it was **p** up by its roots in .... Eze 19:12
have **p** my sword out from its .... Eze 21:5
a sword is **p** out of its holder. .... Eze 21:28
The little horn **p** out three of .... Da 7:8
It had **p** out three of the other. .... Da 7:20
worshiped him, was **p** down. .... Da 8:11
the Temple being **p** down, and the .... Da 8:13
kingdom will be **p** up and given .... Da 11:4
a burning stick **p** from a fire, ... Am 4:11
and they will not be **p** out again .... Am 9:15
burning stick **p** from the fire." .... Zch 3:2
Red horses **p** the first chariot. .... Zch 6:2
horses **p** the second chariot. .... Zch 6:2
horses **p** the third chariot, ... Zch 6:3
horses **p** the fourth chariot. .... Zch 6:3
chariot **p** by the black horses .... Zch 6:6
as the weeds are **p** up and burned .... Mt 13:40
the fishermen **p** the net to the................ Mt 13:48
will be **p** up by the roots. .... Mt 15:13
for his sword and **p** it out. .... Mt 26:51
standing nearby **p** out his sword.............. Mk 14:47
p it out and struck the servant .... Jn 18:10
into the boat and **p** the net to .... Jn 21:11
So they **p** up the anchor, ... Ac 27:13
are **p** away from him by their 1Ti 5:11
fruit that are **p** out of the .... Jud 1:12

PULLING
as if you were **p** them out of a 1Ki 8:51

PUNCH
doorframe and **p** a hole through.............. Ex 21:6

PUNISH
I will **p** the world for its evil .... Is 13:11
time the LORD will **p** Leviathan, ... Is 27:1
Shouldn't I **p** the people of .... Je 5:9
do and will **p** them for their .... Je 14:10
I will **p** her for all the times .... Hos 2:13

PUNISHED
He has not **p** us as our sins..................... Ps 103:10
them back to Jerusalem to be **p**.............. Ac 22:5
I often **p** them and tried to make .... Ac 26:11

PUNISHMENT
This **p** is more than I can stand! .... Ge 4:13
person to be put to death as **p**, ... Ex 23:7
When terrible **p** passes by, ... Is 28:15

I will change your **p** into peace, ... Is 60:17
like this the **p** it deserves?"................... Je 9:9
give them the **p** they deserve. .... Je 11:20
brought your time of **p** near; .... Eze 22:4
The time of **p** has come, the time .... Hos 9:7
off the day of **p**, but you bring .... Am 6:3
So you will have a worse **p**. .... Mt 23:14
they should have a much worse **p**. .... Heb 10:29
That **p** is especially for those 2Pe 2:10

PUNISHMENTS
will choose their **p**, and I will .... Is 66:4
my four terrible **p** against it—................. Eze 14:21

PUNON
left Zalmonah and camped at **P**. .... Nu 33:42
They left **P** and camped at Oboth. .... Nu 33:43

PUR
P (that is, the lot) was thrown................. Est 3:7
had thrown the **P** (that is, the .... Est 9:24
which comes from the word "**P**".............. Est 9:26

PURAH
take your servant **P** with you. .... Jdg 7:10
and his servant **P** went down to .... Jdg 7:11

PURE
Ark inside and out with **p** gold, ... Ex 25:11
make a lid of **p** gold for the Ark .... Ex 25:17
Cover it with **p** gold, and put a .... Ex 25:24
jars and cups, out of **p** gold. .... Ex 25:29
Hammer **p** gold to make a .... Ex 25:31
piece, hammered out of **p** gold. .... Ex 25:36
trays must be made of **p** gold.................. Ex 25:38
pounds of **p** gold to make .... Ex 25:39
Israel to bring you **p** olive oil,................. Ex 27:20
two chains of **p** gold, twisted .... Ex 28:14
Make chains of **p** gold, twisted .... Ex 28:22
Make a strip of **p** gold and carve .... Ex 28:36
and its corners with **p** gold, ... Ex 30:3
galbanum, and **p** frankincense. .... Ex 30:34
to it to keep it **p** and holy. .... Ex 30:35
the **p** gold lampstand and .... Ex 31:8
and out, with **p** gold, and he put.............. Ex 37:2
he made a lid of **p** gold that was.............. Ex 37:6
covered it with **p** gold and put .... Ex 37:11
He made of **p** gold all the things.............. Ex 37:16
he made the lampstand of **p** gold, ... Ex 37:17
were all one piece of **p**, ... Ex 37:22
He made seven **p** gold lamps for .... Ex 37:23
and he made **p** gold wick trimmers .... Ex 37:23
pounds of **p** gold to make .... Ex 37:24
and the corners with **p** gold, ... Ex 37:26
the priests and the **p**, ... Ex 37:29
They made chains of **p** gold, ... Ex 39:15
made bells of **p** gold and hung .... Ex 39:25
They made a strip of **p** gold, ... Ex 39:30
the **p** gold lampstand with its .... Ex 39:37
of the altar, to make it **p**....................... Le 8:15
to bring you **p** oil from crushed .... Le 24:2
the lampstands of **p** gold before .... Le 24:4
Put **p** incense on each row as the .... Le 24:7
if she is not **p** and if she has .... Nu 5:27
woman has not sinned, she is **p**.............. Nu 5:28
Make the Levites **p**, and present .... Nu 8:15
their sins so they would be **p**. .... Nu 8:21
your God with joy and a **p** heart, ... Dt 28:47
You are **p** to those who are pure, ... 2Sa 22:27
You are pure to those who are **p**, ... 2Sa 22:27
the LORD's words are **p**......................... 2Sa 22:31
gallons of **p** olive oil every 1Ki 5:11
covered this room with **p** gold, ... 1Ki 6:20
of the Temple with **p** gold, ... 1Ki 6:21
the lampstands of **p** gold (five 1Ki 7:49
the **p** gold bowls, wick trimmers, ... 1Ki 7:50

of Lebanon, were made of **p** gold. 1Ki 10:21
made of **p** gold or silver. 2Ki 25:15
they made all the holy things **p**. 1Ch 23:28
told how much **p** gold should be 1Ch 28:17
and how much **p** gold should be 1Ch 28:18
pounds of **p** gold from Ophir 1Ch 29:4
thousand pounds of **p** silver. 1Ch 29:4
inside of the porch with **p** gold. 2Ch 3:4
and covered them with **p** gold. 2Ch 3:5
thousand pounds of **p** gold...................... 2Ch 3:8
and their lamps of **p** gold, ... 2Ch 4:20
lamps, and tongs of **p** gold;................... 2Ch 4:21
the **p** gold wick trimmers, small 2Ch 4:22
and covered it with **p** gold. 2Ch 9:17
of Lebanon, were made of **p** gold. 2Ch 9:20
Judah and the Temple **p** again. 2Ch 34:8
and Levites made themselves **p**, ... Ne 12:30
and the wall of Jerusalem **p**. .... Ne 12:30
of their God in making things **p**............... Ne 12:45
Can a person be **p** before his .... Job 4:17
can anyone be **p**? How can someone .... Job 15:14
heavens are not **p** in his eyes. .... Job 15:15
How much less **p** is one who is .... Job 15:16
cruel, and my prayer is **p**. .... Job 16:17
no one born to a woman can be **p**. .... Job 25:4
the stars are not **p** in his eyes. .... Job 25:5
and places where gold is made **p**. .... Job 28:1
in gold or said to **p** gold, ' .... Job 31:24
said, 'I am **p** and without sin .... Job 33:9
LORD's words are **p**, like silver .... Ps 12:6
You are **p** to those who are pure, ... Ps 18:26
You are pure to those who are **p**, ... Ps 18:26
The LORD's words are **p**. .... Ps 18:30
The commands of the LORD are **p**; .... Ps 19:8
Then I can be **p** and innocent of.............. Ps 19:13
with clean hands and **p** hearts, ... Ps 24:4
Create in me a **p** heart, God, and .... Ps 51:10
to those who have **p** hearts. .... Ps 73:1
So why have I kept my heart **p?** .... Ps 73:13
are those who live **p** lives, ... Ps 119:1
a young person live a **p** life? .... Ps 119:9
a good person are like **p** silver, ... Pr 10:20
Whoever loves **p** thoughts and .... Pr 22:11
Some people think they are **p**, ... Pr 30:12
I am not **p**, and I live among .... Is 6:5
live among people who are not **p**, ... Is 6:5
be harder to find than **p** gold;................. Is 13:12
I have made you **p**, but not by .... Is 48:10
by fire, as silver is made **p**. .... Is 48:10
and who are not **p** will not enter .... Is 52:1
there and make yourselves **p**.................... Is 52:11
holy and **p** to go to worship .... Is 66:17
The **p** metal does not come out; .... Je 6:29
was made of **p** gold or silver. .... Je 52:19
how the **p** gold has dulled! .... La 4:1
make the altar **p** and ready for .... Eze 43:20
make the altar **p** and ready for .... Eze 43:22
making the altar **p** and ready,................ Eze 43:23
make the altar **p** and ready for .... Eze 43:26
make the Temple **p** and ready for .... Eze 45:18
make the Temple **p** and ready for .... Eze 45:20
the statue was made of **p** gold. .... Da 2:32
be made clean, **p**, and spotless, ... Da 12:10
of all nations **p** speech so that .... Zph 3:9
and make them **p** like gold and .... Mal 3:3
blessed whose thoughts are **p**, ... Mt 5:8
perfume, made of **p** nard. .... Mk 14:3
Moses taught about being made **p**,........... Lk 2:22
things to make themselves **p**. .... Jn 11:55
perfume made from **p** nard. .... Jn 12:3
he made their hearts **p**. .... Ac 15:9
servants of God by our **p** lives, ... 2Co 6:6
so we should make ourselves **p**— 2Co 7:1

want to give you as his **p** bride. 2Co 11:2
from your true and **p** following 2Co 11:3
not being **p**, taking part .... Gal 5:19
church could be **p** and without .... Eph 5:27
that you will be **p** and without .... Php 1:10
and right and **p** and beautiful .... Php 4:8
peace, make you **p**, belonging.................. 1Th 5:23
comes from a **p** heart and a good 1Ti 1:5
your faith, and your **p** life. 1Ti 4:12
Always treat them in a **p** way.................. 1Ti 5:2
sins of others. Keep yourself **p**. 1Ti 5:22
trust in the Lord from **p** hearts. 2Ti 2:22
those who are **p**, all things are .... Tit 1:15
all things are **p**, but to those .... Tit 1:15
do not believe, nothing is **p**. .... Tit 1:15
to be wise and **p**, to be good .... Tit 2:5
and to make us **p** people who .... Tit 2:14
holy, sinless, **p**, not influenced .... Heb 7:26
our consciences **p** from useless .... Heb 9:14
have been washed with **p** water............... Heb 10:22
should keep their marriage **p**................... Heb 13:4
God accepts as **p** and without................. Jam 1:27
from God is first of all **p**,...................... Jam 3:17
same time, make your thinking **p**. .... Jam 4:8
to prove that your faith is **p**. 1Pe 1:7
be proved to be **p** by fire but 1Pe 1:7
was like a **p** and perfect lamb. 1Pe 1:19
should want the **p** and simple 1Pe 2:2
will see the **p** lives you live 1Pe 3:2
Christ is **p**, and all who have 1Jn 3:3
keep themselves **p** like Christ. 1Jn 3:3
me gold made **p** in fire so you .... Rev 3:18
because they kept themselves **p**............... Rev 14:4
and the city was made of **p** gold, ... Rev 21:18
of pure gold, as **p** as glass. .... Rev 21:18
was made of **p** gold as clear as .... Rev 21:21

PURER
Our princes were **p** than snow, ... La 4:7
made stronger and **p** and without .... Da 11:35

PUREST
be bought with the **p** gold. .... Job 28:19
more than gold, even the **p** gold. .... Ps 19:10
commands more than the **p** gold. .... Ps 119:127
gold, better than the **p** silver. .... Pr 8:19

PURIFIED
Bathsheba had **p** herself from her 2Sa 11:4
We have **p** the entire Temple of 2Ch 29:18
I ordered the rooms to be **p**, ... Ne 13:9
So I **p** them of everything that .... Ne 13:30
pure, like silver **p** by fire, ... Ps 12:6
like silver **p** seven times over. .... Ps 12:6
you have **p** us like silver........................ Ps 66:10
the scum left when silver is **p**; .... Is 1:22
I have **p** you by giving you .... Is 48:10
in the furnace when silver is **p**. .... Eze 22:18
to the truth has **p** your souls, ... 1Pe 1:22

PURIFIES
someone who heats and **p** silver, ... Mal 3:3

PURIFY
But also **p** those things with the .... Nu 31:23
the Temple of the LORD to **p** it. 2Ch 29:15
the Temple of the LORD to **p** it, ... 2Ch 29:16
the Levites to **p** themselves and .... Ne 13:22
he will **p** the Levites and make .... Mal 3:3

PURIFYING
test with fire, **p** them like .... Zch 13:9
will be like a **p** fire and like .... Mal 3:2

PURIM
So these days were called **P**, ... Est 9:26
These days of **P** should always be .... Est 9:28

P

this second letter about **P**. .... Est 9:29
up these days of **P** at the chosen.............. Est 9:31
letter set up the rules for **P**,.................... Est 9:32

PURITY

This **p** of faith is worth more 1Pe 1:7
But the **p** of your faith will 1Pe 1:7

PURPLE

blue, **p**, and red thread; .... Ex 25:4
and blue, **p**, and red thread.................... Ex 26:1
and blue, **p**, and red thread.................... Ex 26:31
and blue, **p**, and red thread.................... Ex 26:36
with blue, **p**, and red thread .... Ex 27:16
gold and blue, **p** and red thread,.............. Ex 28:5
gold and blue, **p** and red thread,.............. Ex 28:6
gold and blue, **p** and red thread,.............. Ex 28:8
gold and blue, **p** and red thread,.............. Ex 28:15
of blue, **p**, and red thread, ... Ex 28:33
blue, **p** and red thread, and fine .... Ex 35:6
who had blue, **p**, and red thread, ... Ex 35:23
make the blue, **p**, and red thread .... Ex 35:25
the blue, **p**, and red thread................... Ex 35:35
of blue, **p**, and red cloth, ... Ex 36:8
of blue, **p**, and red thread .... Ex 36:35
of blue, **p**, and red thread .... Ex 36:37
made of blue, **p**, and red thread .... Ex 38:18
the blue, **p**, and red thread .... Ex 38:23
used blue, **p**, and red thread .... Ex 39:1
and blue, **p**, and red thread.................... Ex 39:2
the blue, **p**, and red thread,................... Ex 39:3
and blue, **p**, and red thread................... Ex 39:5
and blue, **p**, and red thread................... Ex 39:8
of blue, **p**, and red thread, ... Ex 39:24
and blue, **p**, and red thread.................... Ex 39:29
and spread a **p** cloth over it. .... Nu 4:13
and **p** robes worn by the kings of .... Jdg 8:26
iron, and with **p**, red, and blue 2Ch 2:7
wood, and with **p**, blue, and red 2Ch 2:14
of blue, **p**, and red thread 2Ch 3:14
curtains and **p** drapes that were .... Est 1:6
pillars by white and **p** cords. .... Est 1:6
He also had a **p** robe made of the .... Est 8:15
covered with **p** cloth that the .... Sng 3:10
and your hair is like **p** cloth; .... Sng 7:5
They put blue and **p** clothes on .... Je 10:9
deck were blue and **p** and came .... Eze 27:7
for turquoise, **p** cloth, cloth................... Eze 27:16
will receive **p** clothes fit for .... Da 5:7
will give you **p** clothes fit for .... Da 5:16
be dressed in **p** clothes and to .... Da 5:29
They put a **p** robe on Jesus and .... Mk 15:17
took off the **p** robe and put his .... Mk 15:20
and put a **p** robe around him. .... Jn 19:2
crown of thorns and the **p** robe. .... Jn 19:5
whose job was selling **p** cloth. .... Ac 16:14
was dressed in **p** and red and was .... Rev 17:4
fine linen, **p** cloth, silk, red .... Rev 18:12
in fine linen, **p** and red cloth, ... Rev 18:16

PURPOSE

and murders another person on **p**, ... Ex 21:14
only for its very special **p**. .... Ex 30:36
out of Egypt for an evil **p**. .... Ex 32:12
is given for the **p** of being .... Le 27:29
anyone who sins on **p** is against.............. Nu 15:30
him beforehand or kill him on **p**. .... Jos 20:5
that makes my **p** unclear by .... Job 38:2
that made my **p** unclear by saying .... Job 42:3
body and one spirit for his **p**— .... Mal 2:15
kind of thinking and the same **p**. 1Co 1:10
one who waters have the same **p**, ... 1Co 3:8
The **p** of all these things should 1Co 14:26
but only if their **p** is good. .... Gal 4:18
let us know his secret **p**. .... Eph 1:9

His **p** was to make the two groups .... Eph 2:15
also Christ's **p** to end the .... Eph 2:16
p was that through the church .... Eph 3:10
agrees with the **p** God had since.............. Eph 3:11
are standing strong with one **p**, ... Php 1:27
love, and having one mind and **p**. .... Php 2:2
The **p** of this command is for 1Ti 1:5
because of God's **p** and grace. 2Ti 1:9
know the Lord's **p** for him in the .... Jam 5:11
The Son of God came for this **p**:.............. 1Jn 3:8
of these kings have the same **p**, ... Rev 17:13
carry out his **p** by agreeing to................ Rev 17:17

PURPOSES

known the secret **p** of people's 1Co 4:5
things are used for special **p**, ... 2Ti 2:20
evil will be used for special **p**............... 2Ti 2:21
clearly that his **p** never change, ... Heb 6:17

PURSE

put it into a **p** full of holes." .... Hag 1:6
Don't carry a **p**, a bag, or .... Lk 10:4
When I sent you out without a **p**, ... Lk 22:35
now if you have a **p** or a bag, ... Lk 22:36

PURSES

robes, capes, shawls, and **p**, ... Is 3:22
for yourselves **p** that will not .... Lk 12:33

PUSH

let the army of Ai **p** them back. .... Jos 8:15
The LORD will **p** them out ahead .... Jos 23:5
but you would **p** me into a dirty .... Job 9:31
p needy people off the path; .... Job 24:4
Do not **p** me away or leave me .... Ps 27:9
You let our enemies **p** us back, ... Ps 44:10
will **p** you away from me just as.............. Je 7:15
You **p** with your side and with .... Eze 34:21
and asked him to **p** off a little................ Lk 5:3

PUSHED

Then he **p** as hard as he could, ... Jdg 16:30
So Joab **p** the sword into Amasa's 2Sa 20:10
These rooms were **p** against the.............. 1Ki 6:6
your help we **p** back our enemies .... Ps 44:5
We have been **p** down into the .... Ps 44:25
from me just as I **p** away your .... Je 7:15
because the LORD **p** them down. .... Je 46:15
Then he **p** her back into the .... Zch 5:8
Jesus and **p** very close around .... Mk 5:24
hurting the other **p** Moses away .... Ac 7:27
and it is **p** by strong winds..................... Jam 3:4

PUSHING

They started **p** him back and .... Ge 19:9
all the sick were **p** toward him .... Mk 3:10
many people are **p** against you! .... Mk 5:31
you and are **p** against you." .... Lk 8:45

PUT

God **p** all these in the sky to .... Ge 1:17
p the man he had formed into it. .... Ge 2:8
God **p** the tree that gives life .... Ge 2:9
The LORD God **p** the man in the .... Ge 2:15
this, a curse will be **p** on you. .... Ge 3:14
So I will **p** a curse on the .... Ge 3:17
Then the LORD **p** a mark on Cain .... Ge 4:15
P a door in the side of the boat. .... Ge 6:16
Cush, Mizraim, **P**, and Canaan. .... Ge 10:6
Hagar **p** her son under a bush. .... Ge 21:15
Abraham also **p** seven female................. Ge 21:28
Why did you **p** these seven female .... Ge 21:29
P your hand under my leg. .... Ge 24:2
So the servant **p** his hand under.............. Ge 24:9
'Please **p** your jar down so I can.............. Ge 24:14
' Then I **p** the ring in her nose .... Ge 24:47
or his wife will be **p** to death." .... Ge 26:11

in the house and **p** them on the	Ge 27:15
the goats and **p** them on Jacob's	Ge 27:16
Then they would **p** the stone back	Ge 29:3
p the branches in front of the	Ge 30:38
p the branches before their	Ge 30:41
Jacob did not **p** the branches	Ge 30:42
So Jacob **p** his children and his	Ge 31:17
P it in front of your relatives	Ge 31:37
rocks that I have **p** between us	Ge 31:51
hip and **p** it out of joint.	Ge 32:25
Jacob **p** the slave girls with	Ge 33:2
meet Jacob and **p** his arms around	Ge 33:4
P away the foreign gods you	Ge 35:2
his clothes and **p** on rough cloth	Ge 37:34
her face and **p** on the clothes	Ge 38:19
birth, one baby **p** his hand out.	Ge 38:28
He **p** Joseph in charge of the	Ge 39:4
When Joseph was **p** in charge of	Ge 39:5
He has **p** me in charge of	Ge 39:8
Joseph and **p** him into the prison	Ge 39:20
the king's prisoners were **p**.	Ge 39:20
he **p** them in the prison of the	Ge 40:3
of the guard **p** the two prisoners	Ge 40:4
to deserve being **p** in prison."	Ge 40:15
once again he **p** the king's cup	Ge 40:21
and you **p** us in prison in the	Ge 41:10
and he shaved, **p** on clean	Ge 41:14
I will **p** you in charge of my	Ge 41:40
have **p** you in charge of all the	Ge 41:41
and he **p** it on Joseph's finger.	Ge 41:42
and he **p** a gold chain around	Ge 41:42
the king **p** Joseph in charge of	Ge 41:43
Then Joseph **p** them all in prison	Ge 42:17
with grain and to **p** the money	Ge 42:25
So the brothers **p** the grain on	Ge 42:26
for the grain has been **p** back.	Ge 42:28
You may **p** my two sons to death	Ge 42:37
money that was **p** in our sacks	Ge 43:18
don't know who **p** that money in	Ge 43:22
must have **p** the money in your	Ge 43:23
and **p** each man's money into his	Ge 44:1
P my silver cup in the sack of	Ge 44:2
Then they **p** their sacks back on	Ge 44:13
p them in charge of my sheep and	Ge 47:6
you love me, **p** your hand under	Ge 47:29
the boys and **p** his arms around	Ge 48:10
He **p** Ephraim on his right side	Ge 48:13
his arms and **p** his right hand	Ge 48:14
p his left hand on the head of	Ge 48:14
that his father **p** his right hand	Ge 48:17
P your right hand on his head."	Ge 48:18
he will **p** his back to the load	Ge 49:15
He **p** his feet back on the bed,	Ge 49:33
and then they **p** him in a coffin	Ge 50:26
They **p** slave masters over them,	Ex 1:11
She **p** the baby in the basket.	Ex 2:3
Then she **p** the basket among the	Ex 2:3
You should **p** those gifts on your	Ex 3:22
"**P** your hand inside your coat."	Ex 4:6
So Moses **p** his hand inside his	Ex 4:6
Now **p** your hand inside your coat	Ex 4:7
So Moses **p** his hand inside his	Ex 4:7
and his sons, **p** them on a donkey	Ex 4:20
The Egyptians **p** them in piles,	Ex 8:14
the blood and **p** it on the sides	Ex 12:7
p the jar of manna in front of	Ex 16:34
but when Moses **p** his hands down,	Ex 17:11
men **p** a large rock under him,	Ex 17:12
the mountain must be **p** to death	Ex 19:12
kills him must be **p** to death.	Ex 21:12
on purpose, **p** him to death, even	Ex 21:14
his mother must be **p** to death.	Ex 21:15
he is caught must be **p** to death.	Ex 21:16
or mother must be **p** to death	Ex 21:17
owner must also be **p** to death.	Ex 21:29
P to death any woman who does	Ex 22:18
P to death anyone who has sexual	Ex 22:19
honest person to be **p** to death	Ex 23:7
Moses **p** half of the blood of	Ex 24:6
jewels to be **p** on the holy vest	Ex 25:7
p a gold strip all around it.	Ex 25:11
P the poles through the rings on	Ex 25:14
Then **p** in the Ark the Agreement	Ex 25:16
p one on each end of the lid.	Ex 25:18
P this lid on top of the Ark,	Ex 25:21
and **p** in the Ark the Agreement	Ex 25:21
and **p** a gold strip around it.	Ex 25:24
and **p** a gold strip around it.	Ex 25:25
P the rings close to the frame	Ex 25:27
On this table **p** the bread that	Ex 25:30
P a bud under each pair of	Ex 25:35
small oil lamps and **p** them on	Ex 25:37
bronze hooks and **p** them in the	Ex 26:11
and **p** the Ark of the Agreement	Ex 26:33
P the lid on the Ark of the	Ex 26:34
p the table on the north side of	Ex 26:35
P the lampstand on the south	Ex 26:35
and **p** a bronze ring at each of	Ex 27:4
P the screen inside the altar,	Ex 27:5
P the poles through the rings on	Ex 27:7
P gold around the stones to hold	Ex 28:11
Then **p** the two stones on the two	Ex 28:12
P four rows of beautiful gems on	Ex 28:17
P gold around these jewels to	Ex 28:20
gold rings and **p** them on the two	Ex 28:23
gold rings and **p** them at the two	Ex 28:26
P them close to the seam above	Ex 28:27
p the Urim and Thummim inside	Ex 28:30
p it on the front of the turban.	Ex 28:37
P these clothes on your brother	Ex 28:41
P these in one basket, and bring	Ex 29:3
Then **p** on him the holy vest and	Ex 29:5
P the turban on his head, and	Ex 29:6
p the holy crown on the turban.	Ex 29:6
his sons and **p** the inner robes	Ex 29:8
P the headbands on their heads,	Ex 29:9
and his sons must **p** their hands	Ex 29:10
your finger to **p** some of the	Ex 29:12
and his sons **p** their hands on	Ex 29:15
and his sons **p** their hands on	Ex 29:19
P the blood on the bottom of the	Ex 29:20
which you **p** before the LORD.	Ex 29:23
P all of these in the hands of	Ex 29:24
p a gold strip all around the	Ex 30:3
P the altar of incense in front	Ex 30:6
P the bowl and stand between the	Ex 30:18
the altar, and **p** water in the	Ex 30:18
special oil must be **p** on people	Ex 30:25
P this oil on the Meeting Tent	Ex 30:26
p the oil on the altar for burnt	Ex 30:28
P the oil on Aaron and his sons	Ex 30:30
It is to be **p** on people and	Ex 30:31
and **p** it in front of the Ark of	Ex 30:36
cut jewels and **p** them in metal,	Ex 31:5
that person must be **p** to death;	Ex 31:14
Sabbath day must be **p** to death.	Ex 31:15
'Every man must **p** on his sword	Ex 32:27
and none of them **p** on jewelry.	Ex 33:4
I will **p** you in a large crack in	Ex 33:22
he **p** a covering over his face.	Ex 34:33
on that day must be **p** to death.	Ex 35:2
jewels to be **p** on the holy vest	Ex 35:9
other jewels to **p** on the holy	Ex 35:27
and jewels and **p** them in metal,	Ex 35:33
of goat hair, to **p** over the Holy	Ex 36:14
and he **p** a gold strip around it.	Ex 37:2

He **p** the poles through the rings .... Ex 37:5
pure gold and **p** a gold strip .... Ex 37:11
and he **p** a gold strip around it. .... Ex 37:12
The rings were **p** close to the .... Ex 37:14
he **p** gold trim around the altar. .... Ex 37:26
two gold rings and **p** them below .... Ex 37:27
the altar and **p** it inside the.................... Ex 38:4
he **p** them at the four corners .... Ex 38:5
He **p** the poles through the rings .... Ex 38:7
They **p** gold around the onyx .... Ex 39:6
Then they **p** four rows of it. .... Ex 39:10
Gold was **p** around these jewels .... Ex 39:13
They **p** the two gold rings on the .... Ex 39:16
Then they **p** two gold chains in .... Ex 39:17
gold rings and **p** them at the .... Ex 39:19
P the Ark of the Agreement in it .... Ex 40:3
P the gold altar for burning .... Ex 40:5
p the curtain at the entrance .... Ex 40:5
P the altar of burnt offerings .... Ex 40:6
P the bowl between the Meeting............. Ex 40:7
the altar, and **p** water in it. .... Ex 40:7
and **p** the curtain at the entry .... Ex 40:8
p the holy clothes on Aaron. .... Ex 40:13
sons and **p** the inner robes .... Ex 40:14
the Holy Tent, he **p** the bases in .... Ex 40:18
he **p** the frames on the bases. .... Ex 40:18
Next he **p** the crossbars through............. Ex 40:18
Holy Tent and **p** the covering .... Ex 40:19
Moses **p** the stone tablets that .... Ex 40:20
He **p** the poles through the rings .... Ex 40:20
of the Ark and **p** the lid on it. .... Ex 40:20
Moses **p** the table in the Meeting .... Ex 40:22
Then he **p** the bread on the table .... Ex 40:23
Moses **p** the lampstand in the .... Ex 40:24
Then he **p** the lamps on the .... Ex 40:25
Moses **p** the gold altar for .... Ex 40:26
He **p** the altar for burnt .... Ex 40:29
Moses **p** the bowl between the .... Ex 40:30
he **p** water in it for washing. .... Ex 40:30
and he **p** up the curtain at the................. Ex 40:33
He must **p** his hand on the .... Le 1:4
when they have **p** wood and fire............. Le 1:7
pour oil on it, **p** incense on it, ... Le 2:1
You must also **p** salt on all your .... Le 2:13
P oil and incense on it; .... Le 2:15
person must **p** his hand on the .... Le 3:2
and **p** his hand on its head. .... Le 3:8
and **p** his hand on its head..................... Le 3:13
of the LORD, **p** his hand on its .... Le 4:4
priest must also **p** some of the .... Le 4:7
of people must **p** their hands .... Le 4:15
Then he must **p** some of the blood .... Le 4:18
The ruler must **p** his hand on the .... Le 4:24
his finger and **p** it on the...................... Le 4:25
He must **p** his hand on the .... Le 4:29
his finger and **p** it on the....................... Le 4:30
He must **p** his hand on the .... Le 4:33
his finger and **p** it on the....................... Le 4:34
He must not **p** oil or incense on .... Le 5:11
The priest must **p** on his linen .... Le 6:10
on the altar and **p** them beside .... Le 6:10
those clothes and **p** on others.................. Le 6:11
The priest must **p** more firewood .... Le 6:12
He **p** the inner robe on Aaron and .... Le 8:7
Then Moses **p** the outer robe on .... Le 8:7
Then Moses **p** the chest covering .... Le 8:8
covering on him and **p** the Urim............... Le 8:8
He also **p** the turban on Aaron's............... Le 8:9
He **p** the strip of gold, the holy .... Le 8:9
Then Moses **p** the special oil on .... Le 8:10
He **p** the inner robes on them, ... Le 8:13
around them, and **p** headbands on .... Le 8:13
and his sons **p** their hands on................. Le 8:14

with his finger **p** some of it on .... Le 8:15
and his sons **p** their hands on................. Le 8:18
and his sons **p** their hands on................. Le 8:22
sheep and **p** some of its blood .... Le 8:23
He **p** some of the blood on the .... Le 8:24
yeast that is **p** before the LORD .... Le 8:26
p these pieces of bread on the .... Le 8:26
these things he **p** in the hands .... Le 8:27
in the blood and **p** it on the...................... Le 9:9
Aaron's sons **p** them on the .... Le 9:20
burning incense, **p** fire in them, ... Le 10:1
But if you **p** water on some seeds .... Le 11:38
and he must **p** that piece of..................... Le 13:50
offering and **p** it on the bottom .... Le 14:14
He will also **p** some of it on the .... Le 14:14
The priest will **p** some oil from .... Le 14:17
He will **p** the rest of the oil .... Le 14:18
and **p** it on the bottom of the .... Le 14:25
The priest will **p** some of this .... Le 14:25
his hand and **p** it on the bottom .... Le 14:28
He will also **p** some of it on the .... Le 14:28
priest must **p** the rest of the .... Le 14:29
Then the owner must **p** new stones .... Le 14:42
and plaster and **p** in new stones .... Le 14:43
plaster have been **p** in a house, ... Le 14:48
must **p** on the holy linen inner .... Le 16:4
must **p** the incense on the fire................. Le 16:13
goat's blood and **p** it on the .... Le 16:18
He will **p** both his hands on the .... Le 16:21
way Aaron will **p** the people's .... Le 16:21
clothes he had **p** on before he................. Le 16:23
holy place and **p** on his regular .... Le 16:24
He must **p** on the holy linen .... Le 16:32
a deaf person or **p** something in.............. Le 19:14
that would **p** your neighbor's .... Le 19:16
they are not to be **p** to death, ... Le 19:20
who died or **p** tattoo marks.................... Le 19:28
or mother must be **p** to death.................. Le 20:9
adultery and must be **p** to death. .... Le 20:10
wife must be **p** to death. .... Le 20:11
both of them must be **p** to death. .... Le 20:12
They must be **p** to death........................ Le 20:13
animal, he must be **p** to death. .... Le 20:15
They must be **p** to death........................ Le 20:16
must be **p** to death. .... Le 20:27
P them in two rows on the golden .... Le 24:6
P pure incense on each row as .... Le 24:7
day Aaron will **p** the bread in.................. Le 24:8
heard him must **p** their hands on .... Le 24:14
the LORD must be **p** to death;.................. Le 24:16
LORD, they must be **p** to death. .... Le 24:16
person must be **p** to death. .... Le 24:17
person must be **p** to death. .... Le 24:21
Don't **p** stone statues in your .... Le 26:1
must not try to **p** another animal .... Le 27:10
back; he must be **p** to death. .... Le 27:29
Instead **p** the Levites in charge .... Nu 1:50
Holy Tent will be **p** to death. .... Nu 1:51
holy things must be **p** to death."............... Nu 3:10
Holy Place was to be **p** to death. .... Nu 3:38
this they must **p** a covering made .... Nu 4:6
over that, and **p** the poles in .... Nu 4:6
They must **p** the plates, pans, ... Nu 4:7
they must **p** a red cloth over .... Nu 4:8
fine leather, and **p** the poles in .... Nu 4:8
leather and **p** all these things .... Nu 4:10
fine leather, and **p** the poles in .... Nu 4:11
fine leather and **p** these things .... Nu 4:12
and **p** them on the bronze altar. .... Nu 4:14
over it and **p** the poles in place .... Nu 4:14
and he will **p** some dirt from the .... Nu 5:17
will then **p** on her the curse .... Nu 5:21
hair will be **p** in the fire that .... Nu 6:18

'P the seven lamps where they .... Nu 8:2
Israelites should **p** their hands .... Nu 8:10
The Levites will **p** their hands .... Nu 8:12
care about me, **p** me to death, ... Nu 11:15
so **p** her outside the camp for .... Nu 12:14
So Miriam was **p** outside of the .... Nu 12:15
If you **p** these people to death .... Nu 14:15
P a blue thread in each one of .... Nu 15:38
So why do you **p** yourselves above .... Nu 16:3
Tomorrow **p** fire and incense in .... Nu 16:7
Will you **p** out the eyes of these .... Nu 16:14
your pan and **p** incense in it; .... Nu 16:17
his pan and **p** burning incense .... Nu 16:18
flat sheets to **p** on the altar, ... Nu 16:39
and **p** fire from the altar and .... Nu 16:46
P them in the Meeting Tent in .... Nu 17:4
Moses took **p** before the Lᴏʀᴅ in .... Nu 17:7
P Aaron's walking stick back in .... Nu 17:10
Holy Place will be **p** to death." .... Nu 18:7
the priest must **p** some of its .... Nu 19:4
the cow and **p** them in a clean .... Nu 19:9
clothes and **p** them on his son .... Nu 20:26
clothes and **p** them on Aaron's .... Nu 20:28
snake, and **p** it on a pole. .... Nu 21:8
bronze snake and **p** it on a pole. .... Nu 21:9
So come and **p** a curse on them, ... Nu 22:6
and if you **p** a curse on someone, ... Nu 22:6
So come and **p** a curse on them, ... Nu 22:11
Don't **p** a curse on those people, ... Nu 22:12
Come and **p** a curse on these .... Nu 22:17
morning and **p** a saddle on his .... Nu 22:21
p a curse on the people of Jacob .... Nu 23:7
Each of you must **p** to death your .... Nu 25:5
woman who was **p** to death was .... Nu 25:15
is in him. **P** your hand on him, ... Nu 27:18
and he **p** his hands on him and .... Nu 27:23
P any gold, silver, bronze, iron, ... Nu 31:22
Then they **p** it in the Meeting .... Nu 31:54
murderer. He must be **p** to death. .... Nu 35:16
murderer. He must be **p** to death. .... Nu 35:17
murderer. He must be **p** to death. .... Nu 35:18
person must **p** the murderer to .... Nu 35:19
murderer and must be **p** to death. .... Nu 35:21
murderer may be **p** to death only .... Nu 35:30
No one may be **p** to death with .... Nu 35:30
who should be **p** to death. .... Nu 35:31
A murderer must be **p** to death. .... Nu 35:31
the murderer to be **p** to death. .... Nu 35:33
Then all of you **p** on weapons, ... Dt 1:41
and you will **p** the new tablets .... Dt 10:2
I **p** the tablets in the Ark I had .... Dt 10:5
will **p** grass in the fields for .... Dt 11:15
You must **p** them to death. .... Dt 13:9
and **p** it in the middle of the .... Dt 13:16
before the person is **p** to death; .... Dt 17:6
person should not be **p** to death. .... Dt 17:6
your God must be **p** to death. .... Dt 17:12
he must be **p** to death and his .... Dt 21:22
then **p** these tassels on the four .... Dt 22:12
of the town must **p** her to death .... Dt 22:21
city gate and **p** them to death .... Dt 22:24
with her must be **p** to death. .... Dt 22:25
to **p** a curse on you. .... Dt 23:4
do not **p** any grapes into your .... Dt 23:24
must not be **p** to death if their .... Dt 24:16
must not be **p** to death if their .... Dt 24:16
P the food in a basket and go to .... Dt 26:2
the Lᴏʀᴅ will **p** a load on you .... Dt 28:48
their land and **p** them in another .... Dt 29:28
your God will **p** all these curses .... Dt 30:7
Teachings and **p** it beside the .... Dt 31:26
Moses had **p** his hands on him .... Dt 34:9
against you will be **p** to death. .... Jos 1:18

the rocks and **p** them down where .... Jos 4:3
with them and **p** them down where .... Jos 4:8
Joshua also **p** twelve rocks in .... Jos 4:9
They **p** all of her family in a .... Jos 6:23
and they **p** them on the backs of .... Jos 9:4
They **p** old sandals on their feet .... Jos 9:5
P some men there to guard it, ... Jos 10:18
P your feet on the necks of .... Jos 10:24
came close and **p** their feet on .... Jos 10:24
Heber had **p** up his tent by the .... Jdg 4:11
Then he **p** the meat into a basket .... Jdg 6:19
P the meat and the bread without .... Jdg 6:20
I will **p** some wool on the .... Jdg 6:37
which he **p** in his hometown of .... Jdg 8:27
They **p** men on the hilltops in .... Jdg 9:25
some branches and **p** them on his .... Jdg 9:48
He **p** them on his shoulders and .... Jdg 16:3
where they **p** bronze chains on .... Jdg 16:21
So he **p** her on his donkey and .... Jdg 19:28
so that we can **p** them to death. .... Jdg 20:13
an altar and **p** burnt offerings. .... Jdg 21:4
Wash yourself, **p** on perfume, ... Ru 3:3
Boaz then **p** it on her head and .... Ru 3:15
had decided to **p** them to death. 1Sa 2:25
his clothes and **p** dust on his 1Sa 4:12
temple and **p** it next to Dagon. 1Sa 5:2
they **p** Dagon back in his place. 1Sa 5:3
P the Ark of the Lᴏʀᴅ on the 1Sa 6:8
They **p** the Ark of the Lᴏʀᴅ and 1Sa 6:11
and they **p** both on the large 1Sa 6:15
rock on which they **p** the Ark of 1Sa 6:18
the Israelites **p** away their 1Sa 7:4
the thigh and **p** it on the table 1Sa 9:24
in a book and **p** it before the 1Sa 10:25
No one will be **p** to death today. 1Sa 11:13
do and have **p** a king over you. 1Sa 12:1
The Lᴏʀᴅ has **p** him over you. 1Sa 12:13
to Ahijah, "**P** your hand down! 1Sa 14:19
the oath Saul had **p** on the army, ... 1Sa 14:27
P to death men and women, ... 1Sa 15:3
where he has **p** up a monument in 1Sa 15:12
Saul **p** his own clothes on David. 1Sa 17:38
He **p** a bronze helmet on his head 1Sa 17:38
p on Saul's sword and tried 1Sa 17:39
all the armor Saul had **p** on him. 1Sa 17:39
He **p** them in his shepherd's bag 1Sa 17:40
from his bag, **p** it into his 1Sa 17:49
to Jerusalem and **p** Goliath's 1Sa 17:54
Then Saul **p** David over the 1Sa 18:5
David won't be **p** to death." 1Sa 19:6
and **p** goats' hair at its head. 1Sa 19:13
Lᴏʀᴅ **p** you in my power in the 1Sa 24:10
to them, "**P** on your swords!" 1Sa 25:13
So they **p** on their swords, ... 1Sa 25:13
swords, and David **p** on his also. 1Sa 25:13
of pressed figs and **p** all these 1Sa 25:18
Lᴏʀᴅ had **p** them sound asleep. 1Sa 26:12
Then Saul **p** on other clothes to 1Sa 28:8
She **p** the food before them, ... 1Sa 28:25
p Saul's armor in the temple 1Sa 31:10
red dresses and **p** on gold 2Sa 1:24
clothes and **p** on rough cloth 2Sa 3:31
more I must **p** you evil men to 2Sa 4:11
They **p** the Ark of God on a new 2Sa 6:3
David **p** up a tent for the Ark of 2Sa 6:17
the Israelites **p** it in its place 2Sa 6:17
Then David **p** groups of soldiers 2Sa 8:6
He **p** groups of soldiers all over 2Sa 8:14
p the rest of the army under 2Sa 10:10
P Uriah on the front lines where 2Sa 11:15
were and **p** Uriah there. 2Sa 11:16
floor, washed himself, **p** lotions 2Sa 12:20
Tamar **p** ashes on her head and 2Sa 13:19

They **p** the weak prisoners on................. 2Ch 28:15
made altars and **p** them on every 2Ch 28:24
of the LORD and **p** them in the 2Ch 29:16
But we have **p** them back and made 2Ch 29:19
and the people **p** their hands 2Ch 29:23
King Hezekiah **p** the Levites in 2Ch 29:25
and they **p** all of them in piles. 2Ch 31:6
of the wall and **p** towers on it. 2Ch 32:5
Hezekiah **p** army commanders over 2Ch 32:6
an idol and **p** it in the Temple 2Ch 33:7
Manasseh, **p** hooks in him, ... 2Ch 33:11
Then he **p** commanders in all the 2Ch 33:14
anger, which will not be **p** out.' 2Ch 34:25
P the Holy Ark in the Temple 2Ch 35:3
his chariot and **p** him in another 2Ch 35:24
Jehoiakim, **p** bronze chains 2Ch 36:6
and **p** them in his own palace. 2Ch 36:7
kingdom and to **p** it in writing. .... Ezr 1:1
Jerusalem and **p** in the temple .... Ezr 1:7
Jerusalem and had **p** them in the .... Ezr 5:14
and **p** them back in the Temple in .... Ezr 5:15
of God should be **p** back in their .... Ezr 6:5
they are to be **p** back in the .... Ezr 6:5
Then they **p** the priests and the .... Ezr 6:18
taken away, or be **p** in jail. .... Ezr 7:26
He rebuilt it, **p** a roof over it, ... Ne 3:15
So I **p** people behind the lowest .... Ne 4:13
and I **p** families together with................ Ne 4:13
p my brother Hanani, along with .... Ne 7:2
and **p** some at guard posts and .... Ne 7:3
rough cloth and **p** dust on their .... Ne 9:1
kings you have **p** over us because .... Ne 9:37
our God to **p** in the storerooms .... Ne 10:38
hired Balaam to **p** a curse on .... Ne 13:2
and singers and **p** them back at .... Ne 13:11
I **p** these men in charge of the .... Ne 13:13
I **p** my servants at the gates so .... Ne 13:19
those people, **p** curses on them, ... Ne 13:25
quarters and **p** under the care .... Est 2:3
in Susa and **p** under the care .... Est 2:8
palace and **p** under the care .... Est 2:8
he **p** a royal crown on her head .... Est 2:17
they will **p** it into the royal .... Est 3:9
p on rough cloth and ashes, ... Est 4:1
for Mordecai to **p** on instead of .... Est 4:4
enters must be **p** to death unless .... Est 4:11
third day Esther **p** on her royal .... Est 5:1
Let the servants the robe on .... Est 6:9
and he **p** the robe on Mordecai. .... Est 6:11
Esther **p** Mordecai in charge of .... Est 8:2
You have **p** a wall around him, ... Job 1:10
p painful sores on Job's body,................ Job 2:7
their robes and **p** dirt on their .... Job 2:12
days of the year or **p** it in any................ Job 3:6
and my misery **p** on scales...................... Job 6:2
P away the sin that is in your .... Job 11:14
chains that kings **p** on and puts .... Job 12:18
Why should I **p** myself in danger .... Job 13:14
You **p** my feet in chains and keep .... Job 13:27
alone until we **p** in our time .... Job 14:6
it will bud and **p** out new shoots............. Job 14:9
of the wicked will be **p** out,................... Job 18:5
were first **p** on the earth. .... Job 20:4
p your hand over your mouth in.............. Job 21:5
p on right living as if it were .... Job 29:14
I have not **p** my trust in gold or .... Job 31:24
I would **p** it on like a crown. .... Job 31:36
the earth or **p** him in charge .... Job 34:13
who **p** its cornerstone in place .... Job 38:6
when I **p** limits on the sea and .... Job 38:10
on the sea and **p** its doors and .... Job 38:10
Who **p** wisdom inside the mind or .... Job 38:36
so I will **p** my hand over my .... Job 40:4

Can anyone **p** hooks in its nose? .... Job 40:24
you **p** a cord through its nose .... Job 41:2
would a bird or **p** it on a leash .... Job 41:5
you **p** one hand on it, you will .... Job 41:8
You **p** them in charge of .... Ps 8:6
You **p** all things under their .... Ps 8:6
the orphans and **p** an end to .... Ps 10:18
You **p** good things before him and .... Ps 21:3
All you who **p** your hope in the .... Ps 31:24
those who **p** their hope in his .... Ps 33:18
to us as we **p** our hope in you................. Ps 33:22
I **p** on clothes of sadness and .... Ps 35:13
He **p** a new song in my mouth, ... Ps 40:3
I should **p** my hope in God and .... Ps 42:5
I should **p** my hope in God and .... Ps 42:11
I should **p** my hope in God and .... Ps 43:5
P on your sword, powerful .... Ps 45:3
for us and **p** them under our .... Ps 47:3
don't **p** your trust in them. .... Ps 62:10
us be trapped and **p** a heavy load .... Ps 66:11
p poison in my food and gave................. Ps 69:21
a necklace and **p** on violence as .... Ps 73:6
You have **p** them in danger; .... Ps 73:18
I let them **p** down their baskets. .... Ps 81:6
I will **p** Egypt and Babylonia on .... Ps 87:4
You have **p** the evil we have done .... Ps 90:8
He has **p** his angels in charge of............. Ps 91:11
They **p** chains around his feet................. Ps 105:18
He loved to **p** curses on others, ... Ps 109:17
side until I **p** your enemies .... Ps 110:1
I **p** my hope in your word. .... Ps 119:74
have almost **p** me in the grave .... Ps 119:87
p your hope in the LORD because .... Ps 130:7
p your hope in the LORD now and........... Ps 131:3
and have **p** your hand on me. .... Ps 139:5
When I was **p** together there, ... Ps 139:15
not **p** your trust in princes or .... Ps 146:3
He **p** them in place forever and .... Ps 148:6
will **p** those kings in chains .... Ps 149:8
the mountains were **p** in place. .... Pr 8:25
there when God **p** the skies in .... Pr 8:27
clouds above and **p** the deep .... Pr 8:28
angry king can **p** someone to .... Pr 16:14
so that you will **p** your trust .... Pr 22:19
die like a flame that is **p** out. .... Pr 24:20
Lazy people may **p** their hands in .... Pr 26:15
but no one can **p** up with .... Pr 27:4
P on nice clothes and make .... Ec 9:8
against it and **p** his armies all................ Ec 9:14
crown his mother **p** on his head .... Sng 3:11
and don't want to **p** it on again. .... Sng 5:3
My lover **p** his hand through the .... Sng 5:4
P me like a seal on your heart, ... Sng 8:6
water cannot **p** out the flame .... Sng 8:7
we will **p** silver towers on her. .... Sng 8:9
be able to **p** out that fire." .... Is 1:31
So the Lord will **p** sores on the .... Is 3:17
we will **p** great cedars there. .... Is 9:10
the wicked will be **p** to death.................. Is 11:4
child will be able to **p** his hand .... Is 11:8
No Arab will **p** a tent there; .... Is 13:20
I will **p** my throne above God's .... Is 14:13
because I have **p** an end to .... Is 16:10
your robe and **p** it on him and .... Is 22:21
I will **p** the key to the house of .... Is 22:22
I will **p** a stone in the ground .... Is 28:16
I will **p** armies all around you, ... Is 29:3
but they will be **p** to shame, ... Is 30:5
nice clothes and **p** rough cloth .... Is 32:11
his clothes and **p** on rough cloth............. Is 37:1
I am going to **p** a spirit in the .... Is 37:7
were frightened and **p** to shame. .... Is 37:27
will **p** my hook in your nose and .... Is 37:29

from figs and **p** it on Hezekiah's.............. Is 38:21
I will **p** pine, fir, and cypress .... Is 41:19
I have **p** my Spirit upon him, ... Is 42:1
of grass or **p** out even a weak.................. Is 42:3
destroyed as a flame is **p** out................... Is 43:17
honor me when I **p** water in the .... Is 43:20
idols will be **p** to great shame; .... Is 45:16
again will Israel be **p** to shame................ Is 45:17
They **p** it on their shoulders and.............. Is 46:7
But the LORD has **p** on him the .... Is 53:6
family. He was **p** to death; he .... Is 53:8
people you have **p** in prison .... Is 58:6
He **p** the helmet of salvation on .... Is 59:17
p on his clothes for punishing .... Is 59:17
Lord GOD has **p** his Spirit in me .... Is 61:1
I have **p** guards on the walls to .... Is 62:6
is the one who **p** his Holy Spirit .... Is 63:11
Lord GOD will **p** you to death................. Is 65:15
I will **p** a mark on some of the .... Is 66:19
Today I have **p** you in charge of .... Je 1:10
no one will be able to **p** it out, ... Je 4:4
p on rough cloth, show how sad............. Je 4:8
do you **p** on your finest dress .... Je 4:30
Why do you **p** color around your .... Je 4:30
I will **p** problems in front of .... Je 6:21
p on rough cloth and roll in the .... Je 6:26
hot fire that no one can **p** out. .... Je 7:20
They **p** blue and purple clothes .... Je 10:9
one is left to **p** up my tent .... Je 10:20
You have **p** the evil people here .... Je 12:2
linen belt and **p** it around your .... Je 13:1
LORD told me, and **p** it around my........... Je 13:2
And it will not be **p** out.'" .... Je 17:27
the men from Judah be **p** to death .... Je 18:21
that cannot be **p** back together .... Je 19:11
a fire that no one can **p** out, ... Je 21:12
p it on the back of your neck................... Je 27:2
the nations who **p** themselves .... Je 27:11
P yourself under the control of .... Je 27:12
king of Babylon has **p** on Judah. .... Je 28:2
king of Babylon **p** on Judah.'" .... Je 28:4
p that yoke on all the nations .... Je 28:11
I will **p** a yoke of iron on the .... Je 28:14
p iron rings around his neck. .... Je 29:26
P up signs to show you the way .... Je 31:21
I will **p** my teachings in their .... Je 31:33
king of Judah had **p** Jeremiah in .... Je 32:3
and **p** them in a clay jar so they .... Je 32:14
They **p** their hateful idols in .... Je 32:34
Then I **p** some bowls full of wine .... Je 35:5
The officers **p** the scroll in the .... Je 36:20
had not yet been **p** into prison. .... Je 37:4
Then they **p** him in jail in the .... Je 37:15
So those people **p** Jeremiah into............. Je 37:16
for Jeremiah to be **p** under guard .... Je 37:21
Jeremiah must be **p** to death! .... Je 38:4
Jeremiah and **p** him into the well .... Je 38:6
that the officers had **p** Jeremiah.............. Je 38:7
P these old rags and worn-out .... Je 38:12
Then he **p** out Zedekiah's eyes. .... Je 39:7
He **p** bronze chains on Zedekiah .... Je 39:7
of Babylon had **p** Gedaliah son .... Je 40:7
and **p** what you harvest in your .... Je 40:10
son of Nethaniah **p** dead bodies .... Je 41:9
of the guard had **p** Gedaliah son .... Je 43:6
battle and **p** on your helmets! .... Je 46:4
your spears. **P** on your armor! .... Je 46:4
of Cush and **P** who carry shields, ... Je 46:9
let us **p** an end to that nation!' .... Je 48:2
P on your rough cloth to show .... Je 49:3
Hamath and Arpad are **p** to shame, ... Je 49:23
The god Bel will be **p** to shame, ... Je 50:2
gods will be **p** to shame, ... Je 50:2

even let them **p** on their armor. .... Je 51:3
P the watchmen in their places, ... Je 51:12
will **p** my hand out against you. .... Je 51:25
Then he **p** out Zedekiah's eyes, ... Je 52:11
and **p** bronze chains on him, ... Je 52:11
So Jehoiachin **p** away his prison .... Je 52:33
their heads and **p** on rough cloth .... La 2:10
he **p** heavy chains on me. .... La 3:7
stubborn, and **p** your curse on .... La 3:65
entered me and **p** me on my feet. .... Eze 2:2
yourself a brick, **p** it in front .... Eze 4:1
and **p** heavy logs in place to .... Eze 4:2
I will **p** ropes on you so you .... Eze 4:8
seeds, and **p** them in one bowl .... Eze 4:9
have **p** her at the center of the .... Eze 5:5
They will **p** on rough cloth to .... Eze 7:18
through Jerusalem and **p** a mark .... Eze 9:4
living creature **p** out his hand................. Eze 10:7
and **p** it in the hands of the man.............. Eze 10:7
and I will **p** inside them a new .... Eze 11:19
among them will **p** his things on .... Eze 12:12
wall on which you **p** whitewash............. Eze 13:14
They **p** up evil things that cause .... Eze 14:3
idols and **p** up evil things .... Eze 14:4
off of you, and **p** oil on you. .... Eze 16:9
I **p** beautiful clothes made with .... Eze 16:10
on you and **p** sandals of fine .... Eze 16:10
I **p** jewelry on you: bracelets on .... Eze 16:11
I will **p** you to death because I .... Eze 16:38
I will **p** an end to your sexual .... Eze 16:41
so he will surely be **p** to death. .... Eze 18:13
Then they **p** him into a cage with .... Eze 19:9
They **p** him into prison so his .... Eze 19:9
destroy them or **p** an end to them .... Eze 20:17
that burn will not be **p** out. .... Eze 20:47
It will not be **p** out.'" .... Eze 20:48
The sword will be **p** on the necks .... Eze 21:29
P the sword back in its holder. .... Eze 21:30
I am going to **p** you together .... Eze 22:19
People as silver, copper, iron, ... Eze 22:20
my hot anger and **p** you together .... Eze 22:20
I will **p** you together and make .... Eze 22:21
I will **p** a stop to the sinful .... Eze 23:27
their eyes, and **p** on jewelry. .... Eze 23:40
which they **p** my incense and my .... Eze 23:41
They **p** bracelets on the wrists .... Eze 23:42
So I will **p** an end to sexual .... Eze 23:48
Lord GOD says: **P** on the pot; put .... Eze 24:3
p it on and pour water in it. .... Eze 24:3
P in the pieces of meat, the..................... Eze 24:4
I **p** the blood she spilled on the .... Eze 24:8
and **p** your sandals on your feet. .... Eze 24:17
and **P** were warriors in your navy .... Eze 27:10
they **p** on rough cloth to show .... Eze 27:31
I **p** you on the holy mountain of .... Eze 28:14
But I will **p** hooks in your jaws, ... Eze 29:4
Cush, **P**, Lydia, Arabia, Libya,................. Eze 30:5
strong and **p** my sword in his .... Eze 30:24
I am the LORD when I **p** my sword .... Eze 30:25
they will not **p** their tops among............. Eze 31:14
graves were **p** in the deepest .... Eze 32:23
the sick or **p** bandages on those .... Eze 34:4
p bandages on those that were .... Eze 34:16
Then I will **p** over them one .... Eze 34:23
and I will **p** a new way of .... Eze 36:26
will **p** my Spirit inside you and .... Eze 36:27
of the LORD and **p** me down in the .... Eze 37:1
will **p** muscles on you and flesh .... Eze 37:6
Then I will **p** breath in you so................. Eze 37:6
And I will **p** my Spirit inside .... Eze 37:14
Then I will **p** you in your own................. Eze 37:14
and I will **p** it with the stick .... Eze 37:19
I will **p** them in their land and .... Eze 37:26

Then I will **p** my Temple among .... Eze 37:26
you around and **p** hooks in your............. Eze 38:4
Cush, and **P** will be with them .... Eze 38:5
bone is to **p** a marker by it...................... Eze 39:15
because I will **p** my Spirit into .... Eze 39:29
of Israel and **p** me down on a .... Eze 40:2
the priests **p** their tools which .... Eze 40:42
inches wide were **p** up on all the .... Eze 40:43
offering was **p** on the tables. .... Eze 40:43
There they will **p** the most holy .... Eze 42:13
After they **p** on other clothes,............... Eze 42:14
bull's blood and **p** it on the .... Eze 43:20
yourselves but **p** foreigners in .... Eze 44:8
will **p** them in charge of taking .... Eze 44:14
holy rooms and **p** on other .... Eze 44:19
sin offering and **p** it on the .... Eze 45:19
to Babylonia and **p** in the temple .... Da 1:2
Don't **p** the wise men of Babylon .... Da 2:24
of Babylon and **p** him in charge .... Da 2:48
p this man in charge of all the .... Da 5:11
a gold chain **p** around his neck. .... Da 5:29
king planned to **p** Daniel in .... Da 6:3
officers to **p** special seals .... Da 6:17
thrones were **p** in their places, ... Da 7:9
I fasted, **p** on rough cloth, ... Da 9:3
against God; to **p** an end to sin; .... Da 9:24
a commander will **p** an end to the .... Da 11:18
In the future I will **p** an end to .... Hos 1:4
I will **p** an end to all her .... Hos 2:11
She **p** on her rings and jewelry .... Hos 2:13
days he will **p** new life in us; .... Hos 6:2
P the trumpet to your lips and .... Hos 8:1
they **p** up better stone pillars .... Hos 10:1
I will **p** a yoke on her neck and .... Hos 10:11
p on your rough cloth and cry to .... Joe 1:13
Don't let them be **p** to shame;................ Joe 2:17
and you **p** my precious treasures .... Joe 3:5
will be no one to **p** it out. .... Am 5:6
You **p** off the day of punishment, ... Am 6:3
I will **p** a plumb line among my .... Am 7:8
they **p** on rough cloth to show .... Jnh 3:5
will **p** them together like sheep .... Mic 2:12
They will **p** their hands over .... Mic 7:16
and the shield is **p** into place................. Nah 2:5
P and Libya supported her. .... Nah 3:9
of her leaders were **p** in chains. .... Nah 3:10
So how can you **p** up with those............. Hab 1:13
p on clothes, but you are not .... Hag 1:6
as if you had **p** it into a purse .... Hag 1:6
"**P** a clean turban on his head." .... Zch 3:5
So they **p** a clean turban on his .... Zch 3:5
I **p** this stone in front of .... Zch 3:9
the basket and **p** the lid back .... Zch 5:8
and **p** it on the head of Joshua .... Zch 6:11
and **p** the human spirit within: .... Zch 12:1
as easily as they **p** on clothes," .... Mal 2:16
I will come and **p** a curse on the............. Mal 4:6
He will **p** the good part of the................. Mt 3:12
a fire that cannot be **p** out." .... Mt 3:12
of Jerusalem and **p** him on a high .... Mt 4:5
'He has **p** his angels in charge .... Mt 4:6
that John had been **p** in prison, ... Mt 4:12
They **p** it on a lampstand so the .... Mt 5:15
you to a guard to **p** you in jail. .... Mt 5:25
don't **p** on a sad face like the .... Mt 6:16
and have them **p** ashes on. .... Mt 10:21
rough cloth and **p** ashes on..................... Mt 11:21
I will **p** my Spirit upon him, ... Mt 12:18
of grass or **p** out even a weak .... Mt 12:20
a net that was **p** into the lake .... Mt 13:47
sat down and **p** the good fish............... Mt 13:48
him up, and **p** him into prison .... Mt 14:3
or mother must be **p** to death.' .... Mt 15:4

not what people **p** into their .... Mt 15:11
They **p** them at Jesus' feet, ... Mt 15:30
I will **p** up three tents here— .... Mt 17:4
How long must I **p** up with you?............. Mt 17:17
was very angry and **p** the servant .... Mt 18:34
so he could **p** his hands on them .... Mt 19:13
After Jesus **p** his hands on the .... Mt 19:15
He **p** a wall around it and dug a .... Mt 21:33
until I **p** your enemies under .... Mt 22:44
So you should have **p** my gold in .... Mt 25:27
Son of Man will **p** the sheep on .... Mt 25:33
P your sword back in its place. .... Mt 26:52
clothes and **p** a red robe on him. .... Mt 27:28
made a crown, **p** it on his head, ... Mt 27:29
and **p** a stick in his right hand. .... Mt 27:29
the robe and **p** his own clothes .... Mt 27:31
They **p** a sign above Jesus' head .... Mt 27:37
He **p** Jesus' body in a new tomb .... Mt 27:60
After John was **p** in prison,.................... Mk 1:14
should be **p** into new leather .... Mk 2:22
You **p** the lamp on a lampstand. .... Mk 4:21
Please come and **p** your hands on .... Mk 5:23
demons out and **p** olive oil on............... Mk 6:13
arrest John and **p** him in prison .... Mk 6:17
John's body and **p** it in a tomb. .... Mk 6:29
or mother must be **p** to death.' .... Mk 7:10
nothing people **p** into their .... Mk 7:15
begged Jesus to **p** his hand on .... Mk 7:32
He **p** his fingers in the man's .... Mk 7:33
the man's eyes and **p** his hands .... Mk 8:23
Again Jesus **p** his hands on the .... Mk 8:25
How long must I **p** up with you?............. Mk 9:19
die; the fire is never **p** out. .... Mk 9:44
die; the fire is never **p** out. .... Mk 9:46
die; the fire is never **p** out. .... Mk 9:48
his arms, **p** his hands on them, ... Mk 10:16
to Jesus and **p** their coats on it .... Mk 11:7
He **p** a wall around it and dug a .... Mk 12:1
until I **p** your enemies under .... Mk 12:36
the people **p** in their money. .... Mk 12:41
widow came and **p** in two small .... Mk 12:42
and cause them to be **p** to death. .... Mk 13:12
They **p** a purple robe on Jesus .... Mk 15:17
robe and **p** his own clothes .... Mk 15:20
They also **p** two robbers on .... Mk 15:27
"They **p** him with criminals." .... Mk 15:28
He **p** the body in a tomb that was .... Mk 15:46
spices to **p** on Jesus' body. .... Mk 16:1
He will **p** the good part of the................. Lk 3:17
a fire that cannot be **p** out." .... Lk 3:17
even worse: He **p** John in prison. .... Lk 3:20
to Jerusalem and **p** him on a high .... Lk 4:9
'He has **p** his angels in charge .... Lk 4:10
The Lord has **p** his Spirit in me, ... Lk 4:18
and **p** your nets in the water to .... Lk 5:4
But you say to **p** the nets in the .... Lk 5:5
him in and **p** him down before .... Lk 5:18
wine must be **p** into new leather .... Lk 5:38
You did not **p** oil on my head,................ Lk 7:46
stay with you and **p** up with you? .... Lk 9:41
rough cloth and **p** ashes on.................... Lk 10:13
Then he **p** the hurt man on his .... Lk 10:34
around it and **p** on some .... Lk 13:8
Jesus **p** his hands on her, and............... Lk 13:13
best clothes and **p** them on him. .... Lk 15:22
p a ring on his finger and .... Lk 15:22
Why then didn't you **p** my money .... Lk 19:23
colt's back, and **p** Jesus on it. .... Lk 19:35
until I **p** your enemies under .... Lk 20:43
synagogues and **p** you in jail .... Lk 21:12
out with Jesus to be **p** to death. .... Lk 23:32
and **p** it in a tomb that was cut .... Lk 23:53
before John was **p** into prison. .... Jn 3:24

God the Father has **p** his power." .... Jn 6:27
mud with it and **p** the mud on the .... Jn 9:6
some mud and **p** it on my eyes. .... Jn 9:11
answered, "He **p** mud on my eyes, ... Jn 9:15
woman who later **p** perfume on the .... Jn 11:2
fear they would be **p** out of the .... Jn 12:42
he **p** on his clothes and sat down .... Jn 13:12
People will **p** you out of their .... Jn 16:2
to Peter, "**P** your sword back .... Jn 18:11
allowed to **p** anyone to death, ... Jn 18:31
branches and **p** it on Jesus' head .... Jn 19:2
Jesus' head and **p** a purple robe .... Jn 19:2
a sign and **p** it on the cross .... Jn 19:19
p the sponge on a branch of a .... Jn 19:29
know where they have **p** him." .... Jn 20:2
know where they have **p** him." .... Jn 20:13
me where you **p** him, and I will .... Jn 20:15
his hands and **p** my finger where .... Jn 20:25
nails were and **p** my hand into .... Jn 20:25
to Thomas, "**P** your finger here .... Jn 20:27
P your hand here in my side. .... Jn 20:27
you will **p** out your hands and .... Jn 21:18
They **p** the names of two men .... Ac 1:23
p him to death by nailing him .... Ac 2:23
until I **p** your enemies under .... Ac 2:35
and John and **p** them in jail. .... Ac 4:3
the apostles and **p** them in jail. .... Ac 5:18
The men you **p** in jail are .... Ac 5:25
We will **p** them in charge of this .... Ac 6:3
Then they **p** these men before the .... Ac 6:6
of Egypt and **p** him in charge of .... Ac 7:10
to Shechem and **p** in a grave .... Ac 7:16
When they **p** Moses outside, ... Ac 7:21
was washed and **p** in a room .... Ac 9:37
he **p** him in jail and handed him .... Ac 12:4
dressed and **p** on your sandals .... Ac 12:8
"**P** on your coat and follow me." .... Ac 12:8
chosen day Herod **p** on his royal .... Ac 12:21
for Jesus to be **p** to death, ... Ac 13:28
Paul and Barnabas **p** them in the .... Ac 14:23
believers had **p** them into God's .... Ac 14:26
in Antioch **p** Paul into the .... Ac 15:40
p them far inside the jail and .... Ac 16:24
and the others **p** up a sum of .... Ac 17:9
had used and **p** them on the sick .... Ac 19:12
They **p** a man named Alexander in .... Ac 19:33
and **p** his arms around him. .... Ac 20:10
and women and **p** them in jail. .... Ac 22:4
synagogue I **p** the believers .... Ac 22:19
Paul away and **p** him in the army .... Ac 23:10
me the power to **p** many of God's .... Ac 26:10
man should die or be **p** in jail." .... Ac 26:31
to Italy, so he **p** us on it. .... Ac 27:6
and **p** his hands on the man and .... Ac 28:8
I will **p** in Jerusalem a stone .... Rm 9:33
God is able to **p** them back where .... Rm 11:23
Christ we are **p** right with God, ... 1Co 1:30
has been **p** on the foundation 1Co 3:14
to me that God has **p** us apostles 1Co 4:9
they hurt us, we **p** up with it. 1Co 4:12
this should be **p** out of your 1Co 5:2
p up with everything ourselves 1Co 9:12
anything that is **p** before you. 1Co 10:27
But God **p** the body together and 1Co 12:24
says that God **p** all things under 1Co 15:27
the One who **p** everything under 1Co 15:27
has been **p** under the Son, ... 1Co 15:28
he will **p** himself under God, ... 1Co 15:28
who had **p** all things under him. 1Co 15:28
Why do we **p** ourselves in danger 1Co 15:30
of you should **p** aside money as 1Co 16:2
We have **p** our hope in him, ... 2Co 1:10
He **p** his mark on us to show that 2Co 1:22

he **p** his Spirit in our hearts 2Co 1:22
who **p** a covering over his face 2Co 3:13
so he **p** guards around the city. 2Co 11:32
p our faith in Christ Jesus, ... Gal 2:16
was the law that **p** me to death, ... Gal 2:19
I was **p** to death on the cross .... Gal 2:20
away the curse the law **p** on us. .... Gal 3:13
with us and **p** himself under that .... Gal 3:13
God **p** his special mark of .... Eph 1:13
the dead and **p** him at his right .... Eph 1:20
has **p** Christ over all rulers, ... Eph 1:21
God **p** everything under his power .... Eph 1:22
P on the full armor of God so .... Eph 6:11
why you need to **p** on God's full .... Eph 6:13
do not **p** trust in ourselves or .... Php 3:3
be able to **p** trust in myself .... Php 3:4
So **p** all evil things out of your .... Col 3:5
But now also **p** these things out .... Col 3:8
be against and **p** himself above 2Th 2:4
But do not **p** younger widows on 1Ti 5:11
side until I **p** your enemies .... Heb 1:13
p all things under their control. .... Heb 2:8
When God **p** everything under .... Heb 2:8
I will **p** my teachings in their .... Heb 8:10
enemies to be **p** under his power. .... Heb 10:13
I will **p** my teachings in their .... Heb 10:16
He was **p** to death without mercy. .... Heb 10:28
Others were **p** in chains and .... Heb 11:36
the joy that God **p** before him. .... Heb 12:2
must be **p** to death with stones. .... Heb 12:20
So **p** out of your life every evil .... Jam 1:21
When we **p** bits into the mouths .... Jam 3:3
I will **p** a stone in the ground 1Pe 2:6
them to hell and **p** them in caves 2Pe 2:4
He **p** his right hand on me and .... Rev 1:17
know you do not **p** up with the .... Rev 2:2
the devil will **p** some of you in .... Rev 2:10
that I will not **p** any other load .... Rev 2:24
have **p** an open door before you, ... Rev 3:8
me medicine to **p** on your eyes so .... Rev 3:18
They **p** their crowns down before .... Rev 4:10
The angel **p** this offering on the .... Rev 8:3
He **p** his right foot on the sea .... Rev 10:2
p the breath of life into the .... Rev 11:11
person will be **p** in pain with .... Rev 14:10

PUTEOLI
and a day later we came to **P**. .... Ac 28:13

PUTHITES
Ithrites, **P**, Shumathites, and 1Ch 2:53

PUTIEL
Aaron married a daughter of **P**, ... Ex 6:25

PUTS
If your father **p** a curse on you, ... Ge 27:13
like it or **p** it on someone who .... Ex 30:33
body in water before he **p** them .... Le 16:4
'The man who **p** on his armor 1Ki 20:11
he **p** even more blame on people .... Job 4:19
comes along and **p** you in prison .... Job 11:10
anyone he **p** in prison cannot be .... Job 12:14
kings put on and **p** a garment on .... Job 12:18
pieces and **p** others in their .... Job 34:24
its strength or **p** a flowing mane .... Job 39:19
lazy person **p** his hand in the .... Pr 19:24
that Assyria **p** on you will be .... Is 10:27
into his house and **p** his hand on .... Am 5:19
the person **p** it on a lampstand .... Lk 8:16
a lamp and **p** it in a secret .... Lk 11:33
he happily **p** it on his shoulders .... Lk 15:5
rule until he **p** all enemies 1Co 15:25
p her hope in God and continues 1Ti 5:5
to accept them and **p** them out of 3Jn 1:10

PUTTING

I am **p** my rainbow in the clouds .... Ge 9:13
p them with its head and its .... Ex 29:17
service to God by **p** blood on its .... Ex 30:10
p the lamps so they lighted the .... Nu 8:3
back for **p** out my two eyes!" .... Jdg 16:28
Micah's house, **p** their little.................... Jdg 18:21
p the meat on the wood but not 1Ki 18:23
p his mouth on the boy's mouth, ... 2Ki 4:34
responsible for **p** the holy bread.............. 1Ch 23:29
and they are **p** timbers in the .... Ezr 5:8
priests are **p** their seals on it. .... Ne 9:38
I am **p** my words in your mouth. .... Je 1:9
idols or by **p** up the things that .... Eze 14:7
p caulk in your ship's seams. .... Eze 27:9
name unclean by **p** their doorway .... Eze 43:8
entrance and **p** soldiers there .... Mt 27:66
sick people by **p** his hands on.................. Mk 6:5
P his hands on each sick person, ... Lk 4:40
some rich people **p** their gifts .... Lk 21:1
a poor widow **p** two small copper .... Lk 21:2
and women and **p** them in jail. .... Ac 8:3
testing God by **p** a heavy load .... Ac 15:10
Now I am **p** you in the care of .... Ac 20:32
sticks and was **p** them on the .... Ac 28:3

PYRRHUS

with him were Sopater son of **P**, ... Ac 20:4

Q

QUAIL

out and gathered **q** all that day, ... Nu 11:32
brought them **q** and filled them .... Ps 105:40

QUARREL

"Don't **q** on the way home." .... Ge 45:24
to them, "Why do you **q** with me? .... Ex 17:2
Did he ever **q** or fight with the .... Jdg 11:25
control their tempers stop a **q**. .... Pr 15:18
Starting a **q** is like a leak in a................ Pr 17:14
someone else's **q** as you pass by.............. Pr 26:17
priests, when they **q** with you. .... Hos 4:4
Lord must not **q** but must be kind 2Ti 2:24
and argue and **q** about the law. .... Tit 3:9

QUARRELED

So they **q** with Moses and said, ... Ex 17:2
it Meribah, because they **q**..................... Ex 17:7

QUARRELING

such as murder, **q**, or attack, ... Dt 17:8
decide cases of **q** and attacks................ Dt 21:5
have a feast where there is **q**. .... Pr 17:1
and a **q** wife is like dripping .... Pr 19:13
inside the house with a **q** wife. .... Pr 21:9
than with a **q** and complaining .... Pr 21:19
inside the house with a **q** wife. .... Pr 25:24
and without gossip, **q** will stop. .... Pr 26:20
A **q** wife is as bothersome as a .... Pr 27:15
is jealousy and **q** among you, ... 1Co 3:3

QUARRELS

The words of fools start **q**. .... Pr 18:6
but avoiding **q** will bring you .... Pr 20:3
Then fighting, **q**, and insults .... Pr 22:10
that there are **q** among you. 1Co 1:11
and constant **q** from those who 1Ti 6:5
you know they grow into **q**. 2Ti 2:23

QUARRELSOME

a **q** person keeps an argument .... Pr 26:21

QUARRY

at the stone **q** from which you .... Is 51:1

QUART

mixed with one **q** of oil from .... Ex 29:40
Pour out a **q** of wine as a drink .... Ex 29:40
must also offer a **q** of wine as a .... Le 23:13
mixed with one **q** of olive oil. .... Nu 15:4
also prepare a **q** of wine as a .... Nu 15:5
mixed with one **q** of oil from .... Nu 28:5
Offer one **q** of wine with each .... Nu 28:7
lamb it will be one **q** of wine. .... Nu 28:14
two-thirds of a **q** of water every .... Eze 4:11
A **q** of wheat for a day's pay, ... Rev 6:6

QUARTERS

to the women's **q** and put under .... Est 2:3
the best part of the women's **q**. .... Est 2:9
from the women's **q** to the king's .... Est 2:13
another part of the women's **q**. .... Est 2:14

QUARTS

prepare twenty **q** of fine flour, ... Ge 18:6
about two **q** for every person in .... Ex 16:16
offer also two **q** of fine flour .... Ex 29:40
Also take four **q** of olive oil, ... Ex 30:24
bring about two **q** of fine flour .... Le 5:11
must bring two **q** of fine flour.................. Le 6:20
also take six **q** of fine flour .... Le 14:10
four **q** of fine flour mixed with .... Le 23:13
four **q** of flour for each loaf. .... Le 24:5
her of two **q** of barley flour. .... Nu 5:15
offering of two **q** of fine flour,............... Nu 28:5
lambs offer two **q** of flour. .... Nu 28:29
offering of six **q** of fine flour .... Nu 29:3
and with twenty **q** of flour, ... Jdg 6:19
hold about thirteen **q** of seed.................. 1Ki 18:32
tomorrow seven **q** of fine flour 2Ki 7:1
and one-third **q** of grain and one .... Eze 46:14
three **q** of barley for a day's .... Rev 6:6

QUARTUS

treasurer, and our brother **Q**. .... Rm 16:23

QUARTZ

a ruby, topaz, and yellow **q**; .... Ex 28:17
a ruby, a topaz, and a yellow **q**; .... Ex 39:10
emerald, yellow **q**, onyx, and .... Eze 28:13
body was like shiny yellow **q**................... Da 10:6

QUEEN

When the **q** of Sheba heard about 1Ki 10:1
removed her from being **q** mother........... 1Ki 15:13
When the **q** of Sheba heard about 2Ch 9:1
from being **q** mother, because she 2Ch 15:16
The **q** was sitting next to the .... Ne 2:6
Q Vashti also gave a banquet for .... Est 1:9
become **q** in place of Vashti. .... Est 2:4
inside to beg **Q** Esther to save .... Est 7:7
the Jew and **Q** Esther had sent .... Est 9:31
be called the **q** of kingdoms. .... Is 47:5
offer them to the **Q** Goddess. .... Je 7:18
to the king and the **q** mother: .... Je 13:18
the king and the **q** mother; .... Je 29:2
sacrifices to the **Q** Goddess, ... Je 44:17
was like a **q** of all the other .... La 1:1
very beautiful and became a **q**. .... Eze 16:13
the **Q** of the South will stand up.............. Mt 12:42
Judgment Day the **Q** of the South .... Lk 11:31
of Candace, the **q** of the .... Ac 8:27
'I am a **q** sitting on my throne. .... Rev 18:7

QUEENS

may be sixty **q** and eighty slave .... Sng 6:8
the **q** and the slave women also .... Sng 6:9
the kings and **q** of Judah did?.................. Je 44:9

QUESTION

Israelites asked the LORD a **q**. .... Jdg 20:27
They asked this **q** because they .... Jdg 21:5

me one **q.**" The woman said, ... 2Sa 14:18
told him to, who can **q** him?" 2Sa 16:10
will answer your **q** about what I .... Est 5:8
You **q** me about my children. .... Is 45:11
in other nations this **q:** ' .... Je 18:13
powerful hand or **q** what he does. .... Da 4:35
their men to ask the LORD a **q.** .... Zch 7:2
I also will ask you a **q.** .... Mt 21:24
again about the **q** of divorce. .... Mk 10:10
So Pilate asked Jesus another **q,** .... Mk 15:4
sent us to you with this **q:** ' .... Lk 7:20
to show the importance of his **q,** .... Lk 10:29
But they would not answer his **q.** .... Lk 14:4
I will also ask you a **q.** .... Lk 20:3
asked Philip this **q** to test him, ... Jn 6:6
preparing to **q** Paul moved away .... Ac 22:29
beings have no right to **q** God. .... Rm 9:20

QUESTIONED
He **q** us carefully about .... Ge 43:7
because my innocence is being **q.** .... Job 6:29
q me without finding anything .... Ps 17:3
But I have **q** him before you all, ... Lk 23:14
The high priest **q** them, ... Ac 5:27
So he **q** the guards and ordered .... Ac 12:19

QUESTIONING
with Adonijah by **q** what he did............... 1Ki 1:6
are you **q** us about a good thing .... Ac 4:9

QUESTIONS
' We just answered his **q.** .... Ge 43:7
came to test him with hard **q.** 1Ki 10:1
and Solomon answered all her **q.** 1Ki 10:3
Without asking **q,** God breaks .... Job 34:24
enough to ask him any more **q.** .... Mt 22:46
to Jesus and began to ask him **q.** .... Mk 8:11
to them and asking them **q.** .... Lk 2:46
are going to ask him more **q.** .... Ac 23:20
By asking him **q** yourself, you .... Ac 24:8
Do not ask **q** about it. 1Co 10:25
Do not ask **q** about it. 1Co 10:27

QUICK
to do evil and are **q** to kill. .... Pr 1:16
feet that are **q** to do evil, ... Pr 6:18
fools are careless and **q** to act. .... Pr 14:16
a person with a **q** temper sins a .... Pr 29:22
be too **q** to leave the king. .... Ec 8:3
They take **q,** short steps, making .... Is 3:16
The new king will be like a **q.** .... Is 14:29
Go, **q** messengers, to a people .... Is 18:2
I will be **q** to testify against .... Mal 3:5
they will bring **q** ruin on 2Pe 2:1

QUICK-TEMPERED
friends with **q** people or spend .... Pr 22:24

QUICKER
they will dry up **q** than grass. .... Job 8:12
leopards and **q** than wolves at .... Hab 1:8

QUICKLY
You had **q** turned away from what .... Dt 9:16
become angry **q,** because getting .... Ec 7:9
become friends **q,** before you go............... Mt 5:25
go **q** and tell his followers, ' .... Mt 28:7
they saw her stand and leave **q,** .... Jn 11:31
thing that you will do—do it **q.**" .... Jn 13:27
they will be destroyed **q.** 1Th 5:3
pains that come **q** to a woman 1Th 5:3
to spread **q** and that people 2Th 3:1
selfish, or becoming angry **q.** .... Tit 1:7
go away and **q** forget what they .... Jam 1:24
will come to you **q** and fight .... Rev 2:16

QUIET
the whole world rests and is **q.** .... Is 14:7
I cannot keep **q,** because I have .... Je 4:19
It is now **q** in the streets of .... Je 33:10
warned the blind men to be **q,** .... Mt 20:31
the evil spirit, "Be **q!** .... Mk 1:25
wind and said to the waves, "**Q!** .... Mk 4:39
warned the blind man to be **q,** .... Mk 10:48
the evil spirit, "Be **q!** .... Lk 4:35
warned the blind man to be **q.** .... Lk 18:39
We cannot keep **q.** We must speak .... Ac 4:20
language, they became very **q.** .... Ac 22:2
should be **q** in the church 1Co 14:28
should keep **q** in the church 1Co 14:34
that we can have **q** and peaceful............... 1Ti 2:2
of a gentle and **q** spirit that..................... 1Pe 3:4

QUIETLY
and waited **q** for my advice. .... Job 29:21
these things **q** as you go to bed .... Ps 4:4
I will **q** watch from where I...................... Is 18:4
good to wait **q** for the LORD to .... La 3:26
they want to make us go away **q.** .... Ac 16:37
Christ to work **q** and earn their 2Th 3:12
by listening **q** and being ready 1Ti 2:11
over a man, but to listen **q,** 1Ti 2:12

QUIETNESS
I have no peace or **q.** .... Job 3:26

QUIETS
With his power he **q** the sea; .... Job 26:12

QUIRINIUS
was taken while **Q** was governor .... Lk 2:2

QUIT
now you want them to **q** working!" .... Ex 5:5
You have **q** following me and have............ 1Ki 14:9
I did not **q** until they were .... Ps 18:37
Q punishing me; your beating is............... Ps 39:10
new strength, so you did not **q.** .... Is 57:10
is because Judah **q** following my .... Je 9:13
and those who **q** following the .... Zph 1:6

QUITE
have told me **q** plainly that 1Co 1:11

QUITS
The person who **q** doing what is............... Pr 15:10

R

RAAMAH
Havilah, Sabtah, **R,** and Sabteca. .... Ge 10:7
The sons of **R** were Sheba and .... Ge 10:7
Havilah, Sabta, **R,** and Sabteca. 1Ch 1:9
of Sheba and **R** became merchants .... Eze 27:22

RAAMAH'S
R sons were Sheba and Dedan. 1Ch 1:9

RAAMIAH
Nehemiah, Azariah, **R,** Nahamani,............ Ne 7:7

RABBAH
and attacked the city of **R.** 2Sa 11:1
the city wall of **R** that will .... Am 1:14

RABBI
They said, "**R,** where are you .... Jn 1:38
"**R**" means "Teacher." .... Jn 1:38

RABBIM
Heshbon near the gate of Bath **R.** .... Sng 7:4

RABBIT
The **r** chews the cud but does not .... Le 11:6

RABBITH
R, Kishion, Ebez,.................................... Jos 19:20

RABBITS
not eat camels, **r,** or rock .... Dt 14:7

RABBONI
in the Hebrew language, "**R.**" .... Jn 20:16

RACAL
R, the cities of the 1Sa 30:29

RACE
an athlete eager to run a **r.** .... Ps 19:5
does not always win the **r,** .... Ec 9:11
how can you **r** against horses? .... Je 12:5
The chariots **r** through the .... Nah 2:4
know that in a **r** all the runners 1Co 9:24
You were running a good **r.** .... Gal 5:7
not wasted. I ran the **r** and won. .... Php 2:16
have finished the **r,** I have kept 2Ti 4:7
let us run the **r** that is before .... Heb 12:1
Those from every **r** of people, ... Rev 11:9

RACED
He **r** on the wings of the wind. 2Sa 22:11
He **r** on the wings of the wind. .... Ps 18:10

RACES
the horse **r** over the ground; .... Job 39:24
sits, are peoples, **r,** nations, ... Rev 17:15

RACHEL
Then Jacob kissed **R** and cried. .... Ge 29:11
was Leah, and the younger was **R.** .... Ge 29:16
Jacob loved **R,** so he said to .... Ge 29:18
seven years so he could marry **R.** .... Ge 29:20
R said, "I wish the LORD would........... Ge 30:24
R was buried on the road to .... Ge 35:19
your home, like **R** and Leah, who .... Ru 4:11
R crying for her children. .... Je 31:15
R crying for her children. .... Mt 2:18

RACING
tired while **r** against people, ... Je 12:5

RADDAI
was Nethanel, his fifth was **R,** 1Ch 2:14

RAFTS
bring it on **r** by sea to Joppa 2Ch 2:16

RAGE
of the LORD's anger and **r,** .... Dt 9:19
go, and how you **r** against me. 2Ki 19:27
Because you **r** against me, and 2Ki 19:28
go, and how you **r** against me. .... Is 37:28
Because you **r** against me, and .... Is 37:29
In my anger and **r,** I will pay .... Mic 5:15

RAGING
sank like lead in the **r** water. .... Ex 15:10
mountains shake at the **r** sea. .... Ps 46:3

RAGS
too much and end up wearing **r.** .... Pr 23:21
them away like filthy **r** and say, ... Is 30:22
He took some old **r** and worn-out .... Je 38:11
he let those **r** down with some .... Je 38:11
Put these old **r** and worn-out .... Je 38:12

RAHAB
house of a prostitute named **R.** .... Jos 2:1
You crushed the sea monster **R;** .... Ps 89:10
that country **R** the Do-Nothing. .... Is 30:7
you cut **R** into pieces and killed .... Is 51:9
Boaz's mother was **R.**) Boaz was .... Mt 1:5
by faith that **R,** the prostitute .... Heb 11:31
example is **R,** a prostitute, who .... Jam 2:25

RAHAM
Shema was the father of **R,** 1Ch 2:44

RAID
had gone out to **r** the Israelites 2Ki 5:2

RAIDED
David and his men **r** the people 1Sa 27:8
Amalekites had **r** southern Judah 1Sa 30:1
had **r** the southern area of the 1Sa 30:14

RAIDING
camp and those in the **r** party. 1Sa 14:15
"Where did you go **r** today?" 1Sa 27:10
The LORD sent **r** parties from 2Ki 24:2

RAIDS
the Philistine camp to make **r.** 1Sa 13:17

RAIN
not yet made it **r** on the land. .... Ge 2:5
now I will send **r** on the earth. .... Ge 7:4
When the king saw that the **r,** .... Ex 9:34
to fall like **r** from the sky for .... Ex 16:4
land that drinks **r** from heaven. .... Dt 11:11
he will send **r** on your land at .... Dt 11:14
My teaching will drop like **r;** .... Dt 32:2
the LORD to send thunder and **r.** 1Sa 12:17
be no dew or **r** on the mountains 2Sa 1:21
no **r** or dew will fall during the 1Ki 17:1
because a heavy **r** is coming." 1Ki 18:41
they would for **r** and drank in my .... Job 29:23
the earth and turns them into **r.** .... Job 36:27
sends the lightning with the **r.** .... Ps 135:7
are full of **r,** they will shower .... Ec 11:3
the **r** clouds will never seem to .... Ec 12:2
to hide from the storm and **r.** .... Is 4:6
above, make victory fall like **r;** .... Is 45:8
R and snow fall from the sky and .... Is 55:10
He will come to us like **r,** .... Hos 6:3
I held back the **r** from you three........... Am 4:7
Ask the LORD for **r** during the .... Zch 10:1
and he sends **r** to those who do .... Mt 5:45
He prayed that it would not **r,** .... Jam 5:17
the **r** came down from the sky, ... Jam 5:18
They are clouds without **r,** .... Jud 1:12

RAINBOW
I am putting my **r** in the clouds .... Ge 9:13
earth and **r** appears in them, ... Ge 9:14
the **r** appears in the clouds, ... Ge 9:16
The **r** is a sign of the agreement .... Ge 9:17
looked like the **r** in the clouds .... Eze 1:28
the throne was a **r** the color of .... Rev 4:3
a cloud with a **r** over his head. .... Rev 10:1

RAINED
the skies **r,** and the clouds .... Jdg 5:4
He **r** manna down on them to eat; .... Ps 78:24
He **r** meat on them like dust. .... Ps 78:27
It **r** hard, the floods came, and .... Mt 7:25
It **r** hard, the floods came, and .... Mt 7:27
fire and sulfur **r** down from the .... Lk 17:29

RAINING
meeting and because it was **r.** .... Ezr 10:9
Because it was **r** and very cold, ... Ac 28:2
the sky from **r** during the time .... Rev 11:6

RAINS
I will give you **r** at the right .... Le 26:4
from mountain **r** and stay near .... Job 24:8
for the heavy **r** and sets a path .... Job 38:25
The autumn **r** fill it with pools .... Ps 84:6
the **r** are over and gone. .... Sng 2:11
have not been any spring **r.** .... Je 3:3
and spring **r** in their seasons .... Je 5:24
will cause the **r** to come when it .... Eze 34:26
rain during the springtime **r.** .... Zch 10:1
receive the autumn and spring **r.** .... Jam 5:7

RAINSTORM
attack like a **r** beating against .... Is 25:4

RAINY

here, and it's the r season. .... Ezr 10:13
a continual dripping on a r day. .... Pr 27:15
in the clouds on a r day. .... Eze 1:28
you say that it will be a r day, ... Mt 16:3

RAISE

to live in tents and r cattle. .... Ge 4:20
Tell Aaron to r his walking .... Ex 8:16
R your hand toward the sky. .... Ex 9:22
I will r my hands to the LORD in .... Ex 9:29
R your hand over the land of .... Ex 10:12
R your hand toward the sky, ... Ex 10:21
R your walking stick and hold it .... Ex 14:16
I r my hand toward heaven and .... Dt 32:40
and we will r a flag in the name .... Ps 20:5
I r my voice in praise and tell .... Ps 26:7
I r my hands toward your Most .... Ps 28:2
They r their young near your .... Ps 84:3
LORD, the seas r, the seas raise .... Ps 93:3
raise, the seas r their voice. .... Ps 93:3
The seas r up their pounding .... Ps 93:3
R your hands in the Temple and .... Ps 134:2
When you r your arms to me in .... Is 1:15
with a rod and r a stick against .... Is 10:24
He will r his stick over the .... Is 10:26
will r a banner as a sign for .... Is 11:12
R a flag on the bare mountain. .... Is 13:2
R your hand to signal them to .... Is 13:2
because he will r his hand to .... Is 19:16
I will r my banner for all the .... Is 49:22
R the banner as a sign for the .... Is 62:10
R the signal flag toward .... Je 4:6
R the warning flag over the town .... Je 6:1
because I will r my hand and .... Je 6:12
when I will r up a good branch .... Je 23:5
will r his shields against you. .... Eze 26:8
day he will r us up so that we .... Hos 6:2
will no longer r swords against .... Mic 4:3
So you will r your fist in .... Mic 5:9
the sick, r the dead to life .... Mt 10:8
I must r them all on the last .... Jn 6:39
and I will r them on the last .... Jn 6:40
and I will r that person up on .... Jn 6:44
will r them up on the last day. .... Jn 6:54
for God to r people from the .... Ac 26:8
will also r us from the dead. 1Co 6:14
God will also r us with Jesus. 2Co 4:14
God used to r Christ from the .... Eph 1:20
but r them with the training and .... Eph 6:4
God will r with Jesus those who 1Th 4:14
that God could r the dead, ... Heb 11:19

RAISED

When Moses r his walking stick .... Ex 9:23
He r his hands to the LORD, ... Ex 9:33
the Most High r his voice. 2Sa 22:14
When the angel r his arm toward 2Sa 24:16
their arm is r to do harm, ... Job 38:15
Every valley should be r up, ... Is 40:4
and the roads will be r up. .... Is 49:11
Temple had a r base all around .... Eze 41:8
It was r up on one of its sides .... Da 7:5
hear, the dead are r to life, ... Mt 11:5
and then be r from the dead .... Mt 16:21
had died were r from the dead. .... Mt 27:52
after Jesus was r from the dead .... Mt 27:53
hear, the dead are r to life, ... Lk 7:22
But after Jesus was r to glory, ... Jn 12:16
Jesus when he r Lazarus from .... Jn 12:17
One whom God r from the dead. .... Ac 2:32
God has r up his servant Jesus .... Ac 3:26
but God r him from the dead. .... Ac 4:10
Jesus was truly r from the dead. .... Ac 4:33

God of our ancestors, r Jesus up .... Ac 5:30
as Christ was r from the dead .... Rm 6:4
God r Jesus from the dead, ... Rm 8:11
but he was also r from the dead, ... Rm 8:34
heart that God r Jesus from the .... Rm 10:9
By his power God has r the Lord 1Co 6:14
that Christ was r from the dead, ... 1Co 15:12
with the dead who are r to life. 1Co 15:42
God r the Lord Jesus from the 2Co 4:14
And he r us up with Christ and .... Eph 2:6
and you were r up with him .... Col 2:12
they could be r from the dead to .... Heb 11:35
who r Christ from the dead and 1Pe 1:21
Christ was r from the dead. 1Pe 3:21
among those r from the dead. .... Rev 1:5
and on the land r his right hand .... Rev 10:5

RAISES

and he r them to life again. 1Sa 2:6
The LORD r the poor up from the 1Sa 2:8
she r her voice in the city .... Pr 1:20
understanding r her voice. .... Pr 8:1
r a banner for the nations far .... Is 5:26
When the LORD r his hand to .... Is 14:27
as the Father r the dead and .... Jn 5:21
who r people from the dead. 2Co 1:9
thing that r itself against 2Co 10:5

RAISIN

groan for the r cakes they had .... Is 16:7
and love to eat the r cakes." .... Hos 3:1

RAISING

children, by r Jesus from the .... Ac 13:33
this to everyone by r that man .... Ac 17:31
works such as r her children, ... 1Ti 5:10
about the r of the dead and .... Heb 6:2
This is the first r of the dead. .... Rev 20:5
in this first r of the dead. .... Rev 20:6

RAISINS

grape juice or eat grapes or r. .... Nu 6:3
cakes of r, and two hundred 1Sa 25:18
fig cake and two clusters of r. 1Sa 30:12
and a cake of r to every 2Sa 6:19
hundred cakes of r, one hundred 2Sa 16:1
fig cakes, r, wine, oil, cows 1Ch 12:40
and r to every Israelite man and 1Ch 16:3
me with r, and refresh me .... Sng 2:5

RAKEM

Sheresh's sons were Ulam and **R.** 1Ch 7:16

RAKKATH

Zer, Hammath, **R,** Kinnereth, ... Jos 19:35

RAKKON

Me Jarkon, **R,** and the area near .... Jos 19:46

RAM

Hezron was the father of **R,** .... Ru 4:19
were Jerahmeel, **R,** and Caleb. 1Ch 2:9
R was Amminadab's father, and 1Ch 2:10
sons were **R,** Bunah, Oren, Ozem, ... 1Ch 2:25
R was Jerahmeel's first son. 1Ch 2:25
first son, **R,** had sons. 1Ch 2:27
the family of **R,** became very .... Job 32:2
Hezron was the father of **R.** .... Mt 1:3
R was the father of Amminadab. .... Mt 1:4

RAMAH

together and met Samuel at **R.** 1Sa 8:4
buried him at his home in **R.** 1Sa 25:1
was heard in **R** of painful crying .... Je 31:15
was heard in **R** of painful crying .... Mt 2:18

RAMATH

from Heshbon to **R** Mizpah and .... Jos 13:26
So that place was named **R** Lehi. .... Jdg 15:17

RAMATHAIM
of Jeroham from **R** in the 1Sa 1:1

RAMESES
in Egypt, near the city of **R.** .... Ge 47:11
Pithom and **R** as supply centers .... Ex 1:11
traveled from **R** to Succoth. .... Ex 12:37
Israelites left **R** and marched .... Nu 33:3
Israelites left **R** and camped at .... Nu 33:5

RAMIAH
R, Izziah, Malkijah, Mijamin, ... Ezr 10:25

RAMOTH
R in Gilead was for the Gadites; .... Dt 4:43
prophet, went to **R** in Gilead. 2Ki 9:4
son of Ahab to **R** in Gilead, ... 2Ch 22:5

RAMP
or build a **r** to attack the city 2Ki 19:32
or build a **r** to attack the city .... Is 37:33
build an attack **r** to the top of .... Je 6:6

RAMPS
He will build **r** to the tops of .... Da 11:15

RAN
he **r** from his tent to meet them. .... Ge 18:2
But Esau **r** to meet Jacob and put .... Ge 33:4
r to Eli and said, "I am here. 1Sa 3:5
Then David **r** and stood beside 1Sa 17:51
So the water **r** off the altar and 1Ki 18:35
they **r** to tell their message. .... Je 23:21
herdsmen **r** away and went into .... Mt 8:33
They **r** to tell Jesus' followers .... Mt 28:8
Peter got up and **r** to the tomb. .... Lk 24:12
she **r** to Simon Peter and the .... Jn 20:2
other follower **r** faster than .... Jn 20:4
Together they **r**, took Paul, and .... Ac 21:30
and soldiers and **r** to the place .... Ac 21:32
not wasted. I **r** the race and won .... Php 2:16
The woman **r** away into the desert .... Rev 12:6
Then every island **r** away, and .... Rev 16:20
Earth and sky **r** away from him .... Rev 20:11

RANK
of the next **r** and the 2Ki 23:4
Zephaniah the priest next in **r**, ... 2Ki 25:18
the highest **r** in the kingdom. .... Est 1:14
gave him a new **r** that was higher .... Est 3:1
Zephaniah the priest next in **r**, ... Je 52:24

RANKS
He **r** higher than everything that .... Col 1:15

RANSOM
have to pay a **r** for their lives .... Pr 13:8
his life as a **r** for many people. .... Mt 20:28
his life as a **r** for many people. .... Mk 10:45

RAPED
be robbed and their wives **r**. .... Is 13:16

RAPHA
of the sons of **R**, had a bronze 2Sa 21:16
another one of the sons of **R**. 2Sa 21:18
also was one of the sons of **R**. 2Sa 21:20
four sons of **R** from Gath were 2Sa 21:22
Eshton was the father of Beth **R**, ... 1Ch 4:12
his fourth, and **R** was his fifth 1Ch 8:2
also was one of the sons of **R**. 1Ch 20:6
descendants of **R** from Gath were 1Ch 20:8

RAPHAH
of Binea. **R** was Binea's son 1Ch 8:37

RAPHAH'S
Eleasah was **R** son, and Azel was 1Ch 8:37

RAPHU
of Benjamin, Palti son of **R**; .... Nu 13:9

RARE
fill a home with **r** and beautiful .... Pr 24:4

RASH
a swelling or a **r** or a bright .... Le 13:2
is only a **r**. The person must .... Le 13:6
But if the **r** spreads again after .... Le 13:7
and if the **r** has spread on the .... Le 13:8
disease is only a harmless **r**. .... Le 13:39

RASHES
swellings, **r**, or bright spots on .... Le 14:56

RATS
moles, **r**, all kinds of great .... Le 11:29
skin and five gold models of **r**. 1Sa 6:4
growths and the **r** that are 1Sa 6:5
box with the gold **r** and models 1Sa 6:11
also sent gold models of **r**. 1Sa 6:18
The number of **r** matched the 1Sa 6:18
meat of pigs and **r** and other .... Is 66:17

RATTLES
tambourines, **r**, and cymbals. 2Sa 6:5
The bag of arrows **r** against the .... Job 39:23

RATTLING
there was a noise and a **r**. .... Eze 37:7

RAVEN
sent out a **r**. It flew here and .... Ge 8:7
any kind of **r**, ... Le 11:15
any kind of **r**, ... Dt 14:14
hair is wavy and black like a **r**. .... Sng 5:11

RAVENS
I have commanded **r** to bring you 1Ki 17:4
and owls and **r** will live there. .... Is 34:11

RAW
not eat the lamb **r** or boiled in .... Ex 12:9
skin looks **r** in the swelling, ... Le 13:10
meat from you, only **r** meat." 1Sa 2:15
and every shoulder was rubbed **r**. .... Eze 29:18

RAYS
R of light shine from his hand, ... Hab 3:4
the sun, with healing in its **r**. .... Mal 4:2

RAZOR
ever cut his hair with a **r**." 1Sa 1:11
Your tongue is like a sharp **r**, ... Ps 52:2
use it like a **r** to punish Judah .... Is 7:20
like a barber's **r** to shave your .... Eze 5:1

REACHES
Our guilt even **r** up to the sky. .... Ezr 9:6
your love **r** to the heavens, ... Ps 36:5
Your great love **r** to the skies, ... Ps 57:10
your justice **r** to the skies. .... Ps 71:19
Your great love **r** to the skies, ... Ps 108:4
his glory **r** to the skies. .... Ps 113:4
it **r** to the clouds.' .... Je 51:9
Jerusalem **r** out her hands, ... La 1:17
Your power **r** to the far parts of .... Da 4:22
the LORD's terrible anger **r** you, ... Zph 2:2

READ
Agreement and **r** it so the people .... Ex 24:7
all the time and **r** from it every .... Dt 17:19
Water Gate Ezra **r** the Teachings .... Ne 8:3
They **r** from the Book of the .... Ne 8:8
R from the scroll to all the .... Je 36:6
but they could not **r** the writing .... Da 5:8
And have you not **r** in the law of .... Mt 12:5
always did, and stood up to **r**. .... Lk 4:16
Many of the people **r** the sign, ... Jn 19:20
which are a Jewish Sabbath day. .... Ac 13:27
And it is still **r** in the .... Ac 15:21
hearts, known and **r** by everyone. 2Co 3:2
when they **r** the law of Moses, ... 2Co 3:15

After this letter is r to you, ... Col 4:16
continue to r the Scriptures to 1Ti 4:13

READING

After you finish r this scroll, ... Je 51:63
I, Daniel, was r the Scriptures. .... Da 9:2
in his chariot r from the Book .... Ac 8:28
he heard the man r from Isaiah .... Ac 8:30
you understand what you are r?" .... Ac 8:30
of Scripture he was r was this: .... Ac 8:32

READS

so whoever r it can run to tell................. Hab 2:2
is the one who r the words of .... Rev 1:3

READY

the people, "Be r in three days. .... Ex 19:15
other half was r with spears, ... Ne 4:16
They are like lions r to kill;..................... Ps 17:12
you are always r to be merciful, ... Ps 51:1
but they are r to attack me. .... Ps 59:4
you are getting r to attack. .... Ps 83:2
Jeremiah, get r. Stand up and .... Je 1:17
Court was r to begin, and the .... Da 7:10
The LORD was r to bring the .... Da 9:14
The wedding feast is r. .... Mt 22:8
also must be r, because the Son .... Mt 24:44
make a people r for the coming .... Lk 1:17
to make everything r for him. .... Lk 9:52
Be dressed, r for service, and .... Lk 12:35
I am not only r to be tied up in .... Ac 21:13
They are always r to kill people .... Rm 3:15
like a woman r to give birth. .... Rm 8:22
who is always r to help. 2Co 8:22
am now r to visit you the third 2Co 12:14
Be r at all times, and tell........................ 2Ti 4:2
must be r to welcome guests .... Tit 1:8
obey them, to be r to do good, ... Tit 3:1
and worn out is r to disappear............... Heb 8:13
Always be r to answer everyone............... 1Pe 3:15
who is r to judge the living and 1Pe 4:5
woman who was r to give birth so .... Rev 12:4
Lamb's bride has made herself r. .... Rev 19:7

REAIAH

R was Shobal's son. Reaiah was............... 1Ch 4:2
R was the father of Jahath, ... 1Ch 4:2
Shimei's son. R was Micah's son 1Ch 5:5
Giddel, Gahar, R,................................. Ezr 2:47
R, Rezin, Nekoda, ... Ne 7:50

REAIAH'S

was Micah's son. Baal was R son. 1Ch 5:5

REALLY

The Lord r has risen from the................. Lk 24:34

REAP

his ground and r his harvest. 1Sa 8:12

REAR

six frames for the r or west end .... Ex 26:22
frames for each corner at the r. .... Ex 26:23
frames at the r of the Tent, ... Ex 26:25
on the west end, at the r........................ Ex 26:27
length of each side and r. .... Ex 26:28
six frames for the r or west end .... Ex 36:27
at the r of the Holy Tent........................ Ex 36:28
west end, at the r of the Tent. .... Ex 36:32
of each side and r of the Tent. .... Ex 36:33
ones were the r guard for all .... Nu 10:25
and those in the r into the .... Joe 2:20

REARED

have not r young men or women." .... Is 23:4
So who r these children?........................ Is 49:21

REASON

want to destroy me for no r. .... Ps 69:4
about me and attack me for no r. .... Ps 109:3
Leaders attack me for no r,..................... Ps 119:161
realized the r people work hard .... Ec 4:4
good r, the young women love .... Sng 1:4
For this r I will make him a .... Is 53:12
And this is the r: God lives .... Is 57:15
give you good r to be afraid .... Je 1:17
looking for a r to accuse Jesus, ... Mt 12:10
his wife for any r he chooses?" .... Mt 19:3
For this r the baby will be holy .... Lk 1:35
I can find no r to kill him. .... Lk 23:22
I found no r to order his death. .... Ac 25:25
There is no r why this man .... Ac 26:31
So do we have a r to brag about .... Rm 3:27
he did, he had a r to brag. .... Rm 4:2
I have greater r for trusting .... Php 3:4
there is no r to praise you for 1Pe 2:20
For this r the Good News was................. 1Pe 4:6
The r the people in the world do 1Jn 3:1
our God into a r for sexual sin. .... Jud 1:4

REASONABLE

speaking to you as to r people; 1Co 10:15

REASONED

like a child, I r like a child..................... 1Co 13:11

REASONS

but the LORD will judge your r. .... Pr 16:2
but the LORD judges your r. .... Pr 21:2
they offer them for the wrong r. .... Pr 21:27
tried to find r to accuse Daniel .... Da 6:4
and your holy city for these r: .... Da 9:24
are different r why some men................. Mt 19:12
Christ for selfish and wrong r, ... Php 1:17
whether for right or wrong r, ... Php 1:18
not come from lies or wrong r, ... 1Th 2:3

REBA

Zur, Hur, and R, who were the .... Nu 31:8
Evi, Rekem, Zur, Hur, and R. .... Jos 13:21

REBEKAH

eating. But R loved Jacob. .... Ge 25:28
much sorrow to Isaac and R. .... Ge 26:35

REBEL

prison who was a r and had .... Mk 15:7

REBELS

Your rulers are r and friends of .... Is 1:23

REBUILD

He will r my city and set my .... Is 45:13
They will r the old ruins and .... Is 61:4
says, "If they r them, I will .... Mal 1:4
But I will r its ruins, and I .... Ac 15:16

REBUILDING

We are r the Temple that a great............... Ezr 5:11
and that you are r the wall..................... Ne 6:6
places and for r the roads and .... Is 58:12

REBUILDS

The LORD r Jerusalem; .... Ps 147:2

REBUILT

The people of Dan r the city and .... Jdg 18:28
worshiped, but Manasseh r them. 2Ki 21:3
order for this Temple to be r. .... Ezr 5:13
Let the Temple be r as a place .... Ezr 6:3

RECAH

These people were from R. 1Ch 4:12

RECALL

We continually r before God our 1Th 1:3

RECEIVE

my son Isaac should r it all." .... Ge 21:10
Why did my mother's knees r me, ... Job 3:12
They will r a blessing from the .... Ps 24:5
Let him r gold from Sheba. .... Ps 72:15
later you will r me in honor. .... Ps 73:24
who plan evil will r trouble. .... Pr 22:8
explain it will r purple clothes .... Da 5:7
High God will r the power to .... Da 7:18
accepts him will r the reward .... Mt 10:41
person is good will r the reward .... Mt 10:41
R the kingdom God has prepared .... Mt 25:34
will r a greater punishment. .... Mk 12:40
Give, and you will r. .... Lk 6:38
Yes, everyone who asks will r. .... Lk 11:10
will r a greater punishment. .... Lk 20:47
in Jesus would r the Spirit. .... Jn 7:39
the Son of Man to r his glory. .... Jn 12:23
Ask and you will r, so that your .... Jn 16:24
and said, "R the Holy Spirit. .... Jn 20:22
Wait here to r the promise from .... Ac 1:4
comes to you, you will r power. .... Ac 1:8
And you will r the gift of the .... Ac 2:38
"Lord Jesus, r my spirit." .... Ac 7:59
we will r blessings from God .... Rm 8:17
they also can r mercy from him. .... Rm 11:31
Now we did not r the spirit of 1Co 2:12
if you did not r it as a gift? 1Co 4:7
How did you r the Holy Spirit? .... Gal 3:2
the free woman should r it all." .... Gal 4:30
God can now r the blessings he .... Heb 9:15
what God wants and r what he has .... Heb 10:36
faith and to r the kingdom God .... Jam 2:5
you do not r because the reason .... Jam 4:3
so that you might r a blessing. 1Pe 3:9
but that you r your full reward. 2Jn 1:8
to r glory and honor and power, ... Rev 4:11
was killed is worthy to r power, ... Rev 5:12
but they will r power to rule .... Rev 17:12
you will not r the disasters .... Rev 18:4
who win the victory will r this, ... Rev 21:7
that they will r the right to .... Rev 22:14

RECEIVED

He r more honor than the Thirty, ... 2Sa 23:23
the punishment I should have r. .... Job 33:27
You r gifts from the people, ... Ps 68:18
tired of the advice you have r. .... Is 47:13
get their pay, each r one coin. .... Mt 20:9
one of them also r one coin. .... Mt 20:10
I would have r my gold back with .... Mt 25:27
that you have r the things you .... Mk 11:24
until you have r that power from .... Lk 24:49
from him we all r one gift after .... Jn 1:16
people gods who r God's message, ... Jn 10:35
have r the agreement God made .... Ac 3:25
The man who r the miracle of. .... Ac 4:22
people, they r the Holy Spirit .... Ac 8:17
bodies they r the punishment .... Rm 1:27
his descendants r the promise .... Rm 4:13
many people r God's gift of life .... Rm 5:15
The Spirit we r does not make us .... Rm 8:15
but we r the Spirit that is from 1Co 2:12
same teaching I r from the Lord: 1Co 11:23
I passed on to you what I r, ... 1Co 15:3
you r the Spirit because you .... Gal 3:2
what you learned and r from me, ... Php 4:9
r that same promise from God. .... Heb 11:9
was right, r God's promises, ... Heb 11:33
Women r their dead relatives .... Heb 11:35
Each of you has r a gift to use 1Pe 4:10
To you who have r a faith as 2Pe 1:1
when he r honor and glory from 2Pe 1:17

RECEIVES

not die before he r a fair trial .... Nu 35:12
he r nothing from your hand. .... Job 35:7
Now the Son of Man r his glory, ... Jn 13:31
and God r glory through him. .... Jn 13:31
If God r glory through him, ... Jn 13:32
it, and it r God's blessings. .... Heb 6:7
that Levi, who r a tenth, also .... Heb 7:9
name except the one who r it. .... Rev 2:17

RECEIVING

have the hope of r the life that .... Tit 3:7
are r the goal of your faith— 1Pe 1:9

RECENTLY

had r moved to Corinth from .... Ac 18:2

RECKLESS

some worthless, r men, who .... Jdg 9:4
the noise of a r crowd in the .... Eze 23:42

RECOGNIZE

was still too dark to r anyone. .... Ru 3:14
clothes so no one will r me. 1Ki 22:30
clothes so no one will r me. 2Ch 18:29
they almost didn't r him. .... Job 2:12
he goes by me, I do not r him. .... Job 9:11
and even fools r it. .... Pr 14:33
and Israel doesn't r us. .... Is 63:16
come, and they did not r him. .... Mt 17:12
you did not r the time when God .... Lk 19:44
they were allowed to r Jesus. .... Lk 24:31
You should r the value of people 1Co 16:18

RECOGNIZED

Judah r them and said, "She is .... Ge 38:26
they r the voice of the young .... Jdg 18:3
of Israel r me as their king 1Ki 2:15
Obadiah r Elijah, so he bowed 1Ki 18:7
he can be r as one truly sent by .... Je 28:9
When the people there r Jesus, ... Mt 14:35
saw them leave and r them. .... Mk 6:33
people immediately r Jesus. .... Mk 6:54
road and how they r Jesus when .... Lk 24:35
When she r Peter's voice, she .... Ac 12:14

RECOGNIZES

no one r them in the streets. .... La 4:8

RECOGNIZING

but they were kept from r him. .... Lk 24:16
the cup without r the body eat 1Co 11:29

RECOMMEND

I r to you our sister Phoebe, ... Rm 16:1

RECOVER

if I will r from my injuries." 2Ki 1:2
if I will r from my sickness. 2Ki 8:8
asks if he will r from his 2Ki 8:9
You will surely r,' but the LORD 2Ki 8:10
told me that you will surely r." 2Ki 8:14

RECOVERED

He r the valuable things and 1Sa 30:19
them any of the things we r. 1Sa 30:22

RED

The first baby was born r. .... Ge 25:25
Let me eat some of that r soup, ... Ge 25:30
the locusts away into the R Sea. .... Ex 10:19
sheepskins that are dyed r; .... Ex 25:5
He commanded the R Sea, and it .... Ps 106:9
parted the water of the R Sea. .... Ps 136:13
stare at the wine when it is r, ... Pr 23:31
Though your sins are deep r, ... Is 1:18

R

clothes bright **r** as if you had .... Is 63:2
I saw a man riding a **r** horse. .... Zch 1:8
R horses pulled the first .... Zch 6:2
weather, because the sky is **r**. .... Mt 16:2
crossed the **R** Sea as if it were .... Heb 11:29
another horse came out, a **r** one. .... Rev 6:4
was a giant **r** dragon with seven.............. Rev 12:3

RED-WHITE
if there is a **r** sore on his bald.................. Le 13:42
his bald head or forehead is **r**, ... Le 13:43

REDDER
Their bodies were **r** than rubies;.............. La 4:7

REED
to see? A **r** blown by the wind? .... Mt 11:7
to see? A **r** blown by the wind? .... Lk 7:24

REEDS
basket made of **r** and covered it .... Ex 2:3
which will be like **r** swaying in 1Ki 14:15
and **r** cannot grow tall without .... Job 8:11
on the water in boats made of **r**............... Is 18:2

REELAIAH
Seraiah, **R**, Mordecai, Bilshan .... Ezr 2:2

REFER
These rules **r** to earthly things .... Col 2:22

REFLECTION
we see a dim **r**, as if we were 1Co 13:12

REFLECTS
As water **r** your face, so your .... Pr 27:19
The Son **r** the glory of God and .... Heb 1:3

REFRESH
R yourself by eating something. .... Jdg 19:5
father said, "**R** yourself. .... Jdg 19:8
r those who send them, ... Pr 25:13
raisins, and **r** me with apples,.................. Sng 2:5
R my heart in Christ. .... Phm 1:20

REFRESHED
house and the foreigner be **r**. .... Ex 23:12
you **r** your tired land. .... Ps 68:9
They have **r** my spirit and yours. 1Co 16:18
to God's people has **r** them. .... Phm 1:7

REFUSE
If you **r** to let my people go, ... Ex 10:4
he couldn't **r** them anymore, ... 2Ki 2:17
them, because they **r** to work................... Pr 21:25
But if you **r** to obey and if you .... Is 1:20
These people **r** to accept the .... Is 8:6
Those who **r**, let them refuse, ... Eze 3:27
for those who **r** to follow it. 1Ti 1:9
others, will **r** to forgive, will 2Ti 3:3
and do not **r** to listen when God .... Heb 12:25

REFUSED
to save him, but we **r** to listen. .... Ge 42:21
day of the month he **r** to eat. 1Sa 20:34
king's officers **r** to kill the 1Sa 22:17
with God and **r** to live by his .... Ps 78:10
But now you have **r** and rejected .... Ps 89:38
have **r** to obey the teachings .... Is 5:24
You people have **r** to accept this .... Is 30:12
but they **r** to learn what is .... Je 5:3
should be **r** if it is accepted.................... 1Ti 4:4
r to be called the son of the .... Heb 11:24
Others **r** to listen to him when .... Heb 12:25
r to obey God long ago in the 1Pe 3:20
But the people **r** to change their .... Rev 16:9
they **r** to change their hearts .... Rev 16:11

REFUSES
stubborn and **r** to let the people .... Ex 7:14
but the one who **r** to take .... Pr 28:16

If he **r** to listen to them, ... Mt 18:17
If he **r** to listen to the church, ... Mt 18:17

REFUSING
r to obey all my commands, ... Le 26:15
the LORD and **r** to follow him? .... Jos 22:18
R to listen to what Neco said at 2Ch 35:22
have turned away, **r** to obey you. .... Da 9:11
over their mouths, **r** to listen. .... Mic 7:16
R to eat does not make us less 1Co 8:8

REGAIN
you so you can **r** your strength. .... Ge 18:5
people will **r** southern Judah .... Ob 1:19
They will **r** the lands of Ephraim .... Ob 1:19

REGAINED
way you have **r** your innocence. 2Co 7:11

REGARDLESS
or rough cloth, **r** of its use. .... Le 11:32

REGEM
sons were **R**, Jotham, Geshan, ... 1Ch 2:47

REGEM-MELECH
sent Sharezer, **R**, and their men .... Zch 7:2

REGION
Jair from the **r** of Gilead became .... Jdg 10:3
Jordan River in the **r** of Gilead, ... Jdg 10:8
It was the **r** of Gad, Reuben, and 2Ki 10:33

REGIONS
listed by their families and **r**, ... Ge 36:40
the **r** of Geshur and of the .... Jos 13:2
and all of you **r** of Philistia! .... Joe 3:4
went through the **r** of Galatia .... Ac 18:23
from town to town in these **r**, ... Ac 18:23

REGISTER
so I could **r** them by families .... Ne 7:5
must list their names in a **r**. .... Lk 2:1

REGISTERED
went to their own towns to be **r**............... Lk 2:3
Joseph **r** with Mary, to whom he .... Lk 2:5

REGISTRATION
This was the first **r**;............................... Lk 2:2
Galilee at the time of the **r**. .... Ac 5:37

REGULAR
They are to be the **r** share which .... Ex 29:28
They took their **r** places in the 2Ch 30:16
they had **r** sacrifices every day, ... Ezr 3:5
the **r** grain offerings and burnt .... Ne 10:33
the altar at **r** times and that .... Ne 13:31
the feasts and **r** times of .... Eze 46:11
be decided at the **r** town meeting .... Ac 19:39

REGULARLY
the trumpets **r** before the Ark.................. 1Ch 16:6

REGULATED
orders, which **r** them day by day. .... Ne 11:23

REHABIAH
Eliezer's first son was **R**.......................... 1Ch 23:17
other sons, but **R** had many sons. 1Ch 23:17
Isshiah was the first son of **R**.................. 1Ch 24:21
Eliezer's son **R**, Rehabiah's son 1Ch 26:25

REHABIAH'S
son Rehabiah, **R** son Jeshaiah, ... 1Ch 26:25

REHOB
all the way to **R** by Lebo Hamath. .... Nu 13:21
it went to Abdon, **R**, Hammon, and .... Jos 19:28
Ummah, Aphek, and **R**. There were .... Jos 19:30
Helkath, and **R**, and the pastures .... Jos 21:31
Aczib, Helbah, Aphek, and **R**. .... Jdg 1:31
was in a valley near Beth **R**. .... Jdg 18:28
defeated Hadadezer son of **R**,.................. 2Sa 8:3

taken from Hadadezer son of **R**,............... 2Sa 8:12
soldiers from Beth **R** and Zobah. 2Sa 10:6
Zobah and **R** and the men from 2Sa 10:8
Mica, **R**, Hashabiah, ... Ne 10:11

REHOBOAM
R went to Shechem, where all the 1Ki 12:1
When **R** arrived in Jerusalem, ... 1Ki 12:21
Solomon was the father of **R**. .... Mt 1:7
R was the father of Abijah...................... Mt 1:7

REHOBOTH
of Nineveh, **R** Ir, and Calah. .... Ge 10:11
He was from **R** on the Euphrates .... Ge 36:37
He was from **R** by the river. 1Ch 1:48

REHUM
Mispar, Bigvai, **R**, and Baanah. .... Ezr 2:2
R the governor and Shimshai the .... Ezr 4:8
letter is from **R** the governor, ... Ezr 4:9
To **R** the governor and Shimshai .... Ezr 4:17
sent was read to **R** and Shimshai .... Ezr 4:23
working under **R** son of Bani................... Ne 3:17
R, Hashabnah, Maaseiah, ... Ne 10:25
Shecaniah, **R**, Meremoth, ... Ne 12:3

REI
prophet, Shimei, **R**, and King 1Ki 1:8

REINS
must be led with bits and **r**, ... Ps 32:9

REJECT
make the people curse and **r** you. .... Nu 5:21
baby, her people will **r** her. .... Nu 5:27
food must not **r** the one who eats .... Rm 14:3
of people who **r** the truth. .... Tit 1:14
They **r** God's authority and speak .... Jud 1:8

REJECTED
They have not **r** you. 1Sa 8:7
You have **r** the LORD's command. 1Sa 15:23
that the builders **r** became the .... Ps 118:22
our gods' will be **r** in disgrace. .... Is 42:17
so I **r** those who belonged to me. .... Is 47:9
He was hated and **r** by people. .... Is 53:3
you completely **r** the nation of .... Je 14:19
But Israel has **r** what is good, ... Hos 8:3
that the builders **r** became the .... Mt 21:42
things and be **r** by the people .... Lk 17:25
the stone that you builders **r**, ... Ac 4:11
man the two men of Israel **r**, ... Ac 7:35
They **r** him and wanted to go back........... Ac 7:39
people have **r** this, and their 1Ti 1:19
that the builders **r** has become 1Pe 2:7

REJECTING
sinning and **r** the LORD, turning .... Is 59:13
people, you are **r** what God said. .... Mk 7:13

REJECTS
Now he **r** you as king." 1Sa 15:23
now he **r** you as king of Israel. 1Sa 15:26
then that place **r** it and says, '................. Job 8:18

REJOICE
r before the LORD your God. .... Dt 12:12
Everyone should **r**: you, your .... Dt 12:12
R in the LORD your God's .... Dt 12:18
R before the LORD your God at .... Dt 16:11
should **r**: you, your sons .... Dt 16:11
should **r** at your Feast: .... Dt 16:14
foreigners among you should **r**, ... Dt 26:11
eat them and **r** before the LORD.............. Dt 27:7
of the Philistines will **r**. 2Sa 1:20
Let the skies **r** and the earth be 1Ch 16:31
fields and everything in them **r**. 1Ch 16:32
and I **r** to see their giving. 1Ch 29:17
I will **r** because you saved me. .... Ps 9:14

against me will **r** that I've been .... Ps 13:4
Then the people of Jacob will **r**, ... Ps 14:7
So I **r** and am glad. Even my body .... Ps 16:9
will be glad and **r** in your love, ... Ps 31:7
r and be happy in the LORD. .... Ps 32:11
r in him, because we trust his................... Ps 33:21
Then I will **r** in the LORD; .... Ps 35:9
and all the towns of Judah **r**, ... Ps 48:11
Then the people of Jacob will **r**, ... Ps 53:6
But the king will **r** in his God. .... Ps 63:11
So let us **r** because of what he .... Ps 66:6
be glad and should **r** before God; .... Ps 68:3
name is the LORD. **R** before him. .... Ps 68:4
who worship you **r** and be glad. .... Ps 70:4
Your people would **r** in you. .... Ps 85:6
your name they **r** and continually .... Ps 89:16
will sing and **r** all our lives. .... Ps 90:14
Let the skies **r** and the earth be .... Ps 96:11
fields and everything in them **r**. .... Ps 96:12
Let the earth **r**; faraway lands................. Ps 97:1
glad, and the towns of Judah **r**. .... Ps 97:8
R in the LORD, you who do right. .... Ps 97:12
Let us **r** and be glad today! .... Ps 118:24
who respect you **r** when they see .... Ps 119:74
of Jerusalem **r** because of their .... Ps 149:2
who worship him **r** in his glory. .... Ps 149:5
We will **r** and be happy with you; .... Sng 1:4
They **r** and are glad to do my .... Is 13:3
the cedar trees of Lebanon **r**. .... Is 14:8
you will not **r** any longer, ... Is 23:12
we will **r** and be happy when he.............. Is 25:9
they will **r** in the Holy One of .... Is 29:19
but shout and **r** together,........................ Is 52:9
so your God will **r** over you. .... Is 62:5
Then I will **r** over Jerusalem and .... Is 65:19
be honored so we may see you **r**,' .... Is 66:5
Jerusalem, **r**. All you people who .... Is 66:10
Israel, do not **r**; don't shout..................... Hos 9:1
I will **r** in God my Savior. .... Hab 3:18
be happy and **r** with all your .... Zph 3:14
save you. He will **r** over you. .... Zph 3:17
R greatly, people of Jerusalem! .... Zch 9:9
children will see it and **r**; .... Zch 10:7
R and be glad, because you have .... Mt 5:12
So I am glad, and I **r**. .... Ac 2:26
on the earth will **r** and be happy .... Rev 11:10
So **r**, you heavens and all who .... Rev 12:12
Let us **r** and be happy and give .... Rev 19:7

REJOICED
people **r** to see their leaders 1Ch 29:9
was to her, and they **r** with her. .... Lk 1:58
Then Jesus **r** in the Holy Spirit .... Lk 10:21
the entire crowd **r** at all the .... Lk 13:17

REJOICES
r like an athlete eager to run .... Ps 19:5
the king **r** because of your .... Ps 21:1
all that I am **r** in my God. .... Is 61:10
As a man **r** over his new wife, ... Is 62:5
So he **r** and sings for joy. .... Hab 1:15
my heart **r** in God my Savior, ... Lk 1:47
in evil but **r** over the truth. 1Co 13:6

REJOICING
sadness, but we are always **r**. 2Co 6:10

REKEM
killed were Evi, **R**, Zur, Hur, ... Nu 31:8
including Evi, **R**, Zur, Hur, and .... Jos 13:21
R, Irpeel, Taralah, ... Jos 18:27
Korah, Tappuah, **R**, and Shema. 1Ch 2:43
R was the father of Shammai. 1Ch 2:44

R

RELATED

person was only **r** to him by .... Le 21:4
the king how he was **r** to her. .... Est 8:1

RELATIVE

Naomi had a rich **r** named Boaz, ... Ru 2:1
that I am a **r** who is to take .... Ru 3:12
Elizabeth, your **r**, is also .... Lk 1:36
servant was a **r** of the man whose .... Jn 18:26

RELATIVES

neighbors and **r** heard how good .... Lk 1:58
your other **r**, and your rich .... Lk 14:12
brothers, **r**, and friends will .... Lk 21:16
his **r** and close friends. .... Ac 10:24
their dead **r** raised back to life .... Heb 11:35

RELAX

tonight. **R** and enjoy yourself. .... Jdg 19:6
said to myself, "**R**, because the .... Ps 116:7

RELEASE

Pilate had to **r** one prisoner to .... Lk 23:17

RELEASED

he **r** from prison the chief .... Ge 40:20
When the land is **r** at the year .... Le 27:21
No soldier is **r** in times of war, ... Ec 8:8
tell the prisoners they are **r**. .... Is 61:1

RELIABLE

advice was as **r** as God's own 2Sa 16:23
Absalom thought it was that **r**. 2Sa 16:23
you true and **r** words so that you .... Pr 22:21
some men to be **r** witnesses: .... Is 8:2

RELIEF

and a little **r** from our slavery. .... Ezr 9:8
and my words would bring you **r**. .... Job 16:5
I must speak so I will feel **r**; .... Job 32:20
they beg for **r** from powerful .... Job 35:9

RELIEVE

people may go to **r** themselves. .... Dt 23:12
you, and when you **r** yourself, ... Dt 23:13
and he went in to **r** himself. 1Sa 24:3

RELIEVING

thought the king was **r** himself. .... Jdg 3:24

RELIGION

a follower of the Jewish **r** .... Ac 6:5
about their own **r** and about a .... Ac 25:19
my past life in the Jewish **r**. .... Gal 1:13
a leader in the Jewish **r**, ... Gal 1:14
they are only part of a human **r**. .... Col 2:23
Their "**r**" is worth nothing. .... Jam 1:26
R that God accepts as pure and .... Jam 1:27

RELIGIOUS

who hold **r** feasts for the god .... Is 65:11
I cannot stand your **r** meetings. .... Am 5:21
a good and **r** man named Joseph .... Lk 23:50
with a Jew about **r** washing. .... Jn 3:25
Since the **r** leaders did not want .... Jn 19:31
There were some **r** Jews staying. .... Ac 2:5
And some **r** people buried Stephen .... Ac 8:2
Cornelius was a **r** man. .... Ac 10:2
a **r** man who worked for him. .... Ac 10:7
of the important **r** women and the .... Ac 13:50
you are very **r** in all things. .... Ac 17:22
to me. He was a **r** man; he obeyed .... Ac 22:12
speaking against this **r** group." .... Ac 28:22
and drinking or about a **r** feast, ... Col 2:16
stand and do their **r** service, ... Heb 10:11
think they are **r** but say things .... Jam 1:26

REMAIN

will not **r** in human beings .... Ge 6:3
and will **r** only in the Nile. .... Ex 8:9
They will **r** only in the Nile." .... Ex 8:11

You only need to **r** calm; .... Ex 14:14
in her house should **r** alive. .... Jos 6:17
is that you **r** brave and fight 1Sa 18:17
let no evil **r** in your tent. .... Job 11:14
be destroyed, but you will **r**. .... Ps 102:26
their children will **r** with you." .... Ps 102:28
who are innocent will **r** in it. .... Pr 2:21
people will not **r** in the land. .... Pr 10:30
The people who **r** will be like a .... Is 6:13
All who **r** in the land will go .... Is 7:22
be destroyed; only ruins will **r**. .... Is 17:1
there your fine chariots will **r**. .... Is 22:18
while you **r** patient with them. .... Je 15:15
How long will they **r** unclean? .... Hos 8:5
people of Jerusalem will **r** safe. .... Zch 12:6
R in me, and I will remain in .... Jn 15:4
in me, and I will **r** in you. .... Jn 15:4
alone but must **r** in the vine. .... Jn 15:4
fruit alone but must **r** in me. .... Jn 15:4
If any **r** in me and I remain in. .... Jn 15:5
remain in me and I **r** in them, ... Jn 15:5
If any do not **r** in me, they are .... Jn 15:6
If you **r** in me and follow my .... Jn 15:7
loved me. Now **r** in my love. .... Jn 15:9
commands, and I **r** in his love. .... Jn 15:10
commands, you will **r** in my love. .... Jn 15:10
but Silas decided to **r** there .... Ac 15:34
be destroyed, but you will **r**. .... Heb 1:11
that cannot be shaken will **r**. .... Heb 12:27

REMAINED

and have **r** there until now. .... Ge 32:4
The gnats **r** on the people and .... Ex 8:18
over the Tent, they **r** camped. .... Nu 9:18
There **r** from what the soldiers .... Nu 31:32
home, but ten thousand **r**. .... Jdg 7:3
' She came and has **r** here, ... Ru 2:7
of them had **r** loyal to Saul's 1Ch 12:29
They **r** there as slaves until the 2Ch 36:20
to make sure the Sabbath **r** holy. .... Ne 13:22
one escaped or **r** alive on the .... La 2:22
to them and **r** unable to speak. .... Lk 1:22

REMAINING

said to Aaron and his **r** sons, ... Le 10:12
and Ithamar, Aaron's **r** sons. .... Le 10:16
sure that the **r** men of Benjamin .... Jdg 21:7
R calm solves great problems. .... Ec 10:4
earth because of the **r** sounds of. .... Rev 8:13

REMAINS

in it. He **r** loyal forever. .... Ps 146:6
with understanding **r** calm. .... Pr 14:17
saying you see, your guilt **r**." .... Jn 9:41
never dies, it **r** only a single .... Jn 12:24
the new life from God **r** in them. 1Jn 3:9

REMALIAH

Pekah son of **R** was one of 2Ki 15:25
Pekah son of **R** became king over 2Ki 15:27
Pekah son of **R** and attacked 2Ki 15:30
year Pekah son of **R** was king of 2Ki 15:32
Pekah son of **R** against Judah. 2Ki 15:37
year Pekah son of **R** was king of 2Ki 16:1
king of Aram and Pekah son of **R**, ... 2Ki 16:5
of Pekah son of **R** killed one 2Ch 28:6
king of Aram and Pekah son of **R**, ... Is 7:1
and Pekah son of **R**, scare you. .... Is 7:4
by its weak king, the son of **R**. .... Is 7:9
of Rezin and Pekah son of **R**. .... Is 8:6

REMEMBER

I will **r** my agreement between me .... Ge 9:15
served wine did not **r** Joseph. .... Ge 40:23
Now I **r** something I promised to .... Ge 41:9
to the people, "**R** this day, the. .... Ex 13:3

R to keep the Sabbath holy. .... Ex 20:8
R that you were slaves in Egypt .... Dt 5:15
R this and do not forget it: .... Dt 9:7
R the old days. Think of the .... Dt 32:7
R me and don't forget me. 1Sa 1:11
R the miracles he has done, ... 1Ch 16:12
R the Lord, who is great and .... Ne 4:14
R to be kind to me, my God, for .... Ne 5:19
R me, my God, for this. .... Ne 13:14
were brought. **R** me, my God; be .... Ne 13:31
May he **r** all your offerings and .... Ps 20:3
Do not **r** the sins and wrong .... Ps 25:7
When I **r** these things, I speak .... Ps 42:4
I **r** you where the Jordan River .... Ps 42:6
I **r** you while I'm lying in bed;.............. Ps 63:6
I **r** what the LORD did; .... Ps 77:11
R the miracles he has done; .... Ps 105:5
LORD, I **r** you at night, and I .... Ps 119:55
of my mouth if I do not **r** you,.............. Ps 137:6
their need and **r** their misery no............. Pr 31:7
R your Creator while you are .... Ec 12:1
please **r** that I have always .... Is 38:3
I will not **r** your sins. .... Is 43:25
R what happened long ago. .... Is 46:9
don't **r** our sins forever. .... Is 64:9
R me and take care of me. .... Je 15:15
I will not **r** their sins anymore. .... Je 31:34
r my suffering and my misery, ... La 3:19
you are angry, **r** to be kind................... Hab 3:2
that he would **r** his holy promise .... Lk 1:72
R Lot's wife. .... Lk 17:32
r me when you come into your .... Lk 23:42
R what I told you: A servant is .... Jn 15:20
taught you to **r** the words Jesus .... Ac 20:35
us was to **r** to help the poor—............... Gal 2:10
R that in the past you were .... Eph 2:12
my own hand. **R** me in prison. .... Col 4:18
I **r** your true faith. 2Ti 1:5
I will not **r** their sins anymore. .... Heb 8:12
R your leaders who taught God's .... Heb 13:7
So **r** where you were before you............. Rev 2:5

REMEMBERED

But God **r** Noah and all the wild............. Ge 8:1
but he **r** what Abraham had asked. .... Ge 19:29
Joseph **r** his dreams about his .... Ge 42:9
and he **r** the agreement he had .... Ex 2:24
has **r** his love and his loyalty .... Ps 98:3
He **r** his holy promise to his .... Ps 105:42
Good people will always be **r**. .... Ps 112:6
He **r** us when we were in trouble. .... Ps 136:23
and cried when we **r** Jerusalem. .... Ps 137:1
then his people **r** what happened .... Is 63:11
had almost gone, I **r** the LORD. .... Jnh 2:7
And Peter **r** what Jesus had told............. Mt 26:75
Then the women **r** what Jesus had .... Lk 24:8
God **r** the sins of Babylon the .... Rev 16:19

REMEMBERING

trumpet for a special time of **r**. .... Le 23:24
people of Israel, **r** to show them .... Lk 1:54
R that you cried for me, I want 2Ti 1:4

REMEMBERS

he **r** that we are dust. .... Ps 103:14
He **r** his agreement forever. .... Ps 111:5
The LORD **r** us and will bless us. .... Ps 115:12

REMEMBRANCE

for jealousy, an offering of **r**. .... Nu 5:15
will hand her the offering of **r**, ... Nu 5:18

REMETH

R, En Gannim, En Haddah, and .... Jos 19:21

REMIND

is why I **r** you to keep using 2Ti 1:6
R the believers to yield to the .... Tit 3:1

REMINDER

your hand or a **r** on your .... Ex 13:9
your hand and a **r** on your .... Ex 13:16
a continual **r** before the LORD. .... Ex 28:29
things will be a **r** of the LORD's .... Is 55:13
this **r** will never be destroyed................. Is 55:13

REMINDERS

the holy vest as **r** of the twelve .... Ex 28:12
of the LORD as **r** of the sons of .... Ex 28:12
as **r** of the twelve sons of .... Ex 39:7

REMOVE

you are to **r** all the yeast from .... Ex 12:15
he will **r** with the kidneys. .... Le 3:4
So **r** evil from your house. .... Job 22:23
when you **r** those who do evil, ... Ps 125:5
R the scum from the silver,................... Pr 25:4
I will **r** the hedge, and it will .... Is 5:5
R your veil and your nice skirts............. Is 47:2
'Soon I will **r** you from the .... Je 28:16
built more altars to **r** sin, ... Hos 8:11
We should **r** from our lives .... Heb 12:1

REMOVED

Noah **r** the covering of the boat .... Ge 8:13
of worship to gods were not **r**. 1Ki 15:14
until the LORD **r** the Israelites 2Ki 17:23
He **r** the places where gods were 2Ki 18:4
So Josiah **r** idol worship from................. 2Ch 34:5
my honor and the crown from my .... Job 19:9
wicked will be **r** from the land, ... Pr 2:22
Assyria puts on you will be **r**, ... Is 10:27
but that weight will be **r**....................... Is 14:25
I have **r** your sins like a cloud................. Is 44:22
evil is not **r** from my people. .... Je 6:29
anger he has **r** all the strength .... La 2:3
Its heavy rust cannot be **r**, ... Eze 24:12

REMOVES

this way the priest **r** the sins .... Le 4:20
way the priest **r** the ruler's sin .... Le 4:26
other for the goat that **r** sin. .... Le 16:8
the desert as a goat that **r** sin............... Le 16:10
It is the blood that **r** the sins, ... Le 17:11
This **r** sin so they will belong .... Nu 6:11
sin offering which **r** your sins, ... Nu 29:11

REMOVING

That law for **r** the sins of the .... Le 16:34
and legs and **r** Judah's beard................. Is 7:20

RENAMED

They **r** Nebo and Baal Meon when .... Nu 32:38

RENTAL

the **r** price covers the loss. .... Ex 22:15

RENTED

the animal was **r**, the rental .... Ex 22:15
He **r** the vineyards for others to .... Sng 8:11
and everyone who **r** had to pay .... Sng 8:11
years in his own **r** house and .... Ac 28:30

REPAID

he has not **r** us for the evil we .... Ps 103:10
with them, and you will be **r**. .... Lk 14:12
But you will be **r** when the good............. Lk 14:14

REPAIR

and carpenters to **r** the Temple 2Ch 24:12
down houses to **r** the walls with .... Is 22:10
ruins, 'I will **r** you.' .... Is 44:26
They will **r** the ruined cities .... Is 61:4

REPAIRED

son of Besodeiah r the Old Gate. ....Ne 3:6
the wall was r by Rephaiah son ....Ne 3:9
Then the holy place will be r." ....Da 8:14

REPAIRS

of Hakkoz, made r next to them. ....Ne 3:4
made r next to Meremoth ....Ne 3:4
of Baana made r next to ....Ne 3:4

REPAY

is not the way to r the LORD, ...Dt 32:6
wrong; I will r them. Soon their ....Dt 32:35
because he will r you for the ....Dt 32:43
of Benjamin to r them for the ....Jdg 20:10
May the LORD r you with children 1Sa 2:20
my misery and r me with 2Sa 16:12
But see how they r us for not 2Ch 20:11
They r me with evil for the good ....Ps 35:12
They r me with evil for the good ....Ps 38:20
R those around us seven times ....Ps 79:12
them, but they r me with evil..................Ps 109:5
instead, I will r you in full. ....Is 65:6
I will r you for what you have.................Eze 16:43
them as a promise to r a loan, ...Eze 33:15
I will r them for the wrong they ....Hos 4:9
I will r them," says the Lord. ....Rm 12:19
family and to r their parents 1Ti 5:4
do wrong; I will r them." And he ....Heb 10:30
Do not do wrong to r a wrong, ...1Pe 3:9
do not insult to r an insult. 1Pe 3:9
But r with a blessing, because 1Pe 3:9
I will r each of you for what ....Rev 2:23
and I will r each one of you for ....Rev 22:12

REPEAT

asked David to r his promise of 1Sa 20:17
our side? (Let Israel r this.)....................Ps 124:1
my life. (Let Israel r this.) ....Ps 129:1
so that you are ready to r them. ....Pr 22:18

REPEATED

Jephthah r all of his words in ....Jdg 11:11
he r their words to the LORD...................1Sa 8:21

REPEATS

A fool who r his foolishness is ....Pr 26:11
around and r the same pattern ....Ec 1:6

REPHAEL

were Othni, R, Obed, Elzabad, ...1Ch 26:7

REPHAH

R was Ephraim's son. Resheph was 1Ch 7:25

REPHAH'S

son. Resheph was R son. Telah 1Ch 7:25

REPHAIAH

the sons of R, Arnan, Obadiah 1Ch 3:21
Neariah, R, and Uzziel, led....................1Ch 4:42
were Uzzi, R, Jeriel, Jahmai 1Ch 7:2
father. R was Binea's son 1Ch 9:43
was repaired by R son of Hur, ...Ne 3:9

REPHAIAH'S

Eleasah was R son, and Azel was 1Ch 9:43

REPHAIM

north side of the Valley of R. ....Jos 18:16
and camped in the Valley of R. 2Sa 5:18
and camped at the Valley of R. 2Sa 5:22
had camped in the Valley of R. 2Sa 23:13
had camped in the Valley of R. 1Ch 11:15
the people in the Valley of R. 1Ch 14:9
harvest in the Valley of R. ....Is 17:5

REPHAITES

and defeated the R in Ashteroth..............Ge 14:5
Hittites, Perizzites, R, ...Ge 15:20
The Emites were thought to be R, ...Dt 2:11

thought to be a land of the R, ...Dt 2:20
of Bashan was left of the few R. ....Dt 3:11
was called the land of the R. ....Dt 3:13
was one of the last of the R. ....Jos 12:4
Og was one of the last of the R, ...Jos 13:12
of the Perizzites and the R.....................Jos 17:15
one of the descendants of the R..............1Ch 20:4

REPHAN

of the star god R that you made ....Ac 7:43

REPHIDIM

They camped at R, but there was ....Ex 17:1
At R the Amalekites came and ....Ex 17:8
When they left R, they came to ....Ex 19:2
They left Alush and camped at R, ...Nu 33:14
They left R and camped in the ....Nu 33:15

REPLACE

people the Levites could not r. ....Nu 3:49
of Samaria to r the Israelites. 2Ki 17:24
have sons to r your fathers. ....Ps 45:16
let another man r him as leader................Ps 109:8
them a crown to r their ashes, ...Is 61:3
of gladness to r their sorrow, ...Is 61:3
of praise to r their spirit ....Is 61:3
'Let another man r him as leader. ....Ac 1:20

REPLACED

holy bread was r with hot bread. 1Sa 21:6
Felix was r by Porcius Festus as ....Ac 24:27

REPLACES

and a maid who r her mistress. ....Pr 30:23

REPLIED

you from Ephraim?" If he r no, ...Jdg 12:5
said, and he r, "I have been 2Sa 3:8
Jehoshaphat r, "I will go with..................2Ki 3:7

REPORT

Israelites a bad r about the ....Nu 13:32
given a bad r about the land..................Nu 14:36
men who gave a very bad r died; ....Nu 14:37
are spreading a bad r about you. 1Sa 2:24
the young man who brought the r, ...2Sa 1:13
He will hear a r that will make 2Ki 19:7
king received a r that Tirhakah, ...2Ki 19:9
do not need to r how they use 2Ki 22:7
stopped until a r could go to ....Ezr 5:5
was said in the r they sent to ....Ezr 5:7
A r is going around to all the ....Ne 6:6
When the r was investigated, ...Est 2:23
and have him r what he sees. ....Is 21:6
He will hear a r that will make ....Is 37:7
king received a r that Tirhakah, ...Is 37:9
R this to the nations. ....Je 4:16
have tried to r on the things ....Lk 1:1
me a r of what you have done..................Lk 16:2

REPORTED

The men r to them and showed ....Nu 13:26
went and r this to the people 1Sa 17:31
also r to them what he himself 2Sa 17:15
The servants came back and r, ...2Ki 6:13
The lookout r, "The messenger 2Ki 9:18
The lookout r, "The second man..............2Ki 9:20
to the king and r to Josiah, ...2Ki 22:9
to the king and r to Josiah, ...2Ch 34:16
went back and r to Esther ....Est 4:9
at Susa was r to the king. ....Est 9:11
the writing case at his side r, ...Eze 9:11
went back and r to the leaders. ....Ac 5:22
went to the commander and r it. ....Ac 22:30

REPORTS

his father bad r about his ....Ge 37:2
When they hear r about you, ...Dt 2:25

'We have heard r about it.' .... Job 28:22
heard the r about Jesus. .... Mt 14:1

REPTILE
wild animal, bird, r, and fish, ... Jam 3:7

REPTILES
lizards, sand r, and chameleons................ Le 11:30
kinds of animals, r, and birds. .... Ac 10:12
wild beasts, r, and birds.......................... Ac 11:6

REQUEST
listen to my prayer and my r, ... 1Ki 8:28
listen to my prayer and my r, ... 2Ch 6:19

REQUIRED
according to the number r. .... Nu 29:18
according to the number r. .... Nu 29:21
according to the number r. .... Nu 29:24
according to the number r. .... Nu 29:27
according to the number r. .... Nu 29:30
according to the number r. .... Nu 29:33
according to the number r. .... Nu 29:37
hands in the way r by their .... Mk 7:3

RESCUE
about me, "God won't r him." .... Ps 3:2
Save me and r me from those who .... Ps 7:1
likes you, maybe he will r you." .... Ps 22:8
R me from the lion's mouth; .... Ps 22:21
r me from my enemies. .... Ps 69:18
do what is right, save and r me; .... Ps 71:2
I will r them and honor them. .... Ps 91:15
See my suffering and r me,...................... Ps 119:153
LORD, r me from evil people; .... Ps 140:1
Save me and r me out of this sea .... Ps 144:7
r me from these foreigners...................... Ps 144:11
r those who are about to be .... Pr 24:11
He will r them from those who .... Is 19:20
I will r you and save you," .... Je 15:20
people and r you from these .... Je 15:21
will save you and r you from his .... Je 42:11
Will I r them from death? .... Hos 13:14
will r us from the Assyrians .... Mic 5:6

RESCUED
of Egypt and had r them from the 2Ki 17:7
to you for help and were r. .... Ps 22:5
you, LORD, because you r me. .... Ps 30:1
the people you love will be r. .... Ps 60:5
the people you love will be r. .... Ps 108:6
He r me from Herod and from all .... Ac 12:11

RESCUES
God r and saves people and does .... Da 6:27

RESEN
He also built R, the great city .... Ge 10:12

RESHEPH
Ephraim's son. R was Rephah's 1Ch 7:25

RESHEPH'S
son. Telah was R son. Tahan was 1Ch 7:25

RESIN
r, onycha, galbanum, and pure .... Ex 30:34

RESOURCEFUL
person will escape by being r.................. Pr 11:9

RESPECT
in the sea will r and fear you.................. Ge 9:2
low before Joseph to show him r. .... Ge 43:28
his secrets to those who r him; .... Ps 25:14
they r you as long as the sun .... Ps 72:5
did not r the One who planned .... Is 22:11
to greet them with r in the .... Mk 12:38
to be greeted with r in the .... Lk 11:43
all the other guests will r you. .... Lk 14:10
everyone felt great r for God. .... Ac 2:43

All the people r him. .... Ac 10:22
who do not r the Son of God, ... Heb 10:29
pleases him with r and fear, ... Heb 12:28
But you show no r to the poor. .... Jam 2:6
people, all who r you, great and .... Rev 11:18
Everyone will r you, Lord, and .... Rev 15:4

RESPECTABLE
more r parts of our body need 1Co 12:24

RESPECTED
the most r man in his family. .... Ge 34:19

RESPECTFUL
who are always r will be happy, ... Pr 28:14

RESPECTING
he has commanded you and r him............ Dt 8:6
Does God punish you for r him?.............. Job 22:4
By r the LORD you will avoid................ Pr 16:6
R the LORD and not being proud .... Pr 22:4
R the Lord by the way they lived, ... Ac 9:31

RESPECTS
Everyone in your house r him. 1Sa 22:14
how the man who r the LORD will .... Ps 128:4
Whoever r the LORD will have a .... Pr 10:27
a woman who r the LORD should .... Pr 31:30
No one r other people. .... Is 33:8
No one r the priests or honors .... La 4:16

RESPOND
If anyone greets you, don't r. 2Ki 4:29
Then I can r to any insult. .... Pr 27:11
they understand, they won't r. .... Pr 29:19
There she will r as when she was .... Hos 2:15

REST
You may r under the tree, ... Ge 18:4
the LORD's holy day of r. .... Ex 16:23
on the seventh day you must r. .... Ex 23:12
lets your ox and your donkey r, ... Ex 23:12
the seventh day is a day of r, ... Ex 31:15
on the seventh day you must r— .... Ex 34:21
he will give you r from all your .... Dt 12:10
The ones he loves r with him." .... Dt 33:12
given to the r of the families .... Jos 17:6
the r got down on their knees................ Jdg 7:6
Gideon sent the r of Israel to .... Jdg 7:8
few moments to r in the shelter. .... Ru 2:7
Boaz will not r until he has...................... Ru 3:18
Joab put the r of the army under 2Sa 10:10
from the r of the Temple 1Ki 6:16
he would give r to his people 1Ki 8:56
and the r of the people. 1Ki 12:23
a son, a man of peace and r. 1Ch 22:9
I will give him r from all his 1Ch 22:9
are the names of the r of Levi's 1Ch 24:20
and the r of the Jewish people .... Ezr 6:16
have led the r of the Israelites................ Ezr 9:2
and the r of the people: .... Ne 4:14
they done in the r of the king's .... Est 9:12
I have no r, only trouble." .... Job 3:26
He lets me r in green pastures. .... Ps 23:2
Then I would fly away and r. .... Ps 55:6
find r in God; only he can save .... Ps 62:1
find r in God; only he gives me .... Ps 62:5
have troubles like the r of us; .... Ps 73:5
You give them r from times of .... Ps 94:13
'They will never enter my r.'" .... Ps 95:11
your hands and lie down to r.................. Pr 24:33
the LORD will r upon that king. .... Is 11:2
to them, "Here is a place of r;................ Is 28:12
there and find a place of r. .... Is 34:14
which cannot r, whose waves toss .... Is 57:20
gave the people a place to r. .... Is 63:14
you will find r for yourselves.................. Je 6:16

of my suffering and cannot r.'" .... Je 45:3
can his sword r when the LORD .... Je 47:7
We are tired and find no r. .... La 5:5
will get your r, and at the end .... Da 12:13
loads, and I will give you r. .... Mt 11:28
Man has no place to r his head." .... Lk 9:58
looking for a place to r. .... Lk 11:24
into Macedonia, we had no r. 2Co 7:5
he will give r to you who are 2Th 1:7
'They will never enter my r.'" .... Heb 3:11
not lead the people into that r, ... Heb 4:8
that the r for God's people .... Heb 4:9
will r from their hard work, ... Rev 14:13

RESTED

doing, so he r from all his work .... Ge 2:2
On the seventh day he r. .... Ex 20:11
day I did not work; I r.'" .... Ex 31:17
bowl r on the backs of twelve 1Ki 7:25
After he went to his room and r, ... 2Ki 4:11
On the Sabbath day they r, ... Lk 23:56
seventh day God r from all his .... Heb 4:4

RESTING

was a ladder r on the earth .... Ge 28:12
This is my r place forever. .... Ps 132:14
of Ammon a r place for sheep .... Eze 25:5
Are you still sleeping and r? .... Mt 26:45
Are you still sleeping and r? .... Mk 14:41

RESTORE

the old ruins and r the places .... Is 61:4
made you want to r yourselves. 2Co 7:11

RESTS

guards Israel never r or sleeps. .... Ps 121:4
the whole world r and is quiet. .... Is 14:7

RESULT

As a r, I will do this to you: .... Le 26:16
As a r, Jesus could not enter a .... Mk 1:45
As a r, they became full of .... Rm 1:24
It was not the r of your own .... Eph 2:9

RESULTS

will enjoy the r of their own .... Eze 18:20
will suffer the r of their own .... Eze 18:20

RESURRECTION

again in the r on the last day. .... Jn 11:24
her, "I am the r and the life. .... Jn 11:25

RETELL

They will r your mighty acts, ... Ps 145:4

RETIRE

they must r from their jobs and .... Nu 8:25

RETURN

Later you will r to the ground, ... Ge 3:19
die, you will r to the dust." .... Ge 3:19
and then he left to r home. .... Ge 31:55
away, you must r it to him. .... Ex 23:4
Then Moses would r to the camp, ... Ex 33:11
and we will not r home until .... Nu 32:18
the people to r to their tents, ... Dt 5:30
you, "Don't r that way again." .... Dt 17:16
children will r to the LORD your .... Dt 30:2
ready to leave Moab and r home. .... Ru 1:6
if you r to the city, you can 2Sa 15:34
In r it is my wish that you give 1Ki 5:9
I will r to my own country." 1Ki 11:21
anything nor to r on the same 1Ki 13:9
and did not r on the same road 1Ki 13:10
there or r on the same road 1Ki 13:17
will make him r to his own 2Ki 19:7
and water until I r safely from 2Ch 18:26
But if you r to me and obey my .... Ne 1:9
warned them to r to your .... Ne 9:29

go to the grave and never r. .... Job 7:9
I will not r from the land of .... Job 10:21
I go on the journey of no r. .... Job 16:22
It will r to the way it was when .... Job 33:25
LORD, r and save me; save me .... Ps 6:4
long before you r and show .... Ps 90:13
those who respect you r to me, ... Ps 119:79
LORD, r our prisoners again, as .... Ps 126:4
out the seeds will r singing and .... Ps 126:6
gives evil in r for good will .... Pr 17:13
after a while you will get a r. .... Ec 11:1
spirit will r to God who gave .... Ec 12:7
people did not r to the one who .... Is 9:13
be left alive to r to the LORD. .... Is 10:22
the LORD has freed will r there .... Is 35:10
They should r to the LORD so he .... Is 55:7
sky and don't r without watering .... Is 55:10
They will not r to me empty. .... Is 55:11
If you will r, Israel, then .... Je 4:1
change your heart and r to me, ... Je 15:19
I will r them to the land I gave .... Je 30:3
will r to what they were before. .... Eze 16:55
action and then r to his own .... Da 11:28
he will r and show his anger .... Da 11:30
of Israel will r to the LORD .... Hos 3:5
their deeds and r to their God. .... Hos 5:4
Israel will r to being captives .... Hos 9:3
You must r to your God; .... Hos 12:6
Israel, r to the LORD your God, ... Hos 14:1
I will r to Jerusalem and live .... Zch 8:3
r to your place of safety. .... Zch 9:12
their children will live and r. .... Zch 10:9
R to me, and I will return to you, ... Mal 3:7
in Egypt until I tell you to r." .... Mt 2:13
people of Israel r to the Lord .... Lk 1:16
but he did not insult them in r. 1Pe 2:23
But if they r to evil things and 2Pe 2:20

RETURNED

he left, and Abraham r home. .... Ge 18:33
Then Abraham r to his servants. .... Ge 22:19
The messengers r to Jacob and .... Ge 32:6
So Tamar r to her father's home. .... Ge 38:11
money that was r to you in your .... Ge 43:12
the donkeys and r to the city. .... Ge 44:13
You have r from killing, my son. .... Ge 49:9
his father, he r to Egypt, along .... Ge 50:14
next day Moses r and saw two .... Ex 2:13
Then Moses r to the LORD and .... Ex 5:22
the land, the men r to the camp. .... Nu 13:25
they r to the city without .... Jos 2:22
two months she r to her father, ... Jdg 11:39
r from Moab and arrived at .... Ru 1:22
The Israelites r after chasing 1Sa 17:53
he and the men r home. 1Sa 18:6
and all his army r to Jerusalem. 1Ch 20:3
Then he r to Jerusalem. 1Ch 21:4
made king, he r from Egypt. 2Ch 10:2
the Israelites r to their own 2Ch 31:1
the area who r from captivity, ... Ezr 2:1
of those who had r first. .... Ne 7:5
the area who r from captivity, ... Ne 7:6
They r to Jerusalem and Judah, ... Ne 7:6
When the king r from the palace .... Est 7:8
and when Joab r and defeated .... Ps 59:17
and power and r the glory to my .... Da 4:36
to your ancestors, who r to me. .... Zch 1:6
talking with me r and woke me up .... Zch 4:1
three months and then r home. .... Lk 1:56
Holy Spirit, r from the Jordan .... Lk 4:1
Jesus r to Galilee in the power .... Lk 4:14
the apostles r, they told Jesus .... Lk 9:10
So the servant r and told his .... Lk 14:21

When he **r** home, he said, 'Call .... Lk 19:15
happened, they **r** home, beating .... Lk 23:48
him and **r** to Jerusalem very .... Lk 24:52
ate some food, his strength **r**. .... Ac 9:19
Jerusalem, they **r** to Antioch, ... Ac 12:25
Paul and Barnabas **r** to Lystra, ... Ac 14:21
Later, when I **r** to Jerusalem, I .... Ac 22:17

RETURNING
As he was **r**, the king of Sodom .... Ge 14:17
The people are **r** to you like .... Is 60:8
he himself was **r** there soon. .... Ac 25:4

RETURNS
r to darkness without even a name. .... Ec 6:4
when the LORD **r** to Jerusalem. .... Is 52:8
anyone but **r** what was given as .... Eze 18:7

REU
years old, his son **R** was born. .... Ge 11:18
When **R** was 32 years old, his son .... Ge 11:20
R lived 207 years and had other .... Ge 11:21
Eber, Peleg, **R,** 1Ch 1:25
the son of **R.** Reu was the son.................. Lk 3:35
the son of Reu. **R** was the son................. Lk 3:35

REUBEN
She named him **R,** because she .... Ge 29:32
R, his first son, then Simeon, ... Ge 35:23
When **R** came back to the well and .... Ge 37:29
R was Jacob's first son. .... Ge 46:8
R, Simeon, Levi, Judah, ... Ex 1:2
from the tribe of **R,** Shammua son .... Nu 13:4
The tribe of **R,** the first son..................... Nu 26:5
tribes of Gad, **R,** and East .... Nu 32:33
Gad, **R,** and East Manasseh have .... Jos 18:7
region of Gad, **R,** and Manasseh. 2Ki 10:33
the tribe of **R** twelve thousand, ... Rev 7:5

REUBENITE
of Eliab the **R,** when the ground............... Dt 11:6
son of Shiza the **R,** who was the............... 1Ch 11:42

REUBENITES
I gave the **R** and the Gadites the.............. Dt 3:16
desert high plain was for the **R;** .... Dt 4:43
The **R** thought hard about what .... Jdg 5:15

REUEL
for Esau. Basemath gave him **R,**............... Ge 36:4
and Esau, and **R,** son of Basemath .... Ge 36:10
R had four sons: Nahath, Zerah,............... Ge 36:13
Esau's son **R** was the father of .... Ge 36:17
that came from **R** in the land of .... Ge 36:17
went back to their father **R,** .... Ex 2:18
was the son of **R** the Midianite, ... Nu 10:29
were Eliphaz, **R,** Jeush, Jalam, ... 1Ch 1:35
Reuel's son, and **R** was Ibnijah's 1Ch 9:8

REUEL'S
R sons were Nahath, Zerah, ... 1Ch 1:37
Shephatiah was **R** son, and Reuel 1Ch 9:8

REUMAH
other sons by his slave woman **R.** .... Ge 22:24

REVELATION
of wisdom and **r** so that you will .... Eph 1:17
This is the **r** of Jesus Christ, ... Rev 1:1

REVELATIONS
visions and **r** from the Lord. 2Co 12:1

REVENGE
down to get **r** for the families 2Ki 10:13
have no pity when he gets **r**. .... Pr 6:34
my enemies took **r** on me and made .... La 3:60
To stir up my anger and **r,** .... Eze 24:8
'Edom took **r** on the people of .... Eze 25:12
people Israel to take **r** on Edom............... Eze 25:14
will know what my **r** feels like, ... Eze 25:14

taken **r** with hateful hearts...................... Eze 25:15
and do great acts of **r** to them. .... Eze 25:17
LORD when I take **r** on them.'" .... Eze 25:17

REWARD
and I will give you a great **r**." .... Ge 15:1
Keeping them brings great **r**. .... Ps 19:11
and their **r** will last forever. .... Ps 37:18
from the LORD; babies are a **r**. .... Ps 127:3
head, and the LORD will **r** you. .... Pr 25:22
what is the **r** for being wise?".................. Ec 2:15
God will decide my **r**." .... Is 49:4
have a great **r** waiting for you.................. Mt 5:12
who love you, you will get no **r**. .... Mt 5:46
will have no **r** from your Father .... Mt 6:1
already have their full **r**. .... Mt 6:2
in secret, and he will **r** you. .... Mt 6:4
will receive the **r** of a prophet. .... Mt 10:41
will truly get their **r**." .... Mt 10:42
will **r** them for what they have .... Mt 16:27
you have a great **r** in heaven. .... Lk 6:23
the builder will get a **r**. 1Co 3:14
So what **r** do I get? This is my 1Co 9:18
receive your **r** from the Lord, ... Col 3:24
the past, which has a great **r**. .... Heb 10:35
he was looking for God's **r**...................... Heb 11:26
I will bring my **r** with me, ... Rev 22:12

REWARDED
People will be **r** for what they.................. Pr 18:20
You will be **r** for your work!" .... Je 31:16
each will be **r** for his own work............... 1Co 3:8

REWARDS
The LORD **r** us for the things we 1Sa 26:23
There really are **r** for doing .... Ps 58:11
give those **r** to someone else. .... Da 5:17
and that he **r** those who truly .... Heb 11:6

REZEPH
Haran, and **R,** and the people.................. 2Ki 19:12
Haran, and **R,** and the people.................. Is 37:12

REZIN
R king of Aram and Pekah son of 2Ki 16:5

RHEGIUM
From there we sailed to **R**. .... Ac 28:13

RHESA
Joanan was the son of **R**. .... Lk 3:27
R was the son of Zerubbabel. .... Lk 3:27

RHODA
girl named **R** came to answer it................ Ac 12:13

RHODES
People of **R** became merchants .... Eze 27:15
The next day we reached **R,** .... Ac 21:1

RIB
the place where he took the **r**. .... Ge 2:21
God used the **r** from the man to .... Ge 2:22

RIBAI
Ithai son of **R** from Gibeah in 2Sa 23:29
Ithai son of **R** from Gibeah in 1Ch 11:31

RIBBON
of the holy vest with blue **r,** .... Ex 28:28
Use blue **r** to tie it to the .... Ex 28:37
They used a blue **r** and tied the .... Ex 39:21
to the turban with a blue **r,**...................... Ex 39:31

RIBLAH
to the king of Babylon at **R**. 2Ki 25:20
There at **R,** in the land of 2Ki 25:21

RIBS
God removed one of the man's **r**. .... Ge 2:21
and had three **r** in its mouth .... Da 7:5

R

RICH

Abram was very **r** in cattle,......................Ge 13:2
cannot say, 'I made Abram **r.**'....................Ge 14:23
poor, and others he makes **r.**.................1Sa 2:7
was **r,** but the other was poor...................2Sa 12:1
great and small, **r** and poor ....Ps 49:2
lots of money protects the **r,** ....Pr 10:15
pretend to be **r** but really have ....Pr 13:7
The **r** may have to pay a ransom ....Pr 13:8
The **r** and the poor are alike in ....Pr 22:2
men, and he died with the **r.** ....Is 53:9
The **r** must not brag about their ....Je 9:23
be hard for a **r** person to enter ....Mt 19:23
than for a **r** person to enter...................Mt 19:24
That evening a **r** man named ....Mt 27:57
and sent the **r** away with nothing ....Lk 1:53
There was a **r** man who had some ....Lk 12:16
and are not **r** toward God."....................Lk 12:21
make known his **r** glory to the ....Rm 9:23
failure brought **r** blessings for ....Rm 11:12
think you are **r.** You think you 1Co 4:8
making many people **r** in faith. 2Co 6:10
You know that Christ was **r,** 2Co 8:9
of sins. How **r** is God's grace, ...Eph 1:7
will know how **r** and glorious are ....Eph 1:18
same way the **r** will die while ....Jam 1:11
the world to be **r** with faith and ....Jam 2:5
The **r** are always trying to ....Jam 2:6
You **r** people, listen! Cry and be ....Jam 5:1
are poor, but really you are **r!**...............Rev 2:9
You say, 'I am **r,** and I have....................Rev 3:17

RICHER

always at ease, and getting **r.** ....Ps 73:12
gives to others will get **r;**......................Pr 11:25
He will be much **r** than all the ....Da 11:2
people became **r,** they built more ....Hos 10:1
receive much **r** blessings when ....Rm 11:12

RICHES

a long life, or **r** for yourself, ...1Ki 3:11
did not ask for: **r** and honor. 1Ki 3:13
money and brag about their **r.** ....Ps 49:6
you gain more **r,** don't put your ....Ps 62:10
rules as people enjoy great **r.** ....Ps 119:14
you will give your **r** to others,...............Pr 5:9
R and honor are mine to give. ....Pr 8:18
R will not help when it's time ....Pr 11:4
who trust in **r** will be ruined,................Pr 11:28
important than having great **r.** ....Pr 22:1
R will not go on forever, nor do ....Pr 27:24
except to look at their **r.** ....Ec 5:11
they will lose their **r.** ....Je 17:11
serve both God and worldly **r.** ....Mt 6:24
with his **r** was not dressed ....Mt 6:29
Yes, God's **r** are very great, and ....Rm 11:33
the very great **r** of his grace ....Eph 2:7
Good News about the **r** of Christ, ...Eph 3:8
his wonderful **r** in Christ Jesus ....Php 4:19
God, not in their uncertain **r.** 1Ti 6:17
Your **r** have rotted, and your ....Jam 5:2
All these **r** have been destroyed ....Rev 18:17

RICHEST

The **r** areas will feel safe, ...Da 11:24

RICHLY

Lord your God will **r** bless you..............Dt 15:4
Stephen was **r** blessed by God who ....Ac 6:8
of Christ live in you **r.**.........................Col 3:16
r gives us everything to enjoy. 1Ti 6:17
God poured out **r** upon us that ....Tit 3:6
peace, and love be yours **r.** ....Jud 1:2

RIDDLE

to them, "Let me tell you a **r.** ....Jdg 14:12
give a **r** and tell a story to the.................Eze 17:2

RIDDLES

words of the wise and their **r.** ....Pr 1:6

RIDE

You who **r** on white donkeys and ....Jdg 5:10
six thousand men to **r** in them. 1Sa 13:5
are for your family to **r.** 2Sa 16:2
I will **r** it so I can go with 2Sa 19:26
and you **r** on the wings of the................Ps 104:3
seen servants **r** horses while ....Ec 10:7
"We will **r** away on fast horses."...............Is 30:16
for Paul to **r** so he can be taken ....Ac 23:24

RIDER

the **r** is thrown off backward. ....Ge 49:17
horse and its **r** into the sea. ....Ex 15:1
horse and its **r** into the sea." ....Ex 15:21

RIDERS

horses and **r** fell dead..............................Ps 76:6
I use you to smash horses and **r.** ....Je 51:21
you are full of horses and **r,** ....Eze 39:20
the chariots and their **r.** ....Hag 2:22
horses will fall with their **r,**...................Hag 2:22
horses and their **r** I saw in the ....Rev 9:17
and their **r,** and the bodies ....Rev 19:18

RIDES

who **r** through the skies to help ....Dt 33:26
who **r** on the clouds in his ....Dt 33:26
way for him who **r** through the ....Ps 68:4
to the one who **r** through the ....Ps 68:33
this woman and the beast she **r—** ....Rev 17:7

RIDING

unclean sits when **r** will become..............Le 15:9
Balaam was **r** his donkey, and he ....Nu 22:22
and the men **r** in them were 2Sa 1:6
As Absalom was **r** his mule, ...2Sa 18:9
with me except the one I was **r.** ....Ne 2:12
animal I was **r** to pass through. ....Ne 2:14
hurried out, **r** on the royal ....Est 8:14
They will come **r** in chariots and ....Je 17:25
r in chariots and on horses. ....Je 22:4
soldiers come **r** on their horses ....Je 50:42
and lieutenants **r** on horseback. ....Eze 23:6
and lieutenants **r** horses. ....Eze 23:12
important men and all **r** horses. ....Eze 23:23
trading saddle blankets for **r.** ....Eze 27:20
a mighty army, all **r** on horses. ....Eze 38:15
I saw a man **r** a red horse. ....Zch 1:8
He is gentle and **r** on a donkey, ...Zch 9:9
He is gentle and **r** on a donkey, ...Mt 21:5

RIGHT

make a helper who is **r** for him." ....Ge 2:18
a helper that was **r** for him. ....Ge 2:20
to the left, I will go to the ....Ge 13:9
If you go to the **r,** I will go to ....Ge 13:9
that faith made him **r** with God. ....Ge 15:6
Let the Lord decide who is **r—** ....Ge 16:5
Obey me and do what is **r.** ....Ge 17:1
to you at the **r** time a year from ....Ge 18:14
them to, to live **r** and be fair. ....Ge 18:19
Won't you do what is **r?**........................Ge 18:25
know she is the **r** one for your ....Ge 24:14
he led me on the **r** road to get................Ge 24:48
Jacob is the **r** name for him. ....Ge 27:36
but it is not **r** for you to work ....Ge 29:15
decide which one of us is **r.**...................Ge 31:37
and the flocks are all **r.** ....Ge 37:14
She is more in the **r** than I. ....Ge 38:26
is there with our father **r** now, ...Ge 42:13

R

divided to the **r** and to the left 2Ki 2:14
She said, "It will be all **r**." 2Ki 4:23
her and ask, 'Are you all **r**? 2Ki 4:26
Is your husband all **r**? 2Ki 4:26
Is the boy all **r**?'" She 2Ki 4:26
answered, "Everything is all **r**." 2Ki 4:26
He asked, "Is everything all **r**?" 2Ki 5:21
said, "Everything is all **r**. 2Ki 5:22
This is not the **r** road or the 2Ki 6:19
the right road or the **r** city. 2Ki 6:19
Let's go **r** now and tell the 2Ki 7:9
to Jehu, "Is everything all **r**? 2Ki 9:11
in obeying what I said was **r**. 2Ki 10:30
the LORD said was **r** as long as 2Ki 12:2
on the **r** side as the people came 2Ki 12:9
did what the LORD said was **r**. 2Ki 14:3
He did what the LORD said was **r**, ... 2Ki 15:3
did what the LORD said was **r**, ... 2Ki 15:34
the LORD his God said was **r**................. 2Ki 16:2
did what the LORD said was **r**, ... 2Ki 18:3
have done what you said was **r**." 2Ki 20:3
did what the LORD said was **r**. 2Ki 22:2
did not stop doing what was **r**. 2Ki 22:2
group stood by Heman's **r** side. 1Ch 6:39
either their **r** or left hands to 1Ch 12:2
they knew the **r** time to do it. 1Ch 12:32
it was the **r** thing to do. 1Ch 13:4
what was fair and **r** for all his 1Ch 18:14
will do what he thinks is **r**." 1Ch 19:13
happy when people do what is **r**. 1Ch 29:17
lead these people in the **r** way, ... 2Ch 1:10
Teach them to do what is **r**................... 2Ch 6:27
their prayers, and do what is **r**. 2Ch 6:35
home in heaven and do what is **r**. 2Ch 6:39
"The LORD does what is **r**." 2Ch 12:6
his sons the **r** to rule Israel 2Ch 13:5
his God said was good and **r**. 2Ch 14:2
on his **r** and on his left. 2Ch 18:18
be with those who do what is **r**." 2Ch 19:11
he did what the LORD said was **r**. 2Ch 20:32
the LORD said was **r** as long as 2Ch 24:2
did what the LORD said was **r**, ... 2Ch 25:2
He did what the LORD said was **r**, ... 2Ch 26:4
don't have the **r** to burn incense 2Ch 26:18
did what the LORD said was **r**, ... 2Ch 27:2
not do what the LORD said was **r**. 2Ch 28:1
did what the LORD said was **r**, ... 2Ch 29:2
what was good and **r** and obedient....... 2Ch 31:20
He did what the LORD said was **r**. 2Ch 34:2
did not stop doing what was **r**. 2Ch 34:2
They offered the **r** number of .... Ezr 3:4
a loud voice, "Ezra, you're **r**! .... Ezr 10:12
What you are doing is not **r**. .... Ne 5:9
olive trees, and houses **r** now................ Ne 5:11
On his **r** were Mattithiah, Shema, ... Ne 8:4
because you do what is **r**. .... Ne 9:8
went to the **r** on top of the wall .... Ne 12:31
would know the **r** thing to do................ Est 1:13
is not **r** for you to allow them .... Est 3:8
think it is the **r** thing to do,................. Est 8:5
city have the **r** to gather .... Est 8:11
do it in the **r** way and at the .... Est 9:27
said to Satan, "All **r**, then. .... Job 1:12
said to Satan, "All **r**, then. .... Job 2:6
'Can a human be more **r** than God? ...... Job 4:17
of grain gathered at the **r** time. .... Job 5:26
difference between **r** and wrong. .... Job 6:30
does not make wrong what is **r**. .... Job 8:3
can anyone be **r** in the presence .... Job 9:2
Even if I were **r**, I could not .... Job 9:15
Even if I were **r**, my own mouth .... Job 9:20
Even if I am **r**, I cannot lift my .... Job 10:15
Is this talker in the **r**? .... Job 11:2

teachings are **r**, and I am clean .... Job 11:4
even though I am **r** and innocent! .... Job 12:4
think it **r** that those people .... Job 12:5
and I know I will be proved **r**................. Job 13:18
those who do **r** will continue to .... Job 17:9
do right will continue to do **r**, ... Job 17:9
on the ground, **r** in their path. .... Job 18:10
I will never agree you are **r**; .... Job 27:5
I will insist that I am **r**; .... Job 27:6
I put on **r** living as if it were .... Job 29:14
On my **r** side they rise up like a .... Job 30:12
away from doing what is **r**. .... Job 31:7
because he was so sure he was **r**. .... Job 32:1
claimed he was **r** instead of God. .... Job 32:2
ones who understand what is **r**. .... Job 32:9
you are not **r** in saying this, ... Job 33:12
will set things **r** for him again. .... Job 33:26
'I sinned and twisted what was **r**, ... Job 33:27
because I want to prove you **r**. .... Job 33:32
decide for ourselves what is **r**, ... Job 34:4
will never twist what is **r**. .... Job 34:12
govern who hates what is **r**? .... Job 34:17
'God will show that I am **r**,' .... Job 35:2
I will show that my Maker is **r**. .... Job 36:3
watches over those who do **r**; .... Job 36:7
is always **r** and never punishes .... Job 37:23
and know the **r** time for them to........... Job 39:2
me to make yourself look **r**? .... Job 40:8
not said what is **r** about me, ... Job 42:7
not said what is **r** about me, ... Job 42:8
my God who does what is **r**. .... Ps 4:1
Do what is **r** as a sacrifice to .... Ps 5:8
show me the **r** thing to do. .... Ps 5:8
bless those who do what is **r**; .... Ps 5:12
because I am **r**, because I have .... Ps 7:8
God, you do what is **r**............................ Ps 7:9
and help those who do what is **r**. .... Ps 7:9
saves those whose hearts are **r**. .... Ps 7:10
judges by what is **r**, and God is .... Ps 7:11
LORD because he does what is **r**. .... Ps 7:17
throne and judged by what was **r**. .... Ps 9:4
The LORD tests those who do **r**, ... Ps 11:5
does what is **r**, and he loves .... Ps 11:7
is with those who do what is **r**. .... Ps 14:5
innocent and who do what is **r**. .... Ps 15:2
at your **r** hand I will find...................... Ps 16:11
You will judge that I am **r**; .... Ps 17:2
I have lived **r**, I will see your .... Ps 17:15
me because I did what was **r**. .... Ps 18:20
me because I did what was **r**, ... Ps 18:24
I did what the LORD said was **r**............. Ps 18:24
You support me with your **r** hand. .... Ps 18:35
The orders of the LORD are **r**; .... Ps 19:8
they are completely **r**. .... Ps 19:9
him with his strong **r** hand. .... Ps 20:6
tell that he does what is **r**. .... Ps 22:31
on paths that are **r** for the good .... Ps 23:3
saves them will declare them **r**. .... Ps 24:5
The LORD is good and **r**; .... Ps 25:8
he points sinners to the **r** way. .... Ps 25:8
who are humble how to do **r**, ... Ps 25:9
to do what is **r** because I have .... Ps 27:11
me because you do what is **r**. .... Ps 31:1
speak against those who do **r**................. Ps 31:18
Sing all you whose hearts are **r**. .... Ps 32:11
the LORD, you who do what is **r**; .... Ps 33:1
and everything he does is **r**. .... Ps 33:4
He loves what is **r** and fair;.................... Ps 33:5
who do what is **r** may have many .... Ps 34:19
little and be **r** than to have .... Ps 37:16
LORD supports those who do **r**. .... Ps 37:17
but those who do **r** give freely .... Ps 37:21
victory for what is true and **r**. .... Ps 45:4

You love **r** and hate evil, so God .... Ps 45:7
stands at your **r** side wearing .... Ps 45:9
Your **r** hand is full of goodness. .... Ps 48:10
even the skies say he is **r**. .... Ps 50:6
are **r** when you speak and fair .... Ps 51:4
and make my spirit **r** again. .... Ps 51:10
be pleased with **r** sacrifices and .... Ps 51:19
wrong more than **r** and lies more .... Ps 52:3
Those who do **r** will see this and .... Ps 52:6
you rulers really say what is **r**? .... Ps 58:1
are rewards for doing what is **r**. .... Ps 58:11
you support me with your **r** hand. .... Ps 63:8
those who do **r** should be glad .... Ps 68:3
with those who do what is **r**. .... Ps 69:28
do what is **r**, save and rescue .... Ps 71:2
will tell how you do what is **r**................. Ps 71:15
that only you do what is **r**. .... Ps 71:16
decide what is **r** for the poor. .... Ps 72:2
your **r** hand is lifted up. .... Ps 89:13
is built on what is **r** and fair. .... Ps 89:14
we have done **r** in front of you; .... Ps 90:8
even ten thousand **r** beside you, ... Ps 91:7
people who do **r** and sentence to .... Ps 94:21
is built on what is **r** and fair. .... Ps 97:2
Light shines on those who do **r**; .... Ps 97:11
in the Lord, you who do **r**. .... Ps 97:12
his **r** hand and holy arm he has .... Ps 98:1
is fair and **r** for the people .... Ps 99:4
to her; the **r** time has come. .... Ps 102:13
does what is **r** and fair for all .... Ps 103:6
them their food at the **r** time. .... Ps 104:27
words proved that Joseph was **r**............... Ps 105:19
those who do **r**, who do what is .... Ps 106:3
did what was **r**, and it will be .... Ps 106:31
Sit by me at my **r** side until I .... Ps 110:1
They were made true and **r**. .... Ps 111:8
they do are **r** and will continue .... Ps 112:9
Lord is kind and does what is **r**; .... Ps 116:5
the tents of those who do **r**: .... Ps 118:15
you because your laws are **r**. .... Ps 119:62
your laws are **r** and that it was .... Ps 119:75
and that it was **r** for you to .... Ps 119:75
I have done what is fair and **r**. .... Ps 119:121
you do what is **r**, and your laws .... Ps 119:137
commanded are **r** and completely .... Ps 119:138
not rule over those who do **r**. .... Ps 125:3
people who do **r** might use their .... Ps 125:3
But the Lord does what is **r**; .... Ps 129:4
May your priests do what is **r**. .... Ps 132:9
let my **r** hand lose its skill. .... Ps 137:5
With your **r** hand you would hold .... Ps 139:10
no one alive is **r** before you. .... Ps 143:2
give it to them at the **r** time. .... Ps 145:15
Everything the Lord does is **r**. .... Ps 145:17
The Lord loves those who do **r**. .... Ps 146:8
what is honest and fair and **r**. .... Pr 1:3
out a net **r** where the birds .... Pr 1:17
is the good and **r** thing to do. .... Pr 2:9
do what is **r** but what is evil .... Pr 2:13
you be good and do what is **r**................. Pr 2:20
With her **r** hand wisdom offers .... Pr 3:16
the home of those who do **r**. .... Pr 3:33
I am leading you on the **r** path. .... Pr 4:11
your eyes focused on what is **r**, ... Pr 4:25
you do, and always do what is **r**............. Pr 4:26
say, and what I tell you is **r**. .... Pr 8:6
knowledge may our words are **r**. .... Pr 8:9
I do what is **r** and follow the .... Pr 8:20
but **r** living will save you from .... Pr 10:2
people know the **r** thing to say, ... Pr 10:32
but **r** living will save you from .... Pr 11:4
Doing **r** brings freedom to honest .... Pr 11:6
those who do **r** will be set free .... Pr 11:21

Those who do **r** only wish for .... Pr 11:23
Fools think they are doing **r**, ... Pr 12:15
Doing what is **r** is the way to .... Pr 12:28
Doing what is **r** protects the .... Pr 13:6
one makes everything **r**. .... Pr 13:17
honest people work at being **r**. .... Pr 14:9
people think they are doing **r**,............... Pr 14:12
at the door of those who do **r**............... Pr 14:19
but those who do **r** are protected .... Pr 14:32
Doing what is **r** makes a nation .... Pr 14:34
he loves those who do what is **r**............. Pr 15:9
what is **r** will be punished, ... Pr 15:10
understanding does what is **r**................. Pr 15:21
Saying the **r** word at the right................ Pr 15:23
right word at the **r** time is so .... Pr 15:23
the prayers of those who do **r**. .... Pr 15:29
You may believe you are doing **r**, ... Pr 16:2
to be poor and **r** than to be .... Pr 16:8
people think they are doing **r**,............... Pr 16:25
those who do **r** can run to him .... Pr 18:10
one side of a story seems **r**,................. Pr 18:17
and he will make things **r**. .... Pr 20:22
You may believe you are doing **r**, ... Pr 21:2
Doing what is **r** and fair is more............. Pr 21:3
they refuse to do what is **r**. .... Pr 21:7
lives, but honest people do **r**. .... Pr 21:8
who is always **r**, watches the .... Pr 21:12
instead of those who do **r**. .... Pr 21:18
tries to live **r** and be loyal .... Pr 21:21
children to live the **r** way, ... Pr 22:6
may be taken **r** out from under .... Pr 22:27
pleased if you speak what is **r**. .... Pr 23:16
Keep your mind on what is **r**. .... Pr 23:19
The **r** word spoken at the right .... Pr 25:11
word spoken at the **r** time is as .... Pr 25:11
and try to kill those who do **r**............... Pr 29:10
but those who do **r** will see them .... Pr 29:16
everything just **r** and on time,............... Ec 3:11
where there should have been **r**,............... Ec 3:16
Don't be too **r**, and don't be too .... Ec 7:16
person does the **r** thing at the .... Ec 8:5
the right thing at the **r** time. .... Ec 8:5
There is a **r** time and a right .... Ec 8:6
right time and a **r** way for .... Ec 8:6
people are not punished **r** away,............... Ec 8:11
those who are **r** and those who .... Ec 9:2
heart of the wise leads to **r**,................... Ec 10:2
for just the **r** words to write .... Ec 12:10
and his **r** arm holds me tight. .... Sng 2:6
and his **r** arm holds me tight. .... Sng 8:3
the City That Is **R** with God, ... Is 1:26
doing what is **r**, her people who .... Is 1:27
do what is **r** that things will .... Is 3:10
turn you away from what is **r**................. Is 3:12
gives you the **r** to crush my..................... Is 3:15
He hoped for **r** living, but there .... Is 5:7
himself holy by doing what is **r**. .... Is 5:16
will grab something on the **r**,.................. Is 9:20
judge fairly and do what is **r**. .... Is 16:5
for those who are **r** with God;................. Is 26:7
will learn the **r** way of living. .... Is 26:9
I will water it at the **r** time. .... Is 27:3
him and shows him the **r** way. .... Is 28:26
way—to the **r** or to the left— .... Is 30:21
you saying, "This is the **r** way. .... Is 30:21
the poor person is in the **r**. .... Is 32:7
does what is **r** and speaks what .... Is 33:15
is right and speaks what is **r**, ... Is 33:15
have done what you said was **r**." .... Is 38:3
Who taught him the **r** way? .... Is 40:14
together to decide who is **r**.................... Is 41:1
you with my **r** hand that saves .... Is 41:10
holds your **r** hand, and I tell .... Is 41:13

so we could say, 'He was r'? .... Is 41:26
you to do r, and I will hold .... Is 42:6
witnesses to prove they were r. .... Is 43:9
Let's meet and decide what is r. .... Is 43:26
have done and show you are r. .... Is 43:26
I hold your r hand and will help............... Is 45:1
the truth; I say what is r. .... Is 45:19
who are far from what is r. .... Is 46:12
soon do the things that are r. .... Is 46:13
With my r hand I spread out the.............. Is 48:13
At the r time I will hear your .... Is 49:8
who try to live r and follow the .... Is 51:1
soon show that I do what is r. .... Is 51:5
know what is r should listen to .... Is 51:7
make many people r with God; .... Is 53:11
out to the r and to the left. .... Is 54:3
and do what is r, because my .... Is 56:1
will know that I do what is r. .... Is 56:1
who are r with God may die, ... Is 57:1
Those who do r are being taken .... Is 57:1
a nation that does what is r, ... Is 58:2
have kept away from what is r. .... Is 59:14
you will be ruled by what is r.................... Is 60:17
your people will do what is r. .... Is 60:21
I, the LORD, speak what is r. .... Is 63:1
led Moses by the r hand with his .... Is 63:12
the r things we have done are................. Is 64:6
R in front of me they continue .... Is 65:3
he was leading you in the r way? .... Je 2:17
honest, and r way, then the...................... Je 4:2
they refused to learn what is r. .... Je 5:3
have the harvest at the r time.' .... Je 5:24
'It's all r, it's all right. .... Je 6:14
It's all right, it's all r.' .... Je 6:14
' But really, it is not all r........................... Je 6:14
your lives and do what is r! .... Je 7:3
your lives and do what is r....................... Je 7:5
but they do not say what is r. .... Je 8:6
the sky know the r times to do .... Je 8:7
"It's all r, it's all right............................... Je 8:11
It's all right, it's all r." .... Je 8:11
But really, it is not all r. .... Je 8:11
I do things that are r on earth. .... Je 9:24
case to you, you are always r.................. Je 12:1
each one the r payment for what .... Je 17:10
your ways and do what is r.' .... Je 18:11
Do what is fair and r. .... Je 22:3
He did what was r and fair,...................... Je 22:15
were a signet ring on my r hand, ... Je 22:24
what is fair and r in the land. .... Je 23:5
The LORD Does What Is **R**. .... Je 23:6
me what you think is good and r. .... Je 26:14
is your r and your duty to buy .... Je 32:7
It is your r and duty to buy it .... Je 32:8
what is fair and r in the land. .... Je 33:15
The LORD Does What Is **R**." .... Je 33:16
will always come at the r times. .... Je 33:20
hearts and did what I say is r.................... Je 34:15
'The LORD has shown us to be r. .... Je 51:10
The LORD is r, but I refused to .... La 1:18
city those who did what was r. .... La 4:13
of a lion on the r side and the.................. Eze 1:10
those who do r may turn away .... Eze 3:20
a second time, on your r side................... Eze 4:6
those who did r to be sad, ... Eze 13:22
because they did what was r. .... Eze 14:20
and does what is fair and r. .... Eze 18:5
son has done what is fair and r. .... Eze 18:19
Those who do r will enjoy the .... Eze 18:20
rules and do what is fair and r. .... Eze 18:21
they have done what is r, ... Eze 18:22
and do what is fair and r, ... Eze 18:27
the wicked and those who do r. .... Eze 21:3

the wicked and those who do r, ... Eze 21:4
Sword, cut on the r side;......................... Eze 21:16
The lot in his r hand tells him.................. Eze 21:22
comes who has a r to be king. .... Eze 21:27
Then I will give him that r.' .... Eze 21:27
give them the r to punish you, ... Eze 23:24
men who do r will punish them .... Eze 23:45
Your life was r and good from .... Eze 28:15
of those who do r will not save .... Eze 33:12
and do what is r and honest. .... Eze 33:14
They now do what is r and fair, ... Eze 33:16
evil and do what is r and fair, ... Eze 33:19
your arrows from your r hand. .... Eze 39:3
and do what is r and fair. .... Eze 45:9
Stop sinning and do what is r. .... Da 4:27
he does is r and fair, ... Da 4:37
are good and r, but we are full .... Da 9:7
LORD our God is r in everything .... Da 9:14
you do what is r, but please do .... Da 9:16
At the r time the king of the .... Da 11:29
Then, at the r time, the end.................... Da 11:35
others to live r will shine like .... Da 12:3
they are r in front of me......................... Hos 7:2
The LORD's ways are r. .... Hos 14:9
Because he does what is r, ... Joe 2:23
don't know how to do what is r,'' .... Am 3:10
throw on the ground what is r. .... Am 5:7
people who do r, you take money .... Am 5:12
changed what is r into a bitter .... Am 6:12
Seer, go back r now to Judah................. Am 7:12
you think it is r for you to be .... Jnh 4:4
you think it is r for you to be .... Jnh 4:9
It is r for me to be angry! .... Jnh 4:9
who do not know r from wrong,.............. Jnh 4:11
the person who does what is r. .... Mic 2:7
fairness and twist what is r. .... Mic 3:9
r to rule will come again to you.............. Mic 4:8
know the LORD does what is r!'' .... Mic 6:5
to do what is r to other people, ... Mic 6:8
bring about what is r for me. .... Mic 7:9
and I will see him set things r. .... Mic 7:9
those who are r with God will .... Hab 2:4
from the LORD's r hand is coming........... Hab 2:16
laws. Do what is r. Learn to be .... Zph 2:3
it can't be taught to do r......................... Zph 3:2
people say the r time has not .... Hag 1:2
Is it r for you to be living in .... Hag 1:4
you who live r in Babylon." .... Zch 2:7
Joshua's r side to accuse him................. Zch 3:1
one on the r of the bowl and the............ Zch 4:3
olive trees on the r and left.................... Zch 4:11
'Do what is r and true. .... Zch 7:9
He does what is r, and he saves............. Zch 9:9
strike his arm and his r eye. .... Zch 11:17
and his r eye will go blind." .... Zch 11:17
people around them left and r. .... Zch 12:6
to the LORD in the r way. .... Mal 3:3
If your r eye causes you to sin, ... Mt 5:29
your r hand causes you to sin, ... Mt 5:30
slaps you on the r cheek, ... Mt 5:39
to those who do r and to those .... Mt 5:45
torture us before the r time?'' .... Mt 8:29
proved to be r by what she does. .... Mt 11:19
it r to heal on the Sabbath day? .... Mt 12:10
of your words will prove you r, ... Mt 12:37
Isaiah was r when he said about .... Mt 15:7
It is not r to take the .... Mt 15:26
They are r to say that Elijah is .... Mt 17:11
Is it r for a man to divorce his .... Mt 19:3
will sit at your r side and the .... Mt 20:21
who will sit at my r or my left; .... Mt 20:23
to show you the r way to live.................. Mt 21:32
it r to pay taxes to Caesar or .... Mt 22:17

Sit by me at my **r** side, until I .... Mt 22:44
their food at the **r** time? .... Mt 24:45
the sheep on his **r** and the goats .... Mt 25:33
say to the people on his **r**, ' .... Mt 25:34
spirit wants to do what is **r**, ... Mt 26:41
sitting at the **r** hand of God, ... Mt 26:64
and put a stick in his **r** hand. .... Mt 27:29
on the **r** and the other on the .... Mt 27:38
He said, "The **r** time has come. .... Mk 1:15
hole in the roof **r** above where .... Mk 2:4
clothed, and in his **r** mind. .... Mk 5:15
the girl stood **r** up and began .... Mk 5:42
the Baptist **r** now on a platter. .... Mk 6:25
Isaiah was **r** when he spoke about .... Mk 7:6
It is not **r** to take the .... Mk 7:27
Then **r** away he got into a boat .... Mk 8:10
They are **r** to say that Elijah .... Mk 9:12
Is it **r** for a man to divorce his .... Mk 10:2
of us sit at your **r** side and one .... Mk 10:37
who will sit at my **r** or my left; .... Mk 10:40
was not the **r** season for figs. .... Mk 11:13
it **r** to pay taxes to Caesar or .... Mk 12:14
You were **r** when you said God is .... Mk 12:32
Sit by me at my **r** side, until I .... Mk 12:36
spirit wants to do what is **r**, ... Mk 14:38
sitting at the **r** hand of God, ... Mk 14:62
one on the **r**, and the other .... Mk 15:27
robe and sitting on the **r** side, ... Mk 16:5
and he sat at the **r** side of God. .... Mk 16:19
standing on the **r** side of the .... Lk 1:11
back to the **r** way of thinking .... Lk 1:17
of the crowd **r** before Jesus. .... Lk 5:19
a crippled **r** hand was there. .... Lk 6:6
proved to be **r** by what it does. .... Lk 7:35
said to Simon, "You are **r**." .... Lk 7:43
clothed and in his **r** mind, ... Lk 8:35
said to him, "Your answer is **r**. .... Lk 10:28
their food at the **r** time? .... Lk 12:42
decide for yourselves what is **r**? .... Lk 12:57
it cannot be **r** for a prophet to .... Lk 13:33
Is it **r** or wrong to heal on the .... Lk 14:3
give what is **r** to his people who .... Lk 18:7
went home, he was **r** with God, ... Lk 18:14
is it **r** for us to pay taxes to .... Lk 20:22
Lord, "Sit by me at my **r** side, ... Lk 20:42
priest and cut off his **r** ear. .... Lk 22:50
will sit at the **r** hand of the .... Lk 22:69
on his **r** and the other on his .... Lk 23:33
himself stood **r** in the middle .... Lk 24:36
him he gave the **r** to become .... Jn 1:12
you have the **r** to do these .... Jn 2:18
You are **r** to say you have no .... Jn 4:17
The **r** time for me has not yet .... Jn 7:6
come, but any time is **r** for you. .... Jn 7:6
because the **r** time for me has .... Jn 7:8
but judge by what is really **r**." .... Jn 7:24
it was not yet the **r** time. .... Jn 7:30
because the **r** time for him had .... Jn 8:20
a demon in you. Are we not **r**?" .... Jn 8:48
I have the **r** to give my life, ... Jn 10:18
I have the **r** to take it back. .... Jn 10:18
only asleep, he will be all **r**." .... Jn 11:12
It was **r** for her to save this .... Jn 12:7
that nothing is going **r** for us. .... Jn 12:19
and you are **r**, because that is .... Jn 13:13
sin, about being **r** with God, and .... Jn 16:8
them that being **r** with God comes .... Jn 16:10
priest, cutting off his **r** ear. .... Jn 18:10
came and stood **r** in the middle .... Jn 20:19
in and stood **r** in the middle .... Jn 20:26
your net on the **r** side of the .... Jn 21:6
it happened **r** here among you. .... Ac 2:22
and is now at God's **r** side. .... Ac 2:33

Lord, "Sit by me at my **r** side, ... Ac 2:34
took the man's **r** hand and lifted .... Ac 3:7
all things will be made **r** again. .... Ac 3:21
God raised to be on his **r** side, ... Ac 5:31
It is not **r** for us to stop our .... Ac 6:2
Jesus standing at God's **r** side. .... Ac 7:55
Man standing at God's **r** side." .... Ac 7:56
your heart is not **r** before God. .... Ac 8:21
worships him and does what is **r**. .... Ac 10:35
R then three men who were sent .... Ac 11:11
enemy of everything that is **r**! .... Ac 13:10
heaven and crops at the **r** times, ... Ac 14:17
that are not **r** for us as Romans .... Ac 16:21
you have the **r** to beat a Roman .... Ac 22:25
are being made **r** through your .... Ac 24:2
Way of Jesus is not the **r** way. .... Ac 24:14
what I believe is **r** before God .... Ac 24:16
when Paul spoke about living **r**, ... Ac 24:25
God makes people **r** with himself— .... Rm 1:17
those who are **r** with God will .... Rm 1:17
we know that his judging is **r**. .... Rm 2:2
will see God's **r** judgments. .... Rm 2:5
does not make people **r** with God. .... Rm 2:13
the law who will be **r** with him. .... Rm 2:13
they know what is **r** and wrong, ... Rm 2:15
thoughts tell them they did **r**. .... Rm 2:15
people what is **r** and teach those .... Rm 2:20
be shown to be **r** when you speak, ... Rm 3:4
more clearly that God is **r**. .... Rm 3:5
one who always does what is **r**, ... Rm 3:10
no one can be made **r** with God by .... Rm 3:20
make people **r** with him without .... Rm 3:21
God makes people **r** with himself .... Rm 3:22
need to be made **r** with God by .... Rm 3:24
always does what is **r** and fair, ... Rm 3:25
today that he does what is **r**. .... Rm 3:26
he could make **r** any person who .... Rm 3:26
person is made **r** with God .... Rm 3:28
will make Jews **r** with him by .... Rm 3:30
are not Jews with him through .... Rm 3:30
was made **r** by the things he .... Rm 4:2
that faith made him **r** with God." .... Rm 4:3
that will make them **r** with God. .... Rm 4:5
even evil people **r** in his sight. .... Rm 4:5
and that makes them **r** with him. .... Rm 4:5
makes people **r** with himself. .... Rm 4:6
that faith made him **r** with God. .... Rm 4:9
that he was **r** with God through .... Rm 4:11
accepted as being **r** with God. .... Rm 4:11
through being **r** with God by his .... Rm 4:13
that faith made him **r** with God." .... Rm 4:22
the dead to make us **r** with God. .... Rm 4:25
have been made **r** with God by our .... Rm 5:1
at the **r** time, Christ died .... Rm 5:6
we have been made **r** with God by .... Rm 5:9
and it makes people **r** with God .... Rm 5:16
of being made **r** with him will .... Rm 5:17
did makes all people **r** with God. .... Rm 5:18
God, and many will be made **r**. .... Rm 5:19
by making people **r** with him. .... Rm 5:21
which makes you **r** with him. .... Rm 6:16
command is holy and **r** and good. .... Rm 7:12
Christ made you **r** with God. .... Rm 8:10
called, he also made **r** with him; .... Rm 8:30
and those he made **r**, he also .... Rm 8:30
God is the One who makes them **r**. .... Rm 8:33
and now he is on God's **r** side, ... Rm 8:34
Moses and the **r** way of worship .... Rm 9:4
At the **r** time I will return, ... Rm 9:9
have no **r** to question God. .... Rm 9:20
to make themselves **r** with God, ... Rm 9:30
were made **r** with God because .... Rm 9:30
to make themselves **r** with God. .... Rm 9:31

R

make themselves r by the things .... Rm 9:32
trusting in God to make them r. .... Rm 9:32
but they do not know the r way. .... Rm 10:2
God makes people r with him, ... Rm 10:3
make themselves r in their own .... Rm 10:3
God's way of making people r. .... Rm 10:3
in him may be r with God. .... Rm 10:4
about being made r by following .... Rm 10:5
being made r through faith: .... Rm 10:6
and so we are made r with God. .... Rm 10:10
tried to be r with God, ... Rm 11:7
God chose did become r with him. .... Rm 11:7
to do what everyone thinks is r. .... Rm 12:17
Those who do r do not have to .... Rm 13:3
Then do what is r, and they will .... Rm 13:3
but because you know it is r. .... Rm 13:5
us live in a r way, like people .... Rm 13:13
believes it is r to eat all .... Rm 14:2
believes it is r to eat only .... Rm 14:2
that it is r to eat any kind .... Rm 14:3
things are living r with God, ... Rm 14:17
All foods are all r to eat, ... Rm 14:20
they think is r without feeling .... Rm 14:22
being sure it is r are wrong .... Rm 14:23
they did not believe it was r. .... Rm 14:23
believing it is r is a sin. .... Rm 14:23
In Christ we are put r with God, ... 1Co 1:30
not make me r before the Lord 1Co 4:4
do not judge before the r time; 1Co 4:5
judges who are not r with God? 1Co 6:1
God's people decide who is r? 1Co 6:1
and you were made r with God in 1Co 6:11
I want you to live in the r way, ... 1Co 7:35
not doing the r thing with the 1Co 7:36
he is doing the r thing. 1Co 7:37
man who marries his girl does r, ... 1Co 7:38
not have the r to eat and drink? 1Co 9:4
Do we not have the r to bring a 1Co 9:5
others have the r to get 1Co 9:12
you, surely we have this r, too. 1Co 9:12
Is it r for a woman to pray to 1Co 11:13
judged ourselves in the r way, ... 1Co 11:31
be done in a r and orderly way. 1Co 14:40
raised to life in the r order. 1Co 15:23
back to your r way of thinking 1Co 15:34
makes people r with God has much 2Co 3:9
we have our r minds, it is for 2Co 5:13
we could become r with God. 2Co 5:21
At the r time I heard your 2Co 6:2
you that the "r time" is now, ... 2Co 6:2
We use our r living to defend 2Co 6:7
made you want to do the r thing. 2Co 7:11
and you showed that I was r. 2Co 7:14
Lord accepts as r and also what 2Co 8:21
and also what people think is r. 2Co 8:21
he does are r and will continue 2Co 9:9
servants who work for what is r. 2Co 11:15
important that you do what is r, ... 2Co 13:7
a person is made r with God not .... Gal 2:16
might be made r with God because .... Gal 2:16
no one can be made r with God by .... Gal 2:16
trying to be made r with God, ... Gal 2:17
law could make us r with God. .... Gal 2:21
that faith made him r with God." .... Gal 3:6
non-Jewish people r through .... Gal 3:8
law to make them r are under a .... Gal 3:10
no one can be made r with God by .... Gal 3:11
Those who are r with God will .... Gal 3:11
law could make us r with God. .... Gal 3:21
could be made r with God through .... Gal 3:24
But when the r time came, God .... Gal 4:4
to be made r with God through .... Gal 5:4
from being made r with God, ... Gal 5:5

gently help make him r again. .... Gal 6:1
life at the r time if we do not .... Gal 6:9
plan, when the r time came, that .... Eph 1:10
and put him at his r side in the .... Eph 1:20
we all have the r to come to the .... Eph 2:18
things are not r for God's holy .... Eph 5:3
These things are not r for you. .... Eph 5:4
of goodness, r living, and truth .... Eph 5:9
this is the r thing to do. .... Eph 6:1
protection of r living on your .... Eph 6:14
I know that I am r to think like .... Php 1:7
whether for r or wrong reasons, ... Php 1:18
Now I am r with God, not because .... Php 3:9
my faith to make me r with him. .... Php 3:9
and honorable and r and pure and .... Php 4:8
is sitting at the r hand of God. .... Col 3:1
because this is the r thing to .... Col 3:18
This is only r, because your 2Th 1:3
that God is r in his judgment. 2Th 1:5
God will do what is r. 2Th 1:6
so he will appear at the r time. 2Th 2:6
We had the r to ask you to help 2Th 3:9
faith and do what you know is r. 1Ti 1:19
proof that came at the r time. 1Ti 2:6
which is r for women who say 1Ti 2:10
human body, proved r in spirit, ... 1Ti 3:16
live in the r way, serve God, ... 1Ti 6:11
make that happen at the r time. 1Ti 6:15
what I know is r as my ancestors 2Ti 1:3
the true teaching in the r way. 2Ti 2:15
Try hard to live r and to have 2Ti 2:22
and for teaching how to live r. 2Ti 3:16
a crown for being r with God. 2Ti 4:8
At the r time God let the world .... Tit 1:3
be wise, live r, and be holy .... Tit 1:8
in a wise and r way and in a way .... Tit 2:12
deeds we did to be r with him. .... Tit 3:5
Being made r with God by his .... Tit 3:7
and order you to do what is r. .... Phm 1:8
sat down at the r side of God, ... Heb 1:3
You love r and hate evil, so God .... Heb 1:9
Sit by me at my r side until I .... Heb 1:13
knows nothing about r teaching. .... Heb 5:13
who sits on the r side of God's .... Heb 8:1
time at just the r time to take .... Heb 9:26
sat down at the r side of God. .... Heb 10:12
Those who are r with me will .... Heb 10:38
who are made r with God through .... Heb 11:7
did what was r, received God's .... Heb 11:33
sitting at the r side of God's .... Heb 12:2
we start living in the r way. .... Heb 12:11
Keep on the r path, so the weak .... Heb 12:13
always want to do the r thing. .... Heb 13:18
you live the r kind of life God .... Jam 1:20
obey this law, you are doing r. .... Jam 2:8
was made r with God by what he .... Jam 2:21
that faith made him r with God." .... Jam 2:23
people are made r with God by .... Jam 2:24
who was made r with God by .... Jam 2:25
it by living r and doing good .... Jam 3:13
So it is not r for you to judge .... Jam 4:12
who knows the r thing to do, ... Jam 4:17
and to praise those who do r, ... 1Pe 2:14
and start living for what is r. 1Pe 2:24
always do what is r and are not 1Pe 3:6
even if you suffer for doing r, ... 1Pe 3:14
and is at God's r side ruling 1Pe 3:22
they continue to do what is r. 1Pe 4:19
you up when the r time comes. 1Pe 5:6
grace, will make everything r. 1Pe 5:10
Jesus Christ does what is r. 2Pe 1:1
I think it is r for me to help 2Pe 1:13
preached about being r with God, ... 2Pe 2:5

teachers left the **r** road and 2Pe 2:15
never known the **r** way than to 2Pe 2:21
can trust God to do what is **r**. 1Jn 1:9
the One who does what is **r**. 1Jn 2:1
that all who do **r** are God's 1Jn 2:29
a person must do what is **r**. 1Jn 3:7
not do what is **r** are not God's 1Jn 3:10
held seven stars in his **r** hand, ... Rev 1:16
put his hand on me and said, ... Rev 1:17
you saw in my **r** hand and the .... Rev 1:20
stars in his **r** hand and walks .... Rev 2:1
is something you do that is **r**: .... Rev 2:6
I will give the **r** to eat the .... Rev 2:7
be eager to do **r**, and change .... Rev 3:19
scroll in the **r** hand of the One .... Rev 5:1
scroll from the **r** hand of the .... Rev 5:7
He put his **r** foot on the sea and .... Rev 10:2
raised his **r** hand to heaven, ... Rev 10:5
a mark on their **r** hand or on .... Rev 13:16
the Lord does is **r** and true, ... Rev 15:3
because the **r** things you have. .... Rev 15:4
You are **r** to decide to punish .... Rev 16:5
evil people is **r** and fair." .... Rev 16:7
his judgments are true and **r**. .... Rev 19:2
and he is **r** when he judges and .... Rev 19:11
whoever is doing **r** continue to .... Rev 22:11
is doing right continue to do **r**. .... Rev 22:11
receive the **r** to eat the fruit .... Rev 22:14

RIGHT-LIVING
way plant a good crop of **r**. .... Jam 3:18

RIGHTEOUS
earth praising God, the **R** One. .... Is 24:16
to see the **R** One, and to hear .... Ac 22:14
Since you know that Christ is **r**, ... 1Jn 2:29
way. Christ is **r**. So to be like 1Jn 3:7

RIGHTLY
he could judge **r** and so he could .... Rm 3:26
continue to live and stand **r**, ... 1Ti 4:16
judge who judges **r**, will give 2Ti 4:8
One who judges **r**, take care of 1Pe 2:23

RIGHTS
sell me your **r** as the firstborn .... Ge 25:31
cared about his **r** as the .... Ge 25:34
so he has the **r** that belong to .... Dt 21:17
explained the **r** and duties 1Sa 10:25
taken away my **r**, the Almighty, ... Job 27:2
but he gives the poor their **r**. .... Job 36:6
defend the **r** of the poor and .... Ps 82:3
not take away the **r** of the needy .... Pr 22:22
of those who take away their **r**. .... Pr 22:23
the needy from getting their **r**. .... Pr 31:5
defend the **r** of all those who .... Pr 31:8
and defend the **r** of the poor and .... Pr 31:9
treated fairly or given their **r**. .... Ec 5:8
Stand up for the **r** of widows." .... Is 1:17
they rob my people of their **r**. .... Is 10:2
'Give my **r** against my enemy.' .... Lk 18:3
I will see that she gets her **r**. .... Lk 18:5
not have full **r** over her own 1Co 7:4
not have full **r** over his own 1Co 7:4
I have not used any of these **r**. 1Co 9:15
do not use my full **r** in my work 1Co 9:18

RIM
altar, under its **r**, halfway up .... Ex 27:5
altar, under its **r**, halfway up .... Ex 38:4
outer edge of the bowl was a **r**. 1Ki 7:24
Under this **r** were two rows of 1Ki 7:24
The **r** of the bowl was like the 1Ki 7:26
was like the **r** of a cup or like 1Ki 7:26
bulls under the **r** of the bowl— 2Ch 4:3
The **r** of the bowl was like the 2Ch 4:5

was like the **r** of a cup or like 2Ch 4:5
and its **r** is about nine inches .... Eze 43:13
r around the altar is ten and .... Eze 43:17
the ledge, and all around the **r**. .... Eze 43:20

RIMMON
Rithmah and camped at **R** Perez. .... Nu 33:19
They left **R** Perez and camped at .... Nu 33:20
Lebaoth, Shilhim, Ain, and **R**. .... Jos 15:32
towns of Ain, **R**, Ether, and .... Jos 19:7
and Eth Kazin, ending at **R**. .... Jos 19:13
Jehud, Bene Berak, Gath **R**, ... Jos 19:45
and Gath **R**. There were four .... Jos 21:24
and Gath **R** and the pastures .... Jos 21:25
the desert to the rock of **R**, ... Jdg 20:45
to the rock of **R** in the desert, ... Jdg 20:47
who were at the rock of **R**, ... Jdg 21:13
were the sons of **R** of Beeroth, ... 2Sa 4:5
Baanah, sons of **R** from Beeroth, ... 2Sa 4:5
the sons of **R** of Beeroth, ... 2Sa 4:9
into the temple of **R** to worship, ... 2Ki 5:18
were Etam, Ain, **R**, Token, and 1Ch 4:32
Aijalon, and Gath **R**. 1Ch 6:69
in En **R**, Zorah, Jarmuth, ... Ne 11:29
crying for Hadad **R** in the plain .... Zch 12:11
from Geba to **R** will be turned .... Zch 14:10

RIMMONO
Jokneam, Kartah, **R**, and Tabor. 1Ch 6:77

RIMS
the axles, **r**, spokes, and hubs 1Ki 7:33
r of the wheels were high and .... Eze 1:18

RING
Rebekah a gold **r** weighing .... Ge 24:22
own finger his **r** with the royal .... Ge 41:42
a piece of silver and a gold **r**. .... Job 42:11
is like a gold **r** in a pig's .... Pr 11:22
used his signet **r** and the rings .... Da 6:17
a **r** on his finger and sandals .... Lk 15:22
nice clothes and a gold **r**. .... Jam 2:2

RINGING
The **r** of the bells will be heard .... Ex 28:35

RINGS
poles through the **r** on the sides .... Ex 25:14
ring and the **r** of his royal .... Da 6:17
She put on her **r** and jewelry and .... Hos 2:13

RINNAH
sons were Amnon, **R**, Ben-Hanan, ... 1Ch 4:20

RINSED
be scrubbed and **r** with water. .... Le 6:28

RIOT
the people might cause a **r**." .... Mt 26:5
this and that a **r** was starting, ... Mt 27:24
the people might cause a **r**." .... Mk 14:2
had committed murder during a **r**. .... Mk 15:7
for his part in a **r** in the city .... Lk 23:19
formed a mob, and started a **r**. .... Ac 17:5

RIOTING
was in jail for **r** and murder, ... Lk 23:25
today and say that we are **r**. .... Ac 19:40

RIOTS
special day of **r** and confusion. .... Is 22:5
When you hear about wars and **r**, ... Lk 21:9
upset with us and start **r**. 2Co 6:5

RIP
They will **r** me to pieces, and no .... Ps 7:2

RIPE
pulled off before they are **r**, ... Job 15:33
will be no harvest or **r** fruit. .... Is 16:9
tool, because the harvest is **r**. .... Joe 3:13

R

are like fig trees with **r** fruit. .... Nah 3:12
the fruit of the earth is **r**." .... Rev 14:15
vine, because its grapes are **r**." .... Rev 14:18

RIPEN
But both wheat crops **r** later, ... Ex 9:32
like figs that **r** early in the .... Je 24:2

RIPENED
blossom, and then the grapes **r**. .... Ge 40:10
the barley had **r**, so these crops .... Ex 9:31

RIPHATH
were Ashkenaz, **R**, and Togarmah. .... Ge 10:3
were Ashkenaz, **R**, and Togarmah. 1Ch 1:6

RIPPED
them and **r** open all their 2Ki 15:16
pregnant women will be **r** open." .... Hos 13:16
They **r** open the pregnant women .... Am 1:13

RIPPING
of her cubs, **r** their bodies open .... Hos 13:8

RISE
but a mist would **r** up from the .... Ge 2:6
continued to **r**, and the boat .... Ge 7:18
It continued to **r** until it was .... Ge 7:20
r and eat the food that your son .... Ge 27:31
the people would **r** and stand at .... Ex 33:8
camp, Moses said, "**R** up, LORD!" .... Nu 10:35
The people **r** up like a lioness; .... Nu 23:24
a ruler will **r** from Israel....................... Nu 24:17
let their enemies **r** up again." .... Dt 33:11
smoke began to **r** from the city. .... Jdg 20:40
so they couldn't **r** up again. 2Sa 22:39
Now, **r**, LORD God, and come to.............. 2Ch 6:41
melting ice and **r** with melting .... Job 6:16
we lie down and do not **r** again; .... Job 14:12
earth will **r** up against them. .... Job 20:27
right side they **r** up like a mob. .... Job 30:12
r up! My God, come save me! .... Ps 3:7
LORD, **r** up in your anger; .... Ps 7:6
r up and judge the nations....................... Ps 9:19
r up and punish the wicked. .... Ps 10:12
says, "I will now **r** up, because .... Ps 12:5
LORD, **r** up, face the enemy, and .... Ps 17:13
so they couldn't **r** up again. .... Ps 18:38
When troubles **r** like a flood, ... Ps 32:6
and armor. **R** up and help me. .... Ps 35:2
Let God **r** up and scatter his .... Ps 68:1
Lord, when you **r** up, they will .... Ps 73:20
roar as they **r** against you .... Ps 74:23
Do their spirits **r** up and praise .... Ps 88:10
R up, Judge of the earth, and .... Ps 94:2
R, LORD, and come to your .... Ps 132:8
If I **r** with the sun in the east .... Ps 139:9
hate those who **r** up against you............. Ps 139:21
be for people who **r** early in the .... Is 5:11
it will fall and never **r** again. .... Is 24:20
ghosts will not **r** from death. .... Is 26:14
their bodies will **r** from death. .... Is 26:19
He wants to **r** and comfort you. .... Is 30:18
He will **r** up and fight against................ Is 31:2
stink will **r** from the bodies, ... Is 34:3
the smoke will **r** from Edom .... Is 34:10
They will **r** up as an eagle in .... Is 40:31
together and will never **r** again. .... Is 43:17
He makes clouds **r** in the sky all............. Je 10:13
'I will **r** up and cover the earth. .... Je 46:8
He makes clouds **r** in the sky all............ Je 51:16
and will not **r** again because .... Je 51:64
end you will **r** to receive your .... Da 12:13
and she will not **r** up again. .... Am 5:2
whole land will **r** like the Nile; .... Am 8:8
mountains of the sea start to **r**, ... Jnh 2:6
the sun to **r** on good people .... Mt 5:45

until it made all the dough **r**." .... Mt 13:33
would not **r** from the dead. .... Mt 22:23
when people **r** from the dead, ... Mt 22:28
When people **r** from the dead, ... Mt 22:30
But after I **r** from the dead, ... Mt 26:32
days I will **r** from the dead.' .... Mt 27:63
killed and then **r** from the dead .... Mk 8:31
days, he will **r** from the dead." .... Mk 9:31
day, he will **r** to life again.".................... Mk 10:34
would not **r** from the dead. .... Mk 12:18
when people **r** from the dead, ... Mk 12:23
When people **r** from the dead, ... Mk 12:25
But after I **r** from the dead, ... Mk 14:28
the fall and **r** of many in Israel .... Lk 2:34
until it made all the dough **r**." .... Lk 13:21
good people **r** from the dead." .... Lk 14:14
day, he will **r** to life again.".................... Lk 18:33
would not **r** from the dead, ... Lk 20:27
be when people **r** from the dead?" .... Lk 20:33
r from the dead on the third day. .... Lk 24:7
would suffer and **r** from the dead .... Lk 24:46
did good will **r** and have life .... Jn 5:29
who did evil will **r** to be judged .... Jn 5:29
brother will **r** again." .... Jn 11:23
that he will **r** and live again .... Jn 11:24
that Jesus must **r** from the dead.............. Jn 20:9
that people will **r** from the dead .... Ac 4:2
die and then **r** from the dead. .... Ac 17:3
own group will **r** up and twist.............. Ac 20:30
people will **r** from the dead. .... Ac 23:6
people will **r** from the dead. .... Ac 23:8
people will **r** from the dead!' .... Ac 24:21
as the first to **r** from the dead, ... Ac 26:23
the whole batch of dough **r**." 1Co 5:6
the whole batch of dough **r**." .... Gal 5:9
R from death, and Christ will .... Eph 5:14
in Christ will **r** first. 1Th 4:16
pain will **r** forever and ever .... Rev 14:11
smoke will **r** forever and ever. .... Rev 19:3

RISEN
God has **r** with a shout of joy; .... Ps 47:5
the LORD has **r** as the trumpets .... Ps 47:5
the water has **r** to my neck. .... Ps 69:1
The sea has **r** over Babylon; .... Je 51:42
The water had **r** too high; .... Eze 47:5
who has **r** from the dead. .... Mt 14:2
Son of Man had **r** from the dead. .... Mt 17:9
that he has **r** from the dead. .... Mt 27:64
has **r** from the dead as he said .... Mt 28:6
'Jesus has **r** from the dead. .... Mt 28:7
who has **r** from the dead. .... Mk 6:14
Now he has **r** from the dead!" .... Mk 6:16
Son of Man had **r** from the dead. .... Mk 9:9
He has **r** from the dead; .... Mk 16:6
after he had **r** from the dead. .... Mk 16:14
Baptist has **r** from the dead." .... Lk 9:7
long ago has **r** from the dead." .... Lk 9:8
he has **r** from the dead. .... Lk 24:6
Lord really has **r** from the dead!............... Lk 24:34

RISES
where the sun **r**, and they will .... Nu 2:3
The sun **r** at one end of the sky .... Ps 19:6
where the sun **r** to where it sets .... Ps 65:8
When the sun **r**, they leave and .... Ps 104:22
where the sun **r** to where it sets .... Ps 113:3
sun **r**, the sun sets, and then .... Ec 1:5
back to where it **r** again....................... Ec 1:5
The sun will grow dark as it **r**, ... Is 13:10
river, which **r** to the throat..................... Is 30:28
The enemy **r** up like a cloud, ... Je 4:13
Egypt **r** up like the Nile River, ... Je 46:8
The whole land **r** like the Nile .... Am 9:5

still dark, or when the sun **r.** .... Mk 13:35
The sun **r** with burning heat and .... Jam 1:11
morning star **r** in your hearts. 2Pe 1:19

RISING

and saw smoke **r** from the land, ... Ge 19:28
and the smoke **r** from the .... Ex 20:18
saw smoke **r** from their city. .... Jos 8:20
and saw the smoke **r** from it, ... Jos 8:21
you be as strong as the **r** sun!" .... Jdg 5:31
earth from the **r** to the setting................. Ps 50:1
be like water **r** over the banks .... Is 8:7
pass through it, **r** to Judah's .... Is 8:8
you were as bright as the **r** sun! .... Is 14:12
your voice **r** from the ground .... Is 29:4
Who is this, **r** up like the Nile .... Je 46:7
in the north like **r** waters. .... Je 47:2
cloud of incense was **r.** .... Eze 8:11
to you about **r** from the dead. .... Mt 22:31
he meant about **r** from the dead. .... Mk 9:10
about people **r** from the dead................. Mk 12:26
the Christ **r** from the dead. .... Ac 2:31
Jesus and his **r** from the dead. .... Ac 17:18
with him by **r** from the dead as .... Rm 6:5
but the **r** from death also comes 1Co 15:21
saying that the **r** from the dead 2Ti 2:18

RISK

We **r** our lives to get our food; .... La 5:9

RISKED

people of Zebulun **r** their lives, ... Jdg 5:18
for you and **r** his life to save .... Jdg 9:17
I **r** my own life and went against .... Jdg 12:3
David **r** his life when he killed 1Sa 19:5
I have **r** my life and done what 1Sa 28:21
of the men who **r** their lives!" 2Sa 23:17
of the men who **r** their lives to 1Ch 11:19
who **r** their own lives to save .... Rm 16:4
r his life to give me the help .... Php 2:30

RISSAH

left Libnah and camped at **R.** .... Nu 33:21
They left **R** and camped at .... Nu 33:22

RITHMAH

left Hazeroth and camped at **R.** .... Nu 33:18
They left **R** and camped at Rimmon .... Nu 33:19

RIVER

A **r** flowed through Eden and .... Ge 2:10
the land between the **r** of Egypt .... Ge 15:18
Egypt and the great **r** Euphrates. .... Ge 15:18
must throw him into the Nile **R,** .... Ex 1:22
died, and the **r** began to stink, ... Ex 7:21
cross the Jordan **R** into the land.............. Dt 2:29
on the shores of the Jabbok **R,** .... Dt 2:37
other side of the **r** and led him .... Jos 24:3
from the Euphrates **R** to the land 1Ki 4:21
west of the Euphrates **R—** 1Ki 4:24
There is a **r** that brings joy to .... Ps 46:4
people crossed the **r** on foot. .... Ps 66:6
from the Euphrates **R** to the ends .... Ps 72:8
of water from the Euphrates **R.** .... Is 8:7
by the Kebar **R** among the people .... Eze 1:1
it was now a **r** that I could not .... Eze 47:5
baptized by him in the Jordan **R.** .... Mk 1:5
tied at the great **r** Euphrates." .... Rev 9:14
showed me the **r** of the water .... Rev 22:1

RIVERS

Pharpar, the **r** of Damascus, are 2Ki 5:12
the deadly **r** overwhelmed me. .... Ps 18:4
and made the flowing **r** run dry. .... Ps 74:15
He turned their **r** to blood so no .... Ps 78:44
By the **r** in Babylon we sat and .... Ps 137:1
All the **r** flow to the sea, ... Ec 1:7

Their land is divided by **r.** .... Is 18:2
the desert and **r** in the dry land .... Is 43:20
your legs and cross the **r.** .... Is 47:2
with ten thousand **r** of oil? .... Mic 6:7
r of living water will flow out .... Jn 7:38
and have been in danger from **r,**.............. 2Co 11:26
on a third of the **r** and on the .... Rev 8:10
bowl on the **r** and the springs .... Rev 16:4

RIZIA

sons were Arah, Hanniel, and **R.** 1Ch 7:39

RIZPAH

once had a slave woman named **R,**........... 2Sa 3:7
sons of **R** and Saul. 2Sa 21:8
R was the daughter of Aiah. 2Sa 21:8
Aiah's daughter **R** took the rough 2Sa 21:10
David what Aiah's daughter **R,** 2Sa 21:11

ROAD

sitting by the **r** heard that .... Mt 20:30
spread their coats on the **r.** .... Mt 21:8
Seeing a fig tree beside the **r,** .... Mt 21:19
of Timaeus was sitting by the **r.** .... Mk 10:46
a priest was going down that **r.** .... Lk 10:31
to us on the **r** and explained .... Lk 24:32
the Lord on the **r** and the Lord .... Ac 9:27
them escape by a different **r.** .... Jam 2:25
left the right **r** and lost their 2Pe 2:15

ROAM

growl and **r** around the city. .... Ps 59:6
growl and **r** around the city. .... Ps 59:14

ROAMED

This cub **r** among the lions. .... Eze 19:6

ROAMS

It **r** the hills looking for .... Job 39:8

ROAR

even if the oceans **r** and foam, ... Ps 46:3
don't forget their **r** as they .... Ps 74:23
The lions **r** as they attack. .... Ps 104:21
'The LORD will **r** from heaven and........... Je 25:30
He will **r** loudly against his..................... Je 25:30
the waters in the skies **r.** .... Je 51:16
people **r** like young lions........................ Je 51:38
forest does not **r** unless it has................. Am 3:4
of the **r** and fury of the sea. .... Lk 21:25

ROARED

Enemies have **r** like lions at .... Je 2:15
The lion has **r**! Who wouldn't be .... Am 3:8

ROARING

young lion came **r** toward Samson! .... Jdg 14:5
r lions they open their mouths .... Ps 22:13
around like a **r** lion looking for 1Pe 5:8
loudly like the **r** of a lion. .... Rev 10:3

ROARS

over the dead animal and **r.** .... Is 31:4
When he **r**, his children will .... Hos 11:10

ROAST

night they must **r** the lamb over .... Ex 12:8
R the whole lamb over a fire— .... Ex 12:9
R the meat and eat it at the..................... Dt 16:7
Give the priest some meat to **r.** 1Sa 2:15

ROASTED

of new grain **r** in the fire. .... Le 2:14
any new grain, **r** grain, or bread.............. Le 23:14
made without yeast and **r** grain. .... Jos 5:11
Boaz handed her some **r** grain, ... Ru 2:14
barley, flour, **r** grain, beans, ... 2Sa 17:28
The Levites **r** the Passover 2Ch 35:13

R

ROB

cheat your neighbor or r him.	Le 19:13
Philistines tonight and r them.	1Sa 14:36
of Moabites would r the land	2Ki 13:20
don't r the place where they	Pr 24:15
and they r my people of their	Is 10:2
He does not r other people.	Eze 18:7
He will r the countries he	Da 11:24
they r them even of their	Mic 2:2
you r them of their safety;	Mic 2:8
that their slaves will r them."	Zch 2:9
capture the city and r the	Zch 14:2
Should a person r God? But you	Mal 3:8

ROBBED

as a bear that is r of its cubs.	2Sa 17:8
You ask, 'How have we r you?'	Mal 3:8

ROBBER

other way, is a thief and a r.	Jn 10:1
go free!" (Barabbas was a r.)	Jn 18:40

ROBBERS

Two r were crucified beside	Mt 27:38
before me were thieves and r.	Jn 10:8
the greedy, or r, or those who	1Co 5:10

ROBE

vest, an outer r, a woven inner	Ex 28:4
in the inner r and the outer.	Ex 29:5
Saul caught his r, and it tore.	1Sa 15:27
cut off a corner of Saul's r.	1Sa 24:4
a special r with long sleeves	2Sa 13:18
bring a royal r that the king	Est 6:8
up and tore his r and shaved his	Job 1:20
His long r filled the Temple.	Is 6:1
I will take your r and put it on	Is 22:21
clothes and put a red r on him.	Mt 27:28
wearing a white r and sitting	Mk 16:5
him in a kingly r and sent him	Lk 23:11
and put a purple r around him.	Jn 19:2
given a white r and was told to	Rev 6:11
dressed in a r dipped in blood	Rev 19:13
his r and on his upper leg was	Rev 19:16

ROBES

dressed in their r, stood with	Ezr 3:10
put on her royal r and stood in	Est 5:1
and tore their r and put dirt on	Job 2:12
and on to the collar of his r.	Ps 133:2
their fine r, capes, shawls, and	Is 3:22
they must wear linen r.	Eze 44:17
while still wearing their r,	Da 3:21
burned, their r were not burned	Da 3:27
day Herod put on his royal r,	Ac 12:21
wearing white r and holding palm	Rev 7:9
these people dressed in white r?	Rev 7:13
washed their r and made them	Rev 7:14
who wash their r so that they	Rev 22:14

ROBS

A child who r his father and	Pr 19:26
Whoever r father or mother and	Pr 28:24

ROCK

took a large r and set it up	Ge 31:45
here is the r I set up on end.	Ge 31:51
rocks and this r set on end will	Ge 31:52
Jacob set up a r on her grave to	Ge 35:20
her. That r is still there.	Ge 35:20
the Shepherd, the R of Israel.	Ge 49:24
sank to the bottom like a r.	Ex 15:5
they will be as still as a r.	Ex 15:16
of you on a r at Mount Sinai.	Ex 17:6
Hit that r with the stick,	Ex 17:6
the men put a large r under him,	Ex 17:12
other with a r or with his fist	Ex 21:18

me where you may stand on a r.	Ex 33:21
crack in the r and cover you	Ex 33:22
The r badger chews the cud but	Le 11:5
Speak to that r in front of them	Nu 20:8
bring the water out from that r,	Nu 20:8
the people in front of the r,	Nu 20:10
to bring water out of this r?"	Nu 20:10
hand and hit the r twice with	Nu 20:11
who takes a r and kills a person	Nu 35:17
might drop a r on someone he	Nu 35:23
He gave you water from a solid r	Dt 8:15
camels, rabbits, or r badgers.	Dt 14:7
He is like a r; what he does is	Dt 32:4
bringing oil from the solid r.	Dt 32:13
rejected the R who saved them.	Dt 32:15
You left God who is the R,	Dt 32:18
unless their R has sold them,	Dt 32:30
r of these people is not like	Dt 32:31
these people is not like our R;	Dt 32:31
Where is the r they trusted?	Dt 32:37
Each of you bring back one r,	Jos 4:5
one r for each of the twelve	Jos 4:8
yeast on that r over there.	Jdg 6:20
up from the r and completely	Jdg 6:21
Oreb at the R of Oreb and Zeeb	Jdg 7:25
young goat on a r and offered	Jdg 13:19
in a cave in the r of Etam.	Jdg 15:8
the cave in the r of Etam and	Jdg 15:11
him up from the cave in the r.	Jdg 15:13
the desert to the r of Rimmon,	Jdg 20:45
ran to the r of Rimmon in the	Jdg 20:47
who were at the r of Rimmon,	Jdg 21:13
there is no R like our God.	1Sa 2:2
and stopped near a large r.	1Sa 6:14
they put both on the large r.	1Sa 6:15
large r on which they put the	1Sa 6:18
began. Wait by the r Ezel.	1Sa 20:19
to the side of the r as if I am	1Sa 20:20
from the south side of the r.	1Sa 20:41
and went down to a r and stayed	1Sa 23:25
call this place R of Parting.	1Sa 23:28
came to the great r at Gibeon,	2Sa 20:8
and put it on a r for herself.	2Sa 21:10
The LORD is my r, my fortress,	2Sa 22:2
My God is my r. I can run to him	2Sa 22:3
Who is the R? Only our God.	2Sa 22:32
lives! May my R be praised!	2Sa 22:47
Praise God, the R, who saves me!	2Sa 22:47
the R of Israel said to me: '	2Sa 23:3
only wood and r statues that	2Ki 19:18
to him at the r by the cave near	1Ch 11:15
brought them water from the r.	Ne 9:15
and a r can be moved from its	Job 14:18
tunnels through the r and see	Job 28:10
Its chest is as hard as a r,	Job 41:24
The LORD is my r, my protection,	Ps 18:2
My God is my r. I can run to him	Ps 18:2
Who is the R? Only our God.	Ps 18:31
lives! May my R be praised.	Ps 18:46
LORD, you are my R, the one who	Ps 19:14
LORD, my R, I call out to you	Ps 28:1
Be my r of protection, a strong	Ps 31:2
You are my r and my protection.	Ps 31:3
stood me on a r and made my feet	Ps 40:2
say to God, my R, "Why have you	Ps 42:9
He is my r and my salvation.	Ps 62:2
He is my r and my salvation.	Ps 62:6
He is my mighty r and my	Ps 62:7
you are my r and my strong,	Ps 71:3
out of the r and caused water	Ps 78:16
When he hit the r, water poured	Ps 78:20
remember that God was their R,	Ps 78:35
my God, the R, my Savior.'	Ps 89:26

will not hit your foot on a **r**. .... Ps 91:12
is my **R**, and there is no wrong .... Ps 92:15
God is the **r** of my protection................. Ps 94:22
praises to the **R** who saves us. .... Ps 95:1
split the **r**, and water flowed .... Ps 105:41
He turned a **r** into a pool of .... Ps 114:8
a hard **r** into a spring of water. .... Ps 114:8
the LORD, my **R**, who trains me .... Ps 144:1
the way a snake slides over a **r**, ... Pr 30:19
R badgers are not very powerful, ... Pr 30:26
hiding in the cracks of the **r**, ... Sng 2:14
like a **r** that makes them fall. .... Is 8:14
people will fall over this **r**. .... Is 8:15
Midian at the **r** of Oreb. .... Is 10:26
carving out a tomb from the **r**? .... Is 22:16
because he is our **R** forever. .... Is 26:4
this important and precious **r**.............. Is 28:16
of the LORD, to the **R** of Israel. .... Is 30:29
from a large **r** in a hot land. .... Is 32:2
only wood and **r** statues that .... Is 37:19
of no other **R**; I am the only .... Is 44:8
water flow from a **r** for them. .... Is 48:21
He split the **r**, and water flowed .... Is 48:21
at the **r** from which you were .... Is 51:1
became more stubborn than a **r**; .... Je 5:3
like a hammer that smashes a **r**? .... Je 23:29
poured the blood on the bare **r**. .... Eze 24:7
on the bare **r** so it will not be .... Eze 24:8
her ruins and make her a bare **r**. .... Eze 26:4
make you a bare **r**, and you will .... Eze 26:14
you saw a **r** cut free, but no .... Da 2:34
no human being touched the **r**. .... Da 2:34
Then the **r** that hit the statue .... Da 2:35
you saw a **r** cut from a mountain, ... Da 2:45
The **r** broke the iron, bronze, ... Da 2:45
to put special seals on the **r**. .... Da 6:17
move the **r** and bring Daniel .... Da 6:17
R, you picked them to punish. .... Hab 1:12
hearts as hard as **r** and would .... Zch 7:12
I will make it like a heavy **r**; .... Zch 12:3
not hit your foot on a **r**.'" .... Mt 4:6
man who built his house on **r**............... Mt 7:24
fall, because it was built on **r**.............. Mt 7:25
this **r** I will build my church, ... Mt 16:18
he had cut out of a wall of **r**, ... Mt 27:60
that was cut out of a wall of **r**. .... Mk 15:46
tell this **r** to become bread." .... Lk 4:3
not hit your foot on a **r**.'" .... Lk 4:11
and laid the foundation on **r**. .... Lk 6:48
Some seed fell on **r**, and when it.............. Lk 8:6
that fell on **r** is like those who .... Lk 8:13
that was cut out of a wall of **r**. .... Lk 23:53
or make from gold, silver, or **r**. .... Ac 17:29
to stumble, a **r** that makes them .... Rm 9:33
that spiritual **r** that followed 1Co 10:4
them, and that **r** was Christ. 1Co 10:4
this important and precious **r**.............. 1Pe 2:6
a **r** that makes them fall." 1Pe 2:8

ROCKS

bushes, among the **r**, and in pits.............. 1Sa 13:6
apart and large **r** to break in 1Ki 19:11
do not run on **r**, and people do .... Am 6:12
earth shook and **r** broke apart. .... Mt 27:51
for Abraham from these **r**. .... Lk 3:8
afraid that we would hit the **r**, ... Ac 27:29
and in the **r** on the mountains. .... Rev 6:15
to the mountains and the **r**,.................. Rev 6:16

ROCKY

the **r** peak is its protected .... Job 39:28
caves in the **r** cliffs and will .... Is 2:19
bodies to be buried in a **r** pit. .... Is 14:19
sacrifice them in the **r** places. .... Is 57:5

a dry and **r** land, through .... Je 2:6
Some seed fell on **r** ground, ... Mt 13:5
the seed that fell on **r** ground? .... Mt 13:20
Some seed fell on **r** ground where .... Mk 4:5
the seed planted on **r** ground. .... Mk 4:16

ROD

spear was like a weaver's **r**, ... 1Sa 17:7
was as large as a weaver's **r**. 2Sa 21:19
spear as large as a weaver's **r**. 1Ch 11:23
was as large as a weaver's **r**. 1Ch 20:5
rule over them with an iron **r**.................. Ps 2:9
Your **r** and your shepherd's staff .... Ps 23:4
sins with a **r** and their wrongs .... Ps 89:32
backs and the **r** the enemy used .... Is 9:4
use him like a **r** to show my .... Is 10:5
beat you with a **r** and raise a .... Is 10:24
he will strike Assyria with a **r**. .... Is 30:31
LORD punishes Assyria with a **r**, ... Is 30:32
comes from the **r** of the LORD's.............. La 3:1
you were only beaten with a **r**. .... Eze 21:10
to the **r** of punishment; .... Mic 6:9
Aaron's **r** that once grew leaves,.............. Heb 9:4
rule over them with an iron **r**,.................. Rev 2:27
a measuring stick like a **r**, ... Rev 11:1
all the nations with an iron **r**. .... Rev 12:5
will rule them with a **r** of iron. .... Rev 19:15
had a measuring **r** made of gold.............. Rev 21:15
measured the city with the **r**. .... Rev 21:16

RODANIM

Tarshish, Kittim, and **R**. .... Ge 10:4
Tarshish, Kittim, and **R**. 1Ch 1:7

RODE

thousand men who **r** in chariots, ... 2Sa 8:4
He **r** a creature with wings and 2Sa 22:11
The horseman **r** out to meet Jehu. 2Ki 9:18
He **r** a creature with wings and .... Ps 18:10
As Jesus **r** toward Jerusalem, ... Lk 19:36
crown, and he **r** out, determined.............. Rev 6:2

RODS

and had them beaten with **r**. .... Ac 16:22
times I was beaten with **r**. 2Co 11:25

ROE

deer, gazelle, **r** deer, wild .... Dt 14:5

ROGEL

En Shemesh and stopped at En **R**. .... Jos 15:7
of the Jebusite city to En **R**. .... Jos 18:16
Ahimaaz were waiting at En **R**. 2Sa 17:17
Zoheleth near the spring of **R**. 1Ki 1:9

ROGELIM

Barzillai was from **R** in Gilead. 2Sa 17:27
came down from **R** to cross the 2Sa 19:31

ROHGAH

sons were **R**, Hubbah, and Aram 1Ch 7:34

ROI

Bered, was called Beer Lahai **R**.............. Ge 16:14
left Beer Lahai **R** and was living .... Ge 24:62
was now living at Beer Lahai **R**. .... Ge 25:11

ROLL

shepherds would **r** the stone away .... Ge 29:3
Then we will **r** away the stone .... Ge 29:8
R a large stone over here now!".............. 1Sa 14:33
and they **r** in among the ruins. .... Job 30:14
Whoever tries to **r** a boulder .... Pr 26:27
r you tightly into a ball and .... Is 22:18
rough cloth and **r** in the ashes .... Je 6:26
R around in the dust, leaders of .... Je 25:34
will fall and **r** around in its .... Je 48:26
I will **r** you off the cliffs, ... Je 51:25
their heads and **r** in ashes to .... Eze 27:30

R

R in the dust at Beth Ophrah. .... Mic 1:10
Who will **r** away for us the stone .... Mk 16:3

ROLLED

to the well and **r** the stone from .... Ge 29:10
of barley bread **r** into the camp .... Jdg 7:13
Boaz was startled and **r** over. .... Ru 3:8
this woman **r** over on her baby 1Ki 3:19
off his coat, **r** it up, and hit 2Ki 2:8
the sky will be **r** up like a .... Is 34:4
and he **r** a very large stone to .... Mt 27:60
and **r** the stone away from the .... Mt 28:2
fell down and **r** on the ground, ... Mk 9:20
Then he **r** a very large stone to .... Mk 15:46
stone had already been **r** away, ... Mk 16:4
They found the stone **r** away from .... Lk 24:2
as a scroll when it is **r** up, ... Rev 6:14

ROLLS

the cloth a weaver **r** up and cuts .... Is 38:12
it goes back and **r** in the mud." 2Pe 2:22

ROMAMTI-EZER

Giddalti, **R,** Joshbekashah, ... 1Ch 25:4
twelve men were chosen from **R,** 1Ch 25:31

ROMAN

This man is a **R** citizen." .... Ac 22:26

ROMANS

Then the **R** will come and take .... Jn 11:48
not right for us as **R** to do." .... Ac 16:21
R do not hand him over until he .... Ac 25:16
in Jerusalem and given to the **R.** .... Ac 28:17

ROME

You must do the same in **R.**" .... Ac 23:11
When he came to **R,** he looked 2Ti 1:17

ROOF

from the edge of the **r** down. .... Ge 6:16
curtain from the hooks in the **r,** .... Ex 26:33
edge of the **r** so you will not .... Dt 22:8
around on the **r** of his palace. 2Sa 11:2
stick to the **r** of my mouth if I. .... Ps 137:6
a hole in the **r** right above .... Mk 2:4
went up on the **r** and lowered the .... Lk 5:19
who is on the **r** and whose .... Lk 17:31
was going up to the **r** to pray. .... Ac 10:9

ROOM

and the main **r** of the Temple. 1Ki 7:50
on the bed in the **r** where he was 1Ki 17:19
in an upstairs **r** in his house, ... Da 6:10
should come from his **r,** .... Joe 2:16
isn't enough **r** for them all. .... Zch 10:10
go into your **r** and close the .... Mt 6:6
there was no **r** in the house, ... Mk 2:2
is my guest **r** in which I can .... Mk 14:14
commanded, but we still have **r**.' .... Lk 14:22
the upstairs **r** where they were .... Ac 1:13
prepare a **r** for me in which to .... Phm 1:22

ROOMS

Make **r** in it and cover it inside .... Ge 6:14
his upper **r** above the skies .... Am 9:6
there were no **r** left in the inn, ... Lk 2:7
There are many **r** in my Father's .... Jn 14:2

ROOMY

was large and **r,** but there were .... Ne 7:4

ROOSTER

before the **r** crows you will say .... Mt 26:34
before the **r** crows twice you .... Mk 14:30
wasn't true. At once a **r** crowed. .... Jn 18:27

ROOT

that take **r,** they will grow 2Ki 19:30
and ate the **r** of the broom tree .... Job 30:4
we took **r** and filled the land. .... Ps 80:9

that take **r,** they will grow .... Is 37:31
like a **r** growing in a dry land. .... Is 53:2
its **r** is dying, and it has no .... Hos 9:16
so that roots a **r** or branch will .... Mal 4:1
that you do not support the **r,** .... Rm 11:18
root, but the **r** supports you. .... Rm 11:18

ROOTS

a plant whose **r** rot and whose .... Is 5:24
be like a plant with good **r;** .... Is 27:6
stump and its **r** in the ground .... Da 4:15
stump and its **r** in the ground .... Da 4:23
of the tree and its **r** were left .... Da 4:26
Lebanon, their **r** will be firm. .... Hos 14:5
dry and dead, even to the **r.** .... Mk 11:20
If the **r** of a tree are holy, ... Rm 11:16
Keep your **r** deep in him and have .... Col 2:7

ROPE

so she used a **r** to let the men .... Jos 2:15
within two **r** lengths were killed 2Sa 8:2
within the next **r** length were 2Sa 8:2
or tie its tongue down with a **r?** .... Job 41:1
a **r** that is woven of three .... Ec 4:12
they lowered a **r** with a weight .... Ac 27:28

ROPES

with two new **r** and led him up .... Jdg 15:13
officers used **r** to lower .... Je 38:6
up with the **r** and lifted him out .... Je 38:13

ROSE

and as it **r** it lifted the boat .... Ge 7:17
water **r** so much that even the .... Ge 7:19
Abraham, God **r** and left him. .... Ge 17:22
Abraham **r** and bowed to the .... Ge 23:7
Jacob **r** early in the morning and .... Ge 28:18
night Jacob **r** and crossed the .... Ge 32:22
Then the sun **r** as he was leaving .... Ge 32:31
The smoke **r** from the mountain .... Ex 19:18
When the cloud **r** from the Holy .... Ex 40:36
in that place until the cloud **r.** .... Ex 40:37
Mount Sinai and **r** like the sun .... Dt 33:2
When Ruth **r** and went back to .... Ru 2:15
people of Ashdod **r** early the 1Sa 5:3
The next morning when they **r,** 1Sa 5:4
The mountains **r;** the valleys .... Ps 104:8
I am a **r** in the Plain of Sharon, ... Sng 2:1
But the next day when the sun **r,** .... Jnh 4:7
As the sun **r** higher in the sky, ... Jnh 4:8
noise, and its waves **r** high. .... Hab 3:10
But when the sun **r,** the plants .... Mt 13:6
But when the sun **r,** the plants .... Mk 4:6
Jesus **r** from the dead early .... Mk 16:9
Christ died and **r** from the dead .... Rm 14:9
Jesus died and that he **r** again. 1Th 4:14
Jesus Christ **r** from the dead. 1Pe 1:3

ROSH

Naaman, Ehi, **R,** Muppim, Huppim, ... Ge 46:21

ROT

left alive will **r** away in their .... Le 26:39
They will also **r** away because of .... Le 26:39
will not let your holy one **r.** .... Ps 16:10
bodies will **r** in a grave far .... Ps 49:14
but jealousy will **r** your bones. .... Pr 14:30
whose roots **r** and whose flower .... Is 5:24
All the water plants will **r;** .... Is 19:6
he finds a tree that will not **r.** .... Is 40:20
and their fish **r** because there .... Is 50:2
but you must **r** away in your sins .... Eze 24:23
like a **r** to the people of Judah. .... Hos 5:12
Their bodies will **r** and stink. .... Joe 2:20
flesh will **r** away while they .... Zch 14:12
Their eyes will **r** in their .... Zch 14:12
tongues will **r** in their mouths. .... Zch 14:12

ROTTED (cont.)

will not let your Holy One r. .... Ac 2:27
the grave. His body did not r.' .... Ac 2:31
will not let your Holy One r.' .... Ac 13:35
and his body did r in the grave. .... Ac 13:36
the dead did not r in the grave. .... Ac 13:37

ROTTED

their bodies r on the ground. .... Ps 83:10
Your riches have r, and your .... Jam 5:2

ROTTEN

wears out like something r, ... Job 13:28
is terrible and r and drinks up .... Job 15:16
metal as if it were r wood. .... Job 41:27
basket had figs too r to eat. .... Je 24:2
r figs are too rotten to eat. .... Je 24:3
rotten figs are too r to eat.'' .... Je 24:3
the bad figs are too r to eat.' .... Je 24:8
will be like those r figs. .... Je 24:8
bad figs that are too r to eat. .... Je 29:17

ROUGH

The r ground should be made .... Is 40:4
and r roads should be made .... Lk 3:5

ROUGHLY

took him away r and unfairly. .... Is 53:8

ROUND

made from bronze a large r bowl, ... 1Ki 7:23
The opening of the bowl was r, ... 1Ki 7:31
frame, which was square, not r. 1Ki 7:31
and its back was r at the top. 1Ki 10:19
made from bronze a large r bowl, ... 2Ch 4:2
Your r thighs are like jewels .... Sng 7:1
navel is like a r drinking cup .... Sng 7:2

ROW

The first r must have a ruby, ... Ex 28:17
In the first r there was a ruby, ... Ex 39:10
lampstand with its lamps in a r, ... Ex 39:37
the LORD, six loaves in each r. .... Le 24:6
on each r as the memorial .... Le 24:7
Ziba had a r of donkeys loaded 2Sa 16:1
and one r of cedar boards. 1Ki 6:36
with fifteen beams in each r, ... 1Ki 7:3
blocks and one r of cedar beams. 1Ki 7:12
to the plowed r with a harness .... Job 39:10
and Arvad used oars to r you. .... Eze 27:8
All the men who r leave their .... Eze 27:29
The r of rooms along the outer .... Eze 42:8
men tried to r the ship back to .... Jnh 1:13
struggling hard to r the boat, ... Mk 6:48

ROWED

men who r you brought you out .... Eze 27:26
When they had r the boat about .... Jn 6:19

ROWS

they put four r of beautiful .... Ex 39:10

ROYAL

I am speaking of r things. .... Ps 45:1
Judah holds my r scepter. .... Ps 60:7
Judah holds my r scepter. .... Ps 108:8
this great Babylon as my r home. .... Da 4:30
Your r power has been taken away .... Da 4:31
Listen, r family, because you .... Hos 5:1
day Herod put on his r robes, ... Ac 12:21
This r law is found in the .... Jam 2:8
chosen people, r priests, a holy 1Pe 2:9

RUBBED

will no longer be r with oil. 2Sa 1:21
You were not r with salt or .... Eze 16:4
Every soldier's head was r bare, ... Eze 29:18
and every shoulder was r raw. .... Eze 29:18
heads of grain, r them in their .... Lk 6:1

RUBBING

them many times and r them with .... Lk 7:38

RUBIES

wisdom is much greater than r. .... Job 28:18
Wisdom is more precious than r; .... Pr 3:15
Wisdom is more precious than r. .... Pr 8:11
There is gold and plenty of r, ... Pr 20:15
she is worth more than r. .... Pr 31:10
I will use r to build your walls .... Is 54:12
Their bodies were redder than r; .... La 4:7
on, fine linen, coral, and r. .... Eze 27:16

RUBY

The first row must have a r, ... Ex 28:17
In the first row there was a r, ... Ex 39:10
r, topaz, and emerald, yellow .... Eze 28:13

RUDDER

But a very small r controls that .... Jam 3:4

RUDDERS

ropes that were holding the r. .... Ac 27:40

RUDE

but the rich give r answers. .... Pr 18:23
are r and conceited and brag .... Rm 1:30
Love is not r, is not selfish, ... 1Co 13:5

RUE

your mint, your r, and every .... Lk 11:42

RUFUS

the father of Alexander and R, ... Mk 15:21
Greetings to R, who is a special .... Rm 16:13

RUG

and she covered him with a r. .... Jdg 4:18

RUGGED

and the r ground should be made .... Is 40:4

RUGS

they spread the r; they eat and .... Is 21:5

RUIN

won't fear the r that comes to .... Pr 3:25
talk will lead to your r. .... Pr 10:10
friends may r you, but a real .... Pr 18:24
wicked and brings r on every .... Pr 21:12
It will be an empty r forever.' .... Je 51:62
they go they cause r and misery. .... Rm 3:16
be set free from r to have the .... Rm 8:21
trap them and cause their r; .... Rm 11:9
things that r and destroy people 1Ti 6:9
like that can r many of you. .... Heb 12:15

RUINED

The r city will be empty, and .... Is 24:10
it will be completely r. .... Is 60:12
it will not be r or destroyed. .... Is 60:18
will repair the r cities that .... Is 61:4
The fields are r; the ground is .... Joe 1:10
and the wine bags will be r. .... Mt 9:17
and the leather bags will be r. .... Lk 5:37
She has been r, because all the .... Rev 18:3

RUINING

Egypt flies were r the land. .... Ex 8:24
out from Egypt are r themselves. .... Dt 9:12
the rats that are r the country, ... 1Sa 6:5
You are r the Sabbath day. .... Ne 13:17
at Israel by r the Sabbath day. .... Ne 13:18
r you because of your sins. .... Mic 6:13

RUINS

rebuild the old r and restore .... Is 61:4
city of Jerusalem a heap of r, ... Je 9:11
and leave them in r forever. .... Je 25:9
be rebuilt on its hill of r, ... Je 30:18
that they become r where no one .... Je 34:22
rebuild its r as it was before .... Am 9:11

R

Samaria a pile of **r** in the open .... Mic 1:6
while the Temple is still in **r**?" .... Hag 1:4
rebuild its **r**, and I will set .... Ac 15:16

RULE
light to **r** the day and made.................... Ge 1:16
but he will **r** over you." .... Ge 3:16
you, but you must **r** over it." .... Ge 4:7
I will not **r** over you, nor will .... Jdg 8:23
you will **r** over your enemies. .... Ps 110:2
He made the sun to **r** the day. .... Ps 136:8
when he has many people to **r**, ... Pr 14:28
servant will **r** over the master's .... Pr 17:2
children will **r** over you. .... Is 3:4
cruelly, and women **r** over them. .... Is 3:12
with power to **r** all the people. .... Is 40:10
But you **r** forever, LORD. .... La 5:19
part, will **r** over the earth. .... Da 2:39
Christ must **r** until he puts all 1Co 15:25
to those who follow this **r**— .... Gal 6:16
By his power to **r** all things, ... Php 3:21
with you, we gave you this **r**: 2Th 3:10
we will also **r** with him. 2Ti 2:12
You will **r** your kingdom with .... Heb 1:8
left that they did not **r**. .... Heb 2:8
The old **r** is now set aside, ... Heb 7:18
'You will **r** over them with an .... Rev 2:27
a son who will **r** all the nations .... Rev 12:5

RULED
are the kings who **r** in the land .... Ge 36:31
ago when the judges **r** Israel, ... Ru 1:1
He **r** nations in anger and .... Is 14:6

RULER
live, God made you **r** over them............... Da 2:38
made him **r** over the whole area .... Da 2:48
Most High God is **r** over every .... Da 4:25
third highest **r** in the kingdom. .... Da 5:7
that time the **r** of Israel will .... Mic 5:4
A **r** will come from you who will .... Mt 2:6
Beelzebul, the **r** of demons, to .... Mt 12:24
time Herod, the **r** of Galilee, ... Mt 14:1
power from the **r** of demons to .... Mk 3:22
Pontius Pilate, the **r** of Judea; .... Lk 3:1
now the **r** of this world will be .... Jn 12:31
because the **r** of this world is .... Jn 14:30
'Who made you our **r** and judge? .... Ac 7:27
He is the **r** of the kings of the .... Rev 1:5
the **r** of all God has made, ... Rev 3:14

RULERS
r, learn this lesson. .... Ps 2:10
is the kind of mistake **r** make: .... Ec 10:5
your **r** are like those of Sodom, ... Is 1:10
know that the **r** of the .... Mt 20:25
The other nations have **r**. .... Mk 10:42
has brought down **r** from their .... Lk 1:52
the leading priests and the **r**. .... Lk 23:13
The next day the **r**, the elders, ... Ac 4:5
R of the people and you elders, ... Ac 4:8
Silas to the Roman **r** and said, ... Ac 16:20
right do not have to fear the **r;** .... Rm 13:3
None of the **r** of this world 1Co 2:8
against the **r** and authorities .... Eph 6:12
authority of **r** and government .... Tit 3:1
to be the **r** of the new world .... Heb 2:5
the earth, the **r**, the generals, ... Rev 6:15

RULES
is King, and he **r** the nations. .... Ps 22:28
know that God **r** over Israel and.............. Ps 59:13
his kingdom **r** over everything .... Ps 103:19
the Most High God **r** over every .... Da 4:17
one in heaven **r** your kingdom. .... Da 4:26

To the King that **r** forever, ... 1Ti 1:17
obey all the **r** in order to win. 2Ti 2:5

RULING
nor angels, nor **r** spirits, ... Rm 8:38
comes from the **r** spirits of this .... Col 2:8
made free from the **r** spirits of .... Col 2:20
yet see them **r** over everything. .... Heb 2:8
God's right side **r** over angels, ... 1Pe 3:22

RUMAH
of Pedaiah, who was from **R**. 2Ki 23:36

RUMBLING
voice and to the **r** that comes .... Job 37:2
and the **r** of chariot wheels. .... Je 47:3
heard a loud **r** sound behind me, ... Eze 3:12
It was a loud **r** sound. .... Eze 3:13
noise of chariots **r** over the .... Joe 2:5

RUMOR
One **r** comes this year, and .... Je 51:46
and **r** will be added to rumor. .... Eze 7:26
and rumor will be added to **r**. .... Eze 7:26

RUMORS
r will spread through the land, ... Je 51:46
There will be **r** of terrible .... Je 51:46

RUN
and fifty men to **r** before him.................. 2Sa 15:1
Don't let any of them **r** away!" 1Ki 18:40
of Israel to **r** away from Abijah 2Ch 13:15
I can **r** to him for safety. .... Ps 18:2
an athlete eager to **r** a race. .... Ps 19:5
your thoughts **r** your life. .... Pr 4:23
who do right can **r** to him for .... Pr 18:10
They **r** after them, begging, but .... Pr 19:7
they will **r** and not need rest; .... Is 40:31
Come, let's **r** to the strong, ... Je 8:14
I didn't **r** away from being the .... Je 17:16
r to you for safety in times of .... Je 17:17
animals under the tree **r** away, ... Da 4:14
Horses do not **r** on rocks, and................ Am 6:12
in a race all the runners **r**, ... 1Co 9:24
r away from all those things. 1Ti 6:11
But **r** away from the evil desires 2Ti 2:22
So let us **r** the race that is .... Heb 12:1
and the devil will **r** from you. .... Jam 4:7
but death will **r** away from them. .... Rev 9:6

RUNNER
Asahel was a fast **r**, as fast as.................. 2Sa 2:18
My days go by faster than a **r;** .... Job 9:25
fastest **r** does not always win .... Ec 9:11
escape, not even the fastest **r**................. Am 2:14

RUNNERS
The fast **r** cannot run away; .... Je 46:6
and even fast **r** will not get .... Am 2:15
that in a race all the **r** run, ... 1Co 9:24

RUNNING
head and **r** down his beard. .... Ps 133:2
like a deer **r** from a hunter,.................... Pr 6:5
do all this **r** in and out of my .... Is 1:12
like water **r** down a hillside. .... Mic 1:4
together, and **r** over, it will .... Lk 6:38
They were both **r**, but the other .... Jn 20:4
You were **r** a good race. .... Gal 5:7

RUNS
he **r** at me like a soldier. .... Job 16:14
is strong, and **r** from nothing, ... Pr 30:30
like a spring that never **r** dry. .... Is 58:11
season that **r** from place to .... Je 2:23
side the border **r** south from a .... Eze 47:18
up, and the olive oil **r** out. .... Joe 1:10
like someone who **r** from a lion .... Am 5:19

valley that **r** east and west. .... Zch 14:4
in heaven that never **r** out, ... Lk 12:33
he **r** away and leaves the sheep .... Jn 10:12
man **r** away because he is only .... Jn 10:13

RUSH
of the LORD will **r** upon you with 1Sa 10:6
the streets and **r** back and forth .... Nah 2:4

RUSHED
His soldiers **r** out like a storm................. Hab 3:14
the whole herd **r** down the hill .... Mt 8:32
r down the hill into the lake .... Mk 5:13

RUSHES
the Jordan River **r** to its mouth. .... Job 40:23

RUSHING
and **r** waters wash away the dirt. .... Job 14:19
His breath is like a **r** river, ... Is 30:28
Like locusts **r** about, they will.................. Is 33:4
like the roar of **r** water, ... Eze 43:2
But like a **r** flood, he will .... Nah 1:8
with fear. The **r** water flowed.................. Hab 3:10

RUST
iron that became covered with **r**. .... Je 6:28
rusty pot whose **r** will not come .... Eze 24:6
then melt and its **r** burn away. .... Eze 24:11
Its heavy **r** cannot be removed, ... Eze 24:12
where moths and **r** will destroy .... Mt 6:19
by moths or **r** and where thieves .... Mt 6:20
and that **r** will be a proof that................. Jam 5:3

RUSTED
Your gold and silver have **r**, ... Jam 5:3

RUSTY
will be for the **r** pot whose rust .... Eze 24:6

RUTH
But **R** said, "Don't beg me to .... Ru 1:16
Naomi and her daughter-in-law **R**, ... Ru 1:22

RUTH'S
Naomi, **R** mother-in-law, said .... Ru 3:1

S

SABACHTHANI
loud voice, "Eli, Eli, lama **s**?" .... Mt 27:46
voice, "Eloi, Eloi, lama **s**." .... Mk 15:34

SABBATH
because tomorrow is the **S**,.................... Ex 16:23
Remember to keep the **S** holy. .... Ex 20:8
blessed the **S** day and made it .... Ex 20:11
during the **S** day must be put .... Ex 31:15
a **S** of rest to honor the LORD. .... Ex 35:2
is a **S** to the LORD in all your................. Le 23:3
This is the **S** that you bring the .... Le 23:15
man gathering wood on the **S** day. .... Nu 15:32
the New Moon or the **S** day." 2Ki 4:23
off duty on the **S** must protect 2Ki 11:7
goods or grain to sell on the **S**, ... Ne 10:31
law about the **S** and not do what .... Is 58:13
some fields of grain on a **S** day. .... Mt 12:1
is unlawful to do on the **S** day." .... Mt 12:2
of Man is Lord of the **S** day." .... Mt 12:8
The **S** day was made to help .... Mk 2:27
The day after the **S** day, Mary.................. Mk 16:1
On the **S** day he went to the .... Lk 4:16
a baby boy on a **S** day. .... Jn 7:22
which are read every **S** day. .... Ac 13:27
a New Moon Festival, or a **S** day. .... Col 2:16

SABBATHS
must keep the rules about my **S**,.................... Ex 31:13
the laws about **S**, and respect my .... Le 19:30

Remember my **S**, and respect my .... Le 26:2
your New Moons, **S**, and other .... Is 1:13
New Moon festivals, and her **S**. .... Hos 2:11

SABEAN
them to the **S** people far away. .... Joe 3:8

SABEANS
when the **S** attacked and carried .... Job 1:15
The **S** will walk behind you, ... Is 45:14

SABTA
were Seba, Havilah, **S**, Raamah,............... 1Ch 1:9

SABTAH
were Seba, Havilah, **S**, Raamah,............... Ge 10:7

SABTECA
Havilah, Sabtah, Raamah, and **S**. .... Ge 10:7
Havilah, Sabta, Raamah, and **S**. 1Ch 1:9

SACAR
Ahiam son of **S** the Hararite; 1Ch 11:35
Joah was third, **S** was fourth, ... 1Ch 26:4

SACK
opened his **s** to get food for his .... Ge 42:27
found the cup in Benjamin's **s**. .... Ge 44:12

SACKS
As the brothers emptied their **s**, ... Ge 42:35
who put that money in our **s**." .... Ge 43:22
gathered old **s** and old leather .... Jos 9:4

SACRED
on the slopes of the **s** mountain................. Is 14:13

SACRIFICE
is the Passover **s** to honor the................. Ex 12:27
fat from the **s** for the next day .... Ex 23:18
the blood of a **s** to me with .... Ex 34:25
leave any of the **s** of the Feast................. Ex 34:25
he must make a **s** by fire to the .... Le 3:3
who offers the **s** to remove sins .... Le 7:7
the **s** should be eaten the same .... Le 7:16
part of it as his **s** to the LORD. .... Le 7:29
offers a burnt offering or **s**,.................... Le 17:8
bull as a burnt offering or **s**, ... Nu 15:8
to offer a great **s** to their god .... Jdg 16:23
had killed the bull for the **s**, ... 1Sa 1:25
because he must bless the **s**. 1Sa 9:13
It is better to obey than to **s**. 1Sa 15:22
take anything you want for a **s**. 2Sa 24:22
went to Gibeon to offer a **s**, ... 1Ki 3:4
At the time for the evening **s**, ... 1Ki 18:36
LORD came down and burned the **s**, ... 1Ki 18:38
offering or **s** to any other gods 2Ki 5:17
I have a great **s** for Baal........................ 2Ki 10:19
the burnt offering and of the **s**. 2Ki 16:15
offered a **s** of twenty-two 2Ch 7:5
the Levites to **s** to the LORD,.................. 2Ch 11:16
agreement with me, using a **s**." .... Ps 50:5
The **s** God wants is a broken .... Ps 51:17
about the time of the evening **s**, ... Da 9:21
from offering the daily **s**, ... Da 11:31
The daily **s** to be stopped. .... Da 12:11
they cannot **s** it in the Temple. .... Hos 9:4
Though people **s** bulls at Gilgal, ... Hos 12:11
those calf idols and **s** to them." .... Hos 13:2
they offered a **s** to the LORD and .... Jnh 1:16
Joseph also went to offer a **s**, ... Lk 2:24
your lives as a living **s** to him. .... Rm 12:1
offering and **s** to God............................ Eph 5:2
sweet-smelling **s** offered to God .... Php 4:18
offered as a **s** one time to take .... Heb 9:28
holy through the **s** Christ made .... Heb 10:10
Christ offered one **s** for sins, ... Heb 10:12
With one **s** he made perfect .... Heb 10:14
is no longer any **s** for sins. .... Heb 10:26

S

God a better **s** than Cain did. .... Heb 11:4
offer to God our **s** of praise, ... Heb 13:15

SACRIFICED

your children to be **s** to Molech, ... Le 18:21
bull that had been **s** on it. .... Jdg 6:28
So Manoah **s** a young goat on a .... Jdg 13:19
Today he has **s** many cows, fat 1Ki 1:25
the Ark and **s** so many sheep 1Ki 8:5
meat that had been **s** to lifeless .... Ps 106:28
our Passover lamb, has been **s**. 1Co 5:7
that the food **s** to an idol is 1Co 10:19
I say that what is **s** to idols is 1Co 10:20

SACRIFICES

offering and other **s** to God. .... Ex 18:12
it and offered **s** to it. .... Ex 32:8
left from the **s** offered by fire .... Le 10:12
blood of your **s** should be poured .... Dt 12:27
Who ate the fat from their **s,** .... Dt 32:38
offerings and accept all your **s.** .... Ps 20:3
pleased by **s,** or I would give .... Ps 51:16
and daughters as **s** to demons. .... Ps 106:37
as **s** to the idols of Canaan.................... Ps 106:38
Let them offer **s** to thank him. .... Ps 107:22
I do not want all these **s.** .... Is 1:11
bringing me worthless **s!**......................... Is 1:13
brought me your **s** of sheep nor .... Is 43:23
the daily **s** that were offered .... Da 8:11
They offered **s** to the Baals and .... Hos 11:2
Offer your **s** every morning, ... Am 4:4
did not bring me **s** and offerings .... Am 5:25
you bring blind animals as **s,** .... Mal 1:8
more than I want animal **s.'** .... Mt 9:13
more than I want animal **s.'** .... Mt 12:7
animals and **s** we offer to God. .... Mk 12:33
they brought **s** to it and were .... Ac 7:41
those who eat the **s** share in the 1Co 10:18
to offer gifts and **s** for sins...................... Heb 5:1
must offer **s** for his own sins .... Heb 5:3
who had to offer **s** every day, ... Heb 7:27
to be made clean by animal **s.** .... Heb 9:23
You do not want **s** and offerings, ... Heb 10:5
often offering the same **s.** .... Heb 10:11
because such **s** please God...................... Heb 13:16
who offer spiritual **s** to God. 1Pe 2:5

SACRIFICING

they have been **s** in the open .... Le 17:5
were still **s** at altars in many 1Ki 3:2
s them to Adrammelech and 2Ki 17:31
more than **s** a bull with horns................. Ps 69:31
the animals they were **s** to God. .... Lk 13:1
take away all sin by **s** himself. .... Heb 9:26

SAD

she was not **s** anymore. 1Sa 1:18
your face look **s** even though you .... Ne 2:2

SADDENED

I may be **s** by many of those who 2Co 12:21

SADDLE

her camel's **s** and was sitting .... Ge 31:34

SADDLED

in the morning and **s** his donkey. .... Ge 22:3
took his two **s** donkeys and his .... Jdg 19:10
he **s** his donkey and went to his 2Sa 17:23
So they **s** the donkey, and he 1Ki 13:13
Then she **s** the donkey and said 2Ki 4:24

SADDUCEES

Pharisees and **S** came to the .... Mt 3:7
S, who believed people would................. Lk 20:27
group called the **S**) became very.............. Ac 5:17
The **S** do not believe in angels .... Ac 23:8

SADLY

We call out **s** like the doves. .... Is 59:11
They will cry for you and **s** say, ... Je 34:5
I cry **s** for Moab, for everyone .... Je 48:31
My heart cries **s** for Moab like a............. Je 48:36
cry **s** because the town of Ai is .... Je 49:3

SAFE

He took me to a **s** place. 2Sa 22:20
Good people will always be **s,**................. Pr 10:30
Innocent people will be kept **s,** .... Pr 28:18
tomb and made it **s** from thieves .... Mt 27:66
house, his possessions are **s.** .... Lk 11:21
keep them **s** by the power of your .... Jn 17:11
be kept **s** and without fault when 1Th 5:23
The Son of God keeps them **s,** 1Jn 5:18
been kept **s** in Jesus Christ: .... Jud 1:1

SAFELY

and arrived **s** at the city of .... Ge 33:18
I return **s** from the battle. 1Ki 22:27
if you come back **s** from battle, ... 1Ki 22:28
own nets, but let me pass by **s.** .... Ps 141:10
my people will be able to eat **s,** .... Is 14:30
be taken to Governor Felix **s.**" .... Ac 23:24
the people made it **s** to land. .... Ac 27:44
wisdom and knowledge are **s** kept. .... Col 2:3
will bring me **s** to his heavenly 2Ti 4:18

SAFER

It is **s** to avoid such promises.................. Pr 11:15

SAFEST

gathered in the **s** room of the .... Jdg 9:46
them against the **s** room of the .... Jdg 9:49

SAFETY

I can run to him for **s.** .... Ps 18:2
my place of **s** in times of......................... Ps 59:16
Let me find **s** in the shelter of................. Ps 61:4
Be my place of **s** where I can .... Ps 71:3
Doing evil brings no **s** at all, ... Pr 12:3
will be able to lie down in **s.** .... Is 14:30
The Israelites will live in **s,** .... Mic 5:4
return to your place of **s**......................... Zch 9:12
us who came to God for **s.** .... Heb 6:18

SAIL

Ships will **s** from the shores of .... Nu 24:24
trading ships to **s** to Ophir for 1Ki 22:48
Geber, so they never set **s.** 1Ki 22:48
some men to **s** with his men, ... 1Ki 22:49
they could not **s** out to trade. 2Ch 20:37
no powerful ship will **s** on them. .... Is 33:21
you people who **s** on the seas and .... Is 42:10
Your **s** of linen with designs .... Eze 27:7
He was ready to **s** for Syria, ... Ac 20:3
that we would **s** for Italy. .... Ac 27:1
and was about to **s** to different .... Ac 27:2
and it was now dangerous to **s,** .... Ac 27:9
it and could not **s** against it. .... Ac 27:15
lowered the **s** and let the wind .... Ac 27:17
beach and wanted to **s** the ship .... Ac 27:39
raised the front **s** into the wind .... Ac 27:40

SAILED

The ships **s** to Ophir and brought 1Ki 9:28
his followers **s** across the lake .... Lk 8:26
From there they **s** to the island .... Ac 13:4
and those with him **s** from Paphos .... Ac 13:13
there they **s** away to Antioch .... Ac 14:26
took Mark and **s** to Cyprus, ... Ac 15:39
We left Troas and **s** straight to .... Ac 16:11
The next day we **s** to Neapolis. .... Ac 16:11
Then he left and **s** for Syria, ... Ac 18:18
And so he **s** away from Ephesus. .... Ac 18:21
We **s** from Philippi after the .... Ac 20:6

ahead of Paul and s for the city .... Ac 20:13
We s from Mitylene and the next .... Ac 20:15
The following day we s to Samos, ... Ac 20:15
we s straight to the island of .... Ac 21:1
so we went aboard and s away. .... Ac 21:2
We s near the island of Cyprus, ... Ac 21:3
the north, but we s on to Syria. .... Ac 21:3
We left Sidon and s close to the .... Ac 27:4
We s slowly for many days. .... Ac 27:7
So we s by the south side of the .... Ac 27:7
we s very close to the island .... Ac 27:13
should not have s from Crete.................. Ac 27:21
the wind and s toward the beach. .... Ac 27:40
From there we s to Rhegium. .... Ac 28:13

SAILING
While they were s, Jesus fell .... Lk 8:23
S past it was hard. Then we came .... Ac 27:8
lives of everyone s with you.' .... Ac 27:24

SAILORS
had skilled s, so he sent them............... 1Ki 9:27
his own men, who were skilled s. 2Ch 8:18
S have made you rich........................... Is 23:2
the s of Tyre brought grain from............. Is 23:3
You s from other lands, hear: .... Is 33:23
men who were s on your deck................. Eze 27:8
sea and their s came alongside .... Eze 27:9
seamen, your s, your workers, ... Eze 27:27
with fear when your s cry out. .... Eze 27:28
seamen and the s of other ships .... Eze 27:29
The s were afraid, and each man .... Jnh 1:5
midnight the s thought we were.............. Ac 27:27
The s were afraid that we would............. Ac 27:29
Some of the s wanted to leave .... Ac 27:30
daylight came, the s saw land. .... Ac 27:39
passenger, the s, and all those .... Rev 18:17

SAILS
if you're on top of a ship's s. .... Pr 23:34
the way a ship s on the sea, ... Pr 30:19
The s are not spread open. .... Is 33:23

SAINTS
he called the s and the widows .... Ac 9:41

SAKE
to the LORD for Israel's s, ... 1Sa 7:9
For his own s, the LORD won't 1Sa 12:22
that person for Jonathan's s!"................. 2Sa 9:1
for your father Jonathan's s. 2Sa 9:7
with young Absalom for my s." 2Sa 18:5
do this for the s of my servant 1Ki 11:32
city for my s and for the sake................. 2Ki 19:34
my sake and for the s of David, ... 2Ki 19:34
the city for my s and for the 2Ki 20:6
sake and for the s of my servant 2Ki 20:6
thing for my s and because you 1Ch 17:19
together. For my s, fast; do not .... Est 4:16
For the s of your name, LORD, ... Ps 25:11
LORD saved them for his own s, ... Ps 106:8
For the s of the Temple of the................. Ps 122:9
For the s of your servant David, ... Ps 132:10
city for my s and for David, ... Is 37:35
erases all your sins, for my s; .... Is 43:25
But for my own s I will be .... Is 48:9
this for myself, for my own s. .... Is 48:11
Jerusalem's s I will not stop .... Is 62:1
For our s come back to us, ... Is 63:17
For your s, do not hate us. .... Je 14:21
I acted for the s of my name so .... Eze 20:9
I acted for the s of my name so .... Eze 20:14
I acted for the s of my name so .... Eze 20:22
with you for the s of my name, ... Eze 20:44
to act, but not for your s. .... Eze 36:22
not going to do this for your s, ... Eze 36:32

for your s do good things for .... Da 9:17
For your s, don't wait, because .... Da 9:19
for the s of your own rules..................... Mt 15:6
That voice was for your s, ... Jn 12:30
For their s, I am making myself .... Jn 17:19
We are fools for Christ's s, ... 1Co 4:10
in these last times for your s. 1Pe 1:20
For the Lord's s, yield to the 1Pe 2:13

SAKES
glad for your s I was not there .... Jn 11:15

SAKKUTH
king, the god S, and Kaiwan your .... Am 5:26

SALAMIS
they came to S, they preached .... Ac 13:5

SALARY
hired worker's s all night until .... Le 19:13
in the army and pays his own s............... 1Co 9:7

SALE
received from the s of family .... Dt 18:8
and made no profit on the s.................... Ps 44:12

SALECAH
of Bashan as far as S and Edrei,............. Dt 3:10
Mount Hermon, S, and all the .... Jos 12:5
Hermon and Bashan as far as S. .... Jos 13:11
area of Bashan all the way to S............... 1Ch 5:11

SALEM
king of S brought out bread .... Ge 14:18
was the king of S and a priest .... Heb 7:1
and he is king of S, which means .... Heb 7:2

SALIM
in Aenon, near S, because there.............. Jn 3:23

SALLAI
Following him were Gabbai and S,........... Ne 11:8

SALLU
there was S son of Meshullam. 1Ch 9:7
There was S son of Meshullam. .... Ne 11:7
S, Amok, Hilkiah, and Jedaiah. .... Ne 12:7

SALLU'S
Kallai, from S family; .... Ne 12:20

SALMA'S
S descendants were Bethlehem, ... 1Ch 2:54

SALMON
who was the father of S. .... Ru 4:20
S was the father of Boaz, who .... Ru 4:21
Nahshon was the father of S, ... 1Ch 2:11
Nahshon was the father of S. .... Mt 1:4
S was the father of Boaz. .... Mt 1:5
Boaz was the son of S. .... Lk 3:32
S was the son of Nahshon. .... Lk 3:32

SALMONE
of the island of Crete near S. .... Ac 27:7

SALOME
Mary Magdalene, S, and Mary the .... Mk 15:40
and S bought some sweet-smelling........... Mk 16:1

SALT
did, she became a pillar of s. .... Ge 19:26
s to it to keep it pure and holy. .... Ex 30:35
must also put s on all your .... Le 2:13
S stands for your agreement with .... Le 2:13
You must add s to all your .... Le 2:13
agreement of s before the LORD .... Nu 18:19
but burning cinders and s. .... Dt 29:23
the City of S, and En Gedi. .... Jos 15:62
down and threw s over the ruins. .... Jdg 9:45
Arameans in the Valley of S. 2Sa 8:13
me a new bowl and put s in it." 2Ki 2:20
spring and threw the s in it. 2Ki 2:21
Edomites in the Valley of S. 2Ki 14:7

S

Edomites in the Valley of **S.** 1Ch 18:12
forever by an agreement of **s.** 2Ch 13:5
the Valley of **S** in the country 2Ch 25:11
or wheat, **s,** wine, or olive .... Ezr 6:9
give him as much **s** as he wants. .... Ezr 7:22
food is not eaten without **s,**.................... Job 6:6
Edomites at the Valley of **S.** .... Ps 59:11
not rubbed with **s** or wrapped in .... Eze 16:4
are to throw **s** on them and offer .... Eze 43:24
they will be left for **s.** .... Eze 47:11
of weeds, a pit of **s,** and a ruin .... Zph 2:9
You are the **s** of the earth. .... Mt 5:13
But if the **s** loses its salty .... Mt 5:13
S is good, but if the salt loses .... Mk 9:50
but if the **s** loses its salty .... Mk 9:50
So, be full of **s,** and have peace .... Mk 9:50
S is good, but if it loses its .... Lk 14:34

SALTED
person will be **s** with fire. .... Mk 9:49

SALTY
made fertile land **s,** because the .... Ps 107:34
if the salt loses its **s** taste, ... Mt 5:13
it cannot be made **s** again. .... Mt 5:13
if the salt loses its **s** taste, ... Mk 9:50
you cannot make it **s** again. .... Mk 9:50
but if it loses its **s** taste, ... Lk 14:34
you cannot make it **s** again. .... Lk 14:34
a well full of **s** water cannot .... Jam 3:12

SALU
woman was named Zimri son of **S.** .... Nu 25:14

SALVATION
LORD, I wait for your **s.** .... Ge 49:18
accomplish my **s** and satisfy all 2Sa 23:5
Let your priests receive your **s,** 2Ch 6:41
This is my **s.** The wicked cannot.............. Job 13:16
and fill me with songs of **s.**..................... Ps 32:7
speak about your loyalty and **s.** .... Ps 40:10
Give me back the joy of your **s** .... Ps 51:12
God of my **s,** and I will sing .... Ps 51:14
He is my rock and my **s.** .... Ps 62:2
He is my rock and my **s.** .... Ps 62:6
My honor and **s** come from God. .... Ps 62:7
who love your **s** always say, ... Ps 70:4
tell about your **s** all day long, ... Ps 71:15
You belong to the earth. .... Ps 74:12
I will lift up the cup of **s,** .... Ps 116:13
looking for your **s** and for your .... Ps 119:123
I will cover her priests with **s,**................. Ps 132:16
receive your **s** with joy as you .... Is 12:3
We don't bring **s** to the land or .... Is 26:18
He is full of **s,** wisdom, and .... Is 33:6
it, and let **s** grow, and let........................ Is 45:8
that **s** will continue forever. .... Is 45:17
I will bring **s** soon. .... Is 46:13
On the day of **s** I will help you. .... Is 49:8
But my **s** will continue forever, ... Is 51:6
and my **s** will continue from now .... Is 51:8
who announces **s** and says to .... Is 52:7
earth will see the **s** of our God. .... Is 52:10
because my **s** will come to you .... Is 56:1
to be saved, but **s** is far away. .... Is 59:11
put the helmet of **s** on his head. .... Is 59:17
name your walls **S** and your gates .... Is 60:18
with clothes of **s** and wrapped me .... Is 61:10
until her **s** burns bright like a .... Is 62:1
Surely the **s** of Israel comes .... Je 3:23
S comes from the LORD!" .... Jnh 2:9
my own eyes I have seen your **s,** .... Lk 2:30
know about the **s** of God!'" .... Lk 3:6
S has come to this house today, ... Lk 19:9
because **s** comes from the Jews. .... Jn 4:22

news about this **s** has been sent .... Ac 13:26
also sent his **s** to all nations, ... Ac 28:28
failure brought **s** to those who .... Rm 11:11
because our **s** is nearer now than .... Rm 13:11
it is for your comfort and **s,** 2Co 1:6
On the day of **s** I helped you." 2Co 6:2
and the "day of **s**" is now. 2Co 6:2
This leads to **s,** and you cannot 2Co 7:10
the Good News about your **s**— .... Eph 1:13
Accept God's **s** as your helmet, ... Eph 6:17
to complete your **s** with fear and .... Php 2:12
and the hope of **s** should be our 1Th 5:8
but to have **s** through our Lord 1Th 5:9
can have the **s** that is in Christ 2Ti 2:10
With that **s** comes glory that 2Ti 2:10
wisdom leads to **s** through faith 2Ti 3:15
help those who will receive **s.**................. Heb 1:14
if we ignore this great **s.** .... Heb 2:3
himself first told about this **s,**................. Heb 2:3
people to **s** perfect through..................... Heb 2:10
give eternal **s** to all who obey .... Heb 5:9
you that will lead to your **s.** .... Heb 6:9
but to bring **s** to those who are .... Heb 9:28
faith until **s** is shown to you 1Pe 1:5
your faith—the **s** of your souls. 1Pe 1:9
and tried to learn about this **s.** 1Pe 1:10
By it you can mature in your **s,** 1Pe 2:2
you about the **s** we all share. .... Jud 1:3
a loud voice, "**S** belongs to our .... Rev 7:10
The **s** and the power and the .... Rev 12:10
S, glory, and power belong to .... Rev 19:1

SAMARIA
the hill of **S** from Shemer for 1Ki 16:24
and called it **S** after the name................ 1Ki 16:24
Go to Ahab king of Israel in **S.** 1Ki 21:18
Israel is led by the city of **S,** .... Is 7:9
the area between **S** and Galilee. .... Lk 17:11
to go through the country of **S.** .... Jn 4:4
In **S** Jesus came to the town .... Jn 4:5
all of Judea, in **S,** and in every .... Ac 1:8

SAMARITAN
Then a **S** traveling down the road .... Lk 10:33
The **S** went to him, poured olive............. Lk 10:34
the **S** brought out two coins, ... Lk 10:35
And this man was a **S.** .... Lk 17:16
Is this **S** the only one who came............. Lk 17:18
When a **S** woman came to the well .... Jn 4:7
Jewish man and I am a **S** woman." .... Jn 4:9
say you are a **S** and have a demon .... Jn 8:48
prayed that the **S** believers .... Ac 8:15
went through many **S** towns and .... Ac 8:25

SAMARITANS
temples had been built by the **S.**............. 2Ki 17:29
or to any town where the **S** live............... Mt 10:5
people are not friends with **S.**................. Jn 4:9
S worship something you don't .... Jn 4:22
Many of the **S** in that town .... Jn 4:39
When the **S** came to Jesus, they .... Jn 4:40

SAMGAR
of the district of **S**; .... Je 39:3

SAMLAH
When Hadad died, **S** became king............. Ge 36:36
When **S** died, Shaul became king. .... Ge 36:37
When Hadad died, **S** became king............. 1Ch 1:47
When **S** died, Shaul became king. 1Ch 1:48

SAMOS
following day we sailed to **S,** .... Ac 20:15

SAMOTHRACE
straight to the island of **S.** .... Ac 16:11

SAMSON

wheat harvest, **S** went to visit .... Jdg 15:1
Delilah said to **S**, "Tell me why .... Jdg 16:6
Then **S** turned to the two center .... Jdg 16:29
Gideon, Barak, **S**, Jephthah, ... Heb 11:32

SAMUEL

She named him **S**, saying, "His 1Sa 1:20
The boy **S** served the LORD under 1Sa 3:1
as he had before, "**S**, Samuel!" 1Sa 3:10
S continued as judge of Israel 1Sa 7:15
Then **S** left and went to Ramah, ... 1Sa 15:34
had seven of his sons pass by **S**. 1Sa 16:10
asked, "Where are **S** and David?" 1Sa 19:22
Now **S** died, and all the 1Sa 25:1
He answered, "Bring up **S**." 1Sa 28:11
the woman saw **S**, she screamed. 1Sa 28:12
in the records of **S** the seer, ... 1Ch 29:29
S, and all the other prophets .... Ac 3:24
until the time of **S** the prophet. .... Ac 13:20
Jephthah, David, **S**, and the .... Heb 11:32

SAMUEL'S

year **S** mother made a little 1Sa 2:19
not let any of **S** messages fail 1Sa 3:19
the Philistines all **S** life. 1Sa 7:13
But **S** sons did not live as he 1Sa 8:3
S sons were Joel, the first son, ... 1Ch 6:28
was Joel's son. Joel was **S** son. 1Ch 6:33

SANBALLAT

When **S** the Horonite and Tobiah .... Ne 2:10
But when **S** the Horonite, Tobiah .... Ne 2:19
When **S** heard we were rebuilding .... Ne 4:1
who was next to **S**, said, "If a .... Ne 4:3
the insults of **S** and Tobiah back .... Ne 4:4
But **S**, Tobiah, the Arabs, the .... Ne 4:7
Then **S**, Tobiah, Geshem the Arab, ... Ne 6:1
So **S** and Geshem sent me this .... Ne 6:2
S and Geshem sent the same .... Ne 6:4
The fifth time **S** sent his helper .... Ne 6:5
that Tobiah and **S** had paid him .... Ne 6:12
Tobiah and **S** and what they have .... Ne 6:14
a daughter of **S** the Horonite, ... Ne 13:28

SAND

sky and the **s** on the seashore .... Ge 22:17
many as the **s** of the seashore. .... Ge 32:12
and hid his body in the **s**. .... Ex 2:12
as grains of **s** on the seashore. 1Ki 4:20
more than all the grains of **s**. .... Ps 139:18
man who built his house on **s**. .... Mt 7:26
like the grains of **s** by the sea. .... Rm 9:27

SANDAL

a thread or a **s** strap so that .... Ge 14:23
took off his **s** and gave it to .... Ru 4:7
" and he took off his **s**. .... Ru 4:8
and their **s** straps are not .... Is 5:27

SANDALS

Take off your **s**, because you are .... Ex 3:5
your clothes nor **s** wore out. .... Dt 29:5
the poor to buy a pair of **s**. .... Am 2:6
for the price of a pair of **s**. .... Am 8:6
whose **s** I am not good enough to .... Mt 3:11
I am not worthy to untie his **s**.' .... Ac 13:25

SANDBANK

But the ship hit a **s**. .... Ac 27:41

SANDBANKS

ship would hit the **s** of Syrtis, ... Ac 27:17

SANG

they **s** to the LORD: .... Ezr 3:11
morning stars **s** together and all .... Job 38:7

SANK

and they **s** to the bottom like a .... Ex 15:5
They **s** like lead in the raging .... Ex 15:10
Even the handle **s** in, and the .... Jdg 3:22
Jael's feet he **s**. He fell, and .... Jdg 5:27
At her feet he **s**. He fell. Where .... Jdg 5:27
Where Sisera **s**, there he fell, ... Jdg 5:27
the valleys **s**. The water went .... Ps 104:8
Jeremiah **s** down into the mud. .... Je 38:6
else on board **s** into the sea .... Eze 27:27

SANNAH

Dannah, Kiriath **S** (also called .... Jos 15:49

SANSANNAH

Ziklag, Madmannah, **S**, ... Jos 15:31

SAPH

the Hushathite killed **S**, ... 2Sa 21:18

SAPPHIRA

and his wife **S** sold some land. .... Ac 5:1
S answered, "Yes, that was the .... Ac 5:8
that moment **S** fell down by his .... Ac 5:10

SAPPHIRE

were paved with blue **s** stones, ... Ex 24:10
turquoise, a **s**, and an emerald; .... Ex 28:18
turquoise, a **s**, and an emerald; .... Ex 39:11
or with valuable onyx or **s** gems. .... Job 28:16
It looked like a **s** gem. .... Eze 1:26
like a **s** gem which looked .... Eze 10:1
onyx, and jasper, **s**, turquoise, ... Eze 28:13
the second was **s**, the third was .... Rev 21:19

SAPPHIRES

S are found in rocks, and gold .... Job 28:6
like shiny ivory covered with **s**. .... Sng 5:14
build your foundations with **s**. .... Is 54:11
they looked like **s**. .... La 4:7

SARAH

name of Sarai, your wife, to **S**. .... Ge 17:15
S your wife will have a son, ... Ge 17:19
to Abraham, "Why did **S** laugh? .... Ge 18:13
LORD cared for **S** as he had said .... Ge 21:1
Isaac, the son **S** gave birth to. .... Ge 21:3
S lived to be one hundred .... Ge 23:1
ancestor, and **S**, who gave birth .... Is 51:2
and **S** could not have children. .... Heb 11:11
S obeyed Abraham, her husband, ... 1Pe 3:6
children of **S** if you always do 1Pe 3:6

SARAI

wife was named **S**, and Nahor's .... Ge 11:29
S was not able to have children. .... Ge 11:30
Abram said to **S**, "You are .... Ge 16:6

SARDIS

Thyatira, **S**, Philadelphia, ... Rev 1:11
to the angel of the church in **S**: .... Rev 3:1
a few there in **S** who have kept .... Rev 3:4

SARGON

S king of Assyria sent a .... Is 20:1

SARID

of Zebulun went as far as **S**. .... Jos 19:10
It went from **S** to the area of .... Jos 19:12

SAT

a short distance and **s** down. .... Ge 21:16
She **s** there and began to cry. .... Ge 21:16
the brothers **s** down to eat. .... Ge 37:25
Then she **s** down by the gate of .... Ge 38:14
strength and **s** up on his bed. .... Ge 48:2
There he **s** down near a well. .... Ex 2:15
of the king who **s** on the throne .... Ex 12:29
rock under him, and he **s** on it. .... Ex 17:12
They **s** down to eat and drink, ... Ex 32:6
the fluid **s** on must wash his .... Le 15:6

S

she has s on must wash his..................... Le 15:22
woman's bed or something she s .... Le 15:23
the LORD came and s down under .... Jdg 6:11
So the two men s down to eat and .... Jdg 19:6
square of the city and s down, ... Jdg 19:15
There they s down and cried to .... Jdg 20:26
of Bethel and s before God until.............. Jdg 21:2
So Ruth s down beside the .... Ru 2:14
the city gate and s there until .... Ru 4:1
So the man came over and s down. .... Ru 4:1
Sit down here!" So they s down. .... Ru 4:2
came, the king s down to eat. 1Sa 20:24
He s where he always sat, near 1Sa 20:25
he always s, near the wall. 1Sa 20:25
Jonathan s across from him, ... 1Sa 20:25
him, and Abner s next to Saul, ... 1Sa 20:25
the ground and s on the bed. 1Sa 28:23
Abner's group s on one side of 2Sa 2:13
Joab's group s on the other. 2Sa 2:13
David went in and s in front of 2Sa 7:18
bowed down, and s on the throne. 1Ki 2:19
Then she s down at his right 1Ki 2:19
He s down under a bush and asked 1Ki 19:4
Two troublemakers s across from 1Ki 21:13
the king s on the royal throne. 2Ki 11:19
David went in and s in front of 1Ch 17:16
Then Solomon s on the LORD's 1Ch 29:23
and beard, and s down in shock. .... Ezr 9:3
I s there in shock until the .... Ezr 9:4
tenth month they s down to study .... Ezr 10:16
I s down and cried for several .... Ne 1:4
king and Haman s down to drink, ... Est 3:15
and he s in ashes in misery. .... Job 2:8
Then they s on the ground with .... Job 2:13
you s on your throne and judged .... Ps 9:4
Some s in gloom and darkness; .... Ps 107:10
Babylon we s and cried when we .... Ps 137:1
You have s by the road waiting .... Je 3:2
I never s with the crowd as they.............. Je 15:17
I s by myself, because you were .... Je 15:17
Jerusalem and s down at the .... Je 39:3
I s there seven days where these .... Eze 3:15
to me and s down in front of me. .... Eze 14:1
the LORD and s down in front .... Eze 20:1
s on a fine bed with a table..................... Eze 23:41
Eternal One, s on his throne. .... Da 7:9
on rough cloth, and s in ashes. .... Da 9:3
rough cloth and s in ashes to .... Jnh 3:6
Jonah went out and s down east.............. Jnh 4:5
for himself and s in the shade, ... Jnh 4:5
he went up on a hill and s down. .... Mt 5:1
of the house and s by the lake. .... Mt 13:1
he got into a boat and s down, ... Mt 13:2
They s down and put all the good .... Mt 13:48
went up on a hill and s there. .... Mt 15:29
on them, and Jesus s on them. .... Mt 21:7
Every day I s in the Temple..................... Mt 26:55
and he s down with the guards to .... Mt 26:58
The soldiers s there and .... Mt 27:36
Then he s on the stone. .... Mt 28:2
so he s down in a boat near the .... Mk 4:1
So they s in groups of fifty or .... Mk 6:40
Jesus s down and called the .... Mk 9:35
coats on it, and Jesus s on it. .... Mk 11:7
Jesus s near the Temple money .... Mk 12:41
There he s with the guards, ... Mk 14:54
he s at the right side of God. .... Mk 16:19
to the assistant, and s down. .... Lk 4:20
Then Jesus s down and continued .... Lk 5:3
And the son s up and began to .... Lk 7:15
house and s at the table.......................... Lk 7:36
this, and all the people s down. .... Lk 9:15
went in and s at the table. .... Lk 11:37

of the courtyard and s together, ... Lk 22:55
sat together, Peter s with them. .... Lk 22:55
so he s down beside the well. .... Jn 4:6
on a hill and s down there with .... Jn 6:3
five thousand men s down there. ....,..... Jn 6:10
him, and he s and taught them. .... Jn 8:2
Jesus found a colt and s on it................... Jn 12:14
on his clothes and s down again. .... Jn 13:12
Jesus out and s down on the .... Jn 19:13
when she saw Peter, she s up................... Ac 9:40
royal robes, s on his throne, ... Ac 12:21
into the synagogue and s down. .... Ac 13:14
In Lystra there s a man who had .... Ac 14:8
we s down and talked with them. .... Ac 16:13
The next day I s on the judge's .... Ac 25:17
They s down to eat and drink, ... 1Co 10:7
he s down at the right side of .... Heb 1:3
s down at the right side of God. .... Heb 10:12
the victory and s down with my .... Rev 3:21
The One who s on the throne .... Rev 4:3

SATAN

S was against Israel, and he 1Ch 21:1
the LORD, and S was with him. .... Job 1:6
LORD said to S, "Where have you .... Job 1:7
S answered the LORD, "I have .... Job 1:7
the LORD said to S, "Have you .... Job 1:8
But S answered the LORD, "Job............... Job 1:9
The LORD said to S, "All right, ... Job 1:12
Then S left the LORD's .... Job 1:12
the LORD, and S was with them............... Job 2:1
LORD said to S, "Where have you .... Job 2:2
S answered the LORD, "I have .... Job 2:2
the LORD said to S, "Have you .... Job 2:3
for another!" S answered. "A man .... Job 2:4
The LORD said to S, "All right, ... Job 2:6
So S left the LORD's presence. .... Job 2:7
And S was standing by Joshua's .... Zch 3:1
LORD said to S, "The LORD says .... Zch 3:2
The LORD says no to you, S! .... Zch 3:2
the devil, "Go away from me, S!............... Mt 4:10
And if S forces out himself, ... Mt 12:26
then S is divided against......................... Mt 12:26
to Peter, "Go away from me, S! .... Mt 16:23
forty days and was tempted by S. .... Mk 1:13
S will not force himself out of .... Mk 3:23
And if S is against himself and .... Mk 3:26
continue; that is the end of S. .... Mk 3:26
but S quickly comes and takes .... Mk 4:15
He said, "Go away from me, S! .... Mk 8:33
I saw S fall like lightning from .... Lk 10:18
So if S is divided against .... Lk 11:18
has been held by S for eighteen .... Lk 13:16
S entered Judas Iscariot, one of .... Lk 22:3
S has asked to test all of you .... Lk 22:31
took the bread, S entered him. .... Jn 13:27
why did you let S rule your..................... Ac 5:3
from the power of S and to God. .... Ac 26:18
will soon defeat S and give you .... Rm 16:20
then hand this man over to S.................... 1Co 5:5
again so S cannot tempt you 1Co 7:5
did this so that S would not win 2Co 2:11
Even S changes himself to look 2Co 11:14
problem was a messenger from S, ... 2Co 12:7
than one, but S stopped us. 1Th 2:18
will come by the power of S. 2Th 2:9
given them to S so they will 1Ti 1:20
already turned away to follow S. 1Ti 5:15
a synagogue that belongs to S. .... Rev 2:9
It is where S has his throne. .... Rev 2:13
in your city, where S lives. .... Rev 2:13
that belongs to S say they are................. Rev 3:9
old snake called the devil or S, ... Rev 12:9

snake who is the devil and **S,** .... Rev 20:2
S will be set free from his .... Rev 20:7
and **S,** who tricked them, was .... Rev 20:10

SATAN'S
know very well what **S** plans are. 2Co 2:11
surprise us if **S** servants also 2Co 11:15
what some call **S** deep secrets. .... Rev 2:24
And **S** army marched across the............. Rev 20:9

SATISFACTION
they will give you **s.** .... Pr 29:17

SATISFIED
When Moses heard this, he was **s.** .... Le 10:20
This plan is King Hezekiah and 2Ch 30:4
will see your likeness and be **s.** .... Ps 17:15
the LORD will live and be **s,** .... Pr 19:23
three things that are never **s,** .... Pr 30:15
but was never **s** with what he had .... Ec 4:8
wealth will not be **s** with it.................... Ec 5:10
he will see life and be **s.** .... Is 53:11
hungry dogs that are never **s.** .... Is 56:11
take comfort from her and be **s,** .... Is 66:11
Your father was **s** to have food .... Je 22:15
them, and then I will be **s.** .... Eze 5:13
because you could not be **s.** .... Eze 16:28
with them, you still were not **s.** .... Eze 16:28
and they became full and **s.** .... Hos 13:6
those who are **s** with themselves, ... Zph 1:12
justice, for they will be **s.** .... Mt 5:6
should be **s** to become like .... Mt 10:25
should be **s** to become like .... Mt 10:25
All the people ate and were **s.**.............. Mt 14:20
All the people ate and were **s.**.............. Mt 15:37
All the people ate and were **s.**.............. Mk 6:42
All the people ate and were **s.**.............. Mk 8:8
Be **s** with the pay you get." .... Lk 3:14
blessed, because you will be **s.** .... Lk 6:21
all ate and were **s,** and what was .... Lk 9:17
you ate the bread and were **s.**............... Jn 6:26
learned to be **s** with the things .... Php 4:11
if we are **s** with what we have. 1Ti 6:6
clothes, we will be **s** with that. 1Ti 6:8
and be **s** with what you have. .... Heb 13:5
their desire for sin is never **s.** 2Pe 2:14

SATISFIES
He **s** me with good things and .... Ps 103:5
s the thirsty and fills up the .... Ps 107:9
will enjoy the rich food that **s.** .... Is 55:2
until it **s** its thirst for their .... Je 46:10

SATISFY
salvation and **s** all my desires. 2Sa 23:5
sends rain to **s** the empty land .... Job 38:27
the female lion to **s** the hunger .... Job 38:39
and you **s** all living things. .... Ps 145:16
that doesn't really **s** you? .... Is 55:2
they want to do is **s** themselves. .... Is 56:11
will **s** your needs in dry lands................. Is 58:11
It will not **s** their hunger or.................... Eze 7:19
but even this did not **s** you.................... Eze 16:29
food will only **s** their hunger; .... Hos 9:4
we will **s** him and save you from .... Mt 28:14
If they plant to **s** their sinful .... Gal 6:8

SATISFYING
age, after a long and **s** life. .... Ge 25:8
forget about **s** your sinful self................ Rm 13:14

SAUCE
our bread and dip it in our **s.**" .... Ru 2:14

SAUL
a son named **S,** who was a fine 1Sa 9:2
S stood a head taller than any 1Sa 9:2
Kish said to **S,** his son, "Take 1Sa 9:3

S went through the mountains of 1Sa 9:4
the area of Zuph, **S** said to his 1Sa 9:5
S said to his servant, "If we go 1Sa 9:7
Again the servant answered **S.** 1Sa 9:8
S said to his servant, "That's a 1Sa 9:10
As **S** and the servant were going 1Sa 9:11
S and the servant asked them, ... 1Sa 9:11
S and the servant went up to the 1Sa 9:14
The day before **S** came, the LORD 1Sa 9:15
Samuel first saw **S,** the LORD 1Sa 9:17
S approached Samuel at the gate 1Sa 9:18
S answered, "But I am from the 1Sa 9:21
Samuel took **S** and his servant 1Sa 9:22
it on the table in front of **S.**................... 1Sa 9:24
So **S** ate with Samuel that 1Sa 9:24
talked with **S** on the roof of his 1Sa 9:25
Samuel called to **S** on the roof. 1Sa 9:26
So **S** got up and went out of the 1Sa 9:26
As **S,** his servant, and Samuel 1Sa 9:27
Samuel said to **S,** "Tell the 1Sa 9:27
He kissed **S** and said, "The LORD 1Sa 10:1
When **S** turned to leave Samuel,............. 1Sa 10:9
When **S** and his servant arrived 1Sa 10:10
S met a group of prophets. 1Sa 10:10
who had known **S** before saw him 1Sa 10:11
Is even **S** one of the prophets?" 1Sa 10:11
"Is even **S** one of the prophets?" 1Sa 10:12
When **S** finished prophesying, ... 1Sa 10:13
S said, "We were looking for 1Sa 10:14
S answered, "He told us the 1Sa 10:16
But **S** did not tell his uncle 1Sa 10:16
and **S** son of Kish was picked. 1Sa 10:21
But when they looked for **S,** 1Sa 10:21
the LORD, "Has **S** come here yet?" 1Sa 10:22
When **S** stood among the people, ... 1Sa 10:23
S also went to his home in 1Sa 10:26
disapproved of **S** and refused to 1Sa 10:27
gifts to him. But **S** kept quiet. 1Sa 10:27
to Gibeah where **S** lived and told 1Sa 11:4
S was coming home from plowing 1Sa 11:5
Then they told **S** what the 1Sa 11:5
When **S** heard their words, God's 1Sa 11:6
does not follow **S** and Samuel." 1Sa 11:7
S gathered the people together 1Sa 11:8
The next morning **S** divided his 1Sa 11:11
Who didn't want **S** as king? 1Sa 11:12
But **S** said, "No! No one will be 1Sa 11:13
LORD, the people made **S** king. 1Sa 11:15
and **S** and all the Israelites had 1Sa 11:15
S was thirty years old when he 1Sa 13:1
S chose three thousand men from 1Sa 13:2
S sent the other men in the army 1Sa 13:2
S said, "Let the Hebrews hear 1Sa 13:3
S has defeated the Philistine 1Sa 13:4
were called to join **S** at Gilgal. 1Sa 13:4
But **S** stayed at Gilgal, and all 1Sa 13:7
S waited seven days, because 1Sa 13:8
So **S** said, "Bring me the whole 1Sa 13:9
Then **S** offered the whole burnt 1Sa 13:9
arrived, and **S** went to greet him 1Sa 13:10
S answered, "I saw the soldiers 1Sa 13:11
S counted the men who were still 1Sa 13:15
S and his son Jonathan and the 1Sa 13:16
soldiers with **S** and Jonathan had 1Sa 13:22
Only **S** and his son Jonathan had 1Sa 13:22
S was sitting under a 1Sa 14:2
S said to his army, "Check to 1Sa 14:17
So **S** said to Ahijah the priest, ... 1Sa 14:18
While **S** was talking to the 1Sa 14:19
Then **S** said to Ahijah, "Put your 1Sa 14:19
Then **S** gathered his army and 1Sa 14:20
Israelites with **S** and Jonathan. 1Sa 14:21
day because **S** had made an oath 1Sa 14:24

S

not heard the oath **S** had put on 1Sa 14:27
Someone said to **S**, "Look! 1Sa 14:33
S said, "You have sinned! 1Sa 14:33
Then **S** built an altar to the..................... 1Sa 14:35
S said, "Let's go after the 1Sa 14:36
So **S** asked God, "Should I chase 1Sa 14:37
did not answer **S** at that time.................... 1Sa 14:37
Then **S** said to all the leaders 1Sa 14:38
Then **S** said to all the 1Sa 14:40
Then **S** prayed to the LORD, ... 1Sa 14:41
And **S** and Jonathan were picked; 1Sa 14:41
S said, "Now let us discover if 1Sa 14:42
S said to Jonathan, "Tell me 1Sa 14:43
Jonathan told **S**, "I only tasted 1Sa 14:43
S said, "Jonathan, if you don't 1Sa 14:44
But the soldiers said to **S**, ... 1Sa 14:45
Then **S** stopped chasing the 1Sa 14:46
When **S** became king over Israel, ... 1Sa 14:47
Everywhere **S** went he defeated 1Sa 14:47
Samuel said to **S**, "The LORD sent 1Sa 15:1
So **S** called the army together at 1Sa 15:4
S went to the city of Amalek 1Sa 15:5
Then **S** defeated the Amalekites. 1Sa 15:7
S and the army let Agag live, ... 1Sa 15:9
I am sorry I made **S** king, ... 1Sa 15:11
got up and went to meet **S**. 1Sa 15:12
told Samuel, "**S** has gone to 1Sa 15:12
came to **S**, Saul said, "May 1Sa 15:13
came to Saul, **S** said, "May the 1Sa 15:13
S answered, "The soldiers took 1Sa 15:15
Samuel said to **S**, "Stop! 1Sa 15:16
S answered, "Tell me." 1Sa 15:16
S said, "But I did obey the LORD. 1Sa 15:20
Then **S** said to Samuel, "I have 1Sa 15:24
Samuel said to **S**, "I won't go 1Sa 15:26
to leave, **S** caught his robe 1Sa 15:27
S answered, "I have sinned. 1Sa 15:30
So Samuel went back with **S**, ... 1Sa 15:31
with Saul, and **S** worshiped the 1Sa 15:31
S went up to his home in Gibeah. 1Sa 15:34
Samuel never saw **S** again the 1Sa 15:35
his life, but he was sad for **S**. 1Sa 15:35
he had made **S** king of Israel................... 1Sa 15:35
continue to feel sorry for **S**? 1Sa 16:1
S will hear the news and will 1Sa 16:2
the LORD's Spirit had left **S**, ... 1Sa 16:14
So **S** said to his servants, ... 1Sa 16:17
Then **S** sent messengers to Jesse, ... 1Sa 16:19
them with his son David to **S**.................. 1Sa 16:20
David came to **S**, he began to 1Sa 16:21
S liked David and made him the 1Sa 16:21
S sent a message to Jesse, ... 1Sa 16:22
evil spirit from God troubled **S**, ... 1Sa 16:23
leave him, and **S** would feel 1Sa 16:23
S and the Israelites gathered in 1Sa 17:2
When **S** and the Israelites heard.............. 1Sa 17:11
sons followed **S** to the war..................... 1Sa 17:13
three oldest sons followed **S**, ... 1Sa 17:14
and forth from **S** to Bethlehem, ... 1Sa 17:15
brothers are with **S** and the army 1Sa 17:31
what David said was told to **S**, ... 1Sa 17:31
David said to **S**, "Don't let 1Sa 17:32
S answered, "You can't go out 1Sa 17:33
David said to **S**, "I, your 1Sa 17:34
S said to David, "Go, and may 1Sa 17:37
S put his own clothes on David. 1Sa 17:38
all the armor **S** had put on him. 1Sa 17:39
He said to **S**, "I can't go in 1Sa 17:39
When **S** saw David go out to meet 1Sa 17:55
to meet Goliath, **S** asked Abner, ... 1Sa 17:55
Goliath, Abner brought him to **S**. 1Sa 17:57
S asked him, "Young man, who is 1Sa 17:58
David finished talking with **S**, ... 1Sa 18:1

S kept David with him from that 1Sa 18:2
S sent David to fight in 1Sa 18:5
Then **S** put David over the 1Sa 18:5
towns of Israel to meet King **S**. 1Sa 18:6
S has killed thousands of his 1Sa 18:7
song upset **S**, and he became 1Sa 18:8
So **S** watched David closely from 1Sa 18:9
spirit from God rushed upon **S**, ... 1Sa 18:10
but **S** had a spear in his hand. 1Sa 18:10
was with David but had left **S**. 1Sa 18:12
So **S** was afraid of David. 1Sa 18:12
When **S** saw that David was very 1Sa 18:15
S said to David, "Here is my 1Sa 18:17
S thought, "I won't have to 1Sa 18:17
David answered **S**, saying, "Who 1Sa 18:18
S gave her instead to Adriel of 1Sa 18:19
they told **S**, he was pleased. 1Sa 18:20
So **S** said to David a second 1Sa 18:21
And **S** ordered his servants to 1Sa 18:22
S said, "Tell David, 'The king 1Sa 18:25
S planned to let the.............................. 1Sa 18:25
foreskins to **S** so he could be 1Sa 18:27
Then **S** gave him his daughter 1Sa 18:27
S saw that the LORD was with 1Sa 18:28
S told his son Jonathan and all 1Sa 19:1
My father **S** is looking for a 1Sa 19:2
Jonathan talked to **S** his father, ... 1Sa 19:4
S listened to Jonathan and then 1Sa 19:6
brought David to **S**, and David 1Sa 19:7
and David was with **S** as before. 1Sa 19:7
LORD rushed upon **S** as he was 1Sa 19:9
S tried to pin David to the wall 1Sa 19:10
S sent messengers to David's 1Sa 19:11
S sent messengers to take David 1Sa 19:14
S sent them back to see David, ... 1Sa 19:15
S said to Michal, "Why did you 1Sa 19:17
Michal answered **S**, "David told 1Sa 19:17
After David had escaped from **S**, ... 1Sa 19:18
everything **S** had done to him. 1Sa 19:18
S heard that David was in Naioth 1Sa 19:19
When **S** heard the news, he sent............. 1Sa 19:21
S himself went to Ramah, ... 1Sa 19:22
When **S** went to Naioth at Ramah, ... 1Sa 19:23
"Is even **S** one of the prophets?" 1Sa 19:24
Abner sat next to **S**, but David's.............. 1Sa 20:25
That day **S** said nothing........................ 1Sa 20:26
So **S** said to Jonathan, "Why 1Sa 20:27
Then **S** became very angry with 1Sa 20:30
Then **S** threw his spear at 1Sa 20:33
ran away from **S** and went to 1Sa 21:10
'**S** has killed thousands of his 1Sa 21:11
S heard that David and his men 1Sa 22:6
S was sitting under the tamarisk 1Sa 22:6
S said to them, "Listen, men of 1Sa 22:7
said to Ahimelech, "Listen now, ... 1Sa 22:12
S said, "Why are you and Jesse's 1Sa 22:13
He told David that **S** had killed 1Sa 22:21
I knew he would surely tell **S**. 1Sa 22:22
Someone told **S** that David was 1Sa 23:7
S said, "God has handed David 1Sa 23:7
S called all his army together................ 1Sa 23:8
David learned **S** was making evil 1Sa 23:9
have heard that **S** plans to come.............. 1Sa 23:10
of Keilah hand me over to **S**? 1Sa 23:11
Will **S** come down to Keilah, ... 1Sa 23:11
answered, "**S** will come down. 1Sa 23:11
hand me and my men over to **S**?" 1Sa 23:12
When **S** found out that David had 1Sa 23:13
Every day **S** looked for David, ... 1Sa 23:14
he learned that **S** was coming to 1Sa 23:15
Even my father **S** knows this." 1Sa 23:17
from Ziph went to **S** at Gibeah 1Sa 23:19
S answered, "The LORD bless you........... 1Sa 23:21

S

In Jerusalem S was still .... Ac 9:1
Then if S found any followers of .... Ac 9:2
So S headed toward Damascus. .... Ac 9:3
S fell to the ground and heard a .... Ac 9:4
a voice saying to him, "S, Saul! .... Ac 9:4
a voice saying to him, "Saul, S! .... Ac 9:4
S said, "Who are you, Lord?" .... Ac 9:5
traveling with S stood there but .... Ac 9:7
S got up from the ground and.................. Ac 9:8
those with S took his hand and .... Ac 9:8
For three days S could not see .... Ac 9:9
for a man named S from the city .... Ac 9:11
S has seen a vision in which a .... Ac 9:12
I have chosen S for an important .... Ac 9:15
He laid his hands on S and said, ... Ac 9:17
said, "Brother S, the Lord Jesus .... Ac 9:17
Then S got up and was baptized. .... Ac 9:18
S stayed with the followers of................ Ac 9:19
But S grew more powerful...................... Ac 9:22
days, they made plans to kill S. .... Ac 9:23
but S learned about their plan. .... Ac 9:24
followers of S helped him leave .... Ac 9:25
When S went to Jerusalem, he .... Ac 9:26
accepted S and took him to .... Ac 9:27
to them that S had seen the Lord .... Ac 9:27
and the Lord had spoken to S. .... Ac 9:27
them how boldly S had preached .... Ac 9:27
And so S stayed with the .... Ac 9:28
they took S to Caesarea and from .... Ac 9:30
city of Tarsus to look for S,.................. Ac 11:25
when he found S, he brought him .... Ac 11:26
a whole year S and Barnabas met .... Ac 11:26
and gave it to Barnabas and S, ... Ac 11:30
Barnabas and S finished their .... Ac 12:25
with Herod, the ruler), and S.................. Ac 13:1
Barnabas and S to do a special .... Ac 13:2
on Barnabas and S and sent them .... Ac 13:3
Barnabas and S, sent out by the.............. Ac 13:4
Barnabas and S to come to him,............. Ac 13:7
But S, who was also called Paul, ... Ac 13:9
so God gave them S son of Kish. .... Ac 13:21
S was from the tribe of Benjamin .... Ac 13:21
voice saying, 'S, Saul, why are .... Ac 22:7
saying, 'Saul, S, why are you .... Ac 22:7
said, 'Brother S, see again!' .... Ac 22:13
saying, 'S, Saul, why are you .... Ac 26:14
saying, 'Saul, S, why are you .... Ac 26:14

SAUL'S

Now the donkeys of S father, ... 1Sa 9:3
oil and poured it on S head. 1Sa 10:1
Samuel, God changed S heart. 1Sa 10:9
S uncle asked him and his 1Sa 10:14
S uncle asked, "Please tell me. 1Sa 10:15
One day Jonathan, S son, said to 1Sa 14:1
S guards were at Gibeah in the 1Sa 14:16
S sons were Jonathan, Ishvi, and 1Sa 14:49
S wife was Ahinoam daughter of 1Sa 14:50
was Abner son of Ner, S uncle. 1Sa 14:50
S father Kish and Abner's father 1Sa 14:51
S life he fought hard against 1Sa 14:52
S servants said to him, "See, an 1Sa 16:15
and you are S servants! 1Sa 17:8
In S time Jesse was an old man........... 1Sa 17:12
David put on S sword and tried 1Sa 17:39
which pleased S officers and all 1Sa 18:5
time came for S daughter Merab 1Sa 18:19
Now S other daughter, Michal, ... 1Sa 18:20
S servants said these words to 1Sa 18:23
When S servants told him what 1Sa 18:24
When S servants told this to 1Sa 18:26
more skillful than S officers. 1Sa 18:30
So S spear went into the wall, ... 1Sa 19:10

the Spirit of God entered S men, ... 1Sa 19:20
One of S servants happened to be 1Sa 21:7
the chief of S shepherds....................... 1Sa 21:7
standing there with S officers, ... 1Sa 22:9
But S son Jonathan went to David 1Sa 23:16
cut off a corner of S robe. 1Sa 24:4
had cut off a corner of S robe. 1Sa 24:5
S daughter Michal was also 1Sa 25:44
the commander of S army, were.............. 1Sa 26:5
go down into S camp with me?".............. 1Sa 26:6
and Abishai went into S camp. 1Sa 26:7
water jug that are near S head. 1Sa 26:11
water jug that were near S head, ... 1Sa 26:12
of the mountain far from S camp. 1Sa 26:13
But S officer refused, because 1Sa 31:4
They cut off S head and took off 1Sa 31:9
They put S armor in the temple 1Sa 31:10
a young man from S camp came to 2Sa 1:2
S shield will no longer be 2Sa 1:21
S sword did not fail to wound.............. 2Sa 1:22
Ner was the commander of S army. 2Sa 2:8
Abner took S son Ish-Bosheth to 2Sa 2:8
S son Ish-Bosheth was forty 2Sa 2:10
who supported S family and those 2Sa 3:1
supporters of S family became 2Sa 3:1
the supporters of S family and 2Sa 3:6
you bring S daughter Michal 2Sa 3:13
messengers to S son Ish-Bosheth, ... 2Sa 3:14
were captains in S army came to 2Sa 4:2
S son Jonathan had a son named 2Sa 4:4
S daughter Michal looked out the 2Sa 6:16
but S daughter Michal came out............. 2Sa 6:20
father or anyone from S family. 2Sa 6:21
And S daughter Michal had no 2Sa 6:23
anyone still left in S family? 2Sa 9:1
named Ziba from S family.................... 2Sa 9:2
Is anyone left in S family? 2Sa 9:3
David called S servant Ziba. 2Sa 9:9
He was from S family group, ... 2Sa 16:5
the people in S family you 2Sa 16:8
took S place as king, but now.............. 2Sa 16:8
the servant from S family, ... 2Sa 19:17
Mephibosheth, S grandson, also.............. 2Sa 19:24
five sons of S daughter Merab. 2Sa 21:8
Rizpah, S slave woman, was 2Sa 21:11
the bodies of S seven sons who 2Sa 21:13
in the tomb of S father Kish. 2Sa 21:14
Kish was S father. Saul was 1Ch 9:39
But S officer refused, because 1Ch 10:4
stripped S body and took his 1Ch 10:9
Philistines put S armor in the.............. 1Ch 10:10
They were S relatives from the 1Ch 12:2
Benjamin, who were S relatives.............. 1Ch 12:29
loyal to S family until then 1Ch 12:29
S daughter Michal watched from a........... 1Ch 15:29
fish scales fell from S eyes,.................... Ac 9:18

SAVAGE

Some s animal has eaten him. .... Ge 37:33

SAVE

Surely you will s the city for .... Ge 18:24
I will s the whole city because .... Ge 18:26
s me from my brother Esau. .... Ge 32:11
Reuben planned to s Joseph later .... Ge 37:22
and he begged us to s him, ... Ge 42:21
of you to s people's lives. .... Ge 45:5
into good to s the lives of many .... Ge 50:20
I have come down to s them from .... Ex 3:8
have done nothing to s them." .... Ex 5:23
I will s you from the hard work .... Ex 6:6
will see the LORD s you today. .... Ex 14:13
S the rest of the food until .... Ex 16:23
'S two quarts of this food for .... Ex 16:32

and s it for your descendants." .... Ex 16:33
You must not s any of the fat .... Ex 23:18
of you and will s you from your .... Nu 10:9
he tried to s my honor among................ Nu 25:11
But s for yourselves the girls .... Nu 31:18
Be sure to s one-tenth of all .... Dt 14:22
S all the first male animals..................... Dt 15:19
cities in order to s his life. .... Dt 19:4
of these cities to s his life. .... Dt 19:5
your enemies and to s you." .... Dt 20:4
but no one was there to s her.................. Dt 22:27
wife comes to s her husband .... Dt 25:11
day, and no one will s you. .... Dt 28:29
enemies, and no one will s you. .... Dt 28:31
to live. S us from death.".......................... Jos 2:13
and help us! S us! All the .... Jos 10:6
sent judges to s them from their............. Jdg 2:18
the LORD sent someone to s them............ Jdg 3:9
he sent someone to s them..................... Jdg 3:15
with your strength and s Israel .... Jdg 6:14
Lord, how can I s Israel?......................... Jdg 6:15
said you would help me s Israel............... Jdg 6:36
you will use me to s Israel, ... Jdg 6:37
will s you and hand Midian over .... Jdg 7:7
his life to s you from the power .... Jdg 9:17
another judge came to s Israel. .... Jdg 10:1
So I refuse to s you again. .... Jdg 10:13
Let them s you when you are in .... Jdg 10:14
want, but please s us today!" .... Jdg 10:15
He will begin to s Israel from .... Jdg 13:5
was no one to s the people of .... Jdg 18:28
God will s us from our enemies. 1Sa 4:3
Who can s us from these powerful 1Sa 4:8
Then he will s you from the 1Sa 7:3
to s us from the Philistines! 1Sa 7:8
He will s my people from the 1Sa 9:16
said, "How can this man s us?" 1Sa 10:27
But now s us from our enemies, ... 1Sa 12:10
They can't help you or s you. 1Sa 12:21
attack it and s the sheep from 1Sa 17:35
and a bear will s me from this 1Sa 17:37
swords or spears to s people. 1Sa 17:47
Attack them, and s Keilah." 1Sa 23:2
am right. May he s me from you!" 1Sa 24:15
my life and s me from all 1Sa 26:24
I will s my people Israel from 2Sa 3:18
Perhaps he will s me from those............. 2Sa 14:16
You s the humble, but you bring.............. 2Sa 22:28
but no one came to s them...................... 2Sa 22:42
advise you to s yourself and 1Ki 1:12
He gave Israel a man to s them, ... 2Ki 13:5
Come and s me from the king 2Ki 16:7
s you from all your enemies. 2Ki 17:39
he can't s you from my power. 2Ki 18:29
'The LORD will surely s us. 2Ki 18:30
he says, 'The LORD will s us.'.................. 2Ki 18:32
did not s Samaria from my power. 2Ki 18:34
can the LORD s Jerusalem from my 2Ki 18:35
the gods of those people s them? 2Ki 19:12
s us from the king's power so 2Ki 19:19
will defend and s this city for 2Ki 19:34
I will s you and this city from 2Ki 20:6
Say to him, "S us, God our 1Ch 16:35
us back and s us from other 1Ch 16:35
them but will s them soon. 2Ch 12:7
Then you will hear and s us.' 2Ch 20:9
and you will see the LORD s you. 2Ch 20:17
not even s their own people 2Ch 25:15
our God will s us from the king 2Ch 32:11
nations could not s their people 2Ch 32:13
their gods could s them from me. 2Ch 32:14
your god cannot s you from my 2Ch 32:14
has been able to s his people 2Ch 32:15

less able to s you from me." 2Ch 32:15
nations could not s their people 2Ch 32:17
won't be able to s his people 2Ch 32:17
will help and s the Jewish .... Est 4:14
beg Queen Esther to s his life. .... Est 7:7
all he has to s his own life. .... Job 2:4
He will s you from six troubles; .... Job 5:19
in battle he will s you from the .... Job 5:20
S me from the enemy's power. .... Job 6:23
but no one can s me from your .... Job 10:7
God does this to s people from .... Job 33:18
and say: 'S him from death. .... Job 33:24
which I s for times of trouble,................ Job 38:23
are strong enough to s yourself. .... Job 40:14
up! My God, come s me! You have .... Ps 3:7
The LORD can s his people. .... Ps 3:8
LORD, return and s me; save me .... Ps 6:4
s me because of your kindness. .... Ps 6:4
S me and rescue me from those .... Ps 7:1
to pieces, and no one can s me. .... Ps 7:2
S me, LORD, because the good .... Ps 12:1
your power s you those who trust .... Ps 17:7
S me from the wicked with your .... Ps 17:13
s me by your power from those .... Ps 17:14
You s the humble, but you bring.............. Ps 18:27
but no one came to s them...................... Ps 18:41
LORD, s the king! Answer us when .... Ps 20:9
he is so happy when you s him! .... Ps 21:1
Maybe he will s you. If he likes .... Ps 22:8
S me from the sword; save my .... Ps 22:20
s my life from the dogs. .... Ps 22:20
s me from the horns of the bulls. .... Ps 22:21
me and s me. I trust you, ... Ps 25:20
s Israel from all their troubles! .... Ps 25:22
so s me and have mercy on me. .... Ps 26:11
S your people and bless those .... Ps 28:9
S me because you do what is .... Ps 31:1
Listen to me and s me quickly. .... Ps 31:2
a strong city to s me. .... Ps 31:2
S me, LORD, God of truth. .... Ps 31:5
S me from my enemies and from .... Ps 31:15
S me because of your love. .... Ps 31:16
they can't s by their strength. .... Ps 33:17
Tell me, "I will s you.".......................... Ps 35:3
You s the weak from the strong,.............. Ps 35:10
S my life from their attacks; .... Ps 35:17
s me from these people who are .... Ps 35:17
S me from all my sins. Don't let .... Ps 39:8
Please, LORD, s me. Hurry, LORD,........... Ps 40:13
comes, the LORD will s them................... Ps 41:1
S me from liars and those who do .... Ps 43:1
me, and my sword can't s me................... Ps 44:6
Because of your love, s us. .... Ps 44:26
But God will s my life and will .... Ps 49:15
I will s you, and you will honor .... Ps 50:15
apart, and no one will s you. .... Ps 50:22
will s those who do that." .... Ps 50:23
s me from the guilt of murder, ... Ps 51:14
s me because of who you are................... Ps 54:1
help, and the LORD will s me. .... Ps 55:16
God, s me from my enemies. .... Ps 59:1
S me from those who do evil and .... Ps 59:2
Answer us and s us by your power......... Ps 60:5
rest in God; only he can s me. .... Ps 62:1
will learn that you can s................... Ps 67:2
God, s me, because the water has .... Ps 69:1
You are truly able to s. .... Ps 69:13
S me from those who hate me and .... Ps 69:14
Come near and s me; rescue me.............. Ps 69:18
God, s me and protect me. .... Ps 69:29
God will s Jerusalem and rebuild .... Ps 69:35
God, come quickly and s me. .... Ps 70:1
You help me and s me. LORD, do .... Ps 70:5

S

what is right, **s** and rescue me; .... Ps 71:2
me; listen to me and **s** me. .... Ps 71:2
the command to **s** me, because you .... Ps 71:3
s me from the power of the..................... Ps 71:4
because no one will **s** him." .... Ps 71:11
to the poor and **s** the needy and .... Ps 72:4
out and will **s** the needy when .... Ps 72:12
and he will **s** their lives. .... Ps 72:13
He will **s** them from cruel people .... Ps 72:14
to judge and to **s** the needy..................... Ps 76:9
had not trusted him to **s** them. .... Ps 78:22
S us and forgive our sins so .... Ps 79:9
great power to **s** those sentenced .... Ps 79:11
your strength, and come to **s** us............... Ps 80:2
S the weak and helpless;...................... Ps 82:4
show us your love, and **s** us. .... Ps 85:7
will soon **s** those who respect .... Ps 85:9
My God, **s** me, your servant who .... Ps 86:2
S me, the son of your female .... Ps 86:16
God will **s** you from hidden traps .... Ps 91:3
Whoever loves me, I will **s**..................... Ps 91:14
and they will see how I can **s**." .... Ps 91:16
has made known his power to **s**; .... Ps 98:2
have seen God's power to **s**. .... Ps 98:3
help me when you **s** them. .... Ps 106:4
s us and bring us back from .... Ps 106:47
Answer us and **s** us by your power........... Ps 108:6
Because your love is good, **s** me. .... Ps 109:21
because you are loving, **s** me. .... Ps 109:26
I said, "Please, LORD, **s** me!" .... Ps 116:4
LORD, **s** us; please, LORD, ... Ps 118:25
and **s** me as you have promised................ Ps 119:41
from waiting for you to **s** me, ... Ps 119:81
I am yours. **S** me. I want to obey .... Ps 119:94
S me from harmful people so I .... Ps 119:134
S me so I can obey your rules. .... Ps 119:146
Argue my case and **s** me. .... Ps 119:154
I am waiting for you to **s** me, ... Ps 119:166
to my prayer; **s** me as you .... Ps 119:170
I want you to **s** me, LORD. .... Ps 119:174
s me from liars and from those .... Ps 120:2
he is loving and able to **s**. .... Ps 130:7
He will **s** Israel from all their .... Ps 130:8
reach down and **s** me by your................. Ps 138:7
S me from those who are chasing .... Ps 142:6
LORD, **s** me from my enemies; .... Ps 143:9
In your goodness **s** me from my .... Ps 143:11
S me and rescue me out of this .... Ps 144:7
You **s** your servant David from .... Ps 144:10
S me, rescue me from those .... Ps 144:11
other people, who cannot **s** you............... Ps 146:3
will **s** you from the unfaithful .... Pr 2:16
living will **s** you from death. .... Pr 10:2
living will **s** you from death. .... Pr 11:4
lots of good advice will **s** it. .... Pr 11:14
of good people will **s** them..................... Pr 12:6
that can **s** people from death .... Pr 13:14
that can **s** people from death .... Pr 14:27
you will **s** them from death. .... Pr 23:14
S those who are being led to .... Pr 24:11
because it can **s** whoever has it. .... Ec 7:12
used his wisdom to **s** his town. .... Ec 9:15
trusting in people to **s** you, ... Is 2:22
no one will try to **s** his brother .... Is 9:19
someone to **s** and defend them .... Is 19:20
so they would **s** us from the king .... Is 20:6
two walls to **s** water from the .... Is 22:11
him, and he has come to **s** us................. Is 25:9
They think horses will **s** them. .... Is 31:1
and strong horsemen will **s** them. .... Is 31:1
He will defend and **s** it; .... Is 31:5
pass over' and **s** Jerusalem." .... Is 31:5
S us when we are in trouble. .... Is 33:2

LORD is our king. He will **s** us. .... Is 33:22
they did, but he will **s** you." .... Is 35:4
you, because he can't **s** you. .... Is 36:14
'The LORD will surely **s** us. .... Is 36:15
saying, 'The LORD will **s** us.' .... Is 36:18
did not **s** Samaria from my power. .... Is 36:19
can the LORD **s** Jerusalem from my .... Is 36:20
the gods of those people **s** them? .... Is 37:12
s us from the king's power so .... Is 37:20
will defend and **s** this city for .... Is 37:35
I will **s** you and this city from................ Is 38:6
and there is no one to **s** them................ Is 42:22
other nations to **s** your life..................... Is 43:4
No one can **s** people from my .... Is 43:13
says, "You are my god. **S** me!" .... Is 44:17
He cannot **s** himself or say,................... Is 44:20
pray to a god who cannot **s** them. .... Is 45:20
cannot **s** themselves but will .... Is 46:2
I will carry you and **s** you. .... Is 46:4
It cannot **s** them from their..................... Is 46:7
I will **s** Jerusalem and bring .... Is 46:13
them **s** you from what is about .... Is 47:13
They cannot **s** themselves from .... Is 47:14
will be no one left to **s** you." .... Is 47:15
and I will **s** your children. .... Is 49:25
think I am not able to **s** you? .... Is 50:2
I not have the power to **s** you? .... Is 50:2
I will soon **s** you. I will use my .... Is 51:5
LORD's power is enough to **s** you. .... Is 59:1
his own power to **s** the people; .... Is 59:16
I have the power to **s** you." .... Is 63:1
the time has come for me to **s**. .... Is 63:4
my own power to **s** my people; .... Is 63:5
He sent his own angel to **s** them. .... Is 63:9
they say, 'Come and **s** us!' .... Je 2:27
them come and **s** you when you are .... Je 2:28
who is not able to **s** anyone? .... Je 14:9
I will rescue you and **s** you," .... Je 15:20
I will **s** you from these wicked .... Je 15:21
S me, and I will truly be saved. .... Je 17:14
the city will **s** his life as if .... Je 21:9
S the person who has been robbed............ Je 21:12
S the one who has been robbed .... Je 22:3
I will soon **s** you from that .... Je 30:10
I will **s** your family from that .... Je 30:10
I am with you and will **s** you," .... Je 30:11
'LORD, **s** your people, those who .... Je 31:7
But I will **s** you on that day, ... Je 39:17
will surely **s** you, Ebed-Melech. .... Je 39:18
I will **s** you and rescue you from .... Je 42:11
I will surely **s** you from those .... Je 46:27
his treasures will **s** him. .... Je 49:4
Do not **s** any of them, because .... Je 50:14
from Babylon and **s** your lives! .... Je 51:6
wait quietly for the LORD to **s**. .... La 3:26
our towers for a nation to **s** us. .... La 4:17
and no one can **s** us from them. .... La 5:8
they will not **s** their lives. .... Eze 7:13
gold will not **s** them from the .... Eze 7:19
But I will **s** a few of them from .... Eze 12:16
but try to **s** your own lives. .... Eze 13:18
off your veils and **s** my people .... Eze 13:21
and I will **s** my people from your .... Eze 13:23
could **s** only themselves, ... Eze 14:14
they could not **s** their own sons .... Eze 14:16
They could **s** only themselves, ... Eze 14:16
they could not **s** their sons or .... Eze 14:18
They could **s** only themselves. .... Eze 14:18
they could not **s** their son or .... Eze 14:20
They could **s** only themselves............... Eze 14:20
right, they will **s** their lives. .... Eze 18:27
right will not **s** them when they .... Eze 33:12
will **s** them from all the places .... Eze 34:12

So I will s my flock; they will .... Eze 34:22
captivity and s them from the................. Eze 34:27
So I will s you from all your .... Eze 36:29
I will s them from all the ways .... Eze 37:23
will be able to s you from my .... Da 3:15
serve is able to s us from the .... Da 3:17
He will s us from your power,................. Da 3:17
But even if God does not s us, ... Da 3:18
other god can s his people like .... Da 3:29
He wanted to s Daniel, and he .... Da 6:14
to think of a way to s him. .... Da 6:14
you serve all the time s you!" .... Da 6:16
able to s you from the lions? .... Da 6:20
and none could s another animal .... Da 8:4
No one was able to s the sheep .... Da 8:7
I will s them, but not by using .... Hos 1:7
Lᴏʀᴅ their God, will s them." .... Hos 1:7
and no one will s her from me. .... Hos 2:10
no one will be able to s them................. Hos 5:14
I want to s them, but they have .... Hos 7:13
Can he s you in any of your .... Hos 13:10
Will I s them from the place of .... Hos 13:14
Assyria cannot s us, nor will we............. Hos 14:3
not be able to s themselves. .... Am 2:14
A shepherd might s from a lion's .... Am 3:12
won't be able to s yourselves.................. Mic 2:3
pieces, and no one can s them. .... Mic 5:8
store up, but s nothing, and .... Mic 6:14
I will wait for God to s me; .... Mic 7:7
violence, but you do not s us! .... Hab 1:2
You came out to s your people, ... Hab 3:13
people, to s your chosen one .... Hab 3:13
silver nor gold will s them. .... Zph 1:18
the mighty One will s you. .... Zph 3:17
I will s my people who cannot .... Zph 3:19
I will s my people from .... Zch 8:7
But I will s you, and you will .... Zch 8:13
their God will s them as if his................. Zch 9:16
people of Judah and s the people .... Zch 10:6
will s them, and they will grow .... Zch 10:8
I will not s anyone from them. .... Zch 11:6
The Lᴏʀᴅ will s the homes of .... Zch 12:7
because he will s his people .... Mt 1:21
but s us from the Evil One. .... Mt 6:13
woke him, saying, "Lord, s us! .... Mt 8:25
He shouted, "Lord, s me!" .... Mt 14:30
God s you from those things, ... Mt 16:22
who want to s their lives will .... Mt 16:25
of Man came to s lost people. .... Mt 18:11
three days. So s yourself! Come .... Mt 27:40
others, but he can't s himself!................. Mt 27:42
God, so let God s him now, if .... Mt 27:43
if Elijah will come to s him." .... Mt 27:49
him and s you from trouble." .... Mt 28:14
to do evil, to s a life or to .... Mk 3:4
who want to s their lives will .... Mk 8:35
So s yourself! Come down from .... Mk 15:30
people, but he can't s himself. .... Mk 15:31
promised he would s us from our .... Lk 1:71
he would s us from the power................. Lk 1:74
to s a life or to destroy it?" .... Lk 6:9
who want to s their lives will .... Lk 9:24
souls of people but to s them." .... Lk 9:56
give up their lives will s them. .... Lk 17:33
to find lost people and s them." .... Lk 19:10
time when God came to s you." .... Lk 19:44
faith you will s your lives. .... Lk 21:19
Let him s himself if he is God's .... Lk 23:35
king of the Jews, s yourself!" .... Lk 23:37
Then s yourself and us." .... Lk 23:39
but to s the world through him. .... Jn 3:17
the one you hoped would s you. .... Jn 5:45
for her to s this perfume for .... Jn 12:7

'Father, s me from this time' .... Jn 12:27
the world, but to s the world. .... Jn 12:47
S yourselves from the evil of .... Ac 2:40
the only One who can s people. .... Ac 4:12
in the world is able to s us." .... Ac 4:12
God was asking him to s them,................. Ac 7:25
and have come down to s them. .... Ac 7:34
trusting in him to s you.' .... Ac 22:16
you that he will s the lives of .... Ac 27:24
power God uses to s everyone who .... Rm 1:16
believes—to s the Jews first, ... Rm 1:16
first, and then to s non-Jews. .... Rm 1:16
people will die to s the life of .... Rm 5:7
he will s us through his Son's................. Rm 5:10
will s me from this body that .... Rm 7:24
their own lives to s my life................. Rm 16:4
foolish to s those who believe................. 1Co 1:21
maybe you will s your husband. 1Co 7:16
maybe you will s your wife. 1Co 7:16
people so I could s some of them 1Co 9:22
S it up so you will not have to 1Co 16:2
and he will continue to s us. 2Co 1:10
in him, and he will s us again. 2Co 1:10
not have to s up to give to 2Co 12:14
Parents should s to give to 2Co 12:14
me and gave himself to s me. .... Gal 2:20
You did not s yourselves; .... Eph 2:8
into the world to s sinners, ... 1Ti 1:15
you will s both yourself and 1Ti 4:16
The Lord will s me when anyone 2Ti 4:18
that can s everyone has come. .... Tit 2:11
One who could s him from death, ... Heb 5:7
able always to s those who come .... Heb 7:25
a large boat to s his family................. Heb 11:7
in your hearts, which can s you................. Jam 1:21
Can faith like that s them? .... Jam 2:14
only One who can s and destroy. .... Jam 4:12
wrong way will s that sinner's .... Jam 5:20
knows how to s those who serve 2Pe 2:9
out of the fire, and s them. .... Jud 1:23

SAVED

kind to me and have s my life. .... Ge 19:19
So God s Lot's life, but he .... Ge 19:29
to God, and his son was s. .... Ge 22:13
Haven't you s a blessing for me? .... Ge 27:36
camp can run away and be s." .... Ge 32:8
to face, but my life was s." .... Ge 32:30
heard their plan and s Joseph, ... Ge 37:21
food should be s to use during .... Ge 41:36
said, "You have s our lives. .... Ge 47:25
the Angel who s me from all my................. Ge 48:16
Egyptians, he s our homes.'" .... Ex 12:27
day the Lᴏʀᴅ s the Israelites .... Ex 14:30
me sing; he has s me. He is my .... Ex 15:2
and lead the people you have s. .... Ex 15:13
the people s it until the next .... Ex 16:24
He s me from the king of Egypt." .... Ex 18:4
way and how the Lᴏʀᴅ had s them. .... Ex 18:8
for Israel when he had s them .... Ex 18:9
He has s you from the Egyptians .... Ex 18:10
and he has s the people from the .... Ex 18:10
has s the Israelites from my .... Nu 25:11
life could be s by running to .... Dt 4:42
out of Egypt and s you from the .... Dt 13:5
and the Lᴏʀᴅ your God s you. .... Dt 15:15
people Israel, whom you have s................. Dt 21:8
Lᴏʀᴅ your God s you from there. .... Dt 24:18
rejected the Rock who s them. .... Dt 32:15
you are a people s by the Lᴏʀᴅ. .... Dt 33:29
the Lᴏʀᴅ and must be s for him." .... Jos 6:19
These were s for the Lᴏʀᴅ. .... Jos 6:24
Joshua s Rahab the prostitute, ... Jos 6:25

S

So Joshua s their lives by not .... Jos 9:26
I s you and brought you out of .... Jos 24:10
who s the Israelites from the .... Jdg 2:16
brother, s the Israelites. .... Jdg 3:9
Shamgar son of Anath s Israel. .... Jdg 3:31
I s you from the Egyptians and .... Jdg 6:9
to brag that they s themselves. .... Jdg 7:2
You s us from the Midianites. .... Jdg 8:22
who had s them from all their .... Jdg 8:34
cried out to me, and I s you. .... Jdg 10:12
This is the meat s for you. 1Sa 9:24
I s you from Egypt's control and 1Sa 10:18
up tomorrow, you will be s.'" 1Sa 11:9
Today the LORD has s Israel!" 1Sa 11:13
s you from your enemies around 1Sa 12:11
the LORD s the Israelites that................. 1Sa 14:23
the LORD lives who has s Israel, ... 1Sa 14:39
So the army s Jonathan, and he 1Sa 14:45
He s the Israelites from their 1Sa 14:48
They s the best sheep and cattle 1Sa 15:15
LORD who s me from a lion and 1Sa 17:37
Philistines and s the people of 1Sa 23:5
he has s me from all trouble! 2Sa 4:9
of Israel and s you from Saul................. 2Sa 12:7
him the LORD has s him from his 2Sa 18:19
They s your life and the lives 2Sa 19:5
The king s us from the 2Sa 19:9
Philistine and s David's life. 2Sa 21:17
when the LORD s him from Saul 2Sa 22:1
and I will be s from my enemies. 2Sa 22:4
s me from my powerful enemies, ... 2Sa 22:18
he delights in me, he s me. 2Sa 22:20
You s me when my people attacked 2Sa 22:44
You s me from violent people. 2Sa 22:49
The LORD has s me from all 1Ki 1:29
so he s the Israelites through 2Ki 14:27
of any other nation s his people 2Ki 18:33
countries has s his people from 2Ki 18:35
so do not think you will be s. 2Ki 19:11
So the LORD s Hezekiah and the 2Ch 32:22
whom you have s with your great .... Ne 1:10
them saviors who s them from the .... Ne 9:27
you s them again and again. .... Ne 9:28
the warning that s the king." .... Est 7:9
all the years s up for them...................... Job 15:20
' then the humble will be s...................... Job 22:29
escape and be s because your................. Job 22:30
and I would be s forever by my .... Job 23:7
because I s the poor who called .... Job 29:12
I will rejoice because you s me. .... Ps 9:14
heart is happy because you s me. .... Ps 13:5
the LORD had s him from Saul .... Ps 17:15
and I will be s from my enemies. .... Ps 18:3
s me from my powerful enemies, ... Ps 18:17
he delights in me, he s me. .... Ps 18:19
s me when the people attacked .... Ps 18:43
You s me from violent people. .... Ps 18:48
they trusted, and you s them. .... Ps 22:4
No king is s by his great army. .... Ps 33:16
He s me from all that I feared. .... Ps 34:4
heard him and s him from all his .... Ps 34:6
You s us from our foes, and you .... Ps 44:7
You have s me from all my .... Ps 54:7
you have s me from death. .... Ps 56:13
praises to you. You have s me. .... Ps 71:23
You s us, and we are your very .... Ps 74:2
power you have s your people, ... Ps 77:15
that God Most High had s them............. Ps 78:35
or the time he s them from the .... Ps 78:42
us your kindness so we can be s. .... Ps 80:3
us your kindness so we can be s. .... Ps 80:7
us your kindness so we can be s. .... Ps 80:19
you called, and I s you. .... Ps 81:7

You have s me from death. .... Ps 86:13
But the LORD s them for his own .... Ps 106:8
He s them from those who hated .... Ps 106:10
He s them from their enemies, ... Ps 106:10
They forgot the God who s them, ... Ps 106:21
LORD s his people many times, ... Ps 106:43
whom the LORD has s should say. .... Ps 107:2
He has s them from the enemy .... Ps 107:2
and he s them from their .... Ps 107:6
and he s them from their .... Ps 107:13
and he s them from their .... Ps 107:19
so they were s from dying. .... Ps 107:20
and he s them from their .... Ps 107:28
when I was helpless, he s me................. Ps 116:6
LORD, you s me from death. .... Ps 116:8
and a song. He has s me. .... Ps 118:14
for answering me. You have s me. .... Ps 118:21
Help me, and I will be s......................... Ps 119:117
people are far from being s, ... Ps 119:155
good person is s from trouble; .... Pr 11:8
s is a curse to its owners. .... Ec 5:13
pleases God will be s from them, ... Ec 7:26
I have s them for you, my lover, ... Sng 7:13
and makes me sing. He has s me." .... Is 12:2
up what they have s and carry it .... Is 15:7
profits will be s for the LORD. .... Is 23:18
hope they will be s by the king .... Is 30:2
me and trust me, you will be s............... Is 30:15
of any other nation s his people .... Is 36:18
countries has s his people from .... Is 36:20
so do not think you will be s. .... Is 37:11
The LORD s me, so we will play.............. Is 38:20
be afraid, because I have s you. .... Is 43:1
spoken to you, s you, and told .... Is 43:12
back to me because I s you." .... Is 44:22
The LORD s the people of Jacob! .... Is 44:23
his glory when s Israel. .... Is 44:23
LORD says, who s you, who formed .... Is 44:24
Israel will be s by the LORD, ... Is 45:17
everywhere, follow me and be s. .... Is 45:22
The LORD has s his servants,................. Is 48:20
over the world the way to be s." .... Is 49:6
soldiers have taken will be s. .... Is 49:25
people to cross over and be s................. Is 51:10
so you will be s without cost." .... Is 52:3
his people. He has s Jerusalem. .... Is 52:9
want to be s, but salvation is .... Is 59:11
Holy People, the S People of the............. Is 62:12
not lie to me." So he s them. .... Is 63:8
love and kindness, he s them. .... Is 63:9
the one who has always s us." .... Is 63:16
disobeyed, so how can we be s? .... Is 64:5
send some of these s people to .... Is 66:19
So the s people will tell the..................... Is 66:19
hearts so that you can be s. .... Je 4:14
ended, and we have not been s." .... Je 8:20
you have s Israel in times of .... Je 14:8
I have s you for a good reason. .... Je 15:11
Save me, and I will truly be s................. Je 17:14
In his time Judah will be s, ... Je 23:6
but they will be s from it." .... Je 30:7
At that time Judah will be s, ... Je 33:16
of Babylon, your life will be s. .... Je 38:17
you, and your life will be s..................... Je 38:20
army officers s the captives .... Je 41:16
But you will have s your life. .... Eze 3:19
And you will have s your life." .... Eze 3:21
which would have s their lives. .... Eze 13:22
and silver and have s it in your .... Eze 28:4
would have s their own lives. .... Eze 33:5
But you have s your life. .... Eze 33:9
his angel and s his servants .... Da 3:28
He is the one who s Daniel from .... Da 6:27

of Ammon will be **s** from him. ....Da 11:41
but your people will be **s**. ....Da 12:1
written in God's book will be **s**. ....Da 12:1
who calls on the LORD will be **s**, ...Joe 2:32
will be people who will be **s**, ...Joe 2:32
Israelites in Samaria will be **s**— ....Am 3:12
but you **s** me from the pit of ....Jnh 2:6
you will be **s** from that place ....Mic 4:10
faith until the end will be **s**. ....Mt 10:22
things and old things he has **s**." ....Mt 13:52
and asked, "Then who can be **s**?" ....Mt 19:25
faith until the end will be **s**. ....Mt 24:13
They said, "He **s** others, but he ....Mt 27:42
each other, "Then who can be **s**?" ....Mk 10:26
faith until the end will be **s**. ....Mk 13:13
each other, "He **s** other people, ...Mk 15:31
and is baptized will be **s**, ...Mk 16:16
they will be **s** by having their ....Lk 1:77
you are **s** from your sins. ....Lk 7:50
they cannot believe it and be **s**. ....Lk 8:12
will only a few people be **s**?" ....Lk 13:23
they asked, "Then who can be **s**?" ....Lk 18:26
of Jesus, saying, "He **s** others. ....Lk 23:35
you have **s** the best wine till ....Jn 2:10
I tell you this so you can be **s**............Jn 5:34
me will be **s** and will be able ....Jn 10:9
calls on the Lord will be **s**.' ....Ac 2:21
who were being **s** to the group ....Ac 2:47
and **s** him from all his troubles. ....Ac 7:10
and all your family will be **s**.' ....Ac 11:14
the world the way to be **s**.'" ....Ac 13:47
You cannot be **s** if you are not ....Ac 15:1
they too will be **s** by the grace ....Ac 15:11
telling you how you can be **s**." ....Ac 16:17
Men, what must I do to be **s**?" ....Ac 16:30
Lord Jesus and you will be **s**— ....Ac 16:31
you are not **s**, it will be your ....Ac 18:6
went with my soldiers and **s** him. ....Ac 23:27
I do not ask to be **s** from death. ....Ac 25:11
today would be **s** and be like me— ....Ac 26:29
we lost all hope of being **s**. ....Ac 27:20
ship, your lives cannot be **s**." ....Ac 27:31
will surely be **s** from God's ....Rm 5:9
were **s**, and we have this hope. ....Rm 8:24
only a few of them will be **s**, ...Rm 10:1
is for all the Jews to be **s**. ....Rm 10:1
from the dead, you will be **s**. ....Rm 10:9
we believe, and so we are **s**. ....Rm 10:10
calls on the Lord will be **s**." ....Rm 10:13
way, help some of them to be **s**. ....Rm 11:14
is how all Israel will be **s**. ....Rm 11:26
Pray that I will be **s** from the ....Rm 15:31
who are being **s** it is the power 1Co 1:18
builder will be **s**, but it will 1Co 3:15
his spirit will be **s** on the day 1Co 5:5
most people so they can be **s**. 1Co 10:33
And you are being **s** by it if you 1Co 15:2
s us from these great dangers. 2Co 1:10
who are being **s** and among those 2Co 2:15
but to those who are being **s**, ...2Co 2:15
You have been **s** by God's grace. ....Eph 2:5
you have been **s** by grace through ....Eph 2:8
but that you will be **s** by God. ....Php 1:28
are not Jews so they may be **s**. 1Th 2:16
the truth, they would be **s**. 2Th 2:10
you from the beginning to be **s**. 2Th 2:13
You are **s** by the Spirit that 2Th 2:13
call you to be **s** so you can 2Th 2:14
all people to be **s** and to know 1Ti 2:4
But she will be **s** through having 1Ti 2:15
s us and made us his holy people. 2Ti 1:9
but the Lord **s** me from all those 2Ti 3:11
I was **s** from the lion's mouth. 2Ti 4:17

insist on circumcision to be **s**..............Tit 1:10
he **s** us because of his mercy. ....Tit 3:5
He **s** us through the washing that ....Tit 3:5
the way to be **s** did not enter, ...Heb 4:6
people who have faith and are **s**. ....Heb 10:39
fires and were **s** from being ....Heb 11:34
You **s** your treasure for the last ....Jam 5:3
But you were **s** from that useless 1Pe 1:18
eight in all—were **s** by water. 1Pe 3:20
hard for a good person to be **s**, ...1Pe 4:18
But God **s** Noah, who preached 2Pe 2:5
But he **s** Lot from those cities. 2Pe 2:7
that we are **s** because our Lord 2Pe 3:15
that the Lord **s** his people by ....Jud 1:5

SAVES
he **s** those whose hearts are ....Ps 7:10
he **s** those whose spirits have ....Ps 34:18

SAVING
You seem far from **s** me, far away ....Ps 22:1
They love you for **s** them. ....Ps 40:16
I thank God for **s** me through ....Rm 7:25
they will be **s** a treasure for 1Ti 6:19

SAVIOR
is my rock, my fortress, my **S**. 2Sa 22:2
Save us, God our **S**, and bring us 1Ch 16:35
is my rock, my protection, my **S**. ....Ps 18:2
and teach me, my God, my **S**...............Ps 25:5
or leave me alone, God, my **S**. ....Ps 27:9
come and help me, my Lord and **S**. ....Ps 38:22
You are my helper and **s**. ....Ps 40:17
God and keep praising him, my **S** ....Ps 42:5
praising him, my **S** and my God. ....Ps 42:11
praising him, my **S** and my God. ....Ps 43:5
us in amazing ways, God our **S**. ....Ps 65:5
the Lord, God our **S**, who helps ....Ps 68:19
our **S**, help us so people will ....Ps 79:9
God our **S**, bring us back again..............Ps 85:4
father, my God, the Rock, my **S**.' ....Ps 89:26
God, my mighty **s**, you protect me ....Ps 140:7
He is my defender and my **S**. ....Ps 144:2
the Holy One of Israel, your **S**. ....Is 43:3
am the LORD; I am the only **S**. ....Is 43:11
God and **S** of Israel, you are a ....Is 45:15
God. I am the **S**. There is no ....Is 45:21
Our **S** is named the LORD ....Is 47:4
Then a **S** will come to Jerusalem ....Is 59:20
Look, your **S** is coming. ....Is 62:11
I will rejoice in God my **S**. ....Hab 3:18
my heart rejoices in God my **S**, ...Lk 1:47
us a powerful **S** from the family ....Lk 1:69
Today your **S** was born in the ....Lk 2:11
really is the **S** of the world." ....Jn 4:42
his right side, as Leader and **S**. ....Ac 5:31
God sent to be a ruler and **s**, ...Ac 7:35
to be its **S**, as he promised..................Ac 13:23
realize that Jesus was the **S**. ....Ac 13:27
The **S** will come from Jerusalem; ....Rm 11:26
And he is the **S** of the body, ...Eph 5:23
and we are waiting for our **S**, ...Php 3:20
of God our **S** and Christ Jesus 1Ti 1:1
good, and it pleases God our **S**, ...1Ti 2:3
God who is the **S** of all people, ...1Ti 4:10
coming of our **S** Christ Jesus..................2Ti 1:10
by the command of God our **S**. ....Tit 1:3
Father and Christ Jesus our **S**. ....Tit 1:4
of God our **S** attractive. ....Tit 2:10
great God and **S** Jesus Christ ....Tit 2:13
and love of God our **S** was shown, ...Tit 3:4
through Jesus Christ our **S**. ....Tit 3:6
our God and **S** Jesus Christ does 2Pe 1:1
of our Lord and **S** Jesus Christ. 2Pe 1:11
our Lord and **S** Jesus Christ. 2Pe 2:20

S

our Lord and **S** gave us through 2Pe 3:2
of our Lord and **S** Jesus Christ. 2Pe 3:18
Son to be the **S** of the world. 1Jn 4:14

SAVIORS

and gave them **s** who saved them .... Ne 9:27

SAWS

and forced them to work with **s,** 2Sa 12:31
and forced them to work with **s,** 1Ch 20:3

SCABS

is covered with worms and **s,** .... Job 7:5

SCALES

if the animal has fins and **s,** .... Le 11:9
and does not have fins and **s—** .... Le 11:10
that does not have fins and **s.** .... Le 11:12
anything that has fins and **s,** .... Dt 14:9
that does not have fins and **s.** .... Dt 14:10
weighed and my misery put on **s.** .... Job 6:2
let God weigh me on honest **s.** .... Job 31:6
On the **s,** they weigh nothing; .... Ps 62:9
The LORD hates dishonest **s,** .... Pr 11:1
wants honest balances and **s;** .... Pr 16:11
and dishonest **s** do not please .... Pr 20:23
dust of the earth and **s** to weigh .... Is 40:12
the dust on his measuring **s.** .... Is 40:15
no more than fine dust on his **s.** .... Is 40:15
and weigh their silver on the **s.** .... Is 46:6
weighed out the silver on the **s.** .... Je 32:10
Then take **s** and weigh and divide .... Eze 5:1
must have honest **s,** an honest .... Eze 45:10
weighed on the **s** and found not .... Da 5:27
The merchants use dishonest **s;** .... Hos 12:7
we can change the **s** to cheat the .... Am 8:5
others with wrong weights and **s?** .... Mic 6:11
like fish **s** fell from Saul's .... Ac 9:18
held a pair of **s** in his hand. .... Rev 6:5

SCALP

a sore on the **s** or on the chin, ... Le 13:29

SCAR

it is only the **s** from the old .... Le 13:23
spot is only a **s** from the burn. .... Le 13:28

SCARE

will be no one to **s** them away. .... Dt 28:26
things you have seen will **s** you. .... Dt 28:67
wanted to **s** the people away so 2Ch 32:18
Our enemies were trying to **s** us, ... Ne 6:9
lie down, and no one will **s** you. .... Job 11:19
His bright glory would **s** you, ... Job 13:11
Pekah son of Remaliah, **s** you. .... Is 7:4
you will be able to **s** someone. .... Is 47:12
They **s** and frighten people. .... Hab 1:7
have come to **s** and throw down .... Zch 1:21
I am trying to **s** you with my 2Co 10:9

SCARECROWS

are like **s** in melon fields; .... Je 10:5

SCARED

My scream **s** him and he ran away, ... Ge 39:15
And Moab was **s** of so many .... Nu 22:3
that they were **s** and too afraid .... Jos 5:1
words, they were very **s.** 1Sa 17:11
I am **s** and shaking, and terror .... Ps 55:5

SCARES

It **s** people with its proud .... Job 39:20

SCARLET

Though your sins are like **s,** .... Is 1:18

SCARS

I have **s** on my body that show I .... Gal 6:17

SCARVES

their **s,** ankle chains, the cloth .... Is 3:20

SCATTER

will **s** the people who cut their .... Je 49:32
and the sheep will **s.**' .... Mt 26:31
and the sheep will **s.**' .... Mk 14:27

SCATTERED

we will not be **s** over all the .... Ge 11:4
So the LORD **s** them from there .... Ge 11:8
army of Israel **s** over the hills 1Ki 22:17
you have rejected us and **s** us. .... Ps 60:1
The Almighty **s** kings like snow .... Ps 68:14
your power you **s** your enemies. .... Ps 89:10
and all who do evil will be **s.** .... Ps 92:9
You have **s** my people and forced .... Je 23:2
all those nations where I **s** you, ... Je 30:11
They were **s** all over the face of .... Eze 34:6
care of his **s** flock when it is .... Eze 34:12
'I **s** them like a hurricane to .... Zch 7:14
I have **s** them among the nations, ... Zch 10:9
has **s** the people who are proud .... Lk 1:51
they were **s,** they told people .... Ac 8:4
people who are **s** everywhere .... Jam 1:1

SCATTERING

are **s** and destroying my people, ... Je 23:1

SCATTERS

nations large and then **s** them. .... Job 12:23
Watch how God **s** his lightning .... Job 36:30
with water and **s** his lightning .... Job 37:11
like wool and **s** the frost like .... Ps 147:16
plants the dill and **s** the cumin. .... Is 28:25
attacks the sheep and **s** them. .... Jn 10:12

SCEPTER

the king holds out his gold **s.** .... Est 4:11
her the gold **s** that was in his .... Est 5:2
held out the gold **s** to Esther. .... Est 8:4
Judah holds my royal **s.** .... Ps 60:7
Judah holds my royal **s.** .... Ps 108:8
has broken the **s** of evil rulers .... Is 14:5
good enough for a king's **s.** .... Eze 19:11
could become a **s** for a king.' .... Eze 19:14

SCEPTERS

With their **s** and poles, they dug .... Nu 21:18

SCEVA

Seven sons of **S,** a leading .... Ac 19:14

SCHOOL

This man has never studied in **s.** .... Jn 7:15
he went to the **s** of a man named .... Ac 19:9

SCOLD

God would surely **s** you if you .... Job 13:10
I do not **s** you for your .... Ps 50:8
But I will **s** you and accuse you .... Ps 50:21
You **s** proud people; those who .... Ps 119:21

SCOLDED

but his father **s** him, saying, ... Ge 37:10
But Jesus turned and **s** them. .... Lk 9:55

SCORCHING

and dry it up with a **s** wind. .... Is 11:15

SCORPION

cross south of **S** Pass, and go .... Nu 34:4
and went south of **S** Pass to Zin. .... Jos 15:3
Amorites was from **S** Pass to Sela .... Jdg 1:36
an egg, would you give them a **s?** .... Lk 11:12
like the pain a **s** gives when it .... Rev 9:5

SCORPIONS

power to walk on snakes and **s,** .... Lk 10:19
given the power to sting like **s.** .... Rev 9:3
had tails with stingers like **s,** .... Rev 9:10

SCOUTS

sent out **s** who told him that 1Ki 20:17

SCRAP
bones or a **s** of an ear of his .... Am 3:12

SCRAPE
of broken pottery to **s** himself, ... Job 2:8
I will also **s** away her ruins and .... Eze 26:4

SCRAPED
all the inside of the house **s**. .... Le 14:41
plaster they **s** off the walls, ... Le 14:41

SCRAPS
off used to eat **s** that fell from .... Jdg 1:7

SCREAM
My **s** scared him and he ran away, ... Ge 39:15
a city and did not **s** for help. .... Dt 22:24
I **s** for help but I get no .... Job 19:7

SCREAMED
relations with me, but I **s**. .... Ge 39:14
When he came near me, I **s**. .... Ge 39:18
girl in the country and she **s**, ... Dt 22:27
the woman saw Samuel, she **s**. 1Sa 28:12
Athaliah tore her clothes and **s**, ... 2Ki 11:14
Athaliah tore her clothes and **s**, ... 2Ch 23:13
The evil spirit **s** and caused the .... Mk 9:26

SCREAMING
s and cutting himself with stones. .... Mk 5:5

SCREAMS
them heard their **s** and ran away, ... Nu 16:34
be no war, no **s** in our streets. .... Ps 144:14
my son, and suddenly he **s**. .... Lk 9:39

SCREECH
horned owls, **s** owls, sea gulls, ... Le 11:16
horned owls, **s** owls, sea gulls, ... Dt 14:15

SCREEN
a large bronze **s** to hold the .... Ex 27:4
Put the **s** inside the altar, ... Ex 27:5
burnt offering and its bronze **s**, ... Ex 35:16
a large bronze **s** to hold the .... Ex 38:4
at the four corners of the **s**. .... Ex 38:5
make the altar and the bronze **s**, ... Ex 38:30
the bronze altar and its **s**, ... Ex 39:39

SCRIPTURE
S says, 'I want kindness more .... Mt 12:7
why does the **S** say that the Son .... Mk 9:12
Surely you have read this **S**: ' .... Mk 12:10
And the **S** came true that says, ... Mk 15:28
The **S** says, 'He was treated like .... Lk 22:37
I tell you this **s** must have its .... Lk 22:37
believed the **S** and the words .... Jn 2:22
person's heart, as the **S** says." .... Jn 7:38
The **S** says that the Christ will .... Jn 7:42
This **S** called those people gods .... Jn 10:35
message, and **S** is always true. .... Jn 10:35
This was as the **S** says, ... Jn 12:14
bring about what the **S** said: ' .... Jn 13:18
so that the **S** would come true .... Jn 17:12
so that this **S** would come true: .... Jn 19:24
So that the **S** would come true, ... Jn 19:28
to make the **S** come true: .... Jn 19:36
And another **S** says, "They will .... Jn 19:37
The portion of **S** he was reading .... Ac 8:32
and starting with this same **S**, ... Ac 8:35
the **S** says, "But those who are .... Rm 1:17
because the **S** says, "Abraham .... Rm 4:3
As the **S** says, "I loved Jacob, ... Rm 9:13
The **S** says to the king of Egypt: .... Rm 9:17
As the **S** says in Hosea: .... Rm 9:25
As it is written in the **S**: .... Rm 9:33
is what the **S** says about being .... Rm 10:6
This is what the **S** says: .... Rm 10:8
the **S** says, "Anyone who trusts .... Rm 10:11

That **S** says "anyone" because .... Rm 10:12
as the **S** says, "Anyone who calls .... Rm 10:13
Yes, they heard—as the **S** says: .... Rm 10:18
know what the **S** says about .... Rm 11:2
the **S** says, "Who has known the .... Rm 11:34
The **S** also says, "Be happy, you .... Rm 15:10
Again the **S** says, "All you who .... Rm 15:11
So, as the **S** says, "If people 1Co 1:31
one can judge him. The **S** says: 1Co 2:15
that **S** was written for us, ... 1Co 9:10
The **S** says that God put all 1Co 15:27
this **S** will be made true: 1Co 15:54
beforehand, as the **S** says: .... Gal 3:8
But what does the **S** say? .... Gal 4:30
The **S** says, "So a man will leave .... Eph 5:31
because the **S** says: 1Ti 5:18
All **S** is inspired by God and is 2Ti 3:16
This is what the **S** says: .... Heb 3:15
And again in the **S** God said, ... Heb 4:5
later in the same **S** used before: .... Heb 4:7
And in another **S** God says, ... Heb 5:6
continues living, as the **S** says. .... Heb 7:8
In this **S** he first said, "You do .... Heb 10:8
the **S** says that he was a man who .... Heb 11:5
full meaning of the **S** that says: .... Jam 2:23
Do you think the **S** means nothing .... Jam 4:5
grace, as the **S** says, "God is .... Jam 4:6
The **S** says, "All people are like 1Pe 1:24
The **S** says: "I will put a stone 1Pe 2:6
The **S** says, "A person must do 1Pe 3:10

SCRIPTURES
who explain the **S** have written .... Je 8:8
I, Daniel, was reading the **S**. .... Da 9:2
wrote about this in the **S**: .... Mt 2:5
written in the **S**, 'A person .... Mt 4:4
it is written in the **S**: ' .... Mt 4:6
also says in the **S**, 'Do not test .... Mt 4:7
is written in the **S**, 'You must .... Mt 4:10
Surely you have read in the **S**: .... Mt 19:4
written in the **S**, 'My Temple .... Mt 21:13
Haven't you read in the **S**, ' .... Mt 21:16
you have read this in the **S**: ' .... Mt 21:42
you don't know what the **S** say, ... Mt 22:29
boxes holding **S** that they wear, ... Mt 23:5
Man will die, just as the **S** say. .... Mt 26:24
it is written in the **S**: ' .... Mt 26:31
to bring about what the **S** say." .... Mt 26:54
as the **S** said it would happen. .... Mk 9:13
written in the **S**, 'My Temple .... Mk 11:17
Don't you know what the **S** say, ... Mk 12:24
Man will die, just as the **S** say. .... Mk 14:21
it is written in the **S**: ' .... Mk 14:27
to make the **S** come true." .... Mk 14:49
It is written in the **S**: ' .... Lk 4:4
It is written in the **S**: ' .... Lk 4:8
It is written in the **S**: ' .... Lk 4:10
But it also says in the **S**: .... Lk 4:12
written in the **S**, 'My Temple .... Lk 19:46
all that is written in the **S**. .... Lk 21:22
written about himself in the **S**. .... Lk 24:27
road and explained the **S** to us." .... Lk 24:32
so they could understand the **S**. .... Lk 24:45
what was written in the **S**: .... Jn 2:17
study the **S** because you think .... Jn 5:39
This is written in the **S**: ' .... Jn 6:31
Study the **S**, and you will learn .... Jn 7:52
from the **S** that Jesus must .... Jn 20:9
to him all that the **S** had said, ... Ac 13:29
his fellow Jews about the **S**. .... Ac 17:2
and studied the **S** every day to .... Ac 17:11
speaker who knew the **S** well. .... Ac 18:24
proving with the **S** that Jesus is .... Ac 18:28

S

written in the **s**, 'You must not .... Ac 23:5
as it is written in the Holy **S**. .... Rm 1:2
just as the **S** say: .... Rm 2:24
is false. As the **S** say: "So you .... Rm 3:4
As the **S** say: "There is no one .... Rm 3:10
As it is written in the **S**: .... Rm 4:17
As it is written in the **S**: .... Rm 8:36
As it is written in the **S**: .... Rm 11:8
It is written in the **S**: .... Rm 11:26
it is written in the **S**: .... Rm 14:11
It was as the **S** said: .... Rm 15:3
The **S** give us patience and .... Rm 15:4
It is written in the **S**: .... Rm 15:9
But it is written in the **S**: .... Rm 15:21
It is written in the **S**: 1Co 1:19
But as it is written in the **S**: 1Co 2:9
is written in the **S**, "He catches 1Co 3:19
It is also written in the **S**, ... 1Co 3:20
only what is written in the **S**." 1Co 4:6
written in the **S**, "The two will 1Co 6:16
Just as it is written in the **S**: 1Co 10:7
It is written in the **S**: 1Co 14:21
died for our sins, as the **S** say; 1Co 15:3
on the third day as the **S** say; 1Co 15:4
It is written in the **S**: 1Co 15:45
written in the **S**, "I believed, ... 2Co 4:13
As it is written in the **S**, ... 2Co 8:15
It is written in the **S**: 2Co 9:9
The **S** say the same thing about .... Gal 3:6
The **S**, telling what would happen .... Gal 3:8
because the **S** say, "Anyone will .... Gal 3:10
because the **S** say, "Those who .... Gal 3:11
written in the **S**, "Anyone whose .... Gal 3:13
S showed that the whole world .... Gal 3:22
The **S** say that Abraham had two .... Gal 4:22
It is written in the **S**: .... Gal 4:27
That is why it says in the **S**, ... Eph 4:8
to read the **S** to the people, ... 1Ti 4:13
known the Holy **S** which are able 2Ti 3:15
Using the **S**, the person who 2Ti 3:17
written in the **S**, "Why are .... Heb 2:6
In the **S** he talked about the .... Heb 4:4
royal law is found in the **S**: .... Jam 2:8
It is written in the **S**: 1Pe 1:16
No prophecy in the **S** ever comes 2Pe 1:20
falsely explain the other **S**, ... 2Pe 3:16

SCROLL
write these curses on a **s**, ... Nu 5:23
teachings on a **s** for himself, ... Dt 17:18
They described in a **s** each town.............. Jos 18:9
A **s** was found in Ecbatana, ... Ezr 6:2
written down, written on a **s**. .... Job 19:23
Take a large **s** and write on it .... Is 8:1
write this on a **s**, so that for .... Is 30:8
sky will be rolled up like a **s**. .... Is 34:4
at the LORD's **s** and read what is .... Is 34:16
Get a **s**. Write on it all the .... Je 36:2
wrote those messages on the **s**. .... Je 36:4
from the **s** to all the people .... Je 36:6
wrote on the **s** as I spoke them .... Je 36:6
read aloud the **s** that had the .... Je 36:8
people there the **s** containing .... Je 36:10
He read the **s** in the Temple of .... Je 36:10
the LORD that were on the **s**. .... Je 36:11
read to the people from the **s**. .... Je 36:13
Bring the **s** that you read to the .... Je 36:14
Neriah took the **s** and went with .... Je 36:14
sit down and read the **s** to us." .... Je 36:15
So Baruch read the **s** to them. .... Je 36:15
these words you wrote on the **s?**.............. Je 36:17
them down with ink on this **s**." .... Je 36:18
officers put the **s** in the room .... Je 36:20

and told him all about the **s**. .... Je 36:20
sent Jehudi to get the **s**. .... Je 36:21
brought the **s** from the room .... Je 36:21
off of the **s** with a penknife. .... Je 36:23
whole **s** was burned in the fire. .... Je 36:23
Jehoiakim out of burning the **s**, ... Je 36:25
burned the **s** where Baruch had .... Je 36:27
Get another **s**. Write all the .... Je 36:28
on the first **s** that Jehoiakim .... Je 36:28
You burned up that **s** and said, ... Je 36:29
took another **s** and gave it to .... Je 36:32
wrote on the **s** the same words .... Je 36:32
were on the **s** Jehoiakim king .... Je 36:32
were added to the second **s**. .... Je 36:32
and Baruch wrote them on a **s**: .... Je 45:1
written on a **s** all the terrible .... Je 51:60
After you finish reading this **s**, ... Je 51:63
out to me, and a **s** was in it. .... Eze 2:9
He opened the **s** in front of me. .... Eze 2:10
find; eat this **s**. Then go and .... Eze 3:1
and he gave me the **s** to eat. .... Eze 3:2
this **s** which I am giving you, ... Eze 3:3
up again and saw a flying **s**. .... Zch 5:1
I see a flying **s**, thirty feet .... Zch 5:2
The **s** will stay in that person's .... Zch 5:4
Then I saw a **s** in the right hand.............. Rev 5:1
The **s** had writing on both sides .... Rev 5:1
break the seals and open the **s?**" .... Rev 5:2
could open the **s** or look inside. .... Rev 5:3
to open the **s** or look inside. .... Rev 5:4
able to open the **s** and its seven .... Rev 5:5
and took the **s** from the right .... Rev 5:7
he took the **s**, the four living .... Rev 5:8
to take the **s** and to open its .... Rev 5:9
disappeared as a **s** when it is .... Rev 6:14
holding a small **s** open in his .... Rev 10:2
and take the open **s** that is in .... Rev 10:8
told him to give me the small **s**. .... Rev 10:9
to me, "Take the **s** and eat it. .... Rev 10:9
took the small **s** from the .... Rev 10:10

SCRUB
with soap and **s** my hands with .... Job 9:30

SCRUBBED
must be **s** and rinsed with water. .... Le 6:28

SCUM
Remove the **s** from the silver, ... Pr 25:4
become like the **s** left when .... Is 1:22
made us like **s** and trash among.............. La 3:45
become useless like **s** to me. .... Eze 22:18
you have become useless like **s**, ... Eze 22:19
The dirty **s** stuck inside it may .... Eze 24:11

SCYTHIANS
people who are foreigners, or **S**............... Col 3:11

SEA
the large **s** animals and every .... Ge 1:21
thing that moves in the **s**. .... Ge 1:21
s is filled with these living .... Ge 1:21
the fish in the **s** and the birds .... Ge 1:26
the fish in the **s** and over the .... Ge 1:28
every fish in the **s** will respect .... Ge 9:2
Mediterranean **S** came from these .... Ge 10:5
of Siddim (now the Dead **S**). .... Ge 14:3
Zebulun will live near the **s**. .... Ge 49:13
the locusts away into the Red **S**.............. Ex 10:19
the desert toward the Red **S**. .... Ex 13:18
between Migdol and the Red **S**. .... Ex 14:2
Zephon, on the shore of the **s**. .... Ex 14:2
they were camped by the Red **S**,.............. Ex 14:9
it over the **s** so that the sea .... Ex 14:16
the sea so that the **s** will split .... Ex 14:16
Moses held his hand over the **s**. .... Ex 14:21

drove back the s with a strong .... Ex 14:21
making the s become dry ground. .... Ex 14:21
went through the s on dry land, ... Ex 14:22
followed them into the s......................... Ex 14:23
hand over the s so that the .... Ex 14:26
raised his hand over the s, ... Ex 14:27
at dawn the s returned to its .... Ex 14:27
LORD swept them away into the s........... Ex 14:27
the Israelites into the s. .... Ex 14:28
crossed the s on dry land, ... Ex 14:29
horse and its rider into the s. .... Ex 15:1
Egypt he has thrown into the s. .... Ex 15:4
are drowned in the Red S. .... Ex 15:4
solid in the middle of the s..................... Ex 15:8
and covered them with the s. .... Ex 15:10
king of Egypt went into the s,................ Ex 15:19
them with water from the s. .... Ex 15:19
through the s on dry land. .... Ex 15:19
horse and its rider into the s." .... Ex 15:21
from the Red S into the Desert .... Ex 15:22
the earth, the s, and everything .... Ex 20:11
land from the Red S to the .... Ex 23:31
Red Sea to the Mediterranean S, ... Ex 23:31
live in the s or in a river,....................... Le 11:9
lives in the s or in a river .... Le 11:10
screech owls, s gulls, any kind .... Le 11:16
animals in the s and those that .... Le 11:46
we caught all the fish in the s, ... Nu 11:22
sent a strong wind from the s, ... Nu 11:31
live near the s and along the .... Nu 13:29
desert road toward the Red S." .... Nu 14:25
on the road toward the Red S, ... Nu 21:4
through the s into the desert. .... Nu 33:8
Elim and camped near the Red S. .... Nu 33:10
They left the Red S and camped.............. Nu 33:11
at the south end of the Dead S, ... Nu 34:3
will end at the Mediterranean S. .... Nu 34:5
will be the Mediterranean S. .... Nu 34:6
Mediterranean S and go to Mount .... Nu 34:7
River and end at the Dead S. .... Nu 34:12
desert road toward the Red S." .... Dt 1:40
desert road toward the Red S, ... Dt 2:1
to the Dead S west of Mount .... Dt 3:17
far as the Dead S below Mount .... Dt 4:49
them in the Red S as they were .... Dt 11:4
River to the Mediterranean S................... Dt 11:24
screech owls, s gulls, any kind .... Dt 14:15
not on the other side of the S................. Dt 30:13
will go across the s and get it? .... Dt 30:13
well from all that is in the s, ... Dt 33:19
as far as the Mediterranean S, ... Dt 34:2
Mediterranean S in the west will .... Jos 1:4
dried up the Red S when you came .... Jos 2:10
flowing down to the S of Arabah .... Jos 3:16
the Dead S) was completely .... Jos 3:16
as the LORD did to the Red S. .... Jos 4:23
the Mediterranean S heard that .... Jos 5:1
the whole Mediterranean S coast. .... Jos 9:1
from Lake Galilee to the Dead S. .... Jos 12:3
at the south end of the Dead S .... Jos 15:2
and then to the Mediterranean S. .... Jos 15:4
was the shore of the Dead S, ... Jos 15:5
at the bay of the s at the mouth .... Jos 15:5
on to Jabneel, ending at the s. .... Jos 15:11
Mediterranean S was the western .... Jos 15:12
coast of the Mediterranean S.................. Jos 15:47
to Gezer and ended at the s. .... Jos 16:3
and then to the S. From .... Jos 16:6
Kanah Ravine and ended at the s. .... Jos 16:8
of the ravine and went to the s. .... Jos 17:9
Mediterranean S was the western .... Jos 17:10
the north shore of the Dead S, ... Jos 18:19
Jordan River flows into the s................... Jos 18:19

toward Hosah, ending at the s. .... Jos 19:29
the Mediterranean S in the west, ... Jos 23:4
came to the Red S, and the .... Jos 24:6
and made the s to cover them. .... Jos 24:7
desert to the Red S and then to .... Jdg 11:16
as grains of sand by the s. 2Sa 17:11
the valleys of the s appeared, ... 2Sa 22:16
them down from Lebanon to the s........... 1Ki 5:9
bowl, which was called the S.................. 1Ki 7:23
Elath on the shore of the Red S,............. 1Ki 9:26
had many trading ships at s, ... 1Ki 10:22
"Go and look toward the s." 1Ki 18:43
human fist, coming from the s." 1Ki 18:44
from Lebo Hamath to the Dead S. 2Ki 14:25
was called the S, off the bronze 2Ki 16:17
was called the S, in the Temple 2Ki 25:13
Let the s and everything in it 1Ch 16:32
was called the S, the pillars, ... 1Ch 18:8
bring it on rafts by s to Joppa. 2Ch 2:16
bowl, which was called the S. 2Ch 4:2
Elath near the Red S in the land.............. 2Ch 8:17
the other side of the Dead S. 2Ch 20:2
heard them cry out at the Red S. .... Ne 9:9
divided the s in front of our .... Ne 9:11
to wake up the s monster .... Job 3:8
I am not the s or the sea .... Job 7:12
am not the sea or the s monster.............. Job 7:12
and walks on the waves of the s. .... Job 9:8
the earth and wider than the s. .... Job 11:9
let the fish of the s tell you. .... Job 12:8
With his power he quiets the s; .... Job 26:12
destroys Rahab, the s monster. .... Job 26:12
' the s says, 'It's not in me.'..................... Job 28:14
up the deepest parts of the s. .... Job 36:30
to keep the s in when it broke .... Job 38:8
a coat for the s and wrapped it .... Job 38:9
limits on the s and put its .... Job 38:10
I said to the s, 'You may come .... Job 38:11
to where the s begins or walked.............. Job 38:16
in the valleys under the s? .... Job 38:16
It makes the deep s bubble like .... Job 41:31
it stirs up the s like a pot of .... Job 41:31
that makes the s look as if it .... Job 41:32
fish in the s, and everything .... Ps 8:8
the valleys of the s appeared, ... Ps 18:15
's voice is heard over the s...................... Ps 29:3
the water of the s into a heap. .... Ps 33:7
the mountains fall into the s, ... Ps 46:2
shake at the raging s. .... Ps 46:3
and beyond the s trust you...................... Ps 65:5
He turned the s into dry land.................. Ps 66:6
back from the depths of the s. .... Ps 68:22
his kingdom go from s to sea,.................. Ps 72:8
his kingdom go from sea to s,................. Ps 72:8
split open the s by your power .... Ps 74:13
the heads of the s monster..................... Ps 74:13
way through the s and paths .... Ps 77:19
divided the Red S and led them .... Ps 78:13
as many as the sand of the s. .... Ps 78:27
their enemies drowned in the s. .... Ps 78:53
reached the Mediterranean S,.................. Ps 80:11
rule the mighty s and calm the .... Ps 89:9
You crushed the s monster Rahab; .... Ps 89:10
power over the s and control .... Ps 89:25
The s is his because he made it, ... Ps 95:5
let the s and everything in it .... Ps 96:11
Let the s and everything in it .... Ps 98:7
Look at the s, so big and wide, ... Ps 104:25
and there is the s monster .... Ps 104:26
turned against you at the Red S............... Ps 106:7
the Red S, and it dried up .... Ps 106:9
through the deep s as if it were .... Ps 106:9
and amazing things by the Red S. .... Ps 106:22

S

went out to **s** in ships and did .... Ps 107:23
The Red **S** looked and ran away; .... Ps 114:3
S, why did you run away? .... Ps 114:5
parted the water of the Red **S**. .... Ps 136:13
his army drowned in the Red **S**. .... Ps 136:15
settle in the west beyond the **s**, ... Ps 139:9
me out of this **s** of enemies, ... Ps 144:7
the **s** and everything in it. .... Ps 146:6
you large **s** animals and all the .... Ps 148:7
ordered the **s** not to go beyond .... Pr 8:29
the way a ship sails on the **s**, ... Pr 30:19
All the rivers flow to the **s**, ... Ec 1:7
but the **s** never becomes full. .... Ec 1:7
roar like the waves of the **s**. .... Is 5:30
the Mediterranean **S** to the land .... Is 9:1
the grains of sand by the **s**. .... Is 10:22
as the **s** is full of water. .... Is 11:9
and all the islands of the **s**. .... Is 11:11
will dry up the Red **S** of Egypt. .... Is 11:15
they had spread as far as the **s**. .... Is 16:8
is like the noise from the **s**. .... Is 17:12
sends messengers across the **s**; .... Is 18:2
The **s** will become dry, and the .... Is 19:5
who live near the **s** will say, ' .... Is 20:6
about the Desert by the **S**: .... Is 21:1
traveled the **s** to bring grain .... Is 23:3
city of the **s**, be ashamed, ... Is 23:4
be ashamed, because the **s** says: .... Is 23:4
living near the **s** should be sad. .... Is 23:6
his hand over the **s** and made its .... Is 23:11
if you cross the **s** to Cyprus, ... Is 23:12
People in the islands of the **s**, ... Is 24:15
will kill the monster in the **s**. .... Is 27:1
road through the **s** and a path .... Is 43:16
to you like the waves of the **s**. .... Is 48:18
to shout and the **s** becomes dry. .... Is 50:2
and killed that **s** monster. .... Is 51:9
dried up the **s** and the waters .... Is 51:10
parts of the **s** into a road for .... Is 51:10
who stirs the **s** and makes the .... Is 51:15
people are like the angry **s**, ... Is 57:20
the people through the **s**, ... Is 63:11
Go across the **s** to the island of .... Je 2:10
to be a border for the **s**, ... Je 5:22
than grains of sand in the **s**. .... Je 15:8
is called the **S**, the stands that .... Je 27:19
in the faraway lands by the **s**: ' .... Je 31:10
He stirs up the **s** so that its .... Je 31:35
like Mount Carmel by the **s**. .... Je 46:18
spread all the way to the **s**, ... Je 48:32
sea, as far as the **s** of Jazer. .... Je 48:32
heard all the way to the Red **S**. .... Je 49:21
are troubled like the tossing **s**. .... Je 49:23
is loud like the roaring **s**. .... Je 50:42
dry up Babylon's **s** and make her .... Je 51:36
The **s** has risen over Babylon; .... Je 51:42
bowl, called the **S**, which were .... Je 52:17
called the **S** with the twelve .... Je 52:20
Your ruin is as deep as the **s**. .... La 2:13
like the roaring sound of the **s**, ... Eze 1:24
coast of the Mediterranean **S**. .... Eze 25:16
like the **s** beating its waves on .... Eze 26:3
wood, and trash into the **s**. .... Eze 26:12
You have lost your **s** power! .... Eze 26:17
islands of the **s** are afraid .... Eze 26:18
Mediterranean **S** will cover you. .... Eze 26:19
Mediterranean **S** and is a place .... Eze 27:3
the ships of the **s** and their .... Eze 27:9
· cargo in the middle of the **s**. .... Eze 27:25
pieces in the middle of the **s**. .... Eze 27:26
sank into the **s** on the day your .... Eze 27:27
like Tyre, surrounded by the **s**." .... Eze 27:32
broken by the **s** and have sunk to .... Eze 27:34

like those who are killed at **s**. .... Eze 28:8
The fish of the **s**, the birds of .... Eze 38:20
Travelers, east of the Dead **S**. .... Eze 39:11
reach to the Mediterranean **S**. .... Eze 45:7
When it enters the Dead **S**, ... Eze 47:8
goes the Dead **S** will become .... Eze 47:9
will stand by the Dead **S**. .... Eze 47:10
kinds of fish in the Dead **S**, ... Eze 47:10
many as in the Mediterranean **S**. .... Eze 47:10
start at the Mediterranean **S**. .... Eze 47:15
Mediterranean **S** east to the town .... Eze 47:17
the town of Tamar on the Dead **S**. .... Eze 47:18
of Egypt to the Mediterranean **S**. .... Eze 47:19
the Mediterranean **S** will be the .... Eze 47:20
go from the **s** through Hethlon .... Eze 48:1
Mediterranean **S** on the west side .... Eze 48:1
of it to the Mediterranean **S**. .... Eze 48:21
Mediterranean **S** on the west side .... Eze 48:23
on the Dead **S** to the waters .... Eze 48:28
of Egypt to the Mediterranean **S**. .... Eze 48:28
which made the **s** very rough. .... Da 7:2
huge animals come up from the **s**, ... Da 7:3
Mediterranean **S** and will capture .... Da 11:18
between the **s** and the beautiful .... Da 11:45
the grains of sand of the **s**, ... Hos 1:10
and the fish of the **s** are dying. .... Hos 4:3
will be forced into the Dead **S**, ... Joe 2:20
rear into the Mediterranean **S**. .... Joe 2:20
the waters of the **s** to pour out .... Am 5:8
the valley south of the Dead **S**." .... Am 6:14
Mediterranean **S** to the Dead Sea .... Am 8:12
Mediterranean Sea to the Dead **S**, ... Am 8:12
from me at the bottom of the **s**, ... Am 9:3
waters of the **s** and pours them .... Am 9:6
LORD sent a great wind on the **s**, ... Jnh 1:4
which made the **s** so stormy that .... Jnh 1:4
ship into the **s** to make the ship .... Jnh 1:5
who made the **s** and the land." .... Jnh 1:9
the waves of the **s** were becoming .... Jnh 1:11
to make the **s** calm down for us? .... Jnh 1:11
me into the **s**, and then it will .... Jnh 1:12
because the **s** was becoming more .... Jnh 1:13
Jonah and threw him into the **s**, ... Jnh 1:15
the sea, and the **s** became calm. .... Jnh 1:15
threw me into the **s**, down, down .... Jnh 2:3
sea, down, down into the deep **s**. .... Jnh 2:3
waters of the **s** closed around my .... Jnh 2:5
The deep **s** was all around me; .... Jnh 2:5
of the **s** start to rise, ... Jnh 2:6
and from **s** to sea and mountain .... Mic 7:12
and from sea to **s** and mountain .... Mic 7:12
into the deepest part of the **s**. .... Mic 7:19
speaks to the **s** and makes it dry .... Nah 1:4
treat people like fish in the **s**, ... Hab 1:14
like **s** animals without a leader. .... Hab 1:14
just as water covers the **s**, ... Hab 2:14
angry with the **s** when you rode .... Hab 3:8
The **s** made a loud noise, and its .... Hab 3:10
through the **s** with your horses, ... Hab 3:15
the air and the fish of the **s**. .... Zph 1:3
who live by the Mediterranean **S**, ... Zph 2:5
The land by the Mediterranean **S**, ... Zph 2:6
earth, the **s** and the dry land. .... Hag 2:6
and destroy her power on the **s**. .... Zch 9:4
kingdom will go from **s** to sea, ... Zch 9:10
kingdom will go from sea to **s**, ... Zch 9:10
come through the **s** of trouble. .... Zch 10:11
The waves of the **s** will be calm, ... Zch 10:11
it will flow east to the Dead **S**, ... Zch 14:8
west to the Mediterranean **S**. .... Zch 14:8
land of Naphtali along the **s**, ... Mt 4:15
neck and be drowned in the **s**. .... Mt 18:6
mountain, 'Go, fall into the **s**.' .... Mt 21:21

across land and **s** to find one .... Mt 23:15
neck and be drowned in the **s.** .... Mk 9:42
mountain, 'Go, fall into the **s.**' .... Mk 11:23
thrown into the **s** with a large.............. Lk 17:2
up and plant yourself in the **s,**' .... Lk 17:6
of the roar and fury of the **s.** .... Lk 21:25
the earth, the **s,** and everything .... Ac 4:24
in Egypt, at the Red **S,** and then.............. Ac 7:36
and has a house beside the **s.**" .... Ac 10:6
and has a house beside the **s.**'.............. Ac 10:32
the earth, the **s,** and everything .... Ac 14:15
We went across the **s** by Cilicia .... Ac 27:5
around in the Adriatic **S.**...................... Ac 27:27
throwing the grain into the **s.** .... Ac 27:38
and left the anchors in the **s.** .... Ac 27:40
not die in the **s,** but Justice .... Ac 28:4
the grains of sand by the **s.**...................... Rm 9:27
and all went through the **s.** 1Co 10:1
Moses in the cloud and in the **s.** 1Co 10:2
a night and a day in the **s.** 2Co 11:25
no one lives, and on the **s.** 2Co 11:26
crossed the Red **S** as if it were .... Heb 11:29
doubts is like a wave in the **s,**.................. Jam 1:6
are like wild waves of the **s,** .... Jud 1:13
that looked like a **s** of glass, ... Rev 4:6
the earth and in the **s** saying:.............. Rev 5:13
land or on the **s** or on any tree. .... Rev 7:1
to harm the earth and the **s.** .... Rev 7:2
the land or the **s** or the trees .... Rev 7:3
fire, was thrown into the **s.** .... Rev 8:8
a third of the **s** became blood, ... Rev 8:8
the living things in the **s** died, ... Rev 8:9
foot on the **s** and his left foot .... Rev 10:2
standing on the **s** and on the .... Rev 10:5
and the **s** and all that is in it. .... Rev 10:6
on the **s** and on the land. .... Rev 10:8
for the earth and the **s,** .... Rev 12:12
a beast coming up out of the **s.** .... Rev 13:1
earth, and the **s,** and the .... Rev 14:7
looked like a **s** of glass mixed.............. Rev 15:2
were standing by the **s** of glass. .... Rev 15:2
poured out his bowl on the **s,** .... Rev 16:3
living thing in the **s** died. .... Rev 16:3
Every **s** captain, every .... Rev 18:17
living from the **s** stood far away .... Rev 18:17
had ships on the **s** became rich .... Rev 18:19
grain, and threw it into the **s.** .... Rev 18:21
The **s** gave up the dead who were .... Rev 20:13
and there was no **s** anymore. .... Rev 21:1

SEACOAST
southern area, the **s,** the land .... Dt 1:7
Lebanon to the **s** town of Joppa.............. Ezr 3:7
even from the cities on the **s.** .... Est 10:1
to attack Ashkelon and the **s.**" .... Je 47:7
live along the **s** will shake with .... Eze 26:15
leaders of the **s** will get down .... Eze 26:16
of many lands along the **s.** ' .... Eze 27:3
the **s** cities of Tyre and Sidon.................. Lk 6:17

SEAL
Give me your **s** and its cord, ... Ge 38:18
get back his **s** and the walking .... Ge 38:20
Look at this **s** and its cord and .... Ge 38:25
his ring with the royal **s** on it,.............. Ge 41:42
carves words and designs on a **s.** .... Ex 28:11
stones as you would carve a **s.** .... Ex 28:21
on it as you would carve a **s:** '.............. Ex 28:36
carves words and designs on a **s.** .... Ex 39:6
jewels as a person carves a **s.** .... Ex 39:14
as one might carve on a **s:** .... Ex 39:30
and used his own **s** to seal them. 1Ki 21:8
and used his own seal to **s** them. 1Ki 21:8
Then **s** the order with the king's.............. Est 8:8

like clay being pressed by a **s;** .... Job 38:14
Put me like a **s** on your heart,.............. Sng 8:6
heart, like a **s** on your arm...................... Sng 8:6
S up the teaching while my .... Is 8:16
will sign and **s** their agreements.............. Je 32:44
But **s** up the vision, because .... Da 8:26
close up the book and **s** it. .... Da 12:4
words are written on the **s:** 2Ti 2:19
the Lamb opened the second **s,** .... Rev 6:3
the Lamb opened the third **s,** .... Rev 6:5
the Lamb opened the fourth **s,** .... Rev 6:7
the Lamb opened the fifth **s,** .... Rev 6:9
the Lamb opened the sixth **s,** .... Rev 6:12
east who had the **s** of the living .... Rev 7:2
the Lamb opened the seventh **s,** .... Rev 8:1

SEALED
are the men who **s** the agreement: .... Ne 10:1
These are the Levites who **s** it: .... Ne 10:9
the people who **s** the agreement: .... Ne 10:14
Xerxes and **s** with his signet .... Est 3:12
name and **s** with his signet .... Est 8:8
King Xerxes and **s** the letters .... Est 8:10
that are tightly **s** together. .... Job 41:15
of a book that is closed and **s.** .... Is 29:11
read the book, because it is **s.**" .... Is 29:11
the record and **s** it and had some .... Je 32:10
the one that was **s** that had the .... Je 32:11
and the one that was not **s.** .... Je 32:11
the **s** copy and the copy that was .... Je 32:14
and the copy that was not **s**—.................. Je 32:14
closed up and **s** until the time .... Da 12:9
that is **s** with the blood 1Co 11:25

SEALING
safe from thieves by **s** the stone .... Mt 27:66

SEALS
are putting their **s** on it."...................... Ne 9:38
to put special **s** on the rock. .... Da 6:17
was kept closed with seven **s.** .... Rev 5:1
to break the **s** and open the .... Rev 5:2
the scroll and its seven **s.**" .... Rev 5:5
the scroll and to open its **s,** .... Rev 5:9
opened the first of the seven **s.** .... Rev 6:1

SEAM
close to the **s** above the woven .... Ex 28:27
vest, near the **s,** just above .... Ex 39:20

SEAMEN
goods, your **s,** your sailors,.............. Eze 27:27
the **s** and the sailors of other .... Eze 27:29

SEAMS
clothes must be torn at the **s,** .... Le 13:45
putting caulk in your ship's **s.**.................. Eze 27:9

SEARCH
a part of the country to **s;** 1Ki 18:6
to every country to **s** for you. 1Ki 18:10
who will **s** everywhere in your 1Ki 20:6
We suggest you **s** the records of .... Ezr 4:15
let a **s** be made in the royal .... Ezr 5:17
an order to **s** the records kept.................. Ezr 6:1
Let a **s** be made for beautiful .... Est 2:2
They **s** for death more than for .... Job 3:21
Then you will **s** for me, but I .... Job 7:21
I have done and **s** for my sin. .... Job 10:6
Can you **s** the limits of the .... Job 11:7
bring lights and **s** deep into the .... Job 28:3
They **s** for places where rivers .... Job 28:11
are my God. I **s** for you. I .... Ps 63:1
S for it like silver, and hunt .... Pr 2:4
S the public squares of the city. .... Je 5:1
You will **s** for me. And when you .... Je 29:13
And when you **s** for me with all .... Je 29:13

did not s for my flock............................Eze 34:8
s for my sheep and take care ....Eze 34:11
will s for the lost, bring back ....Eze 34:16
are finished, they will still s. ....Eze 39:14
They will s for the word of the ....Am 8:12
will s Jerusalem with lamps. ....Zph 1:12
S, and you will find. ....Mt 7:7
S, and you will find. ....Lk 11:9
you are; don't go away and s. ....Lk 17:23
him and perhaps s all around for ....Ac 17:27

SEARCHED
The servant s the sacks, going ....Ge 44:12
the records were s, and some 1Ch 26:31
These people s for their family ....Ezr 2:62
I ordered the records to be s, ...Ezr 4:19
These people s for their family ....Ne 7:64
went after and s for and ....Je 8:2
strayed away or s for the lost. ....Eze 34:4
and no one s or looked for them. ....Eze 34:6
The prophets s carefully and 1Pe 1:10

SEARCHES
The LORD s all the earth for 2Ch 16:9
inside people and s through ....Pr 20:27
things, who s for the truth, I ....Je 5:1
Everyone who s will find. ....Mt 7:8
The one who s will find. ....Lk 11:10
The Spirit s out all things, ...1Co 2:10
am the One who s hearts and ....Rev 2:23

SEARCHING
After s everywhere in Israel for 1Ki 1:3
While I was s, I did not find ....Ec 7:28

SEAS
that was gathered together "s." ....Ge 1:10
the water of the s, and let the ....Ge 1:22
the s and everything in them; ....Ne 9:6
heavier than the sand of the s. ....Job 6:3
You stopped the roaring s, ...Ps 65:7
the s and everything in them. ....Ps 69:34
LORD, the s raise, the seas ....Ps 93:3
seas raise, the s raise their ....Ps 93:3
The s raise up their pounding.................Ps 93:3
borders for the s that they ....Ps 104:9
in the s and the deep oceans. ....Ps 135:6
spread out the earth on the s. ....Ps 136:6
sail on the s and you animals ....Is 42:10
across the s will be given to ....Is 60:5
people had great power on the s. ....Eze 26:17
You were at home on the high s. ....Eze 27:4
brought you out into the high s, ...Eze 27:26
you traded went out over the s, ...Eze 27:33
a god in the middle of the s." ....Eze 28:2
are like a crocodile in the s. ....Eze 32:2

SEASHORE
the sky and the sand on the s, ...Ge 22:17
as many as the sand of the s. ....Ge 32:12
as much as the sand of the s— ....Ge 41:49
Egyptians lying dead on the s. ....Ex 14:30
as grains of sand on the s. ....Jos 11:4
people of Asher stayed at the s, ...Jdg 5:17
as the grains of sand on the s! ....Jdg 7:12
as the grains of sand on the s. 1Sa 13:5
as grains of sand on the s. 1Ki 4:20
as the grains of sand on the s. 1Ki 4:29
of sand on the s that no one can............Je 33:22
sand on the s, they could not ....Heb 11:12
And the dragon stood on the s. ....Rev 12:18
they will be like sand on the s. ....Rev 20:8

SEASON
during the s when the flocks ....Ge 31:10
the planting s and the harvest ....Ex 34:21
season and the harvest s. ....Ex 34:21

give you rains at the right s; ....Le 26:4
was the s for the first grapes. ....Nu 13:20
the harvest s at the beginning.................2Sa 21:9
here, and it's the rainy s.....................Ezr 10:13
they stop flowing in the dry s; ....Job 6:17
The tree produces fruit in s, ...Ps 1:3
on earth has its special s. ....Ec 3:1
she-camel in mating s that runs ....Je 2:23
figs that ripen early in the s. ....Je 24:2
it was not the right s for figs. ....Mk 11:13

SEASONS
used for signs, s, days, and ....Ge 1:14
You made the moon to mark the s,...........Ps 104:19
and spring rains in their s, ...Je 5:24
the times and s of the year.....................Da 2:21
days, months, s, and years.....................Gal 4:10

SEAT
this is the mercy s. Make it ....Ex 25:17
Your s will be empty, so my 1Sa 20:18
S two troublemakers across from 1Ki 21:10
and gave him a s of honor above 2Ki 25:28
The s was covered with purple ....Sng 3:10
and gave him a s of honor above ....Je 52:32
sitting there on the judge's s, ...Mt 27:19
don't take the most important s,.............Lk 14:8
'Give this person your s.'.....................Lk 14:9
go sit in a s that is not...........................Lk 14:10
on the judge's s at the place ....Jn 19:13
was seated on the judge's s.................Ac 25:6
at Caesar's judgment s now, ...Ac 25:10
on the judge's s and commanded ....Ac 25:17
Christ and gave us a s with him ....Eph 2:6
sit here in this good s." ....Jam 2:3

SEATED
brothers were s in front of him ....Ge 43:33
and then they s the king on the 2Ch 23:20
Festus was s on the judge's seat ....Ac 25:6

SEATS
honor above the s of the other 2Ki 25:28
He s them with princes, the ....Ps 113:8
honor above the s of the other ....Je 52:32
the most important s at feasts................Mt 23:6
most important s in the ....Mk 12:39
most important s in the ....Lk 11:43
most important s in the ....Lk 20:46

SEAWEED
s was wrapped around my head. ....Jnh 2:5

SEBA
of Cush were S, Havilah, Sabtah ....Ge 10:7
sons were S, Havilah, Sabta 1Ch 1:9
kings of Sheba and S bring their ....Ps 72:10
I gave Cush and S to make you ....Is 43:3
tall people of S will come to ....Is 45:14

SECACAH
Beth Arabah, Middin, S, ...Jos 15:61

SECOND
to Abraham from heaven a s time ....Ge 22:15
and the s year you will eat what...............2Ki 19:29
s angel said to him, "Run and ....Zch 2:4
horses pulled the s chariot.....................Zch 6:2
can a person be born a s time?" ....Jn 3:4
That was the s miracle Jesus did ....Jn 4:54
the first and s guards and came ....Ac 12:10
Behind the s curtain was a room ....Heb 9:3
priest could go into the s room, ...Heb 9:7
And he will come a s time, ...Heb 9:28
will not be hurt by the s death. ....Rev 2:11
The lake of fire is the s death. ....Rev 20:14

SECOND-FLOOR
stairs went up to the s rooms..................1Ki 6:8

SECRECY
given in s will quiet great .... Pr 21:14

SECRET
the LORD our God has kept s, ... Dt 29:29
not find out the s of Samson's .... Jdg 16:9
Forgive me for my s sins. .... Ps 19:12
you clearly see our s sins. .... Ps 90:8
food eaten in s tastes better." .... Pr 9:17
even what is done in s, the good .... Ec 12:14
God explained the s to Daniel in .... Da 2:19
Your giving should be done in s. .... Mt 6:4
s thing will be made known. .... Lk 8:17
puts it in a s place or under .... Lk 11:33
was a s follower of Jesus, ... Jn 19:38
about what those people do in s. .... Eph 5:12

SECRETARIES
Levites worked as s, officers, ... 2Ch 34:13
month, the royal s were called, ... Est 3:12
time the king's s were called. .... Est 8:9
s wrote out all of Mordecai's .... Est 8:9

SECRETARY
Seraiah was the royal s. 2Sa 8:17
Sheba was the royal s. 2Sa 20:25
the king's royal s and the high 2Ki 12:10
was the royal s, and Joah son 2Ki 18:18
was the royal s, and Joah son 2Ki 18:37
the royal s, and the older 2Ki 19:2
of Meshullam, was the royal s. 2Ki 22:3
said to Shaphan the royal s, ... 2Ki 22:8
the royal s went to the king 2Ki 22:9
the royal s told the king, ... 2Ki 22:10
Shaphan the royal s, and Asaiah 2Ki 22:12
He took the royal s who selected 2Ki 25:19
Shavsha was the royal s. 1Ch 18:16
the tribe of Levi, was the s. 1Ch 24:6
king's royal s and the leading 2Ch 24:11
Jeiel the royal s and Maaseiah 2Ch 26:11
said to Shaphan the royal s, ... 2Ch 34:15
the royal s told the king, ... 2Ch 34:18
Shaphan the royal s, and Asaiah, ... 2Ch 34:20
the governor's s wrote a letter .... Ezr 4:8
Shimshai the s, and their fellow .... Ezr 4:9
the governor and Shimshai the s, ... Ezr 4:17
Shimshai the s and the others. .... Ezr 4:23
was the royal s, and Joah son .... Is 36:3
was the royal s, and Joah son .... Is 36:22
the royal s, and the older .... Is 37:2
son of Shaphan, a royal s. .... Je 36:10
Elishama the royal s; .... Je 36:12
room of Elishama the royal s. .... Je 36:20
the royal s and read it to .... Je 36:21
arrest Baruch the s and Jeremiah .... Je 36:26
to Baruch son of Neriah, his s. .... Je 36:32
house of Jonathan the royal s, ... Je 37:15
house of Jonathan the royal s, ... Je 37:20
the royal s who selected people .... Je 52:25

SECRETARY'S
down to the royal s room in the .... Je 36:12

SECRETLY
did you run away s and trick me? .... Ge 31:27
idol or statue and s sets it up, ... Dt 27:15
cursed who kills a neighbor s." .... Dt 27:24
will eat them s while the enemy .... Dt 28:57
Joshua son of Nun s sent out two .... Jos 2:1
accepted money s to make wrong 1Sa 8:3
Did I ever s accept money to 1Sa 12:3
Jabesh Gilead had s taken them 2Sa 21:12
s sinning against the LORD their 2Ki 17:9
s keeping my guilt to myself. .... Job 31:33
If anyone s says things against .... Ps 101:5
but he is s planning to attack .... Je 9:8

I will cry s because of your .... Je 13:17
so he planned to divorce her s. .... Mt 1:19
So they s urged some men to say, ... Ac 6:11
had come into our group s. .... Gal 2:4
They will s teach things that 2Pe 2:1
Some people have s entered your .... Jud 1:4

SECRETS
and tell you the s of wisdom, ... Job 11:6
Can you understand the s of God? .... Job 11:7
LORD tells his s to those who .... Ps 25:14
can't keep s, but a trustworthy .... Pr 11:13
can't keep s, so avoid people .... Pr 20:19
and learn the s of the earth. .... Je 31:37
you important s you have never .... Je 33:3
Don't keep any s from us. .... Je 38:25
think you can find out all s. .... Eze 28:3
He makes known s that are deep .... Da 2:22
dreams and s and could answer .... Da 5:12
to know the s about the kingdom .... Mt 13:11
but others cannot know these s. .... Mt 13:11
to know the s about the kingdom .... Lk 8:10
things, even the deep s of God. 1Co 2:10
ones God has trusted with his s. 1Co 4:1
what some call Satan's deep s. .... Rev 2:24

SECTION
bowl-shaped s and next to the 1Ki 7:20
taking care of his own s." .... Je 6:3

SECTIONS
Manasseh had ten s of land west .... Jos 17:5
the Jordan River and two more s, ... Jos 17:5

SECU
went to Ramah, to the well at S. 1Sa 19:22

SECUNDUS
Aristarchus and S, from the city .... Ac 20:4

SECURITY
be peace and s in my lifetime." 2Ki 20:19
to pure gold, 'You are my s.' .... Job 31:24
a good person has safety and s. .... Pr 12:3
respect the LORD will have s, ... Pr 14:26
be peace and s in my lifetime." .... Is 39:8

SEED
Every s will produce more of its .... Ge 1:11
Each s grew its own kind of .... Ge 1:12
Isaac planted s in that land, ... Ge 26:12
Give us s to plant so that we .... Ge 47:19
I will give you s and you can .... Ge 47:23
to use as s for the field and as .... Ge 47:24
falls on a s to be planted, ... Le 11:37
planted, that s is still clean. .... Le 11:37
with two different kinds of s. .... Le 19:19
may plant s in your field for .... Le 25:3
must not plant s in your field .... Le 25:4
success when you plant your s, ... Le 26:16
on how much s is needed to plant .... Le 27:16
six bushels of barley s needed. .... Le 27:16
to plant your s and water it, ... Dt 11:10
will plant much s in your field, ... Dt 28:38
hold about thirteen quarts of s. 1Ki 18:32
ten bushels of s will grow only .... Is 5:10
special vine, as a very good s. .... Je 2:21
eagle took some s from the land .... Eze 17:5
So the s became a vine, and its .... Eze 17:6
and s will be planted in you. .... Eze 36:9
farmer went out to plant his s. .... Mt 13:3
planting, some s fell by the .... Mt 13:4
Some s fell on rocky ground, ... Mt 13:5
That s grew very fast, because .... Mt 13:5
Some other s fell among thorny .... Mt 13:7
Some other s fell on good ground .... Mt 13:8
What is the s that fell by the .... Mt 13:19

That **s** is like the person who .... Mt 13:19
And what is the **s** that fell on .... Mt 13:20
That **s** is like the person who .... Mt 13:20
what is the **s** that fell among .... Mt 13:22
That **s** is like the person who .... Mt 13:22
But what is the **s** that fell on .... Mt 13:23
That **s** is like the person who .... Mt 13:23
who planted good **s** in his field. .... Mt 13:24
planted good **s** in your field. .... Mt 13:27
is like a mustard **s** that a man .... Mt 13:31
That **s** is the smallest of all .... Mt 13:32
the good **s** in the field is .... Mt 13:37
and the good **s** are all of God's .... Mt 13:38
planted the bad **s** is the devil. .... Mt 13:39
faith is as big as a mustard **s**, ... Mt 17:20
where you did not sow any **s**. .... Mt 25:24
crops where I did not sow any **s**. .... Mt 25:26
farmer went out to plant his **s**. .... Mk 4:3
planting, some **s** fell by the .... Mk 4:4
s fell on rocky ground where .... Mk 4:5
That **s** grew very fast, because .... Mk 4:5
Some other **s** fell among thorny .... Mk 4:7
Some other **s** fell on good ground .... Mk 4:8
are like the **s** planted on rocky .... Mk 4:16
are like the **s** planted among .... Mk 4:18
are like the **s** planted in the .... Mk 4:20
who plants **s** in the ground. .... Mk 4:26
or awake, the **s** still grows, ... Mk 4:27
of God is like a mustard **s**, ... Mk 4:31
the smallest **s** you plant in the .... Mk 4:31
this **s** grows and becomes the .... Mk 4:32
farmer went out to plant his **s**. .... Lk 8:5
planting, some **s** fell by the .... Lk 8:5
walked on the **s**, and the birds .... Lk 8:5
Some **s** fell on rock, and when it .... Lk 8:6
Some **s** fell among thorny weeds, ... Lk 8:7
And some **s** fell on good ground............ Lk 8:8
means: The **s** is God's message .... Lk 8:11
The **s** that fell beside the road.................. Lk 8:12
The **s** that fell on rock is like .... Lk 8:13
The **s** that fell among the thorny .... Lk 8:14
And the **s** that fell on the good .... Lk 8:15
like a mustard **s** that a man .... Lk 13:19
The **s** grows and becomes a tree, ... Lk 13:19
were the size of a mustard **s**, ... Lk 17:6
it remains only a single **s**. .... Jn 12:24
I planted the **s**, and Apollos 1Co 3:6
planted spiritual **s** among you, ... 1Co 15:36
When you sow a **s**, it must die in 1Co 15:36
What you sow is only a bare **s**, ... 1Co 15:37
each kind of **s** its own body. 1Co 15:38
One who gives **s** to the farmer 2Co 9:10
give you all the **s** you need and 2Co 9:10

SEEDS

make grain for **s** and others to .... Ge 1:11
to make fruits with **s** in them.................. Ge 1:11
with grain for **s** and trees that .... Ge 1:12
that made fruits with **s** in them. .... Ge 1:12
have grain for **s** and all the.................... Ge 1:29
whose fruits have **s** in them. .... Ge 1:29
small white and tasted like .... Ex 16:31
put water on some **s** and a dead, ... Le 11:38
Don't plant **s**, or harvest the .... Le 25:11
we don't plant **s** or gather crops .... Le 25:20
even the **s** or the skin. .... Nu 6:4
manna was like small white **s**. .... Nu 11:7
kinds of **s** in your vineyard. .... Dt 22:9
They planted **s** in the fields and .... Ps 107:37
they carry out the **s** will return .... Ps 126:6
weather will never plant **s**; .... Ec 11:4
send rain for the **s** you plant .... Is 30:23
as you plant **s** near every stream .... Is 32:20

ground, like **s** that are planted .... Is 40:24
making **s** for the farmer and .... Is 55:10
causes the **s** planted in it to .... Is 61:11
and don't plant **s** among thorns.............. Je 4:3
houses, plant **s**, or plant .... Je 35:7
peas, and millet **s**, and put them.............. Eze 4:9
we planted fig **s**, they lie dry .... Joe 1:17
Do you have **s** for crops still in .... Hag 2:19
will plant their **s** in peace, ... Zch 8:12
seed is the smallest of all **s**, ... Mt 13:32
ground and die to make many **s**. .... Jn 12:24

SEEING

It is like **s** the face of God, ... Ge 33:10
without anyone **s** what happened. .... Ex 22:10
You are **s** the shadows of the .... Jdg 9:36
full years without **s** King David. 2Sa 14:28
fly away without my **s** any joy. .... Job 9:25
just **s** it overwhelms people. .... Job 41:9
but after **s** them does not do .... Eze 18:14
S a fig tree beside the road, ... Mt 21:19
Even after **s** this, you still .... Mt 21:32
S a fig tree in leaf from far .... Mk 11:13
S that Jesus gave good answers .... Mk 12:28
S their faith, Jesus said, ... Lk 5:20
and thought they were **s** a ghost. .... Lk 24:37
went, washed, and came back **s**.............. Jn 9:7
believe without **s** me will be .... Jn 20:29
thought he might be **s** a vision. .... Ac 12:9
S the crowd, the Jewish people .... Ac 13:45
of Cyprus, **s** it to the north,.................... Ac 21:3

SEEK

let those who **s** the Lord be 1Ch 16:10
will pray and **s** me and stop 2Ch 7:14
let those who **s** the Lord be .... Ps 105:3
those who enjoy them **s** them. .... Ps 111:2
who are uneducated, **s** wisdom. .... Pr 8:5
and those who **s** me find me. .... Pr 8:17
to do good. **S** justice. Punish .... Is 1:17
They don't **s** justice for the .... Is 1:23
of Judah sent you to **s** my help. .... Je 37:7
hope in him, to those who **s** him. .... La 3:25
S first God's kingdom and what .... Mt 6:33
s God's kingdom, and all your .... Lk 12:31
You should **s** after love, and you.............. 1Co 14:1
s most of all to have the gifts 1Co 14:12

SEEKING

A woman will go **s** a man.".................... Je 31:22
too is actively **s** such people to .... Jn 4:23

SEEM

the spot does not **s** deeper than .... Le 13:4
it and it does not **s** deeper than .... Le 13:31
the sore does not **s** deeper than .... Le 13:32
it does not **s** deeper than the .... Le 13:34
makes wise people **s** blind, ... Dt 16:19
It will **s** as if the Midianites .... Jdg 6:16
all our trouble **s** unimportant to .... Ne 9:32
No wonder my words **s** careless. .... Job 6:3
you began with **s** unimportant, ... Job 8:7
darkness will **s** like morning. .... Job 11:17
and when things **s** to be going .... Job 15:21
Even though they **s** strong, ... Job 24:22
which you **s** to want more than .... Job 36:21
You **s** far from saving me, far .... Ps 22:1
Evil people **s** to do well, but .... Ps 92:7
man's wife may **s** sweet as honey; .... Pr 5:3
Even fools **s** to be wise if they .... Pr 17:28
It can **s** to grow wings and fly .... Pr 23:5
their jaws **s** full of knives. .... Pr 30:14
but they never **s** to get enough .... Ec 6:7
clouds will never **s** to go away. .... Ec 12:2
They **s** to be bathed in cream and .... Sng 5:12

farmland will **s** like a forest. .... Is 29:17
by on the road don't **s** to care. .... La 1:12
It may **s** like a long time,...................... Hab 2:3
it **s** like nothing to you?' .... Hag 2:3
with those who **s** unimportant. .... Rm 12:16
You **s** to think God's church is 1Co 11:22
the body that **s** to be the weaker............. 1Co 12:22
s to be dying, but we continue 2Co 6:9
you by arguments that **s** good, ... Col 2:4
They **s** to be wise, but they are .... Col 2:23

SEEMS

and the sore **s** deeper than the .... Le 13:3
If the spot **s** deeper than the .... Le 13:20
If the white spot **s** deeper than .... Le 13:25
If it **s** deeper than the skin and .... Le 13:30
people as it **s** best to you. .... Est 8:8
in the valley is sweet to them. .... Job 21:33
one side of a story **s** right, ... Pr 18:17
He **s** to be telling us about some............. Ac 17:18
But it **s** to me that God has put 1Co 4:9
and if it **s** good for me to go 1Co 16:4
even if it **s** we have failed. 2Co 13:7

SEEN

I have **s** that you are the best .... Ge 7:1
of the mountains could be **s**. .... Ge 8:5
"Have I really **s** God who sees me?" .... Ge 16:13
she had said and had **s** the ring .... Ge 24:30
The LORD has **s** my troubles. .... Ge 29:32
I have **s** that your father is not .... Ge 31:5
I have **s** all the wrong things .... Ge 31:12
I have **s** God face to face, ... Ge 32:30
cows I have **s** in all the land .... Ge 41:19
and I haven't **s** him since. .... Ge 44:28
him about everything you have **s**. .... Ge 45:13
because I have **s** your face and I............. Ge 46:30
I have **s** the troubles my people .... Ex 3:7
and I have **s** the way the .... Ex 3:9
and I have **s** what has happened............... Ex 3:16
them and had **s** their troubles, ... Ex 4:31
or ancestors have ever **s**— .... Ex 10:6
one of you has **s** what I did to................ Ex 19:4
yourselves have **s** that I talked .... Ex 20:22
Moses, "I have **s** these people, ... Ex 32:9
But my face must not be **s**." .... Ex 33:23
with you or even be **s** any place .... Ex 34:3
what he has **s** or what he knows.............. Le 5:1
'I have **s** something like mildew .... Le 14:35
He has even **s** the form of the................ Nu 12:8
that you were **s** face to face. .... Nu 14:14
into the land he has already **s**, ... Nu 14:24
After you have **s** it, you will .... Nu 27:13
You have **s** for yourself all that .... Dt 3:21
You have **s** for yourselves what .... Dt 4:3
forget the things you have **s**. .... Dt 4:9
Today we have **s** that a person .... Dt 5:24
nor your ancestors had ever **s**. .... Dt 8:3
your ancestors had never **s**. .... Dt 8:16
you have **s** with your own eyes. .... Dt 10:21
you have **s** will scare you. .... Dt 28:67
You have **s** everything the LORD .... Dt 29:2
have **s** what the LORD has done............... Jos 23:3
Joshua who had **s** what the LORD .... Jos 24:31
and who had **s** what great things .... Jdg 2:7
I have **s** the angel of the LORD .... Jdg 6:22
said, "We have **s** God, so we will .... Jdg 13:22
We have **s** the land, and it .... Jdg 18:9
I have **s** the suffering of my 1Sa 9:16
I have **s** a son of Jesse of 1Sa 16:18
David and his men had been **s**. 1Sa 22:6
staying and who has **s** him there. 1Sa 23:22
You have **s** something with your.............. 1Sa 24:10
did not want to be **s** going into 2Sa 17:17

tell the king what you have **s**." 2Sa 18:21
foundations of the earth were **s**. 2Sa 22:16
I have come and **s** it with my own 1Ki 10:7
in or been **s** since that time. 1Ki 10:12
lived and told what they had **s**. 1Ki 13:25
I will be **s** by Ahab today." 1Ki 18:15
The LORD had **s** the troubles of 2Ki 13:4
The LORD had **s** how the 2Ki 14:26
your prayer and **s** your tears, ... 2Ki 20:5
all the hated gods **s** in the land 2Ki 23:24
I have come and **s** it with my own 2Ch 9:6
Judah had ever **s** such beautiful 2Ch 9:11
But God has **s** the cruel way you 2Ch 28:9
leaders who had **s** the first .... Ezr 3:12
what they had **s** and what .... Est 9:26
I have **s** a fool succeed, but I .... Job 5:3
Now my eyes have **s** all this; .... Job 13:1
I will tell you what I have **s**. .... Job 15:17
You have all **s** this yourselves. .... Job 27:12
the falcon has not **s** it................. Job 28:7
Everybody has **s** it; people look .... Job 36:25
Have you **s** the gates of the deep .... Job 38:17
of the snow or **s** the storehouses .... Job 38:22
but now my eyes have **s** you. .... Job 42:5
foundations of the earth were **s**. .... Ps 18:15
I have never **s** good people left .... Ps 37:25
and now we have **s** that God will .... Ps 48:8
I have **s** my enemies defeated. .... Ps 54:7
I have **s** you in the Temple and .... Ps 63:2
Temple and have **s** your strength .... Ps 63:2
have **s** your victory march; .... Ps 68:24
but your footprints were not **s**. .... Ps 77:19
his glory will be **s** in our land. .... Ps 85:9
We have **s** years of trouble................. Ps 90:15
the earth have **s** God's power to .... Ps 98:3
there his glory will be **s**. .... Ps 102:16
I thought about what I had **s**; .... Pr 24:32
Because of something you have **s**, ... Pr 25:7
they have not **s** the evil that is .... Ec 4:3
I have **s** real misery here on .... Ec 5:13
I have **s** what is best for people .... Ec 5:18
I have **s** something else wrong .... Ec 6:1
life I have **s** both of these: .... Ec 7:15
have **s** good people die in spite .... Ec 7:15
I have **s** servants ride horses .... Ec 10:7
"Have you **s** the one I love?" .... Sng 3:3
pure, but I have **s** the King, the .... Is 6:5
now they have **s** a great light.................. Is 9:2
I have **s** a terrible vision....................... Is 21:2
your prayer and **s** your tears. .... Is 38:5
Israel, you have **s** much, but you .... Is 42:20
I have **s** what they have done,............... Is 57:18
No one has ever **s** a God besides .... Is 64:4
no one has **s** that happen. .... Is 66:8
what I have done nor **s** my glory. .... Is 66:19
to me, "You have **s** correctly. .... Je 1:12
I have **s** the terrible things you .... Je 13:27
And I have **s** the prophets of .... Je 23:14
they have **s** her nakedness....................... La 1:8
We have finally **s** it happen." .... La 2:16
am a man who has **s** the suffering .... La 3:1
you have **s** how I have been .... La 3:59
You have **s** how my enemies took .... La 3:60
to be **s** by all who pass by. .... Eze 5:14
there, as I had **s** on the plain. .... Eze 8:4
have you **s** what the elders of .... Eze 8:12
Have you **s** each man in the room .... Eze 8:12
hand could be **s** under the wings .... Eze 10:8
I had **s** by the Kebar River. .... Eze 10:15
creatures I had **s** under the God .... Eze 10:20
as the ones I had **s** by the Kebar. .... Eze 10:22
then the vision I had **s** ended.................. Eze 11:24
and have not **s** a vision from me! .... Eze 13:3

S

a son who has s all his father's .... Eze 18:14
it was s, because it was tall..................... Eze 19:11
idols you have s and liked. .... Eze 20:7
sins are s in all the things .... Eze 21:24
the vision I had s when the LORD .... Eze 43:3
the vision I had s by the Kebar .... Eze 43:3
sky and could be s from anywhere........... Da 4:11
and it could be s from all over .... Da 4:20
from any animal I had s before, ... Da 7:7
two horns that I had s standing .... Da 8:6
I had s him in my last vision. .... Da 9:21
I have s horrible things in .... Hos 6:10
have s Israel, like Tyre, given .... Hos 9:13
that they had s in the east went .... Mt 2:9
front of people to be s by them. .... Mt 6:1
to your Father who cannot be s. .... Mt 6:6
We have never s anything like .... Mt 9:33
what they had s until the Son .... Mt 17:9
he will be s by everyone, like .... Mt 24:27
have never s anything like this! .... Mk 2:12
what they had s until the Son .... Mk 9:9
She said that she had s him, ... Mk 16:11
those who had s him after he had .... Mk 16:14
and they knew he had s a vision .... Lk 1:22
When they had s him, they told .... Lk 2:17
everything they had s and heard. .... Lk 2:20
eyes I have s your salvation, ... Lk 2:30
"Today we have s amazing things!" .... Lk 5:26
at that time what they had s. .... Lk 9:36
for all the miracles they had s. .... Lk 19:37
us that they had s a vision of .... Lk 24:23
No one has ever s God. But God.............. Jn 1:18
I have s this happen, and I tell .... Jn 1:34
we tell about what we have s, ... Jn 3:11
tells what he has s and heard, ... Jn 3:32
They had s all the things he did .... Jn 4:45
his voice or s what he looks .... Jn 5:37
you have s me and still don't .... Jn 6:36
No one has s the Father except .... Jn 6:46
only he has s the Father. .... Jn 6:46
You have never s Abraham! .... Jn 8:57
who had earlier s this man .... Jn 9:8
said to him, "You have s him. .... Jn 9:37
know him, and you have s him." .... Jn 14:7
Whoever has s me has seen the .... Jn 14:9
has seen me has s the Father. .... Jn 14:9
now they have s what I have done .... Jn 15:24
Father and not being s anymore. .... Jn 16:10
about what we have s and heard." .... Ac 4:20
I have s the troubles my people .... Ac 7:34
what they had s Jesus do and .... Ac 8:25
Saul has s a vision in which a .... Ac 9:12
them that Saul had s the Lord on .... Ac 9:27
He has s that you give to the .... Ac 10:4
prayer and has s that you give .... Ac 10:31
to life and caused him to be s, ... Ac 10:40
After Paul had s the vision,.................... Ac 16:10
because they had s Trophimus, ... Ac 21:29
about what you have s and heard. .... Ac 22:15
that you have s and the things .... Ac 26:16
small and great, what I have s. .... Ac 26:22
They have s the glory of God,................. Rm 9:4
No one has ever s this, and no 1Co 2:9
their work will be clearly s, ... 1Co 3:13
I have s Jesus our Lord. 1Co 9:1
Spirit can be s in each person, ... 1Co 12:7
and that he was s by Peter and 1Co 15:5
Jesus was s by more than five 1Co 15:6
Then he was s by James and later 1Co 15:7
Last of all he was s by me— 1Co 15:8
can also be s in our bodies.................... 2Co 4:10
of Jesus can be s in our bodies 2Co 4:11
that can be s rather than what 2Co 5:12

earth, things s and unseen, all .... Col 1:16
and others who have never s me. .... Col 2:1
who cannot be s, the only God, ... 1Ti 1:17
in spirit, and s by angels. 1Ti 3:16
progress may be s by everyone. 1Ti 4:15
sins of others are s only later.................. 1Ti 5:24
are not easily s cannot stay 1Ti 5:25
one has ever s God, or can see 1Ti 6:16
by something that cannot be s. .... Heb 11:3
You have not s Christ, but still 1Pe 1:8
examined and s how good the Lord 1Pe 2:3
I have s Christ's sufferings,..................... 1Pe 5:1
we have s with our own eyes, ... 1Jn 1:1
to you what we have s and heard, ... 1Jn 1:3
No one has ever s God, but if we 1Jn 4:12
We have s and can testify that 1Jn 4:14
whom they have s, cannot love 1Jn 4:20
God, whom they have never s. 1Jn 4:20
has told everything he has s. .... Rev 1:2
people could be s in his temple. .... Rev 11:19

SEER

would say, "Let's go to the s."................. 1Sa 9:9
in the past he was called a s. 1Sa 9:9
asked them, "Is the s here?" 1Sa 9:11
begin eating until the s comes, ... 1Sa 9:13
Samuel answered, "I am the s. 1Sa 9:19
the priest, "Aren't you a s? 2Sa 15:27
who was a prophet and David's s. 2Sa 24:11
prophet and s to warn Israel 2Ki 17:13
and Samuel the s chose these men........... 1Ch 9:22
said to Gad, who was David's s, ... 1Ch 21:9
were sons of Heman, David's s. 1Ch 25:5
had been given by Samuel the s, ... 1Ch 26:28
in the records of Samuel the s, ... 1Ch 29:29
and the records of Gad the s. 1Ch 29:29
in the visions of Iddo the s,..................... 2Ch 9:29
the prophet and Iddo the s,..................... 2Ch 12:15
time Hanani the s came to Asa 2Ch 16:7
Hanani the s because of what.................. 2Ch 16:10
son of Hanani, a s, went out 2Ch 19:2
was the king's s, and Nathan was 2Ch 29:25
David and Asaph the s had used. 2Ch 29:30
and Jeduthun, the king's s. 2Ch 35:15
said to Amos, "S, go back right .... Am 7:12

SEER'S

tell me where the s house is." 1Sa 9:18

SEERS

what the s said to him in the 2Ch 33:18
written in the book of the s. 2Ch 33:19
heads. (The s are your heads.................... Is 29:10
They tell the s, "Don't see any .... Is 30:10
The s will be ashamed; .... Mic 3:7

SEGUB

and it cost the life of S, ... 1Ki 16:34
and she had a son named S. 1Ch 2:21
S was the father of Jair. 1Ch 2:22

SEIR

the area called S in the country .... Ge 32:3
were the sons of S the Horite,................. Ge 36:20
These sons of S were the leaders .... Ge 36:21
on the Mount S road takes eleven .... Dt 1:2
west and went toward Mount S. .... Jos 15:10
Mount S and all Edom, you will .... Eze 35:15

SEIR'S

S sons were Lotan, Shobal,..................... 1Ch 1:38

SEIRAH

by the statues and went to S. .... Jdg 3:26

SEIZE

said this, they tried to s him. .... Jn 7:30

SEIZED
who had s a well of water .... Ge 21:25
' I s him and killed him at 2Sa 4:10

SEIZES
An evil spirit s my son, and .... Lk 9:39

SELA
Scorpion Pass to S and beyond. .... Jdg 1:36
He also took the city of S. 2Ki 14:7
Send a lamb from S through the .... Is 16:1
living in S should sing for .... Is 42:11

SELECTED
secretary who s people for the 2Ki 25:19
secretary who s people for the .... Je 52:25

SELED
Nadab's sons were S and Appaim. 1Ch 2:30
S died without having children. 1Ch 2:30

SELEUCIA
Spirit, went to the city of S. .... Ac 13:4

SELF-CONTROL
They teach wisdom and s; .... Pr 1:2
wisdom, s, and understanding. .... Pr 23:23
living right, s, and the time .... Ac 24:25
you because of a lack of s. 1Co 7:5
the games use s so they can win 1Co 9:25
gentleness, s. There is no law .... Gal 5:23
we should be alert and have s. 1Th 5:6
clothes that show respect and s, ... 1Ti 2:9
love, and holiness, with s. 1Ti 2:15
spirit of power and love and s. 2Ti 1:7
minds for service and have s. 1Pe 1:13
and to your knowledge, add s; 2Pe 1:6
and to your s, add patience; 2Pe 1:6

SELF-CONTROLLED
to be wise and s and will teach .... Pr 1:3
He must be s, wise, respected by 1Ti 3:2
They must be s and trustworthy 1Ti 3:11
live right, and be holy and s. .... Tit 1:8
men to be s, serious, wise, ... Tit 2:2

SELFISH
not be s or greedy toward them. .... Dt 15:7
They are s and brag about .... Ps 17:10
do not control their s desires. .... Ps 73:7
greed kills s people. .... Pr 1:19
people are s and hate all good .... Pr 18:1
Don't eat the food of s people; .... Pr 23:6
S people are always worrying. .... Pr 23:7
S people are in a hurry to get .... Pr 28:22
hearts desire their s profits. .... Eze 33:31
But other people are s. .... Rm 2:8
not rude, is not s, and does not 1Co 13:5
jealousy, anger, s fighting, ... 2Co 12:20
angry, being s, making people .... Gal 5:20
given up their old s feelings .... Gal 5:24
about Christ for s and wrong .... Php 1:17
wrong, being s, or becoming .... Tit 1:7
But if you are s and have bitter .... Jam 3:14
come from the s desires that war .... Jam 4:1

SELFISHNESS
and nothing escapes their s. .... Job 20:20
of sin, evil, s, and hatred. .... Rm 1:29
do not let s or pride be your .... Php 2:3
we had no s to hide from you. 1Th 2:5
jealousy and s are, there will .... Jam 3:16

SELL
You must s me your rights as the .... Ge 25:31
s him to those Ishmaelites. .... Ge 37:27
s the oil and pay what you owe. 2Ki 4:7
they s people who have done .... Am 2:6
be over so we can s grain? .... Am 8:5

will even s the wheat that was .... Am 8:6
then go and s your possessions .... Mt 19:21
same sex, who s slaves, who tell. 1Ti 1:10
one could buy or s without this .... Rev 13:17

SELLER
buyer be happy or the s be sad, ... Eze 7:12

SELLERS
twice traders and s of all kinds .... Ne 13:20
to buyers and s, to those who .... Is 24:2
S will not return to the land .... Eze 7:13
be any buyers or s in the Temple .... Zch 14:21

SELLS
If a man s his daughter as a .... Ex 21:7
clothes and s them and provides .... Pr 31:24

SEMAKIAH
Obed, Elzabad, Elihu, and S. 1Ch 26:7
and S were skilled workers. 1Ch 26:7

SEMEIN
Mattathias was the son of S. .... Lk 3:26
S was the son of Josech. .... Lk 3:26

SEMEN
If s goes out from a man, ... Le 15:16
with a woman and s comes out, ... Le 15:18
unclean from s coming out of his .... Le 15:32
a dead body, from his own s, ... Le 22:4

SENAAH
of S—3,630. .... Ezr 2:35
of S—3,930. .... Ne 7:38

SEND
' The LORD will s his angel .... Ge 24:7
I will s you a young goat from .... Ge 38:17
Please, Lord, s someone else." .... Ex 4:13
I will s swarms of flies into .... Ex 8:21
will s terror ahead of you that .... Ex 23:28
I will s an angel to lead you, ... Ex 33:2
s me to the city in Judah where .... Ne 2:5
It pleased the king to s me, ... Ne 2:6
S some to people who have none, ... Ne 8:10
he s you help from his Temple .... Ps 20:2
S me your light and truth to .... Ps 43:3
You s rain to the plowed fields; .... Ps 65:10
S the lightning and scatter my .... Ps 144:6
voice, saying, "Whom can I s? .... Is 6:8
So I said, "Here I am. S me!" .... Is 6:8
deaf than the messenger I s. .... Is 42:19
' You must go everywhere I s you, ... Je 1:7
I did not s them. They say, ... Je 14:15
and I will s my anger against .... Eze 7:3
I will s fire on Magog and those .... Eze 39:6
So I will s a fire on the walls .... Am 1:7
says, "I will s my messenger, ... Mal 3:1
But I will s you Elijah the .... Mal 4:5
that he will s more workers to .... Mt 9:38
'I will s my messenger ahead of .... Mt 11:10
S the people away so they can go .... Mt 14:15
loud trumpet to s his angels all .... Mt 24:31
begged Jesus, "S us into the .... Mk 5:12
and got ready to s them out two .... Mk 6:7
in pieces and s him away to be .... Lk 12:46
I will s you what my Father has .... Lk 24:49
God did not s his Son into the .... Jn 3:17
I will s the Helper to you. .... Jn 16:7
Father sent me, I now s you." .... Jn 20:21
'S some men to Joppa and invite .... Ac 11:13
Christ did not s me to baptize. 1Co 1:17
Lord Jesus to s Timothy to you .... Php 2:19
and s Timothy to you. Timothy, ... 1Th 3:2
in a book and s it to the seven .... Rev 1:11

S

SENDING

and he **s** rain to those who do.................. Mt 5:45
together with me, **s** greetings,.................. Rm 16:21
Christ Jesus, **s** greetings to you .... Phm 1:23
like you, **s** you greetings. 1Pe 5:13

SENEH

on the other side was named **S**. 1Sa 14:4

SENIR

but the Amorites call it **S**. .... Dt 3:9
to Baal Hermon, **S**, and Mount 1Ch 5:23
tops of Mount **S** and Mount Hermon .... Sng 4:8

SENNACHERIB

S king of Assyria attacked all.................. 2Ki 18:13
Hezekiah knew that **S** had come to 2Ch 32:2

SENSE

Israel has no **s**; they do not .... Dt 32:28
it make more **s** just to do it? 2Ki 5:13
not give it a share of good **s**. .... Job 39:17
knowledge and **s** to the young. .... Pr 1:4
Good **s** will protect you; .... Pr 2:11
hold on to wisdom and good **s**. .... Pr 3:21
to use good **s**, and watch what .... Pr 5:2
takes part in adultery has no **s**; .... Pr 6:32
with good **s** know what I say .... Pr 8:9
also have knowledge and good **s**. .... Pr 8:12
I have good **s** and advice, and I .... Pr 8:14
without good **s** find fault with.................. Pr 11:12
without good **s** is like a gold .... Pr 11:22
wise person acts with good **s**,.................. Pr 13:16
are selfish and hate all good **s**. .... Pr 18:1
not use good **s** will end up among .... Pr 21:16
vineyard of someone with no **s**. .... Pr 24:30
foolish people who have no **s**.................. Je 5:21
would no longer have a **s** of sin............... Heb 10:2

SENSELESS

I was **s** and stupid. .... Ps 73:22

SENSIBLE

Be **s**, and then we can talk...................... Job 18:2
seven people who give **s** answers. .... Pr 26:16
My words are true and **s**. .... Ac 26:25

SENT

he **s** out a raven. It flew here .... Ge 8:7
Then Noah **s** out a dove to find .... Ge 8:8
days Noah again **s** out the dove .... Ge 8:10
days later he **s** the dove out .... Ge 8:12
But the LORD **s** terrible diseases .... Ge 12:17
the king **s** for Abram and said, ... Ge 12:18
so he has **s** us to destroy it." .... Ge 19:13
The LORD **s** a rain of burning .... Ge 19:24
he **s** some servants to take her. .... Ge 20:2
them to Hagar and **s** her away. .... Ge 21:14
then **s** them to the East to be .... Ge 25:6
good to you and **s** you away in .... Ge 26:29
Then Isaac **s** them away, and they .... Ge 26:31
So she **s** for Jacob and said to .... Ge 27:42
So Isaac **s** Jacob to Northwest .... Ge 28:5
Jacob and **s** him to Northwest .... Ge 28:6
I could have **s** you away with joy .... Ge 31:27
you would have **s** me away with............... Ge 31:42
Jacob **s** messengers to Esau, ... Ge 32:3
He **s** them as a gift to you, ... Ge 32:18
So Jacob **s** the gifts to Esau, ... Ge 32:21
s his family and everything he .... Ge 32:23
Joseph's father **s** him from the .... Ge 37:14
Judah **s** his friend Hirah with .... Ge 38:20
I **s** her the goat as I promised, ... Ge 38:23
she **s** a message to her .... Ge 38:25
he **s** for all the magicians and.................. Ge 41:8
brothers were **s** away with their .... Ge 44:3
God **s** me here ahead of you to .... Ge 45:5

So God **s** me here ahead of you to .... Ge 45:7
So it was not you who **s** me here, ... Ge 45:8
Joseph also **s** his father ten.................... Ge 45:23
Joseph had **s** to carry him back .... Ge 45:27
wagons the king of Egypt had **s**. .... Ge 46:5
Jacob **s** Judah ahead of him to .... Ge 46:28
So they **s** a message to Joseph .... Ge 50:16
king of Egypt **s** for the nurses .... Ex 1:18
she **s** her slave girl to get it. .... Ex 2:5
of your ancestors **s** me to you.' .... Ex 3:13
tell them, 'I AM **s** me to you.'" .... Ex 3:14
of Jacob. He **s** me to you.' This .... Ex 3:15
to him when he **s** him to Egypt. .... Ex 4:28
Is this why you **s** me here? .... Ex 5:22
God of the Hebrews, **s** me to you. .... Ex 7:16
the frogs he had **s** to the king. .... Ex 8:12
king **s** people to see what had.................. Ex 9:7
the LORD **s** thunder and hail,.................. Ex 9:23
The king **s** for Moses and Aaron .... Ex 9:27
When the king **s** the people out .... Ex 13:17
Moses had **s** his wife Zipporah .... Ex 18:2
Jethro had **s** a message ahead to .... Ex 18:6
So Moses **s** his father-in-law on .... Ex 18:27
Then Moses **s** young Israelite men .... Ex 24:5
Then Moses **s** this command .... Ex 36:6
this goat will be **s** out into the .... Le 16:10
LORD's command and **s** those .... Nu 5:4
LORD **s** a strong wind from the .... Nu 11:31
s command and **s** the Israelite .... Nu 13:3
the men Moses **s** to explore the .... Nu 13:16
Moses **s** them to explore Canaan .... Nu 13:17
went to the land where you **s** us, ... Nu 13:27
The men Moses had **s** to explore .... Nu 14:36
that the LORD has **s** me to do all .... Nu 16:28
Moses **s** messengers to the king .... Nu 20:14
he heard us and **s** an angel to .... Nu 20:16
So the LORD **s** them poisonous .... Nu 21:6
The Israelites **s** messengers to .... Nu 21:21
After Moses **s** spies to the town .... Nu 21:32
He **s** messengers to Balaam son of .... Nu 22:5
s them to me with this message:............... Nu 22:10
So Balak **s** other leaders—this .... Nu 22:15
When you **s** messengers to me, ... Nu 24:12
Moses **s** those men to war; .... Nu 31:6
I **s** them from Kadesh Barnea to .... Nu 32:8
The spies we **s** have made us .... Dt 1:28
s messengers from the desert of .... Dt 2:26
Then the LORD **s** you away from .... Dt 9:23
must not be **s** to war or be given .... Dt 24:5
your God has **s** you away to other .... Dt 30:1
and **s** him to do signs and .... Dt 34:11
of Nun secretly **s** out two spies .... Jos 2:1
king of Jericho **s** this message .... Jos 2:3
So she **s** them away, and they .... Jos 2:21
hid the two spies we **s** out. .... Jos 6:17
the men he had **s** to spy out .... Jos 6:25
Joshua **s** some men from Jericho .... Jos 7:2
So Joshua **s** men who ran to the............... Jos 7:22
men and **s** them out at night. .... Jos 8:3
Then Joshua **s** them to wait in .... Jos 8:9
king of Jerusalem **s** a message to .... Jos 10:3
The Gibeonites **s** this message to .... Jos 10:6
he **s** messages to Jobab king of .... Jos 11:1
s messages to the kings in the .... Jos 11:2
He **s** a message to the king of.................. Jos 11:2
He **s** messages to the Amorites, ... Jos 11:3
Jabin also **s** one to the Hivites, ... Jos 11:3
s me to look at the land where .... Jos 14:7
as I was the day Moses **s** me out, ... Jos 14:11
And he **s** them to their homes and .... Jos 22:7
The Israelites **s** Phinehas son of .... Jos 22:13
They also **s** one leader from each .... Jos 22:14
Then I **s** Moses and Aaron to .... Jos 24:5

king s for Balaam son of Beor .... Jos 24:9
I s terror ahead of you to force .... Jos 24:12
Then Joshua s the people back to .... Jos 24:28
They s some spies to Bethel .... Jdg 1:23
Then Joshua s the people back to .... Jdg 2:6
for them and s judges to save .... Jdg 2:18
the LORD s someone to save them. .... Jdg 3:9
he s someone to save them. .... Jdg 3:15
Israel s Ehud to give Eglon king .... Jdg 3:15
Ehud s away the people who had .... Jdg 3:18
Then he s all of his servants .... Jdg 3:19
Deborah s a message to Barak son .... Jdg 4:6
the LORD s a prophet to them. .... Jdg 6:8
He s messengers to all of .... Jdg 6:35
He also s messengers to the .... Jdg 6:35
Gideon s the rest of Israel to .... Jdg 7:8
Gideon s messengers through all .... Jdg 7:24
God s an evil spirit to make .... Jdg 9:23
So God s the evil spirit to .... Jdg 9:24
He s secret messengers to .... Jdg 9:31
Jephthah s messengers to the .... Jdg 11:12
Jephthah s the messengers to the .... Jdg 11:14
Israel s messengers to the king .... Jdg 11:17
s the same message to the king .... Jdg 11:17
Then Israel s messengers to .... Jdg 11:19
So he s her away for two .... Jdg 11:38
they s thirty friends to be with .... Jdg 14:11
s a message to the Philistine .... Jdg 16:18
slave woman and s her outside to .... Jdg 19:25
Then he s a part to each area of .... Jdg 19:29
parts and s one part to each .... Jdg 20:6
of Israel s men throughout .... Jdg 20:12
of Israelites s twelve thousand .... Jdg 21:10
of Israelites s a message to .... Jdg 21:13
So the people s men to Shiloh. 1Sa 4:4
the Philistines s the Ark of God 1Sa 5:10
Philistines had s these gold 1Sa 6:17
They s one model for each 1Sa 6:17
Philistines also s gold models 1Sa 6:18
Then they s messengers to the 1Sa 6:21
So the LORD s Moses and Aaron, ... 1Sa 12:8
So the LORD s Gideon, Barak, ... 1Sa 12:11
day the LORD s thunder and rain 1Sa 12:18
Saul s the other men in the army 1Sa 13:2
The LORD s me to appoint you 1Sa 15:1
And he s you on a mission 1Sa 15:18
So Jesse s and had his youngest 1Sa 16:12
Then Saul s messengers to Jesse, ... 1Sa 16:19
and he s them with his son David 1Sa 16:20
Saul s a message to Jesse, ... 1Sa 16:22
to Saul, and he s for David. 1Sa 17:31
Saul s David to fight in 1Sa 18:5
He s David away and made him 1Sa 18:13
Saul s messengers to David's 1Sa 19:11
Saul s messengers to take David 1Sa 19:14
Saul s them back to see David, ... 1Sa 19:15
So he s messengers to capture 1Sa 19:20
the news, he s more messengers, ... 1Sa 19:21
Then he s messengers a third 1Sa 19:21
Then the king s for the priest 1Sa 22:11
So he s ten young men and told 1Sa 25:5
David s messengers from the 1Sa 25:14
didn't see the men you s. 1Sa 25:25
of Israel, who s you to meet me. 1Sa 25:32
Then David s a message to 1Sa 25:39
David s us to take you so you 1Sa 25:40
he s out spies and learned for 1Sa 26:4
he s some of the things he had 1Sa 30:26
David also s some things to the 1Sa 30:27
Then they s messengers through 1Sa 31:9
So David s messengers to the men 2Sa 2:5
Then Abner s messengers to ask 2Sa 3:12
David s messengers to Saul's 2Sa 3:14

So Ish-Bosheth s men to take 2Sa 3:15
Abner s this message to the 2Sa 3:17
he s messengers after Abner, ... 2Sa 3:26
the city of Tyre s messengers to 2Sa 5:11
So Toi s his son Joram to greet 2Sa 8:10
So David s his messengers to 2Sa 10:2
David's then to study the city 2Sa 10:3
the hips. Then he s them away. 2Sa 10:4
he s messengers to meet his 2Sa 10:5
he s Joab with the whole army. 2Sa 10:7
Israel and s them out to fight 2Sa 10:9
Then he s them out to fight the 2Sa 10:10
Hadadezer s messengers to bring 2Sa 10:16
to war, David s out Joab, his 2Sa 11:1
So David s his servants to find 2Sa 11:3
So David s messengers to bring 2Sa 11:4
pregnant and s a word to David, ... 2Sa 11:5
So David s a message to Joab: 2Sa 11:6
And Joab s Uriah to David. 2Sa 11:6
and the king s a gift to him. 2Sa 11:8
to Joab and s it by Uriah. 2Sa 11:14
Then Joab s David a complete 2Sa 11:18
David's servants to bring her to 2Sa 11:27
The LORD s Nathan to David. 2Sa 12:1
The LORD s word through Nathan 2Sa 12:25
Joab s messengers to David and 2Sa 12:27
David s for Tamar in the palace, ... 2Sa 13:7
So Joab s messengers to Tekoa to 2Sa 14:2
who have been s away will not 2Sa 14:14
Then Absalom s for Joab so he 2Sa 14:29
Absalom s a message a second 2Sa 14:29
to Joab, "I s a message to you 2Sa 14:32
But he s secret messengers 2Sa 15:10
sacrifices, he s for Ahithophel, ... 2Sa 15:12
He s the troops out in three 2Sa 18:2
When Joab s me, I saw some great 2Sa 18:29
King David s a message to Zadok 2Sa 19:11
s a message to the king that 2Sa 19:14
should tell the LORD who s me." 2Sa 24:13
So the LORD s a terrible disease 2Sa 24:15
King David s Zadok the priest, ... 1Ki 1:44
King Solomon s some men to get 1Ki 1:53
Next the king s for Shimei. 1Ki 2:36
Solomon s for Shimei and said, ... 1Ki 2:42
The king s his servants to get a 1Ki 3:24
of all nations s them to him, ... 1Ki 4:34
he s his messengers to Solomon. 1Ki 5:1
Solomon s this message back to 1Ki 5:2
Then Hiram s back this message 1Ki 5:8
I received the message you s, ... 1Ki 5:8
He s a group of ten thousand men 1Ki 5:14
King Solomon s to Tyre and had 1Ki 7:13
day Solomon s the people home. 1Ki 8:66
Hiram had s Solomon about nine 1Ki 9:14
so he s them to serve in these 1Ki 9:27
After the people s for him, ... 1Ki 12:3
Rehoboam s him to the people 1Ki 12:18
So the LORD s a lion to kill 1Ki 13:26
Then he s them to Ben-Hadad son 1Ki 15:18
so he s the commanders of his 1Ki 15:20
King Ahab s for Obadiah, who was 1Ki 18:3
the king has s people to every 1Ki 18:10
So Jezebel s a messenger to 1Ki 19:2
The king s messengers into the 1Ki 20:2
Then Ben-Hadad s another message 1Ki 20:10
Ben-Hadad s out scouts who told 1Ki 20:17
Then she s them to the elders 1Ki 21:8
Then the leaders s a message to 1Ki 21:14
He s messengers and told them, ... 2Ki 1:2
the messengers s by the king. 2Ki 1:3
to the king who s you and tell 2Ki 1:6
Then he s a captain with his 2Ki 1:9
Ahaziah s another captain and 2Ki 1:11

Ahaziah then **s** a third captain 2Ki 1:13
'You have **s** messengers to ask 2Ki 1:16
the LORD has **s** me to Jericho." 2Ki 2:4
The LORD has **s** me to the Jordan 2Ki 2:6
So they **s** fifty men who looked 2Ki 2:17
He also **s** messengers to 2Ki 3:7
he **s** the king this message: 2Ki 5:8
Elisha **s** Naaman a messenger who 2Ki 5:10
master has **s** me. He said, 'Two 2Ki 5:22
s a message to the king of 2Ki 6:9
the king **s** horses, chariots, ... 2Ki 6:14
drank, the king **s** them away, and 2Ki 6:23
king **s** a messenger to Elisha, ... 2Ki 6:32
king **s** them after the Aramean 2Ki 7:14
king of Aram **s** me to you. 2Ki 8:9
Then Joram **s** out a second 2Ki 9:19
letters and **s** them to Samaria 2Ki 10:1
the guardians **s** a message to 2Ki 10:5
in baskets and **s** them to Jehu at 2Ki 10:7
Then Jehu **s** word through all 2Ki 10:21
year Jehoiada **s** for the 2Ki 11:4
Joash **s** all this treasure to 2Ki 12:18
Amaziah **s** messengers to Jehoash 2Ki 14:8
in Lebanon **s** a message to a 2Ki 14:9
but they **s** men after him to 2Ki 14:19
Ahaz **s** messengers to 2Ki 16:7
and he **s** these as a gift to the 2Ki 16:8
captured it and **s** all its people 2Ki 16:9
and he **s** plans and a pattern of 2Ki 16:10
King Ahaz had **s** him from 2Ki 16:11
so he **s** lions among them which 2Ki 17:25
You **s** foreigners into the cities 2Ki 17:26
is why he has **s** lions among them 2Ki 17:26
king of Judah **s** a message to the 2Ki 18:14
of Assyria **s** out his supreme 2Ki 18:17
so the king **s** Eliakim, Shebna, ... 2Ki 18:18
He **s** me to speak also to those 2Ki 18:27
Hezekiah **s** Eliakim, the palace 2Ki 19:2
king of Assyria **s** his field 2Ki 19:4
he **s** messengers to Hezekiah, ... 2Ki 19:9
Isaiah son of Amoz **s** a message 2Ki 19:20
You have **s** your messengers to 2Ki 19:23
He **s** letters and a gift to 2Ki 20:12
s Shaphan to the Temple of the 2Ki 22:3
Tell the man who **s** you to me, ... 2Ki 22:15
who **s** you to ask the LORD, ' 2Ki 22:18
sight, as I have **s** Israel away. 2Ki 23:27
The LORD **s** raiding parties from 2Ki 24:2
home when the LORD **s** Judah and 1Ch 6:15
Then they **s** messengers through 1Ch 10:9
the city of Tyre **s** messengers to 1Ch 14:1
He also **s** cedar logs, ... 1Ch 14:1
Toi **s** his son Hadoram to greet 1Ch 18:10
So David **s** messengers to 1Ch 19:2
David **s** them to study the land 1Ch 19:3
the hips. Then he **s** them away. 1Ch 19:4
he **s** messengers to meet them, ... 1Ch 19:5
and the Ammonites **s** about 1Ch 19:6
he **s** Joab with the whole army. 1Ch 19:8
Israel and **s** them out to fight 1Ch 19:10
they **s** messengers to bring other 1Ch 19:16
should tell the LORD who **s** me." 1Ch 21:12
So the LORD **s** a terrible disease 1Ch 21:14
God **s** an angel to destroy 1Ch 21:15
Solomon **s** this message to Hiram 2Ch 2:3
month Solomon **s** the people home, ... 2Ch 7:10
and Solomon **s** Israelites to live 2Ch 8:2
Hiram **s** ships to Solomon that 2Ch 8:18
ships that he **s** out to trade, ... 2Ch 9:21
After the people **s** for him, ... 2Ch 10:3
When Rehoboam **s** him to the 2Ch 10:18
But Jeroboam had **s** some troops 2Ch 13:13
Then he **s** it with messengers to 2Ch 16:2

King Asa and **s** the commanders 2Ch 16:4
Jehoshaphat **s** his officers to 2Ch 17:7
Jehoshaphat **s** with them these 2Ch 17:8
He also **s** the priests Elishama 2Ch 17:8
the priest **s** out the commanders 2Ch 23:14
though the LORD **s** prophets to 2Ch 24:19
and **s** all the valuable things to 2Ch 24:23
So Amaziah **s** the Israelite army 2Ch 25:10
so he **s** a prophet to him who 2Ch 25:15
Then he **s** a message to Jehoash 2Ch 25:17
in Lebanon **s** a message to a 2Ch 25:18
but they **s** men after him to 2Ch 25:27
King Hezekiah **s** messages to all 2Ch 30:1
Then he **s** his officers to 2Ch 32:9
Then the LORD **s** an angel who 2Ch 32:21
of Babylon **s** messengers to 2Ch 32:31
He **s** Shaphan son of Azaliah, ... 2Ch 34:8
those the king **s** with him went 2Ch 34:22
Tell the man who **s** you to me, ... 2Ch 34:23
who **s** you to ask the LORD, ' 2Ch 34:26
But Neco **s** messengers to Josiah, ... 2Ch 35:21
Nebuchadnezzar **s** for Jehoiachin 2Ch 36:10
s prophets again and again to 2Ch 36:15
the letter they **s** to Artaxerxes. .... Ezr 4:11
King Artaxerxes **s** this answer: .... Ezr 4:17
The letter you **s** to us has been .... Ezr 4:18
King Artaxerxes **s** was read to .... Ezr 4:23
letter that was **s** to King Darius .... Ezr 5:6
in the report they **s** to him: .... Ezr 5:7
you are **s** by the king and the .... Ezr 7:14
be killed, or **s** away, or have .... Ezr 7:26
s these men to Iddo, the leader .... Ezr 8:17
I **s** them to bring servants to us .... Ezr 8:17
They **s** an order in Judah and .... Ezr 10:7
king had also **s** army officers .... Ne 2:9
and Geshem **s** me this message: .... Ne 6:2
So I **s** messengers to them with .... Ne 6:3
and Geshem **s** the same message to .... Ne 6:4
and each time I **s** back the same .... Ne 6:4
time Sanballat **s** his helper to .... Ne 6:5
So I **s** him back this answer: .... Ne 6:8
that God had not **s** him but that .... Ne 6:12
people of Judah **s** many letters .... Ne 6:17
So Tobiah **s** letters to frighten .... Ne 6:19
Horonite, so I **s** him away from .... Ne 13:28
s letters to all the states of .... Est 1:22
Letters were **s** by messengers to .... Est 3:13
s clothes for Mordecai to put .... Est 4:4
Then Mordecai **s** back word to .... Est 4:13
Then Esther **s** this answer to .... Est 4:15
Haman the Agagite **s** messages to .... Est 8:5
Then he **s** the king's orders by .... Est 8:10
order was to be **s** out as a law .... Est 8:13
Then he **s** letters to all the .... Est 9:20
he **s** out written orders that the .... Est 9:25
Mordecai **s** letters to all the .... Est 9:30
Queen Esther had **s** out the order .... Est 9:31
The Babylonians **s** three groups .... Job 1:17
But you **s** widows away .... Job 22:9
Evil people will be **s** away, ... Ps 37:9
those he curses will be **s** away. .... Ps 37:22
you will see the wicked **s** away. .... Ps 37:34
David when Saul **s** men to watch .... Ps 58:11
God, you **s** much rain; you .... Ps 68:9
s them all the food they could .... Ps 78:25
He **s** the east wind from heaven .... Ps 78:26
He **s** flies that bit the people. .... Ps 78:45
He **s** frogs that destroyed them. .... Ps 78:45
He **s** his strong anger against .... Ps 78:49
Then he **s** a man ahead of them— .... Ps 105:17
The king of Egypt **s** for Joseph .... Ps 105:20
Then he **s** his servant Moses, ... Ps 105:26
The LORD **s** darkness and made the .... Ps 105:28

like rain and s lightning .... Ps 105:32
but he also s a terrible disease .... Ps 106:15
She has s out her servant girls, ... Pr 9:3
will be s against them. .... Pr 17:11
The Lord s a message against the .... Is 9:8
will know that God has s it. .... Is 9:9
pride has been s down to the .... Is 14:11
king of Assyria s a military .... Is 20:1
king of Assyria s out his field .... Is 36:2
He s me to speak also to those .... Is 36:12
Hezekiah s Eliakim, the palace .... Is 37:2
king of Assyria s his field .... Is 37:4
he s messengers to Hezekiah, ... Is 37:9
Isaiah son of Amoz s a message.............. Is 37:21
You have s your messengers to .... Is 37:24
He s letters and a gift to .... Is 39:1
s a messenger to Jerusalem with .... Is 41:27
the Lord GOD has s me with his............. Is 48:16
me, your mother was s away. .... Is 50:1
You have s your messengers to .... Is 57:9
He has s me to comfort those .... Is 61:1
He has s me to announce the time .... Is 61:2
He has s me to comfort all those .... Is 61:2
He s his own angel to save them. .... Is 63:9
Egypt, I have s my servants, ... Je 7:25
where he had s them . . . ' And I............. Je 16:15
the Lord had s him to prophesy, ... Je 19:14
king of Judah s Pashhur son .... Je 21:1
thrown out and s into a foreign .... Je 22:28
I s my people to other .... Je 23:3
where he had s them away . . . ' .... Je 23:8
'I s the people of Judah out of................. Je 24:5
The Lord has s all his servants............... Je 25:4
I have s them to you again and .... Je 26:5
The Lord s me to say everything .... Je 26:12
The Lord truly s me to you to .... Je 26:15
King Jehoiakim s Elnathan son .... Je 26:22
as one truly s by the Lord." .... Je 28:9
the prophet s from Jerusalem to .... Je 29:1
He s it to all the other people .... Je 29:1
letter was s after all these .... Je 29:2
king of Judah s Elasah son of................. Je 29:3
all those people I s away from .... Je 29:4
city where I s you as captives................. Je 29:7
places I have s you as captives, ... Je 29:14
I s my message to them again and .... Je 29:19
s letters in your name to all .... Je 29:25
Jeremiah has s this message to .... Je 29:28
I s all my servants the prophets .... Je 35:15
Then the officers s a man named .... Je 36:14
King Jehoiakim s Jehudi to get .... Je 36:21
Now King Zedekiah s Jehucal son .... Je 37:3
king of Judah s you to seek my .... Je 37:7
King Zedekiah s for Jeremiah .... Je 37:17
King Zedekiah s someone to get .... Je 38:14
Nebuchadnezzar s these men for .... Je 39:13
has s Ishmael son of Nethaniah .... Je 40:14
You s me to ask the Lord for .... Je 42:9
You s me to the Lord your God, ... Je 42:20
in all that he s me to tell you. .... Je 42:21
their God had s him to tell them............. Je 43:1
I s all my servants, the .... Je 44:4
has been s among the nations. .... Je 49:14
He s fire from above that went .... La 1:13
are not being s to people whose .... Eze 3:5
You are being s to Israel. .... Eze 3:5
are not being s to many nations .... Eze 3:6
If I had s you to them, they................... Eze 3:6
s the people far away among the .... Eze 11:16
when the Lord has not s them. .... Eze 13:6
It s out its branches from the .... Eze 17:7
with them and s messengers to .... Eze 23:16
They even s for men from far .... Eze 23:40

after a messenger was s to them. .... Eze 23:40
of the tree and s their streams .... Eze 31:4
because I s them into captivity .... Eze 39:28
men were s to look for Daniel .... Da 2:13
Their God has s his angel and .... Da 3:28
Nebuchadnezzar s this letter to .... Da 4:1
So God s the hand that wrote on .... Da 5:24
My God s his angel to close the .... Da 6:22
because I have been s to you." .... Da 10:11
for help and s to the great king .... Hos 5:13
he has s the fall rain and the .... Joe 2:23
Though I s my great army against .... Joe 2:25
You s my people to that faraway .... Joe 3:7
I s disasters against you, ... Am 4:10
s this message to Jeroboam king .... Am 7:10
has been s among the nations................. Ob 1:1
But the Lord s a great wind on.............. Jnh 1:4
He s this announcement through .... Jnh 3:7
God s a worm to attack the plant .... Jnh 4:7
God s a very hot east wind to .... Jnh 4:8
together those who were s away, ... Mic 4:6
nation of those who were s away. .... Mic 4:7
I s Moses, Aaron, and Miriam to .... Mic 6:4
he has s your enemies away. .... Zph 3:15
the Lord their God had s him. .... Hag 1:12
the ones the Lord s through all .... Zch 1:10
has honored me and s me against .... Zch 2:8
that the Lord All-Powerful s me. .... Zch 2:9
All-Powerful has s me to you. .... Zch 2:11
All-Powerful has s me to you. .... Zch 4:9
All-Powerful has s me to you. .... Zch 6:15
The city of Bethel s Sharezer, ... Zch 7:2
the words he s by his Spirit .... Zch 7:12
disease he s the other nations................. Zch 14:18
He s the wise men to Bethlehem, ... Mt 2:8
Jesus s out these twelve men .... Mt 10:5
also accepts the One who s me. .... Mt 10:40
So John s some of his followers .... Mt 11:2
He s soldiers to the prison to .... Mt 14:10
After he had s them away, he .... Mt 14:23
God s me only to the lost sheep, ... Mt 15:24
Then he s them into the vineyard .... Mt 20:2
From there Jesus s two of his .... Mt 21:1
he s his servants to the farmers .... Mt 21:34
So the man s some other servants .... Mt 21:36
more than he s the first time. .... Mt 21:36
the king s his servants to tell .... Mt 22:3
Then the king s other servants, ... Mt 22:4
was furious and s his army to................. Mt 22:7
They s some of their own .... Mt 22:16
to death those who are s to you. .... Mt 23:37
who had been s from the leading .... Mt 26:47
his wife s this message to him: .... Mt 27:19
Then the Spirit s Jesus into the .... Mk 1:12
they s someone in to tell him to .... Mk 3:31
the king s a soldier to bring .... Mk 6:27
had eaten, Jesus s them home. .... Mk 8:9
me accepts the One who s me." .... Mk 9:37
From there Jesus s two of his .... Mk 11:1
he s a servant to the farmers to .... Mk 12:2
and beat him and s him away .... Mk 12:3
Then the man s another servant. .... Mk 12:4
So the man s another servant, ... Mk 12:5
The man s many other servants; .... Mk 12:5
He s him last of all, saying, ' .... Mk 12:6
Jewish leaders s some Pharisees .... Mk 12:13
Jesus s two of his followers and .... Mk 14:13
who had been s from the leading .... Mk 14:43
who s me to talk to you and to .... Lk 1:19
God s the angel Gabriel to .... Lk 1:26
good things and s the rich away .... Lk 1:53
Augustus Caesar s an order that............. Lk 2:1
He has s me to tell the captives .... Lk 4:18

S

God s me to free those who have .... Lk 4:18
Elijah was s to none of those .... Lk 4:26
too. This is why I was s." .... Lk 4:43
s some Jewish elders to him to .... Lk 7:3
the officer s friends to say, ... Lk 7:6
who had been s to Jesus went .... Lk 7:10
and s them to the Lord to ask, ... Lk 7:19
the Baptist s us to you with .... Lk 7:20
but Jesus s him away, saying, ... Lk 8:38
He s the apostles out to tell .... Lk 9:2
me accepts the One who s me, ... Lk 9:48
He s some messengers ahead of .... Lk 9:52
others and s them out in pairs .... Lk 10:1
to accept the One who s me." .... Lk 10:16
to death those who are s to you. .... Lk 13:34
man, healed him, and s him away. .... Lk 14:4
man s his servant to tell the .... Lk 14:17
the citizens there who s the son .... Lk 15:15
So they s a group to follow him .... Lk 19:14
he s out two of his followers. .... Lk 19:29
he s a servant to the farmers to .... Lk 20:10
beat the servant and s him away .... Lk 20:10
Then he s another servant. .... Lk 20:11
and s him away empty-handed. .... Lk 20:11
So the man s a third servant. .... Lk 20:12
Jesus and s some spies who .... Lk 20:20
When I s you out without a...................... Lk 22:35
Pilate s Jesus to Herod, ... Lk 23:7
a kingly robe and s him back to .... Lk 23:11
with him; he s him back to us. .... Lk 23:15
man named John who was s by God. .... Jn 1:6
in Jerusalem s priests and .... Jn 1:19
answer to tell those who s us. .... Jn 1:22
who had been s asked John: .... Jn 1:24
you are a teacher s from God, ... Jn 3:2
I am the one s to prepare the .... Jn 3:28
One whom God s speaks the words .... Jn 3:34
what the One who s me wants me .... Jn 4:34
I s you to harvest a crop that .... Jn 4:38
not honor the Father who s him. .... Jn 5:23
in the One who s me has eternal .... Jn 5:24
try to please the One who s me. .... Jn 5:30
You have s people to John, ... Jn 5:33
prove that the Father s me. .... Jn 5:36
himself who s me has given proof .... Jn 5:37
believe in the One the Father s. .... Jn 5:38
is this: Believe the One he s." .... Jn 6:29
what the One who s me wants me .... Jn 6:39
The Father is the One who s me. .... Jn 6:44
living Father s me, and I live .... Jn 6:57
but they come from him who s me. .... Jn 7:16
to the one who s them speak the .... Jn 7:18
I was s by the One who is true, ... Jn 7:28
I am from him, and he s me." .... Jn 7:29
and the Pharisees s some Temple .... Jn 7:32
go back to the One who s me. .... Jn 7:33
The Father who s me is with me. .... Jn 8:16
the Father who s me is the other .... Jn 8:18
heard from the One who s me, ... Jn 8:26
The One who s me is with me. .... Jn 8:29
by my own authority; God s me. .... Jn 8:42
the work of the One who s me. .... Jn 9:4
means S.) So the man went, ... Jn 9:7
So they s for the man's parents .... Jn 9:18
God chose and s into the world. .... Jn 10:36
and Martha s someone to tell .... Jn 11:3
them to believe that you s me." .... Jn 11:42
believing in the One who was s. .... Jn 12:44
sees me sees the One who s me. .... Jn 12:45
The Father who s me told me what........... Jn 12:49
greater than the one who s him. .... Jn 13:16
also accepts the One who s me." .... Jn 13:20
it is from my Father, who s me. .... Jn 14:24

do not know the One who s me. .... Jn 15:21
going back to the One who s me. .... Jn 16:5
Jesus Christ, the One you s. .... Jn 17:3
and they believed that you s me. .... Jn 17:8
I have s them into the world, ... Jn 17:18
just as you s me into the world. .... Jn 17:18
will believe that you s me. .... Jn 17:21
know that you s me and that you .... Jn 17:23
and these people know you s me. .... Jn 17:25
Annas s Jesus, who was still .... Jn 18:24
As the Father s me, I now send .... Jn 20:21
Jesus and s him to you first .... Ac 3:26
They s some men to the jail to .... Ac 5:21
s him to this place where you .... Ac 7:4
in Egypt, he s his sons there. .... Ac 7:12
Then Joseph s messengers to .... Ac 7:14
the same man God s to be a ruler .... Ac 7:35
they s Peter and John to them. .... Ac 8:14
Saul, the Lord Jesus s me. .... Ac 9:17
s me so that you can see again .... Ac 9:17
and from there s him to Tarsus. .... Ac 9:30
they s two messengers to Peter. .... Ac 9:38
Peter s everyone out of the room .... Ac 9:40
to them and s them to Joppa. .... Ac 10:8
men Cornelius s had found .... Ac 10:17
because I have s them to you." .... Ac 10:20
tell me why you s for me." .... Ac 10:29
So I s for you immediately, ... Ac 10:33
that God has s to the people .... Ac 10:36
three men who were s to me from .... Ac 11:11
so they s Barnabas to Antioch. .... Ac 11:22
Lord really s his angel to me .... Ac 12:11
and Saul and s them out. .... Ac 13:3
and Saul, s out by the Holy...................... Ac 13:4
of the synagogue s a message to .... Ac 13:15
this salvation has been s to us. .... Ac 13:26
care and had s them out to do .... Ac 14:26
They s the following letter with .... Ac 15:23
and Silas were s off in peace .... Ac 15:33
back to those who had s them .... Ac 15:33
Roman officers the police to .... Ac 16:35
officers have s an order to let .... Ac 16:36
the believers s Paul and Silas .... Ac 17:10
believers quickly s Paul away to.............. Ac 17:14
Paul s Timothy and Erastus, ... Ac 19:22
friends of Paul s him a message, ... Ac 19:31
Paul s for the followers to come .... Ac 20:1
from Miletus Paul s to Ephesus .... Ac 20:17
have already s a letter to the .... Ac 21:25
The commander s the young man .... Ac 23:22
to kill Paul, I s him to you at .... Ac 23:30
he often s for Paul and talked.................. Ac 24:26
later Paul s for the leaders .... Ac 28:17
God has also s his salvation to .... Ac 28:28
God s him to die in our place to .... Rm 3:25
He s his own Son to earth with .... Rm 8:3
them, that person must be s. .... Rm 10:15
And he s me to preach the Good 1Co 1:17
letter from Christ s through us. 2Co 3:3
So we have been s to speak for 2Co 5:20
they are s from the churches, ... 2Co 8:23
s to beat me and keep me from 2Co 12:7
of the messengers I s to you? 2Co 12:17
and I s our brother with him. 2Co 12:18
nor was I s from human beings. .... Gal 1:1
Jewish people s from James came .... Gal 2:12
God s his Son who was born of a .... Gal 4:4
God s the Spirit of his Son into .... Gal 4:6
have been s to preach this Good.............. Eph 6:20
I needed help, you s him to me. .... Php 2:25
Several times you s me things I .... Php 4:16
We s him to strengthen and 1Th 3:2
I s Timothy to you so I could 1Th 3:5

God s me to tell about the 2Ti 1:1
I s Tychicus to Ephesus. 2Ti 4:12
I was s to help the faith of .... Tit 1:1
God and are s to help those who .... Heb 1:14
who was s to us and is the high .... Heb 3:1
Spirit who was s from heaven— 1Pe 1:12
leaders who are s by him to 1Pe 2:14
s them to hell and put them in 2Pe 2:4
He s one and only Son into 1Jn 4:9
He s his Son to die in our place 1Jn 4:10
that the Father s his Son to be 1Jn 4:14
And Jesus s his angel to show it............... Rev 1:1
of God that were s into all the .... Rev 5:6
s his angel to show his servants .... Rev 22:6
s my angel to tell you these .... Rev 22:16

SENTENCE
There he passed s on Zedekiah. 2Ki 25:6
who do right and s to death the .... Ps 94:21
passed his s on Zedekiah. .... Je 39:5
There he passed s on Zedekiah. .... Je 52:9
the holy ones declared the s. .... Da 4:17
asking me to s him to death. .... Ac 25:15

SENTENCED
power to save those s to die. .... Ps 79:11
and he freed those s to die...................... Ps 102:20
him over to be s to death, ... Lk 24:20
last place, like those s to die. 1Co 4:9

SEORIM
was Harim. The fourth was S. 1Ch 24:8

SEPARATE
so no one should s them." .... Mt 19:6
and he will s them into two .... Mt 25:32
so no one should s them." .... Mk 10:9
Can anything s us from the love............... Rm 8:35
ever be able to s us from the .... Rm 8:39
people, and be s, says the Lord. 2Co 6:17

SEPARATED
evil that has s you from your .... Is 59:2
Lord, let him be s from God—lost 1Co 16:22
and he s himself from them. .... Gal 2:12
They were s as if there were a .... Eph 2:14
At one time you were s from God. .... Col 1:21
though we were s from you for a 1Th 2:17
Maybe Onesimus was s from you .... Phm 1:15

SEPARATES
The farmer s the wheat from the .... Is 28:28
groups as a shepherd s the sheep .... Mt 25:32

SEPARATING
was s some wheat from the chaff .... Jdg 6:11
Araunah was s the wheat from the........... 1Ch 21:20
s the good grain from the chaff. .... Mt 3:12
s the good grain from the chaff. .... Lk 3:17

SEPHAR
between Mesha and S in the hill............... Ge 10:30

SEPHARAD
and live in S will take back..................... Ob 1:20

SEPHARVAIM
and S and put them in the cities............... 2Ki 17:24
and Anammelech, the gods of S. 2Ki 17:31
are the gods of S, Hena, and 2Ki 18:34
the kings of S, Hena, and Ivvah 2Ki 19:13
Where are the gods of S? .... Is 36:19
the kings of S, Hena, and Ivvah .... Is 37:13

SEPHARVITES
The S burned their children in 2Ki 17:31

SEPHER
Debir had been called Kiriath S. .... Jos 15:15
captures the city of Kiriath S." .... Jos 15:16

Debir had been called Kiriath S. .... Jdg 1:11
captures the city of Kiriath S." .... Jdg 1:12

SERAH
Beriah, and their sister was S. .... Ge 46:17
also had a daughter named S. .... Nu 26:46
Timnath S in the mountains of .... Jos 19:50
in his own land at Timnath S,............... Jos 24:30
land at Timnath S in the .... Jdg 2:9
and Beriah. Their sister was S. 1Ch 7:30

SERED
sons were S, Elon, and Jahleel .... Ge 46:14
From S came the Seredite family .... Nu 26:26

SEREDITE
Sered came the S family group; .... Nu 26:26

SERGIUS
always stayed close to S Paulus,............... Ac 13:7

SERIOUS
will have long and s diseases,.................. Dt 28:59
earth that causes s problems for............... Ec 6:1
heal my people's s injuries as.................. Je 6:14
heal my people's s injuries as .... Je 8:11
had such a s argument about this .... Ac 15:39
there was some s trouble in .... Ac 19:23
I was very s about serving God,............... Ac 22:3
making s charges against him, ... Ac 25:7
but not of any s crime as I .... Ac 25:18
It has made you very s. 2Co 7:11
self-controlled, s, wise, strong .... Tit 2:2

SERIOUSLY
have been s hurt, even though I .... Job 34:6

SERIOUSNESS
teach, do it with honesty and s. .... Tit 2:7

SERUG
years old, his son S was born. .... Ge 11:20
When S was 30 years old, his son .... Ge 11:22
S lived 200 years and had other .... Ge 11:23
S, Nahor, Terah, ... 1Ch 1:26
Nahor was the son of S. .... Lk 3:35
the son of Serug. S was the son .... Lk 3:35

SERVANT
stay awhile with me, your s. .... Ge 18:3
gave it to a s, who hurried to .... Ge 18:7
and his s girls so they could .... Ge 20:17
Abraham said to his oldest s, ... Ge 24:2
The s said to him, "What if this .... Ge 24:5
So the s put his hand under his .... Ge 24:9
The s took ten of Abraham's .... Ge 24:10
The s said, "LORD, God of my .... Ge 24:12
one for your s Isaac and that .... Ge 24:14
Before the s had finished .... Ge 24:15
The s ran to her and said, ... Ge 24:17
The s quietly watched her. .... Ge 24:21
The s bowed and worshiped the .... Ge 24:26
who ran out to Abraham's s, ... Ge 24:29
So Abraham's s went into the.................. Ge 24:32
to Abraham's s so he and the men .... Ge 24:32
Then Laban gave the s food, ... Ge 24:33
food, but the s said, "I will .... Ge 24:33
He said, "I am Abraham's s. .... Ge 24:34
When Abraham's s heard these .... Ge 24:52
The s and the men with him ate .... Ge 24:54
morning, the s said, "Now let me .... Ge 24:54
But the s said to them, "Do not .... Ge 24:56
go with Abraham's s and his men. .... Ge 24:59
Then Rebekah and her s girls got .... Ge 24:61
and followed the s and his men. .... Ge 24:61
So the s took Rebekah and left. .... Ge 24:61
asked the s, "Who is that man .... Ge 24:65
The s answered, "That is my .... Ge 24:65
The s told Isaac everything that .... Ge 24:66

S

Egyptian **s**, was Ishmael's .... Ge 25:12
because of my **s** Abraham." .... Ge 26:24
I will send a **s** to bring you .... Ge 27:45
to his daughter to be her **s**. .... Ge 29:24
his daughter Rachel to be her **s**. .... Ge 29:29
is what Jacob, your **s**, says: .... Ge 32:4
To the **s** with the first group of .... Ge 32:17
you and ask, 'Whose **s** are you? .... Ge 32:17
'They belong to your **s** Jacob. .... Ge 32:18
Jacob ordered the second **s**, ... Ge 32:19
the third **s**, and all the other .... Ge 32:19
'Your **s** Jacob is coming behind us. .... Ge 32:20
has been good to me, your **s**." .... Ge 33:5
you go on ahead of me, your **s**. .... Ge 33:14
him to be his personal **s**. .... Ge 39:4
a **s** of the captain of the guard, ... Ge 41:12
said to his **s** in charge of his .... Ge 43:16
The **s** did as Joseph told him and .... Ge 43:17
brothers went to the **s** in charge .... Ge 43:19
But the **s** answered, "It's all .... Ge 43:23
Then the **s** brought Simeon out .... Ge 43:23
The **s** led the men into Joseph's .... Ge 43:24
answered, "Your **s**, our father, ... Ge 43:28
command to the **s** in charge of .... Ge 44:1
The **s** did what Joseph told him. .... Ge 44:2
said to the **s** in charge of his .... Ge 44:4
So the **s** caught up with the .... Ge 44:6
But the brothers said to the **s**, ... Ge 44:7
The **s** said, "We will do as you .... Ge 44:10
The **s** searched the sacks, going .... Ge 44:12
and her **s** girls were walking .... Ex 2:5
trusted him and his **s** Moses. .... Ex 14:31
give a person as a **s** to the LORD .... Le 27:2
me, your **s**, this trouble? .... Nu 11:11
is not true with my **s** Moses. .... Nu 12:7
to speak against my **s** Moses." .... Nu 12:8
my **s** Caleb thinks differently .... Nu 14:24
show me, your **s**, how great you .... Dt 3:24
Then Moses, the **s** of the LORD, ... Dt 34:5
After Moses, the **s** of the LORD, ... Jos 1:1
LORD said, "My **s** Moses is dead. .... Jos 1:2
teachings my **s** Moses gave you. .... Jos 1:7
what Moses, the **s** of the LORD, ... Jos 1:13
that Moses, the **s** of the LORD, ... Jos 1:15
have a command for me, his **s**?" .... Jos 5:14
the LORD's **s**, had commanded. .... Jos 8:31
way the LORD's **s** Moses had .... Jos 8:33
commanded his **s** Moses to give .... Jos 9:24
as Moses, the **s** of the LORD, had .... Jos 11:12
commanded his **s** Moses to do this .... Jos 11:15
The LORD's **s** Moses and the .... Jos 12:6
LORD's **s** Moses had given them .... Jos 13:8
the LORD's **s**, sent me to look .... Jos 14:7
Moses, the **s** of the LORD, gave .... Jos 18:7
the LORD's **s**, told you to do. .... Jos 22:2
Moses, the LORD's **s**, gave you, ... Jos 22:4
Moses, the LORD's **s**, gave you: .... Jos 22:5
son of Nun, the **s** of the LORD, ... Jdg 2:8
wisest of her **s** ladies answer .... Jdg 5:29
take your **s** Purah with you. .... Jdg 7:10
Gideon and his **s** Purah went down .... Jdg 7:11
You gave me, your **s**, this great .... Jdg 15:18
said to the **s** holding his hand, ... Jdg 16:26
with him his **s** and two donkeys. .... Jdg 19:3
and his **s** got up to leave, ... Jdg 19:9
So the **s** said to his master, ... Jdg 19:11
me, the young woman, and my **s**. .... Jdg 19:19
Then Boaz asked his **s** in charge .... Ru 2:5
s answered, "She is the young .... Ru 2:6
to me, your **s**, though I am not .... Ru 3:9
said, "I am Ruth, your **s** girl. .... Ru 3:9
The priest's **s** would then come 1Sa 2:13
the priest's **s** would come to the 1Sa 2:15

the priest's **s** would answer, ... 1Sa 2:16
I am your **s** and I am listening.' 1Sa 3:9
I am your **s** and I am listening." 1Sa 3:10
but he and the **s** could not find 1Sa 9:4
said to his **s**, "Let's go back 1Sa 9:5
the **s** answered, "A man of God 1Sa 9:6
Saul said to his **s**, "If we go 1Sa 9:7
Again the **s** answered Saul. 1Sa 9:8
said to his **s**, "That's a good 1Sa 9:10
As Saul and the **s** were going up 1Sa 9:11
Saul and the **s** asked them, ... 1Sa 9:11
Saul and the **s** went up to the 1Sa 9:14
you and your **s** are to eat with 1Sa 9:19
Saul and his **s** into a large room 1Sa 9:22
As Saul, his **s**, and Samuel were 1Sa 9:27
Tell the **s** to go on ahead of us, ... 1Sa 9:27
Saul and his **s** arrived at Gibeah 1Sa 10:10
uncle asked him and his **s**, ... 1Sa 10:14
I, your **s**, will go and fight 1Sa 17:32
to Saul, "I, your **s**, have been 1Sa 17:34
I, your **s**, have killed both a 1Sa 17:36
the son of your **s** Jesse of 1Sa 17:58
wrong to your **s** David since he 1Sa 19:4
be loyal to me, your **s**. 1Sa 20:8
encouraged my **s** to ambush me 1Sa 22:8
have no other **s** who is as loyal 1Sa 22:14
I, your **s**, know nothing about 1Sa 22:15
God of Israel, tell me, your **s**!" 1Sa 23:11
I, your **s**, didn't see the men 1Sa 25:25
ground and said, "I am your **s**. 1Sa 25:41
what I, your **s**, can do!" 1Sa 28:2
I, your **s**, have obeyed you. 1Sa 28:21
Through my **s** David, I will save 2Sa 3:18
in front of the **s** girls of your 2Sa 6:20
Go and tell my **s** David, 'This is 2Sa 7:5
You must tell my **s** David, ... 2Sa 7:8
you know me, your **s**, so well! 2Sa 7:20
about my family and me, your **s**. 2Sa 7:25
the family of your **s** David will 2Sa 7:26
' So I, your **s**, am brave enough 2Sa 7:27
these good things to me, your **s**. 2Sa 7:28
there was a **s** named Ziba from 2Sa 9:2
He answered, "Yes, I am your **s**." 2Sa 9:2
said, "I am your **s**," 2Sa 9:6
being very kind to me, your **s**! 2Sa 9:8
King David called Saul's **s** Ziba. 2Sa 9:9
David, "I, your **s**, will do 2Sa 9:11
A **s** answered, "That woman is 2Sa 11:3
s Uriah the Hittite also died. 2Sa 11:21
s Uriah the Hittite also died. 2Sa 11:24
his young **s** back in and said 2Sa 13:17
So his **s** led her out of the room 2Sa 13:18
Your **s** Joab did tell me to say 2Sa 14:19
Absalom, 'I am your **s**, my king. 2Sa 15:34
Ziba, Mephibosheth's **s**, met him. 2Sa 16:1
so a **s** girl would go out to them 2Sa 17:17
Ziba, the **s** from Saul's family, ... 2Sa 19:17
My master, my **s** Ziba tricked me! 2Sa 19:26
But here is Kimham, your **s**. 2Sa 19:37
me, your **s**, because I have 2Sa 24:10
invite me, your own **s**, or Zadok 1Ki 1:26
You were very kind to your **s**, ... 1Ki 3:6
have made me, your **s**, king in my 1Ki 3:7
I, your **s**, am here among your 1Ki 3:8
you made to your **s** David, ... 1Ki 8:24
you made to your **s** David, ... 1Ki 8:25
you made to your **s** David, ... 1Ki 8:26
my request, because I am your **s**. 1Ki 8:28
this prayer your **s** prays to you 1Ki 8:28
Moses your **s** when you brought 1Ki 8:53
he gave through his **s** Moses. 1Ki 8:56
right for his **s** and his people 1Ki 8:59
had done for his **s** David and his 1Ki 8:66

of David, my **s,** and because 1Ki 11:13
the sake of my **s** David and for 1Ki 11:32
his life because of my **s,** David, ... 1Ki 11:34
David, my **s,** in Jerusalem, the 1Ki 11:36
be like a **s** to them today. 1Ki 12:7
But you are not like my **s** David, ... 1Ki 14:8
the LORD had said through his **s,** 1Ki 14:18
through his **s** Ahijah from Shiloh 1Ki 15:29
of Israel and that I am your **s.** 1Ki 18:36
Then Elijah said to his **s,** 1Ki 18:43
The **s** went and looked. 1Ki 18:43
seventh time, the **s** said, "I see 1Ki 18:44
Elijah told the **s,** "Go to Ahab............. 1Ki 18:44
his life, taking his **s** with him............ 1Ki 19:3
Judah, Elijah left his **s** there. 1Ki 19:3
said, "Your **s** Ben-Hadad says, ... 1Ki 20:32
is here. He was Elijah's **s.**" 2Ki 3:11
Elisha, "Your **s,** my husband, is 2Ki 4:1
he said to his **s** Gehazi, "Call 2Ki 4:12
When the **s** had called her, ... 2Ki 4:12
had told his **s,** "Now say to her, ... 2Ki 4:13
God, don't lie to me, your **s!**" 2Ki 4:16
The father said to his **s,** 2Ki 4:19
The **s** took him to his mother, ... 2Ki 4:20
the donkey and said to her **s,** 2Ki 4:24
he said to his **s** Gehazi, "Look, ... 2Ki 4:25
he said to his **s,** "Put the large 2Ki 4:38
Elisha's **s** asked, "How can I 2Ki 4:43
I am sending my **s** Naaman to you 2Ki 5:6
the **s** of Elisha the man of God, ... 2Ki 5:20
Elisha's **s** got up early, and 2Ki 6:15
The **s** said to Elisha, "Oh, my 2Ki 6:15
with Gehazi, the **s** of the man of.......... 2Ki 8:4
Judah because of his **s** David.............. 2Ki 8:19
Then the **s** got Joram's chariot 2Ki 9:21
this through his **s** Elijah the 2Ki 9:36
has spoken through his **s** Elijah,.......... 2Ki 10:10
said through his **s** Jonah son of 2Ki 14:25
I am your **s** and your friend. 2Ki 16:7
Shalmaneser's **s** and had made 2Ki 17:3
the LORD's **s,** had commanded. 2Ki 18:12
for the sake of David, my **s.'**" 2Ki 19:34
for the sake of my **s** David.'" 2Ki 20:6
teachings my **s** Moses gave them." 2Ki 21:8
and Asaiah the king's **s.** 2Ki 22:12
s for three years 2Ki 24:1
had a **s** from Egypt named Jarha. 1Ch 2:34
his daughter marry his **s** Jarha,........... 1Ch 2:35
Moses, God's **s,** had commanded. 1Ch 6:49
are the descendants of his **s,** 1Ch 16:13
tell David my **s,** 'This is what 1Ch 17:4
Now, tell my **s** David: 1Ch 17:7
to you for honoring me, your **s?** 1Ch 17:18
about my family and me, your **s.** 1Ch 17:23
the family of your **s** David will 1Ch 17:24
So I, your **s,** am brave enough to 1Ch 17:25
these good things to me, your **s.** 1Ch 17:26
me, your **s,** because I have 1Ch 21:8
Moses the LORD's **s** had made in 2Ch 1:3
you made to your **s** David, ... 2Ch 6:15
you made to your **s** David, ... 2Ch 6:16
that promise you made to your **s.** 2Ch 6:17
my request, because I am your **s.** 2Ch 6:19
this prayer your **s** prays to you. 2Ch 6:19
your love for your **s** David." 2Ch 6:42
the LORD's **s,** and the people 2Ch 24:6
Moses, the **s** of God, had made 2Ch 24:9
the LORD God and his **s** Hezekiah. 2Ch 32:16
and Asaiah, the king's **s.**................. 2Ch 34:20
that I, your **s,** am praying to .... Ne 1:6
and laws you gave your **s** Moses. .... Ne 1:7
what you taught your **s** Moses, ... Ne 1:8
prayer of your **s** and the prayers........... Ne 1:11

Give me, your **s,** success today; .... Ne 1:11
teachings through your **s** Moses. .... Ne 9:14
through Moses the **s** of God, ... Ne 10:29
He gave her seven **s** girls chosen .... Est 2:9
and her seven **s** girls to the.............. Est 2:9
Esther's **s** girls and eunuchs .... Est 4:4
I and my **s** girls will also fast........... Est 4:16
Have you noticed my **s** Job? .... Job 1:8
Have you noticed my **s** Job? .... Job 2:3
I call for my **s,** but he does not .... Job 19:16
right about me, as my **s** Job did........... Job 42:7
and go to my **s** Job, and offer............. Job 42:8
My **s** Job will pray for you, ... Job 42:8
about me, as my **s** Job did." .... Job 42:8
By the LORD's **s,** David. .... Ps 17:15
By them your **s** is warned. .... Ps 19:11
not turn your **s** away in anger; .... Ps 27:9
your kindness to me, your **s.** .... Ps 31:16
Of David, the **s** of the LORD. .... Ps 35:28
Do not hide from me, your **s.** .... Ps 69:17
David to be his **s** and took him .... Ps 78:70
save me, your **s** who trusts in .... Ps 86:2
to me, your **s,** because I give my .... Ps 86:4
Give me, your **s,** strength. .... Ps 86:16
me, the son of your female **s.** .... Ps 86:16
I made a promise to my **s** David. .... Ps 89:3
I have found my **s** David; .... Ps 89:20
with your **s** and thrown his .... Ps 89:39
how they insulted your **s;** .... Ps 89:50
descendants of his **s** Abraham, ... Ps 105:6
he sent his **s** Moses, and Aaron .... Ps 105:26
holy promise to his **s** Abraham. .... Ps 105:42
Then I, your **s,** will be glad. .... Ps 109:28
LORD, I am your **s;** I am your............... Ps 116:16
I am your **s** and the son of your .... Ps 116:16
and the son of your female **s.** .... Ps 116:16
to me, your **s,** so I can live, ... Ps 119:17
me, I, your **s,** will think about........... Ps 119:23
to me, your **s,** so you will be .... Ps 119:38
your promise to me, your **s;** .... Ps 119:49
done good things for your **s,** .... Ps 119:65
as you promised me, your **s.** .... Ps 119:76
that you will help me, your **s.** .... Ps 119:122
love to me, your **s,** and teach me .... Ps 119:124
I am your **s.** Give me wisdom so I .... Ps 119:125
your kindness to me, your **s.** .... Ps 119:135
proven, so I, your **s,** love them. .... Ps 119:140
Look for your **s,** because I have .... Ps 119:176
and a female **s** depends on her .... Ps 123:2
For the sake of your **s** David, ... Ps 132:10
judge me, your **s,** because no one .... Ps 143:2
trouble me, because I am your **s.** .... Ps 143:12
You save your **s** David from cruel .... Ps 144:10
She has sent out her **s** girls, ... Pr 9:3
A fool will be a **s** to the wise. .... Pr 11:29
but has a **s** is better off than .... Pr 12:9
A king is pleased with a wise **s,** .... Pr 14:35
A wise **s** will rule over the .... Pr 17:2
to make your **s** girls healthy. .... Pr 27:27
Words alone cannot correct a **s,** .... Pr 29:19
s who becomes a king, a foolish .... Pr 30:22
family and feeds her **s** girls. .... Pr 31:15
might hear your **s** insulting you........... Ec 7:21
Isaiah my **s** has walked around .... Is 20:3
Go to this **s** Shebna, the manager .... Is 22:15
I will call for my **s** Eliakim son .... Is 22:20
my sake and for David, my **s.'**" .... Is 37:35
Here is my **s,** the one I support. .... Is 42:1
blind than my **s** Israel or more .... Is 42:19
blind than the **s** of the LORD. .... Is 42:19
my witnesses and the **s** I chose. .... Is 43:10
told me, "Israel, you are my **s.** .... Is 49:3
body of my mother to be his **s,** .... Is 49:5

S

an important s to me to bring .... Is 49:6
the people, to the s of rulers. .... Is 49:7
fears the LORD and obeys his s? .... Is 50:10
"See, my s will act wisely. .... Is 52:13
My good s will make many people .... Is 53:11
along with my s Nebuchadnezzar .... Je 25:9
king of Babylon, my s. .... Je 27:6
kings will make Babylon their s. .... Je 27:7
then would my s David not have .... Je 33:21
descendants to my s David and to .... Je 33:22
of David my s rule over .... Je 33:26
a Cushite and a s in the palace, ... Je 38:7
I will soon send for my s, ... Je 43:10
special guards and s of the king .... Je 52:12
the land I gave to my s Jacob. .... Eze 28:25
them one shepherd, my s David. .... Eze 34:23
and my s David will be a ruler .... Eze 34:24
My s David will be their king, ... Eze 37:24
the land I gave to my s Jacob, ... Eze 37:25
David my s will be their king, ... Eze 37:25
will belong to the s only until .... Eze 46:17
be the king's s until the first .... Da 1:21
Daniel, "Daniel, s of the living .... Da 6:20
of Moses, the s of God, because .... Da 9:11
hear the prayers of your s. .... Da 9:17
can I, your s, talk with you? .... Da 10:17
Shealtiel, my s,' says the LORD .... Hag 2:23
to bring my s called the Branch .... Zch 3:8
and a s honors his master.". .... Mal 1:6
the teaching of Moses my s, ... Mal 4:4
said, "Lord, my s is at home in .... Mt 8:6
it, and my s will be healed. .... Mt 8:8
I say to my s, 'Do this,' and my .... Mt 8:9
Do this,' and my s does it. .... Mt 8:9
Your s will be healed just as .... Mt 8:13
And his s was healed that same .... Mt 8:13
and a s is not better than his .... Mt 10:24
s should be satisfied to become .... Mt 10:25
Here is my s whom I have chosen. .... Mt 12:18
a s who owed him several million .... Mt 18:24
But the s did not have enough .... Mt 18:25
everything the s owned should be .... Mt 18:25
to pay the king what the s owed. .... Mt 18:25
But the s fell on his knees and .... Mt 18:26
sorry for his s and told him he .... Mt 18:27
Then he let the s go free. .... Mt 18:27
same s found another servant. .... Mt 18:28
found another s who owed him a .... Mt 18:28
s grabbed him around the neck .... Mt 18:28
The other s fell on his knees .... Mt 18:29
But the first s refused to be. .... Mt 18:30
threw the other s into prison .... Mt 18:30
called his s in and said, ' .... Mt 18:32
in and said, 'You evil s! .... Mt 18:32
showed mercy to that other s, ... Mt 18:33
and put the s in prison to be .... Mt 18:34
serve the rest of you like a s. .... Mt 20:26
killed a third s with stones. .... Mt 21:35
is your s is the greatest .... Mt 23:11
wise and loyal s that the master .... Mt 24:45
and finds the s doing his work, ... Mt 24:46
his work, the s will be blessed. .... Mt 24:46
will choose that s to take care .... Mt 24:47
that evil s thinks to himself. .... Mt 24:48
come when that s is not ready .... Mt 24:50
He gave one s five bags of gold, ... Mt 25:15
another s two bags of gold, ... Mt 25:15
and a third s one bag of gold, ... Mt 25:15
The s who got five bags went .... Mt 25:16
the s who had two bags invested .... Mt 25:17
But the s who got one bag went .... Mt 25:18
The s who was given five bags of .... Mt 25:20
You are a good and loyal s. .... Mt 25:21

Then the s who had been given .... Mt 25:22
You are a good and loyal s. .... Mt 25:23
Then the s who had been given .... Mt 25:24
'You are a wicked and lazy s! .... Mt 25:26
gold from that s and give it to .... Mt 25:28
it to the s who has ten bags .... Mt 25:28
'Throw that useless s outside, ... Mt 25:30
He struck the s of the high .... Mt 26:51
a s girl came to him and said, ... Mt 26:69
be last of all and s of all." .... Mk 9:35
serve the rest of you like a s. .... Mk 10:43
sent a s to the farmers to get .... Mk 12:2
grabbed the s and beat him .... Mk 12:3
Then the man sent another s. .... Mk 12:4
So the man sent another s, ... Mk 12:5
man tells the s guarding the .... Mk 13:34
and struck the s of the high .... Mk 14:47
a s girl of the high priest came .... Mk 14:66
The s girl saw Peter there, ... Mk 14:69
said, "I am the s of the Lord. .... Lk 1:38
concern for his humble s girl. .... Lk 1:48
He has helped his s, the people .... Lk 1:54
the family of God's s David. .... Lk 1:69
let me, your s, die in peace as. .... Lk 2:29
officer who had a s who was very .... Lk 7:2
s was so sick he was nearly dead. .... Lk 7:2
Jesus to come and heal his s. .... Lk 7:3
it, and my s will be healed. .... Lk 7:7
I say to my s, 'Do this,' and my .... Lk 7:8
Do this,' and my s does it." .... Lk 7:8
they found the s in good health. .... Lk 7:10
and trusted s that the master .... Lk 12:42
and finds the s doing his work, ... Lk 12:43
his work, the s will be blessed. .... Lk 12:43
will choose that s to take care .... Lk 12:44
But suppose the s thinks to. .... Lk 12:45
come when that s is not ready .... Lk 12:46
The s who knows what his master .... Lk 12:47
But the s who does not know what. ...... Lk 12:48
But the s answered, 'Master, let .... Lk 13:8
the man sent his s to tell the .... Lk 14:17
So the s returned and told his. .... Lk 14:21
the s said to him, 'Master, ... Lk 14:22
The master said to the s, ' .... Lk 14:23
The s said, 'Your brother has .... Lk 15:27
No s can serve two masters. .... Lk 16:13
The s will hate one master and .... Lk 16:13
one of you has a s who has been .... Lk 17:7
When the s comes in from working ...... Lk 17:7
The s does not get any special .... Lk 17:9
and gave a coin to each s. .... Lk 19:13
The first s came and said, ... Lk 19:16
king said to the s, 'Excellent! .... Lk 19:17
You are a good s. Since I can .... Lk 19:17
The second s said, 'Sir, I .... Lk 19:18
said to this s, 'You can rule .... Lk 19:19
Then another s came in and said .... Lk 19:20
Then the king said to the s, ' .... Lk 19:22
by your own words, you evil s. .... Lk 19:22
away from this s and give it to .... Lk 19:24
give it to the s who earned ten .... Lk 19:24
that s already has ten coins.' .... Lk 19:25
sent a s to the farmers to get .... Lk 20:10
they beat the s and sent him .... Lk 20:10
Then he sent another s. .... Lk 20:11
beat this s also, and showed .... Lk 20:11
So the man sent a third s. .... Lk 20:12
the leader should be like the s. ...... Lk 22:26
but I am like a s among you. .... Lk 22:27
them struck the s of the high .... Lk 22:50
A s girl saw Peter sitting there ..... Lk 22:56
Then my s will be with me .... Jn 12:26
a s is not greater than his .... Jn 13:16

S

738

family became Mephibosheth's s. 2Sa 9:12
sent out Joab, his s, and all..................... 2Sa 11:1
David sent his s to find out who 2Sa 11:3
on the city wall shot at your s, ... 2Sa 11:24
David sent s to bring her to his 2Sa 11:27
David's s were afraid to tell 2Sa 12:18
When David saw his s whispering,............ 2Sa 12:19
His s gave him some food, and he 2Sa 12:20
David's s said to him, "Why are 2Sa 12:21
He said to his s, "All of you, ... 2Sa 13:9
Then Absalom instructed his s, ... 2Sa 13:28
All his s standing nearby tore.................. 2Sa 13:31
and all his s began crying also 2Sa 13:36
Then Absalom said to his s, ... 2Sa 14:30
So Absalom's s set fire to 2Sa 14:30
"Why did your s burn my field?" 2Sa 14:31
All the king's s passed by him—.............. 2Sa 15:18
of figs are for the s to eat. 2Sa 16:2
Absalom's s came to the woman at 2Sa 17:20
Absalom's s then went to look 2Sa 17:20
After Absalom's s left, Jonathan.............. 2Sa 17:21
Now go out and encourage your s............. 2Sa 19:7
sons and twenty s with him. 2Sa 19:17
king and his s coming to him.................. 2Sa 24:20
although his s covered him with............... 1Ki 1:1
The s told the king, "Nathan the 1Ki 1:23
we are your s, why didn't you............... 1Ki 1:27
Take my s with you and put my 1Ki 1:33
He told some s to bring another 1Ki 2:19
king sent his s to get a sword. 1Ki 3:24
My s will work with yours, ... 1Ki 5:6
My s will bring them down from 1Ki 5:9
love with your s who truly 1Ki 8:23
and forgive the sins of your s, ... 1Ki 8:36
a large group of s and camels.................. 1Ki 10:2
the palace s, and their good 1Ki 10:5
She saw the s who served him at 1Ki 10:5
she and her s returned to her 1Ki 10:13
and the lives of your fifty s. 2Ki 1:13
Send me one of the s and one of 2Ki 4:22
Naaman's s came near and said to............ 2Ki 5:13
them to two of his s to carry 2Ki 5:23
from Naaman's s and put them 2Ki 5:24
Then he let Naaman's s go,..................... 2Ki 5:24
sheep, oxen, male s, or female 2Ki 5:26
male servants, or female s. 2Ki 5:26
The s came back and reported, ... 2Ki 6:13
the deaths of my s the prophets 2Ki 9:7
all the LORD's s who were 2Ki 9:7
Ahaziah's s carried his body in 2Ki 9:28
Two or three s looked out the 2Ki 9:32
"We are your s," they said. 2Ki 10:5
there are no s of the LORD with.............. 2Ki 10:23
you through my s the prophets." 2Ki 17:13
through all his s the prophets. 2Ki 17:23
the words the s of the king of................. 2Ki 19:6
they will become s in the palace............. 2Ki 20:18
said through his s the prophets, ... 2Ki 21:10
Josiah's s carried his body in a 2Ki 23:30
through his s the prophets. 2Ki 24:2
Jehoiachin's mother, s, nobles, ... 2Ki 24:12
priests, Levites, and Temple s. 1Ch 9:2
of Moab became s of David and 1Ch 18:2
became David's s and gave him 1Ch 18:6
all the Edomites became his s. 1Ch 18:13
all the Israelites are your s.................... 1Ch 21:3
I know your s are experienced at 2Ch 2:8
and my s will help them....................... 2Ch 2:8
will give your s who cut the 2Ch 2:10
Now send my s the wheat, barley, ... 2Ch 2:15
love with your s who truly 2Ch 6:14
and forgive the sins of your s, ... 2Ch 6:27
a large group of s with her and 2Ch 9:1

the palace s and their good..................... 2Ch 9:4
s who served Solomon his wine 2Ch 9:4
she and her s returned to her 2Ch 9:12
become Shishak's s so they may 2Ch 12:8
him, to be his s, and to burn 2Ch 29:11
He told his s, "Take me away 2Ch 35:23
These are the Temple s: .... Ezr 2:43
descendants of the s of Solomon: .... Ezr 2:55
The Temple s and the descendants........... Ezr 2:58
descendants of the s of Solomon .... Ezr 2:58
male and female s and the 200 .... Ezr 2:65
and Temple s, along with some .... Ezr 2:70
From your s who live in .... Ezr 4:11
We are the s of the God of .... Ezr 5:11
gatekeepers, and Temple s..................... Ezr 7:7
Temple s, and other workers .... Ezr 7:24
are the Temple s in Casiphia. .... Ezr 8:17
sent them to bring s to us for .... Ezr 8:17
hundred twenty of the Temple s, ... Ezr 8:20
through your s the prophets. .... Ezr 9:11
to you day and night for your s, ... Ne 1:6
They are your s and your people, ... Ne 1:10
prayers of your s who love to .... Ne 1:11
his s, will start rebuilding, ... Ne 2:20
The Temple s who lived on the .... Ne 3:26
of the Temple s and the traders, ... Ne 3:31
These are the Temple s: .... Ne 7:46
descendants of the s of Solomon: .... Ne 7:57
The Temple s and the descendants........... Ne 7:60
of the s of Solomon totaled.................... Ne 7:60
male and female s and the 245 .... Ne 7:67
the Temple s, and all the other .... Ne 7:73
singers, Temple s, all those who .... Ne 10:28
Levites, Temple s, and........................... Ne 11:3
and descendants of Solomon's s. .... Ne 11:3
The Temple s lived on the hill.................. Ne 11:21
I put my s at the gates no .... Ne 13:19
the king's personal s suggested, ... Est 2:2
The king's personal s answered,.............. Est 6:3
The king's personal s said, ... Est 6:5
Have the s bring a royal robe .... Est 6:8
the s put the robe on the man .... Est 6:9
s came in and covered Haman's .... Est 7:8
He also had a large number of s. .... Job 1:3
They killed the s with swords, ... Job 1:15
burned up the sheep and the s, ... Job 1:16
your camels and killed the s. .... Job 1:17
and my female s treat me like.................. Job 19:15
The s of my house have always .... Job 31:31
But the LORD saves his s' lives; .... Ps 34:22
who loves to see his s do well." .... Ps 35:27
of his s will inherit that .... Ps 69:36
the bodies of your s as food to .... Ps 79:2
punish those who kill your s. .... Ps 79:10
and show kindness to your s?.................. Ps 90:13
Show your s the wonderful things .... Ps 90:16
innocent lives will be my s...................... Ps 101:6
Your s love even her stones; .... Ps 102:14
you are his s who do what he .... Ps 103:21
and flames of fire are your s. .... Ps 104:4
and to make plans against his s.............. Ps 105:25
Praise him, you s of the LORD; .... Ps 113:1
LORD, all you s of the LORD, you .... Ps 134:1
praise him, you s of the LORD, ... Ps 135:1
against the king and his s. .... Ps 135:9
people and has mercy on his s. .... Ps 135:14
a gift to his s, the Israelites.................... Ps 136:22
and borrowers are s to lenders. .... Pr 22:7
you spoil your s when they are .... Pr 29:21
things about s to their masters .... Pr 30:10
I have seen s ride horses while .... Ec 10:7
princes walk like s on foot..................... Ec 10:7
the words the s of the king of................. Is 37:6

they will become **s** in the palace .... Is 39:7
People of Israel, you are my **s**. .... Is 41:8
I said, 'You are my **s**.' .... Is 41:9
People of Jacob, you are my **s**. .... Is 44:1
of Jacob, my **s**, don't be afraid. .... Is 44:2
Israel, remember you are my **s**. .... Is 44:21
I made you, and you are my **s**. .... Is 44:21
the messages of my **s** come true; .... Is 44:26
I do these things for my **s**, ... Is 45:4
The LORD has saved his **s**, ... Is 48:20
the good things my **s** receive. .... Is 54:17
will be named the **s** of our God. .... Is 61:6
back to us, your **s**, who belong .... Is 63:17
will do the same thing to my **s**— .... Is 65:8
my **s** will live there. .... Is 65:9
My **s** will eat, but you evil .... Is 65:13
My **s** will drink, but you evil .... Is 65:13
My **s** will be happy, but you evil .... Is 65:13
My **s** will shout for joy because .... Is 65:14
will be like curses to my **s**, ... Is 65:15
will call his **s** by another name .... Is 65:15
The LORD's **s** will see his power, ... Is 66:14
I have sent my **s**, the prophets, ... Je 7:25
men send their **s** to get water. .... Je 14:3
sent all his **s** the prophets to .... Je 25:4
of Egypt, his **s**, his officers, ... Je 25:19
to what my **s** the prophets say .... Je 26:5
again and again through my **s**, ... Je 29:19
of Jacob, my **s**, don't be afraid. .... Je 30:10
I sent all my **s** the prophets to .... Je 35:15
and his **s** heard everything .... Je 36:24
and his children and his **s**, ... Je 36:31
Zedekiah, his **s**, and the people .... Je 37:2
sent all my **s** the prophets, to .... Je 44:4
of Jacob, my **s**, don't be afraid; .... Je 46:27
of Jacob, my **s**, do not be afraid .... Je 46:28
spoke through my **s**, the prophets .... Eze 38:17
are to be **s** in my Holy Place .... Eze 44:11
from his land to any of his **s**, ... Eze 46:17
they would become **s** of the king .... Da 1:5
you want to treat us, your **s**." .... Da 1:13
young men became the king's **s**.............. Da 1:19
tell us, your **s**, your dream. .... Da 2:4
Tell us, your **s**, the dream, and .... Da 2:7
S of the Most High God, come here! .... Da 3:26
and saved his **s** from the fire! .... Da 3:28
and told his **s** to lift Daniel .... Da 6:23
We did not listen to your **s**, ... Da 9:6
he gave us through his **s**, ... Da 9:10
priests, the **s** of the LORD, are .... Joe 1:9
S of the altar, cry out loud. .... Joe 1:13
S of my God, keep your rough .... Joe 1:13
the LORD's **s**, should cry between .... Joe 2:17
his plans to his **s** the prophets. .... Am 3:7
and laws to my **s** the prophets, ... Zch 1:6
Then the man's **s** came to him and.......... Mt 13:27
' The **s** asked, 'Do you want us .... Mt 13:28
he said to his **s**, "Jesus is John .... Mt 14:2
the money his **s** owed him. .... Mt 18:23
When the other **s** saw what had .... Mt 18:31
he sent his **s** to the farmers to .... Mt 21:34
But the farmers grabbed the **s**, ... Mt 21:35
some other **s** to the farmers, ... Mt 21:36
same thing to the **s** that they .... Mt 21:36
the king sent his **s** to tell the .... Mt 22:3
Then the king sent other **s**, ... Mt 22:4
listen to the **s** and left to do .... Mt 22:5
the other people grabbed the **s**, ... Mt 22:6
king said to his **s**, 'The wedding .... Mt 22:8
So the **s** went into the streets .... Mt 22:10
told some **s**, 'Tie this man's'.................... Mt 22:13
give the other **s** their food at .... Mt 24:45
beat the other **s** and eat and get .... Mt 24:49

called for his **s** and told them .... Mt 25:14
and asked the **s** what they did .... Mt 25:19
So the master told his other **s**, ... Mt 25:28
The man sent many other **s**; .... Mk 12:5
and lets his **s** take care of it, ... Mk 13:34
Be like **s** who are waiting for .... Lk 12:36
the **s** immediately open the door .... Lk 12:36
serve and tell the **s** to sit at .... Lk 12:37
Those **s** will be blessed when he.............. Lk 12:38
give the other **s** their food at .... Lk 12:42
he begins to beat the other **s**, ... Lk 12:45
All of my father's **s** have plenty .... Lk 15:17
let me be like one of your **s**."' .... Lk 15:19
But the father said to his **s**, ' .... Lk 15:22
to one of the **s** and asked what .... Lk 15:26
should say, 'We are unworthy **s**; .... Lk 17:10
ten of his **s** and gave a coin .... Lk 19:13
'Call those **s** who have my money .... Lk 19:15
His mother said to the **s**,........................ Jn 2:5
said to the **s**, "Fill the jars .... Jn 2:7
but the **s** who had brought the .... Jn 2:9
way the man's **s** came and met him .... Jn 4:51
longer call you **s**, because a .... Jn 15:15
so the **s** and guards had built a .... Jn 18:18
One of the **s** of the high priest .... Jn 18:26
s would have fought to keep me .... Jn 18:36
help us, your **s**, to speak your.................... Ac 4:29
two of his **s** and a soldier, ... Ac 10:7
These men are **s** of the Most High .... Ac 16:17
We are only **s** of God who helped 1Co 3:5
think of us as **s** of Christ, ... 1Co 4:1
us able to be **s** of a new 2Co 3:6
that we are your **s** for Jesus. 2Co 4:5
way we show we are **s** of God: 2Co 6:4
We show we are **s** of God by our 2Co 6:6
us if Satan's **s** also make........................ 2Co 11:15
look like **s** who work for what is 2Co 11:15
and Timothy, **s** of Christ Jesus. .... Php 1:1
makes his **s** become like flames .... Heb 1:7
to do evil. Live as **s** of God...................... 1Pe 2:16
Be good **s** of God's various gifts 1Pe 4:10
to show his **s** what must soon .... Rev 1:1
of their fellow **s** and brothers .... Rev 6:11
the Good News God told to his **s**, ... Rev 10:7
to reward your **s** the prophets................ Rev 11:18
back for the death of his **s**." .... Rev 19:2
and God's **s** will worship him. .... Rev 22:3
to show his **s** the things that .... Rev 22:6

SERVE

But he said, 'I **s** the LORD, who .... Ge 24:40
the older will **s** the younger." .... Ge 25:23
nations **s** you and peoples bow .... Ge 27:29
But you must **s** me another seven .... Ge 29:27
will **s** the king his wine just .... Ge 40:13
himself and said, "**S** the meal." .... Ge 43:31
will stay and **s** the Egyptians.' .... Ex 14:12
must not worship or **s** any idol; .... Ex 20:5
he will **s** you for six years. .... Ex 21:2
the slave will **s** that master all .... Ex 21:6
Israelites to **s** me as priests. .... Ex 28:1
so that he may **s** me as a priest. .... Ex 28:3
Then they may **s** me as priests. .... Ex 28:4
me so they may **s** me as priests. .... Ex 28:41
near the altar to **s** as priests .... Ex 28:43
and his sons to **s** me as priests. .... Ex 29:1
Meeting Tent is in the Holy .... Ex 29:30
so they may **s** me as priests. .... Ex 29:44
the altar to **s** as priests and.................... Ex 30:20
that they may **s** me as priests. .... Ex 30:30
to wear when they **s** as priests. .... Ex 31:10
to wear when they **s** as priests." .... Ex 35:19
so that he may **s** me as a priest. .... Ex 40:13

they may also **s** me as priests. .... Ex 40:15
or older who will **s** in the army .... Nu 1:3
were able to **s** in the army were .... Nu 1:20
were able to **s** in the army were .... Nu 1:22
were able to **s** in the army were .... Nu 1:24
were able to **s** in the army were .... Nu 1:26
were able to **s** in the army were .... Nu 1:28
were able to **s** in the army were .... Nu 1:30
were able to **s** in the army were .... Nu 1:32
were able to **s** in the army were .... Nu 1:34
were able to **s** in the army were .... Nu 1:36
were able to **s** in the army were .... Nu 1:38
were able to **s** in the army were .... Nu 1:40
were able to **s** in the army were .... Nu 1:42
was able to **s** in the army was................ Nu 1:45
were appointed to **s** as priests. .... Nu 3:3
Meeting Tent and **s** the people of .... Nu 3:8
and his sons to **s** as priests, ... Nu 3:10
all who come to **s** in the Meeting .... Nu 4:3
as they **s** in the Meeting .... Nu 4:31
that they may **s** the Israelites .... Nu 8:19
all the Israelites and **s** them. .... Nu 16:9
you and your sons **s** in the Tent .... Nu 18:2
and your sons may **s** as priests. .... Nu 18:7
Only you may **s** at the altar or .... Nu 18:7
or older who will **s** in the army .... Nu 26:2
must not worship or **s** any idol, ... Dt 5:9
They were to **s** the Lord and to .... Dt 10:8
S the Lord your God with your .... Dt 10:12
the Lord your God and **s** him. .... Dt 10:20
your God and **s** him with your .... Dt 11:13
turn away to and worship other .... Dt 11:16
places where they **s** their gods, ... Dt 12:2
say, "Let's **s** other gods" (gods .... Dt 13:2
S only the Lord your God. .... Dt 13:4
S him and be loyal to him. .... Dt 13:4
try to lead you to **s** other gods—........... Dt 13:6
that person will **s** you for six .... Dt 15:12
to stand and **s** the Lord always. .... Dt 18:5
he wants to **s** the Lord there, ... Dt 18:6
he may **s** the Lord his God. .... Dt 18:7
Levites who **s** there before .... Dt 18:7
your God to **s** him and to give .... Dt 21:5
not follow other gods or **s** them............. Dt 28:14
where you will **s** other gods made .... Dt 28:36
but you did not **s** the Lord your .... Dt 28:47
so you will **s** the enemies the .... Dt 28:48
There you will **s** other gods of .... Dt 28:64
God to go and **s** the gods of .... Dt 29:18
are led to bow and **s** other gods,........... Dt 30:17
turn to other gods and **s** them. .... Dt 31:20
old enough to **s** in the army died .... Jos 5:4
and their work is to **s** the Lord. .... Jos 18:7
follow him and **s** him the very .... Jos 22:5
Don't **s** or worship them. .... Jos 23:7
If you go and **s** other gods and .... Jos 23:16
respect the Lord and **s** him fully .... Jos 24:14
River and in Egypt. **S** the Lord. .... Jos 24:14
if you don't want to **s** the Lord, ... Jos 24:15
today whom you will **s**. .... Jos 24:15
You may **s** the gods that your .... Jos 24:15
or you may **s** the gods of the .... Jos 24:15
my family, we will **s** the Lord."............. Jos 24:15
the Lord to **s** other gods! .... Jos 24:16
we will **s** the Lord, because he .... Jos 24:18
You are not able to **s** the Lord, ... Jos 24:19
leave the Lord and **s** other gods, ... Jos 24:20
"No! We will **s** the Lord." .... Jos 24:21
you have chosen to **s** the Lord." .... Jos 24:22
We will **s** the Lord our God, ... Jos 24:24
Abimelech that we should **s** him? .... Jdg 9:28
We should **s** the men of Hamor, ... Jdg 9:28
Why should we **s** Abimelech?................ Jdg 9:28

Abimelech that we should **s** him?' .... Jdg 9:38
continued to **s** the Lord under 1Sa 2:11
family would **s** me always.'..................... 1Sa 2:30
and he will always **s** before my 1Sa 2:35
to the Lord and **s** only him. 1Sa 7:3
and make them **s** with his 1Sa 8:11
with us, and we will **s** you." 1Sa 11:1
our enemies, and we will **s** you.'............. 1Sa 12:10
must honor the Lord and **s** him. 1Sa 12:14
S the Lord with all your heart. 1Sa 12:20
Lord and truly **s** him with all 1Sa 12:24
came to Saul, he began to **s** him. 1Sa 16:21
David stay and **s** me because I 1Sa 16:22
I'm ready to **s** you and to wash 1Sa 25:41
told me, 'Go and **s** other gods.' 1Sa 26:19
He will **s** me forever." 1Sa 27:12
to have you **s** in my army. 1Sa 29:6
father, but now I will **s** you.' 2Sa 15:34
So whom should I **s** now? 2Sa 16:19
I will **s** you as I served him." 2Sa 16:19
People I never knew **s** me. 2Sa 22:44
But you must **s** me as your father 1Ki 9:4
not **s** or worship other gods. 1Ki 9:6
he sent them to **s** in these ships 1Ki 9:27
as he did. Then we will **s** you." 1Ki 12:4
If you **s** them and give them a 1Ki 12:7
answer, they will **s** you always." 1Ki 12:7
in Bethel to **s** at the places 1Ki 12:32
Ahab began to **s** Baal and worship........... 1Ki 16:31
I **s** the Lord, the God of Israel, ... 1Ki 17:1
lives, whom I **s**, I will be seen................. 1Ki 18:15
lives, whom I **s**, I tell you the 2Ki 3:14
as the Lord lives whom I **s**, ... 2Ki 5:16
but Jehu will **s** Baal much. 2Ki 10:18
money from the people you **s**,............... 2Ki 12:7
not allowed to **s** at the Lord's 2Ki 23:9
objects used to **s** in the Temple. 2Ki 25:14
in the land and **s** the king of 2Ki 25:24
men ready to **s** in the army, ... 1Ch 7:4
men ready to **s** in the army. 1Ch 7:11
soldiers ready to **s** in the army. 1Ch 7:40
the Lord and to **s** him forever." 1Ch 15:2
the Levites to **s** before the Ark 1Ch 16:4
They were to **s** there every day. 1Ch 16:37
other Levites to **s** with them. 1Ch 16:38
Lord, and to **s** him as priests. 1Ch 23:13
Their job was to **s** in the Temple........... 1Ch 23:28
many Levites should **s** each time. 1Ch 23:31
were chosen to **s** as priests. 1Ch 24:5
groups chosen to **s** in the Temple 1Ch 24:19
family was to **s** at the Temple. 1Ch 25:8
S him completely and willingly, ... 1Ch 28:9
people want to **s** you always, ... 1Ch 29:18
son Solomon a desire to **s** you. 1Ch 29:19
themselves ready to **s** the Lord. 2Ch 5:11
But you must **s** me as your father 2Ch 7:17
not **s** or worship other gods. 2Ch 7:19
their groups to **s** at each gate,............... 2Ch 8:14
as he did. Then we will **s** you." 2Ch 10:4
answer, they will **s** you always." 2Ch 10:7
to let them **s** as priests to 2Ch 11:14
The priests who **s** the Lord are............... 2Ch 13:10
had volunteered to **s** the Lord. 2Ch 17:16
You must always **s** the Lord 2Ch 19:9
Levites will **s** as officers for 2Ch 19:11
the priests and Levites who **s**................. 2Ch 23:6
been made ready to **s** the Lord, ... 2Ch 23:6
before him, to **s** him, to be his 2Ch 29:11
themselves ready to **s** the Lord, ... 2Ch 30:3
S the Lord your God so he will 2Ch 30:8
themselves ready to **s** the Lord. 2Ch 31:18
all these things to **s** the Lord, ... 2Ch 32:1
people of Judah to **s** the Lord, ... 2Ch 33:16

in Israel to **s** the LORD their 2Ch 34:33
Now **s** the LORD your God and his 2Ch 35:3
certain time to **s** God in the .... Ezr 6:18
wine servers to **s** each man what .... Est 1:8
chosen by the king to **s** her. .... Est 4:5
Almighty that we should **s** him? .... Job 21:15
If they obey and **s** him, the rest .... Job 36:11
wild ox agree to **s** you and stay .... Job 39:9
People I never knew **s** me. .... Ps 18:43
people in the future will **s** him; .... Ps 22:30
to him and all nations **s** him. .... Ps 72:11
S the LORD with joy; come before .... Ps 100:2
and kingdoms will **s** the LORD. .... Ps 102:22
laws, because all things **s** you. .... Ps 119:91
you who **s** at night in the Temple .... Ps 134:1
to the people who **s** the LORD, ... Is 23:18
the LORD called me to **s** him. .... Is 49:1
and love him, to **s** him, to obey .... Is 56:6
and their kings will **s** you. .... Is 60:10
that doesn't **s** you will be .... Is 60:12
and said, 'I will not **s** you!' .... Je 2:20
So now you will **s** foreigners in .... Je 5:19
gods to **s** and worship them. .... Je 13:10
Then you may **s** me. And if you .... Je 15:19
There you can **s** other gods day .... Je 16:13
other gods to **s** them or to .... Je 25:6
will have to **s** many nations and .... Je 25:14
nations will **s** Nebuchadnezzar .... Je 27:7
refuse to **s** Nebuchadnezzar .... Je 27:8
of Babylon and **s** him I will let .... Je 27:11
the king of Babylon and **s** him, ... Je 27:12
those who do not **s** the king of .... Je 27:13
But **s** the king of Babylon, ... Je 27:17
to make them **s** Nebuchadnezzar .... Je 28:14
They will **s** the LORD their God .... Je 30:9
of Levi who **s** me in the Temple .... Je 33:22
not follow other gods to **s** them. .... Je 35:15
Jonadab son of Recab to **s** me.'" .... Je 35:19
be afraid to **s** the Babylonians .... Je 40:9
in the land and **s** the king of .... Je 40:9
objects used to **s** in the Temple. .... Je 52:18
those who want to **s** their evil .... Eze 11:21
of Israel, go **s** your idols for .... Eze 20:39
Israel will **s** me in the land, ... Eze 20:40
the priests who **s** in the Temple .... Eze 40:45
the priests who **s** at the altar. .... Eze 40:46
come near the LORD to **s** him." .... Eze 40:46
and who come near me to **s** me, ... Eze 43:19
the Temple and **s** in the Temple .... Eze 44:11
before the people to **s** them. .... Eze 44:11
come near me to **s** as priests, ... Eze 44:13
so they may come near to **s** me. .... Eze 44:16
my table to **s** me and take care .... Eze 44:16
not wear wool to **s** at the gates .... Eze 44:17
courtyard to **s** in the Temple, ... Eze 44:27
the priests who **s** in the Temple, ... Eze 45:4
come near to the LORD to **s** him. .... Eze 45:4
the Levites, who **s** in the Temple. .... Eze 45:5
and able to **s** in his palace. .... Da 1:4
They do not **s** your gods and do .... Da 3:12
that you do not **s** my gods nor .... Da 3:14
the God we **s** is able to save us .... Da 3:17
We will not **s** your gods or .... Da 3:18
die rather than **s** or worship any .... Da 3:28
May the God you **s** all the time .... Da 6:16
nation, and language will **s** him. .... Da 7:14
will respect and **s** them.' .... Da 7:27
you do as I tell you and **s** me, ... Zch 3:7
appointed to **s** the Lord of all .... Zch 4:14
said, 'It is useless to **s** God. .... Mal 3:14
those who **s** God and those who .... Mal 3:18
Lord your God and **s** only him.'" .... Mt 4:10
No one can **s** two masters. .... Mt 6:24

cannot **s** both God and worldly .... Mt 6:24
stood up and began to **s** Jesus. .... Mt 8:15
among you must **s** the rest of you .... Mt 20:26
among you must **s** the rest of you .... Mt 20:27
He came to **s** others and to give .... Mt 20:28
among you must **s** the rest of you .... Mk 10:43
among you must **s** all of you like .... Mk 10:44
He came to **s** others and to give .... Mk 10:45
to those who worship and **s** him. .... Lk 1:50
so we could **s** him without fear, ... Lk 1:74
Lord your God and **s** only him.'" .... Lk 4:8
dress himself to **s** and tell the .... Lk 12:37
the table, and he will **s** them. .... Lk 12:37
No servant can **s** two masters. .... Lk 16:13
cannot **s** both God and worldly .... Lk 16:13
get yourself ready and **s** me. .... Lk 17:8
People always **s** the best wine .... Jn 2:10
awhile, they **s** the cheaper wine. .... Jn 2:10
myself ready to **s** so that they .... Jn 17:19
God's word in order to **s** tables. .... Ac 6:2
their lives to **s** our Lord Jesus .... Ac 15:26
receive as they **s** God day and .... Ac 26:7
whom I **s** with my whole heart by .... Rm 1:9
the parts of your body to **s** sin, ... Rm 6:13
now we **s** God in a new way with .... Rm 7:6
the gift of serving should **s**. .... Rm 12:7
and those who **s** at the altar get 1Co 9:13
ways to **s** but the same Lord 1Co 12:5
to serve but the same Lord to **s**. 1Co 12:5
their money so I could **s** you. 2Co 11:8
S each other with love. .... Gal 5:13
favor, but as them honestly, ... Col 3:22
Then let them **s** as deacons if 1Ti 3:10
Those who **s** well as deacons are 1Ti 3:13
but train yourself to **s** God. 1Ti 4:7
They should **s** their masters even 1Ti 6:2
shows the true way to **s** God. 1Ti 6:3
the right way, **s** God, have faith 1Ti 6:11
I **s** him, doing what I know is 2Ti 1:3
as if they **s** God but will not 2Ti 3:5
that shows people how to **s** God. .... Tit 1:1
in a way that shows we **s** God. .... Tit 2:12
are spirits who **s** God and are .... Heb 1:14
acts so we may **s** the living God. .... Heb 9:14
the priests who **s** in the Holy .... Heb 13:10
a gift to use to **s** others. 1Pe 4:10
serves should **s** with the 1Pe 4:11
it because you are happy to **s**, ... 1Pe 5:2
we need to live and to **s** God. 2Pe 1:3
save those who **s** him when 2Pe 2:9
live holy lives and **s** God, ... 2Pe 3:11
of priests who **s** God his Father. .... Rev 1:6
of the people who **s** our God." .... Rev 7:3
miracles to **s** the first beast. .... Rev 13:14
you who **s** him and all you who .... Rev 19:5

SERVED
had **s** Kedorlaomer for twelve .... Ge 14:4
know that I have **s** you well." .... Ge 30:26
the man who **s** wine to the king .... Ge 40:1
his officer who **s** him wine and .... Ge 40:2
king's officer who **s** him wine. .... Ge 40:5
the man who **s** wine to the king .... Ge 40:9
the chief officer who **s** his wine .... Ge 40:20
chief officer who **s** wine his old .... Ge 40:21
the officer who **s** wine did not .... Ge 40:23
officer who **s** wine to the king .... Ge 41:9
So they **s** Joseph at one table, ... Ge 43:32
Abraham and Isaac **s** our God, ... Ge 48:15
the doctors who **s** him to prepare .... Ge 50:2
Remember the men who **s** you— .... Ex 32:13
the women who **s** at the entrance .... Ex 38:8
wear when they **s** in the Holy .... Ex 39:1

S

outer robe when he s as priest, ... Ex 39:26
wear when they s in the Holy .... Ex 39:41
wore when they s as priests. .... Ex 39:41
and Ithamar s as priests during .... Nu 3:4
they s you six years and did .... Dt 15:18
person may have s other gods and .... Dt 17:3
They went and s other gods and............... Dt 29:26
The Israelites s the LORD during .... Jos 24:31
The people s the LORD during the .... Jdg 2:7
Israel also s their gods. .... Jdg 3:6
their God and s the idols of .... Jdg 3:7
his sons s as priests for the..................... Jdg 18:30
s before the Ark of the Agreement. .... Jdg 20:28
the sons of Eli, s as priests of 1Sa 1:3
the women who s at the entrance 1Sa 2:22
The boy Samuel s the LORD under 1Sa 3:1
and they s only the LORD. 1Sa 7:4
And Samuel s as judge of Israel 1Sa 7:6
they left me and s other gods.................. 1Sa 8:8
left the LORD and s the Baals 1Sa 12:10
who had s the Philistines 1Sa 14:21
He s Saul king of Israel, but he 1Sa 29:3
the kings who s Hadadezer saw 2Sa 10:19
with the Israelites and s them. 2Sa 10:19
Next she took the pan and s him, ... 2Sa 13:9
In the past I s your father, ... 2Sa 15:34
In the past I s your father. 2Sa 16:19
I will serve you as I s him."...................... 2Sa 16:19
cared for the king and s him. 1Ki 1:4
They worshiped and s those gods, ... 1Ki 9:9
the servants who s him at feasts.............. 1Ki 10:5
him and who s as his advisers. 1Ki 12:8
I have always s you as well as I 1Ki 19:10
I have always s you as well as I 1Ki 19:14
worshiped and s the god Baal, ... 1Ki 22:53
little girl s Naaman's wife. 2Ki 5:2
to them, "Ahab s Baal a little,................. 2Ki 10:18
They s idols when the LORD had 2Ki 17:12
the stars of the sky and s Baal. 2Ki 17:16
LORD but also s their own gods, ... 2Ki 17:33
the stars of the sky and s them. 2Ki 21:3
They s by making music at the 1Ch 6:32
and they s until Solomon built 1Ch 6:32
other Levites s by doing their 1Ch 6:48
priests who s with him in front 1Ch 16:39
officers who s at his side. 1Ch 18:17
When those who s Hadadezer saw 1Ch 19:19
made peace with David and s him........... 1Ch 19:19
They s in the LORD's Temple.................. 1Ch 23:24
s before the LORD every day. 1Ch 23:31
and Ithamar s as the priests. 1Ch 24:2
of the men who s in this way:................. 1Ch 25:1
Asaph's sons who s were Zaccur, ... 1Ch 25:2
sons who s were Gedaliah, ... 1Ch 25:3
Heman's sons who s were Bukkiah, ... 1Ch 25:4
and they s in the Temple of the 1Ch 26:12
the Israelites who s the king in 1Ch 27:1
gods and worshiped and s them, ... 2Ch 7:22
servants who s Solomon his wine 2Ch 9:4
him and who s as his advisers. 2Ch 10:8
these soldiers s King 2Ch 17:19
relatives who s Ahaziah,........................ 2Ch 22:8
priests who s the LORD followed 2Ch 26:17
the stars of the sky and s them. 2Ch 33:3
them as they s in the Temple 2Ch 35:2
was the one who s wine to the .... Ne 1:11
They s in the days of Joiakim .... Ne 12:26
They also s in the days of .... Ne 12:26
the priests and Levites who s.................. Ne 12:44
and singers who s had gone back .... Ne 13:10
Wine was s in gold cups of .... Est 1:7
to the seven eunuchs who s him— .... Est 1:10
the LORD and s foreign idols .... Je 5:19

people loved and s and went .... Je 8:2
other gods and s and worshiped............... Je 16:11
worshiped and s other gods.'" .... Je 22:9
I s this wine to the people of .... Je 25:18
after he has s you for six years .... Je 34:14
Son of Man did not come to be s. .... Mt 20:28
Son of Man did not come to be s. .... Mk 10:45
beginning and s God by telling .... Lk 1:2
'I have s you like a slave for .... Lk 15:29
Martha s the food, and Lazarus .... Jn 12:2
you know I always s the Lord.................. Ac 20:19
who s in the emperor's army,.................. Ac 27:1
worshiped and s what had been .... Rm 1:25
I s God by teaching his Good .... Rm 15:16
You know he has s with me in .... Php 2:22
They s with me in telling the .... Php 4:3
that tribe ever s as a priest at .... Heb 7:13

SERVERS

He told the wine s to serve each............... Est 1:8

SERVES

this robe when he s as priest. .... Ex 28:35
not invite Solomon, who s you. 1Ki 1:19
the money from the people he s............... 2Ki 12:5
mercy to his child who s him, ... Mal 3:17
Whoever s me must follow me. .... Jn 12:26
will honor anyone who s me. .... Jn 12:26
Anyone who s Christ by living .... Rm 14:18
soldier ever s in the army and 1Co 9:7
else who works and s with them. 1Co 16:16
News, as a son s his father....................... Php 2:22
works and s with me in the army .... Php 2:25
the person who s God will be 2Ti 3:17
Our high priest s in the Most .... Heb 8:2
Anyone who s should serve with 1Pe 4:11

SERVICE

prepare themselves for s to God, ... Ex 19:14
their clothes are given to my s. .... Ex 29:21
things for the s in the Meeting .... Ex 30:16
been given for s to the LORD.................. Ex 32:29
and things to the LORD's s." .... Nu 4:16
he gave it for s to the LORD by .... Nu 7:1
love for the Temple and its s. .... Ne 13:14
their time of s is finished, ... Is 40:2
yourselves to the s of the LORD, ... Je 4:4
time you will be called for s. .... Eze 38:8
pure and ready for God's s. .... Eze 43:20
for the special s and stood in .... Da 3:3
When his time of s at the Temple .... Lk 1:23
ready for s, and have your .... Lk 12:35
they are offering s to God. .... Jn 16:2
ready for your s through your .... Jn 17:17
ready for their s of the truth. .... Jn 17:19
day for the afternoon prayer s. .... Ac 3:1
officer in the s of Candace,..................... Ac 8:27
we might be used in s to God.................. Rm 7:4
to the s of God's people. 1Co 16:15
in this s for God's people. 2Co 8:4
because of his s in preaching 2Co 8:18
are doing this s to bring glory 2Co 9:12
This s you do not only helps the.............. 2Co 9:12
could not give in your s to me. .... Php 2:30
high priest in s to God. .... Heb 2:17
stand and do their religious s, ... Heb 10:11
them that their s was not for 1Pe 1:12
your minds for s and have 1Pe 1:13
to your patience, add s for God; 2Pe 1:6
and to your s for God, add 2Pe 1:7
They started out in s to Christ, ... 3Jn 1:5
your faith, your s, and your .... Rev 2:19
sisters in the s of Christ who .... Rev 6:11

SERVICES

utensils used in the Temple s. 1Ch 9:28
things used in its s anymore.". 1Ch 23:26
with the s at the Temple of the 1Ch 23:32
stood across from them in the s. .... Ne 12:9

SERVING

when he began s the king of .... Ge 41:46
things used for s in the Holy .... Nu 4:12
things used for s at the altar— .... Nu 4:14
you this gift of s as a priest, ... Nu 18:7
work they do s at the Meeting .... Nu 18:21
from me, to begin s other gods. .... Dt 7:4
yourselves completely to s him, ... Dt 10:16
who is there s the LORD your God .... Dt 17:12
left the LORD and stopped s him. .... Jdg 10:6
boy Samuel grew up s the LORD. 1Sa 2:21
because in always s you, they 1Ki 10:8
s as king for twenty-two years. 1Ki 14:20
of Assyria and stopped s him. 2Ki 18:7
responsible for s in the Temple 1Ch 9:13
was their way of s in the Temple 1Ch 25:6
of the divisions s the king, ... 1Ch 28:1
all the work of s in the Temple 1Ch 28:13
because in always s you, they 2Ch 9:7
may learn that s me is different 2Ch 12:8
is different than s the kings of 2Ch 12:8
priests who are s in the Temple. .... Ne 10:36
and where the priests who are s, ... Ne 10:39
of the eunuchs there s the king, ... Est 7:9
Enjoy s the LORD, and he will .... Ps 37:4
does not give itself to s me." .... Je 9:26
be priests s me in the Temple. .... Je 33:21
must learn that s clothes there .... Eze 42:14
not given themselves to s me. .... Eze 44:7
themselves to s me may not enter .... Eze 44:9
take off their s clothes before .... Eze 44:19
the holy duty of s the LORD. .... Eze 48:11
thousands of angels were s him, ... Da 7:10
left her, and she began s them. .... Mk 1:31
day Zechariah was s as a priest .... Lk 1:8
she got up and began s them. .... Lk 4:39
at the table or the one s? .... Lk 22:27
I was very serious about s God, ... Ac 22:3
has the gift of s should serve. .... Rm 12:7
s the Lord with all your heart. .... Rm 12:11
people are not s our Lord Christ. .... Rm 16:18
Are they s Christ? I am serving 2Co 11:23
Christ? I am s him more. (I am 2Co 11:23
holy people for the work of s, ... Eph 4:12
who is greedy is s a false god. .... Eph 5:5
Work as if you were s the Lord, ... Eph 6:7
as if you were s only men and .... Eph 6:7
lives as a sacrifice in s God. .... Php 2:17
This is really s a false God. .... Col 3:5
You are s the Lord Christ. .... Col 3:24
idols and began s the living and 1Th 1:9
and gave me this work of s him. 1Ti 1:12
but s God helps you in every way 1Ti 4:8
They think that s God is a way 1Ti 6:5
S God does make us very rich, ... 1Ti 6:6
so no one s in the army wastes 2Ti 2:4
he will never stop s as priest. .... Heb 7:24

SETH

She named him S and said, ... Ge 4:25
S also had a son, and they named .... Ge 4:26
and image, and Adam named him S. .... Ge 5:3
After S was born, Adam lived 800 .... Ge 5:4
When S was 105 years old, he had .... Ge 5:6
S lived 807 years and had other .... Ge 5:7
So S lived a total of 912 years, ... Ge 5:8
Adam was the father of S. 1Ch 1:1
S was the father of Enosh. 1Ch 1:1

Enosh was the son of S. .... Lk 3:38
the son of Seth. S was the son .... Lk 3:38

SETHUR

of Asher, S son of Michael; .... Nu 13:13

SETS

to join the two s of curtains so .... Ex 26:6
to join the two s of cloth .... Ex 36:18
Don't carry two s of weights .... Dt 25:13
have two different s of measures .... Dt 25:14
or statue and secretly s it up, ... Dt 27:15
and the one who s up the gates .... Jos 6:26
anything else before the sun s!" 2Sa 3:35
he s them on thrones with kings .... Job 36:7
the heavy rains and s a path for .... Job 38:25
Its breath s coals on fire, ... Job 41:21
the sun rises to where it s. .... Ps 65:8
s his people free. He made his .... Ps 111:9
the sun rises to where it s. .... Ps 113:3
The LORD s the prisoners free. .... Ps 146:7
sun rises, the sun s, and then .... Ec 1:5
and he s anyone he chooses over .... Da 5:21
he s their foundations on the .... Am 9:6

SETTING

the rules for s her free are .... Ex 21:7
the rules for s the male slaves .... Ex 21:7
Moses finished s up the Holy .... Nu 7:1
the wood but not s fire to it. 1Ki 18:23
answers by s fire to his wood 1Ki 18:24
its boards and s its doors, ... Ne 3:3
rebuilding it and s its doors, ... Ne 3:13
from the rising to the s sun. .... Ps 50:1
talk about s traps, thinking. .... Ps 64:5
neighbors are s a trap for them. .... Pr 29:5

SETTINGS

made of wood and onyx for the s. 1Ch 29:2

SETTLE

will allow you to s in the land. .... Ge 46:34
Take over the land and s there, ... Nu 33:53
to her to s their arguments. .... Jdg 4:5
the king to s would come here 2Sa 15:2
of the LORD and s problems 2Ch 19:8
of Israel s there in tents. .... Ps 78:55
had the hungry s there so they .... Ps 107:36
in the east and s in the west .... Ps 139:9
Don't let liars s in the land. .... Ps 140:11
Throwing lots can s arguments .... Pr 18:18
He will s arguments among the .... Is 2:4
live there or s there again. .... Is 13:20
will s them in their own land. .... Is 14:1
He will s his argument with .... Is 27:8
Build houses and s in the land. .... Je 29:5
so build houses and s down. .... Je 29:28
to go to Egypt and s there, ... Je 44:12
They are like wine left to s; .... Je 48:11
people s in Gad's towns? .... Je 49:1
s them again in their homes, ... Hos 11:11
try hard to s it on the way. .... Lk 12:58

SETTLED

land of Babylonia and s there. .... Ge 11:2
the city of Haran, they s there. .... Ge 11:31
land of Egypt and s everywhere. .... Ex 10:14
came to the land where they s— .... Ex 16:35
because the cloud had s on it, ... Ex 40:35
where they had s and all their .... Nu 31:10
of Manasseh, and they s there. .... Nu 32:40
they came to Moab, they s there. .... Ru 1:2
went to Damascus and s there, ... 1Ki 11:24
He s them in Halah, in Gozan on 2Ki 17:6
to Assyria and s them in Halah, ... 2Ki 18:11
Philistines came and s in them. 1Ch 10:7
until a priest had s this matter .... Ezr 2:63

S

the Israelites s in their .... Ezr 2:70
s in their own towns as well. .... Ezr 2:70
Israelites were s in their .... Ezr 3:1
their countries and s in the .... Ezr 4:10
until a priest s this matter .... Ne 7:65
these people all s in their own .... Ne 7:73
Israelites were s in their own .... Ne 7:73
So they s from Beersheba all the .... Ne 11:30
Levites from Judah s in the land.............. Ne 11:36
Your people s there. .... Ps 68:10

SETTLEMENT
that lead to the s of Ar. .... Nu 21:15

SETTLEMENTS
according to their s and camps. .... Ge 25:16
s of Kedar should praise him................... Is 42:11

SETTLERS
a prophet from the s in Gilead. 1Ki 17:1

SEVEN
that person s times more." .... Ge 4:15
killer is punished s times, ... Ge 4:24
Take with you s pairs, each male .... Ge 7:2
Take s pairs of all the birds of .... Ge 7:3
S days from now I will send rain .... Ge 7:4
S days later the flood started.................. Ge 7:10
After s days Noah again sent out .... Ge 8:10
S days later he sent the dove .... Ge 8:12
Abraham also put s female lambs .... Ge 21:28
did you put these s female lambs .... Ge 21:29
I will work s years for you." .... Ge 29:18
worked for Laban s years so he .... Ge 29:20
After s years Jacob said to .... Ge 29:21
must serve me another s years.".............. Ge 29:27
for Laban another s years. .... Ge 29:30
After s days Laban found him in .... Ge 31:23
on the ground s times as he was............. Ge 33:3
He saw s fat and beautiful cows .... Ge 41:2
Then s more cows came up out of .... Ge 41:3
stood beside the s beautiful .... Ge 41:3
The s thin and ugly cows ate the .... Ge 41:4
ugly cows ate the s beautiful .... Ge 41:4
his dream he saw s full and good .... Ge 41:5
s more heads of grain sprang up, ... Ge 41:6
of grain ate the s full and good .... Ge 41:7
I saw s fat and beautiful cows................. Ge 41:18
Then I saw s more cows come out .... Ge 41:19
cows ate the first s fat cows, ... Ge 41:20
after they had eaten the s cows, ... Ge 41:21
I saw s full and good heads of .... Ge 41:22
s more heads of grain sprang .... Ge 41:23
thin heads ate the s good heads.............. Ge 41:24
The s good cows stand for seven .... Ge 41:26
good cows stand for s years, ... Ge 41:26
and the s good heads of grain................. Ge 41:26
of grain stand for s years. .... Ge 41:26
The s thin and ugly cows stand .... Ge 41:27
and ugly cows stand for s years, ... Ge 41:27
and the s thin heads of grain .... Ge 41:27
stand for s years of hunger. .... Ge 41:27
You will have s years of good .... Ge 41:29
But after those s years, there .... Ge 41:30
will come s years of hunger .... Ge 41:30
grown during the s good years. .... Ge 41:34
use during the s years of hunger .... Ge 41:36
during the s years of hunger. .... Ge 41:36
During the s good years, the .... Ge 41:47
during those s years of good .... Ge 41:48
The s years of good crops came .... Ge 41:53
the s years of hunger began, ... Ge 41:54
clothes and about s and one-half .... Ge 45:22
There were s persons in this .... Ge 46:25
of sorrow continued for s days.............. Ge 50:10

in Midian who had s daughters. .... Ex 2:16
S days passed after the LORD .... Ex 7:25
made without yeast for s days. .... Ex 12:15
for the full s days of the feast .... Ex 12:15
For s days there must not be any .... Ex 12:19
For s days you must eat bread .... Ex 13:6
So for s days you must not eat .... Ex 13:7
with their mothers for s days,............... Ex 22:30
For s days you must eat bread .... Ex 23:15
Then make s small oil lamps and .... Ex 25:37
s and one-half feet long and .... Ex 27:1
long and s and one-half feet .... Ex 27:1
around it s and one-half feet .... Ex 27:18
wear these clothes for s days................... Ex 29:30
spend s days appointing them. .... Ex 29:35
Spend s days making the altar .... Ex 29:37
For s days you must eat bread .... Ex 34:18
He made s pure gold lamps for .... Ex 37:23
s and one-half feet long and .... Ex 38:1
long and s and one-half feet .... Ex 38:1
long and s and one-half feet .... Ex 38:18
and sprinkle it s times before .... Le 4:6
must sprinkle it s times before .... Le 4:17
some oil on the altar s times, ... Le 8:11
of appointing will last s days;.................. Le 8:33
Tent day and night for s days................... Le 8:35
will become unclean for s days, ... Le 12:2
from other people for s days. .... Le 13:4
separated for s more days. .... Le 13:5
from other people for s days. .... Le 13:21
from other people for s days. .... Le 13:26
from other people for s days. .... Le 13:31
other people for s more days. .... Le 13:33
in a separate place for s days.................. Le 13:50
the clothing for s more days. .... Le 13:54
sprinkle the blood s times on .... Le 14:7
his tent for the first s days. .... Le 14:8
some of the oil s times before................. Le 14:16
his left hand s times before..................... Le 14:27
close up the house for s days................... Le 14:38
the blood on the house s times. .... Le 14:51
he must count s days for himself .... Le 15:13
she is unclean for s days; .... Le 15:19
he will be unclean for s days; .... Le 15:24
she must wait s days, and after .... Le 15:28
the blood s times in front .... Le 16:14
on the altar s times to make .... Le 16:19
it must stay s days with its .... Le 22:27
made without yeast for s days. .... Le 23:6
For s days you will bring an .... Le 23:8
Count s full weeks from the .... Le 23:15
and s male lambs that are one .... Le 23:18
LORD will continue for s days............... Le 23:34
to the LORD each day for s days. .... Le 23:36
the LORD's festival for s days. .... Le 23:39
the LORD your God for s days. .... Le 23:40
the LORD for s days each year. .... Le 23:41
Live in shelters for s days. .... Le 23:42
Count off s groups of seven .... Le 25:8
off seven groups of s years, ... Le 25:8
there will be s years of rest..................... Le 25:8
will punish you s times more for .... Le 26:18
I will beat you s times harder.................. Le 26:21
will punish you s more times for .... Le 26:24
will punish you s more times for .... Le 26:28
their head s days later to be .... Nu 6:9
'Put the s lamps where they can .... Nu 8:2
have been shamed for s days,................... Nu 12:14
her outside the camp for s days.............. Nu 12:14
outside of the camp for s days, ... Nu 12:15
had been built s years before .... Nu 13:22
and sprinkle it s times toward .... Nu 19:4
body will be unclean for s days. .... Nu 19:11

it will be unclean for s days. .... Nu 19:14
will be unclean for s days. .... Nu 19:16
Balak, "Build me s altars here, ... Nu 23:1
and prepare s bulls and seven .... Nu 23:1
bulls and s male sheep for me." .... Nu 23:1
I have prepared s altars, ... Nu 23:4
There Balak built s altars and................ Nu 23:14
Build me s altars here and .... Nu 23:29
prepare for me s bulls and seven .... Nu 23:29
seven bulls and s male sheep." .... Nu 23:29
and s male lambs a year old, ... Nu 28:11
For s days, you may eat only .... Nu 28:17
and s male lambs a year old. .... Nu 28:19
each of the s lambs, it must .... Nu 28:21
by fire each day for s days,.................... Nu 28:24
and s male lambs a year old. .... Nu 28:27
each of the s lambs offer two .... Nu 28:29
and s male lambs a year old. .... Nu 29:2
each of the s lambs offer two .... Nu 29:4
and s male lambs a year old. .... Nu 29:8
each of the s lambs it must be .... Nu 29:10
festival to the LORD for s days. .... Nu 29:12
the seventh day offer s bulls, ... Nu 29:32
and s male lambs a year old. .... Nu 29:36
outside the camp for s days. .... Nu 31:19
s nations that are stronger than .... Dt 7:1
At the end of every s years, ... Dt 15:1
But for s days eat bread made .... Dt 16:3
in your land for s days. .... Dt 16:4
Count s weeks from the time you .... Dt 16:9
Feast of Shelters for s days, ... Dt 16:13
your God for s days at the place............. Dt 16:15
run from you in s directions. .... Dt 28:7
run from them in s directions. .... Dt 28:25
Have s priests carry trumpets................. Jos 6:4
around the city s times and have .... Jos 6:4
Tell s priests to carry trumpets .... Jos 6:6
the s priests began marching .... Jos 6:8
They carried the s trumpets and.............. Jos 6:8
The s priests carried the seven .... Jos 6:13
priests carried the s trumpets .... Jos 6:13
marched around the city s times. .... Jos 6:15
were still s tribes of Israel .... Jos 18:2
divide the land into s parts. .... Jos 18:5
describe the s parts of land................. Jos 18:6
each town in the s parts of the .... Jos 18:9
So for s years the LORD handed .... Jdg 6:1
and a second bull s years old................. Jdg 6:25
Ibzan judged Israel for s years. .... Jdg 12:9
during the s days of the feast .... Jdg 14:12
the rest of the s days of the.................. Jdg 14:17
tie me up with s new bowstrings .... Jdg 16:7
brought Delilah s new bowstrings .... Jdg 16:8
weave the s braids of my hair................ Jdg 16:13
Delilah wove the s braids of his .... Jdg 16:13
to shave off the s braids of .... Jdg 16:19
S hundred of these trained .... Jdg 20:16
is better for you than s sons, ... Ru 4:15
not have children now has s, ... 1Sa 2:5
of God in their land s months. 1Sa 6:1
But you must wait s days. 1Sa 10:8
Give us s days to send........................ 1Sa 11:3
Saul waited s days, because 1Sa 13:8
Jesse had s of his sons pass by 1Sa 16:10
of Jabesh fasted for s days.................. 1Sa 31:13
in Hebron for s years and six 2Sa 2:11
in Hebron for s years and six 2Sa 5:5
s thousand men who rode in 2Sa 8:4
David killed s hundred Aramean 2Sa 10:18
So bring s of his sons to us. 2Sa 21:6
David gave these s sons to the 2Sa 21:9
All s sons died together. 2Sa 21:9
bodies of Saul's s sons who were 2Sa 21:13

weighing about s and one-half 2Sa 21:16
s years in Hebron and........................ 1Ki 2:11
floor were s and one-half feet................ 1Ki 6:6
bottom floor was s and one-half........... 1Ki 6:10
wing was s and one-half feet 1Ki 6:24
had spent s years building it 1Ki 6:38
that were s and one-half feet 1Ki 7:16
made a net of s chains for each 1Ki 7:17
and s and one-half feet deep. 1Ki 7:23
before the LORD for s days, ... 1Ki 8:65
seven days, then s more days,............... 1Ki 8:65
contained about s and one-half 1Ki 10:16
He had s hundred wives who were........... 1Ki 11:3
and ruled in Tirzah s days. 1Ki 16:15
again. This happened s times................ 1Ki 18:43
I have s thousand people left in 1Ki 19:18
about s thousand people in all. 1Ki 20:15
from each other for s days................... 1Ki 20:29
After they had marched s days, ... 2Ki 3:9
took s hundred men with swords 2Ki 3:26
The boy sneezed s times and 2Ki 4:35
with him about s hundred fifty 2Ki 5:5
in the Jordan River s times. 2Ki 5:10
dipped in the Jordan s times, ... 2Ki 5:14
time tomorrow s quarts of fine 2Ki 7:1
So s quarts of fine flour were 2Ki 7:16
of barley and s quarts of fine 2Ki 7:18
food that will last s years." 2Ki 8:1
of the Philistines for s years. 2Ki 8:2
After s years she returned from 2Ki 8:3
Joash was s years old when he 2Ki 11:21
also took all s thousand 2Ki 24:16
David ruled for s and one-half 1Ch 3:4
Elioenai had s sons: Hodaviah, ... 1Ch 3:24
s relatives in their families 1Ch 5:13
thousand s hundred sixty 1Ch 5:18
one thousand s hundred sixty............... 1Ch 9:13
the gatekeepers for s days. 1Ch 9:25
of Jabesh fasted for s days.................. 1Ch 10:12
was about s and one-half feet 1Ch 11:23
sacrificed s bulls and seven 1Ch 15:26
seven bulls and s male sheep................ 1Ch 15:26
s thousand men who rode in 1Ch 18:4
David killed s thousand Aramean 1Ch 19:18
supplied about s and one-half............... 1Ch 22:14
about s hundred fifty thousand 1Ch 29:7
and about s million five hundred 1Ch 29:7
s years in Hebron and....................... 1Ch 29:27
one creature was s and one-half............. 2Ch 3:11
was also s and one-half feet 2Ch 3:11
and was also s and one-half feet............ 2Ch 3:12
and it was also s and one-half 2Ch 3:12
pillar was over s feet tall. 2Ch 3:15
and s and one-half feet deep. 2Ch 4:2
bronze platform s and one-half 2Ch 6:13
feet long, s and one-half feet 2Ch 6:13
and s and one-half feet high, ... 2Ch 6:13
the festival for s days.......................... 2Ch 7:8
s days they celebrated giving 2Ch 7:9
the festival for s days......................... 2Ch 7:9
contained about s and one-half 2Ch 9:15
young bull and s male sheep can 2Ch 13:9
to the LORD s hundred bulls 2Ch 15:11
bulls and s thousand sheep................. 2Ch 15:11
Joash was s years old when he 2Ch 24:1
of three hundred s thousand five 2Ch 26:13
They brought s bulls, seven male 2Ch 29:21
seven bulls, s male sheep, seven 2Ch 29:21
male sheep, s lambs, and seven 2Ch 29:21
seven lambs, and s male goats............. 2Ch 29:21
Bread for s days with great joy 2Ch 30:21
people ate the feast for s days, ... 2Ch 30:22
agreed to stay s more days, ... 2Ch 30:23

S

with joy for **s** more days. 2Ch 30:23
bulls and **s** thousand sheep to.................2Ch 30:24
of Unleavened Bread for **s** days.................2Ch 35:17
For **s** days they celebrated the ....Ezr 6:22
the king and the **s** people who ....Ezr 7:14
celebrated the feast for **s** days, ...Ne 8:18
of the palace garden for **s** days, ...Est 1:5
a command to the **s** eunuchs who ....Est 1:10
s of the important men of Persia ....Est 1:14
These **s** had special privileges ....Est 1:14
He gave her **s** servant girls ....Est 2:9
her and her **s** servant girls to ....Est 2:9
Then I will pay **s** hundred fifty ....Est 3:9
had **s** sons and three daughters.................Job 1:2
He owned **s** thousand sheep, ...Job 1:3
ground with Job **s** days and seven ....Job 2:13
Job seven days and **s** nights. ....Job 2:13
After **s** days Job cried out and ....Job 3:1
even **s** troubles will not harm ....Job 5:19
Now take **s** bulls and seven male ....Job 42:8
seven bulls and **s** male sheep,.................Job 42:8
Job also had **s** sons and three.................Job 42:13
silver purified **s** times over.....................Ps 12:6
those around us **s** times over for.............Ps 79:12
S times a day I praise you for ....Ps 119:164
There are **s** things he cannot ....Pr 6:16
he must pay back **s** times what he ....Pr 6:31
she has made its **s** columns. ....Pr 9:1
be bothered by trouble **s** times, ...Pr 24:16
is wiser than **s** people who give ....Pr 26:16
At that time **s** women will grab ....Is 4:1
divide it into **s** small rivers so.................Is 11:15
the sun will be **s** times brighter ....Is 30:26
now, like the light of **s** days. ....Is 30:26
a woman with **s** sons felt faint ....Je 15:9
weighing out **s** ounces of silver ....Je 32:9
'At the end of every **s** years, ...Je 34:14
pillar was about **s** and one-half ....Je 52:22
s people who advised the king, ...Je 52:25
I sat there **s** days where these.................Eze 3:15
After **s** days the LORD spoke his ....Eze 3:16
burn in their fires for **s** years.................Eze 39:9
burying them for **s** months to ....Eze 39:12
After the **s** months are finished, ...Eze 39:14
S steps went up to the gateway, ...Eze 40:22
S steps went up to this gateway. ....Eze 40:26
were side rooms **s** feet wide all ....Eze 41:5
It measures **s** feet from the ....Eze 43:14
on the altar is **s** feet high, ...Eze 43:15
every day for **s** days as a sin ....Eze 43:25
For **s** days the priests are to ....Eze 43:26
these **s** days, on the eighth ....Eze 43:27
again, he must wait **s** days....................Eze 44:26
will be about **s** miles long and ....Eze 45:1
a part about **s** miles long and ....Eze 45:3
Another area about **s** miles long.............Eze 45:5
wide and about **s** miles long, ...Eze 45:6
be a feast of the **s** days when you ....Eze 45:21
During the **s** days of the feast ....Eze 45:23
he must offer **s** bulls and seven ....Eze 45:23
seven bulls and **s** male sheep ....Eze 45:23
every day of the **s** days of the ....Eze 45:23
the same things for **s** days: ....Eze 45:25
will be about **s** miles wide and ....Eze 48:8
LORD will be about **s** miles long ....Eze 48:9
have land about **s** miles long ....Eze 48:10
have a share about **s** miles long ....Eze 48:13
will be about **s** miles and its ....Eze 48:13
miles wide and **s** miles long. ....Eze 48:15
will be square, **s** miles by seven ....Eze 48:20
square, seven miles by **s** miles. ....Eze 48:20
to be heated **s** times hotter than ....Da 3:19
mind of an animal for **s** years. ....Da 4:16

like a wild animal for **s** years.' ....Da 4:23
S years will pass, and then you ....Da 4:25
S years will pass before you ....Da 4:32
with many people for **s** years.................Da 9:27
We will set up **s** shepherds,....................Mic 5:5
of Joshua, a stone with **s** sides. ....Zch 3:9
And there are **s** lamps and also ....Zch 4:2
and also **s** places for wicks. ....Zch 4:2
are the **s** eyes of the LORD, ...Zch 4:10
out and brings **s** other spirits ....Mt 12:45
They answered, "**S**, and a few ....Mt 15:34
took the **s** loaves of bread and ....Mt 15:36
followers filled **s** baskets with ....Mt 15:37
the **s** loaves of bread that fed ....Mt 16:10
forgive him as many as **s** times?" ....Mt 18:21
forgive him more than **s** times. ....Mt 18:22
he wrongs you seventy times **s**. ....Mt 18:22
Once there were **s** brothers among.............Mt 22:25
Since all **s** men had married her, ...Mt 22:28
you have?" They answered, "**S**."...............Mk 8:5
Then he took the **s** loaves, ...Mk 8:6
followers filled **s** baskets with ....Mk 8:8
when I divided **s** loaves of bread ....Mk 8:20
of food?" They answered, "**S**." ....Mk 8:20
Once there were **s** brothers. ....Mk 12:20
All **s** brothers married her and ....Mk 12:22
Since all **s** brothers had married ....Mk 12:23
had forced **s** demons out of her. ....Mk 16:9
once been married for **s** years. ....Lk 2:36
from whom **s** demons had gone out; ....Lk 8:2
out and brings **s** other spirits ....Lk 11:26
against you **s** times in one day ....Lk 17:4
Once there were **s** brothers. ....Lk 20:29
happened with all **s** brothers; ....Lk 20:31
Since all **s** brothers had married ....Lk 20:33
about **s** miles from Jerusalem. ....Lk 24:13
choose **s** of your own men who are ....Ac 6:3
so they chose these **s** men: ....Ac 6:5
God destroyed **s** nations in the ....Ac 13:19
S sons of Sceva, a leading ....Ac 19:14
where we stayed for **s** days. ....Ac 20:6
and stayed with them for **s** days. ....Ac 21:4
one of the **s** helpers, and stayed ....Ac 21:8
the **s** days were almost over, ...Ac 21:27
I have left **s** thousand people ....Rm 11:4
marched around them for **s** days. ....Heb 11:30
and **s** other people with him. 2Pe 2:5
To the **s** churches in Asia: ....Rev 1:4
from the **s** spirits before his ....Rev 1:4
and send it to the **s** churches: ....Rev 1:11
I turned, I saw **s** golden ....Rev 1:12
He held **s** stars in his right ....Rev 1:16
secret of the **s** stars that you ....Rev 1:20
hand and the **s** golden lampstands ....Rev 1:20
The **s** lampstands are the seven ....Rev 1:20
lampstands are the **s** churches, ...Rev 1:20
and the **s** stars are the angels ....Rev 1:20
the angels of the **s** churches. ....Rev 1:20
One who holds the **s** stars in his.............Rev 2:1
walks among the **s** golden ....Rev 2:1
The One who has the **s** spirits.................Rev 3:1
and the **s** stars says this ....Rev 3:1
Before the throne **s** lamps were ....Rev 4:5
which are the **s** spirits of God. ....Rev 4:5
was kept closed with **s** seals. ....Rev 5:1
the scroll and its **s** seals." ....Rev 5:5
He had **s** horns and seven eyes, ...Rev 5:6
He had seven horns and **s** eyes, ...Rev 5:6
which are the **s** spirits of God ....Rev 5:6
opened the first of the **s** seals. ....Rev 6:1
And I saw the **s** angels who stand ....Rev 8:2
to whom were given **s** trumpets.............Rev 8:2
Then the **s** angels who had the ....Rev 8:6

who had the **s** trumpets prepared .... Rev 8:6
the voices of **s** thunders spoke. .... Rev 10:3
When the **s** thunders spoke, ... Rev 10:4
hidden what the **s** thunders said. .... Rev 10:4
S thousand people were killed in .... Rev 11:13
dragon with **s** heads and seven .... Rev 12:3
seven heads and **s** crowns on each .... Rev 12:3
It had ten horns and **s** heads, ... Rev 13:1
There were **s** angels bringing .... Rev 15:1
angels bringing **s** disasters..................... Rev 15:1
And the **s** angels bringing the................. Rev 15:6
bringing the **s** disasters came .... Rev 15:6
to the **s** angels seven golden .... Rev 15:7
the seven angels **s** golden bowls.............. Rev 15:7
the temple until the **s** disasters .... Rev 15:8
disasters of the **s** angels were .... Rev 15:8
temple saying to the **s** angels,............... Rev 16:1
pour out the **s** bowls of God's .... Rev 16:1
Then one of the **s** angels who had .... Rev 17:1
angels who had the **s** bowls came .... Rev 17:1
it had **s** heads and ten horns. .... Rev 17:3
one with **s** heads and ten horns............... Rev 17:7
The **s** heads on the beast are .... Rev 17:9
the beast are **s** mountains where .... Rev 17:9
they are **s** kings. Five of the .... Rev 17:10
He belongs to the first **s** kings, ... Rev 17:11
Then one of the **s** angels who had .... Rev 21:9
angels who had the **s** bowls full .... Rev 21:9
full of the **s** last troubles .... Rev 21:9

SEVENTEEN
was a young man, **s** years old. .... Ge 37:2
Jacob lived in Egypt **s** years, ... Ge 47:28
ruled in Jerusalem for **s** years. 1Ki 14:21
Jehoahaz ruled **s** years, ... 2Ki 13:1
They had **s** thousand two hundred 1Ch 7:11
There were **s** hundred skilled men 1Ch 26:30
it held about **s** thousand five 2Ch 4:5
king in Jerusalem for **s** years................... 2Ch 12:13
which was **s** and one-half feet .... Eze 40:11
The entrance was **s** and one-half .... Eze 41:2
which was **s** and one-half feet .... Eze 42:4

SEVENTEENTH
On the **s** day of the second month .... Ge 7:11
Jehoshaphat's **s** year as king 1Ki 22:51
of Judah in the **s** year Pekah son 2Ki 16:1
The **s** was Hezir. 1Ch 24:15
S, twelve men were chosen from 1Ch 25:24

SEVENTH
By the **s** day God finished the................. Ge 2:2
God blessed the **s** day and made .... Ge 2:3
but the **s** day is a day of rest .... Ex 20:10
On the **s** day he rested. .... Ex 20:11
but on the **s** day you must rest. .... Ex 23:12
but the **s** day is a day of rest, ... Ex 31:15
But during the **s** year, you must .... Le 25:4
In the **s** year of King Artaxerxes .... Ezr 7:7
about the **s** day of the week .... Heb 4:4
the **s** descendant from Adam,................. Jud 1:14

SEVENTY
family of Jacob in Egypt was **s.** .... Ge 46:27
was a total of **s** people who were .... Ex 1:5
of water and **s** palm trees. .... Ex 15:27
and **s** of the elders of Israel .... Ex 24:1
There were only **s** of your .... Dt 10:22
had **s** sons of his own, because .... Jdg 8:30
Our lifetime is **s** years or, ... Ps 90:10
the king of Babylon for **s** years. .... Je 25:11
But when the **s** years have .... Je 25:12
will be powerful for **s** years. .... Je 29:10
be empty ruins for **s** years. .... Da 9:2
with them for **s** years now." .... Zch 1:12

'For **s** years you fasted and .... Zch 7:5
if he wrongs you **s** times seven. .... Mt 18:22
soldiers, **s** horsemen, and two................. Ac 23:23

SEVENTY-FIVE
to be one hundred **s** years old. .... Ge 25:7
s pounds of pure gold to make .... Ex 25:39
his relatives (**s** persons .... Ac 7:14

SEVENTY-FOUR
gave him about **s** thousand pounds 2Ki 15:19
sent about **s** thousand pounds 1Ch 19:6

SEVENTY-ONE
There were **s** hundred men from 1Ch 12:25

SEVENTY-SEVEN
will be punished **s** times." .... Ge 4:24
the names of **s** officers and..................... Jdg 8:14
s hundred sheep and 2Ch 17:11
sheep and **s** hundred goats. 2Ch 17:11
male sheep, and **s** lambs. .... Ezr 8:35

SEVENTY-SIX
were two hundred **s** people on the .... Ac 27:37

SEVENTY-TWO
the Lord chose **s** others and sent .... Lk 10:1
When the **s** came back, they were .... Lk 10:17

SEW
apart and a time to **s** together. .... Ec 3:7

SEWAGE
And they made it into a **s** pit, ... 2Ki 10:27

SEWED
they **s** fig leaves together and .... Ge 3:7

SEWING
and also skilled at **s** the blue, ... Ex 38:23

SEWN
cloth belt with designs **s** on it. .... Ex 28:39
s by a person who could sew well. .... Ex 38:18
a woven collar **s** around it so it .... Ex 39:23
and designs were **s** onto it, ... Ex 39:29

SEWS
No one **s** a patch of unshrunk.................. Mt 9:16
No one **s** a patch of unshrunk.................. Mk 2:21

SEXUAL
is if she has **s** relations with .... Mt 5:32
if his wife has **s** relations with .... Mt 19:9
blood, and any kind of **s** sin. .... Ac 15:29
Do not take part in **s** sin.'" .... Ac 21:25
they became full of **s** sin, ... Rm 1:24
that there is **s** sin among you.................. 1Co 5:1
body is not for **s** sin but for 1Co 6:13
So run away from **s** sin. 1Co 6:18
But because **s** sin is a danger,................. 1Co 7:2
and to stay away from **s** sins. 1Th 4:3
were full of **s** sin and people .... Jud 1:7
and by taking part in **s** sins. .... Rev 2:14
from their **s** sins or stealing. .... Rev 9:21

SEXUALLY
associate with those who sin **s**. 1Co 5:9
magic, who sin **s**, who murder, ... Rev 22:15

SHAALABBIN
S, Aijalon, Ithlah, ... Jos 19:42

SHAALBIM
in Mount Heres, Aijalon, and **S**. .... Jdg 1:35
of Makaz, **S**, Beth Shemesh, ... 1Ki 4:9

SHAALBONITE
Eliahba the **S**; the sons of 2Sa 23:32
the Baharumite; Eliahba the **S**; 1Ch 11:33

SHAALIM
They went into the land of **S**, ... 1Sa 9:4

S

SHAAPH

Geshan, Pelet, Ephah, and **S**.	1Ch 2:47
S, and Sheva. Shaaph was the	1Ch 2:49
S was the father of Madmannah.	1Ch 2:49

SHAARAIM

S, Adithaim, and Gederah (also	Jos 15:36
lay on the **S** road as far as	1Sa 17:52
Hazar Susim, Beth Biri, and **S**.	1Ch 4:31

SHAASHGAZ

be placed under the care of **S**,	Est 2:14

SHABBETHAI

S the Levite were against the	Ezr 10:15
Jamin, Akkub, **S**, Hodiah,	Ne 8:7
And there were **S** and Jozabad,	Ne 11:16

SHADE

come and find shelter in my **s**!	Jdg 9:15
trees, palms, and **s** trees.	Ne 8:15
the mountains with our **s**.	Ps 80:10
The LORD is the **s** that protects	Ps 121:5
from our enemies as **s** protects	Is 16:3
like **s** that protects them from	Is 25:4
his covering for **s** above them.	Je 43:10
nations lived in the tree's **s**.	Eze 31:6
earth left the **s** of that tree.	Eze 31:12
lived under the great tree's **s**.	Eze 31:17
trees, because their **s** is nice.	Hos 4:13
for himself and sat in the **s**,	Jnh 4:5
which gave him **s** and helped him	Jnh 4:6
birds can make nests in its **s**."	Mk 4:32

SHADED

branches that **s** the forest.	Eze 31:3

SHADES

Your cloth **s** over the deck were	Eze 27:7

SHADOW

Do you want the **s** to go forward	2Ki 20:9
easy for the **s** to go forward ten	2Ki 20:10
brought the **s** ten steps back	2Ki 20:11
Our time on earth is like a **s**.	1Ch 29:15
Our days on earth are only a **s**.	Job 8:9
like a passing **s** that does not	Job 14:2
and my body is as thin as a **s**.	Job 17:7
place or deep **s** where those who	Job 34:22
lotus plants hide it in their **s**;	Job 40:22
me under the **s** of your wings.	Ps 17:8
people in the **s** of your wings.	Ps 36:7
hide under the **s** of your wings	Ps 57:1
My days are like a passing **s**;	Ps 102:11
I am dying like an evening **s**;	Ps 109:23
short life passes like a **s**.	Ec 6:12
Like a **s**, they will not last.	Ec 8:13
I enjoy sitting in his **s**;	Sng 2:3
like a cool **s** from a large rock	Is 32:2
The sun has made a **s** go down the	Is 38:8
So the **s** made by the sun went	Is 38:8
He hid me in the **s** of his hand.	Is 49:2
I sit in the **s** of trouble now,	Mic 7:8
in darkness, in the **s** of death.	Lk 1:79
least his **s** might fall on them.	Ac 5:15
were like a **s** of what was to	Col 2:17
only a copy and a **s** of what is	Heb 8:5

SHADOWS

are seeing the **s** of the	Jdg 9:36
The **s** just look like people."	Jdg 9:36
slave wishing for the evening **s**,	Job 7:2
brings dark **s** into the light.	Job 12:22
People are like **s** moving about.	Ps 39:6
their lives are like passing **s**.	Ps 144:4
day dawns and the **s** disappear.	Sng 2:17
day dawns and the **s** disappear,	Sng 4:6
the evening **s** are growing long.	Je 6:4

covered with the **s** of death,	Mt 4:16
change like their shifting **s**.	Jam 1:17

SHADRACH

Hananiah's was **S**, Mishael's was	Da 1:7
Daniel asked the king to make **S**,	Da 2:49
Their names are **S**, Meshach, and	Da 3:12
very angry and called for **S**,	Da 3:13
said, "**S**, Meshach,	Da 3:14
S, Meshach, and Abednego	Da 3:16
was furious with **S**,	Da 3:19
in his army to tie up **S**,	Da 3:20
So **S**, Meshach, and Abednego were	Da 3:21
the strong soldiers who threw **S**,	Da 3:22
Firmly tied, **S**, Meshach, and	Da 3:23
and shouted, "**S**, Meshach,	Da 3:26
So **S**, Meshach, and Abednego	Da 3:26
Praise the God of **S**, Meshach,	Da 3:28
anything against the God of **S**,	Da 3:29
king promoted **S**, Meshach, and	Da 3:30

SHAGEE

Jonathan son of **S** the Hararite;	1Ch 11:34

SHAHAR

S on the hill in the valley,	Jos 13:19

SHAHAZUMAH

called Tabor, **S**, and Beth	Jos 19:22

SHAKE

men of Moab will **s** with fear;	Ex 15:15
you, they will **s** with fear, and	Dt 2:25
I did before and **s** myself free."	Jdg 16:20
of joy that made the ground **s**.	1Sa 4:5
of heaven began to **s**.	2Sa 22:8
way may God **s** out everyone who	Ne 5:13
May God **s** him out of his house	Ne 5:13
because they **s** their fists at	Job 15:25
you and **s** my head at you.	Job 16:4
foundations **s** when he thunders	Job 26:11
its edges and **s** evil people out	Job 38:13
when they **s** a spear at it.	Job 41:29
of the mountains began to **s**.	Ps 18:7
their tongues and **s** their heads.	Ps 22:7
nations; people **s** their heads.	Ps 44:14
or the mountains **s** at the raging	Ps 46:3
Nations tremble and kingdoms **s**.	Ps 46:6
You made the earth **s** and crack.	Ps 60:2
who see them will **s** their heads.	Ps 64:8
earth with all its people may **s**,	Ps 75:3
Let the peoples **s** with fear.	Ps 99:1
with wings. Let the earth **s**.	Ps 99:1
look at me and **s** their heads.	Ps 109:25
s with fear before the Lord,	Ps 114:7
I **s** in fear of you; I respect	Ps 119:120
your arms will **s** and your legs	Ec 12:3
when he stands to **s** the earth.	Is 2:19
when he stands to **s** the earth.	Is 2:21
the frame around the door to **s**,	Is 6:4
They will **s** their fist at Mount	Is 10:32
make the sky **s**, and the earth	Is 13:13
I see causes me to **s** with fear.	Is 21:3
foundations of the earth will **s**.	Is 24:18
the earth will **s** violently.	Is 24:19
it will **s** like a hut in a storm.	Is 24:20
but you should **s** with fear.	Is 32:11
separated from God **s** with fear.	Is 33:14
away on the earth, **s** with fear.	Is 41:5
Now **s** off the dust and stand up.	Is 52:2
nations will **s** with fear when	Is 64:2
happened and **s** with great fear!	Je 2:12
You should **s** with fear in my	Je 5:22
They will **s** their heads as they	Je 18:16
fun of it and **s** their heads when	Je 19:8
All my bones **s**. I'm like someone	Je 23:9

Edom's fall, the earth will **s**. ....Je 49:21
will **s** their heads when they ....Je 50:13
capture, the earth will **s**. ....Je 50:46
of Jerusalem and **s** their heads. ....La 2:15
who own land will **s** with fear. ....Eze 7:27
s with fear as you drink your ....Eze 12:18
I will **s** my fist at you for................Eze 22:13
Your walls will **s** at the noise ....Eze 26:10
seacoast will **s** with fear when ....Eze 26:15
on the shore **s** with fear when ....Eze 27:28
made the nations **s** with fear at ....Eze 31:16
They will **s** every moment on the ....Eze 32:10
the earth will **s** with fear................Eze 38:20
live in the land **s** with fear, ...Joe 2:1
see them, nations **s** with fear, ...Joe 2:6
Before them, earth and sky **s**. ....Joe 2:10
the sky and the earth will **s**. ....Joe 3:16
whole land will **s** because of it, ...Am 8:8
the bottom of the doors will **s**. ....Am 9:1
The mountains **s** in front of him, ...Nah 1:5
all who live in it **s** with fear. ....Nah 1:5
and make you **s** with fear. ....Hab 2:7
and the nations **s** with fear................Hab 3:6
bones feel weak, and my legs **s**. ....Hab 3:16
will make fun and **s** their fists. ....Zph 2:15
I will once again **s** the heavens ....Hag 2:6
I will **s** all the nations, and ....Hag 2:7
'I am going to **s** the heavens and ....Hag 2:21
I will **s** my hand against them so ....Zch 2:9
people of Gaza will **s** with fear, ...Zch 9:5
that place and **s** its dust off................Mt 10:14
S its dust off your feet as a ....Mk 6:11
but it could not **s** it, because ....Lk 6:48
s the dust off of your feet as ....Lk 9:5
' Moses began to **s** with fear and ....Ac 7:32
Once again I will **s** not only the ....Heb 12:26

SHAKEN
person be **s** out and emptied! ....Ne 5:13
city, and so it will not be **s**. ....Ps 46:5
I am **s** off like a locust. ....Ps 109:23
it will be **s**, and then it will ....Am 8:8
the tree is **s**, the figs fall ....Nah 3:12
of the heavens will be **s**.' ....Mt 24:29
of the heavens will be **s**.' ....Mk 13:25
Pressed down, **s** together, and ....Lk 6:38
powers of the heavens will be **s**. ....Lk 21:26
where they were meeting was **s**................Ac 4:31
that can be **s**—will be destroyed................Heb 12:27
that cannot be **s** will remain. ....Heb 12:27
have a kingdom that cannot be **s**. ....Heb 12:28

SHAKES
He **s** the earth out of its place................Job 9:6
terribly afraid and my body **s**. ....Job 21:6
The LORD's voice **s** the desert; ....Ps 29:8
the LORD **s** the Desert of Kadesh. ....Ps 29:8
The LORD's voice **s** the oaks and ....Ps 29:9
be afraid even if the earth **s**, ...Ps 46:2
looks at the earth, and it **s**. ....Ps 104:32
The ground **s** from the neighing ....Je 8:16
The earth **s** when he is angry, ...Je 10:10
The land **s** and moves in pain, ...Je 51:29
the land, and the land **s**. ....Am 9:5
He stands and **s** the earth. ....Hab 3:6

SHAKING
in his army were **s** with fear. 1Sa 13:7
all my bones were **s**. ....Job 4:14
I am scared and **s**, and terror ....Ps 55:5
Heal its breaks because it is **s**. ....Ps 60:2
they are **s** with fear. ....Is 15:4
worried, and I am **s** with fear. ....Is 21:4
the mountains, and they were **s**. ....Je 4:24
I was so afraid that I was **s**. ....Da 10:10

I stood up, but I was still **s**. ....Da 10:11
be like someone **s** grain through................Am 9:9
S with fear, she told him the ....Mk 5:33
were confused and **s** with fear, ...Mk 16:8
came forward, **s**, and fell down ....Lk 8:47
inside and, **s** with fear, fell ....Ac 16:29
Moses said, "I am **s** with fear." ....Heb 12:21

SHALISHA
of Ephraim and the land of **S**,................1Sa 9:4

SHALISHAH
man from Baal **S** came to Elisha, ...2Ki 4:42

SHALLEKETH
Gate and the **S** Gate on the upper 1Ch 26:16

SHALLUM
S son of Jabesh made plans 2Ki 15:10
Then **S** became king in his place. 2Ki 15:10
S son of Jabesh became king 2Ki 15:13
S ruled for a month in Samaria................2Ki 15:13
and attacked **S** son of Jabesh 2Ki 15:14
other acts of **S** and his secret 2Ki 15:15
was the wife of **S** son of Tikvah,................2Ki 22:14
Sismai was the father of **S**. 1Ch 2:40
S was the father of Jekamiah, ...1Ch 2:41
Zedekiah, and his fourth was **S**. 1Ch 3:15
Shaul's son was **S**. Shallum's son 1Ch 4:25
Zadok was the father of **S**. 1Ch 6:12
S was the father of Hilkiah. 1Ch 6:13
Of the gatekeepers there were **S**, ...1Ch 9:17
relatives. **S** was their leader. 1Ch 9:17
S was Kore's son. Kore was 1Ch 9:19
S and his relatives from the 1Ch 9:19
He was the first son of **S**, ...1Ch 9:31
Jehizkiah son of **S**, and Amasa 2Ch 28:12
was the wife of **S** son of Tikvah,................2Ch 34:22
descendants of **S**, Ater, Talmon, ...Ezr 2:42
the son of **S**, the son of Zadok, ...Ezr 7:2
gatekeepers: **S**, Telem, and Uri ....Ezr 10:24
S, Amariah, and Joseph................Ezr 10:42
Next to them **S** son of Hallohesh, ...Ne 3:12
descendants of **S**, Ater, Talmon, ...Ne 7:45
of your uncle **S**, will come to ....Je 32:7
the room of Maaseiah son of **S**, ...Je 35:4

SHALLUM'S
him and became king in **S** place. 2Ki 15:14
was Shallum. **S** son was Mibsam. 1Ch 4:25

SHALLUN
S son of Col-Hozeh, the ruler of ....Ne 3:15
Next to **S** was Nehemiah son of ....Ne 3:16

SHALMAI
Hagab, **S**, Hanan, ...Ezr 2:46
Lebana, Hagaba, **S**,................Ne 7:48

SHALMAN
the time King **S** destroyed Beth ....Hos 10:14

SHALMANESER
S king of Assyria came to attack 2Ki 17:3
the payments, to **S** that he had 2Ki 17:3
stopped giving **S** the payments, ...2Ki 17:4
S king of Assyria surrounded................2Ki 18:9

SHALMANESER'S
Hoshea had been **S** servant and 2Ki 17:3

SHAMA
S and Jeiel sons of Hotham the 1Ch 11:44

SHAME
I could never get rid of my **s**! 2Sa 13:13
will you turn my honor into **s**? ....Ps 4:2
Cover them with **s** and disgrace, ...Ps 35:26
I carry this **s**, and my face is ....Ps 69:7
You see my **s** and disgrace................Ps 69:19
be covered with **s** and disgrace. ....Ps 71:13

S

Take away the **s** I fear, because .... Ps 119:39
Jerusalem be turned back in **s.** .... Ps 129:5
his mother brings **s** and disgrace .... Pr 19:26
but they will be put to **s,** .... Is 30:5
but don't bring **s** to me. .... Je 17:18
but we are full of **s** today— .... Da 9:7
wake up to find **s** and disgrace .... Da 12:2
No more will I **s** you among the .... Joe 2:19
and the kingdoms your **s.** .... Nah 3:5
the Lord has taken away that **s.**" .... Lk 1:25
but you bring **s** to God by .... Rm 2:23
of the world to **s** the wise, ... 1Co 1:27
say this to **s** you. Surely there 1Co 6:5
They have lost all feeling of **s,** .... Eph 4:19
he accepted the **s** as if it were.............. Heb 12:2
and have people see their **s.**" .... Rev 16:15

SHAMEFUL
incense to that **s** god Baal as .... Je 11:13
Men did **s** things with other men, ... Rm 1:27
But since it is **s** for a woman to 1Co 11:6
It is **s** for a woman to speak in 1Co 14:35
It is **s** even to talk about what................ Eph 5:12

SHAMEFULLY
while another has **s** made his .... Eze 22:11

SHAMES
a prostitute, she **s** her father. .... Le 21:9

SHAMGAR
S son of Anath saved Israel. .... Jdg 3:31
S killed six hundred Philistines .... Jdg 3:31
In the days of **S** son of Anath, ... Jdg 5:6

SHAMHUTH
fifth month, was **S,** from Izrah's 1Ch 27:8

SHAMING
again and are **s** him in front .... Heb 6:6

SHAMIR
the mountains: **S,** Jattir, Socoh, ... Jos 15:48
the city of **S** in the mountains................. Jdg 10:1
he died and was buried in **S.** .... Jdg 10:2
was Micah. Micah's son was **S.** 1Ch 24:24

SHAMMA
Bezer, Hod, **S,** Shilshah, Ithran, ... 1Ch 7:37

SHAMMAH
Nahath, Zerah, **S,** and Mizzah. .... Ge 36:13
Nahath, Zerah, **S,** and Mizzah. .... Ge 36:17
Then Jesse had **S** pass by. 1Sa 16:9
Abinadab, and the third was **S.** 1Sa 17:13
Next there was **S** son of Agee the 2Sa 23:11
but **S** stood in the middle of the 2Sa 23:12
S the Harodite; Elika the....................... 2Sa 23:25
son of **S** the Hararite; 2Sa 23:33
Nahath, Zerah, **S,** and Mizzah. 1Ch 1:37

SHAMMAI
Onam's sons were **S** and Jada. 1Ch 2:28
Rekem was the father of **S.**.............. 1Ch 2:44
S was the father of Maon, and 1Ch 2:45

SHAMMAI'S
S sons were Nadab and Abishur. 1Ch 2:28
Jada was **S** brother, and Jada's 1Ch 2:32

SHAMMOTH
S the Harorite; Helez the 1Ch 11:27

SHAMMUA
of Reuben, **S** son of Zaccur; .... Nu 13:4
S, Shobab, Nathan, Solomon,.......... 2Sa 5:14
S, Shobab, Nathan, and Solomon— 1Ch 3:5
S, Shobab, Nathan, Solomon,.................. 1Ch 14:4
And there was Abda son of **S.** .... Ne 11:17
S was the son of Galal, the son .... Ne 11:17
S, from Bilgah's family; .... Ne 12:18

SHAMSHERAI
sons were **S,** Shehariah, ... 1Ch 8:26

SHAN
Beth **S** and its small towns;.................... Jos 17:11
weapons in Beth **S** and all the .... Jos 17:16
living in the cities of Beth **S,** .... Jdg 1:27
his body on the wall of Beth **S.** 1Sa 31:10
all night and came to Beth **S.** 1Sa 31:12
wall of Beth **S** and brought them 1Sa 31:12
square of Beth **S** after they had 2Sa 21:12
and all of Beth **S** next to 1Ki 4:12
from Beth **S** to Abel Meholah 1Ki 4:12
land were the towns of Beth **S,** 1Ch 7:29

SHAPHAM
the main leader, **S** was second, ... 1Ch 5:12
Zabdi, from **S,** was in charge of 1Ch 27:27

SHAPHAN
he sent **S** to the Temple of the 2Ki 22:3
S son of Azaliah, the son of 2Ki 22:3
priest said to **S** the royal 2Ki 22:8

SHAPHAT
tribe of Simeon, **S** son of Hori; .... Nu 13:5
on Elisha son of **S** from Abel 1Ki 19:16
Elisha son of **S** plowing a field 1Ki 19:19
Elisha son of **S** is here. 2Ki 3:11
of Elisha son of **S** isn't cut off................ 2Ki 6:31
Igal, Bariah, Neariah, and **S.** 1Ch 3:22
then Janai and **S** were leaders 1Ch 5:12
S son of Adlai was in charge of 1Ch 27:29

SHAPHIR
and ashamed, you who live in **S.** .... Mic 1:11

SHARAI
Macnadebai, Shashai, **S,**........................ Ezr 10:40

SHARAR
Ahiam son of **S** the Hararite; 2Sa 23:33

SHARE
We have no **s** in David! 2Sa 20:1
king, "We have no **s** in David! 1Ki 12:16
S your food with the hungry and .... Is 58:7
of God should **s** all the good .... Gal 6:6
something to **s** with those who .... Eph 4:28
to be generous and ready to **s.** 1Ti 6:18
S in the troubles we have like a 2Ti 2:3
to others, and **s** with them, ... Heb 13:16

SHARED
shouldn't be **s** with strangers.................. Pr 5:17
are not Jews have **s** in the Jews'............... Rm 15:27
gift, and **s** in the Holy Spirit .... Heb 6:4
sometimes you **s** with those who .... Heb 10:33
with her and **s** her wealth will .... Rev 18:9

SHARES
older son two **s** of everything he.............. Dt 21:17
not giving the Levites their **s.** .... Ne 13:10
wide as one of the tribes' **s.** .... Eze 48:8
tribes of Israel to be their **s,**" .... Eze 48:29
body; her husband **s** them. And 1Co 7:4
his own body; his wife **s** them. 1Co 7:4

SHAREZER
Adrammelech and **S** killed him 2Ki 19:37
Adrammelech and **S** killed him .... Is 37:38
The city of Bethel sent **S,** .... Zch 7:2

SHARING
teaching, **s,** breaking bread, ... Ac 2:42
hope we have of **s** God's glory. .... Rm 5:2
which is a **s** in the blood of.................... 1Co 10:16
that we break is a **s** in the body 1Co 10:16
same thoughts, **s** the same love, ... Php 2:2
happy that you are **s** in Christ's 1Pe 4:13

SHARON

in the Plain of **S** all the way to 1Ch 5:16
Shitrai, from **S**, was in charge 1Ch 27:29
that fed in the Plain of **S**. 1Ch 27:29
I am a rose in the Plain of **S**, ... Sng 2:1
The Plain of **S** is dry like the .... Is 33:9
of Carmel and the Plain of **S**. .... Is 35:2
the Plain of **S** will be a field .... Is 65:10
on the Plain of **S** saw him and .... Ac 9:35

SHARP

the slave's ear using a **s** tool. .... Ex 21:6
will be like **s** hooks in your .... Nu 33:55
with a **s** stick used to .... Jdg 3:31
whips that have **s** points.'" 1Ki 12:11
with whips that have **s** points." 1Ki 12:14
whips that have **s** points.'" 2Ch 10:11
with whips that have **s** points." 2Ch 10:14
Your **s** arrows will enter the .... Ps 45:5
Your tongue is like a **s** razor, ... Ps 52:2
their tongues as **s** as swords. .... Ps 57:4
you with the **s** arrows of a .... Ps 120:4
their tongues **s** as a snake's; .... Ps 140:3
a club, a sword, or a **s** arrow. .... Pr 25:18
people are like **s** sticks used to .... Ec 12:11
Their arrows are **s**, and all of .... Is 5:28
board with many **s** teeth. .... Is 41:15
made my tongue like a **s** sword. .... Is 49:2
He made me like a **s** arrow. .... Is 49:2
Their tongues are like **s** arrows. .... Je 9:8
human, take a **s** sword, and use .... Eze 5:1
a sword, made **s** and polished. .... Eze 21:9
It is made **s** for the killing. .... Eze 21:10
It is made **s** and polished, ... Eze 21:11
branches or **s** stickers to hurt .... Eze 28:24
and a **s** double-edged sword came .... Rev 1:16
One who has the **s**, double-edged .... Rev 2:12
his head and a **s** sickle in his .... Rev 14:14
and he also had a **s** sickle. .... Rev 14:17
to the angel with the **s** sickle, ... Rev 14:18
Take your **s** sickle and gather .... Rev 14:18
mouth comes a **s** sword that he .... Rev 19:15

SHARPEN

I will **s** my flashing sword, ... Dt 32:41
lives, God will **s** his sword; .... Ps 7:12
They **s** their tongues like swords .... Ps 64:3
S the arrows! Pick up your .... Je 51:11

SHARPENED

hoes, axes, and sickles **s**. 1Sa 13:20

SHARPENING

of silver for **s** plows and hoes. 1Sa 13:21
an ounce of silver for **s** picks, ... 1Sa 13:21

SHARPENS

As iron **s** iron, so people can .... Pr 27:17

SHARPER

and working and is **s** than a .... Heb 4:12

SHARUHEN

Beth Lebaoth, and **S**. .... Jos 19:6

SHASHAI

Macnadebai, **S**, Sharai, ... Ezr 10:40

SHASHAK

sons were Ahio, **S**, Jeremoth, ... 1Ch 8:14

SHASHAK'S

S sons were Ishpan, Eber, Eliel, ... 1Ch 8:22

SHATTERED

city will be disgraced and **s**. .... Je 48:1
Moab is **s**! The people are .... Je 48:39
how broken and **s** that hammer is .... Je 50:23

SHAUL

When Samlah died, **S** became king. .... Ge 36:37
When **S** died, Baal-Hanan son of .... Ge 36:38
Jakin, Zohar, and **S** (Simeon's .... Ge 46:10
Jakin, Zohar, and **S**, the son of .... Ex 6:15
from **S** came the Shaulite family .... Nu 26:13
When Samlah died, not **s** became king. 1Ch 1:48
When **S** died, Baal-Hanan son of 1Ch 1:49
Jamin, Jarib, Zerah, and **S**. 1Ch 4:24
Uzziah, and Uzziah's son was **S**. 1Ch 6:24

SHAUL'S

S son was Shallum. Shallum's son 1Ch 4:25

SHAULITE

Shaul came the **S** family group. .... Nu 26:13

SHAVE

the person must **s** himself, ... Le 13:33
he must not **s** the sore place. .... Le 13:33
his clothes, **s** off all his hair .... Le 14:8
day he must **s** off all his hair— .... Le 14:9
Priests must not **s** their heads, ... Le 21:5
or **s** off the edges of their .... Le 21:5
So they must **s** their head seven .... Nu 6:9
Meeting Tent and **s** off their .... Nu 6:18
and have them **s** their bodies and .... Nu 8:7
cut yourselves or **s** your heads .... Dt 14:1
where she must **s** her head and .... Dt 21:12
in a man to **s** off the seven .... Jdg 16:19
to **s** their heads and wear rough .... Is 22:12
cut himself or **s** his head to .... Je 16:6
will be sad and **s** their heads. .... Je 47:5
barber's razor to **s** your head .... Eze 5:1
They **s** their heads for you, ... Eze 27:31
They must not **s** their heads or .... Eze 44:20
I will make you **s** your heads as .... Am 8:10
so they can **s** their heads. .... Ac 21:24
off her hair or to **s** her head, ... 1Co 11:6

SHAVED

prison, and he **s**, put on clean .... Ge 41:14
If someone **s** my head, I would .... Jdg 16:17
shame them he **s** off half their 2Sa 10:4
To shame them he **s** their beards 1Ch 19:4
his robe and **s** his head to show .... Job 1:20
beard has been **s** to show how sad .... Is 15:2
and Samaria had **s** off their .... Je 41:5
head has been **s** and every beard .... Je 48:37
and all their heads will be **s**. .... Eze 7:18
as a woman who has her head **s**. 1Co 11:5

SHAVEH

and the Emites in **S** Kiriathaim. .... Ge 14:5
to meet him in the Valley of **S**. .... Ge 14:17

SHAVING

be as if the Lord is **s** the hair .... Is 7:20
you by **s** the top of your .... Je 2:16

SHAVSHA

S was the royal secretary. 1Ch 18:16

SHAWL

me your **s** and hold it open. .... Ru 3:15
So Ruth held her **s** open, ... Ru 3:15

SHAWLS

robes, capes, **s**, and purses, ... Is 3:22
dresses, turbans, and long **s**. .... Is 3:23

SHE'S

S very upset, and the LORD has 2Ki 4:27

SHE-CAMEL

are like a **s** in mating season .... Je 2:23

SHEAL

Adaiah, Jashub, **S**, and Jeremoth. .... Ezr 10:29

SHEALTIEL

as a prisoner. His sons were **S**, ... 1Ch 3:17
Zerubbabel son of **S** and began to .... Ezr 3:2
Zerubbabel son of **S**, Jeshua son .... Ezr 3:8
son of **S** and Jeshua son .... Ezr 5:2
son of **S** and with Jeshua. .... Ne 12:1
the LORD to Zerubbabel son of **S**, ... Hag 1:1
son of **S** and Joshua son .... Hag 1:12
stirred up Zerubbabel son of **S**, ... Hag 1:14
Speak to Zerubbabel son of **S**, ... Hag 2:2
son of **S**, my servant,' .... Hag 2:23
Jehoiachin was the father of **S**. .... Mt 1:12
S was the grandfather of........................ Mt 1:12
was the grandson of **S**. .... Lk 3:27
S was the son of Neri............................ Lk 3:27

SHEAR-JASHUB

You and your son **S** should go and .... Is 7:3

SHEARED

white like newly **s** sheep just .... Sng 4:2

SHEARIAH

Bokeru, Ishmael, **S**, Obadiah, and 1Ch 8:38
Bokeru, Ishmael, **S**, Obadiah, and 1Ch 9:44

SHEBA

sons of Raamah were **S** and Dedan. .... Ge 10:7
Obal, Abimael, **S**, ... Ge 10:28
was the father of **S** and Dedan. .... Ge 25:3
also called **S**), Moladah, ... Jos 19:2
troublemaker named **S** son of................ 2Sa 20:1
and followed **S** son of Bicri. 2Sa 20:2
S son of Bicri is more dangerous 2Sa 20:6
to chase **S** son of Bicri. 2Sa 20:7
to chase **S** son of Bicri. 2Sa 20:10
Joab to chase **S** son of Bicri. 2Sa 20:13
S went through all the tribes of 2Sa 20:14
who is named **S** son of Bicri. 2Sa 20:21
off the head of **S** son of Bicri 2Sa 20:22
S was the royal secretary. 2Sa 20:25
When the queen of **S** heard about 1Ki 10:1
The queen of **S** learned that 1Ki 10:4
than the queen of **S** gave to King 1Ki 10:10
the queen of **S** everything she.............. 1Ki 10:13
Raamah's sons were **S** and Dedan........... 1Ch 1:9
Obal, Abimael, **S**, ... 1Ch 1:22
Jokshan's sons were **S** and Dedan.......... 1Ch 1:32
Meshullam, **S**, Jorai, Jacan, Zia 1Ch 5:13
When the queen of **S** heard about 2Ch 9:1
The queen of **S** saw that Solomon 2Ch 9:3
as the queen of **S** gave to King 2Ch 9:9
the queen of **S** everything she.............. 2Ch 9:12
the traders of **S** look hopefully. .... Job 6:19
the kings of **S** and Seba bring .... Ps 72:10
Let him receive gold from **S**. .... Ps 72:15
will come from **S** bringing gold .... Is 60:6
of incense from the land of **S**? .... Je 6:20
The merchants of **S** and Raamah .... Eze 27:22
the traders of **S**, Asshur, and .... Eze 27:23
S, Dedan, and the traders of .... Eze 38:13

SHEBANIAH

The priests **S**, Joshaphat, ... 1Ch 15:24
Bani, Kadmiel, **S**, Bunni,...................... Ne 9:4
Hodiah, **S**, and Pethahiah. .... Ne 9:5
Hattush, **S**, Malluch, ... Ne 10:4
S, Hodiah, Kelita, Pelaiah, Hanan, ... Ne 10:10
Zaccur, Sherebiah, **S**, ... Ne 10:12

SHEBAT

is the month of **S**, in Darius's .... Zch 1:7

SHEBER

was the mother of **S**, Tirhanah, ... 1Ch 2:48

SHEBNA

sent Eliakim, **S**, and Joah out to 2Ki 18:18
S was the royal secretary, ... 2Ki 18:18
son of Hilkiah, **S**, and Joah said 2Ki 18:26
Then Eliakim, **S**, and Joah tore 2Ki 18:37
S was the royal secretary, ... 2Ki 18:37
palace manager, and **S**, the royal 2Ki 19:2
to this servant **S**, the manager .... Is 22:15
Eliakim, **S**, and Joah went out to .... Is 36:3
S was the royal secretary, ... Is 36:3
Then Eliakim, **S**, and Joah said.............. Is 36:11
Then Eliakim, **S**, and Joah tore .... Is 36:22
S was the royal secretary, ... Is 36:22
palace manager, and **S**, the royal .... Is 37:2

SHECANIAH

Rephaiah, Arnan, Obadiah, and **S**............. 1Ch 3:21
was Jeshua. The tenth was **S**. 1Ch 24:11
and **S** helped Kore in the towns 2Ch 31:15
of the descendants of **S**. .... Ezr 8:3
S son of Jahaziel, with three .... Ezr 8:5
Then **S** son of Jehiel the Elamite .... Ezr 10:2
him, Shemaiah son of **S**, the .... Ne 3:29
the son-in-law of **S** son of Arah.............. Ne 6:18
S, Rehum, Meremoth, ... Ne 12:3

SHECANIAH'S

S son was Shemaiah. 1Ch 3:22
Joseph, from **S** family; .... Ne 12:14

SHECHEM

as the great tree of Moreh at **S**. .... Ge 12:6
traveled from **S** to the mountain.............. Ge 12:8
at the city of **S** in the land of .... Ge 33:18
father of **S** for one hundred .... Ge 33:19
When **S** son of Hamor the Hivite, ... Ge 34:2
S fell in love with Dinah, ... Ge 34:3
learned how **S** had disgraced his .... Ge 34:5
Hamor father of **S** went to talk .... Ge 34:6
very angry that **S** had done such .... Ge 34:7
My son **S** is deeply in love with .... Ge 34:8
S also talked to Jacob and to .... Ge 34:11
sons answered **S** and his father .... Ge 34:13
because **S** had disgraced their .... Ge 34:13
seemed fair to Hamor and **S**. .... Ge 34:18
So **S** quickly went to be .... Ge 34:19
Now **S** was the most respected man .... Ge 34:19
So Hamor and **S** went to the gate .... Ge 34:20
They agreed with Hamor and **S**,.............. Ge 34:24
Hamor and his son **S** and then .... Ge 34:26
back for what **S** had done to .... Ge 34:27
great tree near the town of **S**. .... Ge 35:4
brothers went to **S** to graze.................. Ge 37:12
Go to **S** where your brothers are .... Ge 37:13
When Joseph came to **S**,...................... Ge 37:14
the land of **S** that I took from .... Ge 48:22
S came the Shechemite family .... Nu 26:31
Helek, Asriel, **S**, Hepher, and .... Jos 17:2
Asher and Micmethath, near **S**. .... Jos 17:7
S in the mountains of Ephraim; .... Jos 20:7
S in the mountains of Ephraim .... Jos 21:21
tribes of Israel together at **S**. .... Jos 24:1
On that day at **S** Joshua made an .... Jos 24:25
buried them at **S**, in the land .... Jos 24:32
Hamor was the father of **S**). .... Jos 24:32
a slave woman who lived in **S**, ... Jdg 8:31
to his uncles in the city of **S**. .... Jdg 9:1
the leaders of **S**, 'Is it better .... Jdg 9:2
all the leaders of **S** about this. .... Jdg 9:3
the leaders of **S** gave Abimelech............ Jdg 9:4
the leaders of **S** and Beth Millo .... Jdg 9:6
the great tree standing in **S**. .... Jdg 9:6
you leaders of **S**, so that God .... Jdg 9:7
the leaders of **S** just because he .... Jdg 9:18
you leaders of **S** and Beth Millo! .... Jdg 9:20

the leaders of S and Beth Millo .... Jdg 9:20
and the leaders of S so that the .... Jdg 9:23
the leaders of S turned against .... Jdg 9:23
the leaders of S had helped him. .... Jdg 9:24
The leaders of S were against.................. Jdg 9:25
and his brothers moved into S, ... Jdg 9:26
the leaders of S trusted him. .... Jdg 9:26
Ebed said, "We are the men of S. .... Jdg 9:28
the ruler of S, heard what Gaal .... Jdg 9:30
Gaal's brothers have come to S, ... Jdg 9:31
and hid near S in four groups. .... Jdg 9:34
led the men of S out to fight .... Jdg 9:39
and his brothers to leave S. .... Jdg 9:41
day the people of S went out to .... Jdg 9:42
the city of S all day until they.................. Jdg 9:45
in the Tower of S heard what had .... Jdg 9:46
heard what had happened to S, ... Jdg 9:46
Tower of S had gathered there. .... Jdg 9:47
went up Mount Zalmon, near S. .... Jdg 9:48
at the Tower of S also died— .... Jdg 9:49
the men of S for the evil they .... Jdg 9:57
road that goes from Bethel to S, ... Jdg 21:19
Rehoboam went to S, where all 1Ki 12:1
Jeroboam made S in the mountains 1Ki 12:25
They received S, one of the...................... 1Ch 6:67
were Ahian, S, Likhi, and Aniam 1Ch 7:19
and S and the villages near it. 1Ch 7:28
Rehoboam went to S, where all 2Ch 10:1
I will divide S and measure off .... Ps 60:6
I will divide S and measure off .... Ps 108:7
Those men from S, Shiloh, and .... Je 41:5
on the road to S and do wicked .... Hos 6:9
were moved to S and put in .... Ac 7:16
from the sons of Hamor in S. .... Ac 7:16

SHECHEM'S

Dinah out of S house and left. .... Ge 34:26
the men of Hamor, S father. .... Jdg 9:28

SHECHEMITE

Shechem came the S family group; .... Nu 26:31

SHED

loudly for her or s any tears. .... Eze 24:16

SHEDEUR

tribe of Reuben—Elizur son of S; .... Nu 1:5
of Reuben is Elizur son of S. .... Nu 2:10
Elizur son of S was the .... Nu 10:18

SHEEP

gave Abram s, cattle, male and .... Ge 12:16
three-year-old male s, a dove, ... Ge 15:9
Abimelech gave Abraham some s, ... Ge 20:14
Abimelech some s and cattle, ... Ge 21:27
and saw a male s caught in a .... Ge 22:13
and took the s and killed it. .... Ge 22:13
has given him many flocks of s, ... Ge 24:35
three flocks of s lying nearby,................. Ge 29:2
from the well and water the s. .... Ge 29:3
is coming now with his s." .... Ge 29:6
time for the s to be gathered .... Ge 29:7
of the well and water the s." .... Ge 29:8
Rachel came with her father's s,............. Ge 29:9
was her job to care for the s. .... Ge 29:9
daughter Rachel and Laban's s, ... Ge 29:10
its mouth and watered Laban's s. .... Ge 29:10
every speckled or spotted s, ... Ge 30:32
on them), and all the black s. .... Ge 30:35
gone to cut the wool from his s, ... Ge 31:19
of the male s from your flocks. .... Ge 31:38
hundred female s and twenty male........... Ge 32:14
female sheep and twenty male s, ... Ge 32:14
cutting the wool from his s. .... Ge 38:12
to cut the wool from his s. .... Ge 38:13
in charge of my s and cattle." .... Ge 47:6

their horses, s, goats, cattle, ... Ge 47:17
goats, and s to become sick. .... Ex 9:3
a young s or a young goat. .... Ex 12:5
as well as a large number of s, ... Ex 12:38
your s and your cattle .... Ex 20:24
a bull or a s and kills or sells .... Ex 22:1
stole and four s for the one..................... Ex 22:1
sheep for the one s he stole. .... Ex 22:1
whether ox, donkey, s, clothing, ... Ex 22:9
his donkey, ox, s, or some other .... Ex 22:10
same with your bulls and your s. .... Ex 22:30
and two male s that have nothing .... Ex 29:1
with the bull and two male s. .... Ex 29:3
of the male s, and have Aaron .... Ex 29:15
Burn the whole s on the altar; .... Ex 29:18
the other male s, and have Aaron .... Ex 29:19
take the fat from the male s, ... Ex 29:22
This is the male s to be used in .... Ex 29:22
of the male s used to appoint .... Ex 29:26
thigh of the s that were used .... Ex 29:27
Take the male s used to appoint .... Ex 29:31
the meat of the s and the bread .... Ex 29:32
the meat from that s or any of .... Ex 29:34
burnt offering is a s or a goat .... Le 1:10
flock a male s that has nothing .... Le 5:15
using the male s as the penalty .... Le 5:16
priest a male s from the flock, ... Le 5:18
priest—a male s from the flock, ... Le 6:6
fat from cattle, s, or goats. .... Le 7:23
sin offering and the two male s, ... Le 8:2
brought the male s of the burnt .... Le 8:18
cut the male s into pieces and................. Le 8:20
the whole s on the altar as .... Le 8:21
Moses brought the other male s,............. Le 8:22
Moses killed the s and put some............. Le 8:23
and right thigh of the male s. .... Le 8:26
share of the male s used in .... Le 8:29
calf and a male s that have .... Le 9:2
and the male s will be a whole .... Le 9:2
bull and a male s for fellowship .... Le 9:4
and the male s as the fellowship.............. Le 9:18
fat of the bull and the male s— .... Le 9:19
breasts of the bull and the s .... Le 9:20
and a male s for a whole burnt .... Le 16:3
and one male s for a burnt .... Le 16:5
bring a male s as his penalty .... Le 19:21
will offer the s as a penalty..................... Le 19:22
it—a bull, a s, or a goat—so it................ Le 22:19
When an ox, a s, or a goat is .... Le 22:27
same day, either an ox or a s. .... Le 22:28
bull, two male s, and seven male .... Le 23:18
must blow the horn of a male s; .... Le 25:9
is a cow or a s, it is the LORD' .... Le 27:26
sacrifice a male s to remove the .... Nu 5:8
and a male s that has nothing................. Nu 6:14
kill the male s as a fellowship................. Nu 6:17
boiled shoulder from the male s. .... Nu 6:19
and the thigh from the male s. .... Nu 6:20
twelve male s, and twelve male .... Nu 7:87
sixty male s, sixty male goats .... Nu 7:88
If you are giving a male s, ... Nu 15:6
Prepare each bull or male s, ... Nu 15:11
the firstborn ox or s or goat. .... Nu 18:17
cattle and s as a sacrifice .... Nu 22:40
bulls and seven male s for me." .... Nu 23:1
a bull and a male s on each of .... Nu 23:2
and a male s on each altar." .... Nu 23:4
bull and a male s on each altar. .... Nu 23:14
seven bulls and seven male s." .... Nu 23:29
bull and a male s on each altar. .... Nu 23:30
them out like s and bring them .... Nu 27:17
must not be like s without a .... Nu 27:17
bulls, one male s, and seven .... Nu 28:11

S

grain offering with the male **s**. .... Nu 28:12
with the male **s** it will be one .... Nu 28:14
bulls, one male **s**, and seven .... Nu 28:19
With the male **s** it must be four .... Nu 28:20
bulls, one male **s**, and seven .... Nu 28:27
With the male **s**, it must be four .... Nu 28:28
bull, one male **s**, and seven male .... Nu 29:2
the male **s** offer four quarts, ... Nu 29:3
bull, one male **s**, and seven male .... Nu 29:8
With the male **s** it must be four .... Nu 29:9
bulls, two male **s**, and fourteen .... Nu 29:13
the two male **s** it must be four .... Nu 29:14
bulls, two male **s**, and fourteen .... Nu 29:17
for the bulls, **s**, and lambs, ... Nu 29:18
bulls, two male **s**, and fourteen .... Nu 29:20
for the bulls, **s**, and lambs, ... Nu 29:21
bulls, two male **s**, and fourteen .... Nu 29:23
for the bulls, **s**, and lambs, ... Nu 29:24
bulls, two male **s**, and fourteen .... Nu 29:26
for the bulls, **s**, and lambs, ... Nu 29:27
bulls, two male **s**, and fourteen .... Nu 29:29
for the bulls, **s**, and lambs, ... Nu 29:30
bulls, two male **s**, and fourteen .... Nu 29:32
for the bulls, **s**, and lambs, ... Nu 29:33
bull, one male **s**, and seven male .... Nu 29:36
bull, the male **s**, and the lambs, ... Nu 29:37
people, cattle, donkeys, or **s**. .... Nu 31:28
cattle, donkeys, **s**, or other .... Nu 31:30
soldiers had taken 675,000 **s**, ... Nu 31:32
who went to war got 337,000 **s**, ... Nu 31:36
The people got 337,500 **s**, ... Nu 31:43
And they built **s** pens. .... Nu 32:36
you may eat: oxen, **s**, goats, ... Dt 14:4
ibex, antelope, and mountain **s**. .... Dt 14:5
you wish—cattle, **s**, wine, beer, ... Dt 14:26
the first lamb born to your **s**. .... Dt 15:19
an ox or **s** has something wrong............... Dt 17:1
a bull or **s** as a sacrifice, ... Dt 18:3
first wool you cut from your **s**. .... Dt 18:4
ox or **s** wandering away, ... Dt 22:1
Your **s** will be given to your .... Dt 28:31
there were fat **s** and goats. .... Dt 32:14
There were **s** and goats from .... Dt 32:14
horns of male **s** and have them .... Jos 6:4
and old, cattle, **s**, and donkeys. .... Jos 6:21
cattle, donkeys, **s**, tent, and................... Jos 7:24
the music played for your **s**? .... Jdg 5:16
to eat, and no **s**, cattle, or .... Jdg 6:4
They had taken **s**, cattle, and 1Sa 14:32
bring his ox and **s** to me and 1Sa 14:34
babies, cattle and **s**, camels and 1Sa 15:3
with the best **s**, fat cattle, ... 1Sa 15:9
cattle mooing and **s** bleating?" 1Sa 15:14
saved the best **s** and cattle to 1Sa 15:15
took the best **s** and cattle to 1Sa 15:21
God than to offer the fat of **s**. 1Sa 15:22
He is out taking care of the **s**." 1Sa 16:11
son David, who is with the **s**." 1Sa 16:19
he took care of his father's **s**. 1Sa 17:15
David left the **s** with another 1Sa 17:20
care of those few **s** of yours in 1Sa 17:28
have been keeping my father's **s**. 1Sa 17:34
and took a **s** from the flock, ... 1Sa 17:34
and save the **s** from its mouth. 1Sa 17:35
babies, cattle, donkeys, and **s**. 1Sa 22:19
Saul came to the **s** pens beside 1Sa 24:3
three thousand **s** and a thousand 1Sa 25:2
the wool off his **s** at Carmel. 1Sa 25:2
was cutting the wool from his **s**............... 1Sa 25:4
cutting the wool from your **s**. 1Sa 25:7
were with them caring for the **s**............... 1Sa 25:16
wine, five cooked **s**, a bushel of 1Sa 25:18
sure none of his **s** was missing. 1Sa 25:21

men and women and took their **s**, ... 1Sa 27:9
David took all the **s** and cattle, ... 1Sa 30:20
from tending the **s** and made you 2Sa 7:8
rich man had many **s** and cattle............... 2Sa 12:2
take one of his own **s** or cattle. 2Sa 12:4
to cut the wool from his **s**. 2Sa 13:23
milk curds, **s**, and cheese made 2Sa 17:29
people only followed me like **s**. 2Sa 24:17
Then Adonijah killed some **s**, ... 1Ki 1:9
calves, and **s** for sacrifices. 1Ki 1:19
fat calves, and **s**, and he has 1Ki 1:25
one hundred **s**, three kinds 1Ki 4:23
so many **s** and cattle no one 1Ki 8:5
twenty thousand **s** as fellowship............... 1Ki 8:63
the hills like **s** without a 1Ki 22:17
Mesha king of Moab raised **s**................... 2Ki 3:4
wool of one hundred thousand **s**. 2Ki 3:4
olives, grapes, **s**, oxen, male 2Ki 5:26
two hundred fifty thousand **s**,................... 1Ch 5:21
steal cows and **s** and were killed 1Ch 7:21
oil, cows, and **s**, because the 1Ch 12:40
seven bulls and seven male **s**. 1Ch 15:26
from tending the **s** and made you 1Ch 17:7
people only followed me like **s**. 1Ch 21:17
thousand male **s**, and a thousand 1Ch 29:21
so many **s** and bulls no one 2Ch 5:6
one hundred twenty thousand **s**............... 2Ch 7:5
and seven male **s** can become a 2Ch 13:9
and took many **s** and camels. 2Ch 14:15
and seven thousand **s** and goats 2Ch 15:11
hundred and seventy-seven 2Ch 17:11
sacrificed many **s** and cattle as 2Ch 18:2
the hills like **s** without a 2Ch 18:16
seven male **s**, seven lambs, ... 2Ch 29:21
They killed the **s** and sprinkled 2Ch 29:22
hundred male **s**, and two hundred 2Ch 29:32
and three thousand **s** and goats. 2Ch 29:33
seven thousand **s** to the people. 2Ch 30:24
ten thousand **s** to the people. 2Ch 30:24
their cattle and **s** and one-tenth 2Ch 31:6
the cattle and pens for the **s**. 2Ch 32:28
thirty thousand **s** and goats to 2Ch 35:7
five thousand **s** and goats and 2Ch 35:9
young bulls, male **s**, or lambs .... Ezr 6:9
two hundred male **s**, and four................... Ezr 6:17
buy bulls, male **s**, and lambs, ... Ezr 7:17
ninety-six male **s**, and .... Ezr 8:35
brought a male **s** from the flock .... Ezr 10:19
to work and rebuild the **S** Gate. .... Ne 3:1
of the wall and the **S** Gate. .... Ne 3:32
one ox, six good **s**, and birds. .... Ne 5:18
as far as the **S** Gate and stopped .... Ne 12:39
He owned seven thousand **s**, ... Job 1:3
burned up the **s** and the servants .... Job 1:16
fathers sit with my **s** dogs. .... Job 30:1
him with the wool of my **s**. .... Job 31:20
seven bulls and seven male **s**,................... Job 42:8
Job had fourteen thousand **s**, ... Job 42:12
all the **s**, the cattle, and the.................... Ps 8:7
gave us away like **s** to be eaten .... Ps 44:11
no more than **s** to be killed. .... Ps 44:22
Like **s**, they must die, and death............... Ps 49:14
and I will offer **s**, bulls, and .... Ps 66:15
with us, the **s** of your pasture? .... Ps 74:1
people out like **s** and he guided .... Ps 78:52
and took him from the **s** pens. .... Ps 78:70
tending the **s** so he could lead .... Ps 78:71
people, the **s** of your flock. .... Ps 79:13
care of, the **s** that he tends..................... Ps 95:7
are his people, the **s** he tends................. Ps 100:3
families grow like flocks of **s**................... Ps 107:41
danced like **s** and the hills like .... Ps 114:4
why did you dance like **s**? .... Ps 114:6

I have wandered like a lost **s**. .... Ps 119:176
Let our **s** in the fields have .... Ps 144:13
you know how your **s** are doing, ... Pr 27:23
love, where do you feed your **s**? .... Sng 1:7
for you near your friend's **s**, ... Sng 1:7
to follow the **s** and feed your .... Sng 1:8
like newly sheared **s** just coming .... Sng 4:2
are white like **s** just coming .... Sng 6:6
of male **s** and fat from fine .... Is 1:11
Then the **s** will go anywhere they .... Is 5:17
one young cow and two **s** alive. .... Is 7:21
Only a son and cattle will go to .... Is 7:25
hunted deer or like **s** who have .... Is 13:14
no shepherd will bring **s** there. .... Is 13:20
They kill the cattle and the **s**; .... Is 22:13
and **s** will go there to eat. .... Is 32:14
the fat from the kidneys of **s**. .... Is 34:6
sacrifices of **s** nor honored me .... Is 43:23
all have wandered away like **s**; .... Is 53:6
a **s** is quiet while its wool is .... Is 53:7
All the **s** from Kedar will be .... Is 60:7
the **s** from Nebaioth will be .... Is 60:7
will come to tend your **s**...................... Is 61:5
Those who kill **s** as a sacrifice .... Is 66:3
away like **s** to be butchered .... Je 12:3
oil, young **s**, and young cows .... Je 31:12
count their **s** as the sheep walk .... Je 33:13
sheep as the **s** walk in front .... Je 33:13
to attack a strong pen for **s**, ... Je 49:19
My people have been like lost **s**.............. Je 50:6
like a flock of **s** that are .... Je 50:17
to attack a strong pen for **s**, ... Je 50:44
like **s** and goats waiting to be .... Je 51:40
count you like **s** and will bring .... Eze 20:37
of Ammon a resting place for **s**. .... Eze 25:5
received lambs, male **s**, and .... Eze 27:21
kill the fat **s**, but you do not .... Eze 34:3
ruled the **s** with cruel force. .... Eze 34:4
The **s** were scattered, because .... Eze 34:5
happened to my **s** and will not .... Eze 34:10
search for my **s** and take care............... Eze 34:11
found, I will take care of my **s**. .... Eze 34:12
will destroy those **s** that are .... Eze 34:16
I will tend the **s** with fairness................ Eze 34:16
judge between one **s** and another, ... Eze 34:17
between the male **s** and the male .... Eze 34:17
the fat **s** and the thin sheep. .... Eze 34:20
the fat sheep and the thin **s**. .... Eze 34:20
all the weak **s** with your horns .... Eze 34:21
judge between one **s** and another. .... Eze 34:22
peace with my **s** and will remove .... Eze 34:25
Then the **s** will live safely in .... Eze 34:25
And the **s** will be safe on their .... Eze 34:27
You, my human **s**, are the sheep I .... Eze 34:31
sheep, are the **s** I care for, and .... Eze 34:31
male **s**, lambs, goats, and bulls. .... Eze 39:18
and a male **s** from the flock, ... Eze 43:23
bull and male **s** from the flock, ... Eze 43:25
should give one **s** from each .... Eze 45:15
and seven male **s** that have .... Eze 45:23
and one-half bushel for each **s**. .... Eze 45:24
them and a male **s** that has.................... Eze 46:4
grain offering with the male **s**, ... Eze 46:6
lambs and a male **s** that have .... Eze 46:6
one-half bushel with the male **s**............. Eze 46:7
must be offered with a male **s**. .... Eze 46:11
and saw a male **s** standing beside .... Da 8:3
I watched the **s** charge to the .... Da 8:4
goat charged the **s** with the two .... Da 8:6
goat attack the **s** and break the .... Da 8:7
The **s** was not strong enough to .... Da 8:7
goat knocked the **s** to the ground .... Da 8:7
to save the **s** from the goat,................... Da 8:7

You saw a male **s** with two horns, ... Da 8:20
he tended **s** to pay for her. .... Hos 12:12
even the flocks of **s** suffer. .... Joe 1:18
or a scrap of an ear of his **s**. .... Am 3:12
them together like **s** in a pen, ... Mic 2:12
a young lion in a flock of **s**: .... Mic 5:8
pleased with a thousand male **s**? .... Mic 6:7
There may be no **s** in the pens .... Hab 3:17
for shepherds, and pens for **s**................. Zph 2:6
they will let their **s** eat grass. .... Zph 2:7
them as if his people were **s**. .... Zch 9:16
So the people are like lost **s**. .... Zch 10:2
don't feel sorry for their **s**. .... Zch 11:5
will not care for the dying **s**, ... Zch 11:16
will eat the best **s** and tear off .... Zch 11:16
and the **s** will scatter, ... Zch 13:7
to you looking gentle like **s**, ... Mt 7:15
helpless, like **s** without a...................... Mt 9:36
of Israel, who are like lost **s**. .... Mt 10:6
you out like **s** among wolves. .... Mt 10:16
any of you has a **s**, and it falls .... Mt 12:11
is more important than a **s**? .... Mt 12:12
God sent me only to the lost **s**, ... Mt 15:24
a man has a hundred **s** but one of .... Mt 18:12
but one of the **s** gets lost, ... Mt 18:12
and go to look for the lost **s**. .... Mt 18:12
about that one **s** than about .... Mt 18:13
separates the **s** from the goats. .... Mt 25:32
Man will put the **s** on his right .... Mt 25:33
and the **s** will scatter.' .... Mt 26:31
they were like **s** without a .... Mk 6:34
and the **s** will scatter.' .... Mk 14:27
fields nearby watching their **s**. .... Lk 2:8
shepherds went back to their **s**, ... Lk 2:20
you out like **s** among wolves. .... Lk 10:3
has a hundred **s** but loses one................ Lk 15:4
ninety-nine **s** in the open field .... Lk 15:4
for the lost **s** until he finds it .... Lk 15:4
me because I found my lost **s**.' .... Lk 15:6
the ground or caring for the **s**. .... Lk 17:7
selling cattle, **s**, and doves. .... Jn 2:14
them, both the **s** and cattle, to .... Jn 2:15
This pool is near the **S** Gate. .... Jn 5:2
door is the shepherd of the **s**. .... Jn 10:2
And the **s** listen to the voice of .... Jn 10:3
He calls his own **s** by name and .... Jn 10:3
When he brings all his **s** out, ... Jn 10:4
truth, I am the door for the **s**. .... Jn 10:7
The **s** did not listen to them. .... Jn 10:8
gives his life for the **s**. .... Jn 10:11
paid to keep the **s** is different .... Jn 10:12
away and leaves the **s** alone. .... Jn 10:12
attacks the **s** and scatters them. .... Jn 10:12
not really care about the **s**. .... Jn 10:13
know my **s**, and my sheep know me, ... Jn 10:14
know my sheep, and my **s** know me, ... Jn 10:14
I give my life for the **s**. .... Jn 10:15
I have other **s** that are not in .... Jn 10:16
because you are not my **s**. .... Jn 10:26
My **s** listen to my voice; .... Jn 10:27
My Father gave my **s** to me. .... Jn 10:29
can steal my **s** out of my........................ Jn 10:29
Jesus said, "Take care of my **s**." .... Jn 21:16
He said to him, "Feed my **s**. .... Jn 21:17
He was like a **s** being led to be .... Ac 8:32
no more than **s** to be killed." .... Rm 8:36
wore the skins of **s** and goats. .... Heb 11:37
You were like **s** that wandered 1Pe 2:25
wheat, cattle, **s**, horses, ... Rev 18:13

S

SHEEP'S
blowing trumpets and s horns. 2Ch 15:14
the trumpets and the s horns; .... Ps 98:6
sheep and break the s two horns. .... Da 8:7

SHEEPFOLD
Why did you stay by the s? .... Jdg 5:16
not enter the s by the door, ... Jn 10:1

SHEEPSKINS
s that are dyed red; .... Ex 25:5
Holy Tent from s colored red, ... Ex 26:14
and male s that are colored red. .... Ex 35:7
goat hair or male s colored red .... Ex 35:23
one made of male s colored red .... Ex 36:19
made of male s colored red, ... Ex 39:34

SHEERAH
Ephraim's daughter was S. 1Ch 7:24
Upper Beth Horon, and Uzzen S. 1Ch 7:24

SHEET
are to show the s to the elders .... Dt 22:17
wife spread a s over the opening 2Sa 17:19
like a big s being lowered to .... Ac 10:11
and at once the s was taken back .... Ac 10:16
like a big s being lowered .... Ac 11:5

SHEETS
the gold into s and then cut it .... Ex 39:3
them into flat s that will be .... Nu 16:38
hammered into flat s to put on .... Nu 16:39
These s were to remind the .... Nu 16:40
bed with colored s from Egypt. .... Pr 7:16

SHEHARIAH
were Shamsherai, S, Athaliah, ... 1Ch 8:26

SHEKEL
The s will be worth twenty .... Eze 45:12

SHEKELS
a mina will be worth sixty s. .... Eze 45:12

SHELAH
Arphaxad was the father of S, ... Ge 10:24
years old, his son S was born. .... Ge 11:12
When S was 30 years old, his son .... Ge 11:14
S lived 403 years and had other .... Ge 11:15
had another son and named him S. .... Ge 38:5
until my young son S grows up." .... Ge 38:11
was afraid that S also would die .... Ge 38:11
younger son S had grown up, ... Ge 38:14
her to my son S as I promised." .... Ge 38:26
were Er, Onan, S, Perez, and .... Ge 46:12
From S came the Shelanite family .... Nu 26:20
Arphaxad was the father of S, ... 1Ch 1:18
line included Shem, Arphaxad, S, ... 1Ch 1:24
sons were Er, Onan, and S. 1Ch 2:3
These sons of S were potters. 1Ch 4:23
of Zechariah, a descendant of S. .... Ne 11:5
Eber was the son of S. .... Lk 3:35
S was the son of Cainan. .... Lk 3:36

SHELANITE
Shelah came the S family group; .... Nu 26:20

SHELEMIAH
S, Nathan, Adaiah, ... Ezr 10:39
Azarel, S, Shemariah, ... Ezr 10:41
Hananiah son of S, and Hanun, ... Ne 3:30
S the priest, Zadok the teacher, ... Ne 13:13
Nethaniah was the son of S, ... Je 36:14
and S son of Abdeel to arrest .... Je 36:26
Jehucal son of S and the priest .... Je 37:3
Irijah son of S son of Hananiah .... Je 37:13
Jehucal son of S, and Pashhur .... Je 38:1

SHELEPH
of Almodad, S, Hazarmaveth, ... Ge 10:26
of Almodad, S, Hazarmaveth, ... 1Ch 1:20

SHELESH
were Zophah, Imna, S, and Amal. 1Ch 7:35

SHELISHIYAH
they run to Eglath S. .... Is 15:5
away as Horonaim and Eglath S. .... Je 48:34

SHELLS
of white marble, s, and gems. .... Est 1:6

SHELOMI
tribe of Asher, Ahihud son of S; .... Nu 34:27

SHELOMITH
name was S, the daughter .... Le 24:11
and their sister was S. 1Ch 3:19
Izhar's first son was S. 1Ch 23:18
son Zicri, and Zicri's son S. 1Ch 26:25
S and his relatives were 1Ch 26:26
S and his relatives took care of 1Ch 26:28
Abijah, Attai, Ziza, and S. 2Ch 11:20
S son of Josiphiah, with one .... Ezr 8:10

SHELOMOTH
sons were S, Haziel, and Haran 1Ch 23:9
there was S, and Jahath was 1Ch 24:22
Jahath was a descendant of S. 1Ch 24:22

SHELTER
come and find s in my shade! .... Jdg 9:15
a few moments to rest in the s." .... Ru 2:7
wings you have come for s." .... Ru 2:12
made darkness his s, surrounded 2Sa 22:12
rocks because they have no s. .... Job 24:8
his covering, his s around him, ... Ps 18:11
he will keep me safe in his s. .... Ps 27:5
You s them from evil words. .... Ps 31:20
safety in the s of your wings. .... Ps 61:4
like an empty s in a vineyard, ... Is 1:8
You are like a s from storms, ... Is 25:4
will be like a s from the wind, ... Is 32:2
again or to set up a s for me. .... Je 10:20
and live in the s of the tree's .... Eze 17:23
animals found s under the tree, ... Da 4:12
There he made a s for himself .... Jnh 4:5

SHELTERS
himself and s for his animals .... Ge 33:17
the Feast of S in the fall, ... Ex 23:16
the Feast of S in the fall. .... Ex 34:22
seventh month is the Feast of S. .... Le 23:34
Live in s for seven days. .... Le 23:42
born in Israel must live in s .... Le 23:42
Israel live in s during the time .... Le 23:43
the Feast of S for seven days, ... Dt 16:13
of Weeks, and the Feast of S. .... Dt 16:16
of Weeks, and the Feast of S. 2Ch 8:13
they celebrated the Feast of S. .... Ezr 3:4
the Feast of S, they had regular .... Ezr 3:5
were to live in s during the .... Ne 8:14
Make s with them, as it is .... Ne 8:15
They built s on their roofs, ... Ne 8:16
captivity built s and lived in .... Ne 8:17
you celebrate the Feast of S, ... Eze 45:25
and to celebrate the Feast of S. .... Zch 14:16
not celebrate the Feast of S. .... Zch 14:18
go to celebrate the Feast of S. .... Zch 14:19
It was time for the Feast of S. .... Jn 7:2

SHELUMIEL
tribe of Simeon—S son of .... Nu 1:6
of Simeon is S son of .... Nu 2:12
S son of Zurishaddai was over .... Nu 10:19

SHELVES
Double s three inches wide were .... Eze 40:43

SHEM

he became the father of **S**, ... Ge 5:32
had three sons: **S**, Ham, and .... Ge 6:10
wife, his sons **S**, Ham, and .... Ge 7:13
out of the boat with him were **S**, ... Ge 9:18
Then **S** and Japheth got a coat .... Ge 9:23
LORD, the God of **S**, be praised!.............. Ge 9:26
This is the family history of **S**, ... Ge 10:1
S, Japheth's older brother, also .... Ge 10:21
The sons of **S** were Elam, Asshur, ... Ge 10:22
the people from the family of **S**, ... Ge 10:31
This is the family history of **S**. .... Ge 11:10
the flood, when **S** was 100 years...... Ge 11:10
S lived 500 years and had other .... Ge 11:11
of Noah were **S**, Ham, and Japheth 1Ch 1:4
The family line included **S**,................. 1Ch 1:24
Arphaxad was the son of **S**. .... Lk 3:36
the son of Shem. **S** was the son .... Lk 3:36

SHEM'S

May Canaan be **S** slave. .... Ge 9:26
May Japheth live in **S** tents, ... Ge 9:27
S sons were Elam, Asshur, ... 1Ch 1:17

SHEMA

Amam, **S**, Moladah, ... Jos 15:26
Korah, Tappuah, Rekem, and **S**. 1Ch 2:43
S was the father of Raham,.................... 1Ch 2:44
was the son of **S**, and Shema was 1Ch 5:8
son of Shema, and **S** was the son 1Ch 5:8
Mattithiah, **S**, Anaiah, Uriah, ... Ne 8:4

SHEMAAH

and Joash were sons of **S**, ... 1Ch 12:3

SHEMAIAH

But God spoke his word to **S**, ... 1Ki 12:22

SHEMARIAH

Jerimoth, Bealiah, and **S**. 1Ch 12:5
Jeush, **S**, and Zaham. 2Ch 11:19
Benjamin, Malluch, and **S**. .... Ezr 10:32
Azarel, Shelemiah, **S**, ... Ezr 10:41

SHEMEBER

of Admah, **S** king of Zeboiim, ... Ge 14:2

SHEMER

of Samaria from **S** for about one 1Ki 16:24
name of its earlier owner, **S**. 1Ki 16:24
S was Mahli's son. Mahli was.................. 1Ch 6:47

SHEMER'S

was Bani's son. Bani was **S** son............. 1Ch 6:46

SHEMIDA

S came the Shemidaite family .... Nu 26:32
Asriel, Shechem, Hepher, and **S**. .... Jos 17:2
The sons of **S** were Ahian, ... 1Ch 7:19

SHEMIDAITE

Shemida came the **S** family group;........... Nu 26:32

SHEMINITH

Upon the **s**. A psalm of David. .... Ps 5:12
music. Upon the **s**. A psalm of .... Ps 11:7

SHEMIRAMOTH

Jaaziel, **S**, Jehiel, Unni, ... 1Ch 15:18
Jaaziel, **S**, Jehiel, Unni, ... 1Ch 15:20
were Jaaziel, **S**, Jehiel, ... 1Ch 16:5
Zebadiah, Asahel, **S**, Jehonathan, ... 2Ch 17:8

SHEMUEL

of Simeon, **S** son of Ammihud; .... Nu 34:20

SHEN

set it up between Mizpah and **S**.............. 1Sa 7:12

SHENAZZAR

Pedaiah, **S**, Jekamiah, Hoshama............ 1Ch 3:18

SHEPHAM

begin at Hazar Enan and go to **S**. .... Nu 34:10
From **S** the border will go east .... Nu 34:11

SHEPHATIAH

fifth son was **S**, whose mother 2Sa 3:4
fifth son was **S**, whose mother 1Ch 3:3
there was Meshullam son of **S**. 1Ch 9:8
S was Reuel's son, and Reuel was 1Ch 9:8
There was **S** from Haruph. 1Ch 12:5
S son of Maacah was over the 1Ch 27:16
Azariahu, Michael, and **S**. 2Ch 21:2
the descendants of **S**—372; .... Ezr 2:4
S, Hattil, Pokereth-Hazzebaim, ... Ezr 2:57
From the descendants of **S**:.................... Ezr 8:8
the descendants of **S**—372; .... Ne 7:9
S, Hattil, Pokereth-Hazzebaim, ... Ne 7:59
was the son of **S**, the son of .... Ne 11:4
S son of Mattan, Gedaliah son of .... Je 38:1

SHEPHER

and camped at Mount **S**........................ Nu 33:23
They left Mount **S** and camped at .... Nu 33:24

SHEPHERD

and like a **s** God has led me all .... Ge 48:15
and his strength from the **S**, ... Ge 49:24
not be like sheep without a **s**." .... Nu 27:17
left the sheep with another **s**. 1Sa 17:20
'You will be a **s** for my people. 2Sa 5:2
hills like sheep without a **s**.................... 1Ki 22:17
'You will be the **s** for my people 1Ch 11:2
hills like sheep without a **s**.................... 2Ch 18:16
The LORD is my **s**; I have .... Ps 23:1
Be their **s** and carry them .... Ps 28:9
and death will be their **s**. .... Ps 49:14
S of Israel, listen to us. .... Ps 80:1
teachings that come from one **S**. .... Ec 12:11
or like sheep who have no **s**. .... Is 13:14
no **s** will bring sheep there.................... Is 13:20
care of his people like a **s**. .... Is 40:11
'He is my **s** and will do all that .... Is 44:28
each **s** taking care of his own .... Je 6:3
from being the **s** you wanted. .... Je 17:16
watch over his people like a **s**.' .... Je 31:10
As a **s** wraps himself in his.................... Je 43:12
there was no **s**, and they became .... Eze 34:5
because the flock has no **s**. .... Eze 34:8
As a **s** takes care of his .... Eze 34:12
Then I will put over them one **s**,.............. Eze 34:23
and tend them and be their **s**. .... Eze 34:23
and they will all have one **s**. .... Eze 37:24
A **s** might save from a lion's .... Am 3:12
living as a **s**, and I take care .... Am 7:14
s your people with your stick;................. Mic 7:14
abused, because there is no **s**................. Zch 10:2
take care of you like a **s**........................ Zch 11:9
used by a foolish **s** again,...................... Zch 11:15
to get a new **s** for the country. .... Zch 11:16
for the useless **s** who abandoned .... Zch 11:17
Sword, hit the **s**. Attack the man .... Zch 13:7
Kill the **s**, and the sheep will .... Zch 13:7
will be like a **s** for my people .... Mt 2:6
like sheep without a **s**. .... Mt 9:36
two groups as a **s** separates the .... Mt 25:32
'I will kill the **s**, and the .... Mt 26:31
were like sheep without a **s**. .... Mk 6:34
'I will kill the **s**, and the .... Mk 14:27
the door is the **s** of the sheep................. Jn 10:2
listen to the voice of the **s**. .... Jn 10:3
I am the good **s**. The good .... Jn 10:11
good **s** gives his life for the.................... Jn 10:11
from the **s** who owns them..................... Jn 10:12
I am the good **s**. I know my .... Jn 10:14
will be one flock and one **s**. .... Jn 10:16

S

come back to the **S** and Overseer 1Pe 2:25
s God's flock, for whom you are.............. 1Pe 5:2
the Chief **S,** comes, you will 1Pe 5:4
of the throne will be their **s.** .... Rev 7:17

SHEPHERD'S
them in his **s** bag and grabbed 1Sa 17:40
rod and your **s** staff comfort me .... Ps 23:4
Like a **s** tent, my home has been .... Is 38:12

SHEPHERDS
your servants, are **s,** just as .... Ge 47:3
Some **s** came and chased the girls .... Ex 2:17
blow all your **s** away and send .... Je 22:22
I use you to smash **s** and flocks............. Je 51:23
of Israel, who are like **s.** .... Eze 34:2
I am against the **s.** .... Eze 34:10
of the **s** will become dry .... Am 1:2
some **s** were in the fields nearby .... Lk 2:8

SHEPHO
Manahath, Ebal, **S,** and Onam. .... Ge 36:23
Manahath, Ebal, **S,** and Onam. 1Ch 1:40

SHEPHUPHAN
Gera, **S,** and Huram. 1Ch 8:5

SHEREBIAH
so Iddo's relatives gave us **S,** .... Ezr 8:18
who were leaders, **S,** Hashabiah, ... Ezr 8:24
Jeshua, Bani, **S,** Jamin, Akkub, ... Ne 8:7
Bunni, **S,** Bani, and Kenani..................... Ne 9:4
Hashabneiah, **S,** Hodiah, ... Ne 9:5
Zaccur, **S,** Shebaniah,........................... Ne 10:12
Binnui, Kadmiel, **S,** Judah, and .... Ne 12:8
were Hashabiah, **S,** Jeshua son of .... Ne 12:24

SHEREBIAH'S
And they brought **S** sons and .... Ezr 8:18

SHERESH
Peresh's brother was named **S.** 1Ch 7:16

SHERESH'S
S sons were Ulam and Rakem. 1Ch 7:16

SHESHAI
where Ahiman, **S,** and Talmai, ... Nu 13:22
S, Ahiman, and Talmai, the..................... Jos 15:14
And they defeated **S,** Ahiman, and........... Jdg 1:10

SHESHAN
who became the father of **S.** 1Ch 2:31
S was the father of Ahlai. 1Ch 2:31
S did not have any sons, only 1Ch 2:34
S let his daughter marry his 1Ch 2:35

SHESHBAZZAR
them and count them out for **S,** .... Ezr 1:8
S brought all these things along.............. Ezr 1:11
Then King Cyrus gave them to **S,** .... Ezr 5:14
So **S** came and laid the .... Ezr 5:16

SHETH
the skulls of the sons of **S.** .... Nu 24:17

SHETHAR
to were Carshena, **S,** Admatha, ... Est 1:14

SHETHAR-BOZENAI
and **S,** and their fellow .... Ezr 5:3
Trans-Euphrates, **S,** and the .... Ezr 5:6
of Trans-Euphrates, **S,** and all................. Ezr 6:6
Trans-Euphrates, **S,** and their .... Ezr 6:13

SHEVA
Shaaph, and **S.** Shaaph was the 1Ch 2:49
S was the father of Macbenah and 1Ch 2:49

SHIBAH
Isaac named it **S** and that city .... Ge 26:33

SHIBBOLETH
say to him, "Say the word '**S.**'" .... Jdg 12:6

SHIELD
He is your **s** and helper, your .... Dt 33:29
could find a **s** or a spear among .... Jdg 5:8
carried his **s** walked in front 1Sa 17:7
who held his **s** walked in front 1Sa 17:41
warrior's **s** was dishonored. 2Sa 1:21
s will no longer be rubbed 2Sa 1:21
He is my **s** and my saving 2Sa 22:3
is a **s** to those who trust him. 2Sa 22:31
protect me with your saving **s.** 2Sa 22:36
Each **s** is so close to the next .... Job 41:16
LORD, you are my **s,** my wonderful .... Ps 3:3
protect them like a soldier's **s.** .... Ps 5:12
God protects me like a **s;**...................... Ps 7:10
He is my **s** and my saving .... Ps 18:2
is a **s** to those who trust him. .... Ps 18:30
protect me with your saving **s.** .... Ps 18:35
The LORD is my strength and **s.**.............. Ps 28:7
our help, our **s** to protect us. .... Ps 33:20
Pick up the **s** and armor........................ Ps 35:2
look at our **s;** be kind to your .... Ps 84:9
LORD God is like a sun and **s;** .... Ps 84:11
Our king, our **s,** belongs to the .... Ps 89:18
will be your **s** and protection. .... Ps 91:4
are my hiding place and my **s;** .... Ps 119:114
my Savior, my **s** and my .... Ps 144:2
Like a **s** he protects the .... Pr 2:7
each **s** belongs to a strong .... Sng 4:4
and the **s** is put into place. .... Nah 2:5
And also use the **s** of faith with .... Eph 6:16

SHIELDS
hundred large **s** of hammered gold........... 1Ki 10:16
made bronze **s** to put in their 1Ki 14:27
with spears, **s,** bows, and armor.............. Ne 4:16

SHIFTING
not change like their **s** shadows............... Jam 1:17

SHIGGAION
s of David which he sang to the .... Ps 6:10

SHIGIONOTH
of Habakkuk the prophet, on **s.** .... Hab 3:1

SHIHOR
the area from the **S** River at the .... Jos 13:3
Mount Carmel and **S** Libnath. .... Jos 19:26
the **S** River in Egypt to Lebo 1Ch 13:5
and drink from the **S** River. .... Je 2:18

SHIKKERON
it turned toward **S** and went past .... Jos 15:11

SHILHI
name was Azubah daughter of **S.** 1Ki 22:42
name was Azubah daughter of **S.** 2Ch 20:31

SHILHIM
Lebaoth, **S,** Ain, and Rimmon. .... Jos 15:32

SHILLEM
Jahziel, Guni, Jezer, and **S.**..................... Ge 46:24
S came the Shillemite family .... Nu 26:49
Jahziel, Guni, Jezer, and **S.**..................... 1Ch 7:13

SHILLEMITE
Shillem came the **S** family group. .... Nu 26:49

SHILOAH
of the pool of **S** and are .... Is 8:6

SHILOH
Judah will rule until **S** comes,................. Ge 49:10
who was still at the camp at **S.** .... Jos 18:9
the Holy Tent of God was in **S.** .... Jdg 18:31
to the house of the LORD at **S,** 1Sa 1:24
of Eli, the LORD's priest in **S.**................... 1Sa 14:3
He left his dwelling at **S,**....................... Ps 78:60
to the town of **S,** where I first .... Je 7:12
I destroyed my Holy Tent at **S.** .... Je 26:6

SHILONITE
the S people there were Asaiah 1Ch 9:5
in the prophecy of Ahijah the S, ... 2Ch 9:29

SHILSHAH
Hod, Shamma, S, Ithran, and 1Ch 7:37

SHIMEA
was Abinadab, his third was S, ... 1Ch 2:13
Uzzah's son was S. Shimea's son 1Ch 6:30
S was Michael's son. Michael was 1Ch 6:40
Jonathan son of S, David's 1Ch 20:7

SHIMEA'S
S son was Haggiah, and Haggiah's 1Ch 6:30
son. Berekiah was S son. 1Ch 6:39

SHIMEAH
a friend named Jonadab son of S, ... 2Sa 13:3
Jonadab son of S, David's 2Sa 13:32
Jonathan son of S, David's 2Sa 21:21
Mikloth was the father of S. 1Ch 8:32

SHIMEAM'S
Mikloth was S father. 1Ch 9:38

SHIMEATH
Jozabad son of S and Jehozabad 2Ki 12:21
was the son of S, a woman from 2Ch 24:26

SHIMEATHITES
Tirathites, S, and Sucathites 1Ch 2:55

SHIMEI
but S followed on the nearby 2Sa 16:13
S should die because he cursed 2Sa 19:21
So Solomon sent for S and said, ... 1Ki 2:42

SHIMEON
Ishijah, Malkijah, Shemaiah, S, ... Ezr 10:31

SHIMON'S
S sons were Amnon, Rinnah, ... 1Ch 4:20

SHIMRATH
Adaiah, Beraiah, and S. 1Ch 8:21

SHIMRI
son of S; Joha, Jediael's 1Ch 11:45
S was chosen to be in charge.................. 1Ch 26:10
family there were S and Jeiel. 2Ch 29:13

SHIMRITH
And Jehozabad was the son of S, ... 2Ch 24:26

SHIMRON
were Tola, Puah, Jashub, and S. .... Ge 46:13
S came the Shimronite family .... Nu 26:24
the king of S, and to the king .... Jos 11:1
S Meron, Acshaph, ... Jos 12:20
of Kattath, Nahalal, S, Idalah, ... Jos 19:15
Tola, Puah, Jashub, and S. 1Ch 7:1

SHIMRONITE
Shimron came the S family group. .... Nu 26:24

SHIMSHAI
governor and S the governor's .... Ezr 4:8
the governor, S the secretary, ... Ezr 4:9
governor and S the secretary, ... Ezr 4:17
to Rehum and S the secretary .... Ezr 4:23

SHINAB
of Gomorrah, S king of Admah, ... Ge 14:2

SHINE
in the sky to s on the earth, ... Ge 1:17
Don't let light s on it. .... Job 3:4
the sun not to s and shuts off .... Job 9:7
and light will s on your ways. .... Job 22:28
goodness will s like the sun, ... Ps 37:6
will s down from heaven. .... Ps 85:11
oil that makes our faces s. .... Ps 104:15
shame, but his crown will s." .... Ps 132:18
a light to s for all people. .... Is 42:6

your light will s like the dawn, ... Is 58:8
light will s in the darkness .... Is 58:10
get up and s, because your light .... Is 60:1
you will s with happiness; .... Is 60:5
faces will s with happiness .... Je 31:12
LORD makes the sun s in the day .... Je 31:35
moon and stars to s at night. .... Je 31:35
See how the gold has lost its s, ... La 4:1
cloud, and the moon will not s. .... Eze 32:7
its brightness made the earth s. .... Eze 43:2
wise people will s like the .... Da 12:3
live right will s like stars. .... Da 12:3
Rays of light s from his hand, ... Hab 3:4
They will s in his land like .... Zch 9:16
goodness will s on you like the .... Mal 4:2
but a light will s on them." .... Mt 4:16
good people will s like the sun .... Mt 13:43
It will s on those who live in .... Lk 1:79
then you will s bright, as when .... Lk 11:36
again, he will s like lightning, ... Lk 17:24
because the sun did not s. .... Lk 23:45
the light s out of the darkness! 2Co 4:6
made his light s in our hearts 2Co 4:6
and Christ will s on you." .... Eph 5:14
among whom you s like stars in .... Php 2:15
lamp will never s in you again, ... Rev 18:23
the sun or the moon to s on it, ... Rev 21:23

SHINED
God's lamp s on my head, and I .... Job 29:3
but a light has s on them. .... Is 9:2
among the gems that s like fire. .... Eze 28:14
among the gems that s like fire. .... Eze 28:16
and a light s in the cell. .... Ac 12:7

SHINES
His light s on all people. .... Job 25:3
God s from Jerusalem, whose .... Ps 50:2
long as the sun s and as long as .... Ps 72:5
remembered as long as the sun s. .... Ps 72:17
Light s on those who do right; .... Ps 97:11
A light s in the dark for honest .... Ps 112:4
young woman that s out like the .... Sng 6:10
the glory of the LORD s on you. .... Is 60:1
the LORD s on you, and people .... Is 60:2
her goodness s like a bright .... Is 62:1
the light s for all the people .... Mt 5:15
as when a lamp s on you." .... Lk 11:36
The Light s in the darkness, ... Jn 1:5

SHINING
his face was s because he had .... Ex 34:29
saw that Moses' face was s, ... Ex 34:30
see that Moses' face was s. .... Ex 34:35
the sun was on the water. 2Ki 3:22
it leaves a s path in the water .... Job 41:32
Praise him, all you s stars. .... Ps 148:3
your walls and s jewels for the .... Is 54:12
wheels looked like s chrysolite. .... Eze 10:9
make all the s lights in the sky .... Eze 32:8
dark, and the stars stop s. .... Joe 2:10
and the stars will stop s. .... Joe 3:15
swords are s, spears are .... Nah 3:3
and the gleam of your s spear. .... Hab 3:11
He was s as bright as lightning, ... Mt 28:3
His clothes became s white, ... Mk 9:3
of the Lord was s around them, ... Lk 2:9
and his clothes became s white. .... Lk 9:29
service, and have your lamps s. .... Lk 12:35
two men in s clothes suddenly .... Lk 24:4
was like a burning and s lamp, ... Jn 5:35
before we wearing s clothes. .... Ac 10:30
a light s in a dark place, ... 2Pe 1:19
and the true light is already s. 1Jn 2:8
like the sun s at its brightest .... Rev 1:16

S

fire and feet like **s** bronze, ... Rev 2:18
s linen and wore golden bands .... Rev 15:6
and red and was **s** with the gold, ... Rev 17:4
cloth, and she was **s** with gold, ... Rev 18:16
It was **s** with the glory of God .... Rev 21:11
It was **s** like crystal and was .... Rev 22:1

SHINY
mind are like a **s** coating on a................ Pr 26:23
His body is like **s** ivory covered .... Sng 5:14
you saw a huge, **s,** and .... Da 2:31
body was like **s** yellow quartz. .... Da 10:6
and legs were **s** like polished .... Da 10:6

SHION
Hapharaim, **S,** Anaharath, ... Jos 19:19

SHIP
the way a **s** sails on the sea, ... Pr 30:19
he found a **s** that was going .... Jnh 1:3
But the **s** hit a sandbank. .... Ac 27:41

SHIPHRAH
nurses, named **S** and Puah, helped........... Ex 1:15

SHIPHTAN
son of Joseph, Kemuel son of **S;** .... Nu 34:24

SHIPS
send you back to Egypt in **s,** .... Dt 28:68
why did you stay by the **s?** .... Jdg 5:17
also built **s** at Ezion Geber,..................... 1Ki 9:26
also had many trading **s** at sea, ... 1Ki 10:22
built trading **s** to sail to Ophir 1Ki 22:48
with Ahaziah to build trading **s,** 2Ch 20:36
out to sea in **s** and did business .... Ps 107:23
You trading **s,** cry! The houses .... Is 23:1
All the **s** of the sea and their .... Eze 27:9

SHIPWRECKED
and their faith has been **s.** 1Ti 1:19

SHIRT
you in court and take your **s,** .... Mt 5:40
not stop him from taking your **s.** .... Lk 6:29
They also took his long **s,** .... Jn 19:23

SHIRTS
you thirty linen **s** and thirty .... Jdg 14:12
me thirty linen **s** and thirty.................... Jdg 14:13
you have two **s,** share with the .... Lk 3:11
showed him the **s** and coats .... Ac 9:39

SHISHA
Ahijah, sons of **S,** recorded what 1Ki 4:3

SHISHAK
to Egypt, to **S** king of Egypt, ... 1Ki 11:40
S king of Egypt attacked....................... 1Ki 14:25
S king of Egypt attacked........................ 2Ch 12:2
S had twelve hundred chariots 2Ch 12:3
S captured the strong, walled................. 2Ch 12:4
because they were afraid of **S.** 2Ch 12:5
leave you to face **S** alone.' " 2Ch 12:5
I will not use **S** to punish 2Ch 12:7
S king of Egypt attacked....................... 2Ch 12:9

SHISHAK'S
will become **S** servants so they 2Ch 12:8

SHITRAI
S, from Sharon, was in charge of 1Ch 27:29

SHITTAH
city of Beth **S** toward Zererah. .... Jdg 7:22

SHIZA
Adina son of **S** the Reubenite, ... 1Ch 11:42

SHOA
men from Pekod, **S,** and Koa will .... Eze 23:23

SHOBAB
Shammua, **S,** Nathan, Solomon,............. 2Sa 5:14
sons were Jesher, **S,** and Ardon.............. 1Ch 2:18
Shammua, **S,** Nathan, and Solomon— 1Ch 3:5
Shammua, **S,** Nathan, Solomon,............. 1Ch 14:4

SHOBACH
leader was **S,** the commander................. 2Sa 10:16
He also killed **S,** the commander 2Sa 10:18

SHOBAI
Akkub, Hatita, and **S**—139..................... Ezr 2:42
Akkub, Hatita, and **S**—138..................... Ne 7:45

SHOBAL
Lotan, **S,** Zibeon, Anah, ... Ge 36:20
The sons of **S** were Alvan, ... Ge 36:23
Lotan, **S,** Zibeon, Anah, ... Ge 36:29
were Lotan, **S,** Zibeon, Anah,.................. 1Ch 1:38
S was the father of Kiriath 1Ch 2:52
Hezron, Carmi, Hur, and **S**...................... 1Ch 4:1

SHOBAL'S
S sons were Alvan, Manahath, ... 1Ch 1:40
S descendants were Haroeh, ... 1Ch 2:52
Reaiah was **S** son. Reaiah was the 1Ch 4:2

SHOBEK
Hallohesh, Pilha, **S,**............................... Ne 10:24

SHOBI
S, Makir, and Barzillai were at 2Sa 17:27
S son of Nahash was from the 2Sa 17:27

SHOHAM
son of Merari had sons named **S,** 1Ch 24:27

SHOMER
Shimeath and Jehozabad son of **S**........... 2Ki 12:21
of Japhlet, **S,** Hotham, and their.............. 1Ch 7:32
Japhlet's brother was **S.** 1Ch 7:34

SHOMER'S
S sons were Rohgah, Hubbah, and........... 1Ch 7:34
S brother was Hotham. 1Ch 7:35

SHOOK
and the whole mountain **s** wildly. .... Ex 19:18
they **s** with fear and stood far................. Ex 20:18
Edom, the earth **s,** the skies .... Jdg 5:4
The mountains **s** before the LORD,........... Jdg 5:5
ground itself **s!** God had caused 1Sa 14:15
elders of Bethlehem **s** with fear. 1Sa 16:4
Ahimelech **s** with fear when he 1Sa 21:1
The earth trembled and **s.** 2Sa 22:8
made so much noise the ground **s.** 1Ki 1:40
I **s** out the folds of my robe..................... Ne 5:13
The earth trembled and **s.** .... Ps 18:7
The ground **s** and the sky poured .... Ps 68:8
the deep waters **s** with fear. .... Ps 77:16
The earth trembled and **s.** .... Ps 77:18
They **s** with fear like trees of .... Is 7:2
on earth, who **s** the kingdoms, ... Is 14:16
you **s** your head and acted as if .... Je 48:27
saw you and **s** with fear. .... Hab 3:10
Jesus and **s** their heads, ... Mt 27:39
earth **s** and rocks broke apart. .... Mt 27:51
the tomb **s** with fear because .... Mt 28:4
The evil spirit **s** the man .... Mk 1:26
Jesus and **s** their heads, ... Mk 15:29
Paul and Barnabas **s** the dust off .... Ac 13:51
earthquake that **s** the foundation .... Ac 16:26
So he **s** off the dust from his .... Ac 18:6
Paul **s** the snake off into the .... Ac 28:5
before, his voice **s** the earth, ... Heb 12:26

SHOOT
violently and **s** at him angrily, ... Ge 49:23
they will **s** them with arrows. .... Nu 24:8
upon them and **s** my arrows at .... Dt 32:23

day I will s three arrows to 1Sa 20:20
"Run and find the arrows I s." 1Sa 20:36
know they would s arrows from 2Sa 11:20
him, saying, "S Ahaziah, too!" 2Ki 9:27
Elisha said, "S," and Jehoash 2Ki 13:17
city or even s an arrow here. 2Ki 19:32
or left hands to s arrows or to 1Ch 12:2
were used to s arrows and large 2Ch 26:15
its mouth; sparks of fire s out. .... Job 41:19
They s from dark places at those .... Ps 11:2
like swords and s bitter words .... Ps 64:3
places they s at innocent people .... Ps 64:4
they s suddenly and are not .... Ps 64:4
But God will s them with arrows; .... Ps 64:7
bow that does not s straight. .... Ps 78:57
You planted this s with your own .... Ps 80:15
S your arrows and force them .... Ps 144:6
of their bows are ready to s. .... Is 5:28
soldiers will s the young men .... Is 13:18
bows ready to s, from a hard .... Is 21:15
city or even s an arrow here. .... Is 37:33
S your arrows at Babylon! .... Je 50:14
prepare their bows to s. .... Je 51:3
prepared to s his bow, and his .... La 2:4
prepared to s his bow and made............. La 3:12
like a loose bow that can't s. .... Hos 7:16
arrows will s like lightning. .... Zch 9:14

SHOOTING
rock as if I am s at a target. 1Sa 20:20
like an archer s at just...................... Pr 26:10
Like a madman s deadly, burning .... Pr 26:10
s lies from their mouths like .... Je 9:3

SHOOTS
and put out new s like a plant. .... Job 14:9
and our s went to the Euphrates............. Ps 80:11

SHOPHACH
leader was S, the commander................ 1Ch 19:16
He also killed S, the commander 1Ch 19:18

SHOPHAN
Atroth S, Jazer, Jogbehah, ... Nu 32:35

SHOPS
And you may put s in Damascus, ... 1Ki 20:34

SHORE
His s will be a safe place for .... Ge 49:13
Zephon, on the s of the sea. .... Ex 14:2
hidden in the sand on the s." .... Dt 33:19
stopped at the s of the Jordan................ Jos 13:23
was the s of the Dead Sea, ... Jos 15:5
at the north s of the Dead Sea, ... Jos 18:19
them along the s to the place 1Ki 5:9
Elath on the s of the Red Sea, ... 1Ki 9:26
that its waves crash on the s. .... Je 31:35
villages on the s across from .... Eze 26:6
your villages on the s across .... Eze 26:8
people on the s shake with fear .... Eze 27:28
of other ships stand on the s. .... Eze 27:29
who live along the s are shocked .... Eze 27:35
while the people stood on the s. .... Mt 13:2
pulled the net to the s........................ Mt 13:48
they came to s at Gennesaret................ Mt 14:34
along the s of Lake Galilee. .... Mt 15:29
sat down in a boat near the s................. Mk 4:1
on the s close to the water. .... Mk 4:1
they came to s at Gennesaret and .... Mk 6:53
two boats at the s of the lake................. Lk 5:2
brought their boats to the s, ... Lk 5:11
morning Jesus stood on the s,............... Jn 21:4
followers went to s in the boat, ... Jn 21:8
They were not very far from s, ... Jn 21:8
out of the boat and onto the s, ... Jn 21:9
and pulled the net to the s. .... Jn 21:11

SHORES
will sail from the s of Cyprus .... Nu 24:24
on the s of the Jabbok River, ... Dt 2:37
its waves on your island s. .... Eze 26:3

SHORT
Remember how s my life is. .... Ps 89:47
because he was too s to see .... Lk 19:3
and fallen s of God's glorious .... Rm 3:23
thing that lasts only a s time, ... 1Co 9:25
us for a s time in the way they .... Heb 12:10
he comes, he must stay a s time. .... Rev 17:10
must be set free for a s time. .... Rev 20:3

SHORTAGE
was a s of food in the land.................... Ru 1:1
was a s of food that lasted 2Sa 21:1
are the reason for this s, ... 2Sa 21:1
there was a s of food in the................... 2Ki 4:38
was a s of food in Samaria. 2Ki 6:25

SHORTEST
though that was the s way. .... Ex 13:17

SHOT
with stones or s with arrows. .... Ex 19:13
Jonathan s an arrow beyond him. 1Sa 20:36
The archers s him, and he was 1Sa 31:3
the city wall s at your servants 2Sa 11:24
s his arrows and scattered his 2Sa 22:15
a soldier s an arrow, but he............... 1Ki 22:34
drew his bow and s Joram between 2Ki 9:24
said, "Shoot," and Jehoash s................. 2Ki 13:17
and the archers s him with their............. 1Ch 10:3
a soldier s an arrow which hit 2Ch 18:33
King Josiah was s by archers................... 2Ch 35:23
s his arrows and scattered his .... Ps 18:14
and s through the liver with an .... Pr 7:23
He s me in the kidneys with the .... La 3:13

SHOULDER
carrying her water jar on her s. .... Ge 24:15
the jar from her s and gave him .... Ge 24:18
with her water jar on her s. .... Ge 24:45
the jar from her s and said, ' .... Ge 24:46
will be a pair of s straps tied .... Ex 28:7
tied together over each s. .... Ex 28:7
gold pieces on the s straps in .... Ex 28:25
bottom of the s straps in the .... Ex 28:27
They made the s straps for the .... Ex 39:4
and tied together over each s................... Ex 39:4
the gems on the s straps of the .... Ex 39:7
pieces to the two s straps in .... Ex 39:18
bottom of the s straps in front .... Ex 39:20
them a boiled s from the male .... Nu 6:19
giving them the s, the cheeks,................. Dt 18:3
Israel, and carry it on your s. .... Jos 4:5
arm fall off my s and be broken .... Job 31:22
would wear the writing on my s; .... Job 31:36
his things on his s in the dark .... Eze 12:6
and every s was rubbed raw. .... Eze 29:18
with your side and with your s, ... Eze 34:21

SHOULDERS
carrying it on both their s, ... Ge 9:23
and carried them on their s. .... Ex 12:34
names on his s in the presence .... Ex 28:12
were on your s and let you walk.............. Le 26:13
the holy things on their s. .... Nu 7:9
branches and put them on his s............... Jdg 9:48
put them on his s and carried................. Jdg 16:3
and shot Joram between his s. 2Ki 9:24
carry the Ark of God on their s, ... 1Ch 15:15
to place on your s anymore. 2Ch 35:3
I took the load off their s; .... Ps 81:6
put it on their s and carry it. .... Is 46:7
carry your daughters on their s. .... Is 49:22

S

them onto your **s** with the people .... Eze 12:6
them on my **s** as the people .... Eze 12:7
best pieces—the legs and the **s.** .... Eze 24:4
and tore open their **s.** .... Eze 29:7
he happily puts it on his **s** .... Lk 15:5

SHOULDN'T

we **s** give them any of the things 1Sa 30:22
King Ahab, you **s** say that!" 1Ki 22:8
King Ahab, you **s** say that!" 2Ch 18:7
on my head. I **s** refuse it. But I .... Ps 141:5
yours alone and **s** be shared with .... Pr 5:17
It **s** snow in summer or rain at .... Pr 26:1
S I punish the people of Judah .... Je 5:9
S I give a nation such as this .... Je 5:9
S I punish the people of Judah .... Je 5:29
S I give a nation such as this .... Je 5:29
S I punish the people for doing .... Je 9:9
S I give a nation like this the .... Je 9:9
Then **s** I show concern for the .... Jnh 4:11
S I drink the cup the Father .... Jn 18:11

SHOUT

It is not a **s** of victory; .... Ex 32:18
all the people give a loud **s.** .... Jos 6:5
He said, "Don't **s.** Don't say a .... Jos 6:10
the day I tell you. Then **s.**" .... Jos 6:10
command: "Now, **s**! The LORD has .... Jos 6:16
the trumpets and the people's **s,** .... Jos 6:20
Then **s**, 'For the LORD and for .... Jdg 7:18
gave a great **s** of joy that made 1Sa 4:5
Philistines heard Israel's **s,** 1Sa 4:6
the trumpet and **s**, 'Long live 1Ki 1:34
the sea and everything in it **s;** 1Ch 16:32
with no **s** of joy to be heard. .... Job 3:7
longer hear the **s** of the slave .... Job 3:18
I **s**, 'I have been wronged!' .... Job 19:7
face and will **s** with happiness. .... Job 33:26
Can you **s** an order to the clouds .... Job 38:34
it does not hear the drivers **s.** .... Job 39:7
and we will **s** for joy when you .... Ps 20:5
my friends sing and **s** for joy. .... Ps 35:27
you people. **S** to God with joy. .... Ps 47:1
God has risen with a **s** of joy; .... Ps 47:5
at Edom. I **s** at Philistia." .... Ps 60:8
on earth, with **s** for joy to God! .... Ps 66:1
I will **s** for joy when I sing .... Ps 71:23
s out loud to the God of Jacob. .... Ps 81:1
Let's **s** praises to the Rock who .... Ps 95:1
the sea and everything in it **s.** .... Ps 96:11
S with joy to the LORD, all the .... Ps 98:4
s for joy to the LORD the King. .... Ps 98:6
the sea and everything in it **s;** .... Ps 98:7
S to the LORD, all the earth. .... Ps 100:1
at Edom. I **s** at Philistia." .... Ps 108:9
Let them **s** his praise with their .... Ps 149:6
Their **s** is like the roar of a .... Is 5:29
S and sing for joy, you people. .... Is 12:6
The people **s** for joy. From the .... Is 24:14
can't talk now will **s** with joy. .... Is 35:6
S out loud the good news. .... Is 40:9
S it out and don't be afraid. .... Is 40:9
they should **s** from the .... Is 42:11
He will **s** out the battle cry and .... Is 42:13
Babylonians will **s** their cries .... Is 43:14
Earth, **s** for joy, even in your .... Is 44:23
Mountains, **s** with joy, because .... Is 49:13
I need only to **s** and the sea .... Is 50:2
and have heard God's angry **s.** .... Is 51:20
but **s** and rejoice together, ... Is 52:9
Start singing and **s** for joy. .... Is 54:1
The LORD says, "**S** out loud. .... Is 58:1
S out loud like a trumpet. .... Is 58:1
servants will **s** for joy because .... Is 65:14

' **S** out loud and say, 'Come .... Je 4:5
Every time I speak, I **s.** .... Je 20:8
heaven and will **s** from his Holy .... Je 25:30
will **s** like people who walk on .... Je 25:30
will **s** against all who live on .... Je 25:30
of Ephraim **s** this message: ' .... Je 31:6
S for Israel, the greatest of .... Je 31:7
Sing your praises and **s** this: ' .... Je 31:7
of Jerusalem and **s** for joy. .... Je 31:12
Men will **s** to them, 'Terror on .... Je 49:29
around Babylon, **s** the war cry! .... Je 50:15
over you and **s** their victory.' .... Je 51:14
They will **s** and laugh. .... Je 51:39
is in them will **s** for joy about .... Je 51:48
They will **s** because the army .... Je 51:48
Even if they **s** in my ears, ... Eze 8:18
S and yell, human, because the .... Eze 21:12
to **s** the battle cry and give the .... Eze 21:22
don't **s** for joy as the other .... Hos 9:1
They used to **s** for joy about its .... Hos 10:5
s a warning on my holy mountain. .... Joe 2:1
food to eat, they **s**, 'Peace!' .... Mic 3:5
Israel, **s** for joy! Jerusalem .... Zph 3:14
S and be glad, Jerusalem. .... Zch 2:10
S for joy, people of Jerusalem! .... Zch 9:9
will drink and **s** like drunks. .... Zch 9:15
ear you should **s** from the .... Mt 10:27
by, he began to **s**, "Jesus, Son .... Mk 10:47
continued to **s**, demanding that .... Lk 23:23
cross began to **s** insults at .... Lk 23:39
But I did **s** one thing when I .... Ac 24:21
Start singing and **s** for joy. .... Gal 4:27
Never **s** angrily or say things to .... Eph 4:31

SHOUTED

The Egyptians **s**, "Let's get away .... Ex 14:25
they **s** with joy and bowed .... Le 9:24
blew the trumpets, the people **s.** .... Jos 6:20
Then they **s**, "A sword for the .... Jdg 7:20
He **s** to the people: .... Jdg 9:7
men with Micah **s** at the Danites, ... Jdg 18:23
They **s** to the old man who owned .... Jdg 19:22
Then the people **s**, "Long live 1Sa 10:24
the camp **s** to Jonathan and his 1Sa 14:12
stood and **s** to the Israelite 1Sa 17:8
He **s** things against Israel as 1Sa 17:23
of Israel and Judah **s** and chased 1Sa 17:52
Then he **s**, "Hurry! Go quickly! 1Sa 20:38
of the cave, he **s** to Saul, "My 1Sa 24:8
David's **s** to the army and to Abner 1Sa 26:14
Abner **s** to Joab, "Must the sword 2Sa 2:26
the Israelites **s** with joy and 2Sa 6:15
He **s** the news to the king. 2Sa 18:25
But a wise woman **s** out from the 2Sa 20:16
the people **s**, "Long live King 1Ki 1:39
Elisha saw it and **s**, "My father! 2Ki 2:12
to eat it, they **s**, "Man of God, ... 2Ki 4:40
the gatekeepers **s** out and told 2Ki 7:11
They blew the trumpet and **s**, ... 2Ki 9:13
commander stood and **s** loudly in 2Ki 18:28
They **s**, blew horns and trumpets, ... 1Ch 15:28
When they **s**, God caused Jeroboam 2Ch 13:15
poured olive oil on him and **s**, ... 2Ch 23:11
the king's officers **s** in Hebrew, ... 2Ch 32:18
then all the people **s** loudly, ... Ezr 3:11
the people of Susa **s** for joy. .... Est 8:15
people **s** at them as if they were .... Job 30:5
and all the angels **s** with joy? .... Job 38:7
against you **s** in your meeting. .... Ps 74:4
commander stood and **s** loudly in .... Is 36:13
are unclean," people **s** at them. .... La 4:15
Then he **s** with a loud voice in .... Eze 9:1
the ground and **s** with a loud .... Eze 11:13

of the blazing furnace and **s**, ... Da 3:26
They **s**, "What do you want with .... Mt 8:29
He **s**, "Lord, save me!" .... Mt 14:30
going by, so they **s**, "Lord, Son .... Mt 20:30
quiet, but they **s** even more, ... Mt 20:31
But they **s** louder, "Crucify him! .... Mt 27:23
had an evil spirit in him. He **s**, ... Mk 1:23
they fell down before him and **s**, ... Mk 3:11
The man **s** in a loud voice, ... Mk 5:7
quiet, but he **s** even more, "Son .... Mk 10:48
They **s**, "Crucify him!" .... Mk 15:13
But they **s** even louder, ... Mk 15:14
evil spirit **s** in a loud voice, ... Lk 4:33
A man in the crowd **s** to him, ... Lk 9:38
room will be **s** from the .... Lk 12:3
But the blind man **s** even more, ... Lk 18:39
But the people **s** together, ... Lk 23:18
But they **s** again, "Crucify him! .... Lk 23:21
They **s** back, "No, not him! .... Jn 18:40
saw Jesus, they **s**, "Crucify him! .... Jn 19:6
They **s**, "Take him away! .... Jn 19:15
Then they **s** loudly and covered .... Ac 7:57
They **s**, "This is the voice of a .... Ac 12:22
s in the Lycaonian language, ... Ac 14:11
Paul **s**, "Don't hurt yourself! .... Ac 16:28
they became very angry and **s**, ... Ac 19:28
they all **s** the same thing for .... Ac 19:34
They **s**, "People of Israel, help .... Ac 21:28
They **s**, threw off their coats, ... Ac 22:23
this, Paul **s** to them, "My .... Ac 23:6
These souls **s** in a loud voice, ... Rev 6:10
he **s** loudly like the roaring .... Rev 10:3
And when he **s**, the voices of a .... Rev 10:3
He **s** in a powerful voice: .... Rev 18:2

SHOUTING

heard the sound of the people **s**, ... Ex 32:17
must warn other people by **s**, ' .... Le 13:45
Midianites began **s** and running .... Jdg 7:21
came to meet him, **s** for joy. .... Jdg 15:14
What's all this **s** in the Hebrew 1Sa 4:6
positions, **s** their war cry. 1Sa 17:20
Playing flutes and **s** for joy, ... 1Ki 1:40
went into the city, **s** with joy. 1Ki 1:45
until noon, **s** "Baal, answer us! 1Ki 18:26
But Jehoshaphat began **s**. 1Ki 22:32
s with a loud voice and blowing 2Ch 15:14
Jehoshaphat began **s**, and the 2Ch 18:31
other people were **s** with joy. .... Ezr 3:12
the joyful **s** and the sad crying .... Ezr 3:13
is like a woman **s** in the street; .... Pr 1:20
calls to you like someone **s**; .... Pr 8:1
I am **s** to all people. .... Pr 8:4
as if it were **s** with joy. .... Is 35:2
Your guards are **s**. They are all .... Is 52:8
They are all **s** for joy! .... Is 52:8
s words of war against the .... Je 4:16
I am always **s** about violence and .... Je 20:8
hear the sound of the leaders **s**. .... Je 25:36
be no happy **s** on the mountains. .... Eze 7:7
topmost stone, **s**, 'It's .... Zch 4:7
She is following us and **s**." .... Mt 15:23
behind him, **s**, "Praise to the .... Mt 21:9
and behind him, **s**, "Praise God! .... Mk 11:9
of many people, **s**, "You are the .... Lk 4:41
began joyfully **s** praise to God .... Lk 19:37
to meet Jesus, **s**, "Praise God! .... Jn 12:13
They ran in among the people, **s**, ... Ac 14:14
Paul and us, **s**, "These men are .... Ac 16:17
Some people were **s** one thing, ... Ac 19:32
thing, and some were **s** another. .... Ac 19:32
of all this confusion and **s**, ... Ac 21:34
following them, **s**, "Kill him!" .... Ac 21:36

Then they began **s**, "Get rid of .... Ac 22:22
the people were **s** against him .... Ac 22:24
s that he should not live any .... Ac 25:24
They were **s** in a loud voice, ... Rev 7:10

SHOUTS

and your lips with **s** of joy. .... Job 8:21
it hears the **s** of commanders and .... Job 39:25
God **s** and the earth crumbles. .... Ps 46:6
Everything **s** and sings for joy. .... Ps 65:13
S of joy and victory come from .... Ps 118:15
noisy street and **s** at the city .... Pr 1:21
people die, there are **s** of joy. .... Pr 11:10
the fool only **s** or laughs, ... Pr 29:9
better than the **s** of a foolish .... Ec 9:17
There will be no **s** of joy, ... Is 16:9
and no songs or **s** of joy in the .... Is 16:10
I have put an end to **s** of joy. .... Is 16:10
Tell this news with **s** of joy to .... Is 48:20
I have heard the **s** of war. .... Je 4:19
on the grapes with **s** of joy. .... Je 48:33
There are **s**, but not shouts of .... Je 48:33
are shouts, but not **s** of joy. .... Je 48:33
ears and ignore my gasps and **s**." .... La 3:56
The LORD **s** out orders to his .... Joe 2:11

SHOVE

person might **s** someone or throw .... Nu 35:20
person might suddenly **s** someone, ... Nu 35:22

SHOVELS

the ashes, the **s**, the bowls for .... Ex 27:3
pots, **s**, bowls for sprinkling .... Ex 38:3
forks, the **s**, and the bowls— .... Nu 4:14
made bowls, **s**, and small bowls 1Ki 7:40
pots, **s**, small bowls, and all 1Ki 7:45
took the pots, **s**, wick trimmers, ... 2Ki 25:14
made bowls, **s**, and small bowls 2Ch 4:11
the pots, **s**, forks, and all the 2Ch 4:16
have to use **s** and pitchforks .... Is 30:24
took the pots, **s**, wick trimmers, ... Je 52:18

SHOW

and go to the land I will **s** you. .... Ge 12:1
your foreskin to **s** that you are .... Ge 17:11
be marked to **s** that you are part .... Ge 17:13
Please **s** this kindness to my .... Ge 24:12
anything, **s** it to everyone. .... Ge 31:37
his clothes to **s** he was upset. .... Ge 37:29
rough cloth to **s** that he was .... Ge 37:34
before Joseph to **s** him respect. .... Ge 43:28
clothes to **s** they were afraid .... Ge 44:13
And how can we **s** we are not .... Ge 44:16
you when you **s** them this second .... Ex 4:8
S them to the king of Egypt. .... Ex 4:21
s you my power so that my name .... Ex 9:16
so I could **s** them my powerful .... Ex 10:1
I **s** kindness to thousands who .... Ex 20:6
in it by the plan I will **s** you. .... Ex 25:9
clothes to **s** that he belongs to .... Ex 28:3
This will **s** that Aaron and his .... Ex 29:21
s me your plans so that I may .... Ex 33:13
Now, please **s** me your glory." .... Ex 33:18
I will **s** kindness to anyone to .... Ex 33:19
to whom I want to **s** kindness, ... Ex 33:19
and I will **s** mercy to anyone to .... Ex 33:19
to whom I want to **s** mercy. .... Ex 33:19
offering to **s** his thanks, ... Le 7:12
which he gives to **s** thanks. .... Le 7:13
Don't **s** sadness by tearing your .... Le 10:6
this would **s** that you do not .... Le 18:21
or you will **s** that you don't .... Le 19:12
You must not **s** special favor to .... Le 19:15
cut your body to **s** sadness for .... Le 19:28
S respect to old people; .... Le 19:32

S

S respect also to your God......................Le 19:32
to their God and s respect for ....Le 21:6
So he must not s his sadness by ....Le 21:10
respect them to s that you ....Le 22:2
S respect for my holy name. ....Le 22:32
Then I will s kindness to you ....Le 26:9
I will s my great anger; ....Le 26:28
must go in and s each Kohathite..............Nu 4:19
May the LORD s you his kindness ....Nu 6:25
s myself to them in visions; ....Nu 12:6
So s your strength now, Lord..................Nu 14:17
the LORD will s who belongs to ....Nu 16:5
have begun to s me, your servant ....Dt 3:24
in order to s the other nations ....Dt 4:6
with them or s them any mercy. ....Dt 7:2
agreement and s his love to you ....Dt 7:12
say they will s you a miracle ....Dt 13:1
your heads to s your sadness...................Dt 14:1
a gift that will s how much the ....Dt 16:17
person who does not s respect ....Dt 17:12
and they will not s disrespect ....Dt 17:13
S no mercy. You must remove from ....Dt 19:13
S no mercy. A life must be paid ....Dt 19:21
her parents are to s the sheet ....Dt 22:17
gives you a coat to s he will ....Dt 24:12
off her hand. S her no mercy. ....Dt 25:12
that you will s kindness to my ....Jos 2:12
their heads to s their sorrow. ....Jos 7:6
because I will s you what the ....Jos 10:25
S us a way into the city, ...Jdg 1:24
I will s you the man you are ....Jdg 4:22
his clothes to s his sorrow. ....Jdg 11:35
they did not s respect for 1Sa 2:17
continued to s himself at Shiloh 1Sa 3:21
his head to s his great sadness. 1Sa 4:12
must appoint the one I s you." 1Sa 16:3
some proof to s me that they are 1Sa 17:18
s me the kindness of the LORD 1Sa 20:14
support me and s that I am right 1Sa 24:15
you did not s the Amalekites how 1Sa 28:18
To s his sadness, his clothes 2Sa 1:2
his clothes to s his sorrow, ...2Sa 1:11
rough cloth to s how sad you are 2Sa 3:31
I want to s kindness to that...................2Sa 9:1
I want to s God's kindness to 2Sa 9:3
s how upset she was, Tamar put 2Sa 13:19
on the ground to s his sadness. 2Sa 13:31
the ground to s respect and said..............2Sa 14:4
s that you are guilty for not 2Sa 14:13
on his head to s how sad he was. 2Sa 15:32
was worn to s sadness and put 2Sa 21:10
head to s he was the king. 1Ki 1:39
Adonijah must s that he is a man 1Ki 1:52
have captured them s them mercy. 1Ki 8:50
S these people that you 1Ki 18:36
in rough cloth to s our sadness, ...1Ki 20:31
rough cloth to s how sad and 1Ki 21:27
tore them to s how sad he was. 2Ki 2:12
his clothes to s how upset he 2Ki 5:7
his clothes to s his sadness. 2Ki 6:30
their clothes to s how upset 2Ki 18:37
rough cloth to s how sad he was. 2Ki 19:1
the sign from the LORD to s you: 2Ki 20:9
clothes to s how upset he was. 2Ki 22:11
your clothes to s how upset you 2Ki 22:19
groups of Issachar s there were 1Ch 7:5
family histories s that all 1Ch 8:28
rough cloth to s their grief. 1Ch 21:16
can make any design you s him................2Ch 2:14
offerings, to s thanks to him." 2Ch 29:31
offerings to s thanks to God. 2Ch 33:16
clothes to s how upset he was. 2Ch 34:19
your clothes to s how upset you 2Ch 34:27

this king to s kindness to me." ....Ne 1:11
their heads to s their sadness. ....Ne 9:1
was to come to s her beauty to ....Est 1:11
not bow down or s him honor. ....Est 3:2
and ashes to s how sad they were ....Est 4:3
wanted Hathach to s it to Esther ....Est 4:8
angels came to s themselves ....Job 1:6
his head to s how sad he was. ....Job 1:20
angels came to s themselves ....Job 2:1
They wanted to s their concern ....Job 2:11
their heads to s how sad they ....Job 2:12
S me where I have been wrong. ....Job 6:24
a lion and again s your terrible ....Job 10:16
S me my wrong and my sin. ....Job 13:23
over my skin to s my sadness and ....Job 16:15
The heavens will s their guilt,.................Job 20:27
children and s no kindness to..................Job 24:21
can s that my words are worth ....Job 24:25
I sign my name to s I have told ....Job 31:35
had no answer to s that Job was..............Job 32:3
only God will s Job to be wrong, ...Job 32:13
words s he does not understand. ....Job 34:35
'God will s that I am right,' ....Job 35:2
and I will s you that there is ....Job 36:2
I will s that my Maker is right. ....Job 36:3
water his earth and s his love. ....Job 37:13
S that you are loyal to his son, ...Ps 2:12
s me the right thing to do. ....Ps 5:8
S me clearly how you want me to ....Ps 5:8
me your ways. S me how to live. ....Ps 25:4
my hands to s I am innocent, ...Ps 26:6
S your kindness to me, your ....Ps 31:16
you wise and s you where to go...............Ps 32:8
s your love to us as we put our ....Ps 33:22
hole in my ear to s that my body ....Ps 40:6
S your glory and majesty. ....Ps 45:3
an offering to s thanks to God. ....Ps 50:14
bring me offerings to s thanks. ....Ps 50:23
By your strength s that I am ....Ps 54:1
bless us and s us your kindness ....Ps 67:1
s the mighty power you have used ....Ps 68:28
the wicked, 'Don't s your power. ....Ps 75:4
He found a way to s his anger. ....Ps 78:50
S your mercy to us soon, because ....Ps 79:8
with wings. S your greatness ....Ps 80:1
S us your kindness so we can be ....Ps 80:3
S us your kindness so we can be ....Ps 80:7
S us your kindness so we can be ....Ps 80:19
long will you s greater kindness...............Ps 82:2
LORD, s us your love, and save ....Ps 85:7
S me a sign of your goodness. ....Ps 86:17
Do you s your miracles for the ....Ps 88:10
return and s kindness to your..................Ps 90:13
S your servants the wonderful ....Ps 90:16
s your greatness to their ....Ps 90:16
s your greatness and punish! ....Ps 94:1
own sake, to s his great power ....Ps 106:8
even his prayers s his guilt.....................Ps 109:7
Let no one s him love or have..................Ps 109:12
an offering to s thanks to you, ...Ps 116:17
LORD, s me your love, and save ....Ps 119:41
S your love to me, your servant,...............Ps 119:124
S your kindness to me, your ....Ps 119:135
we wait for him to s us mercy. ....Ps 123:2
S me what I should do, because ....Ps 143:8
Fools quickly s that they are ....Pr 12:16
fools s how foolish they are. ....Pr 13:16
quick tempers their ....Pr 14:29
happiness will s in your eyes. ....Pr 15:30
their actions s if they are ....Pr 20:11
than to have love and not s it..................Pr 27:5
people and to s them they are..................Ec 3:18
the road, they s they are not ....Ec 10:3

they s everyone how stupid they.............. Ec 10:3
S me your face, and let me hear.............. Sng 2:14
the holy God will s himself holy.............. Is 5:16
nor will he s mercy to the.............. Is 9:17
him like a rod to s my anger; .... Is 10:5
stars will not s their light; .... Is 13:10
will s no mercy on children, ... Is 13:18
The LORD will s mercy to the.................. Is 14:1
shaved to s how sad Moab is. .... Is 15:2
rough cloth to s their sadness. .... Is 15:3
Let them s you what the LORD .... Is 19:12
the LORD will s himself to the .... Is 19:21
even if you s them kindness. .... Is 26:10
S them your strong love for your .... Is 26:11
earth will s the blood of the .... Is 26:21
LORD wants to s his mercy to you .... Is 30:18
your waist to s your sadness. .... Is 32:11
stand up and s my greatness. .... Is 33:10
will s its happiness, as if it .... Is 35:2
their clothes to s how upset .... Is 36:22
rough cloth to s how sad he was. .... Is 37:1
the sign from the LORD to s you: .... Is 38:7
What will s that I will go up to .... Is 38:22
have done and s you are right. .... Is 43:26
I s that the signs of the lying .... Is 44:25
I will s my glory through you." .... Is 49:3
all nations to s people all over .... Is 49:6
will s mercy to those who live.................. Is 51:3
I will soon s that I do what is .... Is 51:5
The LORD will s his holy power.............. Is 52:10
but I will s you mercy with .... Is 54:8
You will s that those who speak .... Is 54:17
makes me want to s you mercy?.............. Is 57:6
lie in ashes to s their sadness. .... Is 58:5
our sins s we are wrong........................ Is 59:12
He will s his anger to those who.............. Is 59:18
my own hands to s my greatness. .... Is 60:21
the LORD will s his kindness .... Is 61:2
by the LORD to s his greatness. .... Is 61:3
in Jerusalem to s respect to the .... Je 3:17
rough cloth, s how sad you are .... Je 4:8
They are cruel and s no mercy. .... Je 6:23
the ashes to s how sad you are .... Je 6:26
pity on them or s mercy that .... Je 13:14
the dead or to s your sorrow for .... Je 16:5
his head to s sorrow for them. .... Je 16:6
help you or s you any favors. .... Je 16:13
The LORD will s him that he can .... Je 17:7
offerings to s thanks to God. .... Je 17:26
will not s any mercy or pity .... Je 21:7
Put up signs to s you the way .... Je 31:21
You s love and kindness to .... Je 32:18
their clothes to s their sorrow. .... Je 36:24
same way I will s my anger .... Je 42:18
to Elam and s them how angry I.............. Je 49:3
in Elam to s that I am king, ... Je 49:38
rough cloth to s their sadness. .... La 2:10
no pity, and I will s no mercy.................. Eze 5:11
I will s no pity, and I will not .... Eze 7:9
rough cloth to s how sad they.................. Eze 7:18
Their faces will s their shame, ... Eze 7:18
no pity, nor will I s mercy. .... Eze 8:18
pity anyone, and don't s mercy. .... Eze 9:5
no pity, nor will I s mercy. .... Eze 9:10
you I will s how holy I am so .... Eze 20:41
one sign to s the road he can .... Eze 21:20
other sign to s the road to .... Eze 21:20
and s how afraid they are. .... Eze 26:16
roll in ashes to s they are sad. .... Eze 27:30
rough cloth to s they are upset. .... Eze 27:31
and their faces s their fear. .... Eze 27:35
and I will s my glory among you. .... Eze 28:22

will s my holiness by defeating .... Eze 28:22
I will s my holiness when the .... Eze 28:25
in black to s her sadness about .... Eze 31:15
punish you and s the Israelites .... Eze 35:11
Then I will s how great I am. .... Eze 38:23
I will s my holiness, and I will .... Eze 38:23
I will s my glory among the .... Eze 39:21
use my people to s many nations .... Eze 39:27
to all that I will s you,...................... Eze 40:4
S them its exits and entrances, ... Eze 43:11
of heaven would s them mercy and .... Da 2:18
by my power to s my glory and my .... Da 4:30
s my sadness, I fasted, put on .... Da 9:3
you s us mercy and forgive us .... Da 9:9
will return and s his anger .... Da 11:30
the North will s his power in .... Da 11:42
But I will s pity to the people .... Hos 1:7
So I will s her nakedness to her .... Hos 2:10
I will s you my love and mercy. .... Hos 2:19
and I will s pity to the one I .... Hos 2:23
s your love to a woman loved by .... Hos 3:1
I will s them no mercy. .... Hos 13:14
You s mercy to orphans." .... Hos 14:3
cloth and cry to s your sadness. .... Joe 1:13
on all night to s your sadness. .... Joe 1:13
is not enough to s you are sad; .... Joe 2:13
I will s miracles in the sky and .... Joe 2:30
as a sacrifice to s your thanks, ... Am 4:5
Israel to s how crooked they .... Am 7:8
rough cloth to s your sadness; .... Am 8:10
rough cloth to s their sadness. .... Jnh 3:5
sat in ashes to s how upset he .... Jnh 3:6
Then shouldn't I s concern for .... Jnh 4:11
your hair to s you are sad for .... Mic 1:16
Egypt, I will s them miracles." .... Mic 7:15
your face and s the nations your .... Nah 3:5
day that God will s his anger, ... Zph 1:18
"I'll s you what they are." .... Zch 1:9
it be before you s mercy to .... Zch 1:12
each other and s no respect for .... Mal 2:10
obey his laws and to s the LORD .... Mal 3:14
I will s mercy to my people. .... Mal 3:17
things that s you really have .... Mt 3:8
with water to s that your hearts .... Mt 3:11
blessed who s mercy to others .... Mt 5:7
for God will s mercy to them.................. Mt 5:7
look sad to s people they are .... Mt 6:16
But go and s yourself to the .... Mt 8:4
This will s the people what I .... Mt 8:4
to s they had changed. .... Mt 11:21
and they will s that you are .... Mt 12:41
She will s that you are guilty, ... Mt 12:42
So they s that the things Isaiah .... Mt 13:14
'These people s honor to me with .... Mt 15:8
asked him to s them a miracle .... Mt 16:1
people love to s their power .... Mt 20:25
John came to s you the right way .... Mt 21:32
S me a coin used for paying the .... Mt 22:19
and you s honor to the graves of .... Mt 23:29
came up to s him the Temple's .... Mt 24:1
But go and s yourself to the .... Mk 1:44
This will s the people what I .... Mk 1:44
How can I s you what the kingdom .... Mk 4:30
'These people s honor to me with .... Mk 7:6
rulers love to s their power.................... Mk 10:42
owner will s you a large room .... Mk 14:15
God will s his mercy forever and .... Lk 1:50
remembering to s them mercy .... Lk 1:54
things that s you really have .... Lk 3:8
the Lord will s his kindness." .... Lk 4:19
but go and s yourself to the .... Lk 5:14
This will s the people what I .... Lk 5:14
S mercy, just as your Father .... Lk 6:36

S

I will s you what everyone is .... Lk 6:47
to s they had changed. .... Lk 10:13
wanting to s the importance of .... Lk 10:29
She will s they are guilty, ... Lk 11:31
and they will s that you are .... Lk 11:32
And now you s that you approve .... Lk 11:48
I will s you the one to fear. .... Lk 12:5
and s yourselves to the priests. .... Lk 17:14
S me a coin. Whose image and .... Lk 20:24
Then he will s you a large, ... Lk 22:12
S us a miracle to prove you have .... Jn 2:18
because it will s all the evil .... Jn 3:20
the Father will s the Son even.................. Jn 5:20
doing these things, s yourself .... Jn 7:4
in my Father's name s who I am. .... Jn 10:25
said this to s how he would die .... Jn 12:33
to him, "Lord, s us the Father. .... Jn 14:8
do you say, 'S us the Father'? .... Jn 14:9
them and will s myself to them." .... Jn 14:21
do you plan to s yourself to us .... Jn 14:22
much fruit and s that you are my .... Jn 15:8
a person can s is to die for his .... Jn 15:13
like, and I will s them again. .... Jn 17:26
wrong, then s what it was. .... Jn 18:23
said this to s how Peter would .... Jn 21:19
I will s miracles in the sky and .... Ac 2:19
S us your power to heal. .... Ac 4:30
go to the land I will s you.' .... Ac 7:3
I will s him how much he must .... Ac 9:16
you will s people all over the .... Ac 13:47
Bernice appeared with great s, ... Ac 25:23
the things that I will s you. .... Ac 26:16
do things to s they really had .... Ac 26:20
and they s no kindness or mercy .... Rm 1:31
They s that in their hearts they .... Rm 2:15
And they s this by their .... Rm 2:15
think you can s foolish people .... Rm 2:20
will s that you are guilty........................ Rm 2:27
God gave Jesus to s today that .... Rm 3:26
circumcised to s that he was .... Rm 4:11
was used to s that sin is very .... Rm 7:13
for God to s his children's .... Rm 8:19
I will s kindness to anyone to .... Rm 9:15
to whom I want to s kindness, ... Rm 9:15
and I will s mercy to anyone to .... Rm 9:15
to whom I want to s mercy." .... Rm 9:15
to whom he decides to s mercy; .... Rm 9:16
to s my power in you so that my............. Rm 9:17
mercy where he wants to s mercy, ... Rm 9:18
He wanted to s his anger and to .... Rm 9:22
' And I will s my love to those .... Rm 9:25
so that he can s mercy to all. .... Rm 11:32
S respect and honor to them all............. Rm 13:7
of the Jews to s that God's .... Rm 15:8
words or a s of human wisdom. 1Co 2:1
work to s what sort of work 1Co 3:13
valuable must s they are worthy............. 1Co 4:3
We are like a s for the whole 1Co 4:9
now I will s you the best way 1Co 12:31
mark on us to s that we are his 2Co 1:22
beg you to s that you love him. 2Co 2:8
You s that you are a letter from 2Co 3:3
We all s the Lord's glory, ... 2Co 3:18
every way we s we are servants 2Co 6:4
We s we are servants of God by 2Co 6:6
the Lord and to s that we really 2Co 8:19
So s these men the proof of your 2Co 8:24
will s the same authority that 2Co 10:11
that we s in our letters. 2Co 10:11
the things that s I am weak. 2Co 11:30
It was given to s that the wrong .... Gal 3:19
for people to s interest in you, ... Gal 4:18
on my body that s I belong to .... Gal 6:17

time he could s the very great.................. Eph 2:7
the Spirit to s that God will..................... Eph 4:30
But s that they are wrong. .... Eph 5:11
to s the greatness of Christ in .... Php 1:20
was no way for you to s it. .... Php 4:10
have this to s they are from me. 2Th 3:17
Christ Jesus could s that he has 1Ti 1:16
proper clothes that s respect 1Ti 2:9
a yoke should s full respect to 1Ti 6:1
should not s their masters any 1Ti 6:2
May the Lord s mercy to the 2Ti 1:16
and they s those who are .... Tit 1:9
but their actions s they do not .... Tit 1:16
them but should s their masters .... Tit 2:10
uses this to s that the way .... Heb 9:8
begin without blood to s death. .... Heb 9:18
without blood to s death. .... Heb 9:22
each other to s love and do good .... Heb 10:24
they s they are looking for a .... Heb 11:14
again" clearly s us that .... Heb 12:27
your patience is itself perfectly .... Jam 1:4
You s special attention to the .... Jam 2:3
you s no respect to the poor. .... Jam 2:6
So you must s mercy to others, ... Jam 2:13
or God will not s mercy to you .... Jam 2:13
S me your faith without doing .... Jam 2:18
I will s you my faith by what .... Jam 2:18
Then they should s it by living .... Jam 3:13
S respect for all people: 1Pe 2:17
But s them respect, because God 1Pe 3:7
S mercy to some people who have .... Jud 1:22
S mercy mixed with fear to..................... Jud 1:23
to s his servants what must soon .... Rev 1:1
his angel to s it to his servant................. Rev 1:1
I will s you what must happen .... Rev 4:1
rough cloth to s their sadness." .... Rev 11:3
and I will s you the punishment .... Rev 17:1
and I will s you the bride, ... Rev 21:9
sent his angel to s his servants .... Rev 22:6

SHOWED

The LORD s us great and terrible .... Dt 6:22
there the LORD s him all the .... Dt 34:1
because you s kindness to the 1Sa 15:6
that the LORD s me two baskets .... Je 24:1
This is what the Lord GOD s me: .... Am 7:1
high mountain and s him all the............... Mt 4:8
took Jesus and s him all the .... Lk 4:5
"The one who s him mercy." .... Lk 10:37
he s them his hands and feet................... Lk 24:40
s them his hands and his side. .... Jn 20:20
third time Jesus s himself to .... Jn 21:14
s me the holy city, Jerusalem,................. Rev 21:10

SHOWER

and to the s, 'Be a heavy rain................... Job 37:6
his kindness is like a spring s. .... Pr 16:15
rain, they will s on the earth. .... Ec 11:3

SHOWERS

will be like s on the grass; .... Dt 32:2
clouds, and s fall on people. .... Job 36:28
like s that water the earth. .... Ps 72:6
have the power to send down s?............... Je 14:22
had rain or s when God is angry. .... Eze 22:24
there will be s to bless them. .... Eze 34:26
sends the s and gives everyone .... Zch 10:1

SHOWING

God is s the king what he is .... Ge 41:28
Egyptians are s great sorrow!" .... Ge 50:11
must never stop s your kindness 1Sa 20:15
God was s kindness to me. .... Ne 2:8
King Xerxes was s off the great .... Est 1:4
can't keep from s how foolish................. Pr 12:23

I have continued s you kindness. .... Je 31:3
and Jerusalem, s them their .... Eze 23:36
with the sword, s them no mercy. .... Am 1:11
people without s mercy? .... Hab 1:17
people will stop s their love .... Mt 24:12
proved he is real by s kindness, ... Ac 14:17
s them that Jesus is the Christ. .... Ac 18:5
the gift of s mercy to others .... Rm 12:8
truth plainly, s everyone who we 2Co 4:2
know his secret by s it to me. .... Eph 3:3
of grace, s how generous he is. .... Eph 4:7
things without s favor of any 1Ti 5:21
for s people what is wrong in 2Ti 3:16
what the Spirit was s them, ... 1Pe 1:11

SHOWN
Holy Tent by the plan s to you .... Ex 26:30
as you were s on the mountain. .... Ex 27:8
and the miracles he had s them.............. Ps 78:11
glory will be s through the Son. .... Jn 14:13
And my glory is s through them. .... Jn 17:10
But God has s me that I should .... Ac 10:28
Yes, God has s himself to them. .... Rm 1:19
through angels was s to be true,............. Heb 2:2
Must you be s that faith that .... Jam 2:20

SHOWS
He s those who are humble how to ..... Ps 25:9
The LORD s his true love every .... Ps 42:8
are a God who s mercy and is .... Ps 86:15
As a parent s mercy to his child .... Mal 3:17
The way you talk s it." .... Mt 26:73
So God s mercy where he wants to .... Rm 9:18
and this s that you are not 1Co 3:3
and this s that none of them 1Jn 2:19

SHRINK
the patch will s and pull away .... Mt 9:16
the patch will s and pull away—.............. Mk 2:21

SHUA
the daughter of a man named S,........... Ge 38:2
wife, the daughter of S, died. .... Ge 38:12
the daughter of S, was their 1Ch 2:3
Hotham, and their sister S..................... 1Ch 7:32

SHUAH
Medan, Midian, Ishbak, and S. .... Ge 25:2
Medan, Midian, Ishbak, and S. 1Ch 1:32

SHUAL
Hazar S, Beersheba, Biziothiah,............. Jos 15:28
Hazar S, Balah, Ezem, ... Jos 19:3
Ophrah road in the land of S. 1Sa 13:17
in Beersheba, Moladah, Hazar S, ... 1Ch 4:28
Suah, Harnepher, S and Imrah, ... 1Ch 7:36
Hazar S, Beersheba and its..................... Ne 11:27

SHUBAEL
Gershom's first son was S. 1Ch 23:16
S was a descendant of Amram, ... 1Ch 24:20
Jehdeiah was a descendant of S. 1Ch 24:20
Mattaniah, Uzziel, S, Jerimoth, ... 1Ch 25:4
twelve men were chosen from S, ... 1Ch 25:20
S, the descendant of Gershom, ... 1Ch 26:24

SHUBAEL'S
These were S relatives from 1Ch 26:25

SHUHAH'S
Kelub, S brother, was the father............. 1Ch 4:11

SHUHAM
From S came the Shuhamite family .... Nu 26:42

SHUHAMITE
Shuham came the S family group. .... Nu 26:42
of men in the S family group of .... Nu 26:43

SHUHITE
Bildad the S, and Zophar .... Job 2:11
Then Bildad the S answered: .... Job 8:1
Then Bildad the S answered: .... Job 18:1
Then Bildad the S answered: .... Job 25:1
Bildad the S, and Zophar .... Job 42:9

SHULAM
back, come back, woman of S. .... Sng 6:13
the woman of S as you would at.............. Sng 6:13

SHUMATHITES
Puthites, S, and Mishraites. 1Ch 2:53

SHUNAM
Abishag from S and brought her 1Ki 1:3
the girl from S, was caring for 1Ki 1:15

SHUNAMMITE
me Abishag the S to be my wife." 1Ki 2:17
Allow Abishag the S to marry 1Ki 2:21
Gehazi, "Call the S woman." 2Ki 4:12
Look, there's the S woman! 2Ki 4:25
Gehazi and said, "Call the S!" 2Ki 4:36

SHUNEM
included Jezreel, Kesulloth, S, ... Jos 19:18
together and made camp at S. 1Sa 28:4
day Elisha went to S, where an 2Ki 4:8

SHUNI
Zephon, Haggi, S, Ezbon, Eri, ... Ge 46:16
S came the Shunite family group; .... Nu 26:15

SHUNITE
Shuni came the S family group; .... Nu 26:15

SHUPHAM
S came the Shuphamite family .... Nu 26:39

SHUPHAMITE
Shupham came the S family group; .... Nu 26:39

SHUPPIM
S and Hosah were chosen for the 1Ch 26:16

SHUPPITES
The S and Huppites were 1Ch 7:12
a wife from the Huppites and S............... 1Ch 7:15

SHUR
in the desert, by the road to S. .... Ge 16:7
awhile between Kadesh and S. .... Ge 20:1
lived from Havilah to S, ... Ge 25:18
Red Sea into the Desert of S. .... Ex 15:22
all the way from Havilah to S, ... 1Sa 15:7
that reached to S and Egypt. 1Sa 27:8

SHUT
you and will s the heavens so it .... Dt 11:17
your house and s the door behind 2Ki 4:4
Elisha and the door behind 2Ki 4:5
Then she s the door and left. 2Ki 4:21
entered the room and s the door, ... 2Ki 4:33
arrives, s the door and hold 2Ki 6:32
They s the doors of the porch of.............. 2Ch 29:7
have them s and bolt the doors. .... Ne 7:3
the doors be s at sunset before .... Ne 13:19
the daytime they s themselves up .... Job 24:16
Who s the doors to keep the sea............... Job 38:8
the mouths of liars will be s. .... Ps 63:11
have planned evil, s your mouth. .... Pr 30:32
people dumb. S their ears. Cover .... Is 6:10
they will be s up in prison. .... Is 24:22
your rooms and s your doors .... Is 26:20
be amazed and s their mouths. .... Is 52:15
He s me in so I could not get .... La 3:7
s yourself up in your house. .... Eze 3:24
Temple area, but the gate was s.............. Eze 44:1
to me, "This gate will stay s; .... Eze 44:2
through it. So it must stay s. .... Eze 44:2

S

will stay **s** on the six working .... Eze 46:1
will not be **s** until evening. .... Eze 46:2
the gate will be **s** after he has .... Eze 46:12
will not spring **s** if there is .... Am 3:5
will hate you, **s** you out, insult .... Lk 6:22
promises, and **s** the mouths of .... Heb 11:33
will never be **s** on any day, ... Rev 21:25

SHUTHELAH
From **S** came the Shuthelahite .... Nu 26:35
was the family group from **S**: .... Nu 26:36
Ephraim's son was **S**. 1Ch 7:20
Zabad's son was **S**. 1Ch 7:21

SHUTHELAH'S
S son was Bered. 1Ch 7:20

SHUTHELAHITE
came the **S** family group; .... Nu 26:35

SHUTS
not to shine and **s** off the light .... Job 9:7

SHUTTERS
house I looked out through the **s** .... Pr 7:6

SIA
Keros, **S**, Padon, ... Ne 7:47

SIAHA
Keros, **S**, Padon, ... Ezr 2:44

SIBBECAI
S the Hushathite killed Saph, ... 2Sa 21:18
S the Hushathite; Ilai the 1Ch 11:29
S the Hushathite killed Sippai, ... 1Ch 20:4
for the eighth month, was **S**. 1Ch 27:11

SIBBOLETH
Ephraim said, "**S**," the men of .... Jdg 12:6

SIBMAH
Nebo, Baal Meon, and **S**. .... Nu 32:38
Kiriathaim, **S**, Zereth Shahar on .... Jos 13:19
and the vines of **S** cannot grow .... Is 16:8
Jazer for the grapevines of **S**. .... Is 16:9
the grapevines of the town of **S**. .... Je 48:32

SIBRAIM
and **S** on the border between .... Eze 47:16

SICK
became so **s** he almost died. 2Ki 20:1
sad even though you are not **s**? .... Ne 2:2
and your whole heart is **s**. .... Is 1:5
tears, and I am **s** to my stomach. .... La 2:11
bring crippled and **s** animals, ... Mal 1:8
people brought all the **s** to him. .... Mt 4:24
mother-in-law was **s** in bed with .... Mt 8:14
them, and he healed all the **s**. .... Mt 8:16
who need a doctor, but the **s**. .... Mt 9:12
Heal the **s**, raise the dead to .... Mt 10:8
I was **s**, and you cared for me. .... Mt 25:36
oil on many **s** people and healed .... Mk 6:13
will touch the **s**, and the sick .... Mk 16:18
Lazarus, the man who was now **s**. .... Jn 11:2
in your group are **s** and weak, ... 1Co 11:30
Yes, he was **s**, and nearly died, ... Php 2:27
Anyone who is **s** should call the .... Jam 5:14
will make the **s** person well; .... Jam 5:15

SICKLE
neighbor's grain with your **s**. .... Dt 23:25
head and a sharp **s** in his hand. .... Rev 14:14
Take your **s** and harvest from the .... Rev 14:15
swung his **s** over the earth, ... Rev 14:16
and he also had a sharp **s**. .... Rev 14:17
to the angel with the sharp **s**, ... Rev 14:18
Take your sharp **s** and gather the .... Rev 14:18
swung his **s** over the earth. .... Rev 14:19

SICKLES
hoes, axes, and **s** sharpened. 1Sa 13:20

SICKNESS
I will take away **s** from you. .... Ex 23:25
a terrible **s** that came while .... Nu 11:33
them a terrible **s** and get rid of .... Nu 14:12
killed them with a terrible **s**. .... Nu 14:37
the **s** has already started." .... Nu 16:46
where the **s** had already started .... Nu 16:47
living, and the **s** stopped there. .... Nu 16:48
14,700 people died from that **s**, ... Nu 16:49
The terrible **s** had been stopped. .... Nu 16:50
Then the terrible **s** among the .... Nu 25:8
This **s** had killed twenty-four .... Nu 25:9
killed when the **s** came because .... Nu 25:18
After the great **s**, the LORD said .... Nu 26:1
a terrible **s** struck the LORD' .... Nu 31:16
every disease and **s** not written .... Dt 28:61
the same **s** has come on you 1Sa 6:4
LORD has given us this great **s**. 1Sa 6:9
Our **s** just happened by chance." 1Sa 6:9
or a great **s** will spread among 1Ki 8:37
if I will recover from my **s**." 2Ki 8:8
if he will recover from his **s**." 2Ki 8:9
or a great **s** will spread among 2Ch 6:28
war, punishment, **s**, or hunger, ... 2Ch 20:9
in the dark or **s** that strikes at .... Ps 91:6
to live can get you through **s**, ... Pr 18:14
who has lost much weight from **s**. .... Is 17:4
a **s** will kill all the plants. .... Is 17:11
I can see the **s** and hurts of .... Je 6:7
I told myself, "This is my **s**; .... Je 10:19
city, I see much **s**, because the .... Je 14:18
Where is your **s**, death? .... Hos 13:14
S goes before him, and disease .... Hab 3:5
every kind of disease and **s**. .... Mt 10:1
you are free from your **s**." .... Lk 13:12
freed from her **s** on a Sabbath .... Lk 13:16
pool was healed from any **s** he .... Jn 5:4
This **s** will not end in death. .... Jn 11:4
Though my **s** was a trouble for .... Gal 4:14
spread like a **s** inside the body. 2Ti 2:17

SICKNESSES
on you any of the **s** I brought .... Ex 15:26
and long and miserable **s**. .... Dt 28:59
I may send **s** to my people. 2Ch 7:13
all the people's diseases and **s**. .... Mt 4:23
all kinds of diseases and **s**. .... Mt 9:35
who had different kinds of **s**, ... Mk 1:34
and to be healed of their **s**, ... Lk 5:15
and to be healed of their **s**, ... Lk 6:18
healed many people of their **s**, ... Lk 7:21
been healed of **s** and evil .... Lk 8:2
and the ability to heal **s**. .... Lk 9:1
great earthquakes, **s**, and a lack .... Lk 21:11
stomach and your frequent **s**. 1Ti 5:23

SIDDIM
their armies in the Valley of **S** .... Ge 14:3
out to fight in the Valley of **S**. .... Ge 14:8
tar pits in the Valley of **S**. .... Ge 14:10

SIDE
Aaron on one **s** and Hur on the .... Ex 17:12
not take his **s** just because he .... Ex 23:3
out on the **s** of the altar. .... Le 1:15
on the other **s** of the Euphrates .... Jos 24:2
takes Baal's **s** will be killed. .... Jdg 6:31
the enemy across to the other **s**. .... Jdg 8:4
Philistine camp on the other **s**." 1Sa 14:1
she sat down at his right **s**. 1Ki 2:19
also built some **s** rooms against 1Ki 6:5
and said, "Who is on my **s**? 2Ki 9:32

his sword at his s as he worked. .... Ne 4:18
choose his s against mine; .... Job 13:8
your s one thousand people may .... Ps 91:7
me at my right s until I put .... Ps 110:1
They surrounded me on every s, ... Ps 118:11
the LORD had not been on our s? .... Ps 124:1
Terror on every s! Tell on him! .... Je 20:10
Then lie down on your left s, ... Eze 4:4
a second time, on your right s. .... Eze 4:6
standing on my s of the river, ... Da 12:5
other was standing on the far s. .... Da 12:5
to the other s of the lake to .... Mk 5:1
robe and sitting on the right s, ... Mk 16:5
on the right s of the incense .... Lk 1:11
he walked by on the other s. .... Lk 10:31
by on the other s of the road. .... Lk 10:32
Lord, "Sit by me at my right s, ... Lk 20:42
on the other s of the Jordan .... Jn 1:28
on the right s of God's throne. .... Heb 8:1
sat down at the right s of God. .... Heb 10:12
at the right s of God's throne. .... Heb 12:2
is at God's right s ruling over 1Pe 3:22
life was on each s of the river. .... Rev 22:2

SIDES

the hair on the s of your heads .... Le 19:27
your eyes and thorns in your s. .... Nu 33:55
from the far s of the earth. .... Je 6:22
bird attacked on all s by hawks. .... Je 12:9
and will hold you in on all s. .... Lk 19:43
writing on both s and was kept .... Rev 5:1

SIDON

Canaan was the father of S, ... Ge 10:15
They chased them to Greater S, ... Jos 11:8
gods of Aram, S, Moab, and Ammon .... Jdg 10:6
you merchants of S, be silent. .... Is 23:2
went to the area of Tyre and S. .... Mt 15:21
seacoast cities of Tyre and S. .... Lk 6:17

SIDONIAN

called Sirion by the S people, ... Dt 3:9
worshiped the S god Ashtoreth, ... 1Ki 11:33

SIDONIANS

The S are living in the hill .... Jos 13:6
S, Amalekites, and Maonites were .... Jdg 10:12
long way from the S and had no .... Jdg 18:7
Edomites, S, and Hittites. 1Ki 11:1
the hated goddess of the S. 2Ki 23:13
north and all the S are there. .... Eze 32:30

SIFTING

as if he is s them through .... Is 30:28

SIFTS

of you as a farmer s his wheat. .... Lk 22:31

SIGHED

he s and said to the man, ... Mk 7:34
Jesus s deeply and said, "Why do .... Mk 8:12

SIGHT

gives a person s or blindness? .... Ex 4:11
in plain s of Moses and all .... Nu 25:6
of Canaan in the s of Israel. .... Dt 28:65
I will send Judah out of my s, ... Jdg 4:23
and I am clean in God's s.' 2Ki 23:27
s has grown weak because of my .... Job 11:4
the north, I catch no s of him; .... Job 17:7
is gone. I am losing my s. .... Job 23:9
the LORD is precious in his s. .... Ps 38:10
The LORD gives s to the blind. .... Ps 116:15
Don't let them out of your s. .... Ps 146:8
that I must remove it from my s. .... Pr 3:21
did to Jerusalem in your s," .... Je 32:31
shocked at the s of each other, ... Je 51:24
.... Eze 4:17

in the s of the nations. .... Eze 22:16
he gave s to many blind people. .... Lk 7:21
to people is hateful in God's s. .... Lk 16:15
asked, "How did you get your s?" .... Jn 9:10
man, "How did you get your s?" .... Jn 9:15
of anyone giving s to a man born .... Jn 9:32
a cloud hid him from their s. .... Ac 1:9
even evil people right in his s. .... Rm 4:5
not make us better in God's s. 1Co 8:8
of people we are in God's s. 2Co 4:2
In the s of God, who gives life 1Ti 6:13

SIGHTS

war, and great s, by his great .... Dt 4:34
Your eyes will see strange s, ... Pr 23:33

SIGN

This is the s of the agreement .... Ge 9:12
clouds as the s of the agreement .... Ge 9:13
rainbow is a s of the agreement .... Ge 9:17
blood will be a s on the houses .... Ex 12:13
they will be a s between you and .... Ex 31:13
day will be a s between me .... Ex 31:17
they will be a s to the .... Nu 16:38
tie them to your hands as a s. .... Dt 6:8
tie them to your hands as a s; .... Dt 11:18
will show you a miracle or a s. .... Dt 13:1
The miracle or s might even .... Dt 13:2
They will be a s among you. .... Jos 4:6
as a s to destroy the city, ... Jos 8:26
I will give you a s. 1Sa 2:34
This will be the s for us." 1Sa 14:10
is the LORD's s that this will 1Ki 13:3
This was the s the LORD had told 1Ki 13:5
men had wanted a s from Ahab. 1Ki 20:33
I will give you this s: 2Ki 19:29
What will be the s that the LORD 2Ki 20:8
This is the s from the LORD to 2Ki 20:9
spoke to him and gave him a s. 2Ch 32:24
about a strange s that had 2Ch 32:31
Here I s my name to show I have .... Job 31:35
Show me a s of your goodness. .... Ps 86:17
there is no s of where it was .... Ps 103:16
Ask for a s from the LORD your .... Is 7:11
may be a s from as deep as the .... Is 7:11
ask for a s or test the LORD. .... Is 7:12
Lord himself will give you a s: .... Is 7:14
a banner as a s for all nations, ... Is 11:12
This will be the a s a witness .... Is 19:20
three years as a s against Egypt .... Is 20:3
this as a s for the people, ... Is 30:8
I will give you this s: .... Is 37:30
This is the s from the LORD to .... Is 38:7
Isaiah, "What will be the s? .... Is 38:22
will be the s of my agreement. .... Is 42:6
Another will s his name 'I am .... Is 44:5
will be the s of my agreement. .... Is 49:8
banner as a s for the people. .... Is 62:10
They will s and seal their .... Je 32:44
I will give you a s that I will .... Je 44:29
attack. This is a s to Israel. .... Eze 4:3
have made you a s to the people .... Eze 12:6
Say, 'I am a s to you.' .... Eze 12:11
make them a s and an example, ... Eze 14:8
Sabbaths to be a s between us so .... Eze 20:12
they will be a s between me and .... Eze 20:20
Mark one s to show the road he .... Eze 21:20
the other s to show the road .... Eze 21:20
So you will be a s for them, ... Eze 24:27
The s will stay there until the .... Eze 39:15
the law and s your name to it .... Da 6:8
Didn't you s a law that says no .... Da 6:12
see you work a miracle as a s." .... Mt 12:38
want to see a miracle for a s. .... Mt 12:39

S

But no **s** will be given to them, ... Mt 12:39
the **s** of the prophet Jonah. .... Mt 12:39
people ask for a miracle as a **s**, ... Mt 16:4
they will not be given any **s**, ... Mt 16:4
sign, except the **s** of Jonah." .... Mt 16:4
will be the **s** that it is time .... Mt 24:3
the **s** of the Son of Man will .... Mt 24:30
They put a **s** above Jesus' head .... Mt 27:37
people ask for a miracle as a **s**? .... Mk 8:12
no **s** will be given to you." .... Mk 8:12
what will be the **s** that they are .... Mk 13:4
There was a **s** with this charge .... Mk 15:26
will be a **s** from God that many .... Lk 2:34
to give them a **s** from heaven.................. Lk 11:16
want to see a miracle for a **s**, ... Lk 11:29
but no **s** will be given them, ... Lk 11:29
them, except the **s** of Jonah. .... Lk 11:29
Jonah was a **s** for those people .... Lk 11:30
Man will be a **s** for the people .... Lk 11:30
What will be the **s** that they are .... Lk 21:7
Pilate wrote a **s** and put it on .... Jn 19:19
The **s** was written in Hebrew, ... Jn 19:20
Many of the people read the **s**, ... Jn 19:20
the **s** of which was circumcision. .... Ac 7:8
Peter made a **s** with his hand to .... Ac 12:17
governor made a **s** for Paul to.................. Ac 24:10
languages is a **s** for those 1Co 14:22
we mark with a **s** the foreheads .... Rev 7:3
people were marked with the **s**. .... Rev 7:4
thousand were marked with the **s**, ... Rev 7:5
thousand were marked with the **s**. .... Rev 7:8
not have the **s** of God on their .... Rev 9:4

SIGNAL

had set up a **s** with the men in .... Jdg 20:38
your hand to **s** them to enter .... Is 13:2
lift my hand to **s** the nations; .... Is 49:22
Raise the **s** flag toward .... Je 4:6
had planned to give them a **s**,.................. Mt 26:48
Judas had planned a **s** for them,.............. Mk 14:44

SIGNED

some letters, **s** Ahab's name to 1Ki 21:8
I **s** the record and sealed it and .... Je 32:10
other witnesses who **s** the record .... Je 32:12
So King Darius **s** the law. .... Da 6:9
O king, or to the law you **s**...................... Da 6:13

SIGNET

bracelets, **s** rings, earrings,...................... Nu 31:50
king took his **s** ring off and .... Est 3:10
and sealed with his **s** ring. .... Est 3:12
took off his **s** ring that he had .... Est 8:2
order with the king's **s** ring, ... Est 8:8
and sealed with his **s** ring can .... Est 8:8
letters with the king's **s** ring. .... Est 8:10
their **s** rings, nose rings, ... Is 3:21
if you were a **s** ring on my right .... Je 22:24
the king used his **s** ring and the .... Da 6:17
you important like my **s** ring, ... Hag 2:23

SIGNS

These lights will be used for **s**, ... Ge 1:14
learn things by a **s** and dreams?" .... Ge 44:15
the future by **s** or black magic. .... Le 19:26
it with tests, **s**, miracles, war, ... Dt 4:34
and terrible **s** and miracles, ... Dt 6:22
the troubles, **s**, and miracles he .... Dt 7:19
his **s** and the things he did in .... Dt 11:3
try to explain the meaning of **s**. .... Dt 18:10
great terrors, **s**, and miracles. .... Dt 26:8
curses will be **s** and miracles to .... Dt 28:46
great troubles, **s**, and miracles. .... Dt 29:3
sent him to do **s** and miracles .... Dt 34:11
these **s** happen, do whatever 1Sa 10:7

All these **s** came true that day. 1Sa 10:9
by explaining **s** and dreams, ... 2Ki 21:6
by explaining **s** and dreams. 2Ch 33:6
You did **s** and miracles against .... Ne 9:10
do not see any **s**. There are no .... Ps 74:9
forgot the **s** he did in Egypt .... Ps 78:43
They did many **s** among the .... Ps 105:27
He did many **s** and miracles in .... Ps 135:9
and making **s** with their fingers.............. Pr 6:13
We are **s** and proofs for the...................... Is 8:18
I show that the **s** of the lying .... Is 44:25
afraid of special **s** in the sky, ... Je 10:2
of Israel, fix the road **s**. .... Je 31:21
Put up **s** to show you the way .... Je 31:21
of Egypt using **s** and miracles.................. Je 32:21
make **s** where the road divides .... Eze 21:19
from this place all **s** of Baal, ... Zph 1:4
You see these **s** in the sky and .... Mt 16:3
He could only make **s** to them and ....Lk 1:22
Then they made **s** to his father .... Lk 1:62
events and great **s** will come .... Lk 21:11
There will be **s** in the sun, ... Lk 21:25
people must see **s** and miracles .... Jn 4:48
and **s** he did through Jesus. .... Ac 2:22
were doing many miracles and **s**, ... Ac 2:43
apostles did many **s** and miracles .... Ac 5:12
miracles and **s** among the people. .... Ac 6:8
worked miracles and **s** in Egypt, ... Ac 7:36
power to work miracles and **s**. .... Ac 14:3
the miracles and **s** that God did .... Ac 15:12
I am an apostle—**s**, wonders, ... 2Co 12:12
false miracles, **s**, and wonders. 2Th 2:9
wonders, great **s**, many kinds .... Heb 2:4

SIHON

Israelites sent messengers to **S**, ... Nu 21:21
But King **S** would not let the .... Nu 21:23
Heshbon was the city where **S**, ... Nu 21:26
daughters were captured by **S**, ... Nu 21:29
Do to him what you did to **S**, ... Nu 21:34
land had been the kingdom of **S**, ... Nu 32:33
the LORD had defeated **S** and Og. .... Dt 1:4
S was king of the Amorite people .... Dt 1:4
power to defeat **S** the Amorite, ... Dt 2:24
Kedemoth to **S** king of Heshbon. .... Dt 2:26
But **S** king of Heshbon would not .... Dt 2:30
The LORD wanted you to defeat **S**, ... Dt 2:30
begun to give **S** and his country .... Dt 2:31
Then **S** and all his army came out .... Dt 2:32
the LORD our God gave **S** to us. .... Dt 2:33
what you did to **S** king of the .... Dt 3:2
the cities of **S** king of Heshbon. .... Dt 3:6
Jordan River, in the land of **S**. .... Dt 4:46
S king of the Amorites ruled in .... Dt 4:46
S king of Heshbon and Og king of .... Dt 29:7
nations what he did to **S** and Og, ... Dt 31:4
how you destroyed **S** and Og,.................. Jos 2:10
S king of Heshbon and Og king of .... Jos 9:10
S king of the Amorites lived in .... Jos 12:2
S ruled over half the land of .... Jos 12:2
the border of **S** king of Heshbon .... Jos 12:5
the towns ruled by **S** king of the.............. Jos 13:10
all the area that **S** king of the .... Jos 13:21
together with **S** and lived in .... Jos 13:21
the other land **S** king of Heshbon .... Jos 13:27
sent messengers to **S** king of the .... Jdg 11:19
But **S** did not trust the ....Jdg 11:20
handed **S** and his army over to .... Jdg 11:21
been the country of **S** king of 1Ki 4:19
the country of **S** king of Heshbon .... Ne 9:22
S king of the Amorites, Og king.............. Ps 135:11
He defeated **S** king of the .... Ps 136:19
the hometown of **S** king of Moab. .... Je 48:45

SIHON'S

and rebuild it; rebuild **S** city. .... Nu 21:27
flames came from **S** city. .... Nu 21:28

SILAS

chose Judas Barsabbas and **S**, ... Ac 15:22
So we are sending Judas and **S**, ... Ac 15:27
Judas and **S**, who were also .... Ac 15:32
time Judas and **S** were sent off .... Ac 15:33
but **S** decided to remain there. .... Ac 15:34
but Paul chose **S** and left. .... Ac 15:40
Paul and **S** and dragged them. .... Ac 16:19
brought Paul and **S** to the Roman .... Ac 16:20
of Paul and **S** and had them .... Ac 16:22
Then Paul and **S** were thrown into .... Ac 16:23
midnight Paul and **S** were praying .... Ac 16:25
fell down before Paul and **S**. .... Ac 16:29
Paul and **S** told the message of .... Ac 16:32
took Paul and **S** and washed their .... Ac 16:33
took Paul and **S** home and gave .... Ac 16:34
that Paul and **S** were Roman .... Ac 16:38
told Paul and **S** they were sorry .... Ac 16:39
Paul and **S** traveled through .... Ac 17:1
convinced and joined Paul and **S**, ... Ac 17:4
for Paul and **S**, wanting to bring. .... Ac 17:5
sent Paul and **S** to Berea where. .... Ac 17:10
what Paul and **S** said and studied .... Ac 17:11
S and Timothy stayed in Berea. .... Ac 17:14
Paul back to **S** and Timothy for .... Ac 17:15
was waiting for **S** and Timothy .... Ac 17:16
S and Timothy came from .... Ac 18:5
S and Timothy and I preached 2Co 1:19
From Paul, **S**, and Timothy. 1Th 1:1
From Paul, **S**, and Timothy. 2Th 1:1
short letter with the help of **S**, ... 1Pe 5:12

SILENCE

And so you **s** your enemies and .... Ps 8:2
So **s** their lying lips. .... Ps 31:18
Let them be shamed into **s**. .... Ps 40:15
s the songs of those who have .... Is 25:5
sit on the ground in **s**. .... La 2:10
bodies thrown everywhere! **S**!" .... Am 8:3
When there was **s**, he spoke to .... Ac 21:40
there was **s** in heaven for about .... Rev 8:1

SILENCED

people will be **s** in darkness. 1Sa 2:9
those who are unfair are **s**. .... Job 5:16
when the land is **s** by the hot, ... Job 37:17
of Madmen, you will also be **s**. .... Je 48:2

SILENT

Before I finished my **s** prayer, ... Ge 24:45
we have good news, but we are **s**. 2Ki 7:9
The people were **s**. They didn't 2Ki 18:36
people be **s** and takes away .... Job 12:20
I call at night; I am not **s**. .... Ps 22:2
If you are **s**, I will be like .... Ps 28:1
I will sing to you and not be **s**. .... Ps 30:12
and lie **s** in the grave. .... Ps 31:17
you know my lips are not **s**. .... Ps 40:9
God comes, and he will not be **s**. .... Ps 50:3
and the earth was afraid and **s**. .... Ps 76:8
God, do not be **s** or still. .... Ps 83:1
God, I praise you. Do not be **s**. .... Ps 109:1
those in the grave are **s**. .... Ps 115:17
is a time to be **s** and a time to. .... Ec 3:7
Be **s**, you who live on the island .... Is 23:2
you merchants of Sidon, be **s**. .... Is 23:2
The people were **s**. They didn't .... Is 36:21
They must not be **s** day or night. .... Is 62:6
Will you be **s** and punish us .... Is 64:12
city of Ashkelon will be made **s**. .... Je 47:5
sounds of the city become **s**. .... Je 51:55

of your mouth so you will be **s**. .... Eze 3:26
You will speak and be **s** no more. .... Eze 24:27
the one who says to a **s** stone, ' .... Hab 2:19
should be **s** in his presence. .... Hab 2:20
s before the Lord GOD, because .... Zph 1:7
Be **s**, everyone, in the presence .... Zch 2:13
at his answer, they became **s**. .... Lk 20:26

SILENTLY

Groan **s**; do not cry loudly for. .... Eze 24:17

SILK

Your lips are like red **s** thread, ... Sng 4:3
linen and covered you with **s**. .... Eze 16:10
of fine linen, **s**, and beautiful .... Eze 16:13
purple cloth, **s**, red cloth; .... Rev 18:12

SILLA

Millo on the road down to **S**. 2Ki 12:20

SILLY

get control of **s** women who are 2Ti 3:6

SILOAM

of the Pool of **S** next to the. .... Ne 3:15
the tower of **S** fell on them? .... Lk 13:4
"Go and wash in the Pool of **S**." .... Jn 9:7
of Siloam." (**S** means Sent.) So .... Jn 9:7
he told me to go to **S** and wash. .... Jn 9:11

SILVER

rich in cattle, **s**, and gold. .... Ge 13:2
pounds of **s** to make up for any .... Ge 20:16
land is worth ten pounds of **s**, ... Ge 23:15
pounds of **s**, and they counted .... Ge 23:16
herds of cattle, **s** and gold, ... Ge 24:35
Rebekah gold and **s** jewelry and. .... Ge 24:53
for one hundred pieces of **s**. .... Ge 33:19
for eight ounces of **s**. .... Ge 37:28
Put my **s** cup in the sack of the .... Ge 44:2
would not steal **s** or gold from .... Ge 44:8
you find that **s** cup in the sack .... Ge 44:9
seven and one-half pounds of **s**. .... Ge 45:22
house for gifts—**s**, gold, and .... Ex 3:22
for things made of **s** and gold." .... Ex 11:2
things made of **s** and gold and .... Ex 12:35
not use gold or **s** to make idols .... Ex 20:23
twelve ounces of **s**, and the bull .... Ex 21:32
from them: gold, **s**, bronze; .... Ex 25:3
have two **s** bases to go under .... Ex 26:19
You must make forty **s** bases for .... Ex 26:19
and forty **s** bases for them— .... Ex 26:21
there will be sixteen **s** bases— .... Ex 26:25
and set them in four **s** bases. .... Ex 26:32
curtains with **s** hooks and bands .... Ex 27:10
curtains on **s** hooks and bands .... Ex 27:11
must have **s** bands and hooks. .... Ex 27:17
pay one-fifth of an ounce of **s**. .... Ex 30:13
made from gold, **s**, and bronze, ... Ex 31:4
to the LORD: gold, **s**, bronze, ... Ex 35:5
who could give **s** or bronze. .... Ex 35:24
be made of gold, **s**, and bronze, ... Ex 35:32
made forty **s** bases that went .... Ex 36:24
forty **s** bases—two to go under .... Ex 36:26
frames and sixteen **s** bases— .... Ex 36:30
as well as four **s** bases in which .... Ex 36:36
hung on **s** hooks and bands .... Ex 38:10
and it hung on **s** hooks and bands .... Ex 38:11
was held up by **s** hooks and bands. .... Ex 38:12
on the posts were made of **s**, ... Ex 38:17
posts were covered with **s** also. .... Ex 38:17
in the courtyard had **s** bands. .... Ex 38:17
on the posts were made of **s**, ... Ex 38:19
the posts were covered with **s**. .... Ex 38:19
The **s** was given by the members .... Ex 38:25
pay one-fifth of an ounce of **s**, ... Ex 38:26
this **s**, 7,500 pounds were used .... Ex 38:27

S

-five hundred pounds of s, ... 2Ch 27:5
He made treasuries for his s, ... 2Ch 32:27
hundred pounds of s and about 2Ch 36:3
Give them s and gold, supplies .... Ezr 1:4
them things made of s and gold,.............. Ezr 1:6
one thousand s dishes, ... Ezr 1:9
hundred ten matching s bowls, ... Ezr 1:10
hundred pieces of gold and s.................... Ezr 1:11
pounds of s, and 100 pieces .... Ezr 2:69
the gold and s bowls and pans .... Ezr 5:14
these gold and s bowls and pans, ... Ezr 5:15
The gold and s utensils from the .... Ezr 6:5
with you the s and gold that .... Ezr 7:15
Also take the s and gold you .... Ezr 7:16
may spend the s and gold left................ Ezr 7:18
-five hundred pounds of s, ... Ezr 7:22
the offering of s and gold .... Ezr 8:25
fifty thousand pounds of s, ... Ezr 8:26
hundred pounds of s objects, ... Ezr 8:26
The s and gold are gifts to the .... Ezr 8:28
and Levites accepted the s,..................... Ezr 8:30
fourth day we weighed out the s, ... Ezr 8:33
one pound of s from each person .... Ne 5:15
pounds of s to the treasury .... Ne 7:71
2,250 pounds of s, and 67 pieces........... Ne 7:72
of an ounce of s each year. .... Ne 10:32
were tied to s rings on marble .... Est 1:6
were gold and s couches on a .... Est 1:6
pounds of s to those who do .... Est 3:9
their houses with gold and s. .... Job 3:15
gold and the best s for you. .... Job 22:25
may heap up s like piles of dirt .... Job 27:16
innocent will divide up their s. .... Job 27:17
people dig s and places where .... Job 28:1
its cost cannot be weighed in s. .... Job 28:15
a piece of s and a gold ring. .... Job 42:11
are pure, like s purified by .... Ps 12:6
s purified seven times over..................... Ps 12:6
you have purified us like s. .... Ps 66:10
they will bring you their s. .... Ps 68:30
carried with them s and gold.................. Ps 105:37
idols are made of s and gold, ... Ps 115:4
of pieces of gold and s. .... Ps 119:72
nations are made of s and gold, ... Ps 135:15
for it like s, and hunt for it .... Pr 2:4
Wisdom is worth more than s; .... Pr 3:14
my teachings instead of s, ... Pr 8:10
gold, better than the purest s. .... Pr 8:19
a good person are like pure s,................ Pr 10:20
understanding rather than s! .... Pr 16:16
A hot furnace tests s and gold, ... Pr 17:3
of is better than s or gold. .... Pr 22:1
Remove the scum from the s, ... Pr 25:4
so the s can be used by the .... Pr 25:4
as gold apples in a s bowl. .... Pr 25:11
A hot furnace tests s and gold, ... Pr 27:21
I also gathered s and gold for .... Ec 2:8
snap like a s chain or break .... Ec 12:6
you gold earrings with s hooks. .... Sng 1:11
its posts of s and its braces.................... Sng 3:10
we will put s towers on her. .... Sng 8:9
pounds of s for the fruit......................... Sng 8:11
pounds of s are for you, ... Sng 8:12
scum left when s is purified; .... Is 1:22
has been filled with s and gold; .... Is 2:7
away their gold and s idols, ... Is 2:20
about twenty-five pounds of s. .... Is 7:23
not care about s or delight in .... Is 13:17
statues covered with s and gold,............ Is 30:22
worshiping idols of gold and s, ... Is 31:7
the s, gold, spices, expensive .... Is 39:2
gold and makes s chains for it. .... Is 40:19
and weigh their s on the scales. .... Is 46:6

not by fire, as s is made pure................... Is 48:10
lands, and with them s and gold. .... Is 60:9
of bronze, s in place of iron .... Is 60:17
will be called rejected s, ... Je 6:30
their idols with s and gold. .... Je 10:4
Hammered s is brought from .... Je 10:9
out seven ounces of s for him. .... Je 32:9
weighed out the s on the scales. .... Je 32:10
'Buy the field with s and call .... Je 32:25
that was made of pure gold or s. .... Je 52:19
throw their s into the streets .... Eze 7:19
Their s and gold will not save................ Eze 7:19
So you wore gold and s. .... Eze 16:13
my gold and s I had given you .... Eze 16:17
the furnace when s is purified. .... Eze 22:18
put s, copper, iron, lead, ... Eze 22:20
As s is melted in a furnace,.................... Eze 22:22
They traded your goods for s,................ Eze 27:12
gained gold and s and have saved .... Eze 28:4
to carry away s and gold and to .... Eze 38:13
chest and arms were made of s. .... Da 2:32
clay, bronze, s, and gold broke .... Da 2:35
bronze, clay, s, and gold to .... Da 2:45
the gold and s cups that his .... Da 5:2
made from gold, s, bronze, iron,............ Da 5:4
You praised the gods of s, ... Da 5:23
things made of s and gold back .... Da 11:8
god of power with gold and s, ... Da 11:38
of gold and s and all the riches .... Da 11:43
I gave her much s and gold, ... Hos 2:8
six ounces of s and ten bushels .... Hos 3:2
They made their s and gold into .... Hos 8:4
grow over their s treasures, ... Hos 9:6
They make idols of their s, ... Hos 13:2
You took my s and gold, and you .... Joe 3:5
For s, they sell people who have .... Am 2:6
We will buy poor people for s, ... Am 8:6
Take the s! Take the gold! There .... Nah 2:9
statue covered with gold and s; .... Hab 2:19
all the s traders will be gone. .... Zph 1:11
neither their s nor gold will .... Zph 1:18
'The s is mine, and the gold is .... Hag 2:8
Take s and gold from Heldai, ... Zch 6:10
the s and gold into a crown, ... Zch 6:11
She has piled up s like dust and .... Zch 9:3
they paid me thirty pieces of s. .... Zch 11:12
thirty pieces of s and threw .... Zch 11:13
them like s, testing them like .... Zch 13:9
much gold, s, and clothes. .... Zch 14:14
who heats and purifies s, ... Mal 3:3
make them pure like gold and s............. Mal 3:3
with you—gold or s or copper. .... Mt 10:9
they gave him thirty s coins. .... Mt 26:15
took the thirty s coins back to .... Mt 27:3
picked up the s coins in the .... Mt 27:6
They took thirty s coins. .... Mt 27:9
used those thirty s coins to buy .... Mt 27:10
Suppose a woman has ten s coins, ... Lk 15:8
I don't have any s or gold, ... Ac 3:6
or make from gold, s, or rock. .... Ac 17:29
about fifty thousand s coins. .... Ac 19:19
who worked with s, made little .... Ac 19:24
made little s models that looked............. Ac 19:24
using gold, s, jewels, wood,................... 1Co 3:12
only things made of gold and s, ... 2Ti 2:20
Your gold and s have rusted, ... Jam 5:3
that ruins like gold or s, ... 1Pe 1:18
made of gold, s, bronze, stone, ... Rev 9:20
of gold, s, jewels, pearls .... Rev 18:12

SILVERSMITH

five pounds and gave it to a s. .... Jdg 17:4
the silver can be used by the s. .... Pr 25:4

S

SIMEON

She named him **S** and said, ... Ge 29:33
of Jacob's sons, **S** and Levi .... Ge 34:25
Then Jacob said to **S** and Levi, ... Ge 34:30
first son, then **S**, Levi, Judah, ... Ge 35:23
He took **S** and tied him up while .... Ge 42:24
Joseph is gone, **S** is gone, and .... Ge 42:36
he will allow **S** and Benjamin to.............. Ge 43:14
servant brought **S** out to them. .... Ge 43:23
as Reuben and **S** are my sons. .... Ge 48:5
S and Levi are brothers who used .... Ge 49:5
Reuben, **S**, Levi, Judah, ... Ex 1:2
are the family groups of **S**. .... Ex 6:15
from the tribe of **S**—Shelumiel .... Nu 1:6
The tribe of **S** was counted; .... Nu 1:22
The tribe of **S** totaled 59,300 .... Nu 1:23
them the tribe of **S** will camp.............. Nu 2:12
the people of **S** is Shelumiel son.............. Nu 2:12
the division of the tribe of **S**. .... Nu 10:19
from the tribe of **S**, Shaphat son.............. Nu 13:5
of a family in the tribe of **S**. .... Nu 25:14
family groups in the tribe of **S**: .... Nu 26:12
were the family groups of **S**, ... Nu 26:14
from the tribe of **S**, Shemuel son .... Nu 34:20
S, Levi, Judah, Issachar, Joseph .... Dt 27:12
was given to the tribe of **S**.................... Jos 19:1
family groups in the tribe of **S**. .... Jos 19:8
areas of Judah, **S**, and Benjamin. .... Jos 21:4
from the lands of Judah and **S**. .... Jos 21:9
of Judah said to the men of **S**, ... Jdg 1:3
So the men of **S** went with them. .... Jdg 1:3
men of Judah and the men of **S**,.............. Jdg 1:17
were Reuben, **S**, Levi, Judah, ... 1Ch 2:1
of Judah, **S**, and Benjamin,..................... 1Ch 6:65
seventy-one hundred men from **S**. 1Ch 12:25
Maacah was over the tribe of **S**. 1Ch 27:16
and **S** who were living in Judah................ 2Ch 15:9
and **S** all the way to Naphtali, ... 2Ch 34:6
Benjamin's land, **S** will have one .... Eze 48:24
a man named **S** who was a good .... Lk 2:25
S had been told by the Holy .... Lk 2:26
The Spirit led **S** to the Temple. .... Lk 2:27
S took the baby in his arms and.............. Lk 2:28
amazed at what **S** had said about .... Lk 2:33
Then **S** blessed them and said to .... Lk 2:34
Levi was the son of **S**............................ Lk 3:30
S was the son of Judah. .... Lk 3:30
Barnabas, **S** (also called Niger), ... Ac 13:1
the tribe of **S** twelve thousand, ... Rev 7:7

SIMEON'S

S sons were Jemuel, Jamin, Ohad, ... Ge 46:10
S son by a Canaanite woman .... Ge 46:10
S sons were Jemuel, Jamin, Ohad, ... Ex 6:15
S sons were Nemuel, Jamin, Jarib,........... 1Ch 4:24
South of **S** land, Issachar will................. Eze 48:25
S Gate, Issachar's Gate, and .... Eze 48:33

SIMEONITES

The land of the **S** was taken from .... Jos 19:9
the **S** received part of their .... Jos 19:9
hundred of the **S** and attacked 1Ch 4:42
until now these **S** have lived in 1Ch 4:43

SIMILAR

And many **s** words were added to .... Je 36:32
A **s** disease will strike the .... Zch 14:15

SIMON

two brothers, **S** (called Peter) .... Mt 4:18
So **S** and Andrew immediately left........... Mt 4:20
S (also called Peter) and his .... Mt 10:2
S the Zealot and Judas Iscariot, ... Mt 10:4
are James, Joseph, **S**, and Judas. .... Mt 13:55
S Peter answered, "You are the .... Mt 16:16

You are blessed, **S** son of Jonah, ... Mt 16:17
in Bethany at the house of **S**, ... Mt 26:6
from Cyrene, named **S**, to carry .... Mt 27:32
he saw **S** and his brother Andrew .... Mk 1:16
So **S** and Andrew immediately left........... Mk 1:18
to the home of **S** and Andrew. .... Mk 1:29
S and his friends went to look .... Mk 1:36
S (Jesus named him Peter),..................... Mk 3:16
Thaddaeus, **S** the Zealot, ... Mk 3:18
of James, Joseph, Judas, and **S**. .... Mk 6:3
in Bethany at the house of **S**, ... Mk 14:3
said to Peter, "**S**, are you...................... Mk 14:37
A man named **S** from Cyrene, ... Mk 15:21
soldiers forced **S** to carry the .... Mk 15:21
and went to the home of **S**.................... Lk 4:38
the one that belonged to **S**,.................... Lk 5:3
he said to **S**, "Take the boat .... Lk 5:4
S answered, "Master, we worked .... Lk 5:5
When **S** Peter saw what had .... Lk 5:8
Jesus said to **S**, "Don't be .... Lk 5:10
S (Jesus named him Peter), his .... Lk 6:14
son of Alphaeus, **S** (called the .... Lk 6:15
the Pharisee, "**S**, I have .... Lk 7:40
S said, "Teacher, tell me." .... Lk 7:40
S, the Pharisee, answered, "I .... Lk 7:43
Jesus said to **S**, "You are right. .... Lk 7:43
toward the woman and said to **S**, ... Lk 7:44
S, Simon, Satan has asked to .... Lk 22:31
Simon, **S**, Satan has asked to .... Lk 22:31
led Jesus away, **S**, a man from .... Lk 23:26
He showed himself to **S**." .... Lk 24:34
was Andrew, **S** Peter's brother. .... Jn 1:40
his brother **S** and say to him, ... Jn 1:41
Then Andrew took **S** to Jesus. .... Jn 1:42
said, "You are **S** son of John. .... Jn 1:42
Andrew, **S** Peter's brother, ... Jn 6:8
S Peter answered him, "Lord, who........... Jn 6:68
Judas, the son of **S** Iscariot. .... Jn 6:71
the son of **S**, to turn against .... Jn 13:2
Jesus came to **S** Peter, who said .... Jn 13:6
S Peter answered, "Lord, then .... Jn 13:9
S Peter motioned to him to ask .... Jn 13:24
to Judas Iscariot, the son of **S**. .... Jn 13:26
S Peter asked Jesus, "Lord, ... Jn 13:36
S Peter, who had a sword, pulled .... Jn 18:10
S Peter and another one of Jesus' .... Jn 18:15
As **S** Peter was standing and .... Jn 18:25
she ran to **S** Peter and the .... Jn 20:2
S Peter arrived and went into .... Jn 20:6
S Peter, Thomas (called Didymus),........... Jn 21:2
S Peter said, "I am going out to .... Jn 21:3
S Peter went into the boat and .... Jn 21:11
Jesus said to **S** Peter, "Simon .... Jn 21:15
Simon Peter, "**S** son of John, do .... Jn 21:15
Jesus said, "**S** son of John, do .... Jn 21:16
time he said, "**S** son of John, do .... Jn 21:17
son of Alphaeus, **S** (known as the .... Ac 1:13
was a man named **S** in that city............... Ac 8:9
S had practiced magic and amazed .... Ac 8:9
attention to **S**, saying, "This .... Ac 8:10
S had amazed them with his magic .... Ac 8:11
S himself believed, and after he .... Ac 8:13
things Philip did, **S** was amazed. .... Ac 8:13
S saw that the Spirit was given .... Ac 8:18
S answered, "Both of you pray .... Ac 8:24
a man named **S** who was a tanner .... Ac 9:43
back a man named **S** who is also .... Ac 10:5
man, also named **S**, who is a .... Ac 10:6
"Is **S** Peter staying here?" .... Ac 10:18
Joppa and ask **S** Peter to come. .... Ac 10:32
man, also named **S**, who is a .... Ac 10:32
and invite **S** Peter to come..................... Ac 11:13

S has told us how God showed his .... Ac 15:14
From **S** Peter, a servant and 2Pe 1:1

SIMON'S

S mother-in-law was sick in bed.............. Mk 1:30
S mother-in-law was sick with a............. Lk 4:38
the sons of Zebedee, **S** partners................ Lk 5:10
sent had found **S** house and were .... Ac 10:17

SIMPLE

can decide the **s** cases........................... Ex 18:22
decided the **s** cases themselves .... Ex 18:26
want the pure and **s** teaching.................. 1Pe 2:2

SIMPLY

but the wicked **s** pour out evil. .... Pr 15:28
Do you believe **s** because I told .... Jn 1:50
God, not **s** a human teaching. 1Th 4:8

SIN

not do them well, **s** is ready to .... Ge 4:7
S wants you, but you must rule .... Ge 4:7
allow you to **s** against me and .... Ge 20:6
have been guilty of a great **s**." .... Ge 26:10
thing? It is a **s** against God." .... Ge 39:9
Now forgive my **s** this time. .... Ex 10:17
and came to the Desert of **S**, ... Ex 16:1
the Desert of **S** and traveled .... Ex 17:1
respect him so you will not **s**." .... Ex 20:20
they will make you **s** against me. .... Ex 23:33
is an offering to take away **s**. .... Ex 29:14
them to do such a terrible **s**?"................. Ex 32:21
You have done a terrible **s**. .... Ex 32:30
please forgive them of this **s**. .... Ex 32:32
of the people who **s** against me. .... Ex 32:33
I will punish them for their **s**." .... Ex 32:34
for evil, for **s**, and for turning................ Ex 34:7
but forgive our evil and our **s**. .... Ex 34:9
the person's **s** so he will belong .... Le 1:4
as a **s** offering for the sin he .... Le 4:3
offering for the **s** he has done. .... Le 4:3
from the bull of the **s** offering— .... Le 4:8
about the **s** they have done, ... Le 4:14
a young bull as a **s** offering and .... Le 4:14
first bull of the **s** offering. .... Le 4:20
This is the **s** offering for the .... Le 4:21
When he learns about his **s**, ... Le 4:23
the LORD ; it is a **s** offering. .... Le 4:24
blood of the **s** offering on his .... Le 4:25
the ruler's **s** so he belongs to .... Le 4:26
the person learns about his **s**,................. Le 4:28
it as an offering for his **s**. .... Le 4:28
person's **s** so he will belong .... Le 4:31
a lamb as his offering for **s**, ... Le 4:32
and kill it as a **s** offering in................... Le 4:33
blood from the **s** offering on his .... Le 4:34
the court, he is guilty of **s**. .... Le 5:1
be unclean and guilty of **s**. .... Le 5:2
to the LORD as a penalty for **s**; .... Le 5:6
person's **s** so he will belong .... Le 5:6
LORD as the penalty for his **s**. .... Le 5:7
bird must be for a **s** offering, ... Le 5:7
the one for the **s** offering. .... Le 5:8
the blood from the **s** offering on .... Le 5:9
the altar; it is a **s** offering. .... Le 5:9
the person's **s** so he will belong .... Le 5:10
fine flour as an offering for **s**. .... Le 5:11
because it is a **s** offering. .... Le 5:11
to the LORD; it is a **s** offering. .... Le 5:12
left of the **s** offering belongs .... Le 5:13
pay for the **s** he did against .... Le 5:16
the person's **s** so he will belong .... Le 5:16
He is responsible for his **s**. .... Le 5:17
will remove the **s** so the person .... Le 5:18
A person might **s** against the .... Le 6:2

or he might do some other **s**. .... Le 6:3
these things, he is guilty of **s**. .... Le 6:4
person's **s** so he will belong .... Le 6:7
like the **s** offering and the .... Le 6:17
teachings about the **s** offering: .... Le 6:25
The **s** offering must be killed in .... Le 6:25
who offers the **s** offering must .... Le 6:26
the meat of the **s** offering must .... Le 6:27
the blood of the **s** offering is .... Le 6:30
used to remove **s** in the Holy .... Le 6:30
that **s** offering must be burned .... Le 6:30
is like the **s** offering in that.................... Le 7:7
the meat will be guilty of **s**..................... Le 7:18
grain offering, the **s** offering, ... Le 7:37
the bull of the **s** offering and .... Le 8:2
the bull for the **s** offering, ... Le 8:14
The calf for the **s** offering, ... Le 9:2
a male goat for a **s** offering and .... Le 9:3
altar and offer **s** offerings and .... Le 9:7
bull calf as a **s** offering for .... Le 9:8
liver from the **s** offering and .... Le 9:10
of the people's **s** offering and .... Le 9:15
offered it for the **s** offering,................. Le 9:15
had done the first **s** offering. .... Le 9:15
offering the **s** offering, ... Le 9:22
for the goat of the **s** offering, ... Le 10:16
brought their **s** offering and .... Le 10:19
if I ate the **s** offering today?" .... Le 10:19
young pigeon for a **s** offering. .... Le 12:6
and one for a **s** offering. .... Le 12:8
where the **s** offering and the .... Le 14:13
offering is like the **s** offering— .... Le 14:13
offer the **s** offering to make .... Le 14:19
One bird is for a **s** offering and .... Le 14:22
the birds for a **s** offering and .... Le 14:31
one for a **s** offering and the .... Le 15:15
offer one bird for a **s** offering .... Le 15:30
offer a bull for a **s** offering .... Le 16:3
goats for a **s** offering and one................ Le 16:5
the bull for the **s** offering for .... Le 16:6
for the goat that removes **s**. .... Le 16:8
will offer it as a **s** offering. .... Le 16:9
chosen by lot to remove the **s**, ... Le 16:10
remove Israel's **s** so they will .... Le 16:10
desert as a goat that removes **s**. .... Le 16:10
the bull as a **s** offering for .... Le 16:11
the bull for the **s** offering for .... Le 16:11
the goat of the **s** offering for .... Le 16:15
burn the fat of the **s** offering .... Le 16:25
the goat for the **s** offerings,................. Le 16:27
he will be guilty of **s**.'" .... Le 17:16
a woman. That is a hateful **s**. .... Le 18:22
it then will be guilty of **s**, ... Le 19:8
before the LORD for the man's **s**, ... Le 19:22
he will be forgiven for his **s**. .... Le 19:22
be filled with all kinds of **s**..................... Le 19:29
two men have done a hateful **s**. .... Le 20:13
sister, and he is guilty of **s**. .... Le 20:17
of you are guilty of this **s**. .... Le 20:19
children; they are guilty of **s**. .... Le 20:20
male goat for a **s** offering and .... Le 23:19
you clean from **s** so you will .... Le 23:28
his God, he is guilty of **s**. .... Le 24:15
more you **s**, the more you will .... Le 26:21
accept punishment for their **s**, ... Le 26:41
Her **s** might be kept hidden from .... Nu 5:13
will offer one as a **s** offering .... Nu 6:11
This removes **s** so they will..................... Nu 6:11
wrong with it, as a **s** offering,................ Nu 6:14
the LORD and make the **s** offering........... Nu 6:16
male goats for a **s** offering .... Nu 7:87
young bull for a **s** offering..................... Nu 8:8
one bull will be a **s** offering to .... Nu 8:12

S

and must be punished for the **s.** .... Nu 9:13
forgive us for our foolish **s.** .... Nu 12:11
He forgives **s** and law breaking. .... Nu 14:18
When parents **s,** he will also .... Nu 14:18
these people's **s,** just as you .... Nu 14:19
a male goat as a **s** offering. .... Nu 15:24
will remove that **s** for all the .... Nu 15:25
by fire and a **s** offering. .... Nu 15:25
be brought for a **s** offering. .... Nu 15:27
will remove the **s** of the person .... Nu 15:28
the people and remove their **s.** .... Nu 16:46
the incense to remove their **s.** .... Nu 16:47
they are grain or **s** or penalty .... Nu 18:9
or they will die for their **s.** .... Nu 18:22
If you do not **s** against the holy .... Nu 18:32
ceremony to cleanse away **s.** .... Nu 19:9
He hates **s** as much as I do.................... Nu 25:11
he died because of his own **s,** .... Nu 27:3
bring a **s** offering of one goat .... Nu 28:15
Bring one goat as a **s** offering, ... Nu 28:22
male goat for a **s** offering to .... Nu 29:5
one male goat as a **s** offering.................. Nu 29:11
addition to the **s** offering which .... Nu 29:11
one male goat as a **s** offering in .... Nu 29:16
one male goat as a **s** offering,................. Nu 29:19
one male goat as a **s** offering, ... Nu 29:22
one male goat as a **s** offering, ... Nu 29:25
one male goat as a **s** offering, ... Nu 29:28
one male goat as a **s** offering, ... Nu 29:31
one male goat as a **s** offering, ... Nu 29:34
one male goat as a **s** offering,................. Nu 29:38
you will be punished for your **s.** .... Nu 32:23
and camped in the Desert of **S.** .... Nu 33:11
the Desert of **S** and camped at .... Nu 33:12
way to remove the **s** of killing................. Nu 35:33
Don't **s** by making idols of any .... Dt 4:16
If people **s** against me and hate .... Dt 5:9
don't look at their **s** and evil. .... Dt 9:27
he will find you guilty of **s.** .... Dt 15:9
accuse a person of a crime or **s.** .... Dt 19:15
you will **s** against the LORD your .... Dt 20:18
remove this **s** from your people .... Dt 21:8
guilty of a **s** worthy of death, ... Dt 21:22
not done a **s** worthy of death. .... Dt 22:26
from you. Do not be guilty of **s.** .... Dt 23:21
Don't bring this **s** into the land .... Dt 24:4
and you will be guilty of **s.** .... Dt 24:15
person must die for his own **s.** .... Dt 24:16
he will remove the **s** of his land .... Dt 32:43
suffer long because of that **s,** .... Jos 22:17
Achan died because of his **s,** .... Jos 22:20
If you turn against him and **s,**................. Jos 24:19
saw that the **s** of the servants 1Sa 2:17
you **s** against someone, God can 1Sa 2:25
But if you **s** against the LORD 1Sa 2:25
Don't **s** against the LORD by 1Sa 14:34
find out what **s** has been done 1Sa 14:38
if my son Jonathan did the **s,** 1Sa 14:39
is as bad as the **s** of sorcery. 1Sa 15:23
is as bad as the **s** of worshiping 1Sa 15:23
Now, I beg you, forgive my **s.** 1Sa 15:25
How did I **s** against your father?.............. 1Sa 20:1
The LORD has taken away your **s.** 2Sa 12:13
the Israelites, **s** against you, ... 1Ki 8:33
When they **s** against you, you................ 1Ki 8:35
people will also **s** against you. 1Ki 8:46
This became a very great **s,** 1Ki 12:30
and this **s** caused its ruin and 1Ki 13:34
he made the people of Israel **s.** 1Ki 14:16
led the people of Israel to **s,** 1Ki 15:26
led the people of Israel to **s,** 1Ki 15:30
led the people of Israel to **s,** 1Ki 15:34
have led my people Israel to **s.** 1Ki 16:2

led the people of Israel to **s,** 1Ki 16:13
led the people of Israel to **s,** 1Ki 16:19
led the people of Israel to **s,** 1Ki 16:26
remind me of my **s** and to kill my 1Ki 17:18
led the people of Israel to **s.'** 1Ki 21:22
people of Israel into more **s.** 1Ki 22:52
he continued to **s** like Jeroboam 2Ki 3:3
Nebat who had led Israel to **s.** 2Ki 3:3
led Israel to **s** by worshiping 2Ki 10:29
by which he had led Israel to **s.** 2Ki 10:31
offerings and **s** offerings was 2Ki 12:16
Jeroboam had led Israel to **s,** 2Ki 13:2
had led Israel to **s,** and they 2Ki 13:6
Jeroboam had led Israel to **s,** 2Ki 13:11
of Nebat had led Israel to **s,** 2Ki 14:24
led the people of Israel to **s,** 2Ki 15:9
of Nebat had led Israel to **s,** 2Ki 15:18
of Nebat had led Israel to **s,** 2Ki 15:24
of Nebat had led Israel to **s,** 2Ki 15:28
LORD and led them to **s** greatly................ 2Ki 17:21
led Judah to **s** with his idols. 2Ki 21:11
was besides the **s** he led Judah 2Ki 21:16
as king, even the **s** he did, are 2Ki 21:17
Nebat, who had led Israel to **s.** 2Ki 23:15
will make Israel guilty of **s.''** 1Ch 21:3
the Israelites, **s** against you, ... 2Ch 6:24
Forgive the **s** of your people 2Ch 6:25
When they **s** against you, you................ 2Ch 6:26
people will also **s** against you. 2Ch 6:36
forgive their **s,** and I will heal................ 2Ch 7:14
people not to **s** against the LORD 2Ch 19:10
the people of Jerusalem to **s,** 2Ch 21:11
and Jerusalem to **s** against God,.............. 2Ch 21:13
be guilty of **s** against the LORD 2Ch 28:13
will make our **s** and guilt even................ 2Ch 28:13
led the people of Judah to **s,** 2Ch 28:19
to remove the **s** of the people 2Ch 29:21
goats for the **s** offering before 2Ch 29:23
offering and **s** offering should 2Ch 29:24
For a **s** offering there were .... Ezr 8:35
me so I would do this and **s.** .... Ne 6:13
made King Solomon of Israel **s.** .... Ne 13:26
but foreign women made him **s.** .... Ne 13:26
this Job did not **s** or blame God................ Job 1:22
Job did not **s** in what he said .... Job 2:10
I have done and search for my **s.** .... Job 10:6
not let my **s** go unpunished. .... Job 10:14
even forgotten some of your **s.** .... Job 11:6
Put away the **s** that is in your .... Job 11:14
Show me my wrong and my **s.** .... Job 13:23
you will not keep track of my **s.** .... Job 14:16
and you will cover up my **s.** .... Job 14:17
Your **s** teaches your mouth what .... Job 15:5
not dirty with **s** will grow .... Job 17:9
be shameful, a **s** to be punished............. Job 31:11
not let my mouth **s** by cursing my .... Job 31:30
not hidden my **s** as others do,................ Job 31:33
said, 'I am pure and without **s;** .... Job 33:9
but I will not **s** anymore......................... Job 34:31
now adds to his **s** by turning .... Job 34:37
you **s,** it does nothing to God;................ Job 35:6
When you are angry, do not **s.** .... Ps 4:4
their tongues for **s** and evil. .... Ps 10:7
but those who **s** without excuse .... Ps 25:3
with those who hide their **s.** .... Ps 26:4
S speaks to the wicked in their .... Ps 36:1
don't see their **s** and hate it. .... Ps 36:2
are not healthy because of my **s.** .... Ps 38:3
my guilt; I am troubled by my **s**............... Ps 38:18
and will not **s** by what I say. .... Ps 39:1
after David's **s** with Bathsheba. .... Ps 50:23
wrongs, and I can't forget my **s.** .... Ps 51:3
brought into this world in **s.** .... Ps 51:5

In s my mother gave birth to me.	Ps 51:5
Take away my s, and I will be	Ps 51:7
that is broken and sorry for s.	Ps 51:17
They s by what they say;	Ps 59:12
they s with their words.	Ps 59:12
had known of any s in my heart,	Ps 66:18
of those who continue to s.	Ps 68:21
continued to s against him;	Ps 78:17
so I would not s against you.	Ps 119:11
don't let any s control me.	Ps 119:133
sinners try to lead you into s,	Pr 1:10
talk a lot, you are sure to s;	Pr 10:19
Fools don't care if they s,	Pr 14:9
It is a s to hate your neighbor,	Pr 14:21
but s will bring disgrace to any	Pr 14:34
truth brings forgiveness of s.	Pr 16:6
someone's s makes a friend,	Pr 17:9
gossiping about the s breaks up	Pr 17:9
loves to argue loves to s.	Pr 17:19
and evil actions are s.	Pr 21:4
but some will s for only a piece	Pr 28:21
are trapped by their own s,	Pr 29:6
there is much s, but those who	Pr 29:16
let your words cause you to s,	Ec 5:6
a nation of s, a people loaded	Is 1:4
they are proud of their s.	Is 3:9
lips. Your s is taken away."	Is 6:7
Its s is like a heavy weight on	Is 24:20
twice for every s they did."	Is 40:2
Jacob who have turned from s,"	Is 59:20
All of us are dirty with s.	Is 64:6
you have to do is admit your s—	Je 3:13
What s have we done against the	Je 16:10
s is not hidden from my eyes.	Je 16:17
The s of the people of Judah is	Je 17:1
person will die for his own s;	Je 31:30
a thing and cause Judah to s.	Je 32:35
but I will wash away that s.	Je 33:8
ways, they will die in their s.	Eze 3:18
will die because of their s.	Eze 3:19
will die because of their s,	Eze 3:20
those good people not to s,	Eze 3:21
and they do not s, they will	Eze 3:21
as the years of the people's s.	Eze 4:5
of Israel's s on you for three	Eze 4:5
a day for each year of their s.	Eze 4:6
become weak because of their s.	Eze 4:17
the valleys about their own s.	Eze 7:16
it caused them to fall into s.	Eze 7:19
The s of the people of Israel	Eze 9:9
things that cause people to s.	Eze 14:3
cause people to s and then come	Eze 14:4
things that cause people to s.	Eze 14:7
of a country s against me by not	Eze 14:13
and partners in sexual s.	Eze 16:26
This was the s of your sister	Eze 16:49
will not die for his father's s;	Eze 18:17
So he will die for his own s.	Eze 18:18
punished for the father's s?'	Eze 18:19
be punished for a parent's s,	Eze 18:20
not be punished for a child's s.	Eze 18:20
your sinning so s will not bring	Eze 18:30
it is really proof of their s,	Eze 21:23
sins and the s of worshiping	Eze 23:49
from your s until my anger	Eze 24:13
of their s in turning to Egypt	Eze 29:16
died because of their own s.	Eze 33:6
will not save them when they s.	Eze 33:12
If good people s, they will not	Eze 33:12
that give life and do not s,	Eze 33:15
the ways they s and turn against	Eze 37:23
burnt offerings, s offerings,	Eze 40:39
grain offerings, s offerings,	Eze 42:13

a young bull as a s offering to	Eze 43:19
the bull for the s offering and	Eze 43:21
wrong with it for a s offering.	Eze 43:22
for seven days as a s offering.	Eze 43:25
must be punished for their s.	Eze 44:10
will be punished for their s,	Eze 44:12
he must offer a s offering for	Eze 44:27
grain offerings, s offerings,	Eze 44:29
will supply the s offerings,	Eze 45:17
blood from this s offering and	Eze 45:19
of the land as a s offering.	Eze 45:22
goat every day as a s offering.	Eze 45:23
s offerings, burnt offerings,	Eze 45:25
offering and s offering and bake	Eze 46:20
to put an end to s; to take away	Da 9:24
the more they s against me.	Hos 4:7
priests live off the s offerings	Hos 4:8
the people to s more and more.	Hos 4:8
will stumble because of their s,	Hos 5:5
Israel, Israel's s will go away,	Hos 7:1
built more altars to remove s,	Hos 8:11
gone deep into s as the people	Hos 9:9
Take away all our s and kindly	Hos 14:2
to the city of Bethel and s;	Am 4:4
come to Gilgal and s even more.	Am 4:4
this is because of Jacob's s,	Mic 1:5
What is the place of Jacob's s?	Mic 1:5
my very own child for my s?"	Mic 6:7
those who are guilty of s;	Mic 7:18
have taken away your s from you,	Zch 3:4
take away the s of this land.'	Zch 3:9
of their s and uncleanness."	Zch 13:1
and wants to s sexually with her	Mt 5:28
done that s with the woman.	Mt 5:28
your right eye causes you to s,	Mt 5:29
your right hand causes you to s,	Mt 5:30
for every s and everything	Mt 12:31
who cause s and all who do evil.	Mt 13:41
someone causes that child to s,	Mt 18:6
the things that cause them to s.	Mt 18:7
or your foot causes you to s,	Mt 18:8
If your eye causes you to s,	Mt 18:9
will complete the s that your	Mt 23:32
is guilty of a s that continues	Mk 3:29
someone causes that child to s,	Mk 9:42
If your hand causes you to s,	Mk 9:43
If your foot causes you to s,	Mk 9:45
If your eye causes you to s,	Mk 9:47
because of his s with Herodias,	Lk 3:19
are ungrateful and full of s.	Lk 6:35
cause people to s will happen,	Lk 17:1
one of these little ones to s.	Lk 17:2
takes away the s of the world!	Jn 1:29
go now, but don't s anymore."	Jn 8:11
lives in s is a slave to sin.	Jn 8:34
lives in sin is a slave to s.	Jn 8:34
you prove that I am guilty of s?	Jn 8:46
whose s caused this man to be	Jn 9:2
his own s or his parents' sin?"	Jn 9:2
his own sin or his parents' s?"	Jn 9:2
not this man's s or his parents'	Jn 9:3
or his parents' s that made him	Jn 9:3
You were born full of s!	Jn 9:34
you would not be guilty of s.	Jn 9:41
they would not be guilty of s,	Jn 15:22
they have no excuse for their s.	Jn 15:22
they would not be guilty of s.	Jn 15:24
of the world the truth about s,	Jn 16:8
to them that s is not believing	Jn 16:9
you is guilty of a greater s."	Jn 19:11
not hold this s against them."	Ac 7:60
bitter jealousy and ruled by s."	Ac 8:23
kind of sexual s, eating animals	Ac 15:20

S

blood, and any kind of sexual **s**. .... Ac 15:29
Do not take part in sexual **s**.'" .... Ac 21:25
they became full of sexual **s**, ... Rm 1:24
are filled with every kind of **s**, ... Rm 1:29
but you are guilty of that **s**. .... Rm 2:22
not Jews are all guilty of **s**. .... Rm 3:9
The law only shows us our **s**. .... Rm 3:20
made free from **s** through Jesus .... Rm 3:24
S came into the world because of .... Rm 5:12
man did, and with **s** came death. .... Rm 5:12
S was in the world before the .... Rm 5:13
but **s** is not counted against us .... Rm 5:13
free gift is not like Adam's **s**. .... Rm 5:15
of the **s** of that one man. .... Rm 5:15
So as one **s** of Adam brought the .... Rm 5:18
The law came to make **s** worse. .... Rm 5:20
But when **s** grew worse, God's .... Rm 5:20
S once used death to rule us, ... Rm 5:21
can we continue living with **s**? .... Rm 6:2
and we would not be slaves to **s**. .... Rm 6:6
defeat the power of **s** one time— .... Rm 6:10
to the power of **s** and alive with .... Rm 6:11
do not let **s** control your life .... Rm 6:12
parts of your body to serve **s**, ... Rm 6:13
S will not be your master, ... Rm 6:14
Should we **s** because we are under .... Rm 6:15
You can follow **s**, which brings .... Rm 6:16
the past you were slaves to **s**— .... Rm 6:17
slaves to sin—**s** controlled you. .... Rm 6:17
You were made free from **s**, ... Rm 6:18
body to be slaves to **s** and evil; .... Rm 6:19
the past you were slaves to **s**, ... Rm 6:20
are free from **s** and have become .... Rm 6:22
The payment for **s** is death. .... Rm 6:23
am saying that **s** and the law are .... Rm 7:7
way I could learn what **s** meant. .... Rm 7:7
And **s** found a way to use that .... Rm 7:8
without the law, **s** has no power. .... Rm 7:8
to me, then **s** began to live, ... Rm 7:9
S found a way to fool me by .... Rm 7:11
S used something that is good to .... Rm 7:13
could see what **s** is really like .... Rm 7:13
to show that **s** is very evil. .... Rm 7:13
spiritual since **s** rules me as if .... Rm 7:14
s living in me that does them. .... Rm 7:17
It is **s** living in me that does .... Rm 7:20
in my body is the law of **s**, ... Rm 7:23
I am a slave to the law of **s**. .... Rm 7:25
the law that brings **s** and death. .... Rm 8:2
life that others use for **s**. .... Rm 8:3
his Son to be an offering for **s**, ... Rm 8:3
used a human life to destroy **s**. .... Rm 8:3
always be dead because of **s**. .... Rm 8:10
will make another Christian **s**. .... Rm 14:13
that causes someone else to **s**. .... Rm 14:20
your brother or sister to **s**. .... Rm 14:21
believing it is right is a **s**. .... Rm 14:23
and have been set free from **s**. 1Co 1:30
there is sexual **s** among you. 1Co 5:1
man who did that as if I were 1Co 5:3
the yeast of **s** and wickedness. 1Co 5:8
with those who **s** sexually. 1Co 5:9
of this world who **s** sexually, ... 1Co 5:10
in Christ but who **s** sexually, ... 1Co 5:11
not for sexual **s** but for the 1Co 6:13
So run away from sexual **s**. 1Co 6:18
Every other **s** people do is 1Co 6:18
but those who **s** sexually sin 1Co 6:18
who sin sexually **s** against their 1Co 6:18
because sexual **s** is a danger, ... 1Co 7:2
should get married. It is no **s**. 1Co 7:36
weak in faith to fall into **s**. 1Co 8:9
When you **s** against your brothers 1Co 8:12

eat causes them to fall into **s**, ... 1Co 8:13
will not cause any of them to **s**. 1Co 8:13
their **s** will be shown to them, ... 1Co 14:24
Death's power to hurt is **s**, ... 1Co 15:56
and the power of **s** is the law. 1Co 15:56
people guilty of **s** had glory, ... 2Co 3:9
Christ had no **s**, but God made 2Co 5:21
made him become **s** so that in 2Co 5:21
time someone is led into **s**. 2Co 11:29
mean that Christ encourages **s**? .... Gal 2:17
the whole world is bound by **s**. .... Gal 3:22
you might be tempted to **s**, ... Gal 6:1
angry, do not **s**, and be sure to .... Eph 4:26
must be no sexual **s** among you, ... Eph 5:3
with no evil or **s** or any other .... Eph 5:27
for sexual **s** like the people 1Th 4:5
does not want us to live in **s**. 1Th 4:7
who are full of **s** and are led by 2Ti 3:6
who are full of **s** and do not .... Tit 1:15
because **s** has tricked you. .... Heb 3:13
that we are, but he did not **s**. .... Heb 4:15
he set us free from **s** forever. .... Heb 9:12
could be set free from **s**. .... Heb 9:15
take away all **s** by sacrificing .... Heb 9:26
not to offer himself for **s**, ... Heb 9:28
no longer have a sense of **s**. .... Heb 10:2
of enjoying **s** for a short time. .... Heb 11:25
the way and the **s** that so easily .... Heb 12:1
You are struggling against **s**, ... Heb 12:4
and try to live free from **s**. .... Heb 12:14
part in sexual **s** or is like Esau .... Heb 12:16
desire leads to **s**, and then the .... Jam 1:15
and then the **s** grows and brings .... Jam 1:15
clean **s** out of your lives. .... Jam 4:8
stop living for **s** and start 1Pe 2:24
in the body is finished with **s**. 1Pe 4:1
their desire for **s** is never 2Pe 2:14
weak people into the trap of **s**, ... 2Pe 2:14
lead people into the trap of **s**— 2Pe 2:18
to be without **s** and without 2Pe 3:14
Son, cleanses us from every **s**. 1Jn 1:7
say we have no **s**, we are fooling 1Jn 1:8
letter to you so you will not **s**. 1Jn 2:1
if anyone does **s**, we have a 1Jn 2:1
s is against God's law. 1Jn 3:4
that there is no **s** in Christ. 1Jn 3:5
continues to **s** belongs to the 1Jn 3:8
s that does not lead to eternal. 1Jn 5:16
people whose **s** does not lead to 1Jn 5:16
There is **s** that leads to death. 1Jn 5:16
person should pray about that **s**. 1Jn 5:16
wrong is always **s**, but there is 1Jn 5:17
there is **s** that does not lead 1Jn 5:17
children do not continue to **s**. 1Jn 5:18
God into a reason for sexual **s**. .... Jud 1:4
full of sexual **s** and people who .... Jud 1:7
make themselves filthy with **s**. .... Jud 1:8
clothes which are dirty from **s**. .... Jud 1:23
of Israel to **s** by eating food .... Rev 2:14
heart and turn away from her **s**, ... Rev 2:21
from the wine of her sexual **s**." .... Rev 17:2
the uncleanness of her sexual **s**. .... Rev 17:4
of the desire of her sexual **s**. .... Rev 18:3
earth evil with her sexual **s**. .... Rev 19:2
who kill, who **s** sexually, who do .... Rev 21:8
evil magic, who **s** sexually, who .... Rev 22:15

SIN'S
is made free from **s** control. .... Rm 6:7

SINAI
he came to **S**, the mountain .... Ex 3:1
he met Moses at **S**, the mountain .... Ex 4:27
which was between Elim and **S**; .... Ex 16:1

of you on a rock at Mount **S**. .... Ex 17:6
they reached the Desert of **S**. .... Ex 19:1
to the Desert of **S** and camped .... Ex 19:2
will come down on Mount **S**, ... Ex 19:11
Mount **S** was covered with smoke, ... Ex 19:18
came down on top of Mount **S**, ... Ex 19:20
cannot come up on Mount **S**, ... Ex 19:23
Moses went up to **S**, the mountain .... Ex 24:13
the LORD came down on Mount **S**, ... Ex 24:16
speaking to Moses on Mount **S**, ... Ex 31:18
off their jewelry at Mount **S**. .... Ex 33:6
and then come up on Mount **S**. .... Ex 34:2
next morning he went up Mount **S**, ... Ex 34:4
Moses came down from Mount **S**, ... Ex 34:29
LORD had given him on Mount **S**. .... Ex 34:32
Moses on Mount **S** on the day he .... Le 7:38
to the LORD in the **S** Desert. .... Le 7:38
LORD said to Moses at Mount **S**, ... Le 25:1
through Moses at Mount **S**. .... Le 26:46
Moses at Mount **S** for the people .... Le 27:34
Meeting Tent in the Desert of **S**. .... Nu 1:1
they were in the Desert of **S**. .... Nu 1:19
LORD talked to Moses on Mount **S**. .... Nu 3:1
the LORD in the Desert of **S**. .... Nu 3:4
to Moses in the Desert of **S**, ... Nu 3:14
in the Desert of **S** in the first .... Nu 9:1
in the Desert of **S** at twilight .... Nu 9:5
the Desert of **S** and continued .... Nu 10:12
Israelites in the Desert of **S**, ... Nu 26:64
offering which began at Mount **S**; .... Nu 28:6
and camped in the Desert of **S**. .... Nu 33:15
the Desert of **S** and camped at .... Nu 33:16
trip from Mount **S** to Kadesh .... Dt 1:2
spoke to us at Mount **S** and said, ... Dt 1:6
we left Mount **S** and went toward .... Dt 1:19
the LORD your God at Mount **S**. .... Dt 4:10
to you from the fire at Mount **S**, ... Dt 4:15
an Agreement with us at Mount **S**............. Dt 5:2
Mount **S** you made the LORD angry— ...... Dt 9:8
you were gathered at Mount **S**. .... Dt 18:16
had made with them at Mount **S**. .... Dt 29:1
came from Mount **S** and rose like .... Dt 33:2
God of Mount **S**, before the LORD .... Jdg 5:5
had put in the Ark at Mount **S**. 1Ki 8:9
days and nights to Mount **S**, ... 1Ki 19:8
had put in the Ark at Mount **S**, ... 2Ch 5:10
came down to Mount **S** and spoke .... Ne 9:13
the God of Mount **S**, before God, ... Ps 68:8
comes from Mount **S** to his holy .... Ps 68:17
calf at Mount **S** and worshiped .... Ps 106:19
gave to him on Mount **S** for all .... Mal 4:4
was in the desert near Mount **S**................. Ac 7:30
that spoke to him at Mount **S**,................. Ac 7:38
law that God made on Mount **S**,............... Gal 4:24
is like Mount **S** in Arabia and is .... Gal 4:25

SINCERE

honest and **s** when you made .... Jdg 9:16
been honest and **s** to Gideon and .... Jdg 9:19
he was fair and **s**. You must obey 1Ki 9:4
I am **s** in saying what I know. .... Job 33:3
but you are not honest or **s**. .... Is 48:1
who acted as if they were **s**. .... Lk 20:20
an honest and **s** heart from God. 2Co 1:12
and respect and from a **s** heart, ... Eph 6:5
to God with a **s** heart and a sure .... Heb 10:22

SINCERELY

LORD and serve him fully and **s**. .... Jos 24:14
he had told her everything **s**, ... Jdg 16:18

SINFUL

You **s** people are making the LORD .... Nu 32:14
I took that **s** calf idol you had .... Dt 9:21
They will keep you from **s** women .... Pr 6:24

Making foolish plans is **s**, ... Pr 24:9
have shown how **s** you are by .... Eze 21:24
to do the **s** things you had .... Eze 23:21
a stop to the **s** life you began .... Eze 23:27
know about the **s** things you did. .... Eze 23:29
By your **s** action you have .... Eze 24:13
Because of the **s** things they .... Hos 9:15
watching the **s** kingdom Israel. .... Am 9:8
Evil and **s** people are the ones .... Mt 12:39
Evil and **s** people ask for a .... Mt 16:4
to be handed over to **s** people. .... Mt 26:45
lying, doing **s** things, jealousy, ... Mk 7:22
are living in a **s** and evil time................. Mk 8:38
to be handed over to **s** people. .... Mk 14:41
from me, Lord. I am a **s** man!" .... Lk 5:8
A **s** woman in the town learned .... Lk 7:37
they were more **s** than all others .... Lk 13:2
they were more **s** than all the .... Lk 13:4
must be handed over to **s** people, ... Lk 24:7
and let them go their **s** way, ... Rm 1:24
We died to our old **s** lives, ... Rm 6:2
so that our **s** selves would have .... Rm 6:6
do what your **s** self wants to do. .... Rm 6:12
we were ruled by our **s** selves. .... Rm 7:5
made us want to do **s** things that .... Rm 7:5
of me that is earthly and **s**. .... Rm 7:18
but in my **s** self I am a slave to .... Rm 7:25
was made weak by our **s** selves. .... Rm 8:3
not live following our **s** selves, ... Rm 8:4
following their **s** selves think .... Rm 8:5
things that their **s** selves want. .... Rm 8:5
is controlled by the **s** self, ... Rm 8:6
is controlled by the **s** self, ... Rm 8:7
ruled by their **s** selves cannot .... Rm 8:8
are not ruled by your **s** selves. .... Rm 8:9
be ruled by our **s** selves or live .... Rm 8:12
live the way our **s** selves want. .... Rm 8:12
wrong things your **s** selves want, ... Rm 8:13
about satisfying your **s** self. .... Rm 13:14
So his **s** self will be destroyed, ... 1Co 5:5
to do what pleases your **s** self. .... Gal 5:13
not do what your **s** selves want. .... Gal 5:16
s selves want what is against .... Gal 5:17
what is against our **s** selves. .... Gal 5:17
wrong things the **s** self does are .... Gal 5:19
crucified their own **s** selves. .... Gal 5:24
plant to satisfy their **s** selves, ... Gal 6:8
their **s** selves will bring them .... Gal 6:8
to please our **s** selves and doing............. Eph 2:3
because we were **s** by nature. .... Eph 2:3
from the power of your **s** self.................. Col 2:11
from the power of your **s** self,................. Col 2:13
the evil desires of the **s** self. .... Col 2:23
Your old **s** self has died, and .... Col 3:3
have left your old **s** life and .... Col 3:9
who are against God and are **s**, ... 1Ti 3:9
that such people are evil and **s**; .... Tit 3:11
evil things their **s** selves want..................... 2Pe 2:10
wanting to please our **s** selves, ... 1Jn 2:16
wanting the **s** things we see, ... 1Jn 2:16
who did not do **s** things with .... Rev 14:4

SING

I will **s** to the LORD, because he............... Ex 15:1
me strength and makes me **s**; .... Ex 15:2
S to the LORD, because he is .... Ex 15:21
out water, well! **S** about it. .... Nu 21:17
Then have them **s** it, because it .... Dt 31:19
I myself will **s** to the LORD. .... Jdg 5:3
Wake up, wake up, **s** a song! .... Jdg 5:12
the man they dance and **s** about, ... 1Sa 21:11
Israelites dance and **s** about, ... 1Sa 29:5
I will **s** praises to your name. 2Sa 22:50

S

cymbals and to s happy songs. 1Ch 15:16
S to him; sing praises to him. 1Ch 16:9
Sing to him; s praises to him. 1Ch 16:9
S to the LORD, all the earth. 1Ch 16:23
the forest will s for joy before................ 1Ch 16:33
They will s because he is coming 1Ch 16:33
chosen by name to s praises to 1Ch 16:41
they began to s and praise God, ... 2Ch 20:22
in Israel to s these songs that 2Ch 35:25
They s to the music of.......................... Job 21:12
and I made the widow's heart s.............. Job 29:13
harp is tuned to s a sad song, ... Job 30:31
let them s glad songs forever. .... Ps 5:11
I s praises to the LORD Most .... Ps 7:17
and babies to s praises to you................... Ps 8:2
I will s praises to your name. .... Ps 9:2
S praises to the LORD who is .... Ps 9:11
I s to the LORD because he has .... Ps 13:6
I will s praises to your name. .... Ps 18:49
We s and praise your greatness. .... Ps 21:13
I will s and praise the LORD. .... Ps 27:6
S praises to the LORD, you who .... Ps 30:4
I will s to you and not be .... Ps 30:12
S all you whose hearts are right. .... Ps 32:11
S to the LORD, you who do what .... Ps 33:1
S a new song to him; play well .... Ps 33:3
May my friends s and shout for .... Ps 35:27
S praises to God. Sing praises. .... Ps 47:6
praises to God. S praises. Sing .... Ps 47:6
Sing praises. S praises to our .... Ps 47:6
praises to our King. S praises. .... Ps 47:6
so s a song of praise to him. .... Ps 47:7
I will s about your goodness. .... Ps 51:14
I will s and praise you. .... Ps 57:7
I will s songs of praise about .... Ps 57:9
I will s about your strength. .... Ps 59:16
I will s about your love. .... Ps 59:16
I will s praises to you............................ Ps 59:17
lips will s, and my mouth will................. Ps 63:5
Because of your protection, I s. .... Ps 63:7
S about his glory! Make his .... Ps 66:2
They s praises to your name." .... Ps 66:4
our God; loudly s his praise. .... Ps 66:8
be glad and s because you judge .... Ps 67:4
S to God; sing praises to his .... Ps 68:4
Sing to God; s praises to his .... Ps 68:4
Kingdoms of the earth, s to God; .... Ps 68:32
s praises to the Lord. .... Ps 68:32
S to the one who rides through .... Ps 68:33
I will s to you with the lyre, ... Ps 71:22
for joy when I s praises to you. .... Ps 71:23
I will s praise to the God of.................... Ps 75:9
S for joy to God, our strength; .... Ps 81:1
will dance and s, "All good .... Ps 87:7
I will always s about the LORD's .... Ps 89:1
Mount Hermon s for joy at your .... Ps 89:12
Then we will s and rejoice all................. Ps 90:14
to s praises to God Most High. .... Ps 92:1
I will s for joy about what your .... Ps 92:4
let's s for joy to the LORD. .... Ps 95:1
Let's s songs to him, ... Ps 95:2
S to the LORD a new song;...................... Ps 96:1
s to the LORD, all the earth. .... Ps 96:1
S to the LORD and praise his .... Ps 96:2
of the forest will s for joy .... Ps 96:12
S to the LORD a new song,...................... Ps 98:1
the world and everyone in it s. .... Ps 98:7
the mountains s together for joy............. Ps 98:8
Let them s before the LORD, ... Ps 98:9
I will s of your love and .... Ps 101:1
LORD, I will s praises to you. .... Ps 101:1
they s among the tree branches................ Ps 104:12
will s to the LORD all my life; .... Ps 104:33

I will s praises to my God as .... Ps 104:33
S to him; sing praises to him. .... Ps 105:2
Sing to him; s praises to him. .... Ps 105:2
I will s and praise you with all .... Ps 108:1
I will s songs of praise about .... Ps 108:3
s about your demands wherever I .... Ps 119:54
Let me s about your promises, ... Ps 119:172
crops will s at harvest time .... Ps 126:5
May your people s for joy. .... Ps 132:9
me will really s for joy. .... Ps 132:16
s praises to him, because it is .... Ps 135:3
who captured us asked us to s; .... Ps 137:3
"S us a song about Jerusalem!" .... Ps 137:3
But we cannot s songs about the .... Ps 137:4
I will s to you before the gods. .... Ps 138:1
They will s about what the LORD .... Ps 138:5
I will s a new song to you; .... Ps 144:9
goodness and will s about your .... Ps 145:7
I will s praises to my God as .... Ps 146:2
It is good to s praises to our .... Ps 147:1
S praises to the LORD; praise.................. Ps 147:7
S a new song to the LORD;...................... Ps 149:1
s his praise in the meeting of .... Ps 149:1
should s praises to him with .... Ps 149:3
Let them s for joy even in bed! .... Ps 149:5
good people can s and be happy. .... Pr 29:6
The time has come to s; .... Sng 2:12
I will s for my friend a song .... Is 5:1
me strength and makes me s. .... Is 12:2
S praise to the LORD, because he .... Is 12:5
Shout and s for joy, you people .... Is 12:6
Israel will s this song about .... Is 14:4
Now the people begin to s. .... Is 14:7
harp well. S your song often .... Is 23:16
no longer s while they drink .... Is 24:9
time people will s this song in .... Is 26:1
time people will s about the .... Is 27:2
You will s happy songs as on the .... Is 30:29
died cannot s praises to you; .... Is 38:18
S a new song to the LORD;...................... Is 42:10
s his praise everywhere on the .... Is 42:10
living in Sela should s for joy; .... Is 42:11
I made will s songs to praise me............... Is 43:21
s for joy because the LORD did .... Is 44:23
S, you mountains, with thanks to .... Is 44:23
S, too, you trees in the forest!.................. Is 44:23
will give thanks and s songs. .... Is 51:3
The LORD says, "S, Jerusalem. .... Is 54:1
and they will s praises to the .... Is 60:6
mountains and s a funeral song .... Je 9:10
S to the LORD! Praise the LORD! .... Je 20:13
places will s songs of praise. .... Je 30:19
Be happy and s for the people of .... Je 31:7
S your praises and shout this: ' .... Je 31:7
the young men no longer s. .... La 5:14
S a funeral song for the leaders .... Eze 19:1
s a funeral song for the city of .... Eze 27:2
crying they s a funeral song .... Eze 27:32
s a funeral song for the king of .... Eze 28:12
s a funeral song about the king .... Eze 32:2
song people will s for Egypt. .... Eze 32:16
women of the nations will s it; .... Eze 32:16
they will s a funeral song for .... Eze 32:16
funeral song that I s about you, ... Am 5:1
fun of you and s this sad song .... Mic 2:4
S, Jerusalem. Israel, shout for .... Zph 3:14
will s and be joyful about you. .... Zph 3:17
and babies to s praises'?" .... Mt 21:16
I will s praises to your name." .... Rm 15:9
you people, s praises to him. .... Rm 15:11
I will s with my spirit, but I.................... 1Co 14:15
but I will also s with my mind. 1Co 14:15
who is happy should s praises. .... Jam 5:13

SINGER

he is the sweet s of Israel: 2Sa 23:1
family there was Heman the s. 1Ch 6:33
more than a s who sings love .... Eze 33:32

SINGERS

sound of the s at the watering .... Jdg 5:11
the voices of men and women s................ 2Sa 19:35
brothers as s to play their 1Ch 15:16
The s Heman, Asaph, and Ethan 1Ch 15:19
and all the s wore robes of fine 1Ch 15:27
chose men to be s to the LORD.............. 2Ch 20:21
The s were playing musical 2Ch 23:13
people worshiped, the s sang,.................. 2Ch 29:28
The Levite s from Asaph's family 2Ch 35:15
the men and women s remember and 2Ch 35:25
These are the s: the descendants .... Ezr 2:41
male and female s they had with .... Ezr 2:65
Levites, s, gatekeepers, ... Ezr 2:70
Levites, s, gatekeepers, ... Ezr 7:7
Levites, s, gatekeepers, ... Ezr 7:24
Among the s: Eliashib. Among the........... Ezr 10:24
the gatekeepers, s, and Levites .... Ne 7:1
These are the s: the descendants .... Ne 7:44
245 male and female s with them. .... Ne 7:67
gatekeepers, the s, the Temple .... Ne 7:73
gatekeepers, s, Temple servants,.............. Ne 10:28
the gatekeepers, and s stay. .... Ne 10:39
who were the s responsible for .... Ne 11:22
The s were under the king's .... Ne 11:23
together s from all around .... Ne 12:28
The s had built villages for .... Ne 12:29
The s and gatekeepers also did .... Ne 12:45
a leader of the s and of the..................... Ne 12:46
to the s and gatekeepers .... Ne 12:47
to the Levites, s, and .... Ne 13:5
the Levites and s who served had .... Ne 13:10
the Levites and s and put them .... Ne 13:11
The s are in front and the .... Ps 68:25
male and female s and all the................. Ec 2:8

SINGING

away with joy and s and with the .... Ge 31:27
is the sound of s that I hear." .... Ex 32:18
they were s and playing lyres 1Ch 13:8
Kenaniah was in charge of the s, ... 1Ch 15:22
the man in charge of the s, ... 1Ch 15:27
the job of s praises to the LORD.............. 1Ch 16:7
with much joy and s as David had 2Ch 23:18
the s to the LORD also began. 2Ch 29:27
with harps and the sound of s. .... Ps 98:5
come before him with s. .... Ps 100:2
joy, his chosen ones with s...................... Ps 105:43
seeds will return s and carrying .... Ps 126:6
S songs to someone who is sad is .... Pr 25:20
wake up when a bird starts s,.................. Ec 12:4
but you will barely hear s. .... Ec 12:4
Start s and shout for joy........................ Is 54:1
They will begin s a funeral song.............. Eze 26:17
After s a hymn, they went out to .... Mt 26:30
After s a hymn, they went out to .... Mk 14:26
praying and s songs to God as .... Ac 16:25
Start s and shout for joy........................ Gal 4:27
s and making music in your .... Eph 5:19
instruct each other by s psalms, ... Col 3:16

SINGLE

not lose even a s hair from his 1Ki 1:52
It was to happen on a s day—.................. Est 3:13
anything good. Not a s person. .... Ps 53:3
to you suddenly, in a s day..................... Is 47:9
dies, it remains only a s seed................... Jn 12:24
he sold all that for a s meal. .... Heb 12:16
having been made from a s pearl. .... Rev 21:21

SINGS

Everything shouts and s for joy. .... Ps 65:13
you and s praises to you. .... Ps 66:4
than a singer who s love songs .... Eze 33:32
So he rejoices and s for joy. .... Hab 1:15

SINITES

Hivites, Arkites, S, ... Ge 10:17
Hivites, Arkites, S, ... 1Ch 1:15

SINK

the mud, and do not let me s. .... Ps 69:14
way Babylon will s and will not .... Je 51:64
he became afraid and began to s. .... Mt 14:30

SINKING

I'm s down into the mud, and .... Ps 69:2
so full that they were almost s. .... Lk 5:7

SINLESS

He is holy, s, pure, not .... Heb 7:26

SINNED

wrong and have s and done evil .... Ge 50:17
told them, "This time I have s. .... Ex 9:27
had stopped, he s again, and he .... Ex 9:34
I have s against the LORD your .... Ex 10:16
then they got up and s sexually. .... Ex 32:6
terribly these people have s! .... Ex 32:31
things, he must tell how he s. .... Le 5:5
the person s without knowing .... Le 5:18
They s because they showed the.............. Le 20:18
against me and s against me, ... Le 26:40
jealousy and suspects she has s— .... Nu 5:14
and if she has s against her .... Nu 5:27
But if the woman has not s, ... Nu 5:28
had s because they were near................... Nu 6:11
mountains, saying, "We have s. .... Nu 14:40
the person who s accidentally. .... Nu 15:28
Only one man has really s." .... Nu 16:22
these men who s and lost their .... Nu 16:38
We s when we grumbled at you and .... Nu 21:7
angel of the LORD, "I have s; .... Nu 22:34
because the people s at Peor."................... Nu 25:18
people who had s against the .... Nu 32:23
We have s against the LORD, ... Dt 1:41
I saw you had s against the LORD .... Dt 9:16
You had s by doing what the LORD .... Dt 9:18
You both s against me at the .... Dt 32:51
The Israelites have s; .... Jos 7:11
I have s against the LORD, ... Jos 7:20
Israelites again s and worshiped .... Jdg 2:19
LORD, "We have s against you. .... Jdg 10:10
said to the LORD, "We have s. .... Jdg 10:15
have not s against you, but you .... Jdg 11:27
"We have s against the LORD." 1Sa 7:6
the LORD and said, 'We have s. 1Sa 12:10
Saul said, "You have s! 1Sa 14:33
Saul said to Samuel, "I have s. 1Sa 15:24
Saul answered, "I have s. 1Sa 15:30
Then Saul said, "I have s. 1Sa 26:21
"I have s against the LORD." 2Sa 12:13
If I have s, he can put me to 2Sa 14:32
know I have s. That is why I am 2Sa 19:20
I have s greatly by what I have 2Sa 24:10
am the one who s and did wrong. 2Sa 24:17
prisoners, saying, 'We have s.................. 1Ki 8:47
way the family of Jeroboam s, ... 1Ki 13:34
Jeroboam s, and then he made the........... 1Ki 14:16
time when David s against Uriah 1Ki 15:5
and Nadab s in the same way as 1Ki 15:26
Jeroboam had s very much and had 1Ki 15:30
and Baasha s in the same way as 1Ki 15:34
and his son Elah s and led the 1Ki 16:13
because he had s by doing what 1Ki 16:19
and Zimri s in the same way as 1Ki 16:19

S

and Omri **s** in the same way as 1Ki 16:26
s in the same ways as Jeroboam............... 1Ki 16:31
Ahab **s** terribly by worshiping 1Ki 21:26
Israelites had **s** against the 2Ki 17:7
But they **s** against the God that 1Ch 5:25
I have **s** greatly by what I have 1Ch 21:8
am the one who **s** and did wrong. 1Ch 21:17
prisoners, saying, 'We have **s**................... 2Ch 6:37
people who have **s** against you. 2Ch 6:39
you also have **s** against the LORD 2Ch 28:10
Instead, Amon **s** even more. 2Ch 33:23
or two, because we have **s** badly. .... Ezr 10:13
family and I have **s** against you. .... Ne 1:6
but they **s** against your laws. .... Ne 9:29
may have **s** and cursed God .... Job 1:5
If I have **s**, what have I done to .... Job 7:20
Your children **s** against God, ... Job 8:4
If I **s**, you would watch me and .... Job 10:14
Even if I have **s**, it is my worry .... Job 19:4
'I **s** and twisted what was right, ... Job 33:27
even though I have not **s**.' .... Job 34:6
that they have **s** in their pride. .... Job 36:9
I have not **s** with my mouth. .... Ps 17:3
proud as much as they have **s**. .... Ps 31:23
because I have **s** against you." .... Ps 41:4
the only one I have **s** against; .... Ps 51:4
but I have not **s** or done wrong, ... Ps 59:3
We have **s** just as our ancestors .... Ps 106:6
silver, which you **s** by making. .... Is 31:7
because we **s** against him. .... Is 42:24
first father **s**, and your leaders .... Is 43:27
forgiveness for those who **s**." .... Is 53:12
But you were angry because we **s**. .... Is 64:5
of the people who **s** against me. .... Is 66:24
because you say, 'I have not **s**.' .... Je 2:35
We have **s** against the LORD our .... Je 3:25
people of Judah have **s** greatly. .... Je 5:6
We have **s** against the LORD, ... Je 8:14
because my people have **s**. .... Je 9:7
we have **s** against you. .... Je 14:7
We have **s** against you. .... Je 14:20
of Judah have **s** throughout .... Je 15:13
because you **s** by worshiping .... Je 17:3
They **s** against me, but I will .... Je 33:8
people of Judah **s** against the .... Je 40:3
You **s** against the LORD. .... Je 44:23
Those people **s** against the LORD, ... Je 50:7
Babylon has **s** against the LORD. .... Je 50:14
Jerusalem **s** terribly, so she has .... La 1:8
We have **s** and turned against .... La 3:42
her prophets **s** and her priests .... La 4:13
Our ancestors **s** against you, ... La 5:7
How terrible it is because we **s**. .... La 5:16
ancestors have **s** against me .... Eze 2:3
They have **s**, so they will die .... Eze 18:24
learned to be cruel, and you **s**. .... Eze 28:16
for anyone who has **s** by accident .... Eze 45:20
But we have **s** and done wrong. .... Da 9:5
because we have **s** against you. .... Da 9:8
God, because we **s** against you. .... Da 9:11
we have **s** and have done wrong. .... Da 9:15
You have **s** very much, and your............... Hos 9:7
you have **s** since the time of .... Hos 10:9
But they **s** by worshiping Baal, ... Hos 13:1
of Israel how they have **s**. .... Mic 3:8
I **s** against the LORD, so he was .... Mic 7:9
they have **s** against the LORD.................. Zph 1:17
forgiven those who **s** against us............... Mt 6:12
saying, "I **s**; I handed over to .... Mt 27:4
s against God and against you. .... Lk 15:18
I have **s** against God and against .... Lk 15:21
here who has never **s** can throw .... Jn 8:7
Everyone has **s** and fallen short .... Rm 3:23

must die—because everyone **s**. .... Rm 5:12
those who had not **s** by breaking .... Rm 5:14
After Adam **s** once, he was judged............ Rm 5:16
man **s**, and so death ruled all .... Rm 5:17
decide to marry, you have not **s**. 1Co 7:28
decides to marry, she has not **s**. 1Co 7:28
they got up and **s** sexually." 1Co 10:7
those who have **s** because they 2Co 12:21
a warning to those who had **s**. 2Co 13:2
He was angry with those who **s**,............... Heb 3:17
the person has **s**, the sins will............... Jam 5:15
He had never **s**, and he had never 1Pe 2:22
When angels **s**, God did not let 2Pe 2:4
say we have not **s**, we make God 1Jn 1:10
of the earth **s** sexually with her .... Rev 17:2
the earth have **s** sexually with .... Rev 18:3
of the earth who **s** sexually with............... Rev 18:9

SINNER

but doing evil ruins the **s**. .... Pr 13:6
but a **s** will be caught by them. .... Ec 7:26
Though a **s** might do a hundred .... Ec 8:12
a good person as happen to a **s**, ... Ec 9:2
but one **s** can destroy much good. .... Ec 9:18
will be thought of as a **s**........................ Is 65:20
the woman touching him is a **s**!" .... Lk 7:39
heaven over one **s** who changes .... Lk 15:7
of God when one **s** changes his .... Lk 15:10
God, have mercy on me, a **s**.' .... Lk 18:13
"Jesus is staying with a **s**!" .... Lk 19:7
A man who is a **s** can't do .... Jn 9:16
We know that this man is a **s**." .... Jn 9:24
I don't know if he is a **s**. .... Jn 9:25
So why am I judged a **s**?" .... Rm 3:7
was tricked and became a **s**. 1Ti 2:14
who brings a **s** back from the .... Jam 5:20
and the **s** will surely be lost! 1Pe 4:18
and God will give the **s** life. 1Jn 5:16

SINNER'S

but a **s** wealth is stored up for .... Pr 13:22
will save that **s** soul from death .... Jam 5:20

SINNERS

grave quickly takes away the **s**. .... Job 24:19
don't go where **s** go, who don't .... Ps 1:1
S will not worship with God's................... Ps 1:5
he points to the right way. .... Ps 25:8
me with those **s** or take my life .... Ps 26:9
But **s** will be destroyed; .... Ps 37:38
and **s** will turn back to you. .... Ps 51:13
Let **s** be destroyed from the .... Ps 104:35
if **s** try to lead you into sin,..................... Pr 1:10
But **s** will fall into their own .... Pr 1:18
wicked and the **s** will be .... Pr 11:31
Trouble always comes to **s**, ... Pr 13:21
Don't envy **s**, but always respect .... Pr 23:17
But **s** will get only the work of .... Ec 2:26
But **s** and those who turn against .... Is 1:28
land and the **s** who live in it. .... Is 13:9
The **s** in Jerusalem are afraid; .... Is 33:14
will die because they were **s**, ... Eze 33:8
will die because they were **s**. .... Eze 33:9
All the **s** among my people will .... Am 9:10
collectors and "**s**" came and ate .... Mt 9:10
eat with tax collectors and **s**?" .... Mt 9:11
good people but to invite **s**." .... Mt 9:13
friend of tax collectors and **s**.'............... Mt 11:19
collectors and "**s**" were eating .... Mk 2:15
with the tax collectors and "**s**," .... Mk 2:16
eat with tax collectors and **s**?" .... Mk 2:16
good people but to invite **s**." .... Mk 2:17
with tax collectors and **s**?" .... Lk 5:30
people but **s** to change their .... Lk 5:32
s love the people who love them. .... Lk 6:32

should you get? Even **s** do that! .... Lk 6:33
Even **s** lend to other sinners so .... Lk 6:34
lend to other **s** so that they can .... Lk 6:34
friend of tax collectors and s!' .... Lk 7:34
collectors and **s** all came to.................... Lk 15:1
man welcomes **s** and even eats .... Lk 15:2
that God does not listen to **s**, ... Jn 9:31
law and who are **s** will be lost, ... Rm 2:12
the law and are **s** will be judged............... Rm 2:12
for us while we were still **s**. .... Rm 5:8
God, and many became **s**. .... Rm 5:19
were not born as non-Jewish "s," .... Gal 2:15
it became clear that we are **s**, ... Gal 2:17
came into the world to save **s**, ... 1Ti 1:15
the worst of all **s**, Christ Jesus 1Ti 1:16
influenced by **s**, and he is .... Heb 7:26
You **s**, clean sin out of your.................... Jam 4:8
punish the **s** who are against .... Jud 1:15

SINNING
and were always **s** against the .... Ge 13:13
that is really **s** against the .... Nu 5:6
they didn't know they were **s**.................. Nu 15:25
the men began **s** sexually with .... Nu 25:1
you will be **s** against the LORD; .... Nu 32:23
but you are **s** against me by .... Jdg 11:27
would be **s** against the LORD. 1Sa 12:23
The men are **s** against the LORD. 1Sa 14:33
they will stop **s** when you make 1Ki 8:35
secretly **s** against the LORD 2Ki 17:9
they will stop **s** when you make 2Ch 6:26
I don't gain anything by not **s**.' .... Job 35:3
But they kept on **s**; they did not .... Ps 78:32
s and rejecting the LORD. .... Is 59:13
They have become tired from **s**. .... Je 9:5
so the people don't stop **s**. .... Je 23:14
stop all your **s** so sin will not .... Eze 18:30
' they may stop **s** and do what is............... Eze 33:14
Stop **s** and do what is right. .... Da 4:27
We have not stopped **s**. .... Da 9:13
they have become altars for **s**. .... Hos 8:11
people there have continued **s**. .... Hos 10:9
still keep on **s** more and more. .... Hos 13:2
they kept many people from **s**. .... Mal 2:6
change their lives and stop **s**. .... Mt 11:20
its people would have stopped **s**, ... Mt 11:21
and if he is sorry and stops **s**,............... Lk 17:3
Stop **s** so that something worse .... Jn 5:14
should continue **s** so that God .... Rm 6:1
you are also **s** against Christ. 1Co 8:12
be guilty of **s** against the body 1Co 11:27
way of thinking and stop **s**...................... 1Co 15:34
sexual **s**, doing evil, letting .... Col 3:5
who continue **s** that they are 1Ti 5:20
decide to go on **s** after we have .... Heb 10:26
than another, you are **s**. .... Jam 2:9
to do, but does not do it, is **s**. .... Jam 4:17
talk, told Balaam he was **s**. 2Pe 2:16
in Christ does not go on **s**. 1Jn 3:6
who goes on **s** has never really 1Jn 3:8
The devil has been **s** since the 1Jn 3:8
children do not continue **s**, ... 1Jn 3:9
They are not able to go on **s**, ... 1Jn 3:9
sees a brother or sister **s**....................... 1Jn 5:16

SINS
to remove their **s** and to make .... Ex 29:33
to remove the **s** of Aaron and his .... Ex 29:36
the animal offered to remove **s**. .... Ex 30:10
so your **s** will be removed.".................... Ex 32:30
'When a person **s** by accident and .... Le 4:2
appointed priest **s** so that he .... Le 4:3
nation of Israel **s** accidentally................. Le 4:13
removes the **s** of the people so .... Le 4:20

If a ruler **s** by accident and .... Le 4:22
in the community **s** by accident .... Le 4:27
person's **s** so he will belong .... Le 4:35
the person's **s** so he will belong .... Le 5:13
accidentally **s** and does .... Le 5:15
If a person **s** and does something .... Le 5:17
LORD by doing one of these **s**: .... Le 6:2
him for the **s** that made him .... Le 6:7
to remove **s** will get the meat .... Le 7:7
to remove your **s** so you will .... Le 8:34
remove your **s** and the people's .... Le 9:7
and the people's **s** so you will.................. Le 9:7
to remove their **s** for them so .... Le 9:7
to remove their **s** so they will .... Le 10:17
to remove **s** from him and his .... Le 16:6
to remove the **s** from him and his .... Le 16:11
be clean from the **s** and crimes .... Le 16:16
acts to remove **s** from himself, ... Le 16:17
from all the **s** of the Israelites .... Le 16:19
over it all the **s** and crimes of .... Le 16:21
put the people's **s** on the goat's .... Le 16:21
all the people's **s** to a lonely .... Le 16:22
to remove **s** from himself and the .... Le 16:24
to remove **s**, into the desert.................... Le 16:26
All your **s** will be removed...................... Le 16:30
also remove the **s** of the priests .... Le 16:33
for removing the **s** of the .... Le 16:34
to remove your **s** so you will .... Le 17:11
is the blood that removes the **s**, ... Le 17:11
because they did these **s**, ... Le 18:24
and I punished it for its **s**, ... Le 18:25
not do any of these hateful **s**. .... Le 18:26
these hateful **s** must be cut off .... Le 18:29
these hateful **s** that were done .... Le 18:30
to remove the **s** of the man so he .... Le 19:22
Because they did all these **s**, ... Le 20:23
you seven times more for your **s**. .... Le 26:18
you seven more times for your **s**. .... Le 26:24
you seven more times for your **s**. .... Le 26:28
countries because of their **s**. .... Le 26:39
because of their ancestors' **s**. .... Le 26:39
confess their **s** and the sins.................... Le 26:40
sins and the **s** of their .... Le 26:40
the punishment for their **s**. .... Le 26:43
remove the **s** of the Levites so .... Nu 8:12
the Israelites' **s** so they will.................... Nu 8:19
removed their **s** so they would be .... Nu 8:21
you will suffer for your **s**—..................... Nu 14:34
one person **s** without meaning .... Nu 15:27
for everyone who **s** accidentally— .... Nu 15:29
But anyone who **s** on purpose is .... Nu 15:30
destroyed because of their **s**.".................. Nu 16:26
for any **s** against it. .... Nu 18:23
He removed the **s** of the .... Nu 25:13
to remove your **s** so you will .... Nu 28:22
to remove your **s** so you will .... Nu 28:30
to remove your **s** so you will .... Nu 29:5
offering which removes your **s**, ... Nu 29:11
to remove our **s** so we will .... Nu 31:50
added to all our **s** the evil of 1Sa 12:19
When he **s**, I will use other 2Sa 7:14
Forgive the **s** of your people 1Ki 8:34
and forgive the **s** of your....................... 1Ki 8:36
Everyone **s**, so your people will 1Ki 8:46
sorry for their **s** when they are 1Ki 8:47
of all their **s** and for turning 1Ki 8:50
s made the LORD very angry,.................. 1Ki 14:22
did all the same **s** his father 1Ki 15:3
Their **s** have made me angry, ... 1Ki 16:2
did not stop doing these same **s**............... 2Ki 3:3
stop doing the **s** Jeroboam son 2Ki 10:29
doing the same **s** Jeroboam had 2Ki 10:31
did the same **s** Jeroboam son of 2Ki 13:2

S

did not stop doing these same **s**............... 2Ki 13:2
doing the same **s** that the family............... 2Ki 13:6
they continued doing those **s**. 2Ki 13:6
doing the same **s** Jeroboam son 2Ki 13:11
Each must die for his own **s**." 2Ki 14:6
did not stop doing the same **s**. 2Ki 14:24
did not stop doing the same **s**. 2Ki 15:9
did not stop doing the same **s**. 2Ki 15:18
did not stop doing the same **s**. 2Ki 15:24
did not stop doing the same **s**. 2Ki 15:28
same hateful **s** as the nations 2Ki 16:3
to do all the **s** Jeroboam did. 2Ki 17:22
They did not stop doing these **s** 2Ki 17:22
of all the **s** of Manasseh. 2Ki 24:3
LORD would not forgive these **s**. 2Ki 24:4
the Israelites' **s** so they could 1Ch 6:49
the people's **s** were removed. 1Ch 28:11
and forgive the **s** of your 2Ch 6:27
Everyone **s**, so your people will 2Ch 6:36
sorry for their **s** when they are 2Ch 6:37
Each must die for his own **s**." 2Ch 25:4
same hateful **s** as the nations 2Ch 28:3
remove the **s** of the Israelites 2Ch 29:24
pity for him, his **s**, his 2Ch 33:19
to forgive the **s** of all Israel, ... Ezr 6:17
because our **s** are so many. .... Ezr 9:6
Because of our **s**, we, our kings, ... Ezr 9:7
I confess the **s** we Israelites .... Ne 1:6
take away their **s** so that you .... Ne 4:5
confessed their **s** and their .... Ne 9:2
sins and their ancestors' **s**. .... Ne 9:2
confessed their **s** and worshiped............... Ne 9:3
put over us because of our **s**. .... Ne 9:37
remove the **s** of the Israelites .... Ne 10:33
my wrongs and forgive my **s**? .... Job 7:21
he punished them for their **s**. .... Job 8:4
evil things and **s** have I done? .... Job 13:23
make me suffer for my boyhood **s**. .... Job 13:26
limits and your **s** have no end. .... Job 22:5
have been **s** to be punished, ... Job 31:28
for his **s** and so he may .... Job 33:30
even if your **s** are many, they do............... Job 35:6
away because their **s** are many; .... Ps 5:10
Forgive me for my secret **s**. .... Ps 19:12
Keep me from the **s** of pride; .... Ps 19:13
innocent of the greatest of **s**. .... Ps 19:13
remember the **s** and wrong things .... Ps 25:7
name, LORD, forgive my many **s**. .... Ps 25:11
and take away all my **s**. .... Ps 25:18
the person whose **s** are forgiven, ... Ps 32:1
I confessed my **s** to you and .... Ps 32:5
will confess my **s** to the LORD," .... Ps 32:5
me from all my **s**. Don't let .... Ps 39:8
and punish people for their **s**; .... Ps 39:11
and sacrifices to take away **s**. .... Ps 40:6
My **s** have caught me so that I .... Ps 40:12
I have more **s** than hairs on my .... Ps 40:12
face from my **s** and wipe out all .... Ps 51:9
us, but you forgive our **s**. .... Ps 65:3
He forgave their **s** and did not .... Ps 78:38
Don't punish us for our past **s**. .... Ps 79:8
and forgive our **s** so people will .... Ps 79:9
people and covered their **s**. .... Ps 85:2
I will punish their **s** with a rod .... Ps 89:32
you clearly see our secret **s**. .... Ps 90:8
for their **s** and will destroy .... Ps 94:23
forgives all my **s** and heals all .... Ps 103:3
us as our **s** should be punished .... Ps 103:10
has taken our **s** away from us as .... Ps 103:12
people became unholy by their **s**; .... Ps 106:39
don't let the **s** of his mother be .... Ps 109:14
LORD, always remember their **s**. .... Ps 109:15
punished people for all their **s**, ... Ps 130:3

save Israel from all their **s**. .... Ps 130:8
ropes of his **s** will tie him up .... Pr 5:22
If you hide your **s**, you will not .... Pr 28:13
with a quick temper **s** a lot. .... Pr 29:22
always does good and never **s**. .... Ec 7:20
Though your **s** are like scarlet, ... Is 1:18
Though your **s** are deep red, ... Is 1:18
their guilt and **s** behind them as .... Is 5:18
and wicked people for their **s**. .... Is 13:11
people of the world for their **s**. .... Is 26:21
this is how its **s** will be taken .... Is 27:9
more and more **s** to themselves. .... Is 30:1
will have their **s** forgiven. .... Is 33:24
me die but threw my **s** far away............... Is 38:17
that they have paid for their **s**, ... Is 40:2
me down with your many **s**; .... Is 43:24
the One who erases all your **s**, ... Is 43:25
I will not remember your **s**. .... Is 43:25
swept away your **s** like a big .... Is 44:22
removed your **s** like a cloud that .... Is 44:22
punished for the **s** of my people. .... Is 53:8
he will carry away their **s**. .... Is 53:11
carried away the **s** of many............... Is 53:12
family of Jacob about their **s**. .... Is 58:1
Your **s** cause him to turn away .... Is 59:2
our **s** show we are wrong. .... Is 59:12
and our **s**, like the wind, ... Is 64:6
and have let our **s** destroy us. .... Is 64:7
don't remember our **s** forever. .... Is 64:9
you for your **s** and your .... Is 65:7
sins and your ancestors' **s**," .... Is 65:7
Your **s** have kept you from .... Je 5:25
know how to blush about their **s**. .... Je 6:15
know how to blush about their **s**. .... Je 8:12
to the same s their ancestors .... Je 11:10
happened because of your many **s**............... Je 13:22
Because of your **s**, your skirt .... Je 13:22
that we suffer because of our **s**. .... Je 14:7
will punish them for their **s**." .... Je 14:10
twice for every one of their **s**, ... Je 16:18
Their **s** were cut with a hard .... Je 17:1
s were cut into the corners .... Je 17:1
or erase their **s** from your mind. .... Je 18:23
great and your **s** were so many. .... Je 30:14
guilt, because of your many **s**. .... Je 30:15
not remember their **s** anymore."............... Je 31:34
children for their parents' **s**. .... Je 32:18
them for the **s** and the evil .... Je 36:3
will try to find Judah's **s**,............... Je 50:20
sins, but no **s** will be found, ... Je 50:20
and I will forgive their **s**............... Je 50:20
killed because of Babylon's **s**............... Je 51:6
is punishing her for her many **s**. .... La 1:5
dirty by her **s** and did not think .... La 1:9
has noticed my **s**; they are tied .... La 1:14
done to me because of all my **s**. .... La 1:22
not point out your **s** to keep you............... La 2:14
when he is punished for his **s**. .... La 3:39
LORD will punish the **s** of Edom; .... La 4:22
we suffer because of their **s**. .... La 5:7
Because of their **s**, they will .... Eze 7:13
anymore with all their **s**............... Eze 14:11
your sexual **s** were not enough .... Eze 16:20
your hateful acts and sexual **s**, ... Eze 16:22
your sexual **s** became worse and .... Eze 16:23
Your sexual **s** became even worse, ... Eze 16:26
many more sexual **s** in Babylonia, ... Eze 16:29
in your sexual **s** with them as............... Eze 16:36
put an end to your sexual **s**, ... Eze 16:41
you add sexual **s** to all your .... Eze 16:43
did not do half the **s** you do; .... Eze 16:51
Your **s** were even more terrible .... Eze 16:52
to your sisters in their **s**. .... Eze 16:54

your terrible **s** and for actions .... Eze 16:58
The person who **s** is the one who .... Eze 18:4
who has seen all his father's **s,** .... Eze 18:14
The person who **s** is the one who .... Eze 18:20
doing all the **s** they have done .... Eze 18:21
Their **s** will be forgotten............ Eze 18:22
will die because of their **s.** .... Eze 18:24
doing all the **s** they had done,............ Eze 18:28
rid of all the **s** you have done,............ Eze 18:31
s are seen in all the things .... Eze 21:24
and they take part in sexual **s.** .... Eze 22:9
things you did. Your sexual **s** .... Eze 23:29
be punished for your sexual **s.**" .... Eze 23:35
their sexual **s** with her. .... Eze 23:43
an end to sexual **s** in the land. .... Eze 23:48
do the sexual **s** you have done. .... Eze 23:48
for your sexual **s** and the sin .... Eze 23:49
rot away in your **s** and groan to .... Eze 24:23
your many **s** and dishonest............ Eze 28:18
and **s** are hurting us. .... Eze 33:10
be punished for any of their **s.** .... Eze 33:16
because of your **s** and for .... Eze 36:31
I cleanse you from all your **s:** .... Eze 36:33
which I hate, or by their **s.** .... Eze 37:23
their uncleanness and their **s,** .... Eze 39:24
their sexual **s** or with the dead .... Eze 43:7
their sexual **s** and take the dead .... Eze 43:9
they will be ashamed of their **s.** .... Eze 43:10
to remove **s** so you will belong .... Eze 45:15
to pay for the **s** of Israel. .... Eze 45:17
and told him about all of our **s.** .... Da 9:4
Because of our **s** and the evil .... Da 9:16
confessing my **s** and the sins of .... Da 9:20
my sins and the **s** of the people .... Da 9:20
for their **s** of adultery. .... Hos 4:14
he will punish them for their **s.** .... Hos 8:13
has come, the time to pay for **s.** .... Hos 9:7
and he will punish their **s.** .... Hos 9:9
the places where Israel **s.** .... Hos 10:8
be punished for their double **s.** .... Hos 10:10
because of the **s** they have done. .... Hos 12:8
The **s** of Israel are on record, ... Hos 13:12
because your **s** have made you .... Hos 14:1
will punish you for all your **s.**" .... Am 3:2
I punish Israel for their **s,** .... Am 3:14
many crimes, your terrible **s.** .... Am 5:12
not overlook their **s** anymore............ Am 8:2
because of the **s** of the nation .... Mic 1:5
Jerusalem's **s** started in you; .... Mic 1:13
Israel's **s** were found in you. .... Mic 1:13
ruining you because of your **s.** .... Mic 6:13
look at the **s** of your people .... Mic 7:18
you will conquer our **s.** .... Mic 7:19
away all our **s** into the deepest .... Mic 7:19
the people's **s** in all the land. .... Zch 5:6
save his people from their **s.**" .... Mt 1:21
confessed their **s,** and he............ Mt 3:6
us for our **s,** just as we have .... Mt 6:12
you forgive others for their **s,** .... Mt 6:14
also forgive you for your **s.** .... Mt 6:14
heaven will not forgive your **s.** .... Mt 6:15
young man. Your **s** are forgiven." .... Mt 9:2
say, 'Your **s** are forgiven,' or .... Mt 9:5
on earth to forgive **s.**" .... Mt 9:6
sexual **s,** stealing, lying .... Mt 15:19
fellow believer **s** against you, ... Mt 18:15
my fellow believer **s** against me,............ Mt 18:21
out for many to forgive their **s.** .... Mt 26:28
lives for the forgiveness of **s.** .... Mk 1:4
confessed their **s** and were .... Mk 1:5
Young man, your **s** are forgiven." .... Mk 2:5
Only God can forgive **s.**"............ Mk 2:7
man, 'Your **s** are forgiven,' or .... Mk 2:9

on earth to forgive **s.**" .... Mk 2:10
all **s** that people do and all the .... Mk 3:28
thoughts, sexual **s,** stealing, ... Mk 7:21
heaven will also forgive your **s.** .... Mk 11:25
heaven will not forgive your **s.** .... Mk 11:26
by having their **s** forgiven. .... Lk 1:77
lives for the forgiveness of **s.** .... Lk 3:3
Friend, your **s** are forgiven." .... Lk 5:20
Only God can forgive **s.**"............ Lk 5:21
say, 'Your **s** are forgiven,' or .... Lk 5:23
on earth to forgive **s.**" .... Lk 5:24
that her many **s** are forgiven, ... Lk 7:47
to her, "Your **s** are forgiven." .... Lk 7:48
is this who even forgives **s?**" .... Lk 7:49
you are saved from your **s.** .... Lk 7:50
Forgive us for our **s,** because we............ Lk 11:4
another follower **s,** warn him, ... Lk 17:3
If he **s** against you seven times .... Lk 17:4
forgiveness of **s** would be .... Lk 24:47
but you will die in your **s.** .... Jn 8:21
that you would die in your **s.** .... Jn 8:24
will die in your **s** if you don't .... Jn 8:24
If you forgive anyone his **s,**............ Jn 20:23
for the forgiveness of your **s.** .... Ac 2:38
and he will forgive your **s.** .... Ac 3:19
lives and have their **s** forgiven. .... Ac 5:31
of their **s** through Jesus' .... Ac 10:43
and wash your **s** away, trusting .... Ac 22:16
Then their **s** can be forgiven, ... Ac 26:18
in our place to take away our **s.** .... Rm 3:25
not punish people for their **s.** .... Rm 3:25
are they whose **s** are forgiven, ... Rm 4:7
was given to die for our **s,** .... Rm 4:25
free gift came after many **s,** .... Rm 5:16
why does God blame us for our **s?** .... Rm 9:19
when I take away their **s.**" .... Rm 11:27
be no sexual **s** of any kind, ... Rm 13:13
must not take part in sexual **s,** 1Co 10:8
of them died because of their **s.** 1Co 10:8
that Christ died for our **s,** 1Co 15:3
you are still guilty of your **s.** 1Co 15:17
hold the world guilty of its **s.** 2Co 5:19
their sexual **s** and the shameful 2Co 12:21
himself for our **s** to free us .... Gal 1:4
pure, taking part in sexual **s,** .... Gal 5:19
and so we have forgiveness of **s.** .... Eph 1:7
because of your **s** and the things .... Eph 2:1
and of God who **s** sexually,............ Eph 5:5
Son paid for our **s,** and in him .... Col 1:14
because of your **s** and because .... Col 2:13
and he forgave all our **s.** .... Col 2:13
increasing their **s** to the limit............ 1Th 2:16
and to stay away from sexual **s.** 1Th 4:3
who take part in sexual **s,** 1Ti 1:10
don't share in the **s** of others. 1Ti 5:22
The **s** of some people are easy to 1Ti 5:24
the **s** of others are seen only 1Ti 5:24
their own **s** prove them wrong. .... Tit 3:11
made people clean from their **s,** .... Heb 1:3
place to take away their **s.** .... Heb 2:17
gifts and sacrifices for **s.**............ Heb 5:1
for his own **s** and also for the .... Heb 5:3
also for the **s** of the people............ Heb 5:3
for their own **s,** and then for .... Heb 7:27
then for the **s** of the people. .... Heb 7:27
not remember their **s** anymore."............ Heb 8:12
himself and for **s** the people did .... Heb 9:7
and **s** cannot be forgiven without .... Heb 9:22
take away the **s** of many people............ Heb 9:28
them of their **s** every year, ... Heb 10:3
bulls and goats to take away **s.** .... Heb 10:4
and offerings to take away **s.** .... Heb 10:6
and offerings to take away **s.**" .... Heb 10:8

S

can never take away **s**. .... Heb 10:11
offered one sacrifice for **s**, ... Heb 10:12
Their **s** and the evil things they .... Heb 10:17
more need for a sacrifice for **s**. .... Heb 10:18
no longer any sacrifice for **s**. .... Heb 10:26
those who take part in sexual **s**. .... Heb 13:4
he offers this blood for **s**. .... Heb 13:11
sinned, the **s** will be forgiven................... Jam 5:15
Confess your **s** to each other and .... Jam 5:16
will cause many **s** to be forgiven .... Jam 5:20
Christ carried our **s** in his body 1Pe 2:24
himself suffered for **s** once...................... 1Pe 3:18
You were guilty of sexual **s**, ... 1Pe 4:3
forgive each other for many **s**. 1Pe 4:8
was made clean from his past **s**............... 2Pe 1:9
we confess our **s**, he will........................ 1Jn 1:9
forgive our **s**, because we can 1Jn 1:9
in our place to take away our **s**, ... 1Jn 2:2
and not only our **s** but the sins 1Jn 2:2
sins but the **s** of all people. 1Jn 2:2
because your **s** are forgiven 1Jn 2:12
The person who **s** breaks God's 1Jn 3:4
to take away **s** and that there is 1Jn 3:5
in our place to take away our **s**. 1Jn 4:10
free from our **s** with the blood .... Rev 1:5
and by taking part in sexual **s**. .... Rev 2:14
part in sexual **s** and to eat food .... Rev 2:20
from their sexual **s** or stealing. .... Rev 9:21
God remembered the **s** of Babylon .... Rev 16:19
you will not share in her **s**, ... Rev 18:4
Her **s** have piled up as high as .... Rev 18:5

SIPHMOTH
Aroer, **S**, Eshtemoa, ... 1Sa 30:28

SIPPAI
the Hushathite killed **S**, ... 1Ch 20:4

SIR
and said, "**S**, if you think well .... Ge 18:3
to one of them, "**S**, please don't .... Ge 19:18
S, you are a great leader among.............. Ge 23:6
No, **s**. I will give you the land .... Ge 23:11
S, the land is worth ten pounds .... Ge 23:15
Rebekah said, "Drink, **s**." .... Ge 24:18
Laban said, "**S**, you are welcome .... Ge 24:31
Gideon said, "**S**, if the LORD is .... Jdg 6:13
I can continue to please you, **s**. .... Ru 2:13
answered, "No, **s**, I have not 1Sa 1:15
as you live, **s**, I am the same 1Sa 1:26
I asked, "What are these, **s**?" .... Zch 1:9
with me, "**S**, what are these? .... Zch 4:4
what they are?" "No, **s**," I said. .... Zch 4:5
what they are?" "No, **s**," I said. .... Zch 4:13
with me, "What are these, **s**?" .... Zch 6:4
answered, 'Yes, **s**, I will go and .... Mt 21:30
back and say, 'S, sir, open the .... Mt 25:11
and said, 'Sir, **s**, open the door .... Mt 25:11
They said, "We remember that .... Mt 27:63
door and say, 'S, open the door .... Lk 13:25
came and said, 'S, I earned ten .... Lk 19:16
servant said, 'S, I earned five .... Lk 19:18
to the king, 'S, here is your.................... Lk 19:20
They said, 'But **s**, that servant................ Lk 19:25
woman said, "**S**, where will you .... Jn 4:11
said to him, "**S**, give me this .... Jn 4:15
woman said, "**S**, I can see that .... Jn 4:19
officer said, "**S**, come before my.............. Jn 4:49
answered, "**S**, there is no one .... Jn 5:7
people said, "**S**, give us this .... Jn 6:34
She answered, "No one, **s**." .... Jn 8:11
the Son of Man, **s**, so that I can .... Jn 9:36
and said, "**S**, we would like to .... Jn 12:21
him, "Did you take him away, **s**? .... Jn 20:15
I answered, "You know, **s**." .... Rev 7:14

SIRAH
him back from the well of **S**. 2Sa 3:26

SIRION
is called **S** by the Sidonian .... Dt 3:9

SIRS
Lot said, "**S**, please come to my .... Ge 19:2

SISERA
S, who lived in Harosheth .... Jdg 4:2
I will make **S**, the commander of .... Jdg 4:7
I will hand **S** over to you.'"..................... Jdg 4:7
LORD will let a woman defeat **S**." .... Jdg 4:9
When **S** was told that Barak son .... Jdg 4:12
S gathered his nine hundred iron .... Jdg 4:13
day the LORD will hand over **S**. .... Jdg 4:14
the LORD confused **S** and his army .... Jdg 4:15
but **S** left his chariot and ran .... Jdg 4:15
But **S** himself ran away to the................. Jdg 4:17
out to meet **S** and said to him.................. Jdg 4:18
So **S** went into Jael's tent, ... Jdg 4:18
S said to Jael, "I am thirsty. .... Jdg 4:19
a hammer and quietly went to **S**. .... Jdg 4:21
into the ground. And so **S** died. .... Jdg 4:21
came by Jael's tent, chasing **S**. .... Jdg 4:22
tent, and there **S** lay dead, with .... Jdg 4:22
from their paths, they fought **S**. .... Jdg 5:20
S asked for water, but Jael gave .... Jdg 5:25
hammer. She hit **S**! She smashed .... Jdg 5:26
Where **S** sank, there he fell, ... Jdg 5:27
Maybe **S** is taking pieces of dyed .... Jdg 5:30
handed them over as slaves to **S**, ... 1Sa 12:9
Barkos, **S**, Temah, ... Ezr 2:53
Barkos, **S**, Temah, ... Ne 7:55
what you did to **S** and Jabin at .... Ps 83:9

SISERA'S
his men chased **S** chariots and .... Jdg 4:16
swords they killed all of **S** men; .... Jdg 4:16
peg through the side of **S** head .... Jdg 4:21
Kishon River swept **S** men away, ... Jdg 5:21
galloping go **S** mighty horses. .... Jdg 5:22
S mother looked out through the .... Jdg 5:28
'Why is **S** chariot so late in .... Jdg 5:28
and **S** mother says to herself, ... Jdg 5:29

SISMAI
Eleasah was the father of **S**. 1Ch 2:40
S was the father of Shallum. 1Ch 2:40

SISTER
them you are my **s** so that things .... Ge 12:13
And it is true that she is my **s**. .... Ge 20:12
She is my **s**," because he was .... Ge 26:7
had disgraced their **s** Dinah. .... Ge 34:13
Then the baby's **s** asked the .... Ex 2:7
Then Aaron's **s** Miriam, a .... Ex 15:20
has sexual relations with his **s**, ... Dt 27:22
s, my bride, you have thrilled .... Sng 4:9
Open to me, my **s**, my darling, my .... Sng 5:2
have a little **s**, and her breasts .... Sng 8:8
true brother and **s** and mother .... Mt 12:50
Mary and her **s** Martha lived. .... Jn 11:1
I recommend to you our **s** Phoebe, ... Rm 16:1
A brother or **s** in Christ might .... Jam 2:15
of your chosen **s** greet you...................... 2Jn 1:13

SISTER-IN-LAW
your **s** is going back to her own .... Ru 1:15

SISTERS
invited their **s** to eat and drink .... Job 1:4
brothers and came to his house .... Job 42:11
and your **s**, 'you have been .... Hos 2:1
brothers, **s**, father, mother, ... Mt 19:29
brothers, **s**, mother, father, ... Mk 10:29

SIT

them when you **s** at home and walk .... Dt 6:7
them when you **s** at home and walk .... Dt 11:19
S by me at my right side until I .... Ps 110:1
If you **s** down to eat with a .... Pr 23:1
I will **s** on the mountain of the .... Is 14:13
them out like a tent to **s** under. .... Is 40:22
Everyone will **s** under his own .... Mic 4:4
the west and will **s** and eat with .... Mt 8:11
the people to **s** down on the .... Mt 14:19
Son of Man will **s** on his great .... Mt 19:28
of my sons will **s** at your right .... Mt 20:21
choose who will **s** at my right or .... Mt 20:23
S by me at my right side, ... Mt 22:44
south and will **s** down at the .... Lk 13:29
choosing the best places to **s**, ... Lk 14:7
go **s** in a seat that is not .... Lk 14:10
Take your bill, **s** down quickly, ... Lk 16:6
S by me at my right side, ... Ac 2:34
S by me at my right side until I .... Heb 1:13
s here in this good seat." .... Jam 2:3

SITE

moved from one tent **s** to another 1Ch 17:5
of God on the same **s** as before. .... Ezr 2:68

SITHRI

were Mishael, Elzaphan, and **S**. .... Ex 6:22

SITS

the king, who **s** on his throne, ... Ex 11:5
But the one who is in heaven .... Ps 2:4
She **s** at the door of her house .... Pr 9:14
God **s** on his throne above the .... Is 40:22
mountains where the woman **s**. .... Rev 17:9
the prostitute **s**, are peoples, ... Rev 17:15
God, who **s** on the throne. .... Rev 19:4

SITTING

Abraham was **s** at the entrance of .... Ge 18:1
as Lot was **s** near the city gate .... Ge 19:1
I was **s** in my house with the .... Eze 8:1
I saw women **s** and crying for.................. Eze 8:14
a man named Matthew **s** in the tax .... Mt 9:9
the Son of Man **s** at the right .... Mt 26:64
a white robe and **s** on the right .... Mk 16:5
they found Jesus **s** in the Temple .... Lk 2:46
found the man **s** at Jesus' feet, ... Lk 8:35
s on the colt of a donkey." .... Jn 12:15
of the followers **s** next to Jesus .... Jn 13:23
s where Jesus' body had been, ... Jn 20:12
whole house where they were **s**.............. Ac 2:2
he was **s** in his chariot reading .... Ac 8:28
Eutychus was **s** in the window. .... Ac 20:9
where Christ is **s** at the right .... Col 3:1
twenty-four elders **s** on them.................. Rev 4:4

SIVAN

of the third month, which is **S**. .... Est 8:9

SIX

done during **s** days each week, ... Ex 20:9
reason is that in **s** days the .... Ex 20:11
he will serve you for **s** years. .... Ex 21:2
s on one stone and six on the .... Ex 28:10
David and the **s** hundred men with 1Sa 30:9
for seven years and **s** months. 2Sa 2:11
had **s** fingers on each hand and 2Sa 21:20
The throne had **s** steps on it, ... 1Ki 10:19
There are **s** things the LORD .... Pr 6:16
make only **s** gallons of wine, ... Is 5:10
Each creature had **s** wings:...................... Is 6:2
S days later, Jesus took Peter,.................. Mt 17:1
there were **s** stone water jars .... Jn 2:6
These **s** believers here also went .... Ac 11:12
creatures had **s** wings and was .... Rev 4:8

SIXTEEN

There were **s** persons in this .... Ge 46:18
there will be **s** silver bases— .... Ex 26:25
eight frames and **s** silver bases— .... Ex 36:30
There were **s** towns and their .... Jos 15:41
There were **s** towns and their .... Jos 19:22
Jehoash ruled **s** years,............................ 2Ki 13:10
Uzziah was **s** years old. 2Ki 14:21
Uzziah was **s** years old when he.............. 2Ki 15:2
and he ruled **s** years in 2Ki 15:33
and he ruled **s** years in 2Ki 16:2
Shimei had **s** sons and six 1Ch 4:27
s leaders from Eleazar's family 1Ch 24:4
twenty-two sons and **s** daughters. 2Ch 13:21
Uzziah was **s** years old. 2Ch 26:1
Uzziah was **s** years old when he.............. 2Ch 26:3
and he ruled **s** years in 2Ch 27:1
he ruled **s** years in Jerusalem. 2Ch 27:8
and he ruled **s** years in 2Ch 28:1
to be guarded by **s** soldiers. .... Ac 12:4

SIXTEENTH

was Bilgah. The **s** was Immer. 1Ch 24:14
S, twelve men were chosen from 1Ch 25:23
finished on the **s** day of the.................... 2Ch 29:17

SIXTH

came. This was the **s** day. .... Ge 1:31
Elizabeth's **s** month of pregnancy .... Lk 1:26
the Lamb opened the **s** seal, ... Rev 6:12
Then the **s** angel blew his .... Rev 9:13
voice said to the **s** angel who .... Rev 9:14
The **s** angel poured out his bowl .... Rev 16:12
was onyx, the **s** was carnelian, ... Rev 21:20

SIXTY

Isaac was **s** years old when they.............. Ge 25:26
more, some made **s** times more, ... Mt 13:8
more, some made **s** times more, ... Mk 4:8
must be at least **s** years old. 1Ti 5:9

SIXTY-EIGHT

There were **s** hundred men with 1Ch 12:24
Obed-Edom and **s** other Levites to 1Ch 16:38

SIXTY-FIVE

Within **s** years Israel will no .... Is 7:8

SIXTY-SIX

who went to Egypt was **s**, ... Ge 46:26
It will be **s** days before she .... Le 12:5

SIXTY-TWO

Obed-Edom had **s** descendants in 1Ch 26:8
about **s** thousand bushels of 2Ch 27:5
and about **s** thousand bushels of 2Ch 27:5
king when he was **s** years old. .... Da 5:31

SKILL

of God and have given him the **s**, ... Ex 31:3
of God and has given him the **s**,.............. Ex 35:31
given him the **s** to do all kinds .... Ex 35:35
let my right hand lose its **s**...................... Ps 137:5
knowledge, and **s**, but they will .... Ec 2:21
Through your great **s** in trading,............ Eze 28:5
spoke to him with wisdom and **s**, ... Da 2:14
Tyre and Sidon, with their **s**. .... Zch 9:2

SKILLED

grew up, Esau became a **s** hunter. .... Ge 25:27
if any of them are **s** shepherds, ... Ge 47:6
I have never been a **s** speaker. .... Ex 4:10
family of Levi, is a **s** speaker. .... Ex 4:14
Have a **s** craftsman sew designs .... Ex 26:1
and have a **s** craftsman sew .... Ex 26:31
Tell all the **s** craftsmen to whom............ Ex 28:3
s craftsmen are to make it. .... Ex 28:6
Let all the **s** workers come and .... Ex 35:10
Every **s** woman used her hands to .... Ex 35:25

S

SKILLFUL

women who were **s** and wanted to .... Ex 35:26
and every **s** person will do the .... Ex 36:1
to do all the **s** work needed to .... Ex 36:1
all the other **s** people to whom .... Ex 36:2
So all the **s** workers left the .... Ex 36:4
Then the **s** workers made the Holy............ Ex 36:8
A **s** craftsman sewed designs of .... Ex 36:35
designer and also **s** at sewing................. Ex 38:23
This was done by **s** craftsmen. .... Ex 39:3
The **s** craftsmen made the chest .... Ex 39:8
They are **s** fighters. ....Jos 17:16
Your father is a **s** fighter. 2Sa 17:8
and had been **s** in making things 1Ki 7:14
was also very **s** and experienced 1Ki 7:14
Hiram had **s** sailors, so he sent 1Ki 9:27
and bows. They were **s** in war. 1Ch 5:18
for war and **s** with shields 1Ch 12:8
people **s** in every kind of work. 1Ch 22:15
They are **s** in working with gold, ... 1Ch 22:16
trained and **s** in making music 1Ch 25:7
and Semakiah were **s** workers. 1Ch 26:7
relatives who were **s** workers. 1Ch 26:9
seventeen hundred **s** men in 1Ch 26:30
who were **s** men and leaders 1Ch 26:32
Every **s** worker is ready to help 1Ch 28:21
S men may use the gold and 1Ch 29:5
send me a man **s** in working with 2Ch 2:7
will work with my **s** craftsmen in 2Ch 2:7
I will send you a **s** and wise man 2Ch 2:13
Huram-Abi is **s** in working with 2Ch 2:14
He is **s** in making engravings and 2Ch 2:14
his own men, who were **s** sailors. 2Ch 8:18
ready to fight and **s** with spears 2Ch 25:5
Levites were all **s** musicians. 2Ch 34:12
is like the pen of a **s** writer. .... Ps 45:1
you see people **s** in their work? .... Pr 22:29
the counselors, the **s** craftsmen, ... Is 3:3
Then he finds a **s** craftsman to .... Is 40:20
things are made by **s** workers. .... Je 10:9
the **s** craftsmen who were left............... Je 52:15
your **s** men were the sailors on .... Eze 27:8
Where is the **s** talker of this 1Co 1:20

SKILLFUL

David was more **s** than Saul's................. 1Sa 18:30
and guided them with **s** hands. .... Ps 78:72
They are **s** at doing evil, but .... Je 4:22

SKILLFULLY

on him with its **s** woven belt. .... Ex 29:5
The **s** woven belt was made in the .... Ex 39:5
He tied the **s** woven belt around .... Le 8:7

SKILLS

I have given **s** to all the .... Ex 31:6
to whom the LORD had given **s**,.............. Ex 36:2

SKIN

up the man's **s** at the place .... Ge 2:21
bull's meat, **s**, and intestines .... Ex 29:14
that he will **s** the animal and .... Le 1:6
may also have the **s** from it. .... Le 7:8
it is a harmful **s** disease. .... Le 13:11
even the seeds or the **s**. .... Nu 6:4
"One **s** for another!" Satan..................... Job 2:4
and my **s** is broken and full of .... Job 7:5
I am nothing but **s** and bones; .... Job 19:20
escaped by the **s** of my teeth. .... Job 19:20
Even after my **s** has been .... Job 19:26
My **s** has become black and peels .... Job 30:30
of my grief, my **s** hangs on my .... Ps 102:5
Cush change the color of his **s**? .... Je 13:23
out my flesh and **s** and broke my .... La 3:4

SKINNED

Then the Levites **s** the animals 2Ch 35:11

SKINS

from animal **s** for the man and .... Ge 3:21
She also took the **s** of the goats .... Ge 27:16
the animals' **s**, bodies, and .... Le 16:27
Some wore the **s** of sheep and .... Heb 11:37

SKIPPING

the mountains, **s** over the hills. .... Sng 2:8

SKIRT

s was torn off and your body .... Je 13:22

SKIRTS

your veil and your nice **s**. .... Is 47:2
I will pull your **s** up over your .... Je 13:26

SKULL

on his head, crushing his **s**. .... Jdg 9:53
They found only her **s**, feet, and 2Ki 9:35
which means the Place of the **S**............... Mt 27:33
which means the Place of the **S**............... Mk 15:22
came to a place called the **S**, ... Lk 23:33
place called The Place of the **S**, ... Jn 19:17

SKULLS

and smash the **s** of the sons of .... Nu 24:17
hairy **s** of those who continue................. Ps 68:21

SKY

a dependable witness in the **s**." .... Ps 89:37
weather, because the **s** is red. .... Mt 16:2
because the **s** is dark and red. .... Mt 16:3
as there are stars in the **s**. .... Heb 11:12

SLAP

The **s** of a friend can be trusted .... Pr 27:6
should let anyone **s** his cheek; .... La 3:30

SLAPPED

to Micaiah and **s** him in the face 1Ki 22:24
to Micaiah and **s** him in the face 2Ch 18:23
with their fists. Others **s** him. .... Mt 26:67

SLAPS

If someone **s** you on the right .... Mt 5:39
If anyone **s** you on one cheek, ... Lk 6:29

SLAVE

But if your **s** says to you, ... Dt 15:16
Joseph, who was sold as a **s**. .... Ps 105:17
like someone who was born a **s**? .... Je 2:14
was to keep a fellow Jew as a **s**. .... Je 34:9
serve the rest of you like a **s**. .... Mt 20:27
must serve all of you like a **s**. .... Mk 10:44
who lives in sin is a **s** to sin. .... Jn 8:34
If you were a **s** when God called............... 1Co 7:21
I make myself a **s** to all people 1Co 9:19
and Greek, **s** and free person,................. Gal 3:28
So now you are not a **s**; .... Gal 4:7
mother of one son was a **s** woman, ... Gal 4:22
son from the **s** woman was born.............. Gal 4:23
longer as a **s**, but better than .... Phm 1:16
but better than a **s**, as a loved .... Phm 1:16
poor, free and **s**, to have a mark .... Rev 13:16
all people—free, **s**, small, and .... Rev 19:18

SLAVE'S

the **s** master gives him a wife, ... Ex 21:4
then the **s** master must take him .... Ex 21:6
hole through the **s** ear using a .... Ex 21:6

SLAVERY

and their **s** was hard. .... Ex 6:9
brought them out of **s** in Egypt. .... Le 25:42
freed you from the land of **s**, ... Dt 7:8
you out of Egypt, the land of **s**. .... Jdg 6:8
your people from **s** in Egypt. 2Sa 7:23
your people from **s** in Egypt. 1Ch 17:21
and a little relief from our **s**. .... Ezr 9:8
a leader to take them back to **s**. .... Ne 9:17
Inside it is nothing but **s**. .... Je 6:6

of Egypt and freed you from **s;** .... Mic 6:4
go back into the **s** of the law. .... Gal 5:1

SLAVES
will make them **s** and be cruel to .... Ge 15:13
They must not become **s** again. .... Le 25:42
Your men and women **s** must come .... Le 25:44
you can make them **s** forever................... Le 25:46
We were **s** to the king of Egypt, ... Dt 6:21
been sold as male and female **s,** .... Est 7:4
male and female **s** and no longer .... Je 34:10
us and we would not be **s** to sin. .... Rm 6:6
like **s** to obey someone .... Rm 6:16
In the past you were **s** to sin— .... Rm 6:17
and now you are **s** to goodness. .... Rm 6:18
sin and have become **s** of God. .... Rm 6:22
so do not become **s** of people................... 1Co 7:23
Some of us are **s**, and some are 1Co 12:13

SLAYS
and jealousy **s** the stupid. .... Job 5:2

SLEEP
caused the man to **s** very deeply, ... Ge 2:21
down, Abram fell into a deep **s.** .... Ge 15:12
laid his head on it to go to **s.** .... Ge 28:11
Jacob woke from his **s** and said, ... Ge 28:16
you may **s** with Jacob tonight." .... Ge 30:15
I was cold and could not **s.** .... Ge 31:40
He has nothing else to **s** in...................... Ex 22:27
neighbor needs that coat to **s.** .... Dt 24:13
spies went to **s** for the night, ... Jos 2:8
very tired, he was in a deep **s.** .... Jdg 4:21
got Samson to **s,** lying in her .... Jdg 16:19
know where he lies down to **s.** .... Ru 3:4
good and went to **s** lying beside .... Ru 3:7
Then he went back to **s.** 1Ki 19:6
same night the king could not **s.**............... Est 6:1
when people in deep **s.** .... Job 4:13
when people are in a deep **s,** .... Job 33:15
I can lie down and go to **s,** .... Ps 3:5
I go to bed and **s** in peace, ... Ps 4:8
While people **s,** you take their .... Ps 90:5
The LORD gives **s** to those he.................. Ps 127:2
close my eyes, or let myself **s** .... Ps 132:4
lie down, you will **s** in peace. .... Pr 3:24
they cannot **s** until they do evil .... Pr 4:16
Don't go to **s** or even rest your .... Pr 6:4
You **s** a little; you take a nap. .... Pr 6:10
They will guard you when you **s.** .... Pr 6:22
but those who **s** through the .... Pr 10:5
Lazy people **s** a lot, and idle .... Pr 19:15
If you love to **s,** you will be .... Pr 20:13
desire for **s** will kill them, ... Pr 21:25
They **s** too much and end up .... Pr 23:21
You **s** a little; you take a nap. .... Pr 24:33
Those who work hard **s** in peace; .... Ec 5:12
about their wealth and cannot **s.** .... Ec 5:12
I **s,** but my heart is awake. .... Sng 5:2
The soldiers will **s** at Geba...................... Is 10:29
who tried to **s** on a bed that was.............. Is 28:20
has made you go into a deep **s.** .... Is 29:10
down and dream and love to **s.** .... Is 56:10
My **s** had been very pleasant. .... Je 31:26
they will **s** forever and never .... Je 51:39
Then they will **s** forever and .... Je 51:57
the desert will **s** in the woods. .... Eze 34:25
to him, and he could not **s.** .... Da 6:18
fell into a deep **s** with my face .... Da 8:18
fell into a deep **s** with my face .... Da 10:9
night they will **s** in the houses .... Zph 2:7
became sleepy and went to **s.** .... Mt 25:5
find places to **s** and something .... Lk 9:12
was falling into a deep **s.** .... Ac 20:9
for you to wake up from your **s,** .... Rm 13:11

that those who **s** in death will.................. 1Co 15:20
We will not all **s** in death, ... 1Co 15:51
sometimes we get no **s** or food. 2Co 6:5
and many times I did not **s.** 2Co 11:27
Those who **s,** sleep at night. 1Th 5:7
Those who sleep, **s** at night. 1Th 5:7

SLEEPER
said: "Wake up, **s!** Rise from .... Eph 5:14

SLEEPING
Noah was **s** because of the wine. .... Ge 9:24
the land on which you are now **s.** .... Ge 28:13
of Saul's army, were **s.** 1Sa 26:5
Saul was **s** in the middle of the 1Sa 26:5
and the army were **s** around Saul. 1Sa 26:7
Maybe he is **s** so you will have 1Ki 18:27
Why are you **s**? Get up! Don't................. Ps 44:23
When will you get up from **s**?................. Pr 6:9
day and night and hardly ever **s.** .... Ec 8:16
came and said, "Why are you **s**?.............. Jnh 1:6
the boat, but Jesus was **s.** .... Mt 8:24
Are you still **s** and resting? .... Mt 26:45
s with his head on a cushion. .... Mk 4:38
back suddenly and find you **s.** .... Mk 13:36
to Peter, "Simon, are you **s**? .... Mk 14:37
Are you still **s** and resting? .... Mk 14:41
two people will be **s** in one bed; .... Lk 17:34
said to them, "Why are you **s**? .... Lk 22:46
he meant Lazarus was really **s.** .... Jn 11:13
was **s** between two soldiers, ... Ac 12:6
be like other people who are **s,** 1Th 5:6

SLEEPS
He who guards you never **s.** .... Ps 121:3
guards Israel never rests or **s.**................... Ps 121:4

SLEEPY
of them gets **s** and falls asleep .... Is 5:27
they became **s** and went to sleep. .... Mt 25:5
and the others were very **s,**..................... Lk 9:32

SLEET
and their sycamore trees with **s.**............... Ps 78:47

SLEEVES
a special robe with long **s.** .... Ge 37:3
pulled off his robe with long **s** .... Ge 37:23
a special robe with long **s,** 2Sa 13:18

SLEPT
who have never **s** with a man. .... Ge 19:8
stone he had **s** on and set it up .... Ge 28:18
So Jacob **s** with her that night. .... Ge 30:16
The king **s** again and dreamed a .... Ge 41:5
While Samson **s,** Delilah wove .... Jdg 16:13
and ate, drank, and **s** there. .... Jdg 19:4
he **s** outside the door of the 2Sa 11:9
Uriah again **s** with the king's 2Sa 11:13
from his cup and **s** in his arms. 2Sa 12:3
He **s** with her and had sexual 2Sa 12:24
lay down under the tree and **s.** 1Ki 19:5
and even **s** in the rough cloth to 1Ki 21:27
young, she had **s** with men, and .... Eze 23:8

SLICES
veil are like **s** of a pomegranate .... Sng 4:3
veil are like **s** of a pomegranate .... Sng 6:7

SLIDE
s poles through them to carry.................. Ex 30:4

SLIDES
the way a snake **s** over a rock, ... Pr 30:19

SLING
of whom could **s** a stone at a .... Jdg 20:16
bag and grabbed his **s.** 1Sa 17:40
put it into his **s,** and slung it. 1Sa 17:49
with only a **s** and a stone. 1Sa 17:50

S

he would throw a stone from a **s**. 1Sa 25:29
to shoot arrows or to **s** rocks. 1Ch 12:2

SLINGS
bows, and stones for their **s**. 2Ch 26:14
stones from **s** are like chaff to .... Job 41:28

SLINGSHOT
is like tying a stone in a **s**. .... Pr 26:8

SLINGSHOTS
but the men with **s** surrounded it 2Ki 3:25
will destroy the enemy with **s**. .... Zch 9:15

SLIP
their foot will **s**, because their .... Dt 32:35
and before you **s** and fall on the .... Je 13:16

SLIPPED
but Jesus often **s** away to be .... Lk 5:16

SLIPPERY
road be dark and **s** as the angel .... Ps 35:6
His words are **s** like butter, ... Ps 55:21

SLOPE
There was a steep **s** on each side 1Sa 14:4

SLOPES
and the **s** of the ravines that .... Nu 21:15
the western hills, and the **s**. .... Jos 10:40
south to the **s** of Pisgah. .... Jos 12:3
Valley, the **s**, the desert, ... Jos 12:8
on the **s** of the sacred mountain. .... Is 14:13

SLOW
he will not be **s** to pay back .... Dt 7:10
God, do not be **s** to pay it, ... Dt 23:21
Don't **s** down for me unless I 2Ki 4:24
to God, don't be **s** to keep it. .... Ec 5:4
he will not be **s** to answer them. .... Lk 18:7
You are foolish and **s** to believe .... Lk 24:25
you are so **s** to understand. .... Heb 5:11
to listen and to speak. .... Jam 1:19
The Lord is not **s** in doing what 2Pe 3:9

SLOW-MOVING
to accept the **s** waters of the .... Is 8:6

SLOWLY
I will follow you **s** and let the .... Ge 33:14
speak **s** and can't find the best .... Ex 4:10
I will force those people out **s**, ... Ex 23:30
your eyes and **s** kill you. .... Le 26:16
We sailed **s** for many days. .... Ac 27:7

SLOWNESS
way some people understand **s**. 2Pe 3:9

SLUNG
put it into his sling, and **s** it. 1Sa 17:49

SMALL
roasted grain, beans, **s** peas, ... 2Sa 17:28
said, "I see a **s** cloud, the size 1Ki 18:44
great and **s** are in the grave .... Job 3:19
large and **s** that cannot be .... Ps 104:25
Powerful people will be like **s**, ... Is 1:31
These **s** trees have been chopped .... Is 9:10
Evil is like a **s** fire. .... Is 9:18
this? It is too **s** already!" .... Am 7:2
this? It is too **s** already." .... Am 7:5
not think that **s** beginnings are .... Zch 4:10
followers also had a few **s** fish. .... Mk 8:7
all people, **s** and great, what I. .... Ac 26:22
we went below a **s** island named .... Ac 27:16
a very **s** rudder controls that .... Jam 3:4
dead, great and **s**, standing. .... Rev 20:12

SMART
the people who are wise and **s**. .... Mt 11:25
the people who are wise and **s**. .... Lk 10:21

the governor and a **s** man. .... Ac 13:7
Do not think how **s** you are. .... Rm 12:16

SMARTER
who makes us **s** than the animals .... Job 35:11

SMARTEST
the **s** does not always become. .... Ec 9:11

SMEAR
But you **s** me with lies. .... Job 13:4
I will **s** your faces with the .... Mal 2:3

SMELL
The **s** of my son is like the .... Ge 27:27
have noses, but they cannot **s**. .... Ps 115:6
they didn't even **s** like smoke! .... Da 3:27
And the sweet **s** from the perfume .... Jn 12:3
ear, it would not be able to **s**. 1Co 12:17
are the sweet **s** of Christ among 2Co 2:15
are the **s** of death that brings 2Co 2:16
we are the **s** of life that brings 2Co 2:16

SMELLED
When Isaac **s** Esau's clothes, ... Ge 27:27

SMELLS
' It **s** the battle from far away; .... Job 39:25
Who is this that **s** like myrrh, ... Sng 3:6
your perfume **s** better than any .... Sng 4:10
and let its sweet **s** flow out. .... Sng 4:16

SMILE
the look on my face and **s**,' .... Job 9:27
Happiness makes a person **s**, ... Pr 15:13

SMILED
I **s** at them when they doubted, ... Job 29:24

SMILING
A **s** king can give people life; .... Pr 16:15

SMOKE
Valley and saw **s** rising from the. .... Ge 19:28
the land, like **s** from a furnace. .... Ge 19:28
Mount Sinai was covered with **s**, ... Ex 19:18
s rose from the mountain like. .... Ex 19:18
mountain like **s** from a furnace, ... Ex 19:18
the lightning and the **s** rising .... Ex 20:18
they saw **s** rising from their .... Jos 8:20
and saw the **s** rising from it, ... Jos 8:21
up a cloud of **s** from the city. .... Jdg 20:38
then a cloud of **s** began to rise .... Jdg 20:40
whole city was going up in **s**. .... Jdg 20:40
S came out of his nose, and 2Sa 22:9
S pours out of its nose, as if .... Job 41:20
S came out of his nose, and .... Ps 18:8
they will disappear like **s**. .... Ps 37:20
them away as **s** is driven away .... Ps 68:2
My life is passing away like **s**, ... Ps 102:3
the mountains, and they **s**. .... Ps 104:32
like a wine bag going up in **s**, ... Ps 119:83
the mountains so they will **s**. .... Ps 144:5
on the teeth or **s** in the eyes. .... Pr 10:26
of the desert like a cloud of **s**? .... Sng 3:6
with a cloud of **s** during the day .... Is 4:5
as the Temple filled with **s**. .... Is 6:4
they all go up in a column of **s**. .... Is 9:18
a fire with thick clouds of **s**. .... Is 30:27
the **s** will rise from Edom .... Is 34:10
will disappear like clouds of **s**. .... Is 51:6
people are like **s** in my nose. .... Is 65:5
they didn't even smell like **s**! .... Da 3:27
like **s** going out a window. .... Hos 13:3
blood, fire, and thick **s**. .... Joe 2:30
will burn up your chariots in **s**, ... Nah 2:13
blood, fire, and thick **s**. .... Ac 2:19
The **s** from the incense went up .... Rev 8:4
and **s** came up from the hole like .... Rev 9:2

the hole like **s** from a big .... Rev 9:2
because of the **s** from the hole. .... Rev 9:2
down to the earth out of the **s**, ... Rev 9:3
lions, with fire, **s**, and sulfur .... Rev 9:17
the fire, the **s**, and the sulfur. .... Rev 9:18
the **s** from their burning pain .... Rev 14:11
was filled with **s** from the glory .... Rev 15:8
will see the **s** from her burning. .... Rev 18:9
As they saw the **s** from her .... Rev 18:18
s will rise forever and ever...................... Rev 19:3

SMOKING
Suddenly a **s** firepot and a .... Ge 15:17

SMOOTH
Esau is a hairy man, and I am **s!** .... Ge 27:11
and chose five **s** stones from 1Sa 17:40
they may be as **s** as olive oil. .... Pr 5:3
life is like a **s** highway. .... Pr 15:19
the way of life **s** for those .... Is 26:7
He makes the ground flat and **s**............. Is 28:25
rugged ground should be made **s**. .... Is 40:4
them, and the rough ground **s**. .... Is 42:16
You take the **s** rocks from the................. Is 57:6
rough roads should be made **s**. .... Lk 3:5

SMOOTH-SKINNED
to a people who are tall and **s**, ... Is 18:2
the people who are tall and **s**,................. Is 18:7

SMOOTHER
His words are **s** than oil, but .... Ps 55:21

SMOOTHLY
in the cup, when it goes down **s**............. Pr 23:31
rivers to run as **s** as olive oil, ... Eze 32:14

SMOOTHS
the workman who **s** the metal with .... Is 41:7

SMYRNA
to Ephesus, **S**, Pergamum, ... Rev 1:11
to the angel of the church in **S**: .... Rev 2:8

SNAILS
Let them be like **s** that melt as .... Ps 58:8

SNAKE
Now the **s** was the most clever of .... Ge 3:1
One day the **s** said to the woman, ... Ge 3:1
The woman answered the **s**, ... Ge 3:2
But the **s** said to the woman, ... Ge 3:4
answered, "The **s** tricked me, so............. Ge 3:13
The LORD God said to the **s**, ... Ge 3:14
Dan will be like a **s** by the side .... Ge 49:17
a dangerous **s** lying near the .... Ge 49:17
That **s** bites a horse's leg, ... Ge 49:17
the ground, and it became a **s**. .... Ex 4:3
a snake. Moses ran from the **s**, ... Ex 4:3
out and grab the **s** by its tail."................ Ex 4:4
out and took hold of the **s**, ... Ex 4:4
king, and it will become a **s**." .... Ex 7:9
his officers, and it became a **s**. .... Ex 7:10
walking stick that became a **s**. .... Ex 7:15
Make a bronze **s**, and put it on a .... Nu 21:8
Moses made a bronze **s** and put it .... Nu 21:9
Then when a **s** bit anyone, that .... Nu 21:9
at the bronze **s** and lived. .... Nu 21:9
their wine is like **s** poison,..................... Dt 32:33
the bronze **s** Moses had made. 2Ki 18:4
the poison of a **s** inside them. .... Job 20:14
His hand stabs the fleeing **s**. .... Job 26:13
the music of the **s** charmer no .... Ps 58:5
their words are like **s** poison. .... Ps 140:3
it bites like a **s** with poison in................. Pr 23:32
the way **s** slides over a rock, ... Pr 30:19
a wall might be bitten by a **s**; .... Ec 10:8
If a **s** bites the tamer before it................ Ec 10:11
into the nest of a poisonous **s**. .... Is 11:8

He is like a **s** that will give .... Is 14:29
birth to another dangerous **s**. .... Is 14:29
quick, dangerous **s** to bite you. .... Is 14:29
punish Leviathan, the gliding **s**. .... Is 27:1
the coiled **s**, with his great .... Is 27:1
open, a poisonous **s** comes out. .... Is 59:5
and a **s** on the ground will not .... Is 65:25
like a hissing **s** that is trying .... Je 46:22
like a giant **s** that swallowed .... Je 51:34
and then is bitten by a **s**....................... Am 5:19
I will command a **s** to bite them. .... Am 9:3
will crawl in the dust like a **s**,............... Mic 7:17
a fish, would you give them a **s?**............ Mt 7:10
you would give them a **s** instead? .... Lk 11:11
lifted up the **s** in the desert, ... Jn 3:14
a poisonous **s** came out because............. Ac 28:3
island saw the **s** hanging from .... Ac 28:4
Paul shook the **s** off into the .... Ac 28:5
Their words are like **s** poison." .... Rm 3:13
tricked by the **s** with his evil 2Co 11:3
is that old **s** called the devil .... Rev 12:9
one-half years, away from the **s**............. Rev 12:14
Then the **s** poured water out of .... Rev 12:15
that old **s** who is the devil and .... Rev 20:2

SNAKE'S
and the **s** fangs will kill them.................. Job 20:16
make their tongues sharp as a **s**; .... Ps 140:3

SNAKES
and their sticks became **s**. .... Ex 7:12
the LORD sent them poisonous **s**; .... Nu 21:6
LORD will take away these **s**." .... Nu 21:7
had poisonous **s** and stinging .... Dt 8:15
and gliding, poisonous **s**. .... Dt 32:24
They will suck the poison of **s**, ... Job 20:16
They are like poisonous **s**, ... Ps 58:4
will step on strong lions and **s**. .... Ps 91:13
poisonous **s** and darting snakes.............. Is 30:6
poisonous snakes and darting **s**............. Is 30:6
evil like eggs from poisonous **s**. .... Is 59:5
poisonous **s** to attack you. .... Je 8:17
These **s** cannot be charmed, ... Je 8:17
saw them, he said, "You are **s!** .... Mt 3:7
as clever as **s** and as innocent. .... Mt 10:16
You **s!** You are evil people, so................. Mt 12:34
You are **s!** A family of poisonous .... Mt 23:33
A family of poisonous **s!**........................ Mt 23:33
will pick up **s** and drink poison .... Mk 16:18
John, he said, "You are all **s!** .... Lk 3:7
to walk on **s** and scorpions, ... Lk 10:19
people, birds, animals, and **s**. .... Rm 1:23
they were killed by **s**. 1Co 10:9
tails were like **s** with heads, ... Rev 9:19

SNAP
your life will **s** like a silver .... Ec 12:6

SNATCHED
evil people and **s** the captives .... Job 29:17
s me up and threw me into the .... Job 30:22

SNATCHES
If he **s** something away, no one .... Job 9:12
and a storm **s** them away in the .... Job 27:20

SNEAK
some troops to **s** behind Judah's............. 2Ch 13:13

SNEEZED
The boy **s** seven times and opened 2Ki 4:35

SNIFF
bare hills and **s** the wind like .... Je 14:6
and you **s** at it in disgust," .... Mal 1:13

SNIFFS
in the desert and **s** the wind at .... Je 2:24

S

SNORTING

scares people with its proud s. .... Job 39:20
the s of the enemy's horses is .... Je 8:16
acts of adultery and your s, ... Je 13:27

SNORTS

blows, the horse s, 'Aha!' .... Job 39:25
When it s, flashes of light are .... Job 41:18

SNOUT

like a gold ring in a pig's s.................... Pr 11:22

SNOW

Miriam, she was as white as s; .... Nu 12:10
disease and was as white as s. 2Ki 5:27
ice and rise with melting s...................... Job 6:16
and dryness quickly melt the s, ... Job 24:19
He says to the s, 'Fall on the .... Job 37:6
the storehouse of the s or seen .... Job 38:22
and I will be whiter than s....................... Ps 51:7
kings like s on Mount Zalmon. .... Ps 68:14
He spreads the s like wool and .... Ps 147:16
lightning and hail, s and mist, ... Ps 148:8
the coolness of s in the .... Pr 25:13
It shouldn't s in summer or rain .... Pr 26:1
they can be as white as s. .... Is 1:18
Rain and s fall from the sky and .... Is 55:10
s on the mountains of Lebanon .... Je 18:14
Our princes were purer than s, ... La 4:7
His clothes were white like s, ... Da 7:9
and his clothes were white as s. .... Mt 28:3
wool, as white as s, and his .... Rev 1:14

SNOWS

about her family when it s,.................... Pr 31:21

SNOWY

and killed a lion on a s day. 2Sa 23:20
and killed a lion on a s day. 1Ch 11:22

SO-CALLED

above any s god or anything 2Th 2:4

SOAKED

They are s from mountain rains .... Job 24:8
my bed is s from my crying. .... Ps 6:6
the soldiers s a sponge in it, ... Jn 19:29

SOAP

wash myself with s and scrub my .... Job 9:30
scrub my hands with strong s, ... Job 9:30
all your wrongs as if with s; .... Is 1:25
with cleanser and use much s, ... Je 2:22
fire and like laundry s. .... Mal 3:2

SOB

They cry and s for you; they cry .... Eze 27:31

SOCKETS

Their eyes will rot in their s, ... Zch 14:12

SOCO

Beth Zur, S, Adullam, ... 2Ch 11:7
Gederoth, S, Timnah, and Gimzo 2Ch 28:18

SOCOH

Jarmuth, Adullam, S, Azekah, ... Jos 15:35
mountains: Shamir, Jattir, S, ... Jos 15:48
met at S in Judah and camped 1Sa 17:1
Dammim between S and Azekah. 1Sa 17:1
of Arubboth, S, and all the land 1Ki 4:10

SODA

day or pouring vinegar on s. .... Pr 25:20

SODI

of Zebulun, Gaddiel son of S; .... Nu 13:10

SODOM

and then to S, Gomorrah, Admah .... Ge 10:19
LORD destroyed S and Gomorrah............ Ge 13:10
Jordan Valley, very near to S. .... Ge 13:12
the people of S were very evil.................. Ge 13:13

Bera king of S, Birsha king of .... Ge 14:2
At that time the kings of S,..................... Ge 14:8
When the kings of S and Gomorrah .... Ge 14:10
the people of S and Gomorrah .... Ge 14:11
nephew who was living in S, ... Ge 14:12
the king of S came out to meet .... Ge 14:17
The king of S said to Abram, ... Ge 14:21
But Abram said to the king of S, ... Ge 14:22
leave and started out toward S. .... Ge 18:16
the people of S and Gomorrah. .... Ge 18:20
men turned and went toward S, ... Ge 18:22
good people in the city of S, ... Ge 18:26
angels came to S in the evening .... Ge 19:1
every part of S surrounded Lot's .... Ge 19:4
I cannot destroy S until you are .... Ge 19:22
from the sky on S and Gomorrah .... Ge 19:24
down toward S and Gomorrah .... Ge 19:28
It is like S and Gomorrah, ... Dt 29:23
vine comes from S, and their .... Dt 32:32
the cities of S and Gomorrah.................. Is 1:9
your rulers are like those of S, ... Is 1:10
the people of S, they are proud .... Is 3:9
destroy it like S and Gomorrah. .... Is 13:19
people are like the city of S. .... Je 23:14
the cities of S and Gomorrah .... Je 49:18
the cities of S and Gomorrah .... Je 50:40
been punished more than S was. .... La 4:6
S was destroyed suddenly, and no .... La 4:6
sister is S, who lived south .... Eze 16:46
Your sister S and her daughters .... Eze 16:48
was the sin of your sister S: .... Eze 16:49
S and her daughters were proud .... Eze 16:50
give back to S and her daughters .... Eze 16:53
S with her daughters and Samaria........... Eze 16:55
sister S when you were proud, ... Eze 16:56
as I destroyed S and Gomorrah. .... Am 4:11
Moab will be destroyed like S, ... Zph 2:9
for the towns of S and Gomorrah .... Mt 10:15
I did in you had happened in S, ... Mt 11:23
be better for S than for you." .... Mt 11:24
for the people of S than for the .... Lk 10:12
day Lot left S, fire and sulfur .... Lk 17:29
the cities of S and Gomorrah." .... Rm 9:29
evil cities of S and Gomorrah 2Pe 2:6
the cities of S and Gomorrah .... Jud 1:7
This city is named S and Egypt, ... Rev 11:8

SOFT

green and s and new leaves .... Mt 24:32
green and s and new leaves .... Mk 13:28

SOFT-SOUNDING

lyre and with the s harp......................... Ps 92:3

SOFTEN

You s the ground with rain, ... Ps 65:10

SOIL

rain and good s so that you will .... Ge 27:28
What about the s? Is it fertile .... Nu 13:20
then please give me some s— 2Ki 5:17
like a healthy tree in good s. .... Ps 37:35
on a hill with very rich s. .... Is 5:1
he does not go on working the s. .... Is 28:24
that work the s will have all .... Is 30:24
a hot and dry land with bad s. .... Je 17:6
no good for the s or for manure; .... Lk 14:35

SOLD

to Jacob and s his part of their .... Ge 25:33
s us to you, and then he spent .... Ge 31:15
out of the well and s him to the .... Ge 37:28
There they s him to Potiphar, ... Ge 37:36
storehouses and s grain to the .... Ge 41:56
was the one who s the grain to .... Ge 42:6
you s as a slave to go to Egypt. .... Ge 45:4

because you s me here. ....Ge 45:5
Every Egyptian s Joseph his ....Ge 47:20
be counted since the land was s. ....Le 25:27
for a full year after it is s, ...Le 25:29
the Levites' cities cannot be s, ...Le 25:34
time from when he s himself up ....Le 25:50
or if it is s to someone else, ...Le 27:20
to the family who s the land. ....Le 27:24
gift cannot be bought back or s. ....Le 27:28
unless their Rock has s them,................Dt 32:30
traders also s horses and 1Ki 10:29
a donkey's head s for about two 2Ki 6:25
of dove's dung s for about two 2Ki 6:25
flour will be s for two-fifths 2Ki 7:1
barley will be s for two-fifths 2Ki 7:1
fine flour were s for two-fifths 2Ki 7:16
of barley were s for two-fifths 2Ki 7:16
Then they s the horses and....................2Ch 1:17
daughters have already been s. ....Ne 5:5
who had been s to foreigners..................Ne 5:8
other things and s them there................Ne 13:16
I have been s to be destroyed ....Est 7:4
If we had been s as male and ....Est 7:4
s your people for nothing and................Ps 44:12
Joseph, who was s as a slave. ....Ps 105:17
Nile Valley and s it to other ....Is 23:3
do you think I s you to pay a ....Is 50:1
evil things you did, I s you. ....Is 50:1
You were not s for a price, ...Is 52:3
Hebrew has s himself to you, ...Je 34:14
land they have s as long as they ....Eze 7:13
ships considered the things you s. ....Eze 27:25
and they s girls to buy wine to ....Joe 3:3
You s the people of Judah and ....Joe 3:6
s all the people of one area....................Am 1:6
s all the people of one area....................Am 1:9
that he went and s everything he ....Mt 13:44
he went and s everything he had ....Mt 13:46
the servant owned should be s, ...Mt 18:25
could have been s for a great ....Mt 26:9
could have been s and the money ....Mk 14:5
Five sparrows are s for only two ....Lk 12:6
Why wasn't it s and the money ....Jn 12:5
owned fields or houses s them, ...Ac 4:34
owned a field, s it, brought the ....Ac 4:37
his wife Sapphira s some land. ....Ac 5:1
Before you s the land, it ....Ac 5:4
even after you s it, you could ....Ac 5:4
Joseph and s him to be a slave ....Ac 7:9
any meat that is s in the meat................1Co 10:25
he s all the meat for a single meal..................Heb 12:16

SOLDIER

each s had taken something for ....Nu 31:53
was a great s, so the lands ....Jos 17:1
Each s is given a girl or two. ....Jdg 5:30
was a strong s from Gilead. ....Jdg 11:1
every Israelite s ran away to 1Sa 4:10
So no Israelite s ate food. 1Sa 14:24
men brought an enemy s to me. 1Ki 20:39
chance, a s shot an arrow, but 1Ki 22:34
of silver to each s of the king 2Ki 15:20
you are a s and have killed 1Ch 28:3
Eliada, a brave s, had two 2Ch 17:17
a s shot an arrow which hit Ahab 2Ch 18:33
he runs at me like a s..............................Job 16:14
s is released in times of war, ...Ec 8:8
the strongest s does not always ....Ec 9:11
shield belongs to a strong s. ....Sng 4:4
will march out like a strong s; ....Is 42:13
Can the wealth a s wins in war ....Is 49:24
be freed from a powerful s? ....Is 49:24
will attack the s next to him. ....Eze 38:21

the weak person say, "I am a s." ....Joe 3:10
I tell one s, 'Go,' and he goes. ....Mt 8:9
I tell another s, 'Come,' and he ....Mt 8:9
king sent a s to bring John's ....Mk 6:27
The s went and cut off John's ....Mk 6:27
to decide what each s would get. ....Mk 15:24
I tell one s, 'Go,' and he goes. ....Lk 7:8
I tell another s, 'Come,' and he ....Lk 7:8
with each s getting one part. ....Jn 19:23
two of his servants and a s, ...Ac 10:7
with the s who guarded him. ....Ac 28:16
No s ever serves in the army and 1Co 9:7
like a good s of Christ Jesus. 2Ti 2:3
s wants to please the enlisting 2Ti 2:4

SOLDIER'S

protect them like a s shield. ....Ps 5:12
Every s head was rubbed bare, ...Eze 29:18

SOLDIERS

Israelite s were killed...........................1Sa 4:10
and I have s under my command. ....Mt 8:9
They paid the s a large amount ....Mt 28:12
The s took Jesus into the ....Mk 15:16
The s made a crown from some ....Jn 19:2
So the s said to each other, ...Jn 19:24
was sleeping between two s, ...Ac 12:6

SOLES

go from the s of your feet to ....Dt 28:35
the s of my feet, I have dried 2Ki 19:24
his head to the s of his feet. ....Job 2:7
You even mark the s of my feet. ....Job 13:27
the s of my feet, I have dried ....Is 37:25

SOLID

waters became s in the middle ....Ex 15:8
spread the s blue cloth over ....Nu 4:6
He gave you water from a s rock ....Dt 8:15
bringing oil from the s rock. ....Dt 32:13
boy is old enough to eat s food, ...1Sa 1:22
I see a s gold lampstand with a ....Zch 4:2
like milk, not s food, because 1Co 3:2
were not able to take s food. 1Co 3:2
You are not ready for s food. ....Heb 5:12
But s food is for those who are ....Heb 5:14

SOLOMON

Shammua, Shobab, Nathan, S, ...2Sa 5:14
another son, whom David named S. 2Sa 12:24
named Solomon. The LORD loved S. 2Sa 12:24
special guard, or his brother S. 1Ki 1:10
that my son S would be king 1Ki 1:13
'Your son S will become king 1Ki 1:17
not invite S, who serves you. 1Ki 1:19
S and I will be treated as 1Ki 1:21
son of Jehoiada, or your son S. 1Ki 1:26
that your son S would be king 1Ki 1:30
and put my son S on my own mule. 1Ki 1:33
and shout, 'Long live King S!' 1Ki 1:34
May he also help S and make King 1Ki 1:37
They put S on King David's mule 1Ki 1:38
shouted, "Long live King S!" 1Ki 1:39
people followed S into the city. 1Ki 1:40
David has made S the new king. 1Ki 1:43
they have put S on the king's 1Ki 1:44
olive oil on S at Gihon to make 1Ki 1:45
S has now become the king. 1Ki 1:46
your God make S even more famous 1Ki 1:47
Adonijah was also afraid of S, ...1Ki 1:50
Then someone told S, "Adonijah 1Ki 1:51
'Tell King S to promise me today 1Ki 1:51
So S answered, "Adonijah must 1Ki 1:52
Then King S sent some men to get............1Ki 1:53
before King S and bowed down................1Ki 1:53
S told him, "Go home." 1Ki 1:53

S

his son **S** his last commands. 1Ki 2:1
S became king after David,.................... 1Ki 2:12
I know King **S** will do anything 1Ki 2:17
went to King **S** to speak to him 1Ki 2:19
When **S** saw her, he stood up to 1Ki 2:19
King **S** answered his mother, ... 1Ki 2:22
Then King **S** swore by the name of........... 1Ki 2:23
Then King **S** gave orders to 1Ki 2:25
King **S** said to Abiathar the 1Ki 2:26
Then **S** removed Abiathar from 1Ki 2:27
told King **S** that Joab had run................. 1Ki 2:29
Then **S** ordered Benaiah to go and 1Ki 2:29
S said to him, "Build a house 1Ki 2:36
Someone told **S** that Shimei had 1Ki 2:41
So **S** sent for Shimei and said, ... 1Ki 2:42
Now **S** was in full control of his 1Ki 2:46
S made an agreement with the 1Ki 3:1
this time **S** was still building 1Ki 3:1
S showed he loved the LORD by 1Ki 3:3
King **S** went to Gibeon to offer a 1Ki 3:4
S answered, "You were very kind 1Ki 3:6
pleased that **S** had asked this. 1Ki 3:10
After **S** woke up from the dream, ... 1Ki 3:15
who were prostitutes came to **S**.............. 1Ki 3:16
Then King **S** said, "One of you 1Ki 3:23
Then King **S** said, "Don't kill 1Ki 3:27
King **S** ruled over all Israel. 1Ki 4:1
S placed twelve governors over 1Ki 4:7
S ruled over all the kingdoms................. 1Ki 4:21
brought **S** the payments he 1Ki 4:21
S needed much food each day to 1Ki 4:22
S controlled all the countries 1Ki 4:24
S had four thousand stalls for 1Ki 4:26
gave King **S** all the food he.................... 1Ki 4:27
God gave **S** great wisdom so he 1Ki 4:29
King **S** became famous in all the 1Ki 4:31
Hiram heard that **S** had been made 1Ki 5:1
he sent his messengers to **S**. 1Ki 5:1
S sent this message back to King 1Ki 5:2
When Hiram heard what **S** asked, ... 1Ki 5:7
sent back this message to **S**: 1Ki 5:8
Hiram gave **S** as much cedar and 1Ki 5:10
And **S** gave Hiram about one 1Ki 5:11
S also gave him about one 1Ki 5:11
The LORD gave **S** wisdom as he had 1Ki 5:12
was peace between Hiram and **S**; 1Ki 5:12
King **S** forced thirty thousand 1Ki 5:13
S forced eighty thousand men to 1Ki 5:15
King **S** commanded them to cut 1Ki 5:17
S began to build the Temple four 1Ki 6:1
S also built some side rooms 1Ki 6:5
S put a roof made from beams and 1Ki 6:9
The LORD said to **S**: 1Ki 6:11
S finished building the Temple. 1Ki 6:14
S prepared the inner room at the 1Ki 6:19
S made two creatures from olive 1Ki 6:23
the fourth year **S** was king over 1Ki 6:37
S had spent seven years building 1Ki 6:38
King **S** also built a palace for 1Ki 7:1
S also built the porch that had 1Ki 7:6
S also built a throne room where 1Ki 7:7
palace where **S** lived was built 1Ki 7:8
S also built the same kind of 1Ki 7:8
S sent to Tyre and had Huram 1Ki 7:13
So he came to King **S** and did all 1Ki 7:14
work for King **S** on the Temple 1Ki 7:40
everything King **S** wanted from 1Ki 7:45
S never weighed the bronze used 1Ki 7:47
S also made all the items for 1Ki 7:48
the work King **S** did for the 1Ki 7:51
S brought in everything his 1Ki 7:51
King **S** called for the elders of 1Ki 8:1
together with King **S** during the.............. 1Ki 8:2

King **S** and all the Israelites 1Ki 8:5
Then **S** said, "The LORD said he 1Ki 8:12
S turned to them and blessed 1Ki 8:14
Then **S** stood facing the LORD's.............. 1Ki 8:22
S prayed this prayer to the LORD, ... 1Ki 8:54
Then King **S** and all Israel with 1Ki 8:62
S killed twenty-two thousand 1Ki 8:63
On that day King **S** made holy the 1Ki 8:64
S and all the Israelites 1Ki 8:65
following day **S** sent the people 1Ki 8:66
S finished building the Temple 1Ki 9:1
King **S** had built two buildings— 1Ki 9:10
that time King **S** gave twenty 1Ki 9:11
Hiram had given **S** all the cedar, ... 1Ki 9:11
see the towns **S** had given him, ... 1Ki 9:12
Hiram had sent **S** about nine 1Ki 9:14
the forced labor **S** used to build 1Ki 9:15
to his daughter, who married **S**. 1Ki 9:16
So **S** rebuilt it.) He also built 1Ki 9:17
King **S** also built cities for 1Ki 9:19
S forced them to work for him as 1Ki 9:21
But **S** did not make slaves of the 1Ki 9:22
the palace that **S** had built for 1Ki 9:24
Then **S** filled in the surrounding............. 1Ki 9:24
times each year **S** offered whole............. 1Ki 9:25
King **S** also built ships at Ezion 1Ki 9:26
pounds of gold to King **S**. 1Ki 9:28
queen of Sheba heard about **S**, ... 1Ki 10:1
she came to **S**, she talked with 1Ki 10:2
S answered all her questions.................. 1Ki 10:3
learned that **S** was very wise.................. 1Ki 10:4
said to King **S**, "What I heard................ 1Ki 10:6
queen of Sheba gave to King **S**. 1Ki 10:10
S used the juniper wood to build 1Ki 10:12
King **S** gave the queen of Sheba 1Ki 10:13
Every year King **S** received about 1Ki 10:14
King **S** made two hundred large............. 1Ki 10:16
King **S** also had many trading 1Ki 10:22
So **S** had more riches and wisdom 1Ki 10:23
to see King **S** and listen to 1Ki 10:24
S had fourteen hundred chariots 1Ki 10:26
In Jerusalem **S** made silver as 1Ki 10:27
King **S** loved many women who were 1Ki 11:1
But **S** fell in love with these 1Ki 11:2
As **S** grew old, his wives caused............... 1Ki 11:4
S worshiped Ashtoreth, the 1Ki 11:5
So **S** did what the LORD said was 1Ki 11:6
S built two places for worship. 1Ki 11:7
S did the same thing for all his 1Ki 11:8
LORD had appeared to **S** twice, ... 1Ki 11:9
The LORD was angry with **S**, ... 1Ki 11:9
he had commanded **S** not to follow 1Ki 11:10
But **S** did not obey the LORD's 1Ki 11:10
the LORD said to **S**, "Because you 1Ki 11:11
Israel all the time **S** was alive. 1Ki 11:25
S was filling in the land and 1Ki 11:27
S saw that this young man was 1Ki 11:28
S put him over all the workers 1Ki 11:28
away from **S** and give you ten 1Ki 11:31
do this because **S** has stopped 1Ki 11:33
S has not obeyed me by doing 1Ki 11:33
all the kingdom away from **S**.................. 1Ki 11:34
S tried to kill Jeroboam, but he 1Ki 11:40
where he stayed until **S** died. 1Ki 11:40
Everything else King **S** did, ... 1Ki 11:41
in the book of the history of **S**. 1Ki 11:41
S ruled in Jerusalem over all 1Ki 11:42
he had gone to escape from **S**. 1Ki 12:2
who had advised **S** during his................. 1Ki 12:6
As son of **S**, Rehoboam wanted to 1Ki 12:21
the gold shields **S** had made. 1Ki 14:26
and his son **S** about the Temple 2Ki 21:7
S king of Israel had built these 2Ki 23:13

gold objects S king of Israel 2Ki 24:13
stands which S had made for 2Ki 25:16
Nathan, and S—the four children 1Ch 3:5
the Temple S built in Jerusalem............... 1Ch 6:10
served until S built the Temple 1Ch 6:32
Shammua, Shobab, Nathan, S, ... 1Ch 14:4
S used this bronze to make.................... 1Ch 18:8
But my son S is young. 1Ch 22:5
for his son S and told him to 1Ch 22:6
name will be S, and I will give 1Ch 22:9
S will build a temple for 1Ch 22:10
S, I have worked hard getting................. 1Ch 22:14
of Israel to help his son S. 1Ch 22:17
made his son S the new king of 1Ch 23:1
he has chosen S to be the new 1Ch 28:5
'Your son S will build my Temple 1Ch 28:6
I have chosen S to be my son, ... 1Ch 28:6
you, my son S, accept the God 1Ch 28:9
S, you must understand this. 1Ch 28:10
gave his son S the plans for 1Ch 28:11
David gave S directions for the 1Ch 28:13
David told S how much gold or 1Ch 28:14
He also gave S the plans for the 1Ch 28:18
David also said to his son S, ... 1Ch 28:20
God chose my son S, who is young 1Ch 29:1
Give my son S a desire to serve 1Ch 29:19
made David's son S king for the............. 1Ch 29:22
olive oil on S to appoint him 1Ch 29:22
Then S sat on the LORD's throne 1Ch 29:23
S was very successful, and all 1Ch 29:23
sons accepted S as king and 1Ch 29:24
The LORD made S great before all........... 1Ch 29:25
and gave S much honor. 1Ch 29:25
Israel before S had such honor. 1Ch 29:25
His son S became king after him. 1Ch 29:28
S, David's son, became a 2Ch 1:1
S spoke to all the people of................... 2Ch 1:2
Then S and all the people with 2Ch 1:3
S and the people worshiped there. 2Ch 1:5
S went up to the bronze altar in 2Ch 1:6
appeared to S and said to him 2Ch 1:7
S answered, "You have been very 2Ch 1:8
God said to S, "You have not 2Ch 1:11
S left the place of worship, ... 2Ch 1:13
There Israel S ruled over Israel. 2Ch 1:13
S had fourteen hundred chariots 2Ch 1:14
In Jerusalem S made silver and 2Ch 1:15
S decided to build a temple as a............. 2Ch 2:1
S sent this message to Hiram 2Ch 2:3
Tyre answered S with this letter 2Ch 2:11
S, because the LORD loves his 2Ch 2:11
S counted all the foreigners 2Ch 2:17
S chose seventy thousand of them 2Ch 2:18
Then S began to build the Temple 2Ch 3:1
S built the Temple on the place 2Ch 3:1
S began building in the second 2Ch 3:2
S used these measurements for 2Ch 3:3
work for King S on the Temple 2Ch 4:11
made for King S for the Temple 2Ch 4:16
S had so many things made that 2Ch 4:18
S also made all the things for 2Ch 4:19
the work S did for the Temple 2Ch 5:1
S called for the elders of...................... 2Ch 5:2
King S and all the Israelites 2Ch 5:6
Then S said, "The LORD said he 2Ch 6:1
S turned to them and blessed 2Ch 6:3
Then S stood facing the LORD's............. 2Ch 6:12
S stood on the platform. 2Ch 6:13
When S finished praying, fire................. 2Ch 7:1
Then King S and all the people 2Ch 7:4
King S offered a sacrifice of 2Ch 7:5
S made holy the middle part of 2Ch 7:7
S and all the Israelites 2Ch 7:8

seventh month S sent the people 2Ch 7:10
good to David, S, and his people 2Ch 7:10
S finished the Temple of the 2Ch 7:11
LORD appeared to S at night and 2Ch 7:12
S had built the Temple of the 2Ch 8:1
S rebuilt the towns that Hiram 2Ch 8:2
and S sent Israelites to live in................ 2Ch 8:2
S also built the town of Tadmor 2Ch 8:4
S forced them to be slave 2Ch 8:8
But S did not make slaves of the 2Ch 8:9
S brought the daughter of the................ 2Ch 8:11
S said, "My wife must not live 2Ch 8:11
Then S offered burnt offerings 2Ch 8:12
S followed his father David's 2Ch 8:14
S went to the towns of Ezion 2Ch 8:17
sent ships to S that were...................... 2Ch 8:18
pounds of gold to King S. 2Ch 8:18
she came to S, she talked with 2Ch 9:1
S answered all her questions................. 2Ch 9:2
Sheba saw that S was very wise. 2Ch 9:3
who served S his wine and their............. 2Ch 9:4
said to King S, "What I heard................ 2Ch 9:5
queen of Sheba gave to King S. 2Ch 9:9
King S used the juniper wood to 2Ch 9:11
King S gave the queen of Sheba 2Ch 9:12
Every year King S received about 2Ch 9:13
King S made two hundred large 2Ch 9:15
King S had many ships that he 2Ch 9:21
S had more riches and wisdom 2Ch 9:22
wanted to see S and listen to 2Ch 9:23
S had four thousand stalls for 2Ch 9:25
S ruled over all the kingdoms 2Ch 9:26
S imported horses from Egypt and........... 2Ch 9:28
Everything else S did, from the 2Ch 9:29
S ruled in Jerusalem over all 2Ch 9:30
Then S died and was buried in 2Ch 9:31
had gone to escape from King S. 2Ch 10:2
who had advised S during his................. 2Ch 10:6
the way David and S had lived. 2Ch 11:17
the gold shields S had made. 2Ch 12:9
the officers of S, David's son, ... 2Ch 13:6
since the time of S son of David 2Ch 30:26
and his son S about the Temple 2Ch 33:7
the Temple that David's son S, ... 2Ch 35:3
and his son S gave you to do. 2Ch 35:4
of the servants of S: .... Ezr 2:55
the servants of S numbered 392............. Ezr 2:58
of the servants of S: .... Ne 7:57
the servants of S totaled 392 .... Ne 7:60
David had commanded his son S. .... Ne 12:45
women made King S of Israel sin. .... Ne 13:26
God loved S and made him king .... Ne 13:26
be ashamed and disgraced. Of S. .... Ps 71:24
for going up to worship. Of S. .... Ps 126:6
wise words of S son of David, ... Pr 1:1
These are the wise words of S: .... Pr 10:1
are more wise sayings of S, ... Pr 25:1
Kedar, like the curtains of S. .... Sng 1:5
King S had a couch made for .... Sng 3:9
go out and see King S. .... Sng 3:11
S had a vineyard at Baal Hamon. .... Sng 8:11
S, the twenty-five pounds of .... Sng 8:12
which King S had made for the .... Je 52:20
David was the father of S. .... Mt 1:6
S was the father of Rehoboam. .... Mt 1:7
you that even S with his riches .... Mt 6:29
someone greater than S is here. .... Mt 12:42
someone greater than S is here. .... Lk 11:31
you that even S with his riches .... Lk 12:27
But S was the one who built the............. Ac 7:47

S

SOLOMON'S

he went to Bathsheba, **S** mother. 1Ki 1:11
and make King **S** throne an even 1Ki 1:37
the oil on **S** head to show he 1Ki 1:39
went to Bathsheba, **S** mother. 1Ki 2:13
heard about King **S** decision, ... 1Ki 3:28
married to Taphath, **S** daughter. 1Ki 4:11
married to Basemath, **S** daughter. 1Ki 4:15
During **S** life Judah and Israel, ... 1Ki 4:25
and straw for **S** chariot and work 1Ki 4:28
came to listen to King **S** wisdom. 1Ki 4:34
they had heard of **S** wisdom. 1Ki 4:34
S and Hiram's builders and the 1Ki 5:18
year of King **S** rule over Israel. 1Ki 6:1
who did the work on **S** projects. 1Ki 9:23
serve in these ships with **S** men. 1Ki 9:27
All of **S** drinking cups, as well 1Ki 10:21
was not valuable in **S** time. 1Ki 10:21
S traders also sold horses and 1Ki 10:29
king of Edom, to become **S** enemy. 1Ki 11:14
another man to be **S** enemy— 1Ki 11:23
of Nebat was one of **S** officers. 1Ki 11:26
will allow **S** son to continue to 1Ki 11:36
Speak to **S** son Rehoboam, the 1Ki 12:23
S son Rehoboam was forty-one 1Ki 14:21
S son was Rehoboam. 1Ch 3:10
had appeared to David, **S** father. 2Ch 3:1
They obeyed all of **S** commands to 2Ch 8:15
All **S** work was done as he had 2Ch 8:16
men went with **S** men to Ophir 2Ch 8:18
of Sheba heard about **S** fame, ... 2Ch 9:1
Hiram's men and **S** men brought 2Ch 9:10
All of **S** drinking cups, as well 2Ch 9:20
In **S** time people did not think 2Ch 9:20
And **S** son Rehoboam became king 2Ch 9:31
Speak to **S** son Rehoboam, the 2Ch 11:3
they supported **S** son Rehoboam 2Ch 11:17
against Rehoboam, **S** son. 2Ch 13:7
and descendants of **S** servants. .... Ne 11:3
S Song of Songs. .... Sng 1:1
it's **S** couch with sixty soldiers .... Sng 3:7
S mother had been Uriah's wife. .... Mt 1:6
to listen to **S** wise teaching. .... Mt 12:42
to listen to **S** wise teaching. .... Lk 11:31
in the Temple in **S** Porch. .... Jn 10:23
and ran to them at **S** Porch. .... Ac 3:11
all meet together on **S** Porch. .... Ac 5:12

SOLVE

the only one to **s** disagreements? .... Ex 18:14
these officers **s** the .... Ex 18:22
but the LORD will **s** them all. .... Ps 34:19
So you must **s** this problem .... Ac 18:15

SOLVED

next day Moses **s** disagreements .... Ex 18:13
with their disagreements **s**." .... Ex 18:23
These officers **s** disagreements .... Ex 18:26
you would not have **s** my riddle!" .... Jdg 14:18
' and the problem would be **s**. 2Sa 20:18
can't be **s** in a day or two .... Ezr 10:13

SOLVES

Remaining calm **s** great problems. .... Ec 10:4

SOLVING

for God's help in **s** their .... Ex 18:15

SOMEDAY

I see someone who will come **s**, ... Nu 24:17
We feared that **s** your people .... Jos 22:24
himself, "Saul will catch me **s**. 1Sa 27:1
S I will go to him, but he 2Sa 12:23
We will all die **s**. We're like 2Sa 14:14
S I will stand up as a witness. .... Zph 3:8

are last now will **s** be first, ... Mt 20:16
are first now will **s** be last." .... Mt 20:16

SON

he named after his **s** Enoch. .... Ge 4:17
Enoch had a **s** named Irad, Irad .... Ge 4:18
and she gave birth to a **s**. .... Ge 4:25
Terah took his **s** Abram, his .... Ge 11:31
pregnant, and you will have a **s**. .... Ge 16:11
gave birth to a **s** for Abram, ... Ge 16:15
the **s** whom Sarah will have at .... Ge 17:21
And Ishmael, his **s**, was thirteen............. Ge 17:25
gave birth to a **s** for Abraham in .... Ge 21:2
Abraham named his **s** Isaac, ... Ge 21:3
old when his **s** Isaac was born. .... Ge 21:5
out this slave woman and her **s**. .... Ge 21:10
Take your only **s**, Isaac, the son .... Ge 22:2
son, Isaac, the **s** you love, and .... Ge 22:2
you did not keep back your **s**, ... Ge 22:12
son, your only **s**, from me, I .... Ge 22:16
a wife for my **s** from my family .... Ge 24:40
son Esau to him and said, "**S**." .... Ge 27:1
Isaac said this to his **s** Esau. .... Ge 27:5
said to her Jacob, "Listen, ... Ge 27:6
he went to Ishmael **s** of Abraham, ... Ge 28:9
that he was the **s** of Rebekah. .... Ge 29:12
news about his sister's **s** Jacob, ... Ge 29:13
pregnant and gave birth to a **s**. .... Ge 29:32
and gave birth to another **s**. .... Ge 29:33
Zilpah gave birth to another **s**, ... Ge 30:12
She gave birth to a fifth **s** .... Ge 30:17
So Leah named her **s** Issachar. .... Ge 30:18
s Joseph has been torn to pieces!" .... Ge 37:33
sad about his **s** for a long time. .... Ge 37:34
be sad about my **s** until the day .... Ge 37:35
So Jacob cried for his **s** Joseph. .... Ge 37:35
My **s** Joseph is still alive, ... Ge 45:28
and each **s** took his own family .... Ex 1:1
Jacob's **s** Joseph was already in .... Ex 1:5
pregnant and gave birth to a **s**. .... Ex 2:2
Israel is my firstborn **s**. .... Ex 4:22
told you to let my **s** go so he .... Ex 4:23
I will kill your firstborn **s**.' " .... Ex 4:23
knife and circumcised her **s**. .... Ex 4:25
she had to circumcise her **s**. .... Ex 4:26
now on when your **s** asks you, ' .... Ex 13:14
The first **s** was named Gershom, ... Ex 18:3
The other **s** was named Eliezer, ... Ex 18:4
helper, Joshua **s** of Nun, did not .... Ex 33:11
chosen Bezalel **s** of Uri the son .... Ex 35:30
Bezalel son of Uri the **s** of Hur, ... Ex 35:30
of her **s** or her daughter .... Le 18:17
mother or father, **s** or daughter, ... Le 21:2
there was a **s** of an Israelite .... Le 24:10
The **s** of the Israelite woman .... Le 24:11
of Dan—Ahiezer **s** of Ammishaddai; .... Nu 1:12
the first **s** born to Israel, ... Nu 1:20
of Ephraim, a **s** of Joseph, was .... Nu 1:32
is Elishama **s** of Ammihud. .... Nu 2:18
is Gamaliel **s** of Pedahzur. .... Nu 2:20
Benjamin is Abidan **s** of Gideoni. .... Nu 2:22
Dan is Ahiezer **s** of Ammishaddai. .... Nu 2:25
was Zuriel **s** of Abihail, ... Nu 3:35
Eleazar **s** of Aaron, the priest, ... Nu 4:16
Ithamar **s** of Aaron, the priest, ... Nu 4:28
Elishama **s** of Ammihud was the .... Nu 10:22
of Issachar, Igal **s** of Joseph; .... Nu 13:7
of Ephraim, Hoshea **s** of Nun; .... Nu 13:8
of Benjamin, Palti **s** of Raphu; .... Nu 13:9
Joshua **s** of Nun and Caleb son of .... Nu 14:6
of Nun and Caleb **s** of Jephunneh, ... Nu 14:6
only Caleb **s** of Jephunneh and .... Nu 14:30
Take Aaron and his **s** Eleazar up .... Nu 20:25

and put them on his s Eleazar. .... Nu 20:26
of Moab, Balak s of Zippor, sent.............. Nu 22:10
Balak s of Zippor says this: .... Nu 22:16
listen. Hear me, s of Zippor. .... Nu 23:18
the message of Balaam s of Beor, ... Nu 24:3
the message of Balaam s of Beor, ... Nu 24:15
Zelophehad was the s of Hepher, ... Nu 27:1
'If a man dies and has no s, ... Nu 27:8
Take Joshua s of Nun, because my .... Nu 27:18
Phinehas s of Eleazar the priest .... Nu 31:6
of Asher, Ahihud s of Shelomi; .... Nu 34:27
you, your s or daughter, your .... Dt 5:14
his s Eleazar became priest in .... Dt 10:6
brother, your s or daughter, ... Dt 13:6
you offer a s or daughter as .... Dt 18:10
not give the s of the wife he .... Dt 21:16
what belongs to the older s, ... Dt 21:16
Our s is stubborn and turns .... Dt 21:20
And they hired Balaam s of Beor, ... Dt 23:4
who was the s of Makir, who was .... Jos 17:3
who was the s of Manasseh. .... Jos 17:3
and to Joshua s of Nun and all .... Jos 17:4
Stone of Bohan s of Reuben. .... Jos 18:17
Joshua s of Nun his land also. .... Jos 19:49
how Achan s of Zerah refused .... Jos 22:20
So Phinehas, s of Eleazar the .... Jos 22:31
children, including his s Isaac. .... Jos 24:3
Othniel s of Kenaz, Caleb's..................... Jdg 1:13
Joshua s of Nun, the servant of .... Jdg 2:8
Othniel s of Kenaz, Caleb's.................... Jdg 3:9
Then Othniel s of Kenaz died. .... Jdg 3:11
s of Gera from the people of .... Jdg 3:15
Shamgar s of Anath saved Israel. .... Jdg 3:31
and Barak s of Abinoam sang .... Jdg 5:1
the days of Shamgar s of Anath, ... Jdg 5:6
your enemies, s of Abinoam! .... Jdg 5:12
Gideon, Joash's s, was .... Jdg 6:11
"Gideon s of Joash did this." .... Jdg 6:29
nor will my s rule over you." .... Jdg 8:23
Gideon s of Joash went to his .... Jdg 8:29
and he had a s by her, whom he .... Jdg 8:31
So Gideon s of Joash died at a .... Jdg 8:32
Abimelech s of Gideon went to .... Jdg 9:1
Gideon's youngest s, Jotham, hid .... Jdg 9:5
the s of my father's slave girl,.......... Jdg 9:18
pregnant and give birth to a s. .... Jdg 13:3
become pregnant and have a s. .... Jdg 13:5
pregnant and will have a s................. Jdg 13:7
gave birth to Judah's s Perez, ... Ru 4:12
and she gave birth to a s. .... Ru 4:13
a man named Elkanah s of Jeroham 1Sa 1:1
in time she gave birth to a s. 1Sa 1:20
to nurse her s until he was old 1Sa 1:23
Kish had a s named Saul, who was 1Sa 9:2
said to Saul, his s, "Take one 1Sa 9:3
"What will I do about my s?"' 1Sa 10:2
What has happened to Kish's s?............. 1Sa 10:11
and Saul s of Kish was picked. 1Sa 10:21
Saul and his s Jonathan and the.............. 1Sa 13:16
Ahijah was a s of Ichabod's 1Sa 14:3
Ichabod was the s of Phinehas, ... 1Sa 14:3
Jesse said to his s David, ... 1Sa 17:17
said, "Find out whose s he is." 1Sa 17:56
I am the s of your servant Jesse 1Sa 17:58
Saul told his s Jonathan and all 1Sa 19:1
Why hasn't the s of Jesse come 1Sa 20:27
He said, "You s of a wicked, ... 1Sa 20:30
on the side of David s of Jesse! 1Sa 20:30
where Saul and Abner s of Ner, ... 1Sa 26:5
and Abishai s of Zeruiah, ... 1Sa 26:6
the army and to Abner s of Ner, ... 1Sa 26:14
Is that your voice, David my s?".............. 1Sa 26:17
Saul and his s Jonathan are dead 2Sa 1:5

Abner s of Ner was the commander 2Sa 2:8
took Saul's s Ish-Bosheth to 2Sa 2:8
Saul's s Ish-Bosheth was forty 2Sa 2:10
Joab s of Zeruiah and David's 2Sa 2:13
for Ish-Bosheth s of Saul, ... 2Sa 2:15
The second s was Kileab, whose.............. 2Sa 3:3
The third s was Absalom, whose 2Sa 3:3
The fourth s was Adonijah,..................... 2Sa 3:4
David had a s named Absalom and 2Sa 13:1
Absalom and a s named Amnon. 2Sa 13:1
named Jonadab s of Shimeah, ... 2Sa 13:3
asked Amnon, "S of the king, why 2Sa 13:4
destruction by killing my s." 2Sa 14:11
lives, no one will hurt your s. 2Sa 14:11
back your s who was forced to 2Sa 14:13
have no s to keep my name alive. 2Sa 18:18
Ahimaaz s of Zadok said to Joab, ... 2Sa 18:19
because the king's s is dead." 2Sa 18:20
But Ahimaaz s of Zadok begged 2Sa 18:22
Joab said, "S, why do you want 2Sa 18:22
runs like Ahimaaz s of Zadok." 2Sa 18:27
cried out, "My s Absalom, my son 2Sa 18:33
Adonijah was the s of King David 1Ki 1:5
spoke with Joab s of Zeruiah and 1Ki 1:7
priest, Benaiah s of Jehoiada,..................... 1Ki 1:8
Haggith's s, has made himself 1Ki 1:11
that my s Solomon would be 1Ki 1:13
'Your s Solomon will become king 1Ki 1:17
living baby is my s, and the 1Ki 3:22
s is alive and your s on is dead. 1Ki 3:23
is alive and your s is dead.'..................... 1Ki 3:23
s is dead and my son is alive. 1Ki 3:23
is dead and my son is alive.'" 1Ki 3:23
was full of love for her s. 1Ki 3:26
will make your s king after you 1Ki 5:5
David a wise s to rule over this 1Ki 5:7
Your s, who comes from your own 1Ki 8:19
away from your s when he becomes 1Ki 11:12
Jeroboam s of Nebat was one of.............. 1Ki 11:26
he was the s of a widow named 1Ki 11:26
the kingdom away from his s,................... 1Ki 11:35
As s of Solomon, Rehoboam wanted 1Ki 12:21
Speak to Solomon's s Rehoboam, ... 1Ki 12:23
will have a s named Josiah. 1Ki 13:2
time Jeroboam's s Abijah became 1Ki 14:1
Ahab s of Omri became king of 1Ki 16:29
Ahab s of Omri did many things 1Ki 16:30
ways as Jeroboam s of Nebat,..................... 1Ki 16:31
his oldest s, to begin work 1Ki 16:34
his youngest s, to build the 1Ki 16:34
through Joshua s of Nun, ... 1Ki 16:34
My s and I will eat it and then 1Ki 17:12
for yourself and your s. 1Ki 17:13
pour oil on Jehu s of Nimshi to 1Ki 19:16
pour oil on Elisha s of Shaphat 1Ki 19:16
and found Elisha s of Shaphat 1Ki 19:19
of King Jeroboam s of Nebat and 1Ki 21:22
of King Baasha s of Ahijah. 1Ki 21:22
year Jehoram s of Jehoshaphat 2Ki 1:17
had no s to take his place. 2Ki 1:17
Joram s of Ahab became king over 2Ki 3:1
like Jeroboam s of Nebat who had 2Ki 3:3
Elisha s of Shaphat is there. 2Ki 3:11
Elisha said, "Pick up your s." 2Ki 4:36
picked up her s and went out..................... 2Ki 4:37
So we boiled my s and ate him. 2Ki 6:29
to visit Joram s of Ahab at 2Ki 8:29
driving like Jehu s of Nimshi..................... 2Ki 9:20
year Joram s of Ahab was king. 2Ki 9:29
he met Jehonadab s of Recab, ... 2Ki 10:15
and Jehonadab s of Recab went 2Ki 10:23
sins Jeroboam s of Nebat had..................... 2Ki 10:29
his servant Jonah s of Amittai, ... 2Ki 14:25

"This is my **S,** whom I love, ... Mt 3:17
If you are the **S** of God, tell. .... Mt 4:3
If you are the **S** of God, jump .... Mt 4:6
but the **S** of Man has no place to .... Mt 8:20
do you want with us, **S** of God? .... Mt 8:29
to you that the **S** of Man has .... Mt 9:6
Have mercy on us, **S** of David!" .... Mt 9:27
James **s** of Zebedee, and his .... Mt 10:2
James **s** of Alphaeus, and .... Mt 10:3
love their **s** or daughter more .... Mt 10:37
The **S** of Man came, eating and .... Mt 11:19
No one knows the **S,** except the .... Mt 11:27
So the **S** of Man is Lord of the .... Mt 12:8
this man is the **S** of David!" .... Mt 12:23
against the **S** of Man can be .... Mt 12:32
S of Man will be in the grave .... Mt 12:40
in the field is the **S** of Man.................... Mt 13:37
The **S** of Man will send out his .... Mt 13:41
He is just the **s** of a carpenter. .... Mt 13:55
"Truly you are the **S** of God!" .... Mt 14:33
out, "Lord, **S** of David, have .... Mt 15:22
do people say the **S** of Man is?" .... Mt 16:13
Christ, the **S** of the living God. .... Mt 16:16
blessed, Simon **s** of Jonah, ... Mt 16:17
S of Man will come again with .... Mt 16:27
The **S** of Man will be turned over .... Mt 20:18
They will give the **S** of Man to .... Mt 20:19
the **S** of Man did not come to be.............. Mt 20:28
shouted, "Lord, **S** of David, have .... Mt 20:30
more, "Lord, **S** of David, have .... Mt 20:31
Praise to the **S** of David! .... Mt 21:9
the Christ? Whose **s** is he?" They .... Mt 22:42
"The Christ is the **S** of David." .... Mt 22:42
so how can the Christ be his **s**?" .... Mt 22:45
of Zechariah **s** of Berakiah, ... Mt 23:35
When the **S** of Man comes, he will .... Mt 24:27
the sign of the **S** of Man will .... Mt 24:30
will see the **S** of Man coming .... Mt 24:30
are the Christ, the **S** of God." .... Mt 26:63
will see the **S** of Man sitting .... Mt 26:64
if you are really the **S** of God!" .... Mt 27:40
said, "I am the **S** of God.'" .... Mt 27:43
"He really was the **S** of God!" .... Mt 27:54
Father and the **S** and the Holy .... Mt 28:19
Jesus Christ, the **S** of God, ... Mk 1:1
You are my **S,** whom I love, and I .... Mk 1:11
to you that the **S** of Man has .... Mk 2:10
a man named Levi **s** of Alphaeus, ... Mk 2:14
the **S** of Man is Lord even of the .... Mk 2:28
shouted, "You are the **S** of God!" .... Mk 3:11
Thomas, James the **s** of Alphaeus, ... Mk 3:18
with me, Jesus, **S** of the Most .... Mk 5:7
the **s** of Mary and the brother of........... Mk 6:3
The **S** of Man will die, just as .... Mk 14:21
who hands the **S** of Man over to.............. Mk 14:21
has come for the **S** of Man to be.............. Mk 14:41
the **S** of the blessed God?" .... Mk 14:61
will see the **S** of Man sitting .... Mk 14:62
man really was the **S** of God!" .... Mk 15:39
James was her youngest **s.** .... Mk 15:40
give birth to a **s,** and you will .... Lk 1:13
pregnant and give birth to a **s,** .... Lk 1:31
be called the **S** of the Most High .... Lk 1:32
and will be called the **S** of God. .... Lk 1:35
pregnant while a **s** though she is .... Lk 1:36
she gave birth to her first **s.** .... Lk 2:7
said to him, "**S,** why did you do .... Lk 2:48
God came to John **s** of Zechariah .... Lk 3:2
You are my **S,** whom I love, and I .... Lk 3:22
that Jesus was Joseph's **s.** .... Lk 3:23
Seth was the **s** of Adam. Adam was .... Lk 3:38
of Adam. Adam was the **s** of God. .... Lk 3:38
Judas **s** of James, and Judas .... Lk 6:16

The **S** of Man will be handed over .... Lk 9:44
The **S** of Man did not come to .... Lk 9:56
but the **S** of Man has no place to .... Lk 9:58
No one knows who the **S** is, ... Lk 10:22
except the **S** and those whom the .... Lk 10:22
whom the **S** chooses to tell. .... Lk 10:22
the **S** of Man will be a sign for .... Lk 11:30
in me, I, the **S** of Man, will say .... Lk 12:8
against the **S** of Man can be .... Lk 12:10
because the **S** of Man will come .... Lk 12:40
father against **s** and son against .... Lk 12:53
The older **s** was in the field, ... Lk 15:25
The older **s** was angry and would .... Lk 15:28
But the older **s** said to his .... Lk 15:29
But your other **s,** who wasted all .... Lk 15:30
said to him, '**S,** you are always .... Lk 15:31
one of the days of the **S** of Man. .... Lk 17:22
When the **S** of Man comes again, ... Lk 17:24
When the **S** of Man comes again, ... Lk 17:26
will be when the **S** of Man comes .... Lk 17:30
But when the **S** of Man comes .... Lk 18:8
about the **S** of Man will happen.............. Lk 18:31
out, "Jesus, **S** of David, have .... Lk 18:38
even more, "**S** of David, have .... Lk 18:39
The **S** of Man came to find lost .... Lk 19:10
so how can the Christ be his **s**?" .... Lk 20:44
will see the **S** of Man coming .... Lk 21:27
to stand before the **S** of Man." .... Lk 21:36
planned for the **S** of Man will .... Lk 22:22
who turns against the **S** of Man." .... Lk 22:22
kiss to give the **S** of Man to his .... Lk 22:48
the **S** of Man will sit at the .... Lk 22:69
"Then are you the **S** of God?" .... Lk 22:70
He said the **S** of Man must be .... Lk 24:7
to the only **S** of the Father— .... Jn 1:14
God the only **S** is very close to .... Jn 1:18
This man is the **S** of God." .... Jn 1:34
said, "You are Simon **s** of John. .... Jn 1:42
He is Jesus, the **s** of Joseph, ... Jn 1:45
Teacher, you are the **S** of God; .... Jn 1:49
coming down' on the **S** of Man." .... Jn 1:51
down from heaven—the **S** of Man. .... Jn 3:13
S of Man must also be lifted up. .... Jn 3:14
one and only **S** so that whoever .... Jn 3:16
not send his **S** into the world .... Jn 3:17
believe in God's **S** are not .... Jn 3:18
in God's one and only **S.** .... Jn 3:18
Father loves the **S** and has given .... Jn 3:35
believe in the **S** have eternal .... Jn 3:36
not obey the **S** will never have .... Jn 3:36
Jacob gave to his **s** Joseph. .... Jn 4:5
Go. Your **s** will live." The man .... Jn 4:50
Father loves the **S** and shows the .... Jn 5:20
and shows the **S** all the things .... Jn 5:20
flesh of the **S** of Man and drink .... Jn 6:53
you to see the **S** of Man going .... Jn 6:62
about Judas, the **s** of Simon .... Jn 6:71
When you lift up the **S** of Man, ... Jn 8:28
but a **s** belongs to the family .... Jn 8:35
So if the **S** makes you free, ... Jn 8:36
Is this your **s** who you say was .... Jn 9:19
this is our **s** and that he was .... Jn 9:20
"Do you believe in the **S** of Man?" .... Jn 9:35
Who is the **S** of Man, sir, so .... Jn 9:36
The **S** of Man is the one talking .... Jn 9:37
because I said, 'I am God's **S**'? .... Jn 10:36
to bring glory to the **S** of God." .... Jn 11:4
Christ, the **S** of God, the One .... Jn 11:27
has come for the **S** of Man to .... Jn 12:23
'The **S** of Man must be lifted up'? .... Jn 12:34
Who is this '**S** of Man'?" .... Jn 12:34
Iscariot, the **s** of Simon, to .... Jn 13:2
Judas Iscariot, the **s** of Simon. .... Jn 13:26

S

Now the **S** of Man receives his .... Jn 13:31
glory to the **S** through himself. .... Jn 13:32
will be shown through the **S**. .... Jn 14:13
glory to your **S** so that the Son .... Jn 17:1
Son so that the **S** can give glory .... Jn 17:1
You gave the **S** power over all .... Jn 17:2
so that the **S** could give eternal .... Jn 17:2
he said he is the **S** of God.".................... Jn 19:7
Dear woman, here is your **s**." .... Jn 19:26
is the Christ, the **S** of God. .... Jn 20:31
Peter, "Simon **s** of John, do you .... Jn 21:15
said, "Simon **s** of John, do you .... Jn 21:16
said, "Simon **s** of John, do you .... Jn 21:17
Matthew, James **s** of Alphaeus, ... Ac 1:13
and Judas **s** of James were there. .... Ac 1:13
so when Abraham had his **s** Isaac, ... Ac 7:8
also circumcised his **s** Jacob, ... Ac 7:8
him as if he were her own **s**. .... Ac 7:21
open and the **S** of Man standing............... Ac 7:56
Jesus Christ is the **S** of God." .... Ac 8:37
saying, "Jesus is the **S** of God." .... Ac 9:20
and said, "You **s** of the devil! .... Ac 13:10
so God gave them Saul **s** of Kish. .... Ac 13:21
found in David **s** of Jesse the .... Ac 13:22
2: 'You are my **S**. Today I have .... Ac 13:33
him were Sopater **s** of Pyrrhus, ... Ac 20:4
with the death of his own **s**. .... Ac 20:28
the Good News about his **S**, ... Rm 1:9
through the death of his **S**. .... Rm 5:10
He sent his own **S** to earth with .... Rm 8:3
By sending his **S** to be an .... Rm 8:3
to be like his **S** so that Jesus .... Rm 8:29
for them to be like his **S**;..................... Rm 8:30
he planned to be like his **S**,.................... Rm 8:30
spare his own **S** but gave him for .... Rm 8:32
and Sarah will have a **s**." .... Rm 9:9
you into fellowship with his **S**, ... 1Co 1:9
you Timothy, my **s** in the Lord. 1Co 4:17
has been put under the **S**, ... 1Co 15:28
The **S** of God, Jesus Christ, that 2Co 1:19
and showed his **s** to me so that I............... Gal 1:16
by faith in the **S** of God who .... Gal 2:20
God sent his **S** who was born of a .... Gal 4:4
Spirit of his **S** into your hearts .... Gal 4:6
out the slave woman and her **s**. .... Gal 4:30
The **s** of the slave woman should .... Gal 4:30
The **s** of the free woman should .... Gal 4:30
same knowledge of the **S** of God. .... Eph 4:13
News, as a **s** serves his father. .... Php 2:22
into the kingdom of his dear **S**. .... Col 1:13
The **S** paid for our sins, and in .... Col 1:14
for God's **S**, whom God raised 1Th 1:10
has spoken to us through his **S**. .... Heb 1:2
of the angels, "You are my **S**. .... Heb 1:5
Father, and he will be my **S**." .... Heb 1:5
But God said this about his **S**: .... Heb 1:8
God said to him, "You are my **S**. .... Heb 5:5
though Jesus was the **S** of God, ... Heb 5:8
are nailing the **S** of God to a .... Heb 6:6
is like the **S** of God;........................... Heb 7:3
who do not respect the **S** of God, ... Heb 10:29
offered his **s** Isaac as a .... Heb 11:17
offer his own **s** as a sacrifice. .... Heb 11:17
be called the **s** of the king of .... Heb 11:24
As the oldest **s**, Esau would have .... Heb 12:16
he offered his **s** Isaac on the .... Jam 2:21
Mark, my **s** in Christ, also 1Pe 5:13
"This is my **S**, whom I love, ... 2Pe 1:17
Balaam was the **s** of Beor, who 2Pe 2:15
God the Father and his **S**, ... 1Jn 1:3
of Jesus, God's **S**, cleanses us................. 1Jn 1:7
one and only **S** into the world 1Jn 4:9
sent his **S** to die in our place 1Jn 4:10

Father sent his **S** to be the 1Jn 4:14
Jesus is the **S** of God has God 1Jn 4:15
that Jesus is the **S** of God. 1Jn 5:5
us the truth about his own **S**. 1Jn 5:9
who believes in the **S** of God has 1Jn 5:10
what God told us about his **S**................. 1Jn 5:10
life, and this life is in his **S**. 1Jn 5:11
Whoever has the **S** has life, ... 1Jn 5:12
not have the **S** of God does not 1Jn 5:12
believe in the **S** of God so you 1Jn 5:13
The **S** of God keeps them safe, ... 1Jn 5:18
know that the **S** of God has come 1Jn 5:20
in the True One and in his **S**, ... 1Jn 5:20
from God the Father and his **S**, ... 2Jn 1:3
has both the Father and the **S**. 2Jn 1:9
who was "like a **S** of Man." .... Rev 1:13
The **S** of God, who has eyes that .... Rev 2:18
gave birth to a **s** who will rule .... Rev 12:5
who had given birth to the **s**. .... Rev 12:13
One who looked like a **S** of Man. .... Rev 14:14

SON'S

me some of your **s** mandrakes." .... Ge 30:14
to take away my **s** mandrakes." .... Ge 30:15
will give me your **s** mandrakes, ... Ge 30:15
for you with my **s** mandrakes." .... Ge 30:16
and see if it is your **s** robe." .... Ge 37:32
over and said, "It is my **s** robe! .... Ge 37:33
This youngest **s** brother is dead,............... Ge 44:20
with your **s** daughter or your .... Le 18:10
she is your **s** wife. Do not have .... Le 18:15
What is his name or his **s** name? .... Pr 30:4
son and then to the **s** children. .... Eze 46:16
will save us through his **S** life. .... Rm 5:10

SON-IN-LAW

the **s** of the man from Timnah, ... Jdg 15:6
woman's father said to his **s**, ... Jdg 19:5
for me to become the king's **s**." 1Sa 18:18
time, "You may become my **s**." 1Sa 18:21
You should be his **s**." 1Sa 18:22
is easy to become the king's **s**? 1Sa 18:23
pleased to become the king's **s**. 1Sa 18:26
so he could be the king's **s**.................... 1Sa 18:27
your own **s** and captain of your 1Sa 22:14
because he was a **s** to Ahab. 2Ki 8:27
he was the **s** of Shecaniah son .... Ne 6:18

SONG

sang this **s** to the LORD:........................ Ex 15:1
Then the Israelites sang this **s**: .... Nu 21:17
write down this **s** and teach it.................. Dt 31:19
s will testify against them, ... Dt 31:21
because the **s** will not be...................... Dt 31:21
Moses wrote down the **s** that day, ... Dt 31:22
spoke this whole **s** for all the .... Dt 31:30
words of this **s** for the people .... Dt 32:44
son of Abinoam sang this **s**: .... Jdg 5:1
Wake up, wake up, sing a **s**! .... Jdg 5:12
The women's **s** upset Saul, and he 1Sa 18:8
sang a funeral **s** about Saul and 2Sa 1:17
of Judah be taught this **s**. 2Sa 1:18
sang this funeral **s** for Abner. 2Sa 3:33
David sang this **s** to the LORD 2Sa 22:1
praised the LORD with this **s**:................. 2Ch 5:13
harp is tuned to sing a sad **s**, ... Job 30:31
David sang this **s** to the LORD .... Ps 17:15
and I praise him with my **s**. .... Ps 28:7
A **s** for giving the Temple to the .... Ps 29:11
Sing a new **s** to him; play well .... Ps 33:3
David's **s** from the time he acted .... Ps 33:22
He put a new **s** in my mouth, ... Ps 40:3
my mouth, a **s** of praise to our .... Ps 40:3
night I have a **s**, and I pray to................. Ps 42:8
A love **s** of the sons of Korah.................. Ps 44:26

so sing a **s** of praise to him. .... Ps 47:7
of music. A psalm of David. A **s.** .... Ps 64:10
director of music. A **s.** A psalm .... Ps 65:13
instruments. A psalm. A **s.** .... Ps 66:20
of music. A psalm of David. A **s.** .... Ps 67:7
praise God in a **s** and will honor .... Ps 69:30
Destroy." A psalm of Asaph. A **s.** .... Ps 74:23
A psalm of Asaph. A **s.** .... Ps 75:10
the nations. A **s.** A psalm of .... Ps 82:8
and comforted me. A **s.** A psalm .... Ps 86:17
from Jerusalem." A **s.** A psalm of .... Ps 87:7
A **s** for the Sabbath day. .... Ps 91:16
Sing to the LORD a new **s**; .... Ps 96:1
the LORD a new **s**, because he has........... Ps 98:1
of the LORD. A **s.** A psalm of .... Ps 107:43
LORD gives me strength and a **s.** .... Ps 118:14
A **s** for going up to worship. .... Ps 120:7
A **s** for going up to worship. .... Ps 121:8
A **s** for going up to worship. .... Ps 122:9
A **s** for going up to worship. .... Ps 123:4
A **s** for going up to worship. .... Ps 124:8
A **s** for going up to worship. .... Ps 125:5
A **s** for going up to worship. .... Ps 126:6
A **s** for going up to worship. .... Ps 127:5
A **s** for going up to worship. .... Ps 128:6
A **s** for going up to worship. .... Ps 129:8
A **s** for going up to worship. .... Ps 130:8
A **s** for going up to worship. .... Ps 131:3
A **s** for going up to worship. .... Ps 132:18
A **s** for going up to worship. .... Ps 133:3
"Sing us a **s** about Jerusalem!" .... Ps 137:3
I will sing a new **s** to you; .... Ps 144:9
Sing a new **s** to the LORD; .... Ps 149:1
Solomon's **S** of Songs. .... Sng 1:1
for my friend a **s** about his .... Is 5:1
will sing this **s** about the king............... Is 14:4
like a harp playing a funeral **s**; .... Is 16:11
like the prostitute in this **s**: .... Is 23:15
well. Sing your **s** often. Then .... Is 23:16
will sing this **s** in Judah: .... Is 26:1
Judah got well, he wrote this **s**: .... Is 38:9
Sing a new **s** to the LORD; .... Is 42:10
will burst into **s** before you, ... Is 55:12
sing a funeral **s** for the empty................ Je 9:10
Teach one another a funeral **s**. .... Je 9:20
make fun of you with this **s**: ' .... Je 38:22
a flute playing a funeral **s**. .... Je 48:36
Sing a funeral **s** for the leaders .... Eze 19:1
is a funeral **s**; it is to be used .... Eze 19:14
is to be used as a funeral **s**." .... Eze 19:14
singing a funeral **s** about you .... Eze 26:17
sing a funeral **s** for the city of.............. Eze 27:2
they sing a funeral **s** for you: .... Eze 27:32
sing a funeral **s** for the king of .... Eze 28:12
sing a funeral **s** about the king .... Eze 32:2
the funeral **s** people will sing .... Eze 32:16
sing a funeral **s** for Egypt and .... Eze 32:16
to this funeral **s** that I sing .... Am 5:1
and sing this sad **s** about you: ' .... Mic 2:4
we sang a sad **s**, but you did not............. Mt 11:17
we sang a sad **s**, but you did not............. Lk 7:32
person has a **s**, and another has 1Co 14:26
all sang a new **s** to the Lamb:................. Rev 5:9
they sang a new **s** before the .... Rev 14:3
learn the new **s** except the one .... Rev 14:3
They sang the **s** of Moses, the................ Rev 15:3
of God, and the **s** of the Lamb: .... Rev 15:3

SONGS

They sang **s** of joy, danced, and 1Sa 18:6
also wrote one thousand five **s**. 1Ki 4:32
and cymbals and to sing happy **s**. 1Ch 15:16
when **s** were sung to God 1Ch 16:42

wrote some sad **s** about Josiah. 2Ch 35:25
and honor Josiah with these **s**. 2Ch 35:25
to sing these **s** that are written 2Ch 35:25
in the collection of sad **s**. 2Ch 35:25
charge of the **s** of thanksgiving. .... Ne 12:8
celebrate with **s** of thanksgiving............. Ne 12:27
singers and of the **s** of praise .... Ne 12:46
Now they make fun of me with **s**; .... Job 30:9
who gives us **s** in the night, ... Job 35:10
let them sing glad **s** forever. .... Ps 5:11
fill me with **s** of salvation. .... Ps 32:7
God's Temple with **s** of praise. .... Ps 42:4
will sing **s** of praise about you .... Ps 57:9
drunkards make up **s** about me. .... Ps 69:12
At night I remember my **s**. .... Ps 77:6
Let's sing **s** to him, ... Ps 95:2
burst into **s** and make music. .... Ps 98:4
his city with **s** of thanksgiving .... Ps 100:4
his courtyards with **s** of praise. .... Ps 100:4
will sing **s** of praise about you .... Ps 108:3
laughter, and we sang happy **s**. .... Ps 126:2
our enemies wanted happy **s**. .... Ps 137:3
we cannot sing **s** about the LORD .... Ps 137:4
Singing **s** to someone who is sad .... Pr 25:20
Solomon's Song of **S**. .... Sng 1:1
orchards and no **s** or shouts of .... Is 16:10
We hear **s** from every part of the .... Is 24:16
you silence the **s** of those who .... Is 25:5
will sing happy **s** as on the .... Is 30:29
so we will play **s** on stringed .... Is 38:20
I made will sing **s** to praise me. .... Is 43:21
will give thanks and sing **s**. .... Is 51:3
places will sing **s** of praise. .... Je 30:19
fun of me with **s** all day long. .... La 3:14
do they make fun of me with **s**. .... La 3:63
Funeral **s**, sad writings, and .... Eze 2:10
So I will stop your **s**; .... Eze 26:13
who sings love **s** and has a .... Eze 33:32
noise of your **s** away from me! .... Am 5:23
You make up **s** on your harps, ... Am 6:5
you compose **s** on musical .... Am 6:5
day the palace **s** will become .... Am 8:3
songs will become funeral **s**," .... Am 8:3
and all your **s** will become songs .... Am 8:10
songs will become **s** of sadness. .... Am 8:10
and singing **s** to God as the .... Ac 16:25
and spiritual **s**, singing and.................. Eph 5:19
spiritual **s** with thankfulness .... Col 3:16

SONS

and had other **s** and daughters. .... Ge 5:4
and had other **s** and daughters. .... Ge 5:7
and had other **s** and daughters. .... Ge 5:10
and had other **s** and daughters. .... Ge 5:13
and had other **s** and daughters. .... Ge 5:16
and had other **s** and daughters. .... Ge 5:19
and had other **s** and daughters. .... Ge 5:22
and had other **s** and daughters. .... Ge 5:26
and had other **s** and daughters. .... Ge 5:30
When the **s** of God saw that these .... Ge 6:2
was when the **s** of God had sexual .... Ge 6:4
He had three **s**: Shem, Ham, and .... Ge 6:10
with you—you, your **s**, your wife, ... Ge 6:18
and your **s'** wives will all go .... Ge 6:18
wife and his **s** and their wives .... Ge 7:7
and his wife, his **s** Shem, Ham, ... Ge 7:13
your wife, your **s**, and their................... Ge 8:16
So Noah went out with his **s**, ... Ge 8:18
his wife, and his **s'** wives. .... Ge 8:18
Noah and his **s** and said to them, ... Ge 9:1
Then God said to Noah and his **s**, ... Ge 9:8
s of Noah who came out of the .... Ge 9:18
These three men were Noah's **s**,.............. Ge 9:19

earth came from these three **s**.	Ge 9:19
Ham, and Japheth, the **s** of Noah.	Ge 10:1
the flood these three men had **s**.	Ge 10:1
The **s** of Japheth were Gomer,	Ge 10:2
The **s** of Gomer were Ashkenaz,	Ge 10:3
The **s** of Javan were Elishah,	Ge 10:4
came from these **s** of Japheth.	Ge 10:5
The **s** of Ham were Cush, Mizraim,	Ge 10:6
s of Cush were Seba, Havilah,	Ge 10:7
The **s** of Raamah were Sheba and	Ge 10:7
these people were the **s** of Ham,	Ge 10:20
older brother, also had **s**.	Ge 10:21
the father of all the **s** of Eber.	Ge 10:21
The **s** of Shem were Elam, Asshur,	Ge 10:22
The **s** of Aram were Uz, Hul,	Ge 10:23
Eber was the father of two **s**—	Ge 10:25
people were the **s** of Joktan.	Ge 10:29
the families from the **s** of Noah,	Ge 10:32
and had other **s** and daughters.	Ge 11:11
and had other **s** and daughters.	Ge 11:13
and had other **s** and daughters.	Ge 11:15
and had other **s** and daughters.	Ge 11:17
and had other **s** and daughters.	Ge 11:19
and had other **s** and daughters.	Ge 11:21
and had other **s** and daughters.	Ge 11:23
and had other **s** and daughters.	Ge 11:25
years old, his **s** Abram, Nahor,	Ge 11:26
any sons-in-law, **s**, daughters,	Ge 19:12
was the mother of these eight **s**,	Ge 22:23
had four other **s** by his slave	Ge 22:24
The **s** of Midian were Ephah,	Ge 25:4
give gifts to the **s** of his other	Ge 25:6
His **s** Isaac and Ishmael buried	Ge 25:9
of Ishmael's **s** in the order they	Ge 25:13
were Ishmael's **s**, and these are	Ge 25:16
your mother's **s** bow down to you	Ge 27:29
both of my **s** on the same day.	Ge 27:45
did not want his **s** to marry.	Ge 28:8
I have given him three **s**."	Ge 29:34
because I have given him six **s**,"	Ge 30:20
told his **s** to watch over them.	Ge 30:35
Jacob heard Laban's **s** talking.	Ge 31:1
slave girls, and his eleven **s**.	Ge 32:22
from the **s** of Hamor father	Ge 33:19
but since his **s** were out in the	Ge 34:5
When Jacob's **s** heard what had	Ge 34:7
Jacob's **s** answered Shechem and	Ge 34:13
of Jacob's **s**, Simeon and Levi.	Ge 34:25
Jacob's **s** came upon the dead.	Ge 34:27
Then Jacob and his **s** left there.	Ge 35:5
about it. Jacob had twelve **s**.	Ge 35:22
He had six **s** by his wife Leah:	Ge 35:23
He had two **s** by his wife Rachel:	Ge 35:24
He had two **s** by Rachel's slave	Ge 35:25
And he had two **s** by Leah's slave	Ge 35:26
These are Jacob's **s** who were	Ge 35:26
and his **s** Esau and Jacob buried	Ge 35:29
These were Esau's **s** who were	Ge 36:5
his wives, his **s**, his daughters,	Ge 36:6
Esau's **s** were Eliphaz, son of	Ge 36:10
Eliphaz had five **s**: Teman, Omar,	Ge 36:11
Reuel had four **s**: Nahath, Zerah,	Ge 36:13
These were the **s** of Esau (also	Ge 36:19
These were the **s** of Seir the	Ge 36:20
These **s** of Seir were the leaders	Ge 36:21
The **s** of Lotan were Hori and	Ge 36:22
The **s** of Shobal were Alvan,	Ge 36:23
The **s** of Zibeon were Aiah and	Ge 36:24
The **s** of Dishon were Hemdan,	Ge 36:26
The **s** of Ezer were Bilhan,	Ge 36:27
s of Dishan were Uz and Aran.	Ge 36:28
the **s** of Bilhah and Zilpah,	Ge 37:2
loved him more than his other **s**.	Ge 37:3
All of his **s** and daughters tried	Ge 37:35
Joseph and Asenath had two **s**.	Ge 41:50
he said to his **s**, "Why are you	Ge 42:1
the **s** of Israel went to Egypt to	Ge 42:5
We are all **s** of the same father.	Ge 42:11
twelve brothers, **s** of the same	Ge 42:13
twelve brothers—**s** of one father.	Ge 42:32
may put my two **s** to death if I	Ge 42:37
my wife Rachel gave me two **s**.	Ge 44:27
So the **s** of Israel did this.	Ge 45:21
The **s** of Israel loaded their	Ge 46:5
his **s** and grandsons, his	Ge 46:7
Reuben's **s** were Hanoch, Pallu,	Ge 46:9
Simeon's **s** were Jemuel, Jamin,	Ge 46:10
Levi's **s** were Gershon, Kohath,	Ge 46:11
Judah's **s** were Er, Onan, Shelah,	Ge 46:12
Perez's **s** were Hezron and Hamul.	Ge 46:12
Issachar's **s** were Tola, Puah,	Ge 46:13
Zebulun's **s** were Sered, Elon,	Ge 46:14
are the **s** of Leah and Jacob	Ge 46:15
Gad's **s** were Zephon, Haggi,	Ge 46:16
Asher's **s** were Imnah, Ishvah,	Ge 46:17
Beriah's **s** were Heber and	Ge 46:17
These are Jacob's **s** by Zilpah,	Ge 46:18
s of Jacob's wife Rachel were	Ge 46:19
Benjamin's **s** were Bela, Beker,	Ge 46:21
These are the **s** of Jacob by his	Ge 46:22
Naphtali's **s** were Jahziel,	Ge 46:24
These are Jacob's **s** by Bilhah,	Ge 46:25
counting the wives of Jacob's **s**.	Ge 46:26
Joseph had two **s** born in Egypt,	Ge 46:27
he took his two **s** Manasseh and	Ge 48:1
Your two **s**, who were born here	Ge 48:5
will be counted as my own **s**.	Ge 48:5
will be my **s** just as Reuben	Ge 48:5
as Reuben and Simeon are my **s**.	Ge 48:5
Israel saw Joseph's **s** and said,	Ge 48:8
They are my **s** that God has given	Ge 48:9
Bring your **s** to me so I may	Ge 48:9
moved his **s** off Israel's lap	Ge 48:12
Then Jacob called his **s** to him.	Ge 49:1
together and listen, **s** of Jacob.	Ge 49:2
the highest position among my **s**,	Ge 49:3
Jacob finished talking to his **s**,	Ge 49:33
So Jacob's **s** did as their father	Ge 50:12
Joseph had the **s** of Israel make	Ge 50:25
he took his **s**, and each son took	Ex 1:1
the names of the **s** of Israel:	Ex 1:1
Moses took his wife and his **s**,	Ex 4:20
first son, Reuben, had four **s**:	Ex 6:14
Simeon's **s** were Jemuel, Jamin,	Ex 6:15
the names of **s** according to	Ex 6:16
Gershon had two **s**, Libni and	Ex 6:17
The **s** of Kohath were Amram,	Ex 6:18
The **s** of Merari were Mahli and	Ex 6:19
Izhar's **s** were Korah, Nepheg,	Ex 6:21
Uzziel's **s** were Mishael,	Ex 6:22
The **s** of Korah were Assir,	Ex 6:24
old people, our **s** and daughters,	Ex 10:9
all the firstborn **s** in the land	Ex 12:29
LORD every firstborn of your **s**.	Ex 13:13
my firstborn **s** from the LORD.'	Ex 13:15
with his two **s**. The first son	Ex 18:3
wife and his two **s** and went to	Ex 18:5
with your wife and her two **s**."	Ex 18:6
gives birth to **s** or daughters,	Ex 21:4
must give me your firstborn **s**.	Ex 22:29
Aaron and his **s** must keep the	Ex 27:21
along with his **s** Nadab, Abihu,	Ex 28:1
your brother Aaron and his **s**.	Ex 28:4
the twelve **s** of Israel on them,	Ex 28:9
the names of the **s** of Israel on	Ex 28:11
of the twelve **s** of Israel.	Ex 28:12

as reminders of the **s** of Israel.	Ex 28:12
of the names of the **s** of Israel.	Ex 28:21
names of the **s** of Israel over	Ex 28:29
and headbands for Aaron's **s**,	Ex 28:40
on your brother Aaron and his **s**,	Ex 28:41
Aaron and his **s** must wear these	Ex 28:43
Aaron and his **s** to serve me as	Ex 29:1
Aaron and his **s** to the entrance	Ex 29:4
Then bring his **s** and put the	Ex 29:8
Aaron and his **s** as priests.	Ex 29:9
Aaron and his **s** must put their	Ex 29:10
Aaron and his **s** put their hands	Ex 29:15
Aaron and his **s** put their hands	Ex 29:19
of Aaron and his **s** and on the	Ex 29:20
and on his **s** and their clothes	Ex 29:21
Aaron and his **s** and their	Ex 29:21
in the hands of Aaron and his **s**,	Ex 29:24
Aaron and his **s** as priests.	Ex 29:27
always give to Aaron and his **s**.	Ex 29:28
Aaron and his **s** must eat the	Ex 29:32
you to do to Aaron and his **s**,	Ex 29:35
Aaron and his **s** so they will be	Ex 29:36
Aaron and his **s** holy so they may	Ex 29:44
Aaron and his **s** must wash their	Ex 30:19
Aaron and his **s** to give them for	Ex 30:30
clothes for his **s** to wear when	Ex 31:10
your wives, **s**, and daughters	Ex 32:2
to kill your own **s** and brothers,	Ex 32:29
as wives for your **s** and those	Ex 34:16
will lead your **s** to do the same	Ex 34:16
buy back all your firstborn **s**.	Ex 34:20
priest and his **s** to wear when	Ex 35:19
the names of the **s** of Israel on	Ex 39:6
of the twelve **s** of Israel.	Ex 39:7
names of the **s** of Israel were	Ex 39:14
fine linen for Aaron and his **s**,	Ex 39:27
and the clothes for his **s**,	Ex 39:41
Aaron and his **s** to the entrance	Ex 40:12
Aaron's **s** and put the inner	Ex 40:14
and Aaron's **s** used this water to	Ex 40:31
and Aaron's **s**, the priests	Le 1:5
and Aaron's **s**, the priests,	Le 1:11
then take it to Aaron's **s**,	Le 2:2
Aaron's **s**, the priests, must	Le 3:2
to Aaron and his **s** from the	Le 7:35
Aaron and his **s** and their	Le 8:2
Aaron and his **s** forward,	Le 8:6
Moses brought Aaron's **s** forward.	Le 8:13
Aaron and his **s** put their hands	Le 8:14
Aaron and his **s** put their hands	Le 8:18
Aaron and his **s** as priests,	Le 8:22
Aaron and his **s** put their hands	Le 8:22
brought Aaron's **s** close to the	Le 8:24
of Aaron and his **s** and presented	Le 8:27
Aaron and his **s** as priests.	Le 8:28
and on Aaron's **s** and their	Le 8:30
his clothes, his **s**, and their	Le 8:30
Moses said to Aaron and his **s**,	Le 8:31
'Aaron and his **s** will eat these	Le 8:31
Aaron and his **s** did everything	Le 8:36
for Aaron and his **s** and for the	Le 9:1
Then his **s** brought the blood to	Le 9:9
His **s** brought the blood to him,	Le 9:12
His **s** brought him the blood,	Le 9:18
Aaron's **s** also brought to Aaron	Le 9:19
s put them on the breasts	Le 9:20
Aaron's **s** Nadab and Abihu took	Le 10:1
about the death of his **s**.	Le 10:3
Uzziel had two **s** named Mishael	Le 10:4
said to Aaron and his other **s**,	Le 10:6
You and your **s** must not drink	Le 10:9
to Aaron and his remaining **s**,	Le 10:12
LORD belongs to you and your **s**.	Le 10:13

you and your **s** and daughters may	Le 10:14
Ithamar, Aaron's remaining **s**.	Le 10:16
priest or to one of Aaron's **s**,	Le 13:2
two of Aaron's **s** had died while	Le 16:1
to Aaron, his **s**, and all the	Le 17:2
Tell these things to Aaron's **s**,	Le 21:1
to Aaron, Aaron's **s**, and all the	Le 21:24
Tell Aaron and his **s**:	Le 22:2
Aaron and his **s** and all the	Le 22:18
will belong to Aaron and his **s**.	Le 24:9
bought it and to his future **s**.	Le 25:30
bodies of your **s** and daughters.	Le 26:29
Aaron had four **s**: Nadab, the	Nu 3:2
were the names of Aaron's **s**,	Nu 3:3
Sinai. They had no **s**. So Eleazar	Nu 3:4
the Levites to Aaron and his **s**;	Nu 3:9
Aaron and his **s** to serve as	Nu 3:10
Levi had three **s**, whose names	Nu 3:17
his **s** camped east of the Holy	Nu 3:38
the firstborn **s** in Israel one	Nu 3:40
of the firstborn **s** of Israel;	Nu 3:41
the firstborn **s** of the	Nu 3:42
the firstborn **s** one month old	Nu 3:43
the firstborn **s** of the	Nu 3:45
more firstborn **s** than Levites,	Nu 3:46
of silver for each of the 273 **s**.	Nu 3:47
Aaron and his **s** as the payment	Nu 3:48
the silver to Aaron and his **s**.	Nu 3:51
Aaron and his **s** must go into the	Nu 4:5
Aaron and his **s** have covered.	Nu 4:15
Aaron and his **s** must go in and	Nu 4:19
Aaron and his **s** are in charge of	Nu 4:27
Aaron and his **s**, 'This is how	Nu 6:23
So Aaron and his **s** will bless	Nu 6:27
of Aaron and his **s** and present	Nu 8:13
Aaron and his **s** so that they may	Nu 8:19
Aaron and his **s** told them what	Nu 8:22
Aaron's **s**, the priests, should	Nu 10:8
were brothers, the **s** of Eliab;	Nu 16:1
and Abiram, the **s** of Eliab, but	Nu 16:12
You, your **s**, and your family	Nu 18:1
you and your **s** are responsible	Nu 18:1
you and your **s** serve in the Tent	Nu 18:2
only you and your **s** may serve as	Nu 18:7
to you and your **s** as your share,	Nu 18:8
be set apart for you and your **s**.	Nu 18:9
to you and your **s** and daughters	Nu 18:11
your **s** and daughters as your	Nu 18:19
His **s** ran away and his daughters	Nu 21:29
Og and his **s** and all his army	Nu 21:35
the skulls of the **s** of Sheth.	Nu 24:17
and Eliab's **s** were Nemuel,	Nu 26:9
Two of Judah's **s**, Er and Onan,	Nu 26:19
son of Hepher had no **s**;	Nu 26:33
Amram had **s** Aaron and Moses	Nu 26:59
of his own sin, and he had no **s**.	Nu 27:3
die out because he had no **s**.	Nu 27:4
were burying their firstborn **s**,	Nu 33:4
him, his **s**, and all his army	Dt 2:33
your daughters marry their **s**,	Dt 7:3
your **s** marry their daughters.	Dt 7:3
the **s** of Eliab the Reubenite,	Dt 11:6
you, your **s** and daughters, your	Dt 12:12
you, your **s** and daughters, your	Dt 12:18
even burn their **s** and daughters	Dt 12:31
you, your **s** and daughters, your	Dt 16:11
you, your **s** and daughters, your	Dt 16:14
priests, the **s** of Levi, should	Dt 21:5
Both wives might have **s** by him.	Dt 21:15
property to his **s** he must not	Dt 21:16
Your **s** and daughters will be	Dt 28:32
You will have **s** and daughters,	Dt 28:41
bodies of the **s** and daughters	Dt 28:53

S

The priests are the s of Levi, ... Dt 31:9
his s and daughters had made him .... Dt 32:19
is the most blessed of the s; .... Dt 33:24
Their s took their places. .... Jos 5:7
But none of the s born on the .... Jos 5:7
the gold, Achan's s, daughters, ... Jos 7:24
of all his s were given this .... Jos 13:31
The s of Joseph had divided into .... Jos 14:4
and Ephraim, s of Joseph, ... Jos 16:4
all the other s of Manasseh son .... Jos 17:2
had no s, but he had five........................ Jos 17:3
received land just as the s did. .... Jos 17:6
belonged to the s of Ephraim.................. Jos 17:8
I gave Isaac two s named Jacob .... Jos 24:4
but Jacob and his s went down to .... Jos 24:4
of silver from the s of Hamor .... Jos 24:32
forced out the three s of Anak. .... Jdg 1:20
to marry the s of those people. .... Jdg 3:6
were my brothers, my mother's s. .... Jdg 8:19
He had seventy s of his own, ... Jdg 8:30
for the seventy s of Gideon to................ Jdg 9:2
brothers, the s of Gideon. .... Jdg 9:5
his seventy s on one stone. .... Jdg 9:18
had killed Gideon's seventy s, ... Jdg 9:24
Isn't he one of Gideon's s, ... Jdg 9:28
Jair had thirty s, who rode .... Jdg 10:4
These thirty s controlled thirty .... Jdg 10:4
Gilead's wife had several s.................... Jdg 11:2
he had no other s or daughters. .... Jdg 11:34
He had thirty s and thirty .... Jdg 12:9
his tribe to be wives for his s................ Jdg 12:9
He had forty s and thirty .... Jdg 12:14
one of his s to be his priest. .... Jdg 17:5
like one of Micah's own s. .... Jdg 17:11
Dan, one of the s of Israel. .... Jdg 18:29
and his s served as priests for .... Jdg 18:30
with his wife and his two s. .... Ru 1:2
and his two s were named Mahlon........... Ru 1:2
and she was left with her two s. .... Ru 1:3
These s married women from Moab. .... Ru 1:4
Naomi and her s had lived in .... Ru 1:4
her husband or her two s. .... Ru 1:5
to me and my s who are now dead. .... Ru 1:8
birth to more s to give you new .... Ru 1:11
and even if I had more s, ... Ru 1:12
what I can pass on to my own s.............. Ru 4:6
is better for you than seven s,............... Ru 4:15
Phinehas, the s of Eli, served 1Sa 1:3
and to her s and daughters. 1Sa 1:4
I mean more to you than ten s?" 1Sa 1:8
Now Eli's s were evil men; 1Sa 2:12
mother of three s and two 1Sa 2:21
everything his s were doing to 1Sa 2:22
and how his s had sexual 1Sa 2:22
Eli said to his s, "Why do you................ 1Sa 2:23
No, my s. The LORD's people are 1Sa 2:24
But Eli's s would not listen to 1Sa 2:25
You honor your s more than me. 1Sa 2:29
your s, Hophni and Phinehas,................ 1Sa 2:34
because he knew his s were evil. 1Sa 3:13
two s, Hophni and Phinehas, ... 1Sa 4:4
and Eli's two s, Hophni and 1Sa 4:11
Your two s are both dead, and 1Sa 4:17
he made his s judges for Israel. 1Sa 8:1
But Samuel's s did not live as................ 1Sa 8:3
and your s don't live as you do. 1Sa 8:5
will take your s and make them 1Sa 8:11
some of your s commanders over 1Sa 8:12
of your other s plows his ground 1Sa 8:12
and my s are here with you. 1Sa 12:2
Saul's s were Jonathan, Ishvi,............... 1Sa 14:49
father Ner were s of Abiel..................... 1Sa 14:51
chosen one of his s to be king." 1Sa 16:1

Jesse and his s apart to the.................... 1Sa 16:5
seven of his s pass by Samuel. 1Sa 16:10
"Are these all the s you have?" 1Sa 16:11
Jesse had eight s. In Saul's 1Sa 17:12
three oldest s followed Saul to 1Sa 17:13
three oldest s followed Saul, ... 1Sa 17:14
you and your s will be with me. 1Sa 28:19
their wives, s, and daughters 1Sa 30:3
because his s and daughters had 1Sa 30:6
young and old, s and daughters............... 1Sa 30:19
hard against Saul and his s, ... 1Sa 31:2
sons, killing his s Jonathan, ... 1Sa 31:2
Saul, his three s, and the....................... 1Sa 31:6
that Saul and his s were dead, ... 1Sa 31:7
and his three s dead on Mount 1Sa 31:8
of Saul and his s from the wall 1Sa 31:12
three s, Joab, Abishai,.......................... 2Sa 2:18
S were born to David at Hebron. 2Sa 3:2
These s were born to David at 2Sa 3:5
These s of Zeruiah are too much 2Sa 3:39
They were the s of Rimmon of 2Sa 4:2
Recab and Baanah, s of Rimmon 2Sa 4:5
the s of Rimmon of Beeroth, ... 2Sa 4:9
More s and daughters were born 2Sa 5:13
the names of the s born to David 2Sa 5:14
Uzzah and Ahio, s of Abinadab,.............. 2Sa 6:3
one of your s the next king, ... 2Sa 7:12
And David's s were priests. 2Sa 8:18
You, your s, and your servants 2Sa 9:10
Ziba had fifteen s and twenty 2Sa 9:10
if he were one of the king's s.................. 2Sa 9:11
all the king's s to come also. 2Sa 13:23
the king's s go with Absalom.................. 2Sa 13:27
of David's other s got on their 2Sa 13:29
While the king's s were on their.............. 2Sa 13:30
has killed all of the king's s! 2Sa 13:30
young men, your s, are killed. 2Sa 13:32
all of the king's s are dead. 2Sa 13:33
The king's s are coming!" 2Sa 13:35
the king's s arrived, crying 2Sa 13:36
had two s. They were out in the 2Sa 14:6
had three s and one daughter 2Sa 14:27
not concern you, s of Zeruiah! 2Sa 16:10
life and the lives of your s,.................... 2Sa 19:5
his fifteen s and twenty 2Sa 19:17
not concern you, s of Zeruiah! 2Sa 19:22
So bring seven of his s to us. 2Sa 21:6
Mephibosheth, s of Rizpah and 2Sa 21:8
took the five s of Saul's 2Sa 21:8
the father of Merab's five s. 2Sa 21:8
gave these seven s to the....................... 2Sa 21:9
All seven s died together. 2Sa 21:9
the rain fell on her s' bodies. 2Sa 21:10
of the sky touch her s' bodies, ... 2Sa 21:10
Saul's seven s who were hanged 2Sa 21:13
one of the s of Rapha, had a 2Sa 21:16
another one of the s of Rapha. 2Sa 21:18
also was one of the s of Rapha. 2Sa 21:20
These four s of Rapha from Gath 2Sa 21:22
Shaalbonite; the s of Jashen; 2Sa 23:32
the other s of King David, ... 1Ki 1:9
you to save yourself and your s............... 1Ki 1:12
And he has invited all your s,................. 1Ki 1:19
he has invited all your other s, ... 1Ki 1:25
made one of my s the king and 1Ki 1:48
Ahijah, s of Shisha, recorded 1Ki 4:3
and Darda—the three s of Mahol. 1Ki 4:31
'If your s are careful to obey 1Ki 8:25
His s came and told him what the 1Ki 13:11
So his s showed him the road.................. 1Ki 13:12
told his s to put a saddle 1Ki 13:13
Then the prophet said to his s, ... 1Ki 13:27
he said to his s, "When I die, ... 1Ki 13:31

tribes, the number of Jacob's s.	1Ki 18:31
the door behind you and your s.	2Ki 4:4
the door behind her and her s.	2Ki 4:5
You and your s can live on what	2Ki 4:7
the blood of Naboth and his s,	2Ki 9:26
Ahab had seventy s in Samaria.	2Ki 10:1
the guardians of the s of Ahab.	2Ki 10:1
have your master's s with you,	2Ki 10:2
person among your master's s,	2Ki 10:3
your master's s and come to me	2Ki 10:6
Now the seventy s of the king's	2Ki 10:6
took the king's s and killed all	2Ki 10:7
the heads of the king's s."	2Ki 10:8
among the other s of the king	2Ki 11:2
Your s down to your	2Ki 15:12
They made their s and daughters	2Ki 17:17
his s Adrammelech and Sharezer	2Ki 19:37
Zedekiah's s as he watched.	2Ki 25:7
s of Noah were Shem, Ham, and	1Ch 1:4
Japheth's s were Gomer, Magog,	1Ch 1:5
s were Ashkenaz, Riphath,	1Ch 1:6
s were Elishah, Tarshish,	1Ch 1:7
Ham's s were Cush, Mizraim, Put,	1Ch 1:8
Cush's s were Seba, Havilah,	1Ch 1:9
Raamah's s were Sheba and Dedan.	1Ch 1:9
Shem's s were Elam, Asshur,	1Ch 1:17
Aram's s were Uz, Hul, Gether,	1Ch 1:17
had two s. One son was named	1Ch 1:19
All these were Joktan's s.	1Ch 1:23
Abraham's s were Isaac and	1Ch 1:28
These were the s of Isaac and	1Ch 1:29
His other s were Kedar, Adbeel,	1Ch 1:29
Kedemah. These were Ishmael's s.	1Ch 1:31
s were Sheba and Dedan.	1Ch 1:32
Midian's s were Ephah, Epher,	1Ch 1:33
and Isaac's s were Esau and	1Ch 1:34
Esau's s were Eliphaz, Reuel,	1Ch 1:35
Eliphaz's s were Teman, Omar,	1Ch 1:36
Reuel's s were Nahath, Zerah,	1Ch 1:37
Seir's s were Lotan, Shobal,	1Ch 1:38
Lotan's s were Hori and Homam,	1Ch 1:39
Shobal's s were Alvan, Manahath,	1Ch 1:40
Zibeon's s were Aiah and Anah.	1Ch 1:40
Dishon's s were Hemdan, Eshban,	1Ch 1:41
Ezer's s were Bilhan, Zaavan,	1Ch 1:42
Dishan's s were Uz and Aran.	1Ch 1:42
The s of Israel were Reuben,	1Ch 2:1
Judah's s were Er, Onan, and	1Ch 2:3
the father, so Judah had five s.	1Ch 2:4
Perez's s were Hezron and Hamul.	1Ch 2:5
Zerah had five s: Zimri, Ethan,	1Ch 2:6
Hezron's s were Jerahmeel,	1Ch 2:9
Zeruiah's three s were Abishai,	1Ch 2:16
and Azubah's s were Jesher,	1Ch 2:18
Jerahmeel's s were Ram, Bunah,	1Ch 2:25
first son, Ram, had s.	1Ch 2:27
Onam's s were Shammai and Jada.	1Ch 2:28
Shammai's s were Nadab and	1Ch 2:28
their s were Ahban and Molid.	1Ch 2:29
Nadab's s were Seled and Appaim.	1Ch 2:30
and Jada's s were Jether and	1Ch 2:32
Jonathan's s were Peleth and	1Ch 2:33
Sheshan did not have any s,	1Ch 2:34
Hebron's s were Korah, Tappuah,	1Ch 2:43
Jahdai's s were Regem, Jotham,	1Ch 2:47
These are David's s who were	1Ch 3:1
These six s of David were born	1Ch 3:4
These were all of David's s,	1Ch 3:9
were Josiah's s: His first son	1Ch 3:15
prisoner. His s were Shealtiel,	1Ch 3:17
Pedaiah's s were Zerubbabel and	1Ch 3:19
Zerubbabel's s were Meshullam	1Ch 3:19
also had five other s:	1Ch 3:20

Jeshaiah, and the s of Rephaiah,	1Ch 3:21
Shemaiah's s were Hattush,	1Ch 3:22
Neariah had three s: Elioenai,	1Ch 3:23
Elioenai had seven s: Hodaviah,	1Ch 3:24
The s of Ashhur and Naarah were	1Ch 4:6
Helah's s were Zereth, Zohar,	1Ch 4:7
The s of Kenaz were Othniel and	1Ch 4:13
Othniel's s were Hathath and	1Ch 4:13
Caleb's s were Iru, Elah, and	1Ch 4:15
s were Ziph, Ziphah,	1Ch 4:16
The s of Hodiah's wife were	1Ch 4:19
Shimon's s were Amnon, Rinnah,	1Ch 4:20
Ishi's s were Zoheth and	1Ch 4:20
These s of Shelah were potters.	1Ch 4:23
Simeon's s were Nemuel, Jamin,	1Ch 4:24
had sixteen s and six daughters	1Ch 4:27
Ishi's s, Pelatiah, Neariah,	1Ch 4:42
were given to Joseph's s.	1Ch 5:1
Reuben's s were Hanoch, Pallu,	1Ch 5:3
Levi's s were Gershon, Kohath,	1Ch 6:1
Kohath's s were Amram, Izhar,	1Ch 6:2
Aaron's s were Nadab, Abihu,	1Ch 6:3
Levi's s were Gershon, Kohath,	1Ch 6:16
names of Gershon's s were Libni	1Ch 6:17
Kohath's s were Amram, Izhar,	1Ch 6:18
Merari's s were Mahli and Mushi.	1Ch 6:19
s were Amasai and Ahimoth.	1Ch 6:25
Samuel's s were Joel, the first	1Ch 6:28
are the musicians and their s:	1Ch 6:33
These were Aaron's s: Eleazar	1Ch 6:50
Issachar had four s: Tola, Puah,	1Ch 7:1
Tola's s were Uzzi, Rephaiah,	1Ch 7:2
Izrahiah's s were Michael,	1Ch 7:3
had three s: Bela, Beker,	1Ch 7:6
Bela had five s: Ezbon, Uzzi,	1Ch 7:7
Beker's s were Zemirah, Joash,	1Ch 7:8
They all were Beker's s.	1Ch 7:8
Bilhan's s were Jeush, Benjamin,	1Ch 7:10
All these s of Jediael were	1Ch 7:11
Naphtali's s were Jahziel,	1Ch 7:13
Sheresh's s were Ulam and Rakem.	1Ch 7:16
These were the s of Gilead,	1Ch 7:17
The s of Shemida were Ahian,	1Ch 7:19
Asher's s were Imnah, Ishvah,	1Ch 7:30
Beriah's s were Heber and	1Ch 7:31
Japhlet's s were Pasach, Bimhal,	1Ch 7:33
Shomer's s were Rohgah, Hubbah,	1Ch 7:34
Hotham's s were Zophah, Imna,	1Ch 7:35
Zophah's s were Suah, Harnepher,	1Ch 7:36
Jether's s were Jephunneh,	1Ch 7:38
Ulla's s were Arah, Hanniel, and	1Ch 7:39
s were Addar, Gera, Abihud,	1Ch 8:3
Beriah's s were Ahio, Shashak,	1Ch 8:14
Elpaal's s were Zebadiah,	1Ch 8:17
Shimei's s were Jakim, Zicri,	1Ch 8:19
Shashak's s were Ishpan, Eber,	1Ch 8:22
Jeroham's s were Shamsherai,	1Ch 8:26
other s were Zur, Kish, Baal,	1Ch 8:30
These s also lived near their	1Ch 8:32
Micah's s were Pithon, Melech,	1Ch 8:35
Azel had six s: Azrikam, Bokeru,	1Ch 8:38
All these were Azel's s.	1Ch 8:38
Ulam's s were mighty warriors	1Ch 8:40
They had many s and grandsons—	1Ch 8:40
there were Asaiah and his s.	1Ch 9:5
other s were Zur, Kish, Baal,	1Ch 9:36
Micah's s were Pithon, Melech,	1Ch 9:41
Azel had six s: Azrikam, Bokeru,	1Ch 9:44
and Hanan. They were Azel's s.	1Ch 9:44
hard against Saul and his s,	1Ch 10:2
sons, killing his s Jonathan,	1Ch 10:2
So Saul and three of his s died;	1Ch 10:6
that Saul and his s were dead,	1Ch 10:7

S

Saul and his s dead on Mount	1Ch 10:8
of Saul and his s and brought	1Ch 10:12
the s of Hashem the Gizonite;	1Ch 11:34
Shama and Jeiel s of Hotham the	1Ch 11:44
and Joshaviah, Elnaam's s;	1Ch 11:46
and Joash were s of Shemaah,	1Ch 12:3
and Pelet, the s of Azmaveth.	1Ch 12:3
and Zebadiah, the s of Jeroham,	1Ch 12:7
and had more s and daughters.	1Ch 14:3
Jeduthun's s guarded the gates.	1Ch 16:42
make one of your s the new king,	1Ch 17:11
And David's s were important	1Ch 18:17
also was one of the s of Rapha.	1Ch 20:6
Araunah's four s who were with	1Ch 21:20
that were led by Levi's three s:	1Ch 23:6
Ladan had three s. His first son	1Ch 23:8
and his other s were Zetham and	1Ch 23:8
Shimei's s were Shelomoth,	1Ch 23:9
These three s were leaders of	1Ch 23:9
Shimei had four s: Jahath, Ziza,	1Ch 23:10
Kohath had four s: Amram, Izhar,	1Ch 23:12
Amram's s were Aaron and Moses.	1Ch 23:13
and his s were counted as part	1Ch 23:14
' s were Gershom and Eliezer.	1Ch 23:15
had no other s, but Rehabiah had	1Ch 23:17
sons, but Rehabiah had many s.	1Ch 23:17
Merari's s were Mahli and Mushi.	1Ch 23:21
Mahli's s were Eleazar and Kish.	1Ch 23:21
Eleazar died without s;	1Ch 23:22
their cousins, the s of Kish.	1Ch 23:22
Mushi's three s were Mahli,	1Ch 23:23
were the groups of Aaron's s:	1Ch 24:1
Aaron's s were Nadab, Abihu,	1Ch 24:1
father did, and they had no s.	1Ch 24:2
of Marari had s named Shoham,	1Ch 24:27
but Eleazar did not have any s.	1Ch 24:28
Mushi's s were Mahli, Eder, and	1Ch 24:30
chose some of the s of Asaph,	1Ch 25:1
s who served were Zaccur,	1Ch 25:2
and Asaph directed his s.	1Ch 25:2
Jeduthun's s who served were	1Ch 25:3
Heman's s who served were	1Ch 25:5
All these were s of Heman,	1Ch 25:5
strong, so Heman had many s.	1Ch 25:5
gave him fourteen s and three	1Ch 25:5
all his s in making music	1Ch 25:6
Gedaliah, his s and relatives.	1Ch 25:9
Zaccur, his s and relatives.	1Ch 25:10
from Izri, his s and relatives.	1Ch 25:11
Nethaniah, his s and relatives.	1Ch 25:12
Bukkiah, his s and relatives.	1Ch 25:13
Jesarelah, his s and relatives.	1Ch 25:14
Jeshaiah, his s and relatives.	1Ch 25:15
Mattaniah, his s and relatives.	1Ch 25:16
Shimei, his s and relatives.	1Ch 25:17
Azarel, his s and relatives.	1Ch 25:18
Hashabiah, his s and relatives.	1Ch 25:19
Shubael, his s and relatives.	1Ch 25:20
Mattithiah, his s and relatives.	1Ch 25:21
Jerimoth, his s and relatives.	1Ch 25:22
Hananiah, his s and relatives.	1Ch 25:23
his s and relatives.	1Ch 25:24
Hanani, his s and relatives.	1Ch 25:25
Mallothi, his s and relatives.	1Ch 25:26
Eliathah, his s and relatives.	1Ch 25:27
Hothir, his s and relatives.	1Ch 25:28
Giddalti, his s and relatives.	1Ch 25:29
Mahazioth, his s and relatives.	1Ch 25:30
his s and relatives.	1Ch 25:31
Meshelemiah had s. Zechariah was	1Ch 26:2
Obed-Edom had s. Shemaiah was	1Ch 26:4
son Shemaiah also had s.	1Ch 26:6
s were Othni, Rephael,	1Ch 26:7
They and their s and relatives	1Ch 26:8
Meshelemiah had s and relatives	1Ch 26:9
the Merari family, Hosah had s.	1Ch 26:10
had thirteen s and relatives.	1Ch 26:11
and Obed-Edom's s were chosen to	1Ch 26:15
His s were Zetham and Joel his	1Ch 26:22
He and his s worked outside the	1Ch 26:29
took care of the king's s.	1Ch 27:32
belonged to the king and his s,	1Ch 28:1
The LORD has given me many s,	1Ch 28:5
and from those s he has chosen	1Ch 28:5
King David's s accepted Solomon	1Ch 29:24
and all their s and relatives—	2Ch 5:12
'If your s are careful to obey	2Ch 6:16
Jeroboam and his s refused to	2Ch 11:14
Mahalath gave Rehoboam these s:	2Ch 11:19
of twenty-eight s and sixty	2Ch 11:21
He spread his s through all the	2Ch 11:23
plenty of supplies to his s,	2Ch 11:23
David and his s the right to	2Ch 13:5
which belongs to David's s.	2Ch 13:8
the LORD's priests, Aaron's s.	2Ch 13:9
serve the LORD are Aaron's s,	2Ch 13:10
of twenty-two s and sixteen	2Ch 13:21
They were the s of Jehoshaphat	2Ch 21:2
gave his s many gifts of silver	2Ch 21:3
as well as his s and wives.	2Ch 21:17
killed all of Jehoram's older s.	2Ch 22:1
of Judah and the s of Ahaziah's	2Ch 22:8
among the other s of the king	2Ch 22:11
Jehoiada and his s brought out	2Ch 23:11
and Joash had s and daughters.	2Ch 24:3
In the past the s of wicked	2Ch 24:7
story of Joash's s, the great	2Ch 24:27
took women, s and daughters,	2Ch 28:8
were killed in battle and our s,	2Ch 29:9
My s, don't waste any more time.	2Ch 29:11
babies, wives, s, and daughters	2Ch 31:18
of his own s killed him with	2Ch 32:21
Jeshua and his s and brothers;	Ezr 3:9
Kadmiel and his s who were the	Ezr 3:9
and the s of Henadad and their	Ezr 3:9
and their s and brothers.	Ezr 3:9
Levites, the s of Asaph, stood	Ezr 3:10
the life of the king and his s.	Ezr 6:10
angry with the king and his s.	Ezr 7:23
Sherebiah's s and brothers,	Ezr 8:18
men and their s have married	Ezr 9:2
your daughters marry their s,	Ezr 9:12
their daughters marry your s.	Ezr 9:12
The s of Hassenaah rebuilt the	Ne 3:3
brothers, your s and daughters,	Ne 4:14
We have many s and daughters in	Ne 5:2
and our s are like their sons.	Ne 5:5
and our sons are like their s.	Ne 5:5
to sell our s and daughters as	Ne 5:5
Binnui of the s of Henadad,	Ne 10:9
wives and their s and daughters	Ne 10:28
nor to let our s marry their	Ne 10:30
our firstborn s and cattle	Ne 10:36
marry the s of foreigners	Ne 13:25
wives for your s or yourselves.	Ne 13:25
One of Joiada's s married a	Ne 13:28
he was and how many s he had.	Est 5:11
the ten s of Haman, son of	Est 9:10
have also killed Haman's ten s.	Est 9:12
of Haman's ten s be hanged	Est 9:13
bodies of the ten s of Haman	Est 9:14
Haman and his s should be hanged	Est 9:25
had seven s and three daughters.	Job 1:2
s took turns holding feasts	Job 1:4
One day Job's s and daughters	Job 1:13
Your s and daughters were eating	Job 1:18

Job also had seven **s** and three .... Job 42:13
They have many **s** and leave much .... Ps 17:14
A maskil of the **s** of Korah. .... Ps 41:13
A maskil of the **s** of Korah. .... Ps 43:5
A love song of the **s** of Korah. .... Ps 44:26
You will have **s** to replace your .... Ps 45:16
A psalm of the **s** of Korah. .... Ps 45:17
A psalm of the **s** of Korah. .... Ps 46:11
A psalm of the **s** of Korah. .... Ps 47:9
A psalm of the **s** of Korah. .... Ps 48:14
all the firstborn **s** in Egypt, ... Ps 78:51
You are all **s** of God Most High. .... Ps 82:6
A psalm of the **s** of Korah. .... Ps 83:18
A psalm of the **s** of Korah. .... Ps 84:12
A psalm of the **s** of Korah. .... Ps 86:17
A psalm of the **s** of Korah. .... Ps 87:7
all the firstborn **s** in the land, ... Ps 105:36
killed their **s** and daughters as .... Ps 106:37
their own **s** and daughters, ... Ps 106:38
If your **s** keep my agreement and .... Ps 132:12
their **s** after them will rule .... Ps 132:12
the firstborn **s** in Egypt the .... Ps 135:8
firstborn **s** of the Egyptians. .... Ps 136:10
Let our **s** in their youth grow .... Ps 144:12
Now, my **s**, listen to me, and .... Pr 5:7
Now, my **s**, listen to me; .... Pr 7:24
his **s** Adrammelech and Sharezer .... Is 37:38
Bring my **s** from far away and my .... Is 43:6
will bring your **s** back to you in .... Is 49:22
Your **s** are coming from far away, ... Is 60:4
herds, their **s** and daughters. .... Je 3:24
will eat your **s** and daughters .... Je 5:17
Fathers and **s** will stumble over .... Je 6:21
their own **s** and daughters as .... Je 7:31
Their **s** and daughters will die .... Je 11:22
fathers and **s** alike, says the .... Je 13:14
wives, or their **s**, or their .... Je 14:16
woman with seven **s** felt faint .... Je 15:9
married or have **s** or daughters .... Je 16:2
this about the **s** and daughters .... Je 16:3
of their own **s** and daughters, ... Je 19:9
and have **s** and daughters. .... Je 29:6
wives for your **s**, and let your .... Je 29:6
also may have **s** and daughters .... Je 29:6
burn their **s** and daughters as .... Je 32:35
brothers and **s** and the whole .... Je 35:3
the room of the **s** of Hanan son .... Je 35:4
nor our wives, **s**, or daughters .... Je 35:8
killed Zedekiah's **s** and all the .... Je 39:6
and Jonathan **s** of Kareah, ... Je 40:8
the **s** of Ephai the Netophathite, ... Je 40:8
Your **s** have been taken captive, ... Je 48:46
Zedekiah's **s** as he watched. .... Je 52:10
save their own **s** or daughters. .... Eze 14:16
not save their **s** or daughters. .... Eze 14:18
some **s** and daughters will be led .... Eze 14:22
also took your **s** and daughters .... Eze 16:20
wives and had **s** and daughters. .... Eze 23:4
took away her **s** and daughters. .... Eze 23:10
take away your **s** and daughters, ... Eze 23:25
them kill their **s** and daughters .... Eze 23:47
your **s** and daughters that you .... Eze 24:21
away their **s** and daughters also. .... Eze 24:25
from his land to any of his **s**, ... Eze 46:16
the ruler's **s** may keep a gift .... Eze 46:17
must give his **s** some of his own .... Eze 46:18
The **s** of the king of the North .... Da 11:10
Your **s** and daughters will .... Joe 2:28
will sell your **s** and daughters .... Joe 3:8
Fathers and **s** have sexual .... Am 2:7
and your **s** and daughters will be .... Am 7:17
and the king's **s** and all those .... Zph 1:8
and John, the **s** of Zebedee. .... Mt 4:21

came to Jesus with her **s**. .... Mt 20:20
one of my **s** will sit at your .... Mt 20:21
The **s** answered, "Yes, we can." .... Mt 20:22
this: A man had two **s**. He went .... Mt 21:28
of the two **s** obeyed his father? .... Mt 21:31
and the two **s** of Zebedee with .... Mt 26:37
and John, the **s** of Zebedee. .... Mk 1:19
John, the **s** of Zebedee (Jesus .... Mk 3:17
which means "S of Thunder" .... Mk 3:17
James and John, **s** of Zebedee, ... Mk 10:35
and John, the **s** of Zebedee, ... Lk 5:10
Jesus said, "A man had two **s**. .... Lk 15:11
the property between his two **s**. .... Lk 15:12
along with his **s** and flocks?" .... Jn 4:12
Galilee, the two **s** of Zebedee, ... Jn 21:2
Your **s** and daughters will .... Ac 2:17
Jacob did the same for his **s**, ... Ac 7:8
Jacob's **s** became jealous of .... Ac 7:9
Jacob's **s**, our ancestors, could .... Ac 7:11
in Egypt, he sent his **s** there. .... Ac 7:12
Egypt, where he and his **s** died. .... Ac 7:15
of money from the **s** of Hamor in .... Ac 7:16
lived in Midian, he had two **s**. .... Ac 7:29
s of the family of Abraham, ... Ac 13:26
Seven **s** of Sceva, a leading .... Ac 19:14
Rebekah's **s** had the same father, ... Rm 9:10
you will be my **s** and daughters, ... 2Co 6:18
say that Abraham had two **s**. .... Gal 4:22
blessed each one of Joseph's **s**. .... Heb 11:21
kill the firstborn **s** of Israel. .... Heb 11:28

SONS-IN-LAW

Do you have any **s**, sons, ... Ge 19:12
to his future **s** who were pledged .... Ge 19:14

SOON

As **s** as Jesus was baptized, ... Mt 3:16
S after the trouble of those .... Mt 24:29
'My master will not come back **s**,' .... Mt 24:48
As **s** as Jesus and his followers .... Mk 1:29
S afterwards Jesus went to a .... Lk 7:11
which he would **s** bring about in .... Lk 9:31
'My master will not come back **s**,' .... Lk 12:45
know it will **s** be destroyed. .... Lk 21:20
As **s** as Judas took the bread, ... Jn 13:27
to Abraham was **s** to come true, ... Ac 7:17
S he began to preach about Jesus .... Ac 9:20
come to him as **s** as they could. .... Ac 17:15
himself was returning there **s**. .... Ac 25:4
brings peace will **s** defeat Satan .... Rm 16:20
come to you very **s** if the Lord 1Co 4:19
its present form will **s** be gone. 1Co 7:31
Jesus to send Timothy to you **s**. .... Php 2:19
will help me to come to you **s**. .... Php 2:24
and kind. The Lord is coming **s**. .... Php 4:5
are gone as **s** as they are used .... Col 2:22
I hope I can come to you **s**, ... 1Ti 3:14
to come to me as **s** as you can, ... 2Ti 4:9
God will send me back to you **s**. .... Heb 13:19
If he arrives **s**, we will both .... Heb 13:23
because the Lord is coming **s**. .... Jam 5:8
I know I must **s** leave this body, ... 2Pe 1:14
hope to see you **s** and talk face 3Jn 1:14
his servants what must **s** happen. .... Rev 1:1
I am coming **s**. Continue strong .... Rev 3:11
The third trouble is coming **s**. .... Rev 11:14
her baby as **s** as it was born. .... Rev 12:4
But **s** it will come up out of the .... Rev 17:8
the things that must happen **s**. .... Rev 22:6
I am coming **s**! Blessed is the .... Rev 22:7
I am coming **s**! I will bring my .... Rev 22:12
says, "Yes, I am coming **s**," .... Rev 22:20

SOPATER

with him were **S** son of Pyrrhus, ... Ac 20:4

S

SOPHERETH

descendants of Sotai, **S**, Perida, ... Ne 7:57

SORCERY

is as bad as the sin of **s**. 1Sa 15:23

SORE

If the **s** looks like a harmful .... Le 13:2
look at the **s** on the person's .... Le 13:3
the hair in the **s** has become .... Le 13:3
and the **s** seems deeper than the............. Le 13:3
sees that the **s** has not changed .... Le 13:5
If the **s** has faded and has not............... Le 13:6
is clean. The **s** is only a rash. .... Le 13:6
when the person has an open **s**, ... Le 13:14
When the priest sees the open **s**, ... Le 13:15
The open **s** is not clean; .... Le 13:15
If the open **s** becomes white .... Le 13:16
the open **s** becomes white or red, ... Le 13:24
or a woman gets a **s** on the scalp .... Le 13:29
a priest must look at the **s**. .... Le 13:30
the priest must look at the **s**. .... Le 13:32
and the **s** does not seem deeper .... Le 13:32
he must not shave the **s** place. .... Le 13:33
the priest must look at the **s**. .... Le 13:34
But if the **s** spreads on the skin .... Le 13:35
If the **s** has spread on the skin .... Le 13:36
priest thinks the **s** has stopped .... Le 13:37
growing in it, the **s** has healed. .... Le 13:37
a red-white **s** on his bald head .... Le 13:42
swelling of the **s** on his bald .... Le 13:43
because of the **s** on his head. .... Le 13:44
will give you boils on your .... Dt 28:35
fever, and my whole body is **s**. .... Ps 38:7
my throat is **s**. My eyes are .... Ps 69:3

SOREK

who lived in the Valley of **S**. .... Jdg 16:4

SORES

out and become **s** on the skin .... Ex 9:9
break out and become **s** on people .... Ex 9:10
and if the **s** have become white, ... Le 13:17
the person with the **s** is clean. .... Le 13:17
that has running **s** or any sort .... Le 22:22
bad growths, **s**, and itches that .... Dt 28:27
someone with **s** or with a skin 2Sa 3:29
He put painful **s** on Job's body, ... Job 2:7
my skin is broken and full of **s**. .... Job 7:5
My **s** stink and become infected .... Ps 38:5
and open **s** that are not cleaned .... Is 1:6
the Lord will put **s** on the heads .... Is 3:17
case and no cure for your **s**. .... Je 30:13
whose body was covered with **s**,............. Lk 16:20
dogs would come and lick his **s**. .... Lk 16:21
ugly and painful **s** came upon all .... Rev 16:2
their pain and the **s** they had, ... Rev 16:11

SORROW

women brought much **s** to Isaac.............. Ge 26:35
Judah had gotten over his **s**, ... Ge 38:12
cause the great **s** that kills our .... Ge 44:31
had a time of **s** for Jacob that .... Ge 50:3
When this time of **s** had ended, ... Ge 50:4
Joseph's time of **s** continued for .... Ge 50:10
Egyptians are showing great **s**!"............. Ge 50:11
place is named **S** of the .... Ge 50:11
the holy part while I was in **s**............. Dt 26:14
Joshua tore his clothes in **s**. .... Jos 7:6
on their heads to show their **s**. .... Jos 7:6
tore his clothes to show his **s**. .... Jdg 11:35
tore his clothes to show his **s**,................ 2Sa 1:11
is a day of **s** and punishment 2Ki 19:3
You changed my **s** into dancing. .... Ps 30:11
and showed my **s** by fasting. .... Ps 35:13
us as much joy as you gave us **s**. .... Ps 90:15

in the end she will bring you **s**, ... Pr 5:4
wealth, and no **s** comes with it. .... Pr 10:22
and cause their mother great **s**. .... Pr 17:25
knowledge also gains more **s**.................. Ec 1:18
work is full of pain and **s**, ... Ec 2:23
are days full of sadness and **s**, ... Ec 5:17
S is better than laughter,...................... Ec 7:3
My heart cries with **s** for Moab. .... Is 15:5
it will make Egypt hurt with **s**. .... Is 23:5
has given you **s** and hurt like .... Is 30:20
and **s** and sadness will go far .... Is 35:10
is a day of **s** and punishment .... Is 37:3
will shout their cries of **s**. .... Is 43:14
all sadness and **s** will be gone .... Is 51:11
of gladness to replace their **s**,............. Is 61:3
dead or to show your **s** for them, ... Je 16:5
his head to show **s** for them. .... Je 16:6
I have known in trouble and **s**, ... Je 20:18
I beat my breast with **s**. .... Je 31:19
their clothes to show their **s** .... Je 36:24
LORD has given me **s** along with .... Je 45:3
their heads to the ground in **s**. .... La 2:10
and my misery, my **s** and trouble. .... La 3:19
he brings **s**, he also has mercy .... La 3:32
heart is full of **s**, to the point .... Mt 26:38
heart is full of **s**, to the point .... Mk 14:34
God would take away Israel's **s**,............. Lk 2:25
I have great **s** and always feel............... Rm 9:2
because your **s** made you change 2Co 7:9
The kind of **s** God wants makes 2Co 7:10
But the kind of **s** the world has 2Co 7:10
See what this **s**—the sorrow God 2Co 7:11
the **s** God wanted you to have— 2Co 7:11
have caused themselves much **s**.............. 1Ti 6:10

SORROWFULLY

this, he left **s**, because he was................ Mt 19:22
and he left **s**, because he was .... Mk 10:22

SORROWING

and to help the **s** people of .... Is 61:3

SORRY

was **s** he had made human beings .... Ge 6:6
I am **s** I have made them." .... Ge 6:7
so she felt **s** for him and said,................. Ex 2:6
you refuse to be **s** for what you .... Ex 10:3
people are **s** for what they did .... Le 26:41
Do not feel **s** for them, and do .... Dt 7:16
not listen or feel **s** for them, ... Dt 13:8
you mercy and feel **s** for you, ... Dt 13:17
people or feel **s** for the young. .... Dt 28:50
He will feel **s** for you, and he .... Dt 30:3
So the LORD felt **s** for them and .... Jdg 2:18
he felt **s** for them when he saw .... Jdg 10:16
Israelites felt **s** for their .... Jdg 21:6
of Israel felt **s** for the .... Jdg 21:15
I am **s** I made Saul king, because 1Sa 15:11
LORD was very **s** he had made Saul 1Sa 15:35
you continue to feel **s** for Saul? 1Sa 16:1
LORD will feel **s** for me and let 2Sa 12:22
LORD felt very **s** about the.................... 2Sa 24:16
the people will become truly **s**. 1Ki 8:38
people will be **s** for their sins 1Ki 8:47
They will be **s** and pray to you 1Ki 8:47
Ahab is now **s** for what he has 1Ki 21:29
you became **s** for what you had 2Ki 22:19
it and felt very **s** about the 1Ch 21:15
the people will become truly **s**. 2Ch 6:29
people will be **s** for their sins 2Ch 6:37
They will be **s** and pray to you 2Ch 6:37
Rehoboam were **s** for what they............. 2Ch 12:6
saw they were **s** for what they 2Ch 12:7
The king and the leaders are **s**. 2Ch 12:7
Rehoboam was **s** for what he had 2Ch 12:12

and Zebulun were **s** for what they 2Ch 30:11
Jerusalem were **s** and stopped 2Ch 32:26
you became **s** for what you had 2Ch 34:27
body and feel **s** for themselves." .... Job 14:22
that is broken and **s** for sin. .... Ps 51:17
and he felt **s** for them because .... Ps 106:45
they feel **s** for little ones. .... Is 13:18
but no one will feel **s** for you. .... Is 51:19
people to be **s** for what they .... Is 58:5
They do not feel **s** about their .... Je 8:6
I will feel **s** for them again. .... Je 12:15
will not feel **s** or have pity on .... Je 13:14
would not feel **s** for the people .... Je 15:1
Who will feel **s** for you, ... Je 15:5
I am **s** that you gave birth to me .... Je 15:10
or pity or feel **s** for them!' .... Je 21:7
Don't feel **s** for the young men .... Je 51:3
No one felt **s** enough for you to .... Eze 16:5
have not been **s** for what you .... Da 5:22
land and felt **s** for his people. .... Joe 2:18
don't feel **s** for their sheep. .... Zch 11:5
I don't feel **s** anymore for the .... Zch 11:6
that we were **s** for what we did. .... Mal 3:14
he felt **s** for them because they .... Mt 9:36
they were **s** and changed their .... Mt 12:41
He felt **s** for them and healed .... Mt 14:14
I feel **s** for these people, ... Mt 15:32
master felt **s** for his servant .... Mt 18:27
had happened, they were very **s**. .... Mt 18:31
Jesus felt **s** for the blind men .... Mt 20:34
he was very **s** for what he had .... Mt 27:3
Jesus felt **s** for the man, so he .... Mk 1:41
He felt **s** for them, because they .... Mk 6:34
I feel **s** for these people, ... Mk 8:2
he felt very **s** for her and said, ... Lk 7:13
the man, he felt very **s** for him. .... Lk 10:33
they were **s** and changed their .... Lk 11:32
saw him and felt **s** for his son. .... Lk 15:20
if he is **s** and stops sinning, ... Lk 17:3
and says that he is **s** each time, ... Lk 17:4
Silas they were **s** and took them .... Ac 16:39
you are very **s** for what you did 2Co 2:4
you sad, I am not **s** I wrote it. 2Co 7:8
first I was **s**, because it made 2Co 7:8
and you cannot be **s** for that. 2Co 7:10

SORT

sores or any **s** of skin disease. .... Le 22:22
to show what **s** of work it was. 1Co 3:13

SORTS

A wise king **s** out the evil .... Pr 20:26

SOSIPATER

Jason, and **S**, my relatives. .... Rm 16:21

SOSTHENES

they all grabbed **S**, the leader .... Ac 18:17
Also from **S**, our brother in 1Co 1:1

SOTAI

descendants of **S**, Hassophereth, ... Ezr 2:55
descendants of **S**, Sophereth, ... Ne 7:57

SOUL

heart, all your **s**, and all your .... Dt 6:5
your sight weak, and your **s** sad. .... Dt 28:65
March on, my **s**, with strength! .... Jdg 5:21
all his heart, **s**, and strength, ... 2Ki 23:25
Wake up, my **s**. Wake up, harp and .... Ps 57:8
My **s** wants to be with you at .... Is 26:9
have had these troubles in my **s**, ... Is 38:15
After his **s** suffers many things, ... Is 53:11
your **s** will enjoy the rich food .... Is 55:2
the body but cannot kill the **s**. .... Mt 10:28
can destroy the **s** and the body .... Mt 10:28
heart, all your **s**, and all your .... Mt 22:37

all your **s**, all your mind, ... Mk 12:30
Mary said, "My **s** praises the .... Lk 1:46
heart, all your **s**, all your .... Lk 10:27
that makes body or **s** unclean. 2Co 7:1
self—spirit, **s**, and body—be kept 1Th 5:23
where the **s** and the spirit are .... Heb 4:12
hope as an anchor for the **s**, ... Heb 6:19
save that sinner's **s** from death .... Jam 5:20
to do that fight against your **s**. 1Pe 2:11
I know your **s** is doing fine, ... 3Jn 1:2

SOULS

Our **s** want to remember you and .... Is 26:8
world if they lose their **s**. .... Mt 16:26
pay enough to buy back their **s**. .... Mt 16:26
world if they lose their **s**. .... Mk 8:36
pay enough to buy back their **s**. .... Mk 8:37
destroy the **s** of people but to .... Lk 9:56
they are responsible for your **s**. .... Heb 13:17
faith—the salvation of your **s**. 1Pe 1:9
the truth has purified your **s**, ... 1Pe 1:22
Shepherd and Overseer of your **s**. 1Pe 2:25
trust their **s** to the faithful 1Pe 4:19
the altar the **s** of those who had .... Rev 6:9
These **s** shouted in a loud voice, ... Rev 6:10
And I saw the **s** of those who had .... Rev 20:4

SOUND

The **s** from the trumpet became .... Ex 19:19
Joshua heard the **s** of the people .... Ex 32:17
is the **s** of singing that I hear. .... Ex 32:18
by the **s** of a leaf being .... Le 26:36
loud **s** will tell them to move. .... Nu 10:6
heard the **s** of words, but you .... Dt 4:12
When you hear that **s**, have all .... Jos 6:5
At the **s** of the trumpets and the .... Jos 6:20
Listen to the **s** of the singers .... Jdg 5:11
the LORD had put them **s** asleep. 1Sa 26:12
When you hear the **s** of marching 2Sa 5:24
he heard the **s** from the trumpet 1Ki 1:41
But there was no **s**, and no one 1Ki 18:26
there was a quiet, gentle **s**. 1Ki 19:12
The **s** of his master's feet is 2Ki 6:32
army to hear the **s** of chariots, ... 2Ki 7:6
When you hear the **s** of marching 1Ch 14:15
you hear the **s** of the trumpet, ... Ne 4:20
The **s** of happiness in Jerusalem .... Ne 12:43
the **s** of the flute makes them .... Job 21:12
At the **s** of his thunder, my .... Job 37:1
when he thunders with a great **s**. .... Job 37:4
Hear the **s** of my prayer, when I .... Ps 28:2
The **s** of the water is loud; .... Ps 93:4
with harps and the **s** of singing. .... Ps 98:5
mountains, the **s** of many people. .... Is 13:4
the **s** of nations gathering .... Is 13:4
is filled with the **s** of wings. .... Is 18:1
You will hear a trumpet **s**. .... Is 18:3
escape from the **s** of terror will .... Is 24:18
It will **s** like the voice of a .... Is 29:4
have heard the **s** of the trumpet .... Je 4:19
At the **s** of the horsemen and the .... Je 4:29
It is the **s** of Jerusalem gasping .... Je 4:31
for the **s** of the war trumpet! .... Je 6:17
They **s** like the roaring ocean .... Je 6:23
Listen to the **s** of my people. .... Je 8:19
The **s** of loud crying is heard .... Je 9:19
and the **s** of people grinding .... Je 25:10
I hear the **s** of the leaders .... Je 25:36
There will be the **s** of laughter. .... Je 30:19
will hear the **s** of the running .... Je 47:3
At the **s** of Edom's fall, the .... Je 49:21
the **s** is loud like the roaring .... Je 50:42
At the **s** of Babylon's capture, ... Je 50:46
I heard the **s** of their wings, ... Eze 1:24

like the roaring **s** of the sea, ... Eze 1:24
a roaring **s** like a noisy army. .... Eze 1:24
a loud rumbling **s** behind me, ... Eze 3:12
other and the **s** of the wheels .... Eze 3:13
It was a loud rumbling **s**. .... Eze 3:13
The **s** of the wings of the living .... Eze 10:5
terrified by the **s** of his roar. .... Eze 19:7
with fear at the **s** of the tree .... Eze 31:16
they hear the **s** of the trumpet .... Eze 33:4
They heard the **s** of the trumpet .... Eze 33:5
you hear the **s** of the horns, ... Da 3:5
they heard the **s** of the horns, ... Da 3:7
again hear the **s** of the horns, ... Da 3:15
the **s** of whips and the noise .... Nah 3:2
lips tremble when I hear the **s**. .... Hab 3:16
the **s** of music and dancing. .... Lk 15:25
to and you hear the **s** of it, ... Jn 3:8
he went **s** asleep and fell to the .... Ac 20:9
trumpet does not give a clear **s**, ... 1Co 14:8
trumpet will **s**, and those who 1Co 15:52
want to make it **s** worse than it 2Co 2:5
are powerful and **s** important, ... 2Co 10:10
or to the **s** of a voice like .... Heb 12:19
the **s** of their wings was like .... Rev 9:9
And I heard a **s** from heaven like .... Rev 14:2
and like the **s** of loud thunder. .... Rev 14:2
The **s** I heard was like people .... Rev 14:2
The **s** of grinding grain will .... Rev 18:22

SOUNDED
sang together **s** like one person 2Ch 5:13
has risen as the trumpets **s**. .... Ps 47:5
Your thunder **s** in the whirlwind. .... Ps 77:18
It **s** like the roar of rushing .... Eze 43:2
and his voice **s** like the roar of .... Da 10:6
because it **s** like nonsense. .... Lk 24:11
behind me that **s** like a trumpet. .... Rev 1:10
before, that **s** like a trumpet, ... Rev 4:1
something that **s** like a voice .... Rev 6:6
I heard what **s** like a great many .... Rev 19:1
I heard what **s** like a great many .... Rev 19:6

SOUNDING
and again, **s** like waterfalls .... Ps 42:7

SOUNDS
Your voice **s** like Jacob's voice, ... Ge 27:22
"It **s** like war down in the camp." .... Ex 32:17
are **s** of his chariots' horses .... Jdg 5:28
I make sad **s** as I eat; .... Job 3:24
Terrible **s** fill their ears, ... Job 15:21
Make me hear **s** of joy and .... Ps 51:8
No **s** come from their throats. .... Ps 115:7
The happy **s** of wild parties will .... Is 24:8
in that city the **s** of crying and .... Is 65:19
s of violence and destruction .... Je 6:7
end the happy **s** of the bride .... Je 7:34
will be no happy **s** in the cities .... Je 7:34
will soon stop the **s** of joy and .... Je 16:9
and the happy **s** of brides .... Je 16:9
bring an end to the **s** of joy and .... Je 25:10
the **s** of brides and bridegrooms, ... Je 25:10
There will be **s** of joy and .... Je 33:11
and the happy **s** of brides .... Je 33:11
There will be the **s** of people .... Je 33:11
S of people crying are heard in .... Je 51:54
S of people destroying things .... Je 51:54
making the loud **s** of the city .... Je 51:55
the middle of the **s** of war and .... Am 2:2
and make sad **s** like the owls do .... Mic 1:8
message that **s** foolish to save 1Co 1:21
lifeless things that make **s**— 1Co 14:7
are all kinds of **s** in the world, ... 1Co 14:10
blinks—when the last trumpet **s**. 1Co 15:52
the remaining **s** of the trumpets .... Rev 8:13

SOUP
boiling a pot of vegetable **s**. .... Ge 25:29
Let me eat some of that red **s**, ... Ge 25:30
gave Esau bread and vegetable **s**, ... Ge 25:34
are full of **s** made from meat .... Is 65:4

SOUR
food will turn **s** in their .... Job 20:14
who think **s** is sweet and sweet .... Is 5:20
sour is sweet and sweet is **s**. .... Is 5:20
'The parents have eaten **s** grapes, ... Je 31:29
their teeth from the **s** taste.' .... Je 31:29
person who eats **s** grapes will .... Je 31:30
'The parents have eaten **s** grapes, ... Eze 18:2
their teeth from the **s** taste'? .... Eze 18:2
It will be **s** in your stomach, ... Rev 10:9
ate it, it was **s** in my stomach. .... Rev 10:10

SOURCE
they showed the **s** of her blood. .... Le 20:18

SOUTH
and east, north and **s**, and all .... Ge 28:14
he turns to the **s**, I cannot see .... Job 23:9
is silenced by the hot, **s** wind. .... Job 37:17
The wind blows to the **s**; .... Ec 1:6
It grew to the **s**, the east, and .... Da 8:9
will attack the king of the **S**, ... Da 11:9
the Queen of the **S** will stand up .... Mt 12:42
the Queen of the **S** will stand up .... Lk 11:31
wind begin to blow from the **s**, ... Lk 12:55
north, three on the **s**, and three .... Rev 21:13

SOUTHEAST
large bowl in the **s** corner of 1Ki 7:39
large bowl in the **s** corner of 2Ch 4:10

SOUTHWEST
which faced **s** and northwest. .... Ac 27:12

SOW
of cattle or **s** your field with .... Le 19:19
where you did not **s** any seed. .... Mt 25:24
where I did not **s** any seed. .... Mt 25:26
When you **s** a seed, it must die 1Co 15:36
And when you **s** it, it does not 1Co 15:37
What you **s** is only a bare seed, ... 1Co 15:37

SPACE
keep some **s** between each herd. .... Ge 32:16
sky out over empty **s** and hangs .... Job 26:7
balconies took more **s** from them. .... Eze 42:5
will be an open **s** around the .... Eze 45:2

SPAIN
to visit you on my way to **S**. .... Rm 15:24
I will leave for **S** and stop and .... Rm 15:28

SPANK
If you **s** them, they won't die. .... Pr 23:13
you **s** them, you will save them .... Pr 23:14

SPARE
Don't take money to **s** the life .... Nu 35:31
protect them and **s** their life .... Ps 41:2
did not **s** his own Son but gave .... Rm 8:32

SPARED
not kill you if you had **s** them." .... Jdg 8:19
The LORD **s** me because I did what 2Sa 22:21
it is the wicked who are **s**. .... Job 21:30
The LORD **s** me because I did what .... Ps 18:20
you **s** me from going down to the .... Ps 30:3

SPARES
from death and **s** their lives .... Ps 33:19

SPARK
is like the last **s** of a fire. 2Sa 14:7

SPARKLE
with one **s** from your necklace. .... Sng 4:9

SPARKLED
calf's hoofs and s like polished .... Eze 1:7
a dome that s like ice and was .... Eze 1:22

SPARKLES
is red, when it s in the cup, ... Pr 23:31

SPARKLING
will not admire the s streams or .... Job 20:17
They looked like s chrysolite. .... Eze 1:16

SPARKS
as surely as s fly upward. .... Job 5:7
from its mouth; s of fire shoot .... Job 41:19
and their works will be like s. .... Is 1:31

SPARROWS
The s have found a home, and the .... Ps 84:3
they are like s or swallows that .... Pr 26:2
Two s cost only a penny, but not .... Mt 10:29
are worth much more than many s. .... Mt 10:31
Five s are sold for only two .... Lk 12:6
are worth much more than many s. .... Lk 12:7

SPAT
people there s in Jesus' face .... Mt 26:67
They s on Jesus. Then they took .... Mt 27:30

SPEAK
been brave to s to the Lord. .... Ge 18:27
been brave to s to the Lord. .... Ge 18:31
dead wife here, s to Ephron, the .... Ge 23:8
and could not s to him politely. .... Ge 37:4
please let me s plainly to you, ... Ge 44:18
talking to you, I cannot s well. .... Ex 4:10
I s slowly and can't find the .... Ex 4:10
someone deaf or not able to s? .... Ex 4:11
I will help you s, and I will .... Ex 4:12
You will s to Aaron and tell him .... Ex 4:15
both of you to s and will teach .... Ex 4:15
Aaron will s to the people for .... Ex 4:16
God says, and he will s for you. .... Ex 4:16
will remind you to s the LORD's. .... Ex 13:9
S to the whole community of the .... Ex 16:9
You must s to God for the people .... Ex 18:19
in a thick cloud and s to you. .... Ex 19:9
to Moses, "S to us yourself, ... Ex 20:19
But don't let God s to us, ... Ex 20:19
You must not s against God or .... Ex 22:28
meet you there and s to you. .... Ex 29:42
before the LORD to s with him, ... Ex 34:34
he went in to s with the LORD. .... Ex 34:35
S to Aaron, his sons, and all .... Le 17:2
if they s against the LORD, ... Le 24:16
S to the people of Israel and .... Le 27:2
Meeting Tent to s with the LORD, ... Nu 7:89
S to Aaron and tell him, ... Nu 8:2
come down and s with you there. .... Nu 11:17
Doesn't he also s through us?" .... Nu 12:2
I will s to them in dreams. .... Nu 12:6
I s face to face with him— .... Nu 12:8
be afraid to s against my— .... Nu 12:8
S to the Israelites and say to .... Nu 15:2
S to the Israelites and tell .... Nu 15:38
as a group to s to Moses and .... Nu 16:3
S to the people of Israel and .... Nu 17:2
S to the Levites and tell them: .... Nu 18:26
S to that rock in front of them .... Nu 20:8
S to the Israelites and tell .... Nu 33:51
and earth to s against you this .... Dt 4:26
ever heard God s from a fire .... Dt 4:33
you heard him s from the fire. .... Dt 4:36
hear the LORD our God s anymore. .... Dt 5:25
This prophet will s for me; .... Dt 18:19
must come and s to the army .... Dt 20:2
Hear, heavens, and I will s. .... Dt 32:1
I heard you s a curse about the .... Jdg 17:2

Now, all you Israelites, s up. .... Jdg 20:7
bragging, don't s proud words. 1Sa 2:3
the LORD did not s directly to 1Sa 3:1
calls you again, say, 'S, LORD. 1Sa 3:9
Samuel said, "S, LORD. 1Sa 3:10
he think he can s against the 1Sa 17:26
and king." The king said, "S." 2Sa 14:12
S to the elders of Judah. 2Sa 19:11
"You may s," she said. 1Ki 2:14
"I will s to the king for you." 1Ki 2:18
to King Solomon to s to him for 1Ki 2:19
of Israel and s evil about them. 1Ki 9:7
S to Solomon's son Rehoboam, ... 1Ki 12:23
man of God to s against the 1Ki 13:2
they heard Naboth s against God 1Ki 21:10
they had heard him s against God 1Ki 21:13
to tell you to s only the truth 1Ki 22:16
left me to s through you?" 1Ki 22:24
Do you want me to s to the king. 2Ki 4:13
you what you s in your bedroom. 2Ki 6:12
Please s to us in the Aramaic 2Ki 18:26
Don't s to us in Hebrew, because 2Ki 18:26
He sent me to s also to those 2Ki 18:27
to the Holy Tent to s with God, ... 1Ch 21:30
fun of it and s evil about it. 2Ch 7:20
S to Solomon's son Rehoboam, ... 2Ch 11:3
to tell you to s only the truth 2Ch 18:15
left me to s through you?" 2Ch 18:23
and they couldn't s the language .... Ne 13:24
they will s in the same way to .... Est 1:18
If someone tried to s with you, ... Job 4:2
I will s out in the suffering of .... Job 7:11
tell you and s about what they .... Job 8:10
Then I could s without being .... Job 9:35
will s because I am so unhappy. .... Job 10:1
I wish God would s and open his .... Job 11:5
S to the earth, and it will .... Job 12:8
But I want to s to the Almighty .... Job 13:3
should not s evil in the name .... Job 13:7
you cannot s God's truth by .... Job 13:7
Be quiet and let me s. .... Job 13:13
or let me s, and you answer. .... Job 13:22
Why do you s out your anger .... Job 15:13
I also could s as you do if you .... Job 16:4
Even if I s, my pain is not .... Job 16:6
and if I don't s, it still does .... Job 16:6
People might s against their .... Job 17:5
patient while I s. After I have .... Job 21:3
my lips will not s evil, and my .... Job 27:4
Job continued to s: .... Job 29:1
people should s, and those who .... Job 32:7
are quiet, must I wait to s? .... Job 32:16
I too will s and tell what I .... Job 32:17
the spirit in me causes me to s. .... Job 32:18
I must s so I will feel relief; .... Job 32:20
open my mouth and am ready to s. .... Job 33:2
God does s—sometimes one way and .... Job 33:14
may be an angel to s for him, ... Job 33:23
be quiet, and I will s. .... Job 33:31
s up, because I want to prove .... Job 33:32
who understand s, and the wise .... Job 34:34
God be told that I want to s? .... Job 37:20
you for mercy and s to you with .... Job 41:3
I will s about Leviathan's arms .... Job 41:12
said, 'Listen now, and I will s. .... Job 42:4
Such people s the truth from .... Ps 15:2
idols or even s their names. .... Ps 16:4
prayer, because I s the truth. .... Ps 17:1
it cannot s about your truth. .... Ps 30:9
and hatred they s against those .... Ps 31:18
They s against me and say, ... Ps 35:21
Good people s with wisdom, ... Ps 37:30
Like the mute, I cannot s. .... Ps 38:13

I s about your loyalty and .... Ps 40:10
these things, I s with a broken .... Ps 42:4
You s against your brother and .... Ps 50:20
right when you s and fair when .... Ps 51:4
let me s so I may praise you. .... Ps 51:15
make fun of others and s evil;................. Ps 73:8
they s of hurting others. .... Ps 73:8
I will s using stories; .... Ps 78:2
no one can s all his praise. .... Ps 106:2
to those who s evil against me. .... Ps 109:20
have mouths, but they cannot s. .... Ps 115:5
Even if princes s against me, ... Ps 119:23
me s your praise, because you .... Ps 119:171
have mouths, but they cannot s. .... Ps 135:16
when they hear the words you s. .... Ps 138:4
and will s about your power .... Ps 145:11
They will s to you when you are.............. Pr 6:22
say is true, I refuse to s evil. .... Pr 8:7
people s with understanding, ... Pr 10:13
use knowledge when they s, ... Pr 15:2
if they don't s, they appear to .... Pr 17:28
will be rewarded by how they s. .... Pr 18:20
Those who s with care will be .... Pr 18:21
a few people s with knowledge. .... Pr 20:15
a truthful witness will s on. .... Pr 21:28
Don't s to fools; they will only .... Pr 23:9
pleased if you s what is right.................. Pr 23:16
fools when they s foolishly,.................... Pr 26:4
fools when they s foolishly,.................... Pr 26:5
see people who s too quickly? .... Pr 29:20
people want to s to a ruler, ... Pr 29:26
S up for those who cannot speak .... Pr 31:8
who cannot s for themselves; .... Pr 31:8
S up and judge fairly, and .... Pr 31:9
Her children s well of her. .... Pr 31:28
to be silent and a time to s.................... Ec 3:7
before you s, and be careful .... Ec 5:2
do not s the word of the LORD, ... Is 8:20
the prophets who s lies were the .... Is 9:15
evil; they all s lies. But the .... Is 9:17
cities in Egypt will s Hebrew, ... Is 19:18
languages to s to these people. .... Is 28:11
down and will s from the ground; .... Is 29:4
who cannot s clearly now will .... Is 32:4
then be able to s clearly and .... Is 32:4
Please s to us in the Aramaic .... Is 36:11
Don't s to us in Hebrew, because .... Is 36:11
He sent me to s also to those .... Is 36:12
S kindly to the people of........................ Is 40:2
Come to me and s; we will meet .... Is 41:1
cry out or yell or s loudly in .... Is 42:2
I did not s in secret or hide my .... Is 45:19
am the LORD, and I s the truth; .... Is 45:19
let people s evil against me, ... Is 48:11
All day long they s against me. .... Is 52:5
that those who s against you are .... Is 54:17
thing is true of the words I s. .... Is 55:11
I will continue to s for her; .... Is 62:1
I, the LORD, s what is right. .... Is 63:1
Lord GOD, I don't know how to s. .... Je 1:6
Go and s to the people of .... Je 2:2
Go and s this message toward the .... Je 3:12
people there s a language you .... Je 5:15
The prophets s lies, and the .... Je 5:31
whom can I s? Whom can I warn? .... Je 6:10
did not s to them and give them .... Je 7:22
Their mouths s lies. Everyone................ Je 9:8
their mouths they s well of you, ... Je 12:2
or appoint men or s to them. .... Je 14:14
the prophets s will be thrown .... Je 14:16
s this message to the people of .... Je 14:17
And if you s things that have .... Je 15:19
words, then you may s for me. .... Je 15:19

when I will s about a nation .... Je 18:7
when I will s about a nation .... Je 18:9
There s the words I tell you. .... Je 19:2
I did not command or s about; .... Je 19:5
Every time I s, I shout. .... Je 20:8
will not s anymore in his name. .... Je 20:9
I did not s to them, but they .... Je 23:21
my message s it truthfully! .... Je 23:28
only message you s is your own .... Je 23:36
how you should s to the prophets .... Je 23:37
insult them and s evil of them. .... Je 25:18
Yes, I often s against Israel, ... Je 31:20
And he will s to the king of .... Je 32:4
Mizpah and will s for you before .... Je 40:10
nations will s evil of you. .... Je 42:18
Other nations will s evil of you .... Je 44:8
nations will s evil about them. .... Je 44:12
that city and s evil of it. .... Je 49:13
S the whole message and say: ' .... Je 50:2
their mouths to s against you.................. La 2:16
Nobody can s and have it happen .... La 3:37
their mouths and s against us. .... La 3:46
your feet so I may s with you." .... Eze 2:1
But s my words to them......................... Eze 2:7
Then go and s to the people of .... Eze 3:1
Israel, and s my words to them. .... Eze 3:4
all the words I will s to you, ... Eze 3:10
If you don't s out to warn the .... Eze 3:18
There I will s to you." .... Eze 3:22
But when I s to you, I will open .... Eze 3:27
but I, the LORD, will s. .... Eze 12:25
So s to them and tell them, ' .... Eze 14:4
have tricked that prophet to s. .... Eze 14:9
s to the elders of Israel and................... Eze 20:3
s to the people of Israel. .... Eze 20:27
Jerusalem and s against the holy .... Eze 21:2
will s and be silent no more. .... Eze 24:27
S to Tyre, which has ports for................. Eze 27:3
let you, Ezekiel, s to them. .... Eze 29:21
mighty ones will s about the .... Eze 32:21
s to your people and say to them: .... Eze 33:2
' but you don't s to warn the .... Eze 33:8
to me. I could s; I was not .... Eze 33:22
I s in hot anger against the .... Eze 36:5
I s against the people of Edom, ... Eze 36:5
I s in my jealous anger, because .... Eze 36:6
S to every kind of bird and wild .... Eze 39:17
Then s to those who refuse to .... Eze 44:6
and those who s every language.............. Da 4:1
king will s against the Most .... Da 7:25
about the words I will s to you, ... Da 10:11
bowed facedown and could not s. .... Da 10:15
my mouth and started to s. .... Da 10:16
said, "Master, s, since you have .... Da 10:19
desert and s tenderly to her. .... Hos 2:14
"At that time I will s to you," .... Hos 2:21
I will s to the skies, and they .... Hos 2:21
those who s in court against .... Am 5:10
makes idols that can't even s!................ Hab 2:18
all of them will s the name of................ Zph 3:9
S to Zerubbabel son of .... Hag 2:2
leave the man, he was able to s. .... Mt 9:33
I will s using stories; .... Mt 13:35
could not s, and many others.................. Mt 15:30
who could not s before were now .... Mt 15:31
speak before were now able to s. .... Mt 15:31
before he could s, Jesus said to .... Mt 17:25
would not allow the demons to s, ... Mk 1:34
can't talk he makes able to s." .... Mk 7:37
people unable to hear or s, ... Mk 9:25
They will s in new languages.................. Mk 16:17
not be able to s until the day .... Lk 1:20
he could not s to them, and they.............. Lk 1:22

them and remained unable to s. .... Lk 1:22
and would not allow them to s, ... Lk 4:41
People s the things that are in .... Lk 6:45
use stories to s to other people .... Lk 8:10
man who had been unable to s, ... Lk 11:14
some people to s to him and ask .... Lk 14:32
they heard John s about him was .... Jn 1:40
from my Father and s for him, ... Jn 5:43
one who sent them s the truth, ... Jn 7:18
But because I s the truth, ... Jn 8:45
is old enough to s for himself." .... Jn 9:21
but because you s against God. .... Jn 10:33
do you say that I s against God .... Jn 10:36
He will not s his own words, ... Jn 16:13
he will s only what he hears, ... Jn 16:13
I will s to you in plain words .... Jn 16:25
said, "You refuse to s to me? .... Jn 19:10
and they began to s different .... Ac 2:4
and John were not afraid to s, ... Ac 4:13
told them not to s or to teach .... Ac 4:18
must s about what we have seen .... Ac 4:20
to s your word without fear. .... Ac 4:29
told them not to s in the name .... Ac 5:40
helping him to s with wisdom, ... Ac 6:10
We heard Stephen s against Moses .... Ac 6:11
Philip began to s, and starting .... Ac 8:35
Peter began to s: "I really .... Ac 10:34
encourage the people, please s." .... Ac 13:15
We must s the message of God to .... Ac 13:46
man was listening to Paul s, ... Ac 14:9
Apollos began to s very boldly .... Ac 18:26
commander said, "Do you s Greek? .... Ac 21:37
Please, let me s to the people." .... Ac 21:39
angel or a spirit did s to him." .... Ac 23:9
made a plan for Paul to s, ... Ac 24:10
may now s to defend yourself. .... Ac 26:1
raised his hand and began to s. .... Ac 26:1
to make them s against Jesus. .... Ac 26:11
and I can s freely to him. .... Ac 26:26
who are not Jews s against God's .... Rm 2:24
be shown to be right when you s, ... Rm 3:4
I s a wisdom to those who are 1Co 2:6
s God's secret wisdom, which he 1Co 2:7
And we s about these things, ... 1Co 2:13
we s nice words about them. 1Co 4:13
idols—things that could not s. 1Co 12:2
the ability to s with wisdom, ... 1Co 12:8
the ability to s with knowledge. 1Co 12:8
the ability to s in different 1Co 12:10
and those who can s in different 1Co 12:28
all s in different languages 1Co 12:30
may s in different languages of 1Co 13:1
The ones who s in different 1Co 14:4
who can only s in different 1Co 14:5
Unless you s clearly with your 1Co 14:9
thank God that I s in different 1Co 14:18
I would rather s five words I 1Co 14:19
I will s to these people 1Co 14:21
or not more than three, who s. 1Co 14:27
They should s one after the 1Co 14:27
then those who s in a different 1Co 14:28
They should s only to themselves 1Co 14:28
two or three prophets should s, ... 1Co 14:29
They are not allowed to s, ... 1Co 14:34
for a woman to s in the church 1Co 14:35
in Christ we s the truth before 2Co 2:17
We believe, and so we s. 2Co 4:13
have been sent to s for Christ. 2Co 5:20
We s for Christ when we beg you 2Co 5:20
are liars, but we s the truth. 2Co 6:8
I s to you as if you were my 2Co 6:13
and you must not s foolishly or .... Eph 5:4
S to each other with psalms, ... Eph 5:19

Also pray for me that when I s, ... Eph 6:19
Good News I will s without fear, ... Eph 6:20
not afraid to s the word of God .... Php 1:14
Pray that I can s in a way that .... Col 4:4
But we s the Good News because 1Th 2:4
When we s, we are not trying to 1Th 2:4
tell lies, who s falsely, and 1Ti 1:10
will learn not to s against God. 1Ti 1:20
They must not s evil of others. 1Ti 3:11
not s angrily to an older man, ... 1Ti 5:1
so no one will s against God's 1Ti 6:1
S the truth so that you cannot .... Tit 2:8
to s no evil about anyone, ... Tit 3:2
from lips that s his name. .... Heb 13:15
willing to listen and slow to s. .... Jam 1:19
the ones who s against Jesus, ... Jam 2:7
If you s against your fellow .... Jam 4:11
that those who s evil of your 1Pe 3:16
speaks should s words from God. 1Pe 4:11
are not afraid to s against the 2Pe 2:10
these people s against things 2Pe 2:12
We also s well of him, and you 3Jn 1:12
authority and s against the .... Jud 1:8
these people s against things .... Jud 1:10
were not afraid to s my name. .... Rev 3:8
used its mouth to s against God, ... Rev 13:6
one so that the idol could s. .... Rev 13:15

SPEAKER

I have never been a skilled s. .... Ex 4:10
family of Levi, is a skilled s. .... Ex 4:14
me either. I am not a good s." .... Ex 6:12
answered, "I am not a good s. .... Ex 6:30
He is a good s and handsome, ... 1Sa 16:18
and you are an excellent s, ... Ps 45:2
because he was the main s. .... Ac 14:12
and was a good s who knew the .... Ac 18:24
the first s should stop 1Co 14:30
be a trained s, but I do have 2Co 11:6

SPEAKING

the LORD finished s to Abraham, ... Ge 18:33
was still s when another .... Job 1:16
I am s of royal things. .... Ps 45:1
stop your mouth from s evil, ... Ps 50:19
the ground and heard a voice s. .... Eze 1:28
king and began s against the men .... Da 3:8
Then I heard a holy angel s. .... Da 8:13
lying, and s evil of others. .... Mt 15:19
s by the power of the Holy .... Mt 22:43
comes, s only for himself, ... Jn 5:43
You are s clearly to us now and .... Jn 16:29
one heard them s in his own .... Ac 2:6
I heard a voice s to me in the .... Ac 26:14
if I come to you s in different 1Co 14:6
has the gift of s in a different 1Co 14:13
S the truth with love, we will .... Eph 4:15
gave you in our s and in our 2Th 2:15
who work hard by s and teaching, ... 1Ti 5:17
fighting, s against others, ... 1Ti 6:4
not s against others or enslaved .... Tit 2:3
through his faith he is still s. .... Heb 11:4
judging and s against the law .... Jam 4:11

SPEAKS

face as a man s with his friend .... Ex 33:11
listen when he s will answer to .... Dt 18:19
or if a prophet s in the name of .... Dt 18:20
I have one who s for me in .... Job 16:19
The one who s for me is my .... Job 16:20
Sin s to the wicked in their .... Ps 36:1
and my heart s with .... Ps 49:3
The God of gods, the LORD, s. .... Ps 50:1
Anyone who s against the Son of .... Mt 12:32
The mouth s the things that are .... Mt 12:34

S

anyone who s against the Holy .... Mk 3:29
witnesses who s about myself, ... Jn 8:18
sent me, and he s the truth." .... Jn 8:26
Spirit himself s to God for us,.............. Rm 8:26
the Spirit s to God for his .... Rm 8:27
and everyone s in different 1Co 14:23
Another s in a different 1Co 14:26
if anyone s in a different..................... 1Co 14:27
not refuse to listen when God s. .... Heb 12:25
Anyone who s should speak words 1Pe 4:11

SPEAR

left the meeting and got his s................. Nu 25:7
and drove his s through both .... Nu 25:8
Hold your s toward Ai, because .... Jos 8:18
Joshua held his s toward the .... Jos 8:18
Joshua had held his s toward Ai, ... Jos 8:26
a shield or a s among the forty .... Jdg 5:8
he had a bronze s on his back. 1Sa 17:6
part of his larger s was like a 1Sa 17:7
but Saul had a s in his hand. 1Sa 18:10
He threw the s, thinking, "I'll 1Sa 18:11
house with his s in his hand. 1Sa 19:9
David to the wall with his s, ... 1Sa 19:10
So Saul's s went into the wall, ... 1Sa 19:10
Saul threw his s at Jonathan, ... 1Sa 20:33
Do you have a s or sword here? 1Sa 21:8
He had a s in his hand. 1Sa 22:6
the camp with his s stuck in the 1Sa 26:7
Saul to the ground with my s................. 1Sa 26:8
Take the s and water jug that 1Sa 26:11
David took the s and water jug 1Sa 26:12
are the king's s and water jug................. 1Sa 26:16
David answered, "Here is your s. 1Sa 26:22
I saw Saul leaning on his s. 2Sa 1:6
So using the back end of his s, ... 2Sa 2:23
and the s came out of his back. 2Sa 2:23
His s was as large as a weaver's............ 2Sa 21:19
with his s and killed them. 2Sa 23:18
who had a s in his hand. 2Sa 23:21
but he grabbed the s from the................. 2Sa 23:21
and killed him with his own s. 2Sa 23:21
He used his s to fight three................... 1Ch 11:11
with his s and killed them. 1Ch 11:20
feet tall and had a s as large 1Ch 11:23
but he grabbed the s from the................. 1Ch 11:23
and killed him with his own s. 1Ch 11:23
His s was as large as a weaver's............ 1Ch 20:5
when they shake a s at it. .... Job 41:29
and the gleam of your shining s. .... Hab 3:11
the enemy's own s you stabbed .... Hab 3:14
stuck his s into Jesus' side,..................... Jn 19:34

SPEARHEAD

had a bronze s weighing about 2Sa 21:16

SPEARS

might make swords and s."..................... 1Sa 13:19
and Jonathan had no swords or s. 1Sa 13:22
to me using a sword and two s. 1Sa 17:45
need swords or s to save people. 1Sa 17:47
Joab took three s and stabbed 2Sa 18:14
with swords and s until their 1Ki 18:28
commanders the s and shields 2Ki 11:10
and skilled with shields and s. 1Ch 12:8
They carried shields and s. 1Ch 12:24
them who carried shields and s.............. 1Ch 12:34
put shields and s in all the 2Ch 11:12
carried large shields and s..................... 2Ch 14:8
hundred men the s and the large 2Ch 23:9
and skilled with s and shields. 2Ch 25:5
army shields, s, helmets, armor 2Ch 26:14
with their swords, s, and bows. .... Ne 4:13
The other half was ready with s, ... Ne 4:16
the men holding s from sunrise .... Ne 4:21

with the flashing s and swords. .... Job 39:23
or fill its head with fishing s? .... Job 41:7
nor the arrows, darts, and s. .... Job 41:26
Lift up your s, both large and .... Ps 35:3
all bows and s and burns up .... Ps 46:9
teeth are like s and arrows,................... Ps 57:4
plows and their s into hooks for.............. Is 2:4
The soldiers carry bows and s. .... Je 6:23
Polish your s. Put on your armor .... Je 46:4
Their armies have bows and s. .... Je 50:42
and arrows, war clubs, and s................. Eze 39:9
and make s from your hooks for .... Joe 3:10
blades and their s into hooks .... Mic 4:3
are shining, s are gleaming! .... Nah 3:3
hundred men with s ready to .... Ac 23:23

SPECIAL

and the s olive oil poured on a .... Ex 25:6
to make s clothes for Aaron— .... Ex 28:3
Take the s olive oil and pour it .... Ex 29:7
what you gain and your s gifts; .... Dt 12:6
an offering as a s gift to him, ... Dt 16:10
favorites or give s favors to..................... Dt 33:9
Naphtali enjoys s kindnesses,................. Dt 33:23
things are used for s purposes, ... 2Ti 2:20
will be used for s purposes. 2Ti 2:21
food and drink and s washings. .... Heb 9:10
You show s attention to the one .... Jam 2:3
Christ gave you a s gift that is 1Jn 2:27
spots in your s Christian meals .... Jud 1:12

SPECIALLY

LORD, like land s given to him. .... Le 27:21

SPECKLED

will take every s or spotted..................... Ge 30:32
and every spotted or s goat. .... Ge 30:32
goat that isn't s or spotted or .... Ge 30:33
the s and spotted female goats .... Ge 30:35
were streaked, s, or spotted. .... Ge 30:39
have all the s animals as your................. Ge 31:8
gave birth to s young ones....................... Ge 31:8
were streaked, s, or spotted. .... Ge 31:10
the streaked, s, or spotted male .... Ge 31:12
to me like a s bird attacked..................... Je 12:9

SPEECH

They have no s or words; .... Ps 19:3
to people whose s you can't .... Eze 3:5
many nations whose s you can't.............. Eze 3:6
I was not without s anymore. .... Eze 33:22
all nations pure s so that all .... Zph 3:9
When I began my s, the Holy .... Ac 11:15
and made a s to the people. .... Ac 12:21
hypocrisy, jealousy, and evil s. 1Pe 2:1

SPEECHES

words or make s that have no................. Job 15:3
your long-winded s never end? .... Job 16:3
I could make great s against you .... Job 16:4
When will you stop these s? .... Job 18:2

SPEED

children set the s at which we .... Ge 33:14

SPEND

to my house and s the night. .... Ge 19:2
will s the night in the city's..................... Ge 19:2
me and my men to s the night?".............. Ge 24:23
a place for you to s the night." .... Ge 24:25
her or even s time with her. .... Ge 39:10
and have them s today and..................... Ex 19:10
s seven days appointing them. .... Ex 29:35
S seven days making the altar .... Ex 29:37
and s it on things for the....................... Ex 30:16
went in to s the night with her. .... Jdg 16:1
S the night here and enjoy .... Jdg 19:9

and s the night here." .... Jdg 19:11
Ramah so we can s the night in .... Jdg 19:13
stopped there to s the night. .... Jdg 19:15
them home to s the night. .... Jdg 19:15
but don't s the night in the .... Jdg 19:20
in Benjamin to s the night. .... Jdg 20:4
fellow Jews may s the silver and .... Ezr 7:18
They s the night naked, because............. Job 24:7
stranger ever had to s the night .... Job 31:32
I do not s time with liars, ... Ps 26:4
S time with the wise and you .... Pr 13:20
people or s time with those who............. Pr 22:24
friends they have to help s it. .... Ec 5:11
into the country and s the night .... Sng 7:11
Why s your money on something .... Is 55:2
the graves and s their nights .... Is 65:4
where travelers s the night— .... Je 9:2
If you s more money on him, ... Lk 10:35
Be careful not to s your time .... Lk 21:34
men to come in and s the night. .... Ac 10:23
Tell them not to s their time on 1Ti 1:4

SPENDING
Why are you s the night by the .... Ne 13:21

SPENDS
who do evil and s time with .... Job 34:8

SPENT
and drank and s the night there .... Ge 24:54
he s the night there because the .... Ge 28:11
and then he s all of the money .... Ge 31:15
s the night on the mountain. .... Ge 31:54
My life has been s wandering................. Ge 47:9
house, where they s the night. .... Jdg 18:2
Solomon had s seven years.................... 1Ki 6:38
to know how the money was s, ... 2Ki 12:15
They s three days there with 1Ch 12:39
kinds of goods s the night .... Ne 13:20
and my years are s in crying. .... Ps 31:10
from Dedan s the night near .... Is 21:13
They s much time in houses of .... Je 5:7
Bethany, where he s the night. .... Mt 21:17
doctors and had s all the money.............. Mk 5:26
he s the night praying to God. .... Lk 6:12
After he had s everything, ... Lk 15:14
They s their time learning the................. Ac 2:42
Paul s all his time telling...................... Ac 18:5
of those times I s a night and a 2Co 11:25
We s our lives doing evil and .... Tit 3:3

SPICE
smells better than any s......................... Sng 4:10
gathered my myrrh with my s. .... Sng 5:1
cinnamon, s, incense, myrrh, ... Rev 18:13

SPICED
you a drink of s wine from my .... Sng 8:2

SPICES
Their camels were carrying s,................. Ge 37:25
some honey, s, myrrh, pistachio .... Ge 43:11
s for sweet-smelling incense, ... Ex 25:6
Take the finest s: twelve pounds .... Ex 30:23
Take these sweet-smelling s: .... Ex 30:34
s for the special olive oil used................. Ex 35:8
also brought s and olive oil for .... Ex 35:28
They are like s planted by the................. Nu 24:6
servants and camels carrying s, ... 1Ki 10:2
of gold and many s and jewels. 1Ki 10:10
brought more s than the queen 1Ki 10:10
clothes, weapons, s, horses, and 1Ki 10:25
the silver, gold, s, expensive 2Ki 20:13
wine, oil, incense, and s,...................... 1Ch 9:29
took care of mixing the s. 1Ch 9:30
-smelling s in his presence..................... 2Ch 2:4
with her and camels carrying s, ... 2Ch 9:1

of gold and many s and jewels. 2Ch 9:9
ever given such s as the queen 2Ch 9:9
clothes, weapons, s, horses, and.............. 2Ch 9:24
bed filled with s and different................. 2Ch 16:14
gold, gems, s, shields, and 2Ch 32:27
it is full of wine mixed with s. .... Ps 75:8
myrrh, incense, and other s? .... Sng 3:6
and aloes—all the best s....................... Sng 4:14
His cheeks are like beds of s; .... Sng 5:13
garden, to the beds of s, to .... Sng 6:2
on the mountains where s grow............... Sng 8:14
the silver, gold, s, expensive .... Is 39:2
Mix in the s, and let the bones .... Eze 24:10
your goods for all the best s, ... Eze 27:22
-smelling s to put on Jesus'..................... Mk 16:1
left to prepare s and perfumes. .... Lk 23:56
the s they had prepared......................... Lk 24:1
it with the s in pieces of linen .... Jn 19:40

SPIDER'S
what they trust is like a s web. .... Job 8:14
They lean on the s web, but it............... Job 8:15
wicked build are like a s web,................. Job 27:18
lies as they would spin a s web. .... Is 59:5

SPIED
two men who had s out the land, ... Jos 6:22

SPIES
He said to them, "You are s! .... Ge 42:9
We are honest men, not s."..................... Ge 42:11
can see I was right! You are s! .... Ge 42:14
as the king lives, you are s."................... Ge 42:16
that we were honest men, not s............... Ge 42:31
you are not s but honest men.................. Ge 42:34
After Moses sent s to the town .... Nu 21:32
The s we sent have made us .... Dt 1:28
sent out two s from Acacia and .... Jos 2:1
looking for the s on the road .... Jos 2:7
Before the s went to sleep for .... Jos 2:8
Rahab hid the two s we sent out. .... Jos 6:17
They sent some s to Bethel .... Jdg 1:23
s saw a man coming out of the .... Jdg 1:24
The five s went into the house .... Jdg 18:17
When the s went into Micah's .... Jdg 18:18
he sent out s and learned for 1Sa 26:4
and sent some s who acted as if .... Lk 20:20
So the s asked Jesus, "Teacher, ... Lk 20:21
They came in like s to overturn .... Gal 2:4
welcomed the s and was not .... Heb 11:31
She welcomed the s into her home............ Jam 2:25

SPILL
Don't s any blood. Throw him .... Ge 37:22
insides to s onto the ground. 2Sa 20:10
the wine will s, and the wine .... Mt 9:17
bags, the wine will s out, and .... Lk 5:37
over, it will s into your lap. .... Lk 6:38

SPILLED
like water s on the ground; 2Sa 14:14
They have s blood like water all .... Ps 79:3
the blood she s on the bare rock.............. Eze 24:8

SPILLING
full and the barrels are s over, ... Joe 3:13

SPILLS
he s my blood on the ground. .... Job 16:13

SPIN
as they would s a spider's web. .... Is 59:5

SPIRIT
and God's S was moving over the .... Ge 1:2
My S will not remain in human .... Ge 6:3
God's s is in him!" .... Ge 41:38
with the S of God and have .... Ex 31:3
Bezalel with the S of God and .... Ex 35:31

S

some of the **S** that is in you, ... Nu 11:17
took some of the **S** Moses had, ... Nu 11:25
With the **S** in them, they .... Nu 11:25
the **S** was also given to them, ... Nu 11:26
give his **S** to all of them!" .... Nu 11:29
S of God took control of him, ... Nu 24:2
of Nun, because my **S** is in him. .... Nu 27:18
The **S** of the LORD entered .... Jdg 3:10
But the **S** of the LORD entered .... Jdg 6:34
sent an evil **s** to make trouble .... Jdg 9:23
sent the evil **s** to punish them. .... Jdg 9:24
Then the **S** of the LORD entered .... Jdg 11:29
The **S** of the LORD began to work .... Jdg 13:25
The **S** of the LORD entered Samson .... Jdg 14:6
Then the **S** of the LORD entered .... Jdg 14:19
Then the **S** of the LORD entered .... Jdg 15:14
Then the **S** of the LORD will rush 1Sa 10:6
The **S** of God rushed upon him, ... 1Sa 10:10
God's **S** rushed upon him with 1Sa 11:6
the LORD's **S** worked in David. 1Sa 16:13
But the LORD's **S** had left Saul, ... 1Sa 16:14
and an evil **s** from the LORD 1Sa 16:14
s from God is troubling you. 1Sa 16:15
Then the evil **s** from God troubles 1Sa 16:16
the evil **s** from God troubled 1Sa 16:23
Then the evil **s** would leave him, ... 1Sa 16:23
day an evil **s** from God roamed 1Sa 18:10
again an evil **s** from the LORD 1Sa 19:9
So the **S** of God entered Saul's 1Sa 19:20
the **S** of God also rushed upon 1Sa 19:23
to her, "Talk to a **s** for me. 1Sa 28:8
I see a **s** coming up out of the 1Sa 28:13
The LORD's **S** spoke through me, ... 2Sa 23:2
The **S** of the LORD may carry you 1Ki 18:12
Then one **s** came and stood before 1Ki 22:21
The **s** answered, 'I will go to 1Ki 22:22
Has the LORD's **s** left me to 1Ki 22:24
me a double share of your **s**." 2Ki 2:9
now has the **s** Elijah had." 2Ki 2:15
the **S** of the LORD has taken 2Ki 2:16
said to him, "My **s** was with you. 2Ki 5:26
am going to put a **s** in the king 2Ki 19:7
Then the **S** entered Amasai, ... 1Ch 12:18
The **S** of God entered Azariah son 2Ch 15:1
Then one **s** came and stood before 2Ch 18:20
The **s** answered, 'I will go to 2Ch 18:21
Has the LORD's **S** left me to 2Ch 18:23
Then the **S** of the LORD entered 2Ch 20:14
Then the **S** of God entered 2Ch 24:20
gave your good **S** to teach them. .... Ne 9:20
warned them by your **S** through .... Ne 9:30
A **s** glided past my face, and the .... Job 4:15
The **s** stopped, but I could not .... Job 4:16
my **s** drinks in their poison; .... Job 6:4
out in the suffering of my **s**. .... Job 7:11
My **s** is broken; the days of my .... Job 17:1
have broken the **s** of those who .... Job 31:39
But it is the **s** in a person, ... Job 32:8
and the **s** in me causes me to .... Job 32:18
The **S** of God created me, and the .... Job 33:4
and make my **s** right again. .... Ps 51:10
take your Holy **S** away from me. .... Ps 51:11
strong by giving me a willing **s**. .... Ps 51:12
God wants to a broken **s**. .... Ps 51:17
turned against the **S** of God, ... Ps 106:33
I go to get away from your **S**? .... Ps 139:7
Let your good **S** lead me on level .... Ps 143:10
but dishonest words crush the **s**. .... Pr 15:4
sadness can break a person's **s**. .... Pr 15:13
but a broken **s** drains your .... Pr 17:22
no one can live with a broken **s**. .... Pr 18:14
that the human **s** goes up to God .... Ec 3:21
God and that the **s** of an animal .... Ec 3:21

your **s** will return to God who .... Ec 12:7
the city with the **s** of fairness .... Is 4:4
of fairness and the **s** of fire. .... Is 4:4
The **S** of the LORD will rest upon .... Is 11:2
The **S** will give him wisdom and .... Is 11:2
The **S** will teach him to know and .... Is 11:2
and my **s** wants to be with you at .... Is 26:9
nations, without asking my **S**. .... Is 30:1
are only animals and are not **s**. .... Is 31:3
God pours his **S** from above upon .... Is 32:15
so his **S** will gather them .... Is 34:16
am going to put a **s** in the king .... Is 37:7
Because of you, my **s** also lives; .... Is 38:16
I have put my **S** upon him, and he .... Is 42:1
will pour out my **S** into your .... Is 44:3
Lord GOD has sent me with his **S**. .... Is 48:16
S and my words that I give you .... Is 59:21
Lord GOD has put his **S** in me, ... Is 61:1
to replace their **s** of sadness. .... Is 61:3
and made his Holy **S** very sad. .... Is 63:10
who put his Holy **S** among them, ... Is 63:11
S of the LORD gave the people .... Is 63:14
Wherever the **s** would go, the .... Eze 1:12
Wherever the **s** would go, the .... Eze 1:20
because the **s** of the living .... Eze 1:20
because the **s** of the living .... Eze 1:21
the **S** entered me and put me on .... Eze 2:2
Then the **S** lifted me up, and I .... Eze 3:12
the **S** lifted me up and took me .... Eze 3:14
Then the **S** entered me and made .... Eze 3:24
The **S** lifted me up between the .... Eze 8:3
because the **s** of the living .... Eze 10:17
The **S** lifted me up and brought .... Eze 11:1
Then the **S** of the LORD entered .... Eze 11:5
The **S** lifted me up and brought .... Eze 11:24
a vision given by the **S** of God, ... Eze 11:24
I will put my **S** inside you and .... Eze 36:27
me out by the **S** of the LORD and .... Eze 37:1
And I will put my **S** inside you, ... Eze 37:14
I will put my **S** into the people .... Eze 39:29
Then the **S** picked me up and .... Eze 43:5
because the **s** of the holy gods .... Da 4:8
I know that the **s** of the holy .... Da 4:9
because the **s** of the holy gods .... Da 4:18
who has the **s** of the holy gods. .... Da 5:11
heard that the **s** of the gods is. .... Da 5:14
will pour out my **S** on all kinds .... Joe 2:28
will pour out my **S** also on male .... Joe 2:29
power, with the **S** of the LORD, ... Mic 3:8
and my **S** is still with you. .... Hag 2:5
but by my **S**,' says the LORD .... Zch 4:6
have caused my **s** to rest in the .... Zch 6:8
he sent by his **S** through the .... Zch 7:12
and put the human **s** within: .... Zch 12:1
in Jerusalem a **s** of kindness and .... Zch 12:10
body and one **s** for his purpose— .... Mal 2:15
by the power of the Holy **S**. .... Mt 1:18
baby in her is from the Holy **S**. .... Mt 1:20
you with the Holy **S** and fire. .... Mt 3:11
and he saw God's **S** coming down .... Mt 3:16
Then the **S** led Jesus into the .... Mt 4:1
speaking but the **S** of your .... Mt 10:20
I am gentle and humble in **s**, ... Mt 11:29
I will put my **S** upon him, and he .... Mt 12:18
power of God's **S** to force out .... Mt 12:28
against the Holy **S** will not be .... Mt 12:31
against the Holy **S** will not be .... Mt 12:32
When an evil **s** comes out of a .... Mt 12:43
the **s** says, 'I will go back to .... Mt 12:44
' When the **s** comes back, it .... Mt 12:44
Then the evil **s** goes and .... Mt 12:45
That kind of **s** comes out only if .... Mt 17:21
by the power of the Holy **S**, ... Mt 22:43

The **s** wants to do what is right, ... Mt 26:41
and the Son and the Holy **S**. .... Mt 28:19
baptize you with the Holy **S**." .... Mk 1:8
The Holy **S** came down on him like .... Mk 1:10
Then the **S** sent Jesus into the .... Mk 1:12
who had an evil **s** in him. .... Mk 1:23
Jesus commanded the evil **s**, ... Mk 1:25
The evil **s** shook the man .... Mk 1:26
against the Holy **S** will never be .... Mk 3:29
he had an evil **s** inside him. .... Mk 3:30
a man with an evil **s** came to him .... Mk 5:2
to him, "You evil **s**, come out of .... Mk 5:8
had an evil **s** in her heard that .... Mk 7:25
He has an evil **s** in him that .... Mk 9:17
the **s** attacks him, it throws .... Mk 9:18
to force the evil **s** out, ... Mk 9:18
As soon as the evil **s** saw Jesus, ... Mk 9:20
The **s** often throws him into a .... Mk 9:22
ordered the evil **s**, saying, "You .... Mk 9:25
You **s** that makes people unable .... Mk 9:25
The evil **s** screamed and caused .... Mk 9:26
again. Then the **s** came out. The .... Mk 9:26
we force that evil **s** out?" .... Mk 9:28
That kind of **s** can only be .... Mk 9:29
speaking by the Holy **S**, said: ' .... Mk 12:36
it will be the Holy **S**. .... Mk 13:11
The **s** wants to do what is right, ... Mk 14:38
will be filled with the Holy **S**. .... Lk 1:15
the Lord in **s** and power like .... Lk 1:17
The Holy **S** will come upon you, ... Lk 1:35
was filled with the Holy **S**. .... Lk 1:41
with the Holy **S** and prophesied: .... Lk 1:67
grew up and became strong in **s**. .... Lk 1:80
and the Holy **S** was in him. .... Lk 2:25
told by the Holy **S** that he would .... Lk 2:26
The **S** led Simeon to the Temple. .... Lk 2:27
you with the Holy **S** and fire. .... Lk 3:16
and the Holy **S** came down on him .... Lk 3:22
filled with the Holy **S**, returned .... Lk 4:1
The **S** led Jesus into the desert .... Lk 4:1
in the power of the Holy **S**, ... Lk 4:14
The Lord has put his **S** in me, ... Lk 4:18
him an evil **s** shouted in a loud .... Lk 4:33
Jesus commanded the evil **s**, ... Lk 4:35
The evil **s** threw the man down .... Lk 4:35
commanding the evil **s** to come .... Lk 8:29
s came back into her, and she .... Lk 8:55
An evil **s** seizes my son, and .... Lk 9:39
The evil **s** keeps on hurting him .... Lk 9:39
to force the evil **s** out, ... Lk 9:40
to the evil **s** and healed the boy .... Lk 9:42
what kind of **s** you belong to. .... Lk 9:55
rejoiced in the Holy **S** and said, ... Lk 10:21
give the Holy **S** to those who ask .... Lk 11:13
When an evil **s** comes out of a .... Lk 11:24
Then the evil **s** goes out and .... Lk 11:26
against the Holy **S** will not be .... Lk 12:10
time the Holy **S** will teach you .... Lk 12:12
had an evil **s** in her that made .... Lk 13:11
are born from water and the **S**, ... Jn 3:5
spiritual life comes from the **S**. .... Jn 3:6
person who is born from the **S**." .... Jn 3:8
God gives him the **S** fully. .... Jn 3:34
the Father in **s** and truth, ... Jn 4:23
God is **s**, and those who worship .... Jn 4:24
must worship in **s** and truth." .... Jn 4:24
It is the **S** that gives life. .... Jn 6:63
The words I told you are **s**, ... Jn 6:63
was talking about the Holy **S**. .... Jn 7:39
The **S** had not yet been given, ... Jn 7:39
in Jesus would receive the **S**. .... Jn 7:39
the **S** of truth. The world cannot .... Jn 14:17
is the Holy **S** whom the Father .... Jn 14:26

he is the **S** of truth who comes .... Jn 15:26
But when the **S** of truth comes, ... Jn 16:13
The **S** of truth will bring glory .... Jn 16:14
I said that the **S** will take what .... Jn 16:15
and said, "Receive the Holy **S**. .... Jn 20:22
with the help of the Holy **S**, ... Ac 1:2
be baptized with the Holy **S**." .... Ac 1:5
when the Holy **S** comes to you, ... Ac 1:8
were all filled with the Holy **S**, ... Ac 2:4
the Holy **S** was giving them. .... Ac 2:4
will pour out my **S** on all kinds .... Ac 2:17
pour out my **S** also on my male .... Ac 2:18
given the Holy **S** to Jesus as he .... Ac 2:33
So Jesus has poured out that **S**, ... Ac 2:33
receive the gift of the Holy **S**. .... Ac 2:38
with the Holy **S**, said to them, ... Ac 4:8
the Holy **S**, through our father .... Ac 4:25
were all filled with the Holy **S**, ... Ac 4:31
united in their hearts and **s**. .... Ac 4:32
to the Holy **S** and to keep for .... Ac 5:3
agree to test the **S** of the Lord? .... Ac 5:9
The Holy **S**, whom God has given .... Ac 5:32
of the **S** and full of wisdom. .... Ac 6:3
faith and full of the Holy **S** .... Ac 6:5
But the **S** was helping him to .... Ac 6:10
the Holy **S** is trying to tell .... Ac 7:51
Stephen was full of the Holy **S**. .... Ac 7:55
Lord Jesus, receive my **s**." .... Ac 7:59
might receive the Holy **S**. .... Ac 8:15
but the Holy **S** had not yet come .... Ac 8:16
they received the Holy **S**. .... Ac 8:17
Simon saw that the **S** was given .... Ac 8:18
hands will receive the Holy **S**." .... Ac 8:19
S said to Philip, "Go to that .... Ac 8:29
the **S** of the Lord took Philip .... Ac 8:39
and be filled with the Holy **S**." .... Ac 9:17
being encouraged by the Holy **S**, ... Ac 9:31
the vision, the **S** said to him, ... Ac 10:19
gave him the Holy **S** and power. .... Ac 10:38
Holy **S** came down on all those .... Ac 10:44
of the Holy **S** had been given .... Ac 10:45
the Holy **S** just as we did!" .... Ac 10:47
The **S** told me to go with them .... Ac 11:12
the Holy **S** came on them just as .... Ac 11:15
be baptized with the Holy **S**.' .... Ac 11:16
with the help of the Holy **S**. .... Ac 11:28
time the Holy **S** said to them, ... Ac 13:2
out by the Holy **S**, went to the .... Ac 13:4
was filled with the Holy **S**. .... Ac 13:9
filled with joy and the Holy **S**. .... Ac 13:52
to us by giving them the Holy **S**, ... Ac 15:8
the Holy **S** that you should .... Ac 15:28
since the Holy **S** did not let .... Ac 16:6
the **S** of Jesus did not let them. .... Ac 16:7
She had a special **s** in her, ... Ac 16:16
so he turned and said to the **s**, ... Ac 16:18
Immediately, the **s** came out. .... Ac 16:18
the Holy **S** when you believed? .... Ac 19:2
never even heard of a Holy **S**." .... Ac 19:2
and the Holy **S** came upon them. .... Ac 19:6
one time an evil **s** said to them, ... Ac 19:15
had the evil **s** jumped on them. .... Ac 19:16
must obey the Holy **S** and go to .... Ac 20:22
city the Holy **S** tells me that .... Ac 20:23
people the Holy **S** has given to .... Ac 20:28
the Holy **S** they warned Paul .... Ac 21:4
said, "The Holy **S** says, 'This is .... Ac 21:11
angel or a **s** did speak to him. .... Ac 23:9
The Holy **S** spoke the truth to .... Ac 28:25
is done in the heart by the **S**, ... Rm 2:29
us his love through the Holy **S**, ... Rm 5:5
God in a new way with the **S**, ... Rm 7:6
law of the **S** that brings life .... Rm 8:2

but we live following the **S.** .... Rm 8:4
following the **S** are thinking .... Rm 8:5
things the **S** wants them to do. .... Rm 8:5
thinking is controlled by the **S,** .... Rm 8:6
ruled by the **S,** if that Spirit .... Rm 8:9
if that **S** of God really lives in .... Rm 8:9
not have the **S** of Christ does .... Rm 8:9
then the **S** gives you life, ... Rm 8:10
and if God's **S** is living in you, ... Rm 8:11
life through his **S** that lives in .... Rm 8:11
those who let God's **S** lead them. .... Rm 8:14
The **S** we received does not make .... Rm 8:15
that **S** we cry out, "Father." .... Rm 8:15
And the **S** himself joins with our .... Rm 8:16
We have the **S** as the first part .... Rm 8:23
S helps us with our weakness. .... Rm 8:26
But the **S** himself speaks to God .... Rm 8:26
what is in the mind of the **S,** .... Rm 8:27
because the **S** speaks to God for .... Rm 8:27
is ruled by the Holy **S,** .... Rm 9:1
peace, and joy in the Holy **S.** .... Rm 14:17
by the power of the Holy **S.** .... Rm 15:13
made holy by the Holy **S.** .... Rm 15:16
of the power of the Holy **S.** .... Rm 15:19
love that the Holy **S** gives us. .... Rm 15:30
of the power that the **S** gives. 1Co 2:4
us these things through the **S.** 1Co 2:10
The **S** searches out all things, ... 1Co 2:10
Only a person's **s** that lives 1Co 2:11
of God except the **S** of God. 1Co 2:11
not receive the **s** of the world, ... 1Co 2:12
we received the **S** that is from 1Co 2:12
with words taught us by the **S.** 1Co 2:13
not have the **S** does not accept 1Co 2:14
that come from the **S** of God. 1Co 2:14
be judged to be true by the **S.** 1Co 2:14
I would to people without the **S—** 1Co 3:1
and that God's **S** lives in you? 1Co 3:16
person, but I am with you in **s.** 1Co 5:3
with you in **s** with the power 1Co 5:4
and his **s** will be saved on the 1Co 5:5
Christ and in the **S** of our God. 1Co 6:11
the Lord is one **s** with the Lord. 1Co 6:17
for the Holy **S** who is in you. 1Co 6:19
received the Holy **S** from God. 1Co 6:19
wants to be holy in body and **s.** 1Co 7:34
I believe I also have God's **S.** 1Co 7:40
with the help of God's **S** says, ... 1Co 12:3
without the help of the Holy **S.** 1Co 12:3
they are all from the same **S.** 1Co 12:4
Something from the **S** can be seen .:........ 1Co 12:7
The **S** gives one person the 1Co 12:8
and the same **S** gives another 1Co 12:8
The same **S** gives faith to one 1Co 12:9
one **S** gives gifts of healing. 1Co 12:9
S gives to another person the 1Co 12:10
The **S** gives one person the 1Co 12:10
One **S,** the same Spirit, does all 1Co 12:11
the same **S,** does all these 1Co 12:11
and the **S** decides what to give 1Co 12:11
into one body through one **S.** 1Co 12:13
all made to share in the one **S.** 1Co 12:13
secret things through the **S.** 1Co 14:2
language, my **s** is praying, but 1Co 14:14
pray with my **s,** but I will also 1Co 14:15
sing with my **s,** but I will also 1Co 14:15
If you praise God with your **s,** 1Co 14:16
Adam became a **s** that gives life. 1Co 15:45
have refreshed my **s** and yours. 1Co 16:18
and he put his **S** in our hearts 2Co 1:22
ink but with the **S** of the living 2Co 3:3
written law, but it is of the **S.** 2Co 3:6
death, but the **S** gives life. 2Co 3:6

that brings the **S** has even more 2Co 3:8
The Lord is the **S,** and where the 2Co 3:17
and where the **S** of the Lord is, ... 2Co 3:17
from the Lord, who is the **S.** 2Co 3:18
but our **s** inside us is made new 2Co 4:16
has given us the **S** to be a 2Co 5:5
by the Holy **S,** by true love, ... 2Co 6:6
to accept a **s** or gospel that is 2Co 11:4
from the **S** and Good News you 2Co 11:4
same thing and with the same **s.** 2Co 12:18
of the Holy **S** be with you all. 2Co 13:14
How did you receive the Holy **S?** .... Gal 3:2
you receive the **S** by following .... Gal 3:2
you received the **S** because you .... Gal 3:2
your life in Christ by the **S.** .... Gal 3:3
God give you the **S** and work .... Gal 3:5
receive the **S** that God promised .... Gal 3:14
God sent the **S** of his Son into .... Gal 4:6
hearts, and the **S** cries out, ... Gal 4:6
and by the **S** we wait eagerly for .... Gal 5:5
Live by following the **S.** .... Gal 5:16
want what is against the **S,** .... Gal 5:17
and the **S** wants what is against .... Gal 5:17
But if the **S** is leading you, ... Gal 5:18
But the **S** produces the fruit of .... Gal 5:22
We get our new life from the **S,** .... Gal 5:25
so we should follow the **S.** .... Gal 5:25
if they plant to please the **S,** .... Gal 6:8
receive eternal life from the **S.** .... Gal 6:8
Jesus Christ be with your **s.** .... Gal 6:18
giving you the Holy **S** that he .... Eph 1:13
Holy **S** is the guarantee that .... Eph 1:14
to give you a **s** of wisdom and .... Eph 1:17
That same **s** is now working in .... Eph 2:2
to come to the Father in one **S.** .... Eph 2:18
where God lives through the **S.** .... Eph 2:22
now, through the **S,** God has .... Eph 3:5
strong inwardly through his **S.** .... Eph 3:16
with peace through the **S,** .... Eph 4:3
There is one body and one **S,** .... Eph 4:4
And do not make the Holy **S** sad. .... Eph 4:30
The **S** is God's proof that you .... Eph 4:30
gave you the **S** to show that God .... Eph 4:30
you, but be filled with the **S.** .... Eph 5:18
and take the sword of the **S,** .... Eph 6:17
Pray in the **S** at all times with .... Eph 6:18
for me and for the **S** of Jesus Christ .... Php 1:19
Do we share together in the **s?** .... Php 2:1
We worship God through his **S,** .... Php 3:3
love you have from the Holy **S.** .... Col 1:8
with the Holy **S,** and with sure 1Th 1:5
joy that comes from the Holy **S.** 1Th 1:6
the One who gives us his Holy **S.** 1Th 4:8
back the work of the Holy **S.** 1Th 5:19
whole self—**s,** soul, and body— 1Th 5:23
saved by the **S** that makes you 2Th 2:13
proved right in **s,** and seen by 1Ti 3:16
Now the Holy **S** clearly says that 1Ti 4:1
did not give us a **s** that makes 2Ti 1:7
us afraid but a **s** of power and 2Ti 1:7
of the Holy **S** who lives in us 2Ti 1:14
The Lord be with your **s.** 2Ti 4:22
new people through the Holy **S.** .... Tit 3:5
us that Holy **S** through Jesus .... Tit 3:6
Jesus Christ be with your **s.** .... Phm 1:25
people gifts through the Holy **S,** .... Heb 2:4
So it is as the Holy **S** says: .... Heb 3:7
the soul and the **s** are joined, ... Heb 4:12
gift, and shared in the Holy **S.** .... Heb 6:4
Holy **S** uses this to show that .... Heb 9:8
the eternal **S** as a perfect .... Heb 9:14
The Holy **S** also tells us about .... Heb 10:15
who insult the **S** of God's grace? .... Heb 10:29

that does not have a **s** is dead, ... Jam 2:26
The **S** that God made to live in .... Jam 4:5
The **S** of Christ was in the 1Pe 1:11
about what the **S** was showing 1Pe 1:11
help of the Holy **S** who was sent 1Pe 1:12
and quiet **s** that will never 1Pe 3:4
but he was made alive in the **s**. 1Pe 3:18
in the **s** he went and preached 1Pe 3:19
live in the **s** as God lives. 1Pe 4:6
the glorious **S**, the Spirit of 1Pe 4:14
Spirit, the **S** of God, is with 1Pe 4:14
led by the Holy **S** spoke words 2Pe 1:21
us because of the **S** God gave us. 1Jn 3:24
So do not believe every **s**, ... 1Jn 4:1
is how you can know God's **S**: 1Jn 4:2
Every **s** who confesses that Jesus 1Jn 4:2
And every **s** who refuses to say 1Jn 4:3
It is the **s** of the enemy of 1Jn 4:3
because God's **S**, who is in you, ... 1Jn 4:4
how we know the **S** that is true 1Jn 4:6
is true and the **s** that is false. 1Jn 4:6
in us, because he gave us his **S**. 1Jn 4:13
the **S** says that this is true, ... 1Jn 5:6
because the **S** is the truth. 1Jn 5:6
the **S**, the water, and the blood; 1Jn 5:8
world, who do not have the **S**. .... Jud 1:19
up, praying in the Holy **S**. .... Jud 1:20
the Lord's day I was in the **S**, ... Rev 1:10
listen to what the **S** says to the .... Rev 2:7
listen to what the **S** says to the .... Rev 2:11
listen to what the **S** says to the .... Rev 2:17
listen to what the **S** says to the .... Rev 2:29
listen to what the **S** says to the .... Rev 3:6
listen to what the **S** says to the .... Rev 3:13
listen to what the **S** says to the .... Rev 3:22
Immediately I was in the **S**, ... Rev 4:2
The **S** says, "Yes, they will .... Rev 14:13
me away by the **S** to the desert. .... Rev 17:3
and a prison for every evil **s**, ... Rev 18:2
Jesus is the **s** that gives all .... Rev 19:10
me away by the **S** to a very large .... Rev 21:10
The **S** and the bride say, "Come!" .... Rev 22:17

SPIRIT'S
if you use the **S** help to stop .... Rm 8:13
people, which is the **S** work. 1Pe 1:2

SPIRITS
God over the **s** of all people. .... Nu 16:22
the God of the **s** of all people. .... Nu 27:16
talk with the **s** of dead people. .... Dt 18:11
The **s** of the dead tremble, ... Job 26:5
those whose **s** have been crushed .... Ps 34:18
God breaks the **s** of great .... Ps 76:12
Do their **s** rise up and praise .... Ps 88:10
It wakes the **s** of the dead, ... Is 14:9
their idols and **s** of the dead, ... Is 19:3
because your **s** will be broken. .... Is 65:14
These are the four **s** of heaven. .... Zch 6:5
and unclean **s** from the land. .... Zch 13:2
drive out evil **s** and to heal .... Mt 10:1
seven other **s** even more evil .... Mt 12:45
even gives commands to evil **s**, ... Mk 1:27
When evil **s** saw Jesus, they fell .... Mk 3:11
Legion, because we are many **s**." .... Mk 5:9
The evil **s** left the man and went............... Mk 5:13
used to have the many evil **s**, ... Mk 5:15
gave them authority over evil **s**. .... Mk 6:7
and power he commands evil **s**, ... Lk 4:36
who were troubled by evil **s**. .... Lk 6:18
and evil **s**, and he gave sight .... Lk 7:21
healed of sicknesses and evil **s**: .... Lk 8:2
happy because the **s** obey you but .... Lk 10:20
seven other **s** more evil than it .... Lk 11:26

who were bothered by evil **s**, ... Ac 5:16
these people had evil **s** in them, ... Ac 8:7
Philip made the evil **s** leave. .... Ac 8:7
s made a loud noise when they .... Ac 8:7
healed and evil **s** left them. .... Ac 19:12
and making evil **s** go out of .... Ac 19:13
Jesus to force the evil **s** out. .... Ac 19:13
in angels or **s** or that people .... Ac 23:8
joins with our **s** to say we are .... Rm 8:16
nor ruling **s**, nothing now, ... Rm 8:38
between good and evil **s**..................... 1Co 12:10
The **s** of prophets are under the 1Co 14:32
from the ruling **s** of this world, ... Col 2:8
from the ruling **s** of the world, ... Col 2:20
They will follow **s** that lie and 1Ti 4:1
the angels are **s** who serve God .... Heb 1:14
Father of our **s** so we will have .... Heb 12:9
and to the **s** of good people who............ Heb 12:23
and preached to the **s** in prison 1Pe 3:19
test the **s** to see if they are 1Jn 4:1
from the seven **s** before his..................... Rev 1:4
has the seven **s** and the seven .... Rev 3:1
which are the seven **s** of God............ Rev 4:5
are the seven **s** of God that were .... Rev 5:6
saw three evil **s** that looked .... Rev 16:13
These evil **s** are the spirits of .... Rev 16:14
spirits are the **s** of demons,..................... Rev 16:14
Then the evil **s** gathered the .... Rev 16:16
God of the **s** of the prophets, ... Rev 22:6

SPIRITUAL
you say the **s** person is crazy .... Hos 9:7
who realize their **s** poverty,..................... Mt 5:3
own kind than **s** people are. .... Lk 16:8
s life comes from the Spirit. .... Jn 3:6
give you some **s** gift to make you .... Rm 1:11
which brings **s** death, or you can .... Rm 6:16
We know that the law is **s**, ... Rm 7:14
but I am not **s** since sin rules .... Rm 7:14
which is the **s** way for you to .... Rm 12:1
shared in the Jews' **s** blessings, ... 1Co 2:13
And so we explain **s** truths to 1Co 2:13
spiritual truths to **s** people...................... 1Co 2:13
s person is able to judge all 1Co 2:15
to you as I talk to **s** people...................... 1Co 3:1
are still not **s**, because you are 1Co 3:3
this shows that you are not **s**. 1Co 3:3
we planted **s** seed among you, ... 1Co 9:11
They all ate the same **s** food, ... 1Co 10:3
and all drank the same **s** drink. 1Co 10:4
drank from that **s** rock that..................... 1Co 10:4
you to understand about **s** gifts. 1Co 12:1
truly want to have the **s** gifts, ... 1Co 14:1
you want **s** gifts very much, ... 1Co 14:12
are prophets or **s** persons should 1Co 14:37
it is raised, it is a **s** body...................... 1Co 15:44
and there is also a **s** body. 1Co 15:44
s did not come first, but the 1Co 15:46
but the physical and then the **s**. 1Co 15:46
you who are **s** should go to that .... Gal 6:1
has given us every **s** blessing .... Eph 1:3
hymns, and **s** songs, singing .... Eph 5:19
against the **s** powers of evil in .... Eph 6:12
and understanding in **s** things .... Col 1:9
God stripped the **s** rulers and .... Col 2:15
and **s** songs with thankfulness in .... Col 3:16
the world. It is not **s**; it is .... Jam 3:15
be used to build a **s** temple— 1Pe 2:5
who offer **s** sacrifices to God 1Pe 2:5
Egypt, which has a **s** meaning. .... Rev 11:8

SPIRITUALLY
help you grow **s** as I have helped .... Rm 1:13
selves want, you will die **s**. .... Rm 8:13

SPIT

the past you were s dead because .... Eph 2:1
Though we were s dead because of .... Eph 2:5
of us who are s mature should .... Php 3:15
When you were s dead because of .... Col 2:13
grow to be s mature and have.................. Col 4:12
that God has made them s rich. .... Jam 1:9
shown them that they are s poor. .... Jam 1:10

SPIT

If her father had s in her face, ... Nu 12:14
of his sandals and s in his face .... Dt 25:9
the gate and let s run down his 1Sa 21:13
curse word; people s in my face............... Job 17:6
but they will s them out; .... Job 20:15
they make fun of me and s at me. .... Is 50:6
best things. Then he s us out. .... Je 51:34
will make him s out what he has .... Je 51:44
ears and then s and touched .... Mk 7:33
Then he s on the man's eyes and .... Mk 8:23
will laugh at him and s on him. .... Mk 10:34
there began to s at Jesus. .... Mk 14:65
They s on him and made fun of .... Mk 15:19
at him, insult him, s on him, ... Lk 18:32
he s on the ground and made some .... Jn 9:6
ready to s you out of my mouth............... Rev 3:16

SPITE

believe me in s of the miracles .... Nu 14:11
In s of all this Job did not .... Job 2:10
In s of all their hard work, ... Ec 5:15
people die in s of their .... Ec 7:15
a long time in s of their evil. .... Ec 7:15
to you, in s of all your magic .... Is 47:9
in s of your powerful tricks. .... Is 47:9

SPITS

the body fluid s on someone who .... Le 15:8

SPITTING

they do not mind s in my face. .... Job 30:10

SPLASH

You s around in your streams and .... Eze 32:2

SPLASHED

Some of her blood s on the wall............... 2Ki 9:33
Blood s on my clothes, and I .... Is 63:3

SPLENDID

You are more s than the hills .... Ps 76:4
What he does is glorious and s, ... Ps 111:3

SPLENDOR

the LORD and the s of our God............... Is 35:2
of the world and all their s..................... Mt 4:8

SPLINTERED

Egypt is like a s walking stick. 2Ki 18:21
Egypt is like a s walking stick. .... Is 36:6
you s and tore open their .... Eze 29:7

SPLIT

the underground springs s open, ... Ge 7:11
the sea will s and the people .... Ex 14:16
dry ground. The water was s, ... Ex 14:21
animal that has s hoofs .... Le 11:3
the cud or only have s hoofs, ... Le 11:4
cud but does not have a s hoof; .... Le 11:4
cud but does not have a s hoof; .... Le 11:5
cud but does not have a s hoof; .... Le 11:6
Now the pig has a s hoof that is .... Le 11:7
Some animals have s hoofs, ... Le 11:26
the ground under the men s open. .... Nu 16:31
that has a s hoof and chews .... Dt 14:6
but they do not have s hoofs, ... Dt 14:7
they have s hoofs, but they do .... Dt 14:8
to the ground and s open their 2Ki 8:12
them off so that they s open. 2Ch 25:12
You s open the sea by your power .... Ps 74:13

He s the rocks in the desert and .... Ps 78:15
God s the rock, and water flowed .... Ps 105:41
the earth will s open; .... Is 24:19
He s the rock, and water flowed............... Is 48:21
Selah You s the earth with .... Hab 3:9
Mount of Olives will s in two,.................. Zch 14:4
other and not be s into groups. 1Co 1:10
The great city s into three .... Rev 16:19

SPOIL

Don't let murder s your land. .... Nu 35:33
so do not s it with murder.'" .... Nu 35:34
If you s your servants when they .... Pr 29:21
little foolishness as s wisdom. .... Ec 10:1

SPOILED

there have s it by the evil .... Ezr 9:11
destroyed or be s or lose their 1Pe 1:4

SPOILS

Don't work for the food that s. .... Jn 6:27

SPOKE

the whole world s one language, ... Ge 11:1
the LORD s his word to Abram in .... Ge 15:1
Then the LORD s his word to .... Ge 15:4
a name to the LORD who s to her: .... Ge 16:13
But one night God s to Abimelech .... Ge 20:3
The angel of God s to me in that .... Ge 31:11
your father s to me and warned .... Ge 31:29
Dinah, and he s kindly to her. .... Ge 34:3
their city and s to the men of .... Ge 34:20
time he went back and s to them. .... Ge 42:24
of that land unkindly to us. .... Ge 42:30
house and s to him at the door .... Ge 43:19
During the night God s to Israel............... Ge 46:2
Joseph s to the king's officers.................. Ge 50:4
his brothers and s kind words to .... Ge 50:21
the LORD s to Moses and Aaron .... Ex 6:13
The LORD s to Moses in the land .... Ex 6:28
when they s to the king. .... Ex 7:7
The LORD s to Moses and Aaron in .... Ex 12:1
Then Moses s, and the voice of .... Ex 19:19
Then God s all these words: .... Ex 20:1
while the LORD s with Moses. .... Ex 33:9
The LORD s to Moses face to face .... Ex 33:11
called to Moses and s to him .... Le 1:1
Then Moses s to the people and .... Le 8:5
that time the LORD s to Moses. .... Le 16:1
Take the one who s against me .... Le 24:14
Then Moses s to the people of .... Le 24:23
The LORD s to Moses in the .... Nu 1:1
In this way the LORD s with him. .... Nu 7:89
LORD s to Moses in the Desert .... Nu 9:1
in the cloud and s to Moses. .... Nu 11:25
So the LORD suddenly s to Moses,........... Nu 12:4
So Moses s to the Israelites. .... Nu 17:6
the priest s to the people......................... Nu 26:3
Moses s with the leaders of the .... Nu 30:1
The LORD s to Moses and said, ... Nu 31:1
Jericho, the LORD s to Moses. .... Nu 33:50
LORD s to Moses on the plains .... Nu 35:1
LORD our God s to us at Mount .... Dt 1:6
The LORD s to you from the fire. .... Dt 4:12
Since the LORD s to you from the .... Dt 4:15
He s to you from heaven to teach .... Dt 4:36
The LORD s to you face to face .... Dt 5:4
The LORD s these commands to all .... Dt 5:22
who were priests s to all Israel .... Dt 27:9
Moses went and s these words to .... Dt 31:1
And Moses s this whole song for .... Dt 31:30
and they s all the words of this .... Dt 32:44
The LORD s to Moses again that .... Dt 32:48
the LORD s to Joshua son of Nun, ... Jos 1:1
Then he s to the Israelites: .... Jos 4:21

was here the LORD s to us today. .... Jos 24:27
uncles s to all the leaders .... Jdg 9:3
you the man who s to my wife?" .... Jdg 13:11
Samuel s to the whole group of 1Sa 7:8
But no one in the army s. 1Sa 14:39
the LORD s his word to Samuel:.............. 1Sa 15:10
Mizpah in Moab and s to the king 1Sa 22:3
day the LORD s of when he said 1Sa 24:4
night the LORD s his word to 2Sa 7:4
woman from Tekoa s to the king. 2Sa 14:4
people of Judah s even more 2Sa 19:43
Then the woman s very wisely to 2Sa 20:22
together and s to them. 2Sa 21:2
The LORD s strongly. The wind 2Sa 22:16
The LORD's Spirit s through me, ... 2Sa 23:2
The God of Israel s; the Rock of 2Sa 23:3
the LORD s his word to Gad, ... 2Sa 24:11
Adonijah s with Joab son of 1Ki 1:7
his life he s three thousand................... 1Ki 4:32
You s it with your own mouth and 1Ki 8:24
King Rehoboam s cruel words to 1Ki 12:13
But God s his word to Shemaiah, ... 1Ki 12:22
the LORD s his word to the old 1Ki 13:20
him the LORD s against the altar 1Ki 13:32
What the LORD s through him will 1Ki 13:32
Jehu son of Hanani s the word of 1Ki 16:1
The LORD s his word against 1Ki 16:7
The LORD also s against Baasha 1Ki 16:7
the LORD s his word to Elijah: 1Ki 17:2
the LORD s his word to Elijah, ... 1Ki 17:8
the LORD s his word to Elijah: 1Ki 18:1
Then the LORD s his word to him: 1Ki 19:9
this time the LORD s his word to 1Ki 21:17
LORD s his word to Elijah the 1Ki 21:28
Elisha s to the woman whose son 2Ki 8:1
the LORD s to him by Isaiah: 2Ki 20:4
Evil-Merodach s kindly to 2Ki 25:28
that night God s his word to 1Ch 17:3
When he s against Israel, ... 1Ch 20:7
But the LORD s his word to me, ' 1Ch 22:8
Solomon s to all the people of 2Ch 1:2
You s it with your own mouth and 2Ch 6:15
King Rehoboam s cruel words to 2Ch 10:13
But the LORD s his word to 2Ch 11:2
the LORD s his word to Shemaiah,......... 2Ch 12:7
town of Mareshah s against 2Ch 20:37
the prophet s, Amaziah said to 2Ch 25:16
They s against him, saying, "The 2Ch 32:17
s about the God of Jerusalem 2Ch 32:19
the LORD s to him and gave him a.......... 2Ch 32:24
The LORD s to Manasseh and his 2Ch 33:10
The prophet Jeremiah s messages 2Ch 36:12
these Levites s: Jeshua, Kadmiel .... Ne 9:5
Mount Sinai and s from heaven to .... Ne 9:13
of Egypt.' They s against you.................. Ne 9:18
prophets and s against you. .... Ne 9:26
So King Xerxes s with the wise .... Est 1:13
Once again Esther s to the king............. Est 8:3
his people and s up for the .... Est 10:3
who heard me s well of me, ... Job 29:11
speaking, they s no more. .... Job 29:22
I waited while you three s, ... Job 32:11
I s one time, but I will not .... Job 40:5
I even s two times, but I will .... Job 40:5
Then the LORD s to Job from the .... Job 40:6
' Surely I s of things I did not .... Job 42:3
You s strongly against the .... Ps 9:5
LORD, you s strongly. The wind .... Ps 18:15
He s, and it happened. .... Ps 33:9
it, my anger burned. So I s:................... Ps 39:3
Jacob, when you s strongly, ... Ps 76:6
Then they s against God, saying, ... Ps 78:19
you s to those who worship you. .... Ps 89:19

He s to them from the pillar of .... Ps 99:7
The LORD s and flies came, ... Ps 105:31
He s and grasshoppers came; .... Ps 105:34
so Moses s without stopping to .... Ps 106:33
He s, and a storm came up, which .... Ps 107:25
My lover s and said to me, ... Sng 2:10
When he s, he took my breath .... Sng 5:6
Then the LORD s to Ahaz again, ... Is 7:10
Again the LORD s to me, saying, ... Is 8:5
The LORD s to me with his great .... Is 8:11
Then the LORD s through Isaiah .... Is 20:2
the LORD s his word to Isaiah: .... Is 38:4
I s to you, but you wouldn't .... Is 65:12
I s to them, but they did not .... Is 66:4
The LORD s his word to Jeremiah .... Je 1:2
LORD also s to Jeremiah while .... Je 1:3
The LORD s his word to me, ... Je 1:4
The LORD s his word to me, ... Je 1:11
The LORD s his word to me again:......... Je 1:13
The LORD s his word to me, ... Je 2:1
that the LORD s to Jeremiah: .... Je 7:1
I s to you again and again, ... Je 7:13
that the LORD s to Jeremiah: .... Je 11:1
Then the LORD s his word to me a........... Je 13:3
Then the LORD s his word to me. .... Je 13:8
the LORD s to Jeremiah about .... Je 14:1
Then the LORD s his word to me: .... Je 16:1
the word the LORD s to Jeremiah: .... Je 18:1
Then the LORD s his word to me: .... Je 18:5
that the LORD s to Jeremiah. .... Je 21:1
Then the LORD s his word to me: .... Je 24:4
the prophet s to all the people .... Je 25:2
Then Jeremiah s these words to .... Je 26:12
The LORD s his word to Jeremiah .... Je 27:1
s to me in the Temple of the .... Je 28:1
Jeremiah s to the prophet .... Je 28:5
The LORD s his word to Jeremiah .... Je 28:12
the LORD s his word to Jeremiah: .... Je 29:30
that the LORD s to Jeremiah. .... Je 30:1
LORD s this message about the .... Je 30:4
the word the LORD s to Jeremiah .... Je 32:1
The LORD s this word to me: .... Je 32:6
Then the LORD s this word to .... Je 32:26
the LORD s his word to him a .... Je 33:1
The LORD s his word to Jeremiah,.......... Je 33:19
The LORD s his word to Jeremiah, ... Je 33:23
The LORD s his word to Jeremiah .... Je 34:1
The LORD s his word to Jeremiah. .... Je 34:8
the LORD s his word to Jeremiah: .... Je 34:12
the LORD s his word to Jeremiah, ... Je 35:1
the LORD s his word to Jeremiah: .... Je 35:12
I s to those people, but they .... Je 35:17
The LORD s this word to Jeremiah........... Je 36:1
from when I first s to you, ... Je 36:2
Jeremiah s the messages the LORD .... Je 36:4
the scroll as I s them to you. .... Je 36:6
Jeremiah s them all to me, ... Je 36:18
the LORD s his word to Jeremiah .... Je 36:27
As Jeremiah s, Baruch wrote on............. Je 36:32
The LORD s his word to Jeremiah .... Je 37:6
the LORD s his word to him: .... Je 39:15
The LORD s his word to Jeremiah .... Je 40:1
son of Kareah s to Gedaliah .... Je 40:15
days later the LORD s his word .... Je 42:7
Tahpanhes the LORD s his word to .... Je 43:8
from the LORD that you s to us............... Je 44:16
Jeremiah s to all the people—............... Je 44:20
The LORD s this word to Jeremiah........... Je 46:1
message the LORD s to Jeremiah .... Je 46:13
the LORD s his word to Jeremiah .... Je 47:1
When you s about Israel, you .... Je 48:27
the LORD s this word to Jeremiah .... Je 49:34
message the LORD s to Babylon............. Je 50:1

S

Evil-Merodach s kindly to .... Je 52:32
The LORD s his word to Ezekiel.............. Eze 1:3
While he s to me, the Spirit .... Eze 2:2
days the LORD s his word to me .... Eze 3:16
He s to me and said, "Go, shut .... Eze 3:24
Again the LORD s his word to me,........... Eze 6:1
Again the LORD s his word to me,........... Eze 7:1
The LORD s his word to me, ... Eze 11:14
Again the LORD s his word to me, ... Eze 12:1
the LORD s his word to me, ... Eze 12:8
The LORD s his word to me, ... Eze 12:17
The LORD s his word to me, ... Eze 12:21
The LORD s his word to me, ... Eze 12:26
The LORD s his word to me, ... Eze 13:1
you prophets s things that are .... Eze 13:8
Then the LORD s his word to me, ... Eze 14:2
The LORD s his word to me, ... Eze 14:12
The LORD s his word to me, ... Eze 15:1
The LORD s his word to me, ... Eze 16:1
The LORD s his word to me, ... Eze 17:1
Then the LORD s his word to me, ... Eze 17:11
The LORD s his word to me, ... Eze 18:1
The LORD s his word to me, ... Eze 20:2
Your ancestors s against me by .... Eze 20:27
Now the LORD s his word to me, ... Eze 20:45
Then the LORD s his word to me, ... Eze 21:1
The LORD s his word to me, ... Eze 21:8
The LORD s his word to me, ... Eze 21:18
The LORD s his word to me, ... Eze 22:1
The LORD s his word to me, ... Eze 22:17
The LORD s his word to me, ... Eze 22:23
The LORD s his word to me, ... Eze 23:1
The LORD s his word to me in the .... Eze 24:1
Then the LORD s his word to me, ... Eze 24:15
So I s to the people in the .... Eze 24:18
The LORD s his word to me. .... Eze 24:20
The LORD s his word to me, ... Eze 25:1
The LORD s his word to me, ... Eze 26:1
The LORD s his word to me, ... Eze 27:1
The LORD s his word to me, ... Eze 28:1
The LORD s his word to me, ... Eze 28:11
The LORD s his word to me, ... Eze 28:20
The LORD s his word to me, ... Eze 29:1
The LORD s his word to me, ... Eze 29:17
The LORD s his word to me, ... Eze 30:1
The LORD s his word to me, ... Eze 30:20
The LORD s his word to me, ... Eze 31:1
The LORD s his word to me, ... Eze 32:1
The LORD s his word to me, ... Eze 32:17
The LORD s his word to me, ... Eze 33:1
Then the LORD s his word to me, ... Eze 33:23
The LORD s his word to me, ... Eze 34:1
The LORD s his word to me, ... Eze 35:1
The LORD s his word to me again,........... Eze 36:16
The LORD s his word to me, ... Eze 37:15
The LORD s his word to me, ... Eze 38:1
one about whom I s in past days. .... Eze 38:17
I s through my servants, the .... Eze 38:17
But Daniel s to him with wisdom .... Da 2:14
and those who s every language.............. Da 3:7
He s very loudly and said, '................. Da 4:14
and those who s every language.............. Da 5:19
to those who s every language in .... Da 6:25
who s for you to our kings,..................... Da 9:6
When he s to me, I became.................... Da 10:19
of the two men s to him and .... Da 12:6
The LORD s his word to Hosea son .... Hos 1:1
at Bethel and s with him there. .... Hos 12:4
s to the prophets and gave them.............. Hos 12:10
The LORD s his word to Joel son .... Joe 1:1
The LORD s his word to Jonah son .... Jnh 1:1
Then the LORD s to the fish, ... Jnh 2:10
The LORD s his word to Jonah .... Jnh 3:1

The prophet Haggai s the word of .... Hag 1:1
Haggai the prophet s the word of .... Hag 1:3
the LORD s his word through .... Hag 2:1
LORD s his word to Haggai the .... Hag 2:10
the LORD s his word a second .... Hag 2:20
the LORD s his word to the.................... Zch 1:1
The LORD s his word to the .... Zch 1:7
Then they s to the LORD's angel, ... Zch 1:11
Then the LORD s his word to me .... Zch 4:8
The LORD s his word to me, ... Zch 6:9
LORD s his word to Zechariah. .... Zch 7:1
All-Powerful s his word to me, ... Zch 7:4
And the LORD s his word to .... Zch 7:8
LORD All-Powerful s his word, ... Zch 8:1
The prophets s these words when .... Zch 8:9
All-Powerful s his word to me................ Zch 8:18
true teachings and s no lies. .... Mal 2:6
the LORD s with each other .... Mal 3:16
angel of the Lord s to Joseph in .... Mt 2:19
me, 'Lord, Lord, we s for you,................. Mt 7:22
s and the demons left them, ... Mt 8:16
But Jesus quickly s to them, ... Mt 14:27
Daniel the prophet s about 'a .... Mt 24:15
quickly Jesus s to them and said .... Mk 6:50
was right when he s about you .... Mk 7:6
his tongue so that he s clearly. .... Mk 7:35
thanked God and s about Jesus to .... Lk 2:38
But John s against Herod, the............... Lk 3:19
All the people s well of Jesus .... Lk 4:22
at the words of grace he s. .... Lk 4:22
because he s with authority. .... Lk 4:32
been unable to speak, then s. .... Lk 11:14
Jesus s first to his followers, ... Lk 12:1
John s freely and did not refuse .... Jn 1:20
the one you s about so much?................. Jn 3:26
We know that God s to Moses, ... Jn 9:29
Jesus' glory and s about him. .... Jn 12:41
s to the girl at the door, ... Jn 18:16
and he s to them about the .... Ac 1:3
a loud voice he s to the crowd: .... Ac 2:14
ago when he s through his holy .... Ac 3:21
prophets who s for God after .... Ac 3:24
and they s God's word without .... Ac 4:31
the angel that s to him at Mount.............. Ac 7:38
where God s to our ancestors .... Ac 7:44
The Lord s to Ananias in a .... Ac 9:10
the Jewish people who s Greek,.............. Ac 9:29
the angel who s to Cornelius .... Ac 10:7
A holy angel s to Cornelius, ... Ac 10:22
the voice from heaven s again, ' .... Ac 11:9
Antioch, they s also to Greeks, ... Ac 11:20
stood up and s with the help of .... Ac 11:28
Paul and Barnabas s very boldly, ... Ac 13:46
They s so well that a great many .... Ac 14:1
long time and s bravely for the .... Ac 14:3
but Gallio s, saying, "I would .... Ac 18:14
excited when he s and taught the .... Ac 18:25
synagogue and s out boldly for .... Ac 19:8
bread, and Paul s to the group. .... Ac 20:7
He s to them a long time, until .... Ac 20:11
building, he s to the commander .... Ac 21:37
he s to them in the Hebrew.................... Ac 21:40
afraid when Paul s about living .... Ac 24:25
He s to them all day long. .... Ac 28:23
The Holy Spirit s the truth to .... Ac 28:25
"I believed, so I s." 2Co 4:13
I s to Peter in front of them.................... Gal 2:14
In the past I s against Christ 1Ti 1:13
In the past God s to our .... Heb 1:1
teaching God s through angels .... Heb 2:2
He s about that day through .... Heb 4:7
God s later about another .... Heb 4:8
s about the Israelites leaving .... Heb 11:22

he **s** before, his voice shook .... Heb 12:26
the prophets who **s** for the Lord. .... Jam 5:10
Holy Spirit **s** words from God. 2Pe 1:21
It **s** with a man's voice and 2Pe 2:16
the holy prophets **s** in the past, ... 2Pe 3:2
same voice that **s** to me before, ... Rev 4:1
the voices of seven thunders **s.** .... Rev 10:3
When the seven thunders **s,** .... Rev 10:4
a lamb, but it **s** like a dragon. .... Rev 13:11
seven bowls came and **s** to me. .... Rev 17:1

SPOKEN

I, the LORD, have **s,** and I will .... Nu 14:35
So the curse **s** by Jotham, the .... Jdg 9:57
when the LORD has **s** against me .... Ru 1:21
LORD had not **s** directly to him 1Sa 3:7
because he has **s** against the 1Sa 17:36
You have **s** against him. 1Sa 17:45
by the birds. The LORD has **s.**'" 1Ki 14:11
the LORD has not **s** through me. 1Ki 22:28
The LORD has **s** through his 2Ki 10:6
of Assyria have **s** against me. 2Ki 19:6
insulted me and **s** against me;.............. 2Ki 19:22
the LORD has not **s** through me. 2Ch 18:27
LORD's message **s** by Jeremiah 2Ch 36:22
LORD's message **s** by Jeremiah .... Ezr 1:1
when words are **s** gently to you? .... Job 15:11
left the commands he has **s;** .... Job 23:12
Job has not **s** his words against .... Job 32:14
Then the time he had **s** of came,............ Ps 105:19
and liars have **s** against me, ... Ps 109:2
about all the laws you have **s.** .... Ps 119:13
know that I have **s** correctly: .... Ps 141:6
S words can be like deep water, ... Pr 18:4
The right word **s** at the right .... Pr 25:11
A wise saying **s** by a fool is as .... Pr 26:7
wise saying **s** by a fool is like .... Pr 26:9
LORD, the God of Israel, has **s.** .... Is 21:17
from the earth. The LORD has **s.** .... Is 25:8
of Assyria have **s** against me. .... Is 37:6
insulted me and **s** against me;.............. Is 37:23
I myself have **s** to you, saved .... Is 43:12
I have **s;** I have called him. I .... Is 48:15
the beginning I have **s** openly. .... Is 48:16
Truth is not **s** in the streets; .... Is 59:14
because I have **s** and will not .... Je 4:28
because the LORD has **s** to you. .... Je 13:15
The LORD has **s** his word to me .... Je 25:3
I have **s** messages from the LORD .... Je 25:3
They have also **s** lies and said............... Je 29:23
all the words I have **s** to you. .... Je 30:2
the words I have **s** to you about .... Je 36:2
the words Jeremiah had **s** to him. .... Je 36:27
the LORD had **s** through Jeremiah .... Je 37:2
know that I, the LORD, have **s.** .... Eze 5:13
anger. I, the LORD, have **s.** .... Eze 5:15
I, the LORD, have **s.**" .... Eze 5:17
Jerusalem have **s** about your own .... Eze 11:15
are lies, because I have not **s.** .... Eze 13:7
know that I, the LORD, have **s.** .... Eze 17:21
I have **s,** and I will do it.'" .... Eze 17:24
I, the LORD, have **s.**" .... Eze 21:17
because I, the LORD, have **s.'** .... Eze 21:32
LORD, have **s,** and I will act.'" .... Eze 22:14
says' when the LORD has not **s.** .... Eze 22:28
I have **s,** says the Lord GOD. .... Eze 23:34
I, the LORD, have **s.** .... Eze 24:14
city of Tyre has **s** against .... Eze 26:2
I have **s,** says the Lord GOD. .... Eze 26:5
the LORD, have **s,** says the Lord............. Eze 26:14
I have **s,** says the Lord GOD.'" .... Eze 28:10
foreigners. I, the LORD, have **s.** .... Eze 30:12
among them. I, the LORD, have **s.** .... Eze 34:24

the LORD, have **s,** and I will do .... Eze 36:36
the LORD, have **s** and done it, ... Eze 37:14
because I have **s,** says the Lord .... Eze 39:5
but they have **s** lies against me. .... Hos 7:13
that the LORD has **s** against you, ... Am 3:1
The Lord GOD has **s.** Who will not .... Am 3:8
the words I have **s** will never be .... Lk 21:33
other person who has ever **s!**" .... Jn 7:46
said, "An angel has **s** to him." .... Jn 12:29
of the words I have **s** to you. .... Jn 15:3
If I had not come and **s** to them,............. Jn 15:22
I have **s** openly to everyone. .... Jn 18:20
and after they had **s** the message .... Ac 8:25
road and the Lord had **s** to Saul. .... Ac 9:27
the gift to interpret what is **s.** 1Co 14:13
We have **s** freely to you in 2Co 6:11
days God has **s** to us through his .... Heb 1:2
Their judgment **s** against them 2Pe 2:3

SPOKES

axles, rims, **s,** and hubs—were 1Ki 7:33

SPOKESMAN

of Meshezabel was the king's **s.** .... Ne 11:24

SPONGE

ran and got a **s** and filled it .... Mt 27:48
Someone there ran and got a **s,** .... Mk 15:36
the soldiers soaked a **s** in it, ... Jn 19:29
the **s** on a branch of a hyssop .... Jn 19:29

SPOT

and the slave dies on the **s,** .... Ex 21:20
or a rash or a bright **s.** .... Le 13:2
there is a white **s** on a person's .... Le 13:4
but the **s** does not seem deeper .... Le 13:4
hair from the **s** has not turned .... Le 13:4
swelling or a bright red **s,** .... Le 13:19
If the **s** seems deeper than the .... Le 13:20
The **s** is a harmful skin disease .... Le 13:20
looks at the **s** and there are no .... Le 13:21
in it and the **s** is not deeper .... Le 13:21
If the **s** spreads on the skin, ... Le 13:22
if the bright **s** does not spread .... Le 13:23
If the white **s** seems deeper than .... Le 13:25
hair at that **s** has become white .... Le 13:25
looks at the **s** and there is no .... Le 13:26
no white hair in the bright **s,** .... Le 13:26
and the **s** is no deeper than the .... Le 13:26
If the **s** has spread on the skin, ... Le 13:27
if the bright **s** has not spread .... Le 13:28
because the **s** is only a scar .... Le 13:28
is no healthy **s** from the bottom .... Is 1:6

SPOTLESS

pure, and **s,** but the wicked.................... Da 12:10

SPOTS

goats that had streaks or **s,**................... Ge 30:35
a woman has white **s** on the skin, ... Le 13:38
If the **s** on the skin are dull.................. Le 13:39
rashes, or bright **s** on the skin; .... Le 14:56
Can a leopard change his **s?** .... Je 13:23
like dirty **s** and stains among 2Pe 2:13
are like dirty **s** in your special .... Jud 1:12

SPOTTED

take every speckled or **s** sheep .... Ge 30:32
and every **s** or speckled goat. .... Ge 30:32
speckled or **s** or any lamb that .... Ge 30:33
the speckled and **s** female goats .... Ge 30:35
were streaked, speckled, or **s.**................ Ge 30:39
were streaked, speckled, or **s.**................ Ge 31:10
or **s** male goats are mating...................... Ge 31:12
s horses pulled the fourth .... Zch 6:3
and the **s** horses will go to the .... Zch 6:6

S

SPRANG

seven more heads of grain s up, ... Ge 41:6
heads of grain s up after them, ... Ge 41:23
sword but s to life again......................... Rev 13:14

SPREAD

Moses s the cloth over the Holy .... Ex 40:19
and it has not s on the skin, ... Le 13:5
s out a net beside the road;..................... Ps 140:5
is useless to s out a net right .... Pr 1:17
use their words to s knowledge, ... Pr 15:7
this army will s its wings like .... Is 8:8
He s the letter out before the .... Is 37:14
s out the earth and everything .... Is 42:5
men left and s the news about .... Mt 9:31
Many people s their coats on the .... Mt 21:8
Many people s their coats on the .... Mk 11:8
word of God was continuing to s. .... Ac 6:7
continued to s and reach people. .... Ac 12:24
God uses us to s his knowledge 2Co 2:14
teaching will s like a sickness................. 2Ti 2:17
the Passover and s the blood on .... Heb 11:28
woman Jezebel s false teachings. .... Rev 2:20

SPREADING

thinks the sore has stopped s,................ Le 13:37
green or red, it is a s mildew. .... Le 13:49
because the mildew is s. .... Le 13:52
or knitted), the mildew is s. .... Le 13:57
LORD's people are s a bad report 1Sa 2:24
We are s out along the wall so .... Ne 4:19
of the moon, s his clouds over .... Job 26:9
myself and s out the earth all .... Is 44:24
the sky and s its wings over .... Je 48:40
down and s its wings over .... Je 49:22
s them among the countries. .... Eze 29:12
s them among the countries. .... Eze 30:23
s them among the countries. .... Eze 30:26
They will be like s branches, ... Hos 14:6
to keep it from s among the .... Ac 4:17
of the Lord was s through the................. Ac 13:49
of the Lord kept s and growing. .... Ac 19:20

SPREADS

man starts a fire that s through .... Ex 22:6
But if the rash s again after .... Le 13:7
the skin disease s all over a .... Le 13:12
If the spot s on the skin. .... Le 13:32
But if the sore s on the skin .... Le 13:35
like a skin disease that s, ... Le 13:43
has a skin disease that s, ... Le 13:45
It s its wings to catch them and .... Dt 32:11
how God s out the clouds .... Job 36:29
flies and s its wings toward .... Job 39:26
He s the snow like wool and .... Ps 147:16
of my perfume s out to the king .... Sng 1:12
of cloth and s them out like .... Is 40:22
tongue s its evil through the .... Jam 3:6

SPRING

found Hagar beside a s of water.............. Ge 16:7
the s, when the kings normally 2Sa 11:1
drank in my words like s rain. .... Job 29:23
of Baca, they make it like a s................. Ps 84:6
a hard rock into a s of water. .... Ps 114:8
his kindness is like a s shower. .... Pr 16:15
like a muddy s or a dirty well................. Pr 25:26
be like a broken pitcher at a s, ... Ec 12:6
like a walled-in s, a closed-up................. Sng 4:12
like a s that never runs dry. .... Is 58:11
from me, the s of living water. .... Je 2:13
bad water flow from the same s? .... Jam 3:11
receive the autumn and s rains. .... Jam 5:7
water from the s of the water .... Rev 21:6

SPRINGS

there were twelve s of water and .... Nu 33:9
also give me s of water." .... Jos 15:19
and the dry ground will have s. .... Is 35:7
will dry up his s and wells of .... Hos 13:15
the rivers and the s of water, ... Rev 16:4

SPRINGTIME

would rob the land in the s. 2Ki 13:20
for rain during the s rains. .... Zch 10:1

SPRINKLE

its blood and s it on all four .... Ex 29:16
Then s the rest of the blood .... Ex 29:20
S this on Aaron and his clothes .... Ex 29:21
its blood and s it on all sides .... Le 1:5
must s its blood on all sides of .... Le 1:11
must s the blood on all sides of .... Le 3:2
priests must s its blood on all .... Le 3:8
priests must s its blood on all .... Le 3:13
the blood and s it seven times................. Le 4:6
he must s it seven times before .... Le 4:17
He must s the blood from the sin .... Le 5:9
the priest must s its blood on .... Le 7:2
priest will s the blood seven .... Le 14:7
finger he will s some of the oil .... Le 14:16
he will s some of the oil from .... Le 14:27
The priest will s the blood on .... Le 14:51
from the bull and s it with his................. Le 16:14
finger he will s the blood seven .... Le 16:14
he will s some of the blood on .... Le 16:19
the priest will s the blood from .... Le 17:6
S the cleansing water on them, ... Nu 8:7
S their blood on the altar and................. Nu 18:17
his finger and s it seven times .... Nu 19:4
then he must s it over the tent .... Nu 19:18
He must also s the people who .... Nu 19:18
who is clean must s this water .... Nu 19:19
Those who s the cleansing water .... Nu 19:21
S on the altar all the blood of................. 2Ki 16:15
I will s clean water on you,..................... Eze 36:25
offerings and to s blood on it.................. Eze 43:18
hyssop plant to s it on the book .... Heb 9:19

SPRINKLED

and he s the other half of the .... Ex 24:6
the bowls and s it on the people .... Ex 24:8
the blood is s on any clothes, ... Le 6:27
He s some oil on the altar seven............. Le 8:11
killed it and s the blood on all .... Le 8:19
Then he s blood on all sides of .... Le 8:24
and he s them on Aaron and .... Le 8:30
and he s it on all sides of the .... Le 9:12
and he s it on all sides of the .... Le 9:18
water is not s on them, ... Nu 19:13
they were not s with the .... Nu 19:20
He also s the blood of his 2Ki 16:13
the bulls and s their blood 2Ch 29:22
the sheep and s their blood..................... 2Ch 29:22
the lambs and s their blood 2Ch 29:22
priests, who s it on the altar. 2Ch 30:16
Then he s the powder on the 2Ch 34:4
priests, who s it on the altar. 2Ch 35:11
of a cow are s on the people who .... Heb 9:13
Moses s the blood on the Holy .... Heb 9:21
have come to the s blood that................. Heb 12:24

SPRINKLES

to the priest who s the blood .... Le 7:14

SPRINKLING

the bowls for s blood, the meat .... Ex 27:3
bowls for s blood, meat forks .... Ex 38:3
s the altar and all its tools .... Le 8:11
s it on the lid and in front of .... Le 16:15
a bowl used for s blood at the................. Zch 9:15

SPROUT

the grass s from the ground. 2Sa 23:4
like a stump that will s again." .... Is 6:13
cause the plants to s and grow, ... Is 55:10
a good branch s from David's .... Je 33:15

SPROUTED

It s and became a low vine that .... Eze 17:6
the wheat s and the heads of .... Mt 13:26

SPY

men before us to s out the land. .... Dt 1:22
here tonight to s out the land." .... Jos 2:2
have come to s out our whole .... Jos 2:3
he had sent to s out Jericho. .... Jos 6:25
"Go to Ai and s out the area." .... Jos 7:2
So the men went to s on Ai. .... Jos 7:2
and Eshtaol to s out and explore .... Jdg 18:2
the city and s it out and 2Sa 10:3
and capture it and s it out." 1Ch 19:3

SPYING

accused us of s on his country, ... Ge 42:30

SQUARE

night in the city's public s." .... Ge 19:2
should be s—seven and one-half .... Ex 27:1
came to the public s of the city .... Jdg 19:15
gate and sit in the public s. .... Job 29:7
The city was built in a s, ... Rev 21:16

SQUARES

raises her voice in the city s. .... Pr 1:20

STACHYS

greetings to my dear friend S. .... Rm 16:9

STACK

fire burning a s of wood or like .... Zch 12:6

STACKED

grain or grain that has been s, ... Ex 22:6

STAFF

your shepherd's s comfort me. .... Ps 23:4

STAIN

still see the s of your guilt," .... Je 2:22

STAINED

every uniform s with blood has .... Is 9:5
clothes, and I s all my clothing .... Is 63:3

STAINS

dirty spots and s among you. 2Pe 2:13

STAIRS

s went up to the second-floor 1Ki 6:8
s went on to the third-floor 1Ki 6:8
and put it on the s for Jehu. 2Ki 9:13
Levites were standing on the s: .... Ne 9:4

STAIRWAY

back up the s of Ahaz that it 2Ki 20:11
a shadow go down the s of Ahaz, ... Is 38:8
and its s had eight steps. .... Eze 40:31
and its s had eight steps. .... Eze 40:34
and its s had eight steps. .... Eze 40:37
s went up from the lowest story .... Eze 41:7
covered by a roof over the s. .... Eze 41:26

STAKES

hang them on s in the presence 2Sa 21:6
and hung them on s on a hill 2Sa 21:9
seven sons who were hanged on s. 2Sa 21:13
ropes longer and its s stronger, ... Is 54:2

STALK

heads of grain growing on one s. .... Ge 41:5
heads of grain growing on one s. .... Ge 41:22
the branch and s in one day. .... Is 9:14
made out of a weak s of grass. .... Eze 29:6
Like a s with no head of grain, ... Hos 8:7

STALKS

among the tall s of grass at the .... Ex 2:3
for dry s to use for straw. .... Ex 5:12
there under s of flax that she .... Jos 2:6
of a roaring fire burning dry s. .... Joe 2:5
of Esau will be like dry s. .... Ob 1:18

STALLIONS

like a mare among the king's s. .... Sng 1:9

STALLS

four thousand s for his chariot 1Ki 4:26
had four thousand s for horses 2Ch 9:25
and oil and s for all the cattle 2Ch 32:28
bulls from your s or goats from .... Ps 50:9

STAMP

Clap your hands, s your feet, ... Eze 6:11

STAMPED

your hands and s your feet; .... Eze 25:6

STAND

could not s before Moses, ... Ex 9:11
S still and you will see the .... Ex 14:13
Tomorrow I will s on the top of .... Ex 17:9
enough to s up against your .... Le 26:37
S up, Balak, and listen. .... Nu 23:18
If something cannot s the fire, ... Nu 31:23
your tribes to s and serve the .... Dt 18:5
arguing must s in the presence .... Dt 19:17
tribes must s on Mount Gerizim .... Dt 27:12
River, and s in the water." .... Jos 3:8
Sun, s still over Gibeon. .... Jos 10:12
Today I s and dare the army of 1Sa 17:10
of you must s around the king 2Ki 11:8
Just s strong in your places, ... 2Ch 20:17
S up and praise the LORD your .... Ne 9:5
end he will s upon the earth. .... Job 19:25
fun of you cannot s before you. .... Ps 5:5
s up against my enemies' anger. .... Ps 7:6
he helps me s on the steep .... Ps 18:33
I s in a safe place. LORD, I .... Ps 26:12
one can s against you when you .... Ps 76:7
you who s in the LORD's Temple .... Ps 135:2
are seven things he cannot s: .... Pr 6:16
of Jesse will s as a banner for .... Is 11:10
will see you and s to honor you; .... Is 49:7
s up on your feet so I may speak .... Eze 2:1
walls and to s before me where .... Eze 22:30
he could not s up because his .... Da 5:6
No animal could s before him, ... Da 8:4
protects your people, will s up. .... Da 12:1
No one can s up against it! .... Joe 2:11
These horns s for the nations .... Zch 1:21
that day he will s on the Mount .... Zch 14:4
from Nineveh will s up with you .... Mt 12:41
of the South will s up with you .... Mt 12:42
forced her to s before the .... Jn 8:3
they saw her s and leave quickly .... Jn 11:31
and able to s here before you .... Ac 4:10
Go s in the Temple and tell the .... Ac 5:20
am very blessed to s before you .... Ac 26:2
We will all s before God to be .... Rm 14:10
brothers and sisters, s strong. 1Co 15:58
made us free. So s strong. Do .... Gal 5:1
you will be able to s strong. .... Eph 6:13
So s strong, with the belt of .... Eph 6:14
of peace to help you s strong. .... Eph 6:15
s strong in the Lord as I have .... Php 4:1
full if you s strong in the Lord 1Th 3:8
the poor person, "S over there," .... Jam 2:3
S strong in that grace. 1Pe 5:12
I s at the door and knock. .... Rev 3:20

S

STANDARD

line and goodness as the **s**. .... Is 28:17
short of God's glorious **s,** .... Rm 3:23

STANDARDS

You judge by human **s**. .... Jn 8:15

STANDING

up and saw three men **s** near him. .... Ge 18:2
we are **s** at your gates. .... Ps 122:2
s in front of the LORD's angel. .... Zch 3:1
and brothers are **s** outside, ... Mt 12:47
some people **s** here will see the .... Mt 16:28
some people **s** here will see the .... Mk 9:1
God and Jesus **s** at God's right .... Ac 7:55
by **s** strong in your faith........................ 1Pe 5:9
great and small, **s** before the .... Rev 20:12

STANDS

foot platform **s** near Haman's.................. Est 7:9
Your bride **s** at your right side .... Ps 45:9
made the earth, and it still **s**. .... Ps 119:90
it in its place, and there it **s;** .... Is 46:7
the bridegroom **s** by and listens .... Jn 3:29
put on the foundation still **s,** 1Co 3:14
This beast **s** before the first .... Rev 13:12

STAR

A **s** will come from Jacob; .... Nu 24:17
morning **s,** you have fallen .... Is 14:12
who made the **s** groups Pleiades............... Am 5:8
and the **s** gods you have made. .... Am 5:26
saw his **s** in the east and have .... Mt 2:2
exact time they first saw the **s**. .... Mt 2:7
The **s** that they had seen in the .... Mt 2:9
When the wise men saw the **s,** .... Mt 2:10
idols of the **s** god Rephan that .... Ac 7:43
And each **s** is different in its 1Co 15:41
and the morning **s** rises in your 2Pe 1:19
also give him the morning **s**. .... Rev 2:28
and a large **s**, burning like .... Rev 8:10
The name of the **s** is Wormwood. .... Rev 8:11
and I saw a **s** fall from the sky .... Rev 9:1
The **s** was given the key to the .... Rev 9:1
and I am the bright morning **s**." .... Rev 22:16

STARE

people look and **s** at me........................ Ps 22:17
Don't **s** at the wine when it is .... Pr 23:31
Those who see you **s** at you. .... Is 14:16
I will make people **s** at you. .... Nah 3:6

STARED

Hazael **s** at Elisha until he felt 2Ki 8:11
Cornelius **s** at the angel. .... Ac 10:4

STARES

my enemy **s** at me with his angry .... Job 16:9

STARS

the night. He also made the **s**. .... Ge 1:16
are so many **s** you cannot count.............. Ge 15:5
be as many as the **s** in the sky .... Ge 22:17
and eleven **s** bowing down to me." .... Ge 37:9
sun, moon, and **s,** and everything .... Dt 4:19
The **s** fought from heaven; .... Jdg 5:20
the morning **s** sang together .... Job 38:7
see the moon and **s,** which you .... Ps 8:3
the moon and **s** to rule the night.............. Ps 136:9
He counts the **s** and names each .... Ps 147:4
Praise him, all you shining **s**. .... Ps 148:3
put my throne above God's **s**. .... Is 14:13
will shine like **s** forever and .... Da 12:3
The **s** will fall from the sky. .... Mt 24:29
beauty, and the **s** have another. 1Co 15:41
They are like **s** that wander in .... Jud 1:13
And the **s** in the sky fell to the .... Rev 6:13
a third of the **s** were struck. .... Rev 8:12

START

evil plans, who always **s** fights. .... Ps 140:2
The words of fools **s** quarrels.................. Pr 18:6

STARTLE

Terrible things **s** them from .... Job 18:11

STARTLED

Boaz was **s** and rolled over. .... Ru 3:8
Zechariah was **s** and frightened. .... Lk 1:12
Mary was very **s** by what the .... Lk 1:29

STARTS

Suppose a man **s** a fire that .... Ex 22:6
someone who **s** arguments among .... Pr 6:19
wake up when a bird **s** singing, ... Ec 12:4
He also **s** a fire to bake his .... Is 44:15
to a son before the pain **s**. .... Is 66:7
up both ends and **s** to burn the .... Eze 15:4
pool when the water **s** moving. .... Jn 5:7
and it **s** a fire that influences .... Jam 3:6

STARVATION

like an oven; we burn with **s**. .... La 5:10
people by war, by **s,** by disease, ... Rev 6:8

STARVE

all that you have will not **s**.' .... Ge 45:11
this desert to **s** us to death." .... Ex 16:3
will make you **s** so that you will .... Dt 28:53
you and make you **s** in all your .... Dt 28:55
will make you **s** in all your .... Dt 28:57
because you will **s** to death. .... Ec 4:5
in war, or they will **s** to death. .... Je 16:4
their children **s,** and let their .... Je 18:21
the city, he will **s** to death.".................. Je 38:9
They **s** in pain and die, because .... La 4:9

STARVED

They will be **s** and sick, ... Dt 32:24

STARVING

They know we are **s**. 2Ki 7:12
foods are now **s** in the streets. .... La 4:5

STATE

writing of each **s** and in the .... Est 1:22
in every **s** of his kingdom to .... Est 2:3
soldiers in each **s** and to the .... Est 3:12
writing of each **s** and in the .... Est 3:12
a law in every **s** so all the .... Est 3:14
of the soldiers in each **s,** .... Est 8:9
writing of each **s** and in the .... Est 8:9
the army of any **s** or people who .... Est 8:11
be sent out as a law in every **s**. .... Est 8:13
order went to every **s** and city, ... Est 8:17
In every **s** and city to which the .... Est 8:17
family, in every **s,** and in every .... Est 9:28
to accept their **s** in life and .... Ec 5:19

STATES

-seven **s** from India to Cush. .... Est 1:1
to all the **s** of the kingdom .... Est 1:22
in all the **s** of your kingdom. .... Est 3:8
of the royal **s** know that no man.............. Est 4:11
twenty-seven **s** that reached .... Est 8:9
All the important men of the **s,** .... Est 9:3
twenty-seven **s** of the kingdom .... Est 9:30

STEADY

kept his hands **s** until the sun.................. Ex 17:12
reached out to **s** the Ark of God. 2Sa 6:6
out his hand to **s** the Ark. 1Ch 13:9
me on a rock and made my feet **s**. .... Ps 40:2
My heart is **s,** God; my heart is .... Ps 57:7
God; my heart is **s**. I will sing .... Ps 57:7
I am the one who holds it **s**. .... Ps 75:3
I will **s** him with my hand and .... Ps 89:21
God, my heart is **s**. I will sing .... Ps 108:1

their hearts are s because they .... Ps 112:7
strong and the weak knees s. .... Is 35:3

STEAL

but why did you s my idols?" .... Ge 31:30
You must not s. .... Ex 20:15
You must not s. .... Dt 5:19
thieves can break in and s them. .... Mt 6:19
must not s; you must not tell .... Mt 19:18
A thief comes to s and kill and .... Jn 10:10
They should not s from them but .... Tit 2:10

STEALING

against Keilah and s grain from 1Sa 23:1
trust in force. S is of no use. .... Ps 62:10
your enemies are s everything .... Is 1:7
I hate s and everything that is .... Is 61:8
when someone catches him s................. Je 2:26
They keep s words from each .... Je 23:30
fist at you for s money and for .... Eze 22:13
s and adultery are everywhere. .... Hos 4:2
sexual sins, s, lying, and...................... Mt 15:19
sins, s, murder, adultery,...................... Mk 7:21
Those who are s must stop .... Eph 4:28
must stop s and start working .... Eph 4:28
from their sexual sins or s. .... Rev 9:21

STEALS

If a man s a bull or a sheep and .... Ex 22:1
who passes by s from us. .... Ps 80:12
who passes by s from him. .... Ps 89:41
a thief when he s because he is .... Pr 6:30
He s and refuses to return what .... Eze 18:12
for the one that s many things. .... Hab 2:6

STEEP

There was a s slope on each side 1Sa 14:4
me stand on the s mountains.................. 2Sa 22:34
me stand on the s mountains................... Ps 18:33
I can walk on the s mountains. .... Hab 3:19

STEP

Everywhere you s will be yours............... Dt 11:24
When they s into the water, ... Jos 3:13
refuse to s on the doorsill 1Sa 5:5
I am only a s away from death!" 1Sa 20:3
said, "S over here and wait. 2Sa 18:30
one lion at each end of each s. 1Ki 10:20
one lion at each end of each s. 2Ch 9:19
side and chase them at every s. .... Job 18:11
me, they would s aside, and the .... Job 29:8
ways and counts every s I take. .... Job 31:4
explain to God every s I took,................. Job 31:37
he sees every s they take. .... Job 34:21
a foot might s on them and crush .... Job 39:15
you will s on strong lions and................. Ps 91:13
You will s on your olives, ... Mic 6:15

STEPHANAS

I also baptized the family of S, ... 1Co 1:16
the family of S were the first 1Co 16:15
I am happy that S, Fortunatus, ... 1Co 16:17

STEPHEN

S (a man with great faith and .... Ac 6:5
S was richly blessed by God who .... Ac 6:8
They all came and argued with S. .... Ac 6:9
We heard S speak against Moses .... Ac 6:11
and grabbed S and brought him.............. Ac 6:12
people to tell lies about S, ... Ac 6:13
were watching S closely and saw .... Ac 6:15
The high priest said to S, ... Ac 7:1
S answered, "Brothers and .... Ac 7:2
S continued speaking:........................... Ac 7:51
were grinding their teeth at S. .... Ac 7:54
But S was full of the Holy .... Ac 7:55
their ears and all ran at S. .... Ac 7:57

lies against S left their coats .... Ac 7:58
throwing stones, S prayed, "Lord .... Ac 7:59
After S said this, he died. .... Ac 7:60
that the killing of S was good. .... Ac 8:1
people buried S and cried loudly .... Ac 8:2
persecuted after S was killed.................. Ac 11:19
also know I was there when S, ... Ac 22:20

STEPPED

offering, he s down from the .... Le 9:22
the river and s into the water,................ Jos 3:15
So Ahimaaz s aside and stood 2Sa 18:30
Joab s forward, his sword fell................ 2Sa 20:8
the followers s out of the boat .... Jn 21:9

STEPPING

that they were s on each other. .... Lk 12:1

STEPS

must not go up to my altar on s,............. Ex 20:26
of the LORD had walked six s, ... 2Sa 6:13
The throne had six s on it, ... 1Ki 10:19
Twelve lions stood on the six s, ... 1Ki 10:20
go forward ten s or back ten 2Ki 20:9
ten steps or back ten s?"...................... 2Ki 20:9
the shadow to go forward ten s. 2Ki 20:10
Instead, let it go back ten s." 2Ki 20:10
the shadow ten s back up the 2Ki 20:11
wood to build s for the Temple 2Ch 9:11
throne had six s on it and a 2Ch 9:18
Twelve lions stood on the six s, ... 2Ch 9:19
the way to the s that went down.............. Ne 3:15
straight up the s to the highest .... Ne 12:37
will count my s, but you will .... Job 14:16
Their strong s will grow weak; .... Job 18:7
have closely followed his s;................... Job 23:11
When people's s follow the LORD, ... Ps 37:23
They watch my s, hoping to kill .... Ps 56:6
Guide my s as you promised; .... Ps 119:133
her s are headed straight to the .... Pr 5:5
quick, short s, making noise .... Is 3:16
I will make it go back ten s.'"................. Is 38:8
back up the ten s it had gone .... Is 38:8
went up its s and measured the .... Eze 40:6
Seven s went up to the gateway, ... Eze 40:22
Seven s went up to this gateway. .... Eze 40:26
and its stairway had eight s. .... Eze 40:31
and its stairway had eight s. .... Eze 40:34
and its stairway had eight s. .... Eze 40:37
with ten s leading up to it. .... Eze 40:49
stories like s and had balconies .... Eze 42:3
Its s are on the east side." .... Eze 43:17
Paul came to the s, the soldiers .... Ac 21:35
Paul stood on the s and waved .... Ac 21:40

STEW

and boil some s for these men." 2Ki 4:38
poured out the s for the others 2Ki 4:40

STICK

that were hidden now s out. .... Job 33:21
take a s and write on it, ' .... Eze 37:16
I will take the s for Joseph and .... Eze 37:19

STICKERS

branches and s all around you, ... Eze 2:6
or sharp s to hurt Israel......................... Eze 28:24

STICKING

all the fish s to your sides. .... Eze 29:4

STICKS

their walking s on the ground, ... Ex 7:12
and their s became snakes..................... Ex 7:12
get twelve walking s from them— .... Nu 17:2
the walking s from the LORD's .... Nu 17:9
and the s used to guide oxen. 1Sa 13:21
and my tongue s to the top of my .... Ps 22:15

are like sharp **s** used to guide .... Ec 12:11
barely burning **s** that are ready .... Is 7:4
Hold the **s** on which you wrote .... Eze 37:20
they ask those **s** of wood to .... Hos 4:12
Then I took two **s**; I called one .... Zch 11:7
your town that **s** to our feet we .... Lk 10:11
a pile of **s** and was putting .... Ac 28:3

STICKY
destruction, out of the **s** mud. .... Ps 40:2

STIFF
his teeth, and becomes very **s.** .... Mk 9:18

STILL
Will you **s** destroy it? .... Ge 18:24
Joseph is **s** alive and is the .... Ge 45:26
Stand **s** and you will see the .... Ex 14:13
Sun, stand **s** over Gibeon. .... Jos 10:12
It **s** stands at Ophrah, where the.............. Jdg 6:24
There are **s** too many men. .... Jdg 7:4
Ahab answered, "Is he **s** alive? 1Ki 20:32
messenger was **s** speaking when .... Job 1:16
messenger was **s** speaking when .... Job 1:17
messenger was **s** speaking when .... Job 1:18
While they are **s** growing and not .... Job 8:12
pray to you while they **s** can. .... Ps 32:6
Be **s** and know that I am God. .... Ps 46:10
While they were **s** eating, and.............. Ps 78:30
they will **s** produce fruit;....................... Ps 92:14
made the earth, and it **s** stands. .... Ps 119:90
When I wake up, I am **s** with you. .... Ps 139:18
tent will **s** be standing. .... Pr 14:11
only the LORD will **s** be praised. .... Is 2:11
But the LORD is **s** angry; .... Is 5:25
But the LORD was **s** angry;.................... Is 9:12
But the LORD is **s** angry; .... Is 9:17
but they will **s** be hungry. .... Is 9:20
But the LORD is **s** angry; .... Is 10:4
to your holder. Stop and be **s.**' .... Je 47:6
The words were **s** in his mouth .... Da 4:31
When I was **s** in my own country .... Jnh 4:2
sun and moon stood **s** in the sky; .... Hab 3:11
s others say you are Jeremiah .... Mt 16:14
s refused to change your ways .... Mt 21:32
Quiet! Be **s**!" Then the wind .... Mk 4:39
Are you **s** sleeping and resting? .... Mk 14:41
There is **s** more thing you .... Lk 18:22
while Peter was **s** speaking, ... Lk 22:60
While they **s** could not believe .... Lk 24:41
Do you **s** not know me, Philip? .... Jn 14:9
But they are **s** in the world..................... Jn 17:11
apostles who were **s** in Jerusalem .... Ac 8:14
Jerusalem Saul was **s** threatening .... Ac 9:1
for us while we were **s** sinners. .... Rm 5:8
while her husband is **s** alive, ... Rm 7:3
You are **s** not spiritual, because 1Co 3:3
you are **s** guilty of your sins. 1Co 15:17
that you are **s** helping them. .... Heb 6:10
old Holy Tent was **s** being used. .... Heb 9:8
his faith he is **s** speaking. .... Heb 11:4
die while they are **s** taking care .... Jam 1:11
were **s** some of their fellow..................... Rev 6:11
there are **s** two other troubles.................. Rev 9:12
disasters **s** did not change .... Rev 9:20

STILLED
He **s** the storm and calmed the .... Ps 107:29

STING
the power to **s** like scorpions. .... Rev 9:3

STINGERS
had tails with **s** like scorpions, ... Rev 9:10

STINGING
poisonous snakes and **s** insects. .... Dt 8:15

STINGS
gives when it **s** someone. .... Rev 9:5

STINK
and the river will begin to **s.** .... Ex 7:18
river began to **s,** so the .... Ex 7:21
the whole country began to **s.**.................. Ex 8:14
full of worms and began to **s,** .... Ex 16:20
it began to **s** or have worms in .... Ex 16:24
My sores **s** and become infected.............. Ps 38:5
flies can make even perfume **s.** .... Ec 10:1
perfume, they will **s.** .... Is 3:24
The canals will **s;** the streams.................. Is 19:6
The **s** will rise from the bodies, ... Is 34:3
Their bodies will rot and **s.** .... Joe 2:20
you smell the **s** from all the .... Am 4:10

STIR
and fight and **s** up trouble. .... Ne 4:8
and did not **s** up all his anger .... Ps 78:38
To **s** up my anger and revenge, ... Eze 24:8
your streams and **s** up the water .... Eze 32:2
of a human will not **s** the water, ... Eze 32:13
will **s** up everyone against the .... Da 11:2
he will use to **s** up his strength .... Da 11:25
does not need to **s** up the fire.................. Hos 7:4

STIRRED
has **s** up their enemies against .... Is 9:11
The LORD has **s** up the kings of.............. Je 51:11
While they are **s** up, I will give .... Je 51:39
It has **s** itself up against you! .... Eze 7:6
The LORD **s** up Zerubbabel son of............ Hag 1:14
to the pool and **s** up the water. .... Jn 5:4
But the Jewish people **s** up some .... Ac 13:50

STIRRING
Just as **s** milk makes butter, ... Pr 30:33
so **s** up anger causes trouble." .... Pr 30:33
your horses, **s** the great waters .... Hab 3:15
s up his people everywhere in .... Ac 24:5
in the Temple or **s** up the people.............. Ac 24:12

STIRS
it **s** up the sea like a pot of .... Job 41:31
Hatred **s** up trouble, but love .... Pr 10:12
s the sea and makes the waves .... Is 51:15
s up the sea so that its waves .... Je 31:35
my love for you **s** up my pity. .... Hos 11:8

STOIC
the Epicurean and **S** philosophers .... Ac 17:18

STOLE
the night and **s** the body while .... Mt 28:13
box, and he often **s** from it..................... Jn 12:6

STOLEN
that Rachel had **s** Laban's idols............... Ge 31:32
animal that was **s** during the day .... Ge 31:39
to my friend or **s** without reason .... Ps 7:4
fill our houses with **s** goods. .... Pr 1:13
S water is sweeter, and food .... Pr 9:17

STOMACH
He will make your **s** get big, ... Nu 5:21
but Joab stabbed him in the **s,** 2Sa 3:27
goes into the **s** and then goes .... Mt 15:17
into the mind, but into the **s.** .... Mk 7:19
Food is for the **s,** and the 1Co 6:13
stomach, and the **s** for food," 1Co 6:13

STOMACHS
those that crawl on their **s,** .... Le 11:42
food will turn sour in your **s,** .... Job 20:14
When the wicked fill their **s,** .... Job 20:23
their hunger or fill their **s,** .... Eze 7:19
S ache, and everyone's face .... Nah 2:10

STONE

found a s and laid his head on	Ge 28:11
and took the s he had slept	Ge 28:18
This s which I have set up on	Ge 28:22
A large s covered the mouth of the	Ge 29:2
would roll the s away from the	Ge 29:3
would put the s back in its	Ge 29:3
roll away the s from the mouth	Ge 29:8
and rolled the s from its mouth	Ge 29:10
olive oil on the s you set up on	Ge 31:13
Jacob set up a s on edge in that	Ge 35:14
wooden buckets and in s jars."	Ex 7:19
almost ready to s me to death."	Ex 17:4
into pieces the s pillars they	Ex 23:24
one s for each of the twelve	Ex 24:4
I will give you two s tablets.	Ex 24:12
the two s tablets behind it	Ex 26:33
six on one s and six on the	Ex 28:10
gave him the two s tablets with	Ex 31:18
he had the two s tablets with	Ex 32:15
written on both sides of each s,	Ex 32:15
threw down the s tablets that he	Ex 32:19
Cut two more s tablets like the	Ex 34:1
So Moses cut two s tablets like	Ex 34:4
the two s tablets with him.	Ex 34:4
break their s pillars, and cut	Ex 34:13
Commandments—on the s tablets.	Ex 34:28
carrying the two s tablets of	Ex 34:29
to cut designs in metal and s.	Ex 35:35
cut designs into metal and s;	Ex 38:23
Moses put the s tablets that had	Ex 40:20
You must s them to death;	Le 20:27
Don't put s statues in your land	Le 26:1
he wrote them on two s tablets.	Dt 4:13
of wood and s, that cannot see	Dt 4:28
he wrote them on two s tablets,	Dt 5:22
smash their holy s pillars,	Dt 7:5
to receive the s tablets,	Dt 9:9
The LORD gave me two s tablets,	Dt 9:10
LORD gave me the two s tablets,	Dt 9:11
and the two s tablets with the	Dt 9:15
I took the two s tablets and	Dt 9:17
Cut two s tablets like the first	Dt 10:1
and I cut out two s tablets like	Dt 10:3
smash their holy s pillars,	Dt 12:3
do not set up holy s pillars.	Dt 16:22
Do not move the s that marks a	Dt 19:14
cursed who moves the s that	Dt 27:17
other gods made of wood and s.	Dt 28:36
serve other gods of wood and s,	Dt 28:64
of wood, s, silver, and gold.	Dt 29:17
Beth Arabah to the great S of Bohan son	Jos 15:6
down to the great S of Bohan son	Jos 18:17
he took a large s and set it up	Jos 24:26
to all the people, "See this s!	Jos 24:27
He killed them all on one s.	Jdg 9:5
his seventy sons on one s.	Jdg 9:18
a grinding s on his head,	Jdg 9:53
could sling s at a hair and	Jdg 20:16
Samuel took a s and set it up	1Sa 7:12
He named the s Ebenezer, saying,	1Sa 7:12
Roll a large s over here now!"	1Sa 14:33
He took a s from his bag, put it	1Sa 17:49
s hit the Philistine and went	1Sa 17:49
with only a sling and a s.	1Sa 17:50
he would throw a s from a sling.	1Sa 25:29
stopped, and he became like s.	1Sa 25:37
She threw a large s for grinding	2Sa 11:21
Not a s will be left!"	2Sa 17:13
at the S of Zoheleth near	1Ki 1:9
country, cutting s, and he had	1Ki 5:15
blocks of fine s to be used for	1Ki 5:17
were made with blocks of fine s.	1Ki 7:9

was made with blocks of s.	1Ki 7:9
with large blocks of fine s,	1Ki 7:10
of fine s and cedar beams.	1Ki 7:11
three rows of s blocks and one	1Ki 7:12
the Ark were two s tablets that	1Ki 8:9
The people built s pillars and	1Ki 14:23
one s for each of the twelve	1Ki 18:31
he removed the s pillars his	2Ki 3:2
tore down the s pillar of Baal,	2Ki 10:27
buy timber and cut s to repair	2Ki 12:12
up, and he put it on a s base.	2Ki 16:17
They put up s pillars to gods	2Ki 17:10
He smashed the s pillars and cut	2Ki 18:4
buy timber and cut s to repair	2Ki 22:6
to pieces the s pillars they	2Ki 23:14
be weighed, and wood and s.	1Ch 22:14
men to cut s in the hill country	2Ch 2:2
bronze, iron, s, and wood, and	2Ch 2:14
of them to cut s in the	2Ch 2:18
the Ark were two s tablets that	2Ch 5:10
He smashed the s pillars that	2Ch 14:3
smashed the s pillars used to	2Ch 31:1
builders to buy cut s and wood.	2Ch 34:11
climbed up on the s wall they	Ne 4:3
like a s thrown into mighty.	Ne 9:11
I do not have the strength of s;	Job 6:12
lead, or carved into s forever.	Job 19:24
the water becomes hard as s,	Job 38:30
even as hard as a grinding s.	Job 41:24
The s that the builders rejected	Ps 118:22
Don't move an old s that marks a	Pr 22:28
Don't move an old s that marks a	Pr 23:10
and the s walls had fallen down.	Pr 24:31
like tying a s in a slingshot.	Pr 26:8
S is heavy, and sand is weighty,	Pr 27:3
I will break down the s wall,	Is 5:5
he will be like a s that causes	Is 8:14
I will put a s in the ground in	Is 28:16
ground in Jerusalem, a tested s.	Is 28:16
look at the s quarry from which	Is 51:1
and to idols of s, 'You gave	Je 2:27
idols made of s and wood.	Je 3:9
point into the s that is their.	Je 17:1
He will destroy the s pillars in	Je 43:13
tie a s to it and throw it into	Je 51:63
my way with a s wall and led me	La 3:9
as a diamond, harder than s.	Eze 3:9
heart of s from their bodies	Eze 11:19
idols made of wood and s."	Eze 20:32
hearts of s from your bodies,	Eze 36:26
made of cut s for the burnt	Eze 40:42
they faced the s pavement of the	Eze 42:3
A s wall was around each of the	Eze 46:23
built in each of the s walls.	Eze 46:23
bronze, iron, wood, and s.	Da 5:4
and s that are really not gods;	Da 5:23
A big s was brought and placed	Da 6:17
sacrifices or holy s pillars,	Hos 3:4
put up better s pillars to honor	Hos 10:1
destroy their holy s pillars.	Hos 10:2
like piles of s in a plowed	Hos 12:11
built fancy houses of cut s,	Am 5:11
not even a tiny s falls through.	Am 9:9
of gods and the s pillars you	Mic 5:13
one who says to a silent s, '	Hab 2:19
crows will sit on the s pillars.	Zph 2:14
I put this s in front of Joshua,	Zch 3:9
of Joshua, a s with seven sides	Zch 3:9
he will bring out the topmost s,	Zch 4:7
of you would give them a s?	Mt 7:9
have a large s tied around the	Mt 18:6
'The s that the builders	Mt 21:42
falls on this s will be broken,	Mt 21:44

S

and on whomever that s falls, ... Mt 21:44
prophets and s to death those .... Mt 23:37
not one s will be left on .... Mt 24:2
Every s will be thrown down to .... Mt 24:2
rolled a very large s to block .... Mt 27:60
by sealing the s in the entrance .... Mt 27:66
and rolled the s away from the .... Mt 28:2
entrance. Then he sat on the s. .... Mt 28:2
have a large s tied around his .... Mk 9:42
'The s that the builders .... Mk 12:10
Not one s will be left on .... Mk 13:2
Every s will be thrown down to .... Mk 13:2
rolled a very large s to block .... Mk 15:46
away for us the s that covers .... Mk 16:3
saw that the s had already been .... Mk 16:4
prophets and s to death those .... Lk 13:34
with a large s around your neck .... Lk 17:2
and not one s will be left on .... Lk 19:44
the people will s us to death, ... Lk 20:6
'The s that the builders .... Lk 20:17
falls on that s will be broken, ... Lk 20:18
come when not one s will be left .... Lk 21:6
Every s will be thrown down." .... Lk 21:6
found the s rolled away from .... Lk 24:2
there were six s water jars that .... Jn 2:6
commands that we s to death .... Jn 8:5
can throw the first s at her." .... Jn 8:7
there tried to s you to death .... Jn 11:8
a cave with a large s covering .... Jn 11:38
Jesus said, "Move the s away." .... Jn 11:39
they moved the s away from the .... Jn 11:41
the place called The S Pavement. .... Jn 19:13
that the large s had been moved .... Jn 20:1
is 'the s that you builders .... Ac 4:11
people would s them to death. .... Ac 5:26
Barnabas and to s them to death. .... Ac 14:5
Artemis and her holy s that fell .... Ac 19:35
stumbled over the s that causes .... Rm 9:32
in Jerusalem a s that causes .... Rm 9:33
is not written on s tablets but 2Co 3:3
death was written in words on s. 2Co 3:7
important s in that building, ... Eph 2:20
and the s tablets of the old .... Heb 9:4
Lord Jesus, the "s" that lives. 1Pe 2:4
the world did not want this s, ... 1Pe 2:4
but he was the s God chose, ... 1Pe 2:4
I will put a s in the ground in 1Pe 2:6
This s is worth much to you who 1Pe 2:7
the s that the builders rejected 1Pe 2:7
he is "a s that causes people to 1Pe 2:8
victory a white s with a new .... Rev 2:17
silver, bronze, s, and wood— .... Rev 9:20
angel picked up a large s, ... Rev 18:21

STONE'S
Jesus went about a s throw away .... Lk 22:41

STONECUTTERS
cedar logs, carpenters, and s. 2Sa 5:11
well as the bricklayers and s. 2Ki 12:12
David chose s to cut stones to 1Ch 22:2
many workmen—s, bricklayers, ... 1Ch 22:15

STONED
the bull must be s to death, ... Ex 21:29
bull must also be s to death. .... Ex 21:32
the camp and s him to death, ... Nu 15:36
time I was almost s to death. 2Co 11:25
They were s to death, they were .... Heb 11:37

STONES
they used bricks instead of s, ... Ge 11:3
set up a pile of s to remind us .... Ge 31:44
will throw s at us and kill us. .... Ex 8:26
with s or shot with arrows. .... Ex 19:13

you use s to make an altar for .... Ex 20:25
don't use s that you have shaped .... Ex 20:25
that bull by throwing s at it, ... Ex 21:28
set up twelve s, one stone for .... Ex 24:4
were paved with blue sapphire s, ... Ex 24:10
onyx s, and other jewels to be .... Ex 25:7
Take two onyx s and write the .... Ex 28:9
Israel on these s in the same .... Ex 28:11
gold around the s to hold them .... Ex 28:11
Then put the two s on the two .... Ex 28:12
two gold pieces to hold the s .... Ex 28:13
two gold pieces that hold the s. .... Ex 28:14
on each of the s as you would .... Ex 28:21
the first two s which you broke. .... Ex 34:1
onyx s, and other jewels to be .... Ex 35:9
brought onyx s and other jewels .... Ex 35:27
to cut s and jewels and put them .... Ex 35:33
around the onyx s and then wrote .... Ex 39:6
tear out the s with the mildew .... Le 14:40
must put new s in the walls, ... Le 14:42
taken away the old s and plaster .... Le 14:43
and put in new s and plaster. .... Le 14:43
remove all its s, plaster, and .... Le 14:45
after new s and plaster have .... Le 14:48
throw s at him and kill him. .... Le 20:2
must throw s at him and kill .... Le 24:14
kill him by throwing s at him. .... Le 24:16
killed him by throwing s at him. .... Le 24:23
or crush it between s. .... Nu 11:8
about killing them with s. .... Nu 14:10
him by throwing s at him outside .... Nu 15:35
You must throw s at them until .... Dt 13:10
gates and throw s at that person .... Dt 17:5
first to throw s at the person, ... Dt 17:7
town must throw s at him until .... Dt 21:21
to death by throwing s at her. .... Dt 22:21
to death by throwing s at them. .... Dt 22:24
not take his two s for grinding .... Dt 24:6
up some large s and cover them .... Dt 27:2
set up these s on Mount Ebal, ... Dt 27:4
an altar of s there to the LORD .... Dt 27:5
use any iron tool to cut the s; .... Dt 27:5
your God with s from the field. .... Dt 27:6
of these teachings on the s." .... Dt 27:8
from flint s and circumcise .... Jos 5:2
from flint s and circumcised .... Jos 5:3
people threw s at Achan and his .... Jos 7:25
It was made from uncut s; .... Jos 8:31
of Moses on s for all the people .... Jos 8:32
your God with its s in the right .... Jdg 5:3
five smooth s from a stream. 1Sa 17:40
to kill David with s, ... 1Sa 30:6
He threw s at David and his 2Sa 16:6
and throwing s and dirt at him. 2Sa 16:13
and filled the pit with many s. 2Sa 18:17
thousand men to carry the s. 1Ki 5:15
Byblos carved the s and prepared 1Ki 5:18
prepared the s and the logs for 1Ki 5:18
The s were prepared at the same 1Ki 6:7
Since these s were the only ones 1Ki 6:7
could not see the s of the wall, ... 1Ki 6:18
three rows of cut s and one row 1Ki 6:36
These fine s went from the 1Ki 7:9
these foundation s were other 1Ki 7:11
as common as s and cedar trees 1Ki 10:27
they threw s at him until he 1Ki 12:18
away all the s and wood Baasha 1Ki 15:22
He took twelve s, one stone for 1Ki 18:31
Elijah used these s to rebuild 1Ki 18:32
the wood, the s, and the ground 1Ki 18:38
the city and kill him with s." 1Ki 21:10
the city and killed him with s. 1Ki 21:13
city with its s still in place, ... 2Ki 3:25

broke the s of the altar into 2Ki 23:15
stonecutters to cut s to be used 1Ch 22:2
colors, valuable s, and white 1Ch 29:2
plentiful as s and cedar trees 2Ch 1:15
as common as s and cedar trees 2Ch 9:27
they threw s at him until he 2Ch 10:18
command they threw s at him in 2Ch 24:21
bows, and s for their slings. 2Ch 26:14
that Temple with large s, ... Ezr 5:8
layers of large s and then one .... Ezr 6:4
Can they bring s back to life .... Ne 4:2
with the s in the field, ... Job 5:23
look for a place among the s. .... Job 8:17
washes over s and wears them .... Job 14:19
s from slings are like chaff to .... Job 41:28
Your servants love even her s; .... Ps 102:14
the decorated s in the Temple. .... Ps 144:12
because those s were set up by .... Pr 22:28
to throw away s and a time to .... Ec 3:5
tower, built with rows of s. .... Sng 4:4
the field of s and planted the .... Is 5:2
we will build again with cut s. .... Is 9:10
repair the walls with their s. .... Is 22:10
must use large s to grind grain .... Is 47:2
rebuild you with turquoise s, ... Is 54:11
Move all the s off the road. .... Is 62:10
Take some large s. Bury them in .... Je 43:9
over these s I have buried, ... Je 43:10
only ruins and piles of s today. .... Je 44:6
me in a pit; they threw s at me. .... La 3:53
s of the Temple are scattered .... La 4:1
you to throw s at you and to cut .... Eze 16:40
kill them by throwing s at them, ... Eze 23:47
will throw your s, wood, and .... Eze 26:12
and a pavement of s all around .... Eze 40:17
your houses into piles of s. .... Da 2:5
house turned into a pile of s. .... Da 3:29
I will pour her s down into the .... Mic 1:6
The s of the walls will cry out .... Hab 2:11
started laying s on top of .... Hag 2:15
stones on top of s to build the .... Hag 2:15
it with its wood and s.'" .... Zch 5:4
killed a third servant with s. .... Mt 21:35
and cutting himself with s. .... Mk 5:5
are! How big the s are!" .... Mk 13:1
then the s would cry out." .... Lk 19:40
with beautiful s and gifts .... Lk 21:5
picked up s to throw at him .... Jn 8:59
picked up s to kill Jesus. .... Jn 10:31
began to throw s at him to kill .... Ac 7:58
While they were throwing s, ... Ac 7:59
So they threw s at him and .... Ac 14:19
it must be put to death with s." .... Heb 12:20
You also are like living s, ... 1Pe 2:5
throne looked like precious s, ... Rev 4:3
built on twelve foundation s, ... Rev 21:14
and on the s were written the .... Rev 21:14
The foundation s of the city .... Rev 21:19

STONEWORKERS
And they hired s and carpenters 2Ch 24:12

STOOD
Abraham s there before the LORD. .... Ge 18:22
where he had s before the LORD. .... Ge 19:27
My bundle s up, and your bundles .... Ge 37:7
to Egypt and s before Joseph. .... Ge 43:15
baby's sister s a short distance .... Ex 2:4
and they s at the foot of the .... Ex 19:17
the cloud s over the entrance of .... Dt 31:15
the commander s and shouted 2Ki 18:28
king s by the pillar and made 2Ki 23:3
The Levites also s every morning 1Ch 23:30
Ezra the priest s up and said to .... Ezr 10:10

the teacher s on a high wooden .... Ne 8:4
opened it, all the people s up. .... Ne 8:5
the hair on my body s on end. .... Job 4:15
He s me on a rock and made my .... Ps 40:2
s up to judge and to save the .... Ps 76:9
s before him and stopped God's .... Ps 106:23
creatures of fire s above him. .... Is 6:2
Remember that I s before you and .... Je 18:20
men went in and s by the bronze .... Eze 9:2
millions of angels s before him. .... Da 7:10
he said this, I s up, but I was .... Da 10:11
The Lord s by a straight wall, ... Am 7:7
sun and moon s still in the sky .... Hab 3:11
Then she s up and began to serve .... Mt 8:15
he always did, and s up to read. .... Lk 4:16
Pharisee s alone and prayed, ' .... Lk 18:11
But Zacchaeus s and said to the .... Lk 19:8
clothes suddenly s beside them. .... Lk 24:4
Jesus himself s right in the .... Lk 24:36
Jesus came and s right in the .... Jn 20:19
white clothes s beside them. .... Ac 1:10
He jumped up, s on his feet, and .... Ac 3:8
The man s and begged, "Come over ...... Ac 16:9
so Paul s on the steps and waved .... Ac 21:40
when he s before Pontius 1Ti 6:13

STOOPED
You have s to make me great. 2Sa 22:36
You have s to make me great. .... Ps 18:35

STOPPED
underground springs s flowing, ... Ge 8:2
So they s up all the wells the .... Ge 26:15
and the sickness s there. .... Nu 16:48
and the moon s until the people .... Jos 10:13
people who were carrying it s. .... Lk 7:14
They s, and it became calm. .... Lk 8:24
and instantly her bleeding s. .... Lk 8:44
men s having natural sex and .... Rm 1:27
and he never s believing. .... Rm 4:20
people must be s, because they .... Tit 1:11
sacrifices would have already s. .... Heb 10:2
s great fires and were saved .... Heb 11:34
man's voice and s the prophet's 2Pe 2:16

STOPPING
that everyone was s to look at 2Sa 20:12
They insulted me without s. .... Ps 35:15
Moses spoke without s to think. .... Ps 106:33
S her is like stopping the wind .... Pr 27:16
her is like s the wind or trying .... Pr 27:16
tears night and day, without s. .... Je 14:17
flow continually, without s, ... La 3:49
is s me from being baptized? .... Ac 8:36
know what is that Man of Evil 2Th 2:6
is one who is s that power. 2Th 2:7

STOPS
if he s fearing the Almighty. .... Job 6:14
he s everyone from working so .... Job 37:7
He s wars everywhere on the .... Ps 46:9
be like a spring that s flowing? .... Je 15:18
in him that s him from talking. .... Mk 9:17
if he is sorry and s sinning, ... Lk 17:3
My Father never s working, ... Jn 5:17
This s all excuses and brings .... Rm 3:19
of faith that s all bragging, ... Rm 3:27
he even s those who do want to 3Jn 1:10

STORAGE
other towns for s and all the 2Ch 8:6
He built s buildings for grain, ... 2Ch 32:28
what you harvest in your s jars. .... Je 40:10

STORE
of food and s it on the boat .... Ge 6:21
authority they should s the .... Ge 41:35

crop and s it in your towns. .... Dt 14:28
but they s up food in the summer .... Pr 6:8
they s up food in the summer.................. Pr 30:25
They will s their food in .... Is 10:28
You will s up, but save nothing, ... Mic 6:14
what you s up, the sword will .... Mic 6:14
Don't s treasures for yourselves .... Mt 6:19
But s your treasures in heaven .... Mt 6:20
or harvest or s food in barns, ... Mt 6:26
and there I will s all my grain................ Lk 12:18
be for those who s up things for .... Lk 12:21

STORED
of good crops and s the food in .... Ge 41:48
every city he s grain that had .... Ge 41:48
Joseph s much grain, as much as .... Ge 41:49
ancestors have s up until this 2Ki 20:17
Naphtali where treasures were s. 2Ch 16:4
storm comes from where it was s; .... Job 37:9
that you have s up for those who .... Ps 31:19
wealth is s up for good people .... Pr 13:22
s up water in the lower pool. .... Is 22:9
ancestors have s up until this .... Is 39:6
wealth that is s away and the .... Is 45:3
are on record, s away, waiting .... Hos 13:12
the good they s in their hearts .... Lk 6:45
the evil they s in their hearts .... Lk 6:45
good things s to last for many .... Lk 12:19

STOREHOUSE
up his heavenly s so that the .... Dt 28:12
sons were chosen to guard the s. 1Ch 26:15
Levites at a time guarded the s. 1Ch 26:17
ever gone into the s of the snow.............. Job 38:22
Bring to the s a full tenth of .... Mal 3:10

STOREHOUSES
opened the s and sold grain to .... Ge 41:56
and I have it locked in my s. .... Dt 32:34
showed them what was in his s: 2Ki 20:13
was in charge of the royal s. 1Ch 27:25
charge of the s in the country, ... 1Ch 27:25
the snow or seen the s for hail, ... Job 38:22
brings out the wind from his s. .... Ps 135:7
messengers what was in his s: .... Is 39:2
brings out the wind from his s. .... Je 10:13
Break open her s of grain. .... Je 50:26
brings out the wind from his s. .... Je 51:16

STOREROOM
room under the s in the palace. .... Je 38:11
opened up his s and brought out .... Je 50:25

STOREROOMS
buildings, its s, its upper 1Ch 28:11
to prepare the s in the Temple 2Ch 31:11
priests at the s of the Temple .... Ne 10:37
to put in the s of the treasury.................. Ne 10:38
to bring to the s the gifts of .... Ne 10:39
who guarded the s next to the .... Ne 12:25
men to be in charge of the s. .... Ne 12:44
was in charge of the Temple s, ... Ne 13:4
Tobiah use one of the large s. .... Ne 13:5
brought to the s a tenth of .... Ne 13:12
these men in charge of the s: .... Ne 13:13
and have saved it in your s. .... Eze 28:4
The s for grain have been broken .... Joe 1:17
they don't have s or barns, ... Lk 12:24

STORES
He s up wisdom for those who are .... Pr 2:7

STORIES
not spread false s against other .... Le 19:16
you never listened to their s? .... Job 21:29
I will speak using s; .... Ps 78:2
can understand wise words and s, ... Pr 1:6

me, 'He is only telling s.' " .... Eze 20:49
rooms were on three different s,............. Eze 41:6
built in three s like steps and .... Eze 42:3
and second s of the building .... Eze 42:5
The rooms were on three s. .... Eze 42:6
those on the first and second s. .... Eze 42:6
Then Jesus used s to teach them .... Mt 13:3
Why do you use s to teach the .... Mt 13:10
This is why I use s to teach the .... Mt 13:13
Jesus used s to tell all these .... Mt 13:34
he always used s to teach them. .... Mt 13:34
I will speak using s; .... Mt 13:35
finished teaching with these s, ... Mt 13:53
and the Pharisees heard these s,............. Mt 21:45
again used s to teach them. .... Mt 22:1
about wars and s of wars that................. Mt 24:6
together and taught them with s. .... Mk 3:23
them many things, using s. .... Mk 4:2
him asked him about the s. .... Mk 4:10
I tell everything by using s .... Mk 4:11
Jesus used many s like these to .... Mk 4:33
He always used s to teach them............... Mk 4:34
Jesus began to use s to teach .... Mk 12:1
about wars and s of wars that................. Mk 13:7
and s about him spread all .... Lk 4:14
But I use s to speak to other .... Lk 8:10
these things indirectly in s....................... Jn 16:25
I will not use s like that to .... Jn 16:25
are not using s that are hard to .... Jn 16:29
their time on s that are not 1Ti 1:4
follow foolish s that disagree 1Ti 4:7
will begin to follow false s....................... 2Ti 4:4
Jewish false s and the commands .... Tit 1:14
just clever s that someone 2Pe 1:16

STORING
built cities for s grain and 1Ki 9:19
was in charge of s the wine that.............. 1Ch 27:27
in charge of s the olive oil. 1Ch 27:28
as towns for s grain and 2Ch 8:4
towns for s supplies in Judah................... 2Ch 17:12
gathering and s wealth that they .... Ec 2:26

STORK
not like the feathers of the s. .... Job 39:13
wings were like those of a s, ... Zch 5:9

STORK'S
the s home is in the fir trees. .... Ps 104:17

STORKS
s, any kind of heron, hoopoes, ... Le 11:19
s, any kind of heron, the .... Dt 14:18
The s, doves, swifts, and .... Je 8:7

STORM
crush me with a s and multiply .... Job 9:17
chaff that is blown away by a s?.............. Job 21:18
a s snatches them away in the .... Job 27:20
and tossed me about in the s. .... Job 30:22
thunder announces the coming s, ... Job 36:33
The s comes from where it was .... Job 37:9
LORD answered Job from the s................. Job 38:1
LORD spoke to Job from the s: .... Job 40:6
and a powerful s surrounds him. .... Ps 50:3
far away from the wind and s." .... Ps 55:8
them with your s, and frighten .... Ps 83:15
He spoke, and a s came up, which .... Ps 107:25
The s was so bad that they lost .... Ps 107:26
He stilled the s and calmed the .... Ps 107:29
comes over you like a s, ... Pr 1:27
A s will blow the evil person .... Pr 10:25
if you're in a s on the ocean, ... Pr 23:34
to hide from the s and rain. .... Is 4:6
tumbleweeds blown away by a s. .... Is 17:13
it will shake like a hut in a s. .... Is 24:20

a s of hail and strong wind, ... Is 28:2
like a great s with much rain .... Is 30:30
safe place in a s, like streams .... Is 32:2
of a strong s he will set that .... Je 11:16
a s, my punishment will blow .... Je 22:22
the LORD will come like a s. .... Je 23:19
like a powerful s from the .... Je 25:32
It is a s from the LORD! .... Je 30:23
will come like a s crashing down .... Je 30:23
You will come like a s. .... Eze 38:9
but they will harvest a s. .... Hos 8:7
this great s has come on you. .... Jnh 1:12
out like a s to scatter us. .... Hab 3:14
A great s arose on the lake so............... Mt 8:24
The next day the s was blowing .... Ac 27:18
days, and the s was very bad, we .... Ac 27:20
water and clouds blown by a s. 2Pe 2:17

STORMS
You are like a shelter from s, ... Is 25:4
noises, with s, strong winds, ... Is 29:6
S have hurt you, and you have .... Is 54:11
there are whirlwinds and s, ... Nah 1:3
march in the s of the south. .... Zch 9:14
to darkness, sadness, and s. .... Heb 12:18

STORMY
mighty sea and calm the s waves. .... Ps 89:9
and s winds that obey him, ... Ps 148:8
I saw a s wind coming from the .... Eze 1:4
and a s wind will break the wall. .... Eze 13:11
break the wall with a s wind. .... Eze 13:13
a s day with strong winds. .... Am 1:14
made the sea so s that the ship .... Jnh 1:4
the sea was becoming more s. .... Jnh 1:13

STRAIGHT
people can go s into the city." .... Jos 6:5
everyone ran s into the city. .... Jos 6:20
Then send the cart s on its way. 1Sa 6:8
Then the cows went s toward Beth 1Sa 6:12
Abner, going s toward him. 2Sa 2:19
waters flow s down to the west 2Ch 32:30
Fountain Gate s up the steps to .... Ne 12:37
had been carried s from birth to .... Job 10:19
You made us unable to walk s, ... Ps 60:3
bow that does not shoot s. .... Ps 78:57
led them on a s road to a city .... Ps 107:7
look s ahead to what is good. .... Pr 4:25
steps are headed s to the grave. .... Pr 5:5
is crooked, you can't make it s. .... Ec 1:15
Make a s road in the dry lands .... Is 40:3
drank it and could not walk s. .... Is 51:22
the Corner Gate s to the hill of .... Je 31:39
Their legs were s. Their feet .... Eze 1:7
moved, but each went s ahead. .... Eze 1:9
Each went s ahead. Wherever the .... Eze 1:12
stretched out s toward one .... Eze 1:23
They each went s ahead. .... Eze 10:22
They all march s ahead and do .... Joe 2:7
You will go s out of the city .... Am 4:3
The Lord stood by a s wall, ... Am 7:7
Make the road s for him.'" .... Mt 3:3
Make the road s for him.'" .... Mk 1:3
So Judas went s to Jesus and .... Mk 14:45
Make the road s for him. .... Lk 3:4
with turns should be made s, ... Lk 3:5
she could not stand up s. .... Lk 13:11
able to stand up s and began .... Lk 13:13
turned and looked s at Peter. .... Lk 22:61
'Make the road s for the Lord.' .... Jn 1:23
John looked s at him and said .... Ac 3:4
Get up and go to S Street. .... Ac 9:11
He looked s at Elymas .... Ac 13:9
looked s at him and saw that .... Ac 14:9

Troas and sailed s to the island .... Ac 16:11
sailed s to the island of Cos. .... Ac 21:1

STRAIGHTEN
No one can s what he has bent. .... Ec 7:13

STRAIN
will cry out and s like a woman .... Is 42:14
of Jerusalem, s and be in pain. .... Mic 4:10

STRAINER
through the s of destruction. .... Is 30:28
shaking grain through a s, ... Am 9:9

STRAINING
past and s toward what is ahead, ... Php 3:13

STRANGE
will go closer to this s thing. .... Ex 3:3
him about a s sign that had 2Ch 32:31
Your eyes will see s sights, ... Pr 23:33
LORD will use s words and.................... Is 28:11
He will do his work, his s work. .... Is 28:21
will finish his job, his s job. .... Is 28:21
whose s language you couldn't .... Is 33:19
the teachings are s and foreign. .... Hos 8:12
This is a very s thing. .... Jn 9:30
people who use s words and 1Co 14:21
all kinds of s teachings lead .... Heb 13:9
think it is s that you do not do 1Pe 4:4
that something s is happening to 1Pe 4:12

STRANGER
the land of Canaan now as a s, ... Ge 17:8
man Lot came to our city as a s,............. Ge 19:9
where you have lived as a s— .... Ge 21:23
Abraham lived as a s in the land .... Ge 21:34
I am only a s and a foreigner .... Ge 23:4
where you are now living as a s, ... Ge 28:4
Moses was a s in a land that was .... Ex 2:22
"I am a s in a foreign country." .... Ex 18:3
as you would a s or foreigner. .... Le 25:35
servants treat me like a s; .... Job 19:15
No s ever had to spend the night .... Job 31:32
I am like a s to my closest .... Ps 69:8
I am a s on earth. Do not hide .... Ps 119:19
until he pays what the s owes. .... Pr 20:16
come from a s and not from your .... Pr 27:2
until he pays what the s owes. .... Pr 27:13
a s enjoys them instead. .... Ec 6:2
away from him as if he were a s. .... Is 1:4
are you like a s in the land,.................. Je 14:8
But they will never follow a s. .... Jn 10:5
land of Midian where he was a s. .... Ac 7:29

STRANGER'S
who promises to pay a s debts, ... Pr 20:16
who promises to pay a s loan,............... Pr 27:13

STRANGERS
descendants will be s and travel .... Ge 15:13
He has treated us like s. .... Ge 31:15
It is also for s, orphans, and .... Dt 14:29
your town, the s, orphans, and .... Dt 16:11
the Levites, s, orphans, and .... Dt 16:14
and they were s in the land. 1Ch 16:19
We are like foreigners and s, ... 1Ch 29:15
and my friends have become s. .... Job 19:13
I took the side of s who were in .... Job 29:16
S turn against me, and cruel .... Ps 54:3
They were s in the land. .... Ps 105:12
let s steal everything he has .... Ps 109:11
S will enjoy your wealth, and .... Pr 5:10
and shouldn't be shared with s. .... Pr 5:17
and s cannot share your joy. .... Pr 14:10
You must not be hard on s, ... Je 7:6
because s have gone into the .... Je 51:51
land has been turned over to s; .... La 5:2

S

you over to s and punish you. .... Eze 11:9
s instead of your husband. .... Eze 16:32
and s will never even go through .... Joe 3:17
helping while s carried Israel's .... Ob 1:11
as a place to bury s who died in .... Mt 27:7
will be s in a land they .... Ac 7:6
Bring s in need into your homes. .... Rm 12:13
not foreigners or s any longer, ... Eph 2:19
welcoming s, washing the feet 1Ti 5:10
like visitors and s on earth..................... Heb 11:13
to welcome s, because some who .... Heb 13:2
foreigners and s in this world. 1Pe 2:11

STRANGLED
eating animals that have been s,............. Ac 15:20
any animals that have been s,................. Ac 15:29
or animals that have been s. .... Ac 21:25

STRAP
or a sandal s so that you cannot.............. Ge 14:23

STRAPS
pair of shoulder s tied together .... Ex 28:7
on the two s of the holy vest .... Ex 28:12
on the shoulder s in the front .... Ex 28:25
of the shoulder s in the front .... Ex 28:27
the shoulder s for the holy vest .... Ex 39:4
on the shoulder s of the holy .... Ex 39:7
the two shoulder s in the front .... Ex 39:18
the shoulder s in front of the .... Ex 39:20
their sandal s are not broken................. Is 5:27
Make a yoke out of s and poles, ... Je 27:2

STRAW
camels and gave them s and food, ... Ge 24:32
give the people s to make bricks .... Ex 5:7
for dry stalks to use for s. .... Ex 5:12
as fire burns s or dry grass. .... Is 5:24
enemy Moab like s that is .... Is 25:10
But they are like s; fire will.................... Is 47:14
jewels, wood, grass, or s, ... 1Co 3:12

STRAY
Do not s from it either from the .... Jos 23:6
old, they will not s from it. .... Pr 22:6
way and let me s and left me .... La 3:11
Then we will not s away from the .... Heb 2:1

STRAYED
I haven't s from your orders. .... Ps 119:110
those who s away or searched .... Eze 34:4
bring back those that s away, ... Eze 34:16

STREAKED
the young that were born were s, ... Ge 30:39
them face the s and dark animals .... Ge 30:40
have all the s animals as your................. Ge 31:8
flocks gave birth to s babies. .... Ge 31:8
goats who were mating were s, ... Ge 31:10
Only the s, speckled, or spotted .... Ge 31:12

STREAKS
male goats that had s or spots, ... Ge 30:35

STREAM
that sends its roots by a s. .... Je 17:8
an overflowing s and will cover .... Je 47:2
flow like a never-ending s. .... Am 5:24

STREAMBEDS
lived in dried up s, in caves, ... Job 30:6

STREAMING
a flock of goats s down Mount .... Sng 4:1
a flock of goats s down Mount .... Sng 6:5
all nations will come s to it. .... Is 2:2
other nations will come s to it. .... Mic 4:1

STREAMS
a place with s of water. .... Dt 10:7
They are like s that do not .... Job 6:15

s that sometimes run over. .... Job 6:15
the sparkling s or the rivers .... Job 20:17
trees by the s surround it. .... Job 40:22
a deer thirsts for s of water, ... Ps 42:1
the springs and s and made the .... Ps 74:15
He brought s out of the rock and .... Ps 78:16
as you bring s to the desert. .... Ps 126:4
flies from Egypt's faraway s. .... Is 7:18
the s of Egypt will decrease and............. Is 19:6
hill will have s filled with .... Is 30:25
like s of water in a dry land, ... Is 32:2
a place with s and wide rivers .... Is 33:21
and s will flow in the dry land. .... Is 35:6
and make s flow on dry land. .... Is 44:3
trees growing beside s of water. .... Is 44:4
I will make your s become dry!' .... Is 44:27
s of water will flow from our .... Je 9:18
cool, flowing s do not dry up. .... Je 18:14
those people by s of water on an .... Je 31:9
S of tears flow from my eyes, ... La 3:48
I will make the s of the Nile .... Eze 30:12
and sent their s to all other..................... Eze 31:4
around in your s and stir up the .... Eze 32:2
The s of water have dried up, ... Joe 1:20
or were you angry at the s? .... Hab 3:8

STREET
down and lie on every s corner, ... Is 51:20
you were like a s for them to .... Is 51:23
walked on, like mud in the s." .... Mic 7:10
to death at every s corner. .... Nah 3:10
Get up and go to Straight S. .... Ac 9:11
And the s of the city was made .... Rev 21:21
the middle of the s of the city.................. Rev 22:2

STREETS
it in the s of Ashkelon. 2Sa 1:20
Don't pour your water in the s; .... Pr 5:16
around on the corners of the s. .... Pr 7:12
There's a lion in the s!" .... Pr 26:13
be deaf to the noise in the s, ... Ec 12:4
the city, in the s and squares, ... Sng 3:2
Truth is not spoken in the s; .... Is 59:14
and on the s so that people will .... Mt 6:2
will hear his voice in the s. .... Mt 12:19

STRENGTH
you so you can regain your s................... Ge 18:5
daytime the sun took away my s, ... Ge 31:40
he used all his s and sat up on .... Ge 48:2
my first son, you are my s. .... Ge 49:3
of Jacob and his s from the..................... Ge 49:24
LORD gives me s and makes me .... Ex 15:2
With your s you will guide them.............. Ex 15:13
they see your s, they will be as .... Ex 15:16
with your great power and s. .... Ex 32:11
So show your s now, Lord. .... Nu 14:17
You have great s, and no other .... Dt 3:24
by his great power and s. .... Dt 4:34
of Egypt himself by his great s. .... Dt 4:37
there by his great power and s. .... Dt 5:15
all your soul, and all your s. .... Dt 6:5
great power and s brought you .... Dt 7:19
because of my own power and s," .... Dt 8:17
Egypt by your great power and s. .... Dt 9:26
with your great power and s." .... Dt 9:29
his majesty, his mighty s, his s, ... Dt 11:2
with his great power and s,..................... Dt 26:8
will see that their s is gone, ... Dt 32:36
March on, my soul, with s! .... Jdg 5:21
Go with your s and save Israel .... Jdg 6:14
out the secret of Samson's s. .... Jdg 16:9
me the secret of your great s." .... Jdg 16:15
I would lose my s and be as weak .... Jdg 16:17
him weak, and his s left him. .... Jdg 16:19

please give me **s** one more time .... Jdg 16:28
have enough **s** to go on your way. 1Sa 28:22
David found **s** in the LORD his 1Sa 30:6
He is my shield and my saving **s,** 2Sa 22:3
You gave me **s** in battle. 2Sa 22:40
the north pillar In Him Is **S.** 1Ki 7:21
of Egypt with great power and **s.** 2Ki 17:36
heart, soul, and **s,** following 2Ki 23:25
With all their **s** they were 1Ch 13:8
Depend on the LORD and his **s;** 1Ch 16:11
the power and **s** to make anyone 1Ch 29:12
the north pillar In Him Is **S.** 2Ch 3:17
the Agreement that shows your **s.** 2Ch 6:41
have power and **s,** so no one can 2Ch 20:6
with your great **s** and power. .... Ne 1:10
by his power and **s** are written .... Est 10:2
to the grave with all your **s,** .... Job 5:26
I do not have the **s** to wait. .... Job 6:11
I do not have the **s** of stone; .... Job 6:12
or give **s** to those who do .... Job 8:20
it comes to **s,** God is stronger .... Job 9:19
taken away my **s** and destroyed my .... Job 16:7
Hunger takes away their **s,** .... Job 18:12
They had the **s** of their youth in .... Job 20:11
while he still has all his **s,** .... Job 21:23
and I will always have great **s.'** .... Job 29:20
have for their **s** since they had .... Job 30:2
they had lost their **s** to work? .... Job 30:2
has taken away my **s** and made me .... Job 30:11
all your great **s** will keep you .... Job 36:19
He has great **s;** he is always .... Job 37:23
for its great **s** and leave your .... Job 39:11
horse its **s** or puts a flowing .... Job 39:19
enjoying its **s,** and charges .... Job 39:21
at the **s** it has in its body; .... Job 40:16
great **s** and well-formed body.................. Job 41:12
There is great **s** in its neck..................... Job 41:22
because the LORD gives me **s.** .... Ps 3:5
I love you, LORD. You are my **s.** .... Ps 18:1
He is my shield and my saving **s,** .... Ps 18:2
You gave me **s** in battle. .... Ps 18:39
they give new **s.** The rules of .... Ps 19:7
king rejoices because of your **s;** .... Ps 21:1
My **s** is gone, like water poured .... Ps 22:14
My **s** has dried up like a clay .... Ps 22:15
away. You are my **s;** hurry to .... Ps 22:19
gives me new **s.** He leads me on.............. Ps 23:3
The LORD is my **s** and shield. .... Ps 28:7
The LORD gives **s** to his people;.............. Ps 29:11
My troubles are using up my **s,** .... Ps 31:10
My **s** was gone as in the summer .... Ps 32:4
warrior escapes by his great **s.** .... Ps 33:16
they can't save by their great **s.** .... Ps 33:17
he is their **s** in times of .... Ps 37:39
heart pounds, and my **s** is gone. .... Ps 38:10
will give them **s** when they are .... Ps 41:3
me **s** so I can pay them back. .... Ps 41:10
God, you are my **s.** Why have you .... Ps 43:2
it was your great power and **s.** .... Ps 44:3
God is our protection and our **s.** .... Ps 46:1
By your **s** show that I am .... Ps 54:1
God, my **s,** I am looking to you, ... Ps 59:9
But I will sing about your **s.** .... Ps 59:16
God, my **s,** I will sing praises .... Ps 59:17
and have seen your **s** and glory. .... Ps 63:2
made the mountains by your **s;** .... Ps 65:6
gives his people **s** and power. .... Ps 68:35
not leave me when my **s** is gone. .... Ps 71:9
become weak, but God is my **s.** .... Ps 73:26
warrior had the **s** to stop it. .... Ps 76:5
Use your **s,** and come to save us. .... Ps 80:2
Sing for joy to God, our **s;** .... Ps 81:1
those whose **s** comes from you, ... Ps 84:5

Give me, your servant, **s.** .... Ps 86:16
I am like a man with no **s.** .... Ps 88:4
their glorious **s,** and in your .... Ps 89:17
I have given **s** to a warrior; .... Ps 89:19
You have given **s** to his enemies .... Ps 89:42
in majesty and armed with **s.** .... Ps 93:1
give us bread that gives us **s.** .... Ps 104:15
Depend on the LORD and his **s;** .... Ps 105:4
The LORD gives me **s** and a song. .... Ps 118:14
with the Ark that shows your **s.** .... Ps 132:8
it with his great power and **s.** .... Ps 136:12
with the **s** of a horse or with .... Ps 147:10
Praise him for his **s;** .... Ps 150:2
Patience is better than **s.** .... Pr 16:32
a broken spirit drains your **s.** .... Pr 17:22
The young glory in their **s,** .... Pr 20:29
with knowledge have great **s.** .... Pr 24:5
waste your **s** on women or your .... Pr 31:3
think wisdom is better than **s.** .... Ec 9:16
eat only at mealtime and for **s,** .... Ec 10:17
will not have **s** enough to last. .... Is 7:9
The **s** of Assyria will be burned .... Is 10:16
and fairness will give him **s,** .... Is 11:5
LORD gives me **s** and makes me .... Is 12:2
decide cases and **s** to those who............. Is 28:6
Give us **s** every morning. .... Is 33:2
gives **s** to those who are tired .... Is 40:29
and I will get my **s** from my God. .... Is 49:5
and use your **s,** powerful LORD.............. Is 51:9
You found new **s,** so you did not............. Is 57:10
lands and give **s** to your bones. .... Is 58:11
his own goodness gave him **s.**................. Is 59:16
must not brag about their **s.** .... Je 9:23
you are my **s** and my protection, ... Je 16:19
them about my power and my **s.**............. Je 16:21
who depend on humans for **s,**................. Je 17:5
you with my great power and **s.** .... Je 21:5
with my great power and **s.** .... Je 27:5
give rest and **s** to those who are .... Je 31:25
and your great power and **s.** .... Je 32:21
Moab's **s** has been cut off, ... Je 48:25
Elam's bow, its greatest **s.** .... Je 49:35
Their **s** is gone, and they have .... Je 51:30
has turned my **s** into weakness. .... La 1:14
no one who can give me **s** again. .... La 1:16
has removed all the **s** of Israel; .... La 2:3
said, "My **s** is gone, and I have .... La 3:18
great power and **s** and anger to .... Eze 20:33
great power and **s** and anger I .... Eze 20:34
You think it gives you **s.** .... Eze 24:21
that gives them **s** and joy, ... Eze 24:25
Their **s** frightened people, ... Eze 32:30
a kingdom, power, **s,** and glory. .... Da 2:37
some of the **s** of iron in it, ... Da 2:41
glory, and the **s** of a king. .... Da 7:14
lost my **s,** my face turned white .... Da 10:8
My **s** is gone, and it is hard for .... Da 10:17
touched me again and gave me **s.** .... Da 10:18
since you have given me **s.**" .... Da 10:19
to stir up his **s** and courage. .... Da 11:25
North will worship power and **s,** .... Da 11:38
nations have eaten up his **s,** .... Hos 7:9
I trained them and gave them **s,** .... Hos 7:15
leaders brag about their **s,** .... Hos 7:16
taken Karnaim by our own **s.**" .... Am 6:13
with justice and **s,** to tell the .... Mic 3:8
with the LORD's **s** and with the .... Mic 5:4
Get ready. Gather all your **s!** .... Nah 2:1
and Egypt gave her endless **s;**................ Nah 3:9
of worshiping their own **s.**"................... Hab 1:11
The Lord GOD is my **s.** .... Hab 3:19
by your own **s** or by your own .... Zch 4:6
His arm will lose all its **s,** .... Zch 11:17

S

has been going forward in **s**, ... Mt 11:12
and pray for **s** against .... Mt 26:41
all your mind, and all your **s.**' .... Mk 12:30
all his mind, and all his **s.** .... Mk 12:33
and pray for **s** against .... Mk 14:38
soul, all your **s**, and all your .... Lk 10:27
"Pray for **s** against temptation." .... Lk 22:40
up and pray for **s** against .... Lk 22:46
ate some food, his **s** returned.................. Ac 9:19
giving **s** to the churches .... Ac 15:41
giving **s** to all the followers. .... Ac 18:23
able to give you **s**, and it will .... Ac 20:32
You now share the **s** and life of .... Rm 11:17
of God is stronger than human **s.** 1Co 1:25
to people to give them **s**,....................... 1Co 14:3
that were beyond our own **s.** 2Co 1:8
power is the same as the great **s**............. Eph 1:19
your life in Christ give you **s?** .... Php 2:1
Christ, because he gives me **s.** .... Php 4:13
Christ's great **s** that works so .... Col 1:29
other and give each other **s**, ... 1Th 5:11
will give you **s** and will protect 2Th 3:3
Lord, who gave me **s**, because he 1Ti 1:12
who gives us the **s** to do that, ... 2Ti 1:8
and gave me **s** so I could fully 2Ti 4:17
They give us **s** to hold on to the .... Heb 6:18
serve with the **s** God gives so 1Pe 4:11
you have little **s**, but you have .... Rev 3:8
wisdom, and **s**, honor, glory, ... Rev 5:12
and **s** belong to our God forever............. Rev 7:12
with all its **s** in the cup of his .... Rev 14:10

STRENGTHEN

go home now and **s** your army and 1Ki 20:22
s the one you have chosen for .... Ps 80:17
God Most High will **s** her." .... Ps 87:5
my hand and **s** him with my arm .... Ps 89:21
S me with raisins, and refresh .... Sng 2:5
I will **s** the people of Judah and .... Zch 10:6
heaven appeared to him to **s** him. .... Lk 22:43
many things to **s** the followers .... Ac 20:2
will **s** you with his own great .... Col 1:11
We sent him to **s** and encourage.............. 1Th 3:2
to the people, **s** them, and teach 1Ti 4:13
s yourselves with the same way 1Pe 4:11
S yourselves so that you will 1Pe 4:2
S what you have left before it .... Rev 3:2

STRENGTHENED

Horesh and **s** his faith in God. 1Sa 23:16
first one and **s** the area that 2Ch 32:5
and you have **s** those who could............. Job 4:4
your own hands and **s** this child. .... Ps 80:15
Then he will be **s.** .... Ps 110:7
He has **s** your enemies. .... La 2:17
I want them to be **s** and joined .... Col 2:2
not stumble but rather be **s.** .... Heb 12:13
should be **s** by God's grace, ... Heb 13:9

STRENGTHENS

A wise woman **s** her family, ... Pr 14:1

STRETCH

your hand and **s** your hand over.............. Ex 7:19
I will **s** the measuring line of 2Ki 21:13
cannot **s** out the sky like God .... Job 37:18
You **s** out the skies like a tent. .... Ps 104:2
They will **s** from the road along .... Is 9:1
The LORD will **s** out his arm, ... Is 31:3
s it out and make it wider. .... Is 54:2
to **s** out the skies. .... Je 10:12
line will **s** from the Corner .... Je 31:39
to **s** out the skies. .... Je 51:15
I will **s** out my hand against you.............. Eze 35:3
with ivory and **s** out on your .... Am 6:4

STRETCHED

He **s** himself out on top of the.................. 2Ki 4:34
Who **s** a ruler across it? .... Job 38:5
when he **s** the horizon over the .... Pr 8:27
The LORD has **s** his hand over the .... Is 23:11
the skies and **s** them out. .... Is 42:5
my own hands I **s** out the skies, ... Is 45:12
who **s** out the skies and made the .... Is 51:13
He **s** out a net for my feet and .... La 1:13
creatures were **s** out straight .... Eze 1:23
and saw a hand **s** out to me, ... Eze 2:9
It **s** out the shape of a hand and .... Eze 8:3
LORD says, who **s** out the skies,.............. Zch 12:1

STRETCHES

he **s** out and lies down to rest, ... Ge 49:9
He alone **s** out the skies and .... Job 9:8
God **s** the northern sky out over.............. Job 26:7
veil that **s** over all peoples; .... Is 25:7
see the land that **s** far away. .... Is 33:17
He **s** out the skies like a piece.................. Is 40:22

STRETCHING

east of Egypt **s** toward Assyria. .... Ge 25:18
s out the skies by myself and .... Is 44:24

STRICT

The king's command was very **s**, ... Da 3:22
They make **s** rules and try to .... Mt 23:4
Jesus gave them **s** orders not to .... Mk 5:43
You make **s** rules that are very .... Lk 11:46
We gave you **s** orders not to .... Ac 5:28
God is kind and also very **s.** .... Rm 11:22
I had a **s** view of the law, ... Php 3:5

STRICTLY

who teach will be judged more **s.** .... Jam 3:1

STRIKE

I will **s** Egypt with all the .... Ex 3:20
I will **s** the water of the Nile .... Ex 7:17
his walking stick and **s** the dust .... Ex 8:16
you used to **s** the Nile River. .... Ex 17:5
disaster will **s** the Israelites.................... Nu 8:19
Whom will you **s** next?" 1Sa 6:20
said to him, "**S** the ground." 2Ki 13:18
that set day to **s** back at their .... Est 8:13
and commands it to **s** its target. .... Job 36:32
So let ruin **s** them suddenly. .... Ps 35:8
So trouble will **s** them in an .... Pr 6:15
raised to **s** down the people .... Is 5:25
raised to **s** down the people .... Is 9:17
raised to **s** down the people .... Is 9:21
raised to **s** down the people .... Is 10:4
raise his hand to **s** them down. .... Is 19:16
because he will **s** Assyria with a.............. Is 30:31
the north and **s** all the people .... Je 1:14
Let the sword **s** two or three .... Eze 21:14
A sword will **s** his arm and his .... Zch 11:17
disease will **s** the horses,...................... Zch 14:15
we **s** them with our swords?" .... Lk 22:49

STRIKES

the tongue that **s** like a whip, ... Job 5:21
dark or sickness that **s** at noon. .... Ps 91:6
make fun when disaster **s** you, ... Pr 1:26
when trouble **s** you like a .... Pr 1:27

STRIKING

s each other with their swords! 1Sa 14:20

STRING

nurse tied a red **s** on his hand .... Ge 38:28
with the red **s** on his hand was .... Ge 38:30
a piece of red **s**, and a hyssop.................. Le 14:4
wood, the red **s**, and the hyssop;.............. Le 14:6
a piece of red **s**, and a hyssop.................. Le 14:49
and the red **s**, and he will dip .... Le 14:51

and the red s to make the house .... Le 14:52
and a red s and throw them onto .... Nu 19:6
like pieces of burned s. .... Jdg 16:9
he will s his bow and take aim. .... Ps 7:12
the wicked s their bows; .... Ps 11:2

STRINGED
tambourines and s instruments. 1Sa 18:6
With s instruments. .... Ps 3:8
With s instruments. .... Ps 5:12
With s instruments. .... Ps 53:6
With s instruments. .... Ps 54:7
With s instruments. .... Ps 60:12
With s instruments. .... Ps 66:20
With s instruments. .... Ps 75:10
praise him with s instruments .... Ps 150:4
will play songs on s instruments .... Is 38:20
On my s instruments. .... Hab 3:19

STRINGS
like burned s and fell off his .... Jdg 15:14
woven of three s is hard to .... Ec 4:12
to untie the s of his sandals." .... Jn 1:27

STRIP
and put a gold s all around it. .... Ex 25:11
and put a gold s around it. .... Ex 25:24
and put a gold s around it. .... Ex 25:25
Make a s of pure gold and carve .... Ex 28:36
and put a gold s all around the .... Ex 30:3
beneath the gold s on opposite .... Ex 30:4
and he put a gold s around it. .... Ex 37:2
gold and put a gold s around it. .... Ex 37:11
and he put a gold s around it. .... Ex 37:12
They made a s of pure gold, ... Ex 39:30
He put the s of gold, the holy .... Le 8:9
A s of bronze around the top of 1Ki 7:35
came to s the dead soldiers, ... 1Ch 10:8
But I will s Edom bare. .... Je 49:10
and I will s you naked in front .... Eze 16:37
roots and s off its fruit. .... Eze 17:9
S off its leaves and scatter its .... Da 4:14
I will s her naked and leave her .... Hos 2:3
the valley and s her down to her .... Mic 1:6
they s the land and then fly .... Nah 3:16

STRIPES
branches had white s on them. .... Ge 30:37

STRIPPED
Hezekiah s all the gold that 2Ki 18:16
Philistines s Saul's body and 1Ch 10:9
soldiers were s as they lay .... Ps 76:5
land will be s bare because .... Eze 12:19
They s her naked and took away .... Eze 23:10
It has s all the bark off my .... Joe 1:7
God s the spiritual rulers and .... Col 2:15

STRIPS
then cut it into long, thin s. .... Ex 39:3
the oaks and s the leaves off .... Ps 29:9
in and saw the s of linen cloth .... Jn 20:5
and saw the s of linen lying .... Jn 20:6
place from the s of linen. .... Jn 20:7

STRONG
became very s, and the country .... Ex 1:7
many and too s for us to handle! .... Ex 1:9
the people who live there are s. .... Nu 13:28
the people, "Be s and brave, ... Dt 31:7
Joshua, be s and brave! .... Jos 1:6
of the s comes something sweet .... Jdg 14:14
Be a good and s leader. 1Ki 2:2
I will make your kingdom s. 1Ki 9:5
He wants to make them s. 2Ch 16:9
of the LORD will make you s." .... Ne 8:10
because they were too s for me. .... Ps 18:17

saves him with his s right hand. .... Ps 20:6
Like the s bulls of Bashan, ... Ps 22:12
The LORD, s and mighty. .... Ps 24:8
are not very s, but they store .... Pr 30:25
with energy, and her arms are s. .... Pr 31:17
She is s and is respected by the .... Pr 31:25
But God is s and will buy them .... Je 50:34
were hurt, and make the weak s. .... Eze 34:16
But when he was s, his big horn .... Da 8:8
decisions about s nations that .... Mic 4:3
to enter a s person's house .... Mt 12:29
must first tie up the s person. .... Mt 12:29
grew up and became s in spirit. .... Lk 1:80
When a s person with many .... Lk 11:21
who are s in faith should help .... Rm 15:1
We are weak, but you are s. 1Co 4:10
I am weak, then I am truly s. 2Co 12:10
s in the Lord and in his great .... Eph 6:10
stand s and continue to believe 2Th 2:15
be s in the grace we have in 2Ti 2:1
were weak, and yet were made s. .... Heb 11:34

STRONGER
they are s than we are." .... Nu 13:31
What is s than a lion?" .... Jdg 14:18
They were s than lions. 2Sa 1:23
weakness of God is s than human 1Co 1:25
We are not s than he is, are we? 1Co 10:22

STRONGEST
saw where its s defenders were 2Sa 11:16
s soldier does not always win .... Ec 9:11
some of the s soldiers in his .... Da 3:20

STRONGHOLD
as David was hiding in the s. 1Sa 22:4
to David, "Don't stay in the s. 1Sa 22:5
the news, he went down to the s. 2Sa 5:17
At that time David was in the s, ... 2Sa 23:14
At that time David was in a s, ... 1Ch 11:16
David at his s in the desert. 1Ch 12:8
also came to David at his s. 1Ch 12:16

STRONGHOLDS
palaces and destroyed all her s. .... La 2:5
hiding in the s and caves will .... Eze 33:27
the land and pull down your s; .... Am 3:11

STRONGLY
of that country s warned us, ' .... Ge 43:3
border, which was s defended. .... Nu 21:24
The LORD spoke s. The wind blew 2Sa 22:16
I s advise you to save yourself 1Ki 1:12
Would he not argue s against me? .... Job 23:6
are joined s to one another; .... Job 41:17
You spoke s against the foreign .... Ps 9:5
LORD, you spoke s. The wind blew .... Ps 18:15
when you spoke s and .... Ps 76:6
they will know how s I felt. .... Eze 5:13
warned them s, saying, "Don't .... Mt 9:30
at once, but he warned him s, ... Mk 1:43
But Jesus s warned them not to .... Mk 3:12
there, s accusing Jesus. .... Lk 23:10
He argued very s with the Jews .... Ac 18:28
I s encouraged him to visit you 1Co 16:12
because he fought s against our 2Ti 4:15

STRUCK
They s those outside the door .... Ge 19:11
he s Jacob's hip and put it out .... Ge 32:25
walking stick and s the water in .... Ex 7:20
was in his hand and s the dust .... Ex 8:17
sickness the LORD's people .... Nu 31:16
in the fields and s them down. .... Jdg 9:44
great defeat Jephthah s them .... Jdg 11:33
men of Gilead s them down .... Jdg 12:4
are the ones who s the Egyptians 1Sa 4:8

S

STRUGGLE

in the city were **s** with terror 1Sa 5:11
the LORD had **s** them down. 1Sa 6:19
Jonathan **s** down the Philistines 1Sa 14:13
later the LORD **s** Nabal and he 1Sa 25:38
Absalom and **s** him and killed him 2Sa 18:15
So Jehoash the **s** the ground three 2Ki 13:18
should have **s** five or six times! 2Ki 13:19
you would have **s** Aram until you 2Ki 13:19
The LORD **s** Uzziah with a skin 2Ki 15:5
Abijah's army is Israel so that 2Ch 13:17
LORD **s** Jeroboam, and he died. 2Ch 13:20
They are **s** down, and then they .... Job 34:20
You have **s** my enemies on the .... Ps 3:7
they will suddenly be **s** down. .... Ps 64:7
he **s** down the best young men of .... Ps 78:31
He **s** down his enemies and .... Ps 78:66
He **s** down their grapevines and .... Ps 105:33
to the one who had **s** them; .... Is 9:13
of Babylon **s** people in anger .... Is 14:6
the king who **s** you is now dead. .... Is 14:29
Disasters **s** them,'" says the .... Je 2:3
You **s** the people of Judah, ... Je 5:3
He **s** the servant of the high .... Mt 26:51
out his sword and **s** the servant .... Mk 14:47
And one of them **s** the servant of .... Lk 22:50
pulled it out and **s** the servant .... Jn 18:10
angel **s** Peter on the side and .... Ac 12:7
and a third of the stars were **s**. .... Rev 8:12

STRUGGLE

But when you **s**, you will break .... Ge 27:40
so why should I **s** for no reason? .... Job 9:29
All my days are a **s**; .... Job 14:14
help those who **s** under the .... Mt 23:4
I work and **s**, using Christ's .... Col 1:29
This is why we work and **s**: 1Ti 4:10
You had a hard **s** with many .... Heb 10:32

STRUGGLED

the babies **s** inside her. .... Ge 25:22
I have **s** hard with my sister, ... Ge 30:8

STRUGGLES

stayed with me through my **s**. .... Lk 22:28
you, you saw the **s** I had, and .... Php 1:30
about the **s** I am having now. .... Php 1:30
are having the same kind of **s**. .... Php 1:30
but your **s** have not yet caused .... Heb 12:4

STRUGGLING

their work and **s** here on earth? .... Ec 2:22
you will always be **s** for more, ... Ec 4:6
saw his followers **s** hard to row .... Mk 6:48
You are **s** against sin, but your .... Heb 12:4

STRUT

are three things that **s** proudly, ... Pr 30:29

STUBBORN

of Egypt was **s** and refused to .... Ex 13:15
Our son is **s** and turns against .... Dt 21:20
people who are **s** and who do not .... Eze 2:4

STUBBORNLY

They **s** charge at God with thick, ... Job 15:26
They **s** do only what they want to .... Je 13:10

STUCK

corner that **s** out like a horn .... Ex 37:25
with his spear **s** in the ground 1Sa 26:7
tired his hand **s** to his sword. 2Sa 23:10
if their tongues **s** to the roof .... Job 29:10
is like a thorn **s** in the hand .... Pr 26:9
your feet were **s** in the mud, ... Je 38:22
The dirty scum **s** inside it may .... Eze 24:11
Now I will make you get **s**, ... Am 2:13
wagon loaded with grain gets **s**. .... Am 2:13

STUDENT

teacher and the **s**, had to throw 1Ch 25:8
teaches me to listen like a **s**. .... Is 50:4
A **s** is not better than his. .... Mt 10:24
s should be satisfied to become .... Mt 10:25
A **s** is not better than the .... Lk 6:40
but the **s** who has been fully .... Lk 6:40
I was a **s** of Gamaliel, who .... Ac 22:3

STUDIED

I **s** and tried very hard to find .... Ec 7:25
thought about, **s**, and set in. .... Ec 12:9
that people had written and **s**. .... Da 1:17
Since I myself have **s** everything .... Lk 1:3
This man has never **s** in school. .... Jn 7:15
Silas said and **s** the Scriptures .... Ac 17:11

STUDY

S it day and night to be sure to .... Jos 1:8
send them out to **s** the land. .... Jos 18:4
Go and **s** the land and describe .... Jos 18:8
sent them to **s** the city and spy 2Sa 10:3
David sent them to **s** the land 1Ch 19:3
they sat down to **s** each case. .... Ezr 10:16
They gathered to **s** the words of .... Ne 8:13
ashamed when I **s** your commands. .... Ps 119:6
your orders and **s** your ways. .... Ps 119:15
and too much **s** will make you .... Ec 12:12
So let those who **s** the sky— .... Is 47:13
You carefully **s** the Scriptures. .... Jn 5:39
S the Scriptures, and you will. .... Jn 7:52
much **s** has driven you crazy!" .... Ac 26:24
carefully **s** God's perfect law .... Jam 1:25
and they continue to **s** it. .... Jam 1:25

STUMBLE

me like a deer that does not **s**; 2Sa 22:34
he makes them **s** like drunks. .... Job 12:25
me like a deer that does not **s**; .... Ps 18:33
If they **s**, they will not fall, ... Ps 37:24
even see what makes them **s**. .... Pr 4:19
a stone that causes people to **s**, ... Is 8:14
The earth will **s** around like .... Is 24:20
they **s** from drinking too much .... Is 28:7
They **s** from too much beer. .... Is 28:7
judges **s** when they make their .... Is 28:7
and the one who helps will **s**, ... Is 31:3
a desert, the people did not **s**. .... Is 63:13
and sons will **s** over them .... Je 6:21
If you **s** in a country that is .... Je 12:5
my anger and **s** about and act .... Je 25:16
even road where they will not **s**. .... Je 31:9
They **s** and fall in the north, ... Je 46:6
Proud Babylon will **s** and fall, ... Je 50:32
Israel will **s** because of their .... Hos 5:5
of Judah will **s** with them. .... Hos 5:5
officers, but they **s** on the way. .... Nah 2:5
People **s** over the dead bodies. .... Nah 3:3
that does not **s** so I can walk .... Hab 3:19
who do not **s** in their faith .... Mt 11:6
you will all **s** in your faith .... Mt 26:31
else may **s** in their faith .... Mt 26:33
You will all **s** in your faith, ... Mk 14:27
else may **s** in their faith, ... Mk 14:29
who do not **s** in their faith .... Lk 7:23
will not **s**, because he can see .... Jn 11:9
stone that causes people to **s**. .... Rm 9:32
a stone that causes people to **s**, ... Rm 9:33
them to **s** and be paid back. .... Rm 11:9
the Jews to **s** and is foolishness 1Co 1:23
the weak will not **s** but rather. .... Heb 12:13
a stone that causes people to **s**, ... 1Pe 2:8

They s because they do not..................... 1Pe 2:8
cause anyone to s in his faith.................. 1Jn 2:10

STUMBLED
floor of Nacon, the oxen s. 2Sa 6:6
Kidon, the oxen s, and Uzzah 1Ch 13:9
Not one of his people s. .... Ps 105:37
They s, and no one helped. .... Ps 107:12
They s and fell like people who .... Ps 107:27
happen because Jerusalem has s, ... Is 3:8
drank the whole cup until you s. .... Is 51:17
idols and have s in what they do .... Je 18:15
They s again and again and fell .... Je 46:16
and boys s under loads of wood. .... La 5:13
s over the stone that causes .... Rm 9:32

STUMBLES
s because there is no light to .... Jn 11:10

STUMBLING
like drunk people s in their own .... Is 19:14

STUMP
and its s dies in the dirt, ... Job 14:8
an oak tree whose s is left when.............. Is 6:13
be like a s that will sprout .... Is 6:13
will grow from a s of a tree; .... Is 11:1
But leave the s and its roots in .... Da 4:15
But leave the s and its roots in .... Da 4:23
Since the s of the tree and its .... Da 4:26
waste and made my fig tree a s. .... Joe 1:7

SUAH
sons were S, Harnepher, Shual 1Ch 7:36

SUBTRACT
Then he will s that number from .... Le 27:18

SUCATHITES
and S and were from the Kenite.............. 1Ch 2:55

SUCCESS
will not have s when you plant .... Le 26:16
their peace or s as long as you .... Dt 23:6
will give you s, and there will................. Dt 30:5
today I offer you life and s,.................... Dt 30:15
Power is not the key to s. 1Sa 2:9
He had great s in everything he 1Sa 18:14
me when the LORD brings you s." 1Sa 25:31
he had s in everything he did.................. 2Ki 18:7
son of Jesse. S, success to you. 1Ch 12:18
Jesse. Success, s to you. 1Ch 12:18
S to those who help you, because 1Ch 12:18
you obey them, you will have s. 1Ch 22:13
He had s in doing everything he.............. 2Ch 7:11
So they built and had s. 2Ch 14:7
obeyed the LORD, God gave him s. 2Ch 26:5
his work for God. So he had s. 2Ch 31:21
not wish for their peace or s. .... Ezr 9:12
Give me, your servant, s today; .... Ne 1:11
God of heaven will give us s. .... Ne 2:20
trick others so they have no s. .... Job 5:12
because s has been taken away .... Job 6:13
The s of the wicked is not their .... Job 21:16
the LORD gave him s again. .... Job 42:10
Give us s in what we do; .... Ps 90:17
yes, give us s in what we do. .... Ps 90:17
LORD give you s, and may he give............ Ps 115:14
he give you and your children s.............. Ps 115:14
please, LORD, give us s. .... Ps 118:25
you do, and he will give you s. .... Pr 3:6
So are wealth and lasting s. .... Pr 8:18
but good people enjoy s. .... Pr 13:21
an evil heart will find no s, ... Pr 17:20
loyal finds life, s, and honor. .... Pr 21:21
all our s is because of what you .... Is 26:12
do not have s, and all their .... Je 10:21

SUCCESSES
did and all his s are written 1Ki 16:27
these wars and his s are written 1Ki 22:45

SUCCOTH
traveled from Rameses to S. .... Ex 12:37
and measure off the Valley of S............... Ps 60:6

SUCK
will s the poison of snakes,..................... Job 20:16

SUDDEN
If the whip brings s death, ... Job 9:23
you and s danger frightens .... Job 22:10
won't be afraid of s trouble; .... Pr 3:25
like a s flood of water pouring .... Is 28:2

SUDDENLY
many times will s be hurt beyond .... Pr 29:1
S, the Lord you are looking for .... Mal 3:1
seizes my son, and s he screams. .... Lk 9:39
that day might come on you s, ... Lk 21:34
S a noise like a strong, blowing .... Ac 2:2
from heaven s flashed around.................. Ac 9:3

SUE
So people s each other in court; .... Hos 10:4
someone wants to s you in court .... Mt 5:40

SUFFER
Son of Man must s many things............... Mk 8:31
that the Christ would s and rise .... Lk 24:46
that his Christ would s and die. .... Ac 3:18
how much he must s for my name." .... Ac 9:16
We must s many things to enter .... Ac 14:22
But we must s as Christ suffered .... Rm 8:17
up, the builder will s loss. 1Co 3:15
choose us to s his anger but to 1Th 5:9
But s with me for the Good News. 2Ti 1:8
He chose to s with God's people.............. Heb 11:25
But if you s for doing good, ... 1Pe 2:20
Do not s for murder, theft, or 1Pe 4:15

SUFFERED
because I s for the foolish .... Je 31:19
She had s very much from many .... Mk 5:26
and the people s very much. .... Ac 7:11
he himself s and was tempted. .... Heb 2:18
So Jesus also s outside the city .... Heb 13:12
because Christ s for you and 1Pe 2:21
person who has s in the body is 1Pe 4:1
and have s troubles for my .... Rev 2:3

SUFFERING
take away this cup of s. .... Lk 22:42
the honor of s disgrace for .... Ac 5:41
trouble and s to everyone who .... Rm 2:9
to salvation perfect through s. .... Heb 2:10
is having the same kinds of s.................. 1Pe 5:9
of us share with Christ in s, ... Rev 1:9

SUFFERINGS
I would have died from my s. .... Ps 119:92
The s we have now are nothing .... Rm 8:18
or problems or s or hunger or .... Rm 8:35
share in the many s of Christ.................. 2Co 1:5
patiently the same s we have.................. 2Co 1:6
that you share in our s and also 2Co 1:7
hard times, s, and all kinds.................... 2Co 12:10
because of the s I am having for.............. Eph 3:13
My s are for your glory. .... Eph 3:13
share in his s and become like .... Php 3:10
I am happy in my s for you. .... Col 1:24
had a hard struggle with many s, ... Heb 10:32
So hold on through your s, ... Heb 12:7
advance about the s of Christ 1Pe 1:11
glory that would follow those s. 1Pe 1:11
in Christ's s so that you will 1Pe 4:13
seen Christ's s, and I will 1Pe 5:1

S

SUFFERS

After his soul **s** many things, ... Is 53:11
where she **s** and works hard. .... La 1:3
and Jerusalem **s** terribly. .... La 1:4
If one part of the body **s,** 1Co 12:26

SUGGEST

This is what I **s:** Gather all the 2Sa 17:11
We **s** you search the records of .... Ezr 4:15

SUGGESTED

what Ahithophel had **s** to Absalom 2Sa 17:15
to them what he himself had **s.** 2Sa 17:15
Israel promise to do what was **s;** .... Ezr 10:5
captives did what was **s.** .... Ezr 10:16
so King Xerxes did as Memucan **s.** .... Est 1:21
the king's personal servants **s,** .... Est 2:2
what Hegai **s** she should take .... Est 2:15
leave out anything you have **s.**" .... Est 6:10

SUGGESTION

liked this **s,** so he ordered .... Est 5:14

SUITABLE

I must find a **s** home for you, ... Ru 3:1

SUKKITES

of Libyans, **S,** and Cushites 2Ch 12:3

SULFUR

rain of burning **s** down from the............. Ge 19:24
and **s** is scattered over their .... Job 18:15
and burning **s** on the wicked. .... Ps 11:6
stream of burning **s** and set it .... Is 30:33
Its dirt will be like burning **s.** .... Is 34:9
hailstones and burning **s** on Gog, ... Eze 38:22
fire and **s** rained down from the .... Lk 17:29
dark blue, and yellow like **s.** .... Rev 9:17
s coming out of their mouths. .... Rev 9:17
the fire, the smoke, and the **s.** .... Rev 9:18
with burning **s** before the holy .... Rev 14:10
lake of fire that burns with **s.** .... Rev 19:20
lake of burning **s** with the beast .... Rev 20:10
place in the lake of burning **s.** .... Rev 21:8

SUM

had bought for a **s** of money from .... Ac 7:16
the others put up a **s** of money. .... Ac 17:9

SUMMER

cold and hot, **s** and winter, day .... Ge 8:22
in the room above his **s** palace. .... Jdg 3:20
was gone as in the **s** heat. .... Ps 32:4
you created **s** and winter. .... Ps 74:17
food in the **s** and gather their .... Pr 6:8
shouldn't snow in **s** or rain at .... Pr 26:1
but they store up food in the **s.** .... Pr 30:25
Birds will feed on them all **s,** .... Is 18:6
will be like the first fig of **s.** .... Is 28:4
and no **s** fruit to gather. .... Is 32:10
s has ended, and we have not .... Je 8:20
the wine, the **s** fruit, and the .... Je 40:10
harvest of wine and **s** fruit. .... Je 40:12
together with the **s** house. .... Am 3:15
showed me: a basket of **s** fruit. .... Am 8:1
I said, "A basket of **s** fruit." .... Am 8:2
and all the **s** fruit has been .... Mic 7:1
It will flow **s** and winter. .... Zch 14:8
appear, you know **s** is near. .... Mt 24:32
appear, you know **s** is near. .... Mk 13:28
appear, you know that **s** is near. .... Lk 21:30

SUMMERTIME

the coolness of snow in the **s.** .... Pr 25:13
on a threshing floor in the **s;** .... Da 2:35

SUMS

people gave large **s** of money. .... Mk 12:41

SUN

As the **s** was going down, Abram .... Ge 15:12
best fruits that the **s** brings, ... Dt 33:14
S, stand still over Gibeon. .... Jos 10:12
else before the **s** sets!" 2Sa 3:35
were for the worship of the **s.** 2Ki 23:11
sky is like a home for the **s.** .... Ps 19:4
the rising to the setting **s.** .... Ps 50:1
LORD God is like a **s** and shield; .... Ps 84:11
and the **s** always knows when to .... Ps 104:19
When the **s** rises, they leave and .... Ps 104:22
that protects you from the **s.** .... Ps 121:5
If I rise with the **s** in the east .... Ps 139:9
Praise him, **s** and moon. Praise .... Ps 148:3
The **s** rises, the sun sets, and .... Ec 1:5
sun rises, the **s** sets, and then .... Ec 1:5
never saw the **s** and never knew .... Ec 6:5
from the **s,** moon, and stars .... Ec 12:2
When the **s** comes up, the king of .... Hos 10:15
The **s** and the moon will become .... Joe 3:15
will shine on you like the **s,** .... Mal 4:2
He causes the **s** to rise on good .... Mt 5:45
face became bright like the **s,** .... Mt 17:2
days, 'the **s** will grow dark, ... Mt 24:29
The **s** will become dark, the moon .... Ac 2:20
not need the **s** or the moon to .... Rev 21:23
of a lamp or the light of the **s,** .... Rev 22:5

SUNG

when songs were **s** to God. 1Ch 16:42
about which people have **s.** .... Job 36:24

SUNK

sea and have **s** to the bottom. .... Eze 27:34

SUNRISE

Tent, toward the **s,** in front .... Nu 3:38
spears from **s** till the stars .... Ne 4:21
to the brightness of your **s.** .... Is 60:3
Like the light at **s,** a great and .... Joe 2:2
soon after **s,** the women were .... Mk 16:2

SUNSET

must give it back to him by **s,** .... Ex 22:26
to the west, toward the **s.** .... Dt 11:30
and at **s** he may come back into .... Dt 23:11
the coat back at **s,** because your .... Dt 24:13
Pay them each day before **s,** .... Dt 24:15
At **s** Joshua told his men to take............. Jos 8:29
At **s** Joshua told his men to take............. Jos 10:27
Before **s** on the seventh day of .... Jdg 14:18
fought them from **s** until the 1Sa 30:17
Near **s** a cry went out through 1Ki 22:36
evening. Then he died at **s.** 2Ch 18:34
doors be shut at **s** before the .... Ne 13:19
dawn and **s** many people are .... Job 4:20
hard until **s** trying to think .... Da 6:14
and quicker than wolves at **s.** .... Hab 1:8
At **s** you say we will have good .... Mt 16:2

SUNSHINE

He is like **s** after a rain that 2Sa 23:4
plants in the **s** that spread .... Job 8:16
S is sweet; it is good to see .... Ec 11:7
like heat in the **s,** like the dew .... Is 18:4
will be bright like **s** at noon. .... Is 58:10

SUPERVISOR

of Hilkiah, the **s** in the Temple. .... Ne 11:11

SUPERVISORS

hundred fifty **s** over the people 1Ki 9:23
the money to the **s** of the work 2Ki 22:5
workers and **s** at the Temple." 2Ki 22:9
Shimei were over these **s:** 2Ch 31:13
gave it to the **s** of the work 2Ch 34:10
Their **s** were Jahath and Obadiah, ... 2Ch 34:12

it to the s and the workers." 2Ch 34:17
would not work under their s. .... Ne 3:5
the king choose s in every state .... Est 2:3
chose three men as s over those .... Da 6:2
and Daniel was one of the s. .... Da 6:2
The s were to ensure that the .... Da 6:2
than the other s and governors, ... Da 6:3
the other s and governors tried .... Da 6:4
So the s and governors went as a .... Da 6:6
The s, assistant governors, ... Da 6:7

SUPH
were in the desert area near S, ... Dt 1:1

SUPHAH
. . . and Waheb in S, and the .... Nu 21:14

SUPPER
same way, after s, Jesus took .... Lk 22:20
Jesus at the s and had said, ... Jn 21:20
not really eating the Lord's S................. 1Co 11:20

SUPPLIED
David s a large amount of iron 1Ch 22:3
He also s more bronze than could 1Ch 22:3
and he s more cedar logs than 1Ch 22:4
have s about seven and one-half.............. 1Ch 22:14

SUPPLIES
the people, 'Get your s ready. .... Jos 1:11
These will find s for the army. .... Jdg 20:10
the man who kept the s and ran 1Sa 17:22
hundred men stayed with the s. 1Sa 25:13
stayed with the s as for the one 1Sa 30:24
grain and s and cities for 1Ki 9:19
towns for storing grain and s................. 2Ch 8:4
he put commanders and s of food, ... 2Ch 11:11
He gave plenty of s to his sons, ... 2Ch 11:23
towns for storing s in Judah. 2Ch 17:12
He kept many s in the towns of 2Ch 17:13
found many s, much clothing,................. 2Ch 20:25
silver and gold, s and cattle, ... Ezr 1:4
gold, along with s, cattle, ... Ezr 1:6
and gather their s at harvest. .... Pr 6:8

SUPPLY
and Rameses as s centers for the .... Ex 1:11
and have captured its water s. 2Sa 12:27
to cut off the s of bread to .... Eze 4:16
I will cut off your s of food. .... Eze 5:16
cut off their s of food and send .... Eze 14:13
responsibility to s the burnt .... Eze 45:17
The ruler will s the sin .... Eze 45:17
the ruler will s the same things .... Eze 45:25

SUPPORT
land could not s both of them................. Ge 13:6
the boards that s the whole temple........... Hab 2:11
that you do not s the root, ... Rm 11:18
s and foundation of the truth.................. 1Ti 3:15
strong and s you and keep you 1Pe 5:10

SUPPORTED
long time you have s the other .... Jos 22:3
pillars that s the whole temple. .... Jdg 16:29
me, but the LORD has s me! 1Sa 25:39
Put and Libya s her. .... Nah 3:9

SUPPORTERS
The s of David's family became 2Sa 3:1
the s of Saul's family became 2Sa 3:1
war between the s of Saul's 2Sa 3:6
family and the s of David's.................... 2Sa 3:6
main leader among the s of Saul. 2Sa 3:6

SUPPOSE
S two men are fighting and hit a .... Ex 21:22
I s the whole world would not be .... Jn 21:25
S one of you who has knowledge 1Co 8:10

S someone comes into your church .... Jam 2:2
S someone has enough to live and 1Jn 3:17

SUPPOSED
Judah were s to give up eating .... Je 36:9
death to those who are s to die. .... Je 43:11
People who were s to be his good .... Da 11:26

SUPREME
the LORD is s, he takes care .... Ps 138:6

SUR
of you will be at the S Gate, ... 2Ki 11:6

SURE
know for s that you will be................... Nu 32:23
s promise that he will not take .... Ps 132:11
He makes s that justice is done, ... Pr 2:8
watching to make s my words come .... Je 1:12
who makes s we have the harvest .... Je 5:24
the holy and s blessings that I .... Ac 13:34
for the soul, s and strong. .... Heb 6:19

SURFACE
his feet was a s that looked as .... Ex 24:10
red and goes into the wall's s, ... Le 14:37
and even the s of the ocean is................ Job 38:30
he will ruin the s of the land .... Is 24:1

SURRENDER
The LORD will s Zebah and .... Jdg 8:7
the LORD did not s David to him. 1Sa 23:14
'If you s to the officers of the .... Je 38:17
you refuse to s to the officers .... Je 38:18
if you refuse to s to the .... Je 38:21

SURRENDERED
king of Judah s to the king of................ 2Ki 24:12
those who had s to the king of 2Ki 25:11
who had s to him earlier, ... Je 39:9
Babylon has s, her towers have .... Je 50:15
those who had s to the king of .... Je 52:15

SURRENDERS
of Jerusalem and s to the .... Je 21:9
But everyone who s to the .... Je 38:2

SURROUND
me, from my enemies who s me. .... Ps 17:9

SURROUNDED
part of Sodom s Lot's house. .... Ge 19:4
men of the city s the house and .... Jdg 19:22
shelter, s by fog and clouds. 2Sa 22:12
around him, s by fog and clouds............. Ps 18:11
People have s me like angry .... Ps 22:12
Israel has s me with lies;...................... Hos 11:12
because we are s and attacked. .... Mic 5:1
We are s by a great cloud of .... Heb 12:1

SURROUNDS
the LORD s his people now and .... Ps 125:2
This sword s the people to be .... Eze 21:14

SURVIVE
no one can s his strong anger. .... Nah 1:6
no one can s when he comes. .... Mal 3:2

SURVIVED
into the sea. Not one of them s. .... Ex 14:28

SUSAH
Ziklag, Beth Marcaboth, Hazar S, ... Jos 19:5

SUSANNA
Herod's house); S; and many .... Lk 8:3

SUSI
of Joseph), Gaddi son of S;................... Nu 13:11

SUSIM
Marcaboth, Hazar S, Beth Biri, ... 1Ch 4:31

S

SUSPECTS

jealousy and s she has sinned— .... Nu 5:14
jealous because he s his wife. .... Nu 5:30

SWALLOW

The ground will open and s them. .... Nu 16:30
The earth will s us, too!" .... Nu 16:34
me alone even long enough to s? .... Job 7:19
your anger you will s them up, ... Ps 21:9
the deep water s me or the grave .... Ps 69:15
Let's s them alive, as death .... Pr 1:12
let's s them whole, as the grave .... Pr 1:12
caused a big fish to s Jonah, ... Jnh 1:17
when the wicked s up people who .... Hab 1:13

SWALLOWED

But Aaron's stick s theirs. .... Ex 7:12
and the earth s our enemies. .... Ex 15:12
earth opened and s them and all .... Nu 16:32
opened up and s them and Korah; .... Nu 26:10
the ground opened up and s them, ... Dt 11:6
have s riches, but they will .... Job 20:15
Would a person ask to be s up? .... Job 37:20
up and s Dathan and closed .... Ps 106:17
they would have s us alive. .... Ps 124:3
like a giant snake that s us. .... Je 51:34
make him spit out what he has s. .... Je 51:44
The Lord s up without mercy all .... La 2:2
like an enemy; he s up Israel. .... La 2:5
He s up all her palaces and .... La 2:5
They say, "We have s you up. .... La 2:16

SWALLOWING

its mouth and s the river that .... Rev 12:16

SWALLOWS

a home, and the s have nests. .... Ps 84:3
sparrows or s that fly around .... Pr 26:2
of a drink and then s a camel! .... Mt 23:24

SWAMP

cannot grow where there is no s, ... Job 8:11
by the tall grass in the s. .... Job 40:21

SWAMPLANDS

captured, and the s are burning. .... Je 51:32

SWAMPS

fit only for owls and for s. .... Is 14:23
But its s and marshes will not .... Eze 47:11

SWARM

creatures that s on the earth, ... Ge 7:21
lion and found a s of bees and .... Jdg 14:8
surrounded me like a s of bees, ... Ps 118:12
will be like a s of locusts. .... Je 51:14
they are like a s of locusts. .... Je 51:27
He was forming a s of locusts, ... Am 7:1

SWARMING

have left, the s locusts have .... Joe 1:4
what the s locusts have left, ... Joe 1:4
those s locusts and hopping .... Joe 2:25
grow in number like s locusts! .... Nah 3:15

SWARMS

I will send s of flies into your .... Ex 8:21
and great s of flies came into .... Ex 8:24
S of flies covered all the .... Ex 10:14
animals like s of locusts to .... Jdg 6:5
are like s of locusts that .... Nah 3:17

SWAY

it and go and s over the other .... Jdg 9:9
and go and s over the other .... Jdg 9:11
it and go and s over the trees?' .... Jdg 9:13

SWAYING

be like reeds s in the water. 1Ki 14:15
swinging and s from ropes. .... Job 28:4

SWEAR

You s by the LORD's name and .... Is 48:1
But I tell you, never s an oath. .... Mt 5:34
place a curse on himself and s, ... Mt 26:74
place a curse on himself and s, ... Mk 14:71
than themselves when they s. .... Heb 6:16

SWEARS

If he s an oath that he is not 1Ki 8:31
If he s an oath that he is not 2Ch 6:22
The person who s by the altar is .... Mt 23:20
the person who s by the Temple .... Mt 23:21
The person who s by heaven is .... Mt 23:22

SWEAT

will s and work hard for your .... Ge 3:19
His s was like drops of blood .... Lk 22:44

SWEEP

I will s Babylon as with a broom .... Is 14:23
will light a lamp, s the house, ... Lk 15:8

SWEEPS

clever traps and s away the .... Job 5:13
because it s them out of their .... Job 27:21

SWEET

two handfuls of s incense that .... Le 16:12
stop making my s and good fruit .... Jdg 9:11
the strong comes something s." .... Jdg 14:14
he is the s singer of Israel: 2Sa 23:1
enjoy good food and s drinks. .... Ne 8:10
Your promises are s to me, ... Ps 119:103
man's wife may seem s as honey; .... Pr 5:3
made my bed smell s with myrrh, ... Pr 7:17
food may taste s at first, ... Pr 20:17
from the honeycomb tastes s. .... Pr 24:13
his fruit is s to my taste. .... Sng 2:3
His mouth is s to kiss, and I .... Sng 5:16
think sour is s and sweet is .... Is 5:20
And the s smell from the perfume .... Jn 12:3
We are the s smell of Christ 2Co 2:15
mouth it will be s as honey." .... Rev 10:9
my mouth it tasted s as honey, ... Rev 10:10

SWEET-SMELLING

himself for us as a s offering .... Eph 5:2
It is like a s sacrifice offered .... Php 4:18

SWEETER

and said, "What is s than honey? .... Jdg 14:18
They are s than honey, even the .... Ps 19:10
sweet to me, s than honey in my .... Ps 119:103
Stolen water is s, and food .... Pr 9:17

SWEETLY

wine go down s for my lover; .... Sng 7:9

SWELL

out, and your feet did not s. .... Dt 8:4
out, and their feet did not s. .... Ne 9:21
Paul would s up or fall down .... Ac 28:6

SWELLING

have on his skin a s or a rash .... Le 13:2
there is a white s in the skin, ... Le 13:10
and the skin looks raw in the s, ... Le 13:10
is a white s or a bright red .... Le 13:19
it is the s from the burn. .... Le 13:28
If the s of the sore on his bald .... Le 13:43
disease, fever, s, heat, lack of .... Dt 28:22

SWELLINGS

s, rashes, or bright spots on .... Le 14:56

SWEPT

the LORD s them away into the .... Ex 14:27
The Kishon River s Sisera's men .... Jdg 5:21
attackers that s down and stole .... Job 1:17
s away on the day of God's anger. .... Job 20:28
they are s away by terrors. .... Ps 73:19

They would have **s** us away like a .... Ps 124:5
I have **s** away your sins like a .... Is 44:22
army will be **s** away in defeat; .... Da 11:26
They will be **s** away as if by a .... Hos 4:19
wheat that was **s** up from the .... Am 8:6
still empty, **s** clean, and made .... Mt 12:44
finds that house **s** clean and .... Lk 11:25
His tail **s** a third of the stars .... Rev 12:4

SWIFTLY

They will come **s** like birds from .... Hos 11:11

SWIFTS

storks, doves, **s**, and thrushes .... Je 8:7

SWIM

of them could **s** away and escape. .... Ac 27:42
everyone who could **s** to jump .... Ac 27:43
the water first and **s** to land. .... Ac 27:43

SWIMMING

in it like a person who is **s**. .... Is 25:11
it was deep enough for **s**; .... Eze 47:5

SWIMS

When it **s**, it leaves a shining .... Job 41:32

SWING

will not **s** out from the holy .... Ex 28:28
would not **s** out from the holy .... Ex 39:21
you when I **s** my sword in front .... Eze 32:10
two pieces that would **s** open. .... Eze 41:24
S the cutting tool, because the .... Joe 3:13

SWINGING

far from people, **s** and swaying .... Job 28:4

SWINGS

to cut wood and **s** an ax to cut .... Dt 19:5
better than the person who **s** it. .... Is 10:15

SWIRL

his command they **s** around over .... Job 37:12

SWIRLING

It will come **s** down on the heads .... Je 23:19

SWOOP

it will **s** down like an eagle. .... Dt 28:49

SWOOPING

like eagles **s** down to feed. .... Job 9:26
is like an eagle **s** down and .... Je 49:22
like an eagle **s** down for food .... Hab 1:8

SWOOPS

The enemy **s** down on the LORD's .... Hos 8:1

SWORD

angels and a **s** of fire that .... Ge 3:24
You will live by using your **s**, ... Ge 27:40
people with my **s** and my bow." .... Ge 48:22
I'll pull out my **s**, and my hand .... Ex 15:9
must put on his **s** and go through .... Le 26:7
them, killing them with your **s**. .... Le 26:7
and kill them with your **s**. .... Le 26:8
pull out my **s** and destroy you .... Le 26:33
were chasing them with a **s**, ... Le 26:36
were chasing them with a **s**, ... Le 26:37
was killed by a **s** or who died .... Nu 19:16
the road with a **s** in his hand, ... Nu 22:23
I wish I had a **s** in my hand! .... Nu 22:29
in the road with his **s** drawn. .... Nu 22:31
Balaam son of Beor with a **s**. .... Nu 31:8
must kill with a **s** everyone who .... Dt 13:15
well as the animals, with a **s**. .... Dt 13:15
In the streets the **s** will kill; .... Dt 32:25
I will sharpen my flashing **s**, ... Dt 32:41
my **s** will eat their flesh. .... Dt 32:42
and helper, your glorious **s**. .... Dt 33:29
of him with a **s** in his hand. .... Jos 5:13
with the **s** every living thing .... Jos 6:21

made himself a **s** with two edges, ... Jdg 3:16
took out the **s** that was tied to .... Jdg 3:21
Then he stabbed the **s** deep into .... Jdg 3:21
king's fat covered the whole **s**, ... Jdg 3:22
so Ehud left the **s** in Eglon. .... Jdg 3:22
LORD defeated them with the **s**, ... Jdg 4:15
is about the **s** of Gideon son .... Jdg 7:14
"A **s** for the LORD and for Gideon!" .... Jdg 7:20
so he did not take out his **s**. .... Jdg 8:20
Take out your **s** and kill me. .... Jdg 9:54
all of Agag's army with the **s**. 1Sa 15:8
Your **s** made other mothers lose 1Sa 15:33
on Saul's **s** and tried to walk 1Sa 17:39
to me using a **s** and two spears. 1Sa 17:45
not even have a **s** in his hand. 1Sa 17:50
took Goliath's **s** out of its 1Sa 17:51
including his **s**, bow, and belt. 1Sa 18:4
Do you have a spear or **s** here? 1Sa 21:8
I left without my **s** or any other 1Sa 21:8
The **s** of Goliath the Philistine, ... 1Sa 21:9
no other **s** here but that one. 1Sa 21:9
There is no other **s** like it. 1Sa 21:9
and gave him the **s** of Goliath 1Sa 22:10
You gave him bread and a **s**! 1Sa 22:13
With the **s** he killed men, women, ... 1Sa 22:19
Pull out your **s** and kill me. 1Sa 31:4
took his own **s** and threw himself 1Sa 31:4
he threw himself on his own **s**, ... 1Sa 31:5
Saul's **s** did not fail to wound 2Sa 1:22
Joab, "Must the **s** kill forever? 2Sa 2:26
The **s** kills everyone the same. 2Sa 11:25
with the **s** of the Ammonites 2Sa 12:9
your family who will die by a **s**, ... 2Sa 12:10
that held his **s** in its case. 2Sa 20:8
his **s** fell out of its case. 2Sa 20:8
watching the **s** in Joab's hand. 2Sa 20:10
Joab pushed the **s** into Amasa's 2Sa 20:10
and one-half pounds and a new **s**. 2Sa 21:16
tired his hand stuck to his **s**. 2Sa 23:10
could use the **s** and five hundred 2Sa 24:9
sent his servants to get a **s** 1Ki 3:24
all the prophets with a **s**. 1Ki 19:1
who escapes from Hazael's **s**, ... 1Ki 19:17
who escapes from Jehu's **s** 1Ki 19:17
captured with your **s** and bow. 2Ki 6:22
Baal with the **s** and threw their 2Ki 10:25
and kill with a **s** anyone who 2Ki 11:15
death with the **s** at the palace. 2Ki 11:20
him to die by the **s** there.'" 2Ki 9:7
Sharezer killed him with a **s**. 2Ki 19:37
Pull out your **s** and stab me. 1Ch 10:4
took his own **s** and threw himself 1Ch 10:4
himself on his own **s** and died. 1Ch 10:5
of Israel who could use the **s**, ... 1Ch 21:5
in Judah who could use the **s**. 1Ch 21:5
holding his **s** drawn and pointed 1Ch 21:16
angel to put his **s** back into its 1Ch 21:27
the angel of the LORD and his **s**. 1Ch 21:30
brothers with a **s** and also 2Ch 21:4
with a **s** anyone who follows her. 2Ch 23:14
been put to death with the **s**. 2Ch 23:21
own sons killed him with a **s**. 2Ch 32:21
punished by the **s** and captivity. .... Ezr 9:7
builder wore his **s** at his side .... Ne 4:18
he will save you from the **s**. .... Job 5:20
that they will die by the **s**. .... Job 15:22
be afraid of the **s** yourselves. .... Job 19:29
will bring punishment by the **s**. .... Job 19:29
but the **s** will kill them. .... Job 27:14
will die by the **s**, and they will .... Job 36:12
it does not run away from the **s**. .... Job 39:22
The **s** that hits it does not hurt .... Job 41:26
lives, God will sharpen his **s**; .... Ps 7:12

S

me from the wicked with your **s**. .... Ps 17:13
Save me from the **s**; save my life .... Ps 22:20
help me, and my **s** can't save me. .... Ps 44:6
Put on your **s**, powerful warrior................ Ps 45:3
Their priests fell by the **s**, ... Ps 78:64
You have made his **s** useless; .... Ps 89:43
you pain like a two-edged **s**. .... Pr 5:4
Careless words stab like a **s**, ... Pr 12:18
as a club, a **s**, or a sharp arrow .... Pr 25:18
Every man wears a **s** at his side .... Sng 3:8
caught will be killed with a **s**.................. Is 13:15
great and hard and powerful **s**. .... Is 27:1
Assyria will be defeated by a **s**, ... Is 31:8
but not the **s** of a person; .... Is 31:8
but not by a person's **s**. .... Is 31:8
will run away from the **s** of God, ... Is 31:8
The LORD's **s** in the sky is .... Is 34:5
LORD's **s** will be covered with .... Is 34:6
him to die by the **s** there.'" .... Is 37:7
Sharezer killed him with a **s**. .... Is 37:38
He uses his **s**, and kings become .... Is 41:2
made my tongue like a sharp **s**. .... Is 49:2
and I will punish you with my **s**............... Is 65:12
destroy many people with his **s**; .... Is 66:16
' but now the **s** is pointing at .... Je 4:10
Judah with the **s** until they are .... Je 9:16
an enemy's **s** or from hunger. .... Je 14:13
hunger and from an enemy's **s**. .... Je 14:15
hunger and from an enemy's **s**. .... Je 14:16
the evil people with a **s**,'" .... Je 25:31
who had Uriah killed with a **s**. .... Je 26:23
by the enemy's **s** found help .... Je 31:2
You will not be killed with a **s**. .... Je 34:4
You will not die from a **s**, ... Je 39:18
the son of Shaphan, with a **s**. .... Je 41:2
who are to be killed with a **s**. .... Je 43:11
killed by the **s** and will come .... Je 44:28
The **s** will kill until it is .... Je 46:10
get away from our enemy's **s**!' .... Je 46:16
You cry, 'S of the LORD, how .... Je 47:6
But how can his **s** rest when the............. Je 47:7
silenced. The **s** will chase you. .... Je 48:2
holds back his **s** from killing. .... Je 48:10
I will send a **s** to chase Elam .... Je 49:37
Let a **s** kill the people living .... Je 50:35
Let a **s** kill her false prophets, ... Je 50:36
Let a **s** kill her warriors, ... Je 50:36
Let a **s** kill her horses and .... Je 50:37
Let a **s** attack her treasures, ... Je 50:37
a **s** attack her waters so they .... Je 50:38
Out in the streets, the **s** kills; .... La 1:20
men have been killed by the **s**. .... La 2:21
take a sharp **s**, and use it like .... Eze 5:1
how I will chase them with a **s**. .... Eze 5:2
fall dead by the **s** outside your .... Eze 5:12
as I chase them with a **s**......................... Eze 5:12
will bring the **s** against you to .... Eze 5:17
I will bring a **s** against you, ... Eze 6:3
The **s** is outside, and disease .... Eze 7:15
in the field will die by the **s**. .... Eze 7:15
have feared the **s**, but I will................... Eze 11:8
I will bring a **s** against you, ... Eze 11:8
You will die by the **s**. .... Eze 11:10
and I will chase them with a **s**. .... Eze 12:14
them from the **s** and from hunger .... Eze 12:16
who escape will die by the **s**, ... Eze 17:21
I will pull my **s** out of its .... Eze 21:3
my **s** will come out from its .... Eze 21:4
have pulled my **s** out from its .... Eze 21:5
My **s** will not go back in again.' .... Eze 21:5
A **s**, a sword, made sharp and................ Eze 21:9
A sword, a **s**, made sharp and................ Eze 21:9
horrible punishment by the **s**.................. Eze 21:10

The **s** should be polished. .... Eze 21:11
because the **s** is meant for my .... Eze 21:12
They will be killed by the **s**, ... Eze 21:12
Let the **s** strike two or three .... Eze 21:14
It is a **s** meant for killing, ... Eze 21:14
a **s** meant for much killing..................... Eze 21:14
This **s** surrounds the people to .... Eze 21:14
the killing **s** at all their city.................. Eze 21:15
The **s** is made to flash like .... Eze 21:15
S, cut on the right side; .... Eze 21:16
of Babylon and his **s** can follow. .... Eze 21:19
he can take with his **s** to Rabbah .... Eze 21:20
s, a sword is pulled out of its .... Eze 21:28
a **s** is pulled out of its holder. .... Eze 21:28
The **s** will be put on the necks .... Eze 21:29
Put the **s** back in its holder. .... Eze 21:30
Then they killed her with a **s**. .... Eze 23:10
will fall dead by the **s**........................... Eze 24:21
will kill your army with the **s**,............... Eze 26:11
enough to hold a **s** in war. .... Eze 30:21
I will make the **s** fall from his .... Eze 30:22
strong and put my **s** in his hand. .... Eze 30:24
when I put my **s** into the hand .... Eze 30:25
when I swing my **s** in front of .... Eze 32:10
s of the king of Babylon will .... Eze 32:11
killed in war. The **s** is ready; .... Eze 32:20
depend on your **s** and do terrible .... Eze 33:26
Everyone's **s** will attack the .... Eze 38:21
bow and the **s** and the weapons .... Hos 2:18
with the **s**, showing them no .... Am 1:11
Jeroboam's family with the **s**." .... Am 7:9
'Jeroboam will die by the **s**, ... Am 7:11
left alive I will kill with a **s**. .... Am 9:1
will command the **s** to kill them. .... Am 9:4
my people will die by the **s**— .... Am 9:10
store up, the **s** will destroy. .... Mic 6:14
and the **s** will kill your young................ Nah 2:13
you up. The **s** will kill you; .... Nah 3:15
also will be killed by my **s**." .... Zph 2:12
will use you like a warrior's **s**. .... Zch 9:13
A **s** will strike his arm and his .... Zch 11:17
S, hit the shepherd. Attack the .... Zch 13:7
come to bring peace, but a **s**. .... Mt 10:34
reached for his **s** and pulled it .... Mt 26:51
Put your **s** back in its place. .... Mt 26:52
pulled out his **s** and struck .... Mk 14:47
be killed by the **s** and taken as .... Lk 21:24
don't have a **s**, sell your coat .... Lk 22:36
Peter, who had a **s**, pulled it .... Jn 18:10
said to Peter, "Put your **s** back. .... Jn 18:11
of John, to be killed by the **s**. .... Ac 12:2
he got his **s** and was about to .... Ac 16:27
and take the **s** of the Spirit, ... Eph 6:17
sharper than a double-edged **s**. .... Heb 4:12
double-edged **s** came out of his .... Rev 1:16
sharp, double-edged **s** says this: .... Rev 2:12
them with the **s** that comes out .... Rev 2:16
other, and he was given a big **s**. .... Rev 6:4
you are to be killed with the **s**, ... Rev 13:10
you will be killed with the **s**. .... Rev 13:10
by the deadly **s** but sprang to .... Rev 13:14
comes a sharp **s** that he will use............ Rev 19:15
killed with the **s** that came out .... Rev 19:21

SWORDS

took their **s** and made a surprise .... Ge 34:25
who used their **s** to do violence. .... Ge 49:5
this land to be killed with **s**? .... Nu 14:3
who will kill you with **s**........................ Nu 14:43
will come and meet you with **s**."........... Nu 20:18
kill all the men with your **s**, ... Dt 20:13
than by the Israelites' **s**. .... Jos 10:11
land without using **s** and bows. .... Jos 24:12

with their s and burned the city .... Jdg 1:8
attacked with s the people in .... Jdg 1:25
With their s they killed all of .... Jdg 4:16
fight each other with their s! .... Jdg 7:22
with their s and then burned .... Jdg 18:27
were 400,000 soldiers with s. .... Jdg 20:2
who were trained with s.......................... Jdg 20:15
400,000 soldiers with s. .... Jdg 20:17
all of whom carried s. .... Jdg 20:25
Benjaminites, all armed with s. .... Jdg 20:35
in the city with their s. .... Jdg 20:37
whom had fought bravely with s. .... Jdg 20:46
to kill the people with their s,............... Jdg 21:10
might make s and spears." 1Sa 13:19
and Jonathan had no s or spears. 1Sa 13:22
each other with their s! 1Sa 14:20
does not need s or spears to 1Sa 17:47
said to them, "Put on your s!" 1Sa 25:13
put on their s, and David put 1Sa 25:13
themselves with s and spears 1Ki 18:28
and killed your prophets with s. 1Ki 19:10
and killed your prophets with s. 1Ki 19:14
men with s to try to break 2Ki 3:26
and kill their young men with s............... 2Ki 8:12
perfumes, his s and shields, and 2Ki 20:13
carried shields and s and bows. 1Ch 5:18
as they chase you with their s. 1Ch 21:12
families together with their s,................ Ne 4:13
And, with their s, the Jewish .... Est 9:5
They killed the servants with s, ... Job 1:15
with the flashing spears and s. .... Job 39:23
draw their s and bend their .... Ps 37:14
But their s will stab their own .... Ps 37:15
It wasn't their s that took the .... Ps 44:3
their tongues as sharp as s. .... Ps 57:4
be killed with s and eaten by .... Ps 63:10
tongues like s and shoot bitter .... Ps 64:3
shields, the s, and the weapons .... Ps 76:3
your servant David from cruel s. .... Ps 144:10
two-edged s in their hands...................... Ps 149:6
Some people have teeth like s; .... Pr 30:14
all carry s and have been .... Sng 3:8
destroyed by your enemies' s." .... Is 1:20
will make their s into plows and............. Is 2:4
your men will be killed with s, ... Is 3:25
were running from s, from swords .... Is 21:15
swords, from s ready to kill, ... Is 21:15
but not with s, nor did they die .... Is 22:2
perfumes, his s and shields, and............. Is 39:2
With your s you killed your .... Je 2:30
destroy with their s the strong, ... Je 5:17
roads, because the enemy has s............... Je 6:25
will attack this country with s. .... Je 14:15
I see people killed by s. .... Je 14:18
their enemies kill them with s. .... Je 18:21
men be killed with s in battle.................. Je 18:21
I will have them killed with s................... Je 19:7
killing your friends with s. .... Je 20:4
and then will kill them with s. .... Je 20:4
Jerusalem, using s, hunger, and .... Je 44:13
will die from s or hunger until .... Je 44:27
escaped being killed with s, ... Je 51:50
you into pieces with their s. .... Eze 16:40
them cut them down with their s. .... Eze 23:47
pull out their s and destroy all .... Eze 28:7
pull out their s against Egypt .... Eze 30:11
to fall by the s of mighty...................... Eze 32:12
had their s laid under their.................... Eze 32:27
small shields and all having s. .... Eze 38:4
But they will be killed with s,................ Da 11:33
but not by using bows or s,................... Hos 1:7
they will be killed with s, ... Hos 7:16
Make s from your plows, and make .... Joe 3:10

I killed your young men with s, ... Am 4:10
daughters will be killed with s. .... Am 7:17
hammer their s into plow blades .... Mic 4:3
no longer raise s against other .... Mic 4:3
the Assyrians with their s; .... Mic 5:6
of Assyria with their s drawn. .... Mic 5:6
are charging, s are shining, ... Nah 3:3
people kill each other with s.' .... Hag 2:22
people carrying s and clubs who .... Mt 26:47
who use s will be killed with .... Mt 26:52
swords will be killed with s. .... Mt 26:52
to get me with s and clubs as if .... Mt 26:55
people carrying s and clubs who .... Mk 14:43
to get me with s and clubs as if .... Mk 14:48
Look, Lord, here are two s." .... Lk 22:38
we strike them with our s?" .... Lk 22:49
came out here with s and clubs .... Lk 22:52
saved from being killed with s. .... Heb 11:34
and they were killed with s. .... Heb 11:37

SWORE

morning the men s an oath to.................. Ge 26:31
and he s that I would not cross .... Dt 4:21
ancestors, which he s to them. .... Dt 4:31
So the LORD s they would not see .... Jos 5:6
the Israelites s an oath to keep .... Jos 9:15
breaking the oath we s to them. .... Jos 9:20
We s before the LORD that we .... Jdg 21:7
them, because we s, 'Anyone who .... Jdg 21:18
So I s to Eli's family, 'Your 1Sa 3:14
Then King Solomon s by the name........... 1Ki 2:23
So he s to them that they would .... Ps 106:26
in the desert I s to the .... Eze 20:15
in the desert I s to the.......................... Eze 20:23
himself when he s to Abraham, ... Heb 6:13

SWORN

LORD had s to them this would .... Jdg 2:15
Mizpah the men of Israel had s, ... Jdg 21:1
they had s that anyone who .... Jdg 21:5
'I have s by my great name: .... Je 44:26
The LORD has s by his name,................... Am 8:7

SWUNG

on the cloud s his sickle over .... Rev 14:16
Then the angel s his sickle over .... Rev 14:19

SYCAMORE

the olive trees and s trees in 1Ch 27:28
hail and their s trees with .... Ps 78:47
and I take care of s trees. .... Am 7:14
he climbed a s tree so he could .... Lk 19:4

SYCHAR

Jesus came to the town called S, ... Jn 4:5

SYMBOL

It is a s of the people's sins...................... Zch 5:6
should have a s of authority on 1Co 11:10

SYMBOLS

They are s of what will happen. .... Zch 3:8
They are s of the two who have .... Zch 4:14

SYMPATHY

I looked for s, but there was .... Ps 69:20

SYNAGOGUE

and taught the people in the s, ... Mt 13:54
He went to the s and began to .... Mk 1:21
A leader of the s, named Jairus,.............. Mk 5:22
people, and he built us a s." .... Lk 7:5
teaching in the s in Capernaum................ Jn 6:59
they would be put out of the s. .... Jn 12:42
Barnabas went as usual to the s. .... Ac 14:1
are a s that belongs to Satan. .... Rev 2:9
Those in the s that belongs to................ Rev 3:9

S

SYNAGOGUES

seats at feasts and in the s. .... Mt 23:6
in the s and forcing out .... Mk 1:39
will put you out of their s. .... Jn 16:2
letters to the s in the city .... Ac 9:2
people in the s or in the city. .... Ac 24:12

SYNTYCHE

I ask Euodia and S to agree in .... Php 4:2

SYRACUSE

We stopped at S for three days. .... Ac 28:12

SYRIA

about Jesus spread all over S, ... Mt 4:24
Greek, born in Phoenicia, in S. .... Mk 7:26
Quirinius was governor of S. .... Lk 2:2
who was from the country of S." .... Lk 4:27
in Antioch, S, and Cilicia: .... Ac 15:23
he went through S and Cilicia. .... Ac 15:41
Then he left and sailed for S, ... Ac 18:18
He was ready to sail for S, ... Ac 20:3
go back through Macedonia to S. .... Ac 20:3
north, but we sailed on to S. .... Ac 21:3
to the areas of S and Cilicia. .... Gal 1:21

SYRTIS

would hit the sandbanks of S, ... Ac 27:17

SYSTEM

law concerning the s of priests .... Heb 7:11
be made perfect through that s. .... Heb 7:11
open while the s of the old Holy .... Heb 9:8
ends the first s of sacrifices .... Heb 10:9
so he can set up the new s. .... Heb 10:9

T

T

having fun doesn't accomplish .... Ec 2:2

TAANACH

T, Megiddo, ... Jos 12:21
who lived in T and its small .... Jos 17:11
gave them T and Gath Rimmon .... Jos 21:25
of Beth Shan, T, Dor, Ibleam, ... Jdg 1:27
the kings of Canaan fought at T, ... Jdg 5:19
son of Ahilud was governor of T, ... 1Ki 4:12
of Beth Shan, T, Megiddo, and 1Ch 7:29

TAANATH

eastward toward T Shiloh and .... Jos 16:6

TABALIAH

was his second son, T was third, ... 1Ch 26:11

TABBAOTH

descendants of Ziha, Hasupha, T, ... Ezr 2:43
descendants of Ziha, Hasupha, T, ... Ne 7:46

TABBATH

Meholah, near the city of T. .... Jdg 7:22

TABEEL

Mithredath, T, and those with .... Ezr 4:7
make the son of T the new king .... Is 7:6

TABERAH

So that place was called T, ... Nu 11:3
also made the LORD angry at T, ... Dt 9:22

TABITHA

there was a follower named T .... Ac 9:36
Peter was in Lydda, T became .... Ac 9:37
shirts and coats T had made when .... Ac 9:39
body and said, "T, stand up." .... Ac 9:40
showed them that T was alive. .... Ac 9:41

TABLE

So they served Joseph at one t, ... Ge 43:32
his brothers at another t, ... Ge 43:32

who ate with him at another t. .... Ge 43:32
from Joseph's t was taken to .... Ge 43:34
Make a t out of acacia wood, ... Ex 25:23
corners of the t where the four .... Ex 25:26
frame around the top of the t, ... Ex 25:27
carry the t with these poles. .... Ex 25:28
the plates and bowls for the t, ... Ex 25:29
On this t put the bread that .... Ex 25:30
put the t on the north side of .... Ex 26:35
the Holy Tent across from the t. .... Ex 26:35
on the t and all its dishes, ... Ex 30:27
includes the t and everything .... Ex 31:8
the t, and its poles, all the .... Ex 35:13
the things that go with the t, ... Ex 35:13
he made the t of acacia wood; .... Ex 37:10
rings for the t and attached .... Ex 37:13
corners of the t where the four .... Ex 37:13
frame around the top of the t, ... Ex 37:14
for carrying the t were made of .... Ex 37:15
things that were used on the t: .... Ex 37:16
the t, all its containers, and .... Ex 39:36
Bring in the t and arrange .... Ex 40:4
on the t that should be .... Ex 40:4
Moses put the t in the Meeting .... Ex 40:22
bread on the t before the LORD .... Ex 40:23
the Holy Tent across from the t. .... Ex 40:24
on the golden t before the LORD, ... Le 24:6
the Ark, the t, the lampstand, ... Nu 3:31
cloth over the t for the bread .... Nu 4:7
for drink offerings on the t; .... Nu 4:7
that is always there on the t. .... Nu 4:7
eat scraps that fell from my t. .... Jdg 1:7
them a choice place at the t. 1Sa 9:22
put it on the t in front of Saul 1Sa 9:24
has not come to the king's t." 1Sa 20:29
was very angry and left the t. 1Sa 20:34
you will always eat at my t." 2Sa 9:7
will always eat at my t." 2Sa 9:10
ate at David's t as if he were 2Sa 9:11
he always ate at the king's t. 2Sa 9:13
people who eat at your own t. 2Sa 19:28
and allow them to eat at your t. 1Ki 2:7
all the people who ate at his t: 1Ki 4:22
person who ate at the king's t. 1Ki 4:27
golden t which held the bread 1Ki 7:48
the food on his t, his many 1Ki 10:5
they were sitting at the t, ... 1Ki 13:20
who eat at Jezebel's t." 1Ki 18:19
We can put a t, a chair, and a 2Ki 4:10
life, he ate at the king's t. 2Ki 25:29
was put on the t every Sabbath 1Ch 9:32
putting the holy bread on the t, ... 1Ch 23:29
be used for each t that held the 1Ch 28:16
the food on his t, his many 2Ch 9:4
on the special t in the Temple. 2Ch 13:11
and the t for the holy bread and 2Ch 29:18
people and officers at my t, ... Ne 5:17
bread that is set out on the t; .... Ne 10:33
he has set your t full of the .... Job 36:16
who ate at my t, has even turned .... Ps 41:9
and wine; she has set her t. .... Pr 9:2
They set the t; they spread the .... Is 21:5
Every t is covered with vomit, ... Is 28:8
life, he ate at the king's t. .... Je 52:33
fine bed with a t set before it, ... Eze 23:41
At my t you are to eat until you .... Eze 39:20
This is the t that is in the .... Eze 41:22
may come near my t to serve me .... Eze 44:16
at the same t and lie to each .... Da 11:27
fall from their masters' t." .... Mt 15:27
sitting at the t with his twelve .... Mt 26:20
the dogs under the t can eat the .... Mk 7:28
the right side of the incense t. .... Lk 1:11

T

and you will be like the t. .... Dt 28:44
Its t is like a cedar tree; .... Job 40:17
cut off Israel's head and t, ... Is 9:14
who speak lies were the t. .... Is 9:15
His t swept a third of the stars .... Rev 12:4

TAILS

time, tied their t together, and .... Jdg 15:4
a torch to the t of each pair .... Jdg 15:4
The locusts had t with stingers .... Rev 9:10
and in their t was their power .... Rev 9:10
in their mouths and in their t; .... Rev 9:19
their t were like snakes with .... Rev 9:19

TAKE

is your wife. T her and leave!" .... Ge 12:19
Then God said, "T your only son, ... Ge 22:2
should I t your son with me back .... Ge 24:5
Don't t my son back there. .... Ge 24:6
must not t my son back there. .... Ge 24:8
T off your sandals, because you .... Ex 3:5
and t some of the elders of .... Ex 17:5
not want to t your neighbor's .... Ex 20:17
he may t his wife with him. .... Ex 21:3
and they must t care of it and.............. Nu 1:50
will t a handful of the grain, ... Nu 5:26
T the Levites away from the .... Nu 8:6
I will t you to another place. .... Nu 23:27
said to Moses, "T Joshua son of .... Nu 27:18
groups should t a count of the .... Nu 31:26
crossing the Jordan River to t. .... Dt 4:26
not want to t your neighbor's .... Dt 5:21
not judge unfairly or t sides. .... Dt 16:19
t the man or woman who has done .... Dt 17:5
army answered, "T off your .... Jos 5:15
Don't t any of the things that .... Jos 6:18
one who should t care of us." .... Ru 2:20
is supposed to t care of me." .... Ru 3:9
who is to t care of you, ... Ru 3:12
will t your sons and make them 1Sa 8:11
He will t others to make weapons 1Sa 8:12
He will t your daughters to make 1Sa 8:13
He will t your best fields, ... 1Sa 8:14
but only to t weapons and armor 2Sa 23:10
you may t anything you want for 2Sa 24:22
a widow there to t care of you." 1Ki 17:9
want they will t and carry off.' 1Ki 20:6
who lives to t it off who has 1Ki 20:11
Then t Naboth out of the city 1Ki 21:10
you may go and t for yourself................ 1Ki 21:15
Then Jehu said, "T them alive!" 2Ki 10:14
Should we t only good things .... Job 2:10
danger and t my life in my own .... Job 13:14
But God knows the way that I t, ... Job 23:10
Wicked people t other people's .... Job 24:2
Maker would quickly t me away. .... Job 32:22
should decide to t away life and .... Job 34:14
will string his bow and t aim. .... Ps 7:12
Why do you t care of human .... Ps 8:4
lend and do not t money to hurt.............. Ps 15:5
troubles, and t away all my sins .... Ps 25:18
those sinners or t my life with .... Ps 26:9
leave me, the LORD will t me .... Ps 27:10
and he will t care of you. .... Ps 37:5
from you or t your Holy Spirit .... Ps 51:11
people sleep, you t their lives. .... Ps 90:5
do not t me in the middle of my .... Ps 102:24
When you t away their breath, ... Ps 104:29
promise that he will not t back. .... Ps 132:11
T away my desire to do evil or .... Ps 141:4
and it will t care of you. .... Pr 4:6
a little; you t a nap. You fold .... Pr 6:10
t the road of understanding. .... Pr 9:6
Good people t care of their..................... Pr 12:10

will t all the worthless things .... Is 1:25
Please, t away our shame." .... Is 4:1
not let idols t the praise that .... Is 42:8
Who let robbers t Israel away? .... Is 42:24
nations and t away other kings' .... Is 45:1
return to me, I will t you back. .... Je 15:19
let your enemies t you as their .... Je 17:4
Babylon did not t these away .... Je 27:20
T me back so that I may come .... Je 31:18
I will not t pity on her .... Hos 2:4
come back and t away my grain at........... Hos 2:9
T away all our sin and kindly .... Hos 14:2
Sepharad will t back the cities .... Ob 1:20
you people who will t your land, ... Mic 1:15
against those who t part in evil .... Mal 3:5
be afraid to t Mary as your wife .... Mt 1:20
T the child and his mother and .... Mt 2:13
arrest you and t you to court .... Mt 10:17
been trying to t it by force. .... Mt 11:12
is not right to t the children's .... Mt 15:26
T that coin and give it to the .... Mt 17:27
You t away widows' houses, ... Mt 23:14
that servant to t care of .... Mt 24:47
but they did not t more oil for .... Mt 25:3
and told them to t care of his .... Mt 25:14
'T the bag of gold from that .... Mt 25:28
and said, "T this bread and eat .... Mt 26:26
T some soldiers and go guard the .... Mt 27:65
his followers and said, "T it; .... Mk 14:22
T away this cup of suffering. .... Mk 14:36
Elijah will come to t him down .... Mk 15:36
said to them, "T nothing for .... Lk 9:3
and said, 'T care of this man. .... Lk 10:35
that servant to t care of .... Lk 12:44
enemy might t you to the judge .... Lk 12:58
that they are about to t place?" .... Lk 21:7
T this cup and share it among .... Lk 22:17
t away this cup of suffering. .... Lk 22:42
to come and t him by force .... Jn 6:15
so that I can t it back again. .... Jn 10:17
because he will t what I have to .... Jn 16:14
said to him, 'T off your sandals .... Ac 7:33
of Jesus and t them back to .... Ac 9:21
people when I t away their sins. .... Rm 11:27
We must not t part in sexual 1Co 10:8
It will t only a second—as 1Co 15:52
you approve to t your gift to 1Co 16:3
three times to t this problem 2Co 12:8
and t the sword of the Spirit, ... Eph 6:17
Why do you t care of human .... Heb 2:6
bulls and goats to t away sins. .... Heb 10:4
judges rightly, t care of him. 1Pe 2:23
They t pleasure in openly doing 2Pe 2:13
T others out of the fire, and .... Jud 1:23
to you and will t away your .... Rev 2:5
T your sharp sickle and gather .... Rev 14:18
They will t everything she has .... Rev 17:16
God will t away that one's share .... Rev 22:19

TAKEN

because she was t out of man." .... Ge 2:23
because you were t from it...................... Ge 3:19
said, "God has t away my shame," .... Ge 30:23
Then the Holy Tent was t down, ... Nu 10:17
and children will be t away. .... Nu 14:3
The LORD has t away your sin. 2Sa 12:13
He had t care of the king when 2Sa 19:32
for you before I am t from you?" 2Ki 2:9
you see me when I am t from you, ... 2Ki 2:10
of the LORD has t Elijah up and.............. 2Ki 2:16
to me, and he has t them away. .... Job 1:21
your guilt is t away, because .... Is 6:7
your lips. Your sin is t away." .... Is 6:7

you have t away their heavy load .... Is 9:4
will all be t, because the LORD .... Is 24:3
is how its sins will be t away: .... Is 27:9
rest of my life t away from me?" .... Is 38:10
nation has t away my people for.............. Is 52:5
Good people are t away, but no .... Is 57:1
You will be t prisoner by the .... Je 38:23
They had Jeremiah t out of the .... Je 39:14
animals had been t from them, ... Da 7:12
of the king will be t away, ... Da 7:26
will be t, and the other will..................... Mt 24:40
everything t away from them.' .... Mt 25:29
the Lord has t away that shame.............. Lk 1:25
it was t while Quirinius was .... Lk 2:2
They have t away my Lord,.................... Jn 20:13
the day he was t up into heaven. .... Ac 1:2
whom you saw t up from you into .... Ac 1:11
That covering is t away only 2Co 3:14
that Enoch was t to heaven so he .... Heb 11:5
because God had t him away. .... Heb 11:5
she would be t care of for three .... Rev 12:14

TAKES

when the LORD t you into the .... Ex 13:11
If a man t the cover off a pit, ... Ex 21:33
Anyone who t a rock and kills a .... Nu 35:17
Mount Seir road t eleven days. .... Dt 1:2
be cursed who t money to murder .... Dt 27:25
LORD t his place in court and .... Is 3:13
He t care of his people like a .... Is 40:11
As a shepherd t care of his .... Eze 34:12
when someone t something that.............. Lk 6:30
devil comes and t it away from .... Lk 8:12
who t away the sin of the world! .... Jn 1:29
No one t it away from me; .... Jn 10:18
No person t care of a flock 1Co 9:7
This t wisdom. Let the one who .... Rev 13:18
And if anyone t away from the .... Rev 22:19

TAKING

even t what grew among the .... Job 5:5
T gifts to important people will .... Pr 18:16
is sad is like t away his coat .... Pr 25:20
them in charge of t care of the .... Eze 44:14
People will still be t the place .... Am 5:13
Will he keep on t riches with .... Hab 1:17
"Where are they t the basket?" .... Zch 5:10
you why you are t the donkeys, ... Mt 21:3
T hold of the girl's hand,....................... Mk 5:41
If your enemy is t you to court, ... Lk 12:58
and t the followers with him, ... Ac 19:9
t their money so I could serve................ 2Co 11:8
not being pure, t part in sexual .... Gal 5:19
room without t blood with him, ... Heb 9:7
they are still t care of .... Jam 1:11
to idols and by t part in sexual .... Rev 2:14

TALENTED

and the t one does not always .... Ec 9:11

TALITHA

hand, he said to her, "T, koum!"............. Mk 5:41

TALL

Anakites, who are strong and t. .... Dt 9:2
a people who are t and .... Is 18:2

TALLER

are stronger and t than we are. .... Dt 1:28
stood a head t than any other................. 1Sa 9:2

TALLEST

cut down its t cedars and its 2Ki 19:23
cut down its t cedars and its .... Is 37:24

TALMAI

Sheshai, and T, the descendants.............. Nu 13:22
Ahiman, and T, the descendants.............. Jos 15:14

defeated Sheshai, Ahiman, and T. .... Jdg 1:10
mother was Maacah daughter of T, ... 2Sa 3:3
ran away to T son of Ammihud, ... 2Sa 13:37
mother was Maacah daughter of T, ... 1Ch 3:2

TALMON

Shallum, Akkub, T, Ahiman, and 1Ch 9:17
Shallum, Ater, T, Akkub, Hatita,........... Ezr 2:42
Shallum, Ater, T, Akkub, Hatita,........... Ne 7:45
were Akkub, T, and others with .... Ne 11:19
Meshullam, T, and Akkub. .... Ne 12:25

TAMAR

Amorites who lived in Hazazon T. .... Ge 14:7
a girl named T to be the wife .... Ge 38:6
relations with T he did not .... Ge 38:9
it impossible for T to become .... Ge 38:9
said to his daughter-in-law T, ... Ge 38:11
So T returned to her father's .... Ge 38:11
T learned that Judah, her .... Ge 38:13
He did not know that she was T, ... Ge 38:16
T answered, "Give me your seal............... Ge 38:18
Then Judah and T had sexual................. Ge 38:18
and T became pregnant......................... Ge 38:18
When T went home, she took off .... Ge 38:19
someone told Judah, "T, your .... Ge 38:24
the people went to bring T out, ... Ge 38:25
time came for T to give birth,............... Ge 38:27
at a place named Baal T........................ Jdg 20:33
As T gave birth to Judah's son .... Ru 4:12
had a beautiful sister named T, ... 2Sa 13:1
T was a virgin. Amnon made 2Sa 13:2
him, "I love T, the sister of my 2Sa 13:4
let my sister T come in and give.............. 2Sa 13:5
Please let my sister T come in. 2Sa 13:6
David sent for T in the palace, ... 2Sa 13:7
So T went to her brother Amnon's 2Sa 13:8
T took some dough and pressed it 2Sa 13:8
Amnon said to T, "Bring the food 2Sa 13:10
T took the cakes she had made 2Sa 13:10
T said to him, "No, brother! 2Sa 13:12
After that, Amnon hated T..................... 2Sa 13:15
T said to him, "No! Sending me 2Sa 13:16
T was wearing a special robe 2Sa 13:18
T put ashes on her head and tore 2Sa 13:19
So T lived in her brother........................ 2Sa 13:20
for disgracing his sister T. 2Sa 13:22
his sister T to have sexual 2Sa 13:32
His daughter's name was also T, ... 2Sa 14:27
daughter-in-law T gave birth to 1Ch 2:4
also had a daughter named T.................. 1Ch 3:9
They are already in Hazazon T!" 2Ch 20:2
T is also called En Gedi. 2Ch 20:2
the town of T on the Dead Sea. .... Eze 47:18
go east from T all the way to .... Eze 47:19
go east from T on the Dead Sea .... Eze 48:28
Their mother was T.) Perez was .... Mt 1:3

TAMAR'S

Absalom, T brother, said to her, ... 2Sa 13:20

TAMARISK

planted a tree at Beersheba .... Ge 21:33
under the t tree on the hill 1Sa 22:6
them under the t tree in Jabesh............... 1Sa 31:13

TAMBOURINE

took a t in her hand. .... Ex 15:20
him, playing a t and dancing. .... Jdg 11:34

TAMBOURINES

with the music of t and harps. .... Ge 31:27
her, playing t and dancing. .... Ex 15:20
be playing harps, t, flutes, and 1Sa 10:5
and played t and stringed 1Sa 18:6
lyres, harps, t, rattles, and 2Sa 6:5
lyres, harps, t, cymbals, ... 1Ch 13:8

T

to the music of t and harps, ...Job 21:12
middle are the girls with the t. ....Ps 68:25
music. Play the t. Play pleasant ....Ps 81:2
praises to him with the t animals. ....Ps 149:3
Praise him with t and dancing; ....Ps 150:4
lyres, harps, t, flutes, and ....Is 5:12
happy music of the t will end..................Is 24:8
to the music of t and harps; ....Is 30:32
pick up your t again and dance ....Je 31:4

TAME

Let there be t animals and small ....Ge 1:24
animals, the t animals, and all ....Ge 1:25
sky, over the t animals, over ....Ge 1:26
gave names to all the t animals, ...Ge 2:20
no other animal, t or wild, will ....Ge 3:14
every kind of wild and t animal,..............Ge 7:14
all the birds, t animals, wild ....Ge 7:21
the wild and t animals with him..............Ge 8:1
the t and the wild animals, ...Ge 9:10
a wild donkey can be born t. ....Job 11:12
People can t every kind of wild ....Jam 3:7
but no one can t the tongue. ....Jam 3:8

TAMED

bites the tamer before it is t, ...Ec 10:11
and fish, and they have t them, ...Jam 3:7

TAMER

a snake bites the t before it is.................Ec 10:11
it is tamed, what good is the t? ....Ec 10:11

TAMMUZ

women sitting and crying for T. ....Eze 8:14

TAN

My lover is healthy and t, ...Sng 5:10

TANGLED

will be like t thorns or like ....Nah 1:10

TANHUMETH

Seraiah son of T the 2Ki 25:23
Seraiah son of T, the sons of ....Je 40:8

TANNED

was a fine boy, t, and handsome. 1Sa 16:12
was only a boy, t and handsome, ...1Sa 17:42

TANNER

a man named Simon who was a t. ....Ac 9:43
is a t and has a house beside ....Ac 10:6
is a t and has a house beside ....Ac 10:32

TAPHATH

He was married to T, Solomon's..............1Ki 4:11

TAPPING

their eyes, t with their feet ....Pr 6:13

TAPPUAH

T, Hepher, ...Jos 12:17
Zanoah, En Gannim, T, Enam, ...Jos 15:34
Janim, Beth T, Aphekah,.......................Jos 15:53
border went from T west to Kanah...........Jos 16:8
went south to the En T area, ...Jos 17:7
except for the town of T........................Jos 17:8
sons were Korah, T, Rekem, and 1Ch 2:43

TAR

it inside and outside with t....................Ge 6:14
stones, t instead of mortar. ....Ge 11:3
There were many t pits in the.................Ge 14:10
soldiers fell into the t pits, ...Ge 14:10
covered it with t so that it ....Ex 2:3
rivers will be like hot t. ....Is 34:9
Its land will be like burning t..................Is 34:9

TARALAH

Rekem, Irpeel, T,................................Jos 18:27

TAREA

Pithon, Melech, T, and Ahaz. 1Ch 8:35

TARGET

rock as if I am shooting at a t. 1Sa 20:20
Why have you made me your t? ....Job 7:20
He has made me his t;..........................Job 16:12
and commands it to strike its t. ....Job 36:32
made me the t for his arrows..................La 3:12

TARSHISH

Javan were Elishah, T, Kittim, ...Ge 10:4
sons were Elishah, T, Kittim, ...1Ch 1:7
Zethan, T, and Ahishahar. 1Ch 7:10
Admatha, T, Meres, Marsena,.................Est 1:14
the kings of T and the faraway ....Ps 72:10
You ships should return to T. ....Is 23:6
land, people of T, like the Nile ....Is 23:10
to T, Libya, Lud (the land of ....Is 66:19
is brought from T and gold from ....Je 10:9
People of T became traders for ....Eze 27:12
the traders of T, with all its...................Eze 38:13
from the LORD by going to T...................Jnh 1:3
that was going to the city of T. ....Jnh 1:3
planning to go to T to run away ....Jnh 1:3
is why I quickly ran away to T. ....Jnh 4:2

TARSUS

named Saul from the city of T. ....Ac 9:11
and from there sent him to T. ....Ac 9:30
the city of T to look for Saul, ...Ac 11:25
I am a Jew from T in the country ....Ac 21:39
born in T in the country of ....Ac 22:3

TARTAK

Avvites worshiped Nibhaz and T. 2Ki 17:31

TASK

People have a hard t on earth, ...Job 7:1
finished their t in Jerusalem, ...Ac 12:25

TASSELS

thread in each one of these t. ....Nu 15:38
will have these t to look at to ....Nu 15:39
then put these t on the four ....Dt 22:12

TASTE

I am too old to t what I eat or.................2Sa 19:35
Evil may t sweet in their ....Job 20:12
food may t sweet at first, ...Pr 20:17
his fruit is sweet to my t........................Sng 2:3
The beer will t bitter to those ....Is 24:9
their teeth from the sour t.'....................Je 31:29
So they t as they did before, ...Je 48:11
their teeth from the sour t'? ....Eze 18:2
what is right into a bitter t.....................Am 6:12
will be allowed to t anything. ....Jnh 3:7
if the salt loses its salty t, ...Mt 5:13
if the salt loses its salty t, ...Mk 9:50
but if it loses its salty t, ...Lk 14:34
this," "Don't t that," "Don't ....Col 2:21

TASTED

white seeds and t like wafers ....Ex 16:31
t like bread baked with olive oil. ....Nu 11:8
The men of Israel t the bread,.................Jos 9:14
I only t a little honey from the 1Sa 14:43
He t the wine but refused to ....Mt 27:34
When he t it, the water had ....Jn 2:9
When Jesus t the vinegar, he ....Jn 19:30
In my mouth it t sweet as honey, ...Rev 10:10

TASTELESS

T food is not eaten without salt, ...Job 6:6

TASTES

words as the tongue t food......................Job 12:11
words as the tongue t food......................Job 34:3
food eaten in secret t better." ....Pr 9:17
from the honeycomb t sweet. ....Pr 24:13
not even honey t good, but when ....Pr 27:7
even something bitter t sweet. ....Pr 27:7

TASTING
feel after just t a little of 1Sa 14:29

TASTY
you prepare the t food that I .... Ge 27:4
and prepare some t food for me .... Ge 27:7
gave Jacob the t food and the.................. Ge 27:17
prepared some t food and brought .... Ge 27:31
let me eat t food with those .... Ps 141:4
gossip are like t bits of food. .... Pr 18:8
gossip are like t bits of food; .... Pr 26:22

TATTENAI
At that time **T,** the governor of .... Ezr 5:3
was sent to King Darius by **T,**.................. Ezr 5:6
Now then, **T,** governor of .... Ezr 6:6
So, **T,** the governor of .... Ezr 6:13

TATTOO
who died or put t marks on .... Le 19:28

TAUGHT
Remember what you t your servant .... Ne 1:8
the message his mother t him: .... Pr 31:1
very wise and t the people what .... Ec 12:9
It was I who t Israel to walk, ... Hos 11:3
They t the true teachings and .... Mal 2:6
He t like a person who had.................... Mt 7:29
law who has been t about the .... Mt 13:52
to his hometown and t the people .... Mt 13:54
the things they had done and t. .... Mk 6:30
and he t them as he usually did............... Mk 10:1
pray as John t his followers." .... Lk 11:1
to him, and he sat and t them. .... Jn 8:2
only what the Father has t me. .... Jn 8:28
If I still t circumcision, ... Gal 5:11
so you were t the truth that is................. Eph 4:21
were t to leave your old self— .... Eph 4:22
But you were t to be made new in .... Eph 4:23
and they have t their hearts to 2Pe 2:14
in Christ, as his gift t you. 1Jn 2:27
He t Balak how to cause the .... Rev 2:14
who have the message Jesus t. .... Rev 12:17

TAX
Even the t collectors do that. .... Mt 5:46
teacher eat with t collectors .... Mt 9:11
and Matthew, the t collector; .... Mt 10:3
the Temple t came to Peter..................... Mt 17:24
a very important t collector, ... Lk 19:2
you owe any kind of t, pay it. .... Rm 13:7

TAXED
Menahem t Israel to pay about 2Ki 15:20
Jehoiakim t the land and took 2Ki 23:35

TAXES
right to pay t to Caesar or not? .... Mt 22:17
This is also why you pay t. .... Rm 13:6

TEACH
and I will t you what to say." .... Ex 4:12
and t them the right way to live .... Ex 18:20
T them to your children, and .... Dt 6:7
T them well to your children, ... Dt 11:19
No one can t knowledge to God; .... Job 21:22
many years should t wisdom.'.................. Job 32:7
your truth, and t me, my God, my .... Ps 25:5
LORD, t me your ways, and guide .... Ps 27:11
Then I will t your ways to those .... Ps 51:13
T us how short our lives really .... Ps 90:12
you t them from your law. .... Ps 94:12
Then God will t us his ways, ... Is 2:3
longer have to t their neighbors .... Je 31:34
Ashpenaz was to t them the .... Da 1:4
and that you t the truth about................. Mt 22:16
t us to pray as John taught his .... Lk 11:1
the Helper will t you everything .... Jn 14:26

Jesus began to do and t .... Ac 1:1
just as I t it in all the 1Co 4:17
in order to t others than 1Co 14:19
I was chosen to t those who are 1Ti 2:7
allow a woman to t or to have 1Ti 2:12
welcome guests, and able to t. 1Ti 3:2
You should t people whom you can 2Ti 2:2
must gently t those who disagree 2Ti 2:25

TEACHER
a t of the law came to Jesus .... Mt 8:19
Why does your t eat with tax .... Mt 9:11
is not better than his t, ... Mt 10:24
But you must not be called 'T,' .... Mt 23:8
asked, "Good t, what must I do .... Mk 10:17
and said, "T, we know you are .... Jn 3:2
are an important t in Israel, ... Jn 3:10

TEACHERS
than all my t, because I think .... Ps 119:99
in the Temple with the t, ... Lk 2:46
to prophets, and third to t. 1Co 12:28
find many more t who please them 2Ti 4:3
you should be t, but you need .... Heb 5:12
not many of you should become t, ... Jam 3:1
have some false t in your group............... 2Pe 2:1
Many false t are in the world 2Jn 1:7

TEACHES
right, and he t them his ways................... Ps 25:9
the wise person t others how to .... Pr 11:30
any command and t other people .... Mt 5:19
commands and t other people to .... Mt 5:19
nature itself t you that wearing 1Co 11:14
This story t something else: .... Gal 4:24
It t us not to live against God .... Tit 2:12
that grace t us to live in the .... Tit 2:12
His gift t you about everything, ... 1Jn 2:27

TEACHING
in Galilee, t in the synagogues, ... Mt 4:23
the people were amazed at his t, ... Mt 7:28
they were amazed at Jesus' t. .... Mt 22:33
Every day I sat in the Temple t, ... Mt 26:55
The people were amazed at his t, ... Mk 1:22
obeys my t will never die.' .... Jn 8:52
love me, they will obey my t. .... Jn 14:23
they continued t the people..................... Ac 5:42
has the gift of t should teach. .... Rm 12:7
false and empty t that is only .... Col 2:8
Let the t of Christ live in you .... Col 3:16
you accepted the t with the joy 1Th 1:6
great patience and careful t, ... 2Ti 4:2

TEAM
a field with a t of oxen. 1Ki 19:19
was plowing with the twelfth t. 1Ki 19:19
a chariot with a t of horses." .... Is 21:9

TEAMS
owned twelve t of oxen and was.............. 1Ki 19:19
five hundred t of oxen, and five .... Job 1:3
camels, a thousand t of oxen, ... Job 42:12
sees chariots and t of horses, ... Is 21:7

TEAR
is a time to t apart and a time.................. Ec 3:7
I will t down my barns and build .... Lk 12:18
We should not t this into parts. .... Jn 19:24
were so many, the net did not t. .... Jn 21:11
people would t Paul to pieces. .... Ac 23:10
build you up, not to t you down............... 2Co 10:8
build you up, not to t you down. 2Co 13:10
away every t from their eyes. .... Rev 7:17
away every t from their eyes .... Rev 21:4

TEARING

show sadness by t your clothes	Le 10:6
go uncombed or t his clothes.	Le 21:10
was as easy as t apart a young	Jdg 14:6
Like wolves t a dead animal,	Eze 22:27
T your clothes is not enough to	Joe 2:13
each other t and each other	Gal 5:15

TEARS

night my bed is wet with t;	Ps 6:6
You have kept a list of my t.	Ps 56:8
and my t fall into my drinks.	Ps 102:9
T stream from my eyes, because	Ps 119:136
I saw their t and that they had	Ec 4:1
your prayer and seen your t.	Is 38:5
my eyes like a fountain of t!	Je 9:1
to wash his feet with her t,	Lk 7:38
feet with her t and dried them	Lk 7:44
heart, and I wrote with many t.	2Co 2:4
loud cries and t to the One who	Heb 5:7

TEASE

Peninnah would t Hannah and	1Sa 1:6

TEBAH

names were T, Gaham, Tahash,	Ge 22:24
of bronze from T and Berothai,	2Sa 8:8
made of bronze from T and Cun,	1Ch 18:8

TEBETH

the month of T, during Xerxes'	Est 2:16

TEETH

escaped by the skin of my t.	Job 19:20
break the t in their mouths!	Ps 58:6
Your t are white like newly	Sng 4:2
their t from the sour taste.	Je 31:29
their t from the sour taste'	Eze 18:2
It had large iron t. It crushed	Da 7:7
boards that had iron t.	Am 1:3
and grind their t with pain."	Mt 8:12
cry and grind their t with pain.	Mt 13:42
and their t were like lions'	Rev 9:8

TEHINNAH

of Beth Rapha, Paseah, and T.	1Ch 4:12
T was the father of the people	1Ch 4:12

TEKEL

'Mene, mene, t, and parsin.'	Da 5:25
T: You have been weighed on the	Da 5:27

TEKOA

messengers to T to bring a wise	2Sa 14:2
the woman from T spoke to the	2Sa 14:4
The woman of T said to him,	2Sa 14:9
Ira son of Ikkesh from T;	2Sa 23:26
Ashhur became the father of T.	1Ch 2:24
Ira son of Ikkesh from T;	1Ch 11:28
of Ikkesh from the town of T.	1Ch 27:9
cities of Bethlehem, Etam, T,	2Ch 11:6
into the Desert of T early in	2Ch 20:20
The people from T made repairs	Ne 3:5
leading men of T would not work	Ne 3:5
people of T repaired the wall	Ne 3:27
war trumpet in the town of T!	Je 6:1
shepherds from the town of T.	Am 1:1

TEKOA'S

T father was Ashhur.	1Ch 4:5

TEL

of Eden living in T Assar.	2Ki 19:12
from the towns of T Melah,	Ezr 2:59
of Tel Melah, T Harsha, Kerub,	Ezr 2:59
from the towns of T Melah,	Ne 7:61
of Tel Melah, T Harsha, Kerub,	Ne 7:61
of Eden living in T Assar.	Is 37:12
by the Kebar River at T Abib.	Eze 3:15

TELAH

Rephah's son. T was Resheph's	1Ch 7:25

TELAH'S

Resheph's son. Tahan was T son.	1Ch 7:25

TELAIM

called the army together at T.	1Sa 15:4

TELEM

Ziph, T, Bealoth,	Jos 15:24
Shallum, T, and Uri.	Ezr 10:24

TEMA

Hadad, T, Jetur, Naphish, and	Ge 25:15
Mishma, Dumah, Massa, Hadad, T,	1Ch 1:30
travelers from T look for water,	Job 6:19
the people of T gave food to	Is 21:14
people of Dedan and T and Buz;	Je 25:23

TEMAH

Barkos, Sisera, T,	Ezr 2:53
Barkos, Sisera, T,	Ne 7:55

TEMAN

T, Omar, Zepho, Gatam, and Kenaz.	Ge 36:11
these leaders: T, Omar, Zepho,	Ge 36:15
Kenaz, T, Mibzar,	Ge 36:42
sons were T, Omar, Zepho, Gatam	1Ch 1:36
Kenaz, T, Mibzar,	1Ch 1:53
no more wisdom in the town of T?	Je 49:7
to the people in the town of T.	Je 49:20
the way from T to Dedan as they	Eze 25:13
on the city of T that will even	Am 1:12
Then, city of T, your best	Ob 1:9
is coming from T; the Holy One	Hab 3:3

TEMANITE

Eliphaz the T, Bildad the	Job 2:11
Then Eliphaz the T answered:	Job 4:1
Then Eliphaz the T answered:	Job 15:1
Then Eliphaz the T answered:	Job 22:1
he said to Eliphaz the T,	Job 42:7
So Eliphaz the T, Bildad the	Job 42:9

TEMANITES

He was from the land of the T.	Ge 36:34
He was from the land of the T.	1Ch 1:45

TEMENI

Hepher, T, and Haahashtari	1Ch 4:6

TEMPER

with a quick t does foolish	Pr 14:17
Controlling your t is better	Pr 16:32
with a quick t sins a lot.	Pr 29:22
anger, bad t, doing or saying	Col 3:8

TEMPERS

people with quick t show their	Pr 14:29
with quick t cause trouble,	Pr 15:18
control their t stop a quarrel.	Pr 15:18
with quick t will have to pay	Pr 19:19
time with those who have bad t.	Pr 22:24
Foolish people lose their t,	Pr 29:11

TEMPLE

the safest room of the t.	Jdg 9:49
that hold up the t so I can lean	Jdg 16:26
Now the t was full of men and	Jdg 16:27
that supported the whole t.	Jdg 16:29
causing the t to fall on the	Jdg 16:30
They came into the t of Baal,	2Ki 10:21
any damage they find in the t."	2Ki 12:5
a priest in the T Solomon built	1Ch 6:10
from far away to pray at this T.	2Ch 6:32
The LORD's glory filled the T.	2Ch 7:1
not enter the T of the LORD,	2Ch 7:2
seen the first T cried when they	Ezr 3:12
rebuilding the T that a great	Ezr 5:11
The LORD is in his holy t;	Ps 11:4

From his t he heard my voice;................. Ps 18:6
look with my own eyes at his T. .... Ps 27:4
His long robe filled the T. ....Is 6:1
This is the T of the LORD. .... Je 7:4
taken from the T of God in .... Da 5:3
hope to see your Holy T again.' .... Jnh 2:4
on which the T stands will be .... Mic 3:12
The LORD is in his Holy T;.................... Hab 2:20
great the T was before it was .... Hag 2:3
looking for will come to his T; .... Mal 3:1
him on a high place of the T. .... Mt 4:5
priests in the T break this law .... Mt 12:5
here that is greater than the T. .... Mt 12:6
threw the money into the T. .... Mt 27:5
curtain in the T was torn into .... Mt 27:51
opposite the T, he was alone .... Mk 13:3
between the altar and the T. .... Lk 11:51
and cattle, to leave the T. .... Jn 2:15
love for your T completely .... Jn 2:17
Destroy this t, and I will build .... Jn 2:19
went to the T at three o'clock .... Ac 3:1
you are God's t and that God's 1Co 3:16
your body is a t for the Holy 1Co 6:19
and become a holy t in the Lord. .... Eph 2:21
The t was filled with smoke from .... Rev 15:8
I did not see a t in the city, ... Rev 21:22
and the Lamb are the city's t. .... Rev 21:22

TEMPLE'S
put gold on the T ceiling beams,........... 2Ch 3:7
in and out of my T rooms? .... Is 1:3
up to show him the T buildings. .... Mt 24:1

TEMPLES
Jeroboam built t on the places 1Ki 12:31
and in the t where gods were 2Ki 17:29
These t had been built by the 2Ki 17:29
had built t for worshiping 2Ki 23:19
all those t and did the same 2Ki 23:19
set fire to the t of the gods of .... Je 43:12
will burn down the t of the gods........... Je 43:13
my precious treasures in your t. .... Joe 3:5
lies in the t of their gods. .... Zph 1:9
not live in t built by human.................. Ac 17:24
idols, but you steal from t. .... Rm 2:22

TEMPT
devil came to Jesus to t him, ... Mt 4:3
so Satan cannot t you because of 1Co 7:5
Evil cannot t God, and God .... Jam 1:13
God himself does not t anyone. .... Jam 1:13

TEMPTATION
life and the t of wealth stop .... Mt 13:22
and pray for strength against t. .... Mt 26:41
of this life, the t of wealth, ... Mk 4:19
and pray for strength against t. .... Mk 14:38
"Pray for strength against t." .... Lk 22:40
pray for strength against t." .... Lk 22:46
The only t that has come to you 1Co 10:13
rich bring t to themselves 1Ti 6:9

TEMPTED
the desert to be t by the devil.............. Mt 4:1
And do not cause us to be t, ... Mt 6:13
forty days and was t by Satan.............. Mk 1:13
the devil t Jesus for forty .... Lk 4:2
the devil had t Jesus in every .... Lk 4:13
And do not cause us to be t.'" .... Lk 11:4
permit you to be t more than you 1Co 10:13
But when you are t, he will also 1Co 10:13
because you might be t to sin, ... Gal 6:1
was afraid the devil had t you, ... 1Th 3:5
now he can help those who are t, ... Heb 2:18
he himself suffered and was t. .... Heb 2:18
He was t in every way that we .... Heb 4:15

When people are t and still.................... Jam 1:12
When people are t, they should .... Jam 1:13
But people are t when their own .... Jam 1:14

TEMPTING
should not say, "God is t me." .... Jam 1:13

TEN
What if you find t there?" .... Ge 18:32
me and changed my pay t times. .... Ge 31:7
he was one hundred t years old.............. Ge 50:22
Agreement—the T Commandments— ..... Ex 34:28
you will chase t thousand men. .... Le 26:8
t women will be able to cook all.............. Le 26:26
me and tested me t times. .... Nu 14:22
at the age of one hundred t. .... Jos 24:29
I mean more to you than t sons?" 1Sa 1:8
he left t slave women to take 2Sa 15:16
shadow to go forward t steps................. 2Ki 20:10
You have insulted me t times now .... Job 19:3
or even t thousand right beside .... Ps 91:7
stronger than t leaders in a................... Ec 7:19
the best of t thousand men. .... Sng 5:10
will make it go back t steps.'" .... Is 38:8
give us this test for t days: .... Da 1:12
They were t times better than................ Da 1:20
seen before, and it had t horns. .... Da 7:7
know about the t horns on its................ Da 7:20
The t horns are ten kings who .... Da 7:24
pleased with t thousand rivers .... Mic 6:7
will be like t bridesmaids who .... Mt 25:1
servant who has t bags of gold. .... Mt 25:28
a woman has t silver coins,................... Lk 15:8
t men who had a skin disease met .... Lk 17:12
It had t horns and seven heads, ... Rev 13:1

TEN-ACRE
At that time a t vineyard will .... Is 5:10

TEN-STRINGED
make music for him on a t lyre. .... Ps 33:2
you with the t lyre and with .... Ps 92:3
will play to you on the t harp................. Ps 144:9

TEND
me and made me t the vineyards, ... Sng 1:6
the vineyards for others to t, ... Sng 8:11
are for those who t the fruit. .... Sng 8:12
will come to t your sheep. .... Is 61:5
countries will t your fields .... Is 61:5
not let them t the flock anymore .... Eze 34:10
will t the sheep with fairness................ Eze 34:16
feed them and t them and be .... Eze 34:23
t the flock of people who belong .... Mic 7:14

TENDED
so I haven't t my own vineyard! .... Sng 1:6
he t sheep to pay for her. .... Hos 12:12

TENDER
the field, like t, young grass, ... 2Ki 19:26
the field, like t, young grass, ... Is 37:27
longer be called t or beautiful. .... Is 47:1
You eat t lambs and fattened .... Am 6:4

TENDERLY
holding his wife Rebekah t. .... Ge 26:8
the desert and speak t to her. .... Hos 2:14

TENDERNESS
you look at it with love and t................. Eze 24:21

TENDING
pasture and from t the sheep and 2Sa 7:8
pasture and from t the sheep and 1Ch 17:7
him from t the sheep so he .... Ps 78:71
took me away from t the flock .... Am 7:15

TENDS

care of, the sheep that he t.....................Ps 95:7
are his people, the sheep he t. ....Ps 100:3
Whoever t a fig tree gets to eat ....Pr 27:18

TENS

hundreds, fifties, and t. ....Ex 18:21
hundreds, fifties, and t. ....Ex 18:25
has killed t of thousands." 1Sa 18:7
David has killed t of thousands, ...1Sa 18:8
has killed t of thousands.' 1Sa 21:11
has killed t of thousands.' 1Sa 29:5
thousands and t of thousands.................Ps 144:13

TENT

drunk and lay naked in his t. ....Ge 9:21
Bethel and set up his t there. ....Ge 12:8
of the entrance of the Holy T, ...Ex 40:6
On the day the Holy T, the Tent ....Nu 9:15
men who ran to the t and found ....Jos 7:22
took a t peg and a hammer and ....Jdg 4:21
reached out and took the t peg. ....Jdg 5:26
It hit the t so hard that the ....Jdg 7:13
the t we live in here on earth— 2Co 5:1
serve in the Holy T cannot eat ....Heb 13:10
the temple (the T of the ....Rev 15:5

TENTH

first day of the t month the...................Ge 8:5
Melchizedek a t of everything he ....Ge 14:20
that on the t day of this month ....Ex 12:3
On the t day of the seventh...................Le 16:29
will be on the t day of the ....Le 23:27
will be on the t day of the ....Le 25:9
person wants to get back that t, ...Le 27:31
will take every t animal from a ....Le 27:32
Israel give me a t of what they ....Nu 18:21
will give that t to the Levites ....Nu 18:21
give a t of everything ....Nu 18:24
will give that t to the Levites ....Nu 18:24
will receive a t of everything ....Nu 18:26
you must give a t of that back ....Nu 18:26
When you receive a t from the ....Nu 18:28
you will give a t of that to ....Nu 18:28
meeting on the t day of the ....Nu 29:7
bring a t of what you gain and ....Dt 12:6
offerings of a t of what you...................Dt 12:11
LORD, eat the t of your grain, ...Dt 14:23
so much you cannot carry a t, ...Dt 14:24
Bring a t of all your harvest ....Dt 26:12
year to give a t of your harvest ....Dt 26:12
Jordan on the t day of the first ....Jos 4:19
on the t day of the tenth month...............2Ki 25:1
on the tenth day of the t month.............2Ki 25:1
Jeremiah was t, and Macbannai...............1Ch 12:13
was Jeshua. The t was Shecaniah. 1Ch 24:11
T, twelve men were chosen from 1Ch 25:17
The t commander, for the tenth 1Ch 27:13
for the t month, was Maharai 1Ch 27:13
first day of the t month they ....Ezr 10:16
will bring a t of our crops to ....Ne 10:37
receive the t of the people's ....Ne 10:38
must bring a t of all they ....Ne 10:38
and the t offerings of grain, ...Ne 13:5
storerooms a t of their crops, ...Ne 13:12
the royal palace in the t month, ...Est 2:16
Jeremiah in the t year Zedekiah...............Je 32:1
was during the t month of the ....Je 39:1
ninth year, t month, and tenth ....Je 52:4
tenth month, and t day as king. ....Je 52:4
on the t day of the fifth ....Je 52:12
on the t day of the month. ....Eze 20:1
captivity, in the t month, on ....Eze 24:1
on the t day of the month. ....Eze 24:1
It was the t year of our ....Eze 29:1

captivity, in the t month, on ....Eze 29:1
on the fifth day of the t month. ....Eze 33:21
on the t day of the month. ....Eze 40:1
will always be a t of a homer, ...Eze 45:11
will always be a t of a homer. ....Eze 45:11
are to offer is a t of a bath ....Eze 45:14
and t months will become good,.............Zch 8:19
and the t of your crops. ....Mal 3:8
a full t of what you earn ....Mal 3:10
gave him a t of everything he ....Heb 7:2
gave him a t of everything that ....Heb 7:4
collect a t from the people— ....Heb 7:5
he collected a t from Abraham. ....Heb 7:6
receive a t, even though they ....Heb 7:8
who received a t from Abraham, ...Heb 7:8
who receives a t, also paid it ....Heb 7:9
Abraham paid Melchizedek a t. ....Heb 7:9
and a t of the city was...........................Rev 11:13
topaz, the t was chrysoprase, ...Rev 21:20

TENTMAKERS

they were t, just as he was,.....................Ac 18:3

TENTS

to live in t and raise cattle. ....Ge 4:20
Your t are beautiful, people of ....Nu 24:5
were getting drunk in their t. 1Ki 20:16
the camp, all around the t. ....Ps 78:28
of Israel settle there in t.......................Ps 78:55
in their t and did not obey ....Ps 106:25
come from the t of those who do ....Ps 118:15
I will put up three t here—.....................Mt 17:4
us make three t—one for you, one ....Mk 9:5
us make three t—one for you, one ....Lk 9:33
He lived in t with Isaac and ....Heb 11:9

TERAH

years old, his son T was born. ....Ge 11:24
After T was 70 years old, his ....Ge 11:26
This is the family history of T. ....Ge 11:27
T was the father of Abram,.....................Ge 11:27
his father, T, was still alive ....Ge 11:28
T took his son Abram, his ....Ge 11:31
T lived to be 205 years old,...................Ge 11:32
left Tahath and camped at T. ....Nu 33:27
They left T and camped at ....Nu 33:28
T, the father of Abraham and ....Jos 24:2
Serug, Nahor, T, ...1Ch 1:26
Abraham was the son of T.....................Lk 3:34
T was the son of Nahor.........................Lk 3:34

TERESH

Now Bigthana and T were two of ....Est 2:21
the king about Bigthana and T, ...Est 6:2

TERMS

let us think in human t: ....Gal 3:15

TERRACES

and all the t out to the Kidron ....Je 31:40

TERRIBLE

that large and t desert you saw, ...Dt 1:19
and say, "The t day is coming." ....Eze 30:2
the most t in the world. ....Eze 32:12
that was cruel, t, and very ....Da 7:7

TERRIFIED

truly, Moab was t by them. ....Nu 22:3
and they will be t of you." ....Dt 2:25
were t because they knew ....Jdg 20:41
trouble hits you, and you are t. ....Job 4:5
we are t by your hot anger. ....Ps 90:7
Shiloah and are t of Rezin and ....Is 8:6
this punishment will be t." ....Is 28:19
will be t when they see ....Is 31:9
Let them be t, but keep me from ....Je 17:18
will not be afraid or t again, ...Je 23:4

TERRIFIES
That army is t, and the soldiers .... Je 46:5
in it were t by the sound of his .... Eze 19:7
fearful and t and thought she .... Lk 24:37

TERRIFIES
the Almighty t me. .... Job 23:16

TERRIFY
dreams and t me with visions .... Job 7:14
Worry and suffering t them; .... Job 15:24
I will t Elam in front of their .... Je 49:37
I wanted to t them so they would .... Eze 20:26

TERRIFYING
great and t day of the LORD' .... Mal 4:5

TERROR
t will take hold of the .... Ex 15:14
T and horror will fall on them. .... Ex 15:16
I will send t ahead of you that .... Ex 23:28
will also send t among them so .... Dt 7:20
T will be in your heart, ... Dt 28:67
in their homes there will be t. .... Dt 32:25
I sent t ahead of you to force .... Jos 24:12
struck with t because God was 1Sa 5:11
filled with t before the king .... Est 7:6
so his t would no longer .... Job 9:34
the wicked are filled with t, ... Ps 14:5
insults. T is all around me. .... Ps 31:13
filled with t where there had .... Ps 53:5
the t of death has attacked me. .... Ps 55:4
and shaking, and t grips me. .... Ps 55:5
meaning and their years in t. .... Ps 78:33
from the sound of t will fall .... Is 24:18
think about the t of the past; .... Is 33:18
There is t on every side. .... Je 6:25
heal us, but only t has come. .... Je 8:15
of healing, but only t came. .... Je 14:19
Don't be a t to me. I run to you .... Je 17:17
terrified, but keep me from t. .... Je 17:18
name for you is T on Every Side. .... Je 20:3
soon make you a t to yourself. .... Je 20:4
about me: "T on every side! Tell .... Je 20:10
You brought great t on everyone. .... Je 32:21
There is t on every side!" .... Je 46:5
I will soon bring t on you from .... Je 49:5
to them, 'T on every side!' .... Je 49:29
and they will be full of t. .... Je 50:36
be a warning and a t to them. .... Eze 5:15
anger, a day of t and trouble, a .... Zph 1:15

TERRORS
using great t, signs, and .... Dt 26:8
God's t are gathered against me. .... Job 6:4
stop frightening me with your t. .... Job 13:21
off to Death, the King of T. .... Job 18:14
T will come over them; .... Job 20:25
friends with the t of darkness. .... Job 24:17
they are swept away by t. .... Ps 73:19
suffer from your t, and I am .... Ps 88:15
and your t have destroyed me. .... Ps 88:16
There are t, holes, and traps .... Is 24:17
You invited t to come against me .... La 2:22

TERTIUS
I am T, and I am writing this .... Rm 16:22

TERTULLUS
the elders and a lawyer named T. .... Ac 24:1
and T began to accuse him, ... Ac 24:2

TEST
because God has come to t you. .... Ex 20:20
not t the LORD your God as you .... Dt 6:16
away your pride and to t you, ... Dt 8:16
I will use them to t Israel, ... Jdg 2:22
wanted to t the Israelites who .... Jdg 3:1
in the land to t the Israelites— .... Jdg 3:4

Please let me make one more t. .... Jdg 6:39
and I will t them for you there. .... Jdg 7:4
she came to t him with hard 1Ki 10:1
that you t people's hearts. 1Ch 29:17
to Jerusalem to t him with hard 2Ch 9:1
alone to t him so he could 2Ch 32:31
morning and t them every moment .... Job 7:18
try me and t me; look closely .... Ps 26:2
They decided to t God by asking .... Ps 78:18
t me and know my anxious .... Ps 139:23
the way it is to t people and to .... Ec 3:18
used wisdom to t all these .... Ec 7:23
ask for a sign or t the LORD." .... Is 7:12
observe their ways and t them. .... Je 6:27
I will t the people of Judah as .... Je 9:7
know how to t peoples' hearts. .... Je 11:20
You see me and t my thoughts .... Je 12:3
a person's heart and t the mind. .... Je 17:10
All-Powerful, you t good people; .... Je 20:12
The t will come. And Judah, ... Eze 21:13
give us this t for ten days: .... Da 1:12
agreed to t them for ten days. .... Da 1:14
that is left I will t with fire, ... Zch 13:9
T me in this," says the LORD .... Mal 3:10
'Do not t the Lord your God.'" .... Mt 4:7
Jesus this question to him: .... Mt 22:35
'Do not t the Lord your God.'" .... Lk 4:12
on the law stood up to t Jesus, ... Lk 10:25
wanting to t Jesus, asked him .... Lk 11:16
has asked to t all of you as .... Lk 22:31
Philip this question to him, ... Jn 6:6
husband agree to t the Spirit .... Ac 5:9
the fire will t everyone's work 1Co 3:13
We must not t Christ as some of 1Co 10:9
I wrote you to t you and to see 2Co 2:9
T yourselves to see if you are 2Co 13:5
is in you—unless you fail the t. 2Co 13:5
ourselves have not failed the t. 2Co 13:6
see that we have passed the t, ... 2Co 13:7
But t everything. Keep what is 1Th 5:21
T them first. Then let them 1Ti 3:10
these troubles your faith, ... Jam 1:3
which now comes to you. 1Pe 4:12
but t the spirits to see if they 1Jn 4:1
some of you in prison to t you, ... Rev 2:10
whole world to t those who live .... Rev 3:10

TESTED
things God t Abraham's faith .... Ge 22:1
there he t their loyalty to him. .... Ex 15:25
the Israelites t the LORD when .... Ex 17:7
disobeyed me and t me ten times. .... Nu 14:22
which t you like a furnace for .... Dt 4:20
you t him at Massah and argued .... Dt 33:8
when he has t me, I will come .... Job 23:10
he set wisdom up and t it. .... Job 28:27
wish Job would be t completely, ... Job 34:36
you have t me all night. .... Ps 17:3
God, you have t us; you have .... Ps 66:10
and again they t God and brought .... Ps 78:41
they t God and turned against .... Ps 78:56
I t you at the waters of Meribah .... Ps 81:7
your ancestors t me and tried me .... Ps 95:9
desert, and they t God there. .... Ps 106:14
and people are t by the praise .... Pr 27:21
ground in Jerusalem, a t stone. .... Is 28:16
who was t and proved that he .... Rm 16:10
They have been t by great 2Co 8:2
because God t us and trusted 1Th 2:4
when you t God in the desert. .... Heb 3:8
tried me and t me and saw the .... Heb 3:9
when God t him, offered his .... Heb 11:17
have t those who say they are .... Rev 2:2

TESTIFIED
because we t of him that he 1Co 15:15
who heard him t it was true. .... Heb 2:3
God also t to the truth of the .... Heb 2:4

TESTIFIES
Israel's pride t against them. .... Hos 5:5

TESTIFY
this song will t against them, ... Dt 31:21
and earth to t against them. .... Dt 31:28
you must t against me before the 1Sa 12:3
your own lips t against you. .... Job 15:6
Men without mercy stand up to t. .... Ps 35:11
Israel, I will t against you. .... Ps 50:7
Don't t against your neighbor .... Pr 24:28
If they have to t in court, ... Pr 29:24
will be quick to t against those .... Mal 3:5
I am ready to t that you would .... Gal 4:15
seen and can t that the Father 1Jn 4:14

TESTING
Why are you t the LORD?" .... Ex 17:2
away your pride and t you, ... Dt 8:2
The LORD your God is t you, ... Dt 13:3
like silver, t them like gold. .... Zch 13:9
now why are you t God by putting .... Ac 15:10

TESTS
He did it with t, signs, ... Dt 4:34
The ear t words as the tongue .... Job 12:11
The ear t words as the tongue .... Job 34:3
The LORD t those who do right, ... Ps 11:5
A hot furnace t silver and gold, ... Pr 17:3
and gold, but the LORD t hearts. .... Pr 17:3
A hot furnace t silver and gold, ... Pr 27:21
you like a worker who t metal, ... Je 6:27
as a person t metal in a fire. .... Je 9:7
but God, who t our hearts. 1Th 2:4

THADDAEUS
James son of Alphaeus, and T; .... Mt 10:3
son of Alphaeus, T, Simon the .... Mk 3:18

THANK
"No, t you," said Jacob. .... Ge 33:15
offering is given to t the LORD, ... Le 7:15
T the LORD because he is good. 1Ch 16:34
Then we will t you and will 1Ch 16:35
t you and praise your glorious 1Ch 29:13
they said, "T the LORD, because 2Ch 20:21
sacrifices and t offerings, ... 2Ch 29:31
Hezekiah did not t God for his 2Ch 32:25
will t you forever for what you .... Ps 52:9
I will t you, LORD, because you .... Ps 54:6
give you my offerings to t you, ... Ps 56:12
God, we t you; we thank you .... Ps 75:1
we t you because you are near. .... Ps 75:1
flock. We will t you always; .... Ps 79:13
T him and praise his name. .... Ps 100:4
T the LORD because he is good. .... Ps 106:1
Then we will t you and will .... Ps 106:47
T the LORD because he is good. .... Ps 107:1
them offer sacrifices to t him. .... Ps 107:22
I will t the LORD very much; .... Ps 109:30
I will t the LORD with all my .... Ps 111:1
T the LORD because he is good. .... Ps 118:1
I will come in and t the LORD. .... Ps 118:19
LORD, I t you for answering me. .... Ps 118:21
are my God, and I will t you; .... Ps 118:28
T the LORD because he is good. .... Ps 118:29
I get up to t you because your .... Ps 119:62
I will t you with all my heart; .... Ps 138:1
and I will t you for your love .... Ps 138:2
t you and praise you, God of my .... Da 2:23
kneel down to pray and t God, ... Da 6:10
will praise and t you while I .... Jnh 2:9

one who came back to t God?" .... Lk 17:18
I t you that I am not like other .... Lk 18:11
said, "Father, I t you that you .... Jn 11:41
to say that I t my God through .... Rm 1:8
not give glory to God or t him. .... Rm 1:21
But t God, you fully obeyed the .... Rm 6:17
I t God for saving me through .... Rm 7:25
always t my God for you because 1Co 1:4
I t God because in Christ you 1Co 1:5
I t God I did not baptize any of 1Co 1:14
of something for which I t God? 1Co 10:30
t God that I speak in different 1Co 14:18
But we t God! He gives us the 1Co 15:57
t God because he gave Titus the 2Co 8:16
t my God every time I remember .... Php 1:3
I t God for the help you gave me .... Php 1:5
prayers for you we always t God, ... Col 1:3
We always t God for all of you 1Th 1:2
And we t him that you continue 1Th 1:3
we always t God because when you 1Th 2:13
We cannot t him enough for all 1Th 3:9
We must always t God for you, ... 2Th 1:3
So we must always t God for you. 2Th 2:13
I t Christ Jesus our Lord, ... 1Ti 1:12
I t God as I always mention you 2Ti 1:3
I always t my God when I mention .... Phm 1:4

THANKED
I bowed my head and t the LORD. .... Ge 24:48
They were pleased and t God. .... Jos 22:33
as they praised and t the LORD. 2Ch 5:13
They worshiped and t the LORD, ... 2Ch 7:3
heaven, he t God for the food. .... Mt 14:19
took some bread and t God for it .... Mt 26:26
took a cup and t God for it and .... Mt 26:27
to heaven, he t God for the food .... Mk 6:41
took some bread and t God for it .... Mk 14:22
took a cup and t God for it and .... Mk 14:23
the baby in his arms and t God: .... Lk 2:28
she t God and spoke about Jesus .... Lk 2:38
to heaven, he t God for the food .... Lk 9:16
down at Jesus' feet and t him. .... Lk 17:16
loaves of bread, t God for them, ... Jn 6:11
some bread and t God for it .... Ac 27:35
he was encouraged and t God. .... Ac 28:15

THANKFUL
wild animals will be t to me— .... Is 43:20
place, and we are t for them. .... Ac 24:3
I am t to them, and all the .... Rm 16:4
-Jewish churches are t as well. .... Rm 16:4
were taught, and always be t. .... Col 2:7
body to have peace. Always be t. .... Col 3:15
they need and being t to him. 1Ti 2:1
parents or be t or be the kind 2Ti 3:2
So let us be t, because we have .... Heb 12:28

THANKFULNESS
I eat the meal with t, why am I 1Co 10:30
songs with t in your hearts to .... Col 3:16

THANKING
praising God and t him for .... Lk 2:20
and he followed Jesus, t God. .... Lk 18:43
You may be t God in a good way, ... 1Co 14:17
keeping alert, and always t God. .... Col 4:2

THANKS
offering to show his t, ... Le 7:12
which he gives to show t. .... Le 7:13
offering of t to the LORD, ... Le 22:29
and giving t and praising 1Ch 16:4
Give t to the LORD and pray to 1Ch 16:8
morning and gave t and praise to 1Ch 23:30
a harp to give t and praise to 1Ch 25:3
offerings, to show t to him." 2Ch 29:31

and to give t and praise at the 2Ch 31:2
and offerings to show t to God. 2Ch 33:16
two large choruses to give t. .... Ne 12:31
an offering to show t to God. .... Ps 50:14
bring me offerings to show t. .... Ps 50:23
and will honor him by giving t. .... Ps 69:30
our God is holy. A psalm of t. .... Ps 99:9
Give t to the LORD and pray to .... Ps 105:1
Let them give t to the LORD for .... Ps 107:8
Let them give t to the LORD for .... Ps 107:15
Let them give t to the LORD for .... Ps 107:21
Let them give t to the LORD for .... Ps 107:31
an offering to show t to you, ... Ps 116:17
Give t to the LORD because he is .... Ps 136:1
Give t to the God of gods. .... Ps 136:2
Give t to the Lord of lords. .... Ps 136:3
Give t to the God of heaven. .... Ps 136:26
you mountains, with t to God. .... Is 44:23
they will give t and sing songs. .... Is 51:3
and offerings to show t to God. .... Je 17:26
offerings of t to the LORD. .... Je 33:11
as a sacrifice to show your t, ... Am 4:5
and the fish and gave t to God. .... Mt 15:36
seven loaves, gave t to God, and .... Mk 8:6
After Jesus gave t for the fish, ... Mk 8:7
get any special t for doing what .... Lk 17:9
a cup, gave t, and said, "Take .... Lk 22:17
some bread, gave t, broke it, ... Lk 22:19
some bread, gave t, divided it, ... Lk 24:30
after the Lord had given t. .... Jn 6:23
Lord, and they give t to God. .... Rm 14:6
Lord, and they give t to God. .... Rm 14:6
We give t for the cup of 1Co 10:16
and gave t for it. Then he broke 1Co 11:24
say amen to your prayer of t, ... 1Co 14:16
many people will give t for us— 2Co 1:11
t be to God, who always leads 2Co 2:14
bring increasing t to God for 2Co 4:15
cause many to give t to God. 2Co 9:11
also brings many more t to God. 2Co 9:12
T be to God for his gift that is 2Co 9:15
stopped giving t to God for you. .... Eph 1:16
you should be giving t to God. .... Eph 5:4
Always give t to God the Father .... Eph 5:20
you need, always giving t. .... Php 4:6
joyfully give t to the Father .... Col 1:12
give t to God the Father through .... Col 3:17
and give t whatever happens. 1Th 5:18
to be eaten with t by people who 1Ti 4:3
if it is accepted with t, ... 1Ti 4:4
and t to the One who sits on the .... Rev 4:9
glory, wisdom, t, honor, power, ... Rev 7:12
We give t to you, Lord God .... Rev 11:17

THANKSGIVING

With praise and t, they sang to .... Ezr 3:11
led the people in t and prayer. .... Ne 11:17
in charge of the songs of t. .... Ne 12:8
and gave praise and t to God. .... Ne 12:24
with songs of t and with the .... Ne 12:27
songs of praise and t to God. .... Ne 12:46
Let's come to him with t. .... Ps 95:2
city with songs of t and into .... Ps 100:4

THAT'S

want to walk through. T all." .... Nu 20:19
you said, "T a good thing to do. .... Dt 1:14
The LORD said to me, "T enough. .... Dt 3:26
to his servant, "T a good idea. 1Sa 9:10
T why they are so weak." 1Sa 14:28
T why I called for you. 1Sa 28:15
T why he has done this to you 1Sa 28:18
They answered, "T not true. 2Ki 9:12
T why the young women love you. .... Sng 1:3

said to Irijah, "T not true! .... Je 37:14
because t why you have been .... Eze 40:4
T your problem, not ours." .... Mt 27:4
and resting? T enough. The time .... Mk 14:41

THEATER

with Paul, and ran to the t. .... Ac 19:29
him not to go into the t. .... Ac 19:31

THEBES

Amon, the god of the city of T. .... Je 46:25
a fire in Zoan and punish T. .... Eze 30:14
great numbers of people in T. .... Eze 30:15
The walls of T will be broken .... Eze 30:16
are no better than T, who sits .... Nah 3:8
But T was captured and went into .... Nah 3:10

THEBEZ

Abimelech went to the city of T. .... Jdg 9:50
and killed him there in T. 2Sa 11:21

THEFT

for murder, t, or any other 1Pe 4:15

THEOPHILUS

most excellent T, it seemed good .... Lk 1:3
To T. The first book I wrote was .... Ac 1:1

THERE'S

and t no water to drink .... Nu 20:5
T no reason to kill him!" 1Sa 19:5
T no other sword here but that 1Sa 21:9
Gehazi, "Look, t the Shunammite 2Ki 4:25
Man of God, t death in the pot!" 2Ki 4:40
person says, "T a lion outside! .... Pr 22:13
person says, "T a lion in the .... Pr 26:13
T a lion in the streets!" .... Pr 26:13

THESSALONICA

and came to T where there was .... Ac 17:1
to listen than the people in T. .... Ac 17:11
the people in T learned that .... Ac 17:13
Secundus, from the city of T; .... Ac 20:4
from the city of T in Macedonia, ... Ac 27:2
things I needed when I was in T. .... Php 4:16
the church in T, the church in 1Th 1:1
To the church in T in God our 2Th 1:1
world, left me and went to T. 2Ti 4:10

THEUDAS

Remember when T appeared? .... Ac 5:36

THEY'RE

T eating meat without draining 1Sa 14:33
T saying, 'When the Israelites 2Ki 7:12

THICK

to you in a t cloud and speak .... Ex 19:9
and lightning with a t cloud on .... Ex 19:16
it went under the t branches of 2Sa 18:9
of the bowl were four inches t, ... 1Ki 7:26
of the bowl were four inches t, ... 2Ch 4:5
Let t darkness cover its light. .... Job 3:5
Let t darkness capture that .... Job 3:6
stubbornly charge at God with t, ... Job 15:26
of the wicked are t with fat, ... Job 15:27
T clouds cover him so he cannot .... Job 22:14
by the t darkness that covers my .... Job 23:17
up the waters in his t clouds, ... Job 26:8
the mines for ore in t darkness. .... Job 28:3
T, dark clouds surround him. .... Ps 97:2
become dark in this t cloud. .... Is 5:30
a fire with t clouds of smoke .... Is 30:27
hide in the t bushes and climb .... Je 4:29
you do in the t thornbushes .... Je 12:5
he will turn it into t darkness; .... Je 13:16
coming up from the t bushes near .... Je 49:19
coming up from the t bushes near .... Je 50:44
Babylon's t wall will be .... Je 51:58

T

THICKNESS

each pillar was three inches t. .... Je 52:21
tall among the t branches. .... Eze 19:11
and one-half feet t and ten and .... Eze 40:5
rooms were about nine feet t. .... Eze 40:7
were three and one-half feet t. .... Eze 40:9
Each was about nine feet t..................... Eze 40:48
each ten and one-half feet t. .... Eze 41:1
was three and one-half feet t................... Eze 41:3
each more than twelve feet t. .... Eze 41:3
was ten and one-half feet t..................... Eze 41:5
it was ten and one-half feet t. .... Eze 41:8
rooms was about nine feet t. .... Eze 41:9
nine feet t and one hundred .... Eze 41:12
blood, fire, and t smoke. .... Joe 2:30
blood, fire, and t smoke. .... Ac 2:19

THICKNESS

each room were the same t. .... Eze 40:10

THIEF

If the t is caught, he must pay .... Ex 22:7
But if the t is never found, ... Ex 22:8
When you see a t, you join him. .... Ps 50:18
don't hate a t when he steals .... Pr 6:30
A t is ashamed when someone .... Je 2:26
side says every t will be taken .... Zch 5:3
time of night a t was coming, ... Mt 24:43
watch and not let the t break .... Mt 24:43
knew what time a t was coming, ... Lk 12:39
not allow the t to enter his .... Lk 12:39
other way, is a t and a robber. .... Jn 10:1
A t comes to steal and kill and .... Jn 10:10
he said this because he was a t. .... Jn 12:6
a t that comes in the night. 1Th 5:2
will not surprise you like a t. 1Th 5:4
of the Lord will come like a t.................. 2Pe 3:10
will come like a t, and you will .... Rev 3:3
I will come as a t comes!........................ Rev 16:15

THIEVES

At night they go about like t. .... Job 24:14
at them as if they were t. .... Job 30:5
Partners of t are their own .... Pr 29:24
are rebels and friends of t. .... Is 1:23
but they weren't t you caught .... Je 2:34
in the middle of a gang of t. .... Je 48:27
T break into houses, and robbers .... Hos 7:1
entering through windows like t. .... Joe 2:9
t came to you, if robbers came .... Ob 1:5
the houses of t and those who .... Zch 5:4
destroy them and t can break................. Mt 6:19
or rust and where t cannot break .... Mt 6:20
made it safe from t by sealing .... Mt 27:66
where t can't steal and moths................ Lk 12:33
before me were t and robbers. .... Jn 10:8
from rivers, t, my own people, ... 2Co 11:26

THIGH

around them, and the right t. .... Ex 29:22
breast and the t of the sheep .... Ex 29:27
give the right t from the .... Le 7:32
the breast and the t from the .... Le 7:34
with their fat, and the right t................... Le 8:25
fat and right t of the male .... Le 8:26
and the right t before the LORD .... Le 9:21
the breast and t of the........................... Le 10:14
along with the t and the breast .... Le 10:15
breast and the t from the male .... Nu 6:20
and the right t will be yours. .... Nu 18:18
the cook took the t and put it 1Sa 9:24

THIGHS

muscles of its t are woven .... Job 40:17
Your round t are like jewels .... Sng 7:1

THIN

river, but they were t and ugly. .... Ge 41:3
seven t and ugly cows ate the .... Ge 41:4
they were t and burned by the .... Ge 41:6
The t heads of grain ate the .... Ge 41:7
that were t and lean and ugly— .... Ge 41:19
these t and ugly cows ate the .... Ge 41:20
looked just as t and ugly as .... Ge 41:21
these heads were t and ugly and .... Ge 41:23
Then the t heads ate the seven .... Ge 41:24
The seven t and ugly cows stand .... Ge 41:27
and the seven t heads of grain .... Ge 41:27
t flakes like frost were on the .... Ex 16:14
then cut it into long, t strips. .... Ex 39:3
hair around it is t and yellow,................. Le 13:30
You have made me t and weak, ... Job 16:8
and my body is as t as a shadow. .... Job 17:7
They were t from hunger and .... Job 30:3
becomes so t there is almost .... Job 33:21
fasting, and I have grown t. .... Ps 109:24
the fat sheep and the t sheep. .... Eze 34:20

THINK

Don't t that I have come to .... Mt 5:17
Don't t that I came to bring .... Mt 10:34
comes from the way they t;...................... Mt 15:18
things people t are important." .... Mt 16:23
because you t they give you .... Jn 5:39
Do not t you are better than you .... Rm 12:3
Do not t how smart you are. .... Rm 12:16
I t it is good for you to stay.................... 1Co 7:26
He must t about two things— 1Co 7:34
If you t you know something, ... 1Co 8:2
t only about earthly things...................... Php 3:19
Do not t that something strange 1Pe 4:12

THINKS

The lazy person t he is wiser .... Pr 26:16
If a man t he is not doing the 1Co 7:36
of Christ as the world t, ... 2Co 5:16
but those the Lord t are good. 2Co 10:18
If anyone t he is important when .... Gal 6:3
If anyone t he has a reason to .... Php 3:4
like Esau and never t about God. .... Heb 12:16
but if he t of God and can stand 1Pe 2:19

THINNER

of each room was t than the wall 1Ki 6:6

THIRD

came. This was the t day. .... Ge 1:13
The t river, named Tigris, flows .... Ge 2:14
On the t day Abraham looked up .... Ge 22:4
The t son is Kemuel (the father .... Ge 22:21
servant, the t servant, and all .... Ge 32:19
Esau's t wife was Oholibamah the .... Ge 36:14
Kezib when this t son was born............. Ge 38:5
the t day Joseph said to them, ... Ge 42:18
On the morning of the t day, ... Ex 19:16
the t must have a jacinth, ... Ex 28:19
in the t there was a jacinth, ... Ex 39:12
sacrifice is left on the t day, ... Le 7:17
eaten on the t day will not be .... Le 7:18
But if any is left on the t day, ... Le 19:6
any of it is eaten on the t day,................. Le 19:7
will be the t group to march .... Nu 2:24
water on the t day and on the................. Nu 19:12
themselves on the t day and the .... Nu 19:12
unclean people on the t day and............. Nu 19:19
On the t day offer eleven .... Nu 29:20
the t and seventh days you and .... Nu 31:19
At the end of every t year, ... Dt 14:28
of all your harvest the t year .... Dt 26:12
lived and on the t day came to .... Jos 9:17
The t part of the land was given .... Jos 19:10

This is the t time you have made .... Jdg 16:15
at Gibeah on the t day, ... Jdg 20:30
called Samuel for the t time. 1Sa 3:8
the t will have a leather bag 1Sa 10:3
The t group went on the border 1Sa 13:18
Abinadab, and the t was Shammah. 1Sa 17:13
he sent messengers a t time, ... 1Sa 19:21
the field until the t evening. 1Sa 20:5
On the t day go to the place 1Sa 20:19
On the t day I will shoot three 1Sa 20:20
On the t day, when David and his 1Sa 30:1
On the t day a young man from 2Sa 1:2
The t son was Absalom, whose 2Sa 3:3
of Zeruiah commanded another t. 2Sa 18:2
from Gath commanded the last t. 2Sa 18:2
during Asa's t year as king of 1Ki 15:28
during Asa's t year as king.................. 1Ki 15:33
During the t year without rain, ... 1Ki 18:1
said, "Do it a t time," and they 1Ki 18:34
and they did it the t time. 1Ki 18:34
During the t year Jehoshaphat 1Ki 22:2
then sent a t captain with his 2Ki 1:13
The t captain came and fell down 2Ki 1:13
A t of you who go on duty on the 2Ki 11:5
A t of you will be at the Sur 2Ki 11:6
another t will be at the gate 2Ki 11:6
king during the t year Hoshea 2Ki 18:1
But in the t year, plant grain 2Ki 19:29
of the LORD on the t day?" 2Ki 20:8
was Abinadab, his t was Shimea, ... 1Ch 2:13
The t son was Absalom, whose 1Ch 3:2
Jehoiakim, his t was Zedekiah, ... 1Ch 3:15
second son, Aharah was his t, ... 1Ch 8:1
Jeush, and Eliphelet was his t. 1Ch 8:39
second in command. Eliab was t, ... 1Ch 12:9
was Amariah, his t was Jahaziel, ... 1Ch 23:19
The t was Harim. The fourth was 1Ch 24:8
Jahaziel was his t, and Jekameam 1Ch 24:23
T, twelve men were chosen from 1Ch 25:10
Zebadiah was t, Jathniel was 1Ch 26:2
second, Joah was t, Sacar was 1Ch 26:4
Tabaliah was t, and Zechariah 1Ch 26:11
The t commander, for the third 1Ch 27:5
for the t month, was Benaiah 1Ch 27:5
in Jerusalem in the t month on 2Ch 15:10
During the t year of his rule, ... 2Ch 17:7
A t of you will guard the doors. 2Ch 23:4
A t of you will be at the king's 2Ch 23:5
and a t of you will be at the 2Ch 23:5
the piles in the t month and 2Ch 31:7
finished on the t day of the .... Ezr 6:15
In the t year of his rule, ... Est 1:3
On the t day Esther put on her .... Est 5:1
twenty-third day of the t month,............ Est 8:9
The t messenger was still .... Job 1:18
the t daughter Keren-Happuch. .... Job 42:14
But in the t year, plant grain .... Is 37:30
bring him to the t entrance to................ Je 38:14
t of you will die by disease or................ Eze 5:12
A t will fall dead by the sword .... Eze 5:12
And a t I will scatter in every .... Eze 5:12
the t was the face of a lion,................... Eze 10:14
captivity, in the t month, on .... Eze 31:1
During the t year that Jehoiakim .... Da 1:1
Next a t kingdom, the bronze................. Da 2:39
that person the t highest ruler .... Da 5:7
will become the t highest ruler .... Da 5:16
Daniel was the t highest ruler............... Da 5:29
During the t year of King .... Da 8:1
During Cyrus' t year as king of .... Da 10:1
on the t day he will raise us up .... Hos 6:2
horses pulled the t chariot,................... Zch 6:3
The t that is left I will test .... Zch 13:9

from the dead on the t day...................... Mt 16:21
But on the t day he will be .... Mt 17:23
But on the t day, he will be .... Mt 20:19
and then killed a t servant with .... Mt 21:35
happened to the t brother and .... Mt 22:26
and a t servant one bag of gold, ... Mt 25:15
went away and prayed a t time, ... Mt 26:44
guarded closely till the t day. .... Mt 27:64
But on the t day, he will rise .... Mk 10:34
happened with the t brother. .... Mk 12:21
After Jesus prayed a t time, ... Mk 14:41
Then, on the t day, I will reach .... Lk 13:32
A t person said, 'I just got .... Lk 14:20
But on the t day, he will rise .... Lk 18:33
So the man sent a t servant. .... Lk 20:12
And the t brother married the .... Lk 20:31
A t time Pilate said to them, ... Lk 23:22
from the dead on the t day." .... Lk 24:7
it is now the t day since this .... Lk 24:21
rise from the dead on the t day .... Lk 24:46
This was now the t time Jesus .... Jn 21:14
A t time he said, "Simon son of .... Jn 21:17
Jesus asked him the t time,.................... Jn 21:17
Yet, on the t day, God raised .... Ac 10:40
to the ground from the t floor. .... Ac 20:9
to prophets, and t to teachers. 1Co 12:28
to life on the t day as the 1Co 15:4
up to the t heaven fourteen.................... 2Co 12:2
ready to visit you the t time, ... 2Co 12:14
will come to you for the t time. 2Co 13:1
The t had a face like a man. .... Rev 4:7
When the Lamb opened the t seal, ... Rev 6:5
I heard the t living creature .... Rev 6:5
a t of the earth, and all the .... Rev 8:7
and a t of the trees were burned.............. Rev 8:7
And a t of the sea became blood, ... Rev 8:8
a t of the living things in the .... Rev 8:9
and a t of the ships were........................ Rev 8:9
Then the t angel blew his .... Rev 8:10
It fell on a t of the rivers and .... Rev 8:10
And a t of all the water became .... Rev 8:11
his trumpet, and a t of the sun, ... Rev 8:12
of the sun, and a t of the moon, ... Rev 8:12
a t of the stars were struck. .... Rev 8:12
So a t of them became dark, ... Rev 8:12
and a t of the day was without .... Rev 8:12
could kill a t of all people .... Rev 9:15
A t of all the people on earth .... Rev 9:18
The t trouble is coming soon. .... Rev 11:14
tail swept a t of the stars out .... Rev 12:4
a t angel followed the first .... Rev 14:9
The t angel poured out his bowl .... Rev 16:4
sapphire, the t was chalcedony, ... Rev 21:19

THIRD-FLOOR
stairs went on to the t rooms. 1Ki 6:8

THIRST
and our farm animals with t?" .... Ex 17:3
Do I have to die of t now? .... Jdg 15:18
you will die from hunger and t. 2Ch 32:11
of water, so I t for you, God. .... Ps 42:1
I t for the living God. .... Ps 42:2
I t for you like someone in a .... Ps 63:1
land needs rain, I t for you,................... Ps 143:6
the common people will die of t. .... Is 5:13
Their tongues are dry with t. .... Is 41:17
is no water; they die of t. .... Is 50:2
satisfies its t for their blood .... Je 46:10
and I will kill her with t........................ Hos 2:3
People weak from t went from .... Am 4:8
men will become weak from t. .... Am 8:13
who hunger and t after justice, ... Mt 5:6

THIRSTS

a deer t for streams of water, ... Ps 42:1

THIRSTY

people were very t for water, ... Ex 17:3
will be hungry, t, naked, and .... Dt 28:48
Sisera said to Jael, "I am t. .... Jdg 4:19
Samson was very t, so he cried .... Jdg 15:18
When you are t, you may go and .... Ru 2:9
and tired and t in the desert." 2Sa 17:29
When they were t, you brought .... Ne 9:15
eat and water when they were t. .... Ne 9:20
and t people want his wealth. .... Job 5:5
get wine, but they still go t. .... Job 24:11
were hungry and t, and they were .... Ps 107:5
He satisfies the t and fills up .... Ps 107:9
If he is t, give him a drink. .... Pr 25:21
They gave water to t travelers; .... Is 21:14
will be like a t man who dreams .... Is 29:8
awakens, he is still weak and t. .... Is 29:8
the hungry or let t people drink .... Is 32:6
water for the t land and make .... Is 44:3
not become t when he led them .... Is 48:21
They will not be hungry or t, ... Is 49:10
you who are t, come and drink .... Is 55:1
but you evil people will be t. .... Is 65:13
babies are so t their tongues .... La 4:4
the desert, in a dry and t land. .... Eze 19:13
hungry for bread or t for water, ... Am 8:11
You drink, but you are still t. .... Hag 1:6
I was t, and you gave me .... Mt 25:35
t and give you something to drink? .... Mt 25:37
I was t, and you gave me nothing .... Mt 25:42
you hungry or t or alone and .... Mt 25:44
this water will be t again, ... Jn 4:13
water I give will never be t. .... Jn 4:14
I will never be t again and will .... Jn 4:15
believes in me will never be t. .... Jn 6:35
Let anyone who is t come to me .... Jn 7:37
come true, he said, "I am t." .... Jn 19:28
if he is t, give him a drink. .... Rm 12:20
hungry and t, and many times 2Co 11:27
and they will never be t again. .... Rev 7:16
of life to anyone who is t. .... Rev 21:6
Let whoever is t come; .... Rev 22:17

THIRTEEN

was t years old when he was .... Ge 17:25
t young bulls, two male sheep, ... Nu 29:13
With each of the t bulls offer a .... Nu 29:14
it was more than t feet long and .... Dt 3:11
There were t towns and their .... Jos 19:6
were given t towns in the areas .... Jos 21:4
were given t towns in the land .... Jos 21:6
So these t towns with their .... Jos 21:19
groups received t towns and the .... Jos 21:33
took him t years to finish it. 1Ki 7:1
to hold about t quarts of seed. 1Ki 18:32
and t quarts of barley will be 2Ki 7:1
and t quarts of barley were sold 2Ki 7:16
T quarts of barley and seven 2Ki 7:18
received a total of t towns. 1Ch 6:60
group received t towns from the 1Ch 6:62
Hosah had t sons and relatives. 1Ch 26:11

THIRTEENTH

but in the t year, they all .... Ge 14:4
The t was Huppah. 1Ch 24:13
T, twelve men were chosen from 1Ch 25:20
On the t day of the first month, ... Est 3:12
the t day of the twelfth month, ... Est 3:13
Xerxes was the t day of the .... Est 8:12
to be done on the t day of the .... Est 9:1
happened on the t day of the .... Est 9:17
Susa met on the t and fourteenth .... Est 9:18

---

during the t year that Josiah .... Je 1:2
since the t year of Josiah .... Je 25:3

THIRTIETH

It was the t year, on the fifth .... Eze 1:1

THIRTY

you find only t good people in .... Ge 18:30
If I find t good people there, ... Ge 18:30
t female camels and their young, ... Ge 32:15
Joseph was t years old when he .... Ge 41:46
—only one hundred t years. .... Ge 47:9
Egypt for four hundred t years; .... Ex 12:40
the four hundred t years ended, ... Ex 12:41
is to be a curtain t feet wide, ... Ex 27:16
The curtain was t feet long and .... Ex 38:18
the men from t to fifty years .... Nu 4:3
the men from t to fifty years .... Nu 4:23
the men from t to fifty years .... Nu 4:30
men from t to fifty years old .... Nu 4:35
men from t to fifty years old .... Nu 4:39
men from t to fifty years old .... Nu 4:43
the men from t to fifty who were .... Nu 4:47
Israel cried for him for t days. .... Nu 20:29
cried for Moses for t days, ... Dt 34:8
Then he chose t thousand of his .... Jos 8:3
Jair had t sons, who rode thirty .... Jdg 10:4
thirty sons, who rode t donkeys .... Jdg 10:4
These t sons controlled thirty .... Jdg 10:4
controlled t towns in Gilead .... Jdg 10:4
He had t sons and thirty .... Jdg 12:9
had thirty sons and t daughters. .... Jdg 12:9
and he brought t women who were .... Jdg 12:9
had forty sons and t grandsons, ... Jdg 12:14
they sent t friends to be with .... Jdg 14:11
I will give you t linen shirts .... Jdg 14:12
linen shirts and t changes of .... Jdg 14:12
you must give me t linen shirts .... Jdg 14:13
linen shirts and t changes of .... Jdg 14:13
and killed t of its men and took .... Jdg 14:19
About t Israelites were killed— .... Jdg 20:31
had killed about t Israelites. .... Jdg 20:39
because t thousand Israelite 1Sa 4:10
About t guests were there. 1Sa 9:22
from Israel and t thousand men 1Sa 11:8
Saul was t years old when he 1Sa 13:1
David was t years old when he 2Sa 5:4
of Israel—t thousand of them. 2Sa 6:1
three of the T, David's chief 2Sa 23:13
received more honor than the T, ... 2Sa 23:23
following men were among the T: 2Sa 23:24
Solomon forced t thousand men 1Ki 5:13
ninety feet long, t feet wide, ... 1Ki 6:2
feet deep and t feet wide. 1Ki 6:3
A room t feet long was built in 1Ki 6:16
This inner room was t feet long, ... 1Ki 6:20
thirty feet long, t feet wide, ... 1Ki 6:20
feet wide, and t feet high. 1Ki 6:20
about two hundred t gallons. 1Ki 7:38
three of the T, David's chief 1Ch 11:15
received more honor than the T, ... 1Ch 11:25
Reubenites, and his t soldiers; 1Ch 11:42
was one of the T. In fact, he 1Ch 12:4
he was the leader of the T. 1Ch 12:4
leader of the T, and he said: 1Ch 12:18
were one hundred t people from 1Ch 15:7
Levites who were t years old and 1Ch 23:3
who was one of the T soldiers. 1Ch 27:6
feet long and t feet wide, ... 2Ch 3:3
the Temple was t feet long and 2Ch 3:4
feet long and t feet high. 2Ch 3:4
It was t feet long and thirty 2Ch 3:8
feet long and t feet wide, ... 2Ch 3:8
creatures were t feet across. 2Ch 3:11

wings were t feet across...................... 2Ch 3:13
made a bronze altar t feet long, ... 2Ch 4:1
thirty feet long, t feet wide,.................... 2Ch 4:1
he was one hundred t years old........... 2Ch 24:15
the Israelites t thousand sheep 2Ch 35:7
He listed t gold dishes, one .... Ezr 1:9
t gold bowls, four hundred ten .... Ezr 1:10
to go to the king for t days." .... Est 4:11
have written t sayings for you, ... Pr 22:20
Take t men from the palace and .... Je 38:10
T rooms were along the edge of .... Eze 40:17
with t rooms on each side...................... Eze 41:6
the next t days no one should................. Da 6:7
during the next t days will be .... Da 6:12
t feet long and fifteen feet wide............... Zch 5:2
So they paid me t pieces of.................... Zch 11:12
So I took the t pieces of silver .... Zch 11:13
and some made t times more.................... Mt 13:8
and sometimes t times more." .... Mt 13:23
they gave him t silver coins. .... Mt 26:15
So he took the t silver coins .... Mt 27:3
They took t silver coins. .... Mt 27:9
They used those t silver coins. .... Mt 27:10
Some plants made t times more, ... Mk 4:8
fruit—sometimes t times more, ... Mk 4:20
he was about t years old. .... Lk 3:23
held about twenty or t gallons. .... Jn 2:6
came four hundred t years later,............. Gal 3:17

THIRTY-EIGHT
had been t years from the time .... Dt 2:14
there were t thousand Levites. 1Ch 23:3
who had been sick for t years. .... Jn 5:5

THIRTY-EIGHTH
during Asa's t year as king.................... 1Ki 16:29
during Uzziah's t year as king 2Ki 15:8

THIRTY-FIFTH
war until the t year of Asa's 2Ch 15:19

THIRTY-FIRST
during the t year Asa was king 1Ki 16:23

THIRTY-FIVE
he collected t pounds of silver, ... Nu 3:50
Jehoshaphat was t years old when 1Ki 22:42
was t years old when he became 2Ch 20:31
which was about t feet wide. .... Eze 40:14
The porch was t feet long and .... Eze 40:49
feet long and t feet wide. .... Eze 41:2
It was t feet long and .... Eze 41:4
feet long and t feet wide. .... Eze 41:4
It was t feet wide and went all .... Eze 41:10
There was t feet of the inner .... Eze 42:3

THIRTY-FOUR
thousand t fighting men........................ 1Ch 7:7
back about t thousand pounds 2Ch 8:18
years and four hundred t years. .... Da 9:25
the four hundred t years the .... Da 9:26

THIRTY-NINE
punishment of t lashes with a................. 2Co 11:24

THIRTY-NINTH
during Uzziah's t year as king 2Ki 15:13
during Uzziah's t year as king 2Ki 15:17
In the t year of his rule, ... 2Ch 16:12

THIRTY-ONE
The total number of kings was t. .... Jos 12:24
and he ruled t years in 2Ki 22:1
he ruled t years in Jerusalem.................. 2Ch 34:1

THIRTY-SECOND
twelve years, until his t year. .... Ne 5:14
Babylon in the t year he was .... Ne 13:6

THIRTY-SEVEN
one hundred t years and then .... Ge 25:17
Levi lived one hundred t years. .... Ex 6:16
Amram lived one hundred t years. .... Ex 6:20
There were t in all. 2Sa 23:39
was held in Babylon for t years. 2Ki 25:27
There were t hundred with him. 1Ch 12:27
had t thousand soldiers with 1Ch 12:34
prison in Babylon for t years. .... Je 52:31
four hundred t feet on the north............. Eze 48:17
hundred t feet on the south, ... Eze 48:17
four hundred t feet on the east, ... Eze 48:17
four hundred t feet on the west. .... Eze 48:17

THIRTY-SEVENTH
during Joash's t year as king of 2Ki 13:10
In the t year Evil-Merodach 2Ki 25:27

THIRTY-SIX
of acacia wood, t inches long,.................. Ex 25:23
and make it t inches high. .... Ex 30:2
it was t inches long, eighteen .... Ex 37:10
wide—and it was t inches high. .... Ex 37:25
of Ai killed about t Israelites .... Jos 7:5
shows they had t thousand men 1Ch 7:4
and t hundred men to direct the 2Ch 2:2
and t hundred of them to direct 2Ch 2:18

THIRTY-SIXTH
In the t year of Asa's rule, ... 2Ch 16:1

THIRTY-THREE
There were t persons in this .... Ge 46:15
lived one hundred t years. .... Ex 6:18
Then it will be t days before .... Le 12:4
Judah in Jerusalem for t years. 2Sa 5:5
in Hebron and t years in 1Ki 2:11
There were also t hundred men 1Ki 5:16
ruled in Jerusalem t years. 1Ch 3:4
in Hebron and t years in 1Ch 29:27

THIRTY-TWO
back about t thousand pounds 1Ki 9:28
There were t kings with their 1Ki 20:1
two hundred t of them. 1Ki 20:15
and the t rulers helping 1Ki 20:16
Don't allow the t rulers to 1Ki 20:24
had ordered his t chariot 1Ki 22:31
Jehoram was t years old when he 2Ki 8:17
Ammonites hired t thousand 1Ch 19:7
He was t years old when he began 2Ch 21:5
Jehoram was t years old when he 2Ch 21:20

THOMAS
T and Matthew, the tax collector; .... Mt 10:3
Matthew, T, James the son .... Mk 3:18
Matthew, T, James son of .... Lk 6:15
Then T (the one called Didymus) .... Jn 11:16
T said to Jesus, "Lord, we don't .... Jn 14:5
T (called Didymus), who was one .... Jn 20:24
other followers kept telling T,................. Jn 20:25
But T said, "I will not believe .... Jn 20:25
again, and T was with them. .... Jn 20:26
Then he said to T, "Put your .... Jn 20:27
T said to him, "My Lord and my .... Jn 20:28
Simon Peter, T (called Didymus), ... Jn 21:2
Andrew, Philip, T, Bartholomew, ... Ac 1:13

THORN
a fool is like a t stuck in the .... Pr 26:9

THORNBUSH
all the trees said to the t, ' .... Jdg 9:14
But the t said to the trees, ... Jdg 9:15
come out of the t and burn up .... Jdg 9:15
A t in Lebanon sent a message to 2Ki 14:9
walking on and crushing the t. 2Ki 14:9
A t in Lebanon sent a message to 2Ch 25:18

walking on and crushing the **t**. 2Ch 25:18
the best of them is like a **t;** .... Mic 7:4

THORNBUSHES

through the **t** to his neighbor's .... Ex 22:6
by the **t** and watering holes. .... Is 7:19
builds a wall of **t** in war, ... Is 27:4
will burn quickly like dry **t.**" .... Is 33:12
trees will grow where **t** were. .... Is 55:13
do in the thick **t** along the .... Je 12:5
So I will block her road with **t;** .... Hos 2:6
come from **t,** and figs don't..................... Mt 7:16
People don't gather figs from **t,** .... Lk 6:44

THORNS

will produce **t** and weeds for you .... Ge 3:18
your eyes and **t** in your sides.................... Nu 33:55
on your back and **t** in your eyes, ... Jos 23:13
whip your skin with **t** and briers .... Jdg 8:7
punished them with **t** and briers.............. Jdg 8:16
thrown away like **t** that cannot 2Sa 23:6
taking what grew among the **t,** .... Job 5:5
then let **t** come up instead of .... Job 31:40
than burning **t** can heat a pot. .... Ps 58:9
they died as quickly as **t** burn. .... Ps 118:12
life is like a patch of **t,** .... Pr 15:19
paths covered with **t** and traps. .... Pr 22:5
T had grown up everywhere. .... Pr 24:31
the crackling of **t** in a cooking .... Ec 7:6
darling is like a lily among **t!** .... Sng 2:2
and weeds and **t** will grow there. .... Is 5:6
will become full of weeds and **t.** .... Is 7:23
will be filled with weeds and **t.** .... Is 7:25
First, it burns weeds and **t.** .... Is 9:18
suddenly burns the weeds and **t.** .... Is 10:17
in which only **t** and weeds now .... Is 32:13
T will take over the strong .... Is 34:13
and don't plant seeds among **t.** .... Je 4:3
but they have harvested only **t.** .... Je 12:13
and **t** will drive them out of .... Hos 9:6
T and weeds will grow up and .... Hos 10:8
be like tangled **t** or like people .... Nah 1:10
the crown of **t** and the purple .... Jn 19:5
land that grows **t** and weeds and .... Heb 6:8

THORNY

they may be like **t** branches and.............. Eze 2:6
nations are like **t** branches or .... Eze 28:24
figs don't come from **t** weeds.................... Mt 7:16
other seed fell among **t** weeds, ... Mt 13:7
that fell among the **t** weeds? .... Mt 13:22
Using **t** branches, they made a .... Mt 27:29
other seed fell among **t** weeds, ... Mk 4:7
seed planted among the **t** weeds. .... Mk 4:18
Jesus and used **t** branches to .... Mk 15:17
Some seed fell among **t** weeds, ... Lk 8:7
fell among the **t** weeds is like .... Lk 8:14
crown from some **t** branches and .... Jn 19:2

THOROUGHLY

King Ahab **t** defeated the Aramean 1Ki 20:21

THOUGHTLESSLY

the name of the LORD your God **t;**........... Ex 20:7
the name of the LORD your God **t,**........... Dt 5:11
Your enemies use your name **t.** .... Ps 139:20

THOUGHTS

Their **t** are evil even when they .... Ge 8:21
Beware of evil **t.** Don't think, ... Dt 15:9
My troubled **t** cause me to .... Job 20:2
very well your **t** and your plans .... Job 21:27
You know our **t** and feelings. .... Ps 7:9
is no room for God in their **t.** .... Ps 10:4
hope my words and **t** please you. .... Ps 19:14
How deep are your **t!** .... Ps 92:5
He knows their **t** are just a puff .... Ps 94:11

May my **t** please him; .... Ps 104:34
You know my **t** before I think................. Ps 139:2
your **t** are precious to me. .... Ps 139:17
test me and know my anxious **t.**............... Ps 139:23
because your **t** run your life. .... Pr 4:23
evil person's **t** are worth very .... Pr 10:20
no knowledge in the **t** of fools. .... Pr 15:7
knows the **t** of the living. .... Pr 15:11
LORD hates evil **t** but is pleased.............. Pr 15:26
People's **t** can be like a deep .... Pr 20:5
and searches through their **t.** .... Pr 20:27
looks, proud **t,** and evil actions .... Pr 21:4
loves pure **t** and kind words .... Pr 22:11
their minds are full of evil **t.** .... Pr 26:25
and foolish **t** while they live .... Ec 9:3
they should stop their evil **t.** .... Is 55:7
My **t** are not like your thoughts................ Is 55:8
My thoughts are not like your **t.** .... Is 55:8
ways and my **t** higher than your.............. Is 55:9
my thoughts higher than your **t.** .... Is 55:9
They think evil **t.** Everywhere.................. Is 59:7
they have evil **t** and do evil .... Is 66:18
see me and test my **t** about you. .... Je 12:3
words and **t** of my enemies are .... La 3:62
and makes his **t** known to people. .... Am 4:13
are blessed whose **t** are pure, ... Mt 5:8
their **t**, Jesus said, "Why .... Mt 9:4
Why are you thinking evil **t?** .... Mt 9:4
Out of the mind come evil **t,** .... Mt 15:19
evil **t**, sexual sins, stealing, ... Mk 7:21
so that the **t** of many will be .... Lk 2:35
knowing their **t,** he said to them.............. Lk 11:17
Satan rule your **t** to lie to the .... Ac 5:3
who knows the **t** of everyone,.................. Ac 15:8
Sometimes their **t** tell them they.............. Rm 2:15
sometimes their **t** tell them they .... Rm 2:15
will judge people's secret **t.**..................... Rm 2:16
Who knows the **t** that another 1Co 2:11
lives within him knows his **t.** 1Co 2:11
No one knows the **t** of God except 1Co 2:11
He knows their **t** are just a puff 1Co 3:20
Their **t** are worth nothing. .... Eph 4:17
very happy by having the same **t,** .... Php 2:2
letting evil **t** control you,........................ Col 3:5
our **t** settle with you........................... 1Th 2:17
And it judges the **t** and feelings .... Heb 4:12
and with evil **t** you are deciding .... Jam 2:4
people whose **t** are only of this .... Jud 1:19

THOUSAND

about six hundred **t** men walking, ... Ex 12:37
of you will chase ten **t** men. .... Le 26:8
of love for a **t** lifetimes for .... Dt 7:9
person cannot chase a **t** people, ... Dt 32:30
cannot fight ten **t** unless their................. Dt 32:30
and about three **t** men and women........... Jdg 16:27
horses and twelve **t** horses..................... 1Ki 4:26
he spoke three **t** wise sayings.................. 1Ki 4:32
I have seven **t** people left in 1Ki 19:18
about seven **t** people in all. 1Ki 20:15
commanders of a **t** soldiers went 1Ch 15:25
captured two **t** of his chariots, ... 1Ch 18:4
hundred fifty **t** pounds of silver .... Est 3:9
He owned seven **t** sheep, three .... Job 1:3
Job had fourteen **t** sheep, six .... Job 42:12
is better than a **t** days anywhere.............. Ps 84:10
a **t** years is like the passing of .... Ps 90:4
your side one **t** people may die, ... Ps 91:7
or even ten **t** right beside you, ... Ps 91:7
and tan, the best of ten **t** men. .... Sng 5:10
and a **t** of your men will run .... Is 30:17
big banquet for a **t** royal guests .... Da 5:1
If a **t** soldiers leave a city, ... Am 5:3

hundred twenty **t** people who do .... Jnh 4:11
were about five **t** men there who .... Mt 14:21
were about four **t** men there who .... Mt 15:38
About three **t** people were added .... Ac 2:41
now about five **t** in the group .... Ac 4:4
have left seven **t** people in .... Rm 11:4
day twenty-three **t** of them died 1Co 10:8
Lord one day is as a **t** years, ... 2Pe 3:8
forty-four **t** people who had his .... Rev 14:1
and tied him up for a **t** years. .... Rev 20:2
rule with him for a **t** years. .... Rev 20:6
When the **t** years are over, ... Rev 20:7

THOUSANDS

I show kindness to **t** who love me .... Ex 20:6
and is kind to **t** of people. .... Ex 34:7
came with **t** of angels from the .... Dt 33:2
Saul has killed **t** of his enemies 1Sa 18:7
but David has killed tens of **t**." 1Sa 18:7
more to me than **t** of pieces of .... Ps 119:72
and kindness to **t** of people, ... Je 32:18
So many **t** of people had gathered .... Lk 12:1
see that number of our people .... Ac 21:20
to teach others than **t** of words 1Co 14:19
You have come to **t** of angels .... Heb 12:22
coming with many **t** of his holy .... Jud 1:14
were **t** and thousands of angels, ... Rev 5:11
were thousands and **t** of angels, ... Rev 5:11

THREAD

not keep even a **t** or a sandal .... Ge 14:23
blue, purple, and red **t**; .... Ex 25:4
and blue, purple, and red **t**. .... Ex 26:1
purple, and red **t**, and have a .... Ex 26:31
and blue, purple, and red **t**. .... Ex 26:36
with blue, purple, and red **t**. .... Ex 27:16
and red **t**, and fine linen. .... Ex 28:5
purple and red **t**, and fine linen .... Ex 28:6
and red **t**, and fine linen. .... Ex 28:8
and red **t**, and fine linen. .... Ex 28:15
purple, and red **t**, and hang them .... Ex 28:33
and red **t**, and fine linen, ... Ex 35:6
and red **t**, and fine linen .... Ex 35:23
and red **t**, and fine linen .... Ex 35:25
to help made **t** of the goat hair. .... Ex 35:26
the blue, purple, and red **t**. .... Ex 35:35
and red **t**, and fine linen .... Ex 36:35
and red **t**, and fine linen .... Ex 36:37
and red **t**, and fine linen .... Ex 38:18
and red **t**, and fine linen .... Ex 38:23
and red **t** to make woven clothes .... Ex 39:1
and red **t**, and fine linen .... Ex 39:2
and red **t**, and fine linen .... Ex 39:3
and red **t**, and fine linen. .... Ex 39:5
and red **t**, and fine linen. .... Ex 39:8
purple, and red **t**, and fine .... Ex 39:24
purple, and red **t**, and designs .... Ex 39:29
several pieces of **t** together and .... Nu 15:38
a blue **t** in each one of these .... Nu 15:38
several pieces of **t** together; .... Dt 22:12
with purple, red, and blue **t**. 2Ch 2:7
blue, and red **t**, and expensive 2Ch 2:14
purple, and red **t**, and expensive 2Ch 3:14
She makes **t** with her hands and .... Pr 31:19
Your lips are like red silk **t**, ... Sng 4:3

THREADS

as easily as if they were **t**. .... Jdg 16:12

THREAT

the **t** of death has passed. 1Sa 15:32

THREATEN

slaves. Do not **t** them. Remember .... Eph 6:9
suffered, but he did not **t**. 1Pe 2:23

THREATENING

in the army were **t** to kill David 1Sa 30:6
Saul was still **t** the followers .... Ac 9:1

THREATENS

and no danger **t** my people. 1Ki 5:4
to the One who **t** to punish. .... Mic 6:9

THREATS

are full of curses, lies, and **t**; .... Ps 10:7
will make **t**, and a thousand .... Is 30:17
will make **t**, and all of you .... Is 30:17
of Moab and the **t** of the people .... Zph 2:8
now, Lord, listen to their **t**. .... Ac 4:29

THREE

He had **t** sons: Shem, Ham, and .... Ge 6:10
up and saw **t** men standing near.............. Ge 18:2
a place that was **t** days' journey .... Ge 30:36
T days later Laban learned that .... Ge 31:22
was, she hid him for **t** months. .... Ex 2:2
Let us travel **t** days into the .... Ex 3:18
So **t** times during every year all .... Ex 23:17
enough crops for **t** years. .... Le 25:21
you hit your donkey **t** times? .... Nu 22:32
Give **t** cities east of the Jordan .... Nu 35:14
must be two or **t** witnesses that .... Dt 17:6
be proved by two or **t** witnesses............. Dt 19:15
But he kept **t** hundred men and .... Jdg 7:8
For **t** hundred years the .... Jdg 11:26
and about **t** thousand men and .... Jdg 16:27
Once, **t** of the Thirty, David's 2Sa 23:13
So the **t** warriors broke through 2Sa 23:16
things that the **t** warriors did. 2Sa 23:17
and was more honored than the **T**........... 2Sa 23:19
I offer you **t** choices. 2Sa 24:12
life he spoke **t** thousand wise 1Ki 4:32
families and **t** hundred slave 1Ki 11:3
For **t** years there was peace 1Ki 22:1
and attacked it for **t** years. 2Ki 17:5
king in Jerusalem for **t** months. 2Ki 23:31
and he was king **t** months in 2Ki 24:8
had seven sons and **t** daughters.............. Job 1:2
sheep, **t** thousand camels .... Job 1:3
Now Job had **t** friends: .... Job 2:11
' There are **t** things that are .... Pr 30:15
Two or **t** olives are left in the .... Is 17:6
barefoot for **t** years as a sign .... Is 20:3
Even if **t** great men like Noah, ... Eze 14:14
we tie up only **t** men and throw .... Da 3:24
T times each day Daniel would .... Da 6:10
sides and had **t** ribs in its .... Da 7:5
of your crops every **t** days. .... Am 4:4
rain from you **t** months before .... Am 4:7
inside the fish **t** days and three .... Jnh 1:17
grave three days and **t** nights.................. Mt 12:40
Between and six o'clock in the.............. Mt 14:25
I will put up **t** tents here— .... Mt 17:4
proved by two or **t** witnesses.'............... Mt 18:16
because if two or **t** people come .... Mt 18:20
you will say **t** times that you .... Mt 26:34
'After **t** days I will rise from .... Mt 27:63
for about **t** months and then .... Lk 1:56
in Israel for **t** and one-half .... Lk 4:25
will build it again in **t** days." .... Jn 2:19
About **t** thousand people were .... Ac 2:41
t days Saul could not see and .... Ac 9:9
This happened **t** times, and at.............. Ac 10:16
remember that for **t** years, ... Ac 20:31
So these **t** things continue 1Co 13:13
or not more than **t**, who speak. 1Co 14:27
T different times I was beaten 2Co 11:25
t years I went to Jerusalem.................... Gal 1:18
hid him for **t** months after he .... Heb 11:23
the land for **t** and a half years! .... Jam 5:17

THREE-DAY

So there are t witnesses: 1Jn 5:7
on the south, and t on the west. .... Rev 21:13

THREE-DAY

Let us make a t journey into the .... Ex 8:27

THREE-FOURTHS

weighed about one and t pounds. .... Nu 7:85

THREE-QUARTER

about one and t pounds of silver .... Jdg 9:4

THREE-YEAR-OLD

Abram, "Bring me a t cow, a .... Ge 15:9
three-year-old cow, a t goat, a .... Ge 15:9
goat, a t male sheep, a dove, ... Ge 15:9
along with a t bull, one-half 1Sa 1:24

THRESH

young cow that likes to t grain. .... Hos 10:11

THRESHING

came to the t floor of Atad, ... Ge 50:10
sadness at the t floor of Atad .... Ge 50:11
Your t will continue until the .... Le 26:5
your offering from the t floor. .... Nu 15:20
harvest from the t floor and .... Dt 16:13
put some wool on the t floor. .... Jdg 6:37
will be working at the t floor. .... Ru 3:2
and go down to the t floor. .... Ru 3:3
went down to the t floor and did .... Ru 3:6
woman came here to the t floor." .... Ru 3:14
tree at the t floor near Gibeah. 1Sa 14:2
grain from the t floors." 1Sa 23:1
came to the t floor of Nacon, ... 2Sa 6:6
was then by the t floor of 2Sa 24:16
the LORD on the t floor of 2Sa 24:18
To buy the t floor from you so I 2Sa 24:21
offering and the t boards and 2Sa 24:22
David bought the t floor and the 2Sa 24:24
on their thrones at the t floor, ... 1Ki 22:10
Can I get help from the t floor 2Ki 6:27
came to the t floor of Kidon, ... 1Ch 13:9
standing at the t floor of 1Ch 21:15
the LORD on the t floor of 1Ch 21:18
he left the t floor and bowed 1Ch 21:21
Sell me your t floor so I can 1Ch 21:22
to David, "Take this t floor. 1Ch 21:23
the t boards for the wood, ... 1Ch 21:23
him on the t floor of Araunah, ... 1Ch 21:28
prepared on the t floor of 2Ch 3:1
on their thrones at the t floor, ... 2Ch 18:9
and gather it to your t floor? .... Job 39:12
trail in the mud like a t board. .... Job 41:30
like grain on the t floor. .... Is 21:10
you like a new t board with many .... Is 41:15
of Babylon is like a t floor, ... Je 51:33
became like chaff on a t floor .... Da 2:35
of prostitutes on every t floor. .... Hos 9:1
the t floor and the winepress .... Hos 9:2
chaff blown from the t floor, ... Hos 13:3
And the t floors will be full of .... Joe 2:24
of Gilead with t boards that had .... Am 1:3
bundles of grain to the t floor. .... Mic 4:12

THREW

They t their walking sticks on .... Ex 7:12
So they t Jezebel down, and the 2Ki 9:33
When they t lots, the lot .... Jnh 1:7
up Jonah and t him into the sea, ... Jnh 1:15
He t the other servant into .... Mt 18:30
So Judas t the money into the .... Mt 27:5
and t him out of the vineyard. .... Mk 12:8
The evil spirit t the man down .... Lk 4:35
demon t him on the ground and .... Lk 9:42
he t him into the bottomless .... Rev 20:3

THRILLED

my bride, you have t my heart; .... Sng 4:9
have t my heart with a glance .... Sng 4:9
He is t that he gets to hear the .... Jn 3:29
followers were t when they saw .... Jn 20:20

THROAT

My t prefers to be choked; .... Job 7:15
for help; my t is sore. My eyes .... Ps 69:3
through it, rising to Judah's t. .... Is 8:8
river, which rises to the t. .... Is 30:28
are bare or until your t is dry. .... Je 2:25
of the sea closed around my t. .... Jnh 2:5

THROATS

Their t are like open graves; .... Ps 5:9
No sounds come from their t. .... Ps 115:7
the sword is pointing at our t!" .... Je 4:10
Their t are like open graves; .... Rm 3:13

THRONE

Judah will always be on the t. .... Ge 49:10
who sits on his t, to the .... Ex 11:5
sat on the t to the firstborn .... Ex 12:29
my hands toward the LORD's t. .... Ex 17:16
and receive a t of honor. 1Sa 2:8
whose t is between the gold 2Sa 6:2
Your t will last forever.' " 2Sa 7:16
you and your t are innocent." 2Sa 14:9
would rule on your t after you. 1Ki 1:13
me, and he will rule on my t.' 1Ki 1:17
and that he will rule on your t? 1Ki 1:24
and rule on my t in my place." 1Ki 1:30
will sit on my t and rule in my 1Ki 1:35
King Solomon's t an even greater 1Ki 1:37
an even greater t than yours." 1Ki 1:37
bowed down, and sat on the t. 1Ki 2:19
bring another t for his mother. 1Ki 2:19
given me the t that belonged to 1Ki 2:24
his family, and his t forever." 1Ki 2:33
also built a t room where he 1Ki 7:7
king built a large t of ivory 1Ki 10:18
The t had six steps on it, ... 1Ki 10:19
sitting on his t with his 1Ki 22:19
the king sat on the royal t. 2Ki 11:19
took his place on the t. 2Ki 13:13
the platform for the royal t, ... 2Ki 16:18
whose t is between the gold 2Ki 19:15
God's t is between the golden, ... 1Ch 13:6
on the LORD's t as king and took 1Ch 29:23
has put you on his t to rule for 2Ch 9:8
king built a large t of ivory 2Ch 9:17
The t had six steps on it and a 2Ch 9:18
sitting on his t with his 2Ch 18:18
they seated the king on the t. 2Ch 23:20
on his royal t in the hall, ... Est 5:1
you sat on your t and judged by .... Ps 9:4
He sits on his t to judge, ... Ps 9:7
LORD sits on his t in heaven. .... Ps 11:4
praises of Israel are your t. .... Ps 22:3
From his t he watches all who .... Ps 33:14
your t will last forever and .... Ps 45:6
God sits on his holy t. .... Ps 47:8
You sit on your t between the .... Ps 80:1
have thrown his t to the ground. .... Ps 89:44
LORD has set his t in heaven, ... Ps 103:19
rule on your t forever and ever. .... Ps 132:12
a king sits on his t to judge, ... Pr 20:8
Lord sitting on a very high t. .... Is 6:1
king on David's t and over .... Is 9:7
I will put my t above God's .... Is 14:13
whose t is between the gold .... Is 37:16
God sits on his t above the .... Is 40:22
Heaven is my t, and the earth is .... Is 66:1
Jerusalem The T of the LORD, ... Je 3:17

the kings who sit on David's **t,** .... Je 13:13
the honor from your glorious **t.** .... Je 14:21
honored as a glorious **t** for God. .... Je 17:12
sit on David's **t** will come .... Je 17:25
Judah, who rules from David's **t.** .... Je 22:2
sit on David's **t** will come .... Je 22:4
will set on the **t** of David or.................... Je 22:30
sitting on David's **t** now and all .... Je 29:16
sit on the **t** of the family .... Je 33:17
ruling as king on David's **t.**.................... Je 33:21
will not sit on David's **t.** .... Je 36:30
I will set his **t** over these .... Je 43:10
will set up my **t** in Elam to show .... Je 49:38
something that looked like a **t.** .... Eze 1:26
And on the **t** was a shape like a .... Eze 1:26
gem which looked like a **t.** .... Eze 10:1
I sit on the **t** of a god in .... Eze 28:2
this is my **t** and the place where .... Eze 43:7
so he was taken off his royal **t.** .... Da 5:20
the Eternal One, sat on his **t.** .... Da 7:9
t was made from fire, and the................. Da 7:9
wheels of his **t** were blazing .... Da 7:9
got up from his **t,** took off his .... Jnh 3:6
man will sit on his **t** and rule,................ Zch 6:13
other will be a priest on his **t.**............... Zch 6:13
because heaven is God's **t.** .... Mt 5:34
of Man will sit on his great **t.** .... Mt 19:28
using God's **t** and the One who .... Mt 23:22
and the One who sits on that **t.** .... Mt 23:22
be King and sit on his great **t.**.............. Mt 25:31
give him the **t** of King David, ... Lk 1:32
'Heaven is my **t,** and the earth .... Ac 7:49
robes, sat on his **t,** and made a .... Ac 12:21
your **t** will last forever and .... Heb 1:8
before God's **t** where there is .... Heb 4:16
right side of God's **t** in heaven. .... Heb 8:1
at the right side of God's **t.** .... Heb 12:2
the seven spirits before his **t,** .... Rev 1:4
It is where Satan has his **t.** .... Rev 2:13
with me on my **t** in the same way .... Rev 3:21
down with my Father on his **t.** .... Rev 3:21
and before me was a **t** in heaven, ... Rev 4:2
One who sat on the **t** looked like .... Rev 4:3
All around the **t** was a rainbow .... Rev 4:3
Around the **t** there were .... Rev 4:4
and thunder came from the **t.** .... Rev 4:5
Before the **t** seven lamps were .... Rev 4:5
Also before the **t** there was.................... Rev 4:6
around the **t** were four living .... Rev 4:6
to the One who sits on the **t,** .... Rev 4:9
the One who sits on the **t,** .... Rev 4:10
down before the **t** and say: .... Rev 4:10
of the One sitting on the **t.** .... Rev 5:1
center of the **t** and in the....................... Rev 5:6
of the One sitting on the **t.** .... Rev 5:7
of many angels around the **t,** .... Rev 5:11
sits on the **t** and to the Lamb .... Rev 5:13
who sits on the **t** and from the .... Rev 6:16
before the **t** and before the Lamb .... Rev 7:9
who sits on the **t,** and to the .... Rev 7:10
around the **t** and the elders................... Rev 7:11
before the **t** and worshiped God, ... Rev 7:11
they are before the **t** of God. .... Rev 7:15
sits on the **t** will be present.................. Rev 7:15
center of the **t** will be their .... Rev 7:17
the golden altar before the **t.** .... Rev 8:3
taken up to God and to his **t.** .... Rev 12:5
his power and his **t** and great .... Rev 13:2
song before the **t** and before the............. Rev 14:3
his bowl on the **t** of the beast,............... Rev 16:10
out of the temple from the **t,** .... Rev 16:17
'I am a queen sitting on my **t.**................. Rev 18:7
God, who sits on the **t.** .... Rev 19:4

Then a voice came from the **t,** .... Rev 19:5
a great white **t** and the One who .... Rev 20:11
small, standing before the **t.** .... Rev 20:12
I heard a loud voice from the **t,** .... Rev 21:3
who was sitting on the **t** said, ... Rev 21:5
The One on the **t** said to me, ... Rev 21:6
flowing from the **t** of God and .... Rev 22:1
t of God and of the Lamb will................ Rev 22:3

THRONES
on their **t** at the threshing 1Ki 22:10
on their **t** at the threshing 2Ch 18:9
he sets them on **t** with kings and .... Job 36:7
David set their **t** to judge the .... Ps 122:5
up from their **t** to greet you. .... Is 14:9
and set up their **t** near the .... Je 1:15
down from your **t,** because your............. Je 13:18
will get down from their **t,** .... Eze 26:16
t were put in their places, ... Da 7:9
me will also sit on twelve **t,** .... Mt 19:28
rulers from their **t** and raised .... Lk 1:52
you will sit on **t,** judging the .... Lk 22:30
other **t** with twenty-four .... Rev 4:4
who sit on their **t** before God,............... Rev 11:16
Then I saw some **t** and people .... Rev 20:4

THROW
and a time to **t** things away. .... Ec 3:6
If you will **t** away your idols .... Je 4:1
Cut off your hair and **t** it away. .... Je 7:29
me up, and **t** me into the sea .... Jnh 1:12
"**T** the money to the potter." .... Zch 11:13
take it out and **t** it away. .... Mt 5:29
angels will **t** the evil people .... Mt 13:50
sin, cut it off and **t** it away. .... Mt 18:8
planned to **t** him off the edge,............... Lk 4:29
officer might **t** you into jail. .... Lk 12:58
a stone's **t** away from them. .... Lk 22:41
sinned can **t** the first stone .... Jn 8:7
picked up stones to **t** at him. .... Jn 8:59
T out the slave woman and her .... Gal 4:30
So I will **t** her on a bed of .... Rev 2:22

THROWN
be cut down and **t** into the fire. .... Mt 3:10
to be **t** out and walked on. .... Mt 5:13
your whole body **t** into hell. .... Mt 5:29
but tomorrow is **t** into the fire. .... Mt 6:30
stone will be **t** down to the .... Mt 24:2
two feet and be **t** into hell. .... Mk 9:45
stone will be **t** down to the .... Mk 13:2
but you yourselves **t** outside. .... Lk 13:28
heard that they had **t** him out, ... Jn 9:35
of this world will be **t** down. .... Jn 12:31
a branch that is **t** away and then .... Jn 15:6
Paul and Silas were **t** into jail, ... Ac 16:23
and he has not **t** his people out. .... Rm 11:2
We are beaten and **t** into prison............. 2Co 6:5
put in chains and **t** into prison. .... Heb 11:36
goes back to what it has **t** up," 2Pe 2:22
with fire, was **t** into the sea. .... Rev 8:8
giant dragon was **t** down out of .... Rev 12:9
his angels was **t** down to the .... Rev 12:9
before our God, has been **t** down. .... Rev 12:10
saw he had been **t** down to the .... Rev 12:13
city of Babylon will be **t** down, ... Rev 18:21
and the beast were **t** alive into .... Rev 19:20
was **t** into the lake of burning................ Rev 20:10
and Hades were **t** into the lake .... Rev 20:14
book of life was **t** into the lake .... Rev 20:15

THROWS
He **t** me into the mud, and I .... Job 30:19
but he **t** the wicked to the .... Ps 147:6
He **t** down hail like rocks. .... Ps 147:17

T

He t lots with arrows and asks .... Eze 21:21
attacks him, it t him on the .... Mk 9:18
spirit often t him into a fire .... Mk 9:22

THRUSHES
and t know when it is time to .... Je 8:7

THUMB
some on the t of Aaron's right .... Le 8:23
of it on the t of the person's .... Le 14:14
some on the t of the person's .... Le 14:17
blood on the t of the person's .... Le 14:25
of it on the t of the person's ....Le 14:28

THUMBS
sons and on the t of their right .... Ex 29:20
some on the t of their right .... Le 8:24
they cut off his t and big toes. .... Jdg 1:6
kings whose t and big toes had .... Jdg 1:7

THUMMIM
the Urim and T inside the chest .... Ex 28:30
the Urim and the T in the chest .... Le 8:8
your T and Urim belong to Levi, ... Dt 33:8
matter by using the Urim and T .... Ezr 2:63
matter by using the Urim and T .... Ne 7:65

THUNDER
sky, the LORD sent t and hail, ... Ex 9:23
had enough of God's t and hail. .... Ex 9:28
and the t and hail will stop. .... Ex 9:29
and the t and rain stopped. .... Ex 9:33
rain, hail, and t had stopped, ... Ex 9:34
there was t and lightning with a .... Ex 19:16
heard the t and the trumpet .... Ex 20:18
will t in heaven against them 1Sa 2:10
against them with loud t. 1Sa 7:10
for the LORD to send t and rain. 1Sa 12:17
day the LORD sent t and rain. 1Sa 12:18
or how he sends t from where he .... Job 36:29
t announces the coming storm, ... Job 36:33
sound of his t, my heart pounds .... Job 37:1
Listen to the t of God's voice .... Job 37:2
Can your voice t like his? .... Job 40:9
Your t sounded in the whirlwind. .... Ps 77:18
I answered you with t .... Ps 81:7
All-Powerful will come with t, ... Is 29:6
voice will t from that city, ... Joe 3:16
which means "Sons of T"), ... Mk 3:17
heard the voice, said it was t. .... Jn 12:29
and noises and t came from the .... Rev 4:5
say with a voice like t, ... Rev 6:1
of lightning, t and loud noises, ... Rev 8:5
noises, t, an earthquake, ... Rev 11:19
and like the sound of loud t. .... Rev 14:2
lightning, noises, t, and a big .... Rev 16:18
and like the noise of loud t. .... Rev 19:6

THUNDERED
But the LORD t against them with 1Sa 7:10
The LORD t from heaven; 2Sa 22:14
The LORD t from heaven; .... Ps 18:13
rain. The sky t. Your lightning .... Ps 77:17
When you t your orders, it .... Ps 104:7

THUNDERING
could understand God's t power?" .... Job 26:14
He speaks with a t voice. .... Ps 68:33

THUNDERS
shake when he t at them. .... Job 26:11
the roar when he t with a great .... Job 37:4
God's voice t in wonderful ways; .... Job 37:5
The glorious God t; .... Ps 29:3
the LORD t over the ocean. .... Ps 29:3
When he t, the waters in the .... Je 10:13
When he t, the waters in the .... Je 51:16
the voices of seven t spoke. .... Rev 10:3

the seven t spoke, I started .... Rev 10:4
hidden what the seven t said, ... Rev 10:4

THUNDERSTORM
set a path for a t to follow, ... Job 28:26
rains and sets a path for the t? .... Job 38:25

THYATIRA
from the city of T whose job was .... Ac 16:14
Smyrna, Pergamum, T, Sardis, ... Rev 1:11
to the angel of the church in T: .... Rev 2:18
others of you in T have not .... Rev 2:24

TIBERIAS
Lake Galilee (or, Lake T). .... Jn 6:1
boats came from T and landed .... Jn 6:23

TIBERIUS
year of the rule of T Caesar. .... Lk 3:1

TIBNI
people wanted T son of Ginath to 1Ki 16:21
followers of T son of Ginath, ... 1Ki 16:22
of Ginath, so T died, and Omri 1Ki 16:22

TIDAL
of Elam, and T was king of Goiim .... Ge 14:1
king of Elam, T king of Goiim, ... Ge 14:9

TIE
We will just t you up and give .... Jdg 15:13
off the ropes that t us down." .... Ps 2:3
ropes of his sins will t him up. .... Pr 5:22
t a stone to it and throw it .... Je 51:63

TIED
find a donkey t there with its .... Mt 21:2

TIES
He t his donkey to a grapevine, ... Ge 49:11
trouble, like ropes, t them up, ... Job 36:8
had broken their t with him. .... Je 5:5
unless he first t up the strong .... Mk 3:27

TIGHT
by the heel and hold them t. .... Job 18:9
and his right arm holds me t. .... Sng 2:6
and his right arm holds me t. .... Sng 8:3

TIGHTEN
the cloth, and t it with a pin. .... Jdg 16:13

TIGHTENED
who t his clothes around him and 1Ki 18:46

TIGHTER
ropes around you will become t .... Is 28:22

TIGHTLY
but Ruth held on to her t. .... Ru 1:14
back that are t sealed together .... Job 41:15
folds of its skin are t joined; .... Job 41:23
and roll you t into a ball and .... Is 22:18
belt is wrapped t around a .... Je 13:11
many colors, and t wound ropes. .... Eze 27:24
They do not hold t to Christ, ... Col 2:19

TIGLATH-PILESER
T king of Assyria. 2Ki 15:29
messengers to T king of Assyria, ... 2Ki 16:7
to meet T king of Assyria 2Ki 16:10
T king of Assyria captured him 1Ch 5:6
Pul was also called T. 1Ch 5:26
T king of Assyria came to Ahaz, ... 2Ch 28:20

TIGRIS
third river, named T, flows out .... Ge 2:14
beside the great T River. .... Da 10:4

TIKVAH
the wife of Shallum son of T, ... 2Ki 22:14
the wife of Shallum son of T, ... 2Ch 34:22
Jahzeiah son of T, Meshullam, ... Ezr 10:15

TILES
floor set with t of white marble .... Est 1:6

TILON
Amnon, Rinnah, Ben-Hanan, and T. 1Ch 4:20

TIMAEUS
Bartimaeus son of T was sitting .... Mk 10:46

TIMBER
money to buy t and cut stone to 2Ki 12:12
money to buy t and cut stone to 2Ki 22:6
telling him to give me t? .... Ne 2:8

TIMBERS
they are putting t in the walls. .... Ezr 5:8
stones and then one layer of t. .... Ezr 6:4

TIME
have at this same t next year." .... Ge 17:21
Abraham from heaven a second t .... Ge 22:15
At this t Isaac had left Beer .... Ge 24:62
When the t came, Rebekah gave .... Ge 25:24
So at this t tomorrow, I will .... Ex 9:18
at the set t during the month .... Ex 23:15
Each t you offer a lamb as a .... Nu 15:5
was the king of Moab at this t. .... Nu 22:4
this t there were more of them, ... Nu 22:15
The seventh t around the priests .... Jos 6:16
At the t of the wheat harvest, ... Jdg 15:1
called Samuel for the third t. 1Sa 3:8
at Kiriath Jearim a long t— 1Sa 7:2
she finished her t of sadness, ... 2Sa 11:27
it a third t," and they did it 1Ki 18:34
At that t Tattenai, the governor .... Ezr 5:3
had a certain t to serve God .... Ezr 6:18
king to send me, so I set a t. .... Ne 2:6
If you keep quiet at this t, ... Est 4:14
away before their t was up, ... Job 22:16
I do not spend t with liars, ... Ps 26:4
song from the t he acted crazy .... Ps 33:22
I'm only here a short t. .... Ps 39:12
in danger of death all the t. .... Ps 44:22
People, trust God all the t. .... Ps 62:8
have been our king for a long t. .... Ps 74:12
say, "I set the t for trial, and .... Ps 75:2
the t he had spoken of came, ... Ps 105:19
desire for your laws all the t. .... Ps 119:20
family and never wastes her t. .... Pr 31:27
There is a t for everything, ... Ec 3:1
There is a t to be born and a .... Ec 3:2
everything just right and on t, ... Ec 3:11
foolish. Why die before your t? .... Ec 7:17
is a right t and a right way .... Ec 8:6
T and chance happen to everyone. .... Ec 9:11
The t has come to sing; .... Sng 2:12
Like the t you defeated Midian, ... Is 9:4
A long t ago I told you things .... Is 46:10
So a long t ago I told you about .... Is 48:5
At the right t I will hear your .... Is 49:8
t of destruction is coming; .... Je 46:21
At that t people will try to .... Je 50:20
live for a certain period of t. .... Da 7:12
then the t came for them to .... Da 7:22
is about the t of the end." .... Da 8:17
happen in the t of God's anger. .... Da 8:19
until the t of the end comes .... Da 11:35
sealed until the t of the end. .... Da 12:9
at harvest t and my new wine .... Hos 2:9
sinned since the t of Gibeah, ... Hos 10:9
will be like the t King Shalman .... Hos 10:14
quiet, because it is a bad t. .... Am 5:13
and stop doing harm all the t. .... Jnh 3:8
them the exact t they first saw .... Mt 2:7
torture us before the right t?" .... Mt 8:29
The chosen t is near. I will .... Mt 26:18

He said, "The right t has come. .... Mk 1:15
When it was t for Elizabeth to .... Lk 1:57
At that t some people were there .... Lk 13:1
a person be born a second t?" .... Jn 3:4
The right t for me has not yet .... Jn 7:6
A third t he said, "Simon son of .... Jn 21:17
this t there was a meeting .... Ac 1:15
always used their t to talk .... Ac 17:21
at the right t, Christ died for .... Rm 5:6
we live in an important t. .... Rm 13:11
do not judge before the right t; 1Co 4:5
We do not have much t left. 1Co 7:29
person not born at the normal t. 1Co 15:8
At the right t I heard your 2Co 6:2
you that the "right t" is now, ... 2Co 6:2
But when the right t came, ... Gal 4:4
for all future t he could show .... Eph 2:7
and in Christ Jesus for all t, ... Eph 3:21
proof that came at the right t. 1Ti 2:6
Christ Jesus before t began, ... 2Ti 1:9
and the t has come for me to 2Ti 4:6
David a long t later in the same .... Heb 4:7
and for all t when he offered .... Heb 7:27
until the t of God's new way. .... Heb 9:10
a sacrifice one t to take away .... Heb 9:28
do not have t to tell you about .... Heb 11:32
You can see it for a short t, ... Jam 4:14
is shown to you at the end of t. 1Pe 1:5
for a short t different kinds 1Pe 1:6
world would be like at that t. 1Pe 1:11
you up when the right t comes. 1Pe 5:6
he hears us every t we ask him, ... 1Jn 5:14
The t is near when all of this .... Rev 1:3
knows he does not have much t." .... Rev 12:12
because the t has come for God .... Rev 14:7
because the t is near for all. .... Rev 22:10

TIMES
He has tricked me these two t. .... Ge 27:36
me and changed my pay ten t. .... Ge 31:7
the ground seven t as he was .... Ge 33:3
So three t during every year all .... Ex 23:17
announce at the t set for them. .... Le 23:4
punish you seven t more for your .... Le 26:18
you hit your donkey three t? .... Nu 22:32
the city seven t and have the .... Jos 6:4
ground before Jonathan three t. 1Sa 20:41
sneezed seven t and opened his 2Ki 4:35
in the Jordan River seven t. 2Ki 5:10
he defends them in t of trouble. .... Ps 9:9
their lives in t of hunger. .... Ps 33:19
I will praise the LORD at all t; .... Ps 34:1
Many t he held back his anger .... Ps 78:38
Seven t a day I praise you for .... Ps 119:164
be bothered by trouble seven t, ... Pr 24:16
Because of the t she turned. .... Is 50:1
They were ten t better than all .... Da 1:20
be heated seven t hotter than .... Da 3:19
Three t each day Daniel would .... Da 6:10
to his God three t every day." .... Da 6:13
try to change t and laws that .... Da 7:25
and sometimes thirty t more." .... Mt 13:23
forgive him more than seven t. .... Mt 18:22
will say three t that you don't .... Mt 26:34
I will pay back four t more." .... Lk 19:8
will say three t that you don't .... Lk 22:34
authority to decide dates and t. .... Ac 1:7
happened three t, and at once .... Ac 10:16
This happened three t. .... Ac 11:10
heaven and crops at the right t, ... Ac 14:17
insults, hard t, sufferings, and 2Co 12:10
lived in other t were not told .... Eph 3:5
in the later t some people will 1Ti 4:1

Be ready at all **t,** and tell..........................2Ti 4:2
control yourself at all **t,** 2Ti 4:5
to their own masters at all **t,** ....Tit 2:9
the prophets many **t** and in many ....Heb 1:1
did not offer himself many **t.** ....Heb 9:25
to suffer many **t** since the world..............Heb 9:26
in these last **t** for your sake. 1Pe 1:20
In the last **t** there will be........................Jud 1:18
earth as many **t** as they want..................Rev 11:6
produces fruit twelve **t** a year, ...Rev 22:2

TIMNA
also had a slave woman named **T,** ....Ge 36:12
and **T** and Eliphaz gave birth to ....Ge 36:12
Hori and Homam. (**T** was Lotan's ....Ge 36:22
names were **T,** Alvah, Jetheth, ...Ge 36:40
Gatam, Kenaz, **T,** and Amalek. 1Ch 1:36
and Homam, and his sister was **T.** 1Ch 1:39
family groups of Edom were **T,** 1Ch 1:51

TIMNAH
he went to **T** to his men who were ....Ge 38:12
was going to **T** to cut the wool ....Ge 38:13
gate of Enaim on the road to **T.** ....Ge 38:14
From there it went past **T** ....Jos 15:10
Gibeah, and **T.** There were ten ....Jos 15:57
Elon, **T,** Ekron, ...Jos 19:43
to the city of **T** where he saw ....Jdg 14:1
I saw a Philistine woman in **T.** ....Jdg 14:2
with his father and mother to **T,** ....Jdg 14:5
son-in-law of the man from **T,** ....Jdg 15:6
Gederoth, Soco, **T,** and Gimzo, ...2Ch 28:18

TIMNATH
T Serah in the mountains of ....Jos 19:50
him in his own land at **T** Serah, ...Jos 24:30
his own land at **T** Serah in the ....Jdg 2:9

TIMON
Procorus, Nicanor, **T,** Parmenas,..............Ac 6:5

TIMOTHY
where a follower named **T** lived. ....Ac 16:1
Iconium respected **T** and said..................Ac 16:2
wanted **T** to travel with him, ...Ac 16:3
Paul circumcised **T** to please his..............Ac 16:3
but Silas and **T** stayed in Berea. ....Ac 17:14
to Silas and **T** for them to come ....Ac 17:15
for Silas and **T** in Athens, ...Ac 17:16
Silas and **T** came from Macedonia ....Ac 18:5
Paul sent **T** and Erastus, two of ....Ac 19:22
from Derbe; **T;** and Tychicus ....Ac 20:4
T, a worker together with me,..................Rm 16:21
is why I am sending to you **T,**..................1Co 4:17
I love **T,** and he is faithful. 1Co 4:17
T comes to you, see to it that 1Co 16:10
should treat **T** as unimportant, ...1Co 16:11
Also from **T** our brother in 2Co 1:1
that Silas and **T** and I preached 2Co 1:19
From Paul and **T,** servants of ....Php 1:1
Jesus to send **T** to you soon. ....Php 2:19
I have no one else like **T,**......................Php 2:20
know the kind of person **T** is...................Php 2:22
Also from **T,** our brother. ....Col 1:1
From Paul, Silas, and **T.** 1Th 1:1
and send **T** to you. Timothy, our 1Th 3:2
T, our brother, works with us 1Th 3:2
I sent **T** to you so I could learn 1Th 3:5
But **T** now has come back to us 1Th 3:6
From Paul, Silas, and **T.** 2Th 1:1
To **T,** a true child to me because 1Ti 1:2
T, my child, I am giving you a 1Ti 1:18
T, guard what God has trusted to 1Ti 6:20
To **T,** a dear child to me: 2Ti 1:2
You then, **T,** my child, be strong 2Ti 2:1

Jesus, and from **T,** our brother. ....Phm 1:1
our brother **T** has been let out ....Heb 13:23

TIMOTHY'S
T mother was Jewish and a ....Ac 16:1
area knew that **T** father was ....Ac 16:3

TIN
bronze, iron, **t,** or lead— ....Nu 31:22
the copper, **t,** iron, and lead ....Eze 22:18
and **t** together inside a furnace ....Eze 22:20
for silver, iron, **t,** and lead. ....Eze 27:12

TINY
but not even a **t** stone falls ....Am 9:9

TIPHSAH
River—the land from **T** to Gaza..............1Ki 4:24
out from Tirzah and attacked **T,** 2Ki 15:16

TIPPING
boiling water, **t** over from the ....Je 1:13

TIRAS
Javan, Tubal, Meshech, and **T.** ....Ge 10:2
Javan, Tubal, Meshech, and **T.** 1Ch 1:5

TIRATHITES
were called the **T,** Shimeathites,..............1Ch 2:55

TIRHAKAH
king received a report that **T,** 2Ki 19:9
king received a report that **T,** ....Is 37:9

TIRHANAH
She was the mother of Sheber, **T,** 1Ch 2:48

TIRIA
Ziph, Ziphah, **T,** and Asarel. 1Ch 4:16

TIRING
I have done hard and **t** work, ...2Co 11:27

TIRZAH
Noah, Hoglah, Milcah, and **T.**..................Nu 26:33
Noah, Hoglah, Milcah, and **T.** ....Nu 27:1
Mahlah, **T,** Hoglah, Milcah,....................Nu 36:11
T. The total number of kings was ....Jos 12:24
Noah, Hoglah, Milcah, and **T.** ....Jos 17:3
wife left and returned to **T.**....................1Ki 14:17
up Ramah and returned to **T.** 1Ki 15:21
ruled in **T** for twenty-four 1Ki 15:33
Baasha died and was buried in **T,** 1Ki 16:6
Elah ruled in **T** for two years.................1Ki 16:8
Elah while the king was in **T,** 1Ki 16:9
in charge of the palace at **T.** 1Ki 16:9
and ruled in **T** seven days. 1Ki 16:15
left Gibbethon and attacked **T.** 1Ki 16:17
of those years in the city of **T.** 1Ki 16:23
Gadi came up from **T** to Samaria 2Ki 15:14
started out from **T** and attacked 2Ki 15:16
as beautiful as the city of **T,** ....Sng 6:4

TISHBITE
Now Elijah the **T** was a prophet 1Ki 17:1
to the prophet Elijah the **T.**....................1Ki 21:17
spoke his word to Elijah the **T:** 1Ki 21:28
s angel said to Elijah the **T,**....................2Ki 1:3
said, "It was Elijah the **T.**" 2Ki 1:8
his servant Elijah the **T:** ' 2Ki 9:36

TITIUS
moved into the home of **T** Justus, ...Ac 18:7

TITLE
and I give you a **t** of honor even..............Is 45:4
her forehead a **t** was written ....Rev 17:5

TITUS
I did not find my brother **T.** 2Co 2:13
comforted us when **T** came. 2Co 7:6
T told us about your wish to see..............2Co 7:7
to see that **T** was so happy. 2Co 7:13
bragged to **T** about you, and you 2Co 7:14

we bragged about to **T** is true. 2Co 7:14
So we asked **T** to help you finish 2Co 8:6
because he gave **T** the same love 2Co 8:16
T accepted what we asked him to 2Co 8:17
Now about **T**—he is my partner who 2Co 8:23
I asked **T** to go to you, and I 2Co 12:18
T did not cheat you, did he? 2Co 12:18
you know that **T** and I did the 2Co 12:18
Barnabas. I also took **T** with me. .... Gal 2:1
T was with me, but he was not .... Gal 2:3
Galatia, and **T** went to Dalmatia. 2Ti 4:10
To **T**, my true child in the faith .... Tit 1:4

TIZITE
Joha, Jediael's brother, the **T**; 1Ch 11:45

TOAH
T was Zuph's son. Zuph was 1Ch 6:35

TOAH'S
Eliel's son. Eliel was **T** son..................... 1Ch 6:34

TOB
and lived in the land of **T**. .... Jdg 11:3
to bring him back from **T**. .... Jdg 11:5
and twelve thousand men from **T**. 2Sa 10:6
the men from **T** and Maacah were 2Sa 10:8

TOB-ADONIJAH
Adonijah, Tobijah, and **T**. 2Ch 17:8

TOBIAH
of Delaiah, **T**, and Nekoda—652. .... Ezr 2:60
the Horonite and **T** the Ammonite .... Ne 2:10
the Horonite, **T** the Ammonite .... Ne 2:19
T the Ammonite, who was next to .... Ne 4:3
of Sanballat and **T** back on their .... Ne 4:4
But Sanballat, **T**, the Arabs, the .... Ne 4:7
Then Sanballat, **T**, Geshem the .... Ne 6:1
him but that **T** and Sanballat had .... Ne 6:12
remember **T** and Sanballat and .... Ne 6:14
of Judah sent many letters to **T**, ... Ne 6:17
promised to be faithful to **T**, ... Ne 6:18
the good things **T** was doing, ... Ne 6:19
they would tell **T** what I said .... Ne 6:19
T sent letters to frighten me. .... Ne 6:19
of Delaiah, **T**, and Nekoda—642. .... Ne 7:62
storerooms, was friendly with **T**. .... Ne 13:4
Eliashib let **T** use one of the .... Ne 13:5
done by letting **T** have a room .... Ne 13:7

TOBIAH'S
And **T** son Jehohanan had married .... Ne 6:18
so I threw all of **T** goods out of .... Ne 13:8

TOBIJAH
Adonijah, **T**, and Tob-Adonijah. 2Ch 17:8
from Heldai, **T**, and Jedaiah, who .... Zch 6:10
remind Heldai, **T**, Jedaiah, and .... Zch 6:14

TODAY
all of us who are alive here **t**. .... Dt 5:3
t I am letting you choose a .... Dt 11:26
here before the LORD your God **t**, ... Dt 30:15
t I offer you life and success, ... Dt 30:15
T I have become your father. .... Ps 2:7
T listen to what he says. .... Ps 95:7
which is alive **t** but tomorrow is .... Mt 6:30
T your Savior was born in the .... Lk 2:11
"**T** we have seen amazing things!" .... Lk 5:26
T I have become your Father.'................. Ac 13:33
T I have become your Father." .... Heb 1:5
T listen to what he says. .... Heb 3:7
other every day while it is "**t**." .... Heb 3:13
T listen to what he says. .... Heb 3:15
planned another day, called "**t**." .... Heb 4:7
T listen to what he says. .... Heb 4:7
T I have become your Father." .... Heb 5:5

same yesterday, **t**, and forever. .... Heb 13:8
T or tomorrow we will go to some .... Jam 4:13

TODAY'S
write down **t** date, this very .... Eze 24:2
from the evil of **t** people!" .... Ac 2:40

TOE
on the big **t** of his right foot. .... Le 8:23
and on the big **t** of the person's .... Le 14:14
on the big **t** of the person's .... Le 14:17
on the big **t** of the person's .... Le 14:25
on the big **t** of the person's .... Le 14:28
he had, from head to **t**. .... Hab 3:13

TOES
and on the big **t** of their right .... Ex 29:20
some on the big **t** of their right .... Le 8:24
cut off his thumbs and big **t**. .... Jdg 1:6
thumbs and big **t** had been cut .... Jdg 1:7
hand and six **t** on each foot— 2Sa 21:20
-four fingers and **t** in all..................... 2Sa 21:20
hand and six **t** on each foot— 1Ch 20:6
-four fingers and **t** in all........................ 1Ch 20:6
feet and **t** were partly baked .... Da 2:41
The **t** of the statue were partly .... Da 2:42

TOGARMAH
were Ashkenaz, Riphath, and **T**............... Ge 10:3
were Ashkenaz, Riphath, and **T**................ 1Ch 1:6
People of Beth **T** traded your .... Eze 27:14
and the nation of **T** from the far .... Eze 38:6

TOHU
and **T** was the son of Zuph from 1Sa 1:1

TOHU'S
Elihu was **T** son, and Tohu was 1Sa 1:1

TOI
T king of Hamath heard that 2Sa 8:9
So **T** sent his son Joram to greet 2Sa 8:10
had been at war with **T**........................ 2Sa 8:10
T king of Hamath heard that 1Ch 18:9
So **T** sent his son Hadoram to.................. 1Ch 18:10
had been at war with **T**. 1Ch 18:10

TOKEN
Etam, Ain, Rimmon, **T**, and Ashan. 1Ch 4:32

TOLA
sons were **T**, Puah, Jashub,..................... Ge 46:13
From **T** came the Tolaite family .... Nu 26:23
He was **T** son of Puah, the son of .... Jdg 10:1
T was from the people of .... Jdg 10:1
T was a judge for Israel for.................... Jdg 10:2
After **T** died, Jair from the .... Jdg 10:3
T, Puah, Jashub, and Shimron. 1Ch 7:1

TOLA'S
T sons were Uzzi, Rephaiah, ... 1Ch 7:2
family history of **T** descendants,............... 1Ch 7:2

TOLAD
Bilhah, Ezem, **T**, ... 1Ch 4:29

TOLAITE
Tola came the **T** family group; .... Nu 26:23

TOMB
He was buried in the **t** of Joash, ... Jdg 8:32
buried him in the **t** of Manoah, ... Jdg 16:31
near Rachel's **t** on the border 1Sa 10:2
him in the **t** of his father at 2Sa 2:32
it in Abner's **t** at Hebron. 2Sa 4:12
was buried in his father's **t**. 2Sa 17:23
Benjamin in the **t** of Saul's 2Sa 21:14
ancestors in his **t** in Jerusalem. 2Ki 9:28
Asa in the **t** he had made for 2Ch 16:14
could cut out a **t** for your self .... Is 22:16
your **t** in a high place? .... Is 22:16

T

carving out a t from the rock? .... Is 22:16
body in a new t that he had cut .... Mt 27:60
to block the entrance of the t. .... Mt 27:60
Mary were sitting near the t. .... Mt 27:61
order for the t to be guarded .... Mt 27:64
go guard the t the best way you .... Mt 27:65
all went to the t and made it .... Mt 27:66
Mary went to look at the t. .... Mt 28:1
heaven, went to the t, and .... Mt 28:2
guarding the t shook with fear .... Mt 28:4
The women left the t quickly. .... Mt 28:8
been guarding the t went into. .... Mt 28:11
John's body and put it in a t. .... Mk 6:29
the body in a t that was cut out .... Mk 15:46
to block the entrance of the t. .... Mk 15:46
were on their way to the t. .... Mk 16:2
covers the entrance of the t?" .... Mk 16:3
entered the t and saw a young .... Mk 16:5
so they left the t and ran away. .... Mk 16:8
and put it in a t that was cut .... Lk 23:53
t had never been used before. .... Lk 23:53
and saw the t and how Jesus' .... Lk 23:55
women came to the t, bringing .... Lk 24:1
away from the entrance of the t, ... Lk 24:2
women left the t and told all .... Lk 24:9
that had happened at the t. .... Lk 24:10
Peter got up and ran to the t. .... Lk 24:12
this morning they went to the t, ... Lk 24:22
some of our group went to the t, ... Lk 24:24
dead and in the t for four days. .... Jn 11:17
was going to the t to cry there. .... Jn 11:31
very upset, Jesus came to the t. .... Jn 11:38
told him to come out of the t .... Jn 12:17
garden was a new t that had .... Jn 19:41
Jesus in that t because it was .... Jn 19:42
went to the t while it was still .... Jn 20:1
had been moved away from the t, ... Jn 20:1
taken the Lord out of the t, ... Jn 20:2
follower started for the t. .... Jn 20:3
Peter and reached the t first. .... Jn 20:4
and went into the t and saw the .... Jn 20:6
who had reached the t first, ... Jn 20:8
But Mary stood outside the t, ... Jn 20:11
down and looked inside the t. .... Jn 20:11
the cross and laid him in a t. .... Ac 13:29

TOMBS

opposite the t of David and as .... Ne 3:16
keeps watch over their t. .... Job 21:32
remove from their t the bones of .... Je 8:1
You are like t that are painted .... Mt 23:27
Outside, those t look fine, but .... Mt 23:27
You build t for the prophets, ... Mt 23:29
you build t for the prophets .... Lk 11:47
and you build t for them! .... Lk 11:48

TOMORROW

and then t you may continue your .... Ge 19:2
The king answered, "T." .... Ex 8:10
This miracle will happen t.'" .... Ex 8:23
officers, and your people t. .... Ex 8:29
The Lord has set t as the time .... Ex 9:5
So at this time t, I will send a .... Ex 9:18
t I will bring locusts into your .... Ex 10:4
T morning you will see the glory .... Ex 16:7
because t is the Sabbath, ... Ex 16:23
of the food until t morning." .... Ex 16:23
T I will stand on the top of the .... Ex 17:9
spend today and t preparing .... Ex 19:10
and be ready by the day after t. .... Ex 19:11
T there will be a special feast .... Ex 32:5
ready t morning, and then come. .... Ex 34:2
'Make yourselves holy for t, ... Nu 11:18
leave t and follow the desert .... Nu 14:25

T morning the Lord will show who .... Nu 16:5
T put fire and incense in them .... Nu 16:7
must stand before the Lord t. .... Nu 16:16
because t the Lord will do .... Jos 3:5
apart to the Lord for t. .... Jos 7:13
T morning you must be present .... Jos 7:14
at this time t I will give them .... Jos 11:6
angry with everyone in Israel t. .... Jos 22:18
T morning you can get up early .... Jdg 19:9
because t I will hand them over .... Jdg 20:28
this time t I will send you 1Sa 9:16
T morning I will answer all your 1Sa 9:19
'Before the day warms up t, ... 1Sa 11:9
T we will come out to meet you. 1Sa 11:10
t is the New Moon festival. 1Sa 20:5
this same time the day after t, ... 1Sa 20:12
T is the New Moon festival. 1Sa 20:18
T you and your sons will be with 1Sa 28:19
T I'll send you back to the 2Sa 11:12
if by this time t I don't kill 1Ki 19:2
About this time t I will send my 1Ki 20:6
Then we will eat my son t.' 2Ki 6:28
'About this time t seven quarts 2Ki 7:1
about this time t at the gate of 2Ki 7:18
me at Jezreel t about this time. 2Ki 10:6
T go down there and fight those. 2Ch 20:16
out against those people t.'" 2Ch 20:17
Come with Haman t to the banquet .... Est 5:8
And t also the queen has asked .... Est 5:12
to do again t what the king .... Est 9:13
I will give it to you t." .... Pr 3:28
Don't brag about t; .... Pr 27:1
no one knows what t will bring. .... Ec 7:14
drink, because t we will die." .... Is 22:13
And t we will do this again, ... Is 56:12
is alive today but t is thrown .... Mt 6:30
worry about t, because tomorrow .... Mt 6:34
because t will have its own .... Mt 6:34
that the day after t is the day .... Mt 26:2
is alive today but t is thrown .... Lk 12:28
'Today and t I am forcing demons .... Lk 13:32
way today and t and the next day .... Lk 13:33
down to their council meeting t. .... Ac 23:20
said, "T you will hear him. .... Ac 25:22
drink, because t we will die." 1Co 15:32
Today or t we will go to some. .... Jam 4:13
do not know what will happen t! .... Jam 4:14

TONGS

flowers, lamps, and t of gold; 1Ki 7:49
lamps, and t of pure gold; 2Ch 4:21
used a pair of t to take a hot .... Is 6:6

TONGUE

me, and his word was on my t. 2Sa 23:2
from the t that strikes like .... Job 5:21
words as the t tastes food. .... Job 12:11
and my t will not tell a lie. .... Job 27:4
words as the t tastes food. .... Job 34:3
hook or tie its t down with a .... Job 41:1
and my t sticks to the top of my .... Ps 22:15
t is like the pen of a skilled. .... Ps 45:1
evil, and your t makes up lies. .... Ps 50:19
Your t is like a sharp razor, ... Ps 52:2
mouth and praised him with my t. .... Ps 66:17
Let my t stick to the roof of my .... Ps 137:6
Lord, help me control my t; .... Ps 141:3
look, a lying t, hands that .... Pr 6:17
but a liar's t will be stopped. .... Pr 10:31
honey and milk are under your t. .... Sng 4:11
his t is like a burning fire. .... Is 30:27
He made my t like a sharp sword. .... Is 49:2
At whom do you stick out your t? .... Is 57:4
and with your t you say evil .... Is 59:3

I will make your t stick to the .... Eze 3:26
spit and touched the man's t. .... Mk 7:33
to use his t so that he spoke .... Mk 7:35
finger in water and cool my t, ... Lk 16:24
you speak clearly with your t, ... 1Co 14:9
It is the same with the t. .... Jam 3:5
And the t is like a fire. .... Jam 3:6
The t spreads its evil through .... Jam 3:6
The t is set on fire by hell, ... Jam 3:6
but no one can tame the t. .... Jam 3:8

TONGUES

they may hide it under their t. .... Job 20:12
as if their t stuck to the roof .... Job 29:10
they use their t for telling .... Ps 5:9
they use their t for sin and .... Ps 10:7
and cut off those bragging t. .... Ps 12:3
They say, "Our t will help us .... Ps 12:4
out their t and shake their .... Ps 22:7
words that bite and t that lie. .... Ps 52:4
their t as sharp as swords. .... Ps 57:4
They sharpen their t like swords .... Ps 64:3
false, and their t lied to him. .... Ps 78:36
They make their t sharp as a .... Ps 140:3
Their t are dry with thirst. .... Is 41:17
They use their t like a bow, ... Je 9:3
have taught their t to lie. .... Je 9:5
Their t are like sharp arrows. .... Je 9:8
so thirsty their t stick to the .... La 4:4
t will rot in their mouths. .... Zch 14:12
use their t for telling lies. .... Rm 3:13
We use our t to praise our Lord .... Jam 3:9
gnawed their t because of the .... Rev 16:10

TONIGHT

the two men who came to you t? .... Ge 19:5
him drunk again t so you can go .... Ge 19:34
you may sleep with Jacob t." .... Ge 30:15
with me t because I have .... Ge 30:16
'About midnight t I will go .... Ex 11:4
You stay here t as the other men .... Nu 22:19
come here t to spy out the land. .... Jos 2:2
put them down where you stay t." .... Jos 4:3
said to him, "Please stay t. .... Jdg 19:6
hope' and had another husband t, ... Ru 1:12
The t will be working at the .... Ru 3:2
Stay here t, and in the morning .... Ru 3:13
the Philistines t and rob them. 1Sa 14:36
T you must run for your life. 1Sa 19:11
thousand men and chase David t. 2Sa 17:1
him not to stay t at the 2Sa 17:16
man not be left with you by t! 2Sa 19:7
T you will all stumble in your .... Mt 26:31
t before the rooster crows you .... Mt 26:34
t before the rooster crows twice .... Mk 14:30
T your life will be taken from .... Lk 12:20
to leave at nine o'clock t. .... Ac 23:23

TOOK

not be found, because God t him. .... Ge 5:24
So the two men t the hands of .... Ge 19:16
Then Abraham t his knife and was .... Ge 22:10
So Abraham went and t the sheep .... Ge 22:13
Israelites t his land and the .... Dt 4:47
much for myself, so I t them. .... Jos 7:21
Joshua t control of all the land .... Jos 11:23
They t him down to Gaza, where .... Jdg 16:21
with me; I t it." His mother .... Jdg 17:2
and he t off his sandal. .... Ru 4:8
But David t an oath, saying, ... 1Sa 20:3
Joab t him aside into the 2Sa 3:27
of the LORD and t hold of the 1Ki 2:28
So she t my son from my bed 1Ki 3:20
They t or destroyed every 2Ch 36:19
Nebuchadnezzar t them from the .... Ezr 6:5

He t me to a safe place. .... Ps 18:19
t away my clothes of sadness, ... Ps 30:11
his servant and t him from the .... Ps 78:70
on him, and t him to Babylon. .... Je 52:11
lifted me up and t me away. .... Eze 3:14
Then the man t the fire and went .... Eze 10:7
to walk, and t them by the .... Hos 11:3
walk across it t a person three .... Jnh 3:3
angels came and t care of him. .... Mt 4:11
He t our suffering on him and .... Mt 8:17
he t his twelve followers aside .... Mt 20:17
Jesus t some bread and thanked. .... Mt 26:26
These two men t Jesus' body and .... Jn 19:40
They t the apostles and put them .... Ac 5:18
over to be killed, he t bread 1Co 11:23
So I t the small scroll from the .... Rev 10:10

TOOL

the slave's ear using a sharp t. .... Ex 21:6
formed it with a t and made a .... Ex 32:4
use any iron t to cut the stones .... Dt 27:5
no t was ever used on them. .... Jos 8:31
except with a t of iron or wood. 2Sa 23:7
go by faster than a weaver's t, ... Job 7:6
doesn't know he is a t for me. .... Is 10:7
person uses evil like a t. .... Is 32:7
he makes the kind of t he wants. .... Is 54:16
Judah is written with an iron t. .... Je 17:1
Swing the cutting t, because the .... Joe 3:13

TOOLS

who made t out of bronze and .... Ge 4:22
that you have shaped with t. .... Ex 20:25
When you use any t on them, ... Ex 20:25
make all the t and dishes that .... Ex 27:3
on the lampstand and all its t, ... Ex 30:27
offerings and on all its t, ... Ex 30:28
and all its t, the bronze bowl .... Ex 35:16
He made all the t of bronze to .... Ex 38:3
to make all the t for the altar. .... Ex 38:30
a row, and its t, and the olive .... Ex 39:37
and all its t, the bowl and its .... Ex 39:39
offerings and on all its t. .... Ex 40:10
and all its t and the large .... Le 8:11
the t of the Holy Place which .... Nu 3:31
and all its t to prepare them .... Nu 7:1
any other iron t at the Temple. 1Ki 6:7
One workman uses t to heat iron, ... Is 44:12
put their t which they used .... Eze 40:42
when they see Zerubbabel with t, ... Zch 4:10

TOOTH

eye for eye, t for tooth, hand .... Ex 21:24
eye, tooth for t, hand for hand, ... Ex 21:24
master knocks out a t of his .... Ex 21:27
free the slave to pay for the t. .... Ex 21:27
bone, eye for eye, t for tooth. .... Le 24:20
bone, eye for eye, tooth for t. .... Le 24:20
eye for an eye, a t for a tooth, ... Dt 19:21
a tooth for a t, a hand for a .... Dt 19:21
with a broken t or walking with .... Pr 25:19
an eye, and a t for a tooth.' .... Mt 5:38
an eye, and a tooth for a t.' .... Mt 5:38

TOP

whose t will reach high into the .... Ge 11:4
poured olive oil on the t of it. .... Ge 28:18
the t basket were all kinds of .... Ge 40:17
his money in the t of the sack. .... Ge 42:27
Put this lid on t of the Ark, ... Ex 25:21
you will be on t and not on .... Dt 28:13
Moab to the t of Mount Pisgah, ... Dt 34:1
border went to the t of the hill .... Jos 15:8
from the t to the bottom. .... Mt 27:51
leaned on the t of his walking .... Heb 11:21

TOPAZ

must have a ruby, **t**, and yellow .... Ex 28:17
was a ruby, a **t**, and a yellow .... Ex 39:10
The **t** from Cush cannot compare .... Job 28:19
ruby, **t**, and emerald, yellow .... Eze 28:13
the ninth was **t**, the tenth was................. Rev 21:20

TOPHEL

Paran and the towns of **T**, ... Dt 1:1

TOPHETH

Josiah ruined **T**, in the Valley 2Ki 23:10
T has been made ready for a long .... Is 30:33
of worship at **T** in the Valley of .... Je 7:31
call this place **T** or the Valley .... Je 7:32
bury the dead in **T** until there .... Je 7:32
the Valley of Ben Hinnom or **T**, ... Je 19:6
people will be buried here in **T**, ... Je 19:11
I will make this city like **T**. .... Je 19:12
as this place, **T**, because the .... Je 19:13
Jeremiah left **T** where the LORD .... Je 19:14

TOPMOST

he will bring out the **t** stone, ... Zch 4:7

TOPS

tenth month the **t** of the .... Ge 8:5
marching in the **t** of the balsam 2Sa 5:24

TORCH

and a blazing **t** passed between .... Ge 15:17
jar with a burning **t** inside. .... Jdg 7:16
and then tied a **t** to the tails .... Jdg 15:4
burning like a **t**, fell from the .... Rev 8:10

TORCHES

They held the **t** in their left .... Jdg 7:20
After he lit the **t**, he let the .... Jdg 15:5
burning coals of fire or like **t**. .... Eze 1:13
They look like **t**; they run like............... Nah 2:4
They were carrying **t**, lanterns, ... Jn 18:3

TORE

Then Jacob **t** his clothes and put .... Ge 37:34
Saul caught his robe, and it **t**................. 1Sa 15:27
new coat and **t** it into twelve 1Ki 11:30
t the kingdom away from David's 1Ki 14:8
temple of Baal and **t** it down, ... 2Ki 11:18
he got up and **t** his robe and .... Job 1:20
he **t** his clothes and said, ... Mt 26:65
he **t** his clothes and said,........................ Mk 14:63
t off his clothes, beat him, ... Lk 10:30
about it, they **t** their clothes. .... Ac 14:14
The Roman officers **t** the clothes .... Ac 16:22

TORN

Joseph has been **t** to pieces!" .... Ge 37:33
he has been **t** apart by a wild .... Ge 44:28
The LORD has **t** the kingdom of.............. 1Sa 15:28
the LORD, which had been **t** down. 1Ki 18:30
of Israel had **t** his clothes, ... 2Ki 5:8
the Temple was **t** into two pieces .... Mt 27:51
the Temple was **t** into two pieces .... Mk 15:38
in the Temple was **t** in two...................... Lk 23:45

TORNADO

and his chariots come like a **t**. .... Je 4:13

TORTURE

Oh, the **t** in my heart! .... Je 4:19
you come here to **t** us before the .... Mt 8:29
you in God's name not to **t** me!"............... Mk 5:7
I beg you, don't **t** me!" .... Lk 8:28

TORTURED

Others were **t** and refused to .... Heb 11:35

TOSS

is long, and I **t** until dawn. .... Job 7:4
whose waves **t** up waste and mud. .... Is 57:20

TOSSED

me into the wind and **t** me about .... Job 30:22
The ships were **t** as high as the .... Ps 107:26
We will not be **t** about like a .... Eph 4:14

TOSSING

are troubled like the **t** sea. .... Je 49:23
t up their own shameful actions .... Jud 1:13

TOUCH

must not even **t** it, or you will................. Ge 3:3
you to sin against me and **t** her. .... Ge 20:6
Come near so I can **t** you, ... Ge 27:21
and not to **t** the foot of it. .... Ex 19:12
No one is allowed to **t** him..................... Ex 19:13
Or someone might **t** something .... Le 5:2
might **t** human uncleanness—................. Le 5:3
animals or even **t** their dead .... Le 11:8
them or even **t** their dead bodies .... Le 11:11
She must not **t** anything that is .... Le 12:4
close relatives, he may **t** him. .... Le 21:2
way they won't **t** the holy things............. Nu 4:15
they must not **t** them, or they .... Nu 6:7
Don't **t** anything of theirs, ... Nu 16:26
Those who **t** a dead person's body .... Nu 19:11
If those who **t** a dead person's .... Nu 19:13
will not **t** any fields of grain .... Nu 20:17
their meat or **t** their dead .... Dt 14:8
your work and everything you **t**. .... Dt 15:10
because my father won't **t** you. 1Sa 23:17
I wouldn't **t** the king's son even 2Sa 18:12
of the sky **t** her sons' bodies 2Sa 21:10
not let the wild animals **t** them. 2Sa 21:10
No one can **t** them except with a 2Sa 23:7
Don't **t** my chosen people, ... 1Ch 16:22
but you must not **t** Job himself."............... Job 1:12
refuse to **t** it; such food makes .... Job 6:7
their heads may **t** the clouds, ... Job 20:6
Don't **t** my chosen people, ... Ps 105:15
T the mountains so they will .... Ps 144:5
T nothing that is unclean. .... Is 52:11
so no one would **t** their clothes. .... La 4:14
Get away! Don't **t** us!" So they .... La 4:15
don't **t** any who have the mark .... Eze 9:6
They let men **t** and hold their .... Eze 23:3
If I can just **t** his clothes,....................... Mt 9:21
Jesus to let them **t** just the .... Mt 14:36
pushing toward him to **t** him. .... Mk 3:10
If I can just **t** his clothes,........................ Mk 5:28
him to let them **t** just the edge .... Mk 6:56
and begged him to **t** the man. .... Mk 8:22
to Jesus so he could **t** them, ... Mk 10:13
They will **t** the sick, and the .... Mk 16:18
people were trying to **t** Jesus, ... Lk 6:19
Someone did **t** me, because I felt .... Lk 8:46
to Jesus so he could **t** them. .... Lk 18:15
T me and see, because a ghost .... Lk 24:39
But no one was able to **t** him, ... Jn 7:30
but no one was able to **t** him .... Jn 7:44
the Lord will **t** you, and you .... Ac 13:11
T nothing that is unclean, ... 2Co 6:17
"Don't even **t** that thing"? .... Col 2:21
and the Evil One cannot **t** them............... 1Jn 5:18

TOUCHED

t him and said, "Your voice .... Ge 27:22
because Jacob was **t** there. .... Ge 32:32
she **t** Moses' feet with it and .... Ex 4:25
he does not know that he **t** it, ... Le 5:2
if the person the woman's bed .... Le 15:23
as well as anyone who **t** a bone,............... Nu 19:18
anyone or **t** a dead body must .... Nu 31:19
soon as their feet **t** dry land, ... Jos 4:18
continued until it **t** Jericho and .... Jos 16:7
The border **t** Asher's land on the .... Jos 17:10

of their land t the area called .... Jos 19:22
western border t Mount Carmel .... Jos 19:26
The angel of the LORD t the meat .... Jdg 6:21
t the hearts of certain brave 1Sa 10:26
David t the hearts of all the 2Sa 19:14
One creature's wing t one wall, ... 1Ki 6:27
creature's wing t the other wall 1Ki 6:27
an angel came to him and t him. 1Ki 19:5
The angel t him and said, ... 1Ki 19:7
When the man t Elisha's bones, ... 2Ki 13:21
him, because he had t the Ark. 1Ch 13:10
feet long and t the Temple wall. 2Ch 3:11
and it t a wing of the second 2Ch 3:11
second creature t the other side 2Ch 3:12
other wing t the first 2Ch 3:12
forward and t the end of it..................... Est 5:2
The creature t my mouth with the .... Is 6:7
this hot coal has t your lips. .... Is 6:7
out his hand and t my mouth.................. Je 1:9
and their wings t each other. .... Eze 1:9
wings that t one of the other .... Eze 1:11
and they t her breasts and had .... Eze 23:8
There men t and held your young .... Eze 23:21
but no human being t the rock. .... Da 2:34
but no human being t it. .... Da 2:45
top of the tree t the sky and .... Da 4:11
Its top t the sky, and it could .... Da 4:20
the tall tree that t the sky. .... Da 4:22
his feet hardly t the ground. .... Da 8:5
Then he t me and lifted me to my .... Da 8:18
Then a hand t me and set me on .... Da 10:10
who looked like a man t my lips, ... Da 10:16
like a man t me again and gave .... Da 10:18
his hand and t the man and said .... Mt 8:3
Jesus t her hand, and the fever .... Mt 8:15
Jesus and t the edge of his .... Mt 9:20
Jesus t their eyes and said, ... Mt 9:29
and all who t it were healed. .... Mt 14:36
to them and t them and said, ... Mt 17:7
the blind men t their eyes, ... Mt 20:34
out his hand and t him and said, ... Mk 1:41
him in the crowd and t his coat. .... Mk 5:27
and asked, "Who t my clothes?" .... Mk 5:30
And you ask, 'Who t me?'"..................... Mk 5:31
around to see who had t him. .... Mk 5:32
and all who t it were healed. .... Mk 6:56
then spit and t the man's tongue .... Mk 7:33
his hand and t the man and said .... Lk 5:13
He went up and t the coffin, ... Lk 7:14
Jesus and t the edge of his .... Lk 8:44
Then Jesus said, "Who t me?" .... Lk 8:45
people said they had not t him, ... Lk 8:45
why she had t him and how she .... Lk 8:47
Then he t the servant's ear and .... Lk 22:51
that can be t and that is .... Heb 12:18
and we have t with our hands. 1Jn 1:1

TOUCHES

Anyone who t this man or his.................. Ge 26:11
If my father t me, he will know .... Ge 27:12
blood when it t the ground." .... Ex 4:9
Anyone who t the mountain must .... Ex 19:12
anything that t it must be holy .... Ex 29:37
Anything that t these things .... Ex 30:29
Whatever t these offerings shall .... Le 6:18
Whatever t the meat of the sin .... Le 6:27
eat meat that t anything unclean .... Le 7:19
If anyone t something unclean— .... Le 7:21
and anyone who t the dead body .... Le 11:24
and anyone who t the dead body .... Le 11:26
Anyone who t the dead body of .... Le 11:27
anyone who t their dead bodies .... Le 11:31
but anyone who t the dead body.............. Le 11:36

anyone who t its body will be .... Le 11:39
Anyone who t his bed must wash .... Le 15:5
Anyone who t the person who .... Le 15:7
Anyone who t something that was .... Le 15:10
in water and t another person, ... Le 15:11
a body fluid t a clay bowl, ... Le 15:12
If he t a wooden bowl, that bowl .... Le 15:12
anyone who t her will be unclean .... Le 15:19
Anyone who t her bed must wash .... Le 15:21
Anyone who t something she has .... Le 15:22
and her monthly period t him, ... Le 15:24
Whoever t those things will be .... Le 15:27
Anyone who t those things will .... Le 22:6
is outside and t someone who was .... Nu 19:16
or if anyone t a human bone or a .... Nu 19:16
and anyone who t the water will .... Nu 19:21
unclean person t becomes unclean........... Nu 19:22
and whoever t it will be unclean.............. Nu 19:22
He t the mountains, and they .... Ps 104:32
grows until she t the sky, ... Je 51:53
GOD All-Powerful t the land, ... Am 9:5
If that fold t bread, cooked .... Hag 2:12
A person who t a dead body will .... Hag 2:13
If he t any of these foods, ... Hag 2:13
because whoever t you hurts what .... Zch 2:8
even an animal, t the mountain, ... Heb 12:20

TOUCHING

t it will make him unclean. .... Le 7:21
unclean by t a dead person. .... Le 21:1
unclean from t a dead body, ... Le 22:4
from t any unclean crawling .... Le 22:5
or from t an unclean person .... Le 22:5
become unclean by t a dead body. .... Nu 5:2
were unclean from t a dead body. .... Nu 9:6
because of t a dead body. .... Nu 9:7
t Zebulun and the Valley of.................... Jos 19:27
with their wings t each other 1Ki 6:27
living creatures t each other .... Eze 3:13
the woman t him is a sinner! .... Lk 7:39

TOWEL

Taking a t, he wrapped it around .... Jn 13:4
them with the t that was wrapped .... Jn 13:5

TOWER

a city and a t for ourselves,.................... Ge 11:4
city and the t that the people .... Ge 11:5
return and pull down this t." .... Jdg 8:9
pulled down the t of Peniel and .... Jdg 8:17
who were in the T of Shechem .... Jdg 9:46
leaders of the T of Shechem had .... Jdg 9:47
were at the T of Shechem also .... Jdg 9:49
inside the city was a strong t, ... Jdg 9:51
of that city ran to the t. .... Jdg 9:51
climbed up to the roof of the t. .... Jdg 9:51
came to the t to attack it. .... Jdg 9:52
door of the t to set it on fire, ... Jdg 9:52
as far as the T of the Hundred .... Ne 3:1
went on to the T of Hananel .... Ne 3:1
the wall and the T of the Ovens.............. Ne 3:11
bend and by the t on the upper .... Ne 3:25
the east and t that extends .... Ne 3:26
from the great t that extends .... Ne 3:27
went from the T of the Ovens to .... Ne 12:38
the T of Hananel and the Tower .... Ne 12:39
and the T of the Hundred. .... Ne 12:39
like a strong t against my .... Ps 61:3
The LORD is like a strong t; .... Pr 18:10
Your neck is like David's t, ... Sng 4:4
Your neck is like an ivory t. .... Sng 7:4
every tall t and every high, ... Is 2:15
He built a t in the middle of it................ Is 5:2
from the T of Hananel to .... Je 31:38
watch and place myself at the t. .... Hab 2:1

and from the T of Hananel to the .... Zch 14:10
for a winepress and built a t. .... Mt 21:33
for a winepress and built a t. .... Mk 12:1
died when the t of Siloam fell.................. Lk 13:4
want to build a t, you first sit .... Lk 14:28

TOWERS

country, towns, villages, and t. 1Ch 27:25
Let's make t, gates, and bars in 2Ch 14:7
Uzziah built t in Jerusalem at................. 2Ch 26:9
also built t in the desert and 2Ch 26:10
devices on the t and corners 2Ch 26:15
cities and t in the forests. 2Ch 27:4
of the wall and put t on it. 2Ch 32:5
Jerusalem and count its t. .... Ps 48:12
and safety within her strong t." .... Ps 122:7
we will put silver t on her. .... Sng 8:9
and my breasts are like t. .... Sng 8:10
Assyria built t to attack it; .... Is 23:13
you with t and with devices .... Is 29:3
and the t are pulled down. .... Is 30:25
cities and t will be empty. .... Is 32:14
in charge of our defense t?" .... Is 33:18
will take over the strong t, ... Is 34:13
the strong t of Jerusalem!" .... Je 6:5
it burns even the strong t. .... Je 17:27
surrendered, her t have fallen, ... Je 50:15
watch from our t for a nation to .... La 4:17
of Tyre and pull down her t. .... Eze 26:4
down your t with his iron bars. .... Eze 26:9
the strong t of Ben-Hadad. .... Am 1:4
Attack the corner t!' .... Zph 1:16
nations; their t were ruined. I .... Zph 3:6

TOWN

the people in our t know you are .... Ru 3:11
When you enter a city or t,.................... Mt 10:11
the law from every t in Galilee .... Lk 5:17
the t where David lived. .... Jn 7:42

TOWNS

go to other t around here so I .... Mk 1:38

TRACK

I will t him down among all the 1Sa 23:23
you will not keep t of my sin. .... Job 14:16

TRACONITIS

the ruler of Iturea and T;   .... Lk 3:1

TRADE

free to own land and to t here." .... Ge 34:10
live in our land and t here. .... Ge 34:21
ships that he sent out to t, ... 2Ch 9:21
so they could not sail out to t............... 2Ch 20:37
and would t away your friend................. Job 6:27
Tyre, and it will again have t. .... Is 23:17
is a place for t for the people .... Eze 27:3
came alongside to t with you................. Eze 27:9
wealth, your t, your goods, your........... Eze 27:27
your many sins and dishonest t............... Eze 28:18
not to sell or t any of this   .... Eze 48:14

TRADED

when people t or bought back .... Ru 4:7
'The city that t with the .... Eze 26:2
They t your goods for silver, ... Eze 27:12
They t your goods for slaves and .... Eze 27:13
Beth Togarmah t your goods for............. Eze 27:14
They t your goods for turquoise, ... Eze 27:16
They t your goods for wheat from .... Eze 27:17
They t your goods for all the .... Eze 27:22
the goods you t went out over................. Eze 27:33
Because you t with countries far .... Eze 28:16
They t boys for prostitutes, ... Joe 3:3
t the glory of God who lives .... Rm 1:23
They t the truth of God for a .... Rm 1:25

TRADER'S

She is like a t ship, bringing .... Pr 31:14

TRADERS

weight as the t normally did. .... Ge 23:16
So when the Midianite t came by, ... Ge 37:28
gold from the t and merchants, ... 1Ki 10:15
His t bought them in Kue. 1Ki 10:28
Solomon's t also sold horses and 1Ki 10:29
his t bought them in Kue. 2Ch 1:16
gold from t and merchants..................... 2Ch 9:14
the Temple servants and the t, ... Ne 3:31
goldsmiths and the t made .... Ne 3:32
Once or twice t and sellers of .... Ne 13:20
and the t of Sheba look .... Job 6:19
Will t try to bargain with you .... Job 41:6
group of t from Dedan spent the .... Is 21:13
its t were greatly respected.   .... Is 23:8
the land of t, but even this did .... Eze 16:29
and brought it to a land of t, ... Eze 17:4
he planted it in a city of t, ... Eze 17:4
Tarshish became t for you .... Eze 27:12
People of Aram became t for you, ... Eze 27:16
of Kedar became t for you. .... Eze 27:21
and the t of Sheba, Asshur,................... Eze 27:23
workers, your t, your warriors, ... Eze 27:27
The t among the nations hiss at .... Eze 27:36
Dedan, and the t of Tarshish, ... Eze 38:13
Your t are more than the stars .... Nah 3:16
all the silver t will be gone..................... Zph 1:11

TRADING

them alive by t food for their .... Ge 47:17
also had many t ships at sea, ... 1Ki 10:22
built t ships to sail to 1Ki 22:48
with Ahaziah to build t ships,............... 2Ch 20:36
money they made from their t, ... Job 20:18
the large t ships with an east .... Ps 48:7
the t ships and the beautiful .... Is 2:16
about Tyre: You t ships, cry! .... Is 23:1
So be sad, you t ships, because .... Is 23:14
The great t ships will come..................... Is 60:9
They are t their precious things .... La 1:11
Now we can be the t center.   .... Eze 26:2
t saddle blankets for riding. .... Eze 27:20
T ships carried the things you .... Eze 27:25
Through your great skill in t, ... Eze 28:5

TRADITION

the laws of my t more carefully .... Ac 26:5

TRAIL

It leaves a t in the mud like a .... Job 41:30

TRAIN

T children to live the right way, ... Pr 22:6
nor will they t for war anymore............... Is 2:4
they will not t for war anymore............... Mic 4:3
but t yourself to serve God..................... 1Ti 4:7

TRAINED

out his 318 t men who had been .... Ge 14:14
together who were t with swords. .... Jdg 20:15
hundred of these t soldiers were............. Jdg 20:16
of the best t soldiers from all .... Jdg 20:34
brave warriors t for war and 1Ch 12:8
They were t soldiers and knew 1Ch 12:33
forty thousand t soldiers from 1Ch 12:36
relatives were t and skilled.................... 1Ch 25:7
he kept t soldiers in Jerusalem. 2Ch 17:13
had an army of t soldiers. 2Ch 26:11
swords and have been t in war. .... Sng 3:8
a calf that had never been t. .... Je 31:18
arrows are like t soldiers who .... Je 50:9
were to be t for three years, ... Da 1:5
Though I t them and gave them .... Hos 7:15

has been fully t will be like.................... Lk 6:40
I may not be a t speaker, but I 2Co 11:6

TRAINING
had no special t or education................... Ac 4:13
them with the t and teaching .... Eph 6:4
T your body helps you in some 1Ti 4:8

TRAINS
He t my hands for battle so my 2Sa 22:35
He t my hands for battle so my .... Ps 18:34
my Rock, who t me for war, who .... Ps 144:1
me for war, who t me for battle............... Ps 144:1

TRAITOR
I am not a t working for Judah! 2Sa 3:8
but a false witness is a t........................ Pr 14:25
be for you, t, whom no one has .... Is 33:1

TRAITORS
her clothes and screamed, "T! 2Ki 11:14
and screamed, "Traitors! T!" 2Ki 11:14
her clothes and screamed, "T! 2Ch 23:13
and screamed, "Traitors! T!" 2Ch 23:13
Do not give those t any mercy. .... Ps 59:5
I see those t, and I hate them,................. Ps 119:158
I see t turning against you and .... Is 21:2
T turn against people;........................... Is 24:16
But all of them are t. .... Hos 7:4

TRAMPLE
Let him t me into the dust and .... Ps 7:5
to t them down like dirt in the .... Is 10:6
I will t him on my mountains................... Is 14:25
People will t each other in the .... Is 22:5
the city will t it under their..................... Is 26:6
Pigs will only t on them, and .... Mt 7:6
And they will t on the holy city .... Rev 11:2

TRAMPLED
but the people t the officer to 2Ki 7:17
The people t him in the gateway, ... 2Ki 7:20
In your name we t those who came .... Ps 44:5
straw that is t down in the .... Is 25:10
people, will be t underfoot...................... Is 28:3
vineyards and t the plants in my .... Je 12:10
with gravel and t me into the .... La 3:16
They were t in the winepress .... Rev 14:20

TRANS-EUPHRATES
and in other places of the T. .... Ezr 4:10
your servants who live in T. .... Ezr 4:11
will be left with nothing in T. .... Ezr 4:16
to those in other places in T. .... Ezr 4:17
ruled over the whole area of T, ... Ezr 4:20
the governor of T, and........................... Ezr 5:3
the governor of T, ... Ezr 5:6
other important officers of T. .... Ezr 5:6
governor of T, Shethar-Bozenai, ... Ezr 6:6
from taxes collected from T. .... Ezr 6:8
the governor of T, ... Ezr 6:13
in charge of the treasury of T: .... Ezr 7:21
to rule the Jewish people of T. .... Ezr 7:25
and to the governors of T. .... Ezr 8:36
letters for the governors of T. .... Ne 2:7
the governors of T and gave them .... Ne 2:9
were ruled by the governor of T. .... Ne 3:7

TRANSLATED
in the Aramaic language and t. .... Ezr 4:7
to us has been t and read to me............... Ezr 4:18

TRAP
own feasts t them and cause .... Rm 11:9

TRAPS
road; they set t for me. Selah .... Ps 140:5

TRAVEL
t across land and sea to find .... Mt 23:15
He did not want to t in Judea,................. Jn 7:1
wanted Timothy to t with him, ... Ac 16:3
us when we t as do the other 1Co 9:5

TRAVELER
saw the t in the public square................. Jdg 19:17
Then a t stopped to visit the 2Sa 12:4
rich man wanted to feed the t, ... 2Sa 12:4
or like a t who only stays one................. Je 14:8

TRAVELING
While they were t, Jesus asked .... Mk 8:27
while Jesus was t through some .... Lk 8:1
Then a Samaritan t down the road............ Lk 10:33
Jesus and his followers were t, ... Lk 10:38
Large crowds were t with Jesus,............. Lk 14:25
While they were t down the road, ... Ac 8:36
The people t with Saul stood .... Ac 9:7
As Peter was t through all the .... Ac 9:32
people also were t around and .... Ac 19:13
Macedonia and were t with Paul, ... Ac 19:29
me and those who were t with me............ Ac 26:13

TRAVELS
led us where no one t or lives.' .... Je 2:6
of a person, it t through dry .... Mt 12:43
of a person, it t through dry .... Lk 11:24
gone on many t and have been 2Co 11:26

TRAYS
wick trimmers and t must be made .... Ex 25:38
pure gold wick trimmers and t. .... Ex 37:23
trimmers, its t, and all the .... Nu 4:9

TREASURE
sent all this t to Hazael king 2Ki 12:18
death more than for hidden t................... Job 3:21
darkness waits for their t. .... Job 20:26
as if I had found a great t. .... Ps 119:162
and hunt for it like hidden t. .... Pr 2:4
T wisdom, and it will make you .... Pr 4:8
what I say, and t my commands............... Pr 7:1
donkeys and their t on the backs .... Is 30:6
for the LORD is the greatest t. .... Is 33:6
People t them, but they are..................... Is 44:9
evil people in the world as t, ... Eze 7:21
and have taken t and valuable .... Eze 22:25
Did you come to capture t?..................... Eze 38:13
from their t houses everything .... Hos 13:15
t to the Lord of all the earth. .... Mic 4:13
no end to the t—piles of wealth .... Nah 2:9
heart will be where your t is. .... Mt 6:21
heaven is like a t hidden in a .... Mt 13:44
One day a man found the t, ... Mt 13:44
you will have t in heaven. .... Mt 19:21
and you will have t in heaven. .... Mk 10:21
the t in heaven that never runs .... Lk 12:33
heart will be where your t is. .... Lk 12:34
and you will have t in heaven. .... Lk 18:22
We have this t from God, but we 2Co 4:7
like clay jars that hold the t. 2Co 4:7
be saving a t for themselves 1Ti 6:19
saved your t for the last days................... Jam 5:3

TREASURED
I have t his words more than my .... Job 23:12
they will dishonor my t place. .... Eze 7:22
But Mary t these things and .... Lk 2:19

TREASURER
had Mithredath the t bring them .... Ezr 1:8
the city t, and our brother .... Rm 16:23

TREASURES
do well from the t hidden in the .... Dt 33:19
He took the t from the Temple of 1Ki 14:26

took all the t from the Temple 2Ki 24:13
the rooms and t in the Temple 1Ch 9:26
giving my own t of gold and 1Ch 29:3
and took the t from the Temple 2Ch 12:9
in Naphtali where t were stored. 2Ch 16:4
also took the t from the palace 2Ch 25:24
some valuable t from the Temple 2Ch 36:10
and all the t from the Temple of 2Ch 36:18
rock and see all the t there. .... Job 28:10
filling their houses with t. .... Pr 8:21
home with rare and beautiful t. .... Pr 24:4
t from kings and other areas. .... Ec 2:8
there are a great many t there. .... Is 2:7
took all the t from its cities, ... Is 23:13
Your wealth and t I will give to .... Je 15:13
your wealth and t I will give .... Je 17:3
and the t of the kings of Judah. .... Je 20:5
believes his t will save him. .... Je 49:4
attack her t, so they will be................. Je 50:37
water and are rich with many t, ... Je 51:13
as if you were t taken in war. .... Eze 25:7
nations will steal t from Tyre. .... Eze 26:5
wealth and its t as pay for his................ Eze 29:19
I will capture t and take loot. .... Eze 38:12
will take the t of those who .... Eze 39:10
of those who took their t; .... Eze 39:10
The king will get t of gold and .... Da 11:43
will grow over their silver t, ... Hos 9:6
my precious t in your temples. .... Joe 3:5
are filled with t they took by .... Am 3:10
he will take the t out of your .... Am 3:11
will find all your hidden t! .... Ob 1:6
carried Israel's t away. .... Ob 1:11
not take their t in their time .... Ob 1:13
house wicked t and the cursed .... Mic 6:10
gifts and gave him t of gold, ... Mt 2:11
Don't store t for yourselves .... Mt 6:19
But store your t in heaven where .... Mt 6:20
In him all the t of wisdom and .... Col 2:3
than to have all the t of Egypt, ... Heb 11:26

TREASURIES

everything in the t of the........................ 1Ki 7:51
gold from the t of the Temple 1Ki 15:18
was found in the t of the Temple 2Ki 12:18
and he took the t of the palace 2Ki 14:14
LORD and in the t of the palace, ... 2Ki 16:8
of the LORD and in the palace t. 2Ki 18:15
for guarding the t of the Temple.............. 1Ch 26:20
for the t of the Temple........................... 1Ch 26:22
leader responsible for the t. 1Ch 26:24
it, the Temple t, and the 1Ch 28:12
and the t of the holy items used 1Ch 28:12
in the t of God's Temple........................ 2Ch 5:1
as his commands about the t. 2Ch 8:15
gold from the t of the Temple 2Ch 16:2
He made t for his silver, gold,................ 2Ch 32:27

TREASURY

gave them to the t of the Temple 1Ch 29:8
they could to the t to rebuild .... Ezr 2:69
kept in the t in Babylon. .... Ezr 6:1
be paid from the king's t. .... Ezr 6:4
be fully paid from the royal t,................ Ezr 6:8
Use the royal t to pay for .... Ezr 7:20
in charge of the t of.......................... Ezr 7:21
gave to the t about 19 pounds. .... Ne 7:70
of silver to the t for the work................ Ne 7:71
put in the storerooms of the t. .... Ne 10:38
will put it into the royal t." .... Est 3:9
the king's t for the killing .... Est 4:7
of the t, judges, rulers, ... Da 3:2

TREAT

began to t her mistress Sarai .... Ge 16:4
she began to t me badly. .... Ge 16:5
said that you would t me well. .... Ge 32:9
'I will t you well and will make .... Ge 32:12
But I will not t the Israelites .... Ex 8:22
I will t my people differently .... Ex 8:23
the LORD will t Israel's animals.............. Ex 9:4
he must t her as a daughter. .... Ex 21:9
do not t him as a moneylender .... Ex 22:25
I will not t guilty people as .... Ex 23:7
holy, and you must t it as holy. .... Ex 30:32
T it as holy to the LORD. .... Ex 30:37
t them just as you treat your .... Le 19:34
them just as you t your own .... Le 19:34
So you must t clean animals and .... Le 20:25
T him as holy, because he offers.............. Le 21:8
priest must not t these holy .... Le 22:15
' He did not t his brothers as .... Dt 33:9
Why did you t us this way?................ Jdg 8:1
I will also t you well because 2Sa 2:6
Forgive and t each person as he 1Ki 8:39
Forgive and t each person as he 2Ch 6:30
Will you t the words of a........................ Job 6:26
female servants t me like a .... Job 19:15
Lord our God, t us well. .... Ps 90:17
prostitute will t you like a .... Pr 6:26
T wisdom as a sister, and make .... Pr 7:4
Children t my people cruelly, ... Is 3:12
I would be to t you as my own .... Je 3:19
'May the LORD t you like .... Je 29:22
to them, they will t me badly." .... Je 38:19
he will also t you with mercy .... Je 42:12
and do not t them fairly. .... Eze 22:29
They will t you with hate and................ Eze 23:29
I will t you just as you treated .... Eze 35:11
are to t these foreigners the .... Eze 47:22
decide how you want to t us, ... Da 1:13
like Admah or t you like Zeboiim .... Hos 11:8
You t people like fish in the .... Hab 1:14
t him like a person who does .... Mt 18:17
that people will t him as if he .... Mk 9:12
and they will t others cruelly.'................ Lk 11:49
arrest you and t you cruelly. .... Lk 21:12
I t my body hard and make it my 1Co 9:27
none of you should t Timothy as 1Co 16:11
Do not t prophecy as if it were 1Th 5:20
But do not t them as enemies. 2Th 3:15
not let anyone t you as if you 1Ti 4:12
T younger men like brothers, ... 1Ti 5:1
Always t them in a pure way. 1Ti 5:2
not let anyone t you as if you .... Tit 2:15
But if you t one person as being.............. Jam 2:9

TREATED

then they would be t the same. .... Ge 18:25
He has t us like strangers. .... Ge 31:15
to be t like a prostitute. .... Ge 34:31
because he has t her unfairly.................. Ex 21:8
Have you t Gideon as you should? .... Jdg 9:16
this is how they t all the 1Sa 2:14
and I will be t as criminals." 1Ki 1:21
as he should be t because you 1Ki 8:39
you have t me like a very 1Ch 17:17
brother were t the same........................ 1Ch 24:31
as he should be t because you 2Ch 6:30
all people to be t the same,..................... 2Ch 19:7
and their enemies t them badly. .... Ne 9:27
months she was t with oil and .... Est 2:12
have t me badly all my life...................... Ps 129:1
have t me badly all my life,..................... Ps 129:2
they are not t fairly or given .... Ec 5:8
merchants were t like princes, ... Is 23:8

does not care if I am t fairly"? .... Is 40:27
life and was t like a criminal .... Is 53:12
and your body has been t badly............ Je 13:22
They have t Jeremiah the prophet .... Je 38:9
The soldiers t their captives .... Je 50:16
if someone is t unfairly before .... La 3:35
treat you just as you t them. .... Eze 35:11
LORD sees how you t the wife you.......... Mal 2:14
you are t badly in one city, ... Mt 10:23
those who have been t unfairly .... Lk 4:18
'He was t like a criminal,' .... Lk 22:37
was shamed and was t unfairly. .... Ac 8:33
we are t as though we were the 1Co 4:13
the normal way t the other son .... Gal 4:29
You know that we t each of you 1Th 2:11
you are being t badly and are............... 2Th 1:4
those who were being t that way. .... Heb 10:33
were poor, abused, and t badly. .... Heb 11:37

TREATING
Why are you t us, your servants, ... Ex 5:15
the Egyptians are t as slaves, ... Ex 6:5
the king of Aram was t them................. 2Ki 13:4
God is t you as children........................ Heb 12:7

TREATMENTS
let beauty t be given to them. .... Est 2:3
her beauty t and special food .... Est 2:9
months of beauty t that were .... Est 2:12

TREATS
that the LORD t Israel............................ Ex 11:7
If anyone t the Sabbath like any.............. Ex 31:14
and he t me like an enemy. .... Job 19:11
t iron as if it were straw and .... Job 41:27
heaven, and he t everyone alike............... Eph 6:9
the Lord t everyone the same. .... Col 3:25
as a father t his own children. 1Th 2:11

TREATY
not make a peace t with them or .... Dt 7:2
Nahash, "Make a t with us, and 1Sa 11:1
I will make a t with you only if 1Sa 11:2
two kings made a t between 1Ki 5:12
Let there be a t between you and 1Ki 15:19
Break your t with Baasha king of 1Ki 15:19
Let there be a t between you and 2Ch 16:3
Break your t with Baasha king of 2Ch 16:3
of Judah made a t with Ahaziah............... 2Ch 20:35

TREE
every beautiful t and every tree .... Ge 2:9
tree and every t that was good .... Ge 2:9
put the t that gives life and.................. Ge 2:9
life and also the t that gives .... Ge 2:9
fruit from any t in the garden, ... Ge 2:16
the fruit from the t which gives .... Ge 2:17
you ever eat fruit from that t, ... Ge 2:17
fruit from any t in the garden?" .... Ge 3:1
eat fruit from the t that is in .... Ge 3:3
you eat the fruit from that t, ... Ge 3:5
saw that the t was beautiful, ... Ge 3:6
eat fruit from the t from which .... Ge 3:11
she gave me fruit from the t, ... Ge 3:12
ate fruit from the t from which .... Ge 3:17
of the fruit from the t of life, ... Ge 3:22
from getting to the t of life. .... Ge 3:24
far as the great t of Moreh at .... Ge 12:6
You may rest under the t, ... Ge 18:4
he stood under the t near them. .... Ge 18:8
a tamarisk t at Beersheba .... Ge 21:33
under the great t near the town .... Ge 35:4
under the oak t at Bethel, ... Ge 35:8
leaves from every t growing in .... Ex 10:5
was left on any t or plant .... Ex 10:15
and the LORD showed him a t. .... Ex 15:25

threw the t into the water, ... Ex 15:25
After planting a t, wait three .... Le 19:23
from the t will be the LORD' .... Le 19:24
may eat the fruit from the t. .... Le 19:25
The t will then produce more .... Le 19:25
hills and under every green t.................. Dt 12:2
swings an ax to cut down a t. .... Dt 19:5
and his body displayed on a t. .... Dt 21:22
body hanging on the t overnight; .... Dt 21:23
displayed on a t is cursed by .... Dt 21:23
either in a t or on the ground,................ Dt 22:6
king of Ai on a t and left him .... Jos 8:29
down from the t and to throw it .... Jos 8:29
at the large t in Zaanannim, ... Jos 19:33
under the oak t near the LORD's .... Jos 24:26
sit under the Palm T of Deborah, ... Jdg 4:5
by the great t in Zaanannim, ... Jdg 4:11
under the oak t at Ophrah that .... Jdg 6:11
to the angel under the oak t. .... Jdg 6:19
beside the great t standing in .... Jdg 9:6
They said to the olive t, '.................... Jdg 9:8
But the olive t said, 'Men and .... Jdg 9:9
the trees said to the fig t, ' .... Jdg 9:10
But the fig t answered, 'Should .... Jdg 9:11
from the fortune-tellers' t''..................... Jdg 9:37
you reach the big t at Tabor. 1Sa 10:3
a pomegranate t at the threshing 1Sa 14:2
the tamarisk t on the hill at 1Sa 22:6
under the tamarisk t in Jabesh. 1Sa 31:13
thick branches of a large oak t. 2Sa 18:9
head got caught in the t,.................... 2Sa 18:9
Absalom hanging in an oak t!" 2Sa 18:10
was still alive in the oak t, ... 2Sa 18:14
him sitting under an oak t. 1Ki 13:14
hill and under every green t. 1Ki 14:23
lay down under the t and slept. 1Ki 19:5
down every good t and stop up 2Ki 3:19
As one man was cutting down a t, ... 2Ki 6:5
message to a cedar t in Lebanon. 2Ki 14:9
hills, and under every green t. 2Ki 16:4
hill and under every green t. 2Ki 17:10
grapevine and fig t and to drink............... 2Ki 18:31
under the large t in Jabesh. 1Ch 10:12
message to a cedar t in Lebanon. 2Ch 25:18
hills, and under every green t. 2Ch 28:4
went out and got t branches. .... Ne 8:16
fruits of every t to the Temple.................. Ne 10:35
If a t is cut down, there is .... Job 14:7
like an olive t that loses its .... Job 15:33
my hope like a fallen t. .... Job 19:10
and ate the root of the broom t. .... Job 30:4
Its tail is like a cedar t; .... Job 40:17
like a t planted by a river. .... Ps 1:3
The t produces fruit in season, ... Ps 1:3
like a healthy t in good soil. .... Ps 37:35
like an olive t growing in God's .... Ps 52:8
limbs like the mighty cedar t. .... Ps 80:10
they sing among the t branches............... Ps 104:12
every t in the country. .... Ps 105:33
As a t produces fruit, wisdom.................. Pr 3:18
eating fruit from the t of life. .... Pr 13:12
a t gives fruit, healing words .... Pr 15:4
tends a fig t gets to eat its .... Pr 27:18
A t can fall to the north or .... Ec 11:3
like the flowers on an almond t. .... Ec 12:5
is like an apple t in the woods! .... Sng 2:3
You are tall like a palm t, ... Sng 7:7
climb up the palm t and take .... Sng 7:8
under the apple t where you were .... Sng 8:5
be like an oak t whose stump is .... Is 6:13
left when the t is chopped down, ... Is 6:13
chop them down like a great t. .... Is 10:33
will grow from a stump of a t; .... Is 11:1

T

be like an olive t after the .... Is 24:13
or dried-up figs from a fig t. .... Is 34:4
grapevine and fig t and to drink .... Is 36:16
so he finds a t that will not .... Is 40:20
will grow like a t in the grass, ... Is 44:14
he plants a pine t, and the rain .... Is 44:14
he burns the t. He uses some .... Is 44:15
every green t to worship your .... Is 57:5
every green t you lay down as .... Je 2:20
hill and under every green t. .... Je 3:6
every green t and didn't obey .... Je 3:13
vine and no figs on the fig t. .... Je 8:13
called you "a leafy olive t, ... Je 11:16
he will set that t on fire, ... Je 11:16
us destroy the t and its fruit. .... Je 11:19
like a t planted near water that .... Je 17:8
every green t and leafy oak—.................. Eze 6:13
the wood of any t in the forest? .... Eze 15:2
hold of the top of a cedar t. .... Eze 17:3
it to grow like a willow t. .... Eze 17:5
from the top of a cedar t, ... Eze 17:22
and become a great cedar t. .... Eze 17:23
down the high t and make the low .... Eze 17:24
tree and make the low t tall. .... Eze 17:24
up the green t and make the dry .... Eze 17:24
tree and make the dry t grow. .... Eze 17:24
high hill and every leafy t. .... Eze 20:28
took a cedar t from Lebanon to .... Eze 27:5
like a cedar t in Lebanon with .... Eze 31:3
Much water made the t grow;.................. Eze 31:4
bottom of the t and sent their .... Eze 31:4
So the t was taller than all the .... Eze 31:5
the t was great and beautiful, ... Eze 31:7
No t in the garden of God was as .... Eze 31:8
God was as beautiful as this t. .... Eze 31:8
GOD says: The t grew tall. Its .... Eze 31:10
earth left the shade of that t. .... Eze 31:12
of the sky live on the fallen t. .... Eze 31:13
the day when the t went down to .... Eze 31:15
her sadness about the great t,................. Eze 31:15
the sound of the t falling when .... Eze 31:16
with the great t to the place .... Eze 31:17
So no t in Eden is equal to .... Eze 31:18
A palm t was between each carved .... Eze 41:18
toward the palm t on one side. .... Eze 41:19
toward the palm t on the other .... Eze 41:19
in front of me was a t standing .... Da 4:10
The t grew large and strong. .... Da 4:11
The top of the t touched the sky .... Da 4:11
leaves of the t were beautiful.................. Da 4:12
found shelter under the t, ... Da 4:12
'Cut down the t and cut off its .... Da 4:14
animals under the t run away, ... Da 4:14
You saw a t in your dream that .... Da 4:20
O king, you are that t!.......................... Da 4:22
like the tall t that touched the .... Da 4:22
'Cut down the t and destroy it. .... Da 4:23
the stump of the t and its roots .... Da 4:26
the first figs on the fig t. .... Hos 9:10
I am like a green pine t; .... Hos 14:8
waste and made my fig t a stump. .... Joe 1:7
under his own vine and fig t, ... Mic 4:4
When the t is shaken, the figs .... Nah 3:12
and under your own fig t.'" .... Zch 3:10
every t that does not produce .... Mt 3:10
good t produces good fruit,.................... Mt 7:17
but a bad t produces bad fruit. .... Mt 7:17
A good t cannot produce bad .... Mt 7:18
and a bad t cannot produce good .... Mt 7:18
Every t that does not produce................. Mt 7:19
fruit, you must make the t good............. Mt 12:33
If your t is not good, it will .... Mt 12:33
t is known by the kind of fruit .... Mt 12:33

Seeing a fig t beside the road, ... Mt 21:19
but there were no figs on the t, ... Mt 21:19
said to the t, "You will never .... Mt 21:19
The t immediately dried up. .... Mt 21:19
did the fig t dry up so quickly? .... Mt 21:20
I did to this t and even more. .... Mt 21:21
Learn a lesson from the fig t: .... Mt 24:32
Seeing a fig t in leaf from far .... Mk 11:13
said to the t, "May no one ever .... Mk 11:14
they saw the fig t dry and dead, ... Mk 11:20
remembered the t and said to................. Mk 11:21
t you cursed is dry and dead! .... Mk 11:21
Learn a lesson from the fig t: .... Mk 13:28
every t that does not produce .... Lk 3:9
A good t does not produce bad .... Lk 6:43
does a bad t produce good fruit. .... Lk 6:43
t is known by its own fruit...................... Lk 6:44
A man had a fig t planted in his.............. Lk 13:6
looking for some fruit on the t, ... Lk 13:6
fruit on this t for three years .... Lk 13:7
let the t have one more year to .... Lk 13:8
If the t produces fruit next .... Lk 13:9
The seed grows and becomes a t, ... Lk 13:19
could say to this mulberry t, ' .... Lk 17:6
a sycamore t so he could see .... Lk 19:4
Look at the fig t and all the .... Lk 21:29
when you were under the fig t, ... Jn 1:48
you I saw you under the fig t? .... Jn 1:50
If the roots of a t are holy, ... Rm 11:16
from an olive t have been broken .... Rm 11:17
of a wild olive t that has been .... Rm 11:17
has been joined to that first t.................. Rm 11:17
and life of the first t, ... Rm 11:17
I could be joined to their t." .... Rm 11:19
be part of the t only because .... Rm 11:20
natural branches of that t stay, ... Rm 11:21
you will be cut off from the t.................. Rm 11:22
branch to be part of a good t. .... Rm 11:24
from a wild olive t and joined................. Rm 11:24
and joined to a good olive t. .... Rm 11:24
that grew from the good t, ... Rm 11:24
be joined to their own t again. .... Rm 11:24
is displayed on a t is cursed." .... Gal 3:13
can a fig t make olives, ... Jam 3:12
the fruit from the t of life, ... Rev 2:7
from a fig t when the wind .... Rev 6:13
land or on the sea or on any t. .... Rev 7:1
on the earth or any plant or t. .... Rev 9:4
The t of life was on each side .... Rev 22:2
The leaves of the t are for the................. Rev 22:2
fruit from the t of life and may .... Rev 22:14
one's share of the t of life and .... Rev 22:19

TREE'S

the top of the t young branches,............. Eze 17:22
the shelter of the t branches. .... Eze 17:23
made their nests in the t limbs. .... Eze 31:6
nations lived in the t shade. .... Eze 31:6
The t branches fell on the .... Eze 31:12
among the t fallen branches. .... Eze 31:13
lived under the great t shade. .... Eze 31:17
the t branches are holy too. .... Rm 11:16

TREES

for seeds and t that made fruits .... Ge 1:12
and all the t whose fruits have .... Ge 1:29
fruit from the t in the garden.................. Ge 3:2
God among the t in the garden. .... Ge 3:8
live near the great t of Mamre .... Ge 13:18
near the great t of Mamre the................. Ge 14:13
near the great t of Mamre. .... Ge 18:1
and plane t and peeled off some.............. Ge 30:37
broke all the t in the fields...................... Ex 9:25
and all the fruit on the t........................ Ex 10:15

None of the t that are watered .... Eze 31:14
and all the t in the countryside .... Eze 31:15
Then all the t of Eden and the .... Eze 31:16
Eden and the best t of Lebanon,............. Eze 31:16
well-watered t, were comforted .... Eze 31:16
These t had also gone down with .... Eze 31:17
go down to join the t of Eden in .... Eze 31:18
Also the t in the countryside .... Eze 34:27
Carvings of palm t were on each .... Eze 40:16
carvings of palm t measured the .... Eze 40:22
carvings of palm t on its inner .... Eze 40:26
of palm t were on its side .... Eze 40:31
Carvings of palm t were on its .... Eze 40:34
Carvings of palm t were on its .... Eze 40:37
creatures with wings and palm t. .... Eze 41:18
palm t and creatures with wings .... Eze 41:20
Place were palm t and creatures............. Eze 41:25
windows and palm t on both side .... Eze 41:26
saw many t on both sides of the .... Eze 47:7
kinds of fruit t will grow on .... Eze 47:12
The t will have fruit every .... Eze 47:12
fruit from the t will be used .... Eze 47:12
destroy her vines and fig t,..................... Hos 2:12
and other t, because their .... Hos 4:13
Like the cedar t in Lebanon, ... Hos 14:5
the beautiful olive t and the .... Hos 14:6
all the bark off my t and left .... Joe 1:7
and the fig t are dried up. .... Joe 1:12
The pomegranate t, the date palm .... Joe 1:12
date palm t, the apple trees— .... Joe 1:12
trees, the apple t—all the .... Joe 1:12
the t in the field have died. .... Joe 1:12
burned all the t in the field. .... Joe 1:19
The t have given fruit;........................... Joe 2:22
fig t and the grapevines have .... Joe 2:22
from your hooks for trimming t............... Joe 3:10
water to the valley of acacia t. .... Joe 3:18
tall like cedar t and as strong .... Am 2:9
ate your fig and olive t. .... Am 4:9
and I take care of sycamore t. .... Am 7:14
into hooks for trimming t. .... Mic 4:3
are like fig t with ripe fruit. .... Nah 3:12
Fig t may not grow figs, and .... Hab 3:17
Your vines, fig t, pomegranates, ... Hag 2:19
and olive t have not given fruit .... Hag 2:19
among some myrtle t in a ravine, ... Zch 1:8
among the myrtle t explained, ... Zch 1:10
was standing among the myrtle t. .... Zch 1:11
There are two olive t by it, ... Zch 4:3
are the two olive t on the right .... Zch 4:11
so fire may burn your cedar t. .... Zch 11:1
Cry, pine t, because the cedar................. Zch 11:2
because the tall t are ruined. .... Zch 11:2
is now ready to cut down the t, ... Mt 3:10
from the t and spread them .... Mt 21:8
look like t walking around." .... Mk 8:24
is now ready to cut down the t, ... Lk 3:9
fig tree and all the other t. .... Lk 21:29
of palm t and went out to .... Jn 12:13
They are autumn t without fruit .... Jud 1:12
the sea or the t until we mark................. Rev 7:3
a third of the t were burned up. .... Rev 8:7
are the two olive t and the two .... Rev 11:4

TREMBLE
will hear this and t with fear; .... Ex 15:14
afraid and t in their hiding 2Sa 22:46
T before him, everyone on earth. 1Ch 16:30
not stand up or t with fear .... Est 5:9
and makes its foundations t. .... Job 9:6
The spirits of the dead t,....................... Job 26:5
great fear. Be happy, but t. .... Ps 2:11
afraid and t in their hiding .... Ps 18:45

Nations t and kingdoms shake. .... Ps 46:6
T before him, everyone on earth. .... Ps 96:9
when the people see it, they t. .... Ps 97:4
things that make the earth t, ... Pr 30:21
of Egypt will t before him, ... Is 19:1
the sea and made its kingdoms t. .... Is 23:11
feel safe now, but you should t. .... Is 32:11
the mountains will t before you. .... Is 64:1
They will t all over with fear. .... Eze 7:18
Human, t as you eat your food, ... Eze 12:18
the ground and t all the time. .... Eze 26:16
people who live by the coast t, ... Eze 26:18
and Cush will t with fear. .... Eze 30:4
of Cush will t with fear when .... Eze 30:9
Their kings will t with fear .... Eze 32:10
warning in a city, the people t. .... Am 3:6
my lips t when I hear the sound. .... Hab 3:16
that, too, and they t with fear................. Jam 2:19

TREMBLED
Then Isaac t greatly and said,............... Ge 27:33
all the people in the camp t. .... Ex 19:16
The earth t and shook. 2Sa 22:8
They t because the LORD was 2Sa 22:8
Everyone who t in fear at the .... Ezr 9:4
The earth t and shook. .... Ps 18:7
They t because the LORD was .... Ps 18:7
The earth t and shook. .... Ps 77:18
and the mountains t before you.............. Is 64:3
and that the tents of Midian t. .... Hab 3:7

TREMBLES
The earth t when he comes; .... Nah 1:5
these things, and my body t; .... Hab 3:16

TREMBLING
I was t with fear;................................... Job 4:14
All the hills were t. .... Je 4:24
will come t from their holes .... Mic 7:17
I was weak and fearful and t. 1Co 2:3
your salvation with fear and t, ... Php 2:12

TRENCH
streets and a t filled with .... Da 9:25

TRIAL
you must not ruin a fair t. .... Ex 23:2
he receives a fair t in court. .... Nu 35:12
and God has refused me a fair t. .... Job 34:5
Instead of getting a fair t, ... Job 34:6
set the time for t, and I will .... Ps 75:2
the people for t after the....................... Ac 12:4
Herod was to bring him to t, ... Ac 12:6
beat us in public without a t, ... Ac 16:37
I am on t here because I believe .... Ac 23:6
He stopped the t and said, ... Ac 24:22
came here to Caesarea for the t,............. Ac 25:17
Now I am on t because I hope for .... Ac 26:6
Rome to have my t before Caesar. .... Ac 28:19

TRIBAL
names of the t leaders listed .... Ge 25:16

TRIBE
son of Uri from the t of Judah. .... Ex 31:2
from the t of Dan to work .... Ex 31:6
son of Hur, from the t of Judah. .... Ex 35:30
of Ahisamach from the t of Dan, ... Ex 35:34
son of Hur of the t of Judah, ... Ex 38:22
Ahisamach of the t of Dan helped .... Ex 38:23
One man from each t, the leader .... Nu 1:4
from the t of Reuben—Elizur son .... Nu 1:5
from the t of Simeon—Shelumiel .... Nu 1:6
from the t of Judah—Nahshon son........... Nu 1:7
from the t of Issachar—Nethanel .... Nu 1:8
from the t of Zebulun—Eliab son .... Nu 1:9
the t of Ephraim son of Joseph— .... Nu 1:10

T

that should be given to each **t**. ....Jos 18:10
was given to the **t** of Benjamin. ....Jos 18:11
The **t** of Benjamin also received ....Jos 18:25
was given to the **t** of Simeon. ....Jos 19:1
groups in the **t** of Simeon. ....Jos 19:8
was given to the **t** of Zebulun. ....Jos 19:10
was given to the **t** of Issachar. ....Jos 19:17
was given to the **t** of Asher. ....Jos 19:24
was given to the **t** of Naphtali. ....Jos 19:32
land was given to the **t** of Dan. ....Jos 19:40
he was the father of their **t**....................Jos 19:47
leaders of each **t** divided up the ....Jos 19:51
were part of the **t** of Levi. ....Jos 21:4
belonged to the **t** of Benjamin: ....Jos 21:17
towns from the **t** of Ephraim: ....Jos 21:20
The **t** of Dan gave them Eltekeh, ...Jos 21:23
of the Levite **t** were given these ....Jos 21:27
The **t** of Issachar gave them ....Jos 21:28
The **t** of Asher gave them Mishal, ...Jos 21:30
The **t** of Naphtali gave them ....Jos 21:32
The **t** of Zebulun gave them ....Jos 21:34
The **t** of Reuben gave them Bezer, ...Jos 21:36
The **t** of Gad gave them Ramoth in............Jos 21:38
to them, "The **t** of Judah will go ....Jdg 1:2
were not in his **t** to be wives ....Jdg 12:9
Elon from the **t** of Zebulun was a ....Jdg 12:11
named Manoah from the **t** of Dan, ...Jdg 13:2
that time the **t** of Dan was still ....Jdg 18:1
or for a **t** and family group ....Jdg 18:19
priests for the **t** of Dan until ....Jdg 18:30
belongs to the **t** of Benjamin. ....Jdg 19:14
were from the **t** of Benjamin. ....Jdg 19:16
men throughout the **t** of Benjamin ....Jdg 20:12
Which **t** shall be first to attack ....Jdg 20:18
a man from the **t** of Benjamin." ....Jdg 21:1
to us so that one **t** of Israel is ....Jdg 21:3
Did any **t** of Israel not come ....Jdg 21:5
Today one **t** has been cut off ....Jdg 21:6
families so a **t** in Israel will....................Jdg 21:17
a man from the **t** of Benjamin ran 1Sa 4:12
of Abiel from the **t** of Benjamin,...............1Sa 9:1
But I am from the **t** of Benjamin, ...1Sa 9:21
the smallest **t** in Israel. 1Sa 9:21
smallest in the **t** of Benjamin. 1Sa 9:21
the **t** of Benjamin was picked...................1Sa 10:20
belonged to the **t** of Benjamin. 2Sa 4:2
are you the last **t** to bring the 2Sa 19:11
are you the last **t** to bring back 2Sa 19:12
Bicri from the **t** of Benjamin was 2Sa 20:1
a widow from the **t** of Naphtali. 1Ki 7:14
a city in any **t** of Israel where.................1Ki 8:16
I will leave him one **t** to rule. 1Ki 11:13
will allow him to control one **t**. 1Ki 11:32
to rule over one **t** so that there 1Ki 11:36
Only the **t** of Judah continued to 1Ki 12:20
not just from the **t** of Levi. 1Ki 12:31
Ahijah, from the **t** of Issachar, ...1Ki 15:27
Only the **t** of Judah was left. 2Ki 17:18
was a leader of the **t** of Reuben. 1Ch 5:6
people from the **t** of Gad lived 1Ch 5:11
pastures from the **t** of Benjamin: 1Ch 6:60
pastures from the **t** of Ephraim. 1Ch 6:66
From the **t** of Naphtali, the 1Ch 6:76
received from the **t** of Zebulun 1Ch 6:77
From the **t** of Benjamin there was 1Ch 9:7
from the **t** of Levi still stand 1Ch 9:18
from the **t** of Benjamin. 1Ch 12:2
as part of the **t** of Levi. 1Ch 23:14
Nethanel, from the **t** of Levi, ...1Ch 24:6
Zicri was over the **t** of Reuben. 1Ch 27:16
Maacah was over the **t** of Simeon. 1Ch 27:16
Kemuel was over the **t** of Levi. 1Ch 27:17
was over the **t** of Judah. 1Ch 27:18

was over the **t** of Issachar. 1Ch 27:18
was over the **t** of Zebulun. 1Ch 27:19
was over the **t** of Naphtali. 1Ch 27:19
was over the **t** of Ephraim. 1Ch 27:20
was over the **t** of Benjamin. 1Ch 27:21
Jeroham was over the **t** of Dan. 1Ch 27:22
He chose the **t** of Judah to lead, ...1Ch 28:4
a city in any **t** of Israel where.................2Ch 6:5
a leader in the **t** of Judah. 2Ch 19:11
people from the **t** of Ephraim. 2Ch 25:7
one goat for each **t** in Israel. ....Ezr 6:17
was from the **t** of Benjamin, ...Est 2:5
Cush, from the **t** of Benjamin....................Ps 6:10
is the smallest **t**, Benjamin,......................Ps 68:27
did not choose the **t** of Ephraim. ....Ps 78:67
chose the **t** of Judah and Mount ....Ps 78:68
message is to the **t** of Kedar ....Je 49:28
as the land given to each **t**......................Eze 45:7
will let each **t** in the nation ....Eze 45:8
In whatever **t** the foreigner ....Eze 47:23
People of every **t**, nation, and ....Da 7:14
used to fear the **t** of Ephraim;..................Hos 13:1
priests was with the **t** of Levi...................Mal 2:5
agreement with the **t** of Levi!" ....Mal 2:8
of Phanuel in the **t** of Asher. ....Lk 2:36
Saul was from the **t** of Benjamin ....Ac 13:21
Abraham, from the **t** of Benjamin. ....Rm 11:1
of Israel and the **t** of Benjamin. ....Php 3:5
that those in the **t** of Levi who ....Heb 7:5
was not from the **t** of Levi, ...Heb 7:6
of priests from the **t** of Levi, ...Heb 7:11
who belonged to a different **t**...................Heb 7:13
one from that **t** ever served as ....Heb 7:13
Lord came from the **t** of Judah, ...Heb 7:14
priests belonging to that **t**. ....Heb 7:14
The Lion from the **t** of Judah, ...Rev 5:5
people for God from every **t**, ...Rev 5:9
from every **t** of the people ....Rev 7:4
From the **t** of Judah twelve ....Rev 7:5
from the **t** of Reuben twelve ....Rev 7:5
from the **t** of Gad twelve ....Rev 7:5
from the **t** of Asher twelve ....Rev 7:6
from the **t** of Naphtali twelve ....Rev 7:6
from the **t** of Manasseh twelve ....Rev 7:6
from the **t** of Simeon twelve ....Rev 7:7
from the **t** of Levi twelve ....Rev 7:7
from the **t** of Issachar twelve ....Rev 7:7
from the **t** of Zebulun twelve ....Rev 7:8
from the **t** of Joseph twelve....................Rev 7:8
from the **t** of Benjamin twelve ....Rev 7:8
from every nation, **t**, people, ...Rev 7:9
race of people, **t**, language, and ....Rev 11:9
It was given power over every **t**,..............Rev 13:7
every nation, **t**, language, and.................Rev 14:6

TRIBES

them up among the **t** of Jacob and ....Ge 49:7
through all the **t** of Israel. ....Ge 49:7
like the other **t** in Israel. ....Ge 49:16
are the twelve **t** of Israel, ...Ge 49:28
leaders of the **t** of Edom will be ....Ex 15:15
each of the twelve **t** of Israel. ....Ex 24:4
one of the twelve **t** on each of..................Ex 28:21
one of the twelve **t** of Israel. ....Ex 39:14
people to be leaders of their **t**, ...Nu 1:16
The **t** will march out in the same ....Nu 2:17
the **t** camping on the east should ....Nu 10:5
t camping on the south should ....Nu 10:6
the rear guard for all the **t**. ....Nu 10:25
Israelites camped in their **t**, ...Nu 24:2
the leaders of the Israelite **t**. ....Nu 30:1
from each of the **t** of Israel." ....Nu 31:4
the leaders of the **t** of Israel. ....Nu 32:28

gave that land to the t of Gad, ... Nu 32:33
among the nine and one-half t, ... Nu 34:13
The t of Reuben, Gad, and East .... Nu 34:14
two and one-half t received land .... Nu 34:15
The larger t of Israel must give .... Nu 35:8
the smaller t must give fewer .... Nu 35:8
men from other t of Israel, ... Nu 36:3
of the other t will get that .... Nu 36:3
will go to the t of the people .... Nu 36:4
experienced leaders of your t, ... Dt 1:15
made them officers over your t. .... Dt 1:15
leaders of your t and your .... Dt 5:23
place among your t where he is .... Dt 12:5
choose a place in one of your t, ... Dt 12:14
officers for your t in every .... Dt 16:18
out of all your t to stand and .... Dt 18:5
these t must stand on Mount .... Dt 27:12
And these t must stand on Mount .... Dt 27:13
and gave it to the t of Reuben, ... Dt 29:8
them from all the t of Israel .... Dt 29:21
leaders of your t and all your .... Dt 31:28
when the t of Israel came .... Dt 33:5
each of the twelve t of Israel. .... Jos 3:12
each of the twelve t of Israel, ... Jos 4:8
The men from the t of Reuben, ... Jos 4:12
you must be present with your t. .... Jos 7:14
present themselves in their t, ... Jos 7:16
the land among the t of Israel, ... Jos 11:23
that land to the t of Reuben and .... Jos 12:6
the twelve t to be their own .... Jos 12:7
the nine t and West Manasseh. .... Jos 13:7
Manasseh and the t of Reuben and .... Jos 13:8
land to these t on the plains .... Jos 13:32
of all the t of Israel decided .... Jos 14:1
nine-and-a-half t threw lots to .... Jos 14:2
two-and-a-half t their land east .... Jos 14:3
Joseph had divided into two t— .... Jos 14:4
the land to the t of Israel, ... Jos 14:5
people from the t of Joseph said............ Jos 17:14
still seven t of Israel that...................... Jos 18:2
giving it to the different t, ... Jos 19:49
to the different t of Israel. .... Jos 19:51
families of all the t of Israel. .... Jos 21:1
were given from these two t. .... Jos 21:16
the people from the t of Reuben, ... Jos 22:1
the people from the t of Reuben, ... Jos 22:9
altar these three t built at the .... Jos 22:11
very angry at these three t, ... Jos 22:12
each of the ten t at Shiloh. .... Jos 22:14
gathered all the t of Israel .... Jos 24:1
own land among the t of Israel. .... Jdg 18:1
of all the t of Israel took .... Jdg 20:2
men from all the t of Israel, ... Jdg 20:10
The t of Israel sent men .... Jdg 20:12
Which one of the t of Israel did .... Jdg 21:8
had separated them of Israel. .... Jdg 21:15
to their own t and family groups .... Jdg 21:24
from all the t of Israel to be 1Sa 2:28
in your t and family groups. 1Sa 10:19
gathered all the t of Israel, ... 1Sa 10:20
the leader of the t of Israel.................... 1Sa 15:17
Then all the t of Israel came to 2Sa 5:1
I have never said to the t, ... 2Sa 7:7
from one of the t of Israel.".................... 2Sa 15:2
through all the t of Israel. 2Sa 15:10
in all the t of Israel began 2Sa 19:9
We have ten t in the kingdom, ... 2Sa 19:43
through all the t of Israel to 2Sa 20:14
Go through all the t of Israel, ... 2Sa 24:2
heads of the t, and the leaders 1Ki 8:1
workers from the t of Ephraim 1Ki 11:28
from Solomon and give you ten t. 1Ki 11:31
chosen from all the t of Israel. 1Ki 11:32

you to rule over the ten t. 1Ki 11:35
soldiers from the t of Judah and.............. 1Ki 12:21
stone for each of the twelve t,............ 1Ki 18:31
chosen from all the t of Israel. 2Ki 21:7
from the t of Reuben and Gad 1Ch 5:18
The men from the t of Manasseh, ... 1Ch 5:20
towns from the t of Issachar, ... 1Ch 6:62
towns from the t of Reuben, ... 1Ch 6:63
The towns from the t of Judah, ... 1Ch 6:65
People from the t of Judah,...................... 1Ch 9:3
people from the t of Benjamin 1Ch 12:16
did not count the t of Levi and 1Ch 21:6
of directing the t of Reuben, ... 1Ch 26:32
the leaders of the t of Israel. 1Ch 27:16
the leaders of the t of Israel. 1Ch 27:22
There were the leaders of the t, ... 1Ch 28:1
the leaders of the t of Israel, ... 1Ch 29:6
heads of the t, and the leaders 2Ch 5:2
from all the t of Israel who 2Ch 11:16
from all the t of Israel in...................... 2Ch 12:13
and from the t of Ephraim, ... 2Ch 15:9
chosen from all the t of Israel. 2Ch 33:7
He let the t of Israel settle .... Ps 78:55
t go up there, the tribes who .... Ps 122:4
the t who belong to the LORD. .... Ps 122:4
me to bring back the t of Jacob, ... Is 49:6
Joseph and the t of Israel with .... Eze 37:19
the Israelite t by throwing lots .... Eze 45:1
among the twelve t of Israel. .... Eze 47:13
this land among the t of Israel. .... Eze 47:21
the land with the t of Israel. .... Eze 47:22
the areas of the t named here: .... Eze 48:1
wide as one of the t' shares. .... Eze 48:8
from all the t of Israel will .... Eze 48:19
length of the lands of the t,.................. Eze 48:21
the rest of the t will receive: .... Eze 48:23
among the t of Israel to be .... Eze 48:29
named for the t of Israel. .... Eze 48:31
To the t of Israel I tell the .... Hos 5:9
The t of Israel and all people .... Zch 9:1
judging the twelve t of Israel. .... Mt 19:28
judging the twelve t of Israel. .... Lk 22:30
that the twelve t of our people .... Ac 26:7
one of the twelve t of Israel. .... Rev 21:12

TRICKERY

use no t, and we do not change 2Co 4:2

TRIM

he put gold t around the altar. .... Ex 37:26
them below the t on opposite .... Ex 37:27
and you may t your vineyards for .... Le 25:3
your field or t your vineyards. .... Le 25:4

TRIMMED

from your vines that are not t. .... Le 25:5
from the vines that are not t. .... Le 25:11
Then they were t with a saw in 1Ki 7:9
It will not be t or hoed, and .... Is 5:6
keep the hair of their heads t.................. Eze 44:20

TRIMMERS

wick t and trays must be made .... Ex 25:38
made pure gold wick t and trays. .... Ex 37:23
lamps, its wick t, its trays, ... Nu 4:9
gold bowls, wick t, small bowls, ... 1Ki 7:50
cups, wick t, bowls, trumpets 2Ki 12:13
shovels, wick t, dishes, and all 2Ki 25:14
pure gold wick t, small bowls, ... 2Ch 4:22
shovels, wick t, bowls, dishes, ... Je 52:18

TRIMMING

spears into hooks for t trees. .... Is 2:4
from your hooks for t trees. .... Joe 3:10
spears into hooks for t trees. .... Mic 4:3

T

TRIMS

And he t and cleans every branch .... Jn 15:2

TRIP

LORD had made his t successful. .... Ge 24:21
please make my t successful. .... Ge 24:42
LORD has made my t successful. .... Ge 24:56
need for their t back home...................... Ge 42:25
to him during the t to Egypt. .... Ge 42:38
put in our sacks on the first t.................. Ge 43:18
ordered and food for their t. .... Ge 45:21
for his father on his t back...................... Ge 45:23
all he had and started his t. .... Ge 46:1
as if you were going on a t....................... Ex 12:11
to get food ready for their t. .... Ex 12:39
you are away on a t during the .... Nu 9:10
not away on a t but does not eat.............. Nu 9:13
The t from Mount Sinai to Kadesh .... Dt 1:2
desert on the t from Egypt had .... Jos 5:5
sons born on the t from Egypt .... Jos 5:7
cities and their kings on one t, ... Jos 10:42
Uriah, "You came from a long t................ 2Sa 11:10
God for a safe t for ourselves, ... Ezr 8:21
prayed to our God about our t, ... Ezr 8:23
How long will your t take, ... Ne 2:6
people who plan to t me up. .... Ps 140:4
he has gone on a long t. .... Pr 7:19
T and fall, but not from beer. .... Is 29:9
and young people t and fall. .... Is 40:30
of day we t as if it were night .... Is 59:10
are chasing me will t and fall; .... Je 20:11
food and housing on the t. .... Je 51:59
paid for the t and went aboard, ... Jnh 1:3
some farmers and left for a t. .... Mt 21:33
for your t except a walking...................... Mk 6:8
some farmers and left for a t. .... Mk 12:1
is like a man who goes on a t. .... Mk 13:34
nothing for your t, neither a .... Lk 9:3
Jesus was tired from his long t, ... Jn 4:6
This was their first t to Egypt. .... Ac 7:12
continued their t from Perga and .... Ac 13:14
helped them leave on the t,.................... Ac 15:3
we left and continued our t. .... Ac 21:5
We continued our t from Tyre and .... Ac 21:7
be a lot of trouble on this t...................... Ac 27:10
I hope you can help me on my t. .... Rm 15:24
Then you can help me on my t, ... 1Co 16:6
help him on his t in peace so 1Co 16:11
help from you for my t to Judea. 2Co 1:16
continue their t in a way worthy.............. 3Jn 1:6

TRIPOLIS

over the men who came from T, ... Ezr 4:9

TRIPS

could have already made two t." .... Ge 43:10

TRIUMPH

good people t, there is great .... Pr 28:12

TROAS

passed by Mysia and went to T. .... Ac 16:8
We left T and sailed straight to .... Ac 16:11
on ahead and waited for us at T. .... Ac 20:5
days later we met them in T, ... Ac 20:6
When I came to T to preach the 2Co 2:12
good-bye to them at T and went 2Co 2:13
When I was in T, I left my coat 2Ti 4:13

TROOPS

He sent the t out in three 2Sa 18:2
happened to meet David's t. 2Sa 18:9
so the t stopped chasing the 2Sa 18:16
All the t of Judah and half the 2Sa 19:40
and half the t of Israel led 2Sa 19:40
t came back after Eleazar had 2Sa 23:10
Israel's t ran away from the 2Sa 23:11

chariots, and many t to Dothan................ 2Ki 6:14
when he saw Jehu's t coming. 2Ki 9:17
and the commanders of the t,.................. 1Ch 21:2
He brought t of Libyans,........................ 2Ch 12:3
had sent some t to sneak behind 2Ch 13:13
He put t in all the strong, ... 2Ch 17:2
the Israelite t that Amaziah had 2Ch 25:13
Thousands of t may surround me, ... Ps 3:6
with all its t and the nation.................... Eze 38:6
the far north with all its t— .... Eze 38:6
You, all your t, and the many .... Eze 38:9
bring your t together to take .... Eze 38:13
You, all your t, and the nations .... Eze 39:4
heard how many t on horses were .... Rev 9:16

TROPHIMUS

and Tychicus and T, two men from............ Ac 20:4
this because they had seen T, ... Ac 21:29
and I left T sick in Miletus...................... 2Ti 4:20

TROUBLE

you to have much t when you are .... Ge 3:16
you bring this t to my kingdom?.............. Ge 20:9
But he saw the t I had and the .... Ge 31:42
You have caused me a lot of t. .... Ge 34:30
helped me during my time of t. .... Ge 35:3
but she was having much t. .... Ge 35:17
saw his t, and he begged us to .... Ge 42:21
is why we are in this t now." .... Ge 42:21
You have caused me a lot of t." .... Ge 43:6
been short and filled with t— .... Ge 47:9
foremen knew they were in t,.................. Ex 5:19
brought this t on your people? .... Ex 5:22
will this man make t for us? .... Ex 10:7
because it will bring you t. .... Ex 34:12
me, your servant, this t? .... Nu 11:11
the land, they will bring you t. .... Nu 33:55
They will bring t to the land .... Nu 33:55
When he saw our t, hard work, ... Dt 26:7
because their day of t is near,.................. Dt 32:35
will bring t to all of Israel. .... Jos 6:18
son of Zerah to the Valley of T. .... Jos 7:24
why you caused so much t for us, ... Jos 7:25
the LORD will bring t to you." .... Jos 7:25
it is called the Valley of T. .... Jos 7:26
the Danites had t taking their.................. Jos 19:47
gods, he will send you great t. .... Jos 24:20
why are we having so much t? .... Jdg 6:13
they did not cause t anymore.................. Jdg 8:28
spirit to make t between .... Jdg 9:23
causing much t to the people of .... Jdg 10:9
save you when you are in t." .... Jdg 10:14
to me now that you are in t?" .... Jdg 11:7
has given me so much t?" .... Ru 1:21
You will see t in my house. 1Sa 2:32
camp! We're in t! This has never 1Sa 4:7
had much t in giving birth. 1Sa 4:19
of the Ark that you had such t." 1Sa 6:3
saw that they were in t, ... 1Sa 13:6
father has made t for the land! 1Sa 14:29
where you hid when this t began. 1Sa 20:19
who was in t, or who owed money 1Sa 22:2
Terrible t is coming to our 1Sa 25:17
my life and save me from all t." 1Sa 26:24
he has saved me from all t!...................... 2Sa 4:9
'I am bringing t to you from 2Sa 12:11
it would be too much t for you." 2Sa 13:25
In my t I called to the LORD; 2Sa 22:7
attacked me at my time of t, ... 2Sa 22:19
said to Gad, "I am in great t. 2Sa 24:14
LORD has saved me from all t. 1Ki 1:29
and Hadad made t for Israel. 1Ki 11:25
I have not made t in Israel. 1Ki 18:18
made all this t by not obeying 1Ki 18:18

Ben-Hadad is looking for **t**...................... 1Ki 20:7
not cause the **t** to come to him 1Ki 21:29
will bring this **t** to Ahab's 1Ki 21:29
have gone to all this **t** for us. 2Ki 4:13
is trying to start **t** with me." 2Ki 5:7
said to her, "What is your **t**?" 2Ki 6:28
This **t** has come from the LORD. 2Ki 6:33
ask for **t**, or you and Judah 2Ki 14:10
bring so much **t** on Jerusalem 2Ki 21:12
I will bring **t** to this place and 2Ki 22:16
see all the **t** I will bring to 2Ki 22:20
who caused **t** for Israel because 1Ch 2:7
because of the **t** that had 1Ch 7:23
said to Gad, "I am in great **t**. 1Ch 21:13
they were in **t**, they turned to 2Ch 15:4
was much **t** in all the nations 2Ch 15:5
'If **t** comes upon us, or war, ... 2Ch 20:9
cry out to you when we are in **t**. 2Ch 20:9
ask for **t**, or you and Judah 2Ch 25:19
LORD brought **t** on Judah because 2Ch 28:19
he gave Ahaz **t** instead of help. 2Ch 28:20
I will bring **t** to this place and 2Ch 34:24
see all the **t** I will bring to 2Ch 34:28
obey and makes **t** for kings and .... Ezr 4:15
been a place of problems and **t**. .... Ezr 4:19
they are in much **t** and are full .... Ne 1:3
You can see the **t** we have here. .... Ne 2:17
and fight and stir up **t**. .... Ne 4:8
in this time of **t** our ancestors .... Ne 9:27
not let all our **t** seem .... Ne 9:32
This **t** has come to us, to our .... Ne 9:32
please, so we are in much **t**. .... Ne 9:37
good things from God and not **t**?" .... Job 2:10
and did not hide **t** from my eyes. .... Job 3:10
grave the wicked stop making **t**, ... Job 3:17
I have no rest, only **t**." .... Job 3:26
But now **t** comes to you, and you .... Job 4:5
t hits you, and you are .... Job 4:5
who plow evil and plant **t**, ... Job 4:8
and **t** does not grow from the .... Job 5:6
People produce **t** as surely as .... Job 5:7
be kind to him when he is in **t**, ... Job 6:14
Does it make you happy to **t** me? .... Job 10:3
forget your **t** and remember it .... Job 11:16
don't care that others have **t**; .... Job 12:5
a few days and have lots of **t**. .... Job 14:1
who plan **t** and give birth to .... Job 15:35
'We will continue to **t** Job, ... Job 19:28
have plenty, **t** will catch up to .... Job 20:22
How often does **t** come to them? .... Job 21:17
cries when **t** comes to them. .... Job 27:9
side of strangers who were in **t**. .... Job 29:16
cry for help in their time of **t**. .... Job 30:24
I cried for those who were in **t**; .... Job 30:25
fell or laughed when they had **t**. .... Job 31:29
cry out when they are in **t**; .... Job 35:9
in chains, or if **t**, like ropes, ... Job 36:8
the jaws of **t** to an open place .... Job 36:16
strength will keep you out of **t**. .... Job 36:19
which I save for times of **t**, ... Job 38:23
better about the **t** the LORD had .... Job 42:11
easier for me when I am in **t**. .... Ps 4:1
evil and plan **t** and tell lies. .... Ps 7:14
They will get themselves into **t**; .... Ps 7:16
he defends them in times of **t**. .... Ps 9:9
Why do you hide when there is **t**? .... Ps 10:1
in **t** look to you for help. .... Ps 10:14
In my **t** I called to the LORD. .... Ps 18:6
attacked me at my time of **t**, ... Ps 18:18
LORD answer you in times of **t**. .... Ps 20:1
Now **t** is near, and there is no .... Ps 22:11
He does not ignore those in **t**. .... Ps 22:24
when I was in **t**, they gathered .... Ps 35:15

be upset; it only leads to **t**. .... Ps 37:8
not be ashamed when **t** comes. .... Ps 37:19
is their strength in times of **t**. .... Ps 37:39
who want to hurt me plan **t**; .... Ps 38:12
When **t** comes, the LORD will save .... Ps 41:1
He always helps in times of **t**. .... Ps 46:1
Call to me in times of **t**. .... Ps 50:15
and evil and **t** are everywhere .... Ps 55:10
t and lying never leave its .... Ps 55:11
wings until the **t** has passed. .... Ps 57:1
place of safety in times of **t**. .... Ps 59:16
You have given your people **t**. .... Ps 60:3
I promised when I was in **t**. .... Ps 66:14
servant. I am in **t**. Hurry to .... Ps 69:17
for the Lord on the day of **t**. .... Ps 77:2
When you were in **t**, you called, ... Ps 81:7
I call to you in times of **t**, ... Ps 86:7
We have seen years of **t**. .... Ps 90:15
I will be with them in **t**; .... Ps 91:15
from times of **t** until a pit is .... Ps 94:13
hide from me in my time of **t**. .... Ps 102:2
Moses was in **t** because of them .... Ps 106:32
I was in **t**, so I called to the .... Ps 118:5
When I was in **t**, I called to the .... Ps 120:1
am in great **t**, so I call out to .... Ps 130:1
remembered us when we were in **t**. .... Ps 136:23
when I have **t** all around me, ... Ps 138:7
Those around me have planned **t**. .... Ps 140:9
Destroy all those who **t** me, ... Ps 143:12
care of those who are in **t**. .... Ps 145:14
lifts up people who are in **t**. .... Ps 146:8
I will laugh when you are in **t**. .... Pr 1:26
when **t** strikes you like a .... Pr 1:27
when pain and **t** overwhelm you. .... Pr 1:27
You won't be afraid of sudden **t**; .... Pr 3:25
So **t** will strike them in an .... Pr 6:15
A wink may get you into **t**, ... Pr 10:10
Hatred stirs up **t**, but love .... Pr 10:12
The good person is saved from **t**; .... Pr 11:8
people bring **t** on themselves. .... Pr 11:17
looks for evil will find **t**. .... Pr 11:27
Whoever brings **t** to his family .... Pr 11:29
but good people stay out of **t**. .... Pr 12:13
evil person's life is full of **t**. .... Pr 12:21
messenger brings nothing but **t**, ... Pr 13:17
T always comes to sinners, ... Pr 13:21
are careful and stay out of **t**, ... Pr 14:16
evil people get nothing but **t**. .... Pr 15:6
to be wealthy and have much **t**. .... Pr 15:16
with quick tempers cause **t**, ... Pr 15:18
people bring **t** to their families .... Pr 15:27
A useless person causes **t**, ... Pr 16:28
someone's **t** will be punished .... Pr 17:5
people look only for **t**, ... Pr 17:11
good will always have **t** at home. .... Pr 17:13
a brother helps in time of **t**. .... Pr 17:17
brags a lot is asking for **t**. .... Pr 17:19
words are evil will get into **t**. .... Pr 17:20
be satisfied, unbothered by **t**. .... Pr 19:23
say keep themselves out of **t**. .... Pr 21:23
fools keep going and get into **t**. .... Pr 22:3
who plan evil will receive **t**. .... Pr 22:8
Who has **t**? Who has pain? Who .... Pr 23:29
they always talk about making **t**. .... Pr 24:2
If you give up when **t** comes, ... Pr 24:10
be bothered by **t** seven times, ... Pr 24:16
the wicked are overwhelmed by **t**. .... Pr 24:16
when you are in **t** is like eating .... Pr 25:19
family for help when **t** comes. .... Pr 27:10
fools keep going and get into **t**. .... Pr 27:12
are stubborn will get into **t**. .... Pr 28:14
person causes **t**, but the one who .... Pr 28:25
fun of wisdom cause **t** in a city, ... Pr 29:8

T

An angry person causes t; .... Pr 29:22
of people can get you into t, ... Pr 29:25
so stirring up anger causes t." .... Pr 30:33
the days of t come and the years .... Ec 12:1
will not cause me any more t................. Is 1:24
brought much t on themselves. .... Is 3:9
at their land and see only t, ... Is 8:22
remember you when they are in t; .... Is 26:16
Save us when we are in t. .... Is 33:2
force those who t you to eat .... Is 49:26
people who t you and who want............... Is 51:13
If you stop making t for others, ... Is 58:9
They cause t and create more................. Is 59:4
they get into t, they say, 'Come .... Je 2:27
and save you when you are in t!............... Je 2:28
acted has brought this t to you. .... Je 4:18
I will bring t to them so that .... Je 10:18
to me in the time of their t..................... Je 11:14
Won't you have much pain and t, ... Je 13:21
have saved Israel in times of t. .... Je 14:8
you in times of disaster and t.................. Je 15:11
my safe place in times of t..................... Je 16:19
to you for safety in times of t................. Je 17:17
I have known is t and sorrow,.................. Je 20:18
decided to make t for this city .... Je 21:10
a time of great t for the people .... Je 30:7
of Moab have never known t. .... Je 48:11
caught her when she was in t. .... La 1:3
my enemies have heard of my t,............... La 1:21
and my misery, my sorrow and t. .... La 3:19
caused more t than the nations .... Eze 5:7
when they were in t at the time .... Eze 35:5
it will be built in times of t..................... Da 9:25
There will be a time of much t, ... Da 12:1
the Valley of T a door of hope. .... Hos 2:15
their t they will look for me. .... Hos 5:15
plowed evil and harvested t; .... Hos 10:13
you back for those years of t. .... Joe 2:25
When t comes to a city, the Lord .... Am 3:6
will keep watch to give them t, ... Am 9:4
in his time of t or be happy. .... Ob 1:12
in their time of t or laugh at .... Ob 1:13
problems in their time of t..................... Ob 1:13
treasures in their time of t..................... Ob 1:13
their enemy in their time of t................. Ob 1:14
showed that the t had happened............... Jnh 1:7
him, "Tell us, who caused our t?............... Jnh 1:8
because t will come from the .... Mic 1:12
I am planning t against such .... Mic 2:3
those whom I caused to have t. .... Mic 4:6
I sit in the shadow of t now, ... Mic 7:8
giving protection in times of t. .... Nah 1:7
T will not come a second time. .... Nah 1:9
things and make me look at t? .... Hab 1:3
of Cushan were in t and that the .... Hab 3:7
a day of terror and t, a day of .... Zph 1:15
will come through the sea of t. .... Zch 10:11
will bring t to the country, ... Zch 11:6
day has enough t of its own. .... Mt 6:34
has even more t than before. .... Mt 12:45
When t or persecution comes .... Mt 13:21
that time there will be much t. .... Mt 24:21
will be more t than there has .... Mt 24:21
Soon after the t of those days, ... Mt 24:29
him and save you from t." .... Mt 28:14
When t or persecution comes .... Mk 4:17
those days will be full of t. .... Mk 13:19
will be more t than there has .... Mk 13:19
the days after this t comes, ' .... Mk 13:24
Lord, don't t yourself, because .... Lk 7:6
while, but when t comes, they .... Lk 8:13
has even more t than before.".................. Lk 11:26
Pharisees began to give him t, ... Lk 11:53

t will come upon this land, ... Lk 21:23
Jesus makes t with the people .... Lk 23:5
saying he makes t among the .... Lk 23:14
In this world you will have t, ... Jn 16:33
They started t against Paul and .... Ac 13:50
things that t and upset you. .... Ac 15:24
and are making t in our city. .... Ac 16:20
people have made t everywhere .... Ac 17:6
the people and making t. .... Ac 17:13
some serious t in Ephesus about .... Ac 19:23
might see this t today and say .... Ac 19:40
When the t stopped, Paul sent .... Ac 20:1
there was t in the whole city. .... Ac 21:31
who started some t against the .... Ac 21:38
ceremony and had not made any t; .... Ac 24:18
will be a lot of t on this trip. .... Ac 27:10
not have all this t and loss. .... Ac 27:21
He will give t and suffering to .... Rm 2:9
patient when t comes, and pray .... Rm 12:12
The present time is a time of t, ... 1Co 7:26
marry will have t in this life, ... 1Co 7:28
I want you to be free from t. 1Co 7:28
us every time we have t, ... 2Co 1:4
others have t, we can comfort.................. 2Co 1:4
to know about the t we suffered 2Co 1:8
We found t all around us. 2Co 7:5
you, I did not t any of you. 2Co 11:9
my sickness was a t for you, ... Gal 4:14
hating, making t, being jealous, ... Gal 5:20
proud or make t with each other .... Gal 5:26
So do not give me any more t. .... Gal 6:17
wanting to make t for me in .... Php 1:17
this t will bring my freedom. .... Php 1:19
It is no t for me to write the .... Php 3:1
we have much t and suffering, ... 1Th 3:7
He will give t to those who 2Th 1:6
give trouble to those who t you. 2Th 1:6
those in t, and giving her 1Ti 5:10
and begins to cause t among you. .... Heb 12:15
the terrible t which now comes 1Pe 4:12
nor because you t other people. 1Pe 4:15
the time of t that will come.................... Rev 3:10
air cry out in a loud voice, "T! .... Rev 8:13
voice, "Trouble! T! Trouble for .... Rev 8:13
T for those who live on the .... Rev 8:13
The first t is past; .... Rev 9:12
every kind of t to the earth as................. Rev 11:6
The second t is finished. .... Rev 11:14
The third t is coming soon. .... Rev 11:14

TROUBLED

This t Abraham very much because .... Ge 21:11
Don't be t about the boy and the .... Ge 21:12
the king was t about these .... Ge 41:8
I am a deeply t woman, and I was 1Sa 1:15
did not die were t with growths 1Sa 5:12
evil spirit from the Lord t him............... 1Sa 16:14
the evil spirit from God t Saul, ... 1Sa 16:23
feel guilty or t because you................... 1Sa 25:31
Saul said, "I am greatly t. 1Sa 28:15
Hazael king of Aram t Israel. 2Ki 13:22
because God t them with all 2Ch 15:6
the words of a t man as if they .... Job 6:26
My t thoughts cause me to .... Job 20:2
because they t the poor and left .... Job 20:19
enemies will be ashamed and t. .... Ps 6:10
my guilt; I am t by my sin. .... Ps 38:18
am I sad and t by my enemies?"............... Ps 42:9
am I sad and t by my enemies? .... Ps 43:2
and answer me. I am t and upset .... Ps 55:2
and night I am t and upset,..................... Ps 55:17
hold of me. I was t and sad. .... Ps 116:3
Lord will bring t times to you, ... Is 7:17

through the land t and hungry. .... Is 8:21
of the needs of those who are t, ... Is 58:10
and they will not be t anymore. .... Je 31:12
They are t like the tossing sea. .... Je 49:23
I am upset and greatly t. .... La 1:20
My heart is t, because I have .... La 1:20
heard this, he was t, as were .... Mt 2:3
he began to be very sad and t. .... Mt 26:37
him, and it t me very much." .... Mt 27:19
he began to be very sad and t. .... Mk 14:33
who were t by evil spirits. .... Lk 6:18
I feel very t until it is over. .... Lk 12:50
But Jesus said, "Why are you t? .... Lk 24:38
he was upset and was deeply t. .... Jn 11:33
Now I am very t. Should I say, ... Jn 12:27
Jesus said this, he was very t. .... Jn 13:21
Don't let your hearts be t. .... Jn 14:1
let your hearts be t or afraid. .... Jn 14:27
he was t because he saw that the .... Ac 17:16
me, which t me very much. .... Ac 20:19
I was very t and unhappy in my 2Co 2:4
who comforts those who are t, ... 2Co 7:6
to you who are t and to us also 2Th 1:7
those who are t and to do good .... Jam 3:17
t because of the filthy lives 2Pe 2:7

TROUBLEMAKER
get out, you murderer, you t. 2Sa 16:7
happened that a t named Sheba 2Sa 20:1
it you—the biggest t in Israel?" 1Ki 18:17
evil plans will be known as a t. .... Pr 24:8
have found this man to be a t, ... Ac 24:5

TROUBLEMAKERS
Some t among them wanted better .... Nu 11:4
But some t said, "How can this 1Sa 10:27
evil men and t among those who 1Sa 30:22
Seat two t across from him, ... 1Ki 21:10
Two t sat across from Naboth and 1Ki 21:13
but friends of t disgrace their .... Pr 28:7

TROUBLES
save Israel from all their t! .... Ps 25:22
and saved him from all his t. .... Ps 34:6
and forget the t of your body, ... Ec 11:10
Then the t that Assyria puts on .... Is 10:27
caused these t to happen to us. .... Jnh 1:7
and saved him from all his t. .... Ac 7:10
I have seen the t my people have .... Ac 7:34
tells me that t and even jail .... Ac 20:23
two other t that will come. .... Rev 9:12
of the seven last t came to me, ... Rev 21:9

TROUBLING
other kingdoms that were t you.' 1Sa 10:18
evil spirit from God is t you. 1Sa 16:15
Why are you t this woman? .... Mt 26:10
Why are you t her? .... Mk 14:6

TROUGH
the drinking t for the camels. .... Ge 24:20
and laid him in a feeding t. .... Lk 2:7
who was lying in a feeding t. .... Lk 2:16

TROUGHS
to fill the water t for their .... Ex 2:16

TROUSERS
their robes, t, turbans, and .... Da 3:21

TRUE
And it is t that she is my .... Ge 20:12
money to the t owner on the day .... Le 6:5
But even though this is t, ... Le 26:44
this is not t with my servant .... Nu 12:7
he promises, he makes come t. .... Nu 23:19
carefully whether it is t. .... Dt 13:14
If it is t that such a hateful .... Dt 17:4

that it is t before the person .... Dt 17:6
said about his wife are t, ... Dt 22:20
You must have t and honest .... Dt 25:15
we will be kind and t to you." .... Jos 2:14
Achan answered, "It is t! .... Jos 7:20
people of Joseph said, "It is t. .... Jos 17:16
the Israelites; each one came t. .... Jos 21:45
We know the only t altar to the .... Jos 22:29
LORD your God made has come t, ... Jos 23:15
his other promises will come t. .... Jos 23:15
youngest son of Gideon, came t. .... Jdg 9:57
It is t that I am a relative who .... Ru 3:12
messages fail to come t. 1Sa 3:19
knew Samuel was a t prophet of 1Sa 3:20
everything he says comes t. 1Sa 9:6
All these signs came t that day. 1Sa 10:9
It's t that you did wrong, ... 1Sa 12:20
keep this from me? It's not t!" 1Sa 20:2
is especially t when the work is 1Sa 21:5
Isn't that t? Why didn't you 1Sa 26:15
LORD now be loyal and t to you. 2Sa 2:6
are God, and your words are t. 2Sa 7:28
have said about Adonijah is t." 1Ki 1:14
was t for both the main room 1Ki 6:29
know the LORD is the only t God. 1Ki 8:60
as slaves, as is still t today. 1Ki 9:21
achievements and wisdom is t. 1Ki 10:6
him will certainly come t." 1Ki 13:32
was a t follower of the LORD. 1Ki 18:3
LORD is the t God, follow him 1Ki 18:21
Baal is the t God, follow him! 1Ki 18:21
fire to his wood is the t God." 1Ki 18:24
They answered, "That's not t. 2Ki 9:12
about Ahab's family will come t. 2Ki 10:10
and the LORD's word came t. 2Ki 15:12
It is t, LORD, that the kings of 2Ki 19:17
to my father David come t. 2Ch 1:9
workers, as is still t today. 2Ch 8:8
achievements and wisdom is t. 2Ch 9:5
without the t God and without 2Ch 15:3
You know these things are t. 2Ch 29:8
with them. You know this is t. 2Ch 30:7
knew that the LORD is the t God. 2Ch 33:13
spoken by Jeremiah would come t. 2Ch 36:22
spoken by Jeremiah would come t. .... Ezr 1:1
Geshem says it is t, that you .... Ne 6:6
them fair rules and t teachings, ... Ne 9:13
was found to be t, and the two .... Est 2:23
to prove the first letter was t. .... Est 9:29
this, and it is t, so hear it .... Job 5:27
know that this is t, but how can .... Job 9:2
If this is not t, who can prove .... Job 24:25
without knowing what is t; .... Job 34:35
without knowing what is t." .... Job 35:16
by saying things that are not t? .... Job 38:2
saying things that are not t?' .... Job 42:3
t believers are left on earth. .... Ps 12:1
your eyes can see what is t. .... Ps 17:2
The judgments of the LORD are t; .... Ps 19:9
are loving and t for those who .... Ps 25:10
God's word is t, and everything .... Ps 33:4
LORD shows his t love every day. .... Ps 42:8
victory for what is t and right. .... Ps 45:4
and they were not t to him. .... Ps 78:8
They were made t and right. .... Ps 111:8
and your teachings are t. .... Ps 119:142
and all your commands are t. .... Ps 119:151
Your words are t from the start, ... Ps 119:160
teachings will find t peace, ... Ps 119:165
ever say things that are not t. .... Pr 4:24
The same is t if you have sexual .... Pr 6:29
What I say is t, I refuse to .... Pr 8:7
good sense know what I say is t; .... Pr 8:9

that come t are like eating .... Pr 13:12
is so good when wishes come t, ... Pr 13:19
the LORD can make them come t. .... Pr 16:1
I am teaching you t and reliable .... Pr 22:21
you can give t answers to anyone .... Pr 22:21
and your wishes will come t. .... Pr 23:18
and your wishes will come t. .... Pr 24:14
Every word of God is t. .... Pr 30:5
The saying is t: Bad dreams come .... Ec 5:3
write what is dependable and t. .... Ec 12:10
that these things are t. .... Is 7:11
give t peace to those who depend .... Is 26:3
It is t, LORD, that the kings of .... Is 37:18
Then others will say, "It is t." .... Is 43:9
understand that I am the t God. .... Is 43:10
messages of my servants come t; .... Is 44:26
advice of my messengers come t. .... Is 44:26
own power, and my promise is t; .... Is 45:23
make what I have said come t; .... Is 46:11
same thing is t of the words I .... Is 55:11
to make sure my words come t." .... Je 1:12
But the LORD is the only t God. .... Je 10:10
Let's see that message come t!" .... Je 17:15
the message you prophesy come t. .... Je 28:6
peace and that message comes t, ... Je 28:9
said to Irijah, "That's not t! .... Je 37:14
Jerusalem come t through .... Je 39:16
everything come t with your own .... Je 39:16
saying about Ishmael are not t." .... Je 40:16
the LORD be a t and loyal .... Je 42:5
if my word or their word came t. .... Je 44:28
If that were t, why did Molech .... Je 49:1
the LORD, their t resting place, ... Je 50:7
when every vision will come t. .... Eze 12:23
hope their words will come t. .... Eze 13:6
saw visions that do not come t, ... Eze 13:8
says the Lord GOD, this is t. .... Eze 16:48
As surely as I live, this is t: .... Eze 17:19
says the Lord GOD, this is t: .... Eze 18:3
What you want will not come t. .... Eze 20:32
When this comes t, and it surely .... Eze 33:33
dream is t, and you can trust .... Da 2:45
I know this is t, because you .... Da 2:47
is it t that you do not serve my .... Da 3:14
Immediately the words came t. .... Da 4:33
evenings and mornings is t. .... Da 8:26
It was a t message that Daniel .... Da 10:1
for God's promises to come t. .... Da 11:14
and there to find t knowledge." .... Da 12:4
these amazing things come t?" .... Da 12:6
all these things will come t." .... Da 12:7
after all these things come t?" .... Da 12:8
will be t to you as my promised .... Hos 2:20
people are not t, not loyal to .... Hos 4:1
have not been t to the LORD; .... Hos 5:7
those who do not know the t God. .... Hos 7:5
People of Israel, isn't this t?" .... Am 2:11
You will be t to the people of .... Mic 7:20
time for the message to come t, ... Hab 2:3
the message will come t. .... Hab 2:3
'This is also t for the people .... Hag 2:14
'Do what is right and t. .... Zch 7:9
They taught the t teachings and .... Mal 2:6
have children who are t to God. .... Mal 2:15
the prophet Jeremiah came t: .... Mt 2:17
through the prophets came t: .... Mt 2:23
you will be t children of your .... Mt 5:45
is narrow that leads to t life. .... Mt 7:14
their lives will give up t life. .... Mt 10:39
for me will hold on to t life. .... Mt 10:39
If that is t, then what power do .... Mt 12:27
My t brother and sister and .... Mt 12:50
Isaiah said about them are t: ' .... Mt 13:14

their lives will give up t life, ... Mt 16:25
lives for me will have t life...................... Mt 16:25
is t because if two or three .... Mt 18:20
the prophet had said came t: .... Mt 27:9
My t brother and sister and .... Mk 3:35
their lives will give up t life. .... Mk 8:35
the Good News will have t life. .... Mk 8:35
to make the Scriptures come t." .... Mk 14:49
Peter said that it was not t. .... Mk 14:70
the Scripture came t that says, ... Mk 15:28
they told was t by giving them .... Mk 16:20
what you have been taught is t. .... Lk 1:4
I know that what you say is t? .... Lk 1:18
just now, they were coming t!" .... Lk 4:21
their lives will give up t life. .... Lk 9:24
lives for me will have t life...................... Lk 9:24
will trust you with t riches? .... Lk 16:11
what you say and teach is t. .... Lk 20:21
until it is given its t meaning .... Lk 22:16
But Peter said this was not t; .... Lk 22:57
The t Light that gives light to .... Jn 1:9
who follow the t way come to .... Jn 3:21
says has proven that God is t.................. Jn 3:33
coming when the t worshipers .... Jn 4:23
the saying is t, 'One person...................... Jn 4:37
myself, what I say is not t. .... Jn 5:31
things he says about me are t. .... Jn 5:32
giving you the t bread from .... Jn 6:32
My flesh is t food, and my blood .... Jn 6:55
food, and my blood is t drink.................. Jn 6:55
I was sent by the One who is t, ... Jn 7:28
one to say these things are t. .... Jn 8:13
about myself, but they are t. .... Jn 8:14
and Scripture is always t. .... Jn 10:35
John said about this man is t." .... Jn 10:41
world will keep t life forever. .... Jn 12:25
tell you this if it were not t...................... Jn 14:2
I am the t vine; my Father is .... Jn 15:1
in their law would be t: ' .... Jn 15:25
you, the only t God, and that .... Jn 17:3
that the Scripture would come t. .... Jn 17:12
Jesus said before would come t: .... Jn 18:9
what I said is t, why do you hit .... Jn 18:23
Peter said it was not t;........................... Jn 18:25
Again Peter said it wasn't t. .... Jn 18:27
how he would die would come t. .... Jn 18:32
this Scripture would come t: .... Jn 19:24
that the Scripture would come t, ... Jn 19:28
and whatever he says is t. .... Jn 19:35
to make the Scripture come t: .... Jn 19:36
We know that what he says is t. .... Jn 21:24
these things come t in this way. .... Ac 3:18
and we cannot say it is not t. .... Ac 4:16
also proves these things are t." .... Ac 5:32
Stephen, "Are these things t?" .... Ac 7:1
to Abraham was soon to come t, ... Ac 7:17
his house worshiped the t God. .... Ac 10:2
prophets say it is t that all .... Ac 10:43
But she kept on saying it was t, ... Ac 12:15
made them come t when they said .... Ac 13:27
made this promise come t for us, ... Ac 13:33
his grace was t by giving them .... Ac 14:3
find out if these things were t. .... Ac 17:11
no one can say this is not t, ... Ac 19:36
about you is not t and that you .... Ac 21:24
elders can tell you this is t. .... Ac 22:5
if all these things are t." .... Ac 24:8
and said that all of this was t................ Ac 24:9
to them; you know this is t..................... Ac 25:10
But if these charges are not t,................ Ac 25:11
My words are t and sensible. .... Ac 26:25
to have a t knowledge of God. .... Rm 1:28
This is t even though they do .... Rm 2:14

person is not a t Jew if he is .... Rm 2:28
t circumcision is not only on .... Rm 2:28
t circumcision is done in the .... Rm 2:29
continue to be t even when every .... Rm 3:4
This is t for all who believe in .... Rm 3:22
This is t before God, the God .... Rm 4:17
will surely have t life and rule .... Rm 5:17
And that brings t life for all. .... Rm 5:18
That is not t. But the law was .... Rm 7:7
your body, you will have t life. .... Rm 8:13
The t children of God are those .... Rm 8:14
descendants are t children of .... Rm 9:7
are God's t children. .... Rm 9:8
Abraham's t children are those .... Rm 9:8
That is t. But those branches .... Rm 11:20
to the Jewish ancestors are t. .... Rm 15:8
are against the t teaching you .... Rm 16:17
be judged to be t by the Spirit. 1Co 2:14
this were not t, your children 1Co 7:14
is t because woman came from 1Co 11:12
It may be t that there are all 1Co 14:10
As is t in all the churches of 1Co 14:33
That is t, brothers and sisters, ... 1Co 15:31
as it is t that I brag about 1Co 15:31
this Scripture will be made t: 1Co 15:54
to be my witness that this is t: 2Co 1:23
by the Holy Spirit, by t love, ... 2Co 6:6
Everything we said to you was t, ... 2Co 7:14
we bragged about to Titus is t. 2Co 7:14
if your love is t by comparing 2Co 8:8
is t that we brag freely about 2Co 10:8
away from your t and pure 2Co 11:3
men are not t apostles but are 2Co 11:13
It is t that he was weak when he 2Co 13:4
It is t that we are weak in 2Co 13:4
know that the t children of .... Gal 3:7
That would be t only if the law .... Gal 3:21
But now you know the t God. .... Gal 4:9
This is always t, not just when .... Gal 4:18
we have the t hope that comes .... Gal 5:5
you from following the t way? .... Gal 5:7
When you heard the t teaching— .... Eph 1:13
and on earth gets its t name. .... Eph 3:15
you things that are not t, ... Eph 5:6
It is t that some preach about .... Php 1:15
things that are t and honorable .... Php 4:8
a full and t life in Christ, ... Col 2:10
But what is t and real has come .... Col 2:17
you the t knowledge of God. .... Col 3:10
sure knowledge that it is t. 1Th 1:5
serving the living and t God. 1Th 1:9
God knows that this is t. 1Th 2:5
know this is t, and so does God 1Th 2:10
a t child to me because you 1Ti 1:2
that are not t and on long lists 1Ti 1:4
a good conscience and a t faith. 1Ti 1:5
against the t teaching of God. 1Ti 1:10
What I say is t, and you should 1Ti 1:15
What I say is t: Anyone wanting. 1Ti 3:1
What I say is t, and you should 1Ti 4:9
The t widow, who is all alone, ... 1Ti 5:5
agree with the t teaching of our 1Ti 6:3
shows the t way to serve God. 1Ti 6:3
to have the life that is t life. 1Ti 6:19
some have missed the t faith. 1Ti 6:21
I remember your t faith. 2Ti 1:5
the pattern of t teachings that. 2Ti 1:13
teaching is t: If we died with 2Ti 2:11
he must be t to who he is. 2Ti 2:13
and who uses the t teaching in 2Ti 2:15
They have left the t teaching, ... 2Ti 2:18
You know they are t, because you 2Ti 3:14
listen to the t teaching but 2Ti 4:3

t child in the faith we share: .... Tit 1:4
help people by using t teaching, ... Tit 1:9
are against the t teaching that .... Tit 1:9
words that prophet said are t. .... Tit 1:13
to do to follow the t teaching. .... Tit 2:1
teaching is t, and I want you .... Tit 3:8
angels was shown to be t, ... Heb 2:2
heard him testified it was t. .... Heb 2:3
It is still t that some people. .... Heb 4:6
proves that what they say is t, ... Heb 6:16
his promise was t to those who .... Heb 6:17
the t place of worship that was .... Heb 8:2
you are not t children. .... Heb 12:8
you can have t love for your 1Pe 1:22
you women are t children of 1Pe 3:6
the grace that gives t life. 1Pe 3:7
that this is the t grace of God. 1Pe 5:12
they did is like this t saying: 2Pe 2:22
and the t light is already 1Jn 2:8
and it is t, not false. 1Jn 2:27
but by our actions and t caring. 1Jn 3:18
Spirit that is t and the spirit 1Jn 4:6
the Spirit says that this is t, ... 1Jn 5:6
when they say something is t. 1Jn 5:9
so that we can know the T One. 1Jn 5:20
lives are in the T One and in 1Jn 5:20
He is the t God and the eternal 1Jn 5:20
and you know what we say is t. 3Jn 1:12
Jews, but they are not t Jews. .... Rev 2:9
But you are t to me. You did not .... Rev 2:13
what the One who is holy and t, ... Rev 3:7
Jews, but they are not t Jews; .... Rev 3:9
the faithful and t witness, ... Rev 3:14
voice, "Holy and t Lord, how .... Rev 6:10
the Lord does is right and t, ... Rev 15:3
his judgments are t and right. .... Rev 19:2
"These are the t words of God." .... Rev 19:9
horse is called Faithful and T, ... Rev 19:11
words are t and can be trusted. .... Rev 21:5
words can be trusted and are t." .... Rev 22:6
One who says these things are t, ... Rev 22:20

TRUEST
My best and t friend, who ate at .... Ps 41:9

TRULY
is t good to Israel, to those .... Ps 73:1
"T you are the Son of God!" .... Mt 14:33
saying, "T, God is with you." 1Co 14:25
But the t happy people are those .... Jam 1:25
among you who are t wise and .... Jam 3:13
because you t know God and Jesus 2Pe 1:2
God's love has t reached its 1Jn 2:5
in fire so you can be t rich. .... Rev 3:18
on your eyes so you can t see. .... Rev 3:18

TRUMPET
and he blew a t to call the .... Jdg 6:34
gave each man a t and an empty .... Jdg 7:16
Praise him with t blasts; .... Ps 150:3
if the t does not give a clear 1Co 14:8
blinks—when the last t sounds. 1Co 15:52
The t will sound, and those who 1Co 15:52
and with the t call of God. 1Th 4:16
the noise of a t or to the sound .... Heb 12:19
the seventh angel blew his t. .... Rev 11:15

TRUMPETERS
The officers and t were standing 2Ki 11:14
officers and t were standing 2Ch 23:13
and the t blew their trumpets 2Ch 29:28

TRUMPETS
Make two t of hammered silver, ... Nu 10:2
priests carry t made from horns .... Jos 6:4
and to whom were given seven t. .... Rev 8:2

T

had the seven t prepared to blow .... Rev 8:6
sounds of the t that the other .... Rev 8:13
flutes, and t, will never be .... Rev 18:22

TRUST

see that you t God and that you .... Ge 22:12
T him to my care, and I will .... Ge 42:37
with you and will always t you." .... Ex 19:9
I t him to lead all my people. .... Nu 12:7
still did not t the LORD your .... Dt 1:32
You did not t him or obey him. .... Dt 9:23
t in your high, strong walls, ... Dt 28:52
Sihon did not t the Israelites .... Jdg 11:20
' when you don't even t me? .... Jdg 16:15
But the other kings don't t you. 1Sa 29:6
is a shield to those who t him. 2Sa 22:31
says: What can you t in now? 2Ki 18:19
be fooled by the god you t. 2Ki 19:10
nothing to t to help you. 2Ch 32:10
God does not t his angels; .... Job 4:18
what they t is like a spider's .... Job 8:14
places no t in his holy ones, ... Job 15:15
not put my t in gold or said .... Job 31:24
you t the ox to bring in your .... Job 39:12
are those who t him for .... Ps 2:12
to the LORD and t the LORD. .... Ps 4:5
I t in you for protection. .... Ps 7:1
Those who know the LORD t him, ... Ps 9:10
I t in the LORD for protection. .... Ps 11:1
I t in your love. My heart is .... Ps 13:5
me, God, because I t in you. .... Ps 16:1
save those who t you from their .... Ps 17:7
is a shield to those who t him. .... Ps 18:30
Some t in chariots, others in .... Ps 20:7
but we t the LORD our God. .... Ps 20:7
You made me t you while I was .... Ps 22:9
God, I t you. Do not let me be .... Ps 25:2
my Savior. I t you all day long .... Ps 25:5
I t you, so do not let me be .... Ps 25:20
breaks out, I will t the LORD. .... Ps 27:3
I t him, and he helps me. .... Ps 28:7
LORD, I t in you; let me never .... Ps 31:1
gods. I t only in the LORD. .... Ps 31:6
LORD, I t you. I have said, "You .... Ps 31:14
have given to those who t you. .... Ps 31:19
love surrounds those who t him. .... Ps 32:10
because we t his holy name. .... Ps 33:21
T the LORD and do good. .... Ps 37:3
t him, and he will take care of .... Ps 37:5
Wait and t the LORD. Don't be .... Ps 37:7
but those who t the LORD will .... Ps 37:9
because they t in him for .... Ps 37:40
I t you, LORD. You will answer, ... Ps 38:15
Then they will t the LORD. .... Ps 40:3
I don't t my bow to help me, ... Ps 44:6
They t in their money and brag .... Ps 49:6
to those who t in themselves .... Ps 49:13
I t God's love forever and ever. .... Ps 52:8
I will t you because you are .... Ps 52:9
But I will t in you. For .... Ps 55:23
When I am afraid, I will t you. .... Ps 56:3
I t God, so I am not afraid. .... Ps 56:4
t in God. I will not be afraid. .... Ps 56:11
People, t God all the time. .... Ps 62:8
not t in force. Stealing is of .... Ps 62:10
don't put your t in them. .... Ps 62:10
earth and beyond the sea t you. .... Ps 65:5
with the harp. I t you, my God. .... Ps 71:22
they would all t God and would .... Ps 78:7
happy are the people who t you! .... Ps 84:12
You are my God and I t you." .... Ps 91:2
steady because they t the LORD. .... Ps 112:7
and so will those who t them. .... Ps 115:8

Family of Israel, t the LORD; .... Ps 115:9
Family of Aaron, t the LORD; .... Ps 115:10
respect the LORD should t him; .... Ps 115:11
It is better to t the LORD than .... Ps 118:8
trust the LORD than to t people. .... Ps 118:8
It is better to t the LORD than .... Ps 118:9
the LORD than to t princes. .... Ps 118:9
me, because I t what you say. .... Ps 119:42
because I t your commands. .... Ps 119:66
Those who t the LORD are like .... Ps 125:1
to help me, and I t his word. .... Ps 130:5
and so will those who t them. .... Ps 135:18
you for help. I t in you, LORD. .... Ps 141:8
your love, because I t you. .... Ps 143:8
Do not put your t in princes or .... Ps 146:3
with those who t his love. .... Ps 147:11
T the LORD with all your heart, ... Pr 3:5
Those who t in riches will be .... Pr 11:28
Rich people t their wealth to .... Pr 18:11
tear down the defenses they t .... Pr 21:22
you will put your t in the LORD. .... Pr 22:19
Those who t in themselves are .... Pr 28:26
but if you t the LORD, you will .... Pr 29:25
I will t him and not be afraid. .... Is 12:2
They will not t the altars who .... Is 17:8
nor will they t what their hands .... Is 17:8
but you did not t the God who .... Is 22:11
on you, because they t you. .... Is 26:3
So, t the LORD always, because .... Is 26:4
If you come back to me and t me, ... Is 30:15
If you will be calm and t me, ... Is 30:15
But they don't t God, the Holy .... Is 31:1
says: What can you t in now? .... Is 36:4
be fooled by the god you t. .... Is 37:10
die don't t you to help them. .... Is 38:18
the people who t the LORD will .... Is 40:31
far away will t his teachings." .... Is 42:4
those who t in idols, who say .... Is 42:17
Then let him t in the LORD and .... Is 50:10
and t your own light to guide .... Is 50:11
who helps the people who t you. .... Is 64:4
the strong, walled cities you t. .... Je 5:17
Don't t the lies of people who .... Je 7:4
t in that place, which I gave .... Je 7:14
and don't t your own relatives, ... Je 9:4
Don't t them, even when they say .... Je 12:6
on those who t other people, ... Je 17:5
the people of Judah t in lies. .... Je 28:15
You t in the things you do and .... Je 48:7
Your widows also can t in me." .... Je 49:11
and you can t this explanation." .... Da 2:45
and always t in him as your God. .... Hos 12:6
nor will we t in our horses. .... Hos 14:3
your neighbor or t a friend. .... Mic 7:5
It doesn't t the LORD; .... Zph 3:2
and they will t in the LORD. .... Zph 3:12
And do not break your t. .... Mal 2:16
who will t you with true riches? .... Lk 16:11
Since I can t you with small .... Lk 19:17
T in God, and trust in me. .... Jn 14:1
Trust in God, and t in me. .... Jn 14:1
well because of t in Jesus, ... Ac 3:16
those who t in his name! .... Ac 9:21
I t in God that everything will .... Ac 27:25
You t in the law of Moses and .... Rm 2:17
So they must t in him, who makes .... Rm 4:5
blessings to all who t in him, ... Rm 10:12
and peace while you t in him. .... Rm 15:13
show they are worthy of that t. 1Co 4:2
But you can t God, who will not 1Co 10:13
so we would not t in ourselves 2Co 1:9
happy that I can t you fully. 2Co 7:16
I t in the Lord that you will .... Gal 5:10

We do not put t in ourselves or .... Php 3:3
be able to put t in myself. .... Php 3:4
he has a reason to t in himself, ... Php 3:4
You can t the One who calls you 1Th 5:24
whom you can t the things you 2Ti 2:2
those who t in the Lord from 2Ti 2:22
you t those who taught you. 2Ti 3:14
also says, "I will t in God." .... Heb 2:13
because we can t God to do what .... Heb 10:23
God wants should t their souls 1Pe 4:19
because we can t God to do what 1Jn 1:9
has for us, and we t that love................... 1Jn 4:16

TRUSTED
The rules of the LORD can be t; .... Ps 19:7
Our ancestors t you; .... Ps 22:4
they t, and you saved them. .... Ps 22:4
They t you and were not .... Ps 22:5
I have t the LORD and never .... Ps 26:1
I have t you since I was young. .... Ps 71:5
God and had not t him to save .... Ps 78:22
all his orders can be t............................. Ps 111:7
you t me to care for five bags .... Mt 25:20
the first man t and will give .... Lk 11:22
is the wise and t servant that .... Lk 12:42
And from the one t with much, ... Lk 12:48
Whoever can be t with a little.................. Lk 16:10
with God because we t in Christ. .... Gal 2:16
God tested us and t us to do it. 1Th 2:4
because he t me and gave me this 1Ti 1:12
guard what God has t to you. 1Ti 6:20
what he has t me with until that 2Ti 1:12
He t me with that work, and I................. Tit 1:3
they can be fully t so that in .... Tit 2:10
was heard because he t God. .... Heb 5:7
because he t God to do what he .... Heb 11:11
words are true and can be t." .... Rev 21:5
words can be t and are true." .... Rev 22:6

TRUSTING
t him with everything he owned. .... Ge 39:4
Whom are you t for help so that.............. 2Ki 18:20
talk you into t the LORD by 2Ki 18:30
themselves by t what is useless. .... Job 15:31
T unfaithful people when you are .... Pr 25:19
You should stop t in people to .... Is 2:22
Whom are you t for help so that.............. Is 36:5
talk you into t the LORD by .... Is 36:15
look, you are t lies, which is .... Je 7:8
who have stopped t the LORD. .... Je 17:5
to continue t in God's grace. .... Ac 13:43
sins away, t in him to save you. .... Ac 22:16
did instead of t in God to make .... Rm 9:32
law, but by t in Jesus Christ .... Gal 2:16
greater reason for t in myself. .... Php 3:4

TRUSTS
My master t me with everything................ Ge 39:8
let everyone who t you be happy; .... Ps 5:11
The king truly t the LORD. .... Ps 21:7
No one who t you will be .... Ps 25:3
Happy is the person who t him. .... Ps 34:8
no one who t him will be judged .... Ps 34:22
is the person who t the LORD, ... Ps 40:4
your servant who t in you. .... Ps 86:2
who lives nearby and t you. .... Pr 3:29
and whoever t the LORD will be............ Pr 16:20
but the one who t the LORD will .... Pr 28:25
Her husband t her completely. .... Pr 31:11
Anyone who t in it will never be.............. Is 28:16
Anyone who t in me will not be .... Is 49:23
person who t in the LORD will .... Je 17:7
He knows who t in him. .... Nah 1:7
that the master t to give the .... Mt 24:45
He t in God, so let God save him .... Mt 27:43

that the master t to give the .... Lk 12:42
Anyone who t in him will never .... Rm 9:33
Anyone who t in him will never .... Rm 10:11
It always t, always hopes, and 1Co 13:7
Anyone who t in him will never 1Pe 2:6

TRUSTWORTHY
that the kings of Israel are t. 1Ki 20:31
are powerful and completely t. .... Ps 89:8
will look for t people so I can .... Ps 101:6
are right and completely t. .... Ps 119:138
destroy those who are not t. .... Pr 11:3
who are not t will be caught .... Pr 11:6
secrets, but a t person can. .... Pr 11:13
of those who are not t are hard. .... Pr 13:15
but a t one makes everything .... Pr 13:17
it is hard to find a t person. .... Pr 20:6
T messengers refresh those who .... Pr 25:13
because he was t and not lazy or .... Da 6:4
and t in everything................................. 1Ti 3:11
on to the t word just as we .... Tit 1:9

TRUTH
to prove you are telling the t. .... Ge 42:15
see if you are telling the t. .... Ge 42:16
will know you are telling the t, ... Ge 42:20
to Achan, "My son, tell the t. .... Jos 7:19
David said, "Do not hide the t. 2Sa 14:18
speak only the t to me in the 1Ki 22:16
said, "He speaks the LORD's t." 2Ki 3:12
whom I serve, I tell you the t. 2Ki 3:14
speak only the t to me in the 2Ch 18:15
them a message of peace and t. .... Est 9:30
speak God's t by telling lies. .... Job 13:7
name to show I have told the t. .... Job 31:35
mouths do not tell the t; .... Ps 5:9
people speak the t from their .... Ps 15:2
prayer, because I speak the t. .... Ps 17:1
me in your t, and teach me, ... Ps 25:5
your love, and I live by your t. .... Ps 26:3
it cannot speak about your t. .... Ps 30:9
Save me, LORD, God of t. .... Ps 31:5
Live in the land and feed on t. .... Ps 37:3
your love and t from the people .... Ps 40:10
your love and t always protect .... Ps 40:11
me your light and t to guide me.............. Ps 43:3
right and lies more than t. .... Ps 52:3
God sends me his love and t. .... Ps 57:3
the skies, your t to the clouds. .... Ps 57:10
him with your love and t. .... Ps 61:7
Love and t belong to God's .... Ps 85:10
and I will live by your t. .... Ps 86:11
Love and t are in all you do. .... Ps 89:14
His t will be your shield and .... Ps 91:4
fairness and the peoples with t. .... Ps 96:13
skies, your t to the heavens. .... Ps 108:4
much, and his t is everlasting. .... Ps 117:2
I have chosen the way of t; .... Ps 119:30
keep me from speaking your t, ... Ps 119:43
ever forget kindness and t. .... Pr 3:3
An honest witness tells the t, ... Pr 12:17
T will continue forever, but..................... Pr 12:19
Love and t bring forgiveness of .... Pr 16:6
value someone who speaks the t. .... Pr 16:13
Loyalty and t keep a king in .... Pr 20:28
Learn the t and never reject it. .... Pr 23:23
prophets, "Don't tell us the t! .... Is 30:10
am the LORD, and I speak the t;.............. Is 45:19
one tells the t in arguing his .... Is 59:4
T is not spoken in the streets;................. Is 59:14
T cannot be found anywhere,.................. Is 59:15
for the t, I will forgive............................ Je 5:1
don't you look for t in people? .... Je 5:3
They do not tell the t; .... Je 7:28

Lies, not **t,** have grown strong ....Je 9:3
friend, and no one speaks the **t.** ....Je 9:5
T was thrown down to the ground,............Da 8:12
not paid attention to your **t.** ....Da 9:13
is written in the Book of **T.** ....Da 10:21
then, Daniel, I tell you the **t:** ....Da 11:2
tribes of Israel I tell the **t.** ....Hos 5:9
stand those who tell the **t.** ....Am 5:10
they do not tell the **t.** ....Mic 6:12
it will be called the City of **T,** ....Zch 8:3
Tell each other the **t.** ....Zch 8:16
courts judge with **t** and complete ....Zch 8:16
But you must love **t** and peace." ....Zch 8:19
I tell you the **t,** nothing will ....Mt 5:18
I tell you the **t,** you will not...................Mt 5:26
I tell you the **t,** those ....Mt 6:2
I tell you the **t,** they already ....Mt 6:5
I tell you the **t,** those ....Mt 6:16
him, "I tell you the **t,** this is ....Mt 8:10
tell you the **t,** on the Judgment ....Mt 10:15
I tell you the **t,** you will not..................Mt 10:23
I tell you the **t,** John the ....Mt 11:11
I tell you the **t,** many prophets ....Mt 13:17
I tell you the **t,** some people ....Mt 16:28
I tell you the **t,** if your faith...................Mt 17:20
tell you the **t,** you must change ....Mt 18:3
I tell you the **t,** if he finds it ....Mt 18:13
I tell you the **t,** the things you ....Mt 18:18
tell you the **t,** it will be hard ....Mt 19:23
tell you the **t,** when the age to ....Mt 19:28
I tell you the **t,** if you have ....Mt 21:21
I tell you the **t,** the tax...........................Mt 21:31
you teach the **t** about God's way. ....Mt 22:16
I tell you the **t,** all of these ....Mt 23:36
I tell you the **t,** not one stone ....Mt 24:2
I tell you the **t,** all these ....Mt 24:34
tell you the **t,** the master will ....Mt 24:47
tell you the **t,** I don't want you ....Mt 25:12
I tell you the **t,** anything you ....Mt 25:40
I tell you the **t,** anything you ....Mt 25:45
I tell you the **t,** wherever the ....Mt 26:13
tell you the **t,** one of you will ....Mt 26:21
I tell you the **t,** tonight before ....Mt 26:34
I tell you the **t,** all sins that ....Mk 3:28
fear, she told him the whole **t.** ....Mk 5:33
tell you the **t,** no sign will be ....Mk 8:12
I tell you the **t,** some people ....Mk 9:1
I tell you the **t,** whoever gives...................Mk 9:41
tell you the **t,** you must accept ....Mk 10:15
I tell you the **t,** all those who ....Mk 10:29
I tell you the **t,** you can say to...............Mk 11:23
you teach the **t** about God's way...............Mk 12:14
tell you the **t,** this poor widow ....Mk 12:43
I tell you the **t,** all these ....Mk 13:30
I tell you the **t,** wherever the ....Mk 14:9
tell you the **t,** one of you will ....Mk 14:18
I tell you the **t,** I will not ....Mk 14:25
I tell you the **t,** tonight before ....Mk 14:30
I tell you the **t,** a prophet is ....Lk 4:24
tell you the **t,** there were many ....Lk 4:25
I tell you the **t,** some people ....Lk 9:27
tell you the **t,** the master will ....Lk 12:37
tell you the **t,** the master will ....Lk 12:44
tell you the **t,** you must accept ....Lk 18:17
I tell you the **t,** all those who ....Lk 18:29
teach the **t** about God's way. ....Lk 20:21
tell you the **t,** this poor widow ....Lk 21:3
I tell you the **t,** all these ....Lk 21:32
I tell you the **t,** today you will ....Lk 23:43
people the **t** about the Light ....Jn 1:7
people the **t** about the Light. ....Jn 1:8
and he was full of grace and **t.** ....Jn 1:14
John tells the **t** about him and ....Jn 1:15

he was full of grace and **t,** ....Jn 1:16
but grace and **t** came through................Jn 1:17
Here is the **t** John told when the................Jn 1:19
happen, and I tell you the **t:** ....Jn 1:34
I tell you the **t,** you will all ....Jn 1:51
I tell you the **t,** unless you are...................Jn 3:3
I tell you the **t,** unless you are...................Jn 3:5
I tell you the **t,** we talk about ....Jn 3:11
your husband. You told the **t.**" ....Jn 4:18
the Father in spirit and **t,** ....Jn 4:23
must worship in spirit and **t.**" ....Jn 4:24
I tell you the **t,** the Son can do ....Jn 5:19
I tell you the **t,** whoever hears ....Jn 5:24
I tell you the **t,** the time is ....Jn 5:25
John, and he has told you the **t.** ....Jn 5:33
I tell you the **t,** you aren't ....Jn 6:26
I tell you the **t,** it was not ....Jn 6:32
I tell you the **t,** whoever ....Jn 6:47
I tell you the **t,** you must eat ....Jn 6:53
one who sent them speak the **t,** ....Jn 7:18
sent me, and he speaks the **t.**" ....Jn 8:26
will know the **t,** and the truth ....Jn 8:32
and the **t** will make you free." ....Jn 8:32
I tell you the **t,** everyone who ....Jn 8:34
has told you the **t** which I heard...............Jn 8:40
beginning and was against the **t,** ....Jn 8:44
because there is no **t** in him. ....Jn 8:44
But because I speak the **t,** ....Jn 8:45
am telling the **t,** why don't you ....Jn 8:46
I tell you the **t,** whoever obeys ....Jn 8:51
I tell you the **t,** before Abraham ....Jn 8:58
God the glory by telling the **t.**...................Jn 9:24
I tell you the **t,** the person who ....Jn 10:1
I tell you the **t,** I am the door ....Jn 10:7
I tell you the **t,** a grain of ....Jn 12:24
I tell you the **t,** a servant is ....Jn 13:16
tell you the **t,** whoever accepts ....Jn 13:20
tell you the **t,** one of you will ....Jn 13:21
I tell you the **t,** before the ....Jn 13:38
way, and the **t,** and the life....................Jn 14:6
I tell you the **t,** whoever ....Jn 14:12
Spirit of **t.** The world cannot ....Jn 14:17
he is the Spirit of **t** who comes ....Jn 15:26
I tell you the **t,** it is better ....Jn 16:7
of the world the **t** about sin, ...Jn 16:8
But when the Spirit of **t** comes, ...Jn 16:13
he will lead you into all **t.** ....Jn 16:13
The Spirit of **t** will bring glory ....Jn 16:14
I tell you the **t,** you will cry....................Jn 16:20
I tell you the **t,** my Father will...................Jn 16:23
for your service through your **t;** ....Jn 17:17
your truth; your teaching is **t.**..................Jn 17:17
for their service of the **t.** ....Jn 17:19
tell people the **t.** And everyone ....Jn 18:37
belongs to the **t** listens to me." ....Jn 18:37
Pilate said, "What is **t?**" ....Jn 18:38
he knows that he tells the **t,** ....Jn 19:35
I tell you the **t,** when you were ....Jn 21:18
and taught the **t** about Jesus. ....Ac 18:25
up and twist the **t** and will lead ....Ac 20:30
will not accept the **t** about me.' ....Ac 22:18
Spirit spoke the **t** to your ....Ac 28:25
own evil lives they hide the **t.** ....Rm 1:18
They traded the **t** of God for a ....Rm 1:25
They refuse to follow **t** and, ...Rm 2:8
know everything and have all **t.** ....Rm 2:20
because my lie shows God's **t.** ....Rm 3:7
and I am telling you the **t;** ....Rm 9:1
the bread of goodness and **t.** 1Co 5:8
in evil but rejoices over the **t.** 1Co 13:6
I bring you a new **t** or some new 1Co 14:6
Another has a new **t** from God. 1Co 14:26
we speak the **t** before God, ...2Co 2:17

We teach the t plainly, showing 2Co 4:2
people accept the t about us. 2Co 5:11
by speaking the t, and by God's 2Co 6:7
are liars, but we speak the t. 2Co 6:8
this with the t of Christ in me. 2Co 11:10
I would be telling the t. 2Co 12:6
do anything against the t, ...2Co 13:8
the truth, but only for the t. 2Co 13:8
We wanted the t of the Good News ....Gal 2:5
following the t of the Good News ....Gal 2:14
enemy because I tell you the t? ....Gal 4:16
Speaking the t with love, we ....Eph 4:15
taught the t that is in Jesus. ....Eph 4:21
each other the t, because we all ....Eph 4:25
goodness, right living, and t. ....Eph 5:9
the belt of t tied around your ....Eph 6:14
proving the t of the Good News...............Php 1:7
following the t we already have...............Php 3:16
heard the message about the t, ...Col 1:5
understood the t about the grace ....Col 1:6
they refused to love the t. 2Th 2:10
they loved the t, they would be 2Th 2:10
away from the t so they will 2Th 2:11
who did not believe the t, ...2Th 2:12
holy and by your faith in the t. 2Th 2:13
to be saved and to know the t. 1Ti 2:4
am telling the t; I am not lying 1Ti 2:7
to believe and to know the t. 1Ti 2:7
support and foundation of the t. 1Ti 3:15
who believe and know the t. 1Ti 4:3
that disagree with God's t, ...1Ti 4:7
evil minds and have lost the t. 1Ti 6:5
Protect the t that you were 2Ti 1:14
minds so they can accept the t. 2Ti 2:25
able to understand the t fully...................2Ti 3:7
these people are against the t. 2Ti 3:8
listening to the t and will 2Ti 4:4
them know the t that shows ....Tit 1:1
of people who reject the t. ....Tit 1:14
Speak the t so that you cannot ....Tit 2:8
will not stray away from the t. ....Heb 2:1
testified to the t of the...........................Heb 2:4
after we have learned the t, ...Heb 10:26
when you first learned the t. ....Heb 10:32
the word of t so we might be ....Jam 1:18
is a lie that hides the t. ....Jam 3:14
of you wanders away from the t, ...Jam 5:19
obedience to the t has purified 1Pe 1:22
you are very strong in the t, ...2Pe 1:12
evil things about the way of t..................2Pe 2:2
liars and do not follow the t. 1Jn 1:6
and the t is not in us. 1Jn 1:8
and the t is not in that person. 1Jn 2:4
you can see its t in Jesus and 1Jn 2:8
gave you, so you all know the t. 1Jn 2:20
not know the t but because you 1Jn 2:21
but because you do know the t. 1Jn 2:21
that no lie comes from the t. 1Jn 2:21
because the Spirit is the t. 1Jn 5:6
has told us the t about his own 1Jn 5:9
of God has the t that God told 1Jn 5:10
I love all of you in the t, ...2Jn 1:1
those who know the t love you. 2Jn 1:1
because of the t that lives in 2Jn 1:2
will be with us in t and love. 2Jn 1:3
are following the way of t, ...2Jn 1:4
Gaius, whom I love in the t. 3Jn 1:1
told me about the t in your life 3Jn 1:3
you are following the way of t. 3Jn 1:3
are following the way of t. 3Jn 1:4
share in their work for the t. 3Jn 1:8
and the t agrees with what they 3Jn 1:12

TRUTHFUL

been kind and t to him and has ....Ge 24:27
you be kind and t to my master? ....Ge 24:49
You want me to be completely t,..............Ps 51:6
A t witness does not lie, but a...............Pr 14:5
A t witness saves lives, but a ....Pr 14:25
but a t witness will speak on. ....Pr 21:28
A t person will have many ....Pr 28:20
' and you can say it in a t, ...Je 4:2

TRUTHFULLY

who hears my message speak it t! ....Je 23:28
judge, I judge t, because I am ....Jn 8:16

TRUTHS

change the Lord's t into lies. ....Ac 13:10
explain spiritual t to spiritual 1Co 2:13
does not accept the t that come 1Co 2:14
told about the t you have now 1Pe 1:12

TRY

LORD, t me and test me; look................Ps 26:2
all my heart I t to obey you. ....Ps 119:10
I will t to do what you demand ....Ps 119:112
if sinners t to lead you into....................Pr 1:10
T giving them to your governor. ....Mal 1:8
Those who t to hold on to their ....Mt 10:39
rules and t to force people ....Mt 23:4
They will t to fool even the ....Mt 24:24
houses and then to make ....Mk 12:40
They will t to fool even the ....Mk 13:22
don't even t to follow those....................Lk 11:54
T to live in peace with all ....Heb 12:14
and t to live free from sin. ....Heb 12:14
t hard to be certain that you 2Pe 1:10
I will t my best so that you may 2Pe 1:15
T to be at peace with God. 2Pe 3:14

TRYING

and now you are t to take away ....Ge 30:15
a long time, t to capture it, ...Dt 20:19
from Ephraim t to escape would..............Jdg 12:5
Why is he t to kill me?" 1Sa 20:1
at Jonathan, t to kill him. 1Sa 20:33
You are t to trap me and get me 1Sa 28:9
My own son is t to kill me! 2Sa 16:11
the wind or t to grab oil in ....Pr 27:16
LORD is t to teach the people.................Is 28:9
he is t to make them understand ....Is 28:9
Why are you t to trap me? ....Mk 12:15
the law were t to find a trick ....Mk 14:1
hard all night to catch fish, ...Lk 5:5
people were t to touch Jesus, ...Lk 6:19
And Herod kept t to see Jesus. ....Lk 9:9
We are not t to kill you.".......................Jn 7:20
is the man they are t to kill. ....Jn 7:25
and no one is t to stop him. ....Jn 7:26
God, but you are t to kill me. ....Jn 8:40
I am not t to get honor for ....Jn 8:50
Are you t to teach us?" ....Jn 9:34
teaching and are t to make us ....Ac 5:28
Holy Spirit is t to tell you, ...Ac 7:51
Saul was also t to destroy the.................Ac 8:3
in Jerusalem t to destroy those ....Ac 9:21
You who are t to follow God and ....Jam 4:8
If you are t hard to do good, ...1Pe 3:13
people who are t to lead you 1Jn 2:26

TRYPHENA

Greetings to T and Tryphosa, ...Rm 16:12

TRYPHOSA

Greetings to Tryphena and T, ...Rm 16:12

TUB

hid in a large t of flour until ....Mt 13:33
hid in a large t of flour until ....Lk 13:21

TUBAL

Madai, Javan, **T**, Meshech, and .... Ge 10:2
Madai, Javan, **T**, Meshech, and 1Ch 1:5
of archers), **T**, Greece, and all .... Is 66:19
People of Greece, **T**, and Meshech .... Eze 27:13
Meshech and **T** are there with the .... Eze 32:26
of the nations of Meshech and **T**. .... Eze 38:2
chief ruler of Meshech and **T**. .... Eze 38:3
chief ruler of Meshech and **T**. .... Eze 39:1

TUBAL-CAIN

gave birth to **T**, who made tools .... Ge 4:22
The sister of **T** was Naamah. .... Ge 4:22

TUBES

Its bones are like **t** of bronze; .... Job 40:18

TUMBLEWEED

make them like **t**, like chaff .... Ps 83:13

TUMBLEWEEDS

or like **t** blown away by a storm. .... Is 17:13

TUNNEL

you must go through the water **t**. 2Sa 5:8
his work on the **t** to bring water 2Ki 20:20
Miners dig a **t** far from where .... Job 28:4

TUNNELS

They cut **t** through the rock and .... Job 28:10

TURBAN

inner robe, a **t**, and a cloth .... Ex 28:4
blue ribbon to tie it to the **t**; .... Ex 28:37
put it on the front of the **t**. .... Ex 28:37
and make the **t** of fine linen .... Ex 28:39
Put the **t** on his head, and put .... Ex 29:6
and put the holy crown on the **t**............... Ex 29:6
flat piece to the **t** with a blue .... Ex 39:31
also put the **t** on Aaron's head .... Le 8:9
the front of the **t**, as the LORD .... Le 8:9
and he will wear the linen **t**. .... Le 16:4
fairness like a robe and a **t**. .... Job 29:14
Take off the royal **t**, and remove .... Eze 21:26
Tie on your **t**, and put your .... Eze 24:17
"Put a clean **t** on his head." .... Zch 3:5
they put a clean **t** on his head .... Zch 3:5

TURBANS

and they made **t**, headbands, and .... Ex 39:28
linen dresses, **t**, and long .... Is 3:23
waists and on their heads. .... Eze 23:15
Your **t** must stay on your heads, ... Eze 24:23
will wear linen **t** on their heads .... Eze 44:18
robes, trousers, and other .... Da 3:21

TURN

the Israelites to **t** back to Pi .... Ex 14:2
him. Do not **t** against him; he .... Ex 23:21
and I will not **t** away from you. .... Le 26:11
and if you **t** away from my rules .... Le 26:15
If you still **t** against me and .... Le 26:21
and if you still **t** against me, ... Le 26:23
I will also **t** against you. .... Le 26:24
to me and still **t** against me, ... Le 26:27
which made me **t** against them and .... Le 26:41
I will not **t** away from them when .... Le 26:44
Don't **t** against the LORD! .... Nu 14:9
to me, you who **t** against God! .... Nu 20:10
too narrow to **t** left or right. .... Nu 22:26
But you must **t** around and follow .... Dt 1:40
mountains long enough. **T** north .... Dt 2:3
road and not **t** right or left. .... Dt 2:27
people will **t** your children .... Dt 7:4
fooled and will **t** away to serve .... Dt 11:16
said you should **t** against the .... Dt 13:5
They tried to **t** you from doing .... Dt 13:5
because they tried to **t** you away .... Dt 13:10
The LORD will **t** the rain into .... Dt 28:24

But if you **t** away from the LORD .... Dt 30:17
will **t** away from them, and they .... Dt 31:17
I will surely **t** away from them .... Dt 31:18
Then they will **t** to other gods .... Dt 31:20
will **t** away from the commands .... Dt 31:29
I will **t** away from them and see .... Dt 32:20
They **t** away from the fight and .... Jos 7:12
Then we will **t** and run away from .... Jos 8:5
'Why did you **t** against the God .... Jos 22:16
But don't **t** against the LORD and .... Jos 22:19
that you didn't **t** against him. .... Jos 22:31
If you **t** away from the way of .... Jos 23:12
If you **t** against him and sin, ... Jos 24:19
you, but if you **t** against him, ... Jos 24:20
you will not **t** against your God. .... Jos 24:27
and did not **t** right or left. 1Sa 6:12
his word and not **t** against his 1Sa 12:14
and if you **t** against his 1Sa 12:15
but don't **t** away from the LORD. 1Sa 12:20
T to your right or left and 2Sa 2:21
T back and stay with King 2Sa 15:19
T back and take your brothers 2Sa 15:20
You made my enemies **t** back, ... 2Sa 22:41
he caused David to **t** against the 2Sa 24:1
They will truly **t** back to you in 1Ki 8:48
and may he **t** us to himself so we 1Ki 8:58
caused him to **t** away from God 1Ki 11:3
T around and get me out of the 1Ki 22:34
help so that you **t** against him? 2Ki 18:20
I allowed you to **t** to those strong, ... 2Ki 19:25
you have come to **t** me over to my 1Ch 12:17
They came to help **t** the kingdom 1Ch 12:23
But if you **t** away from him, ... 1Ch 28:9
They will truly **t** back to you in 2Ch 6:38
chariot commanders **t** away from 2Ch 18:31
T around and get me out of the 2Ch 18:33
the people to **t** them back to him 2Ch 24:19
He will not **t** away from you if 2Ch 30:9
T the insults of Sanballat and .... Ne 4:4
Everywhere you **t**, the enemy will .... Ne 4:12
are planning to **t** against the .... Ne 6:6
could take her **t** with King .... Est 2:12
Let that day **t** to darkness. .... Job 3:4
You can't **t** to any of the holy .... Job 5:1
Travelers **t** away from their .... Job 6:18
Do you now **t** around and destroy .... Job 10:8
you now **t** me back into dust? .... Job 10:9
growing and will never **t** green. .... Job 15:32
their food will **t** sour in their .... Job 20:14
in his way; I did not **t** aside. .... Job 23:11
to **t** them away from doing wrong .... Job 33:17
together and **t** back into dust .... Job 34:15
don't let much money **t** you away. .... Job 36:18
Be careful not to **t** to evil, ... Job 36:21
long will you **t** my honor into .... Ps 4:2
They will **t** and suddenly leave .... Ps 6:10
My enemies **t** back; they are .... Ps 9:3
But those who **t** to idols will .... Ps 16:4
You made my enemies **t** back, ... Ps 18:40
make them **t** their backs when .... Ps 21:12
They say, "**T** to the LORD for .... Ps 22:8
remember and will **t** to the LORD. .... Ps 22:27
T to me and have mercy on me, ... Ps 25:16
Do not **t** away from me. Do not .... Ps 27:9
Do not **t** your servant away in .... Ps 27:9
plan to harm me **t** back and run .... Ps 35:4
who doesn't **t** to those who are .... Ps 40:4
my teachings and **t** your back on .... Ps 50:17
T your face from my sins and .... Ps 51:9
and sinners will **t** back to you. .... Ps 51:13
Strangers **t** against me, and .... Ps 54:3
evil people **t** away from God; .... Ps 58:3
should not **t** against him. .... Ps 66:7

but those who t against God will .... Ps 68:6
of your great kindness, turn to me. .... Ps 69:16
So their people t to them and .... Ps 73:10
we will not t away from you. .... Ps 80:18
enemies and t my hand against .... Ps 81:14
T to me and have mercy. .... Ps 86:16
You t people back into dust. .... Ps 90:3
I hate those who t against you; .... Ps 101:3
When you t away from them, ... Ps 104:29
breath, they die and t to dust. .... Ps 104:29
they continued to t against him. .... Ps 106:43
Jordan, why did you t back? .... Ps 114:5
light around me t into night." .... Ps 139:11
Don't t away from me, or I will .... Ps 143:7
t off the road of goodness; .... Pr 4:27
officer who in t is cheated by .... Ec 5:8
You will t back into the dust of .... Ec 12:7
disappear. T, my lover. Be like .... Sng 2:17
Which way did your lover t? .... Sng 6:1
T your eyes from me, because .... Sng 6:5
you continue to t against him? .... Is 1:5
to obey and if you t against me, ... Is 1:20
I will t against you and clean .... Is 1:25
and those who t against him will .... Is 1:28
the LORD; they t against him. .... Is 3:8
wrong way and t you away from .... Is 3:12
they will each t and eat their .... Is 9:20
of them will t against Judah. .... Is 9:21
and then I will t my anger to .... Is 10:25
Everyone will t back to his own .... Is 13:14
Traitors t against people; .... Is 24:16
they t against people. .... Is 24:16
others, they will t against you. .... Is 33:1
help so that you t against me? .... Is 36:5
I allowed you to t those strong, ... Is 37:26
will know how they will t out. .... Is 41:22
things, you who t against God. .... Is 46:8
you would surely t against me; .... Is 48:8
You t against God, and you are .... Is 57:4
cause him to t away from you, ... Is 59:2
so why did they t away from me? .... Je 2:5
terrible evil to t away from the .... Je 2:19
then did you t into a wild vine .... Je 2:21
Father' and not t away from me. .... Je 3:19
they refused to t back to God. .... Je 5:3
or I will t my back on you and .... Je 6:8
wrong way, doesn't he t back? .... Je 8:4
and refuse to t around and come .... Je 8:5
but he will t it into thick .... Je 13:16
the people of Judah t you, ... Je 15:19
people and to t your anger away .... Je 18:20
people to t against the LORD. .... Je 28:16
the people to t against me.'" .... Je 29:32
it will t to the place named .... Je 31:39
I will never t away from them; .... Je 32:40
they will never t away from me. .... Je 32:40
then would I t away from Jacob's .... Je 33:26
even they all t and run away .... Je 46:21
did not t when they moved, ... Eze 1:9
are a people who t against me. .... Eze 2:6
not, because they t against me. .... Eze 2:7
Don't t against me as those .... Eze 2:8
are a people who t against me." .... Eze 3:9
and they do not t from their .... Eze 3:19
do right may t away from doing .... Eze 3:20
even though they t against me. .... Eze 3:26
are a people who t against me. .... Eze 3:27
T your face toward the city as .... Eze 4:3
so you cannot t from one side to .... Eze 4:8
will t their wealth into trash. .... Eze 7:22
I will also t away from the .... Eze 7:22
Israel when you t loose your .... Eze 9:8
The wheels did not t about, ... Eze 10:11

did not t their bodies as .... Eze 10:11
and will t against them. .... Eze 15:7
When I t against them, you will .... Eze 15:7
to obey me and who t against me. .... Eze 20:38
ways they sin and t against me, ... Eze 37:23
will t you around and put hooks .... Eze 38:4
I will t my power against the .... Eze 38:12
will t you around and lead you. .... Eze 39:2
I will not t away from them .... Eze 39:29
and I will t your houses into .... Da 2:5
to fight will t against the king .... Da 11:14
the North will t his attention .... Da 11:18
I will t them into a forest, ... Hos 2:12
days they will t in fear to the .... Hos 3:5
their guilt and t back to me. .... Hos 5:15
they will not t back to the LORD .... Hos 7:10
but they really t away from me. .... Hos 7:14
They did not t to the Most High .... Hos 7:16
they refuse to t back to God. .... Hos 11:5
their minds to t away from me. .... Hos 11:7
prophets call them to t to me, ... Hos 11:7
but those who t against God die .... Hos 14:9
Maybe he will t back to you and .... Joe 2:14
Then I will t against the people .... Am 1:8
You t justice upside down, ... Am 5:7
escape alive and t them over to .... Ob 1:14
Everyone must t away from evil .... Jnh 3:8
a daughter will t against her .... Mic 7:6
God and will t in fear before .... Mic 7:17
taken money will t against you. .... Hab 2:7
It's your t to drink and fall to .... Hab 2:16
the LORD will t against the .... Zph 2:13
your enemy might t you over to .... Mt 5:25
t to him the other cheek also. .... Mt 5:39
and dogs will t to attack you. .... Mt 7:6
and they will t against each .... Mt 24:10
for the best time to t Jesus .... Mt 26:16
one of you will t against me." .... Mt 26:21
the one who will t against you, ... Mt 26:22
the one who will t against me. .... Mt 26:23
and they will t him over to the .... Mk 10:33
for the best time to t Jesus .... Mk 14:11
one of you will t against me— .... Mk 14:18
and the judge might t you over .... Lk 12:58
and friends will t against you, ... Lk 21:16
one of you will t against me, ... Lk 22:21
and who would t against him. .... Jn 6:64
he was going to t against Jesus. .... Jn 6:71
who would later t against him, ... Jn 12:4
of Simon, to t against Jesus. .... Jn 13:2
knew who would t against him, ... Jn 13:11
one of you will t against me." .... Jn 13:21
the man who will t against me." .... Jn 13:26
Lord, who will t against you?" .... Jn 21:20
T away from this evil thing you .... Ac 8:22
nations to t to him and live. .... Ac 11:18
telling you to t away from these .... Ac 14:15
things and t to the living God. .... Ac 14:15
the people to t against Paul. .... Ac 14:19
their lives and t to God and .... Ac 20:21
was beginning to t into such a .... Ac 23:10
so that they may t away from .... Ac 26:18
and lives and t to God and do. .... Ac 26:20
So why do you t back to those .... Gal 4:9
to persuade you to t against us .... Gal 4:17
will t against their friends, ... 2Ti 3:4
heart that will t you away from .... Heb 3:12
But if they t back with fear, ... Heb 10:38
not those who t back and are .... Heb 10:39
know it and to t away from the 2Pe 2:21
her heart and t away from her .... Rev 2:21
if they do not t away from the .... Rev 2:22
their hearts and t away from .... Rev 9:20

T

hearts and t away from murder .... Rev 9:21
their hearts and t away from the ...... Rev 16:11

TURNED

They t their faces away so that .... Ge 9:23
year, they all t against him...................... Ge 14:4
Then they t back and went to En .... Ge 14:7
So the men t and went toward .... Ge 18:22
but God t your evil into good to .... Ge 50:20
The king t and went into his .... Ex 7:23
Then Moses t and walked away .... Ex 10:6
They have quickly t away from .... Ex 32:8
from the spot has not t white,.............. Le 13:4
whole body and has t all of the .... Le 13:13
they will admit they t against .... Le 26:40
Tent and Aaron t toward Miriam, ... Nu 12:10
You have t away from the LORD, ... Nu 14:43
person has t against the LORD' .... Nu 15:31
Abiram, and On t against Moses. .... Nu 16:1
they t toward the Meeting Tent, ... Nu 16:42
so the Israelites t back. .... Nu 20:21
donkey saw me and t away from me .... Nu 22:23
If she had not t away, I would................. Nu 22:33
the leaders who t against Moses.............. Nu 26:9
when he t against the LORD. .... Nu 26:9
advice and t the Israelites .... Nu 31:16
we t around, and we traveled .... Dt 2:1
We t off the Jordan Valley road .... Dt 2:8
When we t and went up the road .... Dt 3:1
have quickly t away from what I .... Dt 9:12
I t and came down the mountain .... Dt 9:15
You had quickly t away from what............ Dt 9:16
Then I t and came down the .... Dt 10:5
He t the curse into a blessing .... Dt 23:5
wrong and have t to other gods............. Dt 31:18
running and t against the men .... Jos 8:20
running and t to fight the men .... Jos 8:21
Addar it t and went to Karka.................. Jos 15:3
Debir where it t toward the.................... Jos 15:7
There it t and went toward .... Jos 15:9
Baalah the border t west and .... Jos 15:10
Then it t toward Shikkeron and .... Jos 15:11
Micmethath it t eastward toward .... Jos 16:6
the border t and went south near .... Jos 18:14
There it t north and went to En .... Jos 18:17
Then it t to the east. .... Jos 19:12
the border t and went toward .... Jos 19:13
At Neah it t again and went to .... Jos 19:14
Then it t east and went to Beth .... Jos 19:27
it t and went toward Hosah, ... Jos 19:29
they quickly t away and did not .... Jdg 2:17
he t around and said to Eglon, ... Jdg 3:19
The LORD t to Gideon and said,.............. Jdg 6:14
that the tent t over and fell .... Jdg 7:13
But now you have t against my .... Jdg 9:18
of Shechem t against him. .... Jdg 9:23
Then Samson t to the two center .... Jdg 16:29
who t around and said to Micah, ... Jdg 18:23
so he t and went back home. .... Jdg 18:26
the army of Israel t around in................. Jdg 20:39
Benjaminites t around and saw .... Jdg 20:40
the Israelites t and began to .... Jdg 20:41
When Saul t to leave Samuel,................. 1Sa 10:9
Samuel t to leave, Saul caught 1Sa 15:27
When he t to other people and 1Sa 17:30
was dead, they t and ran. 1Sa 17:51
David has t against me and is................. 1Sa 22:13
He has t against King David. 2Sa 20:1
King Solomon t to them and 1Ki 8:14
but the king t away from........................ 1Ki 11:9
Jeroboam t against the king. 1Ki 11:26
of how Jeroboam t against the 1Ki 11:27
story of how he t against King 1Ki 16:20

down on his bed, t his face to 1Ki 21:4
Israel, so they t to attack him. 1Ki 22:32
Elisha t around, looked at them,............. 2Ki 2:24
king of Moab t against the king 2Ki 3:5
king of Moab has t against me," 2Ki 3:7
Elisha t away and walked around 2Ki 4:35
when the man t from his chariot 2Ki 5:26
Joram t the horses to run away 2Ki 9:23
who t away from Jerusalem. 2Ki 12:18
He t against the king of Assyria 2Ki 18:7
Hezekiah t toward the wall and 2Ki 20:2
When he t around, he saw the 2Ki 23:16
Then he t against Nebuchadnezzar 2Ki 24:1
Zedekiah t against the king of 2Ki 24:20
When he t around, he saw the 1Ch 21:20
King Solomon t to them and 2Ch 6:3
s command and t back and did not 2Ch 11:4
son, t against his master. 2Ch 13:6
the soldiers of Judah t around, ... 2Ch 13:14
in trouble, they t to the LORD, ... 2Ch 15:4
Israel, so they t to attack him. 2Ch 18:31
and he t them back to the LORD, ... 2Ch 19:4
the Israelites t away and did 2Ch 20:10
where the wall t, and he made 2Ch 26:9
They t against the LORD, the God 2Ch 30:7
Zedekiah t against King 2Ch 36:13
I t and went back in through the .... Ne 2:15
stubborn and t against you, ... Ne 9:17
disobedient and t against you................. Ne 9:26
But our God t the curse into a .... Ne 13:2
sadness was t to joy and their .... Est 9:22
the dead was t into celebration .... Est 9:22
God has t me over to evil people .... Job 16:11
those I love have t against me. .... Job 19:19
the lamps of evil people t off?................. Job 21:17
You have t on me without mercy; .... Job 30:21
I have t black, but not by the .... Job 30:28
If I have t away from doing what .... Job 31:7
Many people have t against me............... Ps 3:1
they have t against you. .... Ps 5:10
But all have t away. Together, ... Ps 14:3
But when you t away, I was .... Ps 30:7
He t to me and heard my cry. .... Ps 40:1
my table, has even t against me............. Ps 41:9
hearts haven't t away from you, ... Ps 44:18
But all have t away. Together, ... Ps 53:3
He t the sea into dry land. .... Ps 66:6
from those who t against you. .... Ps 68:18
the desert they t against God .... Ps 78:17
They t against God so often in .... Ps 78:40
He t their rivers to blood so no .... Ps 78:44
tested God and t against God .... Ps 78:56
They t away and were disloyal .... Ps 78:57
have t Jerusalem into ruins. .... Ps 79:1
you t back from your strong .... Ps 85:3
have t his strong cities into .... Ps 89:40
the Egyptians t against what he .... Ps 105:28
so they t against you at the Red .... Ps 106:7
The people t against the Spirit .... Ps 106:33
They had t against the words of .... Ps 107:11
Some fools t against God and................. Ps 107:17
the Jordan River t back. .... Ps 114:3
t a rock into a pool of water, ... Ps 114:8
Jerusalem be t back in shame. .... Ps 129:5
this t out to be like chasing................... Ec 1:17
but they have t against me. .... Is 1:2
and have t away from him as if .... Is 1:4
who t the world into a desert,................. Is 14:17
and they t it into ruins. .... Is 23:13
but joy will have t to sadness;................. Is 24:11
whom no one has t against yet. .... Is 33:1
Hezekiah t toward the wall and .... Is 38:2
you and have not t against you. .... Is 41:9

your leaders have t against me. .... Is 43:27
Even when your hair has t gray, ... Is 46:4
of the times she t against me, ... Is 50:1
and I have not t against him nor .... Is 50:5
them and t away from them .... Is 57:17
We know we have t against God; .... Is 59:12
of Jacob who have t from sin," .... Is 59:20
But they t against him and made .... Is 63:10
because you have t away from us .... Is 64:7
accept people who t against me, ... Is 65:2
hated you and t against you .... Is 66:5
The leaders t against me. .... Je 2:8
They have t away from me, the .... Je 2:13
they have t their backs to me. .... Je 2:27
All of you have t against me," .... Je 2:29
that you t against the LORD your .... Je 3:13
the LORD has not t away from us. .... Je 4:8
because Judah t against me,' " .... Je 4:17
stubborn and have t against me. .... Je 5:23
They have t aside and gone away .... Je 5:23
houses will be t over to others, ... Je 6:12
my people have t against me and .... Je 6:28
He has t his back on them, ... Je 7:29
the wrong way and not t back? .... Je 8:5
They have t my beautiful field .... Je 12:10
They have t my field into a .... Je 12:11
would have t the people from .... Je 23:22
They t their backs to me, not .... Je 32:33
I have t away from this city .... Je 33:5
did evil and t away from me, ... Je 33:8
'The LORD t away from the two .... Je 33:24
Then they t him over to Gedaliah .... Je 39:14
Before Jeremiah t to leave, ... Je 40:5
from Mizpah t around and ran to .... Je 41:14
Zedekiah t against the king of .... Je 52:3
her friends have t against her .... La 1:2
a net for my feet and t me back. .... La 1:13
He has t my strength into .... La 1:14
friends, but they t against me. .... La 1:19
He t his hand against me again .... La 3:3
have sinned and t against you, ... La 3:42
The LORD t loose all of his .... La 4:11
land has been t over to .... La 5:2
our dancing has t to sadness. .... La 5:15
That nation t against me and .... Eze 2:3
a people who have t against me. .... Eze 2:5
to me and t away from me .... Eze 6:9
With their backs to the Temple, ... Eze 8:16
The branches t toward the eagle, ... Eze 17:6
king of Judah t against the king .... Eze 17:15
But they t against me and .... Eze 20:8
the desert Israel t against me. .... Eze 20:13
But the children t against me. .... Eze 20:21
Cut anywhere your blade is t. .... Eze 21:16
me and t your back on me .... Eze 23:35
I t you into ashes on the ground .... Eze 28:18
because they t against me. .... Eze 39:23
So I t away from them and handed .... Eze 39:23
them and t away from them. .... Eze 39:24
and have his house t into a pile .... Da 3:29
His face t white, his knees .... Da 5:6
many people have t against God. .... Da 8:23
Then I t to the Lord God and .... Da 9:3
been wicked and t against you, ... Da 9:5
though we have t against you. .... Da 9:9
your teachings and have t away, ... Da 9:11
my face t white like a dead .... Da 10:8
because they t against me. .... Hos 7:13
agreement and have t against my .... Hos 8:1
their leaders have t against me. .... Hos 9:15
places will be t into ruins, ... Am 7:9
how they have t against God, ... Mic 3:8
and those who t away from the .... Zph 1:6

I had t everyone against his .... Zch 8:10
Rimmon will be t into a plain. .... Zch 14:10
Jesus t and saw the woman and .... Mt 9:22
Iscariot, who t against Jesus. .... Mt 10:4
Son of Man will be t over to the .... Mt 20:18
t over the tables of those who .... Mt 21:12
the man who has t against me." .... Mt 26:46
led him away, and t him over to .... Mt 27:2
knew that they t Jesus in to him .... Mt 27:18
who later t against Jesus. .... Mk 3:19
So he t around in the crowd and .... Mk 5:30
But Jesus t and looked at his .... Mk 8:33
Son of Man will be t over to the .... Mk 10:33
t over the tables of those who .... Mk 11:15
the man who has t against me." .... Mk 14:42
led him away, and t him over to .... Mk 15:1
priests had t Jesus in to him .... Mk 15:10
who later t Jesus over to his .... Lk 6:16
Then Jesus t toward the woman .... Lk 7:44
But Jesus t and scolded them. .... Lk 9:55
Then Jesus t to his followers .... Lk 10:23
and he t and said to them, ... Lk 14:25
He will be t over to those who .... Lk 18:32
Then the Lord t and looked .... Lk 22:61
But Jesus t and said to them, ... Lk 23:28
When Jesus t and saw them .... Jn 1:38
He t over the tables and .... Jn 2:15
at my table has t against me.' .... Jn 13:18
was the one who t against Jesus. .... Jn 18:2
the one who t against Jesus, ... Jn 18:5
The man who t me in to you is .... Jn 19:11
she t around and saw Jesus .... Jn 20:14
Mary t toward Jesus and said in .... Jn 20:16
t and saw that the follower .... Jn 21:20
But God t against them and did .... Ac 7:42
And now you have t against and .... Ac 7:52
saw him and t to the Lord. .... Ac 9:35
Then he t to the body and said, ... Ac 9:40
believed and t to the Lord. .... Ac 11:21
the others and t them against .... Ac 14:2
the other nations had t to God. .... Ac 15:3
so he t and said to the spirit, ... Ac 16:18
convinced and t away many people .... Ac 19:26
they t Paul over to him. .... Ac 23:33
All have t away. Together, ... Rm 3:12
When God t away from the Jews, ... Rm 11:15
But we have t away from secret 2Co 4:2
their hearts or t from their 2Co 12:21
things and t to useless talk. 1Ti 1:6
has t against the faith and is 1Ti 5:8
have already t away to follow 1Ti 5:15
the past when you t against God, ... Heb 3:8
past when you t against God." .... Heb 3:15
and I t away from them, ... Heb 8:9
t to see who was talking to me. .... Rev 1:12
When I t, I saw seven golden .... Rev 1:12

TURNING

wheels of the chariots from t, ... Ex 14:25
not forgive such t against him .... Ex 23:21
for sin, and for t against him, ... Ex 34:7
who are always t against me to .... Nu 17:10
t right or left until we have .... Nu 20:17
And now are you t against the .... Jos 22:18
they are t the city against you! .... Jdg 9:31
If you're t back to the LORD 1Sa 7:3
not done evil by t from my God. 2Sa 22:22
sins and for t against you. 1Ki 8:50
Are you t against the king?" .... Ne 2:19
to his sin by t against God. .... Job 34:37
done evil by t away from my God .... Ps 18:21
Like a door t back and forth on .... Pr 26:14
I see traitors t against you and .... Is 21:2

When you stop t against others, ... Is 33:1
the LORD, t away from our God, ... Is 59:13
of their evil in t away from me. .... Je 1:16
on yourselves by t away from the .... Je 2:17
they are all t against him. .... Je 9:2
everyone's face t white like a .... Je 30:6
would also go, without t. .... Eze 1:12
without t as they went. .... Eze 1:17
you are by t against the LORD .... Eze 21:24
of their sin in t to Egypt for .... Eze 29:16
there was a t away from God, ... Da 8:12
the t away from God that brings.............. Da 8:13
stop people from t against God; .... Da 9:24
of the North, t his pride back .... Da 11:18
T to the crowd that was .... Lk 7:9
to bless you by t each of you .... Ac 3:26
other people who are t to God. .... Ac 15:19
that you are t away so quickly .... Gal 1:6
come until the t away from God 2Th 2:3
God and about t away from those .... Heb 6:1

TURNS

who t against his father and .... Dt 21:18
is stubborn and t against us. .... Dt 21:20
commands or t against you will .... Jos 1:18
a dish and t it upside down. 2Ki 21:13
of our God t away from us." .... Ezr 10:14
Job's sons took t holding feasts .... Job 1:4
knowing it and t them over when .... Job 9:5
as captives and t judges into .... Job 12:17
when he t to the south, I cannot .... Job 23:9
the earth and t them into rain. .... Job 36:27
He t his lightning loose under .... Job 37:3
the lazy person t over and over .... Pr 26:14
Then it t around and repeats the .... Ec 1:6
crying! Moab t away in shame! .... Je 48:39
She groans and t away. .... La 1:8
And Judah t against God, the .... Hos 11:12
people yell, but no one t back. .... Nah 2:8
Roads with t should be made .... Lk 3:5
that one who t against the Son .... Lk 22:22

TURQUOISE

second must have t, a sapphire, ... Ex 28:18
in the second there was a t, ... Ex 39:11
I have given t gems of many 1Ch 29:2
will rebuild you with t stones, ... Is 54:11
They traded your goods for t, ... Eze 27:16
sapphire, t, and chrysolite. .... Eze 28:13

TUSKS

back ivory t and valuable black .... Eze 27:15

TWELFTH

and was plowing with the t team. 1Ki 19:19
Judah during the t year Joram 2Ki 8:25
during Ahaz's t year as king 2Ki 17:1
-seventh day of the t month. 2Ki 25:27
was Eliashib. The t was Jakim. 1Ch 24:12
T, twelve men were chosen from 1Ch 25:19
The t commander, for the twelfth 1Ch 27:15
for the t month, was Heldai 1Ch 27:15
In his t year as king, Josiah 2Ch 34:3
On the t day of the first month .... Ezr 8:31
first month of the t year of .... Est 3:7
So the t month, the month of .... Est 3:7
thirteenth day of the t month, ... Est 3:13
thirteenth day of the t month,.................. Est 8:12
thirteenth day of the t month, ... Est 9:1
twenty-fifth day of the t month. .... Je 52:31
on the t day of the month. .... Eze 29:1
It was in the t year of our .... Eze 32:1
captivity, in the t month, on .... Eze 32:1
It was in the t year of our .... Eze 32:17

It was in the t year of our .... Eze 33:21
jacinth, and the t was amethyst. .... Rev 21:20

TWELVE

served Kedorlaomer for t years, ... Ge 14:4
the father of t great leaders, ... Ge 17:20
about it. Jacob had t sons. .... Ge 35:22
We are ten of t brothers, ... Ge 42:13
that we were ten of t brothers— .... Ge 42:32
are the t tribes of Israel, ... Ge 49:28
there were t springs of water .... Ex 15:27
a new slave, or t ounces of .... Ex 21:32
set up t stones, one stone for .... Ex 24:4
each of the t tribes of Israel. .... Ex 24:4
names of the t sons of Israel .... Ex 28:9
of the t sons of Israel. .... Ex 28:12
There must be t jewels on the .... Ex 28:21
of one of the t tribes on each .... Ex 28:21
t pounds of liquid myrrh, half .... Ex 30:23
and t pounds of cassia. .... Ex 30:24
of the t sons of Israel. .... Ex 39:7
carved on these t jewels as a .... Ex 39:14
of one of the t tribes of Israel .... Ex 39:14
flour and bake t loaves of bread .... Le 24:5
old is about t ounces of silver. .... Le 27:4
and the t leaders of Israel, ... Nu 1:44
six covered carts and t oxen— .... Nu 7:3
t silver plates, twelve silver..................... Nu 7:84
silver plates, t silver bowls, ... Nu 7:84
silver bowls, and t gold dishes. .... Nu 7:84
The t gold dishes filled with .... Nu 7:86
the burnt offering was t bulls, ... Nu 7:87
was twelve bulls, t male sheep, ... Nu 7:87
and t male lambs a year old. .... Nu 7:87
and there were t male goats for .... Nu 7:87
Israel and get t walking sticks .... Nu 17:2
Each of the t leaders gave him a.............. Nu 17:6
give an offering of t bulls, ... Nu 29:17
So t thousand men got ready for .... Nu 31:5
there were t springs of water .... Nu 33:9
so I chose t of your men, one .... Dt 1:23
Now choose t men from among you, ... Jos 3:12
each of the t tribes of Israel. .... Jos 3:12
Choose t men from among the .... Jos 4:2
Tell them to get t rocks from .... Jos 4:3
he called the t men together .... Jos 4:4
Joshua and carried t rocks from.............. Jos 4:8
for each of the t tribes of .... Jos 4:8
Joshua also put t rocks in the .... Jos 4:9
with them the t rocks taken .... Jos 4:20
Ai died that day, t thousand men .... Jos 8:25
among the t tribes to be their .... Jos 12:7
There were t towns and all their.............. Jos 18:24
There were t towns and their .... Jos 19:15
Merari were given t towns in the .... Jos 21:7
Merarite family groups was t.................. Jos 21:40
his slave woman into t parts, ... Jdg 19:29
Israelites sent t thousand .... Jdg 21:10
t from the people of Benjamin 2Sa 2:15
of Saul, and t from David's men.............. 2Sa 2:15
thousand men and t thousand men 2Sa 10:6
Let me choose t thousand men and 2Sa 17:1
Solomon placed t governors over 1Ki 4:7
the names of the t governors: 1Ki 4:8
horses and t thousand horses. 1Ki 4:26
Others were t feet long. 1Ki 7:10
on the backs of t bronze bulls.................. 1Ki 7:25
bowl with t bulls under it; 1Ki 7:44
T lions stood on the six steps, ... 1Ki 10:20
chariots and t thousand horses. 1Ki 10:26
coat and tore it into t pieces. 1Ki 11:30
Omri ruled Israel for t years, ... 1Ki 16:23
He took t stones, one stone for 1Ki 18:31

stone for each of the t tribes, ... 1Ki 18:31
He owned t teams of oxen and was 1Ki 19:19
And Joram ruled t years. 2Ki 3:1
Manasseh was t years old when he 2Ki 21:1
group received t towns from the 1Ch 6:63
two hundred t men were chosen to 1Ch 9:22
were one hundred t people from............. 1Ch 15:10
t men were chosen from Gedaliah, ... 1Ch 25:9
t men were chosen from Zaccur, ... 1Ch 25:10
t men were chosen from Izri, ... 1Ch 25:11
t men were chosen from Nethaniah, ... 1Ch 25:12
t men were chosen from Bukkiah, ... 1Ch 25:13
t men were chosen from Jesarelah, ... 1Ch 25:14
t men were chosen from Jeshaiah, ... 1Ch 25:15
t men were chosen from Mattaniah, ... 1Ch 25:16
t men were chosen from Shimei, ... 1Ch 25:17
t men were chosen from Azarel,............. 1Ch 25:18
t men were chosen from Hashabiah, ... 1Ch 25:19
t men were chosen from Shubael, ... 1Ch 25:20
t men were chosen from 1Ch 25:21
t men were chosen from Jerimoth, ... 1Ch 25:22
t men were chosen from Hananiah, ... 1Ch 25:23
t men were chosen from 1Ch 25:24
t men were chosen from Hanani, ... 1Ch 25:25
t men were chosen from Mallothi, ... 1Ch 25:26
t men were chosen from Eliathah, ... 1Ch 25:27
t men were chosen from Hothir, ... 1Ch 25:28
t men were chosen from Giddalti, ... 1Ch 25:29
t men were chosen from Mahazioth, ... 1Ch 25:30
t men were chosen from 1Ch 25:31
chariots and t thousand horses. 2Ch 1:14
on the backs of t bronze bulls................. 2Ch 4:4
bowl with t bulls under it; 2Ch 4:15
T lions stood on the six steps,................ 2Ch 9:19
and he had t thousand horses. 2Ch 9:25
Shishak had t hundred chariots 2Ch 12:3
Manasseh was t years old when he 2Ch 33:1
they offered t male goats, ... Ezr 6:17
Then I chose t of the priests .... Ezr 8:24
gave them to the t priests I had .... Ezr 8:25
They sacrificed t bulls for all .... Ezr 8:35
there were t male goats. .... Ezr 8:35
governor of Judah for t years, ... Ne 5:14
had to complete t months of .... Est 2:12
and defeated t thousand Edomites .... Ps 59:17
the Sea with the t bronze bulls .... Je 52:20
each more than t feet thick. .... Eze 41:3
among the t tribes of Israel..................... Eze 47:13
T months later as he was walking .... Da 4:29
bleeding for t years came behind .... Mt 9:20
Jesus called his t apostles .... Mt 10:1
are the names of the t apostles: .... Mt 10:2
Jesus sent out these t men with .... Mt 10:5
these things to his t followers, ... Mt 11:1
followers filled t baskets with................. Mt 14:20
me will also sit on t thrones, ... Mt 19:28
judging the t tribes of Israel. .... Mt 19:28
out again about t o'clock and .... Mt 20:5
he took his t followers aside .... Mt 20:17
Then one of the t apostles, ... Mt 26:14
the table with his t followers. .... Mt 26:20
one of the t apostles, came up .... Mt 26:47
me more than t armies of angels. .... Mt 26:53
Jesus chose t and called them, ... Mk 3:14
These are the t men he chose: .... Mk 3:16
the t apostles and others around .... Mk 4:10
had been bleeding for t years. .... Mk 5:25
walking. (She was t years old.) .... Mk 5:42
He called his t followers .... Mk 6:7
followers filled t baskets with................. Mk 6:43
They answered, "T." .... Mk 8:19
called the t apostles to him. .... Mk 9:35
Jesus took the t apostles aside .... Mk 10:32

to Bethany with the t apostles. .... Mk 11:11
One of the t apostles, Judas .... Mk 14:10
went to that house with the t. .... Mk 14:17
is one of the t—the one who dips .... Mk 14:20
one of the t apostles, came up .... Mk 14:43
When he was t years old, they .... Lk 2:42
to him and chose t of them, ... Lk 6:13
The t apostles were with him,................ Lk 8:1
daughter, about t years old, was.............. Lk 8:42
had been bleeding for t years, ... Lk 8:43
Jesus called the t apostles .... Lk 9:1
the t apostles came to Jesus and............. Lk 9:12
gathered up, filling t baskets. .... Lk 9:17
Jesus took the t apostles aside .... Lk 18:31
one of Jesus' t apostles. .... Lk 22:3
judging the t tribes of Israel. .... Lk 22:30
Judas, one of the t apostles, ... Lk 22:47
It was about t o'clock noon. .... Jn 4:6
pieces and filled t baskets with .... Jn 6:13
Jesus asked the t followers, ... Jn 6:67
I chose all t of you, but one of .... Jn 6:70
was one of the t, but later he .... Jn 6:71
Are there not t hours in the .... Jn 11:9
was one of the t, was not with .... Jn 20:24
The t apostles called the whole .... Ac 6:2
the t ancestors of our people. .... Ac 7:8
There were about t people in .... Ac 19:7
in Jerusalem only t days ago. .... Ac 24:11
promise that the t tribes of our .... Ac 26:7
and then by the t apostles. 1Co 15:5
tribe of Judah t thousand were .... Rev 7:5
the tribe of Reuben t thousand, ... Rev 7:5
the tribe of Gad t thousand, ... Rev 7:5
the tribe of Asher t thousand,................ Rev 7:6
tribe of Naphtali t thousand, ... Rev 7:6
tribe of Manasseh t thousand, ... Rev 7:6
the tribe of Simeon t thousand, ... Rev 7:7
the tribe of Levi t thousand, ... Rev 7:7
tribe of Issachar t thousand, ... Rev 7:7
the tribe of Zebulun t thousand, ... Rev 7:8
the tribe of Joseph t thousand, ... Rev 7:8
tribe of Benjamin t thousand .... Rev 7:8
a crown of t stars was on her .... Rev 12:1
high wall with t gates with .... Rev 21:12
twelve gates with t angels at .... Rev 21:12
one of the t tribes of Israel................... Rev 21:12
were built on t foundation .... Rev 21:14
the names of the t apostles of................ Rev 21:14
The t gates were twelve pearls, ... Rev 21:21
The twelve gates were t pearls, ... Rev 21:21
produces fruit t times a year, ... Rev 22:2

TWENTIETH
Agreement on the t day of the .... Nu 10:11
During the t year Jeroboam son 1Ki 15:9
during the t year Jotham son 2Ki 15:30
The t was Jehezkel................................ 1Ch 24:16
T, twelve men were chosen from 1Ch 25:27
It was the t day of the ninth .... Ezr 10:9
month of Kislev in the t year,................ Ne 1:1
Nisan in the t year Artaxerxes .... Ne 2:1
of Judah in the t year of King................ Ne 5:14

TWENTY
it was more than t feet above .... Ge 7:20
prepare t quarts of fine flour, ... Ge 18:6
what if there are t good people .... Ge 18:31
If I find t there, I will not .... Ge 18:31
worked for you now for t years. .... Ge 31:38
a slave for you for t years— .... Ge 31:41
female goats and t male goats, ... Ge 32:14
female sheep and t male sheep, ... Ge 32:14
and ten bulls, t female donkeys, ... Ge 32:15
Make t frames for the south side .... Ex 26:18

Make t more frames for the north .... Ex 26:20
and bands on t bronze posts with .... Ex 27:10
posts with t bronze bases. .... Ex 27:10
and bands on t bronze posts with .... Ex 27:11
posts with t bronze bases. .... Ex 27:11
is counted and is t years old or .... Ex 30:14
They made t frames for the south .... Ex 36:23
that went under the t frames. .... Ex 36:24
They also made t frames for the.............. Ex 36:25
placed on t bronze posts with .... Ex 38:10
posts with t bronze bases. .... Ex 38:10
and bands on t posts with twenty .... Ex 38:11
posts with t bronze bases. .... Ex 38:11
All the men t years old or older .... Ex 38:26
price for a man t to sixty years .... Le 27:3
for a woman t to sixty years .... Le 27:4
for a man five to t years old is .... Le 27:5
count every man t years old or .... Nu 1:3
the men who were t years old or .... Nu 1:18
all the men t years old or older .... Nu 1:20
all the men t years old or older .... Nu 1:22
all the men t years old or older .... Nu 1:24
all the men t years old or older .... Nu 1:26
all the men t years old or older .... Nu 1:28
all the men t years old or older .... Nu 1:30
all the men t years old or older .... Nu 1:32
all the men t years old or older .... Nu 1:34
all the men t years old or older .... Nu 1:36
all the men t years old or older .... Nu 1:38
all the men t years old or older .... Nu 1:40
all the men t years old or older .... Nu 1:42
man of Israel t years old or..................... Nu 1:45
two, five, ten, or even t days, ... Nu 11:19
one of you who is t years old or .... Nu 14:29
the men who are t years old or .... Nu 26:2
Count the men t years old or .... Nu 26:4
Egypt and who are t years old or .... Nu 32:11
am now one hundred t years old, ... Dt 31:2
was one hundred t years old when .... Dt 34:7
people of Israel for t years,..................... Jdg 4:3
and with t quarts of flour, ... Jdg 6:19
one hundred t thousand soldiers .... Jdg 8:10
and t cities as far as the city .... Jdg 11:33
Israel for t years in the days .... Jdg 15:20
people of Israel for t years..................... Jdg 16:31
a long time—t years in all. 1Sa 7:2
killed about t Philistines over 1Sa 14:14
Abner came with t men to David 2Sa 3:20
and t thousand foot soldiers. 2Sa 8:4
had fifteen sons and t servants. 2Sa 9:10
So they hired t thousand Aramean........... 2Sa 10:6
died that day—t thousand men. 2Sa 18:7
fifteen sons and t servants with 2Sa 19:17
After nine months and t days, ... 2Sa 24:8
t cows that were raised in the................. 1Ki 4:23
and one hundred t thousand sheep 1Ki 8:63
By the end of t years, King..................... 1Ki 9:10
Solomon gave t towns in Galilee 1Ki 9:11
bringing him t loaves of barley 2Ki 4:42
of Judah. Pekah ruled t years, ... 2Ki 15:27
Ahaz was t years old when he 2Ki 16:2
family leaders and t thousand 1Ch 7:9
There were t thousand eight 1Ch 12:30
were one hundred t thousand.................. 1Ch 12:37
were one hundred t people from.............. 1Ch 15:5
were two hundred t people from 1Ch 15:6
and t thousand foot soldiers. 1Ch 18:4
person who was t years old or 1Ch 23:24
Levites who were t years old and 1Ch 23:27
the men who were t years old and 1Ch 27:23
two hundred t thousand pounds.............. 1Ch 29:4
five hundred t thousand pounds.............. 1Ch 29:4
one hundred t priests who blew 2Ch 5:12

one hundred t thousand sheep. 2Ch 7:5
By the end of t years, Solomon 2Ch 8:1
the men who were t years old and 2Ch 25:5
Ahaz was t years old when he 2Ch 28:1
one hundred t thousand brave 2Ch 28:6
Levites t years old and older 2Ch 31:17
They chose Levites t years old .... Ezr 3:8
In all there were t men. .... Ezr 8:19
two hundred t of the Temple .... Ezr 8:20
I gave them t gold bowls that .... Ezr 8:27
shekel will be worth t gerahs, ... Eze 45:12
one hundred t governors who................. Da 6:1
one hundred t thousand people .... Jnh 4:11
expecting to find t basketfuls,............... Hag 2:16
jarfuls, but only t were there. .... Hag 2:16
king who has t thousand soldiers .... Lk 14:31
jar held about t or thirty .... Jn 2:6
about one hundred t of them .... Ac 1:15
was one hundred t feet deep. .... Ac 27:28

TWENTY-EIGHT
give you t pounds of silver...................... Jdg 16:5
curse about the t pounds of .... Jdg 17:2
gave the t pounds of silver .... Jdg 17:3
Israel in Samaria for t years. 2Ki 10:36
were t thousand six hundred 1Ch 12:35
the father of t sons and sixty 2Ch 11:21
son of Bebai, with t men. .... Ezr 8:11

TWENTY-FIFTH
on the t day of the month .... Ne 6:15
free on the t day of the twelfth .... Je 52:31
It was the t year of our .... Eze 40:1

TWENTY-FIRST
until the evening of the t day. .... Ex 12:18
The t was Jakin. 1Ch 24:17
T, twelve men were chosen from 1Ch 25:28
On the t day of the seventh .... Hag 2:1

TWENTY-FIVE
brother Abraham t pounds of .... Ge 20:16
Everyone t years old or older .... Nu 8:24
had to pay t pounds of silver .... Sng 8:11
the t pounds of silver are for .... Sng 8:12
are worth about t pounds of .... Is 7:23
There I saw about t men at the .... Eze 8:16
saw t men where the gate opens, ... Eze 11:1

TWENTY-FOUR
t fingers and toes in all. 1Ch 20:6
t thousand Levites will direct 1Ch 23:4
division had t thousand men. 1Ch 27:1
there were t other thrones .... Rev 4:4
thrones with t elders sitting .... Rev 4:4
the t elders bow down before .... Rev 4:10
and the t elders bowed down .... Rev 5:8
Then the t elders, who sit on .... Rev 11:16
Then the t elders and the four .... Rev 19:4

TWENTY-FOURTH
The t was Maaziah............................... 1Ch 24:18
T, twelve men were chosen from 1Ch 25:31
On the t day of that same month, ... Ne 9:1
On the t day of the first month, ... Da 10:4
began on the t day of the sixth .... Hag 1:15
On the t day of the ninth month .... Hag 2:10
'It is the t day of the ninth .... Hag 2:18
Haggai on the t day of the month .... Hag 2:20
It was on the t day of the .... Zch 1:7

TWENTY-NINE
There were t towns and their .... Jos 15:32
thousand silver dishes, t pans, ... Ezr 1:9

TWENTY-ONE
Zedekiah was t years old when he............ 2Ki 24:18

TWENTY-SECOND

The t was Gamul. 1Ch 24:17
T, twelve men were chosen from 1Ch 25:29

TWENTY-SEVEN

to be one hundred t years old. .... Ge 23:1
inches wide, and t inches high. .... Ex 37:10
one t feet tall and eighteen 1Ki 7:15
pillars was about t feet high, ... Je 52:21

TWENTY-SEVENTH

By the t day of the second month .... Ge 8:14
Elah during Asa's t year as king 1Ki 16:10
during Asa's t year as king of................. 1Ki 16:15
during Jeroboam's t year as king 2Ki 15:1
of prison on the t day of the 2Ki 25:27
It was the t year of our .... Eze 29:17

TWENTY-SIX

they had t thousand soldiers 1Ch 7:40
There were t hundred leaders................. 2Ch 26:12
gave the priests t hundred lambs 2Ch 35:8

TWENTY-SIXTH

during Asa's t year as king..................... 1Ki 16:8

TWENTY-THIRD

by the t year Joash was king, ... 2Ki 12:6
during the t year Joash son 2Ki 13:1
The t was Delaiah. 1Ch 24:18
T, twelve men were chosen from 1Ch 25:30
the t day of the seventh month 2Ch 7:10
This was the t day of the third .... Est 8:9
in Nebuchadnezzar's t year, ... Je 52:30

TWENTY-THREE

In one day t thousand of them 1Co 10:8

TWENTY-TWO

David killed t thousand of them. 2Sa 8:5

TWICE

people gathered t as much food— .... Ex 16:22
hit the rock t with his stick. .... Nu 20:11
LORD gave Job t as much as he.............. Job 42:10
the rooster crows t you will say .... Mk 14:30
Before the rooster crows t, ... Mk 14:72
I fast t a week, and I give .... Lk 18:12
first so you could be blessed t. 2Co 1:15
the ground. So they are t dead. .... Jud 1:12
Pay her back t as much as she .... Rev 18:6
for her that is t as strong as .... Rev 18:6

TWIG

cut off a small t from the top .... Eze 17:22

TWIGS

fire that burns t, like a fire .... Is 64:2

TWILIGHT

tell them, 'At t you will eat .... Ex 16:12
the first month, beginning at t. .... Le 23:5
day of this month at t;.......................... Nu 9:3
of Sinai at t on the fourteenth................ Nu 9:5
celebrate it at t on the .... Nu 9:11
morning and the other lamb at t. .... Nu 28:4
Offer the second lamb at t. .... Nu 28:8
So they got up at t and went to 2Ki 7:5
got up and ran away in the t, ... 2Ki 7:7
It was the t of the evening; .... Pr 7:9

TWIN

Each one has a t, and none of .... Sng 4:2
each one has a t, and none of................ Sng 6:6

TWINS

came, Rebekah gave birth to t. .... Ge 25:24
birth, there were t in her body. .... Ge 38:27
two fawns, like t of a gazelle, ... Sng 4:5
two fawns, like t of a gazelle. .... Sng 7:3

TWIST

God does not t justice; .... Job 8:3
will never t what is right. .... Job 34:12
All day long they t my words;................ Ps 56:5
and made all their backs t. .... Eze 29:7
fairness and t what is right. .... Mic 3:9
will rise up and t the truth and .... Ac 20:30

TWISTED

of pure gold, t together like a .... Ex 28:14
of pure gold, t together like .... Ex 28:22
of pure gold, t together like a .... Ex 39:15
'I sinned and t what was right, ... Job 33:27

TWISTING

and t noses makes them bleed, ... Pr 30:33

TWO-AND-A-HALF

given the t tribes their land.................... Jos 14:3

TWO-EDGED

with their t swords in their .... Ps 149:6
causing you pain like a t sword. .... Pr 5:4

TWO-FIFTHS

which weighs t of an ounce. .... Ex 30:13
it weighs t of an ounce. .... Le 27:25
Place, which is t of an ounce. .... Nu 3:47
will be sold for t of an ounce 2Ki 7:1
will be sold for t of an ounce 2Ki 7:1
were sold for t of an ounce 2Ki 7:16
were sold for t of an ounce 2Ki 7:16
will each sell for t of an ounce 2Ki 7:18

TWO-THIRDS

offering and t of a pint of .... Le 14:10
He must also take t of a pint of .... Le 14:21
will drink about t of a quart of .... Eze 4:11
T of the people through all the .... Zch 13:8

TYCHICUS

T and Trophimus, two men from .... Ac 20:4
sending to you T, our brother .... Eph 6:21
T is my dear brother in Christ .... Col 4:7
I sent T to Ephesus.............................. 2Ti 4:12
When I send Artemas or T to you, ... Tit 3:12

TYING

in the field t bundles of wheat .... Ge 37:7
person is like t a stone in a................... Pr 26:8
as the soldiers were t him up,................ Ac 22:25

TYRANNUS

to the school of a man named T............. Ac 19:9

TYRE

to the strong, walled city of T. .... Jos 19:29
of the city of T sent messengers 2Sa 5:11

U

UCAL

is his message to Ithiel and U: .... Pr 30:1

UEL

of Bani: Maadai, Amram, U, ... Ezr 10:34

UGLY

river, but they were thin and u. .... Ge 41:3
seven thin and u cows ate the................ Ge 41:4
that were thin and lean and u—............. Ge 41:19
these thin and u cows ate the .... Ge 41:20
just as thin and u as they did .... Ge 41:21
were thin and u and were burned .... Ge 41:23
seven thin and u cows stand for .... Ge 41:27
Then u and painful sores came .... Rev 16:2

ULAI

I was standing by the U Canal .... Da 8:2
voice calling from the U Canal: .... Da 8:16

ULAM

Shereah's sons were U and Rakem. 1Ch 7:16
first son was U, his second was 1Ch 8:39

ULAM'S

U son was Bedan. These were the 1Ch 7:17
U sons were mighty warriors and 1Ch 8:40

ULLA'S

U sons were Arah, Hanniel, and.............. 1Ch 7:39

UMMAH

U, Aphek, and Rehob. There were .... Jos 19:30

UNABLE

is poor and u to afford these .... Le 14:21
make your body u to give birth .... Nu 5:21
make your body u to give birth .... Nu 5:21
had made her u to have children. 1Sa 1:6
You made us u to walk straight, ... Ps 60:3
became weak and u to breathe. .... Je 15:9
their women u to have children .... Hos 9:14
makes people u to hear or speak .... Mk 9:25
to them and remained u to speak. .... Lk 1:22
the man who had been u to speak,........... Lk 11:14
we were u to help ourselves, ... Rm 5:6
make the wise u to understand." 1Co 1:19

UNAFRAID

you want to be u of the rulers? .... Rm 13:3

UNANSWERED

Should these words go u? .... Job 11:2

UNBELIEVER

Stop being an u and believe." .... Jn 20:27

UNBELIEVERS

and you do this in front of u! 1Co 6:6

UNBELIEVING

u heart that will turn you away .... Heb 3:12

UNBORN

the u baby inside her jumped, ... Lk 1:41

UNBOTHERED

and be satisfied, u by trouble.................. Pr 19:23

UNCERTAIN

in God, not in their u riches. 1Ti 6:17

UNCIRCUMCISED

Who does this u Philistine think.............. 1Sa 17:26
This u Philistine will be like 1Sa 17:36
Then those u men won't make fun 1Sa 31:4
if a man is circumcised or u. .... Gal 6:15
the people the Jews call "u." .... Eph 2:11
who call you "u" call themselves .... Eph 2:11

UNCLE

Aaron's u Uzziel had two sons .... Le 10:4
wife, he has shamed his u. .... Le 20:20
His u, his uncle's son, or any .... Le 25:49
Saul's u asked him and his 1Sa 10:14
Saul's u asked, "Please tell me. 1Sa 10:15
not tell his u what Samuel had 1Sa 10:16
was Abner son of Ner, Saul's u. 1Sa 14:50
Jehoiachin's u, king in 2Ki 24:17
was David's u, and he advised 1Ch 27:32
Jehoiachin's u Zedekiah the king 2Ch 36:10
Mordecai's u, who had been .... Est 2:15
son of your u Shallum, will come .... Je 32:7

UNCLE'S

relations with his u wife,...................... Le 20:20
That man and his u wife will die .... Le 20:20
His uncle, his u son, or any one .... Le 25:49

UNCLEAN

of every kind of u animal. .... Ge 7:2
someone might touch something u, ... Le 5:2
dead body of an u wild animal .... Le 5:2
If anyone touches something u— .... Le 7:21

clean separate from what is u. .... Le 10:10
a split hoof; it is u for you. .... Le 11:4
between u animals and clean .... Le 11:47
will become u for seven days,.................. Le 12:2
mother will be u for two weeks, ... Le 12:5
announce that the person is u; .... Le 13:8
by shouting, 'U, unclean!' .... Le 13:45
on during this time will be u, ... Le 15:20
Pigs are also u for you; .... Dt 14:8
beer or eat anything that is u,.............. Jdg 13:7
or my hands have been made u,............ Job 31:7
Touch nothing that is u. .... Is 52:11
their mouths that makes them u. .... Mt 15:11
from inside and make people u." .... Mk 7:23
not want to make themselves u; .... Jn 18:28
eaten food that is unholy or u." .... Ac 10:14
call any person 'unholy' or 'u.' .... Ac 10:28
anything that is unholy or u.' .... Ac 11:8
which makes it u), any kind of .... Ac 15:20
and has made this holy place u!" .... Ac 21:28
was trying to make the Temple u, ... Ac 24:6
nothing that is u, and I will.................... 2Co 6:17
that makes body or soul u. 2Co 7:1
on the people who are u,........................ Heb 9:13
for every u bird and unclean .... Rev 18:2
every unclean bird and u beast. .... Rev 18:2
Nothing u and no one who does.............. Rev 21:27
Let whoever is u continue to be .... Rev 22:11
is unclean continue to be u. .... Rev 22:11

UNCLEANNESS

Someone might touch human u— .... Le 5:3
something unclean—u that comes .... Le 7:21
the land with u from one end to .... Ezr 9:11
is how I will get rid of your u. .... Eze 22:15
like a woman's u in her time .... Eze 36:17
from all your u and your idols. .... Eze 36:25
I will save you from all your u. .... Eze 36:29
of their u and their sins, ... Eze 39:24
them of their sin and u." .... Zch 13:1
and the u of her sexual sin. .... Rev 17:4

UNCLEAR

my purpose u by saying things .... Job 38:2
made my purpose u by saying .... Job 42:3
The law is only an u picture of .... Heb 10:1

UNCLES

Gideon went to his u in the city .... Jdg 9:1
He said to his u and all of his .... Jdg 9:2
Abimelech's u spoke to all the .... Jdg 9:3

UNCOMBED

clothes or leaving your hair u. .... Le 10:6
he must let his hair stay u, ... Le 13:45
his hair go u or tearing his .... Le 21:10

UNCONTROLLED

But you are u like water, so you .... Ge 49:4
and beer make people loud and u; .... Pr 20:1
God, people are u, but those who .... Pr 29:18

UNCOVER

U your legs and cross the rivers. .... Is 47:2
he will u your evil. .... La 4:22

UNCOVERED

God has u our guilt, so all of .... Ge 44:16
destruction is u before him. .... Job 26:6
me, and you have u yourself. .... Is 57:8
You u your body in your sexual .... Eze 16:36
before your evil was u. .... Eze 16:57
u your bow and commanded many .... Hab 3:9
with her head u brings shame to 1Co 11:5
to pray to God with her head u? 1Co 11:13

UNCOVERS

He u the deep things of darkness .... Job 12:22

UNCUT
It was made from u stones;......................Jos 8:31

UNDERCLOTHES
for them linen u to cover them ....Ex 28:42
wear these u when they enter....................Ex 28:43
headbands, and u of fine linen. ....Ex 39:28
robe and linen u next to his ....Le 6:10
with the linen u next to his ....Le 16:4
on their heads and linen u. ....Eze 44:18

UNDERFOOT
people, will be trampled u. ....Is 28:3

UNDERGROUND
of that year the u springs split ....Ge 7:11
The u springs stopped flowing, ...Ge 8:2
put the deep u springs in place ....Pr 8:28

UNDERSIDE
The u of its body is like broken ....Job 41:30

UNDERSTAND
not be able to u each other." ....Ge 11:7
You won't u their language, ...Dt 28:49
could listen and u had gathered...............Ne 8:2
everyone who could listen and u. ....Ne 8:3
Who could u God's thundering ....Job 26:14
I spoke of things I did not u; ....Job 42:3
Don't the wicked u? ....Ps 14:4
Don't the wicked u? ....Ps 53:4
nothing. You don't u. You walk ....Ps 82:5
it is more than I can u. ....Ps 139:6
Then anyone can u wise words and ....Pr 1:6
Then you will u respect for the ....Pr 2:5
for me, really four I don't u: ....Pr 30:18
and listen, but you will not u. ....Is 6:9
they might really u what they.................Is 6:10
you would u that I am the true ....Is 43:10
doing. They don't u! It is as if ....Is 44:18
Daniel could also u visions and ....Da 1:17
help the others u what is.......................Da 11:33
I did not really u, so I asked, ...Da 12:8
people will not u these things, ...Da 12:10
take away their ability to u. ....Hos 4:11
but they did not u that I had ....Hos 11:3
they might really u what they...............Mt 13:15
this should u what it means. ....Mt 24:15
Don't you u this story? ....Mk 4:13
this should u what it means. ....Mk 13:14
I don't know or u what you are ....Mk 14:68
The people did not u that he was ....Jn 8:27
You don't u what I say, because ....Jn 8:43
You don't u now what I am doing, ...Jn 13:7
"Do you u what you are reading?"...........Ac 8:30
I may u all the secret things of 1Co 13:2
five words I u in order to teach 1Co 14:19
They do not u, and they know ....Eph 4:18
is so great we cannot u it, ...Php 4:7
is by faith we u that the whole ....Heb 11:3
in Paul's letters are hard to u,...............2Pe 3:16
against things they do not u. ....Jud 1:10
You need a wise mind to u this. ....Rev 17:9

UNDERSTANDING
them the wisdom and u to do all ....Ex 36:1
you wisdom and u that is greater 1Ki 3:12
wise, and long life brings u. ....Job 12:12
from, and where does u live? ....Job 28:20
who obey his orders have good u. ....Ps 111:10
I have more u than the elders, ...Ps 119:100
wisdom and u for the foolish ....Ps 119:130
set your mind on u..............................Pr 2:2
and don't depend on your own u. ....Pr 3:5
wisdom, the one who gets u. ....Pr 3:13
the sky in place, using his u. ....Pr 3:19
everything you have, get u....................Pr 4:7

and make u your closest friend. ....Pr 7:4
Wisdom and u will keep you away ....Pr 7:5
and u begins with knowing the ....Pr 9:10
U is like a fountain which gives ....Pr 16:22
a person with u gets knowledge; ....Pr 18:15
is no wisdom, u, or advice that ....Pr 21:30
will give him wisdom and u, ...Is 11:2
and showed him the way to u? ....Is 40:14
they showed much wisdom and u. ....Da 1:20
because his u of the dream ....Da 4:19
amazed at his u and answers...................Lk 2:47
u that God had called us to tell ....Ac 16:10
there without u cannot say amen 1Co 14:16
God, with full wisdom and u, ...Eph 1:8
have greater u in your heart so ....Eph 1:18
knowledge and u with your love; ....Php 1:9
great wisdom and u in spiritual ....Col 1:9
they may be rich in their u......................Col 2:2
you who are truly wise and u? ....Jam 3:13
with your wives in an u way, ...1Pe 3:7
be in agreement, u each other, ...1Pe 3:8
has given us u so that we can 1Jn 5:20
the one who has u find the ....Rev 13:18

UNDERSTANDS
has not given you a mind that u; ....Dt 29:4
that you give me a heart that u, ...1Ki 3:9
He u everything you think.......................1Ch 28:9
Only God u the way to wisdom, ...Job 28:23
No one u how God spreads out the ....Job 36:29
hearts and u everything they ....Ps 33:15
no one u what his life is all.....................Pr 20:24
are taken away, but no one u...................Is 57:1
who hears the teaching and u it. ....Mt 13:23
There is no one who u. ....Rm 3:11
to God. No one u them; they are...............1Co 14:2
is full of pride and u nothing, ...1Ti 6:4

UNDERSTOOD
finally u what they had been ....Ne 8:12
to me and have not u my ways.' ....Ps 95:10
me; you have not u. Even long ....Is 48:8
After I u, I beat my breast with ....Je 31:19
a true message that Daniel u. ....Da 10:1
If you u them, you would not ....Mt 12:7
the followers u that Jesus was ....Mt 16:12
the followers u that Jesus said ....Mt 17:13
at the table u why Jesus said ....Jn 13:28
nor your leaders u what you were ....Ac 3:17
and they u that these men had no ....Ac 4:13
Felix already u much about the ....Ac 24:22
the rulers of this world u it. 1Co 2:8
u that God had given me this ....Gal 2:9
Good News and u the truth about ....Col 1:6
to me and have not u my ways.' ....Heb 3:10
never really u Christ and has 1Jn 3:6

UNDO
unfairly and u their chains. ....Is 58:6
should not u his circumcision. 1Co 7:18

UNEDUCATED
They make the u wise and give ....Pr 1:4
You who are u, seek wisdom. ....Pr 8:5
She says to those who are u, ...Pr 9:4
She says to those who are u, ...Pr 9:16

UNENDING
and be glad even in this u pain, ...Job 6:10

UNFAIR
You must not be u to a poor ....Ex 23:6
Do not be u to a foreigner or an...............Dt 24:17
cursed who is u to foreigners,...............Dt 27:19
those who are u are silenced. ....Job 5:16
mind; do not be u; think again, ...Job 6:29
If I have been u to my male and ....Job 31:13

U

Would you say that I am **u?**.......................Job 40:8
or to be **u** to the innocent ....Pr 18:5
This is also **u** and useless. ....Ec 2:21
be for those who make **u** laws, ...Is 10:1
and you are **u** to your workers. ....Is 58:3
to whom you are **u** and stop their ....Is 58:6
You take **u** interest and profits ....Eze 22:12
those who are **u** to foreigners, ...Mal 3:5
Listen to what the **u** judge said. ....Lk 18:6
about this? Is God **u?** In no way................Rm 9:14
to suffer even when it is **u,** 1Pe 2:19

UNFAIRLY
because he has treated her **u.** ....Ex 21:8
Do not judge **u** or take sides. ....Dt 16:19
taken anything **u** from anyone." 1Sa 12:4
You should not **u** choose his side ....Job 13:8
scold you if you **u** took one....................Job 13:10
right and never punishes **u.** ....Job 37:23
who refuses to take money **u,** ....Is 33:15
Men took him away roughly and **u.** ....Is 53:8
put in prison **u** and undo their ....Is 58:6
take each other to court **u,** ....Is 59:4
is treated **u** before the Most ....La 3:35
people's money **u** and robbed his ....Eze 18:18
those who have been treated **u** ....Lk 4:18
He was shamed and was treated **u.** ....Ac 8:33

UNFAITHFUL
him in being **u** to me by ....Le 20:5
many men to be **u** to their wives. ....Pr 23:28
sexually **u,** not being pure, ...Gal 5:19

UNFAITHFULNESS
his sins, his **u,** the places he 2Ch 33:19
because of the **u** of the captives ....Ezr 9:4
sad about the **u** of the captives ....Ezr 10:6

UNFIT
must not make my Holy Place **u.** ....Le 21:23

UNFORGETTABLE
His miracles are **u.** ....Ps 111:4

UNFRIENDLY
U people are selfish and hate ....Pr 18:1

UNGODLY
are unholy and **u,** who kill their 1Ti 1:9

UNGRATEFUL
who are **u** and full of sin. ....Lk 6:35

UNHAPPY
Why do you look so **u?** ....Ge 4:6
"Why do you look so **u** today?" ....Ge 40:7
given to those who are so **u?** ....Job 3:20
will complain because I am so **u.** ....Job 7:11
I will speak because I am so **u.** ....Job 10:1
person dies with an **u** heart, ...Job 21:25
the Almighty, who has made me **u,** ....Job 27:2
was **u** and angry, and I felt the ....Eze 3:14
But this made Jonah very **u,** ....Jnh 4:1
very troubled and **u** in my heart, ...2Co 2:4

UNHOLY
but the leaders made it **u.** 2Ch 36:14
land was made **u** by their blood...............Ps 106:38
people became **u** by their sins; ....Ps 106:39
I will make your holy rulers **u.** ....Is 43:28
between holy and **u** things,....................Eze 22:26
food that is **u** or unclean." ....Ac 10:14
clean, so don't call them **u!"** ....Ac 10:15
any person 'u' or 'unclean.'......................Ac 10:28
anything that is **u** or unclean.' ....Ac 11:8
clean, so don't call them **u.'**...................Ac 11:9
sinful, who are **u** and ungodly, ...1Ti 1:9

UNIFORM
was wearing his **u,** and at his 2Sa 20:8
battle and every **u** stained with ....Is 9:5

UNIFORMS
wore blue **u.** They were all ....Eze 23:6
all soldiers in beautiful **u—**....................Eze 23:12
will be dressed in beautiful **u.**.................Eze 38:4

UNINVITED
Who would dare to come to me **u?"** ....Je 30:21

UNION
one Pleasant and the other **U,**.................Zch 11:7
second stick, named **U,** to break...............Zch 11:14

UNITE
I will help you **u** all Israel."....................2Sa 3:12

UNITED
mother and be **u** with his wife, ...Ge 2:24
these people are **u,** all speaking ....Ge 11:6
who were attacked **u** their armies ....Ge 14:3
of Israel were **u** and gathered.................Jdg 20:11
God **u** all the people of Judah.................2Ch 30:12
They are **u** in their plan. ....Ps 83:5
will not be **u** as one people. ....Da 2:43
mother and be **u** with his wife, ...Mt 19:5
mother and be **u** with his wife, ...Mk 10:7
believers were **u** in their hearts ....Ac 4:32
mother and be **u** with his wife, ...Eph 5:31

UNITY
you all together in perfect **u.** ....Col 3:14

UNKIND
but an **u** answer will cause more ....Pr 15:1

UNKINDLY
He asked **u,** "Where do you come ....Ge 42:7
of that land spoke **u** to us. ....Ge 42:30
if your father answers you **u?"** 1Sa 20:10
even more **u** than the people 2Sa 19:43

UNKNOWN
But now, **u** to you, Adonijah has...............1Ki 1:18

UNLAWFUL
are doing what is **u** to do on the..............Mt 12:2

UNLEAVENED
celebrate the Feast of **U** Bread, ...Ex 12:17
the Feast of **U** Bread in the way ....Ex 23:15
Celebrate the Feast of **U** Bread. ....Ex 34:18
day of the Feast of **U** Bread, ...Mt 26:17
and the Feast of **U** Bread. ....Mk 14:1
day of the Feast of **U** Bread when ....Mk 14:12
time for the Feast of **U** Bread,.................Lk 22:1
The Day of **U** Bread came when the ....Lk 22:7
time of the Feast of **U** Bread. ....Ac 12:3
after the Feast of **U** Bread. ....Ac 20:6

UNLIKE
U his ancestor David, he did not 2Ki 16:2
U his ancestor David, he did not 2Ch 28:1

UNLOAD
needed to **u** its cargo there. ....Ac 21:3

UNLOADED
After Laban **u** the camels and ....Ge 24:32

UNLOCKED
got the key and **u** them and saw...............Jdg 3:25

UNMARRIED
u sister who is close to him....................Le 21:3
hundred young **u** women in Jabesh ....Jdg 21:12
He had four **u** daughters who had ....Ac 21:9
good for them to stay **u** as I am................1Co 7:8

UNMOVED
Zion, which sits **u** forever. ....Ps 125:1

UNNECESSARY
Who has **u** bruises?.............................Pr 23:29

UNNI
Jehiel, **U**, Eliab, Benaiah, ...1Ch 15:18
Jehiel, **U**, Eliab, Maaseiah, ...1Ch 15:20
and **U**, their relatives, ...Ne 12:9

UNPLOWED
Plow your **u** fields, and don't ....Je 4:3

UNPUNISHED
But you should not leave him **u**. 1Ki 2:9
and would not let my sin go **u**. ....Job 10:14
will not let the guilty go **u**. ....Nah 1:3

UNSANDALED
Israel as the Family of the **U**. ....Dt 25:10

UNSATISFIED
or who was **u** gathered around 1Sa 22:2

UNSEALED
and in his hand was an **u** letter. ....Ne 6:5

UNSEEN
things seen and **u**, all powers,..................Col 1:16

UNSELFISHLY
know I always served the Lord **u**, ...Ac 20:19

UNSHRUNK
sews a patch of **u** cloth over a ....Mt 9:16
sews a patch of **u** cloth over a ....Mk 2:21

UNSTAINED
who have kept their clothes **u**, ...Rev 3:4

UNSUITABLE
make them **u** for use in worship. ....Ex 20:25

UNWANTED
of your grave, like an **u** branch. ....Is 14:19
together, gather, you **u** people. ....Zph 2:1

UNWASHED
eating with **u** hands does not ....Mt 15:20

UNWILLING
were stubborn, **u**, and ....Ne 9:29
but they are **u** to help those who ....Mt 23:4

UNWISE
LORD, you foolish and **u** people. ....Dt 32:6

UNWORTHY
should say, 'We are **u** servants; ....Lk 17:10

UNWRITTEN
obey the **u** laws which have ....Mt 15:2
way required by their **u** laws. ....Mk 7:3
also follow many other **u** laws, ...Mk 7:4
obey the **u** laws which have ....Mk 7:5

UPHAZ
from Tarshish and gold from **U**, ...Je 10:9

UPPER
rings on the two **u** corners of ....Ex 39:16
grain—not even the **u** one—in ....Dt 24:6
gave her the **u** and lower springs ....Jdg 1:15
rebuilt the **U** Gate of the Temple...............2Ki 15:35
from the **u** pool on the road 2Ki 18:17
the direction of the **u** gate, ...Eze 9:2
The **u** rooms rested on the ledges ....Eze 41:6
The **u** ledge is also square, ...Eze 43:17
stomach and the **u** part of its ....Da 2:32
LORD builds his **u** rooms above ....Am 9:6
and on his **u** leg was written ....Rev 19:16

UPRIGHT
wood to make **u** frames for the ....Ex 26:15
to connect the **u** frames of the ....Ex 26:26
they made **u** frames of acacia.................Ex 36:20
to connect the **u** frames of the ....Ex 36:31

UPROAR
waves, and the **u** of the nations. ....Ps 65:7
Their **u** in the LORD's Temple was............La 2:7
So there was a great **u**. ....Ac 23:9

UPSIDE
a dish and turns it **u** down.......................2Ki 21:13
You turn justice **u** down, and you ....Am 5:7

UPSTAIRS
her, carried him **u**, and laid him 1Ki 17:19
bars in his **u** room in Samaria 2Ki 1:2
the roof of the **u** room of Ahaz. 2Ki 23:12
to pray in an **u** room in his ....Da 6:10
you a large room **u** that is ....Mk 14:15
you a large, furnished room **u**. ....Lk 22:12
went to the **u** room where they ....Ac 1:13
was washed and put in a room **u**. ....Ac 9:37
took him to the **u** room where all ....Ac 9:39
were all together in a room **u**,..................Ac 20:8
Then Paul went **u** again, broke ....Ac 20:11

UPSTREAM
the water **u** stopped flowing. ....Jos 3:16

UPWARD
wings should be spread **u**, ...Ex 25:20
creatures' wings were spread **u**, ...Ex 37:9
as surely as sparks fly **u**. ....Job 5:7
LORD, I look **u** to you, you who ....Ps 123:1

UR
Haran died in **U** in Babylonia, ...Ge 11:28
and moved out of **U** of Babylonia. ....Ge 11:31
led you out of **U** of Babylonia so ....Ge 15:7
the Hararite; Eliphal son of **U**; 1Ch 11:35
him out of **U** in Babylonia ....Ne 9:7

URBANUS
Greetings to **U**, a worker........................Rm 16:9

URGE
and **u** the people there to come ....Lk 14:23
Therefore I **u** you who have been ....Eph 4:1

URGED
Naaman **u** him to take the gift, ...2Ki 5:16
and he **u** Gehazi to take it. 2Ki 5:23
they secretly **u** some men to say ....Ac 6:11
encouraged you, we **u** you, and we............1Th 2:12

URI
Bezalel son of **U** from the tribe ....Ex 31:2
tribe of Judah. (**U** was the son ....Ex 31:2
Bezalel son of **U** the son of Hur,..............Ex 35:30
Bezalel son of **U**, the son of Hur ....Ex 38:22
Geber son of **U** was governor of..............1Ki 4:19
was the father of **U**, who was the 1Ch 2:20
altar that Bezalel son of **U**,.....................2Ch 1:5
Shallum, Telem, and **U**. ....Ezr 10:24

URIAH
is the wife of **U** the Hittite." 2Sa 11:3
And **U** the Hittite was one of 2Sa 11:17
U the priest and Zechariah son ....Is 8:2
His name was **U** son of Shemaiah ....Je 26:20

URIAH'S
and Bathsheba, **U** widow, to be 2Sa 12:15
mother had been **U** wife........................Mt 1:6

URIEL
son was **U**. Uriel's son was 1Ch 6:24
group, with **U** as their leader. 1Ch 15:5
U, Asaiah, Joel, Shemaiah, Eliel, ...1Ch 15:11
daughter of **U** from the town 2Ch 13:2

URIEL'S
U son was Uzziah, and Uzziah's...............1Ch 6:24

U

URIM
And put the U and Thummim inside .... Ex 28:30
and put the U and the Thummim .... Le 8:8
from the LORD by using the U. .... Nu 27:21
Thummim and U belong to Levi, ... Dt 33:8
through dreams, U, or prophets.............. 1Sa 28:6
by using the U and Thummim. .... Ezr 2:63
by using the U and Thummim. .... Ne 7:65

URINE
and drink their own u like you.".............. 2Ki 18:27
and drink their own u like you.".............. Is 36:12

USEFUL
become wild and u only as a .... Is 7:24
my power, but I did nothing u. .... Is 49:4
middle, is it u for anything? .... Eze 15:4
be made holy, u to the Master, ... 2Ti 2:21
by God and is u for teaching, ... 2Ti 3:16
now he has become u for both you........... Phm 1:11
help you to be u and productive 2Pe 1:8

USELESS
not listen to their u begging; .... Job 35:13
are the people making u plans? .... Ps 2:1
the enemy. Human help is u, ... Ps 60:11
talk about u family histories .... Tit 3:9
that their lives will not be u. .... Tit 3:14
In the past he was u to you, ... Phm 1:11
because it was weak and u. .... Heb 7:18
pure from u acts so we may serve .... Heb 9:14
you were saved from that u life. 1Pe 1:18

USUAL
do his work as u and was the .... Ge 39:11
his body (the u time it took). .... Ge 50:3
still give the u payment for a .... Ex 22:17
the fat be burned up first as u, ... 1Sa 2:16
things against Israel as u, ... 1Sa 17:23
seven times hotter than u. .... Da 3:19
went as u to the synagogue .... Ac 14:1

USUALLY
of God that u traveled in front .... Ex 14:19
the way men u die—then the LORD .... Nu 16:29
playing the harp as he u did, ... 1Sa 18:10
men the king u talked to were .... Est 1:14
and he taught them as he u did. .... Mk 10:1

UTHAI
There was U son of Ammihud. 1Ch 9:4
U and Zaccur. with seventy men. .... Ezr 8:14

UZ
of Aram were U, Hul, Gether, ... Ge 10:23
first son is U, and the second .... Ge 22:21
sons of Dishan were U and Aran. .... Ge 36:28
Aram's sons were U, Hul, Gether, ... 1Ch 1:17
Dishan's sons were U and Aran. 1Ch 1:42
Job lived in the land of U. .... Job 1:1
all the kings of the land of U; .... Je 25:20
you who live in the land of U................. La 4:21

UZAI
Palal son of U worked across .... Ne 3:25

UZAL
Hadoram, U, Diklah, ... Ge 10:27
Hadoram, U, Diklah, ... 1Ch 1:21

UZZA
his own palace, the garden of U. 2Ki 21:18
in his grave in the garden of U, ... 2Ki 21:26
was the father of U and Ahihud. 1Ch 8:7
U, Paseah, Besai,.............................. Ezr 2:49
Gazzam, U, Paseah, ... Ne 7:51

UZZAH
U and Ahio, sons of Abinadab, ... 2Sa 6:3
So U reached out to steady the 2Sa 6:6

was angry with U and killed him 2Sa 6:7
U died there beside the Ark of 2Sa 6:7
because the LORD had killed U................ 2Sa 6:8
is called the Punishment of U. 2Sa 6:8
was Shimei. Shimei's son was U. 1Ch 6:29
new cart, and U and Ahio guided 1Ch 13:7
and U reached out his hand to 1Ch 13:9
was angry with U and killed him, ... 1Ch 13:10
So U died there in the presence 1Ch 13:10
had punished U in his anger. 1Ch 13:11
is called The Punishment of U. 1Ch 13:11

UZZAH'S
U son was Shimea. Shimea's son 1Ch 6:30

UZZEN
Upper Beth Horon, and U Sheerah. 1Ch 7:24

UZZI
Bukki was the father of U. 1Ch 6:5
U was the father of Zerahiah................... 1Ch 6:6
son. U was Bukki's son. 1Ch 6:51
Tola's sons were U, Rephaiah, ... 1Ch 7:2
Ezbon, U, Uzziel, Jerimoth, and 1Ch 7:7
of Jeroham and Elah son of U. 1Ch 9:8
son of Uzzi. (U was Micri's son. 1Ch 9:8
the son of U, the son of Bukki, ... Ezr 7:4
U son of Bani was appointed over .... Ne 11:22
U was one of Asaph's descendants, ... Ne 11:22
U, from Jedaiah's family; .... Ne 12:19
Shemaiah, Eleazar, U, Jehohanan, ... Ne 12:42

UZZI'S
Bukki's son. Zerahiah was U son. 1Ch 6:51
U son was Izrahiah. Izrahiah's 1Ch 7:3

UZZIA
U the Ashterathite; Shama and 1Ch 11:44

UZZIAH
So King U had the skin disease 2Ch 26:21
In the year that King U died, ... Is 6:1
of Beeri during the time that U, ... Hos 1:1
was at the time U was king of .... Am 1:1
earthquake when U was king of.............. Zch 14:5
Jehoram was the ancestor of U. .... Mt 1:8
U was the father of Jotham. .... Mt 1:9

UZZIEL
Amram, Izhar, Hebron, and U. .... Ex 6:18
Aaron's uncle U had two sons .... Le 10:4
Amram, Izhar, Hebron, and U. .... Nu 3:19
Hebron, and U belonged to Kohath .... Nu 3:27
families was Elizaphan son of U. .... Nu 3:30
Rephaiah, and U, led five 1Ch 4:42
Amram, Izhar, Hebron, and U. 1Ch 6:2
Amram, Izhar, Hebron, and U. 1Ch 6:18
Ezbon, Uzzi, U, Jerimoth, and 1Ch 7:7
Amram, Izhar, Hebron, and U. 1Ch 23:12
Mattaniah, U, Shubael, Jerimoth 1Ch 25:4
of Amram, Izhar, Hebron, and U. 1Ch 26:23
there were Shemaiah and U. 2Ch 29:14
Next to them, U son of Harhaiah, ... Ne 3:8

W

WAFER
made with olive oil, and a w. .... Ex 29:23
a loaf made with oil, and a w.................. Le 8:26
will also give a loaf and a w, ... Nu 6:19

WAFERS
tasted like w made with honey .... Ex 16:31
and w brushed with olive oil. .... Ex 29:2
it may be w made without yeast .... Le 2:4
w made without yeast that have.............. Le 7:12
and w made without yeast spread .... Nu 6:15

WAGES

your **w** be paid in full by the .... Ru 2:12
pay them whatever **w** you decide. 1Ki 5:6
was worth an entire year's **w.**................... Jn 12:5

WAGON

doesn't use a **w** wheel to crush .... Is 28:27
as a **w** loaded with grain gets .... Am 2:13

WAGONS

to take some **w** from Egypt for .... Ge 45:19
gave them **w** as the king had .... Ge 45:21
Jacob saw the **w** Joseph had sent .... Ge 45:27
wives in the **w** the king of Egypt .... Ge 46:5
you load the **w** with many crops.............. Ps 65:11
as people pull **w** with ropes. .... Is 5:18
camels and in chariots and **w.** .... Is 66:20
their weapons, chariots, and **w.** .... Eze 23:24
of horsemen, **w,** and chariots.................. Eze 26:10

WAHEB

. . . and **W** in Suphah, and the .... Nu 21:14

WAIL

A **w** will come from the new area .... Zph 1:10

WAIST

them from the **w** to the upper................. Ex 28:42
and at his **w** he wore a belt that 2Sa 20:8
belt around his **w** and on his 1Ki 2:5
a leather belt around his **w.**" 2Ki 1:8
like a belt around his **w.** .... Is 11:5
cloth around your **w** to show your .... Is 32:11
belt and put it around your **w.** .... Je 13:1
told me, and put it around my **w.** .... Je 13:2
tightly around a person's **w,** .... Je 13:11
wears rough cloth around his **w.**............... Je 48:37
that from the **w** up the shape .... Eze 1:27
From the **w** down it looked like .... Eze 1:27
From the **w** down it looked like .... Eze 8:2
and from the **w** up it looked like.............. Eze 8:2
led me through water up to my **w.** .... Eze 47:4
fine gold wrapped around his **w.** .... Da 10:5
a leather belt around his **w.** .... Mt 3:4
had a leather belt around his **w,** .... Mk 1:6
he wrapped it around his **w.** .... Jn 13:4
tied around your **w** and the .... Eph 6:14

WAISTS

tie cloth belts around their **w.**.................. Ex 29:9
cloth belts worn around their **w,**............... Is 3:20
belts around their **w** and turbans .... Eze 23:15

WAIT

I will **w** for a young woman to .... Ge 24:43
Do not make me **w,** because the .... Ge 24:56
LORD, I **w** for your salvation.................. Ge 49:18
W there, and I will give you two.............. Ex 24:12
W here for us until we come back .... Ex 24:14
bleeding, she must **w** seven days, ... Le 15:28
w three years before using its.................. Le 19:23
to them, "**W,** and I will find .... Nu 9:8
sent them to **w** in ambush between .... Jos 8:9
Why do you **w** so long to take .... Jos 18:3
Please **w** here until I come back.............. Jdg 6:18
"I will **w** until you return." .... Jdg 6:18
something? Don't **w!** Let's go and .... Jdg 18:9
W until this afternoon." .... Jdg 19:8
should you **w** until they were .... Ru 1:13
w here until you see what .... Ru 3:18
But you must **w** seven days. 1Sa 10:8
began. **W** by the rock Ezel. 1Sa 20:19
I will **w** near the crossings into 2Sa 15:28
said, "Step over here and **w.**" 2Sa 18:30
but I will **w** until his son is 1Ki 21:29
Why should I **w** for the LORD any 2Ki 6:33
If we **w** until the sun comes up, ... 2Ki 7:9

the door and run away. Don't **w!**" 2Ki 9:3
let it **w** for daylight that never .... Job 3:9
I do not have the strength to **w.** .... Job 6:11
I will **w** until my change comes. .... Job 14:14
are quiet, must I **w** to speak? .... Job 32:16
him, that you must **w** for him, ... Job 35:14
I need, and I **w** for your answer............... Ps 5:3
They **w** in hiding like a lion. .... Ps 10:9
They **w** to catch poor people; .... Ps 10:9
W for the LORD's help. Be strong .... Ps 27:14
and **w** for the LORD's help. .... Ps 27:14
W and trust the LORD. Don't be .... Ps 37:7
W for the LORD's help and follow .... Ps 37:34
My God, do not **w.** For the .... Ps 40:17
They **w.** They hide. They watch my .... Ps 56:6
me and save me, LORD, do not **w.** .... Ps 70:5
they did not **w** for his advice. .... Ps 106:13
and did not **w** to obey your..................... Ps 119:60
we **w** for him to show us mercy. .... Ps 123:2
I **w** for the LORD to help me, ... Ps 130:5
I **w** for the Lord to help me more .... Ps 130:6
night watchmen **w** for the dawn, ... Ps 130:6
night watchmen **w** for the dawn. .... Ps 130:6
W for the LORD, and he will .... Pr 20:22
Those who **w** for perfect weather .... Ec 11:4
will **w** for the LORD to help us, ... Is 8:17
of Israel. I will **w** for him. .... Is 8:17
w for my power to help them................... Is 51:5
We **w** for the light, but there is .... Is 59:9
lives, and don't **w,** because I am .... Je 4:6
pits, and traps **w** for you, ... Je 48:43
Babylon! Don't **w!** Remember the .... Je 51:50
It is good to **w** quietly for the .... La 3:26
again, he must **w** seven days. .... Eze 44:26
your sake, don't **w,** because your .... Da 9:19
Those who **w** for the end of the .... Da 12:12
You must **w** for me for many days........... Hos 3:3
it does not **w** for human beings;.............. Mic 5:7
I will **w** for God to save me; .... Mic 7:7
I will **w** to see what he will say .... Hab 2:1
I will **w** to learn how God will .... Hab 2:1
but be patient and **w** for it, ... Hab 2:3
But I will **w** patiently for the .... Hab 3:16
Just **w,**" says the LORD. .... Zph 3:8
should we **w** for someone else?" .... Mt 11:3
lamps and went to **w** for the .... Mt 25:1
he left him to **w** until a better .... Lk 4:13
should we **w** for someone else?" .... Lk 7:19
should we **w** for someone else?' .... Lk 7:20
W here to receive the promise .... Ac 1:4
troubles and even jail **w** for me. .... Ac 20:23
Now, why **w** any longer? Get up, ... Ac 22:16
w for God to punish them with .... Rm 12:19
God while you **w** for our Lord 1Co 1:7
w until the Lord comes. 1Co 4:5
to eat, **w** for each other. 1Co 11:33
the Spirit we **w** eagerly for this .... Gal 5:5
you **w** for God's Son, whom God 1Th 1:10
When we could not **w** any longer, ... 1Th 3:1
when I could **w** no longer, I sent............. 1Th 3:5
that while we **w** for our great .... Tit 2:13
as you **w** for and look forward to 2Pe 3:12
God's love as you **w** for the Lord .... Jud 1:21
and was told to **w** a short time .... Rev 6:11
They had to **w** until all of this................. Rev 6:11

WAITED

I **w** patiently for the LORD...................... Ps 40:1
they **w** for the water to move.................. Jn 5:3
But Peter **w** outside near the .... Jn 18:16
on ahead and **w** for us at Troas. .... Ac 20:5
w and watched him for a long .... Ac 28:6
He **w** with patience so that he .... Rm 9:23

those who have **w** with love for 2Ti 4:8
Abraham **w** patiently for this to .... Heb 6:15

WAITING

He was **w** for the time when God .... Lk 2:25
Cornelius was **w** for them and had............ Ac 10:24
also have been **w** with pain .... Rm 8:23
eats without **w** for the others................. 1Co 11:21
But, without **w**, I went away to .... Gal 1:17
were **w** for a better country— .... Heb 11:16
There will be no more **w**! .... Rev 10:6

WAITS

total darkness **w** for their .... Job 20:26
and everyone who **w** for his help .... Is 30:18
And now Christ **w** there for his .... Heb 10:13
patiently **w** for his valuable .... Jam 5:7

WAKE

but I am going there to **w** him." .... Jn 11:11
time for you to **w** up from your .... Rm 13:11
why it is said: "**W** up, sleeper! .... Eph 5:14
they may **w** up and escape from 2Ti 2:26
W up! Strengthen what you have .... Rev 3:2
So you must **w** up, or I will come .... Rev 3:3

WAKES

It **w** the spirits of the dead, ... Is 14:9
Every morning he **w** me......................... Is 50:4

WAKING

It will be like **w** from a dream. .... Ps 73:20

WALK

W through all this land because .... Ge 13:17
to get up and **w** around outside .... Ex 21:19
have wings and **w** on all four .... Le 11:20
have wings and **w** on four feet. .... Le 11:21
have wings and **w** on four feet .... Le 11:23
the animals that **w** on four feet, ... Le 11:27
the animals that **w** on their paws .... Le 11:27
stomachs, that **w** on all four .... Le 11:42
I will **w** with you and be your .... Le 26:12
and let you **w** proudly again. .... Le 26:13
a day's **w** in any direction. .... Nu 11:31
We only want to **w** through. .... Nu 20:19
We only want to **w** through your .... Dt 2:28
at home and **w** along the road, ... Dt 6:7
at home and **w** along the road, ... Dt 11:19
hardly even **w** on the ground, ... Dt 28:56
and you will **w** all over their .... Dt 33:29
and you who **w** along the road, ... Jdg 5:10
sword and tried to **w** around, ... 1Sa 17:39
strong enough to **w** for forty 1Ki 19:8
a net when they **w** into its web. .... Job 18:8
old path where evil people **w**? .... Job 22:15
some animal might **w** on them. .... Job 39:15
Even if I **w** through a very dark .... Ps 23:4
I used to **w** with the crowd and .... Ps 42:4
W around Jerusalem and count its .... Ps 48:12
So I will **w** with God in light .... Ps 56:13
made us unable to **w** straight,................ Ps 60:3
let our enemies **w** on our heads............... Ps 66:12
Like wild pigs they **w** over us; .... Ps 80:13
You **w** in the dark, while the .... Ps 82:5
You will **w** on lions and cobras; .... Ps 91:13
have feet, but they cannot **w**. .... Ps 115:7
So I will **w** with the LORD in the .... Ps 116:9
the path where I **w**, a trap is .... Ps 142:3
But the wicked **w** around in the .... Pr 4:19
They will guide you when you **w**. .... Pr 6:22
and you cannot **w** on hot coals .... Pr 6:28
four that **w** as if they were .... Pr 30:29
but fools **w** around in the dark. .... Ec 2:14
the way fools **w** along the road, ... Ec 10:3
while princes **w** like servants .... Ec 10:7
will be afraid to go for a **w**...................... Ec 12:5

like a grasshopper when you **w**. .... Ec 12:5
They **w** around with their heads .... Is 3:16
soldiers will **w** through Migron. .... Is 10:28
that people can **w** across them .... Is 11:15
a dead body other soldiers **w** .... Is 14:19
your harp around the city .... Is 23:16
by the city will **w** on its ruins; .... Is 26:6
be allowed to **w** on that road; .... Is 35:8
only good people will **w** on it.................. Is 35:8
will **w** and not become tired. .... Is 40:31
So you will **w** on mountains and .... Is 41:15
you **w** through fire, you will .... Is 43:2
The Sabeans will **w** behind you, ... Is 45:14
That person may **w** in the dark .... Is 50:10
w in the light of your fires, ... Is 50:11
it and could not **w** straight...................... Is 51:22
'Bow down so we can **w** over you.' .... Is 51:23
back like dirt for them to **w** .... Is 51:23
Your God will **w** before you, ... Is 58:8
W up and down the streets of .... Je 5:1
the good way is, and **w** on it. .... Je 6:16
'We will not **w** on the good way.' .... Je 6:16
the fields or **w** down the roads, ... Je 6:25
Since they cannot **w**, they must .... Je 10:5
They **w** along back roads and on .... Je 18:15
like people who **w** on grapes to .... Je 25:30
as the sheep **w** in front of them .... Je 33:13
could not even **w** in the streets. .... La 4:18
and **w** away like a captive in the .... Eze 12:3
or animal will **w** through it, ... Eze 29:11
people Israel to **w** on you and................ Eze 36:12
It will **w** on and crush the whole .... Da 7:23
It was I who taught Israel to **w**, ... Hos 11:3
w on them as you would walk on .... Joe 3:13
as you would **w** on grapes to get .... Joe 3:13
They **w** on poor people as if they .... Am 2:7
will not **w** together unless .... Am 3:3
You **w** on poor people, forcing .... Am 5:11
you who **w** on helpless people, ... Am 8:4
to **w** across it took a person .... Jnh 3:3
is coming down to **w** on the tops .... Mic 1:3
You will no longer **w** proudly,................ Mic 2:3
our country and **w** over our large .... Mic 5:5
when they **w** over our borders. .... Mic 5:6
stumble so I can **w** on the steep .... Hab 3:19
they will **w** around like the .... Zph 1:17
people who cannot **w** and gather .... Zph 3:19
to tell him, 'Stand up and **w**'? .... Mt 9:5
crippled can **w**, and people with .... Mt 11:5
The lame could **w**, and the blind............ Mt 15:31
Stand up. Take your mat and **w**? .... Mk 2:9
he wanted to **w** past the boat................ Mk 6:48
They like to **w** around wearing .... Mk 12:38
or to say, 'Stand up and **w**'? .... Lk 5:23
crippled can **w**, and people with .... Lk 7:22
given you power to **w** on snakes............... Lk 10:19
people **w** on without knowing. .... Lk 11:44
They like to **w** around wearing .... Lk 20:46
' cross and to **w** behind him. .... Lk 23:26
are talking about while you **w**?"............... Lk 24:17
Pick up your mat and **w**." .... Jn 5:8
up his mat and began to **w**..................... Jn 5:9
'Pick up your mat and **w**.' " .... Jn 5:11
you to pick up your mat and **w**?" .... Jn 5:12
so **w** while you have the light. .... Jn 12:35
If you **w** in the darkness, you .... Jn 12:35
from Nazareth, stand up and **w**!" .... Ac 3:6
on his feet, and began to **w**. .... Ac 3:8
goodness that made this man **w**............... Ac 3:12
live with them and **w** with them. 2Co 6:16
so they will **w** with me and will .... Rev 3:4
that cannot see or hear or **w**. .... Rev 9:20

they will not w around naked .... Rev 16:15
the people of the world will w, ... Rev 21:24

WALKED

Enoch w with God 300 years more .... Ge 5:22
Enoch w with God; one day Enoch .... Ge 5:24
of his time, and he w with God. .... Ge 6:9
they w backwards into the tent .... Ge 9:23
Abraham w along with them a .... Ge 18:16
Jacob owned w ahead of them. .... Ge 31:18
people w ahead of his chariot .... Ge 41:43
Moses turned and w away from the .... Ex 10:6
the Israelites w through the sea .... Ex 15:19
and she w close to one wall, ... Nu 22:25
Hahiroth and w through the sea .... Nu 33:8
his descendants the land he w .... Dt 1:36
people of Israel w across the .... Jos 3:17
and armed men w behind the Ark .... Jos 6:9
other soldiers w behind the Ark .... Jos 6:13
his hands and w along eating it. .... Jdg 14:9
his shield w in front of him. 1Sa 17:7
his shield w in front of him. 1Sa 17:41
And he w on, prophesying until 1Sa 19:23
Ark of the LORD had w six steps, ... 2Sa 6:13
from his bed and w around on the 2Sa 11:2
them out and w on them like mud 2Sa 22:43
Then Elijah w for a whole day 1Ki 19:4
away and w around the room 2Ki 4:35
As he w along the wall, the 2Ki 6:30
they w through on dry ground. .... Ne 9:11
the teacher w in front of them. .... Ne 12:36
day Mordecai w back and forth .... Est 2:11
live, where no one has ever w; .... Job 28:4
Proud animals have not w there, ... Job 28:8
and I w through darkness by his .... Job 29:3
sea begins or w in the valleys .... Job 38:16
friendship and w together to .... Ps 55:14
I haven't w away from your laws, ... Ps 119:102
the stone wall, and it will be w .... Is 5:5
Isaiah obeyed and w around naked .... Is 20:2
my servant has w around naked .... Is 20:3
as if you had w on the grapes to .... Is 63:2
I have w in the winepress alone, ... Is 63:3
I was angry and w on the nations .... Is 63:3
I was angry, I w on the nations. .... Is 63:6
our enemies have w on your holy .... Is 63:18
before me and w between the .... Je 34:18
to meet them, crying as he w. .... Je 41:6
You w among the gems that shined .... Eze 28:14
and then it w on whatever was .... Da 7:7
killed and then w on whatever .... Da 7:19
ground and then w all over him. .... Da 8:7
to the ground and w on them! .... Da 8:10
the army of heaven being w on? .... Da 8:13
the city and w for one day, ... Jnh 3:4
They will get w on, like mud in .... Mic 7:10
to be thrown out and w on. .... Mt 5:13
the boat and w on the water to .... Mt 14:29
People w by and insulted Jesus .... Mt 27:39
and w out while everyone was .... Mk 2:12
People w by and insulted Jesus .... Mk 15:29
Jesus w through the crowd and .... Lk 4:30
People w on the seed, and the .... Lk 8:5
the man, he w by on the other .... Lk 10:31
he w by on the other side of the .... Lk 10:32
When they had w down one street, ... Ac 12:10
Elymas, and he w around, trying .... Ac 13:11
born crippled; he had never w. .... Ac 14:8

WALKING

the LORD God w in the garden .... Ge 3:8
Ahijah heard her w to the door, ... 1Ki 14:6
tooth or w with a crippled .... Pr 25:19
roads, no one w in the paths. .... Is 33:8

I see four men w around in the .... Da 3:25
later as he was w on the roof of .... Da 4:29
As Jesus was w by Lake Galilee, ... Mt 4:18
came to them, w on the water. .... Mt 14:25
saw him w on the water, ... Mt 14:26
left the Temple and was w away, ... Mt 24:1
After w a little farther away .... Mk 14:35
they were w in the country, ... Mk 16:12
w and jumping and praising God. .... Ac 3:8
on the top of his w stick .... Heb 11:21

WALKS

out the skies and w on the waves .... Job 9:8
see us as he w around high up .... Job 22:14
comes back or w the path of life .... Pr 2:19
He w on kings as if they were .... Is 41:25
just as a potter w on the clay. .... Is 41:25
to everyone who w on the earth. .... Is 42:5
No one w on the grapes with .... Je 48:33
other, because each w in line. .... Joe 2:8
into darkness and w over the .... Am 4:13
If anyone w in the daylight, ... Jn 11:9
But if anyone w at night, he .... Jn 11:10
right hand and w among the seven .... Rev 2:1

WALKWAY

along the edge of the paved w. .... Eze 40:17

WALL

whose branches grow over the w. .... Ge 49:22
with a w of water on their right .... Ex 14:22
with a w of water on their right .... Ex 14:29
The moving water stood like a w; .... Ex 15:8
Make a w of curtains to form a .... Ex 27:9
should have a w of fine linen .... Ex 27:9
must have a w of curtains .... Ex 27:12
posts and ten bases on that w. .... Ex 27:12
there is to be a w of curtains .... Ex 27:14
is also to be a w of curtains .... Ex 27:15
with a w of curtains around it .... Ex 27:18
Holy Tent and the w around the .... Ex 27:19
Then he made a w of curtains to .... Ex 38:9
north side the w of curtains was .... Ex 38:11
the w of curtains was .... Ex 38:12
entry there was a w of curtains .... Ex 38:14
there was also a w of curtains .... Ex 38:15
bases for the w of curtains .... Ex 38:31
and she walked close to one w, ... Nu 22:25
hundred feet from the city w. .... Nu 35:4
direction outside the city w— .... Nu 35:5
build a low w around the edge of .... Dt 22:8
in was built on the city w, ... Jos 2:15
"I'll pin David to the w." 1Sa 18:11
David to the w with his spear, ... 1Sa 19:10
So Saul's spear went into the w, ... 1Sa 19:10
where he always sat, near the w. 1Sa 20:25
were like a w around us while 1Sa 25:16
his body on the w of Beth Shan 1Sa 31:10
his sons from the w of Beth Shan 1Sa 31:12
shoot arrows from the city w? 2Sa 11:20
It was a woman on the city w. 2Sa 11:21
Why did you go so near the w?' 2Sa 11:21
on the city w shot at your 2Sa 11:24
on the city w saw many people 2Sa 13:34
dirt up against the city w, ... 2Sa 20:15
be thrown over the w to you." 2Sa 20:21
and threw it over the w to Joab. 2Sa 20:22
God's help I can jump over a w. 2Sa 22:30
as well as a w around Jerusalem. 1Ki 3:1
Temple w that formed the side 1Ki 6:6
thinner than the w in the room 1Ki 6:6
pushed against the Temple w, ... 1Ki 6:6
main beams built into this w. 1Ki 6:6
not see the stones of the w, ... 1Ki 6:18
creature's wing touched one w, ... 1Ki 6:27

the other **w** with their wings 1Ki 6:27
and build the **w** around Jerusalem 1Ki 9:15
repairing the **w** of Jerusalem, ... 1Ki 11:27
where a city **w** fell on 1Ki 20:30
his face to the **w**, and refused 1Ki 21:4
as a burnt offering on the **w**. 2Ki 3:27
Israel was passing by on the **w**, ... 2Ki 6:26
walked along the **w**, the people 2Ki 6:30
splashed on the **w** and on the 2Ki 9:33
broke down the **w** of Jerusalem 2Ki 14:13
on the city **w** can hear you." 2Ki 18:26
sitting on the **w** who will have 2Ki 18:27
turned toward the **w** and prayed............. 2Ki 20:2
going to the **w** that was around 1Ch 11:8
long and touched the Temple **w**. 2Ch 3:11
broke down the **w** of Jerusalem,............. 2Ch 25:23
and where the **w** turned, and he 2Ch 26:9
added greatly to the **w** at Ophel............. 2Ch 27:3
parts of the **w** and put towers................ 2Ch 32:5
built another **w** outside the 2Ch 32:5
who were on the city **w**. 2Ch 32:18
rebuilt the outer **w** of Jerusalem............. 2Ch 33:14
down Jerusalem's **w** and burned 2Ch 36:19
has given us a **w** to protect us .... Ezr 9:9
The **w** around Jerusalem is broken........... Ne 1:3
and for the city **w**, and for the .... Ne 2:8
at night, inspecting the **w**. .... Ne 2:15
rebuild the **w** of Jerusalem so................ Ne 2:17
of Jericho built part of the **w**, ... Ne 3:2
Jerusalem as far as the Broad **W**. .... Ne 3:8
next part of the **w** was repaired .... Ne 3:9
part of the **w** and the Tower .... Ne 3:11
of the **w** to the Trash Gate. .... Ne 3:13
also repaired the **w** of the Pool .... Ne 3:15
repaired another part of the **w**. .... Ne 3:19
worked hard on the **w** that went............. Ne 3:20
repaired the **w** that went from .... Ne 3:21
Henadad repaired the **w** that went .... Ne 3:24
repaired the **w** from the great................ Ne 3:27
the palace to the **w** of Ophel. .... Ne 3:27
on another part of the **w**. .... Ne 3:30
room above the corner of the **w**............. Ne 3:31
corner of the **w** and the Sheep .... Ne 3:32
heard we were rebuilding the **w**,............. Ne 4:1
Will they rebuild the **w**? .... Ne 4:2
up on the stone **w** they are .... Ne 4:3
So we rebuilt the **w** to half its................ Ne 4:6
in the **w** were being closed. .... Ne 4:7
trash we cannot rebuild the **w**." .... Ne 4:10
the lowest places along the **w**— .... Ne 4:13
So we all went back to the **w**, ... Ne 4:15
half my people worked on the **w**. .... Ne 4:16
who were building the **w**. .... Ne 4:17
out along the **w** so that we are .... Ne 4:19
I worked on the **w**, as did all my............. Ne 5:16
had rebuilt the **w** and that there............. Ne 6:1
that you are rebuilding the **w**................ Ne 6:6
the **w** will not be finished.".................... Ne 6:9
The **w** of Jerusalem was completed .... Ne 6:15
After the **w** had been rebuilt and .... Ne 7:1
When the **w** of Jerusalem was .... Ne 12:27
with joy the gift of the **w**. .... Ne 12:27
and the **w** of Jerusalem pure................ Ne 12:30
of Judah go up on top of the **w**, ... Ne 12:31
to the right on top of the **w**, ... Ne 12:31
part of the **w** by the older part .... Ne 12:37
them on top of the **w** with half .... Ne 12:38
of the Ovens to the Broad **W**, ... Ne 12:38
you spending the night by the **w**? .... Ne 13:21
You have put a **w** around him, ... Job 1:10
as if through a hole in the **w**, ... Job 30:14
God's help I can jump over a **w**............... Ps 18:29
like a leaning **w**, like a fence .... Ps 62:3

the water stand up like a **w**. .... Ps 78:13
knocks down a **w** might be bitten .... Ec 10:8
behind our **w** peeking through .... Sng 2:9
guards on the **w** took away my .... Sng 5:7
she is a **w**, we will put silver .... Sng 8:9
am a **w**, and my breasts are like .... Sng 8:10
tower and every high, strong **w**, ... Is 2:15
I will break down the stone **w**, ... Is 5:5
rainstorm beating against the **w**, ... Is 25:4
anyone builds a **w** of thornbushes .... Is 27:4
be like a high **w** with cracks in .... Is 30:13
on the city **w** can hear you." .... Is 36:11
sitting on the **w** who will have .... Is 36:12
turned toward the **w** and prayed............. Is 38:2
blind feeling our way along a **w**............... Is 59:10
an iron pillar, a bronze **w**. .... Je 1:18
as strong as a **w** to this people, ... Je 15:20
as strong as a **w** of bronze. .... Je 15:20
who are all around the city **w**. .... Je 21:4
the city **w** was broken through. .... Je 39:2
even the **w** around the city will .... Je 51:44
Babylon's thick **w** will be .... Je 51:58
Then the city **w** was broken .... Je 52:7
The **w** of each pillar was three .... Je 52:21
to destroy the **w** around .... La 2:8
He measured the **w** and did not .... La 2:8
W of Jerusalem, let your tears .... La 2:18
my way with a stone **w** and led me .... La 3:9
it up like an iron **w** between you .... Eze 4:3
I looked, I saw a hole in the **w**. .... Eze 8:7
me, "Human, dig through the **w**." .... Eze 8:8
I dug through the **w** and saw an .... Eze 8:8
carved on the **w** all around. .... Eze 8:10
through the **w** while they watch .... Eze 12:5
dug through the **w** with my hands............ Eze 12:7
through the **w** to bring him out .... Eze 12:12
broken places or repaired the **w**. .... Eze 13:5
When the people build a weak **w**, ... Eze 13:10
cover a weak **w** with whitewash............ Eze 13:11
wind will break the **w** down. .... Eze 13:11
When the **w** has fallen, people .... Eze 13:12
whitewash you used on the **w**?" .... Eze 13:12
I will break the **w** with a stormy............. Eze 13:13
hailstones will destroy the **w**. .... Eze 13:13
tear down the **w** on which you put .... Eze 13:14
And when the **w** falls, you will .... Eze 13:14
my anger on the **w** and against .... Eze 13:15
tell you, "The **w** is gone, and .... Eze 13:15
of Babylonian men on a **w**. .... Eze 23:14
every **w** will fall to the ground. .... Eze 38:20
I saw a **w** that surrounded the .... Eze 40:5
So the man measured the **w**, ... Eze 40:5
there was a low **w** about....................... Eze 40:12
on each side **w** of the rooms. .... Eze 40:16
from the outer **w** to the inner .... Eze 40:19
the outer wall to the inner **w**. .... Eze 40:19
as the gateways in the outer **w**. .... Eze 40:28
as the gateways in the outer **w**. .... Eze 40:29
by each side **w** of the porch, ... Eze 40:40
each side **w** of the porch. .... Eze 40:48
measured the **w** of the Temple, ... Eze 41:5
outer **w** of the side rooms was .... Eze 41:9
The **w** around the building was .... Eze 41:12
feet from one **w** to the other. .... Eze 41:15
the part of the **w** above the.................... Eze 41:17
There was a **w** outside parallel .... Eze 42:7
at the start of the **w** beside the .... Eze 42:10
open end of a path beside the **w**, ... Eze 42:12
Temple area had a **w** all around .... Eze 42:20
doorpost so only a **w** separated .... Eze 43:8
A stone **w** was around each of the .... Eze 46:23
the south side **w** of the Temple .... Eze 47:1
writing on the plaster of the **w**, ... Da 5:5

the writing on the **w** means." .... Da 5:12
writing on the **w** and explain it .... Da 5:16
writing on the **w** for you and .... Da 5:17
the hand that wrote on the **w**. .... Da 5:24
that were written on the **w**: ' .... Da 5:25
I will build a **w** around her so................. Hos 2:6
climb over the **w** like warriors. .... Joe 2:7
They run at the **w** and climb into .... Joe 2:9
on the city of Rabbah that .... Am 1:14
and puts his hand on the **w**, ... Am 5:19
The Lord stood by a straight **w**, ... Am 7:7
to the city **w**, and the shield .... Nah 2:5
waters were like a **w** around her. .... Nah 3:8
will be a **w** of fire around it,' .... Zch 2:5
built a strong **w** for herself. .... Zch 9:3
He put a **w** around it and dug a .... Mt 21:33
he had cut out of a **w** of rock,................. Mt 27:60
He put a **w** around it and dug a .... Mk 12:1
that was cut out of a **w** of rock. .... Mk 15:46
will build a **w** around you and .... Lk 19:43
that was cut out of a **w** of rock. .... Lk 23:53
an opening in the city **w**.......................... Ac 9:25
You are like a **w** that has been .... Ac 23:3
through a hole in the city **w**. 2Co 11:33
if there were a **w** between them,.............. Eph 2:14
broke down that **w** of hate by .... Eph 2:14
had a great high **w** with twelve .... Rev 21:12
the city, its gates, and its **w**. .... Rev 21:15
The angel also measured the **w**. .... Rev 21:17
w was made of jasper, and the .... Rev 21:18

WALL'S

red and goes into the **w** surface,.............. Le 14:37
will see the **w** foundation. .... Eze 13:14

WALLED

sells a home in a **w** city, ... Le 25:29
cities are **w** and very large.................... Nu 13:28
be in strong, **w** cities, safe .... Nu 32:17
These were strong, **w** cities. .... Nu 32:36
back to their strong, **w** cities. .... Jos 10:20
to the strong, **w** city of Tyre. .... Jos 19:29
w cities inside these borders .... Jos 19:35
w cities and country villages. 1Sa 6:18
w city and called the City of 2Sa 5:9
before he finds **w** cities and 2Sa 20:6
w city of Tyre and to all the 2Sa 24:7
w cities with bronze bars on 1Ki 4:13
w cities and every important town. 2Ki 3:19
w cities with fire and kill 2Ki 8:12
to the strong, **w** city. 2Ki 17:9
and the strong, **w** cities. 2Ki 18:8
w cities of Judah and captured 2Ki 18:13
w cities into piles of rocks. 2Ki 19:25
in the strong, **w** city, which is 1Ch 11:7
w cities in Judah and Benjamin............... 2Ch 11:23
them to every strong, **w** city. 2Ch 11:23
w cities of Judah and came as 2Ch 12:4
w cities in Judah during the 2Ch 14:6
the strong, **w** cities of Judah 2Ch 17:2
w cities and towns for storing 2Ch 17:12
w cities through all of Judah. 2Ch 17:19
the strong, **w** cities of Judah. 2Ch 19:5
them strong, **w** cities in Judah. 2Ch 21:3
well as **w** cities and towers in 2Ch 27:4
the strong, **w** cities, hoping to............... 2Ch 32:1
the strong, **w** cities in Judah 2Ch 33:14
w cities and fertile land. .... Ne 9:25
bring me to the strong, **w** city? .... Ps 60:9
my rock and my strong, **w** city. .... Ps 71:3
bring me to the strong, **w** city? .... Ps 108:10
me like a strong, **w** city, and he .... Ps 144:2
to win back than a **w** city, ... Pr 18:19
w cities of Israel will be .... Is 17:3

Canaan's strong, **w** cities be .... Is 23:11
w city will be empty like a .... Is 27:10
he would be in a high, **w** city. .... Is 33:16
will grow in the **w** cities........................ Is 34:13
w cities of Judah and captured .... Is 36:1
w cities into piles of rocks. .... Is 37:26
escape to the strong, **w** cities!' .... Je 4:5
the strong, **w** cities you trust. .... Je 5:17
run to the strong, **w** cities. .... Je 8:14
w cities left in the land of .... Je 34:7
destroyed your strong, **w** cities. .... Je 48:18
w cities will be defeated........................ Je 48:41
w city and will fight and win. .... Da 11:7
w city of the king of the South. .... Da 11:10
will capture a strong, **w** city. .... Da 11:15
w cities of his own country, ... Da 11:19
w cities with the help of a .... Da 11:39
has built many strong, **w** cities. .... Hos 8:14
w cities will be destroyed. .... Hos 10:14
he ruins the strong, **w** city. .... Am 5:9
w cities and build dirt piles to .... Hab 1:10
'Attack the strong, **w** cities!'.................. Zph 1:16

WALLED-IN

locked up, like a **w** spring, a .... Sng 4:12

WALLS

with high **w** and gates with bars. .... Dt 3:5
Rebuild the **w** of Jerusalem. .... Ps 51:18
peace within her **w** and safety .... Ps 122:7
I always think about your **w**. .... Is 49:16
will name your **w** Salvation and .... Is 60:18
put guards on the **w** to watch. .... Is 62:6
all the city **w** around Jerusalem .... Je 1:15
will become a city without **w**, ... Zch 2:4
faith that the **w** of Jericho fell.............. Heb 11:30

WANDER

and makes them **w** through a .... Job 12:24
Make his children **w** around, ... Ps 109:10
They will **w** from the .... Am 8:12
night he would **w** around the .... Mk 5:5
like stars that **w** in the sky..................... Jud 1:13

WANDERED

the time we all **w** in the desert. .... Jos 14:10
flock **w** over all the mountains .... Eze 34:6
They **w** in deserts and mountains, ... Heb 11:38
You were like sheep that **w** away, ... 1Pe 2:25

WANDERERS

in the land where you are **w**.' .... Je 35:7

WANDERING

a man found him **w** in the field .... Ge 37:15

WANDERS

if one of you **w** away from the .... Jam 5:19

WANT

Where do you **w** us to prepare for .... Mt 26:17
Whom do you **w** me to set free: .... Mt 27:17
"What do you **w** me to do for you?" .... Lk 18:41
He said, "Lord, I **w** to see.".................... Lk 18:41
Why do you **w** to hear it again? .... Jn 9:27
you **w** to become his followers, ... Jn 9:27
did not **w** to obey Moses. .... Ac 7:39
and said, "What do you **w**, Lord?" .... Ac 10:4
of Jesse the kind of man I **w**. .... Ac 13:22
I **w** you to know that I planned .... Rm 1:13
I **w** you to understand about 1Co 12:1
I **w** you brothers and sisters to .... Php 1:12

WANTED

my Sabbaths and **w** to worship .... Eze 20:16
Many times I **w** to gather your .... Mt 23:37
Many times I **w** to gather your .... Lk 13:34
We **w** very much to see you and 1Th 2:17

We **w** to come to you. I, Paul, ... 1Th 2:18
good things you **w** are gone from .... Rev 18:14

WANTING

W more is useless—like chasing.............. Ec 6:9
came to Jesus, **w** to trick him. .... Mt 16:1
w to bring them out to the people. .... Ac 17:5
But not **w** to take any more of .... Ac 24:4
sinful way, **w** only to do evil. .... Rm 1:24
w the sinful things we see, ... 1Jn 2:16

WANTS

to someone who **w** to borrow from........... Mt 5:42
people choose to do what God **w**, ... Jn 7:17

WAR

kings went to **w** against several .... Ge 14:2
if you had captured them in a **w**. .... Ge 31:26
if there is a **w**, they might join .... Ex 1:10
kill us with a disease or in **w**." .... Ex 5:3
prepared his **w** chariot and took............. Ex 14:6
be very angry and kill you in **w**. .... Ex 22:24
sounds like **w** down in the camp. .... Ex 32:17
Get some men ready for **w**. .... Nu 31:3
Send to **w** a thousand men from............. Nu 31:4
thousand men got ready for **w**, ... Nu 31:5
Moses sent those men to **w**; .... Nu 31:6
men, who returned from **w**..................... Nu 31:14
the soldiers who had gone to **w**, ... Nu 31:21
who went to **w** and the rest .... Nu 31:27
From the soldiers who went to **w**, ... Nu 31:28
who went to **w** got 337,000 sheep, ... Nu 31:36
brothers go to **w** while you stay .... Nu 32:6
Then we will prepare for **w**. .... Nu 32:17
Do not go to **w** against them. .... Dt 2:5
Don't go to **w** against them, ... Dt 2:9
them or go to **w** against them, ... Dt 2:19
signs, miracles, **w**, and great .... Dt 4:34
When you go to **w** against your .... Dt 20:1
so don't make **w** against them. .... Dt 20:19
When you go to **w** against your .... Dt 21:10
you are camped in time of **w**, ... Dt 23:9
not be sent to **w** or be given any............. Dt 24:5
men must dress for **w** and cross .... Jos 1:14
were dressed for **w**, and they .... Jos 4:12
prepared for **w** passed before .... Jos 4:13
the people not to give a **w** cry. .... Jos 6:10
other cities were defeated in **w**. .... Jos 11:19
When he went to **w**, the LORD .... Jdg 3:10
gathered for **w** and camped in .... Jdg 10:17
Ammonites made **w** against Israel,........... Jdg 11:5
against me by making **w** on me............... Jdg 11:27
Zorah and Eshtaol ready for **w**. .... Jdg 18:11
wearing their weapons of **w**. .... Jdg 18:16
men armed for **w** stood by the .... Jdg 18:17
wives for Benjamin during the **w**, ... Jdg 21:22
make weapons of **w** and equipment 1Sa 8:12
Make **w** on them until all of them 1Sa 15:18
gathered their armies for **w**. 1Sa 17:1
sons followed Saul to the **w**. 1Sa 17:13
positions, shouting their **w** cry. 1Sa 17:20
When **w** broke out again, David 1Sa 19:8
The weapons of **w** are gone." 2Sa 1:27
There was a long **w** between the 2Sa 3:1
During the **w** between the 2Sa 3:6
of his family be killed in **w**. 2Sa 3:29
had been at **w** with Toi. 2Sa 8:10
kings normally went out to **w**, ... 2Sa 11:1
were, and how the **w** was going. 2Sa 11:7
a complete account of the **w**. 2Sa 11:18
David what happened in the **w**. 2Sa 11:19
Again there was **w** between the 2Sa 21:15
as if he and they were at **w**, ... 1Ki 2:5
must not go to **w** against your 1Ki 12:24
There was **w** between Rehoboam and 1Ki 14:30

There was **w** between Abijam and 1Ki 15:6
there was **w** between Abijam and 1Ki 15:7
There was **w** between Asa and 1Ki 15:16
There was **w** between Asa king of 1Ki 15:32
also had prepared for **w**........................ 1Ki 20:27
Should I go to **w** against Ramoth 1Ki 22:6
of Aram was at **w** with Israel.................. 2Ki 6:8
including his **w** against Amaziah 2Ki 13:12
During a **w** Hazael had taken some 2Ki 13:25
including his **w** against Amaziah 2Ki 14:15
battle plans and power for **w**, ... 2Ki 18:20
strong and able to fight in **w**, ... 2Ki 24:16
people fought a **w** against the................ 1Ch 5:10
bows. They were skilled in **w**.................. 1Ch 5:18
They started a **w** against the 1Ch 5:19
Gad prayed to God during the **w**, ... 1Ch 5:20
king of Assyria want to go to **w**............... 1Ch 5:26
trained for **w** and skilled with 1Ch 12:8
They were warriors ready for **w**. 1Ch 12:25
use every kind of weapon of **w**. 1Ch 12:33
from Dan, who were ready for **w**. 1Ch 12:35
Asher, who were ready for **w**. 1Ch 12:36
men were ready to go to **w**.................... 1Ch 12:38
had been at **w** with Toi. 1Ch 18:10
w broke out with the Philistines. 1Ch 20:4
must not go to **w** against your 2Ch 11:4
And there was **w** between Abijah 2Ch 13:2
to call us to **w** against you. 2Ch 13:12
He had no **w** in these years, ... 2Ch 14:6
There was no more **w** until the 2Ch 15:19
did not start a **w** against 2Ch 17:10
eighty thousand men armed for **w**........... 2Ch 17:18
Should we go to **w** against Ramoth 2Ch 18:5
to start a **w** with Jehoshaphat. 2Ch 20:1
comes upon us, or **w**, punishment, ... 2Ch 20:9
kingdom was not at **w**. 2Ch 20:30
can make yourself strong for **w**, ... 2Ch 25:8
let fight in the **w** were robbing 2Ch 25:13
Uzziah fought a **w** against the 2Ch 26:6
soldiers coming home from **w**. 2Ch 28:12
should not be **w** between us. 2Ch 35:21
for days of **w** and battle? .... Job 38:23
w breaks out, I will trust the .... Ps 27:3
butter, but **w** is in his heart.................... Ps 55:21
divide the wealth taken in **w**. .... Ps 68:12
those nations that love **w**. .... Ps 68:30
swords, and the weapons of **w**. .... Ps 76:3
When I talk peace, they want **w**. .... Ps 120:7
trains me for **w**, who trains me .... Ps 144:1
Let there be no **w**, no screams in .... Ps 144:14
you go to **w**, get the advice of .... Pr 20:18
need advice when you go to **w**. .... Pr 24:6
is a time for **w** and a time for .... Ec 3:8
is released in times of **w**,....................... Ec 8:8
is better than weapons of **w**, ... Ec 9:18
and have been trained in **w**. .... Sng 3:8
will they train for **w** anymore. .... Is 2:4
and your heroes will die in **w**. .... Is 3:25
taking what they have won in **w**. .... Is 9:3
people in **w** and would not let .... Is 14:17
a wall of thornbushes in **w**,.................... Is 27:4
away the things you stole in **w**. .... Is 33:4
battle plans and power for **w**, ... Is 36:5
like a man ready to fight a **w**.................. Is 42:13
soldier wins in **w** be taken away............. Is 49:24
shouting words of **w** against the............. Je 4:16
I have heard the shouts of **w**. .... Je 4:19
long must I look at the **w** flag? .... Je 4:21
must I listen to the **w** trumpet? .... Je 4:21
We will never see **w** or hunger! .... Je 5:12
Blow the **w** trumpet in the town .... Je 6:1
for the sound of the **w** trumpet!'............. Je 6:17
Their young men will die in **w**. .... Je 11:22

the people of Judah with w, ... Je 14:12
to die in w will die in war .... Je 15:2
to die in war will die in w. .... Je 15:2
I will send w to kill, dogs to .... Je 15:3
They will die in w, or they will .... Je 16:4
have weapons of w in your hands .... Je 21:4
Jerusalem will be killed in w. .... Je 21:7
will die in w or from hunger .... Je 21:9
as if it were a prize won in w. .... Je 21:9
I will send w, hunger, and .... Je 24:10
because of the w I am going to .... Je 25:16
up because of the w I am sending .... Je 25:27
I am sending w on all the people .... Je 25:29
of the terrible w he brought, ... Je 25:38
I will punish them with w, ... Je 27:8
you and your people die from w, ... Je 27:13
They prophesied that w, hunger, ... Je 28:8
I will soon send w, hunger, and .... Je 29:17
will chase them with w, hunger, ... Je 29:18
from you in w will have their .... Je 30:16
Because of w, hunger, and .... Je 32:24
saying, 'Because of w, hunger, ... Je 32:36
says the LORD, to w, to terrible .... Je 34:17
in Jerusalem will die from w, ... Je 38:2
we will not see w, or hear the .... Je 42:14
or hear the trumpets of w, ... Je 42:14
are afraid of w, but it will .... Je 42:16
will die in w or from hunger .... Je 42:17
but you will die there by w, ... Je 42:22
he will bring w to those who are ...... Je 43:11
will be killed in w or die from ...... Je 44:12
will be killed in w or die from ...... Je 44:12
been killed in w and by hunger." .... Je 44:18
'Get ready for w, because the .... Je 46:14
herds of cattle as w prizes. .... Je 49:32
their places for w against it, ... Je 50:9
not return from w with empty .... Je 50:9
positions for w against Babylon, ... Je 50:14
around Babylon, shout the w cry! .... Je 50:15
You are my w club, my battle .... Je 51:20
killed in the w were better off .... La 4:9
They will die by w, hunger, and .... Eze 6:11
one who is nearby will die in w. .... Eze 6:12
as loot from w and to the most .... Eze 7:21
I might bring a w against that .... Eze 14:17
'Let a w be fought in that land,' .... Eze 14:17
against it—w, hunger, wild .... Eze 14:21
help the king of Judah in the w. .... Eze 17:17
you were treasures taken in w. .... Eze 25:7
island will be destroyed by w. .... Eze 26:6
for work horses, w horses, and .... Eze 27:14
with Egypt will fall dead in w. .... Eze 30:5
will fall dead in w from Migdol .... Eze 30:6
Bubastis will fall dead in w, ... Eze 30:17
enough to hold a sword in w. .... Eze 30:21
he uses it in w against Egypt. .... Eze 30:25
were killed in w and those among .... Eze 31:17
those who were killed in w. .... Eze 31:18
fall among those killed in w. .... Eze 32:20
those killed in w, have come .... Eze 32:21
around. All were killed in w, ... Eze 32:22
of them have been killed in w. .... Eze 32:23
All of them were killed in w. .... Eze 32:24
Elam with all those killed in w. .... Eze 32:25
people are unclean, killed in w. .... Eze 32:25
and have been killed in w. .... Eze 32:26
their weapons of w to the place .... Eze 32:27
unclean, who were killed in w. .... Eze 32:28
in death with those killed in w, ... Eze 32:29
lying with those killed in w. .... Eze 32:30
these who have been killed in w. .... Eze 32:31
all his soldiers killed in w, ... Eze 32:31
were killed in w, says the Lord .... Eze 32:32

I bring a w against a land. .... Eze 33:2
in Israel will be killed in w. .... Eze 33:27
be defeated in w when they were .... Eze 35:5
Those killed in w will fall on .... Eze 35:8
that has been rebuilt from w. .... Eze 38:8
I will call for a w against Gog .... Eze 38:21
bows and arrows, w clubs, and .... Eze 39:9
until all of them died in w. .... Eze 39:23
began making w against God's .... Da 7:21
and w will continue until the .... Da 9:26
a vision about a great w. .... Da 10:1
of the North will prepare for w. .... Da 11:10
powerful army and prepare for w. .... Da 11:25
or horsemen, or weapons of w. .... Hos 1:7
the sword and the weapons of w, ... Hos 2:18
But w will surely overwhelm them .... Hos 10:9
W will sweep through their. .... Hos 11:6
people of Israel will die in w; .... Hos 13:16
and they run like w horses. .... Joe 2:4
nations: Prepare for w! Wake up .... Joe 3:9
Let all the men of w come near .... Joe 3:9
of the sounds of w and trumpets. .... Am 2:2
of their safety; you plan w. .... Mic 2:8
call for a holy w against that .... Mic 3:5
will not train for w anymore. .... Mic 4:3
water before the long w begins. .... Nah 3:14
bows used in w will be broken. .... Zch 9:10
them like my proud w horses. .... Zch 10:3
LORD will go to w against those .... Zch 14:3
which makes w against the law .... Rm 7:23
And in a w, if the trumpet does 1Co 14:8
desires that w within you. .... Jam 4:1
the earth to kill people by w, ... Rev 6:8
pit will fight a w against them. .... Rev 11:7
Then there was a w in heaven. .... Rev 12:7
off to make w against all her .... Rev 12:17
Who can make w against it?" .... Rev 13:4
power to make w against God's .... Rev 13:7
They will make w against the .... Rev 17:14
when he judges and makes w. .... Rev 19:11
together to make w against the .... Rev 19:19

WARDEN
the prison w to like Joseph. .... Ge 39:21
prison w chose Joseph to take .... Ge 39:22
The w paid no attention to .... Ge 39:23

WARM
only cover to keep his body w. .... Ex 22:27
come to you it was w and fresh, ... Jos 9:12
blankets, he could not keep w. 1Ki 1:1
close to you and keep you w." 1Ki 1:2
Soon the boy's skin became w. 2Ki 4:34
and lets them w in the sand. .... Job 39:14
fine clothes to keep them w. .... Pr 31:21
they will be w, but a person .... Ec 4:11
a person alone will not be w. .... Ec 4:11
for a fire to keep himself w. .... Is 44:15
the wood to keep himself w. .... Is 44:16
Good! Now I am w. I can see .... Is 44:16
but you are not w enough. .... Hag 1:6
I hope you stay w and get plenty .... Jam 2:16

WARMED
because I w him with the wool of .... Job 31:20

WARMING
with the guards, w himself by .... Mk 14:54
She saw Peter w himself at the .... Mk 14:67
around it, w themselves. .... Jn 18:18
standing with them, w himself. .... Jn 18:18
was standing and w himself, ... Jn 18:25

WARMS
'Before the day w up tomorrow, ... 1Sa 11:9

WARMTH

coals that give **w** nor like a .... Is 47:14

WARN

If you **w** the wicked and they do .... Eze 3:19
But if you **w** the wicked to stop .... Eze 33:9
follower sins, **w** him, and if he .... Lk 17:3
we must **w** them not to talk to .... Ac 4:17
to **w** those who do not work. 1Th 5:14
W them as fellow believers. 2Th 3:15
I **w** everyone who hears the words .... Rev 22:18

WARNED

of that country strongly **w** us, ' .... Ge 43:3
By them your servant is **w**. .... Ps 19:11
God **w** the wise men in a dream .... Mt 2:12
After being **w** in a dream, he .... Mt 2:22
Who **w** you to run away from God's .... Mt 3:7
This is why God **w** Moses when he .... Heb 8:5
to him when he **w** them on earth, ... Heb 12:25

WARNING

because they believed the **w**. .... Eze 3:21
a trumpet blows a **w** in a city, ... Am 3:6
off your feet as a **w** to them." .... Mk 6:11
leave the town, as a **w** to them." .... Lk 9:5
I never stopped **w** each of you, ... Ac 20:31
to give you a **w** as my own dear 1Co 4:14
I gave a **w** to those who had 2Co 13:2
I give a **w** to all the others. 2Co 13:2
that the others will have a **w**. 1Ti 5:20
w people in God's presence not 2Ti 2:14
After a first and second **w**, ... Tit 3:10

WARNINGS

they refused to listen to his **w**. 2Ki 17:15
commands and **w** you gave them. .... Ne 9:34
ears and frightens them with **w** .... Job 33:16
He does not change his **w**. .... Is 31:2
ears, so they cannot hear my **w**. .... Je 6:10
people refuse to listen to my **w**. .... Je 13:10
the **w** written in this book. .... Je 25:13
heard God's **w** about things he .... Heb 11:7

WARNS

Then the LORD **w** them and .... Ps 2:5
to God who **w** us from heaven. .... Heb 12:25

WARS

the Book of the **W** of the LORD .... Nu 21:14
not fought in the **w** of Canaan. .... Jdg 3:1
fought in those **w** how to fight. .... Jdg 3:2
had to fight many **w** with the 1Ki 5:3
fought **w** and continued to rule 1Ki 14:19
Jehoshaphat fought many **w**, ... 1Ki 22:45
these **w** and his successes are 1Ki 22:45
You have fought many **w**. 1Ch 22:8
they had taken in **w** to be used 1Ch 26:27
There were **w** between Rehoboam 2Ch 12:15
so from now on you will have **w**." 2Ch 16:9
king and all his **w** are written 2Ch 27:7
He stops **w** everywhere on the .... Ps 46:9
brought terrible **w** against us .... Is 42:25
will hear about **w** and stories of .... Mt 24:6
stories of **w** that are coming, ... Mt 24:6
you hear about **w** and stories of .... Mk 13:7
stories of **w** that are coming, ... Mk 13:7
When you hear about **w** and riots, ... Lk 21:9

WASH

so all of you can **w** your feet. .... Ge 18:4
There you can **w** your feet, ... Ge 19:2
into pieces and **w** its inner .... Ex 29:17
the desert must **w** his clothes .... Le 16:26
W yourself, put on perfume, ... Ru 3:3
serve you and to **w** the feet of 1Sa 25:41
Go and **w** in the Jordan River 2Ki 5:10

W away all my guilt and make me .... Ps 51:2
W me, and I will be whiter than .... Ps 51:7
W yourselves and make yourselves .... Is 1:16
They don't **w** their hands before .... Mt 15:2
She began to **w** his feet with her .... Lk 7:38
"Go and **w** in the Pool of Siloam." .... Jn 9:7
and began to **w** the followers' .... Jn 13:5
you will never **w** my feet." .... Jn 13:8
you also should **w** each other's .... Jn 13:14
baptized, and **w** your sins away, ... Ac 22:16
are those who **w** their robes so .... Rev 22:14

WASHBOWL

Moab is like my **w**. I throw my .... Ps 60:8
Moab is like my **w**. I throw my .... Ps 108:9

WASHED

water, and they **w** their feet. .... Ge 43:24
Then he **w** his face and came out. .... Ge 43:31
God, and they **w** their clothes. .... Ex 19:14
I have **w** my feet and don't want .... Sng 5:3
They will be **w** away as if in a .... Is 28:17
some water and **w** his hands in .... Mt 27:24
but she **w** my feet with her tears .... Lk 7:44
the man went, **w**, and came back .... Jn 9:7
I went and **w**, and then I could .... Jn 9:11
on my eyes, I **w**, and now I see. .... Jn 9:15
Teacher, have **w** your feet, you .... Jn 13:14
like that, but you were **w** clean. 1Co 6:11
have been **w** with pure water. .... Heb 10:22
After a pig is **w**, it goes back 2Pe 2:22
They have **w** their robes and made .... Rev 7:14

WASHES

unless he **w** with water. .... Le 22:6
A mountain **w** away and crumbles; .... Job 14:18
Water **w** over stones and wears .... Job 14:19

WASHING

such as the **w** of cups, pitchers .... Mk 7:4
left them and were **w** their nets .... Lk 5:2
Jews used in their **w** ceremony. .... Jn 2:6
with a Jew about religious **w**. .... Jn 3:25
he had finished **w** their feet, ... Jn 13:12
church clean by **w** it with water .... Eph 5:26
w the feet of God's people, ... 1Ti 5:10
through the **w** that made us new .... Tit 3:5
not the **w** of dirt from the body, ... 1Pe 3:21

WASHINGS

food and drink and special **w** .... Heb 9:10

WASTE

become empty, your cities a **w**. .... Le 26:33
"I won't **w** time here with you!" 2Sa 18:14
My sons, don't **w** any more time. 2Ch 29:11
fools **w** everything they have. .... Pr 21:20
of prostitutes **w** their money. .... Pr 29:3
Don't **w** your strength on women .... Pr 31:3
whose waves toss up **w** and mud. .... Is 57:20
my grapevine a **w** and made my fig .... Joe 1:7
They asked, "Why **w** that perfume? .... Mt 26:8
each other, "Why **w** that perfume? .... Mk 14:4
and don't **w** time talking with .... Lk 10:4
Why should it **w** the ground?' .... Lk 13:7
for the trial, I did not **w** time. .... Ac 25:17
they learn to fritter their time, ... 1Ti 5:13
And they not only **w** their time 1Ti 5:13

WASTED

If we had not **w** all this time, ... Ge 43:10
you will have **w** your kind words .... Pr 23:8
land empty and **w** from the desert .... Eze 6:14
There he **w** his money in foolish .... Lk 15:13
who **w** all your money on .... Lk 15:30
and bread so that nothing is **w**." .... Jn 6:12
and his grace to me was not **w**. 1Co 15:10

work in the Lord is never **w**. 1Co 15:58
the work I am now doing to be **w**. .... Gal 2:2
Were all your experiences **w?** .... Gal 3:4
that my work for you has been **w**. .... Gal 4:11
happy because my work was not **w**. .... Php 2:16
our hard work would have been **w**. 1Th 3:5
In the past you **w** too much time 1Pe 4:3

WASTEFUL
having made and **w** parties, ... Gal 5:21
many wild and **w** things they do, ... 1Pe 4:4

WASTELAND
was an empty **w** for seventy years 2Ch 36:21
God will make it an empty **w;** .... Is 34:11

WASTES
her family and never **w** her time. .... Pr 31:27
like a sick person who **w** away. .... Is 10:18
in the army **w** time with everyday 2Ti 2:4

WATCH
and I cannot **w** this happen." .... Ge 21:16
He told his sons to **w** over them. .... Ge 30:35
Let the LORD **w** over us while we .... Ge 31:49
give birth to their babies, **w!** .... Ex 1:16
LORD kept **w** to bring them out .... Ex 12:42
are to keep **w** to honor the LORD .... Ex 12:42
May the LORD **w** over you and give .... Nu 6:26
give him his orders as they **w**. .... Nu 27:19
W out and don't forget the .... Dt 4:9
did not see him, **w** yourselves................. Dt 4:15
but continue to **w** and be ready. .... Jos 8:4
told the men, "**W** me and do what .... Jdg 7:17
the middle **w** of the night. .... Jdg 7:19
W for the young women from.................. Jdg 21:21
W to see into which fields they .... Ru 2:9
W him so you will know where he .... Ru 3:4
said to Samuel, "**W**, I am going 1Sa 3:11
W the cart. If it goes toward 1Sa 6:9
down here just to **w** the battle." 1Sa 17:28
to kill you. **W** out in the 1Sa 19:2
David's house to **w** it and to 1Sa 19:11
While you **w**, I will take your 2Sa 12:11
of me so I can **w** and eat it from.............. 2Sa 13:5
special cakes for me while I **w**. 2Sa 13:6
his servants, "**W** Amnon. 2Sa 13:28
day please **w** over this Temple 1Ki 8:29
forever and will **w** over it and................. 1Ki 9:3
night please **w** over this Temple 2Ch 6:20
I will always **w** over it and love 2Ch 7:16
said to them, "**W** what you do, ... 2Ch 19:6
W what you do, because the LORD 2Ch 19:7
guards to **w** for them day .... Ne 4:9
you would **w** me and would not let.......... Job 10:14
and keep close **w** wherever I go.............. Job 13:27
do you need to **w** me like this? .... Job 14:3
surround me; I **w** them insult me. .... Job 17:2
them; they **w** them grow up. .... Job 21:8
someone keeps **w** over their tombs .... Job 21:32
Good people can **w** and be glad;.............. Job 22:19
of adultery **w** for the night,.................... Job 24:15
do so that everyone else can **w**, ... Job 34:26
W how God scatters his lightning .... Job 36:30
Do you **w** when the deer gives .... Job 39:1
they **w** in secret for the .... Ps 10:8
I will guide you and **w** over you. .... Ps 32:8
how long will you **w** this happen? .... Ps 35:17
The wicked **w** for good people so .... Ps 37:32
person, and **w** the honest one. .... Ps 37:37
They **w** my steps, hoping to kill .... Ps 56:6
sent men to **w** David's house to .... Ps 58:11
My love will **w** over him forever, ... Ps 89:28
You will only **w** and see the .... Ps 91:8
charge of you to **w** over you .... Ps 91:11

good sense, and **w** what you say. .... Pr 5:2
Go **w** the ants, you lazy person. .... Pr 6:6
W what they do and be wise. .... Pr 6:6
to me, and **w** closely what I do. .... Pr 23:26
While you **w**, your enemies are .... Is 1:7
W! The Lord GOD All-Powerful .... Is 10:33
I will quietly **w** from where I .... Is 18:4
put guards on the walls to **w**. .... Is 62:6
W what I will do to the people .... Je 6:18
W out for your friends, and .... Je 9:4
You will **w** enemies killing your .... Je 20:4
and he will **w** over his people .... Je 31:10
the way home. **W** the road. Pay .... Je 31:21
But now I will **w** over them to .... Je 31:28
stand next to the road and **w**. .... Je 48:19
We kept **w** from our towers for a .... La 4:17
punish you as the nations **w**. .... Eze 5:8
through the wall while they **w**, ... Eze 12:5
to the many nations that **w**. .... Eze 38:23
rules as they **w** so they will .... Eze 43:11
had ordered a guard to **w** Daniel, ... Da 1:11
food is taken away while we **w**. .... Joe 1:16
I will keep **w** over them, but I.................. Am 9:4
but I will keep **w** to give them .... Am 9:4
the defenses. **W** the road. Get............... Nah 2:1
W them and be amazed and shocked. ...... Hab 1:5
like a guard to **w** and place.................... Hab 2:1
I will **w** over Judah, but I will .... Zch 12:4
owner would **w** and not let the .... Mt 24:43
Stay here and **w** with me." .... Mt 26:38
of death. Stay here and **w**."..................... Mk 14:34
charge of you to **w** over you.' .... Lk 4:10
there to **w** saw what happened .... Lk 23:48
W out for those who do evil, ... Php 3:2
W over them because you want to,........... 1Pe 5:2

WATCHED
kept praying, Eli **w** her mouth. 1Sa 1:12
While the followers **w**, Jesus .... Lk 24:43
They waited and **w** him for a long .... Ac 28:6
in a cloud as their enemies **w**................. Rev 11:12

WATCHER
I done to you, you **w** of humans? .... Job 7:20

WATCHES
cow must be burned while he **w**; .... Nu 19:5
and he **w** it from the beginning .... Dt 11:12
and closely **w** everywhere I go.' .... Job 33:11
God **w** where people go; .... Job 34:21
He always **w** those who do .... Job 36:7
his throne he **w** all who live .... Ps 33:14
The LORD **w** over the lives of the .... Ps 37:18
The LORD **w** over those who follow .... Ps 97:10
The LORD **w** over the foolish; .... Ps 116:6
you do, and he **w** where you go............... Pr 5:21
he **w** both evil and good people.............. Pr 15:3
w the house of the wicked and .... Pr 21:12
She **w** over her family and never .... Pr 31:27
your prayers and **w** over you. .... Hos 14:8

WATCHFUL
the door always to be **w**........................ Mk 13:34

WATCHING
listen to me, **w** at my door every .... Pr 8:34
kept **w** until finally the fourth................. Da 7:11
sees that they were **w** for him. .... Lk 12:37

WATCHMAN
The **w** went up to the roof of the 2Sa 18:24
to me from Edom, "**W**, how much of .... Is 21:11
I now make you a **w** for Israel. .... Eze 3:17
one I have made a **w** for Israel. .... Eze 33:7
Is Israel a **w?** Are God's people .... Hos 9:8

WATCHMEN

more than night **w** wait for the	Ps 130:6
more than night **w** wait for the	Ps 130:6
The **w** found me as they patrolled	Sng 3:3
The **w** found me as they patrolled	Sng 5:7
I set **w** over you and told you, '	Je 6:17
a time when **w** in the mountains	Je 31:6
Put the **w** in their places,	Je 51:12
day that your **w** warned you about	Mic 7:4

WATCHTOWER

standing on the **w** in Jezreel	2Ki 9:17
from the **w** to the strong,	2Ki 17:9
day I stand in the **w** watching;	Is 21:8
And you, **w** of the flocks, hill	Mic 4:8

WATCHTOWERS

including the **w** and the strong,	2Ki 18:8
were in your **w** and hung their	Eze 27:11

WATER

the earth and **w** all the ground.	Ge 2:6
the women come out to get **w**,	Ge 24:11
city are coming out to get **w**.	Ge 24:13
from the well and **w** the sheep.	Ge 29:3
she had pulled him out of the **w**.	Ex 2:10
springs of **w** and seventy palm	Ex 15:27
or in the **w** below the land.	Ex 20:4
that fill the **w** and all other	Le 11:10
wash his clothes and bathe in **w**,	Le 15:5
take some holy **w** in a clay jar,	Nu 5:17
hold the bitter **w** that brings a	Nu 5:18
will make the woman drink the **w**	Nu 5:26
the cleansing **w** on them,	Nu 8:7
branch and dip it into the **w**,	Nu 19:18
will not drink **w** from the wells.	Nu 20:17
or of fish in the **w** below.	Dt 4:18
land with rivers and pools of **w**,	Dt 8:7
had to plant your seed and **w** it,	Dt 11:10
and carry **w** for our people."	Jos 9:21
ground at Lehi, and **w** came out.	Jdg 15:19
and drink from the **w** jugs that	Ru 2:9
must go through the **w** tunnel.	2Sa 5:8
So the **w** ran off the altar and	1Ki 18:35
dried up the **w** in the ditch.	1Ki 18:38
'I have healed this **w**.	2Ki 2:21
head of his ax fell into the **w**.	2Ki 6:5
square by the **W** Gate Ezra read	Ne 8:3
W washes over stones and wears	Job 14:19
drinks up evil as if it were **w**!	Job 15:16
like **w** poured out onto the	Ps 22:14
a deer thirsts for streams of **w**,	Ps 42:1
empty land where there is no **w**.	Ps 63:1
like showers that **w** the earth.	Ps 72:6
the rock, and **w** flowed out;	Ps 105:41
into pools of **w** and dry ground	Ps 107:35
just as you drink **w** from your	Pr 5:15
pour your **w** in the streets;	Pr 5:16
Stolen **w** is sweeter, and food	Pr 9:17
wife is like dripping **w**.	Pr 19:13
As **w** reflects your face, so your	Pr 27:19
like a garden that has much **w**,	Is 58:11
from me, the spring of living **w**.	Je 2:13
and streams of **w** will flow from	Je 9:18
send their servants to get **w**.	Je 14:3
your heart like **w** in prayer to	La 2:19
W came up over my head, and I	La 3:54
We have to buy the **w** we drink;	La 5:4
I saw **w** coming out from under	Eze 47:1
led me through **w** that came up to	Eze 47:4
The **w** had risen too high;	Eze 47:5
to eat and **w** to drink.	Da 1:12
went from town to town for **w**,	Am 4:8
for bread or thirsty for **w**,	Am 8:11
baptize you with **w** to show that	Mt 3:11

a cup of cold **w** because they are	Mt 10:42
me to come to you on the **w**."	Mt 14:28
into the fire or into the **w**.	Mt 17:15
baptize you with **w**, but he will	Mk 1:8
a fire or into **w** to kill him.	Mk 9:22
a jar of **w** will meet you.	Mk 14:13
even the wind and the **w**,	Lk 8:25
dip his finger in **w** and cool my	Lk 16:24
I baptize with **w**, but there is	Jn 1:26
"Fill the jars with **w**."	Jn 2:7
tasted it, the **w** had become wine	Jn 2:9
are born from **w** and the Spirit,	Jn 3:5
came to the well to get some **w**,	Jn 4:7
it is that is asking you for **w**,	Jn 4:10
they waited for the **w** to move.	Jn 5:3
rivers of living **w** will flow out	Jn 7:38
Then he poured **w** into a bowl and	Jn 13:5
at once blood and **w** came out.	Jn 19:34
John baptized people with **w**,	Ac 1:5
officer went down into the **w**,	Ac 8:38
from being baptized with **w**?	Ac 10:47
baptized with **w**, but you will be	Ac 11:16
clean by washing it with **w**.	Eph 5:26
Stop drinking only **w**, but drink	1Ti 5:23
have been washed with pure **w**.	Heb 10:22
Do good and bad **w** flow from the	Jam 3:11
eight in all—were saved by **w**.	1Pe 3:20
was made from **w** and with water.	2Pe 3:5
was made from water and with **w**.	2Pe 3:5
the One who came by **w** and blood.	1Jn 5:6
Spirit, the **w**, and the blood;	1Jn 5:8
the rivers and the springs of **w**,	Rev 16:4
me the river of the **w** of life.	Rev 22:1
may have the **w** of life as a free	Rev 22:17

WATERED

through Eden and **w** the garden.	Ge 2:10
its mouth and **w** Laban's sheep.	Ge 29:10
a healthy vine **w** by a spring,	Ge 49:22
the girls and **w** their flock.	Ex 2:17
water for us and **w** our flock."	Ex 2:19
trees that are **w** well will grow	Eze 31:14
the seed, and Apollos **w** it.	1Co 3:6

WATERFALLS

and again, sounding like **w**.	Ps 42:7

WATERING

of the flocks at the **w** places.	Ge 30:38
of the singers at the **w** holes.	Jdg 5:11
by the thornbushes and **w** holes.	Is 7:19
return without **w** the ground.	Is 55:10
from the **w** places of Israel	Eze 45:15

WATERLESS

prisoners free from the **w** pit.	Zch 9:11

WATERS

to escape the **w** of the flood.	Ge 7:7
And the **w** continued to cover the	Ge 7:24
hand over all the **w** of Egypt,	Ex 8:6
deep **w** covered them, and they	Ex 15:5
your breath, and the **w** piled up.	Ex 15:8
the deep **w** became solid in the	Ex 15:8
These are the **w** of Meribah,	Nu 20:13
my command at the **w** of Meribah.	Nu 20:24
the people at the **w** of Meribah."	Nu 27:14
me at the **w** of Meribah Kadesh	Dt 32:51
with him at the **w** of Meribah.	Dt 33:8
met together at the **w** of Merom,	Jos 11:5
them at the **w** of Merom.	Jos 11:7
continued to the **w** of En Shemesh	Jos 15:7
the spring of the **w** of Nephtoah	Jos 15:9
continued to the **w** of Jericho,	Jos 16:1
went west to the **w** of Nephtoah.	Jos 18:15
at Taanach, by the **w** of Megiddo.	Jdg 5:19

better than all the w of Israel.................2Ki 5:12
and made those w flow straight 2Ch 32:30
a stone thrown into mighty w. ....Ne 9:11
holds back the w, there is no ....Job 12:15
if he lets the w go, they flood ....Job 12:15
rushing w wash away the dirt. ....Job 14:19
who are beneath and in the w. ....Job 26:5
He wraps up the w in his thick ....Job 26:8
and the wide w become frozen. ....Job 37:10
Who w the land where no one ....Job 38:26
He built it on the w and set it ....Ps 24:2
God, the w saw you; they saw you ....Ps 77:16
the deep w shook with fear. ....Ps 77:16
and paths through the deep w, ...Ps 77:19
tested you at the w of Meribah. ....Ps 81:7
the breezes, and the w flow. ....Ps 147:18
heavens and you w above the sky. ....Ps 148:4
can gather up the w in his coat?.............Pr 30:4
the slow-moving w of the pool of ....Is 8:6
stick over the w as he did in ....Is 10:26
When you pass through the w, ...Is 43:2
sea and a path through rough w. ....Is 43:16
I tell the deep w, 'Become dry! ....Is 44:27
the sea and the w of the deep.................Is 51:10
the people through the deep w? ....Is 63:13
he thunders, the w in the skies ....Je 10:13
in the north like rising w. ....Je 47:2
Even the w of Nimrim are dried.............Je 48:34
attack her w so they will be ....Je 50:38
he thunders, the w in the skies ....Je 51:16
bring the deep ocean w over you, ...Eze 26:19
and the great w stopped flowing. ....Eze 31:15
the way to the w of Meribah ....Eze 47:19
Dead Sea to the w of Meribah ....Eze 48:28
spring rain that w the ground." ....Hos 6:3
He calls for the w of the sea to ....Am 5:8
calls for the w of the sea and ....Am 9:6
The w of the sea closed around ....Jnh 2:5
the w were like a wall around ....Nah 3:8
horses, stirring the great w. ....Hab 3:15
and the one who w is not 1Co 3:7
and the one who w have the same 1Co 3:8
to make the w become blood,.................Rev 11:6
heard the angel of the w saying:.............Rev 16:5
the one sitting over many w. ....Rev 17:1
said to me, "The w that you saw, ...Rev 17:15

WATERWAY
came near the w from the upper 2Ki 18:17
Who cuts a w for the heavy rains ....Job 38:25
came near the w from the upper ....Is 36:2

WAVE
thought he would w his hand over 2Ki 5:11
He will w his arm over the ....Is 11:15
doubts is like a w in the sea, ...Jam 1:6

WAVED
Alexander w his hand so he could ....Ac 19:33
on the steps and w his hand to ....Ac 21:40

WAVES
Your w are crashing all around ....Ps 42:7
your powerful w flowed over me. ....Jnh 2:3
was being hit by w, because the ....Mt 14:24
a command to the wind and the w............Lk 8:24
and the w on the lake were.....................Jn 6:18
to break up from the big w. ....Ac 27:41
They are like wild w of the sea, ...Jud 1:13

WAVY
his hair is w and black like a ....Sng 5:11

WAX
heart is like w; it has melted ....Ps 22:14
w melts before a fire, let the ....Ps 68:2

melt like w before the LORD, ...Ps 97:5
crack open, like w near a fire, ...Mic 1:4

WAY
this w Abram and Lot separated. ....Ge 13:11
I have seen the w the Egyptians ....Ex 3:9
The LORD showed them the w; ....Ex 13:21
he showed you which w to go. ....Dt 1:33
Live the w the LORD your God has ....Dt 5:33
the LORD your God that w, ...Dt 12:4
return, you may go on your w." ....Jos 2:16
turn away from the w of the LORD ....Jos 23:12
and in the same w, his other ....Jos 23:15
men on their w to worship God at 1Sa 10:3
them all the w from Gibeon to 2Sa 5:25
Punish him in the w you think is 1Ki 2:6
In this w the family of Jeroboam 1Ki 13:34
in the same w as his father....................1Ki 15:26
It lit the w they were supposed ....Ne 9:12
to get their own w against the ....Job 15:25
has blocked my w so I cannot ....Job 19:8
Their w of thinking is different ....Job 22:18
But God knows the w that I take, ...Job 23:10
He makes my w free from fault.............Ps 18:32
will point them to the best w. ....Ps 25:12
that I cannot see a w to escape. ....Ps 40:12
I have chosen the w of truth; ....Ps 119:30
every evil w so I could obey ....Ps 119:101
In the same w, we depend on the ....Ps 123:2
in an amazing and wonderful w. ....Ps 139:14
In the same w, our bones have ....Ps 141:7
Her house is on the w to death; ....Pr 2:18
guiding you in the w of wisdom, ...Pr 4:11
The w of the good person is like.............Pr 4:18
She is on the w to death;....................Pr 5:5
you by the w she looks at you. ....Pr 6:25
children to live the right w,..................Pr 22:6
the w an eagle flies in the sky, ...Pr 30:19
w a snake slides over a rock, ...Pr 30:19
not judge by the w things look ....Is 11:3
you go the wrong w—to the right ....Is 30:21
the desert the w for the LORD. ....Is 40:3
showed him the w to ....Is 40:14
each of us has gone his own w. ....Is 53:6
They all have gone their own w;..............Is 56:11
road! Prepare the w! Make the ....Is 57:14
feeling our w along a wall. ....Is 59:10
learned the w of the LORD and ....Je 5:4
king who will rule in a wise w; ....Je 23:5
In the same w, their ancestors ....Je 23:27
In the same w Israel will eat ....Eze 4:13
heart and a new w of thinking.................Eze 18:31
'The w of the Lord is not fair.' ....Eze 33:17
'The w of the Lord is not fair.' ....Eze 33:20
He answered, "Go your w, Daniel. ....Da 12:9
her so she cannot find her w. ....Hos 2:6
happen; you wanted it this w." ....Jnh 1:14
who will prepare the w for me. ....Mal 3:1
to the LORD in the right w.....................Mal 3:3
own country by a different w...................Mt 2:12
'Prepare the w for the Lord. ....Mt 3:3
Let it be this w for now. ....Mt 3:15
In the same w, you will know ....Mt 7:20
will prepare the w for you.'....................Mt 11:10
In the same w, the Son of Man ....Mt 12:40
It is the same w with the evil ....Mt 12:45
Jerusalem, he was leading the w. ....Mk 10:32
the same w, the Son of Man did ....Mk 10:45
the son was still a long w off, ...Lk 15:20
teach the truth about God's w. ....Lk 20:21
On the w the man's servants came...........Jn 4:51
but climbs in some other w, ...Jn 10:1
I am the w, and the truth, ...Jn 14:6

any followers of Christ's **W**, ...Ac 9:2
God in a **w** that is against ....Ac 18:13
better understand the **w** of God...............Ac 18:26
of course, there is in every **w**...................Rm 3:2
But God has a **w** to make people ....Rm 3:21
also give you a **w** to escape so 1Co 10:13
will show you the best **w** of all. 1Co 12:31
thing is that in every **w**, ...Php 1:18
to show that the **w** into the Most ....Heb 9:8
a new and living **w** that Jesus................Heb 10:20
have followed the **w** of Cain, ...Jud 1:11

WAYS

hates the evil **w** they worship ....Dt 12:31
refused to change their evil **w**. ....Jdg 2:19
he plans a **w** that those who have 2Sa 14:14
have followed the **w** of the LORD; 2Sa 22:22
not hide the **w** of the Almighty. ....Job 27:11
voice thunders in wonderful **w**; ....Job 37:5
have followed the **w** of the LORD; ....Ps 18:21
The **w** of God are without fault. ....Ps 18:30
tell me your **w**. Show me how to ....Ps 25:4
God is pleased with their **w**. ....Ps 37:23
will teach your **w** to those who ....Ps 51:13
You answer us in amazing **w**, ...Ps 65:5
He showed his **w** to Moses and his...........Ps 103:7
your orders, so I hate lying **w**. ....Ps 119:128
and their **w** are dishonest. ....Pr 2:15
even know that her **w** are wrong. ....Pr 5:6
and bragging, evil **w** and lies.................Pr 8:13
those who follow my **w** are happy. ....Pr 8:32
be paid back for their evil **w**, ...Pr 14:14
found all kinds of **w** to be bad." ....Ec 7:29
Then God will teach us his **w**,................Is 2:3
Your **w** are not like my ways. ....Is 55:8
are my **w** higher than your ways ....Is 55:9
These people choose their own **w**, ...Is 66:3
feel sorry about their wicked **w**, ...Je 8:6
people haven't changed their **w**. ....Je 15:7
your **w** and do what is right.' ....Je 18:11
your wicked **w**! You don't want ....Eze 33:11
so that he can teach us his **w**, ...Mic 4:2
your evil **w** and evil actions. ....Zch 1:4
change your **w** and believe him. ....Mt 21:32
who will change to your **w**......................Mt 23:15
proved in many **w** that he was ....Ac 1:3
separated and went different **w**. ....Ac 15:39
They invent **w** of doing evil. ....Rm 1:30
their stubborn **w** so that he can ....Rm 11:32
God decides or understand his **w**. ....Rm 11:33
times and in many different **w**, ...Heb 1:1
and have not understood my **w**.' ....Heb 3:10
follow their evil **w** and say evil 2Pe 2:2
These are the **w** of the world: 1Jn 2:16
because all the old **w** are gone." ....Rev 21:4

WEAK

would be as **w** as any other man. ....Jdg 16:7
taught and the **w** hands you have ....Job 4:3
My knees are **w** from fasting,................Ps 109:24
strong and the **w** knees steady. ....Is 35:3
more power to those who are **w**..............Is 40:29
is right, but the body is **w**."..................Mt 26:41
faith in God did not become **w**. ....Rm 4:19
the law was made **w** by our sinful ....Rm 8:3
should help the **w** with their ....Rm 15:1
and he chose the **w** things of the 1Co 1:27
We are **w**, but you are strong.................1Co 4:10
Because their conscience is **w**, ...1Co 8:7
This **w** believer for whom Christ 1Co 8:11
those who are **w**, I became weak 1Co 9:22
I became **w** so I could win the 1Co 9:22
in your group are sick and **w**,................1Co 11:30
when I am **w**, then I am truly 2Co 12:10

WEAKEN

into the strong board will **w**. ....Is 22:25

WEAKENED

The ropes on him **w** like burned..............Jdg 15:14

WEAKER

since they are **w** than you. 1Pe 3:7

WEAKEST

group is the **w** in Manasseh, ...Jdg 6:15
It will be the **w** kingdom, and it ....Eze 29:15
killed, particularly the **w** ones. ....Zch 11:7
Then even the **w** of them will be..............Zch 12:8

WEAKLY

All hands will hang **w** with fear,..............Eze 7:17

WEAKNESS

has turned my strength into **w**. ....La 1:14
the Spirit helps us with our **w**. ....Rm 8:26
the **w** of God is stronger than.................1Co 1:25

WEAKNESSES

help the weak with their **w**, ...Rm 15:1
about myself, except about my **w**. 2Co 12:5
very happy to brag about my **w**...............2Co 12:9
reason I am happy when I have **w**, ...2Co 12:10
is able to understand our **w**. ....Heb 4:15
priests who are people with **w**, ...Heb 7:28

WEALTH

took all this **w** from our father ....Ge 31:16
I will also give you more **w**, ...2Ch 1:12
who hate us have taken our **w**. ....Ps 44:10
die and leave their **w** to others. ....Ps 49:10
their **w** won't go down with them. ....Ps 49:17
will be full of **w** and riches, ...Ps 112:3
a hard worker will have great **w**. ....Pr 12:27
people leave their **w** to their ....Pr 13:22
trust their **w** to protect them. ....Pr 18:11
Houses and **w** are inherited from ....Pr 19:14
W can vanish in the wink of an ....Pr 23:5
but their **w** will be given to....................Pr 28:8
to enjoy the **w** and property he ....Ec 5:19

WEAPON

and carried a **w** with the other. ....Ne 4:17

WEAPONS

The **w** of war are gone." 2Sa 1:27
Wisdom is better than **w** of war,..............Ec 9:18
torches, lanterns, and **w**........................Jn 18:3
and take up the **w** used for ....Rm 13:12
We fight with **w** that are 2Co 10:4
Our **w** have power from God that 2Co 10:4

WEAR

Aaron is to **w** their names on his ....Ex 28:12
your clothes did not **w** out, ...Dt 8:4
we drink?' or 'What will we **w**?' ....Mt 6:31
those who **w** fine clothes live in ....Mt 11:8

WEARING

Ahijah who was **w** the holy vest. 1Sa 14:3
old man **w** a coat is coming up. 1Sa 28:14
Tamar was **w** a special robe with 2Sa 13:18
Joab was **w** his uniform, and at 2Sa 20:8
Shiloh, who was **w** a new coat, ...1Ki 11:29
They were all **w** rough cloth when 2Ki 19:2
They were **w** rough cloth to show 1Ch 21:16
w the crown of thorns and the ....Jn 19:5
to the one **w** nice clothes and ....Jam 2:3
w white robes and holding palm ....Rev 7:9
jewels, and pearls she was **w**..................Rev 17:4

WEARY

and the **w** workers are at rest. ....Job 3:17

WEATHER
for perfect w will never plant .... Ec 11:4
you say we will have good w, ... Mt 16:2

WEAVE
very carefully w a belt on the.................. Ex 28:8
they are also able to w things. .... Ex 35:35
w the seven braids of my hair.................. Jdg 16:13
and those who w linen will lose .... Is 19:9
who w cloth will be broken. .... Is 19:10

WEAVER
like the cloth a w rolls up and .... Is 38:12

WEAVER'S
larger spear was like a w rod, ... 1Sa 17:7
spear was as large as a w rod. 2Sa 21:19
had a spear as large as a w rod.............. 1Ch 11:23
spear was as large as a w rod. 1Ch 20:5
days go by faster than a w tool, ... Job 7:6

WEAVES
her hands and w her own cloth. .... Pr 31:19

WEAVING
the women did w for Asherah. 2Ki 23:7

WEB
they trust is like a spider's w. .... Job 8:14
They lean on the spider's w, ... Job 8:15
a net when they walk into its w. .... Job 18:8
build are like a spider's w, ... Job 27:18
as they would spin a spider's w. .... Is 59:5

WEBS
The w they make cannot be used .... Is 59:6
cover yourself with those w. .... Is 59:6

WEDDING
prepared a w feast for his son. .... Mt 22:2
Come to the w feast.' .... Mt 22:4
later there was a w in the town .... Jn 2:1
to the w meal of the Lamb!.................. Rev 19:9

WEEDS
figs don't come from thorny w. .... Mt 7:16
other seed fell among thorny w, ... Mt 13:7
that fell among the thorny w?.................. Mt 13:22
because when you pull up the w, ... Mt 13:29
Let the w and the wheat grow .... Mt 13:30
other seed fell among thorny w, ... Mk 4:7
seed planted among the thorny w. .... Mk 4:18
Some seed fell among thorny w,.............. Lk 8:7
among the thorny w is like those .... Lk 8:14
thorns and w and is worthless .... Heb 6:8

WEEK
the full w of the marriage .... Ge 29:27
first day of the w, soon after .... Mk 16:2
I fast twice a w, and I give .... Lk 18:12
On the first day of the w, ... Ac 20:7
On the first day of every w,.................. 1Co 16:2
about the seventh day of the w: .... Heb 4:4

WEEKS
the Feast of W when you gather.............. Ex 34:22
Count seven w from the time you .... Dt 16:9
had been very sad for three w. .... Da 10:2
any perfumed oil for three w. .... Da 10:3
on each Sabbath day for three w, ... Ac 17:2

WEEP
to come and w and will pay .... Am 5:16
Be sad, cry, and w! Change your .... Jam 4:9

WEEPING
to bring peace are w loudly. .... Is 33:7
and cried out, w and being sad. .... Rev 18:19

WEIGH
W all these by the Holy Place.................. Ex 30:24
and balances should w correctly, ... Le 19:36

it would w about five pounds by.............. 2Sa 14:26
because there was too much to w. 1Ki 7:47
w them in front of the leading .... Ezr 8:29
then let God w me on honest .... Job 31:6
On the scales, they w nothing; .... Ps 62:9
and scales to w the mountains .... Is 40:12
I did not w you down with .... Is 43:23
with gold and w their silver .... Is 46:6
take scales and w and divide the .... Eze 5:1

WEIGHED
He w out the full price, ten .... Ge 23:16
armor that w about one hundred 1Sa 17:5
Instead you have w me down with .... Is 43:24
have been w on the scales and .... Da 5:27

WEIGHING
Rebekah a gold ring w one-fifth.............. Ge 24:22
arm bracelets w about four.................. Ge 24:22
with your w baskets the right .... Le 19:36
a bronze spearhead w about seven.......... 2Sa 21:16
w out seven ounces of silver for .... Je 32:9
each w about a hundred pounds, ... Rev 16:21

WEIGHS
which w two-fifths of an ounce. .... Ex 30:13
it w two-fifths of an ounce. .... Le 27:25
like a load it w me down. .... Ps 38:4

WEIGHT
counted the w as the traders .... Ge 23:16
measure the length or w or.................. Le 19:35
according to a w set by the Holy .... Nu 7:85
to the w set by the Holy .... Nu 7:86
So the total w of all the bronze 1Ki 7:47
that the total w of all the.................. 2Ch 4:18
everything by number and by w, ... Ezr 8:34
the total w was written down. .... Ezr 8:34
do not break under their w. .... Job 26:8
have become a heavy w on me, ... Is 1:14
but that w will be removed. .... Is 14:25
has lost much w from sickness. .... Is 17:4
is like a heavy w on its back; .... Is 24:20
under the w of their rules. .... Mt 23:4
a rope with a w on the end of it .... Ac 27:28

WEIGHTS
Your w and balances should weigh .... Le 19:36
broke the heavy w that were on .... Le 26:13
carry two sets of w with you, ... Dt 25:13
true and honest w and measures .... Dt 25:15
but he is pleased with honest w. .... Pr 11:1
all the w are his work. .... Pr 16:11
dishonest w and dishonest .... Pr 20:10
The Lᴏʀᴅ hates dishonest w,.................. Pr 20:23
others with wrong w and scales? .... Mic 6:11

WEIGHTY
and sand is w, but a complaining .... Pr 27:3

WELCOME
said, "Sir, you are w to come .... Ge 24:31
You are w to stay at my house. .... Jdg 19:20
peacefully to help me, I w you. 1Ch 12:17
to be choked; my bones w death. .... Job 7:15
My words are w to the person who .... Mic 2:7
If the people there w you, ... Mt 10:13
if they don't w you, take back .... Mt 10:13
town refuses to w you or listen .... Mt 10:14
place refuse to w you or listen .... Mk 6:11
were surprised and ran to w him. .... Mk 9:15
people do not w you, shake the .... Lk 9:5
people there would not w him, ... Lk 9:53
a town and the people w you,.................. Lk 10:8
and the people don't w you, ... Lk 10:10
job people will w me into their .... Lk 16:4
W him in the Lord with much joy. .... Php 2:29

about Mark. If he comes, **w** him. .... Col 4:10
ready to **w** guests, and able 1Ti 3:2
must be ready to **w** guests, ... Tit 1:8
w Onesimus as you would welcome .... Phm 1:17
Onesimus as you would **w** me. .... Phm 1:17
Remember to **w** strangers, because .... Heb 13:2
a very great **w** into the eternal 2Pe 1:11
do not **w** or accept that person 2Jn 1:10
you **w** such a person, you share 2Jn 1:11

WELCOMED
They **w** me when I ran away from 1Ki 2:7
So David **w** these men and made 1Ch 12:18
had not **w** the Israelites .... Ne 13:2
Galilee, a crowd **w** him, because .... Lk 8:40
He **w** them and talked with them .... Lk 9:11
will be **w** in those homes that .... Lk 16:9
down quickly and **w** him gladly............. Lk 19:6
Galilee, the people there **w** him........... Jn 4:45
they were **w** by the apostles, ... Ac 15:4
made a fire and **w** all of us. .... Ac 28:2
He **w** us into his home and was .... Ac 28:7
rented house and **w** all people .... Ac 28:30
You **w** him with respect and fear. 2Co 7:15
But you **w** me as an angel from .... Gal 4:14
w the spies and was not killed .... Heb 11:31
done this have **w** angels without .... Heb 13:2
w the spies into her home and .... Jam 2:25

WELCOMES
She **w** the poor and helps the .... Pr 31:20
this man **w** sinners and even eats .... Lk 15:2

WELCOMING
her children, **w** strangers, ... 1Ti 5:10

WELL
God showed Hagar a **w** of water. .... Ge 21:19
There he sat down near a **w**. .... Ex 2:15
you drink water from your own **w**. .... Pr 5:15
a **w** of fresh water flowing down .... Sng 4:15
Jacob's **w** was there. Jesus was .... Jn 4:6

WELL-FED
They are like **w** horses filled .... Je 5:8
will jump around, like **w** calves. .... Mal 4:2

WELL-FORMED
its great strength and **w** body. .... Job 41:12

WELL-KNOWN
w leaders chosen by the .... Nu 16:2

WELL-TRAINED
Israel is like a **w** young cow .... Hos 10:11

WELL-WATERED
They are like **w** plants in the .... Job 8:16
Lebanon, all the **w** trees, were .... Eze 31:16

WEST
was to the **w**, and Ai was to .... Ge 12:8
strong wind blow from the **w**,................ Ex 10:19
of the Amorites **w** of the Jordan .... Jos 5:1
us as far as the east is from **w**. .... Ps 103:12
east and gather you from the **w**. .... Is 43:5
saw a male goat come from the **w**. .... Da 8:5
valley that runs east and **w**. .... Zch 14:4
east and from the **w** and will sit .... Mt 8:11
flashing from the east to the **w**. .... Mt 24:27
see clouds coming up in the **w**, ... Lk 12:54
from the east, **w**, north, and .... Lk 13:29
the south, and three on the **w**. .... Rev 21:13

WESTERN
Your **w** border will be the .... Nu 34:6
the mountains, the **w** hills, the .... Dt 1:7
and on the **w** hills and along .... Jos 9:1
area and the **w** hills.'".......................... Zch 7:7

WET
of your land, both **w** and dry. .... Dt 29:19
around it gets **w** with dew." .... Jdg 6:39
ground around it was **w** with dew. .... Jdg 6:40
rows are not **w** with tears, ... Job 31:38
night my bed is **w** with tears; .... Ps 6:6
My head is **w** with dew, and my .... Sng 5:2
Don't let the belt get **w**."...................... Je 13:1
Let the man become **w** with dew, ... Da 4:15
Let him become **w** with dew and .... Da 4:23
from the sky will make you **w**. .... Da 4:25
an ox. He became **w** from dew. His .... Da 4:33
an ox and became **w** with dew. .... Da 5:21

WHEAT
a land that has **w** and barley, ... Dt 8:8
you the finest **w** and fill you .... Ps 81:16
like a pile of **w** surrounded with............. Sng 7:2
Is straw the same thing as **w**?" .... Je 23:28
so we can bring out **w** to sell? .... Am 8:5
weeds among the **w** and then left. .... Mt 13:25
of you as a farmer sifts his **w**................. Lk 22:31
a grain of **w** must fall to the .... Jn 12:24

WHEEL
spring, or a broken **w** at a well. .... Ec 12:6
him working at the potter's **w**. .... Je 18:3
like one **w** crossways inside .... Eze 1:16

WHEELS
moved, the **w** moved beside them. .... Eze 1:19
And the **w** were lifted up beside............. Eze 1:21
and the **w** of his throne were .... Da 7:9
of whips and the noise of the **w**............. Nah 3:2

WHIP
I will **w** your skin with thorns .... Jdg 8:7
tongue that strikes like a **w**, ... Job 5:21
If the **w** brings sudden death, ... Job 9:23
a rod and their wrongs with a **w**. .... Ps 89:32
W those who make fun of wisdom, ... Pr 19:25
Assyrians with a **w** as he .... Is 10:26
you to court and **w** you in their .... Mt 10:17
Jesus made a **w** out of cords and .... Jn 2:15
of thirty-nine lashes with a **w**. 2Co 11:24

WHIPPED
that Jesus be taken away and **w**............. Jn 19:1

WHIPPINGS
and **w** can change an evil heart............... Pr 20:30

WHIPS
like **w** on your back and thorns .... Jos 23:13
punish him. They will be my **w**. 2Sa 7:14
My father beat you with **w**,.................... 1Ki 12:11
beat you with **w** that have sharp............. 1Ki 12:11
My father beat you with **w**, ... 1Ki 12:14
beat you with **w** that have sharp............ 1Ki 12:14
My father beat you with **w**, ... 2Ch 10:11
beat you with **w** that have sharp............ 2Ch 10:11
My father beat you with **w**, ... 2Ch 10:14
beat you with **w** that have sharp............ 2Ch 10:14
W are for horses, and harnesses .... Pr 26:3
the sound of **w** and the noise .... Nah 3:2
beat him with **w** and crucify him .... Mt 20:19
beaten with **w** and handed over .... Mt 27:26
beat him with **w** and crucify him. .... Mk 10:34
having Jesus made fun of with **w**, ... Mk 15:15
beat him with **w**, and kill him. .... Lk 18:33

WHIRLING
wheels being called "**w** wheels." .... Eze 10:13

WHIRLWIND
Elijah by a **w** up into heaven. 2Ki 2:1
Elijah went up to heaven in a **w**............... 2Ki 2:11
A **w** is what they will get. .... Ps 11:6
Your thunder sounded in the **w**. .... Ps 77:18

trouble strikes you like a **w,** .... Pr 1:27
chariot wheels move like a **w.** .... Is 5:28
will be swept away as if by a **w,** .... Hos 4:19

WHIRLWINDS
goes, there are **w** and storms, ... Nah 1:3

WHISPER
and my ears heard a **w** of it. .... Job 4:12
We only hear a small **w** of him. .... Job 26:14
All my enemies **w** about me and .... Ps 41:7
who **w** and mutter, what to .... Is 8:19
come like a **w** from the dirt. .... Is 29:4

WHISPERED
They **w** to each other, "When dawn .... Jdg 16:2
have talked and **w** against you. .... Eze 36:3
What you hear **w** in your ear you .... Mt 10:27
what you have **w** in an inner room .... Lk 12:3

WHISPERING
When David saw his servants **w,** 2Sa 12:19
I hear many people **w** about me: .... Je 20:10
many people were **w** to each other .... Jn 7:12
heard the crowd **w** these things .... Jn 7:32

WHISTLE
it will **w** at them as they run .... Job 27:23
the Lord will **w** for the .... Is 7:18

WHISTLES
He **w** to call those people from .... Is 5:26

WHITE
all those that had **w** on them .... Ge 30:35
branches had **w** stripes on them. .... Ge 30:37
his teeth are as **w** as the color .... Ge 49:12
it was **w** with a skin disease. .... Ex 4:6
was like small **w** seeds and .... Ex 16:31
w owls, desert owls, ospreys, ... Le 11:18
hair in the sore has become **w,** .... Le 13:3
If there is a **w** spot on a .... Le 13:4
from the spot has not turned **w,** .... Le 13:4
If there is a **w** swelling on the .... Le 13:10
and the hair has become **w,** .... Le 13:10
all of the person's skin **w,** .... Le 13:13
the open sore becomes **w** again, ... Le 13:16
and if the sores have become **w,** .... Le 13:17
is a **w** swelling or a bright .... Le 13:19
and the hair on it has become **w,** .... Le 13:20
and there are no **w** hairs in it .... Le 13:21
the open sore becomes **w** or red, ... Le 13:24
If the **w** spot seems deeper than .... Le 13:25
hair at that spot has become **w,** .... Le 13:25
and there is no **w** hair in the .... Le 13:26
or a woman has **w** spots on the .... Le 13:38
spots on the skin are dull **w,** .... Le 13:39
manna was like small **w** seeds. .... Nu 11:7
Miriam, she was as **w** as snow; .... Nu 12:10
little owls, great owls, **w** owls, ... Dt 14:16
who ride on **w** donkeys and sit .... Jdg 5:10
disease and was as **w** as snow. 2Ki 5:27
valuable stones, and **w** marble. 1Ch 29:2
were dressed in **w** linen and 2Ch 5:12
courtyard had fine **w** curtains .... Est 1:6
pillars by **w** and purple cords .... Est 1:6
set with tiles of **w** marble, ... Est 1:6
of blue and **w** and a large gold .... Est 8:15
is no flavor in the **w** of an egg. .... Job 6:6
sea look as if it had **w** hair. .... Job 41:32
will become **w** like the flowers .... Ec 12:5
Your teeth are **w** like newly .... Sng 4:2
Your teeth are **w** like sheep just .... Sng 6:6
they can be as **w** as snow. .... Is 1:18
red, they can be **w** like wool. .... Is 1:18
face turning **w** like a dead man's .... Je 30:6
His face turned **w,** his knees .... Da 5:6

or let your face be **w** with fear! .... Da 5:10
His clothes were **w** like snow, ... Da 7:9
on his head was **w** like wool. .... Da 7:9
My face became **w** from fear, ... Da 7:28
my face turned **w** like a dead .... Da 10:8
trees and left the branches **w.** .... Joe 1:7
red, brown, and **w** horses behind .... Zch 1:8
W horses pulled the third .... Zch 6:3
The **w** horses will go to the land .... Zch 6:6
on your head become **w** or black. .... Mt 5:36
his clothes became **w** as light. .... Mt 17:2
like tombs that are painted **w.** .... Mt 23:27
and his clothes were **w** as snow. .... Mt 28:3
His clothes became shining **w,** .... Mk 9:3
man wearing a **w** robe and sitting .... Mk 16:5
his clothes became shining **w.** .... Lk 9:29
She saw two angels dressed in **w,** .... Jn 20:12
two men wearing **w** clothes stood .... Ac 1:10
a wall that has been painted **w.** .... Ac 23:3
head and hair were **w** like wool, ... Rev 1:14
like wool, as **w** as snow, and his .... Rev 1:14
the victory a **w** stone with a new .... Rev 2:17
with me and will wear **w** clothes, ... Rev 3:4
be dressed in **w** clothes like .... Rev 3:5
Buy from me **w** clothes so you can .... Rev 3:18
were dressed in **w** and had golden .... Rev 4:4
there before me was a **w** horse. .... Rev 6:2
them was given a **w** robe and was .... Rev 6:11
wearing **w** robes and holding palm .... Rev 7:9
these people dressed in **w** robes? .... Rev 7:13
and made them **w** in the blood .... Rev 7:14
there before me was a **w** cloud, ... Rev 14:14
sitting on the **w** cloud was One .... Rev 14:14
there before me was a **w** horse. .... Rev 19:11
in fine linen, **w** and clean, were .... Rev 19:14
were following him on **w** horses. .... Rev 19:14
I saw a great **w** throne and the .... Rev 20:11

WHITER
and I will be **w** than snow. .... Ps 51:7
than snow, and **w** than milk. .... La 4:7
and his face became even **w.** .... Da 5:9
w than any person could make them .... Mk 9:3

WHITEWASH
cover it with **w** to make it look .... Eze 13:10
a weak wall with **w** that it will .... Eze 13:11
is the **w** you used on the wall? .... Eze 13:12
the wall on which you put **w.** .... Eze 13:14
those who covered it with **w.** .... Eze 13:15
who covered it with **w** are gone. .... Eze 13:15

WHOLE
this time the **w** world spoke one .... Ge 11:1
The **w** land is there in front of .... Ge 13:9
eat that meat for a **w** month. .... Nu 11:20
hand him, his **w** army, and his .... Dt 3:2
and took the **w** area of Argob, ... Dt 3:4
out of Gilgal with his **w** army, ... Jos 10:7
the Lord as a **w** burnt offering. 1Sa 7:9
ancestors, with their **w** being. 2Ch 15:12
him in charge of the **w** world. .... Job 34:13
My **w** being praises the Lord. .... Ps 34:2
and brings joy to the **w** world. .... Ps 48:2
and **w** burnt offerings, ... Ps 51:19
Let his glory fill the **w** world. .... Ps 72:19
enjoying the **w** world, and .... Pr 8:31
Your **w** head is hurt, and your .... Is 1:5
His glory fills the **w** earth." .... Is 6:3
accuse and criticize the **w** land. .... Je 15:10
through the **w** country." .... Je 23:15
This **w** area will be square, ... Eze 48:20
that filled the **w** earth. .... Da 2:35
of the Lord of the **w** world. .... Zch 6:5
will be king over the **w** world. .... Zch 14:9

the w nation has robbed me. .... Mal 3:9
than to have your w body thrown .... Mt 5:29
Then the w town went out to see .... Mt 8:34
to have the w world if they lose .... Mt 16:26
to have the w world if they lose .... Mk 8:36
priests and the w Jewish council .... Mk 14:55
filled the w house where they.................. Ac 2:2
The w church and all the others.............. Ac 5:11
called the w group of followers .... Ac 6:2
The w city became confused. .... Ac 19:29
yeast makes the w batch of dough 1Co 5:6
If the w body were an eye, ... 1Co 12:17
yeast makes the w batch of dough .... Gal 5:9
and that w building is joined .... Eph 2:21
The w body depends on Christ, ... Eph 4:16
you have finished the w fight,................ Eph 6:13
your w self—spirit, soul, and 1Th 5:23
we can control their w bodies. .... Jam 3:3
Evil One controls the w world. 1Jn 5:19
will come to the w world to test .... Rev 3:10

WICK

The w trimmers and trays must be........... Ex 25:38
he made pure gold w trimmers and .... Ex 37:23
its lamps, its w trimmers, its .... Nu 4:9
gold bowls, w trimmers, small 1Ki 7:50
silver cups, w trimmers, bowls, ... 2Ki 12:13
pots, shovels, w trimmers, ... 2Ki 25:14
the pure gold w trimmers, small............ 2Ch 4:22
shovels, w trimmers, bowls, ... Je 52:18

WICKED

earth were very w and that..................... Ge 6:5
done such a w thing to Israel .... Ge 34:7
by this w thing Onan had .... Ge 38:10
You have done a very w thing!'" .... Ge 44:5
don't help a w person by telling .... Ex 23:1
w men of the city surrounded................ Jdg 19:22
Benjamin did this w and terrible .... Jdg 20:6
Hand over the w men in Gibeah so .... Jdg 20:13
you are proud and w at heart. 1Sa 17:28
You son of a w, worthless woman! 1Sa 20:30
Nabal is such a w man that no 1Sa 25:17
W people will no longer bother 2Sa 7:10
Israelites did w things that 2Ki 17:11
did what the LORD said was w, ... 1Ch 2:3
W people will no longer hurt 1Ch 17:9
past the sons of w Athaliah had 2Ch 24:7
people of Judah became more w, ... 2Ch 36:14
marriages with these w people. .... Ezr 9:14
We have been w toward you and .... Ne 1:7
been loyal, but we have been w. .... Ne 9:33
enemy and foe is this w Haman!" .... Est 7:6
In the grave the w stop making .... Job 3:17
What I am saying is not w;..................... Job 6:30
the hope of the w will be gone. .... Job 8:13
tents of the w will be gone." .... Job 8:22
But the w will not be able to .... Job 11:20
The w cannot come before him. .... Job 15:3
not mine, that shows you are w;............. Job 15:6
The w suffer pain all their .... Job 15:20
faces of the w are thick with .... Job 15:27
The w will no longer get rich,................. Job 15:29
breath will carry the w away. .... Job 15:30
The w should not fool themselves .... Job 15:31
and has handed me over to the w. .... Job 16:11
lamp of the w will be put out .... Job 18:5
is what will happen to the w; .... Job 18:21
and the joy of the w lasts only .... Job 20:5
When the w fill their stomachs, ... Job 20:23
The w may run away from an iron .... Job 20:24
success of the w is not their .... Job 21:16
should punish the w themselves.............. Job 21:19
are the tents where the w live?' .... Job 21:28

it is the w who are spared. .... Job 21:30
W people take other people's .... Job 24:2
from the vineyard of the w...................... Job 24:6
hope do the w have when they .... Job 27:8
The w may heap up silver like .... Job 27:16
The houses the w build are like .... Job 27:18
The w are rich when they go to .... Job 27:19
evil and spends time with w men, ... Job 34:8
He keeps the w from ruling and.............. Job 34:30
out, because the w are proud................... Job 35:12
Those who have w hearts hold on .... Job 36:13
are being punished like the w; .... Job 36:17
Crush the w wherever they are. .... Job 40:12
those who don't listen to the w, ... Ps 1:1
But w people are not like that. .... Ps 1:4
So the w will not escape God's .... Ps 1:5
but the w will be destroyed. .... Ps 1:6
have broken the teeth of the w. .... Ps 3:7
a God who is pleased with the w; .... Ps 5:4
those w actions done by evil .... Ps 7:9
is always ready to punish the w............... Ps 7:11
nations and destroyed the w; .... Ps 9:5
the w get trapped by what they .... Ps 9:16
W people will go to the grave, ... Ps 9:17
Proudly the w chase down those .... Ps 10:2
The w people are too proud. .... Ps 10:4
The w think, "God has forgotten .... Ps 10:11
LORD, rise up and punish the w. .... Ps 10:12
Why do w people hate God? .... Ps 10:13
Break the power of w people.................. Ps 10:15
hunters, the w string their bows............. Ps 11:2
but he hates the w and those who .... Ps 11:5
and burning sulfur on the w. .... Ps 11:6
But the w are all around us; .... Ps 12:8
Don't the w understand?........................ Ps 14:4
the w are filled with terror,..................... Ps 14:5
The w upset the plans of the .... Ps 14:6
me from the w who attack me, ... Ps 17:9
me from the w with your sword .... Ps 17:13
and I won't sit with the w. .... Ps 26:5
Don't drag me away with the w,............... Ps 28:3
Let the w be disgraced and lie .... Ps 31:17
W people have many troubles, ... Ps 32:10
Evil will kill the w; .... Ps 34:21
speaks to the w in their hearts .... Ps 36:1
Their words are w lies; .... Ps 36:3
me and the w force me away. .... Ps 36:11
while the w will be no more .... Ps 37:10
The w make evil plans against .... Ps 37:12
But the Lord laughs at the w, ... Ps 37:13
The w draw their swords and bend .... Ps 37:14
power of the w will be broken, ... Ps 37:17
But the w will die. The LORD's .... Ps 37:20
The w borrow and don't pay back,........... Ps 37:21
the children of the w will die................... Ps 37:28
The w watch for good people so.............. Ps 37:32
you will see the w sent away. .... Ps 37:34
I saw a w and cruel man who................... Ps 37:35
in the end the w will die. .... Ps 37:38
them from the w, because they .... Ps 37:40
what I say around w people." .... Ps 39:1
let w fools make fun of me. .... Ps 39:8
God says to the w, "Why do you.............. Ps 50:16
Don't the w understand?........................ Ps 53:4
The w are filled with terror..................... Ps 53:5
says and how the w look at me. .... Ps 55:3
bring down the w to the grave. .... Ps 55:23
feet in the blood of the w. .... Ps 58:10
me from those who plan w things, ... Ps 64:2
They plan w things and say, ... Ps 64:6
let the w be destroyed before .... Ps 68:2
the power of the w and from the .... Ps 71:4
I saw w people doing well. .... Ps 73:3

people are w, always at ease .... Ps 73:12
and to the w, 'Don't show your .... Ps 75:4
drop, and the w drink it all. .... Ps 75:8
take all power away from the w,............. Ps 75:10
show greater kindness to the w? .... Ps 82:2
them from the power of the w. .... Ps 82:4
than live in the homes of the w. .... Ps 84:10
w people will not defeat him. .... Ps 89:22
watch and see the w punished. .... Ps 91:8
W people grow like the grass.................. Ps 92:7
How long will the w be happy? .... Ps 94:3
until a pit is dug for the w. .... Ps 94:13
help me fight against the w? .... Ps 94:16
them from the power of the w. .... Ps 97:10
I will not look at anything w. .... Ps 101:3
will destroy the w in the land. .... Ps 101:8
and let the w live no longer. .... Ps 104:35
and flames burned up the w. .... Ps 106:18
So they became even more w................. Ps 106:43
happy, but the w say nothing................. Ps 107:42
W people and liars have spoken .... Ps 109:2
remember how w his ancestors .... Ps 109:14
The w will see this and become .... Ps 112:10
The wishes of the w will come to .... Ps 112:10
angry with w people who do not .... Ps 119:53
W people have tied me up, but I .... Ps 119:61
W people are waiting to destroy............. Ps 119:95
W people have set a trap for me, ... Ps 119:110
throw away the w of the world .... Ps 119:119
W people are far from being .... Ps 119:155
The w will not rule over those .... Ps 125:3
set me free from those w people. .... Ps 129:4
I wish you would kill the w! .... Ps 139:19
me from the power of w people;............. Ps 140:4
not give the w what they want. .... Ps 140:8
Let the w fall into their own .... Ps 141:10
but he will destroy the w. .... Ps 145:20
but he blocks the way of the w. .... Ps 146:9
he throws the w to the ground. .... Ps 147:6
It will keep you from the w, ... Pr 2:12
But the w will be removed from .... Pr 2:22
the ruin that comes to the w, ... Pr 3:25
Don't follow the ways of the w; .... Pr 4:14
But the w walk around in the .... Pr 4:19
will be caught in his w ways; .... Pr 5:22
Some people are w and no good. .... Pr 6:12
but the w will be overwhelmed by .... Pr 10:6
words of the w contain nothing .... Pr 10:11
but the w will be destroyed by .... Pr 11:5
When the w die, hope dies with .... Pr 11:7
it comes to the w instead. .... Pr 11:8
but the w can destroy it with .... Pr 11:11
but the w can expect to be .... Pr 11:23
and the w and the sinners will .... Pr 11:31
advice of the w will trick you. .... Pr 12:5
The w talk about killing people,............. Pr 12:6
W people die and they are no................. Pr 12:7
kindest acts of the w are cruel. .... Pr 12:10
w want what other evil people .... Pr 12:12
but the w do shameful and .... Pr 13:5
future of the w is like a flame. .... Pr 13:9
A w messenger brings nothing but........... Pr 13:17
eat, but the w go hungry. .... Pr 13:25
The w person's house will be .... Pr 14:11
the w will bow down at the door .... Pr 14:19
The w are ruined by their own .... Pr 14:32
the sacrifice that the w offer, ... Pr 15:8
but the w simply pour out evil. .... Pr 15:28
LORD does not listen to the w, ... Pr 15:29
When the w accept money to do .... Pr 17:23
to honor the w or to be unfair .... Pr 18:5
and w people love what is evil. .... Pr 19:28
violence of the w will destroy................. Pr 21:7

house of the w and brings ruin .... Pr 21:12
W people will suffer instead of .... Pr 21:18
W people are stubborn, but good .... Pr 21:29
Don't be w and attack a good................. Pr 24:15
but the w are overwhelmed by .... Pr 24:16
and don't be jealous of the w................. Pr 24:19
the w will die like a flame that .... Pr 24:20
Don't tell the w that they are .... Pr 24:24
Remove w people from the king's .... Pr 25:5
words from a w mind are like................. Pr 26:23
have been taught praise the w, ... Pr 28:4
innocent than to be rich and w. .... Pr 28:6
but when the w get control, ... Pr 28:12
w ruler is as dangerous to poor .... Pr 28:15
the w get control, everybody .... Pr 28:28
but the w are not concerned. .... Pr 29:7
all his officers will become w................. Pr 29:12
When there are many w people,............. Pr 29:16
and the w hate those who are................. Pr 29:27
Don't be too w, and don't be .... Ec 7:17
by saying crazy and w things. .... Ec 10:13
terrible it will be for the w!..................... Is 3:11
his words the w will be put to................. Is 11:4
its evil and w people for their................. Is 13:11
people will not respect the w................. Is 32:5
A fool does things that are w,................. Is 32:6
The w person uses evil like a .... Is 32:7
was buried with w men, and he .... Is 53:9
The w should stop doing wrong, ... Is 55:7
And Israel's w sister Judah saw .... Je 3:7
make Israel's w sister Judah .... Je 3:8
Israel's w sister didn't even..................... Je 3:10
a better excuse than w Judah. .... Je 3:11
There are w men among my people. ...... Je 5:26
feel sorry about their w ways, ... Je 8:6
will do to all my w neighbors .... Je 12:14
admit that we are w and that our .... Je 14:20
you from these w people and .... Je 15:21
poor from the power of the w. .... Je 20:13
of all the w things you did. .... Je 22:22
on the heads of those w people. .... Je 23:19
them for the w things they did, ... Je 31:34
and will stop doing w things. .... Je 36:3
one will stop doing w things. .... Je 36:7
I say to the w, 'You will surely .... Eze 3:18
out to warn the w to stop their .... Eze 3:18
you warn the w and they do not .... Eze 3:19
evil and give w advice in this .... Eze 11:2
encouraged the w not to stop .... Eze 13:22
the wicked not to stop being w, ... Eze 13:22
But suppose the w stop doing all .... Eze 18:21
do not really want the w to die, ... Eze 18:23
same hateful things the w do................. Eze 18:24
When the w stop being wicked and .... Eze 18:27
stop being w and do what is .... Eze 18:27
you both the w and those who do .... Eze 21:3
cut off the w and those who do .... Eze 21:4
Suppose I say to the w: '..................... Eze 33:8
'W people, you will surely die,' .... Eze 33:8
to warn the w to stop doing .... Eze 33:8
if you warn the w to stop doing .... Eze 33:9
not want any who are w to die. .... Eze 33:11
Stop! Stop your w ways! You .... Eze 33:11
The evil of w people will not .... Eze 33:12
if I say to the w people, '........................ Eze 33:14
But when the w stop doing evil .... Eze 33:19
to tell me lies and w things, ... Da 2:9
Stop doing w things and be kind .... Da 4:27
have been w and turned against............. Da 9:5
but the w will continue to be .... Da 12:10
wicked will continue to be w. .... Da 12:10
Those w people will not .... Da 12:10
road to Shechem and do w things........... Hos 6:9

were very **w** in Gilgal,........................... Hos 9:15
them because of their **w** plans. .... Hos 11:6
still in the **w** house wicked .... Mic 6:10
in the wicked house **w** treasures .... Mic 6:10
the LORD and gives **w** advice. .... Nah 1:11
for you, because you are **w**." .... Nah 1:14
w will not come to attack you................. Nah 1:15
quiet when the **w** swallow up .... Hab 1:13
leader of the **w** ones and took .... Hab 3:13
terrible for the **w**, stubborn..................... Zph 3:1
will say, 'Edom is a **w** country. .... Mal 1:4
crush the **w** like ashes under .... Mal 4:3
'You are a **w** and lazy servant! .... Mt 25:26
them for the **w** things they did, ... Heb 8:12
He held on while **w** people were............. Heb 12:3
the **w** person and the sinner will 1Pe 4:18

WICKEDLY
We have done wrong and acted **w**.'........... 1Ki 8:47
We have done wrong and acted **w**.'........... 2Ch 6:37

WICKEDNESS
so **w** is broken in pieces like a .... Job 24:20
They feast on **w** and cruelty as .... Pr 4:17
will be destroyed by their **w**. .... Pr 11:5
Jerusalem spread **w** through the .... Je 23:15
turn from their **w** or their evil................. Eze 3:19
into a weapon for punishing **w**. .... Eze 7:11
the king happy with their **w**; .... Hos 7:3
will be for people who plan **w**, ... Mic 2:1
said, "The woman stands for **w**." .... Zch 5:8
yeast—the yeast of sin and **w**................ 1Co 5:8

WICKS
and also seven places for **w**. .... Zch 4:2

WIDE
inches long and nine inches **w**— .... Ex 39:9
feet long and six feet **w**! .... Dt 3:11
seven and one-half feet **w**, ... 2Ch 6:13
and nine feet **w** and set it up .... Da 3:1
of your land are **w** open for your .... Nah 3:13
The gate is **w** and the road is .... Mt 7:13
and the road is **w** that leads to .... Mt 7:13
opened his eyes **w** and they were .... Mk 8:25
how **w** and how long and how high .... Eph 3:18
1,500 miles **w**, and 1,500 miles .... Rev 21:16

WIDER
the earth and **w** than the sea. .... Job 11:9
stretch it out and make it **w**. .... Is 54:2
the Temple were **w** on each higher........... Eze 41:7
rooms were **w** on the top story. .... Eze 41:7
stories of the building were **w**. .... Eze 42:5

WIDOW
must not marry a **w**, a divorced .... Le 21:14
If a **w** or divorced woman makes a........... Nu 30:9
of Carmel, the **w** of Nabal. 1Sa 27:3
and Abigail the **w** of Nabal from 1Sa 30:5
I will never be a **w** or lose my................. Is 47:8
but now she is like a **w**. .... La 1:1
and she was a **w** for eighty-four .... Lk 2:37
only to a **w** in Zarephath, ... Lk 4:26
he saw a poor **w** putting two .... Lk 21:2
But if a **w** has children or 1Ti 5:4
I am not a **w**; I will never be .... Rev 18:7

WIDOWED
daughter becomes **w** or divorced, ... Le 22:13

WIDOWS
orphans, and he defends the **w**. .... Ps 68:5
pay and who cheat **w** and orphans, ... Mal 3:5
there were many **w** in Israel .... Lk 4:25
Greek-speaking **w** were not .... Ac 6:1
and for the **w** I say this: 1Co 7:8

care of **w** who are truly widows. 1Ti 5:3
for orphans or **w** who need help, ... Jam 1:27

WIDTH
Its **w** was equal to that of the 1Ki 6:3
measured the **w** of the entrance .... Eze 40:11
The **w** of the gate was about .... Eze 40:11
the length and **w** of the north .... Eze 40:20
same length and **w** and the same .... Eze 42:11
and its full **w** about three miles .... Eze 48:13
its length was equal to its **w**. .... Rev 21:16

WIFE
mother and be united with his **w**, ... Ge 2:24
The man and his **w** were naked,.............. Ge 2:25
the man and his **w** hid from the .... Ge 3:8
listened to what your **w** said, ... Ge 3:17
man named his **w** Eve, because she .... Ge 3:20
man and his **w** and dressed them. .... Ge 3:21
sexual relations with his **w** Eve, ... Ge 4:1
had sexual relations with his **w**, ... Ge 4:17
relations with his **w** Eve again, ... Ge 4:25
sons, your **w**, and your sons' .... Ge 6:18
He and his **w** and his sons and .... Ge 7:7
On that same day Noah and his **w**,.......... Ge 7:13
You and your **w**, your sons, and .... Ge 8:16
his sons, his **w**, and his sons' .... Ge 8:18
Abram's **w** was named Sarai,................. Ge 11:29
and Nahor's **w** was named Milcah. .... Ge 11:29
Sarai (Abram's **w**) and moved out .... Ge 11:31
He took his **w** Sarai, his nephew .... Ge 12:5
he said to his **w** Sarai, "I know .... Ge 12:11
will say, 'This woman is his **w**.' .... Ge 12:12
because of Abram's **w** Sarai. .... Ge 12:17
you tell me Sarai was your **w**? .... Ge 12:18
sister' so that I made her my **w**?............... Ge 12:19
Now, here is your **w**. Take her .... Ge 12:19
so Abram and his **w** left with .... Ge 12:20
So Abram, his **w**, and Lot left .... Ge 13:1
Sarai, Abram's **w**, had no .... Ge 16:1
name of Sarai, your **w**, to Sarah. .... Ge 17:15
Sarah your **w** will have a son, ... Ge 17:19
Where is your **w** Sarah?" .... Ge 18:9
that time your **w** Sarah will have .... Ge 18:10
Take your **w** and your two .... Ge 19:15
hands of Lot, his **w**, and his two............. Ge 19:16
that point Lot's **w** looked back. .... Ge 19:26
people that his **w** Sarah was his .... Ge 20:2
Give Abraham his **w** back. .... Ge 20:7
Sarah, Abraham's **w**, back to him .... Ge 20:14
Abimelech, his **w**, and his .... Ge 20:17
for taking Abraham's **w** Sarah. .... Ge 20:18
mother found a **w** for him in .... Ge 21:21
Nahor and his **w** Milcah have .... Ge 22:20
so that I can bury my dead **w**." .... Ge 23:4
you from burying your dead **w**." .... Ge 23:6
to help me bury my dead **w** here, ... Ge 23:8
as witnesses. Bury your dead **w**." .... Ge 23:11
the land, and bury your dead **w**." .... Ge 23:15
buried his **w** Sarah in the cave .... Ge 23:19
Don't get a **w** for my son from .... Ge 24:3
and get a **w** for my son Isaac." .... Ge 24:4
help you get a **w** for my son .... Ge 24:7
me to find a **w** for his son today .... Ge 24:12
my master's **w**, gave birth to .... Ge 24:36
'Don't get a **w** for my son from .... Ge 24:37
you must get a **w** for my son.'................. Ge 24:38
You will get a **w** for my son from .... Ge 24:40
not give you a **w** for my son, ... Ge 24:41
mother, and she became his **w**. .... Ge 24:67
and his new **w** was Keturah. .... Ge 25:1
buried with his **w** Sarah in the .... Ge 25:10
Isaac's **w** could not have........................ Ge 25:21
w Rebekah was very beautiful, ... Ge 26:7

to tell them she was his **w**. .... Ge 26:7
holding his **w** Rebekah tenderly. .... Ge 26:8
and said, "This woman is your **w**. .... Ge 26:9
sexual relations with your **w**. .... Ge 26:10
this man or his **w** will be put to .... Ge 26:11
Mesopotamia to find a **w** there. .... Ge 28:6
him his daughter Rachel as a **w**.............. Ge 29:28
to Jacob as a **w**, and he had .... Ge 30:4
girl Zilpah to Jacob as a **w**. .... Ge 30:9
He had six sons by his **w** Leah: .... Ge 35:23
He had two sons by his **w** Rachel: .... Ge 35:24
Esau's grandsons by his **w** Adah. .... Ge 36:12
grandsons by his **w** Basemath. .... Ge 36:13
Esau's third **w** was Oholibamah .... Ge 36:14
grandsons of Esau's **w** Basemath. .... Ge 36:17
Esau's **w** Oholibamah gave birth .... Ge 36:18
came from Esau's **w** Oholibamah .... Ge 36:18
Tamar to be the **w** of his first .... Ge 38:6
with your dead brother's **w**. .... Ge 38:8
After a long time Judah's **w**, ... Ge 38:12
some time the **w** of Joseph's .... Ge 39:7
you, because you are his **w**. .... Ge 39:9
His master's **w** grabbed his coat .... Ge 39:12
heard what his **w** said Joseph had .... Ge 39:19
gave Joseph a **w** named Asenath, ... Ge 41:45
Joseph's **w** was Asenath daughter .... Ge 41:50
only son left from my **w** Rachel.............. Ge 42:38
You know that my **w** Rachel gave .... Ge 44:27
sons of Jacob's **w** Rachel were .... Ge 46:19
and Ephraim by his **w** Asenath, ... Ge 46:20
sons of Jacob by his **w** Rachel. .... Ge 46:22
Sarah his **w** are buried there. .... Ge 49:31
and Rebekah his **w** are buried .... Ge 49:31
and I buried my **w** Leah there. .... Ge 49:31
Zipporah to Moses to be his **w**. .... Ex 2:21
Moses took his **w** and his sons, ... Ex 4:20
had sent his **w** Zipporah to .... Ex 18:2
took Moses' **w** and his two sons .... Ex 18:5
with your **w** and her two sons. .... Ex 18:6
must not want his **w** or his male............. Ex 20:17
he must leave without a **w**. .... Ex 21:3
he may take his **w** with him. .... Ex 21:3
slave's master gives him a **w**, ... Ex 21:4
my master, my **w** and my children, ... Ex 21:5
his first **w** from having food .... Ex 21:10
her, and she will become his **w**. .... Ex 22:16
relations with your father's **w**; .... Le 18:8
and his **w** have a daughter, ... Le 18:11
with the **w** of your father's .... Le 18:11
she is your son's **w**. Do not have .... Le 18:15
relations with your brother's **w**. .... Le 18:16
While your **w** is still living,.............. Le 18:18
take her sister as another **w**. .... Le 18:18
your neighbor's **w** and make .... Le 18:20
relations with his neighbor's **w**, ... Le 20:10
relations with his father's **w**, ... Le 20:11
and his father's **w** must be put .... Le 20:11
relations with his uncle's **w**, ... Le 20:20
and his uncle's **w** will die .... Le 20:20
a man to marry his brother's **w**. .... Le 20:21
'A man's **w** might be unfaithful .... Nu 5:12
because he suspects his **w**. .... Nu 5:30
Moses took his **w** Cushite who .... Nu 12:1
whose **w** was named Jochebed. .... Nu 26:59
want to take your neighbor's **w**. .... Dt 5:21
Every husband and **w** will have .... Dt 7:14
or daughter, the **w** you love, or .... Dt 13:6
you may take her as your **w**. .... Dt 21:11
husband, and she will be your **w**. .... Dt 21:13
to the **w** he does not love, ... Dt 21:15
the son of the **w** he loves what .... Dt 21:16
son of the **w** he does not love. .... Dt 21:16
son is from the **w** he does not.............. Dt 21:17

to this man to be his **w**, ... Dt 22:16
will continue to be the man's **w**, ... Dt 22:19
said about his **w** are true, ... Dt 22:20
relations with another man's **w**, ... Dt 22:22
relations with another man's **w**............. Dt 22:24
must not marry his father's **w**; .... Dt 22:30
a year to make his new **w** happy. .... Dt 24:5
one man's **w** comes to save her .... Dt 25:11
relations with his father's **w**, ... Dt 27:20
brother, his **w** whom he loves, ... Dt 28:54
a **w** to the man who attacks and.............. Jos 15:16
Acsah to Othniel to be his **w**. .... Jos 15:17
a **w** to the man who attacks and.............. Jdg 1:12
Acsah to Othniel to be his **w**. .... Jdg 1:13
Deborah, the **w** of Lappidoth, was .... Jdg 4:4
She was the **w** of Heber, one of .... Jdg 4:17
But Jael, the **w** of Heber, took a .... Jdg 4:21
the **w** of Heber the Kenite. .... Jdg 5:24
Gilead's **w** had several sons. .... Jdg 11:2
He had a **w**, but she could not .... Jdg 13:2
appeared to Manoah's **w** and said,.......... Jdg 13:3
Then Manoah's **w** went to him and .... Jdg 13:6
to Manoah's **w** again while she .... Jdg 13:9
got up and followed his **w**. .... Jdg 13:11
you the man who spoke to my **w**?" .... Jdg 13:11
Your **w** must be careful to do .... Jdg 13:13
as Manoah and his **w** watched. .... Jdg 13:19
When Manoah and his **w** saw that, ... Jdg 13:20
But his **w** said to him, "If the .... Jdg 13:23
day they said to Samson's **w**, ... Jdg 14:15
So Samson's **w** went to him, ... Jdg 14:16
Samson's **w** cried for the rest of........... Jdg 14:17
And Samson's **w** was given to his .... Jdg 14:20
Samson went to visit his **w**, ... Jdg 15:1
thought you really hated your **w**, ... Jdg 15:2
gave his **w** to his best man." .... Jdg 15:6
burned Samson's **w** and her father.......... Jdg 15:6
'Anyone who gives a **w** to a man .... Jdg 21:18
Moab with his **w** and his two sons .... Ru 1:2
His **w** was named Naomi, and his .... Ru 1:2
the Moabite, the dead man's **w**. .... Ru 4:5
Moabite who was the **w** of Mahlon, ... Ru 4:10
was the wife of Mahlon, as my **w**. .... Ru 4:10
home as his **w** and had sexual .... Ru 4:13
the meat to his **w** Peninnah and 1Sa 1:4
relations with his **w** Hannah, ... 1Sa 1:19
Eli blessed Elkanah and his **w**, ... 1Sa 2:20
the **w** of Phinehas, was 1Sa 4:19
Saul's **w** was Ahinoam daughter of 1Sa 14:50
his daughter Michal for his **w**. 1Sa 18:27
Michal, David's **w**, warned him, ... 1Sa 19:11
His **w** was named Abigail. 1Sa 25:3
Abigail, Nabal's **w**, "David sent 1Sa 25:14
his **w** told him everything. 1Sa 25:37
Abigail, asking her to be his **w**. 1Sa 25:39
you so you can become his **w**." 1Sa 25:40
And she became David's **w**. 1Sa 25:42
Michal was also David's **w**,................. 1Sa 25:44
each man take his **w** and children 1Sa 30:22
mother was Eglah, David's **w**................ 2Sa 3:5
saying, "Give me my **w** Michal. 2Sa 3:14
is the **w** of Uriah the Hittite." 2Sa 11:3
sexual relations with my **w**!" 2Sa 11:11
became David's **w** and gave birth 2Sa 11:27
and took his **w** to be your wife! 2Sa 12:9
and took his wife to be your **w**! 2Sa 12:9
you took the **w** of Uriah the 2Sa 12:10
David comforted Bathsheba his **w**........... 2Sa 12:24
The man's **w** spread a sheet over 2Sa 17:19
the Shunammite to be my **w**."................ 1Ki 2:17
same kind of palace for his **w**. 1Ki 7:8
Hadad so much he gave Hadad a **w**— 1Ki 11:19
of Tahpenes, the king's **w**. 1Ki 11:19

So Jeroboam said to his **w**, ... 1Ki 14:2
people won't know you are my **w**. 1Ki 14:2
So the king's **w** did as he said 1Ki 14:4
Jeroboam's **w** is coming to ask 1Ki 14:5
said, "Come in, **w** of Jeroboam. 1Ki 14:6
Ahijah said to Jeroboam's **w**, ... 1Ki 14:12
Then Jeroboam's **w** left and 1Ki 14:17
w, Jezebel, came in and asked 1Ki 21:5
because his **w** Jezebel influenced 1Ki 21:25
The **w** of a man from the groups 2Ki 4:1
little girl served Naaman's **w**. 2Ki 5:2
She was the **w** of Shallum son of 2Ki 22:14
Hadad's **w** was named Mehetabel, ... 1Ch 1:50
had children by his **w** Azubah and........... 1Ch 2:18
Ephrathah, his **w** Abijah had his 1Ch 2:24
had another **w**, named Atarah. 1Ch 2:26
Abishur's **w** was named Abihail, ... 1Ch 2:29
Hodiah's **w** was Naham's sister. 1Ch 4:19
sons of Hodiah's **w** were Eshtemoa 1Ch 4:19
Makir took a **w** from the Huppites 1Ch 7:15
Makir's **w** Maacah had a son whom 1Ch 7:16
relations with his **w** again. 1Ch 7:23
leader. His **w** was named Maacah. 1Ch 8:29
leader. His **w** was named Maacah. 1Ch 9:35
My **w** must not live in King 2Ch 8:11
sister and the **w** of Jehoiada the............. 2Ch 22:11
She was the **w** of Shallum son of 2Ch 34:22
together his friends and his **w**, ... Est 5:10
Then Haman's **w**, Zeresh, and all .... Est 5:14
He told his **w**, Zeresh, and all .... Est 6:13
Haman's **w** and the men who gave........... Est 6:13
Job's **w** said to him, "Why are .... Job 2:9
My **w** can't stand my breath, ... Job 19:17
at my neighbor's door for his **w**,.............. Job 31:9
let my **w** grind another man's.................. Job 31:10
orphans and his **w** a widow. .... Ps 109:9
Your **w** will give you many .... Ps 128:3
the unfaithful **w** who tries to .... Pr 2:16
another man's **w** may seem sweet .... Pr 5:3
Be faithful to your own **w**, ... Pr 5:15
happy with the **w** you married .... Pr 5:18
a woman who is not your **w**. .... Pr 5:20
of another man's unfaithful **w**. .... Pr 6:24
relations with another man's **w**. .... Pr 6:29
unfaithful **w** and her pleasing. .... Pr 7:5
A good **w** is like a crown for her .... Pr 12:4
a disgraceful **w** is like a .... Pr 12:4
When a man finds a **w**, he finds .... Pr 18:22
a quarreling **w** is like dripping .... Pr 19:13
but a wise **w** is a gift from the .... Pr 19:14
the house with a quarreling **w**. .... Pr 21:9
a quarreling and complaining **w**. .... Pr 21:19
an unfaithful **w** are like a deep .... Pr 22:14
an unfaithful **w** is like a narrow .... Pr 23:27
the house with a quarreling **w**. .... Pr 25:24
A quarreling **w** is as bothersome .... Pr 27:15
It is hard to find a good **w**, ... Pr 31:10
Enjoy life with the **w** you love. .... Ec 9:9
You were like a **w** who married .... Is 54:6
a man rejoices over his new **w**, ... Is 62:5
divorces his **w** and she leaves................. Je 3:1
were like an unfaithful **w** to me............... Je 5:7
each one wants another man's **w**. .... Je 5:8
A husband and his **w** will both be .... Je 6:11
You are a **w** who is guilty of .... Eze 16:32
his neighbor's **w** or with a woman .... Eze 18:6
relations with his neighbor's **w**. .... Eze 18:11
relations with his neighbor's **w**. .... Eze 18:15
act with his neighbor's **w**, ... Eze 22:11
While still my **w**, Samaria had .... Eze 23:5
going to take your **w** from you, ... Eze 24:16
and my **w** died in the evening. .... Eze 24:18
relations with his neighbor's **w**. .... Eze 33:26

his daughters as a **w** to the king............... Da 11:17
because she is no longer my **w**, ... Hos 2:2
behaving like an unfaithful **w**. .... Hos 2:2
where he worked to get a **w**; .... Hos 12:12
'Your **w** will become a prostitute .... Am 7:17
say anything, even to your **w**. .... Mic 7:5
you treated the **w** you married .... Mal 2:14
promise to the **w** you married................... Mal 2:15
mother had been Uriah's **w**. .... Mt 1:6
afraid to take Mary as your **w**, ... Mt 1:20
Joseph took Mary as his **w**,.................... Mt 1:24
who divorces his **w** must give her .... Mt 5:31
divorces his **w** forces her to be .... Mt 5:32
to divorce his **w** is if she has .... Mt 5:32
who had been the **w** of Philip, ... Mt 14:3
the servant's **w** and children. .... Mt 18:25
to divorce his **w** for any reason .... Mt 19:3
mother and be united with his **w**, ... Mt 19:5
to divorce his **w** by giving her .... Mt 19:7
who divorces his **w** and marries .... Mt 19:9
to divorce his **w** is if his wife .... Mt 19:9
his wife is if his **w** has sexual .... Mt 19:9
reason a man can divorce his **w**,............... Mt 19:10
Then the **w** of Zebedee came to .... Mt 20:20
the dead, whose **w** will she be?".............. Mt 22:28
his **w** sent this message to him: .... Mt 27:19
prison in order to please his **w**, ... Mk 6:17
She had been the **w** of Philip,.............. Mk 6:17
be married to your brother's **w**.".............. Mk 6:18
for a man to divorce his **w**?" .... Mk 10:2
mother and be united with his **w**, ... Mk 10:7
who divorces his **w** and marries .... Mk 10:11
leaving a **w** but no children, ... Mk 12:19
the dead, whose **w** will she be?".............. Mk 12:23
Zechariah's **w**, Elizabeth, came .... Lk 1:5
Your **w**, Elizabeth, will give .... Lk 1:13
old man, and my **w** is old, too." .... Lk 1:18
Zechariah's **w**, Elizabeth, became .... Lk 1:24
Herodias, the **w** of Herod's .... Lk 3:19
Joanna, the **w** of Cuza (the .... Lk 8:3
father, mother, **w**, children, ... Lk 14:26
a man divorces his **w** and marries .... Lk 16:18
Remember Lot's **w**. .... Lk 17:32
and leaves a **w** but no children, ... Lk 20:28
whose **w** will she be when people .... Lk 20:33
sister, Mary the **w** of Clopas, ... Jn 19:25
Ananias and his **w** Sapphira sold .... Ac 5:1
his **w** knew about this and agreed .... Ac 5:2
three hours later his **w** came .... Ac 5:7
Aquila and his **w**, Priscilla, had .... Ac 18:2
some days Felix came with his **w**, ... Ac 24:24
A man there has his father's **w**. 1Co 5:1
each man should have his own **w**, ... 1Co 7:2
should give his **w** all that he 1Co 7:3
all that he owes her as his **w**. 1Co 7:3
the **w** should give her husband 1Co 7:3
The **w** does not have full rights 1Co 7:4
his own body; his **w** shares them. 1Co 7:4
w should not leave her husband. 1Co 7:10
should not divorce his **w**. 1Co 7:11
Christian man has a **w** who is not 1Co 7:12
holy through his believing **w**. 1Co 7:14
And the **w** who is not a believer 1Co 7:14
W, you don't know; maybe you 1Co 7:16
maybe you will save your **w**. 1Co 7:16
If you have a **w**, do not try to 1Co 7:27
married, do not try to find a **w**. 1Co 7:27
world, trying to please his **w**, ... 1Co 7:33
pleasing his **w** and pleasing the 1Co 7:34
a believing **w** with us when we 1Co 9:5
husband is the head of the **w**,................... Eph 5:23
who loves his **w** loves himself. .... Eph 5:28
mother and be united with his **w**, ... Eph 5:31

WIFE'S

you must love his **w** as he loves .... Eph 5:33
a **w** must respect her husband. .... Eph 5:33
and he must have only one **w**. 1Ti 3:2
must have only one **w** and be good 1Ti 3:12
have only one **w**, and must have............... Tit 1:6
and husband and **w** should keep .... Heb 13:4
the bride, the **w** of the Lamb." .... Rev 21:9

WIFE'S

the side of his **w** body and went .... Ge 23:3
w name was Mehetabel daughter .... Ge 36:39
I'm going to my **w** room," but her .... Jdg 15:1

WILD

Ishmael will be like a **w** donkey............... Ge 16:12
father that a **w** animal killed .... Ge 37:20
in this place where **w** dogs live, ... Ps 44:19
will become **w** and useful only .... Is 7:24
houses will be full of **w** dogs. .... Is 13:21
he ate locusts and **w** honey. .... Mt 3:4
He was with the **w** animals, ... Mk 1:13
saw animals, **w** beasts, reptiles .... Ac 11:6
branch of a **w** olive tree that .... Rm 11:17
and by the **w** animals of the .... Rev 6:8

WILDLY

and the whole mountain shook **w**. .... Ex 19:18
that the people were acting **w**. .... Ex 32:25
paws **w**, enjoying its strength, ... Job 39:21

WILL

or you **w** show that you don't .... Le 19:12
I **w** tell about your goodness in .... Ps 40:9
me live so people **w** praise you. .... Ps 143:11
w be forced away from people. .... Da 4:32
you **w** live with the wild animals .... Da 4:32
in heaven **w** also forgive you .... Mt 6:14
are our Lord' **w** enter the .... Mt 7:21
that what you want **w** be done." .... Mt 26:42
'I **w** send my messenger ahead of .... Lk 7:27
you **w** say three times that you .... Lk 22:34
I said, 'A man **w** come after me, ... Jn 1:30
he **w** explain everything to us." .... Jn 4:25
before you **w** believe in me." .... Jn 4:48
who did evil **w** rise to be judged............... Jn 5:29
they **w** know that my teaching .... Jn 7:17
what the Lord wants **w** be done." .... Ac 21:14
I pray that I **w** be allowed to .... Rm 1:10
So one of you **w** ask me:............... Rm 9:19
you **w** be able to decide what .... Rm 12:2
Jesus **w** keep you strong until............... 1Co 1:8
your "doing" **w** be equal to your 2Co 8:11
that we **w** receive what God .... Eph 1:14
so that you **w** know him better. .... Eph 1:17
also that you **w** have greater .... Eph 1:18
wine, which **w** ruin you, but be .... Eph 5:18
live in a way that **w** please God,............... 1Th 4:1
The Lord **w** punish people who do 1Th 4:6
the agreement I **w** make with them .... Heb 10:16
lives that they **w** see the good............... 1Pe 2:12
you do and **w** give glory to God 1Pe 2:12
so that you **w** live here on earth 1Pe 4:2
But they **w** have to explain this 1Pe 4:5
I **w** try my best so that you may 2Pe 1:15
the light and **w** not cause anyone 1Jn 2:10
you **w** stay in the Son and in the 1Jn 2:24
of God so you **w** know you have............... 1Jn 5:13
and God **w** give the sinner life. 1Jn 5:16

WILLING

You were **w** to kill your own sons .... Ex 32:29
everyone who is **w** bring this .... Ex 35:5
anyone who was **w** also brought 2Ch 29:31
If you are **w** and if I have .... Ne 2:5
If you are **w**, give me letters .... Ne 2:7
the people were **w** to work............... Ne 4:6

strong by giving me a **w** spirit. .... Ps 51:12
accept my **w** praise and teach me .... Ps 119:108
the one who is **w** to sell it. .... Pr 11:26
If you become **w** and obey me, ... Is 1:19
You are even **w** to kill innocent .... Je 22:17
will not be **w** to listen to you, ... Eze 3:7
they are not **w** to listen to me. .... Eze 3:7
They were **w** to die rather than .... Da 3:28
Whoever is not **w** to carry the .... Mt 10:38
They must be **w** even to give up .... Mt 16:24
They must be **w** even to give up .... Mk 8:34
They must be **w** to give up their .... Lk 9:23
Whoever is not **w** to carry his............... Lk 14:27
if you are **w**, take away this .... Lk 22:42
people were more **w** to listen .... Ac 17:11
are very **w** to accept a spirit 2Co 11:4
always be **w** to listen and slow .... Jam 1:19
people should be **w** to be under 1Pe 5:5

WILLOW

it to grow like a **w** tree. .... Eze 17:5

WILLS

when that man **w** his property to .... Dt 21:16

WILTED

a desert that is **w** and dead. .... Je 12:11

WIN

Israelites would **w** the fight, ... Ex 17:11
down, the Amalekites would **w**. .... Ex 17:11
LORD's command? You will not **w**! .... Nu 14:41
will give you the power to **w**. .... Jos 8:7
Peniel, "After I **w** the victory, ... Jdg 8:9
and the LORD helps me **w**, ... Jdg 11:9
flat land, and then we will **w**, ... 1Ki 20:23
flat land, and then we will **w**." 1Ki 20:25
Attack Ramoth in Gilead and **w**,............... 1Ki 22:12
Micaiah answered, "Attack and **w**!............... 1Ki 22:15
Don't let anyone **w** against you." 2Ch 14:11
Attack Ramoth in Gilead and **w**,............... 2Ch 18:11
are saying King Ahab will **w**. 2Ch 18:12
Micaiah answered, "Attack and **w**!............... 2Ch 18:14
a Jew, you cannot **w** against him. .... Est 6:13
Do not let them **w** over me. .... Job 17:4
when I knew I could **w** in court............... Job 31:21
Our tongues will help us **w**. .... Ps 12:4
long will my enemy **w** over me? .... Ps 13:2
but we march forward and **w**............... Ps 20:8
your majesty the victory for .... Ps 45:4
Temple, "When I **w**, I will divide............... Ps 60:6
but we can **w** with God's help. .... Ps 60:12
Temple, "When I **w**, I will divide. .... Ps 108:7
but we can **w** with God's help. .... Ps 108:13
harder to **w** back than a walled .... Pr 18:19
lots of good advice, you will **w**. .... Pr 24:6
does not always **w** the race, ... Ec 9:11
does not always **w** the battle, ... Ec 9:11
beach, but they can't **w** over it. .... Je 5:22
will let those **w** who want to .... Je 21:7
Then I will **w** back my people............... Eze 14:5
city and will fight and **w**. .... Da 11:7
he makes justice the **w** the victory. .... Mt 12:20
and you will **w** your case."............... Rm 3:4
people to **w** as many as I can............... 1Co 9:19
became like a Jew to **w** the Jews. 1Co 9:20
I did this to **w** those who are 1Co 9:20
I did this to **w** those people who............... 1Co 9:21
weak so I could **w** the weak. 1Co 9:22
one gets the prize. So run to **w**! 1Co 9:24
so they can **w** a crown. 1Co 9:25
Satan would not **w** anything from 2Co 2:11
all the rules in order to **w**. 2Ti 2:5
those who **w** the victory I will .... Rev 2:7
Those who **w** the victory will not .... Rev 2:11

Those who **w** the victory will be .... Rev 3:5
make those who **w** the victory .... Rev 3:12
Those who **w** the victory will sit .... Rev 3:21
determined to **w** the victory. .... Rev 6:2
Those who **w** the victory will .... Rev 21:7

WIND

He made a **w** blow over the earth, ... Ge 8:1
and burned by the hot east **w.** .... Ge 41:6
were burned by the hot east **w.** .... Ge 41:23
the hot east **w** stand for seven .... Ge 41:27
LORD caused a strong **w** to blow .... Ex 10:13
east **w** had brought the locusts. .... Ex 10:13
So the LORD changed the **w.** .... Ex 10:19
a very strong **w** blow from the .... Ex 10:19
the sea with a strong east **w,** .... Ex 14:21
of a leaf being blown by the **w.** .... Le 26:36
sent a strong **w** from the sea, ... Nu 11:31
He raced on the wings of the **w.** 2Sa 22:11
The **w** blew from his nose. 2Sa 22:16
The **w** began to blow, and soon a 1Ki 18:45
a very strong **w** blew until it 1Ki 19:11
But the LORD was not in the **w.** 1Ki 19:11
After the **w,** there was an 1Ki 19:11
says you won't see **w** or rain, ... 2Ki 3:17
is burned by the **w** before it can 2Ki 19:26
Suddenly a great **w** came from the .... Job 1:19
man as if they were only **w?** .... Job 6:26
Your words are no more than **w.** .... Job 8:2
a leaf that is blown by the **w;** .... Job 13:25
his stomach with the hot east **w.** .... Job 15:2
straw in the **w** or like chaff .... Job 21:18
The east **w** will carry them away, ... Job 27:21
w will hit them without mercy .... Job 27:22
be as if the **w** is clapping its .... Job 27:23
gave power to the **w** and measured .... Job 28:25
honor away as if by a great **w,** .... Job 30:15
threw me into the **w** and tossed .... Job 30:22
is silenced by the hot, south **w.** .... Job 37:17
sky after the **w** has blown all .... Job 37:21
chaff that the **w** blows away. .... Ps 1:4
He raced on the wings of the **w.** .... Ps 18:10
The **w** blew from your nose. .... Ps 18:15
into pieces, like dust in the **w.** .... Ps 18:42
blown by the **w** as the angel .... Ps 35:5
trading ships with an east **w.** .... Ps 48:7
far away from the **w** and storm." .... Ps 55:8
smoke is driven away by the **w.** .... Ps 68:2
He sent the east **w** from heaven .... Ps 78:26
led the south **w** by his power. .... Ps 78:26
like a **w** that blows and does not .... Ps 78:39
like chaff blown away by the **w.** .... Ps 83:13
and frighten them with your **w.** .... Ps 83:15
thoughts are just a puff of **w.** .... Ps 94:11
After the **w** blows, the flower is .... Ps 103:16
you ride on the wings of the **w.** .... Ps 104:3
He brings out the **w** from his .... Ps 135:7
be left with nothing but the **w.** .... Pr 11:29
like clouds and **w** that give no .... Pr 25:14
As the north **w** brings rain, ... Pr 25:23
stopping the **w** or trying to grab .... Pr 27:16
Who can hold the **w** in his hand? .... Pr 30:4
The **w** blows to the south; .... Ec 1:6
all useless, like chasing the **w.** .... Ec 1:14
out to be like chasing the **w.** .... Ec 1:17
was useless, like chasing the **w.** .... Ec 2:11
is useless, like chasing the **w.** .... Ec 2:17
is useless, like chasing the **w.** .... Ec 2:26
is useless, like chasing the **w.** .... Ec 4:4
and that is like chasing the **w.** .... Ec 4:6
are useless, like chasing the **w.** .... Ec 4:16
do they gain from chasing the **w?** .... Ec 5:16
is useless—like chasing the **w.** .... Ec 6:9

control the **w** or stop his own .... Ec 8:8
know where the **w** will blow, ... Ec 11:5
north **w.** Come, south wind. .... Sng 4:16
wind. Come, south **w.** Blow on my .... Sng 4:16
of the forest blown by the **w.** .... Is 7:2
dry it up with a scorching **w.** .... Is 11:15
the hills being blown by the **w,** .... Is 17:13
the desert like **w** blowing in the .... Is 21:1
We gave birth, but only to **w.** .... Is 26:18
a hot desert **w,** he will drive it .... Is 27:8
a storm of hail and strong **w,** .... Is 28:2
be like a shelter from the **w,** .... Is 32:2
A destructive **w** will burn you .... Is 33:11
is burned by the **w** before it can .... Is 37:27
and the **w** blows them away like .... Is 40:24
and the **w** will carry them away; .... Is 41:16
nor the desert **w** will hurt them. .... Is 49:10
The **w** will blow them all away; .... Is 57:13
just a puff of **w** will take them .... Is 57:13
sins, like the **w,** have carried .... Is 64:6
and sniffs the **w** at mating time. .... Je 2:24
A hot **w** blows from the bare .... Je 4:11
is not a gentle **w** to separate .... Je 4:11
I feel a stronger **w** than that. .... Je 4:12
prophets are like an empty **w;** .... Je 5:13
and brings out the **w** from his .... Je 10:13
is blown away by the desert **w.** .... Je 13:24
and sniff the **w** like wild dogs. .... Je 14:6
a strong east **w,** I will scatter .... Je 18:17
a destroying **w** to blow against .... Je 51:1
Babylon like a **w** that blows .... Je 51:2
and brings out the **w** from his .... Je 51:16
I saw a stormy **w** coming from the .... Eze 1:4
And scatter one-third to the **w.** .... Eze 5:2
and a stormy **w** will break the .... Eze 13:11
break the wall with a stormy **w.** .... Eze 13:13
die when the east **w** hits it in .... Eze 17:10
will be scattered to every **w.** .... Eze 17:21
The east **w** dried it up. .... Eze 19:12
but the east **w** broke you to .... Eze 27:26
said to me, "Prophesy to the **w.** .... Eze 37:9
and say to the **w,** 'This is what .... Eze 37:9
W, come from the four winds, and .... Eze 37:9
the **w** blew them away, and there .... Da 2:35
In the vision the **w** was blowing .... Da 7:2
plans are like planting the **w,** .... Hos 8:7
is as useless as chasing the **w;** .... Hos 12:1
he chases the east **w** all day. .... Hos 12:1
will send a **w** from the east, ... Hos 13:15
and creates the **w** and makes his .... Am 4:13
LORD sent a great **w** on the sea, ... Jnh 1:4
Since the **w** and the waves of the .... Jnh 1:11
sent a very hot east **w** to blow, ... Jnh 4:8
they leave like the **w** and move .... Hab 1:11
out with the **w** in their wings. .... Zch 5:9
command to the **w** and the waves, ... Mt 8:26
the **w** and the waves obey him! .... Mt 8:27
to see? A reed blown by the **w?** .... Mt 11:7
the **w** was blowing against .... Mt 14:24
Peter saw the **w** and the waves, ... Mt 14:30
the boat, the **w** became calm. .... Mt 14:32
A very strong **w** came up on the .... Mk 4:37
and commanded the **w** and said to .... Mk 4:39
Then the **w** stopped, and it .... Mk 4:39
the **w** and the waves obey him! .... Mk 4:41
the **w** was blowing against .... Mk 6:48
them, and the **w** became calm. .... Mk 6:51
to see? A reed blown by the **w?** .... Lk 7:24
A very strong **w** blew up on the .... Lk 8:23
command to the **w** and the waves. .... Lk 8:24
even the **w** and the water, ... Lk 8:25
you feel the **w** begin to blow .... Lk 12:55
w blows where it wants to and .... Jn 3:8

charge of storing the **w** that 1Ch 27:27
fifteen thousand gallons of **w**, ... 2Ch 2:10
barley, oil, and **w** you promised. 2Ch 2:15
Solomon his **w** and their good 2Ch 9:4
of food, oil, and **w** in them. 2Ch 11:11
their grain, new **w**, oil, honey, ... 2Ch 31:5
for grain, new **w**, and oil and 2Ch 32:28
also gave food, **w**, and oil to .... Ezr 3:7
or wheat, salt, **w**, or olive oil. .... Ezr 6:9
gallons of **w**, and six hundred .... Ezr 7:22
one who served **w** to the king. .... Ne 1:11
He wanted some **w**, so I took some .... Ne 2:1
money, grain, new **w**, and oil." .... Ne 5:11
person, along with food and **w**. .... Ne 5:15
days there were all kinds of **w**. .... Ne 5:18
trees, and our new **w** and oil. .... Ne 10:37
gifts of grain, new **w**, and oil. .... Ne 10:39
of grain, new **w**, and olive oil .... Ne 13:5
crops, new **w**, and olive oil. .... Ne 13:12
they were bringing loads of **w**, ... Ne 13:15
W was served in gold cups of .... Est 1:7
was plenty of the king's **w**, ... Est 1:7
He told the **w** servers to serve .... Est 1:8
he had been drinking much **w**. .... Est 1:10
were drinking **w**, the king said .... Est 5:6
were drinking **w** on the second .... Est 7:2
got up, left his **w**, and went out .... Est 7:7
eating and drinking **w** together .... Job 1:13
eating and drinking **w** together .... Job 1:18
to get oil and grapes to get **w**, ... Job 24:11
am like **w** that has been bottled .... Job 32:19
burst like a new leather **w** bag. .... Job 32:19
with all their grain and new **w**. .... Ps 4:7
like people drunk with **w**. .... Ps 60:3
it is full of **w** mixed with .... Ps 75:8
a man who had been drunk with **w**. .... Ps 78:65
You give us **w** that makes happy .... Ps 104:15
though I am like a **w** bag going .... Ps 119:83
and your **w** barrels will overflow .... Pr 3:10
will overflow with new **w**. .... Pr 3:10
eating bread and drinking **w**. .... Pr 4:17
She has prepared her food and **w**; .... Pr 9:2
and drink the **w** I have prepared. .... Pr 9:5
W and beer make people loud and .... Pr 20:1
whoever loves **w** and perfume will .... Pr 21:17
drink too much **w** or eat too much .... Pr 23:20
is people who drink too much **w**, ... Pr 23:30
stare at the **w** when it is red, ... Pr 23:31
Kings should not drink **w**, ... Pr 31:4
are dying and **w** to those who are .... Pr 31:6
myself up with **w** while my mind .... Ec 2:3
drink your **w** and be happy, ... Ec 9:7
you feel good, **w** makes you feel. .... Ec 10:19
your love is better than **w**. .... Sng 1:2
we praise your love more than **w**. .... Sng 1:4
Your love is better than **w**. .... Sng 4:10
I have drunk my **w** and my milk. .... Sng 5:1
cup always filled with **w**. .... Sng 7:2
and your mouth like the best **w**. .... Sng 7:9
Let this **w** go down sweetly for .... Sng 7:9
a drink of spiced **w** from my .... Sng 8:2
you are like **w** mixed with water. .... Is 1:22
will make only six gallons of **w**, ... Is 5:10
at night, becoming drunk with **w**. .... Is 5:11
tambourines, flutes, and **w**. .... Is 5:12
for drinking **w** and are champions .... Is 5:22
No one makes **w** in the .... Is 16:10
eat the food and drink the **w**. .... Is 22:13
The new **w** will be bad, and the .... Is 24:7
sing while they drink their **w**. .... Is 24:9
in the streets will ask for **w**, ... Is 24:11
with all the best food and **w**, ... Is 25:6
and wine, the finest meat and **w**. .... Is 25:6

those leaders are drunk with **w**; .... Is 28:7
with beer and are filled with **w**. .... Is 28:7
Become drunk, but not from **w**. .... Is 29:9
a land with grain and new **w**, ... Is 36:17
will be the **w** that makes them .... Is 49:26
punishment was like **w** in a cup. .... Is 51:17
The LORD made you drink that **w**; .... Is 51:17
who are drunk but not from **w**. .... Is 51:21
I gave you is like a cup of **w**. .... Is 51:22
buy **w** and milk without money .... Is 55:1
say, "Come, let's drink some **w**; .... Is 56:12
drink the new **w** that you have .... Is 62:8
will drink the **w** in the courts .... Is 62:9
walked on the grapes to make **w**?" .... Is 63:2
for holding **w** should be filled. .... Je 13:12
wine should be filled with **w**.' .... Je 13:12
we know all **w** bags should be .... Je 13:12
bags should be filled with **w**.' .... Je 13:12
who has been overcome with **w**. .... Je 23:9
My anger is like the **w** in a cup. .... Je 25:15
I served this **w** to the people of .... Je 25:18
who walk on grapes to make **w**; .... Je 25:30
the grain, new **w**, oil, young .... Je 31:12
and offer them **w** to drink." .... Je 35:2
bowls full of **w** and some cups .... Je 35:5
I said to them, "Drink some **w**." .... Je 35:5
men answered, "We never drink **w**. .... Je 35:6
descendants must never drink **w**. .... Je 35:6
sons, or daughters ever drink **w**. .... Je 35:8
his descendants not to drink **w**, ... Je 35:14
do not drink **w**. But I, the LORD. .... Je 35:14
Harvest the **w**, the summer fruit, ... Je 40:10
harvest of **w** and summer fruit .... Je 40:12
They are like **w** left to settle; .... Je 48:11
stopped the flow of **w** from the .... Je 48:33
The nations drank Babylon's **w**, ... Je 51:7
"Where is the grain and **w**?" .... La 2:12
may drink **w** when they enter. .... Eze 44:21
amount of food and **w** every day, ... Da 1:5
food or drink his **w** because that .... Da 1:8
the king's special food and **w**, ... Da 1:16
guests and drank **w** with them. .... Da 5:1
Belshazzar was drinking his **w**, ... Da 5:2
slave women drank **w** from them. .... Da 5:23
meat, or drink any **w**, or use any .... Da 10:3
wool and flax, **w** and olive oil.' .... Hos 2:5
gave her grain, new **w**, and oil. .... Hos 2:8
time and my new **w** when it is .... Hos 2:9
produce grain, new **w**, and oil; .... Hos 2:22
old and new **w**, which take away .... Hos 4:11
The rulers become crazy with **w**; .... Hos 7:5
to ask for grain and new **w**, ... Hos 7:14
and there won't be enough new **w**. .... Hos 9:2
give offerings of **w** to the LORD; .... Hos 9:4
as famous as the **w** of Lebanon. .... Hos 14:7
All you people who drink **w**, ... Joe 1:5
because your **w** has been taken .... Joe 1:5
the new **w** is dried up, ... Joe 1:10
you grain, new **w**, and olive oil, ... Joe 2:19
with new **w** and olive oil. .... Joe 2:24
sold girls to buy **w** to drink. .... Joe 3:3
On that day **w** will drip from the .... Joe 3:18
that money they buy **w** to drink .... Am 2:8
the Nazirites drink **w** and told .... Am 2:12
will not drink the **w** from them. .... Am 5:11
You drink **w** by the bowlful and .... Am 6:6
W will drip from the mountains .... Am 9:13
and drink the **w** from them; .... Am 9:14
you if you give him **w** and beer. .... Mic 2:11
you will not drink the new **w**. .... Mic 6:15
like people drunk from their **w**; .... Nah 1:10
Just as **w** can trick a person, ... Hab 2:5
from the jug of **w** until they are .... Hab 2:15

will not drink any w from them................ Zph 1:13
grain, the new w, the olive oil, ... Hag 1:11
cooked food, w, olive oil, or .... Hag 2:12
to come to the w vat to take out .... Hag 2:16
and the young women on new w. .... Zch 9:17
glad as when they have drunk w. .... Zch 10:7
pour new w into old leather .... Mt 9:17
will break, the w will spill. .... Mt 9:17
and the w bags will be ruined. .... Mt 9:17
always pour new w into new wine .... Mt 9:17
pour new wine into new w bags. .... Mt 9:17
too much and drinks too much w, ... Mt 11:19
gave Jesus w mixed with gall to .... Mt 27:34
He tasted the w but refused to .... Mt 27:34
pours new w into old leather .... Mk 2:22
the new w will break the bags, ... Mk 2:22
and the w will be ruined along .... Mk 2:22
But new w should be put into new .... Mk 2:22
to give Jesus w mixed with myrrh .... Mk 15:23
He will never drink w or beer, ... Lk 1:15
pours new w into old leather .... Lk 5:37
the new w will break the bags, ... Lk 5:37
the bags, the w will spill out, ... Lk 5:37
New w must be put into new .... Lk 5:38
drinking old w wants new wine,............... Lk 5:39
drinking old wine wants new w,............... Lk 5:39
says, 'The old w is better.'"................... Lk 5:39
did not eat bread or drink w, ... Lk 7:33
too much and drinks too much w, ... Lk 7:34
olive oil and w on his wounds, ... Lk 10:34
When all the w was gone, Jesus' .... Jn 2:3
to him, "They have no more w." .... Jn 2:3
it, the water had become w. .... Jn 2:9
He did not know where the w came .... Jn 2:9
always serve the best w first. .... Jn 2:10
they serve the cheaper w. .... Jn 2:10
have saved the best w till now." .... Jn 2:10
he had changed the water into w. .... Jn 4:46
"They have had too much w."................. Ac 2:13
meat or drink w or do anything .... Rm 14:21
be drunk with w, which will ruin .... Eph 5:18
drink too much w or like to 1Ti 3:3
drink too much w or try to get 1Ti 3:8
drink a little w to help your 1Ti 5:23
They must not drink too much w, ... Tit 1:7
or enslaved to too much w, ... Tit 2:3
not damage the olive oil and w!" .... Rev 6:6
nations drink the w of the anger .... Rev 14:8
will drink the w of God's anger, ... Rev 14:10
with the w of his terrible .... Rev 16:19
from the w of her sexual sin. .... Rev 17:2
have drunk the w of the desire .... Rev 18:3
Prepare w for her that is twice .... Rev 18:6
strong as the w she prepared for .... Rev 18:6
frankincense, w, olive oil, fine .... Rev 18:13
crush the w in the winepress .... Rev 19:15

WINEPRESS

from the threshing floor and w. .... Dt 16:13
the chaff in a w to keep the .... Jdg 6:11
Oreb and Zeeb at the w of Zeeb, ... Jdg 7:25
threshing floor or from the w?" 2Ki 6:27
of it and cut out a w as well. .... Is 5:2
I have walked in the w alone, ... Is 63:3
As if in a w, the Lord has .... La 1:15
floor and the w will not feed .... Hos 9:2
because the w is full and the .... Joe 3:13
dug a hole for a w and built a.............. Mt 21:33
dug a hole for a w and built a.............. Mk 12:1
into the great w of God's anger. .... Rev 14:19
trampled in the w outside the................. Rev 14:20
out of the w as high as horses .... Rev 14:20
wine in the w of the terrible .... Rev 19:15

WINEPRESSES

working in the w on the Sabbath .... Ne 13:15
No one makes wine in the w, ... Is 16:10
the flow of wine from the w. .... Je 48:33
of Hananel to the king's w...................... Zch 14:10

WING

Each w was seven and one-half 1Ki 6:24
from the end of one w to the end 1Ki 6:24
One creature's w touched one 1Ki 6:27
other creature's w touched the 1Ki 6:27
One w of one creature was seven 2Ch 3:11
creature's other w was also 2Ch 3:11
and it touched a w of the second 2Ch 3:11
One w of the second creature................. 2Ch 3:12
creature's other w touched the 2Ch 3:12
touched the first creature's w,................. 2Ch 3:12

WINGED

lid between the two w creatures............... Ex 25:22
of locusts, w locusts, crickets .... Le 11:22
between the golden, w creatures 1Ch 13:6

WINGS

of Egypt, as if on eagle's w. .... Ex 19:4
to make two creatures with w, ... Ex 25:18
creatures' w should be spread .... Ex 25:20
creatures with w on the pieces .... Ex 26:1
of creatures with w on it. .... Ex 26:31
with w on the curtains. .... Ex 36:8
of creatures with w on it. .... Ex 36:35
creatures with w and attached .... Ex 37:7
The creatures' w were spread................. Ex 37:9
open by its w without dividing .... Le 1:17
that have w and walk on all .... Le 11:20
that have w and walk on four .... Le 11:21
that have w and walk on four .... Le 11:23
creatures with w that were above .... Nu 7:89
insects with w are unclean for .... Dt 14:19
Other things with w are clean, ... Dt 14:20
It spreads its w to catch them .... Dt 32:11
under whose w you have come for .... Ru 2:12
the gold creatures with w. 1Sa 4:4
the gold creatures with w. 2Sa 6:2
rode a creature with w and flew. 2Sa 22:11
He raced on the w of the wind. 2Sa 22:11
and had two w. Each wing was 1Ki 6:24
Place with their w spread out. 1Ki 6:27
wall with their w touching each 1Ki 6:27
pictures of creatures with w, ... 1Ki 6:29
Creatures with w, as well as 1Ki 6:32
pictures of creatures with w, ... 1Ki 6:35
bulls, and creatures with w. 1Ki 7:29
carvings of creatures with w, ... 1Ki 7:36
the w of the golden creatures. 1Ki 8:6
The w of these creatures were 1Ki 8:7
the gold creatures with w, ... 2Ki 19:15
that spread their w over the Ark 1Ch 28:18
creatures with w on the walls. 2Ch 3:7
creatures with w for the Most................. 2Ch 3:10
The w of the gold creatures were 2Ch 3:11
creatures' w were thirty feet 2Ch 3:13
of creatures with w in it......................... 2Ch 3:14
the w of the golden creatures. 2Ch 5:7
The w of these creatures were 2Ch 5:8
The w of the ostrich flap........................ Job 39:13
and spreads its w toward the .... Job 39:26
me under the shadow of your w. .... Ps 17:8
rode a creature with w and flew. .... Ps 18:10
He raced on the w of the wind. .... Ps 18:10
people in the shadow of your w.............. Ps 36:7
I wish I had w like a dove. .... Ps 55:6
shadow of your w until the .... Ps 57:1
in the shelter of your w. .... Ps 61:4
the gold creatures with w. .... Ps 80:1

and under his **w** you can hide. .... Ps 91:4
the gold creatures with **w**. .... Ps 99:1
you ride on the **w**. .... Ps 104:3
can seem to grow **w** and fly away .... Pr 23:5
Each creature had six **w:** .... Is 6:2
It used two **w** to cover its face, ... Is 6:2
its face, two **w** to cover its .... Is 6:2
its feet, and two **w** for flying. .... Is 6:2
will spread its **w** like a bird .... Is 8:8
is filled with the sound of **w**. .... Is 18:1
their young under their **w**. .... Is 34:15
the gold creatures with **w**, ... Is 37:16
Give **w** to Moab, because she will .... Je 48:9
and spreading its **w** over Moab. .... Je 48:40
spreading its **w** over the city .... Je 49:22
them had four faces and four **w**. .... Eze 1:6
hands under their **w** on their .... Eze 1:8
four of them had faces and **w**, ... Eze 1:8
and their **w** touched each other. .... Eze 1:9
Their **w** were spread out above. .... Eze 1:11
Each had two **w** that touched one .... Eze 1:11
and two **w** that covered its .... Eze 1:11
the dome the **w** of the living .... Eze 1:23
had two **w** covering its body. .... Eze 1:23
I heard the sound of their **w**, ... Eze 1:24
stopped, they lowered their **w**. .... Eze 1:24
stopped, they lowered their **w**. .... Eze 1:25
I heard the sound of the living .... Eze 3:13
from above the creatures with **w**, ... Eze 9:3
The sound of the **w** of the living............. Eze 10:5
seen under the **w** of the living .... Eze 10:8
hands, their **w**, and the wheels .... Eze 10:12
the face of a creature with **w**. .... Eze 10:14
lifted their **w** to fly up........................... Eze 10:16
spread their **w** and flew up .... Eze 10:19
one had four faces and four **w**, ... Eze 10:21
and under their **w** were things .... Eze 10:21
lifted their **w** with the wheels .... Eze 11:22
eagle with big **w** and long .... Eze 17:3
eagle with big **w** and many.................... Eze 17:7
creatures with **w** and palm trees. .... Eze 41:18
creatures with **w** were carved. .... Eze 41:20
palm trees and creatures with **w**, ... Eze 41:25
a lion, but had **w** like an eagle. .... Da 7:4
until its **w** were torn off. .... Da 7:4
with four **w** on its back that .... Da 7:6
that looked like a bird's **w**. .... Da 7:6
out with the wind in their **w**. .... Zch 5:9
Their **w** were like those of a .... Zch 5:9
gathers her chicks under her **w**, ... Mt 23:37
gathers her chicks under her **w**, ... Lk 13:34
whose **w** reached over the lid. .... Heb 9:5
had six **w** and was covered.................... Rev 4:8
sound of their **w** was like the .... Rev 9:9
given the two **w** of a great eagle............... Rev 12:14

WINK

A **w** may get you into trouble, ... Pr 10:10
can vanish in the **w** of an eye. .... Pr 23:5

WINKING

w with their eyes, tapping with .... Pr 6:13

WINKS

Someone who **w** is planning evil, ... Pr 16:30

WINNING

said, "We are **w** as before!" .... Jdg 20:32
saying, "We are **w**, as in the .... Jdg 20:39
David, "The men of Ammon were **w**. 2Sa 11:23
kept him from **w** and have thrown .... Ps 89:44

WINS

The wisdom of the wise **w** praise, ... Pr 12:8
a soldier **w** in war be taken .... Is 49:24
money to decide who **w** in court. .... Mic 3:11

---

to everyone who **w** the victory. .... Rev 2:17
to each one who **w** the victory a............. Rev 2:17
to everyone who **w** the victory .... Rev 2:26

WINTER

hot, summer and **w**, day and night .... Ge 8:22
you created summer and **w**. .... Ps 74:17
Look, the **w** is past; the rains .... Sng 2:11
animals will eat them that **w**." .... Is 18:6
was sitting in the **w** apartment. .... Je 36:22
I will tear down the **w** house, ... Am 3:15
It will flow summer and **w**. .... Zch 14:8
will not be **w** or a Sabbath day .... Mt 24:20
things will not happen in **w**, ... Mk 13:18
at Jerusalem. It was **w**, ... Jn 10:22
for the ship to stay for the **w**, ... Ac 27:12
and stay there for the **w**. .... Ac 27:12
you for a time or even all **w**. 1Co 16:6
you can to come to me before **w**. 2Ti 4:21
decided to stay there this **w**. .... Tit 3:12

WIPE

and I will **w** off from the earth .... Ge 7:4
then **w** the blood on the sides.................. Ex 12:22
and that you won't **w** out my name 1Sa 24:21
I will **w** out Jerusalem as the 2Ki 21:13
and completely **w** out all the .... Est 3:13
and completely **w** out the army of .... Est 8:11
to be merciful, **w** out all my .... Ps 51:1
my sins and **w** out all my guilt .... Ps 51:9
w their names from the book of............... Ps 69:28
Lord GOD will **w** away every tear .... Is 25:8
I will **w** you out of the lands so .... Eze 25:7
our feet we **w** off against you. .... Lk 10:11
And God will **w** away every tear .... Rev 7:17
He will **w** away every tear from .... Rev 21:4

WIPED

be killed and completely **w** out. .... Est 7:4
w out their names forever and .... Ps 9:5
the sins of his mother be **w** out. .... Ps 109:14
things you made will be **w** out. .... Eze 6:6
on the Lord and **w** his feet with .... Jn 11:2
and then she **w** his feet with her .... Jn 12:3

WIPES

a person **w** a dish and turns it 2Ki 21:13

WISDOM

I have given **w** to make special .... Ex 28:3
he gave them the **w** and .... Ex 36:1
that you have **w** and .... Dt 4:6
of Nun was then filled with **w**, ... Dt 34:9
May you be blessed for your **w**. 1Sa 25:33
asked for **w** to make the right.................. 1Ki 3:11
I will give you **w** and 1Ki 3:12
They saw he had **w** from God to.............. 1Ki 3:28
gave Solomon great **w** so he could 1Ki 4:29
His **w** was as hard to measure as 1Ki 4:29
w was greater than any wisdom 1Ki 4:30
greater than any **w** of the East, ... 1Ki 4:30
of the East, or any **w** in Egypt. 1Ki 4:30
to listen to King Solomon's **w**. 1Ki 4:34
they had heard of Solomon's **w**. 1Ki 4:34
LORD gave Solomon **w** as he had 1Ki 5:12
your achievements and **w** is true. 1Ki 10:6
Your **w** and wealth are much 1Ki 10:7
they are able to hear your **w**. 1Ki 10:8
more riches and **w** than all the 1Ki 10:23
listen to the **w** God had given.................. 1Ki 10:24
did, and the **w** he showed, is 1Ki 11:41
LORD give you **w** and............................ 1Ch 22:12
Now give me **w** and knowledge so I 2Ch 1:10
have asked for **w** and knowledge 2Ch 1:11
I will give you **w** and knowledge. 2Ch 1:12
one with **w** and understanding, ... 2Ch 2:12

your achievements and w is true. 2Ch 9:5
told even half of your great w! 2Ch 9:6
they are able to hear your w. 2Ch 9:7
more riches and w than all the 2Ch 9:22
listen to the w God had given 2Ch 9:23
use the w you have from your God........... Ezr 7:25
up, and they die without w.' .... Job 4:21
God's w is deep, and his power .... Job 9:4
and tell you the secrets of w, ... Job 11:6
wisdom, because w has two sides. .... Job 11:6
when you die, w will die with .... Job 12:2
But only God has w and power, ... Job 12:13
and takes away the w of elders. .... Job 12:20
But you limit w to yourself. .... Job 15:8
advice lacks w! You have shown .... Job 26:3
by his w he destroys Rahab, ... Job 26:12
But where can w be found, ... Job 28:12
not understand the value of w; .... Job 28:13
W cannot be bought with gold, ... Job 28:15
W cannot be bought with fine .... Job 28:16
are not as valuable as w,...................... Job 28:17
the price of w is much greater .... Job 28:18
from Cush cannot compare to w; .... Job 28:19
So where does w come from, ... Job 28:20
God understands the way to w, ... Job 28:23
he looked at w and decided its .... Job 28:27
he set w up and tested it. .... Job 28:27
'The fear of the Lord is w; .... Job 28:28
many years should teach w.' .... Job 32:7
Don't say, 'We have found w; .... Job 32:13
quiet, and I will teach you w." .... Job 33:33
Who put w inside the mind or .... Job 38:36
Who has the w to count the .... Job 38:37
God did not give the ostrich w; .... Job 39:17
it through your w that the hawk .... Job 39:26
people speak with w, and they .... Ps 37:30
truthful, so teach me w. .... Ps 51:6
with your w you made them all. .... Ps 104:24
W begins with respect for the................. Ps 111:10
Teach me w and knowledge because .... Ps 119:66
Give me w so I can understand .... Ps 119:125
your words gives w and .... Ps 119:130
With his w he made the skies. .... Ps 136:5
They teach w and self-control; .... Pr 1:2
but fools hate w and discipline. .... Pr 1:7
W is like a woman shouting in .... Pr 1:20
you make fun of w and hate .... Pr 1:22
Listen carefully to w; .... Pr 2:2
Cry out for w, and beg for .... Pr 2:3
Only the Lord gives w; .... Pr 2:6
He stores up w for those who are .... Pr 2:7
W will come into your mind, ... Pr 2:10
But w will help you be good and .... Pr 2:20
Don't depend on your own w. .... Pr 3:7
Happy is the person who finds w, ... Pr 3:13
W is worth more than silver; .... Pr 3:14
W is more precious than rubies;.............. Pr 3:15
her right hand w offers you a .... Pr 3:16
W will make your life pleasant .... Pr 3:17
w gives life to those who use it, ... Pr 3:18
made the earth, using his w. .... Pr 3:19
hold on to w and good sense. .... Pr 3:21
Get w and understanding. .... Pr 4:5
Hold on to w, and it will take .... Pr 4:6
W is the most important thing; .... Pr 4:7
thing; so get w. If it costs .... Pr 4:7
Treasure w, and it will make you .... Pr 4:8
am guiding you in the way of w,............. Pr 4:11
My son, pay attention to my w; .... Pr 5:1
Treat w as a sister, and make .... Pr 7:4
W and understanding will keep .... Pr 7:5
I noticed one of them had no w. .... Pr 7:7
W calls to you like someone .... Pr 8:1

You who are uneducated, seek w. .... Pr 8:5
W is more precious than rubies................ Pr 8:11
I am w, and I have good .... Pr 8:12
I, w, was with the Lord when he .... Pr 8:22
W has built her house; .... Pr 9:1
someone who makes fun of w, ... Pr 9:7
correct those who make fun of w, ... Pr 9:8
W begins with respect for the .... Pr 9:10
w will add years to your life. .... Pr 9:11
wise person is rewarded by w, ... Pr 9:12
fun of w will suffer for it. .... Pr 9:12
does not have w or knowledge. .... Pr 9:13
people without w should be .... Pr 10:13
die because they don't have w. .... Pr 10:21
The w of the wise wins praise, ... Pr 12:8
makes fun of w won't listen to .... Pr 13:1
make fun of w look for it and............... Pr 14:6
W lives in those with .... Pr 14:33
who make fun of w don't like to............. Pr 15:12
A person without w enjoys being .... Pr 15:21
for the Lord will teach you w. .... Pr 15:33
It is better to get w than gold,............... Pr 16:16
a fool any good to try to buy w, ... Pr 17:16
is always looking for w, ... Pr 17:24
but w is like a flowing stream. .... Pr 18:4
Those who get w do themselves a .... Pr 19:8
Whip those who make fun of w, ... Pr 19:25
foolish people will gain some w............... Pr 19:25
who make fun of w will be .... Pr 19:29
can find the w there. .... Pr 20:5
punish those who make fun of w, ... Pr 21:11
foolish person may gain some w. .... Pr 21:11
There is no w, understanding, or .... Pr 21:30
of the one who makes fun of w. .... Pr 22:10
Get w, self-control, and .... Pr 23:23
takes w to have a good family, ... Pr 24:3
people cannot understand w. .... Pr 24:7
and making fun of w is hateful. .... Pr 24:9
the same way, w is pleasing to .... Pr 24:14
A ruler without w will be cruel,.............. Pr 28:16
Those who love w make their................. Pr 29:3
who make fun of w cause trouble .... Pr 29:8
to use my w to learn about .... Ec 1:13
I know what w and knowledge .... Ec 1:16
find out about w and knowledge .... Ec 1:17
With much w comes much .... Ec 1:18
My w helped me in all this..................... Ec 2:9
can work hard using all their w, ... Ec 2:21
God will give them w, knowledge, ... Ec 2:26
W is better when it comes with .... Ec 7:11
W is like money: they both help. .... Ec 7:12
But w is better, because it can .... Ec 7:12
W makes a person stronger than .... Ec 7:19
I used w to test all these .... Ec 7:23
and tried very hard to find w, ... Ec 7:25
things mean. W brings happiness .... Ec 8:1
no knowledge, and no w. .... Ec 9:10
who used his w to save his town .... Ec 9:15
I still think w is better than .... Ec 9:16
the poor man's w and stopped .... Ec 9:16
W is better than weapons of war, ... Ec 9:18
little foolishness can spoil w. .... Ec 10:1
by my w I have defeated many .... Is 10:13
will give him w and.............................. Is 11:2
he will give w to the judges who .... Is 28:6
wise men will lose their w; .... Is 29:14
of salvation, w, and knowledge. .... Is 33:6
understand how great his w is. .... Is 40:28
' Your w and knowledge have .... Is 47:10
must not brag about their w. .... Je 9:23
He used his w to build the world .... Je 10:12
Is there no more w in the town .... Je 49:7
Have they lost their w? .... Je 49:7

He used his **w** to build the world .... Je 51:15
Through your **w** and understanding .... Eze 28:4
all that your **w** has built,........................ Eze 28:7
full of **w** and perfect in beauty. .... Eze 28:12
ruined your **w** because of your .... Eze 28:17
four young men **w** and the ability .... Da 1:17
they showed much **w** and .... Da 1:20
spoke to him with **w** and skill, ... Da 2:14
because he has **w** and power. .... Da 2:20
He gives **w** to those who are wise .... Da 2:21
you have given me **w** and power. .... Da 2:23
I have greater **w** than any other .... Da 2:30
knowledge, and **w** like the gods. .... Da 5:11
to give you **w** and to help you................ Da 9:22
' But **w** is proved to be right by .... Mt 11:19
man get this **w** and this power to .... Mt 13:54
What is this **w** that has been .... Mk 6:2
He was filled with **w**, and God's .... Lk 2:40
But **w** is proved to be right by .... Lk 7:35
This is why in his **w** God said, ' .... Lk 11:49
give you the **w** to say things .... Lk 21:15
of the Spirit and full of **w**. .... Ac 6:3
was helping him to speak with **w**, ... Ac 6:10
because of the **w** God gave him............... Ac 7:10
and his **w** and knowledge have no .... Rm 11:33
words of human **w** so that the 1Co 1:17
cause the wise to lose their **w**; 1Co 1:19
God has made the **w** of the world 1Co 1:20
the **w** of God the world did not 1Co 1:21
not know God through its own **w**. 1Co 1:21
miracles, and the Greeks want **w**. 1Co 1:22
of God and the **w** of God to those 1Co 1:24
of God is wiser than human **w**, ... 1Co 1:25
in the way the world judges **w**. 1Co 1:26
has become for us **w** from God. 1Co 1:30
words or a show of human **w**.................. 1Co 2:1
words of human **w** that persuade 1Co 2:4
God's power and not in human **w**. 1Co 2:5
I speak a **w** to those who are 1Co 2:6
this **w** is not from this world 1Co 2:6
God's secret **w**, which he has 1Co 2:7
planned this **w** for our glory. 1Co 2:7
us by human **w** but with words 1Co 2:13
because the **w** of this world is 1Co 3:19
the ability to speak with **w**,.................... 1Co 12:8
by the kind of **w** the world has. 2Co 1:12
with full **w** and understanding, ... Eph 1:8
you a spirit of **w** and revelation .... Eph 1:17
world will now know God's **w**, ... Eph 3:10
also have great **w** and .... Col 1:9
using all **w** to warn and to teach .... Col 1:28
the treasures of **w** and knowledge .... Col 2:3
Use all **w** to teach and instruct .... Col 3:16
And that **w** leads to salvation 2Ti 3:15
But if any of you needs **w**, ... Jam 1:5
and will give you **w** without .... Jam 1:5
a gentleness that comes from **w**............. Jam 3:13
That kind of "**w**" does not come............. Jam 3:15
But the **w** that comes from God is .... Jam 3:17
This **w** is always ready to help .... Jam 3:17
with the **w** that God gave him. 2Pe 3:15
power, wealth, **w**, and strength, ... Rev 5:12
Praise, glory, **w**, thanks, honor, ... Rev 7:12
This takes **w**. Let the one who .... Rev 13:18

WISE

and that it would make her **w**. .... Ge 3:6
magicians and **w** men of Egypt. .... Ge 41:8
man who is very **w** and .... Ge 41:33
is no one as **w** and understanding .... Ge 41:39
king called in his **w** men and his .... Ex 7:11
w men who have understanding and .... Dt 1:13
So I took the **w** and experienced .... Dt 1:15

Israel is **w** and understanding. .... Dt 4:6
of payment makes **w** people seem .... Dt 16:19
wish they were **w** and understood .... Dt 32:29
you will be **w** and successful in .... Jos 1:8
She was **w** and beautiful, but 1Sa 25:3
to bring a **w** woman from there 2Sa 14:2
you are **w** like an angel of God 2Sa 14:20
But a **w** woman shouted out from 2Sa 20:16
You are a **w** man, and you will 1Ki 2:9
three thousand **w** sayings and 1Ki 4:32
given David a **w** son to rule over 1Ki 5:7
learned that Solomon was very **w**. 1Ki 10:4
He was a **w** counselor and was 1Ch 26:14
Jonathan was a **w** man and a 1Ch 27:32
He has given King David a **w** son, ... 2Ch 2:12
you a skilled and **w** man named 2Ch 2:13
saw that Solomon was very **w**. 2Ch 9:3
a **w** man from the descendants of .... Ezr 8:18
spoke with the **w** men who would .... Est 1:13
w men the king usually talked .... Est 1:14
kings and **w** men of the earth................. Job 3:14
He catches the **w** in their own .... Job 5:13
cannot become **w** any more than .... Job 11:12
are the only **w** people and that .... Job 12:2
Older people are **w**, and long .... Job 12:12
God leads the **w** away as captives .... Job 12:17
then you would really be **w**! .... Job 13:5
Your **w** sayings are worth no more........... Job 13:12
A **w** person would not answer with .... Job 15:2
are things **w** men have told; .... Job 15:18
I do not find a **w** person among .... Job 17:10
Can even a **w** person do him good? .... Job 22:2
not just older people who are **w**; .... Job 32:9
Hear my words, you **w** men; .... Job 34:2
and the **w** who hear me say, ... Job 34:34
those who say they are **w**." .... Job 37:24
So, kings, be **w**; rulers, learn .... Ps 2:10
they make plain people **w**. .... Ps 19:7
I will make you **w** and show you .... Ps 32:8
they are no longer **w** or good................... Ps 36:3
What I say is **w**, and my heart .... Ps 49:3
pay attention to a **w** saying; .... Ps 49:4
See, even **w** people die. .... Ps 49:10
people to see if anyone was **w**, ... Ps 53:2
really are so that we may be **w**. .... Ps 90:12
He taught the older men to be **w**. .... Ps 105:22
Whoever is **w** will remember these .... Ps 107:43
These are the **w** words of Solomon .... Pr 1:1
help you understand **w** words. .... Pr 1:2
you how to be **w** and .... Pr 1:3
the uneducated **w** and give .... Pr 1:4
W people can also listen and .... Pr 1:5
can understand **w** words and .... Pr 1:6
the words of the **w** and their .... Pr 1:6
W people will receive honor, ... Pr 3:35
Watch what they do and be **w**. .... Pr 6:6
my teaching, and you will be **w**;.............. Pr 8:33
But correct the **w**, and they will .... Pr 9:8
the **w**, and they will become .... Pr 9:9
The **w** person is rewarded by .... Pr 9:12
are the **w** words of Solomon: .... Pr 10:1
W children make their father .... Pr 10:1
who gather crops on time are **w**, ... Pr 10:5
The **w** do what they are told, ... Pr 10:8
W people speak with .... Pr 10:13
The **w** don't tell everything they .... Pr 10:14
if you are **w**, you will keep .... Pr 10:19
enjoys doing what is **w**. .... Pr 10:23
A good person says **w** things,.................. Pr 10:31
to shame; it is **w** to be humble. .... Pr 11:2
fool will be a servant to the **w**. .... Pr 11:29
the **w** person teaches others how .... Pr 11:30
The wisdom of the **w** wins praise, ... Pr 12:8

chases empty dreams is not **w**. .... Pr 12:11
but the **w** listen to advice. .... Pr 12:15
upset, but the **w** ignore insults. .... Pr 12:16
but **w** words bring healing........................ Pr 12:18
W people keep what they know to .... Pr 12:23
W children take their parents' .... Pr 13:1
but those who take advice are **w**. .... Pr 13:10
teaching of a **w** person gives .... Pr 13:14
Every **w** person acts with good .... Pr 13:16
time with the **w** and you will .... Pr 13:20
the wise and you will become **w**, ... Pr 13:20
w woman strengthens her family. .... Pr 14:1
the words of the **w** will protect .... Pr 14:3
A **w** person will understand what .... Pr 14:8
but the **w** think about what they........... Pr 14:15
W people are careful and stay .... Pr 14:16
but the **w** are rewarded with .... Pr 14:18
W people are rewarded with .... Pr 14:24
is pleased with a **w** servant, ... Pr 14:35
W people use knowledge when they .... Pr 15:2
who accepts correction is **w**. .... Pr 15:5
W people use their words to .... Pr 15:7
will not ask the **w** for advice. .... Pr 15:12
W children make their father .... Pr 15:20
W people's lives get better and .... Pr 15:24
you will live among the **w**. .... Pr 15:31
so a **w** person will try to make .... Pr 16:14
The **w** are known for their .... Pr 16:21
W people's minds tell them what .... Pr 16:23
A **w** servant will rule over the .... Pr 17:2
w person will learn more from a .... Pr 17:10
have the ability to be **w**. .... Pr 17:16
It is not **w** to promise to pay .... Pr 17:18
The **w** say very little, and those .... Pr 17:27
fools seem to be **w** if they keep .... Pr 17:28
the **w** person listens to learn .... Pr 18:15
The **w** are patient; they will be .... Pr 19:11
but a **w** wife is a gift from the................ Pr 19:14
and in the end you will be **w**. .... Pr 19:20
is not **w** to get drunk on them. .... Pr 20:1
A **w** king sorts out the evil .... Pr 20:26
you teach the **w**, they will get .... Pr 21:11
W people's houses are full of .... Pr 21:20
w person can defeat a city full .... Pr 21:22
The **w** see danger ahead and avoid .... Pr 22:3
carefully to what **w** people say; .... Pr 22:17
be **w** enough to control yourself. .... Pr 23:4
will only ignore your **w** words. .... Pr 23:9
if you are **w**, then I will be .... Pr 23:15
Listen, my child, and be **w**. .... Pr 23:19
parents who have **w** children are .... Pr 23:24
W people have great power, ... Pr 24:5
These are also sayings of the **w**:........... Pr 24:23
These are more **w** sayings of .... Pr 25:1
A **w** warning to someone who will........... Pr 25:12
will think they are really **w**. .... Pr 26:5
w saying spoken by a fool is as .... Pr 26:7
A **w** saying spoken by a fool is .... Pr 26:9
for those who think they are **w**. .... Pr 26:12
Be **w**, my child, and make me................. Pr 27:11
The **w** see danger ahead and avoid .... Pr 27:12
they have been taught are **w**, ... Pr 28:7
people may think they are **w**, ... Pr 28:11
but **w** people calm anger down. .... Pr 29:8
When a **w** person takes a foolish .... Pr 29:9
but **w** people control theirs. .... Pr 29:11
and punishment make children **w**, ... Pr 29:15
I have not learned to be **w**, ... Pr 30:3
are small, but they are very **w**: .... Pr 30:24
She speaks **w** words and teaches .... Pr 31:26
become very **w** and am now wiser .... Ec 1:16
to think again about being **w**, ... Ec 2:12
I saw that being **w** is certainly .... Ec 2:13

W people see where they are .... Ec 2:14
I saw that both **w** and foolish .... Ec 2:14
what is the reward for being **w**?" .... Ec 2:15
"Being **w** is also useless." .... Ec 2:15
The **w** person and the fool will .... Ec 2:16
know if he will be **w** or foolish. .... Ec 2:19
poor but **w** boy is better than a .... Ec 4:13
In this way a **w** person is no .... Ec 6:8
A **w** person thinks about death, ... Ec 7:4
criticized by a **w** person than to .... Ec 7:5
Even **w** people are fools if they .... Ec 7:7
It is not **w** to ask such .... Ec 7:10
too right, and don't be too **w**. .... Ec 7:16
I wanted to be **w**, but it was too .... Ec 7:23
one is like the **w** person who can .... Ec 8:1
A **w** person does the right thing............. Ec 8:5
Even if **w** people say they .... Ec 8:17
people and **w** people and what .... Ec 9:1
saw something **w** here on earth .... Ec 9:13
was a poor but **w** man in the town .... Ec 9:15
quiet words of a **w** person are .... Ec 9:17
heart of the **w** leads to right, ... Ec 10:2
road, they show they are not **w**; .... Ec 10:3
Being **w** will make it easier. .... Ec 10:10
The words of the **w** bring them .... Ec 10:12
Teacher was very **w** and taught .... Ec 12:9
set in order many **w** teachings. .... Ec 12:9
Words from **w** people are like................ Ec 12:11
they are **w** teachings that come .... Ec 12:11
think they are **w** and believe .... Is 5:21
the **w** men who advise the king of .... Is 19:11
can you say to him, 'I am **w**'? .... Is 19:11
Egypt, where are your **w** men? .... Is 19:12
wonderful advice, who is very **w**. .... Is 28:29
Their **w** men will lose their..................... Is 29:14
their **w** men will not be able to .... Is 29:14
But he is **w** and can bring them .... Is 31:2
even the **w**; they think they..................... Is 44:25
saying, "We are **w**, because we .... Je 8:8
These **w** teachers refused to .... Je 8:9
so they are not really **w** at all. .... Je 8:9
What person is **w** enough to .... Je 9:12
The **w** must not brag about their .... Je 9:23
Of all the **w** people among the .... Je 10:7
none of them is as **w** as you. .... Je 10:7
Those **w** people are stupid and .... Je 10:8
the advice from the **w** teachers .... Je 18:18
a king who will rule in a **w** way;........... Je 23:5
Can the **w** men of Edom no longer........... Je 49:7
and her officers and **w** men! .... Je 50:35
rulers and **w** men drunk, ... Je 51:57
who uses **w** sayings will say .... Eze 16:44
You think you are as **w** as a god, ... Eze 28:2
You think you are **w** like a god, ... Eze 28:6
wizards, and **w** men, because he .... Da 2:2
The **w** men answered the king in .... Da 2:4
the **w** men said to the king, ... Da 2:7
The **w** men answered the king, ... Da 2:10
magicians, or **w** men to do this; .... Da 2:10
that all the **w** men of Babylon be .... Da 2:12
to kill the **w** men was announced .... Da 2:13
to kill the **w** men of Babylon. .... Da 2:14
with the other **w** men of Babylon. .... Da 2:18
those who are **w** and knowledge to .... Da 2:21
to kill the **w** men of Babylon. .... Da 2:24
Don't put the **w** men of Babylon. .... Da 2:24
answered, "No **w** man, magician, ... Da 2:27
of all the **w** men of Babylon. .... Da 2:48
ordered all the **w** men of Babylon .... Da 4:6
magicians, and **w** men came, and I .... Da 4:7
None of the **w** men in my kingdom .... Da 4:18
magicians, **w** men, and wizards .... Da 5:7
Then all the king's **w** men came............... Da 5:8

man in charge of all the **w** men, ... Da 5:11
He was very **w** and had knowledge .... Da 5:12
that you are very **w** and have .... Da 5:14
The **w** men and magicians were .... Da 5:15
Those who are **w** will help the .... Da 11:33
When the **w** ones are suffering, ... Da 11:34
many who join the **w** ones will .... Da 11:34
Some of the **w** ones will be..................... Da 11:35
The **w** people will shine like the .... Da 12:3
but the **w** will understand them.............. Da 12:10
A **w** person will know these .... Hos 14:9
such times the **w** person will .... Am 5:13
destroy the **w** people from Edom, ... Ob 1:8
and the **w** person honors him. .... Mic 6:9
some **w** men from the east came to .... Mt 2:1
with the **w** men and learned .... Mt 2:7
He sent the **w** men to Bethlehem, ... Mt 2:8
After the **w** men heard the king,............. Mt 2:9
When the **w** men saw the star, ... Mt 2:10
God warned the **w** men in a dream .... Mt 2:12
saw that the **w** men had tricked .... Mt 2:16
time he learned from the **w** men. .... Mt 2:16
them is like a **w** man who built .... Mt 7:24
the people who are **w** and smart. .... Mt 11:25
listen to Solomon's **w** teaching. .... Mt 12:42
prophets and **w** men and teachers .... Mt 23:34
Who is the **w** and loyal servant .... Mt 24:45
were foolish and five were **w**. .... Mt 25:2
The **w** bridesmaids took their.................. Mt 25:4
foolish ones said to the **w**, '................... Mt 25:8
The **w** bridesmaids answered, ' .... Mt 25:9
the people who are **w** and smart. .... Lk 10:21
listen to Solomon's **w** teaching. .... Lk 11:31
Who is the **w** and trusted servant .... Lk 12:42
made right through your **w** help. .... Ac 24:2
Greeks, the **w** and the foolish. .... Rm 1:14
they were **w**, but they became .... Rm 1:22
want you to be **w** in what is good .... Rm 16:19
To the only **w** God be glory..................... Rm 16:27
I will cause the **w** to lose their 1Co 1:19
I will make the **w** unable to 1Co 1:19
Where is the **w** person? Where is 1Co 1:20
many of you were **w** in the way 1Co 1:26
of the world to shame the **w**, ... 1Co 1:27
think you are **w** in this world,................. 1Co 3:18
so that you can become truly **w**, ... 1Co 3:18
those who are **w** in their own 1Co 3:19
Lord knows what **w** people think. 1Co 3:20
but you are very **w** in Christ. 1Co 4:10
among you **w** enough to judge 1Co 6:5
You are **w**, so you will gladly be 2Co 11:19
live like those who are not **w**, ... Eph 5:15
They seem to be **w**, but they are .... Col 2:23
Be **w** in the way you act with .... Col 4:5
be self-controlled, **w**, respected 1Ti 3:2
which are able to make you **w**. 2Ti 3:15
what is good, be **w**, live right,.............. Tit 1:8
serious, **w**, strong in faith, in .... Tit 2:2
to be **w** and pure, to be good .... Tit 2:5
encourage young men to be **w**. .... Tit 2:6
present age in a **w** and right way .... Tit 2:12
who are truly **w** and .... Jam 3:13
You need a **w** mind to understand .... Rev 17:9

WISELY

woman spoke very **w** to all the 2Sa 20:22
Rehoboam acted **w**. He spread his 2Ch 11:23
If you live **w**, you will live a .... Pr 9:11
those who live **w** will be kept .... Pr 28:26
my mind was still thinking **w**................... Ec 2:3
See, my servant will act **w**. .... Is 52:13
saw that the man answered him **w**, ... Mk 12:34
who are not wise, but live **w**. .... Eph 5:15

WISER

He was **w** than anyone on earth. 1Ki 4:31
He was even **w** than Ethan the 1Ki 4:31
the earth and **w** than the birds .... Job 35:11
make me **w** than my enemies. .... Ps 119:98
I am **w** than all my teachers, ... Ps 119:99
and they will become even **w**;................. Pr 9:9
thinks he is **w** than seven people .... Pr 26:16
wise and am now **w** than anyone .... Ec 1:16
You think you are **w** than Daniel. .... Eze 28:3
Jesus became **w** and grew .... Lk 2:52
of God is **w** than human wisdom, ... 1Co 1:25

WISEST

The **w** of her servant ladies .... Jdg 5:29
him in the way you think is **w**, ... 1Ki 2:6
the **w** does not always have food, ... Ec 9:11

WISH

I **w** the LORD would give me .... Ge 30:24
to Moses, "Go! I **w** you well." .... Ex 4:18
I **w** all the LORD's people could .... Nu 11:29
I **w** the LORD would give his .... Nu 11:29
We **w** we had died in Egypt or in .... Nu 14:2
I **w** I had a sword in my hand! .... Nu 22:29
You may marry anyone you **w**, ... Nu 36:6
I **w** their hearts would always................. Dt 5:29
Do not **w** for the silver and gold.............. Dt 7:25
silver to buy anything you **w**— .... Dt 14:26
wine, beer, or anything you **w**. .... Dt 14:26
do not **w** that you didn't have .... Dt 15:10
Don't **w** for their peace or .... Dt 23:6
may eat as many grapes as you **w**, ... Dt 23:24
will say, "I **w** it were evening, ... Dt 28:67
will say, "I **w** it were morning. .... Dt 28:67
w they were wise and understood .... Dt 32:29
I **w** they could see what will .... Dt 32:29
answered, "Go! I **w** you well. May 1Sa 1:17
I **w** someone would make me judge 2Sa 15:4
I **w** I had died and not you....................... 2Sa 18:33
will do for him anything you **w**, ... 2Sa 19:38
do anything for you that you **w**." 2Sa 19:38
I **w** someone would get me water 2Sa 23:15
return it is my **w** that you give 1Ki 5:9
I **w** my master would meet the 2Ki 5:3
I **w** someone would get me water 1Ch 11:17
Do not **w** for their peace or .... Ezr 9:12
I **w** my suffering could be .... Job 6:2
How I **w** that I might have what I .... Job 6:8
How I **w** God would crush me and .... Job 6:9
I **w** there were someone to make .... Job 9:33
I **w** I had died before anyone saw .... Job 10:18
I **w** I had never lived, but had .... Job 10:19
I **w** God would speak and open his .... Job 11:5
I **w** you would just stop talking; .... Job 13:5
I **w** you would hide me in the .... Job 14:13
w you would set a time and then .... Job 14:13
How I **w** my words were written .... Job 19:23
w they were carved with an iron .... Job 19:24
w I knew where to find God so I .... Job 23:3
I **w** the Almighty would set a .... Job 24:1
How I **w** for the months that have .... Job 29:2
I **w** for the days when I was .... Job 29:4
How I **w** a court would hear my .... Job 31:35
I **w** Job would be tested .... Job 34:36
w for the night when people .... Job 36:20
can say what we **w**; no one is our .... Ps 12:4
good you **w** for Jerusalem. .... Ps 51:18
I **w** I had wings like a dove. .... Ps 55:6
w my people would listen to me; .... Ps 81:13
I **w** Israel would live my way. .... Ps 81:13
I **w** I were more loyal in obeying .... Ps 119:5
LORD our God, I **w** good for her. .... Ps 122:9
I **w** you would kill the wicked! .... Ps 139:19

who do right only **w** for good, ... Pr 11:23
All day long they **w** for more, ... Pr 21:26
it. I **w** I could wake up. .... Pr 23:35
I **w** you were like my brother who .... Sng 8:1
are not dead will **w** they were, ... Je 8:3
w my head were like a spring of .... Je 9:1
I **w** I had a place in the desert— .... Je 9:2
open to you. Go wherever you **w**." .... Je 40:4
I **w** you peace and great wealth! .... Da 4:1
I **w** the dream were about your .... Da 4:19
and I **w** its meaning were for .... Da 4:19
I **w** you great peace and wealth. .... Da 6:25
I **w** one of you would close the .... Mal 1:10
and I can give it to anyone I **w**. .... Lk 4:6
and I **w** it were already burning! .... Lk 12:49
I **w** you knew today what would .... Lk 19:42
not by its own **w** but because God .... Rm 8:20
I **w** I could help my Jewish .... Rm 9:3
would even **w** that I were cursed .... Rm 9:3
W good for those who harm you; .... Rm 12:14
w them well and do not curse them. .... Rm 12:14
I **w** you really were kings so we 1Co 4:8
I **w** that everyone were like me, ... 1Co 7:7
I **w** all of you had the gift of 1Co 14:5
more, I **w** you would prophesy. 1Co 14:5
us about your **w** to see me and 2Co 7:7
they will **w** they could be with 2Co 9:14
I **w** you would be patient with me 2Co 11:1
I **w** I could be with you now and .... Gal 4:20
I **w** the people who are bothering .... Gal 5:12
I **w** that you were hot or cold! .... Rev 3:15

WISHED
to drink as much as they **w**. .... Est 1:8
could order the princes as he **w**. .... Ps 105:22
very weak and he were dead. .... Jnh 4:8
back the peace you **w** for them. .... Mt 10:13
them to do with him as they **w**. .... Lk 23:25

WISHES
if the king **w**, let a search be .... Ezr 5:17
my kingdom who **w** may go with you ..... Ezr 7:13
over as you want and as God **w**. .... Ezr 7:18
The **w** of the wicked will come to .... Ps 112:10
But **w** that come true are like .... Pr 13:12
It is so good when **w** come true, ... Pr 13:19
and your **w** will come true. .... Pr 23:18
and your **w** will come true. .... Pr 24:14
carry out his **w** against Babylon. .... Is 48:14
to you very soon if the Lord **w**. 1Co 4:19
whoever **w** may have the water of .... Rev 22:17

WISHFUL
magic, and their own **w** thinking. .... Je 14:14
from their own **w** thinking. .... Je 23:26

WISHING
like a slave **w** for the evening .... Job 7:2
rules instead of **w** for riches. .... Ps 119:36

WITCHCRAFT
Don't let anyone use magic or **w**, ... Dt 18:10
to people who use magic and **w**, ... Dt 18:14
worships idols and uses **w**." 2Ki 9:22
out the future by magic and **w**. 2Ki 17:17
magic and **w** and told the future. 2Ch 33:6
with her prostitution and her **w**. .... Nah 3:4
gods, doing **w**, hating, making .... Gal 5:20

WITNESS
that God is our **w** even if no one .... Ge 31:50
If you are a **w** in court, don't .... Ex 23:1
you are a **w** in court, you must .... Ex 23:2
be put to death with only one **w**. .... Nu 35:30
there is only one **w**, the person .... Dt 17:6
One **w** is not enough to accuse a .... Dt 19:15
If a **w** lies and accuses a person .... Dt 19:16

The **w** who is a liar, lying about .... Dt 19:18
it will be my **w** against them. .... Dt 31:19
stay there as a **w** against you. .... Dt 31:26
The Lord is a **w** to what you have 1Sa 12:5
king is also a **w** today that you 1Sa 12:5
"He is our **w**," they said. 1Sa 12:5
The Lord is a **w** between you and 1Sa 20:23
Lord will be a **w** between you and 1Sa 20:42
a dependable **w** in the sky." .... Ps 89:37
a **w** who lies, and someone who .... Pr 6:19
An honest **w** tells the truth, ... Pr 12:17
but a dishonest **w** tells lies. .... Pr 12:17
A truthful **w** does not lie, ... Pr 14:5
but a false **w** tells nothing but .... Pr 14:5
A truthful **w** saves lives, but a .... Pr 14:25
but a false **w** is a traitor. .... Pr 14:25
A **w** who lies will not go free; .... Pr 19:5
A **w** who lies will not go free, ... Pr 19:9
An evil **w** makes fun of fairness, ... Pr 19:28
A lying **w** will be forgotten, ... Pr 21:28
but a truthful **w** will speak on. .... Pr 21:28
be a sign and a **w** to the Lord .... Is 19:20
come this will be a **w** forever. .... Is 30:8
I made David a **w** of my power for .... Is 55:4
I am a **w** to it," says the Lord. .... Je 29:23
it and had some people **w** it. .... Je 32:10
true and loyal **w** against us if .... Je 42:5
God will be a **w** against you, ... Mic 1:2
Someday I will stand up as a **w**. .... Zph 3:8
who sent me is the other **w**." .... Jn 8:18
You will be his **w** to all people, ... Ac 22:15
Stephen, your **w**, was killed. .... Ac 22:20
you to be my servant and my **w**— .... Ac 26:16
Just as our **w** about Christ has 1Co 1:6
ask God to be my **w** that this is 2Co 1:23
is the faithful **w**, the first. .... Rev 1:5
my faithful **w** who was killed in .... Rev 2:13
and true **w**, the ruler of all .... Rev 3:14

WITNESSES
can be the **w** that I am buying .... Ge 23:9
in it, with these people as **w**. .... Ge 23:11
in front of the Hittite **w**. .... Ge 23:16
Your relatives will be my **w**. .... Ge 31:32
to death only if there are **w**. .... Nu 35:30
two or three **w** that it is true .... Dt 17:6
The **w** must be the first to throw .... Dt 17:7
be proved by two or three **w**. .... Dt 19:15
I ask heaven and earth to be **w**. .... Dt 30:19
You are your own **w** that you have .... Jos 24:22
the people, "You are **w** today. .... Ru 4:9
his hometown. You are **w** today." .... Ru 4:10
the city gate said, "We are **w**. .... Ru 4:11
You bring new **w** against me and .... Job 10:17
some men to be reliable **w**: .... Is 8:2
to believe the proof from **w**. .... Is 33:8
them bring their **w** to prove they .... Is 43:9
You are my **w** and the servant I .... Is 43:10
are my **w**, and I am God," says .... Is 43:12
You are my **w**. There is no other. .... Is 44:8
people are **w** for the statues .... Is 44:9
and pay attention, you **w**. .... Je 6:18
other **w** who signed the record .... Je 32:12
with silver and call in **w**.' .... Je 32:25
their agreements and call in **w**. .... Je 32:44
Listen and be **w** against the .... Am 3:13
be proved by two or three **w**.' .... Mt 18:16
We don't need any more **w**; .... Mt 26:65
said, "We don't need any more **w**! .... Mk 14:63
said, "Why do we need **w** now? .... Lk 22:71
You are **w** of these things. .... Lk 24:48
that when two **w** say the same .... Jn 8:17
I am one of the **w** who speaks .... Jn 8:18

You will be my w—in Jerusalem, ... Ac 1:8
And we are all w to this.................. Ac 2:32
from the dead. We are w to this.............. Ac 3:15
only by the w God had already .... Ac 10:41
And we are those w who ate and .... Ac 10:41
are now his w to the people. .... Ac 13:31
be proved by two or three w.".............. 2Co 13:1
elder, without two or three w.................. 1Ti 5:19
good confession before many w. 1Ti 6:12
proof given by two or three w. .... Heb 10:28
So there are three w: 1Jn 5:7
and these three w agree.................. 1Jn 5:8
power to my two w to prophesy .... Rev 11:3
These two w are the two olive .... Rev 11:4
These w have the power to stop .... Rev 11:6
When the two w have finished .... Rev 11:7
The bodies of the two w will lie .... Rev 11:8
bodies of the two w for three .... Rev 11:9

WIVES

Lamech said to his w: .... Ge 4:23
You w of Lamech, listen to what .... Ge 4:23
your sons' w will all go into .... Ge 6:18
sons and their w went into the .... Ge 7:7
and their w went into the boat. .... Ge 7:13
and their w should go out of the.............. Ge 8:16
sons, his wife, and his sons' w. .... Ge 8:18
to the sons of his other w, ... Ge 25:6
already had w, but he went to.............. Ge 28:9
Give me my w and my children and .... Ge 30:26
children and his w on camels, ... Ge 31:17
taking with him his two w, ... Ge 32:22
to our men as w and take our................. Ge 34:9
our women for your men as w. .... Ge 34:9
even their w and children and .... Ge 34:29
Esau took his w, his sons, his .... Ge 36:6
Zilpah, his father's w, cared .... Ge 37:2
and their w and to bring their .... Ge 45:19
and their w in the wagons the .... Ge 46:5
counting the w of Jacob's sons. .... Ge 46:26
with many babies born to your w, ... Ge 49:25
Then your will become widows, ... Ex 22:24
the gold earrings that your w,.............. Ex 32:2
daughters as w for your sons .... Ex 34:16
Our w and children will be taken .... Nu 14:3
their tents with their w, ... Nu 16:27
to Moses for husbands and w, ... Nu 30:16
Our children, w, and all our .... Nu 32:26
Your w, your young children, and .... Dt 3:19
The king must not have many w, ... Dt 17:17
might have two w, one he loves .... Dt 21:15
Both w might have sons by him.............. Dt 21:15
your w and children and the .... Dt 29:11
Your w, children, and animals .... Jos 1:14
his own, because he had many w. .... Jdg 8:30
his tribe to be w for his sons. .... Jdg 12:9
men of Benjamin will have w?" .... Jdg 21:7
Where can we get w for the men .... Jdg 21:16
We did not get w for Benjamin .... Jdg 21:22
Elkanah had two w named Hannah 1Sa 1:2
So they were both David's w. 1Sa 25:43
David had his two w with him— 1Sa 27:3
had been burned and their w,.............. 1Sa 30:3
two w had also been taken— 1Sa 30:5
David got his two w back and 1Sa 30:18
up to Hebron with his two w: 2Sa 2:2
slave women and w in Jerusalem. 2Sa 5:13
gave you his kingdom and his w. 2Sa 12:8
I will take your w from you and 2Sa 12:11
sexual relations with your w, ... 2Sa 12:11
daughters, w, and slave women 2Sa 19:5
seven hundred w who were from 1Ki 11:3
His w caused him to turn away 1Ki 11:3

his w caused him to follow other 1Ki 11:4
all his foreign w so they could 1Ki 11:8
best of your w and children.' 1Ki 20:3
gold, your w and your children. 1Ki 20:5
he said I had to give him my w, ... 1Ki 20:7
as the king's mother and his w, ... 2Ki 24:15
Ashhur had two w named Helah and........ 1Ch 4:5
they had many w and children. 1Ch 7:4
his other w and slave women. 2Ch 11:21
had eighteen w and sixty slave 2Ch 11:21
and he also found w for them. 2Ch 11:23
their babies, w, and children. 2Ch 20:13
your children, w, and everything 2Ch 21:14
as well as his sons and w. 2Ch 21:17
Jehoiada chose two w for Joash, ... 2Ch 24:3
and w were taken captive. 2Ch 29:9
Levites' babies, w, sons, and 2Ch 31:18
you and from your non-Jewish w.".......... Ezr 10:11
all promised to divorce their w, ... Ezr 10:19
of them had children by these w. .... Ezr 10:44
your w, and your homes........................Ne 4:14
men and their w complained .... Ne 5:1
and also their w and their sons .... Ne 10:28
of foreigners as w for your sons.............. Ne 13:25
God when you marry foreign w." .... Ne 13:27
All the w of the important men .... Est 1:17
Today the w of the important men .... Est 1:18
men to be unfaithful to their w. .... Pr 23:28
be robbed and their w raped. .... Is 13:16
along with their fields and w, ... Je 6:12
I will give their w to other men .... Je 8:10
them, or their w, or their sons, ... Je 14:16
Let their w lose their children .... Je 18:21
Find w for your sons, and let .... Je 29:6
with their neighbors' w. .... Je 29:23
Neither we nor our w, sons, or .... Je 35:8
All your w and children will be .... Je 38:23
the evil you and your w did? .... Je 44:9
You and your w did what you said .... Je 44:25
their fathers' w and with women .... Eze 22:10
They became my w and had sons .... Eze 23:4
guests, his w, and his slave .... Da 5:2
guests, his w, and his slave .... Da 5:3
guests, your w, and your slave .... Da 5:23
They, their w, and their .... Da 6:24
and their w by themselves, ... Zch 12:12
and their w by themselves, ... Zch 12:12
and their w by themselves, ... Zch 12:13
and their w by themselves, ... Zch 12:13
and their w by themselves. .... Zch 12:14
made husbands and w to become .... Mal 2:15
to divorce your w because you .... Mt 19:8
have left houses, w, brothers, ... Lk 18:29
those who have w should live as 1Co 7:29
should live as if they had no w. 1Co 7:29
W, yield to your husbands, as.............. Eph 5:22
so you w should yield to your.................. Eph 5:24
love your w as Christ loved the .... Eph 5:25
should love their w as they love .... Eph 5:28
W, yield to the authority of.................. Col 3:18
love your w and be gentle with .... Col 3:19
you w should yield to your 1Pe 3:1
by the way their w live. 1Pe 3:1
live with your w in an 1Pe 3:7

WIZARDS

magicians, w, and wise men, ... Da 2:2
and w of Babylon and said to .... Da 5:7
-tellers, magicians, and w. .... Da 5:11

WOKE

When he w up and learned what .... Ge 9:24
Then Jacob w from his sleep and .... Ge 28:16
fat cows. Then the king w up................... Ge 41:4

Then the king **w** up again, and he	Ge 41:7
in the beginning. Then I **w** up.	Ge 41:21
Samson **w** up and pulled out the	Jdg 16:14
He **w** up and thought, "I'll	Jdg 16:20
them or knew about it or **w** up,	1Sa 26:12
After Solomon **w** up from the	1Ki 3:15
I **w** you under the apple tree	Sng 8:5
I, Jeremiah, **w** up and looked	Je 31:26
me returned and **w** me up as if I	Zch 4:1
When Joseph **w** up, he did what	Mt 1:24
followers went to him and **w** him,	Mt 8:25
the bridesmaids **w** up and got	Mt 25:7
Jesus **w** and left the house.	Mk 1:35
His followers **w** him and said,	Mk 4:38
went to Jesus and **w** him,	Lk 8:24
Peter on the side and **w** him up.	Ac 12:7
The jailer **w** up and saw that the	Ac 16:27

WOLF

Benjamin is like a hungry **w**.	Ge 49:27
A **w** from the desert will kill	Je 5:6
When the worker sees a **w** coming,	Jn 10:12
Then the **w** attacks the sheep and	Jn 10:12

WOLVES

Then **w** will live in peace with	Is 11:6
W will howl within the strong	Is 13:22
W and lambs will eat together in	Is 65:25
Like **w** tearing a dead animal,	Eze 22:27
and quicker than **w** at sunset.	Hab 1:8
are like hungry **w** that attack	Zph 3:3
are really dangerous like **w**.	Mt 7:15
you out like sheep among **w**.	Mt 10:16
you out like sheep among **w**.	Lk 10:3
come like wild **w** and try to	Ac 20:29

WOMAN

rib from the man to make a **w**,	Ge 2:22
he brought the **w** to the man.	Ge 2:22
But the snake said to the **w**,	Ge 3:4
You gave this **w** to me and she	Ge 3:12
you and the **w** enemies to each	Ge 3:15
God said to the **w**, "I will cause	Ge 3:16
with a man as you would a **w**.	Le 18:22
firstborn of every Israelite **w**.	Nu 8:16
a Midianite **w** his brothers	Nu 25:6
both the **w** and the man who had	Dt 22:22
will let a **w** defeat Sisera."	Jdg 4:9
to say, 'A **w** killed Abimelech.	Jdg 9:54
young Moabite **w** who came back	Ru 2:6
our town know you are a good **w**.	Ru 3:11
Find me a **w** who is a medium so I	1Sa 28:7
When the **w** saw Samuel, she	1Sa 28:12
on the roof, he saw a **w** bathing	2Sa 11:2
to bring a wise **w** from there.	2Sa 14:2
a wise **w** shouted out from the	2Sa 20:16
for a young **w** to care for you	1Ki 1:2
Give the baby to the first **w**,	1Ki 3:27
Gehazi, "Call the Shunammite **w**."	2Ki 4:12
or unimportant, a man or **w**.	2Ch 15:13
son of Shimeath, a **w** from Ammon.	2Ch 24:26
son of Shimrith, a **w** from Moab.	2Ch 24:26
a non-Jewish **w** meet with the	Ezr 10:14
that no man or **w** may go to the	Est 4:11
are talking like a foolish **w**.	Job 2:10
can someone born to a **w** be good?	Job 15:14
hurt like a **w** having a baby.	Ps 48:6
children to the **w** who has none	Ps 113:9
Wisdom is like a **w** shouting in	Pr 1:20
Stay away from such a **w**.	Pr 5:8
give your love to just any **w**.	Pr 5:16
captive by a **w** who takes part	Pr 5:20
Don't fondle a **w** who is not your	Pr 5:20
and a **w** who takes part in	Pr 6:26
Foolishness is like a loud **w**;	Pr 9:13

A kind **w** gets respect, but cruel	Pr 11:16
but a foolish **w** destroys hers by	Pr 14:1
way a man and a **w** fall in love.	Pr 30:19
is the way of a **w** who takes part	Pr 30:20
a hated **w** who gets married,	Pr 30:23
but a **w** who respects the LORD	Pr 31:30
Can a **w** forget the baby she	Is 49:15
You are like a **w** who never gave	Is 54:1
groan like a **w** giving birth to	Je 22:23
in pain like a **w** having a baby?	Je 30:6
A **w** will go seeking a man."	Je 31:22
running away and the **w** escaping.	Je 48:19
like a **w** who is having a baby.	Je 48:41
love to a **w** loved by someone	Hos 3:1
like a **w** trying to give birth?	Mic 4:9
like a **w** trying to give birth,	Mic 4:10
looks at a **w** and wants to sin	Mt 5:28
done that sin with the **w**.	Mt 5:28
that divorced **w** is guilty of	Mt 5:32
Then a **w** who had been bleeding	Mt 9:20
answered, "**W**, you have great	Mt 15:28
And the **w** who divorces her	Mk 10:12
a **w** approached him with an	Mk 14:3
they got very angry with the **w**.	Mk 14:5
This **w** did the only thing she	Mk 14:8
what this **w** has done will be	Mk 14:9
you more than any other **w**,	Lk 1:42
A sinful **w** in the town learned	Lk 7:37
know that the **w** touching him is	Lk 7:39
toward the **w** and said to Simon	Lk 7:44
A **w** named Martha let Jesus stay	Lk 10:38
Suppose a **w** has ten silver	Lk 15:8
he said, "**W**, I don't know him."	Lk 22:57
Dear **w**, why come to me	Jn 2:4
a Samaritan **w** came to the well	Jn 4:7
The **w** said, "I am surprised that	Jn 4:9
man and I a Samaritan **w**."	Jn 4:9
Jesus said, "Believe me, **w**.	Jn 4:21
brought a **w** who had been caught	Jn 8:3
this **w** was caught having sexual	Jn 8:4
to death every **w** who does this.	Jn 8:5
alone with the **w** standing before	Jn 8:9
asked her, "**W**, where are they	Jn 8:10
They asked her, "**W**, why are you	Jn 20:13
Jesus asked her, "**W**, why are you	Jn 20:15
listeners was a **w** named Lydia	Ac 16:14
Areopagus, a **w** named Damaris,	Ac 17:34
a **w** must stay married to her	Rm 7:2
like a **w** ready to give birth.	Rm 8:22
have sexual relations with a **w**.	1Co 7:1
and each **w** should have her own	1Co 7:2
if a Christian **w** has a husband	1Co 7:13
the Christian man or **w** is free.	1Co 7:15
the head of a **w** is the man,	1Co 11:3
But every **w** who prays or	1Co 11:5
the same as a **w** who has her head	1Co 11:5
If a **w** does not cover her head,	1Co 11:6
shameful for a **w** to cut off her	1Co 11:6
of God. But **w** is man's glory.	1Co 11:7
not come from **w**, but woman came	1Co 11:8
it right for a **w** to pray to God	1Co 11:13
It is shameful for a **w** to speak	1Co 14:35
was born of a **w** and lived under	Gal 4:4
Let a **w** learn by listening	1Ti 2:11
do not allow a **w** to teach or to	1Ti 2:12
but the **w** was tricked and became	1Ti 2:14
a **w** must be at least sixty years	1Ti 5:9
If any **w** who is a believer has	1Ti 5:16
they look at a **w** they want her,	2Pe 2:14
You let that **w** Jezebel spread	Rev 2:20
There I saw a **w** sitting on a red	Rev 17:3
The **w** was dressed in purple and	Rev 17:4
I saw that the **w** was drunk with	Rev 17:6

When I saw the **w**, I was very .... Rev 17:6
secret of this **w** and the beast .... Rev 17:7
mountains where the **w** sits. .... Rev 17:9
The **w** you saw is the great city .... Rev 17:18

WOMAN'S

amount the **w** husband says .... Ex 21:22
touched the **w** bed or something .... Le 15:23
with this **w** granddaughter, ... Le 18:17
A **w** husband may make her keep or .... Nu 30:13
the young **w** father, asked him to .... Jdg 19:4
but the **w** father said to his .... Jdg 19:5
The **w** father said, "Refresh .... Jdg 19:8
the young **w** father, said, "It's .... Jdg 19:9
day Elisha came to the **w** house. 2Ki 4:11
When the king heard the **w** words,......... 2Ki 6:30
ways were like a **w** uncleanness............. Eze 36:17
that moment the **w** daughter was .... Mt 15:28
But long hair is a **w** glory. 1Co 11:15

WOMB

I die when I came out of the **w**? .... Job 3:11
God made me in my mother's **w**, ... Job 31:15
I was still in my mother's **w**. .... Is 49:1
I made you in your mother's **w**, ... Je 1:5
come out of its mother's **w**..................... Hos 13:13
enter his mother's **w** again. .... Jn 3:4

WOMBS

both of us in our mothers' **w**. .... Job 31:15

WOMEN

married two **w**, Adah and Zillah. .... Ge 4:19
These **w** gave birth to children, ... Ge 6:4
the **w** and the other people, ... Ge 14:16
the age when **w** normally have .... Ge 18:11
on the earth **w** and men marry, ... Ge 19:31
kept all the **w** in Abimelech's .... Ge 20:18
the **w** come out to get water, ... Ge 24:11
two Hittite **w**—Judith daughter .... Ge 26:34
These **w** brought much sorrow to .... Ge 26:35
Isaac, "I am tired of Hittite **w**................. Ge 27:46
of these Hittite **w** here in this .... Ge 27:46
his sons to marry Canaanite **w**. .... Ge 28:8
Now **w** will call me happy," .... Ge 30:13
where the two slave **w** stayed, ... Ge 31:33
my daughters or marry other **w**............... Ge 31:50
up and saw the **w** and children, ... Ge 33:5
out to visit the **w** of the land. .... Ge 34:1
Give your **w** to our men as wives .... Ge 34:9
and take our **w** for your men as .... Ge 34:9
Then your men can marry our **w**, ... Ge 34:16
and our men can marry your **w**, ... Ge 34:16
us marry their **w**, and we can let .... Ge 34:21
and we can let them marry our **w**. .... Ge 34:21
Esau married **w** from the land of .... Ge 36:2
the Israelite **w** give birth to................... Ex 1:15
the Hebrew **w** give birth to..................... Ex 1:16
The Hebrew **w** are much stronger .... Ex 1:19
stronger than the Egyptian **w**. .... Ex 1:19
may take your **w** and children .... Ex 10:24
the men and **w** of Israel to ask .... Ex 11:2
including the **w** and children.................. Ex 12:37
All the **w** followed her, playing .... Ex 15:20
of your **w** will have her baby .... Ex 23:26
and all **w** will have children. .... Ex 23:26
All the men and **w** who wanted to .... Ex 35:22
All the **w** who were skilled and .... Ex 35:26
All the men and **w** of Israel who .... Ex 35:29
belonged to the **w** who served at .... Ex 38:8
and the two **w** in fire so that .... Le 20:14
for your men and **w** servants,................. Le 25:6
Your men and **w** slaves must .... Le 25:44
ten **w** will be able to cook all .... Le 26:26
both men and **w** outside the camp .... Nu 5:3

'If men or **w** want to promise to .... Nu 6:2
sinning sexually with Moabite **w**. .... Nu 25:1
The **w** invited them to their .... Nu 25:2
the Midianite **w** and children,................... Nu 31:9
Why did you let the **w** live? .... Nu 31:15
all the Midianite **w** who have had .... Nu 31:17
and 32,000 **w** who had not had .... Nu 31:35
as the men, **w**, and children. .... Dt 2:34
all the men, **w**, and children, ... Dt 3:6
don't make statues—of men or **w**, ... Dt 4:16
Take the **w**, children, and .... Dt 20:14
the men, **w**, children, and .... Dt 31:12
Young men and **w** will die, and so .... Dt 32:25
city—men and **w**, young and old, ... Jos 6:21
day, twelve thousand men and **w**, ... Jos 8:25
together—men, **w**, and children— .... Jos 8:35
above all **w** who live in tents .... Jdg 5:24
about a thousand men and **w**.................. Jdg 9:49
all the men, **w**, and leaders of................. Jdg 9:51
year the young **w** of Israel would .... Jdg 11:40
he brought thirty **w** who were not .... Jdg 12:9
temple was full of men and **w**. .... Jdg 16:27
men and **w** were on the roof .... Jdg 16:27
swords, even the **w** and children. .... Jdg 21:10
young unmarried **w** in Jabesh .... Jdg 21:12
gave them the **w** from Jabesh .... Jdg 21:14
but there were not enough **w**. .... Jdg 21:14
The **w** of Benjamin have been .... Jdg 21:16
for the young **w** from Shiloh to .... Jdg 21:21
the young Shiloh **w** and return to .... Jdg 21:21
did not give the **w** to the men .... Jdg 21:22
While the young **w** were dancing, ... Jdg 21:23
These sons married **w** from Moab............ Ru 1:4
Naomi kissed the **w** good-bye, ... Ru 1:9
The **w** cried together out loud.................. Ru 1:14
The **w** of the town said, "Is this .... Ru 1:19
closely behind my **w** workers. .... Ru 2:8
working with his **w** workers. .... Ru 2:22
whose young **w** you worked with, ... Ru 3:2
The **w** told Naomi, "Praise the .... Ru 4:14
with the **w** who served at 1Sa 2:22
the **w** who helped her said,................... 1Sa 4:20
met some young **w** coming out to 1Sa 9:11
The young **w** answered, "Yes, he's 1Sa 9:12
to death men and **w**, children and 1Sa 15:3
W came out from all the towns of 1Sa 18:6
The **w** say David has killed tens 1Sa 18:8
have kept themselves from **w**." 1Sa 21:4
No **w** have been near us for days. 1Sa 21:5
he killed men, **w**, children, ... 1Sa 22:19
all the men and **w** and took their 1Sa 27:9
captured the **w** and everyone,................. 1Sa 30:2
the Philistine **w** will be happy. 2Sa 1:20
better than the love of **w**. 2Sa 1:26
himself more slave **w** and wives.............. 2Sa 5:13
every Israelite, both men and **w**............... 2Sa 6:19
he left ten slave **w** to take care 2Sa 15:16
some of his slave **w** to take care............... 2Sa 16:21
with his father's slave **w**......................... 2Sa 16:22
daughters, wives, and slave **w**. 2Sa 19:5
the voices of men and **w** singers. 2Sa 19:35
ten of his slave **w** there to take 2Sa 20:3
One day two **w** who were 1Ki 3:16
one of the **w** said, "My master, ... 1Ki 3:17
So the two **w** argued before the 1Ki 3:22
Solomon loved many **w** who were 1Ki 11:1
as well as the **w** of the Moabites, ... 1Ki 11:1
fell in love with these **w**. 1Ki 11:2
hundred slave **w** who gave birth.............. 1Ki 11:3
split open their pregnant **w**." 2Ki 8:12
open all their pregnant **w**. 2Ki 15:16
where the **w** did weaving for 2Ki 23:7
for those born to his slave **w**. 1Ch 3:9

married more **w** in Jerusalem 1Ch 14:3
his other wives and slave **w**. 2Ch 11:21
and sixty slave **w** and was the 2Ch 11:21
married fourteen **w** and was the 2Ch 13:21
They took **w**, sons and daughters, ... 2Ch 28:8
all the men and **w** singers 2Ch 35:25
no mercy on the young men or **w**, ... 2Ch 36:17
their sons have married these **w**. .... Ezr 9:2
Israelite men, **w**, and children .... Ezr 10:1
God by marrying **w** from the .... Ezr 10:2
away all these **w** and their .... Ezr 10:3
and have married non-Jewish **w**. .... Ezr 10:10
who had married non-Jewish **w**. .... Ezr 10:17
who had married foreign **w**: .... Ezr 10:18
these married non-Jewish **w**: .... Ezr 10:25
men had married non-Jewish **w**,.............. Ezr 10:44
Men, **w**, and all who could listen .... Ne 8:2
noon to the men, **w**, and everyone .... Ne 8:3
The **w** and children were happy................ Ne 12:43
who had married **w** from Ashdod, ... Ne 13:23
Foreign **w** made King Solomon of .... Ne 13:26
but foreign **w** made him sin. .... Ne 13:26
a banquet for the **w** in the royal .... Est 1:9
all the **w** will respect their .... Est 1:20
eunuch in charge of the **w**. .... Est 2:3
who was in charge of the **w**. .... Est 2:8
where the king's **w** lived to find .... Est 2:11
that were ordered for the **w**. .... Est 2:12
eunuch in charge of the slave **w**.............. Est 2:14
who was in charge of the **w**. .... Est 2:15
young and old, **w** and little .... Est 3:13
the same to the **w** and children .... Est 8:11
of us born to **w** live only a few .... Job 14:1
people abuse **w** who cannot have .... Job 24:21
were no other **w** in all the land .... Job 42:15
are among your honored **w**. .... Ps 45:9
and the young **w** had no one to .... Ps 78:63
young men and **w**, old people and .... Ps 148:12
keep you from sinful **w** and from .... Pr 6:24
your strength on **w** or your time.............. Pr 31:3
are many fine **w**, but you are .... Pr 31:29
and all the **w** a man could ever .... Ec 2:8
found that some **w** are worse than .... Ec 7:26
That's why the young **w** love you. .... Sng 1:3
reason, the young **w** love you. .... Sng 1:4
dark but lovely, **w** of Jerusalem, ... Sng 1:5
You are the most beautiful of **w**. .... Sng 1:8
Among the young **w**, my darling is........... Sng 2:2
W of Jerusalem, promise me by .... Sng 2:7
W of Jerusalem, promise me by .... Sng 3:5
cloth that the **w** of Jerusalem .... Sng 3:10
W of Jerusalem, go out and see .... Sng 3:11
Promise me, **w** of Jerusalem, if .... Sng 5:8
lovers, most beautiful of **w**? .... Sng 5:9
lover gone, most beautiful of **w**?.............. Sng 6:1
and eighty slave **w** and so many.............. Sng 6:8
The young **w** saw her and called .... Sng 6:9
the slave **w** also praised her. .... Sng 6:9
W of Jerusalem, promise not to .... Sng 8:4
cruelly, and **w** rule over them. .... Is 3:12
The **w** of Jerusalem are proud. .... Is 3:16
heads of those **w** in Jerusalem, ... Is 3:17
that time seven **w** will grab one .... Is 4:1
filth from the **w** of Jerusalem.................. Is 4:4
those men and **w** from the other............. Is 14:2
The **w** of Moab try to cross the .... Is 16:2
the Egyptians will be like **w**. .... Is 19:16
have not reared young men or **w**." .... Is 23:4
to **w** slaves and their women .... Is 24:2
slaves and their **w** masters,................... Is 24:2
so **w** will use them for firewood. .... Is 27:11
You **w** who are calm now, stand up .... Is 32:9
You **w** who feel safe now, hear .... Is 32:9

You **w** feel safe now, but after................. Is 32:10
W, you are calm now, but you .... Is 32:11
W, you feel safe now, but you .... Is 32:11
Even the worst **w** can learn evil .... Je 2:33
The **w** make the dough for cakes .... Je 7:18
Call for the **w** who cry at .... Je 9:17
Send for those **w** who are good at .... Je 9:17
Now, **w** of Judah, listen to the............... Je 9:20
Some of the **w** are pregnant, ... Je 31:8
Then young **w** of Israel will be .... Je 31:13
All the **w** left in the palace of .... Je 38:22
Your **w** will make fun of you with .... Je 38:22
men, **w**, and children who were .... Je 40:7
were soldiers, **w**, children, ... Je 41:16
away the men, **w**, and children, ... Je 43:6
are cutting off the men and **w**, ... Je 44:7
them were many **w** of Judah who .... Je 44:15
The **w** said, "Our husbands knew .... Je 44:19
—men and **w**—who answered him. .... Je 44:20
said to all those men and **w**, ... Je 44:24
they will be like frightened **w**. .... Je 50:37
I use you to smash men and **w**. .... Je 51:22
to smash young men and young **w**. .... Je 51:22
have become like frightened **w**. .... Je 51:30
her young **w** are suffering, ... La 1:4
young **w** and men have gone into .... La 1:18
The young **w** of Jerusalem bow .... La 2:10
W eat their own babies, the .... La 2:20
My young **w** and young men have .... La 2:21
to all the **w** of my city. .... La 3:51
own hands kind **w** cook their own .... La 4:10
enemy abused the **w** of Jerusalem .... La 5:11
where I saw **w** sitting and crying .... Eze 8:14
young men and **w**, little children .... Eze 9:6
and older **w**, but don't touch .... Eze 9:6
look toward the **w** among your .... Eze 13:17
it will be for **w** who sew magic .... Eze 13:18
the Philistine **w**, who were .... Eze 16:27
punish you as **w** guilty of .... Eze 16:38
punish you in front of many **w**. .... Eze 16:41
now the Edomite **w** and their .... Eze 16:57
the Philistine **w** humiliate you. .... Eze 16:57
and with **w** who are unclean, ... Eze 22:10
caused many **w** to become widows. .... Eze 22:25
W everywhere began talking about .... Eze 23:10
and Jerusalem, these shameful **w**. .... Eze 23:44
as they punish **w** who take part .... Eze 23:45
Then all **w** will be warned, ... Eze 23:48
The **w** of the nations will sing................ Eze 32:16
with the **w** of the powerful .... Eze 32:18
not marry widows or divorced **w**. .... Eze 44:22
and his slave **w** could drink from .... Da 5:2
and his slave **w** drank from them. .... Da 5:3
and your slave **w** drank wine from........... Da 5:23
or the god that **w** worship. .... Da 11:37
Make their **w** unable to have .... Hos 9:14
their pregnant **w** will be ripped .... Hos 13:16
the pregnant **w** in Gilead so they .... Am 1:13
beautiful young **w** and the young .... Am 8:13
You've forced the **w** of my people .... Mic 2:9
are all **w**! The gates of your .... Nah 3:13
up and saw two **w** going out with .... Zch 5:9
Old men and old **w** will again sit .... Zch 8:4
and the young **w** on new wine. .... Zch 9:17
rob the houses and attack the **w**. .... Zch 14:2
of Judah married **w** who worship .... Mal 2:11
not counting **w** and children. .... Mt 14:21
who ate, besides **w** and children. .... Mt 15:38
will be for **w** who are pregnant .... Mt 24:19
w will be grinding grain with .... Mt 24:41
Many **w** who had followed Jesus .... Mt 27:55
said to the **w**, "Don't be afraid .... Mt 28:5
The **w** left the tomb quickly. .... Mt 28:8

The **w** came up to him, took hold .... Mt 28:9
While the **w** went to tell Jesus' .... Mt 28:11
will be for **w** who are pregnant .... Mk 13:17
Some **w** were standing at a .... Mk 15:40
These **w** had followed Jesus in .... Mk 15:41
Many other **w** were also there who .... Mk 15:41
w were on their way to the tomb. .... Mk 16:2
Then the **w** looked and saw that .... Mk 16:4
The **w** entered the tomb and saw a .... Mk 16:5
The **w** were confused and shaking .... Mk 16:8
and also some **w** who had been .... Lk 8:2
These **w** used their own money to .... Lk 8:3
servants, men and **w**, and to eat .... Lk 12:45
will be two **w** grinding grain .... Lk 17:35
will be for **w** who are pregnant .... Lk 21:23
including some **w** who were sad .... Lk 23:27
said to them, "**W** of Jerusalem, ... Lk 23:28
are the **w** who cannot have .... Lk 23:29
including the **w** who had followed .... Lk 23:49
The **w** who had come from Galilee .... Lk 23:55
the **w** left to prepare spices .... Lk 23:56
at dawn, the **w** came to the tomb .... Lk 24:1
The **w** were very afraid and bowed .... Lk 24:5
Then the **w** remembered what Jesus .... Lk 24:8
The **w** left the tomb and told all .... Lk 24:9
and some other **w** who told the .... Lk 24:10
But they did not believe the **w**, ... Lk 24:11
And today some **w** among us amazed ...... Lk 24:22
found it just as the **w** said, ... Lk 24:24
praying together with some **w**, ... Ac 1:14
and more men and **w** believed in .... Ac 5:14
out men and **w** and putting them .... Ac 8:3
men and **w** believed Philip and .... Ac 8:12
Way, men or **w**, he would arrest .... Ac 9:2
religious **w** and the leaders .... Ac 13:50
Some **w** had gathered there, ... Ac 16:13
God and many of the important **w** .... Ac 17:4
many important Greek **w** and men. .... Ac 17:12
even the **w** and children, came .... Ac 21:5
arrested men and **w** and put them .... Ac 22:4
W stopped having natural sex and .... Rm 1:26
started having sex with other **w** .... Rm 1:26
w who work very hard for the .... Rm 16:12
But in the Lord **w** are not 1Co 11:11
men are not independent of **w**. 1Co 11:11
w should keep quiet in the 1Co 14:34
The two **w** are like the two .... Gal 4:24
you were serving only men and **w** .... Eph 6:7
friend, to help these **w**. .... Php 4:3
w should wear proper clothes 1Ti 2:9
which is right for **w** who say 1Ti 2:10
w must be respected by others. 1Ti 3:11
like mothers, and younger 1Ti 5:2
and younger **w** like sisters. 1Ti 5:2
control of silly **w** who are full 2Ti 3:6
These **w** are always learning new 2Ti 3:7
older **w** to be holy in their .... Tit 2:3
teach the young **w** to love their .... Tit 2:4
W received their dead relatives .... Heb 11:35
way the holy **w** who lived long 1Pe 3:5
And you **w** are true children of 1Pe 3:6
did not do sinful things with **w**, ... Rev 14:4

WOMEN'S

a man must not wear **w** clothes .... Dt 22:5
The **w** song upset Saul, and he 1Sa 18:8
be taken to the **w** quarters and .... Est 2:3
the best part of the **w** quarters. .... Est 2:9
with her from the **w** quarters to .... Est 2:13
another part of the **w** quarters. .... Est 2:14
Their hair was like **w** hair, ... Rev 9:8

WON

Mamre their share of what we **w**, ... Ge 14:24
with my sister, and I have **w**." .... Ge 30:8
with people, and you have **w**." .... Ge 32:28
and say, 'We have **w**! .... Dt 32:27
but the Israelites **w** them back, ... 1Sa 7:14
and the LORD **w** a great victory 1Sa 19:5
army had **w** the battle that 2Sa 19:2
after Eleazar had **w** the battle, ... 2Sa 23:10
in a mountain area, Israel **w**. 1Ki 20:23
Jeroboam **w** back Israel's border 2Ki 14:25
and how he **w** back from Judah 2Ki 14:28
And the people of Judah **w**, ... 2Ch 13:18
my enemy will say, "I have **w**!" .... Ps 13:4
holy arm he has **w** the victory. .... Ps 98:1
of the LORD has **w** the victory; .... Ps 118:16
taking what they have **w** in war .... Is 9:3
and by this you **w** for yourself .... Is 63:14
stronger than I am, so you **w**. .... Je 20:7
as if it were a prize **w** in war. .... Je 21:9
because the enemy has **w**." .... La 1:9
because the enemy has **w**." .... La 1:16
wrestled with the angel and **w**, ... Hos 12:4
wasted. I ran the race and **w**. .... Php 2:16
he **w** the victory and showed the .... Col 2:15
everything that he **w** in battle. .... Heb 7:4
same way that I **w** the victory .... Rev 3:21
has **w** the victory so that he is .... Rev 5:5
those who had **w** the victory over .... Rev 15:2

WONDER

No **w** my words seem careless. .... Job 6:3
great God who causes fear and **w**. .... Da 9:4
will you make us **w** about you? .... Jn 10:24
You can **w**, and then die. .... Ac 13:41
And then a great **w** appeared in .... Rev 12:1
Then another **w** appeared in .... Rev 12:3
I saw another **w** in heaven that .... Rev 15:1

WONDERED

angel said and **w** what this .... Lk 1:29
people who heard about them **w**, ... Lk 1:66
they **w** if John might be the one. .... Lk 3:15
were confused and **w** what was .... Ac 5:24
very upset and **w** what had .... Ac 12:18

WONDERFUL

When she saw how **w** the baby was, ... Ex 2:2
LORD, will do **w** things for you. .... Ex 34:10
do all the **w** things he promised .... Dt 1:11
great God, who is strong and **w**. .... Dt 10:17
done great and **w** things for you, ... Dt 10:21
glorious and **w** name of the LORD .... Dt 28:58
land with **w** dew from heaven .... Dt 33:13
did great and **w** things for all .... Dt 34:12
the **w** things he did for you! 1Sa 12:24
love to me was **w**, better than 2Sa 1:26
did great and **w** miracles for 2Sa 7:23
truly built a **w** Temple for you— 1Ki 8:13
have done this **w** thing for my 1Ch 17:19
the great and **w** things you did 1Ch 17:21
to build will be large and **w**. 2Ch 2:9
I have built a **w** Temple for you— 2Ch 6:2
him because he is holy and **w**. 2Ch 20:21
Blessed be your **w** name. .... Ne 9:5
It is more **w** than all blessing .... Ne 9:5
the great and mighty and **w** God. .... Ne 9:32
God's voice thunders in **w** ways; .... Job 37:5
of things too **w** for me to know. .... Job 42:3
my **w** God who gives me courage. .... Ps 3:3
name is the most **w** name in all .... Ps 8:1
name is the most **w** name in all .... Ps 8:9
they are the **w** ones I enjoy. .... Ps 16:3
Your love is **w**. By your power .... Ps 17:7
love to me was **w** when my city .... Ps 31:21

The LORD Most High is w. .... Ps 47:2
God, you are w in your Temple. .... Ps 68:35
God, how w you are! .... Ps 76:4
w things are said about you. .... Ps 87:3
servants the w things you do; .... Ps 90:16
everlasting. He is holy and w. .... Ps 111:9
did this, and it is w to us. .... Ps 118:23
Your rules are w. That is why I .... Ps 119:129
made me in an amazing and w way. .... Ps 139:14
What you have done is w. .... Ps 139:14
w majesty, and glory. .... Ps 145:5
He is more w than heaven and .... Ps 148:13
as w as an army flying flags. .... Sng 6:10
His name will be W Counselor, ... Is 9:6
like a w crown of flowers for .... Is 28:5
who gives w advice, who is very.............. Is 28:29
The LORD made his teachings w, ... Is 42:21
who does w things for you. .... Is 60:9
the right hand with his w power, ... Is 63:12
you won for yourself w fame. .... Is 63:14
at us from your w and holy home .... Is 63:15
you in our holy and w Temple, ... Is 64:11
did miracles and w things in the .... Je 32:20
You had a w life, as if you were .... Eze 28:13
done miracles and w things for .... Da 4:2
His w acts are great, and his .... Da 4:3
LORD has surely done a w thing!"........... Joe 2:21
the LORD has done a w thing. .... Joe 2:21
Jesus was doing w things and .... Mt 21:15
did this, and it is w to us.' .... Mt 21:42
did this, and it is w to us.'" .... Mk 12:11
at all the w things Jesus was .... Lk 13:17
the dead by the w power of the .... Rm 6:4
gift that is too w for words...................... 2Co 9:15
proud of the w things that were 2Co 12:7
to God because of his w grace. .... Eph 1:6
will use his w riches in Christ .... Php 4:19
to tell about the w acts of God, ... 1Pe 2:9
of darkness into his w light. 1Pe 2:9
You do great and w things,..................... Rev 15:3

WONDERFULLY

You are w holy, amazingly .... Ex 15:11

WONDERING

everyone was w about all that .... Lk 9:43
w what is happening to the world, ... Lk 21:26
While they were w about this, ... Lk 24:4
w about what had happened. .... Lk 24:12
While Peter was w what this .... Ac 10:17

WONDERS

he has done, his w, and his 1Ch 16:12
God does w that cannot be .... Job 5:9
He does w that cannot be .... Job 9:10
in Egypt and his w in the fields .... Ps 78:43
his w and his decisions. .... Ps 105:5
Egyptians and worked in Egypt.............. Ps 105:27
perform great w and miracles. .... Mt 24:24
perform great w and miracles. .... Mk 13:22
by the miracles, w, and signs he .... Ac 2:22
apostle—signs, w, and miracles. 2Co 12:12
false miracles, signs, and w. 2Th 2:9
truth of the message by using w, ... Heb 2:4

WOOD

boat of cypress w for yourself. .... Ge 6:14
After he cut the w for the .... Ge 22:3
Abraham took the w for the .... Ge 22:6
We have the fire and the w,.................... Ge 22:7
laid the w on it and then tied .... Ge 22:9
laid him on the w on the altar. .... Ge 22:9
red; fine leather, acacia w; .... Ex 25:5
Use acacia w and build an Ark .... Ex 25:10
from acacia w and cover them .... Ex 25:13

Make a table out of acacia w, ... Ex 25:23
Make the poles out of acacia w, ... Ex 25:28
Use acacia w to make upright .... Ex 26:15
crossbars of acacia w to connect .... Ex 26:26
posts of acacia w that are .... Ex 26:32
posts of acacia w covered with .... Ex 26:37
Make an altar of acacia w, ... Ex 27:1
pans for carrying the burning w. .... Ex 27:3
screen to hold the burning w, ... Ex 27:4
poles of acacia w for the altar, ... Ex 27:6
out of acacia w for burning .... Ex 30:1
from acacia w and cover them .... Ex 30:5
metal, to carve w, and to do all .... Ex 31:5
bring fine leather, acacia w, ... Ex 35:7
who had acacia w to be used in .... Ex 35:24
metal, to carve w, and to do all .... Ex 35:33
of acacia w for the Holy Tent.................. Ex 36:20
crossbars of acacia w to connect .... Ex 36:31
posts of acacia w for it and.................... Ex 36:36
made the Ark of acacia w; .... Ex 37:1
poles of acacia w and covered .... Ex 37:4
he made the table of acacia w; .... Ex 37:10
of acacia w and were covered................. Ex 37:15
of incense out of acacia w. .... Ex 37:25
poles of acacia w and covered .... Ex 37:28
burnt offerings out of acacia w. .... Ex 38:1
hold the burning w for the altar .... Ex 38:4
poles of acacia w and covered .... Ex 38:6
when they have put w and fire on .... Le 1:7
pieces on the w that is on the .... Le 1:8
on the w that is on the fire of .... Le 1:12
on the w which is on the fire. .... Le 1:17
that is on the w of the fire. .... Le 3:5
burn it on a w fire on the pile................ Le 4:12
includes anything made from w,............ Le 11:32
piece of cedar w, a piece of red .... Le 14:4
of cedar w, the red string, ... Le 14:6
plaster, and w, and take them to............ Le 14:45
piece of cedar w, a piece of red .... Le 14:49
alive, the cedar w, the hyssop, ... Le 14:51
bird, the cedar w, the hyssop, ... Le 14:52
gathering w on the Sabbath day. .... Nu 15:32
him gathering w brought him to............ Nu 15:33
of leather, goat hair, or w." .... Nu 31:20
a piece of w and kills someone .... Nu 35:18
gods made of w and stone, that .... Dt 4:28
I made the Ark out of acacia w, ... Dt 10:3
neighbor to cut w and swings an .... Dt 19:5
other gods made of w and stone. .... Dt 28:36
serve other gods of w and stone, ... Dt 28:64
your w and carry your water. .... Dt 29:11
their hateful idols made of w,................. Dt 29:17
they will cut w and carry water .... Jos 9:21
have to cut w and carry water .... Jos 9:23
They cut w and carried water for .... Jos 9:27
the w from the Asherah idol. .... Jdg 6:26
chopped up the w of the cart. 1Sa 6:14
in a palace made of cedar w, ... 2Sa 7:2
except with a tool of iron or w. 2Sa 23:7
boards and the yokes for the w. 2Sa 24:22
from olive w and placed them 1Ki 6:23
made from olive w were placed at 1Ki 6:31
the two olive w doors that were 1Ki 6:32
door frame made of olive w. 1Ki 6:33
as much juniper w and jewels. 1Ki 10:11
used the juniper w to build 1Ki 10:12
Such fine juniper w has not been 1Ki 10:12
the stones and w Baasha had 1Ki 15:22
a widow gathering w for a fire. 1Ki 17:10
to gather some w so I could go 1Ki 17:12
let them put the meat on the w, ... 1Ki 18:23
meat on the w but not setting................ 1Ki 18:23
fire to his w is the true God." 1Ki 18:24

Elijah put the **w** on the altar, ... 1Ki 18:33
and laid the pieces on the **w**. 1Ki 18:33
it on the meat and on the **w**." 1Ki 18:34
sacrifice, the **w**, the stones, ... 1Ki 18:38
were only **w** and rock statues 2Ki 19:18
the threshing boards for the **w**, ... 1Ch 21:23
be weighed, and **w** and stone.................. 1Ch 22:14
I have given **w** for the things 1Ch 29:2
things made of **w** and onyx for 1Ch 29:2
Send me a lot of **w**, because the 2Ch 2:9
who cut the **w** one hundred 2Ch 2:10
stone, and **w**, and with purple.............. 2Ch 2:14
cut as much **w** from Lebanon as.............. 2Ch 2:16
Ophir, juniper **w**, and jewels. 2Ch 9:10
the juniper **w** to build steps 2Ch 9:11
the rocks and **w** that Baasha had 2Ch 16:6
builders to buy cut stone and **w**.............. 2Ch 34:11
The **w** was used to rebuild the 2Ch 34:11
w beam is to be pulled from his .... Ezr 6:11
must bring **w** to the Temple. .... Ne 10:34
w is for burning on the altar .... Ne 10:34
also made sure **w** was brought for .... Ne 13:31
metal as if it were rotten **w**. .... Job 41:27
and with burning coals of **w**. .... Ps 120:4
Without **w**, a fire will go out, ... Pr 26:20
as charcoal and **w** keep a fire.................. Pr 26:21
ceiling is made of juniper **w**. .... Sng 1:17
for himself of **w** from Lebanon. .... Sng 3:9
dry pieces of **w**, and their works.............. Is 1:31
and wide with much **w** and fire.............. Is 30:33
were only **w** and rock statues.................. Is 37:19
and a compass to draw on the **w**. .... Is 44:13
makes the **w** look exactly like .... Is 44:13
uses some of the **w** for a fire to .... Is 44:15
part of the **w** to make a god, ... Is 44:15
burns half of the **w** in the fire. .... Is 44:16
also burns the **w** to keep himself .... Is 44:16
a statue from the **w** that is left .... Is 44:17
burned half of the **w** in the fire .... Is 44:19
And I used the **w** that was left .... Is 44:19
I am worshiping a block of **w**!" .... Is 44:19
carry idols of **w** don't know what .... Is 45:20
in place of **w**, iron in place .... Is 60:17
"I see a stick of almond **w**." .... Je 1:11
say to things of **w**, 'You are my .... Je 2:27
idols made of stone and **w**. .... Je 3:9
will be like **w** that it burns up. .... Je 5:14
children gather **w**, and the .... Je 7:18
use the **w** to make a fire.................. Je 7:18
idols are just **w** cut from the .... Je 10:3
large blocks of **w** at the Upper .... Je 20:2
Jeremiah out of the blocks of **w**,.............. Je 20:3
and uses cedar **w** for the walls, ... Je 22:14
their bones; it is as dry as **w**. .... La 4:8
boys stumbled under loads of **w**. .... La 5:13
is the **w** of the vine better than .... Eze 15:2
better than the **w** of any tree .... Eze 15:2
Can **w** be taken from the vine to .... Eze 15:3
have given the **w** of the vine as .... Eze 15:6
idols made of **w** and stone." .... Eze 20:32
flock, and pile **w** under the pot. .... Eze 24:5
pile the **w** high for burning. .... Eze 24:9
up the **w** and light the fire. .... Eze 24:10
throw your stones, **w**, and trash .... Eze 26:12
black **w** as your payment. .... Eze 27:15
need to take **w** from the field .... Eze 39:10
had **w** panels on the walls. .... Eze 41:16
the Temple had **w** panels on the .... Eze 41:16
The **w** covered all the walls from .... Eze 41:16
an altar of **w**. It was more than .... Eze 41:22
corners, base, and sides were **w**.............. Eze 41:22
And there was a **w** roof over the .... Eze 41:25
bronze, iron, **w**, and stone. .... Da 5:4

bronze, iron, **w**, and stone that .... Da 5:23
sticks of **w** to advise them! .... Hos 4:12
be like a chip of **w** floating on .... Hos 10:7
bring back **w**, and build the .... Hag 1:8
it with its **w** and stones.' " .... Zch 5:4
a stack of **w** or like a fire .... Zch 12:6
big piece of **w** in your own eye? .... Mt 7:3
big piece of **w** in your own eye. .... Mt 7:4
take the **w** out of your own eye. .... Mt 7:5
big piece of **w** in your own eye? .... Lk 6:41
big piece of **w** in your own eye! .... Lk 6:42
take the **w** out of your own eye. .... Lk 6:42
down between large blocks of **w**. .... Ac 16:24
silver, jewels, **w**, grass, or 1Co 3:12
also things made of **w** and clay. 2Ti 2:20
stone, and **w**—things that cannot .... Rev 9:20
kinds of citron **w** and all kinds .... Rev 18:12
expensive **w**, bronze, iron, ... Rev 18:12

WOODEN

in **w** buckets and in stone jars. .... Ex 7:19
he touches a **w** bowl, that bowl .... Le 15:12
the mountain. Also make a **w** Ark............. Dt 10:1
Do not set up a **w** Asherah idol .... Dt 16:21
The **w** part of his larger spear 1Sa 17:7
They were playing **w** instruments: 2Sa 6:5
He used their **w** yoke for a fire. 1Ki 6:41
down through the **w** bars in his 2Ki 1:2
and the **w** and metal idols. 2Ch 34:3
idols and the **w** and metal idols 2Ch 34:4
stood on a high **w** platform that .... Ne 8:4
and my **w** and metal statues made .... Is 48:5
come from worthless **w** idols. .... Je 10:8
have broken a **w** yoke, but I will.............. Je 28:13
hands and feet between **w** blocks, ... Je 29:26
My people ask **w** idols for .... Hos 4:12
one who says to a **w** statue, ' .... Hab 2:19
the **w** boards of the buildings .... Zph 2:14
to follow using **w** boards or .... Ac 27:44

WOODS

Now the army went into the **w**, ... 1Sa 14:25
came out of the **w** and tore.................. 2Ki 2:24
is like an apple tree in the **w**! .... Sng 2:3
the desert and sleep in the **w**. .... Eze 34:25

WOOL

to cut the **w** from his sheep, ... Ge 31:19
cutting the **w** from his sheep. .... Ge 38:12
to cut the **w** from his sheep. .... Ge 38:13
be clothing made of linen or **w** .... Le 13:47
or knitted, **w** or linen, or made .... Le 13:52
not cut off the **w** from the first .... Dt 15:19
as the first **w** you cut from your .... Dt 18:4
clothes made of **w** and linen .... Dt 22:11
I will put some **w** on the .... Jdg 6:37
is dew only on the **w** but all of .... Jdg 6:37
next morning and squeezed the **w**,.......... Jdg 6:38
Let only the **w** be dry while the .... Jdg 6:39
Just the **w** was dry, but the .... Jdg 6:40
was cutting the **w** off his sheep 1Sa 25:2
cutting the **w** from his sheep. 1Sa 25:4
cutting the **w** from your sheep 1Sa 25:7
for my servants who cut the **w**. 1Sa 25:11
to cut the **w** from his sheep. 2Sa 13:23
I have men coming to cut the **w**.............. 2Sa 13:24
lambs and the **w** of one hundred 2Ki 3:4
him with the **w** of my sheep. .... Job 31:20
the snow like **w** and scatters .... Ps 147:16
Make clothes from the lambs' **w**, ... Pr 27:26
She looks for **w** and flax and .... Pr 31:13
red, they can be white like **w**.................. Is 1:18
will eat them as if they were **w**. .... Is 51:8
quiet while its **w** is being cut; .... Is 53:7
clothe yourselves with the **w**. .... Eze 34:3

They must not wear **w** to serve at .... Eze 44:17
on his head was white like **w**. .... Da 7:9
food and water, and flax, wine .... Hos 2:5
take back my **w** and linen that .... Hos 2:9
quiet while its **w** is being cut; .... Ac 8:32
Then he used red **w** and a branch .... Heb 9:19
head and hair were white like **w**, ... Rev 1:14

WORD

the LORD spoke his **w** to Abram in .... Ge 15:1
the LORD spoke his **w** to Abram: .... Ge 15:4
respected the **w** of the LORD .... Ex 9:20
the LORD's **w** and has not obeyed .... Nu 15:31
No, the **w** is very near you. .... Dt 30:14
protected your **w** and guarded .... Dt 33:9
Don't say a **w** until the day I .... Jos 6:10
brave enough to say a **w** against .... Jos 10:21
"Say the **w** 'Shibboleth.'" .... Jdg 12:6
could not say that **w** correctly. .... Jdg 12:6
Don't say a **w**. Come with us .... Jdg 18:19
himself to Samuel through his **w**. 1Sa 3:21
You must obey his **w** and not turn 1Sa 12:14
the LORD spoke his **w** to Samuel: 1Sa 15:10
I will send **w** to you and let you 1Sa 20:12
the LORD spoke his **w** to Nathan, ... 2Sa 7:4
pregnant and sent **w** to David, ... 2Sa 11:5
The LORD sent **w** through Nathan 2Sa 12:25
did not say a **w**, good or bad, to 2Sa 13:22
was as reliable as God's own **w**. 2Sa 16:23
and his **w** was on my tongue. 2Sa 23:2
the LORD spoke his **w** to Gad, ... 2Sa 24:11
But God spoke his **w** to Shemaiah, ... 1Ki 12:22
LORD spoke his **w** to the old 1Ki 13:20
Hanani spoke the **w** of the LORD 1Ki 16:1
LORD spoke his **w** against Baasha 1Ki 16:7
the LORD spoke his **w** to Elijah: 1Ki 17:2
the LORD spoke his **w** to Elijah, ... 1Ki 17:8
the LORD spoke his **w** to Elijah: 1Ki 18:1
the LORD spoke his **w** to him: 1Ki 19:9
LORD spoke his **w** to the prophet 1Ki 21:17
The LORD spoke his **w** to Elijah. 1Ki 21:28
said, "Listen to the LORD's **w**. 2Ki 7:1
Then Jehu sent **w** through all 2Ki 10:21
and the LORD's **w** came true. 2Ki 15:12
the LORD spoke his **w** to Isaiah: 2Ki 20:4
night God spoke his **w** to Nathan, ... 1Ch 17:3
the LORD spoke his **w** to me, ' 1Ch 22:8
LORD spoke his **w** to Shemaiah, ... 2Ch 11:2
LORD spoke his **w** to Shemaiah, ... 2Ch 12:7
did not obey the LORD's **w**; 2Ch 34:21
in fear at the **w** of the God of .... Ezr 9:4
Mordecai sent back **w** to Esther: .... Est 4:13
which comes from the **w** "Pur" .... Est 9:26
No one said a **w** to him because .... Job 2:13
A **w** was brought to me in secret, ... Job 4:12
God has made my name a curse **w**; .... Job 17:6
you have said; I heard every **w**. .... Job 33:8
God's **w** is true, and everything .... Ps 33:4
I praise God for his **w**. .... Ps 56:4
I praise God for his **w** to me; .... Ps 56:10
I praise the LORD for his **w**. .... Ps 56:10
a pure life? By obeying your **w**. .... Ps 119:9
and I will not forget your **w**. .... Ps 119:16
can live, so I can obey your **w**. .... Ps 119:17
things. Let me live by your **w**. .... Ps 119:37
wrong, but now I obey your **w**. .... Ps 119:67
because I put my hope in your **w**. .... Ps 119:74
save me, but I hope in your **w**. .... Ps 119:81
LORD, your **w** is everlasting; .... Ps 119:89
evil way so I could obey your **w**. .... Ps 119:101
w is like a lamp for my feet .... Ps 119:105
LORD, give me life by your **w**. .... Ps 119:107
and my shield; I hope in your **w**. .... Ps 119:114

and cry out. I hope in your **w**. .... Ps 119:147
Let your **w** help me understand. .... Ps 119:169
to help me, and I trust his **w**. .... Ps 130:5
name and your **w** greater than .... Ps 138:2
before I say a **w**, you already .... Ps 139:4
He gave his **w** to Jacob, his laws .... Ps 147:19
but a kind **w** cheers you up. .... Pr 12:25
Saying the right **w** at the right .... Pr 15:23
The right **w** spoken at the right .... Pr 25:11
and a gentle **w** can get through .... Pr 25:15
Where there is no **w** from God, ... Pr 29:18
Every **w** of God is true. .... Pr 30:5
Hear the **w** of the LORD; .... Is 1:10
do not speak the **w** of the LORD, ... Is 8:20
the LORD spoke his **w** to Isaiah: .... Is 38:4
but the **w** of our God will live .... Is 40:8
punished, but he didn't say a **w**. .... Is 53:7
or stubborn and who fear my **w**. .... Is 66:2
LORD spoke his **w** to Jeremiah .... Je 1:2
The LORD spoke his **w** to me, ... Je 1:4
The LORD spoke his **w** to me, ... Je 1:11
LORD spoke his **w** to me again: .... Je 1:13
The LORD spoke his **w** to me, ... Je 2:1
Hear the **w** of the LORD, family .... Je 2:4
attention to the **w** of the LORD: .... Je 2:31
the **w** of God is not in them. .... Je 5:13
don't like the **w** of the LORD; .... Je 6:10
is the **w** that the LORD spoke .... Je 7:1
Hear the **w** of the LORD, ... Je 7:2
to listen to the **w** of the LORD, ... Je 8:9
listen to the **w** of the LORD ; .... Je 9:20
LORD spoke his **w** to me a second .... Je 13:3
Then the LORD spoke his **w** to me. .... Je 13:8
Then the LORD spoke his **w** to me: .... Je 16:1
Where is the **w** from the LORD? .... Je 17:15
'Hear the **w** of the LORD, kings .... Je 17:20
This is the **w** the LORD spoke to .... Je 18:1
Then the LORD spoke his **w** to me: .... Je 18:5
is the **w** that the LORD spoke .... Je 21:1
'Hear the **w** of the LORD. .... Je 21:11
'Hear the **w** of the LORD, king of .... Je 22:2
Judah, hear the **w** of the LORD! .... Je 22:29
Then the LORD spoke his **w** to me: .... Je 24:4
has spoken his **w** to me again .... Je 25:3
you to say; don't leave out a **w**. .... Je 26:2
spoke his **w** to Jeremiah soon .... Je 27:1
LORD spoke his **w** to Jeremiah .... Je 28:12
LORD spoke his **w** to Jeremiah: .... Je 29:30
This is the **w** the LORD spoke to .... Je 32:1
The LORD spoke this **w** to me: .... Je 32:6
LORD spoke this **w** to Jeremiah: .... Je 32:26
LORD spoke his **w** to him a second .... Je 33:1
LORD spoke his **w** to Jeremiah, ... Je 33:19
LORD spoke his **w** to Jeremiah, ... Je 33:23
spoke his **w** to Jeremiah when .... Je 34:1
LORD spoke his **w** to Jeremiah. .... Je 34:8
LORD spoke his **w** to Jeremiah: .... Je 34:12
LORD spoke his **w** to Jeremiah, ... Je 35:1
LORD spoke his **w** to Jeremiah: .... Je 35:12
LORD spoke this **w** to Jeremiah .... Je 36:1
LORD spoke his **w** to Jeremiah: .... Je 36:27
The LORD spoke his **w** to Jeremiah .... Je 37:6
the LORD spoke his **w** to him: .... Je 39:15
LORD spoke his **w** to Jeremiah .... Je 40:1
LORD spoke his **w** to Jeremiah. .... Je 42:7
You will become a curse **w**, ... Je 42:18
LORD spoke his **w** to Jeremiah: .... Je 43:8
They will become a curse **w**, ... Je 44:12
Egypt, hear the **w** of the LORD: .... Je 44:24
But hear the **w** of the LORD. .... Je 44:26
will know if my **w** or their word .... Je 44:28
if my word or their **w** came true. .... Je 44:28
LORD spoke this **w** to Jeremiah .... Je 46:1

the LORD spoke his w to Jeremiah ....Je 47:1
LORD spoke this w to Jeremiah ....Je 49:34
he has kept his w that he ....La 2:17
LORD spoke his w to Ezekiel son ....Eze 1:3
LORD spoke his w to me again. ....Eze 3:16
time you hear a w from my mouth, ...Eze 3:17
the LORD spoke his w to me, ...Eze 6:1
listen to the w of the Lord GOD...............Eze 6:3
the LORD spoke his w to me, ...Eze 7:1
The LORD spoke his w to me, ...Eze 11:14
the LORD spoke his w to me, ...Eze 12:1
the LORD spoke his w to me, ...Eze 12:8
The LORD spoke his w to me, ...Eze 12:17
The LORD spoke his w to me, ...Eze 12:21
time I will say the w and do it, ...Eze 12:25
The LORD spoke his w to me, ...Eze 12:26
The LORD spoke his w to me, ...Eze 13:1
'Listen to the w of the LORD. ....Eze 13:2
Then the LORD spoke his w to me, ...Eze 14:2
The LORD spoke his w to me, ...Eze 14:12
The LORD spoke his w to me, ...Eze 15:1
The LORD spoke his w to me, ...Eze 16:1
hear the w of the LORD..........................Eze 16:35
The LORD spoke his w to me, ...Eze 17:1
Then the LORD spoke his w to me, ...Eze 17:11
The LORD spoke his w to me, ...Eze 18:1
The LORD spoke his w to me, ...Eze 20:2
Now the LORD spoke his w to me,...........Eze 20:45
'Hear the w of the LORD. ....Eze 20:47
Then the LORD spoke his w to me, ...Eze 21:1
The LORD spoke his w to me, ...Eze 21:8
The LORD spoke his w to me, ...Eze 21:18
The LORD spoke his w to me, ...Eze 22:1
The LORD spoke his w to me, ...Eze 22:17
The LORD spoke his w to me, ...Eze 22:23
The LORD spoke his w to me, ...Eze 23:1
LORD spoke his w to me in the ....Eze 24:1
Then the LORD spoke his w to me, ...Eze 24:15
The LORD spoke his w to me. ....Eze 24:20
The LORD spoke his w to me, ...Eze 25:1
'Hear the w of the Lord GOD...................Eze 25:3
The LORD spoke his w to me, ...Eze 26:1
The LORD spoke his w to me, ...Eze 27:1
The LORD spoke his w to me, ...Eze 28:1
The LORD spoke his w to me, ...Eze 28:11
The LORD spoke his w to me, ...Eze 28:20
The LORD spoke his w to me, ...Eze 29:1
The LORD spoke his w to me, ...Eze 29:17
The LORD spoke his w to me, ...Eze 30:1
The LORD spoke his w to me, ...Eze 30:20
The LORD spoke his w to me, ...Eze 31:1
The LORD spoke his w to me, ...Eze 32:1
The LORD spoke his w to me, ...Eze 32:17
The LORD spoke his w to me, ...Eze 33:1
If you hear a w from my mouth,..............Eze 33:7
Then the LORD spoke his w to me, ...Eze 33:23
The LORD spoke his w to me, ...Eze 34:1
hear the w of the LORD. ....Eze 34:7
hear the w of the LORD. ....Eze 34:9
The LORD spoke his w to me, ...Eze 35:1
Israel, hear the w of the LORD. ....Eze 36:1
hear the w of the Lord GOD. ....Eze 36:4
LORD spoke his w to me again, ...Eze 36:16
bones, hear the w of the LORD. ....Eze 37:4
The LORD spoke his w to me, ...Eze 37:15
The LORD spoke his w to me, ...Eze 38:1
LORD spoke his w to Hosea son ....Hos 1:1
The LORD spoke his w to Joel son...........Joe 1:1
Listen to this w that the LORD ....Am 3:1
So listen to the LORD's w. ....Am 7:16
search for the w of the LORD, ...Am 8:12
LORD spoke his w to Jonah son..............Jnh 1:1
LORD spoke his w to Jonah again ....Jnh 3:1

the w of the LORD came to Micah, ...Mic 1:1
w of the LORD from that city...................Mic 4:2
This is the w of the LORD that ....Zph 1:1
w of the LORD is against you, ...Zph 2:5
Haggai spoke the w of the LORD ....Hag 1:1
prophet spoke the w of the LORD: ....Hag 1:3
LORD spoke his w through Haggai ....Hag 2:1
the LORD spoke his w to Haggai ....Hag 2:10
LORD spoke his w a second time ....Hag 2:20
LORD spoke his w to the prophet ....Zch 1:1
LORD spoke his w to the prophet ....Zch 1:7
This is the w of the LORD to ....Zch 4:6
LORD spoke his w to me again, ...Zch 4:8
The LORD spoke his w to me, ...Zch 6:9
LORD spoke his w to Zechariah. ....Zch 7:1
All-Powerful spoke his w to me,..............Zch 7:4
LORD spoke his w to Zechariah. ....Zch 7:8
LORD All-Powerful spoke his w, ...Zch 8:1
spoke his w to me again. ....Zch 8:18
message is the w of the LORD. ....Zch 9:1
message is the w of the LORD to ....Zch 12:1
message is the w of the LORD ....Mal 1:1
the w of God came to John son of ....Lk 3:2
around him to hear the w of God. ....Lk 5:1
the beginning there was the W. ....Jn 1:1
The W was with God, and the Word ....Jn 1:1
was with God, and the W was God. ....Jn 1:1
The W was in the world, and the ....Jn 1:10
The W became a human and lived ....Jn 1:14
w I have taught will be their ....Jn 12:48
to speak your w without fear...................Ac 4:29
they spoke God's w without fear. ....Ac 4:31
teaching God's w in order to ....Ac 6:2
pray and to teach the w of God." ....Ac 6:4
The w of God was continuing to..............Ac 6:7
had accepted the w of God, ...Ac 8:14
came to hear the w of the Lord. ....Ac 13:44
preaching the w of God in Berea ....Ac 17:13
teaching God's w to the people. ....Ac 18:11
in Asia heard the w of the Lord...............Ac 19:10
way the w of the Lord kept..................Ac 19:20
says: "The w is near you; it is..................Rm 10:8
We do not sell the w of God for 2Co 2:17
Christ used the w to make the ....Eph 5:26
Spirit, which is the w of God. ....Eph 6:17
afraid to speak the w of God. ....Php 1:14
you accepted it as the w of God,..............1Th 2:13
the trustworthy w just as we ....Tit 1:9
together with his powerful w...................Heb 1:3
God's w is alive and working and ....Heb 4:12
found out how good God's w is, ...Heb 6:5
but the w of God's oath came.................Heb 7:28
begged not to hear another w. ....Heb 12:19
life through the w of truth so ....Jam 1:18
but the w of the Lord will live 1Pe 1:25
And this is the w that was 1Pe 1:25
anyone's saying a w to them. 1Pe 3:1
By the w of God heaven was made, ...2Pe 3:5
that same w of God is keeping 2Pe 3:7
you about the W that gives life. 1Jn 1:1
seen. It is the w of God; it is ....Rev 1:2
I had preached the w of God and ....Rev 1:9
faithful to the w of God and to ....Rev 6:9
and his name is the W of God. ....Rev 19:13

WORDS

and everyone used the same w. ....Ge 11:1
Abraham's servant heard these w, ...Ge 24:52
Esau heard the w of his father, ...Ge 27:34
and spoke kind w to them. ....Ge 50:21
and can't find the best w." ....Ex 4:10
tell the Israelites these w." ....Ex 19:6
told them all the w the LORD had ....Ex 19:7

Then God spoke all these **w:** .... Ex 20:1
all the LORD's **w** and laws for .... Ex 24:3
down all the **w** of the LORD. .... Ex 24:4
with you about all these **w.**" .... Ex 24:8
a person carves **w** and designs .... Ex 28:11
and carve these **w** on it as you .... Ex 28:36
write the same **w** on them that .... Ex 34:1
Write down these **w,** because with .... Ex 34:27
because with these **w** I have made .... Ex 34:27
wrote the **w** of the Agreement— .... Ex 34:28
as a person carves **w** and designs .... Ex 39:6
and carved these **w** in the gold, ... Ex 39:30
the **w** off into the bitter water, ... Nu 5:23
He said, "Listen to my **w:** .... Nu 12:6
of a man who hears the **w** of God. .... Nu 24:4
of a man who hears the **w** of God. .... Nu 24:16
the sound of **w,** but you did not .... Dt 4:12
the tablets the same **w** that were .... Dt 10:2
Remember my **w** with your whole .... Dt 11:18
it changes the **w** of good people. .... Dt 16:19
write all the **w** of these .... Dt 27:3
clearly all the **w** of these .... Dt 27:8
agree with the **w** of these .... Dt 27:26
These are the **w** of that .... Dt 29:1
went and spoke these **w** to all .... Dt 31:1
writing all the **w** of the .... Dt 31:24
my **w** will fall like dew. .... Dt 32:2
spoke all the **w** of this song for .... Dt 32:44
speaking these **w** to all Israel, ... Dt 32:45
to all the **w** I have said to you .... Dt 32:46
not be unimportant **w** for you, ... Dt 32:47
By these **w** you will live a long .... Dt 32:47
listen to the **w** of the LORD your .... Jos 3:9
read all the **w** of the teachings, ... Jos 8:34
These **w** are written in the Book .... Jos 10:13
repeated all of his **w** in front .... Jdg 11:11
kind and encouraging to me, ... Ru 2:13
bragging, don't speak proud **w.** 1Sa 2:3
he repeated their **w** to the LORD. 1Sa 8:21
Saul heard their **w,** God's Spirit 1Sa 11:6
the LORD's commands and your **w.** 1Sa 15:24
heard the Philistine's **w,** 1Sa 17:11
servants said these **w** to David, ... 1Sa 18:23
to these **w** and was very much 1Sa 21:12
used these **w** to stop his men 1Sa 24:7
David finished saying these **w,** 1Sa 24:16
have heard your **w,** and I will do 1Sa 25:35
are God, and your **w** are true. 2Sa 7:28
Encourage Joab with these **w.**" 2Sa 11:25
go to the king and say these **w.**" 2Sa 14:3
'May the **w** of my master the king 2Sa 14:17
king and told him Absalom's **w.** 2Sa 14:33
the LORD's **w** are pure. 2Sa 22:31
These are the last **w** of David. 2Sa 23:1
Rehoboam spoke cruel **w** to them, ... 1Ki 12:13
Remember my **w,** all you people!" 1Ki 22:28
the king heard the woman's **w,** 2Ki 6:30
war, but your **w** mean nothing. 2Ki 18:20
frightened by the **w** the servants 2Ki 19:6
Listen to the **w** Sennacherib has 2Ki 19:16
I have heard your proud **w,** 2Ki 19:28
Listen to the **w** of the LORD: 2Ki 20:16
"These **w** from the LORD are good." 2Ki 20:19
the king heard the **w** of the Book 2Ki 22:11
about the **w** in the book that 2Ki 22:13
did not obey the **w** of this book; 2Ki 22:13
says about the **w** you heard: 2Ki 22:18
When you heard my **w** against this 2Ki 22:19
to them all the **w** of the Book 2Ki 23:2
and to obey the **w** of the 2Ki 23:3
was to obey the **w** of the 2Ki 23:24
Rehoboam spoke cruel **w** to them, ... 2Ch 10:13
he heard these **w** and the message 2Ch 15:8

Remember my **w,** all you people!" 2Ch 18:27
using the **w** David and Asaph the 2Ch 29:30
by the **w** of Hezekiah king 2Ch 32:8
king heard the **w** of the 2Ch 34:19
about the **w** in the book that 2Ch 34:21
says about the **w** you heard: 2Ch 34:26
When you heard my **w** against this 2Ch 34:27
to them all the **w** in the Book 2Ch 34:30
and to obey the **w** of the 2Ch 34:31
These are the **w** of Nehemiah son .... Ne 1:1
listened to the **w** of the .... Ne 8:9
to study the **w** of the Teachings. .... Ne 8:13
Your **w** have comforted those who .... Job 4:4
No wonder my **w** seem careless. .... Job 6:3
reject the **w** of the Holy One. .... Job 6:10
Honest **w** are painful, but your .... Job 6:25
you treat the **w** of a troubled .... Job 6:26
Your **w** are no more than wind. .... Job 8:2
even find **w** to argue with him? .... Job 9:14
Should these **w** go unanswered? .... Job 11:2
The ear tests **w** as the tongue .... Job 12:11
Listen carefully to my **w;** .... Job 13:17
answer with empty **w** or fill his .... Job 15:2
with useless **w** or make speeches .... Job 15:3
you use **w** to trick others. .... Job 15:5
even when **w** are spoken gently to .... Job 15:11
Why do these **w** pour out of your .... Job 15:13
and my **w** would bring you relief. .... Job 16:5
me and crush me with your **w?** .... Job 19:2
How I wish my **w** were written .... Job 19:23
Listen carefully to my **w,** .... Job 21:2
and keep his **w** in your heart. .... Job 22:22
treasured his **w** more than my own .... Job 23:12
that my **w** are worth nothing? .... Job 24:25
Who has helped you say these **w?** .... Job 26:4
My **w** fell very gently on their .... Job 29:22
and drank in my **w** like spring .... Job 29:23
The **w** of Job are finished. .... Job 31:40
While you looked for **w** to use, ... Job 32:11
has not spoken his **w** against me, ... Job 32:14
no more to say; **w** have failed .... Job 32:15
am full of **w,** and the spirit in .... Job 32:18
Now, Job, listen to my **w.** .... Job 33:1
My **w** come from an honest heart, ... Job 33:3
Hear my **w,** you wise men; .... Job 34:2
The ear tests **w** as the tongue .... Job 34:3
w show he does not understand. .... Job 34:35
saying many **w** without knowing .... Job 35:16
be sure that my **w** are not false; .... Job 36:4
and speak to you with gentle **w?** .... Job 41:3
listen to my **w.** Understand my .... Ps 5:1
The LORD's **w** are pure, like .... Ps 12:6
The LORD's **w** are pure. .... Ps 18:30
They have no speech or **w;** .... Ps 19:3
their **w** go everywhere on earth. .... Ps 19:4
I hope my **w** and thoughts please .... Ps 19:14
You shelter them from evil **w,** .... Ps 31:20
Their **w** are not friendly but are .... Ps 35:20
Their **w** are wicked lies; .... Ps 36:3
Beautiful **w** fill my mind. .... Ps 45:1
You love **w** that bite and tongues .... Ps 52:4
destroy and confuse their **w,** .... Ps 55:9
His **w** are slippery like butter, ... Ps 55:21
His **w** are smoother than oil, ... Ps 55:21
All day long they twist my **w;** .... Ps 56:5
they sin with their **w.** .... Ps 59:12
and shoot bitter **w** like arrows. .... Ps 64:3
Their own **w** will be used against .... Ps 64:8
their **w** were false, and their .... Ps 78:36
They are full of proud **w;** .... Ps 94:4
and the LORD's **w** proved that .... Ps 105:19
against the **w** of God and had .... Ps 107:11
have taken your **w** to heart so I .... Ps 119:11

I have promised to obey your w............... Ps 119:57
Learning your w gives wisdom and .... Ps 119:130
enemies have forgotten your w. .... Ps 119:139
Your w are true from the start, ... Ps 119:160
when they hear the w you speak. .... Ps 138:4
their w are like snake poison.................. Ps 140:3
are the wise w of Solomon son .... Pr 1:1
will help you understand wise w. .... Pr 1:2
can find good advice in these w............. Pr 1:5
understand wise w and stories, ... Pr 1:6
the w of the wise and their .... Pr 1:6
from those whose w are bad, ... Pr 2:12
into adultery with pleasing w.................. Pr 2:16
Hold on to my w with all your .... Pr 4:4
Don't forget or ignore my w. .... Pr 4:5
My child, pay attention to my w; .... Pr 4:20
Don't ever forget my w; .... Pr 4:21
listen to my w of understanding. .... Pr 5:1
The w of another man's wife may .... Pr 5:3
might be caught by your own w............. Pr 6:2
Keep their w in mind forever as .... Pr 6:21
the pleasing w of another man's.............. Pr 6:24
wife and her pleasing w........................ Pr 7:5
her clever w she made him give .... Pr 7:21
by her pleasing w she led him .... Pr 7:21
knowledge know my w are right. .... Pr 8:9
These are the wise w of Solomon: .... Pr 10:1
w of a good person give life, ... Pr 10:11
but the w of the wicked contain .... Pr 10:11
The w of a good person are like .... Pr 10:20
Good people's w will help many............. Pr 10:21
an evil person can destroy .... Pr 11:9
can destroy it with their w..................... Pr 11:11
but the w of good people will .... Pr 12:6
Careless w stab like a sword, ... Pr 12:18
sword, but wise w bring healing. .... Pr 12:18
be punished for their proud w, ... Pr 14:3
but the w of the wise will .... Pr 14:3
fruit, healing w give life,........................ Pr 15:4
dishonest w crush the spirit. .... Pr 15:4
people use their w to spread .... Pr 15:7
but is pleased with kind w. .... Pr 15:26
The w of a king are like a .... Pr 16:10
pleasant w make them better .... Pr 16:21
Pleasant w are like a honeycomb, ... Pr 16:24
and their w are like a burning .... Pr 16:27
Evil people listen to evil w. .... Pr 17:4
Liars pay attention to cruel w. .... Pr 17:4
the person whose w are evil will .... Pr 17:20
Spoken w can be like deep water, ... Pr 18:4
The w of fools start quarrels. .... Pr 18:6
The w of fools will ruin them;................. Pr 18:7
their own w will trap them. .... Pr 18:7
The w of a gossip are like tasty .... Pr 18:8
and kind w will have even .... Pr 22:11
but he destroys false w. .... Pr 22:12
The w of an unfaithful wife are .... Pr 22:14
and reliable w so that you can .... Pr 22:21
will have wasted your kind w. .... Pr 23:8
will only ignore your wise w. .... Pr 23:9
carefully to w of knowledge. .... Pr 23:12
The w of a gossip are like tasty .... Pr 26:22
Kind w from a wicked mind are .... Pr 26:23
try to fool you with their w, ... Pr 26:24
People's w may be kind, but .... Pr 26:25
W alone cannot correct a servant, ... Pr 29:19
These are the w of Agur son of .... Pr 30:1
Do not add to his w, or he will .... Pr 30:6
These are the w of King Lemuel, ... Pr 31:1
She speaks wise w and teaches .... Pr 31:26
These are the w of the Teacher, ... Ec 1:1
W come again and again to our .... Ec 1:8
so say only a few w to God. .... Ec 5:2

and too many w come from foolish .... Ec 5:3
Don't let your w cause you to .... Ec 5:6
angry with your w and will..................... Ec 5:6
The quiet w of a wise person are .... Ec 9:17
The w of the wise bring them .... Ec 10:12
but the w of a fool will destroy .... Ec 10:12
little bird might carry your w; .... Ec 10:20
just the right w to write what .... Ec 12:10
W from wise people are like .... Ec 12:11
so their w are worth nothing. .... Is 8:20
and by his w the wicked will be .... Is 11:4
will use strange w and foreign .... Is 28:11
So the w of the LORD will be, ... Is 28:13
your w will come like a whisper............... Is 29:4
is like the w of a book that is .... Is 29:11
deaf will hear the w in a book. .... Is 29:18
war, but your w mean nothing. .... Is 36:5
frightened by the w the servants .... Is 37:6
to all the w Sennacherib has .... Is 37:17
I have heard your proud w,..................... Is 37:29
Listen to the w of the LORD .... Is 39:5
"These w from the LORD are good." .... Is 39:8
secret or hide my w in some dark .... Is 45:19
give you the w I want you to say .... Is 51:16
thing is true of the w I speak................... Is 55:11
stop using cruel w and pointing .... Is 58:9
Spirit and my w that I give you .... Is 59:21
who obey the w of the LORD,................. Is 66:5
These are the w of Jeremiah son .... Je 1:1
I am putting my w in your mouth. .... Je 1:9
to make sure my w come true." .... Je 1:12
shouting at war against the .... Je 4:16
the w I give you will be like .... Je 5:14
ears to hear the w of his mouth.............. Je 9:20
These are the w that the LORD .... Je 11:1
Listen to the w of this .... Je 11:2
not obey the w of this agreement .... Je 11:3
'Listen to the w of this .... Je 11:6
These are the w that the LORD .... Je 14:1
w came to me, and I listened .... Je 15:16
Your w made me very happy, ... Je 15:16
not useless w, then you may .... Je 15:19
and the w of the prophets .... Je 18:18
There speak the w I tell you. .... Je 19:2
of the LORD and his holy w. .... Je 23:9
keep stealing w from each other .... Je 23:30
use their own w and pretend it .... Je 23:31
message you speak is your own w.............. Je 23:36
have changed the w of our God,.............. Je 23:36
If you use these w, this is what .... Je 23:38
I told you not to use those w, ... Je 23:38
against them with all these w. .... Je 25:30
speaking these w in the Temple .... Je 26:7
spoke these w to all the .... Je 26:12
These are the w that the LORD .... Je 30:1
a book all the w I have spoken .... Je 30:2
towns will again use these w: ' .... Je 31:23
These are the w of the LORD,................. Je 33:2
on it all the w I have spoken to .... Je 36:2
which are the w you wrote on the .... Je 36:6
scroll containing Jeremiah's w. .... Je 36:10
the officers heard all the w, ... Je 36:16
tell the king about these w." .... Je 36:16
you get all these w you wrote .... Je 36:17
written all the w Jeremiah had .... Je 36:27
Write all the w on it that were .... Je 36:28
the scroll the same w that were .... Je 36:32
And many similar w were added to .... Je 36:32
not listen to the w the LORD had .... Je 37:2
I will make my w about Jerusalem........... Je 39:16
all these w about Babylon. .... Je 51:60
The w of Jeremiah end here. .... Je 51:64
The w and thoughts of my enemies .... La 3:62

afraid of the people or their **w**. .... Eze 2:6
of their **w** or their looks, ... Eze 2:6
But speak my **w** to them. .... Eze 2:7
w about troubles were written .... Eze 2:10
Israel, and speak my **w** to them. .... Eze 3:4
whose **w** you cannot understand. .... Eze 3:6
believe all the **w** I will speak .... Eze 3:10
None of my **w** will be delayed .... Eze 12:28
hope their **w** will come true. .... Eze 13:6
were my people and hear your **w**, ... Eze 33:31
They hear your **w**, but they will .... Eze 33:32
The **w** were still in his mouth .... Da 4:31
Immediately the **w** came true. .... Da 4:33
These are the **w** that were .... Da 5:25
This is what the **w** mean: .... Da 5:26
about the **w** I will speak to you .... Da 10:11
the LORD and say these **w** to him: .... Hos 14:2
These are the **w** of Amos, one of .... Am 1:1
this land can't hold all his **w**. .... Am 7:10
be hungry for **w** from the LORD. .... Am 8:11
My **w** are welcome to the person .... Mic 2:7
won't trick people with their **w**. .... Zph 3:13
I commanded my **w** and laws to my .... Zch 1:6
and his **w** were comforting and .... Zch 1:13
not hear the **w** he sent by his .... Zch 7:12
who are hearing these **w** today. .... Zch 8:9
spoke these **w** when the .... Zch 8:9
have tired the LORD with your **w**. .... Mal 2:17
them because of their many **w**. .... Mt 6:7
who hears my **w** and obeys them is .... Mt 7:24
who hears my **w** and does not obey .... Mt 7:26
really know what those **w** mean. .... Mt 12:7
The **w** you have said will be used .... Mt 12:37
Some of your **w** will prove you .... Mt 12:37
some of your **w** will prove you .... Mt 12:37
people show honor to me with **w**, ... Mt 15:8
but the **w** I have said will never .... Mt 24:35
answered, "Those are your **w**. .... Mt 26:64
answered, "Those are your **w**." .... Mt 27:11
people show honor to me with **w**, ... Mk 7:6
but the **w** I have said will never .... Mk 13:31
answered, "Those are your **w**." .... Mk 15:2
you heard these **w** just now, ... Lk 4:21
amazed at the **w** of grace he .... Lk 4:22
to me and hears my **w** and obeys. .... Lk 6:47
one who hears my **w** and does not .... Lk 6:49
will condemn you by your own **w**, ... Lk 19:22
but the **w** I have spoken will .... Lk 21:33
answered, "Those are your **w**." .... Lk 23:3
the cross these **w** were written: .... Lk 23:38
them in the **w** of the prophet .... Jn 1:23
and the **w** Jesus had said. .... Jn 2:22
God sent speaks the **w** of God, ... Jn 3:34
The **w** I told you are spirit, ... Jn 6:63
You have the **w** that give eternal .... Jn 6:68
When the people heard Jesus' **w**, ... Jn 7:40
The **w** he says are greater than .... Jn 7:46
greater than the **w** of any other .... Jn 7:46
because of these **w** of Jesus. .... Jn 10:19
who hears my **w** and does not obey .... Jn 12:47
in me and do not accept my **w**. .... Jn 12:48
The **w** I say to you don't come .... Jn 14:10
because of the **w** I have spoken .... Jn 15:3
He will not speak his own **w**, ... Jn 16:13
you in plain **w** about the Father. .... Jn 16:25
so that the **w** Jesus said before .... Jn 18:9
of Israel, listen to these **w**: .... Ac 2:22
warned them with many other **w**. .... Ac 2:40
and his **w** were so strong that .... Ac 6:10
By the **w** he will say to you, ... Ac 11:14
I remembered the **w** of the Lord. .... Ac 11:16
understand the **w** that the .... Ac 13:27
Even with these **w**, they were .... Ac 14:18

The **w** of the prophets agree with .... Ac 15:15
that had these **w** written on it: .... Ac 17:23
questions about **w** and names— .... Ac 18:15
to remember the **w** Jesus said: ' .... Ac 20:35
One, and to hear **w** from him. .... Ac 22:14
be kind and listen to our few **w**. .... Ac 24:4
My **w** are true and sensible. .... Ac 26:25
Their **w** are like snake poison. .... Rm 3:13
Those **w** ("God accepted Abraham's .... Rm 4:23
feelings that **w** cannot explain. .... Rm 8:26
w go everywhere on earth." .... Rm 10:18
and fine **w** to fool the minds .... Rm 16:18
without using **w** of human wisdom 1Co 1:17
secret with fancy **w** or a show of 1Co 2:1
were not with **w** of human wisdom 1Co 2:4
not with **w** taught us by human 1Co 2:13
human wisdom but with **w** taught 1Co 2:13
we speak nice **w** about them. 1Co 4:13
others with **w**, or get drunk, ... 1Co 5:11
rather speak five **w** I understand 1Co 14:19
thousands of **w** in a different 1Co 14:19
who use strange **w** and foreign 1Co 14:21
death was written in **w** on stone. 2Co 3:7
you in this will not be empty **w**. 2Co 9:3
that is too wonderful for **w**. 2Co 9:15
In other **w**, the law was our .... Gal 3:24
what will help others become .... Eph 4:23
God will give me **w** so that I can .... Eph 6:19
and using evil **w** when you talk. .... Col 3:8
to you came not only with **w**, ... 1Th 1:5
of God, not the **w** of humans. 1Th 2:13
each other with these **w**. 1Th 4:18
from the false **w** of liars whose 1Ti 4:2
strong by the **w** of the faith. 1Ti 4:6
to the believers with your **w**, ... 1Ti 4:12
arguing and fighting about **w**. 1Ti 6:4
presence not to argue about **w**. 2Ti 2:14
These **w** are written on the seal: 2Ti 2:19
w that prophet said are true. .... Tit 1:13
the encouraging **w** that call you .... Heb 12:5
The **w** "once again" clearly show .... Heb 12:27
needs, your **w** are worth nothing. .... Jam 2:16
speaks should speak **w** from God. 1Pe 4:11
Holy Spirit spoke **w** from God. 2Pe 1:21
They brag with **w** that mean 2Pe 2:18
think about the **w** the holy 2Pe 3:2
people not only with **w** and talk, ... 1Jn 3:18
who reads the **w** of God's message. .... Rev 1:3
to say proud **w** and words against .... Rev 13:5
proud words and **w** against God, ... Rev 13:5
"These are the true **w** of God." .... Rev 19:9
because these **w** are true and can .... Rev 21:5
w can be trusted and are true. .... Rev 22:6
one who obeys the **w** of prophecy .... Rev 22:7
who obey the **w** in this book. .... Rev 22:9
keep secret the **w** of prophecy in .... Rev 22:10
who hears the **w** of the prophecy .... Rev 22:18
anyone adds anything to these **w**, ... Rev 22:18
away from the **w** of this book .... Rev 22:19

WORE

priest **w** this outer robe when .... Ex 39:26
which they **w** when they served as .... Ex 39:41
your clothes nor sandals **w** out. .... Dt 29:5
on their feet and **w** old clothes, ... Jos 9:5
The Ishmaelites **w** gold earrings. .... Jdg 8:24
As a boy he **w** a linen holy vest. 1Sa 2:18
He **w** bronze protectors on his 1Sa 17:6
men who **w** the linen holy vest 1Sa 22:18
daughters who **w** this kind of robe. 2Sa 13:18
at his waist he **w** a belt that 2Sa 20:8
rough cloth and **w** ropes on their 1Ki 20:32
So Ahab **w** other clothes and 1Ki 22:30

a hairy man and **w** a leather belt 2Ki 1:8
all the singers **w** robes of fine 1Ch 15:27
also **w** a robe of fine linen 1Ch 15:27
So Ahab **w** other clothes, ... 2Ch 18:29
He **w** different clothes so no one 2Ch 35:22
Each builder **w** his sword at his .... Ne 4:18
and they **w** rough cloth and put .... Ne 9:1
I **w** fairness like a robe and a .... Job 29:14
others as often as he **w** clothes. .... Ps 109:18
He **w** out my flesh and skin and .... La 3:4
So you **w** gold and silver. .... Eze 16:13
w blue uniforms. They were all .... Eze 23:6
men on a wall. They **w** red .... Eze 23:14
and he **w** a leather belt around .... Mt 3:4
John **w** clothes made from camel's .... Mk 1:6
Some **w** the skins of sheep and .... Heb 11:37
heads they **w** what looked like .... Rev 9:7
linen and **w** golden bands tied .... Rev 15:6

WORK

God finished the **w** he had been .... Ge 2:2
so he rested from all his **w**. .... Ge 2:2
rested from all the **w** he had .... Ge 2:3
of Eden to care for it and **w** it. .... Ge 2:15
you will have to **w** very hard for .... Ge 3:17
will sweat and **w** hard for your .... Ge 3:19
garden of Eden to **w** the ground .... Ge 3:23
cursed in your **w** with the ground .... Ge 4:11
You will **w** the ground, but it .... Ge 4:12
He will comfort us in our **w**, ... Ge 5:29
for you to **w** for me without .... Ge 29:15
I will **w** seven years for you." .... Ge 29:18
I promised to **w** for you is over. .... Ge 29:21
I had and the hard **w** I did, ... Ge 31:42
house to do his **w** as usual and .... Ge 39:11
allow you to return to your **w**. .... Ge 40:13
he will ask, 'What **w** do you do?' .... Ge 46:33
brothers, "What **w** do you do?" .... Ge 47:3
the king paid them for their **w**. .... Ge 47:22
forced the Israelites to **w**, ... Ex 1:12
the Israelites to **w** hard to make .... Ex 1:14
do all kinds of **w** in the fields. .... Ex 1:14
to them in all their painful **w**. .... Ex 1:14
they were forced to **w** very hard. .... Ex 2:11
they were forced to **w** very hard. .... Ex 2:23
the people away from their **w**? .... Ex 5:4
these people **w** harder and keep .... Ex 5:9
forcing the people to **w** harder. .... Ex 5:13
for the **w** the people did. .... Ex 5:14
don't want to **w**! That is why you .... Ex 5:17
Now, go back to **w**! We will not .... Ex 5:18
from the hard **w** the Egyptians .... Ex 6:6
from the hard **w** the Egyptians .... Ex 6:7
must not do any **w** on these days; .... Ex 12:16
the only **w** you may do is to .... Ex 12:16
This is too much **w** for you; .... Ex 18:18
they will share the **w** with you. .... Ex 18:22
W and get everything done during .... Ex 20:9
On that day no one may do any **w**: .... Ex 20:10
You should **w** six days a week, ... Ex 23:12
knowledge to do all kinds of **w**. .... Ex 31:3
wood, and to do all kinds of **w**. .... Ex 31:5
tribe of Dan to **w** with Bezalel. .... Ex 31:6
On the seventh day I did not **w**; .... Ex 31:17
people with you will see my **w**. .... Ex 34:10
You must **w** for six days, but on .... Ex 34:21
You are to **w** for six days, ... Ex 35:2
to be used in the **w** brought it. .... Ex 35:24
LORD for all the **w** the LORD had .... Ex 35:29
knowledge to do all kinds of **w**. .... Ex 35:31
wood, and to do all kinds of **w**. .... Ex 35:33
the skill to do all kinds of **w**. .... Ex 35:35
person will do the **w** the LORD .... Ex 36:1

the skilled **w** needed to build .... Ex 36:1
they wanted to help with the **w**. .... Ex 36:2
left the **w** they were doing .... Ex 36:4
we need to do the **w** the LORD .... Ex 36:5
than enough to do all the **w**. .... Ex 36:7
So all the **w** on the Meeting Tent .... Ex 39:32
done all this **w** just as the LORD .... Ex 39:42
at all the **w** and saw they had .... Ex 39:43
So Moses finished the **w**. .... Ex 40:33
and you must not do any **w**. .... Le 16:29
with you must not **w** either. .... Le 16:29
There are six days for you to **w**, ... Le 23:3
must not do any **w**. It is a .... Le 23:3
and you must not do any **w**. .... Le 23:7
must not do any regular **w**.' " .... Le 23:8
you must not do any **w** that day. .... Le 23:21
Do not do any **w**, and bring an .... Le 23:25
Do not do any **w** on that day, ... Le 23:28
You must not do any **w** at all; .... Le 23:31
the first day; do not do any **w**. .... Le 23:35
a holy meeting; do not do any **w**. .... Le 23:36
not make him **w** like a slave. .... Le 25:39
You will **w** hard, but it will not .... Le 26:20
doing the **w** in the Holy Tent. .... Nu 3:7
by doing the **w** in the Holy Tent. .... Nu 3:8
and all the **w** connected with .... Nu 3:26
and all the **w** connected with .... Nu 3:31
and all the **w** connected with .... Nu 3:36
This is the **w** of the Gershonite .... Nu 4:28
the priest, will direct their **w**. .... Nu 4:28
all who **w** at the Meeting Tent. .... Nu 4:30
is the **w** the Merarite family .... Nu 4:33
priest, will direct their **w**." .... Nu 4:33
old who were to **w** at the Meeting .... Nu 4:35
who were given **w** at the Meeting .... Nu 4:39
old who were to **w** at the Meeting .... Nu 4:43
who were given **w** at the Meeting .... Nu 4:47
was given his **w** and told what to .... Nu 4:49
use them in the **w** of the Meeting .... Nu 7:5
which they needed for their **w**. .... Nu 7:7
which they needed for their **w**. .... Nu 7:8
directed the **w** of all of them. .... Nu 7:8
ready to do the **w** of the LORD. .... Nu 8:11
may come to **w** at the Meeting .... Nu 8:15
came to the Meeting Tent to **w**, ... Nu 8:22
from their jobs and not **w** again. .... Nu 8:25
with their **w** at the Meeting. .... Nu 8:26
must not do the **w** themselves. .... Nu 8:26
to do the **w** in the LORD's .... Nu 16:9
to do all the **w** that needs to be .... Nu 18:3
They must do the **w** at the Tent, ... Nu 18:4
to the LORD, to **w** at the Meeting .... Nu 18:6
for the **w** they do serving .... Nu 18:21
Levites should **w** in the Meeting .... Nu 18:23
pay for your **w** in the Meeting .... Nu 18:31
tricks will **w** on the people of .... Nu 23:23
no magic will **w** against Israel. .... Nu 23:23
festival, and don't **w** that day. .... Nu 28:18
meeting, and don't **w** that day. .... Nu 28:25
holy meeting. Don't **w** that day. .... Nu 28:26
month, and don't **w** on that day. .... Nu 29:1
day do not eat and do not **w**. .... Nu 29:7
month, and do not **w** on that day. .... Nu 29:12
and do not **w** on that day. .... Nu 29:35
continued to **w** against them to .... Dt 2:15
may **w** and get everything done .... Dt 5:13
On that day no one may do any **w**: .... Dt 5:14
bless you and all the **w** you do. .... Dt 14:29
will bless your **w** and everything .... Dt 15:10
did twice the **w** of a hired .... Dt 15:18
Do not **w** the first calf born to .... Dt 15:19
your God, and do not **w** that day. .... Dt 16:8
harvest and all the **w** you do, ... Dt 16:15

your slaves and **w** for you. .... Dt 20:11
us suffer and **w** very hard. .... Dt 26:6
trouble, hard **w,** and suffering, ... Dt 26:7
land and hard **w** have produced. .... Dt 28:33
vineyards and **w** hard in them, ... Dt 28:39
be pleased with the **w** they do. .... Dt 33:11
the Canaanites to **w** for them, ... Jos 17:13
their **w** is to serve the LORD. .... Jos 18:7
where you did not have to **w.** .... Jos 24:13
the Canaanites to **w** as slaves, ... Jdg 1:28
Zebulun made them **w** as slaves. .... Jdg 1:30
made the Amorites **w** as slaves. .... Jdg 1:35
LORD began to **w** in Samson while .... Jdg 13:25
in from his **w** in the fields. .... Jdg 19:16
Ruth rose and went back to **w,** .... Ru 2:15
Where did you **w?** Blessed be .... Ru 2:19
If you **w** in another field, ... Ru 2:22
of food now must **w** for food, ... 1Sa 2:5
and use them all for his own **w.** 1Sa 8:16
even when we do ordinary **w.** 1Sa 21:5
true when the **w** is holy." 1Sa 21:5
and forced them to **w** with saws, ... 2Sa 12:31
who were forced to do hard **w.** 2Sa 20:24
Solomon's chariot and **w** horses; 1Ki 4:28
My servants will **w** with yours, ... 1Ki 5:6
men of Israel to help in this **w.** 1Ki 5:13
thousand men to **w** in the hill 1Ki 5:15
W began on the Temple in Ziv, ... 1Ki 6:37
and experienced in bronze **w.** 1Ki 7:14
and did all the bronze **w.** 1Ki 7:14
So the **w** on the pillars was.................... 1Ki 7:22
all his **w** for King Solomon 1Ki 7:40
Finally the **w** King Solomon did 1Ki 7:51
could not continue their **w,** 1Ki 8:11
forced them to **w** for him as 1Ki 9:21
important officers over the **w.** 1Ki 9:23
who did the **w** on Solomon's 1Ki 9:23
he finished the **w** on the Temple. 1Ki 9:25
father forced us to **w** very hard. 1Ki 12:4
don't make us **w** as hard as he 1Ki 12:4
'Don't make us **w** as hard as your 1Ki 12:9
father forced us to **w** very hard. 1Ki 12:10
Now make our **w** easier.' 1Ki 12:10
forced you to **w** hard, but I will 1Ki 12:11
I will make you **w** even harder. 1Ki 12:11
My father forced you to **w** hard, ... 1Ki 12:14
I will make you **w** even harder. 1Ki 12:14
son, to begin **w** on the city, and 1Ki 16:34
charge of the **w** on the Temple. 2Ki 12:11
victories, his **w** on the pool, ... 2Ki 20:20
his **w** on the tunnel to bring 2Ki 20:20
of the **w** on the Temple 2Ki 22:5
They began their **w** after the Ark 1Ch 6:31
followed the rules for their **w.** 1Ch 6:32
own special **w** in the Holy Tent 1Ch 6:48
did all the **w** in the Most Holy 1Ch 6:49
not do other **w** in the Temple................. 1Ch 9:33
and forced them to **w** with saws, ... 1Ch 20:3
skilled in every kind of **w.** 1Ch 22:15
begin the **w,** and may the LORD 1Ch 22:16
will direct the **w** of the Temple 1Ch 23:4
The **w** was divided by lots among 1Ch 24:6
for the LORD's **w** and the king's 1Ch 26:30
in God's **w** and the king's 1Ch 26:32
him about all the **w** of serving 1Ch 28:13
strong and brave, and do the **w.** 1Ch 28:20
until all the **w** for the Temple 1Ch 28:20
for all the **w** on the Temple 1Ch 28:21
to help you with all the **w.** 1Ch 28:21
to know, but the **w** is important............... 1Ch 29:1
for all the gold and silver **w.** 1Ch 29:5
for the king's **w** gave their 1Ch 29:6
He will **w** with my skilled 2Ch 2:7

he finished his **w** for King 2Ch 4:11
Finally all the **w** Solomon did................. 2Ch 5:1
not continue their **w** because of 2Ch 5:14
stood ready to do their **w.** 2Ch 7:6
the priests do their daily **w.** 2Ch 8:14
All Solomon's **w** was done as he 2Ch 8:16
father forced us to **w** very hard. 2Ch 10:4
and don't make us **w** as he did. 2Ch 10:4
'Don't make us **w** as hard as your 2Ch 10:9
father forced us to **w** very hard. 2Ch 10:10
Now make our **w** easier.' 2Ch 10:10
forced you to **w** hard, but I will 2Ch 10:11
I will make you **w** even harder. 2Ch 10:11
My father forced you to **w** hard, ... 2Ch 10:14
I will make you **w** even harder. 2Ch 10:14
get a reward for your good **w."** 2Ch 15:7
up Ramah and left his **w.** 2Ch 16:5
hired people to **w** with iron and 2Ch 24:12
and the **w** to repair the Temple 2Ch 24:13
the Levites who started to **w.** 2Ch 29:12
them until the **w** was finished................. 2Ch 29:34
himself fully to his **w** for God. 2Ch 31:21
of the **w** on the Temple 2Ch 34:10
The men did their **w** well. 2Ch 34:12
to Jerusalem began to **w.** .... Ezr 3:8
in charge of the **w** of building................. Ezr 3:9
order for those men to stop **w.** .... Ezr 4:21
So the **w** on the Temple of God in .... Ezr 4:24
until now the **w** has been going .... Ezr 5:16
not bother the **w** on that Temple............. Ezr 6:7
Do this so the **w** will not stop. .... Ezr 6:8
them in the **w** on the Temple .... Ezr 6:22
the others who would do the **w.** .... Ne 2:16
So they began to **w** hard. .... Ne 2:18
priests went to **w** and rebuilt .... Ne 3:1
of Tekoa would not **w** under their .... Ne 3:5
the people were willing to **w.** .... Ne 4:6
and kill them and stop the **w."** .... Ne 4:11
to the wall, each to his own **w.** .... Ne 4:15
did their **w** with one hand .... Ne 4:17
we continued to **w** with half the .... Ne 4:21
am doing a great **w,** and I can't .... Ne 6:3
don't want the **w** to stop while I .... Ne 6:3
They will get too weak to **w.** .... Ne 6:9
that the **w** had been done with .... Ne 6:16
family leaders gave to the **w.** .... Ne 7:70
to the treasury for the **w.** .... Ne 7:71
and for the **w** of the Temple of .... Ne 10:33
in all the towns where we **w.** .... Ne 10:37
who did the **w** for the Temple. .... Ne 11:12
in charge of the **w** outside the .... Ne 11:16
about me, the **w** of your hands? .... Job 10:3
When he is at **w** in the north, ... Job 23:9
they **w** far from people, swinging .... Job 28:4
had lost their strength to **w?** .... Job 30:2
up my road and **w** to destroy me, ... Job 30:13
to praise his **w,** about which .... Job 36:24
knows it is the **w** of God. .... Job 37:7
leave your heavy **w** for it to do? .... Job 39:11
care that its **w** is for nothing, ... Job 39:16
you, but their traps won't **w.** .... Ps 21:11
Look for peace and **w** for it. .... Ps 34:14
All their **w** is for nothing; .... Ps 39:6
are full of hard **w** and pain. .... Ps 90:10
people go to **w** and work until .... Ps 104:23
go to work and **w** until evening............... Ps 104:23
he broke their pride by hard **w.** .... Ps 107:12
an evil person **w** against him,................. Ps 109:5
and gold, the **w** of human hands. .... Ps 115:4
You will enjoy what you **w** for, ... Ps 128:2
and gold, the **w** of human hands. .... Ps 135:15
the LORD when he began his **w,**............... Pr 8:22
Those who **w** their land will have .... Pr 12:11

had sent them out to do this w. .... Ac 14:26
not continue with them in the w. .... Ac 15:38
Because of his w, every Jew and .... Ac 19:10
who did this w made much money. .... Ac 19:24
who did the same kind of w. .... Ac 19:25
and those who w with him have a .... Ac 19:38
w that the Lord Jesus gave me— .... Ac 20:24
that you should w as I did and .... Ac 20:35
me the special w of an apostle, ... Rm 1:5
and obey. I do this w for him................... Rm 1:5
When people w, their pay is not .... Rm 4:4
cannot do any w that will make .... Rm 4:5
since I have that w, I will make .... Rm 11:13
Do not be lazy but w hard, ... Rm 12:11
and give their time to their w................. Rm 13:6
of food destroy the w of God. .... Rm 14:20
have finished that part of my w. .... Rm 15:19
to build on the w someone else .... Rm 15:20
Now I have finished my w here. .... Rm 15:23
to help me in my w by praying to .... Rm 15:30
who w together with me in Christ .... Rm 16:3
women who w very hard for the.............. Rm 16:12
of us did the w God gave us to 1Co 3:5
will be rewarded for his own w. 1Co 3:8
their w will be clearly seen, ... 1Co 3:13
test everyone's w to show what 1Co 3:13
to show what sort of w it was. 1Co 3:13
We w hard with our own hands for 1Co 4:12
is busy with the Lord's w, ... 1Co 7:32
is busy with the Lord's w. 1Co 7:34
an example of my w in the Lord. 1Co 9:1
ones who must w to earn our 1Co 9:6
some of the grain for their w." 1Co 9:10
that those who w at the Temple 1Co 9:13
get their living from this w...................... 1Co 9:14
full rights in my w of preaching 1Co 9:18
fully to the w of the Lord, ... 1Co 15:58
know that your w in the Lord is 1Co 15:58
and growing w has been given to 1Co 16:9
So who is able to do this w? 2Co 2:16
that we can do this w ourselves............... 2Co 3:5
gave us this w to do, so we 2Co 4:1
God gave us the w of telling 2Co 5:18
anyone to find fault with our w, ... 2Co 6:3
We w hard, and sometimes we get 2Co 6:5
this special w of grace since he 2Co 8:6
So now finish the w you started. 2Co 8:11
enough to give to every good w. 2Co 9:8
outside the w that was given us 2Co 10:13
bragging to the w that God gave 2Co 10:13
this includes our w with you. 2Co 10:13
bragging to the w that is ours, ... 2Co 10:15
you will help our w to grow much 2Co 10:15
to brag about w that has already 2Co 10:16
say that the w they brag about 2Co 11:12
servants who w for what is right 2Co 11:15
I have done hard and tiring w, ... 2Co 11:27
me apart for his w even before I............... Gal 1:15
not want my past w and the work .... Gal 2:2
work and the w I am now doing to........... Gal 2:2
had been given the w of telling .... Gal 2:7
Peter had the w of telling the .... Gal 2:7
the power to w as an apostle for .... Gal 2:8
me the power to w as an apostle .... Gal 2:8
the Spirit and w miracles among .... Gal 3:5
that my w for you has been .... Gal 4:11
God gave me this w to tell you .... Eph 3:2
God gave me the w of telling all.............. Eph 3:9
some to have the w of caring for .... Eph 4:11
people for the w of serving, ... Eph 4:12
This w must continue until we .... Eph 4:13
does its own w to make the whole .... Eph 4:16
Do your w with enthusiasm. .... Eph 6:7

W as if you were serving the .... Eph 6:7
servant of the Lord's w. .... Eph 6:21
God began doing a good w in you,........... Php 1:6
God gave me the w of defending .... Php 1:16
will be able to w for the Lord. .... Php 1:22
that you w together as one for .... Php 1:27
because my w was not wasted. .... Php 2:16
not in the w of Jesus Christ. .... Php 2:21
almost died for the w of Christ. .... Php 2:30
fruit in every good w and grow .... Col 1:10
me a special w to do that helps .... Col 1:25
and that w is to tell fully the .... Col 1:25
To do this, I w and struggle, ... Col 1:29
to know how hard I w for you, ... Col 2:1
In all the w you are doing, ... Col 3:23
you are doing, w the best you................. Col 3:23
W as if you were doing it for .... Col 3:23
believers who w with me for .... Col 4:11
to finish the w the Lord gave .... Col 4:17
faith and the w you have done 1Th 1:3
our hard w and difficulties 1Th 2:9
our hard w would have been 1Th 3:5
and do your own w as we have 1Th 4:11
those who w hard among you, ... 1Th 5:12
love because of the w they do. 1Th 5:13
to warn those who do not w. 1Th 5:14
not hold back the w of the Holy 1Th 5:19
who refuses to w and does not 2Th 3:6
refuses to w should not eat." 2Th 3:10
in your group refuse to w. 2Th 3:11
Jesus Christ to w quietly and 2Th 3:12
not help God's w, which is done 1Ti 1:4
gave me this w of serving him. 1Ti 1:12
an overseer desires a good w................... 1Ti 3:1
This is why we w and struggle: 1Ti 4:10
those who w hard by speaking 1Ti 5:17
Master, ready to do any good w............... 2Ti 2:21
is needed to do every good w................... 2Ti 3:17
do the w of telling the Good 2Ti 4:5
he can help me in my w here................... 2Ti 4:11
He trusted me with that w, ... Tit 1:3
But God's w was finished from .... Heb 4:3
will rest from his w as God did. .... Heb 4:10
is given the w of going before .... Heb 5:1
one chooses himself for this w. .... Heb 5:4
a good crop for those who w it, ... Heb 6:7
will not forget the w you did .... Heb 6:10
the same hard w all your lives .... Heb 6:11
priest has the w of offering...................... Heb 8:3
The w they do as priests is only .... Heb 8:5
But the priestly w that has been .... Heb 8:6
greater than the w that was .... Heb 8:6
they will do this w with joy, ... Heb 13:17
help you to make their w hard. .... Heb 13:17
People who w for peace in a .... Jam 3:18
people, which is the Spirit's w. 1Pe 1:2
judges each person's w equally. 1Pe 1:17
look for peace and w for it. 1Pe 3:11
to destroy the devil's w. 1Jn 3:8
person, you share in the evil w. 2Jn 1:11
share in their w for the truth. 3Jn 1:8
you w hard and never give up. .... Rev 2:2
will rest from their hard w,...................... Rev 14:13

WORKED

So Jacob w for Laban seven years .... Ge 29:20
I w hard for you so that I could .... Ge 29:25
Jacob w for Laban for another .... Ge 29:30
know that I have w hard for you, ... Ge 30:29
know that I have w as hard as I .... Ge 31:6
I have w for you now for twenty............... Ge 31:38
I w like a slave for you for .... Ge 31:41
They w the gold into the blue, ... Ex 39:3

groups who **w** at the Meeting .... Nu 4:37
groups who **w** at the Meeting .... Nu 4:41
it and that has never been **w**. .... Nu 19:2
things for which you have **w**, ... Dt 12:7
about the things you have **w** for. .... Dt 12:18
that has never **w** or worn a yoke, ... Dt 21:3
and the Canaanites **w** as slaves. .... Jdg 1:33
whose field she had **w**.......................... Ru 2:19
The man I **w** with today is named .... Ru 2:19
whose young women you **w** with, ... Ru 3:2
the LORD's Spirit **w** in David. 1Sa 16:13
Each group **w** in Lebanon one 1Ki 5:14
the builders who **w** on the Temple 2Ki 12:11
and Gederah and **w** for the king. 1Ch 4:23
have **w** hard getting many of the 1Ch 22:14
relatives also **w** in the Temple. 1Ch 26:12
He and his sons **w** outside the 1Ch 26:29
the people who **w** on the Temple 2Ch 24:12
The people **w** hard, and the work 2Ch 24:13
He had people who **w** his fields 2Ch 26:10
Some Levites **w** as secretaries, ... 2Ch 34:13
The priests **w** until night, ... 2Ch 35:14
Ezra had **w** hard to know and obey .... Ezr 7:10
They **w** as far as the Tower of................. Ne 3:1
He **w** across from the way up to .... Ne 3:19
son of Zabbai **w** hard on the wall .... Ne 3:20
Next to him **w** the priests from .... Ne 3:22
Palal son of Uzai **w** across from .... Ne 3:25
They **w** toward the east and the .... Ne 3:26
He **w** as far as the house of the .... Ne 3:31
half my people **w** on the wall.................. Ne 4:16
his sword at his side as he **w**. .... Ne 4:18
I **w** on the wall, as did all my .... Ne 5:16
because he **w** for the good of his .... Est 10:3
back what they **w** for without................. Job 20:18
spirit of those who **w** the land, ... Job 31:39
and what they **w** for to locusts. .... Ps 78:46
Egyptians and **w** wonders in Egypt .... Ps 105:27
received what others had **w** for. .... Ps 105:44
steal everything he has **w** for................... Ps 109:11
and what you **w** so hard for will.............. Pr 5:10
the things I had **w** for here on .... Ec 2:18
for which I **w** so hard here on .... Ec 2:19
get the things for which they **w**. .... Ec 2:21
He always **w** hard but was never .... Ec 4:8
everything you have **w** for. .... Ec 5:6
People once **w** and grew food on .... Is 7:25
You have **w** with these people, ... Is 47:15
I have **w** hard for nothing; .... Is 49:4
wine that you have **w** to make. .... Is 62:8
everything our ancestors **w** for— .... Je 3:24
They have **w** hard until they were .... Je 12:13
take away everything you **w** for,............. Eze 23:29
he **w** hard until sunset trying .... Da 6:14
where he **w** to get a wife; .... Hos 12:12
So they came and **w** on the Temple .... Hag 1:14
hired last and **w** only one hour. .... Mt 20:12
you paid us who **w** hard all day .... Mt 20:12
we **w** hard all night trying to .... Lk 5:5
w miracles and signs in Egypt, ... Ac 7:36
a religious man who **w** for him. .... Ac 10:7
with them and **w** with them. .... Ac 18:3
Demetrius, who **w** with silver, ... Ac 19:24
You know I always **w** to take care .... Ac 20:34
Mary, who **w** very hard for you. .... Rm 16:6
who also has **w** very hard for the .... Rm 16:12
I **w** harder than all the other 1Co 15:10
I have **w** much harder than they. 2Co 11:23
and others who **w** with me,.................... Php 4:3
I know he has **w** hard for you and .... Col 4:13
We **w** night and day so we would 1Th 2:9
We **w** very hard night and day so 2Th 3:8
but we **w** to take care of 2Th 3:9

the things he did **w** together. .... Jam 2:22
lose everything you have **w** for, ... 2Jn 1:8

WORKER

nor a hired **w** may eat it.......................... Ex 12:45
powerful, a **w** of miracles. .... Ex 15:11
or a hired **w** must not eat it. .... Le 22:10
be like a hired **w** and a visitor .... Le 25:40
this young man was a good **w**. 1Ki 11:28
Every skilled **w** is ready to help 1Ch 28:21
but a hard **w** will become rich. .... Pr 10:4
but a hard **w** will have great .... Pr 12:27
you like a **w** who tests metal .... Je 6:27
shaped by a **w** with his chisel. .... Je 10:3
A **w** should be given his pay. .... Lk 10:7
The **w** who is paid to keep the .... Jn 10:12
When the **w** sees a wolf coming, ... Jn 10:12
he is only a paid **w** and does not .... Jn 10:13
a **w** together with me for Christ............... Rm 16:9
Timothy, a **w** together with me, ... Rm 16:21
"A **w** should be given his pay................... 1Ti 5:18
a **w** who is not ashamed and who 2Ti 2:15
our dear friend and **w** with us; .... Phm 1:1
to Archippus, a **w** with us; .... Phm 1:2

WORKER'S

keep a hired **w** salary all night .... Le 19:13

WORKERS

These **w** will make all these .... Ex 31:11
all the skilled **w** come and make .... Ex 35:10
all the skilled **w** left the work .... Ex 36:4
Then the skilled **w** made the Holy .... Ex 36:8
Then the **w** made another tent of .... Ex 36:14
The **w** sewed five curtains .... Ex 36:16
The **w** made two gold pieces and .... Ex 39:16
for your hired **w**, and for the .... Le 25:6
grain that he **w** cutting the .... Ru 2:3
Bethlehem and greeted his **w**,................. Ru 2:4
And the **w** answered, "May the .... Ru 2:4
his servant in charge of the **w**, ... Ru 2:5
me follow the **w** cutting grain.................. Ru 2:7
closely behind my women **w**. .... Ru 2:8
So Ruth sat down beside the **w**. .... Ru 2:14
commanded his **w**, "Let her gather........... Ru 2:15
close to my **w** until they have .... Ru 2:21
working with his women **w**. .... Ru 2:22
closely with the **w** of Boaz,..................... Ru 2:23
hundred men who directed the **w**, ... 1Ki 5:16
over all the **w** from the tribes 1Ki 11:28
They paid the money to the **w**, ... 2Ki 12:14
because the **w** were honest. 2Ki 12:15
They must pay the **w** who repair 2Ki 22:5
it to the **w** and supervisors 2Ki 22:9
all the craftsmen and metal **w**. 2Ki 24:14
thousand craftsmen and metal **w**. 2Ki 24:16
and Semakiah were skilled **w**. 1Ch 26:7
were capable men and strong **w**. 1Ch 26:8
relatives who were skilled **w**. 1Ch 26:9
of the field **w** who farmed the................. 1Ch 27:26
hundred men to direct the **w**. 2Ch 2:2
them to direct the **w** and to keep 2Ch 2:18
forced them to be slave **w**, ... 2Ch 8:8
the **w** finished, they brought 2Ch 24:14
and they paid the **w** who rebuilt............. 2Ch 34:10
in charge of the **w** who carried 2Ch 34:13
loads and all the other **w**. 2Ch 34:13
to the supervisors and the **w**." 2Ch 34:17
their fellow **w**—the judges and .... Ezr 4:9
all their fellow **w** living in .... Ezr 4:17
and their fellow **w** went to the .... Ezr 5:3
their fellow **w** carried out King .... Ezr 6:13
and other **w** in this Temple of................. Ezr 7:24
Judah said, "The **w** are getting .... Ne 4:10
brothers, my **w**, nor the guards .... Ne 4:23

and the weary **w** are at rest. .... Job 3:17
Hard **w** will become leaders, ... Pr 12:24
w' hunger helps them, because .... Pr 16:26
The **w** cut the wheat. .... Is 17:5
The **w** help each other and say to .... Is 41:6
and you are unfair to your **w**. .... Is 58:3
things are made by skilled **w**. .... Je 10:9
If **w** came and picked the grapes .... Je 49:9
W of Byblos were with you, ... Eze 27:9
sailors, your **w**, your traders, ... Eze 27:27
to grow food for the city **w**.................. Eze 48:18
The city **w** from all the tribes .... Eze 48:19
If **w** came and picked the grapes .... Ob 1:5
those who cheat **w** of their pay .... Mal 3:5
but only a few **w** to help harvest .... Mt 9:37
will send more **w** to gather his .... Mt 9:38
W should be given what they need. .... Mt 10:10
harvest time I will tell the **w**, ... Mt 13:30
and the **w** who gather are God's.............. Mt 13:39
agreed to pay the **w** one coin for .... Mt 20:2
said to the boss of all the **w**, ' .... Mt 20:8
Call the **w** and pay them. .... Mt 20:8
When the **w** who were hired at .... Mt 20:9
When the **w** who were hired first .... Mt 20:10
said to one of those **w**, ' .... Mt 20:13
with the hired **w** and followed .... Mk 1:20
but there are only a few **w**. .... Lk 10:2
will send more **w** to help gather .... Lk 10:2
are God's **w**, working together; 1Co 3:9
But we are **w** with you for your 2Co 1:24
We are **w** together with God, ... 2Co 6:1
true apostles but are **w** who lie. 2Co 11:13
pure, to be good **w** at home, to .... Tit 2:5
and Luke, **w** together with me .... Phm 1:24
not give the **w** who mowed your.............. Jam 5:4
cries of the **w** have been heard .... Jam 5:4

WORKING

forced me to stop **w** the ground,.............. Ge 4:14
I have earned them by **w** for you, ... Ge 30:26
now you want them to quit **w**!" .... Ex 5:5
six days for **w**, but the seventh .... Ex 31:15
When an ox is **w** in the grain,.............. Dt 25:4
you to continue **w** with his women........... Ru 2:22
So Ruth continued **w** closely with .... Ru 2:23
he will be **w** at the threshing .... Ru 3:2
I am not a traitor **w** for Judah! 2Sa 3:4
plans were **w** very well. 2Sa 15:12
me who of us is **w** for the king 2Ki 6:11
because they are **w** honestly."................ 2Ki 22:7
They are skilled in **w** with gold, ... 1Ch 22:16
me a man skilled in **w** with gold, ... 2Ch 2:7
is skilled in **w** with gold, ... 2Ch 2:14
and to keep the people **w**. 2Ch 2:18
Jozadak started **w** again to.................. Ezr 5:2
of the men **w** on this building?" .... Ezr 5:4
They are **w** very hard and are.................. Ezr 5:8
w under Rehum son of Bani. .... Ne 4:16
w in front of his own house. .... Ne 3:28
people were already **w** very hard. .... Ne 5:18
people in Judah **w** in the........................ Ne 13:15
everyone from **w** so everyone .... Job 37:7
the builders are **w** for nothing. .... Ps 127:1
stay up late, **w** for a living. .... Ps 127:2
For whom am I **w** so hard? .... Ec 4:8
get more done by **w** together. .... Ec 4:9
w day and night and hardly ever .... Ec 8:16
there is no **w**, no planning, no .... Ec 9:10
he does not go on **w** the soil. .... Is 28:24
and saw him **w** at the potter's.................. Je 18:3
as a reward for **w** hard for me, ... Eze 29:20
stay shut on the six **w** days, ... Eze 46:1
people finished **w** on the........................ Hag 2:18

work with me is **w** against me. .... Mt 12:30
workers one coin for **w** that day. .... Mt 20:2
work with me is **w** against me. .... Lk 11:23
comes in from **w** in the field, ... Lk 17:7
never stops **w**, and so I keep .... Jn 5:17
working, and so I keep **w**, too." .... Jn 5:17
I see another law **w** in my body,.............. Rm 7:23
That other law **w** in my body is .... Rm 7:23
Rulers are **w** for God and give .... Rm 13:6
are God's workers, **w** together; 1Co 3:9
When an ox is **w** in the grain,.............. 1Co 9:9
are many people **w** against me. 1Co 16:9
because he is **w** for the Lord 1Co 16:10
So death is **w** in us, but life is.................. 2Co 4:12
in us, but life is **w** in you. 2Co 4:12
partner who is **w** with me to help 2Co 8:23
people are **w** hard to persuade .... Gal 4:17
same spirit is now **w** in those .... Eph 2:2
With God's power **w** in us, God .... Eph 3:20
must stop stealing and start **w**. .... Eph 4:28
Keep on **w** to complete your .... Php 2:12
because God is **w** in you to help.............. Php 2:13
evil is already **w** in the world,.................. 2Th 2:7
When an ox is **w** in the grain,.............. 1Ti 5:18
is alive and **w** and is sharper .... Heb 4:12

WORKMAN

and the **w** who smooths the metal .... Is 41:7
One **w** uses tools to heat iron,.................. Is 44:12
Another **w** uses a line and a .... Is 44:13
w makes the wood look exactly .... Is 44:13
No **w** doing any job will ever be .... Rev 18:22

WORKMAN'S

hand reached for the **w** hammer. .... Jdg 5:26

WORKMEN

You have many **w**—stonecutters, ... 1Ch 22:15
at night and **w** during the day." .... Ne 4:22
The **w** who made them will be .... Is 44:11

WORKS

anyone who **w** on the Sabbath day........... Ex 31:14
Anyone who **w** during the Sabbath .... Ex 31:15
Anyone who **w** on that day must be .... Ex 35:2
If anyone **w** on this day, I will.................. Le 23:30
only a small part of God's **w**. .... Job 26:14
is one of the first of God's **w**, ... Job 40:19
Say to God, "Your **w** are amazing! .... Ps 66:3
and tell about your powerful **w**, ... Ps 71:16
like you and no **w** like yours. .... Ps 86:8
the one he **w** for like vinegar .... Pr 10:26
and their **w** will be like sparks. .... Is 1:31
iron, and he **w** over hot coals.................. Is 44:12
where she suffers and **w** hard. .... La 1:3
Build battle **w** against the city .... Eze 4:2
many good **w** from the Father. .... Jn 10:32
of these good **w** are you killing .... Jn 10:32
I did **w** among them that no one.............. Jn 15:24
If I had not done these **w**, ... Jn 15:24
in everything God **w** for the good .... Rm 8:28
and the one who **w** in the grain 1Co 9:10
ways that God **w** through people 1Co 12:6
God **w** in all of us in everything 1Co 12:6
anyone else who **w** and serves 1Co 16:16
of faith that **w** through love. .... Gal 5:6
us to do good **w**, which God .... Eph 2:10
w and serves with me in the army .... Php 2:25
He **w** together with us and is a .... Col 1:7
strength that **w** so powerfully in.............. Col 1:29
message which **w** in you who.................. 1Th 2:13
w with us for God and helps us 1Th 3:2
and perform the **w** that come from........... 2Th 1:11
must be known for her good **w**— 1Ti 5:10
w such as raising her children, ... 1Ti 5:10

The farmer who **w** hard should be 2Ti 2:6
day God rested from all his **w**." .... Heb 4:4

WORLD

he had done in creating the **w**. .... Ge 2:3
time the whole **w** spoke one .... Ge 11:1
the language of the whole **w**. .... Ge 11:9
out from there over the whole **w**. .... Ge 11:9
in that part of the **w**. .... Ge 41:56
part of the **w** came to Joseph .... Ge 41:57
in that part of the **w**. .... Ge 41:57
people in the **w** afraid of you. .... Dt 2:25
and the **w** will forget who they .... Dt 7:24
make the whole **w** forget who they .... Dt 9:14
LORD owns the **w** and everything .... Dt 10:14
the end of the **w**, and it will .... Dt 28:49
of the whole **w** will go ahead .... Jos 3:11
the Master of the whole **w**, ... Jos 3:13
the LORD set the **w** upon them. 1Sa 2:8
Then all the **w** will know there 1Sa 17:46
people of the **w** will know the.................. 1Ki 8:60
destroy Israel from the **w**, ... 2Ki 14:27
His laws are for all the **w**. 1Ch 16:14
he is coming to judge the **w**. 1Ch 16:33
the people of the **w** worshiped, ... 2Ch 32:19
and chased out of the **w**........................ Job 18:18
him in charge of the whole **w**. .... Job 34:13
he will judge the **w** in fairness; .... Ps 9:8
for the godly people in the **w**, ... Ps 16:3
goes out through all the **w**; .... Ps 19:4
in it—the **w** and all its people. .... Ps 24:1
the whole **w** should fear him. .... Ps 33:8
he makes the **w** forget them. .... Ps 34:16
and brings joy to the whole **w**. .... Ps 48:2
was brought into this **w** in sin. .... Ps 51:5
is a God who judges the **w**." .... Ps 58:11
so the **w** will learn your ways, ... Ps 67:2
Let his glory fill the whole **w**. .... Ps 72:19
Lightning lit up the **w**............................ Ps 77:18
while the **w** is falling apart. .... Ps 82:5
You made the **w** and everything in .... Ps 89:11
you created the earth and the **w**, ... Ps 90:2
The **w** is set, and it cannot be .... Ps 93:1
He is coming to judge the **w**; .... Ps 96:13
will judge the **w** with fairness............... Ps 96:13
His lightning lights up the **w**; .... Ps 97:4
let the **w** and everyone in it .... Ps 98:7
he is coming to judge the **w**. .... Ps 98:9
He will judge the **w** fairly; .... Ps 98:9
His laws are for all the **w**. .... Ps 105:7
defeat rulers all over the **w**. .... Ps 110:6
the wicked of the **w** like trash. .... Ps 119:119
even before the **w** began. .... Pr 8:23
the whole **w**, and delighted .... Pr 8:31
happening in the **w** of the dead, ... Pr 15:11
come into this **w** with nothing, ... Ec 5:15
Let all the **w** know what he has .... Is 12:5
I will punish the **w** for its evil .... Is 13:11
the whole **w** rests and is quiet. .... Is 14:7
the dead, the leaders of the **w**. .... Is 14:9
who turned the **w** into a desert, ... Is 14:17
again fill the **w** with their .... Is 14:21
All you people of the **w**, look!.................. Is 18:3
Everyone who lives in the **w**, ... Is 18:3
the **w** will grow weak and die; .... Is 24:4
The people of the **w** are guilty, ... Is 24:6
people of the **w** will learn the .... Is 26:9
even if they live in a good **w**; .... Is 26:10
or make new people for the **w**. .... Is 26:18
people of the **w** for their sins.................. Is 26:21
Then the **w** will be filled with .... Is 27:6
the **w** and everything in it. .... Is 34:1
judges of this **w** worth nothing. .... Is 40:23

forever, who created all the **w**. .... Is 40:28
he brings justice to the **w**. .... Is 42:4
all over the **w** the way to be .... Is 49:6
I would never flood the **w** again. .... Is 54:9
wisdom to build the **w** and his .... Je 10:12
you from all over the **w** and say,............... Je 16:19
people all over the **w** will curse .... Je 26:6
on all the nations of the **w**, ... Je 28:11
together from all around the **w**. .... Je 50:41
wisdom to build the **w** and his .... Je 51:15
people of the **w** could not .... La 4:12
people in the **w** as treasure, ... Eze 7:21
land, the best land in the **w**. .... Eze 20:6
land, the best land in the **w**. .... Eze 20:15
any place in the **w** of the living .... Eze 26:20
the most terrible in the **w**. .... Eze 32:12
live at the center of the **w**."................... Eze 38:12
every language in all the **w**: .... Da 4:1
spoke every language in the **w**: .... Da 6:25
destroy people all over the **w**.................. Da 7:23
toward the four parts of the **w**. .... Da 11:4
of the best nation in the **w**; .... Am 6:1
the **w** and all who live in it .... Nah 1:5
that will burn up the whole **w**; .... Zph 1:18
that will burn up the whole **w**. .... Zph 3:8
of the Lord of the whole **w**. .... Zch 6:5
will be king over the whole **w**. .... Zch 14:9
kingdoms of the **w** and all their .... Mt 4:8
light that gives light to the **w**. .... Mt 5:14
secret since the **w** was made." .... Mt 13:35
The field is the **w**, and the good .... Mt 13:38
to have the whole **w** if they lose .... Mt 16:26
the people of the **w** because of .... Mt 18:7
God made the **w**, 'he made them .... Mt 19:4
be more and more evil in the **w**, ... Mt 24:12
will be preached in all the **w**, ... Mt 24:14
beginning of the **w** until now, ... Mt 24:21
the peoples of the **w** will cry. .... Mt 24:30
people from every part of the **w**............... Mt 24:31
of the **w** will be gathered .... Mt 25:32
for you since the **w** was made. .... Mt 25:34
News is preached in all the **w**, ... Mt 26:13
of all people in the **w**. .... Mt 28:19
to have the whole **w** if they lose .... Mk 8:36
God made the **w**, 'he made them .... Mk 10:6
Here in this **w** they will have a .... Mk 10:30
when God made the **w**, until now, ... Mk 13:19
News is preached in all the **w**, ... Mk 14:9
everywhere in the **w**, and tell .... Mk 16:15
in the **w** and told the Good .... Mk 16:20
kingdoms of the **w** in an instant. .... Lk 4:5
to have the whole **w** if they.................... Lk 9:25
since the beginning of the **w**— .... Lk 11:50
people in the **w** are trying to .... Lk 12:30
I came to set fire to the **w**, ... Lk 12:49
what is happening to the **w**, ... Lk 21:26
to all was coming into the **w**! .... Jn 1:9
Word was in the **w**, and the world .... Jn 1:10
and the **w** was made by him, ... Jn 1:10
but the **w** did not know him. .... Jn 1:10
He came to the **w** that was his .... Jn 1:11
who takes away the sin of the **w**! .... Jn 1:29
God loved the **w** so much that he .... Jn 3:16
his Son into the **w** to judge the .... Jn 3:17
the world to judge the **w** guilty, ... Jn 3:17
but to save the **w** through him. .... Jn 3:17
The Light has come into the **w**, ... Jn 3:19
really is the Savior of the **w**." .... Jn 4:42
who is coming into the **w**." .... Jn 6:14
heaven and gives life to the **w**." .... Jn 6:33
up so that the **w** may have life." .... Jn 6:51
things, show yourself to the **w**." .... Jn 7:4
The **w** cannot hate you, but it .... Jn 7:7

"I am the light of the **w**. ....Jn 8:12
belong to this **w,** but I don't ....Jn 8:23
but I don't belong to this **w**. ....Jn 8:23
I am in the **w,** I am the light ....Jn 9:5
world, I am the light of the **w**." ....Jn 9:5
I came into this **w** so that the ....Jn 9:39
so that the **w** could be judged. ....Jn 9:39
God chose and sent into the **w**. ....Jn 10:36
God, the One coming to the **w**." ....Jn 11:27
The whole **w** is following him." ....Jn 12:19
lives in this **w** will keep true ....Jn 12:25
the time for the **w** to be judged; ....Jn 12:31
ruler of this **w** will be thrown ....Jn 12:31
light into the **w** so that whoever ....Jn 12:46
I did not come to judge the **w,** ....Jn 12:47
the world, but to save the **w**. ....Jn 12:47
to leave this **w** and go back to ....Jn 13:1
those who were his own in the **w,** ....Jn 13:1
The **w** cannot accept him, because ....Jn 14:17
while the **w** will not see me ....Jn 14:19
and not to the rest of the **w**?" ....Jn 14:22
give it to you as the **w** does. ....Jn 14:27
the ruler of this **w** is coming. ....Jn 14:30
but the **w** must know that I love ....Jn 14:31
If the **w** hates you, remember ....Jn 15:18
belonged to the **w,** it would love ....Jn 15:19
I have chosen you out of the **w,** ....Jn 15:19
That is why the **w** hates you. ....Jn 15:19
people of the **w** the truth about ....Jn 16:8
the ruler of this **w** was judged. ....Jn 16:11
be sad, but the **w** will be happy. ....Jn 16:20
child has been born into the **w**. ....Jn 16:21
came from the Father into the **w**. ....Jn 16:28
am leaving the **w** and going back ....Jn 16:28
In this **w** you will have trouble, ...Jn 16:33
I have defeated the **w**." ....Jn 16:33
with you before the **w** was made. ....Jn 17:5
to those you gave me from the **w**. ....Jn 17:6
people in the **w** but for those ....Jn 17:9
not stay in the **w** any longer. ....Jn 17:11
But they are still in the **w**. ....Jn 17:11
am still in the **w** so that these...............Jn 17:13
the **w** has hated them, because ....Jn 17:14
they don't belong to the **w,** ....Jn 17:14
just as I don't belong to the **w**. ....Jn 17:14
them out of the **w** but to keep..............Jn 17:15
They don't belong to the **w,** ....Jn 17:16
just as I don't belong to the **w**. ....Jn 17:16
I have sent them into the **w,** ....Jn 17:18
just as you sent me into the **w**. ....Jn 17:18
Then the **w** will believe that you............Jn 17:21
Then the **w** will know that you ....Jn 17:23
loved me before the **w** was made. ....Jn 17:24
The **w** does not know you, but I ....Jn 17:25
does not belong to this **w**. ....Jn 18:36
belonged to this **w,** my servants ....Jn 18:36
I was born and came into the **w:** ....Jn 18:37
the whole **w** would not be big ....Jn 21:25
and in every part of the **w**." ....Ac 1:8
from every country in the **w**. ....Ac 2:5
else in the **w** is able to save ....Ac 4:12
time is coming to the whole **w**. ....Ac 11:28
all over the **w** the way to be ....Ac 13:47
trouble everywhere in the **w,** ....Ac 17:6
made the whole **w** and everything ....Ac 17:24
who live everywhere in the **w**. ....Ac 17:26
people in the **w** to change their ....Ac 17:30
judge all the **w** with fairness, ...Ac 17:31
Asia and the whole **w** worships." ....Ac 19:27
his people everywhere in the **w**. ....Ac 24:5
time when God will judge the **w**. ....Ac 24:25
in the **w** are talking about ....Rm 1:8
beginning of the **w** those things ....Rm 1:20

us, he could not judge the **w**. ....Rm 3:6
brings the whole **w** under God's..........Rm 3:19
that they would get the whole **w**. ....Rm 4:13
came into the **w** because of what ....Rm 5:12
Sin was in the **w** before the law ....Rm 5:13
Not only the **w,** but we also have ....Rm 8:23
knew them before he made the **w,** ....Rm 8:29
in the whole **w** will ever be able ....Rm 8:39
go down into the **w** below?'" ....Rm 10:7
went out through all the **w;**.................Rm 10:18
rich blessings for the **w,** ....Rm 11:12
surely the **w** will receive much ....Rm 11:12
with other people in the **w**. ....Rm 11:15
Do not be shaped by this **w;** ....Rm 12:2
is the skilled talker of this **w?**.................1Co 1:20
the wisdom of the **w** foolish. 1Co 1:20
of God the **w** did not know God 1Co 1:21
in the way the **w** judges wisdom. 1Co 1:26
things of the **w** to shame the 1Co 1:27
weak things of the **w** to shame 1Co 1:27
He chose what the **w** thinks is 1Co 1:28
and what the **w** looks down on and 1Co 1:28
destroy what the **w** thinks is 1Co 1:28
is not from this **w** or from the.................1Co 2:6
or from the rulers of this **w,** 1Co 2:6
Before the **w** began, God planned 1Co 2:7
rulers of this **w** understood it..................1Co 2:8
not receive the spirit of the **w,** 1Co 2:12
are acting like people of the **w**. 1Co 3:3
are acting like people of the **w**. 1Co 3:4
think you are wise in this **w,** 1Co 3:18
wisdom of this **w** is foolishness 1Co 3:19
the **w,** life, death, the present,...............1Co 3:22
a show for the whole **w** to see—..............1Co 4:9
we were the garbage of the **w**—..............1Co 4:13
those of this **w** who sin sexually...............1Co 5:10
you would have to leave this **w**. 1Co 5:10
God's people will judge the **w**. 1Co 6:2
So if you are to judge the **w,** 1Co 6:2
things of the **w** should live as 1Co 7:31
because this **w** in its present 1Co 7:31
is busy with things of the **w,** 1Co 7:33
is busy with things of the **w,** 1Co 7:34
idol is really nothing in the **w,** 1Co 8:4
be destroyed along with the **w**. 1Co 11:32
all kinds of sounds in the **w,** 1Co 14:10
more than anyone else in the **w**.............1Co 15:19
we have done in the **w,** 2Co 1:12
by the kind of wisdom the **w** has. 2Co 1:12
I make plans as the **w** does, ...2Co 1:17
who rules this **w** has blinded 2Co 4:4
think of anyone as the **w** does. 2Co 5:16
of Christ as the **w** thinks, ...2Co 5:16
peace between the **w** and himself. 2Co 5:19
did not hold the **w** guilty of its 2Co 5:19
sorrow the **w** has brings death. 2Co 7:10
do live in the **w,** but we do not 2Co 10:3
in the same way the **w** fights. 2Co 10:3
different from those the **w** uses. 2Co 10:4
about their lives in the **w**. 2Co 11:18
free us from this evil **w** we live ....Gal 1:4
the whole **w** is bound by sin. ....Gal 3:22
to the useless rules of this **w**. ....Gal 4:3
of Jesus my **w** was crucified, ...Gal 6:14
crucified, and I died to the **w**. ....Gal 6:14
blessing in the heavenly **w**. ....Eph 1:3
us before the **w** was made so that ....Eph 1:4
right side in the heavenly **w**. ....Eph 1:20
not only in this **w** but also in ....Eph 1:21
you lived the way the **w** lives,.................Eph 2:2
in the heavenly **w** will now know ....Eph 3:10
of evil in the heavenly **w**. ....Eph 6:12
shine like stars in the dark **w**...................Php 2:15

in the w that Good News is.....................Col 1:6
been told to everyone in the w, ...Col 1:23
the ruling spirits of this w, ...Col 2:8
and showed the w that they were ....Col 2:15
the ruling spirits of the w, ...Col 2:20
belong to this w by following ....Col 2:20
is already working in the w, ...2Th 2:7
came into the w to save sinners,...............1Ti 1:15
in by the w, and taken up 1Ti 3:16
We brought nothing into the w, ...1Ti 6:7
of this w not to be proud. 1Ti 6:17
who loved this w, left me and 2Ti 4:10
God let the w know about that ....Tit 1:3
evil things the w wants to do....................Tit 2:12
and through him he made the w. ....Heb 1:2
his firstborn Son into the w, ...Heb 1:6
of the new w that was coming, ...Heb 2:5
from the time he made the w....................Heb 4:3
in all the w can be hidden ....Heb 4:13
the powers of his new w...........................Heb 6:5
and does not belong to this w. ....Heb 9:11
many times since the w was made. ....Heb 9:26
So when Christ came into the w, ...Heb 10:5
that the whole w was made by ....Heb 11:3
showed that the w was wrong, ...Heb 11:7
The w was not good enough for ....Heb 11:38
scattered everywhere in the w: ....Jam 1:1
poor in the w to be rich with ....Jam 2:5
is a whole w of evil among the ....Jam 3:6
come from God but from the w. ....Jam 3:15
that loving the w is the same as ....Jam 4:4
a friend of the w becomes God's ....Jam 4:4
God and the w at the same time, ...Jam 4:8
and what the w would be like at..............1Pe 1:11
chosen before the w was made, ...1Pe 1:20
was shown to the w in these last 1Pe 1:20
people of the w did not want 1Pe 2:4
and strangers in this w. 1Pe 2:11
who have authority in this w: 1Pe 2:13
all over the w is having the.....................1Pe 5:9
and the w will not ruin you with 2Pe 1:4
punished the w long ago when he 2Pe 2:5
a flood to the w that was full 2Pe 2:5
the evil in the w by knowing our 2Pe 2:20
but the w continues the way it 2Pe 3:3
Then the w was flooded and 2Pe 3:6
Do not love the w or the things 1Jn 2:15
world or the things in the w. 1Jn 2:15
If you love the w, the love of 1Jn 2:15
These are the ways of the w: 1Jn 2:16
but all of them come from the w. 1Jn 2:16
The w and everything that people 1Jn 2:17
people in the w do not know us 1Jn 3:1
the people of the w hate you. 1Jn 3:13
have gone out into the w. 1Jn 4:1
and now he is already in the w. 1Jn 4:3
than the devil, who is in the w. 1Jn 4:4
belong to the w, so what they 1Jn 4:5
so what they say is from the w, ...1Jn 4:5
and the w listens to them. 1Jn 4:5
Son into the w so that we could 1Jn 4:9
Son to be the Savior of the w..................1Jn 4:14
in this w we are like him. 1Jn 4:17
a child of God conquers the w. 1Jn 5:4
the victory that conquers the w— 1Jn 5:4
who conquers the w is the person 1Jn 5:5
Evil One controls the whole w. 1Jn 5:19
are in the w now who do not 2Jn 1:7
thoughts are only of this w, ...Jud 1:19
to the whole w to test those who ....Rev 3:10
that were sent into all the w. ....Rev 5:6
to rule the w now belongs to ....Rev 11:15
The people of the w were angry,..............Rev 11:18

Satan, who tricks the whole w. ....Rev 12:9
Then the whole w was amazed and ....Rev 13:3
of the w whose names are ....Rev 13:8
of the whole w to gather them ....Rev 16:14
since the beginning of the w. ....Rev 17:8
the people of the w will walk,..................Rev 21:24

WORLD'S
he can see by this w light. ....Jn 11:9
the powers of this w darkness, ...Eph 6:12
free from the w evil influence. ....Jam 1:27
were the w great people,........................Rev 18:23

WORLDLY
serve both God and w riches. ....Mt 6:24
w people are more clever with ....Lk 16:8
yourselves using w riches so ....Lk 16:9
cannot be trusted with w riches,.............Lk 16:11
serve both God and w riches." ....Lk 16:13
or worrying about w things. ....Lk 21:34
They think we live in a w way, ...2Co 10:2

WORM
and to the w, 'You are my mother ....Job 17:14
But I am like a w instead of a.................Ps 22:6
even though you are weak as a w. ....Is 41:14
God sent a w to attack the plant.............Jnh 4:7
In hell the w does not die; ....Mk 9:44
In hell the w does not die; ....Mk 9:46
In hell the w does not die; ....Mk 9:48

WORMS
It became full of w and began to ....Ex 16:20
began to stink or have w in it. ....Ex 16:24
because the w will eat them. ....Dt 28:39
is covered with w and scabs, ...Job 7:5
other, and w cover them both ....Job 21:26
and w will eat their bodies......................Job 24:20
like insects. They are only w!" ....Job 25:6
and w cover your body like a ....Is 14:11
and w will eat them as if they................Is 51:8
The w that eat them will never ....Is 66:24
and he was eaten by w and died. ....Ac 12:23

WORMWOOD
The name of the star is W. ....Rev 8:11

WORN
outer robe to be w under the ....Ex 28:31
outer robe to be w under the ....Ex 39:22
has never worked or a w yoke, ...Dt 21:3
When you were tired and w out, ...Dt 25:18
and sandals are w out from the ....Jos 9:13
and purple robes w by the kings ....Jdg 8:26
cloth that was w to show sadness 2Sa 21:10
that the king himself has w. ....Est 6:8
so upset I am w out, because my ....Ps 119:139
the cloth belts w around their..................Is 3:20
who have never w your name. ....Is 63:19
one who was w out by her acts ....Eze 23:43
They would have w rough cloth ....Mt 11:21
long time he had w no clothes ....Lk 8:27
They would have w rough cloth ....Lk 10:13
bother me until I am w out.' " ....Lk 18:5
that is old and w out is ready ....Heb 8:13

WORN-OUT
old rags and w clothes from that ....Je 38:11
old rags and w clothes under ....Je 38:12

WORRIED
Jacob was very afraid and w. ....Ge 32:7
morning, he saw they were w. ....Ge 40:6
Now don't be w or angry with ....Ge 45:5
The LORD will make your mind w, ...Dt 28:65
they became w because he still ....Jdg 3:25
because he was w about the Ark 1Sa 4:13
Don't be afraid or w because of 2Ch 32:7

me. I am very w. They dug a pit .... Ps 57:6
I was very w, but you comforted .... Ps 94:19
I am w, and I am shaking with .... Is 21:4
who are now w will be able to .... Is 32:4
And you are w about hunger, ... Je 42:16
he came near the den, he was w. .... Da 6:20
I, Daniel, was w. The visions .... Da 7:15
from Israel are w about the .... Hos 10:5
and I were very w about you and .... Lk 2:48
you are w and upset about many .... Lk 10:41
is w because you heard that he .... Php 2:26

WORRIES

Give your w to the LORD, and he .... Ps 55:22
tomorrow will have its own w. .... Mt 6:34
but lets w about this life .... Mt 13:22
but the w of this life, the .... Mk 4:19
but they let the w, riches, and .... Lk 8:14
Give all your w to him, because 1Pe 5:7

WORRY

them not to w about bringing .... Ge 45:20
so don't be afraid and don't w." .... Dt 1:21
Don't be afraid and don't w." .... Dt 31:8
who helped her said, "Don't w! 1Sa 4:20
Don't w about the donkeys you 1Sa 9:20
"Don't w," Elijah said to her. 1Ki 17:13
W and suffering terrify them; .... Job 15:24
I have sinned, it is my w alone. .... Job 19:4
How long must I w and feel sad .... Ps 13:2
W is a heavy load, but a kind .... Pr 12:25
She does not w about her family .... Pr 31:21
But rich people w about their .... Ec 5:12
They do not w about how short .... Ec 5:20
Don't w, and forget the troubles .... Ec 11:10
calm and don't w. Don't let .... Is 7:4
So don't w, because I am with .... Is 41:10
afraid! Don't w! I have always .... Is 44:8
It does not w in a year when no .... Je 17:8
and they will w as they eat. .... Eze 4:16
don't w about the food or drink .... Mt 6:25
And why do you w about clothes? .... Mt 6:28
Don't w and say, 'What will we .... Mt 6:31
So don't w about tomorrow, ... Mt 6:34
don't w about what to say or how .... Mt 10:19
don't w ahead of time about what .... Mk 13:11
don't w about how to defend .... Lk 12:11
don't w about the food you need .... Lk 12:22
then why w about the big things? .... Lk 12:26
minds not to w ahead of time .... Lk 21:14
He said, "Don't w. He is alive .... Ac 20:10
I want you to be free from w. 1Co 7:32
not w about anything, but pray .... Php 4:6

WORRYING

and will start w about us." 1Sa 9:5
his donkeys and is w about you 1Sa 10:2
are always w about how much .... Pr 23:7
Bad dreams come from too much w, ... Ec 5:3
time to your life by w about it. .... Mt 6:27
time to your life by w about it. .... Lk 12:25
will drink, and don't keep w. .... Lk 12:29
or w about worldly things. .... Lk 21:34
and I can stop w about you. .... Php 2:28

WORSHIP

and I will go over there and w, ... Ge 22:5
all of you will w me on this .... Ex 3:12
to let my son go so he may w me. .... Ex 4:23
my people go w me in the desert .... Ex 7:16
Let my people go to w me. .... Ex 8:1
my people go so they can w me .... Ex 8:20
Let my people go to w me. .... Ex 9:1
Let my people go to w me. .... Ex 9:13
Let my people go to w me. .... Ex 10:3

Israelites go to w the LORD .... Ex 10:7
Go and w the LORD your God. .... Ex 10:8
the men may go and w the LORD, ... Ex 10:11
of you may go and w the LORD .... Ex 10:24
the animals to w the LORD our .... Ex 10:26
we will need to w the LORD until .... Ex 10:26
have asked; go and w the LORD. .... Ex 12:31
must not w or serve any idol, ... Ex 20:5
do not w these gods in addition .... Ex 20:23
W me in every place that I .... Ex 20:24
them unsuitable for use in w. .... Ex 20:25
one is to come to w me without .... Ex 23:15
must come to w the LORD God. .... Ex 23:17
down to their gods or w them. .... Ex 23:24
the stone pillars they use in w. .... Ex 23:24
If you w the LORD your God, ... Ex 23:25
If you w their gods, you will be .... Ex 23:33
come up to me and w me from a .... Ex 24:1
w any other god, because I, ... Ex 34:14
they w their gods, they will .... Ex 34:15
sons and those daughters w gods, ... Ex 34:16
Do not w idols or make statues .... Le 19:4
began to w Baal of Peor, ... Nu 25:3
Wreck all of their places of w. .... Nu 33:52
But don't bow down and w them, ... Dt 4:19
There you will w gods made by .... Dt 4:28
or anything to w that looks like .... Dt 5:8
must not w or serve any idol, ... Dt 5:9
You must w him and make your .... Dt 6:13
not w other gods as the people .... Dt 6:14
you, and if you w other gods, he .... Dt 6:15
them, and do not w their gods, ... Dt 7:16
other gods and w them and bow .... Dt 8:19
away to serve and w other gods. .... Dt 11:16
and do not w other gods you do .... Dt 11:28
w the LORD your God that way, ... Dt 12:4
Do not w the way we have been .... Dt 12:8
say, "How do these nations w? .... Dt 12:30
Don't w the LORD your God that .... Dt 12:31
the evil ways they w their gods. .... Dt 12:31
not known) "and let's w them." .... Dt 13:2
"Let's go and w other gods." .... Dt 13:6
"Let's go and w other gods." .... Dt 13:13
into the meeting to w the LORD. .... Dt 23:1
into the meeting to w the LORD. .... Dt 23:2
into the meeting to w the LORD, ... Dt 23:3
into the meeting to w the LORD. .... Dt 23:8
me but will w the foreign gods .... Dt 31:16
say, 'You cannot w the LORD, the .... Jos 22:24
You cannot w the LORD.' .... Jos 22:25
after us that we w the LORD with .... Jos 22:27
Don't serve or w them. .... Jos 23:7
and serve other gods and w them, ... Jos 23:16
They began to w the gods of the .... Jdg 2:12
but do not w their gods.' .... Jdg 6:10
an altar there to w the LORD and .... Jdg 6:24
went up to Shiloh to w the LORD 1Sa 1:3
a sacrifice at the place of w. 1Sa 9:12
up to the place of w to eat. 1Sa 9:13
on his way up to the place of w. 1Sa 9:14
Go with me to the place of w. 1Sa 9:19
from the place of w and went to 1Sa 9:25
on their way to w God at Bethel 1Sa 10:3
come down from the place of w. 1Sa 10:5
he entered the place of w. 1Sa 10:13
are of no use, so don't w them. 1Sa 12:21
with me so I may w the LORD." 1Sa 15:25
that I can w the LORD your God. 1Sa 15:30
went into the LORD's house to w. 2Sa 12:20
I will w him in Hebron.'" 2Sa 15:8
where people used to w God, ... 2Sa 15:32
bowed down on his bed to w God, ... 1Ki 1:47
Temple for the w of the LORD had 1Ki 3:2

at altars in many places of **w**. 1Ki 3:2
other places of **w** were still 1Ki 3:3
the most important place of **w**. 1Ki 3:4
this Temple as a place to **w** you. 1Ki 8:43
must not serve or **w** other gods. 1Ki 9:6
Solomon built two places for **w**. 1Ki 11:7
One was a place to **w** Chemosh, ... 1Ki 11:7
other was a place to **w** Molech. 1Ki 11:7
you to go to Jerusalem to **w**," 1Ki 12:28
far as Dan to **w** the calf there. 1Ki 12:30
temples on the places of **w**. 1Ki 12:31
at the places of **w** he had made. 1Ki 12:32
the places of **w** now make their 1Ki 13:2
the places of **w** in the towns 1Ki 13:32
the places of **w** from among all 1Ki 13:33
the places of **w** was allowed to 1Ki 13:33
they set up idols to **w** Asherah. 1Ki 14:15
and places to **w** gods and Asherah 1Ki 14:23
at the **w** places to leave 1Ki 15:12
The places of **w** to gods were not 1Ki 15:14
began to serve Baal and **w** him. 1Ki 16:31
in the places of **w** from the days 1Ki 22:46
into the temple of Rimmon to **w**, ... 2Ki 5:18
and all the people who **w** Baal. 2Ki 10:19
Jehu destroyed Baal **w** in Israel, ... 2Ki 10:28
built places to **w** gods in all 2Ki 17:9
first they did not **w** the LORD, ... 2Ki 17:25
They do not **w** the LORD nor obey 2Ki 17:34
down to them or **w** them or offer 2Ki 17:35
W the LORD who brought you up 2Ki 17:36
Instead **w** the LORD your God, ... 2Ki 17:39
s altars and the places of **w**. 2Ki 18:22
You must **w** only at this one 2Ki 18:22
built altars to **w** the stars in 2Ki 21:5
the places of **w** at the entrance 2Ki 23:8
were for the **w** of the sun. 2Ki 23:11
that were for sun **w** also 2Ki 23:11
the place of **w** made by Jeroboam 2Ki 23:15
priests of those places of **w**; 2Ki 23:20
of leading the **w** and giving 1Ch 16:4
W the LORD because he is holy 1Ch 16:29
at the place of **w** in Gibeon. 1Ch 16:39
in Gibeon at the place of **w**. 1Ch 21:29
build a temple for **w** to me, ... 1Ch 22:8
will build a temple for **w** to me. 1Ch 22:19
the Temple for **w** to the LORD. 1Ch 22:19
build your Temple for **w** to you. 1Ch 29:16
to the place of **w** at the town 2Ch 1:3
Solomon left the place of **w**, ... 2Ch 1:13
a place to **w** the LORD and also 2Ch 2:1
this Temple as a place to **w** you. 2Ch 6:33
the altar for the **w** of God. 2Ch 7:9
must not serve or **w** other gods. 2Ch 7:19
the places of **w** and for the goat 2Ch 11:15
the places of **w** to gods were not 2Ch 15:17
built places to **w** gods on the 2Ch 21:11
began to **w** the Asherah idols 2Ch 24:18
and started to **w** them himself. 2Ch 25:14
He made metal idols to **w** Baal. 2Ch 28:2
sacrifices to **w** other gods. 2Ch 28:25
stone pillars used to **w** gods. 2Ch 31:1
offerings, to **w**, and to give 2Ch 31:2
LORD's places of **w** and altars. 2Ch 32:12
that you must **w** and burn incense 2Ch 32:12
built altars to **w** the stars in 2Ch 33:5
sacrifices at the places of **w**, ... 2Ch 33:17
Josiah removed idol **w** from Judah 2Ch 34:5
that day for the **w** of the LORD, ... 2Ch 35:16
like you and want to **w** your God. .... Ezr 4:2
in order to **w** the LORD, ... Ezr 6:21
the utensils for **w** in the Temple .... Ezr 7:19
be allowed in the meeting to **w**. .... Ne 13:1
down to the ground to **w** God. .... Job 1:20

for God and limit the **w** of him. .... Job 15:4
the sun and moon a kiss of **w**. .... Job 31:27
Sinners will not **w** with God's .... Ps 1:5
I can **w** in your holy Temple. .... Ps 5:7
those nations that do not **w** you .... Ps 10:16
of the nations will **w** him .... Ps 22:27
people on earth will eat and **w**. .... Ps 22:29
heart said of you, "Go, **w** him." .... Ps 27:8
So I come to **w** you, LORD. .... Ps 27:8
w the LORD because he is holy. .... Ps 29:2
I hate those who **w** false gods. .... Ps 31:6
All the earth should **w** the LORD; .... Ps 33:8
I will teach you to **w** the LORD. .... Ps 34:11
will not leave those who **w** him. .... Ps 37:28
people will see this and **w** him. .... Ps 40:3
or to those who **w** false gods. .... Ps 40:4
around, you who **w** me, who have .... Ps 50:5
With those who **w** you, I will .... Ps 52:9
Be encouraged, you who **w** God. .... Ps 69:32
let all those who **w** you rejoice .... Ps 70:4
should come to the God we **w**. .... Ps 76:11
by building places to **w** gods; .... Ps 78:58
of those who **w** you to the wild .... Ps 79:2
you must not **w** any false god. .... Ps 81:9
peace for those who **w** him. .... Ps 85:8
Protect me, because I **w** you. .... Ps 86:2
have made will come and **w** you. .... Ps 86:9
you spoke to those who **w** you. .... Ps 89:19
Come, let's **w** him and bow down. .... Ps 95:6
W the LORD because he is holy. .... Ps 96:9
Those who **w** idols should be .... Ps 97:7
All the gods should **w** the LORD. .... Ps 97:7
our God, and **w** at the Temple, ... Ps 99:5
and **w** at his holy mountain, ... Ps 99:9
A psalm for going up to **w**. .... Ps 119:176
A song for going up to **w**. .... Ps 120:7
A song for going up to **w**. .... Ps 121:8
A song for going up to **w**. .... Ps 122:9
A song for going up to **w**. .... Ps 123:4
A song for going up to **w**. .... Ps 124:8
A song for going up to **w**. .... Ps 125:5
A song for going up to **w**. .... Ps 126:6
A song for going up to **w**. .... Ps 127:5
A song for going up to **w**. .... Ps 128:6
A song for going up to **w**. .... Ps 129:8
A song for going up to **w**. .... Ps 130:8
A song for going up to **w**. .... Ps 131:3
Let's **w** at his footstool. .... Ps 132:7
and those who **w** me will really .... Ps 132:16
A song for going up to **w**. .... Ps 132:18
A song for going up to **w**. .... Ps 133:3
Let those who **w** him rejoice in .... Ps 149:5
God is honored by all who **w** him. .... Ps 149:9
when you go to **w** at the Temple. .... Ec 5:1
The people **w** these idols they .... Is 2:8
they made for themselves to **w**; .... Is 2:20
those kingdoms that **w** idols, ... Is 10:10
Praise the LORD and **w** him. .... Is 12:4
go to the places of **w** to cry. .... Is 15:2
their places of **w** and will try .... Is 16:12
They will **w** God and offer many .... Is 19:21
Assyrians will **w** God together. .... Is 19:23
will come and **w** the LORD on that .... Is 27:13
These people **w** me with their .... Is 29:13
Their **w** is based on nothing but .... Is 29:13
s altars and the places of **w**. .... Is 36:7
must **w** only at this one altar. .... Is 36:7
Those who **w** you should be hated .... Is 41:24
Then they bow down and **w** it. .... Is 46:6
who do not **w** God and who are .... Is 52:1
the LORD's things used in **w**, ... Is 52:11
the LORD to **w** him and love him .... Is 56:6
every green tree to **w** your gods. .... Is 57:5

offerings on them to w them, ... Is 57:6
mountain, who w the god Luck, ... Is 65:11
are like those who w idols. .... Is 66:3
and pure to go to w their gods .... Is 66:17
will come to w me every Sabbath .... Is 66:23
It was foolish to w idols on the .... Je 3:23
these gates to w the LORD, ... Je 7:2
built places of w at Topheth .... Je 7:31
other gods to serve and w them.............. Je 13:10
the places of w in your country, ... Je 17:3
places on hilltops to w Baal, ... Je 19:5
gods to serve them or to w them. .... Je 25:6
are coming to w at the Temple .... Je 26:2
Jerusalem to w the LORD our God! .... Je 31:6
built places to w Baal so they .... Je 32:35
truly want to w me all their .... Je 32:39
out drink offerings to w her, ... Je 44:17
the places of w and from burning .... Je 48:35
The people who w Chemosh have .... Je 48:46
destroy your places of idol w.................. Eze 6:3
places of idol w will be ruined; .... Eze 6:6
me and desired to w their idols. .... Eze 6:9
these people want to w idols. .... Eze 14:3
Israel want to w idols and put .... Eze 14:4
me by wanting to w idols or by .... Eze 14:7
made your places of w colorful. .... Eze 16:16
yourself a place to w gods. .... Eze 16:24
a place of w in every city .... Eze 16:24
a place of w at the beginning .... Eze 16:25
built your place to w gods at .... Eze 16:31
made places of w in every city .... Eze 16:31
your places of w and destroy .... Eze 16:39
other places where you w gods. .... Eze 16:39
eat at the mountain places of w. .... Eze 18:6
at the mountain places of w. .... Eze 18:11
eat at the mountain places of w. .... Eze 18:15
and wanted to w their idols. .... Eze 20:16
high place where you go to w?'" .... Eze 20:29
We want to w idols made of wood .... Eze 20:32
at the mountain places of w, ... Eze 22:9
your places of w through your .... Eze 28:18
old places to w gods have become .... Eze 36:2
helped the people to w their idols .... Eze 44:12
The ruler will w at the entrance .... Eze 46:2
the land will w at the entrance .... Eze 46:3
the north gate to w must go out .... Eze 46:9
times of w one-half bushel .... Eze 46:11
bow down and w the gold statue .... Da 3:5
bow down and w will immediately .... Da 3:6
bow down and w the gold statue. .... Da 3:10
and do not w the gold statue .... Da 3:12
my gods nor w the gold statue I .... Da 3:14
you bow down and w the statue I .... Da 3:15
But if you do not w it, you will .... Da 3:15
your gods or w the gold statue .... Da 3:18
than serve or w any god other .... Da 3:28
that you always w been able to .... Da 6:20
or the god that women w. .... Da 11:37
of the North will w power and .... Da 11:38
which his ancestors did not w. .... Da 11:38
even though they w other gods .... Hos 3:1
have chosen to w idols, ... Hos 4:17
They will come to w the LORD, ... Hos 5:6
So their false w will destroy .... Hos 5:7
places of false w will be .... Hos 10:8
as you used to do on w days. .... Hos 12:9
As they w at their altars,....................... Am 2:8
descendants will be destroyed .... Am 7:9
People who w useless idols give .... Jnh 2:8
What is Judah's place of idol w? .... Mic 1:5
pillars you w so that you will .... Mic 5:13
will no longer w what your hands .... Mic 5:13
net and burns incense to w it,................ Hab 1:16

destroy those who w the stars .... Zph 1:5
those who w and make promises .... Zph 1:5
I will punish those who w Dagon, ... Zph 1:9
places will w him wherever they .... Zph 2:11
it doesn't w its God. .... Zph 3:2
of the LORD and w me together. .... Zph 3:9
nations will come to w the LORD .... Zch 8:22
year after year to w the King, ... Zch 14:16
go to Jerusalem to w the King, ... Zch 14:17
women who w foreign gods. .... Mal 2:11
east and have come to w him." .... Mt 2:2
tell me so I can w him too." .... Mt 2:8
If you will bow down and w me,.............. Mt 4:9
'You must w the Lord your God .... Mt 4:10
Their w of me is worthless..................... Mt 15:9
Their w of me is worthless..................... Mk 7:7
to those who w and serve him. .... Lk 1:50
If you w me, then it will be .... Lk 4:7
'You must w the Lord your God .... Lk 4:8
the place where people must w." .... Jn 4:20
will you actually w the Father. .... Jn 4:21
You Samaritans w something you .... Jn 4:22
what we w, because salvation................ Jn 4:22
worshipers will w the Father in .... Jn 4:23
seeking such people to w him. .... Jn 4:23
and those who w him must worship .... Jn 4:24
worship him must w in spirit and .... Jn 4:24
Jerusalem to w at the Passover .... Jn 12:20
and will w me in this place. .... Ac 7:7
you the tent to w Molech and the .... Ac 7:43
god Rephan that you made to w. .... Ac 7:43
He had gone to Jerusalem to w. .... Ac 8:27
Israelites and you who w God, ... Ac 13:16
and others who w God, listen! .... Ac 13:26
had changed to w God followed .... Ac 13:43
city, I saw the objects you w. .... Ac 17:23
You w a god that you don't know, ... Ac 17:23
people to w God in a way that .... Ac 18:13
that I went to w in Jerusalem .... Ac 24:11
w the God of our ancestors as a .... Ac 24:14
from the God I belong to and w. .... Ac 27:23
forever for the w of idols made .... Rm 1:23
right way of w and his promises. .... Rm 9:4
the spiritual way for you to w. .... Rm 12:1
robbers, or those who w idols. 1Co 5:11
are greedy, or w idols, or abuse 1Co 5:11
Do not w idols, as some of them 1Co 10:7
run away from the w of idols.................. 1Co 10:14
and led away to w idols— 1Co 12:2
will bow down and w God saying, ... 1Co 14:25
We w God through his Spirit, ... Php 3:3
humiliate yourself and w angels. .... Col 2:18
god or anything that people w. 2Th 2:4
full of w and respect for God.................. 1Ti 2:2
for women who say they w God. 1Ti 2:10
of our life of w is great: 1Ti 3:16
"Let all God's angels w him." .... Heb 1:6
true place of w that was made .... Heb 8:2
had rules for w and a place on .... Heb 9:1
and a place on earth for w...................... Heb 9:1
the first room every day to w. .... Heb 9:6
over all the things used in w. .... Heb 9:21
those who come near to w God. .... Heb 10:1
We should w God in a way that .... Heb 12:28
parties, and hateful idol w. 1Pe 4:3
and they w him who lives forever .... Rev 4:10
They w him day and night in his .... Rev 7:15
live on earth will w the beast— .... Rev 13:8
on earth the first beast .... Rev 13:12
all who will not w the image of .... Rev 13:15
So w God who made the heavens, ... Rev 14:7
those who w the beast and his .... Rev 14:11
nations will come and w you, ... Rev 15:4

at the angel's feet to **w** him, ... Rev 19:10
but he said to me, "Do not **w** me! .... Rev 19:10
W God, because the message about ..... Rev 19:10
evil magic, who **w** idols, and who .... Rev 21:8
and God's servants will **w** him. .... Rev 22:3
I bowed down to **w** at the feet of .... Rev 22:8
angel said to me, "Do not **w** me! .... Rev 22:9
the words in this book. **W** God!" .... Rev 22:9
who murder, who **w** idols, and who ..... Rev 22:15

WORSHIPED

altar to the LORD and **w** him.................. Ge 12:8
So he **w** the LORD there. .... Ge 13:4
The servant bowed and **w** the LORD .... Ge 24:26
an altar and **w** the LORD there. .... Ge 26:25
the God whom his father Isaac **w**. .... Ge 31:53
Then Israel **w** as he leaned on .... Ge 47:31
they bowed down and **w** him.................. Ex 4:31
bowed down and **w** the LORD. .... Ex 12:27
and they have **w** it and offered .... Ex 32:8
they stood and **w**, each person at .... Ex 33:10
bowed to the ground and **w**. .... Ex 34:8
where gods are **w** and cut down .... Le 26:30
ate food there and **w** these gods. .... Nu 25:2
your tribes where he is to be **w**. .... Dt 12:5
a place where he is to be **w**. .... Dt 12:11
LORD your God chooses to be **w**. .... Dt 12:18
he is to be **w** that is too far .... Dt 12:21
will choose where he is to be **w**. .... Dt 14:23
choose to be **w** is too far away .... Dt 14:24
place he will choose to be **w**. .... Dt 15:20
the LORD will choose to be **w**. .... Dt 16:2
place he will choose to be **w**. .... Dt 16:6
place he will choose to be **w**. .... Dt 16:11
your God will choose to be **w**................. Dt 26:2
Abraham and Nahor, **w** other gods. .... Jos 24:2
your ancestors **w** on the other .... Jos 24:14
your ancestors **w** when they lived .... Jos 24:15
and they **w** the Baal idols. .... Jdg 2:11
LORD **w** Baal and Ashtoreth. .... Jdg 2:13
to God but **w** other gods instead............. Jdg 2:17
again sinned and **w** other gods. .... Jdg 2:19
and what it meant, he **w** God.................. Jdg 7:15
were unfaithful to God and **w** it,.............. Jdg 8:27
They **w** Baal and Ashtoreth, ... Jdg 10:6
our God and **w** the Baal idols. .... Jdg 10:10
me again and have **w** other gods. .... Jdg 10:13
and they **w** the LORD again. .... Jdg 10:16
family got up and **w** the LORD. 1Sa 1:19
And he **w** the LORD there. 1Sa 1:28
with Saul, and Saul **w** the LORD. 1Sa 15:31
have said, 'I will be **w** there.' 1Ki 8:29
I will be **w** there forever and 1Ki 9:3
They **w** and served those gods, ... 1Ki 9:9
Solomon **w** Ashtoreth, the goddess 1Ki 11:5
me and has **w** the Sidonian god 1Ki 11:33
the city where I chose to be **w**. 1Ki 11:36
the place where he would be **w**. 1Ki 14:21
because they **w** worthless idols. 1Ki 16:26
which was the way they **w**. 1Ki 18:28
the places where gods were **w**, ... 1Ki 22:43
Ahaziah **w** and served the god 1Ki 22:53
where gods were **w** were not 2Ki 12:3
where gods were **w** were not 2Ki 14:4
where gods were **w** were not 2Ki 15:4
where gods were **w** were not 2Ki 15:35
at the places where gods were **w**, ... 2Ki 16:4
incense everywhere gods were **w**, ... 2Ki 17:11
They **w** useless idols and became 2Ki 17:15
They **w** all the stars of the sky 2Ki 17:16
the temples where gods were **w**............. 2Ki 17:29
The people from Cuthah **w** Nergal. 2Ki 17:30
The people of Hamath **w** Ashima. 2Ki 17:30

The Avvites **w** Nibhaz and Tartak. 2Ki 17:31
the places where gods were **w**. 2Ki 17:32
the LORD but also **w** their idols, ... 2Ki 17:41
the places where gods were **w**. 2Ki 18:4
the places where gods were **w**, ... 2Ki 21:3
Manasseh also **w** all the stars of............ 2Ki 21:3
"I will be **w** in Jerusalem," 2Ki 21:4
I will be **w** forever in this 2Ki 21:7
he **w** the idols his father had 2Ki 21:21
the idols his father had **w**, ... 2Ki 21:21
where gods were **w** in the cities 2Ki 23:5
the places where gods were **w**, ... 2Ki 23:8
where gods were **w** were not 2Ki 23:9
where gods were **w** east of 2Ki 23:13
pieces the stone pillars they **w**, ... 2Ki 23:14
I said, 'I will be **w** there.'" 2Ki 23:27
God that their ancestors had **w**. 1Ch 5:25
Solomon and the people **w** there. 2Ch 1:5
as the place I am to be **w**, ... 2Ch 6:6
you have said you would be **w**. 2Ch 6:20
They **w** and thanked the LORD, ... 2Ch 7:3
So I will be **w** there forever. 2Ch 7:16
gods and **w** and served them, ... 2Ch 7:22
Israel in which he was to be **w**. 2Ch 12:13
the places where gods were **w**. 2Ch 14:3
gods were **w** and the incense 2Ch 14:5
where you have chosen to be **w**. 2Ch 20:9
down before the LORD and **w** him. 2Ch 20:18
where gods were **w** were not 2Ch 20:33
the idols they **w** and started to 2Ch 25:14
at the places where gods were **w**, ... 2Ch 28:4
All the people **w**, the singers 2Ch 29:28
with him bowed down and **w**.................. 2Ch 29:29
with joy and bowed down and **w**. 2Ch 29:30
gods the people of the world **w**, ... 2Ch 32:19
the places where gods were **w**, ... 2Ch 33:3
Asherah idols and **w** all the 2Ch 33:3
will be **w** in Jerusalem forever, ... 2Ch 33:4
I will be **w** forever in this 2Ch 33:7
Amon **w** and offered sacrifices to 2Ch 33:22
as the place he is to be **w**. .... Ezr 6:12
to where I have chosen to be **w**.'............. Ne 1:9
bowed down and **w** the LORD with .... Ne 8:6
sins and **w** the LORD their God............... Ne 9:3
who have not **w** idols, who have.............. Ps 24:4
where God was **w** in the land. .... Ps 74:8
Sinai and **w** a metal statue...................... Ps 106:19
They **w** other nations' idols and .... Ps 106:36
because you have **w** gods under .... Is 1:29
because you have **w** idols in your .... Is 1:29
Our ancestors **w** you in our holy .... Is 64:11
other gods and **w** idols they had............. Je 1:16
Your ancestors **w** useless idols .... Je 2:5
of Baal and **w** useless idols. .... Je 2:8
I have not **w** the Baal idols'? .... Je 2:23
because she **w** idols made of .... Je 3:9
your God and **w** gods under every .... Je 3:13
where I have chosen to be **w**?................ Je 7:10
chosen to be **w** is nothing more .... Je 7:11
I first made a place to be **w**. .... Je 7:12
chosen to be **w** in Jerusalem. .... Je 7:14
chosen to be **w** and have made it .... Je 7:30
after and searched for and **w**.................. Je 8:2
and followed and **w** other gods .... Je 11:10
gods and served and **w** them................. Je 16:11
the people **w** gods on the roofs .... Je 19:13
They **w** the stars and burned .... Je 19:13
They **w** and served other gods.'" .... Je 22:9
ancestors forgot me and **w** Baal. .... Je 23:27
where I have chosen to be **w**, ... Je 32:34
where I have chosen to be **w**. .... Je 34:15
my Sabbaths and **w** the idols of .... Eze 20:24
bowed down and **w** the gold statue .... Da 3:7

the place where people **w** him, ... Da 8:11
his ancestors **w** or the god that .... Da 11:37
as hateful as the thing they **w**. .... Hos 9:10
and they bowed down and **w** him. .... Mt 2:11
in the boat with Jesus and said, ... Mt 14:33
hold of his feet, and **w** him. .... Mt 28:9
they saw Jesus and **w** him, ... Mt 28:17
never left the Temple but **w** God, ... Lk 2:37
They **w** him and returned to .... Lk 24:52
ancestors **w** on this mountain, ... Jn 4:20
Then the man **w** Jesus. .... Jn 9:38
in his house **w** the true God. .... Ac 10:2
fell at his feet, and **w** him. .... Ac 10:25
w God, and he opened her mind............... Ac 16:14
of the Greeks who **w** God and many .... Ac 17:4
Jews and the Greeks who **w** God. .... Ac 17:17
the synagogue. This man **w** God. .... Ac 18:7
They **w** and served what had been .... Rm 1:25
Then he **w** as he leaned on the .... Heb 11:21
and the elders bowed down and **w**. .... Rev 5:14
before the throne and **w** God, ... Rev 7:11
down on their faces and **w** God. .... Rev 11:16
People **w** the dragon because he.............. Rev 13:4
And they also **w** the beast, ... Rev 13:4
of the beast and who **w** his idol. .... Rev 16:2
creatures bowed down and **w** God, ... Rev 19:4
of the beast and **w** his idol...................... Rev 19:20
They had not **w** the beast or his .... Rev 20:4

WORSHIPER

the conscience of the **w** perfect. .... Heb 9:9

WORSHIPERS

have become **w** of Baal of Peor. .... Nu 25:5
he could destroy the **w** of Baal. 2Ki 10:19
and all the **w** of Baal came; 2Ki 10:21
robes for all the **w** of Baal." 2Ki 10:22
Jehu said to the **w** of Baal, ... 2Ki 10:23
sure there are only **w** of Baal." 2Ki 10:23
Then the **w** of Baal went in to.................. 2Ki 10:24
Go in and kill the **w** of Baal. 2Ki 10:25
killed the **w** of Baal with........................ 2Ki 10:25
these **w** will see me do what I.................. Ps 22:25
do not let your **w** be disgraced .... Ps 69:6
and Samuel was among his **w**. .... Ps 99:6
when the true **w** will worship .... Jn 4:23
The **w** would be made clean, ... Heb 10:2

WORSHIPING

unfaithful to me by **w** Molech. .... Le 20:5
our children stop **w** the LORD. .... Jos 22:25
is as bad as the sin of **w** idols. 1Sa 15:23
a temple for **w** the LORD his God 1Ki 5:3
will build a temple for **w** me.' 1Ki 5:5
temple for **w** the LORD my God. 1Ki 5:5
in Samaria for **w** Baal and put an 1Ki 16:32
also made an idol for **w** Asherah. 1Ki 16:33
Ahab sinned terribly by **w** idols,.............. 1Ki 21:26
Israel to sin by **w** the golden 2Ki 10:29
Sennacherib was **w** in the temple 2Ki 19:37
built temples for **w** gods in the 2Ki 23:19
They began **w** the gods of the.................. 1Ch 5:25
a temple for **w** the LORD my God. 1Ch 22:7
not build a temple for **w** me, ... 1Ch 28:3
a temple for **w** the LORD my God, ... 2Ch 2:4
the places for **w** gods and the 2Ch 17:6
things for **w** the Baal idols....................... 2Ch 24:7
leaders stopped **w** in the Temple 2Ch 24:18
LORD and stopped **w** at the Temple 2Ch 29:6
and places for **w** gods in all of 2Ch 31:1
places he built for **w** gods and 2Ch 33:19
the places for **w** gods, the 2Ch 34:3
thought about the **w** the sun in its .... Job 31:26
They joined in **w** Baal at Peor................... Ps 106:28
of you will stop **w** idols of gold .... Is 31:7

Sennacherib was **w** in the temple .... Is 37:38
I am **w** a block of wood!" .... Is 44:19
people make me angry by **w** idols,........... Je 8:19
because you sinned by **w** there. .... Je 17:3
angry by **w** idols that are the .... Je 25:6
me angry by **w** idols that were .... Je 25:7
me angry by **w** idols made with .... Je 32:30
incense and **w** other gods that .... Je 44:3
east and were **w** the sun in the .... Eze 8:16
answer them myself for **w** idols............... Eze 14:4
and lives, and stop **w** idols...................... Eze 14:6
unclean by **w** their idols........................ Eze 23:30
sins and the sin of **w** idols...................... Eze 23:49
Peor, they began **w** an idol, and .... Hos 9:10
But they sinned by **w** Baal, ... Hos 13:1
are guilty of **w** their own .... Hab 1:11
bowing on their knees and **w** him. .... Mk 15:19
from Galilee while they were **w**............... Lk 13:1
try to stop them from **w** the sun, ... Ac 7:42
They were all **w** the Lord and.................. Ac 13:2
w gods, doing witchcraft, hating, ... Gal 5:20
you stopped **w** idols and began 1Th 1:9
did not stop **w** demons and idols .... Rev 9:20
and count the people **w** there. .... Rev 11:1

WORSHIPS

mother Jezebel **w** idols and uses 2Ki 9:22
The heavenly army **w** you. .... Ne 9:6
All the earth **w** you and sings.................. Ps 66:4
to make a god, and then he **w** it! .... Is 44:15
He bows down to it and **w** it. .... Is 44:17
No one **w** you or even asks you to .... Is 64:7
to anyone who **w** and obeys him. .... Jn 9:31
to arrest everyone who **w** you." .... Ac 9:14
a good man; he **w** God. All the .... Ac 10:22
anyone who **w** him and does what .... Ac 10:35
in Asia and the whole world **w**.".............. Ac 19:27
If anyone **w** the beast and his .... Rev 14:9

WORTH

the land is **w** ten pounds of..................... Ge 23:15
as much as the object is **w**...................... Ex 22:9
it and that is **w** the correct .... Le 5:18
it and that is **w** the correct .... Le 6:6
But you're **w** ten thousand of us! 2Sa 18:3
I will pay you what it is **w**." 1Ki 21:2
wise sayings are **w** no more than .... Job 13:12
that my words are **w** nothing?" .... Job 24:25
jasper are not **w** talking about, ... Job 28:18
at wisdom and decided its **w**; .... Job 28:27
They are **w** more than gold, ... Ps 19:10
think we are **w** no more than .... Ps 44:22
teachings are **w** more to me than .... Ps 119:72
Wisdom is **w** more than silver; .... Pr 3:14
thoughts are **w** very little. .... Pr 10:20
because she is **w** more than .... Pr 31:10
which are **w** about twenty-five .... Is 7:23
so their words are **w** nothing.................. Is 8:20
all the nations are **w** nothing;................. Is 40:17
judges of this world **w** nothing. .... Is 40:23
do anything; they are **w** nothing. .... Is 41:29
idols, but they are **w** nothing. .... Is 44:9
will decide what my work is **w**; .... Is 49:4
God for idols **w** nothing......................... Je 2:11
of other people are **w** nothing .... Je 10:3
They are **w** nothing; people make .... Je 10:15
if you speak things that have **w**, ... Je 15:19
They are **w** nothing; people make .... Je 51:18
they were false and **w** nothing. .... La 2:14
shekel will be **w** twenty gerahs, ... Eze 45:12
a mina will be **w** sixty shekels. .... Eze 45:12
of Gilead are evil, **w** nothing. .... Hos 12:11
comfort they give is **w** nothing. .... Zch 10:2
how little they thought I was **w**. .... Zch 11:13

WORTHLESS

unclean, and the food has no **w**.' .... Mal 1:12
that you are **w** much more than .... Mt 6:26
You are **w** much more than many .... Mt 10:31
little children are **w** nothing. .... Mt 18:10
pay you what your work is **w**.' .... Mt 20:4
the Israelites thought he was **w**. .... Mt 27:9
which were only **w** a few cents. .... Mk 12:42
It was **w** a full year's work....................... Mk 14:5
You are **w** much more than many .... Lk 12:7
you are **w** much more than birds. .... Lk 12:24
myself, that honor is **w** nothing................ Jn 8:54
perfume was **w** an entire year's .... Jn 12:5
Those books were **w** about fifty .... Ac 19:19
think we are **w** no more than .... Rm 8:36
then our preaching is **w** nothing, ... 1Co 15:14
and your faith is **w** nothing. 1Co 15:14
I am **w** nothing, but those "great 2Co 12:11
are not **w** any more than I 2Co 12:11
Their thoughts are **w** nothing. .... Eph 4:17
which are not **w** anything. .... Eph 5:11
think they are **w** nothing because .... Php 3:7
things are **w** nothing compared .... Php 3:8
things are **w** nothing and will................. Tit 3:9
Lord's discipline is **w** nothing, ... Heb 12:5
Their "religion" is **w** nothing................. Jam 1:26
their faith is **w** nothing. .... Jam 2:14
needs, your words are **w** nothing. .... Jam 2:16
that does nothing is **w** nothing? .... Jam 2:20
of faith is **w** more than gold, ... 1Pe 1:7
This stone is **w** much to you who 1Pe 2:7

WORTHLESS

jealous and **w** idols to make me .... Dt 32:21
used the silver to hire some **w**, ... Jdg 9:4
There some **w** men began to follow .... Jdg 11:3
You son of a wicked, **w** woman! 1Sa 20:30
attention to this **w** man Nabal. 1Sa 25:25
angry because of their **w** idols. 1Ki 16:13
because they worshiped **w** idols. 1Ki 16:26
Then **w**, evil men joined Jeroboam 2Ch 13:7
You are **w** doctors, all of you! .... Job 13:4
They are **w** people without names .... Job 30:8
kings, 'You are **w**,' or to .... Job 34:18
me from looking at **w** things. .... Ps 119:37
bringing me **w** sacrifices! .... Is 1:13
take all the **w** things out of you .... Is 1:25
come from **w** wooden idols. .... Je 10:8
idolatries, **w** magic, and their .... Je 14:14
burn incense to **w** idols and have .... Je 18:15
Their worship of me is **w**. .... Mt 15:9
It is **w** to have the whole world .... Mt 16:26
Their worship of me is **w**. .... Mk 7:7
It is **w** to have the whole world .... Mk 8:36
It is **w** to have the whole world .... Lk 9:25
from these **w** things and turn .... Ac 14:15
have their own **w** thinking and to .... Rm 1:28
the law, then faith is **w**. .... Rm 4:14
God's promise to Abraham is **w**,.............. Rm 4:14
and now I know they are **w** trash. .... Php 3:8
who talk about **w** things and lead .... Tit 1:10
grows thorns and weeds and is **w**. .... Heb 6:8
past you were living in a **w** way,.............. 1Pe 1:18

WORTHY

I am not **w** of the kindness and .... Ge 32:10
because he is **w** of great honor. .... Ex 15:1
because he is **w** of great honor; .... Ex 15:21
is guilty of a sin **w** of death, ... Dt 21:22
has not done a sin **w** of death. .... Dt 22:26
I am not **w** of a reward from you, ... 2Sa 19:36
LORD, who is **w** of praise, and I................ 2Sa 22:4
best and most **w** person among 2Ki 10:3
I am not **w**; I cannot answer you .... Job 40:4
LORD, who is **w** of praise, and I................ Ps 18:3

is great and **w** of our praise; .... Ps 145:3
I am not **w** for you to come into .... Mt 8:8
some **w** person there and stay .... Mt 10:11
love me are not **w** to be my...................... Mt 10:37
me are not **w** to be my followers. .... Mt 10:37
and follow me is not **w** of me................... Mt 10:38
but they were not **w** to come. .... Mt 22:8
This officer is **w** of your help.................. Lk 7:4
I am not **w** to have you come .... Lk 7:6
I am no longer **w** to be called .... Lk 15:19
I am no longer **w** to be called .... Lk 15:21
those who will be **w** to be raised .... Lk 20:35
them, the one **w** of destruction, ... Jn 17:12
I am not **w** to untie his sandals. .... Ac 13:25
yourselves not **w** of having .... Ac 13:46
no charge was **w** of jail or death .... Ac 23:29
show they are **w** of that trust................... 1Co 4:2
way that is not **w** of it will be 1Co 11:27
that are good and **w** of praise. .... Php 4:8
to be counted **w** of his kingdom 2Th 1:5
their trip in a way **w** of God. 3Jn 1:6
clothes, because they are **w**. .... Rev 3:4
You are **w**, our Lord and God, to .... Rev 4:11
Who is **w** to break the seals and............... Rev 5:2
no one who was **w** to open the .... Rev 5:4
You are **w** to take the scroll and .... Rev 5:9
was killed is **w** to receive power.............. Rev 5:12

WOULDN'T

It **w** be right to do that, ... Ex 8:26
I **w** harm the LORD's appointed 1Sa 26:23
I **w** touch the king's son even if 2Sa 18:12
I **w** even look at you or notice 2Ki 3:14
great thing, **w** you have done it 2Ki 5:13
You **w** kill people whom you 2Ki 6:22
You **w** let the Israelites enter 2Ch 20:10
spoke to you, but you **w** listen. .... Is 65:12
w the land become completely .... Je 3:1
but they **w** listen or learn. .... Je 32:33
Anyone who **w** do this was to be .... Da 3:11
has roared! Who **w** be afraid? The .... Am 3:8
' But they **w** listen or pay .... Zch 1:4
He **w** accept you," says the LORD .... Mal 1:8
we **w** have brought him to you.".............. Jn 18:30

WOUND

burn for burn, **w** for wound, and .... Ex 21:25
burn, wound for **w**, and bruise .... Ex 21:25
not fail to **w** many strong men 2Sa 1:22
heal from the **w** he had received 2Ki 8:29
My **w** cannot be healed. .... Je 10:19
people have a **w** that cannot be .... Je 30:12
colors, and tightly **w** ropes...................... Eze 27:24
Samaria's **w** cannot be healed .... Mic 1:9
Nothing can heal your **w**; .... Nah 3:19
as if it had been killed by a **w**, ... Rev 13:3
but this death **w** was healed. .... Rev 13:3
had the death **w** that was healed. .... Rev 13:12

WOUNDED

shot him, and he was badly **w**. 1Sa 31:3
The Arameans **w** Joram......................... 2Ki 8:28
Jezreel, because he had been **w**............... 2Ki 8:29
Ahaziah was **w** in his chariot on 2Ki 9:27
him with their arrows and **w** him. 1Ch 10:3
The Arameans **w** Joram......................... 2Ch 22:5
Jezreel because he had been **w**. 2Ch 22:6
left, Joash was badly **w**. 2Ch 24:25
me away because I am badly **w**." 2Ch 35:23
Your arrows have **w** me, and your .... Ps 38:2
the pain of those you have **w**. .... Ps 69:26
But he was **w** for the wrong we .... Is 53:5
W people will cry with pain all .... Je 51:52
They faint like **w** soldiers in .... La 2:12
Those who are **w** in Sidon will .... Eze 28:23

He has **w** us, but he will bandage .... Hos 6:1
farmers **w** him and threw him out............ Lk 20:12
the one that was **w** by the deadly .... Rev 13:14

WOUNDING
a man for **w** me, a young man .... Ge 4:23

WOUNDS
heal from the **w** he received at 2Ch 22:6
and multiply my **w** for no reason. .... Job 9:17
Because of my **w**, my friends and .... Ps 38:11
over my back, making long **w**. .... Ps 129:3
and bandages their **w**. .... Ps 147:3
covered with **w**, hurts, and open............ Is 1:6
we are healed because of his **w**. .... Is 53:5
and your **w** will quickly heal. .... Is 58:8
as if they were small **w**. .... Je 6:14
as if they were small **w**. .... Je 8:11
its illness and Judah saw its **w**, ... Hos 5:13
cannot heal you or cure your **w**. .... Hos 5:13
but he will bandage our **w**. .... Hos 6:1
olive oil and wine on his **w**, ... Lk 10:34
and Silas and washed their **w**. .... Ac 16:33
you are healed because of his **w**. 1Pe 2:24

WOVE
They **w** inner robes of fine linen............ Ex 39:27
Delilah **w** the seven braids of .... Jdg 16:13
women of Jerusalem **w** with love. .... Sng 3:10

WOVEN
an outer robe, a **w** inner robe, a .... Ex 28:4
above the **w** belt of the holy .... Ex 28:27
it to the **w** belt so the chest............ Ex 28:28
with a **w** collar around the hole .... Ex 28:32
Make the **w** inner robe of fine .... Ex 28:39
Also make **w** inner robes, cloth .... Ex 28:40
him with its skillfully **w** belt. .... Ex 29:5
They will make the **w** clothes and .... Ex 31:10
red thread to make **w** clothes for .... Ex 39:1
The skillfully **w** belt was made .... Ex 39:5
above the **w** belt of the holy .... Ex 39:20
connecting it to the **w** belt. .... Ex 39:21
It was **w** only of blue cloth............ Ex 39:22
with a **w** collar sewn around it .... Ex 39:23
the skillfully **w** belt around him .... Le 8:7
(either **w** or knitted), or of .... Le 13:48
w or knitted material is green .... Le 13:49
the cloth (either **w** or knitted)............ Le 13:51
matter if it is **w** or knitted, ... Le 13:52
either knitted or **w**) or leather, ... Le 13:53
or cloth (either **w** or knitted). .... Le 13:56
or cloth (either **w** or knitted), ... Le 13:57
the cloth (either **w** or knitted) .... Le 13:58
cloth (either **w** or knitted) or .... Le 13:59
of wool and linen **w** together. .... Dt 22:11
of its thighs are **w** together. .... Job 40:17
Her gown is **w** with gold. .... Ps 45:13
rope that is **w** of three strings............ Ec 4:12
piece of cloth, **w** from top to .... Jn 19:23

WRAP
Then they must **w** everything in .... Nu 4:10
Holy Place and **w** them in a blue .... Nu 4:12
They **w** their roots around a pile .... Job 8:17
clothes and **w** around him like .... Ps 109:19
too narrow to **w** around himself. .... Is 28:20
will **w** Egypt around him. .... Je 43:12

WRAPPED
w the bowls for making dough .... Ex 12:34
It is **w** in a cloth behind the 1Sa 21:9
The ropes of death **w** around me. 2Sa 22:6
prophet **w** his face in a cloth 1Ki 20:38
for the sea and **w** it in dark .... Job 38:9
The ropes of death **w** around me. .... Ps 18:5
for punishing and **w** himself in .... Is 59:17

salvation and **w** me with a coat .... Is 61:10
As a belt is **w** tightly around a .... Je 13:11
I **w** the families of Israel and .... Je 13:11
You **w** yourself in anger and .... La 3:43
You **w** yourself in a cloud, ... La 3:44
rubbed with salt or **w** in cloths. .... Eze 16:4
w you in fine linen and covered .... Eze 16:10
has not been **w** with a bandage, ... Eze 30:21
of fine gold **w** around his waist. .... Da 10:5
seaweed was **w** around my head. .... Jnh 2:5
the body and **w** it in a clean .... Mt 27:59
cross, and **w** it in the linen............ Mk 15:46
she **w** the baby with pieces of............ Lk 2:7
will find a baby **w** in pieces of .... Lk 2:12
your coin which I **w** in a piece .... Lk 19:20
from the cross, **w** it in cloth, ... Lk 23:53
that Jesus' body had been **w** .... Lk 24:12
his hands and feet he **w** with pieces .... Jn 11:44
a towel, he **w** it around his .... Jn 13:4
the towel that was **w** around him. .... Jn 13:5
Jesus' body and **w** it with the .... Jn 19:40
he **w** his coat around himself............ Jn 21:7

WRAPS
He **w** up the waters in his thick .... Job 26:8
As a shepherd **w** himself in his .... Je 43:12

WRECK
W all of their places of worship............ Nu 33:52

WRECKED
the ships were **w** at Ezion Geber, ... 1Ki 22:48
The ships were **w** so they could 2Ch 20:37
the enemy **w** everything in the .... Ps 74:3
sea on the day your ship was **w**............ Eze 27:27
times I was in ships that **w**, ... 2Co 11:25

WRESTLED
a man came and **w** with him until .... Ge 32:24
because you have **w** with God and .... Ge 32:28
grew to be a man, he **w** with God. .... Hos 12:3
When Jacob **w** with the angel and .... Hos 12:4

WRISTS
you from the chains on your **w**. .... Je 40:4
charms on their **w** and make veils .... Eze 13:18
bracelets on the **w** of the two .... Eze 23:42

WRITE
W about this battle in a book so............ Ex 17:14
two onyx stones and **w** the names .... Ex 28:9
W the names in order, from the .... Ex 28:10
and I will **w** the same words on .... Ex 34:1
said to Moses, "**W** down these .... Ex 34:27
The priest should **w** these curses .... Nu 5:23
W the name of each man on his .... Nu 17:2
stick from Levi, **w** Aaron's name. .... Nu 17:3
W them down and tie them to your .... Dt 6:8
and **w** them on your doors and .... Dt 6:9
I will **w** on the tablets the same .... Dt 10:2
W them down and tie them to your .... Dt 11:18
W them on your doors and gates .... Dt 11:20
he should **w** a copy of the .... Dt 17:18
w all the words of these .... Dt 27:3
Then **w** clearly all the words of .... Dt 27:8
Now **w** down this song and teach .... Dt 31:19
let the king **w** us and tell us .... Ezr 5:17
w another order to the Jewish .... Est 8:8
You **w** down cruel things against .... Job 13:26
one who accuses me **w** it down. .... Job 31:35
W these things for the future so .... Ps 102:18
W them on your heart as if on a............ Pr 3:3
w them on your heart as if on a .... Pr 7:3
right words to **w** what is .... Ec 12:10
a large scroll and **w** on it with .... Is 8:1
and those who **w** laws that make .... Is 10:1
Now **w** this on a sign for the .... Is 30:8

for the people, **w** this on a .... Is 30:8
W this down in the record about .... Je 22:30
w in a book all the words I have .... Je 30:2
their minds and **w** them on their .... Je 31:33
W on it all the words I have .... Je 36:2
W everything from when I first .... Je 36:2
you **w** down what Jeremiah said .... Je 36:17
W all the words on it that were .... Je 36:28
did you **w** on it 'the king of.................... Je 36:29
Human, **w** down today's date, this .... Eze 24:2
take a stick and **w** on it, ' .... Eze 37:16
another stick and **w** on it, ' .... Eze 37:16
W the rules as they watch so .... Eze 43:11
answered me: "**W** down the vision; .... Hab 2:2
w it clearly on clay tablets so .... Hab 2:2
allowed a man to **w** out divorce .... Mk 10:4
good for me to **w** it out for you. .... Lk 1:3
and **w** four hundred gallons.' .... Lk 16:6
your bill and **w** eight hundred .... Lk 16:7
Pilate, "Don't **w**, 'The King of .... Jn 19:21
But **w**, 'This man said, "I am .... Jn 19:21
asked him to **w** letters to the .... Ac 9:2
we should **w** a letter to them .... Ac 15:20
definite to **w** the emperor about .... Ac 25:26
him and give me something to **w**. .... Ac 25:26
Now I **w** about people who are not........... 1Co 7:25
Now I will **w** about meat that is 1Co 8:1
I will **w** about the collection 1Co 16:1
I did not **w** to make you sad, ... 2Co 2:4
do not need to **w** you about this 2Co 9:1
these things I **w** are not lies. .... Gal 1:20
letters I use to **w** this myself. .... Gal 6:11
for me to **w** the same things .... Php 3:1
greet you and **w** this with my own .... Col 4:18
do not need to **w** you about 1Th 4:9
do not need to **w** you about times 1Th 5:1
from me. This is the way I **w**. 2Th 3:17
w this letter, knowing that you .... Phm 1:21
their minds and **w** them on their .... Heb 8:10
their hearts and **w** them on their .... Heb 10:16
We **w** you now about what has 1Jn 1:1
We **w** to you about the Word that 1Jn 1:1
We **w** this to you so we may be 1Jn 1:4
I **w** this letter to you so you 1Jn 2:1
I **w** to you, dear children, ... 1Jn 2:12
I **w** to you, fathers, because you 1Jn 2:13
w to you, young people, because 1Jn 2:13
w to you, children, because you 1Jn 2:14
I **w** to you, fathers, because you 1Jn 2:14
w to you, young people, because 1Jn 2:14
I do not **w** to you because you do 1Jn 2:21
I **w** this letter to you who 1Jn 5:13
I have many things to **w** to you, ... 2Jn 1:12
many things I want to **w** you, ... 3Jn 1:13
wanted very much to **w** you about .... Jud 1:3
I felt the need to **w** you about .... Jud 1:3
W what you see in a book and .... Rev 1:11
So **w** the things you see, what is .... Rev 1:19
W this to the angel of the .... Rev 2:1
W this to the angel of the .... Rev 2:8
W this to the angel of the .... Rev 2:12
W this to the angel of the .... Rev 2:18
W this to the angel of the .... Rev 3:1
W this to the angel of the .... Rev 3:7
I will **w** them the name of my .... Rev 3:12
will also **w** on them my new name. .... Rev 3:12
W this to the angel of the .... Rev 3:14
thunders spoke, I started to **w**. .... Rev 10:4
said, and do not **w** them down." .... Rev 10:4
from heaven saying, "**W** this: .... Rev 14:13
the angel said to me, "**W** this:.............. Rev 19:9
Then he said, "**W** this, because .... Rev 21:5

WRITER
is like the pen of a skilled **w**. .... Ps 45:1

WRITES
He **w** out divorce papers for her, ... Dt 24:1
So he **w** out divorce papers for .... Dt 24:3
Moses **w** about being made right .... Rm 10:5
He **w** about this in all his 2Pe 3:16

WRITING
Moses finished **w** all the words .... Dt 31:24
describe in **w** the land their .... Jos 18:4
parts of land in **w** and bring .... Jos 18:6
the land and describe it in **w**. .... Jos 18:8
kingdom and to put it in **w**..................... Ezr 1:1
we are **w** to let the king know. .... Ezr 4:14
we are making an agreement in **w**,........... Ne 9:38
kingdom in the **w** of each state .... Est 1:22
written in the **w** of each state .... Est 3:12
wrote in the **w** of each state .... Est 8:9
in their own **w** and language.................. Est 8:9
w them a message of peace and .... Est 9:30
would wear the **w** on my shoulder .... Job 31:36
People are always **w** books, ... Ec 12:12
in linen with a **w** case at his .... Eze 9:2
who had the **w** case at his side. .... Eze 9:3
linen with the **w** case at his .... Eze 9:11
and began **w** on the plaster .... Da 5:5
can read this **w** and explain it .... Da 5:7
not read the **w** or tell the king .... Da 5:8
you what the **w** on the wall means .... Da 5:12
me to read this **w** and to explain .... Da 5:15
Read this **w** on the wall and .... Da 5:16
will read the **w** on the wall for .... Da 5:17
asked for a **w** tablet and wrote, ... Lk 1:63
over and started **w** on the ground .... Jn 8:6
I am **w** this letter from Paul. .... Rm 16:22
am **w** this to give you a warning 1Co 4:14
I am **w** to tell you that you must.............. 1Co 5:11
And I am not **w** this now to get 1Co 9:15
that what I am **w** to you is the 1Co 14:37
am **w** this greeting with my own 1Co 16:21
I am **w** this while I am away from 2Co 13:10
I am **w** these things to you now. 1Ti 3:14
am **w** this with my own hand. .... Phm 1:19
I am not **w** a new command to you 1Jn 2:7
But also I am **w** a new command to 1Jn 2:8
I am **w** this letter about those 1Jn 2:26
The scroll had **w** on both sides .... Rev 5:1

WRITINGS
Those **w** tell what David did as 1Ch 29:30
recorded in the **w** of the prophet 2Ch 13:22
songs, sad **w**, and words about .... Eze 2:10
the language and **w** of the .... Da 1:4
law and the **w** of the prophets .... Mt 22:40
Moses and the **w** of the prophets .... Lk 16:16
Moses and the **w** of the prophets .... Lk 16:29
Moses and the **w** of the prophets .... Ac 13:15
of Moses and the prophets' **w**, ... Ac 28:23
through the **w** of the prophets. .... Rm 16:26

WRITTEN
commands I have **w** to instruct .... Ex 24:12
with the Agreement **w** on them, ... Ex 31:18
written on them, **w** by the finger .... Ex 31:18
commands were **w** on both sides .... Ex 32:15
God himself had **w** the commands .... Ex 32:16
which you have **w** the names of .... Ex 32:32
had the Agreement **w** on them .... Ex 40:20
which God had **w** on with his own .... Dt 9:10
these tablets he had **w** before— .... Dt 10:4
that are **w** in this book. .... Dt 28:58
and sickness not **w** in this Book .... Dt 28:61
all the curses **w** in this book .... Dt 29:20

your names are **w** in heaven." .... Lk 10:20
said, "What is **w** in the law? .... Lk 10:26
It is **w** in the Scriptures, ... Lk 19:46
all that is **w** in the Scriptures .... Lk 21:22
It was **w** about me, and it is .... Lk 22:37
of the cross these words were **w**: .... Lk 23:38
that had been **w** about himself .... Lk 24:27
that everything **w** about me must .... Lk 24:44
It is **w** that the Christ would .... Lk 24:46
what was **w** in the Scriptures: .... Jn 2:17
This is **w** in the Scriptures: ' .... Jn 6:31
It is **w** in the prophets, 'They .... Jn 6:45
It is **w** in your law that God .... Jn 10:34
this had been **w** about him and .... Jn 12:16
so that what is **w** in their law .... Jn 15:25
The sign was **w** in Hebrew, in .... Jn 19:20
What I have **w**, I have written." .... Jn 19:22
What I have written, I have **w**." .... Jn 19:22
that are not **w** in this book .... Jn 20:30
But these are **w** so that you may .... Jn 20:31
and who has now **w** them down. .... Jn 21:24
every one of them were **w** down, ... Jn 21:25
all the books that would be **w**. .... Jn 21:25
Psalms," Peter said, "this is **w**: .... Ac 1:20
' And it is also **w**: ' .... Ac 1:20
This is what is **w** in the book of .... Ac 7:42
that had these words **w** on it: .... Ac 17:23
It is **w** in the Scriptures, ' .... Ac 23:5
Moses and that is **w** in the books .... Ac 24:14
it is **w** in the Holy Scriptures. .... Rm 1:2
You Jews have the **w** law and .... Rm 2:27
by the Spirit, not by the **w** law. .... Rm 2:29
As it is **w** in the Scriptures: .... Rm 4:17
were **w** not only for Abraham .... Rm 4:23
not in the old way with **w** rules. .... Rm 7:6
As it is **w** in the Scriptures, ... Rm 8:36
As it is **w** in the Scripture: .... Rm 9:33
It is **w**, "How beautiful is the .... Rm 10:15
As it is **w** in the Scriptures: .... Rm 11:8
It is **w** in the Scriptures: .... Rm 11:26
anger. It is **w**: "I will punish .... Rm 12:19
because it is **w** in the .... Rm 14:11
that was **w** in the past was .... Rm 15:4
in the past was **w** to teach us. .... Rm 15:4
It is **w** in the Scriptures: .... Rm 15:9
But I have **w** to you very openly .... Rm 15:15
But it is **w** in the Scriptures: .... Rm 15:21
It is **w** in the Scriptures: 1Co 1:19
as it is **w** in the Scriptures: 1Co 2:9
It is **w** in the Scriptures, ... 1Co 3:19
It is also **w** in the Scriptures, ... 1Co 3:20
what is **w** in the Scriptures. 1Co 4:6
It is **w** in the Scriptures, ... 1Co 6:16
It is **w** in the law of Moses: 1Co 9:9
that Scripture was **w** for us, ... 1Co 9:10
Just as it is **w** in the 1Co 10:7
They were **w** down to teach us, ... 1Co 10:11
It is **w** in the Scriptures: 1Co 14:21
It is **w** in the Scriptures: 1Co 15:45
are our letter, **w** on our hearts, ... 2Co 3:2
letter is not **w** with ink but 2Co 3:3
It is not **w** on stone tablets but 2Co 3:3
new agreement is not a **w** law, ... 2Co 3:6
The **w** law brings death, but the 2Co 3:6
death was **w** in words on stone 2Co 3:7
It is **w** in the Scriptures, ... 2Co 4:13
As it is **w** in the Scriptures, ... 2Co 8:15
It is **w** in the Scriptures: 2Co 9:9
always obey what is **w** in the .... Gal 3:10
It is **w** in the Scriptures, ... Gal 3:13
It is **w** in the Scriptures: .... Gal 4:27
already **w** a little about this. .... Eph 3:3
whose names are **w** in the book of ...... Php 4:3

These words are **w** on the seal: 2Ti 2:19
the ones **w** on parchment. 2Ti 4:13
It is **w** in the Scriptures, ... Heb 2:6
It is **w** about me in the book. .... Heb 10:7
whose names are **w** in heaven. .... Heb 12:23
message I have **w** to encourage .... Heb 13:22
It is **w** in the Scriptures: 1Pe 1:16
letter I have **w** you to help your 2Pe 3:1
message and do what is **w** in it. .... Rev 1:3
stone with a new name **w** on it. .... Rev 2:17
against God was **w** on each head. .... Rev 13:1
names are not **w** in the Lamb's .... Rev 13:8
his Father's name **w** on their .... Rev 14:1
with names against God **w** on it, ... Rev 17:3
a title was **w** that was secret. .... Rev 17:5
This is what was **w**: THE GREAT .... Rev 17:5
have not been **w** in the book of .... Rev 17:8
He has a name **w** on him, which no .... Rev 19:12
his upper leg was **w** this name: .... Rev 19:16
done, which was **w** in the books. .... Rev 20:12
name was not found **w** in the book .... Rev 20:15
each gate was **w** the name of one .... Rev 21:12
on the stones were **w** the names .... Rev 21:14
whose names are **w** in the Lamb's .... Rev 21:27
his name will be **w** on their .... Rev 22:4
disasters **w** about in this book. .... Rev 22:18
which are **w** about in this book. .... Rev 22:19

WRONG

know I was doing anything **w**." .... Ge 20:5
What **w** did I do against you? .... Ge 20:9
make up for any **w** that people .... Ge 20:16
He said, "What is **w**, Hagar? .... Ge 21:17
seen all the **w** things Laban has .... Ge 31:12
and said, "What **w** have I done? .... Ge 31:36
It was **w** for him to have sexual .... Ge 34:7
You are doing it **w**, Father. .... Ge 48:18
We did many **w** things to him. .... Ge 50:15
'You have done **w** and have sinned .... Ge 50:17
we beg you to forgive our **w**. .... Ge 50:17
to the one that was in the **w**, ... Ex 2:13
I and my people are in the **w**. .... Ex 9:27
male that has nothing **w** with it. .... Ex 12:5
You must not do **w** just because .... Ex 23:2
if anything is **w** with the gifts .... Ex 28:38
be guilty of **w**, and they will .... Ex 28:43
that have nothing **w** with them. .... Ex 29:1
people are always ready to do **w**, ... Ex 32:22
male that has nothing **w** with it. .... Le 1:3
male that has nothing **w** with it. .... Le 1:10
it must have nothing **w** with it. .... Le 3:1
it must have nothing **w** with it. .... Le 3:6
one that has nothing **w** with it, ... Le 4:3
that has nothing **w** with it as .... Le 4:23
that has nothing **w** with it as .... Le 4:28
that has nothing **w** with it. .... Le 4:32
that has nothing **w** with it. .... Le 5:15
has nothing **w** with it and that .... Le 5:18
The person is guilty of doing **w**, ... Le 5:19
have anything **w** with it and that .... Le 6:6
that have nothing **w** with them, ... Le 9:2
it must have nothing **w** with it. .... Le 9:3
that have nothing **w** with them .... Le 14:10
lamb that has nothing **w** with it .... Le 14:10
by any of these **w** things. .... Le 18:24
your neighbor does something **w**, ... Le 19:17
about the **w** things people do .... Le 19:18
have something **w** with them, ... Le 21:17
has something **w** with him must .... Le 21:18
something **w** with their eyes, ... Le 21:20
has something **w** with him, ... Le 21:21
He has something **w** with him; .... Le 21:21
he has something **w** with him. .... Le 21:23

things the LORD said were w, ... 2Ch 33:6
of Judah and Jerusalem to do w. 2Ch 33:9
He did what the LORD said was w, ... 2Ch 33:22
the LORD his God said was w. 2Ch 36:5
He did what the LORD said was w. 2Ch 36:9
the LORD his God said was w. 2Ch 36:12
has not done w to the king alone .... Est 1:16
She has also done w to all the .... Est 1:16
Show me where I have been w. .... Job 6:24
difference between right and w. .... Job 6:30
does not make w what is right. .... Job 8:3
my own mouth would say I was w;........... Job 9:20
No one can accuse me of doing w. .... Job 13:19
Show me my w and my sin. .... Job 13:23
and this shows I have done w. .... Job 16:8
are upset with those who do w. .... Job 17:8
thoughts and your plans to w me. .... Job 21:27
God accuses no one of doing w. .... Job 24:12
not true, who can prove I am w? .... Job 24:25
my foes like those who are w............... Job 27:7
and disaster for those who do w. .... Job 31:3
will know I have done nothing w. .... Job 31:6
has been led by my eyes to do w, ... Job 31:7
answer to show that Job was w, ... Job 32:3
not one of you has proved Job w; .... Job 32:12
only God will show Job to be w,............ Job 32:13
away from doing w and to keep .... Job 33:17
God can never do w! It is .... Job 34:10
Truly God will never do w; .... Job 34:12
If I have done w, I will not do .... Job 34:32
say to God, 'You have done w.' .... Job 36:23
Have my hands done something w? .... Ps 7:3
Have I done w to my friend or .... Ps 7:4
I have done no w, God Most High. .... Ps 7:8
everyone loves what is w. .... Ps 12:8
They do no w to their neighbors.............. Ps 15:3
me without finding anything w; .... Ps 17:3
the sins and w things I did when .... Ps 25:7
hands, and they do w for money. .... Ps 26:10
be jealous of those who do w,................ Ps 37:1
than to have much and be w. .... Ps 37:16
I have done what you say is w. .... Ps 51:4
your ways to those who do w,................ Ps 51:13
You love w more than right and .... Ps 52:3
but I have not sinned or done w, ... Ps 59:3
have done nothing w, but they .... Ps 59:4
encourage each other to do w. .... Ps 64:5
you know what I have done w; .... Ps 69:5
I kept my hands from doing w? .... Ps 73:13
Rock, and there is no w in him. .... Ps 92:15
who want to do w stay away from .... Ps 101:4
did. We have done w; we have .... Ps 106:6
They don't do what is w; .... Ps 119:3
suffered, I did w, but now I...................Ps 119:67
leave me to those who do w me. .... Ps 119:121
Don't let proud people w me. .... Ps 119:122
or to join others in doing w. .... Ps 141:4
enjoy doing w and are happy to .... Pr 2:14
they do is w, and their ways .... Pr 2:15
the LORD and refuse to do w. .... Pr 3:7
The LORD hates those who do w, ... Pr 3:32
even know that her ways are w. .... Pr 5:6
accept no payment for the w; .... Pr 6:35
words she led him into doing w............... Pr 7:21
gotten by doing w have no value, ... Pr 10:2
A foolish person enjoys doing w, ... Pr 10:23
person is easily led to do w. .... Pr 12:26
can't be paid to do w will live. .... Pr 15:27
Kings hate those who do w, ... Pr 16:12
neighbors and lead them to do w. .... Pr 16:29
grins is planning something w. .... Pr 16:30
money to do w there can be no .... Pr 17:23
I have never done anything w." .... Pr 20:9

pay you back for the w you did." .... Pr 20:22
offer them for the w reasons. .... Pr 21:27
when your neighbor proves you w? .... Pr 25:8
people to do w will be ruined .... Pr 28:10
understanding will prove them w. .... Pr 28:11
says, "It's not w," is just like .... Pr 28:24
'I haven't done anything w.' .... Pr 30:20
have been right, there was w. .... Ec 3:16
even knowing you are doing w. .... Ec 5:1
something else w here on earth .... Ec 6:1
This is useless and very w. .... Ec 6:2
support something that is w, ... Ec 8:3
are right and those who are w, ... Ec 9:2
is something w that happens here .... Ec 9:3
the heart of a fool leads to w. .... Ec 10:2
something else w that happens .... Ec 10:5
is nothing at all w with you. .... Sng 4:7
I see you do. Stop doing w. .... Is 1:16
all accept money for doing w,............... Is 1:23
filled with w ideas from people .... Is 2:6
for all the w they have done. .... Is 3:11
lead you in the w way and turn .... Is 3:12
led them in the w direction, ... Is 9:16
the king of Egypt give w advice............... Is 19:11
lead that nation the w way. .... Is 19:13
Egypt to wander in the w ways, ... Is 19:14
What is w with you people? .... Is 22:1
People who do w will now .... Is 29:24
If you go the w way—to the right .... Is 30:21
that will lead them the w way. .... Is 30:28
and he says w things about the .... Is 32:6
mind leads him the w way. .... Is 44:20
wants to prove I have done w, ... Is 50:8
he was wounded for the w we did;........... Is 53:5
had done nothing w, and he had .... Is 53:9
who speak against you are w................... Is 54:17
The wicked should stop doing w, ... Is 55:7
your fingers you have done w. .... Is 59:3
have done many w things against .... Is 59:12
our sins show we are w. .... Is 59:12
and everything that is w......................... Is 61:8
made from meat that is w to eat. .... Is 65:4
and the w you have done will .... Je 2:19
is w not to fear me," says the .... Je 2:19
And when someone goes the w way, ... Je 8:4
gone the w way and not turned .... Je 8:5
have we done w? What sin have we .... Je 16:10
but something went w with it. .... Je 18:4
use their power in the w way................... Je 23:10
of Samaria do something w. .... Je 23:13
doing what is w so you can stay .... Je 25:5
tell what is w with all people .... Je 25:31
only the things I said were w................... Je 32:30
led them in the w way and made .... Je 50:6
enemies said, 'We did nothing w. .... Je 50:7
did what the LORD said was w, ... Je 52:2
and led me in the w direction. .... La 3:9
He led me the w way and let me............... La 3:11
my people the w way by saying,............... Eze 13:10
He keeps his hand from doing w. .... Eze 18:8
He keeps his hand from doing w. .... Eze 18:17
did what was w among his people .... Eze 18:18
good and do w and do the same .... Eze 18:24
people stop doing good and do w, ... Eze 18:26
will die, because they did w. .... Eze 18:26
will think this prediction is w, ... Eze 21:23
in you and w the orphans .... Eze 22:7
that has nothing w with it for a .... Eze 43:22
which have nothing w with them. .... Eze 43:23
which have nothing w with them. .... Eze 43:25
bull that has nothing w with it. .... Eze 45:18
that have nothing w with them. .... Eze 45:23
that have nothing w with them .... Eze 46:4

that has nothing w with it. .... Eze 46:4
bull that has nothing w with it. .... Eze 46:6
that have nothing w with them. .... Eze 46:6
that has nothing w with it for a .... Eze 46:13
men who had nothing w with them. .... Da 1:4
find anything w with him or any .... Da 6:4
I never did anything w to you, ... Da 6:22
But we have sinned and done w. .... Da 9:5
we have sinned and have done w. .... Da 9:15
priests are as w as the people, ... Hos 4:9
them for the w they have done. .... Hos 4:9
people who have done nothing w; .... Am 2:6
take money to do w, and you keep .... Am 5:12
who do not know right from w, ... Jnh 4:11
his people the w way of living: .... Mic 3:5
cheat others with w weights and .... Mic 6:11
make me see w things and make .... Hab 1:3
stand to see those who do w. .... Hab 1:13
that becomes rich by doing w, ... Hab 2:9
roof will agree that you are w. .... Hab 2:11
city. He does no w. Every .... Zph 3:5
Israel won't do w or tell lies; .... Zph 3:13
as sacrifices, that is w. .... Mal 1:8
and sick animals, that is w. .... Mal 1:8
that has something w with it. .... Mal 1:14
have caused many people to do w. .... Mal 2:8
do right and to those who do w. .... Mt 5:45
are not w for doing that. .... Mt 12:5
those who have done nothing w. .... Mt 12:7
faith, and your lives are all w. .... Mt 17:17
him in private what he did w. .... Mt 18:15
Jesus in saying something w. .... Mt 22:15
"Why? What w has he done?" .... Mt 27:23
trap him in saying something w. .... Mk 12:13
the dead. You Sadducees are w!" .... Mk 12:27
Jesus had done w so they could .... Mk 14:55
"Why? What w has he done?" .... Mk 15:14
faith, and your lives are all w. .... Lk 9:41
everyone who has done w to us. .... Lk 11:4
to catch him saying something w. .... Lk 11:54
Surely it is not w for her to be .... Lk 13:16
Is it right or w to heal on the .... Lk 14:3
saying something so they could .... Lk 20:20
to stand against or prove w. .... Lk 21:15
Herod found nothing w with him; .... Lk 23:15
them, "Why? What w has he done? .... Lk 23:22
this man has done nothing w." .... Lk 23:41
the Father and say you are w. .... Jn 5:45
one who says you are w is Moses, ... Jn 5:45
If people did w to me, they will .... Jn 15:20
me, they will do w to you, too. .... Jn 15:20
said something w, then show what .... Jn 18:23
What have you done w?" .... Jn 18:35
about a crime or some w. .... Ac 18:14
he was and what he had done w. .... Ac 21:33
We find nothing w with this man. .... Ac 23:9
things that were w by their own .... Ac 23:29
and many w things in our country .... Ac 24:2
I have really done anything w, ... Ac 24:19
if they found any w in me when I .... Ac 24:20
he has really done something w." .... Ac 25:5
done nothing w against the law, ... Ac 25:8
I have done nothing w to them; .... Ac 25:10
something w and the law says .... Ac 25:11
the evil and w things people do .... Rm 1:18
you can judge others, you are w. .... Rm 2:1
judges those who do w things, ... Rm 2:2
those who do w, but you do wrong. .... Rm 2:3
wrong, but you do w yourselves. .... Rm 2:3
they know what is right and w, ... Rm 2:15
thoughts tell them they did w, ... Rm 2:15
When we do w, that shows more .... Rm 3:5
say that God is w to punish us? .... Rm 3:5

but they are w and deserve the .... Rm 3:8
lives to do the w things your .... Rm 8:13
stop doing the w things you do .... Rm 8:13
If someone does w to you, do not .... Rm 12:17
pay him back by doing w to him. .... Rm 12:17
punish others when they w you, ... Rm 12:19
I will punish those who do w; .... Rm 12:19
only those who do w fear them. .... Rm 13:3
But if you do w, then be afraid. .... Rm 13:4
to punish those who do w. .... Rm 13:4
the one who eats all foods is w, ... Rm 14:3
is no food that is w to eat. .... Rm 14:14
person believes something is w, ... Rm 14:14
wrong, that thing is w for him. .... Rm 14:14
by eating food he thinks is w, ... Rm 14:15
but it is w to eat food that .... Rm 14:20
it is right are w because they .... Rm 14:23
there will be no w in you on the 1Co 1:8
I know of no w I have done, ... 1Co 4:4
you yourselves do w and cheat, ... 1Co 6:8
while thinking it is w to do so. 1Co 8:10
them to do what they feel is w, ... 1Co 8:12
it might be thought to be w. 1Co 10:28
I don't mean you think it is w, ... 1Co 10:29
We have not done w to anyone, ... 2Co 7:2
the one who did the w or because 2Co 7:12
Do you think that was w? 2Co 11:7
that you will not do anything w. 2Co 13:7
to his face, because he was w. .... Gal 2:11
would really be w to begin .... Gal 2:18
show that the w things people do .... Gal 3:19
w things the sinful self does .... Gal 5:19
that says these things are w. .... Gal 5:23
in your group does something w, ... Gal 6:1
into following the w path. .... Eph 4:14
But show that they are w. .... Eph 5:11
sin or any other w thing in it. .... Eph 5:27
and without w for the coming .... Php 1:10
for selfish and w reasons, ... Php 1:17
whether for right or w reasons, ... Php 1:18
be innocent and without any w. .... Php 2:15
holy, with no w, and with .... Col 1:22
someone does w to you, forgive .... Col 3:13
anyone who does w will be. .... Col 3:25
will be punished for that w, ... Col 3:25
not come from lies or w reasons, ... 1Th 2:3
do not w or cheat another 1Th 4:6
no one pays back w for wrong, ... 1Th 5:15
no one pays back wrong for w, ... 1Th 5:15
if you find nothing w in them. 1Ti 3:10
sinning that they are w. 1Ti 5:20
to do without w or blame until 1Ti 6:14
to the Lord must stop doing w." 2Ti 2:19
people what is w in their lives, ... 2Ti 3:16
Tell them when they are w. 2Ti 4:2
must not be guilty of doing w, ... Tit 1:6
must not be guilty of doing w, ... Tit 1:7
true teaching that they are w. .... Tit 1:9
and lead others into the w way— .... Tit 1:10
people they are w so they may .... Tit 1:13
them what is w in their lives, ... Tit 2:15
not obey, we were w, and we were .... Tit 3:3
their own sins prove them w. .... Tit 3:11
done anything w to you or if he .... Phm 1:18
and who are doing w things. .... Heb 5:2
been nothing w with the first .... Heb 8:7
something with his people .... Heb 8:8
I will punish those who do w; .... Heb 10:30
showed that the world was w, ... Heb 11:7
lead you into the w way. .... Heb 13:9
evil thing and every kind of w. .... Jam 1:21
If people never said anything w, ... Jam 3:2
because the reason you ask is w. .... Jam 4:3

All of this bragging is w. .... Jam 4:16
will be a proof that you were w. .... Jam 5:3
back from the w way will save .... Jam 5:20
might say that you are doing w. 1Pe 2:12
those who do w and to praise 1Pe 2:14
If you are beaten for doing w, ... 1Pe 2:20
Do not do w to repay a wrong, ... 1Pe 3:9
Do not do wrong to repay a w, ... 1Pe 3:9
than for doing w if that is what 1Pe 3:17
teach things that are w— 2Pe 2:1
loved being paid for doing w. 2Pe 2:15
lead you away by the w they do............... 2Pe 3:17
trying to lead you the w way. 1Jn 2:26
let anyone lead you the w way. 1Jn 3:7
Doing w is always sin, but there............... 1Jn 5:17
to doing the w that Balaam did. .... Jud 1:11
without any w in you and can .... Jud 1:24

WRONGED
it to the person who was w. .... Nu 5:7
that God has w me and pulled his .... Job 19:6
I shout, 'I have been w!' .... Job 19:7
for all who are w by others. .... Ps 103:6
fair for those who have been w. .... Ps 146:7
you have seen how I have been w. .... La 3:59
Why not let yourselves be w? 1Co 6:7

WRONGLY
what was false and led you w. .... La 2:14
their bodies w with each other. .... Rm 1:24

WRONGS
for any w done against .... Nu 18:1
for any w done against .... Nu 18:1
will punish you for those w. 1Ki 2:44
If someone w another person, ... 1Ki 8:31
If someone w another person, ... 2Ch 6:22
you pardon my w and forgive my .... Job 7:21
My w will be closed up in a bag, ... Job 14:17
forgiven, whose w are pardoned. .... Ps 32:1
be merciful, wipe out all my w. .... Ps 51:1
I know about my w, and I can't .... Ps 51:3
a rod and their w with a whip. .... Ps 89:32
you punished them for their w. .... Ps 99:8
but love forgives all w. .... Pr 10:12
away all your w as if with soap; .... Is 1:25
must pay for the w they did to .... Is 34:8
them pay for the w they did, ... Is 35:4
made me tired of your many w. .... Is 43:24
that w others to start a town. .... Hab 2:12
ashamed of the w done against me .... Zph 3:11
him even if he w you seventy .... Mt 18:22
the punishment for those w. .... Rm 1:27
forgiven, whose w are pardoned. .... Rm 4:7
not count up w that have been 1Co 13:5
us from all the w we have done. 1Jn 1:9
turn away from the w she does. .... Rev 2:22
forgotten for w she has done................... Rev 18:5

WROTE
So Moses w down all the words of .... Ex 24:4
And Moses w the words of the .... Ex 34:28
onyx stones and then w the names .... Ex 39:6
he w them on two stone tablets. .... Dt 4:13
Then he w them on two stone. .... Dt 5:22
The LORD w the same things on .... Dt 10:4
So Moses w down these teachings .... Dt 31:9
So Moses w down the song that .... Dt 31:22
There Joshua w the teachings of .... Jos 8:32
Joshua w these things in the .... Jos 24:26
the young man w down for Gideon .... Jdg 8:14
king and then w them in a book............... 1Sa 10:25
morning David w a letter to Joab 2Sa 11:14
the letter David w, "Put Uriah 2Sa 11:15
sayings and also w one thousand 1Ki 4:32

So Jezebel w some letters, ... 1Ki 21:8
The letter she w said: 1Ki 21:9
just as she w in the letters. 1Ki 21:11
Jehu w letters and sent them to 2Ki 10:1
Then Jehu w a second letter, ... 2Ki 10:6
and commands he w for you. 2Ki 17:37
who w and copied important 1Ch 2:55
And they w the history of their 1Ch 4:33
the seer, who w about Jeroboam, ... 2Ch 9:29
and he w letters to the people. 2Ch 30:1
Sennacherib also w letters 2Ch 32:17
Jeremiah w some sad songs about 2Ch 35:25
Jeremiah would come true. He w: 2Ch 36:22
Jeremiah would come true. He w: .... Ezr 1:1
those enemies w a letter against............... Ezr 4:6
and those with them w a letter .... Ezr 4:7
secretary w a letter against..................... Ezr 4:8
and we w down the names of their........... Ezr 5:10
and they w out all of Haman's .... Est 3:12
They w to the king's governors .... Est 3:12
to cancel the letters Haman w. .... Est 8:5
The secretaries w out all of..................... Est 8:9
They w in the writing of each................. Est 8:9
They also w to the Jewish people .... Est 8:9
Mordecai w orders in the name of .... Est 8:10
Mordecai w down everything that .... Est 9:20
w this second letter about Purim. .... Est 9:29
they w to prove the first letter .... Est 9:29
He w to set up these days of .... Est 9:31
Judah got well, he w this song: .... Is 38:9
and Baruch w those messages on .... Je 36:4
the words you w on the scroll as .... Je 36:6
these words you w on the scroll? .... Je 36:17
and I w them down with ink on .... Je 36:18
Baruch w on the scroll the same .... Je 36:32
and Baruch w them on a scroll: .... Je 45:1
on which you w these names in .... Eze 37:20
king watched the hand as it w. .... Da 5:5
the hand that w on the wall. .... Da 5:24
King Darius w a letter to all .... Da 6:25
and he w down what he had .... Da 7:1
The prophet w about this in the .... Mt 2:5
come about as the prophets w." .... Mt 26:56
as the prophet Isaiah w: .... Mk 1:2
w, 'These people show honor to .... Mk 7:6
Moses w that command for you .... Mk 10:5
Moses w that if a man's brother .... Mk 12:19
in which Moses w about the .... Mk 12:26
for a writing tablet and w, ... Lk 1:63
the prophets w about the Son of............... Lk 18:31
Moses w that if a man's brother .... Lk 20:28
he w about the burning bush,................... Lk 20:37
man that Moses w about in the .... Jn 1:45
the prophets also w about him. .... Jn 1:45
me, because Moses w about me............... Jn 5:46
you don't believe what Moses w, ... Jn 5:47
over again and w on the ground. .... Jn 8:8
Pilate w a sign and put it on .... Jn 19:19
The first book I w was about .... Ac 1:1
Joel the prophet w about what is .... Ac 2:16
the words that the prophets w, ... Ac 13:27
helped him and w a letter to .... Ac 18:27
And he w a letter that said:................... Ac 23:25
you believe what the prophets w? .... Ac 26:27
I w you in my earlier letter not 1Co 5:9
the things you w me about..................... 1Co 7:1
w you a letter for this reason:................... 2Co 2:3
When I w to you before, I was 2Co 2:4
heart, and I w with many tears 2Co 2:4
w you to test you and to see if 2Co 2:9
you sad, I am not sorry I w it................... 2Co 7:8
I w that letter, not because of 2Co 7:12
I w the letter so you could see, ... 2Co 7:12

If you read what I **w** then,	Eph 3:4
the letter that I **w** to Laodicea.	Col 4:16
the one who **w** that will is dead.	Heb 9:16
I **w** this short letter with the	1Pe 5:12
I **w** to encourage you and to tell	1Pe 5:12
same thing when he **w** to you with	2Pe 3:15
I **w** something to the church,	3Jn 1:9
ago the prophets **w** about these	Jud 1:4

X

XERXES

When **X** first became king, those	Ezr 4:6
during the time of King **X,**	Est 1:1
those days King **X** ruled from his	Est 1:2
men from all **X'** empire were	Est 1:3
that time King **X** was showing off	Est 1:4
in the royal palace of King **X.**	Est 1:9
banquet, King **X** was very happy,	Est 1:10
King **X** spoke with the wise men	Est 1:13
obeyed the command of King **X,**	Est 1:15
in all the empire of King **X.**	Est 1:16
'King **X** commanded Queen Vashti	Est 1:17
to enter the presence of King **X,**	Est 1:19
King **X** did as Memucan suggested.	Est 1:21
when King **X** was not so angry,	Est 2:1
could take her turn with King **X,**	Est 2:12
was taken to King **X** in the royal	Est 2:16
during **X'** seventh year as king.	Est 2:16
to make plans to kill King **X.**	Est 2:21
King **X** honored Haman son of	Est 3:1
the Jews, in all of **X'** kingdom.	Est 3:6
twelfth year of King **X'** rule—	Est 3:7
Then Haman said to King **X,**	Est 3:8
name of King **X** and sealed with	Est 3:12
Then King **X** asked Queen Esther,	Est 7:5
same day King **X** gave Queen	Est 8:1
King **X** answered Queen Esther and	Est 8:7
in the name of King **X** and sealed	Est 8:10
empire of King **X** was the	Est 8:12
empire of King **X** in order to	Est 9:2
in all the empire of King **X,**	Est 9:20
states of the kingdom of **X,**	Est 9:30
X demanded taxes everywhere,	Est 10:1
great things **X** did by his power	Est 10:2
second in importance to King **X,**	Est 10:3
Darius son of **X** was king over	Da 9:1

Y

YARD

not measure the **y** outside the	Rev 11:2

YARDS

houses, in the **y,** and in the	Ex 8:13
a thousand **y** behind the Ark.	Jos 3:4
the five hundred **y** of the wall.	Ne 3:13
shore, only about a hundred **y.**	Jn 21:8

YEAR

month of that **y** the underground	Ge 7:11
of the first month of that **y,**	Ge 8:13
the thirteenth **y,** they all	Ge 14:4
in the fourteenth **y,** Kedorlaomer	Ge 14:5
have at this same time next **y.**"	Ge 17:21
about this time a **y** from now.	Ge 18:10
at the right time a **y** from now,	Ge 18:14
and that **y** he gathered a great	Ge 26:12
for their farm animals that **y.**	Ge 47:17
The next **y** the people came to	Ge 47:18
first month of the **y** for you.	Ex 12:2

month of the **y** you are to eat	Ex 12:18
the first month of every **y.**	Ex 13:5
this feast every **y** at the right	Ex 13:10
In the seventh **y** you are to set	Ex 21:2
Then during the seventh **y,**	Ex 23:11
Three times each **y** you must hold	Ex 23:14
during every **y** all your males	Ex 23:17
those people out in only one **y.**	Ex 23:29
two lambs that are one **y** old.	Ex 29:38
Once a **y** Aaron must make the	Ex 30:10
is to do this once a **y** from now	Ex 30:10
times each **y** all your males	Ex 34:23
your God three times each **y,**	Ex 34:24
the second **y** after they left	Ex 40:17
must be one **y** old, and it must	Le 9:3
will do these things once a **y.**"	Le 16:34
In the fourth **y** the fruit from	Le 19:24
Then in the fifth **y,** you may eat	Le 19:25
a male lamb, one **y** old, that has	Le 23:12
lambs that are one **y** old and	Le 23:18
the LORD for seven days each **y.**	Le 23:41
the seventh **y,** you must let	Le 25:4
The land will have a **y** of rest.	Le 25:5
produces during that **y** of rest.	Le 25:6
the fiftieth year a special **y,**	Le 25:10
The fiftieth **y** will be a special	Le 25:11
That **y** is Jubilee; it will be a	Le 25:12
the **y** of Jubilee you each must	Le 25:13
what will we eat the seventh **y?**"	Le 25:20
during the sixth **y** that the land	Le 25:21
When you plant in the eighth **y,**	Le 25:22
the harvest of the ninth **y.**	Le 25:22
keep it until the **y** of Jubilee.	Le 25:28
for a full **y** after it is sold,	Le 25:29
house before a full **y** is over,	Le 25:30
with you until the **y** of Jubilee.	Le 25:40
up to the next **y** of Jubilee.	Le 25:50
years before the **y** of Jubilee,	Le 25:51
with the foreigner every **y;**	Le 25:53
him back, at the **y** of Jubilee,	Le 25:54
crops to last for more than a **y.**	Le 26:10
a field at the **y** of Jubilee,	Le 27:17
years to the next **y** of Jubilee.	Le 27:18
is released at the **y** of Jubilee,	Le 27:21
At the **y** of Jubilee, the land	Le 27:24
month in the second **y** after the	Nu 1:1
a male lamb a **y** old as a penalty	Nu 6:12
and twelve male lambs a **y** old.	Nu 7:87
and sixty male lambs a **y** old.	Nu 7:88
month of the second **y** after the	Nu 9:1
for two days, a month, or a **y.**	Nu 9:22
second month of the second **y.**	Nu 10:11
a **y** for each of the forty days	Nu 14:34
male lambs, a **y** old, as a burnt	Nu 28:3
male lambs, a **y** old, that have	Nu 28:9
and seven male lambs a **y** old,	Nu 28:11
be offered each month of the **y.**	Nu 28:14
and seven male lambs a **y** old.	Nu 28:19
and fourteen male lambs a **y** old.	Nu 29:13
n the fortieth **y** after the	Nu 33:38
beginning of the **y** to the end.	Dt 11:12
of all your crops each **y.**	Dt 14:22
At the end of every third **y,**	Dt 14:28
The seventh **y** is near, the year	Dt 15:9
y to cancel what people owe."	Dt 15:9
in the seventh **y** you must let	Dt 15:12
Each **y** you and your family are	Dt 15:20
three times a **y** to the place he	Dt 16:16
stay home for a **y** to make his	Dt 24:5
of all your harvest the third **y**	Dt 26:12
the **y** to give a tenth of your	Dt 26:12
in the land of Canaan that **y.**	Jos 5:12
In the same **y** those people	Jdg 10:8

But in the third **y**, plant grain	Is 37:30
the thirteenth **y** that Josiah son	Je 1:2
the fifth month of his last **y**,	Je 1:3
to happen to them that **y**."	Je 11:23
not worry in a **y** when no rain	Je 17:8
on them in the **y** I punish them,"	Je 23:12
in the fourth **y** that Jehoiakim	Je 25:1
and the first **y** Nebuchadnezzar	Je 25:1
the thirteenth **y** of Josiah son	Je 25:3
was in that same **y**, in the fifth	Je 28:1
fourth **y** as king of Judah	Je 28:1
You will die this **y**, because you	Je 28:16
seventh month of that same **y**.	Je 28:17
in the tenth **y** Zedekiah was king	Je 32:1
the eighteenth **y** of	Je 32:1
the fourth **y** that Jehoiakim	Je 36:1
of the fifth **y** that Jehoiakim	Je 36:9
It was the ninth month of the **y**,	Je 36:22
of the ninth **y** Zedekiah was king	Je 39:1
month in Zedekiah's eleventh **y**.	Je 39:2
was the fourth **y** that Jehoiakim	Je 45:1
in the fourth **y** that Jehoiakim	Je 46:2
will bring the **y** of punishment	Je 48:44
rumor comes this **y**, and another	Je 51:46
and another comes the next **y**.	Je 51:46
the fourth **y** Zedekiah was king	Je 51:59
happened on Zedekiah's ninth **y**,	Je 52:4
Zedekiah's eleventh **y** as king.	Je 52:5
nineteenth **y** as king of Babylon.	Je 52:12
in the seventh **y**, 3,023 Jews;	Je 52:28
Nebuchadnezzar's eighteenth **y**,	Je 52:29
Nebuchadnezzar's twenty-third **y**,	Je 52:30
The **y** Evil-Merodach became king	Je 52:31
the thirtieth **y**, on the fifth	Eze 1:1
month of the fifth **y** that King	Eze 1:2
a day for each **y** of their sin.	Eze 4:6
It was the sixth **y**, on the fifth	Eze 8:1
was the seventh **y** of our	Eze 20:1
me in the ninth **y** of our	Eze 24:1
the eleventh **y** of our captivity	Eze 26:1
was the tenth **y** of our captivity	Eze 29:1
twenty-seventh **y** of our	Eze 29:17
in the eleventh **y** of our	Eze 30:20
in the eleventh **y** of our	Eze 31:1
in the twelfth **y** of our	Eze 32:1
in the twelfth **y** of our	Eze 32:17
in the twelfth **y** of our	Eze 33:21
twenty-fifth **y** of our captivity	Eze 40:1
at the beginning of the **y**,	Eze 40:1
the fourteenth **y** after Jerusalem	Eze 40:1
only until the **y** of freedom.	Eze 46:17
the third **y** that Jehoiakim	Da 1:1
the first **y** Cyrus was king.	Da 1:21
second **y** as king,	Da 2:1
the times and seasons of the **y**.	Da 2:21
first **y** as king of Babylon	Da 7:1
During the third **y** of King	Da 8:1
during the first **y** Darius son of	Da 9:1
During Darius' first **y** as king,	Da 9:2
Cyrus' third **y** as king of Persia	Da 10:1
In the first **y** that Darius the	Da 11:1
in the second **y** that Darius was	Hag 1:1
in the second **y** Darius was king.	Hag 1:15
in the second **y** Darius was king,	Hag 2:10
of the second **y** Darius was king,	Zch 1:1
in Darius's second **y** as king.	Zch 1:7
In the fourth **y** Darius was king,	Zch 7:1
month of each **y** we have shown	Zch 7:3
back to Jerusalem **y** after year	Zch 14:16
year after **y** to worship the King	Zch 14:16
Every **y** at the time of Passover	Mt 27:15
Every **y** at the time of the	Mk 15:6
Every **y** Jesus' parents went to	Lk 2:41

was the fifteenth **y** of the rule	Lk 3:1
have one more **y** to produce fruit	Lk 13:8
the tree produces fruit next **y**,	Lk 13:9
Every **y** at the Passover Feast,	Lk 23:17
to work almost a **y** to buy enough	Jn 6:7
the high priest that **y**.	Jn 11:49
priest that **y**, he was really	Jn 11:51
the high priest that **y**.	Jn 18:13
For a whole **y** Saul and Barnabas	Ac 11:26
stayed there for a **y** and a half,	Ac 18:11
y you were the first to want	2Co 8:10
been ready to give since last **y**.	2Co 9:2
and he did that only once a **y**.	Heb 9:7
once every **y** with blood that	Heb 9:25
the same sacrifices every **y**,	Heb 10:1
them of their sins every **y**,	Heb 10:3
stay there a **y**, do business,	Jam 4:13
and month and **y** so they could	Rev 9:15
produces fruit twelve times a **y**,	Rev 22:2

YEAR-OLD

the entrance a **y** lamb for a	Le 12:6
with them and a **y** female lamb	Le 14:10
must offer a **y** male lamb that	Nu 6:14
a **y** female lamb that has nothing	Nu 6:14
a **y** female goat must be brought	Nu 15:27
you will give a **y** lamb that has	Eze 46:13
burnt offerings, with **y** calves?	Mic 6:6

YEARLY

There is a **y** festival of the	Jdg 21:19
and the three **y** feasts—the Feast	2Ch 8:13
feasts and your other **y** feasts.	Is 1:14
her **y** festivals, her New Moon	Hos 2:11

YEARS

for signs, seasons, days, and **y**.	Ge 1:14
Adam was 130 **y** old, he became	Ge 5:3
Adam lived 800 **y** and had other	Ge 5:4
So Adam lived a total of 930 **y**,	Ge 5:5
Seth was 105 **y** old, he had a son	Ge 5:6
Seth lived 807 **y** and had other	Ge 5:7
So Seth lived a total of 912 **y**,	Ge 5:8
Enosh was 90 **y** old, he had a son	Ge 5:9
Enosh lived 815 **y** and had other	Ge 5:10
So Enosh lived a total of 905 **y**,	Ge 5:11
Kenan was 70 **y** old, he had a son	Ge 5:12
Kenan lived 840 **y** and had other	Ge 5:13
So Kenan lived a total of 910 **y**,	Ge 5:14
When Mahalalel was 65 **y** old,	Ge 5:15
lived 830 **y** and had other sons	Ge 5:16
lived a total of 895 **y**,	Ge 5:17
Jared was 162 **y** old, he had a	Ge 5:18
Jared lived 800 **y** and had other	Ge 5:19
So Jared lived a total of 962 **y**,	Ge 5:20
Enoch was 65 **y** old, he had a son	Ge 5:21
with God 300 **y** more and had	Ge 5:22
So Enoch lived a total of 365 **y**.	Ge 5:23
When Methuselah was 187 **y** old,	Ge 5:25
lived 782 **y** and had other sons	Ge 5:26
lived a total of 969 **y**,	Ge 5:27
Lamech was 595 **y** and had other	Ge 5:30
Lamech lived a total of 777 **y**,	Ge 5:31
Noah was 500 **y** old, he became	Ge 5:32
They will live only 120 **y**."	Ge 6:3
was six hundred **y** old when the	Ge 7:6
When Noah was six hundred **y** old,	Ge 7:11
was six hundred and one **y** old,	Ge 8:13
the flood Noah lived 350 **y**.	Ge 9:28
He lived a total of 950 **y**,	Ge 9:29
Two **y** after the flood, when Shem	Ge 11:10
when Shem was 100 **y** old, his son	Ge 11:10
Shem lived 500 **y** and had other	Ge 11:11
When Arphaxad was 35 **y** old,	Ge 11:12
lived 403 **y** and had other sons	Ge 11:13

Shelah was 30 **y** old, his son	Ge 11:14
Shelah lived 403 **y** and had other	Ge 11:15
When Eber was 34 **y** old, his son	Ge 11:16
Eber lived 430 **y** and had other	Ge 11:17
Peleg was 30 **y** old, his son Reu	Ge 11:18
Peleg lived 209 **y** and had other	Ge 11:19
When Reu was 32 **y** old, his son	Ge 11:20
Reu lived 207 **y** and had other	Ge 11:21
When Serug was 30 **y** old, his son	Ge 11:22
Serug lived 200 **y** and had other	Ge 11:23
When Nahor was 29 **y** old, his son	Ge 11:24
Nahor lived 119 **y** and had other	Ge 11:25
Terah was 70 **y** old, his sons	Ge 11:26
Terah lived to be 205 **y** old,	Ge 11:32
At this time Abram was 75 **y** old.	Ge 12:4
served Kedorlaomer for twelve **y**,	Ge 14:4
to them for four hundred **y**.	Ge 15:13
had lived ten **y** in Canaan that	Ge 16:3
was eighty-six **y** old when Hagar	Ge 16:16
Abram was ninety-nine **y** old,	Ge 17:1
when he is a hundred **y** old?	Ge 17:17
ninety-nine **y** old when he was	Ge 17:24
was thirteen **y** old when he was	Ge 17:25
was one hundred **y** old when his	Ge 21:5
one hundred twenty-seven **y** old.	Ge 23:1
one hundred seventy-five **y** old.	Ge 25:7
thirty-seven **y** and then breathed	Ge 25:17
When Isaac was forty **y** old,	Ge 25:20
Isaac was sixty **y** old when they	Ge 25:26
When Esau was forty **y** old,	Ge 26:34
I will work seven **y** for you."	Ge 29:18
for Laban seven **y** so he could	Ge 29:20
After seven **y** Jacob said to	Ge 29:21
must serve me another seven **y**."	Ge 29:27
for Laban for another seven **y**.	Ge 29:30
worked for you now for twenty **y**.	Ge 31:38
a slave for you for twenty **y**—	Ge 31:41
lived one hundred eighty **y**.	Ge 35:28
a young man, seventeen **y** old.	Ge 37:2
Two **y** later the king dreamed he	Ge 41:1
good cows stand for seven **y**,	Ge 41:26
of grain stand for seven **y**.	Ge 41:26
and ugly cows stand for seven **y**,	Ge 41:27
stand for seven **y** of hunger.	Ge 41:27
will have seven **y** of good crops	Ge 41:29
those seven **y**, there will come	Ge 41:30
will come seven **y** of hunger,	Ge 41:30
grown during the seven good **y**.	Ge 41:34
the good **y** that are coming	Ge 41:35
during the seven **y** of hunger	Ge 41:36
during the seven **y** of hunger."	Ge 41:36
was thirty **y** old when he began	Ge 41:46
the seven good **y**, the crops	Ge 41:47
those seven **y** of good crops	Ge 41:48
Before the seven **y** of hunger came,	Ge 41:50
The seven **y** of good crops came	Ge 41:53
the seven **y** of hunger began,	Ge 41:54
grown on the land for two **y** now,	Ge 45:6
be five more **y** without planting	Ge 45:6
next five **y** of hunger so that	Ge 45:11
only one hundred thirty **y**.	Ge 47:9
lived in Egypt seventeen **y**,	Ge 47:28
one hundred forty-seven **y** old.	Ge 47:28
he was one hundred ten **y** old.	Ge 50:22
he was one hundred ten **y** old.	Ge 50:26
one hundred thirty-seven **y**.	Ex 6:16
one hundred thirty-three **y**.	Ex 6:18
one hundred thirty-seven **y**.	Ex 6:20
Moses was eighty **y** old and Aaron	Ex 7:7
Egypt for four hundred thirty **y**;	Ex 12:40
the four hundred thirty **y** ended,	Ex 12:41
ate manna for forty **y**,	Ex 16:35
he will serve you for six **y**.	Ex 21:2

For six **y** you are to plant and	Ex 23:10
is twenty **y** old or older must	Ex 30:14
the men twenty **y** old or older	Ex 38:26
three **y** before using its fruit.	Le 19:23
seed in your field for six **y**,	Le 25:3
vineyards for six **y** and bring in	Le 25:3
off seven groups of seven **y**,	Le 25:8
of seven years, or forty-nine **y**.	Le 25:8
there will be seven **y** of rest	Le 25:8
the number of **y** since the last	Le 25:15
the number of **y** left for	Le 25:15
there are many **y**, the price will	Le 25:16
But if there are only a few **y**,	Le 25:16
enough crops for three **y**.	Le 25:21
the **y** must be counted since the	Le 25:27
out for a certain number of **y**.	Le 25:50
are still many **y** before the year	Le 25:51
are only a few **y** left until	Le 25:52
twenty to sixty **y** old is about	Le 27:3
twenty to sixty **y** old is about	Le 27:4
five to twenty **y** old is about	Le 27:5
month to five **y** old is about two	Le 27:6
for a man sixty **y** old or older	Le 27:7
the number of **y** to the next year	Le 27:18
must count the **y** to the next	Le 27:23
man twenty **y** old or older who	Nu 1:3
who were twenty **y** old or older	Nu 1:18
men twenty **y** old or older who	Nu 1:20
Israel twenty **y** old or older who	Nu 1:45
men from thirty to fifty **y** old,	Nu 4:3
men from thirty to fifty **y** old,	Nu 4:23
men from thirty to fifty **y** old,	Nu 4:30
thirty to fifty **y** old who were	Nu 4:35
thirty to fifty **y** old who were	Nu 4:39
thirty to fifty **y** old who were	Nu 4:43
twenty-five **y** old or older must	Nu 8:24
been built seven **y** before Zoan	Nu 13:22
you who is twenty **y** old or older	Nu 14:29
be shepherds here for forty **y**.	Nu 14:33
For forty **y** you will suffer for	Nu 14:34
and we lived there for many **y**.	Nu 20:15
which you have ridden for **y**.	Nu 22:30
are twenty **y** old or older who	Nu 26:2
the men twenty **y** old or older,	Nu 26:4
who are twenty **y** old or older	Nu 32:11
in the desert for forty **y**.	Nu 32:13
Aaron was 123 **y** old when he died	Nu 33:39
Forty **y** after the Israelites had	Dt 1:3
with you for the past forty **y**,	Dt 2:7
thirty-eight **y** from the time we	Dt 2:14
in the desert for these forty **y**,	Dt 8:2
these forty **y**, your clothes did	Dt 8:4
At the end of every seven **y**,	Dt 15:1
person will serve you for six **y**.	Dt 15:12
served you six **y** and did twice	Dt 15:18
through the desert for forty **y**,	Dt 29:5
let you live many **y** in the land,	Dt 30:20
am now one hundred twenty **y** old,	Dt 31:2
Think of the **y** already passed.	Dt 32:7
hundred twenty **y** old when he	Dt 34:7
about in the desert for forty **y**.	Jos 5:6
fought against them for many **y**.	Jos 11:18
I was forty **y** old then.	Jos 14:7
for forty-five **y** from the time	Jos 14:10
here I am, eighty-five **y** old.	Jos 14:10
Many **y** passed, and Joshua grew	Jos 23:1
over the Israelites for eight **y**.	Jdg 3:8
land was at peace for forty **y**.	Jdg 3:11
king of Moab for eighteen **y**.	Jdg 3:14
peace in the land for eighty **y**.	Jdg 3:30
people of Israel for twenty **y**,	Jdg 4:3
peace in the land for forty **y**.	Jdg 5:31
So for seven **y** the LORD handed	Jdg 6:1

who were twenty **y** old and older. 2Ch 25:5
lived fifteen **y** after the death 2Ch 25:25
Uzziah was sixteen **y** old. 2Ch 26:1
was sixteen **y** old when he became........... 2Ch 26:3
ruled fifty-two **y** in Jerusalem. 2Ch 26:3
was twenty-five **y** old when he 2Ch 27:1
he ruled sixteen **y** in Jerusalem................ 2Ch 27:1
for three **y** they gave Jotham 2Ch 27:5
was twenty-five **y** old when he 2Ch 27:8
he ruled sixteen **y** in Jerusalem................ 2Ch 27:8
Ahaz was twenty **y** old when he 2Ch 28:1
he ruled sixteen **y** in Jerusalem............... 2Ch 28:1
was twenty-five **y** old when he 2Ch 29:1
twenty-nine **y** in Jerusalem. 2Ch 29:1
the males three **y** old and older 2Ch 31:16
Levites twenty **y** old and older 2Ch 31:17
was twelve **y** old when he became 2Ch 33:1
for fifty-five **y** in Jerusalem. 2Ch 33:1
was twenty-two **y** old when he 2Ch 33:21
was king for two **y** in Jerusalem. 2Ch 33:21
Josiah was eight **y** old when he 2Ch 34:1
ruled thirty-one **y** in Jerusalem. 2Ch 34:1
was twenty-three **y** old when he.............. 2Ch 36:2
was twenty-five **y** old when he 2Ch 36:5
king in Jerusalem for eleven **y**. 2Ch 36:5
eighteen **y** old when he became 2Ch 36:9
was twenty-one **y** old when he 2Ch 36:11
king in Jerusalem for eleven **y**. 2Ch 36:11
for seventy **y** to make up for 2Ch 36:21
up for the **y** of Sabbath rest 2Ch 36:21
Levites twenty **y** old and older .... Ezr 3:8
built and finished many **y** ago. .... Ezr 5:11
governor of Judah for twelve **y**, ... Ne 5:14
them for forty **y** in the desert;............... Ne 9:21
them for many **y** and warned them .... Ne 9:30
and your **y** like our years? .... Job 10:5
and your years like our **y**? .... Job 10:5
during all the **y** saved up for .... Job 15:20
Only a few **y** will pass before I .... Job 16:22
have lived many **y** should teach .... Job 32:7
rest of their **y** will be happy. .... Job 36:11
Have you lived that many **y**? .... Job 38:21
Job lived one hundred forty **y**. .... Job 42:16
was old and had lived many **y**. .... Job 42:17
you gave it to him, so his **y** go .... Ps 21:4
and my **y** are spent in crying.................. Ps 31:10
long life; let him live many **y**. .... Ps 61:6
the old days, the **y** of long ago. .... Ps 77:5
For **y** the power of God Most High .... Ps 77:10
meaning and their **y** in terror.................. Ps 78:33
a thousand **y** is like the passing .... Ps 90:4
Our **y** end with a moan. .... Ps 90:9
Our lifetime is seventy **y** or, ... Ps 90:10
or, if we are strong, eighty **y**. .... Ps 90:10
But the **y** are full of hard work .... Ps 90:10
We have seen **y** of trouble. .... Ps 90:15
with those people for forty **y**, ... Ps 95:10
the middle of my life. Your **y** go .... Ps 102:24
and the best **y** of your life will .... Pr 5:9
wisdom will add **y** to your life. .... Pr 9:11
Even if he lives two thousand **y**, ... Ec 6:6
come and the **y** when you say, ... Ec 12:1
sixty-five **y** Israel will no .... Is 7:8
In three **y** all those people and .... Is 16:14
is three **y** as a hired helper .... Is 16:14
for three **y** as a sign against .... Is 20:3
forget about Tyre for seventy **y**, ... Is 23:15
After seventy **y**, Tyre will be .... Is 23:15
After seventy **y** the LORD will .... Is 23:17
will add fifteen **y** to your life. .... Is 38:5
lives a hundred **y** will be called .... Is 65:20
the eleven **y** that Zedekiah son .... Je 1:3
for these past twenty-three **y**. .... Je 25:3

king of Babylon for seventy **y**. .... Je 25:11
when the seventy **y** have passed, ... Je 25:12
Before two **y** are over, I will .... Je 28:3
it before two **y** are over.'" .... Je 28:11
will be powerful for seventy **y**. .... Je 29:10
'At the end of every seven **y**, ... Je 34:14
he has served you for six **y**.' .... Je 34:14
was twenty-one **y** old when he .... Je 52:1
king in Jerusalem for eleven **y**. .... Je 52:1
in Babylon for thirty-seven **y**. .... Je 52:31
of days as the **y** of the people's .... Eze 4:5
is for a time many **y** from now. .... Eze 12:27
have come to the end of your **y**. .... Eze 22:4
will live in Egypt for forty **y**. .... Eze 29:11
all ruined cities for forty **y**. .... Eze 29:12
forty **y** I will gather Egypt .... Eze 29:13
After those **y** you will come into............. Eze 38:8
for many **y** that I would bring................. Eze 38:17
burn in their fires for seven **y**. .... Eze 39:9
were to be trained for three **y**,.............. Da 1:5
mind of an animal for seven **y**. .... Da 4:16
like a wild animal for seven **y**.' .... Da 4:23
Seven **y** will pass, and then you .... Da 4:25
Seven **y** will pass before you .... Da 4:32
when he was sixty-two **y** old. .... Da 5:31
power for three and one-half **y**. .... Da 7:25
be empty ruins for seventy **y**. .... Da 9:2
hundred ninety **y** for your people .... Da 9:24
be forty-nine **y** and four hundred .... Da 9:25
and four hundred thirty-four **y**. .... Da 9:25
thirty-four **y** the appointed .... Da 9:26
with many people for seven **y**. .... Da 9:27
after three and one-half **y**. .... Da 9:27
Then after a few **y**, a new .... Da 11:6
king of the North for a few **y**. .... Da 11:8
After several **y** he will attack .... Da 11:13
In a few **y** that ruler will be .... Da 11:20
be for three and one-half **y**.................... Da 12:7
you back for those **y** of trouble. .... Joe 2:25
about Israel two **y** before the .... Am 1:1
led you for forty **y** through the .... Am 2:10
in the desert for forty **y**. .... Am 5:25
with them for seventy **y** now." .... Zch 1:12
For **y** in the fifth month of each .... Zch 7:3
'For seventy **y** you fasted and .... Zch 7:5
who were two **y** old or younger. .... Mt 2:16
for twelve **y** came behind Jesus .... Mt 9:20
had been bleeding for twelve **y**. .... Mk 5:25
She was twelve **y** old.) Everyone .... Mk 5:42
once been married for seven **y**. .... Lk 2:36
was a widow for eighty-four **y**. .... Lk 2:37
he was twelve **y** old, they went .... Lk 2:42
he was about thirty **y** old. .... Lk 3:23
Israel for three and one-half **y**, ... Lk 4:25
about twelve **y** old, was dying. .... Lk 8:42
had been bleeding for twelve **y**, ... Lk 8:43
stored to last for many **y**. .... Lk 12:19
fruit on this tree for three **y**, ... Lk 13:7
who, for eighteen **y**, had an evil .... Lk 13:11
held by Satan for eighteen **y**. .... Lk 13:16
slave for many **y** and have always .... Lk 15:29
took forty-six **y** to build this .... Jn 2:20
been sick for thirty-eight **y**. .... Jn 5:5
You are not even fifty **y** old." .... Jn 8:57
was more than forty **y** old. .... Ac 4:22
them for four hundred **y**,....................... Ac 7:6
Moses was about forty **y** old, ... Ac 7:23
Forty **y** later an angel appeared .... Ac 7:30
then in the desert for forty **y**. .... Ac 7:36
in the desert for forty **y**. .... Ac 7:42
his bed for the past eight **y**.................... Ac 9:33
them for forty **y** in the desert................ Ac 13:18
in about four hundred fifty **y**. .... Ac 13:20

YIELDING

and to **y** to their husbands........................ Tit 2:5
Slaves should **y** to their own .... Tit 2:9
believers to **y** to the authority................. Tit 3:1
y to the people who have 1Pe 2:13
y to the authority of your 1Pe 2:18
wives should **y** to your husbands 1Pe 3:1

YIELDING

beautiful, **y** to their own 1Pe 3:5

YIELDS

As the church **y** to Christ, ... Eph 5:24

YOKE

has never worked or worn a **y,** .... Dt 21:3
used their wooden **y** for a fire. 1Ki 19:21
obey me as an ox breaks its **y.** .... Je 2:20
Make a **y** out of straps and .... Je 27:2
'I have broken the **y** the king of .... Je 28:2
I will break the **y** the king of .... Je 28:4
took the **y** off Jeremiah's .... Je 28:10
I will break the **y** of............................... Je 28:11
He put that **y** on all the nations .... Je 28:11
had broken the **y** off of the .... Je 28:12
You have broken a wooden **y,** .... Je 28:13
I will make a **y** of iron in its .... Je 28:13
I will put a **y** of iron on the .... Je 28:14
will break the **y** from their .... Je 30:8
I will put a **y** on her neck and................. Hos 10:11
I lifted the **y** from their neck .... Hos 11:4
slaves under a **y** should show 1Ti 6:1

YOKES

have never had **y** on their necks. 1Sa 6:7
boards and the **y** for the wood. 2Sa 24:22

YOUNG

Have many **y** ones so that you may .... Ge 1:22
wounding me, a **y** man for hitting .... Ge 4:23
them have many **y** ones so that .... Ge 8:17
are evil even when they are **y,**................. Ge 8:21
the food my **y** men have eaten. .... Ge 14:24
sheep, a dove, and a **y** pigeon." .... Ge 15:9
both **y** and old and from every .... Ge 19:4
the men, both **y** and old, could .... Ge 19:11
will wait for a **y** woman to come .... Ge 24:43
bring me two of the best **y** ones.............. Ge 27:9
Then the **y** that were born were .... Ge 30:39
Jacob separated the **y** animals .... Ge 30:40
gave birth to speckled **y** ones................. Ge 31:8
female camels and their **y,** .... Ge 32:15
with my flocks and their **y** ones.............. Ge 33:13
Joseph was a **y** man, seventeen .... Ge 37:2
until my **y** son Shelah grows .... Ge 38:11
I will send you a **y** goat from my .... Ge 38:17
Hirah with the **y** goat to find .... Ge 38:20
A **y** Hebrew man, a servant of the .... Ge 41:12
'That **y** boy cannot leave his .... Ge 44:22
father sees the **y** boy is not .... Ge 44:31
that the **y** boy would be safe .... Ge 44:32
and let the **y** boy go back home .... Ge 44:33
Judah is like a **y** lion. .... Ge 49:9
his **y** donkey to the best branch............... Ge 49:11
and many **y** ones born to your .... Ge 49:25
go with our **y** and old people,.................. Ex 10:9
can be either a **y** sheep or a .... Ex 12:5
a young sheep or a **y** goat. .... Ex 12:5
must not cook a **y** goat in its .... Ex 23:19
Then Moses sent **y** Israelite men .... Ex 24:5
and to sacrifice **y** bulls as .... Ex 24:5
Take one **y** bull and two male................. Ex 29:1
camp, but Moses' **y** helper, ... Ex 33:11
must not cook a **y** goat in its .... Ex 34:26
He must kill the **y** bull before .... Le 1:5
it must be a dove or a **y** pigeon. .... Le 1:14
he must offer a **y** bull to the .... Le 4:3

they must offer a **y** bull as a .... Le 4:14
doves or two **y** pigeons to the .... Le 5:7
and a dove or **y** pigeon for a sin .... Le 12:6
two doves or two **y** pigeons, ... Le 12:8
and two doves or two **y** pigeons, ... Le 14:22
one of the doves or **y** pigeons, ... Le 14:30
doves or two **y** pigeons before .... Le 15:14
two doves or two **y** pigeons and .... Le 15:29
Offer with the bread one **y** bull, ... Le 23:18
doves or two **y** pigeons to the .... Nu 6:10
They must take a **y** bull and the .... Nu 8:8
take a second **y** bull for a sin .... Nu 8:8
A **y** man ran to Moses and said, ... Nu 11:27
Ever since he was a **y** boy, ... Nu 11:28
you prepare a **y** bull as a burnt .... Nu 15:8
sheep, lamb or **y** goat this way. .... Nu 15:11
must offer a **y** bull as a burnt .... Nu 15:24
to get a **y** red cow that does .... Nu 19:2
will be two **y** bulls, one male .... Nu 28:11
a burnt offering of two **y** bulls, ... Nu 28:19
two **y** bulls, one male sheep, and .... Nu 28:27
one **y** bull, one male sheep, and .... Nu 29:2
one **y** bull, one male sheep, and .... Nu 29:8
y bulls, two male sheep, ... Nu 29:13
a **y** woman still living at home .... Nu 30:3
Your wives, your **y** children, and .... Dt 3:19
body must take a **y** cow that has .... Dt 21:3
must break the **y** cow's neck. .... Dt 21:4
hands over the **y** cow whose neck .... Dt 21:6
sitting on the **y** birds or eggs,................. Dt 22:6
mother bird with the **y** birds. .... Dt 22:6
may take the **y** birds, but you .... Dt 22:7
your animals will have many **y,** .... Dt 28:11
people or feel sorry for the **y.** .... Dt 28:50
pour down like rain on **y** plants............... Dt 32:2
nest that flutters over its **y.** .... Dt 32:11
Y men and women will die, and so........... Dt 32:25
and women, **y** and old, cattle,................. Jos 6:21
went in and cooked a **y** goat, ... Jdg 6:19
captured a **y** man from Succoth .... Jdg 8:14
So the **y** man wrote down for .... Jdg 8:14
every year the **y** women of Israel .... Jdg 11:40
we can cook a **y** goat for you." .... Jdg 13:15
sacrificed a **y** goat on a rock .... Jdg 13:19
y lion came roaring toward Samson! .... Jdg 14:5
easy as tearing apart a **y** goat. .... Jdg 14:6
had not plowed with my **y** cow, ... Jdg 14:18
wife, taking a **y** goat with him. .... Jdg 15:1
There was a **y** man who was a .... Jdg 17:7
the voice of the **y** Levite.......................... Jdg 18:3
the **y** woman's father, ... Jdg 19:4
the **y** woman's father, ... Jdg 19:9
wine for me, the **y** woman, and my .... Jdg 19:19
four hundred **y** unmarried women .... Jdg 21:12
for the **y** women from Shiloh .... Jdg 21:21
take one of the **y** Shiloh women............... Jdg 21:21
While the **y** women were dancing, ... Jdg 21:23
She is the **y** Moabite woman who .... Ru 2:6
have warned the **y** men not to .... Ru 2:9
that the **y** men have filled."...................... Ru 2:9
whose **y** women you worked with, ... Ru 3:2
look for a **y** man to marry, ... Ru 3:10
both old and **y** people in Gath 1Sa 5:9
Saul, who was a fine **y** man. 1Sa 9:2
they met some **y** women coming out 1Sa 9:11
The **y** women answered, "Yes, he's 1Sa 9:12
been your leader since I was **y.** 1Sa 12:2
said, "Take a **y** calf with you. 1Sa 16:2
of wine, and a **y** goat, and he 1Sa 16:20
a warrior since he was a **y** man." 1Sa 17:33
who is that **y** man's father?" 1Sa 17:55
asked him, "**Y** man, who is your 1Sa 17:58
He had a **y** boy with him. 1Sa 20:35

So he sent ten y men and told 1Sa 25:5
time, so be kind to my y men. 1Sa 25:8
Let one of your y men come here 1Sa 26:22
everyone, y and old, but they 1Sa 30:2
four hundred y men who rode off 1Sa 30:17
back everyone, y and old, sons 1Sa 30:17
third day a y man from Saul's 2Sa 1:2
The y man answered, "I happened 2Sa 1:6
asked the y man who brought 2Sa 1:13
The y man answered, "I am the 2Sa 1:13
the y men have a contest here. 2Sa 2:14
one of the y men and take his................. 2Sa 2:21
had a y son named Mica. 2Sa 9:12
He called his y servant back in 2Sa 13:17
So Absalom's y men killed Amnon 2Sa 13:29
Don't think all the y men, ... 2Sa 13:32
Bring back the y man Absalom." 2Sa 14:21
Be gentle with y Absalom for my 2Sa 18:5
careful not to hurt y Absalom.' 2Sa 18:12
Ten y men who carried Joab's 2Sa 18:15
asked, "Is y Absalom all right? 2Sa 18:29
"Is y Absalom all right? 2Sa 18:32
to hurt you be like that y man!" 2Sa 18:32
One of Joab's y men stood by................. 2Sa 20:11
When the y man saw that everyone 2Sa 20:12
will look for a y woman to care 1Ki 1:2
Israel for a beautiful y woman, ... 1Ki 1:3
time Hadad was only a y boy,................. 1Ki 11:17
saw that this y man was a good 1Ki 11:28
he asked the y men who had grown 1Ki 12:8
The y men who had grown up with 1Ki 12:10
advice of the y men and said to 1Ki 12:14
'The y officers of the district 1Ki 20:14
So Ahab gathered the y officers 1Ki 20:15
The y officers of the district 1Ki 20:17
The y officers of the district 1Ki 20:19
'Two y men from the groups of 2Ki 5:22
opened the eyes of the y man, ... 2Ki 6:17
kill their y men with swords. 2Ki 8:12
So the y man, the prophet, went............... 2Ki 9:4
The y man said, "For you, ... 2Ki 9:5
Then the y prophet poured the 2Ki 9:6
Then the y prophet opened the 2Ki 9:10
like tender, y grass, like grass................. 2Ki 19:26
He was a strong y warrior,.................... 1Ch 12:28
But my son Solomon is y. 1Ch 22:5
The y and the old, the teacher 1Ch 25:8
a gate to guard. Y and old threw 1Ch 26:13
who is y and hasn't yet learned 1Ch 29:1
he asked the y men who had grown 2Ch 10:8
The y men who had grown up with 2Ch 10:10
advice of the y men and said, ... 2Ch 10:14
He was y and didn't know what to 2Ch 13:7
comes with a y bull and seven 2Ch 13:9
of priests, both y and old. 2Ch 31:15
as king while he was still y, ... 2Ch 34:3
king killed the y men even when 2Ch 36:17
no mercy on the y men or women, ... 2Ch 36:17
they need—y bulls, male sheep .... Ezr 6:9
for beautiful y girls for the .... Est 2:2
every beautiful y girl to the.................... Est 2:3
That meant y and old, women and .... Est 3:13
house fell in on the y people, ... Job 1:19
the y men saw me, they would .... Job 29:8
Since I was y, I have been like .... Job 31:18
I am y, and you are old. .... Job 32:6
to the way it was when he was y. .... Job 33:25
They die while they are still y, ... Job 36:14
satisfy the hunger of the y .... Job 38:39
birds when their y cry out to .... Job 38:41
lie down, their y are born, and .... Job 39:3
Their y ones grow big and strong .... Job 39:4
The ostrich is cruel to its y,.................... Job 39:16

Its y eat blood, and where there .... Job 39:30
wrong things I did when I was y. .... Ps 25:7
I was y, and now I am old, but I .... Ps 37:25
they are still y because evil..................... Ps 55:15
have trusted you since I was y. .... Ps 71:5
have taught me since I was y, ... Ps 71:17
down the best y men of Israel. .... Ps 78:31
The y men died by fire, and the .... Ps 78:63
and the y women had no one to .... Ps 78:63
raise their y near your altars .... Ps 84:3
weak and dying since I was y. .... Ps 88:15
have raised up a y man from my .... Ps 89:19
things and makes me y again, ... Ps 103:5
How can a y person live a pure .... Ps 119:9
who are born to a y man are like .... Ps 127:4
y men and women, old people and........... Ps 148:12
knowledge and sense to the y. .... Pr 1:4
she married when she was y. .... Pr 2:17
I was a y boy in my father's .... Pr 4:3
you married when you were y. .... Pr 5:18
and saw some foolish, y men.................... Pr 7:7
The y glory in their strength, ... Pr 20:29
your servants when they are y, ... Pr 29:21
Y people, enjoy yourselves while .... Ec 11:9
yourselves while you are y;.................... Ec 11:9
be happy while you are y. .... Ec 11:9
your Creator while you are y, ... Ec 12:1
That's why the y women love you. .... Sng 1:3
reason, the y women love you. .... Sng 1:4
sheep and feed your y goats near .... Sng 1:8
Among the y women, my darling is .... Sng 2:2
Among the y men, my lover is .... Sng 2:3
is like a gazelle or a y deer. .... Sng 2:9
There are y figs on the fig .... Sng 2:13
like a gazelle or a y deer on .... Sng 2:17
The y women saw her and called .... Sng 6:9
Who is that y woman that shines .... Sng 6:10
like a gazelle or a y deer on .... Sng 8:14
I will cause y boys to be your .... Is 3:4
Y people will not respect older .... Is 3:5
it is loud like a y lion. .... Is 5:29
to keep only one y cow and two .... Is 7:21
is not happy with the y people, ... Is 9:17
and y bulls will eat together, ... Is 11:6
Their y will lie down to rest .... Is 11:7
shoot the y men with arrows; .... Is 13:18
Old people and y people will be .... Is 20:4
have not reared y men or women." .... Is 23:4
but its y men will be caught and.............. Is 31:8
gather their y under their wings.............. Is 34:15
like tender, y grass, like grass................. Is 37:27
and y people trip and fall. .... Is 40:30
you have used since you were y. .... Is 47:12
been with you since you were y,............... Is 47:15
wife who married y and then her .... Is 54:6
y camels from Midian and Ephah. .... Is 60:6
As a y man marries a woman, ... Is 62:5
hundred years will be called y, ... Is 65:20
birth to children who die y....................... Is 65:23
to me when you were y. nation. .... Je 2:2
You loved me like a y bride. .... Je 2:2
A y woman does not forget her .... Je 2:32
been my friend since I was y. .... Je 3:4
street and on the y men gathered .... Je 6:11
streets and the y men who meet............... Je 9:21
Their y men will die in war. .... Je 11:22
mothers of the y men of Judah. .... Je 15:8
to death and the y men be killed .... Je 18:21
like this since you were y; .... Je 22:21
wine, oil, y sheep, and young .... Je 31:12
oil, young sheep, and y cows. .... Je 31:12
Then y women of Israel will be .... Je 31:13
the y men and old men also. .... Je 31:13

things I did when I was **y**.' ....Je 31:19
Egypt is like a beautiful **y** cow, ...Je 46:20
Her best **y** men will be killed!" ....Je 48:15
drag away the **y** ones of Edom. ....Je 49:20
Surely the **y** men will die in the ....Je 49:26
like a **y** cow in the grain. ....Je 50:11
Kill all the **y** men in Babylon; ....Je 50:27
So her **y** men will be killed in ....Je 50:30
drag away the **y** ones of Babylon. ....Je 50:45
sorry for the **y** men of Babylon. ....Je 51:3
smash old people and **y** people. ....Je 51:22
use you to smash **y** men and young ....Je 51:22
to smash young men and **y** women. ....Je 51:22
people roar like **y** lions; ....Je 51:38
her **y** women are suffering, ...La 1:4
against me to destroy my **y** men. ....La 1:15
y women and men have gone into ....La 1:18
The **y** women of Jerusalem bow ....La 2:10
People and old lie outside on ....La 2:21
My **y** women and young men have ....La 2:21
young women and **y** men have been ....La 2:21
to work hard while he is **y**. ....La 3:27
give their milk to feed their **y**, ...La 4:3
The **y** men ground grain at the ....La 5:13
the **y** men no longer sing. ....La 5:14
the time I was **y** until now I've ....Eze 4:14
old men, **y** men and women, ...Eze 9:6
not remember when you were **y**, ...Eze 16:22
didn't remember when you were **y**, ...Eze 16:43
I made with you when you were **y**, ...Eze 16:60
will also take a **y** branch from ....Eze 17:22
top of the tree's **y** branches, ...Eze 17:22
She lay down among the **y** lions. ....Eze 19:2
While they were **y**, they went to ....Eze 23:3
were all handsome **y** captains ....Eze 23:6
When she was **y**, she had slept ....Eze 23:8
handsome **y** captains and ....Eze 23:12
how she was a **y** prostitute in ....Eze 23:19
touched and held your **y** breasts. ....Eze 23:21
handsome **y** captains and ....Eze 23:23
The **y** men of Heliopolis and ....Eze 30:17
'You are like a **y** lion among the ....Eze 32:2
They will grow and have many **y**. ....Eze 36:11
You must give a **y** bull as a sin ....Eze 43:19
as they did with the **y** bull. ....Eze 43:22
offer a **y** bull and a male sheep ....Eze 43:23
must prepare a **y** bull and male ....Eze 43:25
month take a **y** bull that has ....Eze 45:18
he must offer a **y** bull that has ....Eze 46:6
must be offered with a **y** bull, ...Eze 46:11
wanted only **y** Israelite men who ....Da 1:4
king gave the **y** men a certain ....Da 1:5
The **y** men were to be trained for ....Da 1:5
Among those **y** men were Daniel, ...Da 1:6
worse than other **y** men your age, ...Da 1:10
how the other **y** men look who eat ....Da 1:13
fed than all the **y** men who ate ....Da 1:15
God gave these four **y** men wisdom ....Da 1:17
brought all the **y** men to King ....Da 1:18
none of the **y** men were as good ....Da 1:19
So those four **y** men became the ....Da 1:19
will respond as when she was **y**, ...Hos 2:15
stubborn like a stubborn **y** cow. ....Hos 4:16
Israel, like a **y** lion to Judah. ....Hos 5:14
a well-trained **y** cow that likes ....Hos 10:11
Cry as a **y** woman cries when the ....Joe 1:8
and your **y** men will see visions ....Joe 2:28
and some of your **y** people to be ....Am 2:11
I killed your **y** men with swords, ...Am 4:10
The **y** girl Israel has fallen, ...Am 5:2
time the beautiful **y** women and ....Am 8:13
women and the **y** men will become ....Am 8:13
like a **y** lion in a flock of ....Mic 5:8

place where they feed their **y**? ....Nah 2:11
sword will kill your **y** lions. ....Nah 2:13
Run and tell that **y** man, ...Zch 2:4
y men will grow strong on the ....Zch 9:17
grain and the **y** women on new ....Zch 9:17
or look for the **y** ones, or heal ....Zch 11:16
been a farmer since I was **y**.' ....Zch 13:5
you married when you were **y**. ....Mal 2:14
you married when you were **y**. ....Mal 2:15
man, "Be encouraged, **y** man ....Mt 9:2
The **y** man said, "I have obeyed ....Mt 19:20
But when the **y** man heard this, ...Mt 19:22
paralyzed man, "**Y** man, your sins ....Mk 2:5
This means, "**Y** girl, I tell ....Mk 5:41
answered, "Since he was very **y**. ....Mk 9:21
A **y** man, wearing only a linen ....Mk 14:51
the tomb and saw a **y** man wearing ....Mk 16:5
two doves or two **y** pigeons." ....Lk 2:24
Jesus said, "**Y** man, I tell you, ...Lk 7:14
gave me even a **y** goat to have at ....Lk 15:29
Your **y** men will see visions, ...Ac 2:17
When the **y** men came in and saw ....Ac 5:10
coats with a **y** man named Saul. ....Ac 7:58
A **y** man named Eutychus was ....Ac 20:9
They took the **y** man home alive ....Ac 20:12
Take this **y** man to the ....Ac 23:17
me to bring this **y** man to you. ....Ac 23:18
took the **y** man's hand and led ....Ac 23:19
The **y** man said, "The Jews have ....Ac 23:20
commander sent the **y** man away, ...Ac 23:22
unimportant because you are **y**. 1Ti 4:12
can teach the **y** women to love ....Tit 2:4
encourage **y** men to be wise. ....Tit 2:6
write to you, **y** people, because 1Jn 2:13
write to you, **y** people, because 1Jn 2:14

YOUNGER

older daughter said to the **y**, ...Ge 19:31
older daughter said to the **y**, ...Ge 19:34
and the **y** daughter went and had ....Ge 19:35
The **y** daughter also gave birth ....Ge 19:38
and the older will serve the **y**." ....Ge 25:23
and put them on the **y** son Jacob. ....Ge 27:15
was Leah, and the **y** was Rachel. ....Ge 29:16
me marry your **y** daughter Rachel ....Ge 29:18
do not allow the **y** daughter to ....Ge 29:26
because Judah's **y** son Shelah had ....Ge 38:14
And we have a **y** brother, who was ....Ge 44:20
the head of Ephraim, who was **y**. ....Ge 48:14
But his **y** brother will be ....Ge 48:19
Kenaz, Caleb's **y** brother, ...Jdg 1:13
Kenaz, Caleb's **y** brother, saved ....Jdg 3:9
Her **y** sister is more beautiful. ....Jdg 15:2
his **y** daughter was named Michal. 1Sa 14:49
those who are **y** than I make fun ....Job 30:1
y sister is Sodom, who lived ....Eze 16:46
your older and **y** sisters. ....Eze 16:61
who were two years old or **y**. ....Mt 2:16
The **y** son said to his father, ' ....Lk 15:12
Then the **y** son gathered up all ....Lk 15:13
when you were **y**, you tied your ....Jn 21:18
Treat **y** men like brothers, ...1Ti 5:1
like mothers, and **y** women like 1Ti 5:2
But do not put **y** widows on that 1Ti 5:11
So I want the **y** widows to marry, ...1Ti 5:14
y people should be willing to be 1Pe 5:5

YOUNGEST

up and learned what his **y** son, ...Ge 9:24
Our **y** brother is there with our ....Ge 42:13
place until your **y** brother comes ....Ge 42:15
Then bring your **y** brother back ....Ge 42:20
and that our **y** brother was with ....Ge 42:32
And bring your **y** brother to me ....Ge 42:34

Z

ZAHAM

Azor was the father of **Z**. .... Mt 1:14
Z was the father of Akim. .... Mt 1:14

ZAHAM

Jeush, Shemariah, and **Z**. 2Ch 11:19

ZAIR

and all his chariots went to **Z**. 2Ki 8:21

ZALAPH

the sixth son of **Z**, made repairs .... Ne 3:30

ZALMON

and all his men went up Mount **Z**, ... Jdg 9:48
Z the Ahohite; Maharai the.................... 2Sa 23:28
kings like snow on Mount **Z**. .... Ps 68:14

ZALMONAH

left Mount Hor and camped at **Z**. .... Nu 33:41
They left **Z** and camped at Punon. .... Nu 33:42

ZALMUNNA

chasing Zebah and **Z**, the kings .... Jdg 8:5
haven't caught Zebah and **Z** yet." .... Jdg 8:6
surrender Zebah and **Z** to me. .... Jdg 8:7
Zebah and **Z** and their army were .... Jdg 8:10
and **Z**, the kings of Midian,.................... Jdg 8:12
city, "Here are Zebah and **Z**. .... Jdg 8:15
not caught Zebah and **Z** yet.'" .... Jdg 8:15
Gideon asked Zebah and **Z**, ... Jdg 8:18
Then Zebah and **Z** said to Gideon, ... Jdg 8:21
and killed Zebah and **Z** and took .... Jdg 8:21
what you did to Zebah and **Z**.................... Ps 83:11

ZAMZUMMITES

but the Ammonites called them **Z**. .... Dt 2:20
destroyed the **Z**, and the .... Dt 2:21

ZANOAH

Z, En Gannim, Tappuah, Enam, ... Jos 15:34
Jezreel, Jokdeam, **Z**, ... Jos 15:56
and the people of **Z** repaired the .... Ne 3:13
Z, Adullam and their villages, ... Ne 11:30

ZAPHENATH-PANEAH

The king gave Joseph the name **Z**. .... Ge 41:45

ZAPHON

Succoth, and **Z**, the other land .... Jos 13:27
the river to the town of **Z**. .... Jdg 12:1

ZAREPHATH

Go to **Z** in Sidon and live there. 1Ki 17:9
So Elijah went to **Z**. 1Ki 17:10
Canaanites, all the way to **Z**. .... Ob 1:20
a widow in **Z**, a town in Sidon. .... Lk 4:26

ZARETHAN

away at Adam, a town near **Z**. .... Jos 3:16
and all of Beth Shan next to **Z**. 1Ki 4:12
River between Succoth and **Z**. 1Ki 7:46
River between Succoth and **Z**. 2Ch 4:17

ZATTU

the descendants of **Z**—945;..................... Ezr 2:8
From the descendants of **Z**:..................... Ezr 8:5
From the descendants of **Z**:..................... Ezr 10:27
the descendants of **Z**—845;..................... Ne 7:13
Pahath-Moab, Elam, **Z**, Bani, ... Ne 10:14

ZAZA

sons were Peleth and **Z**. 1Ch 2:33

ZEALOT

Simon the **Z** and Judas Iscariot, ... Mt 10:4
Thaddaeus, Simon the **Z**, ... Mk 3:18
Alphaeus, Simon (called the **Z**), ... Lk 6:15
known as the **Z**), and Judas son .... Ac 1:13

ZEBADIAH

Z, Arad, Eder, ... 1Ch 8:15
sons were **Z**, Meshullam, Hizki 1Ch 8:17
And there were Joelah and **Z**,.................. 1Ch 12:7
was second, **Z** was third,........................ 1Ch 26:2

Asahel's son **Z** took his place as.............. 1Ch 27:7
Nethaniah, **Z**, Asahel,........................... 2Ch 17:8
Z son of Ishmael, a leader in 2Ch 19:11
Z son of Michael, with eighty .... Ezr 8:8
of Immer: Hanani and **Z**. .... Ezr 10:20

ZEBAH

I am chasing **Z** and Zalmunna, ... Jdg 8:5
caught **Z** and Zalmunna yet. .... Jdg 8:6
will surrender **Z** and Zalmunna to .... Jdg 8:7
Z and Zalmunna and their army .... Jdg 8:10
Z and Zalmunna, the kings of .... Jdg 8:12
city, "Here are **Z** and Zalmunna. .... Jdg 8:15
not caught **Z** and Zalmunna yet. .... Jdg 8:15
Gideon asked **Z** and Zalmunna, ... Jdg 8:18
Then **Z** and Zalmunna said to .... Jdg 8:21
got up and killed **Z** and Zalmunna .... Jdg 8:21
what you did to **Z** and Zalmunna. .... Ps 83:11

ZEBEDEE

James and John, the sons of **Z**. .... Mt 4:21
in a boat with their father **Z**, ... Mt 4:21
James son of **Z**, and his brother .... Mt 10:2
Then the wife of **Z** came to Jesus .... Mt 20:20
and the two sons of **Z** with him, ... Mt 26:37
James and John, the sons of **Z**. .... Mk 1:19
the sons of **Z** (Jesus named them .... Mk 3:17
John, sons of **Z**, came to Jesus .... Mk 10:35
the sons of **Z**, Simon's partners .... Lk 5:10
the two sons of **Z**, and two other .... Jn 21:2

ZEBIDAH

mother's name was **Z** daughter of 2Ki 23:36

ZEBINA

Zabad, **Z**, Jaddai, Joel, ... Ezr 10:43

ZEBOIIM

Admah, and **Z**, as far as Lasha. .... Ge 10:19
Shemeber king of **Z**, and the king .... Ge 14:2
Gomorrah, Admah, **Z**, and Bela .... Ge 14:8
and Admah and **Z**, which the LORD .... Dt 29:23
like Admah or treat you like **Z**. .... Hos 11:8

ZEBOIM

the Valley of **Z** toward the 1Sa 13:18
Hadid, **Z**, Neballat, ... Ne 11:34

ZEBUL

sons, and isn't **Z** his officer? .... Jdg 9:28
when **Z**, the ruler of Shechem, ... Jdg 9:30
soldiers, he said to **Z**, "Look! .... Jdg 9:36
But **Z** said, "You are seeing the .... Jdg 9:36
Z said to Gaal, "Where is your .... Jdg 9:38
Z forced Gaal and his brothers .... Jdg 9:41

ZEBULUN

six sons," so she named him **Z**. .... Ge 30:20
Levi, Judah, Issachar, and **Z**. .... Ge 35:23
Z will live near the sea. .... Ge 49:13
Issachar, **Z**, Benjamin,........................... Ex 1:3
from the tribe of **Z**—Eliab son of .... Nu 1:9
The tribe of **Z** was counted; .... Nu 1:30
The tribe of **Z** totaled 57,400 .... Nu 1:31
Next is the tribe of **Z**. .... Nu 2:7
of the people of **Z** is Eliab son .... Nu 2:7
the division of the tribe of **Z**. .... Nu 10:16
from the tribe of **Z**, Gaddiel son .... Nu 13:10
family groups in the tribe of **Z**: .... Nu 26:26
were the family groups of **Z**, ... Nu 26:27
the tribe of **Z**, Elizaphan son .... Nu 34:25
Gad, Asher, **Z**, Dan, and Naphtali .... Dt 27:13
said this about the people of **Z**: .... Dt 33:18
when you go out, **Z**, and be happy .... Dt 33:18
was given to the tribe of **Z**..................... Jos 19:10
family groups of **Z** received some .... Jos 19:10
of **Z** went as far as Sarid. .... Jos 19:10
given to the family groups of **Z**. .... Jos 19:16

touching **Z** and the Valley of .... Jos 19:27
to the area of **Z** on the south, ... Jos 19:34
the areas of Reuben, Gad, and **Z**. .... Jos 21:7
tribe of **Z** gave them Jokneam, ... Jos 21:34
people of **Z** did not force out .... Jdg 1:30
and lived with the people of **Z**, ... Jdg 1:30
but **Z** made them work as slaves. .... Jdg 1:30
of Naphtali and **Z** and lead them .... Jdg 4:6
the people of **Z** and Naphtali .... Jdg 4:10
And from **Z** came those who lead. .... Jdg 5:14
But the people of **Z** risked their .... Jdg 5:18
of Asher, and Naphtali. .... Jdg 6:35
the tribe of **Z** was a judge for .... Jdg 12:11
Elon, the man of **Z**, died and was .... Jdg 12:12
of Aijalon in the land of **Z**. .... Jdg 12:12
Levi, Judah, Issachar, **Z**, ... 1Ch 2:1
tribes of Reuben, Gad, and **Z**. 1Ch 6:63
from the tribe of **Z** the towns 1Ch 6:77
were fifty thousand men from **Z**. 1Ch 12:33
as Issachar, **Z**, and Naphtali, ... 1Ch 12:40
Obadiah was over the tribe of **Z**. 1Ch 27:19
all the way to **Z**, but the people 2Ch 30:10
and **Z** were sorry for what they 2Ch 30:11
leaders of **Z** and of Naphtali. .... Ps 68:27
the lands of **Z** and Naphtali hang .... Is 9:1
Issachar's land, **Z** will have one .... Eze 48:26
in the area near **Z** and Naphtali. .... Mt 4:13
Land of **Z** and land of Naphtali .... Mt 4:15
the tribe of **Z** twelve thousand, ... Rev 7:8

ZECHARIAH

Jeroboam's son **Z** became king in 2Ki 14:29
Z son of Jeroboam was king over 2Ki 15:8
Z did what the LORD said was 2Ki 15:9
Z did not stop doing the same 2Ki 15:9
plans against **Z** and killed him 2Ki 15:10
The other acts of **Z** are written 2Ki 15:11
name was Abijah daughter of **Z**. 2Ki 18:2
Jeiel was the first, then **Z**, ... 1Ch 5:7
Z son of Meshelemiah was the 1Ch 9:21
Gedor, Ahio, **Z**, and Mikloth. 1Ch 9:37
Z, Jaaziel, Shemiramoth, Jehiel, ... 1Ch 15:18
Z, Jaaziel, Shemiramoth, Jehiel, ... 1Ch 15:20
Nethanel, Amasai, **Z**, Benaiah, ... 1Ch 15:24
Z was second to him. 1Ch 16:5
and Isshiah's son was **Z**. 1Ch 24:25
Z was his first son, Jediael was 1Ch 26:2
was third, and **Z** was fourth. 1Ch 26:11
thrown for Meshelemiah's son **Z**. 1Ch 26:14
Iddo son of **Z** was over East 1Ch 27:21
Ben-Hail, Obadiah, **Z**, Nethanel, ... 2Ch 17:7
Z was Benaiah's son. 2Ch 20:14
Azariah, Jehiel, **Z**, Azariahu, ... 2Ch 21:2
of God entered **Z** son of Jehoiada 2Ch 24:20
Z stood before the people and 2Ch 24:20
officers made plans against **Z**. 2Ch 24:21
Joash killed **Z**, Jehoiada's son 2Ch 24:22
Before **Z** died, he said, "May the 2Ch 24:22
he had killed **Z** son of Jehoiada 2Ch 24:25
obeyed God while **Z** was alive, ... 2Ch 26:5
name was Abijah daughter of **Z**. 2Ch 29:1
there were **Z** and Mattaniah. 2Ch 29:13
of Merari, and **Z** and Meshullam, ... 2Ch 34:12
Hilkiah, **Z**, and Jehiel, the 2Ch 35:8
The prophets Haggai and **Z**, ... Ezr 5:1
of Haggai the prophet and **Z**, ... Ezr 6:14
Z, with one hundred fifty men. .... Ezr 8:3
Z son of Bebai, with .... Ezr 8:11
Nathan, **Z**, and Meshullam. .... Ezr 8:16
Mattaniah, **Z**, Jehiel, Abdi, ... Ezr 10:26
Hashbaddanah, **Z**, and Meshullam. .... Ne 8:4
was the son of **Z**, the son of .... Ne 11:4
was the son of **Z**, a descendant .... Ne 11:5

was the son of **Z**, the son of .... Ne 11:12
Z, from Iddo's family; .... Ne 12:16
along with **Z** son of Jonathan. .... Ne 12:35
Elioenai, **Z**, and Hananiah. .... Ne 12:41
priest and **Z** son of Jeberekiah. .... Is 8:2
the prophet **Z** son of Berekiah, ... Zch 1:1
the prophet **Z** son of Berekiah, ... Zch 1:7
the LORD spoke his word to **Z**. .... Zch 7:1
LORD spoke his word to **Z** again, ... Zch 7:8
the murder of **Z** son of Berakiah .... Mt 23:35
a priest named **Z** who belonged to .... Lk 1:5
Z and Elizabeth truly did what .... Lk 1:6
day **Z** was serving as a priest .... Lk 1:8
angel of the Lord appeared to **Z**, ... Lk 1:11
Z was startled and frightened. .... Lk 1:12
to him, "**Z**, don't be afraid. .... Lk 1:13
Z said to the angel, "How can I .... Lk 1:18
still waiting for **Z** and were .... Lk 1:21
When **Z** came outside, he could .... Lk 1:22
to name him **Z** because this was............. Lk 1:59
Z asked for a writing tablet and .... Lk 1:63
Immediately **Z** could talk again, ... Lk 1:64
Z, John's father, was filled .... Lk 1:67
to John son of **Z** in the desert. .... Lk 3:2
of Abel to the killing of **Z**, ... Lk 11:51

ZEDAD

go to Lebo Hamath, and on to **Z**. .... Nu 34:8
Hamath and on to the towns of **Z**, ... Eze 47:15

ZEDEKIAH

Z son of Kenaanah had made some 1Ki 22:11
Then **Z** son of Kenaanah went up 1Ki 22:24
Z said, "Has the LORD's spirit 1Ki 22:24
changed Mattaniah's name to **Z**. 2Ki 24:17
Z was twenty-one years old when 2Ki 24:18
Z did what the LORD said was 2Ki 24:19
Z turned against the king of 2Ki 24:20
Z and his men ran away toward 2Ki 25:4
army chased King **Z** and caught up 2Ki 25:5
they captured **Z** and took him to 2Ki 25:6
There he passed sentence on **Z**. 2Ki 25:6
his third was **Z**, and his fourth 1Ch 3:15
and he was followed by **Z**. 1Ch 3:16
Z son of Kenaanah had made some 2Ch 18:10
Then **Z** son of Kenaanah went up 2Ch 18:23
Z said, "Has the LORD's Spirit 2Ch 18:23
uncle **Z** the king of Judah 2Ch 36:10
Z was twenty-one years old when 2Ch 36:11
Z did what the LORD his God said............ 2Ch 36:12
the LORD, but **Z** did not obey. 2Ch 36:12
Z turned against King 2Ch 36:13
Z became stubborn and refused 2Ch 36:13
governor, son of Hacaliah, **Z**, ... Ne 10:1
years that **Z** son of Josiah was .... Je 1:3
came when **Z** king of Judah sent .... Je 21:1
them, "Tell King **Z** this: .... Je 21:3
I'll hand over **Z** king of Judah, ... Je 21:7
'**Z** king of Judah, his officers, ... Je 24:8
soon after **Z** son of Josiah was .... Je 27:1
to see **Z** king of Judah. .... Je 27:3
same message to **Z** king of Judah. .... Je 27:12
Z king of Judah sent Elasah son............. Je 29:3
Kolaiah and **Z** son of Maaseiah: .... Je 29:21
LORD treat you like **Z** and Ahab. .... Je 29:22
the tenth year **Z** was king of .... Je 32:1
Z king of Judah had put Jeremiah .... Je 32:3
Z had asked, "Why have you .... Je 32:3
Z king of Judah will not escape .... Je 32:4
The king will take **Z** to Babylon, ... Je 32:5
go to **Z** king of Judah and tell................. Je 34:2
But, **Z** king of Judah, listen to .... Je 34:4
this message to **Z** in Jerusalem. .... Je 34:6
This was after King **Z** had made .... Je 34:8

Z

I will hand **Z** king of Judah and .... Je 34:21
of Shaphan; **Z** son of Hananiah .... Je 36:12
had appointed **Z** son of Josiah to .... Je 37:1
Z took the place of Jehoiachin .... Je 37:1
But **Z**, his servants, and the .... Je 37:2
Now King **Z** sent Jehucal son of .... Je 37:3
I know **Z** king of Judah sent you .... Je 37:7
Tell this to King **Z**: '............................... Je 37:7
Then King **Z** sent for Jeremiah .... Je 37:17
Z asked him in private, "Is .... Je 37:17
Z, you will be handed over to .... Je 37:17
Then Jeremiah said to King **Z**, ... Je 37:18
So King **Z** gave orders for .... Je 37:21
King **Z** said to them, "Jeremiah .... Je 38:5
As King **Z** was sitting at the .... Je 38:7
King **Z** commanded Ebed-Melech .... Je 38:10
Then King **Z** sent someone to get .... Je 38:14
said to **Z**, "If I give you .... Je 38:15
But King **Z** made a secret promise .... Je 38:16
Jeremiah said to **Z**, "This is .... Je 38:17
Then King **Z** said to Jeremiah, ... Je 38:19
Then **Z** said to Jeremiah, "Do not .... Je 38:24
said to King **Z** and what he said.............. Je 38:25
the ninth year **Z** was king of .... Je 39:1
When **Z** king of Judah and all his .... Je 39:4
caught up with **Z** in the plains .... Je 39:5
passed his sentence on **Z**. .... Je 39:5
officers of Judah as **Z** watched. .... Je 39:6
chains on **Z** and took him to .... Je 39:7
just as I handed **Z** king of Judah .... Je 44:30
Soon after **Z** became king of .... Je 49:34
to Babylon with **Z** king of Judah .... Je 51:59
the fourth year **Z** was king of .... Je 51:59
Z was twenty-one years old when .... Je 52:1
Z did what the Lord said was .... Je 52:2
Z turned against the king of .... Je 52:3
Z and his men headed toward the .... Je 52:7
army chased King **Z** and caught............... Je 52:8
captured **Z** and took him to .... Je 52:9
There he passed sentence on **Z**. .... Je 52:9
the king kept **Z** in prison there .... Je 52:11

ZEEB
of Midian named Oreb and **Z**. .... Jdg 7:25
of Oreb and **Z** at the winepress .... Jdg 7:25
and Zeeb at the winepress of **Z**, ... Jdg 7:25
heads of Oreb and **Z** to Gideon, ... Jdg 7:25
God let you capture Oreb and **Z**, ... Jdg 8:3
what you did to Oreb and **Z**. .... Ps 83:11

ZEKER
Gedor, Ahio, **Z**, ... 1Ch 8:31

ZELA
son Jonathan at **Z** in Benjamin 2Sa 21:14

ZELAH
Z, Haeleph, the Jebusite city .... Jos 18:28

ZELEK
Z the Ammonite; Naharai the.................. 2Sa 23:37
Z the Ammonite; Naharai the.................. 1Ch 11:39

ZELOPHEHAD
Z son of Hepher had no sons;.................. Nu 26:33
the daughters of **Z** came near. .... Nu 27:1
Z was the son of Hepher, the son .... Nu 27:1
The daughters of **Z** are right; .... Nu 27:7
you to give the land of **Z**, ... Nu 36:2
Z was the son of Hepher, who was........... Jos 17:3
Z had no sons, but he had five .... Jos 17:3
His second son was named **Z**,................. 1Ch 7:15

ZELZAH
on the border of Benjamin at **Z**. 1Sa 10:2

ZEMARAIM
Beth Arabah, **Z**, Bethel, ... Jos 18:22
on Mount **Z** in the mountains 2Ch 13:4

ZEMARITES
Arvadites, **Z**, and Hamathites. .... Ge 10:18
Arvadites, **Z**, and Hamathites. 1Ch 1:16

ZEMIRAH
sons were **Z**, Joash, Eliezer, ... 1Ch 7:8

ZENAN
Z, Hadashah, Migdal Gad, ... Jos 15:37

ZENAS
all you can to help **Z** the lawyer .... Tit 3:13

ZEPHANIAH
Z the priest next in rank, ... 2Ki 25:18
Z was Tahath's son................................ 1Ch 6:36
and the priest **Z** son of Maaseiah .... Je 21:1
to the priest **Z** son of Maaseiah, ... Je 29:25
said to **Z**, 'The Lord has made .... Je 29:26
Z the priest read the letter to .... Je 29:29
and the priest **Z** son of Maaseiah .... Je 37:3
Jehucal and **Z**, I know Zedekiah .... Je 37:7
Z the priest next in rank, ... Je 52:24
came through **Z** while Josiah son .... Zph 1:1
Z was the son of Cushi, who was .... Zph 1:1
to the house of Josiah son of **Z**, ... Zch 6:10
Jedaiah, and Josiah son of **Z**. .... Zch 6:14

ZEPHATH
the Canaanites who lived in **Z**. .... Jdg 1:17

ZEPHATHAH
in the Valley of **Z** at Mareshah. 2Ch 14:10

ZEPHO
Omar, **Z**, Gatam, and Kenaz. .... Ge 36:11
leaders: Teman, Omar, **Z**, Kenaz, ... Ge 36:15
Teman, Omar, **Z**, Gatam, Kenaz,........... 1Ch 1:36

ZEPHON
Gad's sons were **Z**, Haggi, Shuni, ... Ge 46:16
across from Baal **Z**, on the shore .... Ex 14:2
near Pi Hahiroth and Baal **Z**. .... Ex 14:9
From **Z** came the Zephonite family .... Nu 26:15
east of Baal **Z**, and camped near .... Nu 33:7

ZEPHONITE
Zephon came the **Z** family group; .... Nu 26:15

ZER
called Ziddim, **Z**, Hammath, ... Jos 19:35

ZERAH
Nahath, **Z**, Shammah, and Mizzah. .... Ge 36:13
Nahath, **Z**, Shammah, and Mizzah. .... Ge 36:17
Jobab son of **Z** became king. .... Ge 36:33
was born, and they named him **Z**. .... Ge 38:30
Perez, and **Z** (but Er and Onan .... Ge 46:12
from **Z** came the Zerahite family .... Nu 26:13
from **Z** came the Zerahite family .... Nu 26:20
of Zabdi, who was the son of **Z**. .... Jos 7:1
chose the family group of **Z**. .... Jos 7:17
all the families of **Z** presented .... Jos 7:17
of Zabdi, who was the son of **Z**. .... Jos 7:18
led Achan son of **Z** to the Valley.............. Jos 7:24
Achan son of **Z** refused to obey .... Jos 22:20
sons were Nahath, **Z**, Shammah, ... 1Ch 1:37
Jobab son of **Z** became king. 1Ch 1:44
Tamar gave birth to Perez and **Z**. 1Ch 2:4
Z had five sons: Zimri, Ethan, ... 1Ch 2:6
Jamin, Jarib, **Z** and Shaul.................... 1Ch 4:24
Iddo's son was **Z**. And Zerah's 1Ch 6:21
Zerah's son. **Z** was Adaiah's son 1Ch 6:41
Jeuel and other relatives of **Z**. 1Ch 9:6
Then **Z** from Cush came out to 2Ch 14:9
out to fight **Z** and prepared for 2Ch 14:10

was a descendant of **Z**, ... Ne 11:24
was the father of Perez and **Z**. .... Mt 1:3

ZERAHIAH
Uzzi was the father of **Z**......................... 1Ch 6:6
Z was the father of Meraioth. 1Ch 6:6
Bukki's son. **Z** was Uzzi's son. 1Ch 6:51
the son of **Z**, the son of Uzzi, ... Ezr 7:4
son of **Z**, with two hundred.................... Ezr 8:4

ZERAHITE
Zerah came the **Z** family group; .... Nu 26:13
Zerah came the **Z** family group. .... Nu 26:20
Of the **Z** people there were Jeuel 1Ch 9:6

ZERED
went and camped in the **Z** Valley. .... Nu 21:12
get up and cross the **Z** Valley." .... Dt 2:13
until we crossed the **Z** Valley. .... Dt 2:14

ZEREDAH
Ephraimite from the town of **Z**, ... 1Ki 11:26

ZERERAH
city of Beth Shittah toward **Z**................... Jdg 7:22

ZERESH
his friends and his wife, **Z**. .... Est 5:10
Then Haman's wife, **Z**, and all .... Est 5:14
He told his wife, **Z**, and all his .... Est 6:13

ZERETH
Z Shahar on the hill in the .... Jos 13:19
sons were **Z**, Zohar, Ethnan, ... 1Ch 4:7

ZERI
were Gedaliah, **Z**, Jeshaiah, ... 1Ch 25:3

ZEROR
the son of **Z**, who was the son 1Sa 9:1

ZERUAH
was the son of a widow named **Z**. 1Ki 11:26

ZERUBBABEL
sons were **Z** and Shimei........................ 1Ch 3:19
Z also had five other sons: 1Ch 3:20
These people returned with **Z**, ... Ezr 2:2
joined **Z** son of Shealtiel .... Ezr 3:2
in Jerusalem, **Z** son of Shealtiel .... Ezr 3:8
they came to **Z** and the leaders .... Ezr 4:2
But **Z**, Jeshua, and the leaders .... Ezr 4:3
Then **Z** son of Shealtiel and .... Ezr 5:2
These people returned with **Z**, ... Ne 7:7
returned with **Z** son of Shealtiel .... Ne 12:1
in the days of **Z** and Nehemiah. .... Ne 12:47
of the LORD to **Z** son of .... Hag 1:1
Z son of Shealtiel and Joshua.................. Hag 1:12
LORD stirred up **Z** son of .... Hag 1:14
Speak to **Z** son of Shealtiel, ... Hag 2:2
But the LORD says, '**Z**, be brave. .... Hag 2:4
Tell **Z**, the governor of Judah,................ Hag 2:21
will take you, **Z** son of .... Hag 2:23
is the word of the LORD to **Z**: ' .... Zch 4:6
In front of **Z** you will become .... Zch 4:7
Z has laid the foundation of .... Zch 4:9
when they see **Z** with tools, ... Zch 4:10
was the grandfather of **Z**. .... Mt 1:12
Z was the father of Abiud. .... Mt 1:13
Rhesa was the son of **Z**. .... Lk 3:27
Z was the grandson of Shealtiel. .... Lk 3:27

ZERUIAH
Hittite and Abishai son of **Z**, ... 1Sa 26:6
Joab son of **Z** and David's men 2Sa 2:13
These sons of **Z** are too much for 2Sa 3:39
Joab son of **Z** was commander over 2Sa 8:16
Joab son of **Z** knew that King................. 2Sa 14:1
Abishai son of **Z** said to the 2Sa 16:9
does not concern you, sons of **Z**! 2Sa 16:10
of Nahash and sister of **Z**, ... 2Sa 17:25

Abishai son of **Z** commanded.................. 2Sa 18:2
But Abishai son of **Z** said, ... 2Sa 19:21
does not concern you, sons of **Z**! 2Sa 19:22
but Abishai son of **Z** killed the 2Sa 21:17
of Joab son of **Z**, was captain 2Sa 23:18
the armor of Joab son of **Z**; 2Sa 23:37
with Joab son of **Z** and Abiathar 1Ki 1:7
what Joab son of **Z** did to me. 1Ki 2:5
Joab son of **Z** would support him! 1Ki 2:22
sisters were **Z** and Abigail..................... 1Ch 2:16
Joab son of **Z** led the attack, ... 1Ch 11:6
the armor for Joab son of **Z**; 1Ch 11:39
Abishai son of **Z** killed eighteen............. 1Ch 18:12
Joab son of **Z** was commander over 1Ch 18:15
son of Ner, and Joab son of **Z**. 1Ch 26:28
Joab son of **Z** began to count the 1Ch 27:24

ZETHAM
his other sons were **Z** and Joel. 1Ch 23:8
His sons were **Z** and Joel his 1Ch 26:22

ZETHAN
Ehud, Kenaanah, **Z**, Tarshish, and 1Ch 7:10

ZETHAR
Bigtha, Abagtha, **Z**, and Carcas.............. Est 1:10

ZEUS
call Barnabas "**Z**" and Paul .... Ac 14:12
The priest in the temple of **Z**, ... Ac 14:13

ZIA
Jorai, Jacan, **Z**, and Eber. 1Ch 5:13

ZIBA
a servant named **Z** from Saul's 2Sa 9:2
servants called **Z** to him......................... 2Sa 9:2
David said to him, "Are you **Z**?".............. 2Sa 9:2
Z answered the king, "Jonathan.............. 2Sa 9:3
The king asked **Z**, "Where is this 2Sa 9:4
Z answered, "He is at the house.............. 2Sa 9:4
David called Saul's servant **Z**. 2Sa 9:9
Z had fifteen sons and twenty 2Sa 9:10
Z said to King David, "I, your................. 2Sa 9:11
of Olives, **Z**, Mephibosheth's 2Sa 16:1
Z had a row of donkeys loaded 2Sa 16:1
king asked **Z**, "What are these 2Sa 16:2
Z answered, "The donkeys are 2Sa 16:2
Z answered him, "Mephibosheth 2Sa 16:3
the king said to **Z**, "All right. 2Sa 16:4
Z said, "I bow to you. 2Sa 16:4
Z, the servant from Saul's 2Sa 19:17
master, my servant **Z** tricked me! 2Sa 19:26
I said to **Z**, 'I am crippled, so 2Sa 19:26
that you and **Z** will divide the................. 2Sa 19:29
Let **Z** take all the land now that 2Sa 19:30

ZIBEON
Anah, the son of **Z** the Hivite;................ Ge 36:2
Anah was the son of **Z**. .... Ge 36:14
Lotan, Shobal, **Z**, Anah, ... Ge 36:20
sons of **Z** were Aiah and Anah. .... Ge 36:24
Lotan, Shobal, **Z**, Anah, ... Ge 36:29
Lotan, Shobal, **Z**, Anah, Dishon, ... 1Ch 1:38

ZIBIAH
mother's name was **Z**, and she was 2Ki 12:1
mother's name was **Z**, and she was 2Ch 24:1

ZICRI
sons were Korah, Nepheg, and **Z**. .... Ex 6:21
sons were Jakim, **Z**, Zabdi,.................... 1Ch 8:19
Abdon, **Z**, Hanan, ... 1Ch 8:23
Jaareshiah, Elijah, and **Z**. 1Ch 8:27
son, and **Z** was Asaph's son. 1Ch 9:15
Joram's son **Z**, and Zicri's son 1Ch 26:25
Eliezer son of **Z** was over the 1Ch 27:16
Amasiah son of **Z** had volunteered........... 2Ch 17:16
Adaiah, and Elishaphat son of **Z**. 2Ch 23:1

Z

and listen. Hear me, son of Z.................. Nu 23:18
Balak son of Z, prepared to   .... Jos 24:9
any better than Balak son of Z, ... Jdg 11:25

ZIPPORAH
his daughter Z to Moses to be   .... Ex 2:21
Z gave birth to a son. .... Ex 2:22
But Z took a flint knife and   .... Ex 4:25
had sent his wife Z to Jethro, ... Ex 18:2

ZITHERS
flutes, lyres, z, harps, pipes, ... Da 3:5
flutes, lyres, z, pipes, and all   .... Da 3:7
horns, lyres, z, harps, pipes, ... Da 3:10
flutes, lyres, z, harps, pipes, ... Da 3:15

ZIV
second month, the month of Z. 1Ki 6:1
Work began on the Temple in Z,.............. 1Ki 6:37

ZIZ
come up through the Pass of Z. 2Ch 20:16

ZIZA
Jahath, Z, Jeush, and Beriah. 1Ch 23:10
first son, and Z was the second 1Ch 23:11
Abijah, Attai, Z, and Shelomith.............. 2Ch 11:20

ZOAN
seven years before Z in Egypt. .... Nu 13:22
in the fields of Z in Egypt. .... Ps 78:12
his wonders in the fields of Z. .... Ps 78:43
of the city of Z are fools;...................... Is 19:11
The officers of Z have been   .... Is 19:13
Your officers have gone to Z, ... Is 30:4
start a fire in Z and punish .... Eze 30:14

ZOAR
of Egypt in the direction of Z.................. Ge 13:10
Bela. (Bela is also called Z.)   .... Ge 14:2
of Siddim. (Bela is called Z.)   .... Ge 14:8
town is named Z, because it is   .... Ge 19:22
come up when Lot entered Z.   .... Ge 19:23
afraid to continue living in Z, ... Ge 19:30
whole Valley of Jericho up to Z.   .... Dt 34:3
people run away to Z for safety;.............. Is 15:5
be heard from Z as far away as   .... Je 48:34

ZOBAH
Edom, the king of Z, and the 1Sa 14:47
Rehob, king of Z, as he went to 2Sa 8:3
to help Hadadezer king of Z, ... 2Sa 8:5
son of Rehob, king of Z. 2Sa 8:12
soldiers from Beth Rehob and Z. 2Sa 10:6
Arameans from Z and Rehob and 2Sa 10:8
Igal son of Nathan of Z; 2Sa 23:36
his master, Hadadezer king of Z 1Ki 11:23
David defeated the army of Z, ... 1Ki 11:24
king of Z all the way to 1Ch 18:3
to help Hadadezer king of Z, ... 1Ch 18:5
the army of Hadadezer king of Z. 1Ch 18:9
Mesopotamia, Aram Maacah, and Z. 1Ch 19:6
to Hamath Z and captured it. 2Ch 8:3
of Northwest Mesopotamia and Z,.......... Ps 59:17

ZOHAR
to Ephron, the son of Z for me. .... Ge 23:8
was the son of Z the Hittite.   .... Ge 25:9
Jamin, Ohad, Jakin, Z, and Shaul   .... Ge 46:10

Ohad, Jakin, Z, and Shaul, the   .... Ex 6:15
sons were Zereth, Z, Ethnan, ... 1Ch 4:7

ZOHELETH
the Stone of Z near the spring 1Ki 1:9

ZOHETH
sons were Z and Ben-Zoheth. 1Ch 4:20

ZOPHAH
sons were Z, Imna, Shelesh, ... 1Ch 7:35

ZOPHAI
son was Z. Zophai's son was 1Ch 6:26

ZOPHAR
Shuhite, and Z the Naamathite. .... Job 2:11
Then Z the Naamathite answered: .... Job 11:1
Then Z the Naamathite answered: .... Job 20:1
and Z the Naamathite did as the   .... Job 42:9

ZOPHIM
took Balaam to the field of Z,.................. Nu 23:14

ZORAH
hills: Eshtaol, Z, Ashnah, ... Jos 15:33
land included Z, Eshtaol, Ir   .... Jos 19:41
who lived in the city of Z.   .... Jdg 13:2
the cities of Z and Eshtaol. .... Jdg 13:25
the cities of Z and Eshtaol. .... Jdg 16:31
the cities of Z and Eshtaol to   .... Jdg 18:2
men returned to Z and Eshtaol, ... Jdg 18:8
Danites left Z and Eshtaol ready   .... Jdg 18:11
Z, Aijalon, and Hebron. 2Ch 11:10
in En Rimmon, Jarmuth, ... Ne 11:29

ZORATHITE
family groups of the Z people. 1Ch 4:2

ZORATHITES
The Z and the Eshtaolites came 1Ch 2:53

ZORITES
the Manahathites, and the Z. 1Ch 2:54

ZUAR
of Issachar—Nethanel son of Z;   .... Nu 1:8
Issachar is Nethanel son of Z. .... Nu 2:5
Nethanel son of Z was over the   .... Nu 10:15

ZUPH
was from the family of Z. 1Sa 1:1
was the son of Z from the family 1Sa 1:1
they arrived in the area of Z, ... 1Sa 9:5
was Zuph's son. Z was Elkanah's 1Ch 6:35

ZUR
death was Cozbi daughter of Z, ... Nu 25:15
Evi, Rekem, Z, Hur, and Reba, ... Nu 31:8
Evi, Rekem, Z, Hur, and Reba.   .... Jos 13:21
Halhul, Beth Z, Gedor, ... Jos 15:58
Maon was the father of Beth Z. 1Ch 2:45
other sons were Z, Kish, Baal, ... 1Ch 8:30
other sons were Z, Kish, Baal, ... 1Ch 9:36
Beth Z, Soco, Adullam, ... 2Ch 11:7
half of the district of Beth Z. .... Ne 3:16

ZURIEL
families was Z son of Abihail, ... Nu 3:35

ZURISHADDAI
of Simeon—Shelumiel son of Z;   .... Nu 1:6
of Simeon is Shelumiel son of Z.   .... Nu 2:12
Shelumiel son of Z was over the.............. Nu 10:19

ZUZITES
Karnaim, the Z in Ham, and the.............. Ge 14:5

Z